PROFESSIONAL RESPONSIBILITY

STANDARDS, RULES, AND STATUTES

2019–2020 Edition

Selected and Edited

by

JOHN S. DZIENKOWSKI

Professor of Law & Dean John F. Sutton, Jr.
Chair in Lawyering and the Legal Process
University of Texas

444 Cedar Street, Suite 700
St. Paul, MN 55101
1-877-888-1330

Printed in the United States of America

ISBN: 978-1-68467-222-6

PREFACE

In recent years, the American Bar Association (ABA), the states, and other organizations have been active in the promulgation of standards, rules, and statutes that regulate lawyers' conduct. These sources of the law of professional responsibility have significantly affected the manner in which lawyers analyze problems in this area. Similarly, the existence of different formal sources of professional responsibility has altered the way in which lawyers and law students are taught about ethical problems. This collection of Professional Responsibility Standards, Rules, and Statutes is designed to provide teachers and students with easy access to the important sources of professional responsibility.

Beginning with the 1995 edition of Professional Responsibility Standards Rules and Statutes, this book is now published in a full version and an abridged version. The full version will continue to include various sources of professional responsibility including standards for specialized areas of practice and standards for the organized regulation of the profession. The abridged edition will present the ABA versions of the codes governing lawyers and judges as well as several selected rules of procedure and evidence and selected rules from California and New York. The purpose of the two editions is to allow professors to choose which version best fits the class that they plan to teach. This preface will, however, cover materials in both versions.

The full version of Professional Responsibility Standards Rules and Statutes is organized into eight different parts: (1) Codes Regulating Lawyers' Conduct; (2) Code of Judicial Conduct; (3) Rules of Evidence and Procedure that Affect the Legal Profession; (4) Restatement (Third) of the Law Governing Lawyers; (5) Statutes that Affect the Legal Profession; (6) Standards for Specialized Areas of Practice; (7) Standards for the Organized Regulation of Lawyers, and (8) Prior Versions of the ABA Model Rules and the ABA Code of Judicial Conduct. The abridged edition includes the first three parts which focus on the ABA's pronouncements as well as the federal rules of evidence and procedure that influence the legal profession.

In February 2002, the ABA House of Delegates amended the Model Rules to reflect the revisions proposed by the Ethics 2000 Commission. In 2003, the ABA amended the Model Rules to reflect the work of the ABA Commission on Multijurisdictional Practice and the work of the Cheek Commission. In 2012 and 2013, the ABA House of Delegates amended the Model Rules in light of proposals made by the Ethics 20/20 Commission. Where appropriate, the annotations also contain the text of a prior draft of the Model Rules to illustrate a shift in the final ABA position. In light of the fact that the states have made significant modifications to the ABA's version of the Model Rules, it has become desirable to include a section on selected significant state modifications to the Model Rules. Both the full and abridged editions now contain the California and New York state materials.

Both the full and abridged versions include the ABA Model Code of Professional Conduct and the 1908 Canons, as well as the 2018 Code of Judicial Conduct. The unabridged version of this supplement will continue to reproduce the 2001 version of the Model Rules in the annotated format because many court opinions relied upon this language. The unabridged version of this supplement will continue to reproduce the 1990 Code of Judicial Conduct. These prior standards are included to facilitate study of the evolution of professional standards as well as cases and jurisdictions that rely on the prior rules. These two documents are contained in part eight of the unabridged edition.

The full edition contains the text of the sections in the Restatement of Law Governing Lawyers and selected Reporters Comments. This project continues to play a significant role in shaping the law of professional responsibility.

I welcome comments and suggestions on the materials contained in this edition. My E-mail address is jdzienkowski@law.utexas.edu.

PREFACE

The materials are current through May 2019, and this supplement will be updated annually to reflect new and amended statutes and rules.

JOHN S. DZIENKOWSKI

Austin, Texas
May 2019

TABLE OF CONTENTS

Page

PART ONE: CODES AND STANDARDS REGULATING LAWYERS' CONDUCT

PART TWO: CODES OF JUDICIAL CONDUCT

PART THREE: RULES OF EVIDENCE AND PROCEDURE THAT AFFECT THE LEGAL PROFESSION

PART FOUR: RESTATEMENT (THIRD) OF LAW GOVERNING LAWYERS

PART FIVE: STATUTES THAT AFFECT THE LEGAL PROFESSION

PART SIX: STANDARDS FOR SPECIALIZED AREAS OF PRACTICE

PART SEVEN: STANDARDS FOR THE ORGANIZED REGULATION OF LAWYERS

PROFESSIONAL RESPONSIBILITY

STANDARDS, RULES, AND STATUTES

2019–2020 Edition

PART ONE

CODES AND STANDARDS REGULATING LAWYERS' CONDUCT

Table of Contents

Introduction

One of the traditional characteristics of a profession is the attempt to achieve self regulation. Throughout history, professions have enacted codes of conduct to assert control over their members. Various groups within the legal profession have similarly sought to exercise a degree of self regulation by enacting codes of conduct. This part includes several codes and standards which have attempted to regulate the conduct of all lawyers in their practice of law.

The first three codes contained in this section were promulgated by the American Bar Association (ABA), a national voluntary organization of lawyers. The ABA has assumed the primary responsibility for promulgating national ethical standards for the legal profession. In 1908, the ABA enacted 32 Canons of Professional Ethics. Additional canons were added over the years. In 1969, it replaced the Canons with the Model Code of Professional Responsibility. In 1983, the Model Code was replaced with the Model Rules of Professional Conduct. The 1983 version was amended many times by the ABA House of Delegates until the year 2001. That version of the Model Rules is reproduced in the full version of this supplement in part eight.

In 1997, the ABA established an Ethics 2000 Committee to revise the Model Rules in light of developments in law and practice. The ABA House of Delegates adopted a series of revisions in February 2002 to reflect the Ethics 2000 project. In August 2002, the ABA adopted further changes to the Model Rules to reflect the work of the committee on multijurisdictional practice of law. In August 2003, the ABA amended Model Rules 1.6 and 1.13 to reflect the profession's concern for lawyer involvement in financial frauds.

In 2009, the ABA formed the Ethics 20/20 Commission that was charged with modernizing the Model Rules in light of changes in the legal professions around the world. The 20/20 Commission held many hearings and produced several working papers. However, in the end, the Commission produced only two rounds of relatively minor changes that the ABA House of Delegates adopted in 2012 and 2013. Thus, the Ethics 2000 revision of the Model Rules adopted in 2002 and 2003 remains the basis for the current ABA code. Since Ethics 20/20, the House of Delegates has amended the Model Rules several times to reflect changes in law practice and the profession.

Although the ABA's codes of conduct have been influential in shaping the law of professional responsibility, they only have force as a body of rules with its voluntary members. However, the various states and the federal courts have looked to the ABA versions as a basis for regulating lawyers within the jurisdiction. Thus, the ABA's codes have been used as the basis for state and federal codes. With the Model Code, many states adopted the ABA version without many significant changes. However, with the ABA's promulgation of the Model Rules, the states have been less deferential. Many states have made significant modifications to the ABA version. Thus, this part includes a section on significant state modifications to the Model Rules.

A final series of documents in this part reflect a recent trend on the part of the ABA and the states to focus on lawyer professionalism as a basis for regulating lawyers' conduct. The origin of this movement was a study on professionalism commissioned by the ABA. The results of the study identified several reasons for the decline in lawyer professionalism and offered several suggestions to address this problem. The ABA Creed of Professionalism and the ABA Pledge of Professionalism illustrate attempts to implement the suggestions of the Commission on Professionalism. The Texas Creed on Professionalism provides a similar example of a state effort to address this problem. The ABA's Aspirational Goals on Lawyer Advertising provide a more concrete example of urging standards of professionalism in the communication of advertising to the general public.

2019 AMERICAN BAR ASSOCIATION MODEL RULES OF PROFESSIONAL CONDUCT

Annotated to Include Amendments Up to February 2019

CONTENTS

PREAMBLE: A LAWYER'S RESPONSIBILITIES

[1] A lawyer, as a member of the legal profession, is a representative of clients, an officer of the legal system and a public citizen having special responsibility for the quality of justice.

[2] As a representative of clients, a lawyer performs various functions. As advisor, a lawyer provides a client with an informed understanding of the client's legal rights and obligations and explains their practical implications. As advocate, a lawyer zealously asserts the client's position under the rules of the adversary system. As negotiator, a lawyer seeks a result advantageous to the client but consistent with

requirements of honest dealings with others. As an evaluator, a lawyer acts by examining a client's legal affairs and reporting about them to the client or to others.

[3] In addition to these representational functions, a lawyer may serve as a third-party neutral, a nonrepresentational role helping the parties to resolve a dispute or other matter. Some of these Rules apply directly to lawyers who are or have served as third-party neutrals. See, e.g., Rules 1.12 and 2.4. In addition, there are Rules that apply to lawyers who are not active in the practice of law or to practicing lawyers even when they are acting in a nonprofessional capacity. For example, a lawyer who commits fraud in the conduct of a business is subject to discipline for engaging in conduct involving dishonesty, fraud, deceit or misrepresentation. See Rule 8.4.

[4] In all professional functions a lawyer should be competent, prompt and diligent. A lawyer should maintain communication with a client concerning the representation. A lawyer should keep in confidence information relating to representation of a client except so far as disclosure is required or permitted by the Rules of Professional Conduct or other law.

[5] A lawyer's conduct should conform to the requirements of the law, both in professional service to clients and in the lawyer's business and personal affairs. A lawyer should use the law's procedures only for legitimate purposes and not to harass or intimidate others. A lawyer should demonstrate respect for the legal system and for those who serve it, including judges, other lawyers and public officials. While it is a lawyer's duty, when necessary, to challenge the rectitude of official action, it is also a lawyer's duty to uphold legal process.

[6] As a public citizen, a lawyer should seek improvement of the law, access to the legal system, the administration of justice and the quality of service rendered by the legal profession. As a member of a learned profession, a lawyer should cultivate knowledge of the law beyond its use for clients, employ that knowledge in reform of the law and work to strengthen legal education. In addition, a lawyer should further the public's understanding of and confidence in the rule of law and the justice system because legal institutions in a constitutional democracy depend on popular participation and support to maintain their authority. A lawyer should be mindful of deficiencies in the administration of justice and of the fact that the poor, and sometimes persons who are not poor, cannot afford adequate legal assistance. Therefore, all lawyers should devote professional time and resources and use civic influence to ensure equal access to our system of justice for all those who because of economic or social barriers cannot afford or secure adequate legal counsel. A lawyer should aid the legal profession in pursuing these objectives and should help the bar regulate itself in the public interest.

[7] Many of a lawyer's professional responsibilities are prescribed in the Rules of Professional Conduct, as well as substantive and procedural law. However, a lawyer is also guided by personal conscience and the approbation of professional peers. A lawyer should strive to attain the highest level of skill, to improve the law and the legal profession and to exemplify the legal profession's ideals of public service.

[8] A lawyer's responsibilities as a representative of clients, an officer of the legal system and a public citizen are usually harmonious. Thus, when an opposing party is well represented, a lawyer can be a zealous advocate on behalf of a client and at the same time assume that justice is being done. So also, a lawyer can be sure that preserving client confidences ordinarily serves the public interest because people are more likely to seek legal advice, and thereby heed their legal obligations, when they know their communications will be private.

[9] In the nature of law practice, however, conflicting responsibilities are encountered. Virtually all difficult ethical problems arise from conflict between a lawyer's responsibilities to clients, to the legal system and to the lawyer's own interest in remaining an ethical person while earning a satisfactory living. The Rules of Professional Conduct often prescribe terms for resolving such conflicts. Within the framework of these Rules, however, many difficult issues of professional discretion can arise. Such issues must be resolved through the exercise of sensitive professional and moral judgment guided by the basic principles underlying the Rules. These principles include the lawyer's obligation zealously to protect and pursue a client's legitimate interests, within the bounds of the law, while maintaining a professional, courteous and civil attitude toward all persons involved in the legal system.

[10] The legal profession is largely self-governing. Although other professions also have been granted powers of self-government, the legal profession is unique in this respect because of the close relationship

between the profession and the processes of government and law enforcement. This connection is manifested in the fact that ultimate authority over the legal profession is vested largely in the courts.

[11] To the extent that lawyers meet the obligations of their professional calling, the occasion for government regulation is obviated. Self-regulation also helps maintain the legal profession's independence from government domination. An independent legal profession is an important force in preserving government under law, for abuse of legal authority is more readily challenged by a profession whose members are not dependent on government for the right to practice.

[12] The legal profession's relative autonomy carries with it special responsibilities of self-government. The profession has a responsibility to assure that its regulations are conceived in the public interest and not in furtherance of parochial or self-interested concerns of the bar. Every lawyer is responsible for observance of the Rules of Professional Conduct. A lawyer should also aid in securing their observance by other lawyers. Neglect of these responsibilities compromises the independence of the profession and the public interest which it serves.

[13] Lawyers play a vital role in the preservation of society. The fulfillment of this role requires an understanding by lawyers of their relationship to our legal system. The Rules of Professional Conduct, when properly applied, serve to define that relationship.

SCOPE

[14] The Rules of Professional Conduct are rules of reason. They should be interpreted with reference to the purposes of legal representation and of the law itself. Some of the Rules are imperatives, cast in the terms "shall" or "shall not." These define proper conduct for purposes of professional discipline. Others, generally cast in the term "may," are permissive and define areas under the Rules in which the lawyer has discretion to exercise professional judgment. No disciplinary action should be taken when the lawyer chooses not to act or acts within the bounds of such discretion. Other Rules define the nature of relationships between the lawyer and others. The Rules are thus partly obligatory and disciplinary and partly constitutive and descriptive in that they define a lawyer's professional role. Many of the Comments use the term "should." Comments do not add obligations to the Rules but provide guidance for practicing in compliance with the Rules.

[15] The Rules presuppose a larger legal context shaping the lawyer's role. That context includes court rules and statutes relating to matters of licensure, laws defining specific obligations of lawyers and substantive and procedural law in general. The Comments are sometimes used to alert lawyers to their responsibilities under such other law.

[16] Compliance with the Rules, as with all law in an open society, depends primarily upon understanding and voluntary compliance, secondarily upon reinforcement by peer and public opinion and finally, when necessary, upon enforcement through disciplinary proceedings. The Rules do not, however, exhaust the moral and ethical considerations that should inform a lawyer, for no worthwhile human activity can be completely defined by legal rules. The Rules simply provide a framework for the ethical practice of law.

[17] Furthermore, for purposes of determining the lawyer's authority and responsibility, principles of substantive law external to these Rules determine whether a client-lawyer relationship exists. Most of the duties flowing from the client-lawyer relationship attach only after the client has requested the lawyer to render legal services and the lawyer has agreed to do so. But there are some duties, such as that of confidentiality under Rule 1.6, that attach when the lawyer agrees to consider whether a client-lawyer relationship shall be established. See Rule 1.18. Whether a client-lawyer relationship exists for any specific purpose can depend on the circumstances and may be a question of fact.

[18] Under various legal provisions, including constitutional, statutory and common law, the responsibilities of government lawyers may include authority concerning legal matters that ordinarily reposes in the client in private client-lawyer relationships. For example, a lawyer for a government agency may have authority on behalf of the government to decide upon settlement or whether to appeal from an adverse judgment. Such authority in various respects is generally vested in the attorney general and the state's attorney in state government, and their federal counterparts, and the same may be true of other government law officers. Also, lawyers under the supervision of these officers may be authorized to represent

several government agencies in intragovernmental legal controversies in circumstances where a private lawyer could not represent multiple private clients. These Rules do not abrogate any such authority.

[19] Failure to comply with an obligation or prohibition imposed by a Rule is a basis for invoking the disciplinary process. The Rules presuppose that disciplinary assessment of a lawyer's conduct will be made on the basis of the facts and circumstances as they existed at the time of the conduct in question and in recognition of the fact that a lawyer often has to act upon uncertain or incomplete evidence of the situation. Moreover, the Rules presuppose that whether or not discipline should be imposed for a violation, and the severity of a sanction, depend on all the circumstances, such as the willfulness and seriousness of the violation, extenuating factors and whether there have been previous violations.

[20] Violation of a Rule should not itself give rise to a cause of action against a lawyer nor should it create any presumption in such a case that a legal duty has been breached. In addition, violation of a Rule does not necessarily warrant any other nondisciplinary remedy, such as disqualification of a lawyer in pending litigation. The Rules are designed to provide guidance to lawyers and to provide a structure for regulating conduct through disciplinary agencies. They are not designed to be a basis for civil liability. Furthermore, the purpose of the Rules can be subverted when they are invoked by opposing parties as procedural weapons. The fact that a Rule is a just basis for a lawyer's self-assessment, or for sanctioning a lawyer under the administration of a disciplinary authority, does not imply that an antagonist in a collateral proceeding or transaction has standing to seek enforcement of the Rule. Nevertheless, since the Rules do establish standards of conduct by lawyers, a lawyer's violation of a Rule may be evidence of breach of the applicable standard of conduct.

[21] The Comment accompanying each Rule explains and illustrates the meaning and purpose of the Rule. The Preamble and this note on Scope provide general orientation. The Comments are intended as guides to interpretation, but the text of each Rule is authoritative.

CLIENT-LAWYER RELATIONSHIP

Rule 1.0 Terminology

(a) "Belief" or "believes" denotes that the person involved actually supposed the fact in question to be true. A person's belief may be inferred from circumstances.

(b) "Confirmed in writing," when used in reference to the informed consent of a person, denotes informed consent that is given in writing by the person or a writing that a lawyer promptly transmits to the person confirming an oral informed consent. See paragraph (e) for the definition of "informed consent." If it is not feasible to obtain or transmit the writing at the time the person gives informed consent, then the lawyer must obtain or transmit it within a reasonable time thereafter.

(c) "Firm" or "law firm" denotes a lawyer or lawyers in a law partnership, professional corporation, sole proprietorship or other association authorized to practice law; or lawyers employed in a legal services organization or the legal department of a corporation or other organization.

(d) "Fraud" or "fraudulent" denotes conduct that is fraudulent under the substantive or procedural law of the applicable jurisdiction and has a purpose to deceive.

(e) "Informed consent" denotes the agreement by a person to a proposed course of conduct after the lawyer has communicated adequate information and explanation about the material risks of and reasonably available alternatives to the proposed course of conduct.

(f) "Knowingly," "known," or "knows" denotes actual knowledge of the fact in question. A person's knowledge may be inferred from circumstances.

(g) "Partner" denotes a member of a partnership, a shareholder in a law firm organized as a professional corporation, or a member of an association authorized to practice law.

(h) "Reasonable" or "reasonably" when used in relation to conduct by a lawyer denotes the conduct of a reasonably prudent and competent lawyer.

(i) "Reasonable belief" or "reasonably believes" when used in reference to a lawyer denotes that the lawyer believes the matter in question and that the circumstances are such that the belief is reasonable.

(j) "Reasonably should know" when used in reference to a lawyer denotes that a lawyer of reasonable prudence and competence would ascertain the matter in question.

(k) "Screened" denotes the isolation of a lawyer from any participation in a matter through the timely imposition of procedures within a firm that are reasonably adequate under the circumstances to protect information that the isolated lawyer is obligated to protect under these Rules or other law.

(*l*) "Substantial" when used in reference to degree or extent denotes a material matter of clear and weighty importance.

(m) "Tribunal" denotes a court, an arbitrator in a binding arbitration proceeding or a legislative body, administrative agency or other body acting in an adjudicative capacity. A legislative body, administrative agency or other body acts in an adjudicative capacity when a neutral official, after the presentation of evidence or legal argument by a party or parties, will render a binding legal judgment directly affecting a party's interests in a particular matter.

***(n) "Writing" or "written" denotes a tangible or electronic record of a communication or representation, including handwriting, typewriting, printing, photostating, photography, audio or videorecording and electronic communications. A "signed" writing includes an electronic sound, symbol or process attached to or logically associated with a writing and executed or adopted by a person with the intent to sign the writing.**

COMMENT

Confirmed in Writing

[1] If it is not feasible to obtain or transmit a written confirmation at the time the client gives informed consent, then the lawyer must obtain or transmit it within a reasonable time thereafter. If a lawyer has obtained a client's informed consent, the lawyer may act in reliance on that consent so long as it is confirmed in writing within a reasonable time thereafter.

Firm

[2] Whether two or more lawyers constitute a firm within paragraph (c) can depend on the specific facts. For example, two practitioners who share office space and occasionally consult or assist each other ordinarily would not be regarded as constituting a firm. However, if they present themselves to the public in a way that suggests that they are a firm or conduct themselves as a firm, they should be regarded as a firm for purposes of the Rules. The terms of any formal agreement between associated lawyers are relevant in determining whether they are a firm, as is the fact that they have mutual access to information concerning the clients they serve. Furthermore, it is relevant in doubtful cases to consider the underlying purpose of the Rule that is involved. A group of lawyers could be regarded as a firm for purposes of the Rule that the same lawyer should not represent opposing parties in litigation, while it might not be so regarded for purposes of the Rule that information acquired by one lawyer is attributed to another.

[3] With respect to the law department of an organization, including the government, there is ordinarily no question that the members of the department constitute a firm within the meaning of the Rules of Professional Conduct. There can be uncertainty, however, as to the identity of the client. For example, it may not be clear whether the law department of a corporation represents a subsidiary or an

* In August 2012, the ABA House of Delegates amended this provision to change the word "e-mail" to "electronic communications."

ffiliated corporation, as well as the corporation by which the members of the department are directly mployed. A similar question can arise concerning an unincorporated association and its local affiliates.

[4] Similar questions can also arise with respect to lawyers in legal aid and legal services rganizations. Depending upon the structure of the organization, the entire organization or different omponents of it may constitute a firm or firms for purposes of these Rules.

Fraud

[5] When used in these Rules, the terms "fraud" or "fraudulent" refer to conduct that is characterized as such under the substantive or procedural law of the applicable jurisdiction and has a purpose to deceive. This does not include merely negligent misrepresentation or negligent failure to apprise another of relevant nformation. For purposes of these Rules, it is not necessary that anyone has suffered damages or relied on the misrepresentation or failure to inform.

Informed Consent

[6] Many of the Rules of Professional Conduct require the lawyer to obtain the informed consent of a client or other person (e.g., a former client or, under certain circumstances, a prospective client) before accepting or continuing representation or pursuing a course of conduct. See, e.g., Rules 1.2(c), 1.6(a) and 1.7(b). The communication necessary to obtain such consent will vary according to the Rule involved and the circumstances giving rise to the need to obtain informed consent. The lawyer must make reasonable efforts to ensure that the client or other person possesses information reasonably adequate to make an informed decision. Ordinarily, this will require communication that includes a disclosure of the facts and circumstances giving rise to the situation, any explanation reasonably necessary to inform the client or other person of the material advantages and disadvantages of the proposed course of conduct and a discussion of the client's or other person's options and alternatives. In some circumstances it may be appropriate for a lawyer to advise a client or other person to seek the advice of other counsel. A lawyer need not inform a client or other person of facts or implications already known to the client or other person; nevertheless, a lawyer who does not personally inform the client or other person assumes the risk that the client or other person is inadequately informed and the consent is invalid. In determining whether the information and explanation provided are reasonably adequate, relevant factors include whether the client or other person is experienced in legal matters generally and in making decisions of the type involved, and whether the client or other person is independently represented by other counsel in giving the consent. Normally, such persons need less information and explanation than others, and generally a client or other person who is independently represented by other counsel in giving the consent should be assumed to have given informed consent.

[7] Obtaining informed consent will usually require an affirmative response by the client or other person. In general, a lawyer may not assume consent from a client's or other person's silence. Consent may be inferred, however, from the conduct of a client or other person who has reasonably adequate information about the matter. A number of Rules require that a person's consent be confirmed in writing. See Rules 1.7(b) and 1.9(a). For a definition of "writing" and "confirmed in writing," see paragraphs (n) and (b). Other Rules require that a client's consent be obtained in a writing signed by the client. See, e.g., Rules 1.8(a) and (g). For a definition of "signed," see paragraph (n).

Screened

[8] This definition applies to situations where screening of a personally disqualified lawyer is permitted to remove imputation of a conflict of interest under Rules 1.10, 1.11, 1.12 or 1.18.

*[9] The purpose of screening is to assure the affected parties that confidential information known by the personally disqualified lawyer remains protected. The personally disqualified lawyer should acknowledge the obligation not to communicate with any of the other lawyers in the firm with respect to the matter. Similarly, other lawyers in the firm who are working on the matter should be informed that the screening is in place and that they may not communicate with the personally disqualified lawyer with respect to the matter. Additional screening measures that are appropriate for the particular matter will depend on the circumstances. To implement, reinforce and remind all affected lawyers of the presence of the

* In August 2012, the ABA House of Delegates amended this comment to change the word "materials" to the phrase "information, including information in electronic form."

screening, it may be appropriate for the firm to undertake such procedures as a written undertaking by th screened lawyer to avoid any communication with other firm personnel and any contact with any firm file or other information, including information in electronic form, relating to the matter, written notice an instructions to all other firm personnel forbidding any communication with the screened lawyer relating t the matter, denial of access by the screened lawyer to firm files or other information, including informatio in electronic form, relating to the matter and periodic reminders of the screen to the screened lawyer an all other firm personnel.

[10] In order to be effective, screening measures must be implemented as soon as practical after a lawyer or law firm knows or reasonably should know that there is a need for screening.

Rule 1.1 Competence

A lawyer shall provide competent representation to a client. Competent representation requires the legal knowledge, skill, thoroughness and preparation reasonably necessary for the representation.

COMMENT

Legal Knowledge and Skill

[1] In determining whether a lawyer employs the requisite knowledge and skill in a particular matter, relevant factors include the relative complexity and specialized nature of the matter, the lawyer's general experience, the lawyer's training and experience in the field in question, the preparation and study the lawyer is able to give the matter and whether it is feasible to refer the matter to, or associate or consult with, a lawyer of established competence in the field in question. In many instances, the required proficiency is that of a general practitioner. Expertise in a particular field of law may be required in some circumstances.

[2] A lawyer need not necessarily have special training or prior experience to handle legal problems of a type with which the lawyer is unfamiliar. A newly admitted lawyer can be as competent as a practitioner with long experience. Some important legal skills, such as the analysis of precedent, the evaluation of evidence and legal drafting, are required in all legal problems. Perhaps the most fundamental legal skill consists of determining what kind of legal problems a situation may involve, a skill that necessarily transcends any particular specialized knowledge. A lawyer can provide adequate representation in a wholly novel field through necessary study. Competent representation can also be provided through the association of a lawyer of established competence in the field in question.

[3] In an emergency a lawyer may give advice or assistance in a matter in which the lawyer does not have the skill ordinarily required where referral to or consultation or association with another lawyer would be impractical. Even in an emergency, however, assistance should be limited to that reasonably necessary in the circumstances, for ill-considered action under emergency conditions can jeopardize the client's interest.

[4] A lawyer may accept representation where the requisite level of competence can be achieved by reasonable preparation. This applies as well to a lawyer who is appointed as counsel for an unrepresented person. See also Rule 6.2.

Thoroughness and Preparation

[5] Competent handling of a particular matter includes inquiry into and analysis of the factual and legal elements of the problem, and use of methods and procedures meeting the standards of competent practitioners. It also includes adequate preparation. The required attention and preparation are determined in part by what is at stake; major litigation and complex transactions ordinarily require more extensive treatment than matters of lesser complexity and consequence. An agreement between the lawyer and the client regarding the scope of the representation may limit the matters for which the lawyer is responsible. See Rule 1.2(c).

Retaining or Contracting With Other Lawyers*

[6] Before a lawyer retains or contracts with other lawyers outside the lawyer's own firm to provide or assist in the provision of legal services to a client, the lawyer should ordinarily obtain informed consent from the client and must reasonably believe that the other lawyers' services will contribute to the competent and ethical representation of the client. See also Rules 1.2 (allocation of authority), 1.4 (communication with client), 1.5(e) (fee sharing), 1.6 (confidentiality), and 5.5(a) (unauthorized practice of law). The reasonableness of the decision to retain or contract with other lawyers outside the lawyer's own firm will depend upon the circumstances, including the education, experience and reputation of the nonfirm lawyers; the nature of the services assigned to the nonfirm lawyers; and the legal protections, professional conduct rules, and ethical environments of the jurisdictions in which the services will be performed, particularly relating to confidential information.

[7] When lawyers from more than one law firm are providing legal services to the client on a particular matter, the lawyers ordinarily should consult with each other and the client about the scope of their respective representations and the allocation of responsibility among them. See Rule 1.2. When making allocations of responsibility in a matter pending before a tribunal, lawyers and parties may have additional obligations that are a matter of law beyond the scope of these Rules.

Maintaining Competence**

[8] To maintain the requisite knowledge and skill, a lawyer should keep abreast of changes in the law and its practice, including the benefits and risks associated with relevant technology, engage in continuing study and education and comply with all continuing legal education requirements to which the lawyer is subject.

Rule 1.2 Scope of Representation and Allocation of Authority Between Lawyer and Client

(a) Subject to paragraphs (c) and (d), a lawyer shall abide by a client's decisions concerning the objectives of representation and, as required by Rule 1.4, shall consult with the client as to the means by which they are to be pursued. A lawyer may take such action on behalf of the client as is impliedly authorized to carry out the representation. A lawyer shall abide by a client's decision whether to settle a matter. In a criminal case, the lawyer shall abide by the client's decision, after consultation with the lawyer, as to a plea to be entered, whether to waive jury trial and whether the client will testify.

(b) A lawyer's representation of a client, including representation by appointment, does not constitute an endorsement of the client's political, economic, social or moral views or activities.

(c) A lawyer may limit the scope of the representation if the limitation is reasonable under the circumstances and the client gives informed consent.

(d) A lawyer shall not counsel a client to engage, or assist a client, in conduct that the lawyer knows is criminal or fraudulent, but a lawyer may discuss the legal consequences of any proposed course of conduct with a client and may counsel or assist a client to make a good faith effort to determine the validity, scope, meaning or application of the law.

COMMENT

Allocation of Authority between Client and Lawyer

[1] Paragraph (a) confers upon the client the ultimate authority to determine the purposes to be served by legal representation, within the limits imposed by law and the lawyer's professional obligations. The decisions specified in paragraph (a), such as whether to settle a civil matter, must also be made by the

---

* In August 2012, the ABA House of Delegates added new Comments 6 and 7 to address the issue of outsourcing of work to lawyers and nonlawyers outside of the law firm.

** In August 2012, the ABA House of Delegates renumbered Comment 6 as Comment 8 and added a clause to require lawyers to keep abreast of relevant technology.

client. See Rule 1.4(a)(1) for the lawyer's duty to communicate with the client about such decisions. With respect to the means by which the client's objectives are to be pursued, the lawyer shall consult with the client as required by Rule 1.4(a)(2) and may take such action as is impliedly authorized to carry out the representation.

[2] On occasion, however, a lawyer and a client may disagree about the means to be used to accomplish the client's objectives. Clients normally defer to the special knowledge and skill of their lawyer with respect to the means to be used to accomplish their objectives, particularly with respect to technical, legal and tactical matters. Conversely, lawyers usually defer to the client regarding such questions as the expense to be incurred and concern for third persons who might be adversely affected. Because of the varied nature of the matters about which a lawyer and client might disagree and because the actions in question may implicate the interests of a tribunal or other persons, this Rule does not prescribe how such disagreements are to be resolved. Other law, however, may be applicable and should be consulted by the lawyer. The lawyer should also consult with the client and seek a mutually acceptable resolution of the disagreement. If such efforts are unavailing and the lawyer has a fundamental disagreement with the client, the lawyer may withdraw from the representation. See Rule 1.16(b)(4). Conversely, the client may resolve the disagreement by discharging the lawyer. See Rule 1.16(a)(3).

[3] At the outset of a representation, the client may authorize the lawyer to take specific action on the client's behalf without further consultation. Absent a material change in circumstances and subject to Rule 1.4, a lawyer may rely on such an advance authorization. The client may, however, revoke such authority at any time.

[4] In a case in which the client appears to be suffering diminished capacity, the lawyer's duty to abide by the client's decisions is to be guided by reference to Rule 1.14.

Independence from Client's Views or Activities

[5] Legal representation should not be denied to people who are unable to afford legal services, or whose cause is controversial or the subject of popular disapproval. By the same token, representing a client does not constitute approval of the client's views or activities.

Agreements Limiting Scope of Representation

[6] The scope of services to be provided by a lawyer may be limited by agreement with the client or by the terms under which the lawyer's services are made available to the client. When a lawyer has been retained by an insurer to represent an insured, for example, the representation may be limited to matters related to the insurance coverage. A limited representation may be appropriate because the client has limited objectives for the representation. In addition, the terms upon which representation is undertaken may exclude specific means that might otherwise be used to accomplish the client's objectives. Such limitations may exclude actions that the client thinks are too costly or that the lawyer regards as repugnant or imprudent.

[7] Although this Rule affords the lawyer and client substantial latitude to limit the representation, the limitation must be reasonable under the circumstances. If, for example, a client's objective is limited to securing general information about the law the client needs in order to handle a common and typically uncomplicated legal problem, the lawyer and client may agree that the lawyer's services will be limited to a brief telephone consultation. Such a limitation, however, would not be reasonable if the time allotted was not sufficient to yield advice upon which the client could rely. Although an agreement for a limited representation does not exempt a lawyer from the duty to provide competent representation, the limitation is a factor to be considered when determining the legal knowledge, skill, thoroughness and preparation reasonably necessary for the representation. See Rule 1.1.

[8] All agreements concerning a lawyer's representation of a client must accord with the Rules of Professional Conduct and other law. See, e.g., Rules 1.1, 1.8 and 5.6.

Criminal, Fraudulent and Prohibited Transactions

[9] Paragraph (d) prohibits a lawyer from knowingly counseling or assisting a client to commit a crime or fraud. This prohibition, however, does not preclude the lawyer from giving an honest opinion about the actual consequences that appear likely to result from a client's conduct. Nor does the fact that a client uses advice in a course of action that is criminal or fraudulent of itself make a lawyer a party to the course

of action. There is a critical distinction between presenting an analysis of legal aspects of questionable conduct and recommending the means by which a crime or fraud might be committed with impunity.

[10] When the client's course of action has already begun and is continuing, the lawyer's responsibility is especially delicate. The lawyer is required to avoid assisting the client, for example, by drafting or delivering documents that the lawyer knows are fraudulent or by suggesting how the wrongdoing might be concealed. A lawyer may not continue assisting a client in conduct that the lawyer originally supposed was legally proper but then discovers is criminal or fraudulent. The lawyer must, therefore, withdraw from the representation of the client in the matter. See Rule 1.16(a). In some cases, withdrawal alone might be insufficient. It may be necessary for the lawyer to give notice of the fact of withdrawal and to disaffirm any opinion, document, affirmation or the like. See Rule 4.1.

[11] Where the client is a fiduciary, the lawyer may be charged with special obligations in dealings with a beneficiary.

[12] Paragraph (d) applies whether or not the defrauded party is a party to the transaction. Hence, a lawyer must not participate in a transaction to effectuate criminal or fraudulent avoidance of tax liability. Paragraph (d) does not preclude undertaking a criminal defense incident to a general retainer for legal services to a lawful enterprise. The last clause of paragraph (d) recognizes that determining the validity or interpretation of a statute or regulation may require a course of action involving disobedience of the statute or regulation or of the interpretation placed upon it by governmental authorities.

[13] If a lawyer comes to know or reasonably should know that a client expects assistance not permitted by the Rules of Professional Conduct or other law or if the lawyer intends to act contrary to the client's instructions, the lawyer must consult with the client regarding the limitations on the lawyer's conduct. See Rule 1.4(a)(5).

Rule 1.3 Diligence

A lawyer shall act with reasonable diligence and promptness in representing a client.

COMMENT

[1] A lawyer should pursue a matter on behalf of a client despite opposition, obstruction or personal inconvenience to the lawyer, and take whatever lawful and ethical measures are required to vindicate a client's cause or endeavor. A lawyer must also act with commitment and dedication to the interests of the client and with zeal in advocacy upon the client's behalf. A lawyer is not bound, however, to press for every advantage that might be realized for a client. For example, a lawyer may have authority to exercise professional discretion in determining the means by which a matter should be pursued. See Rule 1.2. The lawyer's duty to act with reasonable diligence does not require the use of offensive tactics or preclude the treating of all persons involved in the legal process with courtesy and respect.

[2] A lawyer's work load must be controlled so that each matter can be handled competently.

[3] Perhaps no professional shortcoming is more widely resented than procrastination. A client's interests often can be adversely affected by the passage of time or the change of conditions; in extreme instances, as when a lawyer overlooks a statute of limitations, the client's legal position may be destroyed. Even when the client's interests are not affected in substance, however, unreasonable delay can cause a client needless anxiety and undermine confidence in the lawyer's trustworthiness. A lawyer's duty to act with reasonable promptness, however, does not preclude the lawyer from agreeing to a reasonable request for a postponement that will not prejudice the lawyer's client.

[4] Unless the relationship is terminated as provided in Rule 1.16, a lawyer should carry through to conclusion all matters undertaken for a client. If a lawyer's employment is limited to a specific matter, the relationship terminates when the matter has been resolved. If a lawyer has served a client over a substantial period in a variety of matters, the client sometimes may assume that the lawyer will continue to serve on a continuing basis unless the lawyer gives notice of withdrawal. Doubt about whether a client-lawyer relationship still exists should be clarified by the lawyer, preferably in writing, so that the client will not mistakenly suppose the lawyer is looking after the client's affairs when the lawyer has ceased to do so. For example, if a lawyer has handled a judicial or administrative proceeding that produced a result adverse to the client and the lawyer and the client have not agreed that the lawyer will handle the matter on appeal,

the lawyer must consult with the client about the possibility of appeal before relinquishing responsibility for the matter. See Rule 1.4(a)(2). Whether the lawyer is obligated to prosecute the appeal for the client depends on the scope of the representation the lawyer has agreed to provide to the client. See Rule 1.2.

[5] To prevent neglect of client matters in the event of a sole practitioner's death or disability, the duty of diligence may require that each sole practitioner prepare a plan, in conformity with applicable rules, that designates another competent lawyer to review client files, notify each client of the lawyer's death or disability, and determine whether there is a need for immediate protective action. Cf. Rule 28 of the American Bar Association Model Rules for Lawyer Disciplinary Enforcement (providing for court appointment of a lawyer to inventory files and take other protective action in absence of a plan providing for another lawyer to protect the interests of the clients of a deceased or disabled lawyer).

Rule 1.4 Communication

(a) A lawyer shall:

(1) promptly inform the client of any decision or circumstance with respect to which the client's informed consent, as defined in Rule 1.0(e), is required by these Rules;

(2) reasonably consult with the client about the means by which the client's objectives are to be accomplished;

(3) keep the client reasonably informed about the status of the matter;

(4) promptly comply with reasonable requests for information; and

(5) consult with the client about any relevant limitation on the lawyer's conduct when the lawyer knows that the client expects assistance not permitted by the Rules of Professional Conduct or other law.

(b) A lawyer shall explain a matter to the extent reasonably necessary to permit the client to make informed decisions regarding the representation.

COMMENT

[1] Reasonable communication between the lawyer and the client is necessary for the client effectively to participate in the representation.

Communicating with Client

[2] If these Rules require that a particular decision about the representation be made by the client, paragraph (a)(1) requires that the lawyer promptly consult with and secure the client's consent prior to taking action unless prior discussions with the client have resolved what action the client wants the lawyer to take. For example, a lawyer who receives from opposing counsel an offer of settlement in a civil controversy or a proffered plea bargain in a criminal case must promptly inform the client of its substance unless the client has previously indicated that the proposal will be acceptable or unacceptable or has authorized the lawyer to accept or to reject the offer. See Rule 1.2(a).

[3] Paragraph (a)(2) requires the lawyer to reasonably consult with the client about the means to be used to accomplish the client's objectives. In some situations—depending on both the importance of the action under consideration and the feasibility of consulting with the client—this duty will require consultation prior to taking action. In other circumstances, such as during a trial when an immediate decision must be made, the exigency of the situation may require the lawyer to act without prior consultation. In such cases the lawyer must nonetheless act reasonably to inform the client of actions the lawyer has taken on the client's behalf. Additionally, paragraph (a)(3) requires that the lawyer keep the client reasonably informed about the status of the matter, such as significant developments affecting the timing or the substance of the representation.

*[4] A lawyer's regular communication with clients will minimize the occasions on which a client will need to request information concerning the representation. When a client makes a reasonable request for information, however, paragraph (a)(4) requires prompt compliance with the request, or if a prompt response is not feasible, that the lawyer, or a member of the lawyer's staff, acknowledge receipt of the request and advise the client when a response may be expected. A lawyer should promptly respond to or acknowledge client communications.

Explaining Matters

[5] The client should have sufficient information to participate intelligently in decisions concerning the objectives of the representation and the means by which they are to be pursued, to the extent the client is willing and able to do so. Adequacy of communication depends in part on the kind of advice or assistance that is involved. For example, when there is time to explain a proposal made in a negotiation, the lawyer should review all important provisions with the client before proceeding to an agreement. In litigation a lawyer should explain the general strategy and prospects of success and ordinarily should consult the client on tactics that are likely to result in significant expense or to injure or coerce others. On the other hand, a lawyer ordinarily will not be expected to describe trial or negotiation strategy in detail. The guiding principle is that the lawyer should fulfill reasonable client expectations for information consistent with the duty to act in the client's best interests, and the client's overall requirements as to the character of representation. In certain circumstances, such as when a lawyer asks a client to consent to a representation affected by a conflict of interest, the client must give informed consent, as defined in Rule 1.0(e).

[6] Ordinarily, the information to be provided is that appropriate for a client who is a comprehending and responsible adult. However, fully informing the client according to this standard may be impracticable, for example, where the client is a child or suffers from diminished capacity. See Rule 1.14. When the client is an organization or group, it is often impossible or inappropriate to inform every one of its members about its legal affairs; ordinarily, the lawyer should address communications to the appropriate officials of the organization. See Rule 1.13. Where many routine matters are involved, a system of limited or occasional reporting may be arranged with the client.

Withholding Information

[7] In some circumstances, a lawyer may be justified in delaying transmission of information when the client would be likely to react imprudently to an immediate communication. Thus, a lawyer might withhold a psychiatric diagnosis of a client when the examining psychiatrist indicates that disclosure would harm the client. A lawyer may not withhold information to serve the lawyer's own interest or convenience or the interests or convenience of another person. Rules or court orders governing litigation may provide that information supplied to a lawyer may not be disclosed to the client. Rule 3.4(c) directs compliance with such rules or orders.

Rule 1.5 Fees

(a) A lawyer shall not make an agreement for, charge, or collect an unreasonable fee or an unreasonable amount for expenses. The factors to be considered in determining the reasonableness of a fee include the following:

(1) the time and labor required, the novelty and difficulty of the questions involved, and the skill requisite to perform the legal service properly;

(2) the likelihood, if apparent to the client, that the acceptance of the particular employment will preclude other employment by the lawyer;

(3) the fee customarily charged in the locality for similar legal services;

(4) the amount involved and the results obtained;

(5) the time limitations imposed by the client or by the circumstances;

---

* In August 2012, the ABA House of Delegates deleted a line referring to a duty to return or acknowledge client telephone calls and added a line referring to client communications.

(6) the nature and length of the professional relationship with the client;

(7) the experience, reputation, and ability of the lawyer or lawyers performing the services; and

(8) whether the fee is fixed or contingent.

(b) The scope of the representation and the basis or rate of the fee and expenses for which the client will be responsible shall be communicated to the client, preferably in writing, before or within a reasonable time after commencing the representation, except when the lawyer will charge a regularly represented client on the same basis or rate. Any changes in the basis or rate of the fee or expenses shall also be communicated to the client.

(c) A fee may be contingent on the outcome of the matter for which the service is rendered, except in a matter in which a contingent fee is prohibited by paragraph (d) or other law. A contingent fee agreement shall be in a writing signed by the client and shall state the method by which the fee is to be determined, including the percentage or percentages that shall accrue to the lawyer in the event of settlement, trial or appeal; litigation and other expenses to be deducted from the recovery; and whether such expenses are to be deducted before or after the contingent fee is calculated. The agreement must clearly notify the client of any expenses for which the client will be liable whether or not the client is the prevailing party. Upon conclusion of a contingent fee matter, the lawyer shall provide the client with a written statement stating the outcome of the matter and, if there is a recovery, showing the remittance to the client and the method of its determination.

(d) A lawyer shall not enter into an arrangement for, charge, or collect:

(1) any fee in a domestic relations matter, the payment or amount of which is contingent upon the securing of a divorce or upon the amount of alimony or support, or property settlement in lieu thereof; or

(2) a contingent fee for representing a defendant in a criminal case.

(e) A division of a fee between lawyers who are not in the same firm may be made only if:

(1) the division is in proportion to the services performed by each lawyer or each lawyer assumes joint responsibility for the representation;

(2) the client agrees to the arrangement, including the share each lawyer will receive, and the agreement is confirmed in writing; and

(3) the total fee is reasonable.

COMMENT

Reasonableness of Fee and Expenses

[1] Paragraph (a) requires that lawyers charge fees that are reasonable under the circumstances. The factors specified in (1) through (8) are not exclusive. Nor will each factor be relevant in each instance. Paragraph (a) also requires that expenses for which the client will be charged must be reasonable. A lawyer may seek reimbursement for the cost of services performed in-house, such as copying, or for other expenses incurred in-house, such as telephone charges, either by charging a reasonable amount to which the client has agreed in advance or by charging an amount that reasonably reflects the cost incurred by the lawyer.

Basis or Rate of Fee

[2] When the lawyer has regularly represented a client, they ordinarily will have evolved an understanding concerning the basis or rate of the fee and the expenses for which the client will be responsible. In a new client-lawyer relationship, however, an understanding as to fees and expenses must be promptly established. Generally, it is desirable to furnish the client with at least a simple memorandum or copy of the lawyer's customary fee arrangements that states the general nature of the legal services to be

provided, the basis, rate or total amount of the fee and whether and to what extent the client will be responsible for any costs, expenses or disbursements in the course of the representation. A written statement concerning the terms of the engagement reduces the possibility of misunderstanding.

[3] Contingent fees, like any other fees, are subject to the reasonableness standard of paragraph (a) of this Rule. In determining whether a particular contingent fee is reasonable, or whether it is reasonable to charge any form of contingent fee, a lawyer must consider the factors that are relevant under the circumstances. Applicable law may impose limitations on contingent fees, such as a ceiling on the percentage allowable, or may require a lawyer to offer clients an alternative basis for the fee. Applicable law also may apply to situations other than a contingent fee, for example, government regulations regarding fees in certain tax matters.

Terms of Payment

[4] A lawyer may require advance payment of a fee, but is obliged to return any unearned portion. See Rule 1.16(d). A lawyer may accept property in payment for services, such as an ownership interest in an enterprise, providing this does not involve acquisition of a proprietary interest in the cause of action or subject matter of the litigation contrary to Rule 1.8(i). However, a fee paid in property instead of money may be subject to the requirements of Rule 1.8(a) because such fees often have the essential qualities of a business transaction with the client.

[5] An agreement may not be made whose terms might induce the lawyer improperly to curtail services for the client or perform them in a way contrary to the client's interest. For example, a lawyer should not enter into an agreement whereby services are to be provided only up to a stated amount when it is foreseeable that more extensive services probably will be required, unless the situation is adequately explained to the client. Otherwise, the client might have to bargain for further assistance in the midst of a proceeding or transaction. However, it is proper to define the extent of services in light of the client's ability to pay. A lawyer should not exploit a fee arrangement based primarily on hourly charges by using wasteful procedures.

Prohibited Contingent Fees

[6] Paragraph (d) prohibits a lawyer from charging a contingent fee in a domestic relations matter when payment is contingent upon the securing of a divorce or upon the amount of alimony or support or property settlement to be obtained. This provision does not preclude a contract for a contingent fee for legal representation in connection with the recovery of post-judgment balances due under support, alimony or other financial orders because such contracts do not implicate the same policy concerns.

Division of Fee

[7] A division of fee is a single billing to a client covering the fee of two or more lawyers who are not in the same firm. A division of fee facilitates association of more than one lawyer in a matter in which neither alone could serve the client as well, and most often is used when the fee is contingent and the division is between a referring lawyer and a trial specialist. Paragraph (e) permits the lawyers to divide a fee either on the basis of the proportion of services they render or if each lawyer assumes responsibility for the representation as a whole. In addition, the client must agree to the arrangement, including the share that each lawyer is to receive, and the agreement must be confirmed in writing. Contingent fee agreements must be in a writing signed by the client and must otherwise comply with paragraph (c) of this Rule. Joint responsibility for the representation entails financial and ethical responsibility for the representation as if the lawyers were associated in a partnership. A lawyer should only refer a matter to a lawyer whom the referring lawyer reasonably believes is competent to handle the matter. See Rule 1.1.

[8] Paragraph (e) does not prohibit or regulate division of fees to be received in the future for work done when lawyers were previously associated in a law firm.

Disputes over Fees

[9] If a procedure has been established for resolution of fee disputes, such as an arbitration or mediation procedure established by the bar, the lawyer must comply with the procedure when it is mandatory, and, even when it is voluntary, the lawyer should conscientiously consider submitting to it. Law may prescribe a procedure for determining a lawyer's fee, for example, in representation of an executor or administrator, a class or a person entitled to a reasonable fee as part of the measure of damages. The lawyer

entitled to such a fee and a lawyer representing another party concerned with the fee should comply with the prescribed procedure.

Rule 1.6 Confidentiality of Information*

(a) A lawyer shall not reveal information relating to the representation of a client unless the client gives informed consent, the disclosure is impliedly authorized in order to carry out the representation or the disclosure is permitted by paragraph (b).

(b) A lawyer may reveal information relating to the representation of a client to the extent the lawyer reasonably believes necessary:

(1) to prevent reasonably certain death or substantial bodily harm;

(2) to prevent the client from committing a crime or fraud that is reasonably certain to result in substantial injury to the financial interests or property of another and in furtherance of which the client has used or is using the lawyer's services;

(3) to prevent, mitigate or rectify substantial injury to the financial interests or property of another that is reasonably certain to result or has resulted from the client's commission of a crime or fraud in furtherance of which the client has used the lawyer's services;

(4) to secure legal advice about the lawyer's compliance with these Rules;

(5) to establish a claim or defense on behalf of the lawyer in a controversy between the lawyer and the client, to establish a defense to a criminal charge or civil claim against the lawyer based upon conduct in which the client was involved, or to respond to allegations in any proceeding concerning the lawyer's representation of the client; or

(6) to comply with other law or a court order; or

(7) to detect and resolve conflicts of interest arising from the lawyer's change of employment or from changes in the composition or ownership of a firm, but only if the revealed information would not compromise the attorney-client privilege or otherwise prejudice the client.

(c) A lawyer shall make reasonable efforts to prevent the inadvertent or unauthorized disclosure of, or unauthorized access to, information relating to the representation of a client.

COMMENT

[1] This Rule governs the disclosure by a lawyer of information relating to the representation of a client during the lawyer's representation of the client. See Rule 1.18 for the lawyer's duties with respect to

---

* In August 2003, the ABA House of Delegates modified Model Rule 1.6 by adding new (b)(2) and (b)(3) and modifying some corresponding comments. The original rule text read as follows:

(a) A lawyer shall not reveal information relating to the representation of a client unless the client gives informed consent, the disclosure is impliedly authorized in order to carry out the representation or the disclosure is permitted by paragraph (b).

(b) A lawyer may reveal information relating to the representation of a client to the extent the lawyer reasonably believes necessary:

(1) to prevent reasonably certain death or substantial bodily harm;

(2) to secure legal advice about the lawyer's compliance with these Rules;

(3) to establish a claim or defense on behalf of the lawyer in a controversy between the lawyer and the client, to establish a defense to a criminal charge or civil claim against the lawyer based upon conduct in which the client was involved, or to respond to allegations in any proceeding concerning the lawyer's representation of the client; or

(4) to comply with other law or a court order.

In August 2012, the ABA House of Delegates added a new (b)(7) and (c) to this rule.

information provided to the lawyer by a prospective client, Rule 1.9(c)(2) for the lawyer's duty not to reveal information relating to the lawyer's prior representation of a former client and Rules 1.8(b) and 1.9(c)(1) for the lawyer's duties with respect to the use of such information to the disadvantage of clients and former clients.

[2] A fundamental principle in the client-lawyer relationship is that, in the absence of the client's informed consent, the lawyer must not reveal information relating to the representation. See Rule 1.0(e) for the definition of informed consent. This contributes to the trust that is the hallmark of the client-lawyer relationship. The client is thereby encouraged to seek legal assistance and to communicate fully and frankly with the lawyer even as to embarrassing or legally damaging subject matter. The lawyer needs this information to represent the client effectively and, if necessary, to advise the client to refrain from wrongful conduct. Almost without exception, clients come to lawyers in order to determine their rights and what is, in the complex of laws and regulations, deemed to be legal and correct. Based upon experience, lawyers know that almost all clients follow the advice given, and the law is upheld.

[3] The principle of client-lawyer confidentiality is given effect by related bodies of law: the attorney-client privilege, the work product doctrine and the rule of confidentiality established in professional ethics. The attorney-client privilege and work-product doctrine apply in judicial and other proceedings in which a lawyer may be called as a witness or otherwise required to produce evidence concerning a client. The rule of client-lawyer confidentiality applies in situations other than those where evidence is sought from the lawyer through compulsion of law. The confidentiality rule, for example, applies not only to matters communicated in confidence by the client but also to all information relating to the representation, whatever its source. A lawyer may not disclose such information except as authorized or required by the Rules of Professional Conduct or other law. See also Scope.

[4] Paragraph (a) prohibits a lawyer from revealing information relating to the representation of a client. This prohibition also applies to disclosures by a lawyer that do not in themselves reveal protected information but could reasonably lead to the discovery of such information by a third person. A lawyer's use of a hypothetical to discuss issues relating to the representation is permissible so long as there is no reasonable likelihood that the listener will be able to ascertain the identity of the client or the situation involved.

Authorized Disclosure

[5] Except to the extent that the client's instructions or special circumstances limit that authority, a lawyer is impliedly authorized to make disclosures about a client when appropriate in carrying out the representation. In some situations, for example, a lawyer may be impliedly authorized to admit a fact that cannot properly be disputed or to make a disclosure that facilitates a satisfactory conclusion to a matter. Lawyers in a firm may, in the course of the firm's practice, disclose to each other information relating to a client of the firm, unless the client has instructed that particular information be confined to specified lawyers.

Disclosure Adverse to Client

[6] Although the public interest is usually best served by a strict rule requiring lawyers to preserve the confidentiality of information relating to the representation of their clients, the confidentiality rule is subject to limited exceptions. Paragraph (b)(1) recognizes the overriding value of life and physical integrity and permits disclosure reasonably necessary to prevent reasonably certain death or substantial bodily harm. Such harm is reasonably certain to occur if it will be suffered imminently or if there is a present and substantial threat that a person will suffer such harm at a later date if the lawyer fails to take action necessary to eliminate the threat. Thus, a lawyer who knows that a client has accidentally discharged toxic waste into a town's water supply may reveal this information to the authorities if there is a present and substantial risk that a person who drinks the water will contract a life-threatening or debilitating disease and the lawyer's disclosure is necessary to eliminate the threat or reduce the number of victims.

[7] Paragraph (b)(2) is a limited exception to the rule of confidentiality that permits the lawyer to reveal information to the extent necessary to enable affected persons or appropriate authorities to prevent the client from committing a crime or fraud, as defined in Rule 1.0(d), that is reasonably certain to result in substantial injury to the financial or property interests of another and in furtherance of which the client has used or is using the lawyer's services. Such a serious abuse of the client-lawyer relationship by the client

forfeits the protection of this Rule. The client can, of course, prevent such disclosure by refraining from the wrongful conduct. Although paragraph (b)(2) does not require the lawyer to reveal the client's misconduct, the lawyer may not counsel or assist the client in conduct the lawyer knows is criminal or fraudulent. See Rule 1.2(d). See also Rule 1.16 with respect to the lawyer's obligation or right to withdraw from the representation of the client in such circumstances, and Rule 1.13(c), which permits the lawyer, where the client is an organization, to reveal information relating to the representation in limited circumstances.

[8] Paragraph (b)(3) addresses the situation in which the lawyer does not learn of the client's crime or fraud until after it has been consummated. Although the client no longer has the option of preventing disclosure by refraining from the wrongful conduct, there will be situations in which the loss suffered by the affected person can be prevented, rectified or mitigated. In such situations, the lawyer may disclose information relating to the representation to the extent necessary to enable the affected persons to prevent or mitigate reasonably certain losses or to attempt to recoup their losses. Paragraph (b)(3) does not apply when a person who has committed a crime or fraud thereafter employs a lawyer for representation concerning that offense.

[9] A lawyer's confidentiality obligations do not preclude a lawyer from securing confidential legal advice about the lawyer's personal responsibility to comply with these Rules. In most situations, disclosing information to secure such advice will be impliedly authorized for the lawyer to carry out the representation. Even when the disclosure is not impliedly authorized, paragraph (b)(4) permits such disclosure because of the importance of a lawyer's compliance with the Rules of Professional Conduct.

[10] Where a legal claim or disciplinary charge alleges complicity of the lawyer in a client's conduct or other misconduct of the lawyer involving representation of the client, the lawyer may respond to the extent the lawyer reasonably believes necessary to establish a defense. The same is true with respect to a claim involving the conduct or representation of a former client. Such a charge can arise in a civil, criminal, disciplinary or other proceeding and can be based on a wrong allegedly committed by the lawyer against the client or on a wrong alleged by a third person, for example, a person claiming to have been defrauded by the lawyer and client acting together. The lawyer's right to respond arises when an assertion of such complicity has been made. Paragraph (b)(5) does not require the lawyer to await the commencement of an action or proceeding that charges such complicity, so that the defense may be established by responding directly to a third party who has made such an assertion. The right to defend also applies, of course, where a proceeding has been commenced.

[11] A lawyer entitled to a fee is permitted by paragraph (b)(5) to prove the services rendered in an action to collect it. This aspect of the rule expresses the principle that the beneficiary of a fiduciary relationship may not exploit it to the detriment of the fiduciary.

[12] Other law may require that a lawyer disclose information about a client. Whether such a law supersedes Rule 1.6 is a question of law beyond the scope of these Rules. When disclosure of information relating to the representation appears to be required by other law, the lawyer must discuss the matter with the client to the extent required by Rule 1.4. If, however, the other law supersedes this Rule and requires disclosure, paragraph (b)(6) permits the lawyer to make such disclosures as are necessary to comply with the law.

Detection of Conflicts of Interest*

[13] Paragraph (b)(7) recognizes that lawyers in different firms may need to disclose limited information to each other to detect and resolve conflicts of interest, such as when a lawyer is considering an association with another firm, two or more firms are considering a merger, or a lawyer is considering the purchase of a law practice. See Rule 1.17, Comment [7]. Under these circumstances, lawyers and law firms are permitted to disclose limited information, but only once substantive discussions regarding the new relationship have occurred. Any such disclosure should ordinarily include no more than the identity of the persons and entities involved in a matter, a brief summary of the general issues involved, and information about whether the matter has terminated. Even this limited information, however, should be disclosed only to the extent reasonably necessary to detect and resolve conflicts of interest that might arise from the

---

* In August 2012, the ABA House of Delegates added new Comments 13 and 14 and substantially expanded Comment 18 to reflect the changes made in the text of the rule. Other comments were renumbered to take account of these additions.

possible new relationship. Moreover, the disclosure of any information is prohibited if it would compromise the attorney-client privilege or otherwise prejudice the client (e.g., the fact that a corporate client is seeking advice on a corporate takeover that has not been publicly announced; that a person has consulted a lawyer about the possibility of divorce before the person's intentions are known to the person's spouse; or that a person has consulted a lawyer about a criminal investigation that has not led to a public charge). Under those circumstances, paragraph (a) prohibits disclosure unless the client or former client gives informed consent. A lawyer's fiduciary duty to the lawyer's firm may also govern a lawyer's conduct when exploring an association with another firm and is beyond the scope of these Rules.

[14] Any information disclosed pursuant to paragraph (b)(7) may be used or further disclosed only to the extent necessary to detect and resolve conflicts of interest. Paragraph (b)(7) does not restrict the use of information acquired by means independent of any disclosure pursuant to paragraph (b)(7). Paragraph (b)(7) also does not affect the disclosure of information within a law firm when the disclosure is otherwise authorized, see Comment [5], such as when a lawyer in a firm discloses information to another lawyer in the same firm to detect and resolve conflicts of interest that could arise in connection with undertaking a new representation.

[15] A lawyer may be ordered to reveal information relating to the representation of a client by a court or by another tribunal or governmental entity claiming authority pursuant to other law to compel the disclosure. Absent informed consent of the client to do otherwise, the lawyer should assert on behalf of the client all nonfrivolous claims that the order is not authorized by other law or that the information sought is protected against disclosure by the attorney-client privilege or other applicable law. In the event of an adverse ruling, the lawyer must consult with the client about the possibility of appeal to the extent required by Rule 1.4. Unless review is sought, however, paragraph (b)(64) permits the lawyer to comply with the court's order.

[16] Paragraph (b) permits disclosure only to the extent the lawyer reasonably believes the disclosure is necessary to accomplish one of the purposes specified. Where practicable, the lawyer should first seek to persuade the client to take suitable action to obviate the need for disclosure. In any case, a disclosure adverse to the client's interest should be no greater than the lawyer reasonably believes necessary to accomplish the purpose. If the disclosure will be made in connection with a judicial proceeding, the disclosure should be made in a manner that limits access to the information to the tribunal or other persons having a need to know it and appropriate protective orders or other arrangements should be sought by the lawyer to the fullest extent practicable.

[17] Paragraph (b) permits but does not require the disclosure of information relating to a client's representation to accomplish the purposes specified in paragraphs (b)(1) through (b)(6). In exercising the discretion conferred by this Rule, the lawyer may consider such factors as the nature of the lawyer's relationship with the client and with those who might be injured by the client, the lawyer's own involvement in the transaction and factors that may extenuate the conduct in question. A lawyer's decision not to disclose as permitted by paragraph (b) does not violate this Rule. Disclosure may be required, however, by other Rules. Some Rules require disclosure only if such disclosure would be permitted by paragraph (b). See Rules 1.2(d), 4.1(b), 8.1 and 8.3. Rule 3.3, on the other hand, requires disclosure in some circumstances regardless of whether such disclosure is permitted by this Rule. See Rule 3.3(c).

Acting Competently to Preserve Confidentiality

[18] Paragraph (c) requires a lawyer to act competently to safeguard information relating to the representation of a client against unauthorized access by third parties and against inadvertent or unauthorized disclosure by the lawyer or other persons who are participating in the representation of the client or who are subject to the lawyer's supervision. See Rules 1.1, 5.1 and 5.3. The unauthorized access to, or the inadvertent or unauthorized disclosure of, information relating to the representation of a client does not constitute a violation of paragraph (c) if the lawyer has made reasonable efforts to prevent the access or disclosure. Factors to be considered in determining the reasonableness of the lawyer's efforts include, but are not limited to, the sensitivity of the information, the likelihood of disclosure if additional safeguards are not employed, the cost of employing additional safeguards, the difficulty of implementing the safeguards, and the extent to which the safeguards adversely affect the lawyer's ability to represent clients (e.g., by making a device or important piece of software excessively difficult to use). A client may require the lawyer to implement special security measures not required by this Rule or may give informed consent to forgo

security measures that would otherwise be required by this Rule. Whether a lawyer may be required to take additional steps to safeguard a client's information in order to comply with other law, such as state and federal laws that govern data privacy or that impose notification requirements upon the loss of, or unauthorized access to, electronic information, is beyond the scope of these Rules. For a lawyer's duties when sharing information with nonlawyers outside the lawyer's own firm, see Rule 5.3, Comments [3]–[4].

*[19] When transmitting a communication that includes information relating to the representation of a client, the lawyer must take reasonable precautions to prevent the information from coming into the hands of unintended recipients. This duty, however, does not require that the lawyer use special security measures if the method of communication affords a reasonable expectation of privacy. Special circumstances, however, may warrant special precautions. Factors to be considered in determining the reasonableness of the lawyer's expectation of confidentiality include the sensitivity of the information and the extent to which the privacy of the communication is protected by law or by a confidentiality agreement. A client may require the lawyer to implement special security measures not required by this Rule or may give informed consent to the use of a means of communication that would otherwise be prohibited by this Rule. Whether a lawyer may be required to take additional steps in order to comply with other law, such as state and federal laws that govern data privacy, is beyond the scope of these Rules.

Former Client

[20] The duty of confidentiality continues after the client-lawyer relationship has terminated. See Rule 1.9(c)(2). See Rule 1.9(c)(1) for the prohibition against using such information to the disadvantage of the former client.

Rule 1.7 Conflict of Interest: Current Clients

(a) Except as provided in paragraph (b), a lawyer shall not represent a client if the representation involves a concurrent conflict of interest. A concurrent conflict of interest exists if:

(1) the representation of one client will be directly adverse to another client; or

(2) there is a significant risk that the representation of one or more clients will be materially limited by the lawyer's responsibilities to another client, a former client or a third person or by a personal interest of the lawyer.

(b) Notwithstanding the existence of a concurrent conflict of interest under paragraph (a), a lawyer may represent a client if:

(1) the lawyer reasonably believes that the lawyer will be able to provide competent and diligent representation to each affected client;

(2) the representation is not prohibited by law;

(3) the representation does not involve the assertion of a claim by one client against another client represented by the lawyer in the same litigation or other proceeding before a tribunal; and

(4) each affected client gives informed consent, confirmed in writing.

COMMENT

General Principles

[1] Loyalty and independent judgment are essential elements in the lawyer's relationship to a client. Concurrent conflicts of interest can arise from the lawyer's responsibilities to another client, a former client or a third person or from the lawyer's own interests. For specific Rules regarding certain concurrent conflicts of interest, see Rule 1.8. For former client conflicts of interest, see Rule 1.9. For conflicts of interest involving prospective clients, see Rule 1.18. For definitions of "informed consent" and "confirmed in writing," see Rule 1.0(e) and (b).

---

* In August 2012, the ABA House of Delegates added the last line to renumbered Comment 19.

[2] Resolution of a conflict of interest problem under this Rule requires the lawyer to: 1) clearly identify the client or clients; 2) determine whether a conflict of interest exists; 3) decide whether the representation may be undertaken despite the existence of a conflict, i.e., whether the conflict is consentable; and 4) if so, consult with the clients affected under paragraph (a) and obtain their informed consent, confirmed in writing. The clients affected under paragraph (a) include both of the clients referred to in paragraph (a)(1) and the one or more clients whose representation might be materially limited under paragraph (a)(2).

[3] A conflict of interest may exist before representation is undertaken, in which event the representation must be declined, unless the lawyer obtains the informed consent of each client under the conditions of paragraph (b). To determine whether a conflict of interest exists, a lawyer should adopt reasonable procedures, appropriate for the size and type of firm and practice, to determine in both litigation and non-litigation matters the persons and issues involved. See also Comment to Rule 5.1. Ignorance caused by a failure to institute such procedures will not excuse a lawyer's violation of this Rule. As to whether a client-lawyer relationship exists or, having once been established, is continuing, see Comment to Rule 1.3 and Scope.

[4] If a conflict arises after representation has been undertaken, the lawyer ordinarily must withdraw from the representation, unless the lawyer has obtained the informed consent of the client under the conditions of paragraph (b). See Rule 1.16. Where more than one client is involved, whether the lawyer may continue to represent any of the clients is determined both by the lawyer's ability to comply with duties owed to the former client and by the lawyer's ability to represent adequately the remaining client or clients, given the lawyer's duties to the former client. See Rule 1.9. See also Comments [5] and [29].

[5] Unforeseeable developments, such as changes in corporate and other organizational affiliations or the addition or realignment of parties in litigation, might create conflicts in the midst of a representation, as when a company sued by the lawyer on behalf of one client is bought by another client represented by the lawyer in an unrelated matter. Depending on the circumstances, the lawyer may have the option to withdraw from one of the representations in order to avoid the conflict. The lawyer must seek court approval where necessary and take steps to minimize harm to the clients. See Rule 1.16. The lawyer must continue to protect the confidences of the client from whose representation the lawyer has withdrawn. See Rule 1.9(c).

Identifying Conflicts of Interest: Directly Adverse

[6] Loyalty to a current client prohibits undertaking representation directly adverse to that client without that client's informed consent. Thus, absent consent, a lawyer may not act as an advocate in one matter against a person the lawyer represents in some other matter, even when the matters are wholly unrelated. The client as to whom the representation is directly adverse is likely to feel betrayed, and the resulting damage to the client-lawyer relationship is likely to impair the lawyer's ability to represent the client effectively. In addition, the client on whose behalf the adverse representation is undertaken reasonably may fear that the lawyer will pursue that client's case less effectively out of deference to the other client, i.e., that the representation may be materially limited by the lawyer's interest in retaining the current client. Similarly, a directly adverse conflict may arise when a lawyer is required to cross-examine a client who appears as a witness in a lawsuit involving another client, as when the testimony will be damaging to the client who is represented in the lawsuit. On the other hand, simultaneous representation in unrelated matters of clients whose interests are only economically adverse, such as representation of competing economic enterprises in unrelated litigation, does not ordinarily constitute a conflict of interest and thus may not require consent of the respective clients.

[7] Directly adverse conflicts can also arise in transactional matters. For example, if a lawyer is asked to represent the seller of a business in negotiations with a buyer represented by the lawyer, not in the same transaction but in another, unrelated matter, the lawyer could not undertake the representation without the informed consent of each client.

Identifying Conflicts of Interest: Material Limitation

[8] Even where there is no direct adverseness, a conflict of interest exists if there is a significant risk that a lawyer's ability to consider, recommend or carry out an appropriate course of action for the client will be materially limited as a result of the lawyer's other responsibilities or interests. For example, a lawyer asked to represent several individuals seeking to form a joint venture is likely to be materially limited in

the lawyer's ability to recommend or advocate all possible positions that each might take because of the lawyer's duty of loyalty to the others. The conflict in effect forecloses alternatives that would otherwise be available to the client. The mere possibility of subsequent harm does not itself require disclosure and consent. The critical questions are the likelihood that a difference in interests will eventuate and, if it does, whether it will materially interfere with the lawyer's independent professional judgment in considering alternatives or foreclose courses of action that reasonably should be pursued on behalf of the client.

Lawyer's Responsibilities to Former Clients and Other Third Persons

[9] In addition to conflicts with other current clients, a lawyer's duties of loyalty and independence may be materially limited by responsibilities to former clients under Rule 1.9 or by the lawyer's responsibilities to other persons, such as fiduciary duties arising from a lawyer's service as a trustee, executor or corporate director.

Personal Interest Conflicts

[10] The lawyer's own interests should not be permitted to have an adverse effect on representation of a client. For example, if the probity of a lawyer's own conduct in a transaction is in serious question, it may be difficult or impossible for the lawyer to give a client detached advice. Similarly, when a lawyer has discussions concerning possible employment with an opponent of the lawyer's client, or with a law firm representing the opponent, such discussions could materially limit the lawyer's representation of the client. In addition, a lawyer may not allow related business interests to affect representation, for example, by referring clients to an enterprise in which the lawyer has an undisclosed financial interest. See Rule 1.8 for specific Rules pertaining to a number of personal interest conflicts, including business transactions with clients. See also Rule 1.10 (personal interest conflicts under Rule 1.7 ordinarily are not imputed to other lawyers in a law firm).

[11] When lawyers representing different clients in the same matter or in substantially related matters are closely related by blood or marriage, there may be a significant risk that client confidences will be revealed and that the lawyer's family relationship will interfere with both loyalty and independent professional judgment. As a result, each client is entitled to know of the existence and implications of the relationship between the lawyers before the lawyer agrees to undertake the representation. Thus, a lawyer related to another lawyer, e.g., as parent, child, sibling or spouse, ordinarily may not represent a client in a matter where that lawyer is representing another party, unless each client gives informed consent. The disqualification arising from a close family relationship is personal and ordinarily is not imputed to members of firms with whom the lawyers are associated. See Rule 1.10.

[12] A lawyer is prohibited from engaging in sexual relationships with a client unless the sexual relationship predates the formation of the client-lawyer relationship. See Rule 1.8(j).

Interest of Person Paying for a Lawyer's Service

[13] A lawyer may be paid from a source other than the client, including a co-client, if the client is informed of that fact and consents and the arrangement does not compromise the lawyer's duty of loyalty or independent judgment to the client. See Rule 1.8(f). If acceptance of the payment from any other source presents a significant risk that the lawyer's representation of the client will be materially limited by the lawyer's own interest in accommodating the person paying the lawyer's fee or by the lawyer's responsibilities to a payer who is also a co-client, then the lawyer must comply with the requirements of paragraph (b) before accepting the representation, including determining whether the conflict is consentable and, if so, that the client has adequate information about the material risks of the representation.

Prohibited Representations

[14] Ordinarily, clients may consent to representation notwithstanding a conflict. However, as indicated in paragraph (b), some conflicts are nonconsentable, meaning that the lawyer involved cannot properly ask for such agreement or provide representation on the basis of the client's consent. When the lawyer is representing more than one client, the question of consentability must be resolved as to each client.

[15] Consentability is typically determined by considering whether the interests of the clients will be adequately protected if the clients are permitted to give their informed consent to representation burdened by a conflict of interest. Thus, under paragraph (b)(1), representation is prohibited if in the circumstances

the lawyer cannot reasonably conclude that the lawyer will be able to provide competent and diligent representation. See Rule 1.1 (competence) and Rule 1.3 (diligence).

[16] Paragraph (b)(2) describes conflicts that are nonconsentable because the representation is prohibited by applicable law. For example, in some states substantive law provides that the same lawyer may not represent more than one defendant in a capital case, even with the consent of the clients, and under federal criminal statutes certain representations by a former government lawyer are prohibited, despite the informed consent of the former client. In addition, decisional law in some states limits the ability of a governmental client, such as a municipality, to consent to a conflict of interest.

[17] Paragraph (b)(3) describes conflicts that are nonconsentable because of the institutional interest in vigorous development of each client's position when the clients are aligned directly against each other in the same litigation or other proceeding before a tribunal. Whether clients are aligned directly against each other within the meaning of this paragraph requires examination of the context of the proceeding. Although this paragraph does not preclude a lawyer's multiple representation of adverse parties to a mediation (because mediation is not a proceeding before a "tribunal" under Rule 1.0(m)), such representation may be precluded by paragraph (b)(1).

Informed Consent

[18] Informed consent requires that each affected client be aware of the relevant circumstances and of the material and reasonably foreseeable ways that the conflict could have adverse effects on the interests of that client. See Rule 1.0(e) (informed consent). The information required depends on the nature of the conflict and the nature of the risks involved. When representation of multiple clients in a single matter is undertaken, the information must include the implications of the common representation, including possible effects on loyalty, confidentiality and the attorney-client privilege and the advantages and risks involved. See Comments [30] and [31] (effect of common representation on confidentiality).

[19] Under some circumstances it may be impossible to make the disclosure necessary to obtain consent. For example, when the lawyer represents different clients in related matters and one of the clients refuses to consent to the disclosure necessary to permit the other client to make an informed decision, the lawyer cannot properly ask the latter to consent. In some cases the alternative to common representation can be that each party may have to obtain separate representation with the possibility of incurring additional costs. These costs, along with the benefits of securing separate representation, are factors that may be considered by the affected client in determining whether common representation is in the client's interests.

Consent Confirmed in Writing

[20] Paragraph (b) requires the lawyer to obtain the informed consent of the client, confirmed in writing. Such a writing may consist of a document executed by the client or one that the lawyer promptly records and transmits to the client following an oral consent. See Rule 1.0(b). See also Rule 1.0(n) (writing includes electronic transmission). If it is not feasible to obtain or transmit the writing at the time the client gives informed consent, then the lawyer must obtain or transmit it within a reasonable time thereafter. See Rule 1.0(b). The requirement of a writing does not supplant the need in most cases for the lawyer to talk with the client, to explain the risks and advantages, if any, of representation burdened with a conflict of interest, as well as reasonably available alternatives, and to afford the client a reasonable opportunity to consider the risks and alternatives and to raise questions and concerns. Rather, the writing is required in order to impress upon clients the seriousness of the decision the client is being asked to make and to avoid disputes or ambiguities that might later occur in the absence of a writing.

Revoking Consent

[21] A client who has given consent to a conflict may revoke the consent and, like any other client, may terminate the lawyer's representation at any time. Whether revoking consent to the client's own representation precludes the lawyer from continuing to represent other clients depends on the circumstances, including the nature of the conflict, whether the client revoked consent because of a material change in circumstances, the reasonable expectations of the other clients and whether material detriment to the other clients or the lawyer would result.

Consent to Future Conflict

[22] Whether a lawyer may properly request a client to waive conflicts that might arise in the future is subject to the test of paragraph (b). The effectiveness of such waivers is generally determined by the extent to which the client reasonably understands the material risks that the waiver entails. The more comprehensive the explanation of the types of future representations that might arise and the actual and reasonably foreseeable adverse consequences of those representations, the greater the likelihood that the client will have the requisite understanding. Thus, if the client agrees to consent to a particular type of conflict with which the client is already familiar, then the consent ordinarily will be effective with regard to that type of conflict. If the consent is general and open-ended, then the consent ordinarily will be ineffective, because it is not reasonably likely that the client will have understood the material risks involved. On the other hand, if the client is an experienced user of the legal services involved and is reasonably informed regarding the risk that a conflict may arise, such consent is more likely to be effective, particularly if, e.g., the client is independently represented by other counsel in giving consent and the consent is limited to future conflicts unrelated to the subject of the representation. In any case, advance consent cannot be effective if the circumstances that materialize in the future are such as would make the conflict nonconsentable under paragraph (b).

Conflicts in Litigation

[23] Paragraph (b)(3) prohibits representation of opposing parties in the same litigation, regardless of the clients' consent. On the other hand, simultaneous representation of parties whose interests in litigation may conflict, such as coplaintiffs or codefendants, is governed by paragraph (a)(2). A conflict may exist by reason of substantial discrepancy in the parties' testimony, incompatibility in positions in relation to an opposing party or the fact that there are substantially different possibilities of settlement of the claims or liabilities in question. Such conflicts can arise in criminal cases as well as civil. The potential for conflict of interest in representing multiple defendants in a criminal case is so grave that ordinarily a lawyer should decline to represent more than one codefendant. On the other hand, common representation of persons having similar interests in civil litigation is proper if the requirements of paragraph (b) are met.

[24] Ordinarily a lawyer may take inconsistent legal positions in different tribunals at different times on behalf of different clients. The mere fact that advocating a legal position on behalf of one client might create precedent adverse to the interests of a client represented by the lawyer in an unrelated matter does not create a conflict of interest. A conflict of interest exists, however, if there is a significant risk that a lawyer's action on behalf of one client will materially limit the lawyer's effectiveness in representing another client in a different case; for example, when a decision favoring one client will create a precedent likely to seriously weaken the position taken on behalf of the other client. Factors relevant in determining whether the clients need to be advised of the risk include: where the cases are pending, whether the issue is substantive or procedural, the temporal relationship between the matters, the significance of the issue to the immediate and long-term interests of the clients involved and the clients' reasonable expectations in retaining the lawyer. If there is significant risk of material limitation, then absent informed consent of the affected clients, the lawyer must refuse one of the representations or withdraw from one or both matters.

[25] When a lawyer represents or seeks to represent a class of plaintiffs or defendants in a class-action lawsuit, unnamed members of the class are ordinarily not considered to be clients of the lawyer for purposes of applying paragraph (a)(1) of this Rule. Thus, the lawyer does not typically need to get the consent of such a person before representing a client suing the person in an unrelated matter. Similarly, a lawyer seeking to represent an opponent in a class action does not typically need the consent of an unnamed member of the class whom the lawyer represents in an unrelated matter.

Nonlitigation Conflicts

[26] Conflicts of interest under paragraphs (a)(1) and (a)(2) arise in contexts other than litigation. For a discussion of directly adverse conflicts in transactional matters, see Comment [7]. Relevant factors in determining whether there is significant potential for material limitation include the duration and intimacy of the lawyer's relationship with the client or clients involved, the functions being performed by the lawyer, the likelihood that disagreements will arise and the likely prejudice to the client from the conflict. The question is often one of proximity and degree. See Comment [8].

[27] For example, conflict questions may arise in estate planning and estate administration. A lawyer may be called upon to prepare wills for several family members, such as husband and wife, and, depending upon the circumstances, a conflict of interest may be present. In estate administration the identity of the client may be unclear under the law of a particular jurisdiction. Under one view, the client is the fiduciary; under another view the client is the estate or trust, including its beneficiaries. In order to comply with conflict of interest rules, the lawyer should make clear the lawyer's relationship to the parties involved.

[28] Whether a conflict is consentable depends on the circumstances. For example, a lawyer may not represent multiple parties to a negotiation whose interests are fundamentally antagonistic to each other, but common representation is permissible where the clients are generally aligned in interest even though there is some difference in interest among them. Thus, a lawyer may seek to establish or adjust a relationship between clients on an amicable and mutually advantageous basis; for example, in helping to organize a business in which two or more clients are entrepreneurs, working out the financial reorganization of an enterprise in which two or more clients have an interest or arranging a property distribution in settlement of an estate. The lawyer seeks to resolve potentially adverse interests by developing the parties' mutual interests. Otherwise, each party might have to obtain separate representation, with the possibility of incurring additional cost, complication or even litigation. Given these and other relevant factors, the clients may prefer that the lawyer act for all of them.

Special Considerations in Common Representation

[29] In considering whether to represent multiple clients in the same matter, a lawyer should be mindful that if the common representation fails because the potentially adverse interests cannot be reconciled, the result can be additional cost, embarrassment and recrimination. Ordinarily, the lawyer will be forced to withdraw from representing all of the clients if the common representation fails. In some situations, the risk of failure is so great that multiple representation is plainly impossible. For example, a lawyer cannot undertake common representation of clients where contentious litigation or negotiations between them are imminent or contemplated. Moreover, because the lawyer is required to be impartial between commonly represented clients, representation of multiple clients is improper when it is unlikely that impartiality can be maintained. Generally, if the relationship between the parties has already assumed antagonism, the possibility that the clients' interests can be adequately served by common representation is not very good. Other relevant factors are whether the lawyer subsequently will represent both parties on a continuing basis and whether the situation involves creating or terminating a relationship between the parties.

[30] A particularly important factor in determining the appropriateness of common representation is the effect on client-lawyer confidentiality and the attorney-client privilege. With regard to the attorney-client privilege, the prevailing rule is that, as between commonly represented clients, the privilege does not attach. Hence, it must be assumed that if litigation eventuates between the clients, the privilege will not protect any such communications, and the clients should be so advised.

[31] As to the duty of confidentiality, continued common representation will almost certainly be inadequate if one client asks the lawyer not to disclose to the other client information relevant to the common representation. This is so because the lawyer has an equal duty of loyalty to each client, and each client has the right to be informed of anything bearing on the representation that might affect that client's interests and the right to expect that the lawyer will use that information to that client's benefit. See Rule 1.4. The lawyer should, at the outset of the common representation and as part of the process of obtaining each client's informed consent, advise each client that information will be shared and that the lawyer will have to withdraw if one client decides that some matter material to the representation should be kept from the other. In limited circumstances, it may be appropriate for the lawyer to proceed with the representation when the clients have agreed, after being properly informed, that the lawyer will keep certain information confidential. For example, the lawyer may reasonably conclude that failure to disclose one client's trade secrets to another client will not adversely affect representation involving a joint venture between the clients and agree to keep that information confidential with the informed consent of both clients.

[32] When seeking to establish or adjust a relationship between clients, the lawyer should make clear that the lawyer's role is not that of partisanship normally expected in other circumstances and, thus, that the clients may be required to assume greater responsibility for decisions than when each client is separately

represented. Any limitations on the scope of the representation made necessary as a result of the common representation should be fully explained to the clients at the outset of the representation. See Rule 1.2(c).

[33] Subject to the above limitations, each client in the common representation has the right to loyal and diligent representation and the protection of Rule 1.9 concerning the obligations to a former client. The client also has the right to discharge the lawyer as stated in Rule 1.16.

Organizational Clients

[34] A lawyer who represents a corporation or other organization does not, by virtue of that representation, necessarily represent any constituent or affiliated organization, such as a parent or subsidiary. See Rule 1.13(a). Thus, the lawyer for an organization is not barred from accepting representation adverse to an affiliate in an unrelated matter, unless the circumstances are such that the affiliate should also be considered a client of the lawyer, there is an understanding between the lawyer and the organizational client that the lawyer will avoid representation adverse to the client's affiliates, or the lawyer's obligations to either the organizational client or the new client are likely to limit materially the lawyer's representation of the other client.

[35] A lawyer for a corporation or other organization who is also a member of its board of directors should determine whether the responsibilities of the two roles may conflict. The lawyer may be called on to advise the corporation in matters involving actions of the directors. Consideration should be given to the frequency with which such situations may arise, the potential intensity of the conflict, the effect of the lawyer's resignation from the board and the possibility of the corporation's obtaining legal advice from another lawyer in such situations. If there is material risk that the dual role will compromise the lawyer's independence of professional judgment, the lawyer should not serve as a director or should cease to act as the corporation's lawyer when conflicts of interest arise. The lawyer should advise the other members of the board that in some circumstances matters discussed at board meetings while the lawyer is present in the capacity of director might not be protected by the attorney-client privilege and that conflict of interest considerations might require the lawyer's recusal as a director or might require the lawyer and the lawyer's firm to decline representation of the corporation in a matter.

Rule 1.8 Conflict of Interest: Current Clients: Specific Rules

(a) A lawyer shall not enter into a business transaction with a client or knowingly acquire an ownership, possessory, security or other pecuniary interest adverse to a client unless:

(1) the transaction and terms on which the lawyer acquires the interest are fair and reasonable to the client and are fully disclosed and transmitted in writing in a manner that can be reasonably understood by the client;

(2) the client is advised in writing of the desirability of seeking and is given a reasonable opportunity to seek the advice of independent legal counsel on the transaction; and

(3) the client gives informed consent, in a writing signed by the client, to the essential terms of the transaction and the lawyer's role in the transaction, including whether the lawyer is representing the client in the transaction.

(b) A lawyer shall not use information relating to representation of a client to the disadvantage of the client unless the client gives informed consent, except as permitted or required by these Rules.

(c) A lawyer shall not solicit any substantial gift from a client, including a testamentary gift, or prepare on behalf of a client an instrument giving the lawyer or a person related to the lawyer any substantial gift unless the lawyer or other recipient of the gift is related to the client. For purposes of this paragraph, related persons include a spouse, child, grandchild, parent, grandparent or other relative or individual with whom the lawyer or the client maintains a close, familial relationship.

(d) Prior to the conclusion of representation of a client, a lawyer shall not make or negotiate an agreement giving the lawyer literary or media rights to a portrayal or account based in substantial part on information relating to the representation.

(e) A lawyer shall not provide financial assistance to a client in connection with pending or contemplated litigation, except that:

(1) a lawyer may advance court costs and expenses of litigation, the repayment of which may be contingent on the outcome of the matter; and

(2) a lawyer representing an indigent client may pay court costs and expenses of litigation on behalf of the client.

(f) A lawyer shall not accept compensation for representing a client from one other than the client unless:

(1) the client gives informed consent;

(2) there is no interference with the lawyer's independence of professional judgment or with the client-lawyer relationship; and

(3) information relating to representation of a client is protected as required by Rule 1.6.

(g) A lawyer who represents two or more clients shall not participate in making an aggregate settlement of the claims of or against the clients, or in a criminal case an aggregated agreement as to guilty or nolo contendere pleas, unless each client gives informed consent, in a writing signed by the client. The lawyer's disclosure shall include the existence and nature of all the claims or pleas involved and of the participation of each person in the settlement.

(h) A lawyer shall not:

(1) make an agreement prospectively limiting the lawyer's liability to a client for malpractice unless the client is independently represented in making the agreement; or

(2) settle a claim or potential claim for such liability with an unrepresented client or former client unless that person is advised in writing of the desirability of seeking and is given a reasonable opportunity to seek the advice of independent legal counsel in connection therewith.

(i) A lawyer shall not acquire a proprietary interest in the cause of action or subject matter of litigation the lawyer is conducting for a client, except that the lawyer may:

(1) acquire a lien authorized by law to secure the lawyer's fee or expenses; and

(2) contract with a client for a reasonable contingent fee in a civil case.

(j) A lawyer shall not have sexual relations with a client unless a consensual sexual relationship existed between them when the client-lawyer relationship commenced.

(k) While lawyers are associated in a firm, a prohibition in the foregoing paragraphs (a) through (i) that applies to any one of them shall apply to all of them.

COMMENT

Business Transactions between Client and Lawyer

[1] A lawyer's legal skill and training, together with the relationship of trust and confidence between lawyer and client, create the possibility of overreaching when the lawyer participates in a business, property or financial transaction with a client, for example, a loan or sales transaction or a lawyer investment on behalf of a client. The requirements of paragraph (a) must be met even when the transaction is not closely related to the subject matter of the representation, as when a lawyer drafting a will for a client learns that

the client needs money for unrelated expenses and offers to make a loan to the client. The Rule applies to lawyers engaged in the sale of goods or services related to the practice of law, for example, the sale of title insurance or investment services to existing clients of the lawyer's legal practice. See Rule 5.7. It also applies to lawyers purchasing property from estates they represent. It does not apply to ordinary fee arrangements between client and lawyer, which are governed by Rule 1.5, although its requirements must be met when the lawyer accepts an interest in the client's business or other nonmonetary property as payment of all or part of a fee. In addition, the Rule does not apply to standard commercial transactions between the lawyer and the client for products or services that the client generally markets to others, for example, banking or brokerage services, medical services, products manufactured or distributed by the client, and utilities services. In such transactions, the lawyer has no advantage in dealing with the client, and the restrictions in paragraph (a) are unnecessary and impracticable.

[2] Paragraph (a)(1) requires that the transaction itself be fair to the client and that its essential terms be communicated to the client, in writing, in a manner that can be reasonably understood. Paragraph (a)(2) requires that the client also be advised, in writing, of the desirability of seeking the advice of independent legal counsel. It also requires that the client be given a reasonable opportunity to obtain such advice. Paragraph (a)(3) requires that the lawyer obtain the client's informed consent, in a writing signed by the client, both to the essential terms of the transaction and to the lawyer's role. When necessary, the lawyer should discuss both the material risks of the proposed transaction, including any risk presented by the lawyer's involvement, and the existence of reasonably available alternatives and should explain why the advice of independent legal counsel is desirable. See Rule 1.0(e) (definition of informed consent).

[3] The risk to a client is greatest when the client expects the lawyer to represent the client in the transaction itself or when the lawyer's financial interest otherwise poses a significant risk that the lawyer's representation of the client will be materially limited by the lawyer's financial interest in the transaction. Here the lawyer's role requires that the lawyer must comply, not only with the requirements of paragraph (a), but also with the requirements of Rule 1.7. Under that Rule, the lawyer must disclose the risks associated with the lawyer's dual role as both legal adviser and participant in the transaction, such as the risk that the lawyer will structure the transaction or give legal advice in a way that favors the lawyer's interests at the expense of the client. Moreover, the lawyer must obtain the client's informed consent. In some cases, the lawyer's interest may be such that Rule 1.7 will preclude the lawyer from seeking the client's consent to the transaction.

[4] If the client is independently represented in the transaction, paragraph (a)(2) of this Rule is inapplicable, and the paragraph (a)(1) requirement for full disclosure is satisfied either by a written disclosure by the lawyer involved in the transaction or by the client's independent counsel. The fact that the client was independently represented in the transaction is relevant in determining whether the agreement was fair and reasonable to the client as paragraph (a)(1) further requires.

Use of Information Related to Representation

[5] Use of information relating to the representation to the disadvantage of the client violates the lawyer's duty of loyalty. Paragraph (b) applies when the information is used to benefit either the lawyer or a third person, such as another client or business associate of the lawyer. For example, if a lawyer learns that a client intends to purchase and develop several parcels of land, the lawyer may not use that information to purchase one of the parcels in competition with the client or to recommend that another client make such a purchase. The Rule does not prohibit uses that do not disadvantage the client. For example, a lawyer who learns a government agency's interpretation of trade legislation during the representation of one client may properly use that information to benefit other clients. Paragraph (b) prohibits disadvantageous use of client information unless the client gives informed consent, except as permitted or required by these Rules. See Rules 1.2(d), 1.6, 1.9(c), 3.3, 4.1(b), 8.1 and 8.3.

Gifts to Lawyers

[6] A lawyer may accept a gift from a client, if the transaction meets general standards of fairness. For example, a simple gift such as a present given at a holiday or as a token of appreciation is permitted. If a client offers the lawyer a more substantial gift, paragraph (c) does not prohibit the lawyer from accepting it, although such a gift may be voidable by the client under the doctrine of undue influence, which treats client gifts as presumptively fraudulent. In any event, due to concerns about overreaching and imposition

on clients, a lawyer may not suggest that a substantial gift be made to the lawyer or for the lawyer's benefit, except where the lawyer is related to the client as set forth in paragraph (c).

[7] If effectuation of a substantial gift requires preparing a legal instrument such as a will or conveyance, the client should have the detached advice that another lawyer can provide. The sole exception to this Rule is where the client is a relative of the donee.

[8] This Rule does not prohibit a lawyer from seeking to have the lawyer or a partner or associate of the lawyer named as executor of the client's estate or to another potentially lucrative fiduciary position. Nevertheless, such appointments will be subject to the general conflict of interest provision in Rule 1.7 when there is a significant risk that the lawyer's interest in obtaining the appointment will materially limit the lawyer's independent professional judgment in advising the client concerning the choice of an executor or other fiduciary. In obtaining the client's informed consent to the conflict, the lawyer should advise the client concerning the nature and extent of the lawyer's financial interest in the appointment, as well as the availability of alternative candidates for the position.

Literary Rights

[9] An agreement by which a lawyer acquires literary or media rights concerning the conduct of the representation creates a conflict between the interests of the client and the personal interests of the lawyer. Measures suitable in the representation of the client may detract from the publication value of an account of the representation. Paragraph (d) does not prohibit a lawyer representing a client in a transaction concerning literary property from agreeing that the lawyer's fee shall consist of a share in ownership in the property, if the arrangement conforms to Rule 1.5 and paragraphs (a) and (i).

Financial Assistance

[10] Lawyers may not subsidize lawsuits or administrative proceedings brought on behalf of their clients, including making or guaranteeing loans to their clients for living expenses, because to do so would encourage clients to pursue lawsuits that might not otherwise be brought and because such assistance gives lawyers too great a financial stake in the litigation. These dangers do not warrant a prohibition on a lawyer lending a client court costs and litigation expenses, including the expenses of medical examination and the costs of obtaining and presenting evidence, because these advances are virtually indistinguishable from contingent fees and help ensure access to the courts. Similarly, an exception allowing lawyers representing indigent clients to pay court costs and litigation expenses regardless of whether these funds will be repaid is warranted.

Person Paying for a Lawyer's Services

[11] Lawyers are frequently asked to represent a client under circumstances in which a third person will compensate the lawyer, in whole or in part. The third person might be a relative or friend, an indemnitor (such as a liability insurance company) or a co-client (such as a corporation sued along with one or more of its employees). Because third-party payers frequently have interests that differ from those of the client, including interests in minimizing the amount spent on the representation and in learning how the representation is progressing, lawyers are prohibited from accepting or continuing such representations unless the lawyer determines that there will be no interference with the lawyer's independent professional judgment and there is informed consent from the client. See also Rule 5.4(c) (prohibiting interference with a lawyer's professional judgment by one who recommends, employs or pays the lawyer to render legal services for another).

[12] Sometimes, it will be sufficient for the lawyer to obtain the client's informed consent regarding the fact of the payment and the identity of the third-party payer. If, however, the fee arrangement creates a conflict of interest for the lawyer, then the lawyer must comply with Rule. 1.7. The lawyer must also conform to the requirements of Rule 1.6 concerning confidentiality. Under Rule 1.7(a), a conflict of interest exists if there is significant risk that the lawyer's representation of the client will be materially limited by the lawyer's own interest in the fee arrangement or by the lawyer's responsibilities to the third-party payer (for example, when the third-party payer is a co-client). Under Rule 1.7(b), the lawyer may accept or continue the representation with the informed consent of each affected client, unless the conflict is nonconsentable under that paragraph. Under Rule 1.7(b), the informed consent must be confirmed in writing.

Aggregate Settlements

[13] Differences in willingness to make or accept an offer of settlement are among the risks of common representation of multiple clients by a single lawyer. Under Rule 1.7, this is one of the risks that should be discussed before undertaking the representation, as part of the process of obtaining the clients' informed consent. In addition, Rule 1.2(a) protects each client's right to have the final say in deciding whether to accept or reject an offer of settlement and in deciding whether to enter a guilty or nolo contendere plea in a criminal case. The rule stated in this paragraph is a corollary of both these Rules and provides that, before any settlement offer or plea bargain is made or accepted on behalf of multiple clients, the lawyer must inform each of them about all the material terms of the settlement, including what the other clients will receive or pay if the settlement or plea offer is accepted. See also Rule 1.0(e) (definition of informed consent). Lawyers representing a class of plaintiffs or defendants, or those proceeding derivatively, may not have a full client-lawyer relationship with each member of the class; nevertheless, such lawyers must comply with applicable rules regulating notification of class members and other procedural requirements designed to ensure adequate protection of the entire class.

Limiting Liability and Settling Malpractice Claims

[14] Agreements prospectively limiting a lawyer's liability for malpractice are prohibited unless the client is independently represented in making the agreement because they are likely to undermine competent and diligent representation. Also, many clients are unable to evaluate the desirability of making such an agreement before a dispute has arisen, particularly if they are then represented by the lawyer seeking the agreement. This paragraph does not, however, prohibit a lawyer from entering into an agreement with the client to arbitrate legal malpractice claims, provided such agreements are enforceable and the client is fully informed of the scope and effect of the agreement. Nor does this paragraph limit the ability of lawyers to practice in the form of a limited-liability entity, where permitted by law, provided that each lawyer remains personally liable to the client for his or her own conduct and the firm complies with any conditions required by law, such as provisions requiring client notification or maintenance of adequate liability insurance. Nor does it prohibit an agreement in accordance with Rule 1.2 that defines the scope of the representation, although a definition of scope that makes the obligations of representation illusory will amount to an attempt to limit liability.

[15] Agreements settling a claim or a potential claim for malpractice are not prohibited by this Rule. Nevertheless, in view of the danger that a lawyer will take unfair advantage of an unrepresented client or former client, the lawyer must first advise such a person in writing of the appropriateness of independent representation in connection with such a settlement. In addition, the lawyer must give the client or former client a reasonable opportunity to find and consult independent counsel.

Acquiring Proprietary Interest in Litigation

[16] Paragraph (i) states the traditional general rule that lawyers are prohibited from acquiring a proprietary interest in litigation. Like paragraph (e), the general rule has its basis in common law champerty and maintenance and is designed to avoid giving the lawyer too great an interest in the representation. In addition, when the lawyer acquires an ownership interest in the subject of the representation, it will be more difficult for a client to discharge the lawyer if the client so desires. The Rule is subject to specific exceptions developed in decisional law and continued in these Rules. The exception for certain advances of the costs of litigation is set forth in paragraph (e). In addition, paragraph (i) sets forth exceptions for liens authorized by law to secure the lawyer's fees or expenses and contracts for reasonable contingent fees. The law of each jurisdiction determines which liens are authorized by law. These may include liens granted by statute, liens originating in common law and liens acquired by contract with the client. When a lawyer acquires by contract a security interest in property other than that recovered through the lawyer's efforts in the litigation, such an acquisition is a business or financial transaction with a client and is governed by the requirements of paragraph (a). Contracts for contingent fees in civil cases are governed by Rule 1.5.

Client-Lawyer Sexual Relationships

[17] The relationship between lawyer and client is a fiduciary one in which the lawyer occupies the highest position of trust and confidence. The relationship is almost always unequal; thus, a sexual relationship between lawyer and client can involve unfair exploitation of the lawyer's fiduciary role, in

violation of the lawyer's basic ethical obligation not to use the trust of the client to the client's disadvantage. In addition, such a relationship presents a significant danger that, because of the lawyer's emotional involvement, the lawyer will be unable to represent the client without impairment of the exercise of independent professional judgment. Moreover, a blurred line between the professional and personal relationships may make it difficult to predict to what extent client confidences will be protected by the attorney-client evidentiary privilege, since client confidences are protected by privilege only when they are imparted in the context of the client-lawyer relationship. Because of the significant danger of harm to client interests and because the client's own emotional involvement renders it unlikely that the client could give adequate informed consent, this Rule prohibits the lawyer from having sexual relations with a client regardless of whether the relationship is consensual and regardless of the absence of prejudice to the client.

[18] Sexual relationships that predate the client-lawyer relationship are not prohibited. Issues relating to the exploitation of the fiduciary relationship and client dependency are diminished when the sexual relationship existed prior to the commencement of the client-lawyer relationship. However, before proceeding with the representation in these circumstances, the lawyer should consider whether the lawyer's ability to represent the client will be materially limited by the relationship. See Rule 1.7(a)(2).

[19] When the client is an organization, paragraph (j) of this Rule prohibits a lawyer for the organization (whether inside counsel or outside counsel) from having a sexual relationship with a constituent of the organization who supervises, directs or regularly consults with that lawyer concerning the organization's legal matters.

Imputation of Prohibitions

[20] Under paragraph (k), a prohibition on conduct by an individual lawyer in paragraphs (a) through (i) also applies to all lawyers associated in a firm with the personally prohibited lawyer. For example, one lawyer in a firm may not enter into a business transaction with a client of another member of the firm without complying with paragraph (a), even if the first lawyer is not personally involved in the representation of the client. The prohibition set forth in paragraph (j) is personal and is not applied to associated lawyers.

Rule 1.9 Duties to Former Clients

(a) A lawyer who has formerly represented a client in a matter shall not thereafter represent another person in the same or a substantially related matter in which that person's interests are materially adverse to the interests of the former client unless the former client gives informed consent, confirmed in writing.

(b) A lawyer shall not knowingly represent a person in the same or a substantially related matter in which a firm with which the lawyer formerly was associated had previously represented a client

(1) whose interests are materially adverse to that person; and

(2) about whom the lawyer had acquired information protected by Rules 1.6 and 1.9(c) that is material to the matter;

unless the former client gives informed consent, confirmed in writing.

(c) A lawyer who has formerly represented a client in a matter or whose present or former firm has formerly represented a client in a matter shall not thereafter:

(1) use information relating to the representation to the disadvantage of the former client except as these Rules would permit or require with respect to a client, or when the information has become generally known; or

(2) reveal information relating to the representation except as these Rules would permit or require with respect to a client.

COMMENT

[1] After termination of a client-lawyer relationship, a lawyer has certain continuing duties with respect to confidentiality and conflicts of interest and thus may not represent another client except in conformity with this Rule. Under this Rule, for example, a lawyer could not properly seek to rescind on behalf of a new client a contract drafted on behalf of the former client. So also a lawyer who has prosecuted an accused person could not properly represent the accused in a subsequent civil action against the government concerning the same transaction. Nor could a lawyer who has represented multiple clients in a matter represent one of the clients against the others in the same or a substantially related matter after a dispute arose among the clients in that matter, unless all affected clients give informed consent. See Comment [9]. Current and former government lawyers must comply with this Rule to the extent required by Rule 1.11.

[2] The scope of a "matter" for purposes of this Rule depends on the facts of a particular situation or transaction. The lawyer's involvement in a matter can also be a question of degree. When a lawyer has been directly involved in a specific transaction, subsequent representation of other clients with materially adverse interests in that transaction clearly is prohibited. On the other hand, a lawyer who recurrently handled a type of problem for a former client is not precluded from later representing another client in a factually distinct problem of that type even though the subsequent representation involves a position adverse to the prior client. Similar considerations can apply to the reassignment of military lawyers between defense and prosecution functions within the same military jurisdictions. The underlying question is whether the lawyer was so involved in the matter that the subsequent representation can be justly regarded as a changing of sides in the matter in question.

[3] Matters are "substantially related" for purposes of this Rule if they involve the same transaction or legal dispute or if there otherwise is a substantial risk that confidential factual information as would normally have been obtained in the prior representation would materially advance the client's position in the subsequent matter. For example, a lawyer who has represented a businessperson and learned extensive private financial information about that person may not then represent that person's spouse in seeking a divorce. Similarly, a lawyer who has previously represented a client in securing environmental permits to build a shopping center would be precluded from representing neighbors seeking to oppose rezoning of the property on the basis of environmental considerations; however, the lawyer would not be precluded, on the grounds of substantial relationship, from defending a tenant of the completed shopping center in resisting eviction for nonpayment of rent. Information that has been disclosed to the public or to other parties adverse to the former client ordinarily will not be disqualifying. Information acquired in a prior representation may have been rendered obsolete by the passage of time, a circumstance that may be relevant in determining whether two representations are substantially related. In the case of an organizational client, general knowledge of the client's policies and practices ordinarily will not preclude a subsequent representation; on the other hand, knowledge of specific facts gained in a prior representation that are relevant to the matter in question ordinarily will preclude such a representation. A former client is not required to reveal the confidential information learned by the lawyer in order to establish a substantial risk that the lawyer has confidential information to use in the subsequent matter. A conclusion about the possession of such information may be based on the nature of the services the lawyer provided the former client and information that would in ordinary practice be learned by a lawyer providing such services.

Lawyers Moving Between Firms

[4] When lawyers have been associated within a firm but then end their association, the question of whether a lawyer should undertake representation is more complicated. There are several competing considerations. First, the client previously represented by the former firm must be reasonably assured that the principle of loyalty to the client is not compromised. Second, the rule should not be so broadly cast as to preclude other persons from having reasonable choice of legal counsel. Third, the rule should not unreasonably hamper lawyers from forming new associations and taking on new clients after having left a previous association. In this connection, it should be recognized that today many lawyers practice in firms, that many lawyers to some degree limit their practice to one field or another, and that many move from one association to another several times in their careers. If the concept of imputation were applied with unqualified rigor, the result would be radical curtailment of the opportunity of lawyers to move from one practice setting to another and of the opportunity of clients to change counsel.

[5] Paragraph (b) operates to disqualify the lawyer only when the lawyer involved has actual knowledge of information protected by Rules 1.6 and 1.9(c). Thus, if a lawyer while with one firm acquired no knowledge or information relating to a particular client of the firm, and that lawyer later joined another firm, neither the lawyer individually nor the second firm is disqualified from representing another client in the same or a related matter even though the interests of the two clients conflict. See Rule 1.10(b) for the restrictions on a firm once a lawyer has terminated association with the firm.

[6] Application of paragraph (b) depends on a situation's particular facts, aided by inferences, deductions or working presumptions that reasonably may be made about the way in which lawyers work together. A lawyer may have general access to files of all clients of a law firm and may regularly participate in discussions of their affairs; it should be inferred that such a lawyer in fact is privy to all information about all the firm's clients. In contrast, another lawyer may have access to the files of only a limited number of clients and participate in discussions of the affairs of no other clients; in the absence of information to the contrary, it should be inferred that such a lawyer in fact is privy to information about the clients actually served but not those of other clients. In such an inquiry, the burden of proof should rest upon the firm whose disqualification is sought.

[7] Independent of the question of disqualification of a firm, a lawyer changing professional association has a continuing duty to preserve confidentiality of information about a client formerly represented. See Rules 1.6 and 1.9(c).

[8] Paragraph (c) provides that information acquired by the lawyer in the course of representing a client may not subsequently be used or revealed by the lawyer to the disadvantage of the client. However, the fact that a lawyer has once served a client does not preclude the lawyer from using generally known information about that client when later representing another client.

[9] The provisions of this Rule are for the protection of former clients and can be waived if the client gives informed consent, which consent must be confirmed in writing under paragraphs (a) and (b). See Rule 1.0(e). With regard to the effectiveness of an advance waiver, see Comment [22] to Rule 1.7. With regard to disqualification of a firm with which a lawyer is or was formerly associated, see Rule 1.10.

Rule 1.10 Imputation of Conflicts of Interest: General Rule*

(a) While lawyers are associated in a firm, none of them shall knowingly represent a client when any one of them practicing alone would be prohibited from doing so by Rules 1.7 or 1.9, unless

(1) the prohibition is based upon a personal interest of the disqualified lawyer and does not present a significant risk of materially limiting the representation of the client by the remaining lawyers in the firm; or

(2) the prohibition is based upon Rule 1.9(a), or (b), and arises out of the disqualified lawyer's association with a prior firm, and

(i) the disqualified lawyer is timely screened from any participation in the matter and is apportioned no part of the fee therefrom;

(ii) written notice is promptly given to any affected former client to enable the former client to ascertain compliance with the provisions of this Rule, which shall include a description of the screening procedures employed; a statement of the firm's and of the screened lawyer's compliance with these Rules; a statement that review may be available before a tribunal; and an agreement by the firm to

* In February 2009, the ABA House of Delegates modified Model Rule 1.10(a) by adding the language in (a)(2). This amendment permits a law firm to screen a disqualified lawyer in order to avoid imputation of the screened lawyer's conflict to other attorneys in the firm. After the rule was adopted, critics noted that the February 2009 language did not limit the screening to the migratory lawyer context. Thus, several groups within the ABA proposed a housekeeping amendment, which was adopted by the house of Delegates in August 2009. In 1.10(a)(1), the word "prohibited" was replaced with the word, "disqualified." And, in 1.10(a)(2), a clause was added at the end of the first line: "and arises out of the disqualified lawyer's association with a prior firm."

respond promptly to any written inquiries or objections by the former client about the screening procedures; and

(iii) certifications of compliance with these Rules and with the screening procedures are provided to the former client by the screened lawyer and by a partner of the firm, at reasonable intervals upon the former client's written request and upon termination of the screening procedures.

(b) When a lawyer has terminated an association with a firm, the firm is not prohibited from thereafter representing a person with interests materially adverse to those of a client represented by the formerly associated lawyer and not currently represented by the firm, unless:

(1) the matter is the same or substantially related to that in which the formerly associated lawyer represented the client; and

(2) any lawyer remaining in the firm has information protected by Rules 1.6 and 1.9(c) that is material to the matter.

(c) A disqualification prescribed by this rule may be waived by the affected client under the conditions stated in Rule 1.7.

(d) The disqualification of lawyers associated in a firm with former or current government lawyers is governed by Rule 1.11.

COMMENT*

Definition of "Firm"

[1] For purposes of the Rules of Professional Conduct, the term "firm" denotes lawyers in a law partnership, professional corporation, sole proprietorship or other association authorized to practice law; or lawyers employed in a legal services organization or the legal department of a corporation or other organization. See Rule 1.0(c). Whether two or more lawyers constitute a firm within this definition can depend on the specific facts. See Rule 1.0, Comments [2]–[4].

Principles of Imputed Disqualification

[2] The rule of imputed disqualification stated in paragraph (a) gives effect to the principle of loyalty to the client as it applies to lawyers who practice in a law firm. Such situations can be considered from the premise that a firm of lawyers is essentially one lawyer for purposes of the rules governing loyalty to the client, or from the premise that each lawyer is vicariously bound by the obligation of loyalty owed by each lawyer with whom the lawyer is associated. Paragraph (a)(1) operates only among the lawyers currently associated in a firm. When a lawyer moves from one firm to another, the situation is governed by Rules 1.9(b) and 1.10(a)(2) and 1.10(b).

[3] The rule in paragraph (a) does not prohibit representation where neither questions of client loyalty nor protection of confidential information are presented. Where one lawyer in a firm could not effectively represent a given client because of strong political beliefs, for example, but that lawyer will do no work on the case and the personal beliefs of the lawyer will not materially limit the representation by others in the firm, the firm should not be disqualified. On the other hand, if an opposing party in a case were owned by a lawyer in the law firm, and others in the firm would be materially limited in pursuing the matter because of loyalty to that lawyer, the personal disqualification of the lawyer would be imputed to all others in the firm.

[4] The rule in paragraph (a) also does not prohibit representation by others in the law firm where the person prohibited from involvement in a matter is a nonlawyer, such as a paralegal or legal secretary. Nor does paragraph (a) prohibit representation if the lawyer is prohibited from acting because of events before the person became a lawyer, for example, work that the person did while a law student. Such persons,

* In February 2009, the ABA House of Delegates amended the comments to Model Rule 1.10. Comment 2 was modified to clarify references to (a)(1) and (a)(2) of Rule 1.10. Comments 7–10 are new and old Comments 7–8 are renumbered as 11 and 12.

however, ordinarily must be screened from any personal participation in the matter to avoid communication to others in the firm of confidential information that both the nonlawyers and the firm have a legal duty to protect. See Rules 1.0(k) and 5.3.

[5] Rule 1.10(b) operates to permit a law firm, under certain circumstances, to represent a person with interests directly adverse to those of a client represented by a lawyer who formerly was associated with the firm. The Rule applies regardless of when the formerly associated lawyer represented the client. However, the law firm may not represent a person with interests adverse to those of a present client of the firm, which would violate Rule 1.7. Moreover, the firm may not represent the person where the matter is the same or substantially related to that in which the formerly associated lawyer represented the client and any other lawyer currently in the firm has material information protected by Rules 1.6 and 1.9(c).

[6] Rule 1.10(c) removes imputation with the informed consent of the affected client or former client under the conditions stated in Rule 1.7. The conditions stated in Rule 1.7 require the lawyer to determine that the representation is not prohibited by Rule 1.7(b) and that each affected client or former client has given informed consent to the representation, confirmed in writing. In some cases, the risk may be so severe that the conflict may not be cured by client consent. For a discussion of the effectiveness of client waivers of conflicts that might arise in the future, see Rule 1.7, Comment [22]. For a definition of informed consent, see Rule 1.0(e).

[7] Rule 1.10(a)(2) similarly removes the imputation otherwise required by Rule 1.10(a), but unlike section (c), it does so without requiring that there be informed consent by the former client. Instead, it requires that the procedures laid out in sections (a)(2)(i)-(iii) be followed. A description of effective screening mechanisms appears in Rule 1.0(k). Lawyers should be aware, however, that, even where screening mechanisms have been adopted, tribunals may consider additional factors in ruling upon motions to disqualify a lawyer from pending litigation.

[8] Paragraph (a)(2)(i) does not prohibit the screened lawyer from receiving a salary or partnership share established by prior independent agreement, but that lawyer may not receive compensation directly related to the matter in which the lawyer is disqualified.

[9] The notice required by paragraph (a)(2)(ii) generally should include a description of the screened lawyer's prior representation and be given as soon as practicable after the need for screening becomes apparent. It also should include a statement by the screened lawyer and the firm that the client's material confidential information has not been disclosed or used in violation of the Rules. The notice is intended to enable the former client to evaluate and comment upon the effectiveness of the screening procedures.

[10] The certifications required by paragraph (a)(2)(iii) give the former client assurance that the client's material confidential information has not been disclosed or used inappropriately, either prior to timely implementation of a screen or thereafter. If compliance cannot be certified, the certificate must describe the failure to comply.

[11] Where a lawyer has joined a private firm after having represented the government, imputation is governed by Rule 1.11(b) and (c), not this Rule. Under Rule 1.11(d), where a lawyer represents the government after having served clients in private practice, nongovernmental employment or in another government agency, former-client conflicts are not imputed to government lawyers associated with the individually disqualified lawyer.

[12] Where a lawyer is prohibited from engaging in certain transactions under Rule 1.8, paragraph (k) of that Rule, and not this Rule, determines whether that prohibition also applies to other lawyers associated in a firm with the personally prohibited lawyer.

Rule 1.11 Special Conflicts of Interest for Former and Current Government Officers and Employees

(a) Except as law may otherwise expressly permit, a lawyer who has formerly served as a public officer or employee of the government:

(1) is subject to Rule 1.9(c); and

(2) shall not otherwise represent a client in connection with a matter in which the lawyer participated personally and substantially as a public officer or employee, unless the appropriate government agency gives its informed consent, confirmed in writing, to the representation.

(b) When a lawyer is disqualified from representation under paragraph (a), no lawyer in a firm with which that lawyer is associated may knowingly undertake or continue representation in such a matter unless:

(1) the disqualified lawyer is timely screened from any participation in the matter and is apportioned no part of the fee therefrom; and

(2) written notice is promptly given to the appropriate government agency to enable it to ascertain compliance with the provisions of this rule.

(c) Except as law may otherwise expressly permit, a lawyer having information that the lawyer knows is confidential government information about a person acquired when the lawyer was a public officer or employee, may not represent a private client whose interests are adverse to that person in a matter in which the information could be used to the material disadvantage of that person. As used in this Rule, the term "confidential government information" means information that has been obtained under governmental authority and which, at the time this Rule is applied, the government is prohibited by law from disclosing to the public or has a legal privilege not to disclose and which is not otherwise available to the public. A firm with which that lawyer is associated may undertake or continue representation in the matter only if the disqualified lawyer is timely screened from any participation in the matter and is apportioned no part of the fee therefrom.

(d) Except as law may otherwise expressly permit, a lawyer currently serving as a public officer or employee:

(1) is subject to Rules 1.7 and 1.9; and

(2) shall not:

(i) participate in a matter in which the lawyer participated personally and substantially while in private practice or nongovernmental employment, unless the appropriate government agency gives its informed consent, confirmed in writing; or

(ii) negotiate for private employment with any person who is involved as a party or as lawyer for a party in a matter in which the lawyer is participating personally and substantially, except that a lawyer serving as a law clerk to a judge, other adjudicative officer or arbitrator may negotiate for private employment as permitted by Rule 1.12(b) and subject to the conditions stated in Rule 1.12(b).

(e) As used in this Rule, the term "matter" includes:

(1) any judicial or other proceeding, application, request for a ruling or other determination, contract, claim, controversy, investigation, charge, accusation, arrest or other particular matter involving a specific party or parties, and

(2) any other matter covered by the conflict of interest rules of the appropriate government agency.

COMMENT

[1] A lawyer who has served or is currently serving as a public officer or employee is personally subject to the Rules of Professional Conduct, including the prohibition against concurrent conflicts of interest stated in Rule 1.7. In addition, such a lawyer may be subject to statutes and government regulations

regarding conflict of interest. Such statutes and regulations may circumscribe the extent to which the government agency may give consent under this Rule. See Rule 1.0(e) for the definition of informed consent.

[2] Paragraphs (a)(1), (a)(2) and (d)(1) restate the obligations of an individual lawyer who has served or is currently serving as an officer or employee of the government toward a former government or private client. Rule 1.10 is not applicable to the conflicts of interest addressed by this Rule. Rather, paragraph (b) sets forth a special imputation rule for former government lawyers that provides for screening and notice. Because of the special problems raised by imputation within a government agency, paragraph (d) does not impute the conflicts of a lawyer currently serving as an officer or employee of the government to other associated government officers or employees, although ordinarily it will be prudent to screen such lawyers.

[3] Paragraphs (a)(2) and (d)(2) apply regardless of whether a lawyer is adverse to a former client and are thus designed not only to protect the former client, but also to prevent a lawyer from exploiting public office for the advantage of another client. For example, a lawyer who has pursued a claim on behalf of the government may not pursue the same claim on behalf of a later private client after the lawyer has left government service, except when authorized to do so by the government agency under paragraph (a). Similarly, a lawyer who has pursued a claim on behalf of a private client may not pursue the claim on behalf of the government, except when authorized to do so by paragraph (d). As with paragraphs (a)(1) and (d)(1), Rule 1.10 is not applicable to the conflicts of interest addressed by these paragraphs.

[4] This Rule represents a balancing of interests. On the one hand, where the successive clients are a government agency and another client, public or private, the risk exists that power or discretion vested in that agency might be used for the special benefit of the other client. A lawyer should not be in a position where benefit to the other client might affect performance of the lawyer's professional functions on behalf of the government. Also, unfair advantage could accrue to the other client by reason of access to confidential government information about the client's adversary obtainable only through the lawyer's government service. On the other hand, the rules governing lawyers presently or formerly employed by a government agency should not be so restrictive as to inhibit transfer of employment to and from the government. The government has a legitimate need to attract qualified lawyers as well as to maintain high ethical standards. Thus a former government lawyer is disqualified only from particular matters in which the lawyer participated personally and substantially. The provisions for screening and waiver in paragraph (b) are necessary to prevent the disqualification rule from imposing too severe a deterrent against entering public service. The limitation of disqualification in paragraphs (a)(2) and (d)(2) to matters involving a specific party or parties, rather than extending disqualification to all substantive issues on which the lawyer worked, serves a similar function.

[5] When a lawyer has been employed by one government agency and then moves to a second government agency, it may be appropriate to treat that second agency as another client for purposes of this Rule, as when a lawyer is employed by a city and subsequently is employed by a federal agency. However, because the conflict of interest is governed by paragraph (d), the latter agency is not required to screen the lawyer as paragraph (b) requires a law firm to do. The question of whether two government agencies should be regarded as the same or different clients for conflict of interest purposes is beyond the scope of these Rules. See Rule 1.13 Comment [6].

[6] Paragraphs (b) and (c) contemplate a screening arrangement. See Rule 1.0(k) (requirements for screening procedures). These paragraphs do not prohibit a lawyer from receiving a salary or partnership share established by prior independent agreement, but that lawyer may not receive compensation directly relating the lawyer's compensation to the fee in the matter in which the lawyer is disqualified.

[7] Notice, including a description of the screened lawyer's prior representation and of the screening procedures employed, generally should be given as soon as practicable after the need for screening becomes apparent.

[8] Paragraph (c) operates only when the lawyer in question has knowledge of the information, which means actual knowledge; it does not operate with respect to information that merely could be imputed to the lawyer.

[9] Paragraphs (a) and (d) do not prohibit a lawyer from jointly representing a private party and a government agency when doing so is permitted by Rule 1.7 and is not otherwise prohibited by law.

[10] For purposes of paragraph (e) of this Rule, a "matter" may continue in another form. In determining whether two particular matters are the same, the lawyer should consider the extent to which the matters involve the same basic facts, the same or related parties, and the time elapsed.

Rule 1.12 Former Judge, Arbitrator, Mediator, or Other Third-Party Neutral

(a) Except as stated in paragraph (d), a lawyer shall not represent anyone in connection with a matter in which the lawyer participated personally and substantially as a judge or other adjudicative officer or law clerk to such a person or as an arbitrator, mediator or other third-party neutral, unless all parties to the proceeding give informed consent, confirmed in writing.

(b) A lawyer shall not negotiate for employment with any person who is involved as a party or as lawyer for a party in a matter in which the lawyer is participating personally and substantially as a judge or other adjudicative officer or as an arbitrator, mediator or other third-party neutral. A lawyer serving as a law clerk to a judge or other adjudicative officer may negotiate for employment with a party or lawyer involved in a matter in which the clerk is participating personally and substantially, but only after the lawyer has notified the judge, or other adjudicative officer.

(c) If a lawyer is disqualified by paragraph (a), no lawyer in a firm with which that lawyer is associated may knowingly undertake or continue representation in the matter unless:

(1) the disqualified lawyer is timely screened from any participation in the matter and is apportioned no part of the fee therefrom; and

(2) written notice is promptly given to the parties and any appropriate tribunal to enable them to ascertain compliance with the provisions of this rule.

(d) An arbitrator selected as a partisan of a party in a multimember arbitration panel is not prohibited from subsequently representing that party.

COMMENT

[1] This Rule generally parallels Rule 1.11. The term "personally and substantially" signifies that a judge who was a member of a multimember court, and thereafter left judicial office to practice law, is not prohibited from representing a client in a matter pending in the court, but in which the former judge did not participate. So also the fact that a former judge exercised administrative responsibility in a court does not prevent the former judge from acting as a lawyer in a matter where the judge had previously exercised remote or incidental administrative responsibility that did not affect the merits. Compare the Comment to Rule 1.11. The term "adjudicative officer" includes such officials as judges pro tempore, referees, special masters, hearing officers and other parajudicial officers, and also lawyers who serve as part-time judges. Compliance Canons A(2), B(2) and C of the Model Code of Judicial Conduct provide that a part-time judge, judge pro tempore or retired judge recalled to active service, may not "act as a lawyer in any proceeding in which he served as a judge or in any other proceeding related thereto." Although phrased differently from this Rule, those Rules correspond in meaning.

[2] Like former judges, lawyers who have served as arbitrators, mediators or other third-party neutrals may be asked to represent a client in a matter in which the lawyer participated personally and substantially. This Rule forbids such representation unless all of the parties to the proceedings give their informed consent, confirmed in writing. See Rule 1.0(e) and (b). Other law or codes of ethics governing third-party neutrals may impose more stringent standards of personal or imputed disqualification. See Rule 2.4.

[3] Although lawyers who serve as third-party neutrals do not have information concerning the parties that is protected under Rule 1.6, they typically owe the parties an obligation of confidentiality under law or codes of ethics governing third-party neutrals. Thus, paragraph (c) provides that conflicts of the personally disqualified lawyer will be imputed to other lawyers in a law firm unless the conditions of this paragraph are met.

[4] Requirements for screening procedures are stated in Rule 1.0(k). Paragraph (c)(1) does not prohibit the screened lawyer from receiving a salary or partnership share established by prior independent agreement, but that lawyer may not receive compensation directly related to the matter in which the lawyer is disqualified.

[5] Notice, including a description of the screened lawyer's prior representation and of the screening procedures employed, generally should be given as soon as practicable after the need for screening becomes apparent.

Rule 1.13 Organization as Client*

(a) A lawyer employed or retained by an organization represents the organization acting through its duly authorized constituents.

(b) If a lawyer for an organization knows that an officer, employee or other person associated with the organization is engaged in action, intends to act or refuses to act in a matter related to the representation that is a violation of a legal obligation to the organization, or a violation of law that reasonably might be imputed to the organization, and that is likely to result in substantial injury to the organization, then the lawyer shall proceed as is reasonably necessary in the best interest of the organization. Unless the lawyer reasonably believes that it is not necessary in the best interest of the organization to do so, the lawyer shall refer the matter to higher authority in the organization, including, if warranted by the circumstances, to the highest authority that can act on behalf of the organization as determined by applicable law.

(c) Except as provided in paragraph (d), if,

(1) despite the lawyer's efforts in accordance with paragraph (b), the highest authority that can act on behalf of the organization insists upon or fails to address in a timely and appropriate manner an action, or a refusal to act, that is clearly a violation of law, and

---

* In August 2003, the ABA House of Delegates modified Model Rule 1.13 to respond to the claims that the old rule did not permit lawyers to prevent corporate fraud which had a significant impact on their client's financial well being. The old rule text read as follows:

(a) A lawyer employed or retained by an organization represents the organization acting through its duly authorized constituents.

(b) If a lawyer for an organization knows that an officer, employee or other person associated with the organization is engaged in action, intends to act or refuses to act in a matter related to the representation that is a violation of a legal obligation to the organization, or a violation of law which reasonably might be imputed to the organization, and is likely to result in substantial injury to the organization, the lawyer shall proceed as is reasonably necessary in the best interest of the organization. In determining how to proceed, the lawyer shall give due consideration to the seriousness of the violation and its consequences, the scope and nature of the lawyer's representation, the responsibility in the organization and the apparent motivation of the person involved, the policies of the organization concerning such matters and any other relevant considerations. Any measures taken shall be designed to minimize disruption of the organization and the risk of revealing information relating to the representation to persons outside the organization. Such measures may include among others:

(1) asking for reconsideration of the matter;

(2) advising that a separate legal opinion on the matter be sought for presentation to appropriate authority in the organization; and

(3) referring the matter to higher authority in the organization, including, if warranted by the seriousness of the matter, referral to the highest authority that can act on behalf of the organization as determined by applicable law.

(c) If, despite the lawyer's efforts in accordance with paragraph (b), the highest authority that can act on behalf of the organization insists upon action, or a refusal to act, that is clearly a violation of law and is likely to result in substantial injury to the organization, the lawyer may resign in accordance with Rule 1.16.

(d) In dealing with an organization's directors, officers, employees, members, shareholders or other constituents, a lawyer shall explain the identity of the client when the lawyer knows or reasonably should know that the organization's interests are adverse to those of the constituents with whom the lawyer is dealing.

(e) A lawyer representing an organization may also represent any of its directors, officers, employees, members, shareholders or other constituents, subject to the provisions of Rule 1.7. If the organization's consent to the dual representation is required by Rule 1.7, the consent shall be given by an appropriate official of the organization other than the individual who is to be represented, or by the shareholders.

(2) the lawyer reasonably believes that the violation is reasonably certain to result in substantial injury to the organization,

then the lawyer may reveal information relating to the representation whether or not Rule 1.6 permits such disclosure, but only if and to the extent the lawyer reasonably believes necessary to prevent substantial injury to the organization.

(d) Paragraph (c) shall not apply with respect to information relating to a lawyer's representation of an organization to investigate an alleged violation of law, or to defend the organization or an officer, employee or other constituent associated with the organization against a claim arising out of an alleged violation of law.

(e) A lawyer who reasonably believes that he or she has been discharged because of the lawyer's actions taken pursuant to paragraphs (b) or (c), or who withdraws under circumstances that require or permit the lawyer to take action under either of those paragraphs, shall proceed as the lawyer reasonably believes necessary to assure that the organization's highest authority is informed of the lawyer's discharge or withdrawal.

(f) In dealing with an organization's directors, officers, employees, members, shareholders or other constituents, a lawyer shall explain the identity of the client when the lawyer knows or reasonably should know that the organization's interests are adverse to those of the constituents with whom the lawyer is dealing.

(g) A lawyer representing an organization may also represent any of its directors, officers, employees, members, shareholders or other constituents, subject to the provisions of Rule 1.7. If the organization's consent to the dual representation is required by Rule 1.7, the consent shall be given by an appropriate official of the organization other than the individual who is to be represented, or by the shareholders.

COMMENT

The Entity as the Client

[1] An organizational client is a legal entity, but it cannot act except through its officers, directors, employees, shareholders and other constituents. Officers, directors, employees and shareholders are the constituents of the corporate organizational client. The duties defined in this Comment apply equally to unincorporated associations. "Other constituents" as used in this Comment means the positions equivalent to officers, directors, employees and shareholders held by persons acting for organizational clients that are not corporations.

[2] When one of the constituents of an organizational client communicates with the organization's lawyer in that person's organizational capacity, the communication is protected by Rule 1.6. Thus, by way of example, if an organizational client requests its lawyer to investigate allegations of wrongdoing, interviews made in the course of that investigation between the lawyer and the client's employees or other constituents are covered by Rule 1.6. This does not mean, however, that constituents of an organizational client are the clients of the lawyer. The lawyer may not disclose to such constituents information relating to the representation except for disclosures explicitly or impliedly authorized by the organizational client in order to carry out the representation or as otherwise permitted by Rule 1.6.

[3] When constituents of the organization make decisions for it, the decisions ordinarily must be accepted by the lawyer even if their utility or prudence is doubtful. Decisions concerning policy and operations, including ones entailing serious risk, are not as such in the lawyer's province. Paragraph (b) makes clear, however, that when the lawyer knows that the organization is likely to be substantially injured by action of an officer or other constituent that violates a legal obligation to the organization or is in violation of law that might be imputed to the organization, the lawyer must proceed as is reasonably necessary in the best interest of the organization. As defined in Rule 1.0(f), knowledge can be inferred from circumstances, and a lawyer cannot ignore the obvious.

[4] In determining how to proceed under paragraph (b), the lawyer should give due consideration to the seriousness of the violation and its consequences, the responsibility in the organization and the apparent motivation of the person involved, the policies of the organization concerning such matters, and any other

relevant considerations. Ordinarily, referral to a higher authority would be necessary. In some circumstances, however, it may be appropriate for the lawyer to ask the constituent to reconsider the matter; for example, if the circumstances involve a constituent's innocent misunderstanding of law and subsequent acceptance of the lawyer's advice, the lawyer may reasonably conclude that the best interest of the organization does not require that the matter be referred to higher authority. If a constituent persists in conduct contrary to the lawyer's advice, it will be necessary for the lawyer to take steps to have the matter reviewed by a higher authority in the organization. If the matter is of sufficient seriousness and importance or urgency to the organization, referral to higher authority in the organization may be necessary even if the lawyer has not communicated with the constituent. Any measures taken should, to the extent practicable, minimize the risk of revealing information relating to the representation to persons outside the organization. Even in circumstances where a lawyer is not obligated by Rule 1.13 to proceed, a lawyer may bring to the attention of an organizational client, including its highest authority, matters that the lawyer reasonably believes to be of sufficient importance to warrant doing so in the best interest of the organization.

[5] Paragraph (b) also makes clear that when it is reasonably necessary to enable the organization to address the matter in a timely and appropriate manner, the lawyer must refer the matter to higher authority, including, if warranted by the circumstances, the highest authority that can act on behalf of the organization under applicable law. The organization's highest authority to whom a matter may be referred ordinarily will be the board of directors or similar governing body. However, applicable law may prescribe that under certain conditions the highest authority reposes elsewhere, for example, in the independent directors of a corporation.

Relation to Other Rules

[6] The authority and responsibility provided in this Rule are concurrent with the authority and responsibility provided in other Rules. In particular, this Rule does not limit or expand the lawyer's responsibility under Rules 1.6, 1.8, 1.16, 3.3 or 4.1. Paragraph (c) of this Rule supplements Rule 1.6(b) by providing an additional basis upon which the lawyer may reveal information relating to the representation, but does not modify, restrict, or limit the provisions of Rule 1.6(b)(1)–(6). Under paragraph (c) the lawyer may reveal such information only when the organization's highest authority insists upon or fails to address threatened or ongoing action that is clearly a violation of law, and then only to the extent the lawyer reasonably believes necessary to prevent reasonably certain substantial injury to the organization. It is not necessary that the lawyer's services be used in furtherance of the violation, but it is required that the matter be related to the lawyer's representation of the organization. If the lawyer's services are being used by an organization to further a crime or fraud by the organization, Rules 1.6(b)(2) and 1.6(b)(3) may permit the lawyer to disclose confidential information. In such circumstances Rule 1.2(d) may also be applicable, in which event, withdrawal from the representation under Rule 1.16(a)(1) may be required.

[7] Paragraph (d) makes clear that the authority of a lawyer to disclose information relating to a representation in circumstances described in paragraph (c) does not apply with respect to information relating to a lawyer's engagement by an organization to investigate an alleged violation of law or to defend the organization or an officer, employee or other person associated with the organization against a claim arising out of an alleged violation of law. This is necessary in order to enable organizational clients to enjoy the full benefits of legal counsel in conducting an investigation or defending against a claim.

[8] A lawyer who reasonably believes that he or she has been discharged because of the lawyer's actions taken pursuant to paragraph (b) or (c), or who withdraws in circumstances that require or permit the lawyer to take action under either of these paragraphs, must proceed as the lawyer reasonably believes necessary to assure that the organization's highest authority is informed of the lawyer's discharge or withdrawal.

Government Agency

[9] The duty defined in this Rule applies to governmental organizations. Defining precisely the identity of the client and prescribing the resulting obligations of such lawyers may be more difficult in the government context and is a matter beyond the scope of these Rules. See Scope [18]. Although in some circumstances the client may be a specific agency, it may also be a branch of government, such as the executive branch, or the government as a whole. For example, if the action or failure to act involves the head of a bureau, either the department of which the bureau is a part or the relevant branch of government may be the client for purposes of this Rule. Moreover, in a matter involving the conduct of government officials,

a government lawyer may have authority under applicable law to question such conduct more extensively than that of a lawyer for a private organization in similar circumstances. Thus, when the client is a governmental organization, a different balance may be appropriate between maintaining confidentiality and assuring that the wrongful act is prevented or rectified, for public business is involved. In addition, duties of lawyers employed by the government or lawyers in military service may be defined by statutes and regulation. This Rule does not limit that authority. See Scope.

Clarifying the Lawyer's Role

[10] There are times when the organization's interest may be or become adverse to those of one or more of its constituents. In such circumstances the lawyer should advise any constituent, whose interest the lawyer finds adverse to that of the organization of the conflict or potential conflict of interest, that the lawyer cannot represent such constituent, and that such person may wish to obtain independent representation. Care must be taken to assure that the individual understands that, when there is such adversity of interest, the lawyer for the organization cannot provide legal representation for that constituent individual, and that discussions between the lawyer for the organization and the individual may not be privileged.

[11] Whether such a warning should be given by the lawyer for the organization to any constituent individual may turn on the facts of each case.

Dual Representation

[12] Paragraph (g) recognizes that a lawyer for an organization may also represent a principal officer or major shareholder.

Derivative Actions

[13] Under generally prevailing law, the shareholders or members of a corporation may bring suit to compel the directors to perform their legal obligations in the supervision of the organization. Members of unincorporated associations have essentially the same right. Such an action may be brought nominally by the organization, but usually is, in fact, a legal controversy over management of the organization.

[14] The question can arise whether counsel for the organization may defend such an action. The proposition that the organization is the lawyer's client does not alone resolve the issue. Most derivative actions are a normal incident of an organization's affairs, to be defended by the organization's lawyer like any other suit. However, if the claim involves serious charges of wrongdoing by those in control of the organization, a conflict may arise between the lawyer's duty to the organization and the lawyer's relationship with the board. In those circumstances, Rule 1.7 governs who should represent the directors and the organization.

Rule 1.14 Client with Diminished Capacity

(a) When a client's capacity to make adequately considered decisions in connection with a representation is diminished, whether because of minority, mental impairment or for some other reason, the lawyer shall, as far as reasonably possible, maintain a normal client-lawyer relationship with the client.

(b) When the lawyer reasonably believes that the client has diminished capacity, is at risk of substantial physical, financial or other harm unless action is taken and cannot adequately act in the client's own interest, the lawyer may take reasonably necessary protective action, including consulting with individuals or entities that have the ability to take action to protect the client and, in appropriate cases, seeking the appointment of a guardian ad litem, conservator or guardian.

(c) Information relating to the representation of a client with diminished capacity is protected by Rule 1.6. When taking protective action pursuant to paragraph (b), the lawyer is impliedly authorized under Rule 1.6(a) to reveal information about the client, but only to the extent reasonably necessary to protect the client's interests.

COMMENT

[1] The normal client-lawyer relationship is based on the assumption that the client, when properly advised and assisted, is capable of making decisions about important matters. When the client is a minor or suffers from a diminished mental capacity, however, maintaining the ordinary client-lawyer relationship may not be possible in all respects. In particular, a severely incapacitated person may have no power to make legally binding decisions. Nevertheless, a client with diminished capacity often has the ability to understand, deliberate upon, and reach conclusions about matters affecting the client's own well-being. For example, children as young as five or six years of age, and certainly those of ten or twelve, are regarded as having opinions that are entitled to weight in legal proceedings concerning their custody. So also, it is recognized that some persons of advanced age can be quite capable of handling routine financial matters while needing special legal protection concerning major transactions.

[2] The fact that a client suffers a disability does not diminish the lawyer's obligation to treat the client with attention and respect. Even if the person has a legal representative, the lawyer should as far as possible accord the represented person the status of client, particularly in maintaining communication.

[3] The client may wish to have family members or other persons participate in discussions with the lawyer. When necessary to assist in the representation, the presence of such persons generally does not affect the applicability of the attorney-client evidentiary privilege. Nevertheless, the lawyer must keep the client's interests foremost and, except for protective action authorized under paragraph (b), must to look to the client, and not family members, to make decisions on the client's behalf.

[4] If a legal representative has already been appointed for the client, the lawyer should ordinarily look to the representative for decisions on behalf of the client. In matters involving a minor, whether the lawyer should look to the parents as natural guardians may depend on the type of proceeding or matter in which the lawyer is representing the minor. If the lawyer represents the guardian as distinct from the ward, and is aware that the guardian is acting adversely to the ward's interest, the lawyer may have an obligation to prevent or rectify the guardian's misconduct. See Rule 1.2(d).

Taking Protective Action

[5] If a lawyer reasonably believes that a client is at risk of substantial physical, financial or other harm unless action is taken, and that a normal client-lawyer relationship cannot be maintained as provided in paragraph (a) because the client lacks sufficient capacity to communicate or to make adequately considered decisions in connection with the representation, then paragraph (b) permits the lawyer to take protective measures deemed necessary. Such measures could include: consulting with family members, using a reconsideration period to permit clarification or improvement of circumstances, using voluntary surrogate decisionmaking tools such as durable powers of attorney or consulting with support groups, professional services, adult-protective agencies or other individuals or entities that have the ability to protect the client. In taking any protective action, the lawyer should be guided by such factors as the wishes and values of the client to the extent known, the client's best interests and the goals of intruding into the client's decisionmaking autonomy to the least extent feasible, maximizing client capacities and respecting the client's family and social connections.

[6] In determining the extent of the client's diminished capacity, the lawyer should consider and balance such factors as: the client's ability to articulate reasoning leading to a decision, variability of state of mind and ability to appreciate consequences of a decision; the substantive fairness of a decision; and the consistency of a decision with the known long-term commitments and values of the client. In appropriate circumstances, the lawyer may seek guidance from an appropriate diagnostician.

[7] If a legal representative has not been appointed, the lawyer should consider whether appointment of a guardian ad litem, conservator or guardian is necessary to protect the client's interests. Thus, if a client with diminished capacity has substantial property that should be sold for the client's benefit, effective completion of the transaction may require appointment of a legal representative. In addition, rules of procedure in litigation sometimes provide that minors or persons with diminished capacity must be represented by a guardian or next friend if they do not have a general guardian. In many circumstances, however, appointment of a legal representative may be more expensive or traumatic for the client than circumstances in fact require. Evaluation of such circumstances is a matter entrusted to the professional

judgment of the lawyer. In considering alternatives, however, the lawyer should be aware of any law that requires the lawyer to advocate the least restrictive action on behalf of the client.

Disclosure of the Client's Condition

[8] Disclosure of the client's diminished capacity could adversely affect the client's interests. For example, raising the question of diminished capacity could, in some circumstances, lead to proceedings for involuntary commitment. Information relating to the representation is protected by Rule 1.6. Therefore, unless authorized to do so, the lawyer may not disclose such information. When taking protective action pursuant to paragraph (b), the lawyer is impliedly authorized to make the necessary disclosures, even when the client directs the lawyer to the contrary. Nevertheless, given the risks of disclosure, paragraph (c) limits what the lawyer may disclose in consulting with other individuals or entities or seeking the appointment of a legal representative. At the very least, the lawyer should determine whether it is likely that the person or entity consulted with will act adversely to the client's interests before discussing matters related to the client. The lawyer's position in such cases is an unavoidably difficult one.

Emergency Legal Assistance

[9] In an emergency where the health, safety or a financial interest of a person with seriously diminished capacity is threatened with imminent and irreparable harm, a lawyer may take legal action on behalf of such a person even though the person is unable to establish a client-lawyer relationship or to make or express considered judgments about the matter, when the person or another acting in good faith on that person's behalf has consulted with the lawyer. Even in such an emergency, however, the lawyer should not act unless the lawyer reasonably believes that the person has no other lawyer, agent or other representative available. The lawyer should take legal action on behalf of the person only to the extent reasonably necessary to maintain the status quo or otherwise avoid imminent and irreparable harm. A lawyer who undertakes to represent a person in such an exigent situation has the same duties under these Rules as the lawyer would with respect to a client.

[10] A lawyer who acts on behalf of a person with seriously diminished capacity in an emergency should keep the confidences of the person as if dealing with a client, disclosing them only to the extent necessary to accomplish the intended protective action. The lawyer should disclose to any tribunal involved and to any other counsel involved the nature of his or her relationship with the person. The lawyer should take steps to regularize the relationship or implement other protective solutions as soon as possible. Normally, a lawyer would not seek compensation for such emergency actions taken.

Rule 1.15 Safekeeping Property

(a) A lawyer shall hold property of clients or third persons that is in a lawyer's possession in connection with a representation separate from the lawyer's own property. Funds shall be kept in a separate account maintained in the state where the lawyer's office is situated, or elsewhere with the consent of the client or third person. Other property shall be identified as such and appropriately safeguarded. Complete records of such account funds and other property shall be kept by the lawyer and shall be preserved for a period of [five years] after termination of the representation.

(b) A lawyer may deposit the lawyer's own funds in a client trust account for the sole purpose of paying bank service charges on that account, but only in an amount necessary for that purpose.

(c) A lawyer shall deposit into a client trust account legal fees and expenses that have been paid in advance, to be withdrawn by the lawyer only as fees are earned or expenses incurred.

(d) Upon receiving funds or other property in which a client or third person has an interest, a lawyer shall promptly notify the client or third person. Except as stated in this rule or otherwise permitted by law or by agreement with the client, a lawyer shall promptly deliver to the client or third person any funds or other property that the client or third person is entitled to receive and, upon request by the client or third person, shall promptly render a full accounting regarding such property.

(e) When in the course of representation a lawyer is in possession of property in which two or more persons (one of whom may be the lawyer) claim interests, the property shall be kept separate by the lawyer until the dispute is resolved. The lawyer shall promptly distribute all portions of the property as to which the interests are not in dispute.

COMMENT

[1] A lawyer should hold property of others with the care required of a professional fiduciary. Securities should be kept in a safe deposit box, except when some other form of safekeeping is warranted by special circumstances. All property that is the property of clients or third persons, including prospective clients, must be kept separate from the lawyer's business and personal property and, if monies, in one or more trust accounts. Separate trust accounts may be warranted when administering estate monies or acting in similar fiduciary capacities. A lawyer should maintain on a current basis books and records in accordance with generally accepted accounting practice and comply with any recordkeeping rules established by law or court order. See, e.g., ABA Model Financial Recordkeeping Rule.

[2] While normally it is impermissible to commingle the lawyer's own funds with client funds, paragraph (b) provides that it is permissible when necessary to pay bank service charges on that account. Accurate records must be kept regarding which part of the funds are the lawyer's.

[3] Lawyers often receive funds from which the lawyer's fee will be paid. The lawyer is not required to remit to the client funds that the lawyer reasonably believes represent fees owed. However, a lawyer may not hold funds to coerce a client into accepting the lawyer's contention. The disputed portion of the funds must be kept in a trust account and the lawyer should suggest means for prompt resolution of the dispute, such as arbitration. The undisputed portion of the funds shall be promptly distributed.

[4] Paragraph (e) also recognizes that third parties may have lawful claims against specific funds or other property in a lawyer's custody, such as a client's creditor who has a lien on funds recovered in a personal injury action. A lawyer may have a duty under applicable law to protect such third-party claims against wrongful interference by the client. In such cases, when the third-party claim is not frivolous under applicable law, the lawyer must refuse to surrender the property to the client until the claims are resolved. A lawyer should not unilaterally assume to arbitrate a dispute between the client and the third party, but, when there are substantial grounds for dispute as to the person entitled to the funds, the lawyer may file an action to have a court resolve the dispute.

[5] The obligations of a lawyer under this Rule are independent of those arising from activity other than rendering legal services. For example, a lawyer who serves only as an escrow agent is governed by the applicable law relating to fiduciaries even though the lawyer does not render legal services in the transaction and is not governed by this Rule.

[6] A lawyers' fund for client protection provides a means through the collective efforts of the bar to reimburse persons who have lost money or property as a result of dishonest conduct of a lawyer. Where such a fund has been established, a lawyer must participate where it is mandatory, and, even when it is voluntary, the lawyer should participate.

Rule 1.16 Declining or Terminating Representation

(a) Except as stated in paragraph (c), a lawyer shall not represent a client or, where representation has commenced, shall withdraw from the representation of a client if:

(1) the representation will result in violation of the rules of professional conduct or other law;

(2) the lawyer's physical or mental condition materially impairs the lawyer's ability to represent the client; or

(3) the lawyer is discharged.

(b) Except as stated in paragraph (c), a lawyer may withdraw from representing a client if:

(1) withdrawal can be accomplished without material adverse effect on the interests of the client;

(2) the client persists in a course of action involving the lawyer's services that the lawyer reasonably believes is criminal or fraudulent;

(3) the client has used the lawyer's services to perpetrate a crime or fraud;

(4) the client insists upon taking action that the lawyer considers repugnant or with which the lawyer has a fundamental disagreement;

(5) the client fails substantially to fulfill an obligation to the lawyer regarding the lawyer's services and has been given reasonable warning that the lawyer will withdraw unless the obligation is fulfilled;

(6) the representation will result in an unreasonable financial burden on the lawyer or has been rendered unreasonably difficult by the client; or

(7) other good cause for withdrawal exists.

(c) A lawyer must comply with applicable law requiring notice to or permission of a tribunal when terminating a representation. When ordered to do so by a tribunal, a lawyer shall continue representation notwithstanding good cause for terminating the representation.

(d) Upon termination of representation, a lawyer shall take steps to the extent reasonably practicable to protect a client's interests, such as giving reasonable notice to the client, allowing time for employment of other counsel, surrendering papers and property to which the client is entitled and refunding any advance payment of fee or expense that has not been earned or incurred. The lawyer may retain papers relating to the client to the extent permitted by other law.

COMMENT

[1] A lawyer should not accept representation in a matter unless it can be performed competently, promptly, without improper conflict of interest and to completion. Ordinarily, a representation in a matter is completed when the agreed-upon assistance has been concluded. See Rules 1.2(c) and 6.5. See also Rule 1.3, Comment [4].

Mandatory Withdrawal

[2] A lawyer ordinarily must decline or withdraw from representation if the client demands that the lawyer engage in conduct that is illegal or violates the Rules of Professional Conduct or other law. The lawyer is not obliged to decline or withdraw simply because the client suggests such a course of conduct; a client may make such a suggestion in the hope that a lawyer will not be constrained by a professional obligation.

[3] When a lawyer has been appointed to represent a client, withdrawal ordinarily requires approval of the appointing authority. See also Rule 6.2. Similarly, court approval or notice to the court is often required by applicable law before a lawyer withdraws from pending litigation. Difficulty may be encountered if withdrawal is based on the client's demand that the lawyer engage in unprofessional conduct. The court may request an explanation for the withdrawal, while the lawyer may be bound to keep confidential the facts that would constitute such an explanation. The lawyer's statement that professional considerations require termination of the representation ordinarily should be accepted as sufficient. Lawyers should be mindful of their obligations to both clients and the court under Rules 1.6 and 3.3.

Discharge

[4] A client has a right to discharge a lawyer at any time, with or without cause, subject to liability for payment for the lawyer's services. Where future dispute about the withdrawal may be anticipated, it may be advisable to prepare a written statement reciting the circumstances.

[5] Whether a client can discharge appointed counsel may depend on applicable law. A client seeking to do so should be given a full explanation of the consequences. These consequences may include a decision by the appointing authority that appointment of successor counsel is unjustified, thus requiring self-representation by the client.

[6] If the client has severely diminished capacity, the client may lack the legal capacity to discharge the lawyer, and in any event the discharge may be seriously adverse to the client's interests. The lawyer should make special effort to help the client consider the consequences and may take reasonably necessary protective action as provided in Rule 1.14.

Optional Withdrawal

[7] A lawyer may withdraw from representation in some circumstances. The lawyer has the option to withdraw if it can be accomplished without material adverse effect on the client's interests. Withdrawal is also justified if the client persists in a course of action that the lawyer reasonably believes is criminal or fraudulent, for a lawyer is not required to be associated with such conduct even if the lawyer does not further it. Withdrawal is also permitted if the lawyer's services were misused in the past even if that would materially prejudice the client. The lawyer may also withdraw where the client insists on taking action that the lawyer considers repugnant or with which the lawyer has a fundamental disagreement.

[8] A lawyer may withdraw if the client refuses to abide by the terms of an agreement relating to the representation, such as an agreement concerning fees or court costs or an agreement limiting the objectives of the representation.

Assisting the Client upon Withdrawal

[9] Even if the lawyer has been unfairly discharged by the client, a lawyer must take all reasonable steps to mitigate the consequences to the client. The lawyer may retain papers as security for a fee only to the extent permitted by law. See Rule 1.15.

Rule 1.17 Sale of Law Practice

A lawyer or a law firm may sell or purchase a law practice, or an area of law practice, including good will, if the following conditions are satisfied:

(a) The seller ceases to engage in the private practice of law, or in the area of practice that has been sold, [in the geographic area] [in the jurisdiction] (a jurisdiction may elect either version) in which the practice has been conducted;

(b) The entire practice, or the entire area of practice, is sold to one or more lawyers or law firms;

(c) The seller gives written notice to each of the seller's clients regarding:

(1) the proposed sale;

(2) the client's right to retain other counsel or to take possession of the file; and

(3) the fact that the client's consent to the transfer of the client's files will be presumed if the client does not take any action or does not otherwise object within ninety (90) days of receipt of the notice.

If a client cannot be given notice, the representation of that client may be transferred to the purchaser only upon entry of an order so authorizing by a court having jurisdiction. The seller may disclose to the court in camera information relating to the representation only to the extent necessary to obtain an order authorizing the transfer of a file.

(d) The fees charged clients shall not be increased by reason of the sale.

COMMENT

[1] The practice of law is a profession, not merely a business. Clients are not commodities that can be purchased and sold at will. Pursuant to this Rule, when a lawyer or an entire firm ceases to practice, or ceases to practice in an area of law, and other lawyers or firms take over the representation, the selling

lawyer or firm may obtain compensation for the reasonable value of the practice as may withdrawing partners of law firms. See Rules 5.4 and 5.6.

Termination of Practice by the Seller

[2] The requirement that all of the private practice, or all of an area of practice, be sold is satisfied if the seller in good faith makes the entire practice, or the area of practice, available for sale to the purchasers. The fact that a number of the seller's clients decide not to be represented by the purchasers but take their matters elsewhere, therefore, does not result in a violation. Return to private practice as a result of an unanticipated change in circumstances does not necessarily result in a violation. For example, a lawyer who has sold the practice to accept an appointment to judicial office does not violate the requirement that the sale be attendant to cessation of practice if the lawyer later resumes private practice upon being defeated in a contested or a retention election for the office or resigns from a judiciary position.

[3] The requirement that the seller cease to engage in the private practice of law does not prohibit employment as a lawyer on the staff of a public agency or a legal services entity that provides legal services to the poor, or as in-house counsel to a business.

[4] The Rule permits a sale of an entire practice attendant upon retirement from the private practice of law within the jurisdiction. Its provisions, therefore, accommodate the lawyer who sells the practice on the occasion of moving to another state. Some states are so large that a move from one locale therein to another is tantamount to leaving the jurisdiction in which the lawyer has engaged in the practice of law. To also accommodate lawyers so situated, states may permit the sale of the practice when the lawyer leaves the geographical area rather than the jurisdiction. The alternative desired should be indicated by selecting one of the two provided for in Rule 1.17(a).

[5] This Rule also permits a lawyer or law firm to sell an area of practice. If an area of practice is sold and the lawyer remains in the active practice of law, the lawyer must cease accepting any matters in the area of practice that has been sold, either as counsel or co-counsel or by assuming joint responsibility for a matter in connection with the division of a fee with another lawyer as would otherwise be permitted by Rule 1.5(e). For example, a lawyer with a substantial number of estate planning matters and a substantial number of probate administration cases may sell the estate planning portion of the practice but remain in the practice of law by concentrating on probate administration; however, that practitioner may not thereafter accept any estate planning matters. Although a lawyer who leaves a jurisdiction or geographical area typically would sell the entire practice, this Rule permits the lawyer to limit the sale to one or more areas of the practice, thereby preserving the lawyer's right to continue practice in the areas of the practice that were not sold.

Sale of Entire Practice or Entire Area of Practice

[6] The Rule requires that the seller's entire practice, or an entire area of practice, be sold. The prohibition against sale of less than an entire practice area protects those clients whose matters are less lucrative and who might find it difficult to secure other counsel if a sale could be limited to substantial fee-generating matters. The purchasers are required to undertake all client matters in the practice or practice area, subject to client consent. This requirement is satisfied, however, even if a purchaser is unable to undertake a particular client matter because of a conflict of interest.

Client Confidences, Consent and Notice

*[7] Negotiations between seller and prospective purchaser prior to disclosure of information relating to a specific representation of an identifiable client no more violate the confidentiality provisions of Model Rule 1.6 than do preliminary discussions concerning the possible association of another lawyer or mergers between firms, with respect to which client consent is not required. See Rule 1.6(b)(7). Providing the purchaser access to detailed information relating to the representation, such as the client's file, however, requires client consent. The Rule provides that before such information can be disclosed by the seller to the purchaser the client must be given actual written notice of the contemplated sale, including the identity of the purchaser, and must be told that the decision to consent or make other arrangements must be made within 90 days. If nothing is heard from the client within that time, consent to the sale is presumed.

---

* In August 2012, the ABA House of Delegates amended Comment 7 to reflect the addition of new Rule 1.6(b)(7).

[8] A lawyer or law firm ceasing to practice cannot be required to remain in practice because some clients cannot be given actual notice of the proposed purchase. Since these clients cannot themselves consent to the purchase or direct any other disposition of their files, the Rule requires an order from a court having jurisdiction authorizing their transfer or other disposition. The Court can be expected to determine whether reasonable efforts to locate the client have been exhausted, and whether the absent client's legitimate interests will be served by authorizing the transfer of the file so that the purchaser may continue the representation. Preservation of client confidences requires that the petition for a court order be considered in camera. (A procedure by which such an order can be obtained needs to be established in jurisdictions in which it presently does not exist.)

[9] All elements of client autonomy, including the client's absolute right to discharge a lawyer and transfer the representation to another, survive the sale of the practice or area of practice.

Fee Arrangements Between Client and Purchaser

[10] The sale may not be financed by increases in fees charged the clients of the practice. Existing arrangements between the seller and the client as to fees and the scope of the work must be honored by the purchaser.

Other Applicable Ethical Standards

[11] Lawyers participating in the sale of a law practice or a practice area are subject to the ethical standards applicable to involving another lawyer in the representation of a client. These include, for example, the seller's obligation to exercise competence in identifying a purchaser qualified to assume the practice and the purchaser's obligation to undertake the representation competently (see Rule 1.1); the obligation to avoid disqualifying conflicts, and to secure the client's informed consent for those conflicts that can be agreed to (see Rule 1.7 regarding conflicts and Rule 1.0(e) for the definition of informed consent); and the obligation to protect information relating to the representation (see Rules 1.6 and 1.9).

[12] If approval of the substitution of the purchasing lawyer for the selling lawyer is required by the rules of any tribunal in which a matter is pending, such approval must be obtained before the matter can be included in the sale (see Rule 1.16).

Applicability of the Rule

[13] This Rule applies to the sale of a law practice of a deceased, disabled or disappeared lawyer. Thus, the seller may be represented by a non-lawyer representative not subject to these Rules. Since, however, no lawyer may participate in a sale of a law practice which does not conform to the requirements of this Rule, the representatives of the seller as well as the purchasing lawyer can be expected to see to it that they are met.

[14] Admission to or retirement from a law partnership or professional association, retirement plans and similar arrangements, and a sale of tangible assets of a law practice, do not constitute a sale or purchase governed by this Rule.

[15] This Rule does not apply to the transfers of legal representation between lawyers when such transfers are unrelated to the sale of a practice or an area of practice.

Rule 1.18 Duties to Prospective Client*

(a) A person who consults with a lawyer about the possibility of forming a client-lawyer relationship with respect to a matter is a prospective client.

(b) Even when no client-lawyer relationship ensues, a lawyer who has learned information from a prospective client shall not use or reveal that information, except as Rule 1.9 would permit with respect to information of a former client.

(c) A lawyer subject to paragraph (b) shall not represent a client with interests materially adverse to those of a prospective client in the same or a substantially related

* In August 2012, the ABA House of Delegates amended Rule 1.18(a) and (b) to broaden the definition of a prospective client.

matter if the lawyer received information from the prospective client that could be significantly harmful to that person in the matter, except as provided in paragraph (d). If a lawyer is disqualified from representation under this paragraph, no lawyer in a firm with which that lawyer is associated may knowingly undertake or continue representation in such a matter, except as provided in paragraph (d).

(d) When the lawyer has received disqualifying information as defined in paragraph (c), representation is permissible if:

(1) both the affected client and the prospective client have given informed consent, confirmed in writing, or:

(2) the lawyer who received the information took reasonable measures to avoid exposure to more disqualifying information than was reasonably necessary to determine whether to represent the prospective client; and

(i) the disqualified lawyer is timely screened from any participation in the matter and is apportioned no part of the fee therefrom; and

(ii) written notice is promptly given to the prospective client.

COMMENT*

[1] Prospective clients, like clients, may disclose information to a lawyer, place documents or other property in the lawyer's custody, or rely on the lawyer's advice. A lawyer's consultations with a prospective client usually are limited in time and depth and leave both the prospective client and the lawyer free (and sometimes required) to proceed no further. Hence, prospective clients should receive some but not all of the protection afforded clients.

[2] A person becomes a prospective client by consulting with a lawyer about the possibility of forming a client-lawyer relationship with respect to a matter. Whether communications, including written, oral, or electronic communications, constitute a consultation depends on the circumstances. For example, a consultation is likely to have occurred if a lawyer, either in person or through the lawyer's advertising in any medium, specifically requests or invites the submission of information about a potential representation without clear and reasonably understandable warnings and cautionary statements that limit the lawyer's obligations, and a person provides information in response. See also Comment [4]. In contrast, a consultation does not occur if a person provides information to a lawyer in response to advertising that merely describes the lawyer's education, experience, areas of practice, and contact information, or provides legal information of general interest. Such a person communicates information unilaterally to a lawyer, without any reasonable expectation that the lawyer is willing to discuss the possibility of forming a client-lawyer relationship, and is thus not a "prospective client." Moreover, a person who communicates with a lawyer for the purpose of disqualifying the lawyer is not a "prospective client."

[3] It is often necessary for a prospective client to reveal information to the lawyer during an initial consultation prior to the decision about formation of a client-lawyer relationship. The lawyer often must learn such information to determine whether there is a conflict of interest with an existing client and whether the matter is one that the lawyer is willing to undertake. Paragraph (b) prohibits the lawyer from using or revealing that information, except as permitted by Rule 1.9, even if the client or lawyer decides not to proceed with the representation. The duty exists regardless of how brief the initial conference may be.

[4] In order to avoid acquiring disqualifying information from a prospective client, a lawyer considering whether or not to undertake a new matter should limit the initial consultation to only such information as reasonably appears necessary for that purpose. Where the information indicates that a conflict of interest or other reason for non-representation exists, the lawyer should so inform the prospective client or decline the representation. If the prospective client wishes to retain the lawyer, and if consent is possible under Rule 1.7, then consent from all affected present or former clients must be obtained before accepting the representation.

* In August 2012, the ABA House of Delegates amended Comments 1, 4, and 5 to reflect the change made in the text and substantially added to Comment 2.

[5] A lawyer may condition a consultation with a prospective client on the person's informed consent that no information disclosed during the consultation will prohibit the lawyer from representing a different client in the matter. See Rule 1.0(e) for the definition of informed consent. If the agreement expressly so provides, the prospective client may also consent to the lawyer's subsequent use of information received from the prospective client.

[6] Even in the absence of an agreement, under paragraph (c), the lawyer is not prohibited from representing a client with interests adverse to those of the prospective client in the same or a substantially related matter unless the lawyer has received from the prospective client information that could be significantly harmful if used in the matter.

[7] Under paragraph (c), the prohibition in this Rule is imputed to other lawyers as provided in Rule 1.10, but, under paragraph (d)(1), imputation may be avoided if the lawyer obtains the informed consent, confirmed in writing, of both the prospective and affected clients. In the alternative, imputation may be avoided if the conditions of paragraph (d)(2) are met and all disqualified lawyers are timely screened and written notice is promptly given to the prospective client. See Rule 1.0(k) (requirements for screening procedures). Paragraph (d)(2)(i) does not prohibit the screened lawyer from receiving a salary or partnership share established by prior independent agreement, but that lawyer may not receive compensation directly related to the matter in which the lawyer is disqualified.

[8] Notice, including a general description of the subject matter about which the lawyer was consulted, and of the screening procedures employed, generally should be given as soon as practicable after the need for screening becomes apparent.

[9] For the duty of competence of a lawyer who gives assistance on the merits of a matter to a prospective client, see Rule 1.1. For a lawyer's duties when a prospective client entrusts valuables or papers to the lawyer's care, see Rule 1.15.

COUNSELOR

Rule 2.1 Advisor

In representing a client, a lawyer shall exercise independent professional judgment and render candid advice. In rendering advice, a lawyer may refer not only to law but to other considerations such as moral, economic, social and political factors, that may be relevant to the client's situation.

COMMENT

Scope of Advice

[1] A client is entitled to straightforward advice expressing the lawyer's honest assessment. Legal advice often involves unpleasant facts and alternatives that a client may be disinclined to confront. In presenting advice, a lawyer endeavors to sustain the client's morale and may put advice in as acceptable a form as honesty permits. However, a lawyer should not be deterred from giving candid advice by the prospect that the advice will be unpalatable to the client.

[2] Advice couched in narrow legal terms may be of little value to a client, especially where practical considerations, such as cost or effects on other people, are predominant. Purely technical legal advice, therefore, can sometimes be inadequate. It is proper for a lawyer to refer to relevant moral and ethical considerations in giving advice. Although a lawyer is not a moral advisor as such, moral and ethical considerations impinge upon most legal questions and may decisively influence how the law will be applied.

[3] A client may expressly or impliedly ask the lawyer for purely technical advice. When such a request is made by a client experienced in legal matters, the lawyer may accept it at face value. When such a request is made by a client inexperienced in legal matters, however, the lawyer's responsibility as advisor may include indicating that more may be involved than strictly legal considerations.

[4] Matters that go beyond strictly legal questions may also be in the domain of another profession. Family matters can involve problems within the professional competence of psychiatry, clinical psychology or social work; business matters can involve problems within the competence of the accounting profession

or of financial specialists. Where consultation with a professional in another field is itself something a competent lawyer would recommend, the lawyer should make such a recommendation. At the same time, a lawyer's advice at its best often consists of recommending a course of action in the face of conflicting recommendations of experts.

Offering Advice

[5] In general, a lawyer is not expected to give advice until asked by the client. However, when a lawyer knows that a client proposes a course of action that is likely to result in substantial adverse legal consequences to the client, the lawyer's duty to the client under Rule 1.4 may require that the lawyer offer advice if the client's course of action is related to the representation. Similarly, when a matter is likely to involve litigation, it may be necessary under Rule 1.4 to inform the client of forms of dispute resolution that might constitute reasonable alternatives to litigation. A lawyer ordinarily has no duty to initiate investigation of a client's affairs or to give advice that the client has indicated is unwanted, but a lawyer may initiate advice to a client when doing so appears to be in the client's interest.

Rule 2.2 Intermediary

[Deleted 2002]

Rule 2.3 Evaluation for Use by Third Persons

(a) A lawyer may provide an evaluation of a matter affecting a client for the use of someone other than the client if the lawyer reasonably believes that making the evaluation is compatible with other aspects of the lawyer's relationship with the client.

(b) When the lawyer knows or reasonably should know that the evaluation is likely to affect the client's interests materially and adversely, the lawyer shall not provide the evaluation unless the client gives informed consent.

(c) Except as disclosure is authorized in connection with a report of an evaluation, information relating to the evaluation is otherwise protected by Rule 1.6.

COMMENT

Definition

[1] An evaluation may be performed at the client's direction or when impliedly authorized in order to carry out the representation. See Rule 1.2. Such an evaluation may be for the primary purpose of establishing information for the benefit of third parties; for example, an opinion concerning the title of property rendered at the behest of a vendor for the information of a prospective purchaser, or at the behest of a borrower for the information of a prospective lender. In some situations, the evaluation may be required by a government agency; for example, an opinion concerning the legality of the securities registered for sale under the securities laws. In other instances, the evaluation may be required by a third person, such as a purchaser of a business.

[2] A legal evaluation should be distinguished from an investigation of a person with whom the lawyer does not have a client-lawyer relationship. For example, a lawyer retained by a purchaser to analyze a vendor's title to property does not have a client-lawyer relationship with the vendor. So also, an investigation into a person's affairs by a government lawyer, or by special counsel by a government lawyer, or by special counsel employed by the government, is not an evaluation as that term is used in this Rule. The question is whether the lawyer is retained by the person whose affairs are being examined. When the lawyer is retained by that person, the general rules concerning loyalty to client and preservation of confidences apply, which is not the case if the lawyer is retained by someone else. For this reason, it is essential to identify the person by whom the lawyer is retained. This should be made clear not only to the person under examination, but also to others to whom the results are to be made available.

Duties Owed to Third Person and Client

[3] When the evaluation is intended for the information or use of a third person, a legal duty to that person may or may not arise. That legal question is beyond the scope of this Rule. However, since such an

evaluation involves a departure from the normal client-lawyer relationship, careful analysis of the situation is required. The lawyer must be satisfied as a matter of professional judgment that making the evaluation is compatible with other functions undertaken in behalf of the client. For example, if the lawyer is acting as advocate in defending the client against charges of fraud, it would normally be incompatible with that responsibility for the lawyer to perform an evaluation for others concerning the same or a related transaction. Assuming no such impediment is apparent, however, the lawyer should advise the client of the implications of the evaluation, particularly the lawyer's responsibilities to third persons and the duty to disseminate the findings.

Access to and Disclosure of Information

[4] The quality of an evaluation depends on the freedom and extent of the investigation upon which it is based. Ordinarily a lawyer should have whatever latitude of investigation seems necessary as a matter of professional judgment. Under some circumstances, however, the terms of the evaluation may be limited. For example, certain issues or sources may be categorically excluded, or the scope of search may be limited by time constraints or the noncooperation of persons having relevant information. Any such limitations that are material to the evaluation should be described in the report. If after a lawyer has commenced an evaluation, the client refuses to comply with the terms upon which it was understood the evaluation was to have been made, the lawyer's obligations are determined by law, having reference to the terms of the client's agreement and the surrounding circumstances. In no circumstances is the lawyer permitted to knowingly make a false statement of material fact or law in providing an evaluation under this Rule. See Rule 4.1.

Obtaining Client's Informed Consent

[5] Information relating to an evaluation is protected by Rule 1.6. In many situations, providing an evaluation to a third party poses no significant risk to the client; thus, the lawyer may be impliedly authorized to disclose information to carry out the representation. See Rule 1.6(a). Where, however, it is reasonably likely that providing the evaluation will affect the client's interests materially and adversely, the lawyer must first obtain the client's consent after the client has been adequately informed concerning the important possible effects on the client's interests. See Rules 1.6(a) and 1.0(e).

Financial Auditors' Requests for Information

[6] When a question concerning the legal situation of a client arises at the instance of the client's financial auditor and the question is referred to the lawyer, the lawyer's response may be made in accordance with procedures recognized in the legal profession. Such a procedure is set forth in the American Bar Association Statement of Policy Regarding Lawyers' Responses to Auditors' Requests for Information, adopted in 1975.

Rule 2.4 Lawyer Serving as a Third-Party Neutral

(a) A lawyer serves as a third-party neutral when the lawyer assists two or more persons who are not clients of the lawyer to reach a resolution of a dispute or other matter that has arisen between them. Service as a third-party neutral may include service as an arbitrator, a mediator or in such other capacity as will enable the lawyer to assist the parties to resolve the matter.

(b) A lawyer serving as a third-party neutral shall inform unrepresented parties that the lawyer is not representing them. When the lawyer knows or reasonably should know that a party does not understand the lawyer's role in the matter, the lawyer shall explain the difference between the lawyer's role as a third-party neutral and a lawyer's role as one who represents a client.

COMMENT

[1] Alternative dispute resolution has become a substantial part of the civil justice system. Aside from representing clients in dispute-resolution processes, lawyers often serve as third-party neutrals. A third-party neutral is a person, such as a mediator, arbitrator, conciliator or evaluator, who assists the parties, represented or unrepresented, in the resolution of a dispute or in the arrangement of a transaction. Whether a third-party neutral serves primarily as a facilitator, evaluator or decisionmaker depends on the particular process that is either selected by the parties or mandated by a court.

[2] The role of a third-party neutral is not unique to lawyers, although, in some court-connected contexts, only lawyers are allowed to serve in this role or to handle certain types of cases. In performing this role, the lawyer may be subject to court rules or other law that apply either to third-party neutrals generally or to lawyers serving as third-party neutrals. Lawyer-neutrals may also be subject to various codes of ethics, such as the Code of Ethics for Arbitration in Commercial Disputes prepared by a joint committee of the American Bar Association and the American Arbitration Association or the Model Standards of Conduct for Mediators jointly prepared by the American Bar Association, the American Arbitration Association and the Society of Professionals in Dispute Resolution.

[3] Unlike nonlawyers who serve as third-party neutrals, lawyers serving in this role may experience unique problems as a result of differences between the role of a third-party neutral and a lawyer's service as a client representative. The potential for confusion is significant when the parties are unrepresented in the process. Thus, paragraph (b) requires a lawyer-neutral to inform unrepresented parties that the lawyer is not representing them. For some parties, particularly parties who frequently use dispute-resolution processes, this information will be sufficient. For others, particularly those who are using the process for the first time, more information will be required. Where appropriate, the lawyer should inform unrepresented parties of the important differences between the lawyer's role as third-party neutral and a lawyer's role as a client representative, including the inapplicability of the attorney-client evidentiary privilege. The extent of disclosure required under this paragraph will depend on the particular parties involved and the subject matter of the proceeding, as well as the particular features of the dispute-resolution process selected.

[4] A lawyer who serves as a third-party neutral subsequently may be asked to serve as a lawyer representing a client in the same matter. The conflicts of interest that arise for both the individual lawyer and the lawyer's law firm are addressed in Rule 1.12.

[5] Lawyers who represent clients in alternative dispute-resolution processes are governed by the Rules of Professional Conduct. When the dispute-resolution process takes place before a tribunal, as in binding arbitration (see Rule 1.0(m)), the lawyer's duty of candor is governed by Rule 3.3. Otherwise, the lawyer's duty of candor toward both the third-party neutral and other parties is governed by Rule 4.1.

ADVOCATE

Rule 3.1 Meritorious Claims and Contentions

A lawyer shall not bring or defend a proceeding, or assert or controvert an issue therein, unless there is a basis in law and fact for doing so that is not frivolous, which includes a good faith argument for an extension, modification or reversal of existing law. A lawyer for the defendant in a criminal proceeding, or the respondent in a proceeding that could result in incarceration, may nevertheless so defend the proceeding as to require that every element of the case be established.

COMMENT

[1] The advocate has a duty to use legal procedure for the fullest benefit of the client's cause, but also a duty not to abuse legal procedure. The law, both procedural and substantive, establishes the limits within which an advocate may proceed. However, the law is not always clear and never is static. Accordingly, in determining the proper scope of advocacy, account must be taken of the law's ambiguities and potential for change.

[2] The filing of an action or defense or similar action taken for a client is not frivolous merely because the facts have not first been fully substantiated or because the lawyer expects to develop vital evidence only by discovery. What is required of lawyers, however, is that they inform themselves about the facts of their clients' cases and the applicable law and determine that they can make good faith arguments in support of their clients' positions. Such action is not frivolous even though the lawyer believes that the client's position ultimately will not prevail. The action is frivolous, however, if the lawyer is unable either to make a good faith argument on the merits of the action taken or to support the action taken by a good faith argument for an extension, modification or reversal of existing law.

[3] The lawyer's obligations under this Rule are subordinate to federal or state constitutional law that entitles a defendant in a criminal matter to the assistance of counsel in presenting a claim or contention that otherwise would be prohibited by this Rule.

Rule 3.2 Expediting Litigation

A lawyer shall make reasonable efforts to expedite litigation consistent with the interests of the client.

COMMENT

[1] Dilatory practices bring the administration of justice into disrepute. Although there will be occasions when a lawyer may properly seek a postponement for personal reasons, it is not proper for a lawyer to routinely fail to expedite litigation solely for the convenience of the advocates. Nor will a failure to expedite be reasonable if done for the purpose of frustrating an opposing party's attempt to obtain rightful redress or repose. It is not a justification that similar conduct is often tolerated by the bench and bar. The question is whether a competent lawyer acting in good faith would regard the course of action as having some substantial purpose other than delay. Realizing financial or other benefit from otherwise improper delay in litigation is not a legitimate interest of the client.

Rule 3.3 Candor Toward the Tribunal

(a) A lawyer shall not knowingly:

(1) make a false statement of fact or law to a tribunal or fail to correct a false statement of material fact or law previously made to the tribunal by the lawyer;

(2) fail to disclose to the tribunal legal authority in the controlling jurisdiction known to the lawyer to be directly adverse to the position of the client and not disclosed by opposing counsel; or

(3) offer evidence that the lawyer knows to be false. If a lawyer, the lawyer's client, or a witness called by the lawyer, has offered material evidence and the lawyer comes to know of its falsity, the lawyer shall take reasonable remedial measures, including, if necessary, disclosure to the tribunal. A lawyer may refuse to offer evidence, other than the testimony of a defendant in a criminal matter, that the lawyer reasonably believes is false.

(b) A lawyer who represents a client in an adjudicative proceeding and who knows that a person intends to engage, is engaging or has engaged in criminal or fraudulent conduct related to the proceeding shall take reasonable remedial measures, including, if necessary, disclosure to the tribunal.

(c) The duties stated in paragraphs (a) and (b) continue to the conclusion of the proceeding, and apply even if compliance requires disclosure of information otherwise protected by Rule 1.6.

(d) In an ex parte proceeding, a lawyer shall inform the tribunal of all material facts known to the lawyer that will enable the tribunal to make an informed decision, whether or not the facts are adverse.

COMMENT

[1] This Rule governs the conduct of a lawyer who is representing a client in the proceedings of a tribunal. See Rule 1.0(m) for the definition of "tribunal." It also applies when the lawyer is representing a client in an ancillary proceeding conducted pursuant to the tribunal's adjudicative authority, such as a deposition. Thus, for example, paragraph (a)(3) requires a lawyer to take reasonable remedial measures if the lawyer comes to know that a client who is testifying in a deposition has offered evidence that is false.

[2] This Rule sets forth the special duties of lawyers as officers of the court to avoid conduct that undermines the integrity of the adjudicative process. A lawyer acting as an advocate in an adjudicative

proceeding has an obligation to present the client's case with persuasive force. Performance of that duty while maintaining confidences of the client, however, is qualified by the advocate's duty of candor to the tribunal. Consequently, although a lawyer in an adversary proceeding is not required to present an impartial exposition of the law or to vouch for the evidence submitted in a cause, the lawyer must not allow the tribunal to be misled by false statements of law or fact or evidence that the lawyer knows to be false.

Representations by a Lawyer

[3] An advocate is responsible for pleadings and other documents prepared for litigation, but is usually not required to have personal knowledge of matters asserted therein, for litigation documents ordinarily present assertions by the client, or by someone on the client's behalf, and not assertions by the lawyer. Compare Rule 3.1. However, an assertion purporting to be on the lawyer's own knowledge, as in an affidavit by the lawyer or in a statement in open court, may properly be made only when the lawyer knows the assertion is true or believes it to be true on the basis of a reasonably diligent inquiry. There are circumstances where failure to make a disclosure is the equivalent of an affirmative misrepresentation. The obligation prescribed in Rule 1.2(d) not to counsel a client to commit or assist the client in committing a fraud applies in litigation. Regarding compliance with Rule 1.2(d), see the Comment to that Rule. See also the Comment to Rule 8.4(b).

Legal Argument

[4] Legal argument based on a knowingly false representation of law constitutes dishonesty toward the tribunal. A lawyer is not required to make a disinterested exposition of the law, but must recognize the existence of pertinent legal authorities. Furthermore, as stated in paragraph (a)(2), an advocate has a duty to disclose directly adverse authority in the controlling jurisdiction that has not been disclosed by the opposing party. The underlying concept is that legal argument is a discussion seeking to determine the legal premises properly applicable to the case.

Offering Evidence

[5] Paragraph (a)(3) requires that the lawyer refuse to offer evidence that the lawyer knows to be false, regardless of the client's wishes. This duty is premised on the lawyer's obligation as an officer of the court to prevent the trier of fact from being misled by false evidence. A lawyer does not violate this Rule if the lawyer offers the evidence for the purpose of establishing its falsity.

[6] If a lawyer knows that the client intends to testify falsely or wants the lawyer to introduce false evidence, the lawyer should seek to persuade the client that the evidence should not be offered. If the persuasion is ineffective and the lawyer continues to represent the client, the lawyer must refuse to offer the false evidence. If only a portion of a witness's testimony will be false, the lawyer may call the witness to testify but may not elicit or otherwise permit the witness to present the testimony that the lawyer knows is false.

[7] The duties stated in paragraphs (a) and (b) apply to all lawyers, including defense counsel in criminal cases. In some jurisdictions, however, courts have required counsel to present the accused as a witness or to give a narrative statement if the accused so desires, even if counsel knows that the testimony or statement will be false. The obligation of the advocate under the Rules of Professional Conduct is subordinate to such requirements. See also Comment [9].

[8] The prohibition against offering false evidence only applies if the lawyer knows that the evidence is false. A lawyer's reasonable belief that evidence is false does not preclude its presentation to the trier of fact. A lawyer's knowledge that evidence is false, however, can be inferred from the circumstances. See Rule 1.0(f). Thus, although a lawyer should resolve doubts about the veracity of testimony or other evidence in favor of the client, the lawyer cannot ignore an obvious falsehood.

[9] Although paragraph (a)(3) only prohibits a lawyer from offering evidence the lawyer knows to be false, it permits the lawyer to refuse to offer testimony or other proof that the lawyer reasonably believes is false. Offering such proof may reflect adversely on the lawyer's ability to discriminate in the quality of evidence and thus impair the lawyer's effectiveness as an advocate. Because of the special protections historically provided criminal defendants, however, this Rule does not permit a lawyer to refuse to offer the testimony of such a client where the lawyer reasonably believes but does not know that the testimony will

be false. Unless the lawyer knows the testimony will be false, the lawyer must honor the client's decision to testify. See also Comment [7].

Remedial Measures

[10] Having offered material evidence in the belief that it was true, a lawyer may subsequently come to know that the evidence is false. Or, a lawyer may be surprised when the lawyer's client, or another witness called by the lawyer, offers testimony the lawyer knows to be false, either during the lawyer's direct examination or in response to cross-examination by the opposing lawyer. In such situations or if the lawyer knows of the falsity of testimony elicited from the client during a deposition, the lawyer must take reasonable remedial measures. In such situations, the advocate's proper course is to remonstrate with the client confidentially, advise the client of the lawyer's duty of candor to the tribunal and seek the client's cooperation with respect to the withdrawal or correction of the false statements or evidence. If that fails, the advocate must take further remedial action. If withdrawal from the representation is not permitted or will not undo the effect of the false evidence, the advocate must make such disclosure to the tribunal as is reasonably necessary to remedy the situation, even if doing so requires the lawyer to reveal information that otherwise would be protected by Rule 1.6. It is for the tribunal then to determine what should be done—making a statement about the matter to the trier of fact, ordering a mistrial or perhaps nothing.

[11] The disclosure of a client's false testimony can result in grave consequences to the client, including not only a sense of betrayal but also loss of the case and perhaps a prosecution for perjury. But the alternative is that the lawyer cooperate in deceiving the court, thereby subverting the truth-finding process which the adversary system is designed to implement. See Rule 1.2(d). Furthermore, unless it is clearly understood that the lawyer will act upon the duty to disclose the existence of false evidence, the client can simply reject the lawyer's advice to reveal the false evidence and insist that the lawyer keep silent. Thus the client could in effect coerce the lawyer into being a party to fraud on the court.

Preserving Integrity of Adjudicative Process

[12] Lawyers have a special obligation to protect a tribunal against criminal or fraudulent conduct that undermines the integrity of the adjudicative process, such as bribing, intimidating or otherwise unlawfully communicating with a witness, juror, court official or other participant in the proceeding, unlawfully destroying or concealing documents or other evidence or failing to disclose information to the tribunal when required by law to do so. Thus, paragraph (b) requires a lawyer to take reasonable remedial measures, including disclosure if necessary, whenever the lawyer knows that a person, including the lawyer's client, intends to engage, is engaging or has engaged in criminal or fraudulent conduct related to the proceeding.

Duration of Obligation

[13] A practical time limit on the obligation to rectify false evidence or false statements of law and fact has to be established. The conclusion of the proceeding is a reasonably definite point for the termination of the obligation. A proceeding has concluded within the meaning of this Rule when a final judgment in the proceeding has been affirmed on appeal or the time for review has passed.

Ex Parte Proceedings

[14] Ordinarily, an advocate has the limited responsibility of presenting one side of the matters that a tribunal should consider in reaching a decision; the conflicting position is expected to be presented by the opposing party. However, in any ex parte proceeding, such as an application for a temporary restraining order, there is no balance of presentation by opposing advocates. The object of an ex parte proceeding is nevertheless to yield a substantially just result. The judge has an affirmative responsibility to accord the absent party just consideration. The lawyer for the represented party has the correlative duty to make disclosures of material facts known to the lawyer and that the lawyer reasonably believes are necessary to an informed decision.

Withdrawal

[15] Normally, a lawyer's compliance with the duty of candor imposed by this Rule does not require that the lawyer withdraw from the representation of a client whose interests will be or have been adversely affected by the lawyer's disclosure. The lawyer may, however, be required by Rule 1.16(a) to seek permission of the tribunal to withdraw if the lawyer's compliance with this Rule's duty of candor results in such an

extreme deterioration of the client-lawyer relationship that the lawyer can no longer competently represent the client. Also see Rule 1.16(b) for the circumstances in which a lawyer will be permitted to seek a tribunal's permission to withdraw. In connection with a request for permission to withdraw that is premised on a client's misconduct, a lawyer may reveal information relating to the representation only to the extent reasonably necessary to comply with this Rule or as otherwise permitted by Rule 1.6.

Rule 3.4 Fairness to Opposing Party and Counsel

A lawyer shall not:

(a) unlawfully obstruct another party's access to evidence or unlawfully alter, destroy or conceal a document or other material having potential evidentiary value. A lawyer shall not counsel or assist another person to do any such act;

(b) falsify evidence, counsel or assist a witness to testify falsely, or offer an inducement to a witness that is prohibited by law;

(c) knowingly disobey an obligation under the rules of a tribunal, except for an open refusal based on an assertion that no valid obligation exists;

(d) in pretrial procedure, make a frivolous discovery request or fail to make reasonably diligent effort to comply with a legally proper discovery request by an opposing party;

(e) in trial, allude to any matter that the lawyer does not reasonably believe is relevant or that will not be supported by admissible evidence, assert personal knowledge of facts in issue except when testifying as a witness, or state a personal opinion as to the justness of a cause, the credibility of a witness, the culpability of a civil litigant or the guilt or innocence of an accused; or

(f) request a person other than a client to refrain from voluntarily giving relevant information to another party unless:

(1) the person is a relative or an employee or other agent of a client; and

(2) the lawyer reasonably believes that the person's interests will not be adversely affected by refraining from giving such information.

COMMENT

[1] The procedure of the adversary system contemplates that the evidence in a case is to be marshalled competitively by the contending parties. Fair competition in the adversary system is secured by prohibitions against destruction or concealment of evidence, improperly influencing witnesses, obstructive tactics in discovery procedure, and the like.

[2] Documents and other items of evidence are often essential to establish a claim or defense. Subject to evidentiary privileges, the right of an opposing party, including the government, to obtain evidence through discovery or subpoena is an important procedural right. The exercise of that right can be frustrated if relevant material is altered, concealed or destroyed. Applicable law in many jurisdictions makes it an offense to destroy material for purpose of impairing its availability in a pending proceeding or one whose commencement can be foreseen. Falsifying evidence is also generally a criminal offense. Paragraph (a) applies to evidentiary material generally, including computerized information. Applicable law may permit a lawyer to take temporary possession of physical evidence of client crimes for the purpose of conducting a limited examination that will not alter or destroy material characteristics of the evidence. In such a case, applicable law may require the lawyer to turn the evidence over to the police or other prosecuting authority, depending on the circumstances.

[3] With regard to paragraph (b), it is not improper to pay a witness's expenses or to compensate an expert witness on terms permitted by law. The common law rule in most jurisdictions is that it is improper to pay an occurrence witness any fee for testifying and that it is improper to pay an expert witness a contingent fee.

[4] Paragraph (f) permits a lawyer to advise employees of a client to refrain from giving information to another party, for the employees may identify their interests with those of the client. See also Rule 4.2.

Rule 3.5 Impartiality and Decorum of the Tribunal

A lawyer shall not:

(a) seek to influence a judge, juror, prospective juror or other official by means prohibited by law;

(b) communicate ex parte with such a person during the proceeding unless authorized to do so by law or court order;

(c) communicate with a juror or prospective juror after discharge of the jury if:

(1) the communication is prohibited by law or court order;

(2) the juror has made known to the lawyer a desire not to communicate; or

(3) the communication involves misrepresentation, coercion, duress or harassment; or

(d) engage in conduct intended to disrupt a tribunal.

COMMENT

[1] Many forms of improper influence upon a tribunal are proscribed by criminal law. Others are specified in the ABA Model Code of Judicial Conduct, with which an advocate should be familiar. A lawyer is required to avoid contributing to a violation of such provisions.

[2] During a proceeding a lawyer may not communicate ex parte with persons serving in an official capacity in the proceeding, such as judges, masters or jurors, unless authorized to do so by law or court order.

[3] A lawyer may on occasion want to communicate with a juror or prospective juror after the jury has been discharged. The lawyer may do so unless the communication is prohibited by law or a court order but must respect the desire of the juror not to talk with the lawyer. The lawyer may not engage in improper conduct during the communication.

[4] The advocate's function is to present evidence and argument so that the cause may be decided according to law. Refraining from abusive or obstreperous conduct is a corollary of the advocate's right to speak on behalf of litigants. A lawyer may stand firm against abuse by a judge but should avoid reciprocation; the judge's default is no justification for similar dereliction by an advocate. An advocate can present the cause, protect the record for subsequent review and preserve professional integrity by patient firmness no less effectively than by belligerence or theatrics.

[5] The duty to refrain from disruptive conduct applies to any proceeding of a tribunal, including a deposition. See Rule 1.0(m).

Rule 3.6 Trial Publicity

(a) A lawyer who is participating or has participated in the investigation or litigation of a matter shall not make an extrajudicial statement that the lawyer knows or reasonably should know will be disseminated by means of public communication and will have a substantial likelihood of materially prejudicing an adjudicative proceeding in the matter.

(b) Notwithstanding paragraph (a), a lawyer may state:

(1) the claim, offense or defense involved and, except when prohibited by law, the identity of the persons involved;

(2) information contained in a public record;

(3) that an investigation of a matter is in progress;

(4) the scheduling or result of any step in litigation;

(5) a request for assistance in obtaining evidence and information necessary thereto;

(6) a warning of danger concerning the behavior of a person involved, when there is reason to believe that there exists the likelihood of substantial harm to an individual or to the public interest; and

(7) in a criminal case, in addition to subparagraphs (1) through (6):

(i) the identity, residence, occupation and family status of the accused;

(ii) if the accused has not been apprehended, information necessary to aid in apprehension of that person;

(iii) the fact, time and place of arrest; and

(iv) the identity of investigating and arresting officers or agencies and the length of the investigation.

(c) Notwithstanding paragraph (a), a lawyer may make a statement that a reasonable lawyer would believe is required to protect a client from the substantial undue prejudicial effect of recent publicity not initiated by the lawyer or the lawyer's client. A statement made pursuant to this paragraph shall be limited to such information as is necessary to mitigate the recent adverse publicity.

(d) No lawyer associated in a firm or government agency with a lawyer subject to paragraph (a) shall make a statement prohibited by paragraph (a).

COMMENT

[1] It is difficult to strike a balance between protecting the right to a fair trial and safeguarding the right of free expression. Preserving the right to a fair trial necessarily entails some curtailment of the information that may be disseminated about a party prior to trial, particularly where trial by jury is involved. If there were no such limits, the result would be the practical nullification of the protective effect of the rules of forensic decorum and the exclusionary rules of evidence. On the other hand, there are vital social interests served by the free dissemination of information about events having legal consequences and about legal proceedings themselves. The public has a right to know about threats to its safety and measures aimed at assuring its security. It also has a legitimate interest in the conduct of judicial proceedings, particularly in matters of general public concern. Furthermore, the subject matter of legal proceedings is often of direct significance in debate and deliberation over questions of public policy.

[2] Special rules of confidentiality may validly govern proceedings in juvenile, domestic relations and mental disability proceedings, and perhaps other types of litigation. Rule 3.4(c) requires compliance with such rules.

[3] The Rule sets forth a basic general prohibition against a lawyer's making statements that the lawyer knows or should know will have a substantial likelihood of materially prejudicing an adjudicative proceeding. Recognizing that the public value of informed commentary is great and the likelihood of prejudice to a proceeding by the commentary of a lawyer who is not involved in the proceeding is small, the rule applies only to lawyers who are, or who have been involved in the investigation or litigation of a case, and their associates.

[4] Paragraph (b) identifies specific matters about which a lawyer's statements would not ordinarily be considered to present a substantial likelihood of material prejudice, and should not in any event be considered prohibited by the general prohibition of paragraph (a). Paragraph (b) is not intended to be an exhaustive listing of the subjects upon which a lawyer may make a statement, but statements on other matters may be subject to paragraph (a).

[5] There are, on the other hand, certain subjects that are more likely than not to have a material prejudicial effect on a proceeding, particularly when they refer to a civil matter triable to a jury, a criminal matter, or any other proceeding that could result in incarceration. These subjects relate to:

(1) the character, credibility, reputation or criminal record of a party, suspect in a criminal investigation or witness, or the identity of a witness, or the expected testimony of a party or witness;

(2) in a criminal case or proceeding that could result in incarceration, the possibility of a plea of guilty to the offense or the existence or contents of any confession, admission, or statement given by a defendant or suspect or that person's refusal or failure to make a statement;

(3) the performance or results of any examination or test or the refusal or failure of a person to submit to an examination or test, or the identity or nature of physical evidence expected to be presented;

(4) any opinion as to the guilt or innocence of a defendant or suspect in a criminal case or proceeding that could result in incarceration;

(5) information that the lawyer knows or reasonably should know is likely to be inadmissible as evidence in a trial and that would, if disclosed, create a substantial risk of prejudicing an impartial trial; or

(6) the fact that a defendant has been charged with a crime, unless there is included therein a statement explaining that the charge is merely an accusation and that the defendant is presumed innocent until and unless proven guilty.

[6] Another relevant factor in determining prejudice is the nature of the proceeding involved. Criminal jury trials will be most sensitive to extrajudicial speech. Civil trials may be less sensitive. Non-jury hearings and arbitration proceedings may be even less affected. The Rule will still place limitations on prejudicial comments in these cases, but the likelihood of prejudice may be different depending on the type of proceeding.

[7] Finally, extrajudicial statements that might otherwise raise a question under this Rule may be permissible when they are made in response to statements made publicly by another party, another party's lawyer, or third persons, where a reasonable lawyer would believe a public response is required in order to avoid prejudice to the lawyer's client. When prejudicial statements have been publicly made by others, responsive statements may have the salutary effect of lessening any resulting adverse impact on the adjudicative proceeding. Such responsive statements should be limited to contain only such information as is necessary to mitigate undue prejudice created by the statements made by others.

[8] See Rule 3.8(f) for additional duties of prosecutors in connection with extrajudicial statements about criminal proceedings.

Rule 3.7 Lawyer as Witness

(a) A lawyer shall not act as advocate at a trial in which the lawyer is likely to be a necessary witness unless:

(1) the testimony relates to an uncontested issue;

(2) the testimony relates to the nature and value of legal services rendered in the case; or

(3) disqualification of the lawyer would work substantial hardship on the client.

(b) A lawyer may act as advocate in a trial in which another lawyer in the lawyer's firm is likely to be called as a witness unless precluded from doing so by Rule 1.7 or Rule 1.9.

COMMENT

[1] Combining the roles of advocate and witness can prejudice the tribunal and the opposing party and can also involve a conflict of interest between the lawyer and client.

Advocate-Witness Rule

[2] The tribunal has proper objection when the trier of fact may be confused or misled by a lawyer serving as both advocate and witness. The opposing party has proper objection where the combination of

roles may prejudice that party's rights in the litigation. A witness is required to testify on the basis of personal knowledge, while an advocate is expected to explain and comment on evidence given by others. It may not be clear whether a statement by an advocate-witness should be taken as proof or as an analysis of the proof.

[3] To protect the tribunal, paragraph (a) prohibits a lawyer from simultaneously serving as advocate and necessary witness except in those circumstances specified in paragraphs (a)(1) through (a)(3). Paragraph (a)(1) recognizes that if the testimony will be uncontested, the ambiguities in the dual role are purely theoretical. Paragraph (a)(2) recognizes that where the testimony concerns the extent and value of legal services rendered in the action in which the testimony is offered, permitting the lawyers to testify avoids the need for a second trial with new counsel to resolve that issue. Moreover, in such a situation the judge has firsthand knowledge of the matter in issue; hence, there is less dependence on the adversary process to test the credibility of the testimony.

[4] Apart from these two exceptions, paragraph (a)(3) recognizes that a balancing is required between the interests of the client and those of the tribunal and the opposing party. Whether the tribunal is likely to be misled or the opposing party is likely to suffer prejudice depends on the nature of the case, the importance and probable tenor of the lawyer's testimony, and the probability that the lawyer's testimony will conflict with that of other witnesses. Even if there is risk of such prejudice, in determining whether the lawyer should be disqualified, due regard must be given to the effect of disqualification on the lawyer's client. It is relevant that one or both parties could reasonably foresee that the lawyer would probably be a witness. The conflict of interest principles stated in Rules 1.7, 1.9 and 1.10 have no application to this aspect of the problem.

[5] Because the tribunal is not likely to be misled when a lawyer acts as advocate in a trial in which another lawyer in the lawyer's firm will testify as a necessary witness, paragraph (b) permits the lawyer to do so except in situations involving a conflict of interest.

Conflict of Interest

[6] In determining if it is permissible to act as advocate in a trial in which the lawyer will be a necessary witness, the lawyer must also consider that the dual role may give rise to a conflict of interest that will require compliance with Rules 1.7 or 1.9. For example, if there is likely to be substantial conflict between the testimony of the client and that of the lawyer the representation involves a conflict of interest that requires compliance with Rule 1.7. This would be true even though the lawyer might not be prohibited by paragraph (a) from simultaneously serving as advocate and witness because the lawyer's disqualification would work a substantial hardship on the client. Similarly, a lawyer who might be permitted to simultaneously serve as an advocate and a witness by paragraph (a)(3) might be precluded from doing so by Rule 1.9. The problem can arise whether the lawyer is called as a witness on behalf of the client or is called by the opposing party. Determining whether or not such a conflict exists is primarily the responsibility of the lawyer involved. If there is a conflict of interest, the lawyer must secure the client's informed consent, confirmed in writing. In some cases, the lawyer will be precluded from seeking the client's consent. See Rule 1.7. See Rule 1.0(b) for the definition of "confirmed in writing" and Rule 1.0(e) for the definition of "informed consent."

[7] Paragraph (b) provides that a lawyer is not disqualified from serving as an advocate because a lawyer with whom the lawyer is associated in a firm is precluded from doing so by paragraph (a). If, however, the testifying lawyer would also be disqualified by Rule 1.7 or Rule 1.9 from representing the client in the matter, other lawyers in the firm will be precluded from representing the client by Rule 1.10 unless the client gives informed consent under the conditions stated in Rule 1.7.

Rule 3.8 Special Responsibilities of a Prosecutor*

The prosecutor in a criminal case shall:

(a) refrain from prosecuting a charge that the prosecutor knows is not supported by probable cause;

(b) make reasonable efforts to assure that the accused has been advised of the right to, and the procedure for obtaining, counsel and has been given reasonable opportunity to obtain counsel;

(c) not seek to obtain from an unrepresented accused a waiver of important pretrial rights, such as the right to a preliminary hearing;

(d) make timely disclosure to the defense of all evidence or information known to the prosecutor that tends to negate the guilt of the accused or mitigates the offense, and, in connection with sentencing, disclose to the defense and to the tribunal all unprivileged mitigating information known to the prosecutor, except when the prosecutor is relieved of this responsibility by a protective order of the tribunal;

(e) not subpoena a lawyer in a grand jury or other criminal proceeding to present evidence about a past or present client unless the prosecutor reasonably believes:

(1) the information sought is not protected from disclosure by any applicable privilege;

(2) the evidence sought is essential to the successful completion of an ongoing investigation or prosecution; and

(3) there is no other feasible alternative to obtain the information;

(f) except for statements that are necessary to inform the public of the nature and extent of the prosecutor's action and that serve a legitimate law enforcement purpose, refrain from making extrajudicial comments that have a substantial likelihood of heightening public condemnation of the accused and exercise reasonable care to prevent investigators, law enforcement personnel, employees or other persons assisting or associated with the prosecutor in a criminal case from making an extrajudicial statement that the prosecutor would be prohibited from making under Rule 3.6 or this Rule.

(g) When a prosecutor knows of new, credible and material evidence creating a reasonable likelihood that a convicted defendant did not commit an offense of which the defendant was convicted, the prosecutor shall:

(1) promptly disclose that evidence to an appropriate court or authority, and

(2) if the conviction was obtained in the prosecutor's jurisdiction,

(i) promptly disclose that evidence to the defendant unless a court authorizes delay, and

(ii) undertake further investigation, or make reasonable efforts to cause an investigation, to determine whether the defendant was convicted of an offense that the defendant did not commit.

(h) When a prosecutor knows of clear and convincing evidence establishing that a defendant in the prosecutor's jurisdiction was convicted of an offense that the defendant did not commit, the prosecutor shall seek to remedy the conviction.

---

* In February 2008, the ABA House of Delegates amended Model Rule 3.8 to address concerns that our criminal justice system does not adequately minimize the occurrence of wrongful convictions. The amendment added new sections (g) and (h) and new Comments 7, 8, and 9 and modified Comment 1.

COMMENT

[1] A prosecutor has the responsibility of a minister of justice and not simply that of an advocate. This responsibility carries with it specific obligations to see that the defendant is accorded procedural justice, that guilt is decided upon the basis of sufficient evidence, and that special precautions are taken to prevent and to rectify the conviction of innocent persons. The extent of mandated remedial action is a matter of debate and varies in different jurisdictions. Many jurisdictions have adopted the ABA Standards of Criminal Justice Relating to the Prosecution Function, which are the product of prolonged and careful deliberation by lawyers experienced in both criminal prosecution and defense. Competent representation of the sovereignty may require a prosecutor to undertake some procedural and remedial measures as a matter of obligation. Applicable law may require other measures by the prosecutor and knowing disregard of those obligations or a systematic abuse of prosecutorial discretion could constitute a violation of Rule 8.4.

[2] In some jurisdictions, a defendant may waive a preliminary hearing and thereby lose a valuable opportunity to challenge probable cause. Accordingly, prosecutors should not seek to obtain waivers of preliminary hearings or other important pretrial rights from unrepresented accused persons. Paragraph (c) does not apply, however, to an accused appearing pro se with the approval of the tribunal. Nor does it forbid the lawful questioning of an uncharged suspect who has knowingly waived the rights to counsel and silence.

[3] The exception in paragraph (d) recognizes that a prosecutor may seek an appropriate protective order from the tribunal if disclosure of information to the defense could result in substantial harm to an individual or to the public interest.

[4] Paragraph (e) is intended to limit the issuance of lawyer subpoenas in grand jury and other criminal proceedings to those situations in which there is a genuine need to intrude into the client-lawyer relationship.

[5] Paragraph (f) supplements Rule 3.6, which prohibits extrajudicial statements that have a substantial likelihood of prejudicing an adjudicatory proceeding. In the context of a criminal prosecution, a prosecutor's extrajudicial statement can create the additional problem of increasing public condemnation of the accused. Although the announcement of an indictment, for example, will necessarily have severe consequences for the accused, a prosecutor can, and should, avoid comments which have no legitimate law enforcement purpose and have a substantial likelihood of increasing public opprobrium of the accused. Nothing in this Comment is intended to restrict the statements which a prosecutor may make which comply with Rule 3.6(b) or 3.6(c).

[6] Like other lawyers, prosecutors are subject to Rules 5.1 and 5.3, which relate to responsibilities regarding lawyers and nonlawyers who work for or are associated with the lawyer's office. Paragraph (f) reminds the prosecutor of the importance of these obligations in connection with the unique dangers of improper extrajudicial statements in a criminal case. In addition, paragraph (f) requires a prosecutor to exercise reasonable care to prevent persons assisting or associated with the prosecutor from making improper extrajudicial statements, even when such persons are not under the direct supervision of the prosecutor. Ordinarily, the reasonable care standard will be satisfied if the prosecutor issues the appropriate cautions to law-enforcement personnel and other relevant individuals.

[7] When a prosecutor knows of new, credible and material evidence creating a reasonable likelihood that a person outside the prosecutor's jurisdiction was convicted of a crime that the person did not commit, paragraph (g) requires prompt disclosure to the court or other appropriate authority, such as the chief prosecutor of the jurisdiction where the conviction occurred. If the conviction was obtained in the prosecutor's jurisdiction, paragraph (g) requires the prosecutor to examine the evidence and undertake further investigation to determine whether the defendant is in fact innocent or make reasonable efforts to cause another appropriate authority to undertake the necessary investigation, and to promptly disclose the evidence to the court and, absent court-authorized delay, to the defendant. Consistent with the objectives of Rules 4.2 and 4.3, disclosure to a represented defendant must be made through the defendant's counsel, and, in the case of an unrepresented defendant, would ordinarily be accompanied by a request to a court for the appointment of counsel to assist the defendant in taking such legal measures as may be appropriate.

[8] Under paragraph (h), once the prosecutor knows of clear and convincing evidence that the defendant was convicted of an offense that the defendant did not commit, the prosecutor must seek to remedy the conviction. Necessary steps may include disclosure of the evidence to the defendant, requesting

that the court appoint counsel for an unrepresented indigent defendant and, where appropriate, notifying the court that the prosecutor has knowledge that the defendant did not commit the offense of which the defendant was convicted.

[9] A prosecutor's independent judgment, made in good faith, that the new evidence is not of such nature as to trigger the obligations of sections (g) and (h), though subsequently determined to have been erroneous, does not constitute a violation of this Rule.

Rule 3.9 Advocate in Nonadjudicative Proceedings

A lawyer representing a client before a legislative body or administrative agency in a nonadjudicative proceeding shall disclose that the appearance is in a representative capacity and shall conform to the provisions of Rules 3.3(a) through (c), 3.4(a) through (c), and 3.5.

COMMENT

[1] In representation before bodies such as legislatures, municipal councils, and executive and administrative agencies acting in a rule-making or policy-making capacity, lawyers present facts, formulate issues and advance argument in the matters under consideration. The decision-making body, like a court, should be able to rely on the integrity of the submissions made to it. A lawyer appearing before such a body must deal with it honestly and in conformity with applicable rules of procedure. See Rules 3.3(a) through (c), 3.4(a) through (c) and 3.5.

[2] Lawyers have no exclusive right to appear before nonadjudicative bodies, as they do before a court. The requirements of this Rule therefore may subject lawyers to regulations inapplicable to advocates who are not lawyers. However, legislatures and administrative agencies have a right to expect lawyers to deal with them as they deal with courts.

[3] This Rule only applies when a lawyer represents a client in connection with an official hearing or meeting of a governmental agency or a legislative body to which the lawyer or the lawyer's client is presenting evidence or argument. It does not apply to representation of a client in a negotiation or other bilateral transaction with a governmental agency or in connection with an application for a license or other privilege or the client's compliance with generally applicable reporting requirements, such as the filing of income-tax returns. Nor does it apply to the representation of a client in connection with an investigation or examination of the client's affairs conducted by government investigators or examiners. Representation in such matters is governed by Rules 4.1 through 4.4.

TRANSACTIONS WITH PERSONS OTHER THAN CLIENTS

Rule 4.1 Truthfulness in Statements to Others

In the course of representing a client a lawyer shall not knowingly:

(a) make a false statement of material fact or law to a third person; or

(b) fail to disclose a material fact when disclosure is necessary to avoid assisting a criminal or fraudulent act by a client, unless disclosure is prohibited by Rule 1.6.

COMMENT

Misrepresentation

[1] A lawyer is required to be truthful when dealing with others on a client's behalf, but generally has no affirmative duty to inform an opposing party of relevant facts. A misrepresentation can occur if the lawyer incorporates or affirms a statement of another person that the lawyer knows is false. Misrepresentations can also occur by partially true but misleading statements or omissions that are the equivalent of affirmative false statements. For dishonest conduct that does not amount to a false statement or for misrepresentations by a lawyer other than in the course of representing a client, see Rule 8.4.

Statements of Fact

[2] This Rule refers to statements of fact. Whether a particular statement should be regarded as one of fact can depend on the circumstances. Under generally accepted conventions in negotiation, certain types of statements ordinarily are not taken as statements of material fact. Estimates of price or value placed on the subject of a transaction and a party's intentions as to an acceptable settlement of a claim are ordinarily in this category, and so is the existence of an undisclosed principal except where nondisclosure of the principal would constitute fraud. Lawyers should be mindful of their obligations under applicable law to avoid criminal and tortious misrepresentation.

Crime or Fraud by Client

[3] Under Rule 1.2(d), a lawyer is prohibited from counseling or assisting a client in conduct that the lawyer knows is criminal or fraudulent. Paragraph (b) states a specific application of the principle set forth in Rule 1.2(d) and addresses the situation where a client's crime or fraud takes the form of a lie or misrepresentation. Ordinarily, a lawyer can avoid assisting a client's crime or fraud by withdrawing from the representation. Sometimes it may be necessary for the lawyer to give notice of the fact of withdrawal and to disaffirm an opinion, document, affirmation or the like. In extreme cases, substantive law may require a lawyer to disclose information relating to the representation to avoid being deemed to have assisted the client's crime or fraud. If the lawyer can avoid assisting a client's crime or fraud only by disclosing this information, then under paragraph (b) the lawyer is required to do so, unless the disclosure is prohibited by Rule 1.6.

Rule 4.2 Communication With Person Represented by Counsel

In representing a client, a lawyer shall not communicate about the subject of the representation with a person the lawyer knows to be represented by another lawyer in the matter, unless the lawyer has the consent of the other lawyer or is authorized to do so by law or a court order.

COMMENT

[1] This Rule contributes to the proper functioning of the legal system by protecting a person who has chosen to be represented by a lawyer in a matter against possible overreaching by other lawyers who are participating in the matter, interference by those lawyers with the client-lawyer relationship and the uncounselled disclosure of information relating to the representation.

[2] This Rule applies to communications with any person who is represented by counsel concerning the matter to which the communication relates.

[3] The Rule applies even though the represented person initiates or consents to the communication. A lawyer must immediately terminate communication with a person if, after commencing communication, the lawyer learns that the person is one with whom communication is not permitted by this Rule.

[4] This Rule does not prohibit communication with a represented person, or an employee or agent of such a person, concerning matters outside the representation. For example, the existence of a controversy between a government agency and a private party, or between two organizations, does not prohibit a lawyer for either from communicating with nonlawyer representatives of the other regarding a separate matter. Nor does this Rule preclude communication with a represented person who is seeking advice from a lawyer who is not otherwise representing a client in the matter. A lawyer may not make a communication prohibited by this Rule through the acts of another. See Rule 8.4(a). Parties to a matter may communicate directly with each other, and a lawyer is not prohibited from advising a client concerning a communication that the client is legally entitled to make. Also, a lawyer having independent justification or legal authorization for communicating with a represented person is permitted to do so.

[5] Communications authorized by law may include communications by a lawyer on behalf of a client who is exercising a constitutional or other legal right to communicate with the government. Communications authorized by law may also include investigative activities of lawyers representing governmental entities, directly or through investigative agents, prior to the commencement of criminal or civil enforcement proceedings. When communicating with the accused in a criminal matter, a government lawyer must comply with this Rule in addition to honoring the constitutional rights of the accused. The fact

that a communication does not violate a state or federal constitutional right is insufficient to establish that the communication is permissible under this Rule.

[6] A lawyer who is uncertain whether a communication with a represented person is permissible may seek a court order. A lawyer may also seek a court order in exceptional circumstances to authorize a communication that would otherwise be prohibited by this Rule, for example, where communication with a person represented by counsel is necessary to avoid reasonably certain injury.

[7] In the case of a represented organization, this Rule prohibits communications with a constituent of the organization who supervises, directs or regularly consults with the organization's lawyer concerning the matter or has authority to obligate the organization with respect to the matter or whose act or omission in connection with the matter may be imputed to the organization for purposes of civil or criminal liability. Consent of the organization's lawyer is not required for communication with a former constituent. If a constituent of the organization is represented in the matter by his or her own counsel, the consent by that counsel to a communication will be sufficient for purposes of this Rule. Compare Rule 3.4(f). In communicating with a current or former constituent of an organization, a lawyer must not use methods of obtaining evidence that violate the legal rights of the organization. See Rule 4.4.

[8] The prohibition on communications with a represented person only applies in circumstances where the lawyer knows that the person is in fact represented in the matter to be discussed. This means that the lawyer has actual knowledge of the fact of the representation; but such actual knowledge may be inferred from the circumstances. See Rule 1.0(f). Thus, the lawyer cannot evade the requirement of obtaining the consent of counsel by closing eyes to the obvious.

[9] In the event the person with whom the lawyer communicates is not known to be represented by counsel in the matter, the lawyer's communications are subject to Rule 4.3.

Rule 4.3 Dealing With Unrepresented Person

In dealing on behalf of a client with a person who is not represented by counsel, a lawyer shall not state or imply that the lawyer is disinterested. When the lawyer knows or reasonably should know that the unrepresented person misunderstands the lawyer's role in the matter, the lawyer shall make reasonable efforts to correct the misunderstanding. The lawyer shall not give legal advice to an unrepresented person, other than the advice to secure counsel, if the lawyer knows or reasonably should know that the interests of such a person are or have a reasonable possibility of being in conflict with the interests of the client.

COMMENT

[1] An unrepresented person, particularly one not experienced in dealing with legal matters, might assume that a lawyer is disinterested in loyalties or is a disinterested authority on the law even when the lawyer represents a client. In order to avoid a misunderstanding, a lawyer will typically need to identify the lawyer's client and, where necessary, explain that the client has interests opposed to those of the unrepresented person. For misunderstandings that sometimes arise when a lawyer for an organization deals with an unrepresented constituent, see Rule 1.13(d).

[2] The Rule distinguishes between situations involving unrepresented persons whose interests may be adverse to those of the lawyer's client and those in which the person's interests are not in conflict with the client's. In the former situation, the possibility that the lawyer will compromise the unrepresented person's interests is so great that the Rule prohibits the giving of any advice, apart from the advice to obtain counsel. Whether a lawyer is giving impermissible advice may depend on the experience and sophistication of the unrepresented person, as well as the setting in which the behavior and comments occur. This Rule does not prohibit a lawyer from negotiating the terms of a transaction or settling a dispute with an unrepresented person. So long as the lawyer has explained that the lawyer represents an adverse party and is not representing the person, the lawyer may inform the person of the terms on which the lawyer's client will enter into an agreement or settle a matter, prepare documents that require the person's signature and explain the lawyer's own view of the meaning of the document or the lawyer's view of the underlying legal obligations.

Rule 4.4 Respect for Rights of Third Persons*

(a) In representing a client, a lawyer shall not use means that have no substantial purpose other than to embarrass, delay, or burden a third person, or use methods of obtaining evidence that violate the legal rights of such a person.

(b) A lawyer who receives a document or electronically stored information relating to the representation of the lawyer's client and knows or reasonably should know that the document or electronically stored information was inadvertently sent shall promptly notify the sender.

COMMENT**

[1] Responsibility to a client requires a lawyer to subordinate the interests of others to those of the client, but that responsibility does not imply that a lawyer may disregard the rights of third persons. It is impractical to catalogue all such rights, but they include legal restrictions on methods of obtaining evidence from third persons and unwarranted intrusions into privileged relationships, such as the client-lawyer relationship.

[2] Paragraph (b) recognizes that lawyers sometimes receive a documents or electronically stored information that was mistakenly sent or produced by opposing parties or their lawyers. A document or electronically stored information is inadvertently sent when it is accidentally transmitted, such as when an email or letter is misaddressed or a document or electronically stored information is accidentally included with information that was intentionally transmitted. If a lawyer knows or reasonably should know that such a document or electronically stored information was sent inadvertently, then this Rule requires the lawyer to promptly notify the sender in order to permit that person to take protective measures. Whether the lawyer is required to take additional steps, such as returning or deleting the document or electronically stored information, is a matter of law beyond the scope of these Rules, as is the question of whether the privileged status of a document or electronically stored information has been waived. Similarly, this Rule does not address the legal duties of a lawyer who receives a document or electronically stored information that the lawyer knows or reasonably should know may have been inappropriately obtained by the sending person. For purposes of this Rule, "document or electronically stored information" includes, in addition to paper documents, email and other forms of electronically stored information, including embedded data (commonly referred to as "metadata"), that is subject to being read or put into readable form. Metadata in electronic documents creates an obligation under this Rule only if the receiving lawyer knows or reasonably should know that the metadata was inadvertently sent to the receiving lawyer.

[3] Some lawyers may choose to return a document or delete electronically stored information unread, for example, when the lawyer learns before receiving it that it was inadvertently sent. Where a lawyer is not required by applicable law to do so, the decision to voluntarily return such a document or delete electronically stored information is a matter of professional judgment ordinarily reserved to the lawyer. See Rules 1.2 and 1.4.

LAW FIRMS AND ASSOCIATIONS

Rule 5.1 Responsibilities of Partners, Managers, and Supervisory Lawyers

(a) A partner in a law firm, and a lawyer who individually or together with other lawyers possesses comparable managerial authority in a law firm, shall make reasonable efforts to ensure that the firm has in effect measures giving reasonable assurance that all lawyers in the firm conform to the Rules of Professional Conduct.

---

* In August 2012, the ABA House of Delegates amended Rule 4.4(b) to add the phrase "electronically stored information" to the text.

** In August 2012, the ABA House of Delegates substantially expanded Comment 2 and slightly amended Comment 3 to reflect the addition of "electronically stored information" to the rule.

(b) A lawyer having direct supervisory authority over another lawyer shall make reasonable efforts to ensure that the other lawyer conforms to the Rules of Professional Conduct.

(c) A lawyer shall be responsible for another lawyer's violation of the Rules of Professional Conduct if:

(1) the lawyer orders or, with knowledge of the specific conduct, ratifies the conduct involved; or

(2) the lawyer is a partner or has comparable managerial authority in the law firm in which the other lawyer practices, or has direct supervisory authority over the other lawyer, and knows of the conduct at a time when its consequences can be avoided or mitigated but fails to take reasonable remedial action.

COMMENT

[1] Paragraph (a) applies to lawyers who have managerial authority over the professional work of a firm. See Rule 1.0(c). This includes members of a partnership, the shareholders in a law firm organized as a professional corporation, and members of other associations authorized to practice law; lawyers having comparable managerial authority in a legal services organization or a law department of an enterprise or government agency; and lawyers who have intermediate managerial responsibilities in a firm. Paragraph (b) applies to lawyers who have supervisory authority over the work of other lawyers in a firm.

[2] Paragraph (a) requires lawyers with managerial authority within a firm to make reasonable efforts to establish internal policies and procedures designed to provide reasonable assurance that all lawyers in the firm will conform to the Rules of Professional Conduct. Such policies and procedures include those designed to detect and resolve conflicts of interest, identify dates by which actions must be taken in pending matters, account for client funds and property and ensure that inexperienced lawyers are properly supervised.

[3] Other measures that may be required to fulfill the responsibility prescribed in paragraph (a) can depend on the firm's structure and the nature of its practice. In a small firm of experienced lawyers, informal supervision and periodic review of compliance with the required systems ordinarily will suffice. In a large firm, or in practice situations in which difficult ethical problems frequently arise, more elaborate measures may be necessary. Some firms, for example, have a procedure whereby junior lawyers can make confidential referral of ethical problems directly to a designated senior partner or special committee. See Rule 5.2. Firms, whether large or small, may also rely on continuing legal education in professional ethics. In any event, the ethical atmosphere of a firm can influence the conduct of all its members and the partners may not assume that all lawyers associated with the firm will inevitably conform to the Rules.

[4] Paragraph (c) expresses a general principle of personal responsibility for acts of another. See also Rule 8.4(a).

[5] Paragraph (c)(2) defines the duty of a partner or other lawyer having comparable managerial authority in a law firm, as well as a lawyer who has direct supervisory authority over performance of specific legal work by another lawyer. Whether a lawyer has supervisory authority in particular circumstances is a question of fact. Partners and lawyers with comparable authority have at least indirect responsibility for all work being done by the firm, while a partner or manager in charge of a particular matter ordinarily also has supervisory responsibility for the work of other firm lawyers engaged in the matter. Appropriate remedial action by a partner or managing lawyer would depend on the immediacy of that lawyer's involvement and the seriousness of the misconduct. A supervisor is required to intervene to prevent avoidable consequences of misconduct if the supervisor knows that the misconduct occurred. Thus, if a supervising lawyer knows that a subordinate misrepresented a matter to an opposing party in negotiation, the supervisor as well as the subordinate has a duty to correct the resulting misapprehension.

[6] Professional misconduct by a lawyer under supervision could reveal a violation of paragraph (b) on the part of the supervisory lawyer even though it does not entail a violation of paragraph (c) because there was no direction, ratification or knowledge of the violation.

[7] Apart from this Rule and Rule 8.4(a), a lawyer does not have disciplinary liability for the conduct of a partner, associate or subordinate. Whether a lawyer may be liable civilly or criminally for another lawyer's conduct is a question of law beyond the scope of these Rules.

[8] The duties imposed by this Rule on managing and supervising lawyers do not alter the personal duty of each lawyer in a firm to abide by the Rules of Professional Conduct. See Rule 5.2(a).

Rule 5.2 Responsibilities of a Subordinate Lawyer

(a) A lawyer is bound by the Rules of Professional Conduct notwithstanding that the lawyer acted at the direction of another person.

(b) A subordinate lawyer does not violate the Rules of Professional Conduct if that lawyer acts in accordance with a supervisory lawyer's reasonable resolution of an arguable question of professional duty.

COMMENT

[1] Although a lawyer is not relieved of responsibility for a violation by the fact that the lawyer acted at the direction of a supervisor, that fact may be relevant in determining whether a lawyer had the knowledge required to render conduct a violation of the Rules. For example, if a subordinate filed a frivolous pleading at the direction of a supervisor, the subordinate would not be guilty of a professional violation unless the subordinate knew of the document's frivolous character.

[2] When lawyers in a supervisor-subordinate relationship encounter a matter involving professional judgment as to ethical duty, the supervisor may assume responsibility for making the judgment. Otherwise a consistent course of action or position could not be taken. If the question can reasonably be answered only one way, the duty of both lawyers is clear and they are equally responsible for fulfilling it. However, if the question is reasonably arguable, someone has to decide upon the course of action. That authority ordinarily reposes in the supervisor, and a subordinate may be guided accordingly. For example, if a question arises whether the interests of two clients conflict under Rule 1.7, the supervisor's reasonable resolution of the question should protect the subordinate professionally if the resolution is subsequently challenged.

Rule 5.3 Responsibilities Regarding Nonlawyer Assistance*

With respect to a nonlawyer employed or retained by or associated with a lawyer:

(a) a partner, and a lawyer who individually or together with other lawyers possesses comparable managerial authority in a law firm shall make reasonable efforts to ensure that the firm has in effect measures giving reasonable assurance that the person's conduct is compatible with the professional obligations of the lawyer;

(b) a lawyer having direct supervisory authority over the nonlawyer shall make reasonable efforts to ensure that the person's conduct is compatible with the professional obligations of the lawyer; and

(c) a lawyer shall be responsible for conduct of such a person that would be a violation of the Rules of Professional Conduct if engaged in by a lawyer if:

(1) the lawyer orders or, with the knowledge of the specific conduct, ratifies the conduct involved; or

(2) the lawyer is a partner or has comparable managerial authority in the law firm in which the person is employed, or has direct supervisory authority over the person, and knows of the conduct at a time when its consequences can be avoided or mitigated but fails to take reasonable remedial action.

* In August 2012, the ABA House of Delegates changed the word "Assistants" to "Assistance" in the title of the rule.

COMMENT*

[1] Paragraph (a) requires lawyers with managerial authority within a law firm to make reasonable efforts to ensure that the firm has in effect measures giving reasonable assurance that nonlawyers in the firm and nonlawyers outside the firm who work on firm matters act in a way compatible with the professional obligations of the lawyer. See Comment [6] to Rule 1.1 (retaining lawyers outside the firm) and Comment [1] to Rule 5.1. (responsibilities with respect to lawyers within a firm). Paragraph (b) applies to lawyers who have supervisory authority over such nonlawyers within or outside the firm. Paragraph (c) specifies the circumstances in which a lawyer is responsible for the conduct of such nonlawyers within or outside the firm that would be a violation of the Rules of Professional Conduct if engaged in by a lawyer.

Nonlawyers Within the Firm

[2] Lawyers generally employ assistants in their practice, including secretaries, investigators, law student interns, and paraprofessionals. Such assistants, whether employees or independent contractors, act for the lawyer in rendition of the lawyer's professional services. A lawyer must give such assistants appropriate instruction and supervision concerning the ethical aspects of their employment, particularly regarding the obligation not to disclose information relating to representation of the client, and should be responsible for their work product. The measures employed in supervising nonlawyers should take account of the fact that they do not have legal training and are not subject to professional discipline.

Nonlawyers Outside the Firm

[3] A lawyer may use nonlawyers outside the firm to assist the lawyer in rendering legal services to the client. Examples include the retention of an investigative or paraprofessional service, hiring a document management company to create and maintain a database for complex litigation, sending client documents to a third party for printing or scanning, and using an Internet-based service to store client information. When using such services outside the firm, a lawyer must make reasonable efforts to ensure that the services are provided in a manner that is compatible with the lawyer's professional obligations. The extent of this obligation will depend upon the circumstances, including the education, experience and reputation of the nonlawyer; the nature of the services involved; the terms of any arrangements concerning the protection of client information; and the legal and ethical environments of the jurisdictions in which the services will be performed, particularly with regard to confidentiality. See also Rules 1.1 (competence), 1.2 (allocation of authority), 1.4 (communication with client), 1.6 (confidentiality), 5.4(a) (professional independence of the lawyer), and 5.5(a) (unauthorized practice of law). When retaining or directing a nonlawyer outside the firm, a lawyer should communicate directions appropriate under the circumstances to give reasonable assurance that the nonlawyer's conduct is compatible with the professional obligations of the lawyer.

[4] Where the client directs the selection of a particular nonlawyer service provider outside the firm, the lawyer ordinarily should agree with the client concerning the allocation of responsibility for monitoring as between the client and the lawyer. See Rule 1.2. When making such an allocation in a matter pending before a tribunal, lawyers and parties may have additional obligations that are a matter of law beyond the scope of these Rules.

Rule 5.4 Professional Independence of a Lawyer

(a) A lawyer or law firm shall not share legal fees with a nonlawyer, except that:

(1) an agreement by a lawyer with the lawyer's firm, partner, or associate may provide for the payment of money, over a reasonable period of time after the lawyer's death, to the lawyer's estate or to one or more specified persons;

(2) a lawyer who purchases the practice of a deceased, disabled, or disappeared lawyer may, pursuant to the provisions of Rule 1.17, pay to the estate or other representative of that lawyer the agreed-upon purchase price;

* In August 2012, the ABA House of Delegates reversed the order of the comments and substantially expanded new Comment 1. The ABA also added new Comments 3 and 4.

(3) a lawyer or law firm may include nonlawyer employees in a compensation or retirement plan, even though the plan is based in whole or in part on a profit-sharing arrangement; and

(4) a lawyer may share court-awarded legal fees with a nonprofit organization that employed, retained or recommended employment of the lawyer in the matter.

(b) A lawyer shall not form a partnership with a nonlawyer if any of the activities of the partnership consist of the practice of law.

(c) A lawyer shall not permit a person who recommends, employs, or pays the lawyer to render legal services for another to direct or regulate the lawyer's professional judgment in rendering such legal services.

(d) A lawyer shall not practice with or in the form of a professional corporation or association authorized to practice law for a profit, if:

(1) a nonlawyer owns any interest therein, except that a fiduciary representative of the estate of a lawyer may hold the stock or interest of the lawyer for a reasonable time during administration;

(2) a nonlawyer is a corporate director or officer thereof or occupies the position of similar responsibility in any form of association other than a corporation; or

(3) a nonlawyer has the right to direct or control the professional judgment of a lawyer.

COMMENT

[1] The provisions of this Rule express traditional limitations on sharing fees. These limitations are to protect the lawyer's professional independence of judgment. Where someone other than the client pays the lawyer's fee or salary, or recommends employment of the lawyer, that arrangement does not modify the lawyer's obligation to the client. As stated in paragraph (c), such arrangements should not interfere with the lawyer's professional judgment.

[2] This Rule also expresses traditional limitations on permitting a third party to direct or regulate the lawyer's professional judgment in rendering legal services to another. See also Rule 1.8(f) (lawyer may accept compensation from a third party as long as there is no interference with the lawyer's independent professional judgment and the client gives informed consent).

Rule 5.5 Unauthorized Practice of Law; Multijurisdictional Practice of Law*

(a) A lawyer shall not practice law in a jurisdiction in violation of the regulation of the legal profession in that jurisdiction, or assist another in doing so.

(b) A lawyer who is not admitted to practice in this jurisdiction shall not:

(1) except as authorized by these Rules or other law, establish an office or other systematic and continuous presence in this jurisdiction for the practice of law; or

---

* In August 2002, the ABA adopted the recommendations of the Multijurisdictional Practice of Law Commission and enacted new Model Rule 5.5. The old rule text read as follows:

A lawyer shall not:

(a) practice law in a jurisdiction where doing so violates the regulation of the legal profession in that jurisdiction; or

(b) assist a person who is not a member of the bar in the performance of activity that constitutes the unauthorized practice of law.

In August 2012, the ABA House of Delegates made minor changes to Rule 5.5(d) and Comments 1 and 4. In February 2013, the ABA further amended Rule 5.5(d) to permit foreign lawyers to represent clients on foreign law issues. In February 2016, the ABA amended Rule 5.5(d) and (e) in order to permit foreign licensed attorneys from serving as in-house counsel of an employer client.

(2) hold out to the public or otherwise represent that the lawyer is admitted to practice law in this jurisdiction.

(c) A lawyer admitted in another United States jurisdiction, and not disbarred or suspended from practice in any jurisdiction, may provide legal services on a temporary basis in this jurisdiction that:

(1) are undertaken in association with a lawyer who is admitted to practice in this jurisdiction and who actively participates in the matter;

(2) are in or reasonably related to a pending or potential proceeding before a tribunal in this or another jurisdiction, if the lawyer, or a person the lawyer is assisting, is authorized by law or order to appear in such proceeding or reasonably expects to be so authorized;

(3) are in or reasonably related to a pending or potential arbitration, mediation, or other alternative dispute resolution proceeding in this or another jurisdiction, if the services arise out of or are reasonably related to the lawyer's practice in a jurisdiction in which the lawyer is admitted to practice and are not services for which the forum requires pro hac vice admission; or

(4) are not within paragraphs (c)(2) or (c)(3) and arise out of or are reasonably related to the lawyer's practice in a jurisdiction in which the lawyer is admitted to practice.

(d) A lawyer admitted in another United States jurisdiction or in a foreign jurisdiction, and not disbarred or suspended from practice in any jurisdiction or the equivalent thereof, or a person otherwise lawfully practicing as an in-house counsel under the laws of a foreign jurisdiction, may provide legal services through an office or other systematic and continuous presence in this jurisdiction that:

(1) are provided to the lawyer's employer or its organizational affiliates, are not services for which the forum requires pro hac vice admission; and when performed by a foreign lawyer and requires advice on the law of this or another U.S. jurisdiction or of the United States, such advice shall be based upon the advice of a lawyer who is duly licensed and authorized by the jurisdiction to provide such advice; or

(2) are services that the lawyer is authorized by federal or other law or rule to provide in this jurisdiction.

(e) For purposes of paragraph (d),

(1) the foreign lawyer must be a member in good standing of a recognized legal profession in a foreign jurisdiction, the members of which are admitted to practice as lawyers or counselors at law or the equivalent, and subject to effective regulation and discipline by a duly constituted professional body or a public authority, or,

(2) the person otherwise lawfully practicing as an in-house counsel under the laws of a foreign jurisdiction must be authorized to practice under this rule by, in the exercise of its discretion, [the highest court of this jurisdiction].

COMMENT*

[1] A lawyer may practice law only in a jurisdiction in which the lawyer is authorized to practice. A lawyer may be admitted to practice law in a jurisdiction on a regular basis or may be authorized by court rule or order or by law to practice for a limited purpose or on a restricted basis. Paragraph (a) applies to unauthorized practice of law by a lawyer, whether through the lawyer's direct action or by the lawyer

* In February 2007, the ABA House of Delegates added the last line to Comment 14 of Model Rule 5.5 to address unauthorized practice of law issues created by major disasters. This sentence refers to a standalone Model Rule on Provision of Legal Services Following Determination of a Major Disaster. This rule is reprinted in Part VII of the full edition of this book.

assisting another person. For example, a lawyer may not assist a person in practicing law in violation of the rules governing professional conduct in that person's jurisdiction.

[2] The definition of the practice of law is established by law and varies from one jurisdiction to another. Whatever the definition, limiting the practice of law to members of the bar protects the public against rendition of legal services by unqualified persons. This Rule does not prohibit a lawyer from employing the services of paraprofessionals and delegating functions to them, so long as the lawyer supervises the delegated work and retains responsibility for their work. See Rule 5.3.

[3] A lawyer may provide professional advice and instruction to nonlawyers whose employment requires knowledge of the law; for example, claims adjusters, employees of financial or commercial institutions, social workers, accountants and persons employed in government agencies. Lawyers also may assist independent nonlawyers, such as paraprofessionals, who are authorized by the law of a jurisdiction to provide particular law-related services. In addition, a lawyer may counsel nonlawyers who wish to proceed pro se.

[4] Other than as authorized by law or this Rule, a lawyer who is not admitted to practice generally in this jurisdiction violates paragraph (b)(1) if the lawyer establishes an office or other systematic and continuous presence in this jurisdiction for the practice of law. Presence may be systematic and continuous even if the lawyer is not physically present here. Such a lawyer must not hold out to the public or otherwise represent that the lawyer is admitted to practice law in this jurisdiction. See also Rules 7.1(a) and 7.5(b).

[5] There are occasions in which a lawyer admitted to practice in another United States jurisdiction, and not disbarred or suspended from practice in any jurisdiction, may provide legal services on a temporary basis in this jurisdiction under circumstances that do not create an unreasonable risk to the interests of their clients, the public or the courts. Paragraph (c) identifies four such circumstances. The fact that conduct is not so identified does not imply that the conduct is or is not authorized. With the exception of paragraphs (d)(1) and (d)(2), this Rule does not authorize a U.S. or foreign lawyer to establish an office or other systematic and continuous presence in this jurisdiction without being admitted to practice generally here.

[6] There is no single test to determine whether a lawyer's services are provided on a "temporary basis" in this jurisdiction, and may therefore be permissible under paragraph (c). Services may be "temporary" even though the lawyer provides services in this jurisdiction on a recurring basis, or for an extended period of time, as when the lawyer is representing a client in a single lengthy negotiation or litigation.

[7] Paragraphs (c) and (d) apply to lawyers who are admitted to practice law in any United States jurisdiction, which includes the District of Columbia and any state, territory or commonwealth of the United States. Paragraph (d) also applies to lawyers admitted in a foreign jurisdiction. The word "admitted" in paragraphs (c), (d) and (e) contemplates that the lawyer is authorized to practice in the jurisdiction in which the lawyer is admitted and excludes a lawyer who while technically admitted is not authorized to practice, because, for example, the lawyer is on inactive status.

[8] Paragraph (c)(1) recognizes that the interests of clients and the public are protected if a lawyer admitted only in another jurisdiction associates with a lawyer licensed to practice in this jurisdiction. For this paragraph to apply, however, the lawyer admitted to practice in this jurisdiction must actively participate in and share responsibility for the representation of the client.

[9] Lawyers not admitted to practice generally in a jurisdiction may be authorized by law or order of a tribunal or an administrative agency to appear before the tribunal or agency. This authority may be granted pursuant to formal rules governing admission pro hac vice or pursuant to informal practice of the tribunal or agency. Under paragraph (c)(2), a lawyer does not violate this Rule when the lawyer appears before a tribunal or agency pursuant to such authority. To the extent that a court rule or other law of this jurisdiction requires a lawyer who is not admitted to practice in this jurisdiction to obtain admission pro hac vice before appearing before a tribunal or administrative agency, this Rule requires the lawyer to obtain that authority.

[10] Paragraph (c)(2) also provides that a lawyer rendering services in this jurisdiction on a temporary basis does not violate this Rule when the lawyer engages in conduct in anticipation of a proceeding or hearing in a jurisdiction in which the lawyer is authorized to practice law or in which the lawyer reasonably expects to be admitted pro hac vice. Examples of such conduct include meetings with the client, interviews

of potential witnesses, and the review of documents. Similarly, a lawyer admitted only in another jurisdiction may engage in conduct temporarily in this jurisdiction in connection with pending litigation in another jurisdiction in which the lawyer is or reasonably expects to be authorized to appear, including taking depositions in this jurisdiction.

[11] When a lawyer has been or reasonably expects to be admitted to appear before a court or administrative agency, paragraph (c)(2) also permits conduct by lawyers who are associated with that lawyer in the matter, but who do not expect to appear before the court or administrative agency. For example, subordinate lawyers may conduct research, review documents, and attend meetings with witnesses in support of the lawyer responsible for the litigation.

[12] Paragraph (c)(3) permits a lawyer admitted to practice law in another jurisdiction to perform services on a temporary basis in this jurisdiction if those services are in or reasonably related to a pending or potential arbitration, mediation, or other alternative dispute resolution proceeding in this or another jurisdiction, if the services arise out of or are reasonably related to the lawyer's practice in a jurisdiction in which the lawyer is admitted to practice. The lawyer, however, must obtain admission pro hac vice in the case of a court-annexed arbitration or mediation or otherwise if court rules or law so require.

[13] Paragraph (c)(4) permits a lawyer admitted in another jurisdiction to provide certain legal services on a temporary basis in this jurisdiction that arise out of or are reasonably related to the lawyer's practice in a jurisdiction in which the lawyer is admitted but are not within paragraphs (c)(2) or (c)(3). These services include both legal services and services that nonlawyers may perform but that are considered the practice of law when performed by lawyers.

[14] Paragraphs (c)(3) and (c)(4) require that the services arise out of or be reasonably related to the lawyer's practice in a jurisdiction in which the lawyer is admitted. A variety of factors evidence such a relationship. The lawyer's client may have been previously represented by the lawyer, or may be resident in or have substantial contacts with the jurisdiction in which the lawyer is admitted. The matter, although involving other jurisdictions, may have a significant connection with that jurisdiction. In other cases, significant aspects of the lawyer's work might be conducted in that jurisdiction or a significant aspect of the matter may involve the law of that jurisdiction. The necessary relationship might arise when the client's activities or the legal issues involve multiple jurisdictions, such as when the officers of a multinational corporation survey potential business sites and seek the services of their lawyer in assessing the relative merits of each. In addition, the services may draw on the lawyer's recognized expertise developed through the regular practice of law on behalf of clients in matters involving a particular body of federal, nationally uniform, foreign, or international law. Lawyers desiring to provide *pro bono* legal services on a temporary basis in a jurisdiction that has been affected by a major disaster, but in which they are not otherwise authorized to practice law, as well as lawyers from the affected jurisdiction who seek to practice law temporarily in another jurisdiction, but in which they are not otherwise authorized to practice law, should consult the [*Model Court Rule on Provision of Legal Services Following Determination of Major Disaster*].

[15] Paragraph (d) identifies two circumstances in which a lawyer who is admitted to practice in another United States or foreign jurisdiction, and is not disbarred or suspended from practice in any jurisdiction, or the equivalent thereof, may establish an office or other systematic and continuous presence in this jurisdiction for the practice of law. Pursuant to paragraph (c) of this Rule, a lawyer admitted in any U.S. jurisdiction may also provide legal services in this jurisdiction on a temporary basis. See also Model Rule on Temporary Practice by Foreign Lawyers. Except as provided in paragraphs (d)(1) and (d)(2), a lawyer who is admitted to practice law in another United States or foreign jurisdiction and who establishes an office or other systematic or continuous presence in this jurisdiction must become admitted to practice law generally in this jurisdiction.

[16] Paragraph (d)(1) applies to a U.S. or foreign lawyer who is employed by a client to provide legal services to the client or its organizational affiliates, i.e., entities that control, are controlled by, or are under common control with the employer. This paragraph does not authorize the provision of personal legal services to the employer's officers or employees. The paragraph applies to in-house corporate lawyers, government lawyers and others who are employed to render legal services to the employer. The lawyer's ability to represent the employer outside the jurisdiction in which the lawyer is licensed generally serves the interests of the employer and does not create an unreasonable risk to the client and others because the employer is well situated to assess the lawyer's qualifications and the quality of the lawyer's work. To

further decrease any risk to the client, when advising on the domestic law of a United States jurisdiction or on the law of the United States, the foreign lawyer authorized to practice under paragraph (d)(1) of this Rule needs to base that advice on the advice of a lawyer licensed and authorized by the jurisdiction to provide it.

[17] If an employed lawyer establishes an office or other systematic presence in this jurisdiction for the purpose of rendering legal services to the employer, the lawyer may be subject to registration or other requirements, including assessments for client protection funds and mandatory continuing legal education. See Model Rule for Registration of In-House Counsel.

[18] Paragraph (d)(2) recognizes that a U.S. or foreign lawyer may provide legal services in a jurisdiction in which the lawyer is not licensed when authorized to do so by federal or other law, which includes statute, court rule, executive regulation or judicial precedent. See, e.g., The ABA Model Rule on Practice Pending Admission.

[19] A lawyer who practices law in this jurisdiction pursuant to paragraphs (c) or (d) or otherwise is subject to the disciplinary authority of this jurisdiction. See Rule 8.5(a).

[20] In some circumstances, a lawyer who practices law in this jurisdiction pursuant to paragraphs (c) or (d) may have to inform the client that the lawyer is not licensed to practice law in this jurisdiction. For example, that may be required when the representation occurs primarily in this jurisdiction and requires knowledge of the law of this jurisdiction. See Rule 1.4(b).

[21] Paragraphs (c) and (d) do not authorize communications advertising legal services in this jurisdiction by lawyers who are admitted to practice in other jurisdictions. Whether and how lawyers may communicate the availability of their services in this jurisdiction is governed by Rules 7.1 to 7.5.

Rule 5.6 Restrictions on Right to Practice

A lawyer shall not participate in offering or making:

(a) a partnership, shareholders, operating, employment, or other similar type of agreement that restricts the right of a lawyer to practice after termination of the relationship, except an agreement concerning benefits upon retirement; or

(b) an agreement in which a restriction on the lawyer's right to practice is part of the settlement of a client controversy.

COMMENT

[1] An agreement restricting the right of lawyers to practice after leaving a firm not only limits their professional autonomy but also limits the freedom of clients to choose a lawyer. Paragraph (a) prohibits such agreements except for restrictions incident to provisions concerning retirement benefits for service with the firm.

[2] Paragraph (b) prohibits a lawyer from agreeing not to represent other persons in connection with settling a claim on behalf of a client.

[3] This Rule does not apply to prohibit restrictions that may be included in the terms of the sale of a law practice pursuant to Rule 1.17.

Rule 5.7 Responsibilities Regarding Law-Related Services

(a) A lawyer shall be subject to the Rules of Professional Conduct with respect to the provision of law-related services, as defined in paragraph (b), if the law-related services are provided:

(1) by the lawyer in circumstances that are not distinct from the lawyer's provision of legal services to clients; or

(2) in other circumstances by an entity controlled by the lawyer individually or with others if the lawyer fails to take reasonable measures to assure that a person

obtaining the law-related services knows that the services are not legal services and that the protections of the client-lawyer relationship do not exist.

(b) The term "law-related services" denotes services that might reasonably be performed in conjunction with and in substance are related to the provision of legal services, and that are not prohibited as unauthorized practice of law when provided by a nonlawyer.

COMMENT

[1] When a lawyer performs law-related services or controls an organization that does so, there exists the potential for ethical problems. Principal among these is the possibility that the person for whom the law-related services are performed fails to understand that the services may not carry with them the protections normally afforded as part of the client-lawyer relationship. The recipient of the law-related services may expect, for example, that the protection of client confidences, prohibitions against representation of persons with conflicting interests, and obligations of a lawyer to maintain professional independence apply to the provision of law-related services when that may not be the case.

[2] Rule 5.7 applies to the provision of law-related services by a lawyer even when the lawyer does not provide any legal services to the person for whom the law-related services are performed and whether the law-related services are performed through a law firm or a separate entity. The Rule identifies the circumstances in which all of the Rules of Professional Conduct apply to the provision of law-related services. Even when those circumstances do not exist, however, the conduct of a lawyer involved in the provision of law-related services is subject to those Rules that apply generally to lawyer conduct, regardless of whether the conduct involves the provision of legal services. See, e.g., Rule 8.4.

[3] When law-related services are provided by a lawyer under circumstances that are not distinct from the lawyer's provision of legal services to clients, the lawyer in providing the law-related services must adhere to the requirements of the Rules of Professional Conduct as provided in paragraph (a)(1). Even when the law-related and legal services are provided in circumstances that are distinct from each other, for example through separate entities or different support staff within the law firm, the Rules of Professional Conduct apply to the lawyer as provided in paragraph (a)(2) unless the lawyer takes reasonable measures to assure that the recipient of the law-related services knows that the services are not legal services and that the protections of the client-lawyer relationship do not apply.

[4] Law-related services also may be provided through an entity that is distinct from that through which the lawyer provides legal services. If the lawyer individually or with others has control of such an entity's operations, the Rule requires the lawyer to take reasonable measures to assure that each person using the services of the entity knows that the services provided by the entity are not legal services and that the Rules of Professional Conduct that relate to the client-lawyer relationship do not apply. A lawyer's control of an entity extends to the ability to direct its operation. Whether a lawyer has such control will depend upon the circumstances of the particular case.

[5] When a client-lawyer relationship exists with a person who is referred by a lawyer to a separate law-related service entity controlled by the lawyer, individually or with others, the lawyer must comply with Rule 1.8(a).

[6] In taking the reasonable measures referred to in paragraph (a)(2) to assure that a person using law-related services understands the practical effect or significance of the inapplicability of the Rules of Professional Conduct, the lawyer should communicate to the person receiving the law-related services, in a manner sufficient to assure that the person understands the significance of the fact, that the relationship of the person to the business entity will not be a client-lawyer relationship. The communication should be made before entering into an agreement for provision of or providing law-related services, and preferably should be in writing.

[7] The burden is upon the lawyer to show that the lawyer has taken reasonable measures under the circumstances to communicate the desired understanding. For instance, a sophisticated user of law-related services, such as a publicly held corporation, may require a lesser explanation than someone unaccustomed to making distinctions between legal services and law-related services, such as an individual seeking tax advice from a lawyer-accountant or investigative services in connection with a lawsuit.

[8] Regardless of the sophistication of potential recipients of law-related services, a lawyer should take special care to keep separate the provision of law-related and legal services in order to minimize the risk that the recipient will assume that the law-related services are legal services. The risk of such confusion is especially acute when the lawyer renders both types of services with respect to the same matter. Under some circumstances the legal and law-related services may be so closely entwined that they cannot be distinguished from each other, and the requirement of disclosure and consultation imposed by paragraph (a)(2) of the Rule cannot be met. In such a case a lawyer will be responsible for assuring that both the lawyer's conduct and, to the extent required by Rule 5.3, that of nonlawyer employees in the distinct entity that the lawyer controls complies in all respects with the Rules of Professional Conduct.

[9] A broad range of economic and other interests of clients may be served by lawyers' engaging in the delivery of law-related services. Examples of law-related services include providing title insurance, financial planning, accounting, trust services, real estate counseling, legislative lobbying, economic analysis, social work, psychological counseling, tax preparation, and patent, medical or environmental consulting.

[10] When a lawyer is obliged to accord the recipients of such services the protections of those Rules that apply to the client-lawyer relationship, the lawyer must take special care to heed the proscriptions of the Rules addressing conflict of interest (Rules 1.7 through 1.11, especially Rules 1.7(a)(2) and 1.8(a), (b) and (f)), and to scrupulously adhere to the requirements of Rule 1.6 relating to disclosure of confidential information. The promotion of the law-related services must also in all respects comply with Rules 7.1 through 7.3, dealing with advertising and solicitation. In that regard, lawyers should take special care to identify the obligations that may be imposed as a result of a jurisdiction's decisional law.

[11] When the full protections of all of the Rules of Professional Conduct do not apply to the provision of law-related services, principles of law external to the Rules, for example, the law of principal and agent, govern the legal duties owed to those receiving the services. Those other legal principles may establish a different degree of protection for the recipient with respect to confidentiality of information, conflicts of interest and permissible business relationships with clients. See also Rule 8.4 (Misconduct).

PUBLIC SERVICE

Rule 6.1 Voluntary Pro Bono Publico Service

Every lawyer has a professional responsibility to provide legal services to those unable to pay. A lawyer should aspire to render at least (50) hours of pro bono publico legal services per year. In fulfilling this responsibility, the lawyer should:

(a) provide a substantial majority of the (50) hours of legal services without fee or expectation of fee to:

(1) persons of limited means or

(2) charitable, religious, civic, community, governmental and educational organizations in matters that are designed primarily to address the needs of persons of limited means; and

(b) provide any additional services through:

(1) delivery of legal services at no fee or substantially reduced fee to individuals, groups or organizations seeking to secure or protect civil rights, civil liberties or public rights, or charitable, religious, civic, community, governmental and educational organizations in matters in furtherance of their organizational purposes, where the payment of standard legal fees would significantly deplete the organization's economic resources or would be otherwise inappropriate;

(2) delivery of legal services at a substantially reduced fee to persons of limited means; or

(3) participation in activities for improving the law, the legal system or the legal profession. In addition, a lawyer should voluntarily contribute financial support to organizations that provide legal services to persons of limited means.

COMMENT

[1] Every lawyer, regardless of professional prominence or professional work load, has a responsibility to provide legal services to those unable to pay, and personal involvement in the problems of the disadvantaged can be one of the most rewarding experiences in the life of a lawyer. The American Bar Association urges all lawyers to provide a minimum of 50 hours of pro bono services annually. States, however, may decide to choose a higher or lower number of hours of annual service (which may be expressed as a percentage of a lawyer's professional time) depending upon local needs and local conditions. It is recognized that in some years a lawyer may render greater or fewer hours than the annual standard specified, but during the course of his or her legal career, each lawyer should render on average per year, the number of hours set forth in this Rule. Services can be performed in civil matters or in criminal or quasi-criminal matters for which there is no government obligation to provide funds for legal representation, such as post-conviction death penalty appeal cases.

[2] Paragraphs (a)(1) and (2) recognize the critical need for legal services that exists among persons of limited means by providing that a substantial majority of the legal services rendered annually to the disadvantaged be furnished without fee or expectation of fee. Legal services under these paragraphs consist of a full range of activities, including individual and class representation, the provision of legal advice, legislative lobbying, administrative rule making and the provision of free training or mentoring to those who represent persons of limited means. The variety of these activities should facilitate participation by government lawyers, even when restrictions exist on their engaging in the outside practice of law.

[3] Persons eligible for legal services under paragraphs (a)(1) and (2) are those who qualify for participation in programs funded by the Legal Services Corporation and those whose incomes and financial resources are slightly above the guidelines utilized by such programs but nevertheless, cannot afford counsel. Legal services can be rendered to individuals or to organizations such as homeless shelters, battered women's centers and food pantries that serve those of limited means. The term "governmental organizations" includes, but is not limited to, public protection programs and sections of governmental or public sector agencies.

[4] Because service must be provided without fee or expectation of fee, the intent of the lawyer to render free legal services is essential for the work performed to fall within the meaning of paragraphs (a)(1) and (2). Accordingly, services rendered cannot be considered pro bono if an anticipated fee is uncollected, but the award of statutory attorneys' fees in a case originally accepted as pro bono would not disqualify such services from inclusion under this section. Lawyers who do receive fees in such cases are encouraged to contribute an appropriate portion of such fees to organizations or projects that benefit persons of limited means.

[5] While it is possible for a lawyer to fulfill the annual responsibility to perform pro bono services exclusively through activities described in paragraphs (a)(1) and (2), to the extent that any hours of service remained unfulfilled, the remaining commitment can be met in a variety of ways as set forth in paragraph (b). Constitutional, statutory or regulatory restrictions may prohibit or impede government and public sector lawyers and judges from performing the pro bono services outlined in paragraphs (a)(1) and (2). Accordingly, where those restrictions apply, government and public sector lawyers and judges may fulfill their pro bono responsibility by performing services outlined in paragraph (b).

[6] Paragraph (b)(1) includes the provision of certain types of legal services to those whose incomes and financial resources place them above limited means. It also permits the pro bono lawyer to accept a substantially reduced fee for services. Examples of the types of issues that may be addressed under this paragraph include First Amendment claims, Title VII claims and environmental protection claims. Additionally, a wide range of organizations may be represented, including social service, medical research, cultural and religious groups.

[7] Paragraph (b)(2) covers instances in which lawyers agree to and receive a modest fee for furnishing legal services to persons of limited means. Participation in judicare programs and acceptance of court appointments in which the fee is substantially below a lawyer's usual rate are encouraged under this section.

[8] Paragraph (b)(3) recognizes the value of lawyers engaging in activities that improve the law, the legal system or the legal profession. Serving on bar association committees, serving on boards of pro bono

or legal services programs, taking part in Law Day activities, acting as a continuing legal education instructor, a mediator or an arbitrator and engaging in legislative lobbying to improve the law, the legal system or the profession are a few examples of the many activities that fall within this paragraph.

[9] Because the provision of pro bono services is a professional responsibility, it is the individual ethical commitment of each lawyer. Nevertheless, there may be times when it is not feasible for a lawyer to engage in pro bono services. At such times a lawyer may discharge the pro bono responsibility by providing financial support to organizations providing free legal services to persons of limited means. Such financial support should be reasonably equivalent to the value of the hours of service that would have otherwise been provided. In addition, at times it may be more feasible to satisfy the pro bono responsibility collectively, as by a firm's aggregate pro bono activities.

[10] Because the efforts of individual lawyers are not enough to meet the need for free legal services that exists among persons of limited means, the government and the profession have instituted additional programs to provide those services. Every lawyer should financially support such programs, in addition to either providing direct pro bono services or making financial contributions when pro bono service is not feasible.

[11] Law firms should act reasonably to enable and encourage all lawyers in the firm to provide the pro bono legal services called for by this Rule.

[12] The responsibility set forth in this Rule is not intended to be enforced through disciplinary process.

Rule 6.2 Accepting Appointments

A lawyer shall not seek to avoid appointment by a tribunal to represent a person except for good cause, such as:

(a) representing the client is likely to result in violation of the Rules of Professional Conduct or other law;

(b) representing the client is likely to result in an unreasonable financial burden on the lawyer; or

(c) the client or the cause is so repugnant to the lawyer as to be likely to impair the client-lawyer relationship or the lawyer's ability to represent the client.

COMMENT

[1] A lawyer ordinarily is not obliged to accept a client whose character or cause the lawyer regards as repugnant. The lawyer's freedom to select clients is, however, qualified. All lawyers have a responsibility to assist in providing pro bono publico service. See Rule 6.1. An individual lawyer fulfills this responsibility by accepting a fair share of unpopular matters or indigent or unpopular clients. A lawyer may also be subject to appointment by a court to serve unpopular clients or persons unable to afford legal services.

Appointed Counsel

[2] For good cause a lawyer may seek to decline an appointment to represent a person who cannot afford to retain counsel or whose cause is unpopular. Good cause exists if the lawyer could not handle the matter competently, see Rule 1.1, or if undertaking the representation would result in an improper conflict of interest, for example, when the client or the cause is so repugnant to the lawyer as to be likely to impair the client-lawyer relationship or the lawyer's ability to represent the client. A lawyer may also seek to decline an appointment if acceptance would be unreasonably burdensome, for example, when it would impose a financial sacrifice so great as to be unjust.

[3] An appointed lawyer has the same obligations to the client as retained counsel, including the obligations of loyalty and confidentiality, and is subject to the same limitations on the client-lawyer relationship, such as the obligation to refrain from assisting the client in violation of the Rules.

Rule 6.3 Membership in Legal Services Organizations

A lawyer may serve as a director, officer or member of a legal services organization, apart from the law firm in which the lawyer practices, notwithstanding that the organization serves persons having interests adverse to a client of the lawyer. The lawyer shall not knowingly participate in a decision or action of the organization:

(a) if participating in the decision or action would be incompatible with the lawyer's obligations to a client under Rule 1.7; or

(b) where the decision or action could have a material adverse effect on the representation of a client of the organization whose interests are adverse to a client of the lawyer.

COMMENT

[1] Lawyers should be encouraged to support and participate in legal service organizations. A lawyer who is an officer or a member of such an organization does not thereby have a client-lawyer relationship with persons served by the organization. However, there is potential conflict between the interests of such persons and the interests of the lawyer's clients. If the possibility of such conflict disqualified a lawyer from serving on the board of a legal services organization, the profession's involvement in such organizations would be severely curtailed.

[2] It may be necessary in appropriate cases to reassure a client of the organization that the representation will not be affected by conflicting loyalties of a member of the board. Established, written policies in this respect can enhance the credibility of such assurances.

Rule 6.4 Law Reform Activities Affecting Client Interests

A lawyer may serve as a director, officer or member of an organization involved in reform of the law or its administration notwithstanding that the reform may affect the interests of a client of the lawyer. When the lawyer knows that the interests of a client may be materially benefitted by a decision in which the lawyer participates, the lawyer shall disclose that fact but need not identify the client.

COMMENT

[1] Lawyers involved in organizations seeking law reform generally do not have a client-lawyer relationship with the organization. Otherwise, it might follow that a lawyer could not be involved in a bar association law reform program that might indirectly affect a client. See also Rule 1.2(b). For example, a lawyer specializing in antitrust litigation might be regarded as disqualified from participating in drafting revisions of rules governing that subject. In determining the nature and scope of participation in such activities, a lawyer should be mindful of obligations to clients under other Rules, particularly Rule 1.7. A lawyer is professionally obligated to protect the integrity of the program by making an appropriate disclosure within the organization when the lawyer knows a private client might be materially benefitted.

Rule 6.5 Non-profit and Court-Annexed Limited Legal-Services Programs

(a) A lawyer who, under the auspices of a program sponsored by a nonprofit organization or court, provides short-term limited legal services to a client without expectation by either the lawyer or the client that the lawyer will provide continuing representation in the matter:

(1) is subject to Rules 1.7 and 1.9(a) only if the lawyer knows that the representation of the client involves a conflict of interest; and

(2) is subject to Rule 1.10 only if the lawyer knows that another lawyer associated with the lawyer in a law firm is disqualified by Rule 1.7 or 1.9(a) with respect to the matter.

(b) Except as provided in paragraph (a)(2), Rule 1.10 is inapplicable to a representation governed by this Rule.

COMMENT

[1] Legal services organizations, courts and various nonprofit organizations have established programs through which lawyers provide short-term limited legal services—such as advice or the completion of legal forms—that will assist persons to address their legal problems without further representation by a lawyer. In these programs, such as legal-advice hotlines, advice-only clinics or pro se counseling programs, a client-lawyer relationship is established, but there is no expectation that the lawyer's representation of the client will continue beyond the limited consultation. Such programs are normally operated under circumstances in which ii is not feasible for a lawyer to systematically screen for conflicts of interest as is generally required before undertaking a representation. See, e.g., Rules 1.7, 1.9 and 1.10.

[2] A lawyer who provides short-term limited legal services pursuant to this Rule must secure the clients informed consent to the limited scope of the representation. See Rule 1.2(c). If a short-term limited representation would not be reasonable under the circumstances, the lawyer may offer advice to the client but must also advise the client of the need for further assistance of counsel. Except as provided in this Rule, the Rules of Professional Conduct, including Rules 1.6 and 1.9(c), are applicable to the limited representation.

[3] Because a lawyer who is representing a client in the circumstances addressed by this Rule ordinarily is not able to check systematically for conflicts of interest, paragraph (a) requires compliance with Rules 1.7 or 1.9(a) only if the lawyer knows that the representation presents a conflict of interest for the lawyer, and with Rule 1.10 only if the lawyer knows that another lawyer in the lawyer's firm is disqualified by Rules 1.7 or 1.9(a) in the matter.

[4] Because the limited nature of the services significantly reduces the risk of conflicts of interest with other matters being handled by the lawyer's firm, paragraph (b) provides that Rule 1.10 is inapplicable to a representation governed by this Rule except as provided by paragraph (a)(2). Paragraph (a)(2) requires the participating lawyer to comply with Rule 1.10 when the lawyer knows that the lawyer's firm is disqualified by Rules 1.7 or 1.9(a). By virtue of paragraph (b), however, a lawyer's participation in a short-term limited legal services program will not preclude the lawyer's firm from undertaking or continuing the representation of a client with interests adverse to a client being represented under the program's auspices. Nor will the personal disqualification of a lawyer participating in the program be imputed to other lawyers participating in the program.

[5] If, after commencing a short-term limited representation in accordance with this Rule, a lawyer undertakes to represent the client in the matter on an ongoing basis, Rules 1.7, 1.9(a) and 1.10 become applicable.

INFORMATION ABOUT LEGAL SERVICES

Rule 7.1 Communications Concerning a Lawyer's Services

A lawyer shall not make a false or misleading communication about the lawyer or the lawyer's services. A communication is false or misleading if it contains a material misrepresentation of fact or law, or omits a fact necessary to make the statement considered as a whole not materially misleading.

COMMENT*

[1] This Rule governs all communications about a lawyer's services, including advertising. Whatever means are used to make known a lawyer's services, statements about them must be truthful.

* In August 2012, the ABA House of Delegates amended Comment 3 to change the words, "a prospective client" to "the public."

In August 2018, the ABA House of Delegates amended Comments 1, 2, 3, and 4 and added Comments 5, 6, 7, and 8 as part of a simplification of the advertising rules.

[2] Misleading truthful statements are prohibited by this Rule. A truthful statement is misleading if it omits a fact necessary to make the lawyer's communication considered as a whole not materially misleading. A truthful statement is misleading if a substantial likelihood exists that it will lead a reasonable person to formulate a specific conclusion about the lawyer or the lawyer's services for which there is no reasonable factual foundation. A truthful statement is also misleading if presented in a way that creates a substantial likelihood that a reasonable person would believe the lawyer's communication requires that person to take further action when, in fact, no action is required.

[3] A communication that truthfully reports a lawyer's achievements on behalf of clients or former clients may be misleading if presented so as to lead a reasonable person to form an unjustified expectation that the same results could be obtained for other clients in similar matters without reference to the specific factual and legal circumstances of each client's case. Similarly, an unsubstantiated claim about a lawyer's or law firm's services or fees, or an unsubstantiated comparison of the lawyer's or law firm's services or fees with those of other lawyers or law firms may be misleading if presented with such specificity as would lead a reasonable person to conclude that the comparison or claim can be substantiated. The inclusion of an appropriate disclaimer or qualifying language may preclude a finding that a statement is likely to create unjustified expectations or otherwise mislead the public.

[4] It is professional misconduct for a lawyer to engage in conduct involving dishonesty, fraud, deceit or misrepresentation. Rule 8.4(c). See also Rule 8.4(e) for the prohibition against stating or implying an ability to improperly influence a government agency or official or to achieve results by means that violate the Rules of Professional Conduct or other law.

[5] Firm names, letterhead and professional designations are communications concerning a lawyer's services. A firm may be designated by the names of all or some of its current members, by the names of deceased members where there has been a succession in the firm's identity or by a trade name if it is not false or misleading. A lawyer or law firm also may be designated by a distinctive website address, social media username or comparable professional designation that is not misleading. A law firm name or designation is misleading if it implies a connection with a government agency, with a deceased lawyer who was not a former member of the firm, with a lawyer not associated with the firm or a predecessor firm, with a nonlawyer or with a public or charitable legal services organization. If a firm uses a trade name that includes a geographical name such as "Springfield Legal Clinic," an express statement explaining that it is not a public legal aid organization may be required to avoid a misleading implication. August 20, 2018

[6] A law firm with offices in more than one jurisdiction may use the same name or other professional designation in each jurisdiction.

[7] Lawyers may not imply or hold themselves out as practicing together in one firm when they are not a firm, as defined in Rule 1.0(c), because to do so would be false and misleading.

[8] It is misleading to use the name of a lawyer holding a public office in the name of a law firm, or in communications on the law firm's behalf, during any substantial period in which the lawyer is not actively and regularly practicing with the firm.

Rule 7.2 Communications Concerning a Lawyer's Services: Specific Rules*

(a) A lawyer may communicate information regarding the lawyer's services through any media.

(b) A lawyer shall not compensate, give or promise anything of value to a person for recommending the lawyer's services except that a lawyer may

---

* In November 2002, the ABA added subsection (b)(4) and Comment 8 to permit reciprocal referral agreements between lawyers and others.

In August 2012, the ABA House of Delegates amended Comments 1, 2, 3, 5, 6, and 7 to reflect modern advertising practices.

In August 2018, the ABA House of Delegates re-titled Rule 7.2 from Advertising to the current title, edited the existing text of the rule, and added new sections (b)(5) and (c).

(1) pay the reasonable costs of advertisements or communications permitted by this Rule;

(2) pay the usual charges of a legal service plan or a not-for-profit or qualified lawyer referral service;

(3) pay for a law practice in accordance with Rule 1.17;

(4) refer clients to another lawyer or a nonlawyer professional pursuant to an agreement not otherwise prohibited under these Rules that provides for the other person to refer clients or customers to the lawyer, if

(i) the reciprocal referral agreement is not exclusive, and

(ii) the client is informed of the existence and nature of the agreement; and

(5) give nominal gifts as an expression of appreciation that are neither intended nor reasonably expected to be a form of compensation for recommending a lawyer's services.

(c) A lawyer shall not state or imply that a lawyer is certified as a specialist in a particular field of law, unless:

(1) the lawyer has been certified as a specialist by an organization that has been approved by an appropriate authority of the state or the District of Columbia or a U.S. Territory or that has been accredited by the American Bar Association; and

(2) the name of the certifying organization is clearly identified in the communication.

(d) Any communication made underthis rule must include the name and contact information of at least one lawyer or law firm responsible for its content.

COMMENT*

[1] This Rule permits public dissemination of information concerning a lawyer's or law firm's name, address, email address, website, and telephone number; the kinds of services the lawyer will undertake; the basis on which the lawyer's fees are determined, including prices for specific services and payment and credit arrangements; a lawyer's foreign language ability; names of references and, with their consent, names of clients regularly represented; and other information that might invite the attention of those seeking legal assistance.

Paying Others to Recommend a Lawyer

[2] Except as permitted under paragraphs (b)(1)–(b)(5), lawyers are not permitted to pay others for recommending the lawyer's services. A communication contains a recommendation if it endorses or vouches for a lawyer's credentials, abilities, competence, character, or other professional qualities. Directory listings and group advertisements that list lawyers by practice area, without more, do not constitute impermissible "recommendations."

[3] Paragraph (b)(1) allows a lawyer to pay for advertising and communications permitted by this Rule, including the costs of print directory listings, on-line directory listings, newspaper ads, television and radio airtime, domain-name registrations, sponsorship fees, Internet-based advertisements, and group advertising. A lawyer may compensate employees, agents and vendors who are engaged to provide marketing or client development services, such as publicists, public-relations personnel, business-development staff, television and radio station employees or spokespersons and website designers.

[4] Paragraph (b)(5) permits lawyers to give nominal gifts as an expression of appreciation to a person for recommending the lawyer's services or referring a prospective client. The gift may not be more than a token item as might be given for holidays, or other ordinary social hospitality. A gift is prohibited if offered

* In August 2018, the ABA House of Delegates amended the Comments to Model Rule 7.2 by deleting Comments 1, 3, 4, editing the remaining Comments, and adding new text in Comments 4, 9, 10, 11, and 12.

or given in consideration of any promise, agreement or understanding that such a gift would be forthcoming or that referrals would be made or encouraged in the future.

[5] A lawyer may pay others for generating client leads, such as Internet-based client leads, as long as the lead generator does not recommend the lawyer, any payment to the lead generator is consistent with Rules 1.5(e) (division of fees) and 5.4 (professional independence of the lawyer), and the lead generator's communications are consistent with Rule 7.1 (communications concerning a lawyer's services). To comply with Rule 7.1, a lawyer must not pay a lead generator that states, implies, or creates a reasonable impression that it is recommending the lawyer, is making the referral without payment from the lawyer, or has analyzed a person's legal problems when determining which lawyer should receive the referral. See Comment [2] (definition of "recommendation"). See also Rule 5.3 (duties of lawyers and law firms with respect to the conduct of nonlawyers); Rule 8.4(a) (duty to avoid violating the Rules through the acts of another).

[6] A lawyer may pay the usual charges of a legal service plan or a not-for-profit or qualified lawyer referral service. A legal service plan is a prepaid or group legal service plan or a similar delivery system that assists people who seek to secure legal representation. A lawyer referral service, on the other hand, is any organization that holds itself out to the public as a lawyer referral service. Qualified referral services are consumer-oriented organizations that provide unbiased referrals to lawyers with appropriate experience in the subject matter of the representation and afford other client protections, such as complaint procedures or malpractice insurance requirements. Consequently, this Rule only permits a lawyer to pay the usual charges of a not-for-profit or qualified lawyer referral service. A qualified lawyer referral service is one that is approved by an appropriate regulatory authority as affording adequate protections for the public. See, e.g., the American Bar Association's Model Supreme Court Rules Governing Lawyer Referral Services and Model Lawyer Referral and Information Service Quality Assurance Act.

[7] A lawyer who accepts assignments or referrals from a legal service plan or referrals from a lawyer referral service must act reasonably to assure that the activities of the plan or service are compatible with the lawyer's professional obligations. Legal service plans and lawyer referral services may communicate with the public, but such communication must be in conformity with these Rules. Thus, advertising must not be false or misleading, as would be the case if the communications of a group advertising program or a group legal services plan would mislead the public to think that it was a lawyer referral service sponsored by a state agency or bar association.

[8] A lawyer also may agree to refer clients to another lawyer or a nonlawyer professional, in return for the undertaking of that person to refer clients or customers to the lawyer. Such reciprocal referral arrangements must not interfere with the lawyer's professional judgment as to making referrals or as to providing substantive legal services. See Rules 2.1 and 5.4(c). Except as provided in Rule 1.5(e), a lawyer who receives referrals from a lawyer or nonlawyer professional must not pay anything solely for the referral, but the lawyer does not violate paragraph (b) of this Rule by agreeing to refer clients to the other lawyer or nonlawyer professional, so long as the reciprocal referral agreement is not exclusive and the client is informed of the referral agreement. Conflicts of interest created by such arrangements are governed by Rule 1.7. Reciprocal referral agreements should not be of indefinite duration and should be reviewed periodically to determine whether they comply with these Rules. This Rule does not restrict referrals or divisions of revenues or net income among lawyers within firms comprised of multiple entities.

Communications about Fields of Practice

[9] Paragraph (a) of this Rule permits a lawyer to communicate that the lawyer does or does not practice in particular areas of law. A lawyer is generally permitted to state that the lawyer "concentrates in" or is a "specialist," practices a "specialty," or "specializes in" particular fields based on the lawyer's experience, specialized training or education, but such communications are subject to the "false and misleading" standard applied in Rule 7.1 to communications concerning a lawyer's services.

[10] The Patent and Trademark Office has a long-established policy of designating lawyers practicing before the Office. The designation of Admiralty practice also has a long historical tradition associated with maritime commerce and the federal courts. A lawyer's communications about these practice areas are not prohibited by this Rule.

[11] This Rule permits a lawyer to state that the lawyer is certified as a specialist in a field of law if such certification is granted by an organization approved by an appropriate authority of a state, the District of Columbia or a U.S. Territory or accredited by the American Bar Association or another organization, such as a state supreme court or a state bar association, that has been approved by the authority of the state, the District of Columbia or a U.S. Territory to accredit organizations that certify lawyers as specialists. Certification signifies that an objective entity has recognized an advanced degree of knowledge and experience in the specialty area greater than is suggested by general licensure to practice law. Certifying organizations may be expected to apply standards of experience, knowledge and proficiency to ensure that a lawyer's recognition as a specialist is meaningful and reliable. To ensure that consumers can obtain access to useful information about an organization granting certification, the name of the certifying organization must be included in any communication regarding the certification.

Required Contact Information

[12] This Rule requires that any communication about a lawyer or law firm's services include the name of, and contact information for, the lawyer or law firm. Contact information includes a website address, a telephone number, an email address or a physical office location.

Rule 7.3 Solicitation of Clients*

(a) "Solicitation" or "solicit" denotes a communication initiated by or on behalf of a lawyer or law firm that is directed to a specific person the lawyer knows or reasonably should know needs legal services in a particular matter and that offers to provide, or reasonably can be understood as offering to provide, legal services for that matter.

(b) A lawyer shall solicit professional employment by live person-to-person contact when a significant motive for the lawyer's doing so is the lawyer's or law firm's pecuniary gain, unless the contact is with a:

(1) lawyer; or

(2) person who has a family, close personal, or prior professional relationship with the lawyer or law firm.

(3) person who routinely uses for business purposes the type of legal services offered by the lawyer.

(c) A lawyer shall not solicit professional employment even when not otherwise prohibited by paragraph (a), if:

(1) the target of the solicitation has made known to the lawyer a desire not to be solicited by the lawyer; or

(2) the solicitation involves coercion, duress or harassment.

(d) This Rule does not prohibit communications authorized by law or ordered by a court or other tribunal.

(e) Notwithstanding the prohibitions in this Rule, a lawyer may participate with a prepaid or group legal service plan operated by an organization not owned or directed by the lawyer that uses live person-to-person contact to enroll memberships or sell subscriptions for the plan from persons who are not known to need legal services in a particular matter covered by the plan.

---

* In August 2012, the ABA House of Delegates amended Rule 7.3 to remove the words "prospective client."

In August 2018, the ABA House of Delegates amended Rule 7.3 by adding new sections (a) and (d), deleting (c), and revising the existing language of the other sections. Old section (c) stated "Every written, recorded or electronic communication from a lawyer soliciting professional employment from anyone known to be in need of legal services in a particular matter shall include the words "Advertising Material" on the outside envelope, if any, and at the beginning and ending of any recorded or electronic communication, unless the recipient of the communication is a person specified in paragraphs (a)(1) or (a)(2)."

COMMENT*

[1] Paragraph (b) prohibits a lawyer from soliciting professional employment by live person-to-person contact when a significant motive for the lawyer's doing so is the lawyer's or the law firm's pecuniary gain. A lawyer's communication is not a solicitation if it is directed to the general public, such as through a billboard, an Internet banner advertisement, a website or a television commercial, or if it is in response to a request for information or is automatically generated in response to electronic searches.

[2] "Live person-to-person contact" means in-person, face-to-face, live telephone and other real-time visual or auditory person-to-person communications where the person is subject to a direct personal encounter without time for reflection. Such person-to-person contact does not include chat rooms, text messages or other written communications that recipients may easily disregard. A potential for overreaching exists when a lawyer, seeking pecuniary gain, solicits a person to be in need of legal services. This form of contact subjects a person to the private importuning of the trained advocate in a direct interpersonal encounter. The person, who may already feel overwhelmed by the circumstances giving rise to the need for legal services, may find it difficult to fully evaluate all available alternatives with reasoned judgment and appropriate self-interest in the face of the lawyer's presence and insistence upon an immediate response. The situation is fraught with the possibility of undue influence, intimidation, and over-reaching.

[3] The potential for overreaching inherent in live person-to-person contact justifies its prohibition, since lawyers have alternative means of conveying necessary information. In particular, communications can be mailed or transmitted by email or other electronic means that do not violate other laws. These forms of communication make it possible for a prospective client to be informed about the need for legal services, and about the qualifications of available lawyers and law firms, without subjecting the public to liveperson-to-person persuasion that may overwhelm a person's judgment.

[4] The contents of live person-to-person contact can be disputed and may not be subject to third-party scrutiny. Consequently, they are much more likely to approach (and occasionally cross) the dividing line between accurate representations and those that are false and misleading.

[5] There is far less likelihood that a lawyer would engage in overreaching against a former client, or a person with whom the lawyer has close personal, family, business or professional relationship, or in situations in which the lawyer is motivated by considerations other than the lawyer's pecuniary gain. Nor is there a serious potential for overreaching when the person contacted is a lawyer or is known to routinely use the type of legal services involved for business purposes. Examples include persons who routinely hire outside counsel to represent the entity; entrepreneurs who regularly engage business, employment law or intellectual property lawyers; small business proprietors who routinely hire lawyers for lease or contract issues; and other people who routinely retain lawyers for business transactions or formations. Paragraph (a) is not intended to prohibit a lawyer from participating in constitutionally protected activities of public or charitable legal-service organizations or bona fide political, social, civic, fraternal, employee or trade organizations whose purposes include providing or recommending legal services to their members or beneficiaries.

[6] A solicitation that contains false or misleading information within the meaning of Rule 7.1, that involves coercion, duress or harassment within the meaning of Rule 7.3(c)(2), or that involves contact with someone who has made known to the lawyer a desire not to be solicited by the lawyer within the meaning of Rule 7.3(c)(1) is prohibited. Live, person-to-person contact of individuals who may be especially vulnerable to coercion or duress is ordinarily not appropriate, for example, the elderly, those whose first language is not English, or the disabled.

[7] This Rule does not prohibit a lawyer from contacting representatives of organizations or groups that may be interested in establishing a group or prepaid legal plan for their members, insureds, beneficiaries or other third parties for the purpose of informing such entities of the availability of and details concerning the plan or arrangement which the lawyer or lawyer's firm is willing to offer. This form of

* In August 2012, the ABA House of Delegates added a new Comment 1, renumbered and slightly modified the rest of the comments.

In August 2018, the ABA House of Delegates amended the Comments to Model Rule 7.3 by deleting Comment 8 and adding a new Comment 8. The other comments were edited to reflect the changes in the text of Rule 7.3.

communication is not directed to people who are seeking legal services for themselves. Rather, it is usually addressed to an individual acting in a fiduciary capacity seeking a supplier of legal services for others who may, if they choose, become prospective clients of the lawyer. Under these circumstances, the activity which the lawyer undertakes in communicating with such representatives and the type of information transmitted to the individual are functionally similar to and serve the same purpose as advertising permitted under Rule 7.2.

[8] Communications authorized by law or ordered by a court or tribunal include a notice to potential members of a class in class action litigation.

[9] Paragraph (e) of this Rule permits a lawyer to participate with an organization which uses personal contact to enroll members for its group or prepaid legal service plan, provided that the personal contact is not undertaken by any lawyer who would be a provider of legal services through the plan. The organization must not be owned by or directed (whether as manager or otherwise) by any lawyer or law firm that participates in the plan. For example, paragraph (e) would not permit a lawyer to create an organization controlled directly or indirectly by the lawyer and use the organization for the person-to-person solicitation of legal employment of the lawyer through memberships in the plan or otherwise. The communication permitted by these organizations must not be directed to a person known to need legal services in a particular matter, but must be designed to inform potential plan members generally of another means of affordable legal services. Lawyers who participate in a legal service plan must reasonably assure that the plan sponsors are in compliance with Rules 7.1, 7.2 and 7.3(c).

Rule 7.4 Communication of Fields of Practice and Specialization [Deleted]*

* In August, 2018, the ABA House of Delegates amended Model Rules 7.1 through 7.3 and deleted Rule 7.4. The content of Rule 7.4 was included in the Comments of the amended Model Rule 7.2. The deleted Model Rule 7.4 read as follows:

(a) A lawyer may communicate the fact that the lawyer does or does not practice in particular fields of law.

(b) A lawyer admitted to engage in patent practice before the United States Patent and Trademark Office may use the designation "Patent Attorney" or a substantially similar designation.

(c) A lawyer engaged in Admiralty practice may use the designation "Admiralty," "Proctor in Admiralty" or a substantially similar designation.

(d) A lawyer shall not state or imply that a lawyer is certified as a specialist in a particular field of law, unless:

(1) the lawyer has been certified as a specialist by an organization that has been approved by an appropriate state authority or that has been accredited by the American Bar Association; and

(2) the name of the certifying organization is clearly identified in the communication.

COMMENT

[1] Paragraph (a) of this Rule permits a lawyer to indicate areas of practice in communications about the lawyer's services. If a lawyer practices only in certain fields, or will not accept matters except in a specified field or fields, the lawyer is permitted to so indicate. A lawyer is generally permitted to state that the lawyer is a "specialist," practices a "specialty," or "specializes in" particular fields, but such communications are subject to the "false and misleading" standard applied in Rule 7.1 to communications concerning a lawyer's services.

[2] Paragraph (b) recognizes the long-established policy of the Patent and Trademark Office for the designation of lawyers practicing before the Office. Paragraph (c) recognizes that designation of Admiralty practice has a long historical tradition associated with maritime commerce and the federal courts.

[3] Paragraph (d) permits a lawyer to state that the lawyer is certified as a specialist in a field of law if such certification is granted by an organization approved by an appropriate state authority or accredited by the American Bar Association or another organization, such as a state bar association, that has been approved by the state authority to accredit organizations that certify lawyers as specialists. Certification signifies that an objective entity has recognized an advanced degree of knowledge and experience in the specialty area greater than is suggested by general licensure to practice law. Certifying organizations may be expected to apply standards of experience, knowledge and proficiency to insure that a lawyer's recognition as a specialist is meaningful and reliable. In order to insure that consumers can obtain access to useful information about an organization granting certification, the name of the certifying organization must be included in any communication regarding the certification.

Rule 7.5 Firm Names and Letterheads [Deleted]*

Rule 7.6 Political Contributions to Obtain Government Legal Engagements or Appointments by Judges

A lawyer or law firm shall not accept a government legal engagement or an appointment by a judge if the lawyer or law firm makes a political contribution or solicits political contributions for the purpose of obtaining or being considered for that type of legal engagement or appointment.

COMMENT

[1] Lawyers have a right to participate fully in the political process, which includes making and soliciting political contributions to candidates for judicial and other public office. Nevertheless, when lawyers make or solicit political contributions in order to obtain an engagement for legal work awarded by a government agency, or to obtain appointment by a judge, the public may legitimately question whether the lawyers engaged to perform the work are selected on the basis of competence and merit. In such a circumstance, the integrity of the profession is undermined.

[2] The term "political contribution" denotes any gift, subscription, loan, advance or deposit of anything of value made directly or indirectly to a candidate, incumbent, political party or campaign committee to influence or provide financial support for election to or retention in judicial or other government office. Political contributions in initiative and referendum elections are not included. For purposes of this Rule, the term "political contribution" does not include uncompensated services.

[3] Subject to the exceptions below, (i) the term "government legal engagement" denotes any engagement to provide legal services that a public official has the direct or indirect power to award; and (ii) the term "appointment by a judge" denotes an appointment to a position such as referee, commissioner, special master, receiver, guardian or other similar position that is made by a judge. Those terms do not, however, include (a) substantially uncompensated services; (b) engagements or appointments made on the basis of experience, expertise, professional qualifications and cost following a request for proposal or other process that is free from influence based upon political contributions; and (c) engagements or appointments made on a rotational basis from a list compiled without regard to political contributions.

---

* In August, 2018, the ABA House of Delegated amended Model Rules 7.1 through 7.3 and deleted Model Rule 7.5. The content of Rule 7.5 was included in the Comments of amended Rule 7.1. The old Model Rule 7.5 read as follows:

(a) A lawyer shall not use a firm name, letterhead or other professional designation that violates Rule 7.1. A trade name may be used by a lawyer in private practice if it does not imply a connection with a government agency or with a public or charitable legal services organization and is not otherwise in violation of Rule 7.1.

(b) A law firm with offices in more than one jurisdiction may use the same name or other professional designation in each jurisdiction, but identification of the lawyers in an office of the firm shall indicate the jurisdictional limitations on those not licensed to practice in the jurisdiction where the office is located.

(c) The name of a lawyer holding a public office shall not be used in the name of a law firm, or in communications on its behalf, during any substantial period in which the lawyer is not actively and regularly practicing with the firm.

(d) Lawyers may state or imply that they practice in a partnership or other organization only when that is the fact.

COMMENT

[1] A firm may be designated by the names of all or some of its members, by the names of deceased members where there has been a continuing succession in the firm's identity or by a trade name such as the "ABC Legal Clinic." A lawyer or law firm may also be designated by a distinctive website address or comparable professional designation. Although the United States Supreme Court has held that legislation may prohibit the use of trade names in professional practice, use of such names in law practice is acceptable so long as it is not misleading. If a private firm uses a trade name that includes a geographical name such as "Springfield Legal Clinic," an express disclaimer that it is a public legal aid agency may be required to avoid a misleading implication. It may be observed that any firm name including the name of a deceased partner is, strictly speaking, a trade name. The use of such names to designate law firms has proven a useful means of identification. However, it is misleading to use the name of a lawyer not associated with the firm or a predecessor of the firm, or the name of a nonlawyer.

[2] With regard to paragraph (d), lawyers sharing office facilities, but who are not in fact associated with each other in a law firm, may not denominate themselves as, for example, "Smith and Jones," for that title suggests that they are practicing law together in a firm.

[4] The term "lawyer or law firm" includes a political action committee or other entity owned or controlled by a lawyer or law firm.

[5] Political contributions are for the purpose of obtaining or being considered for a government legal engagement or appointment by a judge if, but for the desire to be considered for the legal engagement or appointment, the lawyer or law firm would not have made or solicited the contributions. The purpose may be determined by an examination of the circumstances in which the contributions occur. For example, one or more contributions that in the aggregate are substantial in relation to other contributions by lawyers or law firms, made for the benefit of an official in a position to influence award of a government legal engagement, and followed by an award of the legal engagement to the contributing or soliciting lawyer or the lawyer's firm would support an inference that the purpose of the contributions was to obtain the engagement, absent other factors that weigh against existence of the proscribed purpose. Those factors may include among others that the contribution or solicitation was made to further a political, social, or economic interest or because of an existing personal, family, or professional relationship with a candidate.

[6] If a lawyer makes or solicits a political contribution under circumstances that constitute bribery or another crime, Rule 8.4(b) is implicated.

MAINTAINING THE INTEGRITY OF THE PROFESSION

Rule 8.1 Bar Admission and Disciplinary Matters

An applicant for admission to the bar, or a lawyer in connection with a bar admission application or in connection with a disciplinary matter, shall not:

(a) knowingly make a false statement of material fact; or

(b) fail to disclose a fact necessary to correct a misapprehension known by the person to have arisen in the matter, or knowingly fail to respond to a lawful demand for information from an admissions or disciplinary authority, except that this rule does not require disclosure of information otherwise protected by Rule 1.6.

COMMENT

[1] The duty imposed by this Rule extends to persons seeking admission to the bar as well as to lawyers. Hence, if a person makes a material false statement in connection with an application for admission, it may be the basis for subsequent disciplinary action if the person is admitted, and in any event may be relevant in a subsequent admission application. The duty imposed by this Rule applies to a lawyer's own admission or discipline as well as that of others. Thus, it is a separate professional offense for a lawyer to knowingly make a misrepresentation or omission in connection with a disciplinary investigation of the lawyer's own conduct. Paragraph (b) of this Rule also requires correction of any prior misstatement in the matter that the applicant or lawyer may have made and affirmative clarification of any misunderstanding on the part of the admissions or disciplinary authority of which the person involved becomes aware.

[2] This Rule is subject to the provisions of the fifth amendment of the United States Constitution and corresponding provisions of state constitutions. A person relying on such a provision in response to a question, however, should do so openly and not use the right of nondisclosure as a justification for failure to comply with this Rule.

[3] A lawyer representing an applicant for admission to the bar, or representing a lawyer who is the subject of a disciplinary inquiry or proceeding, is governed by the rules applicable to the client-lawyer relationship, including Rule 1.6 and, in some cases, Rule 3.3.

Rule 8.2 Judicial and Legal Officials

(a) A lawyer shall not make a statement that the lawyer knows to be false or with reckless disregard as to its truth or falsity concerning the qualifications or integrity of a judge, adjudicatory officer or public legal officer, or of a candidate for election or appointment to judicial or legal office.

(b) A lawyer who is a candidate for judicial office shall comply with the applicable provisions of the Code of Judicial Conduct.

COMMENT

[1] Assessments by lawyers are relied on in evaluating the professional or personal fitness of persons being considered for election or appointment to judicial office and to public legal offices, such as attorney general, prosecuting attorney and public defender. Expressing honest and candid opinions on such matters contributes to improving the administration of justice. Conversely, false statements by a lawyer can unfairly undermine public confidence in the administration of justice.

[2] When a lawyer seeks judicial office, the lawyer should be bound by applicable limitations on political activity.

[3] To maintain the fair and independent administration of justice, lawyers are encouraged to continue traditional efforts to defend judges and courts unjustly criticized.

Rule 8.3 Reporting Professional Misconduct

(a) A lawyer who knows that another lawyer has committed a violation of the Rules of Professional Conduct that raises a substantial question as to that lawyer's honesty, trustworthiness or fitness as a lawyer in other respects, shall inform the appropriate professional authority.

(b) A lawyer who knows that a judge has committed a violation of applicable rules of judicial conduct that raises a substantial question as to the judge's fitness for office shall inform the appropriate authority.

(c) This Rule does not require disclosure of information otherwise protected by Rule 1.6 or information gained by a lawyer or judge while participating in an approved lawyers assistance program.

COMMENT

[1] Self-regulation of the legal profession requires that members of the profession initiate disciplinary investigation when they know of a violation of the Rules of Professional Conduct. Lawyers have a similar obligation with respect to judicial misconduct. An apparently isolated violation may indicate a pattern of misconduct that only a disciplinary investigation can uncover. Reporting a violation is especially important where the victim is unlikely to discover the offense.

[2] A report about misconduct is not required where it would involve violation of Rule 1.6. However, a lawyer should encourage a client to consent to disclosure where prosecution would not substantially prejudice the client's interests.

[3] If a lawyer were obliged to report every violation of the Rules, the failure to report any violation would itself be a professional offense. Such a requirement existed in many jurisdictions but proved to be unenforceable. This Rule limits the reporting obligation to those offenses that a self-regulating profession must vigorously endeavor to prevent. A measure of judgment is, therefore, required in complying with the provisions of this Rule. The term "substantial" refers to the seriousness of the possible offense and not the quantum of evidence of which the lawyer is aware. A report should be made to the bar disciplinary agency unless some other agency, such as a peer review agency, is more appropriate in the circumstances. Similar considerations apply to the reporting of judicial misconduct.

[4] The duty to report professional misconduct does not apply to a lawyer retained to represent a lawyer whose professional conduct is in question. Such a situation is governed by the Rules applicable to the client-lawyer relationship.

[5] Information about a lawyer's or judge's misconduct or fitness may be received by a lawyer in the course of that lawyer's participation in an approved lawyers or judges assistance program. In that circumstance, providing for an exception to the reporting requirements of paragraphs (a) and (b) of this Rule encourages lawyers and judges to seek treatment through such a program. Conversely, without such an exception, lawyers and judges may hesitate to seek assistance from these programs, which may then result

in additional harm to their professional careers and additional injury to the welfare of clients and the public. These Rules do not otherwise address the confidentiality of information received by a lawyer or judge participating in an approved lawyers assistance program; such an obligation, however, may be imposed by the rules of the program or other law.

Rule 8.4 Misconduct*

It is professional misconduct for a lawyer to:

(a) violate or attempt to violate the Rules of Professional Conduct, knowingly assist or induce another to do so, or do so through the acts of another;

(b) commit a criminal act that reflects adversely on the lawyer's honesty, trustworthiness or fitness as a lawyer in other respects;

(c) engage in conduct involving dishonesty, fraud, deceit or misrepresentation;

(d) engage in conduct that is prejudicial to the administration of justice;

(e) state or imply an ability to influence improperly a government agency or official or to achieve results by means that violate the Rules of Professional Conduct or other law; or

(f) knowingly assist a judge or judicial officer in conduct that is a violation of applicable rules of judicial conduct or other law.

(g) engage in conduct that the lawyer knows or reasonably should know is harassment or discrimination on the basis of race, sex, religion, national origin, ethnicity, disability, age, sexual orientation, gender identity, marital status or socioeconomic status in conduct related to the practice of law. This paragraph does not limit the ability of a lawyer to accept, decline or withdraw from a representation in accordance with Rule 1.16. This paragraph does not preclude legitimate advice or advocacy consistent with these Rules.

COMMENT**

[1] Lawyers are subject to discipline when they violate or attempt to violate the Rules of Professional Conduct, knowingly assist or induce another to do so or do so through the acts of another, as when they request or instruct an agent to do so on the lawyer's behalf. Paragraph (a), however, does not prohibit a lawyer from advising a client concerning action the client is legally entitled to take.

[2] Many kinds of illegal conduct reflect adversely on fitness to practice law, such as offenses involving fraud and the offense of willful failure to file an income tax return. However, some kinds of offenses carry no such implication. Traditionally, the distinction was drawn in terms of offenses involving "moral turpitude." That concept can be construed to include offenses concerning some matters of personal morality, such as adultery and comparable offenses, that have no specific connection to fitness for the practice of law. Although a lawyer is personally answerable to the entire criminal law, a lawyer should be professionally answerable only for offenses that indicate lack of those characteristics relevant to law practice. Offenses involving violence, dishonesty, breach of trust, or serious interference with the administration of justice are in that category. A pattern of repeated offenses, even ones of minor significance when considered separately, can indicate indifference to legal obligation.

[3] Discrimination and harassment by lawyers in violation of paragraph (g) undermine confidence in the legal profession and the legal system. Such discrimination includes harmful verbal or physical conduct that manifests bias or prejudice towards others. Harassment includes sexual harassment and derogatory or demeaning verbal or physical conduct. Sexual harassment includes unwelcome sexual advances, requests

---

* In August 2016, the ABA House of Delegates added paragraph (g) to Model Rule 8.4 to address the topic of discriminatory conduct by lawyers.

** In August 2016, the ABA deleted the original Comment 3 and added new Comments 3, 4, and 5, to address the interpretation of new Model Rule 8.4(g). Original Comments 4 and 5 were renumbered to be Comments 6 and 7.

for sexual favors, and other unwelcome verbal or physical conduct of a sexual nature. The substantive law of antidiscrimination and anti-harassment statutes and case law may guide application of paragraph (g).

[4] Conduct related to the practice of law includes representing clients; interacting with witnesses, coworkers, court personnel, lawyers and others while engaged in the practice of law; operating or managing a law firm or law practice; and participating in bar association, business or social activities in connection with the practice of law. Lawyers may engage in conduct undertaken to promote diversity and inclusion without violating this Rule by, for example, implementing initiatives aimed at recruiting, hiring, retaining and advancing diverse employees or sponsoring diverse law student organizations.

[5] A trial judge's finding that peremptory challenges were exercised on a discriminatory basis does not alone establish a violation of paragraph (g). A lawyer does not violate paragraph (g) by limiting the scope or subject matter of the lawyer's practice or by limiting the lawyer's practice to members of underserved populations in accordance with these Rules and other law. A lawyer may charge and collect reasonable fees and expenses for a representation. Rule 1.5(a). Lawyers also should be mindful of their professional obligations under Rule 6.1 to provide legal services to those who are unable to pay, and their obligation under Rule 6.2 not to avoid appointments from a tribunal except for good cause. See Rule 6.2(a), (b) and (c). A lawyer's representation of a client does not constitute an endorsement by the lawyer of the client's views or activities. See Rule 1.2(b).

[6] A lawyer may refuse to comply with an obligation imposed by law upon a good faith belief that no valid obligation exists. The provisions of Rule 1.2(d) concerning a good faith challenge to the validity, scope, meaning or application of the law apply to challenges of legal regulation of the practice of law.

[7] Lawyers holding public office assume legal responsibilities going beyond those of other citizens. A lawyer's abuse of public office can suggest an inability to fulfill the professional role of lawyers. The same is true of abuse of positions of private trust such as trustee, executor, administrator, guardian, agent and officer, director or manager of a corporation or other organization.

Rule 8.5 Disciplinary Authority: Choice of Law*

(a) Disciplinary Authority. A lawyer admitted to practice in this jurisdiction is subject to the disciplinary authority of this jurisdiction, regardless of where the lawyer's conduct occurs. A lawyer not admitted in this jurisdiction is also subject to the disciplinary authority of this jurisdiction if the lawyer provides or offers to provide any legal services in this jurisdiction. A lawyer may be subject to the disciplinary authority of both this jurisdiction and another jurisdiction for the same conduct.

(b) Choice of Law. In any exercise of the disciplinary authority of this jurisdiction, the rules of professional conduct to be applied shall be as follows:

(1) for conduct in connection with a matter pending before a tribunal, the rules of the jurisdiction in which the tribunal sits, unless the rules of the tribunal provide otherwise; and

(2) for any other conduct, the rules of the jurisdiction in which the lawyer's conduct occurred, or, if the predominant effect of the conduct is in a different jurisdiction, the rules of that jurisdiction shall be applied to the conduct. A lawyer shall not be subject to discipline if the lawyer's conduct conforms to the rules of a jurisdiction in which the lawyer reasonably believes the predominant effect of the lawyer's conduct will occur.

COMMENT

Disciplinary Authority

[1] It is longstanding law that the conduct of a lawyer admitted to practice in this jurisdiction is subject to the disciplinary authority of this jurisdiction. Extension of the disciplinary authority of this

* In November 2002, the ABA amended this rule to reflect the recommendations of the multijurisdictional practice of law commission.

jurisdiction to other lawyers who provide or offer to provide legal services in this jurisdiction is for the protection of the citizens of this jurisdiction. Reciprocal enforcement of a jurisdiction's disciplinary findings and sanctions will further advance the purposes of this Rule. See, Rules 6 and 22, ABA Model Rules for Lawyer Disciplinary Enforcement. A lawyer who is subject to the disciplinary authority of this jurisdiction under Rule 8.5(a) appoints an official to be designated by this Court to receive service of process in this jurisdiction. The fact that the lawyer is subject to the disciplinary authority of this jurisdiction may be a factor in determining whether personal jurisdiction may be asserted over the lawyer for civil matters.

Choice of Law*

[2] A lawyer may be potentially subject to more than one set of rules of professional conduct which impose different obligations. The lawyer may be licensed to practice in more than one jurisdiction with differing rules, or may be admitted to practice before a particular court with rules that differ from those of the jurisdiction or jurisdictions in which the lawyer is licensed to practice. Additionally, the lawyer's conduct may involve significant contacts with more than one jurisdiction.

[3] Paragraph (b) seeks to resolve such potential conflicts. Its premise is that minimizing conflicts between rules, as well as uncertainty about which rules are applicable, is in the best interest of both clients and the profession (as well as the bodies having authority to regulate the profession). Accordingly, it takes the approach of (i) providing that any particular conduct of a lawyer shall be subject to only one set of rules of professional conduct, (ii) making the determination of which set of rules applies to particular conduct as straightforward as possible, consistent with recognition of appropriate regulatory interests of relevant jurisdictions, and (iii) providing protection from discipline for lawyers who act reasonably in the face of uncertainty.

[4] Paragraph (b)(1) provides that as to a lawyer's conduct relating to a proceeding pending before a tribunal, the lawyer shall be subject only to the rules of the jurisdiction in which the tribunal sits unless the rules of the tribunal, including its choice of law rule, provide otherwise. As to all other conduct, including conduct in anticipation of a proceeding not yet pending before a tribunal, paragraph (b)(2) provides that a lawyer shall be subject to the rules of the jurisdiction in which the lawyer's conduct occurred, or, if the predominant effect of the conduct is in another jurisdiction, the rules of that jurisdiction shall be applied to the conduct. In the case of conduct in anticipation of a proceeding that is likely to be before a tribunal, the predominant effect of such conduct could be where the conduct occurred, where the tribunal sits or in another jurisdiction.

[5] When a lawyer's conduct involves significant contacts with more than one jurisdiction, it may not be clear whether the predominant effect of the lawyer's conduct will occur in a jurisdiction other than the one in which the conduct occurred. So long as the lawyer's conduct conforms to the rules of a jurisdiction in which the lawyer reasonably believes the predominant effect will occur, the lawyer shall not be subject to discipline under this Rule. With respect to conflicts of interest, in determining a lawyer's reasonable belief under paragraph (b)(2), a written agreement between the lawyer and client that reasonably specifies a particular jurisdiction as within the scope of that paragraph may be considered if the agreement was obtained with the client's informed consent confirmed in the agreement.

[6] If two admitting jurisdictions were to proceed against a lawyer for the same conduct, they should, applying this rule, identify the same governing ethics rules. They should take all appropriate steps to see that they do apply the same rule to the same conduct, and in all events should avoid proceeding against a lawyer on the basis of two inconsistent rules.

[7] The choice of law provision applies to lawyers engaged in transnational practice, unless international law, treaties or other agreements between competent regulatory authorities in the affected jurisdictions provide otherwise.

---

* In February 2013, the ABA House of Delegates added the last line to Comment 5 to allow lawyers and clients to contractually choose a forum's rules of professional responsibility.

INDEX TO ABA MODEL RULES

A

B

C

D

INDEX

J

K

L

M

N

O

INDEX

A CHART COMPARING THE LANGUAGE OF THE STATE CONFIDENTIALITY RULES

I have created this confidentiality chart to allow students to quickly compare any jurisdiction's confidentiality rules with the ABA Model Rules and to locate the rule number for additional research. It does not take into account case law or ethics opinions which may modify these rules and it does not take into account federal and state statutes which may lead to a different result in a specific substantive area. To do so would complicate the usability of the chart and would in fact be misleading. Thus, this chart does not address noisy withdrawal unless such a concept is included in the rule itself, see Arkansas. I also have not included a category based upon Model Rule 4.1—Truthfulness in Statements to Others—because virtually all states' 4.1 rules permit disclosure only to the extent that their confidentiality rules (1.6 and 3.3) allow disclosure. In my opinion, the 4.1 concept is resolved in this chart. I have also chosen to exclude footnotes to increase ease of use. This chart was created by looking up the state ethics rules on the State Ethics Rules subcategory of the Ethics and Professional Responsibility topical database on Westlaw. I checked my research with the excellent chart prepared by the Attorneys' Liability Assurance Society, Inc. An excellent source of state implementation of the ABA Model Rules can be found at http://www.americanbar.org/groups/professional_responsibility/policy.html.

DISCLOSURE

Jurisdiction	To Prevent Serious Bodily Crime	To Prevent Non-Bodily Crime	To Prevent Non-Criminal Fraud	To Rectify Past Crime/Fraud When Lawyer's Services Used	Fraud on Court
ABA 2001 Model Rules	May Reveal 1.6(b)(1)	Must Not 1.6	Must Not 1.6	Must Not 1.6	Must Reveal 3.3(a)(2)
ABA 2019 Model Rules	May Reveal if crime involves reasonably certain death or substantial bodily harm 1.6(b)(1)	May Reveal to prevent client from committing a crime reasonably certain to result in substantial injury to financial interests or property of another and when lawyer's services were used.	May Reveal to prevent client from committing a fraud reasonably certain to result in substantial injury financial interest or property of another and when legal services were used.	May Reveal to prevent, mitigate or rectify substantial injury to the financial interests or property of another that has or is reasonably certain to result from client's commission of a crime or fraud in furtherance of which the client has used the lawyer's services.	Must Take Reasonable Remedial Measures including, if necessary, disclosure to court 3.3(b)
Alabama	May Reveal 1.6(b)(1)	May Reveal 1.6	Must Not 1.6	Must Not 1.6	Must Disclose 3.3(a)(2)
Alaska	May Reveal 1.6(b)(1)	May Reveal 1.6(b)(1)	Must Not 1.6	Shall Not 1.6	Must Disclose 3.3(a)(2)

CONFIDENTIALITY CHART

Jurisdiction	To Prevent Serious Bodily Crime	To Prevent Non-Bodily Crime	To Prevent Non-Criminal Fraud	To Rectify Past Crime/Fraud When Lawyer's Services Used	Fraud on Court
Arizona	Shall Reveal 1.6(b)	May Reveal 1.6(d)(1)	May Reveal 1.6(d)(1)	May Reveal 1.6(d)(2)	Must Disclose 3.3(a)(2)
Arkansas	May Reveal 1.6(b)(1)	May Reveal 1.6(b)(1)	May Reveal 1.6(b)(2)	May Reveal, but allows lawyer to disclose fact of withdrawal and to disavow opinions and documents 1.6(b)(3), 1.6(c)	Must Disclose 3.3
California Statute	May Reveal Bus. Prof. Code § 6068(e)	Must Not Bus. Prof. Code § 6068(e)	Must Not Bus. Prof. Code § 6068(e)	Must Not Bus. Prof. Code § 6068(e)	"shall not seek to mislead judge" Rule 5–200(B)
California Ethics Code	May Reveal 1.6(b)	Must Not 3–1.6	Must Not 1.6	Must Not 1.6	above
Colorado	May Reveal 1.6(b)	May Reveal 1.6(b)	May Reveal 1.6	Must Not 1.6	Must Disclose 3.3(a)(2)
Connecticut	Must Reveal 1.6(b)	Shall Reveal 1.6(c)(2)	May Reveal 1.6	May Reveal 1.6(c)(2)	Must Disclose 3.3(a)(2)
Delaware	May Reveal 1.6(b)(1)	May Reveal 1.6(b)(2)	Must Not 1.6(b)(2)	May Reveal 1.6(b)(3)	Must Disclose 3.3(a)(2)
District of Columbia	May Reveal 1.6(c)(1)	May Reveal 1.6(d)	May Reveal 1.6	May Reveal 1.6	When fraud on court is present or future, lawyer may not participate directly and may use a narrative of client perjury is involved. 3.3(b). When fraud on the court is past, may not reveal if protected by Rule 1.6. 3.3(d)
Florida	Must Reveal 4–1.6(b)(2)	Must Reveal 4–1.6(b)(1)	Must Not 4–1.6	Must Not 4–1.6	Must Disclose 4–3.3(a)(2)

CONFIDENTIALITY CHART

Jurisdiction	To Prevent Serious Bodily Crime	To Prevent Non-Bodily Crime	To Prevent Non-Criminal Fraud	To Rectify Past Crime/Fraud When Lawyer's Services Used	Fraud on Court
Georgia	May Reveal 1.6(b)(1)(ii)	May Reveal 1.6(b)(1)	Must Not 1.6	Must Not 1.6	Must Disclose 3.3(a)(2)
Hawaii	May Reveal 1.6(b)	May Reveal 1.6(b)	May Reveal 1.6(c)(1)	Shall Reveal information which clearly establishes criminal or fraudulent act by client. 1.6(b). May Reveal information which lawyer reasonably believes to have been criminal or fraudulent. 1.6(c)(2)	Must Disclose 3.3(a)(2)
Idaho	May Reveal 1.6(b)(1)	May Reveal 1.6(b)(2)	Must Not 1.6	May Reveal 1.6	Must Disclose 3.3(a)(2)
Illinois	Shall Reveal 1.6(c)	May Reveal 1.6(b)(2)	Must Not 1.6	Must Not 1.6	Must Disclose 3.3(a)(2)
Indiana	May Reveal 1.6(b)(1)	May Reveal 1.6(b)(2)	May Reveal 1.6(b)(2)	May Reveal 1.6(b)(3)	Must Disclose 3.3(a)(2)
Iowa	Shall Reveal 32:1.6(b)(1)	May Reveal 32:1.6(b)(2)	May Reveal 32:1.6(b)(2)	May Reveal 32:1.6(b)(3)	Must Disclose 32:3.3(a)(2)
Kansas	May Reveal 1.6(b)(1)	May Reveal 1.6(b)(1)	Must Not 1.6	Must Not 1.6	Must Disclose 3.3(a)(2)
Kentucky	May Reveal 3.130 (1.6(b)(1))	Must Not 3.130(1.6)	Must Not 3.130 (1.6)	Must Not 3.310 (1.6)	Must Disclose 3.130 (3.3(a)(2))
Louisiana	May Reveal 1.6(b)(1)	May Reveal 1.6(b)(2)	May Reveal 1.6(b)(2)	May Reveal 1.6(b)(3)	Must Reveal 3.3(b)
Maine	May Disclose 1.6(b)(1)	May Disclose 1.6(b)(2)	May Disclose 1.6(b)(2)	May Disclose 1.6(b)(3)	Must Disclose 3.3(a)(2)
Maryland	May Reveal 1.6(b)(1)	May Reveal1.6(b)(2)	May Reveal1.6(b)(2)	May Reveal 1.6(b)(2)	Must Disclose 3.3(a)(2)

CONFIDENTIALITY CHART

Jurisdiction	To Prevent Serious Bodily Crime	To Prevent Non-Bodily Crime	To Prevent Non-Criminal Fraud	To Rectify Past Crime/Fraud When Lawyer's Services Used	Fraud on Court
Massachusetts	May Reveal to prevent death or substantial bodily harm or "wrongful execution or incarceration of another" 1.6(b)(1)	May Reveal 1.6(b)(2)	May Reveal 1.6(b)(3)	May Reveal 1.6(b)(3)	Must Disclose 3.3(a)(2)
Michigan	May Reveal 1.6(c)(4)	May Reveal 1.6(c)(4)	Must Not 1.6	May Reveal 1.6(c)(3)	Must Disclose 3.3(a)(2)
Minnesota	May Reveal 1.6(b)(6)	May Reveal 1.6(b)(3)	May Reveal 1.6(b)(4)	May Reveal 1.6(b)(5)	Must Disclose 3.3(b)
Mississippi	May Reveal 1.6(b)(1)	May Reveal 1.6(b)(2)	Must Reveal 1.6(b)(2)	Must Reveal 1.6(b)(3)	Must Disclose 3.3(a)(2)
Missouri	May Reveal 4–1.6(b)(1)	Must Not 4–1.6	Must Not 4–1.6	Must Not 4–1.6	Must Disclose 4–3.3(a)(2)
Montana	May Reveal 1.6(b)(1)	Must Not 1.6	Must Not 1.6	Must Not 1.6	Must Disclose 3.3(b)
Nebraska	May Reveal 1.6(b)(1)	Must Not 1.6	Must Not 1.6	Must Not 1.6	Must Reveal 3.3(b)
Nevada	Must Reveal 1.6(b)(1)	May Reveal, but shall where practicable first ask client to take suitable action 1.6(b)(2)	May Reveal but shall when practicable first ask client to take suitable action 1.6(b)(2)	May Reveal, but lawyer first shall attempt to persuade client to take corrective action. 1.6(b)(3)	Must Disclose 3.3(b)(2)
New Hampshire	May Reveal 1.6(b)(1)	May Reveal if it is likely to result in substantial injury to the financial interest or property of another 1.6(b)(1)	Must Not 1.6	Must Not 1.6	Must take reasonable remedial measures only if the fraud relates to evidence that the lawyer has offered in the past and the lawyer now realizes that it was false when offered. 3.3(a)(3)

CONFIDENTIALITY CHART

Jurisdiction	To Prevent Serious Bodily Crime	To Prevent Non-Bodily Crime	To Prevent Non-Criminal Fraud	To Rectify Past Crime/Fraud When Lawyer's Services Used	Fraud on Court
New Jersey	Shall Reveal to prevent the client from committing a "criminal, illegal, or fraudulent act" likely to result in "death or substantial bodily harm". 1.6(b)(1)	Shall Reveal to prevent the client from committing a "criminal, illegal, or fraudulent act" likely to result in "substantial injury to the financial interest or property of another". 1.6(b)(1)	Shall Reveal to prevent the client from committing a "criminal, illegal, or fraudulent act" likely to result in "substantial injury to the financial interest or property of another". 1.6(b)(1)	May Reveal 1.6(d)(1)	Must Reveal 1.6(b)(2), 3.3(a)(2)
New Mexico	Should Reveal 16–106(B)	May Reveal 16–106(C)	Must Not 16–106	Must Not 16–106	Must Reveal 16–303(A)(2)
New York	May Reveal 4–101(C)(3)	May Reveal 4–101(C)(3)	Must Not 4–101	Must Not 4–101	When fraud on court is perpetuated by a client, lawyer shall promptly urge client to rectify situation. If fraud is not corrected, lawyer must reveal fraud to court unless it is a client confidence or secret. 7–102(B)(1)
North Carolina	May Reveal 1.6(b)(3)	May Reveal 1.6(b)(2)	Must Not 1.6	May Reveal 1.6(b)(4)	Must Disclose 3.3(a)(2)

CONFIDENTIALITY CHART

Jurisdiction	To Prevent Serious Bodily Crime	To Prevent Non-Bodily Crime	To Prevent Non-Criminal Fraud	To Rectify Past Crime/Fraud When Lawyer's Services Used	Fraud on Court
North Dakota	Must Reveal 1.6(b)	May Reveal 1.6(c)(1)	May Reveal 1.6(c)(1)	May Reveal 1.6(d)	Must Reveal if fraud on court related to evidence that lawyer introduced other than the client's testimony. 3.3(c). Must Not reveal if fraud on the court comes from client's testimony. Lawyer shall urge a client to rectify the fraud and shall attempt to withdraw if client refuses. However, lawyer may not disclose the confidence. 3.3(d)
Ohio	May Reveal 1.6(b)(1)	May Reveal 1.6(b)(2)	Shall Not 1.6	May Reveal 1.6(b)(3)	Must Reveal 3.3(a)(3)
Oklahoma	May Reveal 1.6(b)(1)	May Reveal 1.6(b)(2)	May Reveal 1.6(b)(2)	May Reveal 1.6(b)(3)	Must Disclose 3.3(a)(2)
Oregon	May Reveal 1.6(b)(2)	May Reveal 1.6(b)(1)	Shall Not 1.6	Must Not 1.6	Must Disclose 3.3(b)
Pennsylvania	May Reveal 1.6(c)(1)	May Reveal 1.6(c)(2)	Shall Not 1.6	May Reveal 1.6(c)(3)	Must Disclose 3.3(b)(2), 1.6(b)
Rhode Island	May Reveal 1.6(b)(1)	Must Not 1.6	Must Not 1.6	Must Not 1.6	Must Disclose 3.3(a)(2)
South Carolina	May Reveal 1.6(b)(2)	May Reveal 1.6(b)(1)	May Reveal 1.6(b)(3)	May Reveal 1.6(b)(4)	Must Disclose 3.3(b)(2)
South Dakota	May Reveal 1.6(b)(1)	Shall Not 1.6	Shall Not 1.6	May Reveal 1.6(b)(4)	Must Disclose 3.3(b)(2)

CONFIDENTIALITY CHART

Jurisdiction	To Prevent Serious Bodily Crime	To Prevent Non-Bodily Crime	To Prevent Non-Criminal Fraud	To Rectify Past Crime/Fraud When Lawyer's Services Used	Fraud on Court
Tennessee	Shall Reveal information to prevent reasonably certain death or substantial bodily harm 1.6(c)(1)	May Reveal 1.6(b)(1)	May Reveal. 1.6(b)(2)	May Reveal 1.6(b)(3)	Rule 3.3 has many nuances for dissuading client from committing fraud and allowing for withdrawal. But generally the rule is extremely protective of client confidences.
Texas	Must Reveal 1.05(e)	May Reveal 1.05(c)(7)	May Reveal 1.05(c)(7)	May Reveal 1.05(c)(8)	Shall Disclose 3.03(a)(2)
Utah	May Reveal 1.6(b)(1)	May Reveal crimes likely to result in substantial injury to the financial interests or property of another 1.6(b)(2)	May Reveal non-criminal fraud likely to result in substantial injury to the financial interests or property of another 1.6(b)(3)	May Reveal 1.6(b)(2)	Must Disclose 3.3(b)
Vermont	Must Reveal 1.6(b)(1)	Must Reveal 1.6(b)(2)	Must Reveal 1.6(b)(2)	Must Disclose 1.6(b)(3)	Must Disclose 3.3(a)(2)
Virginia	Shall Promptly Reveal 1.6(c)(1)	Shall Promptly Reveal 1.6(c)(1)	Must Not 1.6	May Reveal 1.6(b)(3)	Shall Promptly Reveal 1.6(c)(2), 3.3(a)(2)

CONFIDENTIALITY CHART

Jurisdiction	To Prevent Serious Bodily Crime	To Prevent Non-Bodily Crime	To Prevent Non-Criminal Fraud	To Rectify Past Crime/Fraud When Lawyer's Services Used	Fraud on Court
Washington	Shall Reveal 1.6(b)(1)	May Reveal 1.6(b)(2)	May Reveal 1.6(b)(3)	May Reveal 1.6(b)(3)	Shall Not Disclose fraud on the court when such information is protected by 1.6 confidentiality. 3.3(a)(2), 3.3(c)
West Virginia	May Reveal 1.6(b)(1)	May Reveal 1.6(b)(2)	May Reveal 1.6	May Reveal 1.6	Must Disclose 3.3(a)(2)
Wisconsin	May Reveal 20:1.6(b)(1)	May Reveal 20:1.6(c)(2)	May Reveal 20:1.6(c)(2)	May Reveal 20:1.6(c)(1)	Must Disclose 20:3.3(a)(2)
Wyoming	May Reveal 1.6(b)(1)	May Reveal 1.6(b)(2)	May Reveal 1.6(b)(2)	May Reveal 1.6(b)(3)	Must Disclose 3.3(a)(2)

SELECTED SIGNIFICANT STATE MODIFICATIONS TO THE ABA MODEL RULES

The ABA Model Rules are designed to serve as a model for the states to consider and adopt. The enactment of the Model Rules caused most of the states to at least reconsider their local codes of ethics. As of the date of this publication, forty-seven states have replaced codes based upon the Model Code and have enacted codes based upon the structure and content of the Model Rules. Every one of these states has in some way amended the Model Rules provisions. Three states (New York, Oregon, and Virginia) have amended their version of the Model Code to reflect certain Model Rules' provisions. One state, California, did not base its code on the Model Code originally and refused to base a 1989 revision on the Model Rules. However, in May 2018, the California Supreme Court adopted a code that is based upon the Model Rules; however, it clearly includes many unique provisions.

In light of the many state modifications to the Model Rules, it is useful to examine selected significant state amendments. Some of these amendments illustrate substantive disagreements with the position adopted by the ABA in the Model Rules. Other modifications reflect local practices that the states have chosen to memorialize in the local code. Still other changes illustrate the desire to be more elaborative with respect to the language in the text. The selected state variations presented in this section fall within each of these categories.

The selected significant state modifications to the ABA Model Rules are presented under the order of the rules and within this framework by alphabetical order of the states. In the advertising section, however, the Texas and Virginia rules are grouped under each state. This section is intended to be illustrative and not exhaustive of the many state modifications. The comments to the state rule are included only if they are relevant to the rule that is illustrated.

TABLE OF CONTENTS

CLIENT-LAWYER RELATIONSHIP

Texas Disciplinary Rule 1.01 *(Modification of Model Rules 1.1 and 1.3)*

[Texas has combined Model Rule 1.1 (competence) and 1.3 (diligence) into one rule.]

RULE 1.01 Competent and Diligent Representation

(a) A lawyer shall not accept or continue employment in a legal matter which the lawyer knows or should know is beyond the lawyer's competence, unless:

(1) another lawyer who is competent to handle the matter is, with the prior informed consent of the client, associated in the matter; or

(2) the advice or assistance of the lawyer is reasonably required in an emergency and the lawyer limits the advice and assistance to that which is reasonably necessary in the circumstances.

(b) In representing a client, a lawyer shall not:

(1) neglect a legal matter entrusted to the lawyer; or

(2) frequently fail to carry out completely the obligations that the lawyer owes to a client or clients.

(c) As used in this Rule, "neglect" signifies inattentiveness involving a conscious disregard for the responsibilities owed to a client or clients.

COMMENT:

Accepting Employment

[1] A lawyer generally should not accept or continue employment in any area of the law in which the lawyer is not and will not be prepared to render competent legal services. "Competence" is defined in Terminology as possession of the legal knowledge, skill, and training reasonably necessary for the representation. Competent representation contemplates appropriate application by the lawyer of that legal knowledge, skill and training, reasonable thoroughness in the study and analysis of the law and facts, and reasonable attentiveness to the responsibilities owed to the client.

[2] In determining whether a matter is beyond a lawyer's competence, relevant factors include the relative complexity and specialized nature of the matter, the lawyer's general experience in the field in question, the preparation and study the lawyer will be able to give the matter, and whether it is feasible either to refer the matter to or associate a lawyer of established competence in the field in question. The required attention and preparation are determined in part by what is at stake; major litigation and complex transactions ordinarily require more elaborate treatment than matters of lesser consequences.

[3] A lawyer may not need to have special training or prior experience to accept employment to handle legal problems of a type with which the lawyer is unfamiliar. Although expertise in a particular field of law may be useful in some circumstances, the appropriate proficiency in many instances is that of a general practitioner. A newly admitted lawyer can be as competent in some matters as a practitioner with long experience. Some important legal skills, such as the analysis of precedent, the evaluation of evidence and legal drafting, are required in all legal problems. Perhaps the most fundamental legal skill consists of determining what kind of legal problems a situation may involve, a skill that necessarily transcends any particular specialized knowledge.

[4] A lawyer possessing the normal skill and training reasonably necessary for the representation of a client in an area of law is not subject to discipline for accepting employment in a matter in which, in order to represent the client properly, the lawyer must become more competent in regard to relevant legal knowledge by additional study and investigation. If the additional study and preparation will result in unusual delay or expense to the client, the lawyer should not accept employment except with the informed consent of the client.

[5] A lawyer offered employment or employed in a matter beyond the lawyer's competence generally must decline or withdraw from the employment or, with the prior informed consent of the client, associate a lawyer who is competent in the matter. Paragraph (a)(2) permits a lawyer, however, to give advice or assistance in an emergency in a matter even though the lawyer does not have the skill ordinarily required if referral to or consultation with another lawyer would be impractical and if the assistance is limited to that which is reasonably necessary in the circumstances.

Competent and Diligent Representation

[6] Having accepted employment, a lawyer should act with competence, commitment and dedication to the interest of the client and with zeal in advocacy upon the client's behalf. A lawyer should feel a moral or professional obligation to pursue a matter on behalf of a client with reasonable diligence and promptness despite opposition, obstruction or personal inconvenience to the lawyer. A lawyer's workload should be controlled so that each matter can be handled with diligence and competence. As provided in paragraph (a), an incompetent lawyer is subject to discipline.

Neglect

[7] Perhaps no professional shortcoming is more widely resented than procrastination. A client's interests often can be adversely affected by the passage of time or the change of conditions; in extreme instances, as when a lawyer overlooks a statute of limitations, the client's legal position may be destroyed. Under paragraph (b), a lawyer is subject to professional discipline for neglecting a particular legal matter as well as for frequent failures to carry out fully the obligations owed to one or more clients. A lawyer who acts in good faith is not subject to discipline, under those provisions for an isolated inadvertent or unskilled act or omission, tactical error, or error of judgment. Because delay can cause a client needless anxiety and

undermine confidence in the lawyer's trustworthiness, there is a duty to communicate reasonably with clients; see Rule 1.03.

Maintaining Competence

[8] Because of the vital role of lawyers in the legal process, each lawyer should strive to become and remain proficient and competent in the practice of law, including the benefits and risks associated with relevant technology. To maintain the requisite knowledge and skill of a competent practitioner, a lawyer should engage in continuing study and education. If a system of peer review has been established, the lawyer should consider making use of it in appropriate circumstances. Isolated instances of faulty conduct or decision should be identified for purposes of additional study or instruction.

Michigan Rule 1.2

[Michigan has amended Model Rule 1.2(a) to read as follows:]

RULE 1.2 Scope of Representation

(a) A lawyer shall seek the lawful objectives of a client through reasonably available means permitted by law and these rules. A lawyer does not violate this rule by acceding to reasonable requests of opposing counsel that do not prejudice the rights of the client, by being punctual in fulfilling all professional commitments, by avoiding offensive tactics. A lawyer shall abide by a client's decision whether to accept an offer of settlement or mediation evaluation of a matter. In a criminal case, the lawyer shall abide by the client's decision, after consultation with the lawyer, as to a plea to be entered, whether to waive jury trial, and whether the client will testify. In representing a client, a lawyer may, where permissible, exercise professional judgment to waive or fail to assert a right or position of the client.

* * *

Florida Rule 4–1.5 *(Modification of Model Rule 1.5)*

[Florida has amended Model Rule 1.5 to read as follows:]

RULE 4–1.5 Fees and Costs for Legal Services

(a) Illegal, Prohibited, or Clearly Excessive Fees and Costs. A lawyer must not enter into an agreement for, charge, or collect an illegal, prohibited, or clearly excessive fee or cost or a fee generated by employment that was obtained through advertising or solicitation not in compliance with the Rules Regulating The Florida Bar. A fee or cost is clearly excessive when:

(1) after a review of the facts, a lawyer of ordinary prudence would be left with a definite and firm conviction that the fee or the cost exceeds a reasonable fee or cost for services provided to such a degree as to constitute clear overreaching or an unconscionable demand by the attorney; or

(2) the fee or cost is sought or secured by the attorney by means of intentional misrepresentation or fraud upon the client, a nonclient party, or any court, as to either entitlement to, or amount of, the fee.

(b) Factors to Be Considered in Determining Reasonable Fee and Costs.

(1) Factors to be considered as guides in determining a reasonable fee include:

(A) the time and labor required, the novelty, complexity, and difficulty of the questions involved, and the skill requisite to perform the legal service properly;

(B) the likelihood that the acceptance of the particular employment will preclude other employment by the lawyer;

(C) the fee, or rate of fee, customarily charged in the locality for legal services of a comparable or similar nature;

(D) the significance of, or amount involved in, the subject matter of the representation, the responsibility involved in the representation, and the results obtained;

(E) the time limitations imposed by the client or by the circumstances and, as between attorney and client, any additional or special time demands or requests of the attorney by the client;

(F) the nature and length of the professional relationship with the client;

(G) the experience, reputation, diligence, and ability of the lawyer or lawyers performing the service and the skill, expertise, or efficiency of effort reflected in the actual providing of such services; and

(H) whether the fee is fixed or contingent, and, if fixed as to amount or rate, then whether the client's ability to pay rested to any significant degree on the outcome of the representation.

(2) Factors to be considered as guides in determining reasonable costs include:

(A) the nature and extent of the disclosure made to the client about the costs;

(B) whether a specific agreement exists between the lawyer and client as to the costs a client is expected to pay and how a cost is calculated that is charged to a client;

(C) the actual amount charged by third party provider of services to the attorney;

(D) whether specific costs can be identified and allocated to an individual client or a reasonable basis exists to estimate the costs charged;

(E) in-house service to a client if the cost is an in-house charge for services; and

(F) the relationship and past course of conduct between the lawyer and the client.

All costs are subject to the test of reasonableness set forth in subdivision (a) above. When the parties have a written contract in which the method is established for charging costs, the costs charged under that contract will be presumed reasonable.

(c) Consideration of All Factors. In determining a reasonable fee, the time devoted to the representation and customary rate of fee need not be the sole or controlling factors. All factors set forth in this rule should be considered, and may be applied, in justification of a fee higher or lower than that which would result from application of only the time and rate factors.

(d) Enforceability of Fee Contracts. Contracts or agreements for attorney's fees between attorney and client will ordinarily be enforceable according to the terms of such contracts or agreements, unless found to be illegal, obtained through advertising or solicitation not in compliance with the Rules Regulating The Florida Bar, prohibited by this rule, or clearly excessive as defined by this rule.

(e) Duty to Communicate Basis or Rate of Fee or Costs to Client and Definitions.

(1) Duty to Communicate. When the lawyer has not regularly represented the client, the basis or rate of the fee and costs must be communicated to the client, preferably in writing, before or within a reasonable time after commencing the representation. A fee for legal services that is nonrefundable in any part must be

confirmed in writing and must explain the intent of the parties as to the nature and amount of the nonrefundable fee. The test of reasonableness found in subdivision (b), above, applies to all fees for legal services without regard to their characterization by the parties.

The fact that a contract may not be in accord with these rules is an issue between the lawyer and client and a matter of professional ethics, but is not the proper basis for an action or defense by an opposing party when fee-shifting litigation is involved.

(2) Definitions.

(A) Retainer. A retainer is a sum of money paid to a lawyer to guarantee the lawyer's future availability. A retainer is not payment for past legal services and is not payment for future services.

(B) Flat Fee. A flat fee is a sum of money paid to a lawyer for all legal services to be provided in the representation. A flat fee may be termed "non-refundable."

(C) Advance Fee. An advanced fee is a sum of money paid to the lawyer against which the lawyer will bill the client as legal services are provided.

(f) Contingent Fees. As to contingent fees:

(1) A fee may be contingent on the outcome of the matter for which the service is rendered, except in a matter in which a contingent fee is prohibited by paragraph (f)(3) or by law. A contingent fee agreement must be in writing and must state the method by which the fee is to be determined, including the percentage or percentages that will accrue to the lawyer in the event of settlement, trial, or appeal, litigation and other expenses to be deducted from the recovery, and whether those expenses are to be deducted before or after the contingent fee is calculated. On conclusion of a contingent fee matter, the lawyer must provide the client with a written statement stating the outcome of the matter and, if there is a recovery, showing the remittance to the client and the method of its determination.

(2) Every lawyer who accepts a retainer or enters into an agreement, express or implied, for compensation for services rendered or to be rendered in any action, claim, or proceeding in which the lawyer's compensation is to be dependent or contingent in whole or in part upon the successful prosecution or settlement must do so only where the fee arrangement is reduced to a written contract, signed by the client, and by a lawyer for the lawyer or for the law firm representing the client. No lawyer or firm may participate in the fee without the consent of the client in writing. Each participating lawyer or law firm shall sign the contract with the client and shall agree to assume joint legal responsibility to the client for the performance of the services in question as if each were partners of the other lawyer or law firm involved. The client must be furnished with a copy of the signed contract and any subsequent notices or consents. All provisions of this rule willl apply to such fee contracts.

(3) A lawyer shall not enter into an arrangement for, charge, or collect:

(A) any fee in a domestic relations matter, the payment or amount of which is contingent upon the securing of a divorce or upon the amount of alimony or support, or property settlement in lieu thereof; or

(B) a contingent fee for representing a defendant in a criminal case.

(4) A lawyer who enters into an arrangement for, charges, or collects any fee in an action or claim for personal injury or for property damages or for death or loss of services resulting from personal injuries based upon tortious conduct of another, including products liability claims, whereby the compensation is to be dependent or

contingent in whole or in part upon the successful prosecution or settlement thereof shall do so only under the following requirements:

(A) The contract must contain the following provisions:

(i) "The undersigned client has, before signing this contract, received and read the statement of client's rights and understands each of the rights set forth in it. The undersigned client has signed the statement and received a signed copy to refer to while being represented by the undersigned lawyer(s)."

(ii) "This contract may be cancelled by written notification to the lawyer at any time within 3 business days of the date the contract was signed, as shown below, and if cancelled the client is not obligated to pay any fees to the attorney for the work performed during that time. If the lawyer has advanced funds to others in representation of the client, the lawyer is entitled to be reimbursed for such amounts that the lawyer has reasonably advanced on behalf of the client."

(B) The contract for representation of a client in a matter set forth in subdivision (f)(4) may provide for a contingent fee arrangement as agreed upon by the client and the lawyer, except as limited by the following provisions:

(i) Without prior court approval as specified below, any contingent fee that exceeds the following standards shall be presumed, unless rebutted, to be clearly excessive:

a. Before the filing of an answer or the demand for appointment of arbitrators or, if no answer is filed or no demand for appointment of arbitrators is made, the expiration of the time period provided for such action:

1. 33⅓% of any recovery up to $1 million; plus

2. 30% of any portion of the recovery between $1 million and $2 million; plus

3. 20% of any portion of the recovery exceeding $2 million.

b. After the filing of an answer or the demand for appointment of arbitrators or, if no answer is filed or no demand for appointment of arbitrators is made, the expiration of the time period provided for such action, through the entry of judgment.

1. 40% of any recovery up to $1 million; plus

2. 30% of any portion of the recovery between $1 million and $2 million; plus

3. 20% of any portion of the recovery exceeding $2 million.

c. If all defendants admit liability at the time of filing their answers and request a trial only on damages:

1. 33⅓% of any recovery up to $1 million; plus

2. 20% of any portion of the recovery between $1 million and $2 million; plus

3. 15% of any portion of the recovery for any amount exceeding $2 million.

d. An additional 5% of any recovery after notice of appeal postjudgment relief or action is required for recovery on the judgment.

(ii) If any client is unable to obtain a lawyer of the client's choice because of the limitations set forth in (f)(4)(B)(i), the client may petition the court in which the matter would be filed, if litigation is necessary, or if that court will not accept jurisdiction for the fee approval, the circuit court in which the cause of action arose, for approval of any fee contract between the client and a lawyer of the client's choosing. Authorization will be given if the court determines the client has a complete understanding of the client's rights and the terms of the proposed contract. The application for authorization of the contract can be filed as a separate proceeding before suit or simultaneously with the filing of a complaint. Proceedings on the petition may occur before service on the defendant and this aspect of the file may be sealed. A petition under this subdivision must contain a certificate showing service on the client and, if the petition is denied, a copy of the petition and order denying the petition must be served on The Florida Bar in Tallahassee by the member of the bar who has filed the petition. Authorization of such a contract does not bar subsequent inquiry as to whether the fee actually claimed or charged is clearly excessive under subdivisions (a) and (b).

(iii) Subject to the provisions of 4–1.5(f)(4)(B)(i) and (ii) a lawyer who enters into an arrangement for, charges, or collects any fee in an action or claim for medical liability in which the compensation is dependent or contingent in whole or in part upon the successful prosecution or settlement must provide the language of article I, section 26 of the Florida Constitution to the client in writing and must orally inform the client that:

a. Unless waived, in any medical liability claim involving a contingency fee, the claimant is entitled to receive no less than 70% of the first $250,000.00 of all damages received by the claimant, exclusive of reasonable and customary costs, whether received by judgment, settlement, or otherwise, and regardless of the number of defendants. The claimant is entitled to 90% of all damages in excess of $250,000.00, exclusive of reasonable and customary costs and regardless of the number of defendants.

b. If a lawyer chooses not to accept the representation of a client under the terms of article I, section 26 of the Florida Constitution, the lawyer shall advise the client, both orally and in writing of alternative terms, if any, under which the lawyer would accept the representation of the client, as well as the client's right to seek representation by another lawyer willing to accept the representation under the terms of article I, section 26 of the Florida Constitution, or a lawyer willing to accept the representation on a fee basis that is not contingent.

c. If any client desires to waive any rights under article I, section 26 of the Florida Constitution in order to obtain a lawyer of the client's choice, a client may do so by waiving such rights in writing, under oath, and in the form provided in this rule. The lawyer must provide each client a copy of the written waiver and must afford each client a full and complete opportunity to understand the rights being waived as set forth in the waiver. A copy of the waiver, signed by each client and lawyer, must be given to each client to retain, and the lawyer must keep a copy in the lawyer's file pertaining to the client. The waiver must be retained by the lawyer with the written fee contract and closing statement under the same conditions and requirements provided in 4–1.5(f)(5).

WAIVER OF THE CONSTITUTIONAL RIGHT PROVIDED IN ARTICLE I, SECTION 26 OF THE FLORIDA CONSTITUTION

On November 2, 2004, voters in the State of Florida approved The Medical Liability Claimant's Compensation Amendment that was identified as Amendment 3 on the ballot. The amendment is set forth below:

The Florida Constitution

Article I, Section 26 is created to read "Claimant's right to fair compensation." In any medical liability claim involving a contingency fee, the claimant is entitled to receive no less than 70% of the first $250,000 in all damages received by the claimant, exclusive of reasonable and customary costs, whether received by judgment, settlement or otherwise, and regardless of the number of defendants. The claimant is entitled to 90% of all damages in excess of $250,000, exclusive of reasonable and customary costs and regardless of the number of defendants. This provision is self-executing and does not require implementing legislation.

The undersigned client understands and acknowledges that (initial each provision):

______ I have been advised that signing this waiver releases an important constitutional right; and

______ I have been advised that I may consult with separate counsel before signing this waiver; and that I may request a hearing before a judge to further explain this waiver; and

______ By signing this waiver I agree to an increase in the attorney fee that might otherwise be owed if the constitutional provision listed above is not waived. Without prior court approval, the increased fee that I agree to may be up to the maximum contingency fee percentages set forth in Rule Regulating The Florida Bar 4–1.5(f)(4)(B)(i). Depending on the circumstances of my case, the maximum agreed upon fee may range from 33⅓% to 40% of any recovery up to $1 million; plus 20% to 30% of any portion of the recovery between $1 million and $2 million; plus 15% to 20% of any recovery exceeding $2 million; and

______ I have three (3) business days following execution of this waiver in which to cancel this waiver; and

______ I wish to engage the legal services of the lawyers or law firms listed below in an action or claim for medical liability the fee for which is contingent in whole or in part upon the successful prosecution or settlement thereof, but I am unable to do so because of the provisions of the constitutional limitation set forth above. In consideration of the lawyers' or law firms' agreements to represent me and my desire to employ the lawyers or law firms listed below, I hereby knowingly, willingly, and voluntarily waive any and all rights and privileges that I may have under the constitutional provision set forth above, as apply to the contingency fee agreement only. Specifically, I waive the percentage restrictions that are the subject of the constitutional provision and confirm the fee percentages set forth in the contingency fee agreement; and

______ I have selected the lawyers or law firms listed below as my counsel of choice in this matter and would not be able to engage their services without this waiver; and I expressly state that this waiver is made freely and voluntarily, with full knowledge of its terms, and that all questions have been answered to my satisfaction.

ACKNOWLEDGMENT BY CLIENT FOR PRESENTATION TO THE COURT

The undersigned client hereby acknowledges, under oath, the following:

I have read and understand this entire waiver of my rights under the constitutional provision set forth above.

I am not under the influence of any substance, drug, or condition (physical, mental, or emotional) that interferes with my understanding of this entire waiver in which I am entering and all the consequences thereof.

I have entered into and signed this waiver freely and voluntarily.

I authorize my lawyers or law firms listed below to present this waiver to the appropriate court, if required for purposes of approval of the contingency fee agreement. Unless the court requires my attendance at a hearing for that purpose, my lawyers or law firms are authorized to provide this waiver to the court for its consideration without my presence.

DATED this ___ day of ______, ___.

By: ______

CLIENT

Sworn to and subscribed before me this ___ day of ______, ___ by ______, who is personally known to me, or has produced the following identification: ______.

______

______

Notary Public

My Commission Expires:

Dated this ___ day of ______, ___.

By: ______

ATTORNEY

(C) Before a lawyer enters into a contingent fee contract for representation of a client in a matter set forth in this rule, the lawyer must provide the client with a copy of the statement of client's rights and must afford the client a full and complete opportunity to understand each of the rights as set forth in it. A copy of the statement, signed by both the client and the lawyer, must be given to the client to retain and the lawyer must keep a copy in the client's file. The statement must be retained by the lawyer with the written fee contract and closing statement under the same conditions and requirements as subdivision (f)(5).

(D) As to lawyers not in the same firm, a division of any fee within subdivision (f)(4) must be on the following basis:

(i) To the lawyer assuming primary responsibility for the legal services on behalf of the client, a minimum of 75% of the total fee.

(ii) To the lawyer assuming secondary responsibility for the legal services on behalf of the client, a maximum of 25% of the total fee. Any fee in excess of 25% will be presumed to be clearly excessive.

(iii) The 25% limitation will not apply to those cases in which 2 or more lawyers or firms accept substantially equal active participation in the providing of legal services. In those circumstances counsel mustapply to the court in which the matter would be filed, if litigation is necessary, or if such court will not accept jurisdiction for the fee division, the circuit court in which the cause of action arose, for authorization of the fee division in excess of 25%, based on a sworn petition signed by all counsel that discloses in detail those services to be performed. The application for authorization of the contract may be filed as a separate proceeding before suit or simultaneously with the filing of a complaint, or within 10 days of execution of a contract for division of fees when new counsel is engaged. Proceedings on these applications may occur before service of process on any party and this aspect of the file may be sealed. Authorization of the contract will not bar subsequent inquiry as to whether the fee actually claimed or charged is clearly excessive. An application under this subdivision must contain a certificate showing service on the client and, if the application is denied, a copy of the petition and order denying the petition must be served on The Florida Bar in Tallahassee by the member of the bar who filed the petition. Counsel may proceed with representation of the client pending court approval.

(iv) The percentages required by this subdivision are applicable after deduction of any fee payable to separate counsel retained especially for appellate purposes.

(5) In the event there is a recovery, on the conclusion of the representation, the lawyer must prepare a closing statement reflecting an itemization of all costs and expenses, together with the amount of fee received by each participating lawyer or law firm. A copy of the closing statement must be executed by all participating lawyers, as well as the client, and each shall receive a copy. Each participating lawyer must retain a copy of the written fee contract and closing statement for 6 years after execution of the closing statement. Any contingent fee contract and closing statement must be available for inspection at reasonable times by the client, by any other person upon judicial order, or by the appropriate disciplinary agency.

(6) In cases in which the client is to receive a recovery that will be paid to the client on a future structured or periodic basis, the contingent fee percentage must be calculated only on the cost of the structured verdict or settlement or, if the cost is unknown, on the present money value of the structured verdict or settlement, whichever is less. If the damages and the fee are to be paid out over the long term future schedule, this limitation does not apply. No attorney may negotiate separately with the defendant for that attorney's fee in a structured verdict or settlement when such separate negotiations would place the attorney in a position of conflict.

(g) Division of Fees Between Lawyers in Different Firms. Subject to the provisions of subdivision (f)(4)(D), a division of fee between lawyers who are not in the same firm may be made only if the total fee is reasonable and:

(1) the division is in proportion to the services performed by each lawyer; or

(2) by written agreement with the client:

(A) each lawyer assumes joint legal responsibility for the representation and agrees to be available for consultation with the client; and

(B) the agreement fully discloses that a division of fees will be made and the basis upon which the division of fees will be made.

(h) Credit Plans. A lawyer or law firm may accept payment under a credit plan. Lawyers may charge clients the actual charge the credit plan imposes on the lawyer for the client's transaction.

(i) Arbitration Clauses. A lawyer must not make an agreement with a potential client prospectively providing for mandatory arbitration of fee disputes without first advising that person in writing that the potential client should consider obtaining independent legal advice as to the advisability of entering into an agreement containing such mandatory arbitration provisions. A lawyer shall not make an agreement containing such mandatory arbitration provisions unless the agreement contains the following language in bold print:

NOTICE: This agreement contains provisions requiring arbitration of fee disputes. Before you sign this agreement you should consider consulting with another lawyer about the advisability of making an agreement with mandatory arbitration requirements. Arbitration proceedings are ways to resolve disputes without use of the court system. By entering into agreements that require arbitration as the way to resolve fee disputes, you give up (waive) your right to go to court to resolve those disputes by a judge or jury. These are important rights that should not be given up without careful consideration.

STATEMENT OF CLIENT'S RIGHTS FOR CONTINGENCY FEES

Before you, the prospective client, arrange a contingent fee agreement with a lawyer, you should understand this statement of your rights as a client. This statement is not a part of the actual contract between you and your lawyer, but, as a prospective client, you should be aware of these rights:

1. There is no legal requirement that a lawyer charge a client a set fee or a percentage of money recovered in a case. You, the client, have the right to talk with your lawyer about the proposed fee and to bargain about the rate or percentage as in any other contract. If you do not reach an agreement with one lawyer you may talk with other lawyers.

2. Any contingent fee contract must be in writing and you have 3 business days to reconsider the contract. You may cancel the contract without any reason if you notify your lawyer in writing within 3 business days of signing the contract. If you withdraw from the contract within the first 3 business days, you do not owe the lawyer a fee although you may be responsible for the lawyer's actual costs during that time. If your lawyer begins to represent you, your lawyer may not withdraw from the case without giving you notice, delivering necessary papers to you, and allowing you time to employ another lawyer. Often, your lawyer must obtain court approval before withdrawing from a case. If you discharge your lawyer without good cause after the 3-day period, you may have to pay a fee for work the lawyer has done.

3. Before hiring a lawyer, you, the client, have the right to know about the lawyer's education, training, and experience. If you ask, the lawyer should tell you specifically about the lawyer's actual experience dealing with cases similar to yours. If you ask, the lawyer should provide information about special training or knowledge and give you this information in writing if you request it.

4. Before signing a contingent fee contract with you, a lawyer must advise you whether the lawyer intends to handle your case alone or whether other lawyers will be helping with the case. If your lawyer intends to refer the case to other lawyers, the lawyer should tell you what kind of fee sharing arrangement will be made with the other lawyers. If lawyers from different law firms will represent you, at least 1 lawyer from each law firm must sign the contingent fee contract.

5. If your lawyer intends to refer your case to another lawyer or counsel with other lawyers, your lawyer should tell you about that at the beginning. If your lawyer takes the case and later decides to refer it to another lawyer or to associate with other lawyers, you should sign a new contract that includes the new lawyers. You, the client, also have the right to consult with each lawyer working on your case and each lawyer is legally responsible to represent your interests and is legally responsible for the acts of the other lawyers involved in the case.

6. You, the client, have the right to know in advance how you will need to pay the expenses and the legal fees at the end of the case. If you pay a deposit in advance for costs, you may ask reasonable questions about how the money will be or has been spent and how much of it remains unspent. Your lawyer should give a reasonable estimate about future necessary costs. If your lawyer agrees to lend or advance you money to prepare or research the case, you have the right to know periodically how much money your lawyer has

spent on your behalf. You also have the right to decide, after consulting with your lawyer, how much money is to be spent to prepare a case. If you pay the expenses, you have the right to decide how much to spend. Your lawyer should also inform you whether the fee will be based on the gross amount recovered or on the amount recovered minus the costs.

7. You, the client, have the right to be told by your lawyer about possible adverse consequences if you lose the case. Those adverse consequences might include money that you might have to pay to your lawyer for costs and liability you might have for attorney's fees to the other side.

8. You, the client, have the right to receive and approve a closing statement at the end of the case before you pay any money. The statement must list all of the financial details of the entire case, including the amount recovered, all expenses, and a precise statement of your lawyer's fee. Until you approve the closing statement your lawyer cannot pay money to anyone, including you, without an appropriate order of the court. You also have the right to have every lawyer or law firm working on your case sign this closing statement.

9. You, the client, have the right to ask your lawyer at reasonable intervals how the case is progressing and to have these questions answered to the best of your lawyer's ability.

10. You, the client, have the right to make the final decision regarding settlement of a case. Your lawyer must notify you of all offers of settlement before and after the trial. Offers during the trial must be immediately communicated and you should consult with your lawyer regarding whether to accept a settlement. However, you must make the final decision to accept or reject a settlement.

11. If at any time you, the client, believe that your lawyer has charged an excessive or illegal fee, you have the right to report the matter to The Florida Bar, the agency that oversees the practice and behavior of all lawyers in Florida. For information on how to reach The Florida Bar, call 850–561–5600, or contact the local bar association. Any disagreement between you and your lawyer about a fee can be taken to court and you may wish to hire another lawyer to help you resolve this disagreement. Usually fee disputes must be handled in a separate lawsuit unless your fee contract provides for arbitration. You can request, but may not require, that a provision for arbitration (under chapter 682, Florida Statutes, or under the fee arbitration rule of the Rules Regulating The Florida Bar) be included in your fee contract.

______________________________	______________________________
Client Signature	Attorney Signature
______________________________	______________________________
Date	Date

COMMENT:

Bases or rate of fees and costs

When the lawyer has regularly represented a client, they ordinarily will have evolved an understanding concerning the basis or rate of the fee. The conduct of the lawyer and client in prior relationships is relevant when analyzing the requirements of this rule. In a new client-lawyer relationship, however, an understanding as to the fee should be promptly established. It is not necessary to recite all the factors that underlie the basis of the fee but only those that are directly involved in its computation. It is sufficient, for example, to state the basic rate is an hourly charge or a fixed amount or an estimated amount, or to identify the factors that may be taken into account in finally fixing the fee. Although hourly billing or a fixed fee may be the most common bases for computing fees in an area of practice, these may not be the only bases for computing fees. A lawyer should, where appropriate, discuss alternative billing methods with the client. When developments occur during the representation that render an earlier estimate substantially inaccurate, a revised estimate should be provided to the client. A written statement concerning the fee reduces the possibility of misunderstanding. Furnishing the client with a simple memorandum or a copy of the lawyer's customary fee schedule is sufficient if the basis or rate of the fee is set forth.

General overhead should be accounted for in a lawyer's fee, whether the lawyer charges hourly, flat, or contingent fees. Filing fees, transcription, and the like should be charged to the client at the actual amount paid by the lawyer. A lawyer may agree with the client to charge a reasonable amount for in-house costs or services. In-house costs include items such as copying, faxing, long distance telephone, and computerized research. In-house services include paralegal services, investigative services, accounting services, and courier services. The lawyer should sufficiently communicate with the client regarding the costs charged to the client so that the client understands the amount of costs being charged or the method for calculation of those costs. Costs appearing in sufficient detail on closing statements and approved by the parties to the transaction should meet the requirements of this rule.

Rule 4–1.8(e) should be consulted regarding a lawyer's providing financial assistance to a client in connection with litigation.

In order to avoid misunderstandings concerning the nature of legal fees, written documentation is required when any aspect of the fee is nonrefundable. A written contract provides a method to resolve misunderstandings and to protect the lawyer in the event of continued misunderstanding. Rule 4–1.5(e) does not require the client to sign a written document memorializing the terms of the fee. A letter from the lawyer to the client setting forth the basis or rate of the fee and the intent of the parties in regard to the nonrefundable nature of the fee is sufficient to meet the requirements of this rule.

All legal fees and contracts for legal fees are subject to the requirements of the Rules Regulating The Florida Bar. In particular, the test for reasonableness of legal fees found in rule 4–1.5(b) applies to all types of legal fees and contracts related to them.

Terms of payment

A lawyer may require advance payment of a fee but is obliged to return any unearned portion. See rule 4–1.16(d). A lawyer is not, however, required to return retainers that, pursuant to an agreement with a client, are not refundable. A nonrefundable retainer or nonrefundable flat fee is the property of the lawyer and should not be held in trust. If a client gives the lawyer a negotiable instrument that represents both an advance on costs plus either a nonrefundable retainer or a nonrefundable flat fee, the entire amount should be deposited into the lawyer's trust account, then the portion representing the earned nonrefundable retainer or nonrefundable flat fee should be withdrawn within a reasonable time. An advance fee must be held in trust until it is earned. Nonrefundable fees are, as all fees, subject to the prohibition against excessive fees.

A lawyer may accept property in payment for services, such as an ownership interest in an enterprise, providing this does not involve acquisition of a proprietary interest in the cause of action or subject matter of the litigation contrary to rule 4–1.8(i). However, a fee paid in property instead of money may be subject to special scrutiny because it involves questions concerning both the value of the services and the lawyer's special knowledge of the value of the property.

An agreement may not be made whose terms might induce the lawyer improperly to curtail services for the client or perform them in a way contrary to the client's interest. For example, a lawyer should not enter into an agreement whereby services are to be provided only up to a stated amount when it is foreseeable that more extensive services probably will be required, unless the situation is adequately explained to the client. Otherwise, the client might have to bargain for further assistance in the midst of a proceeding or transaction. However, it is proper to define the extent of services in light of the client's ability to pay. A lawyer should not exploit a fee arrangement based primarily on hourly charges by using wasteful procedures. When there is doubt whether a contingent fee is consistent with the client's best interest, the lawyer should offer the client alternative bases for the fee and explain their implications. Applicable law may impose limitations on contingent fees, such as a ceiling on the percentage.

Prohibited contingent fees

Subdivision (f)(3)(A) prohibits a lawyer from charging a contingent fee in a domestic relations matter when payment is contingent upon the securing of a divorce or upon the amount of alimony or support or property settlement to be obtained. This provision does not preclude a contract for a contingent fee for legal representation in connection with the recovery of post-judgment balances due under support, alimony, or other financial orders because such contracts do not implicate the same policy concerns.

Contingent fees are prohibited in criminal and certain domestic relations matters. In domestic relations cases, fees that include a bonus provision or additional fee to be determined at a later time and based on results obtained have been held to be impermissible contingency fees and therefore subject to restitution and disciplinary sanction as elsewhere stated in these Rules Regulating The Florida Bar.

Contingent fee regulation

Subdivision (e) is intended to clarify that whether the lawyer' s fee contract complies with these rules is a matter between the lawyer and client and an issue for professional disciplinary enforcement. The rules and subdivision (e) are not intended to be used as procedural weapons or defenses by others. Allowing opposing parties to assert noncompliance with these rules as a defense, including whether the fee is fixed or contingent, allows for potential inequity if the opposing party is allowed to escape responsibility for their actions solely through application of these rules.

Rule 4–1.5(f)(4) should not be construed to apply to actions or claims seeking property or other damages arising in the commercial litigation context.

Rule 4–1.5(f)(4)(B) is intended to apply only to contingent aspects of fee agreements. In the situation where a lawyer and client enter a contract for part noncontingent and part contingent attorney's fees, rule 4–1.5(f)(4)(B) should not be construed to apply to and prohibit or limit the noncontingent portion of the fee agreement. An attorney could properly charge and retain the noncontingent portion of the fee even if the matter was not successfully prosecuted or if the noncontingent portion of the fee exceeded the schedule set forth in rule 4–1.5(f)(4)(B). Rule 4–1.5(f)(4)(B) should, however, be construed to apply to any additional contingent portion of such a contract when considered together with earned noncontingent fees. Thus, under such a contract a lawyer may demand or collect only such additional contingent fees as would not cause the total fees to exceed the schedule set forth in rule 4–1.5(f)(4)(B).

The limitations in rule 4–1.5(f)(4)(B)(i)c are only to be applied in the case where all the defendants admit liability at the time they file their initial answer and the trial is only on the issue of the amount or extent of the loss or the extent of injury suffered by the client. If the trial involves not only the issue of damages but also such questions as proximate cause, affirmative defenses, seat belt defense, or other similar matters, the limitations are not to be applied because of the contingent nature of the case being left for resolution by the trier of fact.

Rule 4–1.5(f)(4)(B)(ii) provides the limitations set forth in subdivision (f)(4)(B)(i) may be waived by the client upon approval by the appropriate judge. This waiver provision may not be used to authorize a lawyer to charge a client a fee that would exceed rule 4–1.5(a) or (b). It is contemplated that this waiver provision will not be necessary except where the client wants to retain a particular lawyer to represent the client or the case involves complex, difficult, or novel questions of law or fact that would justify a contingent fee greater than the schedule but not a contingent fee that would exceed rule 4–1.5(b).

Upon a petition by a client, the trial court reviewing the waiver request must grant that request if the trial court finds the client: (a) understands the right to have the limitations in rule 4–1.5(f)(4)(B) applied in the specific matter; and (b) understands and approves the terms of the proposed contract. The consideration by the trial court of the waiver petition is not to be used as an opportunity for the court to inquire into the merits or details of the particular action or claim that is the subject of the contract.

The proceedings before the trial court and the trial court's decision on a waiver request are to be confidential and not subject to discovery by any of the parties to the action or by any other individual or entity except The Florida Bar. However, terms of the contract approved by the trial court may be subject to discovery if the contract (without court approval) was subject to discovery under applicable case law or rules of evidence.

Rule 4–1.5(f)(4)(B)(iii) is added to acknowledge the provisions of article 1, section 26 of the Florida Constitution, and to create an affirmative obligation on the part of an attorney contemplating a contingency fee contract to notify a potential client with a medical liability claim of the limitations provided in that constitutional provision. This addition to the rule is adopted prior to any judicial interpretation of the meaning or scope of the constitutional provision and this rule is not intended to make any substantive interpretation of the meaning or scope of that provision. The rule also provides that a client who wishes to waive the rights of the constitutional provision, as those rights may relate to attorney's fees, must do so in the form contained in the rule.

Rule 4–1.5(f)(6) prohibits a lawyer from charging the contingent fee percentage on the total, future value of a recovery being paid on a structured or periodic basis. This prohibition does not apply if the lawyer's fee is being paid over the same length of time as the schedule of payments to the client.

Fees that provide for a bonus or additional fees and that otherwise are not prohibited under the Rules Regulating the Florida Bar can be effective tools for structuring fees. For example, a fee contract calling for a flat fee and the payment of a bonus based on the amount of property retained or recovered in a general civil action is not prohibited by these rules. However, the bonus or additional fee must be stated clearly in amount or formula for calculation of the fee (basis or rate). Courts have held that unilateral bonus fees are unenforceable. The test of reasonableness and other requirements of this rule apply to permissible bonus fees.

Division of fee

A division of fee is a single billing to a client covering the fee of 2 or more lawyers who are not in the same firm. A division of fee facilitates association of more than 1 lawyer in a matter in which neither alone could serve the client as well, and most often is used when the fee is contingent and the division is between a referring lawyer and a trial specialist. Subject to the provisions of subdivision (f)(4)(D), subdivision (g) permits the lawyers to divide a fee on either the basis of the proportion of services they render or by agreement between the participating lawyers if all assume responsibility for the representation as a whole and the client is advised and does not object. It does require disclosure to the client of the share that each lawyer is to receive. Joint responsibility for the representation entails the obligations stated in rule 4–5.1 for purposes of the matter involved.

Disputes over fees

Since the fee arbitration rule (Chapter 14) has been established by the bar to provide a procedure for resolution of fee disputes, the lawyer should conscientiously consider submitting to it. Where law prescribes a procedure for determining a lawyer's fee, for example, in representation of an executor or administrator, a class, or a person entitled to a reasonable fee as part of the measure of damages, the lawyer entitled to such a fee and a lawyer representing another party concerned with the fee should comply with the prescribed procedure.

Referral fees and practices

A secondary lawyer shall not be entitled to a fee greater than the limitation set forth in rule 4–1.5(f)(4)(D)(ii) merely because the lawyer agrees to do some or all of the following: (a) consults with the client; (b) answers interrogatories; (c) attends depositions; (d) reviews pleadings; (e) attends the trial; or (f) assumes joint legal responsibility to the client. However, the provisions do not contemplate that a secondary lawyer who does more than the above is necessarily entitled to a larger percentage of the fee than that allowed by the limitation.

The provisions of rule 4–1.5(f)(4)(D)(iii) only apply where the participating lawyers have for purposes of the specific case established a co-counsel relationship. The need for court approval of a referral fee arrangement under rule 4–1.5(f)(4)(D)(iii) should only occur in a small percentage of cases arising under rule 4–1.5(f)(4) and usually occurs prior to the commencement of litigation or at the onset of the representation. However, in those cases in which litigation has been commenced or the representation has already begun, approval of the fee division should be sought within a reasonable period of time after the need for court approval of the fee division arises.

In determining if a co-counsel relationship exists, the court should look to see if the lawyers have established a special partnership agreement for the purpose of the specific case or matter. If such an agreement does exist, it must provide for a sharing of services or responsibility and the fee division is based upon a division of the services to be rendered or the responsibility assumed. It is contemplated that a co-counsel situation would exist where a division of responsibility is based upon, but not limited to, the following: (a) based upon geographic considerations, the lawyers agree to divide the legal work, responsibility, and representation in a convenient fashion. (such a situation would occur when different aspects of a case must be handled in different locations); (b) where the lawyers agree to divide the legal work and representation based upon their particular expertise in the substantive areas of law involved in the litigation; or (c) where the lawyers agree to divide the legal work and representation along established lines of division, such as liability and damages, causation and damages, or other similar factors.

The trial court's responsibility when reviewing an application for authorization of a fee division under rule 4–1.5(f)(4)(D)(iii) is to determine if a co-counsel relationship exists in that particular case. If the court determines a co-counsel relationship exists and authorizes the fee division requested, the court does not have any responsibility to review or approve the specific amount of the fee division agreed upon by the lawyers and the client.

Rule 4–1.5(f)(4)(D)(iv) applies to the situation where appellate counsel is retained during the trial of the case to assist with the appeal of the case. The percentages set forth in subdivision (f)(4)(D) are to be applicable after appellate counsel's fee is established. However, the effect should not be to impose an unreasonable fee on the client.

Credit plans

Credit plans include credit cards.

Kansas Rule 1.5

[Kansas has substituted the following provisions for Model Rule 1.5(c) through (e):]

RULE 1.5

(c) A lawyer's fee shall be reasonable but a court determination that a fee is not reasonable shall not be presumptive evidence of a violation that requires discipline of the attorney.

(d) A fee may be contingent on the outcome of the matter for which the service is rendered, except in a matter in which a contingent fee is prohibited by paragraph (f) or other law. A contingent fee agreement shall be in writing and shall state the method by which the fee is to be determined, including the percentage or percentages that shall accrue to the lawyer in the event of settlement, trial or appeal, and the litigation and other expenses to be deducted from the recovery. All such expenses shall be deducted before the contingent fee is calculated. Upon conclusion of a contingent fee matter, the lawyer shall provide the client with a written statement stating the outcome of the matter and, if there is a recovery, showing the client's share and amount and the method of its determination. The statement shall advise the client of the right to have the fee reviewed as provided in subsection (e).

(e) Upon application by the client, all fee contracts shall be subject to review and approval by the appropriate court having jurisdiction of the matter and the court shall have the authority to determine whether the contract is reasonable. If the court finds the contract is not reasonable, it shall set and allow a reasonable fee.

Texas Disciplinary Rule 1.04

[Texas has modified several subsections of Model Rule 1.5 (fees) to read as follows:]

RULE 1.04 Fees

(f) A division or arrangement for division of a fee between lawyers who are not in the same firm may be made only if:

(1) the division is:

(i) in proportion to the professional services performed by each lawyer; or

(ii) made between lawyers who assume joint responsibility for the representation; and

(2) the client consents in writing to the terms of the arrangement prior to the time of the association or referral proposed, including:

(i) the identity of all lawyers or law firms who will participate in the fee-sharing agreement, and

(ii) whether fees will be divided based on the proportion of services performed or by lawyers agreeing to assume joint responsibility for the representation, and

(iii) the share of the fee that each lawyer or law firm will receive or, if the division is based on the proportion of services performed, the basis on which the division will be made; and

(3) the aggregate fee does not violate paragraph (a).

(g) Every agreement that allows a lawyer or law firm to associate other counsel in the representation of a person, or to refer the person to other counsel for such representation, and that results in such an association with or referral to a different law firm or a lawyer in such a different firm, shall be confirmed by an arrangement conforming to paragraph (f). Consent by a client or a prospective client without knowledge of the information specified in subparagraph (f)(2) does not constitute a confirmation within the meaning of this rule. No attorney shall collect or seek to collect fees or expenses in connection with any such agreement that is not confirmed in that way, except for:

(1) the reasonable value of legal services provided to that person; and

(2) the reasonable and necessary expenses actually incurred on behalf of that person.

(h) Paragraph (f) of this rule does not apply to payment to a former partner or associate pursuant to a separation or retirement agreement, or to a lawyer referral program certified by the State Bar of Texas in accordance with the Texas Lawyer Referral Service Quality Act, Tex. Occ. Code 952.001 et seq., or any amendments or recodifications thereof.

COMMENT:

1. A lawyer in good conscience should not charge or collect more than a reasonable fee, although he may charge less or no fee at all. The determination of the reasonableness of a fee, or of the range of reasonableness, can be a difficult question, and a standard of "reasonableness" is too vague and uncertain to be an appropriate standard in a disciplinary action. For this reason, paragraph (a) adopts, for disciplinary purposes only, a clearer standard: the lawyer is subject to discipline for an illegal fee or an unconscionable fee. Paragraph (a) defines an unconscionable fee in terms of the reasonableness of the fee but in a way to eliminate factual disputes as to the fee's reasonableness. The Rule's "unconscionable" standard, however, does not preclude use of the "reasonableness" standard of paragraph (b) in other settings.

* * *

Division of Fees

10. A division of fees is a single billing to a client covering the fee of two or more lawyers who are not in the same firm. A division of fees facilitates association of more than one lawyer in a matter in which neither alone could serve the client as well, and most often is used when the fee is contingent and the division is between a referring or associating lawyer initially retained by the client and a trial specialist, but it applies in all cases in which two or more lawyers are representing a single client in the same matter, and without regard to whether litigation is involved. Paragraph (f) permits the lawyers to divide a fee either on the basis of the proportion of services they render or if each lawyer assumes joint responsibility for the representation.

11. Contingent fee agreements must be in a writing signed by the client and must otherwise comply with paragraph (d) of this Rule.

12. A division of a fee based on the proportion of services rendered by two or more lawyers contemplates that each lawyer is performing substantial legal services on behalf of the client with respect to the matter. In particular, it requires that each lawyer who participates in the fee have performed services beyond those involved in initially seeking to acquire and being engaged by the client. There must be a reasonable correlation between the amount or value of services rendered and responsibility assumed, and

the share of the fee to be received. However, if each participating lawyer performs substantial legal services on behalf of the client, the agreed division should control even though the division is not directly proportional to actual work performed. If a division of fee is to be based on the proportion of services rendered, the arrangement may provide that the allocation not be made until the end of the representation. When the allocation is deferred until the end of the representation, the terms of the arrangement must include the basis by which the division will be made.

13. Joint responsibility for the representation entails ethical and perhaps financial responsibility for the representation. The ethical responsibility assumed requires that a referring or associating lawyer make reasonable efforts to assure adequacy of representation and to provide adequate client communication. Adequacy of representation requires that the referring or associating lawyer conduct a reasonable investigation of the client's legal matter and refer the matter to a lawyer whom the referring or associating lawyer reasonably believes is competent to handle it. See Rule 1.01. Adequate attorney-client communication requires that a referring or associating lawyer monitor the matter throughout the representation and ensure that the client is informed of those matters that come to that lawyer's attention and that a reasonable lawyer would believe the client should be aware. See Rule 1.03. Attending all depositions and hearings or requiring that copies of all pleadings and correspondence be provided a referring or associating lawyer is not necessary in order to meet the monitoring requirement proposed by this rule. These types of activities may increase the transactional costs, which ultimately the client will bear and unless some benefit will be derived by the client, they should be avoided. The monitoring requirement is only that the referring lawyer be reasonably informed of the matter, respond to client questions, and assist the handling lawyer when necessary. Any referral or association of other counsel should be made based solely on the client's best interest.

14. In the aggregate, the minimum activities that must be undertaken by referring or associating lawyers pursuant to an arrangement for a division of fees are substantially greater than those assumed by a lawyer who forwarded a matter to other counsel, undertook no ongoing obligations with respect to it, and yet received a portion of the handling lawyer's fee once the matter was concluded, as was permitted under the prior version of this rule. Whether such activities, or any additional activities that a lawyer might agree to undertake, suffice to make one lawyer participating in such an arrangement responsible for the professional misconduct of another lawyer who is participating in it and, if so, to what extent, are intended to be resolved by Texas Civil Practice and Remedies Code, ch. 33, or other applicable law.

15. A client must consent in writing to the terms of the arrangement prior to the time of the association or referral proposed. For this consent to be effective, the client must have been advised of at least the key features of that arrangement. Those essential terms, which are specified in subparagraph (f)(2), are 1) the identity of all lawyers or law firms who will participate in the fee-sharing agreement, 2) whether fees will be divided based on the proportion of services performed or by lawyers agreeing to assume joint responsibility for the representation, and 3) the share of the fee that each lawyer or law firm will receive or the basis on which the division will he made if the division is based on proportion of service performed. Consent by a client or prospective client to the referral to or association of other counsel, made prior to any actual such referral or association, but without knowledge of the information specified in subparagraph (f)(2) does not constitute sufficient client confirmation within the meaning of this rule. The referring or associating lawyer or any other lawyer who employs another lawyer to assist in the representation has the primary duty to ensure full disclosure and compliance with this rule.

16. Paragraph (g) facilitates the enforcement of the requirements of paragraph (f). It does so by providing that agreements that authorize an attorney either to refer a person's case to another lawyer, or to associate other counsel in the handling of a client's case, and that actually result in such a referral or association with counsel in a different law firm from the one entering into the agreement, must be confirmed by an arrangement between the person and the lawyers involved that conforms to paragraph (f). As noted there, that arrangement must be presented to and agreed to by the person before the referral or association between the lawyers involved occurs. See subparagraph (f)(2). Because paragraph (g) refers to the party whose matter is involved as a "person" rather than as a "client," it is not possible to evade its requirements by having a referring lawyer not formally enter into an attorney-client relationship with the person involved before referring that person's matter to other counsel. Paragraph (g) does provide, however, for recovery in quantum meruit in instances where its requirements are not met. See subparagraphs (g)(1) and (g)(2).

17. What should be done with any otherwise agreed-to fee that is forfeited in whole or in part due to a lawyer's failure to comply with paragraph (g) is not resolved by these rules.

18. Subparagraph (f)(3) requires that the aggregate fee charged to clients in connection with a given matter by all of the lawyers involved meet the standards of paragraph (a)—that is, not be unconscionable.

Fee Disputes and Determinations

19. If a procedure has been established for resolution of fee disputes, such as an arbitration or mediation procedure established by a bar association, the lawyer should conscientiously consider submitting to it. Law may prescribe a procedure for determining a lawyer's fee, for example, in representation of an executor or administrator, or when a class or a person is entitled to recover a reasonable attorney's fee as part of the measure of damages. All involved lawyers should comply with any prescribed procedures.

Michigan Rule 1.6

[Michigan has modified Model Rule 1.6 to read as follows:]

RULE 1.6 Confidentiality of Information

(a) "Confidence" refers to information protected by the client-lawyer privilege under applicable law, and "secret" refers to other information gained in the professional relationship that the client has requested be held inviolate or the disclosure of which would be embarrassing or would be likely to be detrimental to the client.

(b) Except when permitted under paragraph (c), a lawyer shall not knowingly:

(1) reveal a confidence or secret of a client;

(2) use a confidence or secret of a client to the disadvantage of the client; or

(3) use a confidence or secret of a client for the advantage of the lawyer or of a third person, unless the client consents after full disclosure.

(c) A lawyer may reveal:

(1) confidences or secrets with the consent of the client or clients affected, but only after full disclosure to them;

(2) confidences or secrets when permitted or required by these rules, or when required by law or by court order;

(3) confidences and secrets to the extent reasonably necessary to rectify the consequences of a client's illegal or fraudulent act in the furtherance of which the lawyer's services have been used;

(4) the intention of a client to commit a crime and the information necessary to prevent the crime; and

(5) confidences or secrets necessary to establish or collect a fee, or to defend the lawyer or the lawyer's employees or associates against an accusation of wrongful conduct.

(d) A lawyer shall exercise reasonable care to prevent employees, associates, and others whose services are utilized by the lawyer from disclosing or using confidences or secrets of a client, except that a lawyer may reveal the information allowed by paragraph (c) through an employee.

COMMENT:

The lawyer is part of a judicial system charged with upholding the law. One of the lawyer's functions is to advise clients so that they avoid any violation of the law in the proper exercise of their rights.

The observance of the ethical obligation of a lawyer to hold inviolate confidential information of the client not only facilitates the full development of facts essential to proper representation of the client, but also encourages people to seek early legal assistance.

Almost without exception, clients come to lawyers in order to determine what their rights are and what is, in the maze of laws and regulations, deemed to be legal and correct. The common law recognizes that the client's confidences must be protected from disclosure. Upon the basis of experience, lawyers know that almost all clients follow the advice given and that the law is upheld.

A fundamental principle in the client-lawyer relationship is that the lawyer maintain confidentiality of information relating to the representation. The client is thereby encouraged to communicate fully and frankly with the lawyer even as to embarrassing or legally damaging subject matter.

The principle of confidentiality is given effect in two related bodies of law, the client-lawyer privilege (which includes the work-product doctrine) in the law of evidence and the rule of confidentiality established in professional ethics. The client-lawyer privilege applies in judicial and other proceedings in which a lawyer may be called as a witness or otherwise required to produce evidence concerning a client. The rule of client-lawyer confidentiality applies in situations other than those where evidence is sought from the lawyer through compulsion of law. The confidentiality rule applies to confidences and secrets as defined in the rule. A lawyer may not disclose such information except as authorized or required by the Rules of Professional Conduct or other law. See also Scope, ante.

The requirement of maintaining confidentiality of information relating to representation applies to government lawyers who may disagree with the policy goals that their representation is designed to advance.

Authorized Disclosure. A lawyer is impliedly authorized to make disclosures about a client when appropriate in carrying out the representation, except to the extent that the client's instructions or special circumstances limit that authority. In litigation, for example, a lawyer may disclose information by admitting a fact that cannot properly be disputed, or, in negotiation, by making a disclosure that facilitates a satisfactory conclusion.

Lawyers in a firm may, in the course of the firm's practice, disclose to each other information relating to a client of the firm, unless the client has instructed that particular information be confined to specified lawyers, or unless the disclosure would breach a screen erected within the firm in accordance with Rules 1.10(b), 1.11(a), or 1.12(c).

Disclosure Adverse to Client. The confidentiality rule is subject to limited exceptions. In becoming privy to information about a client, a lawyer may foresee that the client intends to commit a crime. To the extent a lawyer is prohibited from making disclosure, the interests of the potential victim are sacrificed in favor of preserving the client's confidences even though the client's purpose is wrongful. To the extent a lawyer is required or permitted to disclose a client's purposes, the client may be inhibited from revealing facts which would enable the lawyer to counsel against a wrongful course of action. A rule governing disclosure of threatened harm thus involves balancing the interests of one group of potential victims against those of another. On the assumption that lawyers generally fulfill their duty to advise against the commission of deliberately wrongful acts, the public is better protected if full and open communication by the client is encouraged than if it is inhibited.

Generally speaking, information relating to the representation must be kept confidential as stated in paragraph (b). However, when the client is or will be engaged in criminal conduct or the integrity of the lawyer's own conduct is involved, the principle of confidentiality may appropriately yield, depending on the lawyer's knowledge about and relationship to the conduct in question, and the seriousness of that conduct. Several situations must be distinguished.

First, the lawyer may not counsel or assist a client in conduct that is illegal or fraudulent. See Rule 1.2(c). Similarly, a lawyer has a duty under Rule 3.3(a)(4) not to use false evidence. This duty is essentially a special instance of the duty prescribed in Rule 1.2(c) to avoid assisting a client in illegal or fraudulent conduct. The same is true of compliance with Rule 4.1 concerning truthfulness of a lawyer's own representations.

Second, the lawyer may have been innocently involved in past conduct by the client that was criminal or fraudulent. In such a situation the lawyer has not violated Rule 1.2(c), because to "counsel or assist" criminal or fraudulent conduct requires knowing that the conduct is of that character. Even if the involvement was innocent, however, the fact remains that the lawyer's professional services were made the instrument of the client's crime or fraud. The lawyer, therefore, has a legitimate interest in being able to rectify the consequences of such conduct, and has the professional right, although not a professional duty, to rectify the situation. Exercising that right may require revealing information relating to the representation. Paragraph (c)(3) gives the lawyer professional discretion to reveal such information to the extent necessary to accomplish rectification. However, the constitutional rights of defendants in criminal cases may limit the extent to which counsel for a defendant may correct a misrepresentation that is based on information provided by the client. See comment to Rule 3.3.

Third, the lawyer may learn that a client intends prospective conduct that is criminal. Inaction by the lawyer is not a violation of Rule 1.2(c), except in the limited circumstances where failure to act constitutes assisting the client. See comment to Rule 1.2(c). However, the lawyer's knowledge of the client's purpose may enable the lawyer to prevent commission of the prospective crime. If the prospective crime is likely to result in substantial injury, the lawyer may feel a moral obligation to take preventive action. When the threatened injury is grave, such as homicide or serious bodily injury, a lawyer may have an obligation under tort or criminal law to take reasonable preventive measures. Whether the lawyer's concern is based on moral or legal considerations, the interest in preventing the harm may be more compelling than the interest in preserving confidentiality of information relating to the client. As stated in paragraph (c)(4), the lawyer has professional discretion to reveal information in order to prevent a client's criminal act.

It is arguable that the lawyer should have a professional obligation to make a disclosure in order to prevent homicide or serious bodily injury which the lawyer knows is intended by the client. However, it is very difficult for a lawyer to "know" when such a heinous purpose will actually be carried out, for the client may have a change of mind. To require disclosure when the client intends such an act, at the risk of professional discipline if the assessment of the client's purpose turns out to be wrong, would be to impose a penal risk that might interfere with the lawyer's resolution of an inherently difficult moral dilemma.

The lawyer's exercise of discretion requires consideration of such factors as magnitude, proximity, and likelihood of the contemplated wrong; the nature of the lawyer's relationship with the client and with those who might be injured by the client; the lawyer's own involvement in the transaction; and factors that may extenuate the conduct in question. Where practical, the lawyer should seek to persuade the client to take suitable action. In any case, a disclosure adverse to the client's interest should be no greater than the lawyer reasonably believes necessary to the purpose. A lawyer's decision not to make a disclosure permitted by paragraph (c) does not violate this rule.

Where the client is an organization, the lawyer may be in doubt whether contemplated conduct will actually be carried out by the organization. Where necessary to guide conduct in connection with this rule, the lawyer should make an inquiry within the organization as indicated in Rule 1.13(b).

Paragraph (c)(3) does not apply where a lawyer is employed after a crime or fraud has been committed to represent the client in matters ensuing therefrom.

Withdrawal. If the lawyer's services will be used by the client in materially furthering a course of criminal or fraudulent conduct, the lawyer must withdraw, as stated in Rule 1.16(a)(1).

After withdrawal the lawyer is required to refrain from making disclosure of the client's confidences, except as otherwise provided in Rule 1.6. Neither this rule nor Rule 1.8(b) nor Rule 1.16(d) prevents the lawyer from giving notice of the fact of withdrawal, and the lawyer may also withdraw or disaffirm any opinion, document, affirmation, or the like.

Dispute Concerning Lawyer's Conduct. Where a legal claim or disciplinary charge alleges complicity of the lawyer in a client's conduct or other misconduct of the lawyer involving representation of the client, the lawyer may respond to the extent the lawyer reasonably believes necessary to establish a defense. The same is true with respect to a claim involving the conduct or representation of a former client. The lawyer's right to respond arises when an assertion of complicity or other misconduct has been made. Paragraph (c)(5) does not require the lawyer to await the commencement of an action or proceeding that charges complicity or other misconduct, so that the defense may be established by responding directly to a third party who has made such an assertion. The right to defend, of course, applies where a proceeding has been commenced. Where practicable and not prejudicial to the lawyer's ability to establish the defense, the lawyer should advise the client of the third party's assertion and request that the client respond appropriately. In any event, disclosure should be no greater than the lawyer reasonably believes is necessary to vindicate innocence, the disclosure should be made in a manner which limits access to the information to the tribunal or other persons having a need to know it, and appropriate protective orders or other arrangements should be sought by the lawyer to the fullest extent practicable.

If the lawyer is charged with wrongdoing in which the client's conduct is implicated, the rule of confidentiality should not prevent the lawyer from defending against the charge. Such a charge can arise in a civil, criminal, or professional disciplinary proceeding, and can be based on a wrong allegedly committed by the lawyer against the client, or on a wrong alleged by a third person, for example, a person claiming to have been defrauded by the lawyer and client acting together.

A lawyer entitled to a fee is permitted by paragraph (c)(5) to prove the services rendered in an action to collect it. This aspect of the rule expresses the principle that the beneficiary of a fiduciary relationship may not exploit it to the detriment of the fiduciary. As stated above, the lawyer must make every effort practicable to avoid unnecessary disclosure of information relating to a representation, to limit disclosure to those having the need to know it, and to obtain protective orders or make other arrangements minimizing the risk of disclosure.

Disclosures Otherwise Required or Authorized. The scope of the client-lawyer privilege is a question of law. If a lawyer is called as a witness to give testimony concerning a client, absent waiver by the client, paragraph (b)(1) requires the lawyer to invoke the privilege when it is applicable. The lawyer must comply with the final orders of a court or other tribunal of competent jurisdiction requiring the lawyer to give information about the client.

The Rules of Professional Conduct in various circumstances permit or require a lawyer to disclose information relating to the representation. See Rules 2.2, 2.3, 3.3 and 4.1. In addition to these provisions, a lawyer may be obligated or permitted by other provisions of law to give information about a client. Whether another provision of law supersedes Rule 1.6 is a matter of interpretation beyond the scope of these rules, but a presumption should exist against such a supersession.

Former Client. The duty of confidentiality continues after the client-lawyer relationship has terminated. See Rule 1.9.

Texas Disciplinary Rule 1.05 *(Modification of Model Rule 1.6)*

[Texas has modified Model Rule 1.6 (Confidentiality) to read as follows:]

RULE 1.05 Confidentiality of Information

(a) "Confidential information" includes both "privileged information" and "unprivileged client information." "Privileged information" refers to the information of a client protected by the lawyer-client privilege of Rule 503 of the Texas Rules of Evidence or of Rule 503 of the Texas Rules of Criminal Evidence or by the principles of attorney-client privilege governed by Rule 501 of the Federal Rules of Evidence for United States Courts and Magistrates. "Unprivileged client information" means all information relating to a client or furnished by the client, other than privileged information, acquired by the lawyer during the course of or by reason of the representation of the client.

(b) Except as permitted by paragraphs (c) and (d), or as required by paragraphs (e) and (f), a lawyer shall not knowingly:

(1) Reveal confidential information of a client or a former client to:

(i) a person that the client has instructed is not to receive the information; or

(ii) anyone else, other than the client, the client's representatives, or the members, associates, or employees of the lawyer's law firm.

(2) Use confidential information of a client to the disadvantage of the client unless the client consents after consultation.

(3) Use confidential information of a former client to the disadvantage of the former client after the representation is concluded unless the former client consents after consultation or the confidential information has become generally known.

(4) Use privileged information of a client for the advantage of the lawyer or of a third person, unless the client consents after consultation.

(c) A lawyer may reveal confidential information:

(1) When the lawyer has been expressly authorized to do so in order to carry out the representation.

(2) When the client consents after consultation.

(3) To the client, the client's representatives, or the members, associates, and employees of the lawyer's firm, except when otherwise instructed by the client.

(4) When the lawyer has reason to believe it is necessary to do so in order to comply with a court order, a Texas Disciplinary Rule of Professional Conduct, or other law.

(5) To the extent reasonably necessary to enforce a claim or establish a defense on behalf of the lawyer in a controversy between the lawyer and the client.

(6) To establish a defense to a criminal charge, civil claim or disciplinary complaint against the lawyer or the lawyer's associates based upon conduct involving the client or the representation of the client.

(7) When the lawyer has reason to believe it is necessary to do so in order to prevent the client from committing a criminal or fraudulent act.

(8) To the extent revelation reasonably appears necessary to rectify the consequences of a client's criminal or fraudulent act in the commission of which the lawyer's services had been used.

(d) A lawyer also may reveal unprivileged client information:

(1) When impliedly authorized to do so in order to carry out the representation.

(2) When the lawyer has reason to believe it is necessary to do so in order to:

(i) carry out the representation effectively;

(ii) defend the lawyer or the lawyer's employees or associates against a claim of wrongful conduct;

(iii) respond to allegations in any proceeding concerning the lawyer's representation of the client; or

(iv) prove the services rendered to a client, or the reasonable value thereof, or both, in an action against another person or organization responsible for the payment of the fee for services rendered to the client.

(e) When a lawyer has confidential information clearly establishing that a client is likely to commit a criminal or fraudulent act that is likely to result in death or substantial bodily harm to a person, the lawyer shall reveal confidential information to the extent revelation reasonably appears necessary to prevent the client from committing the criminal or fraudulent act.

(f) A lawyer shall reveal confidential information when required to do so by Rule 3.03(a)(2), 3.03(b), or by Rule 4.01(b).

COMMENT:

Confidentiality Generally

1. Both the fiduciary relationship existing between lawyer and client and the proper functioning of the legal system require the preservation by the lawyer of confidential information of one who has employed or sought to employ the lawyer. Free discussion should prevail between lawyer and client in order for the lawyer to be fully informed and for the client to obtain the full benefit of the legal system. The ethical obligation of the lawyer to protect the confidential information of the client not only facilitates the proper representation of the client but also encourages potential clients to seek early legal assistance.

2. Subject to the mandatory disclosure requirements of paragraphs (e) and (f) the lawyer generally should be required to maintain confidentiality of information acquired by the lawyer during the course of or by reason of the representation of the client. This principle involves an ethical obligation not to use the information to the detriment of the client or for the benefit of the lawyer or a third person. In regard to an evaluation of a matter affecting a client for use by a third person, see Rule 2.02.

3. The principle of confidentiality is given effect not only in the Texas Rules of Professional Conduct but also in the law of evidence regarding the attorney-client privilege and in the law of agency. The attorney-client privilege, developed through many decades, provides the client a right to prevent certain confidential communications from being revealed by compulsion of law. Several sound exceptions to confidentiality have been developed in the evidence law of privilege. Exceptions exist in evidence law where the services of the lawyer were sought or used by a client in planning or committing a crime or fraud as well as where issues have arisen as to breach of duty by the lawyer or by the client to the other.

4. Rule 1.05 reinforces the principles of evidence law relating to the attorney-client privilege. Rule 1.05 also furnishes considerable protection to other information falling outside the scope of the privilege. Rule 1.05 extends ethical protection generally to unprivileged information relating to the client or furnished by the client during the course of or by reason of the representation of the client. In this respect Rule 1.05 accords with general fiduciary principles of agency.

5. The requirement of confidentiality applies to government lawyers who may disagree with the policy goals that their representation is designed to advance.

Disclosure for Benefit of Client

6. A lawyer may be expressly authorized to make disclosures to carry out the representation and generally is recognized as having implied-in-fact authority to make disclosures about a client when appropriate in carrying out the representation to the extent that the client's instructions do not limit that authority. In litigation, for example, a lawyer may disclose information by admitting a fact that cannot properly be disputed, or in negotiation by making a disclosure that facilitates a satisfactory conclusion. The effect of Rule 1.05 is to require the lawyer to invoke, for the client, the attorney-client privilege when applicable; but if the court improperly denies the privilege, under paragraph (c)(4) the lawyer may testify as ordered by the court or may test the ruling as permitted by Rule 3.04(d).

7. In the course of a firm's practice, lawyers may disclose to each other and to appropriate employees information relating to a client, unless the client has instructed that particular information be confined to specified lawyers. Subparagraphs (b)(1) and (c)(3) continue these practices concerning disclosure of confidential information within the firm.

Use of Information

8. Following sound principles of agency law, subparagraphs (b)(2) and (4) subject a lawyer to discipline for using information relating to the representation in a manner disadvantageous to the client or beneficial to the lawyer or a third person, absent the informed consent of the client. The duty not to misuse client information continues after the client-lawyer relationship has terminated. Therefore, the lawyer is forbidden by subparagraph (b)(3) to use, in absence of the client's informed consent, confidential information of the former client to the client's disadvantage, unless the information is generally known.

Discretionary Disclosure Adverse to Client

9. In becoming privy to information about a client, a lawyer may foresee that the client intends serious and perhaps irreparable harm. To the extent a lawyer is prohibited from making disclosure, the

interests of the potential victim are sacrificed in favor of preserving the client's information—usually unprivileged information—even though the client's purpose is wrongful. On the other hand, a client who knows or believes that a lawyer is required or permitted to disclose a client's wrongful purposes may be inhibited from revealing facts which would enable the lawyer to counsel effectively against wrongful action. Rule 1.05 thus involves balancing the interests of one group of potential victims against those of another. The criteria provided by the Rule are discussed below.

10. Rule 503(d)(1), Texas Rules of Civil Evidence (Tex.R.Civ.Evid.), and Rule 503(d)(1), Texas Rules of Criminal Evidence (Tex.R.Crim.Evid.), indicate the underlying public policy of furnishing no protection to client information where the client seeks or uses the services of the lawyer to aid in the commission of a crime or fraud. That public policy governs the dictates of Rule 1.05. Where the client is planning or engaging in criminal or fraudulent conduct or where the culpability of the lawyer's conduct is involved, full protection of client information is not justified.

11. Several other situations must be distinguished. First, the lawyer may not counsel or assist a client in conduct that is criminal or fraudulent. See Rule 1.02(c). As noted in the Comment to that Rule, there can be situations where the lawyer may have to reveal information relating to the representation in order to avoid assisting a client's criminal or fraudulent conduct, and sub-paragraph (c)(4) permits doing so. A lawyer's duty under Rule 3.03(a) not to use false or fabricated evidence is a special instance of the duty prescribed in Rule 1.02(c) to avoid assisting a client in criminal or fraudulent conduct, and sub-paragraph (c)(4) permits revealing information necessary to comply with Rule 3.03(a) or (b). The same is true of compliance with Rule 4.01. See also paragraph (f).

12. Second, the lawyer may have been innocently involved in past conduct by the client that was criminal or fraudulent. In such a situation the lawyer has not violated Rule 1.02(c), because to "counsel or assist" criminal or fraudulent conduct requires knowing that the conduct is of that character. Since the lawyer's services were made an instrument of the client's crime or fraud, the lawyer has a legitimate interest both in rectifying the consequences of such conduct and in avoiding charges that the lawyer's participation was culpable. Sub-paragraph (c)(6) and (8) give the lawyer professional discretion to reveal both unprivileged and privileged information in order to serve those interests. See paragraph (g). In view of Tex.R.Civ.Evid. Rule 503(d)(1), and Tex.R.Crim.Evid. 503(d)(1), however, rarely will such information be privileged.

13. Third, the lawyer may learn that a client intends prospective conduct that is criminal or fraudulent. The lawyer's knowledge of the client's purpose may enable the lawyer to prevent commission of the prospective crime or fraud. When the threatened injury is grave, the lawyer's interest in preventing the harm may be more compelling than the interest in preserving confidentiality of information. As stated in subparagraph (c)(7), the lawyer has professional discretion, based on reasonable appearances, to reveal both privileged and unprivileged information in order to prevent the client's commission of any criminal or fraudulent act. In some situations of this sort, disclosure is mandatory. See paragraph (e) and Comments 18–20.

14. The lawyer's exercise of discretion under paragraphs (c) and (d) involves consideration of such factors as the magnitude, proximity, and likelihood of the contemplated wrong, the nature of the lawyer's relationship with the client and with those who might be injured by the client, the lawyer's own involvement in the transaction, and factors that may extenuate the client's conduct in question. In any case, a disclosure adverse to the client's interest should be no greater than the lawyer believes necessary to the purpose. Although preventive action is permitted by paragraphs (c) and (d), failure to take preventive action does not violate those paragraphs. But see paragraphs (e) and (f). *Because these rules do not define standards of civil liability of lawyers for professional conduct, paragraphs (c) and (d) do not create a duty on the lawyer to make any disclosure and no civil liability is intended to arise from the failure to make such disclosure.*

15. A lawyer entitled to a fee necessarily must be permitted to prove the services rendered in an action to collect it, and this necessity is recognized by sub-paragraphs (c)(5) and (d)(2)(iv). This aspect of the rule, in regard to privileged information, expresses the principle that the beneficiary of a fiduciary relationship may not exploit the relationship to the detriment of the fiduciary. Any disclosure by the lawyer, however, should be as protective of the client's interests as possible.

16. If the client is an organization, a lawyer also should refer to Rule 1.12 in order to determine the appropriate conduct in connection with this Rule.

Client Under a Disability

17. In some situations, Rule 1.02(g) requires a lawyer representing a client under a disability to seek the appointment of a legal representative for the client or to seek other orders for the protection of the client. The client may or may not, in a particular matter, effectively consent to the lawyer's revealing to the court confidential information and facts reasonably necessary to secure the desired appointment or order. Nevertheless, the lawyer is authorized by paragraph (c)(4) to reveal such information in order to comply with Rule 1.02(g). See also paragraph 5, Comment to Rule 1.03.

Mandatory Disclosure Adverse to Client

18. Rule 1.05(e) and (f) place upon a lawyer professional obligations in certain situations to make disclosure in order to prevent certain serious crimes by a client or to prevent involvement by the lawyer in a client's crimes or frauds. Except when death or serious bodily harm is likely to result, a lawyer's obligation is to dissuade the client from committing the crime or fraud or to persuade the client to take corrective action; see Rule 1.02(d) and (e).

19. Because it is very difficult for a lawyer to know when a client's criminal or fraudulent purpose actually will be carried out, the lawyer is required by paragraph (e) to act only if the lawyer has information "clearly establishing" the likelihood of such acts and consequences. If the information shows clearly that the client's contemplated crime or fraud is likely to result in death or serious injury, the lawyer must seek to avoid those lamentable results by revealing information necessary to prevent the criminal or fraudulent act. When the threatened crime or fraud is likely to have the less serious result of substantial injury to the financial interests or property of another, the lawyer is not required to reveal preventive information but may do so in conformity to paragraph (c)(7). See also paragraph (f); Rule 1.02(d) and (e); and Rule 3.03(b) and (c).

20. Although a violation of paragraph (e) will subject a lawyer to disciplinary action, the lawyer's decisions whether or how to act should not constitute grounds for discipline unless the lawyer's conduct in the light of those decisions was unreasonable under all existing circumstances as they reasonably appeared to the lawyer. This construction necessarily follows from the fact that paragraph (e) bases the lawyer's affirmative duty to act on how the situation "reasonably appears" to the lawyer, while that imposed by paragraph (f) arises only when a lawyer "knows" that the lawyer's services have been misused by the client. See also Rule 3.03(b).

Withdrawal

21. If the lawyer's services will be used by the client in materially furthering a course of criminal or fraudulent conduct, the lawyer must withdraw, as stated in Rule 1.15(a)(1). After withdrawal, a lawyer's conduct continues to be governed by Rule 1.05. However, the lawyer's duties of disclosure under paragraph (e) of the Rule, insofar as such duties are mandatory, do not survive the end of the relationship even though disclosure remains permissible under paragraphs (6), (7), and (8) if the further requirements of such paragraph are met. Neither this Rule nor Rule 1.15 prevents the lawyer from giving notice of the fact of withdrawal, and no rule forbids the lawyer to withdraw or disaffirm any opinion, document, affirmation, or the like.

Other Rules

22. Various other Texas Rules of Professional Conduct permit or require a lawyer to disclose information relating to the representation. See Rules 1.07, 1.12, 2.02, 3.03 and 4.01. In addition to these provisions, a lawyer may be obligated by other provisions of statutes or other law to give information about a client. Whether another provision of law supersedes Rule 1.05 is a matter of interpretation beyond the scope of these Rules, but sub-paragraph (c)(4) protects the lawyer from discipline who acts on reasonable belief as to the effect of such laws.

***Florida Rule 4–1.7** (Modification of Model Rule 1.7)*

[Florida has modified Model Rule 1.7 (Conflict of Interest) as follows:]

RULE 4–1.7 Conflict of Interest; General Rule

(a) Representing Adverse Interests. Except as provided in subdivision (b), a lawyer must not represent a client if:

(1) the representation of 1 client will be directly adverse to another client; or

(2) there is a substantial risk that the representation of 1 or more clients will be materially limited by the lawyer's responsibilities to another client, a former client or a third person or by a personal interest of the lawyer.

(b) Informed Consent. Notwithstanding the existence of a conflict of interest under subdivision (a), a lawyer may represent a client if:

(1) the lawyer reasonably believes that the lawyer will be able to provide competent and diligent representation to each affected client;

(2) the representation is not prohibited by law;

(3) the representation does not involve the assertion of a position adverse to another client when the lawyer represents both clients in the same proceeding before a tribunal; and

(4) each affected client gives informed consent, confirmed in writing or clearly stated on the record at a hearing.

(c) Explanation to Clients. When representation of multiple clients in a single matter is undertaken, the consultation must include an explanation of the implications of the common representation and the advantages and risks involved.

(d) Lawyers Related by Blood, Adoption, or Marriage. A lawyer related by blood, adoption, or marriage to another lawyer as parent, child, sibling, or spouse must not represent a client in a representation directly adverse to a person who the lawyer knows is represented by the other lawyer except with the client's informed consent, confirmed in writing or clearly stated on the record at a hearing.

(e) Representation of insureds. Upon undertaking the representation of an insured client at the expense of the insurer, a lawyer has a duty to ascertain whether the lawyer will be representing both the insurer and the insured as clients, or only the insured, and to inform both the insured and the insurer regarding the scope of the representation. All other Rules Regulating The Florida Bar related to conflicts of interest apply to the representation as they would in any other situation.

***Texas Disciplinary Rule 1.06** (Modification of Model Rule 1.7)*

[Texas has modified Model Rule 1.7 (Conflict of Interest) as follows:]

RULE 1.06 Conflict of Interest: General Rule

(a) A lawyer shall not represent opposing parties to the same litigation.

(b) In other situations and except to the extent permitted by paragraph (c), a lawyer shall not represent a person if the representation of that person:

(1) involves a substantially related matter in which that person's interests are materially and directly adverse to the interests of another client of the lawyer or the lawyer's firm; or

(2) reasonably appears to be or become adversely limited by the lawyer's or law firm's responsibilities to another client or to a third person or by the lawyer's or law firm's own interests.

(c) A lawyer may represent a client in the circumstances described in (b) if:

(1) the lawyer reasonably believes the representation of each client will not be materially affected; and

(2) each affected or potentially affected client consents to such representation after full disclosure of the existence, nature, implications, and possible adverse consequences of the common representation and the advantages involved, if any.

(d) A lawyer who has represented multiple parties in a matter shall not thereafter represent any of such parties in a dispute among the parties arising out of the matter, unless prior consent is obtained from all such parties to the dispute.

(e) If a lawyer has accepted representation in violation of this Rule, or if multiple representation properly accepted becomes improper under this Rule, the lawyer shall promptly withdraw from one or more representations to the extent necessary for any remaining representation not to be in violation of these Rules.

(f) If a lawyer would be prohibited by this Rule from engaging in particular conduct, no other lawyer while a member or associated with that lawyer's firm may engage in that conduct.

COMMENT:

Loyalty to a Client

1. Loyalty is an essential element in the lawyer's relationship to a client. An impermissible conflict of interest may exist before representation is undertaken, in which event the representation should be declined. If such a conflict arises after representation has been undertaken, the lawyer must take effective action to eliminate the conflict, including withdrawal if necessary to rectify the situation. See also Rule 1.16. When more than one client is involved and the lawyer withdraws because a conflict arises after representation, whether the lawyer may continue to represent any of the clients is determined by this Rule and Rules 1.05 and 1.09. See also Rule 1.07(c). Under this Rule, any conflict that prevents a particular lawyer from undertaking or continuing a representation of a client also prevents any other lawyer who is or becomes a member of or an associate with that lawyer's firm from doing so. See paragraph (f).

2. A fundamental principle recognized by paragraph (a) is that a lawyer may not represent opposing parties in litigation. The term "opposing parties" as used in this Rule contemplates a situation where a judgment favorable to one of the parties will directly impact unfavorably upon the other party. Moreover, as a general proposition loyalty to a client prohibits undertaking representation directly adverse to the representation of that client in a substantially related matter unless that client's fully informed consent is obtained and unless the lawyer reasonably believes that the lawyer's representation will be reasonably protective of that client's interests. Paragraphs (b) and (c) express that general concept.

Conflicts in Litigation

3. Paragraph (a) prohibits representation of opposing parties in litigation. Simultaneous representation of parties whose interests in litigation are not actually directly adverse but where the potential for conflict exists, such as co-plaintiffs or co-defendants, is governed by paragraph (b). An impermissible conflict may exist or develop by reason of substantial discrepancy in the parties' testimony, incompatibility in positions in relation to an opposing party or the fact that there are substantially different possibilities of settlement of the claims or liabilities in question. Such conflicts can arise in criminal cases as well as civil. The potential for conflict of interest in representing multiple defendants in a criminal case is so grave that ordinarily a lawyer should decline to represent more than one co-defendant. On the other hand, common representation of persons having similar interests is proper if the risk of adverse effect is minimal and the requirements of paragraph (b) are met. Compare Rule 1.07 involving intermediation between clients.

Conflict with Lawyer's Own Interests

4. Loyalty to a client is impaired not only by the representation of opposing parties in situations within paragraphs (a) and (b)(1) but also in any situation when a lawyer may not be able to consider, recommend or carry out an appropriate course of action for one client because of the lawyer's own interests or responsibilities to others. The conflict in effect forecloses alternatives that would otherwise be available to the client. Paragraph (b)(2) addresses such situations. A potential possible conflict does not itself necessarily preclude the representation. The critical questions are the likelihood that a conflict exists or will eventuate and, if it does, whether it will materially and adversely affect the lawyer's independent professional judgment in considering alternatives or foreclose courses of action that reasonably should be pursued on behalf of the client. It is for the client to decide whether the client wishes to accommodate the other interest involved. However, the client's consent to the representation by the lawyer of another whose interests are directly adverse is insufficient unless the lawyer also believes that there will be no materially adverse effect upon the interests of either client. See paragraph (c).

5. The lawyer's own interests should not be permitted to have adverse effect on representation of a client, even where paragraph (b)(2) is not violated. For example, a lawyer's need for income should not lead the lawyer to undertake matters that cannot be handled competently and at a reasonable fee. See Rules 1.01 and 1.04. If the probity of a lawyer's own conduct in a transaction is in question, it may be difficult for the lawyer to give a client detached advice. A lawyer should not allow related business interests to affect representation, for example, by referring clients to an enterprise in which the lawyer has an undisclosed interest.

Meaning of Directly Adverse

6. Within the meaning of Rule 1.06(b), the representation of one client is "directly adverse" to the representation of another client if the lawyer's independent judgment on behalf of a client or the lawyer's ability or willingness to consider, recommend or carry out a course of action will be or is reasonably likely to be adversely affected by the lawyer's representation of, or responsibilities to, the other client. The dual representation also is directly adverse if the lawyer reasonably appears to be called upon to espouse adverse positions in the same matter or a related matter. On the other hand, simultaneous representation in unrelated matters of clients whose interests are only generally adverse, such as competing economic enterprises, does not constitute the representation of directly adverse interests. Even when neither paragraph (a) nor (b) is applicable, a lawyer should realize that a business rivalry or personal differences between two clients or potential clients may be so important to one or both that one or the other would consider it contrary to its interests to have the same lawyer as its rival even in unrelated matters; and in those situations a wise lawyer would forego the dual representation.

Full Disclosure and Informed Consent

7. A client under some circumstances may consent to representation notwithstanding a conflict or potential conflict. However, as indicated in paragraph (c)(1), when a disinterested lawyer would conclude that the client should not agree to the representation under the circumstances, the lawyer involved should not ask for such agreement or provide representation on the basis of the client's consent. When more than one client is involved, the question of conflict must be resolved as to each client. Moreover, there may be circumstances where it is impossible to make the full disclosure necessary to obtain informed consent. For example, when the lawyer represents different clients in related matters and one of the clients refuses to consent to the disclosure necessary to permit the other client to make an informed decision, the lawyer cannot properly ask the latter to consent.

8. Disclosure and consent are not formalities. Disclosure sufficient for sophisticated clients may not be sufficient to permit less sophisticated clients to provide fully informed consent. While it is not required that the disclosure and consent be in writing, it would be prudent for the lawyer to provide potential dual clients with at least a written summary of the considerations disclosed.

9. In certain situations, such as in the preparation of loan papers or the preparation of a partnership agreement, a lawyer might have properly undertaken multiple representation and be confronted subsequently by a dispute among those clients in regard to that matter. Paragraph (d) forbids the representation of any of those parties in regard to that dispute unless informed consent is obtained from all of the parties to the dispute who had been represented by the lawyer in that matter.

10. A lawyer may represent parties having antagonistic positions on a legal question that has arisen in different cases, unless representation of either client would be adversely affected. Thus, it is ordinarily not improper to assert such positions in cases pending in different trial courts, but it may be improper to do so in cases pending at the same time in an appellate court.

11. Ordinarily, it is not advisable for a lawyer to act as advocate against a client the lawyer represents in some other matter, even if the other matter is wholly unrelated and even if paragraphs (a), (b), and (d) are not applicable. However, there are circumstances in which a lawyer may act as advocate against a client, for a lawyer is free to do so unless this Rule or another rule of the Texas Rules of Professional Conduct would be violated. For example, a lawyer representing an enterprise with diverse operations may accept employment as an advocate against the enterprise in a matter unrelated to any matter being handled for the enterprise if the representation of one client is not directly adverse to the representation of the other client. The propriety of concurrent representation can depend on the nature of the litigation. For example, a suit charging fraud entails conflict to a degree not involved in a suit for declaratory judgment concerning statutory interpretation.

Interest of Person Paying for a Lawyer's Service

12. A lawyer may be paid from a source other than the client, if the client is informed of that fact and consents and the arrangement does not compromise the lawyer's duty of loyalty to the client. See Rule 1.08(e). For example, when an insurer and its insured have conflicting interests in a matter arising from a liability insurance agreement, and the insurer is required to provide special counsel for the insured, the arrangement should assure the special counsel's professional independence. So also, when a corporation and its directors or employees are involved in a controversy in which they have conflicting interests, the corporation may provide funds for separate legal representation of the directors or employees, if the clients consent after consultation and the arrangement ensures the lawyer's professional independence.

Non-litigation Conflict Situations

13. Conflicts of interest in contexts other than litigation sometimes may be difficult to assess. Relevant factors in determining whether there is potential for adverse effect include the duration and intimacy of the lawyer's relationship with the client or clients involved, the functions being performed by the lawyer, the likelihood that actual conflict will arise and the likely prejudice to the client from the conflict if it does arise. The question is often one of proximity and degree.

14. For example, a lawyer may not represent multiple parties to a negotiation whose interests are fundamentally antagonistic to each other, but common representation may be permissible where the clients are generally aligned in interest even though there is some difference of interest among them.

15. Conflict questions may also arise in estate planning and estate administration. A lawyer may be called upon to prepare wills for several family members, such as husband and wife, and, depending upon the circumstances, a conflict of interest may arise. In estate administration it may be unclear whether the client is the fiduciary or is the estate or trust, including its beneficiaries. The lawyer should make clear the relationship to the parties involved.

16. A lawyer for a corporation or other organization who is also a member of its board of directors should determine whether the responsibilities of the two roles may conflict. The lawyer may be called on to advise the corporation in matters involving actions of the directors. Consideration should be given to the frequency with which such situations may arise, the potential intensity of the conflict, the effect of the lawyer's resignation from the board and the possibility of the corporation's obtaining legal advice from another lawyer in such situations. If there is material risk that the dual role will compromise the lawyer's independence of professional judgment, the lawyer should not serve as a director.

Conflict Charged by an Opposing Party

17. Raising questions of conflict of interest is primarily the responsibility of the lawyer undertaking the representation. In litigation, a court may raise the question when there is reason to infer that the lawyer has neglected the responsibility. In a criminal case, inquiry by the court is generally required when a lawyer represents multiple defendants. Where the conflict is such as clearly to call in question the fair or efficient administration of justice, opposing counsel may properly raise the question. Such an objection should be viewed with great caution, however, for it can be misused as a technique of harassment. See Preamble: Scope.

18. Except when the absolute prohibition of this rule applies or in litigation when a court passes upon issues of conflicting interests in determining a question of disqualification of counsel, resolving questions of conflict of interests may require decisions by all affected clients as well as by the lawyer.

Imputed Conflicts, Nonlawyer Employees, and Lawyers Formerly Employed in a Nonlawyer Role

19. A law firm is not prohibited from representing a client under paragraph (f) merely because a nonlawyer employee of the firm, such as a paralegal or legal secretary, has a conflict of interest arising from prior employment or some other source. Nor is a firm prohibited from representing a client merely because a lawyer of the firm has a conflict of interest arising from events that occurred before the person became a lawyer, such as work that the person did as a law clerk or intern. But the firm must ordinarily screen the person with the conflict from any personal participation in the matter to prevent the person's communicating to others in the firm confidential information that the person and the firm have a legal duty to protect. *See* Rule 5.03; *see also* MODEL RULES PROF'L CONDUCT r. 1.10 cmt. 4 (AM. BAR ASS'N 1983); RESTATEMENT (THIRD) OF THE LAW GOVERNING LAWYERS § 123 cmt. f (AM. LAW INST. 2000).

District of Columbia Rule 1.8

[The District of Columbia has added subsection (i) to Model Rule 1.8]

RULE 1.8 Conflict of Interest: Prohibited Transactions

* * *

(i) A lawyer may acquire and enforce a lien granted by law to secure the lawyer's fees or expenses, but a lawyer shall not impose a lien upon any part of a client's files, except upon the lawyer's own work product, and then only to the extent that the work product has not been paid for. This work product exception shall not apply when the client has become unable to pay, or when withholding the lawyer's work product would present a significant risk to the client of irreparable harm.

COMMENT:

Lawyer's Liens

[16] The substantive law of the District of Columbia has long permitted lawyers to assert and enforce liens against the property of clients. See, e.g., Redevelopment Land Agency v. Dowdey, 618 A.2d 153, 159–60 (D.C.1992), and cases cited therein. Whether a lawyer has a lien on money or property belonging to a client is generally a matter of substantive law as to which the ethics rules take no position. Exceptions to what the common law might otherwise permit are made with respect to contingent fees and retaining liens. See, respectively, Rule 1.5(c) and Rule 1.8(i).

[17] Rule 1.16(d) requires a lawyer to surrender papers and property to which the client is entitled when representation of the client terminates. Paragraph (i) of this Rule states a narrow exception to Rule 1.16(d): a lawyer may retain anything the law permits—including property—except for files. As to files, a lawyer may retain only the lawyer's own work product, and then only if the client has not paid for the work. However, if the client has paid for the work product, the client is entitled to receive it, even if the client has not previously seen or received a copy of the work product. Furthermore, the lawyer may not retain the work product for which the client has not paid, if the client has become unable to pay or if withholding the work product might irreparably harm the client's interest.

[18] Under Rule 1.16(d), for example, a lawyer would be required to return all papers received from a client, such as birth certificates, wills, tax returns, or "green cards." Rule 1.8(i) does not permit retention of such papers to secure payment of any fee due. Only the lawyer's own work product—results of factual investigations, legal research and analysis, and similar materials generated by the lawyer's own effort—could be retained. (The term "work product" as used in paragraph (i) is limited to materials falling within the "work product doctrine," but includes any material generated by the lawyer that would be protected under that doctrine whether or not created in connection with pending or anticipated litigation.) And a lawyer could not withhold all of the work product merely because a portion of the lawyer's fees had not been paid.

[19] There are situations in which withholding the work product would not be permissible because of irreparable harm to the client. The possibility of involuntary incarceration or criminal conviction constitutes one category of irreparable harm. The realistic possibility that a client might irretrievably lose a significant right or become subject to a significant liability because of the withholding of the work product constitutes another category of irreparable harm. On the other hand, the mere fact that the client might have to pay another lawyer to replicate the work product does not, standing alone, constitute irreparable harm. These examples are merely indicative of the meaning of the term "irreparable harm," and are not exhaustive.

Indiana Rule 1.8(l)

[Indiana has added the following provision to Model Rule 1.8.]

RULE 1.8 Conflict of Interest: Prohibited Transactions

* * *

(*l*) A part-time prosecutor or deputy prosecutor authorized by statute to otherwise engage in the practice of law shall refrain from representing a private client in any matter wherein exists an issue upon which said prosecutor has statutory prosecutorial authority or responsibilities. This restriction is not intended to prohibit representation in tort cases in which investigation and any prosecution of infractions has terminated, nor to prohibit representation in family law matters involving no issue subject to prosecutorial authority or responsibilities. Upon a prior, express written limitation of responsibility to exclude prosecutorial authority in matters related to family law, a part-time deputy prosecutor may fully represent private clients in cases involving family law.

Minnesota Rule 1.8(e)(3) & (j)

[Minnesota has added the following provision to Model Rule 1.8:]

RULE 1.8 Conflict of Interest: Prohibited Transactions

* * *

(e) A lawyer shall not provide financial assistance to a client in connection with pending or contemplated litigation, except that:

* * *

(3) a lawyer may guarantee a loan reasonably needed to enable the client to withstand delay in litigation that would otherwise put substantial pressure on the client to settle a case because of financial hardship rather than on the merits, provided the client remains ultimately liable for repayment of the loan without regard to the outcome of the litigation and, further provided, that no promise of such financial assistance was made to the client by the lawyer, or by another in the lawyer's behalf, prior to the employment of that lawyer by that client.

* * *

(j) A lawyer shall not have sexual relations with a current client unless a consensual sexual relationship existed between them when the lawyer-client relationship commenced. For purposes of this paragraph:

(1) "Sexual relations" means sexual intercourse or any other intentional touching of the intimate parts of a person or causing the person to touch the intimate parts of the lawyer.

(2) If the client is an organization, any individual who oversees the representation and gives instructions to the lawyer on behalf of the organization shall be deemed to be the client. In-house attorneys while representing governmental or corporate entities are governed by Rule 1.7(b) rather than by this rule with respect to sexual relations with other employees of the entity they represent.

(3) This paragraph does not prohibit a lawyer from engaging in sexual relations with a client of the lawyer's firm provided that the lawyer has no involvement in the performance of the legal work for the client.

(4) If a party other than the client alleges violation of this paragraph, and the complaint is not summarily dismissed, the Director, in determining whether to investigate the allegation and whether to charge any violation based on the allegations, shall consider the client's statement regarding whether the client would be unduly burdened by the investigation or charge.

Texas Disciplinary Rule 1.09 *(Modification of Model Rule 1.9)*

[Texas has modified Rule 1.9 (Former Client Conflicts) as follows:]

RULE 1.09 Conflict of Interest: Former Client

(a) Without prior consent, a lawyer who personally has formerly represented a client in a matter shall not thereafter represent another person in a matter adverse to the former client:

(1) in which such other person questions the validity of the lawyer's services or work product for the former client; or

(2) if the representation in reasonable probability will involve a violation of Rule 1.05.

(3) if it is the same or a substantially related matter;

(b) Except to the extent authorized by Rule 1.10, when lawyers are or have become members of or associated with a firm, none of them shall knowingly represent a client if any one of them practicing alone would be prohibited from doing so by paragraph (a).

(c) When the association of a lawyer with a firm has terminated, the lawyers who were then associated with that lawyer shall not knowingly represent a client if the lawyer whose association with that firm has terminated would be prohibited from doing so by paragraph (a)(1) or if the representation in reasonable probability will involve a violation of Rule 1.05.

COMMENT:

1. Rule 1.09 addresses the circumstances in which a lawyer in private practice, and other lawyers who were, are or become members of or associated with a firm in which that lawyer practiced or practices, may represent a client against a former client of that lawyer or the lawyer's former firm. Whether a lawyer, or that lawyer's present or former firm, is prohibited from representing a client in a matter by reason of the lawyer's successive government and private employment is governed by Rule 1.10 rather than by this Rule.

2. Paragraph (a) concerns the situation where a lawyer once personally represented a client and now wishes to represent a second client against that former client. Whether such a personal attorney-client relationship existed involves questions of both fact and law that are beyond the scope of these Rules. See Preamble: Scope. Among the relevant factors, however, would be how the former representation actually was conducted within the firm; the nature and scope of the former client's contacts with the firm (including any restrictions the client may have placed on the dissemination of confidential information within the firm); and the size of the firm.

3. Although paragraph (a) does not absolutely prohibit a lawyer from representing a client against a former client, it does provide that the latter representation is improper if any of three circumstances exists, except with prior consent. The first prohibition is against representation adverse to a former client if it is the same or a substantially related matter. The second circumstance is that the lawyer may not represent a client who questions the validity of the lawyer's services or work product for the former client. Thus, for example, a lawyer who drew a will leaving a substantial portion of the testator's property to a designated

beneficiary would violate paragraph (a) by representing the testator's heirs at law in an action seeking to overturn the will.

4. Paragraph (a)'s third limitation on undertaking a representation against a former client is that it may not be done if there is a "reasonable probability" that the representation would cause the lawyer to violate the obligations owed the former client under Rule 1.05. Thus, for example, if there were a reasonable probability that the subsequent representation would involve either an unauthorized disclosure of confidential information under Rule 1.05(b)(1) or an improper use of such information to the disadvantage of the former client under Rule 1.05(b)(3), that representation would be improper under paragraph (a). Whether such a reasonable probability exists in any given case will be a question of fact.

5. Paragraph (b) extends paragraph (a)'s limitations on an individual lawyer's freedom to undertake a representation against that lawyer's former client to all other lawyers who are or become members of or associated with the firm in which that lawyer is practicing. Thus, for example, if a client severs the attorney-client relationship with a lawyer who remains in a firm, the entitlement of that individual lawyer to undertake a representation against that former client is governed by paragraph (a); and all other lawyers who are or become members of or associated with that lawyer's firm are treated in the same manner by paragraph (b). Similarly, if a lawyer severs his or her association with a firm and that firm retains as a client a person whom the lawyer personally represented while with the firm, that lawyer's ability thereafter to undertake a representation against that client is governed by paragraph (a); and all other lawyers who are or become members of or associates with that lawyer's new firm are treated in the same manner by paragraph (b).

6. Paragraph (c) addresses the situation of former partners or associates of a lawyer who once had represented a client when the relationship between the former partners or associates and the lawyer has been terminated. In that situation, the former partners or associates are prohibited from questioning the validity of such lawyer's work product and from undertaking representation which in reasonable probability will involve a violation of Rule 1.05. Such a violation could occur, for example, when the former partners or associates retained materials in their files from the earlier representation of the client that, if disclosed or used in connection with the subsequent representation, would violate Rule 1.05(b)(1) or (b)(3).

7. Thus, the effect of paragraphs (b) and (c) is to extend any inability of a particular lawyer under paragraph (a) to undertake a representation against a former client to all other lawyers who are or become members of or associated with any firm in which that lawyer is practicing. Should those other lawyers cease to be members of the same firm as the lawyer affected by paragraph (a) without themselves coming within its restrictions, they thereafter may undertake the representation against the lawyer's former client unless prevented from doing so by some other of these Rules.

8. Although not required to do so by Rule 1.05 or this Rule, some courts, as a procedural decision, disqualify a lawyer for representing a present client against a former client when the subject matter of the present representation is so closely related to the subject matter of the prior representation that confidences obtained from the former client might be useful in the representation of the present client. See Comment 17 to Rule 1.06. This so-called "substantial relationship" test is defended by asserting that to require a showing that confidences of the first client were in fact used for the benefit of the subsequent client as a condition to procedural disqualification would cause disclosure of the confidences that the court seeks to protect. A lawyer is not subject to discipline under Rule 1.05(b)(1), (3), or (4), however, unless the protected information is actually used. Likewise, a lawyer is not subject to discipline under this Rule unless the new representation by the lawyer in reasonable probability would result in a violation of those provisions.

9. Whether the "substantial relationship" test will continue to be employed as a standard for procedural disqualification is a matter beyond the scope of these Rules. See Preamble: Scope. The possibility that such a disqualification might be sought by the former client or granted by a court, however, is a matter that could be of substantial importance to the present client in deciding whether or not to retain or continue to employ a particular lawyer or law firm as its counsel. Consequently, a lawyer should disclose those possibilities, as well as their potential consequences for the representation, to the present client as soon as the lawyer becomes aware of them; and the client then should be allowed to decide whether or not to obtain new counsel. See Rules 1.03(b) and 1.06(b).

10. This Rule is primarily for the protection of clients and its protections can be waived by them. A waiver is effective only if there is consent after disclosure of the relevant circumstances, including the lawyer's past or intended role on behalf of each client, as appropriate. See Comments 7 and 8 to Rule 1.06.

District of Columbia Rule 1.11

[The District of Columbia has added the following provisions to Model Rule 1.11]

RULE 1.11 Successive Government and Private Employment

* * *

(d) Except as provided in paragraph (e), when any of counsel, lawyer, partner, or associate of a lawyer personally disqualified under paragraph (a) accepts employment in connection with a matter giving rise to the personal disqualification, the following notifications shall be required:

(1) The personally disqualified lawyer shall submit to the public department or agency by which the lawyer was formerly employed and serve on each other party to any pertinent proceeding a signed document attesting that during the period of disqualification the personally disqualified lawyer will not participate in any manner in the matter or the representation, will not discuss the matter or the representation with any partner, associate, or of counsel lawyer, and will not share in any fees for the matter or the representation.

(2) At least one affiliated lawyer shall submit to the same department or agency and serve on the same parties a signed document attesting that all affiliated lawyers are aware of the requirement that the personally disqualified lawyer be screened from participating in or discussing the matter or the representation and describing the procedures being taken to screen the personally disqualified lawyer.

(e) If a client requests in writing that the fact and subject matter of a representation subject to paragraph (d) not be disclosed by submitting the signed statements referred to in paragraph (d), such statements shall be prepared concurrently with undertaking the representation and filed with bar counsel under seal. If at any time thereafter the fact and subject matter of the representation are disclosed to the public or become a part of the public record, the signed statements previously prepared shall be promptly submitted as required by paragraph (d).

(f) Signed documents filed pursuant to paragraph (d) shall be available to the public, except to the extent that a lawyer submitting a signed document demonstrates to the satisfaction of the public department or agency upon which such documents are served that public disclosure is inconsistent with Rule 1.6 or provisions of law.

(g) This Rule applies to any matter involving a specific party or parties.

(h) A lawyer who participates in a program of temporary service to the office of corporation counsel of the kind described in Rule 1.10(e) shall be treated as having served as a public officer or employee for purposes of paragraph (a), and the provisions of paragraphs (b)–(e) shall apply to the lawyer and to lawyers affiliated with the lawyer.

New Hampshire Rule 1.11A

[New Hampshire has added the following provision to address the conduct of lawyer officials:]

RULE 1.11A Conduct of Lawyer-Officials

(a) Definitions. As used in this rule:

lawyer-official **means a lawyer actively engaged in the practice of law, who is a member of a governmental body;**

governmental body means any state or local governmental agency, board, body, council or commission, including any advisory committee established by any of such entities;

related body means a governmental body whose members are appointed or elected by the lawyer-official or the governmental body of which the lawyer-official is a member;

interest means a direct, personal and pecuniary interest, individually or on a client's behalf, in a matter which is under consideration by either the governmental body of which the lawyer-official is a member, or by a related body; and

advisory committee means any committee, council, commission, or other like body whose primary purpose is to consider an issue or issues designated by the appointing authority so as to provide such authority with advice or recommendations concerning the formulation of any public policy or legislation that may be promoted, modified, or opposed by such authority.

(b) No lawyer-official shall:

(1) participate in any hearing, debate, discussion or vote, or in any manner otherwise attempt to influence the outcome of a matter in which the lawyer-official has an interest;

(2) utilize information obtained in such capacity for his or her own personal benefit or that of his or her clients or the clients of the firm with which the lawyer-official is associated;

(3) appear on behalf of a client before any governmental body of which the lawyer-official is a member or any related body;

(4) accept anything of value from any person or organization when the lawyer-official knows or reasonably should know that the offer is for the purpose of influencing the lawyer-official's actions or decisions as a lawyer-official;

(5) use his or her official position to influence or to attempt to influence either the governmental body of which the lawyer is a member or a related body to act in favor of the lawyer-official or the lawyer-official's clients or clients of the firm with which the lawyer-official is associated.

(c) Other lawyers in the firm with which the lawyer-official is associated may appear on behalf of clients before the governmental body of which the lawyer-official is a member, if the lawyer-official publicly disqualifies himself or herself and refrains from participation in the matter in accordance with paragraph (b)(1) of this Rule and otherwise conducts himself or herself with respect to the matter in question in accordance with paragraph (b) of this Rule. Other lawyers in the firm with which the lawyer-official is associated may appear on behalf of clients before a related body, if the lawyer-official conducts himself or herself with respect to the matter in question in accordance with paragraph (b) of this Rule.

Montana Rule 1.17

[Montana has added Rule 1.17 which has no counterpart in the Model Rules]

RULE 1.17 Government Employment

An attorney employed full time by the State of Montana or a political subdivision shall not accept other employment during the course of which it would be possible to use or otherwise rely on information obtained by reason of government employment that is injurious, confidential or privileged and not otherwise discoverable.

COUNSELOR

Oregon Rule 2.4

RULE 2.4 Lawyer Serving as Mediator

(a) A lawyer serving as a mediator:

(1) shall not act as a lawyer for any party against another party in the matter in mediation or in any related proceeding, and

(2) must clearly inform the parties of and obtain the parties' consent to the lawyer's role as mediator.

(b) A lawyer serving as a mediator:

(1) may prepare documents that memorialize and implement the agreement reached in mediation,

(2) shall recommend that each party seek independent legal advice before executing the documents, and

(3) with the consent of all parties, may record or may file the documents in court.

(c) The requirements of Rule 2.4(a)(2) and (b)(2) shall not apply to mediation programs established by operation of law or court order.

ADVOCATE

Kansas Rule 3.5

[Kansas has modified Model Rule 3.5 to read as follows:]

RULE 3.5 Impartiality and Decorum of the Tribunal

A lawyer shall not:

(a) give or lend anything of value to a judge, official, or employee of a tribunal except as permitted by the Kansas Code of Judicial Conduct as it may, from time to time be adopted in Kansas, nor may a lawyer attempt to improperly influence a judge, official or employee of a tribunal, but a lawyer may make a contribution to the campaign fund of a candidate for judicial office in conformity with the Kansas Code of Judicial Conduct;

(b) communicate or cause another to communicate with a member of a jury or the venire from which the jury will be selected about the matters under consideration other than in the course of official proceedings until after the discharge of the jury from further consideration of the case;

(c) communicate or cause another to communicate as to the merits of a cause with a judge or official before whom an adversary proceeding is pending except:

(1) in the course of official proceedings in the cause;

(2) in writing, if the lawyer promptly delivers a copy of the writing to opposing counsel or to the adverse party if unrepresented;

(3) orally upon adequate notice to opposing counsel or the adverse party if unrepresented;

(4) as otherwise authorized by law or court rule;

(d) engage in undignified or discourteous conduct degrading to a tribunal.

TRANSACTIONS WITH PERSONS OTHER THAN CLIENTS

Texas Disciplinary Rule 4.04 *(Modification of Model Rule 4.4)*

[Texas has modified Model Rule 4.4 as follows:]

RULE 4.04 Respect for Rights of Third Persons

* * *

(b) A lawyer shall not present, participate in presenting, or threaten to present:

(1) criminal or disciplinary charges solely to gain an advantage in a civil matter; or

(2) civil, criminal or disciplinary charges against a complainant, a witness, or a potential witness in a bar disciplinary proceeding solely to prevent participation by the complainant, witness or potential witness therein.

LAW FIRMS AND ASSOCIATIONS

District of Columbia Rule 5.4

RULE 5.4 Professional Independence of a Lawyer

(a) A lawyer or law firm shall not share legal fees with a nonlawyer, except that:

(1) an agreement by a lawyer with the lawyer's firm, partner, or associate may provide for the payment of money, over a reasonable period of time after the lawyer's death, to the lawyer's estate or to one or more specified persons;

(2) a lawyer who undertakes to complete unfinished legal business of a deceased lawyer may pay to the estate of the deceased lawyer that proportion of the total compensation which fairly represents the services rendered by the deceased lawyer. A lawyer who purchases the practice of a deceased, disabled, or disappeared lawyer may, pursuant to the provisions of Rule 1.17, pay the estate or other representative of that lawyer the agreed-upon purchase price.

(3) a lawyer or law firm may include nonlawyer employees in a compensation or retirement plan, even though the plan is based in whole or in part on a profit-sharing arrangement; and

(4) sharing of fees is permitted in a partnership or other form of organization which meets the requirements of paragraph (b).

* * *

(b) A lawyer may practice law in a partnership or other form of organization in which a financial interest is held or managerial authority is exercised by an individual nonlawyer who performs professional services which assist the organization in providing legal services to clients, but only if:

(1) the partnership or organization has as its sole purpose providing legal services to clients;

(2) all persons having such managerial authority or holding a financial interest undertake to abide by these rules of professional conduct;

(3) the lawyers who have a financial interest or managerial authority in the partnership or organization undertake to be responsible for the nonlawyer participants to the same extent as if nonlawyer participants were lawyers under rule 5.1;

(4) the foregoing conditions are set forth in writing.

(c) A lawyer shall not permit a person who recommends, employs, or pays the lawyer to render legal services for another to direct or regulate the lawyer's professional judgment in rendering such legal services.

COMMENT:

[1] The provisions of this Rule express traditional limitations on sharing fees with nonlawyers. (On sharing fees among lawyers not in the same firm, see Rule 1.5(e).) These limitations are to protect the lawyer's professional independence of judgment. Where someone other than the client pays the lawyer's fee or salary, or recommends employment of the lawyer, that arrangement does not modify the lawyer's obligation to the client. As stated in paragraph (c), such arrangements should not interfere with the lawyer's professional judgment.

[2] Traditionally, the canons of legal ethics and disciplinary rules prohibited lawyers from practicing law in a partnership that includes nonlawyers or in any other organization where a nonlawyer is a shareholder, director, or officer. Notwithstanding these strictures, the profession implicitly recognized exceptions for lawyers who work for corporate law departments, insurance companies, and legal service organizations.

[3] As the demand increased for a broad range of professional services from a single source, lawyers employed professionals from other disciplines to work for them. So long as the nonlawyers remained employees of the lawyers, these relationships did not violate the disciplinary rules. However, when lawyers and nonlawyers considered forming partnerships and professional corporations to provide a combination of legal and other services to the public, they faced serious obstacles under the former rules.

[4] This Rule rejects an absolute prohibition against lawyers and nonlawyers joining together to provide collaborative services, but continues to impose traditional ethical requirements with respect to the organization thus created. Thus, a lawyer may practice law in an organization where nonlawyers hold a financial interest or exercise managerial authority, but only if the conditions set forth in subparagraphs (b)(1), (b)(2), and (b)(3) are satisfied, and, pursuant to subparagraph (b)(4), satisfaction of these conditions is set forth in a written instrument. The requirement of a writing helps ensure that these important conditions are not overlooked in establishing the organizational structure of entities in which nonlawyers enjoy an ownership or managerial role equivalent to that of a partner in a traditional law firm.

[5] Nonlawyer participants under Rule 5.4 ought not be confused with nonlawyer assistants under Rule 5.3. Nonlawyer participants are persons having managerial authority or financial interests in organizations which provide legal services. Within such organizations, lawyers with financial interests or managerial authority are held responsible for ethical misconduct by nonlawyer participants about which the lawyers know or reasonably should know. This is the same standard of liability contemplated by Rule 5.1, regarding the responsibilities of lawyers with direct supervisory authority over other lawyers.

[6] Nonlawyer assistants under Rule 5.3 do not have managerial authority or financial interests in the organization. Lawyers having direct supervisory authority over nonlawyer assistants are held responsible only for ethical misconduct by assistants about which the lawyers actually know.

[7] As the introductory portion of Subparagraph (b) makes clear, the purpose of liberalizing the rules regarding the possession of a financial interest or the exercise of management authority by a nonlawyer is to permit nonlawyer professionals to work with lawyers in the delivery of legal services without being relegated to the role of an employee. For example, the Rule permits economists to work in a firm with antitrust or public utility practitioners, psychologists or psychiatric social workers to work with family law practitioners to assist in counseling clients, nonlawyer lobbyists to work with lawyers who perform legislative services, certified public accountants to work in conjunction with tax lawyers or others who use accountants' services in performing legal services, and professional managers to serve as office managers, executive directors, or in similar positions. In all of these situations, the professionals may be given financial interests or managerial responsibility, so long as all of the requirements of subparagraph (c) are met.

[8] Subparagraph (b) does not permit an individual or entity to acquire all or any part of the ownership of a law partnership or other form of law practice organization for investment or other purposes. It thus does not permit a corporation, an investment banking firm, an investor, or any other person or entity

to entitle itself to all or any portion of the income or profits of a law firm or other similar organization. Since such an investor would not be an individual performing professional services within the law firm or other organization, the requirements of subparagraph (b) would not be met.

[9] The term "individual" in subparagraph (b) is not intended to preclude the participation in a law firm or other organization by an individual professional corporation in the same manner as lawyers who have incorporated as a professional corporation currently participate in partnerships which include professional corporations.

[10] Some sharing of fees is likely to occur in the kinds of organizations permitted by paragraph (b). Subparagraph (a)(4) makes it clear that such fee-sharing is not prohibited.

* * *

Pennsylvania Rule 5.7

[Pennsylvania has enacted its own Rule 5.7 to govern lawyer involvement in nonlegal services.]

Rule 5.7. Responsibilities Regarding Nonlegal Services

(a) A lawyer who provides nonlegal services to a recipient that are not distinct from legal services provided to that recipient is subject to the Rules of Professional Conduct with respect to the provision of both legal and nonlegal services.

(b) A lawyer who provides nonlegal services to a recipient that are distinct from any legal services provided to the recipient is subject to the Rules of Professional Conduct with respect to the nonlegal services if the lawyer knows or reasonably should know that the recipient might believe that the recipient is receiving the protection of a client-lawyer relationship.

(c) A lawyer who is an owner, controlling party, employee, agent, or is otherwise affiliated with an entity providing nonlegal services to a recipient is subject to the Rules of Professional Conduct with respect to the nonlegal services if the lawyer knows or reasonably should know that the recipient might believe that the recipient is receiving the protection of a client-lawyer relationship.

(d) Paragraph (b) or (c) does not apply if the lawyer makes reasonable efforts to avoid any misunderstanding by the recipient receiving nonlegal services. Those efforts must include advising the recipient that the services are not legal services and that the protection of a client-lawyer relationship does not exist with respect to the provision of nonlegal services to the recipient.

(e) The term "nonlegal services" denotes services that might reasonably be performed in conjunction with and in substance are related to the provision of legal services, and that are not prohibited as unauthorized practice of law when provided by a nonlawyer.

COMMENT:

[1] For many years, lawyers have provided to their clients nonlegal services that are ancillary to the practice of law. Nonlegal services are those that are not prohibited as unauthorized practice of law when provided by a nonlawyer. Examples of nonlegal services include providing title insurance, financial planning, accounting, trust services, real estate counseling, legislative lobbying, economic analysis, social work, psychological counseling, tax return preparation, and patent, medical or environmental consulting. A broad range of economic and other interests of clients may be served by lawyers participating in the delivery of these services.

The Potential for Misunderstanding

[2] Whenever a lawyer directly provides nonlegal services, there exists the potential for ethical problems. Principal among these is the possibility that the person for whom the nonlegal services are performed may fail to understand that the services may not carry with them the protection normally afforded by the client-lawyer relationship. The recipient of the nonlegal services may expect, for example,

that the protection of client confidences, prohibitions against representation of persons with conflicting interests, and obligations of a lawyer to maintain professional independence apply to the provision of nonlegal services when that may not be the case. The risk of such confusion is especially acute when the lawyer renders both types of services with respect to the same matter.

Providing Nonlegal Services That Are Not Distinct From Legal Services

[3] Under some circumstances, the legal and nonlegal services may be so closely entwined that they cannot be distinguished from each other. In this situation, confusion by the recipient as to when the protection of the client-lawyer relationship applies are likely to be unavoidable. Therefore, Rule 5.7(a) requires that the lawyer providing the nonlegal services adhere to all of the requirements of the Rules of Professional Conduct.

[4] In such a case, a lawyer will be responsible for assuring that both the lawyer's conduct and, to the extent required by Rule 5.3, that of nonlawyer employees comply in all respects with the Rules of Professional Conduct. When a lawyer is obliged to accord the recipients of such nonlegal services the protection of those Rules that apply to the client-lawyer relationship, the lawyer must take special care to heed the proscriptions of the Rules addressing conflict of interest (Rules 1.7 through 1.11, especially Rules 1.7(b) and 1.8(a), (b) and (f)), and to scrupulously adhere to the requirements of Rule 1.6 relating to disclosure of confidential information. The promotion of the nonlegal services must also in all respects comply with Rules 7.1 through 7.3, dealing with advertising and solicitation.

[5] Rule 5.7(a) applies to the provision of nonlegal services by a lawyer even when the lawyer does not personally provide any legal services to the person for whom the nonlegal services are performed if the person is also receiving legal services from another lawyer that are not distinct from the nonlegal services.

Avoiding Misunderstanding When A Lawyer Directly Provides Nonlegal Services That Are Distinct From Legal Services

[6] Even when the lawyer believes that his or her provision of nonlegal services is distinct from any legal services provided to the recipient, there is still a risk that the recipient of the nonlegal services will misunderstand the implications of receiving nonlegal services from a lawyer; the recipient might believe that the recipient is receiving the protection of a client-lawyer relationship. Where there is such a risk of misunderstanding, Rule 5.7(b) requires that the lawyer providing the nonlegal services adhere to all the Rules of Professional Conduct, unless exempted by Rule 5.7(d).

Avoiding Misunderstanding When a Lawyer is Indirectly Involved in the Provision of Nonlegal Services

[7] Nonlegal services also may be provided through an entity with which a lawyer is somehow affiliated, for example, as owner, employee, controlling party or agent. In this situation, there is still a risk that the recipient of the nonlegal services might believe that the recipient is receiving the protection of a client-lawyer relationship. Where there is such a risk of misunderstanding, Rule 5.7(c) requires that the lawyer involved with the entity providing nonlegal services adhere to all the Rules of Professional Conduct, unless exempted by Rule 5.7(d).

Avoiding the Application of Paragraphs (b) and (c)

[8] Paragraphs (b) and (c) specify that the Rules of Professional Conduct apply to a lawyer who directly provides or is otherwise involved in the provision of nonlegal services if there is a risk that the recipient might believe that the recipient is receiving the protection of a client-lawyer relationship. Neither the Rules of Professional Conduct nor paragraphs (b) or (c) will apply, however, if pursuant to paragraph (d), the lawyer takes reasonable efforts to avoid any misunderstanding by the recipient. In this respect, Rule 5.7 is analogous to Rule 4.3(c).

[9] In taking the reasonable measures referred to in paragraph (d), the lawyer must communicate to the person receiving the nonlegal services that the relationship will not be a client-lawyer relationship. The communication should be made before entering into an agreement for the provision of nonlegal services, in a manner sufficient to assure that the person understands the significance of the communication, and preferably should be in writing.

[10] The burden is upon the lawyer to show that the lawyer has taken reasonable measures under the circumstances to communicate the desired understanding. For instance, a sophisticated user of nonlegal

services, such as a publicly-held corporation, may require a lesser explanation than someone unaccustomed to making distinctions between legal services and nonlegal services, such as an individual seeking tax advice from a lawyer-accountant or investigative services in connection with a lawsuit.

The Relationship Between Rule 5.7 and Other Rules of Professional Conduct

[11] Even before Rule 5.7 was adopted, a lawyer involved in the provision of nonlegal services was subject to those Rules of Professional Conduct that apply generally. For example, Rule 8.4(c) makes a lawyer responsible for fraud committed with respect to the provision of nonlegal services. Such a lawyer must also comply with Rule 1.8(a). Nothing in this rule is intended to suspend the effect of any otherwise applicable Rule of Professional Conduct such as Rule 1.7(b), Rule 1.8(a) and Rule 8.4(c).

[12] In addition to the Rules of Professional Conduct, principles of law external to the Rules, for example, the law of principal and agent, may govern the legal duties owed by a lawyer to those receiving the nonlegal services.

Pennsylvania Rule 5.8

[Pennsylvania has added a new rule on lawyer involvement in Investment Products]

Rule 5.8. Dealing in Investment Products: Prohibitions and Restrictions

(a) A lawyer shall not broker, offer to sell, sell, or place any investment product unless separately licensed to do so.

(b) A lawyer shall not recommend or offer an investment product to a client or any person with whom the lawyer has a fiduciary relationship, or invest funds belonging to such a person in an investment product, if the lawyer or a person related to the lawyer:

(1) has an interest in compensation paid or provided by a person other than the client or person with whom the lawyer has a fiduciary relationship; or

(2) has an ownership interest in the entity that sponsors, insures, underwrites, manages, or issues the investment product.

(c) For purposes of this Rule:

(1) the term "investment product" includes: an annuity contract; a life insurance contract; a commodity; a swap; an investment fund, including but not limited to a collective trust fund, a common trust fund, a real estate investment fund, and registered investment company; a security, whether or not the security is registered with any federal or state securities regulator; or an investment adviser's, bank's, trust company's, insurance company's, or other financial institution's service as an investment manager or investment adviser;

(2) "person related to the lawyer" includes a spouse, child, grandchild, parent, grandparent or other relative or individual with whom the lawyer maintains a close familial relationship; and

(3) the term "ownership interest" does not include shares of an issuer that has registered the shares under federal securities laws, the issuer's shares are traded on a securities exchange that is registered under federal securities laws, and the lawyer's aggregate interest in shares of all classes is less than one percent of the issuer's outstanding common shares.

EXPLANATORY COMMENT:

[1] Paragraph (a) prohibits a lawyer from brokering, offering to sell, selling, or placing any investment product, as defined in paragraph (c)(1), unless separately licensed to do so. Licensing and registration requirements vary by state. Before offering or selling any investment product in relation to the provision of legal services, a lawyer must consult all applicable federal and state laws to determine eligibility, licensing and regulatory requirements. Paragraph (a) neither addresses the giving of investment

advice nor is intended to supplant or otherwise affect federal and state laws that either require licensing and registration in order to give investment advice or exempt lawyers from their regulatory scheme.

[2] Paragraph (b) prohibits investment situations that are fraught with a potential for a conflict of interest or that provide an opportunity for the lawyer to control or unduly influence the use or management of the funds throughout the course of the investment. Clients who place their trust in their lawyer and assume or expect that the lawyer will protect them from harm are likely to feel deceived if substantial sums of money are lost on investments pursued at the lawyer's recommendation or prompting and the lawyer or a person related to the lawyer either receives compensation or a pecuniary benefit from a person other than the client or has an ownership interest in the entity that sponsors, insures, underwrites, manages, or issues the investment product, even when the reason for the loss is limited to unexpected market conditions. The prohibition of paragraph (b) is not imputed to other lawyers in the lawyer's firm or those lawyers' relatives.

[3] This Rule applies to a lawyer under any circumstance—whether the lawyer is providing legal services, nonlegal services that are not distinct from legal services, or nonlegal services that are distinct from legal services. See Rule 5.7(e) for the meaning of the term "nonlegal services." The prohibition of paragraph (b) is in addition to the restrictions imposed by Rules 1.7(a)(2), 1.8(a) and 5.7.

PUBLIC SERVICE

South Dakota Rule 6.1

[South Dakota has modified Model Rule 6.1 to read as follows:]

RULE 6.1 Voluntary Pro Bono Publico Service

A lawyer should render public interest legal service.

A lawyer may discharge this responsibility by:

(a) providing professional services at no fee or a reduced fee to persons of limited means or to public service or charitable groups or organizations; or

(b) by service without compensation in public interest activities that improve the law, the legal system or the legal profession; or

(c) by financial support for organizations that provide legal services to persons of limited means.

COMMENT:

[1] Every lawyer, regardless of professional prominence or professional work load, has a responsibility to provide legal services to those unable to pay, and personal involvement in the problems of the disadvantaged can be one of the most rewarding experiences in the life of a lawyer. The American Bar Association urges all lawyers to provide a minimum of 50 hours of pro bono services annually. States, however, may decide to choose a higher or lower number of hours of annual service (which may be expressed as a percentage of a lawyer's professional time) depending upon local needs and local conditions. It is recognized that in some years a lawyer may render greater or fewer hours than the annual standard specified, but during the course of his or her legal career, each lawyer should render on average per year, the number of hours set forth in this Rule. Services can be performed in civil matters or in criminal or quasi-criminal matters for which there is no government obligation to provide funds for legal representation, such as post-conviction death penalty appeal cases.

[2] Paragraphs (a)(1) and (2) recognize the critical need for legal services that exists among persons of limited means by providing that a substantial majority of the legal services rendered annually to the disadvantaged be furnished without fee or expectation of fee. Legal services under these paragraphs consist of a full range of activities, including individual and class representation, the provision of legal advice, legislative lobbying, administrative rule making and the provision of free training or mentoring to those who represent persons of limited means. The variety of these activities should facilitate participation by government lawyers, even when restrictions exist on their engaging in the outside practice of law.

[3] Persons eligible for legal services under paragraphs (a)(1) and (2) are those who qualify for participation in programs funded by the Legal Services Corporation and those whose incomes and financial resources are slightly above the guidelines utilized by such programs but nevertheless, cannot afford counsel. Legal services can be rendered to individuals or to organizations such as homeless shelters, battered women's centers and food pantries that serve those of limited means. The term "governmental organizations" includes, but is not limited to, public protection programs and sections of governmental or public sector agencies.

[4] Because service must be provided without fee or expectation of fee, the intent of the lawyer to render free legal services is essential for the work performed to fall within the meaning of paragraphs (a)(1) and (2). Accordingly, services rendered cannot be considered pro bono if an anticipated fee is uncollected, but the award of statutory attorneys' fees in a case originally accepted as pro bono would not disqualify such services from inclusion under this section. Lawyers who do receive fees in such cases are encouraged to contribute an appropriate portion of such fees to organizations or projects that benefit persons of limited means.

[5] While it is possible for a lawyer to fulfill the annual responsibility to perform pro bono services exclusively through activities described in paragraphs (a)(1) and (2), to the extent that any hours of service remained unfulfilled, the remaining commitment can be met in a variety of ways as set forth in paragraph (b). Constitutional, statutory or regulatory restrictions may prohibit or impede government and public sector lawyers and judges from performing the pro bono services outlined in paragraphs (a)(1) and (2). Accordingly, where those restrictions apply, government and public sector lawyers and judges may fulfill their pro bono responsibility by performing services outlined in paragraph (b).

[6] Paragraph (b)(1) includes the provision of certain types of legal services to those whose incomes and financial resources place them above limited means. It also permits the pro bono lawyer to accept a substantially reduced fee for services. Examples of the types of issues that may be addressed under this paragraph include First Amendment claims, Title VII claims and environmental protection claims. Additionally, a wide range of organizations may be represented, including social service, medical research, cultural and religious groups.

[7] Paragraph (b)(2) covers instances in which lawyers agree to and receive a modest fee for furnishing legal services to persons of limited means. Participation in judicare programs and acceptance of court appointments in which the fee is substantially below a lawyer's usual rate are encouraged under this section.

[8] Paragraph (b)(3) recognizes the value of lawyers engaging in activities that improve the law, the legal system or the legal profession. Serving on bar association committees, serving on boards of pro bono or legal services programs, taking part in Law Day activities, acting as a continuing legal education instructor, a mediator or an arbitrator and engaging in legislative lobbying to improve the law, the legal system or the profession are a few examples of the many activities that fall within this paragraph.

[9] Because the provision of pro bono services is a professional responsibility, it is the individual ethical commitment of each lawyer. Nevertheless, there may be times when it is not feasible for a lawyer to engage in pro bono services. At such times a lawyer may discharge the pro bono responsibility by providing financial support to organizations providing free legal services to persons of limited means. Such financial support should be reasonably equivalent to the value of the hours of service that would have otherwise been provided. In addition, at times it may be more feasible to satisfy the pro bono responsibility collectively, as by a firm's aggregate pro bono activities.

[10] Because the efforts of individual lawyers are not enough to meet the need for free legal services that exists among persons of limited means, the government and the profession have instituted additional programs to provide those services. Every lawyer should financially support such programs, in addition to either providing direct pro bono services or making financial contributions when pro bono service is not feasible.

[11] Law firms should act reasonably to enable and encourage all lawyers in the firm to provide the pro bono legal services called for by this Rule.

[12] The responsibility set forth in this Rule is not intended to be enforced through disciplinary process.

INFORMATION ABOUT LEGAL SERVICES

Texas Disciplinary Rules 7.01–7.07

Texas Disciplinary Rule 7.01

RULE 7.01 Firm Names and Letterhead

(a) A lawyer in private practice shall not practice under a trade name, a name that is misleading as to the identity of the lawyer or lawyers practicing under such name, or a firm name containing names other than those of one or more of the lawyers in the firm, except that the names of a professional corporation, professional association, limited liability partnership, or professional limited liability company may contain "P.C.," "L.L.P.," "P.L.L.C.," or similar symbols indicating the nature of the organization, and if otherwise lawful a firm may use as, or continue to include in, its name the name or names of one or more deceased or retired members of the firm or of a predecessor firm in a continuing line of succession. Nothing herein shall prohibit a married woman from practicing under her maiden name.

(b) A firm with offices in more than one jurisdiction may use the same name in each jurisdiction, but identification of the lawyers in an office of the firm shall indicate the jurisdictional limitations on those not licensed to practice in the jurisdiction where the office is located.

(c) The name of a lawyer occupying a judicial, legislative, or public executive or administrative position shall not be used in the name of a firm, or in communications on its behalf, during any substantial period in which the lawyer is not actively and regularly practicing with the firm.

(d) A lawyer shall not hold himself or herself out as being a partner, shareholder, or associate with one or more other lawyers unless they are in fact partners, shareholders, or associates.

(e) A lawyer shall not advertise in the public media or seek professional employment by any communication under a trade or fictitious name, except that a lawyer who practices under a firm name as authorized by paragraph (a) of this Rule may use that name in such advertisement or communication but only if that name is the firm name that appears on the lawyer's letterhead, business cards, office sign, fee contracts, and with the lawyer's signature on pleadings and other legal documents.

(f) A lawyer shall not use a firm name, letterhead, or other professional designation that violates Rule 7.02(a).

COMMENT:

1. A lawyer or law firm may not practice law using a name that is misleading as to the identity of the lawyers practicing under such name, but the continued use of the name of a deceased or retired member of the firm or of a predecessor firm is not considered to be misleading. Trade names are generally considered inherently misleading. Other types of firm names can be misleading as well, such as a firm name that creates the appearance that lawyers are partners or employees of a single law firm when in fact they are merely associated for the purpose of sharing expenses. In such cases, the lawyers involved may not denominate themselves in any manner suggesting such an ongoing professional relationship as, for example, "Smith and Jones" or "Smith and Jones Associates" or "Smith and Associates." Such titles create the false impression that the lawyers named have assumed a joint professional responsibility for clients' legal affairs. See paragraph (d).

2. The practice of law firms having offices in more than one state is commonplace. Although it is not necessary that the name of an interstate firm include Texas lawyers, a letterhead including the name of any lawyer not licensed in Texas must indicate the lawyer is not licensed in Texas.

3. Paragraph (c) is designed to prevent the exploitation of a lawyer's public position for the benefit of the lawyer's firm. Likewise, because it may be misleading under paragraph (a), a lawyer who occupies a judicial, legislative, or public executive or administrative position should not indicate that fact on a letterhead which identifies that person as an attorney in the private practice of law. However, a firm name may include the name of a public official who is actively and regularly practicing law with the firm. But see Rule 7.02(a)(4).

4. With certain limited exceptions, paragraph (a) forbids a lawyer from using a trade name or fictitious name. Paragraph (e) sets out this same prohibition with respect to advertising in public media or written communications seeking professional employment and contains additional restrictions on the use of trade names or fictitious names in those contexts. In a largely overlapping measure, paragraph (f) forbids the use of any such name or designation if it would amount to a "false or misleading communication" under Rule 7.02(a).

(Comment amended by State Bar Board of Directors Jan. 20, 1995.)

Texas Disciplinary Rule 7.02

RULE 7.02 Communications Concerning a Lawyer's Services

(a) A lawyer shall not make or sponsor a false or misleading communication about the qualifications or the services of any lawyer or firm. A communication is false or misleading if it:

(1) contains a material misrepresentation of fact or law, or omits a fact necessary to make the statement considered as a whole not materially misleading;

(2) contains any reference in a public media advertisement to past successes or results obtained unless

(i) the communicating lawyer or member of the law firm served as lead counsel in the matter giving rise to the recovery, or was primarily responsible for the settlement or verdict;

(ii) the amount involved was actually received by the client;

(iii) the reference is accompanied by adequate information regarding the nature of the case or matter and the damages or injuries sustained by the client, and

(iv) if the gross amount received is stated, the attorney's fees and litigation expenses withheld from the amount are stated as well;

(3) is likely to create an unjustified expectation about results the lawyer can achieve, or states or implies that the lawyer can achieve results by means that violate these rules or other law;

(4) compares the lawyer's services with other lawyers' services, unless the comparison can be substantiated by reference to verifiable, objective data;

(5) states or implies that the lawyer is able to influence improperly or upon irrelevant grounds any tribunal, legislative body, or public official; or

(6) designates one or more specific areas of practice in an advertisement in the public media or in a solicitation communication unless the advertising or soliciting lawyer is competent to handle legal matters in each such area of practice; or

(7) uses an actor or model to portray a client of the lawyer or law firm.

(b) Rule 7.02(a)(5) does not require that a lawyer be certified by the Texas Board of Legal Specialization at the time of advertising in a specific area of practice, but such certification shall conclusively establish that such lawyer satisfies the requirements of Rule 7.02(a)(5) with respect to the area(s) of practice in which such lawyer is certified.

(c) A lawyer shall not advertise in the public media or state in a solicitation communication that the lawyer is a specialist, except as permitted under Rule 7.04.

(d) Any statement or disclaimer required by these rules shall be made in each language used in the advertisement or solicitation communication with respect to which such required statement or disclaimer relates; provided however, the mere statement that a particular language is spoken or understood shall not alone result in the need for a statement or disclaimer in that language.

(Former Rule 7.01 adopted eff. Jan. 1, 1990; redesignated and amended to be eff. April 1, 1995; on March 31, 1995, the Texas Supreme Court extended the effective date 120 days after the date of judgment of the U.S. District Court in Texans Against Censorship, Inc. v. State Bar of Texas, 888 F.Supp. 1328 (E.D.Tex. 1995).)

COMMENT:

1. The Rules within Part VII are intended to regulate communications made for the purpose of obtaining professional employment. They are not intended to affect other forms of speech by lawyers, such as political advertisements or political commentary, except insofar as a lawyer's effort to obtain employment is linked to a matter of current public debate.

2. This Rule governs all communications about a lawyer's services, including advertisements regulated by Rule 7.04 and solicitation communications regulated by Rules 7.03 and 7.05. Whatever means are used to make known a lawyer's services, statements about them must be truthful and nondeceptive.

3. Sub-paragraph (a)(1) recognizes that statements can be misleading both by what they contain and what they leave out. Statements that are false or misleading for either reason are prohibited. A truthful statement is misleading if it omits a fact necessary to make the lawyer's communication considered as a whole not materially misleading. A truthful statement is also misleading if there is a substantial likelihood that it will lead a reasonable person to formulate a specific conclusion about the lawyer or the lawyer's services for which there is no reasonable factual foundation.

4. Sub-paragraphs (a)(2) and (3) recognize that statements may create "unjustified expectations". For example, an advertisement that truthfully reports that a lawyer obtained a jury verdict of a certain amount on behalf of a client would nonetheless be misleading if it were to turn out that the verdict was overturned on appeal or later compromised for a substantially reduced amount, and the advertisement did not disclose such facts as well. Even an advertisement that fully and accurately reports a lawyer's achievements on behalf of clients or former clients may be misleading if presented so as to lead a reasonable person to form an unjustified expectation that the same results could be obtained for other clients in similar matters without reference to the specific factual and legal circumstances of each client's case. Those unique circumstances would ordinarily preclude advertisements in the public media and written solicitation communications that discuss the results obtained on behalf of a client, such as the amount of a damage award, the lawyer's record in obtaining favorable settlements or verdicts, as well as those that contain client endorsements.

5. Sub-paragraph (a)(4) recognizes that comparisons of lawyers' services may also be misleading unless those comparisons "can be substantiated by reference to verifiable objective data." Similarly, an unsubstantiated comparison of a lawyer's services or fees with the services or fees of other lawyers may be misleading if presented with such specificity as would lead a reasonable person to conclude that the comparison can be substantiated. Statements comparing a lawyer's services with those of another where the comparisons are not susceptible of precise measurement or verification, such as "we are the toughest lawyers in town", "we will get money for you when other lawyers can't", or "we are the best law firm in Texas if you want a large recovery" can deceive or mislead prospective clients.

6. The inclusion of a disclaimer or qualifying language may preclude a finding that a statement is likely to create unjustified expectations or otherwise mislead a prospective client, but it will not necessarily do so. Unless any such qualifications and disclaimers are both sufficient and displayed with equal prominence to the information to which they pertain, that information can still readily mislead prospective clients into believing that similar results can be obtained for them without reference to their specific factual and legal circumstances. Consequently, in order not to be false, misleading, or deceptive, other of these Rules require that appropriate disclaimers or qualifying language must be presented in the same manner as the communication and with equal prominence. See Rules 7.04(q) and 7.05(a)(2).

7. On the other hand, a simple statement of a lawyer's own qualifications devoid of comparisons to other lawyers does not pose the same risk of being misleading and so does not violate sub-paragraph (a)(4). Similarly, a lawyer making a referral to another lawyer may express a good faith subjective opinion regarding that other lawyer.

8. Thus, this Rule does not prohibit communication of information concerning a lawyer's name or firm name, address and telephone numbers; the basis on which the lawyer's fees are determined, including prices for specific services and payment and credit arrangements; names of references and, with their consent, names of clients regularly represented; and other truthful information that might invite the attention of those seeking legal assistance. When a communication permitted by Rule 7.02 is made in the public media, the lawyer should consult Rule 7.04 for further guidance and restrictions. When a communication permitted by Rule 7.02 is made by a lawyer through a written solicitation, the lawyer should consult Rules 7.03 and 7.05 for further guidance and restrictions.

Communication of Fields of Practice

9. Sub-paragraph (a)(5) prohibits a lawyer from stating or implying that the lawyer has an ability to influence a tribunal, legislative body, or other public official through improper conduct or upon irrelevant grounds. Such conduct brings the profession into disrepute, even though the improper or irrelevant activities referred to are never carried out, and so are prohibited without regard to the lawyer's actual intent to engage in such activities.

10. Paragraphs (a)(6), (b) and (c) of Rule 7.02 regulate communications concerning a lawyer's fields of practice and should be construed together with Rule 7.04 or 7.05, as applicable. If a lawyer in a public media advertisement or in a written solicitation designates one or more specific areas of practice, that designation is at least an implicit representation that the lawyer is qualified in the areas designated. Accordingly, Rule 7.02(a)(5) prohibits the designation of a field of practice unless the communicating lawyer is in fact competent in the area.

11. Typically, one would expect competency to be measured by special education, training, or experience in the particular area of law designated. Because certification by the Texas Board of Legal Specialization involves special education, training, and experience, certification by the Texas Board of Legal Specialization conclusively establishes that a lawyer meets the requirements of Rule 7.02(a)(6) in any area in which the Board has certified the lawyer. However, competency may be established by means other than certification by the Texas Board of Legal Specialization. See Rule 7.04(b).

12. Lawyers who wish to advertise in the public media that they specialize should refer to Rule 7.04(a), (b) and (c). Lawyers who wish to assert a specialty in a written solicitation should refer to Rule 7.05(a)(4) and (b)(1).

Actor Portrayal of Clients

13. Sub-paragraph (a)(7) further protects prospective clients from false, misleading, or deceptive advertisements and solicitations by prohibiting the use of actors to portray clients of a lawyer or law firm. Other rules prohibit the use of actors to portray lawyers in the advertising or soliciting lawyer's firm. See Rules 7.04(g), 7.05(a). The truthfulness of such portrayals is extremely difficult to monitor, and almost inevitably they involve actors whose apparent physical and mental attributes differ in a number of material respects from those of the actual clients portrayed.

Communication in a Second Language

14. The ability of lawyers to communicate in a second language can facilitate the delivery and receipt of legal services. Accordingly, it is in the best interest of the public that potential clients be made aware of a lawyer's language ability. A lawyer may state an ability to communicate in a second language without any further elaboration. However, if a lawyer chooses to communicate with potential clients in a second language, all statements or disclaimers required by the Texas Disciplinary Rules of Professional Conduct must also be made in that language. See paragraph (d). Communicating some information in one language while communicating the rest in another is potentially misleading if the recipient understands only one of the languages.

(Comment amended by State Bar Board of Directors Jan. 20, 1995.)

Texas Disciplinary Rule 7.03

RULE 7.03 Prohibited Solicitations and Payments

(a) A lawyer shall not by in-person contact, or by regulated telephone or other electronic contact as defined in paragraph (f) seek professional employment concerning a matter arising out of a particular occurrence or event, or series of occurrences or events, from a prospective client or nonclient who has not sought the lawyer's advice regarding employment or with whom the lawyer has no family or past or present attorney-client relationship when a significant motive for the lawyer's doing so is the lawyer's pecuniary gain. Notwithstanding the provisions of this paragraph, a lawyer for a qualified nonprofit organization may communicate with the organization's members for the purpose of educating the members to understand the law, to recognize legal problems, to make intelligent selection of counsel, or to use legal services. In those situations where in-person or telephone or other electronic contact is permitted by this paragraph, a lawyer shall not have such a contact with a prospective client if:

(1) the communication involves coercion, duress, fraud, overreaching, intimidation, undue influence, or harassment;

(2) the communication contains information prohibited by Rule 7.02(a); or

(3) the communication contains a false, fraudulent, misleading, deceptive, or unfair statement or claim.

(b) A lawyer shall not pay, give, or offer to pay or give anything of value to a person not licensed to practice law for soliciting prospective clients for, or referring clients or prospective clients to, any lawyer or firm, except that a lawyer may pay reasonable fees for advertising and public relations services rendered in accordance with this Rule and may pay the usual charges of a lawyer referral service that meets the requirements of Occupational Code Title 5, Subtitle B, Chapter 952.

(c) A lawyer, in order to solicit professional employment, shall not pay, give, advance, or offer to pay, give, or advance anything of value, other than actual litigation expenses and other financial assistance as permitted by Rule 1.08(d), to a prospective client or any other person; provided however, this provision does not prohibit the payment of legitimate referral fees as permitted by paragraph (b) of this Rule.

(d) A lawyer shall not enter into an agreement for, charge for, or collect a fee for professional employment obtained in violation of Rule 7.03(a), (b), or (c).

(e) A lawyer shall not participate with or accept referrals from a lawyer referral service unless the lawyer knows or reasonably believes that the lawyer referral service meets the requirements of Occupational Code Title 5, Subtitle B, Chapter 952.

(f) As used in paragraph (a), "regulated telephone or other electronic contact" means any electronic communication initiated by a lawyer or by any person acting on behalf of a lawyer or law firm that will result in the person contacted communicating in a live, interactive manner with any other person by telephone or other electronic means. For purposes of this Rule a website for a lawyer or law firm is not considered a communication initiated by or on behalf of that lawyer or firm.

COMMENT:

1. In many situations, in-person or telephone solicitations by lawyers involve well-known opportunities for abuse of prospective clients. Nonetheless, paragraph (a) unconditionally prohibits those activities only when profit for the lawyer is a significant motive and the solicitation concerns matters arising out of a particular occurrence, event, or series of occurrences or events. The reason for this limited outright ban is that there are circumstances where the dangers of such contacts can be reduced. As long as the conditions of subparagraphs (a)(1) through (a)(3) are not violated by a given contact, a lawyer may engage

in telephone or in-person solicitations when the solicitation is unrelated to a specific occurrence, event, or series of occurrences or events. Similarly, subject to the same restrictions, in-person or telephone solicitations are permitted where the prospective client either has a family or past or present attorney-client relationship with the lawyer or where the potential client had previously contacted the lawyer about possible employment in the matter.

2. In addition, Rule 7.03(a) does not prohibit a lawyer for a qualified non-profit organization from in-person or telephone solicitation of prospective clients for purposes related to that organization. Historically and by law, nonprofit legal aid agencies, unions, and other qualified nonprofit organizations and their lawyers have been permitted to solicit clients in-person or by telephone, and Rule 7.03(a) is not in derogation of their constitutional rights to do so. Attorneys for such nonprofit organizations, however, remain subject to this Rule's general prohibitions against undue influence, intimidation, overreaching, and the like.

Paying for Solicitation

3. Rule 7.03(b) does not prohibit a lawyer from paying standard commercial fees for advertising or public relations services rendered in accordance with these Rules. In addition, a lawyer may pay the fees required by a lawyer referral service that meets the requirements of Article 320(d), Revised Statutes. However, paying, giving, or offering to pay or give anything of value to persons not licensed to practice law who solicit prospective clients for lawyers has always been considered to be against the best interest of both the public and the legal profession. Such actions circumvent these Rules by having a nonlawyer do what a lawyer is ethically proscribed from doing. Accordingly, the practice is forbidden by Rule 7.03(b). As to payments or gifts of value to licensed lawyers for soliciting prospective clients, see Rule 1.04(f).

4. Rule 7.03(c) prohibits a lawyer from paying or giving value directly to a prospective client or any other person as consideration for employment by that client except as permitted by Rule 1.08(d).

5. Paragraph (d) prohibits a lawyer from agreeing to or charging for professional employment obtained in violation of Rule 7.03. Paragraph (e) further requires a lawyer to decline business generated by a lawyer referral service unless the lawyer knows or reasonably believes that service is operated in conformity with statutory requirements.

6. References to "a lawyer" in this and other Rules include lawyers who practice in law firms. A lawyer associated with a firm cannot circumvent these Rules by soliciting or advertising in the name of that firm in a way that violates these Rules. See Rule 7.04(e).

(Comment amended by State Bar Board of Directors Jan. 20, 1995.)

Texas Disciplinary Rule 7.04

RULE 7.04 Advertisements in the Public Media

(a) A lawyer shall not advertise in the public media by stating that the lawyer is a specialist, except as permitted under Rule 7.04(b) or as follows:

(1) A lawyer admitted to practice before the United States Patent Office may use the designation "Patents," "Patent Attorney," or "Patent Lawyer," or any combination of those terms. A lawyer engaged in the trademark practice may use the designation "Trademark," "Trademark Attorney," or "Trademark Lawyer," or any combination of those terms. A lawyer engaged in patent and trademark practice may hold himself or herself out as specializing in "Intellectual Property Law," "Patent, Trademark, Copyright Law and Unfair Competition," or any of those terms.

(2) A lawyer may permit his or her name to be listed in lawyer referral service offices that meet the requirements of Occupational Code Title 5, Subtitle B, Chapter 952, according to the areas of law in which the lawyer will accept referrals.

(3) A lawyer available to practice in a particular area of law or legal service may distribute to other lawyers and publish in legal directories and legal newspapers (whether written or electronic) a listing or an announcement of such availability. The

listing shall not contain a false or misleading representation of special competence or experience, but may contain the kind of information that traditionally has been included in such publications.

(b) A lawyer who advertises in the public media:

(1) shall publish or broadcast the name of at least one lawyer who is responsible for the content of such advertisement; and

(2) shall not include a statement that the lawyer has been certified or designated by an organization as possessing special competence or a statement that the lawyer is a member of an organization the name of which implies that its members possess special competence, except that:

(i) a lawyer who has been awarded a Certificate of Special Competence by the Texas Board of Legal Specialization in the area so advertised, may state with respect to each such area, "Board Certified, [area of specialization]—Texas Board of Legal Specialization;" and

(ii) a lawyer who is a member of an organization the name of which implies that its members possess special competence, or who has been certified or designated by an organization as possessing special competence, may include a factually accurate statement of such membership or may include a factually accurate statement, "Certified [area of specialization] [name of certifying organization]," but such statements may be made only if that organization has been accredited by the Texas Board of Legal Specialization as a bona fide organization that admits to membership or grants certification only on the basis of objective, exacting, publicly available standards (including high standards of individual character, conduct, and reputation) that are reasonably relevant to the special training or special competence that is implied and that are in excess of the level of training and competence generally required for admission to the Bar.

(3) shall, in the case of infomercial or comparable presentation, state that the presentation is an advertisement:

(i) both verbally and in writing at its outset, after any commercial interruption, and at its conclusion; and

(ii) in writing during any portion of the presentation that explains how to contact a lawyer or law firm.

(c) Separate and apart from any other statements, the statements referred to in paragraph (b) shall be displayed conspicuously and in language easily understood by an ordinary consumer.

(d) Subject to the requirements of Rules 7.02 and 7.03 and of paragraphs (a), (b), and (c) of this Rule, a lawyer may, either directly or through a public relations or advertising representative, advertise services in the public media, such as (but not limited to) a telephone directory, legal directory, newspaper or other periodical, outdoor display, radio, television, the internet, or electronic or digital media.

(e) All advertisements in the public media for a lawyer or firm must be reviewed and approved in writing by the lawyer or a lawyer in the firm.

(f) A copy or recording of each advertisement in the public media and relevant approval referred to in paragraph (e), and a record of when and where the advertisement was used, shall be kept by the lawyer or firm for four years after its last dissemination.

(g) In advertisements in the public media, any person who portrays a lawyer whose services or whose firm's services are being advertised, or who narrates an advertisement as if he or she were such a lawyer, shall be one or more of the lawyers whose services are being advertised.

(h) If an advertisement in the public media by a lawyer or firm discloses the willingness or potential willingness of the lawyer or firm to render services on a contingent fee basis, the advertisement must state whether the client will be obligated to pay all or any portion of the court costs and, if a client may be liable for other expenses, this fact must be disclosed. If specific percentage fees or fee ranges of contingent fee work are disclosed in such advertisement, it must also disclose whether the percentage is computed before or after expenses are deducted from the recovery.

(i) A lawyer who advertises in the public media a specific fee or range of fees for a particular service shall conform to the advertised fee or range of fees for the period during which the advertisement is reasonably expected to be in circulation or otherwise expected to be effective in attracting clients, unless the advertisement specifies a shorter period; but in no instance is the lawyer bound to conform to the advertised fee or range of fees for a period of more than one year after the date of publication.

*(j) A lawyer or firm who advertises in the public media must disclose the geographic location, by city or town, of the lawyer's or firm's principal office. A lawyer or firm shall not advertise the existence of any office other than the principal office unless:

(1) that other office is staffed by a lawyer at least three days a week; or

(2) the advertisement discloses the days and times during which a lawyer will be present at that office.

(k) A lawyer may not, directly or indirectly, pay all or a part of the cost of an advertisement in the public media for a lawyer not in the same firm unless such advertisement discloses the name and address of the financing lawyer, the relationship between the advertising lawyer and the financing lawyer, and whether the advertising lawyer is likely to refer cases received through the advertisement to the financing lawyer.

(*l*) If an advertising lawyer knows or should know at the time of an advertisement in the public media that a case or matter will likely be referred to another lawyer or firm, a statement of such fact shall be conspicuously included in such advertisement.

(m) No motto, slogan, or jingle that is false or misleading may be used in any advertisement in the public media.

(n) A lawyer shall not include in any advertisement in the public media the lawyer's association with a lawyer referral service unless the lawyer knows or reasonably believes that the lawyer referral service meets the requirements of Occupational Code Title 5, Subtitle B, Chapter 952.

(*o*) A lawyer may not advertise in the public media as part of an advertising cooperative or venture of two or more lawyers not in the same firm unless each such advertisement:

(1) states that the advertisement is paid for by the cooperating lawyers;

(2) names each of the cooperating lawyers;

(3) sets forth conspicuously the special competency requirements required by Rule 7.04(b) of lawyers who advertise in the public media;

(4) does not state or imply that the lawyers participating in the advertising cooperative or venture possess professional superiority, are able to perform services

* **Publisher's Note:** In Texans Against Censorship, Inc. v. State Bar of Texas, 888 F.Supp. 1328 (E.D.Tex. 1995), the U.S. District Court for the Eastern District of Texas held Rule 7.04(j) unconstitutional as applied to one of the plaintiffs. Affirmed, Texans v. State Bar of Texas, 100 F.3d 953 (5th Cir. 1996).

in a superior manner, or possess special competence in any area of law advertised, except that the advertisement may contain the information permitted by Rule 7.04(b)(2); and

(5) does not otherwise violate the Texas Disciplinary Rules of Professional Conduct.

(p) Each lawyer who advertises in the public media as part of an advertising cooperative or venture shall be individually responsible for:

(1) ensuring that each advertisement does not violate this Rule; and

(2) complying with the filing requirements of Rule 7.07.

(q) If these rules require that specific qualifications, disclaimers, or disclosures of information accompany communications concerning a lawyer's services, the required qualifications, disclaimers, or disclosures must be presented in the same manner as the communication and with equal prominence.

(r) A lawyer who advertises on the internet must display the statements and disclosures required by Rule 7.04.

(Adopted to be eff. April 1, 1995; on March 31, 1995, the Texas Supreme Court extended the effective date 120 days after the date of judgment of the U.S. District Court in Texans Against Censorship, Inc. v. State Bar of Texas, 888 F.Supp. 1328 (E.D.Tex. 1995).)

COMMENT:

1. Neither Rule 7.04 nor Rule 7.05 prohibits communications authorized by law, such as notice to members of a class in class action litigation.

Advertising Areas of Practice and Special Competence

2. Paragraphs (a) and (b) permit a lawyer, under the restrictions set forth, to indicate areas of practice in advertisements about the lawyer's services. See also paragraph (d). The restrictions are designed primarily to require that accurate information be conveyed. These restrictions recognize that a lawyer has a right protected by the United States Constitution to advertise publicly, but that the right may be regulated by reasonable restrictions designed to protect the public from false or misleading information. The restrictions contained in Rule 7.04 are based on the experience of the legal profession in the State of Texas and are designed to curtail what experience has shown to be misleading and deceptive advertising. To ensure accountability, sub-paragraph (b)(1) requires identification of at least one lawyer responsible for the content of the advertisement.

3. Because of long-standing tradition a lawyer admitted to practice before the United States Patent Office may use the designation "patents," "patent attorney" or "patent lawyer" or any combination of those terms. As recognized by paragraph (a)(1), a lawyer engaged in patent and trademark practice may hold himself or herself out as concentrating in "intellectual property law," "patents, or trademarks and related matters," or "patent, trademark, copyright law and unfair competition" or any of those terms.

4. Paragraph (a)(2) recognizes the propriety of listing a lawyer's name in legal directories according to the areas of law in which the lawyer will accept new matters. The same right is given with respect to lawyer referral service offices, but only if those services comply with statutory guidelines. The restriction in paragraph (a)(2) does not prevent a legal aid agency or prepaid legal services plan from advertising legal services provided under its auspices.

5. Paragraph (a)(3) permits advertisements by lawyers to other lawyers in legal directories and legal newspapers, subject to the same requirements of truthfulness that apply to all other forms of lawyer advertising. Such advertisements traditionally contain information about the name, location, telephone numbers, and general availability of a lawyer to work on particular legal matters. Other information may be included so long as it is not false or misleading. Because advertisements in these publications are not available to the general public, lawyers who list various areas of practice are not required to comply with paragraph (b).

6. Some advertisements, sometimes known as tombstone advertisements, mention only such matters as the name of the lawyer or law firm, a listing of lawyers associated with the firm, office addresses and telephone numbers, office and telephone service hours, dates of admission to bars, the acceptance of credit cards, and fees. The content of such advertisements is not the kind of information intended to be regulated by Rule 7.04(b). However, if the advertisement in the public media mentions any area of the law in which the lawyer practices, then, because of the likelihood of misleading material, the lawyer must comply with paragraph (b).

7. Sometimes lawyers choose to advertise in the public media the fact that they have been certified or designated by a particular organization or that they are members of a particular organization. Such statements naturally lead the public to believe that the lawyer possesses special competence in the area of law mentioned. Consequently, in order to ensure that the public will not be misled by such statements, sub-paragraph (b)(2) and paragraph (c) place limited but necessary restrictions upon a lawyer's basic right to advertise those affiliations.

8. Rule 7.04(b)(2) gives lawyers who possess certificates of specialization from the Texas Board of Legal Specialization or other meritorious credentials from organizations approved by the Board the option of stating that fact. If a lawyer mentions in an advertisement in the public media an area of the law in which the lawyer practices and that lawyer has not been awarded a Certificate in the area advertised, then the lawyer must disclaim or, where applicable, state that no certification is available. See sub-paragraph (b)(3). Sub-paragraphs (b)(2) and (b)(3) require that the restrictions set forth be complied with as to each area of law advertised.

9. Paragraph (c) is intended to ensure against misleading or material variations from the statements required by paragraph (b).

10. Paragraphs (e) and (f) provide the advertising lawyer, the Bar, and the public with requisite records should questions arise regarding the propriety of a public media advertisement. Paragraph (e), like paragraph (b)(1), ensures that a particular attorney accepts responsibility for the advertisement. It is in the public interest and in the interest of the legal profession that the records of those advertisements and approvals be maintained.

Examples of Prohibited Advertising

11. Paragraphs (g) through (*o*) regulate conduct that has been found to mislead or be likely to mislead the public. Each paragraph is designed to protect the public and to guard the legal profession against these documented misleading practices while at the same time respecting the constitutional rights of any lawyer to advertise.

12. Paragraph (g) is a limited regulation of video and audio forms of advertising. It prohibits lawyers from misleading the public into believing a nonlawyer portrayor or narrator in the advertisement is one of the lawyers prepared to perform services for the public. It does not prohibit the narration of an advertisement in the third person by an actor, as long as it is clear to those hearing or seeing the advertisement that the actor is not a lawyer prepared to perform services for the public.

13. Contingent fee contracts present unusual opportunities for deception by lawyers or for misunderstanding by the public. By requiring certain disclosures, paragraph (h) safeguards the public from misleading or potentially misleading advertisements that involve representation on a contingent fee basis. The affirmative requirements of paragraph (h) are not triggered solely by the expression of "contingent fee" or "percentage fee" in the advertisement. To the contrary, they encompass advertisements in the public media where the lawyer or firm expresses a mere willingness or potential willingness to render services for a contingent fee. Therefore, statements in an advertisement such as "no fee if no recovery" or "fees in the event of recovery only" are clearly included as a form of advertisement subject to the disclosure requirements of paragraph (h).

14. Paragraphs (i), (j), (k) and (*l*) jointly address the problem of advertising that experience has shown misleads the public concerning the fees that will be charged, the location where services will be provided, or the attorney who will be performing these services. Together they prohibit the same sort of "bait and switch" advertising tactics by lawyers that are universally condemned.

15. Paragraph (i) requires a lawyer who advertises a specific fee or range of fees in the public media to honor those commitments for the period during which the advertisement is reasonably expected to be in circulation or otherwise expected to be effective in attracting clients, unless the advertisement itself specifies a shorter period. In no event, however, is a lawyer required to honor an advertised fee or range of fees for more than one year after publication.

16. Paragraph (j) prohibits advertising the availability of a satellite office that is not staffed by a lawyer at least on a part-time basis. Paragraph (j) does not require, however, that a lawyer or firm identify the particular office as its principal one. Experience has shown that, in the absence of such regulation, members of the public have been misled into employing a lawyer in a distant city who advertises that there is a nearby satellite office, only to learn later that the lawyer is rarely available to the client because the nearby office is seldom open or is staffed only by lay personnel. Paragraph (k) is not intended to restrict the ability of legal services programs to advertise satellite offices in remote parts of the program's service area even if those satellite offices are staffed irregularly by attorneys. Otherwise low-income individuals in and near such communities might be denied access to the only legal services truly available to them.

17. When a lawyer or firm advertises, the public has a right to expect that lawyer or firm will perform the legal services. Experience has shown that attorneys not in the same firm may create a relationship wherein one will finance advertising for the other in return for referrals. Nondisclosure of such a referral relationship is misleading to the public. Accordingly, paragraph (k) prohibits such a relationship between an advertising lawyer and a lawyer who finances the advertising unless the advertisement discloses the nature of the financial relationship between the two lawyers. Paragraph (*l*) addresses the same problem from a different perspective, requiring a lawyer who advertises the availability of legal services and who knows or should know at the time that the advertisement is placed in the media that business will likely be referred to another lawyer or firm, to include a conspicuous statement of that fact in any such advertising. This requirement applies whether or not the lawyer to whom the business is referred is financing the advertisements of the referring lawyer. It does not, however, require disclosure of all possible scenarios under which a referral could occur, such as an unforeseen need to associate with a specialist in accordance with Rule 1.01(a) or the possibility of a referral if a prospective client turns out to have a conflict of interest precluding representation by the advertising lawyer.

18. Paragraph (m) protects the public by forbidding mottos, slogans, and jingles that are false or misleading. There are, however, mottos, slogans, and jingles that are informative rather than false or misleading. Accordingly, paragraph (m) recognizes an advertising lawyer's constitutional right to include appropriate mottos, slogans, and jingles in advertising.

19. Some lawyers choose to band together in a cooperative or joint venture to advertise. Although those arrangements are lawful, the fact that several independent lawyers have joined together in a single advertisement increases the risk of misrepresentation or other forms of inappropriate expression. Special care must be taken to ensure that cooperative advertisements identify each cooperating lawyer, state that each cooperating lawyer is paying for the advertisement, and accurately describe the professional qualifications of each cooperating lawyer. See paragraph (*o*). Furthermore, each cooperating lawyer must comply with the filing requirements of Rule 7.07. See paragraph (p).

(Comment adopted by State Bar Board of Directors Jan. 20, 1995.)

Texas Disciplinary Rule 7.05

RULE 7.05 Prohibited Written, Electronic or Digital Solicitations

(a) A lawyer shall not send, deliver, or transmit, or knowingly permit or knowingly cause another person to send, deliver, or transmit, a written, audio, audiovisual, digital media, recorded telephone message, or other electronic communication to a prospective client for the purpose of obtaining professional employment on behalf of any lawyer or law firm if:

(1) the communication involves coercion, duress, fraud, overreaching, intimidation, undue influence, or harassment;

(2) the communication contains information prohibited by Rule 7.02 or fails to satisfy each of the requirements of Rule 7.04(a) through (c), and (g) through (q) that would be applicable to the communication if it were an advertisement in the public media; or

(3) the communication contains a false, fraudulent, misleading, deceptive, or unfair statement or claim.

(b) Except as provided in paragraph (f) of this Rule, a written, electronic, or digital solicitation communication to prospective clients for the purpose of obtaining professional employment:

(1) shall, in the case of a non-electronically transmitted written communication, be plainly marked "ADVERTISEMENT" on its first page and on the face of the envelope or other packaging used to transmit the communication. If the written communication is in the form of a self-mailing brochure or pamphlet, the word "ADVERTISEMENT" shall be:

(i) in a color that contrasts sharply with the background color; and

(ii) in a size of at least 3/8″ vertically or three times the vertical height of the letters used in the body of such communication, whichever is larger;

(2) shall, in the ease of an electronic mail message, be plainly marked "ADVERTISEMENT" in the subject portion of the electronic mail and at the beginning of the message's text;

(3) shall not be made to resemble legal pleadings or other legal documents;

(4) shall not reveal on the envelope or other packaging or electronic mail subject line used to transmit the communication, or on the outside of a self-mailing brochure or pamphlet, the nature of the legal problem of the prospective client or non-client; and

(5) shall disclose how the lawyer obtained the information prompting the communication to solicit professional employment if such contact was prompted by a specific occurrence involving the recipient of the communication or a family member of such person(s).

(c) Except as provided in paragraph (f) of this Rule, an audio, audio-visual, digital media, recorded telephone message, or other electronic communication sent to prospective clients for the purpose of obtaining professional employment:

(1) shall, in the case of any such communication delivered to the recipient by non-electronic means, plainly and conspicuously state in writing on the outside of any envelope or other packaging used to transmit the communication, that it is an "ADVERTISEMENT";

(2) shall not reveal on any such envelope or other packaging the nature of the legal problem of the prospective client or non-client;

(3) shall disclose, either in the communication itself or in accompanying transmittal message, how the lawyer obtained the information prompting such audio, audiovisual, digital media, recorded telephone message, or other electronic communication to solicit professional employment, if such contact was promoted by a specific occurrence involving the recipient of the communication or a family member of such person(s);

(4) shall, in the case of a recorded audio presentation or a recorded telephone message, plainly state that it is an advertisement prior to any other words being spoken and again at the presentation's or message's conclusion; and

(5) shall, in the case of an audio-visual or digital media presentation, plainly state that the presentation is an advertisement:

(i) both verbally and in writing at the outset of the presentation and again at its conclusion; and

(ii) in writing during any portion of the presentation that explains how to contact a lawyer or law firm.

(d) All written, audio, audio-visual, digital media, recorded telephone message, or other electronic communications made to a prospective client for the purpose of obtaining professional employment of a lawyer or law firm must be reviewed and either signed by or approved in writing by the lawyer or a lawyer in the firm.

(e) A copy of each written, audio, audio-visual, digital media, recorded telephone message, or other electronic solicitation communication, the relevant approval thereof, and a record of the date of each such communication; the name, address, telephone number, or electronic address to which each such communication was sent; and the means by which each such communication was sent shall be kept by the lawyer or firm for four years after its dissemination.

(f) The provisions of paragraphs (b) and (c) of this Rule do not apply to a written audio audiovisual, digital media, recorded telephone message, or other form of electronic solicitation communication:

(1) directed to a family member or a person with whom the lawyer had or has an attorney client relationship;

(2) that is not motivated by or concerned with a particular past occurrence or event or a particular series of past occurrences or events, and also is not motivated by or concerned with the prospective client's specific existing legal problem of which the lawyer is aware;

(3) if the lawyer's use of the communication to secure professional employment was not significantly motivated by a desire for, or by the possibility of obtaining, pecuniary gain; or

(4) that is requested by the prospective client.

COMMENT:

1. Rule 7.03 deals with in-person or telephone contact between a lawyer and a prospective client wherein the lawyer seeks professional employment. Rule 7.04 deals with advertisements in the public media by a lawyer seeking professional employment. This Rule deals with written solicitations between a lawyer and a prospective client. Typical examples are letters or other forms of correspondence addressed to a prospective client.

2. Written solicitations raise more concerns than do comparable written advertisements. Being private, they are more difficult to monitor, and for that reason paragraph (d) requires retention for four years of certain information regarding written solicitations. See also Rule 7.07(a). Paragraph (a) addresses such concerns as well as problems stemming from exceptionally outrageous communications such as written solicitations involving fraud, intimidation, or deceptive and misleading claims. Because receipt of multiple solicitations appears to be most pronounced and vexatious in situations involving accident victims, paragraph (b)(7) requires disclosure of the source of information if the solicitation was prompted by a specific occurrence.

3. Because experience has shown that many written solicitations have been intrusive or misleading by reason of being personalized or being disguised as some form of official communication special prohibitions against such practices are necessary. The requirements of paragraph (b) greatly lessen those dangers of deception and harassment.

4. Newsletters or other works published by a lawyer that are not circulated for the purpose of obtaining professional employment are not within the ambit of paragraph (b).

5. In addition to addressing these special problems posed by written solicitations, Rule 7.05 regulates the content of those communications. It does so by incorporating the standards of Rule 7.02 and those of Rule 7.04 that would apply to the written solicitation were it instead a written advertisement in the public media. See paragraphs (a)(2), (3), and (b)(1). In brief, this approach means that, a lawyer may not include or omit anything from a written solicitation unless the lawyer could do so were the communication a written advertisement in the public media, except for those statements or disclaimers required by Rule 7.04(a)–(c). See sub-paragraph (b)(1).

6. Paragraph (e) provides that none of the restrictions in paragraph (b) apply in certain situations because the dangers of deception, harassment, vexation and overreaching are quite low. For example, a written solicitation may be directed to a family member or a present or a former client, or in response to a request by a prospective client. Similarly, a written solicitation may be used in seeking general employment in commercial matters from a bank or other corporation, when there is neither concern with specific existing legal problems nor concern with a particular past event or series of events. All such communications, however, remain subject to Rule 7.02 and paragraphs (h) through (*o*) of Rule 7.04. See sub-paragraph (a)(2).

7. In addition, paragraph (e) allows such communications in situations not involving the lawyer's pecuniary gain. For purposes of these rules, it is presumed that communications made on behalf of a nonprofit legal aid agency, union, or other qualified nonprofit organization are not motivated by a desire for, or by the possibility of obtaining, pecuniary gain, but that presumption may be rebutted.

(Comment adopted by State Bar Board of Directors Jan. 20, 1995.)

Texas Disciplinary Rule 7.06

RULE 7.06 Prohibited Employment

(a) A lawyer shall not accept or continue employment in a matter when that employment was procured by conduct prohibited by any of Rules 7.01 through 7.05, 8.04(a)(2), or 8.04(a)(9), engaged in by that lawyer personally or by any other person whom the lawyer ordered, encouraged, or knowingly permitted to engage in such conduct.

(b) A lawyer shall not accept or continue employment in a matter when the lawyer knows or reasonably should know that employment was procured by conduct prohibited by any of Rules 7.01 through 7.05, 8.04(a)(2), or 8.04(a)(9), engaged in by any other person or entity that is a shareholder, partner, or member of, an associate in, or of counsel to that lawyer's firm; or by any other person whom any of the foregoing persons or entities ordered, encouraged, or knowingly permitted to engage in such conduct.

(c) A lawyer who has not violated paragraph (a) or (b) in accepting employment in a matter shall not continue employment in that matter once the lawyer knows or reasonably should know that the person procuring the lawyer's employment in the matter engaged in, or ordered, encouraged, or knowingly permitted another to engage in, conduct prohibited by any of Rules 7.01 through 7.05, 8.04(a)(2), or 8.04(a)(9) in connection with the matter unless nothing of value is given thereafter in return for that employment.

A lawyer shall not accept or continue employment when the lawyer knows or reasonably should know that that the person who seeks the lawyer's services does so as a result of conduct prohibited by these rules.

(Former Rule 7.03 adopted eff. Jan. 1, 1990; redesignated and amended to be eff. April 1, 1995; on March 31, 1995, the Texas Supreme Court extended the effective date 120 days after the date of judgment of the U.S. District Court in Texans Against Censorship, Inc. v. State Bar of Texas, 888 F.Supp. 1328 (E.D.Tex. 1995).)

COMMENT:

Selection of a lawyer by a client often is a result of the advice and recommendation of third parties—relatives, friends, acquaintances, business associates and other lawyers. Although that method of referral is perfectly legitimate, the client is best served if the recommendation is disinterested and informed. All lawyers must guard against creating situations where referral from others is the consequence of some form of prohibited compensation or from some form of false or misleading communication, or by virtue of some other violation of these rules. This prohibition on accepting or continuing employment applies even if the lawyer whose services are involved had no direct or indirect involvement with the underlying violation of these Rules, provided that lawyer knows of the violation. See also Rule 7.03(d), forbidding a lawyer to charge or collect a fee where the misconduct involves violations of Rule 7.03(a), (b), or (c).

(Comment amended by State Bar Board of Directors Jan. 20, 1995.)

Texas Disciplinary Rule 7.07

RULE 7.07 Filing Requirements for Public Advertisements and Written, Recorded, Electronic, or Other Digital Solicitations

(a) Except as provided in paragraphs (c) and (e) of this Rule, a lawyer shall file with the Advertising Review Committee of the State Bar of Texas, no later than the mailing or sending by any means, including electronic, of a written, audio, audio-visual, digital or other electronic solicitation communication:

(1) a copy of the written, audio, audio-visual, digital, or other electronic solicitation communication being sent or to be sent to one or more prospective clients for the purpose of obtaining professional employment, together with a representative sample of the envelopes or other packaging in which the communications are enclosed;

(2) a completed lawyer advertising and solicitation communication application form; and

(3) a check or money order payable to the State Bar of Texas for the fee set by the Board of Directors. Such fee shall be for the sole purpose of defraying the expense of enforcing the rules related to such solicitations.

(b) Except as provided in paragraph (e) of this Rule, a lawyer shall file with the Advertising Review Committee of the State Bar of Texas, no later than the first dissemination of an advertisement in the public media, a copy of each of the lawyer's advertisements in the public media. The filing shall include:

(1) a copy of the advertisement in the form in which it appears or will be disseminated appear upon dissemination, such as a videotape, audiotape, DVD, CD, a print copy, or a photograph of outdoor advertising;

(2) a production script of the advertisement setting forth all words used and describing in detail the actions, events, scenes, and background sounds used in such advertisement together with a listing of the names and addresses of persons portrayed or heard to speak, if the advertisement is in or will be in a form in which the advertised message is not fully revealed by a print copy or photograph;

(3) a statement of when and where the advertisement has been, is, or will be used;

(4) a completed lawyer advertising and solicitation communication application form; and

(5) a check or money order payable to the State Bar of Texas for the fee set by the Board of Directors. Such fee shall be for the sole purpose of defraying the expense of enforcing the rules related to such advertisements.

(c) Except as provided in paragraph (e) of this Rule, a lawyer shall file with the Advertising Review Committee of the State Bar of Texas no later than its first posting on the internet or other comparable network of computers information concerning the lawyer's or lawyer's firm's website. As used in this Rule, a "website" means a single or multiple page file, posted on a computer server, which describes a lawyer or law firm's

practice or qualifications, to which public access is provided through publication of a uniform resource locator (URL). The filing shall include:

(1) the intended initial access page of a website;

(2) a completed lawyer advertising and solicitation communication application form; and

(3) a check or money order payable to the State Bar of Texas for the fee set by the Board of Directors. Such fee shall be set for the sole purpose of defraying the expense of enforcing the rules related to such websites.

(d) A lawyer who desires to secure an advance advisory opinion, referred to as a request for pre-approval, concerning compliance of a contemplated written-solicitation communication or advertisement may submit to the Advertising Review Committee, not less than thirty (30) days prior to the date of first dissemination, the material specified in paragraph (a) or (b) or the intended initial access page submitted pursuant to paragraph (c), including the application form and required fee; provided however, it shall not be necessary to submit a videotape or DVD if the videotape or DVD has not then been prepared and the production script submitted reflects in detail and accurately the actions, events, scenes, and background sounds that will be depicted or contained on such videotapes or DVDs, when prepared, as well as the narrative transcript of the verbal and printed portions of such advertisement. If a lawyer submits an advertisement or solicitation communication for pre-approval, a finding of noncompliance by the Advertising Review Committee is not binding in a disciplinary proceeding or disciplinary action, but a finding of compliance is binding in favor of the submitting lawyer as to all materials actually submitted for pre-approval if the representations, statements, materials, facts, and written assurances received in connection therewith are true and are not misleading. The finding of compliance constitutes admissible evidence if offered by a party.

(e) The filing requirements of paragraphs (a), (b), and (c) do not extend to any of the following materials, provided those materials comply with Rule 7.02(a) through (c) and, where applicable, Rule 7.04(a) through (c):

(1) an advertisement in the public media that contains only part or all of the following information:

(i) the name of the lawyer or firm and lawyers associated with the firm, with office addresses, electronic addresses, telephone numbers, office and telephone service hours, telecopier numbers, and a designation of the profession such as “attorney,” “lawyer,” “law office,” or “firm”;

(ii) the particular areas of law in which the lawyer or firm specializes or possesses special competence;

(iii) the particular areas of law in which the lawyer or firm practices or concentrates or to which it limits its practice;

(iv) the date of admission of the lawyer or lawyers to the State Bar of Texas, to particular federal courts, and to the bars of other jurisdictions;

(v) technical and professional licenses granted by this state and other recognized licensing authorities;

(vi) foreign language ability;

(vii) fields of law in which one or more lawyers are certified or designated, provided the statement of this information is in compliance with Rule 7.02(a) through (c);

(viii) identification of prepaid or group legal service plans in which the lawyer participates;

(ix) the acceptance or nonacceptance of credit cards;

(x) any fee for initial consultation and fee schedule;

(xi) other publicly available information concerning legal issues, not prepared or paid for by the firm or any of its lawyers, such as news articles, legal articles, editorial opinions, or other legal developments or events, such as proposed or enacted rules, regulations, or legislation;

(xii) in the case of a website, links to other websites;

(xiii) that the lawyer or firm is a sponsor of a charitable, civic, or community program or event, or is a sponsor of a public service announcement;

(xiv) any disclosure or statement required by these rules; and

(xv) any other information specified from time to time in orders promulgated by the Supreme Court of Texas;

(2) an advertisement in the public media that:

(i) identifies one or more lawyers or a firm as a contributor to a specified charity or as a sponsor of a specified charitable, community, or public interest program, activity, or event; and

(ii) contains no information about the lawyers or firm other than names of the lawyers or firm or both, location of the law offices, and the fact of the sponsorship or contribution;

(3) a listing or entry in a regularly published law list;

(4) an announcement card stating new or changed associations, new offices, or similar changes relating to a lawyer or firm, or a tombstone professional card;

(5) in the case of communications sent, delivered, or transmitted to, rather than accessed by, intended recipients, a newsletter, whether written, digital, or electronic, provided that it is sent, delivered, or transmitted mailed only to:

(i) existing or former clients;

(ii) other lawyers or professionals; or

(iii) members of a nonprofit organization that meets the following conditions: the primary purposes of the organization do not include the rendition of legal services; the recommending, furnishing, paying for, or educating persons regarding legal services is incidental and reasonably related to the primary purposes of the organization; the organization does not derive a financial benefit from the rendition of legal services by a lawyer; and the person for whom the legal services are rendered, and not the organization, is recognized as the client of the lawyer who is recommended, furnished, or paid by the organization;

(6) a solicitation communication that is not motivated by or concerned with a particular past occurrence or event or a particular series of past occurrences or events, and also is not motivated by or concerned with the prospective client's specific existing legal problem of which the lawyer is aware;

(7) a solicitation communication if the lawyer's use of the communication to secure professional employment was not significantly motivated by a desire for, or by the possibility of obtaining, pecuniary gain; or

(8) a solicitation communication that is requested by the prospective client.

(f) If requested by the Advertising Review Committee, a lawyer shall promptly submit information to substantiate statements or representations made or implied in any advertisement in the public media or solicitation communication by which the lawyer seeks paid professional employment.

(Adopted to be eff. April 1, 1995; on March 31, 1995, the Texas Supreme Court extended the effective date 120 days after the date of judgment of the U.S. District Court in Texans Against Censorship, Inc. v. State Bar of Texas, 888 F.Supp. 1328 (E.D.Tex. 1995).)

COMMENT:

1. Rule 7.07 covers the filing requirements for public media advertisements (see Rule 7.04) and written solicitations (see Rule 7.05). Rule 7.07(a) deals with those written solicitations sent by a lawyer to one or more specified prospective clients. Rule 7.07(b) deals with advertisements in the public media. Each provision allows the Bar to charge a fee for reviewing submitted materials, but requires that fee be set solely to defray the expenses of enforcing those provisions.

2. Copies of non-exempt written solicitations or advertisements in the public media must be provided to the Advertising Review Committee of the State Bar of Texas either in advance or concurrently with dissemination, together with the fee required by the State Bar of Texas Board of Directors. Presumably, the Advertising Review Committee will report to the appropriate grievance committee any lawyer whom it finds from the reviewed products has disseminated an advertisement in the public media or written solicitation that violates Rules 7.02, 7.03, 7.04, or 7.05, or, at a minimum, any lawyer whose violation raises a substantial question as to that lawyer's honesty, trustworthiness, or fitness as a lawyer in other respects. See Rule 8.03(a).

3. Paragraphs (a) and (b) do not require that a lawyer submit a copy of each and every written solicitation letter a lawyer sends. If the same form letter is sent to several people, only a representative sample of each form letter, along with a representative sample of the envelopes used to mail the letters, need be filed.

4. A lawyer wishing to do so may secure an advisory opinion from the Advertising Review Committee concerning any proposed advertisement in the public media or any written solicitation in advance of its first use or mailing by complying with Rule 7.07(c). This procedure is intended as a service to those lawyers who want to resolve any possible doubts about their proposed advertisements' or written solicitations' compliance with these Rules before utilizing them. Its use is purely optional. No lawyer is required to obtain advance clearance of any advertisement or written solicitation communication from the State Bar. Although a finding of noncompliance by the Advertising Review Committee is not binding in a disciplinary proceeding, a finding of compliance is binding in favor of the submitting lawyer, as long as the lawyer's presentation to the Advertising Review Committee in connection with that advisory opinion is true and not misleading.

5. Under its Internal Rules and Operating Procedures, the Advertising Review Committee is to complete its evaluations no later than 25 days after the date of receipt of a filing. The only way that the Committee can extend that review period is to: (1) determine that there is reasonable doubt whether the advertisement or written solicitation communication complies with these Rules; (2) conclude that further examination is warranted but cannot be completed within the 25-day period; and (3) advise the lawyer of those determinations in writing within that 25-day period. The Committee's Internal Rules and Operating Procedures also provide that a failure to send such a communication to the lawyer within the 25-day period constitutes approval of the advertisement or written solicitation communication. Consequently, if an attorney submits an advertisement in the public media or written solicitation communication to the Committee for advance approval not less than 30 days prior to the date of first dissemination as required by these Rules, the attorney will receive an assessment of that advertisement or communication before the date of its first intended use.

6. Consistent with the effort to protect the first amendment rights of lawyers while ensuring the right of the public to be free from misleading advertising and the right of the Texas legal profession to maintain its integrity, paragraph (d) exempts certain types of advertisements and written solicitations prepared for the purpose of seeking paid professional employment from the filing requirements of paragraphs (a) and (b). Those types of communications need not be filed at all if they were not prepared to secure paid professional employment.

7. For the most part, the types of exempted advertising listed in subparagraphs (d)(1)–(5) are objective and less likely to result in false, misleading or fraudulent content. Similarly the types of exempted written solicitations listed in subparagraphs (d)(6)–(8) are those found least likely to result in harm to the public. See Rule 7.05(e), and comment 5 to Rule 7.05. The fact that a particular advertisement or written solicitation made by a lawyer is exempted from the filing requirements of this Rule does not exempt a lawyer from the other applicable obligations of these Rules. See generally Rules 7.01 through 7.06.

8. Paragraph (e) does not empower the Advertising Review Committee to seek information from a lawyer to substantiate statements or representations made or implied in advertisements or written communications that do not seek to obtain paid professional employment for that lawyer.

(Comment adopted by State Bar Board of Directors Jan. 20, 1995.)

MAINTAINING THE INTEGRITY OF THE PROFESSION

Texas Disciplinary Rule 8.03

[Texas has modified Model Rule 8.3 to include the following provisions:]

RULE 8.03. Reporting Professional Misconduct

* * *

(e) A lawyer who has been convicted or placed on probation, with or without an adjudication of guilt, by any court for barratry, any felony, or for a misdemeanor involving theft, embezzlement, or fraudulent or reckless misappropriation of money or other property—including a conviction or sentence of probation for attempt, conspiracy, or solicitation—must notify the chief disciplinary counsel within 30 days of the date of the order or judgment. The notice must include a copy of the order or judgment.

(f) A lawyer who has been disciplined by the attorney-regulatory agency of another jurisdiction must notify the chief disciplinary counsel within 30 days of the date of the order or judgment. The notice must include a copy of the order or judgment.

Florida Rule 8.4(d)

[Florida has modified Model Rule 8.4 to read as follows:]

RULE 4–8.4 Misconduct

A lawyer shall not:

* * *

(d) engage in conduct in connection with the practice of law that is prejudicial to the administration of justice, including to knowingly, or through callous indifference, disparage, humiliate, or discriminate against litigants, jurors, witnesses, court personnel, or other lawyers on any basis, including, but not limited to, on account of race, ethnicity, gender, religion, national origin, disability, marital status, sexual orientation, age, socioeconomic status, employment, or physical characteristic;

* * *

(h) willfully refuse, as determined by a court of competent jurisdiction, to timely pay a child support obligation; or

(i) engage in sexual conduct with a client or a representative of a client that exploits or adversely affects the interests of the client or the lawyer-client relationship.

If the sexual conduct commenced after the lawyer-client relationship was formed it shall be presumed that the sexual conduct exploits or adversely affects the interests of the client or the lawyer-client relationship. A lawyer may rebut this presumption by proving

by a preponderance of the evidence that the sexual conduct did not exploit or adversely affect the interests of the client or the lawyer-client relationship.

The prohibition and presumption stated in this rule do not apply to a lawyer in the same firm as another lawyer representing the client if the lawyer involved in the sexual conduct does not personally provide legal services to the client and is screened from access to the file concerning the legal representation.

Minnesota Rule 8.4(g), (h) & (i)

[Minnesota, one of the first states to include a prohibition against discriminatory conduct by lawyers, has amended Model Rule 8.4 to add the following:]

RULE 8.4 Misconduct

It is professional misconduct for a lawyer to:

* * *

(g) harass a person on the basis of sex, race, age, creed, religion, color, national origin, disability, sexual orientation or marital status in connection with a lawyer's professional activities;

(h) commit a discriminatory act, prohibited by federal, state or local statute or ordinance, that reflects adversely on the lawyer's fitness as a lawyer. Whether a discriminatory act reflects adversely on a lawyer's fitness as a lawyer shall be determined after consideration of all the circumstances, including: (1) the seriousness of the act, (2) whether the lawyer knew that it was prohibited by statute or ordinance, (3) whether it was part of a pattern of prohibited conduct, and (4) whether it was committed in connection with the lawyer's professional activities.

(i) refuse to honor a final and binding fee arbitration award after agreeing to arbitrate a fee dispute.

COMMENT—2005:

* * *

[4] Paragraph (g) specifies a particularly egregious type of discriminatory act—harassment on the basis of sex, race, age, creed, religion, color, national origin, disability, sexual preference, or marital status. What constitutes harassment in this context may be determined with reference to antidiscrimination legislation and case law thereunder. This harassment ordinarily involves the active burdening of another, rather than mere passive failure to act properly.

[5] Harassment on the basis of sex, race, age, creed, religion, color, national origin, disability, sexual preference, or marital status may violate either paragraph (g) or paragraph (h). The harassment violates paragraph (g) if the lawyer committed it in connection with the lawyer's professional activities. Harassment, even if not committed in connection with the lawyer's professional activities, violates paragraph (h) if the harassment (1) is prohibited by antidiscrimination legislation and (2) reflects adversely on the lawyer's fitness as a lawyer, determined as specified in paragraph (h).

[6] Paragraph (h) reflects the premise that the concept of human equality lies at the very heart of our legal system. A lawyer whose behavior demonstrates hostility toward or indifference to the policy of equal justice under the law may thereby manifest a lack of character required of members of the legal profession. Therefore, a lawyer's discriminatory act prohibited by statute or ordinance may reflect adversely on his or her fitness as a lawyer even if the unlawful discriminatory act was not committed in connection with the lawyer's professional activities.

[7] Whether an unlawful discriminatory act reflects adversely on fitness as a lawyer is determined after consideration of all relevant circumstances, including the four factors listed in paragraph (h). It is not required that the listed factors be considered equally, nor is the list intended to be exclusive. For example, it would also be relevant that the lawyer reasonably believed that his or her conduct was protected under the state or federal constitution or that the lawyer was acting in a capacity for which the law provides an

exemption from civil liability. See, e.g., Minn.Stat. Section 317A.257 (unpaid director or officer of nonprofit organization acting in good faith and not willfully or recklessly).

[8] A lawyer may refuse to comply with an obligation imposed by law upon a good faith belief that no valid obligation exists. The provisions of Rule 1.2(c)(d) concerning a good faith challenge to the validity, scope, meaning or application of the law apply to challenges of legal regulation of the practice of law.

New Jersey Rule 8.4(g)

[New Jersey has modified Model Rule 8.4 to read as follows:]

RULE 8.4 Misconduct

It is professional misconduct for a lawyer to:

* * *

(g) engage, in a professional capacity, in conduct involving discrimination (except employment discrimination unless resulting in a final agency or judicial determination) because of race, color, religion, age, sex, sexual orientation, national origin, language, marital status, socioeconomic status, or handicap where the conduct is intended or likely to cause harm.

Comment by Supreme Court:

This rule amendment (the addition of paragraph g) is intended to make discriminatory conduct unethical when engaged in by lawyers in their professional capacity. It would, for example, cover activities in the court house, such as a lawyer's treatment of court support staff, as well as conduct more directly related to litigation; activities related to practice outside of the court house, whether or not related to litigation, such as treatment of other attorneys and their staff; bar association and similar activities; and activities in the lawyer's office and firm. Except to the extent that they are closely related to the foregoing, purely private activities are not intended to be covered by this rule amendment, although they may possibly constitute a violation of some other ethical rule. Nor is employment discrimination in hiring, firing, promotion, or partnership status intended to be covered unless it has resulted in either an agency or judicial determination of discriminatory conduct. The Supreme Court believes that existing agencies and courts are better able to deal with such matters, that the disciplinary resources required to investigate and prosecute discrimination in the employment area would be disproportionate to the benefits to the system given remedies available elsewhere, and that limiting ethics proceedings in this area to cases where there has been an adjudication represents a practical resolution of conflicting needs.

"Discrimination" is intended to be construed broadly. It includes sexual harassment, derogatory or demeaning language, and, generally, any conduct towards the named groups that is both harmful and discriminatory.

Case law has already suggested both the area covered by this amendment and the possible direction of future cases. *In re Vincenti*, 114 *N.J.* 275 (554 *A.2d* 470) (1989). The Court believes the administration of justice would be better served, however, by the adoption of this general rule than by a case by case development of the scope of the professional obligation.

While the origin of this rule was a recommendation of the Supreme Court's Task Force on Women in the Courts, the Court concluded that the protection, limited to women and minorities in that recommendation, should be expanded. The groups covered in the initial proposed amendment to the rule are the same as those named in Canon 3A(4) of the Code of Judicial Conduct.

Following the initial publication of this proposed subsection (g) and receipt of various comments and suggestions, the Court revised the proposed amendment by making explicit its intent to limit the rule to conduct by attorneys in a professional capacity, to exclude employment discrimination unless adjudicated, to restrict the scope to conduct intended or likely to cause harm, and to include discrimination because of sexual orientation or socioeconomic status, these categories having been proposed by the ABA's Standing Committee on Ethics and Professional Responsibility as additions to the groups now covered in Canon 3A(4) of the New Jersey Code of Judicial Conduct. That Committee has also proposed that judges require attorneys, in proceedings before a judge, refrain from manifesting by words or conduct any bias or prejudice based on any of these categories. See proposed Canon 3A(6). This revision to the RPC further reflects the Court's intent to cover all discrimination where the attorney intends to cause harm such as inflicting emotional distress or obtaining a tactical advantage and not to cover instances when no harm is intended unless its occurrence is likely regardless of intent, e.g., where discriminatory comments or behavior is repetitive. While obviously the language of the rule cannot explicitly cover every instance of possible discriminatory conduct, the Court believes that, along with existing case law, it sufficiently narrows the breadth of the rule to avoid any suggestion that it is overly broad. See, e.g., *In re Vincenti*, 114 *N.J.* 275 (554 *A.2d* 470) (1989).

District of Columbia Rule 9.1

[The District of Columbia has added the following provision which has no counterpart in the Model Rules:]

NONDISCRIMINATION BY MEMBERS OF THE BAR

RULE 9.1 Nondiscrimination

A lawyer shall not discriminate against any individual in conditions of employment because of the individual's race, color, religion, national origin, sex, age, marital status, sexual orientation, family responsibility, or physical handicap.

COMMENT:

[1] This provision is modeled after the D.C. Human Rights Act, D.C. Code § 2–1402.11 (2001), though in some respects more limited in scope. There are also provisions of federal law that contain certain prohibitions on discrimination in employment. The rule is not intended to create ethical obligations that exceed those imposed on a lawyer by applicable law.

[3] The investigation and adjudication of discrimination claims may involve particular expertise of the kind found within the D.C. Office of Human Rights and the federal Equal Employment Opportunity Commission. Such experience may involve, among other things, methods of analysis of statistical data regarding discrimination claims. These agencies also have, in appropriate circumstances, the power to award remedies to the victims of discrimination, such as reinstatement or back pay, which extend beyond the remedies that are available through the disciplinary process. Remedies available through the disciplinary process include such sanctions as disbarment, suspension, censure, and admonition, but do not extend to monetary awards or other remedies that could alter the employment status to take into account the impact of prior acts of discrimination.

[4] If proceedings are pending before other organizations, such as the D.C. Office of Human Rights or the Equal Employment Opportunity Commission, the processing of complaints by Bar Counsel may be deferred or abated where there is substantial similarity between the complaint filed with Bar Counsel and material allegations involved in such other proceedings. See § 19(d) of Rule XI of the Rules Governing the Bar of the District of Columbia.

Appendix:
States That Have Adopted a Version of the Model Rules*

Alabama—revised for Ethics 2000.

Alaska—revised for Ethics 2000.

Arizona—revised for Ethics 20/20.

Arkansas—revised for Ethics 20/20.

California—revised for Ethics 2000.

Colorado—revised for Ethics 2000.

Connecticut—revised for Ethics 20/20.

Delaware—revised for Ethics 20/20.

District of Columbia—revised for Ethics 2000.

Florida—revised for Ethics 2000.

Georgia

Hawaii

Idaho—revised for Ethics 20/20.

Illinois—revised for Ethics 2000.

Indiana—revised for Ethics 2000.

Iowa—revised for Ethics 2000.

Kansas—revised for Ethics 20/20.

Kentucky—revised for Ethics 2000.

Louisiana—revised for Ethics 20/20.

Maine—revised for Ethics 2000.

Maryland—revised for Ethics 2000.

Massachusetts—revised for Ethics 20/20.

Michigan—revised for Ethics 2000.

Minnesota—revised for Ethics 20/20.

Mississippi—revised for Ethics 2000.

Missouri—revised for Ethics 2000.

Montana—revised for Ethics 2000.

Nebraska—revised for Ethics 2000.

Nevada—revised for Ethics 20/20.

New Hampshire—revised for Ethics 2000.

New Jersey—revised for Ethics 2000.

New Mexico—revised for Ethics 20/20.

New York (Amended version of code to include many Model Rules provisions)

---

* Source: ABA/BNA Manual on Professional Conduct 01:3 (2019) (State Ethics Rules) and ABA Center for Professional Responsibility website. http://www.americanbar.org/content/dam/aba/administrative/professional_responsibility/state_implementation_selected_e20_20_rules.authcheckdam.pdf.

STATE MODIFICATIONS

North Carolina—revised for Ethics 2000.

North Dakota—revised for Ethics 2000.

Ohio—revised for Ethics 20/20.

Oklahoma—revised for Ethics 2000.

Oregon—revised for Ethics 20/20.

Pennsylvania—revised for Ethics 2000.

Rhode Island—revised for Ethics 2000.

South Carolina—revised for Ethics 2000.

South Dakota—revised for Ethics 2000.

Tennessee—revised for Ethics 2000.

Texas

Utah—revised for Ethics 2000.

Vermont—revised for Ethics 2000.

Virginia—revised for Ethics 2000.

Washington—revised for Ethics 2000.

West Virginia—revised for Ethics 20/20.

Wisconsin—revised for Ethics 2000.

Wyoming—revised for Ethics 20/20.

OTHER SELECTED STATE STANDARDS, RULES, AND STATUTES

TABLE OF CONTENTS

Introduction

This section presents a more in depth perspective on how two states have chosen to regulate lawyers. Until 2018, the California Rules of Professional Conduct for governing lawyers' conduct differed substantially from the ABA codes of ethics. In May 2018, the California Supreme Court approved a new set of rules largely based upon the Model Rules. California also has a unique set of court rules to govern multijurisdictional practice. The California approach to regulating lawyer must also consider the legislature's control over lawyers. This form of regulation is contained in the California Business and Professions Code. Selected sections are reproduced below. We include the Disciplinary Rules of the New York Code of Professional Responsibility as an example of a state that continues to retain significant language its old code based rule when it adopted the Model Rules format in 2009.

CALIFORNIA RULES OF PROFESSIONAL CONDUCT (2019)

(Effective November 1, 2018)*

TABLE OF CONTENTS

CLIENT-LAWYER RELATIONSHIP

* Editor's Note. California was long the state with Rules of Professional Conduct that most significantly departed from the format of the ABA Model Rules. On May 10, 2018, the California Supreme Court issued an order approving new Rules of Professional Conduct, which became effective on November 1, 2018. The court's adoption of these 2018 rules overcomes much of the format difference, although as is true in most states, the rules reflect some substantive differences from the ABA Model Rules.

CALIFORNIA RULES

COUNSELOR

ADVOCATE

TRANSACTIONS WITH PERSONS OTHER THAN CLIENTS

LAW FIRMS AND ASSOCIATIONS

PUBLIC SERVICE

INFORMATION ABOUT LEGAL SERVICES

MAINTAINING THE INTEGRITY OF THE PROFESSION

CALIFORNIA RULES OF PROFESSIONAL CONDUCT

CLIENT-LAWYER RELATIONSHIP

Rule 1.0 Purpose and Function of the Rules of Professional Conduct

(a) Purpose.

The following rules are intended to regulate professional conduct of lawyers through discipline. They have been adopted by the Board of Trustees of the State Bar of California and approved by the Supreme Court of California pursuant to Business and Professions Code sections 6076 and 6077 to protect the public, the courts, and the legal profession; protect the integrity of the legal system; and promote the administration of justice and confidence in the legal profession. These rules together with any standards adopted by the Board of Trustees pursuant to these rules shall be binding upon all lawyers.

(b) Function.

(1) A willful violation of any of these rules is a basis for discipline.

(2) The prohibition of certain conduct in these rules is not exclusive. Lawyers are also bound by applicable law including the State Bar Act (Bus. & Prof. Code, § 6000 et seq.) and opinions of California courts.

(3) A violation of a rule does not itself give rise to a cause of action for damages caused by failure to comply with the rule. Nothing in these rules or the Comments to the rules is intended to enlarge or to restrict the law regarding the liability of lawyers to others.

(c) Purpose of Comments.

The comments are not a basis for imposing discipline but are intended only to provide guidance for interpreting and practicing in compliance with the rules.

(d) These rules may be cited and referred to as the "California Rules of Professional Conduct."

Comment

[1] The Rules of Professional Conduct are intended to establish the standards for lawyers for purposes of discipline. (See *Ames v. State Bar* (1973) 8 Cal.3d 910, 917 [106 Cal.Rptr. 489].) Therefore, failure to comply with an obligation or prohibition imposed by a rule is a basis for invoking the disciplinary process. Because the rules are not designed to be a basis for civil liability, a violation of a rule does not itself give rise to a cause of action for enforcement of a rule or for damages caused by failure to comply with the rule. (*Stanley v. Richmond* (1995) 35 Cal.App.4th 1070, 1097 [41 Cal.Rptr.2d 768].) Nevertheless, a lawyer's violation of a rule may be evidence of breach of a lawyer's fiduciary or other substantive legal duty in a non-disciplinary context. (*Ibid.*; see also *Mirabito v. Liccardo* (1992) 4 Cal.App.4th 41, 44 [5 Cal.Rptr.2d 571].) A violation of a rule may have other non-disciplinary consequences. (See, e.g., *Fletcher v. Davis* (2004) 33 Cal.4th 61, 71–72 [14 Cal.Rptr.3d 58] [enforcement of attorney's lien]; *Chambers v. Kay* (2002) 29 Cal.4th 142, 161 [126 Cal.Rptr.2d 536] [enforcement of fee sharing agreement].)

[2] While the rules are intended to regulate professional conduct of lawyers, a violation of a rule can occur when a lawyer is not practicing law or acting in a professional capacity.

[3] A willful violation of a rule does not require that the lawyer intend to violate the rule. (*Phillips v. State Bar* (1989) 49 Cal.3d 944, 952 [264 Cal.Rptr. 346]; and see Bus. & Prof. Code, § 6077.)

[4] In addition to the authorities identified in paragraph (b)(2), opinions of ethics committees in California, although not binding, should be consulted for guidance on proper professional conduct. Ethics opinions and rules and standards promulgated by other jurisdictions and bar associations may also be considered.

[5] The disciplinary standards created by these rules are not intended to address all aspects of a lawyer's professional obligations. A lawyer, as a member of the legal profession, is a representative and advisor of clients, an officer of the legal system and a public citizen having special responsibilities for the quality of justice. A lawyer should be aware of deficiencies in the administration of justice and of the fact that the poor, and sometimes persons* who are not poor cannot afford adequate legal assistance. Therefore, all lawyers are encouraged to devote professional time and resources and use civic influence to ensure equal access to the system of justice for those who because of economic or social barriers cannot afford or secure adequate legal counsel. In meeting this responsibility of the profession, every lawyer should aspire to render at least fifty hours of pro bono publico legal services per year. The lawyer should aim to provide a substantial* majority of such hours to indigent individuals or to nonprofit organizations with a primary purpose of providing services to the poor or on behalf of the poor or disadvantaged. Lawyers may also provide financial support to organizations providing free legal services. (See Bus. & Prof. Code, § 6073.)

Rule 1.0.1 Terminology

(a) "Belief" or "believes" means that the person* involved actually supposes the fact in question to be true. A person's* belief may be inferred from circumstances.

(b) [Reserved]

(c) "Firm" or "law firm" means a law partnership; a professional law corporation; a lawyer acting as a sole proprietorship; an association authorized to practice law; or lawyers employed in a legal services organization or in the legal department, division or office of a corporation, of a government organization, or of another organization.

(d) "Fraud" or "fraudulent" means conduct that is fraudulent under the law of the applicable jurisdiction and has a purpose to deceive.

(e) "Informed consent" means a person's* agreement to a proposed course of conduct after the lawyer has communicated and explained (i) the relevant circumstances and (ii) the material risks, including any actual and reasonably* foreseeable adverse consequences of the proposed course of conduct.

(e-1) "Informed written consent" means that the disclosures and the consent required by paragraph (e) must be in writing.*

(f) "Knowingly," "known," or "knows" means actual knowledge of the fact in question. A person's* knowledge may be inferred from circumstances.

(g) "Partner" means a member of a partnership, a shareholder in a law firm* organized as a professional corporation, or a member of an association authorized to practice law.

(g-1) "Person" has the meaning stated in Evidence Code section 175.

(h) "Reasonable" or "reasonably" when used in relation to conduct by a lawyer means the conduct of a reasonably prudent and competent lawyer.

* An asterisk (*) identifies a word or phrase defined in the terminology rule, rule 1.0.1.

(i) "Reasonable belief" or "reasonably believes" when used in reference to a lawyer means that the lawyer believes the matter in question and that the circumstances are such that the belief is reasonable.

(j) "Reasonably should know" when used in reference to a lawyer means that a lawyer of reasonable prudence and competence would ascertain the matter in question.

(k) "Screened" means the isolation of a lawyer from any participation in a matter, including the timely imposition of procedures within a law firm* that are adequate under the circumstances (i) to protect information that the isolated lawyer is obligated to protect under these rules or other law; and (ii) to protect against other law firm* lawyers and nonlawyer personnel communicating with the lawyer with respect to the matter.

(*l*) "Substantial" when used in reference to degree or extent means a material matter of clear and weighty importance.

(m) "Tribunal" means: (i) a court, an arbitrator, an administrative law judge, or an administrative body acting in an adjudicative capacity and authorized to make a decision that can be binding on the parties involved; or (ii) a special master or other person* to whom a court refers one or more issues and whose decision or recommendation can be binding on the parties if approved by the court.

(n) "Writing" or "written" has the meaning stated in Evidence Code section 250. A "signed" writing includes an electronic sound, symbol, or process attached to or logically associated with a writing and executed, inserted, or adopted by or at the direction of a person* with the intent to sign the writing.

Comment

Firm or Law Firm**

[1] Practitioners who share office space and occasionally consult or assist each other ordinarily would not be regarded as constituting a law firm.* However, if they present themselves to the public in a way that suggests that they are a law firm* or conduct themselves as a law firm,* they may be regarded as a law firm* for purposes of these rules. The terms of any formal agreement between associated lawyers are relevant in determining whether they are a firm,* as is the fact that they have mutual access to information concerning the clients they serve.

[2] The term "of counsel" implies that the lawyer so designated has a relationship with the law firm,* other than as a partner* or associate, or officer or shareholder, that is close, personal, continuous, and regular. Whether a lawyer who is denominated as "of counsel" or by a similar term should be deemed a member of a law firm* for purposes of these rules will also depend on the specific facts. (Compare *People ex rel. Department of Corporations v. Speedee Oil Change Systems, Inc.* (1999) 20 Cal.4th 1135 [86 Cal.Rptr.2d 816] with *Chambers v. Kay* (2002) 29 Cal.4th 142 [126 Cal.Rptr.2d 536].)

*Fraud**

[3] When the terms "fraud"* or "fraudulent"* are used in these rules, it is not necessary that anyone has suffered damages or relied on the misrepresentation or failure to inform because requiring the proof of those elements of fraud* would impede the purpose of certain rules to prevent fraud* or avoid a lawyer assisting in the perpetration of a fraud,* or otherwise frustrate the imposition of discipline on lawyers who engage in fraudulent* conduct. The term "fraud"* or "fraudulent"* when used in these rules does not include merely negligent misrepresentation or negligent failure to apprise another of relevant information.

Informed Consent and Informed Written Consent**

[4] The communication necessary to obtain informed consent* or informed written consent* will vary according to the rule involved and the circumstances giving rise to the need to obtain consent.

* An asterisk (*) identifies a word or phrase defined in the terminology rule, rule 1.0.1.

*Screened**

[5] The purpose of screening* is to assure the affected client, former client, or prospective client that confidential information known* by the personally prohibited lawyer is neither disclosed to other law firm* lawyers or nonlawyer personnel nor used to the detriment of the person* to whom the duty of confidentiality is owed. The personally prohibited lawyer shall acknowledge the obligation not to communicate with any of the other lawyers and nonlawyer personnel in the law firm* with respect to the matter. Similarly, other lawyers and nonlawyer personnel in the law firm* who are working on the matter promptly shall be informed that the screening* is in place and that they may not communicate with the personally prohibited lawyer with respect to the matter. Additional screening* measures that are appropriate for the particular matter will depend on the circumstances. To implement, reinforce and remind all affected law firm* personnel of the presence of the screening,* it may be appropriate for the law firm* to undertake such procedures as a written* undertaking by the personally prohibited lawyer to avoid any communication with other law firm* personnel and any contact with any law firm* files or other materials relating to the matter, written* notice and instructions to all other law firm* personnel forbidding any communication with the personally prohibited lawyer relating to the matter, denial of access by that lawyer to law firm* files or other materials relating to the matter, and periodic reminders of the screen* to the personally prohibited lawyer and all other law firm* personnel.

[6] In order to be effective, screening* measures must be implemented as soon as practical after a lawyer or law firm* knows* or reasonably should know* that there is a need for screening.*

Rule 1.1 Competence

(a) A lawyer shall not intentionally, recklessly, with gross negligence, or repeatedly fail to perform legal services with competence.

(b) For purposes of this rule, "competence" in any legal service shall mean to apply the (i) learning and skill, and (ii) mental, emotional, and physical ability reasonably* necessary for the performance of such service.

(c) If a lawyer does not have sufficient learning and skill when the legal services are undertaken, the lawyer nonetheless may provide competent representation by (i) associating with or, where appropriate, professionally consulting another lawyer whom the lawyer reasonably believes* to be competent, (ii) acquiring sufficient learning and skill before performance is required, or (iii) referring the matter to another lawyer whom the lawyer reasonably believes* to be competent.

(d) In an emergency a lawyer may give advice or assistance in a matter in which the lawyer does not have the skill ordinarily required if referral to, or association or consultation with, another lawyer would be impractical. Assistance in an emergency must be limited to that reasonably* necessary in the circumstances.

Comment

[1] This rule addresses only a lawyer's responsibility for his or her own professional competence. See rules 5.1 and 5.3 with respect to a lawyer's disciplinary responsibility for supervising subordinate lawyers and nonlawyers.

[2] See rule 1.3 with respect to a lawyer's duty to act with reasonable* diligence.

Rule 1.2 Scope of Representation and Allocation of Authority

(a) Subject to rule 1.2.1, a lawyer shall abide by a client's decisions concerning the objectives of representation and, as required by rule 1.4, shall reasonably* consult with the client as to the means by which they are to be pursued. Subject to Business and Professions Code section 6068, subdivision (e)(1) and rule 1.6, a lawyer may take such action on behalf of the client as is impliedly authorized to

* An asterisk (*) identifies a word or phrase defined in the terminology rule, rule 1.0.1.

carry out the representation. A lawyer shall abide by a client's decision whether to settle a matter. Except as otherwise provided by law in a criminal case, the lawyer shall abide by the client's decision, after consultation with the lawyer, as to a plea to be entered, whether to waive jury trial and whether the client will testify.

(b) A lawyer may limit the scope of the representation if the limitation is reasonable* under the circumstances, is not otherwise prohibited by law, and the client gives informed consent.*

Comment

Allocation of Authority between Client and Lawyer

[1] Paragraph (a) confers upon the client the ultimate authority to determine the purposes to be served by legal representation, within the limits imposed by law and the lawyer's professional obligations. (See, e.g., Cal. Const., art. I, § 16; Pen. Code, § 1018.) A lawyer retained to represent a client is authorized to act on behalf of the client, such as in procedural matters and in making certain tactical decisions. A lawyer is not authorized merely by virtue of the lawyer's retention to impair the client's substantive rights or the client's claim itself. (*Blanton v. Womancare, Inc.* (1985) 38 Cal.3d 396, 404 [212 Cal.Rptr. 151, 156].)

[2] At the outset of, or during a representation, the client may authorize the lawyer to take specific action on the client's behalf without further consultation. Absent a material change in circumstances and subject to rule 1.4, a lawyer may rely on such an advance authorization. The client may revoke such authority at any time.

Independence from Client's Views or Activities

[3] A lawyer's representation of a client, including representation by appointment, does not constitute an endorsement of the client's political, economic, social or moral views or activities.

Agreements Limiting Scope of Representation

[4] All agreements concerning a lawyer's representation of a client must accord with the Rules of Professional Conduct and other law. (See, e.g., rules 1.1, 1.8.1, 5.6; see also Cal. Rules of Court, rules 3.35–3.37 [limited scope rules applicable in civil matters generally], 5.425 [limited scope rule applicable in family law matters].)

Rule 1.2.1 Advising or Assisting the Violation of Law

(a) A lawyer shall not counsel a client to engage, or assist a client in conduct that the lawyer knows* is criminal, fraudulent,* or a violation of any law. rule, or ruling of a tribunal.*

(b) Notwithstanding paragraph (a), a lawyer may:

(1) discuss the legal consequences of any proposed course of conduct with a client, and

(2) counsel or assist a client to make a good faith effort to determine the validity, scope, meaning, or application of a law, rule, or ruling of a tribunal.*

Comment

[1] There is a critical distinction under this rule between presenting an analysis of legal aspects of questionable conduct and recommending the means by which a crime or fraud* might be committed with impunity. The fact that a client uses a lawyer's advice in a course of action that is criminal or fraudulent* does not of itself make a lawyer a party to the course of action.

[2] Paragraphs (a) and (b) apply whether or not the client's conduct has already begun and is continuing. In complying with this rule, a lawyer shall not violate the lawyer's duty under Business and Professions Code section 6068, subdivision (a) to uphold the Constitution and laws of the United States and California or the duty of confidentiality as provided in Business and Professions Code

* An asterisk (*) identifies a word or phrase defined in the terminology rule, rule 1.0.1.

section 6068, subdivision (c)(1) and rule 1.6. In some cases, the lawyer's response is limited to the lawyer's right and, where appropriate, duty to resign or withdraw in accordance with rules 1.13 and 1.16.

[3] Paragraph (b) authorizes a lawyer to advise a client in good faith regarding the validity, scope, meaning or application of a law, rule, or ruling of a tribunal* or of the meaning placed upon it by governmental authorities, and of potential consequences to disobedience of the law, rule, or ruling of a tribunal* that the lawyer concludes in good faith to be invalid, as well as legal procedures that may be invoked to obtain a determination of invalidity.

[4] Paragraph (b) also authorizes a lawyer to advise a client on the consequences of violating a law, rule, or ruling of a tribunal* that the client does not contend is unenforceable or unjust in itself, as a means or protesting a law or policy the client finds objectionable. For example, a lawyer may properly advise a client about the consequences of blocking the entrance to a public building as a means of protesting a law or policy the client believes* to be unjust or invalid.

[5] If a lawyer comes to know or reasonably should know that a client expects assistance not permitted by these rules or other law or if the lawyer intends to act contrary to the client's instructions, the lawyer must advise the client regarding the limitations on the lawyer's conduct. (See rule 1.4(a)(4).)

[6] Paragraph (b) permits a lawyer to advise a client regarding the validity, scope, and meaning of California laws that might conflict with federal or tribal law. In the event of such a conflict, the lawyer may assist a client in drafting or administering, or interpreting or complying with California laws, including statutes, regulations, orders, and other state or local provisions, even if the client's actions might violate the conflicting federal or tribal law. If California law conflicts with federal or tribal law, the lawyer must inform the client about related federal or tribal law and policy and under certain circumstances may also be required to provide legal advice to the client regarding the conflict. (See rules 1.1 and 1.4.).

Rule 1.3 Diligence

(a) A lawyer shall not intentionally, repeatedly, recklessly or with gross negligence fail to act with reasonable diligence in representing a client.

(b) For purposes of this rule, "reasonable diligence" shall mean that a lawyer acts with commitment and dedication to the interests of the client and does not neglect or disregard, or unduly delay a legal matter entrusted to the lawyer.

Comment

[1] This rule addresses only a lawyer's responsibility for his or her own professional diligence. See rules 5.1 and 5.3 with respect to a lawyer's disciplinary responsibility for supervising subordinate lawyers and nonlawyers.

[2] See rule 1.1 with respect to a lawyer's duty to perform legal services with competence.

Rule 1.4 Communication with Clients

(a) A lawyer shall:

(1) promptly inform the client of any decision or circumstance with respect to which disclosure or the client's informed consent* is required by these rules or the State Bar Act;

(2) reasonably* consult with the client about the means by which to accomplish the client's objectives in the representation;

* An asterisk (*) identifies a word or phrase defined in the terminology rule, rule 1.0.1.

(3) keep the client reasonably* informed about significant developments relating to the representation, including promptly complying with reasonable* requests for information and copies of significant documents when necessary to keep the client so informed; and

(4) advise the client about any relevant limitation on the lawyer's conduct when the lawyer knows* that the client expects assistance not permitted by the Rules of Professional Conduct or other law.

(b) A lawyer shall explain a matter to the extent reasonably* necessary to permit the client to make informed decisions regarding the representation.

(c) A lawyer may delay transmission of information to a client if the lawyer reasonably believes* that the client would be likely to react in a way that may cause imminent harm to the client or others.

(d) A lawyer's obligation under this rule to provide information and documents is subject to any applicable protective order, non-disclosure agreement, or limitation under statutory or decisional law.

Comment

[1] A lawyer will not be subject to discipline under paragraph (a)(3) of this rule for failing to communicate insignificant or irrelevant information. (See Bus. & Prof. Code, § 6068, subd. (m).) Whether a particular development is significant will generally depend on the surrounding facts and circumstances.

[2] A lawyer may comply with paragraph (a)(3) by providing to the client copies of significant documents by electronic or other means. This rule does not prohibit a lawyer from seeking recovery of the lawyer's expense in any subsequent legal proceeding.

[3] Paragraph (c) applies during a representation and does not alter the obligations applicable at termination of a representation. (See rule 1.16(e)(1).)

[4] This rule is not intended to create, augment, diminish, or eliminate any application of the work product rule. The obligation of the lawyer to provide work product to the client shall be governed by relevant statutory and decisional law.

Rule 1.4.1 Communication of Settlement Offers

(a) A lawyer shall promptly communicate to the lawyer's client:

(1) all terms and conditions of a proposed plea bargain or other dispositive offer made to the client in a criminal matter; and

(2) all amounts, terms, and conditions of any written* offer of settlement made to the client in all other matters.

(b) As used in this rule, "client" includes a person* who possesses the authority to accept an offer of settlement or plea, or, in a class action, all the named representatives of the class.

Comment

An oral offer of settlement made to the client in a civil matter must also be communicated if it is a "significant development" under rule 1.4.

Rule 1.4.2 Disclosure of Professional Liability Insurance

(a) A lawyer who knows* or reasonably should know* that the lawyer does not have professional liability insurance shall inform a client in writing,* at the time of the client's engagement of the lawyer, that the lawyer does not have professional liability insurance.

(b) If notice under paragraph (a) has not been provided at the time of a client's engagement of the lawyer, the lawyer shall inform the client in writing* within thirty days of the date the lawyer knows*

* An asterisk (*) identifies a word or phrase defined in the terminology rule, rule 1.0.1.

or reasonably should know* that the lawyer no longer has professional liability insurance during the representation of the client.

(c) This rule does not apply to:

(1) a lawyer who knows* or reasonably should know* at the time of the client's engagement of the lawyer that the lawyer's legal representation of the client in the matter will not exceed four hours; provided that if the representation subsequently exceeds four hours, the lawyer must comply with paragraphs (a) and (b);

(2) a lawyer who is employed as a government lawyer or in-house counsel when that lawyer is representing or providing legal advice to a client in that capacity;

(3) a lawyer who is rendering legal services in an emergency to avoid foreseeable prejudice to the rights or interests of the client;

(4) a lawyer who has previously advised the client in writing* under paragraph (a) or (b) that the lawyer does not have professional liability insurance.

Comment

[1] The disclosure obligation imposed by paragraph (a) applies with respect to new clients and new engagements with returning clients.

[2] A lawyer may use the following language in making the disclosure required by paragraph (a), and may include that language in a written* fee agreement with the client or in a separate writing:

"Pursuant to rule 1.4.2 of the California Rules of Professional Conduct, I am informing you in writing that I do not have professional liability insurance."

[3] A lawyer may use the following language in making the disclosure required by paragraph (b):

"Pursuant to rule 1.4.2 of the California Rules of Professional Conduct, I am informing you in writing that I no longer have professional liability insurance."

[4] The exception in paragraph (c)(2) for government lawyers and in-house counsels is limited to situations involving direct employment and representation, and does not, for example, apply to outside counsel for a private or governmental entity, or to counsel retained by an insurer to represent an insured. If a lawyer is employed by and provides legal services directly for a private entity or a federal, state or local governmental entity, that entity is presumed to know* whether the lawyer is or is not covered by professional liability insurance.

Rule 1.5 Fees for Legal Services

(a) A lawyer shall not make an agreement for, charge, or collect an unconscionable or illegal fee.

(b) Unconscionability of a fee shall be determined on the basis of all the facts and circumstances existing at the time the agreement is entered into except where the parties contemplate that the fee will be affected by later events. The factors to be considered in determining the unconscionability of a fee include without limitation the following:

(1) whether the lawyer engaged in fraud* or overreaching in negotiating or setting the fee;

(2) whether the lawyer has failed to disclose material facts;

(3) the amount of the fee in proportion to the value of the services performed;

(4) the relative sophistication of the lawyer and the client;

(5) the novelty and difficulty of the questions involved, and the skill requisite to perform the legal service properly;

* An asterisk (*) identifies a word or phrase defined in the terminology rule, rule 1.0.1.

(6) the likelihood, if apparent to the client, that the acceptance of the particular employment will preclude other employment by the lawyer;

(7) the amount involved and the results obtained;

(8) the time limitations imposed by the client or by the circumstances;

(9) the nature and length of the professional relationship with the client;

(10) the experience, reputation, and ability of the lawyer or lawyers performing the services;

(11) whether the fee is fixed or contingent;

(12) the time and labor required; and

(13) whether the client gave informed consent* to the fee.

(c) A lawyer shall not make an agreement for, charge, or collect:

(1) any fee in a family law matter, the payment or amount of which is contingent upon the securing of a dissolution or declaration of nullity of a marriage or upon the amount of spousal or child support, or property settlement in lieu thereof; or

(2) a contingent fee for representing a defendant in a criminal case.

(d) A lawyer may make an agreement for, charge, or collect a fee that is denominated as "earned on receipt" or "non-refundable," or in similar terms, only if the fee is a true retainer and the client agrees in writing* after disclosure that the client will not be entitled to a refund of all or part of the fee charged. A true retainer is a fee that a client pays to a lawyer to ensure the lawyer's availability to the client during a specified period or on a specified matter, but not to any extent as compensation for legal services performed or to be performed.

(e) A lawyer may make an agreement for, charge, or collect a flat fee for specified legal services. A flat fee is a fixed amount that constitutes complete payment for the performance of described services regardless of the amount of work ultimately involved, and which may be paid in whole or in part in advance of the lawyer providing those services.

Comment

Prohibited Contingent Fees

[1] Paragraph (c)(1) does not preclude a contract for a contingent fee for legal representation in connection with the recovery of post-judgment balances due under child or spousal support or other financial orders.

Payment of Fees in Advance of Services

[2] Rule 1.15(a) and (b) govern whether a lawyer must deposit in a trust account a fee paid in advance.

[3] When a lawyer-client relationship terminates, the lawyer must refund the unearned portion of a fee. (See rule 1.16(e)(2).)

Division of Fee

[4] A division of fees among lawyers is governed by rule 1.5.1.

Written Fee Agreements*

[5] Some fee agreements must be in writing* to be enforceable. (See, e.g., Bus. & Prof. Code, §§ 6147 and 6148.)

* An asterisk (*) identifies a word or phrase defined in the terminology rule, rule 1.0.1.

Rule 1.5.1 Fee Divisions Among Lawyers

(a) Lawyers who are not in the same law firm* shall not divide a fee for legal services unless:

(1) the lawyers enter into a written* agreement to divide the fee;

(2) the client has consented in writing,* either at the time the lawyers enter into the agreement to divide the fee or as soon thereafter as reasonably* practicable, after a full written* disclosure to the client of: (i) the fact that a division of fees will be made; (ii) the identity of the lawyers or law firms* that are parties to the division; and (iii) the terms of the division; and

(3) the total fee charged by all lawyers is not increased solely by reason of the agreement to divide fees.

(b) This rule does not apply to a division of fees pursuant to court order.

Comment

The writing* requirements of paragraphs (a)(1) and (a)(2) may be satisfied by one or more writings.*

Rule 1.6 Confidential Information of a Client

(a) A lawyer shall not reveal information protected from disclosure by Business and Professions Code section 6068, subdivision (e)(1) unless the client gives informed consent,* or the disclosure is permitted by paragraph (b) of this rule.

(b) A lawyer may, but is not required to, reveal information protected by Business and Professions Code section 6068, subdivision (e)(1) to the extent that the lawyer reasonably believes* the disclosure is necessary to prevent a criminal act that the lawyer reasonably believes* is likely to result in death of, or substantial* bodily harm to, an individual, as provided in paragraph (c).

(c) Before revealing information protected by Business and Professions Code section 6068, subdivision (e)(1) to prevent a criminal act as provided in paragraph (b), a lawyer shall, if reasonable* under the circumstances:

(1) make a good faith effort to persuade the client: (i) not to commit or to continue the criminal act; or (ii) to pursue a course of conduct that will prevent the threatened death or substantial* bodily harm; or do both (i) and (ii); and

(2) inform the client, at an appropriate time, of the lawyer's ability or decision to reveal information protected by Business and Professions Code section 6068, subdivision (e)(1) as provided in paragraph (b).

(d) In revealing information protected by Business and Professions Code section 6068, subdivision (e)(1) as provided in paragraph (b), the lawyer's disclosure must be no more than is necessary to prevent the criminal act, given the information known* to the lawyer at the time of the disclosure.

(e) A lawyer who does not reveal information permitted by paragraph (b) does not violate this rule.

Comment

Duty of confidentiality

[1] Paragraph (a) relates to a lawyer's obligations under Business and Professions Code section 6068, subdivision (e)(1), which provides it is a duty of a lawyer: "To maintain inviolate the confidence, and at every peril to himself or herself to preserve the secrets, of his or her client." A lawyer's duty to preserve the confidentiality of client information involves public policies of paramount importance. (*In Re Jordan* (1974) 12 Cal.3d 575, 580 [116 Cal.Rptr. 371].) Preserving the confidentiality of client information contributes to the trust that is the hallmark of the lawyer-client relationship. The client is thereby encouraged to seek legal assistance and to communicate fully and frankly with the lawyer even as to embarrassing or detrimental subjects. The lawyer needs this information to represent the

* An asterisk (*) identifies a word or phrase defined in the terminology rule, rule 1.0.1.

client effectively and, if necessary, to advise the client to refrain from wrongful conduct. Almost without exception, clients come to lawyers in order to determine their rights and what is, in the complex of laws and regulations, deemed to be legal and correct. Based upon experience, lawyers know* that almost all clients follow the advice given, and the law is upheld. Paragraph (a) thus recognizes a fundamental principle in the lawyer-client relationship, that, in the absence of the client's informed consent,* a lawyer must not reveal information protected by Business and Professions Code section 6068, subdivision (e)(1). (See, e.g., *Commercial Standard Title Co. v. Superior Court* (1979) 92 Cal.App.3d 934, 945 [155 Cal.Rptr.393].)

Lawyer-client confidentiality encompasses the lawyer-client privilege, the work-product doctrine and ethical standards of confidentiality

[2] The principle of lawyer-client confidentiality applies to information a lawyer acquires by virtue of the representation, whatever its source, and encompasses matters communicated in confidence by the client, and therefore protected by the lawyer-client privilege, matters protected by the work product doctrine, and matters protected under ethical standards of confidentiality, all as established in law, rule and policy. (See *In the Matter of Johnson* (Rev. Dept. 2000) 4 Cal. State Bar Ct. Rptr. 179; *Goldstein v. Lees* (1975) 46 Cal.App.3d 614, 621 [120 Cal.Rptr. 253].) The lawyer-client privilege and work-product doctrine apply in judicial and other proceedings in which a lawyer may be called as a witness or be otherwise compelled to produce evidence concerning a client. A lawyer's ethical duty of confidentiality is not so limited in its scope of protection for the lawyer-client relationship of trust and prevents a lawyer from revealing the client's information even when not subjected to such compulsion. Thus, a lawyer may not reveal such information except with the informed consent* of the client or as authorized or required by the State Bar Act, these rules, or other law.

Narrow exception to duty of confidentiality under this rule

[3] Notwithstanding the important public policies promoted by lawyers adhering to the core duty of confidentiality, the overriding value of life permits disclosures otherwise prohibited by Business and Professions Code section 6068, subdivision (e)(1). Paragraph (b) is based on Business and Professions Code section 6068, subdivision (e)(2), which narrowly permits a lawyer to disclose information protected by Business and Professions Code section 6068, subdivision (e)(1) even without client consent. Evidence Code section 956.5, which relates to the evidentiary lawyer-client privilege, sets forth a similar express exception. Although a lawyer is not permitted to reveal information protected by section 6068, subdivision (e)(1) concerning a client's past, completed criminal acts, the policy favoring the preservation of human life that underlies this exception to the duty of confidentiality and the evidentiary privilege permits disclosure to prevent a future or ongoing criminal act.

Lawyer not subject to discipline for revealing information protected by Business and Professions Code section 6068, subdivision (e)(1) as permitted under this rule

[4] Paragraph (b) reflects a balancing between the interests of preserving client confidentiality and of preventing a criminal act that a lawyer reasonably believes* is likely to result in death or substantial* bodily harm to an individual. A lawyer who reveals information protected by Business and Professions Code section 6068, subdivision (e)(1) as permitted under this rule is not subject to discipline.

No duty to reveal information protected by Business and Professions Code section 6068, subdivision (e)(1)

[5] Neither Business and Professions Code section 6068, subdivision (e)(2) nor paragraph (b) imposes an affirmative obligation on a lawyer to reveal information protected by Business and Professions Code section 6068, subdivision (e)(1) in order to prevent harm. A lawyer may decide not to reveal such information. Whether a lawyer chooses to reveal information protected by section 6068, subdivision (e)(1) as permitted under this rule is a matter for the individual lawyer to decide, based on all the facts and circumstances, such as those discussed in Comment [6] of this rule.

* An asterisk (*) identifies a word or phrase defined in the terminology rule, rule 1.0.1.

Whether to reveal information protected by Business and Professions Code section 6068, subdivision (e) as permitted under paragraph (b)

[6] Disclosure permitted under paragraph (b) is ordinarily a last resort, when no other available action is reasonably* likely to prevent the criminal act. Prior to revealing information protected by Business and Professions Code section 6068, subdivision (e)(1) as permitted by paragraph (b), the lawyer must, if reasonable* under the circumstances, make a good faith effort to persuade the client to take steps to avoid the criminal act or threatened harm. Among the factors to be considered in determining whether to disclose information protected by section 6068, subdivision (e)(1) are the following:

(1) the amount of time that the lawyer has to make a decision about disclosure;

(2) whether the client or a third-party has made similar threats before and whether they have ever acted or attempted to act upon them;

(3) whether the lawyer believes* the lawyer's efforts to persuade the client or a third person* not to engage in the criminal conduct have or have not been successful;

(4) the extent of adverse effect to the client's rights under the Fifth, Sixth and Fourteenth Amendments of the United States Constitution and analogous rights and privacy rights under Article I of the Constitution of the State of California that may result from disclosure contemplated by the lawyer;

(5) the extent of other adverse effects to the client that may result from disclosure contemplated by the lawyer; and

(6) the nature and extent of information that must be disclosed to prevent the criminal act or threatened harm.

A lawyer may also consider whether the prospective harm to the victim or victims is imminent in deciding whether to disclose the information protected by section 6068, subdivision (e)(1). However, the imminence of the harm is not a prerequisite to disclosure and a lawyer may disclose the information protected by section 6068, subdivision (e)(1) without waiting until immediately before the harm is likely to occur.

Whether to counsel client or third person not to commit a criminal act reasonably* likely to result in death or substantial* bodily harm*

[7] Subparagraph (c)(1) provides that before a lawyer may reveal information protected by Business and Professions Code section 6068, subdivision (e)(1), the lawyer must, if reasonable* under the circumstances, make a good faith effort to persuade the client not to commit or to continue the criminal act, or to persuade the client to otherwise pursue a course of conduct that will prevent the threatened death or substantial* bodily harm, including persuading the client to take action to prevent a third person* from committing or continuing a criminal act. If necessary, the client may be persuaded to do both. The interests protected by such counseling are the client's interests in limiting disclosure of information protected by section 6068, subdivision (e) and in taking responsible action to deal with situations attributable to the client. If a client, whether in response to the lawyer's counseling or otherwise, takes corrective action—such as by ceasing the client's own criminal act or by dissuading a third person* from committing or continuing a criminal act before harm is caused—the option for permissive disclosure by the lawyer would cease because the threat posed by the criminal act would no longer be present. When the actor is a nonclient or when the act is deliberate or malicious, the lawyer who contemplates making adverse disclosure of protected information may reasonably* conclude that the compelling interests of the lawyer or others in their own personal safety preclude personal contact with the actor. Before counseling an actor who is a nonclient, the lawyer should, if reasonable* under the circumstances, first advise the client of the lawyer's intended course of action. If a client or another person* has already acted but the intended harm has not yet occurred, the lawyer

---

* An asterisk (*) identifies a word or phrase defined in the terminology rule, rule 1.0.1.

should consider, if reasonable* under the circumstances, efforts to persuade the client or third person* to warn the victim or consider other appropriate action to prevent the harm. Even when the lawyer has concluded that paragraph (b) does not permit the lawyer to reveal information protected by section 6068, subdivision (e)(1), the lawyer nevertheless is permitted to counsel the client as to why it may be in the client's best interest to consent to the attorney's disclosure of that information.

Disclosure of information protected by Business and Professions Code section 6068, subdivision (e)(1) must be no more than is reasonably necessary to prevent the criminal act*

[8] Paragraph (d) requires that disclosure of information protected by Business and Professions Code section 6068, subdivision (e) as permitted by paragraph (b), when made, must be no more extensive than is necessary to prevent the criminal act. Disclosure should allow access to the information to only those persons* who the lawyer reasonably believes* can act to prevent the harm. Under some circumstances, a lawyer may determine that the best course to pursue is to make an anonymous disclosure to the potential victim or relevant law-enforcement authorities. What particular measures are reasonable* depends on the circumstances known* to the lawyer. Relevant circumstances include the time available, whether the victim might be unaware of the threat, the lawyer's prior course of dealings with the client, and the extent of the adverse effect on the client that may result from the disclosure contemplated by the lawyer.

Informing client pursuant to subparagraph (c)(2) of lawyer's ability or decision to reveal information protected by Business and Professions Code section 6068, subdivision (e)(1)

[9] A lawyer is required to keep a client reasonably* informed about significant developments regarding the representation. (See rule 1.4; Bus. & Prof. Code, § 6068, subd. (m).) Paragraph (c)(2), however, recognizes that under certain circumstances, informing a client of the lawyer's ability or decision to reveal information protected by section 6068, subdivision (e)(1) as permitted in paragraph (b) would likely increase the risk of death or substantial* bodily harm, not only to the originally-intended victims of the criminal act, but also to the client or members of the client's family, or to the lawyer or the lawyer's family or associates. Therefore, paragraph (c)(2) requires a lawyer to inform the client of the lawyer's ability or decision to reveal information protected by section 6068, subdivision (e)(1) as permitted in paragraph (b) only if it is reasonable* to do so under the circumstances. Paragraph (c)(2) further recognizes that the appropriate time for the lawyer to inform the client may vary depending upon the circumstances. (See Comment [10] of this rule.) Among the factors to be considered in determining an appropriate time, if any, to inform a client are:

(1) whether the client is an experienced user of legal services;

(2) the frequency of the lawyer's contact with the client;

(3) the nature and length of the professional relationship with the client;

(4) whether the lawyer and client have discussed the lawyer's duty of confidentiality or any exceptions to that duty;

(5) the likelihood that the client's matter will involve information within paragraph (b);

(6) the lawyer's belief,* if applicable, that so informing the client is likely to increase the likelihood that a criminal act likely to result in the death of, or substantial* bodily harm to, an individual; and

(7) the lawyer's belief,* if applicable, that good faith efforts to persuade a client not to act on a threat have failed.

Avoiding a chilling effect on the lawyer-client relationship

[10] The foregoing flexible approach to the lawyer's informing a client of his or her ability or decision to reveal information protected by Business and Professions Code section 6068, subdivision (e)(1) recognizes the concern that informing a client about limits on confidentiality may have a chilling effect

* An asterisk (*) identifies a word or phrase defined in the terminology rule, rule 1.0.1.

on client communication. (See Comment [1].) To avoid that chilling effect, one lawyer may choose to inform the client of the lawyer's ability to reveal information protected by section 6068, subdivision (e)(1) as early as the outset of the representation, while another lawyer may choose to inform a client only at a point when that client has imparted information that comes within paragraph (b), or even choose not to inform a client until such time as the lawyer attempts to counsel the client as contemplated in Comment [7]. In each situation, the lawyer will have satisfied the lawyer's obligation under paragraph (c)(2), and will not be subject to discipline.

Informing client that disclosure has been made; termination of the lawyer-client relationship

[11] When a lawyer has revealed information protected by Business and Professions Code section 6068, subdivision (e) as permitted in paragraph (b), in all but extraordinary cases the relationship between lawyer and client that is based on trust and confidence will have deteriorated so as to make the lawyer's representation of the client impossible. Therefore, when the relationship has deteriorated because of the lawyer's disclosure, the lawyer is required to seek to withdraw from the representation, unless the client has given informed consent* to the lawyer's continued representation. The lawyer normally must inform the client of the fact of the lawyer's disclosure. If the lawyer has a compelling interest in not informing the client, such as to protect the lawyer, the lawyer's family or a third person* from the risk of death or substantial* bodily harm, the lawyer must withdraw from the representation. (See rule 1.16.)

Other consequences of the lawyer's disclosure

[12] Depending upon the circumstances of a lawyer's disclosure of information protected by Business and Professions Code section 6068, subdivision (e)(1) as permitted by this rule, there may be other important issues that a lawyer must address. For example, a lawyer who is likely to testify as a witness in a matter involving a client must comply with rule. 3.7. Similarly, the lawyer must also consider his or her duties of loyalty and competence. (See rules 1.7 and 1.1.)

Other exceptions to confidentiality under California law

[13] This rule is not intended to augment, diminish, or preclude any other exceptions to the duty to preserve information protected by Business and Professions Code section 6068, subdivision (e)(1) recognized under California law.

Rule 1.7 Conflict of Interest: Current Clients

(a) A lawyer shall not, without informed written consent* from each client and compliance with paragraph (d), represent a client if the representation is directly adverse to another client in the same or a separate matter.

(b) A lawyer shall not, without informed written consent* from each affected client and compliance with paragraph (d), represent a client if there is a significant risk the lawyer's representation of the client will be materially limited by the lawyer's responsibilities to or relationships with another client, a former client or a third person,* or by the lawyer's own interests.

(c) Even when a significant risk requiring a lawyer to comply with paragraph (b) is not present, a lawyer shall not represent a client without written* disclosure of the relationship to the client and compliance with paragraph (d) where:

(1) the lawyer has, or knows* that another lawyer in the lawyer's firm* has, a legal, business, financial, professional, or personal relationship with or responsibility to a party or witness in the same matter; or

(2) the lawyer knows* or reasonably should know* that another party's lawyer is a spouse, parent, child, or sibling of the lawyer, lives with the lawyer, is a client of the lawyer or another lawyer in the lawyer's firm,* or has an intimate personal relationship with the lawyer.

* An asterisk (*) identifies a word or phrase defined in the terminology rule, rule 1.0.1.

(d) Representation is permitted under this rule only if the lawyer complies with paragraphs (a), (b), and (c), and:

(1) the lawyer reasonably believes* that the lawyer will be able to provide competent and diligent representation to each affected client;

(2) the representation is not prohibited by law; and

(3) the representation does not involve the assertion of a claim by one client against another client represented by the lawyer in the same litigation or other proceeding before a tribunal.

(e) For purposes of this rule, "matter" includes any judicial or other proceeding, application, request for a ruling or other determination, contract, transaction, claim, controversy, investigation, charge, accusation, arrest, or other deliberation, decision, or action that is focused on the interests of specific persons,* or a discrete and identifiable class of persons.*

Comment

[1] Loyalty and independent judgment are essential elements in the lawyer's relationship to a client. The duty of undivided loyalty to a current client prohibits undertaking representation directly adverse to that client without that client's informed written consent.* Thus, absent consent, a lawyer may not act as an advocate in one matter against a person* the lawyer represents in some other matter, even when the matters are wholly unrelated. (See *Flatt v. Superior Court* (1994) 9 Cal.4th 275 [36 Cal.Rptr.2d 537].) A directly adverse conflict under paragraph (a) can arise in a number of ways, for example, when: (i) a lawyer accepts representation of more than one client in a matter in which the interests of the clients actually conflict; (ii) a lawyer, while representing a client, accepts in another matter the representation of a person* who, in the first matter, is directly adverse to the lawyer's client; or (iii) a lawyer accepts representation of a person* in a matter in which an opposing party is a client of the lawyer or the lawyer's law firm.* Similarly, direct adversity can arise when a lawyer cross-examines a nonparty witness who is the lawyer's client in another matter, if the examination is likely to harm or embarrass the witness. On the other hand, simultaneous representation in unrelated matters of clients whose interests are only economically adverse, such as representation of competing economic enterprises in unrelated litigation, does not ordinarily constitute a conflict of interest and thus may not require informed written consent* of the respective clients.

[2] Paragraphs (a) and (b) apply to all types of legal representations, including the concurrent representation of multiple parties in litigation or in a single transaction or in some other common enterprise or legal relationship. Examples of the latter include the formation of a partnership for several partners* or a corporation for several shareholders, the preparation of a pre-nuptial agreement, or joint or reciprocal wills for a husband and wife, or the resolution of an "uncontested" marital dissolution. If a lawyer initially represents multiple clients with the informed written consent* as required under paragraph (b), and circumstances later develop indicating that direct adversity exists between the clients, the lawyer must obtain further informed written consent* of the clients under paragraph (a).

[3] In *State Farm Mutual Automobile Insurance Company v. Federal Insurance Company* (1999) 72 Cal.App.4th 1422 [86 Cal.Rptr.2d 20], the court held that subparagraph (C)(3) of predecessor rule 3–310 was violated when a lawyer, retained by an insurer to defend one suit, and while that suit was still pending, filed a direct action against the same insurer in an unrelated action without securing the insurer's consent. Notwithstanding *State Farm*, paragraph (a) does not apply with respect to the relationship between an insurer and a lawyer when, in each matter, the insurer's interest is only as an indemnity provider and not as a direct party to the action.

[4] Even where there is no direct adversity, a conflict of interest requiring informed written consent under paragraph (b) exists if there is a significant risk that a lawyer's ability to consider, recommend or carry out an appropriate course of action for the client will be materially limited as a result of the lawyer's other responsibilities, interests, or relationships, whether legal, business, financial,

* An asterisk (*) identifies a word or phrase defined in the terminology rule, rule 1.0.1.

professional, or personal. For example, a lawyer's obligations to two or more clients in the same matter, such as several individuals seeking to form a joint venture, may materially limit the lawyer's ability to recommend or advocate all possible positions that each might take because of the lawyer's duty of loyalty to the other clients. The risk is that the lawyer may not be able to offer alternatives that would otherwise be available to each of the clients. The mere possibility of subsequent harm does not itself require disclosure and informed written consent.* The critical questions are the likelihood that a difference in interests exists or will eventuate and, if it does, whether it will materially interfere with the lawyer's independent professional judgment in considering alternatives or foreclose courses of action that reasonably* should be pursued on behalf of each client. The risk that the lawyer's representation may be materially limited may also arise from present or past relationships between the lawyer, or another member of the lawyer's firm*, with a party, a witness, or another person* who may be affected substantially by the resolution of the matter.

[5] Paragraph (c) requires written* disclosure of any of the specified relationships even if there is not a significant risk the relationship will materially limit the lawyer's representation of the client. However, if the particular circumstances present a significant risk the relationship will materially limit the lawyer's representation of the client, informed written consent* is required under paragraph (b).

[6] Ordinarily paragraphs (a) and (b) will not require informed written consent* simply because a lawyer takes inconsistent legal positions in different tribunals* at different times on behalf of different clients. Advocating a legal position on behalf of a client that might create precedent adverse to the interests of another client represented by a lawyer in an unrelated matter is not sufficient, standing alone, to create a conflict of interest requiring informed written consent.* Informed written consent* may be required, however, if there is a significant risk that: (i) the lawyer may temper the lawyer's advocacy on behalf of one client out of concern about creating precedent adverse to the interest of another client; or (ii) the lawyer's action on behalf of one client will materially limit the lawyer's effectiveness in representing another client in a different case, for example, when a decision favoring one client will create a precedent likely to seriously weaken the position taken on behalf of the other client. Factors relevant in determining whether the clients' informed written consent* is required include: the courts and jurisdictions where the different cases are pending, whether a ruling in one case would have a precedential effect on the other case, whether the legal question is substantive or procedural, the temporal relationship between the matters, the significance of the legal question to the immediate and long-term interests of the clients involved, and the clients' reasonable* expectations in retaining the lawyer.

[7] Other rules and laws may preclude the disclosures necessary to obtain the informed written consent* or provide the information required to permit representation under this rule. (See, e.g., Bus. & Prof. Code, § 6068, subd. (e)(1) and rule 1.6.) If such disclosure is precluded, representation subject to paragraph (a), (b), or (c) of this rule is likewise precluded.

[8] Paragraph (d) imposes conditions that must be satisfied even if informed written consent* is obtained as required by paragraphs (a) or (b) or the lawyer has informed the client in writing* as required by paragraph (c). There are some matters in which the conflicts are such that even informed written consent* may not suffice to permit representation. (See *Woods v. Superior Court* (1983) 149 Cal.App.3d 931 [197 Cal.Rptr. 185]; *Klemm v. Superior Court* (1977) 75 Cal.App.3d 893 [142 Cal.Rptr. 509]; *Ishmael v. Millington* (1966) 241 Cal.App.2d 520 [50 Cal.Rptr. 592].)

[9] This rule does not preclude an informed written consent* to a future conflict in compliance with applicable case law. The effectiveness of an advance consent is generally determined by the extent to which the client reasonably* understands the material risks that the consent entails. The more comprehensive the explanation of the types of future representations that might arise and the actual and reasonably* foreseeable adverse consequences to the client of those representations, the greater the likelihood that the client will have the requisite understanding. The experience and sophistication

* An asterisk (*) identifies a word or phrase defined in the terminology rule, rule 1.0.1.

of the client giving consent, as well as whether the client is independently represented in connection with giving consent, are also relevant in determining whether the client reasonably* understands the risks involved in giving consent. An advance consent cannot be effective if the circumstances that materialize in the future make the conflict nonconsentable under paragraph (d). A lawyer who obtains from a client an advance consent that complies with this rule will have all the duties of a lawyer to that client except as expressly limited by the consent. A lawyer cannot obtain an advance consent to incompetent representation. (See rule 1.8.8.)

[10] A material change in circumstances relevant to application of this rule may trigger a requirement to make new disclosures and, where applicable, obtain new informed written consents.* In the absence of such consents, depending on the circumstances, the lawyer may have the option to withdraw from one or more of the representations in order to avoid the conflict. The lawyer must seek court approval where necessary and take steps to minimize harm to the clients. See rule 1.16. The lawyer must continue to protect the confidences of the clients from whose representation the lawyer has withdrawn. (See rule 1.9(c).)

[11] For special rules governing membership in a legal service organization, see rule 6.3; and for work in conjunction with certain limited legal services programs, see rule 6.5.

Rule 1.8.1 Business Transactions with a Client and Pecuniary Interests Adverse to a Client

A lawyer shall not enter into a business transaction with a client, or knowingly* acquire an ownership, possessory, security or other pecuniary interest adverse to a client, unless each of the following requirements has been satisfied:

(a) the transaction or acquisition and its terms are fair and reasonable* to the client and the terms and the lawyer's role in the transaction or acquisition are fully disclosed and transmitted in writing* to the client in a manner that should reasonably* have been understood by the client;

(b) the client either is represented in the transaction or acquisition by an independent lawyer of the client's choice or the client is advised in writing* to seek the advice of an independent lawyer of the client's choice and is given a reasonable* opportunity to seek that advice; and

(c) the client thereafter provides informed written consent* to the terms of the transaction or acquisition, and to the lawyer's role in it.

Comment

[1] A lawyer has an "other pecuniary interest adverse to a client" within the meaning of this rule when the lawyer possesses a legal right to significantly impair or prejudice the client's rights or interests without court action. (See *Fletcher v. Davis* (2004) 33 Cal.4th 61, 68 [14 Cal.Rptr.3d 58]; see also Bus. & Prof. Code, § 6175.3 [Sale of financial products to elder or dependent adult clients; Disclosure]; Fam. Code, §§ 2033–2034 [Attorney lien on community real property].) However, this rule does not apply to a charging lien given to secure payment of a contingency fee. (See *Plummer v. Day/Eisenberg, LLP* (2010) 184 Cal.App.4th 38 [108 Cal.Rptr.3d 455].)

[2] For purposes of this rule, factors that can be considered in determining whether a lawyer is independent include whether the lawyer: (i) has a financial interest in the transaction or acquisition; and (ii) has a close legal, business, financial, professional or personal relationship with the lawyer seeking the client's consent.

[3] Fairness and reasonableness under paragraph (a) are measured at the time of the transaction or acquisition based on the facts that then exist.

[4] In some circumstances, this rule may apply to a transaction entered into with a former client. (Compare *Hunniecutt v. State Bar* (1988) 44 Cal.3d 362, 370–71 ["[W]hen an attorney enters into a transaction with a former client regarding a fund which resulted from the attorney's representation,

* An asterisk (*) identifies a word or phrase defined in the terminology rule, rule 1.0.1.

it is reasonable to examine the relationship between the parties for indications of special trust resulting therefrom. We conclude that if there is evidence that the client placed his trust in the attorney because of the representation, an attorney-client relationship exists for the purposes of [the predecessor rule) even if the representation has otherwise ended [and] It appears that [the client] became a target of [the lawyer's] solicitation because he knew, through his representation of her, that she had recently received the settlement fund [and the court also found the client to be unsophisticated]."] with *Wallis v. State Bar* (1942) 21 Cal.2d 322 [finding lawyer not subject to discipline for entering into business transaction with a former client where the former client was a sophisticated businesswoman who had actively negotiated for terms she thought desirable, and the transaction was not connected with the matter on which the lawyer previously represented her].)

[5] This rule does not apply to the agreement by which the lawyer is retained by the client, unless the agreement confers on the lawyer an ownership, possessory, security, or other pecuniary interest adverse to the client. Such an agreement is governed, in part, by rule 1.5. This rule also does not apply to an agreement to advance to or deposit with a lawyer a sum to be applied to fees, or costs or other expenses, to be incurred in the future. Such agreements are governed, in part, by rules 1.5 and 1.15.

[6] This rule does not apply: (i) where a lawyer and client each make an investment on terms offered by a third person* to the general public or a significant portion thereof; or (ii) to standard commercial transactions for products or services that a lawyer acquires from a client on the same terms that the client generally markets them to others, where the lawyer has no advantage in dealing with the client.

Rule 1.8.2 Use of Current Client's Information

A lawyer shall not use a client's information protected by Business and Professions Code section 6068, subdivision (e)(1) to the disadvantage of the client unless the client gives informed consent,* except as permitted by these rules or the State Bar Act.

Comment

A lawyer violates the duty of loyalty by using information protected by Business and Professions Code section 6068, subdivision (e)(1) to the disadvantage of a current client.

Rule 1.8.3 Gifts From Client

(a) A lawyer shall not:

(1) solicit a client to make a substantial* gift, including a testamentary gift, to the lawyer or a person* related to the lawyer, unless the lawyer or other recipient of the gift is related to the client, or

(2) prepare on behalf of a client an instrument giving the lawyer or a person* related to the lawyer any substantial* gift, unless (i) the lawyer or other recipient of the gift is related to the client, or (ii) the client has been advised by an independent lawyer who has provided a certificate of independent review that complies with the requirements of Probate Code section 21384.

(b) For purposes of this rule, related persons* include a person* who is "related by blood or affinity" as that term is defined in California Probate Code section 21374, subdivision (a).

Comment

[1] A lawyer or a person* related to a lawyer may accept a gift from the lawyer's client, subject to general standards of fairness and absence of undue influence. A lawyer also does not violate this rule merely by engaging in conduct that might result in a client making a gift, such as by sending the client a wedding announcement. Discipline is appropriate where impermissible influence occurs. (See *Magee v. State Bar* (1962) 58 Cal.2d 423 [24 Cal.Rptr. 839].)

---

* An asterisk (*) identifies a word or phrase defined in the terminology rule, rule 1.0.1.

[2] This rule does not prohibit a lawyer from seeking to have the lawyer or a partner* or associate of the lawyer named as executor of the client's estate or to another potentially lucrative fiduciary position. Such appointments, however, will be subject to rule 1.7(b) and (c).

Rule 1.8.4 [Reserved]

Rule 1.8.5 Payment of Personal or Business Expenses Incurred by or for a Client

(a) A lawyer shall not directly or indirectly pay or agree to pay, guarantee, or represent that the lawyer or lawyer's law firm* will pay the personal or business expenses of a prospective or existing client.

(b) Notwithstanding paragraph (a), a lawyer may:

(1) pay or agree to pay such expenses to third persons,* from funds collected or to be collected for the client as a result of the representation, with the consent of the client;

(2) after the lawyer is retained by the client, agree to lend money to the client based on the client's written* promise to repay the loan, provided the lawyer complies with rules 1.7(b), 1.7(c), and 1.8.1 before making the loan or agreeing to do so;

(3) advance the costs of prosecuting or defending a claim or action, or of otherwise protecting or promoting the client's interests, the repayment of which may be contingent on the outcome of the matter; and

(4) pay the costs of prosecuting or defending a claim or action, or of otherwise protecting or promoting the interests of an indigent person* in a matter in which the lawyer represents the client.

(c) "Costs" within the meaning of paragraphs (b)(3) and (b)(4) are not limited to those costs that are taxable or recoverable under any applicable statute or rule of court but may include any reasonable* expenses of litigation, including court costs, and reasonable* expenses in preparing for litigation or in providing other legal services to the client.

(d) Nothing in this rule shall be deemed to limit the application of rule 1.8.9.

Rule 1.8.6 Compensation from One Other Than Client

A lawyer shall not enter into an agreement for, charge, or accept compensation for representing a client from one other than the client unless:

(a) there is no interference with the lawyer's independent professional judgment or with the lawyer-client relationship;

(b) information is protected as required by Business and Professions Code section 6068, subdivision (e)(1) and rule 1.6; and

(c) the lawyer obtains the client's informed written consent* at or before the time the lawyer has entered into the agreement for, charged, or accepted the compensation, or as soon thereafter as reasonably* practicable, provided that no disclosure or consent is required if:

(1) nondisclosure or the compensation is otherwise authorized by law or a court order; or

(2) the lawyer is rendering legal services on behalf of any public agency or nonprofit organization that provides legal services to other public agencies or the public.

* An asterisk (*) identifies a word or phrase defined in the terminology rule, rule 1.0.1.

Comment

[1] A lawyer's responsibilities in a matter are owed only to the client except where the lawyer also represents the payor in the same matter. With respect to the lawyer's additional duties when representing both the client and the payor in the same matter, see rule 1.7.

[2] A lawyer who is exempt from disclosure and consent requirements under paragraph (c) nevertheless must comply with paragraphs (a) and (b).

[3] This rule is not intended to abrogate existing relationships between insurers and insureds whereby the insurer has the contractual right to unilaterally select counsel for the insured, where there is no conflict of interest. (See *San Diego Navy Federal Credit Union v. Cumis Insurance Society* (1984) 162 Cal.App.3d 358 [208 Cal.Rptr. 494].).

[4] In some limited circumstances, a lawyer might not be able to obtain client consent before the lawyer has entered into an agreement for, charged, or accepted compensation, as required by this rule. This might happen, for example, when a lawyer is retained or paid by a family member on behalf of an incarcerated client or in certain commercial settings, such as when a lawyer is retained by a creditors' committee involved in a corporate debt restructuring and agrees to be compensated for any services to be provided to other similarly situated creditors who have not yet been identified. In such limited situations, paragraph (c) permits the lawyer to comply with this rule as soon thereafter as is reasonably* practicable.

[5] This rule is not intended to alter or diminish a lawyer's obligations under rule 5.4(c).

Rule 1.8.7 Aggregate Settlements

(a) A lawyer who represents two or more clients shall not enter into an aggregate settlement of the claims of or against the clients, or in a criminal case an aggregate agreement as to guilty or nolo contendere pleas, unless each client gives informed written consent.* The lawyer's disclosure shall include the existence and nature of all the claims or pleas involved and of the participation of each person* in the settlement.

(b) This rule does not apply to class action settlements subject to court approval.

Rule 1.8.8 Limiting Liability to Client

A lawyer shall not:

(a) Contract with a client prospectively limiting the lawyer's liability to the client for the lawyer's professional malpractice; or

(b) Settle a claim or potential claim for the lawyer's liability to a client or former client for the lawyer's professional malpractice, unless the client or former client is either:

(1) represented by an independent lawyer concerning the settlement; or

(2) advised in writing* by the lawyer to seek the advice of an independent lawyer of the client's choice regarding the settlement and given a reasonable* opportunity to seek that advice.

Comment

[1] Paragraph (b) does not absolve the lawyer of the obligation to comply with other law. (See, e.g., Bus. & Prof. Code, § 6090.5.)

[2] This rule does not apply to customary qualifications and limitations in legal opinions and memoranda, nor does it prevent a lawyer from reasonably limiting the scope of the lawyer's representation. (See rule 1.2(b).)

---

* An asterisk (*) identifies a word or phrase defined in the terminology rule, rule 1.0.1.

Rule 1.8.9 Purchasing Property at a Foreclosure or a Sale Subject to Judicial Review

(a) A lawyer shall not directly or indirectly purchase property at a probate, foreclosure, receiver's, trustee's, or judicial sale in an action or proceeding in which such lawyer or any lawyer affiliated by reason of personal, business, or professional relationship with that lawyer or with that lawyer's law firm* is acting as a lawyer for a party or as executor, receiver, trustee, administrator, guardian, or conservator.

(b) A lawyer shall not represent the seller at a probate, foreclosure, receiver, trustee, or judicial sale in an action or proceeding in which the purchaser is a spouse or relative of the lawyer or of another lawyer in the lawyer's law firm* or is an employee of the lawyer or the lawyer's law firm.*

(c) This rule does not prohibit a lawyer's participation in transactions that are specifically authorized by and comply with Probate Code sections 9880 through 9885, but such transactions remain subject to the provisions of rules 1.8.1 and 1.7.

Comment

A lawyer may lawfully participate in a transaction involving a probate proceeding which concerns a client by following the process described in Probate Code sections 9880–9885. These provisions, which permit what would otherwise be impermissible self-dealing by specific submissions to and approval by the courts, must be strictly followed in order to avoid violation of this rule.

Rule 1.8.10 Sexual Relations With Current Client

(a) A lawyer shall not engage in sexual relations with a current client who is not the lawyer's spouse or registered domestic partner, unless a consensual sexual relationship existed between them when the lawyer-client relationship commenced.

(b) For purposes of this rule, "sexual relations" means sexual intercourse or the touching of an intimate part of another person* for the purpose of sexual arousal, gratification, or abuse.

(c) If a person* other than the client alleges a violation of this rule, no Notice of Disciplinary Charges may be filed by the State Bar against a lawyer under this rule until the State Bar has attempted to obtain the client's statement regarding, and has considered, whether the client would be unduly burdened by further investigation or a charge.

Comment

[1] Although this rule does not apply to a consensual sexual relationship that exists when a lawyer-client relationship commences, the lawyer nevertheless must comply with all other applicable rules. (See, e.g., rules 1.1, 1.7, and 2.1.)

[2] When the client is an organization, this rule applies to a lawyer for the organization (whether inside counsel or outside counsel) who has sexual relations with a constituent of the organization who supervises, directs or regularly consults with that lawyer concerning the organization's legal matters. (See rule 1.13.)

[3] Business and Professions Code section 6106.9, including the requirement that the complaint be verified, applies to charges under subdivision (a) of that section. This rule and the statute impose different obligations.

Rule 1.8.11 Imputation of Prohibitions Under Rules 1.8.1 to 1.8.9

While lawyers are associated in a law firm,* a prohibition in rules 1.8.1 through 1.8.9 that applies to any one of them shall apply to all of them.

---

* An asterisk (*) identifies a word or phrase defined in the terminology rule, rule 1.0.1.

Comment

A prohibition on conduct by an individual lawyer in rules 1.8.1 through 1.8.9 also applies to all lawyers associated in a law firm* with the personally prohibited lawyer. For example, one lawyer in a law firm* may not enter into a business transaction with a client of another lawyer associated in the law firm* without complying with rule 1.8.1, even if the first lawyer is not personally involved in the representation of the client. This rule does not apply to rule 1.8.10 since the prohibition in that rule is personal and is not applied to associated lawyers.

Rule 1.9 Duties to Former Clients

(a) A lawyer who has formerly represented a client in a matter shall not thereafter represent another person* in the same or a substantially related matter in which that person's* interests are materially adverse to the interests of the former client unless the former client gives informed written consent.*

(b) A lawyer shall not knowingly* represent a person* in the same or a substantially related matter in which a firm* with which the lawyer formerly was associated had previously represented a client

(1) whose interests are materially adverse to that person;* and

(2) about whom the lawyer had acquired information protected by Business and Professions Code section 6068, subdivision (e) and rules 1.6 and 1.9(c) that is material to the matter; unless the former client gives informed written consent.*

(c) A lawyer who has formerly represented a client in a matter or whose present or former firm* has formerly represented a client in a matter shall not thereafter:

(1) use information protected by Business and Professions Code section 6068, subdivision (e) and rule 1.6 acquired by virtue of the representation of the former client to the disadvantage of the former client except as these rules or the State Bar Act would permit with respect to a current client, or when the information has become generally known;* or

(2) reveal information protected by Business and Professions Code section 6068, subdivision (e) and rule 1.6 acquired by virtue of the representation of the former client except as these rules or the State Bar Act permit with respect to a current client.

Comment

[1] After termination of a lawyer-client relationship, the lawyer owes two duties to a former client. The lawyer may not (i) do anything that will injuriously affect the former client in any matter in which the lawyer represented the former client, or (ii) at any time use against the former client knowledge or information acquired by virtue of the previous relationship. (See *Oasis West Realty, LLC v. Goldman* (2011) 51 Cal.4th 811 [124 Cal.Rptr.3d 256]; *Wutchumna Water Co. v. Bailey* (1932) 216 Cal. 564 [15 P.2d 505].) For example, (i) a lawyer could not properly seek to rescind on behalf of a new client a contract drafted on behalf of the former client and (ii) a lawyer who has prosecuted an accused person* could not represent the accused in a subsequent civil action against the government concerning the same matter. (See also Bus. & Prof. Code, § 6131; 18 U.S.C. § 207(a).) These duties exist to preserve a client's trust in the lawyer and to encourage the client's candor in communications with the lawyer.

[2] For what constitutes a "matter" for purposes of this rule, see rule 1.7(e).

[3] Two matters are "the same or substantially related" for purposes of this rule if they involve a substantial* risk of a violation of one of the two duties to a former client described above in Comment [1]. For example, this will occur: (i) if the matters involve the same transaction or legal dispute or other work performed by the lawyer for the former client; or (ii) if the lawyer normally would have obtained information in the prior representation that is protected by Business and Professions Code section 6068, subdivision (e) and rule 1.6, and the lawyer would be expected to use or disclose that information in the subsequent representation because it is material to the subsequent representation.

---

* An asterisk (*) identifies a word or phrase defined in the terminology rule, rule 1.0.1.

[4] Paragraph (b) addresses a lawyer's duties to a client who has become a former client because the lawyer no longer is associated with the law firm* that represents or represented the client. In that situation, the lawyer has a conflict of interest only when the lawyer involved has actual knowledge of information protected by Business and Professions Code section 6068, subdivision (e) and rules 1.6 and 1.9(c). Thus, if a lawyer while with one firm* acquired no knowledge or information relating to a particular client of the firm,* and that lawyer later joined another firm,* neither the lawyer individually nor lawyers in the second firm* would violate this rule by representing another client in the same or a related matter even though the interests of the two clients conflict. See rule 1.10(b) for the restrictions on lawyers in a firm* once a lawyer has terminated association with the firm.*

[5] The fact that information can be discovered in a public record does not, by itself, render that information generally known* under paragraph (c). (See, e.g., *In the Matter of Johnson* (Review Dept. 2000) 4 Cal. State Bar Ct. Rptr. 179.)

[6] With regard to the effectiveness of an advance consent, see rule 1.7, Comment [9]. With regard to imputation of conflicts to lawyers in a firm* with which a lawyer is or was formerly associated, see rule 1.10. Current and former government lawyers must comply with this rule to the extent required by rule 1.11.

Rule 1.10 Imputation Of Conflicts Of Interest: General Rule

(a) While lawyers are associated in a firm,* none of them shall knowingly* represent a client when any one of them practicing alone would be prohibited from doing so by rules 1.7 or 1.9, unless

(1) the prohibition is based on a personal interest of the prohibited lawyer and does not present a significant risk of materially limiting the representation of the client by the remaining lawyers in the firm;* or

(2) the prohibition is based upon rule 1.9(a) or (b) and arises out of the prohibited lawyer's association with a prior firm,* and

(i) the prohibited lawyer did not substantially participate in the same or a substantially related matter;

(ii) the prohibited lawyer is timely screened* from any participation in the matter and is apportioned no part of the fee therefrom; and

(iii) written* notice is promptly given to any affected former client to enable the former client to ascertain compliance with the provisions of this rule, which shall include a description of the screening* procedures employed; and an agreement by the firm* to respond promptly to any written* inquiries or objections by the former client about the screening* procedures.

(b) When a lawyer has terminated an association with a firm,* the firm* is not prohibited from thereafter representing a person* with interests materially adverse to those of a client represented by the formerly associated lawyer and not currently represented by the firm,* unless:

(1) the matter is the same or substantially related to that in which the formerly associated lawyer represented the client; and

(2) any lawyer remaining in the firm* has information protected by Business and Professions Code section 6068, subdivision (e) and rules 1.6 and 1.9(c) that is material to the matter.

(c) A prohibition under this rule may be waived by each affected client under the conditions stated in rule 1.7.

(d) The imputation of a conflict of interest to lawyers associated in a firm* with former or current government lawyers is governed by rule 1.11.

---

* An asterisk (*) identifies a word or phrase defined in the terminology rule, rule 1.0.1.

Comment

[1] In determining whether a prohibited lawyer's previously participation was substantial,* a number of factors should be considered, such as the lawyer's level of responsibility in the prior matter, the duration of the lawyer's participation, the extent to which the lawyer advised or had personal contact with the former client, and the extent to which the lawyer was exposed to confidential information of the former client likely to be material in the current matter.

[2] Paragraph (a) does not prohibit representation by others in the law firm* where the person* prohibited from involvement in a matter is a nonlawyer, such as a paralegal or legal secretary. Nor does paragraph (a) prohibit representation if the lawyer is prohibited from acting because of events before the person* became a lawyer, for example, work that the person* did as a law student. Such persons,* however, ordinarily must be screened* from any personal participation in the matter. (See rules 1.0.1(k) and 5.3.)

[3] Paragraph (a)(2)(ii) does not prohibit the screened* lawyer from receiving a salary or partnership share established by prior independent agreement, but that lawyer may not receive compensation directly related to the matter in which the lawyer is prohibited.

[4] Where a lawyer is prohibited from engaging in certain transactions under rules 1.8.1 through 1.8.9, rule 1.8.11, and not this rule, determines whether that prohibition also applies to other lawyers associated in a firm* with the personally prohibited lawyer.

[5] The responsibilities of managerial and supervisory lawyers prescribed by rules 5.1 and 5.3 apply to screening* arrangements implemented under this rule.

[6] Standards for disqualification, and whether in a particular matter (1) a lawyer's conflict will be imputed to other lawyers in the same firm,* or (2) the use of a timely screen* is effective to avoid that imputation, are also the subject of statutes and case law. (See, e.g., Code Civ. Proc., § 128, subd. (a)(5); Pen. Code, § 1424; *In re Charlisse C.* (2008) 45 Cal.4th 145 [84 Cal.Rptr.3d 597]; *Rhaburn v. Superior Court* (2006) 140 Cal.App.4th 1566 [45 Cal.Rptr.3d 464]; *Kirk v. First American Title Ins. Co.* (2010) 183 Cal.App.4th 776 [108 Cal.Rptr.3d 620].)

Rule 1.11 Special Conflicts of Interest for Former and Current Government Officials and Employees

(a) Except as law may otherwise expressly permit, a lawyer who has formerly served as a public official or employee of the government:

(1) is subject to rule 1.9(c); and

(2) shall not otherwise represent a client in connection with a matter in which the lawyer participated personally and substantially as a public official or employee, unless the appropriate government agency gives its informed written consent* to the representation. This paragraph shall not apply to matters governed by rule 1.12(a).

(b) When a lawyer is prohibited from representation under paragraph (a), no lawyer in a firm* with which that lawyer is associated may knowingly* undertake or continue representation in such a matter unless:

(1) the personally prohibited lawyer is timely screened* from any participation in the matter and is apportioned no part of the fee therefrom; and

(2) written* notice is promptly given to the appropriate government agency to enable it to ascertain compliance with the provisions of this rule

(c) Except as law may otherwise expressly permit, a lawyer who was a public official or employee and, during that employment, acquired information that the lawyer knows* is confidential government information about a person,* may not represent a private client whose interests are

* An asterisk (*) identifies a word or phrase defined in the terminology rule, rule 1.0.1.

adverse to that person* in a matter in which the information could be used to the material disadvantage of that person.* As used in this rule, the term "confidential government information" means information that has been obtained under governmental authority, that, at the time this rule is applied, the government is prohibited by law from disclosing to the public, or has a legal privilege not to disclose, and that is not otherwise available to the public. A firm* with which that lawyer is associated may undertake or continue representation in the matter only if the personally prohibited lawyer is timely screened* from any participation in the matter and is apportioned no part of the fee therefrom.

(d) Except as law may otherwise expressly permit, a lawyer currently serving as a public official or employee:

(1) is subject to rules 1.7 and 1.9; and

(2) shall not:

(i) participate in a matter in which the lawyer participated personally and substantially while in private practice or nongovernmental employment, unless the appropriate government agency gives its informed written consent;* or

(ii) negotiate for private employment with any person* who is involved as a party, or as a lawyer for a party, or with a law firm* for a party, in a matter in which the lawyer is participating personally and substantially, except that a lawyer serving as a law clerk to a judge, other adjudicative officer or arbitrator may negotiate for private employment as permitted by rule 1.12(b) and subject to the conditions stated in rule 1.12(b).

Comment

[1] Rule 1.10 is not applicable to the conflicts of interest addressed by this rule.

[2] For what constitutes a "matter" for purposes of this rule, see rule 1.7(e).

[3] Paragraphs (a)(2) and (d)(2) apply regardless of whether a lawyer is adverse to a former client. Both provisions apply when the former public official or employee of the government has personally and substantially participated in the matter. Personal participation includes both direct participation and the supervision of a subordinate's participation. Substantial* participation requires that the lawyer's involvement be of significance to the matter. Participation may be substantial* even though it is not determinative of the outcome of a particular matter. However, it requires more than official responsibility, knowledge, perfunctory involvement, or involvement on an administrative or peripheral issue. A finding of substantiality should be based not only on the effort devoted to the matter, but also on the importance of the effort. Personal and substantial* participation may occur when, for example, a lawyer participates through decision, approval, disapproval, recommendation, investigation or the rendering of advice in a particular matter.

[4] By requiring a former government lawyer to comply with rule 1.9(c), paragraph (a)(1) protects information obtained while working for the government to the same extent as information learned while representing a private client. This provision applies regardless of whether the lawyer was working in a "legal" capacity. Thus, information learned by the lawyer while in public service in an administrative, policy, or advisory position also is covered by paragraph (a)(1).

[5] Paragraph (c) operates only when the lawyer in question has actual knowledge of the information; it does not operate with respect to information that merely could be imputed to the lawyer.

[6] When a lawyer has been employed by one government agency and then moves to a second government agency, it may be appropriate to treat that second agency as another client for purposes of this rule, as when a lawyer is employed by a city and subsequently is employed by a federal agency. Because conflicts of interest are governed by paragraphs (a) and (b), the latter agency is required to

---

* An asterisk (*) identifies a word or phrase defined in the terminology rule, rule 1.0.1.

screen* the lawyer. Whether two government agencies should be regarded as the same or different clients for conflict of interest purposes is beyond the scope of these rules. (See rule 1.13, Comment [6]; see also *Civil Service Commission v. Superior Court* (1984) 163 Cal.App.3d 70, 76–78 [209 Cal.Rptr. 159].)

[7] Paragraphs (b) and (c) do not prohibit a lawyer from receiving a salary or partnership share established by prior independent agreement, but that lawyer may not receive compensation directly relating the lawyer's compensation to the fee in the matter in which the lawyer is personally prohibited from participating.

[8] Paragraphs (a) and (d) do not prohibit a lawyer from jointly representing a private party and a government agency when doing so is permitted by rule 1.7 and is not otherwise prohibited by law.

[9] A lawyer serving as a public official or employee of the government may participate in a matter in which the lawyer participated substantially while in private practice or non-governmental employment only if: (i) the government agency gives its informed written consent* as required by paragraph (d)(2)(i); and (ii) the former client gives its informed written consent* as required by rule 1.9, to which the lawyer is subject by paragraph (d)(1).

[10] This rule is not intended to address whether in a particular matter: (i) a lawyer's conflict under paragraph (d) will be imputed to other lawyers serving in the same governmental agency; or (ii) the use of a timely screen* will avoid that imputation. The imputation and screening* rules for lawyers moving from private practice into government service under paragraph (d) are left to be addressed by case law and its development. (See *City & County of San Francisco v. Cobra Solutions, Inc.* (2006) 38 Cal.4th 839, 847, 851–54 [43 Cal.Rptr.3d 776]; *City of Santa Barbara v. Superior Court* (2004) 122 Cal.App.4th 17, 26–27 [18 Cal.Rptr.3d 403].) Regarding the standards for recusals of prosecutors in criminal matters, see Penal Code section 1424; *Haraguchi v. Superior Court* (2008) 43 Cal. 4th 706, 711–20 [76 Cal.Rptr.3d 250]; and *Hollywood v. Superior Court* (2008) 43 Cal.4th 721, 727–35 [76 Cal.Rptr.3d 264]. Concerning prohibitions against former prosecutors participating in matters in which they served or participated in as prosecutor, see, e.g., Business and Professions Code section 6131 and 18 United States Code section 207(a).

Rule 1.12 Former Judge, Arbitrator, Mediator, Or Other Third-Party Neutral

(a) Except as stated in paragraph (d), a lawyer shall not represent anyone in connection with a matter in which the lawyer participated personally and substantially as a judge or other adjudicative officer, judicial staff attorney or law clerk to such a person* or as an arbitrator, mediator, or other third-party neutral, unless all parties to the proceeding give informed written consent.*

(b) A lawyer shall not seek employment from any person* who is involved as a party or as lawyer for a party, or with a law firm* for a party, in a matter in which the lawyer is participating personally and substantially as a judge or other adjudicative officer or as an arbitrator, mediator, or other third party neutral. A lawyer serving as a judicial staff attorney or law clerk to a judge or other adjudicative officer may seek employment from a party, or with a lawyer or a law firm* for a party, in a matter in which the staff attorney or clerk is participating personally and substantially, but only with the approval of the court.

(c) If a lawyer is prohibited from representation by paragraph (a), other lawyers in a firm* with which that lawyer is associated may knowingly* undertake or continue representation in the matter only if:

(1) the prohibition does not arise from the lawyer's service as a mediator or settlement judge;

(2) the prohibited lawyer is timely screened* from any participation in the matter and is apportioned no part of the fee therefrom; and

* An asterisk (*) identifies a word or phrase defined in the terminology rule, rule 1.0.1.

(3) written* notice is promptly given to the parties and any appropriate tribunal* to enable them to ascertain compliance with the provisions of this rule.

(d) An arbitrator selected as a partisan of a party in a multimember arbitration panel is not prohibited from subsequently representing that party.

Comment

[1] Paragraphs (a) and (b) apply when a former judge or other adjudicative officer, or a judicial staff attorney or law clerk to such a person,* or an arbitrator, mediator, or other third-party neutral, has personally and substantially participated in the matter. Personal participation includes both direct participation and the supervision of a subordinate's participation, as may occur in a chambers with several staff attorneys or law clerks. Substantial* participation requires that the lawyer's involvement was of significance to the matter. Participation may be substantial* even though it was not determinative of the outcome of a particular case or matter. A finding of substantiality should be based not only on the effort devoted to the matter, but also on the importance of the effort. Personal and substantial* participation may occur when, for example, the lawyer participated through decision, recommendation, or the rendering of advice on a particular case or matter. However, a judge who was a member of a multi-member court, and thereafter left judicial office to practice law, is not prohibited from representing a client in a matter pending in the court, but in which the former judge did not participate, or acquire material confidential information. The fact that a former judge exercised administrative responsibility in a court also does not prevent the former judge from acting as a lawyer in a matter where the judge had previously exercised remote or incidental administrative responsibility that did not affect the merits, such as uncontested procedural duties typically performed by a presiding or supervising judge or justice. The term "adjudicative officer" includes such officials as judges pro tempore, referees, and special masters.

[2] Other law or codes of ethics governing third-party neutrals may impose more stringent standards of personal or imputed disqualification. (See rule 2.4.)

[3] Paragraph (c)(2) does not prohibit the screened* lawyer from receiving a salary or partnership share established by prior independent agreement, but that lawyer may not receive compensation directly related to the matter in which the lawyer is personally prohibited from participating.

Rule 1.13 Organization as Client

(a) A lawyer employed or retained by an organization shall conform his or her representation to the concept that the client is the organization itself, acting through its duly authorized directors, officers, employees, members, shareholders, or other constituents overseeing the particular engagement.

(b) If a lawyer representing an organization knows* that a constituent is acting, intends to act or refuses to act in a matter related to the representation in a manner that the lawyer knows* or reasonably should know* is (i) a violation of a legal obligation to the organization or a violation of law reasonably* imputable to the organization, and (ii) likely to result in substantial* injury to the organization, the lawyer shall proceed as is reasonably* necessary in the best lawful interest of the organization. Unless the lawyer reasonably believes* that it is not necessary in the best lawful interest of the organization to do so, the lawyer shall refer the matter to higher authority in the organization, including, if warranted by the circumstances, to the highest authority that can act on behalf of the organization as determined by applicable law.

(c) In taking any action pursuant to paragraph (b), the lawyer shall not reveal information protected by Business and Professions Code section 6068, subdivision (e).

(d) If, despite the lawyer's actions in accordance with paragraph (b), the highest authority that can act on behalf of the organization insists upon action, or fails to act, in a manner that is a violation of a legal obligation to the organization or a violation of law reasonably* imputable to the organization, and is likely to result in substantial* injury to the organization, the lawyer shall continue to proceed

* An asterisk (*) identifies a word or phrase defined in the terminology rule, rule 1.0.1.

as is reasonably* necessary in the best lawful interests of the organization. The lawyer's response may include the lawyer's right and, where appropriate, duty to resign or withdraw in accordance with rule 1.16.

(e) A lawyer who reasonably believes* that he or she has been discharged because of the lawyer's actions taken pursuant to paragraph (b), or who resigns or withdraws under circumstances described in paragraph (d), shall proceed as the lawyer reasonably believes* necessary to assure that the organization's highest authority is informed of the lawyer's discharge, resignation, or withdrawal.

(f) In dealing with an organization's constituents, a lawyer representing the organization shall explain the identity of the lawyer's client whenever the lawyer knows* or reasonably should know* that the organization's interests are adverse to those of the constituent(s) with whom the lawyer is dealing.

(g) A lawyer representing an organization may also represent any of its constituents, subject to the provisions of rules 1.7, 1.8.2, 1.8.6, and 1.8.7. If the organization's consent to the dual representation is required by any of these rules, the consent shall be given by an appropriate official, constituent, or body of the organization other than the individual who is to be represented, or by the shareholders.

Comment

The Entity as the Client

[1] This rule applies to all forms of private, public and governmental organizations. (See Comment [6].) An organizational client can only act through individuals who are authorized to conduct its affairs. The identity of an organization's constituents will depend on its form, structure, and chosen terminology. For example, in the case of a corporation, constituents include officers, directors, employees and shareholders. In the case of other organizational forms, constituents include the equivalents of officers, directors, employees, and shareholders. For purposes of this rule, any agent or fiduciary authorized to act on behalf of an organization is a constituent of the organization.

[2] A lawyer ordinarily must accept decisions an organization's constituents make on behalf of the organization, even if the lawyer questions their utility or prudence. It is not within the lawyer's province to make decisions on behalf of the organization concerning policy and operations, including ones entailing serious risk. A lawyer, however, has a duty to inform the client of significant developments related to the representation under Business and Professions Code section 6068, subdivision (m) and rule 1.4. Even when a lawyer is not obligated to proceed in accordance with paragraph (b), the lawyer may refer to higher authority, including the organization's highest authority, matters that the lawyer reasonably believes* are sufficiently important to refer in the best interest of the organization subject to Business and Professions Code section 6068, subdivision (e) and rule 1.6.

[3] Paragraph (b) distinguishes between knowledge of the conduct and knowledge of the consequences of that conduct. When a lawyer knows* of the conduct, the lawyer's obligations under paragraph (b) are triggered when the lawyer knows* or reasonably should know* that the conduct is (i) a violation of a legal obligation to the organization, or a violation of law reasonably* imputable to the organization, and (ii) likely to result in substantial* injury to the organization.

[4] In determining how to proceed under paragraph (b), the lawyer should consider the seriousness of the violation and its potential consequences, the responsibility in the organization and the apparent motivation of the person* involved, the policies of the organization concerning such matters, and any other relevant considerations. Ordinarily, referral to a higher authority would be necessary. In some circumstances, however, the lawyer may ask the constituent to reconsider the matter. For example, if the circumstances involve a constituent's innocent misunderstanding of law and subsequent acceptance of the lawyer's advice, the lawyer may reasonably* conclude that the best interest of the organization does not require that the matter be referred to higher authority. If a constituent persists in conduct contrary to the lawyer's advice, it will be necessary for the lawyer to take steps to have the

* An asterisk (*) identifies a word or phrase defined in the terminology rule, rule 1.0.1.

matter reviewed by a higher authority in the organization. If the matter is of sufficient seriousness and importance or urgency to the organization, referral to higher authority in the organization may be necessary even if the lawyer has not communicated with the constituent. For the responsibility of a subordinate lawyer in representing an organization, see rule 5.2.

[5] In determining how to proceed in the best lawful interests of the organization, a lawyer should consider the extent to which the organization should be informed of the circumstances, the actions taken by the organization with respect to the matter and the direction the lawyer has received from the organizational client.

Governmental Organizations

[6] It is beyond the scope of this rule to define precisely the identity of the client and the lawyer's obligations when representing a governmental agency. Although in some circumstances the client may be a specific agency, it may also be a branch of government or the government as a whole. In a matter involving the conduct of government officials, a government lawyer may have authority under applicable law to question such conduct more extensively than that of a lawyer for a private organization in similar circumstances. Duties of lawyers employed by the government or lawyers in military service may be defined by statutes and regulations. In addition, a governmental organization may establish internal organizational rules and procedures that identify an official, agency, organization, or other person* to serve as the designated recipient of whistle-blower reports from the organization's lawyers, consistent with Business and Professions Code section 6068, subdivision (e) and rule 1.6. This rule is not intended to limit that authority.

Rule 1.14 [Reserved]

Rule 1.15 Safekeeping Funds and Property of Clients and Other Persons*

(a) All funds received or held by a lawyer or law firm* for the benefit of a client, or other person* to whom the lawyer owes a contractual, statutory, or other legal duty, including advances for fees, costs and expenses, shall be deposited in one or more identifiable bank accounts labeled "Trust Account" or words of similar import, maintained in the State of California, or, with written* consent of the client, in any other jurisdiction where there is a substantial* relationship between the client or the client's business and the other jurisdiction.

(b) Notwithstanding paragraph (a), a flat fee paid in advance for legal services may be deposited in a lawyer's or law firm's operating account, provided:

(1) the lawyer or law firm* discloses to the client in writing* (i) that the client has a right under paragraph (a) to require that the flat fee be deposited in an identified trust account until the fee is earned, and (ii) that the client is entitled to a refund of any amount of the fee that has not been earned in the event the representation is terminated or the services for which the fee has been paid are not completed; and

(2) if the flat fee exceeds $1,000.00, the client's agreement to deposit the flat fee in the lawyer's operating account and the disclosures required by paragraph (b)(1) are set forth in a writing* signed by the client.

(c) Funds belonging to the lawyer or the law firm shall not be deposited or otherwise commingled with funds held in a trust account except:

(1) funds reasonably* sufficient to pay bank charges; and

(2) funds belonging in part to a client or other person* and in part presently or potentially to the lawyer or the law firm,* in which case the portion belonging to the lawyer or law firm* must be withdrawn at the earliest reasonable* time after the lawyer or law firm's interest in that portion becomes fixed. However, if a client or other person* disputes the lawyer or law firm's right

* An asterisk (*) identifies a word or phrase defined in the terminology rule, rule 1.0.1.

to receive a portion of trust funds, the disputed portion shall not be withdrawn until the dispute is finally resolved.

(d) A lawyer shall:

(1) promptly notify a client or other person* of the receipt of funds, securities, or other property in which the lawyer knows* or reasonably should know* the client or other person* has an interest;

(2) identify and label securities and properties of a client or other person* promptly upon receipt and place them in a safe deposit box or other place of safekeeping as soon as practicable;

(3) maintain complete records of all funds, securities, and other property of a client or other person* coming into the possession of the lawyer or law firm;*

(4) promptly account in writing* to the client or other person* for whom the lawyer holds funds or property;

(5) preserve records of all funds and property held by a lawyer or law firm* under this rule for a period of no less than five years after final appropriate distribution of such funds or property;

(6) comply with any order for an audit of such records issued pursuant to the Rules of Procedure of the State Bar; and

(7) promptly distribute, as requested by the client or other person,* any undisputed funds or property in the possession of the lawyer or law firm* that the client or other person* is entitled to receive.

(e) The Board of Trustees of the State Bar shall have the authority to formulate and adopt standards as to what "records" shall be maintained by lawyers and law firms* in accordance with subparagraph (d)(3). The standards formulated and adopted by the Board, as from time to time amended, shall be effective and binding on all lawyers.

Standards:

Pursuant to this rule, the Board of Trustees of the State Bar adopted the following standards, effective November 1, 2018, as to what "records" shall be maintained by lawyers and law firms* in accordance with paragraph (d)(3).

(1) A lawyer shall, from the date of receipt of funds of the client or other person* through the period ending five years from the date of appropriate disbursement of such funds, maintain:

(a) a written* ledger for each client or other person* on whose behalf funds are held that sets forth:

(i) the name of such client or other person;*

(ii) the date, amount and source of all funds received on behalf of such client or other person;*

(iii) the date, amount, payee and purpose of each disbursement made on behalf of such client or other person;* and

(iv) the current balance for such client or other person;*

(b) a written* journal for each bank account that sets forth:

(i) the name of such account;

(ii) the date, amount and client or other person* affected by each debit and credit; and

(iii) the current balance in such account;

---

* An asterisk (*) identifies a word or phrase defined in the terminology rule, rule 1.0.1.

(c) all bank statements and cancelled checks for each bank account; and

(d) each monthly reconciliation (balancing) of (a), (b), and (c).

(2) A lawyer shall, from the date of receipt of all securities and other properties held for the benefit of client or other person* through the period ending five years from the date of appropriate disbursement of such securities and other properties, maintain a written* journal that specifies:

(a) each item of security and property held;

(b) the person* on whose behalf the security or property is held;

(c) the date of receipt of the security or property;

(d) the date of distribution of the security or property; and

(e) person* to whom the security or property was distributed.

Comment

[1] Whether a lawyer owes a contractual, statutory or other legal duty under paragraph (a) to hold funds on behalf of a person* other than a client in situations where client funds are subject to a third-party lien will depend on the relationship between the lawyer and the third-party, whether the lawyer has assumed a contractual obligation to the third person* and whether the lawyer has an independent obligation to honor the lien under a statute or other law. In certain circumstances, a lawyer may be civilly liable when the lawyer has notice of a lien and disburses funds in contravention of the lien. (See *Kaiser Foundation Health Plan, Inc. v. Aguiluz* (1996) 47 Cal.App.4th 302 [54 Cal.Rptr.2d 665].) However, civil liability by itself does not establish a violation of this rule. (Compare *Johnstone v. State Bar of California* (1966) 64 Cal.2d 153, 155–156 [49 Cal.Rptr. 97] [" 'When an attorney assumes a fiduciary relationship and violates his duty in a manner that would justify disciplinary action if the relationship had been that of attorney and client, he may properly be disciplined for his misconduct.' "] with *Crooks v. State Bar* (1970) 3 Cal.3d 346, 358 [90 Cal.Rptr. 600] [lawyer who agrees to act as escrow or stakeholder for a client and a third-party owes a duty to the nonclient with regard to held funds].)

[2] As used in this rule, "advances for fees" means a payment intended by the client as an advance payment for some or all of the services that the lawyer is expected to perform on the client's behalf. With respect to the difference between a true retainer and a flat fee, which is one type of advance fee, see rule 1.5(d) and (e). Subject to rule 1.5, a lawyer or law firm* may enter into an agreement that defines when or how an advance fee is earned and may be withdrawn from the client trust account.

[3] Absent written* disclosure and the client's agreement in a writing* signed by the client as provided in paragraph (b), a lawyer must deposit a flat fee paid in advance of legal services in the lawyer's trust account. Paragraph (b) does not apply to advance payment for costs and expenses. Paragraph (b) does not alter the lawyer's obligations under paragraph (d) or the lawyer's burden to establish that the fee has been earned.

Rule 1.16 Declining Or Terminating Representation

(a) Except as stated in paragraph (c), a lawyer shall not represent a client or, where representation has commenced, shall withdraw from the representation of a client if:

(1) the lawyer knows* or reasonably should know* that the client is bringing an action, conducting a defense, asserting a position in litigation, or taking an appeal, without probable cause and for the purpose of harassing or maliciously injuring any person;*

(2) the lawyer knows* or reasonably should know* that the representation will result in violation of these rules or of the State Bar Act;

* An asterisk (*) identifies a word or phrase defined in the terminology rule, rule 1.0.1.

(3) the lawyer's mental or physical condition renders it unreasonably difficult to carry out the representation effectively; or

(4) the client discharges the lawyer.

(b) Except as stated in paragraph (c), a lawyer may withdraw from representing a client if:

(1) the client insists upon presenting a claim or defense in litigation, or asserting a position or making a demand in a non-litigation matter, that is not warranted under existing law and cannot be supported by good faith argument for an extension, modification, or reversal of existing law;

(2) the client either seeks to pursue a criminal or fraudulent* course of conduct or has used the lawyer's services to advance a course of conduct that the lawyer reasonably believes* was a crime or fraud;*

(3) the client insists that the lawyer pursue a course of conduct that is criminal or fraudulent;*

(4) the client by other conduct renders it unreasonably difficult for the lawyer to carry out the representation effectively;

(5) the client breaches a material term of an agreement with, or obligation, to the lawyer relating to the representation, and the lawyer has given the client a reasonable* warning after the breach that the lawyer will withdraw unless the client fulfills the agreement or performs the obligation;

(6) the client knowingly* and freely assents to termination of the representation;

(7) the inability to work with co-counsel indicates that the best interests of the client likely will be served by withdrawal;

(8) the lawyer's mental or physical condition renders it difficult for the lawyer to carry out the representation effectively;

(9) a continuation of the representation is likely to result in a violation of these rules or the State Bar Act; or

(10) the lawyer believes* in good faith, in a proceeding pending before a tribunal,* that the tribunal* will find the existence of other good cause for withdrawal.

(c) If permission for termination of a representation is required by the rules of a tribunal,* a lawyer shall not terminate a representation before that tribunal* without its permission.

(d) A lawyer shall not terminate a representation until the lawyer has taken reasonable* steps to avoid reasonably* foreseeable prejudice to the rights of the client, such as giving the client sufficient notice to permit the client to retain other counsel, and complying with paragraph (e).

(e) Upon the termination of a representation for any reason:

(1) subject to any applicable protective order, nondisclosure agreement, statute or regulation, the lawyer promptly shall release to the client, at the request of the client, all client materials and property. "Client materials and property" includes correspondence, pleadings, deposition transcripts, experts' reports and other writings,* exhibits, and physical evidence, whether in tangible, electronic or other form, and other items reasonably* necessary to the client's representation, whether the client has paid for them or not; and

(2) the lawyer promptly shall refund any part of a fee or expense paid in advance that the lawyer has not earned or incurred. This provision is not applicable to a true retainer fee paid solely for the purpose of ensuring the availability of the lawyer for the matter.

* An asterisk (*) identifies a word or phrase defined in the terminology rule, rule 1.0.1.

Comment

[1] This rule applies, without limitation, to a sale of a law practice under rule 1.17. A lawyer can be subject to discipline for improperly threatening to terminate a representation. (See *In the Matter of Shalant* (Review Dept. 2005) 4 Cal. State Bar Ct. Rptr. 829, 837.)

[2] When a lawyer withdraws from the representation of a client in a particular matter under paragraph (a) or (b), the lawyer might not be obligated to withdraw from the representation of the same client in other matters. For example, a lawyer might be obligated under paragraph (a)(1) to withdraw from representing a client because the lawyer has a conflict of interest under rule 1.7, but that conflict might not arise in other representations of the client.

[3] Withdrawal under paragraph (a)(1) is not mandated where a lawyer for the defendant in a criminal proceeding, or the respondent in a proceeding that could result in incarceration, or involuntary commitment or confinement, defends the proceeding by requiring that every element of the case be established. (See rule 3.1(b).)

[4] Lawyers must comply with their obligations to their clients under Business and Professions Code section 6068, subdivision (e) and rule 1.6, and to the courts under rule 3.3 when seeking permission to withdraw under paragraph (c). If a tribunal* denies a lawyer permission to withdraw, the lawyer is obligated to comply with the tribunal's* order. (See Bus. & Prof. Code, §§ 6068, subd. (b) and 6103.) This duty applies even if the lawyer sought permission to withdraw because of a conflict of interest. Regarding withdrawal from limited scope representations that involve court appearances, compliance with applicable California Rules of Court concerning limited scope representation satisfies paragraph (c).

[5] Statutes may prohibit a lawyer from releasing information in the client materials and property under certain circumstances. (See, e.g., Pen. Code, §§ 1054.2 and 1054.10.)

[6] Paragraph (e)(1) does not prohibit a lawyer from making, at the lawyer's own expense, and retaining copies of papers released to the client, or to prohibit a claim for the recovery of the lawyer's expense in any subsequent legal proceeding.

Rule 1.17 Sale of a Law Practice

All or substantially* all of the law practice of a lawyer, living or deceased, including goodwill, may be sold to another lawyer or law firm* subject to all the following conditions:

(a) Fees charged to clients shall not be increased solely by reason of the sale.

(b) If the sale contemplates the transfer of responsibility for work not yet completed or responsibility for client files or information protected by Business and Professions Code section 6068, subdivision (e)(1), then;

(1) if the seller is deceased, or has a conservator or other person* acting in a representative capacity, and no lawyer has been appointed to act for the seller pursuant to Business and Professions Code section 6180.5, then prior to the transfer;

(i) the purchaser shall cause a written* notice to be given to each client whose matter is included in the sale, stating that the interest in the law practice is being transferred to the purchaser; that the client has the right to retain other counsel; that the client may take possession of any client materials and property, as required by rule 1.16(e)(1); and that if no response is received to the notice within 90 days after it is sent, or if the client's rights would be prejudiced by a failure of the purchaser to act during that time, the purchaser may act on behalf of the client until otherwise notified by the client, and

* An asterisk (*) identifies a word or phrase defined in the terminology rule, rule 1.0.1.

(ii) the purchaser shall obtain the written* consent of the client. If reasonable* efforts have been made to locate the client and no response to the paragraph (b)(1)(i) notice is received within 90 days, consent shall be presumed until otherwise notified by the client.

(2) in all other circumstances, not less than 90 days prior to the transfer;

(i) the seller, or the lawyer appointed to act for the seller pursuant to Business and Professions Code section 6180.5, shall cause a written* notice to be given to each client whose matter is included in the sale, stating that the interest in the law practice is being transferred to the purchaser; that the client has the right to retain other counsel; that the client may take possession of any client materials and property, as required by rule 1.16(e)(1); and that if no response is received to the notice within 90 days after it is sent, or if the client's rights would be prejudiced by a failure of the purchaser to act during that time, the purchaser may act on behalf of the client until otherwise notified by the client, and

(ii) the seller, or the lawyer appointed to act for the seller pursuant to Business and Professions Code section 6180.5, shall obtain the written* consent of the client prior to the transfer. If reasonable* efforts have been made to locate the client and no response to the paragraph (b)(2)(i) notice is received within 90 days, consent shall be presumed until otherwise notified by the client.

(c) If substitution is required by the rules of a tribunal* in which a matter is pending, all steps necessary to substitute a lawyer shall be taken.

(d) The purchaser shall comply with the applicable requirements of rules 1.7 and 1.9.

(e) Confidential information shall not be disclosed to a nonlawyer in connection with a sale under this rule.

(f) This rule does not apply to the admission to or retirement from a law firm,* retirement plans and similar arrangements, or sale of tangible assets of a law practice.

Comment

[1] The requirement that the sale be of "all or substantially* all of the law practice of a lawyer" prohibits the sale of only a field or area of practice or the seller's practice in a geographical area or in a particular jurisdiction. The prohibition against the sale of less than all or substantially* all of a practice protects those clients whose matters are less lucrative and who might find it difficult to secure other counsel if a sale could be limited to substantial* fee-generating matters. The purchasers are required to undertake all client matters sold in the transaction, subject to client consent. This requirement is satisfied, however, even if a purchaser is unable to undertake a particular client matter because of a conflict of interest.

[2] Under paragraph (a), the purchaser must honor existing arrangements between the seller and the client as to fees and scope of work and the sale may not be financed by increasing fees charged for client matters transferred through the sale. However, fee increases or other changes to the fee arrangements might be justified by other factors, such as modifications of the purchaser's responsibilities, the passage of time, or reasonable* costs that were not addressed in the original agreement. Any such modifications must comply with rules 1.4 and 1.5 and other relevant provisions of these rules and the State Bar Act.

[3] Transfer of individual client matters, where permitted, is governed by rule 1.5.1. Payment of a fee to a nonlawyer broker for arranging the sale or purchase of a law practice is governed by rule 5.4(a).

* An asterisk (*) identifies a word or phrase defined in the terminology rule, rule 1.0.1.

Rule 1.18 Duties To Prospective Client

(a) A person* who, directly or through an authorized representative, consults a lawyer for the purpose of retaining the lawyer or securing legal service or advice from the lawyer in the lawyer's professional capacity, is a prospective client.

(b) Even when no lawyer-client relationship ensues, a lawyer who has communicated with a prospective client shall not use or reveal information protected by Business and Professions Code section 6068, subdivision (e) and rule 1.6 that the lawyer learned as a result of the consultation, except as rule 1.9 would permit with respect to information of a former client.

(c) A lawyer subject to paragraph (b) shall not represent a client with interests materially adverse to those of a prospective client in the same or a substantially related matter if the lawyer received from the prospective client information protected by Business and Professions Code section 6068, subdivision (e) and rule 1.6 that is material to the matter, except as provided in paragraph (d). If a lawyer is prohibited from representation under this paragraph, no lawyer in a firm* with which that lawyer is associated may knowingly* undertake or continue representation in such a matter, except as provided in paragraph (d).

(d) When the lawyer has received information that prohibits representation as provided in paragraph (c), representation of the affected client is permissible if:

(1) both the affected client and the prospective client have given informed written consent,* or

(2) the lawyer who received the information took reasonable* measures to avoid exposure to more information than was reasonably* necessary to determine whether to represent the prospective client; and

(i) the prohibited lawyer is timely screened* from any participation in the matter and is apportioned no part of the fee therefrom; and

(ii) written* notice is promptly given to the prospective client to enable the prospective client to ascertain compliance with the provisions of this rule.

Comment

[1] As used in this rule, a prospective client includes a person's* authorized representative. A lawyer's discussions with a prospective client can be limited in time and depth and leave both the prospective client and the lawyer free, and sometimes required, to proceed no further. Although a prospective client's information is protected by Business and Professions Code section 6068, subdivision (e) and rule 1.6 the same as that of a client, in limited circumstances provided under paragraph (d), a law firm* is permitted to accept or continue representation of a client with interests adverse to the prospective client. This rule is not intended to limit the application of Evidence Code section 951 (defining "client" within the meaning of the Evidence Code).

[2] Not all persons* who communicate information to a lawyer are entitled to protection under this rule. A person* who by any means communicates information unilaterally to a lawyer, without reasonable* expectation that the lawyer is willing to discuss the possibility of forming a lawyer-client relationship or provide legal advice is not a "prospective client" within the meaning of paragraph (a). In addition, a person* who discloses information to a lawyer after the lawyer has stated his or her unwillingness or inability to consult with the person* (*People v. Gionis* (1995) 9 Cal.4th 1196 [40 Cal.Rptr.2d 456]), or who communicates information to a lawyer without a good faith intention to seek legal advice or representation, is not a prospective client within the meaning of paragraph (a).

[3] In order to avoid acquiring information from a prospective client that would prohibit representation as provided in paragraph (c), a lawyer considering whether or not to undertake a new matter must limit the initial interview to only such information as reasonably* appears necessary for that purpose.

---

* An asterisk (*) identifies a word or phrase defined in the terminology rule, rule 1.0.1.

[4] Under paragraph (c), the prohibition in this rule is imputed to other lawyers in a law firm* as provided in rule 1.10. However, under paragraph (d)(1), the consequences of imputation may be avoided if the informed written consent* of both the prospective and affected clients is obtained. (See rule 1.0.1(e-1) [informed written consent].) In the alternative, imputation may be avoided if the conditions of paragraph (d)(2) are met and all prohibited lawyers are timely screened* and written* notice is promptly given to the prospective client. Paragraph (d)(2)(i) does not prohibit the screened* lawyer from receiving a salary or partnership share established by prior independent agreement, but that lawyer may not receive compensation directly related to the matter in which the lawyer is prohibited.

[5] Notice under paragraph (d)(2)(ii) must include a general description of the subject matter about which the lawyer was consulted, and the screening* procedures employed.

COUNSELOR

Rule 2.1 Advisor

In representing a client, a lawyer shall exercise independent professional judgment and render candid advice.

Comment

[1] A lawyer ordinarily has no duty to initiate investigation of a client's affairs or to give advice that the client has indicated is unwanted, but a lawyer may initiate advice to a client when doing so appears to be in the client's interest.

[2] This rule does not preclude a lawyer who renders advice from referring to considerations other than the law, such as moral, economic, social and political factors that may be relevant to the client's situation.

Rule 2.2 [Reserved]

Rule 2.3 [Reserved]

Rule 2.4 Lawyer as Third-Party Neutral

(a) A lawyer serves as a third-party neutral when the lawyer assists two or more persons* who are not clients of the lawyer to reach a resolution of a dispute, or other matter, that has arisen between them. Service as a third-party neutral may include service as an arbitrator, a mediator or in such other capacity as will enable the lawyer to assist the parties to resolve the matter.

(b) A lawyer serving as a third-party neutral shall inform unrepresented parties that the lawyer is not representing them. When the lawyer knows* or reasonably should know* that a party does not understand the lawyer's role in the matter, the lawyer shall explain the difference between the lawyer's role as a third-party neutral and a lawyer's role as one who represents a client.

Comment

[1] In serving as a third-party neutral, the lawyer may be subject to court rules or other law that apply either to third-party neutrals generally or to lawyers serving as third-party neutrals. Lawyer neutrals may also be subject to various codes of ethics, such as the Judicial Council Standards for Mediators in Court Connected Mediation Programs or the Judicial Council Ethics Standards for Neutral Arbitrators in Contractual Arbitration.

[2] A lawyer who serves as a third-party neutral subsequently may be asked to serve as a lawyer representing a client in the same matter. The conflicts of interest that arise for both the individual lawyer and the lawyer's law firm* are addressed in rule 1.12.

---

* An asterisk (*) identifies a word or phrase defined in the terminology rule, rule 1.0.1.

[3] This rule is not intended to apply to temporary judges, referees or court-appointed arbitrators. (See rule 2.4.1.)

Rule 2.4.1 Lawyer as Temporary Judge, Referee, or Court-Appointed Arbitrator

A lawyer who is serving as a temporary judge, referee, or court-appointed arbitrator, and is subject to canon 6D of the California Code of Judicial Ethics, shall comply with the terms of that canon.

Comment

[1] This rule is intended to permit the State Bar to discipline lawyers who violate applicable portions of the California Code of Judicial Ethics while acting in a judicial capacity pursuant to an order or appointment by a court.

[2] This rule is not intended to apply to a lawyer serving as a third-party neutral in a mediation or a settlement conference, or as a neutral arbitrator pursuant to an arbitration agreement. (See rule 2.4.)

ADVOCATE

Rule 3.1 Meritorious Claims and Contentions

(a) A lawyer shall not:

(1) bring or continue an action, conduct a defense, assert a position in litigation, or take an appeal, without probable cause and for the purpose of harassing or maliciously injuring any person;* or

(2) present a claim or defense in litigation that is not warranted under existing law, unless it can be supported by a good faith argument for an extension, modification, or reversal of the existing law.

(b) A lawyer for the defendant in a criminal proceeding, or the respondent in a proceeding that could result in incarceration, or involuntary commitment or confinement, may nevertheless defend the proceeding by requiring that every element of the case be established.

Rule 3.2 Delay of Litigation

In representing a client, a lawyer shall not use means that have no substantial* purpose other than to delay or prolong the proceeding or to cause needless expense.

Comment

See rule 1.3 with respect to a lawyer's duty to act with reasonable* diligence and rule 3.1(b) with respect to a lawyer's representation of a defendant in a criminal proceeding. See also Business and Professions Code section 6128, subdivision (b).

Rule 3.3 Candor Toward The Tribunal*

(a) A lawyer shall not:

(1) knowingly* make a false statement of fact or law to a tribunal* or fail to correct a false statement of material fact or law previously made to the tribunal* by the lawyer;

(2) fail to disclose to the tribunal* legal authority in the controlling jurisdiction known* to the lawyer to be directly adverse to the position of the client and not disclosed by opposing counsel, or knowingly* misquote to a tribunal* the language of a book, statute, decision or other authority; or

(3) offer evidence that the lawyer knows* to be false. If a lawyer, the lawyer's client, or a witness called by the lawyer, has offered material evidence, and the lawyer comes to know* of its falsity,

* An asterisk (*) identifies a word or phrase defined in the terminology rule, rule 1.0.1.

the lawyer shall take reasonable* remedial measures, including, if necessary, disclosure to the tribunal,* unless disclosure is prohibited by Business and Professions Code section 6068, subdivision (e) and rule 1.6. A lawyer may refuse to offer evidence, other than the testimony of a defendant in a criminal matter, that the lawyer reasonably believes* is false.

(b) A lawyer who represents a client in a proceeding before a tribunal* and who knows* that a person* intends to engage, is engaging or has engaged in criminal or fraudulent* conduct related to the proceeding shall take reasonable* remedial measures to the extent permitted by Business and Professions Code section 6068, subdivision (e) and rule 1.6.

(c) The duties stated in paragraphs (a) and (b) continue to the conclusion of the proceeding.

(d) In an ex parte proceeding where notice to the opposing party in the proceeding is not required or given and the opposing party is not present, a lawyer shall inform the tribunal* of all material facts known* to the lawyer that will enable the tribunal* to make an informed decision, whether or not the facts are adverse to the position of the client.

Comment

[1] This rule governs the conduct of a lawyer in proceedings of a tribunal,* including ancillary proceedings such as a deposition conducted pursuant to a tribunal's* authority. See rule 1.0.1(m) for the definition of "tribunal."

[2] The prohibition in paragraph (a)(1) against making false statements of law or failing to correct a material misstatement of law includes citing as authority a decision that has been overruled or a statute that has been repealed or declared unconstitutional, or failing to correct such a citation previously made to the tribunal* by the lawyer.

Legal Argument

[3] Legal authority in the controlling jurisdiction may include legal authority outside the jurisdiction in which the tribunal* sits, such as a federal statute or case that is determinative of an issue in a state court proceeding or a Supreme Court decision that is binding on a lower court.

[4] The duties stated in paragraphs (a) and (b) apply to all lawyers, including defense counsel in criminal cases. If a lawyer knows* that a client intends to testify falsely or wants the lawyer to introduce false evidence, the lawyer should seek to persuade the client that the evidence should not be offered and, if unsuccessful, must refuse to offer the false evidence. If a criminal defendant insists on testifying, and the lawyer knows* that the testimony will be false, the lawyer may offer the testimony in a narrative form if the lawyer made reasonable* efforts to dissuade the client from the unlawful course of conduct and the lawyer has sought permission from the court to withdraw as required by rule 1.16. (See, e.g., *People v. Johnson* (1998) 62 Cal.App.4th 608 [72 Cal.Rptr.2d 805]; *People v. Jennings* (1999) 70 Cal.App.4th 899 [83 Cal.Rptr.2d 33].) The obligations of a lawyer under these rules and the State Bar Act are subordinate to applicable constitutional provisions.

Remedial Measures

[5] Reasonable* remedial measures under paragraphs (a)(3) and (b) refer to measures that are available under these rules and the State Bar Act, and which a reasonable* lawyer would consider appropriate under the circumstances to comply with the lawyer's duty of candor to the tribunal.* (See, e.g., rules 1.2.1, 1.4(a)(4), 1.16(a), 8.4; Bus. & Prof. Code, §§ 6068, subd. (d), 6128.) Remedial measures also include explaining to the client the lawyer's obligations under this rule and, where applicable, the reasons for the lawyer's decision to seek permission from the tribunal* to withdraw, and remonstrating further with the client to take corrective action that would eliminate the need for the lawyer to withdraw. If the client is an organization, the lawyer should also consider the provisions of rule 1.13. Remedial measures do not include disclosure of client confidential information, which the lawyer is required to protect under Business and Professions Code section 6068, subdivision (e) and rule 1.6.

---

* An asterisk (*) identifies a word or phrase defined in the terminology rule, rule 1.0.1.

Duration of Obligation

[6] A proceeding has concluded within the meaning of this rule when a final judgment in the proceeding has been affirmed on appeal or the time for review has passed. A prosecutor may have obligations that go beyond the scope of this rule. (See, e.g., rule 3.8(f) and (g).)

Ex Parte Communications

[7] Paragraph (d) does not apply to ex parte communications that are not otherwise prohibited by law or the tribunal.*

Withdrawal

[8] A lawyer's compliance with the duty of candor imposed by this rule does not require that the lawyer withdraw from the representation. The lawyer may, however, be required by rule 1.16 to seek permission of the tribunal* to withdraw if the lawyer's compliance with this rule results in a deterioration of the lawyer-client relationship such that the lawyer can no longer competently and diligently represent the client, or where continued employment will result in a violation of these rules. A lawyer must comply with Business and Professions Code section 6068, subdivision (e) and rule 1.6 with respect to a request to withdraw that is premised on a client's misconduct.

[9] In addition to this rule, lawyers remain bound by Business and Professions Code sections 6068, subdivision (d) and 6106.

Rule 3.4 Fairness to Opposing Party and Counsel

A lawyer shall not:

(a) unlawfully obstruct another party's access to evidence, including a witness, or unlawfully alter, destroy or conceal a document or other material having potential evidentiary value. A lawyer shall not counsel or assist another person* to do any such act;

(b) suppress any evidence that the lawyer or the lawyer's client has a legal obligation to reveal or to produce;

(c) falsify evidence, counsel or assist a witness to testify falsely, or offer an inducement to a witness that is prohibited by law;

(d) directly or indirectly pay, offer to pay, or acquiesce in the payment of compensation to a witness contingent upon the content of the witness's testimony or the outcome of the case. Except where prohibited by law, a lawyer may advance, guarantee, or acquiesce in the payment of:

> (1) expenses reasonably* incurred by a witness in attending or testifying;
>
> (2) reasonable* compensation to a witness for loss of time in attending or testifying; or
>
> (3) a reasonable* fee for the professional services of an expert witness;

(e) advise or directly or indirectly cause a person* to secrete himself or herself or to leave the jurisdiction of a tribunal* for the purpose of making that person* unavailable as a witness therein;

(f) knowingly* disobey an obligation under the rules of a tribunal* except for an open refusal based on an assertion that no valid obligation exists; or

(g) in trial, assert personal knowledge of facts in issue except when testifying as a witness, or state a personal opinion as to the guilt or innocence of an accused.

Comment

[1] Paragraph (a) applies to evidentiary material generally, including computerized information. It is a criminal offense to destroy material for purpose of impairing its availability in a pending proceeding or one whose commencement can be foreseen. (See, e.g., Pen. Code, § 135; 18 U.S.C.

* An asterisk (*) identifies a word or phrase defined in the terminology rule, rule 1.0.1.

§§ 1501–1520.) Falsifying evidence is also generally a criminal offense. (See, e.g., Pen. Code, § 132; 18 U.S.C. § 1519.) Applicable law may permit a lawyer to take temporary possession of physical evidence of client crimes for the purpose of conducting a limited examination that will not alter or destroy material characteristics of the evidence. Applicable law may require a lawyer to turn evidence over to the police or other prosecuting authorities, depending on the circumstances. (See *People v. Lee* (1970) 3 Cal.App.3d 514, 526 [83 Cal.Rptr. 715]; *People v. Meredith* (1981) 29 Cal.3d 682 [175 Cal.Rptr. 612].)

[2] A violation of a civil or criminal discovery rule or statute does not by itself establish a violation of this rule. See rule 3.8 for special disclosure responsibilities of a prosecutor.

Rule 3.5 Contact With Judges, Officials, Employees, and Jurors

(a) Except as permitted by statute, an applicable code of judicial ethics or code of judicial conduct, or standards governing employees of a tribunal,* a lawyer shall not directly or indirectly give or lend anything of value to a judge, official, or employee of a tribunal.* This rule does not prohibit a lawyer from contributing to the campaign fund of a judge or judicial officer running for election or confirmation pursuant to applicable law pertaining to such contributions.

(b) Unless permitted to do so by law, an applicable code of judicial ethics or code of judicial conduct, a rule or ruling of a tribunal,* or a court order, a lawyer shall not directly or indirectly communicate with or argue to a judge or judicial officer upon the merits of a contested matter pending before the judge or judicial officer, except:

(1) in open court;

(2) with the consent of all other counsel and any unrepresented parties in the matter;

(3) in the presence of all other counsel and any unrepresented parties in the matter;

(4) in writing* with a copy thereof furnished to all other counsel and any unrepresented parties in the matter; or

(5) in ex parte matters.

(c) As used in this rule, "judge" and "judicial officer" shall also include: (i) administrative law judges; (ii) neutral arbitrators; (iii) State Bar Court judges; (iv) members of an administrative body acting in an adjudicative capacity; and (v) law clerks, research attorneys, or other court personnel who participate in the decision-making process, including referees, special masters, or other persons* to whom a court refers one or more issues and whose decision or recommendation can be binding on the parties if approved by the court.

(d) A lawyer connected with a case shall not communicate directly or indirectly with anyone the lawyer knows* to be a member of the venire from which the jury will be selected for trial of that case.

(e) During trial, a lawyer connected with the case shall not communicate directly or indirectly with any juror.

(f) During trial, a lawyer who is not connected with the case shall not communicate directly or indirectly concerning the case with anyone the lawyer knows* is a juror in the case.

(g) After discharge of the jury from further consideration of a case a lawyer shall not communicate directly or indirectly with a juror if:

(1) the communication is prohibited by law or court order;

(2) the juror has made known to the lawyer a desire not to communicate; or

(3) the communication involves misrepresentation, coercion, or duress, or is intended to harass or embarrass the juror or to influence the juror's actions in future jury service.

* An asterisk (*) identifies a word or phrase defined in the terminology rule, rule 1.0.1.

(h) A lawyer shall not directly or indirectly conduct an out of court investigation of a person* who is either a member of a venire or a juror in a manner likely to influence the state of mind of such person* in connection with present or future jury service.

(i) All restrictions imposed by this rule also apply to communications with, or investigations of, members of the family of a person* who is either a member of a venire or a juror.

(j) A lawyer shall reveal promptly to the court improper conduct by a person* who is either a member of a venire or a juror, or by another toward a person* who is either a member of a venire or a juror or a member of his or her family, of which the lawyer has knowledge.

(k) This rule does not prohibit a lawyer from communicating with persons* who are members of a venire or jurors as a part of the official proceedings.

(*l*) For purposes of this rule, "juror" means any empaneled, discharged, or excused juror.

Comment

[1] An applicable code of judicial ethics or code of judicial conduct under this rule includes the California Code of Judicial Ethics and the Code of Conduct for United States Judges. Regarding employees of a tribunal* not subject to judicial ethics or conduct codes, applicable standards include the Code of Ethics for the Court Employees of California and 5 United States Code section 7353 (Gifts to Federal employees). The statutes applicable to adjudicatory proceedings of state agencies generally are contained in the Administrative Procedure Act (Gov. Code, § 11340 et seq.; see Gov. Code, § 11370 [listing statutes with the act].) State and local agencies also may adopt their own regulations and rules governing communications with members or employees of a tribunal.*

[2] For guidance on permissible communications with a juror in a criminal action after discharge of the jury, see Code of Civil Procedure section 206.

[3] It is improper for a lawyer to communicate with a juror who has been removed, discharged, or excused from an empaneled jury, regardless of whether notice is given to other counsel, until such time as the entire jury has been discharged from further service or unless the communication is part of the official proceedings of the case.

Rule 3.6 Trial Publicity

(a) A lawyer who is participating or has participated in the investigation or litigation of a matter shall not make an extrajudicial statement that the lawyer knows* or reasonably should know* will (i) be disseminated by means of public communication and (ii) have a substantial* likelihood of materially prejudicing an adjudicative proceeding in the matter.

(b) Notwithstanding paragraph (a), but only to the extent permitted by Business and Professions Code section 6068, subdivision (e) and rule 1.6, lawyer may state:

(1) the claim, offense or defense involved and, except when prohibited by law, the identity of the persons* involved;

(2) information contained in a public record;

(3) that an investigation of a matter is in progress;

(4) the scheduling or result of any step in litigation;

(5) a request for assistance in obtaining evidence and information necessary thereto;

(6) a warning of danger concerning the behavior of a person* involved, when there is reason to believe* that there exists the likelihood of substantial* harm to an individual or to the public but only to the extent that dissemination by public communication is reasonably* necessary to protect the individual or the public; and

* An asterisk (*) identifies a word or phrase defined in the terminology rule, rule 1.0.1.

(7) in a criminal case, in addition to subparagraphs (1) through (6):

(i) the identity, general area of residence, and occupation of the accused;

(ii) if the accused has not been apprehended, the information necessary to aid in apprehension of that person;*

(iii) the fact, time, and place of arrest; and

(iv) the identity of investigating and arresting officers or agencies and the length of the investigation.

(c) Notwithstanding paragraph (a), a lawyer may make a statement that a reasonable* lawyer would believe* is required to protect a client from the substantial* undue prejudicial effect of recent publicity not initiated by the lawyer or the lawyer's client. A statement made pursuant to this paragraph shall be limited to such information as is necessary to mitigate the recent adverse publicity.

(d) No lawyer associated in a law firm* or government agency with a lawyer subject to paragraph (a) shall make a statement prohibited by paragraph (a).

Comment

[1] Whether an extrajudicial statement violates this rule depends on many factors, including: (i) whether the extrajudicial statement presents information clearly inadmissible as evidence in the matter for the purpose of proving or disproving a material fact in issue; (ii) whether the extrajudicial statement presents information the lawyer knows* is false, deceptive, or the use of which would violate Business and Professions Code section 6068, subdivision (d) or rule 3.3; (iii) whether the extrajudicial statement violates a lawful "gag" order, or protective order, statute, rule of court, or special rule of confidentiality, for example, in juvenile, domestic, mental disability, and certain criminal proceedings, (see Bus. & Prof. Code, § 6068, subd. (a) and rule 3.4(f), which require compliance with such obligations); and (iv) the timing of the statement.

[2] This rule applies to prosecutors and criminal defense counsel. See rule 3.8(e) for additional duties of prosecutors in connection with extrajudicial statements about criminal proceedings.

Rule 3.7 Lawyer as Witness

(a) A lawyer shall not act as an advocate in a trial in which the lawyer is likely to be a witness unless:

(1) the lawyer's testimony relates to an uncontested issue or matter;

(2) the lawyer's testimony relates to the nature and value of legal services rendered in the case; or

(3) the lawyer has obtained informed written consent* from the client. If the lawyer represents the People or a governmental entity, the consent shall be obtained from the head of the office or a designee of the head of the office by which the lawyer is employed.

(b) A lawyer may act as advocate in a trial in which another lawyer in the lawyer's firm* is likely to be called as a witness unless precluded from doing so by rule 1.7 or rule 1.9.

Comment

[1] This rule applies to a trial before a jury, judge, administrative law judge or arbitrator. This rule does not apply to other adversarial proceedings. This rule also does not apply in non-adversarial proceedings, as where a lawyer testifies on behalf of a client in a hearing before a legislative body.

[2] A lawyer's obligation to obtain informed written consent* may be satisfied when the lawyer makes the required disclosure, and the client gives informed consent* on the record in court before a licensed court reporter or court recorder who prepares a transcript or recording of the disclosure and consent. See definition of "written" in rule 1.0.1(n).

---

* An asterisk (*) identifies a word or phrase defined in the terminology rule, rule 1.0.1.

[3] Notwithstanding a client's informed written consent,* courts retain discretion to take action, up to and including disqualification of a lawyer who seeks to both testify and serve as an advocate, to protect the trier of fact from being misled or the opposing party from being prejudiced. (See, e.g., *Lyle v. Superior Court* (1981) 122 Cal.App.3d 470 [175 Cal.Rptr. 918].)

Rule 3.8 Special Responsibilities of a Prosecutor

The prosecutor in a criminal case shall:

(a) not institute or continue to prosecute a charge that the prosecutor knows* is not supported by probable cause;

(b) make reasonable* efforts to assure that the accused has been advised of the right to, and the procedure for obtaining, counsel and has been given reasonable* opportunity to obtain counsel;

(c) not seek to obtain from an unrepresented accused a waiver of important pretrial rights unless the tribunal* has approved the appearance of the accused in propria persona;

(d) make timely disclosure to the defense of all evidence or information known* to the prosecutor that the prosecutor knows* or reasonably should know* tends to negate the guilt of the accused, mitigate the offense, or mitigate the sentence, except when the prosecutor is relieved of this responsibility by a protective order of the tribunal;* and

(e) exercise reasonable* care to prevent persons* under the supervision or direction of the prosecutor, including investigators, law enforcement personnel, employees or other persons* assisting or associated with the prosecutor in a criminal case from making an extrajudicial statement that the prosecutor would be prohibited from making under rule 3.6.

(f) When a prosecutor knows* of new, credible and material evidence creating a reasonable* likelihood that a convicted defendant did not commit an offense of which the defendant was convicted, the prosecutor shall:

(1) promptly disclose that evidence to an appropriate court or authority, and

(2) if the conviction was obtained in the prosecutor's jurisdiction,

(i) promptly disclose that evidence to the defendant unless a court authorizes delay, and

(ii) undertake further investigation, or make reasonable* efforts to cause an investigation, to determine whether the defendant was convicted of an offense that the defendant did not commit.

(g) When a prosecutor knows* of clear and convincing evidence establishing that a defendant in the prosecutor's jurisdiction was convicted of an offense that the defendant did not commit, the prosecutor shall seek to remedy the conviction.

Comment

[1] A prosecutor has the responsibility of a minister of justice and not simply that of an advocate. This responsibility carries with it specific obligations to see that the defendant is accorded procedural justice, that guilt is decided upon the basis of sufficient evidence, and that special precautions are taken to prevent and to rectify the conviction of innocent persons.* This rule is intended to achieve those results. All lawyers in government service remain bound by rules 3.1 and 3.4.

[2] Paragraph (c) does not forbid the lawful questioning of an uncharged suspect who has knowingly* waived the right to counsel and the right to remain silent. Paragraph (c) also does not forbid prosecutors from seeking from an unrepresented accused a reasonable* waiver of time for initial appearance or preliminary hearing as a means of facilitating the accused's voluntary cooperation in an ongoing law enforcement investigation.

* An asterisk (*) identifies a word or phrase defined in the terminology rule, rule 1.0.1.

[3] The disclosure obligations in paragraph (d) are not limited to evidence or information that is material as defined by *Brady v. Maryland* (1963) 373 U.S. 83 [83 S.Ct. 1194] and its progeny. For example, these obligations include, at a minimum, the duty to disclose impeachment evidence or information that a prosecutor knows* or reasonably should know* casts significant doubt on the accuracy or admissibility of witness testimony on which the prosecution intends to rely. Paragraph (d) does not require disclosure of information protected from disclosure by federal or California laws and rules, as interpreted by case law or court orders. Nothing in this rule is intended to be applied in a manner inconsistent with statutory and constitutional provisions governing discovery in California courts. A disclosure's timeliness will vary with the circumstances, and paragraph (d) is not intended to impose timing requirements different from those established by statutes, procedural rules, court orders, and case law interpreting those authorities and the California and federal constitutions.

[4] The exception in paragraph (d) recognizes that a prosecutor may seek an appropriate protective order from the tribunal* if disclosure of information to the defense could result in substantial* harm to an individual or to the public interest.

[5] Paragraph (e) supplements rule 3.6, which prohibits extrajudicial statements that have a substantial* likelihood of prejudicing an adjudicatory proceeding. Paragraph (e) is not intended to restrict the statements which a prosecutor may make which comply with rule 3.6(b) or 3.6(c).

[6] Prosecutors have a duty to supervise the work of subordinate lawyers and nonlawyer employees or agents. (See rules 5.1 and 5.3.) Ordinarily, the reasonable* care standard of paragraph (e) will be satisfied if the prosecutor issues the appropriate cautions to law enforcement personnel and other relevant individuals.

[7] When a prosecutor knows* of new, credible and material evidence creating a reasonable* likelihood that a person* outside the prosecutor's jurisdiction was convicted of a crime that the person* did not commit, paragraph (f) requires prompt disclosure to the court or other appropriate authority, such as the chief prosecutor of the jurisdiction where the conviction occurred. If the conviction was obtained in the prosecutor's jurisdiction, paragraph (f) requires the prosecutor to examine the evidence and undertake further investigation to determine whether the defendant is in fact innocent or make reasonable* efforts to cause another appropriate authority to undertake the necessary investigation, and to promptly disclose the evidence to the court and, absent court authorized delay, to the defendant. Disclosure to a represented defendant must be made through the defendant's counsel, and, in the case of an unrepresented defendant, would ordinarily be accompanied by a request to a court for the appointment of counsel to assist the defendant in taking such legal measures as may be appropriate. (See rule 4.2.)

[8] Under paragraph (g), once the prosecutor knows* of clear and convincing evidence that the defendant was convicted of an offense that the defendant did not commit, the prosecutor must seek to remedy the conviction. Depending upon the circumstances, steps to remedy the conviction could include disclosure of the evidence to the defendant, requesting that the court appoint counsel for an unrepresented indigent defendant and, where appropriate, notifying the court that the prosecutor has knowledge that the defendant did not commit the offense of which the defendant was convicted.

[9] A prosecutor's independent judgment, made in good faith, that the new evidence is not of such nature as to trigger the obligations of paragraphs (f) and (g), though subsequently determined to have been erroneous, does not constitute a violation of this rule.

Rule 3.9 Advocate in Nonadjudicative Proceedings

A lawyer representing a client before a legislative body or administrative agency in connection with a pending nonadjudicative matter or proceeding shall disclose that the appearance is in a representative capacity, except when the lawyer seeks information from an agency that is available to the public.

* An asterisk (*) identifies a word or phrase defined in the terminology rule, rule 1.0.1.

Comment

This rule only applies when a lawyer represents a client in connection with an official hearing or meeting of a governmental agency or a legislative body to which the lawyer or the lawyer's client is presenting evidence or argument. It does not apply to representation of a client in a negotiation or other bilateral transaction with a governmental agency or in connection with an application for a license or other privilege or the client's compliance with generally applicable reporting requirements, such as the filing of income-tax returns. This rule also does not apply to the representation of a client in connection with an investigation or examination of the client's affairs conducted by government investigators or examiners. Representation in such matters is governed by rules 4.1 through 4.4. This rule does not require a lawyer to disclose a client's identity.

Rule 3.10 Threatening Criminal, Administrative, or Disciplinary Charges

(a) A lawyer shall not threaten to present criminal, administrative, or disciplinary charges to obtain an advantage in a civil dispute.

(b) As used in paragraph (a) of this rule, the term "administrative charges" means the filing or lodging of a complaint with any governmental organization that may order or recommend the loss or suspension of a license, or may impose or recommend the imposition of a fine, pecuniary sanction, or other sanction of a quasi-criminal nature but does not include filing charges with an administrative entity required by law as a condition precedent to maintaining a civil action.

(c) As used in this rule, the term "civil dispute" means a controversy or potential controversy over the rights and duties of two or more persons* under civil law, whether or not an action has been commenced, and includes an administrative proceeding of a quasi-civil nature pending before a federal, state, or local governmental entity.

Comment

[1] Paragraph (a) does not prohibit a statement by a lawyer that the lawyer will present criminal, administrative, or disciplinary charges, unless the statement is made to obtain an advantage in a civil dispute. For example, if a lawyer believes* in good faith that the conduct of the opposing lawyer or party violates criminal or other laws, the lawyer may state that if the conduct continues the lawyer will report it to criminal or administrative authorities. On the other hand, a lawyer could not state or imply that a criminal or administrative action will be pursued unless the opposing party agrees to settle the civil dispute.

[2] This rule does not apply to a threat to bring a civil action. It also does not prohibit actually presenting criminal, administrative or disciplinary charges, even if doing so creates an advantage in a civil dispute. Whether a lawyer's statement violates this rule depends on the specific facts. (See, e.g., *Crane v. State Bar* (1981) 30 Cal.3d 117 [177 Cal.Rptr. 670].) A statement that the lawyer will pursue "all available legal remedies," or words of similar import, does not by itself violate this rule.

[3] This rule does not apply to: (i) a threat to initiate contempt proceedings for a failure to comply with a court order; or (ii) the offer of a civil compromise in accordance with a statute such as Penal Code sections 1377 and 1378.

[4] This rule does not prohibit a government lawyer from offering a global settlement or release-dismissal agreement in connection with related criminal, civil or administrative matters. The government lawyer must have probable cause for initiating or continuing criminal charges. (See rule 3.8(a).)

[5] As used in paragraph (b), "governmental organizations" includes any federal, state, local, and foreign governmental organizations. Paragraph (b) exempts the threat of filing an administrative charge that is a prerequisite to filing a civil complaint on the same transaction or occurrence.

---

* An asterisk (*) identifies a word or phrase defined in the terminology rule, rule 1.0.1.

TRANSACTIONS WITH PERSONS* OTHER THAN CLIENTS

Rule 4.1 Truthfulness in Statements to Others

In the course of representing a client a lawyer shall not knowingly:*

(a) make a false statement of material fact or law to a third person;* or

(b) fail to disclose a material fact to a third person* when disclosure is necessary to avoid assisting a criminal or fraudulent* act by a client, unless disclosure is prohibited by Business and Professions Code section 6068, subdivision (e)(1) or rule 1.6.

Comment

[1] A lawyer is required to be truthful when dealing with others on a client's behalf, but generally has no affirmative duty to inform an opposing party of relevant facts. A misrepresentation can occur if the lawyer incorporates or affirms the truth of a statement of another person* that the lawyer knows* is false. However, in drafting an agreement or other document on behalf of a client, a lawyer does not necessarily affirm or vouch for the truthfulness of representations made by the client in the agreement or document. A nondisclosure can be the equivalent of a false statement of material fact or law under paragraph (a) where a lawyer makes a partially true but misleading material statement or material omission. In addition to this rule, lawyers remain bound by Business and Professions Code section 6106 and rule 8.4.

[2] This rule refers to statements of fact. Whether a particular statement should be regarded as one of fact can depend on the circumstances. For example, in negotiation, certain types of statements ordinarily are not taken as statements of material fact. Estimates of price or value placed on the subject of a transaction and a party's intentions as to an acceptable settlement of a claim are ordinarily in this category, and so is the existence of an undisclosed principal except where nondisclosure of the principal would constitute fraud.*

[3] Under rule 1.2.1, a lawyer is prohibited from counseling or assisting a client in conduct that the lawyer knows* is criminal or fraudulent.* See rule 1.4(a)(4) regarding a lawyer's obligation to consult with the client about limitations on the lawyer's conduct. In some circumstances, a lawyer can avoid assisting a client's crime or fraud* by withdrawing from the representation in compliance with rule 1.16.

[4] Regarding a lawyer's involvement in lawful covert activity in the investigation of violations of law, see rule 8.4, Comment [5].

Rule 4.2 Communication With a Represented Person*

(a) In representing a client, a lawyer shall not communicate directly or indirectly about the subject of the representation with a person* the lawyer knows* to be represented by another lawyer in the matter, unless the lawyer has the consent of the other lawyer.

(b) In the case of a represented corporation, partnership, association, or other private or governmental organization, this rule prohibits communications with:

(1) A current officer, director, partner,*or managing agent of the organization; or

(2) A current employee, member, agent, or other constituent of the organization, if the subject of the communication is any act or omission of such person* in connection with the matter which may be binding upon or imputed to the organization for purposes of civil or criminal liability.

(c) This rule shall not prohibit:

(1) communications with a public official, board, committee, or body; or

(2) communications otherwise authorized by law or a court order.

---

* An asterisk (*) identifies a word or phrase defined in the terminology rule, rule 1.0.1.

(d) For purposes of this rule:

(1) "Managing agent" means an employee, member, agent, or other constituent of an organization with substantial* discretionary authority over decisions that determine organizational policy.

(2) "Public official" means a public officer of the United States government, or of a state, county, city, town, political subdivision, or other governmental organization, with the comparable decision-making authority and responsibilities as the organizational constituents described in paragraph (b)(1).

Comment

[1] This rule applies even though the represented person* initiates or consents to the communication. A lawyer must immediately terminate communication with a person* if, after commencing communication, the lawyer learns that the person* is one with whom communication is not permitted by this rule.

[2] "Subject of the representation," "matter," and "person" are not limited to a litigation context. This rule applies to communications with any person,* whether or not a party to a formal adjudicative proceeding, contract, or negotiation, who is represented by counsel concerning the matter to which the communication relates.

[3] The prohibition against communicating "indirectly" with a person* represented by counsel in paragraph (a) is intended to address situations where a lawyer seeks to communicate with a represented person* through an intermediary such as an agent, investigator or the lawyer's client. This rule, however, does not prevent represented persons* from communicating directly with one another with respect to the subject of the representation, nor does it prohibit a lawyer from advising a client concerning such a communication. A lawyer may also advise a client not to accept or engage in such communications. The rule also does not prohibit a lawyer who is a party to a legal matter from communicating on his or her own behalf with a represented person* in that matter.

[4] This rule does not prohibit communications with a represented person* concerning matters outside the representation. Similarly, a lawyer who knows* that a person* is being provided with limited scope representation is not prohibited from communicating with that person* with respect to matters that are outside the scope of the limited representation. (See, e.g., Cal. Rules of Court, rules 3.35–3.37, 5.425 [Limited Scope Representation].)

[5] This rule does not prohibit communications initiated by a represented person* seeking advice or representation from an independent lawyer of the person's* choice.

[6] If a current constituent of the organization is represented in the matter by his or her own counsel, the consent by that counsel to a communication is sufficient for purposes of this rule.

[7] This rule applies to all forms of governmental and private organizations, such as cities, counties, corporations, partnerships, limited liability companies, and unincorporated associations. When a lawyer communicates on behalf of a client with a governmental organization, or certain employees, members, agents, or other constituents of a governmental organization, however, special considerations exist as a result of the right to petition conferred by the First Amendment of the United States Constitution and article I, section 3 of the California Constitution. Paragraph (c)(1) recognizes these special considerations by generally exempting from application of this rule communications with public boards, committees, and bodies, and with public officials as defined in paragraph (d)(2) of this rule. Communications with a governmental organization constituent who is not a public official, however, will remain subject to this rule when the lawyer knows* the governmental organization is represented in the matter and the communication with that constituent falls within paragraph (b)(2).

[8] Paragraph (c)(2) recognizes that statutory schemes, case law, and court orders may authorize communications between a lawyer and a person* that would otherwise be subject to this rule.

* An asterisk (*) identifies a word or phrase defined in the terminology rule, rule 1.0.1.

Examples of such statutory schemes include those protecting the right of employees to organize and engage in collective bargaining, employee health and safety, and equal employment opportunity. The law also recognizes that prosecutors and other government lawyers are authorized to contact represented persons,* either directly or through investigative agents and informants, in the context of investigative activities, as limited by relevant federal and state constitutions, statutes, rules, and case law. (See, e.g., *United States v. Carona* (9th Cir. 2011) 630 F.3d 917; *United States v. Talao* (9th Cir. 2000) 222 F.3d 1133.) The rule is not intended to preclude communications with represented persons* in the course of such legitimate investigative activities as authorized by law. This rule also is not intended to preclude communications with represented persons* in the course of legitimate investigative activities engaged in, directly or indirectly, by lawyers representing persons* whom the government has accused of or is investigating for crimes, to the extent those investigative activities are authorized by law.

[9] A lawyer who communicates with a represented person* pursuant to paragraph (c) is subject to other restrictions in communicating with the person.* (See, e.g. Bus. & Prof. Code, § 6106; *Snider v. Superior Court* (2003) 113 Cal.App.4th 1187, 1213 [7 Cal.Rptr.3d 119]; *In the Matter of Dale* (2005) 4 Cal. State Bar Ct. Rptr. 798.)

Rule 4.3 Communicating with an Unrepresented Person*

(a) In communicating on behalf of a client with a person* who is not represented by counsel, a lawyer shall not state or imply that the lawyer is disinterested. When the lawyer knows* or reasonably should know* that the unrepresented person* incorrectly believes* the lawyer is disinterested in the matter, the lawyer shall make reasonable* efforts to correct the misunderstanding. If the lawyer knows* or reasonably should know* that the interests of the unrepresented person* are in conflict with the interests of the client, the lawyer shall not give legal advice to that person,* except that the lawyer may, but is not required to, advise the person* to secure counsel.

(b) In communicating on behalf of a client with a person* who is not represented by counsel, a lawyer shall not seek to obtain privileged or other confidential information the lawyer knows* or reasonably should know* the person* may not reveal without violating a duty to another or which the lawyer is not otherwise entitled to receive.

Comment

[1] This rule is intended to protect unrepresented persons,* whatever their interests, from being misled when communicating with a lawyer who is acting for a client.

[2] Paragraph (a) distinguishes between situations in which a lawyer knows* or reasonably should know* that the interests of an unrepresented person* are in conflict with the interests of the lawyer's client and situations in which the lawyer does not. In the former situation, the possibility that the lawyer will compromise the unrepresented person's* interests is so great that the rule prohibits the giving of any legal advice, apart from the advice to obtain counsel. A lawyer does not give legal advice merely by stating a legal position on behalf of the lawyer's client. This rule does not prohibit a lawyer from negotiating the terms of a transaction or settling a dispute with an unrepresented person.* So long as the lawyer discloses that the lawyer represents an adverse party and not the person,* the lawyer may inform the person* of the terms on which the lawyer's client will enter into the agreement or settle the matter, prepare documents that require the person's* signature, and explain the lawyer's own view of the meaning of the document and the underlying legal obligations.

[3] Regarding a lawyer's involvement in lawful covert activity in the investigation of violations of law, see rule 8.4, Comment [5].

* An asterisk (*) identifies a word or phrase defined in the terminology rule, rule 1.0.1.

Rule 4.4 Duties Concerning Inadvertently Transmitted Writings*

Where it is reasonably* apparent to a lawyer who receives a writing* relating to a lawyer's representation of a client that the writing* was inadvertently sent or produced, and the lawyer knows* or reasonably should know* that the writing* is privileged or subject to the work product doctrine, the lawyer shall:

(a) refrain from examining the writing* any more than is necessary to determine that it is privileged or subject to the work product doctrine, and

(b) promptly notify the sender.

Comment

[1] If a lawyer determines this rule applies to a transmitted writing,* the lawyer should return the writing* to the sender, seek to reach agreement with the sender regarding the disposition of the writing,* or seek guidance from a tribunal.* (See *Rico v. Mitsubishi* (2007) 42 Cal.4th 807, 817 [68 Cal.Rptr.3d 758].) In providing notice required by this rule, the lawyer shall comply with rule 4.2.

[2] This rule does not address the legal duties of a lawyer who receives a writing* that the lawyer knows* or reasonably should know* may have been inappropriately disclosed by the sending person.* (See *Clark v. Superior Court* (2011) 196 Cal.App.4th 37 [125 Cal.Rptr.3d 361].)

LAW FIRMS AND ASSOCIATIONS

Rule 5.1 Responsibilities of Managerial and Supervisory Lawyers

(a) A lawyer who individually or together with other lawyers possesses managerial authority in a law firm,* shall make reasonable* efforts to ensure that the firm* has in effect measures giving reasonable* assurance that all lawyers in the firm* comply with these rules and the State Bar Act.

(b) A lawyer having direct supervisory authority over another lawyer, whether or not a member or employee of the same law firm,* shall make reasonable* efforts to ensure that the other lawyer complies with these rules and the State Bar Act.

(c) A lawyer shall be responsible for another lawyer's violation of these rules and the State Bar Act if:

(1) the lawyer orders or, with knowledge of the relevant facts and of the specific conduct, ratifies the conduct involved; or

(2) the lawyer, individually or together with other lawyers, possesses managerial authority in the law firm* in which the other lawyer practices, or has direct supervisory authority over the other lawyer, whether or not a member or employee of the same law firm,* and knows* of the conduct at a time when its consequences can be avoided or mitigated but fails to take reasonable* remedial action.

Comment

Paragraph (a)—Duties Of Managerial Lawyers To Reasonably Assure Compliance with the Rules*

[1] Paragraph (a) requires lawyers with managerial authority within a law firm* to make reasonable* efforts to establish internal policies and procedures designed, for example, to detect and resolve conflicts of interest, identify dates by which actions must be taken in pending matters, account for client funds and property, and ensure that inexperienced lawyers are properly supervised.

[2] Whether particular measures or efforts satisfy the requirements of paragraph (a) might depend upon the law firm's structure and the nature of its practice, including the size of the law firm, whether it has more than one office location or practices in more than one jurisdiction, or whether the firm* or its partners* engage in any ancillary business.

---

* An asterisk (*) identifies a word or phrase defined in the terminology rule, rule 1.0.1.

[3] A partner,* shareholder or other lawyer in a law firm* who has intermediate managerial responsibilities satisfies paragraph (a) if the law firm* has a designated managing lawyer charged with that responsibility, or a management committee or other body that has appropriate managerial authority and is charged with that responsibility. For example, the managing lawyer of an office of a multi-office law firm* would not necessarily be required to promulgate firm-wide policies intended to reasonably* assure that the law firm's lawyers comply with the rules or State Bar Act. However, a lawyer remains responsible to take corrective steps if the lawyer knows* or reasonably should know* that the delegated body or person* is not providing or implementing measures as required by this rule.

[4] Paragraph (a) also requires managerial lawyers to make reasonable* efforts to assure that other lawyers in an agency or department comply with these rules and the State Bar Act. This rule contemplates, for example, the creation and implementation of reasonable* guidelines relating to the assignment of cases and the distribution of workload among lawyers in a public sector legal agency or other legal department. (See, e.g., State Bar of California, Guidelines on Indigent Defense Services Delivery Systems (2006).)

Paragraph (b)—Duties of Supervisory Lawyers

[5] Whether a lawyer has direct supervisory authority over another lawyer in particular circumstances is a question of fact.

Paragraph (c)—Responsibility for Another's Lawyer's Violation

[6] The appropriateness of remedial action under paragraph (c)(2) would depend on the nature and seriousness of the misconduct and the nature and immediacy of its harm. A managerial or supervisory lawyer must intervene to prevent avoidable consequences of misconduct if the lawyer knows* that the misconduct occurred.

[7] A supervisory lawyer violates paragraph (b) by failing to make the efforts required under that paragraph, even if the lawyer does not violate paragraph (c) by knowingly* directing or ratifying the conduct, or where feasible, failing to take reasonable* remedial action.

[8] Paragraphs (a), (b), and (c) create independent bases for discipline. This rule does not impose vicarious responsibility on a lawyer for the acts of another lawyer who is in or outside the law firm.* Apart from paragraph (c) of this rule and rule 8.4(a), a lawyer does not have disciplinary liability for the conduct of a partner,* associate, or subordinate lawyer. The question of whether a lawyer can be liable civilly or criminally for another lawyer's conduct is beyond the scope of these rules.

Rule 5.2 Responsibilities of a Subordinate Lawyer

(a) A lawyer shall comply with these rules and the State Bar Act notwithstanding that the lawyer acts at the direction of another lawyer or other person.*

(b) A subordinate lawyer does not violate these rules or the State Bar Act if that lawyer acts in accordance with a supervisory lawyer's reasonable* resolution of an arguable question of professional duty.

Comment

When lawyers in a supervisor-subordinate relationship encounter a matter involving professional judgment as to the lawyers' responsibilities under these rules or the State Bar Act and the question can reasonably* be answered only one way, the duty of both lawyers is clear and they are equally responsible for fulfilling it. Accordingly, the subordinate lawyer must comply with his or her obligations under paragraph (a). If the question reasonably* can be answered more than one way, the supervisory lawyer may assume responsibility for determining which of the reasonable* alternatives to select, and the subordinate may be guided accordingly. If the subordinate lawyer believes* that the supervisor's proposed resolution of the question of professional duty would result in a violation of these

* An asterisk (*) identifies a word or phrase defined in the terminology rule, rule 1.0.1.

rules or the State Bar Act, the subordinate is obligated to communicate his or her professional judgment regarding the matter to the supervisory lawyer.

Rule 5.3 Responsibilities Regarding Nonlawyer Assistants

With respect to a nonlawyer employed or retained by or associated with a lawyer:

(a) a lawyer who individually or together with other lawyers possesses managerial authority in a law firm,* shall make reasonable* efforts to ensure that the firm* has in effect measures giving reasonable* assurance that the nonlawyer's conduct is compatible with the professional obligations of the lawyer;

(b) a lawyer having direct supervisory authority over the nonlawyer, whether or not an employee of the same law firm,* shall make reasonable* efforts to ensure that the person's* conduct is compatible with the professional obligations of the lawyer; and

(c) a lawyer shall be responsible for conduct of such a person* that would be a violation of these rules or the State Bar Act if engaged in by a lawyer if:

(1) the lawyer orders or, with knowledge of the relevant facts and of the specific conduct, ratifies the conduct involved; or

(2) the lawyer, individually or together with other lawyers, possesses managerial authority in the law firm* in which the person* is employed, or has direct supervisory authority over the person,* whether or not an employee of the same law firm,* and knows* of the conduct at a time when its consequences can be avoided or mitigated but fails to take reasonable* remedial action.

Comment

Lawyers often utilize nonlawyer personnel, including secretaries, investigators, law student interns, and paraprofessionals. Such assistants, whether employees or independent contractors, act for the lawyer in rendition of the lawyer's professional services. A lawyer must give such assistants appropriate instruction and supervision concerning all ethical aspects of their employment. The measures employed in instructing and supervising nonlawyers should take account of the fact that they might not have legal training.

Rule 5.3.1 Employment of Disbarred, Suspended, Resigned, or Involuntarily Inactive Lawyer

(a) For purposes of this rule:

(1) "Employ" means to engage the services of another, including employees, agents, independent contractors and consultants, regardless of whether any compensation is paid;

(2) "Member" means a member of the State Bar of California;

(3) "Involuntarily inactive member" means a member who is ineligible to practice law as a result of action taken pursuant to Business and Professions Code sections 6007, 6203, subdivision (d)(1), or California Rules of Court, rule 9.31(d);

(4) "Resigned member" means a member who has resigned from the State Bar while disciplinary charges are pending; and

(5) "Ineligible person" means a member whose current status with the State Bar of California is disbarred, suspended, resigned, or involuntarily inactive.

(b) A lawyer shall not employ, associate in practice with, or assist a person the lawyer knows* or reasonably should know* is an ineligible person to perform the following on behalf of the lawyer's client:

* An asterisk (*) identifies a word or phrase defined in the terminology rule, rule 1.0.1.

(1) Render legal consultation or advice to the client;

(2) Appear on behalf of a client in any hearing or proceeding or before any judicial officer, arbitrator, mediator, court, public agency, referee, magistrate, commissioner, or hearing officer;

(3) Appear as a representative of the client at a deposition or other discovery matter;

(4) Negotiate or transact any matter for or on behalf of the client with third parties;

(5) Receive, disburse or otherwise handle the client's funds; or

(6) Engage in activities that constitute the practice of law.

(c) A lawyer may employ, associate in practice with, or assist an ineligible person to perform research, drafting or clerical activities, including but not limited to:

(1) Legal work of a preparatory nature, such as legal research, the assemblage of data and other necessary information, drafting of pleadings, briefs, and other similar documents;

(2) Direct communication with the client or third parties regarding matters such as scheduling, billing, updates, confirmation of receipt or sending of correspondence and messages; or

(3) Accompanying an active lawyer in attending a deposition or other discovery matter for the limited purpose of providing clerical assistance to the active lawyer who will appear as the representative of the client.

(d) Prior to or at the time of employing, associating in practice with, or assisting a person* the lawyer knows* or reasonably should know* is an ineligible person, the lawyer shall serve upon the State Bar written* notice of the employment, including a full description of such person's current bar status. The written* notice shall also list the activities prohibited in paragraph (b) and state that the ineligible person will not perform such activities. The lawyer shall serve similar written* notice upon each client on whose specific matter such person* will work, prior to or at the time of employing, associating with, or assisting such person* to work on the client's specific matter. The lawyer shall obtain proof of service of the client's written* notice and shall retain such proof and a true and correct copy of the client's written* notice for two years following termination of the lawyer's employment by the client.

(e) A lawyer may, without client or State Bar notification, employ, associate in practice with, or assist an ineligible person whose sole function is to perform office physical plant or equipment maintenance, courier or delivery services, catering, reception, typing or transcription, or other similar support activities.

(f) When the lawyer no longer employs, associates in practice with, or assists the ineligible person, the lawyer shall promptly serve upon the State Bar written* notice of the termination.

Comment

If the client is an organization, the lawyer shall serve the notice required by paragraph (d) on its highest authorized officer, employee, or constituent overseeing the particular engagement. (See rule 1.13.)

Rule 5.4 Financial and Similar Arrangements with Nonlawyers

(a) A lawyer or law firm* shall not share legal fees directly or indirectly with a nonlawyer or with an organization that is not authorized to practice law, except that:

(1) an agreement by a lawyer with the lawyer's firm,* partner,* or associate may provide for the payment of money or other consideration over a reasonable* period of time after the lawyer's death, to the lawyer's estate or to one or more specified persons;*

(2) a lawyer purchasing the practice of a deceased, disabled or disappeared lawyer may pay the agreed-upon purchase price, pursuant to rule 1.17, to the lawyer's estate or other representative;

(3) a lawyer or law firm* may include nonlawyer employees in a compensation or retirement plan, even though the plan is based in whole or in part on a profit-sharing arrangement, provided the plan does not otherwise violate these rules or the State Bar Act;

(4) a lawyer or law firm* may pay a prescribed registration, referral, or other fee to a lawyer referral service established, sponsored and operated in accordance with the State Bar of California's Minimum Standards for Lawyer Referral Services; or

(5) a lawyer or law firm* may share with or pay a court-awarded legal fee to a nonprofit organization that employed, retained or recommended employment of the lawyer or law firm* in the matter.

(b) A lawyer shall not form a partnership or other organization with a nonlawyer if any of the activities of the partnership or other organization consist of the practice of law.

(c) A lawyer shall not permit a person* who recommends, employs, or pays the lawyer to render legal services for another to direct or regulate the lawyer's independent professional judgment or interfere with the lawyer-client relationship in rendering legal services.

(d) A lawyer shall not practice with or in the form of a professional corporation or other organization authorized to practice law for a profit if:

(1) a nonlawyer owns any interest in it, except that a fiduciary representative of a lawyer's estate may hold the lawyer's stock or other interest for a reasonable* time during administration;

(2) a nonlawyer is a director or officer of the corporation or occupies a position of similar responsibility in any other form of organization; or

(3) a nonlawyer has the right or authority to direct or control the lawyer's independent professional judgment.

(e) The Board of Trustees of the State Bar shall formulate and adopt Minimum Standards for Lawyer Referral Services, which, as from time to time amended, shall be binding on lawyers. A lawyer shall not accept a referral from, or otherwise participate in, a lawyer referral service unless it complies with such Minimum Standards for Lawyer Referral Services.

(f) A lawyer shall not practice with or in the form of a nonprofit legal aid, mutual benefit or advocacy group if the nonprofit organization allows any third person* to interfere with the lawyer's independent professional judgment, or with the lawyer-client relationship, or allows or aids any person* to practice law in violation of these rules or the State Bar Act.

Comment

[1] Paragraph (a) does not prohibit a lawyer or law firm* from paying a bonus to or otherwise compensating a nonlawyer employee from general revenues received for legal services, provided the arrangement does not interfere with the independent professional judgment of the lawyer or lawyers in the firm* and does not violate these rules or the State Bar Act. However, a nonlawyer employee's bonus or other form of compensation may not be based on a percentage or share of fees in specific cases or legal matters.

[2] Paragraph (a) also does not prohibit payment to a nonlawyer third-party for goods and services provided to a lawyer or law firm;* however, the compensation to a nonlawyer third-party may not be determined as a percentage or share of the lawyer's or law firm's overall revenues or tied to fees in particular cases or legal matters. A lawyer may pay to a nonlawyer third-party, such as a collection agency, a percentage of past due or delinquent fees in concluded matters that the third-party collects on the lawyer's behalf.

[3] Paragraph (a)(5) permits a lawyer to share with or pay court-awarded legal fees to nonprofit legal aid, mutual benefit, and advocacy groups that are not engaged in the unauthorized practice of law.

* An asterisk (*) identifies a word or phrase defined in the terminology rule, rule 1.0.1.

(See *Frye v. Tenderloin Housing Clinic, Inc.* (2006) 38 Cal.4th 23 [40 Cal.Rptr.3d 221]; see also rule 6.3.) Regarding a lawyer's contribution of legal fees to a legal services organization, see rule 1.0, Comment [5] on financial support for programs providing pro bono legal services.

[4] This rule is not intended to affect case law regarding the relationship between insurers and lawyers providing legal services to insureds. (See, e.g., *Gafcon, Inc. v. Ponsor Associates* (2002) 98 Cal.App.4th 1388 [120 Cal.Rptr.2d 392].)

[5] Paragraph (c) is not intended to alter or diminish a lawyer's obligations under rule 1.8.6 (Compensation from One Other Than Client).

Rule 5.5 Unauthorized Practice of Law; Multijurisdictional Practice of Law

(a) A lawyer admitted to practice law in California shall not:

(1) practice law in a jurisdiction where to do so would be in violation of regulations of the profession in that jurisdiction; or

(2) knowingly* assist a person* in the unauthorized practice of law in that jurisdiction.

(b) A lawyer who is not admitted to practice law in California shall not:

(1) except as authorized by these rules or other law, establish or maintain a resident office or other systematic or continuous presence in California for the practice of law; or

(2) hold out to the public or otherwise represent that the lawyer is admitted to practice law in California.

Comment

Paragraph (b)(1) prohibits lawyers from practicing law in California unless otherwise entitled to practice law in this state by court rule or other law. (See, e.g., Bus. & Prof. Code, § 6125 et seq.; see also Cal. Rules of Court, rules 9.40 [counsel pro hac vice], 9.41 [appearances by military counsel], 9.42 [certified law students], 9.43 [out-of-state attorney arbitration counsel program], 9.44 [registered foreign legal consultant], 9.45 [registered legal services attorneys], 9.46 [registered in-house counsel], 9.47 [attorneys practicing temporarily in California as part of litigation], 9.48 [non-litigating attorneys temporarily in California to provide legal services].)

Rule 5.6 Restrictions on a Lawyer's Right to Practice

(a) Unless authorized by law, a lawyer shall not participate in offering or making:

(1) a partnership, shareholders, operating, employment, or other similar type of agreement that restricts the right of a lawyer to practice after termination of the relationship, except an agreement that concerns benefits upon retirement; or

(2) an agreement that imposes a restriction on a lawyer's right to practice in connection with a settlement of a client controversy, or otherwise.

(b) A lawyer shall not participate in offering or making an agreement which precludes the reporting of a violation of these rules.

(c) This rule does not prohibit an agreement that is authorized by Business and Professions Code sections 6092.5, subdivision (i) or 6093.

Comment

[1] Concerning the application of paragraph (a)(1), see Business and Professions Code section 16602; *Howard v. Babcock* (1993) 6 Cal.4th 409, 425 [25 Cal.Rptr.2d 80].

---

* An asterisk (*) identifies a word or phrase defined in the terminology rule, rule 1.0.1.

[2] Paragraph (a)(2) prohibits a lawyer from offering or agreeing not to represent other persons* in connection with settling a claim on behalf of a client.

[3] This rule does not prohibit restrictions that may be included in the terms of the sale of a law practice pursuant to rule 1.17.

PUBLIC SERVICE

Rule 6.1 [Reserved]

Rule 6.2 [Reserved]

Rule 6.3 Membership In Legal Services Organization

A lawyer may serve as a director, officer or member of a legal services organization, apart from the law firm* in which the lawyer practices, notwithstanding that the organization serves persons* having interests adverse to a client of the lawyer. The lawyer shall not knowingly* participate in a decision or action of the organization:

(a) if participating in the decision or action would be incompatible with the lawyer's obligations to a client under Business and Professions Code section 6068, subdivision (e)(1) or rules 1.6(a), 1.7, 1.9, or 1.18; or

(b) where the decision or action could have a material adverse effect on the representation of a client of the organization whose interests are adverse to a client of the lawyer.

Comment

Lawyers should support and participate in legal service organizations. A lawyer who is an officer or a member of such an organization does not thereby have a client-lawyer relationship with persons* served by the organization. However, there is potential conflict between the interests of such persons* and the interests of the lawyer's clients. If the possibility of such conflict disqualified a lawyer from serving on the board of a legal services organization, the profession's involvement in such organizations would be severely curtailed.

Rule 6.4 [Reserved]

Rule 6.5 Limited Legal Services Programs

(a) A lawyer who, under the auspices of a program sponsored by a court, government agency, bar association, law school, or nonprofit organization, provides short-term limited legal services to a client without expectation by either the lawyer or the client that the lawyer will provide continuing representation in the matter:

(1) is subject to rules 1.7 and 1.9(a) only if the lawyer knows* that the representation of the client involves a conflict of interest; and

(2) is subject to rule 1.10 only if the lawyer knows* that another lawyer associated with the lawyer in a law firm* is prohibited from representation by rule 1.7 or 1.9(a) with respect to the matter.

(b) Except as provided in paragraph (a)(2), rule 1.10 is inapplicable to a representation governed by this rule.

(c) The personal disqualification of a lawyer participating in the program will not be imputed to other lawyers participating in the program.

* An asterisk (*) identifies a word or phrase defined in the terminology rule, rule 1.0.1.

Comment

[1] Courts, government agencies, bar associations, law schools and various nonprofit organizations have established programs through which lawyers provide short-term limited legal services—such as advice or the completion of legal forms that will assist persons* in addressing their legal problems without further representation by a lawyer. In these programs, such as legal-advice hotlines, advice-only clinics or pro se counseling programs, whenever a lawyer-client relationship is established, there is no expectation that the lawyer's representation of the client will continue beyond that limited consultation. Such programs are normally operated under circumstances in which it is not feasible for a lawyer to systematically screen* for conflicts of interest as is generally required before undertaking a representation.

[2] A lawyer who provides short-term limited legal services pursuant to this rule must secure the client's informed consent* to the limited scope of the representation. (See rule 1.2(b).) If a short-term limited representation would not be reasonable* under the circumstances, the lawyer may offer advice to the client but must also advise the client of the need for further assistance of counsel. Except as provided in this rule, these rules and the State Bar Act, including the lawyer's duty of confidentiality under Business and Professions Code section 6068, subdivision (e)(1) and rules 1.6 and 1.9, are applicable to the limited representation.

[3] A lawyer who is representing a client in the circumstances addressed by this rule ordinarily is not able to check systematically for conflicts of interest. Therefore, paragraph (a)(1) requires compliance with rules 1.7 and 1.9(a) only if the lawyer knows* that the representation presents a conflict of interest for the lawyer. In addition, paragraph (a)(2) imputes conflicts of interest to the lawyer only if the lawyer knows* that another lawyer in the lawyer's law firm* would be disqualified under rules 1.7 or 1.9(a).

[4] Because the limited nature of the services significantly reduces the risk of conflicts of interest with other matters being handled by the lawyer's law firm,* paragraph (b) provides that imputed conflicts of interest are inapplicable to a representation governed by this rule except as provided by paragraph (a)(2). Paragraph (a)(2) imputes conflicts of interest to the participating lawyer when the lawyer knows* that any lawyer in the lawyer's firm* would be disqualified under rules 1.7 or 1.9(a). By virtue of paragraph (b), moreover, a lawyer's participation in a short-term limited legal services program will not be imputed to the lawyer's law firm* or preclude the lawyer's law firm* from undertaking or continuing the representation of a client with interests adverse to a client being represented under the program's auspices. Nor will the personal disqualification of a lawyer participating in the program be imputed to other lawyers participating in the program.

[5] If, after commencing a short-term limited representation in accordance with this rule, a lawyer undertakes to represent the client in the matter on an ongoing basis, rules 1.7, 1.9(a), and 1.10 become applicable.

INFORMATION ABOUT LEGAL SERVICES

Rule 7.1 Communications Concerning a Lawyer's Services

(a) A lawyer shall not make a false or misleading communication about the lawyer or the lawyer's services. A communication is false or misleading if it contains a material misrepresentation of fact or law, or omits a fact necessary to make the communication considered as a whole not materially misleading.

(b) The Board of Trustees of the State Bar may formulate and adopt standards as to communications that will be presumed to violate rule 7.1, 7.2, 7.3, 7.4 or 7.5. The standards shall only be used as presumptions affecting the burden of proof in disciplinary proceedings involving alleged violations of these rules. "Presumption affecting the burden of proof" means that presumption defined in Evidence

* An asterisk (*) identifies a word or phrase defined in the terminology rule, rule 1.0.1.

Code sections 605 and 606. Such standards formulated and adopted by the Board, as from time to time amended, shall be effective and binding on all lawyers.

Comment

[1] This rule governs all communications of any type whatsoever about the lawyer or the lawyer's services, including advertising permitted by rule 7.2. A communication includes any message or offer made by or on behalf of a lawyer concerning the availability for professional employment of a lawyer or a lawyer's law firm* directed to any person.*

[2] A communication that contains an express guarantee or warranty of the result of a particular representation is a false or misleading communication under this rule. (See also Bus. & Prof. Code, § 6157.2, subd. (a).)

[3] This rule prohibits truthful statements that are misleading. A truthful statement is misleading if it omits a fact necessary to make the lawyer's communication considered as a whole not materially misleading. A truthful statement is also misleading if it is presented in a manner that creates a substantial* likelihood that it will lead a reasonable* person* to formulate a specific conclusion about the lawyer or the lawyer's services for which there is no reasonable* factual foundation. Any communication that states or implies "no fee without recovery" is also misleading unless the communication also expressly discloses whether or not the client will be liable for costs.

[4] A communication that truthfully reports a lawyer's achievements on behalf of clients or former clients, or a testimonial about or endorsement of the lawyer, may be misleading if presented so as to lead a reasonable* person* to form an unjustified expectation that the same results could be obtained for other clients in similar matters without reference to the specific factual and legal circumstances of each client's case. Similarly, an unsubstantiated comparison of the lawyer's services or fees with the services or fees of other lawyers may be misleading if presented with such specificity as would lead a reasonable* person* to conclude that the comparison can be substantiated. An appropriate disclaimer or qualifying language often avoids creating unjustified expectations.

[5] This rule prohibits a lawyer from making a communication that states or implies that the lawyer is able to provide legal services in a language other than English unless the lawyer can actually provide legal services in that language or the communication also states in the language of the communication the employment title of the person* who speaks such language.

[6] Rules 7.1 through 7.5 are not the sole basis for regulating communications concerning a lawyer's services. (See, e.g., Bus. & Prof. Code, §§ 6150–6159.2, 17000 et. seq.) Other state or federal laws may also apply.

Rule 7.2 Advertising

(a) Subject to the requirements of rules 7.1 and 7.3, a lawyer may advertise services through any written, recorded or electronic means of communication, including public media.

(b) A lawyer shall not compensate, promise or give anything of value to a person* for the purpose of recommending or securing the services of the lawyer or the lawyer's law firm,* except that a lawyer may:

(1) pay the reasonable* costs of advertisements or communications permitted by this rule;

(2) pay the usual charges of a legal services plan or a qualified lawyer referral service. A qualified lawyer referral service is a lawyer referral service established, sponsored and operated in accordance with the State Bar of California's Minimum Standards for a Lawyer Referral Service in California;

(3) pay for a law practice in accordance with rule 1.17;

* An asterisk (*) identifies a word or phrase defined in the terminology rule, rule 1.0.1.

(4) refer clients to another lawyer or a nonlawyer professional pursuant to an arrangement not otherwise prohibited under these Rules or the State Bar Act that provides for the other person* to refer clients or customers to the lawyer, if:

(i) the reciprocal referral arrangement is not exclusive; and

(ii) the client is informed of the existence and nature of the arrangement;

(5) offer or give a gift or gratuity to a person* having made a recommendation resulting in the employment of the lawyer or the lawyer's law firm,* provided that the gift or gratuity was not offered or given in consideration of any promise, agreement, or understanding that such a gift or gratuity would be forthcoming or that referrals would be made or encouraged in the future.

(c) Any communication made pursuant to this rule shall include the name and address of at least one lawyer or law firm* responsible for its content.

Comment

[1] This rule permits public dissemination of accurate information concerning a lawyer and the lawyer's services, including for example, the lawyer's name or firm* name, the lawyer's contact information; the kinds of services the lawyer will undertake; the basis on which the lawyer's fees are determined, including prices for specific services and payment and credit arrangements; a lawyer's foreign language ability; names of references and, with their consent, names of clients regularly represented; and other information that might invite the attention of those seeking legal assistance. This rule, however, prohibits the dissemination of false or misleading information, for example, an advertisement that sets forth a specific fee or range of fees for a particular service where, in fact, the lawyer charges or intends to charge a greater fee than that stated in the advertisement.

[2] Neither this rule nor rule 7.3 prohibits communications authorized by law, such as court-approved class action notices.

Paying Others to Recommend a Lawyer

[3] Paragraph (b)(1) permits a lawyer to compensate employees, agents, and vendors who are engaged to provide marketing or client-development services, such as publicists, public-relations personnel, business-development staff, and website designers. See rule 5.3 for the duties of lawyers and law firms* with respect to supervising the conduct of nonlawyers who prepare marketing materials and provide client development services.

[4] Paragraph (b)(4) permits a lawyer to make referrals to another lawyer or nonlawyer professional, in return for the undertaking of that person* to refer clients or customers to the lawyer. Such reciprocal referral arrangements must not interfere with the lawyer's professional judgment as to making referrals or as to providing substantive legal services. (See rules 2.1 and 5.4(c).) Conflicts of interest created by arrangements made pursuant to paragraph (b)(4) are governed by rule 1.7. A division of fees between or among lawyers not in the same law firm* is governed by rule 1.5.1.

Rule 7.3 Solicitation of Clients

(a) A lawyer shall not by in-person, live telephone or real-time electronic contact solicit professional employment when a significant motive for doing so is the lawyer's pecuniary gain, unless the person* contacted:

(1) is a lawyer; or

(2) has a family, close personal, or prior professional relationship with the lawyer.

(b) A lawyer shall not solicit professional employment by written,* recorded or electronic communication or by in-person, telephone or real-time electronic contact even when not otherwise prohibited by paragraph (a), if:

* An asterisk (*) identifies a word or phrase defined in the terminology rule, rule 1.0.1.

(1) the person* being solicited has made known* to the lawyer a desire not to be solicited by the lawyer; or

(2) the solicitation is transmitted in any manner which involves intrusion, coercion, duress or harassment.

(c) Every written,* recorded or electronic communication from a lawyer soliciting professional employment from any person* known* to be in need of legal services in a particular matter shall include the word "Advertisement" or words of similar import on the outside envelope, if any, and at the beginning and ending of any recorded or electronic communication, unless the recipient of the communication is a person* specified in paragraphs (a)(1) or (a)(2), or unless it is apparent from the context that the communication is an advertisement.

(d) Notwithstanding the prohibitions in paragraph (a), a lawyer may participate with a prepaid or group legal service plan operated by an organization not owned or directed by the lawyer that uses in-person, live telephone or real-time electronic contact to solicit memberships or subscriptions for the plan from persons* who are not known* to need legal services in a particular matter covered by the plan.

(e) As used in this rule, the terms "solicitation" and "solicit" refer to an oral or written* targeted communication initiated by or on behalf of the lawyer that is directed to a specific person* and that offers to provide, or can reasonably* be understood as offering to provide, legal services.

Comment

[1] A lawyer's communication does not constitute a solicitation if it is directed to the general public, such as through a billboard, an Internet banner advertisement, a website or a television commercial, or if it is in response to a request for information or is automatically generated in response to Internet searches.

[2] Paragraph (a) does not apply to situations in which the lawyer is motivated by considerations other than the lawyer's pecuniary gain. Therefore, paragraph (a) does not prohibit a lawyer from participating in constitutionally protected activities of bona fide public or charitable legal-service organizations, or bona fide political, social, civic, fraternal, employee or trade organizations whose purposes include providing or recommending legal services to its members or beneficiaries. (See, e.g., *In re Primus* (1978) 436 U.S. 412 [98 S.Ct. 1893].)

[3] This rule does not prohibit a lawyer from contacting representatives of organizations or groups that may be interested in establishing a bona fide group or prepaid legal plan for their members, insureds, beneficiaries or other third parties for the purpose of informing such entities of the availability of and details concerning the plan or arrangement which the lawyer or lawyer's firm* is willing to offer.

[4] Lawyers who participate in a legal service plan as permitted under paragraph (d) must comply with rules 7.1, 7.2, and 7.3(b). (See also rules 5.4 and 8.4(a).)

Rule 7.4 Communication of Fields of Practice and Specialization

(a) A lawyer shall not state that the lawyer is a certified specialist in a particular field of law, unless:

(1) the lawyer is currently certified as a specialist by the Board of Legal Specialization, or any other entity accredited by the State Bar to designate specialists pursuant to standards adopted by the Board of Trustees; and

(2) the name of the certifying organization is clearly identified in the communication.

(b) Notwithstanding paragraph (a), a lawyer may communicate the fact that the lawyer does or does not practice in particular fields of law. A lawyer may also communicate that his or her practice

* An asterisk (*) identifies a word or phrase defined in the terminology rule, rule 1.0.1.

specializes in, is limited to, or is concentrated in a particular field of law, subject to the requirements of rule 7.1.

Rule 7.5 Firm* Names and Trade Names

(a) A lawyer shall not use a firm* name, trade name or other professional designation that violates rule 7.1.

(b) A lawyer in private practice shall not use a firm* name, trade name or other professional designation that states or implies a relationship with a government agency or with a public or charitable legal services organization, or otherwise violates rule 7.1.

(c) A lawyer shall not state or imply that the lawyer practices in or has a professional relationship with a law firm* or other organization unless that is the fact.

Comment

The term "other professional designation" includes, but is not limited to, logos, letterheads, URLs, and signature blocks.

MAINTAINING THE INTEGRITY OF THE PROFESSION

Rule 8.1 False Statement Regarding Application for Admission to Practice Law

(a) An applicant for admission to practice law shall not, in connection with that person's* own application for admission, make a statement of material fact that the lawyer knows* to be false, or make such a statement with reckless disregard as to its truth or falsity.

(b) A lawyer shall not, in connection with another person's* application for admission to practice law, make a statement of material fact that the lawyer knows* to be false.

(c) An applicant for admission to practice law, or a lawyer in connection with an application for admission, shall not fail to disclose a fact necessary to correct a statement known* by the applicant or the lawyer to have created a material misapprehension in the matter, except that this rule does not authorize disclosure of information protected by Business and Professions Code section 6068, subdivision (e) and rule 1.6.

(d) As used in this rule, "admission to practice law" includes admission or readmission to membership in the State Bar; reinstatement to active membership in the State Bar; and any similar process relating to admission or certification to practice law in California or elsewhere.

Comment

[1] A person* who makes a false statement in connection with that person's* own application for admission to practice law may be subject to discipline under this rule after that person* has been admitted. (See, e.g., *In re Gossage* (2000) 23 Cal.4th 1080 [99 Cal.Rptr.2d 130].)

[2] A lawyer's duties with respect to a *pro hac vice* application or other application to a court for admission to practice law are governed by rule 3.3.

[3] A lawyer representing an applicant for admission to practice law is governed by the rules applicable to the lawyer-client relationship, including Business and Professions Code section 6068, subdivision (e)(1) and rule 1.6. A lawyer representing a lawyer who is the subject of a disciplinary proceeding is not governed by this rule but is subject to the requirements of rule 3.3.

---

* An asterisk (*) identifies a word or phrase defined in the terminology rule, rule 1.0.1.

Rule 8.1.1 Compliance with Conditions of Discipline and Agreements in Lieu of Discipline

A lawyer shall comply with the terms and conditions attached to any agreement in lieu of discipline, any public or private reproval, or to other discipline administered by the State Bar pursuant to Business and Professions Code sections 6077 and 6078 and California Rules of Court, rule 9.19.

Comment

Other provisions also require a lawyer to comply with agreements in lieu of discipline and conditions of discipline. (See, e.g., Bus. & Prof. Code, § 6068, subds. (k), (*l*).)

Rule 8.2 Judicial Officials

(a) A lawyer shall not make a statement of fact that the lawyer knows* to be false or with reckless disregard as to its truth or falsity concerning the qualifications or integrity of a judge or judicial officer, or of a candidate for election or appointment to judicial office.

(b) A lawyer who is a candidate for judicial office in California shall comply with canon 5 of the California Code of Judicial Ethics. For purposes of this rule, "candidate for judicial office" means a lawyer seeking judicial office by election. The determination of when a lawyer is a candidate for judicial office by election is defined in the terminology section of the California Code of Judicial Ethics. A lawyer's duty to comply with this rule shall end when the lawyer announces withdrawal of the lawyer's candidacy or when the results of the election are final, whichever occurs first.

(c) A lawyer who seeks appointment to judicial office shall comply with canon 5B(1) of the California Code of Judicial Ethics. A lawyer becomes an applicant seeking judicial office by appointment at the time of first submission of an application or personal data questionnaire to the appointing authority. A lawyer's duty to comply with this rule shall end when the lawyer advises the appointing authority of the withdrawal of the lawyer's application.

Comment

To maintain the fair and independent administration of justice, lawyers should defend judges and courts unjustly criticized. Lawyers also are obligated to maintain the respect due to the courts of justice and judicial officers. (See Bus. & Prof. Code, § 6068, subd. (b).)

Rule 8.3 [Reserved]

Rule 8.4 Misconduct

It is professional misconduct for a lawyer to:

(a) violate these rules or the State Bar Act, knowingly* assist, solicit, or induce another to do so, or do so through the acts of another;

(b) commit a criminal act that reflects adversely on the lawyer's honesty, trustworthiness, or fitness as a lawyer in other respects;

(c) engage in conduct involving dishonesty, fraud,* deceit, or reckless or intentional misrepresentation;

(d) engage in conduct that is prejudicial to the administration of justice;

(e) state or imply an ability to influence improperly a government agency or official, or to achieve results by means that violate these rules, the State Bar Act, or other law; or

(f) knowingly* assist, solicit, or induce a judge or judicial officer in conduct that is a violation of an applicable code of judicial ethics or code of judicial conduct, or other law. For purposes of this rule, "judge" and "judicial officer" have the same meaning as in rule 3.5(c).

---

* An asterisk (*) identifies a word or phrase defined in the terminology rule, rule 1.0.1.

Comment

[1] A violation of this rule can occur when a lawyer is acting in propria persona or when a lawyer is not practicing law or acting in a professional capacity.

[2] Paragraph (a) does not prohibit a lawyer from advising a client concerning action the client is legally entitled to take.

[3] A lawyer may be disciplined for criminal acts as set forth in Business and Professions Code sections 6101 et seq., or if the criminal act constitutes "other misconduct warranting discipline" as defined by California Supreme Court case law. (See *In re Kelley* (1990) 52 Cal.3d 487 [276 Cal.Rptr. 375].)

[4] A lawyer may be disciplined under Business and Professions Code section 6106 for acts involving moral turpitude, dishonesty, or corruption, whether intentional, reckless, or grossly negligent.

[5] Paragraph (c) does not apply where a lawyer advises clients or others about, or supervises, lawful covert activity in the investigation of violations of civil or criminal law or constitutional rights, provided the lawyer's conduct is otherwise in compliance with these rules and the State Bar Act.

[6] This rule does not prohibit those activities of a particular lawyer that are protected by the First Amendment to the United States Constitution or by Article I, section 2 of the California Constitution.

Rule 8.4.1 Prohibited Discrimination, Harassment and Retaliation

(a) In representing a client, or in terminating or refusing to accept the representation of any client, a lawyer shall not:

(1) unlawfully harass or unlawfully discriminate against persons* on the basis of any protected characteristic; or

(2) unlawfully retaliate against persons.*

(b) In relation to a law firm's operations, a lawyer shall not:

(1) on the basis of any protected characteristic,

(i) unlawfully discriminate or knowingly* permit unlawful discrimination;

(ii) unlawfully harass or knowingly* permit the unlawful harassment of an employee, an applicant, an unpaid intern or volunteer, or a person* providing services pursuant to a contract; or

(iii) unlawfully refuse to hire or employ a person*, or refuse to select a person* for a training program leading to employment, or bar or discharge a person* from employment or from a training program leading to employment, or discriminate against a person* in compensation or in terms, conditions, or privileges of employment; or

(2) unlawfully retaliate against persons.*

(c) For purposes of this rule:

(1) "protected characteristic" means race, religious creed, color, national origin, ancestry, physical disability, mental disability, medical condition, genetic information, marital status, sex, gender, gender identity, gender expression, sexual orientation, age, military and veteran status, or other category of discrimination prohibited by applicable law, whether the category is actual or perceived;

* An asterisk (*) identifies a word or phrase defined in the terminology rule, rule 1.0.1.

(2) "knowingly permit" means to fail to advocate corrective action where the lawyer knows* of a discriminatory policy or practice that results in the unlawful discrimination or harassment prohibited by paragraph (b);

(3) "unlawfully" and "unlawful" shall be determined by reference to applicable state and federal statutes and decisions making unlawful discrimination or harassment in employment and in offering goods and services to the public; and

(4) "retaliate" means to take adverse action against a person* because that person* has (i) opposed, or (ii) pursued, participated in, or assisted any action alleging, any conduct prohibited by paragraphs (a)(1) or (b)(1) of this rule.

(d) A lawyer who is the subject of a State Bar investigation or State Bar Court proceeding alleging a violation of this rule shall promptly notify the State Bar of any criminal, civil, or administrative action premised, whether in whole or part, on the same conduct that is the subject of the State Bar investigation or State Bar Court proceeding.

(e) Upon being issued a notice of a disciplinary charge under this rule, a lawyer shall:

(1) if the notice is of a disciplinary charge under paragraph (a) of this rule, provide a copy of the notice to the California Department of Fair Employment and Housing and the United States Department of Justice, Coordination and Review Section; or

(2) if the notice is of a disciplinary charge under paragraph (b) of this rule, provide a copy of the notice to the California Department of Fair Employment and Housing and the United States Equal Employment Opportunity Commission.

(f) This rule shall not preclude a lawyer from:

(1) representing a client alleged to have engaged in unlawful discrimination, harassment, or retaliation;

(2) declining or withdrawing from a representation as required or permitted by rule 1.16; or

(3) providing advice and engaging in advocacy as otherwise required or permitted by these rules and the State Bar Act.

Comment

[1] Conduct that violates this rule undermines confidence in the legal profession and our legal system and is contrary to the fundamental principle that all people are created equal. A lawyer may not engage in such conduct through the acts of another. (See rule 8.4(a).) In relation to a law firm's operations, this rule imposes on all law firm* lawyers the responsibility to advocate corrective action to address known* harassing or discriminatory conduct by the firm* or any of its other lawyers or nonlawyer personnel. Law firm* management and supervisorial lawyers retain their separate responsibility under rules 5.1 and 5.3. Neither this rule nor rule 5.1 or 5.3 imposes on the alleged victim of any conduct prohibited by this rule any responsibility to advocate corrective action.

[2] The conduct prohibited by paragraph (a) includes the conduct of a lawyer in a proceeding before a judicial officer. (See Cal. Code Jud. Ethics, canon 3B(6) ["A judge shall require lawyers in proceedings before the judge to refrain from manifesting, by words or conduct, bias or prejudice based upon race, sex, gender, religion, national origin, ethnicity, disability, age, sexual orientation, marital status, socioeconomic status, or political affiliation against parties, witnesses, counsel, or others."].) A lawyer does not violate paragraph (a) by referring to any particular status or group when the reference is relevant to factual or legal issues or arguments in the representation. While both the parties and the court retain discretion to refer such conduct to the State Bar, a court's finding that peremptory challenges were exercised on a discriminatory basis does not alone establish a violation of paragraph (a).

* An asterisk (*) identifies a word or phrase defined in the terminology rule, rule 1.0.1.

[3] A lawyer does not violate this rule by limiting the scope or subject matter of the lawyer's practice or by limiting the lawyer's practice to members of underserved populations. A lawyer also does not violate this rule by otherwise restricting who will be accepted as clients for advocacy-based reasons, as required or permitted by these rules or other law.

[4] This rule does not apply to conduct protected by the First Amendment to the United States Constitution or by Article I, section 2 of the California Constitution.

[5] What constitutes a failure to advocate corrective action under paragraph (c)(2) will depend on the nature and seriousness of the discriminatory policy or practice, the extent to which the lawyer knows* of unlawful discrimination or harassment resulting from that policy or practice, and the nature of the lawyer's relationship to the lawyer or law firm* implementing that policy or practice. For example, a law firm* non-management and nonsupervisorial lawyer who becomes aware that the law firm* is engaging in a discriminatory hiring practice may advocate corrective action by bringing that discriminatory practice to the attention of a law firm* management lawyer who would have responsibility under rule 5.1 or 5.3 to take reasonable* remedial action upon becoming aware of a violation of this rule.

[6] Paragraph (d) ensures that the State Bar and the State Bar Court will be provided with information regarding related proceedings that may be relevant in determining whether a State Bar investigation or a State Bar Court proceeding relating to a violation of this rule should be abated.

[7] Paragraph (e) recognizes the public policy served by enforcement of laws and regulations prohibiting unlawful discrimination, by ensuring that the state and federal agencies with primary responsibility for coordinating the enforcement of those laws and regulations is provided with notice of any allegation of unlawful discrimination, harassment, or retaliation by a lawyer that the State Bar finds has sufficient merit to warrant issuance of a notice of a disciplinary charge.

[8] This rule permits the imposition of discipline for conduct that would not necessarily result in the award of a remedy in a civil or administrative proceeding if such proceeding were filed.

[9] A disciplinary investigation or proceeding for conduct coming within this rule may also be initiated and maintained if such conduct warrants discipline under California Business and Professions Code sections 6106 and 6068, the California Supreme Court's inherent authority to impose discipline, or other disciplinary standard.

Rule 8.5 Disciplinary Authority; Choice of Law

(a) Disciplinary Authority.

A lawyer admitted to practice in California is subject to the disciplinary authority of California, regardless of where the lawyer's conduct occurs. A lawyer not admitted in California is also subject to the disciplinary authority of California if the lawyer provides or offers to provide any legal services in California. A lawyer may be subject to the disciplinary authority of both California and another jurisdiction for the same conduct.

(b) Choice of Law.

In any exercise of the disciplinary authority of California, the rules of professional conduct to be applied shall be as follows:

(1) for conduct in connection with a matter pending before a tribunal,* the rules of the jurisdiction in which the tribunal* sits, unless the rules of the tribunal* provide otherwise; and

(2) for any other conduct, the rules of the jurisdiction in which the lawyer's conduct occurred, or, if the predominant effect of the conduct is in a different jurisdiction, the rules of that jurisdiction shall be applied to the conduct. A lawyer shall not be subject to discipline if the

* An asterisk (*) identifies a word or phrase defined in the terminology rule, rule 1.0.1.

lawyer's conduct conforms to the rules of a jurisdiction in which the lawyer reasonably believes* the predominant effect of the lawyer's conduct will occur.

Comment

Disciplinary Authority

The conduct of a lawyer admitted to practice in California is subject to the disciplinary authority of California. (See Bus. & Prof. Code, §§ 6077, 6100.) Extension of the disciplinary authority of California to other lawyers who provide or offer to provide legal services in California is for the protection of the residents of California. A lawyer disciplined by a disciplinary authority in another jurisdiction may be subject to discipline in California for the same conduct. (See, e.g., § 6049.1.)

CALIFORNIA RULES ON MULTIJURISDICTIONAL PRACTICE

[On April 8, 2004, the California Supreme Court approved several rules on out-of-state lawyers who are practicing in California. In 2007, these rules were renumbered and restructured as follows.]

Rule

Rule 9.45. Registered legal services attorneys

(a) Definitions

The following definitions apply in this rule:

(1) "Qualifying legal services provider" means either of the following, provided that the qualifying legal services provider follows quality-control procedures approved by the State Bar of California:

(A) A nonprofit entity incorporated and operated exclusively in California that as its primary purpose and function provides legal services without charge in civil matters to indigent persons, especially underserved client groups, such as the elderly, persons with disabilities, juveniles, and non-English-speaking persons; or

(B) A program operated exclusively in California by a nonprofit law school approved by the American Bar Association or accredited by the State Bar of California that has operated for at least two years at a cost of at least $20,000 per year as an identifiable law school unit with a primary purpose and function of providing legal services without charge to indigent persons.

(2) "Active member in good standing of the bar of a United States state, jurisdiction, possession, territory, or dependency" means an attorney who:

(A) Is a member in good standing of the entity governing the practice of law in each jurisdiction in which the member is licensed to practice law;

(B) Remains an active member in good standing of the entity governing the practice of law in at least one United States state, jurisdiction, possession, territory, or dependency other than California while practicing law as a registered legal services attorney in California; and

(C) Has not been disbarred, has not resigned with charges pending, or is not suspended from practicing law in any other jurisdiction.

(b) Scope of practice

Subject to all applicable rules, regulations, and statutes, an attorney practicing law under this rule may practice law in California only while working, with or without pay, at a qualifying legal services provider, as defined in this rule, and, at that institution and only on behalf of its clients, may engage, under supervision, in all forms of legal practice that are permissible for a member of the State Bar of California.

(c) Requirements

For an attorney to practice law under this rule, the attorney must:

(1) Be an active member in good standing of the bar of a United States state, jurisdiction, possession, territory, or dependency;

(2) Register with the State Bar of California and file an Application for Determination of Moral Character;

(3) Meet all of the requirements for admission to the State Bar of California, except that the attorney:

(A) Need not take the California bar examination or the Multistate Professional Responsibility Examination; and

(B) May practice law while awaiting the result of his or her Application for Determination of Moral Character;

(4) Comply with the rules adopted by the Board of Governors relating to the State Bar Registered Legal Services Attorney Program;

(5) Practice law exclusively for a single qualifying legal services provider, except that, if so qualified, an attorney may, while practicing under this rule, simultaneously practice law as registered in-house counsel;

(6) Practice law under the supervision of an attorney who is employed by the qualifying legal services provider and who is a member in good standing of the State Bar of California;

(7) Abide by all of the laws and rules that govern members of the State Bar of California, including the Minimum Continuing Legal Education (MCLE) requirements;

(8) Satisfy in his or her first year of practice under this rule all of the MCLE requirements, including ethics education, that members of the State Bar of California must complete every three years; and

(9) Not have taken and failed the California bar examination within five years immediately preceding application to register under this rule.

(d) Application

To qualify to practice law as a registered legal services attorney, the attorney must:

(1) Register as an attorney applicant and file an Application for Determination of Moral Character with the Committee of Bar Examiners;

(2) Submit to the State Bar of California a declaration signed by the attorney agreeing that he or she will be subject to the disciplinary authority of the Supreme Court of California and the State Bar of California and attesting that he or she will not practice law in California other than under supervision at a qualifying legal services provider during the time he or she practices law as a registered legal services attorney in California, except that, if so qualified, the attorney may, while practicing under this rule, simultaneously practice law as registered in-house counsel; and

(3) Submit to the State Bar of California a declaration signed by a qualifying supervisor on behalf of the qualifying legal services provider in California attesting that the applicant will work, with or without pay, as an attorney for the organization; that the applicant will be supervised as specified in this rule; and that the qualifying legal services provider and the supervising attorney assume professional responsibility for any work performed by the applicant under this rule.

(e) Duration of practice

An attorney may practice for no more than a total of three years under this rule.

(f) Application and registration fees

The State Bar of California may set appropriate application fees and initial and annual registration fees to be paid by registered legal services attorneys.

(g) State Bar Registered Legal Services Attorney Program

The State Bar may establish and administer a program for registering California legal services attorneys under rules adopted by the Board of Governors of the State Bar.

(h) Supervision

To meet the requirements of this rule, an attorney supervising a registered legal services attorney:

(1) Must be an active member in good standing of the State Bar of California;

(2) Must have actively practiced law in California and been a member in good standing of the State Bar of California for at least the two years immediately preceding the time of supervision;

(3) Must have practiced law as a full-time occupation for at least four years;

(4) Must not supervise more than two registered legal services attorneys concurrently;

(5) Must assume professional responsibility for any work that the registered legal services attorney performs under the supervising attorney's supervision;

(6) Must assist, counsel, and provide direct supervision of the registered legal services attorney in the activities authorized by this rule and review such activities with the supervised attorney, to the extent required for the protection of the client;

(7) Must read, approve, and personally sign any pleadings, briefs, or other similar documents prepared by the registered legal services attorney before their filing, and must read and approve any documents prepared by the registered legal services attorney for execution by any person who is not a member of the State Bar of California before their submission for execution; and

(8) May, in his or her absence, designate another attorney meeting the requirements of (1) through (7) to provide the supervision required under this rule.

(i) Inherent power of Supreme Court

Nothing in this rule may be construed as affecting the power of the Supreme Court of California to exercise its inherent jurisdiction over the practice of law in California.

(j) Effect of rule on multijurisdictional practice

Nothing in this rule limits the scope of activities permissible under existing law by attorneys who are not members of the State Bar of California.

Rule 9.46. Registered in-house counsel

(a) Definitions

The following definitions apply to terms used in this rule:

(1) "Qualifying institution" means a corporation, a partnership, an association, or other legal entity, including its subsidiaries and organizational affiliates. Neither a

governmental entity nor an entity that provides legal services to others can be a qualifying institution for purposes of this rule. A qualifying institution must:

(A) Employ at least 10 employees full time in California; or

(B) Employ in California an attorney who is an active member in good standing of the State Bar of California.

(2) "Active member in good standing of the bar of a United States state, jurisdiction, possession, territory, or dependency" means an attorney who meets all of the following criteria:

(A) Is a member in good standing of the entity governing the practice of law in each jurisdiction in which the member is licensed to practice law;

(B) Remains an active member in good standing of the entity governing the practice of law in at least one United States state, jurisdiction, possession, territory, or dependency, other than California, while practicing law as registered in-house counsel in California; and

(C) Has not been disbarred, has not resigned with charges pending, or is not suspended from practicing law in any other jurisdiction.

(b) Scope of practice

Subject to all applicable rules, regulations, and statutes, an attorney practicing law under this rule is:

(1) Permitted to provide legal services in California only to the qualifying institution that employs him or her;

(2) Not permitted to make court appearances in California state courts or to engage in any other activities for which *pro hac vice* admission is required if they are performed in California by an attorney who is not a member of the State Bar of California; and

(3) Not permitted to provide personal or individual representation to any customers, shareholders, owners, partners, officers, employees, servants, or agents of the qualifying institution.

(c) Requirements

For an attorney to practice law under this rule, the attorney must:

(1) Be an active member in good standing of the bar of a United States state, jurisdiction, possession, territory, or dependency;

(2) Register with the State Bar of California and file an Application for Determination of Moral Character;

(3) Meet all of the requirements for admission to the State Bar of California, except that the attorney:

(A) Need not take the California bar examination or the Multistate Professional Responsibility Examination; and

(B) May practice law while awaiting the result of his or her Application for Determination of Moral Character;

(4) Comply with the rules adopted by the Board of Governors relating to the State Bar Registered In-House Counsel Program;

(5) Practice law exclusively for a single qualifying institution, except that, while practicing under this rule, the attorney may, if so qualified, simultaneously practice law as a registered legal services attorney;

(6) Abide by all of the laws and rules that govern members of the State Bar of California, including the Minimum Continuing Legal Education (MCLE) requirements;

(7) Satisfy in his or her first year of practice under this rule all of the MCLE requirements, including ethics education, that members of the State Bar of California must complete every three years and, thereafter, satisfy the MCLE requirements applicable to all members of the State Bar; and

(8) Reside in California.

(d) Application

To qualify to practice law as registered in-house counsel, an attorney must:

(1) Register as an attorney applicant and file an Application for Determination of Moral Character with the Committee of Bar Examiners;

(2) Submit to the State Bar of California a declaration signed by the attorney agreeing that he or she will be subject to the disciplinary authority of the Supreme Court of California and the State Bar of California and attesting that he or she will not practice law in California other than on behalf of the qualifying institution during the time he or she is registered in-house counsel in California, except that if so qualified, the attorney may, while practicing under this rule, simultaneously practice law as a registered legal services attorney; and

(3) Submit to the State Bar of California a declaration signed by an officer, a director, or a general counsel of the applicant's employer, on behalf of the applicant's employer, attesting that the applicant is employed as an attorney for the employer, that the nature of the employment conforms to the requirements of this rule, that the employer will notify the State Bar of California within 30 days of the cessation of the applicant's employment in California, and that the person signing the declaration believes, to the best of his or her knowledge after reasonable inquiry, that the applicant qualifies for registration under this rule and is an individual of good moral character.

(e) Duration of practice

A registered in-house counsel must renew his or her registration annually. There is no limitation on the number of years in-house counsel may register under this rule. Registered in-house counsel may practice law under this rule only for as long as he or she remains employed by the same qualifying institution that provided the declaration in support of his or her application. If an attorney practicing law as registered in-house counsel leaves the employment of his or her employer or changes employers, he or she must notify the State Bar of California within 30 days. If an attorney wishes to practice law under this rule for a new employer, he or she must first register as in-house counsel for that employer.

(f) Eligibility

An application to register under this rule may not be denied because:

(1) The attorney applicant has practiced law in California as in-house counsel before the effective date of this rule.

(2) The attorney applicant is practicing law as in-house counsel at or after the effective date of this rule, provided that the attorney applies under this rule within six months of its effective date.

(g) Application and registration fees

The State Bar of California may set appropriate application fees and initial and annual registration fees to be paid by registered in-house counsel.

(h) State Bar Registered In-House Counsel Program

The State Bar must establish and administer a program for registering California in-house counsel under rules adopted by the Board of Governors.

(i) Inherent power of Supreme Court

Nothing in this rule may be construed as affecting the power of the Supreme Court of California to exercise its inherent jurisdiction over the practice of law in California.

(j) Effect of rule on multijurisdictional practice

Nothing in this rule limits the scope of activities permissible under existing law by attorneys who are not members of the State Bar of California.

Rule 9.47. Attorneys practicing law temporarily in California as part of litigation

(a) Definitions

The following definitions apply to the terms used in this rule:

(1) "A formal legal proceeding" means litigation, arbitration, mediation, or a legal action before an administrative decision-maker.

(2) "Authorized to appear" means the attorney is permitted to appear in the proceeding by the rules of the jurisdiction in which the formal legal proceeding is taking place or will be taking place.

(3) "Active member in good standing of the bar of a United States state, jurisdiction, possession, territory, or dependency" means an attorney who meets all of the following criteria:

(A) Is a member in good standing of the entity governing the practice of law in each jurisdiction in which the member is licensed to practice law;

(B) Remains an active member in good standing of the entity governing the practice of law in at least one United States state, jurisdiction, possession, territory, or dependency while practicing law under this rule; and

(C) Has not been disbarred, has not resigned with charges pending, or is not suspended from practicing law in any other jurisdiction.

(b) Requirements

For an attorney to practice law under this rule, the attorney must:

(1) Maintain an office in a United States jurisdiction other than California and in which the attorney is licensed to practice law;

(2) Already be retained by a client in the matter for which the attorney is providing legal services in California, except that the attorney may provide legal advice to a potential client, at the potential client's request, to assist the client in deciding whether to retain the attorney;

(3) Indicate on any Web site or other advertisement that is accessible in California either that the attorney is not a member of the State Bar of California or that the attorney is admitted to practice law only in the states listed; and

(4) Be an active member in good standing of the bar of a United States state, jurisdiction, possession, territory, or dependency.

(c) Permissible activities

An attorney meeting the requirements of this rule, who complies with all applicable rules, regulations, and statutes, is not engaging in the unauthorized practice of law in California if the attorney's services are part of:

(1) A formal legal proceeding that is pending in another jurisdiction and in which the attorney is authorized to appear;

(2) A formal legal proceeding that is anticipated but is not yet pending in California and in which the attorney reasonably expects to be authorized to appear;

(3) A formal legal proceeding that is anticipated but is not yet pending in another jurisdiction and in which the attorney reasonably expects to be authorized to appear; or

(4) A formal legal proceeding that is anticipated or pending and in which the attorney's supervisor is authorized to appear or reasonably expects to be authorized to appear.

The attorney whose anticipated authorization to appear in a formal legal proceeding serves as the basis for practice under this rule must seek that authorization promptly after it becomes possible to do so. Failure to seek that authorization promptly, or denial of that authorization, ends eligibility to practice under this rule.

(d) Restrictions

To qualify to practice law in California under this rule, an attorney must not:

(1) Hold out to the public or otherwise represent that he or she is admitted to practice law in California;

(2) Establish or maintain a resident office or other systematic or continuous presence in California for the practice of law;

(3) Be a resident of California;

(4) Be regularly employed in California;

(5) Regularly engage in substantial business or professional activities in California; or

(6) Have been disbarred, have resigned with charges pending, or be suspended from practicing law in any other jurisdiction.

(e) Conditions

By practicing law in California under this rule, an attorney agrees that he or she is providing legal services in California subject to:

(1) The jurisdiction of the State Bar of California;

(2) The jurisdiction of the courts of this state to the same extent as is a member of the State Bar of California; and

(3) The laws of the State of California relating to the practice of law, the State Bar Rules of Professional Conduct, the rules and regulations of the State Bar of California, and these rules.

(f) Inherent power of Supreme Court

Nothing in this rule may be construed as affecting the power of the Supreme Court of California to exercise its inherent jurisdiction over the practice of law in California.

(g) Effect of rule on multijurisdictional practice

Nothing in this rule limits the scope of activities permissible under existing law by attorneys who are not members of the State Bar of California.

Rule 9.48. Nonlitigating attorneys temporarily in California to provide legal services

(a) Definitions

The following definitions apply to terms used in this rule:

(1) "A transaction or other nonlitigation matter" includes any legal matter other than litigation, arbitration, mediation, or a legal action before an administrative decision-maker.

(2) "Active member in good standing of the bar of a United States state, jurisdiction, possession, territory, or dependency" means an attorney who meets all of the following criteria:

(A) Is a member in good standing of the entity governing the practice of law in each jurisdiction in which the member is licensed to practice law;

(B) Remains an active member in good standing of the entity governing the practice of law in at least one United States state, jurisdiction, possession, territory, or dependency other than California while practicing law under this rule; and

(C) Has not been disbarred, has not resigned with charges pending, or is not suspended from practicing law in any other jurisdiction.

(b) Requirements

For an attorney to practice law under this rule, the attorney must:

(1) Maintain an office in a United States jurisdiction other than California and in which the attorney is licensed to practice law;

(2) Already be retained by a client in the matter for which the attorney is providing legal services in California, except that the attorney may provide legal advice to a potential client, at the potential client's request, to assist the client in deciding whether to retain the attorney;

(3) Indicate on any Web site or other advertisement that is accessible in California either that the attorney is not a member of the State Bar of California or that the attorney is admitted to practice law only in the states listed; and

(4) Be an active member in good standing of the bar of a United States state, jurisdiction, possession, territory, or dependency.

(c) Permissible activities

An attorney who meets the requirements of this rule and who complies with all applicable rules, regulations, and statutes is not engaging in the unauthorized practice of law in California if the attorney:

(1) Provides legal assistance or legal advice in California to a client concerning a transaction or other nonlitigation matter, a material aspect of which is taking place in a jurisdiction other than California and in which the attorney is licensed to provide legal services;

(2) Provides legal assistance or legal advice in California on an issue of federal law or of the law of a jurisdiction other than California to attorneys licensed to practice law in California; or

(3) Is an employee of a client and provides legal assistance or legal advice in California to the client or to the client's subsidiaries or organizational affiliates.

(d) Restrictions

To qualify to practice law in California under this rule, an attorney must not:

(1) Hold out to the public or otherwise represent that he or she is admitted to practice law in California;

(2) Establish or maintain a resident office or other systematic or continuous presence in California for the practice of law;

(3) Be a resident of California;

(4) Be regularly employed in California;

(5) Regularly engage in substantial business or professional activities in California; or

(6) Have been disbarred, have resigned with charges pending, or be suspended from practicing law in any other jurisdiction.

(e) Conditions

By practicing law in California under this rule, an attorney agrees that he or she is providing legal services in California subject to:

(1) The jurisdiction of the State Bar of California;

(2) The jurisdiction of the courts of this state to the same extent as is a member of the State Bar of California; and

(3) The laws of the State of California relating to the practice of law, the State Bar Rules of Professional Conduct, the rules and regulations of the State Bar of California, and these rules.

(f) Scope of practice

An attorney is permitted by this rule to provide legal assistance or legal services concerning only a transaction or other nonlitigation matter.

(g) Inherent power of Supreme Court

Nothing in this rule may be construed as affecting the power of the Supreme Court of California to exercise its inherent jurisdiction over the practice of law in California.

(h) Effect of rule on multijurisdictional practice

Nothing in this rule limits the scope of activities permissible under existing law by attorneys who are not members of the State Bar of California.

CALIFORNIA BUSINESS & PROFESSIONS CODE

(Selected Sections)

CHAPTER 4. ATTORNEYS

TABLE OF CONTENTS

ARTICLE 4. ADMISSION TO THE PRACTICE OF LAW

ARTICLE 8.5 FEE AGREEMENTS

ARTICLE 9. UNLAWFUL SOLICITATION

ARTICLE 9.5 LEGAL ADVERTISING

ARTICLE 13. ARBITRATION OF ATTORNEYS' FEES

ARTICLE 4. ADMISSION TO THE PRACTICE OF LAW

§ 6067. Oath

Every person on his admission shall take an oath to support the Constitution of the United States and the Constitution of the State of California, and faithfully to discharge the duties of any attorney at law to the best of his knowledge and ability. A certificate of the oath shall be indorsed upon his license.

§ 6068. Duties of attorney

It is the duty of an attorney:

(a) To support the Constitution and laws of the United States and of this State.

(b) To maintain the respect due to the courts of justice and judicial officers.

(c) To counsel or maintain such actions, proceedings or defenses only as appear to him legal or just, except the defense of a person charged with a public offense.

(d) To employ, for the purpose of maintaining the causes confided to him or her such means only as are consistent with truth, and never to seek to mislead the judge or any judicial officer by an artifice or false statement of fact or law.

(e)(1) To maintain inviolate the confidence, and at every peril to himself or herself to preserve the secrets, of his or her client.

(2) Notwithstanding paragraph (1), an attorney may, but is not required to, reveal confidential information relating to the representation of a client to the extent that the attorney reasonably believes the disclosure is necessary to prevent a criminal act that the attorney reasonably believes is likely to result in death of, or substantial bodily harm to, an individual.

(f) To advance no fact prejudicial to the honor or reputation of a party or witness, unless required by the justice of the cause with which he or she is charged.

(g) Not to encourage either the commencement or the continuance of an action or proceeding from any corrupt motive of passion or interest.

(h) Never to reject, for any consideration personal to himself or herself, the cause of the defenseless or the oppressed.

(i) To cooperate and participate in any disciplinary investigation or other regulatory or disciplinary proceeding pending against himself or herself. However, this subdivision shall not be construed to deprive an attorney of any privilege guaranteed by the Fifth Amendment to the Constitution of the United States or any other constitutional or statutory privileges. This subdivision shall not be construed to require an attorney to cooperate with a request that requires him or her to waive any constitutional or statutory privilege or to comply with a request for information or other matters within an unreasonable period of time in light of the time constraints of the attorney's practice. Any exercise by an attorney of any constitutional or statutory privilege shall not be used against the attorney in a regulatory or disciplinary proceeding against him or her.

(j) To comply with the requirements of Section 6002.1.

(k) To comply with all conditions attached to any disciplinary probation, including a probation imposed with the concurrence of the attorney.

(*l*) To keep all agreements made in lieu of disciplinary prosecution with the State Bar.

(m) To respond promptly to reasonable status inquiries of clients and to keep clients reasonably informed of significant developments in matters with regard to which the attorney has agreed to provide legal services.

(n) To provide copies to the client of certain documents under time limits and as prescribed in a rule of professional conduct which the board shall adopt.

(*o*) To report to the State Bar, in writing, within 30 days of the time the attorney has knowledge of any of the following:

(1) The filing of three or more lawsuits in a 12-month period against the attorney for malpractice or other wrongful conduct committed in a professional capacity.

(2) The entry of judgment against the attorney in a civil action for fraud, misrepresentation, breach of fiduciary duty, or gross negligence committed in a professional capacity.

(3) The imposition of any judicial sanctions against the attorney, except for sanctions for failure to make discovery or monetary sanctions of less than one thousand dollars ($1,000).

(4) The bringing of an indictment or information charging a felony against the attorney.

(5) The conviction of the attorney, including any verdict of guilty, or plea of guilty or no contest, of a felony, or a misdemeanor committed in the course of the practice of law, or in a manner in which a client of the attorney was the victim, or a necessary element of which, as determined by the statutory or common law definition of the misdemeanor, involves improper conduct of an attorney, including dishonesty or other moral turpitude, or an attempt or a conspiracy or solicitation of another to commit a felony or a misdemeanor of that type.

(6) The imposition of discipline against the attorney by a professional or occupational disciplinary agency or licensing board, whether in California or elsewhere.

(7) Reversal of judgment in a proceeding based in whole or in part upon misconduct, grossly incompetent representation, or wilful misrepresentation by an attorney.

(8) As used in this subdivision, "against the attorney" includes claims and proceedings against any firm of attorneys for the practice of law in which the attorney was a partner at the time of the conduct complained of and any law corporation in which the attorney was a shareholder at the time of the conduct complained of unless the matter has to the attorney's knowledge already been reported by the law firm or corporation.

(9) The State Bar may develop a prescribed form for the making of reports required by this section, usage of which it may require by rule or regulation.

(10) This subdivision is only intended to provide that the failure to report as required herein may serve as a basis of discipline.

§ 6090.5 Settlements; prohibited agreements

(a) It is cause for suspension, disbarment, or other discipline for any member, whether as a party or as an attorney for a party, to agree or seek agreement, that:

(1) The professional misconduct or the terms of a settlement of a claim for professional misconduct shall not be reported to the disciplinary agency.

(2) The plaintiff shall withdraw a disciplinary complaint or shall not cooperate with the investigation or prosecution conducted by the disciplinary agency.

(3) The record of any civil action for professional misconduct shall be sealed from review by the disciplinary agency.

(b) The section applies to all settlements, whether made before or after the commencement of a civil action.

ARTICLE 6. DISCIPLINARY AUTHORITY OF THE COURTS

§ 6100. Disbarment or suspension

For any of the causes provided in this article, arising after an attorney's admission to practice, he or she may be disbarred or suspended by the Supreme Court. Nothing in this article limits the inherent power of the Supreme Court to discipline, including to summarily disbar, any attorney.

§ 6101. Conviction of crime; notice of pendency of action; record of conviction; proceedings

(a) Conviction of a felony or misdemeanor, involving moral turpitude, constitutes a cause for disbarment or suspension.

In any proceeding, whether under this article or otherwise, to disbar or suspend an attorney on account of that conviction, the record of conviction shall be conclusive evidence of guilt of the crime of which he or she has been convicted.

(b) The district attorney, city attorney, or other prosecuting agency shall notify the Office of the State Bar of California of the pendency of an action against an attorney charging a felony or misdemeanor immediately upon obtaining information that the defendant is an attorney. The notice shall identify the attorney and describe the crimes charged and the alleged facts. The prosecuting agency shall also notify the clerk of the court in which the action is pending that the defendant is an attorney, and the clerk shall record prominently in the file that the defendant is an attorney.

(c) The clerk of the court in which an attorney is convicted of a crime shall, within 48 hours after the conviction, transmit a certified copy of the record of conviction to the Office of the State Bar. Within five days of receipt, the Office of the State Bar shall transmit the record of any conviction which involves or may involve moral turpitude to the Supreme Court with such other records and information as may be appropriate to establish the Supreme Court's jurisdiction. The State Bar of California may procure and transmit the record of conviction to the Supreme Court when the clerk has not done so or when the conviction was had in a court other than a court of this state.

(d) The proceedings to disbar or suspend an attorney on account of such a conviction shall be undertaken by the Supreme Court pursuant to the procedure provided in this section and Section 6102, upon the receipt of the certified copy of the record of conviction.

(e) A plea or verdict of guilty, an acceptance of a nolo contendere plea, or a conviction after a plea of nolo contendere is deemed to be a conviction within the meaning of those sections.

§ 6102. Immediate suspension and subsequent disbarment upon conviction of crime; crimes involving moral turpitude or felonies; procedure

(a) Upon the receipt of the certified copy of the record of conviction, if it appears therefrom that the crime of which the attorney was convicted involved or that there is probable cause to believe that it involved moral turpitude or is a felony under the laws of California, the United States, or any state or territory thereof, the Supreme Court shall suspend the attorney until the time for appeal has elapsed, if no appeal has been taken, or until the judgment of conviction has been affirmed on appeal, or has otherwise become final, and until the further order of the court. Upon its own motion or upon good cause shown the court may decline to impose, or may set aside, the suspension when it appears to be in the interest of justice to do so, with due regard being given to maintaining the integrity of and confidence in the profession.

(b) For the purposes of this section, a crime is a felony under the law of California if it is declared to be so specifically or by subdivision (a) of Section 17 of the Penal Code, unless it is charged as a misdemeanor pursuant to paragraph (4) or (5) of subdivision (b) of Section 17 of the Penal Code, irrespective of whether in a particular case the crime may be considered a misdemeanor as a result of postconviction proceedings, including proceedings resulting in punishment or probation set forth in paragraph (1) or (3) of subdivision (b) of Section 17 of the Penal Code.

(c) After the judgment of conviction of an offense specified in subdivision (a) has become final or, irrespective of any subsequent order under Section 1203.4 of the Penal Code or similar statutory provision, an order granting probation has been made suspending the imposition of sentence, the Supreme Court shall summarily disbar the attorney if the offense is a felony under the laws of California, the United States, or any state or territory thereof, and either: (1) an element of the offense is the specific intent to deceive, defraud, steal, or make or suborn a false statement or involved moral turpitude, or (2) the facts and circumstances of the offense involved moral turpitude.

(d) For purposes of this section, a conviction under the laws of another state or territory of the United States shall be deemed a felony if:

(1) The judgment or conviction was entered as a felony irrespective of any subsequent order suspending sentence or granting probation and irrespective of whether the crime may be considered a misdemeanor as a result of postconviction proceedings.

(2) The elements of the offense for which the licensee was convicted would constitute a felony under the laws of the State of California at the time the offense was committed.

(e) Except as provided in subdivision (c), if after adequate notice and opportunity to be heard (which hearing shall not be had until the judgment of conviction has become final or, irrespective of any subsequent order under Section 1203.4 of the Penal Code, an order granting probation has been made suspending the imposition of sentence), the court finds that the crime of which the attorney was convicted, or the circumstances of its commission, involved moral turpitude, it shall enter an order disbarring the attorney or suspending him or her from practice for a limited time, according to the gravity of the crime and the circumstances of the case; otherwise it shall dismiss the proceedings. In determining the extent of the discipline to be imposed in a proceeding pursuant to this article any prior discipline imposed upon the attorney may be considered.

(f) The court may refer the proceedings or any part thereof or issue therein, including the nature or extent of discipline, to the State Bar for hearing, report, and recommendation.

(g) The record of the proceedings resulting in the conviction, including a transcript of the testimony therein, may be received in evidence.

(h) The Supreme Court shall prescribe rules for the practice and procedure in proceedings conducted pursuant to this section and Section 6101.

(i) The other provisions of this article providing a procedure for the disbarment or suspension of an attorney do not apply to proceedings pursuant to this section and Section 6101, unless expressly made applicable.

§ 6103. Disobedience of court order; violation of oath or attorney's duties

A wilful disobedience or violation of an order of the court requiring him to do or forbear an act connected with or in the course of his profession, which he ought in good faith to do or forbear, and any violation of the oath taken by him, or of his duties as such attorney, constitute causes for disbarment or suspension.

§ 6103.5 Written offers of settlement; required communication to client; discovery

(a) A licensee of the State Bar shall promptly communicate to the licensee's client all amounts, terms, and conditions of any written offer of settlement made by or on behalf of an opposing party. As used in this section, "client" includes any person employing the licensee of the State Bar who possesses the authority to accept an offer of settlement, or in a class action, who is a representative of the class.

(b) Any written offer of settlement or any required communication of a settlement offer, as described in subdivision (a), shall be discoverable by either party in any action in which the existence or communication of the offer of settlement is an issue before the trier of fact.

§ 6103.7 Reporting or threatening to report suspected immigration status

It is cause for suspension, disbarment, or other discipline for any licensee of the State Bar to report suspected immigration status or threaten to report suspected immigration status of a witness or party to a civil or administrative action or his or her family member to a federal, state, or local agency because the witness or party exercises or has exercised a right related to his or her employment or hiring of residential real property, broadly interpreted. As used in this section, "family member" means a spouse, parent, sibling, child, uncle, aunt, niece, nephew, cousin, grandparent, or grandchild related by blood, adoption, marriage, or domestic partnership.

§ 6104. Unauthorized appearance

Corruptly or wilfully and without authority appearing as attorney for a party to an action or proceeding constitutes a cause for disbarment or suspension.

§ 6105. Permitting misuse of name

Lending his name to be used as attorney by another person who is not an attorney constitutes a cause for disbarment or suspension.

§ 6106. Moral turpitude, dishonesty or corruption irrespective of criminal conviction

The commission of any act involving moral turpitude, dishonesty or corruption, whether the act is committed in the course of his relations as an attorney or otherwise, and whether the act is a felony or misdemeanor or not, constitutes a cause for disbarment or suspension.

If the act constitutes a felony or misdemeanor, conviction thereof in a criminal proceeding is not a condition precedent to disbarment or suspension from practice therefor.

§ 6106.1 Advocacy of overthrow of government

Advocating the overthrow of the Government of the United States or of this State by force, violence, or other unconstitutional means, constitutes a cause for disbarment or suspension.

§ 6106.5 Insurance claims; fraud

It shall constitute cause for disbarment or suspension for an attorney to engage in any conduct prohibited under Section 1871.4 of the Insurance Code or Section 550 of the Penal Code.

§ 6106.7 Miller-Ayala Athlete Agents Act; violation of requirements

It shall constitute cause for the imposition of discipline of an attorney within the meaning of this chapter for an attorney to violate any provision of the Miller-Ayala Athlete Agents Act (Chapter 2.5 (commencing with Section 18895) of Division 8), or to violate any provision of Chapter 1 (commencing with Section 1500) of Part 6 of Division 2 of the Labor Code, prior to January 1, 1997, or to violate any provision of the law of any other state regulating athlete agents.

§ 6106.8 Sexual involvement between lawyers and clients; rule of professional conduct

(a) The Legislature hereby finds and declares that there is no rule that governs propriety of sexual relationships between lawyers and clients. The Legislature further finds and declares that it is difficult to separate sound judgment from emotion or bias which may result from sexual involvement between a lawyer and his or her client during the period that an attorney-client relationship exists, and that emotional detachment is essential to the lawyer's ability to render competent legal services. Therefore, in order to ensure that a lawyer acts in the best interest of his or her client, a rule of professional conduct governing sexual relations between attorneys and their clients shall be adopted.

(b) With the approval of the Supreme Court, the State Bar shall adopt a rule of professional conduct governing sexual relations between attorneys and their clients in cases involving, but not limited to, probate matters and domestic relations, including dissolution proceedings, child custody cases, and settlement proceedings.

(c) The State Bar shall submit the proposed rule to the Supreme Court for approval no later than January 1, 1991.

(d) Intentional violation of this rule shall constitute a cause for suspension or disbarment.

§ 6106.9 Sexual relations between attorney and client; cause for discipline; complaints to state bar

(a) It shall constitute cause for the imposition of discipline of an attorney within the meaning of this chapter for an attorney to do any of the following:

(1) Expressly or impliedly condition the performance of legal services for a current or prospective client upon the client's willingness to engage in sexual relations with the attorney.

(2) Employ coercion, intimidation, or undue influence in entering into sexual relations with a client.

(3) Continue representation of a client with whom the attorney has sexual relations if the sexual relations cause the attorney to perform legal services incompetently in violation of Rule 3–110 of the Rules of Professional Conduct of the State Bar of California, or if the sexual relations would, or would be likely to, damage or prejudice the client's case.

(b) Subdivision (a) shall not apply to sexual relations between attorneys and their spouses or persons in an equivalent domestic relationship or to ongoing consensual sexual relationships that predate the initiation of the attorney-client relationship.

(c) Where an attorney in a firm has sexual relations with a client but does not participate in the representation of that client, the attorneys in the firm shall not be subject to discipline under this section solely because of the occurrence of those sexual relations.

(d) For the purposes of this section, "sexual relations" means sexual intercourse or the touching of an intimate part of another person for the purpose of sexual arousal, gratification, or abuse.

(e) Any complaint made to the State Bar alleging a violation of subdivision (a) shall be verified under oath by the person making the complaint.

§ 6107. Proceedings upon court's own knowledge or upon information

The proceedings to disbar or suspend an attorney, on grounds other than the conviction of a felony or misdemeanor, involving moral turpitude, may be taken by the court for the matters within its knowledge, or may be taken upon the information of another.

§ 6108. Accusation

If the proceedings are upon the information of another, the accusation shall be in writing and shall state the matters charged, and be verified by the oath of some person, to the effect that the charges therein contained are true.

The verification may be made upon information and belief when the accusation is presented by an organized bar association.

§ 6109. Order to appear and answer; service

Upon receiving the accusation, the court shall make an order requiring the accused to appear and answer it at a specified time, and shall cause a copy of the order and of the accusation to be served upon the accused at least five days before the day appointed in the order.

§ 6110. Citation

The court or judge may direct the service of a citation to the accused, requiring him to appear and answer the accusation, to be made by publication for thirty days in a newspaper of general circulation published in the county in which the proceeding is pending, if it appears by affidavit to the satisfaction of the court or judge that the accused either:

(a) Resides out of the State.

(b) Has departed from the State.

(c) Can not, after due diligence, be found within the State.

(d) Conceals himself to avoid the service of the order to show cause.

The citation shall be:

(a) Directed to the accused.

(b) Recite the date of the filing of the accusation, the name of the accuser, and the general nature of the charges against him.

(c) Require him to appear and answer the accusation at a specified time.

On proof of the publication of the citation as herein required, the court has jurisdiction to proceed to hear the accusation and render judgment with like effect as if an order to show cause and a copy of the accusation had been personally served on the accused.

§ 6111. Appearance; determination upon default

The accused shall appear at the time appointed in the order, and answer the accusation, unless, for sufficient cause, the court assigns another day for that purpose. If he does not appear, the court may proceed and determine the accusation in his absence.

§ 6112. Answer

The accused may answer to the accusation either by objecting to its sufficiency or by denying it.

If he objects to the sufficiency of the accusation, the objection shall be in writing, but need not be in any specific form. It is sufficient if it presents intelligibly the grounds of the objection.

If he denies the accusation, the denial may be oral and without oath, and shall be entered upon the minutes.

§ 6113. Time for answer after objection

If an objection to the sufficiency of the accusation is not sustained, the accused shall answer within the time designated by the court.

§ 6114. Judgment upon plea of guilty or failure to answer; trial upon denial of charges

If the accused pleads guilty, or refuses to answer the accusation, the court shall proceed to judgment of disbarment or suspension.

If he denies the matters charged, the court shall, at such time as it may appoint, proceed to try the accusation.

§ 6115. Reference to take depositions

The court may, in its discretion, order a reference to a committee to take depositions in the matter.

§ 6116. Judgment

When an attorney has been found guilty of the charges made in proceedings not based upon a record of conviction, judgment shall be rendered disbarring the attorney or suspending him from practice for a limited time, according to the gravity of the offense charged.

§ 6117. Effect of disbarment or suspension

During such disbarment or suspension, the attorney shall be precluded from practicing law. When disbarred, his name shall be stricken from the roll of attorneys.

ARTICLE 7. UNLAWFUL PRACTICE OF LAW

§ 6125. Necessity of active membership in state bar

No person shall practice law in California unless the person is an active licensee of the State Bar.

§ 6126. Unauthorized practice, advertising or holding out; penalties

(a) Any person advertising or holding himself or herself out as practicing or entitled to practice law or otherwise practicing law who is not an active member of the State Bar, or otherwise authorized pursuant to statute or court rule to practice law in this state at the time of doing so, is guilty of a misdemeanor punishable by up to one year in a county jail or by a fine of up to one thousand dollars ($1,000), or by both that fine and imprisonment. Upon a second or subsequent conviction, the person shall be confined in a county jail for not less than 90 days, except in an unusual case where the interests of justice would be served by imposition of a lesser sentence or a fine. If the court imposes only a fine or a sentence of less than 90 days for a second or subsequent conviction under this subdivision, the court shall state the reasons for its sentencing choice on the record.

(b) Any person who has been involuntarily enrolled as an inactive member of the State Bar, or has been suspended from membership from the State Bar, or has been disbarred, or has resigned from the State Bar with charges pending, and thereafter practices or attempts to practice law, advertises or holds himself or herself out as practicing or otherwise entitled to practice law, is guilty of a crime punishable by imprisonment pursuant to subdivision (h) of Section 1170 of the Penal Code or in a county jail for a period not to exceed six months. However, any person who has been involuntarily enrolled as an inactive member of the State Bar pursuant to paragraph (1) of subdivision (e) of Section 6007 and who knowingly thereafter practices or attempts to practice law, or advertises or holds himself or herself out as practicing or otherwise entitled to practice law, is guilty of a crime punishable by imprisonment pursuant to subdivision (h) of Section 1170 of the Penal Code or in a county jail for a period not to exceed six months.

(c) The willful failure of a member of the State Bar, or one who has resigned or been disbarred, to comply with an order of the Supreme Court to comply with Rule 9.20 of the California Rules of Court, constitutes a crime punishable by imprisonment in the state prison or county jail.

(d) The penalties provided in this section are cumulative to each other and to any other remedies or penalties provided by law.

§ 6126.3 Jurisdiction of court over unauthorized person's files, records and practice; intervention by the superior court or State Bar; order to show cause; appointment of counsel; notice of cessation of law practice

(a) In addition to any criminal penalties pursuant to Section 6126 or to any contempt proceedings pursuant to Section 6127, the courts of the state shall have the jurisdiction provided in this section when a person advertises or holds himself or herself out as practicing or entitled to practice law, or otherwise practices law, without being an active member of the State Bar or otherwise authorized pursuant to statute or court rule to practice law in this state at the time of doing so.

(b) The State Bar, or the superior court on its own motion, may make application to the superior court for the county where the person described in subdivision (a) maintains or more recently has maintained his or her principal office for the practice of law or where he or she resides, for assumption by the court of jurisdiction over the practice to the extent provided in this section. In any proceeding under this section, the State Bar shall be permitted to intervene and to assume primary responsibility for conducting the action.

(c) An application made pursuant to subdivision (b) shall be verified, and shall state facts showing all of the following:

(1) Probable cause to believe that the facts set forth in subdivision (a) of Section 6126 have occurred.

(2) The interest of the applicant.

(3) Probable cause to believe that the interests of a client or of an interested person or entity will be prejudiced if the proceeding is not maintained.

(d) The application shall be set for hearing, and an order to show cause shall be issued directing the person to show cause why the court should not assume jurisdiction over the practice as provided in this section. A copy of the application and order to show cause shall be served upon the person by personal delivery or, as an alternate method of service, by certified or registered mail, return receipt requested, addressed to the person either at the address at which he or she maintains, or more recently has maintained, his or her principal office or at the address where he or she resides. Service is complete at the time of mailing, but any prescribed period of notice and any right or duty to do any act or make any response within that prescribed period or on a date certain after notice is served by mail shall be extended five days if the place of address is within the State of California, 10 days if the place of address is outside the State of California but within the United States, and 20 days if the place of address is outside the United States. If the State Bar is not the applicant, copies shall also be served upon the Office of the Chief Trial Counsel of the State Bar in similar manner at the time of service on the person who is the subject of the application. The court may prescribe additional or alternative methods of service of the application and order to show cause, and may prescribe methods of notifying and serving notices and process upon other persons and entities in cases not specifically provided herein.

(e) If the court finds that the facts set forth in subdivision (a) of Section 6126 have occurred and that the interests of a client or an interested person or entity will be prejudiced if the proceeding provided herein is not maintained, the court may make an order assuming jurisdiction over the person's practice pursuant to this section. If the person to whom the order to show cause is directed does not appear, the court may make its order upon the verified application or upon such proof as it may require. Thereupon, the court shall appoint one or more active members of the State Bar to act under its direction to mail a notice of cessation of practice, pursuant to subdivision (g), and may order those appointed attorneys to do one or more of the following:

(1) Examine the files and records of the practice and obtain information as to any pending matters that may require attention.

(2) Notify persons and entities who appear to be clients of the person of the occurrence of the event or events stated in subdivision (a) of Section 6126, and inform them that it may be in their best interest to obtain other legal counsel.

(3) Apply for an extension of time pending employment of legal counsel by the client.

(4) With the consent of the client, file notices, motions, and pleadings on behalf of the client where jurisdictional time limits are involved and other legal counsel has not yet been obtained.

(5) Give notice to the depositor and appropriate persons and entities who may be affected, other than clients, of the occurrence of the event or events.

(6) Arrange for the surrender or delivery of clients' papers or property.

(7) Arrange for the appointment of a receiver, where applicable, to take possession and control of any and all bank accounts relating to the affected person's practice.

(8) Do any other acts that the court may direct to carry out the purposes of this section.

The court shall have jurisdiction over the files and records and over the practice of the affected person for the limited purposes of this section, and may make all orders necessary or appropriate to exercise this jurisdiction. The court shall provide a copy of any order issued pursuant to this section to the Office of the Chief Trial Counsel of the State Bar.

(f) Anyone examining the files and records of the practice of the person described in subdivision (a) shall observe any lawyer-client privilege under Sections 950 and 952 of the Evidence Code and shall make disclosure only to the extent necessary to carry out the purposes of this section. That disclosure shall be a disclosure that is reasonably necessary for the accomplishment of the purpose for which the person described in subdivision (a) was consulted. The appointment of a member of the State Bar pursuant to this section shall not affect the lawyer-client privilege, which privilege shall apply to communications by or to the appointed members to the same extent as it would have applied to communications by or to the person described in subdivision (a).

(g) The notice of cessation of law practice shall contain any information that may be required by the court, including, but not limited to, the finding by the court that the facts set forth in subdivision (a) of Section 6126 have occurred and that the court has assumed jurisdiction of the practice. The notice shall be mailed to all clients, to opposing counsel, to courts and agencies in which the person has pending matters with an identification of the matter, to the Office of the Chief Trial Counsel of the State Bar, and to any other person or entity having reason to be informed of the court's assumption of the practice.

(h) Nothing in this section shall authorize the court or an attorney appointed by it pursuant to this section to approve or disapprove of the employment of legal counsel, to fix terms of legal employment, or to supervise or in any way undertake the conduct of the practice, except to the limited extent provided by paragraphs (3) and (4) of subdivision (e).

(i) Unless court approval is first obtained, neither the attorney appointed pursuant to this section, nor his or her corporation, nor any partner or associate of the attorney shall accept employment as an attorney by any client of the affected person on any matter pending at the time of the appointment. Action taken pursuant to paragraphs (3) and (4) of subdivision (e) shall not be deemed employment for purposes of this subdivision.

(j) Upon a finding by the court that it is more likely than not that the application will be granted and that delay in making the orders described in subdivision (e) will result in substantial injury to clients or to others, the court, without notice or upon notice as it shall prescribe, may make interim orders containing any provisions that the court deems appropriate under the circumstances. Such an interim order shall be served in the manner provided in subdivision (d) and, if the application and order to show cause have not yet been served, the application and order to show cause shall be served at the time of serving the interim order.

(k) No person or entity shall incur any liability by reason of the institution or maintenance of a proceeding brought under this section. No person or entity shall incur any liability for an act done or omitted to be done pursuant to order of the court under this section. No person or entity shall be liable for failure to apply for court jurisdiction under this section. Nothing in this section shall affect any obligation otherwise existing between the affected person and any other person or entity.

(*l*) An order pursuant to this section is not appealable and shall not be stayed by petition for a writ, except as ordered by the superior court or by the appellate court.

(m) A member of the State Bar appointed pursuant to this section shall serve without compensation. However, the member may be paid reasonable compensation by the State Bar in cases where the State Bar has determined that the member has devoted extraordinary time and services that were necessary to the performance of the member's duties under this article. All payments of compensation for time and services shall be at the discretion of the State Bar. Any member shall be entitled to reimbursement from the State Bar for necessary expenses incurred in the performance of the member's duties under this article. Upon court approval of expenses or compensation for time and services, the State Bar shall be entitled to reimbursement therefor from the person described in subdivision (a) or his or her estate.

§ 6126.5 Additional remedies and penalties

(a) In addition to any remedies and penalties available in any enforcement action brought in the name of the people of the State of California by the Attorney General, a district attorney, or a city attorney, acting as a public prosecutor, the court shall award relief in the enforcement action for any person who obtained services offered or provided in violation of Section 6125 or 6126 or who purchased any goods, services, or real or personal property in connection with services offered or provided in violation of Section 6125 or 6126 against the person who violated Section 6125 or 6126, or who sold goods, services, or property in connection with that violation. The court shall consider the following relief:

(1) Actual damages.

(2) Restitution of all amounts paid.

(3) The amount of penalties and tax liabilities incurred in connection with the sale or transfer of assets to pay for any goods, services, or property.

(4) Reasonable attorney's fees and costs expended to rectify errors made in the unlawful practice of law.

(5) Prejudgment interest at the legal rate from the date of loss to the date of judgment.

(6) Appropriate equitable relief, including the rescission of sales made in connection with a violation of law.

(b) The relief awarded under paragraphs (1) to (6), inclusive, of subdivision (a) shall be distributed to, or on behalf of, the person for whom it was awarded or, if it is impracticable to do so, shall be distributed as may be directed by the court pursuant to its equitable powers.

(c) The court shall also award the Attorney General, district attorney, or city attorney reasonable attorney's fees and costs and, in the court's discretion, exemplary damages as provided in Section 3294 of the Civil Code.

(d) This section shall not be construed to create, abrogate, or otherwise affect claims, rights, or remedies, if any, that may be held by a person or entity other than those law enforcement agencies described in subdivision (a). The remedies provided in this section are cumulative to each other and to the remedies and penalties provided under other laws.

§ 6127. Contempt of court

The following acts or omissions in respect to the practice of law are contempts of the authority of the courts:

(a) Assuming to be an officer or attorney of a court and acting as such, without authority.

(b) Advertising or holding oneself out as practicing or as entitled to practice law or otherwise practicing law in any court, without being an active member of the State Bar.

Proceedings to adjudge a person in contempt of court under this section are to be taken in accordance with the provisions of Title V of Part III of the Code of Civil Procedure.

§ 6127.5 Law corporation under professional corporation act

Nothing in Sections 6125, 6126 and 6127 shall be deemed to apply to the acts and practices of a law corporation duly certificated pursuant to the Professional Corporation Act, as contained in Part 4 (commencing with Section 13400) of Division 3 of Title 1 of the Corporations Code, and pursuant to Article 10 (commencing with Section 6160) of Chapter 4 of Division 3 of this code, when the law corporation is in compliance with the requirements of (a) the Professional Corporation Act; (b) Article 10 (commencing with Section 6160) of Chapter 4 of Division 3 of this code; and (c) all other statutes and all rules and regulations now or hereafter enacted or adopted pertaining to such corporation and the conduct of its affairs.

§ 6128. Deceit, collusion, delay of suit and improper receipt of money as misdemeanors

Every attorney is guilty of a misdemeanor who either:

(a) Is guilty of any deceit or collusion, or consents to any deceit or collusion, with intent to deceive the court or any party.

(b) Wilfully delays his client's suit with a view to his own gain.

(c) Wilfully receives any money or allowance for or on account of any money which he has not laid out or become answerable for.

Any violation of the provisions of this section is punishable by imprisonment in the county jail not exceeding six months, or by a fine not exceeding two thousand five hundred dollars ($2,500), or by both.

§ 6129. Buying claim as misdemeanor

Every attorney who, either directly or indirectly, buys or is interested in buying any evidence of debt or thing in action, with intent to bring suit thereon, is guilty of a misdemeanor.

Any violation of the provisions of this section is punished by imprisonment in the county jail not exceeding six months, or by a fine not exceeding two thousand five hundred dollars ($2,500), or by both.

§ 6130. Disbarred or suspended attorney suing as assignee

No person, who has been an attorney, shall while a judgment of disbarment or suspension is in force appear on his own behalf as plaintiff in the prosecution of any action where the subject of the action has been assigned to him subsequent to the entry of the judgment of disbarment or suspension and solely for purpose of collection.

§ 6131. Aiding defense where partner or self has acted as public prosecutor; misdemeanor and disbarment

Every attorney is guilty of a misdemeanor and, in addition to the punishment prescribed therefor, shall be disbarred:

(a) Who directly or indirectly advises in relation to, or aids, or promotes the defense of any action or proceeding in any court the prosecution of which is carried on, aided or promoted by any person as district attorney or other public prosecutor with whom such person is directly or indirectly connected as a partner.

(b) Who, having himself prosecuted or in any manner aided or promoted any action or proceeding in any court as district attorney or other public prosecutor, afterwards, directly or indirectly, advises in relation to or takes any part in the defense thereof, as attorney or otherwise, or who takes or receives any valuable consideration from or on behalf of any defendant in any such action upon any understanding or agreement whatever having relation to the defense thereof.

This section does not prohibit an attorney from defending himself in person, as attorney or counsel, when prosecuted, either civilly or criminally.

§ 6132. Firm names; removal of names of attorneys under discipline

Any law firm, partnership, corporation, or association which contains the name of an attorney who is disbarred, or who resigned with charges pending, in its business name shall remove the name of that attorney from its business name, and from all signs, advertisements, letterhead, and other materials containing that name, within 60 days of the disbarment or resignation.

§ 6133. Resigned, suspended or disbarred attorneys; supervision of activities by firms

Any attorney or any law firm, partnership, corporation, or association employing an attorney who has resigned, or who is under actual suspension from the practice of law, or is disbarred, shall not permit that attorney to practice law or so advertise or hold himself or herself out as practicing law and shall supervise him or her in any other assigned duties. A willful violation of this section constitutes a cause for discipline.

ARTICLE 8.5 FEE AGREEMENTS

§ 6146. Limitations; periodic payments

(a) An attorney shall not contract for or collect a contingency fee for representing any person seeking damages in connection with an action for injury or damage against a health care provider based upon such person's alleged professional negligence in excess of the following limits:

(1) Forty percent of the first fifty thousand dollars ($50,000) recovered.

(2) Thirty-three and one-third percent of the next fifty thousand dollars ($50,000) recovered.

(3) Twenty-five percent of the next five hundred thousand dollars ($500,000) recovered.

(4) Fifteen percent of any amount on which the recovery exceeds six hundred thousand dollars ($600,000).

The limitations shall apply regardless of whether the recovery is by settlement, arbitration, or judgment, or whether the person for whom the recovery is made is a responsible adult, an infant, or a person of unsound mind.

(b) If periodic payments are awarded to the plaintiff pursuant to Section 667.7 of the Code of Civil Procedure, the court shall place a total value on these payments based upon the projected life expectancy of the plaintiff and include this amount in computing the total award from which attorney's fees are calculated under this section.

(c) For purposes of this section:

(1) "Recovered" means the net sum recovered after deducting any disbursements or costs incurred in connection with prosecution or settlement of the claim. Costs of medical care incurred by the plaintiff and the attorney's office-overhead costs or charges are not deductible disbursements or costs for such purpose.

(2) "Health care provider" means any person licensed or certified pursuant to Division 2 (commencing with Section 500), or licensed pursuant to the Osteopathic Initiative Act, or the Chiropractic Initiative Act, or licensed pursuant to Chapter 2.5 (commencing with Section 1440) of Division 2 of the Health and Safety Code; and any clinic, health dispensary, or health facility, licensed pursuant to Division 2 (commencing with Section 1200) of the Health and Safety Code. "Health care provider" includes the legal representatives of a health care provider.

(3) "Professional negligence" is a negligent act or omission to act by a health care provider in the rendering of professional services, which act or omission is the proximate cause of a personal injury or wrongful death, provided that the services are within the scope of services for which the provider is licensed and which are not within any restriction imposed by the licensing agency or licensed hospital.

§ 6147. Contingency fee contracts; duplicate copy; contents; effect of noncompliance; recovery of workers' compensation benefits

(a) An attorney who contracts to represent a client on a contingency fee basis shall, at the time the contract is entered into, provide a duplicate copy of the contract, signed by both the attorney and the client, or the client's guardian or representative, to the client, or to the client's guardian or representative. The contract shall be in writing and shall include, but is not limited to, all of the following:

(1) A statement of the contingency fee rate that the client and attorney have agreed upon.

(2) A statement as to how disbursements and costs incurred in connection with the prosecution or settlement of the claim will affect the contingency fee and the client's recovery.

(3) A statement as to what extent, if any, the client could be required to pay any compensation to the attorney for related matters that arise out of their relationship not covered by their contingency fee contract. This may include any amounts collected for the plaintiff by the attorney.

(4) Unless the claim is subject to the provisions of Section 6146, a statement that the fee is not set by law but is negotiable between attorney and client.

(5) If the claim is subject to the provisions of Section 6146, a statement that the rates set forth in that section are the maximum limits for the contingency fee agreement, and that the attorney and client may negotiate a lower rate.

(b) Failure to comply with any provision of this section renders the agreement voidable at the option of the plaintiff, and the attorney shall thereupon be entitled to collect a reasonable fee.

(c) This section shall not apply to contingency fee contracts for the recovery of workers' compensation benefits.

(d) This section shall become operative on January 1, 2000.

§ 6147.5 Contingency fee contracts; recovery of claims between merchants

(a) Sections 6147 and 6148 shall not apply to contingency fee contracts for the recovery of claims between merchants as defined in Section 2104 of the Commercial Code, arising from the sale or lease of goods or services rendered, or money loaned for use, in the conduct of a business or profession if the merchant contracting for legal services employs 10 or more individuals.

(b)(1) In the instances in which no written contract for legal services exists as permitted by subdivision (a), an attorney shall not contract for or collect a contingency fee in excess of the following limits:

(A) Twenty percent of the first three hundred dollars ($300) collected.

(B) Eighteen percent of the next one thousand seven hundred dollars ($1,700) collected.

(C) Thirteen percent of sums collected in excess of two thousand dollars ($2,000).

(2) However, the following minimum charges may be charged and collected:

(A) Twenty-five dollars ($25) in collections of seventy-five dollars ($75) to one hundred twenty-five dollars ($125).

(B) Thirty-three and one-third percent of collections less than seventy-five dollars ($75).

§ 6148. Contracts for services in cases not coming within § 6147; bills rendered by attorney; contents; failure to comply

(a) In any case not coming within Section 6147 in which it is reasonably foreseeable that total expense to a client, including attorney fees will exceed one thousand dollars ($1,000), the contract for services in the case shall be in writing. At the time the contract is entered into, the attorney shall provide a duplicate copy of the contract signed by both the attorney and the client, or the client's guardian or representative, to the client or the client's guardian or representative. The written contract shall contain all of the following:

(1) Any basis of compensation including, but not limited to, hourly rates, statutory fees or flat fees, and other standard rates, fees, and charges applicable to the case.

(2) The general nature of the legal services to be provided to the client.

(3) The respective responsibilities of the attorney and the client as to the performance of the contract.

(b) All bills rendered by an attorney to a client shall clearly state the basis thereof. Bills for the fee portion of the bill shall include the amount, rate, basis for calculation, or other method of determination of the attorney's fees and costs. Bills for the cost and expense portion of the bill shall clearly identify the costs and expenses incurred and the amount of the costs and expenses. Upon request by the client, the attorney shall provide a bill to the client no later than 10 days following the request unless the attorney has provided a bill to the client within 31 days prior to the request, in which case the attorney may provide a bill to the client no later than 31 days following the date the most recent bill was provided. The client is entitled to make similar requests at intervals of no less than 30 days following the initial request. In providing responses to client requests for billing information, the attorney may use billing data that is currently effective on the date of the request, or, if any fees or costs to that date cannot be accurately determined, they shall be described and estimated.

(c) Failure to comply with any provision of this section renders the agreement voidable at the option of the client, and the attorney shall, upon the agreement being voided, be entitled to collect a reasonable fee.

(d) This section shall not apply to any of the following:

(1) Services rendered in an emergency to avoid foreseeable prejudice to the rights or interests of the client or where a writing is otherwise impractical.

(2) An arrangement as to the fee implied by the fact that the attorney's services are of the same general kind as previously rendered to and paid for by the client.

(3) If the client knowingly states in writing, after full disclosure of this section, that a writing concerning fees is not required.

(4) If the client is a corporation.

(e) This section applies prospectively only to fee agreements following its operative date.

(f) This section shall become operative on January 1, 2000.

§ 6149. Written fee contract as confidential communication

A written fee contract shall be deemed to be a confidential communication within the meaning of subdivision (e) of Section 6068 and of Section 952 of the Evidence Code.

§ 6149.5 Third-party liability claim; settlement by insurer; notice to claimant; effect on action or defense

(a) Upon the payment of one hundred dollars ($100) or more in settlement of any third-party liability claim the insurer shall provide written notice to the claimant if both of the following apply:

(1) The claimant is a natural person.

(2) The payment is delivered to the claimant's lawyer or other representative by draft, check, or otherwise.

(b) For purposes of this section, "written notice" includes providing to the claimant a copy of the cover letter sent to the claimant's attorney or other representative that accompanied the settlement payment.

(c) This section shall not create any cause of action for any person against the insurer based upon the insurer's failure to provide the notice to a claimant required by this section. This section shall not create a defense for any party to any cause of action based upon the insurer's failure to provide this notice.

ARTICLE 9. UNLAWFUL SOLICITATION

§ 6150. Relation of article to chapter

This article is a part of Chapter 4 of this division of the Business and Professions Code, but the phrase "this chapter" as used in Chapter 4 does not apply to the provisions of this article unless expressly made applicable.

§ 6151. Definitions

As used in this article:

(a) A runner or capper is any person, firm, association or corporation acting for consideration in any manner or in any capacity as an agent for an attorney at law or law firm, whether the attorney or any member of the law firm is admitted in California or any other jurisdiction, in the solicitation or procurement of business for the attorney at law or law firm as provided in this article.

(b) An agent is one who represents another in dealings with one or more third persons.

§ 6152. Prohibition of solicitation

(a) It is unlawful for:

(1) Any person, in an individual capacity or in a capacity as a public or private employee, or for any firm, corporation, partnership or association to act as a runner or capper for any attorneys or to solicit any business for any attorneys in and about the state prisons, county jails, city jails, city prisons, or other places of detention of persons, city receiving hospitals, city and county receiving hospitals, county hospitals, superior courts, or in any public institution or in any public place or upon any public street or highway or in and about private hospitals, sanitariums or in and about any private institution or upon private property of any character whatsoever.

(2) Any person to solicit another person to commit or join in the commission of a violation of subdivision (a).

(b) A general release from a liability claim obtained from any person during the period of the first physical confinement, whether as an inpatient or outpatient, in a clinic or health facility, as defined in Sections 1203 and 1250 of the Health and Safety Code, as a result of the injury alleged to have given rise to the claim and primarily of treatment of the injury, is presumed fraudulent if the release is executed within 15 days after the commencement of confinement or prior to release from confinement, which ever occurs first.

(c) Nothing in this section shall be construed to prevent the recommendation of professional employment where that recommendation is not prohibited by the Rules of Professional Conduct of the State Bar of California.

(d) Nothing in this section shall be construed to mean that a public defender or assigned counsel may not make known his or her services as a criminal defense attorney to persons unable to afford legal counsel whether those persons are in custody or otherwise.

§ 6153. Violation; penalty

Any person, firm, partnership, association, or corporation violating subdivision (a) of Section 6152 is punishable, upon a first conviction by imprisonment in a county jail for not more than one year or by a fine not exceeding fifteen thousand dollars ($15,000), or by both that imprisonment and fine. Upon a second or subsequent conviction, a person, firm, partnership, association, or corporation is punishable by imprisonment in a county jail for not more than one year, or by imprisonment pursuant to subdivision (h) of Section 1170 of the Penal Code for 2, 3 or 4 years, or by a fine not exceeding fifteen thousand dollars ($15,000), or by both that imprisonment and fine.

Any person employed either as an officer, director, trustee, clerk, servant or agent of this State or of any county or other municipal corporation or subdivision thereof, who is found guilty of violating any of the provisions of this article, shall forfeit the right to his office and employment in addition to any other penalty provided in this article.

§ 6154. Runner or capper used to procure business's void contract; divesting of fees and other compensation; fees recovered from workers' compensation actions

(a) Any contract for professional services secured by any attorney at law or law firm in this state through the services of a runner or capper is void. In any action against any attorney or law firm under the Unfair Practices Act, Chapter 4 (commencing with Section 17000) of Division 7, or Chapter 5 (commencing with Section 17200) of Division 7, any judgment shall include an order divesting the attorney or law firm of any fees and other compensation received pursuant to any such void contract. Those fees and compensation shall be recoverable as additional civil penalties under Chapter 4 (commencing with Section 17000) or Chapter 5 (commencing with Section 17200) of Division 7.

(b) Notwithstanding Section 17206 or any other provision of law, any fees recovered pursuant to subdivision (a) in an action involving professional services related to the provision of workers' compensation shall be allocated as follows: if the action is brought by the Attorney General, one-half of the penalty collected shall be paid to the State General Fund, and one-half of the penalty collected shall be paid to the Workers' Compensation Fraud Account in the Insurance Fund; if the action is brought by a district attorney, one-half of the penalty collected shall be paid to the treasurer of the county in which the judgment was entered, and one-half of the penalty collected shall be paid to the Workers' Compensation Fraud Account in the Insurance Fund; if the action is brought by a city attorney or city prosecutor, one-half of the penalty collected shall be paid to the Workers' Compensation Fraud Account in the Insurance Fund. Moneys deposited into the Workers' Compensation Fraud Account pursuant to this subdivision shall be used in the investigation and prosecution of workers' compensation fraud, as appropriated by the Legislature.

§ 6155. Referral services; conflicts of interest; enforcement; rules and regulations; duration of section

(a) An individual, partnership, corporation, association, or any other entity shall not operate for the direct or indirect purpose, in whole or in part, of referring potential clients to attorneys, and no attorney shall accept a referral of such potential clients, unless all of the following requirements are met:

(1) The service is registered with the State Bar of California and (a) on July 1, 1988, is operated in conformity with minimum standards for a lawyer referral service established by the State Bar, or (b) upon approval by the Supreme Court of minimum standards for a lawyer referral service, is operated in conformity with those standards.

(2) The combined charges to the potential client by the referral service and the attorney to whom the potential client is referred do not exceed the total cost that the client would normally pay if no referral service were involved.

(b) A referral service shall not be owned or operated, in whole or in part, directly or indirectly, by those lawyers to whom, individually or collectively, more than 20 percent of referrals are made. For purposes of this subdivision, a referral service that is owned or operated by a bar association, as defined in the minimum standards, shall be deemed to be owned or operated by its governing committee so long as the governing committee is constituted and functions in the manner prescribed by the minimum standards.

(c) None of the following is a lawyer referral service:

(1) A plan of legal insurance as defined in Section 119.6 of the Insurance Code.

(2) A group or prepaid legal plan, whether operated by a union, trust, mutual benefit or aid association, public or private corporation, or other entity or person, which meets both of the following conditions:

(A) It recommends, furnishes, or pays for legal services to its members or beneficiaries.

(B) It provides telephone advice or personal consultation.

(3) A program having as its purpose the referral of clients to attorneys for representation on a pro bono basis.

(d) The following are in the public interest and do not constitute an unlawful restraint of trade or commerce:

(1) An agreement between a referral service and a participating attorney to eliminate or restrict the attorney's fee for an initial office consultation for each potential client or to provide free or reduced fee services.

(2) Requirements by a referral service that attorneys meet reasonable participation requirements, including experience, education, and training requirements.

(3) Provisions of the minimum standards as approved by the Supreme Court.

(4) Requirements that the application and renewal fees for certification as a lawyer referral service be determined, in whole or in part, by a consideration of any combination of the following factors: a referral service's gross annual revenues, number of panels, number of panel members, amount of fees charged to panel members, or for-profit or nonprofit status; provided that the application and renewal fees do not exceed ten thousand dollars ($10,000) or 1 percent of the gross annual revenues, whichever is less.

(5) Requirements that, to increase access to the justice system for all Californians, lawyer referral services establish separate ongoing activities or arrangements that serve persons of limited means.

(e) A violation or threatened violation of this section may be enjoined by any person.

(f) With the approval of the Supreme Court, the State Bar shall formulate and enforce rules and regulations for carrying out this section, including rules and regulations which do the following:

(1) Establish minimum standards for lawyer referral services. The minimum standards shall include provisions ensuring that panel membership shall be open to all attorneys practicing in the geographical area served who are qualified by virtue of suitable experience, and limiting attorney registration and membership fees to reasonable sums which do not discourage widespread attorney membership.

(2) Require that an entity seeking to qualify as a lawyer referral service register with the State Bar and obtain from the State Bar a certificate of compliance with the minimum standards for lawyer referral services.

(3) Require that the certificate may be obtained, maintained, suspended, or revoked pursuant to procedures set forth in the rules and regulations.

(4) Require the lawyer referral service to pay an application and renewal fee for the certificate in such reasonable amounts as may be determined by the State Bar. The State Bar shall adopt rules authorizing the waiver or reduction of the fees upon a demonstration of financial necessity. The State Bar may require that the application and renewal fees for certification as a lawyer referral service be determined, in whole or in part, by a consideration of any combination of the following factors: a referral service's gross annual revenues, number of panels, number of panel members, amount of fees charged to panel members, or for-profit or nonprofit status;

provided that the application and renewal fees do not exceed ten thousand dollars ($10,000) or 1 percent of the gross annual revenues, whichever is less.

(5) Require that, to increase access to the justice system for all Californians, lawyer referral services establish separate ongoing activities or arrangements that serve persons of limited means.

(6) Require each lawyer who is a member of a certified lawyer referral service to comply with all applicable professional standards, rules, and regulations, and to possess a policy of errors and omissions insurance in an amount not less than one hundred thousand dollars ($100,000) for each occurrence and three hundred thousand dollars ($300,000) aggregate, per year. By rule, the State Bar may provide for alternative proof of financial responsibility to meet this requirement.

(g) Provide that cause for denial of certification or recertification or revocation of certification of a lawyer referral service shall include, but not be limited to:

(1) Noncompliance with the statutes or minimum standards governing lawyer referral services as adopted and from time to time amended.

(2) Sharing common or cross ownership, interests, or operations with any entity which engages in referrals to licensed or unlicensed health care providers.

(3) Direct or indirect consideration regarding referrals between an owner, operator, or member of a lawyer referral service and any licensed or unlicensed health care provider.

(4) Advertising on behalf of attorneys in violation of the Rules of Professional Conduct or the Business and Professions Code.

(h) This section shall not be construed to prohibit attorneys from jointly advertising their services.

(1) Permissible joint advertising, among other things, identifies by name the advertising attorneys or law firms whom the consumer of legal services may select and initiate contact with.

(2) Certifiable referral activity involves, among other things, some person or entity other than the consumer and advertising attorney or law firms which, in person, electronically, or otherwise, refers the consumer to an attorney or law firm not identified in the advertising.

(i) A lawyer referral service certified under this section and operating in full compliance with this section, and in full compliance with the minimum standards and the rules and regulations of the State Bar governing lawyer referral services, shall not be deemed to be in violation of Section 3215 of the Labor Code or Section 750 of the Insurance Code.

(j) The payment by an attorney or law firm member of a certified referral service of the normal fees of that service shall not be deemed to be in violation of Section 3215 of the Labor Code or Section 750 of the Insurance Code, provided that the attorney or law firm member is in full compliance with the minimum standards and the rules and regulations of the State Bar governing lawyer referral services.

(k) Certifications of lawyer referral services issued by the State Bar shall not be transferable.

[Ed. Note: The California Bar has prepared two documents relating to referral services: (1) Minimum Standards for a Lawyer Referral Service in California, and (2) Certification and Renewal Fees for Lawyer Referral Services. These documents are omitted from this publication.]

ARTICLE 9.5 LEGAL ADVERTISING

§ 6157. Definitions

As used in this article, the following definitions apply:

(a) "Licensee" means a licensee in good standing of the State Bar and includes the terms "lawyer" and "attorney" and includes any agent of the licensee and any law firm or law corporation doing business in the State of California.

(b) "Lawyer" means a licensee of the State Bar or a person who is admitted in good standing and eligible to practice before the bar of any United States court or the highest court of the District of Columbia or any state, territory, or insular possession of the United States, or is licensed to practice law in, or is admitted in good standing and eligible to practice before the bar of the highest court of, a foreign country or any political subdivision thereof, and includes any agent of the lawyer, law firm, or law corporation doing business in the state.

(c) "Advertise" or "advertisement" means any communication, disseminated by television or radio, by any print medium, including, but not limited to, newspapers and billboards, or by means of a mailing directed generally to members of the public and not to a specific person, that solicits employment of legal services provided by a licensee, and is directed to the general public and is paid for by, or on the behalf of, an attorney.

(d) "Electronic medium" means television, radio, or computer networks.

§ 6157.1 False, misleading or deceptive statements; prohibition

No advertisement shall contain any false, misleading, or deceptive statement or omit to state any fact necessary to make the statements made, in light of circumstances under which they are made, not false, misleading, or deceptive.

§ 6157.2 Prohibited statements regarding outcome; dramatizations; contingent fee basis representations

No advertisement shall contain or refer to any of the following:

(a) Any guarantee or warranty regarding the outcome of a legal matter as a result of representation by the member.

(b) Statements or symbols stating that the licensee featured in the advertisement can generally obtain immediate cash or quick settlements.

(c)(1) An impersonation of the name, voice, photograph, or electronic image of any person other than the lawyer, directly or implicitly purporting to be that of a lawyer.

(2) An impersonation of the name, voice, photograph, or electronic image of any person directly or implicitly purporting to be a client of the licensee featured in the advertisement, or a dramatization of events, unless disclosure of the impersonation or dramatization is made in the advertisement.

(3) A spokesperson, including a celebrity spokesperson, unless there is a disclosure of the spokesperson's title.

(d) A statement that a licensee offers representation on a contingent basis unless the statement also advises whether a client will be held responsible for any costs advanced by the licensee when no recovery is obtained on behalf of the client. If the client will not be held responsible for costs, no disclosure is required.

§ 6157.3 Advertisements made on behalf of member; required representations

Any advertisement made on behalf of a licensee, which is not paid for by the licensee, shall disclose any business relationship, past or present, between the licensee and the person paying for the advertisement.

§ 6157.4 Lawyer referral service advertising

Any advertisement that is created or disseminated by a lawyer referral service shall disclose whether the attorneys on the organization's referral list, panel, or system, paid any consideration, other than a proportional share of actual cost, to be included on that list, panel, or system.

§ 6157.5 Immigration and naturalization services advertising; member seeking professional employment; application of section

(a) All advertisements published, distributed, or broadcasted by or on behalf of a licensee seeking professional employment for the licensee in providing services relating to immigration or naturalization shall include a statement that he or she is an active licensee of the State Bar, licensed to practice law in this state. If the advertisement seeks employment for a law firm or law corporation employing more than one attorney, the advertisement shall include a statement that all the services relating to immigration and naturalization provided by the firm or corporation shall be provided by an active licensee of the State Bar or by a person under the supervision of an active licensee of the State Bar. This subdivision shall not apply to classified or "yellow pages" listings in a telephone or business directory of three lines or less that state only the name, address, and telephone number of the listed entity.

(b) If the advertisement is in a language other than English, the statement required by subdivision (a) shall be in the same language as the advertisement.

(c) This section shall not apply to licensees employed by public agencies or by nonprofit entities registered with the Secretary of State.

(d) A violation of this section by a licensee shall be cause for discipline by the State Bar.

§ 6158. Electronic media advertising; false, misleading or deceptive message; factual substantiation

In advertising by electronic media, to comply with Sections 6157.1 and 6157.2, the message as a whole may not be false, misleading, or deceptive, and the message as a whole must be factually substantiated. The message means the effect in combination of the spoken word, sound, background, action, symbols, visual image, or any other technique employed to create the message. Factually substantiated means capable of verification by a credible source.

§ 6158.1 False, misleading or deceptive messages; rebuttable presumption

There shall be a rebuttable presumption affecting the burden of producing evidence that the following messages are false, misleading, or deceptive within the meaning of Section 6158:

(a) A message as to the ultimate result of a specific case or cases presented out of context without adequately providing information as to the facts or law giving rise to the result.

(b) The depiction of an event through methods such as the use of displays of injuries, accident scenes, or portrayals of other injurious events which may or may not be accompanied by sound effects and which may give rise to a claim for compensation.

(c) A message referring to or implying money received by or for a client in a particular case or cases, or to potential monetary recovery for a prospective client. A reference to money or monetary recovery includes, but is not limited to, a specific dollar amount, characterization of a sum of money, monetary symbols, or the implication of wealth.

§ 6158.2 Information presumed to be in compliance with article

The following information shall be presumed to be in compliance with this article for purposes of advertising by electronic media, provided the message as a whole is not false, misleading, or deceptive:

(a) Name, including name of law firm, names of professional associates, addresses, telephone numbers, and the designation "lawyer," "attorney," "law firm," or the like.

(b) Fields of practice, limitation of practice, or specialization.

(c) Fees for routine legal services, subject to the requirements of subdivision (d) of Section 6157.2 and the Rules of Professional Conduct.

(d) Date and place of birth.

(e) Date and place of admission to the bar of state and federal courts.

(f) Schools attended, with dates of graduation, degrees, and other scholastic distinctions.

(g) Public or quasi-public offices.

(h) Military service.

(i) Legal authorship.

(j) Legal teaching positions.

(k) Memberships, offices, and committee assignments in bar associations.

(*l*) Memberships and offices in legal fraternities and legal societies.

(m) Technical and professional licenses.

(n) Memberships in scientific, technical, and professional associations and societies.

(*o*) Foreign language ability of the advertising lawyer or a member of lawyer's firm.

§ 6158.3 Electronic media advertising; required disclosures

In addition to any disclosure required by Section 6157.2, Section 6157.3, and the Rules of Professional Conduct, the following disclosure shall appear in advertising by electronic media. Use of the following disclosure alone may not rebut any presumption created in Section 6158.1. If an advertisement in the electronic media conveys a message portraying a result in a particular case or cases, the advertisement must state, in either an oral or printed communication, either of the following disclosures: The advertisement must adequately disclose the factual and legal circumstances that justify the result portrayed in the message, including the basis for liability and the nature of injury or damage sustained, or the advertisement must state that the result portrayed in the advertisement was dependent on the facts of that case, and that the results will differ if based on different facts.

§ 6158.4 Violation; complaint; contents; procedure

(a) Any person claiming a violation of Section 6158, 6158.1, or 6158.3 may file a complaint with the State Bar that states the name of the advertiser, a description of the advertisement claimed to violate these sections, and that specifically identifies the alleged violation. A copy of the complaint shall be served simultaneously upon the advertiser. The advertiser shall have nine days from the date of service of the complaint to voluntarily withdraw from broadcast the advertisement that is the subject of the complaint. If the advertiser elects to withdraw the advertisement, the advertiser shall notify the State Bar of that fact, and no further action may be taken by the complainant. The advertiser shall provide a copy of the complained of advertisement to the State Bar for review within seven days of service of the complaint. Within 21 days of the delivery of the complained of advertisement, the State Bar shall determine whether substantial evidence of a violation of these sections exists. The review shall be conducted by a State Bar attorney who has expertise in the area of lawyer advertising.

(b)(1) Upon a State Bar determination that substantial evidence of a violation exists, if the licencee or certified lawyer referral service withdraws that advertisement from broadcast within 72 hours, no further action may be taken by the complainant.

(2) Upon a State Bar determination that substantial evidence of a violation exists, if the licensee or certified lawyer referral service fails to withdraw the advertisement within 72 hours, a civil enforcement action brought pursuant to subdivision (e) may be commenced within one year of the State Bar decision. If the licensee or certified lawyer referral service withdraws an advertisement upon a State Bar determination that substantial evidence of a violation exists and subsequently rebroadcasts the same advertisement without a finding by the trier of fact in an action brought pursuant to subdivision (c) or (e) that the advertisement does not violate Section 6158, 6158.1, or 6158.3, a civil enforcement action may be commenced within one year of the rebroadcast.

(3) Upon a determination that substantial evidence of a violation does not exist, the complainant is barred from bringing a civil enforcement action pursuant to subdivision (e), but may bring an action for declaratory relief pursuant to subdivision (c).

(c) Any licensee or certified lawyer referral service who was the subject of a complaint and any complainant affected by the decision of the State Bar may bring an action for declaratory relief in the superior court to obtain a judicial declaration of whether Section 6158, 6158.1, or 6158.3 has been violated, and, if applicable, may also request injunctive relief. Any defense otherwise available at law may be raised for the first time in the declaratory relief action, including any constitutional challenge. Any civil enforcement action filed pursuant to subdivision (e) shall be stayed pending the resolution of the declaratory relief action. The action shall be defended by the real party in interest. The State Bar shall not be considered a party to the action unless it elects to intervene in the action.

(1) Upon a State Bar determination that substantial evidence of a violation exists, if the complainant or the licensee or certified lawyer referral service brings an action for declaratory relief to obtain a judicial declaration of whether the advertisement violates Section 6158, 6158.1, or 6158.3, and the court declares that the advertisement violates one or more of the sections, a civil enforcement action pursuant to subdivision (e) may be filed or maintained if the licensee or certified lawyer referral service failed to withdraw the advertisement within 72 hours of the State Bar determination. The decision of the court that an advertisement violates Section 6158, 6158.1, or 6158.3 shall be binding on the issue of whether the advertisement is unlawful in any pending or prospective civil enforcement action brought pursuant to subdivision (e) if that binding effect is supported by the doctrine of collateral estoppel or res judicata.

If, in that declaratory relief action, the court declares that the advertisement does not violate Section 6158, 6158.1, or 6158.3, the licensee or lawyer referral service may broadcast the advertisement. The decision of the court that an advertisement does not violate Section 6158, 6158.1, or 6158.3 shall bar any pending or prospective civil enforcement action brought pursuant to subdivision (e) if that prohibitive effect is supported by the doctrine of collateral estoppel or res judicata.

(2) If, following a State Bar determination that does not find substantial evidence that an advertisement violates Section 6158, 6158.1, or 6158.3, the complainant or the licenseemember or certified lawyer referral service brings an action for declaratory relief to obtain a judicial declaration of whether the advertisement violates Section 6158, 6158.1, or 6158.3, and the court declares that the advertisement violates one or more of the sections, a civil enforcement action pursuant to subdivision (e) may be filed or maintained if the licensee or certified lawyer referral service broadcasts the same advertisement following the decision in the declaratory relief action. The decision of the court that an advertisement violates Section 6158, 6158.1, or 6158.3 shall be binding on the issue of whether the advertisement is unlawful in any pending or prospective civil enforcement action brought pursuant to subdivision (e) if that binding effect is supported by the doctrine of collateral estoppel or res judicata.

If, in that declaratory relief action, the court declares that the advertisement does not violate Section 6158, 6158.1, or 6158.3, the licensee or lawyer referral service may continue broadcast of the advertisement. The decision of the court that an advertisement does not violate Section 6158, 6158.1, or 6158.3 shall bar any pending or prospective civil enforcement action brought pursuant to subdivision (e) if that prohibitive effect is supported by the doctrine of collateral estoppel or res judicata.

(d) The State Bar review procedure shall apply only to licensees and certified referral services. A direct civil enforcement action for a violation of Section 6158, 6158.1, or 6158.3 may be maintained against any other advertiser after first giving 14 days' notice to the advertiser of the alleged violation. If the advertiser does not withdraw from broadcast the advertisement that is the subject of the notice within 14 days of service of the notice, a civil enforcement action pursuant to subdivision (e) may be commenced. The civil enforcement action shall be commenced within one year of the date of the last publication or broadcast of the advertisement that is the subject of the action.

(e) Subject to Section 6158.5, a violation of Section 6158, 6158.1, or 6158.3 shall be cause for a civil enforcement action brought by any person residing within the State of California for an amount up to five thousand dollars ($5,000) for each individual broadcast that violates Section 6158, 6158.1, or 6158.3. Venue shall be in a county where the advertisement was broadcast.

(f) In any civil action brought pursuant to this section, the matter shall be determined according to the law and procedure relating to the trial of civil actions, including trial by jury, if demanded.

(g) The decision of the State Bar pursuant to subdivision (a) shall be admissible in the civil enforcement action brought pursuant to subdivision (e). However, the State Bar shall not be a party or a witness in either a declaratory relief proceeding brought pursuant to subdivision (c) or the civil enforcement action brought pursuant to subdivision (e). Additionally, no direct action may be filed against the State Bar challenging the State Bar's decision pursuant to subdivision (a).

(h) Amounts recovered pursuant to this section shall be paid into the Client Security Fund maintained by the State Bar.

(i) In any civil action brought pursuant to this section, the court shall award attorney's fees pursuant to Section 1021.5 of the Code of Civil Procedure if the court finds that the action has resulted in the enforcement of an important public interest or that a significant benefit has been conferred on the public.

(j) The State Bar shall maintain records of all complainants and complaints filed pursuant to subdivision (a) for a period of seven years. If a complainant files five or more unfounded complaints within seven years, the complainant shall be considered a vexatious litigant for purposes of this section. The State Bar shall require any person deemed a vexatious litigant to post security in the minimum amount of twenty-five thousand dollars ($25,000) prior to considering any complaint filed by that person and shall refrain from taking any action until the security is posted. In any civil action arising from this section brought by a person deemed a vexatious litigant, the defendant may advise the court and trier of fact that the plaintiff is deemed to be a vexatious litigant under the provisions of this section and disclose the basis for this determination.

(k) Nothing in this section shall restrict any other right available under existing law or otherwise available to a citizen seeking redress for false, misleading, or deceptive advertisements.

§ 6158.5 Application of article

This article applies to all lawyers, licensees, law partnerships, law corporations, entities subject to regulation under Section 6155, advertising collectives, cooperatives, or other individuals, including nonlawyers, or groups advertising the availability of legal services. Subdivisions (a) to (k), inclusive, of Section 6158.4 do not apply to qualified legal services projects as defined in Article 14 (commencing with Section 6210) and nonprofit lawyer referral services certified under Section 6155. Sections 6157 to 6158.5, inclusive, do not apply to the media in which the advertising is displayed or to an advertising agency that prepares the contents of an advertisement and is not directly involved in the formation or operation of lawyer advertising collectives or cooperatives, referral services, or other groups existing primarily for the purpose of advertising the availability of legal services or making referrals to attorneys.

§ 6158.7 Violation as cause for discipline by state bar

A violation of Section 6158, 6158.1, or 6158.3 by a licensee shall be cause for discipline by the State Bar. In addition to the existing grounds for initiating a disciplinary proceeding set forth in a statute or in the Rules of Professional Conduct, the State Bar may commence an investigation based upon a complaint filed by a person pursuant to Section 6158.4. The State Bar's decision pursuant to subdivision (a) of Section 6158.4 shall be admissible, but shall not be determinative, in any disciplinary proceeding brought as a result of that complaint.

§ 6159. Report by court of article violators

The court shall report the name, address, and professional license number of any person found in violation of this article to the appropriate professional licensing agency for review and possible disciplinary action.

§ 6159.1 Retention of advertising copy by payor

A true and correct copy of any advertisement made by a person or licensee shall be retained for one year by the person or licensee who pays for an advertisement soliciting employment of legal services.

§ 6159.2 Rights and duties under other laws

(a) Nothing in this article shall be deemed to limit or preclude enforcement of any other provision of law, or of any court rule, or of the State Bar Rules of Professional Conduct.

(b) Nothing in this article shall limit the right of advertising protected under the Constitution of the State of California or of the United States. If any provision of this article is found to violate either Constitution, that provision is severable and the remaining provisions shall be enforceable without the severed provision.

ARTICLE 13. ARBITRATION OF ATTORNEYS' FEES

§ 6200. Establishment of system and procedure; applicability of article; voluntary or mandatory nature; rules; immunity of arbitrator; powers of arbitrator; confidentiality of mediation

(a) The board of trustees shall, by rule, establish, maintain, and administer a system and procedure for the arbitration, and may establish, maintain, and administer a system and procedure for mediation of disputes concerning fees, costs, or both, charged for professional services by licensees of the State Bar or by members of the bar of other jurisdictions. The rules may include provision for a filing fee in the amount as the board may, from time to time, determine.

(b) This article shall not apply to any of the following:

(1) Disputes where a licensee of the State Bar of California is also admitted to practice in another jurisdiction or where an attorney is only admitted to practice in another jurisdiction, and he or she maintains no office in the State of California, and no material portion of the services were rendered in the State of California.

(2) Claims for affirmative relief against the attorney for damages or otherwise based upon alleged malpractice or professional misconduct, except as provided in subdivision (a) of Section 6203.

(3) Disputes where the fee or cost to be paid by the client or on his or her behalf has been determined pursuant to statute or court order.

(c) Unless the client has agreed in writing to arbitration under this article of all disputes concerning fees, costs, or both, arbitration under this article shall be voluntary for a client and shall be mandatory for an attorney if commenced by a client. Mediation under this article shall be voluntary for an attorney and a client.

(d) The board of trustees shall adopt rules to allow arbitration and mediation of attorney fee and cost disputes under this article to proceed under arbitration and mediation systems sponsored by local bar associations in this state. Rules of procedure promulgated by local bar associations are subject to review by the board or a committee designated by the board to ensure that they provide for a fair, impartial, and speedy hearing and award.

(e) In adopting or reviewing rules of arbitration under this section the board shall provide that the panel shall include one attorney member whose area of practice is either, at the option of the client, civil law, if the attorney's representation involved civil law, or criminal law, if the attorney's representation involved criminal law, as follows:

(1) If the panel is composed of three members the panel shall include one attorney member whose area of practice is either, at the option of the client, civil or criminal law, and shall include one lay member.

(2) If the panel is composed of one member, that member shall be an attorney whose area of practice is either, at the option of the client, civil or criminal law.

(f) In any arbitration or mediation conducted pursuant to this article by the State Bar or by a local bar association, pursuant to rules of procedure approved by the board of trustees, an arbitrator or mediator, as well as the arbitrating association and its directors, officers, and employees, shall have the same immunity which attaches in judicial proceedings.

(g) In the conduct of arbitrations under this article the arbitrator or arbitrators may do all of the following:

(1) Take and hear evidence pertaining to the proceeding.

(2) Administer oaths and affirmations.

(3) Issue subpoenas for the attendance of witnesses and the production of books, papers, and documents pertaining to the proceeding.

(h) Participation in mediation is a voluntary consensual process, based on direct negotiations between the attorney and his or her client, and is an extension of the negotiated settlement process. All discussions and offers of settlement are confidential and may not be disclosed in any subsequent arbitration or other proceedings.

§ 6201. Notice to client and state bar; stay of action; right to arbitration; waiver by client

(a) The rules adopted by the board of trustees shall provide that an attorney shall forward a written notice to the client prior to or at the time of service of summons or claim in an action against the client or prior to or at the commencement of any other proceeding against client under a contract between attorney and client which provides for an alternative to arbitration under this article, for recovery of fees, costs, or both. The written notice shall be in the form that the board of trustees prescribes, and shall include a statement of the client's right to arbitration under this article. Failure to give this notice shall be a ground for the dismissal of the action or other proceeding. The notice shall not be required, however, prior to initiating mediation of the dispute.

The rules adopted by the board of trustees shall provide that the client's failure to request arbitration within 30 days after receipt of notice from the attorney shall be deemed a waiver of the client's right to arbitration under the provisions of this article.

(b) If an attorney, or the attorney's assignee, commences an action in any court or any other proceeding and the client is entitled to maintain arbitration under this article, and the dispute is not one to which subdivision (b) of Section 6200 applies, the client may stay the action or other proceeding by serving and filing a request for arbitration in accordance with the rules established by the board of trustees pursuant to subdivision (a) of Section 6200. The request for arbitration shall be served and filed prior to the filing of an answer in the action or equivalent response in the other proceeding; failure to so request arbitration prior to the filing of an answer or equivalent response shall be deemed a waiver of the client's right to arbitration under the provisions of this article if notice of the client's right to arbitration was given pursuant to subdivision (a).

(c) Upon filing and service of the request for arbitration, the action or other proceeding shall be automatically stayed until the award of the arbitrators is issued or the arbitration is otherwise terminated. The stay may be vacated in whole or in part, after a hearing duly noticed by any party or the court, if and to the extent the court finds that the matter is not appropriate for arbitration under the provisions of this article. The action or other proceeding may thereafter proceed subject to the provisions of Section 6204.

(d) A client's right to request or maintain arbitration under the provisions of this article is waived by the client commencing an action or filing any pleading seeking either of the following: (1) Judicial resolution of a fee dispute to which this article applies. (2) Affirmative relief against the attorney for damages or otherwise based upon alleged malpractice or professional misconduct.

(e) If the client waives the right to arbitration under this article, the parties may stipulate to set aside the waiver and to proceed with arbitration.

§ 6203. Award; contents; damages and offset; fees and costs; finality of award; appellate fees and costs; attorney inactive status and penalties

(a) The award shall be in writing and signed by the arbitrators concurring therein. It shall include a determination of all the questions submitted to the arbitrators, the decision of which is necessary in order to determine the controversy. The award shall not include any award to either party for costs or attorney's fees incurred in preparation for or in the course of the fee arbitration proceeding, notwithstanding any contract between the parties providing for such an award or attorney's fees. However, the filing fee paid may be allocated between the parties by the arbitrators. This section shall not preclude an award of costs or attorney's fees to either party by a court pursuant to subdivision (c) of this section or of subdivision (d) of Section 6204. The State Bar, or the local bar association delegated by the State Bar to conduct the arbitration, shall deliver to each of the parties with the award, an original declaration of service of the award.

Evidence relating to claims of malpractice and professional misconduct, shall be admissible only to the extent that those claims bear upon the fees, costs, or both, to which the attorney is entitled. The arbitrators shall not award affirmative relief, in the form of damages or offset or otherwise, for injuries underlying the claim. Nothing in this section shall be construed to prevent the arbitrators from awarding a refund of unearned prepaid fees.

(b) Even if the parties to the arbitration have not agreed in writing to be bound, the arbitration award shall become binding upon the passage of 30 days after service of notice of the award, unless a party has, within the 30 days, sought a trial after arbitration pursuant to Section 6204. If an action has previously been filed in any court, any petition to confirm, correct, or vacate the award shall be to the court in which the action is pending, and may be served by mail on any party who has appeared, as provided in Chapter 4 (commencing with Section 1003) of Title 14 of Part 2 of the Code of Civil Procedure; otherwise it shall be in the same manner as provided in Chapter 4 (commencing with Section 1285) of Title 9 of Part 3 of the Code of Civil Procedure. If no action is pending in any court, the award may be confirmed, corrected, or vacated by petition to the court having jurisdiction over the amount of the arbitration award, but otherwise in the same manner as provided in Chapter 4 (commencing with Section 1285) of Title 9 of Part 3 of the Code of Civil Procedure.

(c) Neither party to the arbitration may recover costs or attorney's fees incurred in preparation for or in the course of the fee arbitration proceeding with the exception of the filing fee paid pursuant to subdivision (a) of this section. However, a court confirming, correcting, or vacating an award under this section may award to the prevailing party reasonable fees and costs including, if applicable, fees or costs on appeal, incurred in obtaining confirmation, correction, or vacation of the award. The party obtaining judgment confirming, correcting, or vacating the award shall be the prevailing party except that, without regard to consideration of who the prevailing party may be, if a party did not appear at the arbitration hearing in the manner provided by the rules adopted by the board of trustees, that party shall not be entitled to attorney's fees or costs upon confirmation, correction, or vacation of the award.

(d)(1) In any matter arbitrated under this article in which the award is binding or has become binding by operation of law or has become a judgment either after confirmation under subdivision (c) or after a trial after arbitration under Section 6204, or in any matter mediated under this article, if: (A) the award, judgment, or agreement reached after mediation includes a refund of fees or costs, or both, to the client and (B) the attorney has not complied with that award, judgment, or agreement the State Bar shall enforce the award, judgment, or agreement by placing the attorney on involuntary inactive status until the refund has been paid.

(2) The State Bar shall provide for an administrative procedure to determine whether an award, judgment, or agreement should be enforced pursuant to this subdivision. An award, judgment, or agreement shall be so enforced if either of the following applies:

(A) The State Bar shows that the attorney has failed to comply with a binding fee arbitration award, judgment, or agreement rendered pursuant to this article.

(B) The attorney has not proposed a payment plan acceptable to the client or the State Bar.

However, the award, judgment, or agreement shall not be so enforced if the attorney has demonstrated that he or she (i) is not personally responsible for making or ensuring payment of the refund, or (ii) is unable to pay the refund.

(3) An attorney who has failed to comply with a binding award, judgment, or agreement shall pay administrative penalties or reasonable costs, or both, as directed by the State Bar. Penalties imposed shall not exceed 20 percent of the amount to be refunded to the client or one thousand dollars ($1,000), whichever is greater. Any penalties or costs, or both, that are not paid shall be added to the license fee of the attorney for the next calendar year.

(4) The board shall terminate the inactive enrollment upon proof that the attorney has complied with the award, judgment, or agreement and upon payment of any costs or penalties, or both, assessed as a result of the attorney's failure to comply.

(5) A request for enforcement under this subdivision shall be made within four years from the date (A) the arbitration award was mailed, (B) the judgment was entered, or (C) the date the agreement was signed. In an arbitrated matter, however, in no event shall a request be made prior to 100 days from the date of the service of a signed copy of the award. In cases where the award is appealed, a request shall not be made prior to 100 days from the date the award has become final as set forth in this section.

ARTICLE 14. FUNDS FOR THE PROVISION OF LEGAL SERVICES TO INDIGENT PERSONS

§ 6210. Legislative findings; purpose

The Legislature finds that, due to insufficient funding, existing programs providing free legal services in civil matters to indigent persons, especially underserved client groups, such as the elderly, the disabled, juveniles, and non-English-speaking persons, do not adequately meet the needs of these persons. It is the purpose of this article to expand the availability and improve the quality of existing free legal services in civil matters to indigent persons, and to initiate new programs that will provide services to them. The Legislature finds that the use of funds collected by the State Bar pursuant to this article for these purposes is in the public interest, is a proper use of the funds, and is consistent with essential public and governmental purposes in the judicial branch of government. The Legislature further finds that the expansion, improvement, and initiation of legal services to indigent persons will aid in the advancement of the science of jurisprudence and the improvement of the administration of justice.

§ 6211. Establishment by attorney by IOLTA account; interest and dividends earned to be paid to state bar; other accounts not prohibited; rules of professional conduct, authority of supreme court or state bar not affected

(a) An attorney or law firm, which in the course of the practice of law receives or disburses trust funds, shall establish and maintain an IOLTA account in which the attorney or law firm shall deposit or invest all client deposits or funds invested for a short period of time. All such client funds may be deposited in a single unsegregated account. The interest and dividends earned on all such accounts shall be paid to the State Bar of California to be used for the purposes set forth in this article.

(b) Nothing in this article shall be construed to prohibit an attorney or law firm from establishing one or more interest bearing bank accounts or other trust investments as may be permitted by the Supreme Court, with the interest or dividends earned on the accounts payable to clients for trust funds not deposited in accordance with subdivision (a).

(c) With the approval of the Supreme Court, the State Bar may formulate and enforce rules of professional conduct pertaining to the use by attorneys or law firms of interest bearing trust accounts for unsegregated client funds pursuant to this article.

(d) Nothing in this article shall be construed as affecting or impairing the disciplinary powers and authority of the Supreme Court or of the State Bar or as modifying the statutes and rules governing the conduct of licensees of the State Bar.

§ 6212. Establishment by attorney of IOLTA account; amount of interest; remittance to state bar; reporting of IOLTA account compliance and other information; statements and reports

An attorney who, or a law firm which, establishes an interest bearing demand trust account pursuant to subdivision (a) of Section 6211 shall comply with all of the following provisions:

(a) The IOLTA account shall be established and maintained with an eligible institution offering or making available an IOLTA account that meets the requirements of this article. The IOLTA account shall be established and maintained consistent with the attorney or law firm's duties of professional responsibility. An eligible financial institution shall have no responsibility for selecting the deposit or investment product chosen for the IOLTA account.

(b) Except as provided in subdivision (f), the rate of interest or dividends payable on any IOLTA account shall not be less than the interest rate or dividends generally paid by the eligible institution to nonattorney customers on accounts of the same type meeting the same minimum balance and other eligibility requirements as the IOLTA account. In determining the interest rate or dividend payable on any IOLTA account, an eligible institution may consider, in addition to the balance in the IOLTA account, risk or other factors customarily considered by the eligible institution when setting the interest rate or dividends for its non-IOLTA accounts, provided that the factors do not discriminate between IOLTA customers and non-IOLTA customers and that these factors do not include the fact that the account is an IOLTA account. The eligible institution shall calculate interest and dividends in accordance with its standard practice for non-IOLTA customers. Nothing in this article shall preclude an eligible institution from paying a higher interest rate or dividend on an IOLTA account or from electing to waive any fees and service charges on an IOLTA account.

(c) Reasonable fees may be deducted from the interest or dividends remitted on an IOLTA account only at the rates and in accordance with the customary practices of the eligible institution for non-IOLTA customers. No other fees or service charges may be deducted from the interest or dividends earned on an IOLTA account. Unless and until the State Bar enacts regulations exempting from compliance with subdivision (a) of Section 6211 those accounts for which maintenance fees exceed the interest or dividends paid, an eligible institution may deduct the fees and service charges in excess of the interest or dividends paid on an IOLTA account from the aggregate interest and dividends remitted to the State Bar. Fees and service charges other than reasonable fees shall be the sole responsibility of, and may only be charged to, the attorney or law firm maintaining the IOLTA account. Fees and charges shall not be assessed against or deducted from the principal of any IOLTA account. It is the intent of the Legislature that the State Bar develop policies so that eligible institutions not incur uncompensated administrative costs in adapting their systems to comply with the provisions of Chapter 422 of the Statutes of 2007 or in making investment products available to IOLTA members.

(d) The attorney or law firm shall report IOLTA account compliance and all other IOLTA account information required by the State Bar in the manner specified by the State Bar.

(e) The eligible institution shall be directed to do all of the following:

(1) To remit interest or dividends on the IOLTA account, less reasonable fees, to the State Bar, at least quarterly.

(2) To transmit to the State Bar with each remittance a statement showing the name of the attorney or law firm for which the remittance is sent, for each account the rate of interest applied or dividend paid, the amount and type of fees deducted, if any, and the average balance for each account for each month of the period for which the report is made.

(3) To transmit to the attorney or law firm customer at the same time a report showing the amount paid to the State Bar for that period, the rate of interest or dividend applied, the amount of fees and service charges deducted, if any, and the average daily account balance for each month of the period for which the report is made.

(f) An eligible institution has no affirmative duty to offer or make investment products available to IOLTA customers. However, if an eligible institution offers or makes investment products available to non-IOLTA customers, in order to remain an IOLTA-eligible institution, it shall make those products available to IOLTA customers or pay an interest rate on the IOLTA deposit account that is comparable to the rate of return or the dividends generally paid on that investment product for similar customers meeting the same minimum balance and other requirements applicable to the investment product. If the eligible institution elects to pay that higher interest rate, the eligible institution may subject the IOLTA deposit account to equivalent fees and charges assessable against the investment product.

§ 6213. Definitions

As used in this article:

(a) "Qualified legal services project" means either of the following:

(1) A nonprofit project incorporated and operated exclusively in California that provides as its primary purpose and function legal services without charge to indigent persons and that has quality control procedures approved by the State Bar of California.

(2) A program operated exclusively in California by a nonprofit law school accredited by the State Bar of California that meets the requirements of subparagraphs (A) and (B).

(A) The program shall have operated for at least two years at a cost of at least twenty thousand dollars ($20,000) per year as an identifiable law school unit with a primary purpose and function of providing legal services without charge to indigent persons.

(B) The program shall have quality control procedures approved by the State Bar of California.

(b) "Qualified support center" means an incorporated nonprofit legal services center that has as its primary purpose and function the provision of legal training, legal technical assistance, or advocacy support without charge and which actually provides through an office in California a significant level of legal training, legal technical assistance, or advocacy support without charge to qualified legal services projects on a statewide basis in California.

(c) "Recipient" means a qualified legal services project or support center receiving financial assistance under this article.

(d) "Indigent person" means a person whose income is (1) 125 percent or less of the current poverty threshold established by the United States Office of Management and Budget, or (2) who is eligible for Supplemental Security Income or free services under the Older Americans Act or Developmentally Disabled Assistance Act. With regard to a project that provides free services of attorneys in private practice without compensation, "indigent person" also means a person whose income is 75 percent or less of the maximum levels of income for lower income households as defined in Section 50079.5 of the Health and Safety Code. For the purpose of this subdivision, the income of a person who is disabled shall be determined after deducting the costs of medical and other disability-related special expenses.

(e) "Fee generating case" means any case or matter that, if undertaken on behalf of an indigent person by an attorney in private practice, reasonably may be expected to result in payment of a fee for legal services from an award to a client, from public funds, or from the opposing party. A case shall not be considered fee generating if adequate representation is unavailable and any of the following circumstances exist:

(1) The recipient has determined that free referral is not possible because of any of the following reasons:

(A) The case has been rejected by the local lawyer referral service, or if there is no such service, by two attorneys in private practice who have experience in the subject matter of the case.

(B) Neither the referral service nor any attorney will consider the case without payment of a consultation fee.

(C) The case if of the type that attorneys in private practice in the area ordinarily do not accept, or do not accept without prepayment of a fee.

(D) Emergency circumstances compel immediate action before referral can be made, but the client is advised that, if appropriate and consistent with professional responsibility, referral will be attempted at a later time.

(2) Recovery of damages is not the principal object of the case and a request for damages is merely ancillary to an action for equitable or other nonpecuniary relief, or inclusion of a counterclaim requesting damages is necessary for effective defense or because of applicable rules governing joinder of counterclaims.

(3) A court has appointed a recipient or an employee of a recipient pursuant to a statute or a court rule or practice of equal applicability to all attorneys in the jurisdiction.

(4) The case involves the rights of a claimant under a publicly supported benefit program for which entitlement to benefit is based on need.

(f) "Legal Services Corporation" means the Legal Services Corporation established under the Legal Services Corporation Act of 1974, (P.L. 93–355; 42 U.S.C. Sec. 2996 et seq.).

(g) "Older Americans Act" means the Older Americans Act of 1965, as amended (P.L. 89–73; 42 U.S.C. Sec. 3001 et seq.).

(h) "Developmentally Disabled Assistance Act" means the Developmentally Disabled Assistance and Bill of Rights Act of 1975, as amended (P.L. 94–103; 42 U.S.C. Sec. 6001 et seq.).

(i) "Supplemental security income recipient" means an individual receiving or eligible to receive payments under Title XVI of the federal Social Security Act, or payments under Chapter 3 (commencing with Section 12000) of Part 3 of Division 9 of the Welfare and Institutions Code.

(j) "IOLTA account" means an account or investment product established and maintained pursuant to subdivision (a) of Section 6211 that is any of the following:

(1) An interest-bearing checking account.

(2) An investment sweep product that is a daily (overnight) financial institution repurchase agreement or an open-end money-market fund.

(3) An investment product authorized by California Supreme Court rule or order.

A daily financial institution repurchase agreement shall be fully collateralized by United States Government Securities or other comparably conservative debt securities, and may be established only with any eligible institution that is "well-capitalized" or "adequately capitalized" as those terms are defined by applicable federal statutes and regulations. An open-end money-market fund shall be invested solely in United States Government Securities or repurchase agreements fully collateralized by United States Government Securities or other comparably conservative debt securities, shall hold itself out as a "money-market fund" as that term is defined by federal statutes and regulations under the Investment Company Act of 1940 (15 U.S.C. Sec. 80a–1 et seq.), and, at the time of the investment, shall have total assets of at least two hundred fifty million dollars ($250,000,000).

(k) "Eligible institution" means either of the following:

(1) A bank, savings and loan, or other financial institution regulated by a federal or state agency that pays interest or dividends in the IOLTA account and carries deposit insurance from an agency of the federal government.

(2) Any other type of financial institution authorized by the Supreme Court.

§ 6214. Qualified legal service projects

(a) Projects meeting the requirements of subdivision (a) of Section 6213 which are funded either in whole or part by the Legal Services Corporation or with Older American Act funds shall be presumed qualified legal services projects for the purpose of this article.

(b) Projects meeting the requirements of subdivision (a) of Section 6213 but not qualifying under the presumption specified in subdivision (a) shall qualify for funds under this article if they meet all of the following additional criteria:

(1) They receive cash funds from other sources in the amount of at least twenty thousand dollars ($20,000) per year to support free legal representation to indigent persons.

(2) They have demonstrated community support for the operation of a viable ongoing program.

(3) They provide one or both of the following special services:

(A) The coordination of the recruitment of substantial numbers of attorneys in private practice to provide free legal representation to indigent persons or to qualified legal services projects in California.

(B) The provision of legal representation, training, or technical assistance on matters concerning special client groups, including the elderly, the disabled, juveniles, and non-English-speaking groups, or on matters of specialized substantive law important to the special client groups.

§ 6214.5 Qualified legal services projects; eligibility for distributions of funds

A law school program that meets the definition of a "qualified legal services project" as defined in paragraph (2) of subdivision (a) of Section 6213, and that applied to the State Bar for funding under this article not later than February 17, 1984, shall be deemed eligible for all distributions of funds made under Section 6216.

§ 6215. Qualified support centers

(a) Support centers satisfying the qualifications specified in subdivision (b) of Section 6213 which were operating an office and providing services in California on December 31, 1980, shall be presumed to be qualified support centers for the purposes of this article.

(b) Support centers not qualifying under the presumption specified in subdivision (a) may qualify as a support center by meeting both of the following additional criteria:

(1) Meeting quality control standards established by the State Bar.

(2) Being deemed to be of special need by a majority of the qualified legal services projects.

§ 6216. Distribution of funds

The State Bar shall distribute all moneys received under the program established by this article for the provision of civil legal services to indigent persons. The funds first shall be distributed 18 months from the effective date of this article, or upon such a date, as shall be determined by the State Bar, that adequate funds are available to initiate the program. Thereafter, the funds shall be distributed on an annual basis. All distributions of funds shall be made in the following order and in the following manner:

(a) To pay the actual administrative costs of the program, including any costs incurred after the adoption of this article and a reasonable reserve therefor.

(b) Eighty-five percent of the funds remaining after payment of administrative costs allocated pursuant to this article shall be distributed to qualified legal services projects. Distribution shall be by a pro rata county-by-county formula based upon the number of persons whose income is 125 percent or less of the current poverty threshold per county. For the purposes of this section, the source of data identifying the number of persons per county shall be the latest available figures from the United States Department of Commerce, Bureau of the Census. Projects from more than one county may pool their funds to operate a joint, multicounty legal services project serving each of their respective counties.

(1)(A) In any county which is served by more than one qualified legal services project, the State Bar shall distribute funds for the county to those projects which apply on a pro rata basis, based upon the amount of their total budget expended in the prior year for legal services in that county as compared to the total expended in the prior year for legal services by all qualified legal services projects applying therefor in the county. In determining the amount of funds to be allocated to a qualified legal services project specified in paragraph (2) of subdivision (a) of Section 6213, the State Bar shall recognize only expenditures attributable to the representation of indigent persons as constituting the budget of the program.

(B) The State Bar shall reserve 10 percent of the funds allocated to the county for distribution to programs meeting the standards of subparagraph (A) of paragraph (3) and paragraphs (1) and (2) of subdivision (b) of Section 6214 and which perform the services described in subparagraph (A) of paragraph (3) of Section 6214 as their principal means of delivering legal services. The State Bar shall distribute the funds for that county to those programs which apply on a pro rata basis, based upon the amount of their total budget expended for free legal services in that county as compared to the total expended for free legal services by all programs meeting the standards of subparagraph (A) of paragraph (3) and paragraphs (1) and (2) of subdivision (b) of Section 6214 in that county. The State Bar shall distribute any funds for which no program has qualified pursuant hereto, in accordance with the provisions of subparagraph (A) of paragraph (1) of this subdivision.

(2) In any county in which there is no qualified legal services projects providing services, the State Bar shall reserve for the remainder of the fiscal year for distribution the pro rata share of funds as provided for by this article. Upon application of a qualified legal services project proposing to provide legal services to the indigent of the county, the State Bar shall distribute the funds to the project. Any funds not so distributed shall be added to the funds to be distributed the following year.

(c) Fifteen percent of the funds remaining after payment of administrative costs allocated for the purposes of this article shall be distributed equally by the State Bar to qualified support centers which apply for the funds. The funds provided to support centers shall be used only for the provision of legal services within California. Qualified support centers that receive funds to provide services to qualified legal services projects from sources other than this article, shall submit and shall have approved by the State Bar a plan assuring that the services funded under this article are in addition to those already funded for qualified legal services projects by other sources.

§ 6217. Maintenance of quality services, professional standards, attorney-client privilege; funds to be expended in accordance with article; interference with attorney prohibited

With respect to the provision of legal assistance under this article, each recipient shall ensure all of the following:

(a) The maintenance of quality service and professional standards.

(b) The expenditure of funds received in accordance with the provisions of this article.

(c) The preservation of the attorney-client privilege in any case, and the protection of the integrity of the adversary process from any impairment in furnishing legal assistance to indigent persons.

(d) That no one shall interfere with any attorney funded in whole or in part by this article in carrying out his or her professional responsibility to his or her client as established by the rules of professional responsibility and this chapter.

§ 6218. Eligibility for services; establishment of guidelines; funds to be expended in accordance with article

All legal services projects and support centers receiving funds pursuant to this article shall adopt financial eligibility guidelines for indigent persons.

(a) Qualified legal services programs shall ensure that funds appropriated pursuant to this article shall be used solely to defray the costs of providing legal services to indigent persons or for such other purposes as set forth in this article.

(b) Funds received pursuant to this article by support centers shall only be used to provide services to qualified legal services projects as defined in subdivision (a) of Section 6213 which are used pursuant to a plan as required by subdivision (c) of Section 6216, or as permitted by Section 6219.

§ 6219. Provision of work opportunities and scholarships for disadvantaged law students

Qualified legal services projects and support centers may use funds provided under this article to provide work opportunities with pay, and where feasible, scholarships for disadvantaged law students to help defray their law school expenses.

§ 6220. Private attorneys providing legal services without charge; support center services

Attorneys in private practice who are providing legal services without charge to indigent persons shall not be disqualified from receiving the services of the qualified support centers.

§ 6221. Services for indigent members of disadvantaged and underserved groups

Qualified legal services projects shall make significant efforts to utilize 20 percent of the funds allocated under this article for increasing the availability of services to the elderly, the disabled, juveniles, or other indigent persons who are members of disadvantaged and underserved groups within their service area.

§ 6222. Financial statements; submission to state bar; state bar report

A recipient of funds allocated pursuant to this article annually shall submit a financial statement to the State Bar, including an audit of the funds by a certified public accountant or a fiscal review approved by the State Bar, a report demonstrating the programs on which they were expended, a report on the recipient's compliance with the requirements of Section 6217, and progress in meeting the service expansion requirements of Section 6221.

The Board of Governors of the State Bar shall include a report of receipts of funds under this article, expenditures for administrative costs, and disbursements of the funds, on a county-by-county basis, in the annual report of State Bar receipts and expenditures required pursuant to Section 6145.

§ 6223. Expenditure of funds; prohibitions

No funds allocated by the State Bar pursuant to this article shall be used for any of the following purposes:

(a) The provision of legal assistance with respect to any fee generating case, except in accordance with guidelines which shall be promulgated by the State Bar.

(b) The provision of legal assistance with respect to any criminal proceeding.

(c) The provision of legal assistance, except to indigent persons or except to provide support services to qualified legal services projects as defined by this article.

§ 6224. State bar; powers; determination of qualifications to receive funds; denial of funds; termination; procedures

The State Bar shall have the power to determine that an applicant for funding is not qualified to receive funding, to deny future funding, or to terminate existing funding because the recipient is not operating in compliance with the requirements or restrictions of this article.

A denial of an application for funding or for future funding or an action by the State Bar to terminate an existing grant of funds under this article shall not become final until the applicant or recipient has been afforded reasonable notice and an opportunity for a timely and fair hearing. Pending final determination of any hearing held with reference to termination of funding, financial assistance shall be continued at its existing level on a month-to-month basis. Hearings for denial shall be conducted by an impartial hearing officer whose decision shall be final. The hearing officer shall render a decision no later than 30 days after the conclusion of the hearing. Specific procedures governing the conduct of the hearings of this section shall be determined by the State Bar pursuant to Section 6225.

§ 6225. Implementation of article; adoption of rules and regulations; procedures

The Board of Trustees of the State Bar shall adopt the regulations and procedures necessary to implement this article and to ensure that the funds allocated herein are utilized to provide civil legal services to indigent persons, especially underserved client groups such as but not limited to the elderly, the disabled, juveniles, and non-English-speaking persons.

In adopting the regulations the Board of Trustees shall comply with the following procedures:

(a) The board shall publish a preliminary draft of the regulations and procedures, which shall be distributed, together with notice of the hearings required by subdivision (b), to commercial banking institutions, to licensees of the State Bar, and to potential recipients of funds.

(b) The board shall hold at least two public hearings, one in southern California and one in northern California where affected and interested parties shall be afforded an opportunity to present oral and written testimony regarding the proposed regulations and procedures.

§ 6226. Implementation of article; resolution

The program authorized by this article shall become operative only upon the adoption of a resolution by the Board of Trustees of the State Bar stating that regulations have been adopted pursuant to Section 6225 which conform the program to all applicable tax and banking statutes, regulations, and rulings.

§ 6227. Credit of state not pledged

Nothing in this article shall create an obligation or pledge of the credit of the State of California or of the State Bar of California. Claims arising by reason of acts done pursuant to this article shall be limited to the moneys generated hereunder.

§ 6228. Severability

If any provision of this article or the application thereof to any group or circumstances is held invalid, such invalidity shall not affect the other provisions or applications of this article which can be given effect without the invalid provision or application, and to this end the provisions of this article are severable.

NEW YORK RULES OF PROFESSIONAL CONDUCT (2019)

(Effective 4/01/09 and as amended through 6/1/19)

[In 2008, New York adopted a set of rules based upon the Model Rules. It is effective on April 1, 2009. The Court amended these rules in 2013, in 2015, in 2017, and in 2018. Ed.]

Table of Contents

Rule 1.0: Terminology

(a) "Advertisement" means any public or private communication made by or on behalf of a lawyer or law firm about that lawyer or law firm's services, the primary purpose of which is for the retention of the lawyer or law firm. It does not include communications to existing clients or other lawyers.

(b) "Belief" or "believes" denotes that the person involved actually believes the fact in question to be true. A person's belief may be inferred from circumstances.

(c) "Computer-accessed communication" means any communication made by or on behalf of a lawyer or law firm that is disseminated through the use of a computer or related electronic device, including, but not limited to, web sites, weblogs, search engines, electronic mail, banner advertisements, pop-up and pop-under advertisements, chat rooms, list servers, instant messaging, or other internet presences, and any attachments or links related thereto.

(d) "Confidential information" is defined in Rule 1.6.

(e) "Confirmed in writing" denotes (i) a writing from the person to the lawyer confirming that the person has given consent, (ii) a writing that the lawyer promptly transmits to the person confirming the person's oral consent, or (iii) a statement by the person made on the record of any proceeding before a tribunal. If it is not feasible to obtain or transmit the writing at the time the person gives oral consent, then the lawyer must obtain or transmit it within a reasonable time thereafter.

(f) "Differing interests" include every interest that will adversely affect either the judgment or the loyalty of a lawyer to a client, whether it be a conflicting, inconsistent, diverse, or other interest.

(g) "Domestic relations matter" denotes representation of a client in a claim, action or proceeding, or preliminary to the filing of a claim, action or proceeding, in either Supreme Court or Family Court, or in any court of appellate jurisdiction, for divorce, separation, annulment, custody, visitation, maintenance, child support or alimony, or to enforce or modify a judgment or order in connection with any such claim, action or proceeding.

(h) "Firm" or "law firm" includes, but is not limited to, a lawyer or lawyers in a law partnership, professional corporation, sole proprietorship or other association authorized to practice law; or lawyers employed in a qualified legal assistance organization, a government law office, or the legal department of a corporation or other organization.

(i) "Fraud" or "fraudulent" denotes conduct that is fraudulent under the substantive or procedural law of the applicable jurisdiction or has a purpose to deceive, provided that it does not include conduct that, although characterized as fraudulent by statute or administrative rule, lacks an element of scienter, deceit, intent to mislead, or knowing failure to correct misrepresentations that can be reasonably expected to induce detrimental reliance by another.

(j) "Informed consent" denotes the agreement by a person to a proposed course of conduct after the lawyer has communicated information adequate for the person to make an informed decision, and after the lawyer has adequately explained to the person the material risks of the proposed course of conduct and reasonably available alternatives.

(k) "Knowingly," "known," "know," or "knows" denotes actual knowledge of the fact in question. A person's knowledge may be inferred from circumstances.

(*l*) "Matter" includes any litigation, judicial or administrative proceeding, case, claim, application, request for a ruling or other determination, contract, controversy, investigation, charge, accusation, arrest, negotiation, arbitration, mediation or any other representation involving a specific party or parties.

(m) "Partner" denotes a member of a partnership, a shareholder in a law firm organized as a professional legal corporation or a member of an association authorized to practice law.

(n) "Person" includes an individual, a corporation, an association, a trust, a partnership, and any other organization or entity.

(*o*) "Professional legal corporation" means a corporation, or an association treated as a corporation, authorized by law to practice law for profit.

(p) "Qualified legal assistance organization" means an office or organization of one of the four types listed in Rule 7.2(b)(1)-(4) that meets all of the requirements thereof.

(q) "Reasonable" or "reasonably," when used in relation to conduct by a lawyer, denotes the conduct of a reasonably prudent and competent lawyer. When used in the context of conflict of interest determinations, "reasonable lawyer" denotes a lawyer acting from the perspective of a reasonably prudent and competent lawyer who is personally disinterested in commencing or continuing the representation.

(r) "Reasonable belief" or "reasonably believes," when used in reference to a lawyer, denotes that the lawyer believes the matter in question and that the circumstances are such that the belief is reasonable.

(s) "Reasonably should know," when used in reference to a lawyer, denotes that a lawyer of reasonable prudence and competence would ascertain the matter in question.

(t) "Screened" or "screening" denotes the isolation of a lawyer from any participation in a matter through the timely imposition of procedures within a firm that are reasonably adequate under the circumstances to protect information that the isolated lawyer or the firm is obligated to protect under these Rules or other law.

(u) "Sexual relations" denotes sexual intercourse or the touching of an intimate part of the lawyer or another person for the purpose of sexual arousal, sexual gratification or sexual abuse.

(v) "State" includes the District of Columbia, Puerto Rico, and other federal territories and possessions.

(w) "Tribunal" denotes a court, an arbitrator in an arbitration proceeding or a legislative body, administrative agency or other body acting in an adjudicative capacity. A legislative body, administrative agency or other body acts in an adjudicative capacity when a neutral official, after the presentation of evidence or legal argument by a party or parties, will render a legal judgment directly affecting a party's interests in a particular matter.

(x) "Writing" or "written" denotes a tangible or electronic record of a communication or representation, including handwriting, typewriting, printing, photocopying, photography, audio or video recording, email or other electronic communication or any other form of recorded communication or recorded representation. A "signed" writing includes an electronic sound, symbol or process attached to or logically associated with a writing and executed or adopted by a person with the intent to sign the writing.

Rule 1.1: Competence

(a) A lawyer should provide competent representation to a client. Competent representation requires the legal knowledge, skill, thoroughness and preparation reasonably necessary for the representation.

(b) A lawyer shall not handle a legal matter that the lawyer knows or should know that the lawyer is not competent to handle, without associating with a lawyer who is competent to handle it.

(c) A lawyer shall not intentionally:

(1) fail to seek the objectives of the client through reasonably available means permitted by law and these Rules; or

(2) prejudice or damage the client during the course of the representation except as permitted or required by these Rules.

Rule 1.2: Scope of Representation and Allocation of Authority Between Client and Lawyer

(a) Subject to the provisions herein, a lawyer shall abide by a client's decisions concerning the objectives of representation and, as required by Rule 1.4, shall consult with the client as to the means by which they are to be pursued. A lawyer shall abide by a client's decision whether to settle a matter. In a criminal case, the lawyer shall abide by the client's decision, after consultation with the lawyer, as to a plea to be entered, whether to waive jury trial and whether the client will testify.

(b) A lawyer's representation of a client, including representation by appointment, does not constitute an endorsement of the client's political, economic, social or moral views or activities.

(c) A lawyer may limit the scope of the representation if the limitation is reasonable under the circumstances, the client gives informed consent and where necessary notice is provided to the tribunal and/or opposing counsel.

(d) A lawyer shall not counsel a client to engage, or assist a client, in conduct that the lawyer knows is illegal or fraudulent, except that the lawyer may discuss the legal consequences of any proposed course of conduct with a client.

(e) A lawyer may exercise professional judgment to waive or fail to assert a right or position of the client, or accede to reasonable requests of opposing counsel, when doing so does not prejudice the rights of the client.

(f) A lawyer may refuse to aid or participate in conduct that the lawyer believes to be unlawful, even though there is some support for an argument that the conduct is legal.

(g) A lawyer does not violate this Rule by being punctual in fulfilling all professional commitments, by avoiding offensive tactics, and by treating with courtesy and consideration all persons involved in the legal process.

Rule 1.3: Diligence

(a) A lawyer shall act with reasonable diligence and promptness in representing a client.

(b) A lawyer shall not neglect a legal matter entrusted to the lawyer.

(c) A lawyer shall not intentionally fail to carry out a contract of employment entered into with a client for professional services, but the lawyer may withdraw as permitted under these Rules.

Rule 1.4: Communication

(a) A lawyer shall:

(1) promptly inform the client of:

(i) any decision or circumstance with respect to which the client's informed consent, as defined in Rule 1.0(j), is required by these Rules;

(ii) any information required by court rule or other law to be communicated to a client; and

(iii) material developments in the matter including settlement or plea offers.

(2) reasonably consult with the client about the means by which the client's objectives are to be accomplished;

(3) keep the client reasonably informed about the status of the matter;

(4) promptly comply with a client's reasonable requests for information; and

(5) consult with the client about any relevant limitation on the lawyer's conduct when the lawyer knows that the client expects assistance not permitted by these Rules or other law.

(b) A lawyer shall explain a matter to the extent reasonably necessary to permit the client to make informed decisions regarding the representation.

Rule 1.5: Fees and Division of Fees

(a) A lawyer shall not make an agreement for, charge, or collect an excessive or illegal fee or expense. A fee is excessive when, after a review of the facts, a reasonable lawyer would be left with a definite and firm conviction that the fee is excessive. The factors to be considered in determining whether a fee is excessive may include the following:

(1) the time and labor required, the novelty and difficulty of the questions involved, and the skill requisite to perform the legal service properly;

(2) the likelihood, if apparent or made known to the client, that the acceptance of the particular employment will preclude other employment by the lawyer;

(3) the fee customarily charged in the locality for similar legal services;

(4) the amount involved and the results obtained;

(5) the time limitations imposed by the client or by circumstances;

(6) the nature and length of the professional relationship with the client;

(7) the experience, reputation and ability of the lawyer or lawyers performing the services; and

(8) whether the fee is fixed or contingent.

(b) A lawyer shall communicate to a client the scope of the representation and the basis or rate of the fee and expenses for which the client will be responsible. This information shall be communicated to the client before or within a reasonable time after commencement of the representation and shall be in writing where required by statute or court rule. This provision shall not apply when the lawyer will charge a regularly represented client on the same basis or rate and perform services that are of the same general kind as previously rendered to and paid for by the client. Any changes in the scope of the representation or the basis or rate of the fee or expenses shall also be communicated to the client.

(c) A fee may be contingent on the outcome of the matter for which the service is rendered, except in a matter in which a contingent fee is prohibited by paragraph (d) or other law. Promptly after a lawyer has been employed in a contingent fee matter, the lawyer shall provide the client with a writing stating the method by which the fee is to be determined, including the percentage or percentages that shall accrue to the lawyer in the event of settlement, trial or appeal; litigation and other expenses to be deducted from the recovery; and whether such expenses are to be deducted before or, if not prohibited by statute or court rule, after the contingent fee is calculated. The writing must clearly notify the client of any expenses for which the client will be liable regardless of whether the client is the prevailing party. Upon conclusion of a contingent fee matter, the lawyer shall provide the client with a writing stating the outcome of the matter and, if there is a recovery, showing the remittance to the client and the method of its determination.

(d) A lawyer shall not enter into an arrangement for, charge or collect:

(1) a contingent fee for representing a defendant in a criminal matter;

(2) a fee prohibited by law or rule of court;

(3) a fee based on fraudulent billing;

(4) a nonrefundable retainer fee; provided that a lawyer may enter into a retainer agreement with a client containing a reasonable minimum fee clause if it defines in plain language and sets forth the circumstances under which such fee may be incurred and how it will be calculated; or

(5) any fee in a domestic relations matter if:

(i) the payment or amount of the fee is contingent upon the securing of a divorce or of obtaining child custody or visitation or is in any way determined by reference to the amount of maintenance, support, equitable distribution, or property settlement;

(ii) a written retainer agreement has not been signed by the lawyer and client setting forth in plain language the nature of the relationship and the details of the fee arrangement; or

(iii) the written retainer agreement includes a security interest, confession of judgment or other lien without prior notice being provided to the client in a signed retainer agreement and approval from a tribunal after notice to the adversary. A lawyer shall not foreclose on a mortgage placed on the marital residence while the spouse who consents to the mortgage remains the titleholder and the residence remains the spouse's primary residence.

(e) In domestic relations matters, a lawyer shall provide a prospective client with a statement of client's rights and responsibilities at the initial conference and prior to the signing of a written retainer agreement.

(f) Where applicable, a lawyer shall resolve fee disputes by arbitration at the election of the client pursuant to a fee arbitration program established by the Chief Administrator of the Courts and approved by the Administrative Board of the Courts.

(g) A lawyer shall not divide a fee for legal services with another lawyer who is not associated in the same law firm unless:

(1) the division is in proportion to the services performed by each lawyer or, by a writing given to the client, each lawyer assumes joint responsibility for the representation;

(2) the client agrees to employment of the other lawyer after a full disclosure that a division of fees will be made, including the share each lawyer will receive, and the client's agreement is confirmed in writing; and

(3) the total fee is not excessive.

(h) Rule 1.5(g) does not prohibit payment to a lawyer formerly associated in a law firm pursuant to a separation or retirement agreement.

Rule 1.6: Confidentiality of Information

(a) A lawyer shall not knowingly reveal confidential information, as defined in this Rule, or use such information to the disadvantage of a client or for the advantage of the lawyer or a third person, unless:

(1) the client gives informed consent, as defined in Rule 1.0(j);

(2) the disclosure is impliedly authorized to advance the best interests of the client and is either reasonable under the circumstances or customary in the professional community; or

(3) the disclosure is permitted by paragraph (b).

"Confidential information" consists of information gained during or relating to the representation of a client, whatever its source, that is (a) protected by the attorney-client privilege, (b) likely to be embarrassing or detrimental to the client if disclosed, or (c) information that the client has requested be kept confidential. "Confidential information" does not ordinarily include (i) a lawyer's legal knowledge or legal research or (ii) information that is generally known in the local community or in the trade, field or profession to which the information relates.

(b) A lawyer may reveal or use confidential information to the extent that the lawyer reasonably believes necessary:

(1) to prevent reasonably certain death or substantial bodily harm;

(2) to prevent the client from committing a crime;

(3) to withdraw a written or oral opinion or representation previously given by the lawyer and reasonably believed by the lawyer still to be relied upon by a third person, where the lawyer has discovered that the opinion or representation was based on materially inaccurate information or is being used to further a crime or fraud;

(4) to secure legal advice about compliance with these Rules or other law by the lawyer, another lawyer associated with the lawyer's firm or the law firm;

(5)(i) defend the lawyer or the lawyer's employees and associates against an accusation of wrongful conduct; or

(ii) to establish or collect a fee; or

(6) when permitted or required under these Rules or to comply with other law or court order.

(c) A lawyer shall make reasonable efforts to prevent the inadvertent or unauthorized disclosure or use of, or unauthorized access to, information protected by Rules 1.6, 1.9(c), or 1.18(b).

Rule 1.7: Conflict of Interest: Current Clients

(a) Except as provided in paragraph (b), a lawyer shall not represent a client if a reasonable lawyer would conclude that either:

(1) the representation will involve the lawyer in representing differing interests; or

(2) there is a significant risk that the lawyer's professional judgment on behalf of a client will be adversely affected by the lawyer's own financial, business, property or other personal interests.

(b) Notwithstanding the existence of a concurrent conflict of interest under paragraph (a), a lawyer may represent a client if:

(1) the lawyer reasonably believes that the lawyer will be able to provide competent and diligent representation to each affected client;

(2) the representation is not prohibited by law;

(3) the representation does not involve the assertion of a claim by one client against another client represented by the lawyer in the same litigation or other proceeding before a tribunal; and

(4) each affected client gives informed consent, confirmed in writing.

Rule 1.8: Current Clients: Specific Conflict of Interest Rules

(a) A lawyer shall not enter into a business transaction with a client if they have differing interests therein and if the client expects the lawyer to exercise professional judgment therein for the protection of the client, unless:

(1) the transaction is fair and reasonable to the client and the terms of the transaction are fully disclosed and transmitted in writing in a manner that can be reasonably understood by the client;

(2) the client is advised in writing of the desirability of seeking, and is given a reasonable opportunity to seek, the advice of independent legal counsel on the transaction; and

(3) the client gives informed consent, in a writing signed by the client, to the essential terms of the transaction and the lawyer's role in the transaction, including whether the lawyer is representing the client in the transaction.

(b) A lawyer shall not use information relating to representation of a client to the disadvantage of the client unless the client gives informed consent, except as permitted or required by these Rules.

(c) A lawyer shall not:

(1) solicit any gift from a client, including a testamentary gift, for the benefit of the lawyer or a person related to the lawyer; or

(2) prepare on behalf of a client an instrument giving the lawyer or a person related to the lawyer any gift, unless the lawyer or other recipient of the gift is related to the client and a reasonable lawyer would conclude that the transaction is fair and reasonable.

For purposes of this paragraph, related persons include a spouse, child, grandchild, parent, grandparent or other relative or individual with whom the lawyer or the client maintains a close, familial relationship.

(d) Prior to conclusion of all aspects of the matter giving rise to the representation or proposed representation of the client or prospective client, a lawyer shall not negotiate or enter into any arrangement or understanding with:

(1) a client or a prospective client by which the lawyer acquires an interest in literary or media rights with respect to the subject matter of the representation or proposed representation; or

(2) any person by which the lawyer transfers or assigns any interest in literary or media rights with respect to the subject matter of the representation of a client or prospective client.

(e) While representing a client in connection with contemplated or pending litigation, a lawyer shall not advance or guarantee financial assistance to the client, except that:

(1) a lawyer may advance court costs and expenses of litigation, the repayment of which may be contingent on the outcome of the matter;

(2) a lawyer representing an indigent or pro bono client may pay court costs and expenses of litigation on behalf of the client; and

(3) a lawyer, in an action in which an attorney's fee is payable in whole or in part as a percentage of the recovery in the action, may pay on the lawyer's own account court costs and expenses of litigation. In such case, the fee paid to the lawyer from the proceeds of the action may include an amount equal to such costs and expenses incurred.

(f) A lawyer shall not accept compensation for representing a client, or anything of value related to the lawyer's representation of the client, from one other than the client unless:

(1) the client gives informed consent;

(2) there is no interference with the lawyer's independent professional judgment or with the client-lawyer relationship; and

(3) the client's confidential information is protected as required by Rule 1.6.

(g) A lawyer who represents two or more clients shall not participate in making an aggregate settlement of the claims of or against the clients, absent court approval, unless each client gives informed consent in a writing signed by the client. The lawyer's disclosure shall include the existence and nature of all the claims involved and of the participation of each person in the settlement.

(h) A lawyer shall not:

(1) make an agreement prospectively limiting the lawyer's liability to a client for malpractice; or

(2) settle a claim or potential claim for such liability with an unrepresented client or former client unless that person is advised in writing of the desirability of seeking, and is given a reasonable opportunity to seek, the advice of independent legal counsel in connection therewith.

(i) A lawyer shall not acquire a proprietary interest in the cause of action or subject matter of litigation the lawyer is conducting for a client, except that the lawyer may:

(1) acquire a lien authorized by law to secure the lawyer's fee or expenses; and

(2) contract with a client for a reasonable contingent fee in a civil matter subject to Rule 1.5(d) or other law or court rule.

(j)(1) A lawyer shall not:

(i) as a condition of entering into or continuing any professional representation by the lawyer or the lawyer's firm, require or demand sexual relations with any person;

(ii) employ coercion, intimidation or undue influence in entering into sexual relations incident to any professional representation by the lawyer or the lawyer's firm; or

(iii) in domestic relations matters, enter into sexual relations with a client during the course of the lawyer's representation of the client.

(2) Rule 1.8(j)(1) shall not apply to sexual relations between lawyers and their spouses or to ongoing consensual sexual relationships that predate the initiation of the client-lawyer relationship.

(k) Where a lawyer in a firm has sexual relations with a client but does not participate in the representation of that client, the lawyers in the firm shall not be subject to discipline under this Rule solely because of the occurrence of such sexual relations.

Rule 1.9: Duties to Former Clients

(a) A lawyer who has formerly represented a client in a matter shall not thereafter represent another person in the same or a substantially related matter in which that person's interests are materially adverse to the interests of the former client unless the former client gives informed consent, confirmed in writing.

(b) Unless the former client gives informed consent, confirmed in writing, a lawyer shall not knowingly represent a person in the same or a substantially related matter in which a firm with which the lawyer formerly was associated had previously represented a client:

(1) whose interests are materially adverse to that person; and

(2) about whom the lawyer had acquired information protected by Rules 1. 6 or paragraph (c) of this Rule that is material to the matter.

(c) A lawyer who has formerly represented a client in a matter or whose present or former firm has formerly represented a client in a matter shall not thereafter:

(1) use confidential information of the former client protected by Rule 1.6 to the disadvantage of the former client, except as these Rules would permit or require with respect to a current client or when the information has become generally known; or

(2) reveal confidential information of the former client protected by Rule 1.6 except as these Rules would permit or require with respect to a current client.

Rule 1.10: Imputation of Conflicts of Interest

(a) While lawyers are associated in a firm, none of them shall knowingly represent a client when any one of them practicing alone would be prohibited from doing so by Rule 1.7, 1.8 or 1.9, except as otherwise provided therein.

(b) When a lawyer has terminated an association with a firm, the firm is prohibited from thereafter representing a person with interests that the firm knows or reasonably should know are materially adverse to those of a client represented by the formerly associated lawyer and not currently represented by the firm if the firm or any lawyer remaining in the firm has information protected by Rule 1.6 or Rule 1.9(c) that is material to the matter.

(c) When a lawyer becomes associated with a firm, the firm may not knowingly represent a client in a matter that is the same as or substantially related to a matter in which the newly associated lawyer, or a firm with which that lawyer was associated, formerly represented a client whose interests are materially adverse to the prospective or current client unless the newly associated lawyer did not acquire any information protected by Rule 1.6 or Rule 1.9(c) that is material to the current matter.

(d) A disqualification prescribed by this Rule may be waived by the affected client or former client under the conditions stated in Rule 1.7.

(e) A law firm shall make a written record of its engagements, at or near the time of each new engagement, and shall implement and maintain a system by which proposed engagements are checked against current and previous engagements when:

(1) the firm agrees to represent a new client;

(2) the firm agrees to represent an existing client in a new matter;

(3) the firm hires or associates with another lawyer; or

(4) an additional party is named or appears in a pending matter.

(f) Substantial failure to keep records or to implement or maintain a conflict-checking system that complies with paragraph (e) shall be a violation thereof regardless of whether there is another violation of these Rules.

(g) Where a violation of paragraph (e) by a law firm is a substantial factor in causing a violation of paragraph (a) by a lawyer, the law firm, as well as the individual lawyer, shall be responsible for the violation of paragraph (a).

(h) A lawyer related to another lawyer as parent, child, sibling or spouse shall not represent in any matter a client whose interests differ from those of another party to the matter who the lawyer knows is represented by the other lawyer unless the client consents to the representation after full disclosure and the lawyer concludes that the lawyer can adequately represent the interests of the client.

Rule 1.11: Special Conflicts of Interest for Former and Current Government Officers and Employees

(a) Except as law may otherwise expressly provide, a lawyer who has formerly served as a public officer or employee of the government:

(1) shall comply with Rule 1.9(c); and

(2) shall not represent a client in connection with a matter in which the lawyer participated personally and substantially as a public officer or employee, unless the appropriate government agency gives its informed consent, confirmed in writing, to the representation. This provision shall not apply to matters governed by Rule 1.12(a).

(b) When a lawyer is disqualified from representation under paragraph (a), no lawyer in a firm with which that lawyer is associated may knowingly undertake or continue representation in such a matter unless:

(1) the firm acts promptly and reasonably to:

(i) notify, as appropriate, lawyers and nonlawyer personnel within the firm that the personally disqualified lawyer is prohibited from participating in the representation of the current client;

(ii) implement effective screening procedures to prevent the flow of information about the matter between the personally disqualified lawyer and the others in the firm;

(iii) ensure that the disqualified lawyer is apportioned no part of the fee therefrom; and

(iv) give written notice to the appropriate government agency to enable it to ascertain compliance with the provisions of this Rule; and

(2) there are no other circumstances in the particular representation that create an appearance of impropriety.

(c) Except as law may otherwise expressly provide, a lawyer having information that the lawyer knows is confidential government information about a person, acquired when the lawyer was a public officer or employee, may not represent a private client whose interests are adverse to that person in a matter in which the information could be used to the material disadvantage of that person. As used in this Rule, the term "confidential government information" means information that has been obtained under governmental authority and that, at the time this Rule is applied, the government is prohibited by law from disclosing to the public or has a legal privilege not to disclose, and that is not otherwise available to the public. A firm with which that lawyer is associated may undertake or continue representation in the matter only if the disqualified lawyer is timely and effectively screened from any participation in the matter in accordance with the provisions of paragraph (b).

(d) Except as law may otherwise expressly provide, a lawyer currently serving as a public officer or employee shall not:

(1) participate in a matter in which the lawyer participated personally and substantially while in private practice or nongovernmental employment, unless under applicable law no one is, or by lawful delegation may be, authorized to act in the lawyer's stead in the matter; or

(2) negotiate for private employment with any person who is involved as a party or as lawyer for a party in a matter in which the lawyer is participating personally and substantially.

(e) As used in this Rule, the term "matter" as defined in Rule 1.0(*l*) does not include or apply to agency rulemaking functions.

(f) A lawyer who holds public office shall not:

(1) use the public position to obtain, or attempt to obtain, a special advantage in legislative matters for the lawyer or for a client under circumstances where the lawyer knows or it is obvious that such action is not in the public interest;

(2) use the public position to influence, or attempt to influence, a tribunal to act in favor of the lawyer or of a client; or

(3) accept anything of value from any person when the lawyer knows or it is obvious that the offer is for the purpose of influencing the lawyer's action as a public official.

Rule 1.12: Specific Conflicts of Interest for Former Judges, Arbitrators, Mediators or Other Third-Party Neutrals

(a) A lawyer shall not accept private employment in a matter upon the merits of which the lawyer has acted in a judicial capacity.

(b) Except as stated in paragraph (e), and unless all parties to the proceeding give informed consent, confirmed in writing, a lawyer shall not represent anyone in connection with a matter in which the lawyer participated personally and substantially as:

(1) an arbitrator, mediator or other third-party neutral; or

(2) a law clerk to a judge or other adjudicative officer or an arbitrator, mediator or other third-party neutral.

(c) A lawyer shall not negotiate for employment with any person who is involved as a party or as lawyer for a party in a matter in which the lawyer is participating personally and substantially as a judge or other adjudicative officer or as an arbitrator, mediator or other third-party neutral.

(d) When a lawyer is disqualified from representation under this Rule, no lawyer in a firm with which that lawyer is associated may knowingly undertake or continue representation in such a matter unless:

(1) the firm acts promptly and reasonably to:

(i) notify, as appropriate, lawyers and nonlawyer personnel within the firm that the personally disqualified lawyer is prohibited from participating in the representation of the current client;

(ii) implement effective screening procedures to prevent the flow of information about the matter between the personally disqualified lawyer and the others in the firm;

(iii) ensure that the disqualified lawyer is apportioned no part of the fee therefrom; and

(iv) give written notice to the parties and any appropriate tribunal to enable it to ascertain compliance with the provisions of this Rule; and

(2) there are no other circumstances in the particular representation that create an appearance of impropriety.

(e) An arbitrator selected as a partisan of a party in a multimember arbitration panel is not prohibited from subsequently representing that party.

Rule 1.13: Organization as Client

(a) When a lawyer employed or retained by an organization is dealing with the organization's directors, officers, employees, members, shareholders or other constituents, and it appears that the organization's interests may differ from those of the constituents with whom the lawyer is dealing, the lawyer shall explain that the lawyer is the lawyer for the organization and not for any of the constituents.

(b) If a lawyer for an organization knows that an officer, employee or other person associated with the organization is engaged in action or intends to act or refuses to act in a matter related to the representation that (i) is a violation of a legal obligation to the organization or a violation of law that reasonably might be imputed to the organization, and (ii) is likely to result in substantial injury to the organization, then the lawyer shall proceed as is reasonably necessary in the best interest of the organization. In determining how to proceed, the lawyer shall give due consideration to the seriousness of the violation and its consequences, the scope and nature of the lawyer's representation, the responsibility in the organization and the apparent motivation of the person involved, the policies of the organization concerning such matters and any other relevant considerations. Any measures taken shall be designed to minimize disruption of the organization and the risk of revealing information relating to the representation to persons outside the organization. Such measures may include, among others:

1. asking reconsideration of the matter;
2. advising that a separate legal opinion on the matter be sought for presentation to an appropriate authority in the organization; and
3. referring the matter to higher authority in the organization, including, if warranted by the seriousness of the matter, referral to the highest authority that can act in behalf of the organization as determined by applicable law.

(c) If, despite the lawyer's efforts in accordance with paragraph (b), the highest authority that can act on behalf of the organization insists upon action, or a refusal to act, that is clearly in violation of law and is likely to result in a substantial injury to the organization, the lawyer may reveal confidential information only if permitted by Rule 1.6, and may resign in accordance with Rule 1.16.

(d) A lawyer representing an organization may also represent any of its directors, officers, employees, members, shareholders or other constituents, subject to the provisions of Rule 1.7. If the organization's consent to the concurrent representation is required by Rule 1.7, the consent shall be given by an appropriate official of the organization other than the individual who is to be represented, or by the shareholders.

Rule 1.14: Client With Diminished Capacity

(a) When a client's capacity to make adequately considered decisions in connection with a representation is diminished, whether because of minority, mental impairment or for some other reason, the lawyer shall, as far as reasonably possible, maintain a conventional relationship with the client.

(b) When the lawyer reasonably believes that the client has diminished capacity, is at risk of substantial physical, financial or other harm unless action is taken and cannot adequately act in the client's own interest, the lawyer may take reasonably necessary protective action, including consulting with individuals or entities that have the ability to take action to protect the client and, in appropriate cases, seeking the appointment of a guardian ad litem, conservator or guardian.

(c) Information relating to the representation of a client with diminished capacity is protected by Rule 1.6. When taking protective action pursuant to paragraph (b), the lawyer is impliedly authorized under Rule 1.6(a) to reveal information about the client, but only to the extent reasonably necessary to protect the client's interests.

Rule 1.15: Preserving Identity of Funds and Property of Others; Fiduciary Responsibility; Commingling and Misappropriation of Client Funds or Property; Maintenance of Bank Accounts; Record Keeping; Examination of Records

(a) Prohibition Against Commingling and Misappropriation of Client Funds or Property.

A lawyer in possession of any funds or other property belonging to another person, where such possession is incident to his or her practice of law, is a fiduciary, and must not misappropriate such funds or property or commingle such funds or property with his or her own.

(b) Separate Accounts.

(1) A lawyer who is in possession of funds belonging to another person incident to the lawyer's practice of law shall maintain such funds in a banking institution within New York State that agrees to provide dishonored check reports in accordance with the provisions of 22 N.Y.C.R.R. Part 1300. "Banking institution" means a state or national bank, trust company, savings bank, savings and loan association or credit union. Such funds shall be maintained, in the lawyer's own name, or in the name of a firm of lawyers of which the lawyer is a member, or in the name of the lawyer or firm of lawyers by whom the lawyer is employed, in a special account or accounts, separate from any business or personal accounts of the lawyer or lawyer's firm, and separate from any accounts that the lawyer may maintain as executor, guardian, trustee or receiver, or in any other fiduciary capacity; into such special account or accounts all funds held in escrow or otherwise entrusted to the lawyer or firm shall be deposited; provided, however, that such funds may be maintained in a banking institution located outside New York State if such banking institution complies with 22 N.Y.C.R.R. Part 1300 and the lawyer has obtained the prior written approval of the person to whom such funds belong specifying the name and address of the office or branch of the banking institution where such funds are to be maintained.

(2) A lawyer or the lawyer's firm shall identify the special bank account or accounts required by Rule 1.15(b)(1) as an "Attorney Special Account," "Attorney Trust Account," or "Attorney Escrow Account," and shall obtain checks and deposit slips that bear such title. Such title may be accompanied by such other descriptive language as the lawyer may deem appropriate, provided that such additional language distinguishes such special account or accounts from other bank accounts that are maintained by the lawyer or the lawyer's firm.

(3) Funds reasonably sufficient to maintain the account or to pay account charges may be deposited therein.

(4) Funds belonging in part to a client or third person and in part currently or potentially to the lawyer or law firm shall be kept in such special account or accounts, but the portion belonging to the lawyer or law firm may be withdrawn when due unless the right of the lawyer or law firm to receive it is disputed by the client or third person, in which event the disputed portion shall not be withdrawn until the dispute is finally resolved.

(c) Notification of Receipt of Property; Safekeeping; Rendering Accounts; Payment or Delivery of Property.

A lawyer shall:

(1) promptly notify a client or third person of the receipt of funds, securities, or other properties in which the client or third person has an interest;

(2) identify and label securities and properties of a client or third person promptly upon receipt and place them in a safe deposit box or other place of safekeeping as soon as practicable;

(3) maintain complete records of all funds, securities, and other properties of a client or third person coming into the possession of the lawyer and render appropriate accounts to the client or third person regarding them; and

(4) promptly pay or deliver to the client or third person as requested by the client or third person the funds, securities, or other properties in the possession of the lawyer that the client or third person is entitled to receive.

(d) Required Bookkeeping Records.

(1) A lawyer shall maintain for seven years after the events that they record:

(i) the records of all deposits in and withdrawals from the accounts specified in Rule 1.15(b) and of any other bank account that concerns or affects the lawyer's practice of law; these records shall specifically identify the date, source and description of each item deposited, as well as the date, payee and purpose of each withdrawal or disbursement;

(ii) a record for special accounts, showing the source of all funds deposited in such accounts, the names of all persons for whom the funds are or were held, the amount of such funds, the description and amounts, and the names of all persons to whom such funds were disbursed;

(iii) copies of all retainer and compensation agreements with clients;

(iv) copies of all statements to clients or other persons showing the disbursement of funds to them or on their behalf;

(v) copies of all bills rendered to clients;

(vi) copies of all records showing payments to lawyers, investigators or other persons, not in the lawyer's regular employ, for services rendered or performed;

(vii) copies of all retainer and closing statements filed with the Office of Court Administration; and

(viii) all checkbooks and check stubs, bank statements, prenumbered canceled checks and duplicate deposit slips.

(2) Lawyers shall make accurate entries of all financial transactions in their records of receipts and disbursements, in their special accounts, in their ledger books or similar records, and in any other books of account kept by them in the regular course of their practice, which entries shall be made at or near the time of the act, condition or event recorded.

(3) For purposes of Rule 1.15(d), a lawyer may satisfy the requirements of maintaining "copies" by maintaining any of the following items: original records, photocopies, microfilm, optical imaging, and any other medium that preserves an image of the document that cannot be altered without detection.

(e) Authorized Signatories.

All special account withdrawals shall be made only to a named payee and not to cash. Such withdrawals shall be made by check or, with the prior written approval of the party entitled to the proceeds, by bank transfer. Only a lawyer admitted to practice law in New York State shall be an authorized signatory of a special account.

(f) Missing Clients.

Whenever any sum of money is payable to a client and the lawyer is unable to locate the client, the lawyer shall apply to the court in which the action was brought if in the unified court system, or, if no action was commenced in the unified court system, to the Supreme Court in the county in which the lawyer maintains an office for the practice of law, for an order directing payment to the lawyer of any fees and disbursements that are owed by the client and the balance, if any, to the Lawyers' Fund for Client Protection for safeguarding and disbursement to persons who are entitled thereto.

(g) Designation of Successor Signatories.

(1) Upon the death of a lawyer who was the sole signatory on an attorney trust, escrow or special account, an application may be made to the Supreme Court for an order designating a successor signatory for such trust, escrow or special account, who shall be a member of the bar in good standing and admitted to the practice of law in New York State.

(2) An application to designate a successor signatory shall be made to the Supreme Court in the judicial district in which the deceased lawyer maintained an office for the practice of law. The application may be made by the legal representative of the deceased lawyer's estate; a lawyer who was affiliated with the deceased lawyer in the practice of law; any person who has a beneficial interest in such trust, escrow or special account; an officer of a city or county bar association; or counsel for an attorney disciplinary committee. No lawyer may charge a legal fee for assisting with an application to designate a successor signatory pursuant to this Rule.

(3) The Supreme Court may designate a successor signatory and may direct the safeguarding of funds from such trust, escrow or special account, and the disbursement of such funds to persons who are entitled thereto, and may order that funds in such account be deposited with the Lawyers' Fund for Client Protection for safeguarding and disbursement to persons who are entitled thereto.

(h) Dissolution of a Firm.

Upon the dissolution of any firm of lawyers, the former partners or members shall make appropriate arrangements for the maintenance, by one of them or by a successor firm, of the records specified in Rule 1.15(d).

(i) Availability of Bookkeeping Records: Records Subject to Production in Disciplinary Investigations and Proceedings.

The financial records required by this Rule shall be located, or made available, at the principal New York State office of the lawyers subject hereto, and any such records shall be produced in response to a notice or subpoena duces tecum issued in connection with a complaint before or any investigation by the appropriate grievance or departmental disciplinary committee, or shall be produced at the direction of the appropriate Appellate Division before any person designated by it. All books and records produced pursuant to this Rule shall be kept confidential, except for the purpose of the particular proceeding, and their contents shall not be disclosed by anyone in violation of the attorney-client privilege.

(j) Disciplinary Action.

A lawyer who does not maintain and keep the accounts and records as specified and required by this Rule, or who does not produce any such records pursuant to this Rule, shall be deemed in violation of these Rules and shall be subject to disciplinary proceedings.

Rule 1.16: Declining or Terminating Representation

(a) A lawyer shall not accept employment on behalf of a person if the lawyer knows or reasonably should know that such person wishes to:

(1) bring a legal action, conduct a defense, or assert a position in a matter, or otherwise have steps taken for such person, merely for the purpose of harassing or maliciously injuring any person; or

(2) present a claim or defense in a matter that is not warranted under existing law, unless it can be supported by a good faith argument for an extension, modification, or reversal of existing law.

(b) Except as stated in paragraph (d), a lawyer shall withdraw from the representation of a client when:

(1) the lawyer knows or reasonably should know that the representation will result in a violation of these Rules or of law;

(2) the lawyer's physical or mental condition materially impairs the lawyer's ability to represent the client;

(3) the lawyer is discharged; or

(4) the lawyer knows or reasonably should know that the client is bringing the legal action, conducting the defense, or asserting a position in the matter, or is otherwise having steps taken, merely for the purpose of harassing or maliciously injuring any person.

(c) Except as stated in paragraph (d), a lawyer may withdraw from representing a client when:

(1) withdrawal can be accomplished without material adverse effect on the interests of the client;

(2) the client persists in a course of action involving the lawyer's services that the lawyer reasonably believes is criminal or fraudulent;

(3) the client has used the lawyer's services to perpetrate a crime or fraud;

(4) the client insists upon taking action with which the lawyer has a fundamental disagreement;

(5) the client deliberately disregards an agreement or obligation to the lawyer as to expenses or fees;

(6) the client insists upon presenting a claim or defense that is not warranted under existing law and cannot be supported by good faith argument for an extension, modification, or reversal of existing law;

(7) the client fails to cooperate in the representation or otherwise renders the representation unreasonably difficult for the lawyer to carry out employment effectively;

(8) the lawyer's inability to work with co-counsel indicates that the best interest of the client likely will be served by withdrawal;

(9) the lawyer's mental or physical condition renders it difficult for the lawyer to carry out the representation effectively;

(10) the client knowingly and freely assents to termination of the employment;

(11) withdrawal is permitted under Rule 1.13(c) or other law;

(12) the lawyer believes in good faith, in a matter pending before a tribunal, that the tribunal will find the existence of other good cause for withdrawal; or

(13) the client insists that the lawyer pursue a course of conduct which is illegal or prohibited under these Rules.

(d) If permission for withdrawal from employment is required by the rules of a tribunal, a lawyer shall not withdraw from employment in a matter before that tribunal without its permission. When ordered to do so by a tribunal, a lawyer shall continue representation notwithstanding good cause for terminating the representation.

(e) Even when withdrawal is otherwise permitted or required, upon termination of representation, a lawyer shall take steps, to the extent reasonably practicable, to avoid foreseeable prejudice to the rights of the client, including giving reasonable notice to the client, allowing time for employment of other counsel, delivering to the client all papers and property to which the client is entitled, promptly refunding any part of a fee paid in advance that has not been earned and complying with applicable laws and rules.

Rule 1.17: Sale of Law Practice

(a) A lawyer retiring from a private practice of law; a law firm, one or more members of which are retiring from the private practice of law with the firm; or the personal representative of a deceased, disabled or missing lawyer, may sell a law practice, including goodwill, to one or more lawyers or law firms, who may purchase the practice. The seller and the buyer may agree on reasonable restrictions on the seller's private practice of law, notwithstanding any other provision of these Rules. Retirement shall include the cessation of the private practice of law in the geographic area, that is, the county and city and any county or city contiguous thereto, in which the practice to be sold has been conducted.

(b) Confidential information.

(1) With respect to each matter subject to the contemplated sale, the seller may provide prospective buyers with any information not protected as confidential information under Rule 1.6.

(2) Notwithstanding Rule 1.6, the seller may provide the prospective buyer with information as to individual clients:

(i) concerning the identity of the client, except as provided in paragraph (b)(6);

(ii) concerning the status and general nature of the matter;

(iii) available in public court files; and

(iv) concerning the financial terms of the client-lawyer relationship and the payment status of the client's account.

(3) Prior to making any disclosure of confidential information that may be permitted under paragraph (b)(2), the seller shall provide the prospective buyer with information regarding the matters involved in the proposed sale sufficient to enable the prospective buyer to determine whether any conflicts of interest exist. Where sufficient information cannot be disclosed without revealing client confidential information, the seller may make the disclosures necessary for the prospective buyer to determine whether any conflict of interest exists, subject to paragraph (b)(6). If the prospective buyer determines that conflicts of interest exist prior to reviewing the information, or determines during the course of review that a conflict of interest exists, the prospective buyer shall not review or continue to review the information unless the seller shall have obtained the consent of the client in accordance with Rule 1.6(a)(1).

(4) Prospective buyers shall maintain the confidentiality of and shall not use any client information received in connection with the proposed sale in the same manner and to the same extent as if the prospective buyers represented the client.

(5) Absent the consent of the client after full disclosure, a seller shall not provide a prospective buyer with information if doing so would cause a violation of the attorney-client privilege.

(6) If the seller has reason to believe that the identity of the client or the fact of the representation itself constitutes confidential information in the circumstances, the seller may not provide such information to a prospective buyer without first advising the client of the identity of the prospective buyer and obtaining the client's consent to the proposed disclosure.

(c) Written notice of the sale shall be given jointly by the seller and the buyer to each of the seller's clients and shall include information regarding:

(1) the client's right to retain other counsel or to take possession of the file;

(2) the fact that the client's consent to the transfer of the client's file or matter to the buyer will be presumed if the client does not take any action or otherwise object within 90 days of the sending of the notice, subject to any court rule or statute requiring express approval by the client or a court;

(3) the fact that agreements between the seller and the seller's clients as to fees will be honored by the buyer;

(4) proposed fee increases, if any, permitted under paragraph (e); and

(5) the identity and background of the buyer or buyers, including principal office address, bar admissions, number of years in practice in New York State, whether the buyer has ever been disciplined for professional misconduct or convicted of a crime, and whether the buyer currently intends to resell the practice.

(d) When the buyer's representation of a client of the seller would give rise to a waivable conflict of interest, the buyer shall not undertake such representation unless the necessary waiver or waivers have been obtained in writing.

(e) The fee charged a client by the buyer shall not be increased by reason of the sale, unless permitted by a retainer agreement with the client or otherwise specifically agreed to by the client.

Rule 1.18: Duties to Prospective Clients

(a) Except as provided in Rule 1.18(c), a person who consults with a lawyer about the possibility of forming a client-lawyer relationship with respect to a matter is a "prospective client."

(b) Even when no client-lawyer relationship ensues, a lawyer who has learned information from a prospective client shall not use or reveal that information, except as Rule 1.9 would permit with respect to information of a former client.

(c) A lawyer subject to paragraph (b) shall not represent a client with interests materially adverse to those of a prospective client in the same or a substantially related matter if the lawyer received information from the prospective client that could be significantly harmful to that person in the matter, except as provided in paragraph (d). If a lawyer is disqualified from representation under this paragraph, no lawyer in a firm with which that lawyer is associated may knowingly undertake or continue representation in such a matter, except as provided in paragraph (d).

(d) When the lawyer has received disqualifying information as defined in paragraph (c), representation is permissible if:

(1) both the affected client and the prospective client have given informed consent, confirmed in writing; or

(2) the lawyer who received the information took reasonable measures to avoid exposure to more disqualifying information than was reasonably necessary to determine whether to represent the prospective client; and

(i) the firm acts promptly and reasonably to notify, as appropriate, lawyers and nonlawyer personnel within the firm that the personally disqualified lawyer is prohibited from participating in the representation of the current client;

(ii) the firm implements effective screening procedures to prevent the flow of information about the matter between the disqualified lawyer and the others in the firm;

(iii) the disqualified lawyer is apportioned no part of the fee therefrom; and

(iv) written notice is promptly given to the prospective client; and

(3) a reasonable lawyer would conclude that the law firm will be able to provide competent and diligent representation in the matter.

(e) A person is not a prospective client within the meaning of paragraph (a) if the person:

(1) communicates information unilaterally to a lawyer, without any reasonable expectation that the lawyer is willing to discuss the possibility of forming a client-lawyer relationship; or

(2) communicates with a lawyer for the purpose of disqualifying the lawyer from handling a materially adverse representation on the same or a substantially related matter.

Rule 2.1: Advisor

In representing a client, a lawyer shall exercise independent professional judgment and render candid advice. In rendering advice, a lawyer may refer not only to law but to other considerations such as moral, economic, social, psychological, and political factors that may be relevant to the client's situation.

[Rule 2.2: Reserved]

Rule 2.3: Evaluation for Use by Third Persons

(a) A lawyer may provide an evaluation of a matter affecting a client for the use of someone other than the client if the lawyer reasonably believes that making the evaluation is compatible with other aspects of the lawyer's relationship with the client.

(b) When the lawyer knows or reasonably should know that the evaluation is likely to affect the client's interests materially and adversely, the lawyer shall not provide the evaluation unless the client gives informed consent.

(c) Unless disclosure is authorized in connection with a report of an evaluation, information relating to the evaluation is protected by Rule 1.6.

Rule 2.4: Lawyer Serving as Third-Party Neutral

(a) A lawyer serves as a "third-party neutral" when the lawyer assists two or more persons who are not clients of the lawyer to reach a resolution of a dispute or other matter that has arisen between them. Service as a third-party neutral may include service as an arbitrator, a mediator or in such other capacity as will enable the lawyer to assist the parties to resolve the matter.

(b) A lawyer serving as a third-party neutral shall inform unrepresented parties that the lawyer is not representing them. When the lawyer knows or reasonably should know that a party does not understand the lawyer's role in the matter, the lawyer shall explain the difference between the lawyer's role as a third-party neutral and a lawyer's role as one who represents a client.

Rule 3.1: Non-Meritorious Claims and Contentions

(a) A lawyer shall not bring or defend a proceeding, or assert or controvert an issue therein, unless there is a basis in law and fact for doing so that is not frivolous. A lawyer for the defendant in a criminal proceeding or for the respondent in a proceeding that could result in incarceration may nevertheless so defend the proceeding as to require that every element of the case be established.

(b) A lawyer's conduct is "frivolous" for purposes of this Rule if:

(1) the lawyer knowingly advances a claim or defense that is unwarranted under existing law, except that the lawyer may advance such claim or defense if it can be supported by good faith argument for an extension, modification, or reversal of existing law;

(2) the conduct has no reasonable purpose other than to delay or prolong the resolution of litigation, in violation of Rule 3.2, or serves merely to harass or maliciously injure another; or

(3) the lawyer knowingly asserts material factual statements that are false.

Rule 3.2: Delay of Litigation

In representing a client, a lawyer shall not use means that have no substantial purpose other than to delay or prolong the proceeding or to cause needless expense.

Rule 3.3: Conduct Before a Tribunal

(a) A lawyer shall not knowingly:

(1) make a false statement of fact or law to a tribunal or fail to correct a false statement of material fact or law previously made to the tribunal by the lawyer;

(2) fail to disclose to the tribunal controlling legal authority known to the lawyer to be directly adverse to the position of the client and not disclosed by opposing counsel; or

(3) offer or use evidence that the lawyer knows to be false. If a lawyer, the lawyer's client, or a witness called by the lawyer has offered material evidence and the lawyer comes to know of its falsity, the lawyer shall take reasonable remedial measures, including, if necessary, disclosure to the tribunal. A lawyer may refuse to offer evidence, other than the testimony of a defendant in a criminal matter, that the lawyer reasonably believes is false.

(b) A lawyer who represents a client before a tribunal and who knows that a person intends to engage, is engaging or has engaged in criminal or fraudulent conduct related to the proceeding shall take reasonable remedial measures, including, if necessary, disclosure to the tribunal.

(c) The duties stated in paragraphs (a) and (b) apply even if compliance requires disclosure of information otherwise protected by Rule 1.6.

(d) In an ex parte proceeding, a lawyer shall inform the tribunal of all material facts known to the lawyer that will enable the tribunal to make an informed decision, whether or not the facts are adverse.

(e) In presenting a matter to a tribunal, a lawyer shall disclose, unless privileged or irrelevant, the identities of the clients the lawyer represents and of the persons who employed the lawyer.

(f) In appearing as a lawyer before a tribunal, a lawyer shall not:

(1) fail to comply with known local customs of courtesy or practice of the bar or a particular tribunal without giving to opposing counsel timely notice of the intent not to comply;

(2) engage in undignified or discourteous conduct;

(3) intentionally or habitually violate any established rule of procedure or of evidence; or

(4) engage in conduct intended to disrupt the tribunal.

Rule 3.4: Fairness to Opposing Party and Counsel

A lawyer shall not:

(a)(1) suppress any evidence that the lawyer or the client has a legal obligation to reveal or produce;

(2) advise or cause a person to hide or leave the jurisdiction of a tribunal for the purpose of making the person unavailable as a witness therein;

(3) conceal or knowingly fail to disclose that which the lawyer is required by law to reveal;

(4) knowingly use perjured testimony or false evidence;

(5) participate in the creation or preservation of evidence when the lawyer knows or it is obvious that the evidence is false; or

(6) knowingly engage in other illegal conduct or conduct contrary to these Rules;

(b) offer an inducement to a witness that is prohibited by law or pay, offer to pay or acquiesce in the payment of compensation to a witness contingent upon the content of the witness's testimony or the outcome of the matter. A lawyer may advance, guarantee or acquiesce in the payment of:

(1) reasonable compensation to a witness for the loss of time in attending, testifying, preparing to testify or otherwise assisting counsel, and reasonable related expenses; or

(2) a reasonable fee for the professional services of an expert witness and reasonable related expenses;

(c) disregard or advise the client to disregard a standing rule of a tribunal or a ruling of a tribunal made in the course of a proceeding, but the lawyer may take appropriate steps in good faith to test the validity of such rule or ruling;

(d) in appearing before a tribunal on behalf of a client:

(1) state or allude to any matter that the lawyer does not reasonably believe is relevant or that will not be supported by admissible evidence;

(2) assert personal knowledge of facts in issue except when testifying as a witness;

(3) assert a personal opinion as to the justness of a cause, the credibility of a witness, the culpability of a civil litigant or the guilt or innocence of an accused but the lawyer may argue, upon analysis of the evidence, for any position or conclusion with respect to the matters stated herein; or

(4) ask any question that the lawyer has no reasonable basis to believe is relevant to the case and that is intended to degrade a witness or other person; or

(e) present, participate in presenting, or threaten to present criminal charges solely to obtain an advantage in a civil matter.

Rule 3.5: Maintaining and Preserving the Impartiality of Tribunals and Jurors

(a) A lawyer shall not:

(1) seek to or cause another person to influence a judge, official or employee of a tribunal by means prohibited by law or give or lend anything of value to such judge, official, or employee of a tribunal when the recipient is prohibited from accepting the gift or loan but a lawyer may make a contribution to the campaign fund of a candidate for judicial office in conformity with Part 100 of the Rules of the Chief Administrator of the Courts;

(2) in an adversarial proceeding communicate or cause another person to do so on the lawyer's behalf, as to the merits of the matter with a judge or official of a tribunal or an employee thereof before whom the matter is pending, except:

(i) in the course of official proceedings in the matter;

(ii) in writing, if the lawyer promptly delivers a copy of the writing to counsel for other parties and to a party who is not represented by a lawyer;

(iii) orally, upon adequate notice to counsel for the other parties and to any party who is not represented by a lawyer; or

(iv) as otherwise authorized by law, or by Part 100 of the Rules of the Chief Administrator of the Courts;

(3) seek to or cause another person to influence a juror or prospective juror by means prohibited by law;

(4) communicate or cause another to communicate with a member of the jury venire from which the jury will be selected for the trial of a case or, during the trial of a case, with any member of the jury unless authorized to do so by law or court order;

(5) communicate with a juror or prospective juror after discharge of the jury if:

(i) the communication is prohibited by law or court order;

(ii) the juror has made known to the lawyer a desire not to communicate;

(iii) the communication involves misrepresentation, coercion, duress or harassment; or

(iv) the communication is an attempt to influence the juror's actions in future jury service; or

(6) conduct a vexatious or harassing investigation of either a member of the venire or a juror or, by financial support or otherwise, cause another to do so.

(b) During the trial of a case a lawyer who is not connected therewith shall not communicate with or cause another to communicate with a juror concerning the case.

(c) All restrictions imposed by this Rule also apply to communications with or investigations of members of a family of a member of the venire or a juror.

(d) A lawyer shall reveal promptly to the court improper conduct by a member of the venire or a juror, or by another toward a member of the venire or a juror or a member of his or her family of which the lawyer has knowledge.

Rule 3.6: Trial Publicity

(a) A lawyer who is participating in or has participated in a criminal or civil matter shall not make an extrajudicial statement that the lawyer knows or reasonably should know will be disseminated by means of public communication and will have a substantial likelihood of materially prejudicing an adjudicative proceeding in the matter.

(b) A statement ordinarily is likely to prejudice materially an adjudicative proceeding when it refers to a civil matter triable to a jury, a criminal matter or any other proceeding that could result in incarceration, and the statement relates to:

(1) the character, credibility, reputation or criminal record of a party, suspect in a criminal investigation or witness, or the identity of a witness or the expected testimony of a party or witness;

(2) in a criminal matter that could result in incarceration, the possibility of a plea of guilty to the offense or the existence or contents of any confession, admission or statement given by a defendant or suspect, or that person's refusal or failure to make a statement;

(3) the performance or results of any examination or test, or the refusal or failure of a person to submit to an examination or test, or the identity or nature of physical evidence expected to be presented;

(4) any opinion as to the guilt or innocence of a defendant or suspect in a criminal matter that could result in incarceration;

(5) information the lawyer knows or reasonably should know is likely to be inadmissible as evidence in a trial and would, if disclosed, create a substantial risk of prejudicing an impartial trial; or

(6) the fact that a defendant has been charged with a crime, unless there is included therein a statement explaining that the charge is merely an accusation and that the defendant is presumed innocent until and unless proven guilty.

(c) Provided that the statement complies with paragraph (a), a lawyer may state the following without elaboration:

(1) the claim, offense or defense and, except when prohibited by law, the identity of the persons involved;

(2) information contained in a public record;

(3) that an investigation of a matter is in progress;

(4) the scheduling or result of any step in litigation;

(5) a request for assistance in obtaining evidence and information necessary thereto;

(6) a warning of danger concerning the behavior of a person involved, when there is reason to believe that there exists the likelihood of substantial harm to an individual or to the public interest; and

(7) in a criminal matter:

(i) the identity, age, residence, occupation and family status of the accused;

(ii) if the accused has not been apprehended, information necessary to aid in apprehension of that person;

(iii) the identity of investigating and arresting officers or agencies and the length of the investigation; and

(iv) the fact, time and place of arrest, resistance, pursuit and use of weapons, and a description of physical evidence seized, other than as contained only in a confession, admission or statement.

(d) Notwithstanding paragraph (a), a lawyer may make a statement that a reasonable lawyer would believe is required to protect a client from the substantial prejudicial effect of recent publicity not initiated by the lawyer or the lawyer's client. A statement made pursuant to this paragraph shall be limited to such information as is necessary to mitigate the recent adverse publicity.

(e) No lawyer associated in a firm or government agency with a lawyer subject to paragraph (a) shall make a statement prohibited by paragraph (a).

Rule 3.7: Lawyer as Witness

(a) A lawyer shall not act as advocate before a tribunal in a matter in which the lawyer is likely to be a witness on a significant issue of fact unless:

(1) the testimony relates solely to an uncontested issue;

(2) the testimony relates solely to the nature and value of legal services rendered in the matter;

(3) disqualification of the lawyer would work substantial hardship on the client;

(4) the testimony will relate solely to a matter of formality, and there is no reason to believe that substantial evidence will be offered in opposition to the testimony; or

(5) the testimony is authorized by the tribunal.

(b) A lawyer may not act as advocate before a tribunal in a matter if:

(1) another lawyer in the lawyer's firm is likely to be called as a witness on a significant issue other than on behalf of the client, and it is apparent that the testimony may be prejudicial to the client; or

(2) the lawyer is precluded from doing so by Rule 1.7 or Rule 1.9.

Rule 3.8: Special Responsibilities of Prosecutors and Other Government Lawyers

(a) A prosecutor or other government lawyer shall not institute, cause to be instituted or maintain a criminal charge when the prosecutor or other government lawyer knows or it is obvious that the charge is not supported by probable cause.

(b) A prosecutor or other government lawyer in criminal litigation shall make timely disclosure to counsel for the defendant or to a defendant who has no counsel of the existence of evidence or information known to the prosecutor or other government lawyer that tends to negate the guilt of the accused, mitigate the degree of the offense, or reduce the sentence, except when relieved of this responsibility by a protective order of a tribunal.

(c) When a prosecutor knows of new, credible and material evidence creating a reasonable likelihood that a convicted defendant did not commit an offense of which the defendant was convicted, the prosecutor shall within a reasonable time: (1) disclose that evidence to an appropriate court or prosecutor's office; or (2) if the conviction was obtained by that prosecutor's office, (A) notify the appropriate court and the defendant that the prosecutor's office possesses such evidence unless a court authorizes delay for good cause shown; (B) disclose that evidence to the defendant unless the disclosure would interfere with an ongoing investigation or endanger the safety of a witness or other person, and a court authorizes delay for good cause shown; and (C) undertake or make reasonable efforts to cause to be undertaken such further inquiry or investigation as may be necessary to provide a reasonable belief that the conviction should or should not be set aside. (d) When a prosecutor knows of clear and convincing evidence establishing that a defendant was convicted, in a prosecution by the prosecutor's office, of an offense that the defendant did not commit, the prosecutor shall seek a remedy consistent with justice, applicable law, and the circumstances of the case. (e) A prosecutor's independent judgment, made in good faith, that the new evidence is not of such nature as to trigger the obligations of sections (c) and (d), though subsequently determined to have been erroneous, does not constitute a violation of this rule.

Rule 3.9: Advocate in Non-Adjudicative Matters

A lawyer communicating in a representative capacity with a legislative body or administrative agency in connection with a pending non-adjudicative matter or proceeding shall disclose that the appearance is in a representative capacity, except when the lawyer seeks information from an agency that is available to the public.

Rule 4.1: Truthfulness in Statements to Others

In the course of representing a client, a lawyer shall not knowingly make a false statement of fact or law to a third person.

Rule 4.2: Communication With Person Represented by Counsel

(a) In representing a client, a lawyer shall not communicate or cause another to communicate about the subject of the representation with a party the lawyer knows to be represented by another lawyer in the matter, unless the lawyer has the prior consent of the other lawyer or is authorized to do so by law.

(b) Notwithstanding the prohibitions of paragraph (a), and unless otherwise prohibited by law, a lawyer may cause a client to communicate with a represented person unless the represented person is not legally competent, and may counsel the client with respect to those communications, provided the lawyer gives reasonable advance notice to the represented person's counsel that such communications will be taking place.

(c) A lawyer who is acting pro se or is represented by counsel in a matter is subject to paragraph (a), but may communicate with a represented person, unless otherwise prohibited by law and unless the represented person is not legally competent, provided the lawyer or the lawyer's counsel gives reasonable advance notice to the represented person's counsel that such communications will be taking place.

Rule 4.3: Communicating With Unrepresented Persons

In communicating on behalf of a client with a person who is not represented by counsel, a lawyer shall not state or imply that the lawyer is disinterested. When the lawyer knows or reasonably should know that the unrepresented person misunderstands the lawyer's role in the matter, the lawyer shall make reasonable efforts to correct the misunderstanding. The lawyer shall not give legal advice to an unrepresented person other than the advice to secure counsel if the lawyer knows or reasonably should know that the interests of such person are or have a reasonable possibility of being in conflict with the interests of the client.

Rule 4.4: Respect for Rights of Third Persons

(a) In representing a client, a lawyer shall not use means that have no substantial purpose other than to embarrass or harm a third person or use methods of obtaining evidence that violate the legal rights of such a person.

(b) A lawyer who receives a document, electronically stored information, or other writing relating to the representation of the lawyer's client and knows or reasonably should know that the document was inadvertently sent shall promptly notify the sender.

Rule 4.5: Communication After Incidents Involving Personal Injury or Wrongful Death

(a) In the event of a specific incident involving potential claims for personal injury or wrongful death, no unsolicited communication shall be made to an individual injured in the incident or to a family member or legal representative of such an individual, by a lawyer or law firm, or by any associate, agent, employee or other representative of a lawyer or law firm representing actual or potential defendants or entities that may defend and/or indemnify said defendants, before the 30th day after the date of the incident, unless a filing must be made within 30 days of the incident as a legal prerequisite to the particular claim, in which case no unsolicited communication shall be made before the 15th day after the date of the incident.

(b) An unsolicited communication by a lawyer or law firm, seeking to represent an injured individual or the legal representative thereof under the circumstance described in paragraph (a) shall comply with Rule 7.3(e).

Rule 5.1: Responsibilities of Law Firms, Partners, Managers and Supervisory Lawyers

(a) A law firm shall make reasonable efforts to ensure that all lawyers in the firm conform to these Rules.

(b)(1) A lawyer with management responsibility in a law firm shall make reasonable efforts to ensure that other lawyers in the law firm conform to these Rules.

(2) A lawyer with direct supervisory authority over another lawyer shall make reasonable efforts to ensure that the supervised lawyer conforms to these Rules.

(c) A law firm shall ensure that the work of partners and associates is adequately supervised, as appropriate. A lawyer with direct supervisory authority over another lawyer shall adequately supervise the work of the other lawyer, as appropriate. In either case, the degree of supervision required is that which is reasonable under the circumstances, taking into account factors such as the experience of the person whose work is being supervised, the amount of work involved in a particular matter, and the likelihood that ethical problems might arise in the course of working on the matter.

(d) A lawyer shall be responsible for a violation of these Rules by another lawyer if:

(1) the lawyer orders or directs the specific conduct or, with knowledge of the specific conduct, ratifies it; or

(2) the lawyer is a partner in a law firm or is a lawyer who individually or together with other lawyers possesses comparable managerial responsibility in a law firm in which the other lawyer practices or is a lawyer who has supervisory authority over the other lawyer; and

(i) knows of such conduct at a time when it could be prevented or its consequences avoided or mitigated but fails to take reasonable remedial action; or

(ii) in the exercise of reasonable management or supervisory authority should have known of the conduct so that reasonable remedial action could have been taken at a time when the consequences of the conduct could have been avoided or mitigated.

Rule 5.2: Responsibilities of a Subordinate Lawyer

(a) A lawyer is bound by these Rules notwithstanding that the lawyer acted at the direction of another person.

(b) A subordinate lawyer does not violate these Rules if that lawyer acts in accordance with a supervisory lawyer's reasonable resolution of an arguable question of professional duty.

Rule 5.3: Lawyer's Responsibility for Conduct of Nonlawyers

(a) A law firm shall ensure that the work of nonlawyers who work for the firm is adequately supervised, as appropriate. A lawyer with direct supervisory authority over a nonlawyer shall adequately supervise the work of the nonlawyer, as appropriate. In either case, the degree of supervision required is that which is reasonable under the circumstances, taking into account factors such as the experience of the person whose work is being supervised, the amount of work involved in a particular matter and the likelihood that ethical problems might arise in the course of working on the matter.

(b) A lawyer shall be responsible for conduct of a nonlawyer employed or retained by or associated with the lawyer that would be a violation of these Rules if engaged in by a lawyer, if:

(1) the lawyer orders or directs the specific conduct or, with knowledge of the specific conduct, ratifies it; or

(2) the lawyer is a partner in a law firm or is a lawyer who individually or together with other lawyers possesses comparable managerial responsibility in a law firm in which the nonlawyer is employed or is a lawyer who has supervisory authority over the nonlawyer; and

(i) knows of such conduct at a time when it could be prevented or its consequences avoided or mitigated but fails to take reasonable remedial action; or

(ii) in the exercise of reasonable management or supervisory authority should have known of the conduct so that reasonable remedial action could have been taken at a time when the consequences of the conduct could have been avoided or mitigated.

Rule 5.4: Professional Independence of a Lawyer

(a) A lawyer or law firm shall not share legal fees with a nonlawyer, except that:

(1) an agreement by a lawyer with the lawyer's firm or another lawyer associated in the firm may provide for the payment of money, over a reasonable period of time after the lawyer's death, to the lawyer's estate or to one or more specified persons;

(2) a lawyer who undertakes to complete unfinished legal business of a deceased lawyer may pay to the estate of the deceased lawyer that portion of the total compensation that fairly represents the services rendered by the deceased lawyer; and

(3) a lawyer or law firm may compensate a nonlawyer employee or include a nonlawyer employee in a retirement plan based in whole or in part on a profit-sharing arrangement.

(b) A lawyer shall not form a partnership with a nonlawyer if any of the activities of the partnership consist of the practice of law.

(c) Unless authorized by law, a lawyer shall not permit a person who recommends, employs or pays the lawyer to render legal service for another to direct or regulate the lawyer's professional judgment in rendering such legal services or to cause the lawyer to compromise the lawyer's duty to maintain the confidential information of the client under Rule 1.6.

(d) A lawyer shall not practice with or in the form of an entity authorized to practice law for profit, if:

(1) a nonlawyer owns any interest therein, except that a fiduciary representative of the estate of a lawyer may hold the stock or interest of the lawyer for a reasonable time during administration;

(2) a nonlawyer is a member, corporate director or officer thereof or occupies a position of similar responsibility in any form of association other than a corporation; or

(3) a nonlawyer has the right to direct or control the professional judgment of a lawyer.

Rule 5.5: Unauthorized Practice of Law

(a) A lawyer shall not practice law in a jurisdiction in violation of the regulation of the legal profession in that jurisdiction.

(b) A lawyer shall not aid a nonlawyer in the unauthorized practice of law.

Rule 5.6: Restrictions on Right to Practice

(a) A lawyer shall not participate in offering or making:

(1) a partnership, shareholder, operating, employment, or other similar type of agreement that restricts the right of a lawyer to practice after termination of the relationship, except an agreement concerning benefits upon retirement; or

(2) an agreement in which a restriction on a lawyer's right to practice is part of the settlement of a client controversy.

(b) This Rule does not prohibit restrictions that may be included in the terms of the sale of a law practice pursuant to Rule 1.17.

Rule 5.7: Responsibilities Regarding Nonlegal Services

(a) With respect to lawyers or law firms providing nonlegal services to clients or other persons:

(1) A lawyer or law firm that provides nonlegal services to a person that are not distinct from legal services being provided to that person by the lawyer or law firm is subject to these Rules with respect to the provision of both legal and nonlegal services.

(2) A lawyer or law firm that provides nonlegal services to a person that are distinct from legal services being provided to that person by the lawyer or law firm is subject to these Rules with respect to the nonlegal services if the person receiving the services could reasonably believe that the nonlegal services are the subject of a client-lawyer relationship.

(3) A lawyer or law firm that is an owner, controlling party or agent of, or that is otherwise affiliated with, an entity that the lawyer or law firm knows to be providing nonlegal services to a person is subject to these Rules with respect to the nonlegal services if the person receiving the services could reasonably believe that the nonlegal services are the subject of a client-lawyer relationship.

(4) For purposes of paragraphs (a)(2) and (a)(3), it will be presumed that the person receiving nonlegal services believes the services to be the subject of a client-lawyer relationship unless the lawyer or law firm has advised the person receiving the services in writing that the services are not legal services and that the protection of a client-lawyer relationship does not exist with respect to the nonlegal services, or if the interest of the lawyer or law firm in the entity providing nonlegal services is *de minimis*.

(b) Notwithstanding the provisions of paragraph (a), a lawyer or law firm that is an owner, controlling party, agent, or is otherwise affiliated with an entity that the lawyer or law firm knows is providing nonlegal services to a person shall not permit any nonlawyer providing such services or affiliated with that entity to direct or regulate the professional judgment of the lawyer or law firm in rendering legal services to any person, or to cause the lawyer or law firm to compromise its duty under Rule 1.6(a) and (c) with respect to the confidential information of a client receiving legal services.

(c) For purposes of this Rule, "nonlegal services" shall mean those services that lawyers may lawfully provide and that are not prohibited as an unauthorized practice of law when provided by a nonlawyer.

Rule 5.8: Contractual Relationship Between Lawyers and Nonlegal Professionals

(a) The practice of law has an essential tradition of complete independence and uncompromised loyalty to those it serves. Recognizing this tradition, clients of lawyers practicing in New York State are guaranteed "independent professional judgment and undivided loyalty uncompromised by conflicts of interest." Indeed, these guarantees represent the very foundation of the profession and allow and foster its continued role as a protector of the system of law. Therefore, a lawyer must remain completely responsible for his or her own independent professional judgment, maintain the confidences and secrets of clients, preserve funds of clients and third parties in his or her control, and otherwise comply with the legal and ethical principles governing lawyers in New York State.

Multi-disciplinary practice between lawyers and nonlawyers is incompatible with the core values of the legal profession and therefore, a strict division between services provided by lawyers and those provided by nonlawyers is essential to protect those values. However, a lawyer or law firm may enter into and maintain a contractual relationship with a nonlegal professional or nonlegal professional service firm for the purpose of offering to the public, on a systematic and continuing basis, legal services performed by the lawyer or law firm as well as other nonlegal professional services, notwithstanding the provisions of Rule 1.7(a), provided that:

(1) the profession of the nonlegal professional or nonlegal professional service firm is included in a list jointly established and maintained by the Appellate Divisions pursuant to Section 1205.3 of the Joint Appellate Division Rules;

(2) the lawyer or law firm neither grants to the nonlegal professional or nonlegal professional service firm, nor permits such person or firm to obtain, hold or exercise, directly or indirectly, any ownership or investment interest in, or managerial or supervisory right, power or position in connection with the practice of law by the lawyer or law firm, nor, as provided in Rule 7.2(a)(1), shares legal fees with a nonlawyer or receives or gives any monetary or other tangible benefit for giving or receiving a referral; and

(3) the fact that the contractual relationship exists is disclosed by the lawyer or law firm to any client of the lawyer or law firm before the client is referred to the nonlegal professional service firm, or to any client of the nonlegal professional service firm before that client receives legal services from the lawyer or law firm; and the client has given informed written consent and has been provided with a copy of the "Statement of Client's Rights In Cooperative Business Arrangements" pursuant to section 1205.4 of the Joint Appellate Divisions Rules.

(b) For purposes of paragraph (a):

(1) each profession on the list maintained pursuant to a Joint Rule of the Appellate Divisions shall have been designated sua sponte, or approved by the Appellate Divisions upon application of a member of a nonlegal profession or nonlegal professional service firm, upon a determination that the profession is composed of individuals who, with respect to their profession:

(a) have been awarded a bachelor's degree or its equivalent from an accredited college or university, or have attained an equivalent combination of educational credit from such a college or university and work experience;

(b) are licensed to practice the profession by an agency of the State of New York or the United States Government; and

(c) are required under penalty of suspension or revocation of license to adhere to a code of ethical conduct that is reasonably comparable to that of the legal profession;

(2) the term "ownership or investment interest" shall mean any such interest in any form of debt or equity, and shall include any interest commonly considered to be an interest accruing to or enjoyed by an owner or investor.

(c) This Rule shall not apply to relationships consisting solely of non-exclusive reciprocal referral agreements or understandings between a lawyer or law firm and a nonlegal professional or nonlegal professional service firm.

Rule 6.1: Voluntary Pro Bono Service

Lawyers are strongly encouraged to provide pro bono legal services to benefit poor persons.

(a) Every lawyer should aspire to:

(1) provide at least 50 hours of pro bono legal services each year to poor persons; and

(2) contribute financially to organizations that provide legal services to poor persons. Lawyers in private practice or employed by a for-profit entity should aspire to contribute annually in an amount at least equivalent to (i) the amount typically billed by the lawyer (or the firm with which the lawyer is associated) for one hour of time; or (ii) if the lawyer's work is performed on a contingency basis, the amount typically billed by lawyers in the community for one hour of time; or (iii) the amount typically paid by the organization employing the lawyer for one hour of the lawyer's time; or (iv) if the lawyer is underemployed, an amount not to exceed one-tenth of one percent of the lawyer's income.

(b) Pro bono legal services that meet this goal are:

(1) professional services rendered in civil matters, and in those criminal matters for which the government is not obliged to provide funds for legal representation, to persons who are financially unable to compensate counsel;

(2) activities related to improving the administration of justice by simplifying the legal process for, or increasing the availability and quality of legal services to, poor persons; and

(3) professional services to charitable, religious, civic and educational organizations in matters designed predominantly to address the needs of poor persons.

(c) Appropriate organizations for financial contributions are:

(1) organizations primarily engaged in the provision of legal services to the poor; and

(2) organizations substantially engaged in the provision of legal services to the poor, provided that the donated funds are to be used for the provision of such legal services.

(d) This Rule is not intended to be enforced through the disciplinary process, and the failure to fulfill the aspirational goals contained herein should be without legal consequence.

[Rule 6.2: Reserved]

Rule 6.3: Membership in a Legal Services Organization

A lawyer may serve as a director, officer or member of a not-for-profit legal services organization, apart from the law firm in which the lawyer practices, notwithstanding that the organization serves persons having interests that differ from those of a client of the lawyer or the lawyer's firm. The lawyer shall not knowingly participate in a decision or action of the organization:

(a) if participating in the decision or action would be incompatible with the lawyer's obligations to a client under Rules 1.7 through 1.13; or

(b) where the decision or action could have a material adverse effect on the representation of a client of the organization whose interests differ from those of a client of the lawyer or the lawyer's firm.

Rule 6.4: Law Reform Activities Affecting Client Interests (Amended 4/22/2010)

A lawyer may serve as a director, officer or member of an organization involved in reform of the law or its administration, notwithstanding that the reform may affect the interests of a client of the lawyer. When the lawyer knows that the interests of a client may be materially benefitted by a decision in which the lawyer actively participates, the lawyer shall disclose that fact to the organization, but need not identify the client. In determining the nature and scope of participation in such activities, a lawyer should be mindful of obligations to clients under other Rules, particularly Rule 1.7.

Rule 6.5: Participation in Limited Pro Bono Legal Service Programs

(a) A lawyer who, under the auspices of a program sponsored by a court, government agency, bar association or not-for-profit legal services organization, provides short-term limited legal services to a client without expectation by either the lawyer or the client that the lawyer will provide continuing representation in the matter:

(1) shall comply with Rules 1.7, 1.8 and 1.9, concerning restrictions on representations where there are or may be conflicts of interest as that term is defined in these Rules, only if the lawyer has actual knowledge at the time of commencement of representation that the representation of the client involves a conflict of interest; and

(2) shall comply with Rule 1.10 only if the lawyer has actual knowledge at the time of commencement of representation that another lawyer associated with the lawyer in a law firm is affected by Rules 1.7, 1.8 and 1.9.

(b) Except as provided in paragraph (a)(2), Rule 1.7 and Rule 1.9 are inapplicable to a representation governed by this Rule.

(c) Short-term limited legal services are services providing legal advice or representation free of charge as part of a program described in paragraph (a) with no expectation that the assistance will continue beyond what is necessary to complete an initial consultation, representation or court appearance.

(d) The lawyer providing short-term limited legal services must secure the client's informed consent to the limited scope of the representation, and such representation shall be subject to the provisions of Rule 1.6.

(e) This Rule shall not apply where the court before which the matter is pending determines that a conflict of interest exists or, if during the course of the representation, the lawyer providing the services becomes aware of the existence of a conflict of interest precluding continued representation.

Rule 7.1: Advertising

(a) A lawyer or law firm shall not use or disseminate or participate in the use or dissemination of any advertisement that:

(1) contains statements or claims that are false, deceptive or misleading; or

(2) violates a Rule.

(b) Subject to the provisions of paragraph (a), an advertisement may include information as to:

(1) legal and nonlegal education, degrees and other scholastic distinctions, dates of admission to any bar; areas of the law in which the lawyer or law firm practices, as authorized by these Rules; public offices and teaching positions held; publications of law related matters authored by the lawyer; memberships in bar associations or other professional societies or

organizations, including offices and committee assignments therein; foreign language fluency; and bona fide professional ratings;

(2) names of clients regularly represented, provided that the client has given prior written consent;

(3) bank references; credit arrangements accepted; prepaid or group legal services programs in which the lawyer or law firm participates; nonlegal services provided by the lawyer or law firm or by an entity owned and controlled by the lawyer or law firm; the existence of contractual relationships between the lawyer or law firm and a nonlegal professional or nonlegal professional service firm, to the extent permitted by Rule 5.8, and the nature and extent of services available through those contractual relationships; and

(4) legal fees for initial consultation; contingent fee rates in civil matters when accompanied by a statement disclosing the information required by paragraph (p); range of fees for legal and nonlegal services, provided that there be available to the public free of charge a written statement clearly describing the scope of each advertised service; hourly rates; and fixed fees for specified legal and nonlegal services.

(c) An advertisement shall not:

(1) include an endorsement of, or testimonial about, a lawyer or law firm from a client with respect to a matter still pending;

(2) include a paid endorsement of, or testimonial about, a lawyer or law firm without disclosing that the person is being compensated therefor;

(3) include the portrayal of a judge, the portrayal of a fictitious law firm, the use of a fictitious name to refer to lawyers not associated together in a law firm, or otherwise imply that lawyers are associated in a law firm if that is not the case;

(4) use actors to portray the lawyer, members of the law firm, or clients, or utilize depictions of fictionalized events or scenes, without disclosure of same;

(5) rely on techniques to obtain attention that demonstrate a clear and intentional lack of relevance to the selection of counsel, including the portrayal of lawyers exhibiting characteristics clearly unrelated to legal competence;

(6) be made to resemble legal documents; or

(7) utilize a nickname, moniker, motto or trade name that implies an ability to obtain results in a matter.

(d) An advertisement that complies with paragraph (e) may contain the following:

(1) statements that are reasonably likely to create an expectation about results the lawyer can achieve;

(2) statements that compare the lawyer's services with the services of other lawyers;

(3) testimonials or endorsements of clients, where not prohibited by paragraph (c)(1), and of former clients; or

(4) statements describing or characterizing the quality of the lawyer's or law firm's services.

(e) It is permissible to provide the information set forth in paragraph (d) provided:

(1) its dissemination does not violate paragraph (a);

(2) it can be factually supported by the lawyer or law firm as of the date on which the advertisement is published or disseminated; and

(3) it is accompanied by the following disclaimer: "Prior results do not guarantee a similar outcome."

(f) Every advertisement other than those appearing in a radio, television or billboard advertisement, in a directory, newspaper, magazine or other periodical (and any web sites related thereto), or made in person pursuant to Rule 7.3(a)(1), shall be labeled "Attorney Advertising" on the first page, or on the home page in the case of a web site. If the communication is in the form of a self-mailing brochure or postcard, the words "Attorney Advertising" shall appear therein. In the case of electronic mail, the subject line shall contain the notation "ATTORNEY ADVERTISING."

(g) A lawyer or law firm shall not utilize:

(1) a pop-up or pop-under advertisement in connection with computer-accessed communications, other than on the lawyer or law firm's own web site or other internet presence; or

(2) meta tags or other hidden computer codes that, if displayed, would violate these Rules.

(h) All advertisements shall include the name, principal law office address and telephone number of the lawyer or law firm whose services are being offered.

(i) Any words or statements required by this Rule to appear in an advertisement must be clearly legible and capable of being read by the average person, if written, and intelligible if spoken aloud. In the case of a web site, the required words or statements shall appear on the home page.

(j) A lawyer or law firm advertising any fixed fee for specified legal services shall, at the time of fee publication, have available to the public a written statement clearly describing the scope of each advertised service, which statement shall be available to the client at the time of retainer for any such service. Such legal services shall include all those services that are recognized as reasonable and necessary under local custom in the area of practice in the community where the services are performed.

(k) All advertisements shall be pre-approved by the lawyer or law firm, and a copy shall be retained for a period of not less than three years following its initial dissemination. Any advertisement contained in a computer-accessed communication shall be retained for a period of not less than one year. A copy of the contents of any web site covered by this Rule shall be preserved upon the initial publication of the web site, any major web site redesign, or a meaningful and extensive content change, but in no event less frequently than once every 90 days.

(*l*) If a lawyer or law firm advertises a range of fees or an hourly rate for services, the lawyer or law firm shall not charge more than the fee advertised for such services. If a lawyer or law firm advertises a fixed fee for specified legal services, or performs services described in a fee schedule, the lawyer or law firm shall not charge more than the fixed fee for such stated legal service as set forth in the advertisement or fee schedule, unless the client agrees in writing that the services performed or to be performed were not legal services referred to or implied in the advertisement or in the fee schedule and, further, that a different fee arrangement shall apply to the transaction.

(m) Unless otherwise specified in the advertisement, if a lawyer publishes any fee information authorized under this Rule in a publication that is published more frequently than once per month, the lawyer shall be bound by any representation made therein for a period of not less than 30 days after such publication. If a lawyer publishes any fee information authorized under this Rule in a publication that is published once per month or less frequently, the lawyer shall be bound by any representation made therein until the publication of the succeeding issue. If a lawyer publishes any fee information authorized under this Rule in a publication that has no fixed date for publication of a succeeding issue, the lawyer shall be bound by any representation made therein for a reasonable period of time after publication, but in no event less than 90 days.

(n) Unless otherwise specified, if a lawyer broadcasts any fee information authorized under this Rule, the lawyer shall be bound by any representation made therein for a period of not less than 30 days after such broadcast.

(*o*) A lawyer shall not compensate or give anything of value to representatives of the press, radio, television or other communication medium in anticipation of or in return for professional publicity in a news item.

(p) All advertisements that contain information about the fees charged by the lawyer or law firm, including those indicating that in the absence of a recovery no fee will be charged, shall comply with the provisions of Judiciary Law § 488(3).

(q) A lawyer may accept employment that results from participation in activities designed to educate the public to recognize legal problems, to make intelligent selection of counsel or to utilize available legal services.

(r) Without affecting the right to accept employment, a lawyer may speak publicly or write for publication on legal topics so long as the lawyer does not undertake to give individual advice.

Rule 7.2: Payment for Referrals

(a) A lawyer shall not compensate or give anything of value to a person or organization to recommend or obtain employment by a client, or as a reward for having made a recommendation resulting in employment by a client, except that:

(1) a lawyer or law firm may refer clients to a nonlegal professional or nonlegal professional service firm pursuant to a contractual relationship with such nonlegal professional or nonlegal professional service firm to provide legal and other professional services on a systematic and continuing basis as permitted by Rule 5.8, provided however that such referral shall not otherwise include any monetary or other tangible consideration or reward for such, or the sharing of legal fees; and

(2) a lawyer may pay the usual and reasonable fees or dues charged by a qualified legal assistance organization or referral fees to another lawyer as permitted by Rule 1.5(g).

(b) A lawyer or the lawyer's partner or associate or any other affiliated lawyer may be recommended, employed or paid by, or may cooperate with one of the following offices or organizations that promote the use of the lawyer's services or those of a partner or associate or any other affiliated lawyer, or request one of the following offices or organizations to recommend or promote the use of the lawyer's services or those of the lawyer's partner or associate, or any other affiliated lawyer as a private practitioner, if there is no interference with the exercise of independent professional judgment on behalf of the client:

(1) a legal aid office or public defender office:

(i) operated or sponsored by a duly accredited law school;

(ii) operated or sponsored by a bona fide, non-profit community organization;

(iii) operated or sponsored by a governmental agency; or

(iv) operated, sponsored, or approved by a bar association;

(2) a military legal assistance office;

(3) a lawyer referral service operated, sponsored or approved by a bar association or authorized by law or court rule; or

(4) any bona fide organization that recommends, furnishes or pays for legal services to its members or beneficiaries provided the following conditions are satisfied:

(i) Neither the lawyer, nor the lawyer's partner, nor associate, nor any other affiliated lawyer nor any nonlawyer, shall have initiated or promoted such organization for the primary purpose of providing financial or other benefit to such lawyer, partner, associate or affiliated lawyer;

(ii) Such organization is not operated for the purpose of procuring legal work or financial benefit for any lawyer as a private practitioner outside of the legal services program of the organization;

(iii) The member or beneficiary to whom the legal services are furnished, and not such organization, is recognized as the client of the lawyer in the matter;

(iv) The legal service plan of such organization provides appropriate relief for any member or beneficiary who asserts a claim that representation by counsel furnished, selected or approved by the organization for the particular matter involved would be unethical, improper or inadequate under the circumstances of the matter involved; and the plan provides an appropriate procedure for seeking such relief;

(v) The lawyer does not know or have cause to know that such organization is in violation of applicable laws, rules of court or other legal requirements that govern its legal service operations; and

(vi) Such organization has filed with the appropriate disciplinary authority, to the extent required by such authority, at least annually a report with respect to its legal service plan, if any, showing its terms, its schedule of benefits, its subscription charges, agreements with counsel and financial results of its legal service activities or, if it has failed to do so, the lawyer does not know or have cause to know of such failure.

Rule 7.3: Solicitation and Recommendation of Professional Employment

(a) A lawyer shall not engage in solicitation:

(1) by in-person or telephone contact, or by real-time or interactive computer-accessed communication unless the recipient is a close friend, relative, former client or existing client; or

(2) by any form of communication if:

(i) the communication or contact violates Rule 4.5, Rule 7.1(a), or paragraph (e) of this Rule;

(ii) the recipient has made known to the lawyer a desire not to be solicited by the lawyer;

(iii) the solicitation involves coercion, duress or harassment;

(iv) the lawyer knows or reasonably should know that the age or the physical, emotional or mental state of the recipient makes it unlikely that the recipient will be able to exercise reasonable judgment in retaining a lawyer; or

(v) the lawyer intends or expects, but does not disclose, that the legal services necessary to handle the matter competently will be performed primarily by another lawyer who is not affiliated with the soliciting lawyer as a partner, associate or of counsel.

(b) For purposes of this Rule, "solicitation" means any advertisement initiated by or on behalf of a lawyer or law firm that is directed to, or targeted at, a specific recipient or group of recipients, or their family members or legal representatives, the primary purpose of which is the retention of the lawyer or law firm, and a significant motive for which is pecuniary gain. It does not include a proposal or other writing prepared and delivered in response to a specific request.

(c) A solicitation directed to a recipient in this State shall be subject to the following provisions:

(1) A copy of the solicitation shall at the time of its dissemination be filed with the attorney disciplinary committee of the judicial district or judicial department wherein the lawyer or law

firm maintains its principal office. Where no such office is maintained, the filing shall be made in the judicial department where the solicitation is targeted. A filing shall consist of:

(i) a copy of the solicitation;

(ii) a transcript of the audio portion of any radio or television solicitation; and

(iii) if the solicitation is in a language other than English, an accurate English-language translation.

(2) Such solicitation shall contain no reference to the fact of filing.

(3) If a solicitation is directed to a predetermined recipient, a list containing the names and addresses of all recipients shall be retained by the lawyer or law firm for a period of not less than three years following the last date of its dissemination.

(4) Solicitations filed pursuant to this subdivision shall be open to public inspection.

(5) The provisions of this paragraph shall not apply to:

(i) a solicitation directed or disseminated to a close friend, relative, or former or existing client;

(ii) a web site maintained by the lawyer or law firm, unless the web site is designed for and directed to or targeted at a prospective client affected by an identifiable actual event or occurrence or by an identifiable prospective defendant; or

(iii) professional cards or other announcements the distribution of which is authorized by Rule 7.5(a).

(d) A written solicitation shall not be sent by a method that requires the recipient to travel to a location other than that at which the recipient ordinarily receives business or personal mail or that requires a signature on the part of the recipient.

(e) No solicitation relating to a specific incident involving potential claims for personal injury or wrongful death shall be disseminated before the 30th day after the date of the incident, unless a filing must be made within 30 days of the incident as a legal prerequisite to the particular claim, in which case no unsolicited communication shall be made before the 15th day after the date of the incident.

(f) Any solicitation made in writing or by computer-accessed communication and directed to a pre-determined recipient, if prompted by a specific occurrence involving or affecting a recipient, shall disclose how the lawyer obtained the identity of the recipient and learned of the recipient's potential legal need.

(g) If a retainer agreement is provided with any solicitation, the top of each page shall be marked "SAMPLE" in red ink in a type size equal to the largest type size used in the agreement and the words "DO NOT SIGN" shall appear on the client signature line.

(h) Any solicitation covered by this section shall include the name, principal law office address and telephone number of the lawyer or law firm whose services are being offered.

(i) The provisions of this Rule shall apply to a lawyer or members of a law firm not admitted to practice in this State who shall solicit retention by residents of this State.

Rule 7.4: Identification of Practice and Specialty

(a) A lawyer or law firm may publicly identify one or more areas of law in which the lawyer or the law firm practices, or may state that the practice of the lawyer or law firm is limited to one or more areas of law, provided that the lawyer or law firm shall not state that the lawyer or law firm is a specialist or specializes in a particular field of law, except as provided in Rule 7.4(c).

(b) A lawyer admitted to engage in patent practice before the United States Patent and Trademark Office may use the designation "Patent Attorney" or a substantially similar designation.

(c) A lawyer may state that the lawyer has been recognized or certified as a specialist only as follows:

(1) A lawyer who is certified as a specialist in a particular area of law or law practice by a private organization approved for that purpose by the American Bar Association may state the fact of certification if, in conjunction therewith, the certifying organization is identified and the following statement is prominently made: "This certification is not granted by any governmental authority;"

(2) A lawyer who is certified as a specialist in a particular area of law or law practice by the authority having jurisdiction over specialization under the laws of another state or territory may state the fact of certification if, in conjunction therewith, the certifying state or territory is identified and the following statement is prominently made: "This certification is not granted by any governmental authority within the State of New York."

(3) A statement is prominently made if:

(i) when written, it is clearly legible and capable of being read by the average person, and is at least two font sizes larger than the largest text used to state the fact of certification; and

(ii) when spoken, it is intelligible to the average person, and is at a cadence no faster, and a level of audibility no lower, than the cadence and level of audibility used to state the fact of certification.

Rule 7.5: Professional Notices, Letterheads, and Signs

(a) A lawyer or law firm may use internet web sites, professional cards, professional announcement cards, office signs, letterheads or similar professional notices or devices, provided the same do not violate any statute or court rule and are in accordance with Rule 7.1, including the following:

(1) a professional card of a lawyer identifying the lawyer by name and as a lawyer, and giving addresses, telephone numbers, the name of the law firm, and any information permitted under Rule 7.1(b) or Rule 7.4. A professional card of a law firm may also give the names of members and associates;

(2) a professional announcement card stating new or changed associations or addresses, change of firm name, or similar matters pertaining to the professional offices of a lawyer or law firm or any nonlegal business conducted by the lawyer or law firm pursuant to Rule 5.7. It may state biographical data, the names of members of the firm and associates, and the names and dates of predecessor firms in a continuing line of succession. It may state the nature of the legal practice if permitted under Rule 7.4;

(3) a sign in or near the office and in the building directory identifying the law office and any nonlegal business conducted by the lawyer or law firm pursuant to Rule 5.7. The sign may state the nature of the legal practice if permitted under Rule 7.4; or

(4) a letterhead identifying the lawyer by name and as a lawyer, and giving addresses, telephone numbers, the name of the law firm, associates and any information permitted under Rule 7.1(b) or Rule 7.4. A letterhead of a law firm may also give the names of members and associates, and names and dates relating to deceased and retired members. A lawyer or law firm may be designated "Of Counsel" on a letterhead if there is a continuing relationship with a lawyer or law firm, other than as a partner or associate. A lawyer or law firm may be designated as "General Counsel" or by similar professional reference on stationery of a client if the lawyer or the firm devotes a substantial amount of professional time in the representation of that client.

The letterhead of a law firm may give the names and dates of predecessor firms in a continuing line of succession.

(b) A lawyer in private practice shall not practice under a trade name, a name that is misleading as to the identity of the lawyer or lawyers practicing under such name, or a firm name containing names other than those of one or more of the lawyers in the firm, except that the name of a professional corporation shall contain "PC" or such symbols permitted by law, the name of a limited liability company or partnership shall contain "LLC," "LLP" or such symbols permitted by law and, if otherwise lawful, a firm may use as, or continue to include in its name the name or names of one or more deceased or retired members of the firm or of a predecessor firm in a continuing line of succession. Such terms as "legal clinic," "legal aid," "legal service office," "legal assistance office," "defender office" and the like may be used only by qualified legal assistance organizations, except that the term "legal clinic" may be used by any lawyer or law firm provided the name of a participating lawyer or firm is incorporated therein. A lawyer or law firm may not include the name of a nonlawyer in its firm name, nor may a lawyer or law firm that has a contractual relationship with a nonlegal professional or nonlegal professional service firm pursuant to Rule 5.8 to provide legal and other professional services on a systematic and continuing basis include in its firm name the name of the nonlegal professional service firm or any individual nonlegal professional affiliated therewith. A lawyer who assumes a judicial, legislative or public executive or administrative post or office shall not permit the lawyer's name to remain in the name of a law firm or to be used in professional notices of the firm during any significant period in which the lawyer is not actively and regularly practicing law as a member of the firm and, during such period, other members of the firm shall not use the lawyer's name in the firm name or in professional notices of the firm.

(c) Lawyers shall not hold themselves out as having a partnership with one or more other lawyers unless they are in fact partners.

(d) A partnership shall not be formed or continued between or among lawyers licensed in different jurisdictions unless all enumerations of the members and associates of the firm on its letterhead and in other permissible listings make clear the jurisdictional limitations on those members and associates of the firm not licensed to practice in all listed jurisdictions; however, the same firm name may be used in each jurisdiction.

(e) A lawyer or law firm may utilize a domain name for an internet web site that does not include the name of the lawyer or law firm provided:

(1) all pages of the web site clearly and conspicuously include the actual name of the lawyer or law firm;

(2) the lawyer or law firm in no way attempts to engage in the practice of law using the domain name;

(3) the domain name does not imply an ability to obtain results in a matter; and

(4) the domain name does not otherwise violate these Rules.

(f) A lawyer or law firm may utilize a telephone number which contains a domain name, nickname, moniker or motto that does not otherwise violate these Rules.

Rule 8.1: Candor in the Bar Admission Process

(a) A lawyer shall be subject to discipline if, in connection with the lawyer's own application for admission to the bar previously filed in this state or in any other jurisdiction, or in connection with the application of another person for admission to the bar, the lawyer knowingly:

(1) has made or failed to correct a false statement of material fact; or

(2) has failed to disclose a material fact requested in connection with a lawful demand for information from an admissions authority.

Rule 8.2: Judicial Officers and Candidates

(a) A lawyer shall not knowingly make a false statement of fact concerning the qualifications, conduct or integrity of a judge or other adjudicatory officer or of a candidate for election or appointment to judicial office.

(b) A lawyer who is a candidate for judicial office shall comply with the applicable provisions of Part 100 of the Rules of the Chief Administrator of the Courts.

Rule 8.3: Reporting Professional Misconduct

(a) A lawyer who knows that another lawyer has committed a violation of the Rules of Professional Conduct that raises a substantial question as to that lawyer's honesty, trustworthiness or fitness as a lawyer shall report such knowledge to a tribunal or other authority empowered to investigate or act upon such violation.

(b) A lawyer who possesses knowledge or evidence concerning another lawyer or a judge shall not fail to respond to a lawful demand for information from a tribunal or other authority empowered to investigate or act upon such conduct.

(c) This Rule does not require disclosure of:

(1) information otherwise protected by Rule 1.6; or

(2) information gained by a lawyer or judge while participating in a bona fide lawyer assistance program.

Rule 8.4: Misconduct

A lawyer or law firm shall not:

(a) violate or attempt to violate the Rules of Professional Conduct, knowingly assist or induce another to do so, or do so through the acts of another;

(b) engage in illegal conduct that adversely reflects on the lawyer's honesty, trustworthiness or fitness as a lawyer;

(c) engage in conduct involving dishonesty, fraud, deceit or misrepresentation;

(d) engage in conduct that is prejudicial to the administration of justice;

(e) state or imply an ability:

(1) to influence improperly or upon irrelevant grounds any tribunal, legislative body or public official; or

(2) to achieve results using means that violate these Rules or other law;

(f) knowingly assist a judge or judicial officer in conduct that is a violation of applicable rules of judicial conduct or other law;

(g) unlawfully discriminate in the practice of law, including in hiring, promoting or otherwise determining conditions of employment on the basis of age, race, creed, color, national origin, sex, disability, marital status, sexual orientation, gender identity, or gender expression. Where there is a tribunal with jurisdiction to hear a complaint, if timely brought, other than a Departmental Disciplinary Committee, a complaint based on unlawful discrimination shall be brought before such tribunal in the first instance. A certified copy of a determination by such a tribunal, which has become final and enforceable and as to which the right to judicial or appellate review has been exhausted, finding that the lawyer has engaged in an unlawful discriminatory practice shall constitute prima facie evidence of professional misconduct in a disciplinary proceeding; or

(h) engage in any other conduct that adversely reflects on the lawyer's fitness as a lawyer.

Rule 8.5: Disciplinary Authority and Choice of Law

(a) A lawyer admitted to practice in this state is subject to the disciplinary authority of this state, regardless of where the lawyer's conduct occurs. A lawyer may be subject to the disciplinary authority of both this state and another jurisdiction where the lawyer is admitted for the same conduct.

(b) In any exercise of the disciplinary authority of this state, the rules of professional conduct to be applied shall be as follows:

(1) For conduct in connection with a proceeding in a court before which a lawyer has been admitted to practice (either generally or for purposes of that proceeding), the rules to be applied shall be the rules of the jurisdiction in which the court sits, unless the rules of the court provide otherwise; and

(2) For any other conduct:

(i) If the lawyer is licensed to practice only in this state, the rules to be applied shall be the rules of this state, and

(ii) If the lawyer is licensed to practice in this state and another jurisdiction, the rules to be applied shall be the rules of the admitting jurisdiction in which the lawyer principally practices; provided, however, that if particular conduct clearly has its predominant effect in another jurisdiction in which the lawyer is licensed to practice, the rules of that jurisdiction shall be applied to that conduct.

AMERICAN BAR ASSOCIATION MODEL CODE OF PROFESSIONAL RESPONSIBILITY

As Amended and in Effect until 1983.

[The Model Code of Professional Responsibility was the product of the Wright Committee's efforts to replace the Canons of Professional Ethics, which had grown from 32 canons in 1908 to 47 canons in 1964. The Model Code was enacted by the ABA in 1969, and subsequently, most states adopted codes of professional responsibility based upon the Model Code. The distinctive feature of the Model Code is its organization into canons, ethical considerations, and disciplinary rules. The canons provided the Model Code with a theoretical structure. Each canon was a general directive to lawyers about the law of professional responsibility. The ethical considerations were more detailed in that they discussed actual fact situations that arose under each canon. Each ethical consideration, however, was only aspirational in nature. Lawyers were supposed to strive to follow the ethical considerations, but they were not considered binding. The disciplinary rules were the provisions that lawyers needed to follow to avoid disciplinary liability. These rules established minimum standards that lawyers were required to follow and standards that were enforced by the disciplinary committees. The ABA replaced the Model Code with the Model Rules of Professional Conduct in 1983. Ed.]

*TABLE OF CONTENTS**

---

* Prepared by Editor.

PREAMBLE AND PRELIMINARY STATEMENT

Preamble[1]

The continued existence of a free and democratic society depends upon recognition of the concept that justice is based upon the rule of law grounded in respect for the dignity of the individual and his capacity

[1] The footnotes are intended merely to enable the reader to relate the provisions of this Code to the ABA Canons of Professional Ethics adopted in 1908, as amended, the Opinions of the ABA Committee on Professional Ethics, and a limited number of other sources; they are not intended to be an annotation of the views taken by the ABA Special

through reason for enlightened self-government.[2] Law so grounded makes justice possible, for only through such law does the dignity of the individual attain respect and protection. Without it, individual rights become subject to unrestrained power, respect for law is destroyed, and rational self-government is impossible.

Lawyers as guardians of the law, play a vital role in the preservation of society. The fulfillment of this role requires an understanding by lawyers of their relationship with and function in our legal system.[3] A consequent obligation of lawyers is to maintain the highest standards of ethical conduct.

In fulfilling his professional responsibilities, a lawyer necessarily assumes various roles that require the performance of many difficult tasks. Not every situation which he may encounter can be foreseen,[4] but fundamental ethical principles are always present to guide him. Within the framework of these principles, a lawyer must with courage and foresight be able and ready to shape the body of the law to the ever-changing relationships of society.[5]

The Code of Professional Responsibility points the way to the aspiring and provides standards by which to judge the transgressor. Each lawyer must find within his own conscience the touchstone against which to test the extent to which his actions should rise above minimum standards. But in the last analysis it is the desire for the respect and confidence of the members of his profession and of the society which he serves that should provide to a lawyer the incentive for the highest possible degree of ethical conduct. The possible loss of that respect and confidence is the ultimate sanction. So long as its practitioners are guided by these principles, the law will continue to be a noble profession. This is its greatness and its strength, which permit of no compromise.

Preliminary Statement

In furtherance of the principles stated in the Preamble, the American Bar Association has promulgated this Code of Professional Responsibility, consisting of three separate but interrelated parts: Canons, Ethical Considerations, and Disciplinary Rules.[6] The Code is designed to be adopted by appropriate agencies both as an inspirational guide to the members of the profession and as a basis for disciplinary action when the conduct of a lawyer falls below the required minimum standards stated in the Disciplinary Rules.

Obviously the Canons, Ethical Considerations, and Disciplinary Rules cannot apply to non-lawyers; however, they do define the type of ethical conduct that the public has a right to expect not only of lawyers but also of their non-professional employees and associates in all matters pertaining to professional

---

Committee on Evaluation of Ethical Standards. Footnotes citing ABA Canons refer to the ABA Canons of Professional Ethics, adopted in 1908, as amended.

2 Cf. ABA Canons, Preamble.

3 "[T]he lawyer stands today in special need of a clear understanding of his obligations and of the vital connection between these obligations and the role his profession plays in society." *Professional Responsibility: Report of the Joint Conference,* 44 A.B.A.J. 1159, 1160 (1958).

4 "No general statement of the responsibilities of the legal profession can encompass all the situations in which the lawyer may be placed. Each position held by him makes its own peculiar demands. These demands the lawyer must clarify for himself in the light of the particular role in which he serves." *Professional Responsibility: Report of the Joint Conference,* 44 A.B.A.J. 1159, 1218 (1958).

5 "The law and its institutions change as social conditions change. They must change if they are to preserve, much less advance, the political and social values from which they derive their purposes and their life. This is true of the most important of legal institutions, the profession of law. The profession, too, must change when conditions change in order to preserve and advance the social values that are its reasons for being." Cheatham, *Availability of Legal Services: The Responsibility of the Individual Lawyer and the Organized Bar,* 12 U.C.L.A.L.Rev. 438, 440 (1965).

6 The Supreme Court of Wisconsin adopted a Code of Judicial Ethics in 1967. "The code is divided into standards and rules, the standards being statements of what the general desirable level of conduct should be, the rules being particular canons, the violation of which shall subject an individual judge to sanctions." In re Promulgation of a Code of Judicial Ethics, 36 Wis.2d 252, 255, 153 N.W.2d 873, 874 (1967).

The portion of the Wisconsin Code of Judicial Ethics entitled "Standards" states that "[t]he following standards set forth the significant qualities of the ideal judge. . . ." Id., 36 Wis.2d at 256, 153 N.W.2d at 875. The portion entitled "Rules" states that "[t]he court promulgates the following rules because the requirements of judicial conduct embodied therein are of sufficient gravity to warrant sanctions if they are not obeyed. . . ." Id., 36 Wis.2d at 259, 153 N.W.2d at 876.

employment. A lawyer should ultimately be responsible for the conduct of his employees and associates in the course of the professional representation of the client.

The Canons are statements of axiomatic norms, expressing in general terms the standards of professional conduct expected of lawyers in their relationships with the public, with the legal system, and with the legal profession. They embody the general concepts from which the Ethical Considerations and the Disciplinary Rules are derived.

The Ethical Considerations are aspirational in character and represent the objectives toward which every member of the profession should strive. They constitute a body of principles upon which the lawyer can rely for guidance in many specific situations.[7]

The Disciplinary Rules, unlike the Ethical Considerations, are mandatory in character. The Disciplinary Rules state the minimum level of conduct below which no lawyer can fall without being subject to disciplinary action. Within the framework of fair trial,[8] the Disciplinary Rules should be uniformly applied to all lawyers,[9] regardless of the nature of their professional activities.[10] The Code makes no attempt to prescribe either disciplinary procedures or penalties[11] for violation of a Disciplinary Rule,[12] nor does it undertake to define standards for civil liability of lawyers for professional conduct. The severity of judgment

---

[7] "Under the conditions of modern practice is it peculiarly necessary that the lawyer should understand, not merely the established standards of professional conduct, but the reasons underlying these standards. Today the lawyer plays a changing and increasingly varied role. In many developing fields the precise contribution of the legal profession is as yet undefined." *Professional Responsibility: Report of the Joint Conference,* 44 A.B.A.J. 1159 (1958).

"A true sense of professional responsibility must derive from an understanding of the reasons that lie back of specific restraints, such as those embodied in the Canons. The grounds for the lawyer's peculiar obligations are to be found in the nature of his calling. The lawyer who seeks a clear understanding of his duties will be led to reflect on the special services his profession renders to society and the services it might render if its full capacities were realized. When the lawyer fully understands the nature of his office, he will then discern what restraints are necessary to keep that office wholesome and effective." *Id.*

[8] "Disbarment, designed to protect the public, is a punishment or penalty imposed on the lawyer. * * * He is accordingly entitled to procedural due process, which includes fair notice of the charge." In re Ruffalo, 390 U.S. 544, 550, 20 L.Ed.2d 117, 122, 88 S.Ct. 1222, 1226 (1968), rehearing denied, 391 U.S. 961, 20 L.Ed.2d 874, 88 S.Ct. 1833 (1968).

"A State cannot exclude a person from the practice of law or from any other occupation in a manner or for reasons that contravene the Due Process or Equal Protection Clause of the Fourteenth Amendment. . . . A State can require high standards of qualification . . . but any qualification must have a rational connection with the applicant's fitness or capacity to practice law." Schware v. Bd. of Bar Examiners, 353 U.S. 232, 239, 1 L.Ed.2d 796, 801–02, 77 S.Ct. 752, 756 (1957).

"[A]n accused lawyer may expect that he will not be condemned out of a capricious self-righteousness or denied the essentials of a fair hearing." Kingsland v. Dorsey, 338 U.S. 318, 320, 94 L.Ed. 123, 126, 70 S.Ct. 123, 124–25 (1949).

"The attorney and counsellor being, by the solemn judicial act of the court, clothed with his office, does not hold it as a matter of grace and favor. The right which it confers upon him to appear for suitors, and to argue causes is something more than a mere indulgence, revocable at the pleasure of the court, or at the command of the legislature. It is a right of which he can only be deprived by the judgment of the court, for moral or professional delinquency." Ex parte Garland, 71 U.S. (4 Wall.) 333, 378–79, 18 L.Ed. 366, 370 (1866).

See generally Comment, *Procedural Due Process and Character Hearings for Bar Applicants,* 15 Stan.L.Rev. 500 (1963).

[9] "The canons of professional ethics must be enforced by the Courts and must be respected by members of the Bar if we are to maintain public confidence in the integrity and impartiality of the administration of justice." In re Meeker, 76 N.M. 354, 357, 414 P.2d 862, 864 (1966), appeal dismissed, 385 U.S. 449 (1967).

[10] See ABA Canon 45.

"The Canons of this Association govern all its members, irrespective of the nature of their practice, and the application of the Canons is not affected by statutes or regulations governing certain activities of lawyers which may prescribe less stringent standards." ABA Comm. on Professional Ethics, Opinions, No. 203 (1940) [hereinafter each Opinion is cited as "ABA Opinion"].

Cf. *ABA Opinion* 152 (1936).

[11] "There is generally no prescribed discipline for any particular type of improper conduct. The disciplinary measures taken are discretionary with the courts, which may disbar, suspend, or merely censure the attorney as the nature of the offense and past indicia of character may warrant." Note, 43 Cornell L.Q. 489, 495 (1958).

[12] The Code seeks only to specify conduct for which a lawyer should be disciplined. Recommendations as to the procedures to be used in disciplinary actions and the gravity of disciplinary measures appropriate for violations of the Code are within the jurisdiction of the American Bar Association Special Committee on Evaluation of Disciplinary Enforcement.

against one found guilty of violating a Disciplinary Rule should be determined by the character of the offense and the attendant circumstances.[13] An enforcing agency, in applying the Disciplinary Rules, may find interpretive guidance in the basic principles embodied in the Canons and in the objectives reflected in the Ethical Considerations.

CANON 1

A Lawyer Should Assist in Maintaining the Integrity and Competence of the Legal Profession

ETHICAL CONSIDERATIONS

EC 1–1 A basic tenet of the professional responsibility of lawyers is that every person in our society should have ready access to the independent professional services of a lawyer of integrity and competence. Maintaining the integrity and improving the competence of the bar to meet the highest standards is the ethical responsibility of every lawyer.

EC 1–2 The public should be protected from those who are not qualified to be lawyers by reason of a deficiency in education[1] or moral standards[2] or of other relevant factors[3] but who nevertheless seek to practice law. To assure the maintenance of high moral and educational standards of the legal profession,

---

[13] "The severity of the judgment of this court should be in proportion to the gravity of the offenses, the moral turpitude involved, and the extent that the defendant's acts and conduct affect his professional qualifications to practice law." Louisiana State Bar Ass'n v. Steiner, 204 La. 1073, 1092–93, 16 So.2d 843, 850 (1944) (Higgins, J., concurring in decree).

"Certainly an erring lawyer who has been disciplined and who having paid the penalty has given satisfactory evidence of repentance and has been rehabilitated and restored to his place at the bar by the court which knows him best ought not to have what amounts to an order of permanent disbarment entered against him by a federal court solely on the basis of an earlier criminal record and without regard to his subsequent rehabilitation and present good character. . . . We think, therefore, that the district court should reconsider the appellant's application for admission and grant it unless the court finds it to be a fact that the appellant is not presently of good moral or professional character." In re Dreier, 258 F.2d 68, 69–70 (3d Cir.1958).

[1] "[W]e cannot conclude that all educational restrictions [on bar admission] are unlawful. We assume that few would deny that a grammar school education requirement, before taking the bar examination, was reasonable. Or that an applicant had to be able to read or write. Once we conclude that *some* restriction is proper, then it becomes a matter of degree—the problem of drawing the line.

. . .

"We conclude the fundamental question here is whether Rule IV, Section 6 of the Rules Pertaining to Admission of Applicants to the State Bar of Arizona is 'arbitrary, capricious and unreasonable.' We conclude an educational requirement of graduation from an accredited law school is not." Hackin v. Lockwood, 361 F.2d 499, 503–04 (9th Cir.1966), cert. denied, 385 U.S. 960, 17 L.Ed.2d 305, 87 S.Ct. 396 (1966).

[2] "Every state in the United States, as a prerequisite for admission to the practice of law, requires that applicants possess 'good moral character.' Although the requirement is of judicial origin, it is now embodied in legislation in most states." Comment, *Procedural Due Process and Character Hearings for Bar Applicants,* 15 Stan.L.Rev. 500 (1963).

"Good character in the members of the bar is essential to the preservation of the integrity of the courts. The duty and power of the court to guard its portals against intrusion by men and women who are mentally and morally dishonest, unfit because of bad character, evidenced by their course of conduct, to participate in the administrative law, would seem to be unquestioned in the matter of preservation of judicial dignity and integrity." In re Monaghan, 126 Vt. 53, 222 A.2d 665, 670 (1966).

"Fundamentally, the question involved in both situations [i.e. admission and disciplinary proceedings] is the same—is the applicant for admission or the attorney sought to be disciplined a fit and proper person to be permitted to practice law, and that usually turns upon whether he has committed or is likely to continue to commit acts of moral turpitude. At the time of oral argument the attorney for respondent frankly conceded that the test for admission and for discipline is and should be the same. We agree with this concession." Hallinan v. Comm. of Bar Examiners, 65 Cal.2d 447, 453, 421 P.2d 76, 81, 55 Cal.Rptr. 228, 233 (1966).

[3] "Proceedings to gain admission to the bar are for the purpose of protecting the public and the courts from the ministrations of persons unfit to practice the profession. Attorneys are officers of the court appointed to assist the court in the administration of justice. Into their hands are committed the property, the liberty and sometimes the lives of their clients. This commitment demands a high degree of intelligence, knowledge of the law, respect for its function in society, sound and faithful judgment and, above all else, integrity of character in private and professional conduct." In re Monaghan, 126 Vt. 53, 222 A.2d 665, 676 (1966) (Holden, C.J., dissenting).

lawyers should affirmatively assist courts and other appropriate bodies in promulgating, enforcing, and improving requirements for admission to the bar.[4] In like manner, the bar has a positive obligation to aid in the continued improvement of all phases of pre-admission and post-admission legal education.

EC 1–3 Before recommending an applicant for admission, a lawyer should satisfy himself that the applicant is of good moral character. Although a lawyer should not become a self-appointed investigator or judge of applicants for admission, he should report to proper officials all unfavorable information he possesses relating to the character or other qualifications of an applicant.[5]

EC 1–4 The integrity of the profession can be maintained only if conduct of lawyers in violation of the Disciplinary Rules is brought to the attention of the proper officials. A lawyer should reveal voluntarily to those officials all unprivileged knowledge of conduct of lawyers which he believes clearly to be in violation of the Disciplinary Rules.[6] A lawyer should, upon request, serve on and assist committees and boards having responsibility for the administration of the Disciplinary Rules.[7]

EC 1–5 A lawyer should maintain high standards of professional conduct and should encourage fellow lawyers to do likewise. He should be temperate and dignified, and he should refrain from all illegal and morally reprehensible conduct.[8] Because of his position in society, even minor violations of law by a lawyer may tend to lessen public confidence in the legal profession. Obedience to law exemplifies respect for law. To lawyers especially, respect for the law should be more than a platitude.

EC 1–6 An applicant for admission to the bar or a lawyer may be unqualified, temporarily or permanently, for other than moral and educational reasons, such as mental or emotional instability. Lawyers should be diligent in taking steps to see that during a period of disqualification such person is not granted a license or, if licensed, is not permitted to practice.[9] In like manner, when the disqualification has terminated, members of the bar should assist such person in being licensed, or, if licensed, in being restored to his full right to practice.

---

[4] "A bar composed of lawyers of good moral character is a worthy objective but it is unnecessary to sacrifice vital freedoms in order to obtain that goal. It is also important both to society and the bar itself that lawyers be unintimidated—free to think, speak, and act as members of an Independent Bar." Konigsberg v. State Bar, 353 U.S. 252, 273, 1 L.Ed.2d 810, 825, 77 S.Ct. 722, 733 (1957).

[5] *See* ABA Canon 29.

[6] ABA Canon 28 designates certain conduct as unprofessional and then states that: "A duty to the public and to the profession devolves upon every member of the Bar having knowledge of such practices upon the part of any practitioner immediately to inform thereof, to the end that the offender may be disbarred." ABA Canon 29 states a broader admonition: "Lawyers should expose without fear or favor before the proper tribunals corrupt or dishonest conduct in the profession."

[7] "It is the obligation of the organized Bar and the individual lawyer to give unstinted cooperation and assistance to the highest court of the state in discharging its function and duty with respect to discipline and in purging the profession of the unworthy." *Report of the Special Committee on Disciplinary Procedures,* 80 A.B.A.Rep. 463, 470 (1955).

[8] Cf. ABA Canon 32.

[9] "We decline, on the present record, to disbar Mr. Sherman or to reprimand him—not because we condone his actions, but because, as heretofore indicated, we are concerned with whether he is mentally responsible for what he has done.

. . .

"The logic of the situation would seem to dictate the conclusion that, if he was mentally responsible for the conduct we have outlined, he should be disbarred; and, if he was not mentally responsible, he should not be permitted to practice law.

"However, the flaw in the logic is that he may have been mentally irresponsible [at the time of his offensive conduct] . . . , and, yet, have sufficiently improved in the almost two and one-half years intervening to be able to capably and competently represent his clients. . . .

. . .

"We would make clear that we are satisfied that a case has been made against Mr. Sherman, warranting a refusal to permit him to further practice law in this state unless he can establish his mental irresponsibility at the time of the offenses charged. The burden of proof is upon him.

"If he establishes such mental irresponsibility, the burden is then upon him to establish his present capability to practice law." In re Sherman, 58 Wash.2d 1, 6–7, 354 P.2d 888, 890 (1960), cert. denied, 371 U.S. 951, 9 L.Ed.2d 499, 83 S.Ct. 506 (1963).

DISCIPLINARY RULES

DR 1-101 Maintaining Integrity and Competence of the Legal Profession.

(A) A lawyer is subject to discipline if he has made a materially false statement in, or if he has deliberately failed to disclose a material fact requested in connection with, his application for admission to the bar.[10]

(B) A lawyer shall not further the application for admission to the bar of another person known by him to be unqualified in respect to character, education, or other relevant attribute.[11]

DR 1-102 Misconduct.

(A) A lawyer shall not:

(1) Violate a Disciplinary Rule.

(2) Circumvent a Disciplinary Rule through actions of another.[12]

(3) Engage in illegal conduct involving moral turpitude.[13]

---

[10] "This Court has the inherent power to revoke a license to practice law in this State, where such license was issued by this Court, and its issuance was procured by the fraudulent concealment, or by the false and fraudulent representation by the applicant of a fact which was manifestly material to the issuance of the license." North Carolina ex rel. Attorney General v. Gorson, 209 N.C. 320, 326, 183 S.E. 392, 395 (1936), cert. denied, 298 U.S. 662, 80 L.Ed. 1387, 56 S.Ct. 752 (1936).

See also Application of Patterson, 318 P.2d 907, 913 (Or.1957), cert. denied, 356 U.S. 947, 2 L.Ed.2d 822, 78 S.Ct. 795 (1958).

[11] See ABA Canon 29.

[12] In *ABA Opinion* 95 (1933), which held that a municipal attorney could not permit police officers to interview persons with claims against the municipality when the attorney knew the claimants to be represented by counsel, the Committee on Professional Ethics said:

"The law officer is, of course, responsible for the acts of those in his department who are under his supervision and control." *Opinion 85.* In re Robinson, 136 N.Y.S. 548 (affirmed 209 N.Y. 354–1912) held that it was a matter of disbarment for an attorney to adopt a general course of approving the unethical conduct of employees of his client, even though he did not actively participate therein.

"'. . . The attorney should not advise or sanction acts by his client which he himself should not do.' *Opinion 75.*"

[13] "The most obvious non-professional ground for disbarment is conviction for a felony. Most states make conviction for a felony grounds for automatic disbarment. Some of these states, including New York, make disbarment mandatory upon conviction for *any* felony, while others require disbarment only for those felonies which involve moral turpitude. There are strong arguments that some felonies, such as involuntary manslaughter, reflect neither on an attorney's fitness, trustworthiness, nor competence and, therefore, should not be grounds for disbarment, but most states tend to disregard these arguments and, following the common law rule, make disbarment mandatory on conviction for any felony." Note, 43 Cornell L.Q. 489, 490 (1958).

"Some states treat conviction for misdemeanors as grounds for automatic disbarment. . . . However, the vast majority, accepting the common law rule, require that the misdemeanor involve moral turpitude. While the definition of moral turpitude may prove difficult, it seems only proper that those minor offenses which do not affect the attorney's fitness to continue in the profession should not be grounds for disbarment. A good example is an assault and battery conviction which would not involve moral turpitude unless done with malice and deliberation." Id. at 491.

"The term 'moral turpitude' has been used in the law for centuries. It has been the subject of many decisions by the courts but has never been clearly defined because of the nature of the term. Perhaps the best general definition of the term 'moral turpitude' is that it imports an act of baseness, vileness or depravity in the duties which one person owes to another or to society in general, which is contrary to the usual, accepted and customary rule of right and duty which a person should follow. 58 C.J.S. at page 1201. Although offenses against revenue laws have been held to be crimes of moral turpitude, it has also been held that the attempt to evade the payment of taxes due to the government or any subdivision thereof, while wrong and unlawful, does not involve moral turpitude. 58 C.J.S. at page 1205." Comm. on Legal Ethics v. Scheer, 149 W.Va. 721, 726–27, 143 S.E.2d 141, 145 (1965).

"The right and power to discipline an attorney, as one of its officers, is inherent in the court. . . . This power is not limited to those instances of misconduct wherein he has been employed, or has acted, in a professional capacity; but, on the contrary, this power may be exercised where his misconduct outside the scope of his professional relations shows him to be an unfit person to practice law." In re Wilson, 391 S.W.2d 914, 917–18 (Mo.1965).

(4) Engage in conduct involving dishonesty, fraud, deceit, or misrepresentation.

(5) Engage in conduct that is prejudicial to the administration of justice.

(6) Engage in any other conduct that adversely reflects on his fitness to practice law.[14]

DR 1–103 Disclosure of Information to Authorities.

(A) A lawyer possessing unprivileged knowledge of a violation of DR 1–102 shall report such knowledge to a tribunal or other authority empowered to investigate or act upon such violation.[15]

(B) A lawyer possessing unprivileged knowledge or evidence concerning another lawyer or a judge shall reveal fully such knowledge or evidence upon proper request of a tribunal or other authority empowered to investigate or act upon the conduct of lawyers or judges.[16]

CANON 2

A Lawyer Should Assist the Legal Profession in Fulfilling Its Duty to Make Legal Counsel Available

Ethical Considerations

EC 2–1 The need of members of the public for legal services[1] is met only if they recognize their legal problems, appreciate the importance of seeking assistance,[2] and are able to obtain the services of acceptable legal counsel.[3] Hence, important functions of the legal profession are to educate laymen to recognize their

---

[14] "It is a fair characterization of the lawyer's responsibility in our society that he stands 'as a shield,' to quote Devlin, J., in defense of right and to ward off wrong. From a profession charged with these responsibilities there must be exacted those qualities of truth-speaking, of a high sense of honor, of granite discretion, of the strictest observance of fiduciary responsibility, that have, throughout the centuries, been compendiously described as 'moral character.' " Schware v. Bd. of Bar Examiners, 353 U.S. 232, 247 L.Ed.2d 796, 806, 77 S.Ct. 752, 761 (1957) (Frankfurter, J., concurring).

"Particularly applicable here is Rule 4.47 providing that 'A lawyer should always maintain his integrity; and shall not willfully commit any act against the interest of the public; nor shall he violate his duty to the courts or his clients; *nor shall he, by any misconduct, commit any offense against the laws of Missouri or the United States of America, which amounts to a crime involving acts done by him contrary to justice, honesty, modesty or good morals;* nor shall he be guilty of any other misconduct whereby, for the protection of the public and those charged with the administration of justice, he should no longer be entrusted with the duties and responsibilities belonging to the office of an attorney.' " In re Wilson, 391 S.W.2d 914, 917 (Mo.1965).

[15] See ABA Canon 29; cf. ABA Canon 28.

[16] Cf. ABA Canons 28 and 29.

[1] "Men have need for more than a system of law; they have need for a system of law which functions, and that means they have need for lawyers." Cheatham, *The Lawyer's Role and Surroundings,* 25 Rocky Mt.L.Rev. 405 (1953).

[2] "Law is not self-applying; men must apply and utilize it in concrete cases. But the ordinary man is incapable. He cannot know the principles of law or the rules guiding the machinery of law administration; he does not know how to formulate his desires with precision and to put them into writing; he is ineffective in the presentation of his claims." Cheatham, *The Lawyer's Role and Surroundings,* 25 Rocky Mt.L.Rev. 405 (1953).

[3] "This need [to provide legal services] was recognized by . . . Mr. [Lewis F.] Powell [Jr., President, American Bar Association, 1963–64], who said: 'Looking at contemporary America realistically, we must admit that despite all our efforts to date (and these have not been insignificant), far too many persons are not able to obtain equal justice under law. This usually results because their poverty or their ignorance has prevented them from obtaining legal counsel.' " Address by E. Clinton Bamberger, Association of American Law Schools 1965 Annual Meeting, Dec. 28, 1965, in Proceedings, Part II, 1965, 61, 63–64 (1965).

"A wide gap separates the need for legal services and its satisfaction, as numerous studies reveal. Looked at from the side of the layman, one reason for the gap is poverty and the consequent inability to pay legal fees. Another set of reasons is ignorance of the need for and the value of legal services, and ignorance of where to find a dependable lawyer. There is fear of the mysterious processes and delays of the law, and there is fear of overreaching and overcharging by lawyers, a fear stimulated by the occasional exposure of shysters." Cheatham, *Availability of Legal Services: The Responsibility of the Individual Lawyer and of the Organized Bar,* 12 U.C.L.A.L.Rev. 438 (1965).

problems, to facilitate the process of intelligent selection of lawyers, and to assist in making legal services fully available.[4]

Recognition of Legal Problems

EC 2–2 The legal profession should assist lay-persons to recognize legal problems because such problems may not be self-revealing and often are not timely noticed. Therefore, lawyers should encourage and participate in educational and public relations programs concerning our legal system with particular reference to legal problems that frequently arise. Preparation of advertisements and professional articles for lay publications[5] and participation in seminars, lectures, and civic programs should be motivated by a desire to educate the public to an awareness of legal needs and to provide information relevant to the selection of the most appropriate counsel rather than to obtain publicity for particular lawyers. The problems of advertising on television require special consideration, due to the style, cost, and transitory nature of such media. If the interests of laypersons in receiving relevant lawyer advertising are not adequately served by print media and radio advertising, and if adequate safeguards to protect the public can reasonably be formulated, television advertising may serve a public interest.

As amended in 1977.

EC 2–3 Whether a lawyer acts properly in volunteering in-person advice to a layperson to seek legal services depends upon the circumstances.[6] The giving of advice that one should take legal action could well be in fulfillment of the duty of the legal profession to assist laypersons in recognizing legal problems.[7] The advice is proper only if motivated by a desire to protect one who does not recognize that he may have legal problems or who is ignorant of his legal rights or obligations. It is improper if motivated by a desire to obtain personal benefit, secure personal publicity, or cause legal action to be taken merely to harass or injure another. A lawyer should not initiate an in-person contact with a non-client, personally or through a representative, for the purpose of being retained to represent him for compensation.

As amended in 1977.

EC 2–4 Since motivation is subjective and often difficult to judge, the motives of a lawyer who volunteers in-person advice likely to produce legal controversy may well be suspect if he receives professional employment or other benefits as a result.[8] A lawyer who volunteers in-person advice that one should obtain

---

4 "It is not only the right but the duty of the profession as a whole to utilize such methods as may be developed to bring the services of its members to those who need them, so long as this can be done ethically and with dignity." *ABA Opinion* 320 (1968).

"[T]here is a responsibility on the bar to make legal services available to those who need them. The maxim, 'privilege brings responsibilities,' can be expanded to read, exclusive privilege to render public service brings responsibility to assure that the service is available to those in need of it." Cheatham, *Availability of Legal Services: The Responsibility of the Individual Lawyer and of the Organized Bar,* 12 U.C.L.A.L.Rev. 438, 443 (1965).

"The obligation to provide legal services for those actually caught up in litigation carries with it the obligation to make preventive legal advice accessible to all. It is among those unaccustomed to business affairs and fearful of the ways of the law that such advice is often most needed. If it is not received in time, the most valiant and skillful representation in court may come too late." *Professional Responsibility: Report of the Joint Conference,* 44 A.B.A.J. 1159, 1216 (1958).

5 "A lawyer may with propriety write articles for publications in which he gives information upon the law. . . ." A.B.A. Canon 40.

6 See ABA Canon 28.

7 This question can assume constitutional dimensions: "We meet at the outset the contention that "solicitation" is wholly outside the area of freedoms protected by the First Amendment. To this contention there are two answers. The first is that a State cannot foreclose the exercise of constitutional rights by mere labels. The second is that abstract discussion is not the only species of communication which the Constitution protects; the First Amendment also protects vigorous advocacy, certainly of lawful ends, against governmental intrusion. . . .

. . .

"However valid may be Virginia's interest in regulating the traditionally illegal practice of barratry, maintenance and champerty, that interest does not justify the prohibition of the NAACP activities disclosed by this record. Malicious intent was of the essence of the common-law offenses of fomenting or stirring up litigation. And whatever may be or may have been true of suits against governments in other countries, the exercise in our own, as in this case of First Amendment rights to enforce Constitutional rights through litigation, as a matter of law, cannot be deemed malicious." NAACP v. Button, 371 U.S. 415, 429, 439–40, 9 L.Ed.2d 405, 415–16, 422, 83 S.Ct. 328, 336, 341 (1963).

8 "It is disreputable for an attorney to breed litigation by seeking out those who have claims for personal injuries or other grounds of action in order to secure them as clients, or to employ agents or runners, or to reward those who bring

the services of a lawyer generally should not himself accept employment, compensation, or other benefit in connection with that matter. However, it is not improper for a lawyer to volunteer such advice and render resulting legal services to close friends, relatives, former clients (in regard to matters germane to former employment), and regular clients.[9]

As amended in 1977.

EC 2–5 A lawyer who writes or speaks for the purpose of educating members of the public to recognize their legal problems should carefully refrain from giving or appearing to give a general solution applicable to all apparently similar individual problems,[10] since slight changes in fact situations may require a material variance in the applicable advice; otherwise, the public may be mislead and misadvised. Talks and writings by lawyers for laypersons should caution them not to attempt to solve individual problems upon the basis of the information contained therein.[11]

As amended in 1977.

Selection of a Lawyer

EC 2–6 Formerly a potential client usually knew the reputations of local lawyers for competency and integrity and therefore could select a practitioner in whom he had confidence. This traditional selection process worked well because it was initiated by the client and the choice was an informed one.

EC 2–7 Changed conditions, however, have seriously restricted the effectiveness of the traditional selection process. Often the reputations of lawyers are not sufficiently known to enable laypersons to make intelligent choices.[12] The law has become increasingly complex and specialized. Few lawyers are willing and competent to deal with every kind of legal matter, and many laypersons have difficulty in determining the competence of lawyers to render different types of legal services. The selection of legal counsel is particularly difficult for transients, persons moving into new areas, persons of limited education or means, and others who have little or no contact with lawyers.[13] Lack of information about the availability of lawyers, the qualifications of particular lawyers, and the expense of legal representation leads laypersons to avoid seeking legal advice.

As amended in 1977.

EC 2–8 Selection of a lawyer by a layperson should be made on an informed basis. Advice and recommendation of third parties—relatives, friends, acquaintances, business associates, or other lawyers—and disclosure of relevant information about the lawyer and his practice may be helpful. A layperson is best served if the recommendation is disinterested and informed. In order that the recommendation be

---

or influence the bringing of business to his office. . . . Moreover, it tends quite easily to the institution of baseless litigation and the manufacture of perjured testimony. From early times, this danger has been recognized in the law by the condemnation of the crime of common barratry, or the stirring up of suits or quarrels between individuals at law or otherwise." In re Ades, 6 F.Supp. 467, 474–75 (D.Mary.1934).

[9] "*Rule 2.*

"§ a. . . .

"[A] member of the State Bar shall not solicit professional employment by

"(1) Volunteering counsel or advice except where ties of blood relationship or trust make it appropriate." Cal.Business and Professions Code § 6076 (West 1962).

[10] "*Rule 18* . . . A member of the State Bar shall not advise inquirers or render opinions to them through or in connection with a newspaper, radio or other publicity medium of any kind in respect to their specific legal problems, whether or not such attorney shall be compensated for his services." Cal.Business and Professions Code § 6076 (West 1962).

[11] "In any case where a member might well apply the advice given in the opinion to his individual affairs, the lawyer rendering the opinion [concerning problems common to members of an association and distributed to the members through a periodic bulletin] should specifically state that this opinion should not be relied on by any member as a basis for handling his individual affairs, but that in every case he should consult his counsel. In the publication of the opinion the association should make a similar statement." *ABA Opinion* 273 (1946).

[12] "A group of recent interrelated changes bears directly on the availability of legal services. . . . [One] change is the constantly accelerating urbanization of the country and the decline of personal and neighborhood knowledge of whom to retain as a professional man." Cheatham, *Availability of Legal Services: The Responsibility of the Individual Lawyer and of the Organized Bar,* 12 U.C.L.A.L.Rev. 438, 440 (1965).

[13] Cf. Cheatham, *A Lawyer When Needed: Legal Services for the Middle Classes,* 63 Colum.L.Rev. 973, 974 (1963).

disinterested, a lawyer should not seek to influence another to recommend his employment. A lawyer should not compensate another person for recommending him, for influencing a prospective client to employ him, or to encourage future recommendations.[14] Advertisements and public communications, whether in law lists, telephone directories, newspapers, other forms of print media, television or radio, should be formulated to convey only information that is necessary to make an appropriate selection. Such information includes: (1) office information, such as, name, including name of law firm and names of professional associates; addresses; telephone numbers; credit card acceptability; fluency in foreign languages; and office hours; (2) relevant biographical information; (3) description of the practice, but only by using designations and definitions authorized by [the agency having jurisdiction of the subject under state law], for example, one or more fields of law in which the lawyer or law firm practices; a statement that practice is limited to one or more fields of law; and/or a statement that the lawyer or law firm specializes in a particular field of law practice, but only by using designations, definitions and standards authorized by [the agency having jurisdiction of the subject under state law]; and (4) permitted fee information. Self-laudation should be avoided.

As amended in 1978.

Selection of a Lawyer: Lawyer Advertising

EC 2–9 The lack of sophistication on the part of many members of the public concerning legal services, the importance of the interests affected by the choice of a lawyer and prior experience with unrestricted lawyer advertising, require that special care be taken by lawyers to avoid misleading the public and to assure that the information set forth in any advertising is relevant to the selection of a lawyer. The lawyer must be mindful that the benefits of lawyer advertising depend upon its reliability and accuracy. Examples of information in lawyer advertising that would be deceptive include misstatements of fact, suggestions that the ingenuity or prior record of a lawyer rather than the justice of the claim are the principal factors likely to determine the result, inclusion of information irrelevant to selecting a lawyer, and representations concerning the quality of service, which cannot be measured or verified. Since lawyer advertising is calculated and not spontaneous, reasonable regulation of lawyer advertising designed to foster compliance with appropriate standards serves the public interest without impeding the flow of useful, meaningful, and relevant information to the public.

As amended in 1977.

EC 2–10 A lawyer should ensure that the information contained in any advertising which the lawyer publishes, broadcasts or causes to be published or broadcast is relevant, is disseminated in an objective and understandable fashion, and would facilitate the prospective client's ability to compare the qualifications of the lawyers available to represent him. A lawyer should strive to communicate such information without undue emphasis upon style and advertising stratagems which serve to hinder rather than to facilitate intelligent selection of counsel. Because technological change is a recurrent feature of communications forms, and because perceptions of what is relevant in lawyer selection may change, lawyer advertising regulations should not be cast in rigid, unchangeable terms. Machinery is therefore available to advertisers and consumers for prompt consideration of proposals to change the rules governing lawyer advertising. The determination of any request for such change should depend upon whether the proposal is necessary in light of existing Code provisions, whether the proposal accords with standards of accuracy, reliability and truthfulness, and whether the proposal would facilitate informed selection of lawyers by potential consumers of legal services. Representatives of lawyers and consumers should be heard in addition to the applicant concerning any proposed change. Any change which is approved should be promulgated in the form of an amendment to the Code so that all lawyers practicing in the jurisdiction may avail themselves of its provisions.

As amended in 1977.

EC 2–11 The name under which a lawyer conducts his practice may be a factor in the selection process.[16] The use of a trade name or an assumed name could mislead laypersons concerning the identity, responsibility, and status of those practicing thereunder.[17] Accordingly, a lawyer in private practice should

[14] See ABA Canon 28.

[16] *Cf. ABA Opinion* 303 (1961).

[17] *See* ABA Canon 33.

practice only under a designation containing his own name, the name of a lawyer employing him, the name of one or more of the lawyers practicing in a partnership, or, if permitted by law, the name of a professional legal corporation, which should be clearly designated as such. For many years some law firms have used a firm name retaining one or more names of deceased or retired partners and such practice is not improper if the firm is a bona fide successor of a firm in which the deceased or retired person was a member, if the use of the name is authorized by law or by contract, and if the public is not misled thereby.[18] However, the name of a partner who withdraws from a firm but continues to practice law should be omitted from the firm name in order to avoid misleading the public.

As amended in 1977.

EC 2–12 A lawyer occupying a judicial, legislative, or public executive or administrative position who has the right to practice law concurrently may allow his name to remain in the name of the firm if he actively continues to practice law as a member thereof. Otherwise, his name should be removed from the firm name,[19] and he should not be identified as a past or present member of the firm; and he should not hold himself out as being a practicing lawyer.

EC 2–13 In order to avoid the possibility of misleading persons with whom he deals, a lawyer should be scrupulous in the representation of his professional status.[20] He should not hold himself out as being a partner or associate of a law firm if he is not one in fact,[21] and thus should not hold himself out as partner or associate if he only shares offices with another lawyer.[22]

EC 2–14 In some instances a lawyer confines his practice to a particular field of law.[23] In the absence of state controls to insure the existence of special competence, a lawyer should not be permitted to hold himself out as a specialist or as having official recognition as a specialist, other than in the fields of admiralty, trademark, and patent law where a holding out as a specialist historically has been permitted. A lawyer may, however, indicate in permitted advertising, if it is factual, a limitation of his practice or one or more particular areas or fields of law in which he practices using designations and definitions authorized for that purpose by [the state agency having jurisdiction]. A lawyer practicing in a jurisdiction which certifies specialists must also be careful not to confuse laypersons as to his status. If a lawyer discloses areas of law

---

18 Id.

"The continued use of a firm name by one or more surviving partners after the death of a member of the firm whose name is in the firm title is expressly permitted by the Canons of Ethics. The reason for this is that all of the partners have by their joint and several efforts over a period of years contributed to the good will attached to the firm name. In the case of a firm having widespread connections, this good will is disturbed by a change in firm name every time a name partner dies, and that reflects a loss in some degree of the good will to the building up of which the surviving partners have contributed their time, skill and labor through a period of years. To avoid this loss the firm name is continued, and to meet the requirements of the Canon the individuals constituting the firm from time to time are listed." *ABA Opinion* 267 (1945).

"Accepted local custom in New York recognizes that the name of a law firm does not necessarily identify the individual members of the firm, and hence the continued use of a firm name after the death of one or more partners is not a deception and is permissible. . . . The continued use of a deceased partner's name in the firm title is not affected by the fact that another partner withdraws from the firm and his name is dropped, or the name of the new partner is added to the firm name." *Opinion* No. 45, Committee on Professional Ethics, New York State Bar Ass'n, 39 N.Y.St.B.J. 455 (1967).

19 Cf. ABA Canon 33 and *ABA Opinion* 315 (1965).

20 Cf. *ABA Opinions* 283 (1950) and 81 (1932).

21 See *ABA Opinion* 316 (1967).

22 "The word 'associates' has a variety of meanings. Principally through custom the word when used on the letterheads of law firms has come to be regarded as describing those who are employees of the firm. Because the word has acquired this special significance in connection with the practice of the law the use of the word to describe lawyer relationships other than employer-employee is likely to be misleading." In re Sussman and Tanner, 241 Ore. 246, 248, 405 P.2d 355, 356 (1965).

According to *ABA Opinion* 310 (1963), use of the term "associates" would be misleading in two situations: (1) where two lawyers are partners and they share both responsibility and liability for the partnership; and (2) where two lawyers practice separately, sharing no responsibility or liability, and only share a suite of offices and some costs.

23 "For a long time, many lawyers have, of necessity, limited their practice to certain branches of law. The increasing complexity of the law and the demand of the public for more expertness on the part of the lawyer has, in the past few years—particularly in the last ten years—brought about specialization on an increasing scale." *Report of the Special Committee on Specialization and Specialized Legal Services,* 79 A.B.A.Rep. 582, 584 (1954).

in which he practices or to which he limits his practice, but is not certified in [the jurisdiction], he, and the designation authorized in [the jurisdiction], should avoid any implication that he is in fact certified.

As amended in 1977.

EC 2–15 The legal profession has developed lawyer referral systems designed to aid individuals who are able to pay fees but need assistance in locating lawyers competent to handle their particular problems. Use of a lawyer referral system enables a layman to avoid an uninformed selection of a lawyer because such a system makes possible the employment of competent lawyers who have indicated an interest in the subject matter involved. Lawyers should support the principle of lawyer referral systems and should encourage the evolution of other ethical plans which aid in the selection of qualified counsel.

Financial Ability to Employ Counsel: Generally

EC 2–16 The legal profession cannot remain a viable force in fulfilling its role in our society unless its members receive adequate compensation for services rendered, and reasonable fees[24] should be charged in appropriate cases to clients able to pay them. Nevertheless, persons unable to pay all or a portion of a reasonable fee should be able to obtain necessary legal services,[25] and lawyers should support and participate in ethical activities designed to achieve that objective.[26]

Financial Ability to Employ Counsel: Persons Able to Pay Reasonable Fees

EC 2–17 The determination of a proper fee requires consideration of the interests of both client and lawyer.[27] A lawyer should not charge more than a reasonable fee,[28] for excessive cost of legal service would deter laymen from utilizing the legal system in protection of their rights. Furthermore, an excessive charge abuses the professional relationship between lawyer and client. On the other hand, adequate compensation is necessary in order to enable the lawyer to serve his client effectively and to preserve the integrity and independence of the profession.[29]

EC 2–18 The determination of the reasonableness of a fee requires consideration of all relevant circumstances,[30] including those stated in the Disciplinary Rules. The fees of a lawyer will vary according to many factors, including the time required, his experience, ability, and reputation, the nature of the employment, the responsibility involved, and the results obtained. It is a commendable and long-standing tradition of the bar that special consideration is given in the fixing of any fee for services rendered a brother lawyer or a member of his immediate family.

As amended in 1974.

EC 2–19 As soon as feasible after a lawyer has been employed, it is desirable that he reach a clear agreement with his client as to the basis of the fee charges to be made. Such a course will not only prevent later misunderstanding but will also work for good relations between the lawyer and the client. It is usually beneficial to reduce to writing the understanding of the parties regarding the fee, particularly when it is contingent. A lawyer should be mindful that many persons who desire to employ him may have had little or no experience with fee charges of lawyers, and for this reason he should explain fully to such persons the reasons for the particular fee arrangement he proposes.

---

[24] See ABA Canon 12.

[25] Cf. ABA Canon 12.

[26] "If there is any fundamental proposition of government on which all would agree, it is that one of the highest goals of society must be to achieve and maintain equality before the law. Yet this ideal remains an empty form of words unless the legal profession is ready to provide adequate representation for those unable to pay the usual fees." *Professional Representation: Report of the Joint Conference,* 44 A.B.A.J. 1159, 1216 (1958).

[27] See ABA Canon 12.

[28] Cf. ABA Canon 12.

[29] "When members of the Bar are induced to render legal services for inadequate compensation as a consequence the quality of the service rendered may be lowered, the welfare of the profession injured and the administration of justice made less efficient." *ABA Opinion* 302 (1961).

[30] See ABA Canon 12.

EC 2–20 Contingent fee arrangements[31] in civil cases have long been commonly accepted in the United States in proceedings to enforce claims. The historical bases of their acceptance are that (1) they often, and in a variety of circumstances, provide the only practical means by which one having a claim against another can economically afford, finance, and obtain the services of a competent lawyer to prosecute his claim, and (2) a successful prosecution of the claim produces a *res* out of which the fee can be paid.[32] Although a lawyer generally should decline to accept employment on a contingent fee basis by one who is able to pay a reasonable fixed fee, it is not necessarily improper for a lawyer, where justified by the particular circumstances of a case, to enter into a contingent fee contract in a civil case with any client who, after being fully informed of all relevant factors, desires that arrangement. Because of the human relationships involved and the unique character of the proceedings, contingent fee arrangements in domestic relation cases are rarely justified. In administrative agency proceedings contingent fee contracts should be governed by the same consideration as in other civil cases. Public policy properly condemns contingent fee arrangements in criminal cases, largely on the ground that legal services in criminal cases do not produce a *res* with which to pay the fee.

EC 2–21 A lawyer should not accept compensation or any thing of value incident to his employment or services from one other than his client without the knowledge and consent of his client after full disclosure.[33]

EC 2–22 Without the consent of his client, a lawyer should not associate in a particular matter another lawyer outside his firm. A fee may properly be divided between lawyers[34] properly associated if the division is in proportion to the services performed and the responsibility assumed by each lawyer[35] and if the total fee is reasonable.

EC 2–23 A lawyer should be zealous in his efforts to avoid controversies over fees with clients[36] and should attempt to resolve amicably any differences on the subject.[37] He should not sue a client for a fee unless necessary to prevent fraud or gross imposition by the client.[38]

---

[31] See ABA Canon 13; see also MacKinnon, Contingent Fees for Legal Services (1964) (A report of the American Bar Foundation).

"A contract for a reasonable contingent fee where sanctioned by law is permitted by *Canon 13,* but the client must remain responsible to the lawyer for expenses advanced by the latter. 'There is to be no barter of the privilege of prosecuting a cause for gain in exchange for the promise of the attorney to prosecute at his own expense.' (Cardozo, C.J. In Matter of Gilman, 251 N.Y. 265, 270–271.)" *ABA Opinion* 246 (1942).

[32] See Comment, Providing Legal Services for the Middle Class in Civil Matters: The Problem, the Duty and a Solution, 26 U.Pitt.L.Rev. 811, 829 (1965).

[33] See ABA Canon 38.

"Of course, as . . . [Informal Opinion 679] points out, there must be full disclosure of the arrangement [that an entity other than the client pays the attorney's fee] by the attorney to the client. . . ." ABA Opinion 320 (1968).

[34] "Only lawyers may share in . . . a division of fees, but . . . it is not necessary that both lawyers be admitted to practice in the same state, so long as the division was based on the division of services or responsibility." ABA Opinion 316 (1967).

[35] See ABA Canon 34.

"We adhere to our previous rulings that where a lawyer merely brings about the employment of another lawyer but renders no service and assumes no responsibility in the matter, a division of the latter's fee is improper. (Opinions 18 and 153).

"It is assumed that the bar, generally, understands what acts or conduct of a lawyer may constitute 'services' to a client within the intendment of Canon 12. Such acts or conduct invariably, if not always involve 'responsibility' on the part of the lawyer, whether the word 'responsibility' be construed to denote the possible resultant legal or moral liability on the part of the lawyer to the client or to others, or the onus of deciding what should or should not be done in behalf of the client. The word 'services' in Canon 12 must be construed in this broad sense and may apply to the selection and retainer of associate counsel as well as to others acts or conduct in the client's behalf." ABA Opinion 204 (1940).

[36] See ABA Canon 14.

[37] Cf. ABA Opinion 320 (1968).

[38] See ABA Canon 14.

"Ours is a learned profession, not a mere money-getting trade. . . . Suits to collect fees should be avoided. Only where the circumstances imperatively require, should resort be had to a suit to compel payment. And where a lawyer does resort to a suit to enforce payment of fees which involves a disclosure, he should carefully avoid any disclosure not clearly necessary to obtaining or defending his rights." ABA Opinion 250 (1943).

But cf. ABA Opinion 320 (1968).

Financial Ability to Employ Counsel: Persons Unable to Pay Reasonable Fees

EC 2–24 A layman whose financial ability is not sufficient to permit payment of any fee cannot obtain legal services, other than in cases where a contingent fee is appropriate, unless the services are provided for him. Even a person of moderate means may be unable to pay a reasonable fee which is large because of the complexity, novelty, or difficulty of the problem or similar factors.[39]

EC 2–25 Historically, the need for legal services of those unable to pay reasonable fees has been met in part by lawyers who donated their services or accepted court appointments on behalf of such individuals. The basic responsibility for providing legal services for those unable to pay ultimately rests upon the individual lawyer, and personal involvement in the problems of the disadvantaged can be one of the most rewarding experiences in the life of a lawyer. Every lawyer, regardless of professional prominence or professional workload, should find time to participate in serving the disadvantaged. The rendition of free legal services to those unable to pay reasonable fees continues to be an obligation of each lawyer, but the efforts of individual lawyers are often not enough to meet the need.[40] Thus it has been necessary for the profession to institute additional programs to provide legal services.[41] Accordingly, legal aid offices,[42] lawyer referral services, and other related programs have been developed, and others will be developed, by the profession.[43] Every lawyer should support all proper efforts to meet this need for legal services.[44]

---

[39] "As a society increases in size, sophistication and technology, the body of laws which is required to control that society also increases in size, scope and complexity. With this growth, the law directly affects more and more facets of individual behavior, creating an expanding need for legal services on the part of the individual members of the society. . . . As legal guidance in social and commercial behavior increasingly becomes necessary, there will come a concurrent demand from the layman that such guidance be made available to him. This demand will not come from those who are able to employ the best legal talent, nor from those who can obtain legal assistance at little or no cost. It will come from the large 'forgotten middle income class,' who can neither afford to pay proportionately large fees nor qualify for ultra-low-cost services. The legal profession must recognize this inevitable demand and consider methods whereby it can be satisfied. If the profession fails to provide such methods, the laity will." Comment, *Providing Legal Services for the Middle Class in Civil Matters: The Problem, the Duty and a Solution,* 26 U.Pitt.L.Rev. 811, 811–12 (1965).

"The issue is not whether we shall do something or do nothing. The demand for ordinary everyday legal justice is so great and the moral nature of the demand is so strong that the issue has become whether we devise, maintain, and support suitable agencies able to satisfy the demand, or by our own default, force the government to take over the job, supplant us, and ultimately dominate us." Smith, *Legal Service Offices for Persons of Moderate Means,* 1949 Wis.L.Rev. 416, 418 (1949).

[40] "Lawyers have peculiar responsibilities for the just administration of the law, and these responsibilities include providing advice and representation for needy persons. To a degree not always appreciated by the public at large, the bar has performed these obligations with zeal and devotion. The Committee is persuaded, however, that a system of justice that attempts, in mid-twentieth century America, to meet the needs of the financially incapacitated accused through primary or exclusive reliance on the uncompensated services of counsel will prove unsuccessful and inadequate. . . . A system of adequate representation, therefore, should be structured and financed in a manner reflecting its public importance. . . . We believe that fees for private appointed counsel should be set by the court within maximum limits established by the statute." Report of the Att'y Gen's Comm. on Poverty and the Administration of Criminal Justice 41–43 (1963).

[41] "At present this representation [of those unable to pay usual fees] is being supplied in some measure through the spontaneous generosity of individual lawyers, through legal aid societies, and—increasingly—through the organized efforts of the Bar. If those who stand in need of this service know of its availability and their need is in fact adequately met, the precise mechanism by which this service is provided becomes of secondary importance. It is of great importance, however, that both the impulse to render this service and the plan for making that impulse effective, should arise within the legal profession itself." *Professional Responsibility: Report of the Joint Conference,* 44 A.B.A.J. 1159, 1216 (1958).

[42] "Free legal clinics carried on by the organized bar are not ethically objectionable. On the contrary, they serve a very worthwhile purpose and should be encouraged." *ABA Opinion* 191 (1939).

[43] "Whereas the American Bar Association believes that it is a fundamental duty of the bar to see to it that all persons requiring legal advice be able to attain it, irrespective of their economic status. . . .

"Resolved, that the Association approves and sponsors the setting up by state and local bar associations of lawyer referral plans and low-cost legal service methods for the purpose of dealing with cases of persons who might not otherwise have the benefit of legal advice. . . ." *Proceedings of the House of Delegates of the American Bar Association,* Oct. 30, 1946, 71 A.B.A.Rep. 103, 109–10 (1946).

[44] "The defense of indigent citizens, without compensation, is carried on throughout the country by lawyers representing legal aid societies, not only with the approval, but with the commendation of those acquainted with the work. Not infrequently services are rendered out of sympathy or for other philanthropic reasons, by individual lawyers

Acceptance and Retention of Employment

EC 2–26 A lawyer is under no obligation to act as advisor or advocate for every person who may wish to become his client; but in furtherance of the objective of the bar to make legal services fully available, a lawyer should not lightly decline proffered employment. The fulfillment of this objective requires acceptance by a lawyer of his share of tendered employment which may be unattractive both to him and the bar generally.[45]

EC 2–27 History is replete with instances of distinguished and sacrificial services by lawyers who have represented unpopular clients and causes. Regardless of his personal feelings, a lawyer should not decline representation because a client or a cause is unpopular or community reaction is adverse.[46]

EC 2–28 The personal preference of a lawyer to avoid adversary alignment against judges, other lawyers,[47] public officials, or influential members of the community does not justify his rejection of tendered employment.

EC 2–29 When a lawyer is appointed by a court or requested by a bar association to undertake representation of a person unable to obtain counsel, whether for financial or other reasons, he should not seek to be excused from undertaking the representation except for compelling reasons.[48] Compelling reasons do not include such factors as the repugnance of the subject matter of the proceeding, the identity[49] or position of a person involved in the case, the belief of the lawyer that the defendant in a criminal proceeding is guilty,[50] or the belief of the lawyer regarding the merits of the civil case.[51]

---

who do not represent legal aid societies. There is nothing whatever in the Canons to prevent a lawyer from performing such an act, nor should there be." *ABA Opinion* 148 (1935).

[45] But cf. ABA Canon 31.

[46] "One of the highest services the lawyer can render to society is to appear in court on behalf of clients whose causes are in disfavor with the general public." *Professional Responsibility: Report of the Joint Conference,* 44 A.B.A.J. 1159, 1216 (1958).

One author proposes the following proposition to be included in "A Proper Oath for Advocates": "I recognize that it is sometimes difficult for clients with unpopular causes to obtain proper legal representation. I will do all that I can to assure that the client with the unpopular cause is properly represented, and that the lawyer representing such a client receives credit from and support of the bar for handling such a matter." Thode, *The Ethical Standard for the Advocate,* 39 Texas L.Rev. 575, 592 (1961).

"§ 6068. . . . It is the duty of an attorney.

. . .

"(h) Never to reject, for any consideration personal to himself, the cause of the defenseless or the oppressed." Cal.Business and Professions Code § 6068 (West 1962). Virtually the same language is found in the Oregon statutes at Ore.Rev.Stats. Ch. 9, § 9.460(8).

See Rostow, *The Lawyer and His Client,* 48 A.B.A.J. 25 and 146 (1962).

[47] See ABA Canons 7 and 29.

"We are of the opinion that it is not professionally improper for a lawyer to accept employment to compel another lawyer to honor the just claim of a layman. On the contrary, it is highly proper that he do so. Unfortunately, there appears to be a widespread feeling among laymen that it is difficult, if not impossible, to obtain justice when they have claims against members of the Bar because other lawyers will not accept employment to proceed against them. The honor of the profession, whose members proudly style themselves officers of the court, must surely be sullied if its members bind themselves by custom to refrain from enforcing just claims of laymen against lawyers." *ABA Opinion* 144 (1935).

[48] ABA Canon 4 uses a slightly different test, saying, "A lawyer assigned as counsel for an indigent prisoner ought not to ask to be excused for any trivial reason. . . ."

[49] Cf. ABA Canon 7.

[50] See ABA Canon 5.

[51] Dr. Johnson's reply to Boswell upon being asked what he thought of "supporting a cause which you know to be bad" was: "Sir, you do not know it to be good or bad till the Judge determines it. I have said that you are to state facts fairly; so that your thinking, or what you call knowing, a cause to be bad, must be from reasoning, must be from supposing your arguments to be weak and inconclusive. But, Sir, that is not enough. An argument which does not convince yourself, may convince the Judge to whom you urge it; and if it does convince him, why, then, Sir, you are wrong, and he is right." 2 Boswell, The Life of Johnson 47–48 (Hill ed. 1887).

EC 2–30 Employment should not be accepted by a lawyer when he is unable to render competent service[52] or when he knows or it is obvious that the person seeking to employ him desires to institute or maintain an action merely for the purpose of harassing or maliciously injuring another.[53] Likewise, a lawyer should decline employment if the intensity of his personal feeling, as distinguished from a community attitude, may impair his effective representation of a prospective client. If a lawyer knows a client has previously obtained counsel, he should not accept employment in the matter unless the other counsel approves[54] or withdraws, or the client terminates the prior employment.[55]

EC 2–31 Full availability of legal counsel requires both that persons be able to obtain counsel and that lawyers who undertake representation complete the work involved. Trial counsel for a convicted defendant should continue to represent his client by advising whether to take an appeal and, if the appeal is prosecuted, by representing him through the appeal unless new counsel is substituted or withdrawal is permitted by the appropriate court.

EC 2–32 A decision by a lawyer to withdraw should be made only on the basis of compelling circumstances,[56] and in a matter pending before a tribunal he must comply with the rules of the tribunal regarding withdrawal. A lawyer should not withdraw without considering carefully and endeavoring to minimize the possible adverse effect on the rights of his client and the possibility of prejudice to his client[57] as a result of his withdrawal. Even when he justifiably withdraws, a lawyer should protect the welfare of his client by giving due notice of his withdrawal,[58] suggesting employment of other counsel, delivering to the client all papers and property to which the client is entitled, cooperating with counsel subsequently employed, and otherwise endeavoring to minimize the possibility of harm. Further, he should refund to the client any compensation not earned during the employment.[59]

EC 2–33 As a part of the legal profession's commitment to the principle that high quality legal services should be available to all, attorneys are encouraged to cooperate with qualified legal assistance organizations providing prepaid legal services. Such participation should at all times be in accordance with the basic tenets of the profession: independence, integrity, competence and devotion to the interests of individual clients. An attorney so participating should make certain that his relationship with a qualified legal assistance organization in no way interferes with his independent, professional representation of the interests of the individual client. An attorney should avoid situations in which officials of the organization who are not lawyers attempt to direct attorneys concerning the manner in which legal services are performed for individual members, and should also avoid situations in which considerations of economy are given undue weight in determining the attorneys employed by an organization or the legal services to be performed for the member or beneficiary rather than competence and quality of service. An attorney interested in maintaining the historic traditions of the profession and preserving the function of a lawyer as a trusted and independent advisor to individual members of society should carefully assess such factors when accepting employment by, or otherwise participating in, a particular qualified legal assistance

---

[52] "The lawyer deciding whether to undertake a case must be able to judge objectively whether he is capable of handling it and whether he can assume its burdens without prejudice to previous commitments. . . ." *Professional Responsibility: Report of the Joint Conference,* 44 A.B.A.J. 1158, 1218 (1958).

[53] "The lawyer must decline to conduct a civil cause or to make a defense when convinced that it is intended merely to harass or to injure the opposite party or to work oppression or wrong." ABA Canon 30.

[54] See ABA Canon 7.

[55] Id.

"From the facts stated we assume that the client has discharged the first attorney and given notice of the discharge. Such being the case, the second attorney may properly accept employment. *Canon 7; Opinions 10, 130, 149." ABA Opinion* 209 (1941).

[56] See ABA Canon 44.

"I will carefully consider, before taking a case, whether it appears that I can fully represent the client within the framework of law. If the decision is in the affirmative, then it will take extreme circumstances to cause me to decide later that I cannot so represent him." Thode, *The Ethical Standard for the Advocate,* 39 Texas L.Rev. 575, 592 (1961) (from "A Proper Oath for Advocates").

[57] *ABA Opinion* 314 (1965) held that a lawyer should not disassociate himself from a cause when "it is obvious that the very act of disassociation would have the effect of violating *Canon 37.*"

[58] ABA Canon 44 enumerates instances in which ". . . the lawyer may be warranted in withdrawing on due notice to the client, allowing him time to employ another lawyer."

[59] *See* ABA Canon 44.

organization, and while so participating should adhere to the highest professional standards of effort and competence.

Added in 1974; amended in 1975.

DISCIPLINARY RULES

DR 2–101 Publicity.

(A) A lawyer shall not, on behalf of himself, his partner, associate or any other lawyer affiliated with him or his firm, use or participate in the use of any form of public communication containing a false, fraudulent, misleading, deceptive, self-laudatory or unfair statement or claim.

(B) In order to facilitate the process of informed selection of a lawyer by potential consumers of legal services, a lawyer may publish or broadcast, subject to DR 2–103, the following information in print media distributed or over television or radio broadcast in the geographic area or areas in which the lawyer resides or maintains offices or in which a significant part of the lawyer's clientele resides, provided that the information disclosed by the lawyer in such publication or broadcast complies with DR 2–101(A), and is presented in a dignified manner:

(1) Name, including name of law firm and names of professional associates; addresses and telephone numbers;

(2) One or more fields of law in which the lawyer or law firm practices, a statement that practice is limited to one or more fields of law, or a statement that the lawyer or law firm specializes in a particular field of law practice, to the extent authorized under DR 2–105;

(3) Date and place of birth;

(4) Date and place of admission to the bar of state and federal courts;

(5) Schools attended, with dates of graduation, degrees and other scholastic distinctions;

(6) Public or quasi-public offices;

(7) Military service;

(8) Legal authorships;

(9) Legal teaching positions;

(10) Memberships, offices, and committee assignments, in bar associations;

(11) Membership and offices in legal fraternities and legal societies;

(12) Technical and professional licenses;

(13) Memberships in scientific, technical and professional associations and societies;

(14) Foreign language ability;

(15) Names and addresses of bank references;

(16) With their written consent, names of clients regularly represented;

(17) Prepaid or group legal services programs in which the lawyer participates;

(18) Whether credit cards or other credit arrangements are accepted;

(19) Office and telephone answering service hours;

(20) Fee for an initial consultation;

(21) Availability upon request of a written schedule of fees and/or an estimate of the fee to be charged for specific services;

(22) Contingent fee rates subject to DR 2–106(C), provided that the statement discloses whether percentages are computed before or after deduction of costs;

(23) Range of fees for services, provided that the statement discloses that the specific fee within the range which will be charged will vary depending upon the particular matter to be handled for each client and the client is entitled without obligation to an estimate of the fee within the range likely to be charged. In print size equivalent to the largest print used in setting forth the fee information;

(24) Hourly rate, provided that the statement discloses that the total fee charged will depend upon the number of hours which must be devoted to the particular matter to be handled for each client and the client is entitled to without obligation an estimate of the fee likely to be charged, in print size at least equivalent to the largest print used in setting forth the fee information;

(25) Fixed fees for specific legal services,* the description of which would not be misunderstood or be deceptive, provided that the statement discloses that the quoted fee will be available only to clients whose matters fall into the services described and that the client is entitled without obligation to a specific estimate of the fee likely to be charged in print size at least equivalent to the largest print used in setting forth the fee information.

(C) Any person desiring to expand the information authorized for disclosure in DR 2–101(B), or to provide for its dissemination through other forums may apply to [the agency having jurisdiction under state law]. Any such application shall be served upon [the agencies having jurisdiction under state law over the regulation of the legal profession and consumer matters] who shall be heard, together with the applicant, on the issue of whether the proposal is necessary in light of the existing provisions of the Code, accords with standards of accuracy, reliability and truthfulness, and would facilitate the process of informed selection of lawyers by potential consumers of legal services. The relief granted in response to any such application shall be promulgated as an amendment to DR 2–101(B), universally applicable to all lawyers.**

(D) If the advertisement is communicated to the public over television or radio, it shall be prerecorded, approved for broadcast by the lawyer, and a recording of the actual transmission shall be retained by the lawyer.

(E) If a lawyer advertises a fee for a service, the lawyer must render that service for no more than the fee advertised.

(F) Unless otherwise specified in the advertisement if a lawyer publishes any fee information authorized under DR 2–101(B) in a publication that is published more frequently than one time per month, the lawyer shall be bound by any representation made therein for a period of not less than 30 days after such publication. If a lawyer publishes any fee information authorized under DR 2–101(B) in a publication that is published once a month or less frequently, he shall be bound by any representation made therein until the publication of the succeeding issue. If a lawyer publishes any fee information authorized under DR 2–101(B) in a publication which has no fixed date for publication of a succeeding issue, the lawyer shall be bound by any representation

* The agency having jurisdiction under state law may desire to issue appropriate guidelines defining "specific legal services."

** The agency having jurisdiction under state law should establish orderly and expeditious procedures for ruling on such applications.

made therein for a reasonable period of time after publication but in no event less than one year.

(G) Unless otherwise specified, if a lawyer broadcasts any fee information authorized under DR 2–101(B), the lawyer shall be bound by any representation made therein for a period of not less than 30 days after such broadcast.

(H) This rule does not prohibit limited and dignified identification of a lawyer as a lawyer as well as by name:

(1) In political advertisements when his professional status is germane to the political campaign or to a political issue.

(2) In public notices when the name and profession of a lawyer are required or authorized by law or are reasonably pertinent for a purpose other than the attraction of potential clients.

(3) In routine reports and announcements of a bona fide business, civic, professional, or political organization in which he serves as a director or officer.

(4) In and on legal documents prepared by him.

(5) In and on legal textbooks, treatises, and other legal publications, and in dignified advertisements thereof.

(I) A lawyer shall not compensate or give any thing of value to representatives of the press, radio, television, or other communication medium in anticipation of or in return for professional publicity in a news item.

As amended in 1974, 1975, 1977 and 1978.

DR 2–102 Professional Notices, Letterheads and Offices.

(A) A lawyer or law firm shall not use or participate in the use of professional cards, professional announcement cards, office signs, letterheads, or similar professional notices or devices, except that the following may be used if they are in dignified form:

(1) A professional card of a lawyer identifying him by name and as a lawyer, and giving his addresses, telephone numbers, the name of his law firm, and any information permitted under DR 2–105. A professional card of a law firm may also give the names of members and associates. Such cards may be used for identification.

(2) A brief professional announcement card stating new or changed associations or addresses, change of firm name, or similar matters pertaining to the professional offices of a lawyer or law firm, which may be mailed to lawyers, clients, former clients, personal friends, and relatives.[64] It shall not state biographical data except to the extent reasonably necessary to identify the lawyer or to explain the change in his association, but it may state the immediate past position of the lawyer.[65] It may give the names and dates of predecessor firms in a continuing line of

---

[64] See *ABA Opinion* 301 (1961).

[65] "[I]t has become commonplace for many lawyers to participate in government service; to deny them the right, upon their return to private practice, to refer to their prior employment in a brief and dignified manner, would place an undue limitation upon a large element of our profession. It is entirely proper for a member of the profession to explain his absence from private practice, where such is the primary purpose of the announcement, by a brief and dignified reference to the prior employment.

". . . [A]ny such announcement should be limited to the immediate past connection of the lawyer with the government, made upon his leaving that position to enter private practice." *ABA Opinion* 301 (1961).

succession. It shall not state the nature of the practice except as permitted under DR 2–105.[66]

(3) A sign on or near the door of the office and in the building directory identifying the law office. The sign shall not state the nature of the practice, except as permitted under DR 2–105.

(4) A letter head of a lawyer identifying him by name and as a lawyer, and giving his addresses, telephone numbers, the name of his law firm, associates and any information permitted under DR 2–105. A letterhead of a law firm may also give the names of members and associates,[67] **and names and dates relating to deceased and retired members.**[68] **A lawyer may be designated "Of Counsel" on a letterhead if he has a continuing relationship with a lawyer or law firm, other than as a partner or associate. A lawyer or law firm may be designated as "General Counsel" or by similar professional reference on stationary of a client if he or the firm devotes a substantial amount of professional time in the representation of that client.**[69] **The letterhead of a law firm may give the names and dates of predecessor firms in a continuing line of succession.**

(B) A lawyer in private practice shall not practice under a trade name, a name that is misleading as to the identity of the lawyer or lawyers practicing under such name, or a firm name containing names other than those of one or more of the lawyers in the firm, except that the name of a professional corporation or professional association may contain "P.C." or "P.A." or similar symbols indicating the nature of the organization, and if otherwise lawful a firm may use as, or continue to include in, its name the name or names of one or more deceased or retired members of the firm or of a predecessor firm in a continuing line of succession.[70] **A lawyer who assumes a judicial, legislative, or public executive or administrative post or office shall not permit his name to remain in the name of a law firm or to be used in professional notices of the firm during any significant period in which he is not actively and regularly practicing law as a member of the firm,**[71] **and during such period other members of the firm shall not use his name in the firm name or in professional notices of the firm.**[72]

(C) A lawyer shall not hold himself out as having a partnership with one or more other lawyers or professional corporations unless they are in fact partners.[74]

---

66 See *ABA Opinion* 251 (1943).

67 "Those lawyers who are working for an individual lawyer or a law firm may be designated on the letterhead and in other appropriate places as 'associates' " *ABA Opinion* 310 (1963).

68 See ABA Canon 33.

69 But see *ABA Opinion* 285 (1951).

70 See ABA Canon 33; cf. *ABA Opinions* 318 (1967), 267 (1945), 219 (1941), 208 (1940), 192 (1939), 97 (1933), and 6 (1925).

71 *ABA Opinion* 318 (1967) held, anything to the contrary in Formal Opinion 315 or in the other opinions cited notwithstanding that: Where a partner whose name appears in the name of a law firm is elected or appointed to high local, state or federal office, which office he intends to occupy only temporarily, at the end of which time he intends to return to his position with the firm, and provided that he is not precluded by holding such office from engaging in the practice of law and does not in fact sever his relationship with the firm but only takes a leave of absence, and provided that there is no local law, statute or custom to the contrary, his name may be retained in the firm name during his term or terms of office, but only if proper precautions are taken not to mislead the public as to his degree of participation in the firm's affairs.

Cf. *ABA Opinion* 143 (1935). New York County Opinion 67, and New York City Opinions 36 and 798; but cf. *ABA Opinion* 192 (1939) and Michigan Opinion 164.

72 Cf. ABA Canon 33.

74 See *ABA Opinion* 277 (1948); cf. ABA Canon 33 and *ABA Opinions* 318 (1967), 126 (1935), 115 (1934), and 106 (1934).

(D) A partnership shall not be formed or continued between or among lawyers licensed in different jurisdictions unless all enumerations of the members and associates of the firm on its letterhead and in other permissible listings make clear the jurisdictional limitations on those members and associates of the firm not licensed to practice in all listed jurisdictions;[75] however, the same firm name may be used in each jurisdiction.

(E) Nothing contained herein shall prohibit a lawyer from using or permitting the use of, in connection with his name, an earned degree or title derived therefrom indicating his training in the law.

As amended in 1976, 1977, 1979 and 1980.

DR 2–103 Recommendation of Professional Employment.[77]

(A) A lawyer shall not, except as authorized in DR 2–101(B), recommend employment as a private practitioner,[78] of himself, his partner, or associate to a layperson who has not sought his advice regarding employment of a lawyer.[79]

(B) A lawyer shall not compensate or give anything of value to a person or organization to recommend or secure his employment[80] by a client, or as a reward for having made a recommendation resulting in his employment[81] by a client, except that he may pay the usual and reasonable fees or dues charged by any of the organizations listed in DR 2–103(D).

(C) A lawyer shall not request a person or organization to recommend or promote the use of his services or those of his partner or associate, or any other lawyer affiliated with him or his firm, as a private practitioner,[83] except as authorized in DR 2–101, and except that

(1) He may request referrals from a lawyer referral service operated, sponsored, or approved by a bar association and may pay its fees incident thereto.[84]

(2) He may cooperate with the legal service activities of any of the offices or organizations enumerated in DR 2–103(D)(1) through (4) and may perform legal services for those to whom he was recommended by it to do such work if:

(a) The person to whom the recommendation is made is a member or beneficiary of such office or organization; and

---

[75] See *ABA Opinions* 318 (1967) and 316 (1967); cf. ABA Canon 33.

[77] Cf. ABA Canon 28.

[78] "We think it clear that a lawyer's seeking employment in an ordinary law office, or appointment to a civil service position, is not prohibited by . . . [Canon 27]." *ABA Opinion* 197 (1939).

[79] "[A] lawyer may not seek from persons not his clients the opportunity to perform . . . a [legal] checkup." *ABA Opinion* 307 (1962).

[80] Cf. *ABA Opinion* 78 (1932).

[81] " 'No financial connection of any kind between the Brotherhood and any lawyer is permissible. No lawyer can properly pay any amount whatsoever to the Brotherhood or any of its departments, officers or members as compensation, reimbursement of expenses or gratuity in connection with the procurement of a case.' " In re Brotherhood of R.R. Trainmen, 13 Ill.2d 391, 398, 150 N.E.2d 163, 167 (1958), quoted in In re Ratner, 194 Kan. 362, 372, 399 P.2d 865, 873 (1956).

See *ABA Opinion* 147 (1935).

[83] "This Court has condemned the practice of ambulance chasing through the media of runners and touters. In similar fashion we have with equal emphasis condemned the practice of direct solicitation by a lawyer. We have classified both offenses as serious breaches of the Canons of Ethics demanding severe treatment of the offending lawyer." State v. Dawson, 111 So.2d 427, 431 (Fla.1959).

[84] "Registrants [of a lawyer referral plan] may be required to contribute to the expense of operating it by a reasonable registration charge or by a reasonable percentage of fees collected by them." *ABA Opinion* 291 (1956).

Cf. *ABA Opinion* 227 (1941).

(b) The lawyer remains free to exercise his independent professional judgment on behalf of his client.

(D) A lawyer or his partner or associate or any other lawyer affiliated with him or his firm may be recommended, employed or paid by, or may cooperate with, one of the following offices or organizations that promote the use of his services or those of his partner or associate or any other lawyer affiliated with him or his firm if there is no interference with the exercise of independent professional judgment in behalf of his client:

(1) A legal aid office or public defender office:

(a) Operated or sponsored by a duly accredited law school.

(b) Operated or sponsored by a bona fide nonprofit community organization.

(c) Operated or sponsored by a governmental agency.

(d) Operated, sponsored, or approved by a bar association.[86]

(2) A military legal assistance office.

(3) A lawyer referral service operated, sponsored, or approved by a bar association.

(4) Any bona fide organization that recommends, furnishes or pays for legal services to its members or beneficiaries[87] provided the following conditions are satisfied:

(a) Such organization, including any affiliate, is so organized and operated that no profit is derived by it from the rendition of legal services by lawyers, and that, if the organization is organized for profit, the legal services are not rendered by lawyers employed, directed, supervised or selected by it except in connection with matters where such organization bears ultimate liability of its member or beneficiary.

(b) Neither the lawyer, nor his partner, nor associate, nor any other lawyer affiliated with him or his firm, nor any non-lawyer, shall have initiated or promoted such organization for the primary purpose of providing financial or other benefit to such lawyer, partner, associate or affiliated lawyer.

(c) Such organization is not operated for the purpose of procuring legal work or financial benefit for any lawyer as a private practitioner outside of the legal services program of the organization.

(d) The member or beneficiary to whom the legal services are furnished, and not such organization, is recognized as the client of the lawyer in the matter.

(e) Any member or beneficiary who is entitled to have legal services furnished or paid for by the organization may, if such member or beneficiary so desires, select counsel other than that furnished, selected or approved by the organization for the particular matter involved; and the legal service plan of such organization provides appropriate relief for any member or beneficiary who asserts a claim that representation by counsel furnished, selected or approved would be unethical, improper or inadequate under the circumstances of the matter involved and the plan provides an appropriate procedure for seeking such relief.

---

86 Cf. *ABA Opinion* 148 (1935).

87 United Mine Workers v. Ill. State Bar Ass'n., 389 U.S. 217, 19 L.Ed.2d 426, 88 S.Ct. 353 (1967); Brotherhood of R.R. Trainmen v. Virginia, 371 U.S. 1, 12 L.Ed.2d 89, 84 S.Ct. 1113 (1964); NAACP v. Button, 371 U.S. 415, 9 L.Ed.2d 405, 83 S.Ct. 328 (1963).

(f) **The lawyer does not know or have cause to know that such organization is in violation of applicable laws, rules of court and other legal requirements that govern its legal service operations.**

(g) **Such organization has filed with the appropriate disciplinary authority at least annually a report with respect to its legal service plan, if any, showing its terms, its schedule of benefits, its subscription charges, agreements with counsel, and financial results of its legal service activities or, if it has failed to do so, the lawyer does not know or have cause to know of such failure.**

(E) **A lawyer shall not accept employment when he knows or it is obvious that the person who seeks his services does so as a result of conduct prohibited under this Disciplinary Rule.**

As amended in 1974, 1975 and 1977.

DR 2-104 Suggestion of Need of Legal Services.[89, 90]

(A) **A lawyer who has given in-person unsolicited advice to a layperson that he should obtain counsel or take legal action shall not accept employment resulting from that advice,[91] except that:**

(1) **A lawyer may accept employment by a close friend, relative, former client (if the advice is germane to the former employment), or one whom the lawyer reasonably believes to be a client.[92]**

(2) **A lawyer may accept employment that results from his participation in activities designed to educate laypersons to recognize legal problems, to make intelligent selection of counsel, or to utilize available legal services if such activities are conducted or sponsored by a qualified legal assistance organization.**

(3) **A lawyer who is recommended, furnished or paid by a qualified legal assistance organization enumerated in DR 2-103(D)(1) through (4) may represent a member or beneficiary thereof, to the extent and under the conditions prescribed therein.**

(4) **Without affecting his right to accept employment, a lawyer may speak publicly or write for publication on legal topics[95] so long as he does not emphasize his own professional experience or reputation and does not undertake to give individual advice.**

---

[89] "If a bar association has embarked on a program of institutional advertising for an annual legal check-up and provides brochures and reprints, it is not improper to have these available in the lawyer's office for persons to read and take." *ABA Opinion* 307 (1962).

Cf. *ABA Opinion* 121 (1934).

[90] ABA Canon 28.

[91] Cf. *ABA Opinions* 229 (1941) and 173 (1937).

[92] "It certainly is not improper for a lawyer to advise his regular clients of new statutes, court decisions, and administrative rulings, which may affect the client's interests, provided the communication is strictly limited to such information. . . .

"When such communications go to concerns or individuals other than regular clients of the lawyer, they are thinly disguised advertisements for professional employment, and are obviously improper." *ABA Opinion* 213 (1941).

"It is our opinion that where the lawyer has no reason to believe that he has been supplanted by another lawyer, it is not only his right, but it might even be his duty to advise his client of any change of fact or law which might defeat the client's testamentary purpose as expressed in the will.

"Periodic notices might be sent to the client for whom a lawyer has drawn a will, suggesting that it might be wise for the client to reexamine his will to determine whether or not there has been any change in his situation requiring a modification of his will." *ABA Opinion* 210 (1941).

Cf. ABA Canon 28.

[95] Cf. *ABA Opinion* 168 (1937).

(5) If success in asserting rights or defenses of his client in litigation in the nature of a class action is dependent upon the joinder of others, a lawyer may accept, but shall not seek, employment from those contacted for the purpose of obtaining their joinder.[96]

As amended in 1974, 1975 and 1977.

DR 2–105 Limitation of Practice.[97]

(A) A lawyer shall not hold himself out publicly as a specialist, as practicing in certain areas of law or as limiting his practice permitted under DR 2–101(B), except as follows:

(1) A lawyer admitted to practice before the United States Patent and Trademark Office may use the designation "Patents," "Patent Attorney," "Patent Lawyer," or "Registered Patent Attorney" or any combination of those terms, on his letterhead and office sign.

(2) A lawyer who publicly discloses fields of law in which the lawyer or the law firm practices or states that his practice is limited to one or more fields of law shall do so by using designations and definitions authorized and approved by [the agency having jurisdiction of the subject under state law].

(3) A lawyer who is certified as a specialist in a particular field of law or law practice by [the authority having jurisdiction under state law over the subject of specialization by lawyers] may hold himself out as such, but only in accordance with the rules prescribed by that authority.[98]

As amended in 1977.

DR 2–106 Fees for Legal Services.[99]

(A) A lawyer shall not enter into an agreement for, charge, or collect an illegal or clearly excessive fee.[100]

(B) A fee is clearly excessive when, after a review of the facts, a lawyer of ordinary prudence would be left with a definite and firm conviction that the fee is in excess of a reasonable fee. Factors to be considered as guides in determining the reasonableness of a fee include the following:

(1) The time and labor required, the novelty and difficulty of the questions involved, and the skill requisite to perform the legal service properly.

(2) The likelihood, if apparent to the client, that the acceptance of the particular employment will preclude other employment by the lawyer.

(3) The fee customarily charged in the locality for similar legal services.

(4) The amount involved and the results obtained.

---

[96] But cf. *ABA Opinion* 111 (1934).

[97] See ABA Canon 45; cf. ABA Canons 43, and 46.

[98] This provision is included to conform to action taken by the ABA House of Delegates at the Mid-Winter Meeting, January, 1969.

[99] See ABA Canon 12.

[100] The charging of a "clearly excessive fee" is a ground for discipline. State ex rel. Nebraska State Bar Ass'n. v. Richards, 165 Neb. 80, 90, 84 N.W.2d 136, 143 (1957).

"An attorney has the right to contract for any fee he chooses so long as it is not excessive (see Opinion 190), and this Committee is not concerned with the amount of such fees unless so excessive as to constitute a misappropriation of the client's funds (see Opinion 27)." *ABA Opinion* 320 (1968).

Cf. *ABA Opinions* 209 (1940), 190 (1939), and 27 (1930) and State ex rel. Lee v. Buchanan, 191 So.2d 33 (Fla.1966).

(5) The time limitations imposed by the client or by the circumstances.

(6) The nature and length of the professional relationship with the client.

(7) The experience, reputation, and ability of the lawyer or lawyers performing the services.

(8) Whether the fee is fixed or contingent.[101]

(C) A lawyer shall not enter into an arrangement for, charge, or collect a contingent fee for representing a defendant in a criminal case.[102]

DR 2–107 Division of Fees Among Lawyers.

(A) A lawyer shall not divide a fee for legal services with another lawyer who is not a partner in or associate of his law firm or law office, unless:

(1) The client consents to employment of the other lawyer after a full disclosure that a division of fees will be made.

(2) The division is made in proportion to the services performed and responsibility assumed by each.[103]

(3) The total fee of the lawyers does not clearly exceed reasonable compensation for all legal services they rendered the client.[104]

(B) This Disciplinary Rule does not prohibit payment to a former partner or associate pursuant to a separation or retirement agreement.

DR 2–108 Agreements Restricting the Practice of a Lawyer.

(A) A lawyer shall not be a party to or participate in a partnership or employment agreement with another lawyer that restricts the right of a lawyer to practice law after the termination of a relationship created by the agreement, except as a condition to payment of retirement benefits.[105]

(B) In connection with the settlement of a controversy or suit, a lawyer shall not enter into an agreement that restricts his right to practice law.

---

[101] Cf. ABA Canon 13; see generally MacKinnon, Contingent Fees for Legal Services (1964) (A Report of the American Bar Foundation).

[102] "Contingent fees, whether in civil or criminal cases, are a special concern of the law. . . .

"In criminal cases, the rule is stricter because of the danger of corrupting justice. The second part of Section 542 of the Restatement [of Contracts] reads: 'A bargain to conduct a criminal case . . . in consideration of a promise of a fee contingent on success is illegal. . . .' " Peyton v. Margiotti, 398 Pa. 86, 156 A.2d 865, 967 (1959).

"The third area of practice in which the use of the contingent fee is generally considered to be prohibited is the prosecution and defense of criminal cases. However, there are so few cases, and these are predominantly old, that it is doubtful that there can be said to be any current law on the subject. . . . In the absence of cases on the validity of contingent fees for defense attorneys, it is necessary to rely on the consensus among commentators that such a fee is void as against public policy. The nature of criminal practice itself makes unlikely the use of contingent fee contracts." MacKinnon, Contingent Fees for Legal Services 52 (1964) (A Report of the American Bar Foundation).

[103] See ABA Canon 34 and *ABA Opinions* 316 (1967) and 294 (1958); see generally *ABA Opinions* 265 (1945), 204 (1940), 190 (1939), 171 (1937), 153 (1936), 97 (1933), 63 (1932), 28 (1930), 27 (1930), and 18 (1930).

[104] "*Canon 12* contemplates that a lawyer's fee should not exceed *the value of the services* rendered. . . .

"*Canon 12* applies, whether joint or separate fees are charged [by associate attorneys]. . . ." *ABA Opinion* 204 (1940).

[105] "[A] general covenant restricting an employed lawyer, after leaving the employment, from practicing in the community for a stated period, appears to this Committee to be an unwarranted restriction on the right of a lawyer to choose where he will practice and inconsistent with our professional status. Accordingly, the Committee is of the opinion it would be improper for the employing lawyer to require the covenant and likewise for the employed lawyer to agree to it." *ABA Opinion* 300 (1961).

DR 2–109 Acceptance of Employment.

(A) A lawyer shall not accept employment on behalf of a person if he knows or it is obvious that such person wishes to:

(1) Bring a legal action, conduct a defense, or assert a position in litigation, or otherwise have steps taken for him, merely for the purpose of harassing or maliciously injuring any person.[106]

(2) Present a claim or defense in litigation that is not warranted under existing law, unless it can be supported by good faith argument for an extension, modification, or reversal of existing law.

DR 2–110 Withdrawal From Employment.[107]

(A) In general.

(1) If permission for withdrawal from employment is required by the rules of a tribunal, a lawyer shall not withdraw from employment in a proceeding before that tribunal without its permission.

(2) In any event, a lawyer shall not withdraw from employment until he has taken reasonable steps to avoid foreseeable prejudice to the rights of his client, including giving due notice to his client, allowing time for employment of other counsel, delivering to the client all papers and property to which the client is entitled, and complying with applicable laws and rules.

(3) A lawyer who withdraws from employment shall refund promptly any part of a fee paid in advance that has not been earned.

(B) Mandatory withdrawal.

A lawyer representing a client before a tribunal, with its permission if required by its rules, shall withdraw from employment, and a lawyer representing a client in other matters shall withdraw from employment, if:

(1) He knows or it is obvious that his client is bringing the legal action, conducting the defense, or asserting a position in the litigation, or is otherwise having steps taken for him, merely for the purpose of harassing or maliciously injuring any person.

(2) He knows or it is obvious that his continued employment will result in violation of a Disciplinary Rule.[108]

(3) His mental or physical condition renders it unreasonably difficult for him to carry out the employment effectively.

(4) He is discharged by his client.

---

[106] See ABA Canon 30.

"*Rule 13.* . . . A member of the State Bar shall not accept employment to prosecute or defend a case solely out of spite, or solely for the purpose of harassing or delaying another. . . ." Cal.Business and Professions Code § 6067 (West 1962).

[107] Cf. ABA Canon 44.

[108] See also Code of Professional Responsibility, DR 5–102 and DR 5–105.

(C) Permissive withdrawal.[109]

If DR 2–110(B) is not applicable, a lawyer may not request permission to withdraw in matters pending before a tribunal, and may not withdraw in other matters, unless such request or such withdrawal is because:

(1) His client:

(a) Insists upon presenting a claim or defense that is not warranted under existing law and cannot be supported by good faith argument for an extension, modification, or reversal of existing law.[110]

(b) Personally seeks to pursue an illegal course of conduct.

(c) Insists that the lawyer pursue a course of conduct that is illegal or that is prohibited under the Disciplinary Rules.

(d) By other conduct renders it unreasonably difficult for the lawyer to carry out his employment effectively.

(e) Insists, in a matter not pending before a tribunal, that the lawyer engage in conduct that is contrary to the judgment and advice of the lawyer but not prohibited under the Disciplinary Rules.

(f) Deliberately disregards an agreement or obligation to the lawyer as to expenses or fees.

(2) His continued employment is likely to result in a violation of a Disciplinary Rule.

(3) His inability to work with co-counsel indicates that the best interests of the client likely will be served by withdrawal.

(4) His mental or physical condition renders it difficult for him to carry out the employment effectively.

(5) His client knowingly and freely assents to termination of his employment.

(6) He believes in good faith, in a proceeding pending before a tribunal, that the tribunal will find the existence of other good cause for withdrawal.

CANON 3

A Lawyer Should Assist in Preventing the Unauthorized Practice of Law

Ethical Considerations

EC 3–1 The prohibition against the practice of law by a layman is grounded in the need of the public for integrity and competence of those who undertake to render legal services. Because of the fiduciary and personal character of the lawyer-client relationship and the inherently complex nature of our legal system, the public can better be assured of the requisite responsibility and competence if the practice of law is confined to those who are subject to the requirements and regulations imposed upon members of the legal profession.

EC 3–2 The sensitive variations in the considerations that bear on legal determinations often make it difficult even for a lawyer to exercise appropriate professional judgment, and it is therefore essential that the personal nature of the relationship of client and lawyer be preserved. Competent professional judgment

---

[109] Cf. ABA Canon 4.

[110] Cf. Anders v. California, 386 U.S. 738, 18 L.Ed.2d 493, 87 S.Ct. 1396 (1967), rehearing denied, 388 U.S. 924, 18 L.Ed.2d 1377, 87 S.Ct. 2094 (1967).

is the product of a trained familiarity with law and legal processes, a disciplined, analytical approach to legal problems, and a firm ethical commitment.

EC 3–3 A non-lawyer who undertakes to handle legal matters is not governed as to integrity or legal competence by the same rules that govern the conduct of a lawyer. A lawyer is not only subject to that regulation but also is committed to high standards of ethical conduct. The public interest is best served in legal matters by a regulated profession committed to such standards.[1] The Disciplinary Rules protect the public in that they prohibit a lawyer from seeking employment by improper overtures, from acting in cases of divided loyalties, and from submitting to the control of others in the exercise of his judgment. Moreover, a person who entrusts legal matters to a lawyer is protected by the attorney-client privilege and by the duty of the lawyer to hold inviolate the confidences and secrets of his client.

EC 3–4 A layman who seeks legal services often is not in a position to judge whether he will receive proper professional attention. The entrustment of a legal matter may well involve the confidences, the reputation, the property, the freedom, or even the life of the client. Proper protection of members of the public demands that no person be permitted to act in the confidential and demanding capacity of a lawyer unless he is subject to the regulations of the legal profession.

EC 3–5 It is neither necessary nor desirable to attempt the formulation of a single, specific definition of what constitutes the practice of law.[2] Functionally, the practice of law relates to the rendition of services for others that call for the professional judgment of a lawyer. The essence of the professional judgment of the lawyer is his educated ability to relate the general body and philosophy of law to a specific legal problem of a client; and thus, the public interest will be better served if only lawyers are permitted to act in matters involving professional judgment. Where this professional judgment is not involved, non-lawyers, such as court clerks, police officers, abstracters, and many governmental employees, may engage in occupations that require a special knowledge of law in certain areas. But the services of a lawyer are essential in the public interest whenever the exercise of professional legal judgment is required.

EC 3–6 A lawyer often delegates tasks to clerks, secretaries, and other lay persons. Such delegation is proper if the lawyer maintains a direct relationship with his client, supervises the delegated work, and has complete professional responsibility for the work product.[3] This delegation enables a lawyer to render legal service more economically and efficiently.

---

[1] "The condemnation of the unauthorized practice of law is designed to protect the public from legal services by persons unskilled in the law. The prohibition of lay intermediaries is intended to insure the loyalty of the lawyer to the client unimpaired by intervening and possibly conflicting interests." Cheatham, *Availability of Legal Services: The Responsibility of the Individual Lawyer and of the Organized Bar,* 12 U.C.L.A.L.Rev. 438, 439 (1965).

[2] "What constitutes unauthorized practice of the law in a particular jurisdiction is a matter for determination by the courts of that jurisdiction." *ABA Opinion* 198 (1939).

"In the light of the historical development of the lawyer's functions, it is impossible to lay down an exhaustive definition of 'the practice of law' by attempting to enumerate every conceivable act performed by lawyers in the normal course of their work." State Bar of Arizona v. Arizona Land Title & Trust Co., 90 Ariz. 76, 87, 366 P.2d 1, 8–9 (1961), modified, 91 Ariz. 293, 371 P.2d 1020 (1962).

[3] "A lawyer can employ lay secretaries, lay investigators, lay detectives, lay researchers, accountants, lay scriveners, nonlawyer draftsmen or nonlawyer researchers. In fact he may employ nonlawyers to do any task for him except counsel clients about law matters, engage directly in the practice of law, appear in court or appear in formal proceedings a part of the judicial process, so long as it is he who takes the work and vouches for it to the client and becomes responsible to the client." *ABA Opinion* 316 (1967).

ABA Opinion 316 (1967) also stated that if a lawyer practices law as part of a law firm which includes lawyers from several states, he may delegate tasks to firm members in other states so long as he "is the person who, on behalf of the firm, vouched for the work of all of the others and, with the client and in the courts, did the legal acts defined by that state as the practice of law."

"A lawyer cannot delegate his professional responsibility to a law student employed in his office. He may avail himself of the assistance of the student in many of the fields of the lawyer's work, such as examination of case law, finding and interviewing witnesses, making collections of claims, examining court records, delivering papers, conveying important messages, and other similar matters. But the student is not permitted, until he is admitted to the Bar, to perform the professional functions of a lawyer, such as conducting court trials, giving professional advice to clients or drawing legal documents for them. The student in all his work must act as agent for the lawyer employing him, who must supervise his work and be responsible for his good conduct." *ABA Opinion* 85 (1932).

EC 3–7 The prohibition against a non-lawyer practicing law does not prevent a layman from representing himself, for then he is ordinarily exposing only himself to possible injury. The purpose of the legal profession is to make educated legal representation available to the public; but anyone who does not wish to avail himself of such representation is not required to do so. Even so, the legal profession should help members of the public to recognize legal problems and to understand why it may be unwise for them to act for themselves in matters having legal consequences.

EC 3–8 Since a lawyer should not aid or encourage a layman to practice law, he should not practice law in association with a layman or otherwise share legal fees with a layman.[4] This does not mean, however, that the pecuniary value of the interest of a deceased lawyer in his firm or practice may not be paid to his estate or specified persons such as his widow or heirs.[5] In like manner, profit-sharing retirement plans of a lawyer or law firm which include non-lawyer office employees are not improper.[6] These limited exceptions to the rule against sharing legal fees with laymen are permissible since they do not aid or encourage laymen to practice law.

EC 3–9 Regulation of the practice of law is accomplished principally by the respective states.[7] Authority to engage in the practice of law conferred in any jurisdiction is not per se a grant of the right to practice elsewhere, and it is improper for a lawyer to engage in practice where he is not permitted by law or by court order to do so. However, the demands of business and the mobility of our society pose distinct problems in the regulation of the practice of law by the states.[8] In furtherance of the public interest, the legal profession should discourage regulation that unreasonably imposes territorial limitations upon the right of a lawyer to handle the legal affairs of his client or upon the opportunity of a client to obtain the services of a lawyer of his choice in all matters including the presentation of a contested matter in a tribunal before which the lawyer is not permanently admitted to practice.[9]

---

4 "No division of fees for legal services is proper, except with another lawyer. . . ." ABA Canon 34. Otherwise, according to *ABA Opinion* 316 (1967), "[t]he Canons of Ethics do not examine into the method by which such persons are remunerated by the lawyer. . . . They may be paid a salary, a per diem charge, a flat fee, a contract price, etc."

See ABA Canons 33 and 47.

5 "Many partnership agreements provide that the active partners, on the death of any one of them, are to make payments to the estate or to the nominee of a deceased partner on a pre-determined formula. It is only where the effect of such an arrangement is to make the estate or nominee a member of the partnership along with the surviving partners that it is prohibited by *Canon 34.* Where the payments are made in accordance with a pre-existing agreement entered into by the deceased partner during his lifetime and providing for a fixed method for determining their amount based upon the value of services rendered during the partner's lifetime and providing for a fixed period over which the payments are to be made, this is not the case. Under these circumstances, whether the payments are considered to be delayed payment of compensation earned but withheld during the partner's lifetime, or whether they are considered to be an approximation of his interest in matters pending at the time of his death, is immaterial. In either event, as Henry S. Drinker says in his book, Legal Ethics, at page 189: 'It would seem, however, that a reasonable agreement to pay the estate a proportion of the receipts for a reasonable period is a proper practical settlement for the lawyer's services to his retirement or death.' " *ABA Opinion* 308 (1963).

6 Cf. ABA Opinion 311 (1964).

7 "That the States have broad power to regulate the practice of law is, of course, beyond question." United Mine Workers v. Ill. State Bar Ass'n, 389 U.S. 217, 222 (1967).

"It is a matter of law, not of ethics, as to where an individual may practice law. Each state has its own rules." *ABA Opinion* 316 (1967).

8 "Much of clients' business crosses state lines. People are mobile, moving from state to state. Many metropolitan areas cross state lines. It is common today to have a single economic and social community involving more than one state. The business of a single client may involve legal problems in several states." *ABA Opinion* 316 (1967).

9 "[W]e reaffirmed the general principle that legal services to New Jersey residents with respect to New Jersey matters may ordinarily be furnished only by New Jersey counsel; but we pointed out that there may be multistate transactions where strict adherence to this thesis would not be in the public interest and that, under the circumstances, it would have been not only more costly to the client but also 'grossly impractical and inefficient' to have had the settlement negotiations conducted by separate lawyers from different states." In re Estate of Waring, 47 N.J. 367, 376, 221 A.2d 193, 197 (1966).

Cf. ABA Opinion 316 (1967).

DISCIPLINARY RULES

DR 3–101 Aiding Unauthorized Practice of Law.[10]

(A) A lawyer shall not aid a non-lawyer in the unauthorized practice of law.[11]

(B) A lawyer shall not practice law in a jurisdiction where to do so would be in violation of regulations of the profession in that jurisdiction.[12]

DR 3–102 Dividing Legal Fees With a Non-lawyer.

(A) A lawyer or law firm shall not share legal fees with a non-lawyer,[13] except that:

(1) An agreement by a lawyer with his firm, partner, or associate may provide for the payment of money, over a reasonable period of time after his death, to his estate or to one or more specified persons.[14]

(2) A lawyer who undertakes to complete unfinished legal business of a deceased lawyer may pay to the estate of the deceased lawyer that proportion of the total compensation which fairly represents the services rendered by the deceased lawyer.

(3) A lawyer or law firm may include non-lawyer employees in a compensation or retirement plan, even though the plan is based in whole or in part on a profit-sharing arrangement [15] providing such plan does not circumvent another disciplinary rule.[16]

As amended in 1980.

DR 3–103 Forming a Partnership With a Non-lawyer.

(A) A lawyer shall not form a partnership with a non-lawyer if any of the activities of the partnership consist of the practice of law.[17]

CANON 4

A Lawyer Should Preserve the Confidences and Secrets of a Client

ETHICAL CONSIDERATIONS

EC 4–1 Both the fiduciary relationship existing between lawyer and client and the proper functioning of the legal system require the preservation by the lawyer of confidences and secrets of one who has employed

---

[10] Conduct permitted by the Disciplinary Rules of Canons 2 and 5 does not violate DR 3–101.

[11] See ABA Canon 47.

[12] It should be noted, however, that a lawyer may engage in conduct, otherwise prohibited by this Disciplinary Rule, where such conduct is authorized by preemptive federal legislation. See Sperry v. Florida, 373 U.S. 379, 10 L.Ed.2d 428, 83 S.Ct. 1322 (1963).

[13] See ABA Canon 34 and *ABA Opinions* 316 (1967), 180 (1938), and 48 (1931).

"The receiving attorney shall not under any guise or form share his fee for legal services with a lay agency, personal or corporate, without prejudice, however, to the right of the lay forwarder to charge and collect from the creditor proper compensation for non-legal services rendered by the law [*sic*] forwarder which are separate and apart from the services performed by the receiving attorney." *ABA Opinion* 294 (1958).

[14] See *ABA Opinion* 266 (1945).

[15] Cf. *ABA Opinion* 311 (1964).

[16] See ABA Informal Opinion 1440 (1979).

[17] See ABA Canon 33; cf. *ABA Opinions* 239 (1942) and 201 (1940).

ABA Opinion 316 (1967) states that lawyers licensed in different jurisdictions may, under certain conditions, enter "into an arrangement for the practice of law" and that a lawyer licensed in State A is not, for such purpose a layman in State B.

or sought to employ him.[1] A client must feel free to discuss whatever he wishes with his lawyer and a lawyer must be equally free to obtain information beyond that volunteered by his client.[2] A lawyer should be fully informed of all the facts of the matter he is handling in order for his client to obtain the full advantage of our legal system. It is for the lawyer in the exercise of his independent professional judgment to separate the relevant and important from the irrelevant and unimportant. The observance of the ethical obligation of a lawyer to hold inviolate the confidences and secrets of his client not only facilitates the full development of facts essential to proper representation of the client but also encourages laymen to seek early legal assistance.

EC 4–2 The obligation to protect confidences and secrets obviously does not preclude a lawyer from revealing information when his client consents after full disclosure,[3] when necessary to perform his professional employment, when permitted by a Disciplinary Rule, or when required by law. Unless the client otherwise directs, a lawyer may disclose the affairs of his client to partners or associates of his firm. It is a matter of common knowledge that the normal operation of a law office exposes confidential professional information to non-lawyer employees of the office, particularly secretaries and those having access to the files; and this obligates a lawyer to exercise care in selecting and training his employees so that the sanctity of all confidences and secrets of his clients may be preserved. If the obligation extends to two or more clients as to the same information, a lawyer should obtain the permission of all before revealing the information. A lawyer must always be sensitive to the rights and wishes of his client and act scrupulously in the making of decisions which may involve the disclosure of information obtained in his professional relationship.[4] Thus, in the absence of consent of his client after full disclosure, a lawyer should not associate another lawyer in the handling of a matter; nor should he, in the absence of consent, seek counsel from another lawyer if there is a reasonable possibility that the identity of the client or his confidences or secrets would be revealed to such lawyer. Both social amenities and professional duty should cause a lawyer to shun indiscreet conversations concerning his clients.

EC 4–3 Unless the client otherwise directs, it is not improper for a lawyer to give limited information from his files to an outside agency necessary for statistical, bookkeeping, accounting, data processing,

---

1 See ABA Canons 6 and 37 and *ABA Opinions* 287 (1953). "The reason underlying the rule with respect to confidential communications between attorney and client is well stated in Mechem on Agency, 2d Ed., Vol. 2, § 2297, as follows: 'The purposes and necessities of the relation between a client and his attorney require, in many cases on the part of the client, the fullest and freest disclosures to the attorney of the client's objects, motives and acts. This disclosure is made in the strictest confidence, relying upon the attorney's honor and fidelity. To permit the attorney to reveal to others what is so disclosed, would be not only a gross violation of a sacred trust upon his part, but it would utterly destroy and prevent the usefulness and benefits to be derived from professional assistance. Based upon considerations of public policy, therefore, the law wisely declares that all confidential communications and disclosures, made by a client to his legal adviser for the purpose of obtaining his professional aid or advice, shall be strictly privileged:—that the attorney shall not be permitted, without the consent of his client,—and much less will he be compelled—to reveal or disclose communications made to him under such circumstances.' " *ABA Opinion* 250 (1943).

"While it is true that complete revelation of relevant facts should be encouraged for trial purposes, nevertheless an attorney's dealings with his client, if both are sincere, and if the dealings involve more than mere technical matters, should be immune to discovery proceedings. There must be freedom from fear of revealment of matters disclosed to an attorney because of the peculiarly intimate relationship existing." Ellis-Foster Co. v. Union Carbide & Carbon Corp., 159 F.Supp. 917, 919 (D.N.J.1958).

Cf. *ABA Opinions* 314 (1965), 274 (1946) and 268 (1945).

2 "While it is the great purpose of law to ascertain the truth, there is the countervailing necessity of insuring the right of every person to freely and fully confer and confide in one having knowledge of the law, and skilled in its practice, in order that the former may have adequate advice and a proper defense. This assistance can be made safely and readily available only when the client is free from the consequences of apprehension of disclosure by reason of the subsequent statements of the skilled lawyer." Baird v. Koerner, 279 F.2d 623, 629–30 (9th Cir.1960).

Cf. *ABA Opinion* 150 (1936).

3 "Where . . . [a client] knowingly and after full disclosure participates in a [legal fee] financing plan which requires the furnishing of certain information to the bank, clearly by his conduct he has waived any privilege as to that information." *ABA Opinion* 320 (1968).

4 "The lawyer must decide when he takes a case whether it is a suitable one for him to undertake and after this decision is made, he is not justified in turning against his client by exposing injurious evidence entrusted to him. . . . [D]oing something intrinsically regrettable, because the only alternative involves worse consequences, is a necessity in every profession." Williston, Life and Law 271 (1940).

Cf. *ABA Opinions* 177 (1938) and 83 (1932).

banking, printing, or other legitimate purposes, provided he exercises due care in the selection of the agency and warns the agency that the information must be kept confidential.

EC 4–4 The attorney-client privilege is more limited than the ethical obligation of a lawyer to guard the confidence and secrets of his client. This ethical precept, unlike the evidentiary privilege, exists without regard to the nature or source of information or the fact that others share the knowledge. A lawyer should endeavor to act in a manner which preserves the evidentiary privilege; for example, he should avoid professional discussions in the presence of persons to whom the privilege does not extend. A lawyer owes an obligation to advise the client of the attorney-client privilege and timely to assert the privilege unless it is waived by the client.

EC 4–5 A lawyer should not use information acquired in the course of the representation of a client to the disadvantage of the client and a lawyer should not use, except with the consent of his client after full disclosure, such information for his own purposes.[5] Likewise, a lawyer should be diligent in his efforts to prevent the misuse of such information by his employees and associates.[6] Care should be exercised by a lawyer to prevent the disclosure of the confidences and secrets of one client to another,[7] and no employment should be accepted that might require such disclosure.

EC 4–6 The obligation of a lawyer to preserve the confidences and secrets of his client continues after the termination of his employment.[8] Thus a lawyer should not attempt to sell a law practice as a going business because, among other reasons, to do so would involve the disclosure of confidences and secrets.[9] A lawyer should also provide for the protection of the confidences and secrets of his client following the termination of the practice of the lawyer, whether termination is due to death, disability, or retirement. For example, a lawyer might provide for the personal papers of the client to be returned to him and for the papers of the lawyer to be delivered to another lawyer or to be destroyed. In determining the method of disposition, the instructions and wishes of the client should be a dominant consideration.

DISCIPLINARY RULES

DR 4–101 Preservation of Confidences and Secrets of a Client.[10]

(A) "Confidence" refers to information protected by the attorney-client privilege under applicable law, and "secret" refers to other information gained in the professional relationship that the client has requested be held inviolate or the disclosure of which would be embarrassing or would be likely to be detrimental to the client.

(B) Except when permitted under DR 4–101(C), a lawyer shall not knowingly:

(1) Reveal a confidence or secret of his client.[11]

---

5 See ABA Canon 11.

6 See ABA Canon 37.

7 See ABA Canons 6 and 37.

"[A]n attorney must not accept professional employment against a client or a former client which will, or even *may* require him to use confidential information obtained by the attorney in the course of his professional relations with such client regarding the subject matter of the employment. . . ." *ABA Opinion* 165 (1936).

8 See ABA Canon 37.

"Confidential communications between an attorney and his client, made because of the relationship and concerning the subject-matter of the attorney's employment, are generally privileged from disclosure without the consent of the client, and this privilege outlasts the attorney's employment. *Canon 37.*" *ABA Opinion* 154 (1936).

9 Cf. *ABA Opinion* 266 (1945).

10 See ABA Canon 37; cf. ABA Canon 6.

11 "§ 6068 . . . It is the duty of an attorney: . . .

"(e) To maintain inviolate the confidence, and at every peril to himself to preserve the secrets, of his client." Cal. Business and Professions Code § 6068 (West 1962). Virtually the same provision is found in the Oregon statutes. Ore.Rev.Stat. ch. 9, § 9.460(5).

"Communications between lawyer and client are privileged (Wigmore on Evidence, 3d Ed., Vol. 8, §§ 2290–2329). The modern theory underlying the privilege is subjective and is to give the client freedom of apprehension in consulting his legal advisor (ibid., § 2290, p. 548). The privilege applies to communications made in seeking legal advice for any purpose

(2) Use a confidence or secret of his client to the disadvantage of the client.

(3) Use a confidence or secret of his client for the advantage of himself[12] or of a third person,[13] unless the client consents after full disclosure.

(C) A lawyer may reveal:

(1) Confidences or secrets with the consent of the client or clients affected, but only after a full disclosure to them.[14]

(2) Confidences or secrets when permitted under Disciplinary Rules or required by law or court order.[15]

(3) The intention of his client to commit a crime[16] and the information necessary to prevent the crime.[17]

(ibid., § 2294, p. 563). The mere circumstance that the advice is given without charge therefore does not nullify the privilege (ibid., § 2303)." *ABA Opinion* 216 (1941).

"It is the duty of an attorney to maintain the confidence and preserve inviolate the secrets of his client. . . ." *ABA Opinion* 155 (1936).

[12] See ABA Canon 11.

"The provision respecting employment is in accord with the general rule announced in the adjudicated cases that a lawyer may not make use of knowledge or information acquired by him through his professional relations with his client, or in the conduct of his client's business, to his own advantage or profit (7 C.J.S., § 125, p. 958; Healy v. Gray, 184 Iowa 111, 168 N.W. 222; Baumgardner v. Hudson, D.C.App., 277 F. 552; Goodrum v. Clement, D.C.App., 277 F. 586)." *ABA Opinion* 250 (1943).

[13] See *ABA Opinion* 177 (1938).

[14] "[A lawyer] may not divulge confidential communications, information, and secrets imparted to him by the client or acquired during their professional relations, unless he is authorized to do so by the client (People v. Gerold, 265 Ill. 448, 107 N.E. 165, 178; Murphy v. Riggs, 238 Mich. 151, 213 N.W. 110, 112; Opinion of this Committee, No. 91)." *ABA Opinion* 202 (1940).

Cf. *ABA Opinion* 91 (1933).

[15] "A defendant in a criminal case when admitted to bail is not only regarded as in the custody of his bail, but he is also in the custody of the law, and admission to bail does not deprive the court of its inherent power to deal with the person of the prisoner. Being in lawful custody, the defendant is guilty of an escape when he gains his liberty before he is delivered in due process of law, and is guilty of a separate offense for which he may be punished. In failing to disclose his client's whereabouts as a fugitive under these circumstances the attorney would not only be aiding his client to escape trial on the charge for which he was indicted, but would likewise be aiding him in evading prosecution for the additional offense of escape.

"It is the opinion of the committee that under such circumstances the attorney's knowledge of his client's whereabouts is not privileged, and that he may be disciplined for failing to disclose that information to the proper authorities. . . ." *ABA Opinion* 155 (1936).

"We held in *Opinion* 155 that a communication by a client to his attorney in respect to the future commission of an unlawful act or to a continuing wrong is not privileged from disclosure. Public policy forbids that the relation of attorney and client should be used to conceal wrongdoing on the part of the client.

. . .

"When an attorney representing a defendant in a criminal case applies on his behalf for probation or suspension of sentence, he represents to the court, by implication at least, that his client will abide by the terms and conditions of the court's order. When that attorney is later advised of a violation of that order, it is his duty to advise his client of the consequences of his act, and endeavor to prevent a continuance of the wrongdoing. If his client thereafter persists in violating the terms and conditions of his probation, it is the duty of the attorney as an officer of the court to advise the proper authorities concerning his client's conduct. Such information, even though coming to the attorney from the client in the course of his professional relations with respect to other matters in which he represents the defendant, is not privileged from disclosure. . . ." *ABA Opinion* 156 (1936).

See *ABA Opinion* 155 (1936).

[16] *ABA Opinion* 314 (1965) indicates that a lawyer must disclose even the confidences of his clients if "the facts in the attorney's possession indicate beyond reasonable doubt that a crime will be committed."

See *ABA Opinion* 155 (1936).

[17] See ABA Canon 37 and *ABA Opinion* 202 (1940).

(4) Confidences or secrets necessary to establish or collect his fee[18] or to defend himself or his employees or associates against an accusation of wrongful conduct.[19]

(D) A lawyer shall exercise reasonable care to prevent his employees, associates, and others whose services are utilized by him from disclosing or using confidences or secrets of a client, except that a lawyer may reveal the information allowed by DR 4–101(C) through an employee.

CANON 5

A Lawyer Should Exercise Independent Professional Judgment on Behalf of a Client

ETHICAL CONSIDERATIONS

EC 5–1 The professional judgment of a lawyer should be exercised, within the bounds of the law, solely for the benefit of his client and free of compromising influences and loyalties.[1] Neither his personal interests, the interests of other clients, nor the desires of third persons should be permitted to dilute his loyalty to his client.

---

[18] Cf. *ABA Opinion* 250 (1943).

[19] See ABA Canon 37 and *ABA Opinions* 202 (1940) and 19 (1930).

"[T]he adjudicated cases recognize an exception to the rule [that a lawyer shall not reveal the confidences of his client], where disclosure is necessary to protect the attorney's interests arising out of the relation of attorney and client in which disclosure was made.

"The exception is stated in Mechem on Agency, 2d Ed., Vol. 2, § 2313, as follows: 'But the attorney may disclose information received from the client when it becomes necessary for his own protection, as if the client should bring an action against the attorney for negligence or misconduct, and it became necessary for the attorney to show what his instructions were, or what was the nature of the duty which the client expected him to perform. So if it became necessary for the attorney to bring an action against the client, the client's privilege could not prevent the attorney from disclosing what was essential as a means of obtaining or defending his own rights.'

"Mr. Jones, in his Commentaries on Evidence, 2d Ed., Vol. 5, § 2165, states the exception thus: 'It has frequently been held that the rule as to privileged communications does not apply when litigation arises between attorney and client to the extent that their communications are relevant to the issue. In such cases, if the disclosure of privileged communications becomes necessary to protect the attorney's rights, he is released from those obligations of secrecy which the law places upon him. He should not, however, disclose more than is necessary for his own protection. It would be a manifest injustice to allow the client to take advantage of the rule of exclusion as to professional confidence to the prejudice of his attorney, or that it should be carried to the extent of depriving the attorney of the means of obtaining or defending his own rights. In such cases the attorney is exempted from the obligations of secrecy.' " *ABA Opinion* 250 (1943).

[1] Cf. ABA Canon 35.

"[A lawyer's] fiduciary duty is of the highest order and he must not represent interests adverse to those of the client. It is true that because of his professional responsibility and the confidence and trust which his client may legitimately repose in him, he must adhere to a high standard of honesty, integrity and good faith in dealing with his client. He is not permitted to take advantage of his position or superior knowledge to impose upon the client; nor to conceal facts or law, nor in any way deceive him without being held responsible therefor." Smoot v. Lund, 13 Utah 2d 168, 172, 369 P.2d 933, 936 (1962).

"When a client engages the services of a lawyer in a given piece of business he is entitled to feel that, until that business is finally disposed of in some manner, he has the undivided loyalty of the one upon whom he looks as his advocate and champion. If, as in this case, he is sued and his home attached by his own attorney, who is representing him in another matter, all feeling of loyalty is necessarily destroyed, and the profession is exposed to the charge that it is interested only in money." Grievance Comm. v. Rattner, 152 Conn. 59, 65, 203 A.2d 82, 84 (1964).

"One of the cardinal principles confronting every attorney in the representation of a client is the requirement of complete loyalty and service in good faith to the best of his ability. In a criminal case the client is entitled to a fair trial, but not a perfect one. These are fundamental requirements of due process under the Fourteenth Amendment. . . . The same principles are applicable in Sixth Amendment cases (not pertinent herein) and suggest that an attorney should have no conflict of interest and that he must devote his full and faithful efforts toward the defense of his client." Johns v. Smyth, 176 F.Supp. 949, 952 (E.D.Va.1959), modified, United States ex rel. Wilkins v. Banmiller, 205 F.Supp. 123, 128 n. 5 (E.D.Pa.1962), aff'd 325 F.2d 514 (3d Cir.1963), cert. denied, 379 U.S. 847, 13 L.Ed.2d 51, 85 S.Ct. 87 (1964).

Interests of a Lawyer That May Affect His Judgment

EC 5–2 A lawyer should not accept proffered employment if his personal interests or desires will, or there is a reasonable probability that they will, affect adversely the advice to be given or services to be rendered the prospective client.[2] After accepting employment, a lawyer carefully should refrain from acquiring a property right or assuming a position that would tend to make his judgment less protective of the interests of his client.

EC 5–3 The self-interest of a lawyer resulting from his ownership of property in which his client also has an interest or which may affect property of his client may interfere with the exercise of free judgment on behalf of his client. If such interference would occur with respect to a prospective client, a lawyer should decline employment proffered by him. After accepting employment, a lawyer should not acquire property rights that would adversely affect his professional judgment in the representation of his client. Even if the property interests of a lawyer do not presently interfere with the exercise of his independent judgment, but the likelihood of interference can reasonably be foreseen by him, a lawyer should explain the situation to his client and should decline employment or withdraw unless the client consents to the continuance of the relationship after full disclosure. A lawyer should not seek to persuade his client to permit him to invest in an undertaking of his client nor make improper use of his professional relationship to influence his client to invest in an enterprise in which the lawyer is interested.

EC 5–4 If, in the course of his representation of a client, a lawyer is permitted to receive from his client a beneficial ownership in publication rights relating to the subject matter of the employment, he may be tempted to subordinate the interests of his client to his own anticipated pecuniary gain. For example, a lawyer in a criminal case who obtains from his client television, radio, motion picture, newspaper, magazine, book, or other publication rights with respect to the case may be influenced, consciously or unconsciously, to a course of conduct that will enhance the value of his publication rights to the prejudice of his client. To prevent these potentially differing interests, such arrangements should be scrupulously avoided prior to the termination of all aspects of the matter giving rise to the employment, even though his employment has previously ended.

EC 5–5 A lawyer should not suggest to his client that a gift be made to himself or for his benefit. If a lawyer accepts a gift from his client, he is peculiarly susceptible to the charge that he unduly influenced or over-reached the client. If a client voluntarily offers to make a gift to his lawyer, the lawyer may accept the gift, but before doing so, he should urge that his client secure disinterested advice from an independent, competent person who is cognizant of all the circumstances.[3] Other than in exceptional circumstances, a

---

[2] "Attorneys must not allow their private interests to conflict with those of their clients. . . . They owe their entire devotion to the interests of their clients." United States v. Anonymous, 215 F.Supp. 111, 113 (E.D.Tenn.1963).

"[T]he court [below] concluded that a firm may not accept any action against a person whom they are presently representing even though there is no relationship between the two cases. In arriving at this conclusion, the court cites an opinion of the Committee on Professional Ethics of the New York County Lawyers' Association which stated in part: 'While under the circumstances . . . there may be no actual conflict of interest . . . "maintenance of public confidence in the Bar requires an attorney who has accepted representation of a client to decline, while representing such client, any employment from an adverse party in any matter even though wholly unrelated to the original retainer." See Question and Answer No. 350, N.Y. County L. Ass'n, Questions and Answer No. 450 (June 21, 1956).' " Grievance Comm. v. Rattner, 152 Conn. 59, 65, 203 A.2d 82, 84 (1964).

[3] "Courts of equity will scrutinize with jealous vigilance transactions between parties occupying fiduciary relations toward each other. . . . A deed will not be held invalid, however, if made by the grantor with full knowledge of its nature and effect, and because of the deliberate, voluntary and intelligent desire of the grantor. . . . Where a fiduciary relation exists, the burden of proof is on the grantee or beneficiary of an instrument executed during the existence of such relationship to show the fairness of the transaction, that it was equitable and just and that it did not proceed from undue influence. . . . The same rule has application where an attorney engages in a transaction with a client during the existence of the relation and is benefited thereby. . . . Conversely, an attorney is not prohibited from dealing with his client or buying his property, and such contracts, if open, fair and honest, when deliberately made, are as valid as contracts between other parties. . . . [I]mportant factors in determining whether a transaction is fair include a showing by the fiduciary (1) that he made a full and frank disclosure of all the relevant information that he had: (2) that the consideration was adequate; and (3) that the principal had independent advice before completing the transaction." McFail v. Braden, 19 Ill.2d 108, 117–18, 166 N.E.2d 46, 52 (1960).

lawyer should insist that an instrument in which his client desires to name him beneficially be prepared by another lawyer selected by the client.[4]

EC 5–6 A lawyer should not consciously influence a client to name him as executor, trustee, or lawyer in an instrument. In those cases where a client wishes to name his lawyer as such, care should be taken by the lawyer to avoid even the appearance of impropriety.[5]

EC 5–7 The possibility of an adverse effect upon the exercise of free judgment by a lawyer on behalf of his client during litigation generally makes it undesirable for the lawyer to acquire a proprietary interest in the cause of his client or otherwise to become financially interested in the outcome of the litigation.[6] However, it is not improper for a lawyer to protect his right to collect a fee for his services by the assertion of legally permissible liens, even though by doing so he may acquire an interest in the outcome of litigation. Although a contingent fee arrangement [7] gives a lawyer a financial interest in the outcome of litigation, a reasonable contingent fee is permissible in civil cases because it may be the only means by which a layman can obtain the services of a lawyer of his choice. But a lawyer, because he is in a better position to evaluate a cause of action, should enter into a continent fee arrangement only in those instances where the arrangement will be beneficial to the client.

EC 5–8 A financial interest in the outcome of litigation also results if monetary advances are made by the lawyer to his client.[8] Although this assistance generally is not encouraged, there are instances when it is not improper to make loans to a client. For example, the advancing or guaranteeing of payment of the costs and expenses of litigation by a lawyer may be the only way a client can enforce his cause of action,[9] but the ultimate liability for such costs and expenses must be that of the client.

EC 5–9 Occasionally a lawyer is called upon to decide in a particular case whether he will be a witness or an advocate. If a lawyer is both counsel and witness, he becomes more easily impeachable for interest and thus may be a less effective witness. Conversely, the opposing counsel may be handicapped in challenging the credibility of the lawyer when the lawyer also appears as an advocate in the case. An advocate who becomes a witness is in the unseemly and ineffective position of arguing his own credibility. The roles of an advocate and of a witness are inconsistent; the function of an advocate is to advance or argue the cause of another, while that of a witness is to state facts objectively.

EC 5–10 Problems incident to the lawyer-witness relationship arise at different stages; they relate either to whether a lawyer should accept employment or should withdraw from employment.[10] Regardless of when the problem arises, his decision is to be governed by the same basic considerations. It is not objectionable for a lawyer who is a potential witness to be an advocate if it is unlikely that he will be called as a witness because his testimony would be merely cumulative or if his testimony will relate only to an uncontested

---

4 See State ex rel. Nebraska State Bar Ass'n v. Richards, 165 Neb. 80, 94–95, 84 N.W.2d 136, 146 (1957).

5 See ABA Canon 9.

6 See ABA Canon 10.

7 See Code of Professional Responsibility, EC 2–20.

8 See ABA Canon 42.

9 "*Rule 3a.* . . . A member of the State Bar shall not directly or indirectly pay or agree to pay, or represent or sanction the representation that he will pay, medical, hospital or nursing bills or other personal expenses incurred by or for a client, prospective or existing; provided this rule shall not prohibit a member:

"(1) with the consent of the client, from paying or agreeing to pay to third persons such expenses from funds collected or to be collected for the client; or

"(2) after he has been employed, from lending money to his client upon the client's promise in writing to repay such loan; or

"(3) from advancing the costs of prosecuting or defending a claim or action. Such costs within the meaning of this subparagraph (3) include all taxable costs or disbursements, costs or investigation and costs of obtaining and presenting evidence." Cal. Business and Professions Code § 6076 (West Supp.1967).

10 "When a lawyer knows, prior to trial, that he will be a necessary witness, except as to merely formal matters such as identification or custody of a document or the like, neither he nor his firm or associates should conduct the trial. If, during the trial, he discovers that the ends of justice require his testimony, he should, from that point on, if feasible and not prejudicial to his client's case, leave further conduct of the trial to other counsel. If circumstances do not permit withdrawal from the conduct of the trial, the lawyer should not argue the credibility of his own testimony." *A Code of Trial Conduct: Promulgated by the American College of Trial Lawyers,* 43 A.B.A.J. 223, 224–25 (1957).

issue.[11] In the exceptional situation where it will be manifestly unfair to the client for the lawyer to refuse employment or to withdraw when he will likely be a witness on a contested issue, he may serve as advocate even though he may be a witness.[12] In making such decision, he should determine the personal or financial sacrifice of the client that may result from his refusal of employment or withdrawal therefrom, the materiality of his testimony, and the effectiveness of his representation in view of his personal involvement. In weighing these factors, it should be clear that refusal or withdrawal will impose an unreasonable hardship upon the client before the lawyer accepts or continues the employment.[13] Where the question arises, doubts should be resolved in favor of the lawyer testifying and against his becoming or continuing as an advocate.[14]

EC 5–11 A lawyer should not permit his personal interests to influence his advice relative to a suggestion by his client that additional counsel be employed.[15] In like manner, his personal interests should not deter him from suggesting that additional counsel be employed; on the contrary, he should be alert to the desirability of recommending additional counsel when, in his judgment, the proper representation of his client requires it. However, a lawyer should advise his client not to employ additional counsel suggested by the client if the lawyer believes that such employment would be a disservice to the client, and he should disclose the reasons for his belief.

EC 5–12 Inability of co-counsel to agree on a matter vital to the representation of their client requires that their disagreement be submitted by them jointly to their client for his resolution, and the decision of the client shall control the action to be taken.[16]

EC 5–13 A lawyer should not maintain membership in or be influenced by any organization of employees that undertakes to prescribe, direct, or suggest when or how he should fulfill his professional obligations to a person or organization that employs him as a lawyer. Although it is not necessarily improper for a lawyer employed by a corporation or similar entity to be a member of an organization of employees, he should be vigilant to safeguard his fidelity as a lawyer to his employer, free from outside influences.

Interests of Multiple Clients

EC 5–14 Maintaining the independence of professional judgment required of a lawyer precludes his acceptance or continuation of employment that will adversely affect his judgment on behalf of or dilute his loyalty to a client.[17] This problem arises whenever a lawyer is asked to represent two or more clients who may have differing interests, whether such interests be conflicting, inconsistent, diverse, or otherwise discordant.[18]

---

[11] Cf. Canon 19: "When a lawyer is a witness for his client, except as to merely formal matters, such as the attestation or custody of an instrument and the like, he should leave the trial of the case to other counsel."

[12] "It is the general rule that a lawyer may not testify in litigation in which he is an advocate unless circumstances arise which could not be anticipated and it is necessary to prevent a miscarriage of justice. In those rare cases where the testimony of an attorney is needed to protect his client's interests, it is not only proper but mandatory that it be forthcoming." Schwartz v. Wenger, 267 Minn. 40, 43–44, 124 N.W.2d 489, 492 (1963).

[13] "The great weight of authority in this country holds that the attorney who acts as counsel and witness, in behalf of his client, in the same cause on a material matter, not of a merely formal character, and not in an emergency, but having knowledge that he would be required to be a witness in ample time to have secured other counsel and given up his service in the case, violates a highly important provision of the Code of Ethics and a rule of professional conduct, but does not commit a legal error in so testifying, as a result of which a new trial will be granted." Erwin M. Jennings Co. v. DiGenova, 107 Conn. 491, 499, 141 A. 866, 869 (1928).

[14] "[C]ases may arise, and in practice often do arise, in which there would be a failure of justice should the attorney withhold his testimony. In such a case it would be a vicious professional sentiment which would deprive the client of the benefit of his attorney's testimony." Connolly v. Straw, 53 Wis. 645, 649, 11 N.W. 17, 19 (1881).

But see Canon 19. "Except when essential to the ends of justice, a lawyer should avoid testifying in court in behalf of his client."

[15] Cf. ABA Canon 7.

[16] See ABA Canon 7.

[17] See ABA Canon 6; cf. *ABA Opinions* 261 (1944), 242 (1942), 142 (1935), and 30 (1931).

[18] The ABA Canons speak of "conflicting interests" rather than "differing interests" but make no attempt to define such other than the statement in Canon 6: "Within the meaning of this canon, a lawyer represents conflicting interests when, in behalf of one client, it is his duty to contend for that which duty to another client requires him to oppose."

EC 5–15 If a lawyer is requested to undertake or to continue representation of multiple clients having potentially differing interests, he must weigh carefully the possibility that his judgment may be impaired or his loyalty divided if he accepts or continues the employment. He should resolve all doubts against the propriety of the representation. A lawyer should never represent in litigation multiple clients with differing interests;[19] and there are few situations in which he would be justified in representing in litigation multiple clients with potentially differing interests. If a lawyer accepted such employment and the interests did become actually differing, he would have to withdraw from employment with likelihood of resulting hardship on the clients; and for this reason it is preferable that he refuse the employment initially. On the other hand, there are many instances in which a lawyer may properly serve multiple clients having potentially differing interests in matters not involving litigation. If the interests vary only slightly, it is generally likely that the lawyer will not be subjected to an adverse influence and that he can retain his independent judgment on behalf of each client; and if the interests become differing, withdrawal is less likely to have a disruptive effect upon the causes of his clients.

EC 5–16 In those instances in which a lawyer is justified in representing two or more clients having differing interests, it is nevertheless essential that each client be given the opportunity to evaluate his need for representation free of any potential conflict and to obtain other counsel if he so desires.[20] Thus before a lawyer may represent multiple clients, he should explain fully to each client the implications of the common representation and should accept or continue employment only if the clients consent.[21] If there are present other circumstances that might cause any of the multiple clients to question the undivided loyalty of the lawyer, he should also advise all of the clients of those circumstances.[22]

EC 5–17 Typically recurring situations involving potentially differing interests are those in which a lawyer is asked to represent co-defendants in a criminal case, co-plaintiffs in a personal injury case, an insured and his insurer,[23] and beneficiaries of the estate of a decedent. Whether a lawyer can fairly and adequately

---

19 "Canon 6 of the Canons of Professional Ethics, adopted by the American Bar Association on September 30, 1937, and by the Pennsylvania Bar Association on January 7, 1938, provides in part that 'It is unprofessional to represent conflicting interests, except by express consent of all concerned given after a full disclosure of the facts. Within the meaning of this Canon, a lawyer represents conflicting interests when, in behalf of one client, it is his duty to contend for that which duty to another client requires him to oppose.' The full disclosure required by this canon contemplates that the possibly adverse effect of the conflict be fully explained by the attorney to the client to be affected and by him thoroughly understood. . . .

"The foregoing canon applies to cases where the circumstances are such that possibly conflicting interests may permissibly be represented by the same attorney. But manifestly, there are instances where the conflicts of interest are so critically adverse as not to admit of one attorney's representing both sides. Such is the situation which this record presents. No one could conscionably contend that the same attorney may represent both the plaintiff and defendant in an adversary action. Yet, that is what is being done in this case." Jedwabny v. Philadelphia Transportation Co., 390 Pa. 231, 235, 135 A.2d 252, 254 (1957), cert. denied, 355 U.S. 966, 2 L.Ed.2d 541, 78 S.Ct. 557 (1958).

20 "Glasser wished the benefit of the undivided assistance of counsel of his own choice. We think that such a desire on the part of an accused should be respected. Irrespective of any conflict of interest, the additional burden of representing another party may conceivably impair counsel's effectiveness.

"To determine the precise degree of prejudice sustained by Glasser as a result of the court's appointment of Stewart as counsel for Kretske is at once difficult and unnecessary. The right to have the assistance of counsel is too fundamental and absolute to allow courts to indulge in nice calculations as to the amount of prejudice arising from its denial." Glasser v. United States, 315 U.S. 60, 75–76, 86 L.Ed. 680, 62 S.Ct. 457, 467 (1942).

21 See ABA Canon 6.

22 Id.

23 Cf. *ABA Opinion* 282 (1950).

"When counsel, although paid by the casualty company, undertakes to represent the policyholder and files his notice of appearance, he owes to his client, the assured, an undeviating and single allegiance. His fealty embraces the requirement to produce in court all witnesses, fact and expert, who are available and necessary for the proper protection of the rights of his client. . . .

". . . The Canons of Professional Ethics make it pellucid that there are not two standards, one applying to counsel privately retained by a client, and the other to counsel paid by an insurance carrier." American Employers Ins. Co. v. Goble Aircraft Specialties, 205 Misc. 1066, 1075, 131 N.Y.S.2d 393, 401 (1954), motion to withdraw appeal granted, 1 App.Div.2d 1008, 154 N.Y.S.2d 835 (1956).

"[C]ounsel, selected by State Farm to defend Dorothy Walker's suit for $50,000 damages, was apprised by Walker that his earlier version of the accident was untrue and that actually the accident occurred because he lost control of his car in passing a Cadillac just ahead. At that point, Walker's counsel should have refused to participate further in view of the conflict of interest between Walker and State Farm. . . . Instead he participated in the ensuing deposition of the

protect the interests of multiple clients in these and similar situations depends upon an analysis of each case. In certain circumstances, there may exist little chance of the judgment of the lawyer being adversely affected by the slight possibility that the interests will become actually differing; in other circumstances, the chance of adverse effect upon his judgment is not unlikely.

EC 5–18 A lawyer employed or retained by a corporation or similar entity owes his allegiance to the entity and not to a stockholder, director, officer, employee, representative, or other person connected with the entity. In advising the entity, a lawyer should keep paramount its interests and his professional judgment should not be influenced by the personal desires of any person or organization. Occasionally a lawyer for an entity is requested by a stockholder, director, officer, employee, representative, or other person connected with the entity to represent him in an individual capacity; in such case the lawyer may serve the individual only if the lawyer is convinced that differing interests are not present.

EC 5–19 A lawyer may represent several clients whose interests are not actually or potentially differing. Nevertheless, he should explain any circumstances that might cause a client to question his undivided loyalty.[24] Regardless of the belief of a lawyer that he may properly represent multiple clients, he must defer to a client who holds the contrary belief and withdraw from representation of that client.

EC 5–20 A lawyer is often asked to serve as an impartial arbitrator or mediator in matters which involve present or former clients. He may serve in either capacity if he first discloses such present or former relationships. After a lawyer has undertaken to act as an impartial arbitrator or mediator, he should not thereafter represent in the dispute any of the parties involved.

Desires of Third Persons

EC 5–21 The obligation of a lawyer to exercise professional judgment solely on behalf of his client requires that he disregard the desires of others that might impair his free judgment.[25] The desires of a third person will seldom adversely affect a lawyer unless that person is in a position to exert strong economic, political, or social pressures upon the lawyer. These influences are often subtle, and a lawyer must be alert to their existence. A lawyer subjected to outside pressures should make full disclosure of them to his client; [26] and if he or his client believes that the effectiveness of his representation has been or will be impaired thereby, the lawyer should take proper steps to withdraw from representation of his client.

EC 5–22 Economic, political, or social pressures by third persons are less likely to impinge upon the independent judgment of a lawyer in a matter in which he is compensated directly by his client and his professional work is exclusively with his client. On the other hand, if a lawyer is compensated from a source other than his client, he may feel a sense of responsibility to someone other than his client.

EC 5–23 A person or organization that pays or furnishes lawyers to represent others possesses a potential power to exert strong pressures against the independent judgment of those lawyers. Some employers may be interested in furthering their own economic, political, or social goals without regard to the professional responsibility of the lawyer to his individual client. Others may be far more concerned with establishment or extension of legal principles than in the immediate protection of the rights of the lawyer's individual client. On some occasions, decisions on priority of work may be made by the employer rather than the lawyer with the result that prosecution of work already undertaken for clients is postponed to their detriment.

Walkers, even took an *ex parte* sworn statement from Mr. Walker in order to advise State Farm what action it should take, and later used the statement against Walker in the District Court. This action appears to contravene an Indiana attorney's duty 'at every peril to himself, to preserve the secrets of his client'. . . ." State Farm Mut. Auto Ins. Co. v. Walker, 382 F.2d 548, 552 (1967), cert. denied, 389 U.S. 1045, 19 L.Ed.2d 837, 88 S.Ct. 789 (1968).

[24] See ABA Canon 6.

[25] See ABA Canon 35.

"Objection to the intervention of a lay intermediary, who may control litigation or otherwise interfere with the rendering of legal services in a confidential relationship, . . . derives from the element of pecuniary gain. Fearful of dangers thought to arise from that element, the courts of several States have sustained regulations aimed at these activities. We intimate no view one way or the other as to the merits of those decisions with respect to the particular arrangements against which they are directed. It is enough that the superficial resemblance in form between those arrangements and that at bar cannot obscure the vital fact that here the entire arrangement employs constitutionally privileged means of expression to secure constitutionally guaranteed civil rights." NAACP v. Button, 371 U.S. 415, 441–42, 9 L.Ed.2d 405, 423–24, 83 S.Ct. 328, 342–43 (1963).

[26] Cf. ABA Canon 38.

Similarly, an employer may seek, consciously or unconsciously, to further its own economic interests through the action of the lawyers employed by it. Since a lawyer must always be free to exercise his professional judgment without regard to the interests or motives of a third person, the lawyer who is employed by one to represent another must constantly guard against erosion of his professional freedom.[27]

EC 5-24 To assist a lawyer in preserving his professional independence, a number of courses are available to him. For example, a lawyer should not practice with or in the form of a professional legal corporation, even though the corporate form is permitted by law,[28] if any director, officer, or stockholder of it is a non-lawyer. Although a lawyer may be employed by a business corporation with non-lawyers serving as directors or officers, and they necessarily have the right to make decisions of business policy, a lawyer must decline to accept direction of his professional judgment from any layman. Various types of legal aid offices are administered by boards of directors composed of lawyers and laymen. A lawyer should not accept employment from such an organization unless the board sets only broad policies and there is no interference in the relationship of the lawyer and the individual client he serves. Where a lawyer is employed by an organization, a written agreement that defines the relationship between him and the organization and provides for his independence is desirable since it may serve to prevent misunderstanding as to their respective roles. Although other innovations in the means of supplying legal counsel may develop, the responsibility of the lawyer to maintain his professional independence remains constant, and the legal profession must insure that changing circumstances do not result in loss of the professional independence of the lawyer.

DISCIPLINARY RULES

DR 5-101 Refusing Employment When the Interests of the Lawyer May Impair His Independent Professional Judgment.

(A) Except with the consent of his client after full disclosure, a lawyer shall not accept employment if the exercise of his professional judgment on behalf of his client will be or reasonably may be affected by his own financial, business, property, or personal interests.[29]

(B) A lawyer shall not accept employment in contemplated or pending litigation if he knows or it is obvious that he or a lawyer in his firm ought to be called as a witness,

---

[27] "Certainly it is true that 'the professional relationship between an attorney and his client is highly personal, involving an intimate appreciation of each individual client's particular problem.' And this Committee does not condone practices which interfere with that relationship. However, the mere fact the lawyer is actually paid by some entity other than the client does not affect that relationship, so long as the lawyer is selected by and is directly responsible to the client. See Informal Opinions 469 and 679. Of course, as the latter decision points out, there must be full disclosure of the arrangement by the attorney to the client. . . ." *ABA Opinion* 320 (1968).

"[A] third party may pay the cost of legal services as long as control remains in the client and the responsibility of the lawyer is solely to the client. Informal Opinions 469 ad [*sic*] 679. See also *Opinion* 237." Id.

[28] *ABA Opinion* 303 (1961) recognized that "[s]tatutory provisions now exist in several states which are designed to make [the practice of law in a form that will be classified as a corporation for federal income tax purposes] legally possible, either as a result of lawyers incorporating or forming associations with various corporate characteristics."

[29] Cf. ABA Canon 6 and *ABA Opinions* 181 (1938), 104 (1934), 103 (1933), 72 (1932), 50 (1931), 49 (1931), and 33 (1931).

"New York County [Opinion] 203. . . . [A lawyer] should not advise a client to employ an investment company in which he is interested, without informing him of this." Drinker, *Legal Ethics* 956 (1953).

"In *Opinions* 72 and 49 this Committee held: The relations of partners in a law firm are such that neither the firm nor any member or associate thereof, may accept any professional employment which any member of the firm cannot properly accept.

"In *Opinion* 16 this Committee held that a member of a law firm could not represent a defendant in a criminal case which was being prosecuted by another member of the firm who was public prosecuting attorney. The Opinion stated that it was clearly unethical for one member of the firm to oppose the interest of the state while another member represented those interests. . . . Since the prosecutor himself could not represent both the public and the defendant, no member of his law firm could either." *ABA Opinion* 296 (1959).

except that he may undertake the employment and he or a lawyer in his firm may testify:

(1) If the testimony will relate solely to an uncontested matter.

(2) If the testimony will relate solely to a matter of formality and there is no reason to believe that substantial evidence will be offered in opposition to the testimony.

(3) If the testimony will relate solely to the nature and value of legal services rendered in the case by the lawyer or his firm to the client.

(4) As to any matter, if refusal would work a substantial hardship on the client because of the distinctive value of the lawyer or his firm as counsel in the particular case.

DR 5-102 Withdrawal as Counsel When the Lawyer Becomes a Witness.[30]

(A) If, after undertaking employment in contemplated or pending litigation, a lawyer learns or it is obvious that he or a lawyer in his firm ought to be called as a witness on behalf of his client, he shall withdraw from the conduct of the trial and his firm, if any, shall not continue representation in the trial, except that he may continue the representation and he or a lawyer in his firm may testify in the circumstances enumerated in DR 5-101(B)(1) through (4).

(B) If, after undertaking employment in contemplated or pending litigation, a lawyer learns or it is obvious that he or a lawyer in his firm may be called as a witness other than on behalf of his client, he may continue the representation until it is apparent that his testimony is or may be prejudicial to his client.[31]

DR 5-103 Avoiding Acquisition of Interest in Litigation.

(A) A lawyer shall not acquire a proprietary interest in the cause of action or subject matter of litigation he is conducting for a client,[32] except that he may:

(1) Acquire a lien granted by law to secure his fee or expenses.

(2) Contract with a client for a reasonable contingent fee in a civil case.[33]

(B) While representing a client in connection with contemplated or pending litigation, a lawyer shall not advance or guarantee financial assistance to his client,[34] except that a lawyer may advance or guarantee the expenses of litigation, including court costs, expenses of investigation, expenses of medical examination, and costs of obtaining and presenting evidence, provided the client remains ultimately liable for such expenses.

DR 5-104 Limiting Business Relations With a Client.

(A) A lawyer shall not enter into a business transaction with a client if they have differing interests therein and if the client expects the lawyer to exercise his professional judgment therein for the protection of the client, unless the client has consented after full disclosure.

---

[30] Cf. ABA Canon 19 and *ABA Opinions* 220 (1941), 185 (1938), 50 (1931), and 33 (1931); but cf. Erwin M. Jennings Co. v. DiGenova, 107 Conn. 491, 498–99, 141 A. 866, 868 (1928).

[31] "This *Canon* [19] *of Ethics* needs no elaboration to be applied to the facts here. Apparently, the object of this precept is to avoid putting a lawyer in the obviously embarrassing predicament of testifying and then having to argue the credibility and effect of his own testimony. It was not designed to permit a lawyer to call opposing counsel as a witness and thereby disqualify him as counsel." Galarowicz v. Ward, 119 Utah 611, 620, 230 P.2d 576, 580 (1951).

[32] ABA Canon 10 and *ABA Opinions* 279 (1949), 246 (1942) and 176 (1938).

[33] See Code of Professional Responsibility, DR 2-106(C).

[34] See ABA Canon 42; cf. *ABA Opinion* 288 (1954).

(B) Prior to conclusion of all aspects of the matter giving rise to his employment, a lawyer shall not enter into any arrangement or understanding with a client or a prospective client by which he acquires an interest in publication rights with respect to the subject matter of his employment or proposed employment.

DR 5–105 Refusing to Accept or Continue Employment if the Interests of Another Client May Impair the Independent Professional Judgment of the Lawyer.

(A) A lawyer shall decline proffered employment if the exercise of his independent professional judgment in behalf of a client will be or is likely to be adversely affected by the acceptance of the proffered employment,[35] or if it would be likely to involve him in representing differing interests, except to the extent permitted under DR 5–105(C).[36]

(B) A lawyer shall not continue multiple employment if the exercise of his independent professional judgment in behalf of a client will be or is likely to be adversely affected by his representation of another client, or if it would be likely to involve him in representing differing interests, except to the extent permitted under DR 5–105(C).[37]

(C) In the situations covered by DR 5–105(A) and (B), a lawyer may represent multiple clients if it is obvious that he can adequately represent the interest of each and if each consents to the representation after full disclosure of the possible effect of such representation on the exercise of his independent professional judgment on behalf of each.

(D) If a lawyer is required to decline employment or to withdraw from employment under a Disciplinary Rule, no partner or associate, or any other lawyer affiliated with him or his firm may accept or continue such employment.

As amended in 1974.

DR 5–106 Settling Similar Claims of Clients.[38]

(A) A lawyer who represents two or more clients shall not make or participate in the making of an aggregate settlement of the claims of or against his clients, unless each client has consented to the settlement after being advised of the existence and nature of all the claims involved in the proposed settlement, of the total amount of the settlement, and of the participation of each person in the settlement.

DR 5–107 Avoiding Influence by Others Than the Client.

(A) Except with the consent of his client after full disclosure, a lawyer shall not:

 (1) Accept compensation for his legal services from one other than his client.

 (2) Accept from one other than his client any thing of value related to his representation of or his employment by his client.[39]

---

[35] See ABA Canon 6; cf. *ABA Opinions* 167 (1937), 60 (1931), and 40 (1931).

[36] *ABA Opinion* 247 (1942) held that an attorney could not investigate a night club shooting on behalf of one of the owner's liability insurers, obtaining the cooperation of the owner, and later represent the injured patron in an action against the owner and a different insurance company unless the attorney obtain the "express consent of all concerned given after a full disclosure of the facts," since to do so would be to represent conflicting interests.

See *ABA Opinions* 247 (1942), 224 (1941), 222 (1941), 218 (1941), 112 (1934), 83 (1932), and 86 (1932).

[37] Cf. *ABA Opinions* 231 (1941) and 160 (1936).

[38] Cf. *ABA Opinions* 243 (1942) and 235 (1941).

[39] See ABA Canon 38.

"A lawyer who receives a commission (whether delayed or not) from a title insurance company or guaranty fund for recommending or selling the insurance to his client, or for work done for the client or the company, without either fully

(B) A lawyer shall not permit a person who recommends, employs, or pays him to render legal services for another to direct or regulate his professional judgment in rendering such legal services.[40]

(C) A lawyer shall not practice with or in the form of a professional corporation or association authorized to practice law for a profit, if:

(1) A non-lawyer owns any interest therein,[41] except that a fiduciary representative of the estate of a lawyer may hold the stock or interest of the lawyer for a reasonable time during administration;

(2) A non-lawyer is a corporate director or officer thereof; [42] or

(3) A non-lawyer has the right to direct or control the professional judgment of a lawyer.[43]

CANON 6

A Lawyer Should Represent a Client Competently

ETHICAL CONSIDERATIONS

EC 6–1 Because of his vital role in the legal process, a lawyer should act with competence and proper care in representing clients. He should strive to become and remain proficient in his practice [1] and should accept employment only in matters which he is or intends to become competent to handle.

---

disclosing to the client his financial interest in the transaction, or crediting the client's bill with the amount thus received, is guilty of unethical conduct." *ABA Opinion* 304 (1962).

[40] See ABA Canon 35; cf. *ABA Opinion* 237 (1941).

"When the lay forwarder, as agent for the creditor, forwards a claim to an attorney, the direct relationship of attorney and client shall then exist between the attorney and the creditor, and the forwarder shall not interpose itself as an intermediary to control the activities of the attorney." *ABA Opinion* 294 (1958).

[41] "Permanent beneficial and voting rights in the organization set up to practice law, whatever its form, must be restricted to lawyers while the organization is engaged in the practice of law." *ABA Opinion* 303 (1961).

[42] "*Canon 33* . . . promulgates underlying principles that must be observed no matter in what form of organization lawyers practice law. Its requirement that no person shall be admitted or held out as a practitioner or member who is not a member of the legal profession duly authorized to practice, and amendable to professional discipline, makes it clear that any centralized management must be in lawyers to avoid a violation of this Canon." *ABA Opinion* 303 (1961).

[43] "There is no intervention of any lay agency between lawyer and client when centralized management provided only by lawyers may give guidance or direction to the services being rendered by a lawyer-member of the organization to a client. The language in *Canon 35* that a lawyer should avoid all relations which direct the performance of his duties by or in the interest of an intermediary refers to lay intermediaries and not lawyer intermediaries with whom he is associated in the practice of law." *ABA Opinion* 303 (1961).

[1] "[W]hen a citizen is faced with the need for a lawyer, he wants, and is entitled to, the best informed counsel he can obtain. Changing times produce changes in our laws and legal procedures. The natural complexities of law require continuing intensive study by a lawyer if he is to render his clients a maximum of efficient service. And, in so doing, he maintains the high standards of the legal profession; and he also increases respect and confidence by the general public." Rochelle & Payne, *The Struggle for Public Understanding,* 25 Texas B.J. 109, 160 (1962).

"We have undergone enormous changes in the last fifty years within the lives of most of the adults living today who may be seeking advice. Most of these changes have been accompanied by changes and developments in the law. . . . Every practicing lawyer encounters these problems and is often perplexed with his own inability to keep up, not only with changes in the law, but also with changes in the lives of his clients and their legal problems.

"To be sure, no client has a right to expect that his lawyer will have all of the answers at the end of his tongue or even in the back of his head at all times. But the client does have the right to expect that the lawyer will have devoted his time and energies to maintaining and improving his competence to know where to look for the answers, to know how to deal with the problems, and to know how to advise to the best of his legal talents and abilities." Levy & Sprague, *Accounting and Law: Is Dual Practice in the Public Interest?*, 52 A.B.A.J. 1110, 1112 (1966).

EC 6–2 A lawyer is aided in attaining and maintaining his competence by keeping abreast of current legal literature and developments, participating in continuing legal education programs,[2] concentrating in particular areas of the law, and by utilizing other available means. He has the additional ethical obligation to assist in improving the legal profession, and he may do so by participating in bar activities intended to advance the quality and standards of members of the profession. Of particular importance is the careful training of his younger associates and the giving of sound guidance to all lawyers who consult him. In short, a lawyer should strive at all levels to aid the legal profession in advancing the highest possible standards of integrity and competence and to meet those standards himself.

EC 6–3 While the licensing of a lawyer is evidence that he has met the standards then prevailing for admission to the bar, a lawyer generally should not accept employment in any area of the law in which he is not qualified.[3] However, he may accept such employment if in good faith he expects to become qualified through study and investigation, as long as such preparation would not result in unreasonable delay or expense to his client. Proper preparation and representation may require the association by the lawyer of professionals in other disciplines. A lawyer offered employment in a matter in which he is not and does not expect to become so qualified should either decline the employment or, with the consent of his client, accept the employment and associate a lawyer who is competent in the matter.

EC 6–4 Having undertaken representation, a lawyer should use proper care to safeguard the interests of his client. If a lawyer has accepted employment in a matter beyond his competence but in which he expected to become competent, he should diligently undertake the work and study necessary to qualify himself. In addition to being qualified to handle a particular matter, his obligation to his client requires him to prepare adequately for and give appropriate attention to his legal work.

EC 6–5 A lawyer should have pride in his professional endeavors. His obligation to act competently calls for higher motivation than that arising from fear of civil liability or disciplinary penalty.

EC 6–6 A lawyer should not seek, by contract or other means, to limit his individual liability to his client for his malpractice. A lawyer who handles the affairs of his client properly has no need to attempt to limit his liability for his professional activities and one who does not handle the affairs of his client properly should not be permitted to do so. A lawyer who is a stockholder in or is associated with a professional legal corporation may, however, limit his liability for malpractice of his associates in the corporation, but only to the extent permitted by law.[4]

DISCIPLINARY RULES

DR 6–101 Failing to Act Competently.

(A) A lawyer shall not:

(1) Handle a legal matter which he knows or should know that he is not competent to handle, without associating with him a lawyer who is competent to handle it.

(2) Handle a legal matter without preparation adequate in the circumstances.

(3) Neglect a legal matter entrusted to him.[5]

---

2 "The whole purpose of continuing legal education, so enthusiastically supported by the ABA, is to make it possible for lawyers to make themselves better lawyers. But there are no nostrums for proficiency in the law; it must come through the hard work of the lawyer himself. To the extent that that work, whether it be in attending institutes or lecture courses, in studying after hours or in the actual day in and day out practice of his profession, can be concentrated within a limited field, the greater the proficiency and expertness that can be developed." *Report of the Special Committee on Specialization and Specialized Legal Education,* 79 A.B.A.Rep. 582, 588 (1954).

3 "If the attorney is not competent to skillfully and properly perform the work, he should not undertake the service." Degen v. Steinbrink, 202 App.Div. 477, 481, 195 N.Y.S. 810, 814 (1922), aff'd mem., 236 N.Y. 669, 142 N.E. 328 (1923).

4 See *ABA Opinion* 303 (1961); cf. Code of Professional Responsibility EC 2–11.

5 The annual report for 1967–1968 of the Committee on Grievances of the Association of the Bar of the City of New York showed a receipt of 2,232 complaints; of the 828 offenses against clients, 76 involved conversion, 49 involved "overreaching," and 452, or more than half of all such offenses, involved neglect. *Annual Report of the Committee on Grievances of the Association of the Bar of the City of New York,* N.Y.L.J., Sept. 12, 1968, at 4, col. 5.

DR 6–102 Limiting Liability to Client.

(A) A lawyer shall not attempt to exonerate himself from or limit his liability to his client for his personal malpractice.

CANON 7

A Lawyer Should Represent a Client Zealously Within the Bounds of the Law

ETHICAL CONSIDERATIONS

EC 7–1 The duty of a lawyer, both to his client[1] and to the legal system, is to represent his client zealously[2] within the bounds of the law,[3] which includes Disciplinary Rules and enforceable professional regulations.[4] The professional responsibility of a lawyer derives from his membership in a profession which has the duty

---

1 "The right to be heard would be, in many cases, of little avail if it did not comprehend the right to be heard by counsel. Even the intelligent and educated layman has small and sometimes no skill in the science of law." Powell v. Alabama, 287 U.S. 45, 68–69, 77 L.Ed. 158, 170, 53 S.Ct. 55, 64 (1932).

2 Cf. ABA Canon 4.

"At times . . . [the tax lawyer] will be wise to discard some arguments and he should exercise discretion to emphasize the arguments which in his judgment are most likely to be persuasive. But this process involves legal judgment rather than moral attitudes. The tax lawyer should put aside private disagreements with Congressional and Treasury policies. His own notions of policy, and his personal view of what the law should be, are irrelevant. The job entrusted to him by his client is to use all his learning and ability to protect his client's rights, not to help in the process of promoting a better tax system. The tax lawyer need not accept his client's economic and social opinions, but the client is paying for technical attention and undivided concentration upon his affairs. He is equally entitled to performance unfettered by his attorney's economic and social predilections." Paul, *The Lawyer is a Tax Advisor,* 25 Rocky Mt.L.Rev. 412, 418 (1953).

3 See ABA Canons 15 and 32.

ABA Canon 5, although only speaking of one accused of crime, imposes a similar obligation on the lawyer: "[T]he lawyer is bound, by all fair and honorable means, to present every defense that the law of the land permits, to the end that no person may be deprived of life or liberty, but by due process of law."

"Any persuasion or pressure on the advocate which deters him from planning and carrying out the litigation on the basis of 'what, within the framework of the law, is best for my client's interest?' interferes with the obligation to represent the client fully within the law.

"This obligation, in its fullest sense, is the heart of the adversary process. Each attorney, as an advocate, acts for and seeks that which in his judgment is best for his client, within the bounds authoritatively established. The advocate does not *decide* what is just in this case—he would be usurping the function of the judge and jury—he acts for and seeks for his client that which he is entitled to under the law. He can do no less and properly represent the client." Thode, *The Ethical Standard for the Advocate,* 39 Texas L.Rev. 575, 584 (1961).

"The [Texas public opinion] survey indicates that distrust of the lawyer can be traced directly to certain factors. Foremost of these is a basic misunderstanding of the function of the lawyer as an advocate in an adversary system.

"Lawyers are accused of taking advantage of 'loopholes' and 'technicalities' to win. Persons who make this charge are unaware, or do not understand, that the lawyer is hired to win, and if he does not exercise every legitimate effort in his client's behalf, then he is betraying a sacred trust." Rochelle & Payne, *The Struggle for Public Understanding,* 25 Texas B.J. 109, 159 (1962).

"The importance of the attorney's undivided allegiance and faithful service to one accused of crime, irrespective of the attorney's personal opinion as to the guilt of his client, lies in Canon 5 of the American Bar Association Canon of Ethics.

"The difficulty lies, of course, in ascertaining whether the attorney has been guilty of an error of judgment, such as an election with respect to trial tactics, or has otherwise been actuated by his conscience or belief that his client should be convicted in any event. All too frequently courts are called upon to review actions of defense counsel which are, at the most, errors of judgment, not properly reviewable on habeas corpus unless the trial is a farce and a mockery of justice which requires the court to intervene. . . . But when defense counsel, in a truly adverse proceeding, admits that his conscience would not permit him to adopt certain customary trial procedures, this extends beyond the realm of judgment and strongly suggests an invasion of constitutional rights." Johns v. Smyth, 176 F.Supp. 949, 952 (E.D.Va.1959), modified, United States ex rel. Wilkins v. Banmiller, 205 F.Supp. 123, 128, n. 5 (E.D. Pa.1962), aff'd 325 F.2d 514 (3d Cir.1963), cert. denied, 379 U.S. 847, 13 L.Ed.2d 51, 85 S.Ct. 87 (1964).

"The adversary system in law administration bears a striking resemblance to the competitive economic system. In each we assume that the individual through partisanship or through self-interest will strive mightily for his side, and that kind of striving we must have. But neither system would be tolerable without restraints and modifications, and at times without outright departures from the system itself. Since the legal profession is entrusted with the system of law administration, a part of its task is to develop in its members appropriate restraints without impairing the values of partisan striving. An accompanying task is to aid in the modification of the adversary system or departure from it in areas to which the system is unsuited." Cheatham, *The Lawyer's Role and Surroundings,* 25 Rocky Mt.L.Rev. 405, 410 (1953).

of assisting members of the public to secure and protect available legal rights and benefits. In our government of laws and not of men, each member of our society is entitled to have his conduct judged and regulated in accordance with the law;[5] to seek any lawful objective[6] through legally permissible means;[7] and to present for adjudication any lawful claim, issue, or defense.

EC 7–2 The bounds of the law in a given case are often difficult to ascertain.[8] The language of legislative enactments and judicial opinions may be uncertain as applied to varying factual situations. The limits and specific meaning of apparently relevant law may be made doubtful by changing or developing constitutional interpretations, inadequately expressed statutes or judicial opinions, and changing public and judicial attitudes. Certainty of law ranges from well-settled rules through areas of conflicting authority to areas without precedent.

EC 7–3 Where the bounds of law are uncertain, the action of a lawyer may depend on whether he is serving as advocate or adviser. A lawyer may serve simultaneously as both advocate and adviser, but the two roles are essentially different.[9] In asserting a position on behalf of his client, an advocate for the most part deals with past conduct and must take the facts as he finds them. By contrast, a lawyer serving as

---

[4] "Rule 4.15 prohibits, in the pursuit of a client's cause, 'any manner of fraud or chicane'; Rule 4.22 requires 'candor and fairness' in the conduct of the lawyer, and forbids the making of knowing misquotations; Rule 4.47 provides that a lawyer 'should always maintain his integrity,' and generally forbids all misconduct injurious to the interests of the public, the courts, or his clients, and acts contrary to 'justice, honesty, modesty or good morals.' Our Commissioner has accurately paraphrased these rules as follows: 'An attorney does not have the duty to do all and whatever he can that may enable him to win his client's cause or to further his client's interest. His duty and efforts in these respects, although they should be prompted by his 'entire devotion' to the interest of his client, must be within and not without the bounds of the law.' " In re Wines, 370 S.W.2d 328, 333 (Mo.1963).

See Note, 38 Texas L.Rev. 107, 110 (1959).

[5] "Under our system of government the process of adjudication is surrounded by safeguards evolved from centuries of experience. These safeguards are not designed merely to lend formality and decorum to the trial of causes. They are predicated on the assumption that to secure for any controversy a truly informed and dispassionate decision is a difficult thing, requiring for its achievement a special summoning and organization of human effort and the adoption of measures to exclude the biases and prejudgments that have free play outside the courtroom. All of this goes for naught if the man with an unpopular cause is unable to find a competent lawyer courageous enough to represent him. His chance to have his day in court loses much of its meaning if his case is handicapped from the outset by the very kind of prejudgment our rules of evidence and procedure are intended to prevent." *Professional Responsibility: Report of the Joint Conference,* 44 A.B.A.J. 1159, 1216 (1958).

[6] "[I]t is . . . [the tax lawyer's] positive duty to show the client how to avail himself to the full of what the law permits. He is not the keeper of the Congressional conscience." Paul, *The Lawyer as a Tax Adviser,* 25 Rocky Mt.L.Rev. 412, 418 (1953).

[7] See ABA Canons 15 and 30.

[8] "The fact that it desired to evade the law, as it is called, is immaterial, because the very meaning of a line in the law is that you intentionally may go as close to it as you can if you do not pass it. . . . It is a matter of proximity and degree as to which minds will differ. . . ." Justice Holmes, in Superior Oil Co. v. Mississippi, 280 U.S. 390, 395–96, 74 L.Ed. 504, 508, 50 S.Ct. 169, 170 (1930).

[9] "Today's lawyers perform two distinct types of functions, and our ethical standards should, but in the main do not, recognize these two functions. Judge Philbrick McCoy recently reported to the American Bar Association the need for a reappraisal of the Canons in light of the new and distinct function of counselor, as distinguished from advocate, which today predominates in the legal profession. . . .

". . . In the first place, any revision of the canons must take into account and speak to this new and now predominant function of the lawyer. . . . It is beyond the scope of this paper to discuss the ethical standards to be applied to the counselor except to state that in my opinion such standards should require a greater recognition and protection for the interest of the public generally than is presently expressed in the canons. Also, the counselor's obligation should extend to requiring him to inform and to impress upon the client a just solution of the problem, considering all interests involved." Thode, *The Ethical Standard for the Advocate,* 39 Texas L.Rev. 575, 578–79 (1961).

"The man who has been called into court to answer for his own actions is entitled to fair hearing. Partisan advocacy plays its essential part in such a hearing, and the lawyer pleading his client's case may properly present it in the most favorable light. A similar resolution of doubts in one direction becomes inappropriate when the lawyer acts as counselor. The reasons that justify and even require partisan advocacy in the trial of a cause do not grant any license to the lawyer to participate as legal advisor in a line of conduct that is immoral, unfair, or of doubtful legality. In saving himself from this unworthy involvement, the lawyer cannot be guided solely by an unreflective inner sense of good faith; he must be at pains to preserve a sufficient detachment from his client's interests so that he remains capable of a sound and objective appraisal of the propriety of what his client proposes to do." *Professional Responsibility: Report of the Joint Conference,* 44 A.B.J. 1159, 1161 (1958).

adviser primarily assists his client in determining the course of future conduct and relationships. While serving as advocate, a lawyer should resolve in favor of his client doubts as to the bounds of the law.[10] In serving a client as adviser, a lawyer in appropriate circumstances should give his professional opinion as to what the ultimate decisions of the courts would likely be as to the applicable law.

Duty of the Lawyer to a Client

EC 7–4 The advocate may urge any permissible construction of the law favorable to his client, without regard to his professional opinion as to the likelihood that the construction will ultimately prevail.[11] His conduct is within the bounds of the law, and therefore permissible, if the position taken is supported by the law or is supportable by a good faith argument for an extension, modification, or reversal of the law. However, a lawyer is not justified in asserting a position in litigation that is frivolous.[12]

EC 7–5 A lawyer as adviser furthers the interest of his client by giving his professional opinion as to what he believes would likely be the ultimate decision of the courts on the matter at hand and by informing his client of the practical effect of such decision.[13] He may continue in the representation of his client even though his client has elected to pursue a course of conduct contrary to the advice of the lawyer so long as he does not thereby knowingly assist the client to engage in illegal conduct or to take a frivolous legal position. A lawyer should never encourage or aid his client to commit criminal acts or counsel his client on how to violate the law and avoid punishment therefor.[14]

---

[10] "[A] lawyer who is asked to advise his client . . . may freely urge the statement of positions most favorable to the client just as long as there is reasonable basis for those positions." *ABA Opinion* 314 (1965).

[11] "The lawyer . . . is not an umpire, but an advocate. He is under no duty to refrain from making every proper argument in support of any legal point because he is not convinced of its inherent soundness. . . . His personal belief in the soundness of his cause or of the authorities supporting it, is irrelevant." *ABA Opinion* 280 (1949).

"Counsel apparently misconceived his role. It was his duty to honorably present his client's contentions in the light most favorable to his client. Instead he presumed to advise the court as to the validity and sufficiency of prisoner's motion, by letter. We therefore conclude that the prisoner had no effective assistance of counsel and remand this case to the District Court with instructions to set aside the Judgment, appoint new counsel to represent the prisoner if he makes no objection thereto, and proceed anew." McCartney v. United States, 343 F.2d 471, 472 (9th Cir.1965).

[12] "Here the court-appointed counsel had the transcript but refused to proceed with the appeal because he found no merit in it. . . . We cannot say that there was a finding of frivolity by either of the California courts or that counsel acted in any greater capacity than merely as *amicus curiae* which was condemned in *Ellis,* supra. Hence California's procedure did not furnish petitioner with counsel acting in the role of an advocate nor did it provide that full consideration and resolution of the matter as is obtained when counsel is acting in that capacity. . . .

"The constitutional requirement of substantial equality and fair process can only be attained where counsel acts in the role of an active advocate in behalf of his client, as opposed to that of *amicus curiae.* The no-merit letter and the procedure it triggers do not reach that dignity. Counsel should, and can with honor and without conflict, be of more assistance to his client and to the court. His role as advocate requires that he support his client's appeal to the best of his ability. Of course, if counsel finds his case to be wholly frivolous, after a conscientious examination of it, he should so advise the court and request permission to withdraw. That request must, however, be accompanied by a brief referring to anything in the record that might arguably support the appeal. A copy of counsel's brief should be furnished the indigent and time allowed him to raise any points that he chooses; the court—not counsel—then proceeds, after a full examination of all the proceedings, to decide whether the case is wholly frivolous. If it so finds it may grant counsel's request to withdraw and dismiss the appeal insofar as federal requirements are concerned, or proceed to a decision on the merits, if state law so requires. On the other hand, if it finds any of the legal points arguable on their merits (and therefore not frivolous) it must, prior to decision afford the indigent the assistance of counsel to argue the appeal." *Anders v. California,* 386 U.S. 738, 744, 18 L.Ed.2d 493, 498, 87 S.Ct. 1396, 1399–1400 (1967), rehearing denied, 388 U.S. 924, 18 L.Ed.2d 1377, 87 S.Ct. 2094 (1967).

See Paul, *The Lawyer As a Tax Adviser,* 25 Rocky Mt.L.Rev. 412, 432 (1953).

[13] See ABA Canon 32.

[14] "For a lawyer to represent a syndicate notoriously engaged in the violation of the law for the purpose of advising the members how to break the law and at the same time escape it, is manifestly improper. While a lawyer may see to it that anyone accused of crime, no matter how serious and flagrant, has a fair trial, and present all available defenses, he may not co-operate in planning violations of the law. There is a sharp distinction, of course, between advising what can lawfully be done and advising how unlawful acts can be done in a way to avoid conviction. Where a lawyer accepts a retainer from an organization, known to be unlawful, and agrees in advance to defend its members when from time to time they are accused of crime arising out of its unlawful activities, this is equally improper."

"See also *Opinion* 155." *ABA Opinion* 281 (1952).

EC 7–6 Whether the proposed action of a lawyer is within the bounds of the law may be a perplexing question when his client is contemplating a course of conduct having legal consequences that vary according to the client's intent, motive, or desires at the time of the action. Often a lawyer is asked to assist his client in developing evidence relevant to the state of mind of the client at a particular time. He may properly assist his client in the development and preservation of evidence of existing motive, intent, or desire; obviously, he may not do anything furthering the creation or preservation of false evidence. In many cases a lawyer may not be certain as to the state of mind of his client, and in those situations he should resolve reasonable doubts in favor of his client.

EC 7–7 In certain areas of legal representation not affecting the merits of the cause or substantially prejudicing the rights of a client, a lawyer is entitled to make decisions on his own. But otherwise the authority to make decisions is exclusively that of the client and, if made within the framework of the law, such decisions are binding on his lawyer. As typical examples in civil cases, it is for the client to decide whether he will accept a settlement offer or whether he will waive his right to plead an affirmative defense. A defense lawyer in a criminal case has the duty to advise his client fully on whether a particular plea to a charge appears to be desirable and as to the prospects of success on appeal, but it is for the client to decide what plea should be entered and whether an appeal should be taken.[15]

EC 7–8 A lawyer should exert his best efforts to insure that decisions of his client are made only after the client has been informed of relevant considerations. A lawyer ought to initiate this decision-making process if the client does not do so. Advice of a lawyer to his client need not be confined to purely legal considerations.[16] A lawyer should advise his client of the possible effect of each legal alternative.[17] A lawyer should bring to bear upon this decision-making process the fullness of his experience as well as his objective viewpoint.[18] In assisting his client to reach a proper decision, it is often desirable for a lawyer to point out those factors which may lead to a decision that is morally just as well as legally permissible.[19] He may emphasize the possibility of harsh consequences that might result from assertion of legally permissible positions. In the final analysis, however, the lawyer should always remember that the decision whether to forego legally available objectives or methods because of non-legal factors is ultimately for the client and not for himself. In the event that the client in a non-adjudicatory matter insists upon a course of conduct that is contrary to the judgment and advice of the lawyer but not prohibited by Disciplinary Rules, the lawyer may withdraw from the employment.[20]

---

[15] See ABA Special Committee on Minimum Standards for the Administration of Criminal Justice, *Standards Relating to Pleas of Guilty,* pp. 69–70 (1968).

[16] "First of all, a truly great lawyer is a wise counselor to all manner of men in the varied crises of their lives when they most need disinterested advice. Effective counseling necessarily involves a thoroughgoing knowledge of the principles of the law not merely as they appear in the books but as they actually operate in action." Vanderbilt, *The Five Functions of the Lawyer: Service to Clients and the Public,* 40 A.B.A.J. 31 (1954).

[17] "A lawyer should endeavor to obtain full knowledge of his client's cause before advising thereon. . . ." ABA Canon 8.

[18] "[I]n devising charters of collaborative effort the lawyer often acts where all of the affected parties are present as participants. But the lawyer also performs a similar function in situations where this is not so, as, for example, in planning estates and drafting wills. Here the instrument defining the terms of collaboration may affect persons not present and often not born. Yet here, too, the good lawyer does not serve merely as a legal conduit for his client's desires, but as a wise counselor, experienced in the art of devising arrangements that will put in workable order the entangled affairs and interests of human beings." *Professional Responsibility: Report of the Joint Conference,* 44 A.B.A.J. 1159, 1162 (1958).

[19] See ABA Canon 8.

"Vital as is the lawyer's role in adjudication, it should not be thought that it is only as an advocate pleading in open court that he contributes to the administration of the law. The most effective realization of the law's aims often takes place in the attorney's office, where litigation is forestalled by anticipating its outcome, where the lawyer's quiet counsel takes the place of public force. Contrary to popular belief, the compliance with the law thus brought about is not generally lip-serving and narrow, for by reminding him of its long-run costs the lawyer often deters his client from a course of conduct technically permissible under existing law, though inconsistent with its underlying spirit and purpose." *Professional Responsibility: Report of the Joint Conference,* 44 A.B.A.J. 1159, 1161 (1958).

[20] "My summation of Judge Sharswood's view of the advocate's duty to the client is that he owes to the client the duty to use all legal means in support of the client's case. However, at the same time Judge Sharswood recognized that many advocates would find this obligation unbearable if applicable without exception. Therefore, the individual lawyer is given the choice of representing his client fully within the bounds set by the law *or of telling his client that he cannot*

EC 7–9 In the exercise of his professional judgment on those decisions which are for his determination in the handling of a legal matter,[21] a lawyer should always act in a manner consistent with the best interests of his client.[22] However, when an action in the best interest of his client seems to him to be unjust, he may ask his client for permission to forego such action.[23]

EC 7–10 The duty of a lawyer to represent his client with zeal does not militate against his concurrent obligation to treat with consideration all persons involved in the legal process and to avoid the infliction of needless harm.

EC 7–11 The responsibilities of a lawyer may vary according to the intelligence, experience, mental condition or age of a client, the obligation of a public officer, or the nature of a particular proceeding. Examples include the representation of an illiterate or an incompetent, service as a public prosecutor or other government lawyer, and appearances before administrative and legislative bodies.

EC 7–12 Any mental or physical condition of a client that renders him incapable of making a considered judgment on his own behalf casts additional responsibilities upon his lawyer. Where an incompetent is acting through a guardian or other legal representative, a lawyer must look to such representative for those decisions which are normally the prerogative of the client to make. If a client under disability has no legal representative, his lawyer may be compelled in court proceedings to make decisions on behalf of the client. If the client is capable of understanding the matter in question or of contributing to the advancement of his interests, regardless of whether he is legally disqualified from performing certain acts, the lawyer should obtain from him all possible aid. If the disability of a client and the lack of a legal representative compel the lawyer to make decisions for his client, the lawyer should consider all circumstances then prevailing and act with care to safeguard and advance the interests of his client. But obviously a lawyer cannot perform any act or make any decision which the law requires his client to perform or make, either acting for himself if competent, or by a duly constituted representative if legally incompetent.

EC 7–13 The responsibility of a public prosecutor differs from that of the usual advocate; his duty is to seek justice, not merely to convict.[24] This special duty exists because: (1) the prosecutor represents the sovereign and therefore should use restraint in the discretionary exercise of governmental powers, such as in the selection of cases to prosecute; (2) during trial the prosecutor is not only an advocate but he also may make decisions normally made by an individual client, and those affecting the public interest should be fair to all; and (3) in our system of criminal justice the accused is to be given the benefit of all reasonable doubts. With respect to evidence and witnesses, the prosecutor has responsibilities different from those of a lawyer in private practice: the prosecutor should make timely disclosure to the defense of available evidence, known to him, that tends to negate the guilt of the accused, mitigate the degree of the offense, or reduce the punishment. Further, a prosecutor should not intentionally avoid pursuit of evidence merely because he believes it will damage the prosecutor's case or aid the accused.

EC 7–14 A government lawyer who has discretionary power relative to litigation should refrain from instituting or continuing litigation that is obviously unfair. A government lawyer not having such discretionary power who believes there is lack of merit in a controversy submitted to him should so advise

---

do so, so that the client may obtain another attorney if he wishes." Thode, *The Ethical Standard for the Advocate,* 39 Texas L.Rev. 575, 582 (1961).

Cf. Code of Professional Responsibility, DR 2–110(C).

[21] See ABA Canon 24.

[22] Thode, *The Ethical Standard for the Advocate,* 39 Texas L.Rev. 575, 592 (1961).

[23] Cf. *ABA Opinions* 253 (1946) and 178 (1938).

[24] See ABA Canon 5 and Berger v. United States, 295 U.S. 78, 79 L.Ed. 1314, 55 S.Ct. 629 (1935).

"The public prosecutor cannot take as a guide for the conduct of his office the standards of an attorney appearing on behalf of an individual client. The freedom elsewhere wisely granted to a partisan advocate must be severely curtailed if the prosecutor's duties are to be properly discharged. The public prosecutor must recall that he occupies a dual role, being obligated, on the one hand, to furnish that adversary element essential to the informed decision of any controversy, but being possessed, on the other, of important governmental powers that are pledged to the accomplishment of one objective only, that of impartial justice. Where the prosecutor is recreant to the trust implicit in his office, he undermines confidence, not only in his profession, but in government and the very ideal of justice itself." *Professional Responsibility: Report of the Joint Conference,* 44 A.B.A.J. 1159, 1218 (1958).

"The prosecuting attorney is the attorney for the state, and it is his primary duty not to convict but to see that justice is done." *ABA Opinion* 150 (1936).

his superiors and recommend the avoidance of unfair litigation. A government lawyer in a civil action or administrative proceeding has the responsibility to seek justice and to develop a full and fair record, and he should not use his position or the economic power of the government to harass parties or to bring about unjust settlements or results.

EC 7–15 The nature and purpose of proceedings before administrative agencies vary widely. The proceedings may be legislative or quasi-judicial, or a combination of both. They may be *ex parte* in character, in which event they may originate either at the instance of the agency or upon motion of an interested party. The scope of an inquiry may be purely investigative or it may be truly adversary looking toward the adjudication of specific rights of a party or of classes of parties. The foregoing are but examples of some of the types of proceedings conducted by administrative agencies. A lawyer appearing before an administrative agency,[25] regardless of the nature of the proceeding it is conducting, has the continuing duty to advance the cause of his client within the bounds of the law.[26] Where the applicable rules of the agency impose specific obligations upon a lawyer, it is his duty to comply therewith, unless the lawyer has a legitimate basis for challenging the validity thereof. In all appearances before administrative agencies, a lawyer should identify himself, his client if identity of his client is not privileged,[27] and the representative nature of his appearance. It is not improper, however, for a lawyer to seek from an agency information available to the public without identifying his client.

EC 7–16 The primary business of a legislative body is to enact laws rather than to adjudicate controversies, although on occasion the activities of a legislative body may take on the characteristics of an adversary proceeding, particularly in investigative and impeachment matters. The role of a lawyer supporting or opposing proposed legislation normally is quite different from his role in representing a person under investigation or on trial by a legislative body. When a lawyer appears in connection with proposed legislation, he seeks to affect the lawmaking process, but when he appears on behalf of a client in investigatory or impeachment proceedings, he is concerned with the protection of the rights of his client. In either event, he should identify himself and his client, if identity of his client is not privileged, and should comply with applicable laws and legislative rules.[28]

EC 7–17 The obligation of loyalty to his client applies only to a lawyer in the discharge of his professional duties and implies no obligation to adopt a personal viewpoint favorable to the interests or desires of his client.[29] While a lawyer must act always with circumspection in order that his conduct will not adversely affect the rights of a client in a matter he is then handling, he may take positions on public issues and espouse legal reforms he favors without regard to the individual views of any client.

EC 7–18 The legal system in its broadest sense functions best when persons in need of legal advice or assistance are represented by their own counsel. For this reason a lawyer should not communicate on the subject matter of the representation of his client with a person he knows to be represented in the matter by a lawyer, unless pursuant to law or rule of court or unless he has the consent of the lawyer for that person.[30]

---

[25] As to appearances before a department of government, Canon 26 provides: "A lawyer openly . . . may render professional services . . . in advocacy of claims before departments of government, upon the same principles of ethics which justify his appearance before the Courts. . . ."

[26] "But as an advocate before a service which itself represents the adversary point of view, where his client's case is fairly arguable, a lawyer is under no duty to disclose its weaknesses, any more than he would be to make such a disclosure to a brother lawyer. The limitations within which he must operate are best expressed in Canon 22. . . ." *ABA Opinion* 314 (1965).

[27] See Baird v. Koerner, 279 F.2d 623 (9th Cir.1960).

[28] See ABA Canon 26.

[29] "Law should be so practiced that the lawyer remains free to make up his own mind how he will vote, what causes he will support, what economic and political philosophy he will espouse. It is one of the glories of the profession that it admits of this freedom. Distinguished examples can be cited of lawyers whose views were at variance from those of their clients, lawyers whose skill and wisdom make them valued advisers to those who had little sympathy with their views as citizens." *Professional Responsibility: Report of the Joint Conference,* 44 A.B.A.J. 1159, 1217 (1958).

"No doubt some tax lawyers feel constrained to abstain from activities on behalf of a better tax system because they think that their clients may object. Clients have no right to object if the tax adviser handles their affairs competently and faithfully and independently of his private views as to tax policy. They buy his expert services, not his private opinions or his silence on issues that gravely affect the public interest." Paul, *The Lawyer as a Tax Adviser,* 25 Rocky Mt.L.Rev. 412, 434 (1953).

[30] See ABA Canon 9.

If one is not represented by counsel, a lawyer representing another may have to deal directly with the unrepresented person; in such an instance, a lawyer should not undertake to give advice to the person who is attempting to represent himself,[31] except that he may advise him to obtain a lawyer.

Duty of the Lawyer to the Adversary System of Justice

EC 7–19 Our legal system provides for the adjudication of disputes governed by the rules of substantive, evidentiary, and procedural law. An adversary presentation counters the natural human tendency to judge too swiftly in terms of the familiar that which is not yet fully known; [32] the advocate, by his zealous preparation and presentation of facts and law, enables the tribunal to come to the hearing with an open and neutral mind and to render impartial judgments.[33] The duty of a lawyer to his client and his duty to the legal system are the same: to represent his client zealously within the bounds of the law.[34]

EC 7–20 In order to function properly, our adjudicative process requires an informed, impartial tribunal capable of administering justice promptly and efficiently [35] according to procedures that command public confidence and respect.[36] Not only must there be competent, adverse presentation of evidence and issues, but a tribunal must be aided by rules appropriate to an effective and dignified process. The procedures under which tribunals operate in our adversary system have been prescribed largely by legislative enactments, court rules and decisions, and administrative rules. Through the years certain concepts of proper professional conduct have become rules of law applicable to the adversary adjudicative process. Many of these concepts are the bases for standards of professional conduct set forth in the Disciplinary Rules.

EC 7–21 The civil adjudicative process is primarily designed for the settlement of disputes between parties, while the criminal process is designed for the protection of society as a whole. Threatening to use, or using, the criminal process to coerce adjustment of private civil claims or controversies is a subversion of that process;[37] further, the person against whom the criminal process is so misused may be deterred from asserting his legal rights and thus the usefulness of the civil process in settling private disputes is impaired. As in all cases of abuse of judicial process, the improper use of criminal process tends to diminish public confidence in our legal system.

EC 7–22 Respect for judicial rulings is essential to the proper administration of justice; however, a litigant or his lawyer may, in good faith and within the framework of the law, take steps to test the correctness of a ruling of a tribunal.[38]

---

31 Id.

32 See *Professional Responsibility: Report of the Joint Conference,* 44 A.B.A.J. 1159, 1160 (1958).

33 "Without the participation of someone who can act responsibly for each of the parties, this essential narrowing of the issues [by exchange of written pleadings or stipulations of counsel] becomes impossible. But here again the true significance of partisan advocacy lies deeper, touching once more the integrity of the adjudicative process itself. It is only through the advocate's participation that the hearing may remain in fact what it purports to be in theory: a public trial of the facts and issues. Each advocate comes to the hearing prepared to present his proofs and arguments, knowing at the same time that his arguments may fail to persuade and that his proof may be rejected as inadequate. . . . The deciding tribunal, on the other hand, comes to the hearing uncommitted. It has not represented to the public that any fact can be proved, that any argument is sound, or that any particular way of stating a litigant's case is the most effective expression of its merits." *Professional Responsibility: Report of the Joint Conference,* 44 A.B.A.J. 1159, 1160–61 (1958).

34 Cf. ABA Canons 15 and 32.

35 Cf. ABA Canon 21.

36 See *Professional Responsibility: Report of the Joint Conference,* 44 A.B.A.J. 1159, 1216 (1958).

37 "We are of the opinion that the letter in question was improper, and that in writing and sending it respondent was guilty of unprofessional conduct. This court has heretofore expressed its disapproval of using threats of criminal prosecution as a means of forcing settlement of civil claims. . . .

"Respondent has been guilty of a violation of a principle which condemns any confusion of threats of criminal prosecution with the enforcement of civil claims. For this misconduct he should be severely censured." Matter of Gelman, 230 App.Div. 524, 527, 245 N.Y.S. 416, 419 (1930).

38 "An attorney has the duty to protect the interests of his client. He has a right to press legitimate argument and to protest an erroneous ruling." Gallagher v. Municipal Court, 31 Cal.2d 784, 796, 192 P.2d 905, 913 (1948).

"There must be protection, however, in the far more frequent case of the attorney who stands on his rights and combats the order in good faith and without disrespect believing with good cause that it is void, for it is here that the independence of the bar becomes valuable." Note, 39 Colum.L.Rev. 433, 438 (1939).

EC 7–23 The complexity of law often makes it difficult for a tribunal to be fully informed unless the pertinent law is presented by the lawyers in the cause. A tribunal that is fully informed on the applicable law is better able to make a fair and accurate determination of the matter before it. The adversary system contemplates that each lawyer will present and argue the existing law in the light most favorable to his client.[39] Where a lawyer knows of legal authority in the controlling jurisdiction directly adverse to the position of his client, he should inform the tribunal of its existence unless his adversary has done so; but, having made such disclosure, he may challenge its soundness in whole or in part.[40]

EC 7–24 In order to bring about just and informed decisions, evidentiary and procedural rules have been established by tribunals to permit the inclusion of relevant evidence and argument and the exclusion of all other considerations. The expression by a lawyer of his personal opinion as to the justness of a cause, as to the credibility of a witness, as to the culpability of a civil litigant, or as to the guilt or innocence of an accused is not a proper subject for argument to the trier of fact.[41] It is improper as to factual matters because admissible evidence possessed by a lawyer should be presented only as sworn testimony. It is improper as to all other matters because, were the rule otherwise, the silence of a lawyer on a given occasion could be construed unfavorably to his client. However, a lawyer may argue, on his analysis of the evidence, for any position or conclusion with respect to any of the foregoing matters.

EC 7–25 Rules of evidence and procedure are designed to lead to just decisions and are part of the framework of the law. Thus while a lawyer may take steps in good faith and within the framework of the law to test the validity of rules, he is not justified in consciously violating such rules and he should be diligent in his efforts to guard against his unintentional violation of them.[42] As examples, a lawyer should subscribe to or verify only those pleadings that he believes are in compliance with applicable law and rules; a lawyer should not make any prefatory statement before a tribunal in regard to the purported facts of the case on trial unless he believes that his statement will be supported by admissible evidence; a lawyer should not ask a witness a question solely for the purpose of harassing or embarrassing him; and a lawyer should not by subterfuge put before a jury matters which it cannot properly consider.

EC 7–26 The law and Disciplinary Rules prohibit the use of fraudulent, false, or perjured testimony or evidence.[43] A lawyer who knowingly[44] participates in introduction of such testimony or evidence is subject to discipline. A lawyer should, however, present any admissible evidence his client desires to have presented unless he knows, or from facts within his knowledge should know, that such testimony or evidence is false, fraudulent, or perjured.[45]

EC 7–27 Because it interferes with the proper administration of justice, a lawyer should not suppress evidence that he or his client has a legal obligation to reveal or produce. In like manner, a lawyer should

---

[39] "Too many do not understand that accomplishment of the layman's abstract ideas of justice is the function of the judge and jury, and that it is the lawyer's sworn duty to portray his client's case in its most favorable light." Rochelle and Payne, *The Struggle for Public Understanding,* 25 Texas B.J. 109, 159 (1962).

[40] "We are of the opinion that this Canon requires the lawyer to disclose such decisions [that are adverse to his client's contentions] to the court. He may, of course, after doing so, challenge the soundness of the decisions or present reasons which he believes would warrant the court in not following them in the pending case." *ABA Opinion* 146 (1935).

Cf. *ABA Opinion* 280 (1949) and Thode, *The Ethical Standard for the Advocate,* 39 Texas L.Rev. 575, 585–86 (1961).

[41] See ABA Canon 15.

"The traditional duty of an advocate is that he honorably uphold the contentions of his client. He should not voluntarily undermine them." Harders v. State of California, 373 F.2d 839, 842 (9th Cir.1967).

[42] See ABA Canon 22.

[43] Id. Cf. ABA Canon 41.

[44] See generally *ABA Opinion* 287 (1953) as to a lawyer's duty when he unknowingly participates in introducing perjured testimony.

[45] "Under any standard of proper ethical conduct an attorney should not sit by silently and permit his client to commit what may have been perjury, and which certainly would mislead the court and the opposing party on a matter vital to the issue under consideration. . . .

. . .

"Respondent next urges that it was his duty to observe the utmost good faith toward his client, and therefore he could not divulge any confidential information. This duty to the client of course does not extend to the point of authorizing collaboration with him in the commission of fraud." In re Carroll, 244 S.W.2d 474, 474–75 (Ky.1951).

not advise or cause a person to secrete himself or to leave the jurisdiction of a tribunal for the purpose of making him unavailable as a witness therein.[46]

EC 7–28 Witnesses should always testify truthfully[47] and should be free from any financial inducements that might tempt them to do otherwise.[48] A lawyer should not pay or agree to pay a non-expert witness an amount in excess of reimbursement for expenses and financial loss incident to his being a witness; however, a lawyer may pay or agree to pay an expert witness a reasonable fee for his services as an expert. But in no event should a lawyer pay or agree to pay a contingent fee to any witness. A lawyer should exercise reasonable diligence to see that his client and lay associates conform to these standards.[49]

EC 7–29 To safeguard the impartiality that is essential to the judicial process, veniremen and jurors should be protected against extraneous influences.[50] When impartiality is present, public confidence in the judicial system is enhanced. There should be no extrajudicial communication with veniremen prior to trial or with jurors during trial by or on behalf of a lawyer connected with the case. Furthermore, a lawyer who is not connected with the case should not communicate with or cause another to communicate with a venireman or a juror about the case. After the trial, communication by a lawyer with jurors is permitted so long as he refrains from asking questions or making comments that tend to harass or embarrass the juror[51] or to influence actions of the juror in future cases. Were a lawyer to be prohibited from communicating after a trial with a juror, he could not ascertain if the verdict might be subject to legal challenge, in which event the invalidity of a verdict might go undetected.[52] When an extrajudicial communication by a lawyer with a juror is permitted by law, it should be made considerately and with deference to the personal feelings of the juror.

EC 7–30 Vexatious or harassing investigations of veniremen or jurors seriously impair the effectiveness of our jury system. For this reason, a lawyer or anyone on his behalf who conducts an investigation of veniremen or jurors should act with circumspection and restraint.

EC 7–31 Communications with or investigations of members of families of veniremen or jurors by a lawyer or by anyone on his behalf are subject to the restrictions imposed upon the lawyer with respect to his communications with or investigations of veniremen and jurors.

EC 7–32 Because of his duty to aid in preserving the integrity of the jury system, a lawyer who learns of improper conduct by or towards a venireman, a juror, or a member of the family of either should make a prompt report to the court regarding such conduct.

---

[46] See ABA Canon 5; cf. *ABA Opinion* 131 (1935).

[47] Cf. ABA Canon 39.

[48] "The prevalence of perjury is a serious menace to the administration of justice, to prevent which no means have as yet been satisfactorily devised. But there certainly can be no greater incentive to perjury than to allow a party to make payments to its opponents witnesses under any guise or on any excuse, and at least attorneys who are officers of the court to aid it in the administration of justice, must keep themselves clear of any connection which in the slightest degree tends to induce witnesses to testify in favor of their clients." In re Robinson, 151 App.Div. 589, 600, 136 N.Y.S. 548, 556–57 (1912), aff'd, 209 N.Y. 354, 103 N.E. 160 (1913).

[49] "It will not do for an attorney who seeks to justify himself against charges of this kind to show that he has escaped criminal responsibility under the Penal Law, nor can he blindly shut his eyes to a system which tends to suborn witnesses, to produce perjured testimony, and to suppress the truth. He has an active affirmative duty to protect the administration of justice from perjury and fraud, and that duty is not performed by allowing his subordinates and assistants to attempt to subvert justice and procure results for his clients based upon false testimony and perjured witnesses." Id., 151 App.Div. at 592, 136 N.Y.S. at 551.

[50] See ABA Canon 23.

[51] "[I]t is unfair to jurors to permit a disappointed litigant to pick over their private associations in search of something to discredit them and their verdict. And it would be unfair to the public too if jurors should understand that they cannot convict a man of means without risking an inquiry of that kind by paid investigators, with, to boot, the distortions an inquiry of that kind can produce." State v. LaFera, 42 N.J. 97, 107, 199 A.2d 630, 636 (1964).

[52] *ABA Opinion* 319 (1968) points out that "[m]any courts today, and the trend is in this direction, allow the testimony of jurors as to all irregularities in and out of the courtroom except those irregularities whose existence can be determined only by exploring the consciousness of a single particular juror, New Jersey v. Kociolek, 20 N.J. 92, 118 A.2d 812 (1955). Model Code of Evidence Rule 301. Certainly as to states in which the testimony and affidavits of jurors may be received in support of or against a motion for new trial, a lawyer, in his obligation to protect his client, must have the tools for ascertaining whether or not grounds for a new trial exist and it is not unethical for him to talk to and question jurors."

EC 7–33 A goal of our legal system is that each party shall have his case, criminal or civil, adjudicated by an impartial tribunal. The attainment of this goal may be defeated by dissemination of news or comments which tend to influence judge or jury.[53] Such news or comments may prevent prospective jurors from being impartial at the outset of the trial [54] and may also interfere with the obligation of jurors to base their verdict solely upon the evidence admitted in the trial.[55] The release by a lawyer of out-of-court statements regarding an anticipated or pending trial may improperly affect the impartiality of the tribunal.[56] For these reasons,

---

[53] Generally see ABA Advisory Committee on Fair Trial and Free Press, Standards Relating to Fair Trial and Free Press (1966).

"[T]he trial court might well have proscribed extrajudicial statements by any lawyer, party, witness, or court official which divulged prejudicial matters. . . . See State v. Van Dwyne, 43 N.J. 369, 389, 204 A.2d 841, 852 (1964), in which the court interpreted Canon 20 of the American Bar Association's Canons of Professional Ethics to prohibit such statements. Being advised of the great public interest in the case, the mass coverage of the press, and the potential prejudicial impact of publicity, the court could also have requested the appropriate city and county officials to promulgate a regulation with respect to dissemination of information about the case by their employees. In addition, reporters who wrote or broadcast prejudicial stories, could have been warned as to the impropriety of publishing material not introduced in the proceedings. . . . In this manner, Sheppard's right to a trial free from outside interference would have been given added protection without corresponding curtailment of the news media. Had the judge, the other officers of the court, and the police placed the interest of justice first, the news media would have soon learned to be content with the task of reporting the case as it unfolded in the courtroom—not pieced together from extrajudicial statements." Sheppard v. Maxwell, 384 U.S. 333, 361–62, 16 L.Ed.2d 600, 619–20, 86 S.Ct. 1507, 1521–22 (1966).

"Court proceedings are held for the solemn purpose of endeavoring to ascertain the truth which is the *sine qua non* of a fair trial. Over the centuries Anglo-American courts have devised careful safeguards by rule and otherwise to protect and facilitate the performance of this high function. As a result, at this time those safeguards do not permit the televising and photographing of a criminal trial, save in two States and there only under restrictions. The federal courts prohibit it by specific rule. This is weighty evidence that our concepts of a fair trial do not tolerate such an indulgence. We have always held that the atmosphere essential to the preservation of a fair trial—the most fundamental of all freedoms—must be maintained at all costs." Estes v. State of Texas, 381 U.S. 532, 540, 14 L.Ed.2d 543, 549, 85 S.Ct. 1628, 1631–32 (1965), rehearing denied, 382 U.S. 875, 15 L.Ed.2d 118, 86 S.Ct. 18 (1965).

[54] "Pretrial can create a major problem for the defendant in a criminal case. Indeed, it may be more harmful than publicity during the trial for it may well set the community opinion as to guilt or innocence. . . . The trial witnesses present at the hearing, as well as the original jury panel, were undoubtedly made aware of the peculiar public importance of the case by the press and television coverage being provided, and by the fact that they themselves were televised live and their pictures rebroadcast on the evening show." Id., 381 U.S. at 536–37, 14 L.Ed.2d at 546–47, 85 S.Ct. at 1629–30.

[55] "The undeviating rule of this Court was expressed by Mr. Justice Holmes over half a century ago in Patterson v. Colorado, 205 U.S. 454, 462 (1907):

"The theory of our system is that the conclusions to be reached in a case will be induced only by evidence and argument in open court, and not by any outside influence, whether of private talk or public print."

Sheppard v. Maxwell, 384 U.S. 333, 351, 16 L.Ed.2d 600, 614, 86 S.Ct. 1507, 1516 (1966).

"The trial judge has a large discretion in ruling on the issue of prejudice resulting from the reading by jurors of news articles concerning the trial. . . . Generalizations beyond that statement are not profitable, because each case must turn on its special facts. We have here the exposure of jurors to information of a character which the trial judge ruled was so prejudicial it could not be directly offered as evidence. The prejudice to the defendant is almost certain to be as great when that evidence reaches the jury through news accounts as when it is a part of the prosecution's evidence. . . . It may indeed be greater for it is then not tempered by protective procedures." Marshall v. United States, 360 U.S. 310, 312–13, 3 L.Ed.2d 1250, 1252, 79 S.Ct. 1171, 1173 (1959).

"The experienced trial lawyer knows that an adverse public opinion is a tremendous disadvantage to the defense of his client. Although grand jurors conduct their deliberations in secret, they are selected from the body of the public. They are likely to know what the general public knows and to reflect the public attitude. Trials are open to the public, and aroused public opinion respecting the merits of a legal controversy creates a court room atmosphere which, without any vocal expression in the presence of the petit jury, makes itself felt and has its effect upon the action of the petit jury. Our fundamental concepts of justice and our American sense of fair play requires that the petit jury shall be composed of persons with fair and impartial minds and without preconceived views as to the merits of the controversy, and that it shall determine the issues presented to it solely upon the evidence adduced at the trial and according to the law given in the instructions of the trial judge.

"While we may doubt that the effect of public opinion would sway or bias the judgment of the trial judge in an equity proceeding, the defendant should not be called upon to run that risk and the trial court should not have his work made more difficult by any dissemination of statements to the public that would be calculated to create a public demand for a particular judgment in a prospective or pending case." *ABA Opinion* 199 (1940).

Cf. Estes v. State of Texas, 381 U.S. 532, 544–45, 14 L.Ed.2d 543, 551, 85 S.Ct. 1628, 1634 (1965), rehearing denied, 381 U.S. 875, 15 L.Ed.2d 118, 86 S.Ct. 18 (1965).

[56] See ABA Canon 20.

standards for permissible and prohibited conduct of a lawyer with respect to trial publicity have been established.

EC 7–34 The impartiality of a public servant in our legal system may be impaired by the receipt of gifts or loans. A lawyer,[57] therefore, is never justified in making a gift or a loan to a judge, a hearing officer, or an official or employee of a tribunal, except as permitted by Section C(4) of Canon 5 of the Code of Judicial Conduct, but a lawyer may make a contribution to the campaign fund of a candidate for judicial office in conformity with Section B(2) under Canon 7 of the Code of Judicial Conduct.[58]

As amended in 1974.

EC 7–35 All litigants and lawyers should have access to tribunals on an equal basis. Generally, in adversary proceedings a lawyer should not communicate with a judge relative to a matter pending before, or which is to be brought before, a tribunal over which he presides in circumstances which might have the effect or give the appearance of granting undue advantage to one party.[59] For example, a lawyer should not communicate with a tribunal by a writing unless a copy thereof is promptly delivered to opposing counsel or to the adverse party if he is not represented by a lawyer. Ordinarily an oral communication by a lawyer with a judge or hearing officer should be made only upon adequate notice to opposing counsel, or, if there is none, to the opposing party. A lawyer should not condone or lend himself to private importunities by another with a judge or hearing officer on behalf of himself or his client.

EC 7–36 Judicial hearings ought to be conducted through dignified and orderly procedures designed to protect the rights of all parties. Although a lawyer has the duty to represent his client zealously, he should not engage in any conduct that offends the dignity and decorum of proceedings.[60] While maintaining his independence, a lawyer should be respectful, courteous, and above-board in his relations with a judge or hearing officer before whom he appears.[61] He should avoid undue solicitude for the comfort or convenience of judge or jury and should avoid any other conduct calculated to gain special consideration.

EC 7–37 In adversary proceedings, clients are litigants and though ill feeling may exist between clients, such ill feeling should not influence a lawyer in his conduct, attitude, and demeanor towards opposing lawyers.[62] A lawyer should not make unfair or derogatory personal reference to opposing counsel. Haranguing and offensive tactics by lawyers interfere with the orderly administration of justice and have no proper place in our legal system.

EC 7–38 A lawyer should be courteous to opposing counsel and should accede to reasonable requests regarding court proceedings, settings, continuances, waiver of procedural formalities, and similar matters which do not prejudice the rights of his client.[63] He should follow local customs of courtesy or practice, unless he gives timely notice to opposing counsel of his intention not to do so.[64] A lawyer should be punctual in fulfilling all professional commitments.[65]

---

[57] Canon 3 observes that a lawyer "deserves rebuke and denunciation for any device or attempt to gain from a Judge special personal consideration or favor."

See ABA Canon 32.

[58] "*Judicial Canon 32* provides:

" 'A judge should not accept any presents or favors from litigants, or from lawyers practicing before him or from others whose interests are likely to be submitted to him for judgment.'

"The language of this Canon is perhaps broad enough to prohibit campaign contributions by lawyers, practicing before the court upon which the candidate hopes to sit. However, we do not think it was intended to prohibit such contributions when the candidate is obligated, by force of circumstances over which he has no control, to conduct a campaign, the expense of which exceeds that which he should reasonably be expected to personally bear!" *ABA Opinion* 226 (1941).

[59] See ABA Canons 3 and 32.

[60] Cf. ABA Canon 18.

[61] See ABA Canons 1 and 3.

[62] See ABA Canon 17.

[63] See ABA Canon 24.

[64] See ABA Canon 25.

[65] See ABA Canon 21.

EC 7–39 In the final analysis, proper functioning of the adversary system depends upon cooperation between lawyers and tribunals in utilizing procedures which will preserve the impartiality of tribunals and make their decisional processes prompt and just, without impinging upon the obligation of lawyers to represent their clients zealously within the framework of the law.

DISCIPLINARY RULES

DR 7–101 Representing a Client Zealously.

(A) A lawyer shall not intentionally:[66]

(1) Fail to seek the lawful objectives of his client through reasonably available means[67] permitted by law and the Disciplinary Rules, except as provided by DR 7–101(B). A lawyer does not violate this Disciplinary Rule, however, by acceding to reasonable requests of opposing counsel which do not prejudice the rights of his client, by being punctual in fulfilling all professional commitments, by avoiding offensive tactics, or by treating with courtesy and consideration all persons involved in the legal process.

(2) Fail to carry out a contract of employment entered into with a client for professional services, but he may withdraw as permitted under DR 2–110, DR 5–102, and DR 5–105.

(3) Prejudice or damage his client during the course of the professional relationship[68] except as required under DR 7–102(B).

(B) In his representation of a client, a lawyer may:

(1) Where permissible, exercise his professional judgment to waive or fail to assert a right or position of his client.

(2) Refuse to aid or participate in conduct that he believes to be unlawful, even though there is some support for an argument that the conduct is legal.

DR 7–102 Representing a Client Within the Bounds of the Law.

(A) In his representation of a client, a lawyer shall not:

(1) File a suit, assert a position, conduct a defense, delay a trial, or take other action on behalf of his client when he knows or when it is obvious that such action would serve merely to harass or maliciously injure another.[69]

(2) Knowingly advance a claim or defense that is unwarranted under existing law, except that he may advance such claim or defense it if can be supported by good faith argument for an extension, modification, or reversal of existing law.

(3) Conceal or knowingly fail to disclose that which he is required by law to reveal.

(4) Knowingly use perjured testimony or false evidence.[70]

(5) Knowingly make a false statement of law or fact.

(6) Participate in the creation or preservation of evidence when he knows or it is obvious that the evidence is false.

---

66 See ABA Canon 15.

67 See ABA Canons 5 and 15; cf. ABA Canons 4 and 32.

68 Cf. ABA Canon 24.

69 See ABA Canon 30.

70 Cf. ABA Canons 22 and 29.

(7) Counsel or assist his client in conduct that the lawyer knows to be illegal or fraudulent.

(8) Knowingly engage in other illegal conduct or conduct contrary to a Disciplinary Rule.

(B) A lawyer who receives information clearly establishing that:

(1) His client has, in the course of the representation, perpetrated a fraud upon a person or tribunal shall promptly call upon his client to rectify the same, and if his client refuses or is unable to do so, he shall reveal the fraud to the affected person or tribunal, except when the information is protected as a privileged communication.[71]

(2) A person other than his client has perpetrated a fraud upon a tribunal shall promptly reveal the fraud to the tribunal.[72]

As amended in 1974.

DR 7–103 Performing the Duty of Public Prosecutor or Other Government Lawyer.[73]

(A) A public prosecutor or other government lawyer shall not institute or cause to be instituted criminal charges when he knows or it is obvious that the charges are not supported by probable cause.

(B) A public prosecutor or other government lawyer in criminal litigation shall make timely disclosure to counsel for the defendant, or to the defendant if he has no counsel, of the existence of evidence, known to the prosecutor or other government lawyer, that tends to negate the guilt of the accused, mitigate the degree of the offense, or reduce the punishment.

DR 7–104 Communicating With One of Adverse Interest.[74]

(A) During the course of his representation of a client a lawyer shall not:

(1) Communicate or cause another to communicate on the subject of the representation with a party he knows to be represented by a lawyer in that matter unless he has the prior consent of the lawyer representing such other party[75] or is authorized by law to do so.

(2) Give advice to a person who is not represented by a lawyer, other than the advice to secure counsel,[76] if the interests of such person are or have a reasonable possibility of being in conflict with the interests of his client.[77]

---

[71] See ABA Canon 41; cf. Hinds v. State Bar, 19 Cal.2d 87, 92–93, 119 P.2d 134, 137 (1941); but see *ABA Opinion* 287 (1953) and Texas Canon 38. Also see Code of Professional Responsibility. DR 4–101(C)(2).

[72] See Precision Inst. Mfg. Co. v. Automotive M.M. Co., 324 U.S. 806, 89 L.Ed. 1381, 65 S.Ct. 993 (1945).

[73] Cf. ABA Canon 5.

[74] "*Rule 12*. . . . A member of the State Bar shall not communicate with a party represented by counsel upon a subject of controversy, in the absence and without the consent of such counsel. This rule shall not apply to communications with a public officer, board, committee or body." Cal. Business and Professions Code § 6076 (West 1962).

[75] See ABA Canon 9; cf. *ABA Opinions* 124 (1934), 108 (1934), 95 (1933), and 75 (1932); also see In re Schwabe, 242 Or. 169, 174–75, 408 P.2d 922, 924 (1965).

"It is clear from the earlier opinions of this committee that *Canon 9* is to be construed literally and does not allow a communication with an opposing party, without the consent of his counsel, though the purpose merely be to investigate the facts. *Opinions 117, 55, 66*," *ABA Opinion* 187 (1938).

[76] Cf. *ABA Opinion* 102 (1933).

[77] Cf. ABA Canon 9 and *ABA Opinion* 58 (1931).

DR 7-105 Threatening Criminal Prosecution.

(A) A lawyer shall not present, participate in presenting, or threaten to present criminal charges solely to obtain an advantage in a civil matter.

DR 7-106 Trial Conduct.

(A) A lawyer shall not disregard or advise his client to disregard a standing rule of a tribunal or a ruling of a tribunal made in the course of a proceeding, but he may take appropriate steps in good faith to test the validity of such rule or ruling.

(B) In presenting a matter to a tribunal, a lawyer shall disclose:[78]

(1) Legal authority in the controlling jurisdiction known to him to be directly adverse to the position of his client and which is not disclosed by opposing counsel.[79]

(2) Unless privileged or irrelevant, the identities of the clients he represents and of the persons who employed him.[80]

(C) In appearing in his professional capacity before a tribunal, a lawyer shall not:

(1) State or allude to any matter that he has no reasonable basis to believe is relevant to the case or that will not be supported by admissible evidence.[81]

(2) Ask any question that he has no reasonable basis to believe is relevant to the case and that is intended to degrade a witness or other person.[82]

---

[78] Cf. Note, 38 Texas L.Rev. 107, 108–09 (1959).

[79] "In the brief summary in the 1947 edition of the Committee's decisions (p. 17), *Opinion 146* was thus summarized: *Opinion 146*—A lawyer should disclose to the court a decision directly adverse to his client's case that is unknown to his adversary.

"We would not confine the Opinion to 'controlling authorities'—i.e., those decisive of the pending case—but, in accordance with the tests hereafter suggested, would apply it to a decision directly adverse to any proposition of law on which the lawyer expressly relies, which would reasonably be considered important by the judge sitting on the case.

* * *

". . . The test in every case should be: Is the decision which opposing counsel has overlooked one which the court should clearly consider in deciding the case? Would a reasonable judge properly feel that a lawyer who advanced, as the law, a proposition adverse to the undisclosed decision, was lacking in candor and fairness to him? Might the judge consider himself misled by an implied representation that the lawyer knew of no adverse authority?" *ABA Opinion* 280 (1949).

[80] "The authorities are substantially uniform against any privilege as applied to the fact of retainer or identity of the client. The privilege is limited to confidential communications, and a retainer is not a confidential communication, although it cannot come into existence without some communication between the attorney and the—at that stage prospective—client." United States v. Pape, 144 F.2d 778, 782 (2d Cir. 1944), cert. denied, 323 U.S. 752 89 L.Ed.2d 602, 65 S.Ct. 86 (1944).

"To be sure, there may be circumstances under which the identification of a client may amount to the prejudicial disclosure of a confidential communication, as where the substance of a disclosure has already been revealed but not its source." Colton v. United States, 306 F.2d 633, 637 (2d Cir. 1962).

[81] See ABA Canon 22; cf. ABA Canon 17.

"The rule allowing counsel when addressing the jury the widest latitude in discussing the evidence and presenting the client's theories falls far short of authorizing the statement by counsel of matter not in evidence, or indulging in argument founded on no proof, or demanding verdicts for purposes other than the just settlement of the matters at issue between the litigants, or appealing to prejudice or passion. The rule confining counsel to legitimate argument is not based on etiquette, but on justice. Its violation is not merely an overstepping of the bounds of propriety, but a violation of a party's rights. The jurors must determine the issues upon the evidence. Counsel's address should help them do this, not tend to lead them astray." Cherry Creek Nat. Bank v. Fidelity & Cas. Co., 207 App.Div. 787, 790–91, 202 N.Y.S. 611, 614 (1924).

[82] Cf. ABA Canon 18.

§ 6068. . . . It is the duty of an attorney:

* * *

(3) Assert his personal knowledge of the facts in issue, except when testifying as a witness.

(4) Assert his personal opinion as to the justness of a cause, as to the credibility of a witness, as to the culpability of a civil litigant, or as to the guilt or innocence of an accused;[83] but he may argue, on his analysis of the evidence, for any position or conclusion with respect to the matters stated herein.

(5) Fail to comply with known local customs of courtesy or practice of the bar or a particular tribunal without giving to opposing counsel timely notice of his intent not to comply.[84]

(6) Engage in undignified or discourteous conduct which is degrading to a tribunal.

(7) Intentionally or habitually violate any established rule of procedure or of evidence.

DR 7–107 Trial Publicity.[85]

(A) A lawyer participating in or associated with the investigation of a criminal matter shall not make or participate in making an extrajudicial statement that a reasonable person would expect to be disseminated by means of public communication and that does more than state without elaboration:

(1) Information contained in a public record.

(2) That the investigation is in progress.

(3) The general scope of the investigation including a description of the offense and, if permitted by law, the identity of the victim.

"(f) To abstain from all offensive personality, and to advance no fact prejudicial to the honor or reputation of a party or witness, unless required by the justice of the cause with which he is charged." Cal.Business and Professions Code § 6068 (West 1962).

[83] "The record in the case at bar was silent concerning the qualities and character of the deceased. It is especially improper, in addressing the jury in a murder case, for the prosecuting attorney to make reference to his knowledge of the good qualities of the deceased where there is no evidence in the record bearing upon his character. . . . A prosecutor should never inject into his argument evidence not introduced at the trial." People v. Dukes, 12 Ill.2d 334, 341, 146 N.E.2d 14, 17–18 (1957).

[84] "A lawyer should not ignore known customs or practice of the Bar or of a particular Court, even when the law permits, without giving timely notice to the opposing counsel." ABA Canon 25.

[85] The provisions of Sections (A), (B), (C), and (D) of this Disciplinary Rule incorporate the fair trial-free press standards which apply to lawyers as adopted by the ABA House of Delegates, Feb. 19, 1968, upon the recommendation of the Fair Trial and Free Press Advisory Committee of the ABA Special Committee on Minimum Standards for the Administration of Criminal Justice.

Cf. ABA Canon 20; see generally ABA Advisory Committee on Fair Trial and Free Press, Standards Relating to Fair Trial and Free Press (1966).

"From the cases coming here we note that unfair and prejudicial news comment on pending trials has become increasingly prevalent. Due process requires that the accused receive a trial by an impartial jury free from outside influences. Given the pervasiveness of modern communications and the difficulty of effacing prejudicial publicity from the minds of the jurors, the trial courts must take strong measures to ensure that the balance is never weighed against the accused. And appellate tribunals have the duty to make an independent evaluation of the circumstances. Of course, there is nothing that prescribes the press from reporting events that transpire in the courtroom. But where there is a reasonable likelihood that prejudicial news prior to trial will prevent a fair trial, the judge should continue the case until the threat abates, or transfer it to another county not so permeated with publicity. . . . The courts must take such steps by rule and regulation that will protect their processes from prejudicial outside interferences. Neither prosecutors, counsel for defense, the accused, witnesses, court staff nor enforcement officers coming under the jurisdiction of the court should be permitted to frustrate its function. Collaboration between counsel and the press as to information affecting the fairness of a criminal trial is not only subject to regulation, but is highly censurable and worthy of disciplinary measures." Sheppard v. Maxwell, 384 U.S. 333, 362–63, 16 L.Ed.2d 600, 620, 86 S.Ct. 1507, 1522 (1966).

(4) A request for assistance in apprehending a suspect or assistance in other matters and the information necessary thereto.

(5) A warning to the public of any dangers.

(B) A lawyer or law firm associated with the prosecution or defense of a criminal matter shall not, from the time of the filing of a complaint, information, or indictment, the issuance of an arrest warrant, or arrest until the commencement of the trial or disposition without trial, make or participate in making an extrajudicial statement that a reasonable person would expect to be disseminated by means of public communication and that relates to:

(1) The character, reputation, or prior criminal record (including arrests, indictments, or other charges of crime) of the accused.

(2) The possibility of a plea of guilty to the offense charged or to a lesser offense.

(3) The existence or contents of any confession, admission, or statement given by the accused or his refusal or failure to make a statement.

(4) The performance or results of any examinations or tests or the refusal or failure of the accused to submit to examinations or tests.

(5) The identity, testimony, or credibility of a prospective witness.

(6) Any opinion as to the guilt or innocence of the accused, the evidence, or the merits of the case.

(C) DR 7–107(B) does not preclude a lawyer during such period from announcing:

(1) The name, age, residence, occupation, and family status of the accused.

(2) If the accused has not been apprehended, any information necessary to aid in his apprehension or to warn the public of any dangers he may present.

(3) A request for assistance in obtaining evidence.

(4) The identity of the victim of the crime.

(5) The fact, time, and place of arrest, resistance, pursuit, and use of weapons.

(6) The identity of investigating and arresting officers or agencies and the length of the investigation.

(7) At the time of seizure, a description of the physical evidence seized, other than a confession, admission, or statement.

(8) The nature, substance, or text of the charge.

(9) Quotations from or references to public records of the court in the case.

(10) The scheduling or result of any step in the judicial proceedings.

(11) That the accused denies the charges made against him.

(D) During the selection of a jury or the trial of a criminal matter, a lawyer or law firm associated with the prosecution or defense of a criminal matter shall not make or participate in making an extra-judicial statement that a reasonable person would expect to be disseminated by means of public communication and that relates to the trial, parties, or issues in the trial or other matters that are reasonably likely to interfere with a fair trial, except that he may quote from or refer without comment to public records of the court in the case.

(E) After the completion of a trial or disposition without trial of a criminal matter and prior to the imposition of sentence, a lawyer or law firm associated with the prosecution or defense shall not make or participate in making an extra-judicial statement that a reasonable person would expect to be disseminated by public communication and that is reasonably likely to affect the imposition of sentence.

(F) The foregoing provisions of DR 7–107 also apply to professional disciplinary proceedings and juvenile disciplinary proceedings when pertinent and consistent with other law applicable to such proceedings.

(G) A lawyer or law firm associated with a civil action shall not during its investigation or litigation make or participate in making an extra-judicial statement, other than a quotation from or reference to public records, that a reasonable person would expect to be disseminated by means of public communication and that relates to:

(1) Evidence regarding the occurrence or transaction involved.

(2) The character, credibility, or criminal record of a party, witness, or prospective witness.

(3) The performance or results of any examinations or tests or the refusal or failure of a party to submit to such.

(4) His opinion as to the merits of the claims or defenses of a party, except as required by law or administrative rule.

(5) Any other matter reasonably likely to interfere with a fair trial of the action.

(H) During the pendency of an administrative proceeding, a lawyer or law firm associated therewith shall not make or participate in making a statement, other than a quotation from or reference to public records, that a reasonable person would expect to be disseminated by means of public communication if it is made outside the official course of the proceeding and relates to:

(1) Evidence regarding the occurrence or transaction involved.

(2) The character, credibility, or criminal record of a party, witness, or prospective witness.

(3) Physical evidence or the performance or results of any examinations or tests or the refusal or failure of a party to submit to such.

(4) His opinion as to the merits of the claims, defenses, or positions of an interested person.

(5) Any other matter reasonably likely to interfere with a fair hearing.

(I) The foregoing provisions of DR 7–107 do not preclude a lawyer from replying to charges of misconduct publicly made against him or from participating in the proceedings of legislative, administrative, or other investigative bodies.

(J) A lawyer shall exercise reasonable care to prevent his employees and associates from making an extra-judicial statement that he would be prohibited from making under DR 7–107.

DR 7–108 Communication With or Investigation of Jurors.

(A) Before the trial of a case a lawyer connected therewith shall not communicate with or cause another to communicate with anyone he knows to be a member of the venire from which the jury will be selected for the trial of the case.

(B) During the trial of a case:

(1) A lawyer connected therewith shall not communicate with or cause another to communicate with any member of the jury.[86]

(2) A lawyer who is not connected therewith shall not communicate with or cause another to communicate with a juror concerning the case.

(C) DR 7-108(A) and (B) do not prohibit a lawyer from communicating with veniremen or jurors in the course of official proceedings.

(D) After discharge of the jury from further consideration of a case with which the lawyer was connected, the lawyer shall not ask questions of or make comments to a member of that jury that are calculated merely to harass or embarrass the juror or to influence his actions in future jury service.[87]

(E) A lawyer shall not conduct or cause, by financial support or otherwise, another to conduct a vexatious or harassing investigation of either a venireman or a juror.

(F) All restrictions imposed by DR 7-108 upon a lawyer also apply to communications with or investigations of members of a family of a venireman or a juror.

(G) A lawyer shall reveal promptly to the court improper conduct by a venireman or a juror, or by another toward a venireman or a juror or a member of his family, of which the lawyer has knowledge.

DR 7-109 Contact With Witnesses.

(A) A lawyer shall not suppress any evidence that he or his client has a legal obligation to reveal or produce.[88]

(B) A lawyer shall not advise or cause a person to secrete himself or to leave the jurisdiction of a tribunal for the purpose of making him unavailable as a witness therein.[89]

(C) A lawyer shall not pay, offer to pay, or acquiesce in the payment of compensation to a witness contingent upon the content of his testimony or the outcome of the case.[90] But a lawyer may advance, guarantee, or acquiesce in the payment of:

(1) Expenses reasonably incurred by a witness in attending or testifying.

(2) Reasonable compensation to a witness for his loss of time in attending or testifying.

(3) A reasonable fee for the professional services of an expert witness.

DR 7-110 Contact With Officials.[91]

(A) A lawyer shall not give or lend any thing of value to a judge, official, or employee of a tribunal, except as permitted by Section C(4) of Canon 5 of the Code of Judicial Conduct, but a lawyer may make a contribution to the campaign fund of a candidate

[86] See ABA Canon 23.

[87] "[I]t would be unethical for a lawyer to harass, entice, induce or exert influence on a juror to obtain his testimony." *ABA Opinion* 319 (1968).

[88] See ABA Canon 5.

[89] Cf. ABA Canon 5.

"*Rule 15*. . . . A member of the State Bar shall not advise a person, whose testimony could establish or tend to establish a material fact, to avoid service of process, or secrete himself, or otherwise to make his testimony unavailable." Cal.Business and Professions Code § 6076 (West 1962).

[90] See In re O'Keefe, 49 Mont. 369, 142 P. 638 (1914).

[91] Cf. ABA Canon 3.

for judicial office in conformity with Section B(2) under Canon 7 of the Code of Judicial Conduct.

(B) In an adversary proceeding, a lawyer shall not communicate, or cause another to communicate, as to the merits of the cause with a judge or an official before whom the proceeding is pending, except:

(1) In the course of official proceedings in the cause.

(2) In writing if he promptly delivers a copy of the writing to opposing counsel or to the adverse party if he is not represented by a lawyer.

(3) Orally upon adequate notice to opposing counsel or to the adverse party if he is not represented by a lawyer.

(4) As otherwise authorized by law, or by Section A(4) under Canon 3 of the Code of Judicial Conduct.[92]

As amended in 1974.

CANON 8

A Lawyer Should Assist in Improving the Legal System

ETHICAL CONSIDERATIONS

EC 8–1 Changes in human affairs and imperfections in human institutions make necessary constant efforts to maintain and improve our legal system.[1] This system should function in a manner that commands public respect and fosters the use of legal remedies to achieve redress of grievances. By reason of education and experience, lawyers are especially qualified to recognize deficiencies in the legal system and to initiate corrective measures therein. Thus they should participate in proposing and supporting legislation and programs to improve the system,[2] without regard to the general interests or desires of clients or former clients.[3]

EC 8–2 Rules of law are deficient if they are not just, understandable, and responsive to the needs of society. If a lawyer believes that the existence or absence of a rule of law, substantive or procedural, causes or contributes to an unjust result, he should endeavor by lawful means to obtain appropriate change in the law. He should encourage the simplification of laws and the repeal or amendment of laws that are

[92] "*Rule 16.* . . . A member of the State Bar shall not, in the absence of opposing counsel, communicate with or argue to a judge or judicial officer except in open court upon the merits of a contested matter pending before such judge or judicial officer; nor shall he, without furnishing opposing counsel with a copy thereof, address a written communication to a judge or judicial officer concerning the merits of a contested matter pending before such judge or judicial officer. This rule shall not apply to ex parte matters." Cal.Business and Professions Code § 6076 (West 1962).

[1] ". . . [Another] task of the great lawyer is to do his part individually and as a member of the organized bar to improve his profession, the courts, and the law. As President Theodore Roosevelt aptly put it, 'Every man owes some of his time to the upbuilding of the profession to which he belongs.' Indeed, this obligation is one of the great things which distinguishes a profession from a business. The soundness and the necessity of President Roosevelt's admonition insofar as it relates to the legal profession cannot be doubted. The advances in natural science and technology are so startling and the velocity of change in business and in social life is so great that the law along with the other social sciences, and even human life itself, is in grave danger of being extinguished by new gods of its own invention if it does not awake from its lethargy." Vanderbilt, *The Five Functions of the Lawyer: Service to Clients and the Public,* 40 A.B.A.J. 31, 31–32 (1954).

[2] See ABA Cannon 29; Cf. Cheatham, *The Lawyer's Role and Surroundings,* 25 Rocky Mt.L.Rev. 405, 406–07 (1953).

"The lawyer tempted by repose should recall the heavy costs paid by his profession when needed legal reform has to be accomplished through the initiative of public-spirited laymen. Where change must be thrust from without upon an unwilling Bar, the public's least flattering picture of the lawyer seems confirmed. The lawyer concerned for the standing of his profession will, therefore, interest himself actively in the improvement of the law. In doing so he will not only help to maintain confidence in the Bar, but will have the satisfaction of meeting a responsibility inhering in the nature of his calling." *Professional Responsibility: Report of the Joint Conference,* 44 A.B.A.J. 1159, 1217 (1958).

[3] See Stayton, *Cum Honore Officium,* 19 Tex.B.J. 765, 766 (1956); *Professional Responsibility: Report of the Joint Conference,* 44 A.B.A.J. 1159, 1162 (1958); and Paul, *The Lawyer as a Tax Adviser,* 25 Rocky Mt.L.Rev. 412, 433–34 (1953).

outmoded.[4] Likewise, legal procedures should be improved whenever experience indicates a change is needed.

EC 8–3 The fair administration of justice requires the availability of competent lawyers. Members of the public should be educated to recognize the existence of legal problems and the resultant need for legal services, and should be provided methods for intelligent selection of counsel. Those persons unable to pay for legal services should be provided needed services. Clients and lawyers should not be penalized by undue geographical restraints upon representation in legal matters, and the bar should address itself to improvements in licensing, reciprocity, and admission procedures consistent with the needs of modern commerce.

EC 8–4 Whenever a lawyer seeks legislative or administrative changes, he should identify the capacity in which he appears, whether on behalf of himself, a client, or the public.[5] A lawyer may advocate such changes on behalf of a client even though he does not agree with them. But when a lawyer purports to act on behalf of the public, he should espouse only those changes which he conscientiously believes to be in the public interest.

EC 8–5 Fraudulent, deceptive, or otherwise illegal conduct by a participant in a proceeding before a tribunal or legislative body is inconsistent with fair administration of justice, and it should never be participated in or condoned by lawyers. Unless constrained by his obligation to preserve the confidences and secrets of his client, a lawyer should reveal to appropriate authorities any knowledge he may have of such improper conduct.

EC 8–6 Judges and administrative officials having adjudicatory powers ought to be persons of integrity, competence, and suitable temperament. Generally, lawyers are qualified, by personal observation or investigation, to evaluate the qualifications of persons seeking or being considered for such public offices, and for this reason they have a special responsibility to aid in the selection of only those who are qualified.[6] It is the duty of lawyers to endeavor to prevent political considerations from outweighing judicial fitness in the selection of judges. Lawyers should protest earnestly against the appointment or election of those who are unsuited for the bench and should strive to have elected[7] or appointed thereto only those who are willing to forego pursuits, whether of a business, political, or other nature, that may interfere with the free and fair consideration of questions presented for adjudication. Adjudicatory officials, not being wholly free to defend themselves, are entitled to receive the support of the bar against unjust criticism.[8] While a lawyer as a citizen has a right to criticize such officials publicly,[9] he should be certain of the merit of his complaint, use appropriate language, and avoid petty criticisms, for unrestrained and intemperate statements tend to

---

[4] "There are few great figures in the history of the Bar who have not concerned themselves with the reform and improvement of the law. The special obligation of the profession with respect to legal reform rests on considerations too obvious to require enumeration. Certainly it is the lawyer who has both the best chance to know when the law is working badly and the special competence to put it in order." *Professional Responsibility: Report of the Joint Conference,* 44 A.B.A.J. 1159, 1217 (1958).

[5] "*Rule 14.* . . . A member of the State Bar shall not communicate with, or appear before, a public officer, board, committee or body, in his professional capacity, without first disclosing that he is an attorney representing interests that may be affected by action of such officer, board, committee or body." Cal.Business and Professions Code § 6076 (West 1962).

[6] See ABA Canon 2.

"Lawyers are better able than laymen to appraise accurately the qualifications of candidates for judicial office. It is proper that they should make that appraisal known to the voters in a proper and dignified manner. A lawyer may with propriety endorse a candidate for judicial office and seek like endorsement from other lawyers. But the lawyer who endorses a judicial candidate or seeks that endorsement from other lawyers should be actuated by a sincere belief in the superior qualifications of the candidate for judicial service and not by personal or selfish motives; and a lawyer should not use or attempt to use the power or prestige of the judicial office to secure such endorsement. On the other hand, the lawyer whose endorsement is sought, if he believes the candidate lacks the essential qualifications for the office or believes the opposing candidate is better qualified, should have the courage and moral stamina to refuse the request for endorsement." *ABA Opinion* 189 (1938).

[7] "[W]e are of the opinion that, whenever a candidate for judicial office merits the endorsement and support of lawyers, the lawyers may make financial contributions toward the campaign if its cost, when reasonably conducted, exceeds that which the candidate would be expected to bear personally." *ABA Opinion* 226 (1941).

[8] See ABA Canon 1.

[9] "Citizens have a right under our constitutional system to criticize governmental officials and agencies. Courts are not, and should not be, immune to such criticism." Konigsberg v. State Bar of California, 353 U.S. 252, 269 (1957).

lessen public confidence in our legal system.[10] Criticisms motivated by reasons other than a desire to improve the legal system are not justified.

EC 8–7 Since lawyers are a vital part of the legal system, they should be persons of integrity, of professional skill, and of dedication to the improvement of the system. Thus a lawyer should aid in establishing, as well as enforcing, standards of conduct adequate to protect the public by insuring that those who practice law are qualified to do so.

EC 8–8 Lawyers often serve as legislators or as holders of other public offices. This is highly desirable, as lawyers are uniquely qualified to make significant contributions to the improvement of the legal system. A lawyer who is a public officer, whether full or part-time, should not engage in activities in which his personal or professional interests are or foreseeably may be in conflict with his official duties.[11]

EC 8–9 The advancement of our legal system is of vital importance in maintaining the rule of law and in facilitating orderly changes; therefore, lawyers should encourage, and should aid in making, needed changes and improvements.

DISCIPLINARY RULES

DR 8–101 Action as a Public Official.

(A) A lawyer who holds public office shall not:

(1) Use his public position to obtain, or attempt to obtain, a special advantage in legislative matters for himself or for a client under circumstances where he knows or it is obvious that such action is not in the public interest.

(2) Use his public position to influence, or attempt to influence, a tribunal to act in favor of himself or of a client.

(3) Accept any thing of value from any person when the lawyer knows or it is obvious that the offer is for the purpose of influencing his action as a public official.

---

[10] "[E]very lawyer, worthy of respect, realizes that public confidence in our courts is the cornerstone of our governmental structure, and will refrain from unjustified attack on the character of the judges, while recognizing the duty to denounce and expose a corrupt or dishonest judge." Kentucky State Bar Ass'n v. Lewis, 282 S.W.2d 321, 326 (Ky.1955).

"We should be the last to deny that Mr. Meeker has the right to uphold the honor of the profession and to expose without fear or favor corrupt or dishonest conduct in the profession, whether the conduct be that of a judge or not. . . . However, this Canon [29] does not permit one to make charges which are false and untrue and unfounded in fact. When one's fancy leads him to make false charges, attacking the character and integrity of others, he does so at his peril. He should not do so without adequate proof of his charges and he is certainly not authorized to make careless, untruthful and vile charges against his professional brethren." In re Meeker, 76 N.M. 354, 364–65, 414 P.2d 862, 869 (1966), appeal dismissed, 385 U.S. 449, 17 L.Ed.2d 510, 87 S.Ct. 613 (1967).

[11] "*Opinions 16, 30, 34, 77, 118* and *134* relate to *Canon 6,* and pass on questions concerning the propriety of the conduct of an attorney who is a public officer, in representing private interests adverse to those of the public body which he represents. The principle applied in those opinions is that an attorney holding public office should avoid all conduct which might lead the layman to conclude that the attorney is utilizing his public position to further his professional success or personal interests." *ABA Opinion* 192 (1939).

"The next question is whether a lawyer-member of a legislative body may appear as counsel or co-counsel at hearings before a zoning board of appeals, or similar tribunal, created by the legislative group of which he is a member. We are of the opinion that he may practice before fact-finding officers, hearing bodies and commissioners, since under our views he may appear as counsel in the courts where his municipality is a party. Decisions made at such hearings are usually subject to administrative review by the courts upon the record there made. It would be inconsistent to say that a lawyer-member of a legislative body could not participate in a hearing at which the record is made, but could appear thereafter when the cause is heard by the courts on administrative review. This is subject to an important exception. He should not appear as counsel where the matter is subject to review by the legislative body of which he is a member. . . . We are of the opinion that where a lawyer does so appear there would be conflict of interests between his duty as an advocate for his client on the one hand and the obligation to his governmental unit on the other." In re Becker, 16 Ill.2d 488, 494–95, 158 N.E.2d 753, 756–57 (1959).

Cf. *ABA Opinions* 186 (1938), 136 (1935), 118 (1934), and 77 (1932).

DR 8–102 Statements Concerning Judges and Other Adjudicatory Officers.[12]

(A) A lawyer shall not knowingly make false statements of fact concerning the qualifications of a candidate for election or appointment to a judicial office.

(B) A lawyer shall not knowingly make false accusations against a judge or other adjudicatory officer.

DR 8–103 Lawyer Candidate for Judicial Office.

(A) A lawyer who is a candidate for judicial office shall comply with the applicable provisions of Canon 7 of the Code of Judicial Conduct.

Added in 1974.

CANON 9

A Lawyer Should Avoid Even the Appearance of Professional Impropriety

ETHICAL CONSIDERATIONS

EC 9–1 Continuation of the American concept that we are to be governed by rules of law requires that the people have faith that justice can be obtained through our legal system.[1] A lawyer should promote public confidence in our system and in the legal profession.[2]

EC 9–2 Public confidence in law and lawyers may be eroded by irresponsible or improper conduct of a lawyer. On occasion, ethical conduct of a lawyer may appear to laymen to be unethical. In order to avoid misunderstandings and hence to maintain confidence, a lawyer should fully and promptly inform his client of material developments in the matters being handled for the client. While a lawyer should guard against otherwise proper conduct that has a tendency to diminish public confidence in the legal system or in the legal profession, his duty to clients or to the public should never be subordinate merely because the full discharge of his obligation may be misunderstood or may tend to subject him or the legal profession to criticism. When explicit ethical guidance does not exist, a lawyer should determine his conduct by acting in a manner that promotes public confidence in the integrity and efficiency of the legal system and the legal profession.[3]

EC 9–3 After a lawyer leaves judicial office or other public employment, he should not accept employment in connection with any matter in which he had substantial responsibility prior to his leaving, since to accept employment would give the appearance of impropriety even if none exists.[4]

EC 9–4 Because the very essence of the legal system is to provide procedures by which matters can be presented in an impartial manner so that they may be decided solely upon the merits, any statement or suggestion by a lawyer that he can or would attempt to circumvent those procedures is detrimental to the legal system and tends to undermine public confidence in it.

EC 9–5 Separation of the funds of a client from those of his lawyer not only serves to protect the client but also avoids even the appearance of impropriety, and therefore commingling of such funds should be avoided.

---

[12] Cf. ABA Canons 1 and 2.

[1] "Integrity is the very breath of justice. Confidence in our law, our courts, and in the administration of justice is our supreme interest. No practice must be permitted to prevail which invites towards the administration of justice a doubt or distrust of its integrity." Erwin M. Jennings Co. v. DiGenova, 107 Conn. 491, 499, 141 A. 866, 868 (1928).

[2] "A lawyer should never be reluctant or too proud to answer unjustified criticism of his profession, of himself, or of his brother lawyer. He should guard the reputation of his profession and of his brothers as zealously as he guards his own." Rochelle and Payne, *The Struggle for Public Understanding,* 25 Texas B.J. 109, 162 (1962).

[3] See ABA Canon 29.

[4] See ABA Canon 36.

EC 9–6 Every lawyer owes a solemn duty to uphold the integrity and honor of his profession; to encourage respect for the law and for the courts and the judges thereof; to observe the Code of Professional Responsibility; to act as a member of a learned profession, one dedicated to public service; to cooperate with his brother lawyers in supporting the organized bar through the devoting of his time, efforts, and financial support as his professional standing and ability reasonably permit; to conduct himself so as to reflect credit on the legal profession and to inspire the confidence, respect, and trust of his clients and of the public; and to strive to avoid not only professional impropriety but also the appearance of impropriety.[5]

EC 9–7 A lawyer has an obligation to the public to participate in collective efforts of the bar to reimburse persons who have lost money or property as a result of the misappropriation or defalcation of another lawyer, and contribution to a clients' security fund is an acceptable method of meeting this obligation.

DISCIPLINARY RULES

DR 9–101 Avoiding Even the Appearance of Impropriety.[6]

(A) A lawyer shall not accept private employment in a matter upon the merits of which he has acted in a judicial capacity.[7]

(B) A lawyer shall not accept private employment in a matter in which he had substantial responsibility while he was a public employee.[8]

---

[5] "As said in Opinion 49 of the Committee on Professional Ethics and Grievances of the American Bar Association, page 134: 'An attorney should not only avoid impropriety but should avoid the appearance of impropriety.' " State ex rel. Nebraska State Bar Ass'n v. Richards, 165 Neb. 80, 93, 84 N.W.2d 136, 145 (1957).

"It would also be preferable that such contribution [to the campaign of a candidate for judicial office] be made to a campaign committee rather than to the candidate personally. In so doing, possible appearances of impropriety would be reduced to a minimum." *ABA Opinion* 226 (1941).

"The lawyer assumes high duties, and has imposed upon him grave responsibilities. He may be the means of much good or much mischief. Interests of vast magnitude are entrusted to him; confidence is reposed in him; life, liberty, character and property should be protected by him. He should guard, with jealous watchfulness, his own reputation, as well as that of his profession." People ex rel. Cutler v. Ford, 54 Ill. 520, 522 (1870), and also quoted in State Board of Law Examiners v. Sheldon, 43 Wyo. 522, 526, 7 P.2d 226, 227 (1932).

See *ABA Opinion* 150 (1936).

[6] Cf. Code of Professional Responsibility, EC 5–6.

[7] See *ABA* Canon 36.

"It is the duty of the judge to rule on questions of law and evidence in misdemeanor cases and examinations in felony cases. That duty calls for impartial and uninfluenced judgment, regardless of the effect on those immediately involved or others who may, directly or indirectly, be affected. Discharge of that duty might be greatly interfered with if the judge, in another capacity, were permitted to hold himself out to employment by those who are to be, or who may be, brought to trial in felony cases, even though he did not conduct the examination. His private interests as a lawyer in building up his clientele, his duty as such zealously to espouse the cause of his private clients and to defend against charges of crime brought by law-enforcement agencies of which he is a part, might prevent, or even destroy, that unbiased judicial judgment which is so essential in the administration of justice.

"In our opinion, acceptance of a judgeship with the duties of conducting misdemeanor trials, and examinations in felony cases to determine whether those accused should be bound over for trial in a higher court, ethically bars the judge from acting as attorney for the defendants upon such trial, whether they were examined by him or by some other judge. Such a practice would not only diminish public confidence in the administration of justice in both courts, but would produce serious conflict between the private interests of the judge as a lawyer, and of his clients, and his duties as a judge in adjudicating important phases of criminal processes in other cases. The public and private duties would be incompatible. The prestige of the judicial office would be diverted to private benefit, and the judicial office would be demeaned thereby." *ABA Opinion* 242 (1942).

"A lawyer, who has previously occupied a judicial position or acted in a judicial capacity, should refrain from accepting employment in any matter involving the same facts as were involved in any specific question which he acted upon in a judicial capacity and, for the same reasons, should also refrain from accepting any employment which might reasonably appear to involve the same facts." *ABA Opinion* 49 (1931).

See *ABA Opinion* 110 (1934).

[8] See *ABA Opinions* 135 (1935) and 134 (1935); cf. ABA Canon 36 and *ABA Opinions* 39 (1931) and 26 (1930). But see *ABA Opinion* 37 (1931).

(C) A lawyer shall not state or imply that he is able to influence improperly or upon irrelevant grounds any tribunal, legislative body,[9] or public official.

DR 9–102 Preserving Identity of Funds and Property of a Client.[10]

(A) All funds of clients paid to a lawyer or law firm, other than advances for costs and expenses, shall be deposited in one or more identifiable bank accounts maintained in the state in which the law office is situated and no funds belonging to the lawyer or law firm shall be deposited therein except as follows:

(1) Funds reasonably sufficient to pay bank charges may be deposited therein.

(2) Funds belonging in part to a client and in part presently or potentially to the lawyer or law firm must be deposited therein, but the portion belonging to the lawyer or law firm may be withdrawn when due unless the right of the lawyer or law firm to receive it is disputed by the client, in which event the disputed portion shall not be withdrawn until the dispute is finally resolved.

(B) A lawyer shall:

(1) Promptly notify a client of the receipt of his funds, securities, or other properties.

(2) Identify and label securities and properties of a client promptly upon receipt and place them in a safe deposit box or other place of safekeeping as soon as practicable.

(3) Maintain complete records of all funds, securities, and other properties of a client coming into the possession of the lawyer and render appropriate accounts to his client regarding them.

(4) Promptly pay or deliver to the client as requested by a client the funds, securities, or other properties in the possession of the lawyer which the client is entitled to receive.

---

9 "[A statement by a governmental department or agency with regard to a lawyer resigning from its staff that includes a laudation of his legal ability] carries implications, probably not founded in fact, that the lawyer's acquaintance and previous relations with the personnel of the administrative agencies of the government place him in an advantageous position in practicing before such agencies. So to imply would not only represent what probably is untrue, but would be highly reprehensible." *ABA Opinion* 184 (1938).

10 See ABA Canon 11.

"*Rule 9.* . . . A member of the State Bar shall not commingle the money or other property of a client with his own; and he shall promptly report to the client the receipt by him of all money and other property belonging to such client. Unless the client otherwise directs in writing, he shall promptly deposit his client's funds in a bank or trust company . . . in a bank account separate from his own account and clearly designated as 'Clients' Funds Account' or 'Trust Funds Account' or words of similar import. Unless the client otherwise directs in writing, securities of a client in bearer form shall be kept by the attorney in a safe deposit box at a bank or trust company, . . . which safe deposit box shall be clearly designated as 'Client's Account' or 'Trust Account' or words of similar import, and be separate from the attorney's own safe deposit box." Cal.Business and Professions Code § 6076 (West 1962).

"[C]ommingling is committed when a client's money is intermingled with that of his attorney and its separate identity lost so that it may be used for the attorney's personal expenses or subjected to claims of his creditors. . . . The rule against commingling was adopted to provide against the probability in some cases, the possibility in many cases, and the danger in all cases that such commingling will result in the loss of clients' money." Black v. State Bar, 57 Cal.2d 219, 225–26, 368 P.2d 118, 122, 18 Cal.Rptr. 518, 522 (1962).

DEFINITIONS*

As used in the Disciplinary Rules of the Code of Professional Responsibility:

(1) "Differing interests" include every interest that will adversely affect either the judgment or the loyalty of a lawyer to a client, whether it be a conflicting, inconsistent, diverse, or other interest.

(2) "Law firm" includes a professional legal corporation.

(3) "Person" includes a corporation, an association, a trust, a partnership, and any other organization or legal entity.

(4) "Professional legal corporation" means a corporation, or an association treated as a corporation, authorized by law to practice law for profit.

(5) "State" includes the District of Columbia, Puerto Rico, and other federal territories and possessions.

(6) "Tribunal" includes all courts and all other adjudicatory bodies.

(7) "A Bar association" includes a bar association of specialists as referred to in DR 2–105(A)(1) or (3).

(8) "Qualified legal assistance organization" means an office or organization of one of the four types listed in DR 2–103(D)(1)–(4), inclusive that meets all the requirements thereof.

As amended in 1974.

* "Confidence" and "secret" are defined in DR 4–101(A).

INDEX TO ABA MODEL CODE

A

B

C

F

G

H

I

J

K

L

M

N

O

P

Q

R

S

T

U

V

W

Z

AMERICAN BAR ASSOCIATION CANONS OF PROFESSIONAL ETHICS

As amended until 1969.

[The ABA adopted 32 Canons of Professional Ethics at its thirty-first annual meeting on August 27, 1908. Between 1908 and 1969, the ABA added Canons 33 through 47. Although the Canons were in effect for 61 years, the general aspirational approach of the Canons proved to be outmoded to regulate the conduct of lawyers in the 1950s and 1960s. The Canons were superseded in 1969 by the Model Code of Professional Responsibility. Ed.]

CANONS OF PROFESSIONAL ETHICS

Preamble.

In America, where the stability of Courts and of all departments of government rests upon the approval of the people, it is peculiarly essential that the system for establishing and dispensing Justice be developed to a high point of efficiency and so maintained that the public shall have absolute confidence in the integrity and impartiality of its administration. The future of the Republic, to a great extent, depends upon our maintenance of Justice pure and unsullied. It cannot be so maintained unless the conduct and the motives of the members of our profession are such as to merit the approval of all just men.

No code or set of rules can be framed, which will particularize all the duties of the lawyer in the varying phases of litigation or in all the relations of professional life. The following canons of ethics are adopted by the American Bar Association as a general guide, yet the enumeration of particular duties should not be construed as a denial of the existence of others equally imperative, though not specifically mentioned.

CANON 1

The Duty of the Lawyer to the Courts

It is the duty of the lawyer to maintain towards the Courts a respectful attitude, not for the sake of the temporary incumbent of the judicial office, but for the maintenance of its supreme importance. Judges, not being wholly free to defend themselves, are peculiarly entitled to receive the support of the Bar against unjust criticism and clamor. Whenever there is proper ground for serious complaint of a judicial officer, it is the right and duty of the lawyer to submit his grievances to the proper authorities. In such cases, but not otherwise, such charges should be encouraged and the person making them should be protected.

CANON 2

The Selection of Judges

It is the duty of the Bar to endeavor to prevent political considerations from outweighing judicial fitness in the selections of Judges. It should protest earnestly and actively against the appointment or election of those who are unsuitable for the Bench; and it should strive to have elevated thereto only those willing to forego other employments, whether of a business, political or other character, which may embarrass their free and fair consideration of questions before them for decision. The aspiration of lawyers for judicial position should be governed by an impartial estimate of their ability to add honor to the office and not by a desire for the distinction the position may bring to themselves.

CANON 3

Attempts to Exert Personal Influence on the Court

Marked attention and unusual hospitality on the part of a lawyer to a Judge, uncalled for by the personal relations of the parties, subject both the Judge and the lawyer to misconstructions of motive and should be avoided. A lawyer should not communicate or argue privately with the Judge as to the merits of a pending cause, and he deserves rebuke and denunciation for any device or attempt to gain from a Judge special personal consideration or favor. A self-respecting independence in the discharge of professional duty, without denial or diminution of the courtesy and respect due the Judge's station, is the only proper foundation for cordial personal and official relations between Bench and Bar.

CANON 4

When Counsel for an Indigent Prisoner

A lawyer assigned as counsel for an indigent prisoner ought not to ask to be excused for any trivial reason, and should always exert his best efforts on his behalf.

CANON 5

The Defense or Prosecution of Those Accused of Crime

It is the right of the lawyer to undertake the defense of a person accused of crime, regardless of his personal opinion as to the guilt of the accused; otherwise innocent persons, victims only of suspicious circumstances, might be denied proper defense. Having undertaken such defense, the lawyer is bound, by all fair and honorable means, to present every defense that the law of the land permits, to the end that no person may be deprived of life or liberty, but by due process of law.

The primary duty of a lawyer engaged in public prosecution is not to convict, but to see that justice is done. The suppression of facts or the secreting of witnesses capable of establishing the innocence of the accused is highly reprehensible.

CANON 6

Adverse Influences and Conflicting Interests

It is the duty of a lawyer at the time of retainer to disclose to the client all the circumstances of his relations to the parties, and any interest in or connection with the controversy, which might influence the client in the selection of counsel.

It is unprofessional to represent conflicting interests, except by express consent of all concerned given after a full disclosure of the facts. Within the meaning of this canon, a lawyer represents conflicting interests when, in behalf of one client, it is his duty to contend for that which duty to another client requires him to oppose.

The obligation to represent the client with undivided fidelity and not to divulge his secrets or confidences forbids also the subsequent acceptance of retainers or employment from others in matters adversely affecting any interest of the client with respect to which confidence has been reposed.

CANON 7

Professional Colleagues and Conflicts of Opinion

A client's proffer of assistance of additional counsel should not be regarded as evidence of want of confidence, but the matter should be left to the determination of the client. A lawyer should decline association as colleague if it is objectionable to the original counsel, but if the lawyer first retained is relieved, another may come into the case.

When lawyers jointly associated in a cause cannot agree as to any matter vital to the interest of the client, the conflict of opinion should be frankly stated to him for his final determination. His decision should be accepted unless the nature of the difference makes it impracticable for the lawyer whose judgment has been overruled to cooperate effectively. In this event it is his duty to ask the client to relieve him.

Efforts, direct or indirect, in any way to encroach upon the professional employment of another lawyer, are unworthy of those who should be brethren at the Bar; but, nevertheless, it is the right of any lawyer, without fear or favor, to give proper advice to those seeking relief against unfaithful or neglectful counsel, generally after communication with the lawyer of whom the complaint is made.

CANON 8

Advising Upon the Merits of a Client's Cause

A lawyer should endeavor to obtain full knowledge of his client's cause before advising thereon, and he is bound to give a candid opinion of the merits and probable result of pending or contemplated litigation. The miscarriages to which justice is subject, by reason of surprises and disappointments in evidence and witnesses, and through mistakes of juries and errors of Courts, even though only occasional, admonish lawyers to beware of bold and confident assurances to clients, especially where the employment may depend upon such assurance. Whenever the controversy will admit of fair adjustment, the client should be advised to avoid or to end the litigation.

CANON 9

Negotiations With Opposite Party

A lawyer should not in any way communicate upon the subject of controversy with a party represented by counsel; much less should he undertake to negotiate or compromise the matter with him, but should deal only with his counsel. It is incumbent upon the lawyer most particularly to avoid everything that may tend to mislead a party not represented by counsel, and he should not undertake to advise him as to the law.

CANON 10

Acquiring Interest in Litigation

The lawyer should not purchase any interest in the subject matter of the litigation which he is conducting.

CANON 11

Dealing With Trust Property

The lawyer should refrain from any action whereby for his personal benefit or gain he abuses or takes advantage of the confidence reposed in him by his client.

Money of the client or collected for the client or other trust property coming into the possession of the lawyer should be reported and accounted for promptly, and should not under any circumstances be commingled with his own or be used by him.

CANON 12

Fixing the Amount of the Fee

In fixing fees, lawyers should avoid charges which overestimate their advice and services, as well as those which undervalue them. A client's ability to pay cannot justify a charge in excess of the value of the service, though his poverty may require a less charge, or even none at all. The reasonable requests of brother lawyers, and of their widows and orphans without ample means, should receive special and kindly consideration.

In determining the amount of the fee, it is proper to consider: (1) the time and labor required, the novelty and difficulty of the questions involved and the skill requisite properly to conduct the cause; (2) whether the acceptance of employment in the particular case will preclude the lawyer's appearance for others in cases likely to arise out of the transaction, and in which there is a reasonable expectation that otherwise he would be employed, or will involve the loss of other employment while employed in the particular case or antagonisms with other clients; (3) the customary charges of the Bar for similar services; (4) the amount involved in the controversy and the benefits resulting to the client from the services; (5) the contingency or the certainty of the compensation; and (6) the character of the employment, whether casual or for an established and constant client. No one of these considerations in itself is controlling. They are mere guides in ascertaining the real value of the service.

In determining the customary charges of the Bar for similar services, it is proper for a lawyer to consider a schedule of minimum fees adopted by a Bar Association, but no lawyer should permit himself to be controlled thereby or to follow it as his sole guide in determining the amount of his fee.

In fixing fees it should never be forgotten that the profession is a branch of the administration of justice and not a mere money-getting trade.

CANON 13

Contingent Fees

A contract for a contingent fee, where sanctioned by law, should be reasonable under all the circumstances of the case, including the risk and uncertainty of the compensation, but should always be subject to the supervision of a court, as to its reasonableness.

CANON 14

Suing a Client for a Fee

Controversies with clients concerning compensation are to be avoided by the lawyer so far as shall be compatible with his self-respect and with his right to receive reasonable recompense for his services; and lawsuits with clients should be resorted to only to prevent injustice, imposition or fraud.

CANON 15

How Far a Lawyer May Go in Supporting a Client's Cause

Nothing operates more certainly to create or to foster popular prejudice against lawyers as a class, and to deprive the profession of that full measure of public esteem and confidence which belongs to the proper discharge of its duties than does the false claim, often set up by the unscrupulous in defense of questionable transactions, that it is the duty of the lawyer to do whatever may enable him to succeed in winning his client's cause.

It is improper for a lawyer to assert in argument his personal belief in his client's innocence or in the justice of his cause.

The lawyer owes "entire devotion to the interest of the client, warm zeal in the maintenance and defense of his rights and the exertion of his utmost learning and ability," to the end that nothing be taken or be withheld from him, save by the rules of law, legally applied. No fear of judicial disfavor or public unpopularity should restrain him from the full discharge of his duty. In the judicial forum the client is entitled to the benefit of any and every remedy and defense that is authorized by the law of the land, and he may expect his lawyer to assert every such remedy or defense. But it is steadfastly to be borne in mind that the great trust of the lawyer is to be performed within and not without the bounds of the law. The office of attorney does not permit, much less does it demand of him for any client, violation of law or any manner of fraud or chicane. He must obey his own conscience and not that of his client.

CANON 16

Restraining Clients From Improprieties

A lawyer should use his best efforts to restrain and to prevent his clients from doing those things which the lawyer himself ought not to do, particularly with reference to their conduct towards Courts, judicial officers, jurors, witnesses and suitors. If a client persists in such wrongdoing the lawyer should terminate their relation.

CANON 17

Ill-Feeling and Personalities Between Advocates

Clients, not lawyers, are the litigants. Whatever may be the ill-feeling existing between clients, it should not be allowed to influence counsel in their conduct and demeanor toward each other or toward suitors in the case. All personalities between counsel should be scrupulously avoided. In the trial of a cause it is indecent to allude to the personal history or the personal peculiarities and idiosyncrasies of counsel on the other side. Personal colloquies between counsel which cause delay and promote unseemly wrangling should also be carefully avoided.

CANON 18

Treatment of Witnesses and Litigants

A lawyer should always treat adverse witnesses and suitors with fairness and due consideration, and he should never minister to the malevolence or prejudices of a client in the trial or conduct of a cause. The client cannot be made the keeper of the lawyer's conscience in professional matters. He has no right to demand that his counsel shall abuse the opposite party or indulge in offensive personalities. Improper speech is not excusable on the ground that it is what the client would say if speaking in his own behalf.

CANON 19

Appearance of Lawyer as Witness for His Client

When a lawyer is a witness for his client, except as to merely formal matters, such as the attestation or custody of an instrument and the like, he should leave the trial of the case to other counsel. Except when essential to the ends of justice, a lawyer should avoid testifying in court in behalf of his client.

CANON 20

Newspaper Discussion of Pending Litigation

Newspaper publications by a lawyer as to pending or anticipated litigation may interfere with a fair trial in the Courts and otherwise prejudice the due administration of justice. Generally they are to be condemned. If the extreme circumstances of a particular case justify a statement to the public, it is unprofessional to make it anonymously. An *ex parte* reference to the facts should not go beyond quotation from the records and papers on file in the court; but even in extreme cases it is better to avoid any *ex parte* statement.

CANON 21

Punctuality and Expedition

It is the duty of the lawyer not only to his client, but also to the Courts and to the public to be punctual in attendance, and to be concise and direct in the trial and disposition of causes.

CANON 22

Candor and Fairness

The conduct of the lawyer before the Court and with other lawyers should be characterized by candor and fairness.

It is not candid or fair for the lawyer knowingly to misquote the contents of a paper, the testimony of a witness, the language or the argument of opposing counsel, or the language of a decision of a textbook; or with knowledge of its invalidity, to cite as authority a decision that has been overruled, or a statute that has been repealed; or in argument to assert as a fact that which has not been proved, or in those jurisdictions where a side has the opening and closing arguments to mislead his opponent by concealing or withholding positions in his opening argument upon which his side then intends to rely.

It is unprofessional and dishonorable to deal other than candidly with the facts in taking the statements of witnesses, in drawing affidavits and other documents, and in the presentation of causes.

A lawyer should not offer evidence which he knows the Court should reject, in order to get the same before the jury by argument for its admissibility, nor should he address to the Judge arguments upon any point not properly calling for determination by him. Neither should he introduce into an argument, addressed to the court, remarks or statements intended to influence the jury or bystanders.

These and all kindred practices are unprofessional and unworthy of an officer of the law charged, as is the lawyer, with the duty of aiding in the administration of justice.

CANON 23

Attitude Toward Jury

All attempts to curry favor with juries by fawning, flattery or pretended solicitude for their personal comfort are unprofessional. Suggestions of counsel, looking to the comfort or convenience of jurors, and propositions to dispense with argument, should be made to the Court out of the jury's hearing. A lawyer must never converse privately with jurors about the case; and both before and during the trial he should avoid communicating with them, even as to matters foreign to the cause.

CANON 24

Right of Lawyer to Control the Incidents of the Trial

As to incidental matters pending the trial, not affecting the merits of the cause, or working substantial prejudice to the rights of the client, such as forcing the opposite lawyer to trial when he is under affliction or bereavement; forcing the trial on a particular day to the injury of the opposite lawyer when no harm will result from a trial at a different time; agreeing to an extension of time for signing a bill of exceptions, cross interrogatories and the like, the lawyer must be allowed to judge. In such matters no client has a right to demand that his counsel shall be illiberal, or that he do anything therein repugnant to his own sense of honor and propriety.

CANON 25

Taking Technical Advantage of Opposite Counsel; Agreements With Him

A lawyer should not ignore known customs or practice of the Bar or of a particular Court, even when the law permits, without giving timely notice to the opposing counsel. As far as possible, important agreements, affecting the rights of clients, should be reduced to writing; but it is dishonorable to avoid performance of an agreement fairly made because it is not reduced to writing, as required by rules of Court.

CANON 26

Professional Advocacy Other Than Before Courts

A lawyer openly, and in his true character may render professional services before legislative or other bodies, regarding proposed legislation and in advocacy of claims before departments of government, upon the same principles of ethics which justify his appearance before the Courts; but it is unprofessional for a lawyer so engaged to conceal his attorneyship, or to employ secret personal solicitations, or to use means other than those addressed to the reason and understanding, to influence action.

CANON 27

Advertising, Direct or Indirect

It is unprofessional to solicit professional employment by circulars, advertisements, through toutors or by personal communications or interviews not warranted by personal relations. Indirect advertisements for professional employment such as furnishing or inspiring newspaper comments, or procuring his photograph to be published in connection with causes in which the lawyer has been or is engaged or concerning the manner of their conduct, the magnitude of the interest involved, the importance of the lawyer's position, and all other like self-laudation, offend the traditions and lower the tone of our profession and are reprehensible; but the customary use of simple professional cards is not improper.

Publication in reputable law lists in a manner consistent with the standards of conduct imposed by these canons of brief biographical and informative data is permissible. Such data must not be misleading and may include only a statement of the lawyer's name and the names of his professional associates; addresses, telephone numbers, cable addresses; branches of the profession practiced; date and place of birth and admission to the bar; schools attended; with dates of graduation, degrees and other educational distinctions; public or quasi-public offices; posts of honor; legal authorships; legal teaching positions; memberships and offices in bar associations and committees thereof, in legal and scientific societies and legal fraternities; foreign language ability; the fact of listings in other reputable law lists; the names and addresses of references; and, with their written consent, the names of clients regularly represented. A certificate of compliance with the Rules and Standards issued by the Standing Committee on Law Lists may be treated as evidence that such list is reputable.

It is not improper for a lawyer who is admitted to practice as a proctor in admiralty to use that designation on his letterhead or shingle or for a lawyer who has complied with the statutory requirements of admission to practice before the patent office, to so use the designation "patent attorney" or "patent lawyer" or "trademark attorney" or "trademark lawyer" or any combination of those terms.

CANON 28

Stirring Up Litigation, Directly or Through Agents

It is unprofessional for a lawyer to volunteer advice to bring a lawsuit, except in rare cases where ties of blood, relationship or trust make it his duty to do so. Stirring up strife and litigation is not only unprofessional, but it is indictable at common law. It is disreputable to hunt up defects in titles or other causes of action and inform thereof in order to be employed to bring suit or collect judgment, or to breed litigation by seeking out those with claims for personal injuries or those having any other grounds of action in order to secure them as clients, or to employ agents or runners for like purposes, or to pay or reward, directly or indirectly, those who bring or influence the bringing of such cases to his office, or to remunerate policemen, court or prison officials, physicians, hospital *attachés* or others who may succeed, under the guise of giving disinterested friendly advice, in influencing the criminal, the sick and the injured, the ignorant or others, to seek his professional services. A duty to the public and to the profession devolves upon every member of the Bar having knowledge of such practices upon the part of any practitioner immediately to inform thereof, to the end that the offender may be disbarred.

CANON 29

Upholding the Honor of the Profession

Lawyers should expose without fear or favor before the proper tribunals corrupt or dishonest conduct in the profession, and should accept without hesitation employment against a member of the Bar who has wronged his client. The counsel upon the trial of a cause in which perjury has been committed owe it to the profession and to the public to bring the matter to the knowledge of the prosecuting authorities. The lawyer should aid in guarding the Bar against the admission to the profession of candidates unfit or unqualified because deficient in either moral character or education. He should strive at all times to uphold the honor and to maintain the dignity of the profession and to improve not only the law but the administration of justice.

CANON 30

Justifiable and Unjustifiable Litigations

The lawyer must decline to conduct a civil cause or to make a defense when convinced that it is intended merely to harass or to injure the opposite party or to work oppression or wrong. But otherwise it is his right, and, having accepted retainer, it becomes his duty to insist upon the judgment of the Court as to the legal merits of his client's claim. His appearance in Court should be deemed equivalent to an assertion on his honor that in his opinion his client's case is one proper for judicial determination.

CANON 31

Responsibility for Litigation

No lawyer is obliged to act either as adviser or advocate for every person who may wish to become his client. He has the right to decline employment. Every lawyer upon his own responsibility must decide what employment he will accept as counsel, what causes he will bring into Court for plaintiffs, what cases he will contest in Court for defendants. The responsibility for advising as to questionable transactions, for bringing questionable suits, for urging questionable defenses, is the lawyer's responsibility. He cannot escape it by urging as an excuse that he is only following his client's instructions.

CANON 32

The Lawyer's Duty in Its Last Analysis

No client, corporate or individual, however powerful, nor any cause, civil or political, however important, is entitled to receive nor should any lawyer render any service or advice involving disloyalty to the law whose ministers we are, or disrespect of the judicial office, which we are bound to uphold, or corruption of any person or persons exercising a public office or private trust, or deception or betrayal of the public. When rendering any such improper service or advice, the lawyer invites and merits stern and just condemnation. Correspondingly, he advances the honor of his profession and the best interests of his client when he renders service or gives advice tending to impress upon the client and his undertaking exact compliance with the strictest principles of moral law. He must also observe and advise his client to observe the statute law, though until a statute shall have been construed and interpreted by competent adjudication, he is free and is entitled to advise as to its validity and as to what he conscientiously believes to be its just meaning and extent. But above all a lawyer will find his highest honor in a deserved reputation for fidelity to private trust and to public duty, as an honest man and as a patriotic and loyal citizen.

CANON 33

Partnerships—Names

Partnerships among lawyers for the practice of their profession are very common and are not to be condemned. In the formation of partnerships and the use of partnership names care should be taken not to violate any law, custom, or rule of court locally applicable. Where partnerships are formed between lawyers who are not all admitted to practice in the courts of the state, care should be taken to avoid any misleading name or representation which would create a false impression as to the professional position or privileges of the member not locally admitted. In the formation of partnerships for the practice of law, no person should be admitted or held out as a practitioner or member who is not a member of the legal profession duly authorized to practice, and amenable to professional discipline. In the selection and use of a firm name, no false, misleading, assumed or trade name should be used. The continued use of the name of a deceased or former partner, when permissible by local custom, is not unethical, but care should be taken that no imposition or deception is practiced through this use. When a member of the firm, on becoming a judge, is precluded from practicing law, his name should not be continued in the firm name.

Partnerships between lawyers and members of other professions or non-professional persons should not be formed or permitted where any part of the partnership's employment consists of the practice of law.

CANON 34

Division of Fees

No division of fees for legal services is proper, except with another lawyer, based upon a division of service or responsibility.

CANON 35

Intermediaries

The professional services of a lawyer should not be controlled or exploited by any lay agency, personal or corporate, which intervenes between client and lawyer. A lawyer's responsibilities and qualifications are individual. He should avoid all relations which direct the performance of his duties by or in the interest of such intermediary. A lawyer's relation to his client should be personal, and the responsibility should be direct to the client. Charitable societies rendering aid to the indigents are not deemed such intermediaries.

A lawyer may accept employment from any organization, such as an association, club or trade organization, to render legal services in any matter in which the organization, as an entity, is interested, but this employment should not include the rendering of legal services to the members of such an organization in respect to their individual affairs.

CANON 36

Retirement From Judicial Position or Public Employment

A lawyer should not accept employment as an advocate in any matter upon the merits of which he has previously acted in a judicial capacity.

A lawyer, having once held public office or having been in the public employ, should not after his retirement accept employment in connection with any matter which he has investigated or passed upon while in such office or employ.

CANON 37

Confidences of a Client

It is the duty of a lawyer to preserve his client's confidences. This duty outlasts the lawyer's employment, and extends as well to his employees; and neither of them should accept employment which involves or may involve the disclosure or use of these confidences, either for the private advantage of the lawyer or his employees or to the disadvantage of the client, without his knowledge and consent, and even though there are other available sources of such information. A lawyer should not continue employment when he discovers that this obligation prevents the performance of his full duty to his former or to his new client.

If a lawyer is accused by his client, he is not precluded from disclosing the truth in respect to the accusation. The announced intention of a client to commit a crime is not included within the confidences which he is bound to respect. He may properly make such disclosures as may be necessary to prevent the act or protect those against whom it is threatened.

CANON 38

Compensation, Commissions and Rebates

A lawyer should accept no compensation, commissions, rebates or other advantages from others without the knowledge and consent of his client after full disclosure.

CANON 39

Witnesses

A lawyer may properly interview any witness or prospective witness for the opposing side in any civil or criminal action without the consent of opposing counsel or party. In doing so, however, he should scrupulously avoid any suggestion calculated to induce the witness to suppress or deviate from the truth, or in any degree to affect his free and untrammeled conduct when appearing at the trial or on the witness stand.

CANON 40

Newspapers

A lawyer may with propriety write articles for publications in which he gives information upon the law; but he should not accept employment from such publications to advise inquirers in respect to their individual rights.

CANON 41

Discovery of Imposition and Deception

When a lawyer discovers that some fraud or deception has been practiced, which has unjustly imposed upon the court or a party, he should endeavor to rectify it; at first by advising his client, and if his client refuses to forego the advantage thus unjustly gained, he should promptly inform the injured person or his counsel, so that they may take appropriate steps.

CANON 42

Expenses of Litigation

A lawyer may not properly agree with a client that the lawyer shall pay or bear the expenses of litigation; he may in good faith advance expenses as a matter of convenience, but subject to reimbursement.

CANON 43

Approved Law Lists

It shall be improper for a lawyer to permit his name to be published in a law list the conduct, management or contents of which are calculated or likely to deceive or injure the public or the profession, or to lower the dignity or standing of the profession.

CANON 44

Withdrawal From Employment as Attorney or Counsel

The right of an attorney or counsel to withdraw from employment, once assumed, arises only from good cause. Even the desire or consent of the client is not always sufficient. The lawyer should not throw up the unfinished task to the detriment of his client except for reasons of honor or self-respect. If the client insists upon an unjust or immoral course in the conduct of his case, or if he persists over the attorney's remonstrance in presenting frivolous defenses, or if he deliberately disregards an agreement or obligation as to fees or expenses, the lawyer may be warranted in withdrawing on due notice to the client, allowing him time to employ another lawyer. So also when a lawyer discovers that his client has no case and the client is determined to continue it; or even if the lawyer finds himself incapable of conducting the case effectively. Sundry other instances may arise in which withdrawal is to be justified. Upon withdrawing from a case after a retainer has been paid, the attorney should refund such part of the retainer as has not been clearly earned.

CANON 45

Specialists

The canons of the American Bar Association apply to all branches of the legal profession; specialists in particular branches are not to be considered as exempt from the application of these principles.

CANON 46

Notice to Local Lawyers

A lawyer available to act as an associate of other lawyers in a particular branch of the law or legal service may send to local lawyers only and publish in his local legal journal, a brief and dignified announcement of his availability to serve other lawyers in connection therewith. The announcement should be in a form which does not constitute a statement or representation of special experience or expertise.

CANON 47

Aiding the Unauthorized Practice of Law

No lawyer shall permit his professional services, or his name, to be used in aid of, or to make possible, the unauthorized practice of law by any lay agency, personal or corporate.

SELECTED STANDARDS ON PROFESSIONALISM AND COURTESY

TABLE OF CONTENTS

ABA REPORT OF COMMISSION ON PROFESSIONALISM (1986)

(Selected Sections)

[The report has been approved for distribution by the House of Delegates of the American Bar Association. However, the views expressed are those of the Commission on Professionalism. They have not been approved by the House of Delegates or the Board of Governors and, accordingly, should not be construed as representing the policy of the Association. Ed.]

* * *

III. THE MEANING OF PROFESSIONALISM

"Professionalism" is an elastic concept the meaning and application of which are hard to pin down. That is perhaps as it should be. The term has a rich, long-standing heritage, and any single definition runs the risk of being too confining.

Yet the term is so important to lawyers that at least a working definition seems essential. Lawyers are proud of being part of one of the "historic" or "learned" professions, along with medicine and the clergy, which have been seen as professions through many centuries.

When he was asked to define a profession, Dean Roscoe Pound of Harvard Law School said:

> The term refers to a group . . . pursuing a learned art as a common calling in the spirit of public service—no less a public service because it may incidentally be a means of livelihood. Pursuit of the learned art in the spirit of a public service is the primary purpose.

The rhetoric may be dated, but the Commission believes the spirit of Dean Pound's definition stands the test of time. The practice of law "in the spirit of a public service" can and ought to be the hallmark of the legal profession.

More recently, others have identified some common elements which distinguish a profession from other occupations. Commission member Professor Eliot Freidson of New York University defines our profession as:

> An occupation whose members have special privileges, such as exclusive licensing, that are justified by the following assumptions:
>
> 1. That its practice requires substantial intellectual training and the use of complex judgments.
> 2. That since clients cannot adequately evaluate the quality of the service, they must trust those they consult.

3. That the client's trust presupposes that the practitioner's self-interest is overbalanced by devotion to serving both the client's interest and the public good, and

4. That the occupation is self-regulating—that is, organized in such a way as to assure the public and the courts that its members are competent, do not violate their client's trust, and transcend their own self-interest.

Again, the Commission suggests that this list of elements is useful in thinking through the issues which follow.

Some may argue on the basis of the cases previously discussed that the legal profession is no longer "special." They might say that lawyers should treat their ideals as archaic, construe the rules of professional conduct as narrowly as possible, and try only to maximize their incomes. The Commission disagrees. Moreover, the testimony we have heard and the surveys we have examined indicate that the public wants the legal profession to maintain its long-held professional ideals. Indeed, the public should expect no less.

We have earlier described the diversity of the Bar, both in terms of demographics and areas of practice. One can properly ask whether any common ideas of professionalism can suffice for such a varied institution. We believe they can. While one must always be conscious of the variety within the legal profession, more unites than separates us.

* * *

The suggestions and conclusions which follow are grouped by the role to be played by each segment of the Bar. In discussing the practicing Bar, we want it to be clear that we are including in that category all lawyers—whether litigators or non-litigators, whether sole practitioners, members or employees of firms, government lawyers or lawyers employed by corporations, educational institutions or other entities.

It is our hope that the recommendations which follow will not be unobserved aspirations, but will represent concrete ways in which lawyers can inspire a rebirth of respect and confidence in themselves, in the services they provide and in the legal system itself. We believe that much can be done. Taken individually, the proposals may not appear substantial, but in the aggregate we believe they can have a significant impact. However, to be effective, they must have the support not only of every part of the legal community, but also of the citizens of this country—the public whose interests lawyers are to serve.

We first present a summary of our recommendations, and then a discussion of each.

IV. SUMMARY OF RECOMMENDATIONS

A. LAW SCHOOLS

1. Law schools should give continuing attention to the form and content of their courses in ethics and professionalism. They should weave ethical and professional issues into courses in both substantive and procedural fields. They should give serious consideration to supplementing courses in ethics and professionalism with a required summer reading list for entering students and with a film or videotape on ethics, along the lines discussed later in this report.

2. Law schools should expose students to promising new methods of dealing with legal problems. Thus, for example, consideration should be given to instruction in such matters as alternative methods of dispute resolution and processes of negotiation.

3. Deans and faculties of law schools should keep in mind that the law school experience provides a student's first exposure to the profession, and that professors inevitably serve as important role models for students. Therefore, the highest standards of ethics and professionalism should be adhered to within law schools.

4. Law schools should adopt codes of student conduct, possibly based on the Model Rules of Professional Conduct. They should report convictions of serious infractions of law school rules to the Character and Fitness Committees, or their equivalent, of states in which the student applies for admission to the Bar.

5. Law schools should retain high admission standards in the face of declining applications and should not lower their standards for graduation.

B. PRACTICING BAR AND BAR ASSOCIATIONS

1. Law firms should help their newly-admitted associates to face the practical and ethical issues which inevitably arise in practice. This can be done in a variety of ways, and small firms or sole practitioners should work together to sponsor programs to facilitate such training. Local bar associations and law schools should assist in such efforts.

2. In order to assure greater competence of practicing lawyers, continuing legal education courses should be strengthened and made mandatory. Where practical, some form of examination in courses taken should be required.

3. The Commission recommends that the American Bar Association prepare a series of six to eight films or videotapes dealing with ethical and professional issues. The tapes should effectively present a wide range of such issues and should use the Socratic approach so effectively used in the Columbia University Media & Society Seminar programs. If feasible, at least one such tape should be designed especially for use in law schools. The tapes also should be made available to state and local bar associations for use in mandatory continuing legal education programs.

4. False, fraudulent or misleading advertising is not constitutionally protected and should be referred to disciplinary authorities for action against offending lawyers. Appropriate measures short of disciplinary action should be considered. Such measures could include requiring an advertisement to contain warnings or disclaimers.

5. The Bar should place increasing emphasis on the role of lawyers as officers of the court, or more broadly, as officers of the system of justice. Lawyers should exercise independent judgment as to how to pursue legal matters. They have a duty to make the system of justice work properly. Ideally, clients should recognize this duty and appreciate the importance to society of maintaining the system of justice.

6. The Bar should study the issue of the participation of law firms and individual lawyers in business activities, certainly where either actual or potential conflicts of interest may be involved.

7. When not representing clients before legislative bodies, lawyers should put aside self-interest and should support legislation that is in the public interest. In addition, the Bar should urge legislative bodies to consider the consequences of proposed legislation on the courts. All too frequently, such legislation, when enacted, inundates the courts with cases never contemplated by the drafters.

8. Fees are a source of misunderstanding between many lawyers and their clients. Further, the amount of fees charged by lawyers in some instances results in bitter criticism of the Bar. The Commission suggests:

a. Fee arrangements between lawyers and their clients should be in writing, where feasible.

b. If, at the end of a lawyer's services in any matter, the client believes that the fee charged was inappropriate, the client should be able to have the matter reviewed by an impartial fee review committee, possibly appointed by the state Supreme Court. All such committees or entities should include lay members.

9. Lawyers and judges should report to the appropriate disciplinary committee or prosecuting attorney any serious misconduct on the part of other lawyers and judges which they believe would support a complaint for discipline or criminal charges.

10. Bar associations should be constantly alert to seek improvements in the system of justice. This should embrace such activities as supporting an expanded use of alternative methods of dispute resolution.

C. JUDGES

1. Trial judges should take a more active role in the conduct of litigation. They should see that cases advance promptly, fairly and without abuse. Granting increased authority to judges runs the risk of arbitrary behavior on their part, but reviewing courts should provide whatever counterbalance is needed.

2. Judges should impose sanctions for abuse of the litigation process. Currently, the Federal Rules of Civil Procedure permit the imposition of sanctions for such abuses, and increasing use is being made of the sanctions to penalize the lawyer or the client, or both. In many state systems, the Supreme Courts have not promulgated such rules. State Supreme Courts should adopt rules similar to Rule 11 of the Federal Rules, so that authority to act is clearly given to trial judges.

3. Merit selection should be the means by which judges are chosen. The Commission believes that a bench of the quality that merit selection can provide is essential to improve our system of justice.

4. State disciplinary agencies under the control of state supreme courts are, in general, insufficiently funded and staffed. They now cannot do much more than deal with charges of theft, neglect or the commission of a felony. Adequate funding should be made available to the disciplinary agencies, enabling them to do a thorough and competent job in pursuing the full range of offenses which occur.

5. State supreme courts control admission to the Bar. They often charge character and fitness committees or their equivalent with the responsibility of reviewing the qualifications of applicants. Adequate funding and authority should be provided to such committees so that they can do a thorough job of investigation.

D. IN GENERAL

All segments of the Bar should:

1. Preserve and develop within the profession integrity, competence, fairness, independence, courage and a devotion to the public interest.
2. Resolve to abide by higher standards of conduct than the minimum required by the Code of Professional Responsibility and the Model Rules of Professional Conduct.
3. Increase the participation of lawyers in *pro bono* activities and help lawyers recognize their obligation to participate.
4. Resist the temptation to make the acquisition of wealth a primary goal of law practice.
5. Encourage innovative methods which simplify and make less expensive the rendering of legal services.
6. Educate the public about legal processes and the legal system.
7. Resolve to employ all the organizational resources necessary in order to assure that the legal profession is effectively self-regulating.

* * *

ABA LAWYER'S CREED OF PROFESSIONALISM (1988)

On August 9th, 1988, the American Bar Association House of Delegates adopted the following resolutions regarding so-called "Codes of Courtesy."

PROFESSIONALISM AND COURTESY

BE IT RESOLVED that the American Bar Association recommends to state and local bar associations that they encourage their members to accept as a guide for their individual conduct, and to comply with, a lawyer's creed of professionalism.

BE IT FURTHER RESOLVED that nothing contained in such a creed shall be deemed to supersede or in any way amend the Model Rules of Professional Conduct or other disciplinary codes, alter existing standards of conduct against which lawyer negligence might be judged or become a basis for the imposition of civil penalty of any kind.

Following is a proposed example of "A Lawyer's Creed of Professionalism."

Preamble

As a lawyer I must strive to make our system of justice work fairly and efficiently. In order to carry out that responsibility, not only will I comply with the letter and spirit of the disciplinary standards applicable to all lawyers, but I will also conduct myself in accordance with the following Creed of Professionalism when dealing with my client, opposing parties, their counsel, the courts and the general public.

A. With respect to my client:

1. I will be loyal and committed to my client's cause, but I will not permit that loyalty and commitment to interfere with my ability to provide my client with objective and independent advice;
2. I will endeavor to achieve my client's lawful objectives in business transactions and in litigation as expeditiously and economically as possible;
3. In appropriate cases, I will counsel my client with respect to mediation, arbitration and other alternative methods of resolving disputes;
4. I will advise my client against pursuing litigation (or any other course of action) that is without merit and against insisting on tactics which are intended to delay resolution of the matter or to harass or drain the financial resources of the opposing party;
5. I will advise my client that civility and courtesy are not to be equated with weakness;
6. While I must abide by my client's decision concerning the objectives of the representation, I nevertheless will counsel my client that a willingness to initiate or engage in settlement discussions is consistent with zealous and effective representation.

B. With respect to opposing parties and their counsel:

1. I will endeavor to be courteous and civil, both in oral and in written communications;
2. I will not knowingly make statements of fact or of law that are untrue;
3. In litigation proceedings I will agree to reasonable requests for extensions of time or for waiver of procedural formalities when the legitimate interests of my client will not be adversely affected;
4. I will endeavor to consult with opposing counsel before scheduling depositions and meetings and before re-scheduling hearings, and I will cooperate with opposing counsel when scheduling changes are requested;
5. I will refrain from utilizing litigation or any other course of conduct to harass the opposing party;
6. I will refrain from engaging in excessive and abusive discovery, and I will comply with all reasonable discovery requests;
7. I will refrain from utilizing delaying tactics;

8. In depositions and other proceedings, and in negotiations, I will conduct myself with dignity, avoid making groundless objections and refrain from engaging in acts of rudeness or disrespect;
9. I will not serve motions and pleadings on the other party, or his counsel, at such a time or in such a manner as will unfairly limit the other party's opportunity to respond;
10. In business transactions I will not quarrel over matters of form or style, but will concentrate on matters of substance and content;
11. I will clearly identify, for other counsel or parties, all changes that I have made in documents submitted to me for review.

C. With respect to the courts and other tribunals:

1. I will be a vigorous and zealous advocate on behalf of my client, while recognizing, as an officer of the court, that excessive zeal may be detrimental to my client's interests as well as to the proper functioning of our system of justice;
2. Where consistent with my client's interests, I will communicate with opposing counsel in an effort to avoid litigation and to resolve litigation that has actually commenced;
3. I will voluntarily withdraw claims or defenses when it becomes apparent that they do not have merit or are superfluous;
4. I will refrain from filing frivolous motions;
5. I will make every effort to agree with other counsel, as early as possible, on a voluntary exchange of information and on a plan for discovery;
6. I will attempt to resolve, by agreement, my objections to matters contained in my opponent's pleadings and discovery requests;
7. When scheduled hearings or depositions have to be cancelled, I will notify opposing counsel, and, if appropriate, the court (or other tribunal) as early as possible;
8. Before dates for hearings or trials are set—or, if that is not feasible, immediately after such dates have been set—I will attempt to verify the availability of key participants and witnesses so that I can promptly notify the court (or other tribunal) and opposing counsel of any likely problem in that regard;
9. In civil matters, I will stipulate to facts as to which there is no genuine dispute;
10. I will endeavor to be punctual in attending court hearings, conferences and depositions;
11. I will at all times be candid with the court.

D. With respect to the public and to our system of justice:

1. I will remember that, in addition to commitment to my client's cause, my responsibilities as a lawyer include a devotion to the public good;
2. I will endeavor to keep myself current in the areas in which I practice and, when necessary, will associate with, or refer my client to, counsel knowledgeable in another field of practice;
3. I will be mindful of the fact that, as a member of a self-regulating profession, it is incumbent on me to report violations by fellow lawyers of any disciplinary rule;
4. I will be mindful of the need to protect the image of the legal profession in the eyes of the public and will be so guided when considering methods and contents of advertising;
5. I will be mindful that the law is a learned profession and that among its desirable goals are devotion to public service, improvement of administration of justice, and the contribution of uncompensated time and civic influence on behalf of those persons who cannot afford adequate legal assistance.

ABA LAWYER'S PLEDGE OF PROFESSIONALISM (1988)

I will remember that the practice of law is first and foremost a profession, and I will subordinate business concerns to professionalism concerns.

I will encourage respect for the law and our legal system through my words and actions.

I will remember my responsibilities to serve as an officer of the court and protector of individual rights.

I will contribute time and resources to public service, public education, charitable, and *pro bono* activities in my community.

I will work with the other participants in the legal system, including judges, opposing counsel and those whose practices are different from mine, to make our legal system more accessible and responsive.

I will resolve matters expeditiously and without unnecessary expense.

I will resolve disputes through negotiation whenever possible.

I will keep my clients well-informed and involved in making the decisions that affect them.

I will continue to expand my knowledge of the law.

I will achieve and maintain proficiency in my practice.

I will be courteous to those with whom I come into contact during the course of my work.

I will honor the spirit and intent, as well as the requirements, of the applicable rules or code of professional conduct for my jurisdiction, and will encourage others to do the same.

THE TEXAS LAWYER'S CREED—A MANDATE FOR PROFESSIONALISM (1989)

Promulgated by the Supreme Court of Texas and the Texas Court of Criminal Appeals (1989)

I am a lawyer; I am entrusted by the People of Texas to preserve and improve our legal system. I am licensed by the Supreme Court of Texas. I must therefore abide by the Texas Disciplinary Rules of Professional Conduct, but I know that Professionalism requires more than merely avoiding the violation of laws and rules. I am committed to this Creed for no other reason than it is right.

I. OUR LEGAL SYSTEM

A lawyer owes to the administration of justice personal dignity, integrity, and independence. A lawyer should always adhere to the highest principles of professionalism.

1. I am passionately proud of my profession. Therefore, "My word is my bond."

2. I am responsible to assure that all persons have access to competent representation regardless of wealth or position in life.

3. I commit myself to an adequate and effective pro bono program.

4. I am obligated to educate my clients, the public, and other lawyers regarding the spirit and letter of this Creed.

5. I will always be conscious of my duty to the judicial system.

SELECTED STANDARDS

II. LAWYER TO CLIENT

A lawyer owes to a client allegiance, learning, skill, and industry. A lawyer shall employ all appropriate means to protect and advance the client's legitimate rights, claims, and objectives. A lawyer shall not be deterred by any real or imagined fear of judicial disfavor or public unpopularity, nor be influenced by mere self-interest.

1. I will advise my client of the contents of this Creed when undertaking representation.

2. I will endeavor to achieve my client's lawful objectives in legal transactions and in litigation as quickly and economically as possible.

3. I will be loyal and committed to my client's lawful objectives, but I will not permit that loyalty and commitment to interfere with my duty to provide objective and independent advice.

4. I will advise my client that civility and courtesy are expected and are not a sign of weakness.

5. I will advise my client of proper and expected behavior.

6. I will treat adverse parties and witnesses with fairness and due consideration. A client has no right to demand that I abuse anyone or indulge in any offensive conduct.

7. I will advise my client that we will not pursue conduct which is intended primarily to harass or drain the financial resources of the opposing party.

8. I will advise my client that we will not pursue tactics which are intended primarily for delay.

9. I will advise my client that we will not pursue any course of action which is without merit.

10. I will advise my client that I reserve the right to determine whether to grant accommodations to opposing counsel in all matters that do not adversely affect my client's lawful objectives. A client has no right to instruct me to refuse reasonable requests made by other counsel.

11. I will advise my client regarding the availability of mediation, arbitration, and other alternative methods of resolving and settling disputes.

III. LAWYER TO LAWYER

A lawyer owes to opposing counsel, in the conduct of legal transactions and the pursuit of litigation, courtesy, candor, cooperation, and scrupulous observance of all agreements and mutual understandings. Ill feelings between clients shall not influence a lawyer's conduct, attitude, or demeanor toward opposing counsel. A lawyer shall not engage in unprofessional conduct in retaliation against other unprofessional conduct.

1. I will be courteous, civil, and prompt in oral and written communications.

2. I will not quarrel over matters of form or style, but I will concentrate on matters of substance.

3. I will identify for other counsel or parties all changes I have made in documents submitted for review.

4. I will attempt to prepare documents which correctly reflect the agreement of the parties. I will not include provisions which have not been agreed upon or omit provisions which are necessary to reflect the agreement of the parties.

5. I will notify opposing counsel, and, if appropriate, the Court or other persons, as soon as practicable, when hearings, depositions, meetings, conferences or closings are cancelled.

6. I will agree to reasonable requests for extensions of time and for waiver of procedural formalities, provided legitimate objectives of my client will not be adversely affected.

7. I will not serve motions or pleadings in any manner that unfairly limits another party's opportunity to respond.

8. I will attempt to resolve by agreement my objections to matters contained in pleadings and discovery requests and responses.

9. I can disagree without being disagreeable. I recognize that effective representation does not require antagonistic or obnoxious behavior. I will neither encourage nor knowingly permit my client or anyone under my control to do anything which would be unethical or improper if done by me.

10. I will not, without good cause, attribute bad motives or unethical conduct to opposing counsel nor bring the profession into disrepute by unfounded accusations of impropriety. I will avoid disparaging personal remarks or acrimony towards opposing counsel, parties and witnesses. I will not be influenced by any ill feeling between clients. I will abstain from any allusion to personal peculiarities or idiosyncrasies of opposing counsel.

11. I will not take advantage, by causing any default or dismissal to be rendered, when I know the identity of an opposing counsel, without first inquiring about that counsel's intention to proceed.

12. I will promptly submit orders to the Court. I will deliver copies to opposing counsel before or contemporaneously with submission to the Court. I will promptly approve the form of orders which accurately reflect the substance of the rulings of the Court.

13. I will not attempt to gain an unfair advantage by sending the Court or its staff correspondence or copies of correspondence.

14. I will not arbitrarily schedule a deposition, Court appearance, or hearing until a good faith effort has been made to schedule it by agreement.

15. I will readily stipulate to undisputed facts in order to avoid needless costs or inconvenience for any party.

16. I will refrain from excessive and abusive discovery.

17. I will comply with all reasonable discovery requests. I will not resist discovery requests which are not objectionable. I will not make objections nor give instructions to a witness for the purpose of delaying or obstructing the discovery process. I will encourage witnesses to respond to all deposition questions which are reasonably understandable. I will neither encourage nor permit my witness to quibble about words where their meaning is reasonably clear.

18. I will not seek Court intervention to obtain discovery which is clearly improper and not discoverable.

19. I will not seek sanctions or disqualification unless it is necessary for protection of my client's lawful objectives or is fully justified by the circumstances.

IV. LAWYER AND JUDGE

Lawyers and judges owe each other respect, diligence, candor, punctuality, and protection against unjust and improper criticism and attack. Lawyers and judges are equally responsible to protect the dignity and independence of the Court and the profession.

1. I will always recognize that the position of judge is the symbol of both the judicial system and administration of justice. I will refrain from conduct that degrades this symbol.

2. I will conduct myself in Court in a professional manner and demonstrate my respect for the Court and the law.

3. I will treat counsel, opposing parties, the Court, and members of the Court staff with courtesy and civility.

4. I will be punctual.

5. I will not engage in any conduct which offends the dignity and decorum of proceedings.

6. I will not knowingly misrepresent, mischaracterize, misquote or miscite facts or authorities to gain an advantage.

7. I will respect the rulings of the Court.

8. I will give the issues in controversy deliberate, impartial and studied analysis and consideration.

9. I will be considerate of the time constraints and pressures imposed upon the Court, Court staff and counsel in efforts to administer justice and resolve disputes.

PART TWO

CODES OF JUDICIAL CONDUCT

TABLE OF CONTENTS

Introduction

As in the case of regulating lawyers' conduct, the ABA has sought to provide standards for regulating judicial conduct. In 1924, the ABA adopted the Canons of Judicial Ethics. During the 1960s, the federal Judicial Conference of the United States developed standards for federal judges. Soon after the ABA adopted the Model Code of Professional Responsibility, the ABA appointed a commission to produce a revised code of conduct for judges. The resulting document is the 1972 Code of Judicial Conduct. In 1990, the ABA replaced the 1972 Code with a new Code of Judicial Conduct. The unabridged edition of this supplement contains the 1990 Code of Judicial Conduct in part eight.

At the February 2007 ABA meeting, the House of Delegates approved a complete revision to the Code of Judicial Conduct. The new code is patterned after the rules and comment approach of the Model Rules. The ABA amended the Code of Judicial Conduct in 2009 and 2010.

In March 2008, the Judicial Conference of the United States approved the Rules for Judicial-Conduct and Judicial-Disability Proceedings. These rules represent the first binding standards for the discipline of Federal Judges on grounds of misconduct disability. The Judicial Conference amended these rules in 2015 and again in 2019.

AMERICAN BAR ASSOCIATION MODEL CODE OF JUDICIAL CONDUCT (2019)

Adopted by the House of Delegates at the February 2007 meeting of the ABA. Amended for housekeeping revisions in 2009. Also amended in August 2010.

TABLE OF CONTENTS

2019 MODEL CODE

CANON 3

A JUDGE SHALL CONDUCT THE JUDGE'S PERSONAL AND EXTRAJUDICIAL ACTIVITIES TO MINIMIZE THE RISK OF CONFLICT WITH THE OBLIGATIONS OF JUDICIAL OFFICE.

RULE 3.1. Extrajudicial Activities in General
RULE 3.2. Appearances Before Governmental Bodies and Consultation With Government Officials
RULE 3.3. Testifying as a Character Witness
RULE 3.4. Appointments to Governmental Positions
RULE 3.5. Use of Nonpublic Information
RULE 3.6. Affiliation With Discriminatory Organizations
RULE 3.7. Participation in Educational, Religious, Charitable, Fraternal, or Civic Organizations and Activities
RULE 3.8. Appointments to Fiduciary Positions
RULE 3.9. Service as Arbitrator or Mediator
RULE 3.10. Practice of Law
RULE 3.11. Financial, Business, or Remunerative Activities
RULE 3.12. Compensation for Extrajudicial Activities
RULE 3.13. Acceptance and Reporting of Gifts, Loans, Bequests, Benefits, or Other Things of Value
RULE 3.14. Reimbursement of Expenses and Waivers of Fees or Charges
RULE 3.15. Reporting Requirements

CANON 4

A JUDGE OR CANDIDATE FOR JUDICIAL OFFICE SHALL NOT ENGAGE IN POLITICAL OR CAMPAIGN ACTIVITY THAT IS INCONSISTENT WITH THE INDEPENDENCE, INTEGRITY, OR IMPARTIALITY OF THE JUDICIARY

RULE 4.1. Political and Campaign Activities of Judges and Judicial Candidates in General
RULE 4.2. Political and Campaign Activities of Judicial Candidates in Public Elections
RULE 4.3. Activities of Candidates for Appointive Judicial Office
RULE 4.4. Campaign Committees
RULE 4.5. Activities of Judges Who Become Candidates for Nonjudicial Office

ABA MODEL CODE OF JUDICIAL CONDUCT (2019)

PREAMBLE

[1] An independent, fair and impartial judiciary is indispensable to our system of justice. The United States legal system is based upon the principle that an independent, impartial, and competent judiciary, composed of men and women of integrity, will interpret and apply the law that governs our society. Thus, the judiciary plays a central role in preserving the principles of justice and the rule of law. Inherent in all the Rules contained in this Code are the precepts that judges, individually and collectively, must respect and honor the judicial office as a public trust and strive to maintain and enhance confidence in the legal system.

[2] Judges should maintain the dignity of judicial office at all times, and avoid both impropriety and the appearance of impropriety in their professional and personal lives. They should aspire at all times to conduct that ensures the greatest possible public confidence in their independence, impartiality, integrity, and competence.

[3] The Model Code of Judicial Conduct establishes standards for the ethical conduct of judges and judicial candidates. It is not intended as an exhaustive guide for the conduct of judges and judicial candidates, who are governed in their judicial and personal conduct by general ethical standards as well as by the Code. The Code is intended, however, to provide guidance and assist judges in maintaining the highest standards of judicial and personal conduct, and to provide a basis for regulating their conduct through disciplinary agencies.

PREAMBLE—REPORTER'S EXPLANATION OF CHANGES†

EXPLANATION OF BLACK LETTER

1. The 1990 Preamble has been essentially dissected, with the objective of describing the general purpose and rationale of the Code in the Preamble, and moving to a new "Scope" section the specific explanation of how the Rules are intended to operate. This approach parallels that taken in the ABA Model Rules of Professional Conduct, whose general format the proposed Rules and Comments also follow.

2. The 1990 Code Preamble language discussing the "degree of discipline to be imposed" in the course of enforcing the Code's provisions has been deleted completely.

3. New language has been added to emphasize that, at all times, judges should avoid both impropriety and the appearance of impropriety in their professional and personal lives and that they should aspire to conduct that ensures the greatest possible public confidence in their independence, integrity, impartiality, and competence.

4. Other changes in language are solely stylistic.

SCOPE

[1] The Model Code of Judicial Conduct consists of four Canons, numbered Rules under each Canon, and Comments that generally follow and explain each Rule. Scope and Terminology sections provide

† The "Reporters' Explanations of Changes" have not been approved by the ABA Joint Commission to Evaluate the Model Code of Judicial Conduct. They have been drafted by the Commission's Reporters, based on the proceedings and record of the Commission, solely to inform the ABA House of Delegates about each of the proposed amendments to the Model Code prior to their being considered at the ABA 2007 Midyear Meeting. THEY ARE NOT TO BE ADOPTED AS PART OF THE MODEL CODE.

additional guidance in interpreting and applying the Code. An Application section establishes when the various Rules apply to a judge or judicial candidate.

[2] The Canons state overarching principles of judicial ethics that all judges must observe. Although a judge may be disciplined only for violating a Rule, the Canons provide important guidance in interpreting the Rules. Where a Rule contains a permissive term, such as "may" or "should," the conduct being addressed is committed to the personal and professional discretion of the judge or candidate in question, and no disciplinary action should be taken for action or inaction within the bounds of such discretion.

[3] The Comments that accompany the Rules serve two functions. First, they provide guidance regarding the purpose, meaning, and proper application of the Rules. They contain explanatory material and, in some instances, provide examples of permitted or prohibited conduct. Comments neither add to nor subtract from the binding obligations set forth in the Rules. Therefore, when a Comment contains the term "must," it does not mean that the Comment itself is binding or enforceable; it signifies that the Rule in question, properly understood, is obligatory as to the conduct at issue.

[4] Second, the Comments identify aspirational goals for judges. To implement fully the principles of this Code as articulated in the Canons, judges should strive to exceed the standards of conduct established by the Rules, holding themselves to the highest ethical standards and seeking to achieve those aspirational goals, thereby enhancing the dignity of the judicial office.

[5] The Rules of the Model Code of Judicial Conduct are rules of reason that should be applied consistent with constitutional requirements, statutes, other court rules, and decisional law, and with due regard for all relevant circumstances. The Rules should not be interpreted to impinge upon the essential independence of judges in making judicial decisions.

[6] Although the black letter of the Rules is binding and enforceable, it is not contemplated that every transgression will result in the imposition of discipline. Whether discipline should be imposed should be determined through a reasonable and reasoned application of the Rules, and should depend upon factors such as the seriousness of the transgression, the facts and circumstances that existed at the time of the transgression, the extent of any pattern of improper activity, whether there have been previous violations, and the effect of the improper activity upon the judicial system or others.

[7] The Code is not designed or intended as a basis for civil or criminal liability. Neither is it intended to be the basis for litigants to seek collateral remedies against each other or to obtain tactical advantages in proceedings before a court.

SCOPE—REPORTER'S EXPLANATION OF CHANGES†

EXPLANATION OF BLACK LETTER

This new Scope section contains the concepts in the 1990 Preamble that explain how the various parts of the Rules are intended to operate. The Scope section indicates that judges may be disciplined only for violating a Rule. With regard to the Canons, or Rule headings, the Scope section explains that the Canons are overarching principles that provide important guidance in interpreting the rules.

TERMINOLOGY

The first time any term listed below is used in a Rule in its defined sense, it is followed by an asterisk (*).

† The "Reporters' Explanations of Changes" have not been approved by the ABA Joint Commission to Evaluate the Model Code of Judicial Conduct. They have been drafted by the Commission's Reporters, based on the proceedings and record of the Commission, solely to inform the ABA House of Delegates about each of the proposed amendments to the Model Code prior to their being considered at the ABA 2007 Midyear Meeting. THEY ARE NOT TO BE ADOPTED AS PART OF THE MODEL CODE.

"Aggregate," in relation to contributions for a candidate, means not only contributions in cash or in kind made directly to a candidate's campaign committee, but also all contributions made indirectly with the understanding that they will be used to support the election of a candidate or to oppose the election of the candidate's opponent. See Rules 2.11 and 4.4.

"Appropriate authority" means the authority having responsibility for initiation of disciplinary process in connection with the violation to be reported. See Rules 2.14 and 2.15.

"Contribution" means both financial and in-kind contributions, such as goods, professional or volunteer services, advertising, and other types of assistance, which, if obtained by the recipient otherwise, would require a financial expenditure. See Rules 2.11, 2.13, 3.7, 4.1, and 4.4.

"De minimis," in the context of interests pertaining to disqualification of a judge, means an insignificant interest that could not raise a reasonable question regarding the judge's impartiality. See Rule 2.11.

"Domestic partner" means a person with whom another person maintains a household and an intimate relationship, other than a person to whom he or she is legally married. See Rules 2.11, 2.13, 3.13, and 3.14.

"Economic interest" means ownership of more than a de minimis legal or equitable interest. Except for situations in which the judge participates in the management of such a legal or equitable interest, or the interest could be substantially affected by the outcome of a proceeding before a judge, it does not include:

(1) an interest in the individual holdings within a mutual or common investment fund;

(2) an interest in securities held by an educational, religious, charitable, fraternal, or civic organization in which the judge or the judge's spouse, domestic partner, parent, or child serves as a director, an officer, an advisor, or other participant;

(3) a deposit in a financial institution or deposits or proprietary interests the judge may maintain as a member of a mutual savings association or credit union, or similar proprietary interests; or

(4) an interest in the issuer of government securities held by the judge.

See Rules 1.3 and 2.11.

"Fiduciary" includes relationships such as executor, administrator, trustee, or guardian. See Rules 2.11, 3.2, and 3.8.

"Impartial," "impartiality," and **"impartially"** mean absence of bias or prejudice in favor of, or against, particular parties or classes of parties, as well as maintenance of an open mind in considering issues that may come before a judge. See Canons 1, 2, and 4, and Rules 1.2, 2.2, 2.10, 2.11, 2.13, 3.1, 3.12, 3.13, 4.1, and 4.2.

"Impending matter" is a matter that is imminent or expected to occur in the near future. See Rules 2.9, 2.10, 3.13, and 4.1.

"Impropriety" includes conduct that violates the law, court rules, or provisions of this Code, and conduct that undermines a judge's independence, integrity, or impartiality. See Canon 1 and Rule 1.2.

"Independence" means a judge's freedom from influence or controls other than those established by law. See Canons 1 and 4, and Rules 1.2, 3.1, 3.12, 3.13, and 4.2.

"Integrity" means probity, fairness, honesty, uprightness, and soundness of character. See Canon 1 and Rule 1.2.

"Judicial candidate" means any person, including a sitting judge, who is seeking selection for or retention in judicial office by election or appointment. A person becomes a candidate for judicial office as soon as he or she makes a public announcement of candidacy, declares or files as a candidate with the election or appointment authority, authorizes or, where permitted, engages in solicitation or acceptance of contributions or support, or is nominated for election or appointment to office. See Rules 2.11, 4.1, 4.2, and 4.4.

"Knowingly," "knowledge," "known," and **"knows"** mean actual knowledge of the fact in question. A person's knowledge may be inferred from circumstances. See Rules 2.11, 2.13, 2.15, 2.16, 3.6, and 4.1.

"Law" encompasses court rules as well as statutes, constitutional provisions, and decisional law. See Rules 1.1, 2.1, 2.2, 2.6, 2.7, 2.9, 3.1, 3.4, 3.9, 3.12, 3.13, 3.14, 3.15, 4.1, 4.2, 4.4, and 4.5.

"Member of the candidate's family" means a spouse, domestic partner, child, grandchild, parent, grandparent, or other relative or person with whom the candidate maintains a close familial relationship.

"Member of the judge's family" means a spouse, domestic partner, child, grandchild, parent, grandparent, or other relative or person with whom the judge maintains a close familial relationship. See Rules 3.7, 3.8, 3.10, and 3.11.

"Member of a judge's family residing in the judge's household" means any relative of a judge by blood or marriage, or a person treated by a judge as a member of the judge's family, who resides in the judge's household. See Rules 2.11 and 3.13.

"Nonpublic information" means information that is not available to the public. Nonpublic information may include, but is not limited to, information that is sealed by statute or court order or impounded or communicated in camera, and information offered in grand jury proceedings, presentencing reports, dependency cases, or psychiatric reports. See Rule 3.5.

"Pending matter" is a matter that has commenced. A matter continues to be pending through any appellate process until final disposition. See Rules 2.9, 2.10, 3.13, and 4.1.

"Personally solicit" means a direct request made by a judge or a judicial candidate for financial support or in-kind services, whether made by letter, telephone, or any other means of communication. See Rule 4.1.

"Political organization" means a political party or other group sponsored by or affiliated with a political party or candidate, the principal purpose of which is to further the election or appointment of candidates for political office. For purposes of this Code, the term does not include a judicial candidate's campaign committee created as authorized by Rule 4.4. See Rules 4.1 and 4.2.

"Public election" includes primary and general elections, partisan elections, nonpartisan elections, and retention elections. See Rules 4.2 and 4.4.

"Third degree of relationship" includes the following persons: great-grandparent, grandparent, parent, uncle, aunt, brother, sister, child, grandchild, great-grandchild, nephew, and niece. See Rule 2.11.

TERMINOLOGY—REPORTER'S EXPLANATION OF CHANGES†

EXPLANATION OF BLACK LETTER

1. The Commission proposes to change the use of asterisks to indicate defined terms, employing them in a Rule only where the defined term is used for the first time. Several commentators observed that the use of asterisks each time a frequently-appearing defined term occurred was more interruptive than useful to the reader.

2. Apart from the addition of "domestic partner" to the definitions of "Member of the candidate's family" and "Member of the judge's family," the following terms are defined in a manner essentially identical to the way they are defined in the 1990 Code (any differences are intended to be purely stylistic):

Aggregate

Appropriate authority

Economic interest

Fiduciary

† The "Reporters' Explanations of Changes" have not been approved by the ABA Joint Commission to Evaluate the Model Code of Judicial Conduct. They have been drafted by the Commission's Reporters, based on the proceedings and record of the Commission, solely to inform the ABA House of Delegates about each of the proposed amendments to the Model Code prior to their being considered at the ABA 2007 Midyear Meeting. THEY ARE NOT TO BE ADOPTED AS PART OF THE MODEL CODE.

Knowingly, knowledge, known, or knows

Law

Member of the candidate's family

Member of the judge's family

Member of the judge's family residing in the judge's household

Nonpublic information

Public election

Third degree of relationship

3. The following terms are no longer contained in the Terminology Section:

"Continuing part-time judge," on the theory that the provision applicable to continuing part-time judges in the Application Section provides a definition already.

"Court personnel," which in the 1990 Code was not, in fact, a definition, but a statement that the term did not include lawyers in a proceeding before the judge. The Commission believed this was too evident to need statement, and otherwise believed that the term "court personnel" is clear enough that it does not need definition. The term "court personnel" has been replaced with "court staff, court officials, and others subject to the judge's direction and control."

"Periodic part-time judge" (on the same theory as applied to "continuing part-time judge"; see above)

"Pro tempore part-time judge" (same reason as above)

"Require," which the Commission believed is easily understood.

The following definitions have been modified:

"De minimis" is defined specifically in the context of "interests pertaining to the disqualification of a judge," because it is only in Rule 2.11 ("Disqualification") that the Commission believes a precise definition of the term need be applied.

"Judicial candidate" is similar to the 1990 Code's term "candidate." The phrase "including a sitting judge" has been added for clarification. The language stating that the term "candidate" applies to a judge who is seeking a non-judicial office has been deleted, consistent with the reformulation of the term being defined.

"Political organization" has been expanded to include the qualifying language "sponsored by or affiliated with a political party or candidate," the principal purpose of which is to further the election or appointment of candidates for political office. In addition, language has been added to clarify that the term is not meant to include a judicial candidate's own campaign committee.

4. The following new defined terms have been added:

"Domestic partner," on the theory that now commonplace "non-traditional" relationships that exist outside marriage are deserving of treatment equal to that afforded marital relationships in evaluating their potential conflict-of-interest implications under the Rules.

"Impartiality," because it is a fundamental goal of the judicial system, and additionally because it has become a defined term in recent decisional law with respect to political activity of judges.

"Impending matter," in order to set temporal limits on the phrase.

"Impropriety," because of its fundamental importance as a concept underlying the importance of appearances created by judges.

"Independence," as a fundamental concept underlying the justice system.

"Integrity," for the same reason as above.

"Pending matter," so as to set temporal limits on the phrase and create greater certainty in the application of the Code's restrictions on judicial speech.

Application

The Application section establishes when the various Rules apply to a judge or judicial candidate.

I. APPLICABILITY OF THIS CODE

(A) The provisions of the Code apply to all full-time judges. Parts II through V of this section identify provisions that apply to four categories of part-time judges only while they are serving as judges, and provisions that do not apply to part-time judges at any time. All other Rules are therefore applicable to part-time judges at all times. The four categories of judicial service in other than a full-time capacity are necessarily defined in general terms because of the widely varying forms of judicial service. Canon 4 applies to judicial candidates.

(B) A judge, within the meaning of this Code, is anyone who is authorized to perform judicial functions, including an officer such as a justice of the peace, magistrate, court commissioner, special master, referee, or member of the administrative law judiciary.[1]

Comment

[1] The Rules in this Code have been formulated to address the ethical obligations of any person who serves a judicial function, and are premised upon the supposition that a uniform system of ethical principles should apply to all those authorized to perform judicial functions.

[2] The determination of which category and, accordingly, which specific Rules apply to an individual judicial officer, depends upon the facts of the particular judicial service.

[3] In recent years many jurisdictions have created what are often called "problem solving" courts, in which judges are authorized by court rules to act in nontraditional ways. For example, judges presiding in drug courts and monitoring the progress of participants in those courts' programs may be authorized and even encouraged to communicate directly with social workers, probation officers, and others outside the context of their usual judicial role as independent decision makers on issues of fact and law. When local rules specifically authorize conduct not otherwise permitted under these Rules, they take precedence over the provisions set forth in the Code. Nevertheless, judges serving on "problem solving" courts shall comply with this Code except to the extent local rules provide and permit otherwise.

APPLICATION—REPORTER'S EXPLANATION OF CHANGES[†]

EXPLANATION OF BLACK LETTER

1. The Commission is proposing a more user-friendly Application section as an alternative to the current version, which is complex and difficult with which to work. The most significant substantive change brings within the definition of "judges" justices of the peace, hearing officers, and "members of the administrative law judiciary."

---

[1] Each jurisdiction should consider the characteristics of particular positions within the administrative law judiciary in adopting, adapting, applying, and enforcing the Code for the administrative law judiciary. *See, e.g.,* Model Code of Judicial Conduct for Federal Administrative Law Judges (1989) and Model Code of Judicial Conduct for State Administrative Law Judges (1995). Both Model Codes are endorsed by the ABA National Conference of Administrative Law Judiciary.

[†] The "Reporters' Explanations of Changes" have not been approved by the ABA Joint Commission to Evaluate the Model Code of Judicial Conduct. They have been drafted by the Commission's Reporters, based on the proceedings and record of the Commission, solely to inform the ABA House of Delegates about each of the proposed amendments to the Model Code prior to their being considered at the ABA 2007 Midyear Meeting. THEY ARE NOT TO BE ADOPTED AS PART OF THE MODEL CODE.

2. The title of Part I, "Applicability of This Code," is clearer and simpler than the title in the 1990 Code. No change in substance is intended.

3. Part I (A) has been revised to make clear which provisions of the Code apply to certain categories of judges or judicial candidates. This is a stylistic change and does not change the substance of the provision. The Commission placed in Part I (A) the sentence, "the four categories of judicial service in other than full-time capacity are necessarily defined in general terms because of the widely varying forms of judicial service," which had been included in Commentary to Section A of the Application Section in the 1990 Code.

4. In Part I (B) of the revised Application, "justice of the peace" and "member of the administrative judiciary" are included as judges "within the meaning of this Code." The application of the Rules to the administrative law judiciary is consistent with policy adopted by the ABA House of Delegates in Report 101B (2001), which provided that members of the administrative law judiciary should be accountable under appropriate ethical standards adapted from the Code in light of the unique characteristics of particular positions in the administrative law judiciary. The rationale for applying the Rules to justices of the peace and members of the administrative law judiciary derives from the fact that they perform essentially the same function as a trial judge hearing a case without a jury.

5. To facilitate easier recognition of the subject matter of the many Rules cited throughout the Application section, parentheticals have been added with the names of each rule cited, eliminating the need to search through the entire Code. This approach is consistent with the format used when citing Rules throughout the rest of the Code.

6. A footnote reference has been revised to state that each jurisdiction "should consider the characteristics of particular members of the administrative law judiciary positions in adopting, adapting, applying and enforcing the Rules for the administrative law judiciary. See, e.g., Model Code of Judicial Conduct for Federal Administrative Law Judges (1989) (endorsed by the National Conference of Administrative Law Judges in February 1989)." The Commission deleted the language that alluded to the executive branch of government in order to avoid difficulties associated with separation of powers issues.

7. The phrase "for service" was added to Part II to explain more fully the meaning of a judge's being "subject to recall." No substantive change is intended.

8. In Parts III, IV and V, the definitions of the various types of part-time judges have been introduced into the text, and deleted from the "Terminology" section of the Code, consistent with the Commission's decision to place terminology within the body of a Rule when that is the only time that it appears.

9. Sections I(D)(2) and I(E)(2) of the 1990 Code were deleted in acknowledgement that this code is not meant to reach the conduct of lawyers, but that of judges. The situations described in both provisions arise under and are to be decided according to the Model Rules of Professional Conduct for lawyers.

10. Part VI, "Time for Compliance," has not changed in substance. Taken directly from Section F of the 1990 Code's Application section, it acknowledges the need to allow new judges to continue to serve as fiduciaries or in a business relationship for a period of up to one year in order to avoid hardship or serious adverse consequences to the beneficiaries of the fiduciary relationship.

EXPLANATION OF COMMENTS

PART I

[1] A new introductory Comment has been added to highlight the fact that it is desirable to have a uniform system of ethical principles that applies to all individuals serving a judicial function.

[2] This Comment clarifies that the category associated with a judicial officer depends on the judicial service.

[3] This new Comment confirms the propriety of using nontraditional methods in "problem solving" courts, such as drug and domestic violence courts, where they are permitted by law, including court rules.

II. Retired Judge Subject to Recall

A retired judge subject to recall for service, who by law is not permitted to practice law, is not required to comply:

(A) with Rule 3.9 (Service as Arbitrator or Mediator), except while serving as a judge

(B) at any time with Rule 3.8(A) (Appointments to Fiduciary Positions).

Comment

[1] For the purposes of this section, as long as a retired judge is subject to being recalled for service, the judge is considered to "perform judicial functions."

III. Continuing Part-Time Judge

A judge who serves repeatedly on a part-time basis by election or under a continuing appointment, including a retired judge subject to recall who is permitted to practice law ("continuing part-time judge"),

(A) is not required to comply:

(1) with Rule 4.1 (Political and Campaign Activities of Judges and Judicial Candidates in General) (A)(1) through (7), except while serving as a judge; or

(2) at any time with Rules 3.4 (Appointments to Governmental Positions), 3.8(A) (Appointments to Fiduciary Positions), 3.9 (Service as Arbitrator or Mediator), 3.10 (Practice of Law), and 3.11(B) (Financial, Business, or Remunerative Activities); and*

(B) shall not practice law in the court on which the judge serves or in any court subject to the appellate jurisdiction of the court on which the judge serves, and shall not act as a lawyer in a proceeding in which the judge has served as a judge or in any other proceeding related thereto.

Comment

[1] When a person who has been a continuing part-time judge is no longer a continuing part-time judge, including a retired judge no longer subject to recall, that person may act as a lawyer in a proceeding in which he or she has served as a judge or in any other proceeding related thereto only with the informed consent of all parties, and pursuant to any applicable Model Rules of Professional Conduct. An adopting jurisdiction should substitute a reference to its applicable rule.

IV. Periodic Part-Time Judge

A periodic part-time judge who serves or expects to serve repeatedly on a part-time basis, but under a separate appointment for each limited period of service or for each matter,

(A) is not required to comply:

(1) with Rule 4.1 (Political and Campaign Activities of Judges and Judicial Candidates in General) (A)(1) through (7), except while serving as a judge; or

(2) at any time with Rules 3.4 (Appointments to Governmental Positions), 3.8(A) (Appointments to Fiduciary Positions), 3.9 (Service as Arbitrator or Mediator), 3.10 (Practice of Law), and 3.11(B) (Financial, Business, or Remunerative Activities); and**

---

* Ed. Note: In August 2010, the ABA House of Delegated Amended III(A) to clarify the rules applicable to continuing part-time judges.

** Ed. Note: In August 2010, the ABA House of Delegates amended IV(A) to clarify the application of the rules to periodic part-time judges.

(B) shall not practice law in the court on which the judge serves or in any court subject to the appellate jurisdiction of the court on which the judge serves, and shall not act as a lawyer in a proceeding in which the judge has served as a judge or in any other proceeding related thereto.

V. PRO TEMPORE PART-TIME JUDGE

A pro tempore part-time judge who serves or expects to serve once or only sporadically on a part-time basis under a separate appointment for each period of service or for each case heard is not required to comply:

(A) except while serving as a judge, with Rules 2.4 (External Influences on Judicial Conduct), 3.2 (Appearances before Governmental Bodies and Consultation with Government Officials), and 4.1 (Political and Campaign Activities of Judges and Judicial Candidates in General) (A)(1) through (7); or

(B) at any time with Rules 3.4 (Appointments to Governmental Positions), 3.8(A) (Appointments to Fiduciary Positions), 3.9 (Service as Arbitrator or Mediator), 3.10 (Practice of Law), and 3.11(B) (Financial, Business, or Remunerative Activities).*

VI. TIME FOR COMPLIANCE

A person to whom this Code becomes applicable shall comply immediately with its provisions, except that those judges to whom Rules 3.8 (Appointments to Fiduciary Positions) and 3.11 (Financial, Business, or Remunerative Activities) apply shall comply with those Rules as soon as reasonably possible, but in no event later than one year after the Code becomes applicable to the judge.

Comment

[1] If serving as a fiduciary when selected as judge, a new judge may, notwithstanding the prohibitions in Rule 3.8, continue to serve as fiduciary, but only for that period of time necessary to avoid serious adverse consequences to the beneficiaries of the fiduciary relationship and in no event longer than one year. Similarly, if engaged at the time of judicial selection in a business activity, a new judge may, notwithstanding the prohibitions in Rule 3.11, continue in that activity for a reasonable period but in no event longer than one year.

CANON 1

A JUDGE SHALL UPHOLD AND PROMOTE THE INDEPENDENCE, INTEGRITY, AND IMPARTIALITY OF THE JUDICIARY, AND SHALL AVOID IMPROPRIETY AND THE APPEARANCE OF IMPROPRIETY.

CANON 1—REPORTER'S EXPLANATION OF CHANGES†

1990 MODEL CODE COMPARISON

Canon 1 is a combination of Canons 1 and 2.

---

* Ed. Note: In August 2010, the ABA House of Delegates amended (A) and (B) to clarify the application of the rules to pro tempore part-time judges.

† The "Reporters' Explanations of Changes" have not been approved by the ABA Joint Commission to Evaluate the Model Code of Judicial Conduct. They have been drafted by the Commission's Reporters, based on the proceedings and record of the Commission, solely to inform the ABA House of Delegates about each of the proposed amendments to the Model Code prior to their being considered at the ABA 2007 Midyear Meeting. THEY ARE NOT TO BE ADOPTED AS PART OF THE MODEL CODE.

2019 MODEL CODE

EXPLANATION OF BLACK LETTER

1. Canon 1 combines most of the subject matter of Canons 1 and 2 in the 1990 Code, addressing both the obligation of judges to uphold the independence, integrity, and impartiality of the judiciary and the obligation to avoid impropriety and its appearance. The admonishment that judges avoid not only impropriety but also its appearance is in the text of Canon 1 and in Rule 1.2.

The decision to combine Canons 1 and 2 in the 1990 Code into a single Canon was based on the premise that they are directed toward essentially the same end: to articulate a limited number of general, overarching principles that should govern a judge's conduct. Former Canons 1 and 2 were inextricably linked: avoiding "impropriety and the appearance of impropriety" in former Canon 2 was instrumental to upholding "the independence and integrity of the judiciary" in former Canon 1. Moreover, the former Code blurred the distinction between its Canons 1 and 2 by including in Canon 2A a duty to act in a manner that "promotes public confidence in the integrity and impartiality of the judiciary," which essentially paraphrased Canon 1's directive to "uphold the integrity and independence of the judiciary." Although one could argue that former Canon 1 was concerned with protecting independence and integrity in fact, while former Canon 2 concentrated upon protecting appearances and public perception, the overlap between them was so great that in the Commission's view preserving the two as discrete Canons was unnecessarily confusing. Accordingly, the two Canons have been combined to underscore the instrumental relationship between them, and thereby reinforce the importance of both.

2. Addition of "promote" to Canon 1

As an overarching objective, the Commission deemed it desirable to speak in terms of an ethical duty to promote as well as uphold judicial independence, integrity and impartiality.

3. "Appearance of impropriety" standard

At the center of the Commission's deliberations over Canon 1 was the "appearance of impropriety." The discussions reflected two competing tensions. On the one hand, a primary purpose of the Code is to advise and inspire judges to adhere to the highest standards of ethical conduct. To preserve public confidence in the courts, it is not enough that judges avoid actual improprieties; they must avoid the appearance of impropriety as well. On the other hand, another purpose of the Rules is to serve as the basis for discipline. To discipline judges for appearing to act improperly—even if they did not act improperly in fact—was considered by some commentators to raise due process issues because of the potential vagueness of the term "impropriety."

To address the concern that a duty to avoid the appearance of impropriety was too vague to be independently enforceable, the Commission's preliminary draft included a comment to the effect that ordinarily, when judges are disciplined for violating their duty to avoid the appearance of impropriety, it is in combination with other, more specific rule violations that give rise to the appearance problem. When the preliminary draft was circulated for public comment in June 2005, that comment was criticized widely for, among other things, diluting the "appearance of impropriety" standard unnecessarily.

Of additional concern was the preliminary draft's deletion of former Canon 2A's directive that "a judge shall . . . act at all times in a manner that promotes public confidence in the integrity and impartiality of the judiciary" (the "act at all times" clause), which had been a rule through which the appearance of impropriety was commonly enforced.

The Commission deleted the offending draft Comment, and restored the "act at all times clause." The Commission had in the interim considered retaining the appearance of impropriety language only in the Canon, and, as a precaution against it being used as a disciplinary standard, included a statement in the Scope Section that the Canons could themselves be enforced only when some Rule was violated. Urgings from legal organizations and the judiciary led the Commission to accept an amendment, during debate in the House of Delegates, that reinstated the obligation of a judge to avoid impropriety and the appearance of impropriety as black letter Rule 1.2. With an enforceable rule thus "on the books," any objections to the non-enforceability of the Canons were withdrawn, and the Scope provision was retained.

4. Use of "independence, integrity, and impartiality"

In the prior Code, "impartiality" did not appear in the titles of Canons 1 or 2, even though it did appear in underlying sections, such as Canon 2A. In the Commission's view, independence, integrity, and impartiality are overarching, fundamental values that the Rules promote, which warrant mention in the title of Canon 1. The term "impartiality" has been added to integrity and independence throughout the Rules, and the Rules have been revised throughout to preserve consistency.

The importance of judicial independence, integrity, and impartiality is underscored by the recurrence of the phrase throughout the Rules. Although it was used in earlier Codes as well, the Commission took pains to ensure that the three terms appear together wherever appropriate, and in the same sequence whenever they are employed.

RULE 1.1 Compliance With the Law

A judge shall comply with the law,* including the Code of Judicial Conduct.

RULE 1.1—REPORTER'S EXPLANATION OF CHANGES†

1990 MODEL CODE COMPARISON

The Rule is the first clause of Canon 2A, combined with a statement from the Commentary to Canon 1A.

EXPLANATION OF BLACK LETTER

1. Creation of a new rule

This Rule reproduces the first clause of former Canon 2A. The former Canon linked the duty to respect and comply with the law to the duty to act at all times in a manner that promoted public confidence in the independence, integrity, and impartiality of the judiciary, which the Commission regarded as distinct and discrete concepts. To be sure, the judge who does not comply with the law diminishes public confidence in judges, but the "act at all times" clause encompasses a far broader range of conduct that deserved to be singled out and articulated at the front of the Canon. The reference to a judge's duty to "respect" the law was deleted because it was believed to be both impossible to define and unnecessary.

2. Addition of "including the Code of Judicial Conduct"

The Commission wanted to leave no room for doubt that the scope of "law" within the meaning of this rule, applies to the Rules themselves.

3. Canon 1A's pronouncement that a judge "should participate in establishing, maintaining and enforcing high standards of conduct" has been revised and moved to the Preamble. The Commission concluded that such hortatory language should not be confused with enforceable standards and that to avoid such confusion, it should not appear in black letter Rules.

EXPLANATION OF COMMENTS

The Commentary to Canon 1A was deleted as unnecessary. Integrity and independence, which were discussed in the deleted comment, are defined terms in the revised Terminology Section.

---

† The "Reporters' Explanations of Changes" have not been approved by the ABA Joint Commission to Evaluate the Model Code of Judicial Conduct. They have been drafted by the Commission's Reporters, based on the proceedings and record of the Commission, solely to inform the ABA House of Delegates about each of the proposed amendments to the Model Code prior to their being considered at the ABA 2007 Midyear Meeting. THEY ARE NOT TO BE ADOPTED AS PART OF THE MODEL CODE.

RULE 1.2 Promoting Confidence in the Judiciary

A judge shall act at all times in a manner that promotes public confidence in the independence,* integrity,* and impartiality* of the judiciary, and shall avoid impropriety and the appearance of impropriety.

Comment

[1] Public confidence in the judiciary is eroded by improper conduct and conduct that creates the appearance of impropriety. This principle applies to both the professional and personal conduct of a judge.

[2] A judge should expect to be the subject of public scrutiny that might be viewed as burdensome if applied to other citizens, and must accept the restrictions imposed by the Code.

[3] Conduct that compromises or appears to compromise the independence, integrity, and impartiality of a judge undermines public confidence in the judiciary. Because it is not practicable to list all such conduct, the Rule is necessarily cast in general terms.

[4] Judges should participate in activities that promote ethical conduct among judges and lawyers, support professionalism within the judiciary and the legal profession, and promote access to justice for all.

[5] Actual improprieties include violations of law, court rules or provisions of this Code. The test for appearance of impropriety is whether the conduct would create in reasonable minds a perception that the judge violated this Code or engaged in other conduct that reflects adversely on the judge's honesty, impartiality, temperament, or fitness to serve as a judge.

[6] A judge should initiate and participate in community outreach activities for the purpose of promoting public understanding of and confidence in the administration of justice._ In conducting such activities, the judge must act in a manner consistent with this Code.

RULE 1.2—REPORTER'S EXPLANATION OF CHANGES†

1990 MODEL CODE COMPARISON

The Rule is Canon 2A.

Comment [1] is based upon the first two sentences of Commentary to Canon 2A, with the first sentence of the second paragraph of Commentary to Canon 2A inserted as a second sentence.

Comment [2] is taken from the first paragraph of Commentary to Canon 2A.

Comment [3] is taken from the first two paragraphs of Commentary to Canon 2A.

The third paragraph of Commentary to Canon 2A was deleted.

Comment [4] is new.

Comment [5] is a reformulation of the second paragraph of Commentary to Canon 2A.

Comment [6] is new.

EXPLANATION OF BLACK LETTER

Creation of a new rule

The first clause of Rule 1.2 is taken from Canon 2. This language was formerly included in the text of Canon 2A and is now a free-standing rule, for reasons explained above in the general discussion of Canon 1.

† The "Reporters' Explanations of Changes" have not been approved by the ABA Joint Commission to Evaluate the Model Code of Judicial Conduct. They have been drafted by the Commission's Reporters, based on the proceedings and record of the Commission, solely to inform the ABA House of Delegates about each of the proposed amendments to the Model Code prior to their being considered at the ABA 2007 Midyear Meeting. THEY ARE NOT TO BE ADOPTED AS PART OF THE MODEL CODE.

The second clause, directing judges to avoid impropriety and the appearance of impropriety was added at the urging of the judiciary and others, to make creating an "appearance of impropriety" an independent basis for discipline.

EXPLANATION OF COMMENTS

[1], [2], [3] The substance of Comments [1], [2], and [3] is derived from Commentary to former Canon 2A. Language from the former Commentary that was deemed self-evident, redundant, or otherwise unnecessary was deleted.

[4] Comment [4] is new. The Commission heard from a number of witnesses who underscored the importance of encouraging judges to promote professionalism among lawyers and judges—to make it clear that doing so was a part of their jobs. Although it was never suggested that judges be subject to discipline for failing to undertake such activities, the Commission agreed that judges should strive to promote professionalism and access to justice and that the aspirational objectives of the Code were well served by including this Comment.

[5] Comment [5] is derived from commentary accompanying Canon 2A of the 1990 Code. It modifies the former commentary's "test" for the appearance of impropriety by stating that an appearance problem arises from the perception that the judge either violated the Code or engaged in other conduct that reflects adversely on the judge's honesty, impartiality, temperament or fitness.

[6] Comment [6] is new, and is designed to encourage judges to participate in community outreach activity. Existing ABA policy encourages judges to engage in such activity as a means to promote public confidence in the courts.

RULE 1.3 Avoiding Abuse of the Prestige of Judicial Office

A judge shall not abuse the prestige of judicial office to advance the personal or economic interests* of the judge or others, or allow others to do so.

Comment

[1] It is improper for a judge to use or attempt to use his or her position to gain personal advantage or deferential treatment of any kind. For example, it would be improper for a judge to allude to his or her judicial status to gain favorable treatment in encounters with traffic officials. Similarly, a judge must not use judicial letterhead to gain an advantage in conducting his or her personal business.

[2] A judge may provide a reference or recommendation for an individual based upon the judge's personal knowledge. The judge may use official letterhead if the judge indicates that the reference is personal and if there is no likelihood that the use of the letterhead would reasonably be perceived as an attempt to exert pressure by reason of the judicial office.

[3] Judges may participate in the process of judicial selection by cooperating with appointing authorities and screening committees, and by responding to inquiries from such entities concerning the professional qualifications of a person being considered for judicial office.

[4] Special considerations arise when judges write or contribute to publications of for-profit entities, whether related or unrelated to the law. A judge shall not permit anyone associated with the publication of such materials to exploit the judge's office in a manner that violates this Rule or other applicable law. In contracts for publication of a judge's writing, the judge shall retain sufficient control over the advertising to avoid such exploitation.

RULE 1.3—REPORTER'S EXPLANATION OF CHANGES†

1990 MODEL CODE COMPARISON:

The Rule and its Comment come from Canon 2B and its Commentary.

EXPLANATION OF BLACK LETTER

1. Creation of separate Rule on abusing prestige of office

This Rule was segregated from former Canon 2B for treatment as a stand-alone Rule because it relates directly to a judge's personal conduct. Former Canon 2B's prohibition on a judge allowing family, social, and political relationships to influence judicial conduct and its prohibition on a judge conveying or allowing others to convey the impression that other persons are in a position to influence the judge related directly to a judge's judicial decision-making responsibilities. For that reason, these provisions belonged more logically in proposed Canon 2. Former Canon 2B's limitation on a judge serving as a character witness, on the other hand, related to a judge's personal conduct and has been moved to Rule 3.3.

2. Substitution of "abuse" for "lend"

The term "abuse" has been substituted for "lend." In the Commission's view, the term "lend" created unnecessary confusion. For example, a judge who wrote a letter of recommendation for a law clerk "lent" the prestige of the judge's office to the recommendation, and some judges told the Commission that they declined to write letters on their clerks' behalf as a consequence. In the Commission's view, however, the problem that Rule 1.3 seeks to address is more accurately characterized as "abuse" of the office.

3. Addition of "economic" interests

Although a judge's "personal" interests might commonly be thought to include "economic" interests, the Commission wanted to avoid any possibility of confusion, and thus made it clear that a judge may not abuse the prestige of office to advance either.

4. Addition of prohibition on others' abuse

The Rule has been revised to prohibit judges from allowing others to abuse the prestige of the judge's office to advance the judge's or others' personal or economic interests. In the Commission's view, judges should not be permitted to look the other way if friends or relatives seek to trade on the judge's position to benefit themselves or others. "Personal" replaced "private" for stylistic reasons not intended to change substantive meaning.

EXPLANATION OF COMMENTS

[1] This Comment elaborates on the core objective underlying the Rule by making plain that a judge should not use his or her position as a judge to gain personal advantage in business or daily life. The last sentence was changed to limit the admonition that a judge should not use his or her judicial letterhead for personal business to situations in which the use of letterhead could "gain advantage." There are times when a judge might draft a personal note on stationery that includes the judge's title that could not conceivably enable the judge to "gain advantage," as, for example, when the judge corresponds with a long-time acquaintance who is well aware of the judge's position. Material from the 1990 comment regarded as too general to be helpful was deleted.

[2] The Commission was in accord that judges should be permitted to use their titles and office letterheads when writing references for people with respect to whom the judge's experience as a judge was relevant. The prohibition on abusing the prestige of judicial office to advance the interests of another is intended to prevent inappropriate exploitation of judges' positions, and there is nothing inappropriate about judges identifying themselves as such when judicial experience is germane to the recommendation. The Comment thus clarifies that a judge may write letters on the basis of a judge's experience on the job (e.g., law clerks)

† The "Reporters' Explanations of Changes" have not been approved by the ABA Joint Commission to Evaluate the Model Code of Judicial Conduct. They have been drafted by the Commission's Reporters, based on the proceedings and record of the Commission, solely to inform the ABA House of Delegates about each of the proposed amendments to the Model Code prior to their being considered at the ABA 2007 Midyear Meeting. THEY ARE NOT TO BE ADOPTED AS PART OF THE MODEL CODE.

or general expertise in the law (e.g., a neighbor applying for admission to law school). This Comment does not admonish judges to avoid writing letters of reference on behalf of someone with respect to whom the judge's status as a judge is irrelevant, rather, it merely advises judges to consider whether their position as a judge might be perceived as exerting pressure by reason of their office and to refrain if it would.

[3] Changes were stylistic and not intended to change substantive meaning.

[4] Deleted material was redundant of the text and otherwise not illuminating.

CANON 2

A JUDGE SHALL PERFORM THE DUTIES OF JUDICIAL OFFICE IMPARTIALLY, COMPETENTLY, AND DILIGENTLY.

CANON 2—REPORTER'S EXPLANATION OF CHANGES†

1990 MODEL CODE COMPARISON

The Canon is former Canon 3.

Canon 2 addresses solely the judge's professional duties as a judge, which constitute part of Canon 3 in the 1990 Code.

EXPLANATION OF BLACK LETTER

Discussion of Canon

This Canon is at the heart of the Rules, in that it governs core judicial functions. It bears emphasis, however, that the judicial function has changed over time and logically reaches such matters as administration, discipline, and some forms of outreach. Judicial activities or conduct, therefore, are not limited to the adjudication of cases, but are intended to reach the broader duties of judicial office. Thus, this Canon on the duties of judicial office includes rules governing judicial discipline, administration, and reporting.

The element of "competence" was added to the Canon in recognition of the importance that competence plays in a judge's discharge of his or her duties.

RULE 2.1 Giving Precedence to the Duties of Judicial Office

The duties of judicial office, as prescribed by law,* shall take precedence over all of a judge's personal and extrajudicial activities.

Comment

[1] To ensure that judges are available to fulfill their judicial duties, judges must conduct their personal and extrajudicial activities to minimize the risk of conflicts that would result in frequent disqualification. See Canon 3.

[2] Although it is not a duty of judicial office unless prescribed by law, judges are encouraged to participate in activities that promote public understanding of and confidence in the justice system.

† The "Reporters' Explanations of Changes" have not been approved by the ABA Joint Commission to Evaluate the Model Code of Judicial Conduct. They have been drafted by the Commission's Reporters, based on the proceedings and record of the Commission, solely to inform the ABA House of Delegates about each of the proposed amendments to the Model Code prior to their being considered at the ABA 2007 Midyear Meeting. THEY ARE NOT TO BE ADOPTED AS PART OF THE MODEL CODE.

RULE 2.1—REPORTER'S EXPLANATION OF CHANGES†

1990 MODEL CODE COMPARISON

The Canon is Canon 3A.

The Comment is new.

EXPLANATION OF BLACK LETTER

1. Deletion of heading

2. Change "judicial duties" to "duties of judicial office"

The wording was changed to emphasize that its application goes beyond adjudicative functions to reach the broader scope of responsibilities that accompany the judicial office.

3. Addition of "shall"

The Commission wanted to make clear that this rule was doing more than making the descriptive point that judicial functions do take precedence; by inserting the term "shall," the Code clearly imposes an ethical duty on judges to give priority to the duties of judicial office.

4. Replace "all the judge's other activities" with "all of a judge's personal and extrajudicial activities"

This change was made to avoid confusion. Judges should give priority to their judicial duties, broadly defined to reach not only adjudication but also the other duties of judicial office (such as administration and discipline), and the Commission wanted to be clear that the matters of secondary importance were limited to personal and extrajudicial activities.

5. Deletion of third sentence

This sentence was deleted as unnecessary.

EXPLANATION OF COMMENTS

[1] New Comment

This Comment has been added to highlight the relationship between Canon 2 and Canon 3: because judges must disqualify themselves from cases in which they have a conflict of interest, they must conduct their extrajudicial activities in ways that minimize their need to disqualify themselves.

[2] New Comment

This comment has been added, along with Comment 6 to Rule 1.2, to underscore the value of judicial outreach. Although undertaking activities that encourage public understanding of and confidence in the justice system is not a duty of judicial office per se, such activities promote public confidence in the courts and to that extent facilitate the courts' mission.

RULE 2.2 Impartiality and Fairness

A judge shall uphold and apply the law,* and shall perform all duties of judicial office fairly and impartially.*

Comment

[1] To ensure impartiality and fairness to all parties, a judge must be objective and open-minded.

[2] Although each judge comes to the bench with a unique background and personal philosophy, a judge must interpret and apply the law without regard to whether the judge approves or disapproves of the law in question.

[3] When applying and interpreting the law, a judge sometimes may make good-faith errors of fact or law. Errors of this kind do not violate this Rule.

[4] It is not a violation of this Rule for a judge to make reasonable accommodations to ensure pro se litigants the opportunity to have their matters fairly heard.

RULE 2.2—REPORTER'S EXPLANATION OF CHANGES†

1990 MODEL CODE COMPARISON

The Rule is the first half of the first sentence of Canon 3B(2).

Comments [1]–[4] are new.

EXPLANATION OF BLACK LETTER

New Rule on upholding the law

This Rule is taken from the first half of the first sentence of Canon 3B(2), which spoke in terms of judges being "faithful" to the law. In its stead, the Commission substituted the phrase "uphold and apply the law." In the Commission's view, "fidelity" lacked clear meaning; the essential point was and remains that judges should interpret and apply the law as they understand it to be written, and the Rule has been revised to make that point more clearly.

Although there is some similarity between this Rule and Rule 1.1, their purposes are fundamentally different. Whereas Rule 1.1 addresses the judge's duty to comply with the law, this Rule directs the judge to follow the rule of law when deciding cases. The duty to follow the law is inextricably linked to a corresponding duty to be fair and impartial. Although the duty to decide cases with impartiality was implicit in numerous provisions in the former Code, it was not stated explicitly. This Rule corrects that oversight and does so by linking the judge's obligation to decide cases with impartiality to a corresponding duty to apply the law.

EXPLANATION OF COMMENTS

[1] This new Comment defines impartiality with reference to the two definitions of impartiality accepted by the Supreme Court in *Republican Party of Minnesota v. White*, lack of bias toward a participant in the judicial process, and open-mindedness.

[2] Comments [2] and [3] were inserted to underscore the distinction between the judge whose honest understanding of the law is influenced by upbringing, education, and life experience, which is neither avoidable nor improper, and the judge who disregards the law.

[3] Comment [3] underscores the point that judges sometime commit good faith errors of fact or law, which does not violate this rule. Rather, the rule is directed at judges who deliberately or repeatedly disregard court orders or other clear requirements of law.

[4] Throughout the life of the Commission, some witnesses urged the Commission to create special rules enabling judges to assist pro se litigants, while others urged the Commission to disregard calls for such rules. This Comment makes clear that judges do not compromise their impartiality when they make reasonable accommodations to pro se litigants who may be completely unfamiliar with the legal system and the litigation process. To the contrary, by leveling the playing field, such judges ensure that pro se litigants receive the fair hearing to which they are entitled. On the other hand, judges should resist unreasonable demands for assistance that might give an unrepresented party an unfair advantage.

---

† The "Reporters' Explanations of Changes" have not been approved by the ABA Joint Commission to Evaluate the Model Code of Judicial Conduct. They have been drafted by the Commission's Reporters, based on the proceedings and record of the Commission, solely to inform the ABA House of Delegates about each of the proposed amendments to the Model Code prior to their being considered at the ABA 2007 Midyear Meeting. THEY ARE NOT TO BE ADOPTED AS PART OF THE MODEL CODE.

RULE 2.3 Bias, Prejudice, and Harassment

(A) A judge shall perform the duties of judicial office, including administrative duties, without bias or prejudice.

(B) A judge shall not, in the performance of judicial duties, by words or conduct manifest bias or prejudice, or engage in harassment, including but not limited to bias, prejudice, or harassment based upon race, sex, gender, religion, national origin, ethnicity, disability, age, sexual orientation, marital status, socioeconomic status, or political affiliation, and shall not permit court staff, court officials, or others subject to the judge's direction and control to do so.

(C) A judge shall require lawyers in proceedings before the court to refrain from manifesting bias or prejudice, or engaging in harassment, based upon attributes including but not limited to race, sex, gender, religion, national origin, ethnicity, disability, age, sexual orientation, marital status, socioeconomic status, or political affiliation, against parties, witnesses, lawyers, or others.

(D) The restrictions of paragraphs (B) and (C) do not preclude judges or lawyers from making legitimate reference to the listed factors, or similar factors, when they are relevant to an issue in a proceeding.

Comment

[1] A judge who manifests bias or prejudice in a proceeding impairs the fairness of the proceeding and brings the judiciary into disrepute.

[2] Examples of manifestations of bias or prejudice include but are not limited to epithets; slurs; demeaning nicknames; negative stereotyping; attempted humor based upon stereotypes; threatening, intimidating, or hostile acts; suggestions of connections between race, ethnicity, or nationality and crime; and irrelevant references to personal characteristics. Even facial expressions and body language can convey to parties and lawyers in the proceeding, jurors, the media, and others an appearance of bias or prejudice. A judge must avoid conduct that may reasonably be perceived as prejudiced or biased.

[3] Harassment, as referred to in paragraphs (B) and (C), is verbal or physical conduct that denigrates or shows hostility or aversion toward a person on bases such as race, sex, gender, religion, national origin, ethnicity, disability, age, sexual orientation, marital status, socioeconomic status, or political affiliation.

[4] Sexual harassment includes but is not limited to sexual advances, requests for sexual favors, and other verbal or physical conduct of a sexual nature that is unwelcome.

RULE 2.3—REPORTER'S EXPLANATION OF CHANGES†

1990 MODEL CODE COMPARISON

Paragraph (A) is taken from the first sentence of Canon 3B(5).

Paragraph (B) is taken from the second sentence of Canon 3B(5).

Paragraph (C) is taken from Canon 3B(6).

Paragraph (D) is taken from Canon 3B(6).

Comment [1] is the second sentence of the second paragraph of Commentary to Canon 3B(5).

† The "Reporters' Explanations of Changes" have not been approved by the ABA Joint Commission to Evaluate the Model Code of Judicial Conduct. They have been drafted by the Commission's Reporters, based on the proceedings and record of the Commission, solely to inform the ABA House of Delegates about each of the proposed amendments to the Model Code prior to their being considered at the ABA 2007 Midyear Meeting. THEY ARE NOT TO BE ADOPTED AS PART OF THE MODEL CODE.

Comment [2] is the third and fourth sentences of the second paragraph of Commentary to Canon 3B(5).

Comments [3] and [4] are new.

The first paragraph of Commentary to Canon 3B(5) was deleted.

EXPLANATION OF BLACK LETTER

1. Paragraphs (B) and (C): Addition of "harassment"

Canon 3B(5) required judges to avoid bias and prejudice, but included nothing in the black letter about harassment, which it relegated to a discussion in the Commentary, limited to sexual harassment. The Commission agreed that harassment was a form of bias or prejudice that the Rules proscribed but wanted to expand it beyond sexual harassment to reach other forms of harassment as well, for which reason it deleted the term "sexual" from the Commentary in an early draft. Witnesses, however, argued that the proposed change could be construed to have an unintended consequence. By deleting the reference to "sexual" harassment per se, the change could be construed as deleting sexual harassment from the range of behaviors barred by the Rules, or at least diminishing its significance. The Commission remained of the view that harassment—including but not limited to sexual harassment—should be proscribed by the Rules. It was, however, persuaded both that sexual harassment deserved special mention, given the significance of the problem, and that harassment per se was sufficiently distinct from bias and prejudice to deserve separate mention in the black letter of the Rule.

2. Paragraphs (B) and (C): Additions to list of factors upon which bias, prejudice, or harassment can be based

Although the Rule prohibits bias, prejudice, or harassment on any basis, it includes an illustrative list, to which four new items were added: gender ("sex" is a term of art employed in sex discrimination statutes, but may not capture bias, prejudice, or harassment against trans-gendered individuals); ethnicity (which the Commission regarded as distinct from national origin; for example, in the case of an Arab-Canadian, discrimination on the basis of Arab ancestry would relate to ethnicity, while discrimination based on Canadian derivation would relate to national origin); marital status (the Commission was made aware of instances in which judges had berated a party for cohabiting or having a child outside of wedlock); and political affiliation (as, for example, when a judge displays animus toward plaintiffs affiliated with a particular political party).

3. Paragraph (D): Legitimate reference to listed factors

When a case before the judge raises issues of bias or prejudice, the judge must be in a position to discuss such issues without fear of violating this rule, for which reason an exception has been created in the text. The substance of this provision formerly was in Canon 3B(6).

EXPLANATION OF COMMENTS

The first paragraph of Commentary to Canon 3B(5) was deleted given the new black letter provision prohibiting harassment and new Comments [2]–[4].

[1] Comment [1] is the second sentence of the second paragraph of Commentary to Canon 3B(5), but with the phrase "on any basis" deleted. The phrase "or prejudice" was added to reach not only favoritism or opposition by a judge to an idea, which is the more common understanding of "bias," but also specially favoring or opposing individuals, which is generally contemplated by the term "prejudice."

[2] The new language was added after several witnesses urged the Commission to provide some illustrations of bias and to better inform judges of what bias entails and what some of the most common bias-related problems are. The list is explicitly non-exclusive and self-explanatory. The last two sentences are taken from the second paragraph of the comment to Canon 3B(5). The terms "in addition to oral communication" and "judicial" were deleted as excess language.

The term "behavior" was replaced with "conduct" in the last sentence for consistency with the rest of the Rules. The last sentence now instructs judges to avoid conduct that may be perceived as "prejudiced or biased" in order to be more comprehensive and consistent with the thrust of the Rule. The addition of the term "reasonably" in the last sentence is consistent with Title VII jurisprudence, which separates the merely vulgar from the deeply offensive.

[3] This new Comment defines harassment and underscores that the prohibition in the black letter includes, but is not limited to, sexual harassment.

[4] This new Comment separately elaborates on the meaning of "sexual harassment." Although the Rule forbids all forms of harassment, witnesses before the Commission were emphatic about the need to single out sexual harassment for special mention, given the nature, extent, and history of the problem.

RULE 2.4 External Influences on Judicial Conduct

(A) A judge shall not be swayed by public clamor or fear of criticism.

(B) A judge shall not permit family, social, political, financial, or other interests or relationships to influence the judge's judicial conduct or judgment.

(C) A judge shall not convey or permit others to convey the impression that any person or organization is in a position to influence the judge.

Comment

[1] An independent judiciary requires that judges decide cases according to the law and facts, without regard to whether particular laws or litigants are popular or unpopular with the public, the media, government officials, or the judge's friends or family. Confidence in the judiciary is eroded if judicial decision making is perceived to be subject to inappropriate outside influences.

RULE 2.4—REPORTER'S EXPLANATION OF CHANGES†

1990 MODEL CODE COMPARISON

Paragraph (A) is the second sentence of Canon 3B(2).

Paragraph (B) is the first sentence of Canon 2B.

Paragraph (C) is the second half of the second sentence of Canon 2B.

Comment [1] is new.

EXPLANATION OF BLACK LETTER

1. Paragraph (B): Addition of "financial"

Paragraph (B) is the first sentence of Canon 2B.

"Financial" relationships were added to the list on influences that judges should avoid. Although the pre-existing rule referred to "other" relationships, the Commission regarded financial relationships as important enough to warrant separate mention.

2. Paragraph (C): Expansion of scope of Rule

The scope of the Rule was expanded slightly. As previously drafted, the Rule forbade a judge from permitting others to convey the impression that "they," meaning the "others," were in a position to influence the judge. As a technical matter, that prohibition did not reach the situation in which "others" conveyed the

---

† The "Reporters' Explanations of Changes" have not been approved by the ABA Joint Commission to Evaluate the Model Code of Judicial Conduct. They have been drafted by the Commission's Reporters, based on the proceedings and record of the Commission, solely to inform the ABA House of Delegates about each of the proposed amendments to the Model Code prior to their being considered at the ABA 2007 Midyear Meeting. THEY ARE NOT TO BE ADOPTED AS PART OF THE MODEL CODE.

impression that a third person was in a position to influence the judge, and the change has been made to cover that scenario.

The Commission felt that the term "special," modifying position, was at best a redundancy and at worst added confusion by creating the impression that there might be persons who are in a position to influence the court.

EXPLANATION OF COMMENTS

[1] Comment [1] is new.

This new Comment is intended to underscore the general purpose underlying paragraphs (A) and (B) by linking the duty not to be swayed by the public, friends, or family to the judge's primary obligation to follow the law and facts impartially.

RULE 2.5 Competence, Diligence, and Cooperation

(A) A judge shall perform judicial and administrative duties, competently and diligently.

(B) A judge shall cooperate with other judges and court officials in the administration of court business.

Comment

[1] Competence in the performance of judicial duties requires the legal knowledge, skill, thoroughness, and preparation reasonably necessary to perform a judge's responsibilities of judicial office.

[2] A judge should seek the necessary docket time, court staff, expertise, and resources to discharge all adjudicative and administrative responsibilities.

[3] Prompt disposition of the court's business requires a judge to devote adequate time to judicial duties, to be punctual in attending court and expeditious in determining matters under submission, and to take reasonable measures to ensure that court officials, litigants, and their lawyers cooperate with the judge to that end.

[4] In disposing of matters promptly and efficiently, a judge must demonstrate due regard for the rights of parties to be heard and to have issues resolved without unnecessary cost or delay. A judge should monitor and supervise cases in ways that reduce or eliminate dilatory practices, avoidable delays, and unnecessary costs.

RULE 2.5—REPORTER'S EXPLANATION OF CHANGES†

1990 MODEL CODE COMPARISON

Part A is taken from Canons 3B(2) and 3C(1). Part B is the second half of Canon 3C(1).

Comments [1] and [2] are new.

Comment [3] is the second paragraph of Commentary to Canon 3B(8).

Comment [4] is the first three sentences of Commentary to 3B(8).

† "Reporters' Explanations of Changes" have not been approved by the ABA Joint Commission to Evaluate the Model Code of Judicial Conduct. They have been drafted by the Commission's Reporters, based on the proceedings and record of the Commission, solely to inform the ABA House of Delegates about each of the proposed amendments to the Model Code prior to their being considered at the ABA 2007 Midyear Meeting. THEY ARE NOT TO BE ADOPTED AS PART OF THE MODEL CODE.

EXPLANATION OF BLACK LETTER

1. New Rule combining duties of competence and diligence

This Rule governs competence, formerly governed by Canon 3B(2), and diligence, formerly governed by Canon 3C and makes the requirements applicable to both adjudicative and administrative duties of a judge. The duty of competence is analogous to a lawyer's professional duty of competence, while the duty to apply the law is discussed elsewhere (the term "fidelity" is no longer used). Corresponding Commentary was moved accordingly. The phrasing was changed from passive to active voice for stylistic reasons.

2. Expansion of Rule

The black letter Rule was clarified to make plain that the duty at issue was one of diligence, and expanded slightly to extend the duty of diligence to all judicial duties and not just "judicial matters," which is generally understood to be limited to case adjudication.

3. Change Rule standard

The obligation to cooperate with others in judicial administration was upgraded from hortatory to mandatory. Efficient and effective administration is a duty of the judicial office, the proper execution of which necessitates cooperation among the judges of the court.

EXPLANATION OF COMMENTS

[1] Comment [1] was added simply to define competence and underscore its fundamental importance in relation to core judicial functions.

[2] New Comment [2] was added to emphasize that the duty to perform judicial and administrative duties competently and diligently requires judges to devote time to proper time management and use of court resources and personnel.

RULE 2.6 Ensuring the Right to Be Heard

(A) A judge shall accord to every person who has a legal interest in a proceeding, or that person's lawyer, the right to be heard according to law.*

(B) A judge may encourage parties to a proceeding and their lawyers to settle matters in dispute but shall not act in a manner that coerces any party into settlement.

Comment

[1] The right to be heard is an essential component of a fair and impartial system of justice. Substantive rights of litigants can be protected only if procedures protecting the right to be heard are observed.

[2] The judge plays an important role in overseeing the settlement of disputes, but should be careful that efforts to further settlement do not undermine any party's right to be heard according to law. The judge should keep in mind the effect that the judge's participation in settlement discussions may have, not only on the judge's own views of the case, but also on the perceptions of the lawyers and the parties if the case remains with the judge after settlement efforts are unsuccessful. Among the factors that a judge should consider when deciding upon an appropriate settlement practice for a case are (1) whether the parties have requested or voluntarily consented to a certain level of participation by the judge in settlement discussions, (2) whether the parties and their counsel are relatively sophisticated in legal matters, (3) whether the case will be tried by the judge or a jury, (4) whether the parties participate with their counsel in settlement discussions, (5) whether any parties are unrepresented by counsel, and (6) whether the matter is civil or criminal.

[3] Judges must be mindful of the effect settlement discussions can have, not only on their objectivity and impartiality, but also on the appearance of their objectivity and impartiality. Despite a judge's best efforts, there may be instances when information obtained during settlement discussions could influence a

judge's decision making during trial, and, in such instances, the judge should consider whether disqualification may be appropriate. See Rule 2.11(A)(1).

RULE 2.6—REPORTER'S EXPLANATION OF CHANGES†

1990 MODEL CODE COMPARISON

Paragraph A of the Rule is 3B(7),

Paragraph B of the Rule is 3B(8) commentary.

Comments [1], [2], and [3] are new.

EXPLANATION OF BLACK LETTER

1. Paragraph (B): New paragraph on settlements

This new paragraph was added in recognition of the fact that out-of-court settlement is a commonly used method of case resolution. It is important for judges to remember that a litigant's right to be heard can inadvertently be impaired by a judge who is overzealous in encouraging an out-of-court resolution. Accordingly, the Rule draws a line between encouraging settlement, which is permitted, and coercing settlement, which is not. The Commission heard testimony from some witnesses who went further, urging the adoption of rules that would prohibit judges from presiding at trial over cases with respect to which they had previously conducted settlement negotiations that ultimately were unsuccessful. Although several members of the Commission agreed that, as a general matter, it was the better practice for judges not to try cases they had attempted to settle given the risk that statements the judge made during settlement negotiations might later be construed as lack of impartiality, the Commission declined to adopt such a rule. The Commission ultimately concluded that such an issue was better left for rules of practice and procedure than ethics.

EXPLANATION OF COMMENTS

[1] New Comment [1] emphasizes what is implicit in the Rule, that judges' duties include ensuring that those entitled have their day in court. In so doing, the Comment underscores the relationship between substantive and procedural justice, i.e. that protection of substantive rights depends in part on respecting procedural rights to be heard.

[2] New Comment [2] provides judges with guidance in conducting settlement talks. It undertakes to sensitize judges to concerns that can arise when they lead settlement discussions and to advise judges on what factors to take into account when deciding how to oversee settlement.

[3] New Comment [3] underscores the point that sometimes events transpiring during settlement talks may bias judges toward a party or create an appearance of bias that necessitates disqualification.

RULE 2.7 Responsibility to Decide

A judge shall hear and decide matters assigned to the judge, except when disqualification is required by Rule 2.11 or other law.*

Comment

[1] Judges must be available to decide the matters that come before the court. Although there are times when disqualification is necessary to protect the rights of litigants and preserve public confidence in

† The "Reporters' Explanations of Changes" have not been approved by the ABA Joint Commission to Evaluate the Model Code of Judicial Conduct. They have been drafted by the Commission's Reporters, based on the proceedings and record of the Commission, solely to inform the ABA House of Delegates about each of the proposed amendments to the Model Code prior to their being considered at the ABA 2007 Midyear Meeting. THEY ARE NOT TO BE ADOPTED AS PART OF THE MODEL CODE.

the independence, integrity, and impartiality of the judiciary, judges must be available to decide matters that come before the courts. Unwarranted disqualification may bring public disfavor to the court and to the judge personally. The dignity of the court, the judge's respect for fulfillment of judicial duties, and a proper concern for the burdens that may be imposed upon the judge's colleagues require that a judge not use disqualification to avoid cases that present difficult, controversial, or unpopular issues.

RULE 2.7—REPORTER'S EXPLANATION OF CHANGES†

1990 MODEL CODE COMPARISON

The Rule is Canon 3B(1).

Comment [1] is new.

EXPLANATION OF BLACK LETTER

Clarification of instances requiring disqualification

1. The Rule is Canon 3B(1), with a slight modification to cross-reference the disqualification rule explicitly and to acknowledge that in some instances disqualification may be required by other law.

EXPLANATION OF COMMENTS

[1] New Comment [1] was added to emphasize that although disqualification remains an important and at times essential option for a judge, it should not be misused as a tool to avoid deciding cases that the judge may regard as unpleasant or unpopular. The effective administration of justice depends on judges remaining available to hear the cases that parties file, and this Comment is intended to remind judges of that concern when they approach issues of disqualification.

RULE 2.8 Decorum, Demeanor, and Communication With Jurors

(A) A judge shall require order and decorum in proceedings before the court.

(B) A judge shall be patient, dignified, and courteous to litigants, jurors, witnesses, lawyers, court staff, court officials, and others with whom the judge deals in an official capacity, and shall require similar conduct of lawyers, court staff, court officials, and others subject to the judge's direction and control.

(C) A judge shall not commend or criticize jurors for their verdict other than in a court order or opinion in a proceeding.

Comment

[1] The duty to hear all proceedings with patience and courtesy is not inconsistent with the duty imposed in Rule 2.5 to dispose promptly of the business of the court. Judges can be efficient and businesslike while being patient and deliberate.

[2] Commending or criticizing jurors for their verdict may imply a judicial expectation in future cases and may impair a juror's ability to be fair and impartial in a subsequent case.

[3] A judge who is not otherwise prohibited by law from doing so may meet with jurors who choose to remain after trial but should be careful not to discuss the merits of the case.

---

† The "Reporters' Explanations of Changes" have not been approved by the ABA Joint Commission to Evaluate the Model Code of Judicial Conduct. They have been drafted by the Commission's Reporters, based on the proceedings and record of the Commission, solely to inform the ABA House of Delegates about each of the proposed amendments to the Model Code prior to their being considered at the ABA 2007 Midyear Meeting. THEY ARE NOT TO BE ADOPTED AS PART OF THE MODEL CODE.

RULE 2.8—REPORTER'S EXPLANATION OF CHANGES†

1990 MODEL CODE COMPARISON

Paragraph (A) is Canon 3B(3).

Paragraph (B) is Canon 3B(4).

Paragraph (C) is the first sentence of Canon 3B(11).

Comment [1] is the Commentary to Canon 3B(4).

Comment [2] is the Commentary to Canon 3B(11).

Comment [3] is new.

EXPLANATION OF BLACK LETTER

1. Paragraph (B): Extension of duty of courtesy

Paragraph (B) is Canon 3B(4), modified to extend the duty of courtesy to court staff, where episodes of abusive behavior occasionally have arisen. "Court officials" was added to be consistent with the list used later in the same paragraph.

2. Paragraph (C): Expressing appreciation to jurors

The Commission moved discussion permitting judges to express appreciation to jurors from the black letter Rule to the Comment on the grounds that it was advice not needed in the black letter.

EXPLANATION OF COMMENTS

[3] New Comment [3] was added in light of the growing recognition that judicial outreach is a valued part of the judicial role and includes outreach to jurors. The Comment makes clear that judges can commend jurors for their service and that the prohibition on judges commending or criticizing the jury for their verdict does not foreclose other communications between judges and jurors. To the contrary, the Commission saw value in creating an opportunity for the judge to learn more about the jury's experience, as long as the merits of the case were not discussed.

RULE 2.9 Ex Parte Communications

(A) A judge shall not initiate, permit, or consider ex parte communications, or consider other communications made to the judge outside the presence of the parties or their lawyers, concerning a pending* or impending matter,* except as follows:

(1) When circumstances require it, ex parte communication for scheduling, administrative, or emergency purposes, which does not address substantive matters, is permitted, provided:

(a) the judge reasonably believes that no party will gain a procedural, substantive, or tactical advantage as a result of the ex parte communication; and

† The "Reporters' Explanations of Changes" have not been approved by the ABA Joint Commission to Evaluate the Model Code of Judicial Conduct. They have been drafted by the Commission's Reporters, based on the proceedings and record of the Commission, solely to inform the ABA House of Delegates about each of the proposed amendments to the Model Code prior to their being considered at the ABA 2007 Midyear Meeting. THEY ARE NOT TO BE ADOPTED AS PART OF THE MODEL CODE.

(b) the judge makes provision promptly to notify all other parties of the substance of the ex parte communication, and gives the parties an opportunity to respond.

(2) A judge may obtain the written advice of a disinterested expert on the law applicable to a proceeding before the judge, if the judge gives advance notice to the parties of the person to be consulted and the subject matter of the advice to be solicited, and affords the parties a reasonable opportunity to object and respond to the notice and to the advice received.

(3) A judge may consult with court staff and court officials whose functions are to aid the judge in carrying out the judge's adjudicative responsibilities, or with other judges, provided the judge makes reasonable efforts to avoid receiving factual information that is not part of the record, and does not abrogate the responsibility personally to decide the matter.

(4) A judge may, with the consent of the parties, confer separately with the parties and their lawyers in an effort to settle matters pending before the judge.

(5) A judge may initiate, permit, or consider any ex parte communication when expressly authorized by law* to do so.

(B) If a judge inadvertently receives an unauthorized ex parte communication bearing upon the substance of a matter, the judge shall make provision promptly to notify the parties of the substance of the communication and provide the parties with an opportunity to respond.

(C) A judge shall not investigate facts in a matter independently, and shall consider only the evidence presented and any facts that may properly be judicially noticed.

(D) A judge shall make reasonable efforts, including providing appropriate supervision, to ensure that this Rule is not violated by court staff, court officials, and others subject to the judge's direction and control.

Comment

[1] To the extent reasonably possible, all parties or their lawyers shall be included in communications with a judge.

[2] Whenever the presence of a party or notice to a party is required by this Rule, it is the party's lawyer, or if the party is unrepresented, the party, who is to be present or to whom notice is to be given.

[3] The proscription against communications concerning a proceeding includes communications with lawyers, law teachers, and other persons who are not participants in the proceeding, except to the limited extent permitted by this Rule.

[4] A judge may initiate, permit, or consider ex parte communications expressly authorized by law, such as when serving on therapeutic or problem-solving courts, mental health courts, or drug courts. In this capacity, judges may assume a more interactive role with parties, treatment providers, probation officers, social workers, and others.

[5] A judge may consult with other judges on pending matters, but must avoid ex parte discussions of a case with judges who have previously been disqualified from hearing the matter, and with judges who have appellate jurisdiction over the matter.

[6] The prohibition against a judge investigating the facts in a matter extends to information available in all mediums, including electronic.

[7] A judge may consult ethics advisory committees, outside counsel, or legal experts concerning the judge's compliance with this Code. Such consultations are not subject to the restrictions of paragraph (A)(2).

RULE 2.9—REPORTER'S EXPLANATION OF CHANGES†

1990 MODEL CODE COMPARISON

Paragraph (A) is the second sentence of Canon 3B(7).

Paragraph (A)(1) is Canon 3B(7)(a).

Paragraph (A)(1)(a) is Canon 3B(7)(a)(i).

Paragraph (A)(1)(b) is Canon 3B(7)(a)(ii).

Paragraph (A)(2) is a modified version of Canon 3B(7)(b).

Paragraph (A)(3) is Canon 3B(7)(c).

Paragraph (A)(4) is Canon 3B(7)(d).

Paragraph (A)(5) is Canon 3B(7)(e).

Paragraph (B) is new.

Paragraph (C) is paragraph 6 of the Commentary to Canon 3B(7).

Paragraph (D) is from the eighth paragraph of Commentary to Canon 3B(7).

Comment [1] is the second paragraph of Commentary to Canon 3B(7).

Comment [2] is the third paragraph of Commentary to Canon 3B(7).

Comment [3] is the first paragraph of Commentary to Canon 3B(7).

Comments [4]–[7] are new.

The fourth, fifth, seventh and ninth paragraphs of Commentary to Canon 3B(7) were deleted.

EXPLANATION OF BLACK LETTER

1. "Issues on the merits" was deleted as duplicative; the Rule's exclusion of "substantive matters" from the scope of permissible ex parte communications would necessarily subsume all "issues on the merits." Replacing "authorized" with "permitted" is stylistic and does not change the substance of the provision.

2. Paragraph (A)(1)(a): Addition of "substantive"

"Substantive" was added in recognition of the fact that a scheduling, administrative, or emergency ex parte communication that is unrelated to substantive matters per se could nonetheless, in some instances, enable a party to gain an inappropriate advantage related to the substance or merits of the case.

3. Paragraph (A)(1)(b): Addition of delegation

Paragraph (A)(1)(b) is Canon 3B(7)(a)(ii), but revised to add the notion that a judge may delegate the notification obligation to others.

4. Paragraph (A)(2): Addition of requirement of advance notice

Paragraph (A)(2) is Canon 3B(7)(b), but modified to add the requirement of advance notice. Under the 1990 Code, a judge could consult with an outside legal expert ex parte before notifying the parties. If such a consultation was problematic for reasons that had not occurred to the judge, post-consultation notification to the parties would come too late to prevent the problem from arising. As revised, the Rule requires the judge to notify the parties before the ex parte contact is made.

5. Paragraph (A)(3): Addition of limitation on consultation

Paragraph (A)(3) is a modified version of Canon 3B(7)(c). The permissibility of a judge's consultation on a case with other court personnel was qualified to include the common sense limitations that the judge

† The "Reporters' Explanations of Changes" have not been approved by the ABA Joint Commission to Evaluate the Model Code of Judicial Conduct. They have been drafted by the Commission's Reporters, based on the proceedings and record of the Commission, solely to inform the ABA House of Delegates about each of the proposed amendments to the Model Code prior to their being considered at the ABA 2007 Midyear Meeting. THEY ARE NOT TO BE ADOPTED AS PART OF THE MODEL CODE.

must not relinquish ultimate responsibility for deciding the case and, in the course of such consultation, should be careful not to acquire improper factual information.

6. Paragraph (B): Creation of new paragraph on inadvertent communications

New Paragraph (B) addresses an issue not covered by the 1990 Code. In situations where a judge inadvertently receives an unauthorized ex parte communication, the new Rule directs the judge to notify all the other parties of the substance of the communication and give them an opportunity to respond. In an age when misdirected faxes and email are common, the need for some provision to deal with inadvertent disclosures of ex parte information impressed the Commission as necessary.

7. Paragraph (C): Creation of new paragraph prohibiting investigation

In the Commission's view, former Commentary prohibiting a judge from undertaking independent factual investigations was largely unsupported by the Rule itself and warranted inclusion as part of the Rule. Moreover, the judge's duty to consider only the evidence presented is a defining feature of the judge's role in an adversarial system and warrants explicit mention in the black letter. The term "must" was replaced with "shall," both for consistency and to make clear that compliance with the proscription is absolute. Specific acknowledgement of the category of evidence or facts that are judicially noticed was considered a beneficial clarification, and was therefore added to this paragraph.

8. Paragraph (D): Creation of new paragraph on avoiding communication through staff

Paragraph (D) was moved to the black letter from the eighth paragraph of Commentary to Canon 3B(7). In the Commission's view, a judge's duty to take steps to avoid violating the Rule against ex parte communications through staff could not be inferred from the black letter of the former Rule.

EXPLANATION OF COMMENTS

[3] Comment [3] is the first paragraph of Commentary to Canon 3B(7), with the addition of "by this Rule," a revision made for stylistic reasons and not intended to change substantive meaning.

[4] New comment dealing with problem-solving and therapeutic courts

The Commission heard a great deal of testimony about therapeutic or problem-solving courts. In these non-traditional courts that hear matters on an increasingly broad array of issues ranging from drugs to juvenile justice, domestic relations, and crime, judges communicate with parties, service providers (such as social workers), and others in ways that can be in tension with traditional rules governing ex parte communications. Several witnesses thus urged the Commission to create special rules for such courts. The Commission was reluctant to do so because therapeutic courts were too many and varied for the Commission to devise rules of general applicability. Instead, the Commission drafted this new Comment, which calls special attention to the exception for ex parte communications authorized by law and notes that this exception enables individual jurisdictions to devise special rules for their therapeutic courts.

[5] New comment regarding judge-to-judge consultations

New Comment [5] was added to clarify that while a judge may consult with other judges about a case, the judge should not consult with judges who have been disqualified from hearing the case. If, for whatever reason, a judge is disqualified from hearing a given matter, it would defeat the purpose of the disqualification rules to permit another judge to confer with the disqualified colleague. In addition, the Comment clarifies that a judge should not consult on a matter with any judge having appellate jurisdiction over the matter.

[6] New Comment containing prohibition against independently investigating facts.

Given the ease with which factual investigation can now be accomplished via electronic databases and the Internet, the risk that a judge or the judge's staff could inadvertently violate Rules 2.9(B) and (C) has heightened considerably. The need for vigilance on the part of judges has increased accordingly.

[7] New Comment regarding judges seeking ex parte guidance regarding compliance with Rules

The Commission wanted to make clear that judges may seek ex parte guidance concerning their compliance with the Code without violating this Rule. Judges routinely consult ethics advisory committees, counsel and outside experts concerning their obligations under the Code in a given context. Because such consultations are not problematic, New Comment [7] was added accordingly.

Deletion of the fourth, fifth, seventh and ninth paragraphs of Commentary to Canon 3B(7)

The Commission deleted the reference to requests for amicus briefs in the fourth paragraph of Canon 3B(7) Commentary as being "often desirable procedures," because it is not an ethical concern.

The fifth paragraph of Canon 3(B)(7) Commentary concerning clearly acceptable purposes for ex parte communications was deleted because it is redundant of the black letter Rule.

The Commission decided to delete Commentary language in the seventh paragraph of Canon 3B(7) authorizing a judge to request that a party submit proposed findings of fact and conclusions of law as long as the other party was given an opportunity to respond to the submission. In the Commission's view, the permissibility of the practice was so free from doubt as to render the Comment unnecessary.

The Commission deleted the ninth paragraph of Canon 3B(7) Commentary. The subject matter, keeping records of communications, is an administrative, rather than an ethical matter.

RULE 2.10 Judicial Statements on Pending and Impending Cases

(A) A judge shall not make any public statement that might reasonably be expected to affect the outcome or impair the fairness of a matter pending* or impending* in any court, or make any nonpublic statement that might substantially interfere with a fair trial or hearing.

(B) A judge shall not, in connection with cases, controversies, or issues that are likely to come before the court, make pledges, promises, or commitments that are inconsistent with the impartial* performance of the adjudicative duties of judicial office.

(C) A judge shall require court staff, court officials, and others subject to the judge's direction and control to refrain from making statements that the judge would be prohibited from making by paragraphs (A) and (B).

(D) Notwithstanding the restrictions in paragraph (A), a judge may make public statements in the course of official duties, may explain court procedures, and may comment on any proceeding in which the judge is a litigant in a personal capacity.

(E) Subject to the requirements of paragraph (A), a judge may respond directly or through a third party to allegations in the media or elsewhere concerning the judge's conduct in a matter.

Comment

[1] This Rule's restrictions on judicial speech are essential to the maintenance of the independence, integrity, and impartiality of the judiciary.

[2] This Rule does not prohibit a judge from commenting on proceedings in which the judge is a litigant in a personal capacity, or represents a *client* as permitted by these Rules. In cases in which the judge is a litigant in an official capacity, such as a writ of mandamus, the judge must not comment publicly.

[3] Depending upon the circumstances, the judge should consider whether it may be preferable for a third party, rather than the judge, to respond or issue statements in connection with allegations concerning the judge's conduct in a matter.

RULE 2.10—REPORTER'S EXPLANATION OF CHANGES†

1990 MODEL CODE COMPARISON

Paragraph (A) is the first sentence of Canon 3B(9).

Paragraph (B) is Canon 3B(10).

Paragraph (C) is the second sentence of Canon 3B(9).

Paragraph (D) is the third and fourth sentences of Canon 3B(9).

Paragraph (E) is new.

Comment [1] is the first sentence of the Commentary to Canon 3B(10).

Comment [2] is new.

Comment [3] is the fifth through seventh sentences of the Commentary to Canon 3B(10).

EXPLANATION OF BLACK LETTER

1. Paragraphs (A) and (C): Separation of former Canon

Former Canon 3B(9) was subdivided into two separate subsections (addressing the judge's statements and the statements of staff, court officers, and others). Paragraph (A) is the first sentence of Canon 3B(9), but was reworded to improve clarity.

In Paragraph (C), the phrase "court personnel" was replaced with "court staff, court officials and others" to broaden the judge's duty to prohibit others from making inappropriate comment on pending and impending cases to include all persons within the judge's control regardless of whether such persons technically qualified as court personnel.

2. In Paragraph (B), "judicial" was inserted before "office" for clarity.

3. Paragraph (E): Adding language concerning responding to media

Judges are justifiably reluctant to speak about pending cases. However, the Commission wanted to make clear that when a judge's conduct is called into question, the judge may respond as long as the response will not affect the fairness of the proceeding.

EXPLANATION OF COMMENTS

Deletion of reference to Model Rules of Professional Conduct

In the Commentary to Canon 3B(10), the cross-reference to the Model Rules of Professional Conduct was deleted as unnecessary.

Substance of Canon 3B(11) and its Commentary moved

The Commission moved Canon 3B(11) and its Commentary, relating to judges commending or criticizing jurors, to Rule 2.8, the Rule devoted to judicial decorum, demeanor, and communication with jurors.

The definitions of "pending" and "impending" in Commentary to Canon 3B(10) were moved to Terminology.

Comment [2] suggests that it may be appropriate in some instances for statements that explain or defend the role or action of a judge in a particular matter to be made by a third person, rather than by the judge. This suggestion reflects a preference for keeping to a minimum the extent to which judges discuss cases directly with the media.

---

† The "Reporters' Explanations of Changes" have not been approved by the ABA Joint Commission to Evaluate the Model Code of Judicial Conduct. They have been drafted by the Commission's Reporters, based on the proceedings and record of the Commission, solely to inform the ABA House of Delegates about each of the proposed amendments to the Model Code prior to their being considered at the ABA 2007 Midyear Meeting. THEY ARE NOT TO BE ADOPTED AS PART OF THE MODEL CODE.

RULE 2.11 Disqualification

(A) A judge shall disqualify himself or herself in any proceeding in which the judge's impartiality* might reasonably be questioned, including but not limited to the following circumstances:

(1) The judge has a personal bias or prejudice concerning a party or a party's lawyer, or personal knowledge* of facts that are in dispute in the proceeding.

(2) The judge knows* that the judge, the judge's spouse or domestic partner,* or a person within the third degree of relationship* to either of them, or the spouse or domestic partner of such a person is:

(a) a party to the proceeding, or an officer, director, general partner, managing member, or trustee of a party;

(b) acting as a lawyer in the proceeding;

(c) a person who has more than a de minimis* interest that could be substantially affected by the proceeding; or

(d) likely to be a material witness in the proceeding.

(3) The judge knows that he or she, individually or as a fiduciary,* or the judge's spouse, domestic partner, parent, or child, or any other member of the judge's family residing in the judge's household,* has an economic interest* in the subject matter in controversy or is a party to the proceeding.

(4) The judge knows or learns by means of a timely motion that a party, a party's lawyer, or the law firm of a party's lawyer has within the previous [insert number] year[s] made aggregate* contributions* to the judge's campaign in an amount that [is greater than $[insert amount] for an individual or $[insert amount] for an entity] [is reasonable and appropriate for an individual or an entity].

(5) The judge, while a judge or a judicial candidate,* has made a public statement, other than in a court proceeding, judicial decision, or opinion, that commits or appears to commit the judge to reach a particular result or rule in a particular way in the proceeding or controversy.

(6) The judge:

(a) served as a lawyer in the matter in controversy, or was associated with a lawyer who participated substantially as a lawyer in the matter during such association;

(b) served in governmental employment, and in such capacity participated personally and substantially as a lawyer or public official concerning the proceeding, or has publicly expressed in such capacity an opinion concerning the merits of the particular matter in controversy;

(c) was a material witness concerning the matter; or

(d) previously presided as a judge over the matter in another court.

(B) A judge shall keep informed about the judge's personal and fiduciary economic interests, and make a reasonable effort to keep informed about the personal economic interests of the judge's spouse or domestic partner and minor children residing in the judge's household.

(C) A judge subject to disqualification under this Rule, other than for bias or prejudice under paragraph (A)(1), may disclose on the record the basis of the judge's disqualification and may ask the parties and their lawyers to consider, outside the presence of the judge and court personnel, whether to waive disqualification. If, following the disclosure, the parties and lawyers agree, without participation by the judge or court personnel, that the judge should not be disqualified, the judge may participate in the proceeding. The agreement shall be incorporated into the record of the proceeding.

Comment

[1] Under this Rule, a judge is disqualified whenever the judge's impartiality might reasonably be questioned, regardless of whether any of the specific provisions of paragraphs (A)(1) through (6) apply. In many jurisdictions, the term "recusal" is used interchangeably with the term "disqualification."

[2] A judge's obligation not to hear or decide matters in which disqualification is required applies regardless of whether a motion to disqualify is filed.

[3] The rule of necessity may override the rule of disqualification. For example, a judge might be required to participate in judicial review of a judicial salary statute, or might be the only judge available in a matter requiring immediate judicial action, such as a hearing on probable cause or a temporary restraining order. In matters that require immediate action, the judge must disclose on the record the basis for possible disqualification and make reasonable efforts to transfer the matter to another judge as soon as practicable.

[4] The fact that a lawyer in a proceeding is affiliated with a law firm with which a relative of the judge is affiliated does not itself disqualify the judge. If, however, the judge's impartiality might reasonably be questioned under paragraph (A), or the relative is known by the judge to have an interest in the law firm that could be substantially affected by the proceeding under paragraph (A)(2)(c), the judge's disqualification is required.

[5] A judge should disclose on the record information that the judge believes the parties or their lawyers might reasonably consider relevant to a possible motion for disqualification, even if the judge believes there is no basis for disqualification.

[6] "Economic interest," as set forth in the Terminology section, means ownership of more than a de minimis legal or equitable interest. Except for situations in which a judge participates in the management of such a legal or equitable interest, or the interest could be substantially affected by the outcome of a proceeding before a judge, it does not include:

(1) an interest in the individual holdings within a mutual or common investment fund;

(2) an interest in securities held by an educational, religious, charitable, fraternal, or civic organization in which the judge or the judge's spouse, domestic partner, parent, or child serves as a director, officer, advisor, or other participant;

(3) a deposit in a financial institution or deposits or proprietary interests the judge may maintain as a member of a mutual savings association or credit union, or similar proprietary interests; or

(4) an interest in the issuer of government securities held by the judge.

RULE 2.11—REPORTER'S EXPLANATION OF CHANGES†

1990 MODEL CODE COMPARISON

Paragraph (A) is Canon 3E(1).

Paragraph (A)(1) is Canon 3E(1)(a).

† The "Reporters' Explanations of Changes" have not been approved by the ABA Joint Commission to Evaluate the Model Code of Judicial Conduct. They have been drafted by the Commission's Reporters, based on the proceedings and record of the Commission, solely to inform the ABA House of Delegates about each of the proposed amendments to the

Paragraph (A)(2) is Canon 3E(1)(d).

Paragraph (A)(2)(a) is Canon 3E(1)(d)(i).

Paragraph (A)(2)(b) is Canon 3E(1)(d)(ii).

Paragraph (A)(2)(c) is Canon 3E(1)(d)(iii).

Paragraph (A)(2)(d) is Canon 3E(1)(d)(iv).

Paragraph (A)(3) is Canon 3E(1)(c).

Paragraph (A)(4) is Canon 3E(1)(e).

Paragraph (A)(5) combines Canons 3E(1)(f), 3E(1)(f)(i), and 3E(1)(f)(ii).

Paragraph (A)(6) is the first two words of Canon 3E(1)(b).

Paragraph (A)(6)(a) is the remainder of the first half of Canon 3E(1)(b).

Paragraph (A)(6)(b) is the Commentary to Canon 3E(1)(b).

Paragraph (A)(6)(c) is the second half of Canon 3E(1)(b).

Paragraph (A)(6)(d) is new.

Paragraph (B) is Canon 3E(2).

Paragraph (C) is Canon 3F.

Comment [1] is the first paragraph of Commentary to Canon 3E(1).

Comment [2] is new.

Comment [3] is the third paragraph of Commentary to Canon 3E(1).

Comment [4] is the Commentary to Canon 3E(1)(f).

Comment [5] is the second paragraph of Commentary to Cannon 3E(1).

Comment [6] is new.

The Commentary to Canon 3F was deleted, as being largely redundant of the black letter and otherwise administrative, rather than ethical, in its recommendations.

EXPLANATION OF BLACK LETTER

Most changes to this Rule and its accompanying Comment are stylistic and structural rather than substantive. Only substantive changes are addressed below.

1. <u>Paragraphs (A)(2), (A)(3), and (B): Addition of "domestic partner"</u>

"Domestic partner" was added to treat domestic partners comparably to spouses for purposes of evaluating economic conflicts.

2. <u>Paragraph (A)(2)(a): Addition of "general partner, managing member"</u>

These additions were made to ensure completeness of the list.

3. In Paragraph (A)(2)(d), "to the judge's knowledge", which is included in former Canon 3E (1) (d) (iv), was deleted as unnecessary.

4. <u>Paragraph (A)(6)(b): New paragraph on government lawyers</u>

Paragraph (A)(6)(b) makes explicit in the black letter what former Canon 3E(1)(b) stated only in Commentary. Judges must not sit on cases concerning matters with which they were involved as government lawyers, for the same reason that they must not sit on cases concerning matters in which they were involved as lawyers, and the Rule has been revised to so state.

Model Code prior to their being considered at the ABA 2007 Midyear Meeting. THEY ARE NOT TO BE ADOPTED AS PART OF THE MODEL CODE.

5. Paragraph A(6)(d): New paragraph on judges sitting on cases they previously heard:

Trial judges sometimes sit by designation on courts of appeal, and vice versa. Such judges should not hear cases over which they presided in a different court, and this Rule makes that clear. This Rule, however, leaves unaffected the propriety of a judge who decided a case on a panel of an appellate court participating in the rehearing of the case en banc with that same court.

EXPLANATION OF COMMENTS

[2] New Comment [2] was added to clarify that the disqualification rules apply regardless of whether a motion to disqualify has been filed. The terms "recusal" and "disqualification" have been defined in different and sometimes inconsistent ways to apply where judges act on their own initiative or pursuant to a motion by a party. This Comment is intended to render such distinctions irrelevant here.

[6] New Comment [6] was added to elaborate on the meaning of "economic interest." Although the term is separately defined in the Terminology section, it is important enough to bear recapitulation here.

RULE 2.12 Supervisory Duties

(A) A judge shall require court staff, court officials, and others subject to the judge's direction and control to act in a manner consistent with the judge's obligations under this Code.

(B) A judge with supervisory authority for the performance of other judges shall take reasonable measures to ensure that those judges properly discharge their judicial responsibilities, including the prompt disposition of matters before them.

Comment

[1] A judge is responsible for his or her own conduct and for the conduct of others, such as staff, when those persons are acting at the judge's direction or control. A judge may not direct court personnel to engage in conduct on the judge's behalf or as the judge's representative when such conduct would violate the Code if undertaken by the judge.

[2] Public confidence in the judicial system depends upon timely justice. To promote the efficient administration of justice, a judge with supervisory authority must take the steps needed to ensure that judges under his or her supervision administer their workloads promptly.

RULE 2.12—REPORTER'S EXPLANATION OF CHANGES†

1990 MODEL CODE COMPARISON

The Rule is Canon 3C(2) and (3).

Comments [1] and [2] are new.

EXPLANATION OF BLACK LETTER

1. Canons 3C(2) and (3) combined

Canons 3C(2) and (3) were combined under a general rubric, "Supervisory Duties."

---

† The "Reporters' Explanations of Changes" have not been approved by the ABA Joint Commission to Evaluate the Model Code of Judicial Conduct. They have been drafted by the Commission's Reporters, based on the proceedings and record of the Commission, solely to inform the ABA House of Delegates about each of the proposed amendments to the Model Code prior to their being considered at the ABA 2007 Midyear Meeting. THEY ARE NOT TO BE ADOPTED AS PART OF THE MODEL CODE.

2. Revision to Court staff standards

Rule 2.12(A) was reworded to reflect a more comprehensive understanding of the standards of conduct required of court personnel. Judges must insist that court staff and officials act in a manner consistent with all of a judge's obligations under the Code and not simply those previously enumerated in Canon 3C(2) relating to diligence, fidelity, and lack of bias or prejudice.

3. Proper discharge of judicial responsibilities of subordinate judges

The Commission reordered the provision to emphasize the importance of the obligation of the supervisory judge to ensure the prompt discharge of judicial responsibilities over all matters.

EXPLANATION OF COMMENTS

[1] New Comment [1] was added to emphasize the critical position judicial staff occupy in the justice system—not only in terms of their relevance to the administration of justice but also in terms of their role in preserving public confidence in the system as a whole. The Comment explains the black letter to underscore that a judge must never direct staff within his or her control to engage in conduct that would violate the Code if undertaken by the judge.

[2] New Comment [2] was added to underscore that public confidence in the courts depends on judges with supervisory authority taking the steps needed to ensure that judges under their supervision administer their workloads both properly and expeditiously.

RULE 2.13 Administrative Appointments

(A) In making administrative appointments, a judge:

(1) shall exercise the power of appointment impartially* and on the basis of merit; and

(2) shall avoid nepotism, favoritism, and unnecessary appointments.

(B) A judge shall not appoint a lawyer to a position if the judge either knows* that the lawyer, or the lawyer's spouse or domestic partner,* has contributed more than $[insert amount] within the prior [insert number] year[s] to the judge's election campaign, or learns of such a contribution* by means of a timely motion by a party or other person properly interested in the matter, unless:

(1) the position is substantially uncompensated;

(2) the lawyer has been selected in rotation from a list of qualified and available lawyers compiled without regard to their having made political contributions; or

(3) the judge or another presiding or administrative judge affirmatively finds that no other lawyer is willing, competent, and able to accept the position.

(C) A judge shall not approve compensation of appointees beyond the fair value of services rendered.

Comment

[1] Appointees of a judge include assigned counsel, officials such as referees, commissioners, special masters, receivers, and guardians, and personnel such as clerks, secretaries, and bailiffs. Consent by the parties to an appointment or an award of compensation does not relieve the judge of the obligation prescribed by paragraph (A).

[2] Unless otherwise defined by law, nepotism is the appointment or hiring of any relative within the third degree of relationship of either the judge or the judge's spouse or domestic partner, or the spouse or domestic partner of such relative.

[3] The rule against making administrative appointments of lawyers who have contributed in excess of a specified dollar amount to a judge's election campaign includes an exception for positions that are substantially uncompensated, such as those for which the lawyer's compensation is limited to reimbursement for out-of-pocket expenses.

RULE 2.13—REPORTER'S EXPLANATION OF CHANGES†

1990 MODEL CODE COMPARISON

Paragraph (A) is taken from Canon 3C(4).

Paragraph (B) is taken from Canon 3C(5).

Paragraph (B)(1) is Canon 3C(5)(a).

Paragraph (B)(2) is Canon 3C(5)(b).

Paragraph (B)(3) is Canon 3C(5)(c).

Paragraph (C) is Canon 3C(4).

Comment [1] is the Commentary to Canon 3C.

Comments [2] and [3] are new.

EXPLANATION OF BLACK LETTER

1. <u>Paragraph (A): Movement of "unnecessary appointments"</u>

The first sentence of former Canon 3C(4) was folded into the Rule for largely stylistic reasons not intended to change substantive meaning.

2. <u>Paragraph (B): Addition of "spouse or domestic partner"</u>

The proscription against the appointment of a lawyer who has contributed a defined amount to the judge's election campaign is extended to the spouse or domestic partner of the lawyer.

EXPLANATION OF COMMENTS

[2] The black letter directs judges to avoid nepotism, and new Comment [2] was added simply to add clarity to the meaning of nepotism with a conventional definition.

[3] The black letter prohibits a judge from awarding appointments to contributors who have given more than a specified amount to the judge's election campaign but creates an exception for "substantially uncompensated" positions. This new Comment clarifies the meaning of "substantially uncompensated" to reach positions in which the appointee is merely reimbursed for out-of-pocket expenses.

RULE 2.14 Disability and Impairment

A judge having a reasonable belief that the performance of a lawyer or another judge is impaired by drugs or alcohol, or by a mental, emotional, or physical condition, shall take appropriate action, which may include a confidential referral to a lawyer or judicial assistance program.

† The "Reporters' Explanations of Changes" have not been approved by the ABA Joint Commission to Evaluate the Model Code of Judicial Conduct. They have been drafted by the Commission's Reporters, based on the proceedings and record of the Commission, solely to inform the ABA House of Delegates about each of the proposed amendments to the Model Code prior to their being considered at the ABA 2007 Midyear Meeting. THEY ARE NOT TO BE ADOPTED AS PART OF THE MODEL CODE.

Comment

[1] "Appropriate action" means action intended and reasonably likely to help the judge or lawyer in question address the problem and prevent harm to the justice system. Depending upon the circumstances, appropriate action may include but is not limited to speaking directly to the impaired person, notifying an individual with supervisory responsibility over the impaired person, or making a referral to an assistance program.

[2] Taking or initiating corrective action by way of referral to an assistance program may satisfy a judge's responsibility under this Rule. Assistance programs have many approaches for offering help to impaired judges and lawyers, such as intervention, counseling, or referral to appropriate health care professionals. Depending upon the gravity of the conduct that has come to the judge's attention, however, the judge may be required to take other action, such as reporting the impaired judge or lawyer to the appropriate authority, agency, or body. See Rule 2.15.

RULE 2.14—REPORTER'S EXPLANATION OF CHANGES†

1990 MODEL CODE COMPARISON

The Rule and Comment are new.

EXPLANATION OF BLACK LETTER

Creation of new Rule on impairment

This is a new Rule, governing a difficult and extremely important issue. Impairment can undermine judicial competence, diligence, and demeanor specifically, and public confidence in the courts generally. The Rule imposes a mandatory obligation to take appropriate action when a judge learns of a colleague's impairment. The objective of this provision is to guide and encourage judges to address impairment problems when they arise.

EXPLANATION OF COMMENTS

[1] This Comment was added to define "appropriate action." There was some concern that disagreement could arise over whether a particular action taken in response to knowledge of impairment was sufficient. This Comment takes a functional approach, by asking whether the action taken would be reasonably likely to rectify the problem.

[2] The Commission was alert to the need for sensitivity when dealing with impairment problems and was careful not to prescribe specific action in response to specific evidence of impairment. Often, referral to a lawyer or judicial assistance referral program may be the most appropriate course, but the Commission recognized that different circumstances may warrant different responses.

RULE 2.15 Responding to Judicial and Lawyer Misconduct

(A) A judge having knowledge* that another judge has committed a violation of this Code that raises a substantial question regarding the judge's honesty, trustworthiness, or fitness as a judge in other respects shall inform the appropriate authority.*

(B) A judge having knowledge that a lawyer has committed a violation of the Rules of Professional Conduct that raises a substantial question regarding the lawyer's

† "Reporters' Explanations of Changes" have not been approved by the ABA Joint Commission to Evaluate the Model Code of Judicial Conduct. They have been drafted by the Commission's Reporters, based on the proceedings and record of the Commission, solely to inform the ABA House of Delegates about each of the proposed amendments to the Model Code prior to their being considered at the ABA 2007 Midyear Meeting. THEY ARE NOT TO BE ADOPTED AS PART OF THE MODEL CODE.

honesty, trustworthiness, or fitness as a lawyer in other respects shall inform the appropriate authority.

(C) A judge who receives information indicating a substantial likelihood that another judge has committed a violation of this Code shall take appropriate action.

(D) A judge who receives information indicating a substantial likelihood that a lawyer has committed a violation of the Rules of Professional Conduct shall take appropriate action.

Comment

[1] Taking action to address known misconduct is a judge's obligation. Paragraphs (A) and (B) impose an obligation on the judge to report to the appropriate disciplinary authority the known misconduct of another judge or a lawyer that raises a substantial question regarding the honesty, trustworthiness, or fitness of that judge or lawyer. Ignoring or denying known misconduct among one's judicial colleagues or members of the legal profession undermines a judge's responsibility to participate in efforts to ensure public respect for the justice system. This Rule limits the reporting obligation to those offenses that an independent judiciary must vigorously endeavor to prevent.

[2] A judge who does not have actual knowledge that another judge or a lawyer may have committed misconduct, but receives information indicating a substantial likelihood of such misconduct, is required to take appropriate action under paragraphs (C) and (D). Appropriate action may include, but is not limited to, communicating directly with the judge who may have violated this Code, communicating with a supervising judge, or reporting the suspected violation to the appropriate authority or other agency or body. Similarly, actions to be taken in response to information indicating that a lawyer has committed a violation of the Rules of Professional Conduct may include but are not limited to communicating directly with the lawyer who may have committed the violation, or reporting the suspected violation to the appropriate authority or other agency or body.

RULE 2.15—REPORTER'S EXPLANATION OF CHANGES†

1990 MODEL CODE COMPARISON

Paragraph (A) is the second sentence of Canon 3D(1).

Paragraph (B) is the second sentence of Canon 3D(2).

Paragraph (C) is the first sentence of Canon 3D(1).

Paragraph (D) is the first sentence of Canon 3D(2).

Comment [1] is new.

Most of Comment [2] is new. The second sentence of the Comment is the Commentary to Canon 3D.

Canon 3D(3) was deleted.

EXPLANATION OF BLACK LETTER

Rules regulating the response to lawyer and judicial misconduct were consolidated to reflect closely related concepts.

1. Paragraph (A): Change to parallel Rule 8.3

The Rule was reworded to parallel the lawyer reporting obligations in Rule 8.3 of the Model Rules of Professional Conduct to require reporting to the "appropriate authority" whenever the judge has knowledge

† The "Reporters' Explanations of Changes" have not been approved by the ABA Joint Commission to Evaluate the Model Code of Judicial Conduct. They have been drafted by the Commission's Reporters, based on the proceedings and record of the Commission, solely to inform the ABA House of Delegates about each of the proposed amendments to the Model Code prior to their being considered at the ABA 2007 Midyear Meeting. THEY ARE NOT TO BE ADOPTED AS PART OF THE MODEL CODE.

of another judge's violation of the Code that raises a substantial question as to the judge's "honesty, trustworthiness, or fitness as a judge in other respects."

2. Paragraphs (B) and (D): Language changes

Changes were made to parallel the obligations by judges to address the misconduct of lawyers.

3. Paragraph (C): Change in duty

Former Canon 3(D)(1) was revised to state that when a judge receives information indicating a substantial likelihood that another judge has violated the Rules, the judge receiving such information shall—no longer should—take "appropriate action." In the Commission's view, in situations where the judge does not "know" but receives information making it substantially likely that another judge has violated the Rules, the judge receiving such information shall take action. The appropriate action would vary with the circumstances. In some instances, it could involve talking to the judge in question or in other instances, taking steps to verify the information received and report it to the appropriate authorities.

4. Deletion of Canon 3D(3)

Former Canon 3D(3) declared that the acts of a judge in the discharge of disciplinary responsibilities were absolutely privileged. Although there was no opposition to the concept that judges should be immune from suit in such situations, the Commission concluded that such a provision was inappropriate for the Model Code of Judicial Conduct. Neither the ABA nor an adopting court is in a position to grant or deny judicial immunity in the context of judicial conduct standards. Accordingly, Canon 3D(3) was viewed as a generalized statement of support for judicial immunity, which, in the Commission's view, was not appropriate for the Code.

EXPLANATION OF COMMENTS

[1] Language was added to underscore the relationship between reporting serious misconduct of judges and lawyers and the judge's responsibility to preserve public confidence in the courts.

[2] Commentary concerning "appropriate action" in response to judicial and lawyer misconduct is consistent with the Commentary in former Canon 3D.

RULE 2.16 Cooperation With Disciplinary Authorities

(A) A judge shall cooperate and be candid and honest with judicial and lawyer disciplinary agencies.

(B) A judge shall not retaliate, directly or indirectly, against a person known* or suspected to have assisted or cooperated with an investigation of a judge or a lawyer.

Comment

[1] Cooperation with investigations and proceedings of judicial and lawyer discipline agencies, as required in paragraph (A), instills confidence in judges' commitment to the integrity of the judicial system and the protection of the public.

RULE 2.16—REPORTER'S EXPLANATION OF CHANGES†

1990 MODEL CODE COMPARISON

The Rule and its Comments are new.

† The "Reporters' Explanations of Changes" have not been approved by the ABA Joint Commission to Evaluate the Model Code of Judicial Conduct. They have been drafted by the Commission's Reporters, based on the proceedings and record of the Commission, solely to inform the ABA House of Delegates about each of the proposed amendments to the

EXPLANATION OF BLACK LETTER

Creation of new Rule

Several witnesses noted that disciplinary authorities often struggle to gain the cooperation of targeted judges in disciplinary matters and the cooperation of judges in lawyer disciplinary proceedings. In the Commission's view, the need for a judge's cooperation in the disciplinary process is paramount. Moreover, for a judge to retaliate against a person for cooperating in disciplinary proceedings against him or her would be patently unethical. This Rule thus serves to address an important omission in the former Code.

CANON 3

A JUDGE SHALL CONDUCT THE JUDGE'S PERSONAL AND EXTRAJUDICIAL ACTIVITIES TO MINIMIZE THE RISK OF CONFLICT WITH THE OBLIGATIONS OF JUDICIAL OFFICE.

CANON 3—REPORTER'S EXPLANATION OF CHANGES†

1990 MODEL CODE COMPARISON

This renumbered Canon 3 is drawn almost exclusively from Canon 4 of the 1990 Code. However, some material involving the "personal" activities of a judge has been repositioned to this Canon from Canon 2 of the 1990 Code.

EXPLANATION OF BLACK LETTER

1. Expanded the reach of this Canon to include "personal" as well as "extrajudicial" activities.

Some activities governed by this Canon, such as accepting gifts or participating in private clubs, are "extrajudicial" in the sense that they are not part of a judge's official duties, yet they are less formal and less public than participating in a seminar or accepting an award. Accordingly, the Commission added the word "personal" to the Canon title to make it more accurate and more complete.

2. Replaced "conflict with judicial obligations" with "conflict with the obligations of judicial office."

No significant substantive change is intended. The substituted phrase is used as a reminder that judges have a variety of duties—including administrative duties—that go with the judicial *office*.

RULE 3.1 Extrajudicial Activities in General

A judge may engage in extrajudicial activities, except as prohibited by law* or this Code. However, when engaging in extrajudicial activities, a judge shall not:

(A) participate in activities that will interfere with the proper performance of the judge's judicial duties;

(B) participate in activities that will lead to frequent disqualification of the judge;

Model Code prior to their being considered at the ABA 2007 Midyear Meeting. THEY ARE NOT TO BE ADOPTED AS PART OF THE MODEL CODE.

† The "Reporters' Explanations of Changes" have not been approved by the ABA Joint Commission to Evaluate the Model Code of Judicial Conduct. They have been drafted by the Commission's Reporters, based on the proceedings and record of the Commission, solely to inform the ABA House of Delegates about each of the proposed amendments to the Model Code prior to their being considered at the ABA 2007 Midyear Meeting. THEY ARE NOT TO BE ADOPTED AS PART OF THE MODEL CODE.

(C) participate in activities that would appear to a reasonable person to undermine the judge's independence,* integrity,* or impartiality;*

(D) engage in conduct that would appear to a reasonable person to be coercive; or

(E) make use of court premises, staff, stationery, equipment, or other resources, except for incidental use for activities that concern the law, the legal system, or the administration of justice, or unless such additional use is permitted by law.

Comment

[1] To the extent that time permits, and judicial independence and impartiality are not compromised, judges are encouraged to engage in appropriate extrajudicial activities. Judges are uniquely qualified to engage in extrajudicial activities that concern the law, the legal system, and the administration of justice, such as by speaking, writing, teaching, or participating in scholarly research projects. In addition, judges are permitted and encouraged to engage in educational, religious, charitable, fraternal or civic extrajudicial activities not conducted for profit, even when the activities do not involve the law. See Rule 3.7.

[2] Participation in both law-related and other extrajudicial activities helps integrate judges into their communities, and furthers public understanding of and respect for courts and the judicial system.

[3] Discriminatory actions and expressions of bias or prejudice by a judge, even outside the judge's official or judicial actions, are likely to appear to a reasonable person to call into question the judge's integrity and impartiality. Examples include jokes or other remarks that demean individuals based upon their race, sex, gender, religion, national origin, ethnicity, disability, age, sexual orientation, or socioeconomic status. For the same reason, a judge's extrajudicial activities must not be conducted in connection or affiliation with an organization that practices invidious discrimination. See Rule 3.6.

[4] While engaged in permitted extrajudicial activities, judges must not coerce others or take action that would reasonably be perceived as coercive. For example, depending upon the circumstances, a judge's solicitation of contributions or memberships for an organization, even as permitted by Rule 3.7(A), might create the risk that the person solicited would feel obligated to respond favorably, or would do so to curry favor with the judge.

RULE 3.1—REPORTER'S EXPLANATION OF CHANGES†

1990 MODEL CODE COMPARISON

To the extent that Rule 3.1 serves as a general list of restrictions upon a judge's participation in extrajudicial activities, it is chiefly derived from Canon 4A. However, the new set of restrictions is somewhat different, as it focuses attention more sharply upon interference with the independence, integrity, and impartiality of judges.

Rule 3.1(A) is essentially the same as Canon 4A(3).

Rule 3.1(B) is new, but is derived from Canon 4A(3), but contains more specific content. See Rule 3.1(A).

Rule 3.1(C) is based upon Canon 4A(1), but with expanded coverage and revised language.

Rule 3.1(D) is new.

Rule 3.1(E) is new, but has some overlap with aspects of Canon 2B ("lend the prestige of judicial office to advance the private interests of the judge or others").

Comment [1] is derived from the first paragraph of the Commentary following Canon 4B, although the subject matter of Canon 4B, Avocational Activities, is not addressed separately.

---

† The "Reporters' Explanations of Changes" have not been approved by the ABA Joint Commission to Evaluate the Model Code of Judicial Conduct. They have been drafted by the Commission's Reporters, based on the proceedings and record of the Commission, solely to inform the ABA House of Delegates about each of the proposed amendments to the Model Code prior to their being considered at the ABA 2007 Midyear Meeting. THEY ARE NOT TO BE ADOPTED AS PART OF THE MODEL CODE.

Comment [2] is based upon the first paragraph of the Commentary following Canon 4A.

Comment [3] is the second paragraph of the Commentary to 4A.

Comment [4] is new.

EXPLANATION OF BLACK LETTER

1. Rule 3.1, lead-in is restructured to permit extrajudicial activities generally, but subject to the listed prohibitions.

The restrictions set forth in Rule 3.1 are generally applicable to all of Canon 3, and are frequently cross-referenced in other Rules within Canon 3.

2. Rule 3.1(A) added the italicized words in "interfere with the proper performance of *the judge's* judicial duties."

3. Rule 3.1(B) is newly added as a specific instance of the prohibition contained in Rule 3.1(A).

One way to interfere with the proper performance of judicial duties is to become involved in extrajudicial activities that will lead to frequent disqualification.

No substantive change is intended.

4. Rule 3.1(C) substituted the phrase "would appear to a reasonable person to undermine" for "cast reasonable doubt on," and broadened coverage from "act impartially" to "the judge's independence, integrity, or impartiality."

The Commission decided that the words "cast reasonable doubt on" are too closely associated with the criminal law, and did not accurately express the proper level of certainty required. The substitute wording makes the standard turn upon the thought processes of a "reasonable person," which is a familiar standard in the law generally and also suggestive of the "might reasonably be questioned" language of 28 U.S.C. § 455. Concern with impairment of a judge's independence, integrity, and impartiality, rather than impartiality alone, is a theme that is prevalent in the Rules.

5. Rule 3.1(D) added a new provision to guard against overt or subtle efforts by a judge to coerce others into participating in extrajudicial activities favored by the judge.

The Commission heard testimony suggesting that coercion of this kind can be a significant problem in small communities with only one judge or a small number of judges, and a small number of lawyers who need to maintain good relations with the judiciary.

6. Rule 3.1(E) added a new prohibition against using court facilities and other resources for a judge's extrajudicial activities, but with an exception for incidental use in connection with a law-related event.

The rationale for the general restriction is that favoring a particular charity or other extrajudicial event by providing access to facilities that are closed to others is an abuse of the prestige of judicial office; see Rule 1.3. The rationale for the exception, however, is that certain activities, such as opening a real courtroom for use in a moot court competition or using a court's conference room for a meeting of a bar association task force that includes the judge, are not abuses of judicial office.

EXPLANATION OF COMMENTS

[1] This Comment was reworded to confirm the special role that judges can play in engaging in extrajudicial activities that involve the law, the legal system, and the administration of justice, but also to approve participation in activities that are *not* law-related, as long as they are undertaken in connection with not-for-profit organizations.

In both instances, the sense of the Comment is to be somewhat more encouraging than was the 1990 Code, so that judges will reach out to the communities of which they are a part, and avoid isolating themselves.

Specific examples in the 1990 Code, both in black letter (avocational activities such as speaking and writing) and in the Commentary (improving criminal and juvenile justice and expressing opposition to the persecution of lawyers and judges in other countries), were removed as unnecessarily restrictive or of insufficiently general application.

[2] This Comment focuses on the positive value of judges being integrated into the activity of the community. The first paragraph of Comment to Canon 4A had addressed that notion implicitly, but spoke in terms of judges not becoming isolated from the communities in which they live.

No substantive change is intended.

[3] This Comment is modified from the second paragraph of the Commentary following Canon 4A.

The cross-reference to Section 2C in the 1990 Code was to the provision on discriminatory organizations, although the Commentary did not make that sufficiently clear. The provision regarding discriminatory organizations has been repositioned to Canon 3; accordingly, the cross-reference is to Rule 3.6.

[4] New Comment [4] fleshes out the intention of Rule 3.1(D), which is also new.

RULE 3.2 Appearances Before Governmental Bodies and Consultation With Government Officials

A judge shall not appear voluntarily at a public hearing before, or otherwise consult with, an executive or a legislative body or official, except:

(A) in connection with matters concerning the law, the legal system, or the administration of justice;

(B) in connection with matters about which the judge acquired knowledge or expertise in the course of the judge's judicial duties; or

(C) when the judge is acting pro se in a matter involving the judge's legal or economic interests, or when the judge is acting in a fiduciary* capacity.

Comment

[1] Judges possess special expertise in matters of law, the legal system, and the administration of justice, and may properly share that expertise with governmental bodies and executive or legislative branch officials.

[2] In appearing before governmental bodies or consulting with government officials, judges must be mindful that they remain subject to other provisions of this Code, such as Rule 1.3, prohibiting judges from using the prestige of office to advance their own or others' interests, Rule 2.10, governing public comment on pending and impending matters, and Rule 3.1(C), prohibiting judges from engaging in extrajudicial activities that would appear to a reasonable person to undermine the judge's independence, integrity, or impartiality.

[3] In general, it would be an unnecessary and unfair burden to prohibit judges from appearing before governmental bodies or consulting with government officials on matters that are likely to affect them as private citizens, such as zoning proposals affecting their real property. In engaging in such activities, however, judges must not refer to their judicial positions, and must otherwise exercise caution to avoid using the prestige of judicial office.

RULE 3.2—REPORTER'S EXPLANATION OF CHANGES†

1990 MODEL CODE COMPARISON

Rule 3.2 is derived from Canon 4C(1). Minor revisions and additions have been made.

Rule 3.2(A) is essentially the same as the middle clause of Canon 4C(1).

† The "Reporters' Explanations of Changes" have not been approved by the ABA Joint Commission to Evaluate the Model Code of Judicial Conduct. They have been drafted by the Commission's Reporters, based on the proceedings and record of the Commission, solely to inform the ABA House of Delegates about each of the proposed amendments to the

Rule 3.2(B) is new.

Rule 3.2(C) is essentially the same as the last clause of Canon 4C(1), but with some minor modifications.

All the Comments are new; Canon 4C(1) had no substantive Commentary.

EXPLANATION OF BLACK LETTER

1. Rule 3.2 lead-in: added the word "voluntarily."

This was a minor but necessary addition, to make clear that judges who are formally summoned to appear before various governmental bodies may not refuse to appear on the ground that it would be "unethical" to do so.

2. Rule 3.2(A): no substantive change is intended.

3. Rule 3.2(B): a new paragraph.

This provision was added to reflect the growing recognition that in the course of carrying out their judicial duties, judges often gain expertise and special insight into legal and social problems and matters of public policy. The point of this provision is to establish that judges are permitted to share this information with other governmental bodies and officials.

4. Rule 3.2(C): modified existing language.

Rule 3.2(C) substituted "the judge's legal or economic interests" for "the judge's interests," and extended the exception to situations in which a judge is "acting in a fiduciary capacity."

EXPLANATION OF COMMENTS

[1] New Comment [1] simply explains the rationale of Rule 3.2(A) and, implicitly, of Rule 3.2(B).

[2] New Comment [2] serves as a reminder that even when it is permissible under Rules 3.2(A) or 3.2(B) for a judge voluntarily to consult with other governmental branch personnel, the judge remains subject to other restrictions of this Code, some of which are given as examples.

[3] New Comment [3] more narrowly describes the types of interests judges may address in their appearances before or consultations with government bodies. Under the original language, the Commission believed a judge might act pro se in connection with any political or social matter that "interested" the judge, which would allow the exception to swallow the rule. Without resorting to legalistic definitions of legally protected interests sufficient to justify formal intervention, the Comment distinguishes between matters that affect judges directly as private citizens and more general causes.

RULE 3.3 Testifying as a Character Witness

A judge shall not testify as a character witness in a judicial, administrative, or other adjudicatory proceeding or otherwise vouch for the character of a person in a legal proceeding, except when duly summoned.

Comment

[1] A judge who, without being subpoenaed, testifies as a character witness abuses the prestige of judicial office to advance the interests of another. See Rule 1.3. Except in unusual circumstances where the demands of justice require, a judge should discourage a party from requiring the judge to testify as a character witness.

Model Code prior to their being considered at the ABA 2007 Midyear Meeting. THEY ARE NOT TO BE ADOPTED AS PART OF THE MODEL CODE.

RULE 3.3—REPORTER'S EXPLANATION OF CHANGES†

1990 MODEL CODE COMPARISON

Rule 3.3 is derived from the last sentence of Canon 2B.

Comment [1] is based upon the last paragraph of the Commentary to Canon 2B.

EXPLANATION OF BLACK LETTER

1. Rule 3.3: substituted the phrase "except when duly summoned" for "testify voluntarily," and added the phrase "otherwise vouch for the character of a person in a legal proceeding." New language, specifying that the Rule applies in all forms of "adjudicatory proceedings," was also added.

Regarding the first revision, similar language ("properly summoned") appeared in the Commentary in the 1990 Code; thus, no substantive change was intended. The Commission added the language about "vouching" because testimony under oath is not the only mode in which judges might abuse the prestige of judicial office when the character of a person is in issue in a legal proceeding.

The remaining addition, "in a judicial, administrative, or other adjudicatory proceeding," is simply a reminder that Rule 3.3 is not limited to civil or criminal trials in courts, but applies whenever testimony is taken on a formal record.

EXPLANATION OF COMMENTS

[1] This Comment is the last sentence of the Commentary to Canon 2B.

Although the Rule permits testifying as a character witness upon receipt of a subpoena or other process, it has always been understood that judges should not encourage a party to issue a sham subpoena for what is in fact voluntary testimony. The Comment goes a step further and suggests that judges should actively discourage parties from compelling their testimony as character witnesses.

RULE 3.4 Appointments to Governmental Positions

A judge shall not accept appointment to a governmental committee, board, commission, or other governmental position, unless it is one that concerns the law, the legal system, or the administration of justice.

Comment

[1] Rule 3.4 implicitly acknowledges the value of judges accepting appointments to entities that concern the law, the legal system, or the administration of justice. Even in such instances, however, a judge should assess the appropriateness of accepting an appointment, paying particular attention to the subject matter of the appointment and the availability and allocation of judicial resources, including the judge's time commitments, and giving due regard to the requirements of the independence and impartiality of the judiciary.

[2] A judge may represent his or her country, state, or locality on ceremonial occasions or in connection with historical, educational, or cultural activities. Such representation does not constitute acceptance of a government position.

---

† The "Reporters' Explanations of Changes" have not been approved by the ABA Joint Commission to Evaluate the Model Code of Judicial Conduct. They have been drafted by the Commission's Reporters, based on the proceedings and record of the Commission, solely to inform the ABA House of Delegates about each of the proposed amendments to the Model Code prior to their being considered at the ABA 2007 Midyear Meeting. THEY ARE NOT TO BE ADOPTED AS PART OF THE MODEL CODE.

RULE 3.4—REPORTER'S EXPLANATION OF CHANGES†

1990 MODEL CODE COMPARISON

Rule 3.4 is derived from the first sentence of Canon 4C(2). It has been recast and simplified.

Comment [1] is based upon the first paragraph of the Commentary to Canon 4C(2), but again reworded and simplified. The second paragraph of the Commentary to Canon 4C(2) was deleted as unnecessary and somewhat confusing.

Comment [2] has been moved into the Comments from the last sentence of the black letter of Canon 4C(2).

EXPLANATION OF BLACK LETTER

1. Rule 3.4: add the word "board" to the list of governmental entities for completeness.

As has been done throughout the revised Code, "improvement in the law," has been changed to "concerns the law," because what constitutes an "improvement" is almost always debatable.

EXPLANATION OF COMMENTS

[1] The Commentary to Canon 4C(2) was modified by removing language that was merely repetitive of the black letter text, and by deleting as infelicitous the reference to the need to "protect" the courts from controversy.

Comment [1] as revised more clearly reflects the point that service on governmental bodies should not be allowed to distract judges from their judicial duties or otherwise compromise their independence, impartiality, or integrity.

[2] New Comment [2] was moved from the black letter text of Canon 4C(2) of the 1990 Code.

In the Commission's view, the provision was of insufficiently general applicability to warrant treatment in the text.

RULE 3.5 Use of Nonpublic Information

A judge shall not intentionally disclose or use nonpublic information* acquired in a judicial capacity for any purpose unrelated to the judge's judicial duties.

Comment

[1] In the course of performing judicial duties, a judge may acquire information of commercial or other value that is unavailable to the public. The judge must not reveal or use such information for personal gain or for any purpose unrelated to his or her judicial duties.

[2] This rule is not intended, however, to affect a judge's ability to act on information as necessary to protect the health or safety of the judge or a member of a judge's family, court personnel, or other judicial officers if consistent with other provisions of this Code.

---

† The "Reporters' Explanations of Changes" have not been approved by the ABA Joint Commission to Evaluate the Model Code of Judicial Conduct. They have been drafted by the Commission's Reporters, based on the proceedings and record of the Commission, solely to inform the ABA House of Delegates about each of the proposed amendments to the Model Code prior to their being considered at the ABA 2007 Midyear Meeting. THEY ARE NOT TO BE ADOPTED AS PART OF THE MODEL CODE.

RULE 3.5—REPORTER'S EXPLANATION OF CHANGES†

1990 MODEL CODE COMPARISON

Rule 3.5 is based upon Canon 3B(12), with minor revisions, including addition of the word "intentionally" in the first line of the black letter text.

Comments [1] and [2] are new.

EXPLANATION OF BLACK LETTER

1. Rule 3.5 includes element of "intentional" conduct:

In the 1990 Code, this provision, Canon 3B(12) was found in the Canon on the performance of *judicial* duties. It was repositioned to Canon 3 on personal and extrajudicial activity, because it is a form of misuse of judicial office for personal gain or advantage. The word "intentionally" was added so as not to impose discipline for mere carelessness.

EXPLANATION OF COMMENTS

[1] New Comment [1] provides a link between using nonpublic information for personal advantage and abuse of judicial office.

[2] New Comment [2] recognizes the unfortunate reality that physical violence has become more common than formerly in and around the courts. If a judge learns of nonpublic information that constitutes a credible threat of violence against court personnel or family members, this Comment contemplates that the judge may take protective measures on the basis of that information.

RULE 3.6 Affiliation With Discriminatory Organizations

(A) A judge shall not hold membership in any organization that practices invidious discrimination on the basis of race, sex, gender, religion, national origin, ethnicity, or sexual orientation.

(B) A judge shall not use the benefits or facilities of an organization if the judge knows* or should know that the organization practices invidious discrimination on one or more of the bases identified in paragraph (A). A judge's attendance at an event in a facility of an organization that the judge is not permitted to join is not a violation of this Rule when the judge's attendance is an isolated event that could not reasonably be perceived as an endorsement of the organization's practices.

Comment

[1] A judge's public manifestation of approval of invidious discrimination on any basis gives rise to the appearance of impropriety and diminishes public confidence in the integrity and impartiality of the judiciary. A judge's membership in an organization that practices invidious discrimination creates the perception that the judge's impartiality is impaired.

[2] An organization is generally said to discriminate invidiously if it arbitrarily excludes from membership on the basis of race, sex, gender, religion, national origin, ethnicity, or sexual orientation persons who would otherwise be eligible for admission. Whether an organization practices invidious discrimination is a complex question to which judges should be attentive. The answer cannot be determined from a mere examination of an organization's current membership rolls, but rather, depends upon how the organization selects members, as well as other relevant factors, such as whether the organization is dedicated to the preservation of religious, ethnic, or cultural values of legitimate common interest to its members, or whether it is an

† The "Reporters' Explanations of Changes" have not been approved by the ABA Joint Commission to Evaluate the Model Code of Judicial Conduct. They have been drafted by the Commission's Reporters, based on the proceedings and record of the Commission, solely to inform the ABA House of Delegates about each of the proposed amendments to the Model Code prior to their being considered at the ABA 2007 Midyear Meeting. THEY ARE NOT TO BE ADOPTED AS PART OF THE MODEL CODE.

intimate, purely private organization whose membership limitations could not constitutionally be prohibited.

[3] When a judge learns that an organization to which the judge belongs engages in invidious discrimination, the judge must resign immediately from the organization.

[4] A judge's membership in a religious organization as a lawful exercise of the freedom of religion is not a violation of this Rule.

[5] This Rule does not apply to national or state military service.

RULE 3.6—REPORTER'S EXPLANATION OF CHANGES†

1990 MODEL CODE COMPARISON

Rule 3.6 is based upon Canon 2C of the 1990 Code and its extensive Commentary. The Commentary was revised substantially, including some substantive changes. Some aspects of the Commentary in the 1990 Code were reworked and moved to the black letter text of Rule 3.6(B).

EXPLANATION OF BLACK LETTER

1. Rule 3.6(A) text is similar to Canon 2C of the 1990 Code.

It does expand the list of prohibited bases of invidious discrimination by adding gender, ethnicity, and sexual orientation.

2. Rule 3.6(B) derives chiefly from the last paragraph of the Commentary to Canon 2C of the 1990 Code, revised to change its focus, and then moved to the black letter text because of its practical importance.

The former Commentary permitted a judge who was already a member of an organization that engaged in invidious discrimination to remain a member for up to one year, if during that year the judge took steps to change the organization's policy. Rule 3.6(B) instead focuses upon the extent to which the judge actually *uses* the benefits or facilities provided by the organization. Building upon ideas found earlier in the Commentary to Canon 2C, the new Rule effectively provides that a judge cannot be the *initiating party* in scheduling an event or taking advantage of the facilities, but is permitted to attend an isolated event that has been scheduled or arranged by someone else, as long as it is clear that merely attending cannot reasonably be seen as an endorsement of the organization and its policies. A hypothetical that informed the Commission's deliberations concerned a wedding reception held at a discriminatory club that the judge could not join according to Rule 3.6(A): the judge could not schedule his or her *own* child's reception at the club, but could attend the reception of a friend or relative's child.

Because Rule 3.6(B) does not allow any active engagement with an organization that practices invidious discrimination, the one-year "grace period" to try to effect change has been eliminated. The Commission concluded that any active involvement would constitute too much of an endorsement of the organization; even good-faith behind-the-scene activities would not sufficiently negate the public's perception of bias.

See Comment [3], which confirms that the lack of any black letter exception regarding membership means that a judge must resign immediately upon learning of the organization's practices.

EXPLANATION OF COMMENTS

[1] This Comment blends the first sentence of the Commentary to Canon 2C of the 1990 Code with language found in the long second paragraph of that Commentary. Revised in part for style and in part for more completeness, the new Comment stresses that support for invidious discrimination generally, and

---

† The "Reporters' Explanations of Changes" have not been approved by the ABA Joint Commission to Evaluate the Model Code of Judicial Conduct. They have been drafted by the Commission's Reporters, based on the proceedings and record of the Commission, solely to inform the ABA House of Delegates about each of the proposed amendments to the Model Code prior to their being considered at the ABA 2007 Midyear Meeting. THEY ARE NOT TO BE ADOPTED AS PART OF THE MODEL CODE.

especially through participation in organizations engaging in it, calls into question a judge's integrity and impartiality, and creates an appearance of impropriety.

[2] Based closely upon the first paragraph of the Commentary to Canon 2C, this Comment provides guidelines—but no hard-and-fast rules—to help determine when an organization engages in invidious discrimination, thus falling under the ban of Rule 3.6(A). The key test is a functional one: whether an excluded applicant (not possessing one of the listed characteristics) *would otherwise be eligible for admission to membership.* In addition, the Comment explains that certain organizations practicing some forms of discrimination cannot be said to be practicing *invidious* or *improper* discrimination, either because the discrimination is based upon rationales that are not socially harmful, or because the members of the organization have a constitutional right to associate without governmental interference.

Although the Commission received a large number of submissions arguing that a particular organization either did or did not practice invidious discrimination, it determined not to cast any judgments in stone. Policies of an organization might change over time, as might the constitutional standard for judging whether an organization is sufficiently "private" to be immune from governmental regulation of its membership policies.

[3] New Comment [3] replaces Commentary in the 1990 Code suggesting that as an alternative to resigning, a judge might instead remain with the organization for up to one year, while attempting to effect change from within. The Commission chose not to add such language to the text of Rule 3.6. Thus, Comment [3] requires immediate resignation to comply with Rule 3.6(A).

[4] The tenor of New Comment [4] was implicit in the Commentary to Canon 2C of the 1990 Code. Comment [4] makes clear that while many religious organizations engage in some forms of discrimination, and some religious organizations may engage in some invidious discrimination, participation by a judge in any bona fide religious organization cannot be prohibited or punished by governmental authorities because of the constitutional guarantee of the free exercise of religion.

[5] New Comment [5] was adopted by the Commission after receiving considerable commentary and after considerable debate. Like religious organizations, military organizations often engage in discrimination and sometimes engage in discrimination that would be found to be invidious in other contexts. The Commission concluded, however, that the practical difficulties involved in enforcing a ban on holding membership in military organizations, and the necessity for uniform rules across the military services, justified an interpretation that service in state and national military organizations does not violate this Rule.

RULE 3.7 Participation in Educational, Religious, Charitable, Fraternal, or Civic Organizations and Activities

(A) Subject to the requirements of Rule 3.1, a judge may participate in activities sponsored by organizations or governmental entities concerned with the law, the legal system, or the administration of justice, and those sponsored by or on behalf of educational, religious, charitable, fraternal, or civic organizations not conducted for profit, including but not limited to the following activities:

(1) assisting such an organization or entity in planning related to fund-raising, and participating in the management and investment of the organization's or entity's funds;

(2) soliciting* contributions* for such an organization or entity, but only from members of the judge's family,* or from judges over whom the judge does not exercise supervisory or appellate authority;

(3) soliciting membership for such an organization or entity, even though the membership dues or fees generated may be used to support the objectives of the organization or entity, but only if the organization or entity is concerned with the law, the legal system, or the administration of justice;

(4) appearing or speaking at, receiving an award or other recognition at, being featured on the program of, and permitting his or her title to be used in connection with an event of such an organization or entity, but if the event serves a fund-raising purpose, the judge may participate only if the event concerns the law, the legal system, or the administration of justice;

(5) making recommendations to such a public or private fund-granting organization or entity in connection with its programs and activities, but only if the organization or entity is concerned with the law, the legal system, or the administration of justice; and

(6) serving as an officer, director, trustee, or nonlegal advisor of such an organization or entity, unless it is likely that the organization or entity:

(a) will be engaged in proceedings that would ordinarily come before the judge; or

(b) will frequently be engaged in adversary proceedings in the court of which the judge is a member, or in any court subject to the appellate jurisdiction of the court of which the judge is a member.

(B) A judge may encourage lawyers to provide pro bono publico legal services.

Comment

[1] The activities permitted by paragraph (A) generally include those sponsored by or undertaken on behalf of public or private not-for-profit educational institutions, and other not-for-profit organizations, including law-related, charitable, and other organizations.

[2] Even for law-related organizations, a judge should consider whether the membership and purposes of the organization, or the nature of the judge's participation in or association with the organization, would conflict with the judge's obligation to refrain from activities that reflect adversely upon a judge's independence, integrity, and impartiality.

[3] Mere attendance at an event, whether or not the event serves a fund-raising purpose, does not constitute a violation of paragraph 4(A). It is also generally permissible for a judge to serve as an usher or a food server or preparer, or to perform similar functions, at fund-raising events sponsored by educational, religious, charitable, fraternal, or civic organizations. Such activities are not solicitation and do not present an element of coercion or abuse the prestige of judicial office.

[4] Identification of a judge's position in educational, religious, charitable, fraternal, or civic organizations on letterhead used for fund-raising or membership solicitation does not violate this Rule. The letterhead may list the judge's title or judicial office if comparable designations are used for other persons.

[5] In addition to appointing lawyers to serve as counsel for indigent parties in individual cases, a judge may promote broader access to justice by encouraging lawyers to participate in pro bono publico legal services, if in doing so the judge does not employ coercion, or abuse the prestige of judicial office. Such encouragement may take many forms, including providing lists of available programs, training lawyers to do pro bono publico legal work, and participating in events recognizing lawyers who have done pro bono publico work.

RULE 3.7—REPORTER'S EXPLANATION OF CHANGES†

1990 MODEL CODE COMPARISON

Rule 3.7(A) and its Comments are based upon Canon 4C(3) and its subparagraphs and their Commentary. The 1990 Code has been thoroughly reorganized in the proposed Code, making line-by-line comparison

† "Reporters' Explanations of Changes" have not been approved by the ABA Joint Commission to Evaluate the Model Code of Judicial Conduct. They have been drafted by the Commission's Reporters, based on the proceedings and

difficult. Virtually all the concepts in Canon 4C(3) have been retained, although some have been made more expansive or more restrictive.

The specific reference in Rule 3.7(B) to pro bono publico legal services is new.

EXPLANATION OF BLACK LETTER

1. Rule 3.7(A) was expanded.

The lead-in to Paragraph (A) added "[s]ubject to the requirements of Rule 3.1," and included law-related public and private organizations and entities, as well as most nonprofit organizations, even if not law-related, within the reach of this paragraph; eliminated specific reference to service as an officer, director, or nonlegal advisor, and placed discussion of those specific situations in the subparagraphs.

This provision is integral to the reorganization of the material on participation in extrajudicial activities, and of Canon 3 generally. Canon 4C(3) of the 1990 Code referred at the outset to service as an officer or a director of various not-for-profit organizations, and then used several subparagraphs to deal with activities in which such officers or directors engaged. The lead-in to Rule 3.7(A) establishes its coverage of essentially the same organizations—public and private, law related and not law related—but then deals in the following subparagraphs with *all* activities related to those organizations, *including* service as an officer or a director.

The opening phrase, "[s]ubject to the requirements of Rule 3.1," is not greatly different in meaning from "subject to the other requirements of this Code," which appeared at the end of Canon 4C(3). Organizationally, however, the specific cross-reference in the proposed Code focuses attention upon particular problems closely associated with extrajudicial and personal activities—such as coercion, undue influence, or interference with the primacy of judicial duties—which is why they were gathered together in a single Rule at the beginning of Canon 3.

2. Rule 3.7(A)(1): repositioned, but substantially the same as the first clause of Canon 4C(3)(b)(i) of the 1990 Code.

The difference, however, as explained above in connection with the lead-in to Rule 3.7(A), is that the 1990 Code allowed these activities (assistance in planning fund-raising and management and investment of an organization's funds) *only* in connection with service as an officer, director, trustee, or nonlegal advisor, or the somewhat nebulous "as a member or otherwise." In the proposed Code, these activities are permissible without more, if participation in the activities of the organization or entity itself is permissible.

3. Rule 3.7(A)(2): substantially the same as the second clause of Canon 4C(3)(b)(i), except added soliciting funds from family members as permissible activity.

The repositioning of this provision into one of the subparagraphs of Rule 3.7(A) has the same significance as described above: it will apply to all judges who engage in this form of extrajudicial activity, not just those who serve as officers, directors, and the like. Judges were already permitted by the 1990 Code to solicit contributions for charities from judges over whom they did not exercise supervisory or appellate authority, because the element of coercion is largely missing, and there is little likelihood that the judge making the contribution would be perceived as attempting to influence the judge making the solicitation. The same rationales support extending permission to judges to solicit this kind of contribution from their own family members.

4. Rule 3.7(A)(3): based upon some aspects of Canon 4C(3)(b)(iii), but with other elements added or deleted or repositioned elsewhere in Canon 3.

The basic idea of prohibiting a judge from soliciting membership in an organization where charging membership dues is essentially a fund-raising device is retained. The rationale is essentially the same as that in the 1990 Code: the risk that persons contacted will feel coerced into joining, or will attempt to curry favor with a sitting judge by joining.

In the proposed Code, however, it is not necessary to advert specifically to the element of coercion—that is covered by the cross-reference to Rule 3.1. Beyond this, the Commission decided to limit the permission

---

record of the Commission, solely to inform the ABA House of Delegates about each of the proposed amendments to the Model Code prior to their being considered at the ABA 2007 Midyear Meeting. THEY ARE NOT TO BE ADOPTED AS PART OF THE MODEL CODE.

granted to solicit membership to membership in law-related organizations—one of several places in Canon 3 where this line is drawn. It was felt that solicitation of membership in a law-related organization, such as a bar association or moot court society, would be perceived as more natural or more appropriate than soliciting membership in a fine arts society or the American Red Cross. This perception is related, at least indirectly, to the thematic requirement of avoiding abuse of the prestige of judicial office. A person who loves opera or is a dedicated member of an environmental protection organization, and who also happens to be a judge, should not use that position as an added reason for someone else to join the cause. On the other hand, it is not inappropriate for judges to use their positions as leaders in the legal community to increase membership in law-related organizations.

5. Rule 3.7(A)(4): a new provision for the Model Code of Judicial Conduct, based upon Commentary to Canons 5B(2) and 5B(3) of the Code of Conduct for United States Judges, and reversing the thrust of Commentary to Canon 4C(3)(b).

The Code of Conduct for United States Judges provides that as a general matter, judges may *not* participate in the fund-raising activities of charitable and other civic organizations other than by attending, which is similar to Commentary in the 1990 Code. In context, however, the federal provision appears to be limited to non-law-related organizations and activities. The Commission adopted the same general stance in Rule 3.7(A)(4), but made the implicit exception explicit: a judge *is* permitted to be a featured speaker or participant at an event that has a fund-raising purpose, *but only if the organization or entity is a law-related one*. The rationale for making this distinction is the same as that for Rule 3.7(A)(3).

6. Rule 3.7(A)(5): essentially the same as Canon 4C(3)(b)(ii) of the 1990 Code.

The one exception is that the authority to make recommendations to fund-granting organizations and entities is not limited to officers, directors, and others directly associated with the organization or entity. This is consistent with the revised organization of Canon 3 generally, and Rule 3.7 specifically, as noted above in connection with the lead-in to Rule 3.7(A) and Rule 3.7(A)(1).

7. Rule 3.7(A)(6): essentially identical to Canon 4C(3)(a) of the 1990 Code.

In the 1990 Code, there was some redundancy between this provision and Canon 4C(3) itself. The main paragraph already dealt generally with service as officer, director, and the like, while subparagraph (a) dealt with restrictions on such service. Rule 3.7(A)(6) makes no substantive change in the combined effect of those two provisions, but makes explicit that service is allowed in both private organizations and public entities, *whether or not they are law related*, as long as the two caveats are satisfied.

Unlike situations in which a judge is soliciting funds or members, participating as an officer or a director does not present the dangers of coercion or abuse of the prestige of judicial office; accordingly, neither the 1990 Code nor the proposed Code differentiate in this area along that axis.

8. Rule 3.7(B): a new provision, encouraging judges to provide leadership in increasing *pro bono publico* lawyering in their respective jurisdictions.

This provision is consistent with the thrust of Rule 3.7(A). It was placed in a separate paragraph because paragraph (A) deals with a large variety of organizations and entities, with varied goals and programs, whereas paragraph (B) refers to specific activities, whether or not conducted in connection with a particular organization or entity.

EXPLANATION OF COMMENTS

[1] New Comment [1] clarifies that the restructuring of Rule 3.7(A) was intended to make it applicable to all public and private not-for-profit organizations and entities. Previously, there was some confusion about the status of public and private universities, including their law schools (which are obviously law-related). Thus, it is permissible, for example, for a judge to serve as a trustee of a private university (rather than merely its law school), as long as it is not conducted for profit.

[2] This Comment is derived from Commentary to Canon 4C(3) of the 1990 Code, but it has been thoroughly revised to provide more clarity. The revised Comment serves as a reminder that participation in law-related activities is permitted more often than is participation in non-law-related activities, *but that even in connection with the former*, other requirements of the proposed Code may counsel caution or even abstention from the activity. Obvious examples include participating in activities sponsored by

organizations that practice invidious discrimination, or serving as the president of a major university (the time commitment associated with the latter making it impossible for a judge to attend to judicial duties).

[3] New Comment [3] is designed to provide a safe harbor for certain minor and noncoercive activities undertaken in connection with an organization's or entity's fund-raising efforts. When a judge donates time to serve food or serve as an usher or other facilitator at an event, the dangers associated with direct solicitation of funds are not present. It is not logical to assume that someone will make a larger donation, merely because a judge is tending the barbeque pit at a charity picnic.

The Commission stopped short, however, of giving as specific examples situations involving the handling of money, such as when a judge serves as ticket-taker or cashier (at a charity bingo night, for example, or a charity auction). At the same time, these activities were not specifically excluded, either. Whether such activities are appropriate depends upon analysis of the overall event, and the significance of the judge's participation. As long as there is no coercion—even subtle and unstated coercion—and as long as the judge's position as a judge is not being exploited, the activity is permissible.

[4] This Comment is based upon parts of the second paragraph of the Commentary to Canon 4C(3)(b) of the 1990 Code, but simplified. Letterhead including a judge's name and position, even when used for fund-raising or membership solicitation purposes, is not coercive and does not abuse the prestige of judicial office, as long as the judge is identified in the same way as other persons on the letterhead. It must be assumed, of course, that the judge's service in some official position in the organization or entity is itself appropriate under other provisions of Rules 3.7 and 3.1.

[5] New Comment [5], responsive to new Rule 3.7(B), makes clear that judges may encourage lawyers to engage in *pro bono publico* service generally, quite apart from situations in which judges may appoint counsel for indigent parties in individual cases. Although the Joint Commission assumed that participation in organizations that promote *pro bono publico* legal services would generally be permissible under rule 3.7(A), it wanted to stress the importance of such service by including a specific provision on this topic.

RULE 3.8 Appointments to Fiduciary Positions

(A) A judge shall not accept appointment to serve in a fiduciary* position, such as executor, administrator, trustee, guardian, attorney in fact, or other personal representative, except for the estate, trust, or person of a member of the judge's family,* and then only if such service will not interfere with the proper performance of judicial duties.

(B) A judge shall not serve in a fiduciary position if the judge as fiduciary will likely be engaged in proceedings that would ordinarily come before the judge, or if the estate, trust, or ward becomes involved in adversary proceedings in the court on which the judge serves, or one under its appellate jurisdiction.

(C) A judge acting in a fiduciary capacity shall be subject to the same restrictions on engaging in financial activities that apply to a judge personally.

(D) If a person who is serving in a fiduciary position becomes a judge, he or she must comply with this Rule as soon as reasonably practicable, but in no event later than [one year] after becoming a judge.

Comment

[1] A judge should recognize that other restrictions imposed by this Code may conflict with a judge's obligations as a fiduciary; in such circumstances, a judge should resign as fiduciary. For example, serving as a fiduciary might require frequent disqualification of a judge under Rule 2.11 because a judge is deemed to have an economic interest in shares of stock held by a trust if the amount of stock held is more than de minimis.

RULE 3.8—REPORTER'S EXPLANATION OF CHANGES†

1990 MODEL CODE COMPARISON

Rule 3.8(A) is essentially identical to Canon 4E(1), with only minor stylistic revisions.

Rule 3.8(B) is essentially identical to Canon 4E(2), also with only minor revisions.

Rule 3.8(C) bears the same relationship to Canon 4E(3).

Rule 3.8(D) is based upon the first paragraph of the Commentary to Canon 4E, but states more directly the time for compliance with the Rule.

Comment [1] is similar to the second paragraph of Commentary to Canon 4E, but recast.

EXPLANATION OF BLACK LETTER

1. Rule 3.8(A): changed the phrase "A judge shall not serve" to "A judge shall not accept appointment to."

No significant substantive change is intended. The new language suggests more of a choice on the judge's part—a choice that must be rejected, except in the case of family members.

2. Rule 3.8(B): changed the phrase "shall not serve as a fiduciary" to "shall not serve in a fiduciary position."

No substantive change is intended, except that serving in a fiduciary *position* connotes a formal appointment and acceptance, as in Rule 3.8(A).

3. Rule 3.8(C): changed the phrase "the same restrictions that apply" to "shall be subject to the same restrictions."

The change is stylistic only.

4. Rule 3.8(D): is new to the black letter text.

It states when a newly elected or appointed judge, who is *already* serving in a fiduciary capacity, must comply with this Rule. The suggested outer limit is one year, but jurisdictions may choose some other time limit.

EXPLANATION OF COMMENTS

[1] This is a slight recasting of the second paragraph of the 1990 Commentary. The Comment serves as a reminder that in addition to the restrictions set forth in Rule 3.8, other provisions of the proposed Code may implicate the permissibility of serving in a fiduciary capacity. For example, if serving as a fiduciary (even for a family member, which is generally permitted) would cause the judge frequently to be disqualified under Rule 2.11, the judge must resign as fiduciary to avoid violation of Rule 3.1(B).

RULE 3.9 Service as Arbitrator or Mediator

A judge shall not act as an arbitrator or a mediator or perform other judicial functions apart from the judge's official duties unless expressly authorized by law.*

Comment

[1] This Rule does not prohibit a judge from participating in arbitration, mediation, or settlement conferences performed as part of assigned judicial duties. Rendering dispute resolution services apart from those duties, whether or not for economic gain, is prohibited unless it is expressly authorized by law.

† The "Reporters' Explanations of Changes" have not been approved by the ABA Joint Commission to Evaluate the Model Code of Judicial Conduct. They have been drafted by the Commission's Reporters, based on the proceedings and record of the Commission, solely to inform the ABA House of Delegates about each of the proposed amendments to the Model Code prior to their being considered at the ABA 2007 Midyear Meeting. THEY ARE NOT TO BE ADOPTED AS PART OF THE MODEL CODE.

RULE 3.9—REPORTER'S EXPLANATION OF CHANGES†

1990 MODEL CODE COMPARISON

Rule 3.9 is based upon Canon 4F, slightly recast.

Comment [1] is the same as the Commentary to Canon 4F, except that an additional sentence was added.

EXPLANATION OF BLACK LETTER

1. Rule 3.9: changed the phrase "in a private capacity" to "apart from the judge's official duties," and slightly revised the text in other respects.

The only substantive change was made in recognition of the fact that a judge could be called upon to provide dispute resolution services *for another governmental entity*. Thus, the phase "in a private capacity" was deemed to be too narrow.

EXPLANATION OF COMMENTS

[1] The first sentence of this Comment is carried forward from the 1990 Commentary. The second sentence explains that the prohibition extends to judges going outside their regular judicial duties to assist in dispute resolution, whether or not for economic gain, unless doing so is expressly authorized by law, such as by court rule.

The Commission heard testimony and received comments on this issue. Some objected that allowing judges to participate in private "rent-a-judge" programs for economic gain would allow judges to trade on their status as judges, thus abusing the prestige of judicial office. Others expressed concern that allowing judges to routinely perform extrajudicial "judicial" services, even without compensation, could create public confusion about the role of the judiciary as an independent branch of the government, thus diminishing respect for the judicial system. Still others were concerned that extrajudicial participation even in *pro bono publico* mediation and arbitration could distract judges from their primary obligations.

Several judges stated their support for permitting judges to provide alternative dispute resolution services to other court systems or to private parties, but without compensation. In their view, this would provide an important public service to the community, demystify the law, and integrate judges into the community as Canon 3 encourages.

The Commission continued the proscription of Canon 4F of the 1990 Code that all such activities are prohibited, whether or not compensation is involved, but that courts or jurisdictions could authorize such activities as conditions warrant.

RULE 3.10 Practice of Law

A judge shall not practice law. A judge may act pro se and may, without compensation, give legal advice to and draft or review documents for a member of the judge's family,* but is prohibited from serving as the family member's lawyer in any forum.

Comment

[1] A judge may act pro se in all legal matters, including matters involving litigation and matters involving appearances before or other dealings with governmental bodies. A judge must not use the prestige of office to advance the judge's personal or family interests. See Rule 1.3.

---

† The "Reporters' Explanations of Changes" have not been approved by the ABA Joint Commission to Evaluate the Model Code of Judicial Conduct. They have been drafted by the Commission's Reporters, based on the proceedings and record of the Commission, solely to inform the ABA House of Delegates about each of the proposed amendments to the Model Code prior to their being considered at the ABA 2007 Midyear Meeting. THEY ARE NOT TO BE ADOPTED AS PART OF THE MODEL CODE.

RULE 3.10—REPORTER'S EXPLANATION OF CHANGES†

1990 MODEL CODE COMPARISON

Rule 3.10 is essentially identical to Canon 4G, with language based upon the second paragraph of Commentary to 4G added as black letter text.

Comment [1] is based upon the first paragraph of the Commentary to Canon 4G.

EXPLANATION OF BLACK LETTER

1. <u>Rule 3.10: blended the two sentences of Canon 4G into one.</u>

2. <u>Commentary from the 1990 Code interpreting Canon 4G as prohibiting a judge from representing a family member has been added to the black letter.</u>

The prohibition against "representing a family member in any court" is a narrower restriction than was "acting as an advocate or negotiator . . . in a legal matter." The Commission took the view that in some informal settings, such as a dispute in a neighborhood association or a purely private and minor commercial dispute, a judge may serve as an "advocate" for a family member without becoming his or her lawyer and thus practicing law in violation of Rule 3.10.

EXPLANATION OF COMMENTS

[1] The first paragraph of the Commentary to Canon 4G was revised slightly and recast. "A judge must not abuse the prestige of office to advance" was replaced with "A judge must not use the prestige of office to advance." No substantive change is intended.

RULE 3.11 Financial, Business, or Remunerative Activities

(A) A judge may hold and manage investments of the judge and members of the judge's family.*

(B) A judge shall not serve as an officer, director, manager, general partner, advisor, or employee of any business entity except that a judge may manage or participate in:

(1) a business closely held by the judge or members of the judge's family; or

(2) a business entity primarily engaged in investment of the financial resources of the judge or members of the judge's family.

(C) A judge shall not engage in financial activities permitted under paragraphs (A) and (B) if they will:

(1) interfere with the proper performance of judicial duties;

(2) lead to frequent disqualification of the judge;

(3) involve the judge in frequent transactions or continuing business relationships with lawyers or other persons likely to come before the court on which the judge serves; or

(4) result in violation of other provisions of this Code.

---

† The "Reporters' Explanations of Changes" have not been approved by the ABA Joint Commission to Evaluate the Model Code of Judicial Conduct. They have been drafted by the Commission's Reporters, based on the proceedings and record of the Commission, solely to inform the ABA House of Delegates about each of the proposed amendments to the Model Code prior to their being considered at the ABA 2007 Midyear Meeting. THEY ARE NOT TO BE ADOPTED AS PART OF THE MODEL CODE.

Comment

[1] Judges are generally permitted to engage in financial activities, including managing real estate and other investments for themselves or for members of their families. Participation in these activities, like participation in other extrajudicial activities, is subject to the requirements of this Code. For example, it would be improper for a judge to spend so much time on business activities that it interferes with the performance of judicial duties. See Rule 2.1. Similarly, it would be improper for a judge to use his or her official title or appear in judicial robes in business advertising, or to conduct his or her business or financial affairs in such a way that disqualification is frequently required. See Rules 1.3 and 2.11.

[2] As soon as practicable without serious financial detriment, the judge must divest himself or herself of investments and other financial interests that might require frequent disqualification or otherwise violate this Rule.

RULE 3.11—REPORTER'S EXPLANATION OF CHANGES†

1990 MODEL CODE COMPARISON

Rule 3.11(A) is derived from Canon 4D(2), excluding the last two clauses.

Rule 3.11(B) is essentially the same as Canon 4D(3).

Rule 3.11(C) combines some new provisions with elements of Canon 4D(1)(b) and Canon 4D(4).

Comment [1] is largely new, but incorporates several aspects of the Commentary to Canon 4D.

Comment [2] is derived from the black letter text of Canon 4D(4).

EXPLANATION OF BLACK LETTER

1. Rule 3.11(A): retained the core language of Canon 4D(2), but deleted the lead-in phrase "subject to the requirements of this Code," as well as the references to "real estate" holdings and "other remunerative activities."

Rule 3.11 represents a reorganization of most of the material governing extrajudicial financial activities found in Canon 4D of the 1990 Code, except for the gift-related provisions in Canon 4D(5).

In Rule 3.11(A), the initial "subject to the requirements of this Code" was deleted as no longer necessary, in light of Rule 3.11(C)(4), as well as Comment [1]. The reference to "real estate" was deemed too specific for inclusion in the black letter text, and moved to Comment [1] as an example of the kinds of investments that a judge might hold or manage. The last clause, "engage in other remunerative activity," was removed as far too broad, and thus inconsistent with other aspects of Rule 3.11. For example, the remunerative activity of being a director or employee of a for-profit business entity is prohibited by Rule 3.11(B), unless the business is closely held by the judge or the judge's family.

2. Rule 3.11(B) is identical to Canon 4D(3) of the 1990 Code, except that the caveat "subject to the requirements of this Code" was eliminated as unnecessary, for the reasons stated immediately above.

The Commission discussed the substantive point of Rule 3.11(B), which is to prohibit judges from engaging in off-bench remunerative activity, except in the case of closely held family businesses, including the investment of financial resources. This exception has been criticized as inconsistent with the rationale for the basic prohibition, and as unfair to judges who do not have family businesses.

Two alternatives were considered, but not adopted. First, it would have been possible to allow judges broadly to engage in remunerative extrajudicial activities, as long as they did not interfere with the performance of judicial duties, lead to frequent disqualification, or otherwise violate the prohibitions found in Rule 3.11(C).

---

† The "Reporters' Explanations of Changes" have not been approved by the ABA Joint Commission to Evaluate the Model Code of Judicial Conduct. They have been drafted by the Commission's Reporters, based on the proceedings and record of the Commission, solely to inform the ABA House of Delegates about each of the proposed amendments to the Model Code prior to their being considered at the ABA 2007 Midyear Meeting. THEY ARE NOT TO BE ADOPTED AS PART OF THE MODEL CODE.

The other possibility would have been to eliminate the family business exception and to require all judges to divest themselves of any interests in the family business when ascending the bench. The Commission elected to maintain the status quo of the 1990 Code as a reasonable middle ground.

3. Rule 3.11(C) is a new provision that gathers in one place some of the caveats about extrajudicial financial activities found throughout Canon 4D of the 1990 Code, while adding additional caveats.

These caveats are meant to apply as restrictions on otherwise permissible activities. The specific language of Rule 3.11(C)(1) is taken from the fourth paragraph of the Commentary to Canon 4D(1); the concept is also drawn in part from the second paragraph of the Commentary to Canon 4D(3): otherwise appropriate business activities (falling within the family business exception) would become improper if "participation requires significant time away from judicial duties."

Rule 3.11(C)(2) is a paraphrase of Canon 4D(4), which requires a judge to minimize the number of cases in which the judge is disqualified. The phraseology used in the proposed Code, "will lead to frequent disqualification of the judge," is used elsewhere in the Code—most significantly for present purposes in Rule 3.1(B).

Rule 3.11(C)(3) is taken from Canon 4D(1)(b), and Rule 3.11(C)(4) is a catchall that makes some other caveats found in Canon 4D unnecessary. For example, the Canon 4D(1)(a) provision, "may reasonably be perceived to exploit the judge's judicial position," was not retained in the proposed Code, because of the prohibition against abusing the prestige of judicial office already found in Rule 1.3.

EXPLANATION OF COMMENTS

[1] New Comment [1] restates the rationale of several of the provisions gathered into Rule 3.11(C), giving some practical examples.

[2] New Comment [2] is essentially the same as the black letter text of Canon 4D(4).

RULE 3.12 Compensation for Extrajudicial Activities

A judge may accept reasonable compensation for extrajudicial activities permitted by this Code or other law* unless such acceptance would appear to a reasonable person to undermine the judge's independence,* integrity,* or impartiality.*

Comment

[1] A judge is permitted to accept honoraria, stipends, fees, wages, salaries, royalties, or other compensation for speaking, teaching, writing, and other extrajudicial activities, provided the compensation is reasonable and commensurate with the task performed. The judge should be mindful, however, that judicial duties must take precedence over other activities. See Rule 2.1.

[2] Compensation derived from extrajudicial activities may be subject to public reporting. See Rule 3.15.

RULE 3.12—REPORTER'S EXPLANATION OF CHANGES†

1990 MODEL CODE COMPARISON

Rule 3.12 is based upon Canon 4H(1), but only as it relates to compensation, not reimbursement of expenses associated with extrajudicial activities. (Reimbursement is governed by Rule 3.14 in the proposed Code.)

† The "Reporters' Explanations of Changes" have not been approved by the ABA Joint Commission to Evaluate the Model Code of Judicial Conduct. They have been drafted by the Commission's Reporters, based on the proceedings and record of the Commission, solely to inform the ABA House of Delegates about each of the proposed amendments to the Model Code prior to their being considered at the ABA 2007 Midyear Meeting. THEY ARE NOT TO BE ADOPTED AS PART OF THE MODEL CODE.

Comment [1] is based upon the black letter text of Canon 4H(1)(a) and some aspects of the Commentary to Canon 4H, but substantially revised.

Comment [2] is new, and serves as a cross-reference to the public reporting provisions of the proposed Code. (Public reporting was addressed in Canon 4H(2), but in connection with compensation only, not reimbursement of expenses. Rule 3.15 addresses all forms of public reporting—compensation, gifts, other things of value, reimbursement of expenses, and waivers of fees.)

EXPLANATION OF BLACK LETTER

1. Rule 3.12: removed references to reimbursement of expenses, and substituted "reasonable compensation" for "shall not exceed for a person who is not a judge would receive for the same activity"; replaced the phrase "give the appearance of influencing the judge's performance of judicial duties or otherwise give the appearance of impropriety" with "would appear to a reasonable person to undermine the judge's independence, integrity, or impartiality."

The Joint Commission completely reorganized the material on compensation, reimbursement for expenses, acceptance of gifts and the like, and public reporting of all these. After the reorganization, Rule 3.12 deals only with compensation for permissible extrajudicial activities. Public reporting of the compensation received, as well as all other reporting, is governed by Rule 3.15.

The language measuring the reasonableness of compensation by what a non-judge would receive was deleted as unsound: if a judge were to be compensated for teaching a law school course on judicial ethics, or giving a lecture on evidentiary rulings, for example, the judge's services would in fact likely be more valuable than those of a non-judge. On the other hand, it was recognized that significant overcompensation could be a mask for an improper gift or an attempt to influence the judge's conduct in office. Accordingly, the language in Canon 4H(1) about appearances was replaced by the language used throughout Canon 3 of the proposed Code: "would appear to a reasonable person to undermine the judge's independence, integrity, or impartiality."

EXPLANATION OF COMMENTS

[1] New Comment [1] is based in part upon some of the language in Canon 4H of the 1990 Code and Rule 3.12 of the proposed Code.

[2] New Comment [2] makes a cross-reference to the public reporting requirement. Some aspects of public reporting were treated in Canon 4H(2), but now all are treated in Rule 3.15.

RULE 3.13 Acceptance and Reporting of Gifts, Loans, Bequests, Benefits, or Other Things of Value

(A) A judge shall not accept any gifts, loans, bequests, benefits, or other things of value, if acceptance is prohibited by law* or would appear to a reasonable person to undermine the judge's independence,* integrity,* or impartiality.*

(B) Unless otherwise prohibited by law, or by paragraph (A), a judge may accept the following without publicly reporting such acceptance:

(1) items with little intrinsic value, such as plaques, certificates, trophies, and greeting cards;

(2) gifts, loans, bequests, benefits, or other things of value from friends, relatives, or other persons, including lawyers, whose appearance or interest in a proceeding pending* or impending* before the judge would in any event require disqualification of the judge under Rule 2.11;

(3) ordinary social hospitality;

(4) commercial or financial opportunities and benefits, including special pricing and discounts, and loans from lending institutions in their regular course of

business, if the same opportunities and benefits or loans are made available on the same terms to similarly situated persons who are not judges;

(5) rewards and prizes given to competitors or participants in random drawings, contests, or other events that are open to persons who are not judges;

(6) scholarships, fellowships, and similar benefits or awards, if they are available to similarly situated persons who are not judges, based upon the same terms and criteria;

(7) books, magazines, journals, audiovisual materials, and other resource materials supplied by publishers on a complimentary basis for official use; or

(8) gifts, awards, or benefits associated with the business, profession, or other separate activity of a spouse, a domestic partner,* or other family member of a judge residing in the judge's household,* but that incidentally benefit the judge.

(C) Unless otherwise prohibited by law or by paragraph (A), a judge may accept the following items, and must report such acceptance to the extent required by Rule 3.15:

(1) gifts incident to a public testimonial;

(2) invitations to the judge and the judge's spouse, domestic partner, or guest to attend without charge:

(a) an event associated with a bar-related function or other activity relating to the law, the legal system, or the administration of justice; or

(b) an event associated with any of the judge's educational, religious, charitable, fraternal or civic activities permitted by this Code, if the same invitation is offered to nonjudges who are engaged in similar ways in the activity as is the judge; and

(3) gifts, loans, bequests, benefits, or other things of value, if the source is a party or other person, including a lawyer, who has come or is likely to come before the judge, or whose interests have come or are likely to come before the judge.

Comment

[1] Whenever a judge accepts a gift or other thing of value without paying fair market value, there is a risk that the benefit might be viewed as intended to influence the judge's decision in a case. Rule 3.13 imposes restrictions upon the acceptance of such benefits, according to the magnitude of the risk. Paragraph (B) identifies circumstances in which the risk that the acceptance would appear to undermine the judge's independence, integrity, or impartiality is low, and explicitly provides that such items need not be publicly reported. As the value of the benefit or the likelihood that the source of the benefit will appear before the judge increases, the judge is either prohibited under paragraph (A) from accepting the gift, or required under paragraph (C) to publicly report it.

[2] Gift-giving between friends and relatives is a common occurrence, and ordinarily does not create an appearance of impropriety or cause reasonable persons to believe that the judge's independence, integrity, or impartiality has been compromised. In addition, when the appearance of friends or relatives in a case would require the judge's disqualification under Rule 2.11, there would be no opportunity for a gift to influence the judge's decision making. Paragraph (B)(2) places no restrictions upon the ability of a judge to accept gifts or other things of value from friends or relatives under these circumstances, and does not require public reporting.

[3] Businesses and financial institutions frequently make available special pricing, discounts, and other benefits, either in connection with a temporary promotion or for preferred customers, based upon longevity of the relationship, volume of business transacted, and other factors. A judge may freely accept such benefits if they are available to the general public, or if the judge qualifies for the special price or discount according to the same criteria as are applied to persons who are not judges. As an example, loans provided at generally prevailing interest rates are not gifts, but a judge could not accept a loan from a financial institution at

below-market interest rates unless the same rate was being made available to the general public for a certain period of time or only to borrowers with specified qualifications that the judge also possesses.

[4] Rule 3.13 applies only to acceptance of gifts or other things of value by a judge. Nonetheless, if a gift or other benefit is given to the judge's spouse, domestic partner, or member of the judge's family residing in the judge's household, it may be viewed as an attempt to evade Rule 3.13 and influence the judge indirectly. Where the gift or benefit is being made primarily to such other persons, and the judge is merely an incidental beneficiary, this concern is reduced. A judge should, however, remind family and household members of the restrictions imposed upon judges, and urge them to take these restrictions into account when making decisions about accepting such gifts or benefits.

[5] Rule 3.13 does not apply to contributions to a judge's campaign for judicial office. Such contributions are governed by other Rules of this Code, including Rules 4.3 and 4.4.

RULE 3.13—REPORTER'S EXPLANATION OF CHANGES†

1990 MODEL CODE COMPARISON

Rule 3.13 is based upon Canon 4D(5), its subsections (a) through (h), and the related Commentary. The Commission thoroughly reorganized this material. In the analysis of the black letter and Comments that follows, the source of the language used in the proposed Code will be identified, where germane.

EXPLANATION OF BLACK LETTER

1. <u>Rule 3.13(A): expanded the universe of coverage to include "other things of value," and linked the overall prohibition of acceptance to what "would appear to a reasonable person to undermine the judge's independence, integrity, or impartiality."</u>

This paragraph has some similarity to Canon 4D(5), but ultimately establishes a different organization and a different mode of analysis. Canon 4D(5) established a general prohibition against a judge accepting gifts or loans or similar items from anyone, but then proceeded to make exceptions in subsections (a) through (h).

Rule 3.13(A) also begins with a list of gifts and things of value that judges are prohibited from accepting. There are no exceptions. The later provisions in Rule 3.13 permit acceptance of some items, sometimes accompanied by public reporting and sometimes not, but in each instance permission is granted only after it has been determined that acceptance has not already been barred by paragraph (A).

This different relationship between earlier and later provisions within Rule 3.13 is characteristic of the Commission's tiered approach to this subject matter. Paragraph (A) establishes a first tier of situations in which acceptance is not permitted at all; paragraph (B) deals with acceptance of items that are not problematic and do not require the transparency of public reporting; and paragraph (C) deals with the tier of items that do not warrant being banned, but must be reported to maintain the public's confidence in the judiciary.

The dividing line between gifts and other items that cannot be accepted at all and those that may be accepted subject to the requirement of public reporting, is when acceptance "would appear to a reasonable person to undermine the judge's independence, integrity, or impartiality." The language is new, and is used thematically throughout Canon 3. It requires judges to evaluate their conduct as would a "reasonable person" subject to later oversight by disciplinary authorities.

2. <u>Rule 3.13(B): established a "tier" of gifts and other things of value that may be accepted without limitation and without public reporting, drawing several items from the exceptions set forth in the</u>

† The "Reporters' Explanations of Changes" have not been approved by the ABA Joint Commission to Evaluate the Model Code of Judicial Conduct. They have been drafted by the Commission's Reporters, based on the proceedings and record of the Commission, solely to inform the ABA House of Delegates about each of the proposed amendments to the Model Code prior to their being considered at the ABA 2007 Midyear Meeting. THEY ARE NOT TO BE ADOPTED AS PART OF THE MODEL CODE.

subsections of Canon 4D(5), but with an eye toward classifying them according to the proposed new organizational scheme.

In the 1990 Code, the exceptions to the basic rule were set out serially, without further classification, and—except in the catchall provision of Canon 4D(5)(h)—without adverting to whether public reporting was a condition of acceptance. The Commission has now gathered in Rule 3.13(B) the items that are sufficiently non-threatening to the integrity of the judicial system as to warrant no further regulation.

For example, subparagraphs (4), (5), and (6) deal with situations in which the listed benefits are equally available to similarly situated persons who are not judges, thus allaying any fears that the benefit is being extended to influence the judge's decision-making or to curry favor with the judge. Subparagraph (2) is similar to Canon 4D(5)(e), but clarifies the category. If a person's appearance or interest in a case pending or impending before a particular judge would require the disqualification of the judge, then any gift or favor from that person could not influence the judge—because by definition the judge would no longer be sitting on the case.

3. Rule 3.13(C): establishes the third "tier" of items that may be accepted by a judge. These items, while not causing a reasonable person to believe that the judge's independence, integrity, or impartiality would be undermined, are of sufficient concern that public reporting is required.

Placement of these items in Rule 3.13(C) rather than paragraphs (A) or (B) represents the Commission's assessment of the level of concern that may attend the acceptance of various benefits. In subparagraph (C)(2)(a), for example, the judgment was made that the gift of a free ticket to attend a law-related event must be reported, so that others might be able to assess whether a particular judge had a particularly close association with a particular bar association or organization. On the other hand, if a judge is invited to attend, free of charge, an event sponsored by a non-law-related organization, the judge cannot accept *at all* unless the additional condition of equal treatment is met. If that condition is met, however, then public reporting should be sufficient to allay concerns about possible lack of impartiality. (This distinction between events and organizations that are or are not law-related is another theme that occurs throughout Canon 3.)

Rule 3.13(C)(3) addresses the same issue as Canon 4D(5)(h), but according to a more discriminating analysis. Under the 1990 Code, a judge cannot accept any gift or favor from a lawyer or party who has come or is likely to come before the judge. (The further requirement of publicly reporting items over $150 appears to apply to other gifts, not the above.) If this means to impose a lifetime ban once a lawyer or the lawyer's firm "has appeared" before the judge, it appears to be more stringent than necessary, and unworkable in practice, as a judge's career lengthens.

Under Rule 3.13(C)(3), the proposed rule provides that such gifts may be accepted as long as they are reported—which will give another party in litigation an opportunity to consider whether disqualification of the judge is required. More important, placement of this item in paragraph (C) assumes that the size of a particular gift or other circumstances will not cause a reasonable person to fear that the judge's impartiality will be impaired. If a reasonable person would take that view, then the gift is wholly impermissible to accept, because it will have failed the test of Rule 3.13(A).

EXPLANATION OF COMMENTS

[1] New Comment [1] explains the three-tiered approach and its rationale.

[2] New Comment [2] explains the classification in Rule 3.13 of gifts and other things of value given to a judge. This subject was treated in both Canon 4D(5)(d) (gifts for special occasions) and Canon 4D(5)(e) (judge would be disqualified in any event), but without an explanation of the rationale. Rule 3.13(B)(2) does not distinguish between different types of gifts from this category of donor, and Comment [2] provides the common rationale.

[3] New Comment [3] provides the rationale for and giving a concrete example of the principle that acceptance of benefits and other things of value that are generally available to non-judges on the same basis as they are available to judges causes no ethical concerns; accordingly, these items may be accepted, without public reporting.

[4] This Comment builds on the introductory language of Canon 4D(5) of the 1990 Code. The point is that while a code of judicial ethics cannot directly bind family members and others close to a judge, it is still prudent for a judge to urge such individuals not to put the judge in a difficult position by accepting gifts and

benefits that the judge could not, because others might perceive the benefit as intended for the judge, but given indirectly.

Comment [4] also adds discussion of a contrasting scenario, which is new. Rule 3.13(B)(8) states that when a gift or other benefit is given to a family member, because of the family member's business or other activities, and the judge benefits merely incidentally, concern that the judge is being influenced or importuned is no longer reasonable, and those gifts need not be reported by the judge. Comment [4] explains the rationale for this new provision.

[5] This Comment paraphrases the first paragraph of the Commentary following Canon 4D(5). The Comment thus makes clear that gifts, donations, or contributions to a judge's campaign for judicial office are governed entirely by Canon 4, which includes regulation of campaign committees.

RULE 3.14 Reimbursement of Expenses and Waivers of Fees or Charges

(A) Unless otherwise prohibited by Rules 3.1 and 3.13(A) or other law,* a judge may accept reimbursement of necessary and reasonable expenses for travel, food, lodging, or other incidental expenses, or a waiver or partial waiver of fees or charges for registration, tuition, and similar items, from sources other than the judge's employing entity, if the expenses or charges are associated with the judge's participation in extrajudicial activities permitted by this Code.

(B) Reimbursement of expenses for necessary travel, food, lodging, or other incidental expenses shall be limited to the actual costs reasonably incurred by the judge and, when appropriate to the occasion, by the judge's spouse, domestic partner,* or guest.

(C) A judge who accepts reimbursement of expenses or waivers or partial waivers of fees or charges on behalf of the judge or the judge's spouse, domestic partner, or guest shall publicly report such acceptance as required by Rule 3.15.

Comment

[1] Educational, civic, religious, fraternal, and charitable organizations often sponsor meetings, seminars, symposia, dinners, awards ceremonies, and similar events. Judges are encouraged to attend educational programs, as both teachers and participants, in law-related and academic disciplines, in furtherance of their duty to remain competent in the law. Participation in a variety of other extrajudicial activity is also permitted and encouraged by this Code.

[2] Not infrequently, sponsoring organizations invite certain judges to attend seminars or other events on a fee-waived or partial-fee-waived basis, and sometimes include reimbursement for necessary travel, food, lodging, or other incidental expenses. A judge's decision whether to accept reimbursement of expenses or a waiver or partial waiver of fees or charges in connection with these or other extrajudicial activities must be based upon an assessment of all the circumstances. The judge must undertake a reasonable inquiry to obtain the information necessary to make an informed judgment about whether acceptance would be consistent with the requirements of this Code.

[3] A judge must assure himself or herself that acceptance of reimbursement or fee waivers would not appear to a reasonable person to undermine the judge's independence, integrity, or impartiality. The factors that a judge should consider when deciding whether to accept reimbursement or a fee waiver for attendance at a particular activity include:

(a) whether the sponsor is an accredited educational institution or bar association rather than a trade association or a for-profit entity;

(b) whether the funding comes largely from numerous contributors rather than from a single entity and is earmarked for programs with specific content;

(c) whether the content is related or unrelated to the subject matter of litigation pending or impending before the judge, or to matters that are likely to come before the judge;

(d) whether the activity is primarily educational rather than recreational, and whether the costs of the event are reasonable and comparable to those associated with similar events sponsored by the judiciary, bar associations, or similar groups;

(e) whether information concerning the activity and its funding sources is available upon inquiry;

(f) whether the sponsor or source of funding is generally associated with particular parties or interests currently appearing or likely to appear in the judge's court, thus possibly requiring disqualification of the judge under Rule 2.11;

(g) whether differing viewpoints are presented; and

(h) whether a broad range of judicial and nonjudicial participants are invited, whether a large number of participants are invited, and whether the program is designed specifically for judges.

RULE 3.14—REPORTER'S EXPLANATION OF CHANGES†

1990 MODEL CODE COMPARISON

Rule 3.14(A) is derived from Canon 4H(1), except that the provisions relating to compensation have been moved to Rule 3.12. Rule 3.14 addresses reimbursement of expenses and waivers of fees or charges only.

Rule 3.14(B) is essentially identical to Canon 4H(1)(b).

Rule 3.14(C) is new as it relates to public reporting of reimbursements and waivers of charges, but is similar to Canon 4(H)(2), which deals with public reporting of compensation received.

Comments [1] through [3] are new.

EXPLANATION OF BLACK LETTER

1. Rule 3.14(A) applies to reimbursement of expenses only, rather than both reimbursement and compensation, but adds waivers of fees and charges as equivalent to reimbursement.

By cross-reference to other Rules it requires judges to consider whether attending an event on a fee-waived or expenses-reimbursed basis would require later disqualification or undermine the judge's independence, integrity, or impartiality. Rule 3.14 and its subparagraph (A) are integral to the total reorganization of Canons 4D and 4H of the 1990 Code. Compensation for extrajudicial activity is no longer linked with reimbursement for expenses, but is addressed separately in Rule 3.12. Reimbursement, in turn, is addressed separately in Rule 3.14. (Other aspects of Canon 4D, such as engaging in financial and business activities, and receipt of gifts and other things of value, are covered by Rules 3.11 and 3.13, respectively.)

The Commission recognized that attendance at tuition-waived and expense-paid seminars and similar events has been a matter of public concern and media attention. It heard much testimony and received numerous comments about the need for more transparency regarding both the amount of fees waived or expenses reimbursed and the nature and sponsorship of the event attended on a cost-free or reduced-cost basis. In response, the Commission elected to treat acceptance of such benefits separately from acceptance of gifts and other things of value generally (see Rule 3.13), and to require public reporting of the benefits received together with other public reporting (see Rule 3.15). The Commission concluded that separating reimbursement and waivers for treatment in this way makes Canon 3 more readable and easier to follow. Moreover, treatment in a separate Rule allows more careful attention to be paid to whether the invitation to attend should be accepted at all.

Although Rule 3.14 applies to events other than privately funded educational seminars, much of the testimony and comments received by the Commission focused upon that subject. In the Commission's view, judicial education of all kinds is of great value; it helps keep judges current on recent developments, alerts

---

† The "Reporters' Explanations of Changes" have not been approved by the ABA Joint Commission to Evaluate the Model Code of Judicial Conduct. They have been drafted by the Commission's Reporters, based on the proceedings and record of the Commission, solely to inform the ABA House of Delegates about each of the proposed amendments to the Model Code prior to their being considered at the ABA 2007 Midyear Meeting. THEY ARE NOT TO BE ADOPTED AS PART OF THE MODEL CODE.

them to future trends, and exposes them to new ways of thinking about the law. Moreover, there was recognition that judicial budgets may not always be adequate to support educational opportunities for judges. For that reason, Rule 3.14—like Canon 4H(1)—permits judges to accept reimbursement for reasonably necessary expenses associated with otherwise permissible extrajudicial activities, and further permits acceptance of waivers of otherwise applicable fees or charges.

A critical aspect of Canon 4H(1) is that permission to accept benefits in connection with extrajudicial activities is conditioned upon the acceptance not giving the appearance of influencing the judge in the performance of judicial duties and not otherwise creating the appearance of impropriety. Rule 3.14 carries this condition forward, for both reimbursements and waivers of fees and charges, but uses language more in harmony with other parts of Canon 3 and the rest of the Model Code. Thus, by cross-referencing Rules 3.1 and 3.13(A), Rule 3.14(A) makes clear that a judge may not accept the proffered benefits if doing so would appear to a reasonable person to undermine the judge's independence, integrity, or impartiality, or if accepting would, for example, lead to frequent disqualification or otherwise interfere with the proper performance of the judge's judicial duties.

2. Rule 3.14(B) is substantially the same as Canon 4H(1)(b) of the 1990 Code.

The exception is that it applies to both reimbursements and waivers of fees and charges, and applies to an accompanying domestic partner as well as to a spouse or guest.

3. Rule 3.14(C) is similar to the public reporting requirement set out in Canon 4H(2).

The exception is that it applies to reimbursements and waivers rather than compensation. In addition, the actual mechanism for reporting is not contained in Rule 3.14(C) itself; the Rule instead cross-references Rule 3.15, which describes all the public reporting required by various Rules in Canon 3.

EXPLANATION OF COMMENTS

[1] New Comment [1] states the rationale for allowing judges to accept these two forms of benefits, and also making clear that Rule 3.14 can apply to any permissible extrajudicial activity, not just privately funded educational programs.

[2] New Comment [2] focuses attention upon educational programs specifically. Not only must a judge consider whether accepting an invitation to attend on an expenses-paid or fee-waived basis would be proper (under Rules 3.1, 3.13(A), and 3.14(A)), but the judge also has an affirmative duty to make reasonable inquiry into the factors that should inform that decision.

Near the end of its deliberations, the Commission became aware of guidelines newly issued by the Judicial Conference of the United States on this subject. The Guidelines delineate a process for helping judges make the inquiry just noted. Any program that wishes to invite judges to attend on a cost-free basis is required to provide considerable information about funding, sponsorship, and program content in advance, and have this information available to judges receiving an invitation. The Commission thought this "pre-registration" approach had merit, but considered the possibility that it would be more difficult to implement throughout all the state jurisdictions, as opposed to in the single federal jurisdiction for which it was designed. Thus the Commission thought it more prudent to wait until the operation of the federal program could be assessed.

[3] New Comment [3] provides guidance to judges in making the determination required by Rule 3.14(A), as explained in Comment [2]. It is founded on revised Advisory Opinion 67 of the Committee on Codes of Conduct of the Judicial Conference of the United States. The factors identified in Opinion 67 can usefully be employed by each judge who has been issued an invitation to attend a cost-free event and is considering whether to accept.

RULE 3.15 Reporting Requirements

(A) A judge shall publicly report the amount or value of:

(1) compensation received for extrajudicial activities as permitted by Rule 3.12;

(2) gifts and other things of value as permitted by Rule 3.13(C), unless the value of such items, alone or in the aggregate with other items received from the same source in the same calendar year, does not exceed $[insert amount]; and

(3) reimbursement of expenses and waiver of fees or charges permitted by Rule 3.14(A), unless the amount of reimbursement or waiver, alone or in the aggregate with other reimbursements or waivers received from the same source in the same calendar year, does not exceed $[insert amount].

(B) When public reporting is required by paragraph (A), a judge shall report the date, place, and nature of the activity for which the judge received any compensation; the description of any gift, loan, bequest, benefit, or other thing of value accepted; and the source of reimbursement of expenses or waiver or partial waiver of fees or charges.

(C) The public report required by paragraph (A) shall be made at least annually, except that for reimbursement of expenses and waiver or partial waiver of fees or charges, the report shall be made within thirty days following the conclusion of the event or program.

(D) Reports made in compliance with this Rule shall be filed as public documents in the office of the clerk of the court on which the judge serves or other office designated by law,* and, when technically feasible, posted by the court or office personnel on the court's website.

RULE 3.15—REPORTER'S EXPLANATION OF CHANGES†

1990 MODEL CODE COMPARISON

Rule 3.15 is based upon Canon 4H(2). However, consistent with the reorganization of Canon 3, this provision is no longer limited to public reporting of compensation received for extrajudicial activities, but includes public reporting of gifts and other things of value accepted pursuant to Rule 3.13, and reimbursement of expenses and waiver or partial waiver of fees and charges accepted pursuant to Rule 3.14.

Technical matters such as what and where to report, on what schedule, and how the information will become transparent to the general public are derived from Canon 4H(2) as well, but with several modifications.

EXPLANATION OF BLACK LETTER

1. <u>Rule 3.15(A) requires that in addition to reporting compensation received, judges must report gifts and other things of value accepted, as well as reimbursements of expenses and waivers of fees and charges.</u>

It deletes a 1990 Code provision on treatment of a spouse's compensation or income in community property states. An important feature of the reorganization of Canon 3 is the gathering of all the public reporting provisions in one place, now Rule 3.15(A), and then cross-referencing this Rule in the Rules where reportable events are discussed.

This organization has the important side effect of removing discussion of monetary limits (if any) from the earlier Rules, and repositioning it in Rule 3.15(A). Thus, for example, Canon 4D(5)(h) of the 1990 Code, which established a reporting threshold of $150 per item, has been recast and moved to Rule 3.15(A)(2). Instead of establishing a threshold amount for all jurisdictions, which might have to be raised periodically in any event on account of inflation, the Commission required establishment of an annual threshold amount that takes into account aggregation of items from the same source. The actual dollar amount, however, was left for each jurisdiction to supply according to conditions there.

---

† "Reporters' Explanations of Changes" have not been approved by the ABA Joint Commission to Evaluate the Model Code of Judicial Conduct. They have been drafted by the Commission's Reporters, based on the proceedings and record of the Commission, solely to inform the ABA House of Delegates about each of the proposed amendments to the Model Code prior to their being considered at the ABA 2007 Midyear Meeting. THEY ARE NOT TO BE ADOPTED AS PART OF THE MODEL CODE.

The reminder in the 1990 Code that community property earned by a judge's spouse is not attributable to the judge for purposes of public reporting was deleted as unnecessary: all the substantive provisions in Canon 3 speak of the judge receiving compensation or receiving gifts or reimbursement of expenses.

Canon 4I of the 1990 Code, which required disclosure of a judge's income and assets in some circumstances, is not included in the proposed Code. The Commission concluded that this form of public reporting is already regulated by statute or court rule in most jurisdictions; thus, its inclusion in a Code of Judicial Conduct is unnecessary.

2. Rule 3.15(B) provides a list of what must be reported when reporting is required under paragraph (A).

3. Rule 3.15(C) addresses the frequency of mandatory public reporting.

The requirement of reporting no less frequently than annually is consistent with Canon 4H(2) of the 1990 Code. Reporting in connection with reimbursements and waivers of fees or charges, however, is required within thirty days of the underlying event, not on a calendar-based schedule.

The Commission borrowed this special reporting requirement from the guidelines recently issued by the Judicial Conference of the United States. Such a requirement can be implemented immediately, is responsive to the need for transparency, and should not be overly burdensome to judges. In situations involving reimbursement in particular, a judge will have to gather receipts for submission to the reimbursing entity, which can be used to satisfy the public reporting requirement. With respect to fee waivers, a judge should be able to obtain a statement of what the fees or charges would have been for a person who was not being offered a waiver. As this requirement becomes better known, it is likely that the sponsoring entity granting the waiver will develop this information and provide the requisite statement as a matter of course.

4. Rule 3.15(D) directs that the reports required by Rule 3.15 be located in a central place and made accessible to the public to ensure transparency.

It tracks Canon 4H(2), except that it calls for posting on the appropriate website when feasible, to facilitate public access. Ordinarily, it is assumed that such posting will be to the court's official website, and will be done by court personnel according to a uniform format, rather than by each reporting judge individually.

CANON 4

A JUDGE OR CANDIDATE FOR JUDICIAL OFFICE SHALL NOT ENGAGE IN POLITICAL OR CAMPAIGN ACTIVITY THAT IS INCONSISTENT WITH THE INDEPENDENCE, INTEGRITY, OR IMPARTIALITY OF THE JUDICIARY.

CANON 4—REPORTER'S EXPLANATION OF CHANGES†

1990 MODEL CODE COMPARISON

Canon 4 of the proposed Code is derived from Canon 5 of the 1990 Code, as amended in 1997, 1999, and 2003—the last time in response to the decision of the U.S. Supreme Court in *Republican Party of Minnesota v. White*, 536 U.S. 765 (2002). Much of the material in Canon 5 was retained, but was reorganized along several axes. The reorganized Canon 4 differentiates more clearly between sitting judges who are and are not also judicial candidates and nonjudges who become candidates. Canon 4 continues to differentiate

† The "Reporters' Explanations of Changes" have not been approved by the ABA Joint Commission to Evaluate the Model Code of Judicial Conduct. They have been drafted by the Commission's Reporters, based on the proceedings and record of the Commission, solely to inform the ABA House of Delegates about each of the proposed amendments to the Model Code prior to their being considered at the ABA 2007 Midyear Meeting. THEY ARE NOT TO BE ADOPTED AS PART OF THE MODEL CODE.

between judicial candidates running in public elections and those seeking appointment, and, within the former category, it further differentiates between partisan, nonpartisan, and retention elections.

EXPLANATION OF BLACK LETTER

1. Replaced "shall refrain from" with "shall not engage in."

The new language is less passive and fits more comfortably with the language of the other three Canons.

2. Replaced "political activity" with "political or campaign activity."

This more accurately reflects the actual content of Canon 4. Canon 5 of the 1990 Code also dealt with more than just "political" activity so the new Canon 4 title has been amplified.

3. Replaced "inappropriate activity" with "activity that is inconsistent with the independence, integrity, or impartiality of the judiciary."

The undefined term "inappropriate" was not sufficiently precise. Concern that the independence, integrity, or impartiality of the judiciary (including candidates who aspire to join the judiciary) will be compromised or undermined is a pervasive theme in the proposed Code.

RULE 4.1 Political and Campaign Activities of Judges and Judicial Candidates in General

(A) Except as permitted by law,* or by Rules 4.2, 4.3, and 4.4, a judge or a judicial candidate* shall not:

(1) act as a leader in, or hold an office in, a political organization;*

(2) make speeches on behalf of a political organization;

(3) publicly endorse or oppose a candidate for any public office;

(4) solicit funds for, pay an assessment to, or make a contribution* to a political organization or a candidate for public office;

(5) attend or purchase tickets for dinners or other events sponsored by a political organization or a candidate for public office;

(6) publicly identify himself or herself as a candidate of a political organization;

(7) seek, accept, or use endorsements from a political organization;

(8) personally solicit* or accept campaign contributions other than through a campaign committee authorized by Rule 4.4;

(9) use or permit the use of campaign contributions for the private benefit of the judge, the candidate, or others;

(10) use court staff, facilities, or other court resources in a campaign for judicial office;

(11) knowingly,* or with reckless disregard for the truth, make any false or misleading statement;

(12) make any statement that would reasonably be expected to affect the outcome or impair the fairness of a matter pending* or impending* in any court; or

(13) in connection with cases, controversies, or issues that are likely to come before the court, make pledges, promises, or commitments that are inconsistent with the impartial* performance of the adjudicative duties of judicial office.

(B) A judge or judicial candidate shall take reasonable measures to ensure that other persons do not undertake, on behalf of the judge or judicial candidate, any activities prohibited under paragraph (A).

Comment

GENERAL CONSIDERATIONS

[1] Even when subject to public election, a judge plays a role different from that of a legislator or executive branch official. Rather than making decisions based upon the expressed views or preferences of the electorate, a judge makes decisions based upon the law and the facts of every case. Therefore, in furtherance of this interest, judges and judicial candidates must, to the greatest extent possible, be free and appear to be free from political influence and political pressure. This Canon imposes narrowly tailored restrictions upon the political and campaign activities of all judges and judicial candidates, taking into account the various methods of selecting judges.

[2] When a person becomes a judicial candidate, this Canon becomes applicable to his or her conduct.

PARTICIPATION IN POLITICAL ACTIVITIES

[3] Public confidence in the independence and impartiality of the judiciary is eroded if judges or judicial candidates are perceived to be subject to political influence. Although judges and judicial candidates may register to vote as members of a political party, they are prohibited by paragraph (A)(1) from assuming leadership roles in political organizations.

[4] Paragraphs (A)(2) and (A)(3) prohibit judges and judicial candidates from making speeches on behalf of political organizations or publicly endorsing or opposing candidates for public office, respectively, to prevent them from abusing the prestige of judicial office to advance the interests of others. See Rule 1.3. These Rules do not prohibit candidates from campaigning on their own behalf, or from endorsing or opposing candidates for the same judicial office for which they are running. See Rules 4.2(B)(2) and 4.2(B)(3).

[5] Although members of the families of judges and judicial candidates are free to engage in their own political activity, including running for public office, there is no "family exception" to the prohibition in paragraph (A)(3) against a judge or candidate publicly endorsing candidates for public office. A judge or judicial candidate must not become involved in, or publicly associated with, a family member's political activity or campaign for public office. To avoid public misunderstanding, judges and judicial candidates should take, and should urge members of their families to take, reasonable steps to avoid any implication that they endorse any family member's candidacy or other political activity.

[6] Judges and judicial candidates retain the right to participate in the political process as voters in both primary and general elections. For purposes of this Canon, participation in a caucus-type election procedure does not constitute public support for or endorsement of a political organization or candidate, and is not prohibited by paragraphs (A)(2) or (A)(3).

STATEMENTS AND COMMENTS MADE DURING A CAMPAIGN FOR JUDICIAL OFFICE

[7] Judicial candidates must be scrupulously fair and accurate in all statements made by them and by their campaign committees. Paragraph (A)(11) obligates candidates and their committees to refrain from making statements that are false or misleading, or that omit facts necessary to make the communication considered as a whole not materially misleading.

[8] Judicial candidates are sometimes the subject of false, misleading, or unfair allegations made by opposing candidates, third parties, or the media. For example, false or misleading statements might be made regarding the identity, present position, experience, qualifications, or judicial rulings of a candidate. In other situations, false or misleading allegations may be made that bear upon a candidate's integrity or fitness for judicial office. As long as the candidate does not violate paragraphs (A)(11), (A)(12), or (A)(13), the candidate may make a factually accurate public response. In addition, when an independent third party has made unwarranted attacks on a candidate's opponent, the candidate may disavow the attacks, and request the third party to cease and desist.

[9] Subject to paragraph (A)(12), a judicial candidate is permitted to respond directly to false, misleading, or unfair allegations made against him or her during a campaign, although it is preferable for someone else to respond if the allegations relate to a pending case.

[10] Paragraph (A)(12) prohibits judicial candidates from making comments that might impair the fairness of pending or impending judicial proceedings. This provision does not restrict arguments or statements to the court or jury by a lawyer who is a judicial candidate, or rulings, statements, or instructions by a judge that may appropriately affect the outcome of a matter.

PLEDGES, PROMISES, OR COMMITMENTS INCONSISTENT WITH IMPARTIAL PERFORMANCE OF THE ADJUDICATIVE DUTIES OF JUDICIAL OFFICE

[11] The role of a judge is different from that of a legislator or executive branch official, even when the judge is subject to public election. Campaigns for judicial office must be conducted differently from campaigns for other offices. The narrowly drafted restrictions upon political and campaign activities of judicial candidates provided in Canon 4 allow candidates to conduct campaigns that provide voters with sufficient information to permit them to distinguish between candidates and make informed electoral choices.

[12] Paragraph (A)(13) makes applicable to both judges and judicial candidates the prohibition that applies to judges in Rule 2.10(B), relating to pledges, promises, or commitments that are inconsistent with the impartial performance of the adjudicative duties of judicial office.

[13] The making of a pledge, promise, or commitment is not dependent upon, or limited to, the use of any specific words or phrases; instead, the totality of the statement must be examined to determine if a reasonable person would believe that the candidate for judicial office has specifically undertaken to reach a particular result. Pledges, promises, or commitments must be contrasted with statements or announcements of personal views on legal, political, or other issues, which are not prohibited. When making such statements, a judge should acknowledge the overarching judicial obligation to apply and uphold the law, without regard to his or her personal views.

[14] A judicial candidate may make campaign promises related to judicial organization, administration, and court management, such as a promise to dispose of a backlog of cases, start court sessions on time, or avoid favoritism in appointments and hiring. A candidate may also pledge to take action outside the courtroom, such as working toward an improved jury selection system, or advocating for more funds to improve the physical plant and amenities of the courthouse.

[15] Judicial candidates may receive questionnaires or requests for interviews from the media and from issue advocacy or other community organizations that seek to learn their views on disputed or controversial legal or political issues. Paragraph (A)(13) does not specifically address judicial responses to such inquiries. Depending upon the wording and format of such questionnaires, candidates' responses might be viewed as pledges, promises, or commitments to perform the adjudicative duties of office other than in an impartial way. To avoid violating paragraph (A)(13), therefore, candidates who respond to media and other inquiries should also give assurances that they will keep an open mind and will carry out their adjudicative duties faithfully and impartially if elected. Candidates who do not respond may state their reasons for not responding, such as the danger that answering might be perceived by a reasonable person as undermining a successful candidate's independence or impartiality, or that it might lead to frequent disqualification. See Rule 2.11.

RULE 4.1—REPORTER'S EXPLANATION OF CHANGES†

1990 MODEL CODE COMPARISON

Rule 4.1(A)(1) is virtually identical to Canon 5A(1)(a).

Rule 4.1(A)(2) is identical to Canon 5A(1)(c).

Rule 4.1(A)(3) is essentially the same as Canon 5A(1)(b).

† The "Reporters' Explanations of Changes" have not been approved by the ABA Joint Commission to Evaluate the Model Code of Judicial Conduct. They have been drafted by the Commission's Reporters, based on the proceedings and record of the Commission, solely to inform the ABA House of Delegates about each of the proposed amendments to the Model Code prior to their being considered at the ABA 2007 Midyear Meeting. THEY ARE NOT TO BE ADOPTED AS PART OF THE MODEL CODE.

Rule 4.1(A)(4) is virtually identical to the first clause of Canon 5A(1)(e).

Rule 4.1(A)(5) is closely patterned on the second clause of Canon 5A(1)(e), and includes the concept embodied in Canon 5A(1)(d), which was eliminated.

Rule 4.1(A)(6) is new, but the prohibition it establishes is removed by later Rules in Canon 4 in some situations.

Rule 4.1(A)(7) is new, and is similar to Rule 4.1(A)(6) in terms of its relationship to other Rules in Canon 4.

Rule 4.1(A)(8) is derived from the first two sentences of Canon 5C(2), but employs different terminology and applies only to solicitation of campaign contributions, not "publicly stated support."

Rule 4.1(A)(9) is essentially identical to the last sentence of Canon 5C(2).

Rule 4.1(A)(10) is new, but is a corollary of one aspect of Canon 2B: lending the prestige—here the trappings—of judicial office to advance a judge's interests.

Rule 4.1(A)(11) is based upon Canon 5A(3)(d)(ii), but substantially revised.

Rule 4.1(A)(12) is new to the Canon on political and campaign activity, but is substantially similar to the first sentence of Canon 3B(9).

Rule 4.1(A)(13) is essentially identical to Canon 5A(3)(d)(i).

Rule 4.1 (B) is based upon elements of Canon 5A(3)(a) and Canon 5A(3)(b), which have been combined and recast.

Comment [1] is new.

Comment [2] is based upon Canon 5E, which has been removed from the black letter text.

Comment [3] is new, but includes a principle taken from the first sentence of the Commentary following Canon 5A(1). See also Comment [6].

Comment [4] is new, but includes reference to the principles embodied in Canon 5C(1)(b), substantially reworded.

Comment [5] is new, but is tangentially related to the Commentary following Canon 5A(3)(a).

Comment [6] is based upon the first sentence of the Commentary following Canon 5A(1), but includes fuller treatment.

Comment [7] is a new Comment, but is based upon Canon 5A(3)(d)(ii), which is now embodied in Rule 4.1(A)(11).

Comment [8] is based upon Canon 5A(3)(e), which has been removed from the black letter text; the new Comment is more detailed and covers slightly more ground.

Comment [9] is new, but also is based upon Canon 5A(3)(e).

Comment [10] is new, but is derived from aspects of Canon 3B(9) and following Commentary.

Comment [11] is new.

Comment [12] is new.

Comment [13] is new.

Comment [14] is based upon the fourth sentence of the Commentary following Canon 5A(3)(d), but provides more detailed treatment, with examples.

Comment [15] is loosely based upon the last paragraph of the Commentary following Canon 5C(2), but provides far more detailed discussion.

EXPLANATION OF BLACK LETTER

1. <u>Rule 4.1(A)'s lead-in added cross-references to specific Rules in Canon 4.</u>

This formulation is critical to the reorganization of Canon 4. Rule 4.1(A) sets out a generally applicable set of prohibitions that apply to all sitting judges and to all judicial candidates (including sitting judges seeking to retain current office or to achieve other judicial office). Rule 4.2 (various forms of public elections), Rule 4.3 (appointment to judicial office), and Rule 4.4 (campaign committees) then selectively eliminate these prohibitions, as appropriate to the specific situation.

2. Rule 4.1(A)(4) replaced "political organization or candidate" with "political organization or a candidate for public office."

No substantive change is intended. The Commission wanted to make clear that the prohibition against soliciting funds or making contributions applies to all candidates for public office, not just candidates for judicial office (as is clear in other provisions of both the 1990 Code and the proposed Code).

3. Rule 4.1(A)(5): made several stylistic revisions in the course of blending Canon 5A(1)(d) and the second clause of Canon 5A(1)(e).

No substantive change is intended. The earlier "attend political gatherings" was eliminated, but the word "attend" was added to the blended Rule. "[D]inners or other events" was substituted for "political party dinners or other functions."

4. Rule 4.1(A)(6) adds a prohibition against a candidate self-identifying as a "candidate of" a political organization.

Canon 5C(1)(a)(ii) of the 1990 Code specifically permitted judges subject to public election to identify themselves at any time as political party *members*. This provision has been eliminated in the proposed Code as unnecessary.

The purpose of Rule 4.1(A)(6) is a different one, however. In the organizational scheme of Canon 4, it is necessary first to prohibit for all judges and judicial candidates what is to be prohibited for any. In the later Rules, exceptions are made as appropriate, leaving in place the general prohibitions that are not singled out for exception. For example, in connection with Rule 4.1(A)(6), see Rule 4.2(C)(1): a candidate running in a partisan public election for judicial office must be permitted to communicate to voters the fact that a particular political organization or party nominated him or her. Thus, because an exception to Rule 4.1(A)(6) appears only in Rule 4.2(C)(1), a candidate running in another type of judicial election is still subject to Rule 4.1(A)(6).

5. Rule 4.1(A)(7): added this provision, which broadly prohibits judicial candidates from seeking, accepting, or using endorsements from political organizations.

As with Rule 4.1(A)(6), the full impact of this new Rule can be judged only by ascertaining the situations in which later Rules in Canon 4 make an exception to it.

6. Rule 4.1(A)(8): retained the language "personally solicit . . . campaign contributions," now defined in the Terminology section; deleted the prohibition against personally soliciting "publicly stated support," and retained the provision permitting contributions to be accepted only through a duly established campaign committee.

The prohibition against seeking "support"—at least from political organizations—is covered (and more broadly) in Rule 4.1(A)(7), and was no longer needed in this Rule.

The Commission was urged to change the operative language (and the definition in the Terminology section) to "solicit campaign contributions in person," to focus more clearly upon the immediacy of the situation and the possibility of coercion. By analogy to the rules regulating lawyer advertising and solicitation, a ban on "in-person" solicitation of campaign contributions would *permit* mailings and similar communications, but would continue to forbid both hand-to-hand transfer of funds and live telephone solicitation. If the original broader language was retained, even a simple mailing to friends and neighbors would be prohibited.

The Commission considered the two possibilities through long debate over many meetings. The Commission was aware that several courts have struck down provisions forbidding "personal solicitation" of campaign funds—often in broad language. Ultimately, the Commission adopted the broader prohibition on the theory that the solicitation of campaign funds in the judicial election context could justify restrictions greater than are permitted for lawyer advertising.

7. Rule 4.1(A)(9) replaces "for the private benefit of the candidate or others" (in Canon 5C(2)) with "for the private benefit of the judge, the candidate, or others."

No substantive changed is intended. Rule 4.1(A) applies to both judges who are *not* currently candidates and to all current judicial candidates.

8. Rule 4.1(A)(10), which prohibits use of official resources for a judge's campaign, breaks little new ground.

Although new to the Canon on political and campaign activity, this provision breaks little new ground. Compare Rule 1.3 (abusing the prestige of judicial office) and Rule 3.1(E) (using official resources in connection with extrajudicial activity).

9. Rule 4.1(A)(11) replaces "knowingly misrepresent the identity, qualifications, present position or other fact" (in Canon 5A(3)(d)(ii)) with "knowingly, or with reckless disregard for the truth, make any false or misleading statement."

Although the 1990 Code language was specific, its precise reach was unclear. The new language used in the proposed Code is established in the law of libel and slander.

10. Rule 4.1(A)(12): added this provision that is new material for Canon 4 on political and campaign activity, but that is a reiteration for emphasis of Rule 2.10(A).

This reiteration is helpful because Rule 2.10(A) can apply only to sitting judges.

11. Rule 4.1(A)(13): replaced "with respect to" (in Canon 5(A)(3)(d)(i)) with "in connection with."

This is a stylistic change only. The language is otherwise identical to policy adopted in 2003 in the wake of the decision in *Republican Party of Minnesota v. White.*

To encourage adoption of an appropriately narrow interpretation of the pledges and promises clause, by disciplinary authorities and by judges and candidates assessing their own conduct, the Commission has included several Comments describing the intended reach of Rule 4.1(A)(13). See Comments [11] through [15]. A judge or candidate who announces his or her personal views on a matter that is likely to come before the court does not compromise impartiality unless the announcement demonstrates a closed mind on the subject, or includes a pledge or a promise to rule in a particular way if the matter comes before the court.

12. Rule 4.1(B) combines in a single Rule, and greatly simplifies, most provisions of Canon 5A(3)(a) and Canon 5A(3)(b).

First, it changes the separate treatment of actions of members of a candidate's family and actions of employees and others who are under the control of a candidate to unitary treatment of actions of "other persons"; second, it explains that the judge or candidate is required to take "reasonable measures" to ensure that these other persons do not undertake action on behalf of the judge or candidate that would otherwise be prohibited; and third, it eliminates the injunction to maintain the dignity appropriate to the judicial office during a judicial campaign.

The Commission concluded that "maintaining appropriate dignity" was too subjective a standard for use in a Rule with potential disciplinary consequences.

No significant substantive changes are intended by other adjustments in the Rule. What constitutes a "reasonable measure" will obviously depend upon whether the person who is attempting to act improperly *on behalf of* the judge or candidate is a family member, an employee, or an appointee.

EXPLANATION OF COMMENTS

[1] New Comment [1] in effect serves as a preamble to Canon 4. Two key points are involved: that states have a compelling interest in the quality of their judiciary and in the regularity of the selection process; and that restrictions on political and campaign-related speech must be narrowly tailored and the least restrictive possible, even when serving such a compelling state interest.

[2] The jurisdictional point of this Comment was originally placed in Canon 5E of the 1990 Code. The Commission concluded that treatment in the black letter text was not required, given that this provision does not establish independent standards of conduct. In transferring this material to a Comment, the Commission also significantly reduced its level of detail. Prior references to the jurisdictional situation when

a candidate is successful or unsuccessful in obtaining judicial office were eliminated as not properly within the scope of this Code.

[3] New Comment [3] explains how restrictions on political participation of judges and judicial candidates were drawn: mere participation in electoral politics does not warrant a restriction, but assuming a leadership role would call into question the judge's or candidate's independence.

[4] New Comment [4] gathers in one place several provisions of Canon 5C(1) of the 1990 Code, and substantially revises the language. Although judicial candidates generally are not permitted to endorse *other* candidates, to avoid abusing the prestige of judicial office, they are nevertheless permitted to campaign on their own behalf. Moreover, although the pros and cons as a matter of policy seemed to be evenly balanced, the Commission elected to retain the traditional exception that permits campaigning for other *judicial candidates* who are effectively running in the same race.

[5] New Comment [5] serves as a reminder that judges and judicial candidates must avoid abusing the prestige of office when their own family members are involved in politics. Thus, while family members are not and cannot be subject to this Code, the people who *are* subject to it must take reasonable steps to ensure that the public does not receive the impression that a judge or judicial candidate is endorsing a family member's candidacy.

[6] This Comment carries forward Commentary from the 1990 Code, noting that judges and judicial candidates do not forfeit the right to vote, and adds a reminder that this principle applies in both general and primary elections. For jurisdictions that employ caucuses rather than secret ballot voting in primary elections, the Commission ultimately concluded that even though a caucus participant may take a public stand in favor of a particular candidate, this should not be counted as a prohibited endorsement, because there is no other way to vote or express a preference in such situations.

[8] This Comment carries forward and expands upon the "right to reply" provision originally found in Canon 5A(3)(e) of the 1990 Code. The last sentence, an aspirational standard, was added to stem increased use of negative campaign ads run by independent groups not controlled by a candidate or the candidate's campaign committee.

[10] New Comment [10] is a reminder that Rule 4.1(A)(12) has brought into the political and electoral context the traditional prohibition against making statements that will improperly influence a trial. Compare Rule 2.10(A). The last sentence of Comment [10] serves as an additional reminder that some statements are *designed* to affect the outcome of a trial, and properly so. A lawyer making a closing argument to a jury and a judge instructing that jury are prime examples.

[11] New Comments [11] and [12] introduce the series of Comments explicating "pledges and promises clause," which is carried forward from Canon 5A(3)(d)(i) of the 1990 Code essentially unchanged.

[13] New Comment [13] describes the fundamental difference between "pledges" and "promises," which are prohibited, and "statements or announcements of personal views," which are permitted and constitutionally protected. The key distinction is between personal statements that are truly personal and that *will not interfere with future decision making*, and improper pledges and promises that commit a judge or judicial candidate to decide a future case in a particular way. A prohibited pledge or promise concerns future decision making.

[14] This Comment is based upon Commentary following Canon 5A(3)(d), but is more complete. It makes the important point that pledges and promises regarding *administration* of the judicial system, as opposed to *decision making in actual cases*, is not prohibited.

[15] The constitutional distinction between (1) making pledges and promises about future decision making, and (2) making statements or announcements about personal views, has emerged in recent years as issue advocacy and other citizen groups (as well as the media) have become more affirmative in issuing questionnaires for judicial candidates to answer. The Commission received testimony and commentary on this issue, and deliberated at length. Comment [15] represents the Commission's understanding of how this issue can and must be resolved.

First, citizens are not subject to the Code of Judicial Conduct, and may inquire of judicial candidates their position on issues. Each citizen is entitled to decide what qualities in a judicial candidate will earn that citizen's vote, and all citizens are entitled to applaud or criticize the answers given, or to comment on a candidate's failure or refusal to answer.

Second, judicial candidates who choose to answer the questionnaires cannot be prevented from doing so, as long as their answers take the form of constitutionally protected statements and announcements of personal views, and do not constitute pledges and promises about future decision making.

Third, and critically important, judicial candidates have the right to refuse to answer, with or without giving reasons, or to answer only in formats that are agreeable to them (assuming they comply with Rule 4.1(A)(13)).

Thus, the Commission took no firm stand on the best response to questionnaires of this kind (and explicitly noted in Comment [15] that the black letter text of Rule 4.1(A)(13) does not provide a clear answer, either). But the principles set forth in this Comment and the previous Comments should assist judicial candidates in formulating their positions on judicial campaign speech.

RULE 4.2 Political and Campaign Activities of Judicial Candidates in Public Elections

(A) A judicial candidate* in a partisan, nonpartisan, or retention public election* shall:

(1) act at all times in a manner consistent with the independence,* integrity,* and impartiality* of the judiciary;

(2) comply with all applicable election, election campaign, and election campaign fund-raising laws and regulations of this jurisdiction;

(3) review and approve the content of all campaign statements and materials produced by the candidate or his or her campaign committee, as authorized by Rule 4.4, before their dissemination; and

(4) take reasonable measures to ensure that other persons do not undertake on behalf of the candidate activities, other than those described in Rule 4.4, that the candidate is prohibited from doing by Rule 4.1.

(B) A candidate for elective judicial office may, unless prohibited by law,* and not earlier than [insert amount of time] before the first applicable primary election, caucus, or general or retention election:

(1) establish a campaign committee pursuant to the provisions of Rule 4.4;

(2) speak on behalf of his or her candidacy through any medium, including but not limited to advertisements, websites, or other campaign literature;

(3) publicly endorse or oppose candidates for the same judicial office for which he or she is running;

(4) attend or purchase tickets for dinners or other events sponsored by a political organization* or a candidate for public office;

(5) seek, accept, or use endorsements from any person or organization other than a partisan political organization; and

(6) contribute to a political organization or candidate for public office, but not more than $[insert amount] to any one organization or candidate.

(C) A judicial candidate in a partisan public election may, unless prohibited by law, and not earlier than [insert amount of time] before the first applicable primary election, caucus, or general election:

(1) identify himself or herself as a candidate of a political organization; and

(2) seek, accept, and use endorsements of a political organization.

Comment

[1] Paragraphs (B) and (C) permit judicial candidates in public elections to engage in some political and campaign activities otherwise prohibited by Rule 4.1. Candidates may not engage in these activities earlier than [insert amount of time] before the first applicable electoral event, such as a caucus or a primary election.

[2] Despite paragraphs (B) and (C), judicial candidates for public election remain subject to many of the provisions of Rule 4.1. For example, a candidate continues to be prohibited from soliciting funds for a political organization, knowingly making false or misleading statements during a campaign, or making certain promises, pledges, or commitments related to future adjudicative duties. See Rule 4.1(A), paragraphs (4), (11), and (13).

[3] In partisan public elections for judicial office, a candidate may be nominated by, affiliated with, or otherwise publicly identified or associated with a political organization, including a political party. This relationship may be maintained throughout the period of the public campaign, and may include use of political party or similar designations on campaign literature and on the ballot.

[4] In nonpartisan public elections or retention elections, paragraph (B)(5) prohibits a candidate from seeking, accepting, or using nominations or endorsements from a partisan political organization.

[5] Judicial candidates are permitted to attend or purchase tickets for dinners and other events sponsored by political organizations.

[6] For purposes of paragraph (B)(3), candidates are considered to be running for the same judicial office if they are competing for a single judgeship or if several judgeships on the same court are to be filled as a result of the election. In endorsing or opposing another candidate for a position on the same court, a judicial candidate must abide by the same rules governing campaign conduct and speech as apply to the candidate's own campaign.

[7] Although judicial candidates in nonpartisan public elections are prohibited from running on a ticket or slate associated with a political organization, they may group themselves into slates or other alliances to conduct their campaigns more effectively. Candidates who have grouped themselves together are considered to be running for the same judicial office if they satisfy the conditions described in Comment [6].

RULE 4.2—REPORTER'S EXPLANATION OF CHANGES†

1990 MODEL CODE COMPARISON

Rule 4.2 is derived from the specific regulation of campaign activity included in Canon 5C, with the exception of provisions concerning campaign committees, which are treated in Rule 4.4. Rule 4.2, in tandem with Rule 4.1, has imposed a logical and tiered organization on this material without making major substantive changes.

The key to understanding the organization of Canon 4 of the proposed Code is to remember that Rule 4.1 applies to all judges (whether or not they are also judicial candidates) and to all judicial candidates (whether or not they are also sitting judges). Rule 4.2 applies only to judicial candidates running in partisan, nonpartisan, or retention public elections. Rule 4.2 adds some restrictions on the activity of judicial candidates that do not appear in Rule 4.1, makes exceptions to some of the restrictions set out in Rule 4.1, and then makes further exceptions that apply only to judicial candidates in partisan elections.

---

† The "Reporters' Explanations of Changes" have not been approved by the ABA Joint Commission to Evaluate the Model Code of Judicial Conduct. They have been drafted by the Commission's Reporters, based on the proceedings and record of the Commission, solely to inform the ABA House of Delegates about each of the proposed amendments to the Model Code prior to their being considered at the ABA 2007 Midyear Meeting. THEY ARE NOT TO BE ADOPTED AS PART OF THE MODEL CODE.

Rule 4.3 applies to the activities of judicial candidates seeking appointive judicial office, but these provisions are relatively straightforward and did not require significant reorganization.

The lead-in to Rule 4.2(A) is similar to that of Canon 5C(1), except that it identifies the three modes of public elections to which this paragraph (and the rest of the Rule) will apply.

Rule 4.2(A)(1) is based upon parts of Canon 5A(3).

Rule 4.2(A)(2) is new as a separate provision, but is consistent with the pervasive statement in the 1990 Code that activities prohibited by law are also prohibited by Canon 5.

Rule 4.2(A)(3) is a new provision, but the requirement that candidates actively take responsibility for campaign literature and other campaign activities is implicit in many provisions of Canon 5 of the 1990 Code.

Rule 4.2(A)(4) is derived from parts of Canon 5A(3)(a)–(c). This material, which governs judicial candidates only, has been repositioned to Rule 4.2.

The lead-in to Rule 4.2(B) is based upon Canon 5C(1), but with a different disposition of the *timing* of the activities that are permitted for judicial candidates. In addition, Rule 4.2(B), like the rest of Rule 4.2, applies only to candidates, whereas Canon 5C(1) applies to sitting judges as well.

Rule 4.2(B)(1) is based upon the second sentence of Canon 5C(2), except that the timing provided for the establishment of campaign committees is different.

Rule 4.2(B)(2) combines and rewords Canons 5C(1)(b)(i)–(b)(iii).

Rule 4.2(B)(3) is virtually identical to Canon 5C(1)(b)(iv).

Rule 4.2(B)(4) is based upon Canon 5C(1)(a)(i), but reworded for consistency with other Rules in Canon 4 of the proposed Code.

Rule 4.2(B)(5) takes the opposite stance from that found in Canon 5C(2), but with an important caveat. The 1990 Code allows judicial candidates to solicit endorsements—"publicly stated support"—only through campaign committees. The proposed Code permits candidates to solicit such support on their own, but not from partisan political organizations.

Rule 4.2(B)(6) is similar to Canon 5C(1)(a)(iii), but establishes dollar limitations (to be supplied by each jurisdiction) on the contributions that can be made.

Rule 4.2(C) and its two subparagraphs permit only candidates in partisan elections to identify themselves as candidates of political organizations' and to seek such organizations' endorsements. Canon 5(C)(1)(a)(ii) had permitted the first of these two activities for candidates in both partisan and non-partisan elections. The 1990 Code did not advert to the distinction between partisan and nonpartisan or retention elections. In furtherance of the organizational scheme of the proposed Code, Rule 4.2(C) states the additional activities that are permitted only for candidates in partisan public elections.

Comments [1] and [2] explain the relationship of Rule 4.2 to Rule 4.1, which is the core of the new organizational scheme. They also explain that a person becomes a judicial candidate according to the definition in the Terminology section, but that the additional activities in which a candidate may engage depend upon the timing counting back from the primary or election in question. The first sentence of Comment [1] is a revision of Commentary to Canon 5C(1).

Comments [3] and [4] are new; the 1990 Code did not distinguish between partisan, nonpartisan, and retention public elections for judicial office.

Comment [5] is similar to Canon 5C(1)(a)(i), but with the important difference that the provision applies *only* to judicial candidates, *while* they are candidates.

Comments [6] and [7] clarify the intended meaning of Rule 4.2(B)(3), which is based upon Canon 5C(1)(b)(iv), and has some similarity to Canon 5C(5). In both instances, the key is to determine when candidates are running for the *same* judicial office.

EXPLANATION OF BLACK LETTER

1. Rule 4.2(A) lead-in: substituted "a judicial candidate in a partisan, nonpartisan, or retention public election" for "a [judge or] candidate subject to public election."

This is an important element of the reorganization of Canon 4 of the proposed Code. By distinguishing between the three modes of public elections, Rule 4.2(A) sets up the possibility of applying further restrictions and permissive provisions to all three modes or to some designated subset, as required. In Rule 4.2(A), for example, obligations *in addition to those already imposed by Rule 4.1* are imposed upon all three types of candidates.

2. Rule 4.2(A)(1): substituted "act at all times in a manner" for "act in a manner," and deleted the requirement that a candidate "shall maintain the dignity appropriate to judicial office."

The first change is stylistic only. The mandatory duty to "maintain dignity" was deleted because it is too subjective.

3. Rule 4.2(A)(2): added this new broad provision that is consistent with the overarching principle that candidates for judicial office must obey applicable laws and regulations.

Some of the specific regulations regarding campaign finance are separately referenced in Rule 4.4, but Rule 4.2(A)(2) might well apply to restrictions on ballot insignia applicable to nonpartisan elections, for example. Thus, although a candidate in a nonpartisan election is not prevented from stating he or she is a member of a particular party, the candidate is prohibited from stating he or she is "the candidate" of that party, if the election laws do not allow party designations on the ballot. Compare Rule 4.1(A)(6), which prohibits all judges and judicial candidates from such self-designation, and Rule 4.2(C)(1), which allows candidates in *partisan* elections to do so.

4. Rule 4.2(A)(3): added the requirement that judicial candidates personally approve the contents of campaign literature and other materials.

The requirement is implicit in several other provisions of Canon 4. For example, if a candidate is prohibited by Rule 4.1(A)(11) from making false or misleading statements in a campaign, it is almost inevitable that the candidate will have a duty to review campaign materials before they are disseminated under his or her name.

5. Rule 4.2(A)(4): substituted "take reasonable measures to ensure" for "shall prohibit," "shall discourage," and "shall encourage to adhere."

The language of the 1990 Code variously applied to employees and officials serving at the pleasure of the candidate (who can be prohibited), others under the direction and control of the candidate (who can be discouraged), and family members (who can be encouraged to assist the candidate in complying with the Rules). What constitutes a "reasonable measure" depends upon circumstances such as those noted above. Rule 4.2(A)(4), which applies only to judicial candidates, is already covered by Rule 4.1(B), which applies to all judges *and* candidates.

6. Rule 4.2(B) lead-in identifies a time period prior to the relevant primary or election, during which certain activities that would or might otherwise be prohibited by Rule 4.1(A) are permitted.

Although the creation of this time period is not new, its use in this Rule to disconnect the status of *being* a judicial candidate from being permitted to engage in the *activities* of a candidate is an important feature of the reorganization of Canon 4. During its deliberations, the Commission was mindful of the need to establish a time period to ensure that a judge elected to a ten-year term could not immediately announce plans to run for reelection, establish a campaign committee, and raise campaign funds for almost ten full years. With the time period in place, the judge can continue to call himself or herself a candidate for ten years, but can raise campaign funds only after the time period has been satisfied, typically one year before the first primary.

7. Rules 4.2(B)(1), 4.2(B)(2), and 4.2(B)(3): retained provisions allowing candidates to establish campaign committees, speak on their own behalf through various communications media, and endorse (or oppose) candidates running for *the same* judicial office.

These activities have traditionally been allowed, and the Commission did not modify these provisions in any substantive ways. It is important to note that permission is granted to all three types of judicial election candidates to engage in these activities, but only during the stated time period.

8. Rule 4.2(B)(4): specifically permitted what Rule 4.1(A)(5) prohibits for both judges and candidates; the permission applies to all candidates, including candidates running in nonpartisan and retention elections.

This is approximately the same result as would be obtained under the 1990 Code, but in a reorganized format. Under Canon 5A(1), judicial candidates are prohibited from attending events of political organizations, unless otherwise permitted. But Canon 5C(1) permits a candidate to "attend political gatherings" *at any time,* which negates the prescription.

In the proposed Code, Rule 4.1(A)(5) generally prohibits attending such political organization functions—as the first layer. Rule 4.2(B)(4) permits an exception, but only during a candidate's candidacy *and after a specific time.*

9. Rule 4.2(B)(5) provides an important distinction between judicial candidates running in partisan and other types of public judicial elections; the full impact of this paragraph depends on other parts of Rule 4.2, especially Rule 4.2(C).

This provision showcases the tiered approach of the proposed Code. According to Rule 4.1(A)(7), judges and candidates may not seek, accept, or use endorsements from a political organization. Rule 4.2(B)(5) continues this prohibition for *all* public election judicial candidates during the time period, because all are permitted to accept endorsements *only* from organizations that are *not* political organizations.

It is only in Rule 4.2(C)(2) that this restriction is finally removed—but for judicial candidates running in partisan elections *only.*

10. Rule 4.2(B)(6) represents an important compromise that allows all candidates for judicial office to make contributions to political organizations or other candidates for public office, but only during the time period.

Under the Canon 5(C)(1)(a)(iii) of the 1990 Code, a judge who was subject to public election at some later time (perhaps ten years away, as in the previous example) and any candidate running in a public election could make such contributions *at any time.* This included candidates running in nonpartisan and retention elections, because the 1990 Code did not distinguish between different modes of public election. Under Rule 4.2(B)(6), all candidates (including sitting judges who become candidates) may make contributions, even to political organizations, but only during the time period.

11. Rule 4.2(C): stated the two exceptions to the earlier prohibitions that apply *only* to judicial candidates in partisan public elections.

This provision permits identification as a candidate of a political organization and acceptance of endorsements from a political organization.

EXPLANATION OF COMMENTS

New Comments [1] through [7] help explain the relationships between the several paragraphs of Rule 4.2, as well as the relationship of this Rule to other Rules in Canon 4, especially Rule 4.1.

RULE 4.3 Activities of Candidates for Appointive Judicial Office

A candidate for appointment to judicial office may:

(A) communicate with the appointing or confirming authority, including any selection, screening, or nominating commission or similar agency; and

(B) seek endorsements for the appointment from any person or organization other than a partisan political organization.

Comment

[1] When seeking support or endorsement, or when communicating directly with an appointing or confirming authority, a candidate for appointive judicial office must not make any pledges, promises, or commitments that are inconsistent with the impartial performance of the adjudicative duties of the office. See Rule 4.1(A)(13).

RULE 4.3—REPORTER'S EXPLANATION OF CHANGES†

1990 MODEL CODE COMPARISON

Rule 4.3(A) is essentially the same as Canon 5B(2)(a)(i), except that it includes a more expansive list of those whom candidates for appointive judicial office may contact.

Rule 4.3(B) is derived from Canon 5B(2)(a)(ii), but it allows candidates to seek endorsements for the appointment from a broader array of persons and organizations.

Comment [1] is new.

EXPLANATION OF BLACK LETTER

1. Rule 4.3(A): added "or confirming authority," and substituted "any selection, screening, or nominating commission or similar agency" for "other agency designated to screen candidates."

The second revision is stylistic only and introduced no substantive change. The Commission added a reference to a "confirming authority," having in mind most obviously the U.S. Senate when sitting to confirm or reject presidential nominations of federal judges. Some state jurisdictions include a similar confirmation process in their overall appointment process, and in those jurisdictions candidates must be allowed to state their qualifications and views to confirming agencies as well as nominating and screening agencies.

2. Rule 4.3(B): greatly relaxed the restrictions on organizations or individuals from whom a candidate for appointive judicial office can seek support for the appointment.

Canon 5B(2)(a) of the 1990 Code limits candidates to seeking support from organizations that "regularly" make recommendations to appointing authorities, and to individuals who have been invited by the appointing (or confirming) authority to provide information.

By eliminating the restriction of obtaining support from only those organizations that regularly make recommendations, the Commission expanded the ability of a candidate to seek endorsement from any person or organization (with the exception of partisan political organizations).

The ability of a candidate to identify his or her own sponsors recognizes the realities in today's world, in which candidates almost universally seek the affirmative support of friends and allies with the appointing authority.

EXPLANATION OF COMMENTS

[1] New Comment [1] serves as a reminder that although candidates for appointive judicial office are not submitting themselves to the voting public, they are submitting themselves to a much smaller "electorate," an appointing authority. It is just as improper in the appointment system to make pledges and promises that are inconsistent with the impartial performance of judicial duties as it is in a campaign for elected office.

---

† The "Reporters' Explanations of Changes" have not been approved by the ABA Joint Commission to Evaluate the Model Code of Judicial Conduct. They have been drafted by the Commission's Reporters, based on the proceedings and record of the Commission, solely to inform the ABA House of Delegates about each of the proposed amendments to the Model Code prior to their being considered at the ABA 2007 Midyear Meeting. THEY ARE NOT TO BE ADOPTED AS PART OF THE MODEL CODE.

RULE 4.4 Campaign Committees

(A) A judicial candidate* subject to public election* may establish a campaign committee to manage and conduct a campaign for the candidate, subject to the provisions of this Code. The candidate is responsible for ensuring that his or her campaign committee complies with applicable provisions of this Code and other applicable law.*

(B) A judicial candidate subject to public election shall direct his or her campaign committee:

(1) to solicit and accept only such campaign contributions* as are reasonable, in any event not to exceed, in the aggregate,* $[insert amount] from any individual or $[insert amount] from any entity or organization;

(2) not to solicit or accept contributions for a candidate's current campaign more than [insert amount of time] before the applicable primary election, caucus, or general or retention election, nor more than [insert number] days after the last election in which the candidate participated; and

(3) to comply with all applicable statutory requirements for disclosure and divestiture of campaign contributions, and to file with [name of appropriate regulatory authority] a report stating the name, address, occupation, and employer of each person who has made campaign contributions to the committee in an aggregate value exceeding $[insert amount]. The report must be filed within [insert number] days following an election, or within such other period as is provided by law.

Comment

[1] Judicial candidates are prohibited from personally soliciting campaign contributions or personally accepting campaign contributions. See Rule 4.1(A)(8). This Rule recognizes that in many jurisdictions, judicial candidates must raise campaign funds to support their candidacies, and permits candidates, other than candidates for appointive judicial office, to establish campaign committees to solicit and accept reasonable financial contributions or in-kind contributions.

[2] Campaign committees may solicit and accept campaign contributions, manage the expenditure of campaign funds, and generally conduct campaigns. Candidates are responsible for compliance with the requirements of election law and other applicable law, and for the activities of their campaign committees.

[3] At the start of a campaign, the candidate must instruct the campaign committee to solicit or accept only such contributions as are reasonable in amount, appropriate under the circumstances, and in conformity with applicable law. Although lawyers and others who might appear before a successful candidate for judicial office are permitted to make campaign contributions, the candidate should instruct his or her campaign committee to be especially cautious in connection with such contributions, so they do not create grounds for disqualification if the candidate is elected to judicial office. See Rule 2.11.

RULE 4.4—REPORTER'S EXPLANATION OF CHANGES†

1990 MODEL CODE COMPARISON

Rule 4.4(A) combines aspects of the second sentence of Canon 5C(2), part of Canon 5C(4), and some of the Commentary following Canon 5C(2).

† The "Reporters' Explanations of Changes" have not been approved by the ABA Joint Commission to Evaluate the Model Code of Judicial Conduct. They have been drafted by the Commission's Reporters, based on the proceedings and record of the Commission, solely to inform the ABA House of Delegates about each of the proposed amendments to the Model Code prior to their being considered at the ABA 2007 Midyear Meeting. THEY ARE NOT TO BE ADOPTED AS PART OF THE MODEL CODE.

Rule 4.4(B)(1) is essentially the same as Canon 5C(3), but also includes an element from Canon 5C(2).

Rule 4.4(B)(2) is essentially the same as the fifth sentence of Canon 5C(2), but with additional language citing compliance with any applicable laws relating to divestiture of campaign funds subsequent to the campaign.

Rule 4.4(B)(3) is based upon Canon 5C(4), but includes an entirely new reference to divestiture of campaign funds.

Comment [1] is based upon the third, fourth, and fifth sentences of the Commentary following Canon 5C(2).

Comment [2] combines aspects of the second sentence of Canon 5C(2) and part of Canon 5C(4).

Comment [3] is partly new, but is based upon aspects of Canon 5C(2) and the following Commentary, plus parts of Canon 5C(4).

EXPLANATION OF BLACK LETTER

1. Rule 4.4(A) makes explicit that campaign committees are permitted only for candidates subject to public election, deleted reference to "committees of responsible persons," and adds a final sentence stating directly the candidate's responsibility for acts of his or her campaign committee.

The placement of the material on campaign committees within Canon 5C of the 1990 Code made it obvious (if not explicit) that these provisions applied only to candidates for elective judicial office (those "subject to public election"). Because Rule 4.4 stands alone in Canon 4, it was necessary to state the point explicitly.

The direction to establish committees composed only of "responsible persons" seemed unnecessary, and was deleted. The last sentence of Rule 4.4(A) is new in this form, but merely makes explicit what is referred to indirectly or assumed throughout Canon 5C of the 1990 Code.

2. Rule 4.4(B)(1) combines and recasts material from both Canon 5C(2) and Canon 5C(3) of the 1990 Code.

No substantive change is intended. This provision establishes that campaign contributions must be "reasonable" in amount (to avoid a suggestion of undue influence) and in addition are subject to aggregate limits (per campaign) for individuals and organizations, limits which each jurisdiction will set according to its conditions and policy choices.

3. Rule 4.4(B)(2) adds the word "current" before the word "campaign," and leaves the post-election time period for ending campaign solicitation open for variation in each jurisdiction.

These are minor adjustments, but could become significant in some settings. The Joint Commission wanted to make it even clearer than in the 1990 Code that the time window for a campaign committee to solicit funds applies to *each* campaign separately. Thus, Rule 4.4(B)(2) specifies that it applies always to a candidate's *current* campaign. More significantly, to prevent the early buildup of campaign funds, the Commission specified that a specific time restriction should be enacted (to be chosen by each jurisdiction) establishing the point at which contributions may be solicited and accepted. The time for continuing to raise campaign funds after the election to pay off debts of the campaign was left to each state to decide.

4. Rule 4.4(B)(3) adds "or within such other period as is provided by law."

Only a minor substantive changed is intended. The Commission, aware that many jurisdictions already have laws regulating elections, including the reporting of campaign contributions and divestiture of the contributions subsequent to a campaign, did not want to interfere with the operation of these laws. In the 1990 Code, possible obligations under law to divest a campaign of its funds were not addressed.

This paragraph recognizes that many jurisdictions already have provisions in their general election and campaign finance laws regarding disclosure and divestiture of campaign funds, and defers to local choices and existing law (if applicable) in setting the specific details.

EXPLANATION OF COMMENT

Comments [1]–[3] explain the operation and rationale for the black letter text of Rule 4.4, borrowing from and recasting both black letter text and Commentary from the 1990 Code.

The treatment of contributions from *lawyers* in Comment [3] builds upon the treatment given in Canon 5C(2) of the 1990 Code, but goes a step further. Canon 5C(2) merely states that solicitation (by a campaign committee) of such contributions is not prohibited whereas Comment [3] to Rule 4.4 urges special caution in light of the enhanced possibility that significant contributions from lawyers (and parties) who might later come before the judge would be a cause for disqualification of the judge under Rule 2.11.

RULE 4.5 Activities of Judges Who Become Candidates for Nonjudicial Office

(A) Upon becoming a candidate for a nonjudicial elective office, a judge shall resign from judicial office, unless permitted by law* to continue to hold judicial office.

(B) Upon becoming a candidate for a nonjudicial appointive office, a judge is not required to resign from judicial office, provided that the judge complies with the other provisions of this Code.

Comment

[1] In campaigns for nonjudicial elective public office, candidates may make pledges, promises, or commitments related to positions they would take and ways they would act if elected to office. Although appropriate in nonjudicial campaigns, this manner of campaigning is inconsistent with the role of a judge, who must remain fair and impartial to all who come before him or her. The potential for misuse of the judicial office, and the political promises that the judge would be compelled to make in the course of campaigning for nonjudicial elective office, together dictate that a judge who wishes to run for such an office must resign upon becoming a candidate.

[2] The "resign to run" rule set forth in paragraph (A) ensures that a judge cannot use the judicial office to promote his or her candidacy, and prevents post-campaign retaliation from the judge in the event the judge is defeated in the election. When a judge is seeking appointive nonjudicial office, however, the dangers are not sufficient to warrant imposing the "resign to run" rule.

RULE 4.5—REPORTER'S EXPLANATION OF CHANGES†

1990 MODEL CODE COMPARISON

Rule 4.5(A) is derived from Canon 5A(2), but has been simplified and reworded.

Rule 4.5(B) is new, but is implicit in and derived from Canon 5A(2).

Comments [1] and [2] are new.

EXPLANATION OF BLACK LETTER

1. Rule 4.5(A) recasts text, substituting "nonjudicial elective office" for "in a primary or in a general election," and deleting the specific exception for state constitutional conventions.

The Commission retained the "resign-to-run" rule with only minor revisions for style and clarity. Canon 5A(2) of the 1990 Code has always been interpreted to apply to elective nonjudicial offices only; the proposed Rule makes that explicit. The Commission also removed the special exception for judges who campaign for election to a state constitutional convention because of the rarity with which such a situation occurs. The remaining language, "unless permitted by law to continue to hold judicial office" should address such situations.

† The "Reporters' Explanations of Changes" have not been approved by the ABA Joint Commission to Evaluate the Model Code of Judicial Conduct. They have been drafted by the Commission's Reporters, based on the proceedings and record of the Commission, solely to inform the ABA House of Delegates about each of the proposed amendments to the Model Code prior to their being considered at the ABA 2007 Midyear Meeting. THEY ARE NOT TO BE ADOPTED AS PART OF THE MODEL CODE.

2. Rule 4.5(B) add a paragraph to clarify what seemed implicit in Canon 5A(2)—that if a judge becomes a candidate for appointment to a nonjudicial office, the judge is not required to resign from judicial office as a general proposition.

The Commission decided to make explicit that the "resign-to-run" rule applies only to nonjudicial elective offices, because it is only there that the dangers justifying the rule (as explained in Comments [1] and [2]) are at their height. In addition, because a sitting judge may become a "candidate" for an appointive non-judicial office—an undefined term in the proposed Code—merely by being considered by an executive branch officer for appointment, the Commission decided it was unwarranted to require automatic resignation. This consideration is especially strong when the executive branch may be considering several nominees for the same position, and when the confirmation process, if any, is both lengthy and of uncertain outcome.

As a fail-safe, the Commission added the reminder that a judge who remains on the bench while a candidate for appointive nonjudicial office must continue to abide by the other provisions of this Code (such as maintaining independence, integrity, and impartiality).

EXPLANATION OF COMMENTS

New Comments [1] and [2] explain the rationale for applying the "resign-to-run" rule to elective nonjudicial offices, but not to appointive ones. The rationale is based chiefly upon the federal decisional law.

RULES FOR JUDICIAL-CONDUCT AND JUDICIAL-DISABILITY PROCEEDINGS

Adopted by the Judicial Conference of the United States on March 11, 2008 and amended on September 17, 2015, and again on March 12, 2019. Effective March 12, 2019.

TABLE OF CONTENTS

ARTICLE VIII. MISCELLANEOUS RULES

§ 310 Overview

Section 320 of this chapter reproduces the Rules for Judicial-Conduct and Judicial-Disability Proceedings. They were adopted on March 11, 2008, and took effect on April 10, 2008. They were amended on September 17, 2015, and again on March 12, 2019.

§ 320 Rules for Judicial-Conduct and Judicial-Disability Proceedings

Preface

These Rules were promulgated by the Judicial Conference of the United States, after public comment, pursuant to 28 U.S.C. §§ 331 and 358, to establish standards and procedures for addressing complaints filed by complainants or identified by chief judges under the Judicial Conduct and Disability Act, 28 U.S.C. §§ 351–364.

ARTICLE I. GENERAL PROVISIONS

1. Scope and Covered Judges

(a) Scope. These Rules govern proceedings under the Judicial Conduct and Disability Act (Act), 28 U.S.C. §§ 351–364, to determine whether a covered judge has engaged in conduct prejudicial to the effective and expeditious administration of the business of the courts or is unable to discharge the duties of office because of mental or physical disability.

(b) Covered Judge. A covered judge is defined under the Act and is limited to judges of United States courts of appeals, judges of United States district courts, judges of United States bankruptcy courts, United States magistrate judges, and judges of the courts specified in 28 U.S.C. § 363.

Commentary on Rule 1

In September 2006, the Judicial Conduct and Disability Act Study Committee ("Breyer Committee"), appointed in 2004 by Chief Justice Rehnquist, presented a report ("Breyer Committee Report"), 239 F.R.D. 116 (Sept. 2006), to Chief Justice Roberts that evaluated implementation of the Judicial Conduct and Disability Act of 1980, 28 U.S.C. §§ 351–364. The Breyer Committee had been formed in response to criticism from the public and Congress regarding the effectiveness of the Act's implementation. The Executive Committee of the Judicial Conference directed its Committee on Judicial Conduct and Disability to consider the Breyer Committee's recommendations and to report on their implementation to the Conference.

The Breyer Committee found that it could not evaluate implementation of the Act without establishing interpretive standards, Breyer Committee Report, 239 F.R.D. at 132, and that a major problem faced by chief judges in implementing the Act was the lack of authoritative interpretive standards. *Id.* at 212–15. The Breyer Committee then established standards to guide its evaluation, some of which were new formulations and some of which were taken from the "Illustrative Rules Governing Complaints of Judicial Misconduct and Disability," discussed below. The principal standards used by the Breyer Committee are in Appendix E of its Report. *Id.* at 238.

Based on the Breyer Committee's findings, the Committee on Judicial Conduct and Disability concluded that there was a need for the Judicial Conference to exercise its power under Section 358 of the Act to fashion standards guiding the various officers and bodies that must exercise responsibility under the Act. To that end, the Committee on Judicial Conduct and Disability proposed rules based largely on Appendix E of the Breyer Committee Report and the Illustrative Rules.

The Illustrative Rules were originally prepared in 1986 by the Special Committee of the Conference of Chief Judges of the United States Courts of Appeals, and were subsequently revised and amended, most recently in 2000, by the predecessor to the Committee on Judicial Conduct and Disability. The Illustrative Rules were adopted, with minor variations, by circuit judicial councils, to govern complaints under the Judicial Conduct and Disability Act.

After being submitted for public comment pursuant to 28 U.S.C. § 358(c), the Judicial Conference promulgated the present Rules on March 11, 2008. They were amended on September 17, 2015, and again on March 12, 2019.

The definition of a covered judge tracks the Judicial Conduct and Disability Act. *See* 28 U.S.C. § 351(d)(1) (defining the term "judge" as "a circuit judge, district judge, bankruptcy judge, or magistrate judge"). As long as the subject of a complaint retains the judicial office and remains a covered judge as defined in Rule 1(b), a complaint must be addressed. *Id.*; 28 U.S.C. §§ 371(b); 372(a).

Rules 8(c) and (d) address the procedures for processing a complaint involving allegations against a person *not* covered by the Act, such as other court personnel, or against both a covered judge and a noncovered person. Court employees seeking to report, or file a claim related to, misconduct or the denial of rights granted under their Employment Dispute Resolution (EDR) plan by other court personnel may wish to consult the Model EDR Plan and the EDR plan for the relevant court, among other resources. *See* Guide to Judiciary Policy, vol. 12, appx. 2B.

2. Construction and Effect

(a) Generally. These Rules are mandatory; they supersede any conflicting judicial-council rules. Judicial councils may promulgate additional rules to implement the Act as long as those rules do not conflict with these Rules.

(b) Exception. A Rule will not apply if, when performing duties authorized by the Act, a chief judge, a special committee, a judicial council, the Committee on Judicial Conduct and Disability, or the Judicial Conference expressly finds that exceptional circumstances render application of that Rule in a particular proceeding manifestly unjust or contrary to the purposes of the Act or these Rules.

Commentary on Rule 2

Unlike the Illustrative Rules, these Rules provide mandatory and nationally uniform provisions governing the substantive and procedural aspects of misconduct and disability proceedings under the Act. The mandatory nature of these Rules is authorized by 28 U.S.C. § 358(a) and (c). Judicial councils retain the power to promulgate rules consistent with these Rules. For example, a local rule may authorize the electronic distribution of materials pursuant to Rule 8(b).

Rule 2(b) recognizes that unforeseen and exceptional circumstances may call for a different approach in particular cases.

3. General Definitions

The following general definitions apply to these Rules. Cognizable misconduct and disability are defined in Rule 4.

(a) Chief Judge. "Chief judge" means the chief judge of a United States court of appeals, of the United States Court of International Trade, or of the United States Court of Federal Claims.

(b) Circuit Clerk. "Circuit clerk" means a clerk of a United States court of appeals, the clerk of the United States Court of International Trade, the clerk of the United States Court of Federal Claims, or the circuit executive of the United States Court of Appeals for the Federal Circuit.

(c) Complaint. A "complaint" is:

(1) a document that, in accordance with Rule 6, is filed by, or on behalf of, any person, including a document filed by an organization; or

(2) information from any source, other than a document described in (c)(1), that gives a chief judge probable cause to believe that a covered judge, as defined in Rule

1(b), has engaged in misconduct or may have a disability, whether or not the information is framed as or is intended to be an allegation of misconduct or disability.

(d) Court of Appeals, District Court, and District Judge. "Court of appeals," "district court," and "district judge," where appropriate, include the United States Court of Federal Claims, the United States Court of International Trade, and the judges thereof.

(e) Judicial Council and Circuit. "Judicial council" and "circuit," where appropriate, include any courts designated in 28 U.S.C. § 363.

(f) Judicial Employee. "Judicial Employee" includes judicial assistants, law clerks, and other court employees, including unpaid staff, such as interns, externs, and other volunteer employees.

(g) Magistrate Judge. "Magistrate judge," where appropriate, includes a special master appointed by the Court of Federal Claims under 42 U.S.C. § 300aa–12(c).

(h) Subject Judge. "Subject judge" means a covered judge, as described in Rule 1(b), who is the subject of a complaint.

Commentary on Rule 3

Rule 3 is derived and adapted from the Breyer Committee Report and the Illustrative Rules.

Unless otherwise specified or the context otherwise indicates, the term "complaint" is used in these Rules to refer both to complaints identified by a chief judge under Rule 5 and to complaints filed by a complainant under Rule 6.

Under the Act, a "complaint" may be filed by "any person" or "identified" by a chief judge. *See* 28 U.S.C. § 351(a), (b). Under Rule 3(c)(1), a complaint may be submitted by, or on behalf of, any person, including a document filed by an organization. Traditional standing requirements do not apply. Individuals or organizations may file a complaint even if they have not been directly injured or aggrieved.

Generally, the word "complaint" brings to mind the commencement of an adversary proceeding in which the contending parties are left to present the evidence and legal arguments, and judges play the role of an essentially passive arbiter. The Act, however, establishes an administrative, inquisitorial process. For example, even absent a complaint filed by a complainant under Rule 6, chief judges are expected in some circumstances to trigger the process—"identify a complaint," *see* 28 U.S.C. § 351(b) and Rule 5—and conduct an investigation without becoming a party. *See* 28 U.S.C. § 352(a); Breyer Committee Report, 239 F.R.D. at 214; Illustrative Rule 2(j). Where the complainant reveals information of misconduct or disability but does not claim it as such, the chief judge is not limited to the "four corners of the complaint" and should proceed under Rule 5 to determine whether identification of a complaint is appropriate. *See* Breyer Committee Report, 239 F.R.D. at 183–84.

An allegation of misconduct or disability filed under Rule 6 is a "complaint," and the Rule so provides in subsection (c)(1). However, both the nature of the process and the use of the term "identify" suggest that the word "complaint" covers more than a document formally triggering the process. The process relies on chief judges considering known information and triggering the process when appropriate. "Identifying" a "complaint," therefore, is best understood as the chief judge's concluding that information known to the judge constitutes probable cause to believe that misconduct occurred or a disability exists, whether or not the information is framed as, or intended to be, an accusation. This definition is codified in subsection (c)(2).

The remaining subsections of Rule 3 provide technical definitions clarifying the application of the Rules.

ARTICLE II. MISCONDUCT AND DISABILITY

4. Misconduct and Disability Definitions

(a) Misconduct Generally. Cognizable Misconduct is conduct prejudicial to the effective and expeditious administration of the business of the courts. Cognizable misconduct includes, but is not limited to, the following:

(1) Violation of Specific Standards of Judicial Conduct. Cognizable misconduct includes:

(A) using the judge's office to obtain special treatment for friends or relatives;

(B) accepting bribes, gifts, or other personal favors related to the judicial office;

(C) engaging in improper ex parte communications with parties or counsel for one side in a case;

(D) engaging in partisan political activity or making inappropriately partisan statements;

(E) soliciting funds for organizations; or

(F) violating rules or standards pertaining to restrictions on outside income or knowingly violating requirements for financial disclosure.

(2) Abusive or Harassing Behavior. Cognizable misconduct includes:

(A) engaging in unwanted, offensive, or abusive sexual conduct, including sexual harassment or assault;

(B) treating litigants, attorneys, judicial employees, or others in a demonstrably egregious and hostile manner; or

(C) creating a hostile work environment for judicial employees.

(3) Discrimination. Cognizable misconduct includes intentional discrimination on the basis of race, color, sex, gender, gender identity, pregnancy, sexual orientation, religion, national origin, age, or disability;

(4) Retaliation. Cognizable misconduct includes retaliating against complainants, witnesses, judicial employees, or others for participating in this complaint process, or for reporting or disclosing judicial misconduct or disability;

(5) Interference or Failure to Comply with the Complaint Process. Cognizable misconduct includes refusing, without good cause shown, to cooperate in the investigation of a complaint or enforcement of a decision rendered under these Rules; or

(6) Failure to Report or Disclose. Cognizable misconduct includes failing to call to the attention of the relevant chief district judge or chief circuit judge any reliable information reasonably likely to constitute judicial misconduct or disability.

A judge who receives such reliable information shall respect a request for confidentiality but shall nonetheless disclose the information to the relevant chief district judge or chief circuit judge, who shall also treat the information as confidential. Certain reliable information may be protected from disclosure by statute or rule. A judge's assurance of confidentiality must yield when there is reliable information of misconduct or disability that threatens the safety or security of any person or that is serious or egregious such that it threatens the integrity and proper functioning of the judiciary.

A person reporting information of misconduct or disability must be informed at the outset of a judge's responsibility to disclose such information to the relevant chief district judge or chief circuit judge.

Reliable information reasonably likely to constitute judicial misconduct or disability related to a chief circuit judge should be called to the attention of the next most-senior active circuit judge. Such information related to a chief district judge should be called to the attention of the chief circuit judge.

(7) Conduct Outside the Performance of Official Duties. Cognizable misconduct includes conduct occurring outside the performance of official duties if the conduct is reasonably likely to have a prejudicial effect on the administration of the business of the courts, including a substantial and widespread lowering of public confidence in the courts among reasonable people.

(b) Conduct Not Constituting Cognizable Misconduct.

(1) Allegations Related to the Merits of a Decision or Procedural Ruling. Cognizable misconduct does not include an allegation that calls into question the correctness of a judge's ruling, including a failure to recuse.

If the decision or ruling is alleged to be the result of an improper motive, *e.g.*, a bribe, ex parte contact, racial or ethnic bias, or improper conduct in rendering a decision or ruling, such as personally derogatory remarks irrelevant to the issues, the complaint is not cognizable to the extent that it calls into question the merits of the decision.

(2) Allegations About Delay. Cognizable misconduct does not include an allegation about delay in rendering a decision or ruling, unless the allegation concerns an improper motive in delaying a particular decision or habitual delay in a significant number of unrelated cases.

(c) Disability. Disability is a temporary or permanent impairment, physical or mental, rendering a judge unable to discharge the duties of the particular judicial office. Examples of disability include substance abuse, the inability to stay awake during court proceedings, or impairment of cognitive abilities that renders the judge unable to function effectively.

Commentary on Rule 4

The phrase "prejudicial to the effective and expeditious administration of the business of the courts" is not subject to precise definition, and subsection (a) therefore provides some specific examples. 28 U.S.C. § 351(a). The Code of Conduct for United States Judges sets forth behavioral guidelines for judges. While the Code's Canons are instructive, ultimately the responsibility for determining what constitutes cognizable misconduct is determined by the Act and these Rules, as interpreted and applied by judicial councils, subject to review and limitations prescribed by the Act and these Rules. *See also* Rule 24 (Public Availability of Decisions).

Even where specific, mandatory rules exist—for example, governing the receipt of gifts by judges, outside earned income, and financial disclosure obligations—the distinction between the misconduct statute and these specific, mandatory rules must be borne in mind. For example, an inadvertent, minor violation of any one of these rules, promptly remedied when called to the attention of the judge, might still be a violation but might not rise to the level of misconduct under the Act. By contrast, a pattern of such violations of the Code might well rise to the level of misconduct.

Rule 4(a)(2)(A) provides expressly that unwanted, offensive, or abusive sexual conduct by a judge, including sexual harassment or assault, constitutes cognizable misconduct. The Rule recognizes that anyone can be a victim of unwanted, offensive, or abusive sexual conduct, regardless of their sex and of the sex of the judge engaging in the misconduct.

Under Rule 4(a)(4), a judge's efforts to retaliate against any person for reporting or disclosing misconduct, or otherwise participating in the complaint process constitute cognizable misconduct. The Rule makes the prohibition against retaliation explicit in the interest of promoting public confidence in the complaint process.

Rules 4(a)(2), (3), and (4) reflect the judiciary's commitment to maintaining a work environment in which all judicial employees are treated with dignity, fairness, and respect, and are free from harassment, discrimination, and retaliation. *See* Code of Conduct for United States Judges, Canon 3A(3) cmt. ("The duty to be respectful includes the responsibility to avoid comment or behavior that could reasonably be interpreted as harassment, prejudice or bias.").

Rule 4(a)(5) provides that a judge's refusal, without good cause shown, to cooperate in the investigation of a complaint or enforcement of a decision rendered under these Rules constitutes cognizable misconduct. While the exercise of rights under the Fifth Amendment to the Constitution would constitute good cause under Rule 4(a)(5), given the fact-specific nature of the inquiry, it is not possible to otherwise anticipate all circumstances that might also constitute good cause. The Commentary on Rule 13 provides additional discussion regarding Rule 4(a)(5). The Rules contemplate that judicial councils will not consider commencing proceedings under Rule 4(a)(5) except as necessary after other means to acquire the information or enforce a decision have been tried or have proven futile.

All judges have a duty to bring to the attention of the relevant chief district judge or chief circuit judge reliable information reasonably likely to constitute judicial misconduct or disability. *See* Rule 4(a)(6). This duty is included within every judge's obligation to assist in addressing allegations of misconduct or disability and to take appropriate action as necessary. Public confidence in the integrity and impartiality of the judiciary is promoted when judges take appropriate action based on reliable information of likely misconduct. Appropriate action depends on the circumstances, but the overarching goal of such action should be to prevent harm to those affected by the misconduct and to prevent recurrence. *See* Code of Conduct for United States Judges, Canon 3B(6) & cmt. These Rules incorporate those principles while allowing for appropriate, expeditious, fair, and effective resolutions of all such complaints.

The formal procedures outlined in these Rules are intended to address serious issues of judicial misconduct and disability. By statute and rule, the chief circuit judge administers the misconduct and disability complaint process, including the authority to investigate an allegation and, if warranted, to identify a formal complaint. *See* Rule 5. Disclosures made to or otherwise brought to the attention of the appropriate chief district judge of reliable information of misconduct or disability that threatens the safety or security of any person or that is serious or egregious such that it threatens the integrity and proper functioning of the judiciary warrant communication to and consultation with the chief circuit judge in light of the chief circuit judge's statutory responsibility for overseeing any required final action.

In practice, however, not all allegations of misconduct or disability will warrant resort to the formal procedures outlined in these Rules because they appear likely to yield to effective, prompt resolution through informal corrective action. In such cases, allegations may initially be addressed to the chief district judge or the chief circuit judge to determine whether informal corrective action will suffice and to initiate such steps as promptly as is reasonable under the circumstances.

A person who seeks to report information of misconduct or disability on a confidential or anonymous basis may proceed through various alternative avenues within the judiciary, including the Office of Judicial Integrity and/or comparable offices within the circuits.

Rule 4(a)(7) reflects that an allegation can meet the statutory standard for misconduct even though the judge's alleged conduct did not occur in the course of the performance of official duties. Furthermore, some conduct specified in Rule 4(a)(1) through 4(a)(6), or not specified within these Rules, might constitute misconduct occurring outside the performance of official duties. The Code of Conduct for United States Judges expressly covers a wide range of extra-official activities, and some of these activities may constitute misconduct under the Act and these Rules. For example, allegations that a judge solicited funds for a charity or other organization or participated in a partisan political event are cognizable under the Act even though they did not occur in the course of the performance of the judge's official duties.

Rule 4(b)(1) tracks the Act, 28 U.S.C. § 352(b)(1)(A)(ii), in excluding from the definition of misconduct allegations "[d]irectly related to the merits of a decision or procedural ruling." This exclusion preserves the independence of judges in the exercise of judicial authority by ensuring that the complaint procedure is not used to collaterally call into question the substance of a judge's decision or procedural ruling. Any allegation that calls into question the correctness of an official decision or procedural ruling of a judge—without more—is merits-related. The phrase "decision or procedural ruling" is not limited to rulings issued in deciding Article III cases or controversies. Thus, a complaint challenging the correctness of a chief judge's determination to dismiss a prior misconduct complaint would be properly dismissed as merits-related—in other words, as challenging the substance of the judge's administrative determination to dismiss the complaint—even though it does not concern the judge's rulings in Article III litigation. Similarly, an allegation that a judge incorrectly declined to approve a Criminal Justice Act voucher is merits-related under this standard.

Conversely, an allegation that a judge conspired with a prosecutor to make a particular ruling is not merits-related, even though it "relates" to a ruling in a colloquial sense. Such an allegation attacks the propriety of conspiring with the prosecutor and goes beyond a challenge to the correctness—"the merits"—of the ruling itself. An allegation that a judge ruled against the complainant because the complainant is a member of a particular racial or ethnic group, or because the judge dislikes the complainant personally, is also not merits-related. Such an allegation attacks the propriety of arriving at rulings with an illicit or improper motive. Similarly, an allegation that a judge used an inappropriate term to refer to a class of people is not merits-related even if the judge used it on the bench or in an opinion; the correctness of the judge's rulings is not at stake. An allegation that a judge treated litigants, attorneys, judicial employees, or others in a demonstrably egregious and hostile manner is also not merits-related.

The existence of an appellate remedy is usually irrelevant to whether an allegation is merits-related. The merits-related ground for dismissal exists to protect judges' independence in making rulings, not to protect or promote the appellate process. A complaint alleging an incorrect ruling is merits-related even though the complainant has no recourse from that ruling. By the same token, an allegation that is otherwise cognizable under the Act should not be dismissed merely because an appellate remedy appears to exist (for example, vacating a ruling that resulted from an improper ex parte communication). However, there may be occasions when appellate and misconduct proceedings overlap, and consideration and disposition of a complaint under these Rules may be properly deferred by the chief judge until the appellate proceedings are concluded to avoid inconsistent decisions.

Because of the special need to protect judges' independence in deciding what to say in an opinion or ruling, a somewhat different standard applies to determine the merits-relatedness of a non-frivolous allegation that a judge's language in a ruling reflected an improper motive. If the judge's language was relevant to the case at hand—for example, a statement that a claim is legally or factually "frivolous"—then the judge's choice of language is presumptively merits-related and excluded, absent evidence apart from the ruling itself suggesting an improper motive. If, on the other hand, the challenged language does not seem relevant on its face, then an additional inquiry under Rule 11(b) is necessary.

With regard to Rule 4(b)(2), a complaint of delay in a single case is excluded as merits-related. Such an allegation may be said to challenge the correctness of an official action of the judge, *i.e.*, assigning a low priority to deciding the particular case. But, an allegation of a habitual pattern of delay in a significant number of unrelated cases, or an allegation of deliberate delay in a single case arising out of an improper motive, is not merits-related.

Rule 4(c) relates to disability and provides only the most general definition, recognizing that a fact-specific approach is the only one available. A mental disability could involve cognitive impairment or any psychiatric or psychological condition that renders the judge unable to discharge the duties of office. Such duties may include those that are administrative. If, for example, the judge is a chief judge, the judicial council, fulfilling its obligation under 28 U.S.C. § 332(d)(1) to make "necessary and appropriate orders for the effective and expeditious administration of justice," may find, under 28 U.S.C. § 45(d) or § 136(e), that the judge is "temporarily unable to perform" his or her chief-judge duties. In that event, an appropriate remedy could involve, under Rule 20(b)(1)(D)(vii), temporary reassignment of chief-judge duties to the next judge statutorily eligible to perform them.

Confidentiality as referenced elsewhere in these Rules is directed toward protecting the fairness and thoroughness of the process by which a complaint is filed or initiated, investigated (in specific circumstances), and ultimately resolved, as specified under these Rules. Nothing in these Rules concerning the confidentiality of the complaint process or the Code of Conduct for Judicial Employees concerning use or disclosure of confidential information received in the course of official duties prevents judicial employees from reporting or disclosing misconduct or disability. *See* Rule 23(c).

ARTICLE III. INITIATION OF COMPLAINT

5. Identification of Complaint

(a) Identification. When a chief judge has information constituting reasonable grounds for inquiry into whether a covered judge has engaged in misconduct or has a disability, the chief judge may conduct an inquiry, as he or she deems appropriate, into the accuracy of the information even if no related complaint has been filed. A chief judge who finds probable cause to believe that misconduct has occurred or that a disability exists may seek an informal resolution that he or she finds satisfactory. If no informal resolution is achieved or is feasible, the chief judge may identify a complaint and, by written order stating the reasons, begin the review provided in Rule 11. If the evidence of misconduct is clear and convincing and no informal resolution is achieved or is feasible, the chief judge must identify a complaint. A chief judge must not decline to identify a complaint merely because the person making the allegation has not filed a complaint under Rule 6. This Rule is subject to Rule 7.

(b) Submission Not Fully Complying with Rule 6. A legible submission in substantial but not full compliance with Rule 6 must be considered as possible grounds for the identification of a complaint under Rule 5(a).

Commentary on Rule 5

This Rule is adapted from the Breyer Committee Report, 239 F.R.D. at 245–46.

The Act authorizes a chief judge, by written order stating reasons, to identify a complaint and thereby dispense with the filing of a written complaint. *See* 28 U.S.C. § 351(b). Under Rule 5, when a chief judge becomes aware of information constituting reasonable grounds to inquire into possible misconduct or disability on the part of a covered judge, and no formal complaint has been filed, the chief judge has the power in his or her discretion to begin an appropriate inquiry. A chief judge's decision whether to informally seek a resolution and/or to identify a complaint is guided by the results of that inquiry. If the chief judge concludes that there is probable cause to believe that misconduct has occurred or a disability exists, the chief judge may seek an informal resolution, if feasible, and if failing in that, may identify a complaint. Discretion is accorded largely for the reasons police officers and prosecutors have discretion in making arrests or bringing charges. The matter may be trivial and isolated, based on marginal evidence, or otherwise highly unlikely to lead to a misconduct or disability finding. On the other hand, if the inquiry leads the chief judge to conclude that there is clear and convincing evidence of misconduct or a disability, and no satisfactory informal resolution has been achieved or is feasible, the chief judge is required to identify a complaint.

An informal resolution is one agreed to by the subject judge and found satisfactory by the chief judge. Because an informal resolution under Rule 5 reached before a complaint is filed under Rule 6 will generally cause a subsequent Rule 6 complaint alleging the identical matter to be concluded, *see* Rule 11(d), the chief judge must be sure that the resolution is fully appropriate before endorsing it. In doing so, the chief judge must balance the seriousness of the matter against the particular judge's alacrity in addressing the issue. The availability of this procedure should encourage attempts at swift remedial action before a formal complaint is filed.

When a chief judge identifies a complaint, a written order stating the reasons for the identification must be provided; this begins the process articulated in Rule 11. Rule 11 provides that once a chief judge has identified a complaint, the chief judge, subject to the disqualification provisions of Rule 25, will perform, with respect to that complaint, all functions assigned to the chief judge for the determination of complaints filed by a complainant.

In high-visibility situations, it may be desirable for a chief judge to identify a complaint without first seeking an informal resolution (and then, if the circumstances warrant, dismiss or conclude the identified complaint without appointment of a special committee) in order to assure the public that the allegations have not been ignored.

A chief judge's decision not to identify a complaint under Rule 5 is not appealable and is subject to Rule 4(b)(1), which excludes merits-related complaints from the definition of misconduct.

A chief judge may not decline to identify a complaint solely on the basis that the unfiled allegations could be raised by one or more persons in a filed complaint, but none of these persons has opted to do so.

Subsection (a) concludes by stating that this Rule is "subject to Rule 7." This is intended to establish that only (i) the chief judge of the home circuit of a potential subject judge, or (ii) the chief judge of a circuit in which misconduct is alleged to have occurred in the course of official business while the potential subject judge was sitting by designation, shall have the power or a duty under this Rule to identify a complaint.

Subsection (b) provides that submissions that do not comply with the requirements of Rule 6(d) must be considered under Rule 5(a). For instance, if a complaint has been filed but the form submitted is unsigned, or the truth of the statements therein are not verified in writing under penalty of perjury, then a chief judge must nevertheless consider the allegations as known information and as a possible basis for the identification of a complaint under the process described in Rule 5(a).

6. Filing of Complaint

(a) Form. A complainant may use the form reproduced in the Appendix to these Rules or a form designated by the rules of the judicial council in the circuit in which the complaint is filed. A complaint form is also available on each court of appeals' website or may be obtained from the circuit clerk or any district court or bankruptcy court within the circuit. A form is not necessary to file a complaint, but the complaint must be written and must include the information described in (b).

(b) Brief Statement of Facts. A complaint must contain a concise statement that details the specific facts on which the claim of misconduct or disability is based. The statement of facts should include a description of:

(1) what happened;

(2) when and where the relevant events happened;

(3) any information that would help an investigator check the facts; and

(4) for an allegation of disability, any additional facts that form the basis of that allegation.

(c) Legibility. A complaint should be typewritten if possible. If not typewritten, it must be legible. An illegible complaint will be returned to the complainant with a request to resubmit it in legible form. If a resubmitted complaint is still illegible, it will not be accepted for filing.

(d) Complainant's Address and Signature; Verification. The complainant must provide a contact address and sign the complaint. The truth of the statements made in the complaint must be verified in writing under penalty of perjury. If any of these requirements are not met, the submission will be accepted, but it will be reviewed under only Rule 5(b).

(e) Number of Copies; Envelope Marking. The complainant shall provide the number of copies of the complaint required by local rule. Each copy should be in an envelope marked "Complaint of Misconduct" or "Complaint of Disability." The envelope must not show the name of any subject judge.

Commentary on Rule 6

The Rule is adapted from the Illustrative Rules and is largely self-explanatory. As discussed in the Commentary on Rule 4 and in Rule 23(c), confidentiality as referenced elsewhere in these Rules does not prevent judicial employees from reporting or disclosing misconduct or disability.

7. Where to Initiate Complaint

(a) Where to File. Except as provided in (b),

(1) a complaint against a judge of a United States court of appeals, a United States district court, a United States bankruptcy court, or a United States magistrate judge must be filed with the circuit clerk in the jurisdiction in which the subject judge holds office.

(2) a complaint against a judge of the United States Court of International Trade or the United States Court of Federal Claims must be filed with the respective clerk of that court.

(3) a complaint against a judge of the United States Court of Appeals for the Federal Circuit must be filed with the circuit executive of that court.

(b) Misconduct in Another Circuit; Transfer. If a complaint alleges misconduct in the course of official business while the subject judge was sitting on a court by designation under 28 U.S.C. §§ 291–293 and 294(d), the complaint may be filed or identified with the circuit clerk of that circuit or of the subject judge's home circuit. The proceeding will continue in the circuit of the first-filed or first-identified complaint. The judicial council of the circuit where the complaint was first filed or first identified may transfer the complaint to the subject judge's home circuit or to the circuit where the alleged misconduct occurred, as the case may be.

Commentary on Rule 7

Title 28 U.S.C. § 351 states that complaints are to be filed with "the clerk of the court of appeals for the circuit." However, in many circuits, this role is filled by circuit executives. Accordingly, the term "circuit clerk," as defined in Rule 3(b) and used throughout these Rules, applies to circuit executives.

Section 351 uses the term "the circuit" in a way that suggests that either the home circuit of the subject judge or the circuit in which misconduct is alleged to have occurred is the proper venue for complaints. With an exception for judges sitting by designation, the Rule requires the filing or identification of a misconduct or disability complaint in the circuit in which the judge holds office, largely based on the administrative perspective of the Act. Given the Act's emphasis on the future conduct of the business of the courts, the circuit in which the judge holds office is the appropriate forum because that circuit is likely best able to influence a judge's future behavior in constructive ways.

However, when judges sit by designation, the non-home circuit has a strong interest in redressing misconduct in the course of official business, and where allegations also involve a member of the bar—ex parte contact between an attorney and a judge, for example—it may often be desirable to have the judicial and bar misconduct proceedings take place in the same venue. Rule 7(b), therefore, allows transfer to, or filing or identification of a complaint in, the non-home circuit. The proceeding may be transferred by the judicial council of the filing or identified circuit to the other circuit.

8. Action by Circuit Clerk

(a) Receipt of Complaint. Upon receiving a complaint against a judge filed under Rule 6 or identified under Rule 5, the circuit clerk must open a file, assign a docket number according to a uniform numbering scheme promulgated by the Committee on Judicial Conduct and Disability, and acknowledge the complaint's receipt.

(b) Distribution of Copies. The circuit clerk must promptly send copies of a complaint filed under Rule 6 to the chief judge or, where the chief judge is disqualified from

considering a complaint, to the judge authorized to act as chief judge under Rule 25(f), and copies of complaints filed under Rule 6 or identified under Rule 5 to each subject judge. The circuit clerk must retain the original complaint. Any further distribution should be as provided by local rule.

(c) Complaint Against Noncovered Person. If the circuit clerk receives a complaint about a person not holding an office described in Rule 1(b), the clerk must not accept the complaint under these Rules.

(d) Complaint Against Judge and Another Noncovered Person. If the circuit clerk receives a complaint about a judge described in Rule 1(b) and a person not holding an office described in Rule 1(b), the clerk must accept the complaint under these Rules only with regard to the judge and must so inform the complainant.

Commentary on Rule 8

This Rule is adapted from the Illustrative Rules and is largely self-explanatory.

The uniform docketing scheme described in subsection (a) should take into account potential problems associated with a complaint that names multiple judges. One solution may be to provide separate docket numbers for each subject judge. Separate docket numbers would help avoid difficulties in tracking cases, particularly if a complaint is dismissed with respect to some, but not all of the named judges.

Complaints against noncovered persons are not to be accepted for processing under these Rules but may, of course, be accepted under other circuit rules or procedures for grievances.

9. Time for Filing or Identifying Complaint

A complaint may be filed or identified at any time. If the passage of time has made an accurate and fair investigation of a complaint impracticable, the complaint must be dismissed under Rule 11(c)(1)(E).

Commentary on Rule 9

This Rule is adapted from the Act, 28 U.S.C. §§ 351, 352(b)(1)(A)(iii), and the Illustrative Rules.

10. Abuse of Complaint Procedure

(a) Abusive Complaints. A complainant who has filed repetitive, harassing, or frivolous complaints, or has otherwise abused the complaint procedure, may be restricted from filing further complaints. After giving the complainant an opportunity to show cause in writing why his or her right to file further complaints should not be limited, the judicial council may prohibit, restrict, or impose conditions on the complainant's use of the complaint procedure. Upon written request of the complainant, the judicial council may revise or withdraw any prohibition, restriction, or condition previously imposed.

(b) Orchestrated Complaints. When many essentially identical complaints from different complainants are received and appear to be part of an orchestrated campaign, the chief judge may recommend that the judicial council issue a written order instructing the circuit clerk to accept only a certain number of such complaints for filing and to refuse to accept additional complaints. The circuit clerk must send a copy of any such order to anyone whose complaint was not accepted.

Commentary on Rule 10

This Rule is adapted from the Illustrative Rules.

Rule 10(a) provides a mechanism for a judicial council to restrict the filing of further complaints by a single complainant who has abused the complaint procedure. In some instances, however, the complaint procedure may be abused in a manner for which the remedy provided in Rule 10(a) may not be appropriate.

For example, some circuits have been inundated with submissions of dozens or hundreds of essentially identical complaints against the same judge or judges, all submitted by different complainants. In many of these instances, persons with grievances against a particular judge or judges used the Internet or other technology to orchestrate mass complaint-filing campaigns against them. If each complaint submitted as part of such a campaign were accepted for filing and processed according to these Rules, there would be a serious drain on court resources without any benefit to the adjudication of the underlying merits.

A judicial council may, therefore, respond to such mass filings under Rule 10(b) by declining to accept repetitive complaints for filing, regardless of the fact that the complaints are nominally submitted by different complainants. When the first complaint or complaints have been dismissed on the merits, and when further, essentially identical submissions follow, the judicial council may issue a second order noting that these are identical or repetitive complaints, directing the circuit clerk not to accept these complaints or any further such complaints for filing, and directing the clerk to send each putative complainant copies of both orders.

ARTICLE IV. REVIEW OF COMPLAINT BY CHIEF JUDGE

11. Chief Judge's Review

(a) Purpose of Chief Judge's Review. When a complaint is identified by the chief judge or is filed, the chief judge must review it unless the chief judge is disqualified under Rule 25, in which case the most-senior active circuit judge not disqualified will review the complaint. If a complaint contains information constituting evidence of misconduct or disability, but the complainant does not claim it as such, the chief judge must treat the complaint as if it did allege misconduct or disability and give notice to the subject judge. After reviewing a complaint, the chief judge must determine whether it should be:

(1) dismissed;

(2) concluded on the ground that voluntary corrective action has been taken;

(3) concluded because intervening events have made action on the complaint no longer necessary; or

(4) referred to a special committee.

(b) Chief Judge's Inquiry. In determining what action to take under Rule 11(a), the chief judge may conduct a limited inquiry. The chief judge, or a designee, may communicate orally or in writing with the complainant, the subject judge, and any others who may have knowledge of the matter, and may obtain and review transcripts and other relevant documents. In conducting the inquiry, the chief judge must not determine any reasonably disputed issue. Any such determination must be left to a special committee appointed under Rule 11(f) and to the judicial council that considers the committee's report.

(c) Dismissal.

(1) Permissible grounds. A complaint may be dismissed in whole or in part to the extent that the chief judge concludes that the complaint:

(A) alleges conduct that, even if true, is not prejudicial to the effective and expeditious administration of the business of the courts and does not indicate a mental or physical disability resulting in the inability to discharge the duties of judicial office;

(B) is directly related to the merits of a decision or procedural ruling;

(C) is frivolous;

(D) is based on allegations lacking sufficient evidence to raise an inference that misconduct has occurred or that a disability exists;

(E) is based on allegations that are incapable of being established through investigation;

(F) has been filed in the wrong circuit under Rule 7; or

(G) is otherwise not appropriate for consideration under the Act.

(2) Impermissible grounds. A complaint must not be dismissed solely because it repeats allegations of a previously dismissed complaint if it also contains material information not previously considered and does not constitute harassment of the subject judge.

(d) Corrective Action. The chief judge may conclude a complaint proceeding in whole or in part if:

(1) an informal resolution under Rule 5 satisfactory to the chief judge was reached before the complaint was filed under Rule 6; or

(2) the chief judge determines that the subject judge has taken appropriate voluntary corrective action that acknowledges and remedies the problems raised by the complaint.

(e) Intervening Events. The chief judge may conclude a complaint proceeding in whole or in part upon determining that intervening events render some or all of the allegations moot or make remedial action impossible as to the subject judge.

(f) Appointment of Special Committee. If some or all of a complaint is not dismissed or concluded, the chief judge must promptly appoint a special committee to investigate the complaint or any relevant portion of it and to make recommendations to the judicial council. Before appointing a special committee, the chief judge must invite the subject judge to respond to the complaint either orally or in writing if the judge was not given an opportunity during the limited inquiry. In the chief judge's discretion, separate complaints may be joined and assigned to a single special committee. Similarly, a single complaint about more than one judge may be severed and more than one special committee appointed.

(g) Notice of Chief Judge's Action; Petition for Review.

(1) When chief judge appoints special committee. If the chief judge appoints a special committee, the chief judge must notify the complainant and the subject judge that the matter has been referred to a committee, notify the complainant of a complainant's rights under Rule 16, and identify the members of the committee. A copy of the order appointing the special committee must be sent to the Committee on Judicial Conduct and Disability.

(2) When chief judge disposes of complaint without appointing special committee. If the chief judge disposes of a complaint under Rule 11(c), (d), or (e), the chief judge must prepare a supporting memorandum that sets forth the reasons for the disposition. If the complaint was initiated by identification under Rule 5, the memorandum must so indicate. Except as authorized by 28 U.S.C. § 360, the memorandum must not include the name of the complainant or of the subject judge. The order and memoranda incorporated by reference in the order must be promptly sent to the complainant, the subject judge, and the Committee on Judicial Conduct and Disability.

(3) Right to petition for review. If the chief judge disposes of a complaint under Rule 11(c), (d), or (e), the complainant and the subject judge must be notified of the right to petition the judicial council for review of the disposition, as provided in Rule 18. If the chief judge so disposes of a complaint that was identified under Rule 5 or

filed by its subject judge, the chief judge must transmit the order and memoranda incorporated by reference in the order to the judicial council for review in accordance with Rule 19. In the event of such a transmission, the subject judge may make a written submission to the judicial council but will have no further right of review except as allowed under Rule 21(b)(1)(B). When a disposition is to be reviewed by the judicial council, the chief judge must promptly transmit all materials obtained in connection with the inquiry under Rule 11(b) to the circuit clerk for transmittal to the council.

(h) Public Availability of Chief Judge's Decision. The chief judge's decision must be made public to the extent, at the time, and in the manner provided in Rule 24.

Commentary on Rule 11

This Rule describes complaint-review actions available either to the chief judge or, where that judge is the subject judge or is otherwise disqualified under Rule 25, such as where the complaint is filed against the chief judge, to the judge designated under Rule 25(f) to perform the chief judge's duties under these Rules. Subsection (a) of this Rule provides that where a complaint has been filed under Rule 6, the ordinary doctrines of waiver do not apply. The chief judge must identify as a complaint any misconduct or disability issues raised by the factual allegations of the complaint even if the complainant makes no such claim with regard to those issues. For example, an allegation limited to misconduct in fact-finding that mentions periods during a trial when the judge was asleep must be treated as a complaint regarding disability. A formal order giving notice of the expanded scope of the proceeding must be given to the subject judge.

Subsection (b) describes the nature of the chief judge's inquiry. It is based largely on the Breyer Committee Report, 239 F.R.D. at 243–45. The Act states that dismissal is appropriate "when a limited inquiry . . . demonstrates that the allegations in the complaint lack any factual foundation or are conclusively refuted by objective evidence." 28 U.S.C. § 352(b)(1)(B). At the same time, however, Section 352(a) states that "[t]he chief judge shall not undertake to make findings of fact about any matter that is reasonably in dispute." These two statutory standards should be read together so that a matter is not "reasonably" in dispute if a limited inquiry shows that the allegations do not constitute misconduct or disability, that they lack any reliable factual foundation, or that they are conclusively refuted by objective evidence.

In conducting a limited inquiry under subsection (b), the chief judge must avoid determinations of reasonably disputed issues, including reasonably disputed issues as to whether the facts alleged constitute misconduct or disability, which are ordinarily left to the judicial council and its special committee. An allegation of fact is ordinarily not "refuted" simply because the subject judge denies it. The limited inquiry must reveal something more in the way of refutation before it is appropriate to dismiss a complaint that is otherwise cognizable. If it is the complainant's word against the subject judge's—in other words, there is simply no other significant evidence of what happened or of the complainant's unreliability—then there must be a special-committee investigation. Such a credibility issue is a matter "reasonably in dispute" within the meaning of the Act.

However, dismissal following a limited inquiry may occur when a complaint refers to transcripts or to witnesses and the chief judge determines that the transcripts and witnesses all support the subject judge. Breyer Committee Report, 239 F.R.D. at 243. For example, consider a complaint alleging that the subject judge said X, and the complaint mentions, or it is independently clear, that five people may have heard what the judge said. *Id.* The chief judge is told by the subject judge and one witness that the judge did not say X, and the chief judge dismisses the complaint without questioning the other four possible witnesses. *Id.* In this example, the matter remains reasonably in dispute. If all five witnesses say the subject judge did not say X, dismissal is appropriate, but if potential witnesses who are reasonably accessible have not been questioned, then the matter remains reasonably in dispute. *Id.*

Similarly, under subsection (c)(1)(A), if it is clear that the conduct or disability alleged, even if true, is not cognizable under these Rules, the complaint should be dismissed. If that issue is reasonably in dispute, however, dismissal under subsection (c)(1)(A) is inappropriate.

Essentially, the standard articulated in subsection (b) is that used to decide motions for summary judgment pursuant to Fed. R. Civ. P. 56. Genuine issues of material fact are not resolved at the summary judgment stage. A material fact is one that "might affect the outcome of the suit under the governing law," and a dispute is "genuine" if "the evidence is such that a reasonable jury could return a verdict for the nonmoving party." *Anderson v. Liberty Lobby*, 477 U.S. 242, 248 (1986). Similarly, the chief judge may not resolve a genuine issue concerning a material fact or the existence of misconduct or a disability when conducting a limited inquiry pursuant to subsection (b).

Subsection (c) describes the grounds on which a complaint may be dismissed. These are adapted from the Act, 28 U.S.C. § 352(b), and the Breyer Committee Report, 239 F.R.D. at 239–45. Subsection (c)(1)(A) permits dismissal of an allegation that, even if true, does not constitute misconduct or disability under the statutory standard. The proper standards are set out in Rule 4 and discussed in the Commentary on that Rule. Subsection (c)(1)(B) permits dismissal of complaints related to the merits of a decision by a subject judge; this standard is also governed by Rule 4 and its accompanying Commentary.

Subsections (c)(1)(C)–(E) implement the statute by allowing dismissal of complaints that are "frivolous, lacking sufficient evidence to raise an inference that misconduct has occurred, or containing allegations which are incapable of being established through investigation." 28 U.S.C. § 352(b)(1)(A)(iii).

Dismissal of a complaint as "frivolous" under Rule 11(c)(1)(C) will generally occur without any inquiry beyond the face of the complaint. For instance, when the allegations are facially incredible or so lacking in indicia of reliability that no further inquiry is warranted, dismissal under this subsection is appropriate.

A complaint warranting dismissal under Rule 11(c)(1)(D) is illustrated by the following example. Consider a complainant who alleges an impropriety and asserts that he knows of it because it was observed and reported to him by a person who is identified. The subject judge denies that the event occurred. When contacted, the source also denies it. In such a case, the chief judge's proper course of action may turn on whether the source had any role in the allegedly improper conduct. If the complaint was based on a lawyer's statement that he or she had an improper ex parte contact with a judge, the lawyer's denial of the impropriety might not be taken as wholly persuasive, and it would be appropriate to conclude that a real factual issue is raised. On the other hand, if the complaint quoted a disinterested third party and that disinterested party denied that the statement had been made, there would be no value in opening a formal investigation. In such a case, it would be appropriate to dismiss the complaint under Rule 11(c)(1)(D).

Rule 11(c)(1)(E) is intended, among other things, to cover situations when no evidence is offered or identified, or when the only identified source is unavailable. Breyer Committee Report, 239 F.R.D. at 243. For example, a complaint alleges that an unnamed attorney told the complainant that the subject judge did X. *Id.* The subject judge denies it. The chief judge requests that the complainant (who does not purport to have observed the subject judge do X) identify the unnamed witness, or that the unnamed witness come forward so that the chief judge can learn the unnamed witness's account. *Id.* The complainant responds that he has spoken with the unnamed witness, that the unnamed witness is an attorney who practices in federal court, and that the unnamed witness is unwilling to be identified or to come forward. *Id.* at 243–44. The allegation is then properly dismissed as containing allegations that are incapable of being established through investigation. *Id.*

If, however, the situation involves a reasonable dispute over credibility, the matter should proceed. For example, the complainant alleges an impropriety and alleges that he or she observed it and that there were no other witnesses; the subject judge denies that the event occurred. Unless the complainant's allegations are facially incredible or so lacking indicia of reliability as to warrant dismissal under Rule 11(c)(1)(C), a special committee must be appointed because there is a material factual question that is reasonably in dispute.

Dismissal is also appropriate when a complaint is filed so long after an alleged event that memory loss, death, or changes to unknown residences prevent a proper investigation.

Subsection (c)(2) indicates that the investigative nature of the process prevents the application of claim preclusion principles where new and material evidence becomes available. However, it also recognizes that at some point a renewed investigation may constitute harassment of the subject judge and should not be undertaken, depending of course on the seriousness of the issues and the weight of the new evidence.

Rule 11(d) implements the Act's provision for dismissal if voluntary appropriate corrective action has been taken. It is largely adapted from the Breyer Committee Report, 239 F.R.D. at 244–45. The Act authorizes the chief judge to conclude the complaint proceedings if "appropriate corrective action has been taken." 28 U.S.C. § 352(b)(2). Under the Rule, action taken after a complaint is filed is "appropriate" when it acknowledges and remedies the problem raised by the complaint. Breyer Committee Report, 239 F.R.D. at 244. Because the Act deals with the conduct of judges, the emphasis is on correction of the judicial conduct that was the subject of the complaint. *Id.* Terminating a complaint based on corrective action is premised on the implicit understanding that voluntary self-correction or redress of misconduct or a disability may be preferable to sanctions. *Id.* The chief judge may facilitate this process by giving the subject judge an objective view of the appearance of the judicial conduct in question and by suggesting appropriate corrective measures. *Id.* Moreover, when corrective action is taken under Rule 5 satisfactory to the chief judge before a complaint is filed, that informal resolution will be sufficient to conclude a subsequent complaint based on identical conduct.

"Corrective action" must be voluntary action taken by the subject judge. Breyer Committee Report, 239 F.R.D. at 244. A remedial action directed by the chief judge or by an appellate court without the participation of the subject judge in formulating the directive or without the subject judge's subsequent agreement to such action does not constitute the requisite voluntary corrective action. *Id.* Neither the chief judge nor an appellate court has authority under the Act to impose a formal remedy or sanction; only the judicial council can impose a formal remedy or sanction under 28 U.S.C. § 354(a)(2). *Id.* Compliance with a previous judicial-council order may serve as corrective action allowing conclusion of a later complaint about the same behavior. *Id.*

Where a subject judge's conduct has resulted in identifiable, particularized harm to the complainant or another individual, appropriate corrective action should include steps taken by that judge to acknowledge and redress the harm, if possible, such as by an apology, recusal from a case, or a pledge to refrain from similar conduct in the future. *Id.* While the Act is generally forward-looking, any corrective action should, to the extent possible, serve to correct a specific harm to an individual, if such harm can reasonably be remedied. *Id.* In some cases, corrective action may not be "appropriate" to justify conclusion of a complaint unless the complainant or other individual harmed is meaningfully apprised of the nature of the corrective action in the chief judge's order, in a direct communication from the subject judge, or otherwise. *Id.*

Voluntary corrective action should be proportionate to any plausible allegations of misconduct in a complaint. The form of corrective action should also be proportionate to any sanctions that the judicial council might impose under Rule 20(b), such as a private or public reprimand or a change in case assignments. Breyer Committee Report, 239 F.R.D at 244–45. In other words, minor corrective action will not suffice to dispose of a serious matter. *Id.*

Rule 11(e) implements Section 352(b)(2) of the Act, which permits the chief judge to "conclude the proceeding," if "action on the complaint is no longer necessary because of intervening events," such as a resignation from judicial office. Ordinarily, stepping down from an administrative post such as chief judge, judicial-council member, or court-committee chair does not constitute an event rendering unnecessary any further action on a complaint alleging judicial misconduct. Breyer Committee Report, 239 F.R.D. at 245. As long as the subject of a complaint retains the judicial office and remains a covered judge as defined in Rule 1(b), a complaint must be addressed. *Id.*; 28 U.S.C. §§ 371(b); 372(a).

Concluding a complaint proceeding, by either the judicial council of the subject judge or the judicial council to which a complaint proceeding has been transferred, precludes remedial action under the Act and these Rules as to the subject judge. But the Judicial Conference and the judicial council of the subject judge have ample authority to assess potential institutional issues related to the complaint as part of their respective responsibilities to promote "the expeditious conduct of court business," 28 U.S.C. § 331, and to "make all necessary and appropriate orders for the effective administration of justice within [each] circuit." *Id.* at § 332(d)(1). Such an assessment might include an analysis of what conditions may have enabled misconduct or prevented its discovery, and what precautionary or curative steps could be undertaken to prevent its recurrence. The judicial council may request that the Committee on Judicial Conduct and Disability transmit its order to relevant Congressional entities.

If a complaint is not disposed of pursuant to Rule 11(c), (d), or (e), a special committee must be appointed. Rule 11(f) states that a subject judge must be invited to respond to the complaint before a special committee is appointed, if no earlier response was invited.

Subject judges receive copies of complaints at the same time that they are referred to the chief judge, and they are free to volunteer responses to them. Under Rule 11(b), the chief judge may request a response if it is thought necessary. However, many complaints are clear candidates for dismissal even if their allegations are accepted as true, and there is no need for the subject judge to devote time to a defense.

The Act requires that the order dismissing a complaint or concluding a proceeding contain a statement of reasons and that a copy of the order be sent to the complainant. 28 U.S.C. § 352(b). Rule 24, dealing with availability of information to the public, contemplates that the order will be made public, usually without disclosing the names of the complainant or the subject judge. If desired for administrative purposes, more identifying information can be included in a non-public version of the order.

When a complaint is disposed of by the chief judge, the statutory purposes are best served by providing the complainant with a full, particularized, but concise explanation, giving reasons for the conclusions reached. *See also* Commentary on Rule 24 (dealing with public availability).

Rule 11(g) provides that the complainant and the subject judge must be notified, in the case of a disposition by the chief judge, of the right to petition the judicial council for review. Because an identified complaint has no "complainant" to petition for review, the chief judge's dispositive order on such a complaint will be transmitted to the judicial council for review. The same will apply where a complaint was filed by its subject judge. A copy of the chief judge's order, and memoranda incorporated by reference in the order, disposing of a complaint must be sent by the circuit clerk to the Committee on Judicial Conduct and Disability.

ARTICLE V. INVESTIGATION AND REPORT BY SPECIAL COMMITTEE

12. Special Committee's Composition

(a) Membership. Except as provided in (e), a special committee appointed under Rule 11(f) must consist of the chief judge and equal numbers of circuit and district judges. These judges may include senior judges. If a complaint is about a district judge, bankruptcy judge, or magistrate judge, then, when possible, the district-judge members of the special committee must be from districts other than the district of the subject judge. For the courts named in 28 U.S.C. § 363, the special committee must be selected from the judges serving on the subject judge's court.

(b) Presiding Officer. When appointing the special committee, the chief judge may serve as the presiding officer or else must designate a committee member as the presiding officer.

(c) Bankruptcy Judge or Magistrate Judge as Adviser. If the subject judge is a bankruptcy judge or magistrate judge, he or she may, within 14 days after being notified of the special committee's appointment, ask the chief judge to designate as a committee adviser another bankruptcy judge or magistrate judge, as the case may be. The chief judge must grant such a request but may otherwise use discretion in naming the adviser. Unless the adviser is a Court of Federal Claims special master appointed under 42 U.S.C. § 300aa–12(c), the adviser must be from a district other than the district of the subject bankruptcy judge or subject magistrate judge. The adviser cannot vote but has the other privileges of a special-committee member.

(d) Provision of Documents. The chief judge must certify to each other member of the special committee and to any adviser copies of the complaint and statement of facts, in whole or relevant part, and any other relevant documents on file.

(e) Continuing Qualification of Special-Committee Member. A member of a special committee may continue to serve on the committee even though the member relinquishes the position of chief judge, active circuit judge, or active district judge, as the case may be, but only if the member continues to hold office under Article III, Section 1, of the Constitution of the United States, or under 28 U.S.C. § 171.

(f) Inability of Special-Committee Member to Complete Service. If a member of a special committee can no longer serve because of death, disability, disqualification, resignation, retirement from office, or other reason, the chief judge must decide whether to appoint a replacement member, either a circuit or district judge as needed under (a). No special committee appointed under these Rules may function with only a single member, and the votes of a two-member committee must be unanimous.

(g) Voting. All actions by a special committee must be by vote of a majority of all members of the committee.

Commentary on Rule 12

This Rule is adapted from the Act and the Illustrative Rules.

Rule 12 leaves the size of a special committee flexible, to be determined on a case-by-case basis. The question the size of a special committee is one that should be weighed with care in view of the potential for consuming the members' time; a large committee should be appointed only if there is a special reason to do so. Rule 12(a) acknowledges the common practice of including senior judges in the membership of a special committee.

Although the Act requires that the chief judge be a member of each special committee, 28 U.S.C. § 353(a)(1), it does not require that the chief judge preside. Accordingly, Rule 12(b) provides that if the chief judge does not preside, he or she must designate another member of the special committee as the presiding officer.

Rule 12(c) provides that the chief judge must appoint a bankruptcy judge or magistrate judge as an adviser to a special committee at the request of a bankruptcy or magistrate subject judge. Subsection (c) also provides that the adviser will have all the privileges of a member of the special committee except a vote. The adviser, therefore, may participate in all deliberations of the special committee, question witnesses at hearings, and write a separate statement to accompany the committee's report to the judicial council.

Rule 12(e) provides that a member of a special committee who remains an Article III judge may continue to serve on the committee even though the member's status otherwise changes. Thus, a special committee that originally consisted of the chief judge and an equal number of circuit and district judges, as required by the law, may continue to function even though changes of status alter that composition. This provision reflects the belief that stability of membership will contribute to the quality of the work of such committees.

Stability of membership is also the principal concern animating Rule 12(f), which deals with the case in which a special committee loses a member before its work is complete. The Rule permits the chief judge to determine whether a replacement member should be appointed. Generally, appointment of a replacement member is desirable in these situations unless the special committee has conducted evidentiary hearings before the vacancy occurs. However, cases may arise in which a special committee is in the late stages of its work, and in which it would be difficult for a new member to play a meaningful role. The Rule also preserves the collegial character of the special-committee process by prohibiting a single surviving member from serving as a committee and by providing that a committee of two surviving members will, in essence, operate under a unanimity rule.

Rule 12(g) provides that actions of a special committee must be by vote of a majority of all the members. All the members of a special committee should participate in committee decisions. In that circumstance, it seems reasonable to require that special-committee decisions be made by a majority of the membership, rather than a majority of some smaller quorum.

13. Conduct of Special-Committee Investigation

(a) Extent and Methods of Special-Committee Investigation. A special committee should determine the appropriate extent and methods of its investigation in light of the allegations in the complaint and the committee's preliminary inquiry. In investigating the alleged misconduct or disability, the special committee should take steps to determine the full scope of the potential misconduct or disability, including whether a pattern of

misconduct or a broader disability exists. The investigation may include use of appropriate experts or other professionals. If, in the course of the investigation, the special committee has cause to believe that the subject judge may have engaged in misconduct or has a disability that is beyond the specific pending complaint, the committee must refer the new matter to the chief judge for a determination of whether action under Rule 5 or Rule 11 is necessary before the committee's investigation is expanded to include the new matter.

(b) Criminal Conduct. If the special committee's investigation concerns conduct that may be a crime, the committee must consult with the appropriate prosecutorial authorities to the extent permitted by the Act to avoid compromising any criminal investigation. The special committee has final authority over the timing and extent of its investigation and the formulation of its recommendations.

(c) Staff. The special committee may arrange for staff assistance to conduct the investigation. It may use existing staff of the judiciary or may hire special staff through the Director of the Administrative Office of the United States Courts.

(d) Delegation of Subpoena Power; Contempt. The chief judge may delegate the authority to exercise the subpoena powers of the special committee. The judicial council or special committee may institute a contempt proceeding under 28 U.S.C. § 332(d) against anyone who fails to comply with a subpoena.

Commentary on Rule 13

This Rule is adapted from the Illustrative Rules.

Rule 13, as well as Rules 14, 15, and 16, are concerned with the way in which the special committee carries out its mission. They reflect the view that the special committee has two roles that are separated in ordinary litigation. First, the special committee has an investigative role of the kind that is characteristically left to executive branch agencies or discovery by civil litigants. 28 U.S.C. § 353(c). Second, it has a formalized fact-finding and recommendation-of-disposition role that is characteristically left to juries, judges, or arbitrators. *Id.* Rule 13 generally governs the investigative stage. Even though the same body has responsibility for both roles under the Act, it is important to distinguish between them in order to ensure that appropriate rights are afforded at appropriate times to the subject judge.

Rule 13(a) includes a provision making clear that the special committee may choose to consult appropriate experts or other professionals if it determines that such a consultation is warranted. If, for example, the special committee has cause to believe that the subject judge may be unable to discharge all of the duties of office by reason of mental or physical disability, the committee could ask the subject judge to respond to inquiries and, if necessary, request the judge to undergo a medical or psychological examination. In advance of any such examination, the special committee may enter into an agreement with the subject judge as to the scope and use that may be made of the examination results. In addition or in the alternative, the special committee may ask to review existing records, including medical records.

The extent of the subject judge's cooperation in the investigation may be taken into account in the consideration of the underlying complaint. If, for example, the subject judge impedes reasonable efforts to confirm or disconfirm the presence of a disability, the special committee may still consider whether the conduct alleged in the complaint and confirmed in the investigation constitutes disability. The same would be true of a complaint alleging misconduct.

The special committee may also consider whether such a judge might be in violation of his or her duty to cooperate in an investigation under these Rules, a duty rooted not only in the Act's definition of misconduct but also in the Code of Conduct for United States Judges, which emphasizes the need to maintain public confidence in the judiciary, *see* Canon 2(A) and Canon 1 cmt., and requires judges to "facilitate the performance of the administrative responsibilities of other judges and court personnel," Canon 3(B)(1). If the special committee finds a breach of the duty to cooperate and believes that the breach may amount to misconduct under Rule 4(a)(5), it should determine, under the final sentence of Rule 13(a), whether that possibility should be referred to the chief judge for consideration of action under Rule 5 or Rule 11. *See also* Commentary on Rule 4.

One of the difficult questions that can arise is the relationship between proceedings under the Act and criminal investigations. Rule 13(b) assigns responsibility for coordination to the special committee in cases in which criminal conduct is suspected, but gives the committee the authority to determine the appropriate pace of its activity in light of any criminal investigation.

Title 28 U.S.C. § 356(a) provides that a special committee will have full subpoena powers as provided in 28 U.S.C. § 332(d). Section 332(d)(1) provides that subpoenas will be issued on behalf of a judicial council by the circuit clerk "at the direction of the chief judge of the circuit or his designee." Rule 13(d) contemplates that, where the chief judge designates someone else as presiding officer of the special committee, the presiding officer also be delegated the authority to direct the circuit clerk to issue subpoenas related to committee proceedings. That is not intended to imply, however, that the decision to use the subpoena power is exercisable by the presiding officer alone. *See* Rule 12(g).

14. Conduct of Special-Committee Hearings

(a) Purpose of Hearings. The special committee may hold hearings to take testimony and receive other evidence, to hear argument, or both. If the special committee is investigating allegations against more than one judge, it may hold joint or separate hearings.

(b) Special-Committee Evidence. Subject to Rule 15, the special committee must obtain material, nonredundant evidence in the form it considers appropriate. In the special committee's discretion, evidence may be obtained by committee members, staff, or both. Witnesses offering testimonial evidence may include the complainant and the subject judge.

(c) Counsel for Witnesses. The subject judge has the right to counsel. The special committee has discretion to decide whether other witnesses may have counsel present when they testify.

(d) Witness Fees. Witness fees must be paid as provided in 28 U.S.C. § 1821.

(e) Oath. All testimony taken at a hearing must be given under oath or affirmation.

(f) Rules of Evidence. The Federal Rules of Evidence do not apply to special-committee hearings.

(g) Record and Transcript. A record and transcript must be made of all hearings.

Commentary on Rule 14

This Rule is adapted from the Act, 28 U.S.C. § 353, and the Illustrative Rules. Rule 14 is concerned with the conduct of fact-finding hearings.

Special-committee hearings will normally be held only after the investigative work has been completed and the committee has concluded that there is sufficient evidence to warrant a formal fact-finding proceeding. Special-committee proceedings are primarily inquisitorial rather than adversarial. Accordingly, the Federal Rules of Evidence do not apply to such hearings. Inevitably, a hearing will have something of an adversary character. Nevertheless, that tendency should be moderated to the extent possible. Even though a proceeding will commonly have investigative and hearing stages, special-committee members should not regard themselves as prosecutors one day and judges the next. Their duty—and that of their staff—is at all times to be impartial seekers of the truth.

Rule 14(b) contemplates that material evidence will be obtained by the special committee and presented in the form of affidavits, live testimony, etc. Staff or others who are organizing the hearings should regard it as their role to present evidence representing the entire picture. With respect to testimonial evidence, the subject judge should normally be called as a special-committee witness. Cases may arise in which the subject judge will not testify voluntarily. In such cases, subpoena powers are available, subject to the normal testimonial privileges. Although Rule 15(c) recognizes the subject judge's statutory right to call witnesses on his or her own behalf, exercise of this right should not usually be necessary.

15. Subject Judge's Rights

(a) Notice.

(1) Generally. The subject judge must receive written notice of:

(A) the appointment of a special committee under Rule 11(f);

(B) the expansion of the scope of an investigation under Rule 13(a);

(C) any hearing under Rule 14, including its purposes, the names of any witnesses the special committee intends to call, and the text of any statements that have been taken from those witnesses.

(2) Suggestion of additional witnesses. The subject judge may suggest additional witnesses to the special committee.

(b) Special-Committee Report. The subject judge must be sent a copy of the special committee's report when it is filed with the judicial council.

(c) Presentation of Evidence. At any hearing held under Rule 14, the subject judge has the right to present evidence, to compel the attendance of witnesses, and to compel the production of documents. At the request of the subject judge, the chief judge or the judge's designee must direct the circuit clerk to issue a subpoena to a witness under 28 U.S.C. § 332(d)(1). The subject judge must be given the opportunity to cross-examine special-committee witnesses, in person or by counsel.

(d) Presentation of Argument. The subject judge may submit written argument to the special committee and must be given a reasonable opportunity to present oral argument at an appropriate stage of the investigation.

(e) Attendance at Hearings. The subject judge has the right to attend any hearing held under Rule 14 and to receive copies of the transcript, of any documents introduced, and of any written arguments submitted by the complainant to the special committee.

(f) Representation by Counsel. The subject judge may choose to be represented by counsel in the exercise of any right enumerated in this Rule. As provided in Rule 20(e), the United States may bear the costs of the representation.

Commentary on Rule 15

This Rule is adapted from the Act and the Illustrative Rules.

The Act states that these Rules must contain provisions requiring that "the judge whose conduct is the subject of a complaint . . . be afforded an opportunity to appear (in person or by counsel) at proceedings conducted by the investigating panel, to present oral and documentary evidence, to compel the attendance of witnesses or the production of documents, to cross-examine witnesses, and to present argument orally or in writing." 28 U.S.C. § 358(b)(2). To implement this provision, Rule 15(e) gives the subject judge the right to attend any hearing held for the purpose of receiving evidence of record or hearing argument under Rule 14.

The Act does not require that the subject judge be permitted to attend all proceedings of the special committee. Accordingly, the Rules do not give a right to attend other proceedings—for example, meetings at which the special committee is engaged in investigative activity, such as interviewing persons to learn whether they ought to be called as witnesses or examining for relevance purposes documents delivered pursuant to a subpoena duces tecum, or meetings in which the committee is deliberating on the evidence or its recommendations.

16. Complainant's Rights in Investigation

(a) Notice. The complainant must receive written notice of the investigation as provided in Rule 11(g)(1). When the special committee's report to the judicial council is filed, the complainant must be notified of the filing. The judicial council may, in its discretion, provide a copy of the report of a special committee to the complainant.

(b) Opportunity to Provide Evidence. If the complainant knows of relevant evidence not already before the special committee, the complainant may briefly explain in writing the basis of that knowledge and the nature of that evidence. If the special committee determines that the complainant has information not already known to the committee that would assist in the committee's investigation, a representative of the committee must interview the complainant.

(c) Presentation of Argument. The complainant may submit written argument to the special committee. In its discretion, the special committee may permit the complainant to offer oral argument.

(d) Representation by Counsel. A complainant may submit written argument through counsel and, if permitted to offer oral argument, may do so through counsel.

Commentary on Rule 16

This Rule is adapted from the Act and the Illustrative Rules.

In accordance with the view of the process as fundamentally administrative and inquisitorial, these Rules do not give the complainant the rights of a party to litigation and leave the complainant's role largely to the discretion of the special committee. However, Rule 16(b) gives the complainant the prerogative to make a brief written submission showing that he or she is aware of relevant evidence not already known to the special committee. (Such a submission may precede any written or oral argument the complainant provides under Rule 16(c), or it may accompany that argument.) If the special committee determines, independently or from the complainant's submission, that the complainant has information that would assist the committee in its investigation, the complainant must be interviewed by a representative of the committee. Such an interview may be in person or by telephone, and the representative of the special committee may be either a member or staff.

Rule 16 does not contemplate that the complainant will ordinarily be permitted to attend proceedings of the special committee except when testifying or presenting oral argument. A special committee may exercise its discretion to permit the complainant to be present at its proceedings, or to permit the complainant, individually or through counsel, to participate in the examination or cross-examination of witnesses.

The Act authorizes an exception to the normal confidentiality provisions where the judicial council in its discretion provides a copy of the report of the special committee to the complainant and to the subject judge. 28 U.S.C. § 360(a)(1). However, the Rules do not entitle the complainant to a copy of the special committee's report.

17. Special-Committee Report

The special committee must file with the judicial council a comprehensive report of its investigation, including findings and recommendations for council action. The report must be accompanied by a statement of the vote by which it was adopted, any separate or dissenting statements of special-committee members, and the record of any hearings held under Rule 14. In addition to being sent to the subject judge under Rule 15(b), a copy of the report and any accompanying statements and documents must be sent to the Committee on Judicial Conduct and Disability.

Commentary on Rule 17

This Rule is adapted from the Illustrative Rules and is self-explanatory. The provision for sending a copy of the special-committee report and accompanying statements and documents to the Committee on

Judicial Conduct and Disability was new at the time the Judicial Conference promulgated the Rules for Judicial-Conduct and Judicial-Disability Proceedings in 2008.

ARTICLE VI. REVIEW BY JUDICIAL COUNCIL

18. Petition for Review of Chief-Judge Disposition Under Rule 11(c), (d), or (e)

(a) Petition for Review. After the chief judge issues an order under Rule 11(c), (d), or (e), the complainant or the subject judge may petition the judicial council of the circuit to review the order. By rules promulgated under 28 U.S.C. § 358, the judicial council may refer a petition for review filed under this Rule to a panel of no fewer than five members of the council, at least two of whom must be district judges.

(b) When to File; Form; Where to File. A petition for review must be filed in the office of the circuit clerk within 42 days after the date of the chief judge's order. The petition for review should be in letter form, addressed to the circuit clerk, and in an envelope marked "Misconduct Petition" or "Disability Petition." The name of the subject judge must not be shown on the envelope. The petition for review should be typewritten or otherwise legible. It should begin with "I hereby petition the judicial council for review of . . ." and state the reasons why the petition should be granted. It must be signed.

(c) Receipt and Distribution of Petition. A circuit clerk who receives a petition for review filed in accordance with this Rule must:

(1) acknowledge its receipt and send a copy to the complainant or subject judge, as the case may be;

(2) promptly distribute to each member of the judicial council, or its relevant panel, except for any member disqualified under Rule 25, or make available in the manner provided by local rule, the following materials:

(A) copies of the complaint;

(B) all materials obtained by the chief judge in connection with the inquiry;

(C) the chief judge's order disposing of the complaint;

(D) any memorandum in support of the chief judge's order;

(E) the petition for review; and

(F) an appropriate ballot; and

(3) send the petition for review to the Committee on Judicial Conduct and Disability. Unless the Committee on Judicial Conduct and Disability requests them, the circuit clerk will not send copies of the materials obtained by the chief judge.

(d) Untimely Petition. The circuit clerk must refuse to accept a petition that is received after the time allowed in (b).

(e) Timely Petition Not in Proper Form. When the circuit clerk receives a petition for review filed within the time allowed but in a form that is improper to a degree that would substantially impair its consideration by the judicial council—such as a document that is ambiguous about whether it is intended to be a petition for review—the circuit clerk must acknowledge its receipt, call the filer's attention to the deficiencies, and give the filer the opportunity to correct the deficiencies within the original time allowed for filing the petition or within 21 days after the date on which a notice of the deficiencies was sent to the complainant, whichever is later. If the deficiencies are corrected within the time allowed, the circuit clerk will proceed according to paragraphs (a) and (c) of this Rule. If the deficiencies are not corrected, the circuit clerk must reject the petition.

Commentary on Rule 18

Rule 18 is adapted largely from the Illustrative Rules.

Subsection (a) permits the subject judge, as well as the complainant, to petition for review of the chief judge's order dismissing a complaint under Rule 11(c), or concluding that appropriate corrective action or intervening events have remedied or mooted the problems raised by the complaint pursuant to Rule 11(d) or (e). Although the subject judge may ostensibly be vindicated by the dismissal or conclusion of a complaint, the chief judge's order may include language disagreeable to the subject judge. For example, an order may dismiss a complaint, but state that the subject judge did in fact engage in misconduct. Accordingly, a subject judge may wish to object to the content of the order and is given the opportunity to petition the judicial council of the circuit for review.

Subsection (b) contains a time limit of 42 days to file a petition for review. It is important to establish a time limit on petitions for review of chief judges' dispositions in order to provide finality to the process. If the complaint requires an investigation, the investigation should proceed; if it does not, the subject judge should know that the matter is closed.

The standards for timely filing under the Federal Rules of Appellate Procedure should be applied to petitions for review. *See* Fed. R. App. P. 25(a)(2)(A), (C).

Rule 18(e) provides for an automatic extension of the time limit imposed under subsection (b) if a person files a petition that is rejected for failure to comply with formal requirements.

19. Judicial-Council Disposition of Petition for Review

(a) Rights of Subject Judge. At any time after a complainant files a petition for review, the subject judge may file a written response with the circuit clerk. The circuit clerk must promptly distribute copies of the response to each member of the judicial council or of the relevant panel, unless that member is disqualified under Rule 25. Copies must also be distributed to the chief judge, to the complainant, and to the Committee on Judicial Conduct and Disability. The subject judge must not otherwise communicate with individual judicial-council members about the matter. The subject judge must be given copies of any communications to the judicial council from the complainant.

(b) Judicial-Council Action. After considering a petition for review and the materials before it, the judicial council may:

(1) affirm the chief judge's disposition by denying the petition;

(2) return the matter to the chief judge with directions to conduct a further inquiry under Rule 11(b) or to identify a complaint under Rule 5;

(3) return the matter to the chief judge with directions to appoint a special committee under Rule 11(f); or

(4) in exceptional circumstances, take other appropriate action.

(c) Notice of Judicial-Council Decision. Copies of the judicial council's order, together with memoranda incorporated by reference in the order and separate concurring or dissenting statements, must be given to the complainant, the subject judge, and the Committee on Judicial Conduct and Disability.

(d) Memorandum of Judicial-Council Decision. If the judicial council's order affirms the chief judge's disposition, a supporting memorandum must be prepared only if the council concludes that there is a need to supplement the chief judge's explanation. A memorandum supporting a judicial-council order must not include the name of the complainant or the subject judge.

(e) Review of Judicial-Council Decision. If the judicial council's decision is adverse to the petitioner, and if no member of the council dissented, the complainant must be notified that he or she has no right to seek review of the decision. If there was a dissent,

the petitioner must be informed that he or she can file a petition for review under Rule 21(b).

(f) Public Availability of Judicial-Council Decision. Materials related to the judicial council's decision must be made public to the extent, at the time, and in the manner set forth in Rule 24.

Commentary on Rule 19

This Rule is adapted largely from the Act and is self-explanatory.

The judicial council should ordinarily review the decision of the chief judge on the merits, treating the petition for review for all practical purposes as an appeal. The judicial council may respond to a petition for review by affirming the chief judge's order, remanding the matter, or, in exceptional cases, taking other appropriate action.

Under Rule 19(b), after considering a petition for review and the materials before it, a judicial council may return a matter to the chief judge to take various actions, including conducting further inquiry under Rule 11(b), identifying a complaint under Rule 5, or appointing a special committee under Rule 11(f).

A petition for review of a judicial council's decision under this Rule may be filed in any matter in which one or more members of the council dissented from the order. *See* Rule 21(b).

20. Judicial-Council Action Following Appointment of Special Committee

(a) Subject Judge's Rights. Within 21 days after the filing of the report of a special committee, the subject judge may send a written response to the members of the judicial council. The subject judge must also be given an opportunity to present argument, personally or through counsel, written or oral, as determined by the judicial council. The subject judge must not otherwise communicate with judicial-council members about the matter.

(b) Judicial-Council Action.

(1) Discretionary actions. Subject to the subject judge's rights set forth in subsection (a), the judicial council may:

(A) dismiss the complaint because:

(i) even if the claim is true, the claimed conduct is not conduct prejudicial to the effective and expeditious administration of the business of the courts and does not indicate a mental or physical disability resulting in inability to discharge the duties of office;

(ii) the complaint is directly related to the merits of a decision or procedural ruling;

(iii) the facts on which the complaint is based have not been established; or

(iv) the complaint is otherwise not appropriate for consideration under 28 U.S.C. §§ 351–364.

(B) conclude the proceeding because appropriate corrective action has been taken or intervening events have made the proceeding unnecessary.

(C) refer the complaint to the Judicial Conference with the judicial council's recommendations for action.

(D) take remedial action to ensure the effective and expeditious administration of the business of the courts, including:

(i) censuring or reprimanding the subject judge, either by private communication or by public announcement;

(ii) ordering that no new cases be assigned to the subject judge for a limited, fixed period;

(iii) in the case of a magistrate judge, ordering the chief judge of the district court to take action specified by the council, including the initiation of removal proceedings under 28 U.S.C. § 631(i) or 42 U.S.C. § 300aa–12(c)(2);

(iv) in the case of a bankruptcy judge, removing the judge from office under 28 U.S.C. § 152(e);

(v) in the case of a circuit or district judge, requesting the judge to retire voluntarily with the provision (if necessary) that ordinary length-of-service requirements be waived;

(vi) in the case of a circuit or district judge who is eligible to retire but does not do so, certifying the disability of the judge under 28 U.S.C. § 372(b) so that an additional judge may be appointed; and

(vii) in the case of a circuit chief judge or district chief judge, finding that the judge is temporarily unable to perform chief-judge duties, with the result that those duties devolve to the next eligible judge in accordance with 28 U.S.C. § 45(d) or § 136(e).

(E) take any combination of actions described in (b)(1)(A)—(D) of this Rule that is within its power.

(2) Mandatory actions. A judicial council must refer a complaint to the Judicial Conference if the council determines that a circuit judge or district judge may have engaged in conduct that:

(A) might constitute ground for impeachment; or

(B) in the interest of justice, is not amenable to resolution by the judicial council.

(c) Inadequate Basis for Decision. If the judicial council finds that a special committee's report, recommendations, and record provide an inadequate basis for decision, it may return the matter to the committee for further investigation and a new report, or it may conduct further investigation. If the judicial council decides to conduct further investigation, the subject judge must be given adequate prior notice in writing of that decision and of the general scope and purpose of the additional investigation. The judicial council's conduct of the additional investigation must generally accord with the procedures and powers set forth in Rules 13 through 16 for the conduct of an investigation by a special committee.

(d) Judicial-Council Vote. Judicial-council action must be taken by a majority of those members of the council who are not disqualified. A decision to remove a bankruptcy judge from office requires a majority vote of all the members of the judicial council.

(e) Recommendation for Fee Reimbursement. If the complaint has been finally dismissed or concluded under (b)(1)(A) or (B) of this Rule, and if the subject judge so requests, the judicial council may recommend that the Director of the Administrative Office use funds appropriated to the judiciary to reimburse the judge for reasonable expenses incurred during the investigation, when those expenses would not have been incurred but for the requirements of the Act and these Rules. Reasonable expenses include attorneys' fees and expenses related to a successful defense or prosecution of a proceeding under Rule 21(a) or (b).

(f) Judicial-Council Order. Judicial-council action must be by written order. Unless the judicial council finds that extraordinary reasons would make it contrary to the interests of justice, the order must be accompanied by a memorandum setting forth the factual determinations on which it is based and the reasons for the council action. Such a memorandum may incorporate all or part of any underlying special-committee report. If the complaint was initiated by identification under Rule 5, the memorandum must so indicate. The order and memoranda incorporated by reference in the order must be provided to the complainant, the subject judge, and the Committee on Judicial Conduct and Disability. The complainant and the subject judge must be notified of any right to review of the judicial council's decision as provided in Rule 21(b). If the complaint was identified under Rule 5 or filed by its subject judge, the judicial council must transmit the order and memoranda incorporated by reference in the order to the Committee on Judicial Conduct and Disability for review in accordance with Rule 21. In the event of such a transmission, the subject judge may make a written submission to the Committee on Judicial Conduct and Disability but will have no further right of review.

Commentary on Rule 20

This Rule is largely adapted from the Illustrative Rules.

Rule 20(a) provides that within 21 days after the filing of the report of a special committee, the subject judge may address a written response to all of the members of the judicial council. The subject judge must also be given an opportunity to present argument to the judicial council, personally or through counsel, or both, at the direction of the council. Whether that argument is written or oral would be for the judicial council to determine. The subject judge may not otherwise communicate with judicial-council members about the matter.

Rule 20(b)(1)(B) allows a judicial council to conclude a proceeding where appropriate corrective action has been taken or intervening events have made the proceeding unnecessary. This provision tracks Rules 11(d) and (e), which provide for similar action by the chief judge. As with Rule 11(d), appropriate corrective action must acknowledge and remedy the problem raised by the complaint. *See* Breyer Committee Report, 239 F.R.D. at 244. And similar to Rule 11(e), although "action on the complaint is no longer necessary because of intervening events," the Judicial Conference and the judicial council of the subject judge may nonetheless be able to take action on potential institutional issues related to the complaint (such as an analysis of what conditions may have enabled misconduct or prevented its discovery, and what precautionary or curative steps could be undertaken to prevent its recurrence). 28 U.S.C. § 352(b)(2).

Rule 20(b)(1)(D) recites the remedial actions enumerated in 28 U.S.C. § 354(a)(2) while making clear that this list is not exhaustive. A judicial council may consider lesser remedies. Some remedies may be unique to senior judges, whose caseloads can be modified by agreement or through statutory designation and certification processes.

Under 28 U.S.C. §§ 45(d) and 136(e), which provide for succession where "a chief judge is temporarily unable to perform his duties as such," the determination whether such an inability exists is not expressly reserved to the chief judge. Nor, indeed, is it assigned to any particular judge or court-governance body. Clearly, however, a chief judge's inability to function as chief could implicate "the effective and expeditious administration of justice," which the judicial council of the circuit must, under 28 U.S.C. § 332(d)(1), "make all necessary and appropriate orders" to secure. For this reason, such reassignment is among a judicial council's remedial options, as subsection (b)(1)(D)(vii) makes clear. Consistent with 28 U.S.C. §§ 45(d) and 136(e), however, any reassignment of chief-judge duties must not outlast the subject judge's inability to perform them. Nor can such reassignment result in any extension of the subject judge's term as chief judge.

Rule 20(c) provides that a judicial council may return a matter to a special committee to augment its findings and report of its investigation to include additional areas of inquiry and investigation to allow the judicial council to reach a complete and fully informed judgment. Rule 20(c) also provides that if the judicial council decides to conduct an additional investigation, the subject judge must be given adequate prior notice in writing of that decision and of the general scope and purpose of the additional investigation. The conduct of the investigation will be generally in accordance with the procedures set forth in Rules 13 through 16 for the conduct of an investigation by a special committee. However, if hearings are held, the judicial council may limit testimony or the presentation of evidence to avoid unnecessary repetition of testimony and evidence before the special committee.

Rule 20(d) provides that judicial-council action must be taken by a majority of those members of the council who are not disqualified, except that a decision to remove a bankruptcy judge from office requires a majority of all the members of the council as required by 28 U.S.C. § 152(e). However, it is inappropriate to apply a similar rule to the less severe actions that a judicial council may take under the Act. If some members of the judicial council are disqualified in the matter, their disqualification should not be given the effect of a vote against council action.

With regard to Rule 20(e), the judicial council, on the request of the subject judge, may recommend to the Director of the Administrative Office that the subject judge be reimbursed for reasonable expenses incurred, including attorneys' fees. The judicial council has the authority to recommend such reimbursement where, after investigation by a special committee, the complaint has been finally dismissed or concluded under subsection (b)(1)(A) or (B) of this Rule. It is contemplated that such reimbursement may be provided for the successful prosecution or defense of a proceeding under Rule 21(a) or (b), in other words, one that results in a Rule 20(b)(1)(A) or (B) dismissal or conclusion.

Rule 20(f) requires that judicial-council action be by order and, normally, that it be supported with a memorandum of factual determinations and reasons. Notice of the action must be given to the complainant and the subject judge, and must include notice of any right to petition for review of the judicial council's decision under Rule 21(b). Because an identified complaint has no "complainant" to petition for review, a judicial council's dispositive order on an identified complaint on which a special committee has been appointed must be transmitted to the Committee on Judicial Conduct and Disability for review. The same will apply where a complaint was filed by its subject judge.

ARTICLE VII. REVIEW BY COMMITTEE ON JUDICIAL CONDUCT AND DISABILITY

21. Committee on Judicial Conduct and Disability

(a) Committee Review. The Committee on Judicial Conduct and Disability, consisting of seven members, considers and disposes of all petitions for review under (b) of this Rule, in conformity with the Committee's jurisdictional statement. Its review of judicial-council orders is for errors of law, clear errors of fact, or abuse of discretion. Its disposition of petitions for review is ordinarily final. The Judicial Conference may, in its sole discretion, review any such Committee decision, but a complainant or subject judge does not have a right to this review.

(b) Reviewable Matters.

(1) Upon petition. A complainant or subject judge may petition the Committee for review of a judicial-council order entered in accordance with:

(A) Rule 20(b)(1)(A), (B), (D), or (E); or

(B) Rule 19(b)(1) or (4) if one or more members of the judicial council dissented from the order.

(2) Upon Committee's initiative. At its initiative and in its sole discretion, the Committee may review any judicial-council order entered under Rule 19(b)(1) or (4), but only to determine whether a special committee should be appointed. Before undertaking the review, the Committee must invite that judicial council to explain why it believes the appointment of a special committee is unnecessary, unless the reasons are clearly stated in the council's order denying the petition for review. If the Committee believes that it would benefit from a submission by the subject judge, it may issue an appropriate request. If the Committee determines that a special

committee should be appointed, the Committee must issue a written decision giving its reasons.

(c) Committee Vote. Any member of the Committee from the same circuit as the subject judge is disqualified from considering or voting on a petition for review related to that subject judge. Committee decisions under (b) of this Rule must be by majority vote of the qualified Committee members. Those members hearing the petition for review should serve in that capacity until final disposition of the petition, whether or not their term of committee membership has ended. If only six members are qualified to consider a petition for review, the Chief Justice shall select an additional judge to join the qualified members to consider the petition. If four or fewer members are qualified to consider a petition for review, the Chief Justice shall select a panel of five judges, including the qualified Committee members, to consider it.

(d) Additional Investigation. Except in extraordinary circumstances, the Committee will not conduct an additional investigation. The Committee may return the matter to the judicial council with directions to undertake an additional investigation. If the Committee conducts an additional investigation, it will exercise the powers of the Judicial Conference under 28 U.S.C. § 331.

(e) Oral Argument; Personal Appearance. There is ordinarily no oral argument or personal appearance before the Committee. In its discretion, the Committee may permit written submissions.

(f) Committee Decision. A Committee decision under this Rule must be transmitted promptly to the Judicial Conference. Other distribution will be by the Administrative Office at the direction of the Committee chair.

(g) Finality. All orders of the Judicial Conference or of the Committee (when the Conference does not exercise its power of review) are final.

Commentary on Rule 21

This Rule is largely self-explanatory.

Rule 21(a) is intended to clarify that the delegation of power to the Committee on Judicial Conduct and Disability to dispose of petitions for review does not preclude review of such dispositions by the Judicial Conference. However, there is no right to such review in any party.

Rules 21(b)(1)(B) and (b)(2) are intended to fill a jurisdictional gap as to review of a dismissal or a conclusion of a complaint under Rule 19(b)(1) or (4). Where one or more members of a judicial council reviewing a petition have dissented, the complainant or the subject judge has the right to petition for review by the Committee. Under Rule 21(b)(2), the Committee may review such a dismissal or conclusion in its sole discretion, whether or not a dissent occurred, and only as to the appointment of a special committee. Any review under Rule 21(b)(2) will be conducted as soon as practicable after the dismissal or conclusion at issue. No party has a right to such review, and such review will be rare.

Rule 21(c) provides for review only by Committee members from circuits other than that of the subject judge. The Rule provides that every petition for review must be considered and voted on by at least five, and if possible by seven, qualified Committee members to avoid the possibility of tie votes. If six, or four or fewer, members are qualified, the Chief Justice shall appoint other judges to join the qualified members to consider the petition for review. To the extent possible, the judges whom the Chief Justice selects to join the qualified members should be drawn from among former members of the Committee.

Under this Rule, all Committee decisions are final in that they are unreviewable unless the Judicial Conference, in its discretion, decides to review a decision. Committee decisions, however, do not necessarily constitute final action on a complaint for purposes of Rule 24.

22. Procedures for Review

(a) Filing Petition for Review. A petition for review of a judicial-council decision on a reviewable matter, as defined in Rule 21(b)(1), may be filed by sending a brief written statement to the Committee on Judicial Conduct and Disability at JCD_PetitionforReview@ao.uscourts.gov or to:

Judicial Conference Committee on Judicial Conduct and Disability

Attn: Office of the General Counsel

Administrative Office of the United States Courts

One Columbus Circle, NE

Washington, D.C. 20544

The Administrative Office will send a copy of the petition for review to the complainant or the subject judge, as the case may be.

(b) Form and Contents of Petition. No particular form is required. The petition for review must contain a short statement of the basic facts underlying the complaint, the history of its consideration before the appropriate judicial council, a copy of the council's decision, and the grounds on which the petitioner seeks review. The petition for review must specify the date and docket number of the judicial-council order for which review is sought. The petitioner may attach any documents or correspondence arising in the course of the proceeding before the judicial council or its special committee. A petition for review should not normally exceed 20 pages plus necessary attachments. A petition for review must be signed by the petitioner or his or her attorney.

(c) Time. A petition for review must be submitted within 42 days after the date of the order for which review is sought.

(d) Action on Receipt of Petition. When a petition for review of a judicial-council decision on a reviewable matter, as defined in Rule 21(b)(1), is submitted in accordance with this Rule, the Administrative Office shall acknowledge its receipt, notify the chair of the Committee on Judicial Conduct and Disability, and distribute the petition to the members of the Committee for their deliberation.

Commentary on Rule 22

Rule 22 is self-explanatory.

ARTICLE VIII. MISCELLANEOUS RULES

23. Confidentiality

(a) Confidentiality Generally. Confidentiality under these Rules is intended to protect the fairness and thoroughness of the process by which a complaint is filed or initiated, investigated (in specific circumstances), and ultimately resolved, as specified under these Rules.

(b) Confidentiality in the Complaint Process.

(1) General Rule. The consideration of a complaint by a chief judge, a special committee, a judicial council, or the Committee on Judicial Conduct and Disability is confidential. Information about this consideration must not be publicly disclosed by any judge or judicial employee, or by any person who records or transcribes testimony except as allowed by these Rules. A chief judge, a judicial council, or the Committee on Judicial Conduct and Disability may disclose the existence of a proceeding under

these Rules when necessary or appropriate to maintain public confidence in the judiciary's ability to redress misconduct or disability.

(2) Files. All files related to a complaint must be separately maintained with appropriate security precautions to ensure confidentiality.

(3) Disclosure in Decisions. Except as otherwise provided in Rule 24, written decisions of a chief judge, a judicial council, or the Committee on Judicial Conduct and Disability, and dissenting opinions or separate statements of members of a council or the Committee may contain information and exhibits that the authors consider appropriate for inclusion, and the information and exhibits may be made public.

(4) Availability to Judicial Conference. On request of the Judicial Conference or its Committee on Judicial Conduct and Disability, the circuit clerk must furnish any requested records related to a complaint. For auditing purposes, the circuit clerk must provide access to the Committee on Judicial Conduct and Disability to records of proceedings under the Act at the site where the records are kept.

(5) Availability to District Court. If the judicial council directs the initiation of proceedings for removal of a magistrate judge under Rule 20(b)(1)(D)(iii), the circuit clerk must provide to the chief judge of the district court copies of the report of the special committee and any other documents and records that were before the council at the time of its decision. On request of the chief judge of the district court, the judicial council may authorize release to that chief judge of any other records relating to the investigation.

(6) Impeachment Proceedings. If the Judicial Conference determines that consideration of impeachment may be warranted, it must transmit the record of all relevant proceedings to the Speaker of the House of Representatives.

(7) Subject Judge's Consent. If both the subject judge and the chief judge consent in writing, any materials from the files may be disclosed to any person. In any such disclosure, the chief judge may require that the identity of the complainant, or of witnesses in an investigation conducted under these Rules, not be revealed.

(8) Disclosure in Special Circumstances. The Judicial Conference, its Committee on Judicial Conduct and Disability, a judicial council, or a chief judge may authorize disclosure of information about the consideration of a complaint, including the papers, documents, and transcripts relating to the investigation, to the extent that disclosure is justified by special circumstances and is not prohibited by the Act. For example, disclosure may be made to judicial researchers engaged in the study or evaluation of experience under the Act and related modes of judicial discipline, but only where the study or evaluation has been specifically approved by the Judicial Conference or by the Committee on Judicial Conduct and Disability. Appropriate steps must be taken to protect the identities of the subject judge, the complainant, and witnesses from public disclosure. Other appropriate safeguards to protect against the dissemination of confidential information may be imposed.

(9) Disclosure of Identity by Subject Judge. Nothing in this Rule precludes the subject judge from acknowledging that he or she is the judge referred to in documents made public under Rule 24.

(10) Assistance and Consultation. Nothing in this Rule prohibits a chief judge, a special committee, a judicial council, or the Judicial Conference or its Committee on Judicial Conduct and Disability, in the performance of any function authorized under the Act or these Rules, from seeking the help of qualified staff or experts or from

consulting other judges who may be helpful regarding the performance of that function.

(c) Disclosure of Misconduct and Disability. Nothing in these Rules and Commentary concerning the confidentiality of the complaint process, or in the Code of Conduct for Judicial Employees concerning the use or disclosure of confidential information received in the course of official duties, prevents a judicial employee from reporting or disclosing misconduct or disability.

Commentary on Rule 23

Rule 23 was adapted from the Illustrative Rules.

The Act applies a rule of confidentiality to "papers, documents, and records of proceedings related to investigations conducted under this chapter" and states that they may not be disclosed "by any person in any proceeding," with enumerated exceptions. 28 U.S.C. § 360(a). Three questions arise: Who is bound by the confidentiality rule, what proceedings are subject to the rule, and who is within the circle of people who may have access to information without breaching the rule?

With regard to the first question, Rule 23(b)(1) provides that judges, employees of the judiciary, and those persons involved in recording proceedings and preparing transcripts are obliged to respect the confidentiality requirement. This of course includes subject judges who do not consent to identification under Rule 23(b)(9).

With regard to the second question, Rule 23(b)(1) applies the rule of confidentiality broadly to consideration of a complaint at any stage.

With regard to the third question, there is no barrier of confidentiality among a chief judge, a judicial council, the Judicial Conference, and the Committee on Judicial Conduct and Disability. Each may have access to any of the confidential records for use in their consideration of a referred matter, a petition for review, or monitoring the administration of the Act. A district court may have similar access if the judicial council orders the district court to initiate proceedings to remove a magistrate judge from office, and Rule 23(b)(5) so provides.

In extraordinary circumstances, a chief judge, a judicial council, or the Committee on Judicial Conduct and Disability may disclose the existence of a proceeding under these Rules. The disclosure of such information in high-visibility or controversial cases is to reassure the public that the judiciary is capable of redressing judicial misconduct or disability. Moreover, the confidentiality requirement does not prevent a chief judge from "communicat[ing] orally or in writing with . . . [persons] who may have knowledge of the matter," as part of a limited inquiry conducted by the chief judge under Rule 11(b).

Rule 23 recognizes that there must be some exceptions to the Act's confidentiality requirement. For example, the Act requires that certain orders and the reasons for them must be made public. 28 U.S.C. § 360(b). Rule 23(b)(3) makes it explicit that written decisions, as well as dissenting opinions and separate statements, may contain references to information that would otherwise be confidential and that such information may be made public. However, subsection (b)(3) is subject to Rule 24(a), which provides the general rule regarding the public availability of decisions. For example, the name of a subject judge cannot be made public in a decision if disclosure of the name is prohibited by that Rule.

The Act makes clear that there is a barrier of confidentiality between the judicial branch and the legislative branch. It provides that material may be disclosed to Congress only if it is believed necessary to an impeachment investigation or trial of a judge. 28 U.S.C. § 360(a)(2). Accordingly, Section 355(b) of the Act requires the Judicial Conference to transmit the record of a proceeding to the House of Representatives if the Conference believes that impeachment of a subject judge may be appropriate. Rule 23(b)(6) implements this requirement.

The Act provides that confidential materials may be disclosed if authorized in writing by the subject judge and by the chief judge. 28 U.S.C. § 360(a)(3). Rule 23(b)(7) implements this requirement. Once the subject judge has consented to the disclosure of confidential materials related to a complaint, the chief judge ordinarily will refuse consent only to the extent necessary to protect the confidentiality interests of the complainant or of witnesses who have testified in investigatory proceedings or who have provided information in response to a limited inquiry undertaken pursuant to Rule 11. It will generally be necessary, therefore, for the chief judge to require that the identities of the complainant or of such witnesses, as well as any identifying information, be shielded in any materials disclosed, except insofar as the chief judge has secured the consent of the complainant or of a particular witness to disclosure, or there is a demonstrated need for disclosure of the information that, in the judgment of the chief judge, outweighs the confidentiality interest of the complainant or of a particular witness (as may be the case where the complainant is delusional or where the complainant or a particular witness has already demonstrated a lack of concern about maintaining the confidentiality of the proceedings).

Rule 23(b)(8) permits disclosure of additional information in circumstances not enumerated. For example, disclosure may be appropriate to permit prosecution for perjury based on testimony given before a special committee, where a special committee discovers evidence of a judge's criminal conduct, to permit disciplinary action by a bar association or other licensing body, or in other appropriate circumstances.

Under subsection (b)(8), where a complainant or other person has publicly released information regarding the existence of a complaint proceeding, the Judicial Conference, the Committee on Judicial Conduct and Disability, a judicial council, or a chief judge may authorize the disclosure of information about the consideration of the complaint, including orders and other materials related to the complaint proceeding, in the interest of assuring the public that the judiciary is acting effectively and expeditiously in addressing the relevant complaint proceeding.

Subsection (b)(8) also permits the authorization of disclosure of information about the consideration of a complaint, including the papers, documents, and transcripts relating to the investigation, to judicial researchers engaged in the study or evaluation of experience under the Act and related modes of judicial discipline. The Rule envisions disclosure of information from the official record of a complaint proceeding to a limited category of persons for appropriately authorized research purposes only, and with appropriate safeguards to protect individual identities in any published research results. In authorizing disclosure, a judicial council may refuse to release particular materials when such release would be contrary to the interests of justice, or when those materials constitute purely internal communications. The Rule does not envision disclosure of purely internal communications between judges and their colleagues and staff.

Under Rule 23(b)(10), any of the specified judges or entities performing a function authorized under these Rules may seek expert or staff assistance or may consult with other judges who may be helpful regarding performance of that function; the confidentiality requirement does not preclude this. A chief judge, for example, may properly seek the advice and assistance of another judge who the chief judge deems to be in the best position to communicate with the subject judge in an attempt to bring about corrective action. As another example, a new chief judge may wish to confer with a predecessor to learn how similar complaints have been handled. In consulting with other judges, of course, a chief judge should disclose information regarding the complaint only to the extent the chief judge deems necessary under the circumstances.

Rule 23(c) provides that confidentiality as referenced in these Rules and Commentary is directed toward protecting the fairness and thoroughness of the process by which a complaint is filed or initiated, investigated (in specific circumstances), and ultimately resolved, as specified under these Rules. Nothing in these Rules concerning the confidentiality of the complaint process or the Code of Conduct for Judicial Employees concerning use or disclosure of confidential information received in the course of official duties prevents judicial employees from reporting or disclosing misconduct or disability.

Judges should bring such matters to the attention of the relevant chief district judge or chief circuit judge in accordance with Rule 4(a)(6). Judges should be mindful of Canon 3(B)(6) of the Code of Conduct for United States Judges, which provides in part that a judge "should take appropriate action upon receipt of reliable information indicating the likelihood that a judge's conduct contravened the Code."

24. Public Availability of Decisions

(a) General Rule; Specific Cases. When final action has been taken on a complaint and it is no longer subject to review as of right, all orders entered by the chief judge and judicial council, including memoranda incorporated by reference in those orders and any

dissenting opinions or separate statements by members of the judicial council, must be made public, with the following exceptions:

(1) if the complaint is finally dismissed under Rule 11(c) without the appointment of a special committee, or if it is concluded under Rule 11(d) because of voluntary corrective action, the publicly available materials generally should not disclose the name of the subject judge without his or her consent.

(2) if the complaint is concluded because of intervening events, or dismissed at any time after a special committee is appointed, the judicial council must determine whether the name of the subject judge should be disclosed.

(3) if the complaint is finally disposed of by a privately communicated censure or reprimand, the publicly available materials must not disclose either the name of the subject judge or the text of the reprimand.

(4) if the complaint is finally disposed of under Rule 20(b)(1)(D) by any remedial action other than private censure or reprimand, the text of the dispositive order must be included in the materials made public, and the name of the subject judge must be disclosed.

(5) the name of the complainant must not be disclosed in materials made public under this Rule unless the chief judge or the judicial council orders disclosure.

(b) Manner of Making Public. The orders described in (a) must be made public by placing the orders on the court's public website and by placing them in a publicly accessible file in the office of the circuit clerk. If the orders appear to have precedential value, the chief judge may cause them to be published. In addition, the Committee on Judicial Conduct and Disability will make available on the judiciary's website, www.uscourts.gov, selected illustrative orders described in paragraph (a), appropriately redacted, to provide additional information to the public on how complaints are addressed under the Act.

(c) Orders of Committee on Judicial Conduct and Disability. Orders of the Committee on Judicial Conduct and Disability constituting final action in a complaint proceeding arising from a particular circuit will be made available to the public in the office of the circuit clerk of the relevant court of appeals. The Committee on Judicial Conduct and Disability will also make such orders available on the judiciary's website, www.uscourts.gov. When authorized by the Committee on Judicial Conduct and Disability, other orders related to complaint proceedings will similarly be made available.

(d) Complaints Referred to Judicial Conference. If a complaint is referred to the Judicial Conference under Rule 20(b)(1)(C) or 20(b)(2), materials relating to the complaint will be made public only if ordered by the Judicial Conference.

Commentary on Rule 24

Rule 24 is adapted from the Illustrative Rules and the recommendations of the Breyer Committee.

The Act requires the circuits to make available only written orders of a judicial council or the Judicial Conference imposing some form of sanction. 28 U.S.C. § 360(b). The Judicial Conference, however, has long recognized the desirability of public availability of a broader range of orders and other materials. In 1994, the Judicial Conference "urge[d] all circuits and courts covered by the Act to submit to the West Publishing Company, for publication in Federal Reporter 3d, and to Lexis all orders issued pursuant to [the Act] that are deemed by the issuing circuit or court to have significant precedential value to other circuits and courts covered by the Act." Report of the Proceedings of the Judicial Conference of the United States, Mar. 1994, at 28. Following this recommendation, the 2000 revision of the Illustrative Rules contained a public availability provision very similar to Rule 24. In 2002, the Judicial Conference again voted to encourage the circuits "to submit non-routine public orders disposing of complaints of judicial misconduct or disability for publication by on-line and print services." Report of the Proceedings of the Judicial Conference of the United

States, Sept. 2002, at 58. The Breyer Committee Report further emphasized that "[p]osting such orders on the judicial branch's public website would not only benefit judges directly, it would also encourage scholarly commentary and analysis of the orders." Breyer Committee Report, 239 F.R.D. at 216. With these considerations in mind, Rule 24 provides for public availability of a wide range of materials.

Rule 24 provides for public availability of orders of a chief judge, a judicial council, and the Committee on Judicial Conduct and Disability, as well as the texts of memoranda incorporated by reference in those orders, together with any dissenting opinions or separate statements by members of the judicial council. No memoranda other than those incorporated by reference in those orders shall be disclosed. However, these orders and memoranda are to be made public only when final action on the complaint has been taken and any right of review has been exhausted. The provision that decisions will be made public only after final action has been taken is designed in part to avoid public disclosure of the existence of pending proceedings. Whether the name of the subject judge is disclosed will then depend on the nature of the final action. If the final action is an order predicated on a finding of misconduct or disability (other than a privately communicated censure or reprimand) the name of the subject judge must be made public. If the final action is dismissal of the complaint, the name of the subject judge must not be disclosed. Rule 24(a)(1) provides that where a proceeding is concluded under Rule 11(d) by the chief judge on the basis of voluntary corrective action, the name of the subject judge generally should not be disclosed, except where the complainant or another person has disclosed the existence of a complaint proceeding to the public. Shielding the name of the subject judge in this circumstance should encourage informal disposition.

If a complaint is dismissed as moot, or because intervening events have made action on the complaint unnecessary, after appointment of a special committee, Rule 24(a)(2) allows the judicial council to determine whether the subject judge will be identified. In such a case, no final decision has been rendered on the merits, but it may be in the public interest—particularly if a judicial officer resigns in the course of an investigation—to make the identity of the subject judge known.

Once a special committee has been appointed, and a proceeding is concluded by the full judicial council on the basis of a remedial order of the council, Rule 24(a)(4) provides for disclosure of the name of the subject judge.

Rule 24(a)(5) provides that the identity of the complainant will be disclosed only if the chief judge so orders. Identifying the complainant when the subject judge is not identified would increase the likelihood that the identity of the subject judge would become publicly known, thus circumventing the policy of nondisclosure. It may not always be practicable to shield the complainant's identity while making public disclosure of the judicial council's order and supporting memoranda; in some circumstances, moreover, the complainant may consent to public identification.

Rule 24(b) makes clear that circuits must post on their external websites all orders required to be made public under Rule 24(a). The judiciary will seek ways to make decisions on complaints filed in their courts more readily accessible to the public through searchable electronic indices.

Matters involving orders issued following a special-committee investigation often involve highly sensitive situations, and it is important that judicial councils have every opportunity to reach a correct and just outcome. This would include the ability to reach informal resolution before a subject judge's identity must be released. But there must also come a point of procedural finality. The date of finality—and thus the time at which other safeguards and rules such as the publication requirement are triggered—is the date on which the judicial council issues a Final Order. *See In re Complaint of Judicial Misconduct*, 751 F.3d 611, 617 (2014) (requiring publication of a judicial council order "[e]ven though the period for review had not yet elapsed" and concluding that "the order was a final decision because the Council had adjudicated the matter on the merits after having received a report from a special investigating committee"). As determined in the cited case, modifications of this kind to a final order are subject to review by the Committee on Judicial Conduct and Disability.

25. Disqualification

(a) General Rule. Any judge is disqualified from participating in any proceeding under these Rules if the judge concludes that circumstances warrant disqualification. If a

complaint is filed by a judge, that judge is disqualified from participating in any consideration of the complaint except to the extent that these Rules provide for a complainant's participation. A chief judge who has identified a complaint under Rule 5 is not automatically disqualified from considering the complaint.

(b) Subject Judge. A subject judge, including a chief judge, is disqualified from considering a complaint except to the extent that these Rules provide for participation by a subject judge.

(c) Chief Judge Disqualified from Considering Petition for Review of Chief Judge's Order. If a petition for review of the chief judge's order entered under Rule 11(c), (d), or (e) is filed with the judicial council in accordance with Rule 18, the chief judge is disqualified from participating in the council's consideration of the petition.

(d) Member of Special Committee Not Disqualified. A member of the judicial council who serves on a special committee, including the chief judge, is not disqualified from participating in council consideration of the committee's report.

(e) Subject Judge's Disqualification After Appointment of Special Committee. Upon appointment of a special committee, the subject judge is disqualified from participating in the identification or consideration of any complaint, related or unrelated to the pending matter, under the Act or these Rules. The disqualification continues until all proceedings on the complaint against the subject judge are finally terminated with no further right of review.

(f) Substitute for Disqualified Chief Judge. If the chief judge is disqualified from performing duties that the Act and these Rules assign to a chief judge (including where a complaint is filed against a chief judge), those duties must be assigned to the most-senior active circuit judge not disqualified. If all circuit judges in regular active service are disqualified, the judicial council may determine whether to request a transfer under Rule 26, or, in the interest of sound judicial administration, to permit the chief judge to dispose of the complaint on the merits. Members of the judicial council who are named in the complaint may participate in this determination if necessary to obtain a quorum of the council.

(g) Judicial-Council Action When Multiple Judges Disqualified. Notwithstanding any other provision in these Rules to the contrary,

(1) a member of the judicial council who is a subject judge may participate in its disposition if:

(A) participation by one or more subject judges is necessary to obtain a quorum of the judicial council;

(B) the judicial council finds that the lack of a quorum is due to the naming of one or more judges in the complaint for the purpose of disqualifying that judge or those judges, or to the naming of one or more judges based on their participation in a decision excluded from the definition of misconduct under Rule 4(b); and

(C) the judicial council votes that it is necessary, appropriate, and in the interest of sound judicial administration that one or more subject judges be eligible to act.

(2) otherwise disqualified members may participate in votes taken under (g)(1)(B) and (g)(1)(C).

(h) Disqualification of Members of Committee on Judicial Conduct and Disability. No member of the Committee on Judicial Conduct and Disability is disqualified from participating in any proceeding under the Act or these Rules because of consultations with

a chief judge, a member of a special committee, or a member of a judicial council about the interpretation or application of the Act or these Rules, unless the member believes that the consultation would prevent fair-minded participation.

Commentary on Rule 25

Rule 25 is adapted from the Illustrative Rules.

Subsection (a) provides the general rule for disqualification. Of course, a judge is not disqualified simply because the subject judge is on the same court. However, this subsection recognizes that there may be cases in which an appearance of bias or prejudice is created by circumstances other than an association with the subject judge as a colleague. For example, a judge may have a familial relationship with a complainant or subject judge. When such circumstances exist, a judge may, in his or her discretion, conclude that disqualification is warranted.

Subsection (e) makes it clear that the disqualification of the subject judge relates only to the subject judge's participation in any proceeding arising under the Act or these Rules. For example, the subject judge cannot initiate complaints by identification, conduct limited inquiries, or choose between dismissal and special-committee investigation as the threshold disposition of a complaint. Likewise, the subject judge cannot participate in any proceeding arising under the Act or these Rules as a member of any special committee, the judicial council of the circuit, the Judicial Conference, or the Committee on Judicial Conduct and Disability. The Illustrative Rule, based on Section 359(a) of the Act, is ambiguous and could be read to disqualify a subject judge from service of any kind on each of the bodies mentioned. This is undoubtedly not the intent of the Act; such a disqualification would be anomalous in light of the Act's allowing a subject judge to continue to decide cases and to continue to exercise the powers of chief circuit or district judge. It would also create a substantial deterrence to the appointment of special committees, particularly where a special committee is needed solely because the chief judge may not decide matters of credibility in his or her review under Rule 11.

While a subject judge is barred by Rule 25(b) from participating in the disposition of the complaint in which he or she is named, Rule 25(e) recognizes that participation in proceedings arising under the Act or these Rules by a judge who is the subject of a special committee investigation may lead to an appearance of self-interest in creating substantive and procedural precedents governing such proceedings. Rule 25(e) bars such participation.

Under the Act, a complaint against the chief judge is to be handled by "that circuit judge in regular active service next senior in date of commission." 28 U.S.C. § 351(c). Rule 25(f) provides that seniority among judges other than the chief judge is to be determined by date of commission, with the result that complaints against the chief judge may be routed to a former chief judge or other judge who was appointed earlier than the chief judge. The Rules do not purport to prescribe who is to preside over meetings of the judicial council. Consequently, where the presiding member of the judicial council is disqualified from participating under these Rules, the order of precedence prescribed by Rule 25(f) for performing "duties that the Act and these Rules assign to a chief judge" does not apply to determine the acting presiding member of the council. That is a matter left to the internal rules or operating practices of each judicial council. In most cases the most senior active circuit judge who is a member of the judicial council and who is not disqualified will preside.

Sometimes a single complaint is filed against a large group of judges. If the normal disqualification rules are observed in such a case, no court of appeals judge can serve as acting chief judge of the circuit, and the judicial council will be without appellate members. Where the complaint is against all circuit and district judges, under normal rules no member of the judicial council can perform the duties assigned to the council under the statute.

A similar problem is created by successive complaints arising out of the same underlying grievance. For example, a complainant files a complaint against a district judge based on alleged misconduct, and the complaint is dismissed by the chief judge under the statute. The complainant may then file a complaint against the chief judge for dismissing the first complaint, and when that complaint is dismissed by the next senior judge, still a third complaint may be filed. The threat is that the complainant will bump down the seniority ladder until, once again, there is no member of the court of appeals who can serve as acting chief judge for the purpose of the next complaint. Similarly, complaints involving the merits of litigation may involve a series of decisions in which many judges participated or in which a rehearing en banc was denied by the court of appeals, and the complaint may name a majority of the judicial council as subject judges.

In recognition that these multiple-judge complaints are virtually always meritless, the judicial council is given discretion to determine: (1) whether it is necessary, appropriate, and in the interest of sound judicial administration to permit the chief judge to dispose of a complaint where it would otherwise be impossible for any active circuit judge in the circuit to act, and (2) whether it is necessary, appropriate, and in the interest of sound judicial administration, after appropriate findings as to need and justification are made, to permit subject judges of the judicial council to participate in the disposition of a petition for review where it would otherwise be impossible to obtain a quorum.

Applying a rule of necessity in these situations is consistent with the appearance of justice. *See, e.g.*, *In re Complaint of Doe*, 2 F.3d 308 (8th Cir. Jud. Council 1993) (invoking the rule of necessity); *In re Complaint of Judicial Misconduct*, No. 91–80464 (9th Cir. Jud. Council 1992) (same). There is no unfairness in permitting the chief judge to dispose of a patently insubstantial complaint that names all active circuit judges in the circuit.

Similarly, there is no unfairness in permitting subject judges, in these circumstances, to participate in the review of the chief judge's dismissal of an insubstantial complaint. The remaining option is to assign the matter to another body. Among other alternatives, the judicial council may request a transfer of the petition under Rule 26. Given the administrative inconvenience and delay involved in these alternatives, it is desirable to request a transfer only if the judicial council determines that the petition for review is substantial enough to warrant such action.

In the unlikely event that a quorum of the judicial council cannot be obtained to consider the report of a special committee, it would normally be necessary to request a transfer under Rule 26.

Rule 25(h) recognizes that the jurisdictional statement of the Committee on Judicial Conduct and Disability contemplates consultation between members of the Committee and judicial participants in proceedings under the Act and these Rules. Such consultation should not automatically preclude participation by a member in that proceeding.

26. Transfer to Another Judicial Council

In exceptional circumstances, a chief judge or a judicial council may ask the Chief Justice to transfer a proceeding based on a complaint identified under Rule 5 or filed under Rule 6 to the judicial council of another circuit. The request for a transfer may be made at any stage of the proceeding before a reference to the Judicial Conference under Rule 20(b)(1)(C) or 20(b)(2) or a petition for review is filed under Rule 22. Upon receiving such a request, the Chief Justice may refuse the request or select the transferee judicial council, which may then exercise the powers of a judicial council under these Rules.

Commentary on Rule 26

Rule 26 implements the Breyer Committee's recommended use of transfers. Breyer Committee Report, 239 F.R.D. at 214–15.

Rule 26 authorizes the transfer of a complaint proceeding to another judicial council selected by the Chief Justice. Such transfers may be appropriate, for example, in the case of a serious complaint where there are multiple disqualifications among the original judicial council, where the issues are highly visible and a local disposition may weaken public confidence in the process, where internal tensions arising in the council as a result of the complaint render disposition by a less involved council appropriate, or where a complaint calls into question policies or governance of the home court of appeals. The power to effect a transfer is lodged in the Chief Justice to avoid disputes in a judicial council over where to transfer a sensitive matter and to ensure that the transferee council accepts the matter.

Upon receipt of a transferred proceeding, the transferee judicial council shall determine the proper stage at which to begin consideration of the complaint—for example, reference to the transferee chief judge, appointment of a special committee, etc.

27. Withdrawal of Complaint or Petition for Review

(a) Complaint Pending Before Chief Judge. With the chief judge's consent, the complainant may withdraw a complaint that is before the chief judge for a decision under Rule 11. The withdrawal of a complaint will not prevent the chief judge from identifying or having to identify a complaint under Rule 5 based on the withdrawn complaint.

(b) Complaint Pending Before Special Committee or Judicial Council. After a complaint has been referred to the special committee for investigation and before the committee files its report, the complainant may withdraw the complaint only with the consent of both the subject judge and either the special committee or the judicial council.

(c) Petition for Review. A petition for review addressed to the judicial council under Rule 18, or the Committee on Judicial Conduct and Disability under Rule 22, may be withdrawn if no action on the petition has been taken.

Commentary on Rule 27

Rule 27 is adapted from the Illustrative Rules and treats the complaint proceeding, once begun, as a matter of public business rather than as the property of the complainant. Accordingly, the chief judge or the judicial council remains responsible for addressing any complaint under the Act, even a complaint that has been formally withdrawn by the complainant.

Under subsection (a), a complaint pending before the chief judge may be withdrawn if the chief judge consents. Where the complaint clearly lacked merit, the chief judge may accordingly be saved the burden of preparing a formal order and supporting memorandum. However, the chief judge may, or be obligated under Rule 5, to identify a complaint based on allegations in a withdrawn complaint.

If the chief judge appoints a special committee, Rule 27(b) provides that the complaint may be withdrawn only with the consent of both the body before which it is pending (the special committee or the judicial council) and the subject judge. Once a complaint has reached the stage of appointment of a special committee, a resolution of the issues may be necessary to preserve public confidence. Moreover, the subject judge is given the right to insist that the matter be resolved on the merits, thereby eliminating any ambiguity that might remain if the proceeding were terminated by withdrawal of the complaint.

With regard to all petitions for review, Rule 27(c) grants the petitioner unrestricted authority to withdraw the petition. It is thought that the public's interest in the proceeding is adequately protected, because there will necessarily have been a decision by the chief judge and often by the judicial council as well in such a case.

28. Availability of Rules and Forms

These Rules and copies of the complaint form as provided in Rule 6(a) must be available without charge in the office of the circuit clerk of each court of appeals, district court, bankruptcy court, or other federal court whose judges are subject to the Act. Each court must also make these Rules, the complaint form, and complaint-filing instructions available on the court's website, or provide an Internet link to these items on the appropriate court of appeals website or on www.uscourts.gov.

29. Effective Date

These Rules will become effective after promulgation by the Judicial Conference of the United States.

Appendix to the Rules: Form AO 310 (Complaint of Judicial Misconduct or Disability)

PART THREE

RULES OF EVIDENCE AND PROCEDURE THAT AFFECT THE LEGAL PROFESSION

TABLE OF CONTENTS

Introduction

Until recently, most courses and casebooks in professional responsibility focused solely on the ABA's model codes of conduct. However, the law which governs and regulates the conduct of lawyers must go far beyond the ABA's pronouncements. One other source of law which affects lawyers' conduct must include rules of evidence, procedure, and court. This part includes rules of evidence and procedure that affect the practice of law.

SELECTED RULES OF EVIDENCE AND PROCEDURE

FEDERAL RULES OF EVIDENCE FOR UNITED STATES COURTS AND MAGISTRATES

Rule 501. Privilege in General

The common law—as interpreted by United States courts in the light of reason and experience—governs a claim of privilege unless any of the following provides otherwise:

- the United States Constitution;
- a federal statute; or
- rules prescribed by the Supreme Court.

But in a civil case, state law governs privilege regarding a claim or defense for which state law supplies the rule of decision.

Rule 502. Attorney-Client Privilege and Work Product; Limitations on Waiver

The following provisions apply, in the circumstances set out, to disclosure of a communication or information covered by the attorney-client privilege or work-product protection.

(a) Disclosure Made in a Federal Proceeding or to a Federal Office or Agency; Scope of a Waiver.—When the disclosure is made in a federal proceeding or to a federal office or agency and waives the attorney-client privilege or work-product protection, the waiver extends to an undisclosed communication or information in a federal or state proceeding only if:

(1) the waiver is intentional;

(2) the disclosed and undisclosed communications or information concern the same subject matter; and

(3) they ought in fairness to be considered together.

(b) Inadvertent Disclosure.—When made in a federal proceeding or to a federal office or agency, the disclosure does not operate as a waiver in a federal or state proceeding if:

(1) the disclosure is inadvertent;

(2) the holder of the privilege or protection took reasonable steps to prevent disclosure; and

(3) the holder promptly took reasonable steps to rectify the error, including (if applicable) following Fed. R. Civ. P. 26(b)(5)(B).

(c) Disclosure Made in a State Proceeding.—When the disclosure is made in a state proceeding and is not the subject of a state-court order concerning waiver, the disclosure does not operate as a waiver in a federal proceeding if the disclosure:

(1) would not be a waiver under this rule if it had been made in a federal proceeding; or

(2) is not a waiver under the law of the state where the disclosure occurred.

(d) Controlling Effect of a Court Order.—A federal court may order that the privilege or protection is not waived by disclosure connected with the litigation pending before the court—in which event the disclosure is also not a waiver in any other federal or state proceeding.

(e) Controlling Effect of a Party Agreement.—An agreement on the effect of disclosure in a federal proceeding is binding only on the parties to the agreement, unless it is incorporated into a court order.

(f) Controlling Effect of this Rule.—Notwithstanding Rules 101 and 1101, this rule applies to state proceedings and to federal court-annexed and federal court-mandated arbitration proceedings, in the circumstances set out in the rule. And notwithstanding Rule 501, this rule applies even if state law provides the rule of decision.

(g) Definitions.—In this rule:

(1) "attorney-client privilege" means the protection that applicable law provides for confidential attorney-client communications; and

(2) "work-product protection" means the protection that applicable law provides for tangible material (or its intangible equivalent) prepared in anticipation of litigation or for trial.

Explanatory Note on Evidence Rule 502 Prepared by the Judicial Conference Advisory Committee on Evidence Rules (Revised 11/28/2007)

This new rule has two major purposes:

1) It resolves some longstanding disputes in the courts about the effect of certain disclosures of communications or information protected by the attorney-client privilege or as work product—specifically those disputes involving inadvertent disclosure and subject matter waiver.

2) It responds to the widespread complaint that litigation costs necessary to protect against waiver of attorney-client privilege or work product have become prohibitive due to the concern that any disclosure (however innocent or minimal) will operate as a subject matter waiver of all protected communications or information. This concern is especially troubling in cases involving electronic discovery. *See, e.g., Hopson v. City of Baltimore,* 232 F.R.D. 228, 244 (D.Md. 2005) (electronic discovery may encompass "millions of documents" and to insist upon "record-by-record pre-production privilege review, on pain of subject matter waiver, would impose upon parties costs of production that bear no proportionality to what is at stake in the litigation").

The rule seeks to provide a predictable, uniform set of standards under which parties can determine the consequences of a disclosure of a communication or information covered by the attorney-client privilege or work-product protection. Parties to litigation need to know, for example, that if they exchange privileged information pursuant to a confidentiality order, the court's order will be enforceable. Moreover, if a federal court's confidentiality order is not enforceable in a state court then the burdensome costs of privilege review and retention are unlikely to be reduced.

The rule makes no attempt to alter federal or state law on whether a communication or information is protected under the attorney-client privilege or work-product immunity as an initial matter. Moreover, while establishing some exceptions to waiver, the rule does not purport to supplant applicable waiver doctrine generally.

The rule governs only certain waivers by disclosure. Other common-law waiver doctrines may result in a finding of waiver even where there is no disclosure of privileged information or work product. *See, e.g., Nguyen v. Excel Corp.,* 197 F.3d 200 (5th Cir. 1999) (reliance on an advice of counsel defense waives the privilege with respect to attorney-client communications pertinent to that defense); *Ryers v. Burleson,* 100 F.R.D. 436 (D.D.C. 1983) (allegation of lawyer malpractice constituted a waiver of confidential communications under the circumstances). The rule is not intended to displace or modify federal common law concerning waiver of privilege or work product where no disclosure has been made.

Subdivision (a). The rule provides that a voluntary disclosure in a federal proceeding or to a federal office or agency, if a waiver, generally results in a waiver only of the communication or information disclosed; a subject matter waiver (of either privilege or work product) is reserved for those unusual situations in which fairness requires a further disclosure of related, protected information, in order to prevent a selective and misleading presentation of evidence to the disadvantage of the adversary. *See, e.g., In re United Mine Workers of America Employee Benefit Plans Litig.*, 159 F.R.D. 307, 312 (D.D.C. 1994) (waiver of work product limited to materials actually disclosed, because the party did not deliberately disclose documents in an attempt to gain a tactical advantage). Thus, subject matter waiver is limited to situations in which a party intentionally puts protected information into the litigation in a selective, misleading and unfair manner. It follows that an inadvertent disclosure of protected information can never result in a subject matter waiver. *See* Rule 502(b). The rule rejects the result in *In re Sealed Case,* 877 F.2d 976 (D.C.Cir. 1989), which held that inadvertent disclosure of documents during discovery automatically constituted a subject matter waiver.

The language concerning subject matter waiver—"ought in fairness"—is taken from Rule 106, because the animating principle is the same. Under both Rules, a party that makes a selective, misleading presentation that is unfair to the adversary opens itself to a more complete and accurate presentation.

To assure protection and predictability, the rule provides that if a disclosure is made at the federal level, the federal rule on subject matter waiver governs subsequent state court determinations on the scope of the waiver by that disclosure.

Subdivision (b). Courts are in conflict over whether an inadvertent disclosure of a communication or information protected as privileged or work product constitutes a waiver. A few courts find that a disclosure must be intentional to be a waiver. Most courts find a waiver only if the disclosing party acted carelessly in disclosing the communication or information and failed to request its return in a timely manner. And a few courts hold that any inadvertent disclosure of a communication or information protected under the attorney-client privilege or as work product constitutes a waiver without regard to the protections taken to avoid such a disclosure. *See generally Hopson v. City of Baltimore,* 232 F.R.D. 228 (D.Md. 2005), for a discussion of this case law.

The rule opts for the middle ground: inadvertent disclosure of protected communications or information in connection with a federal proceeding or to a federal office or agency does not constitute a waiver if the holder took reasonable steps to prevent disclosure and also promptly took reasonable steps to rectify the error. This position is in accord with the majority view on whether inadvertent disclosure is a waiver.

Cases such as *Lois Sportswear, U.S.A., Inc. v. Levi Strauss &* Co., 104 F.R.D. 103, 105 (S.D.N.Y. 1985) and *Hartford Fire Ins. Co. v. Garvey*, 109 F.R.D. 323, 332 (N.D.Cal. 1985), set out a multi-factor test for determining whether inadvertent disclosure is a waiver. The stated factors (none of which is dispositive) are the reasonableness of precautions taken, the time taken to rectify the error, the scope of discovery, the extent of disclosure and the overriding issue of fairness. The rule does not explicitly codify that test, because it is really a set of non-determinative guidelines that vary from case to case. The rule is flexible enough to accommodate any of those listed factors. Other considerations bearing on the reasonableness of a producing party's efforts include the number of documents to be reviewed and the time constraints for production. Depending on the circumstances, a party that uses advanced analytical software applications and linguistic tools in screening for privilege and work product may be found to have taken "reasonable steps" to prevent inadvertent disclosure. The implementation of an efficient system of records management before litigation may also be relevant.

The rule does not require the producing party to engage in a post-production review to determine whether any protected communication or information has been produced by mistake. But the rule does require the producing party to follow up on any obvious indications that a protected communication or information has been produced inadvertently.

The rule applies to inadvertent disclosures made to a federal office or agency, including but not limited to an office or agency that is acting in the course of its regulatory, investigative or enforcement authority. The consequences of waiver, and the concomitant costs of pre-production privilege review, can be as great with respect to disclosures to offices and agencies as they are in litigation.

Subdivision (c). Difficult questions can arise when 1) a disclosure of a communication or information protected by the attorney-client privilege or as work product is made in a state proceeding, 2) the communication or information is offered in a subsequent federal proceeding on the ground that the disclosure waived the privilege or protection, and 3) the state and federal laws are in conflict on the question of waiver. The Committee determined that the proper solution for the federal court is to apply the law that is most protective of privilege and work product. If the state law is more protective (such as where the state law is that an inadvertent disclosure can never be a waiver), the holder of the privilege or protection may well have relied on that law when making the disclosure in the state proceeding. Moreover, applying a more restrictive federal law of waiver could impair the state objective of preserving the privilege or work-product protection for disclosures made in state proceedings. On the other hand, if the federal law is more protective, applying the state law of waiver to determine admissibility in federal court is likely to undermine the federal objective of limiting the costs of production.

The rule does not address the enforceability of a state court confidentiality order in a federal proceeding, as that question is covered both by statutory law and principles of federalism and comity. *See* 28 U.S.C. § 1738 (providing that state judicial proceedings "shall have the same full faith and credit in every court within the United States . . . as they have by law or usage in the courts of such State . . . from which they are taken"). *See also Tucker v. Ohtsu Tire & Rubber Co.,* 191 F.R.D. 495, 499 (D.Md. 2000) (noting that a federal court considering the enforceability of a state confidentiality order is "constrained by principles of comity, courtesy, and . . . federalism"). Thus, a state court order finding no waiver in connection with a disclosure made in a state court proceeding is enforceable under existing law in subsequent federal proceedings.

Subdivision (d). Confidentiality orders are becoming increasingly important in limiting the costs of privilege review and retention, especially in cases involving electronic discovery. But the utility of a confidentiality order in reducing discovery costs is substantially diminished if it provides no protection outside the particular litigation in which the order is entered. Parties are unlikely to be able to reduce the costs of pre-production review for privilege and work product if the consequence of disclosure is that the communications or information could be used by non-parties to the litigation.

There is some dispute on whether a confidentiality order entered in one case is enforceable in other proceedings. *See generally Hopson v. City of Baltimore,* 232 F.R.D. 228 (D.Md. 2005), for a discussion of this case law. The rule provides that when a confidentiality order governing the consequences of disclosure in that case is entered in a federal proceeding, its terms are enforceable against non-parties in any federal or state proceeding. For example, the court order may provide for return of documents without waiver irrespective of the care taken by the disclosing party; the rule contemplates enforcement of "claw-back" and "quick peek" arrangements as a way to avoid the excessive costs of pre-production review for privilege and work product. *See Zubulake v. UBS Warburg LLC,* 216 F.R.D. 280, 290 (S.D.N.Y. 2003) (noting that parties may enter into "so-called 'claw-back' agreements that allow the parties to forego privilege review altogether in favor of an agreement to return inadvertently produced privilege documents"). The rule provides a party with a predictable protection from a court order—predictability that is needed to allow the party to plan in advance to limit the prohibitive costs of privilege and work product review and retention.

Under the rule, a confidentiality order is enforceable whether or not it memorializes an agreement among the parties to the litigation. Party agreement should not be a condition of enforceability of a federal court's order.

Under subdivision (d), a federal court may order that disclosure of privileged or protected information "in connection with" a federal proceeding does not result in waiver. But subdivision (d) does not allow the federal court to enter an order determining the waiver effects of a separate disclosure of the same information in other proceedings, state or federal. If a disclosure has been made in a state proceeding (and is not the subject of a state-court order on waiver), then subdivision (d) is inapplicable. Subdivision (c) would govern the federal court's determination whether the state-court disclosure waived the privilege or protection in the federal proceeding.

Subdivision (e). Subdivision (e) codifies the well-established proposition that parties can enter an agreement to limit the effect of waiver by disclosure between or among them. Of course such an agreement can bind only the parties to the agreement. The rule makes clear that if parties want protection against non-parties from a finding of waiver by disclosure, the agreement must be made part of a court order.

Subdivision (f). The protections against waiver provided by Rule 502 must be applicable when protected communications or information disclosed in federal proceedings are subsequently offered in state proceedings. Otherwise the holders of protected communications and information, and their lawyers, could not rely on the protections provided by the Rule, and the goal of limiting costs in discovery would be substantially undermined. Rule 502(f) is intended to resolve any potential tension between the provisions of Rule 502 that apply to state proceedings and the possible limitations on the applicability of the Federal Rules of Evidence otherwise provided by Rules 101 and 1101.

The rule is intended to apply in all federal court proceedings, including court-annexed and court-ordered arbitrations, without regard to any possible limitations of Rules 101 and 1101. This provision is not intended to raise an inference about the applicability of any other rule of evidence in arbitration proceedings more generally.

The costs of discovery can be equally high for state and federal causes of action, and the rule seeks to limit those costs in all federal proceedings, regardless of whether the claim arises under state or federal law. Accordingly, the rule applies to state law causes of action brought in federal court.

Subdivision (g). The rule's coverage is limited to attorney-client privilege and work product. The operation of waiver by disclosure, as applied to other evidentiary privileges, remains a question of federal common law. Nor does the rule purport to apply to the Fifth Amendment privilege against compelled self-incrimination.

The definition of work product "materials" is intended to include both tangible and intangible information. *See In re Cendant Corp. Sec. Litig.*, 343 F.3d 658, 662 (3d Cir. 2003) ("work product protection extends to both tangible and intangible work product").

Rule 605. Judge's Competency as a Witness

The presiding judge may not testify as a witness at the trial. A party need not object to preserve the issue.

APPENDIX OF DELETED RULES OF EVIDENCE

Rule 503. Lawyer-Client Privilege [Not enacted.]

(a) Definitions. As used in this rule:

(1) A "client" is a person, public officer, or corporation, association, or other organization or entity, either public or private, who is rendered professional legal services by a lawyer, or who consults a lawyer with a view to obtaining professional legal services from him.

(2) A "lawyer" is a person authorized, or reasonably believed by the client to be authorized, to practice law in any state or nation.

(3) A "representative of the lawyer" is one employed to assist the lawyer in the rendition of professional services.

(4) A communication is "confidential" if not intended to be disclosed to third persons other than those to whom disclosure is in furtherance of the rendition of professional legal services to the client or those reasonably necessary for the transmission of the communication.

(b) General rule of privilege. A client has a privilege to refuse to disclose and to prevent any other person from disclosing confidential communications made for the purpose of facilitating the rendition of professional legal services to the client, (1) between himself or his representative and his lawyer or his lawyer's representative, or (2) between his lawyer and the lawyer's representative, or (3) by him or his lawyer to a lawyer representing another in a matter of common interest, or (4) between representatives of the client or between the client and a representative of the client, or (5) between lawyers representing the client.

(c) Who may claim the privilege. The privilege may be claimed by the client, his guardian or conservator, the personal representative of a deceased client, or the successor, trustee, or similar representative of a corporation, association, or other organization, whether or not in existence. The person who was the lawyer at the time of the communication may claim the privilege but only on behalf of the client. His authority to do so is presumed in the absence of evidence to the contrary.

(d) Exceptions. There is no privilege under this rule:

(1) Furtherance of crime or fraud. If the services of the lawyer were sought or obtained to enable or aid anyone to commit or plan to commit what the client knew or reasonably should have known to be a crime or fraud; or

(2) Claimants through same deceased client. As to a communication relevant to an issue between parties who claim through the same deceased client, regardless of whether the claims are by testate or intestate succession or by *inter vivos* transaction; or

(3) Breach of duty by lawyer or client. As to a communication relevant to an issue of breach of duty by the lawyer to his client or by the client to his lawyer; or

(4) Document attested by lawyer. As to a communication relevant to an issue concerning an attested document to which the lawyer is an attesting witness; or

(5) Joint clients. As to a communication relevant to a matter of common interest between two or more clients if the communication was made by any of them to a lawyer retained or consulted in common, when offered in an action between any of the clients.

FEDERAL RULES OF CIVIL PROCEDURE

Rule 11. Signing of Pleadings, Motions, and Other Papers; Representations to Court; Sanctions*

(a) Signature. Every pleading, written motion, and other paper must be signed by at least one attorney of record in the attorney's name—or by a party personally if the party is unrepresented. The paper must state the signer's address, e-mail address, and telephone number. Unless a rule or statute specifically states otherwise, a pleading need not be verified or accompanied by an affidavit. The court must strike an unsigned paper unless the omission is promptly corrected after being called to the attorney's or party's attention.

(b) Representations to the Court. By presenting to the court a pleading, written motion, or other paper—whether by signing, filing, submitting, or later advocating it—an attorney or unrepresented party certifies that to the best of the person's knowledge, information, and belief, formed after an inquiry reasonable under the circumstances:

(1) it is not being presented for any improper purpose, such as to harass, cause unnecessary delay, or needlessly increase the cost of litigation;

(2) the claims, defenses, and other legal contentions are warranted by existing law or by a nonfrivolous argument for extending, modifying, or reversing existing law or for establishing new law;

(3) the factual contentions have evidentiary support or, if specifically so identified, will likely have evidentiary support after a reasonable opportunity for further investigation or discovery; and

(4) the denials of factual contentions are warranted on the evidence or, if specifically so identified, are reasonably based on belief or a lack of information.

(c) Sanctions.

(1) ***In General.*** If, after notice and a reasonable opportunity to respond, the court determines that Rule 11(b) has been violated, the court may impose an appropriate sanction on any attorney, law firm, or party that violated the rule or is responsible for the violation. Absent exceptional circumstances, a law firm must be held jointly responsible for a violation committed by its partner, associate, or employee.

(2) ***Motion for Sanctions.*** A motion for sanctions must be made separately from any other motion and must describe the specific conduct that allegedly violates Rule 11(b). The motion must be served under Rule 5, but it must not be filed or be presented to the court if the challenged paper, claim, defense, contention, or denial is withdrawn or appropriately corrected within 21

---

* [Ed.] This footnote contains the text of Rule 11 prior to the 1993 Amendment.

Every pleading, motion, and other paper of a party represented by an attorney shall be signed by at least one attorney of record in the attorney's individual name, whose address shall be stated. A party who is not represented by an attorney shall sign the party's pleading, motion, or other paper and state the party's address. Except when otherwise specifically provided by rule or statute, pleadings need not be verified or accompanied by affidavit. The rule in equity that the averments of an answer under oath must be overcome by the testimony of two witnesses or of one witness sustained by corroborating circumstances is abolished. The signature of an attorney or party constitutes a certificate by the signer that the signer has read the pleading, motion, or other paper; that to the best of the signer's knowledge, information, and belief formed after reasonable inquiry it is well grounded in fact and is warranted by existing law or a good faith argument for the extension, modification, or reversal of existing law, and that it is not interposed for any improper purpose, such as to harass or to cause unnecessary delay or needless increase in the cost of litigation. If a pleading, motion, or other paper is not signed, it shall be stricken unless it is signed promptly after the omission is called to the attention of the pleader or movant. If a pleading, motion, or other paper is signed in violation of this rule, the court, upon motion or upon its own initiative, shall impose upon the person who signed it, a represented party, or both, an appropriate sanction, which may include an order to pay to the other party or parties the amount of the reasonable expenses incurred because of the filing of the pleading, motion, or other paper, including a reasonable attorney's fee.

days after service or within another time the court sets. If warranted, the court may award to the prevailing party the reasonable expenses, including attorney's fees, incurred for the motion.

(3) ***On the Court's Initiative.*** On its own, the court may order an attorney, law firm, or party to show cause why conduct specifically described in the order has not violated Rule 11(b).

(4) ***Nature of a Sanction.*** A sanction imposed under this rule must be limited to what suffices to deter repetition of the conduct or comparable conduct by others similarly situated. The sanction may include nonmonetary directives; an order to pay a penalty into court; or, if imposed on motion and warranted for effective deterrence, an order directing payment to the movant of part or all of the reasonable attorney's fees and other expenses directly resulting from the violation.

(5) ***Limitations on Monetary Sanctions.*** The court must not impose a monetary sanction:

(A) against a represented party for violating Rule 11(b)(2); or

(B) on its own, unless it issued the show-cause order under Rule 11(c)(3) before voluntary dismissal or settlement of the claims made by or against the party that is, or whose attorneys are, to be sanctioned.

(6) ***Requirements for an Order.*** An order imposing a sanction must describe the sanctioned conduct and explain the basis for the sanction.

(d) Inapplicability to Discovery. This rule does not apply to disclosures and discovery requests, responses, objections, and motions under Rules 26 through 37.

Rule 16. Pretrial Conferences; Scheduling; Management

(a) Purposes of a Pretrial Conference. In any action, the court may order the attorneys and any unrepresented parties to appear for one or more pretrial conferences for such purposes as:

(1) expediting disposition of the action;

(2) establishing early and continuing control so that the case will not be protracted because of lack of management;

(3) discouraging wasteful pretrial activities;

(4) improving the quality of the trial through more thorough preparation; and

(5) facilitating settlement.

(b) Scheduling.

(1) ***Scheduling Order.*** Except in categories of actions exempted by local rule, the district judge—or a magistrate judge when authorized by local rule—must issue a scheduling order:

(A) after receiving the parties' report under Rule 26(f); or

(B) after consulting with the parties' attorneys and any unrepresented parties at a scheduling conference.

(2) ***Time to Issue.*** The judge must issue the scheduling order as soon as practicable, but unless the judge finds good cause for delay, the judge must issue it within the earlier of 90 days after any defendant has been served with the complaint or 60 days after any defendant has appeared.

(3) ***Contents of the Order.***

(A) *Required Contents.* The scheduling order must limit the time to join other parties, amend the pleadings, complete discovery, and file motions.

(B) *Permitted Contents.* The scheduling order may:

(i) modify the timing of disclosures under Rules 26(a) and 26(e)(1);

(ii) modify the extent of discovery;

(iii) provide for disclosure, discovery, or preservation of electronically stored information;

(iv) include any agreements the parties reach for asserting claims of privilege or of protection as trial-preparation material after information is produced, including agreements reached under Federal Rule of Evidence 502;

(v) direct that before moving for an order relating to discovery, the movant must request a conference with the court;

(vi) set dates for pretrial conferences and for trial; and

(vii) include other appropriate matters.

(4) ***Modifying a Schedule.*** A schedule may be modified only for good cause and with the judge's consent.

(c) Attendance and Matters for Consideration at a Pretrial Conference.

(1) ***Attendance.*** A represented party must authorize at least one of its attorneys to make stipulations and admissions about all matters that can reasonably be anticipated for discussion at a pretrial conference. If appropriate, the court may require that a party or its representative be present or reasonably available by other means to consider possible settlement.

(2) ***Matters for Consideration.*** At any pretrial conference, the court may consider and take appropriate action on the following matters:

(A) formulating and simplifying the issues, and eliminating frivolous claims or defenses;

(B) amending the pleadings if necessary or desirable;

(C) obtaining admissions and stipulations about facts and documents to avoid unnecessary proof, and ruling in advance on the admissibility of evidence;

(D) avoiding unnecessary proof and cumulative evidence, and limiting the use of testimony under Federal Rule of Evidence 702;

(E) determining the appropriateness and timing of summary adjudication under Rule 56;

(F) controlling and scheduling discovery, including orders affecting disclosures and discovery under Rule 26 and Rules 29 through 37;

(G) identifying witnesses and documents, scheduling the filing and exchange of any pretrial briefs, and setting dates for further conferences and for trial;

(H) referring matters to a magistrate judge or a master;

(I) settling the case and using special procedures to assist in resolving the dispute when authorized by statute or local rule;

(J) determining the form and content of the pretrial order;

(K) disposing of pending motions;

(L) adopting special procedures for managing potentially difficult or protracted actions that may involve complex issues, multiple parties, difficult legal questions, or unusual proof problems;

(M) ordering a separate trial under Rule 42(b) of a claim, counterclaim, crossclaim, third-party claim, or particular issue;

(N) ordering the presentation of evidence early in the trial on a manageable issue that might, on the evidence, be the basis for a judgment as a matter of law under Rule 50(a) or a judgment on partial findings under Rule 52(c);

(O) establishing a reasonable limit on the time allowed to present evidence; and

(P) facilitating in other ways the just, speedy, and inexpensive disposition of the action.

(d) Pretrial Orders. After any conference under this rule, the court should issue an order reciting the action taken. This order controls the course of the action unless the court modifies it.

(e) Final Pretrial Conference and Orders. The court may hold a final pretrial conference to formulate a trial plan, including a plan to facilitate the admission of evidence. The conference must be held as close to the start of trial as is reasonable, and must be attended by at least one attorney who will conduct the trial for each party and by any unrepresented party. The court may modify the order issued after a final pretrial conference only to prevent manifest injustice.

(f) Sanctions.

(1) ***In General.*** On motion or on its own, the court may issue any just orders, including those authorized by Rule 37(b)(2)(A)(ii)-(vii), if a party or its attorney:

(A) fails to appear at a scheduling or other pretrial conference;

(B) is substantially unprepared to participate—or does not participate in good faith—in the conference; or

(C) fails to obey a scheduling or other pretrial order.

(2) ***Imposing Fees and Costs.*** Instead of or in addition to any other sanction, the court must order the party, its attorney, or both to pay the reasonable expenses—including attorney's fees—incurred because of any noncompliance with this rule, unless the noncompliance was substantially justified or other circumstances make an award of expenses unjust.

Rule 23. Class Actions

(a) Prerequisites. One or more members of a class may sue or be sued as representative parties on behalf of all members only if:

(1) the class is so numerous that joinder of all members is impracticable;

(2) there are questions of law or fact common to the class;

(3) the claims or defenses of the representative parties are typical of the claims or defenses of the class; and

(4) the representative parties will fairly and adequately protect the interests of the class.

(b) Types of Class Actions. A class action may be maintained if Rule 23(a) is satisfied and if:

(1) prosecuting separate actions by or against individual class members would create a risk of:

(A) inconsistent or varying adjudications with respect to individual class members that would establish incompatible standards of conduct for the party opposing the class; or

(B) adjudications with respect to individual class members that, as a practical matter, would be dispositive of the interests of the other members not parties to the individual adjudications or would substantially impair or impede their ability to protect their interests;

(2) the party opposing the class has acted or refused to act on grounds that apply generally to the class, so that final injunctive relief or corresponding declaratory relief is appropriate respecting the class as a whole; or

(3) the court finds that the questions of law or fact common to class members predominate over any questions affecting only individual members, and that a class action is superior to other available methods for fairly and efficiently adjudicating the controversy. The matters pertinent to these findings include:

(A) the class members' interests in individually controlling the prosecution or defense of separate actions;

(B) the extent and nature of any litigation concerning the controversy already begun by or against class members;

(C) the desirability or undesirability of concentrating the litigation of the claims in the particular forum; and

(D) the likely difficulties in managing a class action.

(c) Certification Order; Notice to Class Members; Judgment; Issues Classes; Subclasses.

(1) ***Certification Order.***

(A) *Time to Issue.* At an early practicable time after a person sues or is sued as a class representative, the court must determine by order whether to certify the action as a class action.

(B) *Defining the Class; Appointing Class Counsel.* An order that certifies a class action must define the class and the class claims, issues, or defenses, and must appoint class counsel under Rule 23(g).

(C) *Altering or Amending the Order.* An order that grants or denies class certification may be altered or amended before final judgment.

(2) ***Notice.***

(A) *For (b)(1) or (b)(2) Classes.* For any class certified under Rule 23(b)(1) or (b)(2), the court may direct appropriate notice to the class.

(B) *For (b)(3) Classes.* For any class certified under Rule 23(b)(3)—or upon ordering notice under Rule 23(e)(1) to a class proposed to be certified for purposes of settlement under Rule 23(b)(3)—the court must direct to class members the best notice that is practicable under the circumstances, including individual notice to all members who can be identified through reasonable effort. The notice may be by one or more of the following: United States mail, electronic means, or other appropriate means. The notice must clearly and concisely state in plain, easily understood language:

(i) the nature of the action;

(ii) the definition of the class certified;

(iii) the class claims, issues, or defenses;

(iv) that a class member may enter an appearance through an attorney if the member so desires;

(v) that the court will exclude from the class any member who requests exclusion;

(vi) the time and manner for requesting exclusion; and

(vii) the binding effect of a class judgment on members under Rule 23(c)(3).

(3) ***Judgment.*** Whether or not favorable to the class, the judgment in a class action must:

(A) for any class certified under Rule 23(b)(1) or (b)(2), include and describe those whom the court finds to be class members; and

(B) for any class certified under Rule 23(b)(3), include and specify or describe those to whom the Rule 23(c)(2) notice was directed, who have not requested exclusion, and whom the court finds to be class members.

(4) ***Particular Issues.*** When appropriate, an action may be brought or maintained as a class action with respect to particular issues.

(5) ***Subclasses.*** When appropriate, a class may be divided into subclasses that are each treated as a class under this rule.

(d) Conducting the Action.

(1) ***In General.*** In conducting an action under this rule, the court may issue orders that:

(A) determine the course of proceedings or prescribe measures to prevent undue repetition or complication in presenting evidence or argument;

(B) require—to protect class members and fairly conduct the action—giving appropriate notice to some or all class members of:

(i) any step in the action;

(ii) the proposed extent of the judgment; or

(iii) the members' opportunity to signify whether they consider the representation fair and adequate, to intervene and present claims or defenses, or to otherwise come into the action;

(C) impose conditions on the representative parties or on intervenors;

(D) require that the pleadings be amended to eliminate allegations about representation of absent persons and that the action proceed accordingly; or

(E) deal with similar procedural matters.

(2) ***Combining and Amending Orders.*** An order under Rule 23(d)(1) may be altered or amended from time to time and may be combined with an order under Rule 16.

(e) Settlement, Voluntary Dismissal, or Compromise. The claims, issues, or defenses of a certified class—or a class proposed to be certified for purposes of settlement—may be settled, voluntarily dismissed, or compromised only with the court's approval. The following procedures apply to a proposed settlement, voluntary dismissal, or compromise:

(1) ***Notice to the Class.***

(A) *Information That Parties Must Provide to the Court.* The parties must provide the court with information sufficient to enable it to determine whether to give notice of the proposal to the class.

(B) *Grounds for a Decision to Give Notice.* The court must direct notice in a reasonable manner to all class members who would be bound by the proposal if giving notice is justified by the parties' showing that the court will likely be able to:

(i) approve the proposal under Rule 23(e)(2); and

(ii) certify the class for purposes of judgment on the proposal.

(2) ***Approval of the Proposal.*** If the proposal would bind class members, the court may approve it only after a hearing and only on finding that it is fair, reasonable, and adequate after considering whether:

(A) the class representatives and class counsel have adequately represented the class;

(B) the proposal was negotiated at arm's length;

(C) the relief provided for the class is adequate, taking into account:

(i) the costs, risks, and delay of trial and appeal;

(ii) the effectiveness of any proposed method of distributing relief to the class, including the method of processing class-member claims;

(iii) the terms of any proposed award of attorney's fees, including timing of payment; and

(iv) any agreement required to be identified under Rule 23(e)(3); and

(D) the proposal treats class members equitably relative to each other.

(3) ***Identifying Agreements.*** The parties seeking approval must file a statement identifying any agreement made in connection with the proposal.

(4) ***New Opportunity to Be Excluded.*** If the class action was previously certified under Rule 23(b)(3), the court may refuse to approve a settlement unless it affords a new opportunity to request exclusion to individual class members who had an earlier opportunity to request exclusion but did not do so.

(5) ***Class-Member Objections.***

(A) *In General.* Any class member may object to the proposal if it requires court approval under this subdivision (e) The objection must state whether it applies only to the objector, to a specific subset of the class, or to the entire class, and also state with specificity the grounds for the objection.

(B) *Court Approval Required for Payment in Connection with an Objection.* Unless approved by the court after a hearing, no payment or other consideration may be provided in connection with:

(i) forgoing or withdrawing an objection, or

(ii) forgoing, dismissing, or abandoning an appeal from a judgment approving the proposal.

(C) *Procedure for Approval After an Appeal.* If approval under Rule 23(e)(5)(B) has not been obtained be fore an appeal is docketed in the court of appeals, the procedure of Rule 62.1 applies while the appeal remains pending.

(f) **Appeals.** A court of appeals may permit an appeal from an order granting or denying class-action certification under this rule, but not from an order under Rule 23(e)(1). A party must file a petition for permission to appeal with the circuit clerk within 14 days after the order is entered, or within 45 days after the order is entered if any party is the United States, a United States agency, or a United States officer or employee sued for an act or omission occurring in connection with duties performed on the United States' behalf. An appeal does not stay proceedings in the 118 district court unless the district judge or the court of appeals so orders.

(g) **Class Counsel.**

(1) ***Appointing Class Counsel.*** Unless a statute provides otherwise, a court that certifies a class must appoint class counsel. In appointing class counsel, the court:

(A) must consider:

(i) the work counsel has done in identifying or investigating potential claims in the action;

(ii) counsel's experience in handling class actions, other complex litigation, and the types of claims asserted in the action;

(iii) counsel's knowledge of the applicable law; and

(iv) the resources that counsel will commit to representing the class;

(B) may consider any other matter pertinent to counsel's ability to fairly and adequately represent the interests of the class;

(C) may order potential class counsel to provide information on any subject pertinent to the appointment and to propose terms for attorney's fees and nontaxable costs;

(D) may include in the appointing order provisions about the award of attorney's fees or nontaxable costs under Rule 23(h); and

(E) may make further orders in connection with the appointment.

(2) ***Standard for Appointing Class Counsel.*** When one applicant seeks appointment as class counsel, the court may appoint that applicant only if the applicant is adequate under Rule 23(g)(1) and (4). If more than one adequate applicant seeks appointment, the court must appoint the applicant best able to represent the interests of the class.

(3) ***Interim Counsel.*** The court may designate interim counsel to act on behalf of a putative class before determining whether to certify the action as a class action.

(4) ***Duty of Class Counsel.*** Class counsel must fairly and adequately represent the interests of the class.

(h) Attorney's Fees and Nontaxable Costs. In a certified class action, the court may award reasonable attorney's fees and nontaxable costs that are authorized by law or by the parties' agreement. The following procedures apply:

(1) A claim for an award must be made by motion under Rule 54(d)(2), subject to the provisions of this subdivision (h), at a time the court sets. Notice of the motion must be served on all parties and, for motions by class counsel, directed to class members in a reasonable manner.

(2) A class member, or a party from whom payment is sought, may object to the motion.

(3) The court may hold a hearing and must find the facts and state its legal conclusions under Rule 52(a).

(4) The court may refer issues related to the amount of the award to a special master or a magistrate judge, as provided in Rule 54(d)(2)(D).

Rule 26. General Provisions Governing Discovery; Duty of Disclosure

(a) Required Disclosures.

(1) ***Initial Disclosure.***

(A) *In General.* Except as exempted by Rule 26(a)(1)(B) or as otherwise stipulated or ordered by the court, a party must, without awaiting a discovery request, provide to the other parties:

(i) the name and, if known, the address and telephone number of each individual likely to have discoverable information—along with the subjects of that information—that the disclosing party may use to support its claims or defenses, unless the use would be solely for impeachment;

(ii) a copy—or a description by category and location—of all documents, electronically stored information, and tangible things that the disclosing party has in its possession, custody, or control and may use to support its claims or defenses, unless the use would be solely for impeachment;

(iii) a computation of each category of damages claimed by the disclosing party—who must also make available for inspection and copying as under Rule 34 the documents or other evidentiary material, unless privileged or protected from disclosure, on which each computation is based, including materials bearing on the nature and extent of injuries suffered; and

(iv) for inspection and copying as under Rule 34, any insurance agreement under which an insurance business may be liable to satisfy all or part of a possible judgment in the action or to indemnify or reimburse for payments made to satisfy the judgment.

(B) *Proceedings Exempt from Initial Disclosure.* The following proceedings are exempt from initial disclosure:

(i) an action for review on an administrative record;

(ii) a forfeiture action in rem arising from a federal statute;

(iii) a petition for habeas corpus or any other proceeding to challenge a criminal conviction or sentence;

(iv) an action brought without an attorney by a person in the custody of the United States, a state, or a state subdivision;

(v) an action to enforce or quash an administrative summons or subpoena;

(vi) an action by the United States to recover benefit payments;

(vii) an action by the United States to collect on a student loan guaranteed by the United States;

(viii) a proceeding ancillary to a proceeding in another court; and

(ix) an action to enforce an arbitration award.

(C) *Time for Initial Disclosures—In General.* A party must make the initial disclosures at or within 14 days after the parties' Rule 26(f) conference unless a different time is set by stipulation or court order, or unless a party objects during the conference that initial disclosures are not appropriate in this action and states the objection in the proposed discovery plan. In ruling on the objection, the court must determine what disclosures, if any, are to be made and must set the time for disclosure.

(D) *Time for Initial Disclosures—For Parties Served or Joined Later.* A party that is first served or otherwise joined after the Rule 26(f) conference must make the initial disclosures within 30 days after being served or joined, unless a different time is set by stipulation or court order.

(E) *Basis for Initial Disclosure; Unacceptable Excuses.* A party must make its initial disclosures based on the information then reasonably available to it. A party is not excused from making its disclosures because it has not fully investigated the case or because it challenges the sufficiency of another party's disclosures or because another party has not made its disclosures.

(2) ***Disclosure of Expert Testimony.***

(A) In General. In addition to the disclosures required by Rule 26(a)(1), a party must disclose to the other parties the identity of any witness it may use at trial to present evidence under Federal Rule of Evidence 702, 703, or 705.

(B) Witnesses Who Must Provide a Written Report. Unless otherwise stipulated or ordered by the court, this disclosure must be accompanied by a written report—prepared and signed by the witness—if the witness is one retained or specially employed to provide expert testimony in the case or one whose duties as the party's employee regularly involve giving expert testimony. The report must contain:

(i) a complete statement of all opinions the witness will express and the basis and reasons for them;

(ii) the facts or data considered by the witness in forming them;

(iii) any exhibits that will be used to summarize or support them;

(iv) the witness's qualifications, including a list of all publications authored in the previous 10 years;

(v) a list of all other cases in which, during the previous 4 years, the witness testified as an expert at trial or by deposition; and

(vi) a statement of the compensation to be paid for the study and testimony in the case.

(C) Witnesses Who Do Not Provide a Written Report. Unless otherwise stipulated or ordered by the court, if the witness is not required to provide a written report, this disclosure must state:

(i) the subject matter on which the witness is expected to present evidence under Federal Rule of Evidence 702, 703, or 705; and

(ii) a summary of the facts and opinions to which the witness is expected to testify.

(D) Time to Disclose Expert Testimony. A party must make these disclosures at the times and in the sequence that the court orders. Absent a stipulation or a court order, the disclosures must be made:

(i) at least 90 days before the date set for trial or for the case to be ready for trial; or

(ii) if the evidence is intended solely to contradict or rebut evidence on the same subject matter identified by another party under Rule 26(a)(2)(B) or (C), within 30 days after the other party's disclosure.

(E) Supplementing the Disclosure. The parties must supplement these disclosures when required under Rule 26(e).

(3) ***Pretrial Disclosures.***

(A) *In General.* In addition to the disclosures required by Rule 26(a)(1) and (2), a party must provide to the other parties and promptly file the following information about the evidence that it may present at trial other than solely for impeachment:

(i) the name and, if not previously provided, the address and telephone number of each witness—separately identifying those the party expects to present and those it may call if the need arises;

(ii) the designation of those witnesses whose testimony the party expects to present by deposition and, if not taken stenographically, a transcript of the pertinent parts of the deposition; and

(iii) an identification of each document or other exhibit, including summaries of other evidence—separately identifying those items the party expects to offer and those it may offer if the need arises.

(B) *Time for Pretrial Disclosures; Objections.* Unless the court orders otherwise, these disclosures must be made at least 30 days before trial. Within 14 days after they are made, unless the court sets a different time, a party may serve and promptly file a list of the following objections: any objections to the use under Rule 32(a) of a deposition designated by another party under Rule 26(a)(3)(A)(ii); and any objection, together with the grounds for it, that may be made to the admissibility of materials identified under Rule 26(a)(3)(A)(iii). An objection not so made—except for one under Federal Rule of Evidence 402 or 403—is waived unless excused by the court for good cause.

(4) ***Form of Disclosures.*** Unless the court orders otherwise, all disclosures under Rule 26(a) must be in writing, signed, and served.

(b) Discovery Scope and Limits.

(1) ***Scope in General.*** Unless otherwise limited by court order, the scope of discovery is as follows: Parties may obtain discovery regarding any nonprivileged matter that is relevant to any party's claim or defense and proportional to the needs of the case, considering the importance of the issues at stake in the action, the amount in controversy, the parties' relative access to relevant information, the parties' resources, the importance of the discovery in resolving the issues, and whether the burden or expense of the proposed discovery outweighs its likely benefit. Information within this scope of discovery need not be admissible in evidence to be discoverable.

(2) ***Limitations on Frequency and Extent.***

(A) *When Permitted.* By order, the court may alter the limits in these rules on the number of depositions and interrogatories or on the length of depositions under Rule 30. By order or local rule, the court may also limit the number of requests under Rule 36.

(B) *Specific Limitations on Electronically Stored Information.* A party need not provide discovery of electronically stored information from sources that the party identifies as not reasonably accessible because of undue burden or cost. On motion to compel discovery or for a protective order, the party from whom discovery is sought must show that the information is not reasonably accessible because of undue burden or cost. If that showing is made, the court may nonetheless order discovery from such sources if the requesting party shows good cause, considering the limitations of Rule 26(b)(2)(C). The court may specify conditions for the discovery.

(C) *When Required.* On motion or on its own, the court must limit the frequency or extent of discovery otherwise allowed by these rules or by local rule if it determines that:

(i) the discovery sought is unreasonably cumulative or duplicative, or can be obtained from some other source that is more convenient, less burdensome, or less expensive;

(ii) the party seeking discovery has had ample opportunity to obtain the information by discovery in the action; or

(iii) the proposed discovery is outside the scope permitted by Rule 26(b)(1).

(3) ***Trial Preparation: Materials.***

(A) *Documents and Tangible Things.* Ordinarily, a party may not discover documents and tangible things that are prepared in anticipation of litigation or for trial by or for another party or its representative (including the other party's attorney, consultant, surety, indemnitor, insurer, or agent). But, subject to Rule 26(b)(4), those materials may be discovered if:

(i) they are otherwise discoverable under Rule 26(b)(1); and

(ii) the party shows that it has substantial need for the materials to prepare its case and cannot, without undue hardship, obtain their substantial equivalent by other means.

(B) *Protection Against Disclosure.* If the court orders discovery of those materials, it must protect against disclosure of the mental impressions, conclusions, opinions, or legal theories of a party's attorney or other representative concerning the litigation.

(C) *Previous Statement.* Any party or other person may, on request and without the required showing, obtain the person's own previous statement about the action or its subject matter. If the request is refused, the person may move for a court order, and Rule 37(a)(5) applies to the award of expenses. A previous statement is either:

(i) a written statement that the person has signed or otherwise adopted or approved; or

(ii) a contemporaneous stenographic, mechanical, electrical, or other recording—or a transcription of it—that recites substantially verbatim the person's oral statement.

(4) ***Trial Preparation: Experts.***

(A) *Deposition of an Expert Who May Testify.* A party may depose any person who has been identified as an expert whose opinions may be presented at trial. If Rule 26(a)(2)(B) requires a report from the expert, the deposition may be conducted only after the report is provided.

(B) *Trial-Preparation Protection for Draft Reports or Disclosures.* Rules 26(b)(3)(A) and (B) protect drafts of any report or disclosure required under Rule 26(a)(2), regardless of the form in which the draft is recorded.

(C) *Trial-Preparation Protection for Communications Between a Party's Attorney and Expert Witnesses.* Rules 26(b)(3)(A) and (B) protect communications between the party's attorney and any witness required to provide a report under Rule 26(a)(2)(B), regardless of the form of the communications, except to the extent that the communications:

(i) relate to compensation for the expert's study or testimony;

(ii) identify facts or data that the party's attorney provided and that the expert considered in forming the opinions to be expressed; or

(iii) identify assumptions that the party's attorney provided and that the expert relied on in forming the opinions to be expressed.

(D) *Expert Employed Only for Trial Preparation.* Ordinarily, a party may not, by interrogatories or deposition, discover facts known or opinions held by an expert who has been retained or specially employed by another party in anticipation of litigation or to prepare for trial and who is not expected to be called as a witness at trial. But a party may do so only:

(i) as provided in Rule 35(b); or

(ii) on showing exceptional circumstances under which it is impracticable for the party to obtain facts or opinions on the same subject by other means.

(E) *Payment.* Unless manifest injustice would result, the court must require that the party seeking discovery:

(i) pay the expert a reasonable fee for time spent in responding to discovery under Rule26(b)(4)(A) or (D); and

(ii) for discovery under (D), also pay the other party a fair portion of the fees and expenses it reasonably incurred in obtaining the expert's facts and opinions.

(5) ***Claiming Privilege or Protecting Trial-Preparation Materials.***

(A) *Information Withheld.* When a party withholds information otherwise discoverable by claiming that the information is privileged or subject to protection as trial-preparation material, the party must:

(i) expressly make the claim; and

(ii) describe the nature of the documents, communications, or tangible things not produced or disclosed—and do so in a manner that, without revealing information itself privileged or protected, will enable other parties to assess the claim.

(B) *Information Produced.* If information produced in discovery is subject to a claim of privilege or of protection as trial-preparation material, the party making the claim may notify any party that received the information of the claim and the basis for it. After being notified, a party must promptly return, sequester, or destroy the specified information and any copies it has; must not use or disclose the information until the claim is resolved; must take reasonable steps to retrieve the information if the party disclosed it before being notified; and may promptly present the information to the court under seal for a determination of the claim. The producing party must preserve the information until the claim is resolved.

(c) Protective Orders.

(1) ***In General.*** A party or any person from whom discovery is sought may move for a protective order in the court where the action is pending—or as an alternative on matters relating to a deposition, in the court for the district where the deposition will be taken. The motion must include a certification that the movant has in good faith conferred or attempted to confer with other affected parties in an effort to resolve the dispute without court action. The court may, for good cause, issue an order to protect a party or person from annoyance, embarrassment, oppression, or undue burden or expense, including one or more of the following:

(A) forbidding the disclosure or discovery;

(B) specifying terms, including time and place or the allocation of expenses, for the disclosure or discovery;

(C) prescribing a discovery method other than the one selected by the party seeking discovery;

(D) forbidding inquiry into certain matters, or limiting the scope of disclosure or discovery to certain matters;

(E) designating the persons who may be present while the discovery is conducted;

(F) requiring that a deposition be sealed and opened only on court order;

(G) requiring that a trade secret or other confidential research, development, or commercial information not be revealed or be revealed only in a specified way; and

(H) requiring that the parties simultaneously file specified documents or information in sealed envelopes, to be opened as the court directs.

(2) ***Ordering Discovery.*** If a motion for a protective order is wholly or partly denied, the court may, on just terms, order that any party or person provide or permit discovery.

(3) ***Awarding Expenses.*** Rule 37(a)(5) applies to the award of expenses.

(d) Timing and Sequence of Discovery.

(1) ***Timing.*** A party may not seek discovery from any source before the parties have conferred as required by Rule 26(f), except in a proceeding exempted from initial disclosure under Rule 26(a)(1)(B), or when authorized by these rules, by stipulation, or by court order.

(2) ***Early Rule 34 Requests.***

(A) Time to Deliver. More than 21 days after the summons and complaint are served on a party, a request under Rule 34 may be delivered:

(i) to that party by any other party, and

(ii) by that party to any plaintiff or to any other party that has been served.

(B) ***When Considered Served.*** The request is considered to have been served at the first Rule 26(f) conference.

(3) ***Sequence.*** Unless the parties stipulate or the court orders otherwise for the parties' and witnesses' convenience and in the interests of justice:

(A) methods of discovery may be used in any sequence; and

(B) discovery by one party does not require any other party to delay its discovery.

(e) Supplementing Disclosures and Responses.

(1) ***In General.*** A party who has made a disclosure under Rule 26(a)—or who has responded to an interrogatory, request for production, or request for admission—must supplement or correct its disclosure or response:

(A) in a timely manner if the party learns that in some material respect the disclosure or response is incomplete or incorrect, and if the additional or corrective information has not otherwise been made known to the other parties during the discovery process or in writing; or

(B) as ordered by the court.

(2) ***Expert Witness.*** For an expert whose report must be disclosed under Rule 26(a)(2)(B), the party's duty to supplement extends both to information included in the report and to information given during the expert's deposition. Any additions or changes to this information must be disclosed by the time the party's pretrial disclosures under Rule 26(a)(3) are due.

(f) Conference of the Parties; Planning for Discovery.

(1) ***Conference Timing.*** Except in a proceeding exempted from initial disclosure under Rule 26(a)(1)(B) or when the court orders otherwise, the parties must confer as soon as practicable—and in any event at least 21 days before a scheduling conference is to be held or a scheduling order is due under Rule 16(b).

(2) ***Conference Content; Parties' Responsibilities.*** In conferring, the parties must consider the nature and basis of their claims and defenses and the possibilities for promptly settling or resolving the case; make or arrange for the disclosures required by Rule 26(a)(1); discuss any issues about preserving discoverable information; and develop a proposed discovery plan. The attorneys of record and all unrepresented parties that have appeared in the case are jointly responsible for arranging the conference, for attempting in good faith to agree on the proposed discovery plan, and for submitting to the court within 14 days after the conference a written report outlining the plan. The court may order the parties or attorneys to attend the conference in person.

(3) ***Discovery Plan.*** A discovery plan must state the parties' views and proposals on:

(A) what changes should be made in the timing, form, or requirement for disclosures under Rule 26(a), including a statement of when initial disclosures were made or will be made;

(B) the subjects on which discovery may be needed, when discovery should be completed, and whether discovery should be conducted in phases or be limited to or focused on particular issues;

(C) any issues about disclosure, discovery, or preservation of electronically stored information, including the form or forms in which it should be produced;

(D) any issues about claims of privilege or of protection as trial-preparation materials, including—if the parties agree on a procedure to assert these claims after production—whether to ask the court to include their agreement in an order under Federal Rule of Evidence 502;

(E) what changes should be made in the limitations on discovery imposed under these rules or by local rule, and what other limitations should be imposed; and

(F) any other orders that the court should issue under Rule 26(c) or under Rule 16(b) and(c).

(4) ***Expedited Schedule.*** If necessary to comply with its expedited schedule for Rule 16(b)conferences, a court may by local rule:

(A) require the parties' conference to occur less than 21 days before the scheduling conference is held or a scheduling order is due under Rule 16(b); and

(B) require the written report outlining the discovery plan to be filed less than 14 days after the parties' conference, or excuse the parties from submitting a written report and permit them to report orally on their discovery plan at the Rule 16(b) conference.

(g) Signing Disclosures and Discovery Requests, Responses, and Objections.

(1) ***Signature Required; Effect of Signature.*** Every disclosure under Rule 26(a)(1) or (a)(3) and every discovery request, response, or objection must be signed by at least one attorney of record in the attorney's own name—or by the party personally, if unrepresented—and must state the signer's address, e-mail address, and telephone number. By signing, an attorney or party certifies that to the best of the person's knowledge, information, and belief formed after a reasonable inquiry:

(A) with respect to a disclosure, it is complete and correct as of the time it is made; and

(B) with respect to a discovery request, response, or objection, it is:

(i) consistent with these rules and warranted by existing law or by a nonfrivolous argument for extending, modifying, or reversing existing law, or for establishing new law;

(ii) not interposed for any improper purpose, such as to harass, cause unnecessary delay, or needlessly increase the cost of litigation; and

(iii) neither unreasonable nor unduly burdensome or expensive, considering the needs of the case, prior discovery in the case, the amount in controversy, and the importance of the issues at stake in the action.

(2) ***Failure to Sign.*** Other parties have no duty to act on an unsigned disclosure, request, response, or objection until it is signed, and the court must strike it unless a signature is promptly supplied after the omission is called to the attorney's or party's attention.

(3) ***Sanction for Improper Certification.*** If a certification violates this rule without substantial justification, the court, on motion or on its own, must impose an appropriate sanction on the signer, the party on whose behalf the signer was acting, or both. The sanction may include an order to pay the reasonable expenses, including attorney's fees, caused by the violation.

Rule 37. Failure to Make or Cooperate in Discovery; Sanctions

(a) Motion for an Order Compelling Disclosure or Discovery.

(1) ***In General*** On notice to other parties and all affected persons, a party may move for an order compelling disclosure or discovery. The motion must include a certification that the movant has in good faith conferred or attempted to confer with the person or party failing to make disclosure or discovery in an effort to obtain it without court action.

(2) ***Appropriate Court.*** A motion for an order to a party must be made in the court where the action is pending. A motion for an order to a nonparty must be made in the court where the discovery is or will be taken.

(3) ***Specific Motions.***

(A) *To Compel Disclosure.* If a party fails to make a disclosure required by Rule 26(a), any other party may move to compel disclosure and for appropriate sanctions.

(B) *To Compel a Discovery Response.* A party seeking discovery may move for an order compelling an answer, designation, production, or inspection. This motion may be made if:

(i) a deponent fails to answer a question asked under Rule 30 or 31;

(ii) a corporation or other entity fails to make a designation under Rule 30(b)(6) or 31(a)(4);

(iii) a party fails to answer an interrogatory submitted under Rule 33; or

(iv) a party fails to produce documents or fails to respond that inspection will be permitted—or fails to permit inspection—as requested under Rule 34.

(C) *Related to a Deposition.* When taking an oral deposition, the party asking a question may complete or adjourn the examination before moving for an order.

(4) ***Evasive or Incomplete Disclosure, Answer, or Response.*** For purposes of this subdivision (a), an evasive or incomplete disclosure, answer, or response must be treated as a failure to disclose, answer, or respond.

(5) ***Payment of Expenses; Protective Orders.***

(A) *If the Motion Is Granted (or Disclosure or Discovery Is Provided After Filing).* If the motion is granted—or if the disclosure or requested discovery is provided after the motion was filed—the court must, after giving an opportunity to be heard, require the party or deponent whose conduct necessitated the motion, the party or attorney advising that conduct, or both to pay the movant's reasonable expenses incurred in making the motion, including attorney's fees. But the court must not order this payment if:

(i) the movant filed the motion before attempting in good faith to obtain the disclosure or discovery without court action;

(ii) the opposing party's nondisclosure, response, or objection was substantially justified; or

(iii) other circumstances make an award of expenses unjust.

(B) *If the Motion Is Denied.* If the motion is denied, the court may issue any protective order authorized under Rule 26(c) and must, after giving an opportunity to be heard, require the movant, the attorney filing the motion, or both to pay the party or deponent who opposed the motion its reasonable expenses incurred in opposing the motion, including attorney's fees. But the court must not order this payment if the motion was substantially justified or other circumstances make an award of expenses unjust.

(C) *If the Motion Is Granted in Part and Denied in Part.* If the motion is granted in part and denied in part, the court may issue any protective order authorized under Rule 26(c) and may, after giving an opportunity to be heard, apportion the reasonable expenses for the motion.

(b) Failure to Comply with a Court Order.

(1) ***Sanctions Sought in the District Where the Deposition Is Taken.*** If the court where the discovery is taken orders a deponent to be sworn or to answer a question and the deponent fails to obey, the failure may be treated as contempt of court. If a deposition-related motion is transferred to the court where the action is pending, and that court orders a deponent to be sworn or to answer a question and the deponent fails to obey, the failure may be treated as contempt of either court where the discovery is taken or the court where the action is pending.

(2) ***Sanctions Sought in the District Where the Action Is Pending.***

(A) *For Not Obeying a Discovery Order.* If a party or a party's officer, director, or managing agent—or a witness designated under Rule 30(b)(6) or 31(a)(4)—fails to obey an order to provide or permit discovery, including an order under Rule 26(f), 35, or 37(a), the court where the action is pending may issue further just orders. They may include the following:

(i) directing that the matters embraced in the order or other designated facts be taken as established for purposes of the action, as the prevailing party claims;

(ii) prohibiting the disobedient party from supporting or opposing designated claims or defenses, or from introducing designated matters in evidence;

(iii) striking pleadings in whole or in part;

(iv) staying further proceedings until the order is obeyed;

(v) dismissing the action or proceeding in whole or in part;

(vi) rendering a default judgment against the disobedient party; or

(vii) treating as contempt of court the failure to obey any order except an order to submit to a physical or mental examination.

(B) *For Not Producing a Person for Examination.* If a party fails to comply with an order under Rule 35(a) requiring it to produce another person for examination, the court may issue any of the orders listed in Rule 37(b)(2)(A)(i)-(vi), unless the disobedient party shows that it cannot produce the other person.

(C) *Payment of Expenses.* Instead of or in addition to the orders above, the court must order the disobedient party, the attorney advising that party, or both to pay the reasonable expenses, including attorney's fees, caused by the failure, unless the failure was substantially justified or other circumstances make an award of expenses unjust.

(c) Failure to Disclose, to Supplement an Earlier Response, or to Admit.

(1) ***Failure to Disclose or Supplement.*** If a party fails to provide information or identify a witness as required by Rule 26(a) or (e), the party is not allowed to use that information or witness to supply evidence on a motion, at a hearing, or at a trial, unless the failure was substantially justified or is harmless. In addition to or instead of this sanction, the court, on motion and after giving an opportunity to be heard:

(A) may order payment of the reasonable expenses, including attorney's fees, caused by the failure;

(B) may inform the jury of the party's failure; and

(C) may impose other appropriate sanctions, including any of the orders listed in Rule 37(b)(2)(A)(i)-(vi).

(2) ***Failure to Admit.*** If a party fails to admit what is requested under Rule 36 and if the requesting party later proves a document to be genuine or the matter true, the requesting party may move that the party who failed to admit pay the reasonable expenses, including attorney's fees, incurred in making that proof. The court must so order unless:

(A) the request was held objectionable under Rule 36(a);

(B) the admission sought was of no substantial importance;

(C) the party failing to admit had a reasonable ground to believe that it might prevail on the matter; or

(D) there was other good reason for the failure to admit.

(d) Party's Failure to Attend Its Own Deposition, Serve Answers to Interrogatories, or Respond to a Request for Inspection.

(1) ***In General.***

(A) *Motion; Grounds for Sanctions.* The court where the action is pending may, on motion, order sanctions if:

(i) a party or a party's officer, director, or managing agent—or a person designated under Rule 30(b)(6) or 31(a)(4)—fails, after being served with proper notice, to appear for that person's deposition; or

(ii) a party, after being properly served with interrogatories under Rule 33 or a request for inspection under Rule 34, fails to serve its answers, objections, or written response.

(B) *Certification.* A motion for sanctions for failing to answer or respond must include a certification that the movant has in good faith conferred or attempted to confer with the party failing to act in an effort to obtain the answer or response without court action.

(2) ***Unacceptable Excuse for Failing to Act.*** A failure described in Rule 37(d)(1)(A) is not excused on the ground that the discovery sought was objectionable, unless the party failing to act has a pending motion for a protective order under Rule 26(c).

(3) ***Types of Sanctions.*** Sanctions may include any of the orders listed in Rule 37(b)(2)(A)(i)–(vi). Instead of or in addition to these sanctions, the court must require the party failing to act, the attorney advising that party, or both to pay the reasonable expenses, including attorney's fees, caused by the failure, unless the failure was substantially justified or other circumstances make an award of expenses unjust.

(e) Failure to Preserve Electronically Stored Information. If electronically stored information that should have been preserved in the anticipation or conduct of litigation is lost because a party failed to take reasonable steps to preserve it, and it cannot be restored or replaced through additional discovery, the court:

(1) upon finding prejudice to another party from loss of the information, may order measures no greater than necessary to cure the prejudice; or

(2) only upon finding that the party acted with the intent to deprive another party of the information's use in the litigation may:

(A) presume that the lost information was unfavorable to the party;

(B) instruct the jury that it may or must presume the information was unfavorable to the party; or

(C) dismiss the action or enter a default judgment.

(f) Failure to Participate in Framing a Discovery Plan. If a party or its attorney fails to participate in good faith in developing and submitting a proposed discovery plan as required by Rule 26(f), the court may, after giving an opportunity to be heard, require that party or attorney to pay to any other party the reasonable expenses, including attorney's fees, caused by the failure.

Rule 60. Relief From Judgment or Order

(a) Corrections Based on Clerical Mistakes; Oversights and Omissions. The court may correct a clerical mistake or a mistake arising from oversight or omission whenever one is found in a judgment, order, or other part of the record. The court may do so on motion or on its own, with or without notice. But after an appeal has been docketed in the appellate court and while it is pending, such a mistake may be corrected only with the appellate court's leave.

(b) Grounds for Relief from a Final Judgment, Order, or Proceeding. On motion and just terms, the court may relieve a party or its legal representative from a final judgment, order, or proceeding for the following reasons:

(1) mistake, inadvertence, surprise, or excusable neglect;

(2) newly discovered evidence that, with reasonable diligence, could not have been discovered in time to move for a new trial under Rule 59(b);

(3) fraud (whether previously called intrinsic or extrinsic), misrepresentation, or misconduct by an opposing party;

(4) the judgment is void;

(5) the judgment has been satisfied, released or discharged; it is based on an earlier judgment that has been reversed or vacated; or applying it prospectively is no longer equitable; or

(6) any other reason that justifies relief.

(c) Timing and Effect of the Motion.

(1) ***Timing.*** A motion under Rule 60(b) must be made within a reasonable time—and for reasons (1), (2), and (3) no more than a year after the entry of the judgment or order or the date of the proceeding.

(2) ***Effect on Finality.*** The motion does not affect the judgment's finality or suspend its operation.

(d) Other Powers to Grant Relief. This rule does not limit a court's power to:

(1) entertain an independent action to relieve a party from a judgment, order, or proceeding;

(2) grant relief under 28 U.S.C. § 1655 to a defendant who was not personally notified of the action; or

(3) set aside a judgment for fraud on the court.

(e) Bills and Writs Abolished. The following are abolished: bills of review, bills in the nature of bills of review, and writs of coram nobis, coram vobis, and audita querela.

Rule 63. Judge's Inability to Proceed

If a judge conducting a hearing or trial is unable to proceed, any other judge may proceed upon certifying familiarity with the record and determining that the case may be completed without prejudice to the parties. In a hearing or a nonjury trial, the successor judge must, at a party's request, recall any witness whose testimony is material and disputed and who is available to testify again without undue burden. The successor judge may also recall any other witness.

Rule 68. Offer of Judgment

(a) Making an Offer; Judgment on an Accepted Offer. At least 14 days before the date set for trial, a party defending against a claim may serve on an opposing party an offer to allow judgment on specified terms, with the costs then accrued. If, within 14 days after being served, the opposing party serves written notice accepting the offer, either party may then file the offer and notice of acceptance, plus proof of service. The clerk must then enter judgment.

(b) Unaccepted Offer. An unaccepted offer is considered withdrawn, but it does not preclude a later offer. Evidence of an unaccepted offer is not admissible except in a proceeding to determine costs.

(c) Offer After Liability Is Determined. When one party's liability to another has been determined but the extent of liability remains to be determined by further proceedings, the party held liable may make an offer of judgment. It must be served within a reasonable time—but at least 14 days—before a hearing to determine the extent of liability.

(d) Paying Costs After an Unaccepted Offer. If the judgment that the offeree finally obtains is not more favorable than the unaccepted offer, the offeree must pay the costs incurred after the offer was made.

FEDERAL RULES OF CRIMINAL PROCEDURE

Rule 44. Right to and Appointment of Counsel

(a) Right to Appointed Counsel. A defendant who is unable to obtain counsel is entitled to have counsel appointed to represent the defendant at every stage of the proceeding from initial appearance through appeal, unless the defendant waives this right.

(b) Appointment Procedure. Federal law and local court rules govern the procedure for implementing the right to counsel.

(c) Inquiry Into Joint Representation.

(1) Joint Representation. Joint representation occurs when:

(A) two or more defendants have been charged jointly under Rule 8(b) or have been joined for trial under Rule 13; and

(B) the defendants are represented by the same counsel, or counsel who are associated in law practice.

(2) Court's Responsibilities in Cases of Joint Representation. The court must promptly inquire about the propriety of joint representation and must personally advise each defendant of the right to the effective assistance of counsel, including separate representation. Unless there is good cause to believe that no conflict of interest is likely to arise, the court must take appropriate measures to protect each defendant's right to counsel.

FEDERAL RULES OF APPELLATE PROCEDURE

Rule 38. Damages and Costs for Frivolous Appeals

If a court of appeals determines that an appeal is frivolous, it may, after a separately filed motion or notice from the court and reasonable opportunity to respond, award just damages and single or double costs to the appellee.

Rule 46. Attorneys

(a) Admission to the Bar.

(1) *Eligibility.* An attorney is eligible for admission to the bar of a court of appeals if that attorney is of good moral and professional character and is admitted to practice before the Supreme Court of the United States, the highest court of a state, another United States court of appeals, or a United States district court (including the district courts for Guam, the Northern Mariana Islands, and the Virgin Islands).

(2) *Application.* An applicant must file an application for admission, on a form approved by the court that contains the applicant's personal statement showing eligibility for membership. The applicant must subscribe to the following oath or affirmation:

"I, _______, do solemnly swear (or affirm) that I will conduct myself as an attorney and counselor of this court, uprightly and according to law; and that I will support the Constitution of the United States.

(3) *Admission Procedures.* On written or oral motion of a member of the court's bar, the court will act on the application. An applicant may be admitted by oral motion in open court. But, unless the court orders otherwise, an applicant need not appear before the court to be admitted. Upon admission, an applicant must pay the clerk the fee prescribed by local rule or court order.

(b) Suspension or Disbarment.

(1) *Standard.* A member of the court's bar is subject to suspension or disbarment by the court if the member:

(A) has been suspended or disbarred from practice in any other court; or

(B) is guilty of conduct unbecoming a member of the court's bar.

(2) *Procedure.* The member must be given an opportunity to show good cause, within the time prescribed by the court, why the member should not be suspended or disbarred.

(3) *Order.* The court must enter an appropriate order after the member responds and a hearing is held, if requested, or after the time prescribed for a response expires, if no response is made.

(c) Discipline. A court of appeals may discipline an attorney who practices before it for conduct unbecoming a member of the bar or for failure to comply with any court rule. First, however, the court must afford the attorney reasonable notice, an opportunity to show cause to the contrary, and, if requested, a hearing.

RULES OF THE UNITED STATES SUPREME COURT

Rule 5. Admission to the Bar

1. To qualify for admission to the Bar of this Court, an applicant must have been admitted to practice in the highest court of a State, Commonwealth, Territory or Possession, or the District of Columbia for a period of at least three years immediately before the date of application; must not have been the subject of any adverse disciplinary action pronounced or in effect during that 3-year period; and must appear to the Court to be of good moral and professional character.

2. Each applicant shall file with the Clerk (1) a certificate from the presiding judge, clerk, or other authorized official of that court evidencing the applicant's admission to practice there and the applicant's current good standing, and (2) a completely executed copy of the form approved by this Court and furnished by the Clerk containing (a) the applicant's personal statement, and (b) the statement of two sponsors endorsing the correctness of the applicant's statement, stating that the applicant possesses all the qualifications required for admission, and affirming that the applicant is of good moral and professional character. Both sponsors must be members of the Bar of this Court who personally know, but are not related to, the applicant.

3. If the documents submitted demonstrate that the applicant possesses the necessary qualifications, and if the applicant has signed the oath or affirmation and paid the required fee, the Clerk will notify the applicant of acceptance by the Court as a member of the Bar and issue a certificate of admission. An applicant who so wishes may be admitted in open court on oral motion by a member of the Bar of this Court, provided that all other requirements for admission have been satisfied.

4. Each applicant shall sign the following oath or affirmation: I, _______, do solemnly swear (or affirm) that as an attorney and as a counselor of this Court, I will conduct myself uprightly and according to law, and that I will support the Constitution of the United States.

5. The fee for admission to the Bar and a certificate bearing the seal of the Court is $200, payable to the United States Supreme Court. The Marshal will deposit such fees in a separate fund to be disbursed by the Marshal at the direction of the Chief Justice for the costs of admissions, for the benefit of the Court and its Bar, and for related purposes.

6. The fee for a duplicate certificate of admission to the Bar bearing the seal of the Court is $15, and the fee for a certificate of good standing is $10, payable to the United States Supreme Court. The proceeds will be maintained by the Marshal as provided in paragraph 5 of this Rule.

Rule 6. Argument Pro Hac Vice

1. An attorney not admitted to practice in the highest court of a State, Commonwealth, Territory or Possession, or the District of Columbia for the requisite three years, but otherwise eligible for admission to practice in this Court under Rule 5.1, may be permitted to argue *pro hac vice.*

2. An attorney qualified to practice in the courts of a foreign state may be permitted to argue *pro hac vice.*

3. Oral argument *pro hac vice* is allowed only on motion of the counsel of record for the party on whose behalf leave is requested. The motion shall state concisely the qualifications of the attorney who is to argue *pro hac vice.* It shall be filed with the Clerk, in the form required by Rule 21, no later than the date on which the respondent's or appellee's brief on the merits is due to be filed, and it shall be accompanied by proof of service as required by Rule 29.

Rule 7. Prohibition Against Practice

No employee of this Court shall practice as an attorney or counselor in any court or before any agency of government while employed by the Court; nor shall any person after leaving such employment participate in any professional capacity in any case pending before this Court or in any case being considered for filing in this Court, until two years have elapsed after separation; nor shall a former employee ever participate in any professional capacity in any case that was pending in this Court during the employee's tenure.

Rule 8. Disbarment and Disciplinary Action

1. Whenever a member of the Bar of this Court has been disbarred or suspended from practice in any court of record, or has engaged in conduct unbecoming a member of the Bar of this Court, the Court will enter an order suspending that member from practice before this Court and affording the member an opportunity to show cause, within 40 days, why a disbarment order should not be entered. Upon response, or if no response is timely filed, the Court will enter an appropriate order.

2. After reasonable notice and an opportunity to show cause why disciplinary action should not be taken, and after a hearing if material facts are in dispute, the Court may take any appropriate disciplinary action against any attorney who is admitted to practice before it for conduct unbecoming a member of the Bar or for failure to comply with these Rules or any Rule or order of the Court.

PART FOUR

RESTATEMENT (THIRD) OF LAW GOVERNING LAWYERS

TABLE OF CONTENTS

Introduction

This part includes the text of the sections of the Restatement (Third) of the Law Governing Lawyers and selected comments and illustrations.

RESTATEMENT (THIRD) OF LAW GOVERNING LAWYERS (2000)

[In 1986, the American Law Institute began the process of writing the Restatement of Law Governing Lawyers. This long and difficult task has culminated in the publication of the Restatement (Third) of Law Governing Lawyers in 2000. From the language of the first tentative drafts, courts, commentators, and bar personnel have taken account of the research brought together on this project. Due to space considerations, the entire comments or reporters notes cannot be reprinted. However, selected reporters' comments are reprinted below to the sections which are most pertinent to the courses in professional responsibility. Of course, those who research problems of professional responsibility should consult the two volume work published by the ALI. Ed.]

TABLE OF CONTENTS

CHAPTER 1. REGULATION OF THE LEGAL PROFESSION

TOPIC 1. REGULATION OF LAWYERS—IN GENERAL

Section

TOPIC 2. PROCESS OF PROFESSIONAL REGULATION

TITLE A. ADMISSION TO PRACTICE LAW

TITLE B. AUTHORIZED AND UNAUTHORIZED PRACTICE

TITLE C. PROFESSIONAL DISCIPLINE

TOPIC 3. CIVIL JUDICIAL REMEDIES IN GENERAL

TOPIC 4. LAWYER CRIMINAL OFFENSES

TOPIC 5. LAW-FIRM STRUCTURE AND OPERATION

TITLE A. ASSOCIATION OF LAWYERS IN LAW ORGANIZATIONS

TITLE B. LIMITATIONS ON NONLAWYER INVOLVEMENT IN A LAW FIRM

RESTATEMENT (THIRD) OF LAW GOVERNING LAWYERS

RESTATEMENT (THIRD) OF LAW GOVERNING LAWYERS

CHAPTER 6. REPRESENTING CLIENTS—IN GENERAL

TOPIC 1. LAWYERS FUNCTIONS IN REPRESENTING CLIENTS—IN GENERAL

TOPIC 2. REPRESENTING ORGANIZATIONAL CLIENTS—IN GENERAL

TOPIC 3. LAWYER DEALINGS WITH A NONCLIENT

TITLE A. DEALINGS WITH A NONCLIENT—GENERALLY

TITLE B. CONTACT WITH A REPRESENTED NONCLIENT

TITLE C. DEALINGS WITH AN UNREPRESENTED NONCLIENT

TOPIC 4. LEGISLATIVE AND ADMINISTRATIVE MATTERS

CHAPTER 7. REPRESENTING CLIENTS IN LITIGATION

TOPIC 1. ADVOCACY IN GENERAL

TOPIC 2. LIMITS ON ADVOCACY

TOPIC 3. ADVOCATES AND TRIBUNALS

TOPIC 4. ADVOCATES AND EVIDENCE

CHAPTER 1. REGULATION OF THE LEGAL PROFESSION

TOPIC 1. REGULATION OF LAWYERS—IN GENERAL

§ 1. Regulation of Lawyers—In General

Upon admission to the bar of any jurisdiction, a person becomes a lawyer and is subject to applicable law governing such matters as professional discipline, procedure and evidence, civil remedies, and criminal sanctions.

Comment:

* * *

b. Lawyer codes and background law. Today, as for the last quarter-century, professional discipline of a lawyer in the United States is conducted pursuant to regulations contained in regulatory codes that have been approved in most states by the highest court in the jurisdiction in which the lawyer has been admitted. Such codes are referred to in this Restatement as lawyer codes. Those codes are more or less patterned on model codes published by the American Bar Association, but only the version of the code officially adopted and in force in a jurisdiction regulates the activities of lawyers subject to it. While in most jurisdictions the lawyer code is adopted and subject to revision only through action of the highest court in the state (see Comment *c* hereto), in all jurisdictions at least some legislation is applicable to lawyers and law practice. See, e.g., § 56, Comments *i* and *j* (federal legislation and state consumer-protection laws applicable to lawyers); § 58(3) and Comment *b* thereto (statutes authorizing lawyers to practice in the form of limited-liability partnerships and similar types of law firms); § 68 and following (attorney-client privilege). Federal district courts generally have adopted the lawyer code of the jurisdiction in which the court sits, and all federal courts exercise the power to regulate lawyers appearing before them. Some administrative agencies, primarily within the federal government, have also regulated lawyers practicing before the agency, sometimes through lawyer codes adopted by the agency and specifically applicable to those practitioners. Although uniformity is desirable for many purposes, lawyer codes in fact differ markedly in certain respects from one jurisdiction to another, and no state follows any nationally promulgated bar-association model in all respects.

The legal effect of officially adopted lawyer codes is fundamental and diverse. Lawyer codes are promulgated and applied primarily for the purpose of establishing mandatory standards for the assessment of a lawyer's conduct in the course of a professional-discipline proceeding brought against the lawyer (see Topic 2). Such lawyer codes also typically include commentary containing, among other things, nonbinding advice on how a lawyer may address particular issues or, in general, better practice law. Lawyer-code provisions may also be relevant with respect to the definition of substantive rights or the articulation of factors relevant in granting remedies in other areas. For example, courts have held that lawyer-code provisions may be relevant in determining the reasonableness of a lawyer's fee (see § 34, Comment *d*), in determining questions of fee forfeiture (see § 37, Comment *c*), in defining the appropriate standard of care in legal malpractice (see § 52, Comment *f*), in determining a lawyer's fiduciary duty to a client (see § 48) in determining whether a conflict of interest exists (see § 121, Comment *c*) or has appropriately been consented to by affected clients (see generally § 122), or for the purpose of a motion to disqualify the lawyer. Lawyer-code provisions may also be relevant as an expression of the public policy of the jurisdiction with respect to such issues as the enforceability of transactions entered into in violation of them (e.g. § 47 & Comment *i* thereto).

Lawyer codes in turn reflect other law. Prior to the adoption by states of versions of the 1969 ABA Model Code of Professional Responsibility, many states had no officially adopted lawyer code, although most state bar associations considered the 1908 ABA Canons of Ethics as relevant to guide lawyers. (Some few states had adopted the Canons as explicitly disciplinary rules, although they were not designed for that purpose and in certain respects ill-served it.) There was, however, no regulatory vacuum, for courts had historically asserted plenary power to regulate lawyers (see Comment *c*) and did so through the common-law process. For example, most of the core concepts of lawyer conflicts of interest (see Chapter 8) were already well developed and applied through common-law decisions in disciplinary, disqualification, and legal-malpractice proceedings long before jurisdictions officially adopted lawyer codes stating rules about the same concepts. The drafters of lawyer codes, in turn, have drawn heavily on such decisions in articulating lawyer obligations.

The lawyer codes and much general law remain complementary. The lawyer codes draw much of their moral force and, in many particulars, the detailed description of their rules from preexisting legal requirements and concepts found in the law of torts, contracts, agency, trusts, property, remedies, procedure, evidence, and crimes. Thus, lawyer codes particularize some general legal rules in the particular occupational situation of lawyers but are not exhaustive of those rules. By the same token, lawyer codes often establish the same rules as would apply in a comparable situation involving a nonlawyer professional providing a related service or a rule very like it. The lawyer codes presuppose the general legal background thus referred to and its applicability to lawyers and the rules that make up that background, and they do not preclude application of remedies prescribed by other law. Particular lawyer conduct may violate a lawyer code, tort law, and a criminal statute, or it may have less than all those legal effects. Lawyer codes sometimes differ from other legal provisions with respect to such factors as the following: the specified mental state of the lawyer-actor defined in the standard of conduct; the required presence and kind or degree of harm on the part of the claimant or injured victim of the lawyer's action or nonaction; the possible relevance of reliance by others; and the extent of imputed knowledge, duty, and liability (see Topic 3, Introductory Note)

c. The inherent powers of courts. The highest courts in most states have ruled as a matter of state constitutional law that their power to regulate lawyers is inherent in the judicial function. Thus, the grant of judicial power in a state constitution devolves upon the courts the concomitant regulatory power. The power is said to derive both from the historical role of courts in the United States in regulating lawyers through admission and disbarment and from the traditional practice of courts in England. Admitting lawyers to practice (see § 2), formulating and amending lawyer codes (see Comment *b*), and regulating the system of lawyer discipline (see § 5, Comment *b*) are functions reserved in most states to the highest court of the state. Nonetheless, other tribunals, such as hearing bodies in administrative agencies, perform the important role of implementing the lawyer codes in adjudicating disputes when and to the extent their provisions are relevant (see Comment *b* hereto & Topic 3, Introductory Note).

Beyond affirmative empowerment, some state courts have further held that their constitutional power to regulate lawyers is exclusive of other branches of state government with respect to some matters. On that basis, those courts have held that an attempt by another branch of state government to regulate lawyers is an interference with that judicial power and a violation of the state's constitutionally mandated separation of powers. Some decisions have given effect to an otherwise-invalid statute or regulation on a notion of comity, when the court is persuaded of the wisdom of the enactment and convinced that it does not pose a threat to the court's overall regulation of lawyers.

Federal courts have also affirmed an inherent role in regulating lawyers. That is reflected in enactment of disciplinary rules in each federal court and, often, in creation of a disciplinary apparatus. It is also implicated when federal courts apply provisions of lawyer codes in deciding cases, as in ruling on disqualification motions or requests for fees. There is, however, no body of federal decisional law broadly asserting that federal courts have inherent power to regulate lawyers to the exclusion of the federal legislative and executive branches. Similarly, the regulatory power of federal courts over lawyers practicing before them does not extend into judicial regulation of activities of lawyers appearing before or otherwise dealing with the other branches of the federal government or the public.

d. The role of bar associations. Beginning in the early decades of the 20th century, bar associations have played an increasingly active role in regulating the conduct of lawyers. Together with lawyers who work on disciplinary and similar committees within state-and federal-court systems, bar associations have become the chief embodiment of the concept that lawyers are a self-regulated profession. Self-regulation provides protection of lawyers against political control by the state. However, self-regulation also carries its own risk of under-regulation of lawyers as a whole, regulation (however strict) that is in the interest of lawyers as a group and not the public, or regulation that focuses disproportionately on groups of lawyers disfavored within the controlling bar association or committee.

The three lawyer codes promulgated in this century by the American Bar Association have served as models for regulations adopted in most of the states and the federal courts (see Comment *b*). Even in states—such as California and, to a lesser extent, Texas—in which the form of the lawyer code is markedly different from the ABA models, examination of the code shows significant borrowing in many rules. (By the same token, the two most recent ABA model rules often borrowed from preexisting state codes, such as the code then in effect in California. The 1908 ABA Canons were copied with little change from a preexisting state code.)

In a number of states, membership in the state's bar association is compulsory, in the sense that a lawyer otherwise appropriately admitted to practice must maintain active membership in the bar association as a condition of retention of a valid license to practice law within the jurisdiction. (Such mandatory bars are sometimes called "integrated" bars.) Decisions of the United States Supreme Court have limited the extent to which a member of such a mandatory bar association can be required to pay any portion of dues that supports activities not germane to the organization's functions in providing self-regulation. Those generally include activities of a political or ideological nature not directly connected to the regulation of lawyers and maintenance of the system of justice. Under those decisions, the bar must maintain a system for allocating dues payments for permissible and noncovered purposes and a process to permit lawyers to regain the portion of dues collected for noncovered purposes.

TOPIC 2. PROCESS OF PROFESSIONAL REGULATION

TITLE A. ADMISSION TO PRACTICE LAW

§ 2. Admission to Practice Law

In order to become a lawyer and qualify to practice law in a jurisdiction of admission, a prospective lawyer must comply with requirements of the jurisdiction relating to such matters as education, other demonstration of competence such as success in a bar examination, and character.

TITLE B. AUTHORIZED AND UNAUTHORIZED PRACTICE

§ 3. Jurisdictional Scope of the Practice of Law by a Lawyer

A lawyer currently admitted to practice in a jurisdiction may provide legal services to a client:

(1) at any place within the admitting jurisdiction;

(2) before a tribunal or administrative agency of another jurisdiction or the federal government in compliance with requirements for temporary or regular admission to practice before that tribunal or agency; and

(3) at a place within a jurisdiction in which the lawyer is not admitted to the extent that the lawyer's activities arise out of or are otherwise reasonably related to the lawyer's practice under Subsection (1) or (2).

Comment:

a. *Scope and cross-references.* This Section concerns jurisdictional limits on permissible practice by a lawyer. On choice-of-law issues generally involved in the regulation of lawyers, see § 1, Comment *e*. On jurisdictional and choice-of-law issues involved in lawyer discipline, see § 5, Comment *h*. On unauthorized practice by a nonlawyer or on a lawyer's aiding such unauthorized practice, see § 4.

The state in which a lawyer is admitted is referred to herein as the lawyer's home state. A lawyer who practices law in violation of the rules stated in the Section is susceptible to a variety of sanctions, including professional discipline, injunction, and denial of recovery of fees otherwise earned (see § 49).

b. *Rationale.* As reflected in this Section, jurisdictional limitations on practice applicable to lawyers are primarily a function of state lines (see Introductory Note). For many purposes, lawyers must respect those lines—limiting their general practice to the territory of the one or more jurisdictions in which the lawyer is admitted—although pro hac vice admission (see Comment *e* hereto) and admission to practice in federal courts and before federal agencies (see Comment *e* hereto) authorize extraterritorial practice. Occasionally, proposals are put forward for removal of state-line limitations on practice, as by means of a national bar-admission process. However, local interest in maintaining regulatory control of lawyers practicing locally is strong and historically has prevented adoption of such proposals. Nonetheless, the need to provide effective and efficient legal services to persons and businesses with interstate legal concerns requires that jurisdictions not erect unnecessary barriers to interstate law practice (see Comment *e*).

c. *Required maintenance of a lawyer's admitted status.* In general, only a lawyer who is in current compliance with applicable legal requirements in the admitting jurisdiction (see § 2) for maintaining the lawyer's law license in a currently effective status is qualified to practice law there. Those conditions vary by jurisdiction and can be technical in nature. In some few jurisdictions, for example, maintenance of a valid license is conditioned on maintaining an office within the jurisdiction for the practice of law (see § 2, Comment *f*). Many jurisdictions now require a minimum number of hours per year of qualifying continuing legal education.

A lawyer who was once admitted to practice in a state violates the prohibition against unauthorized practice by continuing to practice law in the state notwithstanding disbarment or suspension, lapse of the lawyer's license to practice in the state (for example, for failure to pay mandatory bar dues or, as indicated above, to comply with applicable continuing-legal-education requirements), resignation, or assumption of nonactive status (as when the lawyer retires or moves to another state). Lapse can occur for failure to file an annual renewal application with self-certification of compliance with the indicated requirements. Any such unauthorized practice by a lawyer is a violation of the state's lawyer code and thus subjects the lawyer to discipline. It may also violate a statutory prohibition in the state against unauthorized practice of law. Such impermissible practice by a lawyer may also lead, among other remedies, to forfeiture of an otherwise valid claim for legal fees (see § 37). When lapse of license for such reasons is not directly related to continuing competence to practice, it does not by itself indicate either legal malpractice or incompetent representation in a criminal-defense representation.

d. Definition of practice by a lawyer. What constitutes the practice of law for the purposes of defining unauthorized practice by a lawyer varies with the reason for which the lawyer is no longer authorized to practice. Either by rule, decisional law, or specific order, a jurisdiction may, for example, prohibit a disbarred or suspended lawyer from functioning as a paralegal in a law firm (compare § 4, Comment *g*), even beyond the prohibition against practicing as a lawyer or holding oneself out as such. The concern is not only that a disbarred lawyer functioning as a paralegal will harm the interests of clients by performing services incompetently, but also that a lawyer who has committed a violation sufficiently serious to warrant substantial discipline and who as a result has been deprived of a law license and the income that it represents is in a position and may be motivated to use such a role as a subterfuge to continue law practice.

e. Extra-jurisdictional law practice by a lawyer. Admission in a state permits a lawyer to maintain an office and otherwise practice law anywhere within its borders. No state today continues the restrictions of former centuries that limited practice to a particular judicial district or county in which a lawyer was admitted.

The rules governing interstate practice by nonlocal lawyers were formed at a time when lawyers conducted very little practice of that nature. Thus, the limitation on legal services threatened by such rules imposed little actual inconvenience. However, as interstate and international commerce, transportation, and communications have expanded, clients have increasingly required a truly interstate and international range of practice by their lawyers. (To a limited extent, many states recognize such needs in the international realm by providing for limited practice in the state by foreign legal consultants. See § 2, Comment *g*.) Applied literally, the old restrictions on practice of law in a state by a lawyer admitted elsewhere could seriously inconvenience clients who have need of such services within the state. Retaining locally admitted counsel would often cause serious delay and expense and could require the client to deal with unfamiliar counsel. Modern communications, including ready electronic connection to much of the law of every state, makes concern about a competent analysis of a distant state's law unfounded. Accordingly, there is much to be said for a rule permitting a lawyer to practice in any state, except for litigation matters or for the purpose of establishing a permanent in-state branch office. Results approaching that rule may arguably be required under the federal interstate commerce clause and the privileges and immunities clause. The approach of the Section is more guarded. However, its primary focus is appropriately on the needs of clients.

The extent to which a lawyer may practice beyond the borders of the lawyer's home state depends on the circumstances in which the lawyer acts in both the lawyer's home state and the other state. At one extreme, it is clear that a lawyer's admission to practice in one jurisdiction does not authorize the lawyer to practice generally in another jurisdiction as if the lawyer were also fully admitted there. Thus, a lawyer admitted in State A may not open an office in State B for the general practice of law there or otherwise engage in the continuous, regular, or repeated representation of clients within the other state.

Certainty is provided in litigated matters by procedures for securing the right to practice elsewhere, although the arrangement is limited to appearances as counsel in individual litigated matters. Apparently all states provide such a procedure for temporary admission of an unadmitted lawyer, usually termed admission pro hac vice. (Compare admission on-motion to the right to practice generally within a jurisdiction as described in § 2, Comment *b*.) Although the decision is sometimes described as discretionary, a court will grant admission pro hac vice if the lawyer applying for admission is in good standing in the bar of another jurisdiction and has complied with applicable requirements (sometimes requiring the association of local counsel), and if no reason is shown why the lawyer cannot be relied upon to provide competent representation to the lawyer's client in conformance with the local lawyer code. Such temporary admission is recognized in Subsection (2). Courts are particularly apt to grant such applications in criminal-defense representations. Some jurisdictions impose limitations, such as a maximum number of such admissions in a specified period. Admission pro hac vice normally permits the lawyer to engage within the jurisdiction in all customary and appropriate activities in conducting the litigation, including appropriate office practice. Activities in contemplation of such admission are also authorized, such as investigating facts or consulting with the client within the jurisdiction prior to drafting a complaint and filing the action.

A lawyer who is properly admitted to practice in a state with respect to litigation pending there, either generally or pro hac vice, may need to conduct proceedings and activities ancillary to the litigation in other states, such as counseling clients, dealing with co-counsel or opposing counsel, conducting depositions, examining documents, interviewing witnesses, negotiating settlements, and the like. Such activities incidental to permissible practice are appropriate and permissible.

Transactional and similar out-of-court representation of clients may raise similar issues, yet there is no equivalent of temporary admission pro hac vice for such representation, as there is in litigation. Even activities that bear close resemblance to in-court litigation, such as representation of clients in arbitration or in administrative hearings, may not include measures for pro hac vice appearance. Some activities are clearly permissible. Thus, a lawyer conducting activities in the lawyer's home state may advise a client about the law of another state, a proceeding in another state, or a transaction there, including conducting research in the law of the other state, advising the client about the application of that law, and drafting legal documents intended to have legal effect there. There is no per se bar against such a lawyer giving a formal opinion based in whole or in part on the law of another jurisdiction, but a lawyer should do so only if the lawyer has adequate familiarity with the relevant law. It is also clearly permissible for a lawyer from a home-state office to direct communications to persons and organizations in other states (in which the lawyer is not separately admitted), by letter, telephone, telecopier, or other forms of electronic communication. On the other hand, as with litigation, it would be impermissible for a lawyer to set up an office for the general practice of nonlitigation law in a jurisdiction in which the lawyer is not admitted as described in § 2.

When other activities of a lawyer in a non-home state are challenged as impermissible for lack of admission to the state's bar, the context in which and purposes for which the lawyer acts should be carefully assessed. Beyond home-state activities, proper representation of clients often requires a lawyer to conduct activities while physically present in one or more other states. Such practice is customary in many areas of legal representation. As stated in Subsection (3), such activities should be recognized as permissible so long as they arise out of or otherwise reasonably relate to the lawyer's practice in a state of admission. In determining that issue, several factors are relevant, including the following: whether the lawyer's client is a regular client of the lawyer or, if a new client, is from the lawyer's home state, has extensive contacts with that state, or contacted the lawyer there; whether a multistate transaction has other significant connections with the lawyer's home state; whether significant aspects of the lawyer's activities are conducted in the lawyer's home state; whether a significant aspect of the matter involves the law of the lawyer's home state; and whether either the activities of the client involve multiple jurisdictions or the legal issues involved are primarily either multistate or federal in nature. Because lawyers in a firm often practice collectively, the activities of all lawyers in the representation of a client are relevant. The customary practices of lawyers who engage in interstate law practice is one appropriate measure of the reasonableness of a lawyer's activities out of state. Association with local counsel may permit a lawyer to conduct in-state activities not otherwise permissible, but such association is not required in most instances of in-state practice. Among other things, the additional expense for the lawyer's client of retaining additional counsel and educating that lawyer about the client's affairs would make such required retention unduly burdensome.

Particularly in the situation of a lawyer representing a multistate or multinational organization, the question of geographical connection may be difficult to assess or establish. Thus, a multinational corporation wishing to select a location in the United States to build a new facility may engage a lawyer to accompany officers of the corporation to survey possible sites in several states, perhaps holding discussions with local governmental officers about such topics as zoning, taxation, environmental requirements, and the like. Such occasional, temporary in-state services, when reasonable and appropriate in performing the lawyer's functions for the client, are a proper aspect of practice and do not constitute impermissible practice in the other state.

Illustrations:

1. Lawyer has an office and is duly licensed to practice law in State A. Lawyer's office is in a community near State B, where Lawyer is not admitted to practice. In the past, several of Lawyer's clients have been residents of State B, and their legal issues sometimes involve research into issues of State B law. In order to provide better service to those clients and to attract business of other clients there, Lawyer rents space, hires nonlawyer assistants, and otherwise prepares premises for the general practice of law at a branch-office location in State B. While representation of residents of State B in Lawyer's office in State A is permissible, Lawyer may not open an office for the general practice of law in State B without obtaining general admission to practice there (see § 2).

2. Same facts as in Illustration 1, except that Lawyer represents a regulated Utility, which operates a power plant in State A near the border with State B. Lawyer's work for Utility principally relates to environmental issues, such as providing advice, obtaining permits, and otherwise complying with federal law and the law of State A. Utility also has occasional issues relating to compliance with the environmental laws of State B because of those same activities. It is permissible for Lawyer to travel to State B to deal with governmental officials with respect to environmental issues arising out of Utility's activities.

3. Same facts as in Illustration 2, except that Lawyer's original work for Utility in State A related to rate-setting proceedings before a utility commission in that state and before the Federal Energy Regulatory Commission. Under recent legislation, Utility may now be able to make retail sales of electricity to consumers in many states. Because of Lawyer's extensive knowledge of Utility's rate-related financial information, Utility has asked Lawyer to take charge of new rate applications in 15 other states, all being states in which Lawyer is not admitted to practice. Lawyer's work in those matters would involve extensive presence and activities in each of the other states until the necessary rates have been established. Although local counsel would often be retained in such matters, Lawyer and other lawyers in Lawyer's firm may permissibly conduct those activities in the other states on behalf of Utility.

4. Lawyer, who practices with a law firm in California, is a nationally known expert in corporate mergers and acquisitions. Utility is a major electricity generator and distributor in the southeastern United States. Under the new legislation referred to in Illustration 3, Utility is considering a hostile takeover of Old Company, an established regional electricity generator and distributor in the northeastern United States. Legal work on the acquisition would require the physical presence of Utility's mergers-and-acquisitions counsel in a number of states in addition to the West Coast state in which Lawyer is admitted, in addition to representation before at least one federal agency in Washington, D.C. Given the multistate and federal nature of the legal work, Lawyer and other members of Lawyer's firm may represent Utility as requested.

5. Lawyer is admitted to practice and has an office in Illinois, where Lawyer practices in the area of trusts and estates, an area involving, among other things, both the law of wills, property, taxation, and trusts of a particular state and federal income, estate, and gift tax law. Client A, whom Lawyer has represented in estate-planning matters, has recently moved to Florida and calls Lawyer from there with a request that leads to Lawyer's preparation of a codicil to A's will, which Lawyer takes to Florida to obtain the necessary signatures. While there, A introduces Lawyer to B, a friend of A, who, after learning of A's estate-planning arrangements from A, wishes Lawyer to prepare a similar estate arrangement for B. Lawyer prepares the necessary documents and conducts legal research in Lawyer's office in Illinois, frequently conferring by telephone and letter with B in Florida. Lawyer then takes the documents to Florida for execution by B and necessary witnesses. Lawyer's activities in Florida on behalf of both A and B were permissible.

f. Multistate practice by inside legal counsel. States have permitted practice within the jurisdiction by inside legal counsel for a corporation or similar organization, even if the lawyer is not locally admitted and even if the lawyer's work consists entirely of in-state activities, when all of the lawyer's work is for the employer-client (compare § 4, Comment *e*) and does not involve appearance in court. Leniency is appropriate because the only concern is with the client-employer, who is presumably in a good position to assess the quality and fitness of the lawyer's work. In the course of such work, the lawyer may deal with outsiders, such as by negotiating with others in settling litigation or directing the activities of lawyers who do enter an appearance for the organization in litigation.

g. Authorized practice in a federal agency or court. A lawyer properly admitted to practice before a federal agency or in a federal court (see § 2, Comment *b*) may practice federal law for a client either at the physical location of the agency or court or in an office in any state, so long as the lawyer's practice arises out of or is reasonably related to the agency's or court's business. Such a basis for authorized practice is recognized in Subsection (2). Thus, a lawyer registered with the United States Patent and Trademark Office could counsel a client from an office anywhere about filing a patent or about assigning the ensuing patent right, matters reasonably related to the lawyer's admission to the agency. (The permissible scope of practice of a nonlawyer patent agent may be less, since admission to the agency does not suggest competence to deal with matters, such as the assignment of patents, beyond the jurisdiction of the agency.)

A lawyer admitted in one state who is admitted to practice in a United States district court located in another state, but who is not otherwise admitted in the second state, can practice law in the state so long as the practice is limited to cases filed in that federal court. Local rules in some few federal district courts additionally require admission to the bar of the sitting state as a condition of admission to the federal court. The requirement is inconsistent with the federal nature of the court's business.

A lawyer or law firm similarly may employ a lawyer or nonlawyer who practices pursuant to such a limited license from a federal agency or court to perform services permissible under the license. Because the person's practice is authorized, the employing lawyer is not engaged in assisting unauthorized practice (compare § 4, Comments *f* & *g*). On the other hand, the employing lawyer or law firm would be so engaged if the unadmitted lawyer or nonlawyer engaged in practice not reasonably related to the work the person is authorized to conduct.

§ 4. Unauthorized Practice by a Nonlawyer

A person not admitted to practice as a lawyer (see § 2) may not engage in the unauthorized practice of law, and a lawyer may not assist a person to do so.

Comment:

a. Scope and cross-references. This Section addresses legal restrictions on the practice of law by a person not admitted to practice as described in § 2. On somewhat similar restrictions on disbarred or suspended lawyers or on lawyers practicing in a jurisdiction in which the lawyer is not admitted, see § 3.

To some, the expression "unauthorized practice of law" by a nonlawyer is incongruous, because it can be taken to imply that nonlawyers may engage in some aspects of law practice, but not others. The phrase has gained near-universal usage in the courts, ethics-committee opinions, and scholarly writing, and it is well understood not to imply any necessary area of permissible practice by a nonlawyer. Moreover, a nonlawyer undoubtedly may engage in some limited forms of law practice, such as self-representation in a civil or criminal matter (see Comment *d*). See also, e.g., § 3, Comment *g*; Comments *c*, *e*, and *g* hereof. It thus would not be accurate for the black letter to state flatly that a nonlawyer may not engage in law practice. On defining unauthorized practice, see Comment *c* hereto.

A nonlawyer who impermissibly engages in the practice of law may be subject to several sanctions, including injunction, contempt, and conviction for crime.

b. Unauthorized practice by a nonlawyer—in general. Courts, typically as the result of lawsuits brought by bar associations, began in the early part of the 20th century to adapt common-law rules to permit bar associations and lawyer-competitors to seek injunctions against some forms of unauthorized practice by nonlawyers. The courts also played a large role in attempting to define and delineate such practice. The primary justification given for unauthorized practice limitations was that of consumer protection—to protect consumers of unauthorized practitioner services against the significant risk of harm believed to be threatened by the nonlawyer practitioner's incompetence or lack of ethical constraints. Delineating the respective areas of permissible and impermissible activities has often been controversial. Some consumer groups and governmental agencies have criticized some restrictions as over-protective, anti-competitive, and costly to consumers.

In the latter part of the 20th century, unauthorized practice restrictions have lessened, to a greater or lesser extent, in most jurisdictions. In some few jurisdictions traditional restraints are apparently still enforced through active programs. In other jurisdictions, enforcement has effectively ceased, and large numbers of lay practitioners perform many traditional legal services. Debate continues about the broad public-policy elements of unauthorized-practice restrictions, including the delineation of lawyer-only practice areas. On areas of nonlawyer practice officially permitted, see Comment *c* hereof.

c. *Delineation of unauthorized practice.* The definitions and tests employed by courts to delineate unauthorized practice by nonlawyers have been vague or conclusory, while jurisdictions have differed significantly in describing what constitutes unauthorized practice in particular areas.

Certain activities, such as the representation of another person in litigation, are generally proscribed. Even in that area, many jurisdictions recognize exceptions for such matters as small-claims and landlord-tenant tribunals and certain proceedings in administrative agencies. Moreover, many jurisdictions have authorized law students and others not admitted in the state to represent indigent persons or others as part of clinical legal-education programs.

Controversy has surrounded many out-of-court activities such as advising on estate planning by bank trust officers, advising on estate planning by insurance agents, stock brokers, or benefit-plan and similar consultants, filling out or providing guidance on forms for property transactions by real-estate agents, title companies, and closing-service companies, and selling books or individual forms containing instructions on self-help legal services or accompanied by personal, nonlawyer assistance on filling them out in connection with legal procedures such as obtaining a marriage dissolution. The position of bar associations has traditionally been that nonlawyer provision of such services denies the person served the benefit of such legal measures as the attorney-client privilege, the benefits of such extraordinary duties as that of confidentiality of client information and the protection against conflicts of interest, and the protection of such measures as those regulating lawyer trust accounts and requiring lawyers to supervise nonlawyer personnel. Several jurisdictions recognize that many such services can be provided by nonlawyers without significant risk of incompetent service, that actual experience in several states with extensive nonlawyer provision of traditional legal services indicates no significant risk of harm to consumers of such services, that persons in need of legal services may be significantly aided in obtaining assistance at a much lower price than would be entailed by segregating out a portion of a transaction to be handled by a lawyer for a fee, and that many persons can ill afford, and most persons are at least inconvenienced by, the typically higher cost of lawyer services. In addition, traditional common-law and statutory consumer-protection measures offer significant protection to consumers of such nonlawyer services.

d. *Pro se appearance.* Every jurisdiction recognizes the right of an individual to proceed "pro se" by providing his or her own representation in any matter, whether or not the person is a lawyer. Because the appearance is personal only, it does not involve an issue of unauthorized practice. The right extends to self-preparation of legal documents and other kinds of out-of-court legal work as well as to in-court representation. In some jurisdictions, tribunals have inaugurated programs to assist persons without counsel in filing necessary papers, with appropriate cautions that court personnel assisting the person do not thereby undertake to provide legal assistance. The United States Supreme Court has held that a person accused of crime in a federal or state prosecution has, as an aspect of the right to the assistance of counsel, the constitutional right to waive counsel and to proceed pro se. In general, however, a person appearing pro se cannot represent any other person or entity, no matter how close the degree of kinship, ownership, or other relationship.

e. *Unauthorized practice for and by entities.* A limitation on pro se representation (see Comment *d*) found in many jurisdictions is that a corporation cannot represent itself in litigation and must accordingly always be represented by counsel. The rule applies, apparently, only to appearances in litigated matters. Thus a nonlawyer officer of a corporation may permissibly draft legal documents, negotiate complex transactions, and perform other tasks for the employing organization, even if the task is typically performed by lawyers for organizations. With respect to litigation, several jurisdictions except representation in certain tribunals, such as landlord-tenant and small-claims courts and in certain administrative proceedings (see Comment *c* hereto), where incorporation (typically of a small owner-operated business) has little bearing on the prerogative of the person to provide self-representation.

Under traditional concepts of unauthorized practice, a lawyer employed by an organization may provide legal services only to the organization as an entity with respect to its own interests and not, for example, to customers of the entity with respect to their own legal matters. Included within the powers of a lawyer retained by an organization (see § 3, Comment *f*) should be the capacity to perform legal services for all entities within the same organizational family. It has proved controversial whether a lawyer employed full time by an insurance company (see § 134) may represent policyholders of the company in covered matters.

f. Lawyer assistance to nonlawyer unauthorized practice. The lawyer codes have traditionally prohibited lawyers from assisting nonlawyers in activities that constitute the unauthorized practice of law. That prohibition is stated in the Section. The limitation supplements requirements that lawyers provide adequate supervision to nonlawyer employees and agents (see Comment *g* hereto; § 11, Comment *e*). By the same token, it has prevented lawyers from sponsoring non-law-firm enterprises in which legal services are provided mainly or entirely by nonlawyers and in which the lawyer gains the profits (see generally § 10).

g. Nonlawyer employees of law firms. For obvious reasons of convenience and better service to clients, lawyers and law firms are empowered to retain nonlawyer personnel to assist firm lawyers in providing legal services to clients. In the course of that work, a nonlawyer may conduct activities that, if conducted by that person alone in representing a client, would constitute unauthorized practice. Those activities are permissible and do not constitute unauthorized practice, so long as the responsible lawyer or law firm provides appropriate supervision (see § 11, Comment *e*), and so long as the nonlawyer is not permitted to own an interest in the law firm, split fees, or exercise management powers with respect to a law-practice aspect of the firm (see § 10).

TITLE C. PROFESSIONAL DISCIPLINE

§ 5. Professional Discipline

(1) A lawyer is subject to professional discipline for violating any provision of an applicable lawyer code.

(2) A lawyer is also subject to professional discipline under Subsection (1) for attempting to commit a violation, knowingly assisting or inducing another to do so, or knowingly doing so through the acts of another.

(3) A lawyer who knows of another lawyer's violation of applicable rules of professional conduct raising a substantial question of the lawyer's honesty or trustworthiness or the lawyer's fitness as a lawyer in some other respect must report that information to appropriate disciplinary authorities.

TOPIC 3. CIVIL JUDICIAL REMEDIES IN GENERAL

§ 6. Jurisdictional Remedies Available to a Client or Nonclient for Lawyer Wrongs

For a lawyer's breach of a duty owed to the lawyer's client or to a nonclient, judicial remedies may be available through judgment or order entered in accordance with the standards applicable to the remedy awarded, including standards concerning limitation of remedies. Judicial remedies include the following:

(1) awarding a sum of money as damages;

(2) providing injunctive relief, including requiring specific performance of a contract or enjoining its nonperformance;

(3) requiring restoration of a specific thing or awarding a sum of money to prevent unjust enrichment;

(4) ordering cancellation or reformation of a contract, deed, or similar instrument;

(5) declaring the rights of the parties, such as determining that an obligation claimed by the lawyer to be owed to the lawyer is not enforceable;

(6) punishing the lawyer for contempt;

(7) enforcing an arbitration award;

(8) disqualifying a lawyer from a representation;

(9) forfeiting a lawyer's fee (see § 37);

(10) denying the admission of evidence wrongfully obtained;

(11) dismissing the claim or defense of a litigant represented by the lawyer;

(12) granting a new trial; and

(13) entering a procedural or other sanction.

Comment:

a. Scope and cross-references. This Section describes judicial relief available to a client or nonclient whose legal rights have been violated by actions of a lawyer. This Restatement does not purport to describe in detail such remedies and rules regarding their implementation (see Introductory Note). Instead, the Section and the following Comments note in general terms the most familiar, applicable remedies and certain circumstances involved in their application to lawyers. This list is not exhaustive, and the availability of one remedy does not necessarily foreclose others. For example, a court awarding a sum of money to prevent unjust enrichment (Subsection (3)) may also impose a constructive trust and order an accounting (see Restatement of Restitution § 160 and Restatement Second, Restitution § 30 (Tentative Draft No. 2, 1984)).

Availability of a particular remedy is subject to customary rules applicable to the remedy, including the general principle that duplicative remedies not be awarded. With respect to limitation of remedies, see Comment *n*.

Generally applicable law defines the elements that must be proved by a party seeking a remedy or seeking to defend against a claim for such a remedy. When the conduct of a lawyer is drawn into question, the provisions of lawyer codes regulating the lawyer with respect to such conduct may be relevant in determining the propriety of the conduct (see § 1, Comment *b*, & § 52, Comment *f*).

b. Damages. The most common kind of case in which damages are allowed is a claim of malpractice by a client against a lawyer. See generally Chapter 4. On the extent of damage remedies available to a nonclient against a lawyer, see generally §§ 51 and 56.

c. Specific performance and other injunctive relief. A lawyer's general undertaking to provide legal services to a client is not specifically enforceable. On the doctrine that a personal-services contract, including a contract to provide legal services, will not be specifically enforced, see Restatement Second, Contracts § 367(1). On the other hand, in litigation matters a court generally has discretion to refuse to permit a lawyer to withdraw to the extent stated in § 32(4) and Comment *d* thereto. The general rule providing limited injunctive relief against a lawyer's breach of a contract to provide personal services exclusively to one client (see id. § 367(2)) would not normally be relevant due to the unenforceability on grounds of public policy of a purported promise by a lawyer not to provide legal services to another client (see § 13). A lawyer employed in a full-time position as employee, such as inside legal counsel to a corporation, government agency, or similar entity, will often function under an agreement or rule requiring the lawyer not to practice law in outside employment. The typical remedy for breach of such an agreement is internal discipline or termination, rather than injunctive relief.

A lawyer may contract with a client to provide nonlegal services, such as when a lawyer and client enter into a business contract that the client seeks to enforce (see § 126). Such a contract is enforceable in accordance with the customary rules governing contracts, including remedies available for breach of such a contract.

Injunctive relief may also be appropriate for a lawyer's violation of noncontractual duties to a client. Thus, a lawyer who fails or refuses to turn over to a client or the client's successor files or other property to which the client is entitled (see § 33(1) & Comment *b* thereto) may be required to do so by injunctive order.

With respect to a nonclient, the instances in which injunctive relief against an opposing lawyer would be appropriate are limited. Nonetheless, when no other suitable remedy is available, it may be appropriate, for example, to enter an injunction against an opposing lawyer's violation of the prohibition against contact with employees of a nonclient (see §§ 99–102).

d. *Preventing unjust enrichment.* A court in a civil action may order a lawyer to return specific property, such as client property wrongfully retained by a lawyer (see § 45). See also § 60(2) (accounting for profits from improper use of confidential information). Disciplinary authorities are also sometimes empowered to order restitution as a disciplinary sanction (see § 5, Comment *j*). On forfeiture of a lawyer's fees, see § 37.

e. *Rescission or reformation of a transaction.* Cancellation of an instrument with otherwise legal effect would be appropriate when, for example, a lawyer obtains a deed to a client's property through undue influence in violation of limitations on business dealings with a client (see § 126) or on client gifts to lawyers (see § 127) or when the instrument was prepared by a lawyer representing clients with substantial conflicts of interests (see § 130). The remedy implements substantive standards applicable to lawyers as an expression of the strong public policy of the jurisdiction.

f. *Declaratory relief.* Under standards otherwise governing the availability of declaratory relief, it may be appropriate for a court to enter an order declaring the respective rights of lawyer and client with respect to a disputed issue or the responsibilities of a lawyer with respect to a nonclient.

g. *Contempt.* An order providing a sanction for civil or criminal contempt may be appropriate for a lawyer's violation of a court injunction or similar order. See Comment *c*; see also § 105. In addition, a lawyer functioning as advocate in a proceeding may be subject to remedies through contempt orders without issuance of a prior judicial order where necessary and appropriate to maintain order in the courtroom or otherwise to prevent significant impairment of the proceedings (see § 105, Comment *e*). Included in such relief may be an appropriate sanction directed toward repairing or punishing harm that the lawyer's contemptuous conduct caused to the lawyer's own client.

h. *Enforcing an arbitration award.* As indicated in § 42, Comment *b*, a lawyer and client may agree to submit a dispute to binding arbitration, and a jurisdiction may require a lawyer to submit to fee arbitration when a client so elects. See also § 54, Comment *b* (malpractice arbitration). As with arbitration awards generally, a court may in an appropriate case enter an order enforcing such an award or denying it enforcement on appropriate grounds. On arbitration awards in a lawyer's favor and against a client or former client, see § 7, Comment *c*.

i. *Disqualification from a representation.* Disqualification of a lawyer and those affiliated with the lawyer from further participation in a pending matter has become the most common remedy for conflicts of interest in litigation (see Chapter 8). Disqualification draws on the inherent power of courts to regulate the conduct of lawyers (see § 1, Comment *c*) as well as the related inherent power of judges to regulate the course of proceedings before them and to issue injunctive and similar directive orders (see Comment *c* hereto). Disqualification, where appropriate, ensures that the case is well presented in court, that confidential information of present or former clients is not misused, and that a client's substantial interest in a lawyer's loyalty is protected. In most instances, determining whether a lawyer should be disqualified involves a balancing of several interests and is appropriate only when less-intrusive remedies are not reasonably available.

The costs imposed on a client deprived of a lawyer's services by disqualification can be substantial. At a minimum, the client is forced to incur the cost of finding a new lawyer not burdened by conflict in whom the client has confidence and educating that lawyer about the facts and issues. The costs of delay in the proceeding are borne by that client in part, but also by the tribunal and society. Disqualification is often the most effective sanction for a conflict of interest and will likely continue to be vigorously applied where necessary to protect the integrity of a proceeding or an important interest of the moving party. In applying it, however, tribunals should be vigilant to prevent its use as a tactic by which one party may impose unwarranted delay, costs, and other burdens on another. In an appropriate case, additional or other remedies may be appropriate, such as professional discipline (see § 5), legal-malpractice recovery (see Chapter 4), fee forfeiture (see § 37 & Comment *d* hereto), rescission or reformation of an instrument (see Comment *d* hereto), various procedural remedies (see Comments *j-m* hereto), or possible criminal sanctions (see § 8). Injunctive relief (see Comment *c* hereto) may be appropriate in a matter not before a tribunal, so that disqualification in a proceeding already underway cannot be sought.

The costs associated with disqualification require that standing to seek disqualification ordinarily be limited to present or former clients who would be adversely affected by the continuing representation, whether or not they are parties to the present litigation. Tribunals should not ordinarily permit parties who are not directly affected to invoke the putative interests of an absent client with whom they are not in privity. However, concerns about the fairness of the processes of tribunals may require that tribunals in some cases raise conflicts issues on their own motion or permit a party who otherwise lacks standing to raise the issue. Particularly in criminal prosecutions (see § 129, Comment *c*), a court may intervene where necessary to protect a defendant against the ineffective assistance of counsel that may result from a conflict of interest.

Concern that motions to disqualify might be used to delay proceedings and harass opposing parties also requires that the motion to disqualify be timely. If a present or former client with knowledge of the conflict fails to take reasonably prompt steps to object or to seek a remedy, disqualification may be precluded. Whether an objection is timely depends on such circumstances as the length of delay from the time when the conflict was reasonably apparent, whether the movant was represented by counsel at relevant times, why the delay occurred, and whether acting now would result in prejudice to the responding party.

A file of the work done on a matter before disqualification by a disqualified lawyer may be provided to a successor lawyer in circumstances in which doing so does not threaten confidential information (see generally § 59) of the successful moving client. The party seeking to justify such a transfer may be required to show both that no impermissible confidential client information is contained in the material transferred, and that the former and new lawyers exchange none in the process of transferring responsibilities for the matter.

Illustration:

1. Lawyer was retained by Defendant to defend a claim for breach of warranty. Lawyer prepared a memorandum of legal research on the question of proper venue and made notes of interviews with three of Defendant's employees who had substantial knowledge of the processes used in manufacture of the product. Shortly thereafter, Lawyer's firm hired New Lawyer, who had been actively working on the case on behalf of Plaintiff at a former firm. Even if Lawyer would be disqualified from continuing to represent Defendant in the case (compare §§ 123–124), the interview notes and memorandum of law could be made available to successor counsel for Defendant because Defendant can show that they were not enhanced or otherwise based on confidential information of Plaintiff revealed by New Lawyer to Lawyer.

When a lawyer undertakes a representation that is later determined to involve a conflict of interest that could not reasonably have been and in fact was not identified at an earlier point (see § 121, Comment *g*), the lawyer is not liable for damages or subject to professional discipline. In such a situation, disqualification may or may not be appropriate (see § 49, Illustration 2).

j. *Denying the admissibility of evidence.* If the admission of evidence on behalf of a party would violate the obligation owed by a lawyer to a client or former client (see generally § 60) or was obtained by a lawyer in violation of the lawyer's obligation not to mislead a nonclient (see § 98), the tribunal may exercise discretion to exclude the evidence, even if the evidence is not otherwise subject to exclusion because of the attorney-client privilege (see § 68 and following) or the work-product immunity (see § 87 and following). Exclusion is proper where it would place the parties in the position they would have occupied if the lawyer had not obtained the confidential information in the first place.

k. *Dismissing a claim or defense.* When a litigant bases an essential element of a claim or defense entirely on confidential client information improperly disclosed by a lawyer (see generally § 60), the tribunal may exercise discretion to dismiss the claim or defense. Such extreme relief is appropriate when no less drastic relief would adequately remedy the disclosure. If, on the other hand, the tribunal finds that the claim or defense would have been made notwithstanding the disclosure, a more appropriate remedy may be disqualification of the revealing lawyer if the lawyer presently represents the responding party and suppression of only such evidence (see Comment *j*) as would not be properly discoverable.

l. *New trial.* Where the determination in a case was affected prejudicially and substantially by a conflict of interest, by a lawyer misuse of confidential information of an objecting client, by a breach of rules governing admissibility of evidence or conduct of the proceeding, or by similarly wrongful conduct of a lawyer, the determination may be reversed and the matter retried. Tribunals are properly reluctant to grant such a remedy. On the other hand, it may be the only effective remedy in a particular case, for example in a criminal case in which a lawyer representing the defendant labored under an impermissible conflict of interest (see § 129). When the complaining party is the client of the offending lawyer in a civil case, tribunals generally relegate the client to such remedies as the client may have directly against the lawyer, concluding that reversal of a determination in favor of an otherwise uninvolved opposing party would be inappropriate (see § 26, Comment *d*).

m. *Procedural or other sanctions.* Most tribunals possess the power to provide sanctions against participants in litigation, including lawyers, who engage in seriously harassing or other sanctionable activities. See generally § 1; see also § 110. Such sanctions include an award of attorney fees to a party injured by the lawyer's conduct, a fine, or a reprimand. In appropriate circumstances, the court may determine that the client was blameless and the lawyer fully blameworthy and accordingly direct that the full weight of a sanction entered against a party be borne only by the lawyer and not by the lawyer's client (see § 110, Comment *g*). Rarely will such relief entail an award from the offending lawyer to that lawyer's own client. However, such an order may be appropriate, for example, when, due to the lawyer's offensive activities, the lawyer's client has retained another lawyer and the court retains jurisdiction to award such a sanction against the predecessor lawyer.

n. *Limitation of remedies.* Applicable rules of the law of remedies may limit relief that otherwise would be available, such as the limitation on recovery of damages for failure to avoid preventable loss. See Restatement Second, Contracts § 350; see also id. §§ 351 (unforeseeability and related limitations), 352 (uncertainty), 353 (losses due to emotional disturbance), and 356 (limitation on liquidated damages and penalties). Similarly, certain remedies may be withheld because precluded by election or affirmance (see id., Ch. 16, Topic 5; see also § 54).

§ 7. Jurisdictional Remedies Available to a Lawyer for Client Wrongs

A lawyer may obtain a remedy based on a present or former client's breach of a duty to the lawyer if the remedy:

(1) is appropriate under applicable law governing the remedy; and

(2) does not put the lawyer in a position prohibited by an applicable lawyer code.

Comment:

a. *Scope and cross-references.* This Section states the general availability of remedies to a lawyer (Subsection (1)), subject to Subsection (2), which recognizes that special limitations on such remedies may be appropriate in view of what the tribunal may properly determine to be overriding considerations arising from appropriate enforcement of a lawyer-code provision applicable to the lawyer. While the discussion herein is limited to remedies, similar considerations may apply to defenses that a lawyer asserts against claims of a client or former client.

b. *Rationale.* A lawyer seeking relief from a present or former client is not in the same position as are most other claimants with respect to responding parties. The relationship between lawyer and client is one in which the lawyer generally owes the client rigorously enforced fiduciary duties, including duties of the utmost good faith and fair dealing (see § 16). Those duties are diminished, but not entirely extinguished, at the end of the representation. While those duties inform many of the substantive rights that a lawyer might assert against a client, it may also be appropriate to take account of the lawyer's fiduciary duties when assessing the suitability of an otherwise-available remedy (e.g., § 41) (fee-collection methods). In view of the predominant role of courts in regulating lawyers (see § 2, Comment *c*), such concepts will be particularly relevant when the remedy in question is discretionary with the court or when a tribunal deals with a novel common-law question of remedy.

Illustrations:

1. In a written contract by which Client retained Lawyer to provide legal services in a personal-injury case, Client agreed to give Lawyer at least 30 days' notice of discharge. Client was a person not experienced in dealings with lawyers, and the representation was a routine personal-injury action. Client later discharged Lawyer without giving prior notice. Lawyer filed suit against Client, seeking damages for Client's violation of the 30-day-notice agreement. Due to Client's right to discharge Lawyer at any time (see § 32), the tribunal should refuse to enforce the 30-day limitation restricting that right.

2. Same facts as in Illustration 1, except that Client is a large organization represented in the negotiations with Lawyer by inside legal counsel. The matter involves an unusual time and capital commitment by Lawyer, necessitating that Lawyer hire additional professional and clerical assistance, terminate representation of other clients, and train office staff to deal with a complex set of technical issues entailed in representing Client. In the circumstances, the 30-day-notice requirement is not unreasonable, as it protects clear and legitimate interests of Lawyer and does not in the circumstances unduly burden Client's right of discharge.

On the right of a discharged inside legal counsel to maintain a suit against a client organization for wrongful dismissal, see § 32, Comment *b*; cf. § 37, Comment *e*.

c. *Public-policy limitations on remedies to lawyer.* As with other considerations of public policy, a tribunal will accord respect to the special rules regulating lawyers, including applicable provisions of a lawyer code, in adjudicating a dispute between a lawyer and a client or former client. Such attention is appropriate both in determining applicable remedial and substantive rules and when dealing with particular defenses, such as defenses of public policy in contract law (see, e.g., Restatement Second, Contracts § 197 et seq.) (unavailability of restitution on public-policy grounds). See § 1, Comment *b*; see, e.g., § 37 (fee forfeiture).

TOPIC 4. LAWYER CRIMINAL OFFENSES

§ 8. Lawyer Criminal Offenses

The traditional and appropriate activities of a lawyer in representing a client in accordance with the requirements of the applicable lawyer code are relevant factors for the tribunal in assessing the propriety of the lawyer's conduct under the criminal law. In other respects, a lawyer is guilty of an offense for an act committed in the course of representing a client to the same extent and on the same basis as would a nonlawyer acting similarly.

TOPIC 5. LAW-FIRM STRUCTURE AND OPERATION

TITLE A. ASSOCIATION OF LAWYERS IN LAW ORGANIZATIONS

§ 9. Law-Practice Organizations—In General

(1) A lawyer may practice as a solo practitioner, as an employee of another lawyer or law firm, or as a member of a law firm constituted as a partnership, professional corporation, or similar entity.

(2) A lawyer employed by an entity described in Subsection (1) is subject to applicable law governing the creation, operation, management, and dissolution of the entity.

(3) Absent an agreement with the firm providing a more permissive rule, a lawyer leaving a law firm may solicit firm clients:

(a) prior to leaving the firm:

(i) only with respect to firm clients on whose matters the lawyer is actively and substantially working; and

(ii) only after the lawyer has adequately and timely informed the firm of the lawyer's intent to contact firm clients for that purpose; and

(b) after ceasing employment in the firm, to the same extent as any other nonfirm lawyer.

TITLE B. LIMITATIONS ON NONLAWYER INVOLVEMENT IN A LAW FIRM

§ 10. Limitations on Nonlawyer Involvement in a Law Firm

(1) A nonlawyer may not own any interest in a law firm, and a nonlawyer may not be empowered to or actually direct or control the professional activities of a lawyer in the firm.

(2) A lawyer may not form a partnership or other business enterprise with a nonlawyer if any of the activities of the enterprise consist of the practice of law.

(3) A lawyer or law firm may not share legal fees with a person not admitted to practice as a lawyer, except that:

(a) an agreement by a lawyer with the lawyer's firm or another lawyer in the firm may provide for payment, over a reasonable period of time after the lawyer's death, to the lawyer's estate or to one or more specified persons;

(b) a lawyer who undertakes to complete unfinished legal business of a deceased lawyer may pay to the estate of the deceased lawyer a portion of the total compensation that fairly represents services rendered by the deceased lawyer; and

(c) a lawyer or law firm may include nonlawyer employees in a compensation or retirement plan, even though the plan is based in whole or in part on a profit-sharing arrangement.

Comment:

a. Scope and cross-references. This Section states several interrelated limitations on the extent to which nonlawyers may own or exercise managerial responsibility in a law firm or share in its fee income and on the correlative extent to which a lawyer may be involved in non-law-firm endeavors, including endeavors some of the activities of which consist of the practice of law. On limitations on the extent to which a nonclient may direct a lawyer's provision of legal services to a client, see § 134. On limitations on fee-splitting among lawyers, see § 47.

b. Rationale. This Section is based on lawyer-code limitations on law-firm structure and practices. Those limitations are prophylactic and are designed to safeguard the professional independence of lawyers. A person entitled to share a lawyer's fees is likely to attempt to influence the lawyer's activities so as to maximize those fees. That could lead to inadequate legal services. The Section should be construed so as to prevent nonlawyer control over lawyers' services, not to implement other goals such as preventing new and useful ways of providing legal services or making sure that nonlawyers do not profit indirectly from legal services in circumstances and under arrangements presenting no significant risk of harm to clients or third persons.

The prohibition of Subsection (3) has no application when a person, such as a spouse, advances an otherwise valid claim on the lawyer's income, net worth, including good will in a law practice, or other wealth (see Principles of the Law of Family Dissolution: Analysis and Recommendations § 4.07) (Proposed Final Draft, Part I, 1997). Jurisdictions disagree as to the permissibility of a sale of the practice of a deceased or retired lawyer and, if permitted, how it may be accomplished.

As indicated in Subsection (3)(a), postdeath distributions to nonlawyers, such as a deceased firm member's spouse or estate, are permissible. Such a distribution may be based on the firm agreement, but it may also be made gratuitously.

c. Nonlawyer ownership or management power in a law firm. As reflected in Subsection (1), the lawyer codes have traditionally prohibited arrangements under which a nonlawyer owns an interest in a law firm or exercises managerial responsibility in a law firm on how legal services are provided. In applying that prohibition, certain areas of nonapplication are recognized. Plainly, a nonlawyer may direct the activities of lawyers when the nonlawyer is a client or an agent of a client in the matter (see § 21(2)), such as a nonlawyer officer of a corporation who directs the activities of a lawyer in the office of inside legal counsel of the organization (see § 96, Comment *d*). A lawyer undertaking to complete unfinished business of a deceased lawyer may agree to pay to the deceased lawyer's estate total compensation that fairly represents the services rendered by that lawyer (see Subsection (3)(b)). Under pension-plan and similar retirement arrangements, it is permissible for nonlawyer personnel of a law firm to share in firm profits (see Subsection (3)(c)).

As with other instances of fee-splitting with a nonlawyer (see Comment *b*), the traditional set of restrictions is intended to protect the professional independence of lawyers. Here also the concern is that permitting such ownership or direction would induce or require lawyers to violate the mandates of the lawyer codes, such as by subjecting the lawyer to the goals and interests of the nonlawyer in ways adverse to the lawyer's duties to a client. As a result, for example, statutes and court rules providing for establishing a law firm as a partnership or professional corporation commonly provide that no principal or partner may be admitted to the partnership or own stock in the corporation who is not a lawyer.

Such restrictions, however, impose costs. One cost is that any kind of capital infusion that would entail granting an ownership or security interest in the law firm itself (as distinguished from its assets) to a nonlawyer investor is prohibited. Perhaps as much as any other constraint, such practical barriers to infusion of capital into law firms significantly limit the ability of law firms to attain what its lawyers may consider to be a more optimal size at which to provide higher-quality and lower-price services to clients. They may also deter law firms from more effectively competing with established law firms and with nonlawyer organizations, such as consulting companies, investment bankers, and accounting firms, to whom clients may turn for more cost-effective law-related services. Further, unlike other persons in many (but not all) occupations, lawyers are unable to realize the present economic value of their reputations, which otherwise could be obtained through sale to investors of stock or other ownership interest.

d. Referral arrangements. Under the rule of Subsection (3), a lawyer may not pay or agree to pay a nonlawyer for referring a client to the lawyer. Such arrangements would give the nonlawyer an incentive to refer to lawyers who will pay the highest referral fee, rather than to lawyers who can provide the most effective services. They also would give the nonlawyer referring person the power and an incentive to influence the lawyer's representation by an explicit or implicit threat to refer no additional clients or by appealing to the lawyer's sense of gratitude for the referral already made. That incentive is not present when the referral comes from a nonprofit referral service. Moreover, a lawyer may pay an advertising, marketing, or similar service for providing professional services in connection with the lawyer's own permissible efforts to advertise for clients. Fee-splitting with a lawyer admitted only in another jurisdiction is subject to § 47 but not to Subsection (3) hereof.

e. Compensation of nonlawyer employees. This Section, of course, does not prohibit a lawyer from providing compensation to secretaries, nonlawyer professionals, and other permanent or temporary employees. That is so even though their compensation indirectly comes from the lawyer's fees and the employees hence have some interest in maximizing the lawyer's fee income. Compare § 47, Comment *b*; on the duty to supervise all such nonlawyer personnel, see § 11. Such compensation may be a percentage of or otherwise contingent on the lawyer's income, so long as the compensation is not contingent on the lawyer's revenue in an individual matter. Thus, under Subsection (3)(c), nonlawyer employees may join in a profit-sharing plan for compensation or retirement. Under tax regulations certain kinds of retirement and similar plans must often be made available to all employees on specified terms of equality.

A lawyer may have business relationships with nonlawyers in non-law practice matters. Thus, a lawyer may serve as co-trustee of a trust or co-executor of an estate and share fees earned for such functions with a nonlawyer co-fiduciary.

f. Nontraditional forms of law practice. The rule against splitting fees with nonlawyers has been one ground for the prohibition of partnerships between lawyers and nonlawyers when the practice of law is an activity of the partnership and for the prohibition of profit-making professional law corporations with stock owned by nonlawyers. This Section does not prohibit a law firm from cooperating with a legally separate partnership or other organization of nonlawyers in providing multi-disciplinary services to clients. The Section allows a lawyer employed and compensated by a nonprofit public-interest organization or a union to remit court-awarded fees to the employing organization, provided that the organization uses the funds only for legal services.

g. Lawyer involvement in ancillary business activities. Ancillary business activities of lawyers can be conducted consistent with the Section and with other applicable requirements. A lawyer may, for example, operate a real-estate agency, insurance agency, title-insurance company, consulting enterprise, or similar business, along with a law practice. So long as each enterprise bills separately and so long as the ancillary enterprise does not engage in the practice of law, involvement of both the lawyer's law practice and the lawyer's ancillary business enterprise in the same matter does not constitute impermissible fee-splitting with a nonlawyer, even if nonlawyers have ownership interests or exercise management powers in the ancillary enterprise.

However, a lawyer's dual practice of law and the ancillary enterprise must be conducted in accordance with applicable legal restrictions, including those of the lawyer codes. Among other things, the lawyer's self-interest in promoting the enterprise must not distort the lawyer's judgment in the provision of legal services to a client, including in making recommendations of the lawyer's own ancillary service. To avoid misleading the client, a lawyer must reveal the lawyer's interest in the ancillary enterprise when it should be reasonably apparent that the client would wish to or should assess that information in determining whether to engage the services of the other business. The lawyer must also, of course, avoid representing a client (or do so only with informed client consent) in a matter in which the ancillary enterprise has an adverse interest of such a kind that it would materially and adversely affect the lawyer's representation of the client (see § 125). The lawyer must also disclose to the client, unless the client is already sufficiently aware, that the client will not have a client-lawyer relationship with the ancillary business and the significance of that fact. Other disclosures may be required in the course of the matter. For example, when circumstances indicate the need to do so to protect an important interest of the client, the lawyer must disclose to the client that the client's communications with personnel of the ancillary enterprise—unlike communications with personnel in the lawyer's law office (see § 70, Comment *g*)—are not protected under the attorney-client privilege. If relevant, the lawyer should also disclose to the client that the ancillary business is not subject to conflict-of-interest rules (see generally Chapter 8) similar to those applicable to law practice.

A lawyer's provision of services to a client through an ancillary business may in some circumstances constitute the rendition of legal services under an applicable lawyer code. As a consequence, the possibly more stringent requirements of the code may control the provision of the ancillary services, such as with respect to the reasonableness of fee charges (§ 34) or confidentiality obligations (§ 60 and following). When those services are distinct and the client understands the significance of the distinction, the ancillary service should not be considered as the rendition of legal services. When those conditions are not met, the lawyer is subject to the lawyer code with respect to all services provided. Whether the services are distinct depends on the client's reasonably apparent understanding concerning such considerations as the nature of the respective ancillary-business and legal services, the physical location at which the services are provided, and the identities and affiliations of lawyer and nonlawyer personnel working on the matter.

h. Sanctions; enforceability of improper agreements. A lawyer who enters a fee-splitting arrangement violating this Section is subject to professional discipline (see § 5) and fee forfeiture (see § 37). Tribunals will not assist such a lawyer to enforce such an arrangement. Whether a nonlawyer may enforce a fee-splitting agreement with a lawyer depends on whether the jurisdiction limits its regulation to lawyers or subjects nonlawyers who enter such agreements to criminal or civil sanctions. With respect to the nonlawyer, a violation of the prohibition of Subsection (2) may constitute unauthorized practice of law, incurring the sanctions applicable to such activity (see § 4).

TITLE C. SUPERVISION OF LAWYERS AND NONLAWYERS WITHIN AN ORGANIZATION

§ 11. A Lawyer's Duty of Supervision

(1) A lawyer who is a partner in a law-firm partnership or a principal in a law firm organized as a corporation or similar entity is subject to professional discipline for failing to make reasonable efforts to ensure that the firm has in effect measures giving reasonable assurance that all lawyers in the firm conform to applicable lawyer-code requirements.

(2) A lawyer who has direct supervisory authority over another lawyer is subject to professional discipline for failing to make reasonable efforts to ensure that the other lawyer conforms to applicable lawyer-code requirements.

(3) A lawyer is subject to professional discipline for another lawyer's violation of the rules of professional conduct if:

(a) the lawyer orders or, with knowledge of the specific conduct, ratifies the conduct involved; or

(b) the lawyer is a partner or principal in the law firm, or has direct supervisory authority over the other lawyer, and knows of the conduct at a time when its consequences can be avoided or mitigated but fails to take reasonable remedial measures.

(4) With respect to a nonlawyer employee of a law firm, the lawyer is subject to professional discipline if either:

(a) the lawyer fails to make reasonable efforts to ensure:

(i) that the firm in which the lawyer practices has in effect measures giving reasonable assurance that the nonlawyer's conduct is compatible with the professional obligations of the lawyer; and

(ii) that conduct of a nonlawyer over whom the lawyer has direct supervisory authority is compatible with the professional obligations of the lawyer; or

(b) the nonlawyer's conduct would be a violation of the applicable lawyer code if engaged in by a lawyer, and

(i) the lawyer orders or, with knowledge of the specific conduct, ratifies the conduct; or

(ii) the lawyer is a partner or principal in the law firm, or has direct supervisory authority over the nonlawyer, and knows of the conduct at a time when its consequences can be avoided or mitigated but fails to take reasonable remedial measures.

§ 12. Duty of a Lawyer Subject to Supervision

(1) For purposes of professional discipline, a lawyer must conform to the requirements of an applicable lawyer code even if the lawyer acted at the direction of another lawyer or other person.

(2) For purposes of professional discipline, a lawyer under the direct supervisory authority of another lawyer does not violate an applicable lawyer code by acting in accordance with the supervisory lawyer's direction based on a reasonable resolution of an arguable question of professional duty.

TITLE D. RESTRICTIONS ON THE RIGHT TO PRACTICE LAW

§ 13. Restrictions on the Right to Practice Law

(1) A lawyer may not offer or enter into a law-firm agreement that restricts the right of the lawyer to practice law after terminating the relationship, except for a restriction incident to the lawyer's retirement from the practice of law.

(2) In settling a client claim, a lawyer may not offer or enter into an agreement that restricts the right of the lawyer to practice law, including the right to represent or take particular action on behalf of other clients.

CHAPTER 2. THE CLIENT-LAWYER RELATIONSHIP

TOPIC 1. CREATING A CLIENT-LAWYER RELATIONSHIP

§ 14. Formation of Client-Lawyer Relationship

A relationship of client and lawyer arises when:

(1) a person manifests to a lawyer the person's intent that the lawyer provide legal services for the person; and either

(a) the lawyer manifests to the person consent to do so; or

(b) the lawyer fails to manifest lack of consent to do so, and the lawyer knows or reasonably should know that the person reasonably relies on the lawyer to provide the services; or

(2) a tribunal with power to do so appoints the lawyer to provide the services.

§ 15. A Lawyer's Duties to a Prospective Client

(1) When a person discusses with a lawyer the possibility of their forming a client-lawyer relationship for a matter and no such relationship ensues, the lawyer must:

(a) not subsequently use or disclose confidential information learned in the consultation, except to the extent permitted with respect to confidential information of a client or former client as stated in §§ 61–67;

(b) protect the person's property in the lawyer's custody as stated in §§ 44–46; and

(c) use reasonable care to the extent the lawyer provides the person legal services.

(2) A lawyer subject to Subsection (1) may not represent a client whose interests are materially adverse to those of a former prospective client in the same or a substantially related matter when the lawyer or another lawyer whose disqualification is imputed to the lawyer under §§ 123 and 124 has received from the prospective client confidential information that could be significantly harmful to the prospective client in the matter, except that such a representation is permissible if:

(a)(i) any personally prohibited lawyer takes reasonable steps to avoid exposure to confidential information other than information appropriate to determine whether to represent the prospective client, and (ii) such lawyer is screened as stated in § 124(2)(b) and (c); or

(b) both the affected client and the prospective client give informed consent to the representation under the limitations and conditions provided in § 122.

Comment:

* * *

b. *Rationale.* Prospective clients are like clients in that they often disclose confidential information to a lawyer, place documents or other property in the lawyer's custody, and rely on the lawyer's advice. But a lawyer's discussions with a prospective client often are limited in time and depth of exploration, do not reflect full consideration of the prospective client's problems, and leave both prospective client and lawyer free (and sometimes required) to proceed no further. Hence, prospective clients should receive some but not all of the protection afforded clients, as indicated in the Section and following Comments.

c. *Confidential information of a prospective client.* It is often necessary for a prospective client to reveal and for the lawyer to learn confidential information (see § 59) during an initial consultation prior to their decision about formation of a client-lawyer relationship. For that reason, the attorney-client privilege attaches to communications of a prospective client (see § 70, Comment *c*). The lawyer must often learn such information to determine whether a conflict of interest exists with an existing client of the lawyer or the lawyer's firm and whether the matter is one that the lawyer is willing to undertake. In all instances, the lawyer must treat that information as confidential in the interest of the prospective client, even if the client or lawyer decides not to proceed with the representation (see Subsection (1)(a); see also § 60(2)). The duty exists regardless of how brief the initial conference may be and regardless of whether screening is instituted under Subsection (2)(a)(ii). The exceptions to the principles of confidentiality and privilege apply to such communications (see §§ 61–67).

Subsection (2) states rules parallel to those governing former-client conflicts under § 132, but it relaxes two analogous former-client rules. First, personal disqualification of a lawyer who deals with a prospective client occurs only when the subsequent matter presents the opportunity to use information obtained from the former prospective client that would be "significantly harmful." In contrast, § 132 applies whenever there is a "substantial risk" of adverse use of the former client's confidential information, regardless of the degree of threatened harm. Second, screening is permitted under Subsection (2)(a) so long as the lawyer takes reasonable steps to limit his or her exposure to confidential information during the initial consultation. In contrast, screening under § 124(2)(a) is permissible only when information obtained in the earlier representation would not likely be of significance in the subsequent representation.

In order to avoid acquiring disqualifying information, a lawyer considering whether or not to undertake a new matter may limit the initial interview to such confidential information as reasonably appears necessary for that purpose. Where that information indicates that a conflict of interest or other reasons for nonrepresentation exists, the lawyer should so inform the prospective client or simply decline the representation. If the prospective client still wishes to retain the lawyer, and if consent is possible under § 122(1), consent from any other affected present or former client should be obtained before further confidential information is elicited. The lawyer may also condition conversations with the prospective client on the person's consent to the lawyer's representation of other clients (see § 122, Comment *d*) or on the prospective client's agreement that any information disclosed during the consultation is not to be treated as confidential (see § 62). The prospective client's informed consent to such an agreement frees the lawyer to represent a client in a matter and to use in that matter, but only if the agreement so provides, confidential information received from the prospective client. A prospective client may also consent to a representation in other ways applicable to a client under § 122.

Even in the absence of such an agreement, when a consultation with a prospective client does not lead to a lawyer's retention the lawyer is not always prohibited from representing a client with interests adverse to those of the prospective client in the same or a substantially related matter. A prospective client's assurance of confidentiality through prophylactic prohibition as broad as that required in the case of a former client under § 132 must yield to a reasonable degree to the need of the legal system and to the interests of the lawyer and of other clients, including the need of a lawyer to obtain information needed to determine whether the lawyer may properly accept the representation without undue risk of prohibitions if no representation ensues. Thus, under Subsection (2), prohibition exists only when the lawyer has received from the prospective client information that could be significantly harmful to the prospective client in the matter. In such an instance and absent the prospective client's consent, the lawyer must withdraw from a substantially related representation commenced before the prospective client communicated with the lawyer and must not represent a client in such a matter in the future, including a client the lawyer ordinarily represents on a continuing basis.

When a tribunal is asked to disqualify a lawyer based on prior dealings with a former prospective client, that person bears the burden of persuading the tribunal that the lawyer received such information. The prohibition is imputed to other lawyers as provided in § 123, but may be avoided if all personally prohibited lawyers are screened as stated in § 124(2)(b) and (2)(c) (see Subsection (2)(a)). In that situation, screening avoids imputation even when the requirements of § 124(2)(a) have not been met. In deciding whether to exercise discretion to require disqualification, a tribunal may consider whether the prospective client disclosed confidential information to the lawyer for the purpose of preventing the lawyer or the lawyer's firm from representing an adverse party rather than in a good-faith endeavor to determine whether to retain the lawyer. The tribunal may also consider whether the disclosure of significantly harmful confidential information resulted from the failure of the lawyer or the prospective client to take precautions reasonable in the circumstances. In addition to screening, Subsection (2)(b) permits representation if both the former prospective client and any affected present client consent.

Illustrations:

1. Person makes an appointment with Lawyer to discuss obtaining a divorce from Person's Spouse. During the initial consultation, Lawyer makes no effort to limit the conversation or obtain any agreement on Person's part to nonconfidentiality. During the course of the one-hour discussion, Person discusses his reasons for seeking a divorce and the nature and extent of his and Spouse's property interests. Because Person considers Lawyer's suggested fee too high, Person retains other counsel. Thereafter, Spouse seeks Lawyer's assistance in defending against Person's divorce action. Lawyer may not accept the representation of Spouse. If Lawyer is screened as provided in§ 124(2)(b) and (c), Lawyer's disqualification is not imputed to other members of Lawyer's firm (see Subsection (2)(a)).

2. The President of Company A makes an appointment with Lawyer, who had not formerly had dealings with Company A. At the outset of the meeting, Lawyer informs President that it will first be necessary to obtain information about Company A and its affiliates and about the general nature of the legal matter to perform a conflicts check pursuant to procedures followed in Lawyer's firm. President supplies that information in a 15-minute meeting, including the information that the matter involves a contract dispute with Company B. The ensuing conflicts check reveals a conflict of interest with another Client of the firm (other than Company B), and Lawyer accordingly declines the representation. Lawyer and the other firm lawyers may continue representing Client (see Subsection (2)(a)).

3. Same facts as Illustration 2, except that Lawyer is later approached by Company B to represent it in its contract dispute with Company A. Both Lawyer and other firm lawyers may accept the representation unless Company A had disclosed to Lawyer confidential information that could be significantly harmful to Company A in the contract dispute. Even if such a disclosure had been made, if Lawyer is screened as provided in § 124(2)(b) and (c), Lawyer's disqualification is not imputed to other members of Lawyer's firm (see Subsection (2)(a)).

4. Same facts as Illustration 2, except that President wishes their first meeting both to discuss conflicts facts and to review Lawyer's preliminary thoughts on the merits of the contract dispute. Lawyer states willingness to do so only if Company A agrees that Lawyer would not be required to keep confidential information revealed during the preliminary discussion. President agrees, and the preliminary discussion ranges over several aspects of the dispute. Lawyer later declines the representation because of a conflict involving another firm client. Thereafter, Lawyer is approached by Company B to represent it in its contract dispute with Company A. Lawyer may accept the representation. Because of President's agreement, Lawyer is not required to keep confidential from Company B information learned during the initial consultation.

d. Protecting a prospective client's property. When prospective clients confide valuables or papers to a lawyer's care, the lawyer is under a duty to safeguard them in the same way as valuables or papers of any person that are in the lawyer's possession as the result of a professional relationship (see §§ 44–46). Ordinarily, if no client-lawyer relationship ensues, the lawyer must promptly return all material received from the prospective client.

e. A lawyer's duty of reasonable care to a prospective client. When a prospective client and a lawyer discuss the possibility of representation, the lawyer might comment on such matters as whether the person has a promising claim or defense, whether the lawyer is appropriate for the matter in question, whether conflicts of interest exist and if so how they might be dealt with, the time within which action must be taken and, if the representation does not proceed, what other lawyer might represent the prospective client. Prospective clients might rely on such advice, and lawyers therefore must use reasonable care in rendering it. The lawyer must also not harm a prospective client through unreasonable delay after indicating that the lawyer might undertake the representation. What care is reasonable depends on the circumstances, including the lawyer's expertise and the time available for consideration (see § 52).

If a lawyer provides advice that is intended to be only tentative or preliminary, the lawyer should so inform the prospective client. Depending on the circumstances, the burden of removing ambiguities rests with the lawyer, particularly as to disclaiming conclusions that the client reasonably assumed from their discussion, for example whether the client has a good claim.

f. Other duties to a prospective client. In addition to duties of confidentiality and care, the lawyer is subject to general law in dealing with a prospective client. The lawyer, for example, may not give the prospective client harmful advice calculated to benefit another client (see §§ 51(2) & 56).

g. Compensation of a lawyer for consultation with a prospective client. In the absence of circumstances indicating otherwise, prospective clients would ordinarily not expect to pay for preliminary discussions with a lawyer. When a client-lawyer relationship does not result, a lawyer is not entitled to be compensated unless that has been expressly agreed or it is otherwise clear from the circumstances that payment will be required.

TOPIC 2. SUMMARY OF THE DUTIES UNDER A CLIENT-LAWYER RELATIONSHIP

§ 16. A Lawyer's Duties to a Client—In General

To the extent consistent with the lawyer's other legal duties and subject to the other provisions of this Restatement, a lawyer must, in matters within the scope of the representation:

(1) proceed in a manner reasonably calculated to advance a client's lawful objectives, as defined by the client after consultation;

(2) act with reasonable competence and diligence;

(3) comply with obligations concerning the client's confidences and property, avoid impermissible conflicting interests, deal honestly with the client, and not employ advantages arising from the client-lawyer relationship in a manner adverse to the client; and

(4) fulfill valid contractual obligations to the client.

Comment:

* * *

b. Rationale. A lawyer is a fiduciary, that is, a person to whom another person's affairs are entrusted in circumstances that often make it difficult or undesirable for that other person to supervise closely the performance of the fiduciary. Assurances of the lawyer's competence, diligence, and loyalty are therefore vital. Lawyers often deal with matters most confidential and vital to the client. A lawyer's work is sometimes complex and technical, often is performed in the client's absence, and often cannot properly be evaluated simply by observing the results. Special safeguards are therefore necessary.

Correlatively, adequate representation is often essential to secure persons their legal rights. Persons are often unable either to know or to secure their rights without a lawyer's help. The law encourages clients to consult lawyers and limits the liability to third persons of lawyers who act vigorously for their clients (see

§§ 51 & 56). Requiring lawyers to protect their clients' interests with competence, diligence, and loyalty furthers those goals.

A lawyer is not required to accept a client, to undertake representation without pay (except when a court has appointed the lawyer), or to remain in a representation when withdrawal is permissible (see §§ 14, 32, 34, & 35). By undertaking a representation, a lawyer does not guarantee success in it, unless the lawyer makes extraordinary representations or warranties or unless the matter is routine and any reasonably competent lawyer could achieve the client's objectives (for example, drafting a deed or setting up a corporation). Lawyers may have duties to others that limit those owed to a client (see Comment *c* hereto).

c. *Goals of a representation.* The lawyer's efforts in a representation must be for the benefit of the client (see Restatement Second, Agency § 387). A client-lawyer relationship is thus different from a partnership entered into for mutual profit; the lawyer may hope to further the lawyer's professional reputation and income through a representation, but may do so only as a by-product of promoting the client's success.

Individual clients define their objectives differently. One litigant might seek the greatest possible personal recovery, another an amicable or speedy resolution of the case, and a third a precedent implementing the client's view of the public interest. The client, not the lawyer, determines the goals to be pursued, subject to the lawyer's duty not to do or assist an unlawful act (see § 94). The lawyer must keep the client informed and consult with the client as is reasonably appropriate to learn the client's decisions (see § 20) and must follow a client's instructions (see § 21(2)). On a lawyer's decisions in the representation, see §§ 22–24.

The lawyer's duties are ordinarily limited to matters covered by the representation. A lawyer who has agreed to write a contract is not required to litigate its validity, even though the client's general objectives may ultimately be aided by resort to litigation (see §§ 14 & 19). Ordinarily the lawyer may not act beyond the scope of contemplated representation without additional authorization from the client (see § 27, Comment *e*). Nevertheless, some of the lawyer's duties survive termination of the representation (see § 33).

The lawyer's legal duties to other persons also limit duties to the client. On the rules governing conflicts of interest, see Chapter 8. A lawyer owes duties to the court or legal system and to an opposing party in litigation (see Chapters 6 & 7) and may owe duties to certain nonclients who might be injured by the lawyer's acts (see § 51). Sometimes a client's duties to other persons, for example as a trustee or class representative, may impose on the lawyer similar consequential duties (see § 14, Comment *f*). A lawyer may not do or assist an unlawful act on behalf of a client (see §§ 23, 32, & 94). Circumstances also exist in which a lawyer may refrain from pursuing the client's goals through means that the lawyer considers lawful but repugnant (see § 23, Comment *c*; § 32).

d. *Duties of competence and diligence.* In pursuing a client's objectives, a lawyer must use reasonable care (see § 52; see also Restatement Second, Agency § 379). The lawyer must be competent to handle the matter, having the appropriate knowledge, skills, time, and professional qualifications. The lawyer must use those capacities diligently, not letting the matter languish but proceeding to perform the services called for by the client's objectives, including appropriate factual research, legal analysis, and exercise of professional judgment. On delay in litigated matters, see § 110. The law seeks to elicit competent and diligent representation through civil liability (see Chapter 4), disciplinary sanctions (see § 5), and such other means as educational and examination requirements for admission to the bar and programs of continued legal education and peer review. Other remedies may be available, such as a new trial in a criminal prosecution because of ineffective assistance of counsel (see § 6).

The Preamble to the ABA Model Rules of Professional Conduct (1983) (see id. § [2]) and EC 7–1 of the ABA Model Code of Professional Responsibility (1969) refer to a lawyer's duty to act "zealously" for a client. The term sets forth a traditional aspiration, but it should not be misunderstood to suggest that lawyers are legally required to function with a certain emotion or style of litigating, negotiating, or counseling. For legal purposes, the term encompasses the duties of competence and diligence.

e. *Duties of loyalty.* The responsibilities entailed in promoting the objectives of the client may be broadly classified as duties of loyalty, but their fulfillment also requires skill in gathering and analyzing information and acting appropriately. In general, they prohibit the lawyer from harming the client. Those duties are enforceable in appropriate circumstances by remedies, such as disqualification, to enforce rules governing conflicts of interest (see § 121, Comment *f*), civil liability (see §§ 50 & 55), and professional discipline (§ 5).

A lawyer may not use or disclose sensitive information about the client, except in appropriate circumstances (see Chapter 5). Likewise, the lawyer must take reasonable measures to safeguard the client's property and papers that come into the lawyer's possession (see §§ 44–46). The rules forbidding conflicts of interest (see Chapter 8) likewise protect against the abuse of client information.

A lawyer must be honest with a client. A lawyer may not obtain unfair contracts or gifts (see §§ 126 & 127) or enter a sexual relationship with a client when that would undermine the client's case, abuse the client's dependence on the lawyer, or create risk to the lawyer's independent judgment, for example when the lawyer represents the client in divorce proceedings (see also, e.g., § 41 (abusive fee-collection methods); see generally Restatement Second, Agency §§ 387–398). A lawyer may not knowingly make false statements to a client and must make disclosures to a client necessary to avoid misleading the client. However, a lawyer's duty of confidentiality to another client may prohibit some disclosures. On the general duty voluntarily to disclose facts to a client, see § 20.

The duties of loyalty are subject to exceptions described elsewhere in this Restatement. Those exceptions typically protect the concerns of third persons and the public or satisfy the practical necessities of the legal system.

f. *Duties defined by contract.* Contracts generally create or define the duties the lawyer owes the client (see Restatement Second, Agency § 376). One or more contracts between client and lawyer may specify the services the lawyer is being retained to provide, the services the lawyer is not obliged to provide, and the goals of the representation. They may address such matters as which lawyers in a law firm will provide the services; what reports are to be provided to the client; whether the lawyer will present a detailed budget for the representation; what arrangements will be made for billing statements for legal services and disbursements; what decisions will be made by the lawyer and what matters decided by the client; and what alternative-dispute-resolution methods the lawyer will explore. Such matters may also be handled by client instructions during the representation (see Topic 3). Various requirements govern client-lawyer contracts (e.g., §§ 18, 19, 22–23, 34–46, 121, & 126–127). A lawyer's intentional failure to fulfill a valid contract may in appropriate circumstances subject the lawyer to professional discipline as well as to contractual remedies.

With respect to contracts between lawyer and client involving business other than fees and disbursements for professional services, see § 126.

§ 17. A Client's Duty to a Lawyer

Subject to the other provisions of this Restatement, in matters covered by the representation a client must:

(1) compensate a lawyer for services and expenses as stated in Chapter 3;

(2) indemnify the lawyer for liability to which the client has exposed the lawyer without the lawyer's fault; and

(3) fulfill any valid contractual obligations to the lawyer.

§ 18. Client-Lawyer Contracts

(1) A contract between a lawyer and client concerning the client-lawyer relationship, including a contract modifying an existing contract, may be enforced by either party if the contract meets other applicable requirements, except that:

(a) if the contract or modification is made beyond a reasonable time after the lawyer has begun to represent the client in the matter (see § 38(1)), the client may avoid it unless the lawyer shows that the contract and the circumstances of its formation were fair and reasonable to the client; and

(b) if the contract is made after the lawyer has finished providing services, the client may avoid it if the client was not informed of facts needed to evaluate the

appropriateness of the lawyer's compensation or other benefits conferred on the lawyer by the contract.

(2) A tribunal should construe a contract between client and lawyer as a reasonable person in the circumstances of the client would have construed it.

§ 19. Agreements Limiting Client or Lawyer Duties

(1) Subject to other requirements stated in this Restatement, a client and lawyer may agree to limit a duty that a lawyer would otherwise owe to the client if:

(a) the client is adequately informed and consents; and

(b) the terms of the limitation are reasonable in the circumstances.

(2) A lawyer may agree to waive a client's duty to pay or other duty owed to the lawyer.

Comment:

* * *

b. *Rationale.* Restrictions on the power of a client to redefine a lawyer's duties are classified as paternalism by some and as necessary protection by others. On the one hand, for some clients the costs of more extensive services may outweigh their benefits. A client might reasonably choose to forgo some of the protection against conflicts of interest, for example, in order to get the help of an especially able or inexpensive lawyer or a lawyer already familiar to the client. The scope of a representation may properly change during a representation, and the lawyer may sometimes be obligated to bring changes of scope to a client's notice (see § 20). In some instances, such as an emergency, a restricted representation may be the only practical way to provide legal services (see Comments *c* and *d* hereto).

On the other hand, there are strong reasons for protecting those who entrust vital concerns and confidential information to lawyers (see § 16, Comment *b*). Clients inexperienced in such limitations may well have difficulty understanding important implications of limiting a lawyer's duty. Not every lawyer who will benefit from the limitation can be trusted to explain its costs and benefits fairly. Also, any attempt to assess the basis of a client's consent could force disclosure of the client's confidences. In the long run, moreover, a restriction could become a standard practice that constricts the rights of clients without compensating benefits. The administration of justice may suffer from distrust of the legal system that may result from such a practice. Those reasons support special scrutiny of noncustomary contracts limiting a lawyer's duties, particularly when the lawyer requests the limitation.

c. *Limiting a representation.* Clients and lawyers may define in reasonable ways the services a lawyer is to provide (see § 16), for example to handle a trial but not any appeal, counsel a client on the tax aspects of a transaction but not other aspects, or advise a client about a representation in which the primary role has been entrusted to another lawyer. Such arrangements are not waivers of a client's right to more extensive services but a definition of the services to be performed. They are therefore treated separately under many lawyer codes as contracts limiting the objectives of the representation. Clients ordinarily understand the implications and possible costs of such arrangements. The scope of many such representations requires no explanation or disclaimer of broader involvement.

Some contracts limiting the scope or objectives of a representation may harm the client, for example if a lawyer insists on agreement that a proposed suit will not include a substantial claim that reasonably should be joined. Section 19(1) hence qualifies the power of client and lawyer to limit the representation. Taken together with requirements stated in other Sections, five safeguards apply.

First, a client must be informed of any significant problems a limitation might entail, and the client must consent (see § 19(1)(a)). For example, if the lawyer is to provide only tax advice, the client must be aware that the transaction may pose non-tax issues as well as being informed of any disadvantages involved in dividing the representation among several lawyers (see also §§ 15 & 20).

Second, any contract limiting the representation is construed from the standpoint of a reasonable client (see § 18(2)).

Third, the fee charged by the lawyer must remain reasonable in view of the limited representation (see § 34).

Fourth, any change made an unreasonably long time after the representation begins must meet the more stringent tests of § 18(1) for postinception contracts or modifications.

Fifth, the terms of the limitation must in all events be reasonable in the circumstances (§ 19(1)(b)). When the client is sophisticated in such waivers, informed consent ordinarily permits the inference that the waiver is reasonable. For other clients, the requirement is met if, in addition to informed consent, the benefits supposedly obtained by the waiver—typically, a reduced legal fee or the ability to retain a particularly able lawyer—could reasonably be considered to outweigh the potential risk posed by the limitation. It is also relevant whether there were special circumstances warranting the limitation and whether it was the client or the lawyer who sought it. Also relevant is the choice available to clients; for example, if most local lawyers, but not lawyers in other communities, insist on the same limitation, client acceptance of the limitation is subject to special scrutiny.

The extent to which alternatives are constrained by circumstances might bear on reasonableness. For example, a client who seeks assistance on a matter on which the statute of limitations is about to run would not reasonably expect extensive investigation and research before the case must be filed. A lawyer may be asked to assist a client concerning an unfamiliar area because other counsel are unavailable. If the lawyer knows or should know that the lawyer lacks competence necessary for the representation, the lawyer must limit assistance to that which the lawyer believes reasonably necessary to deal with the situation.

Reasonableness also requires that limits on a lawyer's work agreed to by client and lawyer not infringe on legal rights of third persons or legal institutions. Hence, a contract limiting a lawyer's role during trial may require the tribunal's approval.

Illustrations:

1. Corporation wishes to hire Law Firm to litigate a substantial suit, proposing a litigation budget. Law Firm explains to Corporation's inside legal counsel that it can litigate the case within that budget but only by conducting limited discovery, which could materially lessen the likelihood of success. Corporation may waive its right to more thorough representation. Corporation will benefit by gaining representation by counsel of its choice at limited expense and could readily have bargained for more thorough and expensive representation.

2. A legal clinic offers for a small fee to have one of its lawyers (a tax specialist) conduct a half-hour review of a client's income-tax return, telling the client of the dangers or opportunities that the review reveals. The tax lawyer makes clear at the outset that the review may fail to find important tax matters and that clients can have a more complete consideration of their returns only if they arrange for a second appointment and agree to pay more. The arrangement is reasonable and permissible. The clients' consent is free and adequately informed, and clients gain the benefit of an inexpensive but expert tax review of a matter that otherwise might well receive no expert review at all.

3. Lawyer offers to provide tax-law advice for an hourly fee lower than most tax lawyers charge. Lawyer has little knowledge of tax law and asks Lawyer's occasional tax clients to agree to waive the requirement of reasonable competence. Such a waiver is invalid, even if clients benefit to some extent from the low price and consent freely and on the basis of adequate information. Moreover, allowing such general waivers would seriously undermine competence requirements essential for protection of the public, with little compensating gain. On prohibitions against limitations of a lawyer's liability, see § 54.

* * *

TOPIC 3. AUTHORITY TO MAKE DECISIONS

§ 20. A Lawyer's Duty to Inform and Consult with a Client

(1) A lawyer must keep a client reasonably informed about the matter and must consult with a client to a reasonable extent concerning decisions to be made by the lawyer under §§ 21–23.

(2) A lawyer must promptly comply with a client's reasonable requests for information.

(3) A lawyer must notify a client of decisions to be made by the client under §§ 21–23 and must explain a matter to the extent reasonably necessary to permit the client to make informed decisions regarding the representation.

§ 21. Allocating the Authority to Decide Between a Client and a Lawyer

As between client and lawyer:

(1) A client and lawyer may agree which of them will make specified decisions, subject to the requirements stated in §§ 18, 19, 22, 23, and other provisions of this Restatement. The agreement may be superseded by another valid agreement.

(2) A client may instruct a lawyer during the representation, subject to the requirements stated in §§ 22, 23, and other provisions of this Restatement.

(3) Subject to Subsections (1) and (2) a lawyer may take any lawful measure within the scope of representation that is reasonably calculated to advance a client's objectives as defined by the client, consulting with the client as required by § 20.

(4) A client may ratify an act of a lawyer that was not previously authorized.

§ 22. Authority Reserved to a Client

(1) As between client and lawyer, subject to Subsection (2) and § 23, the following and comparable decisions are reserved to the client except when the client has validly authorized the lawyer to make the particular decision: whether and on what terms to settle a claim; how a criminal defendant should plead; whether a criminal defendant should waive jury trial; whether a criminal defendant should testify; and whether to appeal in a civil proceeding or criminal prosecution.

(2) A client may not validly authorize a lawyer to make the decisions described in Subsection (1) when other law (such as criminal-procedure rules governing pleas, jury-trial waiver, and defendant testimony) requires the client's personal participation or approval.

(3) Regardless of any contrary contract with a lawyer, a client may revoke a lawyer's authority to make the decisions described in Subsection (1).

§ 23. Authority Reserved to a Lawyer

As between client and lawyer, a lawyer retains authority that may not be overridden by a contract with or an instruction from the client:

(1) to refuse to perform, counsel, or assist future or ongoing acts in the representation that the lawyer reasonably believes to be unlawful;

(2) to make decisions or take actions in the representation that the lawyer reasonably believes to be required by law or an order of a tribunal.

§ 24. A Client with Diminished Capacity

(1) When a client's capacity to make adequately considered decisions in connection with the representation is diminished, whether because of minority, physical illness, mental disability, or other cause, the lawyer must, as far as reasonably possible, maintain a normal client-lawyer relationship with the client and act in the best interests of the client as stated in Subsection (2).

(2) A lawyer representing a client with diminished capacity as described in Subsection (1) and for whom no guardian or other representative is available to act, must,

with respect to a matter within the scope of the representation, pursue the lawyer's reasonable view of the client's objectives or interests as the client would define them if able to make adequately considered decisions on the matter, even if the client expresses no wishes or gives contrary instructions.

(3) If a client with diminished capacity as described in Subsection (1) has a guardian or other person legally entitled to act for the client, the client's lawyer must treat that person as entitled to act with respect to the client's interests in the matter, unless:

(a) the lawyer represents the client in a matter against the interests of that person; or

(b) that person instructs the lawyer to act in a manner that the lawyer knows will violate the person's legal duties toward the client.

(4) A lawyer representing a client with diminished capacity as described in Subsection (1) may seek the appointment of a guardian or take other protective action within the scope of the representation when doing so is practical and will advance the client's objectives or interests, determined as stated in Subsection (2).

Comment:

* * *

b. Rationale. An unimpaired client can define the client's own objectives (see § 19), confer with counsel (see § 20), and make important decisions (see §§ 21 & 22). To the extent a client is incapable of doing so and no other person is empowered to make such decisions, the lawyer's role in making decisions will increase. An alternative is to appoint a guardian for the client, but that may be expensive, not feasible under the circumstances, and embarrassing for the client. In some cases, different views about the client's welfare may be presented by opposing counsel for a tribunal's decision. This Section recognizes that a lawyer must often exercise an informed professional judgment in choosing among those imperfect alternatives. Accordingly, each Subsection applies based on the reasonable belief of the lawyer at the time the lawyer acts on behalf of a client described in Subsection (1).

c. Maintaining a normal client-lawyer relationship so far as possible. Disabilities in making decisions vary from mild to totally incapacitating; they may impair a client's ability to decide matters generally or only with respect to some decisions at some times; and they may be caused by childhood, old age, physical illness, retardation, chemical dependency, mental illness, or other factors. Clients should not be unnecessarily deprived of their right to control their own affairs on account of such disabilities. Lawyers, moreover, should be careful not to construe as proof of disability a client's insistence on a view of the client's welfare that a lawyer considers unwise or otherwise at variance with the lawyer's own views.

When a client with diminished capacity is capable of understanding and communicating, the lawyer should maintain the flow of information and consultation as much as circumstances allow (see § 20). The lawyer should take reasonable steps to elicit the client's own views on decisions necessary to the representation. Sometimes the use of a relative, therapist, or other intermediary may facilitate communication (see §§ 70 & 71). Even when the lawyer is empowered to make decisions for the client (see Comment *d*), the lawyer should, if practical, communicate the proposed decision to the client so that the client will have a chance to comment, remonstrate, or seek help elsewhere. A lawyer may properly withhold from a disabled client information that would harm the client, for example when showing a psychiatric report to a mentally-ill client would be likely to cause the client to attempt suicide, harm another person, or otherwise act unlawfully (see § 20, Comment *b*, & § 46, Comment *c*).

A lawyer for a client with diminished capacity may be retained by a parent, spouse, or other relative of the client. Even when that person is not also a co-client, the lawyer may provide confidential client information to the person to the extent appropriate in providing representation to the client (see § 61). If the disclosure is to be made to a nonclient and there is a significant risk that the information may be used adversely to the client, the lawyer should consult with the client concerning such disclosure.

A client with diminished capacity is entitled to make decisions normally made by clients to the extent that the client is able to do so. The lawyer should adhere, to the extent reasonably possible, to the lawyer's usual function as advocate and agent of the client, not judge or guardian, unless the lawyer's role in the situation is modified by other law. The lawyer should, for example, help the client oppose confinement as a juvenile delinquent even though the lawyer believes that confinement would be in the long-term interests of the client and has unsuccessfully urged the client to accept confinement. Advancing the latter position should be left to opposing counsel.

If a client with diminished capacity owes fiduciary duties to others, the lawyer should be careful to avoid assisting in a violation of those duties (cf. § 51(4)).

d. Deciding for a client with diminished capacity. When a client's disability prevents maintaining a normal client-lawyer relationship and there is no guardian or other legal representative to make decisions for the client, the lawyer may be justified in making decisions with respect to questions within the scope of the representation that would normally be made by the client. A lawyer should act only on a reasonable belief, based on appropriate investigation, that the client is unable to make an adequately considered decision rather than simply being confused or misguided. Because a disability might vary from time to time, the lawyer must reasonably believe that the client is unable to make an adequately considered decision without prejudicial delay.

A lawyer's reasonable belief depends on the circumstances known to the lawyer and discoverable by reasonable investigation. Where practicable and reasonably available, independent professional evaluation of the client's capacity may be sought. If a conflict of interest between client and lawyer is involved (see § 125), disinterested evaluation by another lawyer may be appropriate. Careful consideration is required of the client's circumstances, problems, needs, character, and values, including interests of the client beyond the matter in which the lawyer represents the client. If the client, when able to decide, had expressed views relevant to the decision, the lawyer should follow them unless there is reason to believe that changed circumstances would change those views. The lawyer should also give appropriate weight to the client's presently expressed views.

A lawyer may bring the client's diminished capacity before a tribunal when doing so is reasonably calculated to advance the client's objectives or interests as the client would define them if able to do so rationally. A proceeding seeking appointment of a guardian for the client is one example (see Comment *e*). A lawyer may also raise the issue of the client's incompetence to stand trial in a criminal prosecution or, when a client is incompetent to stand trial, interpose the insanity defense. In such situations, the court and the adversary process provide some check on the lawyer's decision.

In some jurisdictions, if a criminal defendant's competence to stand trial is reasonably arguable, the defendant's lawyer must bring the issue to the court's attention, whether or not the lawyer reasonably believes this to be for the client's benefit. That should not be considered a duty to the client flowing from the representation and is not provided for by this Section.

A lawyer must also make necessary decisions for an incompetent client when it is impractical or undesirable to have a guardian appointed or to take other similar protective measures. For example, when a court appoints a lawyer to represent a young child, it may consider the lawyer to be in effect the child's guardian ad litem. When a client already has a guardian but retains counsel to proceed against that guardian, a court often will not appoint a second guardian to make litigation decisions for the client. Other situations exist in which appointment of a guardian would be too expensive, traumatic, or otherwise undesirable or impractical in the circumstances.

It is often difficult to decide whether the conditions of this Section have been met. A lawyer who acts reasonably and in good faith in perplexing circumstances is not subject to professional discipline or malpractice or similar liability (see Chapter 4). In some situations (for example, when a lawyer discloses a client's diminished capacity to a tribunal against a client's wishes), the lawyer might be required to attempt to withdraw as counsel if the disclosure causes the client effectively to discharge the lawyer (see § 32(2)(c)).

e. Seeking appointment of a guardian. When a client's diminished capacity is severe and no other practical method of protecting the client's best interests is available, a lawyer may petition an appointment of a guardian or other representative to make decisions for the client. A general or limited power of attorney may sometimes be used to avoid the expense and possible embarrassment of a guardianship.

The client might instruct the lawyer to seek appointment of a guardian or take other protective measures. On the use of confidential client information in a guardianship proceeding, see § 61 and § 69, Comment *f*.

A lawyer is not required to seek a guardian for a client whenever the conditions of Subsection (4) are satisfied. For example, it may be clear that the courts will not appoint a guardian or that doing so is not in the client's best interests (see § 16 & Comment *d* hereto).

f. Representing a client for whom a guardian or similar person may act. When a guardian has been appointed, the guardian normally speaks for the client as to matters covered by the guardianship. (When under the law of the jurisdiction a client's power of attorney remains in effect during a disability, the appointee has such authority.) The lawyer therefore should normally follow the decisions of the guardian as if they were those of the client. That principle does not apply when the lawyer is representing the client in proceedings against the guardian, for example, in an attempt to have the guardianship terminated or its terms altered. The law sometimes authorizes the client to bypass a guardian—for example, when a mature minor seeks a court order authorizing her to have an abortion without having to disclose her pregnancy to her parents or guardians. The lawyer may also believe that the guardian is violating fiduciary duties owed to the client and may then seek relief setting aside the guardian's decision or replacing the guardian (see also § 51(4)). If the lawyer believes the guardian to be acting lawfully but inconsistently with the best interests of the client, the lawyer may remonstrate with the guardian or withdraw under § 32(3)(d) (see § 23, Comment *c*).

When a guardian retains a lawyer to represent the guardian, the guardian is the client.

TOPIC 4. A LAWYER'S AUTHORITY TO ACT FOR A CLIENT

§ 25. Appearance Before a Tribunal

A lawyer who enters an appearance before a tribunal on behalf of a person is presumed to represent that person as a client. The presumption may be rebutted.

§ 26. A Lawyer's Actual Authority

A lawyer's act is considered to be that of a client in proceedings before a tribunal or in dealings with third persons when:

(1) the client has expressly or impliedly authorized the act;

(2) authority concerning the act is reserved to the lawyer as stated in § 23; or

(3) the client ratifies the act.

Comment:

a. Scope, cross-references, and terminology. In general, a client is bound by a lawyer's acts in dealings with third persons discussed in this Section or, under § 27, by giving the lawyer an appearance of authority. For situations in which a client may avoid responsibility for authorized acts because of a lawyer's misconduct, see § 29. The word "act" includes failures to act, for example when a lawyer does not object to something done in court.

Although the forms of client approval set forth in this Section might be described as instances of actual authority, agency law has often used finer distinctions. Specific authorization, for example to sell an automobile to a stated person for a stated price, is sometimes called express authority, as opposed to implied authority arising out of a more general delegation of power to act (see Restatement Second, Agency § 7, Comment *c*). An authorization required by law, regardless of the wishes of the principal, is sometimes called inherent authority (see Restatement Second Agency, § 8A); the authority of a lawyer stated in § 26(2) may be so classified. A principal's approval following an agent's act, as provided in § 26(3), is referred to in agency law as ratification (see Restatement Second, Agency § 82). Those terminological matters and other aspects of the authority of an agent are set forth in Restatement Second, Agency, Chapters 1, 3, and 4.

On waiver of the attorney-client privilege by a client who disclaims a lawyer's authority, see § 80(1)(b).

b. Rationale. Legal representation saves the client's time and effort and enables legal work to be delegated to an expert. Lawyers therefore are recognized as agents for their clients in litigation and other legal matters. Indeed, courts commonly will not allow a corporation to participate in litigation through an agent other than a lawyer.

Allowing clients to act through lawyers also subjects clients to obligations and disabilities. With respect to the rights of a third person, the client is bound when a case is lost or a negotiation handled disadvantageously by a lawyer. Attributing the acts of lawyers to their clients is warranted by the fact that, in an important sense, they really are acts authorized by the principal. Much serious activity in business and personal affairs is done through lawyers. The same considerations apply, with qualifications, in holding the client liable for certain wrongs committed by the lawyer (see Comment *d* hereto).

Binding clients to the acts of their lawyers can be unfair in some circumstances. A client might have authorized a lawyer's conduct only in general terms, without contemplating the particular acts that lead to liability. However, it has been regarded as more appropriate for costs flowing from a lawyer's misconduct generally to be borne by the client rather than by an innocent third person. Where the lawyer rather than the client is directly to blame, the client may be able to recover any losses by suing the lawyer, a right not generally accorded to nonclients (see Chapter 4). In practice, however, clients are sometimes unable to control their lawyer's conduct and accordingly may sometimes be excused from the consequences of their lawyer's behavior when that can be done without seriously harming others (see § 29).

c. Forms of client authorization. A client has authorized the act within the meaning of this Section in the circumstances described in §§ 21 and 23. A person dealing with the lawyer might require the lawyer to provide express authority from the lawyer's client. Courts likewise may require such authority, for example ordering a lawyer attending a pretrial conference either to secure settlement authority or to bring the client to the conference.

d. Effects of attributing authorized acts to a client. When a lawyer's act is attributed to a client various legal consequences might follow for the client. If the act consisted of assenting to a contract, the client is bound by the contract (see Restatement Second, Agency, Chapter 6). If the lawyer was authorized to bring or defend a lawsuit, the client is bound by the result. Likewise, the client is bound by authorized lawyer action or inaction during litigation, for example when the lawyer asks a question that elicits an answer harmful to the client or files a frivolous motion.

When a lawyer's act is wrongful and causes injury to a third person, the client as principal is liable as provided by agency law (see Restatement Second, Agency, Chapter 7; see also § 27, Comment *e*).

Illustrations:

1. Seller authorizes Lawyer to negotiate the sale of Seller's factory to Buyer. Lawyer states to Buyer that the factory's foundations are in good condition, knowing that they are not. Because making representations about the factory was within the scope of authority for one authorized to negotiate, Seller is liable to Buyer for misrepresentation and can be required to rescind the sale if the other conditions for rescission have been satisfied. That is so even if Seller did not know about Lawyer's statements or the condition of the foundations (see Restatement Second, Agency §§ 257–259).

2. Same facts as in Illustration 1, except that Lawyer negligently collides with Buyer's automobile while arriving for a negotiating session. Client is not liable to Buyer, unless Lawyer was Seller's employee (for example, because Seller is a corporation and Lawyer is its inside legal counsel) (see Restatement Second, Agency §§ 250 & 251).

A lawyer's conduct may be attributed to a client to determine the client's criminal responsibility. Attribution depends on the criminal law. A client who asks a lawyer to perform a criminal act or assists in its performance is guilty of the lawyer's act as an accomplice (see Model Penal Code § 2.06). A client would be liable as a co-conspirator for crimes committed by a lawyer in pursuit of a criminal conspiracy in which both were engaged. In general, however, criminal liability for another's act is significantly more limited than civil liability.

This Section deals only with the effect of a lawyer's authorized acts on the client, not with their effects on the lawyer. Whether the lawyer can be held liable for contract breaches, torts, and sanctionable litigation behavior is considered in § 30.

e. Ratification by a client. A client may later ratify a lawyer's act for which the lawyer lacked actual authority when it occurred. A client who has ratified a lawyer's act is bound by it. For more detailed consideration, see § 21, Comment *f*, and Restatement Second, Agency, Chapter 4.

§ 27. A Lawyer's Apparent Authority

A lawyer's act is considered to be that of the client in proceedings before a tribunal or in dealings with a third person if the tribunal or third person reasonably assumes that the lawyer is authorized to do the act on the basis of the client's (and not the lawyer's) manifestations of such authorization.

Comment:

a. Scope and cross-references. This Section addresses apparent authority. The concept is employed in this Restatement as defined in Restatement Second, Agency § 8. Because lawyers ordinarily have broad actual authority (see §§ 21 & 23), simply retaining a lawyer confers broad apparent authority on the lawyer unless other facts apparent to the third person show that the lawyer's authority is narrower (see Comment *c*). Such authority arising from the act of retention alone does not extend to matters, such as approving a settlement, reserved for client decision (see § 22). To create apparent authority in such matters, the client must do more than simply retain the lawyer (see Comment *d*). For the effect of a lawyer's discharge or withdrawal on apparent authority, see § 31(3) and Comments *c* and *i* thereto.

b. Rationale. Under the law of agency, a client is bound by the lawyer's act or failure to act when the client has vested the lawyer with apparent authority—an appearance of authority arising from and in accordance with the client's manifestations to third persons (see Restatement Second, Agency § 8). Apparent authority can be identical to, greater, or less than a lawyer's actual authority (see id. Comment *a*). The concepts of actual and apparent authority often lead to similar results. The same acts or statements of a client that confer actual authority can serve to manifest authority to a third person and vice versa. Apparent authority extends beyond actual authority in a lawyer's transactions with third persons when the client has limited the lawyer's actual authority but the limitation has not been disclosed to that person and, instead, the client has manifested to the third person that the lawyer has authority to act in the matter.

Apparent authority exists when and to the extent a client causes a third person to form a reasonable belief that a lawyer is authorized to act for the client. Permitting disavowal would allow clients at their convenience to ratify or disavow their lawyer's acts despite the client's inconsistent manifestation of the lawyer's authority. It would also impose on the third person the burden of proving a fact better known to the client. A client usually can make clear to third persons the limited scope of a lawyer's authority or take care to act in ways that do not manifest authority that the client does not intend.

Recognizing a lawyer as agent creates a risk that a client will be bound by an act the client never intended to authorize. Several safeguards are therefore included in the apparent-authority principle. First, the client must in fact have retained the lawyer or given the third party reason to believe that the client has done so. Second, the client's own acts (including the act of retaining the lawyer) must have warranted a reasonable observer in believing that the client authorized the lawyer to act. Third, the third person must in fact have such a belief. The test thus includes both an objective and a subjective element (see Restatement Second, Agency § 27). In some circumstances courts will take into account the lawyer's lack of actual authority in deciding whether to vacate a default (see § 29). If the client suffers detriment from a lawyer's act performed with apparent but not actual authority, the client can recover from the lawyer for acting beyond the scope of the lawyer's authority (see Comment *f* hereto & § 30; Restatement Second, Agency § 383).

c. Apparent authority created by retention of a lawyer. By retaining a lawyer, a client implies that the lawyer is authorized to act for the client in matters relating to the representation and reasonably appropriate in the circumstances to carry it out. Circumstances known to the third person can narrow the scope of apparent authority thus conferred, for example statements by the client or lawyer that the lawyer is to handle only specified matters (see § 21(2) & Comment *d* thereto). The client can also enlarge the lawyer's apparent authority, for example by acquiescing, to the outsider's knowledge, in the lawyer's taking certain action. In the absence of such variations, a lawyer has apparent authority to do acts that reasonably appear to be calculated to advance the client's objectives in the representation, except for matters reserved to the client under § 22. (For apparent authority with respect to matters reserved to the client, see Comment *d* hereto.)

When a lawyer's apparent authority is in question, what reasonably appears calculated to advance the client's objectives must be determined from the third person's viewpoint. The third person's belief in the lawyer's authority must be reasonable. The same standard applies in a proceeding before a tribunal. However, because of the lawyer's broad actual authority in litigation (see §§ 21 & 23), it will often be unnecessary to conduct a factual inquiry into whether a lawyer had apparent authority in the eyes of either the opposing party or the tribunal.

Illustrations:

1. At Judge's suggestion, Lawyer agrees that both parties to a civil action will waive further discovery and that the trial will begin the next week. Judge does not know, but opposing counsel does, that Lawyer's Client (which has many similar cases) instructs its lawyers in writing not to bring cases to trial without specified discovery, some of which Lawyer has not yet accomplished. Although Lawyer lacked actual authority to waive discovery, Lawyer had apparent authority from Judge's reasonable point of view, and Judge may hold Client to the trial date. Client's remedies are to seek discretionary release from the waiver (see § 29) and to seek to recover any damages from Lawyer for acting beyond authority (see Comment f hereto & § 30).

2. At a pretrial conference in a medical-malpractice case, Lawyer agrees with opposing counsel that neither party will call more than one expert witness at the trial. Opposing counsel is not aware that Lawyer's client (which has many similar cases) instructs its lawyers to present expert testimony from at least two witnesses in every medical-malpractice case involving more than a certain amount in claimed damages. Judge knows of the client's practice but does not inform opposing counsel. The opposing party can hold Lawyer's client to the contract, which Lawyer had apparent authority to make, unless the court releases the parties from the contract (see § 29).

d. *Lawyer's apparent authority to settle and perform other acts reserved to a client.* Generally a client is not bound by a settlement that the client has not authorized a lawyer to make by express, implied, or apparent authority (and that is not validated by later ratification under § 26(3)). Merely retaining a lawyer does not create apparent authority in the lawyer to perform acts governed by § 22. When a lawyer purports to enter a settlement binding on the client but lacks authority to do so, the burden of inconvenience resulting if the client repudiates the settlement is properly left with the opposing party, who should know that settlements are normally subject to approval by the client and who has no manifested contrary indication from the client. The opposing party can protect itself by obtaining clarification of the lawyer's authority. Refusing to uphold a settlement reached without the client's authority means that the case remains open, while upholding such a settlement deprives the client of the right to have the claim resolved on other terms.

Illustrations:

3. Lawyer represents Client in a civil action in which the court orders counsel either to appear at a pretrial conference with authority to settle the case or to arrange for the presence of a person so authorized. Client has not been informed of the order and has not authorized Lawyer to approve a settlement. Lawyer, without disclosing that lack of authority, attends the conference and agrees to a settlement. Client is not bound by the settlement. Lawyer can be subject to disciplinary sanctions, including contempt of court, and liability for damages or sanctions to the opposing party.

4. The same facts as in Illustration 3, except that the opposing party observes that Client is in the courtroom and hears the court's order but leaves as the settlement conference begins without further comment to the court or opposing party. Client's acts create apparent authority in Lawyer to enter the settlement on Client's behalf, and Client is bound by the settlement agreed to by Lawyer.

e. *Effects of attributing to clients acts performed with apparent authority.* A client is liable in tort to a third person when apparent authority manifested by the client aids a lawyer to perform a tortious act injurious to the third person. A client is liable, for example, for misrepresentations and defamatory statements made by a lawyer with apparent authority to make the statements in representing the client (see Restatement Second, Agency § 265, compare § 57(1) (immunity for defamatory statements in the course of litigation)). The lawyer of the client is not considered an employee (servant) of the client unless employed full-or part-time as such an employee (see generally Restatement Second, Agency § 2(2)). The client is therefore not liable for tortious acts committed while the lawyer is acting within the scope of employment but outside the lawyer's actual or apparent authority (see § 26, Comment *d*).

The concept of apparent authority is of little utility in assessing criminal liability of the client. A client who manifested to third persons the lawyer's authority to act for the client might be convicted as an accessory, but only if the client knowingly advanced the criminal enterprise. Similar requirements apply for a client to be convicted as a co-conspirator in crimes committed by a lawyer (see § 26, Comment *d*).

f. *Recovery against a lawyer.* When a client is bound by an act of a lawyer with apparent but not actual authority, a lawyer is subject to liability to the client for any resulting damages to the client, unless the lawyer reasonably believed that the act was authorized by the client (see Restatement Second, Agency § 383, §§ 16, 21, & 22 hereto). The lawyer can also be subject to professional discipline (see § 5) or procedural sanctions (see § 110) for harming the interests of a client through action taken without the client's consent.

If a lawyer's act does not bind the client, the lawyer can be subject to liability to a third person who dealt with the lawyer in good faith. Liability can be based on implied warranty of actual authority or on misrepresentation of the lawyer's authority (see § 30; Restatement Second, Agency §§ 329 & 330). The lawyer is also subject to liability for damages to the client, for example the client's expenses of having the act declared not to be binding (see § 53, Comment *f* (client's recovery of legal fees in such an instance)).

§ 28. A Lawyer's Knowledge; Notification to a Lawyer; and Statements of a Lawyer

(1) Information imparted to a lawyer during and relating to the representation of a client is attributed to the client for the purpose of determining the client's rights and liabilities in matters in which the lawyer represents the client, unless those rights or liabilities require proof of the client's personal knowledge or intentions or the lawyer's legal duties preclude disclosure of the information to the client.

(2) Unless applicable law otherwise provides, a third person may give notification to a client, in a matter in which the client is represented by a lawyer, by giving notification to the client's lawyer, unless the third person knows of circumstances reasonably indicating that the lawyer's authority to receive notification has been abrogated.

(3) A lawyer's unprivileged statement is admissible in evidence against a client as if it were the client's statement if either:

(a) the client authorized the lawyer to make a statement concerning the subject; or

(b) the statement concerns a matter within the scope of the representation and was made by the lawyer during it.

§ 29. A Lawyer's Act or Advice as Mitigating or Avoiding a Client's Responsibility

(1) When a client's intent or mental state is in issue, a tribunal may consider otherwise admissible evidence of a lawyer's advice to the client.

(2) In deciding whether to impose a sanction on a person or to relieve a person from a criminal or civil ruling, default, or judgment, a tribunal may consider otherwise admissible evidence to prove or disprove that the lawyer who represented the person did so inadequately or contrary to the client's instructions.

§ 30. A Lawyer's Liability to a Third Person for Conduct on Behalf of a Client

(1) For improper conduct while representing a client, a lawyer is subject to professional discipline as stated in § 5, to civil liability as stated in Chapter 4, and to prosecution as provided in the criminal law (see § 7).

(2) Unless at the time of contracting the lawyer or third person disclaimed such liability, a lawyer is subject to liability to third persons on contracts the lawyer entered into on behalf of a client if:

(a) the client's existence or identity was not disclosed to the third person; or

(b) the contract is between the lawyer and a third person who provides goods or services used by lawyers and who, as the lawyer knows or reasonably should know, relies on the lawyer's credit.

(3) A lawyer is subject to liability to a third person for damages for loss proximately caused by the lawyer's acting without authority from a client under § 26 if:

(a) the lawyer tortiously misrepresents to the third person that the lawyer has authority to make a contract, conveyance, or affirmation on behalf of the client and the third person reasonably relies on the misrepresentation; or

(b) the lawyer purports to make a contract, conveyance, or affirmation on behalf of the client, unless the lawyer manifests that the lawyer does not warrant that the lawyer is authorized to act or the other party knows that the lawyer is not authorized to act.

TOPIC 5. ENDING A CLIENT-LAWYER RELATIONSHIP

§ 31. Termination of Lawyer's Authority

(1) A lawyer must comply with applicable law requiring notice to or permission of a tribunal when terminating a representation and with an order of a tribunal requiring the representation to continue.

(2) Subject to Subsection (1) and § 33, a lawyer's actual authority to represent a client ends when:

(a) the client discharges the lawyer;

(b) the client dies or, in the case of a corporation or similar organization, loses its capacity to function as such;

(c) the lawyer withdraws;

(d) the lawyer dies or becomes physically or mentally incapable of providing representation, is disbarred or suspended from practicing law, or is ordered by a tribunal to cease representing a client; or

(e) the representation ends as provided by contract or because the lawyer has completed the contemplated services.

(3) A lawyer's apparent authority to act for a client with respect to another person ends when the other person knows or should know of facts from which it can be reasonably inferred that the lawyer lacks actual authority, including knowledge of any event described in Subsection (2).

§ 32. Discharge by a Client and Withdrawal by a Lawyer

(1) Subject to Subsection (5), a client may discharge a lawyer at any time

(2) Subject to Subsection (5), a lawyer may not represent a client or, where representation has commenced, must withdraw from the representation of a client if:

(a) the representation will result in the lawyer's violating rules of professional conduct or other law;

(b) the lawyer's physical or mental condition materially impairs the lawyer's ability to represent the client; or

(c) the client discharges the lawyer.

(3) Subject to Subsections (4) and (5), a lawyer may withdraw from representing a client if:

(a) withdrawal can be accomplished without material adverse effect on the interests of the client;

(b) the lawyer reasonably believes withdrawal is required in circumstances stated in Subsection (2);

(c) the client gives informed consent;

(d) the client persists in a course of action involving the lawyer's services that the lawyer reasonably believes is criminal, fraudulent, or in breach of the client's fiduciary duty;

(e) the lawyer reasonably believes the client has used or threatens to use the lawyer's services to perpetrate a crime or fraud;

(f) the client insists on taking action that the lawyer considers repugnant or imprudent;

(g) the client fails to fulfill a substantial financial or other obligation to the lawyer regarding the lawyer's services and the lawyer has given the client reasonable warning that the lawyer will withdraw unless the client fulfills the obligation;

(h) the representation has been rendered unreasonably difficult by the client or by the irreparable breakdown of the client-lawyer relationship; or

(i) other good cause for withdrawal exists.

(4) In the case of permissive withdrawal under Subsections (3)(f)-(i), a lawyer may not withdraw if the harm that withdrawal would cause significantly exceeds the harm to the lawyer or others in not withdrawing.

(5) Notwithstanding Subsections (1)-(4), a lawyer must comply with applicable law requiring notice to or permission of a tribunal when terminating a representation and with a valid order of a tribunal requiring the representation to continue.

§ 33. A Lawyer's Duties When Representation Terminates

(1) In terminating a representation, a lawyer must take steps to the extent reasonably practicable to protect the client's interests, such as giving notice to the client of the termination, allowing time for employment of other counsel, surrendering papers and property to which the client is entitled, and refunding any advance payment of fee the lawyer has not earned.

(2) Following termination of a representation, a lawyer must:

(a) observe obligations to a former client such as those dealing with client confidences (see Chapter 5), conflicts of interest (see Chapter 8), client property and documents (see §§ 44–46), and fee collection (see § 41);

(b) take no action on behalf of a former client without new authorization and give reasonable notice, to those who might otherwise be misled, that the lawyer lacks authority to act for the client;

(c) take reasonable steps to convey to the former client any material communication the lawyer receives relating to the matter involved in the representation; and

(d) take no unfair advantage of a former client by abusing knowledge or trust acquired by means of the representation.

Comment:

a. *Scope and cross-references.* This Section describes the duties of a lawyer during (see § 33(1)) and after (see § 33(2)) the termination of a client-lawyer relationship. The Section applies regardless of whether client or lawyer initiates the termination or whether termination occurs prematurely or when contemplated. Grounds for termination are set forth in §§ 31 and 32. Former clients owe the duty discussed in Chapter 3 to compensate for services rendered.

b. *Protecting a client's interests when a representation ends.* Ending a representation before a lawyer has completed a matter usually poses special problems for a client. Beyond consultation required before withdrawal (see § 32, Comment *n*), in the process of withdrawal itself a lawyer might be required to consult with the client and engage in other protective measures. New counsel must be found, papers and property retrieved or transferred, imminent deadlines extended, and tribunals and opposing parties notified to deal with new counsel. Lawyers must therefore take reasonably appropriate and practicable measures to protect clients when representation terminates.

What efforts are appropriate and practicable depends on the circumstances, including the subsisting relationship between client and lawyer. The lawyer must ordinarily advise the client of the implications of termination, assist in finding a new lawyer, and devote reasonable efforts to transferring responsibility for the matter. The lawyer must make the client's property and papers available to the client or the client's new lawyer, except to the extent that the lawyer is entitled to retain them. If the client is threatened with an imminent deadline that will expire before new counsel can act, the lawyer must take reasonable steps either to extend the deadline or comply with it (see § 31, Comment *e*). Failure to take such steps can give rise to disciplinary sanctions and malpractice liability. In some situations, the lawyer will be considered still to be the client's representative. Fewer measures usually are required when other lawyers representing the client in the same matter continue to do so (see § 32, Comment *h(ii)*).

c. *Client confidences.* A lawyer's obligation to protect the confidences of a client, addressed in detail in Chapter 5, continues after the representation ends.

d. *Former-client conflicts of interest.* Following termination, the former-client conflict-of-interest rules apply (see § 132). On consent, see Comment *i* hereto and § 122. On a former government lawyer, see § 133.

e. *A former client's property and documents.* The duties of a lawyer to protect and deliver a client's property and documents (see §§ 44–46) continue after the representation ends. Termination entails special duties to deliver to the client property (see § 45, Comment *b*) and documents or copies (see § 46(2)). The lawyer may not keep the client's property or documents in order to secure payment of compensation, except when the lawyer has a valid lien (see § 43) or when the client has not paid for the lawyer's work product (see § 46(3)).

f. *Collecting compensation and returning unearned fees.* The lawyer's efforts to collect compensation are governed by the requirements stated in Chapter 3.

g. *The duty not to act for a former client.* When representation ends a lawyer loses actual authority to act on behalf of the client (see § 31). Purporting to do so subjects the lawyer to discipline and can make the lawyer liable to the former client (see § 27, Comment *f*, & Chapter 4; Restatement Second, Agency § 386) or to third persons who have relied on the lawyer's claimed authority (see § 30(4) & Comment *e* thereto). However the lawyer retains authority to take steps protecting the client's interests (see Comment *b* hereto). The former client can also authorize the lawyer to act, for example by asking the lawyer to convey a request for additional time to opposing counsel.

h. *Conveying communications to a former client.* After termination a lawyer might receive a notice, letter, or other communication intended for a former client. The lawyer must use reasonable efforts to forward the communication. The lawyer ordinarily must also inform the source of the communication that the lawyer no longer represents the former client (see Comment *g* hereto). The lawyer must likewise notify a former client if a third person seeks to obtain material relating to the representation that is still in the lawyer's custody.

A lawyer has no general continuing obligation to pass on to a former client information relating to the former representation. The lawyer might, however, have such an obligation if the lawyer continues to represent the client in other matters or under a continuing relationship. Whether such an obligation exists regarding particular information depends on such factors as the client's reasonable expectations; the scope, magnitude, and duration of the client-lawyer relationship; the evident significance of the information to the client; the burden on the lawyer in making disclosure; and the likelihood that the client will receive the information from another source.

i. *The duty not to take unfair advantage of a former client.* A lawyer may not take unfair advantage of a former client by abusing knowledge or trust acquired through the representation (see §§ 41 & 43; Restatement Second, Agency § 396(d)). For example, a lawyer seeking a former client's consent to a conflict of interest (see § 132) must make adequate disclosure of facts that the former client should know in order to consider whether to consent (see § 122, Comment *c*(*i*)).

CHAPTER 3. CLIENT AND LAWYER: THE FINANCIAL AND PROPERTY RELATIONSHIP

TOPIC 1. LEGAL CONTROLS ON ATTORNEY FEES

§ 34. Reasonable and Lawful Fees

A lawyer may not charge a fee larger than is reasonable in the circumstances or that is prohibited by law.

Comment:

a. *Scope and cross-references.* This Section forbids unlawful fees and unreasonably large fees, while leaving clients and lawyers free to negotiate a broad range of compensation terms. It does not forbid lawyers to serve for low fees or without charge; such service is often in the public interest (see § 38, Comment *c*). Nor does the Section render unenforceable all fee arrangements that might be considered objectionable by some persons, for example, a lawyer's insistence that a needy client pay for the lawyer's services at the lawyer's usual rates. The prohibition on unreasonable payment arrangements is not limited to fees in a narrow sense. It applies also to excessive disbursement or interest charges or improper security interests (see § 43).

The Section applies in two different contexts. First, in fee disputes between lawyer and client, a fee will not be approved to the extent that it violates this Section even though the parties had agreed to the fee. This Section thus applies in proceedings such as suits by lawyers for fees, suits by clients to recover fees already paid, and fee-arbitration proceedings (see § 42). If the parties have not agreed (whether before, during, or after the representation; see § 18) to the basis or amount of the fee, the tribunal will set a fee compensating the lawyer for the fair value of services rendered (see § 39). The fair-value fee will usually be at the lower range of reasonable fees and thus less than a fee for the same services that would be upheld as reasonable if the parties had agreed upon it.

Second, this Section applies when courts or other disciplinary authorities seek to discipline a lawyer for charging unreasonably high fees (see Comment *f* hereto & § 5). In many jurisdictions, authorities have been reluctant to discipline lawyers on such grounds. For a variety of reasons, discipline might be withheld for charging a fee that would nevertheless be set aside as unreasonable in a fee-dispute proceeding. It is therefore important to distinguish between applying this Section in fee disputes (see Comments *b* through *e* hereto) and applying it in disciplinary proceedings (see Comment *f* hereto).

A contract otherwise in compliance with this Section will nevertheless be unenforceable if it violates other restrictions (see §§ 35, 36, & 47), or if the lawyer's misconduct leads to forfeiture of the contractual fee (see §§ 37, 40, & 41). On the lawyer's duty to inform a client of the basis or rate of the fee, see § 38(1).

b. *Rationale.* In general, clients and lawyers are free to contract for the fee that client is to pay (see §§ 18 & 38). Many client-lawyer fee arrangements operate entirely without official scrutiny. A client-lawyer fee arrangement will be set aside when its provisions are unreasonable as to the client (compare Restatement Second, Contracts § 208 (unconscionable contracts)). Courts are concerned to protect clients, particularly those who are unsophisticated in matters of lawyers' compensation, when a lawyer has overreached. Information about fees for legal services is often difficult for prospective clients to obtain. Many clients do not bargain effectively because of their need and inexperience. The services required are often unclear beforehand and difficult to monitor as a lawyer provides them. Lawyers usually encourage their clients to trust them. Lawyers, therefore, owe their clients greater duties than are owed under the general law of contracts.

Moreover, the availability of legal services is often essential if people of limited means are to enjoy legal rights. Those seeking to vindicate their rights through the private bar should not be deterred by the risk of unwarranted fee burdens.

c. *Unenforceable fee contracts.* This Section is typically applied in cases where a client and lawyer agreed on a fee before the lawyer's service began, and the client later challenges that fee. If a fee contract was reached after the lawyer began to serve, it will be enforceable only if it satisfies the standards of § 18. If a tribunal agrees that the fee satisfies those standards, the fee will fall within the range of reasonableness allowed by this Section. If the contract was reached after the services were complete, its validity depends primarily on the circumstances in which the contract was reached (see § 18(1)(b)). In the absence of a fee contract, the tribunal will apply § 39 (see Comment *a* hereto). When a court awards to a prevailing litigant attorney fees payable by an opposing party or out of a common fund, different standards might be used for determining the amount of the fee.

The lawyer codes state factors bearing on the reasonableness of fee arrangements. ABA Model Rules of Professional Conduct, Rule 1.5(a) (1983), and ABA Model Code of Professional Responsibility, DR 2–106(B) (1969), enumerate the following factors: "(1) the time and labor required, the novelty and difficulty of the questions involved, and the skill requisite to perform the legal service properly; (2) the likelihood, if apparent to the client, that the acceptance of the particular employment will preclude other employment by the lawyer; (3) the fee customarily charged in the locality for similar legal services; (4) the amount involved and the results obtained; (5) the time limitations imposed by the client or by the circumstances; (6) the nature and length of the professional relationship with the client; (7) the experience, reputation, and ability of the lawyer or lawyers performing the services; and (8) whether the fee is fixed or contingent." Other factors might also be relevant, such as the client's sophistication, the disclosures made to the client, and the client's ability to pay.

Those factors might be viewed as responding to three questions. First, when the contract was made, did the lawyer afford the client a free and informed choice? Relevant circumstances include whether the client was sophisticated in entering into such arrangements, whether the client was a fiduciary whose beneficiary deserves special protection, whether the client had a reasonable opportunity to seek another lawyer, whether the lawyer adequately explained the probable cost and other implications of the proposed fee contract (see § 38), whether the client understood the alternatives available from this lawyer and others, and whether the lawyer explained the benefits and drawbacks of the proposed legal services without misleading intimations. Fees agreed to by clients sophisticated in entering into such arrangements (such as a fee contract made by inside legal counsel in behalf of a corporation) should almost invariably be found reasonable.

Second, does the contract provide for a fee within the range commonly charged by other lawyers in similar representations? To the extent competition for legal services exists among lawyers in the relevant community, a tribunal can assume that the competition has produced an appropriate level of fee charges. A stated hourly rate, for example, should be compared with the hourly rates charged by lawyers of comparable qualifications for comparable services, and the number of hours claimed should be compared with those commonly invested in similar representations. The percentage in a contingent-fee contract should be compared to percentages commonly used in similar representations for similar services (for example, preparing and trying a novel products-liability claim). Whatever the fee basis, it is also relevant whether accepting the case was likely to foreclose other work or to attract it and whether pursuing the matter at the usual fee was reasonable in light of the client's needs and resources. See § 39, Comment *b*, which discusses the fair-value standard applied in quantum meruit cases and possible defects of a market standard.

Third, was there a subsequent change in circumstances that made the fee contract unreasonable? Although reasonableness is usually assessed as of the time the contract was entered into, later events might be relevant. Some fee contracts make the fee turn on later events. Accordingly, the reasonableness of a fee due under an hourly rate contract, for example, depends on whether the number of hours the lawyer worked was reasonable in light of the matter and client. It is also relevant whether the lawyer provided poor service, such as might make unreasonable a fee that would be appropriate for better services, or services that were better or more successful than normally would have been expected (compare §§ 37 & 40 concerning forfeiture of fees). Finally, events not known or contemplated when the contract was made can render the contract unreasonably favorable to the lawyer or, occasionally, to the client. Compare Restatement Second, Contracts §§ 152–154 and 261–265 (doctrines of mistake, supervening impracticality, supervening frustration). To determine what events client and lawyer contemplated, their contract must be construed in light of its goals and circumstances and in light of the possibilities discussed with the client (see id. §§ 294 & 50). A contingent-fee contract, for example, allocates to the lawyer the risk that the case will require much time and produce no recovery and to the client the risk that the case will require little time and produce a substantial fee. Events within that range of risks, such as a high recovery, do not make unreasonable a contract that was reasonable when made.

Illustration:

1. Bank Clerk is charged with criminal embezzlement and retains Lawyer to defend against the charges for a $15,000 flat fee. The next day another employee confesses to having taken the money, and the prosecutor (not knowing of Lawyer's retention by Bank Clerk) immediately drops the charges against Bank Clerk. Lawyer has done nothing on the case beyond speaking with Bank Clerk. In the absence of special circumstances, such as prior discussion of this possibility or the lawyer having rejected another representation offering a comparable fee in reliance on this engagement, it would be unreasonable for Lawyer to be paid $15,000 for doing so little. Client must pay the fair value of Lawyer's services (see § 39), but more than that is not due and the lawyer must refund the excess if already paid (see § 42). If, however, the prosecutor dropped the charges as the result of a plea bargain negotiated by Lawyer, the rapid disposition would not render unreasonable an otherwise proper $15,000 flat fee. A negotiated disposition without trial is a common event that parties are assumed to contemplate when they agree that the lawyer will receive a flat fee.

d. Reasonable contingent fees; percentage fees. On reasonable contingent fees, see § 35. Fees based on a percentage of the value of the property involved in a decedent's estate or in a real-estate transaction often are predicated on an assumption by the lawyer of the risk that more work than usual will be required. The same might be true of a lump-sum fee. Such fees should therefore be judged in light of the range of lawyer time that matters of the sort and size in question are likely to take. However, unlike contingent fees, percentage fees in such matters usually do not require the lawyer to forgo compensation when the result is unfavorable to the client. If the lawyer does not bear the risk of not being paid, compensation for such a risk is irrelevant in assessing the reasonableness of the fee.

e. Retainer fees. The term "retainer" has been employed to describe different fee arrangements. As used in this Restatement, an "engagement retainer fee" is a fee paid, apart from any other compensation, to ensure that a lawyer will be available for the client if required. An engagement retainer must be distinguished from a lump-sum fee constituting the entire payment for a lawyer's service in a matter and from an advance payment from which fees will be subtracted (see § 38, Comment *g*). A fee is an engagement retainer only if the lawyer is to be additionally compensated for actual work, if any, performed. In some jurisdictions, an engagement retainer is referred to as a "general" or "special" retainer. On the effect of premature termination of the representation on an engagement-retainer fee, see § 40.

An engagement-retainer fee satisfies the requirements of this Section if it bears a reasonable relationship to the income the lawyer sacrifices or expense the lawyer incurs by accepting it, including such costs as turning away other clients (for reasons of time or due to conflicts of interest), hiring new associates so as to be able to take the client's matter, keeping up with the relevant field, and the like. When a client experienced in retaining and compensating lawyers agrees to pay an engagement-retainer fee, the fee will almost invariably be found to fall within the range of reasonableness. Engagement-retainer fees agreed to by clients not so experienced should be more closely scrutinized to ensure that they are no greater than is reasonable and that the engagement-retainer fee is not being used to evade the rules requiring a lawyer to return unearned fees (see § 38, Comment *g*, & § 40, Illustrations 2A & 2B). In some circumstances, large engagement-retainer fees constitute unenforceable liquidated-damage clauses (see Restatement Second, Contracts § 356(1)) or are subject to challenge in the client's bankruptcy proceeding.

f. *The standard for lawyer discipline.* The standards that apply when fees are challenged as unreasonable in fee disputes are also relevant in the discipline of lawyers for charging unreasonably high fees. If a fee would not be set aside in a fee dispute, disciplinary authorities can be expected to find that receiving or charging such a fee does not warrant sanctions for unreasonableness. Disciplinary authorities likewise rely on the list of factors (see Comment *d* hereto) that tribunals refer to in fee disputes. Discipline is also appropriate if the lawyer overreached by deceiving the client, failed to provide all the services in question, or unjustifiably demanded a fee larger than the contract provided. Discipline may also be appropriate if the clear unreasonableness of the fee is demonstrated by other circumstances, including what other lawyers handling such matters charge, the facial unreasonableness of any express fee agreement, limits imposed by statutes, rules, and judicial precedents, previous warnings to the lawyer, evidence that the fee is uniformly deemed to be clearly excessive by responsible practitioners, or other evidence demonstrating the lawyer's gross insensitivity to broadly accepted billing standards.

A lawyer can be disciplined for unreasonably making a large fee claim even though the fee was not collected. In a fee dispute, however, the tribunal is concerned primarily with the reasonableness of the fee the lawyer actually seeks before the tribunal rather than the reasonableness of earlier fee claims made between the parties. On the extent to which a lawyer's abusive fee-collection methods affects the lawyer's entitlement to a fee, see § 41.

g. *Unlawful fees.* A fee that violates a statute or rule regulating the size of fees is impermissible under this Section. General principles governing the enforceability of contracts that violate legal requirements are set forth in Restatement Second, Contracts §§ 178–185. Statutes or rules in some jurisdictions control the percentage of a contingent fee, generally or in particular categories such as worker-compensation claims or medical-malpractice litigation. Other common legislation limits the fees chargeable in proceedings against the government, forbids contingent fees for legislative lobbying, prohibits public defenders or defense counsel paid by the government from accepting payment from their clients, and prohibits lawyers representing wards of the court from accepting payments not approved by the court. A fee for a service a lawyer may not lawfully perform, such as questioning jurors after a trial where that is forbidden (see § 115), is likewise unlawful regardless of the size of the fee (see Restatement Second, Contract §§ 192 & 193). A lawyer may not require a client to pay a fee larger than that contracted for, unless the client validly agrees to the increase.

That a fee contract violates some legal requirement does not necessarily render it unenforceable. The requirement might be one not meant to protect clients or one for which refusal to enforce is an inappropriate sanction. For example, when a lawyer violates a lawyer-code requirement that a fee contract be in writing but the client does not dispute the amount owed under it, that violation alone should not make the contract unenforceable. When only certain parts of a contract between client and lawyer contravene the law, moreover, the lawful parts remain enforceable, except where the lawyer should forfeit the whole fee (see § 37).

§ 35. Contingent-Fee Arrangements

(1) A lawyer may contract with a client for a fee the size or payment of which is contingent on the outcome of a matter, unless the contract violates § 34 or another provision of this Restatement or the size or payment of the fee is:

(a) contingent on success in prosecuting or defending a criminal proceeding; or

(b) contingent on a specified result in a divorce proceeding or a proceeding concerning custody of a child.

(2) Unless the contract construed in the circumstances indicates otherwise, when a lawyer has contracted for a contingent fee, the lawyer is entitled to receive the specified fee only when and to the extent the client receives payment.

Comment:

a. *Scope and cross-references.* This Section complements the general prohibition of unlawful and unreasonably high fees set forth in § 34 and the restrictions on certain other financial arrangements between clients and lawyers set forth in § 36. On a lawyer's duty to inform a client concerning the basis and rate of a fee, see § 38, Comment *b*.

A contingent-fee contract is one providing for a fee the size or payment of which is conditioned on some measure of the client's success. Examples include a contract that a lawyer will receive one-third of a client's recovery and a contract that the lawyer will be paid by the hour but receive a bonus should a stated favorable result occur (see § 34, Comment *a*, & § 35).

b. *Rationale.* Contingent-fee arrangements perform three valuable functions. First, they enable persons who could not otherwise afford counsel to assert their rights, paying their lawyers only if the assertion succeeds. Second, contingent fees give lawyers an additional incentive to seek their clients' success and to encourage only those clients with claims having a substantial likelihood of succeeding. Third, such fees enable a client to share the risk of losing with a lawyer, who is usually better able to assess the risk and to bear it by undertaking similar arrangements in other cases (cf. Restatement Second, Agency § 445).

Although contingent fees were formerly prohibited in the United States and are still prohibited in many other nations, the prohibition reflects circumstances not present in the contemporary United States. Many other nations routinely award attorney fees to the winning party and often have relatively low, standardized and regulated attorney fees, thus providing an alternative means of access to the legal system, which is not generally available here. Those nations might also regard civil litigation as more of an evil and less of an opportunity for the protection of rights than do lawmakers here. Contingent fees are thus criticized there as stirring up litigation and fostering overzealous advocacy.

While many of those criticisms of contingent fees are inapposite in the United States, it remains true that contingent-fee clients are often unsophisticated and inexperienced users of legal services, and their financial position might leave them little choice but to accept whatever contingent-fee arrangements prevail in the locality. It is often difficult even for a careful client or lawyer to estimate in advance how likely it is that a claim will prevail, what the recovery will be, and how much lawyer time will be needed. Finally, standardized contingent-fee arrangements might not take proper account of cases with low risks or high recoveries. Accordingly, courts scrutinize contingent fees with care in determining whether they are reasonable.

The Section forbids contingent-fee arrangements creating certain conflicts of interest that might induce the lawyer to disserve the client's interest or certain public interests. Some such conflicts exist in all fee arrangements. However, some arrangements have been prohibited because their dangers are thought to outweigh their benefits.

c. *Reasonable contingent fees.* A contingent fee may permissibly be greater than what an hourly fee lawyer of similar qualifications would receive for the same representation. A contingent-fee lawyer bears the risk of receiving no pay if the client loses and is entitled to compensation for bearing that risk. Nor is a contingent fee necessarily unreasonable because the lawyer devoted relatively little time to a representation, for the customary terms of such arrangements commit the lawyer to provide necessary effort without extra pay if a relatively large expenditure of the lawyer's time were entailed. However, large fees unearned by either effort or a significant period of risk are unreasonable (see § 34, Comment *c*, & Illustration 1 thereto).

A tribunal will find a contingent fee unreasonable due to a defect in the calculation of risk in two kinds of cases in particular: those in which there was a high likelihood of substantial recovery by trial or settlement, so that the lawyer bore little risk of nonpayment; and those in which the client's recovery was likely to be so large that the lawyer's fee would clearly exceed the sum appropriate to pay for services performed and risks assumed. A lawyer's failure to disclose to the client the general likelihood of recovery, the approximate probable size of any recovery, or the availability of alternative fee systems can also bear upon whether the fee is reasonable.

Illustration:

1. Client seeks Lawyer's help in collecting life-insurance benefits under a $15,000 policy on Client's spouse and agrees to pay a one-third contingent fee. There is no reasonable ground to contest that the benefits are due, the claim has not been contested by the insurer, and when Lawyer presents it the insurer pays without dispute. The $5,000 fee provided by the client-lawyer contract is not reasonable.

d. Reasonable rate and basis of a contingent fee. In addition to unreasonableness due to lack of risk, a contingent fee can also be unreasonable because either the percentage rate is excessive or the base against which the percentage is applied is excessive or otherwise unreasonable. If different from the customary base—the plaintiff's recovery—a contingent base will be unreasonable if it is an inappropriate measure of the lawyer's work and risk and the benefit the client derived from the lawyer's services. Contingent-fee contracts typically contemplate that the client, if successful, will receive a lump-sum award, a stated percentage of which will constitute the lawyer's fees. A client entering a contingent-fee contract reasonably expects that the lawyer will be paid only if and to the extent that the client recovers. For example, when a judgment for the client is entered but not collected, no fee is due unless the contract so provides.

The rule stated in Subsection (2) also requires that, unless the contract indicates otherwise, a contingent-fee lawyer is to receive the specified share of the client's actual-damages recovery. For that purpose, recovery includes damages, restitution, back pay, similar equitable payments, and amounts received in settlement. Unless the contract with the client indicates otherwise, the lawyer is not entitled to the specified percentage of items such as costs and attorney fees that are not usually considered damages. In the absence of prior agreement to the contrary, the amount of the client's recovery is computed net of any offset, such as a recovery by an opposing party on a counterclaim.

Illustrations:

2. Client agrees to pay Lawyer "35 percent of the recovery" in a suit. The court awards Client $20,000 in damages, $500 in costs for disbursements, and $1,000 in attorney fees because of the defendant's discovery abuses. Lawyer is entitled to receive a contingent fee of $7,000 (35% of $20,000), but not 35 percent of the costs' payments. If Lawyer advanced the $500 costs in question, Client must reimburse Lawyer unless their contract validly provides to the contrary (see § 38, Comment e). Whether Lawyer is entitled to recover a portion of the $1,000 attorney-fee award requires both interpretation of the fee contract and consideration of the nature of the fee-shifting award (see § 38(3)(b) & Comment f thereto).

3. Same facts as in Illustration 2, except that Lawyer has also expended $1,500 in disbursements not recoverable from the opposing party as costs but recoverable from Client (see § 38(3)(a) & Comment e thereto). Unless their contract construed in its circumstances provides otherwise, Lawyer is entitled to reimbursement of the $1,500 out of the $20,000 award and to a contingent fee of $6,475, that is, 35 percent of $18,500, the balance of the award.

e. Contingent fees in structured settlements. Under "structured settlements" and some legislation, a claimant will receive regular payments over the claimant's lifetime or some other period rather than receiving a lump sum. If so, under the rule of this Section the lawyer is entitled to receive the stated share of each such payment if and when it is made to the client or (when so provided) for the client's benefit, unless the client-lawyer contract provides otherwise. When a contingent-fee contract provides that the fee is to be paid at once if there is a structured settlement and provides no other method of calculation, the fee should be calculated only on the present value of the settlement.

Illustration:

4. Lawyer brings a personal-injury suit for Client against Defendant under a fee contract stating that, if the suit is settled before trial, Lawyer is to receive a fee equaling "thirty percent of the recovery." Client and Defendant enter a structured settlement under which Defendant is to pay Client $100,000 at once and to buy an annuity (which will in fact cost Defendant $200,000) entitling Client to monthly payments of $1,500 until Client dies. In the absence of a contrary agreement, lawyer is entitled to receive $30,000 when the $100,000 payment is made and $450 (30% of $1,500) if and when each $1,500 payment is made.

f(i). Contingent fees in criminal cases—defense counsel. Contingent fees for defending criminal cases have traditionally been prohibited. The prohibition applies only to representations in a criminal proceeding. It does not forbid a contingent fee for legal work that forestalls a criminal proceeding or work that partly relates to a criminal matter and partly to a noncriminal matter. A lawyer may thus contract for a contingent fee to persuade an administrative agency to terminate an investigation that might have led to civil as well as criminal proceedings or to bring a police-brutality damages suit in which the settlement includes dismissal of criminal charges against the plaintiff.

f(ii). Contingent fees in criminal cases—prosecuting counsel. Fees contingent on success in prosecuting a criminal case violate public policy. Thus, for example, a lawyer in private practice retained to prosecute a criminal contempt should not be compensated contingent on success in the prosecution. A prosecutor whose pay depends on securing a conviction might be tempted to seek convictions more than justice (see § 97). The government does not generally need contingent fees to afford counsel or to transfer to counsel the risk of loss.

g. Contingent fees in divorce or custody cases. Most jurisdictions continue to prohibit fees contingent on securing divorce or child custody. The traditional grounds of the prohibition in divorce cases are that such a fee creates incentives inducing lawyers to discourage reconciliation and encourages bitter and wounding court battles (cf. Restatement Second, Contracts § 190(2)). Since the passage of no-fault divorce legislation, however, public policy does not clearly favor the continuation of a marriage that one spouse wishes to end. Furthermore, in practice, once one spouse retains a lawyer to seek a divorce, a divorce will follow in most cases regardless of the basis of the fee. The principal dispute is likely to be a financial one. The prohibition might hence make it more difficult for the poorer spouse to secure vigorous representation, at least in the relatively rare instances in which law does not provide fee-shifting for the benefit of that client.

The other argument for the prohibition in divorce cases, and the ground for prohibition in custody cases, is that such a fee arrangement is usually unnecessary in order to secure an attorney in a divorce proceeding or custody dispute. The issue usually arises when one or the other spouse has assets, because otherwise there would be no means of paying a contingent fee. If the spouse retaining counsel has assets, no contingent fee is necessary. If it is the other spouse that has assets, the courts will usually require that spouse to pay the first spouse reasonable attorney fees. Again, no contingent fee is necessary.

When either of the two policies supporting the prohibition is inapplicable, the Section should not apply. If, for example, a divorce or custody order has already been finally approved when the fee contract is entered into, there can be little concern that a contingent fee based on the size of the property settlement or child-support payments will discourage reconciliation or custody compromises. (On limitations on post-inception fee contracts, see § 18(1)(a).) In such a situation, the fee is not contingent upon the securing of a divorce or custody order, and this Section does not apply, just as it does not apply to a contingent fee in a property dispute between nondivorcing or already divorced spouses. The prohibition would, however, apply to a contract with a client who is then married that provides for a fee contingent on the amount of the alimony, property disposition, or child-support award but that does not explicitly condition the fee on the grant of a divorce.

§ 36. Forbidden Client-Lawyer Financial Arrangements

(1) A lawyer may not acquire a proprietary interest in the cause of action or subject matter of litigation that the lawyer is conducting for a client, except that the lawyer may:

(a) acquire a lien as provided by § 43 to secure the lawyer's fee or expenses; and

(b) contract with a client for a contingent fee in a civil case except when prohibited as stated in § 35.

(2) A lawyer may not make or guarantee a loan to a client in connection with pending or contemplated litigation that the lawyer is conducting for the client, except that the lawyer may make or guarantee a loan covering court costs and expenses of litigation, the repayment of which to the lawyer may be contingent on the outcome of the matter.

(3) A lawyer may not, before the lawyer ceases to represent a client, make an agreement giving the lawyer literary or media rights to a portrayal or account based in substantial part on information relating to the representation.

§ 37. Partial or Complete Forfeiture of a Lawyer's Compensation

A lawyer engaging in clear and serious violation of duty to a client may be required to forfeit some or all of the lawyer's compensation for the matter. Considerations relevant to the question of forfeiture include the gravity and timing of the violation, its willfulness, its effect on the value of the lawyer's work for the client, any other threatened or actual harm to the client, and the adequacy of other remedies.

Comment:

a. *Scope and cross-references; relation to other doctrines.* Even if a fee is otherwise reasonable (see § 34) and complies with the other requirements of this Chapter, this Section can in some circumstances lead to forfeiture. See also § 41, on abusive fee-collection methods, and § 43, Comments *f* and *g*, discussing the discharge of attorney liens. A client who has already paid a fee subject to forfeiture can sue to recover it (see §§ 33(1) & 42).

A lawyer's improper conduct can reduce or eliminate the fee that the lawyer may reasonably charge under § 34 (see Comment *c* thereof). A lawyer is not entitled to be paid for services rendered in violation of the lawyer's duty to a client or for services needed to alleviate the consequences of the lawyer's misconduct. See Reinstatement Second, Agency § 469 (agent entitled to no compensation for conduct which is disobedient or breach of duty of loyalty to principal). A tribunal will also consider misconduct more broadly, as evidence of the lawyer's lack of competence and loyalty, and hence of the value of the lawyer's services.

Illustration:

1. Lawyer has been retained at an hourly rate to negotiate a contract for Client. Lawyer assures the other parties that Client has consented to a given term, knowing this to be incorrect. Lawyer devotes five hours to working out the details of the term. When Client insists that the term be stricken (see § 22), Lawyer devotes four more hours to explaining to the other parties that Lawyer's lack of authority and Client's rejection of the term requires further negotiations. Lawyer is not entitled to compensation for any of those nine hours of time under either § 34 or § 39. The tribunal, moreover, may properly consider the incident if it bears on the value of such of Lawyer's other time as is otherwise reasonably compensable.

Second, under contract law a lawyer's conduct can render unenforceable the lawyer's fee contract with a client. Thus under contract law the misconduct could constitute a material breach of contract (see § 40) or vitiate the formation of the contract (as in the case of misrepresentations concerning the lawyer's credentials). Alternatively, the contract can be unenforceable because it contains an unlawful provision (see Restatement Second, Contracts §§ 163, 164, 184, 237, 241, & 374; Restatement Second, Agency § 467). In some cases, although the contract is unenforceable on its own terms, the lawyer will still be able to recover the fair value of services rendered (see § 39, Comment *e*).

Third, a lawyer's misconduct can constitute malpractice rendering the lawyer liable for any resulting damage to the client under the common law or, in some jurisdictions, a consumer-protection statute (see § 41, Comment *b*). Malpractice damages can be greater or smaller than the forfeited fees. Conduct constituting malpractice is not always the same as conduct warranting fee forfeiture. A lawyer's negligent legal research, for example, might constitute malpractice, but will not necessarily lead to fee forfeiture. On malpractice liability and measures of damages generally, see § 53. On the duty of an agent to recompense a principal for loss caused by the agent's breach of duty, see Restatement Second, Agency § 401.

b. *Rationale.* The remedy of fee forfeiture presupposes that a lawyer's clear and serious violation of a duty to a client destroys or severely impairs the client-lawyer relationship and thereby the justification of the lawyer's claim to compensation. See Restatement Second, Trusts § 243 (court has discretion to deny or reduce compensation of trustee who commits breach of trust); cf. Restatement Second, Agency § 456(b) (willful and deliberate breach disentitles agent to recover in quantum meruit when agency contract does not apportion compensation). Forfeiture is also a deterrent. The damage that misconduct causes is often difficult to assess. In addition, a tribunal often can determine a forfeiture sanction more easily than a right to compensating damages.

Forfeiture of fees, however, is not justified in each instance in which a lawyer violates a legal duty, nor is total forfeiture always appropriate. Some violations are inadvertent or do not significantly harm the client. Some can be adequately dealt with by the remedies described in Comment *a* or by a partial forfeiture (see Comment *e*). Denying the lawyer all compensation would sometimes be an excessive sanction, giving a windfall to a client. The remedy of this Section should hence be applied with discretion.

c. *Violation of a duty to a client.* This Section provides for forfeiture when a lawyer engages in a clear and serious violation (see Comment *d* hereto) of a duty to the client. The source of the duty can be civil or criminal law, including, for example, the requirements of an applicable lawyer code or the law of malpractice. The misconduct might have occurred when the lawyer was retained, during the representation, or during attempts to collect a fee (see § 41). On improper withdrawal as a ground for forfeiture, see § 40, Comment *e*.

The Section refers only to duties that a lawyer owes to a client, not to those owed to other persons. That a lawyer, for example, harassed an opponent in litigation without harming the client does not warrant relieving the client of any duty to pay the lawyer. On other remedies in such situations, see § 110. But sometimes harassing a nonclient will also violate the lawyer's duty to the client, perhaps exposing the client to demands for sanctions or making the client's cause less likely to prevail. Forfeiture will then be appropriate unless the client is primarily responsible for the breach of duty to a nonclient.

d. *A clear and serious violation—relevant factors.* A lawyer's violation of duty to a client warrants fee forfeiture only if the lawyer's violation was clear. A violation is clear if a reasonable lawyer, knowing the relevant facts and law reasonably accessible to the lawyer, would have known that the conduct was wrongful. The sanction of fee forfeiture should not be applied to a lawyer who could not have been expected to know that conduct was forbidden, for example when the lawyer followed one reasonable interpretation of a client-lawyer contract and another interpretation was later held correct.

To warrant fee forfeiture a lawyer's violation must also be serious. Minor violations do not justify leaving the lawyer entirely unpaid for valuable services rendered to a client, although some such violations will reduce the size of the fee or render the lawyer liable to the client for any harm caused (see Comment *a* hereto).

In approaching the ultimate issue of whether violation of duty warrants fee forfeiture, several factors are relevant. The extent of the misconduct is one factor. Normally, forfeiture is more appropriate for repeated or continuing violations than for a single incident. Whether the breach involved knowing violation or conscious disloyalty to a client is also relevant. See Restatement Second, Agency § 469 (forfeiture for willful and deliberate breach). Forfeiture is generally inappropriate when the lawyer has not done anything willfully blameworthy, for example, when a conflict of interest arises during a representation because of the unexpected act of a client or third person.

Forfeiture should be proportionate to the seriousness of the offense. For example, a lawyer's failure to keep a client's funds segregated in a separate account (see § 44) should not result in forfeiture if the funds are preserved undiminished for the client. But forfeiture is justified for a flagrant violation even though no harm can be proved.

The adequacy of other remedies is also relevant. If, for example, a lawyer improperly withdraws from a representation and is consequently limited to a quantum meruit recovery significantly smaller than the fee contract provided (see § 40), it might be unnecessary to forfeit the quantum meruit recovery as well.

e. *Extent of forfeiture.* Ordinarily, forfeiture extends to all fees for the matter for which the lawyer was retained, such as defending a criminal prosecution or incorporating a corporation. (For a possibly more limited loss of fees under other rules, see Comment *a* hereto.) See § 42 (client's suit for refund of fees already paid). Forfeiture does not extend to a disbursement made by the lawyer to the extent it has conferred a benefit on the client (see § 40, Comment *d*).

Sometimes forfeiture for the entire matter is inappropriate, for example when a lawyer performed valuable services before the misconduct began, and the misconduct was not so grave as to require forfeiture of the fee for all services. Ultimately the question is one of fairness in view of the seriousness of the lawyer's violation and considering the special duties imposed on lawyers, the gravity, timing, and likely consequences to the client of the lawyer's misbehavior, and the connection between the various services performed by the lawyer.

When a lawyer-employee of a client is discharged for misconduct, except in an extreme instance this Section does not warrant forfeiture of all earned salary and pension entitlements otherwise due. The lawyer's loss of employment will itself often be a penalty graver than would be the loss of a fee for a single matter for a nonemployee lawyer. Employers, moreover, are often in a better position to protect themselves against misconduct of their lawyer-employees through supervision and other means. See Comment *a* hereto; Restatement Second, Agency § 401. For an employer's liability for unjust discharge of a lawyer employee, see § 32, Comment *b*.

TOPIC 2. A LAWYER'S CLAIM TO COMPENSATION

§ 38. Client-Lawyer Fee Contracts

(1) Before or within a reasonable time after beginning to represent a client in a matter, a lawyer must communicate to the client, in writing when applicable rules so provide, the basis or rate of the fee, unless the communication is unnecessary for the client because the lawyer has previously represented that client on the same basis or at the same rate.

(2) The validity and construction of a contract between a client and a lawyer concerning the lawyer's fees are governed by § 18.

(3) Unless a contract construed in the circumstances indicates otherwise:

(a) a lawyer may not charge separately for the lawyer's general office and overhead expenses;

(b) payments that the law requires an opposing party or that party's lawyer to pay as attorney-fee awards or sanctions are credited to the client, not the client's lawyer, absent a contrary statute or court order; and

(c) when a lawyer requests and receives a fee payment that is not for services already rendered, that payment is to be credited against whatever fee the lawyer is entitled to collect.

§ 39. A Lawyer's Fee in the Absence of a Contract

If a client and lawyer have not made a valid contract providing for another measure of compensation, a client owes a lawyer who has performed legal services for the client the fair value of the lawyer's services.

Comment:

a. Scope and cross-references. This Section sets forth a lawyer's right to recover a fair fee in quantum meruit for legal services provided to a client when a lawyer and client have not agreed upon another fee. It assumes that a client-lawyer relationship has been created (see § 14). Section 18 specifies requirements for a fee contract (see also § 38). The circumstances might also show that the lawyer was to serve without charge (see § 38, Comment *c*). A fee in quantum meruit may not exceed the applicable legal limits described in Topic 1 of this Chapter. Topic 3 discusses fee-collection procedures, including the various proceedings in which fee disputes can be resolved (see § 42); this Section applies to those proceedings.

A contract gives a client notice of what the fee will be, as required by § 38. A lawyer who fails to give such notice has a weaker claim to a fee whose amount the client might not have anticipated. The reasonableness requirement of § 34 is relevant (a) when a fee contract is challenged as unenforceable because the fee is too large or (b) when disciplinary authorities seek to discipline for a fee that is unreasonably large. The provisions of this Section are relevant but not conclusive when a lawyer faces such charges. However, discipline is inappropriate simply because a lawyer in good faith seeks a larger fee than a tribunal later determines to be due under this Section. If there is no valid fee contract, this Section measures the fee that is due, and a lawyer may then not seek a fee plainly improper under this Section.

The "fair value" fee recoverable under this Section is not measured by the standards applied when a party recovers a reasonable attorney fee from an opposing party under a fee-award statute or doctrine. The latter kind of fee often implicates factors—such as a legislative intent to encourage such suits or to limit fee awards to less than full compensation (for example, when the main purpose of the fee award is to deter misconduct by the fee-paying party)—not present in quantum meruit recovery under this Section.

b. Rationale. The fair-value standard of this Section persists (see Restatement Second, Agency § 443(b)), largely because of the defects of other standards.

b(i). The extent of a right to recover in the absence of a contract. The law permits a lawyer who has not agreed on a fee to recover one. Although both lawyers and clients might be reluctant to discuss fees in advance, both usually expect that some payment will be due. Denying compensation would be unfair to the lawyer and a windfall to the client. Moreover, the parties might have agreed on a measure of compensation, but in a contract unenforceable because it does not meet an applicable legal standard (see Comment *e* hereto)—for example, because it is a contingent-fee contract but is not in writing as a court rule requires. Quantum meruit recovery then provides compensation in circumstances in which it would be contrary to the parties' expectation to deprive the lawyer of all compensation.

b(ii). Measuring fair value. The market value of a lawyer's services is relevant in determining fair value but is not as such the measure of restitutionary recovery. Market value is the basis on which quantum meruit recoveries for other services or goods are often computed (see Restatement of Restitution § 152). When applicable, it assists the tribunal's inquiry, because those active in the market will know the going price and can give evidence about it.

However, some measures of price from a competitive market might be inappropriate. For example, the market price of services for the vigorous litigation of a claim for specific performance of a land-purchase contract might be disproportionate to the value of a particular claim. For some clients, particularly those of small means, paying that price might be a foolish investment. Moreover, a strictly economic calculation of market value presupposes an informed client. But market prices might reflect client ignorance rather than fair bargaining. Where there has been no prior contract as to fee, the lawyer presumably did not adequately explain the cost of pursuing the claim and is thus the proper party to bear the risk of indeterminacy. Hence, the fair-value standard assesses additional considerations and starts with an assumption that the lawyer is entitled to recovery only at the lower range of what otherwise would be a reasonable negotiated fee.

c. Applying the fair-value standard. Assessing the fair value of a lawyer's services might require answers to three questions. What fees are customarily charged by comparable lawyers in the community for similar legal services? What would a fully informed and properly advised client in the client's situation agree to pay for such services? In light of those and other relevant circumstances, what is a fair fee (see Comment *b* hereto)?

In some cases, a standard market rate for a legal service might in fact exist. A lawyer who proves that a standard fee exists in the area should ordinarily be entitled to receive it, unless the client shows that a sophisticated, informed, and properly advised client in the client's situation would have refused to pay the standard fee—for example, because such a client would have decided not to proceed (see Comment *b(ii)* hereto). Similarly, a client should not be required to pay more than the standard fee unless the lawyer shows that, because of the circumstances of the case, a sophisticated, informed, and properly advised client would have agreed to pay a higher fee.

Calculation of an hourly fee might provide guidance. Except in certain areas such as criminal-defense or tort-plaintiff representation, hourly fees are a common contractual basis of payment for legal services. The hourly fee would be that charged by lawyers of similar experience and other credentials in comparable cases, but not more than the standard rate of the lawyer in question for that type of work. The lawyer must show, by records or otherwise, the hours actually and reasonably devoted to the case in view of the importance of the case to the client, the client's financial situation and instructions, and the time that a comparable lawyer would have needed.

The standard rate or hourly fee might be modified by other factors bearing on fairness, including success in the representation and whether the lawyer assumed part of the risk of the client's loss, as in a contingent-fee contract (see § 35). Reference can be made to the factors in § 34, Comment *c*. Concerning expenses and disbursements paid by the lawyer and attorney-fee awards and sanctions collected from an opposing party, the principles of § 38(3)(a) and (b) apply.

A conservative evaluation is usually appropriate in assessing fees under this Section. When a lawyer fails to agree with the client in advance on the fee to be charged, the client should not have to pay as much as some clients might have agreed to pay. A fair-value fee under this Section is thus less than the highest contractual fee that would be upheld as reasonable under § 34.

* * *

§ 40. Fees on Termination

If a client-lawyer relationship ends before the lawyer has completed the services due for a matter and the lawyer's fee has not been forfeited under § 37:

(1) a lawyer who has been discharged or withdraws may recover the lesser of the fair value of the lawyer's services as determined under § 39 and the ratable proportion of the compensation provided by any otherwise enforceable contract between lawyer and client for the services performed; except that

(2) the tribunal may allow such a lawyer to recover the ratable proportion of the compensation provided by such a contract if:

(a) the discharge or withdrawal is not attributable to misconduct of the lawyer;

(b) the lawyer has performed severable services; and

(c) allowing contractual compensation would not burden the client's choice of counsel or the client's ability to replace counsel.

TOPIC 3. FEE-COLLECTION PROCEDURES

§ 41. Fee-Collection Methods

In seeking compensation claimed from a client or former client, a lawyer may not employ collection methods forbidden by law, use confidential information (as defined in Chapter 5) when not permitted under § 65, or harass the client.

§ 42. Remedies and the Burden of Persuasion

(1) A fee dispute between a lawyer and a client may be adjudicated in any appropriate proceeding, including a suit by the lawyer to recover an unpaid fee, a suit for a refund by a client, an arbitration to which both parties consent unless applicable law renders the lawyer's consent unnecessary, or in the court's discretion a proceeding ancillary to a pending suit in which the lawyer performed the services in question.

(2) In any such proceeding the lawyer has the burden of persuading the trier of fact, when relevant, of the existence and terms of any fee contract, the making of any disclosures to the client required to render a contract enforceable, and the extent and value of the lawyer's services.

§ 43. Lawyer Liens

(1) Except as provided in Subsection (2) or by statute or rule, a lawyer does not acquire a lien entitling the lawyer to retain the client's property in the lawyer's possession in order to secure payment of the lawyer's fees and disbursements. A lawyer may decline to deliver to a client or former client an original or copy of any document prepared by the lawyer or at the lawyer's expense if the client or former client has not paid all fees and

disbursements due for the lawyer's work in preparing the document and nondelivery would not unreasonably harm the client or former client.

(2) Unless otherwise provided by statute or rule, client and lawyer may agree that the lawyer shall have a security interest in property of the client recovered for the client through the lawyer's efforts, as follows:

(a) the lawyer may contract in writing with the client for a lien on the proceeds of the representation to secure payment for the lawyer's services and disbursements in that matter;

(b) the lien becomes binding on a third party when the party has notice of the lien;

(c) the lien applies only to the amount of fees and disbursements claimed reasonably and in good faith for the lawyer's services performed in the representation; and

(d) the lawyer may not unreasonably impede the speedy and inexpensive resolution of any dispute concerning those fees and disbursements or the lien.

(3) A tribunal where an action is pending may in its discretion adjudicate any fee or other dispute concerning a lien asserted by a lawyer on property of a party to the action, provide for custody of the property, release all or part of the property to the client or lawyer, and grant such other relief as justice may require.

(4) With respect to property neither in the lawyer's possession nor recovered by the client through the lawyer's efforts, the lawyer may obtain a security interest on property of a client only as provided by other law and consistent with §§ 18 and 126. Acquisition of such a security interest is a business or financial transaction with a client within the meaning of § 126.

TOPIC 4. PROPERTY AND DOCUMENTS OF CLIENTS AND OTHERS

§ 44. Safeguarding and Segregating Property

(1) A lawyer holding funds or other property of a client in connection with a representation, or such funds or other property in which a client claims an interest, must take reasonable steps to safeguard the funds or property. A similar obligation may be imposed by law on funds or other property so held and owned or claimed by a third person. In particular, the lawyer must hold such property separate from the lawyer's property, keep records of it, deposit funds in an account separate from the lawyer's own funds, identify tangible objects, and comply with related requirements imposed by regulatory authorities.

(2) Upon receiving funds or other property in a professional capacity and in which a client or third person owns or claims an interest, a lawyer must promptly notify the client or third person. The lawyer must promptly render a full accounting regarding such property upon request by the client or third person.

§ 45. Surrendering Possession of Property

(1) Except as provided in Subsection (2), a lawyer must promptly deliver, to the client or nonclient so entitled, funds or other property in the lawyer's possession belonging to a client or nonclient.

(2) A lawyer may retain possession of funds or other property of a client or nonclient if:

(a) the client or nonclient consents;

(b) the lawyer's client is entitled to the property, the lawyer appropriately possesses the property for purposes of the representation, and the client has not asked for delivery of the property;

(c) the lawyer has a valid lien on the property (see § 43);

(d) there are substantial grounds for dispute as to the person entitled to the property; or

(e) delivering the property to the client or nonclient would violate a court order or other legal obligation of the lawyer.

§ 46. Documents Relating to a Representation

(1) A lawyer must take reasonable steps to safeguard documents in the lawyer's possession relating to the representation of a client or former client.

(2) On request, a lawyer must allow a client or former client to inspect and copy any document possessed by the lawyer relating to the representation, unless substantial grounds exist to refuse.

(3) Unless a client or former client consents to nondelivery or substantial grounds exist for refusing to make delivery, a lawyer must deliver to the client or former client, at an appropriate time and in any event promptly after the representation ends, such originals and copies of other documents possessed by the lawyer relating to the representation as the client or former client reasonably needs.

(4) Notwithstanding Subsections (2) and (3), a lawyer may decline to deliver to a client or former client an original or copy of any document under circumstances permitted by § 43(1).

TOPIC 5. FEE-SPLITTING WITH A LAWYER NOT IN THE SAME FIRM

§ 47. Fee-Splitting with a Lawyer Not in the Same Firm

A division of fees between lawyers who are not in the same firm may be made only if:

(1) (a) the division is in proportion to the services performed by each lawyer or (b) by agreement with the client, the lawyers assume joint responsibility for the representation;

(2) the client is informed of and does not object to the fact of division, the terms of the division, and the participation of the lawyers involved; and

(3) the total fee is reasonable (see § 34).

CHAPTER 4. LAWYER CIVIL LIABILITY

TOPIC 1. LIABILITY FOR PROFESSIONAL NEGLIGENCE AND BREACH OF FIDUCIARY DUTY

§ 48. Professional Negligence—Elements and Defenses Generally

In addition to the other possible bases of civil liability described in §§ 49, 55, and 56, a lawyer is civilly liable for professional negligence to a person to whom the lawyer owes a duty of care within the meaning of § 50 or § 51, if the lawyer fails to exercise care within

the meaning of § 52 and if that failure is a legal cause of injury within the meaning of § 53, unless the lawyer has a defense within the meaning of § 54.

§ 49. Breach of Fiduciary Duty—Generally

In addition to the other possible bases of civil liability described in §§ 48, 55, and 56, a lawyer is civilly liable to a client if the lawyer breaches a fiduciary duty to the client set forth in § 16(3) and if that failure is a legal cause of injury within the meaning of § 53, unless the lawyer has a defense within the meaning of § 54.

§ 50. Duty of Care to a Client

For purposes of liability under § 48, a lawyer owes a client the duty to exercise care within the meaning of § 52 in pursuing the client's lawful objectives in matters covered by the representation.

§ 51. Duty of Care to Certain Nonclients

For purposes of liability under § 48, a lawyer owes a duty to use care within the meaning of § 52 in each of the following circumstances:

(1) to a prospective client, as stated in § 15;

(2) to a nonclient when and to the extent that:

(a) the lawyer or (with the lawyer's acquiescence) the lawyer's client invites the nonclient to rely on the lawyer's opinion or provision of other legal services, and the nonclient so relies; and

(b) the nonclient is not, under applicable tort law, too remote from the lawyer to be entitled to protection;

(3) to a nonclient when and to the extent that:

(a) the lawyer knows that a client intends as one of the primary objectives of the representation that the lawyer's services benefit the nonclient;

(b) such a duty would not significantly impair the lawyer's performance of obligations to the client; and

(c) the absence of such a duty would make enforcement of those obligations to the client unlikely; and

(4) to a nonclient when and to the extent that:

(a) the lawyer's client is a trustee, guardian, executor, or fiduciary acting primarily to perform similar functions for the nonclient;

(b) the lawyer knows that appropriate action by the lawyer is necessary with respect to a matter within the scope of the representation to prevent or rectify the breach of a fiduciary duty owed by the client to the nonclient, where (i) the breach is a crime or fraud or (ii) the lawyer has assisted or is assisting the breach;

(c) the nonclient is not reasonably able to protect its rights; and

(d) such a duty would not significantly impair the performance of the lawyer's obligations to the client.

Comment:

a. *Scope and cross-references.* This Section sets forth the limited circumstances in which a lawyer owes a duty of care to a nonclient. Compare § 14, describing when one becomes a client, and § 50, which sets forth a lawyer's duty to a client. On the meaning of the term "duty," see § 50, Comment *a*. Even when a duty exists, a lawyer is liable for negligence only if the lawyer violates the duty (see § 52), the violation is the legal cause of damages (see § 53), and no defense is established (see § 54).

As stated in § 54(1), a lawyer is not liable under this Section for any action or inaction the lawyer reasonably believed to be required by law, including a professional rule. As stated in §§ 66(3) and 67(4), a lawyer who takes action or decides not to take action permitted under those Sections is not, solely by reason of such action or inaction, liable for damages.

In appropriate circumstances, a lawyer is also subject to liability to a nonclient on grounds other than negligence (see §§ 48 & 56), for litigation sanctions (see § 110), and for acting without authority (see § 30). On indemnity and contribution, see § 53, Comment *i*. This Section does not consider those liabilities, such as liabilities arising under securities or similar legislation. Nor does the Section consider when a lawyer found liable to a nonclient may recover from a client under such theories as indemnity, contribution, or subrogation. On a client's liability to a nonclient arising out of a lawyer's conduct, see § 26, Comment *d*.

b. *Rationale.* Lawyers regularly act in disputes and transactions involving nonclients who will foreseeably be harmed by inappropriate acts of the lawyers. Holding lawyers liable for such harm is sometimes warranted. Yet it is often difficult to distinguish between harm resulting from inappropriate lawyer conduct on the one hand and, on the other hand, detriment to a nonclient resulting from a lawyer's fulfilling the proper function of helping a client through lawful means. Making lawyers liable to nonclients, moreover, could tend to discourage lawyers from vigorous representation. Hence, a duty of care to nonclients arises only in the limited circumstances described in the Section. Such a duty must be applied in light of those conflicting concerns.

c. *Opposing parties.* A lawyer representing a party in litigation has no duty of care to the opposing party under this Section, and hence no liability for lack of care, except in unusual situations such as when a litigant is provided an opinion letter from opposing counsel as part of a settlement (see Subsection (2) and Comment *e* hereto). Imposing such a duty could discourage vigorous representation of the lawyer's own client through fear of liability to the opponent. Moreover, the opposing party is protected by the rules and procedures of the adversary system and, usually, by counsel. In some circumstances, a lawyer's negligence will entitle an opposing party to relief other than damages, such as vacating a settlement induced by negligent misrepresentation. For a lawyer's liability to sanctions, which may include payments to an opposing party, based on certain litigation misconduct, see § 110. See also § 56, on liability for intentional torts.

Similarly, a lawyer representing a client in an arm's-length business transaction does not owe a duty of care to opposing nonclients, except in the exceptional circumstances described in this Section. On liability for aiding a client's unlawful conduct, see § 56.

Illustration:

1. Lawyer represents Plaintiff in a personal-injury action against Defendant. Because Lawyer fails to conduct an appropriate factual investigation, Lawyer includes a groundless claim in the complaint. Defendant incurs legal expenses in obtaining dismissal of this claim. Lawyer is not liable for negligence to Defendant. Lawyer may, however, be subject to litigation sanctions for having asserted a claim without proper investigation (see § 110). On claims against lawyers for wrongful use of civil proceedings and the like, see § 57(2) and Comment d thereto.

d. *Prospective clients (Subsection (1)).* When a person discusses with a lawyer the possibility of their forming a client-lawyer relationship, and even if no such relationship arises, the lawyer may be liable for failure to use reasonable care to the extent the lawyer advises or provides other legal services for the person (see § 15(2) and the Comments thereto). On duties to a former client, see § 50, Comment *c*.

e. *Inviting reliance of a nonclient (Subsection (2)).* When a lawyer or that lawyer's client (with the lawyer's acquiescence) invites a nonclient to rely on the lawyer's opinion or other legal services, and the nonclient reasonably does so, the lawyer owes a duty to the nonclient to use care (see § 52), unless the jurisdiction's general tort law excludes liability on the ground of remoteness. Accordingly, the nonclient has a claim against the lawyer if the lawyer's negligence with respect to the opinion or other legal services causes injury to the nonclient (see § 95). The lawyer's client typically benefits from the nonclient's reliance, for example, when providing the opinion was called for as a condition to closing under a loan agreement, and recognition of such a claim does not conflict with duties the lawyer properly owed to the client. Allowing the claim tends to benefit future clients in similar situations by giving nonclients reason to rely on similar invitations. See Restatement Second, Torts § 552. If a client is injured by a lawyer's negligence in providing opinions or services to a nonclient, for example because that renders the client liable to the nonclient as the lawyer's principal, the lawyer may have corresponding liability to the client (see § 50).

Clients or lawyers may invite nonclients to rely on a lawyer's legal opinion or services in various circumstances (see § 95). For example, a sales contract for personal property may provide that as a condition to closing the seller's lawyer will provide the buyer with an opinion letter regarding the absence of liens on the property being sold (see id., Illustrations 1 & 2; § 52, Illustration 2). A nonclient may require such an opinion letter as a condition for engaging in a transaction with a lawyer's client. A lawyer's opinion may state the results of a lawyer's investigation and analysis of facts as well as the lawyer's legal conclusions (see § 95). On when a lawyer may properly decline to provide an opinion and on a lawyer's duty when a client insists on nondisclosure, see § 95, Comment d. A lawyer's acquiescence in use of the lawyer's opinion may be manifested either before or after the lawyer renders it.

In some circumstances, reliance by unspecified persons may be expected, as when a lawyer for a borrower writes an opinion letter to the original lender in a bank credit transaction knowing that the letter will be used to solicit other lenders to become participants in syndication of the loan. Whether a subsequent syndication participant can recover for the lawyer's negligence in providing such an opinion letter depends on what, if anything, the letter says about reliance and whether the jurisdiction in question, as a matter of general tort law, adheres to the limitations on duty of Restatement Second, Torts § 552(2) or those of Ultramares Corp. v. Touche, 174 N.E. 441 (N.Y.1931), or has rejected such limitations. To account for such differences in general tort law, Subsection (2) refers to applicable law excluding liability to persons too remote from the lawyer.

When a lawyer owes a duty to a nonclient under this Section, whether the nonclient's cause of action may be asserted in contract or in tort should be determined by reference to the applicable law of professional liability generally. The cause of action ordinarily is in substance identical to a claim for negligent misrepresentation and is subject to rules such as those concerning proof of materiality and reliance (see Restatement Second, Torts §§ 552–554). For liability under securities legislation, see § 56, Comment *i*. Whether the representations are actionable may be affected by the duties of disclosure, if any, that the client owes the nonclient (see § 98, Comment *e*). In the absence of such duties of disclosure, the duty of a lawyer providing an opinion is ordinarily limited to using care to avoid making or adopting misrepresentations. On a lawyer's obligations in furnishing an opinion, see § 95, Comment *c*. On intentionally making or assisting misrepresentations, see § 56, Comment *f*, and § 98.

A lawyer may avoid liability to nonclients under Subsection (2) by making clear that an opinion or representation is directed only to a client and should not be relied on by others. Likewise, a lawyer may limit or avoid liability under Subsection (2) by qualifying a representation, for example by making clear through limiting or disclaiming language in an opinion letter that the lawyer is relying on facts provided by the client without independent investigation by the lawyer (assuming that the lawyer does not know the facts provided by the client to be false, in which case the lawyer would be liable for misrepresentation). The effectiveness of a limitation or disclaimer depends on whether it was reasonable in the circumstances to conclude that those provided with the opinion would receive the limitation or disclaimer and understand its import. The relevant circumstances include customary practices known to the recipient concerning the construction of opinions and whether the recipient is represented by counsel or a similarly experienced agent.

When a nonclient is invited to rely on a lawyer's legal services, other than the lawyer's opinion, the analysis is similar. For example, if the seller's lawyer at a real-estate closing offers to record the deed for the buyer, the lawyer is subject to liability to the buyer for negligence in doing so, even if the buyer did not thereby become a client of the lawyer. When a nonclient is invited to rely on a lawyer's nonlegal services, the lawyer's duty of care is determined by the law applicable to providers of the services in question.

f. A nonclient enforcing a lawyer's duties to a client (Subsection (3)). When a lawyer knows (see Comment *h* hereto) that a client intends a lawyer's services to benefit a third person who is not a client, allowing the nonclient to recover from the lawyer for negligence in performing those services may promote the lawyer's loyal and effective pursuit of the client's objectives. The nonclient, moreover, may be the only person likely to enforce the lawyer's duty to the client, for example because the client has died.

A nonclient's claim under Subsection (3) is recognized only when doing so will both implement the client's intent and serve to fulfill the lawyer's obligations to the client without impairing performance of those obligations in the circumstances of the representation. A duty to a third person hence exists only when the client intends to benefit the third person as one of the primary objectives of the representation, as in the Illustrations below and in Comment *g* hereto. Without adequate evidence of such an intent, upholding a third person's claim could expose lawyers to liability for following a client's instructions in circumstances where it would be difficult to prove what those instructions had been. Threat of such liability would tend to discourage lawyers from following client instructions adversely affecting third persons. When the claim is that the lawyer failed to exercise care in preparing a document, such as a will, for which the law imposes formal or evidentiary requirements, the third person must prove the client's intent by evidence that would satisfy the burden of proof applicable to construction or reformation (as the case may be) of the document. See Restatement Third, Property (Donative Transfers) §§ 11.2 and 12.1 (Tentative Draft No. 1, 1995) (preponderance of evidence to resolve ambiguity in donative instruments; clear and convincing evidence to reform such instruments).

Subsections (3) and (4), although related in their justifications, differ in application. In situations falling under Subsection (3), the client need not owe any preexisting duty to the intended beneficiary. The scope of the intended benefit depends on the client's intent and the lawyer's undertaking. On the other hand, the duty under Subsection (4) typically arises when a lawyer helps a client-fiduciary to carry out a duty of the fiduciary to a beneficiary recognized and defined by trust or other law.

Illustrations:

2. Client retains Lawyer to prepare and help in the drafting and execution of a will leaving Client's estate to Nonclient. Lawyer prepares the will naming Nonclient as the sole beneficiary, but negligently arranges for Client to sign it before an inadequate number of witnesses. Client's intent to benefit Nonclient thus appears on the face of the will executed by Client. After Client dies, the will is held ineffective due to the lack of witnesses, and Nonclient is thereby harmed. Lawyer is subject to liability to Nonclient for negligence in drafting and supervising execution of the will.

3. Same facts as in Illustration 2, except that Lawyer arranges for Client to sign the will before the proper number of witnesses, but Nonclient later alleges that Lawyer negligently wrote the will to name someone other than Nonclient as the legatee. Client's intent to benefit Nonclient thus does not appear on the face of the will. Nonclient can establish the existence of a duty from Lawyer to Nonclient only by producing clear and convincing evidence that Client communicated to Lawyer Client's intent that Nonclient be the legatee. If Lawyer is held liable to Nonclient in situations such as this and the preceding Illustration, applicable principles of law may provide that Lawyer may recover from their unintended recipients the estate assets that should have gone to Nonclient.

4. Same facts as in Illustration 2, except that Lawyer arranges for Client to sign the will before the proper number of witnesses. After Client's death, Heir has the will set aside on the ground that Client was incompetent and then sues Lawyer for expenses imposed on Heir by the will, alleging that Lawyer negligently assisted Client to execute a will despite Client's incompetence. Lawyer is not subject to liability to Heir for negligence. Recognizing a duty by lawyers to heirs to use care in not assisting incompetent clients to execute wills would impair performance of lawyers' duty to assist clients even when the clients' competence might later be challenged. Whether Lawyer is liable to Client's estate or personal representative (due to privity with the lawyer) is beyond the scope of this Restatement. On a lawyer's obligations to a client with diminished capacity, see § 24.

g. A liability insurer's claim for professional negligence. Under Subsection (3), a lawyer designated by an insurer to defend an insured owes a duty of care to the insurer with respect to matters as to which the interests of the insurer and insured are not in conflict, whether or not the insurer is held to be a co-client of the lawyer (see § 134, Comment *f*). For example, if the lawyer negligently fails to oppose a motion for summary judgment against the insured and the insurer must pay the resulting adverse judgment, the insurer has a claim against the lawyer for any proximately caused loss. In such circumstances, the insured and insurer, under the insurance contract, both have a reasonable expectation that the lawyer's services will benefit both insured and insurer. Recognizing that the lawyer owes a duty to the insurer promotes enforcement of the lawyer's obligations to the insured. However, such a duty does not arise when it would significantly impair, in the circumstances of the representation, the lawyer's performance of obligations to the insured. For example, if the lawyer recommends acceptance of a settlement offer just below the policy limits and the insurer accepts the offer, the insurer may not later seek to recover from the lawyer on a claim that a competent lawyer in the circumstances would have advised that the offer be rejected. Allowing recovery in such circumstances would give the lawyer an interest in recommending rejection of a settlement offer beneficial to the insured in order to escape possible liability to the insurer.

h. Duty based on knowledge of a breach of fiduciary duty owed by a client (Subsection (4)). A lawyer representing a client in the client's capacity as a fiduciary (as opposed to the client's personal capacity) may in some circumstances be liable to a beneficiary for a failure to use care to protect the beneficiary. The duty should be recognized only when the requirements of Subsection (4) are met and when action by the lawyer would not violate applicable professional rules (see § 54(1)). The duty arises from the fact that a fiduciary has obligations to the beneficiary that go beyond fair dealing at arm's length. A lawyer is usually so situated as to have special opportunity to observe whether the fiduciary is complying with those obligations. Because fiduciaries are generally obliged to pursue the interests of their beneficiaries, the duty does not subject the lawyer to conflicting or inconsistent duties. A lawyer who knowingly assists a client to violate the client's fiduciary duties is civilly liable, as would be a nonlawyer (see Restatement Second, Trusts § 326). Moreover, to the extent that the lawyer has assisted in creating a risk of injury, it is appropriate to impose a preventive and corrective duty on the lawyer (cf. Restatement Second, Torts § 321).

The duty recognized by Subsection (4) is limited to lawyers representing only a limited category of the persons described as fiduciaries—trustees, executors, guardians, and other fiduciaries acting primarily to fulfill similar functions. Fiduciary responsibility, imposing strict duties to protect specific property for the benefit of specific, designated persons, is the chief end of such relationships. The lawyer is hence less likely to encounter conflicting considerations arising from other responsibilities of the fiduciary-client than are entailed in other relationships in which fiduciary duty is only a part of a broader role. Thus, Subsection (4) does not apply when the client is a partner in a business partnership, a corporate officer or director, or a controlling stockholder.

The scope of a client's fiduciary duties is delimited by the law governing the relationship in question (see, e.g., Restatement Second, Trusts §§ 169–185). Whether and when such law allows a beneficiary to assert derivatively the claim of a trust or other entity against a lawyer is beyond the scope of this Restatement (see Restatement Second, Trusts § 282). Even when a relationship is fiduciary, not all the attendant duties are fiduciary. Thus, violations of duties of loyalty by a fiduciary are ordinarily considered breaches of fiduciary duty, while violations of duties of care are not.

Sometimes a lawyer represents both a fiduciary and the fiduciary's beneficiary and thus may be liable to the beneficiary as a client under § 50 and may incur obligations concerning conflict of interests (see §§ 130–131). A lawyer who represents only the fiduciary may avoid such liability by making clear to the beneficiary that the lawyer represents the fiduciary rather than the beneficiary (compare § 103, Comment *e*).

The duty recognized by Subsection (4) arises only when the lawyer knows that appropriate action by the lawyer is necessary to prevent or mitigate a breach of the client's fiduciary duty. As used in this Subsection and Subsection (3) (see Comment *f*), "know" is the equivalent of the same term defined in ABA Model Rules of Professional Conduct, Terminology § [5] (1983) (". . . 'Knows' denotes actual knowledge of the fact in question. A person's knowledge may be inferred from circumstances."). The concept is functionally the same as the terminology "has reason to know" as defined in Restatement Second, Torts § 12(1) (actor has reason to know when actor "has information from which a person of reasonable intelligence or of the superior intelligence of the actor would infer that the fact in question exists, or that such person would govern his conduct upon the assumption that such facts exists."). The "know" terminology should not be confused with "should know" (see id. § 12(2)). As used in Subsection (3) and (4) "knows" neither assumes nor requires a duty of inquiry.

Generally, a lawyer must follow instruction of the client-fiduciary (see § 21(2) hereto) and may assume in the absence of contrary information that the fiduciary is complying with the law. The duty stated in Subsection (4) applies only to breaches constituting crime or fraud, as determined by applicable law and subject to the limitations set out in § 67, Comment *d*, and § 82, Comment *d*, or those in which the lawyer has assisted or is assisting the fiduciary. A lawyer assists fiduciary breaches, for example, by preparing documents needed to accomplish the fiduciary's wrongful conduct or assisting the fiduciary to conceal such conduct. On the other hand, a lawyer subsequently consulted by a fiduciary to deal with the consequences of a breach of fiduciary duty committed before the consultation began is under no duty to inform the beneficiary of the breach or otherwise to act to rectify it. Such a duty would prevent a person serving as fiduciary from obtaining the effective assistance of counsel with respect to such a past breach.

Liability under Subsection (4) exists only when the beneficiary of the client's fiduciary duty is not reasonably able to protect its rights. That would be so, for example, when the fiduciary client is a guardian for a beneficiary unable (for reasons of youth or incapacity) to manage his or her own affairs. By contrast, for example, a beneficiary of a family voting trust who is in business and has access to the relevant information has no similar need of protection by the trustee's lawyer. In any event, whether or not there is liability under this Section, a lawyer may be liable to a nonclient as stated in § 56.

A lawyer owes no duty to a beneficiary if recognizing such duty would create conflicting or inconsistent duties that might significantly impair the lawyer's performance of obligations to the lawyer's client in the circumstances of the representation. Such impairment might occur, for example, if the lawyer were subject to liability for assisting the fiduciary in an open dispute with a beneficiary or for assisting the fiduciary in exercise of its judgment that would benefit one beneficiary at the expense of another. For similar reasons, a lawyer is not subject to liability to a beneficiary under Subsection (4) for representing the fiduciary in a dispute or negotiation with the beneficiary with respect to a matter affecting the fiduciary's interests.

Under Subsection (4) a lawyer is not liable for failing to take action that the lawyer reasonably believes to be forbidden by professional rules (see § 54(1)). Thus, a lawyer is not liable for failing to disclose confidences when the lawyer reasonably believes that disclosure is forbidden. For example, a lawyer is under no duty to disclose a prospective breach in a jurisdiction that allows disclosure only regarding a crime or fraud threatening imminent death or substantial bodily harm. However, liability could result from failing to attempt to prevent the breach of fiduciary duty through means that do not entail disclosure. In any event, a lawyer's duty under this Section requires only the care set forth in § 52.

Illustrations:

5. Lawyer represents Client in Client's capacity as trustee of an express trust for the benefit of Beneficiary. Client tells Lawyer that Client proposes to transfer trust funds into Client's own account, in circumstances that would constitute embezzlement. Lawyer informs Client that the transfer would be criminal, but Client nevertheless makes the transfer, as Lawyer then knows. Lawyer takes no steps to prevent or rectify the consequences, for example by warning Beneficiary or informing the court to which Client as trustee must make an annual accounting. The jurisdiction's professional rules do not forbid such disclosures (see § 67). Client likewise makes no disclosure. The funds are lost, to the harm of Beneficiary. Lawyer is subject to liability to Beneficiary under this Section.

6. Same facts as in Illustration 5, except that Client asserts to Lawyer that the account to which Client proposes to transfer trust funds is the trust's account. Even though lawyer could have exercised diligence and thereby discovered this to be false, Lawyer does not do so. Lawyer is not liable to the harmed Beneficiary. Lawyer did not owe Beneficiary a duty to use care because Lawyer did not know (although further investigation would have revealed) that appropriate action was necessary to prevent a breach of fiduciary duty by Client.

7. Same facts as in Illustration 5, except that Client proposes to invest trust funds in a way that would be unlawful, but would not constitute a crime or fraud under applicable law. Lawyer's services are not used in consummating the investment. Lawyer does nothing to discourage the investment. Lawyer is not subject to liability to Beneficiary under this Section.

§ 52. Standard of Care

(1) For purposes of liability under §§ 48 and 49, a lawyer who owes a duty of care must exercise the competence and diligence normally exercised by lawyers in similar circumstances.

(2) Proof of a violation of a rule or statute regulating the conduct of lawyers:

(a) does not give rise to an implied cause of action for professional negligence or breach of fiduciary duty;

(b) does not preclude other proof concerning the duty of care in Subsection (1) or the fiduciary duty; and

(c) may be considered by a trier of fact as an aid in understanding and applying the standard of Subsection (1) or § 49 to the extent that (i) the rule or statute was designed for the protection of persons in the position of the claimant and (ii) proof of the content and construction of such a rule or statute is relevant to the claimant's claim.

Comment:

a. Scope and cross-references. This Section defines the duty of care a lawyer owes to clients and to nonclients to whom a duty of care is owed under § 51. A lawyer must exercise such care in pursuing a client's objectives and in fulfilling fiduciary duties owed to a client (see § 50). On the application of the duty to nonclients, see Comment *e* hereto. For a lawyer to be liable for malpractice, the lawyer's violation of this duty must be a legal cause of injury (see § 53) to a person to whom the lawyer owes a duty of care (see §§ 50 & 51), and the lawyer must have established no defense (see § 54). Whether a lawyer has failed to exercise the care required by this Section is not necessarily the same issue as whether the lawyer is subject to professional discipline, litigation sanctions, or other remedies other than legal-malpractice liability. On a lawyer's liability to a client for breach of contract, see § 55. On the applicability of this Section in a client's action for breach of a lawyer's fiduciary duty, see § 49, Comment *d*. On the use of confidential client information by a lawyer defending against a former client's claim of malpractice, see §§ 64 and 80.

b. Competence. The duty of competence set forth in this Section is that generally applicable to practitioners of a profession, that is, "the skill and knowledge normally possessed by members of that profession or trade in good standing . . ." (Restatement Second, Torts § 299A). Informed clients expect services of this kind; it is practical for lawyers to provide them; and the practice of the profession will most often be evidence of what clients need. As is generally true for professions, the legal duty refers to normal professional practice to define the ordinary standard of care for lawyers, rather than referring to that standard as simply evidence of reasonableness.

The competence duty, like that for diligence, does not make the lawyer a guarantor of a successful outcome in the representation (see § 55(1)). It does not expose the lawyer to liability to a client for acting only within the scope of the representation (see § 19 & § 54, Comment *b*) or following the client's instructions (see § 21(2) & § 54, Comment *h*). It does not require a lawyer, in a situation involving the exercise of professional judgment, to employ the same means or select the same options as would other competent lawyers in the many situations in which competent lawyers reasonably exercise professional judgment in different ways. The duty also does not require "average" performance, which would imply that the less skillful part of the profession would automatically be committing malpractice. The duty is one of reasonableness in the circumstances.

A trier of fact applying the standard may consider such circumstances as time pressures, uncertainty about facts or law, the varying means by which different competent lawyers seek to accomplish the same client goal, and the impossibility that all clients will reach their goals. Such factors are especially prevalent in litigation. They warrant caution in evaluating lawyers' decisions, although they do not warrant the view, still occasionally asserted, that all decisions taken in good faith are exempt from malpractice liability. Expert testimony by those knowledgeable about the legal subject matter in question is relevant in applying the standard (see Comment *g* hereto). In appropriate circumstances, a tribunal passing on a motion for summary judgment or directed verdict may determine whether a lawyer has satisfied the duty.

The professional community whose practices and standards are relevant in applying this duty of competence is ordinarily that of lawyers undertaking similar matters in the relevant jurisdiction (typically, a state). (On conflict-of-laws problems, see § 5, Comment *h* (lawyer discipline); § 48, Comment *f*.) The narrower "locality test," under which the standards of a local community governed, has seldom been recognized for lawyers. Restatement Second, Torts § 299A, Comment *g*. The locality test is now generally rejected for all professions, because all professionals can normally obtain access to standard information and facilities, because clients no longer limit themselves to local professionals, and because of the practicalities of proof in malpractice cases (see Comment *g* hereto). In many fields of legal practice, for example the preparation of securities-registration statements or the representation of clients in federal court in litigation under federal legislation, there exists a national practice with national standards. In applying the competence duty, however, it may be appropriate to consider factors such as the unavailability of particular research sources in the community where a lawyer practices in light of the difficulty and probable value in the circumstances of having done further research.

c. *Diligence.* A lawyer must devote reasonable diligence to a representation. The lawyer must perform tasks reasonably appropriate to the representation, including, where appropriate, inquiry into facts, analysis of law, exercise of professional judgment, communication with the client, rendering of practical and ethical advice, and drafting of documents. What kind and extent of effort is appropriate depends on factors such as the scope of the representation (see § 19(1)), the client's instructions (see § 21(2)), the importance of the matter to the client (which may be indicated by the client's own assertions as well as by the matter's probable impact on the client's affairs), the cost of the effort, customary practice, and the time available. A lawyer who informs a client that the lawyer will undertake a specifically described activity is required to do so, as is one properly instructed by a client to take a particular step (see § 21(2)). Circumstances might make it necessary to provide more than one lawyer for a client's matter or to provide appropriate supervision of subordinate lawyers (see § 11) or certain corresponding counsel (see § 58, Comment *e*). When paralegals or other nonlawyers are used, they must be properly supervised. See Restatement Second, Torts § 231, § 58 (vicarious liability of firm and partners); § 11(4) (duty to supervise). Even when a lawyer has been inadequately diligent, the lawyer's breach of duty might not be the legal cause of compensable damage (see § 53), for example if without required investigation the lawyer recommended that the client accept a settlement offer that was in fact a good one.

* * *

§ 53. Causation and Damages

A lawyer is liable under § 48 or § 49 only if the lawyer's breach of a duty of care or breach of fiduciary duty was a legal cause of injury, as determined under generally applicable principles of causation and damages.

Comment:

* * *

b. *Action by a civil litigant: loss of a judgment.* In a lawyer-negligence or fiduciary-breach action brought by one who was the plaintiff in a former and unsuccessful civil action, the plaintiff usually seeks to recover as damages the damages that would have been recovered in the previous action or the additional amount that would have been recovered but for the defendant's misconduct. To do so, the plaintiff must prove by a preponderance of the evidence that, but for the defendant lawyer's misconduct, the plaintiff would have obtained a more favorable judgment in the previous action. The plaintiff must thus prevail in a "trial within a trial." All the issues that would have been litigated in the previous action are litigated between the plaintiff and the plaintiff's former lawyer, with the latter taking the place and bearing the burdens that properly would have fallen on the defendant in the original action. Similarly, the plaintiff bears the burden the plaintiff would have borne in the original trial; in considering whether the plaintiff has carried that burden, however, the trier of fact may consider whether the defendant lawyer's misconduct has made it more difficult for the plaintiff to prove what would have been the result in the original trial. (On a lawyer's right to disclose client confidences when reasonably necessary in defending against a claim, see §§ 64 and 80.) Similar principles apply when a former civil defendant contends that, but for the misconduct of the defendant's former lawyer, the defendant would have secured a better result at trial.

What would have been the result of a previous trial presenting issues of fact normally is an issue for the factfinder in the negligence or fiduciary-breach action. What would have been the result of an appeal in the previous action is, however, an issue of law to be decided by the judge in the negligence or fiduciary-breach action. The judges or jurors who heard or would have heard the original trial or appeal may not be called as witnesses to testify as to how they would have ruled. That would constitute an inappropriate burden on the judiciary and jurors and an unwise personalization of the issue of how a reasonable judge or jury would have ruled.

A plaintiff may show that the defendant's negligence or fiduciary breach caused injury other than the loss of a judgment. For example, a plaintiff may contend that, in a previous action, the plaintiff would have obtained a settlement but for the malpractice of the lawyer who then represented the plaintiff. A plaintiff might contend that the defendant in the previous action made a settlement offer, that the plaintiff's then lawyer negligently failed to inform plaintiff of the offer (see § 20(3)), and that, if informed, plaintiff would have accepted the offer. If the plaintiff can prove this, the plaintiff can recover the difference between what the claimant would have received under the settlement offer and the amount, if any, the claimant in fact received through later settlement or judgment. Similarly, in appropriate circumstances, a plaintiff who can establish that the negligence or fiduciary breach of the plaintiff's former lawyer deprived the plaintiff of a substantial chance of prevailing and that, due to that misconduct, the results of a previous trial cannot be reconstructed, may recover for the loss of that chance in jurisdictions recognizing such a theory of recovery in professional-malpractice cases generally.

The plaintiff in a previous civil action may recover without proving the results of a trial if the party claims damages other than loss of a judgment. For example, a lawyer who negligently discloses a client's trade secret during litigation might be liable for harm to the client's business caused by the disclosure.

Even when a plaintiff would have recovered through trial or settlement in a previous civil action, recovery in the negligence or fiduciary-breach action of what would have been the judgment or settlement in the previous action is precluded in some circumstances. Thus, the lawyer's misconduct will not be the legal cause of loss to the extent that the defendant lawyer can show that the judgment or settlement would have been uncollectible, for example because the previous defendant was insolvent and uninsured. The defendant lawyer bears the burden of coming forward with evidence that this was so. Placement of this burden on the defending lawyer is appropriate because most civil judgments are collectible and because the defendant lawyer was the one who undertook to seek the judgment that the lawyer now calls worthless. The burden of persuading the jury as to collectibility remains upon the plaintiff.

c. Action by a civil litigant: attorney fees that would have been due. When it is shown that a plaintiff would have prevailed in the former civil action but for the lawyer's legal fault, it might be thought that—applying strict causation principles—the damages to be recovered in the legal-malpractice action should be reduced by the fee due the lawyer in the former matter. That is, the plaintiff has lost the net amount recovered after paying that attorney fee. Yet if the net amount were all the plaintiff could recover in the malpractice action, the defendant lawyer would in effect be credited with a fee that the lawyer never earned, and the plaintiff would have to pay two lawyers (the defendant lawyer and the plaintiff's lawyer in the malpractice action) to recover one judgment.

Denial of a fee deduction hence may be an appropriate sanction for the defendant lawyer's misconduct: to the extent that the lawyer defendant did not earn a fee due to the lawyer's misconduct, no such fee may be deducted in calculating the recovery in the malpractice action. The same principles apply to a legal-malpractice plaintiff who was a defendant in a previous civil action. The appropriateness and extent of disallowing deduction of the fee are determined under the standards of § 37 governing fee forfeiture. In some circumstances, those standards allow the lawyer to be credited with fees for services that benefited the client. See § 37, Comment *e*.

Illustration:

1. Plaintiff retains Lawyer to bring a contract action seeking to recover $40,000, at a fee of $150 per hour. After working 10 hours, Lawyer withdraws without cause just before the trial. As a result, Plaintiff's case is dismissed with prejudice. When Plaintiff then sues Lawyer for malpractice and shows that Plaintiff would have prevailed in the contract action but for Lawyer's withdrawal, Plaintiff is entitled to recover $40,000. Lawyer is not entitled to deduct either attorney fees for hours devoted to the case before the withdrawal or hours that would have been devoted to the trial, for both were forfeited by Lawyer's improper and harmful withdrawal (see §§ 37 & 40, Comment e).

d. Action by a criminal defendant. A convicted criminal defendant suing for malpractice must prove both that the lawyer failed to act properly and that, but for that failure, the result would have been different, for example because a double-jeopardy defense would have prevented conviction. Although most jurisdictions addressing the issue have stricter rules, under this Section it is not necessary to prove that the convicted defendant was in fact innocent. As required by most jurisdictions addressing the issue, a convicted defendant seeking damages for malpractice causing a conviction must have had that conviction set aside when process for that relief on the grounds asserted in the malpractice action is available.

A judgment in a postconviction proceeding is binding in the malpractice action to the extent provided by the law of judgments. That law prevents a convicted defendant from relitigating an issue decided in a postconviction proceeding after a full and fair opportunity to litigate, even though the lawyer sued was not a party to that proceeding and is hence not bound by any decision favorable to the defendant. See Restatement Second, Judgements §§ 27–29. Some jurisdictions hold public defenders immune from malpractice suits.

e. *Nonlitigated matters.* Generally applicable principles of causation and damages apply in malpractice actions arising out of a nonlitigated matter. When a lawyer is subject to liability to a nonclient under § 51(2) for negligence in preparing an opinion letter on which the nonclient reasonably relied, recovery is ordinarily governed by the causation and damages rules applicable to negligent misrepresentation actions, unless the lawyer has undertaken greater responsibility to the nonclient (see Restatement Second, Torts § 552B).

f. *Attorney fees as damages.* Like other civil litigants, the winning party in a malpractice action ordinarily cannot recover its attorney fees and other expenses in the malpractice action itself, except to the limited extent that the jurisdiction allows the recovery of court costs. The rule barring fee recovery has exceptions, which may be applicable in a malpractice action in appropriate circumstances. For example, many jurisdictions allow recovery of attorney fees against a plaintiff or defendant that litigates in bad faith (see also § 110, Comment *g* (litigation sanctions)).

The rule barring recovery of fees does not prevent a successful legal-malpractice plaintiff from recovering as damages additional legal expenses reasonably incurred outside the malpractice action itself as a result of a lawyer's misconduct. For example, if a lawyer's negligent title search causes a client to buy land with an unclear title and as a result to incur legal expenses defending the title against a challenger, the client may recover those expenses from the negligent lawyer.

g. *Damages for emotional distress.* General principles applicable to the recovery of damages for emotional distress apply to legal-malpractice actions. In general, such damages are inappropriate in types of cases in which emotional distress is unforeseeable. Thus, emotional-distress damages are ordinarily not recoverable when a lawyer's misconduct causes the client to lose profits from a commercial transaction, but are ordinarily recoverable when misconduct causes a client's imprisonment. The law in some jurisdictions permits recovery for emotional-distress damages only when the defendant lawyer's conduct was clearly culpable (see also § 56, Comment *g*).

h. *Punitive damages.* Whether punitive damages are recoverable in a legal-malpractice action depends on the jurisdiction's generally applicable law. Punitive damages are generally permitted only on a showing of intentional or reckless misconduct by a defendant.

A few decisions allow a plaintiff to recover from a lawyer punitive damages that would have been recovered from the defendant in an underlying action but for the lawyer's misconduct. However, such recovery is not required by the punitive and deterrent purposes of punitive damages. Collecting punitive damages from the lawyer will neither punish nor deter the original tortfeasor and calls for a speculative reconstruction of a hypothetical jury's reaction.

i. *Joint and several liability; contribution; claims against successor counsel.* The principles of joint and several or several liability generally applicable to negligence actions apply to professional-negligence and fiduciary-breach actions (see Chapter 4, Introductory Note). If, for example, a seller and the seller's lawyer both participate in negligent misrepresentations to a buyer, and if the lawyer owes a duty of care to the buyer under § 51(2), general principles of law make the seller and lawyer jointly and severally liable for resulting damages. See also § 56, Comment *d* (liability for advising and assisting clients); Restatement Second, Torts §§ 875–886B. Generally applicable law also governs whether one tortfeasor who has been held liable can obtain contribution or indemnity from another. On a client's obligation to indemnify a lawyer for liabilities to which the client has exposed the lawyer without the lawyer's fault, see § 17(2). On vicarious liability of law firms and their partners for certain torts of firm lawyers, see § 58.

When the damage caused by the negligence or fiduciary breach of a lawyer is increased by the negligence or fiduciary breach of successor counsel retained by the client, the first lawyer is liable to the client for the whole damage if the conditions set forth in Restatement Second, Torts § 447 are satisfied. The successor lawyer is also directly liable to the client for damage caused by that lawyer's negligence or fiduciary breach. The first lawyer, however, may not seek contribution or indemnity from the successor lawyer in the same action in which the successor lawyer represents the client, for that would allow the first lawyer to create or exacerbate a conflict of interest for the second lawyer and force withdrawal of the second lawyer from the action. The first lawyer may, however, dispute liability in the negligence or fiduciary breach action for the portion of the damages caused by the second lawyer on the ground that the conditions of in Restatement Second, Torts § 447 are not satisfied. The client may then choose whether to accept the possibility of such a reduction in damages or to assert a second claim against successor counsel, with the resultant necessity of retaining a third lawyer to proceed against the first two. Regardless of whether the client asserts a second claim, such three-sided disputes may raise problems involving client confidences (see § 52, Comment *h*), conflicts of interest (see § 125), lawyer duties of disclosure (see § 20, Comment *c*), and lawyer witnesses (see § 108) that require lawyers and judges to act carefully to protect the rights of clients and lawyers.

§ 54. Defenses; Prospective Liability Waiver; Settlement with a Client

(1) Except as otherwise provided in this Section, liability under §§ 48 and 49 is subject to the defenses available under generally applicable principles of law governing respectively actions for professional negligence and breach of fiduciary duty. A lawyer is not liable under § 48 or § 49 for any action or inaction the lawyer reasonably believed to be required by law, including a professional rule.

(2) An agreement prospectively limiting a lawyer's liability to a client for malpractice is unenforceable.

(3) The client or former client may rescind an agreement settling a claim by the client or former client against the person's lawyer if:

(a) the client or former client was subjected to improper pressure by the lawyer in reaching the settlement; or

(b) (i) the client or former client was not independently represented in negotiating the settlement, and (ii) the settlement was not fair and reasonable to the client or former client.

(4) For purposes of professional discipline, a lawyer may not:

(a) make an agreement prospectively limiting the lawyer's liability to a client for malpractice; or

(b) settle a claim for such liability with an unrepresented client or former client without first advising that person in writing that independent representation is appropriate in connection therewith.

TOPIC 2. OTHER CIVIL LIABILITY

§ 55. Civil Remedies of a Client Other Than for Malpractice

(1) A lawyer is subject to liability to a client for injury caused by breach of contract in the circumstances and to the extent provided by contract law.

(2) A client is entitled to restitutionary, injunctive, or declaratory remedies against a lawyer in the circumstances and to the extent provided by generally applicable law governing such remedies.

§ 56. Liability to a Client or Nonclient Under General Law

Except as provided in § 57 and in addition to liability under §§ 48–55, a lawyer is subject to liability to a client or nonclient when a nonlawyer would be in similar circumstances.

§ 57. Nonclient Claims—Certain Defenses and Exceptions to Liability

(1) In addition to other absolute or conditional privileges, a lawyer is absolutely privileged to publish matter concerning a nonclient if:

(a) the publication occurs in communications preliminary to a reasonably anticipated proceeding before a tribunal or in the institution or during the course and as a part of such a proceeding;

(b) the lawyer participates as counsel in that proceeding; and

(c) the matter is published to a person who may be involved in the proceeding, and the publication has some relation to the proceeding.

(2) A lawyer representing a client in a civil proceeding or procuring the institution of criminal proceedings by a client is not liable to a nonclient for wrongful use of civil proceedings or for malicious prosecution if the lawyer has probable cause for acting, or if the lawyer acts primarily to help the client obtain a proper adjudication of the client's claim in that proceeding.

(3) A lawyer who advises or assists a client to make or break a contract, to enter or dissolve a legal relationship, or to enter or not enter a contractual relation, is not liable to a nonclient for interference with contract or with prospective contractual relations or with a legal relationship, if the lawyer acts to advance the client's objectives without using wrongful means.

TOPIC 3. VICARIOUS LIABILITY

§ 58. Vicarious Liability

(1) A law firm is subject to civil liability for injury legally caused to a person by any wrongful act or omission of any principal or employee of the firm who was acting in the ordinary course of the firm's business or with actual or apparent authority.

(2) Each of the principals of a law firm organized as a general partnership without limited liability is liable jointly and severally with the firm.

(3) A principal of a law firm organized other than as a general partnership without limited liability as authorized by law is vicariously liable for the acts of another principal or employee of the firm to the extent provided by law.

CHAPTER 5. CONFIDENTIAL CLIENT INFORMATION

TOPIC 1. CONFIDENTIALITY RESPONSIBILITIES OF LAWYERS

TITLE A. A LAWYER'S CONFIDENTIALITY DUTIES

§ 59. Definition of "Confidential Client Information"

Confidential client information consists of information relating to representation of a client, other than information that is generally known.

Comment:

a. *Scope and cross-references.* This Section defines information concerning the representation of a client governed by the confidentiality rule stated in § 60 and for which exceptions are stated in other Sections in this Topic. For the most part, the definition of this Section is relevant to applications of the general duty of confidentiality (see § 60) owed to a current client and to former clients. On the relevance of the definition of confidential information to a determination whether a former matter is "substantially related" to a current matter, see § 132, Comment *d(ii)*.

b. Kinds of confidential client information. A client's approach to a lawyer for legal assistance implies that the client trusts the lawyer to advance and protect the interests of the client (see § 16(1)). The resulting duty of loyalty is the predicate of the duty of confidentiality. The information that a lawyer is obliged to protect and safeguard is called confidential client information in this Restatement.

This definition covers all information relating to representation of a client, whether in oral, documentary, electronic, photographic, or other forms. It covers information gathered from any source, including sources such as third persons whose communications are not protected by the attorney-client privilege (see § 70). It includes work product that the lawyer develops in representing the client, such as the lawyer's notes to a personal file, whether or not the information is immune from discovery as lawyer work product (see Topic 3). It includes information acquired by a lawyer in all client-lawyer relationships (see § 14), including functioning as inside or outside legal counsel, government or private-practice lawyer, counselor or litigator, advocate or intermediary. It applies whether or not the client paid a fee, and whether a lawyer learns the information personally or through an agent, for example information acquired by a lawyer's partners or associate lawyers or by an investigator, paralegal, or secretary. Information acquired by an agent is protected even if it was not thereafter communicated to the lawyer, such as material acquired by an investigator and kept in the investigator's files.

The definition includes information that becomes known by others, so long as the information does not become generally known. See Comment *d* hereto; compare § 71 (condition of attorney-client privilege that communication be made with reasonable expectation of confidentiality); § 79 (waiver of the attorney-client privilege by subsequent disclosure). The fact that information falls outside the attorney-client privilege or work-product immunity does not determine its confidentiality under this Section.

A lawyer may learn information relevant to representation of a client in the course of representing another client, from casual reading or in other accidental ways. On the use of information learned from representation of another client, see § 60, Comment *l*. In the course of representation, a lawyer may learn confidential information about the client that is not necessary for the representation but which is of a personal or proprietary nature or other character such that the client evidently would not wish it disclosed. Such information is confidential under this Section.

c. The time at which information is acquired. Information acquired during the representation or before or after the representation is confidential so long as it is not generally known (see Comment *d* hereto) and relates to the representation. Such information, for example, might be acquired by the lawyer in considering whether to undertake a representation. On the duties of a lawyer with respect to confidential information of a prospective client, see § 15, Comment *c*. Post-representation confidential client information might be acquired, for example, in the form of information on subsequent developments.

Illustrations:

1. Lawyer represents Employer in defending against a claim of employment discrimination by Plaintiff. Plaintiff has joined both Employer and Personnel Director as defending parties. Lawyer extensively confers with Inside Legal Counsel, general counsel of Employer, who provides information about the claim as it relates to Personnel Director. Subsequently, Inside Legal Counsel authorizes Lawyer to represent Personnel Director as a co-client. Information acquired by Lawyer relating to representation of Personnel Director prior to forming the client-lawyer relationship is confidential client information under this Section. On application of the attorney-client privilege, compare § 76 (common-interest arrangements).

2. Lawyer represented Defendant in civil litigation, in which Defendant prevailed. Two years after the representation ended, a Juror in the case writes a letter to Lawyer stating that Defendant approached Juror and several other jurors in a recess during their deliberations and improperly provided them with new evidence that persuaded the jury to find for Defendant. Juror states in the letter that Juror wishes Lawyer to show the letter to the Judge who presided at the trial. Although not subject to the attorney-client privilege (see §§ 70 & 71), the letter relates to Lawyer's representation of Defendant and is thus confidential under this Section. Whether Lawyer may disclose the information is governed by §§ 61–67.

d. Generally known information. Confidential client information does not include information that is generally known. Such information may be employed by lawyer who possesses it in permissibly representing other clients (see § 60, Comments *g* & *h*) and in other contexts where there is a specific justification for doing so (compare Comment *e* hereto). Information might be generally known at the time it is conveyed to the lawyer or might become generally known thereafter. At the same time, the fact that information has become known to some others does not deprive it of protection if it has not become generally known in the relevant sector of the public.

Whether information is generally known depends on all circumstances relevant in obtaining the information. Information contained in books or records in public libraries, public-record depositaries such as government offices, or in publicly accessible electronic-data storage is generally known if the particular information is obtainable through publicly available indexes and similar methods of access. Information is not generally known when a person interested in knowing the information could obtain it only by means of special knowledge or substantial difficulty or expense. Special knowledge includes information about the whereabouts or identity of a person or other source from which the information can be acquired, if those facts are not themselves generally known.

A lawyer may not justify adverse use or disclosure of client information simply because the information has become known to third persons, if it is not otherwise generally known. Moreover, if a current client specifically requests that information of any kind not be used or disclosed in ways otherwise permissible, the lawyer must either honor that request or withdraw from the representation (see § 32; see also §§ 16(2) & 21(2)).

e. Information concerning law, legal institutions, and similar matters. Confidential client information does not include what a lawyer learns about the law, legal institutions such as courts and administrative agencies, and similar public matters in the course of representing clients. Such information is part of the general fund of information available to the lawyer. During legal research of an issue while representing a client, a lawyer may discover a particularly important precedent or devise a novel legal approach that is useful both in the immediate matter and in other representations. The lawyer and other members of the lawyer's firm may use and disclose that information in other representations, so long as they thereby disclose no confidential client information except as permitted by § 60. A lawyer may use such information—about the state of the law, the best way to approach an administrative agency, the preferable way to frame an argument before a particular judge—in a future, otherwise unrelated representation that is adverse to the former client. On the otherwise general prohibition against adverse use or disclosure of confidential information of a former client, see § 132, Comment *f*.

§ 60. A Lawyer's Duty to Safeguard Confidential Client Information

(1) Except as provided in §§ 61–67, during and after representation of a client:

(a) the lawyer may not use or disclose confidential client information as defined in § 59 if there is a reasonable prospect that doing so will adversely affect a material interest of the client or if the client has instructed the lawyer not to use or disclose such information;

(b) the lawyer must take steps reasonable in the circumstances to protect confidential client information against impermissible use or disclosure by the lawyer's associates or agents that may adversely affect a material interest of the client or otherwise than as instructed by the client.

(2) Except as stated in § 62, a lawyer who uses confidential information of a client for the lawyer's pecuniary gain other than in the practice of law must account to the client for any profits made.

Comment:

a. Scope and cross-references. This Section states the principal duties of a lawyer with respect to confidential client information. The first duty is negative—not to use or disclose the information. The second is positive—to safeguard confidential client information in the client's interests. The third duty protects clients against lawyer use or disclosure of confidential information for self-profit (see Comment *j* hereto). The duty not to use or disclose confidential client information is subject to the exceptions provided in §§ 61–67. The duty to safeguard entails the corollary duties to provide adequate supervision of nonlawyer personnel (see § 11) and to assert privileges and other legal protection applicable to confidential client information such as the attorney-client privilege (see § 86(1)(b)) and the work-product immunity (see § 87). See Comment *c* hereto. The duty to safeguard such information is also a principal basis for the rules prohibiting former client conflicts of interest (see Chapter 8, Topic 4). On a lawyer's duty to safeguard confidential information of a prospective client, see § 15.

Remedies for a lawyer's breach of the obligation of § 60 may depend upon the kind of information involved and the nature of the improper use or disclosure. Remedies include exclusion or suppression of the lawyer's attempted testimony in violation of the attorney-client privilege (see § 86), the protection of lawyer work-product against intrusion by third parties (see Topic 3), a client's right to recover damages for negligent (see § 48) or intentional (see § 56) breach of an obligation of confidentiality, professional discipline (see § 5), and the remedies relating to conflicts of interest (see § 6, Comment *i*).

b. Conflicts between protection of confidential client information and other values. The broad prohibition against divulging confidential client information comes at a cost to both lawyers and society. Lawyers sometimes learn information that cannot be disclosed because of the rule of confidentiality but that would be highly useful to other persons. Those may include persons whose personal plight and character are much more sympathetic than those of the lawyer's client or who could accomplish great public good or avoid great public detriment if the information were disclosed. Moreover, the free-speech interests of lawyers is impinged by a broad rule of confidentiality. Nonetheless, despite those costs, the confidentiality rule reflects a considered judgment that high net social value justifies it. It is recognized that the rule better protects legitimate client expectations about communications to their lawyers and that permitting divulgence would be inconsistent with the goal of furthering the lawful objectives of clients (see § 16(1)).

Illustration:

1. Lawyer is appointed to represent Client, a person who has been accused of murder. During confidential conferences between them, Client informs Lawyer that Client in fact committed not only the murder charged but two others as well. Client gives Lawyer sufficient detail to confirm beyond question that Client's story is true. The two other murders involve victims whose bodies have not yet been discovered. Because of similarities between the circumstances of the murders, parents of one of the victims approach Lawyer and beg for any information about their child. Lawyer realizes the personal anguish of the victim's parents and the peace the information that he knows could bring them. Unless Client consents to disclosure (see § 62), Lawyer must respond that Lawyer has no information to give them.

c. Impermissible use or disclosure—in general. A lawyer is prohibited from using or disclosing confidential client information if either of two conditions exists—risk of harm to the client or client instruction.

c(i). Impermissible use or disclosure—a reasonable prospect of adverse effect on a material client interest. The duty of confidentiality is defined in terms of the risk of harm. Subject to exceptions provided in §§ 61–67, use or disclosure of confidential client information is generally prohibited if there is a reasonable prospect that doing so will adversely affect a material interest of the client or prospective client. Although the lawyer codes do not express this limitation, such is the accepted interpretation. For example, under a literal reading of ABA Model Rules of Professional Conduct, Rule 1.6(a) (1983), a lawyer would commit a disciplinary violation by telling an unassociated lawyer in casual conversation the identity of a firm client, even if mention of the client's identity creates no possible risk of harm. Such a strict interpretation goes beyond the proper interpretation of the rule.

What constitutes a reasonable prospect of adverse effect on a material client interest depends on the circumstances. Whether such a prospect exists must be judged from the perspective of a reasonable lawyer based on the specific context of the client matter. Some representations involve highly secret client information; others involve routine information as to which secrecy has little or no material importance. In most representations, some information will be more sensitive than other information. In all representations, the relevant inquiry is whether a lawyer of reasonable caution, considering only the client's objectives, would regard use or disclosure in the circumstances as creating an unreasonable risk of adverse effect either to those objectives or to other interests of the client. For example, a lawyer advising a client on tax planning for a gift that the client intends to keep anonymous from the donee would violate this Section if the lawyer revealed the client's purpose to the donee. If there is a reasonable ground to doubt whether use or disclosure of a client's confidential information would have the described effect, the lawyer should take reasonable steps to ascertain whether adverse effect would result, including consultation with the client when appropriate. Alternatively, the lawyer in such circumstances may obtain client consent to the use or disclosure (see § 62).

Adverse effects include all consequences that a lawyer of reasonable prudence would recognize as risking material frustration of the client's objectives in the representation or material misfortune, disadvantage, or other prejudice to a client in other respects, either during the course of the present representation or in the future. It includes consequences such as financial or physical harm and personal embarrassment that could be caused to a person of normal susceptibility and a normal interest in privacy.

Both use and disclosure adverse to a client are prohibited. As the term is employed in the Section, use of information includes taking the information significantly into account in framing a course of action, such as in making decisions when representing another client or in deciding whether to make a personal investment. Disclosure of information is revealing the information to a person not authorized to receive it and in a form that identifies the client or client matter either expressly or through reasonably ascertainable inference. Revealing information in a way that cannot be linked to the client involved is not a disclosure prohibited by the Section if there is no reasonable likelihood of adverse effect on a material interest of the client. Use of confidential client information can be adverse without disclosure. For example, in representing a subsequent client against the interests of a former client in a related matter, a lawyer who shapes the subsequent representation by employing confidential client information gained about the original client violates the duty of § 60(1) not to use that information, even if the lawyer does not disclose the information to anyone else (see § 132).

c(ii). Impermissible use or disclosure—specific client instructions. Even in the absence of a reasonable prospect of risk of harm to a client, use or disclosure is also prohibited if the affected client instructs the lawyer (see § 21(2)) not to use or disclose information. Such a direction is the client's definition of the client's interests (see § 16(1)), which controls (see § 21(2)). Such an instruction may also limit a lawyer's implied authority to use or disclose confidential client information to advance a client's interests. On the ability of a lawyer to withdraw, see § 32. However, client limitations on a lawyer's authority do not alter a lawyer's obligations under § 63 (using or disclosing confidential client information when required by law or court order) (see § 23). With respect to communications with a third person such as a relative of a client with diminished capacity, see § 24, Comment *c*.

When a fee for a client is paid by a third person (see § 134(1)) and in the absence of different client agreement or instructions, the client and not the third person directs the lawyer with respect to such matters as the treatment of files or other confidential client information. For the special instance of liability insurers, compare § 134, Comment *f*.

d. A lawyer's duty to safeguard confidential client information. A lawyer who acquires confidential client information has a duty to take reasonable steps to secure the information against misuse or inappropriate disclosure, both by the lawyer and by the lawyer's associates or agents to whom the lawyer may permissibly divulge it (see Comment *e*). This requires that client confidential information be acquired, stored, retrieved, and transmitted under systems and controls that are reasonably designed and managed to maintain confidentiality. In responding to a discovery request, for example, a lawyer must exercise reasonable care against the risk that confidential client information not subject to the request is inadvertently disclosed (see § 79). A lawyer should so conduct interviews with clients and others that the benefit of the attorney-client privilege and work-product immunity are preserved (see § 70, Comment *f*). On the release of information to further a client's objectives, including the waiver of claims of privilege or immunity, see § 61, Comment *d*. On asserting objections to attempts to obtain the client's confidential information, see § 63, Comment *b*.

A lawyer must take reasonable steps so that law-office personnel and other agents such as independent investigators properly handle confidential client information. That includes devising and enforcing appropriate policies and practices concerning confidentiality and supervising such personnel in performing those duties (see § 11). A lawyer may act reasonably in relying on other responsible persons in the office or on reputable independent contractors to provide that instruction and supervision (see id.). The reasonableness of specific protective measures depends on such factors as the duties of the agent or other person, the extent to which disclosure would adversely affect the client, the extent of prior training or experience of the person, the existence of other assurances such as adequate supervision by senior employees, and the customs and reputation of independent contractors.

Greater precautions may be necessary when use or disclosure is not directed toward representation of the client (see Comment *f* hereto) or facilitating the lawyer's law practice (see Comment *g*), for example when information is provided to a lawyer outside the firm to assist that lawyer's own representations. A lawyer must not engage in casual or frivolous conversation about a client's matters that creates an unreasonable risk of harm to the interests of the client.

e. Postrepresentation safeguarding. The duty of confidentiality continues so long as the lawyer possesses confidential client information. It extends beyond the end of the representation and beyond the death of the client. Accordingly, a lawyer must take reasonable steps for the future safekeeping of client files, including files in closed matters, or the systematic destruction of nonessential closed files. A lawyer must also take reasonably appropriate steps to provide for return, destruction, or continued safekeeping of client files in the event of the lawyer's retirement, ill health, death, discipline, or other interruption of the lawyer's practice.

f. Divulgence to persons assisting a lawyer in representing a client. A lawyer generally has authority to use or disclose confidential client information to persons assisting the lawyer in representing the client. Those include other lawyers in the same firm and employees such as secretaries and paralegals. A lawyer also may disclose information to independent contractors who assist in the representation, such as investigators, lawyers in other firms, prospective expert witnesses, and public courier companies and photocopy shops, to the extent reasonably appropriate in the client's behalf (see also § 70, Comment *h*). Such disclosures are not permitted contrary to a client's instructions, even within the lawyer's firm (see Comment *c(ii)* hereto), or when screening is required to avoid imputed disqualification of the lawyer's firm (see § 124, Comment *d*, & § 133, Comment *g*).

A lawyer's authority to disclose information for purposes of carrying out the representation is implied and therefore does not require express client consent (see § 21(3)). Agents of a lawyer assisting in representing a client serve as subagents and as such independently owe a duty of confidentiality to the client. See generally Restatement Second, Agency § 428(1) (subagent's general duties to known principals); id.§ 395 (agent's general duty of confidentiality).

g. Divulgence to facilitate law practice. A lawyer may disclose confidential client information for the purpose of facilitating the lawyer's law practice, where no reasonable prospect of harm to the client is thereby created and where appropriate safeguards against impermissible use or disclosure are taken. Thus, disclosure is permitted to other lawyers in the same firm and to employees and agents such as accountants, file clerks, office managers, secretaries, and similar office assistants in the lawyer's firm, and with confidential, independent consultants, such as computer technicians, accountants, bookkeepers, law-practice consultants, and others who assist in furthering the law-practice business of the lawyer or the lawyer's firm. Use or disclosure of confidential client information, if prohibited under § 60, is not permitted for other business purposes, such as aiding investment or business, including one in which the lawyer owns an interest.

h. Divulgence for purpose of professional assistance and development; historical research. When no material risk to a client is entailed, a lawyer may disclose information derived from representing clients for purposes of providing professional assistance to other lawyers, whether informally, as in educational conversations among lawyers, or more formally, as in continuing-legal-education lectures. Thus, a lawyer may confer with another lawyer (whether or not in the same firm) concerning an issue in which the disclosing lawyer has gained experience through representing a client in order to assist the other lawyer in representing that lawyer's own clients.

A lawyer may cooperate with reasonable efforts to obtain information about clients and law practice for public purposes, such as historical research, when no material risk to a client is entailed, such as financial or reputational harm. A lawyer thereby cooperates in furthering public understanding of the law and law practice.

i. Divulgence concerning property dispositions by a deceased client. The attorney-client privilege does not apply to communications relevant to an issue between parties who claim an interest through the same decedent (see § 81). As a corollary, the lawyer may reveal confidential client information to contending heirs or other claimants to an interest through a deceased client, in advance of testifying, if there is a reasonable prospect that doing so would advance the interests of the client-decedent (see § 61). Authority to instruct the lawyer (see Comment *c(ii)* hereto) with respect to such divulgence is determined under the law of succession.

j. A lawyer's self-dealing in confidential client information. Subsection (2) prohibits a lawyer from using or disclosing confidential client information for the lawyer's personal enrichment, regardless of lack of risk of prejudice to the affected client. The duty is removed by client consent (see § 62). The sole remedy of the client for breach of the duty is restitutionary relief in the form of disgorgement of profit (see Restatement Second, Agency § 388, Comment *c*). The lawyer codes differ over whether such self-enriching use or disclosure constitutes a disciplinary violation in the absence of prejudice to the client.

The strict confidentiality duty of the Subsection is warranted for prophylactic purposes. A lawyer who acquires confidential client information as the result of a representation should not be tempted by expectation of profit to risk a possibly incorrect assessment of future harm to a client. There is no important social interest in permitting lawyers to make unconsented use or revelation of confidential client information for self-enrichment in personal transactions.

On limitations on business transactions between a lawyer and client, see § 126.

It is not inconsistent with Subsection (2) for a lawyer to use one client's confidential information for the benefit of another client in the course of representing the other client, even if doing so might also redound to the lawyer's gain, such as by enhancing a contingent-fee recovery. In all such instances, of course, the lawyer may not do so when it would create a material risk of harm to the original client. Thus, if otherwise permissible, a lawyer representing a plaintiff who has acquired extensive confidential information about the manner in which a defendant manufactured a product may employ that information for the benefit of another client with a claim against the same defendant arising out of a defect in the same product.

k. Confidentiality duties to a prospective client. See § 15, Comment c.

l. Use or disclosure of confidential information of co-clients. A lawyer may represent two or more clients in the same matter as co-clients either when there is no conflict of interest between them (see § 121) or when a conflict exists but the co-clients have adequately consented (see § 122). When a conflict of interest exists, as part of the process of obtaining consent, the lawyer is required to inform each co-client of the effect of joint representation upon disclosure of confidential information (see § 122, Comment *c(i)*), including both that all material information will be shared with each co-client during the course of the representation and that a communicating co-client will be unable to assert the attorney-client privilege against the other in the event of later adverse proceedings between them (see § 75).

Sharing of information among the co-clients with respect to the matter involved in the representation is normal and typically expected. As between the co-clients, in many such relationships each co-client is under a fiduciary duty to share all information material to the co-clients' joint enterprise. Such is the law, for example, with respect to members of a partnership. Limitation of the attorney-client privilege as applied to communications of co-clients is based on an assumption that each intends that his or her communications with the lawyer will be shared with the other co-clients but otherwise kept in confidence (see § 75, Comment *d*). Moreover, the common lawyer is required to keep each of the co-clients informed of all information reasonably necessary for the co-client to make decisions in connection with the matter (see § 20). The lawyer's duty extends to communicating information to other co-clients that is adverse to a co-client, whether learned from the lawyer's own investigation or learned in confidence from that co-client.

Co-clients may understand from the circumstances those obligations on the part of the lawyer and their own obligations, or they may explicitly agree to share information. Co-clients can also explicitly agree that the lawyer is not to share certain information, such as described categories of proprietary, financial, or similar information with one or more other co-clients (see § 75, Comment *d*). A lawyer must honor such agreements. If one co-client threatens physical harm or other types of crimes or fraud against the other, an exception to the lawyer's duty of confidentiality may apply (see §§ 66–67).

There is little case authority on the responsibilities of a lawyer when, in the absence of an agreement among the co-clients to restrict sharing of information, one co-client provides to the lawyer material information with the direction that it not be communicated to another co-client. The communicating co-client's expectation that the information be withheld from the other co-client may be manifest from the circumstances, particularly when the communication is clearly antagonistic to the interests of the affected co-client. The lawyer thus confronts a dilemma. If the information is material to the other co-client, failure to communicate it would compromise the lawyer's duties of loyalty, diligence (see § 16(1) & (2)), and communication (see § 20) to that client. On the other hand, sharing the communication with the affected co-client would compromise the communicating client's hope of confidentiality and risks impairing that client's trust in the lawyer.

Such circumstances create a conflict of interest among the co-clients (see § 121 & § 122, Comment *h*). The lawyer cannot continue in the representation without compromising either the duty of communication to the affected co-client or the expectation of confidentiality on the part of the communicating co-client. Moreover, continuing the joint representation without making disclosure may mislead the affected client or otherwise involve the lawyer in assisting the communicating client in a breach of fiduciary duty or other misconduct. Accordingly, the lawyer is required to withdraw unless the communicating client can be persuaded to permit sharing of the communication (see § 32(2)(a)). Following withdrawal, the lawyer may not, without consent of both, represent either co-client adversely to the other with respect to the same or a substantially related matter (see § 121, Comment *e(i)*).

In the course of withdrawal, the lawyer has discretion to warn the affected co-client that a matter seriously and adversely affecting that person's interests has come to light, which the other co-client refuses to permit the lawyer to disclose. Beyond such a limited warning, the lawyer, after consideration of all relevant circumstances, has the further discretion to inform the affected co-client of the specific communication if, in the lawyer's reasonable judgment, the immediacy and magnitude of the risk to the affected co-client outweigh the interest of the communicating client in continued secrecy. In making such determinations, the lawyer may take into account superior legal interests of the lawyer or of affected third persons, such as an interest implicated by a threat of physical harm to the lawyer or another person. See also § 66.

Illustrations:

2. Lawyer has been retained by Husband and Wife to prepare wills pursuant to an arrangement under which each spouse agrees to leave most of their property to the other (compare § 130, Comment c, Illustrations 1–3). Shortly after the wills are executed, Husband (unknown to Wife) asks Lawyer to prepare an inter vivos trust for an illegitimate child whose existence Husband has kept secret from Wife for many years and about whom Husband had not previously informed Lawyer. Husband states that Wife would be distraught at learning of Husband's infidelity and of Husband's years of silence and that disclosure of the information could destroy their marriage. Husband directs Lawyer not to inform Wife. The inter vivos trust that Husband proposes to create would not materially affect Wife's own estate plan or her expected receipt of property under Husband's will, because Husband proposes to use property designated in Husband's will for a personally favored charity. In view of the lack of material effect on Wife, Lawyer may assist Husband to establish and fund the inter vivos trust and refrain from disclosing Husband's information to Wife.

3. Same facts as Illustration 2, except that Husband's proposed inter vivos trust would significantly deplete Husband's estate, to Wife's material detriment and in frustration of the Spouses' intended testamentary arrangements. If Husband refuses to inform Wife or to permit Lawyer to do so, Lawyer must withdraw from representing both Husband and Wife. In the light of all relevant circumstances, Lawyer may exercise discretion whether to inform Wife either that circumstances, which Lawyer has been asked not to reveal, indicate that she should revoke her recent will or to inform Wife of some or all the details of the information that Husband has recently provided so that Wife may protect her interests. Alternatively, Lawyer may inform Wife only that Lawyer is withdrawing because Husband will not permit disclosure of relevant information.

4. Lawyer represents both A and B in forming a business. Before the business is completely formed, A discloses to Lawyer that he has been convicted of defrauding business associates on two recent occasions. The circumstances of the communication from A are such that Lawyer reasonably infers that A believes that B is unaware of that information and does not want it provided to B. Lawyer reasonably believes that B would call off the arrangement with A if B were made aware of the information. Lawyer must first attempt to persuade A either to inform B directly or to permit Lawyer to inform B of the information. Failing that, Lawyer must withdraw from representing both A and B.

In doing so, Lawyer has discretion to warn B that Lawyer has learned in confidence information indicating that B is at significant risk in carrying through with the business arrangement, but that A will not permit Lawyer to disclose that information to B. On the other hand, even if the circumstances do not warrant invoking § 67, Lawyer has the further discretion to inform B of the specific nature of A's communication to B if Lawyer reasonably believes this necessary to protect B's interests in view of the immediacy and magnitude of the threat that Lawyer perceives posed to B.

Even if the co-clients have agreed that the lawyer will keep certain categories of information confidential from one or more other co-clients, in some circumstances it might be evident to the lawyer that the uninformed co-client would not have agreed to nondisclosure had that co-client been aware of the nature of the adverse information. For example, a lawyer's examination of confidential financial information, agreed not to be shown to another co-client to reduce antitrust concerns, could show in fact, contrary to all exterior indications, that the disclosing co-client is insolvent. In view of the co-client's agreement, the lawyer must honor the commitment of confidentiality and not inform the other client, subject to the exceptions described in § 67. The lawyer must, however, withdraw if failure to reveal would mislead the affected client, involve the lawyer in assisting the communicating client in a course of fraud, breach of fiduciary duty, or other unlawful activity, or, as would be true in most such instances, involve the lawyer in representing conflicting interests.

m. *Use or disclosure of confidential information of a nonclient.* A lawyer may come into possession of confidential information of a nonclient, such as that of an opposing party in litigation or in negotiations. Such information may come from the other person or the lawyer or other agent of the person. When the receiving lawyer reasonably concludes that the transmission was authorized, the lawyer may use the information for the client's benefit, for example, where an opposing lawyer has conveyed the information apparently to advance representation (see § 61). Otherwise, the receiving lawyer's responsibilities depend on the circumstances. If the disclosure operates to end legal protection for the information, the lawyer may use it for the benefit of the lawyer's own client and may be required to do so if that would advance the client's lawful objectives (see § 16(1)). That would follow, for example, when an opposing lawyer failed to object to privileged or immune testimony (compare §§ 78, 86(1)(b), & 91(3)). The same legal result may follow when divulgence occurs inadvertently outside of court (see §§ 79 & 91). The receiving lawyer may be required to consult with that lawyer's client (see § 20) about whether to take advantage of the lapse.

If the person whose information was disclosed is entitled to have it suppressed or excluded (see § 79, Comment *c*), the receiving lawyer must either return the information or hold it for disposition after appropriate notification to the opposing person or that person's counsel. A court may suppress material after an inadvertent disclosure that did not amount to a waiver of the attorney-client privilege (see § 79, Comment *h*).

Where deceitful or illegal means were used to obtain the information, the receiving lawyer and that lawyer's client may be liable, among other remedies, for damages for harm caused or for injunctive relief against use or disclosure. The receiving lawyer must take steps to return such confidential client information and to keep it confidential from the lawyer's own client in the interim.

Similarly, if the receiving lawyer is aware that disclosure is being made in breach of trust by a lawyer or other agent of the opposing person, the receiving lawyer must not accept the information. An offending lawyer may be disqualified from further representation in a matter to which the information is relevant if the lawyer's own client would otherwise gain a substantial advantage (see § 6, Comment *i*). A tribunal may also order suppression or exclusion of such information.

TITLE B. USING OR DISCLOSING CONFIDENTIAL CLIENT INFORMATION

§ 61. Using or Disclosing Information to Advance Client Interests

A lawyer may use or disclose confidential client information when the lawyer reasonably believes that doing so will advance the interests of the client in the representation.

§ 62. Using or Disclosing Information with Client Consent

A lawyer may use or disclose confidential client information when the client consents after being adequately informed concerning the use or disclosure

§ 63. Using or Disclosing Information When Required by Law

A lawyer may use or disclose confidential client information when required by law, after the lawyer takes reasonably appropriate steps to assert that the information is privileged or otherwise protected against disclosure

§ 64. Using or Disclosing Information in a Lawyer's Self-Defense

A lawyer may use or disclose confidential client information when and to the extent that the lawyer reasonably believes necessary to defend the lawyer or the lawyer's associate or agent against a charge or threatened charge by any person that the lawyer or such associate or agent acted wrongfully in the course of representing a client.

§ 65. Using or Disclosing Information in a Compensation Dispute

A lawyer may use or disclose confidential client information when and to the extent that the lawyer reasonably believes necessary to permit the lawyer to resolve a dispute with the client concerning compensation or reimbursement that the lawyer reasonably claims the client owes the lawyer

§ 66. Using or Disclosing Information to Prevent Death or Serious Bodily Harm

(1) A lawyer may use or disclose confidential client information when the lawyer reasonably believes that its use or disclosure is necessary to prevent reasonably certain death or serious bodily harm to a person.

(2) Before using or disclosing information under this Section, the lawyer must, if feasible, make a good-faith effort to persuade the client not to act. If the client or another person has already acted, the lawyer must, if feasible, advise the client to warn the victim or to take other action to prevent the harm and advise the client of the lawyer's ability to use or disclose information as provided in this Section and the consequences thereof.

(3) A lawyer who takes action or decides not to take action permitted under this Section is not, solely by reason of such action or inaction, subject to professional discipline, liable for damages to the lawyer's client or any third person, or barred from recovery against a client or third person.

Comment:

a. Scope and cross-references. This Section states an exception to the general duty of confidentiality in § 60(1), recognizing discretion in a lawyer to prevent the consequences of threats to life or personal safety. The rule stated in this Section is distinguishable from financial-harm disclosure under § 67 in three principal ways. First, the threat here need not be the product of a client act (see Comment *c* hereto). Second, the threat need not be created by a criminal or otherwise unlawful act (see id.). Third, the lawyer's services need not have been used to bring about the threatened death or serious bodily harm. As with § 67, a lawyer has discretion under this Section even if the use or disclosure threatens harm to the lawyer's client (see id.).

On cross-references to other Sections, see § 67, Comment *a*.

b. Rationale. The exception recognized by this Section is based on the overriding value of life and physical integrity. Threats to life or body encompassed within this Section may be the product of an act of the client or a nonclient and may be created by wrongful acts, by accident, or by circumstances. See Comment *c*. In all such events, the ultimate threat is the same, and its existence suffices to warrant a lawyer's taking corrective steps to prevent the threatened death or serious bodily harm.

No lawyer code explicitly permits disclosure, as broadly as permitted by Subsection (1), solely on the justification that death or serious bodily harm is threatened, such as where a lawyer becomes aware that a person's life is at risk because of a noncriminal act of a client. There are no reported judicial decisions on the issue. On the other hand, it seems highly unlikely that a court would impose discipline or other liability on a lawyer in an instance within Subsection (1), should the lawyer act reasonably, even in a way that prejudices the client, to remove the threat to life or body. Moreover, seven states do permit (indeed require) disclosure of a client's wrongful violent act to prevent harm.

c. Use or disclosure to prevent death or serious bodily harm. Subsection (1) applies whenever a lawyer has a reasonable basis for believing that use or disclosure of a client's confidential information is necessary to prevent reasonably certain death or serious bodily harm to a person. On what constitutes reasonable belief, see § 67, Comment *h.* A threat within Subsection (1) need not be the product of a client act; an act of a nonclient threatening life or personal safety is also included, as is a threat created through accident or natural causes. It follows that if such a threat is created by a person, whether a client or a nonclient, there is no requirement that the act be criminal or otherwise unlawful.

Illustration:

1. Lawyer is representing Defendant, a responding party in a suit by Plaintiff seeking damages for personal injuries arising out of a vehicle accident. Lawyer asks Doctor, as a consulting expert, to conduct an evaluation of medical evidence submitted by Plaintiff in support of a claim of personal injury. Following the examination, Doctor reports to Lawyer that Plaintiff has an undiagnosed aortal aneurism, which is serious and life-threatening but which can readily be repaired through surgery. Lawyer knows from work on the case that Plaintiff, as well as Plaintiff's treating physician, lawyer, and medical experts, are unaware of the condition. Lawyer is also aware that, if notified of the condition, Plaintiff will likely claim significant additional damages following corrective surgery. Despite Lawyer's urging, Defendant refuses to permit revelation of the condition to Plaintiff. Under this Section, Lawyer has discretion under Subsection (1) to reveal the condition to Plaintiff.

So long as the predicate threat to life or body exists, discretion under Subsection (1) exists notwithstanding that the threat is created by the completed act of a person (including a client) or that the lawyer's information comes from otherwise privileged conversations.

Illustrations:

2. Client seeks legal advice from Lawyer about his dismissal from a maintenance position by Landlord and eviction from his apartment. In expressing his anger about Landlord, Client reveals that Client has set a mechanical device to ignite and burn down the building. Lawyer has reason to believe that there are people living in the building. Despite Lawyer's remonstration, Client refuses to take any action to prevent the fire or to warn others. Despite the risk that calling the fire department or police may result in serious criminal charges against Client, Lawyer has discretion under Subsection (1) to do so.

3. As the result of confidential disclosures at a meeting with engineers employed by Client Corporation, Lawyer reasonably believes that one of the engineers released a toxic substance into a city's water-supply system. Lawyer reasonably believes that the discharge will cause reasonably certain death or serious bodily harm to elderly or ill persons within a short period and that Lawyer's disclosure of the discharge is necessary to permit authorities to remove that threat or lessen the number of its victims. Lawyer's efforts to persuade responsible Client Corporation personnel to take corrective action have been unavailing. Although the act creating the threat has already occurred, Lawyer has discretion to disclose under Subsection (1) for the purpose of preventing the consequences of the act.

In circumstances such as those in Illustration 3, the Section applies even if the act creating the threat of death or serious bodily harm was not a crime or fraud. In other situations, the likelihood that other actors know about and will eliminate the risk may be relevant. Most situations will be intensely fact-sensitive. For example, the character of a threatened act as a crime or fraud suggests a state of mind on the part of the perpetrator that is more threatening to the intended victim than an act that is merely negligent or not wrongful, and thus may more readily warrant the lawyer's conclusion that the risk of harm is great.

Serious bodily harm within the meaning of the Section includes life-threatening illness and injuries and the consequences of events such as imprisonment for a substantial period and child sexual abuse. It also includes a client's threat of suicide.

Illustration:

4. Lawyer advises Manufacturer on product-liability matters. Lawyer had previously advised Manufacturer that use of Component A in a consumer product did not create an unreasonable risk of harm and was in compliance with consumer-protection and other law. Lawyer has now learned that Supplier, unknown to Manufacturer, provided Component A in a form not in compliance with Manufacturer's specifications. Manufacturer promptly altered its production methods so as to avoid any significant risk of harm in products manufactured in the future. There is a slight statistical chance that a consumer using the prior version of the product containing the noncomplying version of Component A might suffer serious bodily harm, but only in a highly unlikely combination of circumstances. Manufacturer's responsible officers have decided not to issue a public notice of the slightly increased risk of harm. Lawyer does not have discretion under this Section to use or disclose Manufacturer's confidential information to make a public warning of the slightly increased risk of harm.

d. A lawyer's reasonable belief. A lawyer's discretion to take appropriate action to prevent death or serious bodily harm under this Section is predicated on the lawyer's reasonable belief that the action is necessary to prevent reasonably certain death or serious bodily harm to a person. Some factors stated in Comment *f* as relevant to a lawyer's choice of appropriate action will also be relevant to the lawyer in assessing whether a situation warranting action exists. Some facts, particularly concerning future acts and probabilities and a client's or third person's subjective state of mind, may be unlikely or difficult for the lawyer to ascertain. Before making disclosure where such facts are ambiguous, the lawyer must make a reasonable effort to determine the relevant facts, taking into account the risks inherent in either action or inaction by the lawyer. As with other matters affecting a lawyer's responsibilities that may arise in the course of representing a client, a lawyer may consult with another lawyer about whether to proceed under this Section.

The Section refers (as does § 67) to a lawyer's reasonable belief that use or disclosure is "necessary" to prevent "reasonably certain" death or serious bodily harm, while ABA Model Rules of Professional Conduct, Rule 1.6(b)(1) (1983) (in its exception dealing with threats of death or bodily harm) refers to "imminent" death or serious bodily harm. The concept of imminence is included in the meaning of the terms "necessary" and "reasonably certain" death or bodily harm in that the need to act must be reasonably believed to exist in view of a present threat of probable death or bodily harm. The concept of imminence is susceptible of an overly narrow interpretation, under which use or disclosure would be precluded until immediately before the threatened death or bodily harm would occur. While such occasions are included within the Section, a lawyer is also permitted to act under the Section whenever the lawyer reasonably believes that intervention is necessary in response to a present threat, even if the death or serious bodily harm appears likely to occur some time in the future. ABA Model Rules of Professional Conduct, Rule 1.6(b)(1) (1983) can be similarly interpreted.

e. Counseling a client. As does § 67(3), Subsection (2) requires counseling with the client, if feasible. The interest protected by such counseling is the client's interest in limiting use or disclosure of confidential information and in taking responsible action to deal with situations that may be of the client's own making or attributable to the client. If a client, whether in response to a lawyer's counseling or otherwise, takes corrective action—such as by ceasing the threatened act before harm is caused—use or disclosure by the lawyer would not be necessary and therefore would not be permissible under this Section. Particularly when the actor is a nonclient or when the act is deliberate or malicious, a lawyer making adverse use or disclosure under this Section may, in the circumstances, reasonably conclude that superior interests of the lawyer or others in their own personal safety preclude personal contact with the actor.

f. Appropriate action. A lawyer's use or disclosure under this Section is a last resort when no other available action is reasonably likely to prevent the threatened death or serious bodily harm. Use or disclosure, when made, should be no more extensive than the lawyer reasonably believes necessary to accomplish the relevant purpose.

Preventive steps that a lawyer may appropriately take include consulting with relatives or friends of the person likely to cause the death or serious bodily harm and with other advisers to that person. (The lawyer may also seek the assistance of such persons in efforts to persuade the person not to act or to warn the threatened victim (see Comment *e* hereto).) A lawyer may also consult with law-enforcement authorities or agencies with jurisdiction over the type of conduct involved in order to prevent it and warn a threatened victim.

What particular measures are reasonable depends on the circumstances known to the lawyer. Relevant circumstances include the degree to which it appears likely that the threatened death or serious bodily harm will actually result, the irreversibility of its consequences once the act has taken place, the time available, whether victims might be unaware of the threat or might rely on the lawyer to protect them, the lawyer's prior course of dealings with the client, and the extent of adverse effect on the client that may result from disclosure contemplated by the lawyer. The lawyer must reasonably believe that the measures are appropriate and that they will entail no more adverse consequences to the client than necessary (see also § 64, Comment *e*).

When a lawyer has taken action under the Section, in all but extraordinary cases the relationship between lawyer and client would have so far deteriorated as to make the lawyer's effective representation of the client impossible. Generally, therefore, the lawyer is required to withdraw from the representation (see § 32(2)(a) & Comment *f* thereto), unless the client gives informed consent to the lawyer's continued representation notwithstanding the lawyer's adverse use or disclosure of information. In any event, the lawyer generally must inform the client of the fact of the lawyer's use or disclosure (see § 20(1)), unless the lawyer has a superior interest in not informing the client, such as to protect the lawyer from wrongful retaliation by the client, to effectuate permissible measures that are not yet complete, or to prevent the client from inflicting further harms on third persons.

g. Effects of a lawyer taking or not taking discretionary remedial action. A lawyer's decision to take action to disclose or not to disclose under this Section is discretionary with the lawyer (compare § 63 (disclosure required by law)). Such action would inevitably conflict to a significant degree with the lawyer's customary role of protecting client interests. Critical facts may be unclear, emotions may be high, and little time may be available in which the lawyer must decide on an appropriate course of action. Subsequent re-examination of the reasonableness of a lawyer's action in the light of later developments would be unwarranted; reasonableness of the lawyer's belief at the time and in the circumstances in which the lawyer acts is alone controlling.

As stated in Subsection (3) and in the corresponding § 67(4), a lawyer who takes action or decides not to take action in a situation described in and consistent with the rule of the Section and § 67 is not, by reason of such action or inaction alone, liable for professional discipline or liable for damages to the client or any third person injured by the client's action. Similarly, a client may not assert as an affirmative defense in a fee or similar suit that the lawyer has or has not taken steps permitted under the Section (see § 37). The same results apply with respect to questions of the vicarious liability (see § 58) of the firm in which the lawyer practices. That is precluded both because of the absence of any violation of duty by the individual lawyer (see § 58(1)) and because vicarious liability would be equally inconsistent with the reasons, stated above, for treating the lawyer's action or inaction as discretionary. Apart from this Section or § 67(4), a lawyer would of course remain liable for otherwise actionable wrongs, such as by participating with a client as a co-principal or accessory in the client's wrongful act (see § 8, Comment *e*).

Because the interests protected by the rule are those of the public and third persons, the discretion of a lawyer to take action consistent with the Section may not be contracted away by agreement between the lawyer and the client or the lawyer and a third person (compare § 23(1)).

§ 67. Using or Disclosing Information to Prevent, Rectify, or Mitigate Substantial Financial Loss

(1) A lawyer may use or disclose confidential client information when the lawyer reasonably believes that its use or disclosure is necessary to prevent a crime or fraud, and:

(a) the crime or fraud threatens substantial financial loss;

(b) the loss has not yet occurred;

(c) the lawyer's client intends to commit the crime or fraud either personally or through a third person; and

(d) the client has employed or is employing the lawyer's services in the matter in which the crime or fraud is committed.

(2) If a crime or fraud described in Subsection (1) has already occurred, a lawyer may use or disclose confidential client information when the lawyer reasonably believes its use or disclosure is necessary to prevent, rectify, or mitigate the loss.

(3) Before using or disclosing information under this Section, the lawyer must, if feasible, make a good-faith effort to persuade the client not to act. If the client or another person has already acted, the lawyer must, if feasible, advise the client to warn the victim or to take other action to prevent, rectify, or mitigate the loss. The lawyer must, if feasible, also advise the client of the lawyer's ability to use or disclose information as provided in this Section and the consequences thereof.

(4) A lawyer who takes action or decides not to take action permitted under this Section is not, solely by reason of such action or inaction, subject to professional discipline, liable for damages to the lawyer's client or any third person, or barred from recovery against a client or third person.

Comment:

a. *Scope and cross-references.* This Section states exceptions to the general confidentiality rule of § 60(1) and recognizes discretion in a lawyer to prevent, mitigate, or rectify the described types of financial loss to another person even if the use or disclosure threatens risk to the lawyer's client. The exception applies when a client intends to commit a criminal or fraudulent act and permits a lawyer, in taking reasonable preventive or corrective measures, to use or disclose confidential client information to prevent the act or to rectify or mitigate it.

Unless this Section or § 66 applies, a lawyer may use or disclose confidential client information only if the client consents (see § 62), if other law so requires (see § 63), or if reasonably necessary in a lawyer's self-defense (see § 64) or in a compensation dispute (see § 65).

On the crime-fraud exception to the attorney-client privilege, see § 82. For a comparison of the Sections, see Comment *c* hereto. On the rule that disclosure under this Section (or § 66) does not constitute waiver by subsequent disclosure for purposes of the attorney-client privilege, see Comment *c* hereto and § 79, Comment *c*.

On a lawyer's nonliability for action or inaction under this Section, see Comment *k* hereto. On a lawyer's liability for certain client harms to described third persons, see §§ 51 and 56.

On a lawyer's general responsibilities with respect to counseling or assisting a client concerning illegal acts, see § 94. See also Comment *i* hereto. On providing information to a client, see generally § 20. On advising an organizational client, see § 96; on advising a governmental client, see § 97. With respect to a lawyer's duties and discretion when dealing with perjury by a client or other witness or with other false evidence, see § 120. A lawyer has the right to withdraw when the lawyer reasonably believes the client is employing the lawyer's assistance to aid wrongful acts, including breaches of fiduciary duty (see § 32(3)(d) & (e)). On a lawyer's duty to withdraw after using or disclosing confidential client information under the Section, see Comment *j* hereto.

b. *Rationale.* The exceptions recognized in this Section reflect a balance between the competing considerations of protecting interests in client confidentiality and lawyer loyalty to clients, on the one hand, and protecting the interests of society and third persons in avoiding substantial financial consequences of crimes or frauds, on the other. The integrity, professional reputation, and financial interests of the lawyer can also be implicated under Subsections (1) and (2) in view of the requirement that the lawyer's services have been employed in commission of the crime or fraud. The exceptions are also justified on the ground that the client is not entitled to the protection of confidentiality when the client knowingly causes substantial financial harm through a crime or fraud and when, as required under Subsections (1) and (2), the client has in effect misused the client-lawyer relationship for that purpose. In most instances of unlawful client acts that threaten such consequences to others, it may be hoped that the client's own sober reflection and the lawyer's counseling (see Comment *i* hereto) will lead the client to refrain from the act or to prevent or mitigate its consequences.

The issues addressed in this Section are variously treated in American jurisdictions. The 1983 ABA Model Rules of Professional Conduct (1983), in Rule 1.6(b), recommended a narrow rule that would permit use or disclosure only in the case of a client's "criminal act that the lawyer believes is likely to result in imminent death or substantial bodily harm . . ." (compare § 66). Some sponsors of that formulation asserted that, despite the absence of explicit permission to act to prevent client fraud, Rule 1.6(b) nonetheless permitted a lawyer to act to prevent a client's crime or fraud as long as the lawyer did not disclose as such the explicit content of communications from the client. In any event, only a small minority of jurisdictions have adopted the apparently restrictive formulation of ABA Model Rule 1.6(b). As indicated in the Reporter's Note, over 40 jurisdictions have rejected the recommended model rule and have broadened the rule so as to permit use or disclosure to prevent substantial financial injury. Seventeen states also permit use or disclosure to rectify past and completed client fraud, which Subsection (2) also permits (see Comment *f* hereto). Lawyer codes in seven states mandate disclosure in at least some circumstances of client fraud; there is no similar requirement in this Section.

The exceptions stated in this Section permit a lawyer to exercise discretion to prevent the described loss to third persons, even though adverse effects might befall the client as a result. The exceptions are extraordinary. The only acts covered under the Section are the described crimes or frauds that threaten substantial financial loss to others. Clients remain protected in consulting a lawyer concerning the legal consequences of any such act in which the lawyer's services were not employed, including acts constituting crimes or frauds.

The discretion recognized in this Section may to an unknowable extent lessen some clients' willingness to consult freely with their lawyers. In this respect, the Section has an effect similar to that of the crime-fraud exception to the attorney-client privilege (see § 82; see also Comment *d* hereto). The social benefits of allowing a lawyer to prevent, mitigate, or rectify substantial financial loss to intended victims of criminal or fraudulent client acts under the described circumstances warrant incurring that additional risk.

Not all crimes and frauds are covered by this Section, but only those that involve a risk of substantial financial loss. The Section applies when a client intends to commit a crime or fraud either personally or through a third person (see Subsection (1)(c)). What constitutes a crime or a fraud is determined under otherwise applicable law. The distinction between acts entailing risks of such loss and other acts that may also be criminal or fraudulent reflects a balance between client confidentiality (see § 60, Comment *b*) and protection of third persons. It could be argued that a lawyer's discretion should be constrained in another manner, for example through case-by-case balancing of those competing interests, perhaps including as a factor the extent to which exercise of the lawyer's discretion would harm the client. Lawyers can be expected to take into account that and other relevant considerations in determining whether to exercise the professional discretion that the Section recognizes. However, the Section does not require that the lawyer exercise discretion only after explicitly making such an evaluation or in any other particular manner.

c. *Comparison with the crime-fraud exception to the attorney-client privilege.* This Section generally corresponds to the crime-fraud exception to the attorney-client privilege (see § 82, Comment *d*). Somewhat different considerations underlie the two rules and they operate in different settings, testimonial and nontestimonial. This Section § 82 both apply to client crimes or frauds. Both apply to acts that a client intends to commit and to acts by a third person whom the client intends to aid.

This Section applies only when the likelihood of financial loss is great and the lawyer reasonably believes that use or revelation is necessary to prevent the crime or fraud or to prevent, rectify, or mitigate the loss it causes (see Comment *f* hereto). In contrast, the crime-fraud exception to the attorney-client privilege stated in § 82 applies without regard to the consequences of the intended act so long as the act itself is a crime or fraud. That exception to the attorney-client privilege applies only when a client consults a lawyer with intention to obtain assistance to commit a crime or fraud or so uses the lawyer's services, whereas the Section applies regardless of the client's intention at the time of consultation (see Comment *g* hereto). The crime-fraud exception to the attorney-client privilege is administered by a tribunal and applies only when a lawyer or another person is called upon to give evidence, whereas the Section concerns action that a lawyer may take on the basis of a reasonable belief and outside of any proceeding and thus without direction from a judicial officer. Finally, this Section is limited to client acts in which a lawyer's services are employed; the crime-fraud exception applies whether or not the lawyer's services are so employed. Due to the several differences in the requirements for this Section and § 82, a finding that a lawyer permissibly used or disclosed confidential client information under this Section and a determination whether § 82 applies must be made independently.

Lawyer disclosure under this Section is taken in the lawyer's personal capacity and not as agent. Accordingly, such disclosure would not constitute disclosure by an agent of the client for purposes of subject-matter waiver of other confidential communications under § 79 (see § 79, Comment *c*).

d. Client crime or fraud. As with the corresponding crime-fraud exception to the attorney-client privilege (see § 82), this Section is limited to acts that under applicable law constitute crimes and frauds. "Fraud" as employed in this Section has the same limited meaning stated in § 82, Comment *d*. As there stated, inaction (through nondisclosure) as well as action may constitute fraud under applicable law. Many acts that will have seriously harmful financial consequences are denominated as crimes or frauds in the law. However, some acts causing financial loss to third persons constitute breaches of other legal obligations, such as intentional torts, breaches of contract, violation of property rights, or violations of statutory, regulatory, or other legal duties that are not crimes or frauds. Some of those acts may be particularly opprobrious in specific instances. However, society has traditionally defined seriously wrongful conduct in terms of crime and fraud. Limiting the exceptions in this Section to crime and fraud is also a matter of practicality, because no other categorical description of harmful acts provides an equally definite limitation on these exceptions to a lawyer's duty of confidentiality.

e. Employment of the lawyer's services in the client's act. Use or disclosure under either Subsection (1) or (2) requires that the lawyer's services are being or were employed in commission of a criminal or fraudulent act. The lawyer's involvement need not be known to or discoverable by the victim or other person. Subsections (1) and (2) apply without regard either to the lawyer's prior knowledge of the client's intended use of the lawyer's services or to when the lawyer forms a reasonable basis for a belief concerning the nature of the client's act. Such employment may occur, for example, when a client has a document prepared by the lawyer for use in a criminal or fraudulent scheme, receives the lawyer's advice concerning the act to assist in carrying it out, asks the lawyer to appear before a court or administrative agency as part of a transaction, or obtains advice that will assist the client in avoiding detection or apprehension for the crime or fraud. It is not necessary that the lawyer's services have been critical to success of the client's act or that the services were specifically requested by the client. It suffices if the services were or are being employed in the commission of the act.

Illustrations:

1. As part of a business transaction, Lawyer on behalf of Client prepares and sends to Victim an opinion letter helpful to Client in completing an aspect of the transaction. At the time of preparing and sending the opinion letter, Lawyer had no reason to believe that the transaction was other than proper, but Lawyer thereafter receives information giving reason to believe the transaction constitutes a crime or fraud by Client within this Section. If the other conditions of the Section are present, Lawyer's opinion letter will have been employed in commission of Client's act, and Lawyer accordingly has discretion to use or disclose confidential information of Client as provided in the Section.

2. Client has put in place a scheme to defraud Victim of substantial funds. After doing so, but before Victim has actually lost any funds, Client seeks Lawyer's assistance in meeting regulatory action and a suit by Victim seeking restitution that might ensue. Despite Lawyer's counseling, Client refuses to warn Victim, return the funds, or take other corrective action. Because Lawyer's services have not been employed in the commission of Client's fraud, Lawyer may not use or disclose Client's confidential information under this Section.

Legal assistance provided only after the client's crime or fraud has already been committed is not within this Section, whether or not loss to the victim has already occurred, if the lawyer's services are not employed for the purposes of a further crime or fraud, such as the crime of obstruction of justice or other unlawful attempt to cover up the prior wrongful act. While applicable law may provide that a completed act is regarded for some purposes as a continuing offense, the limitation of Subsection (1)(d) applies with attention to the time at which the client's acts actually occurred.

Illustrations:

3. Client has been charged by a regulatory agency with participation in a scheme to defraud Victim. Client seeks the assistance of Lawyer in defending against the charges. The loss to Victim has already occurred. During the initial interview and thereafter, Lawyer is provided with ample reason to believe that Client's acts were fraudulent and caused substantial financial loss to Victim. Because Lawyer's services were not employed by Client in committing the fraud, Lawyer does not have discretion under this Section to use or disclose Client's confidential information.

4. The same facts as in Illustration 3, except that the law of the applicable jurisdiction provides that each day during which a wrongdoer in the position of Client fails to make restitution to Victim constitutes a separate offense of the same type as the original wrong. Notwithstanding the continuing-offense law, commission of the fraudulent act of Client has already occurred without use of Lawyer's services. As in Illustration 3, Lawyer does not have discretion under this Section to use or disclose Client's confidential information.

f. Use or disclosure to prevent (Subsection (1)) or to rectify or mitigate (Subsection (2)) a client wrongful act. A lawyer has discretion to use or disclose under this Section when necessary to achieve either of two different purposes—to prevent the act from occurring (Subsection (1)) or to prevent, rectify, or mitigate loss caused by the act (Subsection (2)). Under Subsection (1), a lawyer may take preventive measures even though some act has already occurred, if some material part of the crime or fraud has not yet occurred or has not yet been inflicted on a victim. For example, in a criminal or fraudulent transaction involving more than one step, a lawyer would have discretion to take preventive action under Subsection (1) if some acts remained to be accomplished. Further, if all steps in a transaction to be taken by the client have already occurred, but the intended victim has not taken a final step, such as dispatching funds to the client, action to warn the victim not to take final steps is permissible preventive action within Subsection (1).

Action by the lawyer to prevent, rectify, or mitigate loss under Subsection (2) is in addition to and goes beyond that permitted for preventive purposes under Subsection (1). Actions to prevent, rectify, or mitigate the loss caused by the client's act include correcting or preventing the effects of the client's criminal or fraudulent act, even if the client's crime or fraud has already occurred and regardless of whether its impact has been visited upon the victim. Thus, a lawyer who acquires information from which the lawyer reasonably believes that a client has already defrauded a victim in a scheme in which the lawyer's services were employed may disclose the fraud to the victim when necessary to permit the victim to take possible corrective action, such as to initiate proceedings promptly in order to seize or recover assets fraudulently obtained by the client.

Once use or disclosure of information has been made to prevent, rectify, or mitigate loss under Subsection (2), the lawyer is not further warranted in actively assisting the victim on an ongoing basis in pursuing a remedy against the lawyer's client or in any similar manner aiding the victim or harming the client. Thus, a lawyer is not warranted under this Section in serving as legal counsel for a victim (see also § 132), volunteering to serve as witness in a proceeding by the victim, or cooperating with an administrative agency in obtaining compensation for victims. The lawyer also may not use or disclose information for the purpose of voluntarily assisting a law-enforcement agency to apprehend and prosecute the client, unless the lawyer reasonably believes that such disclosure would be necessary to prevent, rectify, or mitigate the victim's loss. On the rule that disclosure of confidential client information does not constitute waiver of the client's privilege due to subsequent disclosure by an agent, see Comment *c* hereto.

Illustrations:

5. Lawyer has assisted Client in preparing documents by means of which Client will obtain a $5,000,000 loan from Bank. The loan closing occurred on Monday and Bank will make the funds available for Client's use on Wednesday. On Tuesday Client reveals to Lawyer for the first time that Client knowingly obtained the loan by means of a materially false statement of Client's assets. Assuming that the other conditions for application of Subsection (2) are present, while Client's fraudulent act of obtaining the loan has, in large part, already occurred, Lawyer has discretion under the Subsection to use or disclose Client's confidential information to prevent the consequences of the fraud (final release of the funds from Bank) from occurring.

6. The same facts as in Illustration 5, except that Lawyer learned of the fraud on Wednesday after Bank had already released the funds to Client. Under Subsection (2), Lawyer's use or disclosure would be permissible if necessary for the purpose, for example, of enabling Bank to seize assets of Client in its possession or control as an offset against the fraudulently obtained loan or to prevent Client from sending the funds overseas and thereby making it difficult or impossible to trace them.

g. Client's intent. It is not required that the client's requisite intent existed at the time the client consulted the lawyer. For example, the client may form a plan to employ the lawyer's former services in drafting documents in a scheme that the client devises after the lawyer's services have ended. The client need not be aware specifically that the contemplated act was a crime or fraud (see also § 82, Comment *c*). As stated in Subsection (1)(c), the client may act either directly or through a third person. The Section does not apply if the lawyer is aware that the client's purpose had been abandoned, because in that situation disclosure is no longer necessary as required by the Section.

h. A lawyer's reasonable belief. A lawyer's discretion to take appropriate measures to prevent financial loss under this Section or to rectify or mitigate it is predicated on the lawyer's reasonable belief that the client intends to engage in the described crime or fraud and that the lawyer's use or disclosure is necessary to prevent the loss or to rectify or mitigate it. Some facts, particularly concerning future acts and probabilities and a client's subjective state of mind, may be difficult to ascertain. Before making disclosure in such circumstances, the lawyer must make a reasonable effort to determine the relevant facts. As with other matters affecting a lawyer's responsibilities that may arise in the course of representing a client, a lawyer may consult with another lawyer about whether to proceed under the Section. See also § 66, Comment *d*.

i. Counseling a client. When a lawyer becomes aware of a client's intent to pursue a course of action that is criminal or fraudulent, the lawyer may be able, through appeal to the good judgment and moral sense of the client, to persuade the client to abandon the intended course or to make whole any victim of a fraudulent or criminal act (see § 94). Such counseling may avoid difficulties for the client and others. Accordingly, before a lawyer may take remedial action under the Section, the lawyer must consult with the affected client as stated in Subsection (3), if consultation is feasible in view of the imminence of the threatened loss and similar time considerations, the likelihood of the threatened activity and its consequences and the apparent firmness of the client's intentions, any risk to the lawyer or others that may be reasonably apprehended, and other constraints. In the course of consulting with the client, the lawyer must ordinarily inform the client of the lawyer's ability to act pursuant to this Section if the client fails to take corrective action (see § 20), unless the lawyer has a superior interest in not informing the client, such as to protect the lawyer from reasonably apprehended and wrongful retaliation by the client, to effectuate permissible measures that are not yet complete, or to prevent the client from inflicting further financial loss on third persons. If a client, whether in response to a lawyer's counseling or otherwise, takes corrective action—such as by ceasing the threatened act before loss is caused—use or disclosure by the lawyer would not be necessary and therefore would not be permissible under this Section.

j. Appropriate action. A lawyer's use or disclosure of information under the Section is a last resort when no other available action is reasonably likely to prevent the threatened financial loss or to rectify or mitigate it. Use or disclosure, when made, should be no more extensive than the lawyer reasonably believes necessary to accomplish the relevant purpose. On consulting with suitable advisers to a client, the importance of the circumstances known to the lawyer in determining the reasonableness of measures taken, withdrawal by the lawyer, and informing the client after use or disclosure, see § 66, Comment *f*.

In using or disclosing under this Section, the lawyer may also withdraw or disaffirm opinion letters, affidavits, and other legal documents that had been prepared for the client or others that might be employed or that might have been employed in furthering the crime or fraud or contributed to its consequences. In addition, under § 64, a lawyer may take steps that are justified as reasonably appropriate to defend the lawyer and the lawyer's associates against a charge of wrongdoing arising from the representation. Other law may require a lawyer to use or disclose confidential client information in such circumstances (see § 63).

Comment k. Effects of a lawyer taking or not taking discretionary remedial action. The rule of Subsection (4) corresponds to that of § 66(3). See also § 66, Comment *g*.

TOPIC 2. THE ATTORNEY-CLIENT PRIVILEGE

TITLE A. THE SCOPE OF THE PRIVILEGE

§ 68. Attorney-Client Privilege

Except as otherwise provided in this Restatement, the attorney-client privilege may be invoked as provided in § 86 with respect to:

(1) a communication

(2) made between privileged persons

(3) in confidence

(4) for the purpose of obtaining or providing legal assistance for the client.

Comment:

a. Scope and cross-references. This Section states the general formulation of the attorney-client testimonial privilege. It must be read in the context of succeeding Sections that elaborate its four elements: § 69, defining types of communications protected by the privilege; § 70, delineating the privileged persons who may be the source of or receive privileged communications; § 71, defining the requirements of "in confidence"; and § 72, specifying that legal assistance be the purpose of the communication. Applications of the rule with respect to organizational and multiple clients are set out in Title B. The privilege is subject to a number of important waivers, exceptions, and extensions set out in Title C. On invoking the protection of the privilege, see § 86. The legal duty of a lawyer to keep client information confidential is examined in Topic 1.

b. Relationship to other confidentiality principles. The attorney-client privilege and its underlying policies have influenced such related rules as the work-product immunity (see Topic 3), the lawyer's duties respecting confidential client information (see Topic 1), and the immunities of lawyers and clients for injurious statements made in the course of a judicial proceeding (see § 57(1)).

c. Rationale supporting the privilege. The modern attorney-client privilege evolved from an earlier reluctance of English courts to require lawyers to breach the code of a gentleman by being compelled to reveal in court what they had been told by clients. The privilege, such as it was then, belonged to the lawyer. It was a rule congenial with the law, which prevailed in England until the mid-19th century, that made parties to litigation themselves incompetent to testify, whether called as witnesses in their own behalf or by their adversaries. The modern conception of the privilege, reflected in this Restatement, protects clients, not lawyers, and clients have primary authority to determine whether to assert the privilege (see § 86) or waive it (see §§ 78–80).

The rationale for the privilege is that confidentiality enhances the value of client-lawyer communications and hence the efficacy of legal services. The rationale is founded on three related assumptions. First, vindicating rights and complying with obligations under the law and under modern legal processes are matters often too complex and uncertain for a person untrained in the law, so that clients need to consult lawyers. The second assumption is that a client who consults a lawyer needs to disclose all of the facts to the lawyer and must be able to receive in return communications from the lawyer reflecting those facts. It is assumed that, in the absence of such frank and full discussion between client and lawyer, adequate legal assistance cannot be realized. Many legal rules are complex and most are fact-specific in their application. Lawyers are much better situated than nonlawyers to appreciate the effect of legal rules and to identify facts that determine whether a legal rule is applicable. Full disclosure by clients facilitates efficient presentation at trials and other proceedings and in a lawyer's advising functions.

The third assumption supporting the privilege is controversial—that clients would be unwilling to disclose personal, embarrassing, or unpleasant facts unless they could be assured that neither they nor their lawyers could be called later to testify to the communication. Relatedly, it is assumed that lawyers would not feel free in probing client's stories and giving advice unless assured that they would not thereby expose the client to adverse evidentiary risk. Those assumptions cannot be tested but are widely believed by lawyers to be sound. The privilege implies an impairment of the search for truth in some instances.

Recognition of the privilege reflects a judgment that this impairment is outweighed by the social and moral values of confidential consultations. The privilege provides a zone of privacy within which a client may more effectively exercise the full autonomy that the law and legal institutions allow.

The evidentiary consequences of the privilege are indeterminate. If the behavioral assumptions supporting the privilege are well-founded, perhaps the evidence excluded by the privilege would not have come into existence save for the privilege. In any event, testimony concerning out-of-court communications often would be excluded as hearsay, although some of it could come in under exceptions such as that for statements against interest. The privilege also precludes an abusive litigation practice of calling an opposing lawyer as a witness.

Some judicial fact findings undoubtedly have been erroneous because the privilege excluded relevant evidence. The privilege creates tension with the right to confront and cross-examine opposing witnesses. It excuses lawyers from giving relevant testimony and precludes full examination of clients. The privilege no doubt protects wrongdoing in some instances. To that extent the privilege may facilitate serious social harms. The crime-fraud exception to the privilege (see § 82) results in forced disclosure of some such confidential conversations, but certainly not all.

Suggestions have been made that the privilege be conditional, not absolute, and thus inapplicable in cases where extreme need can be shown for admitting evidence of attorney-client communications. The privilege, however, is not subject to ad hoc exceptions. The predictability of a definite rule encourages forthright discussions between client and lawyer. The law accepts the risks of factual error and injustice in individual cases in deference to the values that the privilege vindicates.

d. Source of the law concerning the privilege. In most of the states, the privilege is defined by statute or rule, typically in an evidence code; in a few states, the privilege is common law. In the federal system, the definition of the privilege is left to the common-law process with respect to issues on which federal law applies. Federal Rule of Evidence 501 provides generally that questions of privilege "shall be governed by the principles of the common law as they may be interpreted by the courts of the United States in the light of reason and experience." On elements of a claim or defense as to which state law supplies the rule of decision, however, Rule 501 provides that the federal courts are to apply the attorney-client privilege of the relevant state.

§ 69. Attorney-Client Privilege—"Communication"

A communication within the meaning of § 68 is any expression through which a privileged person, as defined in § 70, undertakes to convey information to another privileged person and any document or other record revealing such an expression.

Comment:

a. Scope and cross-references. This Section defines the concept of "communication" stated in § 68(1). The elements of § 68(2)–(3) are considered in §§ 70–72. On invoking the privilege, see § 86. On the confidentiality responsibilities of lawyers, see §§ 59–67.

b. Communications qualifying for the privilege. A communication can be in any form. Most confidential client communications to a lawyer are written or spoken words, but the privilege applies to communication through technologically enhanced methods such as telephone and telegraph, audio or video tape recording, film, telecopier, and other electronic means. However, communications through a public mode may suggest the absence of a reasonable expectation of confidentiality (see § 71, Comment *e*).

c. Intercepted communications. The communication need not in fact succeed; for example, an intercepted communication is within this Section (see § 71, Comment *c* (eavesdroppers)).

Illustration:

1. Lawyer represents Client in a pending criminal investigation. Lawyer directs Client to make a tape recording detailing everything that Client knows about an unlawful enterprise for Lawyer's review. Client makes the tape recording in secret. A cell mate, after learning of the tape recording, informs the prosecutor who causes the tape to be seized under a subpoena. The attorney-client privilege covers the tape recording.

For the rule where a communication is disclosed to nonprivileged persons, see § 79.

d. Distinction between the content of a communication and knowledge of facts. The attorney-client privilege protects only the content of the communication between privileged persons, not the knowledge of privileged persons about the facts themselves. Although a client cannot be required to testify about communications with a lawyer about a subject, the client may be required to testify about what the client knows concerning the same subject. The client thus may invoke the privilege with respect to the question "Did you tell your lawyer the light was red?" but not with respect to the question "Did you see that the light was red?" Similarly, the privilege does not apply to preexisting documents or other tangible evidence (see Comment *j*), even if they concern the same subject as a privileged communication.

Illustration:

2. Client, a defendant in a breach-of-contract suit, confidentially informs Lawyer about Client's recollection of a course of dealings between Client and a subcontractor, Plaintiff in the pending contract suit. The attorney-client privilege does not prevent Plaintiff from requiring Client to testify at a deposition or trial concerning Client's present recollection of the course of dealings between Client and Plaintiff. Plaintiff may not, however, require Lawyer or Client to testify concerning what Client told Lawyer about those same facts.

e. Communicative client acts. The privilege extends to nonverbal communicative acts intended to convey information. For example, a client may communicate with a lawyer through facial expressions or other communicative bodily motions or gestures (nodding or shaking the head or holding up a certain number of fingers to indicate number) or acting out a recalled incident. On the other hand, the privilege does not extend to a client act simply because the client performed the act in the lawyer's presence. The privilege applies when the purpose in performing the act is to convey information to the lawyer.

Illustrations:

3. Client, charged with a crime, retains Lawyer as defense counsel. Lawyer obtains a police report stating that the perpetrator of the crime had a tattooed right forearm. Lawyer asks Client whether Client's right arm is tattooed. In answer, Client rolls up his right sleeve revealing his forearm. The information that the lawyer thereby acquires derives from a protected communication.

4. The same facts as in Illustration 3, except that, shortly after the crime, Client appears at Lawyer's office wearing a short-sleeved shirt. The observation by Lawyer that Client had a tattoo on his arm is not a communication protected by the privilege.

5. Lawyer represents Client in a divorce and child-custody proceeding. While accompanying Client in a visit to the residence of Client's child, Lawyer observes Client physically break into the premises. Lawyer's knowledge is not protected as a communication from Client.

f. A lawyer's testimony on a client's mental state. A lawyer may have knowledge about a client's mental state based on the client's communications with the lawyer. That knowledge may be relevant, for example, in the context of determining whether an accused is competent to stand trial. The lawyer in such cases is uniquely competent to testify concerning the client's ability to assist in presenting a defense. Testimony may be elicited that concerns the client's mode of thought but not if it would disclose particulars that would tend to incriminate the client. On representing a client with diminished capacity, see § 24.

g. Client identity, the fact of consultation, fee payment, and similar matters. Courts have sometimes asserted that the attorney-client privilege categorically does not apply to such matters as the following: the identity of a client; the fact that the client consulted the lawyer and the general subject matter of the consultation; the identity of a nonclient who retained or paid the lawyer to represent the client; the details of any retainer agreement; the amount of the agreed-upon fee; and the client's whereabouts. Testimony about such matters normally does not reveal the content of communications from the client. However, admissibility of such testimony should be based on the extent to which it reveals the content of a privileged communication. The privilege applies if the testimony directly or by reasonable inference would reveal the content of a confidential communication. But the privilege does not protect clients or lawyers against revealing a lawyer's knowledge about a client solely on the ground that doing so would incriminate the client or otherwise prejudice the client's interests.

Illustration:

6. Client consults Lawyer about Client's taxes. In the consultation, Client communicates to Lawyer Client's name and information indicating that Client owes substantial amounts in back taxes. The fact that Client owes back taxes is not known to the taxing authorities. Lawyer sends a letter to the taxing authorities and encloses a bank draft to cover the back taxes of Client. Lawyer does so to gain an advantage for Client under the tax laws by providing a basis for arguing against the accrual of penalties for continued nonpayment of taxes. Neither Lawyer's letter nor the bank draft reveals the identity of Client. (For the purpose of the Illustration, it is assumed that the client-lawyer communication occurred for the purpose of obtaining legal assistance (see § 72)). In a grand-jury proceeding investigating Client's past failure to pay taxes, Lawyer cannot be required to testify concerning the identity of Client because, on the facts of the Illustration, that testimony would by reasonable inference reveal a confidential communication from Client, Client's communication concerning Client's nonpayment of taxes.

A client also enjoys the constitutional protection against self-incrimination. But this right does not provide a basis on which the client's lawyer can refuse to reveal incriminating information about the client that is not protected by the attorney-client privilege. The precise interaction of the attorney-client and self-incrimination privileges is beyond the scope of this Restatement. Protection may also be provided by the constitutional guarantee of the right to counsel. On the application of the attorney-client privilege to a lawyer's testimony about how the lawyer came into the possession of instrumentalities of crime or the fruits of crime, see § 119.

h. A record of a privileged communication. The privilege applies both to communications when made and to confidential records of such communications, such as a lawyer's note of the conversation. The privilege applies to a record when a communication embodied in the record can be traced to a privileged person as its expressive source (see § 70) and the record was created (see § 71) and preserved (see § 79) in a confidential state.

i. Lawyer communications to a client. Confidential communications by a lawyer to a client are also protected, including a record of a privileged communication such as a memorandum to a confidential file or to another lawyer or other person privileged to receive such a communication under § 71. Some decisions have protected a lawyer communication only if it contains or expressly refers to a client communication. That limitation is rejected here in favor of a broader rule more likely to assure full and frank communication (see § 68, Comment *c*). Moreover, the broader rule avoids difficult questions in determining whether a lawyer's communication itself discloses a client communication. A lawyer communication may also be protected by the work-product immunity (see Topic 3).

Illustration:

7. Lawyer writes a confidential letter to Client offering legal advice on a tax matter on which Client had sought Lawyer's professional assistance. Lawyer's letter is based in part on information that Client supplied to Lawyer, in part on information gathered by Lawyer from third persons, and in part on Lawyer's legal research. Even if each such portion of the letter could be separated from the others, the letter is a communication under this Section, and neither Lawyer nor Client can be made to disclose or testify about any of its contents.

A lawyer may serve as the conduit for information to be conveyed from third persons to the lawyer's client. For most purposes, notice to a lawyer constitutes notice to the lawyer's client (see § 28(1)). In any event, both lawyer and client can be required to testify to the message for which the lawyer served as conduit. Lawyers in such situations serve, not as confidants, but as a communicative link between their clients and opposing parties, courts, and other legal institutions. Were such communications privileged, an opposing party would be required to communicate directly with the client, in derogation of the rule that communications with represented parties must be conducted through their lawyers (see § 99).

j. Preexisting documents and records. A client may communicate information to a lawyer by sending writings or other kinds of documentary or electronic recordings that came into existence prior to the time that the client communicates with the lawyer. The privilege protects the information that the client so communicated but not the preexisting document or record itself. A client-authored document that is not a privileged document when originally composed does not become privileged simply because the client has placed it in the lawyer's hands. However, if a document was a privileged preexisting document and was delivered to the lawyer under circumstances that otherwise would make its communication privileged, it remains privileged in the hands of the lawyer.

Illustrations:

8. Client confidentially delivers Client's business records to Lawyer, who specializes in tax matters, in order to obtain Lawyer's legal advice about taxes. As business records, the documents were not themselves prepared for the purpose of obtaining legal advice and are not protected by another testimonial privilege. They gain no privileged status by the fact that Client delivers them to Lawyer in seeking legal advice.

9. Client possesses a memorandum prepared by Client to communicate with Lawyer A during an earlier representation by Lawyer A. Client takes the memorandum to Lawyer B in confidence to obtain legal services on a different matter. The memorandum qualified as a privileged communication in the earlier matter. While in the hands of Lawyer B, the memorandum remains protected by the attorney-client privilege due to its originally privileged nature.

§ 70. Attorney-Client Privilege—"Privileged Persons"

Privileged persons within the meaning of § 68 are the client (including a prospective client), the client's lawyer, agents of either who facilitate communications between them, and agents of the lawyer who facilitate the representation.

Comment:

a. Scope and cross-references. This Section addresses the requirement of § 68(2) that a confidential communication be "made between privileged persons." On determining which persons in a corporate or other organization qualify as agents for communication, see § 73, Comment *d*. On invoking the privilege, see § 86. See also § 75 (co-client communication) and § 76 (communication in common-interest arrangement).

b. A privileged person as the expressive source. To qualify as privileged, a communication must originate from a person who may make privileged communications and be addressed to persons who may receive them. Those persons are referred to in this Restatement as privileged persons. Client and lawyer are, of course, included. Other privileged persons are those who serve to facilitate communication between client and lawyer and persons who aid the lawyer in representing the client.

The privilege does not extend to communications from nonprivileged persons, even if the client transmits such a person's communication to the lawyer, for example by carrying to the lawyer a document written by a nonprivileged person. Such information may, however, be given a qualified immunity from discovery under the work-product immunity (see § 87). Moreover, if the communication from a nonprivileged person is incorporated in a protected communication from which it cannot be separated, the entire communication is privileged. For example, a lawyer may not be required to testify to what a client had communicated concerning the client's memory of a conversation with a nonprivileged third person.

c. An initial consultation. The privilege protects prospective clients—persons who communicate with a lawyer in an initial consultation but whom the lawyer does not thereafter represent—as well as persons with whom a client-lawyer relationship is established (see § 72(1) & Comment *d* thereof; see also § 15).

d. Third-party payment of a fee. A person who pays a lawyer's fee is not necessarily a client. The relevant question is whether the lawyer undertook to give legal advice or provide other legal assistance to that person (see § 14; see also § 134).

e. Privileged agents for a client or lawyer: in general. The privilege normally applies to communications involving persons who on their own behalf seek legal assistance from a lawyer (see § 72). However, a client need not personally seek legal assistance, but may appoint a third person to do so as the client's agent (e.g., § 134, Comment *f*). Whether a third person is an agent of the client or lawyer or a nonprivileged "stranger" is critical in determining application of the attorney-client privilege. If the third person is an agent for the purpose of the privilege, communications through or in the presence of that person are privileged; if the third person is not an agent, then the communications are not in confidence (see § 71) and are not privileged. Accordingly, a lawyer should allow a nonclient to participate only upon clarifying that person's role and when it reasonably appears that the benefit of that person's presence offsets the risk of a later claim that the presence of a third person forfeited the privilege.

f. A client's agent for communication. A person is a confidential agent for communication if the person's participation is reasonably necessary to facilitate the client's communication with a lawyer or another privileged person and if the client reasonably believes that the person will hold the communication in confidence. Factors that may be relevant in determining whether a third person is an agent for communication include the customary relationship between the client and the asserted agent, the nature of the communication, and the client's need for the third person's presence to communicate effectively with the lawyer or to understand and act upon the lawyer's advice.

Illustrations:

1. The police arrest Client and do not permit Client to communicate directly with Client's regular legal counsel, Lawyer. Client asks Friend, a person whom Client trusts to keep information confidential, to convey to Lawyer the message that Lawyer should not permit the police to search Client's home. Friend is an agent for communication.

2. Client and Lawyer do not speak a language known by the other. Client uses Translator to communicate an otherwise privileged message to Lawyer. Translator is an acquaintance of Client. Translator is an agent for communication.

3. Client regularly employs Secretary to record and transcribe Client's important business letters, including confidential correspondence. Client uses the services of Secretary to prepare a letter to Lawyer. Secretary is an agent for communication.

An agent for communication need not take a direct part in client-lawyer communications, but may be present because of the Client's psychological or other need. A business person may be accompanied by a business associate or expert consultant who can assist the client in interpreting the legal situation.

Illustrations:

4. Client, 16 years old, is represented by Lawyer. Client's parents accompany Client at a meeting with Lawyer concerning a property interest of Client. Client's parents are appropriate agents for communication.

5. Client is advised by Accountant to consult a lawyer about a legal problem involving complex questions of tax accounting. Client, who does not fully understand the nature of the accounting questions, asks Accountant to accompany Client to a consultation with Lawyer so that Accountant can explain the nature of Client's legal matter to Lawyer. Accountant is Client's agent for communication. That would also be true if Accountant were to explain Lawyer's legal advice in business or accounting terms more understandable to Client.

The privilege applies to communications to and from the client disclosed to persons who hire the lawyer as an incident of the lawyer's engagement. Thus, the privilege covers communications by a client-insured to an insurance-company investigator who is to convey the facts to the client's lawyer designated by the insurer, as well as communications from the lawyer for the insured to the insurer in providing a progress report or discussing litigation strategy or settlement (see § 134, Comment *f*). Such situations must be distinguished from communications by an insured to an insurance investigator who will report to the company, to which the privilege does not apply.

g. A lawyer's agent. A lawyer may disclose privileged communications to other office lawyers and with appropriate nonlawyer staff—secretaries, file clerks, computer operators, investigators, office managers, paralegal assistants, telecommunications personnel, and similar law-office assistants. On the duty of a lawyer to protect client information being handled by nonlawyer personnel, see § 60(1)(b). The privilege also extends to communications to and from the client that are disclosed to independent contractors retained by a lawyer, such as an accountant or physician retained by the lawyer to assist in providing legal services to the client and not for the purpose of testifying.

h. An incompetent person as a client. When a client is mentally or physically incapacitated from effectively consulting with a lawyer, a representative may communicate with the incompetent person's lawyer under the protection of the privilege. The privilege also extends to any communications between the incompetent person and the representative relating to the communication with the lawyer.

Illustration:

6. Client is mentally incapacitated, and a court has appointed Guardian as the guardian of the person and property of Client. A question has arisen concerning a right of Client in certain property, and Lawyer is retained to represent the interests of Client in the property. Guardian serves as the agent for communication of Client in discussing the matter with Lawyer.

§ 71. Attorney-Client Privilege—"In Confidence"

A communication is in confidence within the meaning of § 68 if, at the time and in the circumstances of the communication, the communicating person reasonably believes that no one will learn the contents of the communication except a privileged person as defined in § 70 or another person with whom communications are protected under a similar privilege.

Comment:

a. *Scope and cross-references.* This Section considers the requirement of § 68(3) that a communication must be "in confidence." The elements of § 68(1)–(2) and § 68(4) are explained in §§ 69–70 and § 72. Even if the initial communication is in confidence and otherwise qualifies for protection as a privileged communication, its privileged status may be lost by subsequent revelation of the communication (see § 79). On the agency power of a lawyer to waive a privilege by disclosure to a nonprivileged person, see § 79. On the legal responsibilities of lawyers with respect to confidential client information, see generally §§ 60–67. With respect to communications between co-clients, see § 75, and with respect to a communication in a common-interest arrangement, see § 76.

b. *Rationale.* Given the objectives of the attorney-client privilege (see § 68, Comment *c*), a communication must be made in circumstances reasonably indicating that it will be learned only by the lawyer, client, or another privileged person (see § 70). The matter communicated need not itself be secret. For example, a privileged person receiving the communication may have known the same information from another source. The intent of the communicating person to communicate in confidence is relevant but not determinative. Thus, communication in a nonconfidential setting evidences that secrecy was not a consideration even if it is later protested that confidentiality was intended. Extending the privilege to a nonconfidential communication would not further the policy of the privilege and would result in excluding otherwise admissible and relevant evidence (see § 68, Comment *d*). If the communicating person did not intend that the communication be confidential, it is not privileged regardless of the circumstances otherwise attending its transmission.

The presence of a stranger to the lawyer-client relationship does not destroy confidentiality if another privilege protects the communications in the same way as the attorney-client privilege. Thus, in a jurisdiction that recognizes an absolute husband-wife privilege, the presence of a wife at an otherwise confidential meeting between the husband and the husband's lawyer does not destroy the confidentiality required for the attorney-client privilege.

c. *Confidential and nonconfidential communications.* The circumstances must indicate that the communicating persons reasonably believed that the communication would be confidential. Thus, a conversation between lawyer and client in the lawyer's offices is privileged. The same will not necessarily apply to a communication in offices of the client, inasmuch as not all agents of the client are privileged persons within the meaning of § 70 (compare Illustration 1 hereto & Comment *d*). For the delineation of privileged persons in the case of a client that is an organization, see § 73.

The circumstances may indicate that the communicating person knows that a nonprivileged person will learn of it, thus impairing its confidentiality. For example, a client may talk with a lawyer in a loud voice in a public place where nonprivileged persons could readily overhear. Communication over a medium from which it is impossible to exclude other listeners, such as radio, strongly suggests that secrecy is not reasonably expected. Whether the client or other communicating person knew that nonprivileged persons would learn of the communication depends on the specific circumstances. The relevant circumstances are those reasonably evident to the communicating person, not the auditor. Thus, the presence of a surreptitious eavesdropper does not destroy confidentiality.

Illustrations:

1. Client and Lawyer confer in Client's office about a legal matter. Client realizes that occupants of nearby offices can normally hear the sound of voices coming from Client's office but reasonably supposes they cannot intelligibly detect individual words. An occupant of an adjoining office secretly records the conference between Client and Lawyer and is able to make out the contents of their communications. Even if it violates no law in the jurisdiction, the secret recording ordinarily would not be anticipated by persons wishing to confer in confidence. Accordingly, the fact that the eavesdropper overheard the Client-Lawyer communications does not impair their confidential status.

2. During a recess in a trial, Client and Lawyer walk into a courthouse corridor crowded with other persons attending the trial and discuss Client's intended testimony in tones loud enough to be readily overheard by bystanders. As Lawyer knows, the courthouse premises include several areas more appropriate for a confidential conversation than the corridor. The corridor conversation is not in confidence for the purposes of the privilege, and the privilege does not bar examining either Client or Lawyer concerning it.

Confidentiality is a practical requirement. Exigent circumstances may require communications under conditions where ordinary precautions for confidentiality are impossible. The privilege applies if the communicating person has taken reasonable precautions in the circumstances.

Illustration:

3. A jailer requires Client, an incarcerated person, and Lawyer to confer only in a conference area that, as Client and Lawyer know, is sometimes secretly subjected to recorded video surveillance by the jailer. If Client and Lawyer take reasonable precautions to avoid being overheard, the fact that the jailer secretly records their conversation does not deprive it of its confidential character.

d. A communication intended for a nonprivileged person. A client may disclose information to a lawyer intending that it be conveyed to a nonprivileged third person and not intending that the lawyer determine the suitability of thus publishing it. Such a communication is not confidential for purposes of the privilege. Willingness to disclose a communication to nonprivileged persons (compare § 70) without prior review by the lawyer indicates that assurance of confidentiality did not importantly motivate communication.

The critical element is whether the privileged person's evident purpose is that the contents of the communication be made available to a nonprivileged person. Clients do not typically have such a purpose. Rather, a client ordinarily expects the lawyer to release information to nonprivileged persons only after exercising judgment about whether to do so and about the form in which it should be released. In ascertaining purpose, the nature of the legal assistance that the lawyer is providing and the nature of the communication asserted to be confidential are relevant.

A common instance of nonconfidential client-lawyer communications is where a lawyer functions as an attesting witness on a document signed by the lawyer's client. Those circumstances plainly warrant the inference that the lawyer may testify to facts relevant to the attestation, including communications from the client relating to that function.

e. Random dissemination of a communication. Communicating randomly to many auditors indicates that the communicating person was oblivious to secrecy.

Illustration:

4. Client makes an audiotape recording in which Client confesses to committing a crime, remorse for which, Client says on the tape, has led Client to attempt suicide. Client addresses the audio tape to business associates of Client. On the tape, Client mentions that the business associates might wish to provide the tape to Client's Lawyer. Client fails in the suicide attempt and is charged with the crime confessed on the tape. The business associates to whom the tape is addressed give the tape to Lawyer. Client did not intend the message as a confidential communication. It is immaterial

whether or not nonprivileged persons in fact listened to the tape and thus actually learned of the communication.

In many circumstances, including the foregoing Illustration, when a communication is addressed to an audience that includes nonprivileged persons, an additional reason the privilege does not apply is that the client did not communicate to obtain legal assistance (see § 72(2)).

§ 72. Attorney-Client Privilege—Legal Assistance as the Object of Privileged Communication

A communication is made for the purpose of obtaining or providing legal assistance within the meaning of § 68 if it is made to or to assist a person:

(1) who is a lawyer or who the client or prospective client reasonably believes to be a lawyer; and

(2) whom the client or prospective client consults for the purpose of obtaining legal assistance.

TITLE B. THE ATTORNEY-CLIENT PRIVILEGE FOR ORGANIZATIONAL AND MULTIPLE CLIENTS

§ 73. The Privilege for an Organizational Client

When a client is a corporation, unincorporated association, partnership, trust, estate, sole proprietorship, or other for-profit or not-for-profit organization, the attorney-client privilege extends to a communication that:

(1) otherwise qualifies as privileged under §§ 68–72;

(2) is between an agent of the organization and a privileged person as defined in § 70;

(3) concerns a legal matter of interest to the organization; and

(4) is disclosed only to:

(a) privileged persons as defined in § 70; and

(b) other agents of the organization who reasonably need to know of the communication in order to act for the organization.

Comment:

a. Scope and cross-references. This Section states the conditions under which an organization can claim the attorney-client privilege. The requirements of §§ 68–72 must be satisfied, except that this Section recognizes a special class of agents who communicate in behalf of the organizational client (see Comment *d*). The Section also requires that the communication relate to a matter of interest to the organization as such (see Subsection (3) & Comment *f* hereto) and that it be disclosed within the organization only to persons having a reasonable need to know of it (see Subsection (4)(b) & Comment *g* hereto).

Conflicts of interest between an organizational client and its officers and other agents are considered in § 131, Comment *e*. On the application of the privilege to governmental organizations and officers, see § 74.

b. Rationale. The attorney-client privilege encourages organizational clients to have their agents confide in lawyers in order to realize the organization's legal rights and to achieve compliance with law (Comment *d* hereto). Extending the privilege to corporations and other organizations was formerly a matter of doubt but is no longer questioned. However, two pivotal questions must be resolved.

The first is defining the group of persons who can make privileged communications on behalf of an organization. Balance is required. The privilege should cover a sufficiently broad number of organizational communications to realize the organization's policy objectives, but not insulate ordinary intraorganizational communications that may later have importance as evidence. Concern has been expressed, for example, that the privilege would afford organizations "zones of silence" that would be free of evidentiary scrutiny. A subsidiary problem is whether persons who would be nonprivileged occurrence witnesses with respect to communications to a lawyer representing a natural person can be conduits of privileged communications when the client is an organization. That problem has been addressed in terms of the "subject-matter" and "control-group" tests for the privilege (see Comment *d*).

Second is the problem of defining the types of organizations treated as clients for purposes of the privilege. It is now accepted that the privilege applies to corporations, but some decisions have questioned whether the privilege should apply to unincorporated associations, partnerships, or sole proprietorships. Neither logic nor principle supports limiting the organizational privilege to the corporate form (see Comment *c* hereto).

c. Application of the privilege to an organization. As stated in the Section, the privilege applies to all forms of organizations. A corporation with hundreds of employees could as well be a sole proprietorship if its assets were owned by a single person rather than its shares being owned by the same person. It would be anomalous to accord the privilege to a business in corporate form but not if it were organized as a sole proprietorship. In general, an organization under this Section is a group having a recognizable identity as such and some permanency. Thus, an organization under this Section ordinarily would include a law firm, however it may be structured (as a professional corporation, a partnership, a sole proprietorship, or otherwise). The organization need not necessarily be treated as a legal entity for any other legal purpose. The privilege extends as well to charitable, social, fraternal, and other nonprofit organizations such as labor unions and chambers of commerce.

d. An agent of an organizational client. As stated in Subsection (2), the communication must involve an agent of the organization, on one hand, and, on the other, a privileged person within the meaning of § 70, such as the lawyer for the organization. Persons described in Subsection (4)(b) may disclose the communication under a need-to-know limitation (see Comment *g* hereto). The existence of a relationship of principal and agent between the organizational client and the privileged agent is determined according to agency law (see generally Restatement Second, Agency §§ 1–139).

Some decisions apply a "control group" test for determining the scope of the privilege for an organization. That test limits the privilege to communications from persons in the organization who have authority to mold organizational policy or to take action in accordance with the lawyer's advice. The control-group circle excludes many persons within an organization who normally would cooperate with an organization's lawyer. Such a limitation overlooks that the division of functions within an organization often separates decisionmakers from those knowing relevant facts. Such a limitation is unnecessary to prevent abuse of the privilege (see Comment *g*) and significantly frustrates its purpose.

Other decisions apply a "subject matter" test. That test extends the privilege to communications with any lower-echelon employee or agent so long as the communication relates to the subject matter of the representation. In substance, those decisions comport with the need-to-know formulation in this Section (see Comment *g*).

It is not necessary that the agent receive specific direction from the organization to make or receive the communication (see Comment *h*).

Agents of the organization who may make privileged communications under this Section include the organization's officers and employees. For example, a communication by any employee of a corporation to the corporation's lawyer concerning the matter as to which the lawyer was retained to represent the corporation would be privileged, if other conditions of the privilege are satisfied. The concept of agent also includes independent contractors with whom the corporation has a principal-agent relationship and extends to agents of such persons when acting as subagents of the organizational client. For example, a foreign-based corporation may retain a general agency (perhaps a separate corporation) in an American city for the purpose of retaining counsel to represent the interests of the foreign-based corporation. Communications by the general agency would be by an agent for the purpose of this Section.

For purpose of the privilege, when a parent corporation owns controlling interest in a corporate subsidiary, the parent corporation's agents who are responsible for legal matters of the subsidiary are considered agents of the subsidiary. The subsidiary corporation's agents who are responsible for affairs of the parent are also considered agents of the parent for the purpose of the privilege. Directors of a corporation are not its agents for many legal purposes, because they are not subject to the control of the corporation (see Restatement Second, Agency § 14C). However, in communications with the organization's counsel, a director who communicates in the interests and for the benefit of the corporation is its agent for the purposes of this Section. Depending on the circumstances, a director acts in that capacity both when participating in a meeting of directors and when communicating individually with a lawyer for the corporation about the corporation's affairs. Communications to and from nonagent constituents of a corporation, such as shareholders and creditors, are not privileged.

In the case of a partnership, general partners and employees and other agents and subagents of the partnership may serve as agents of the organization for the purpose of making privileged communications (see generally Restatement Second, Agency § 14A). Limited partners who have no other relationship (such as employee) with the limited partnership are analogous to shareholders of a corporation and are not such agents.

In the case of an unincorporated association, agents whose communications may be privileged under this Section include officers and employees and other contractual agents and subagents. Members of an unincorporated association, for example members of a labor union, are not, solely by reason of their status as members, agents of the association for the purposes of this Section. In some situations, for example, involving a small unincorporated association with very active members, the members might be considered agents for the purpose of this Section on the ground that the association functionally is a partnership whose members are like partners.

In the case of an enterprise operated as a sole proprietorship, agents who may make communications privileged under this Section with respect to the proprietorship include employees or contractual agents and subagents of the proprietor.

Communications of a nonagent constituent of the organization may be independently privileged under § 75 where the person is a co-client along with the organization. If the agent of the organization has a conflict of interest with the organization, the lawyer for the organization must not purport to represent both the organization and the agent without consent (see § 131, Comment *c*). The lawyer may not mislead the agent about the nature of the lawyer's loyalty to the organization (see § 103). If a lawyer fails to clarify the lawyer's role as representative solely of the organization and the organization's agent reasonably believes that the lawyer represents the agent, the agent may assert the privilege personally with respect to the agent's own communications (compare § 72(2), Comment *f*; see also § 131, Comment *e*).

The lawyer must also observe limitations on the extent to which a lawyer may communicate with a person of conflicting interests who is not represented by counsel (see § 103) and limitations on communications with persons who are so represented (see § 99 and following).

e. *The temporal relationship of principal-agent.* Under Subsection (2), a person making a privileged communication to a lawyer for an organization must then be acting as agent of the principal-organization. The objective of the organizational privilege is to encourage the organization to have its agents communicate with its lawyer (see Comment d hereto). Generally, that premise implies that persons be agents of the organization at the time of communicating. The privilege may also extend, however, to communications with a person with whom the organization has terminated, for most other purposes, an agency relationship. A former agent is a privileged person under Subsection (2) if, at the time of communicating, the former agent has a continuing legal obligation to the principal-organization to furnish the information to the organization's lawyer. The scope of such a continuing obligation is determined by the law of agency and the terms of the employment contract (see Restatement Second, Agency § 275, Comment *e*, & § 381, Comment *f*). The privilege covers communications with a lawyer for an organization by a retired officer of the organization concerning a matter within the officer's prior responsibilities that is of legal importance to the organization.

Subsection (2) does not include a person with whom the organization established a principal-agent relationship predominantly for the purpose of providing the protection of the privilege to the person's communications, if the person was not an agent at the time of learning the information. For example, communications between the lawyer for an organization and an eyewitness to an event whose communications would not otherwise be privileged cannot be made privileged simply through the organization hiring the person to consult with the organization's lawyer. (As to experts and similar persons employed by a lawyer, see § 70, Comment *g*).

Ordinarily, an agent communicating with an organization's lawyer within this Section will have acquired the information in the course of the agent's work for the organization. However, it is not necessary that the communicated information be so acquired. Thus, a person may communicate under this Section with respect to information learned prior to the relationship or learned outside the person's functions as an agent, so long as the person bears an agency relationship to the principal-organization at the time of the communication and the communication concerns a matter of interest to the organization (see Comment *f*). For example, a chemist for an organization who communicates to the organization's lawyer information about a process that the chemist learned prior to being employed by the organization makes a privileged communication if the other conditions of this Section are satisfied.

f. Limitation to communications relating to the interests of the organization. Subsection (3) requires that the communication relate to a legal matter of interest to the organization. The lawyer must be representing the organization as opposed to the agent who communicates with the lawyer, such as its individual officer or employee. A lawyer representing such an officer or employee, of course, can have privileged communications with that client. But the privilege will not be that of the organization. When a lawyer represents as co-clients both the organization and one of its officers or employees, the privileged nature of communications is determined under § 75. On the conflicts of interest involved in such representations, see § 131, Comment *e*.

g. The need-to-know limitation on disclosing privileged communications. Communications are privileged only if made for the purpose of obtaining legal services (see § 72), and they remain privileged only if neither the client nor an agent of the client subsequently discloses the communication to a nonprivileged person (see § 79; see also § 71, Comment *d*). Those limitations apply to organizational clients as provided in Subsection (4). Communications become, and remain, so protected by the privilege only if the organization does not permit their dissemination to persons other than to privileged persons. Agents of a client to whom confidential communications may be disclosed are generally defined in § 70, Comment *f*, and agents of a lawyer are defined in § 70, Comment *g*. Included among an organizational client's agents for communication are, for example, a secretary who prepares a letter to the organization's lawyer on behalf of a communicating employee.

The need-to-know limitation of Subsection (4)(b) permits disclosing privileged communications to other agents of the organization who reasonably need to know of the privileged communication in order to act for the organization in the matter. Those agents include persons who are responsible for accepting or rejecting a lawyer's advice on behalf of the organization or for acting on legal assistance, such as general legal advice, provided by the lawyer. Access of such persons to privileged communications is not limited to direct exchange with the lawyer. A lawyer may be required to take steps assuring that attorney-client communications will be disseminated only among privileged persons who have a need to know. Persons defined in Subsection (4)(b) may be apprised of privileged communications after they have been made, as by examining records of privileged communications previously made, in order to conduct the affairs of the organization in light of the legal services provided.

Illustration:

1. Lawyer for Organization makes a confidential report to President of Organization, describing Organization's contractual relationship with Supplier, and advising that Organization's contract with Supplier could be terminated without liability. President sends a confidential memorandum to Manager, Organization's purchasing manager, asking whether termination of the contract would nonetheless be inappropriate for business reasons. Because Manager's response would reasonably depend on several aspects of Lawyer's advice, Manager would have need to know the justifying reason for Lawyer's advice that the contract could be terminated. Lawyer's report to President remains privileged notwithstanding that President shared it with Manager.

The need-to-know concept properly extends to all agents of the organization who would be personally held financially or criminally liable for conduct in the matter in question or who would personally benefit from it, such as general partners of a partnership with respect to a claim for or against the partnership. It extends to persons, such as members of a board of directors and senior officers of an organization, whose general management and supervisory responsibilities include wide areas of organizational activities and to lower-echelon agents of the organization whose area of activity is relevant to the legal advice or service rendered.

Dissemination of a communication to persons outside those described in Subsection (4)(b) implies that the protection of confidentiality was not significant (see § 71, Comment *b*). An organization may not immunize documents and other communications generated or circulated for a business or other nonlegal purpose (see § 72).

h. *Directed and volunteered agent communications.* It is not necessary that a superior organizational authority specifically direct an agent to communicate with the organization's lawyer. Unless instructed to the contrary, an agent has authority to volunteer information to a lawyer when reasonably related to the interests of the organization. An agent has similar authority to respond to a request for information from a lawyer for the organization. And the lawyer for the organization ordinarily may seek relevant information directly from employees and other agents without prior direction from superior authorities in the organization.

i. *Inside legal counsel and outside legal counsel.* The privilege under this Section applies without distinction to lawyers who are inside legal counsel or outside legal counsel for an organization (see § 72, Comment *c*). Communications predominantly for a purpose other than obtaining or providing legal services for the organization are not within the privilege (see § 72, Comment *c*). On the credentials of a lawyer for the purposes of the privilege, see § 72(1), Comment *e*.

j. *Invoking and waiving the privilege of an organizational client.* The privilege for organizational clients can be asserted and waived only by a responsible person acting for the organization for this purpose. On waiver, see §§ 78–80. Communications involving an organization's director, officer, or employee may qualify as privileged, but it is a separate question whether such a person has authority to invoke or waive the privilege on behalf of the organization. If the lawyer was representing both the organization and the individual as co-clients, the question of invoking and waiving the privilege is determined under the rule for co-clients (see § 75, Comment *e*). Whether a lawyer has formed a client-lawyer relationship with a person affiliated with the organization, as well as with the organization, is determined under § 14. Communications of such a person who approaches a lawyer for the organization as a prospective client are privileged as provided in § 72. Unless the person's contrary intent is reasonably manifest to a lawyer for the organization, the lawyer acts properly in assuming that a communication from any such person is on behalf and in the interest of the organization and, as such, is privileged in the interest of the organization and not of the individual making the communication. When the person manifests an intention to make a communication privileged against the organization, the lawyer must resist entering into such a client-lawyer relationship and receiving such a communication if doing so would constitute an impermissible conflict of interest (see § 131, Comment *e*).

An agent or former agent may have need for a communication as to which the organization has authority to waive the privilege, for example, when the agent is sued personally. A tribunal may exercise discretion to order production of such a communication for benefit of the agent if the agent establishes three conditions. First, the agent must show that the agent properly came to know the contents of the communication. Second, the agent must show substantial need of the communication. Third, the agent must show that production would create no material risk of prejudice or embarrassment to the organization beyond such evidentiary use as the agent may make of the communication. Such a risk may be controlled by protective orders, redaction, or other measures.

Illustration:

2. Lawyer, representing only Corporation, interviews Employee by electronic mail in connection with reported unlawful activities in Corporation's purchasing department in circumstances providing Corporation with a privilege with respect to their communications. Corporation later dismisses Employee, who sues Corporation, alleging wrongful discharge. Employee files a discovery request seeking all copies of communications between Employee and Lawyer. The tribunal has discretion to order discovery under the conditions stated in the preceding paragraph. In view of the apparent relationship of Employee's statements to possible illegal activities, it is doubtful that Employee could persuade the tribunal that access by Employee would create no material risk that third persons, such as a government agency, would thereby learn of the communication and thus gain a litigation or other advantage with respect to Corporation.

k. Succession in legal control of an organization. When ownership of a corporation or other organization as an entity passes to successors, the transaction carries with it authority concerning asserting or waiving the privilege. After legal control passes in such a transaction, communications from directors, officers, or employees of the acquired organization to lawyers who represent only the predecessor organization, if it maintains a separate existence from the acquiring organization, may no longer be covered by the privilege. When a corporation or other organization has ceased to have a legal existence such that no person can act in its behalf, ordinarily the attorney-client privilege terminates (see generally § 77, Comment *c*).

Illustration:

> 3. X, an officer of Ajax Corporation, communicates in confidence with Lawyer, who represents Ajax, concerning dealings between Ajax and one of its creditors, Vendor Corporation. Ajax later is declared bankrupt and a bankruptcy court appoints Trustee as the trustee in bankruptcy for Ajax. Thereafter, Lawyer is called to the witness stand in litigation between Vendor Corporation and Trustee. Trustee has authority to determine whether the attorney-client privilege should be asserted or waived on behalf of the bankrupt Ajax Corporation with respect to testimony by Lawyer about statements by X. X cannot assert a privilege because X was not a client of Lawyer in the representation. Former officers and directors of Ajax cannot assert the privilege because control of the corporation has passed to Trustee.

A lawyer for an organization is ordinarily authorized to waive the privilege in advancing the interests of the client (see § 61 & § 79, Comment *c*). Otherwise, when called to testify, a lawyer is required to invoke the privilege on behalf of the client (see § 86(1)(b)). On waiver, see §§ 78–80.

§ 74. The Privilege for a Governmental Client

Unless applicable law otherwise provides, the attorney-client privilege extends to a communication of a governmental organization as stated in § 73 and of an individual employee or other agent of a governmental organization as a client with respect to his or her personal interest as stated in §§ 68–72.

Comment:

a. Scope and cross-references. This Section provides that the attorney-client privilege ordinarily applies to governmental agencies as to other organizations as provided in § 73 and to individual governmental employees and other agents who are individually represented as it would for individuals under §§ 68–72.

b. Rationale. The objectives of the attorney-client privilege (see § 68, Comment *c*), including the special objectives relevant to organizational clients (see § 73, Comment *b*), apply in general to governmental clients. The privilege aids government entities and employees in obtaining legal advice founded on a complete and accurate factual picture. Communications from such persons should be correspondingly privileged.

A narrower privilege for governmental clients may be warranted by particular statutory formulations. Open-meeting and open-files statutes reflect a public policy against secrecy in many areas of governmental activity. Moreover, unlike persons in private life, a public agency or employee has no autonomous right of confidentiality in communications relating to governmental business.

Nonetheless, the legal system has recognized the strategic concerns of a public agency or officer in establishing and asserting public legal rights. Even public legal rights are contingent at their boundaries and subject to argumentation and dispute as to their precise extent. Members of the public who assert legal interests against a public agency or officer act not in the general public interest but in their private interest or in what they assert is the public interest. The public acting through its public agencies is entitled to resist claims and contentions that the agency considers legally or factually unwarranted. To that end, a public agency or employee is entitled to engage in confidential communications with counsel to establish and maintain legal positions. Accordingly, courts generally have construed open-meeting, open-files, whistle-blower, and similar statutes as subject to the attorney-client privilege, recognizing that otherwise governments would be at unfair disadvantage in litigation, in handling claims and in negotiations.

A privilege that would cover only litigation, including claims or investigations, would be a plausible alternative. Rule 502(d)(6) of the Revised Uniform Rules of Evidence proposed a governmental-client privilege thus limited, but most states rejected that limitation. Another alternative would be a general but qualified privilege protecting confidential communications unless a tribunal found good cause to require disclosure. The privilege for the government could also be limited to a stated period of time (compare § 77, Reporter's Note to Comment *c*). More particularized rules may be necessary where one agency of government claims the privilege in resisting a demand for information by another. Such rules should take account of the complex considerations of governmental structure, tradition, and regulation that are involved.

This Section, however, states the generally prevailing rule that governmental agencies and employees enjoy the same privilege as nongovernmental counterparts. In any event, information covered by the privilege would, in some situations, be protected from disclosure by such rules as executive privilege or state secrets. Of course, a legislative determination of a need for less confidentiality, for example in a statute that limits attorney-client confidentiality in areas outside of litigation, would prevail over the common-law rule stated in this Section.

c. Application of the general attorney-client-privilege rules to a governmental client. The general requirements of the attorney-client privilege apply with respect to assertedly privileged communications of a governmental client. For example, the privilege extends only to communication for the purpose of obtaining or giving legal assistance (see § 72).

The privilege does not apply to a document that has an independent legal effect as an operative statement of governmental policy. For example, a memorandum by a government lawyer that directs, rather than advises, a governmental officer to act in a certain way is not protected by the privilege. Such a document is a necessarily public statement of public policy and as such is meant to be publicly disseminated (see § 71, Comment *e*).

Communications between a lawyer representing one governmental agency and an employee of another governmental agency are privileged only if the lawyer represents both agencies (see § 75) or if the communication is pursuant to a common-interest arrangement (see § 76).

d. Individual government employees and agents. Employees and agents of a governmental agency may have both official and personal interests in a matter. A police officer sued for damages for the alleged use of excessive force, for example, may be both officially and personally interested in the lawsuit. The officer has the right to consult counsel of the officer's choice with respect to the officer's personal interests. If the officer consults a lawyer retained by the officer's agency or department, the principles of § 73, Comment *j*, determine whether the officer is a co-client with the agency or department (see § 75) or is not a client of the lawyer. Government lawyers may be prohibited from the private practice of law or accepting a matter adverse to the government. Thus, the fact that the common employer of both lawyer and officer is a government agency may affect the reasonableness of the officer's claim of expectation that the lawyer could function as personal counsel for the officer. On the conflict-of-interest limitations on such joint representations, see § 131, Comment *e*. If a lawyer is retained by the agency as separate counsel to represent the personal interests of the employee, for purposes of the privilege the employee is the sole client. As with agents of nongovernmental organizations, the status of a governmental employee or agent as co-client (see § 75), individual client, or nonrepresented communicating agent of the agency sometimes may be difficult to determine. Inquiry in such cases should focus upon the employment relationship of the lawyer and the reasonable belief of the agent at the time of communicating.

e. Invoking and waiving the privilege of a governmental client. The privilege for governmental entities may be asserted or waived by the responsible public official or body. The identity of that responsible person or body is a question of local governmental law. In some states, for example, the state's attorney general decides matters of litigation policy for state agencies, including decisions about the privilege. In other states, such decisions are made by another executive officer or agency in suits in which the attorney general otherwise conducts the litigation. As a general proposition, the official or body that is empowered to assert or forego a claim or defense is entitled to assert or forego the privilege for communications relating to the claim or defense. Waiver of the privilege is determined according to the standards set forth in § 73, Comment *j*. See also Comment *d* hereto.

§ 75. The Privilege of Co-Clients

(1) If two or more persons are jointly represented by the same lawyer in a matter, a communication of either co-client that otherwise qualifies as privileged under §§ 68–72 and relates to matters of common interest is privileged as against third persons, and any co-client may invoke the privilege, unless it has been waived by the client who made the communication.

(2) Unless the co-clients have agreed otherwise, a communication described in Subsection (1) is not privileged as between the co-clients in a subsequent adverse proceeding between them.

Comment:

a. Scope and cross-references. This Section states the attorney-client-privilege rules that apply when co-clients have communications with the same lawyer. The privilege applies only if the other conditions of §§ 68–72 are met, except that Subsection (1) qualifies the requirement of § 71 that the communication be in confidence and Subsection (2) qualifies the rule of § 79 concerning waiver. On invoking the privilege, see § 86. Subsection (2) modifies the normally applicable rules of waiver (see §§ 78–80) in the case of a subsequent proceeding in which the co-clients are adverse. On the duration of the privilege, see § 77. On representation of multiple clients with conflicts of interest, see §§ 121–122 and §§ 128–131. On confidentiality obligations when representing co-clients, see § 60, Comment *l*.

A communication subject to the privilege for co-clients may be made through a client's agents for communication and a lawyer's agents for communication and other agents (see § 70).

b. The co-client privilege. Under Subsection (1), communications by co-clients with their common lawyer retain confidential characteristics as against third persons. The rule recognizes that it may be desirable to have multiple clients represented by the same lawyer.

c. Delimiting co-client situations. Whether a client-lawyer relationship exists between each client and the common lawyer is determined under § 14, specifically whether they have expressly or impliedly agreed to common representation in which confidential information will be shared. A co-client representation can begin with a joint approach to a lawyer or by agreement after separate representations had begun. However, clients of the same lawyer who share a common interest are not necessarily co-clients. Whether individuals have jointly consulted a lawyer or have merely entered concurrent but separate representations is determined by the understanding of the parties and the lawyer in light of the circumstances (see § 14).

Co-client representations must also be distinguished from situations in which a lawyer represents a single client, but another person with allied interests cooperates with the client and the client's lawyer (see § 76).

The scope of the co-client relationship is determined by the extent of the legal matter of common interest. For example, a lawyer might also represent one co-client on other matters separate from the common one. On whether, following the end of a co-client relationship, the lawyer may continue to represent one former co-client adversely to the interests of another, see § 121, Comment *e*. On the confidentiality of communications during a co-client representation, see Comment *d* hereto.

d. The subsequent-proceeding exception to the co-client privilege. As stated in Subsection (2), in a subsequent proceeding in which former co-clients are adverse, one of them may not invoke the attorney-client privilege against the other with respect to communications involving either of them during the co-client relationship. That rule applies whether or not the co-client's communication had been disclosed to the other during the co-client representation, unless they had otherwise agreed.

Rules governing the co-client privilege are premised on an assumption that co-clients usually understand that all information is to be disclosed to all of them. Courts sometimes refer to this as a presumed intent that there should be no confidentiality between co-clients. Fairness and candor between the co-clients and with the lawyer generally precludes the lawyer from keeping information secret from any one of them, unless they have agreed otherwise (see § 60, Comment *l*).

Illustration:

1. Client X and Client Y jointly consult Lawyer about establishing a business, without coming to any agreement about the confidentiality of their communications to Lawyer. X sends a confidential memorandum to Lawyer in which X outlines the proposed business arrangement as X understands it. The joint representation then terminates, and Y knows that X sent the memorandum but not its contents. Subsequently, Y files suit against X to recover damages arising out of the business venture. Although X's memorandum would be privileged against a third person, in the litigation between X and Y the memorandum is not privileged. That result follows although Y never knew the contents of the letter during the joint representation.

Whether communications between the lawyer and a client that occurred before formation of a joint representation are subject to examination depends on the understanding at the time that the new person was joined as a co-client.

Co-clients may agree that the lawyer will not disclose certain confidential communications of one co-client to other co-clients. If the co-clients have so agreed and the co-clients are subsequently involved in adverse proceedings, the communicating client can invoke the privilege with respect to such communications not in fact disclosed to the former co-client seeking to introduce it. In the absence of such an agreement, the lawyer ordinarily is required to convey communications to all interested co-clients (see § 60, Comment *l*). A co-client may also retain additional, separate counsel on the matter of the common representation; communications with such counsel are not subject to this Section.

e. Standing to assert the co-client privilege; waiver. If a third person attempts to gain access to or to introduce a co-client communication, each co-client has standing to assert the privilege. The objecting client need not have been the source of the communication or previously have known about it.

The normal rules of waiver (see §§ 78–80) apply to a co-client's own communications to the common lawyer. Thus, in the absence of an agreement with co-clients to the contrary, each co-client may waive the privilege with respect to that co-client's own communications with the lawyer, so long as the communication relates only to the communicating and waiving client.

One co-client does not have authority to waive the privilege with respect to another co-client's communications to their common lawyer. If a document or other recording embodies communications from two or more co-clients, all those co-clients must join in a waiver, unless a nonwaiving co-client's communication can be redacted from the document.

Disclosure of a co-client communication in the course of subsequent adverse proceeding between co-clients operates as waiver by subsequent disclosure under § 79 with respect to third persons.

§ 76. The Privilege in Common-Interest Arrangements

(1) If two or more clients with a common interest in a litigated or nonlitigated matter are represented by separate lawyers and they agree to exchange information concerning the matter, a communication of any such client that otherwise qualifies as privileged under §§ 68–72 that relates to the matter is privileged as against third persons. Any such client may invoke the privilege, unless it has been waived by the client who made the communication.

(2) Unless the clients have agreed otherwise, a communication described in Subsection (1) is not privileged as between clients described in Subsection (1) in a subsequent adverse proceeding between them.

Comment:

a. Scope and cross-references. This Section states the common-interest attorney-client privilege. The rule differs from the co-client rule of § 75 in that the clients are represented by separate lawyers. Subsection (1) applies only if the other conditions of §§ 68–72 are satisfied, except it qualifies the requirement of § 71 that the communication be in confidence. Subsection (2) modifies the normal rules of waiver (see §§ 78–85) with respect to subsequent adverse proceedings between the clients.

b. Rationale. The rule in this Section permits persons who have common interests to coordinate their positions without destroying the privileged status of their communications with their lawyers. For example, where conflict of interest disqualifies a lawyer from representing two co-defendants in a criminal case (see § 129), the separate lawyers representing them may exchange confidential communications to prepare their defense without loss of the privilege. Clients thus can elect separate representation while maintaining the privilege in cooperating on common elements of interest.

c. Confidentiality and common-interest rules. The common-interest privilege somewhat relaxes the requirement of confidentiality (see § 71) by defining a widened circle of persons to whom clients may disclose privileged communications. As a corollary, the rule also limits what would otherwise be instances of waiver by disclosing a communication (compare § 79). Communications of several commonly interested clients remain confidential against the rest of the world, no matter how many clients are involved. However, the known presence of a stranger negates the privilege for communications made in the stranger's presence.

Exchanging communications may be predicated on an express agreement, but formality is not required. It may pertain to litigation or to other matters. Separately represented clients do not, by the mere fact of cooperation under this Section, impliedly undertake to exchange all information concerning the matter of common interest.

d. The permissible extent of common-interest disclosures. Under the privilege, any member of a client set—a client, the client's agent for communication, the client's lawyer, and the lawyer's agent (see § 70)—can exchange communications with members of a similar client set. However, a communication directly among the clients is not privileged unless made for the purpose of communicating with a privileged person as defined in § 70. A person who is not represented by a lawyer and who is not himself or herself a lawyer cannot participate in a common-interest arrangement within this Section.

e. Extent of common interests. The communication must relate to the common interest, which may be either legal, factual, or strategic in character. The interests of the separately represented clients need not be entirely congruent.

Illustration:

1. Lawyer One separately represents Corporation A and Lawyer Two represents Corporation B in defending a products-liability action brought by a common adversary, Plaintiff X. The two lawyers agree to exchange otherwise privileged communications of their respective clients concerning settlement strategies. Plaintiff Y later sues Corporation A and Corporation B for damages for alleged defects involving the same products and attempts to obtain discovery of the communications between Lawyer One and Lawyer Two. The communications exchanged between the lawyers for Corporation A and Corporation B are privileged and cannot be discovered.

Unlike the relationship between co-clients, the common-interest relationship does not imply an undertaking to disclose all relevant information (compare § 75, Comment *d*). Confidential communications disclosed to only some members of the arrangement remain privileged against other members as well as against the rest of the world.

f. Subsequent adverse proceedings. Disclosing privileged communications to members of a common-interest arrangement waives the privilege as against other members in subsequent adverse proceedings between them, unless they have agreed otherwise. In that respect, the common-interest exception operates in the same way as the exception for subsequent adverse proceedings as between co-clients (see § 75, Comment *d*). Disclosing information does not waive the privilege with respect to other communications that might also be germane to the matter of common interest but that were not in fact disclosed.

There is no waiver between the members exchanging a communication if they have agreed that it will remain privileged as against each other in subsequent adverse proceedings.

g. Standing to assert the privilege; waiver. Any member of a common-interest arrangement may invoke the privilege against third persons, even if the communication in question was not originally made by or addressed to the objecting member.

In the absence of an agreement to the contrary, any member may waive the privilege with respect to that person's own communications. Correlatively, a member is not authorized to waive the privilege for another member's communication. If a document or other recording embodies communications from two or more members, a waiver is effective only if concurred in by all members whose communications are involved, unless an objecting member's communication can be redacted.

TITLE C. DURATION OF THE ATTORNEY-CLIENT PRIVILEGE; WAIVERS AND EXCEPTIONS

§ 77. Duration of the Privilege

Unless waived (see §§ 78–80) or subject to exception (see §§ 81–85), the attorney-client privilege may be invoked as provided in § 86 at any time during or after termination of the relationship between client or prospective client and lawyer.

Comment:

a. *Scope and cross-references.* For limitations on the privilege in subsequent adverse proceedings between co-clients, see § 75(2), and in common-interest arrangements, see § 76(2). The right of the personal representative of a deceased client to assert or waive the privilege is stated in § 86(1)(a).

b. *Termination of the client-lawyer relationship.* The attorney-client privilege continues indefinitely. Termination of the client-lawyer relationship, even for cause, does not terminate the privilege.

c. *Death of a client or cessation of existence of an organization.* The privilege survives the death of the client. A lawyer for a client who has died has a continuing obligation to assert the privilege (see § 63, Comment *b*). On standing to assert the privilege, see § 86, Comments *c* and *d*.

The privilege is subject to exception in a controversy concerning a deceased client's disposition of property (see § 81). When ownership or control of an organizational client is transferred or when the organization ceases to exist, the right to invoke the privilege in behalf of the organization may also shift to others or terminate (see § 73, Comment *k*).

d. *Situations of need and hardship.* The law recognizes no exception to the rule of this Section. Set out below are considerations that may support such an exception, although no court or legislature has adopted it.

It would be desirable that a tribunal be empowered to withhold the privilege of a person then deceased as to a communication that bears on a litigated issue of pivotal significance. The tribunal could balance the interest in confidentiality against any exceptional need for the communication. The tribunal also could consider limiting the proof or sealing the record to limit disclosure. Permitting such disclosure would do little to inhibit clients from confiding in their lawyers. The fortuity of death prevents waiver of the privilege by the client. Appointing a personal representative to consider waiving the privilege simply transforms the issue into one before a probate court. It would be more direct to permit the judge in the proceeding in which the evidence is offered to make a determination based on the relevant factors.

§ 78. Agreement, Disclaimer, or Failure to Object

The attorney-client privilege is waived if the client, the client's lawyer, or another authorized agent of the client:

(1) agrees to waive the privilege;

(2) disclaims protection of the privilege and

(a) another person reasonably relies on the disclaimer to that person's detriment; or

(b) reasons of judicial administration require that the client not be permitted to revoke the disclaimer; or

(3) in a proceeding before a tribunal, fails to object properly to an attempt by another person to give or exact testimony or other evidence of a privileged communication.

Comment:

a. Scope and cross-references. This Section defines the circumstances under which a client loses the protection of the privilege by consent or through conduct inconsistent with maintaining the privilege. On assertion of the privilege, see § 86. On a lawyer's obligation to raise the objection, see § 63, Comment *b*. On the effect of partial disclosure on other communications, see § 79, Comment *c*. See also § 79, Comment *c* (waiver through disclosure by authorized agent). On the effect of waiver on a client's power to raise the privilege on another occasion, see § 79, Comment *i*. On waiver of the lawyer's work-product immunity, see §§ 91–92.

b. Rationale. The attorney-client privilege is personal to the client whose interests it protects. A client can relinquish its protection.

Waiver of the privilege must be contrasted with a lawyer's use or disclosure of confidential client information with client consent under § 62. Under that Section, client consent is effective only if the client is adequately informed (see § 62, Comment *c*). However, because of the interests of third persons and of judicial administration, under this Section the privilege can be lost even though the client is unaware of the privilege or the consequences of waiver (see particularly Comment *e* hereto).

c. Client agreement. Subsection (1) recognizes that the privilege can be waived by consent of a client, the client's lawyer, or another authorized agent. A lawyer generally has implied authority to waive a client's confidentiality rights in the course of representing the client (see § 61). That authority is especially important in litigation, where the lawyer is empowered to deal with evidentiary issues (see § 16(3) & § 26). A lawyer may be required in some circumstances to advise a client concerning waiver (see § 22). Whether a client can contract away the privilege by consent to a conflict of interest is considered in § 122.

Illustration:

> 1. A and B were partners in a business enterprise experiencing financial difficulties. Each retained a lawyer. A agreed to send B communications that he had received from his lawyer analyzing financial arrangements between them if B would forbear from filing suit against A. B delayed filing suit, but A refused to honor his agreement. In subsequent litigation, B seeks discovery of the information communicated to A by A's lawyer. A's agreement waives the protection of the attorney-client privilege.

The power of an agent, such as an employee of an organization, to waive the privilege is determined under the law of agency.

d. Client disclaimer. An announced intention to waive the privilege, not part of an enforceable promise, does not itself waive the privilege. The client ordinarily may rescind the intention, but, as stated in Subsection (2), not if another person reasonably and detrimentally relies on the announcement (see generally Restatement Second, Contracts § 90). So also, a tribunal has discretion to hold a litigant to an announced intention to waive the privilege, even without detrimental reliance.

e. Failure to object to evidence. Failure to object properly to another party's attempt to offer privileged evidence during a proceeding waives the privilege. Reasonable efforts must be exerted to maintain the secrecy of confidential communications, including making timely objection (see § 86) to their disclosure. Waiver by failing to make proper objection is an application of the general rule requiring parties to object contemporaneously to inadmissible evidence. E.g., Federal Rules of Evidence, Rule 103(a)(1).

In pretrial discovery, excessive concern with avoiding waiver can unduly delay and encumber the proceeding. Accordingly, procedural rules commonly permit parties to stipulate that privilege is not waived by failure to object during pretrial discovery (see Federal Rules of Civil Procedure, Rule 29).

§ 79. Subsequent Disclosure

The attorney-client privilege is waived if the client, the client's lawyer, or another authorized agent of the client voluntarily discloses the communication in a nonprivileged communication.

Comment:

a. *Scope and cross-references.* This Section becomes relevant only if the requirements for the privilege (see §§ 68–72) have been satisfied. On waiver in the case of co-clients, see § 75, Comment *c*. Concerning separately represented clients who exchange confidential communications in a common-interest arrangement, see § 76, Comment *f*.

b. *Subsequent disclosure.* Voluntary disclosure of a privileged communication is inconsistent with a later claim that the communication is to be protected. When the disclosure has been made voluntarily, it is unnecessary that there have been detrimental reliance (compare § 78(2)).

c. *Authorized disclosure by a lawyer or other agent.* The privilege is waived if the client's lawyer or another authorized agent of the client discloses the communication acting under actual or apparent authority. A lawyer generally has implied authority to disclose confidential client communications in the course of representing a client (see § 27, Comment *c*; see also § 61). Ratification of the agent's authority has the same effect (see § 26, Comment *e*). Whether a subagent of the client or lawyer has authority to waive is governed by agency law. A file clerk in a law firm, for example, does not have implied authority.

Unauthorized disclosure by a lawyer not in pursuit of the client's interests does not constitute waiver under this Section. For example, disclosure of a client's confidential information to prevent a threat to the life or safety of another (§ 66) or to prevent a client crime or fraud (§ 67) does not constitute waiver within the meaning of this Section, although another basis for finding the privilege inapplicable may apply.

Because of the lawyer's apparent authority to act for the client, a lawyer's failure to consult the client about disclosing privileged information generally will not affect the rights of third persons. A third person may not, however, reasonably rely on acts of an opposing lawyer or other agent constituting manifest disregard of responsibility for the client's interests (see also § 60, Comment *l*, & § 71, Comment *c* (eavesdroppers)). Upon discovery of an agent's wrongful disclosure, the client must promptly take reasonable steps to suppress or recover the wrongfully disclosed communication in order to preserve the privilege.

Illustration:

1. Lawyer sends a confidential memorandum containing privileged communications to Client for Client's review. Lawyer sends it by a reputable document-courier service. An employee of the document-courier service opens the sealed envelope, makes copies, and gives the copies to a government agency. As soon as the existence of the copies is discovered, Lawyer takes reasonable steps to recover them and demands that the document-courier service and the government agency return all communications taken or information gained from them. Even if the document-courier service is considered an agent of Lawyer for some purposes, its employee's actions do not waive Client's privilege in the communications.

d. *A privileged subsequent disclosure.* A subsequent disclosure that is itself privileged does not result in waiver. Thus, a client who discloses a communication protected by the attorney-client privilege to a second lawyer does not waive the privilege if the attorney-client privilege or work-product immunity protects the second communication. So also, showing a confidential letter from the client's lawyer to the client's spouse under circumstances covered by the marital privilege preserves the attorney-client privilege.

e. *Extent of disclosure.* Waiver results only when a nonprivileged person learns the substance of a privileged communication. Knowledge by the nonprivileged person that the client consulted a lawyer does not result in waiver, nor does disclosure of nonprivileged portions of a communication or its general subject matter. Public disclosure of facts that were discussed in confidence with a lawyer does not waive the privilege if the disclosure does not also reveal that they were communicated to the lawyer. See § 69, Comment *d* (distinction between communications and facts).

Illustrations:

2. Client, a defendant in a personal-injury action, makes a privileged communication to Lawyer concerning the circumstances of the accident. In a later judicial proceeding, Client, under questioning by Lawyer, testifies about the occurrence but not about what Client told Lawyer about the same matter. On cross-examination, the lawyer for Plaintiff inquires whether the Client's testimony is

consistent with the account Client gave to Lawyer in confidence. Client's testimony did not waive the privilege.

3. The same facts as in Illustration 2, except that Client states that "I've testified exactly as I told Lawyer just a week after the accident happened. I told Lawyer that the skid marks made by Plaintiff's car were 200 feet long. And I've said the same things here." Such testimony waives the privilege by subsequent disclosure. On the extent of waiver, see Comment *f* hereto.

In the circumstances of Illustration 3, if the client merely testifies that the subject of skid marks was discussed with the client's lawyer, the privilege is not waived.

f. Partial subsequent disclosure and "subject matter" waiver. An initial disclosure resulting in waiver under this Section may consist of disclosure of fewer than all communications between lawyer and client on the subject. The question then arises whether an inquiring party is entitled to access to other relevant communications beyond those actually disclosed. (Similar questions can arise with respect to waiver under § 78 (waiver by agreement, disclaimer, or failure to object) and § 80 (waiver by putting assistance or communication in issue).)

General waiver of all related communications is warranted when a party has selectively offered in evidence before a factfinder only part of a more extensive communication or one of several related communications, and the opposing party seeks to test whether the partial disclosure distorted the context or meaning of the part offered. All authorities agree that in such a situation waiver extends to all otherwise-privileged communications on the same subject matter that are reasonably necessary to make a complete and balanced presentation (compare Federal Rules of Evidence, Rule 106). That breadth of waiver is required by considerations of forensic fairness, to prevent a partial disclosure that would otherwise mislead the factfinder because selectively incomplete. Similar considerations generally apply when the privilege holder makes a partial disclosure in pretrial proceedings, as in support of a motion for summary judgment or during a pretrial hearing on a request for provisional relief.

If partial disclosure occurs in a nontestimonial setting or in the context of pretrial discovery, a clear majority of decisions indicates that a similar broad waiver will be found, even though the disclosure is not intended to obtain advantage as a possibly misleading half-truth in testimony. Although arguably different considerations might apply (because of the absence of opportunity to mislead a factfinder by partial disclosure), courts insist in effect that a party who wishes to assert the privilege take effective steps to protect against even partial disclosure, regardless of the nontestimonial setting. In an appropriate factual setting, waiver may also be supportable on the ground that the partial disclosure was designed to mislead an opposing party in negotiations or was inconsistent with a candid exchange of information in pretrial discovery.

Parties may agree that disclosure of one privileged communication will not be regarded as waiver as to others, and a tribunal may so order, for example in a discovery protective order. Such an agreement or order governs questions of waiver both in the proceeding involved and, with respect to the parties to the agreement, in other proceedings.

g. Voluntary subsequent disclosure. To constitute waiver, a disclosure must be voluntary. The disclosing person need not be aware that the communication was privileged, nor specifically intend to waive the privilege. A disclosure in obedience to legal compulsion or as the product of deception does not constitute waiver.

Illustrations:

4. A burglar ransacks Client's confidential files and carries away copies of communications from Client to Lawyer protected by the attorney-client privilege. The police apprehend the burglar, recover the copies, and examine them in order to identify their owner. Client's right to invoke the privilege is not lost.

5. At a hearing before a tribunal, the presiding officer erroneously overrules Lawyer's objection to a question put to Client that calls for a communication protected by the attorney-client privilege. Client then testifies. By testifying, Client has not waived objection to efforts to elicit additional privileged communications in the litigation nor to claim on appeal that the hearing officer incorrectly

overruled Lawyer's objection. Client also can seek protection of the attorney-client privilege in subsequent litigation.

On resisting disclosure by legal compulsion, see § 86.

h. Inadvertent disclosure. A subsequent disclosure through a voluntary act constitutes a waiver even though not intended to have that effect. It is important to distinguish between inadvertent waiver and a change of heart after voluntary waiver. Waiver does not result if the client or other disclosing person took precautions reasonable in the circumstances to guard against such disclosure. What is reasonable depends on circumstances, including: the relative importance of the communication (the more sensitive the communication, the greater the necessary protective measures); the efficacy of precautions taken and of additional precautions that might have been taken; whether there were externally imposed pressures of time or in the volume of required disclosure; whether disclosure was by act of the client or lawyer or by a third person; and the degree of disclosure to nonprivileged persons.

Once the client knows or reasonably should know that the communication has been disclosed, the client must take prompt and reasonable steps to recover the communication, to reestablish its confidential nature, and to reassert the privilege. Otherwise, apparent acceptance of the disclosure may reflect indifference to confidentiality. Even if fully successful retrieval is impracticable, the client must nonetheless take feasible steps to prevent further distribution.

Illustration:

6. Plaintiff has threatened Client with suit unless Client is able to persuade Plaintiff's lawyers that Client is free from fault. Plaintiff imposes a stringent deadline for Client's showing. Client authorizes Lawyer to produce a large mass of documents. Although reviewed by Lawyer, the documents include a confidential memorandum by Client to Lawyer. The standard procedure of lawyers in the circumstances would not have included reexamining the copies prior to submission. Lawyer's inadvertent disclosure did not waive the privilege. After discovering the mistake, Client must promptly reassert the privilege and demand return of the document.

i. Consequences of client waiver of the privilege. Waiver ordinarily extends to the litigation in or in anticipation of which a disclosure was made and future proceedings as well, whether or not related to the original proceeding. However, if no actual disclosure resulted from the waiver, a client might be in a position to reassert the privilege. For example, inadvertent disclosure of a privileged document in discovery should not preclude subsequent assertion of the privilege against a different opponent in different litigation if the disclosure does not result in the document becoming known to anyone other than the party who received it.

§ 80. Putting Assistance or a Communication in Issue

(1) The attorney-client privilege is waived for any relevant communication if the client asserts as to a material issue in a proceeding that:

(a) the client acted upon the advice of a lawyer or that the advice was otherwise relevant to the legal significance of the client's conduct; or

(b) a lawyer's assistance was ineffective, negligent, or otherwise wrongful.

(2) The attorney-client privilege is waived for a recorded communication if a witness:

(a) employs the communication to aid the witness while testifying; or

(b) employed the communication in preparing to testify, and the tribunal finds that disclosure is required in the interests of justice.

Comment:

a. Scope and cross-references. This Section addresses waiver by interjecting the contents of a confidential communication into litigation. On the exception to the attorney-client privilege in fee suits and for lawyer self-defense, see § 83. On the circumstances in which a client can limit liability or justify an action by relying on legal advice, see § 29.

b. *Putting a privileged communication into issue.* The exceptions stated in Subsection (1) are based on considerations of forensic fairness (compare § 79). If the communication could not be introduced, a client could present the justification of legal advice in an inaccurate, incomplete, and self-serving way. The issue of reliance on legal advice can be interjected through pleadings or testimony. Waiver extends to all communications relevant to the issue asserted by the client. A tribunal may control discovery to postpone or pretermit the issue. For example, if legal advice is presented as an alternative defense, discovery with respect to that issue may be postponed to allow the client opportunity to determine whether to withdraw that defense.

c. *A client attack on a lawyer's services.* A client who contends that a lawyer's assistance was defective waives the privilege with respect to communications relevant to that contention. Waiver affords to interested parties fair opportunity to establish the facts underlying the claim. When the lawyer is a party, the privilege is waived under § 83. Proceedings not involving the lawyer as a party include attacks on a criminal conviction on the ground of ineffective assistance of counsel or on a settlement on the ground that the lawyer lacked authority to bind the client (see §§ 26 & 27).

d. *Using a privileged communication while testifying or preparing to testify.* A witness with consent of or authorized by the client entitled to obtain the privilege might use a privileged communication while testifying or in preparing to testify. An opposing party is permitted to test whether the privileged communication has shaped the testimony. Waiver is automatic when the witness uses the communication in testifying. The standard of permitting review when the presiding officer determines that to be necessary "in the interest of justice" is the formulation employed in the Federal Rules of Evidence (Rule 612(2)). When the witness used the communication to prepare, waiver depends on a determination by the tribunal of whether the witness can recall and testify independent of the communication. Mere review of a privileged communication by a prospective witness does not constitute waiver. The exception should be applied with caution to avoid interfering with legitimate efforts to prepare witnesses for testimony.

If waiver is found, it applies whether the testimony follows or departs from the communication.

§ 81. A Dispute Concerning a Decedent's Disposition of Property

The attorney-client privilege does not apply to a communication from or to a decedent relevant to an issue between parties who claim an interest through the same deceased client, either by testate or intestate succession or by an inter vivos transaction.

§ 82. Client Crime or Fraud

The attorney-client privilege does not apply to a communication occurring when a client:

(a) consults a lawyer for the purpose, later accomplished, of obtaining assistance to engage in a crime or fraud or aiding a third person to do so, or

(b) regardless of the client's purpose at the time of consultation, uses the lawyer's advice or other services to engage in or assist a crime or fraud.

Comment:

a. *Scope and cross-references.* The attorney-client privilege is defined in §§ 68–72. The exception applies to all communications from or to privileged persons (see § 70), if the client's purpose in or use of the consultation is as described. The burden of establishing the elements of the exception is upon a person seeking to overcome the privilege (see § 86(3)).

On a lawyer's responsibilities with respect to counseling a client concerning illegal acts, see § 94. On a lawyer's responsibilities with respect to perjurious or other false evidence, see § 120. A lawyer's duty to safeguard confidential client information (see § 60(1)(b)) is subject to §§ 66–67, permitting a lawyer to use or disclose information as reasonably necessary to prevent (or in some instances to mitigate) certain illegal acts of a client.

b. *Rationale.* When a client consults a lawyer intending to violate elemental legal obligations, there is less social interest in protecting the communication. Correlatively, there is a public interest in preventing clients from attempting to misuse the client-lawyer relationship for seriously harmful ends. Denying protection of the privilege can be founded on the additional moral ground that the client's wrongful intent forfeits the protection. The client can choose whether or not to commit or aid the act after consulting the lawyer and thus is able to avoid exposing secret communications. The exception does not apply to communications about client crimes or frauds that occurred prior to the consultation. Whether a communication relates to past or ongoing or future acts can be a close question. See Comment *e* hereto.

c. Intent of the client and lawyer. The client need not specifically understand that the contemplated act is a crime or fraud. The client's purpose in consulting the lawyer or using the lawyer's services may be inferred from the circumstances. It is irrelevant that the legal service sought by the client (such as drafting an instrument) was itself lawful.

Illustrations:

1. Client is a member of a group engaged in the ongoing enterprise of importing and distributing illegal drugs. Client has agreed with confederates, as part of the consideration for participating in the enterprise, that Client will provide legal representation for the confederates when necessary. Client and Lawyer agree that, for a substantial monthly retainer, Lawyer will stand ready to provide legal services in the event that Client or Client's associates encounter legal difficulties during the operation of the enterprise. In a communication that otherwise qualifies as privileged under § 68, Client informs Lawyer of the identities of confederates in the enterprise. Client continues to engage in the criminal enterprise following the communication. The crime-fraud exception renders nonprivileged the communications between Client and Lawyer, including identification of Client's confederates.

2. Client, who is in financial difficulty, consults Lawyer A concerning the sale of a parcel of real estate owned by Client. Lawyer A provides legal services in connection with the sale. Client then asks Lawyer A to represent Client in petitioning for bankruptcy. Lawyer A advises Client that the bankruptcy petition must list the sale of the real estate because it occurred within the year previous to the date of filing the petition. Client ends the representation. Client shortly thereafter hires Lawyer B. Omitting to tell Lawyer B about the land sale, Client directs Lawyer B to file a bankruptcy petition that does not disclose the proceeds of the sale. In a subsequent proceeding in which Client's fraud in filing the petition is in issue, a tribunal would be warranted in inferring that Client consulted Lawyer A with the purpose of obtaining assistance to defraud creditors in bankruptcy and thus that the communications between Client and Lawyer A concerning report of the land sale in the bankruptcy petition are not privileged. It would also suffice should the tribunal find that Client attempted to use Lawyer A's advice about the required contents of a bankruptcy petition to defraud creditors by withholding information about the land sale from Lawyer B.

A client could intend criminal or fraudulent conduct but not carry through the intended act. The exception should not apply in such circumstances, for it would penalize a client for doing what the privilege is designed to encourage—consulting a lawyer for the purpose of achieving law compliance. By the same token, lawyers might be discouraged from giving full and candid advice to clients about legally questionable courses of action. On the other hand, a client may consult a lawyer about a matter that constitutes a criminal conspiracy but that is later frustrated—and, in that sense, not later accomplished (cf. Subsection (a))—or, similarly, about a criminal attempt. Such a crime is within the exception stated in the Section if its elements are established.

The crime-fraud exception applies regardless of the fact that the client's lawyer is unaware of the client's intent. The exception also applies if the lawyer actively participates in the crime or fraud. However, if a client does not intend to commit a criminal or fraudulent act, the privilege protects the client's communication even if the client's lawyer acts with a criminal or fraudulent intent in giving advice.

Illustration:

3. Lawyer, in complicity with confederates who are not clients, is furthering a scheme to defraud purchasers in a public offering of shares of stock. Client, believing that the stock offering is legitimate and ignorant of facts indicating its wrongful nature, seeks to participate in the offering as an underwriter. In the course of obtaining legal advice from Lawyer, Client conveys communications

to Lawyer that are privileged under § 68. The crime-fraud exception does not prevent Client from asserting the attorney-client privilege, despite Lawyer's complicity in the fraud.

Compare Illustration 1 to this Comment.

d. Kinds of illegal acts included within the exception. The authorities agree that the exception stated in this Section applies to client conduct defined as a crime or fraud. Fraud, for the purpose of the exception, requires a knowing or reckless misrepresentation (or nondisclosure when applicable law requires disclosure) likely to injure another (see Restatement Second, Torts §§ 525–530 (defining elements of fraudulent misrepresentation)).

The evidence codes and judicial decisions are divided on the question of extending the exception to other wrongs such as intentional torts, which, although not criminal or fraudulent, have hallmarks of clear illegality and the threat of serious harm. Legislatures and courts classify illegal acts as crimes and frauds for purposes and policies different from those defining the scope of the privilege. Thus, limiting the exception to crimes and frauds produces an exception narrower than principle and policy would otherwise indicate. Nonetheless, the prevailing view limits the exception to crimes and frauds. The actual instances in which a broader exception might apply are probably few and isolated, and it would be difficult to formulate a broader exception that is not objectionably vague.

Consultation about some acts of civil disobedience is privileged under the Section, for example violations of a law based on a nonfrivolous claim that the law is unconstitutional. The same is true of a communication concerning a contempt sanction necessary to obtain immediate appellate review of an order whose validity is challenged in good faith. (See § 94, Comment *e*, & § 105, Comment *e*.) If, however, the client's position is that the law is valid but there is a superior moral justification for violating it, this Section applies if its conditions are otherwise satisfied.

e. Continuing crimes and frauds. The crime-fraud exception depends on a distinction between past client wrongs and acts that are continuing or will occur in the future. The exception does not apply to communications about client criminal or fraudulent acts that occurred in the past. Communications about past acts are necessary in defending against charges concerning such conduct and, for example, providing background for legal advice concerning a present transaction that is neither criminal nor fraudulent. The possible social costs of denying access to relevant evidence of past acts is accepted in order to realize the enhanced legality and fairness that confidentiality fosters (see § 68, Comment *c*).

The exception does apply to client crimes or frauds that are ongoing or continuing. With respect to past acts that have present consequences, such as the possession of stolen goods, consultation of lawyer and client is privileged if it addresses how the client can rectify the effects of the illegal act—such as by returning the goods to their rightful owner—or defending the client against criminal charges arising out of the offense.

Illustration:

4. Client consults Lawyer about Client's indictment for the crimes of theft and of unlawfully possessing stolen goods. Applicable law treats possession of stolen goods as a continuing offense. Client is hiding the goods in a secret place, knowing that they are stolen. Confidential communications between Client and Lawyer concerning the indictment for theft and possession and the facts underlying those offenses are privileged. Confidential communications concerning ways in which Client can continue to possess the stolen goods, including information supplied by Client about their present location, are not protected by the privilege because of the crime-fraud exception. Confidential communications about ways in which Client might lawfully return the stolen goods to their owner are privileged.

Strict limitation of the exception to ongoing or future crimes and frauds would prohibit a lawyer from testifying that a client confessed to a crime for which an innocent person is on trial. The law of the United Kingdom recognizes an exception in such cases. At least in capital cases, the argument for so extending the exception seems compelling. Compare also § 66 (disclosure to prevent loss of life or serious bodily injury, whether or not risk is created by wrongful client act).

f. Invoking the crime-fraud exception. The crime-fraud exception is relevant only after the attorney-client privilege is successfully invoked. The person seeking access to the communication then must present a prima facie case for the exception. A prima facie case need show only a reasonable basis for concluding that the elements of the exception (see Comment *d*) exist. The showing must be made by evidence other than the contested communication itself. Once a prima facie showing is made, the tribunal has discretion to examine the communication or hear testimony about it in camera, that is, without requiring that the communications be revealed to the party seeking to invoke the exception (see § 86, Comment *f*).

Unless the crime-fraud exception plainly applies to a client-lawyer communication, a lawyer has an obligation to assert the privilege (see § 63, Comment *b*).

g. *Effects of the crime-fraud exception.* A communication to which the crime-fraud exception applies is not privileged under § 68 for any purpose. Evidence of the communication is admissible in the proceeding in which that determination is made or in another proceeding. The privilege still applies, however, to communications that were not for a purpose included within this Section. For example, a client who consulted a lawyer about several different matters on several different occasions could invoke the privilege with respect to consultations concerning matters unrelated to the illegal acts (compare § 79, Comment *e*). With respect to a lawyer's duty not to use or disclose client information even if not privileged, see § 60; compare §§ 66–67.

§ 83. Lawyer Self-Protection

The attorney-client privilege does not apply to a communication that is relevant and reasonably necessary for a lawyer to employ in a proceeding:

(1) to resolve a dispute with a client concerning compensation or reimbursement that the lawyer reasonably claims the client owes the lawyer; or

(2) to defend the lawyer or the lawyer's associate or agent against a charge by any person that the lawyer, associate, or agent acted wrongfully during the course of representing a client.

§ 84. Fiduciary-Lawyer Communications

In a proceeding in which a trustee of an express trust or similar fiduciary is charged with breach of fiduciary duties by a beneficiary, a communication otherwise within § 68 is nonetheless not privileged if the communication:

(a) is relevant to the claimed breach; and

(b) was between the trustee and a lawyer (or other privileged person within the meaning of § 70) who was retained to advise the trustee concerning the administration of the trust.

§ 85. Communications Involving a Fiduciary Within an Organization

In a proceeding involving a dispute between an organizational client and shareholders, members, or other constituents of the organization toward whom the directors, officers, or similar persons managing the organization bear fiduciary responsibilities, the attorney-client privilege of the organization may be withheld from a communication otherwise within § 68 if the tribunal finds that:

(a) those managing the organization are charged with breach of their obligations toward the shareholders, members, or other constituents or toward the organization itself;

(b) the communication occurred prior to the assertion of the charges and relates directly to those charges; and

(c) the need of the requesting party to discover or introduce the communication is sufficiently compelling and the threat to confidentiality sufficiently confined to justify setting the privilege aside.

TITLE D. INVOKING THE PRIVILEGE AND ITS EXCEPTIONS

§ 86. Invoking the Privilege and Its Exceptions

(1) When an attempt is made to introduce in evidence or obtain discovery of a communication privileged under § 68:

(a) A client, a personal representative of an incompetent or deceased client, or a person succeeding to the interest of a client may invoke or waive the privilege, either personally or through counsel or another authorized agent.

(b) A lawyer, an agent of the lawyer, or an agent of a client from whom a privileged communication is sought must invoke the privilege when doing so appears reasonably appropriate, unless the client:

(i) has waived the privilege; or

(ii) has authorized the lawyer or agent to waive it.

(c) Notwithstanding failure to invoke the privilege as specified in Subsections (1)(a) and (1)(b), the tribunal has discretion to invoke the privilege.

(2) A person invoking the privilege must ordinarily object contemporaneously to an attempt to disclose the communication and, if the objection is contested, demonstrate each element of the privilege under § 68.

(3) A person invoking a waiver of or exception to the privilege (§§ 78–85) must assert it and, if the assertion is contested, demonstrate each element of the waiver or exception.

TOPIC 3. THE LAWYER WORK-PRODUCT IMMUNITY

TITLE A. THE SCOPE OF THE LAWYER WORK-PRODUCT IMMUNITY

§ 87. Lawyer Work-Product Immunity

(1) Work product consists of tangible material or its intangible equivalent in unwritten or oral form, other than underlying facts, prepared by a lawyer for litigation then in progress or in reasonable anticipation of future litigation.

(2) Opinion work product consists of the opinions or mental impressions of a lawyer; all other work product is ordinary work product.

(3) Except for material which by applicable law is not so protected, work product is immune from discovery or other compelled disclosure to the extent stated in §§ 88 (ordinary work product) and 89 (opinion work product) when the immunity is invoked as described in § 90.

Comment:

a. Scope and cross-references. This Section defines the work-product immunity as it applies to lawyers. Federal and state discovery rules accord work-product protection to others, including personnel who assist a lawyer, and to litigation preparation of a party and the party's representatives. Application of the immunity with respect to such other persons is beyond the scope of this Restatement.

Section 88 sets forth the standard for overcoming ordinary work-product immunity. The broader protection afforded opinion work product is considered in § 89. Procedures for invoking the immunity and its exceptions are considered in Title B. Title C discusses exceptions to that rule.

b. Rationale. The Federal Rules of Civil Procedure in 1938 provided for notice pleading supplemented by expanded discovery. The Rules sought to eliminate the "sporting" concept of litigation in favor of more accurate factfinding and open truth-seeking. However, the discovery rules presupposed that counsel should be able to work within an area of professional confidentiality, described by the work-product rule. A companion assumption has been that the truth emerges from the adversary presentation of information by opposing sides, in which opposing lawyers competitively develop their own sources of factual and legal information. The work-product doctrine also protects client interests in obtaining diligent assistance from lawyers. A lawyer whose work product would be open to the other side might forgo useful preparatory procedures, for example, note-taking. The immunity also reduces the possibility that a lawyer would have to testify concerning witness statements (compare § 108).

Nonetheless, the work-product immunity is in tension with the purposes of modern discovery by impeding the pretrial exchange of information. The immunity also entails duplication of investigative efforts, perhaps increasing litigation costs. Enforcement of the immunity causes satellite litigation and additional expense.

Protection of lawyer thought processes (see § 89) is at the core of work-product rationale; accordingly, those are accorded the broadest protection. A lawyer's analysis can readily be replicated by an opposing lawyer and, in any event, would usually be inadmissible in evidence. Factual information gathered by a lawyer usually relates directly to controverted issues and generally is discoverable in forms that do not reveal the lawyer's thought processes.

Beyond that, the work-product rules are a set of compromises between openness and secrecy. Thus, under Federal Rule 26(b), the identity of witnesses must be disclosed even if ascertaining their identity has been burdensome or involved confidential consultations with a client. Similarly, under Rule 26(b) statements given by a party to an opposing lawyer are subject to discovery, even though such a statement necessarily reflects the lawyer's thought process in some degree. So also are the opinions of an expert who is expected to testify at trial. A nonparty witness's statement must be produced upon demand by that witness. A party's documents and other records are generally discoverable even if they have been reviewed by counsel. On the other hand, the identity of an expert consulted but who will not testify is protected against discovery, even if that expert's opinion is highly material. So also, the classification systems employed by a lawyer in reviewing a client's documents are not subject to discovery.

c. Applications of the work-product immunity. The work-product immunity operates primarily as a limitation on pretrial discovery, but it can apply to evidence at a trial or hearing. Work-product immunity is also recognized in criminal and administrative proceedings and is incorporated as a limitation on other types of disclosure, for example in the federal Freedom of Information Act. The scope of those applications of the work-product rule is generally beyond the scope of this Restatement.

d. The relationship of the work-product immunity to the attorney-client privilege. The attorney-client privilege is limited to communications between a client and lawyer and certain of their agents (see § 70); in contrast, work product includes many other kinds of materials (see Comment *f*), even when obtained from sources other than the client. Application of the attorney-client privilege absolutely bars discovery or testimonial use; in contrast, the work-product immunity is a qualified protection that, in various circumstances, can be overcome on a proper showing (see §§ 88 & 89). The attorney-client privilege protects communications between client and lawyer regarding all kinds of legal services (see § 72); in contrast, the work-product immunity is limited to materials prepared for or in anticipation of litigation (see Comments *h–j*).

Work-product immunity is also similar to the rule recognized in some jurisdictions that a self-evaluation study and report is immune from discovery. The self-evaluation immunity is not limited to work performed in anticipation of litigation. The scope of self-evaluation and similar immunities is beyond the scope of this Restatement.

e. The source of the law concerning work-product immunity. In the federal system, work-product immunity is recognized both under Rule 26(b)(3) of the Federal Rules of Civil Procedure and as a common-law rule following the decision in *Hickman v. Taylor*. In a few states work-product immunity is established by common law, but in most states it is defined by statute or court rule. Some state statutes mirror Federal Rule of Civil Procedure 26(b)(3), others codify the principles of *Hickman v. Taylor* more broadly; and others codify pre-*Hickman* rules that were not adopted for the federal courts. State courts, in construing their statutes, often look to federal case law in applying work-product immunity.

f. Types of work-product materials. Work product includes tangible materials and intangible equivalents prepared, collected, or assembled by a lawyer. Tangible materials include documents, photographs, diagrams, sketches, questionnaires and surveys, financial and economic analyses, hand-written notes, and material in electronic and other technologically advanced forms, such as stenographic, mechanical, or electronic recordings or transmissions, computer data bases, tapes, and printouts. Intangible work product is equivalent work product in unwritten, oral or remembered form. For example, intangible work product can come into question by a discovery request for a lawyer's recollections derived from oral communications.

A compilation or distillation of non-work-product materials can itself be work product. For example, a lawyer's memorandum analyzing publicly available information constitutes work product. The selection or arrangement of documents that are not themselves protected might reflect mental impressions and legal opinions inherent in making a selection or arrangement. Thus, a lawyer's index of a client's preexisting and discoverable business files will itself be work product if prepared in anticipation of litigation. So also, the manner in which a lawyer has selected certain client files, organized them in pretrial work, and plans to present them at trial is work product.

g. The distinction between protected materials and nonprotected underlying facts. Work-product immunity does not apply to underlying facts of the incident or transaction involved in the litigation, even if the same information is contained in work product. For a comparison to the nonprivileged status accorded to facts under the attorney-client privilege, see § 69, Comment *d*.

The distinction between discoverable underlying facts and nondiscoverable work product can be difficult to draw. Relevant are the form of the question or request, the identity of the person who is to respond, and the form of a responsive answer. Immunity does not attach merely because the underlying fact was discovered through a lawyer's effort or is recorded only in otherwise protected work product, for example, in a lawyer's file memorandum. Immunity does not apply to an interrogatory seeking names of witnesses to the occurrence in question or whether a witness recounts a particular version of events, for example that a traffic light was red or green. On the other hand, an interrogatory seeking the substantially verbatim contents of the witness's unrecorded statement would be objectionable.

h. Anticipation of litigation: kinds of proceedings. The limitation of the work-product immunity to litigation activities is best explained by the origin of the rule in the context of litigation. "Litigation" includes civil and criminal trial proceedings, as well as adversarial proceedings before an administrative agency, an arbitration panel or a claims commission, and alternative-dispute-resolution proceedings such as mediation or mini-trial. It also includes a proceeding such as a grand jury or a coroner's inquiry or an investigative legislative hearing. In general, a proceeding is adversarial when evidence or legal argument is presented by parties contending against each other with respect to legally significant factual issues. Thus, an adversarial rulemaking proceeding is litigation for purposes of the immunity.

i. Anticipation of litigation: the reasonableness standard. Work-product immunity attaches when litigation is then in progress or there is reasonable anticipation of litigation by the lawyer at the time the material was prepared. On what constitutes litigation, see Comment *h* hereto. The fact that litigation did not actually ensue does not affect the immunity.

In one sense, almost all of a lawyer's work anticipates litigation to some degree, because preparing documents or arranging transactions is aimed at avoiding future litigation or enhancing a client's position should litigation occur. However, the immunity covers only material produced when apprehension of litigation was reasonable in the circumstances. The reasonableness of anticipation is determined objectively by considering the factual context in which materials are prepared, the nature of the materials, and the expected role of the lawyer in ensuing litigation.

Illustrations:

1. Employer's Lawyer writes to Physician, setting out circumstances of an employee's death and asking for Physician's opinion as to the cause, stating that Lawyer is preparing for a "possible claim" by the employee's executor for worker-compensation benefits. Lawyer's letter is protected work product.

2. Informed that agents of the Justice Department are questioning Publisher's customers, Lawyer for Publisher prepared a memorandum analyzing the antitrust implications of Publisher's

standard contract form with commercial purchasers. Publisher's employees testify before a grand jury investigating antitrust issues in the publishing industry. Lawyer, reasonably believing there is a risk that the grand jury will indict Publisher, interviews the employees and prepares a debriefing memorandum. Both Lawyer's memorandum analyzing the contract form and Lawyer's debriefing memorandum were prepared in anticipation of litigation. The grand-jury proceeding is itself litigation for this purpose (see Comment *h*).

j. *Future litigation.* If litigation was reasonably anticipated, the immunity is afforded even if litigation occurs in an unanticipated way. For example, work product prepared during or in anticipation of a lawsuit remains immune in a subsequent suit for indemnification, whether or not the indemnification claim could have been anticipated. Work product prepared in anticipation of litigation remains protected in all future litigation.

§ 88. Ordinary Work Product

When work product protection is invoked as described in § 90, ordinary work product (§ 87(2)) is immune from discovery or other compelled disclosure unless either an exception recognized in §§ 91–93 applies or the inquiring party:

(1) has a substantial need for the material in order to prepare for trial; and

(2) is unable without undue hardship to obtain the substantial equivalent of the material by other means.

Comment:

a. *Scope and cross-references.* This Section states the limited immunity of ordinary work product from involuntary disclosure and the need-and-hardship exception. On the much narrower exception for opinion work product, see § 89.

b. *The need-and-hardship exception—in general.* The demonstration of need and hardship operates only when it is first established (see § 90, Comment *b*) that the requested material constitutes protected work product (see § 87). The exception does not provide access if other privileges apply, for example, the attorney-client privilege (see §§ 68–86), the privilege against self-incrimination, or a privilege for proprietary information.

Demonstrating the requisite need and hardship requires the inquiring party to show that the material is relevant to the party's claim or defense, and that the inquiring party will likely be prejudiced in the absence of discovery. As a corollary, it must be shown that substantially equivalent material is not available or, if available, only through cost and effort substantially disproportionate to the amount at stake in the litigation and the value of the information to the inquiring party. The necessary showing is more easily made after other discovery has been completed.

The most common situation involves a prior statement by a witness who is absent, seriously ill, or deceased and thus now unavailable. See Federal Rule of Evidence 804(a). Another common situation concerns statements made contemporaneously with an event. Such statements are often the most reliable recording of recollections of that event and in that sense unique. A third situation is where the passage of time has dulled the memory of the witness.

Illustration:

1. Several witnesses testify before a grand jury investigating the publishing industry. Shortly afterward, Lawyer for Publisher debriefs the witnesses and writes memoranda of those interviews in anticipation of the possible indictment of Publisher and later civil suits. Six years later, Plaintiffs, representing a class of consumers, file an antitrust class action against Publisher and seek discovery of the non-opinion work-product portions of Lawyer's debriefing memoranda. Plaintiffs have been diligent in preparing their case and gathering evidence through other means and demonstrate that the witnesses now are unable to recall the events to which they testified. The court may order the memorandum produced. If the memorandum contains both ordinary and opinion work product, see § 89, Comment *c*.

Substantial need also exists when the material consists of tests performed nearly contemporaneously with a litigated event and substantially equivalent testing is no longer possible.

c. *Material for impeachment.* Need is shown when a requesting party demonstrates that there is likely to be a material discrepancy between a prior statement of a witness reflected in a lawyer's notes and a statement of the same person made later during discovery, such as during a deposition. The discrepancy must be of an impeaching quality. A clear case exists when the witness admits to such a discrepancy. However, the inquiring party may demonstrate a reasonable basis by inference from circumstances. In camera inspection of the statement may be appropriate to determine whether the material should be produced.

d. *Witness statements.* A statement given to a lawyer by a witness is work product. Being ordinary work product, a witness statement may be obtained by an opposing party only upon an appropriate showing of need and hardship. Under the Federal Rules and the law of many states, the person who gives a substantially verbatim statement has the right to obtain a copy of it.

§ 89. Opinion Work Product

When work product protection is invoked as described in § 90, opinion work product (§ 87(2)) is immune from discovery or other compelled disclosure unless either the immunity is waived or an exception applies (§§ 91–93) or extraordinary circumstances justify disclosure.

Comment:

a. *Scope and cross-references.* Opinion work product of a lawyer is defined in § 87(2). Ordinary work product is subject to a general exception for need and hardship (see § 88).

b. *Rationale.* Mental impressions, opinions, conclusions, and legal theories form the core of work product. As impressions formed after the event or transaction in issue, they are also not of the same evidentiary value as percipient witness observation or contemporaneous recording of the event. Disclosure of ordinary work product in cases of need and hardship facilitates trial preparation, but no comparable utility ordinarily attends discovery of a lawyer's theories, conclusions, and other opinions. Strict protection for opinion work product effectuates functioning of the adversary system (see § 87, Comment *b*). Moreover, analysis expressed in opinion work product can be carried out by the requesting party's lawyer.

The protection for opinion work product is qualified by discovery rules requiring disclosure of legal contentions on which a party intends to rely (see Federal Rules of Civil Procedure 33(b) and 36(a), cf. id., Rule 16 (pretrial conference)). Also, an advocate is required under certain circumstances to inform a tribunal of adverse legal authority (see § 111).

c. *Material combining opinion and ordinary work product.* The material sought might contain both ordinary and opinion work product, for example, notes of an interview containing both the recollections of the witness and the thoughts of the lawyer who made the notes. If the tribunal finds that the ordinary work-product material should be produced, it may order production of the notes in redacted form. The tribunal may conduct an in camera inspection to determine whether redaction is appropriate and feasible. If opinion work product is so intertwined in the material that it cannot be redacted without destroying the value of the ordinary work product, the tribunal must balance the need for disclosure against the need for privacy.

d. *The extraordinary-circumstances exception.* The concept of "extraordinary circumstances" has never been intelligibly defined (see Reporter's Note). It apparently signifies unwillingness on the part of tribunals to put the work-product immunity on quite the same footing as the attorney-client privilege.

TITLE B. PROCEDURAL ADMINISTRATION OF THE LAWYER WORK-PRODUCT IMMUNITY

§ 90. Involving the Lawyer Work-Product Immunity and Its Exceptions

(1) Work-product immunity may be invoked by or for a person on whose behalf the work product was prepared.

(2) The person invoking work-product immunity must object and, if the objection is contested, demonstrate each element of the immunity.

(3) Once a claim of work product has been adequately supported, a person entitled to invoke a waiver or exception must assert it and, if the assertion is contested, demonstrate each element of the waiver or exception.

TITLE C. WAIVERS AND EXCEPTIONS TO THE LAWYER WORK-PRODUCT IMMUNITY

§ 91. Voluntary Acts

Work-product immunity is waived if the client, the client's lawyer, or another authorized agent of the client:

(1) agrees to waive the immunity;

(2) disclaims protection of the immunity and:

(a) another person reasonably relies on the disclaimer to that person's detriment; or

(b) reasons of judicial administration require that the client not be permitted to revoke the disclaimer; or

(3) in a proceeding before a tribunal, fails to object properly to an attempt by another person to give or exact testimony or other evidence of work product; or

(4) discloses the material to third persons in circumstances in which there is a significant likelihood that an adversary or potential adversary in anticipated litigation will obtain it.

§ 92. Use of Lawyer Work Product in Litigation

(1) Work-product immunity is waived for any relevant material if the client asserts as to a material issue in a proceeding that:

(a) the client acted upon the advice of a lawyer or that the advice was otherwise relevant to the legal significance of the client's conduct; or

(b) a lawyer's assistance was ineffective, negligent, or otherwise wrongful.

(2) The work-product immunity is waived for recorded material if a witness

(a) employs the material to aid the witness while testifying, or

(b) employed the material in preparing to testify, and the tribunal finds that disclosure is required in the interests of justice.

Comment:

a. Scope and cross-references. This Section parallels the analogous rules governing waiver of the attorney-client privilege by putting legal assistance or privileged communications into issue (see § 80(1)) or using work-product material or privileged communications to assist a witness (see § 80(2)).

b. Putting work product into issue. A party waives work-product protection by putting the protected material into issue, including claims of reliance on counsel and of good faith evidenced by consultation with counsel, or where determining the truth of the party's allegation requires examination of work product. Such waivers, like the analogous waivers of the attorney-client privilege, are based on considerations of fairness (see § 80, Comment *b*). The immunity is not lost if the proceeding in which the claim or defense is asserted, for example in a pleading, ends without other disclosure of the work product (see Comment *f* hereto).

Although discovery of opinion work product is more restricted (see § 89), when the advice or other service of counsel is directly in issue and is evidenced by the lawyer's opinion work product, the balance is struck in favor of disclosure.

c. A client's attack on a lawyer's services. A party who asserts that a lawyer's assistance was defective may not invoke work-product immunity to prevent an opposing party's access to information concerning the claim. See § 80, Comment *c* (analogous waiver of attorney-client privilege). Where the interests of the lawyer and the client conflict (see § 83 & § 90, Comment *c*), the lawyer may not use the work-product protection to deny the client access to relevant work-product materials (see § 90, Comment *c*).

d. Use of work product at a hearing. When a witness has relied on work-product material in testimony, the rules of evidence afford an opposing party the opportunity to examine the relevant portions of the work product. Portions not relevant to the witness's direct examination may be ordered to be redacted.

§ 93. Client Crime or Fraud

Work-product immunity does not apply to materials prepared when a client consults a lawyer for the purpose, later accomplished, of obtaining assistance to engage in a crime or fraud or to aid a third person to do so or uses the materials for such a purpose.

Comment:

a. Scope and cross-references. For the crime-fraud exception to be relevant, the requested materials must qualify as work product under § 87. The crime-fraud exception overcomes protection for both ordinary (see § 88) and opinion (see § 89) work product. The party seeking production need not show need or hardship (compare § 88). On invoking the crime-fraud exception, see § 90, Comment *b*.

For the analogous crime-fraud exception to the attorney-client privilege, see § 82, including the element of accomplishment of the wrongful objective (see § 82, Comment *c*). On the limited circumstances in which a lawyer may disclose a client's intended crime or fraud, see §§ 66–67. On a lawyer's responsibilities with respect to counseling a client concerning illegal acts, see § 94. On a lawyer's responsibilities with respect to false evidence, see § 120.

b. Rationale. Like the crime-fraud exception to the attorney-client privilege (see § 82, Comment *b*), the crime-fraud exception for work-product immunity recognizes that crime and fraud do not warrant such protection. The exception applies to ongoing or future crimes or frauds but not to work product prepared in a representation concerning completed client acts. Whether work product relates to past acts or future or ongoing acts requires close analysis (see § 82, Comment *e*).

c. The intents of the client and the lawyer. To overcome the immunity by use of the crime-fraud exception, the inquiring party must make a sufficient showing that the client's ongoing or future conduct was criminal or fraudulent. The particulars of that showing are the same as for the corresponding exception to the attorney-client privilege (see § 82).

If the client alone has the requisite criminal or fraudulent intent, work-product immunity is lost despite the innocence of the lawyer (see § 82, Comment *c*). The public interest in deterring wrongful acts outweighs the innocent lawyer's interest in privacy. The rule also prevents a client from advancing an illegal scheme through a noncomplicit lawyer. Once the required showing is made, opinion work product of an innocent lawyer is subject to disclosure along with opinion work product of the client and ordinary work product of both client and lawyer. Conversely, the exception does not apply when a lawyer representing an innocent client commits or is complicit in another's crime or fraud (see § 82, Comment c, Illustration 3).

d. Invoking the crime-fraud exception. The crime-fraud exception applies only after a client or lawyer establishes the elements of work-product immunity, as provided in § 90, Comment *b*. The party seeking access to the work product then has the burden of establishing that it falls within the exception (id.; see also § 82, Comment *f*).

CHAPTER 6. REPRESENTING CLIENTS—IN GENERAL

TOPIC 1. LAWYERS FUNCTIONS IN REPRESENTING CLIENTS—IN GENERAL

§ 94. Advising and Assisting a Client—In General

(1) A lawyer who counsels or assists a client to engage in conduct that violates the rights of a third person is subject to liability:

(a) to the third person to the extent stated in §§ 51 and 56–57; and

(b) to the client to the extent stated in §§ 50, 55, and 56.

(2) For purposes of professional discipline, a lawyer may not counsel or assist a client in conduct that the lawyer knows to be criminal or fraudulent or in violation of a court order with the intent of facilitating or encouraging the conduct, but the lawyer may counsel or assist a client in conduct when the lawyer reasonably believes:

(a) that the client's conduct constitutes a good-faith effort to determine the validity, scope, meaning, or application of a law or court order; or

(b) that the client can assert a nonfrivolous argument that the client's conduct will not constitute a crime or fraud or violate a court order.

(3) In counseling a client, a lawyer may address nonlegal aspects of a proposed course of conduct, including moral, reputational, economic, social, political, and business aspects.

§ 95. An Evaluation Undertaken for a Third Person

(1) In furtherance of the objectives of a client in a representation, a lawyer may provide to a nonclient the results of the lawyer's investigation and analysis of facts or the lawyer's professional evaluation or opinion on the matter.

(2) When providing the information, evaluation, or opinion under Subsection (1) is reasonably likely to affect the client's interests materially and adversely, the lawyer must first obtain the client's consent after the client is adequately informed concerning important possible effects on the client's interests.

(3) In providing the information, evaluation, or opinion under Subsection (1), the lawyer must exercise care with respect to the nonclient to the extent stated in § 51(2) and not make false statements prohibited under § 98.

TOPIC 2. REPRESENTING ORGANIZATIONAL CLIENTS—IN GENERAL

§ 96. Representing an Organization as Client

(1) When a lawyer is employed or retained to represent an organization:

(a) the lawyer represents the interests of the organization as defined by its responsible agents acting pursuant to the organization's decision-making procedures; and

(b) subject to Subsection (2), the lawyer must follow instructions in the representation, as stated in § 21(2), given by persons authorized so to act on behalf of the organization.

(2) If a lawyer representing an organization knows of circumstances indicating that a constituent of the organization has engaged in action or intends to act in a way that violates a legal obligation to the organization that will likely cause substantial injury to it,

or that reasonably can be foreseen to be imputable to the organization and likely to result in substantial injury to it, the lawyer must proceed in what the lawyer reasonably believes to be the best interests of the organization.

(3) In the circumstances described in Subsection (2), the lawyer may, in circumstances warranting such steps, ask the constituent to reconsider the matter, recommend that a second legal opinion be sought, and seek review by appropriate supervisory authority within the organization, including referring the matter to the highest authority that can act in behalf of the organization.

Comment:

a. Scope and cross-references. This Section concerns the duties of a lawyer who represents an organization as client and in doing so deals with constituents of the organization. On the definition of organization, see Comment *c*; on the definition of constituent, see Comment *b*. To the extent not inconsistent with § 97, this Section applies to counseling governmental clients.

On forming a client-lawyer relationship with an organizational client, see § 14, Comment *f*. On conflicts of interest involved generally in representing an organization, see § 131; on conflicts involved in representing an organization concurrently with one or more constituents, see § 131, Comments *e* and *f*; on conflicting interests of affiliated organizations, see § 131, Comment *d*. On conflicts of interest that may be involved in providing legal services to an organization while also serving as an officer or director of the organization, see § 135, Comment *d*.

On limitations on advising and assisting a client, see § 94. The attorney-client privilege as applied to corporate and similar clients is considered in § 73.

On disclosing confidential client information with respect to certain unlawful acts of a client, see §§ 66–67. Disclosure under §§ 66–67 differs from action permissible for a lawyer to take under this Section in several respects. First, the purpose of allowing disclosure under §§ 66–67 is to protect third persons or the lawyer, while the purpose of action within the organization under Subsection (2) (see Comments *e* & *f* hereof) is to protect the interests of the organizational client. Second, the crime or fraud warranting disclosure to prevent financial loss under § 67 is that of the client. In situations arising under Subsection (2), a nonclient constituent commits the wrongful act and the client organization is either the victim of the act or is vicariously responsible as a result of the wrongful act of the constituent. Third, permissible disclosure under §§ 66–67 is limited to a future or continuing act of the client (except for disclosure under § 67(2)), and under § 67 is limited to client acts in which the lawyer's legal services were employed by the client. Under Subsection (2), a lawyer may be required to protect the organizational client from past as well as ongoing and future wrongful acts of a constituent (see Comment *e*) and from acts in which the lawyer's services were not employed.

b. Rationale: an organization as client. A lawyer who has been employed or retained to represent an organization as a client owes professional duties of loyalty and competence to the organization. By representing the organization, a lawyer does not thereby also form a client-lawyer relationship with all or any individuals employed by it or who direct its operations or who have an ownership or other beneficial interest in it, such as its shareholders. However additional circumstances may result in a client-lawyer relationship with constituents while the lawyer concurrently represents the organization (see Comment *h* hereto).

A lawyer representing only an organization does not owe duties of care (see § 52), diligence (see § 16), or confidentiality (see § 60) to constituents of the organization. Compare § 132, Comment *g(ii)* (duties of confidentiality to persons about whom lawyer learned confidential information in prior representation of client). Correspondingly, although a lawyer for the organization acts at the direction of its officers, the lawyer for an organization does not possess, solely in that capacity, power to act for officers as their lawyer. Thus, third persons may not reasonably conclude, solely from that capacity, that a lawyer for the organization represents officers individually (compare §§ 26 & 27). Similarly, a lawyer representing only a constituent does not, by virtue of that representation, owe either to the organization employing the constituent or to other constituents obligations that would arise only from a client-lawyer relationship with the organization.

The so-called "entity" theory of organizational representation, stated in Subsection (1), is now universally recognized in American law, for purposes of determining the identity of the direct beneficiary of legal representation of corporations and other forms of organizations. On the definition of organizations within the meaning of this Section, see Comment *c*. Pursuant to the entity theory, the rights and responsibilities of the client-lawyer relationship described in Chapter 2 obtain between the organization and the lawyer.

A lawyer representing an organization deals with individuals such as its officers, directors, and employees, who serve as constituents of the organization. Such individuals acting under the organization's authority retain and direct the lawyer to act on behalf of the organization (see Comment *d* hereto). Nonetheless, personal dealings with such persons do not lessen the lawyer's responsibilities to the organization as client, and the lawyer may not let such dealings hinder the lawyer in the performance of those responsibilities.

A "constituent" of an organization within the meaning of the Section has the same meaning as in Rule 1.13 of the ABA Model Rules of Professional Conduct (1983). A constituent includes an officer, director, or employee of the organization. A shareholder of a stock corporation or a member of a membership corporation is also a constituent within the meaning of this Section, as under Rule 1.13.

A lawyer may represent an organization either as an employee of the organization (inside legal counsel) or as a lawyer in private practice retained by the organization (outside legal counsel). In general, a lawyer's responsibilities to a client organization are the same in both capacities. Special rules for inside legal counsel are stated in § 32, Comment *b*; § 37, Comment *e*; § 58, Comment *c*; and § 123, Comment *d(i)*. However, the nature of the lawyer's work and greater or less access to an organization's channels of information can affect the lawyer's knowledge and thus, for example, the reasonableness of the lawyer's reliance on a constituent of the organization for information and direction.

c. Forms of client organizations. In general, this Section applies to representation of formally constituted organizations. In all events, whether a client-lawyer relationship is formed is to be determined in light of the considerations stated in § 14. Such organizations include for-profit and nonprofit corporations, limited-liability companies, unincorporated associations (such as trade associations and labor unions), general and limited partnerships, professional corporations, business trusts, joint ventures, and similar organizations. An organization client may also be an informal entity such as a social club or an informal group that has established an investment pool. For the purposes of this Section, whether the organization is a formal legal entity is relevant but not determinative. For example, while a sole proprietorship is not treated as an entity for many legal purposes, such an organization may be of sufficient size and complexity to warrant treatment as an organizational client under this Section.

d. The direction of a lawyer's work for a client organization. Persons authorized to act for the organization make decisions about retaining or discharging a lawyer for the organization, determine the scope of the representation, and create an obligation for the organization to compensate the lawyer. As stated in Subsection (1)(b), such persons also direct the activities of the lawyer during the course of the representation (see generally §§ 14, 21, & 38). Unless the lawyer withdraws, the lawyer must follow instructions and implement decisions of those persons, as the lawyer would follow instructions and decisions of an individual client. On advising a client respecting nonlegal considerations, see § 94(3) and Comment *h* thereto. A constituent of the organization authorized to do so may discharge the lawyer. On client discharge generally, see § 32; on withdrawal generally, see § 32(2) and (3). As stated in § 23(1), a lawyer is not bound by a constituent's instruction to a lawyer to perform, counsel, or assist future or ongoing acts that the lawyer reasonably believes to be unlawful. Such an instruction also does not remove the lawyer's duty to protect the best interests of the organizational client as stated in Subsection (2) (see Comments *e* & *f* hereto).

Who within an organization or among related organizations is authorized to direct the activities of a lawyer representing an organization is a question of organizational law beyond the scope of this Restatement. Such law determines whether, for example, an officer of a parent corporation is authorized to direct the activities of a lawyer representing a subsidiary corporation.

e. A constituent's breach of a legal obligation to the client organization. A lawyer representing an organization is required to act with reasonable competence and diligence in the representation (see § 16(2)) and to use care in representing the organizational client (see § 50). The lawyer thus must not knowingly or negligently assist any constituent to breach a legal duty to the organization. However, a lawyer's duty of care to the organization is not limited to avoidance of assisting acts that threaten injury to a client. A lawyer is also required to act diligently and to exercise care by taking steps to prevent reasonably foreseeable harm to a client. Thus, Subsection (2) requires a lawyer to take action to protect the interests of the client organization with respect to certain breaches of legal duty to the organization by a constituent.

The lawyer is not prevented by rules of confidentiality from acting to protect the interests of the organization by disclosing within the organization communications gained from constituents who are not themselves clients. That follows even if disclosure is against the interests of the communicating person, of another constituent whose breach of duty is in issue, or of other constituents (see § 131, Comment *e*). Such disclosure within the organization is subject to direction of a constituent who is authorized to act for the organization in the matter and who is not complicit in the breach (see Comment *d*). The lawyer may withdraw any support that the lawyer may earlier have provided the intended act, such as by withdrawing an opinion letter or draft transaction documents prepared by the lawyer.

Illustration:

1. Lawyer represents Charity, a not-for-profit corporation. Charity promotes medical research through tax-deductible contributions made to it. President as chief executive officer of Charity retained Lawyer to represent Charity as outside general counsel and has extensively communicated in confidence with Lawyer on a variety of matters concerning Charity. President asks Lawyer to draft documents by which Charity would make a gift of a new luxury automobile to a social friend of President. In that and all other work, Lawyer represents only Charity and not President as a client. Lawyer concludes that such a gift would cause financial harm to Charity in violation of President's legal duties to it. Lawyer may not draft the documents. If unable to dissuade President from effecting the gift, Lawyer must take action to protect the interests of Charity (see Subsection (2) & Comment *f*). Lawyer may, for example, communicate with members of Charity's board of directors in endeavoring to prevent the gift from being effectuated.

f. Proceeding in the best interests of the client organization. Within the meaning of Subsection (2), a wrongful act of a constituent threatening substantial injury to a client organization may be of two types. One is an act or failure to act that violates a legal obligation to the organization and that would directly harm the organization, such as by unlawfully converting its assets. The other is an act or failure to act by the constituent that, although perhaps intended to serve an interest of the organization, will foreseeably cause injury to the client, such as by exposing the organization to criminal or civil liability.

In either circumstance, as stated in Subsection (2), if the threatened injury is substantial the lawyer must proceed in what the lawyer reasonably believes to be the best interests of the organization. Those interests are normally defined by appropriate managers of the organization in the exercise of the business and managerial judgment that would be exercised by a person of ordinary prudence in a similar position. The lawyer's duty of care is that of an ordinarily prudent lawyer in such a position (see ALI Principles of Corporate Governance: Analysis and Recommendations § 4.01, at 148–149 (1994)). In the face of threats of substantial injury to the organization of the kind described in Subsection (2), the lawyer must assess the following: the degree and imminence of threatened financial, reputational, and other harms to the organization; the probable results of litigation that might ensue against the organization or for which it would be financially responsible; the costs of taking measures within the organization to prevent or correct the harm; the likely efficaciousness of measures that might be taken; and similar considerations.

The measures that a lawyer may take are those described in Subsection (3), among others. Whether a lawyer has proceeded in the best interests of the organization is determined objectively, on the basis of the circumstances reasonably apparent to the lawyer at the time. Not all lawyers would attempt to resolve a problem defined in Subsection (2) in the same manner. Not all threats to an organization are of the same degree of imminence or substantiality. In some instances the constituent may be acting solely for reasons of self-interest. In others, the constituent may act on the basis of a business judgment whose utility or prudence may be doubtful but that is within the authority of the constituent. The lawyer's assessment of those factors may depend on the constituent's credibility and intentions, based on prior dealings between them and other information available to the lawyer.

The appropriate measures to take are ordinarily a matter for the reasonable judgment of the lawyer, with due regard for the circumstances in which the lawyer must function. Those circumstances include such matters as time and budgetary limitations and limitations of access to additional information and to persons who may otherwise be able to act. If one measure fails, the lawyer must, if the nature of the threat warrants and circumstances permit, take other reasonably available measures. With respect to the lawyer's possible liability to the organizational client, failure to take a particular remedial step is tested under the general standard of § 50. When the lawyer reasonably concludes that any particular step would not likely advance the best interests of the client, the step need not be taken.

Several options are described in Subsection (3). The lawyer may be able to prevent the wrongful act or its harmful consequences by urging reconsideration by the constituent who intends to commit the act. The lawyer may also suggest that the organization obtain a second legal or other expert opinion concerning the questioned activity. It may be appropriate to refer the matter to someone within the organization having authority to prevent the prospective harm, such as an official in the organization senior in authority to the constituent threatening to act. In appropriate circumstances, the lawyer may request intervention by the highest executive authority in the organization or by its governing body, such as a board of directors or the independent directors on the board, or by an owner of a majority of the stock in the organization. In determining how to proceed, the lawyer may be guided by the organization's internal policies and lines of authority or channels of communication.

In a situation arising under Subsection (2), a lawyer does not fulfill the lawyer's duties to the organizational client by withdrawing from the representation without attempting to prevent the constituent's wrongful act. However, the lawyer's threat to withdraw unless corrective action is taken may constitute an effective step in such an attempt.

If a lawyer has attempted appropriately but unsuccessfully to protect the best interests of the organizational client, the lawyer may withdraw if permissible under § 32. Particularly when the lawyer has unsuccessfully sought to enlist assistance from the highest authority within the organization, the lawyer will be warranted in withdrawing either because the client persists in a course of action involving the lawyer's services that the lawyer reasonably believes is criminal or fraudulent (see § 32(3)(d)) or because the client insists on taking action that the lawyer considers repugnant or imprudent (see § 32(3)(f)). On proportionality between certain grounds for withdrawal and possible harm to the organizational client that would be caused by withdrawal, see § 32, Comment *h(i)*. On the circumstances in which a lawyer is required to withdraw, see § 32(2). Following withdrawal, if the lawyer had fulfilled applicable duties prior to withdrawal, the lawyer has no further duty to initiate action to protect the interests of the client organization with respect to the matter. The lawyer continues to be subject to the duties owed to any former client, such as the duty not to become involved in subsequent adverse representations (see § 132) or otherwise to use or disclose the former client's confidential information adversely to the former client (see § 60).

Whether the lawyer may disclose a constituent's breach of legal duty to persons outside the organization is determined primarily under §§ 66–67 (see also §§ 61–64). In limited circumstances, it may clearly appear that limited disclosure to prevent or limit harm would be in the interests of the organizational client and that constituents who purport to forbid disclosure are not authorized to act for the organization. Whether disclosure in such circumstances is warranted is a difficult and rarely encountered issue, on which this Restatement does not take a position.

g. A constituent's breach of fiduciary duty to another constituent. One constituent of an organization may owe fiduciary duties to another such constituent, for example in some instances a majority stockholder to a minority holder. A lawyer representing only the organization has no duty to protect one constituent from another, including from a breach by one constituent of such fiduciary duties, unless the interests of the lawyer's client organization are at risk. On communicating with a nonclient constituent, see § 103, Comment *e*. However, if the lawyer represents as a client either the entity or the constituent owing fiduciary duties, the lawyer may not counsel or assist a breach of any fiduciary obligation owed by the constituent to the organization.

Illustrations:

2. Lawyer represents Client, a closely held corporation, and not any constituent of Client. Under law applicable to the corporation, a majority shareholder owes a fiduciary duty of fair dealing to a minority shareholder in a transaction caused by action of a board of directors whose members have been designated by the majority stockholder. The law provides that the duty is breached if the action detrimentally and substantially affects the value of the minority shareholder's stock. Majority

Shareholder has asked the board of directors of Client, consisting of Majority Shareholder's designees, to adopt a plan for buying back stock of the majority's shareholders in Client. A minority shareholder has protested the plan as unfair to the minority shareholder. Lawyer may advise the board about the position taken by the minority shareholder, but is not obliged to advise against or otherwise seek to prevent action that is consistent with the board's duty to Client.

3. The same facts as in Illustration 2, except that Lawyer has reason to know that the plan violates applicable corporate law and will likely be successfully challenged by minority shareholders in a suit against Client and that Client will likely incur substantial expense as a result. Lawyer owes a duty to Client to take action to protect Client, such as by advising Client's board about the risks of adopting the plan.

On conflicts of interest in cases of intra-organization disagreement, see § 131, Comment *h*.

The foregoing discussion assumes an entity of substantial size and significant degree of organization. On the other hand, in the case of a closely held organization, some decisions have held that a lawyer may owe duties to a nonclient constituent, such as one who owns a minority interest.

h. Relationships with constituent and affiliated organization. Subject to conflict-of-interest considerations addressed in § 131, a lawyer representing a client organization may also represent one or more constituents of the organization, such as an officer or director of the organization (§ 131, Comment *e*) or an organization affiliated with the client (see § 131, Comment *d*). On whether a lawyer has entered into a client-lawyer relationship with a constituent person or an organization affiliated with a client organization, see § 14, Comment *f*. On avoiding misleading a corporate constituent about the role of a lawyer for the organization, see § 103, Comment *e*.

§ 97. Representing a Governmental Client

A lawyer representing a governmental client must proceed in the representation as stated in § 96, except that the lawyer:

(1) possesses such rights and responsibilities as may be defined by law to make decisions on behalf of the governmental client that are within the authority of a client under §§ 22 and 21(2);

(2) except as otherwise provided by law, must proceed as stated in §§ 96(2) and 96(3) with respect to an act of a constituent of the governmental client that violates a legal obligation that will likely cause substantial public or private injury or that reasonably can be foreseen to be imputable to and thus likely result in substantial injury to the client;

(3) if a prosecutor or similar lawyer determining whether to file criminal proceedings or take other steps in such proceedings, must do so only when based on probable cause and the lawyer's belief, formed after due investigation, that there are good factual and legal grounds to support the step taken; and

(4) must observe other applicable restrictions imposed by law on those similarly functioning for the governmental client.

Comment:

a. Scope and cross-references. This Section addresses government lawyers' relationship with their clients. To the extent not inconsistent with this Section, the provisions of § 96 on representing client organizations apply to representing governmental clients. On identifying a lawyer's governmental client, see Comment *c*. Law applicable to governmental organizations determines the appropriate authority of different legal offices of the same government—a matter beyond the scope of this Restatement. On prosecutors and similar government lawyers, see Comment *h*.

This Section covers a lawyer employed full time by a governmental client as well as a lawyer in private practice who provides legal services to a governmental client. With respect to such governmental-representation matters, see Comment *i* hereto.

Many legal rules beyond those stated in the Section apply to a lawyer representing a governmental client. Such a lawyer is required to act in a manner reasonably calculated to advance the lawful objectives of the client entity as defined by persons authorized to instruct the lawyer on behalf of the client. See §§ 16 and 96; see also §§ 16(3) and 112 (duty to protect confidential information of a governmental client); §§ 16(3) and 121 (duty to comply with conflict-of-interest requirements); § 16(2) and Comment *d* thereto (duty to act with reasonable competence and diligence). On the application of the attorney-client privilege to governmental clients, see § 74.

On the civil remedies available to a governmental or any other client with respect to a governmental lawyer's legal malpractice and similar defaults, see § 48 et seq. With respect to some civil remedies, governmental lawyers may be immune from liability with respect to persons other than the lawyer's client (see § 57, Comment *e*).

b. *Rationale.* Although similar in many respects to representation of a client in private practice (see Comment *a* hereto), representation of a governmental client may significantly differ in three principal respects. First, the goals of a governmental client necessarily include pursuit of the public interest, as identified by law and as determined by decisions of government officials in the course of their duties. Second, both government lawyers and governmental officials directing the activities of government lawyers are often subject to greater legal constraint (for example, under state and federal constitutions) than is true of lawyers representing nongovernmental persons or entities. Third, and conversely, a government lawyer may possess powers beyond those possessed by a lawyer representing a nongovernmental client, such as the power to select those persons who will be charged with serious crimes (see Comment *h*). Some government lawyers, such as an elected state attorney general or similar officer, have discretionary powers under law that have no parallel in representation of nongovernmental clients (see Comment *g*).

A lawyer representing a governmental client may also enjoy legal rights with respect to the client that are not possessed by lawyers representing nongovernmental clients. For example, a governmental lawyer in a position for which partisan affiliation is not an appropriate requirement is protected under the federal Constitution against promotion, transfer, recall, and hiring decisions made solely for reasons of political affiliation or support (compare § 32(1) (client may discharge lawyer without cause)).

c. *Identity of a governmental client.* No universal definition of the client of a governmental lawyer is possible. For example, it has been asserted that government lawyers represent the public, or the public interest. However, determining what individual or individuals personify the government requires reference to the need to sustain political and organizational responsibility of governmental officials, as well as the organizational arrangements structured by law within which governmental lawyers work. Those who speak for the governmental client may differ from one representation to another. The identity of the client may also vary depending on the purpose for which the question of identity is posed. For example, when government lawyers negotiate a disputed question of departmental jurisdiction between two federal agencies, it is not helpful to refer to the client of each of the lawyers as "the federal government" or "the public" when considering who is empowered to direct the lawyers' activities. For many purposes, the preferable approach on the question presented is to regard the respective agencies as the clients and to regard the lawyers working for the agencies as subject to the direction of those officers authorized to act in the matter involved in the representation (see Subsection (3)).

Government agencies exist in various forms, ranging from departments or governmental corporations that may sue and be sued in their own names, to divisions of government without such separate legal status, to legislatures or committees of legislatures. If a question arises concerning which of several possible governmental entities a government lawyer represents, the identity of the lawyer's governmental client depends on the circumstances. Relevant are such factors as the terms of retention or other manifestations of the reasonable understanding of the lawyer and the hiring authority involved, the anticipated scope and nature of the lawyer's services, particular regulatory arrangements relevant to the lawyer's work, and the history and traditions of the office (see also § 96, Comment *h*).

A lawyer employed by a governmental agency to represent persons accused of offenses in military court-martial proceedings, in a state-operated public-defender office, or in similar arrangements is properly regarded as representing the individual and not any governmental entity. That would be true despite the fact that for other legal purposes the lawyer is an officer or employee of the government. On the requirement that a lawyer not permit his or her exercise of independent professional judgment to be directed by a nonclient source of the lawyer's fee, see § 134(2) and Comment *d*.

Some litigation involving governmental policy is brought by or against individual governmental officials in their capacity as such, such as is commonly done in mandamus proceedings, habeas corpus proceedings, and agency proceedings brought in the name of the head of the agency or other officer. Proceeding in that form remains the required method of much federal-court litigation against state governmental officials because of the Eleventh Amendment prohibition against suits against a state as such. A lawyer representing a governmental official in such a proceeding is subject to this Section.

When a lawyer is retained to represent a specific individual, either in that person's public (see Comment *b*) or private (nongovernmental) capacity, the person (in the appropriate capacity) is the client, unless the use of the individual's name is merely nominal and the government is the interested party. As described above with respect to multiple agencies, the identity and the specification of the capacity of the person represented by the lawyer is determined by the undertaking and reasonable expectations of both the lawyer and individual (see § 14). A lawyer who represents a governmental official in the person's public capacity must conduct the representation to advance public interests as determined by appropriate governmental officers and not, if different, the personal interests of the occupant of the office (see generally Comment *f*).

* * *

TOPIC 3. LAWYER DEALINGS WITH A NONCLIENT

TITLE A. DEALINGS WITH A NONCLIENT—GENERALLY

§ 98. Statements to a Nonclient

A lawyer communicating on behalf of a client with a nonclient may not:

(1) knowingly make a false statement of material fact or law to the nonclient,

(2) make other statements prohibited by law; or

(3) fail to make a disclosure of information required by law.

Comment:

a. Scope and cross-references. This Section considers misrepresentations by a lawyer in the course of representing a client. Its rules may apply in representing a client in litigation, such as when negotiating a settlement, as well as in nonlitigation situations. On remedies, see Comment *g* hereto and § 51 and § 56, Comment *f*; see also generally § 6. For liability with respect to erroneous statements in an opinion letter or similar evaluation, see § 51(2) and Comment *e* thereto and § 95. On more stringent requirements for statements in some representations of a client before a legislative or administrative body, see § 104. The Section does not purport to state rules of liability under state and federal securities legislation.

On the standard of truthfulness for statements to clients, see §§ 16, 20, and 56. On the standard for communications with a tribunal, see § 120(1)(b). See also § 112 (ex parte and similar proceedings).

On warning a potential victim of certain criminal or fraudulent activities of a client, see §§ 66–67. On a lawyer's right to withdraw when the client engages in criminal or fraudulent conduct, see § 32(3)(d). On a lawyer's duty to protect confidential information of a client, see § 60. A lawyer's obligation not to make statements that mislead an unrepresented nonclient is addressed in § 103.

b. Rationale. A lawyer communicating with a nonclient on behalf of a client is not privileged to make a material misrepresentation of fact or law to the nonclient. See generally Restatement Second, Agency §§ 343 and 348. The law governing misrepresentation by a lawyer includes the criminal law (theft by deception), the law of misrepresentation in tort law and of mistake and fraud in contract law, and procedural law governing statements by an advocate (see § 120, Comment *f*). Compliance with those obligations meets social expectations of honesty and fair dealing and facilitates negotiation and adjudication, which are important professional functions of lawyers. Corresponding duties are stated in lawyer codes, which are generally based on the requirements of criminal and civil law.

This Section applies equally to statements made to a sophisticated person, such as to a lawyer representing another client, as well as to an unsophisticated person. However, the sophistication in similar transactions of a person to whom a representation is made is relevant in determining such issues as the reasonableness of the person's reliance on the representation.

c. Knowing misrepresentation. The law of misrepresentation applies to lawyers. See generally Restatement Second, Contracts § 159 and following; Restatement Second, Torts § 525 and following. For purposes of common-law damage recovery, reckless as well as knowing misrepresentation by a lawyer may be actionable. On negligent misrepresentation, see also § 51(2). A misrepresentation can occur through direct statement or through affirmation of a misrepresentation of another, as when a lawyer knowingly affirms a client's false or misleading statement. A statement can also be false because only partially true. If constrained from conveying specific information to a nonclient, for example due to confidentiality obligations to the lawyer's client, the lawyer must either make no representation or make a representation that is not false.

For purposes of professional discipline, the lawyer codes generally incorporate the definition of misrepresentation employed in the civil law of tort damage liability for knowing misrepresentation, including the elements of falsity, scienter, and materiality. However, for disciplinary purposes, reliance by and injury to another person are not required. The lawyer codes of many jurisdictions also prohibit a lawyer from engaging in "conduct involving dishonesty, fraud, deceit, or misrepresentation" (see § 5, Comment *c*). Some courts have interpreted these provisions to impose a more exacting standard of disclosure than the prohibition against knowing misrepresentation (compare id.).

A knowing misrepresentation may relate to a proposition of fact or law. Certain statements, such as some statements relating to price or value, are considered nonactionable hyperbole or a reflection of the state of mind of the speaker and not misstatements of fact or law (see Restatement Second, Contracts § 168, Restatement Third, Unfair Competition § 3, Comment *d*). Whether a misstatement should be so characterized depends on whether it is reasonably apparent that the person to whom the statement is addressed would regard the statement as one of fact or based on the speaker's knowledge of facts reasonably implied by the statement or as merely an expression of the speaker's state of mind. Assessment depends on the circumstances in which the statement is made, including the past relationship of the negotiating persons, their apparent sophistication, the plausibility of the statement on its face, the phrasing of the statement, related communication between the persons involved, the known negotiating practices of the community in which both are negotiating, and similar circumstances. In general, a lawyer who is known to represent a person in a negotiation will be understood by nonclients to be making nonimpartial statements, in the same manner as would the lawyer's client. Subject to such an understanding, the lawyer is not privileged to make misrepresentations described in this Section.

A lawyer may also be liable under civil or criminal law for aiding and abetting a client's misrepresentation (see § 8). A lawyer representing a client in a transaction with respect to which the client has made a misrepresentation is not free, after the lawyer learns of the misrepresentation, to continue providing assistance to the client as if the misrepresentation had not been made when the lawyer's continued representation of the client would induce the nonclient reasonably to believe that no such misrepresentation has occurred.

Illustration:

1. Client has contracted to sell interests in Client's business to Buyer. As part of the arrangement, Lawyer for Client prepares an offering statement to be presented to Buyer. Lawyer knows that information in the statement, provided by Client, is materially misleading; the information shows Client's business as profitable and growing, but Lawyer knows that its assets are heavily encumbered, business is declining and unprofitable, and the company has substantial debts. Lawyer's knowing actions assisted Client's fraud.

d. Subsequently discovered falsity. A lawyer who has made a representation on behalf of a client reasonably believing it true when made may subsequently come to know of its falsity. An obligation to disclose before consummation of the transaction ordinarily arises, unless the lawyer takes other corrective action. See Restatement Second, Agency § 348, Comment *c*; Restatement Second, Contracts § 161(a) (nondisclosure as equivalent to assertion when person "knows that disclosure of the fact is necessary to prevent some previous assertion from being a misrepresentation or from being fraudulent or material").

Disclosure, being required by law (see § 63), is not prohibited by the general rule of confidentiality (see § 60). Disclosure should not exceed what is required to comply with the disclosure obligation, for example by indicating to recipients that they should not rely on the lawyer's statement. On permissive disclosure to prevent or rectify a client's wrongful act, see §§ 66–67.

e. Affirmative disclosure. In general, a lawyer has no legal duty to make an affirmative disclosure of fact or law when dealing with a nonclient. Applicable statutes, regulations, or common-law rules may require affirmative disclosure in some circumstances, for example disciplinary rules in some states requiring lawyers to disclose a client's intent to commit life-threatening crimes or other wrongful conduct (see § 66, Comment *b*, and Reporter's Note thereto; on permissive disclosure, see §§ 66–67).

On the duty to disclose the lawyer's role as representative of a client to avoid misleading an unrepresented nonclient, see § 103. With respect to a duty to disclose legal authority to a tribunal, see § 111. On the absence of a general duty to disclose facts to a tribunal, see § 120, Comment *b*. See also § 112 on disclosure requirements in ex parte and similar proceedings. On the duty to disclose false evidence to a tribunal, see § 120(2) and Comment *i*.

f. Other wrongful statements. Beyond the law of misrepresentation, other civil or criminal law may constrain a lawyer's statements, for example, the criminal law of extortion. In some jurisdictions, lawyer codes prohibit a lawyer negotiating a civil claim from referring to the prospect of filing criminal charges against the opposing party. On the extent of lawyer liability for defamatory statements concerning nonclients, see § 57(1).

g. Remedies. In general, a lawyer who makes a fraudulent misrepresentation is subject to liability to the injured person when the other elements of the tort are established (see Restatement Second, Agency § 348, see generally § 56). On remedies for nonnegligent misrepresentation, see Restatement Second, Torts § 552C (difference in values represented and those in fact existing). A lawyer's misrepresentation may also be a basis for setting aside or reforming a contract, as well as other contractual remedies (see Restatement Second, Contracts § 345).

The types of misstatements prohibited in the lawyer codes are different in certain important respects from the definitions of false statement for the purposes of many kinds of civil actions, for example because the disciplinary standard does not require third-party reliance or actual harm (see Comment *c* hereto). Conversely, a lawyer's merely negligent misrepresentation (see § 51(2)) may constitute grounds for liability to an injured party but not for discipline for fraud.

TITLE B. CONTACT WITH A REPRESENTED NONCLIENT

§ 99. A Represented Nonclient—The General Anti-Contact Rule

(1) A lawyer representing a client in a matter may not communicate about the subject of the representation with a nonclient whom the lawyer knows to be represented in the matter by another lawyer or with a representative of an organizational nonclient so represented as defined in § 100, unless:

(a) the communication is with a public officer or agency to the extent stated in § 101;

(b) the lawyer is a party and represents no other client in the matter;

(c) the communication is authorized by law;

(d) the communication reasonably responds to an emergency; or

(e) the other lawyer consents.

(2) Subsection (1) does not prohibit the lawyer from assisting the client in otherwise proper communication by the lawyer's client with a represented nonclient.

§ 100. Definition of a Represented Nonclient

Within the meaning of § 99, a represented nonclient includes:

(1) a natural person represented by a lawyer; and:

(2) a current employee or other agent of an organization represented by a lawyer:

(a) if the employee or other agent supervises, directs, or regularly consults with the lawyer concerning the matter or if the agent has power to compromise or settle the matter;

(b) if the acts or omissions of the employee or other agent may be imputed to the organization for purposes of civil or criminal liability in the matter; or

(c) if a statement of the employee or other agent, under applicable rules of evidence, would have the effect of binding the organization with respect to proof of the matter.

§ 101. A Represented Governmental Agency or Officer

(1) Unless otherwise provided by law (see § 99(1)(c)) and except as provided in Subsection (2), the prohibition stated in § 99 against contact with a represented nonclient does not apply to communications with employees of a represented governmental agency or with a governmental officer being represented in the officer's official capacity.

(2) In negotiation or litigation by a lawyer of a specific claim of a client against a governmental agency or against a governmental officer in the officer's official capacity, the prohibition stated in § 99 applies, except that the lawyer may contact any officer of the government if permitted by the agency or with respect to an issue of general policy

§ 102. Information of a Nonclient Known to Be Legally Protected

A lawyer communicating with a nonclient in a situation permitted under § 99 may not seek to obtain information that the lawyer reasonably should know the nonclient may not reveal without violating a duty of confidentiality to another imposed by law.

TITLE C. DEALINGS WITH AN UNREPRESENTED NONCLIENT

§ 103. Dealings with an Unrepresented Nonclient

In the course of representing a client and dealing with a nonclient who is not represented by a lawyer:

(1) the lawyer may not mislead the nonclient, to the prejudice of the nonclient, concerning the identity and interests of the person the lawyer represents; and

(2) when the lawyer knows or reasonably should know that the unrepresented nonclient misunderstands the lawyer's role in the matter, the lawyer must make reasonable efforts to correct the misunderstanding when failure to do so would materially prejudice the nonclient.

Comment:

a. *Scope and cross-references.* This Section states the rule prohibiting a lawyer from misrepresenting material matters concerning the lawyer's representational role when dealing with an unrepresented nonclient. The rule is drawn primarily from the lawyer codes, except that they do not require the element of prejudice to the nonclient. That element is, however, usually required for the purposes of civil liability.

The rule of this Section is a particular application of the general legal prohibitions against misrepresentation stated in § 98. On statements made in the course of representing a client in legislative and administrative matters, see § 104. On dealings with represented nonclients, see § § 99–101. On limitations on the scope of communications with employees and other agents of a represented organization, see § 100, Comment *i,* and § 102. On communications with an unrepresented constituent of a lawyer's own organizational client, see Comment *e* hereto.

On remedies, see Comment *f*. Remedies available for violation of the rules of this Section, where the appropriate additional elements necessary for relief have been shown, are listed in § 99, Comment *n*. In particular, misrepresentation and similar overreaching of an unrepresented nonclient may make rescission appropriate.

b. *Rationale.* Active negotiation by a lawyer with unrepresented nonclients is appropriate in the course of representing a client. In dealing with an unrepresented nonclient, a lawyer's words and actions can result in a duty of care to that person, for example, if the lawyer provides advice (see § 15, Comment *e*, & § 51(2)). Lawyers should in any event be trustworthy. Moreover, by education, training, and practice, lawyers generally possess knowledge and skills not possessed by nonlawyers. Consequently, a lawyer may be in a superior negotiating position when dealing with an unrepresented nonclient, who therefore should be given legal protection against overreaching by a lawyer. E.g., Restatement Second, Contracts § 169(b) (justifiable reliance on assertion of opinion, because of asserting person's special skill, judgment, or objectivity).

This Section states two general requirements. First, the lawyer must not mislead the unrepresented nonclient to that person's detriment concerning the identity and interests of the person whom the lawyer represents. For example, the lawyer may not falsely state or imply that the lawyer represents no one, that the lawyer is disinterestedly protecting the interests of both the client and the unrepresented nonclient, or that the nonclient will suffer no harm by speaking freely. Such a false statement could disarm the unrepresented nonclient and result in unwarranted advantage to the lawyer's client. Second, the lawyer is subject to a duty of disclosure when the lawyer knows or reasonably should know that the unrepresented nonclient misunderstands the lawyer's role in the matter and when failure to correct the misunderstanding would prejudice the nonclient or the nonclient's principal.

Application of the rule of this Section depends significantly on the lawyer's role, the status and role of the unrepresented nonclient, and the context. For example, a lawyer for an employee dealing with an official of an employer in a dispute over compensation may typically assume that the official will understand the lawyer's role once it is stated that the lawyer represents the employee. A lawyer dealing with a sophisticated business person will have less need for caution than when dealing with an unsophisticated nonclient.

c. *A person protected by the rule.* This Section applies to a lawyer's dealings with both unrepresented nonclients of adverse interest and those of apparently congruent interest. The Section applies to a lawyer's work in litigation, transactions, and other matters. It also applies to a lawyer representing a corporation or other organization in dealing with an unrepresented nonclient employee or other constituent of the organization (see Comment *e* hereto).

d. *A transaction on behalf of a client with an unrepresented nonclient.* In a transaction in which only one of the parties is represented, that person is entitled to the benefits of having a lawyer (see Comment *b*). The lawyer may negotiate the terms of a transaction with the unrepresented nonclient and prepare transaction documents that require the signature of that party. The lawyer may advance the lawful interests of the lawyer's client but may not mislead the opposing party as to the lawyer's role. See also § 116, Comment *d* (lawyer has no obligation to inform unrepresented nonclient witness of privilege to refuse to testify or to answer questions that may incriminate).

Formerly, a lawyer-code rule prohibited a lawyer from giving "legal advice" to an unrepresented nonclient. That restriction has now been omitted from most lawyer codes in recognition of the implicit representations that a lawyer necessarily makes in such functions as providing transaction documents to an unrepresented nonclient for signature, seeking originals or copies of documents and other information from the nonclient, and describing the legal effect of actions taken or requested.

Illustrations:

1. Lawyer represents Insurer in a wrongful-death claim asserted by Personal Representative, who is not represented by a lawyer. The claim concerns the death of Decedent assertedly caused by an insured of Insurer. Under applicable law, a settlement by Personal Representative must be approved

by a tribunal. Personal Representative and Insurer's claims manager have agreed on a settlement amount. Lawyer prepares the necessary documents and presents them to Personal Representative for signature. Personal Representative, who is aware that Lawyer represents the interests of Insurer, asks Lawyer why the documents are necessary. Lawyer responds truthfully that to be effective, the documents must be executed and filed for court approval. Lawyer's conduct is permissible under this Section.

2. Lawyer represents the financing Bank in a home sale. Buyer, the borrower, is not represented by another lawyer. Under the terms of the transaction, Buyer is to pay the legal fees of Lawyer. Buyer sends Lawyer a letter stating, "I have several questions about legal issues in the house purchase on which you are representing me." Buyer also has several telephone conversations with Lawyer in which Buyer makes similar statements. In the circumstances, it should be apparent to Lawyer that Buyer is assuming, perhaps mistakenly, that Lawyer represents Buyer in the transaction. It is also apparent that Buyer misunderstands Lawyer's role as lawyer for Bank. Lawyer must inform Buyer that Lawyer represents only Bank and that Buyer should not rely on Lawyer to protect Buyer's interests in the transaction.

e. Dealings with an unrepresented constituent of an organization client. A lawyer for an organizational client, whether inside or outside legal counsel (see § 96), may have important responsibilities in investigating relevant facts within the organization. In doing so, the lawyer may interview constituents of the organization, who in some instances might have interests that differ from those of the organization and might be at personal risk of criminal prosecution or civil penalties. A constituent may mistakenly assume that the lawyer will act to further the personal interests of the constituent, perhaps even against the interests of the organization. Such a mistake on the part of the constituent can occur after an extended period working with the lawyer on matters of common interest to the organization and the constituent, particularly if the lawyer has formerly provided personal counsel to the constituent, and may be more likely to occur with inside legal counsel due to greater personal acquaintanceship. Such an assumption, although erroneous, may be harmless so long as the interests of the constituent and the organization do not materially conflict. However, when those interests do materially conflict, the lawyer's failure to warn the constituent of the nature of the lawyer's role could prejudicially mislead the constituent, impair the interests of the organization, or both.

An adequate clarification may in some instances be required to protect the interest of the organization client in unencumbered representation. Failing to clarify the lawyer's role and the client's interests may redound to the disadvantage of the organization if the lawyer, even if unwittingly, thereby undertakes concurrent representation of both the organization and the constituent. Such a finding could be based in part on a finding that the lawyer's silence had reasonably induced the constituent to believe that the lawyer also represented the constituent. On forming a client-lawyer relationship with a constituent of an organization client, see § 96, Comment *h*; see generally § 14. Among other consequences, the lawyer may be required to withdraw from representing both clients because of the conflict (see § 121, Comment *e(i)*).

The lawyer's duty to clarify the nature of the constituent-lawyer relationship depends on the circumstances, and assessing the nature of such a duty requires balancing several considerations. In general, the lawyer may deal with the unrepresented constituent without warning provided the lawyer reasonably believes, based on information available to the lawyer at the time, that the constituent understands that the lawyer represents the interests of the organization and not the individual interests of the constituent (see § 14(1)(b)). In such a situation, no warning to the nonclient constituent is required even if the constituent provides information or takes other steps against the constituent's own apparent best interests and even if the lawyer, were the lawyer representing only the constituent, would advise the constituent to be more guarded. The absence of a warning in such a situation will often be in the interests of the client organization in assuring that the flow of information and decisionmaking is not impaired by needless warnings to constituents with important responsibilities or information.

When the lawyer does not have a reasonable belief that the constituent is adequately informed, the lawyer must take reasonable steps to correct the constituent's reasonably apparent misunderstanding, particularly when the risk confronting the constituent is severe. For example, the constituent's expression of a belief that the lawyer will keep their conversation confidential from others with decisionmaking authority in the organization or that the interests of the constituent and the organization are the same, when they are not, would normally require a warning by the lawyer. In all events, as required under this

Section, a lawyer must not mislead an unrepresented nonclient about such matters as the lawyer's role and the nature of the client organization's interests with respect to the constituent.

When a constituent is represented by separate counsel in a matter, a lawyer for the organization must comply with limitations on dealing with a represented nonclient (see § 100, Comment *h*).

f. *Remedies.* Professional codes provide for discipline of lawyers (see § 5) for violation of the rule of the Section. A statement of an unrepresented nonclient induced by a lawyer's violation of this Section may be excluded from evidence in a subsequent proceeding. A document or other agreement induced by a lawyer's violation of the Section may be denied legal effect if found to have been obtained through misrepresentation or undue influence or otherwise in violation of public policy. In some situations, a lawyer's activities in violation of this Section may require the lawyer to exercise care to protect the interests of the unrepresented nonclient to the extent stated in other Sections (see § § 14, 51(2), & 56). When necessary in order to remedy or deter particularly egregious violations of this Section, a court may order disqualification of an offending lawyer or law firm.

TOPIC 4. LEGISLATIVE AND ADMINISTRATIVE MATTERS

§ 104. Representing a Client in Legislative and Administrative Matters

A lawyer representing a client before a legislature or administrative agency:

(1) must disclose that the appearance is in a representative capacity and not misrepresent the capacity in which the lawyer appears;

(2) must comply with applicable law and regulations governing such representations; and

(3) except as applicable law otherwise provides:

(a) in an adjudicative proceeding before a government agency or involving such an agency as a participant, has the legal rights and responsibilities of an advocate in a proceeding before a judicial tribunal; and

(b) in other types of proceedings and matters, has the legal rights and responsibilities applicable in the lawyer's dealings with a private person.

CHAPTER 7. REPRESENTING CLIENTS IN LITIGATION

TOPIC 1. ADVOCACY IN GENERAL

§ 105. Complying with Law and Tribunal Rulings

In representing a client in a matter before a tribunal, a lawyer must comply with applicable law, including rules of procedure and evidence and specific tribunal rulings.

§ 106. Dealing with Other Participants in Proceedings

In representing a client in a matter before a tribunal, a lawyer may not use means that have no substantial purpose other than to embarrass, delay, or burden a third person or use methods of obtaining evidence that are prohibited by law.

Comment:

a. *Scope and cross-references.* This Section states the general duty of an advocate to avoid harassing other participants in the proceeding or using means prohibited by law in dealing with them. The rule stated is taken from ABA Model Rules of Professional Conduct, Rule 4.4 (1983). On possible remedies in addition to lawyer discipline, see the Comments hereto and § 57(2) and Comments *d* and *e* thereto (malicious prosecution and similar torts). On the general duties of a lawyer not to file frivolous litigation or take frivolous positions in litigation, see § 110. For restrictions on presenting testimony and other evidence, including dealing with witnesses, see §§ 114–118. On a lawyer's general duty to comply with law and court rulings, see § 105. On the role of a criminal-defense lawyer, see § 110(2) and Comment *f* thereto. On the more-exacting duties of prosecutors, see § 97, Comment *h*. On obligations of candor in dealing with third persons in nonlitigated matters, see § 98. For general restrictions on contacting represented or nonrepresented persons, see §§ 99–103.

b. Investigating and tape recording witnesses. A lawyer may conduct an investigation of a witness to gather information from or about the witness. Such an investigation may legitimately address potentially relevant aspects of the finances, associations, and personal life of the witness. In conducting such investigations personally or through others, however, a lawyer must observe legal constraints on intrusion on privacy. The law of some jurisdictions, for example, prohibits recording conversations with another person without the latter's consent. When secret recording is not prohibited by law, doing so is permissible for lawyers conducting investigations on behalf of their clients, but should be done only when compelling need exists to obtain evidence otherwise unavailable in an equally reliable form. Such a need may exist more readily in a criminal-defense representation. In conducting such an investigation, a lawyer must comply with the limitations of § 99 prohibiting contact with represented person, of § 102 restricting communication with persons who owe certain duties of confidentiality to others, and of § 103 prohibiting misleading an unrepresented person.

c. Calling and examining witness. In general, lawyers make the initial decision concerning which witnesses to call to testify at a deposition or trial. On consultation with a client, see § 20; on interviewing and preparing a witness prior to testimony, see § 116.

Wide latitude is extended to advocates in examining an adverse witness. Limitations are imposed by the rules of evidence, such as the rules of relevance and privilege and through the authority of presiding officers to maintain order and prevent abusive examination. A further restraint on aggressive cross-examination is the risk of incurring antipathy on the part of the presiding officer or jury. A lawyer may also be subject to professional discipline (see § 5) for intimidating or demeaning witnesses in violation of the rule of this Section.

Distinguishing between permissible and impermissible examination is normally left to the discretion of the officer presiding at the hearing. A client may instruct a lawyer how to proceed in examining witnesses, subject to the lawyer's obligations to the tribunal (see § 21(2) & Comment *d* thereto & § 23). A particularly difficult problem is presented when a lawyer has an opportunity to cross-examine a witness with respect to testimony that the lawyer knows to be truthful, including harsh implied criticism of the witness's testimony, character, or capacity for truth-telling. Even if legally permissible, a lawyer would presumably do so only where that would not cause the lawyer to lose credibility with the tribunal or alienate the factfinder. Moreover, a lawyer is never required to conduct such examination, and the lawyer may withdraw if the lawyer's client insists on such a course of action in a setting in which the lawyer considers it imprudent or repugnant (see § 32(3)(f) & Comment *j* thereto).

A lawyer who asks irrelevant or otherwise objectionable questions or employs other means that have no purpose other than to harass the witness may be subjected to judicial sanctions or professional discipline. Rules of permissible questioning under the evidence law applied in a particular tribunal regulate such questions and appropriate judicial responses to them.

A lawyer other than a prosecutor (see § 97, Comment *h*) is not required to inform any nonclient witness or prospective witness of the right to invoke privileges against answering, including the privilege against self-incrimination. On the prohibition against misleading a nonclient witness or other person, see § 99; see also § 103.

d. Opposing counsel and other participants. The professional ideal for the relationship between opposing advocates is that they bear toward each other a respectful and cooperative attitude marked by civility, consistent with their primary responsibilities to their clients. Similar respect and cooperativeness should characterize a lawyer's interactions with all participants in a proceeding. Certain conduct toward other participants, including opposing lawyers, is prohibited, including unlawful physical force or its threat, racial or gender or similar slurs, and charges of wrongdoing made recklessly or knowing them to be without foundation. Also prohibited are legally impermissible forms of partisanship, such as misrepresenting the record (see § 120, Comment *f*). However, a lawyer is permitted to make vigorous argument and to attack an opposing position on all legally available grounds (see § 110). On limitations on calling opposing counsel as a witness, see § 108(4).

e. Embarrassment, delay, or burdening of a third person. Some measure of embarrassment, delay, and burden is inherent in litigation. However, when an advocate lacks a substantial purpose for conduct having those consequences, a disciplinary offense occurs (see § 110). A ruling of a tribunal officer or a standing rule may impose specific time limitations within which prescribed action must be taken; a lawyer ordinarily must comply with them (see § 105). For example, seeking delay in a trial date in order to gather additional relevant evidence is nonfrivolous. On the other hand, delaying a trial solely to permit a client to extract a nuisance-value settlement is an improper purpose. In seeking delay, a lawyer must assert positions only if nonfrivolous under § 110(1), must avoid misstating facts (see § 120(1)(b)) or using evidence known to be false (see § 120(3)), and must comply with court rules and orders (see § 105).

§ 107. Prohibited Forensic Tactics

In representing a client in a matter before a tribunal, a lawyer may not, in the presence of the trier of fact:

(1) state a personal opinion about the justness of a cause, the credibility of a witness, the culpability of a civil litigant, or the guilt or innocence of an accused, but the lawyer may argue any position or conclusion adequately supported by the lawyer's analysis of the evidence; or

(2) allude to any matter that the lawyer does not reasonably believe is relevant or that will not be supported by admissible evidence.

§ 108. An Advocate as a Witness

(1) Except as provided in Subsection (2), a lawyer may not represent a client in a contested hearing or trial of a matter in which:

(a) the lawyer is expected to testify for the lawyer's client; or

(b) the lawyer does not intend to testify but (i) the lawyer's testimony would be material to establishing a claim or defense of the client, and (ii) the client has not consented as stated in § 122 to the lawyer's intention not to testify.

(2) A lawyer may represent a client when the lawyer will testify as stated in Subsection (1)(a) if:

(a) the lawyer's testimony relates to an issue that the lawyer reasonably believes will not be contested or to the nature and value of legal services rendered in the proceeding;

(b) deprivation of the lawyer's services as advocate would work a substantial hardship on the client; or

(c) consent has been given by (i) opposing parties who would be adversely affected by the lawyer's testimony and, (ii) if relevant, the lawyer's client, as stated in § 122 with respect to any conflict of interest between lawyer and client (see § 125) that the lawyer's testimony would create.

(3) A lawyer may not represent a client in a litigated matter pending before a tribunal when the lawyer or a lawyer in the lawyer's firm will give testimony materially adverse to the position of the lawyer's client or materially adverse to a former client of any such lawyer with respect to a matter substantially related to the earlier representation, unless the affected client has consented as stated in § 122 with respect to any conflict of interest between lawyer and client (see § 125) that the testimony would create.

(4) A tribunal should not permit a lawyer to call opposing trial counsel as a witness unless there is a compelling need for the lawyer's testimony.

Comment:

a. *Scope and cross-references.* This Section states rules limiting lawyers who will testify from appearing also as advocates in the same case; it also states a correlative limitation on calling an opposing advocate to the witness stand. The advocate-witness rule, sometimes addresses problems of conflicting interests (see Comment *f*), but generally is a matter of governing improper advocacy. The rule imputing conflicts of interest to other members of a lawyer's firm (see § § 123–124) does not apply generally to an advocate-witness prohibition, except for the situation of adverse testimony referred to in Subsection (3) (see Comment *i*).

On remedies, see Comment *k*. If an advocate testifies, under rules of evidence an opposing party may comment on the interest of the lawyer-witness and urge the factfinder to discredit the lawyer's testimony on that ground. Subsection (4) states a rule of evidence enforceable by a tribunal ruling refusing to permit calling opposing counsel as a witness.

b. *Rationale.* Combining the role of advocate and witness creates several risks. The lawyer's role as witness may hinder effective advocacy on behalf of the client. The combined roles risk confusion on the part of the factfinder and the introduction of both impermissible advocacy from the witness stand and impermissible testimony from counsel table. Concomitantly, an advocate may not interfere with an opposing counsel's function as advocate by calling him or her to the witness stand, except for compelling reasons (see Subsection (4) & Comment *l*). When a lawyer will give testimony adverse to the lawyer's client, a conflict of interest is presented that must either be avoided by withdrawal of the lawyer and the lawyer's firm or, where permitted, consented to by the client as provided in § 122 (see Subsection (3) & Comment *f*).

c. *The basic prohibition against an advocate testifying.* The advocate-witness rule applies in all contested proceedings in which a lawyer appears as both advocate and witness, including trials, hearings on motions for preliminary injunction and for summary judgment, and trial-type hearings before administrative agencies. The rule applies whether the case is being tried to a judge or jury. In trials to a judge, less need may exist for exacting application of the rule in some situations, such as when dealing with contested pretrial matters, particularly where the testimony of the advocate will not be lengthy (see also Comment *g*).

A lawyer serving in a capacity other than that of a courtroom advocate is not precluded from being a witness for the lawyer's client. For example, a lawyer is not subject to the rule who does not appear on a list of counsel, or will not sit at counsel table or otherwise physically appear in support of advocacy. The rule does not require disqualification if the lawyer gives testimony in a proceeding separate from the matter in which the lawyer appears as advocate. Similarly, a lawyer who testifies before a judicial officer concerning only a preliminary motion is not thereby disqualified from serving as advocate at a subsequent trial before a jury.

d. *An advocate appearing pro se.* A lawyer (or any other party) appearing pro se is entitled to testify as a witness, but the lawyer is subject to the Section with respect to representing other co-parties as clients. The tribunal may order separate trials where joinder of the pro se lawyer-litigant with other parties would substantially prejudice a co-party or adverse party. When a lawyer appears as the advocate for a class and claims to be the party representative of the class as well, a tribunal may refuse to permit the litigation to proceed in that form.

e. *The effect of an advocate's announced intent or status as a material witness.* Subsection (1)(a) generally prohibits a lawyer from being both advocate and witness. Prohibition is not affected by the character of the testimony as cumulative.

As recognized in Subsection (1)(b), in certain circumstances a lawyer is a necessary witness and subject to the prohibition against advocacy, regardless of the lawyer's possible inclination not to testify. A lawyer's testimony is material within the meaning of the Subsection when a reasonable lawyer, viewing the circumstances objectively, would conclude that failure of the lawyer to testify would have a substantially adverse effect on the client's cause. The forensic value of evidence must be assessed in practical terms. If other evidence is significantly less probative or credible or the issue is critical and contested, the lawyer's testimony, although cumulative, may be of significant forensic value and thus material.

Illustration:

1. Lawyer One represented Seller in negotiating the sale of Seller's real estate and at the closing of the transaction. In each negotiating session and at the closing, the only parties present were Seller, Lawyer One, Buyer, and Buyer's lawyer. Buyer has now filed suit against Seller to rescind the transaction for fraud, alleging that Seller and Lawyer One made misrepresentations during the negotiations and at the closing. The evidence of what was said is sharply conflicting. Lawyer One would be regarded as a material witness for Seller.

The decision whether a lawyer whose testimony is material should continue in the matter as advocate is one for the client (see § 22). Since the lawyer might be disinclined to testify in order to remain as advocate, a conflict of interest is presented (see § 125). The conflict is consentable when the lawyer can adequately represent the client in the litigation without providing the testimony (see § 122(2)(c)), and when the client gives informed consent to the conflict (see § 122(1)). The client must understand the implications of consent. See also Comment *k* hereto.

f. An advocate's testimony adverse to a client's interest. The advocate-witness rule usually involves intended testimony favorable to the lawyer's client. When the lawyer's testimony would be adverse to an important interest of a present or former client, the broader rule of Subsection (3) applies. In such a representation, a conflict exists between the lawyer's duty to testify truthfully and the client's interest in avoiding adverse testimony (see, e.g., § § 125 & 132). In the absence of client consent, such adverse testimony requires disqualification not only of the lawyer but of the lawyer's firm as well (compare Comment *i*). Although effective client consent removes the conflict between client and lawyer, an opposing party has standing to object to the lawyer's continued advocacy when the advocate personally will testify.

The exceptions, such as that for substantial hardship, see Subsection (2)(b) and Comment *h,* relate only to issues raised by an opposing party's objection to the lawyer's representation and not to whether the lawyer may continue in the representation despite a conflict with the client's interests. Thus, a lawyer whose testimony falls within Subsection (3) may not continue on the attempted justification that the lawyer's testimony relates to an uncontested issue or that the lawyer's services are nonetheless of unique value to the client.

g. The exception for uncontested testimony or to establish the value of legal services (Subsection (2)(a)). An advocate may testify for the lawyer's client to establish a necessary fact that is not significantly contested, for example, to establish the chain of custody or genuineness of a document. Thus, it is customary for advocates to attest to the genuineness of documents when supporting a motion based on facts. Even at a trial, counsel ordinarily may assume that the opposing party will stipulate to apparently uncontested facts. Refusal of an opposing party to do so should not put the advocate's client to the risks and expense of obtaining either other witnesses or other counsel.

The value of legal services rendered in the proceeding may be testified to by an advocate. The exception applies only with respect to legal services rendered in the proceeding in which the testimony will be given and in ancillary proceedings. The exception rests on the need for testimony on such questions by lawyers who participated in providing the services and on the assumption that the issue will normally be tried before a judge in a collateral proceeding rather than before the jury hearing the merits, such as in many fee-shifting situations. However, the exception also applies to jury-tried issues.

h. The exception due to substantial hardship (Subsection (2)(b)). Disqualification of an advocate ordinarily works hardship on the client. Substantial hardship warrants the lawyer in continuing as advocate while also testifying. Relevant factors include the length of time the lawyer has represented the client, the complexity of the issues, the client's economic resources, the lawyer's care in attempting to anticipate or avoid the necessity of testifying, the extent of harm to the lawyer's client and opposing parties from the blending of the roles of advocate and witness, additional expense that disqualification would entail, and the effect of delay upon the interests of the parties and the tribunal.

i. Representation by an advocate affiliated with a testifying lawyer. Any other lawyer in a testifying lawyer's firm may serve as advocate for a party in the proceeding, despite disqualification of one or more firm lawyers as advocates under Subsection (1)(a), so long as the representation would not involve a conflict of interest under Subsection (3). In the typical case in which the lawyer's testimony will be favorable to the client, another firm lawyer may serve as advocate. However, on a lawyer's testimony adverse to the interests of the firm's client, see Comment *f*.

j. Testimony by nonlawyer employee or agent of an advocate. The rule of Subsection (1) does not apply to an advocate's nonlawyer employees or agents who do not sit at counsel table or otherwise visibly function in support of advocacy before the factfinder. The exception applies to paralegals, investigators, secretaries, accountants, or other nonlawyer employees, agents, or independent contractors such as investigators. Under rules of evidence, the relationship between such a witness and an advocate may be shown to impeach the person's testimony.

k. Remedies against violations of the advocate-witness rule. The requirements of Subsections (1) and (3) derive from lawyer-code rules of professional discipline. In addition, if a lawyer enters an appearance to represent a client in circumstances where the lawyer is prohibited from proceeding under Subsection (1), a court may order the lawyer disqualified. Whether disqualification is appropriate "depends on the nature of the case, the importance and probable tenor of the lawyer's testimony, and the probability that the lawyer's testimony will conflict with that of other witnesses. Even if there is a risk of such prejudice, . . . due regard must be given to the effect of disqualification on the lawyer's client." ABA Model Rules of Professional Conduct, Rule 3.7, Comment ¶ [4] (1983). Such a motion should be made promptly after discovery of information indicating the grounds therefor.

When a lawyer's material testimony as a necessary witness (see Comment *e*) would be favorable to the lawyer's client, the lawyer's announced intention not to testify and to continue as advocate should be accepted by the tribunal when it appears that the lawyer's client has adequately consented after appropriate consultation (see generally § 122 & Comment *e* hereto). If the client gives informed consent to the lawyer's not testifying for the client, other parties have no standing to object to the lawyer's failure to testify. If the lawyer proposes to testify, opposing parties have standing to invoke the rules of Subsections (1), (2), and (3). If an opposing party proposes to call the lawyer as a witness, the client or lawyer has standing to invoke the rule of Subsection (4) (see Comment *l* hereto).

When disqualification is impracticable, other appropriate steps may be taken by the tribunal, such as limiting the advocate's reference to the advocate's own testimony in subsequent questioning of other witnesses or in final argument or instructing the jury about the nature of the witness's interest and limitations on the advocate's proper function. When the testimony results in prejudice to the lawyer's client, violation of the rule may also serve as the grounds for forfeiture of the lawyer's fee (see § 37) or reduction or denial of a lawyer's otherwise proper request for court-awarded fees. With respect to a client's recovery against a lawyer for damages caused by the lawyer's violation of this Section, see § 48 and following.

Subsections (1)-(3) are not inflexible rules of evidence. An advocate-witness in violation of the Section is not thereby incompetent to testify in the matter. Nonetheless, rules of evidence typically permit the presiding officer to exclude evidence or testimony whose probative value is substantially outweighed by the risk of unfair prejudice, confusion of the issues, or similar considerations. When the advocate's testimony would be of that character, it may be excluded.

l. Calling an opposing advocate as a witness. As provided in Subsection (4), a lawyer may call opposing counsel to the witness stand only when doing so is justified by compelling need (see also § 106, Comment *e*). A lawyer called as a witness may be seriously disrupted in functioning as an advocate (see Comment *b*). Calling opposing counsel may also create the false impression in the eyes of a jury that the lawyer was improperly involved in the underlying transaction. An adversary who wishes to make an issue of an opposing advocate's role as a prospective witness normally should promptly move for disqualification (see Comment *k*).

§ 109. An Advocate's Public Comment on Pending Litigation

(1) In representing a client in a matter before a tribunal, a lawyer may not make a statement outside the proceeding that a reasonable person would expect to be disseminated by means of public communication when the lawyer knows or reasonably should know that the statement will have a substantial likelihood of materially prejudicing a juror or influencing or intimidating a prospective witness in the proceeding. However, a lawyer may in any event make a statement that is reasonably necessary to mitigate the

impact on the lawyer's client of substantial, undue, and prejudicial publicity recently initiated by one other than the lawyer or the lawyer's client.

(2) A prosecutor must, except for statements necessary to inform the public of the nature and extent of the prosecutor's action and that serve a legitimate law-enforcement purpose, refrain from making extrajudicial comments that have a substantial likelihood of heightening public condemnation of the accused.

TOPIC 2. LIMITS ON ADVOCACY

§ 110. Frivolous Advocacy

(1) A lawyer may not bring or defend a proceeding or assert or controvert an issue therein, unless there is a basis for doing so that is not frivolous, which includes a good-faith argument for an extension, modification, or reversal of existing law.

(2) Notwithstanding Subsection (1), a lawyer for the defendant in a criminal proceeding or the respondent in a proceeding that could result in incarceration may so defend the proceeding as to require that the prosecutor establish every necessary element.

(3) A lawyer may not make a frivolous discovery request, fail to make a reasonably diligent effort to comply with a proper discovery request of another party, or intentionally fail otherwise to comply with applicable procedural requirements concerning discovery.

Comment:

a. *Scope and cross-references.* Subsection (1) states the rule of professional codes requiring that a lawyer have a nonfrivolous basis for steps taken in advocacy for a client. On procedural rules found in most jurisdictions that impose a more exacting requirement, see Comment *c*. Subsection (2) states the more permissive requirement for advocacy in criminal-defense representations. On the requirements that a lawyer not misrepresent the law to a tribunal and that a lawyer cite controlling authority, see § 111. Several Sections in Topic 4 state additional duties in an advocate's dealings with witnesses and evidence. See also § 106 (prohibition against harassing third persons).

b. *Rationale.* Frivolous advocacy inflicts distress, wastes time, and causes increased expense to the tribunal and adversaries and may achieve results for a client that are unjust. Nonetheless, disciplinary enforcement against frivolous litigation is rare. Most bar disciplinary agencies rely on the courts in which litigation occurs to deal with abuse. Tribunals usually sanction only extreme abuse. Administration and interpretation of prohibitions against frivolous litigation should be tempered by concern to avoid overenforcement.

c. *Procedural sanction against unfounded assertions in litigation.* Procedural rules modeled on Rule 11 of the Federal Rules of Civil Procedure impose affirmative obligations going beyond a requirement of minimally plausible position. In addition, courts have inherent power to impose sanctions against frivolous or otherwise abusive litigation tactics (see generally § 1, Comment *b*).

Such procedural rules generally have four elements, although jurisdictions differ on particulars. First, a lawyer may file a pleading, motion, or other paper only after making an inquiry about facts and law that is reasonable in the circumstances. Second, the lawyer's conclusions as to the facts and law must meet an objective, minimal standard of supportability. Third, litigation measures may not be taken for an improper purpose, even in instances in which they are otherwise minimally supportable. Finally, remedies provided for violations may include sanctions such as fee shifting, which in appropriate cases may be imposed directly on an offending lawyer (see Comment *g*).

Federal Rule 11 and corresponding state procedural rules generally are applicable only to positions asserted in writings signed by a lawyer, such as a pleading or motion. Other sources of law may extend a court's power to other activities of an advocate. For example, in the federal system, § 1927 of Title 28 of the United States Code prohibits actions of a lawyer, not limited to writings, that unduly multiply proceedings. A similar authority is conferred on federal appellate courts under Federal Rule of Appellate Procedure 38. Many courts also recognize a residual inherent power to impose sanctions on lawyers for bad-faith litigation.

Detailed consideration of Federal Rule 11 and similar procedural rules is beyond the scope of this Restatement.

d. Frivolous positions in litigation. A frivolous position is one that a lawyer of ordinary competence would recognize as so lacking in merit that there is no substantial possibility that the tribunal would accept it. A nonfrivolous argument includes a good-faith argument for an extension, modification, or reversal of existing law. Whether good faith exists depends on such factors as whether the lawyer in question or another lawyer established a precedent adverse to the position being argued (and, if so, whether the lawyer disclosed that precedent), whether new legal grounds of plausible weight can be advanced, whether new or additional authority supports the lawyer's position, or whether for other reasons, such as a change in the composition of a multi-member court, arguments can be advanced that have a substantially greater chance of success.

Illustrations:

1. The supreme court of a jurisdiction held 10 years ago that only the state legislature could set aside the employment-at-will rule of the state's common law. In a subsequent decision, the same court again referred to the employment-at-will doctrine, stating that "whatever the justice or defects of that rule, we feel presently bound to continue to follow it." In the time since the subsequent decision, the employment-at-will doctrine has been extensively discussed, often critically, in the legal literature, and courts in some jurisdictions have overturned or limited the older decisions. Lawyer now represents an employee at will. Notwithstanding the earlier rulings of the state supreme court, intervening events indicate that a candid attempt to obtain reversal of the employment-at-will doctrine is a nonfrivolous legal position in the jurisdiction. On the other hand, if the state supreme court had unanimously reaffirmed the doctrine in recent months, the action would be frivolous in the absence of reason to believe that there is a substantial possibility that, notwithstanding the recent adverse precedent, the court would reconsider altering its stance.

2. Following unsuccessful litigation in a state court, Lawyer, representing the unsuccessful Claimant in the state-court litigation, filed an action in federal court seeking damages under a federal civil-rights statute, 42 U.S.C. § 1983, against the state-court trial judge, alleging that the judge had denied due process to Claimant in rulings made in the state-court action. The complaint was evidently based on the legal position that the doctrine of absolute judicial immunity should not apply to a case in which a judge has made an egregious error. Although some scholars have criticized the rule, the law is and continues to be well settled that absolute judicial immunity under § 1983 extends to such errors and precludes an action such as that asserted by Claimant. No intervening legal event suggests that any federal court would alter that interpretation. Given the absence of any basis for believing that a substantial possibility exists that an argument against the immunity would be accepted in a federal court, the claim is frivolous.

It may be reasonably doubtful to a lawyer whether existing precedent supports a legal position or whether the lawyer should instead ask a court to extend, modify, or reverse existing law. When an advocate has adequately referred to the relevant authority (see § 111) the rule of this Section is not violated if the lawyer argues that existing precedent supports a legal position even though the tribunal concludes that the argument should more appropriately have been couched as an effort to modify existing law. In any event, a lawyer may not make a false statement of a material proposition of law to the tribunal (see § 111(1)).

e. Abusive discovery practice. As stated in Subsection (3), a lawyer may not, in pretrial procedure, make a frivolous discovery request or fail to make reasonably diligent effort to comply with a proper discovery request of another party. Frivolousness is determined under the standard stated in Comment *d*. Whether a lawyer complying with a discovery request has made a reasonably diligent effort is determined by an objective standard. In any response, the Section permits a lawyer to assert on behalf of the client any nonfrivolous basis for noncompliance. A lawyer must not, for example, delay a discovery response beyond the time permitted by law without adequate justification, provide answers to discovery requests that the lawyer knows to be false and misleading, or knowingly withhold discoverable information in responding to proper requests for such material. Procedural rules (see generally Comment *c*) may impose more stringent standards for making or responding to discovery requests.

f. Advocacy in a criminal-defense representation. The rules in this Section apply generally to criminal-defense lawyers. However, as stated in Subsection (2), a lawyer defending a person accused of crime, even if convinced that the guilt of the offense charged can be proved beyond a reasonable doubt, may require the prosecution to prove every element of the offense, including those facts as to which the lawyer knows the accused can present no effective defense. A criminal-defense lawyer may take any step required or permitted by the constitutional guarantee of the effective assistance of counsel. With respect to propositions of law, a criminal-defense lawyer may make any nonfrivolous argument. Under decisions of the United States Supreme Court, a lawyer representing a convicted person on appeal may be required to file a so-called *Anders* brief in the event the lawyer concludes that there is no nonfrivolous ground on which the appeal can be maintained.

g. Remedies. This Section restates requirements of the lawyer codes, violations of which are sanctioned through professional discipline. Many jurisdictions by legislation or rule provide for fee shifting as a sanction for frivolous advocacy, including sanctions against an advocate, a party, or both and often under standards stricter than those stated in the Section (see Comment *c*). In relatively rare instances, damages may be recovered in an independent action (see generally § 57, Comments *d* & *e*). Under some legislation or rules, an offending lawyer may be fined, reprimanded, otherwise sanctioned, or referred to a disciplinary agency.

Courts generally attempt to impose sanctions for unwarranted litigation on the lawyer or client (see § 29, Comment *d*) in proportion to their relative responsibility. In appropriate circumstances, when a sanction is focused upon a lawyer for deterrence purposes, a tribunal may order that the lawyer not seek reimbursement from a client. Allocating responsibility may be difficult. Achieving precise allocation may entail inquiry into matters that are generally protected by the attorney-client privilege (see § 68 and following) or the work-product immunity (see § 87 and following). In addition, such an inquiry may interject conflicts of interest between lawyer and client with respect to the burdens of the sanction (see Comment *b*). Particularly when the representation is not at an end and the relative fault of lawyer and client is doubtful, the preferable approach is to leave questions of ultimate responsibility between them to resolution after the proceedings are concluded.

§ 111. Disclosure of Legal Authority

In representing a client in a matter before a tribunal, a lawyer may not knowingly:

(1) make a false statement of a material proposition of law to the tribunal; or

(2) fail to disclose to the tribunal legal authority in the controlling jurisdiction known to the lawyer to be directly adverse to the position asserted by the client and not disclosed by opposing counsel.

§ 112. Advocacy in Ex Parte and Other Proceedings

In representing a client in a matter before a tribunal, a lawyer applying for ex parte relief or appearing in another proceeding in which similar special requirements of candor apply must comply with the requirements of § 110 and §§ 118–120 and further:

(1) must not present evidence the lawyer reasonably believes is false;

(2) must disclose all material and relevant facts known to the lawyer that will enable the tribunal to reach an informed decision; and

(3) must comply with any other applicable special requirements of candor imposed by law.

TOPIC 3. ADVOCATES AND TRIBUNALS

§ 113. Improperly Influencing a Judicial Officer

(1) A lawyer may not knowingly communicate ex parte with a judicial officer before whom a proceeding is pending concerning the matter, except as authorized by law.

(2) A lawyer may not make a gift or loan prohibited by law to a judicial officer, attempt to influence the officer otherwise than by legally proper procedures, or state or imply an ability so to influence a judicial officer.

§ 114. A Lawyer's Statements Concerning a Judicial Officer

A lawyer may not knowingly or recklessly make publicly a false statement of fact concerning the qualifications or integrity of an incumbent of a judicial office or a candidate for election to such an office.

§ 115. Lawyer Contact with a Juror

A lawyer may not:

(1) except as allowed by law, communicate with or seek to influence a person known by the lawyer to be a member of a jury pool from which the jury will be drawn;

(2) except as allowed by law, communicate with or seek to influence a member of a jury; or

(3) communicate with a juror who has been excused from further service:

(a) when that would harass the juror or constitute an attempt to influence the juror's actions as a juror in future cases; or

(b) when otherwise prohibited by law.

TOPIC 4. ADVOCATES AND EVIDENCE

§ 116. Interviewing and Preparing a Prospective Witness

(1) A lawyer may interview a witness for the purpose of preparing the witness to testify.

(2) A lawyer may not unlawfully obstruct another party's access to a witness.

(3) A lawyer may not unlawfully induce or assist a prospective witness to evade or ignore process obliging the witness to appear to testify.

(4) A lawyer may not request a person to refrain from voluntarily giving relevant testimony or information to another party, unless:

(a) the person is the lawyer's client in the matter; or

(b) (i) the person is not the lawyer's client but is a relative or employee or other agent of the lawyer or the lawyer's client, and (ii) the lawyer reasonably believes compliance will not materially and adversely affect the person's interests.

Comments:

* * *

b. *Preparing a witness to testify.* Under litigation practice uniformly followed in the United States, a lawyer may interview prospective witnesses prior to their testifying. A prospective witness is generally under no obligation to submit to such an interview. As a practical matter, rules requiring inquiry to support factual allegations in a complaint or other document (see § 110, Comment *c*) may require a lawyer to interview witnesses to gain the necessary factual foundation. Competent preparation for trial (see generally § 52(1)) (general negligence standard might also require pre-testimonial interviews with witnesses).

The work-product immunity (see Chapter 5, Topic 3) and the obligation of confidentiality regarding trial-preparation material (see § 60(1)), result in the process of witness preparation normally being confidential. Compare § 80(2)(b) (loss of confidentiality of material otherwise protected by attorney-client privilege); § 92(1) (same for work-product immunity).

Attempting to induce a witness to testify falsely as to a material fact is a crime, either subornation of perjury or obstruction of justice, and is ground for professional discipline and other remedies (see § 120, Comment *l*). It may also constitute fraud, warranting denial of the attorney-client privilege to client-lawyer communications relating to preparation of the witness (see § 82).

In preparing a witness to testify, a lawyer may invite the witness to provide truthful testimony favorable to the lawyer's client. Preparation consistent with the rule of this Section may include the following: discussing the role of the witness and effective courtroom demeanor; discussing the witness's recollection and probable testimony; revealing to the witness other testimony or evidence that will be presented and asking the witness to reconsider the witness's recollection or recounting of events in that light; discussing the applicability of law to the events in issue; reviewing the factual context into which the witness's observations or opinions will fit; reviewing documents or other physical evidence that may be introduced; and discussing probable lines of hostile cross-examination that the witness should be prepared to meet. Witness preparation may include rehearsal of testimony. A lawyer may suggest choice of words that might be employed to make the witness's meaning clear. However, a lawyer may not assist the witness to testify falsely as to a material fact (see § 120(1)(a)).

* * *

§ 117. Compensating a Witness

A lawyer may not offer or pay to a witness any consideration:

(1) in excess of the reasonable expenses of the witness incurred and the reasonable value of the witness's time spent in providing evidence, except that an expert witness may be offered and paid a noncontingent fee;

(2) contingent on the content of the witness's testimony or the outcome of the litigation; or

(3) otherwise prohibited by law.

§ 118. Falsifying or Destroying Evidence

(1) A lawyer may not falsify documentary or other evidence.

(2) A lawyer may not destroy or obstruct another party's access to documentary or other evidence when doing so would violate a court order or other legal requirements, or counsel or assist a client to do so.

Comment:

a. *Scope and cross-references.* This Section states rules derived from the lawyer code, which in turn are based primarily on criminal-law prohibitions against tampering with evidence. See also § 94(2) (prohibition against counseling or assisting a client to violate a court order) and § 120 (prohibitions against presenting false evidence). On dealing with stolen property, see § 45, Comment *f*. On dealing with evidence of crimes, see § 119. With respect to dealings with a witness, see § 116.

For purposes of Subsection (2), "evidence" is usually defined as documentary or other physical material (including material stored in electronically retrievable form) that a reasonable lawyer would understand may be relevant to an official proceeding. It does not include exhibits and the like that an advocate or client constructs for illustrative purposes at a proceeding, even if the exhibit would be regarded as evidence for some other purpose.

b. *Falsifying documentary and other evidence.* Advocates in the adversary system are primarily responsible for assembling documentary and other evidence to be presented. A lawyer thereby may serve as custodian of evidentiary material, which ordinarily should reach the proceeding in its original condition. A lawyer may not alter such material in any way that impairs its evidentiary value for other parties. Rules of procedure may permit alteration of evidence in the course of reasonable scientific tests by experts.

A lawyer may not forge a document or alter a document with the purpose of misleading another, such as by back-dating the document, removing the document to another file to create a false impression of its provenance, deleting or adding language or other characters to the document so as to alter its effect, or materially changing its physical appearance.

A document, such as an affidavit or declaration, prepared by a lawyer for verification by another person must include only factual statements that the lawyer reasonably believes the person would make if testifying in person before the factfinder. On a submission to a tribunal based on the lawyer's personal knowledge, such as the lawyer's own affidavit or declaration, see § 120.

c. Destroying documentary or other physical evidence. Unlawful destruction or concealment of documents or other evidence during or in anticipation of litigation may subvert fair and full exposition of the facts. On the other hand, it would be intolerable to require retention of all documents and other evidence against the possibility that an adversary in future litigation would wish to examine them. Accordingly, it is presumptively lawful to act pursuant to an established document retention-destruction program that conforms to existing law and is consistently followed, absent a supervening obligation such as a subpoena or other lawful demand for or order relating to the material. On a lawyer's advice to a client on such matters as document retention or suppression, see generally § 94. If the client informs the lawyer that the client intends to destroy a document unlawfully or in violation of a court order, the lawyer must not advise or assist the client to do so (id.).

It may be difficult under applicable criminal law to define the point at which legitimate destruction becomes unlawful obstruction of justice. Under criminal law, a lawyer generally is subject to constraints no different from those imposed on others. Obstruction of justice and similar statutes generally apply only when an official proceeding is ongoing or imminent. For example, The American Law Institute Model Penal Code § 241.7 (1985) provides that the offense of tampering with or fabricating physical evidence occurs only if "an official proceeding or investigation is pending or about to be instituted. . . ."

A lawyer may not destroy evidence or conceal or alter it when a discovery demand, subpoena, or court order has directed the lawyer or the lawyer's client to turn over the evidence. Difficult questions of interpretation can arise with respect to destruction of documents in anticipation of a subpoena or similar process that has not yet issued at the time of destruction. For example, a company manufacturing a product that may cause injuries in the future is not, in the absence of specific prohibition, prohibited from destroying all manufacturing records after a period of time; but difficult questions of interpretation of obstruction-of-justice statutes may arise concerning such practices as culling incriminating documents while leaving others in place. No general statement can accurately describe the legality of record destruction; statutes and decisions in the particular jurisdiction must be consulted. In many jurisdictions, there is no applicable precedent. Legality may turn on such factual questions as the state of mind of the client or a lawyer.

Particular statutes and regulations may impose special obligations to retain records and files and to make them accessible to governmental officials. Procedural law or a tribunal ruling may impose other or additional obligations. For example, a lawyer may not knowingly withhold a document that has been properly requested in discovery unless the lawyer does so in procedurally proper form (see § 110, Comment *e*). Conversely, a lawyer responding to a request for discovery of documents may not mix responsive and nonresponsive documents together in a way designed to obstruct detection of responsive documents (see id.).

Some jurisdictions have recognized an action for damages by a litigant who suffers loss from "spoliation"—an opposing party's or lawyer's unwarranted and injurious suppression of evidence. In some jurisdictions, an unfavorable evidentiary inference may be drawn from failure to produce material that was at one time in the possession and under the control of a party to litigation. The inference may be invoked even in circumstances in which destruction is otherwise lawful. Section 51 does not provide for a lawyer's liability to a nonclient for negligence in such a situation. Falsification or unlawful destruction of evidence may also constitute contempt or may be subject to the tribunal's inherent power to impose a suitable sanction (see § 1, Comment *c*).

§ 119. Physical Evidence of a Client Crime

With respect to physical evidence of a client crime, a lawyer:

(1) may, when reasonably necessary for purposes of the representation, take possession of the evidence and retain it for the time reasonably necessary to examine

it and subject it to tests that do not alter or destroy material characteristics of the evidence; but

(2) following possession under Subsection (1), the lawyer must notify prosecuting authorities of the lawyer's possession of the evidence or turn the evidence over to them.

Comment:

a. Scope and cross-references. This Section states general rules applicable to a lawyer's possession of evidence of client crimes. The rules are derived primarily from scattered decisions dealing with the question and reflect the Institute's view of how a lawyer might appropriately proceed. A lawyer confronted with an issue under the Section should be aware that local law on such questions as a lawyer's ability to remove physical evidence from a site for the purpose of examination may not yet be recognized by applicable decisions. On the obligations of lawyers in dealing with evidence other than evidence of client crime, see § 118. On a lawyer's dealing with stolen property belonging to a third person, see § 45, Comment *f*. On dealing with witnesses, see § 116.

This Section applies to evidence of a client crime, contraband, weapons, and similar implements used in an offense. It also includes such material as documents and material in electronically retrievable form used by the client to plan the offense, documents used in the course of a mail-fraud violation, or transaction documents evidencing a crime.

Witness statements, photographs of the scene of a crime, trial exhibits, and the like prepared by a lawyer or the lawyer's assistants constitute work product and thus are not subject to the Section, even if such material could constitute evidence of a client crime for some purposes, such as if waived. See § 87, Comment *f*, and § 92, Comment *e*; see also § 87, Comment *b*, on the distinction between work-product materials and preexisting documents, such as client files or financial records.

b. Physical evidence of a client crime; retention for reasonably necessary examination. As stated in Subsection (1), a lawyer may legitimately need to possess evidence relating to a crime for the purpose of examining it to prepare a defense. A lawyer has the same privilege as prosecutors to possess and examine such material for the lawful purpose of assisting in the trial of criminal cases. Such an examination may include scientific tests, so long as they do not alter or destroy the value of the evidence for possible use by the prosecution. So long as the lawyer's possession is for that purpose, criminal laws that generally prohibit possession of contraband or other evidence of crimes are inapplicable to the lawyer. Nonetheless, possession of such material otherwise than in strict compliance with the requirements stated in this Section may subject the lawyer to risk of prosecution as an accessory after the fact for accepting evidence that might otherwise be found. A lawyer's office may also thereby be subject to search. In dealing with such evidence, a lawyer may not unlawfully alter, destroy, or conceal it (see § 118). On the prohibition against advising or assisting another person, including the client, to do so, see § 94.

c. Disposition of evidence of a client crime. Once a lawyer's reasonable need for examination of evidence of a client crime has been satisfied, a lawyer's responsibilities with respect to further possession of the evidence are determined under the criminal law and the law affecting confidentiality of client information (see generally Chapter 5). Under the general criminal law, physical evidence of a client crime in possession of the lawyer may not be retained to a point at which its utility as evidence for the prosecution is significantly impaired, such as by waiting until after the trial.

Some decisions have alluded to an additional option—returning the evidence to the site from which it was taken, when that can be accomplished without destroying or altering material characteristics of the evidence. That will often be impossible. The option would also be unavailable when the lawyer reasonably should know that the client or another person will intentionally alter or destroy the evidence.

Evidence subject to this Section will come to the attention of the authorities either through being turned over by the lawyer to them or through notification by the lawyer or another. In the latter case, the authorities may obtain the evidence from the lawyer by proper process. The prosecution and defense should make appropriate arrangements for introduction and authentication of the evidence at trial. Because of the risk of prejudice to the client, that should be done without improperly revealing the source of the evidence to the finder of fact. The parties may also agree that the tribunal may instruct the jury, without revealing the lawyer's involvement, that an appropriate chain of possession links the evidence to the place where it was located before coming into the lawyer's possession. In the absence of agreement to such an instruction by the defense, the prosecutor may offer evidence of the lawyer's possession if necessary to establish the chain of possession.

§ 120. False Testimony or Evidence

(1) A lawyer may not:

(a) knowingly counsel or assist a witness to testify falsely or otherwise to offer false evidence;

(b) knowingly make a false statement of fact to the tribunal;

(c) offer testimony or other evidence as to an issue of fact known by the lawyer to be false.

(2) If a lawyer has offered testimony or other evidence as to a material issue of fact and comes to know of its falsity, the lawyer must take reasonable remedial measures and may disclose confidential client information when necessary to take such a measure.

(3) A lawyer may refuse to offer testimony or other evidence that the lawyer reasonably believes is false, even if the lawyer does not know it to be false.

Comment:

a. Scope and cross-references. Subsections (1) and (2) state limitations on testimony or other evidence that a lawyer may offer (see Comment *d*) before a tribunal, including measures that a lawyer must take on discovering that testimony or other evidence previously offered by the lawyer is false. Under Subsection (3), a lawyer has discretion to offer or to refuse to offer evidence believed to be false, a lesser standard of knowledge than that under Subsections (1) and (2). The rules are drawn from the lawyer codes, although nondisciplinary remedies may also be available. See Comment *l* hereto. With respect to other limitations on a lawyer's advocacy, see Topics 1–4 of this Chapter.

On special duties of candor in ex parte and similar proceedings, see § 112. On the prohibition against false statements of law, see § 111. On special duties of candor applicable to prosecutors in criminal cases, see § 97, Comment *h*.

b. Rationale. An advocate seeks to achieve the client's objectives (see § 16(1)) but in doing so may not distort factfinding by the tribunal by knowingly offering false testimony or other evidence.

A lawyer's discovery that testimony or other evidence is false may occur in circumstances suggesting complicity by the client in preparing or offering it, thus presenting the risk that remedial action by the lawyer can lead to criminal investigation or other adverse consequences for the client. At the very least, remedial action will deprive the client of whatever evidentiary advantage the false evidence would otherwise provide. It has therefore been asserted that remedial action by the lawyer is inconsistent with the requirements of loyalty and confidentiality (see § 60 and following). However, preservation of the integrity of the forum is a superior interest, which would be disserved by a lawyer's knowing offer of false evidence. Moreover, a client has no right to the assistance of counsel in offering such evidence. As indicated in Subsection (2), taking remedial measures required to correct false evidence may necessitate the disclosure of confidential client information otherwise protected under Chapter 5 (see Comment *h* hereto).

The procedural rules concerning burden of proof allocate responsibility for bringing forward evidence. A lawyer might know of testimony or other evidence vital to the other party, but unknown to that party or their advocate. The advocate who knows of the evidence, and who has complied with applicable rules concerning pretrial discovery and other applicable disclosure requirements (see, e.g., § 118), has no legal obligation to reveal the evidence, even though the proceeding thereby may fail to ascertain the facts as the lawyer knows them.

c. A lawyer's knowledge. A lawyer's obligations under Subsection (2) depend on what the lawyer knows and, in the case of Subsection (3), on what the lawyer reasonably believes (see Comment *j*). A lawyer's knowledge may be inferred from the circumstances. Actual knowledge does not include unknown information, even if a reasonable lawyer would have discovered it through inquiry. However, a lawyer may not ignore what is plainly apparent, for example, by refusing to read a document (see § 94, Comment *g*). A lawyer should not conclude that testimony is or will be false unless there is a firm factual basis for doing so. Such a basis exists when facts known to the lawyer or the client's own statements indicate to the lawyer that the testimony or other evidence is false.

d. Offer of false testimony or other false evidence. False testimony includes testimony that a lawyer knows to be false and testimony from a witness who the lawyer knows is only guessing or reciting what the witness has been instructed to say. This Section employs the terms "false testimony" and "false evidence" rather than "perjury" because the latter term defines a crime, which may require elements not relevant for application of the requirements of the Section in other contexts. For example, although a witness who testifies in good faith but contrary to fact lacks the mental state necessary for the crime of perjury, the rule of the Section nevertheless applies to a lawyer who knows that such testimony is false. When a lawyer is charged with the criminal offense of suborning perjury, the more limited definition appropriate to the criminal offense applies.

A lawyer's responsibility for false evidence extends to testimony or other evidence in aid of the lawyer's client offered or similarly sponsored by the lawyer. The responsibility extends to any false testimony elicited by the lawyer, as well as such testimony elicited by another lawyer questioning the lawyer's own client, another witness favorable to the lawyer's client, or a witness whom the lawyer has substantially prepared to testify (see § 116(1)). A lawyer has no responsibility to correct false testimony or other evidence offered by an opposing party or witness. Thus, a plaintiff's lawyer, aware that an adverse witness being examined by the defendant's lawyer is giving false evidence favorable to the plaintiff, is not required to correct it (compare Comment *e*). However, the lawyer may not attempt to reinforce the false evidence, such as by arguing to the factfinder that the false evidence should be accepted as true or otherwise sponsoring or supporting the false evidence (see also Comment *e*).

Illustrations:

1. Lawyer, representing Defendant, knows that a contract between Plaintiff's decedent and Defendant had been superseded by a materially revised version that was executed and retained by Defendant. Plaintiff's Counsel is unaware of the revised contract and has failed to seek information about it in discovery. At trial, Lawyer elicits testimony from Defendant by inquiring about "the contract that you and Plaintiff's decedent signed" and presents Defendant with the original contract, asking, "Is this the contract that you and Plaintiff's decedent signed?" Defendant responds affirmatively. Lawyer has violated Subsection (1)(c).

2. Same facts as in Illustration 1, except that Lawyer does not elicit the testimony there described and Plaintiff's Counsel, mistakenly believing that the revised contract was not in writing, offers an accurate account of its contents through the testimony of a third-party witness. Lawyer successfully objects to the proposed testimony under the jurisdiction's statute of frauds, thereby removing the only evidence known to Plaintiff's Counsel on which the factfinder could find that the original contract was superseded. Defendant offers no additional evidence, and Lawyer does not produce the revised contract. As a result the tribunal enters a directed verdict for Defendant. Lawyer did not violate this Section in making the successful objection, which kept out evidence, or in failing to inform the lawyer for Defendant of the evidence in fact available.

e. Counseling or assisting a witness to offer false testimony or other false evidence. A lawyer may not knowingly counsel or assist a witness to testify falsely or otherwise to offer false evidence as to a material issue of fact (Subsection (1)(a)). With respect to the right of a criminal defendant to testify and application of the rule to criminal-defense counsel, see Comment *i* hereto. If a lawyer knows that a witness will provide truthful evidence as to some matters but false evidence as to others, the lawyer must not elicit the false evidence. On affirmative remedial steps that a lawyer must take when a lawyer knows that a witness has offered false evidence, see Comment *h*.

Illustration:

3. Lawyer, representing as Plaintiffs the officers of a closed financial institution, seeks a preliminary injunction requiring governmental regulators to reopen the institution. Plaintiffs have the burden of establishing that certain documents were executed prior to closure of the institution. Lawyer drafts an affidavit for the signature of the president of the institution, stating that attached as exhibits

are such documents. As Lawyer knows, the exhibits are in fact drafts that were not executed when dated but which have been backdated. Lawyer's offer of the affidavit would violate the rule of Subsection (1)(c).

The prohibitions against false evidence address matters offered in aid of the lawyer's client (see Comment *d*). It is not a violation to elicit from an adversary witness evidence known by the lawyer to be false and apparently adverse to the lawyer's client. The lawyer may have sound tactical reasons for doing so, such as eliciting false testimony for the purpose of later demonstrating its falsity to discredit the witness. Requiring premature disclosure could, under some circumstances, aid the witness in explaining away false testimony or recasting it into a more plausible form.

Illustration:

4. Lawyer, representing Plaintiff, takes the deposition of Witness, who describes the occurrence in question in a way unfavorable to Plaintiff. From other evidence, Lawyer knows that Witness is testifying falsely. Subsequently, the case is settled, and Lawyer never discloses the false nature of Witness's deposition testimony. Lawyer's conduct does not violate this Section.

f. A lawyer's statement of fact to a tribunal. A lawyer may make a submission to a tribunal based on the lawyer's personal knowledge, such as the lawyer's own affidavit or declaration or a representation made on the lawyer's own knowledge. For example, the lawyer may state during a scheduling conference that a conflict exists in the lawyer's trial schedule or state on appeal that certain evidence appears of record. In such statements the lawyer purports to convey information based on personal knowledge. A tribunal or another party should be able to rely on such a statement. Such a statement must have a reasonable basis for belief.

Illustration:

5. Lawyer, representing Accused in defending against criminal charges, files a motion to suppress a purported confession. Lawyer attaches to the motion a copy of a document that appears to be the written confession of Accused. Lawyer states in the motion that Lawyer obtained the document from a police file, but Lawyer takes the position in the motion that other evidence accompanying the motion indicates that the document is a forgery. Because Lawyer purports to be asserting as a personally known fact that the document was obtained from the police file, Lawyer must know from Lawyer's own knowledge that the document is what Lawyer asserts it to be. On the other hand, Lawyer may characterize the document as a forgery based on other evidence so long as Lawyer has a nonfrivolous basis for that position (see § 110(1), Subsection (2) & Comment *d* hereto), even if Lawyer does not personally believe that the document is a forgery.

For the purpose of Subsection (1)(b) a knowing false statement of fact includes a statement on which the lawyer then has insufficient information from which reasonably to conclude that the statement is accurate. A lawyer may make conditional or suppositional statements so long as they are so identified and are neither known to be false nor made without a reasonable basis in fact for their conditional or suppositional character.

Illustration:

6. Lawyer represents A Corporation as defendant in an action seeking damages. Lawyer has filed A Corporation's motion to dismiss for lack of personal jurisdiction. In support of the motion, Lawyer's affidavit states that an attached certificate of a governmental agency of State X is genuine. The certificate states the jurisdiction in which A Corporation is incorporated, a material issue on the motion. Lawyer sought such a certificate from the relevant agency, but the certificate had not arrived by the time for filing the affidavit. Lawyer accordingly prepares what Lawyer reasonably believes is an accurate copy of the certificate and signs it in the name of a governmental official, having seen a telecopied facsimile of the certificate transmitted from the state agency. The certificate arrives the day following the filing of the motion and corresponds to the document attached to Lawyer's affidavit. Lawyer has violated this Section, as well as § 118. Lawyer would not have violated this Section if Lawyer had stated in the affidavit that the attached document was a copy of a document the original of which would be supplied by supplemental submission.

For purposes of professional discipline, the lawyer codes prohibit a lawyer from making only a false statement of "material" fact. A similar condition attaches to the crime of perjury (although often not to the related crime of false swearing or false statements.) However, other procedural or substantive rules may contain no such qualification.

g. Remonstrating with a client or witness. Before taking other steps, a lawyer ordinarily must confidentially remonstrate with the client or witness not to present false evidence or to correct false evidence already presented. Doing so protects against possibly harsher consequences. The form and content of such a remonstration is a matter of judgment. The lawyer must attempt to be persuasive while maintaining the client's trust in the lawyer's loyalty and diligence. If the client insists on offering false evidence, the lawyer must inform the client of the lawyer's duty not to offer false evidence and, if it is offered, to take appropriate remedial action (see Comment *h*).

h. Reasonable remedial measures. A lawyer who has taken appropriate steps to avoid offering false evidence (see Comment *g*) may be required to take additional measures. A lawyer may be surprised by unexpected false evidence given by a witness or may come to know of its falsity only after it has been offered.

If the lawyer's client or the witness refuses to correct the false testimony (see Comment *g*), the lawyer must take steps reasonably calculated to remove the false impression that the evidence may have made on the finder of fact (Subsection (2)). Alternatively, a lawyer could seek a recess and attempt to persuade the witness to correct the false evidence (see Comment *g*). If such steps are unsuccessful, the lawyer must take other steps, such as by moving or stipulating to have the evidence stricken or otherwise withdrawn, or recalling the witness if the witness had already left the stand when the lawyer comes to know of the falsity. Once the false evidence is before the finder of fact, it is not a reasonable remedial measure for the lawyer simply to withdraw from the representation, even if the presiding officer permits withdrawal (see Comment *k* hereto). If no other remedial measure corrects the falsity, the lawyer must inform the opposing party or tribunal of the falsity so that they may take corrective steps.

To the extent necessary in taking reasonable remedial measures under Subsection (2), a lawyer may use or reveal otherwise confidential client information (see § 63). However, the lawyer must proceed so that, consistent with carrying out the measures (including, if necessary, disclosure to the opposing party or tribunal), the lawyer causes the client minimal adverse effects. The lawyer has discretion as to which measures to adopt, so long as they are reasonably calculated to correct the false evidence. If the lawyer makes disclosure to the opposing party or tribunal, thereafter the lawyer must leave further steps to the opposing party or tribunal. Whether testimony concerning client-lawyer communications with respect to the false evidence can be elicited is determined under § 82 (crime-fraud exception to attorney-client privilege). The lawyer's disclosure may give rise to a conflict between the lawyer and client requiring the lawyer to withdraw from the representation (see Comment *k* hereto).

Responsibilities of a lawyer under this Section extend to the end of the proceeding in which the question of false evidence arises. Thus, a lawyer representing a client on appeal from a verdict in a trial continues to carry responsibilities with respect to false evidence offered at trial, particularly evidence discovered to be false after trial (see Comment *i*). If a lawyer is discharged by a client or withdraws, whether or not for reasons associated with the false evidence, the lawyer's obligations under this Section are not thereby terminated. In such an instance, a reasonable remedial measure may consist of disclosing the matter to successor counsel.

Even after the proceeding concludes, the rule stated in other Sections of this Restatement may permit corrective or self-protective action, such as through notification of others of the fact of withdrawal (see §§ 66–67 & 64).

i. False evidence in a criminal-defense representation. The rules stated in the Section generally govern defense counsel in criminal cases. The requirement stated in Comment *g* with respect to remonstrating with a client may often be relevant. However, because of the right to the effective assistance of counsel, withdrawal (see Comment *k*) may be inappropriate in response to threatened client perjury in a criminal case. If defense counsel withdraws, normally it will be necessary for the accused to retain another lawyer or for the court to appoint one, unless the accused proceeds without counsel. Replacement counsel also may have to deal with the same client demand to take the stand to testify falsely. A tribunal may also be concerned that controversy over false evidence may be contrived to delay the proceeding. In criminal cases many courts thus are strongly inclined not to permit withdrawal of defense counsel, particularly if trial is underway or imminent. Withdrawal may be required, however, if the accused denies defense counsel's assertion that presentation of false evidence is threatened.

Some courts permit an accused in such circumstances to give "open narrative" testimony, without requiring defense counsel to take affirmative remedial action as required under Subsection (2). Defense counsel asks only a general question about the events, provides no guidance through additional questions, and does not refer to the false evidence in subsequent argument to the factfinder. Counsel does not otherwise indicate to the presiding officer or opposing counsel that the testimony or other evidence is false, although such indication may be necessary to deal with a prosecutor's objection to use of the open-narrative form of testimony. From the unusual format of examination, prosecutor and presiding officer are likely to understand that the accused is offering false testimony, but an unguided jury may be unaware of or confused about its significance. That solution is not consistent with the rule stated in Subsection (2) or with the requirements of the lawyer codes in most jurisdictions.

However, the defendant may still insist on giving false testimony despite defense counsel's efforts to persuade the defendant not to testify or to testify accurately (see Comment *g*). The accused has the constitutional rights to take the witness stand and to offer evidence in self-defense (see § 22). Unlike counsel in a civil case, who can refuse to call a witness (including a client) who will offer false evidence (see Comment *e*), defense counsel in a criminal case has no authority (beyond persuasion) to prevent a client-accused from taking the witness stand. (Defense counsel does possess that authority with respect to nonclient witnesses and must exercise it consistent with this Section (see § 23).) If the client nonetheless insists on the right to take the stand, defense counsel must accede to the demand of the accused to testify. Thereafter defense counsel may not ask the accused any question if counsel knows that the response would be false. Counsel must also be prepared to take remedial measures, including disclosure, in the event that the accused indeed testifies falsely (see Comment *h*).

In one situation, disclosure of client perjury to the tribunal may not be feasible. When a criminal case is being tried without a jury, informing the judge of perjury by an accused might be tantamount to informing the factfinder of the guilt of the accused. In such an instance, disclosure to the prosecutor might suffice as a remedial measure. The prosecutor may not refer in the judge's presence to the information provided by defense counsel under this Section.

j. *An advocate's discretion to refuse to offer testimony or other evidence reasonably believed to be false.* The rule of Subsection (3) protects a lawyer from forced complicity in violations of the law and protects the tribunal and third persons from erroneous decisions. It also protects the lawyer's reputation as an honest person and as an advocate capable of discriminating between reliable and unreliable evidence. A lawyer may not by agreement with a client surrender the discretion stated in Subsection (3) (see § 23(1)).

The rule of Subsection (3) consists of two elements. First, the lawyer's knowledge is assessed objectively according to a standard of reasonable belief. (In contrast, a firm factual basis is necessary before the mandatory rules stated in Subsections (1) and (2) are applicable (see Comment *c*).) Second, a lawyer who reasonably believes (but does not know) that evidence is false, has discretion to offer or to refuse to offer it.

k. *False evidence and the client-lawyer relationship.* A lawyer's actions in accordance with this Section may impair the trust and respect that otherwise would exist between lawyer and client. A lawyer may be discharged by the client or withdraw from the representation (see § 32).

If a difference between lawyer and client over falsity occurs just before or during trial, a tribunal may refuse to permit a lawyer to withdraw when withdrawal would require the client to proceed without counsel (see § 32(4)).

l. *Remedies.* Violation of Subsections (1) and (2) may be sanctioned through professional discipline. Certain violations may also be remedied through appropriate sanctions in the proceeding (see § 110, Comment *g*). Criminal liability exists for perjury or subornation of perjury. A court may have discretion to disqualify a lawyer who violates a rule of the Section from further representation in the proceeding. Knowing use of perjured testimony may be a basis for granting a new trial or for vacating a judgment or setting aside a settlement based on the false evidence. A litigant has no damage remedy against an opposing lawyer for an alleged perjurious client based solely on violation of this Section. Compare § 57, Comments *d* and *e* (lawyer liability for abuse of process and similar intentional torts).

CHAPTER 8. CONFLICTS OF INTEREST

TOPIC 1. CONFLICTS OF INTERESTS—IN GENERAL

§ 121. The Basic Prohibition of Conflicts of Interests

Unless all affected clients and other necessary persons consent to the representation under the limitations and conditions provided in § 122, a lawyer may not represent a client if the representation would involve a conflict of interest. A conflict of interest is involved if there is a substantial risk that the lawyer's representation of the client would be materially and adversely affected by the lawyer's own interests or by the lawyer's duties to another current client, a former client, or a third person.

Comment:

* * *

b. *Rationale.* The prohibition against lawyer conflicts of interest reflects several competing concerns. First, the law seeks to assure clients that their lawyers will represent them with undivided loyalty. A client is entitled to be represented by a lawyer whom the client can trust. Instilling such confidence is an objective important in itself. For example, the principle underlying the prohibition against a lawyer's filing suit against a present client in an unrelated matter (see § 128, Comment *e*) may also extend to situations, not involving litigation, in which significant impairment of a client's expectation of the lawyer's loyalty would be similarly likely. Contentious dealings, for example involving charges of bad faith against the client whom the lawyer represents in another matter would raise such a concern. So also would negotiating on behalf of one client when a large proportion of the lawyer's other client's net worth is at risk.

Second, the prohibition against conflicts of interest seeks to enhance the effectiveness of legal representation. To the extent that a conflict of interest undermines the independence of the lawyer's professional judgment or inhibits a lawyer from working with appropriate vigor in the client's behalf, the client's expectation of effective representation (see § 16) could be compromised.

Third, a client has a legal right to have the lawyer safeguard the client's confidential information (see § 60). Preventing use of confidential client information against the interests of the client, either to benefit the lawyer's personal interest, in aid of some other client, or to foster an assumed public purpose is facilitated through conflicts rules that reduce the opportunity for such abuse.

Fourth, conflicts rules help ensure that lawyers will not exploit clients, such as by inducing a client to make a gift to the lawyer (see § 127).

Finally, some conflict-of-interest rules protect interests of the legal system in obtaining adequate presentations to tribunals. In the absence of such rules, for example, a lawyer might appear on both sides of the litigation, complicating the process of taking proof and compromising adversary argumentation (see § 128).

On the other hand, avoiding conflicts of interest can impose significant costs on lawyers and clients. Prohibition of conflicts of interest should therefore be no broader than necessary. First, conflict avoidance can make representation more expensive. To the extent that conflict-of-interest rules prevent multiple clients from being represented by a single lawyer, one or both clients will be required to find other lawyers. That might entail uncertainty concerning the successor lawyers' qualifications, usually additional cost, and the inconvenience of separate representation. In matters in which individual claims are small, representation of multiple claimants might be required if the claims are effectively to be considered at all. Second, limitations imposed by conflicts rules can interfere with client expectations. At the very least, one of the clients might be deprived of the services of a lawyer whom the client had a particular reason to retain, perhaps on the basis of a long-time association with the lawyer. In some communities or fields of practice there might be no lawyer who is perfectly conflict-free. Third, obtaining informed consent to conflicted representation itself might compromise important interests. As discussed in § 122, consent to a conflict of interest requires that each affected client give consent based on adequate information. The process of obtaining informed consent is not only potentially time-consuming; it might also be impractical because it would require the disclosure of information that the clients would prefer not to have disclosed, for example, the subject matter about which they have consulted the lawyer. Fourth, conflicts prohibitions interfere with lawyers' own freedom to practice according to their own best judgment of appropriate professional behavior. It is appropriate to give significant weight to the freedom and professionalism of lawyers in the formulation of legal rules governing conflicts.

c. *The general conflict-of-interest standard.* The standard adopted in this Chapter answers the four questions to which any conflicts-of-interest standard must respond. Those are (i) What kind of effect is prohibited? (ii) How significant must the effect be? (iii) What probability must there be that the effect will occur? (iv) From whose perspective are conflicts of interest to be determined? The standard adopted here incorporates elements common to all three of the major lawyer codes developed in this century. It casts the answer to each question in terms of factual predicates and practical consequences that are reasonably susceptible of objective assessment by lawyers subject to the rules, by clients whom the rules affect, and by tribunals.

c(i). Prohibited effects. Unless there is risk that the lawyer's representation would be affected "adversely," there is no conflict of interest. The 1969 Code of Professional Responsibility uses the term "differing interests" to define situations that a lawyer must treat as an actual or potential conflict. However, this standard can be interpreted over-inclusively. Two clients rarely have interests that are entirely identical. If the term "differing" interests were given its broadest meaning, a lawyer might almost never be able to represent two clients without the client's consent.

"Adverse" effect relates to the quality of the representation, not necessarily the quality of the result obtained in a given case. The standard refers to the incentives faced by the lawyer before or during the representation because it often cannot be foretold what the actual result would have been if the representation had been conflict-free.

Illustration:

1. Lawyer has been retained by A and B, each a competitor for a single broadcast license, to assist each of them in obtaining the license from Agency. Such work often requires advocacy by the lawyer for an applicant before Agency. Lawyer's representation will have an adverse effect on both A and B as that term is used in this Section. Even though either A or B might obtain the license and thus arguably not have been adversely affected by the joint representation, Lawyer will have duties to A that restrict Lawyer's ability to urge B's application and vice versa. In most instances, informed consent of both A and B would not suffice to allow the dual representation (see § 122).

c(ii). "Materially" adverse effect. Materiality of a possible conflict is determined by reference to obligations necessarily assumed by the lawyer (see § 16), or assumed by agreement with the client either in the retainer agreement (see § 19) or in the course of the representation (see § 21). An otherwise immaterial conflict could be considered material if, for example, a client had made clear that the client considered the possible conflict a serious and substantial matter.

Illustration:

2. Lawyer is asked by Client A to represent Client A in an aspect of the hostile takeover by Client A of Lawyer's corporate Client B. Success in such a venture would have a material adverse effect on Client B and hence involves a conflict of interest within the meaning of this Section. Whether informed consent of both A and B would be sufficient to allow the dual representation in this situation is considered in § 122.

c(iii). Likelihood of effect. There is no conflict of interest within the meaning of this Section unless there is a "substantial risk" that a material adverse effect will occur. In many cases the material adverse effect on the representation will be immediate, actual, and apparent. Other situations, however, might present a risk that is only potential or contingent. In this context, "substantial risk" means that in the circumstances the risk is significant and plausible, even if it is not certain or even probable that it will occur. The standard requires more than a mere possibility of adverse effect.

Illustration:

3. Clients A and B have come to Lawyer for help in organizing a new business. Lawyer is satisfied that both clients are committed to forming the enterprise and that an agreement can be prepared that will embody their common undertaking. Nonetheless, because a substantial risk of

future conflict exists in any such arrangement, Lawyer must explain to the clients that because of future economic uncertainties inherent in any such undertaking, the clients' interests could differ in material ways in the future. Lawyer must obtain informed consent pursuant to § 122 before undertaking the common representation.

Some conflicts can be eliminated by an agreement limiting the scope of the lawyer's representation if the limitation can be given effect without rendering the remaining representation objectively inadequate (see § 19 & § 122, Comment *g(iv)*).

Illustration:

4. Lawyer has been retained by Client to represent Client in general business matters. Client has a distribution contract with Manufacturer, and there is a chance that disputes could arise under the contract. Lawyer represents Manufacturer in local real-estate matters completely unrelated to Client's business. An agreement between Lawyer and Client that the scope of Lawyer's representation of Client will not extend to dealing with disputes with Manufacturer would eliminate the conflict posed by the chance otherwise of representing Client in matters adverse to Manufacturer (see § 128). Such an agreement would not require the consent of Manufacturer.

General antagonism between clients does not necessarily mean that a lawyer would be engaged in conflicted representations by representing the clients in separate, unrelated matters. A conflict for a lawyer ordinarily exists only when there is conflict in the interests of the clients that are involved in the matters being handled by the lawyer or when unrelated representations are of such a nature that the lawyer's relationship with one or both clients likely would be adversely affected.

Illustration:

5. For many years Law Firm has represented Bank in mortgage foreclosures and does so currently. Other lawyers in Law Firm have continuously represented Manufacturer as outside general counsel and do so currently. Bank and Manufacturer entered into an agreement under which Bank would loan a sum of money to Manufacturer. Lawyers from Law Firm did not represent either client in negotiating the loan agreement. A dispute arose between the parties to the agreement, and Manufacturer announced that it would file suit against Bank for breach of the loan contract. Absent client consent as provided in § 122, Law Firm lawyers may not represent either Bank or Manufacturer in the litigation (see § 128(2)). Law Firm may not withdraw from representing either client in order to file or defend a suit on the loan agreement against the other (see § 132, Comment *c*). Law Firm may, however, continue to provide legal services to both clients in matters unrelated to the litigation because as to those matters the clients' interests are not in conflict.

c(iv). The perspective for determining conflict of interest. This Section employs an objective standard by which to assess the adverseness, materiality, and substantiality of the risk of the effect on representation. The standard of this Section is not the "appearance of impropriety" standard formerly used by some courts to define the scope of impermissible conflicts. That standard could prohibit not only conflicts as defined in this Section, but also situations that might appear improper to an uninformed observer or even an interested party.

The propriety of the lawyer's action should be determined based only on facts and circumstances that the lawyer knew or should have known at the time of undertaking or continuing a representation. It should not be evaluated in light of information that became known only later and that could not reasonably have been anticipated.

The standard of this Section allows consideration in a given situation of the social value of the lawyer's behavior alleged to constitute the conflict. For example, a lawyer's statement about a matter of public importance might conflict with a client's objectives, but the public importance of free expression is a factor to be considered in limiting the possible reach of the relevant conflicts rule (see § 125, Comment *e*).

Whether there is adverseness, materiality, and substantiality in a given circumstance is often dependent on specific circumstances that are ambiguous and the subject of conflicting evidence. Accordingly, there are necessarily circumstances in which the lawyer's avoidance of a representation is permissible but not obligatory. A lawyer also would be justified in withdrawing from some representations in circumstances in which it would be improper to disqualify the lawyer or the lawyer's firm.

d. Representation of a client. The prohibition of conflicts of interest ordinarily restricts a lawyer's activities only where those activities materially and adversely affect the lawyer's ability to represent a client including such an effect on a client's reasonable expectation of the lawyer's loyalty. The formation of a client-lawyer relationship is considered in § 14. Obligations to nonclients might be imposed on a lawyer by other principles of law, see § 135. That a formal client-lawyer relationship has come to an end does not terminate all conflict-of-interest restrictions, such as the prohibition against a lawyer accepting representation contrary to the interest of a former client (see § 132).

For purposes of identifying conflicts of interest, a lawyer's client is ordinarily the person or entity that consents to the formation of the client-lawyer relationship, see § 14. For example, when a lawyer is retained by Corporation A, Corporation A is ordinarily the lawyer's client; neither individual officers of Corporation A nor other corporations in which Corporation A has an ownership interest, that hold an ownership interest in Corporation A, or in which a major shareholder in Corporation A has an ownership interest, are thereby considered to be the lawyer's client.

In some situations, however, the financial or personal relationship between the lawyer's client and other persons or entities might be such that the lawyer's obligations to the client will extend to those other persons or entities as well. That will be true, for example, where financial loss or benefit to the nonclient person or entity will have a direct, adverse impact on the client.

Illustrations:

6. Lawyer represents Corporation A in local real-estate transactions. Lawyer has been asked to represent Plaintiff in a products-liability action against Corporation B claiming substantial damages. Corporation B is a wholly owned subsidiary of Corporation A; any judgment obtained against Corporation B will have a material adverse impact on the value of Corporation B's assets and on the value of the assets of Corporation A. Just as Lawyer could not file suit against Corporation A on behalf of another client, even in a matter unrelated to the subject of Lawyer's representation of Corporation A (see § 128, Comment *e*), Lawyer may not represent Plaintiff in the suit against Corporation B without the consent of both Plaintiff and Corporation A under the limitations and conditions provided in § 122.

7. The same facts as in Illustration 6, except that Corporation B is not a subsidiary of Corporation A. Instead, 51 percent of the stock of Corporation A and 60 percent of the stock of Corporation B are owned by X Corporation. The remainder of the stock in both Corporation A and Corporation B is held by the public. Lawyer does not represent X Corporation. The circumstances are such that an adverse judgment against Corporation B will have no material adverse impact on the financial position of Corporation A. No conflict of interest is presented; Lawyer may represent Plaintiff in the suit against Corporation B.

Similar problems could arise where the client and nonclient are individuals and representation adverse to the nonclient could have direct material effect on the client's interest. Such a situation would exist, for example, where a lawyer representing one spouse was asked to bring suit against the other, or where a lawyer representing one holder of an interest in property was asked by someone else to bring suit against the other holder in circumstances where the suit could materially and adversely affect the interest of the lawyer's client.

In yet other situations, the conflict of interest arises because the circumstances indicate that the confidence that a client reasonably reposes in the loyalty of a lawyer would be compromised due to the lawyer's relationship with another client or person whose interests would be adversely affected by the representation.

Illustration:

8. The same facts as in Illustration 7, except that one-half of Lawyer's practice consists of work for Corporation A. Plaintiff could reasonably believe that Lawyer's concern about a possible adverse reaction by Corporation A to the suit against Corporation B will inhibit Lawyer's pursuit of Plaintiff's case against Corporation B (see §§ 125 & 128). Lawyer may not represent Plaintiff in the suit against Corporation B unless Plaintiff consents to the representation under the limitations and conditions provided in § 122. Because Lawyer's representation of Corporation A is assumed in Illustration 7 not to be adversely affected by the representation of Plaintiff, the consent of Corporation A to the representation is not required.

Significant control of the nonclient by the client also might suffice to require a lawyer to treat the nonclient as if it were a client in determining whether a conflict of interest exists in a lawyer's representation of another client with interests adverse to the nonclient.

Illustration:

9. The same facts as in Illustration 7, except that X Corporation has elected a majority of the Directors of Corporation B and has approved its key officers. Officers of X Corporation regularly supervise decisions made by Corporation B, and Lawyer has regularly advised X Corporation on products-liability issues affecting all of the corporations in which X Corporation owns an interest. X Corporation has used that advice to give direction about minimizing claims exposure to Corporation B. Although Lawyer does not represent Corporation B, Lawyer's earlier assistance to X Corporation on products-liability matters was substantially related to the suit that Plaintiff has asked Lawyer to file against Corporation B (see § 132). Lawyer may not represent Plaintiff in the suit against Corporation B unless Plaintiff, X Corporation, and Corporation B consent to the representation under the limitations and conditions provided in § 122. In the circumstances, informed consent on behalf of Corporation B may be provided by officers of X Corporation who direct the legal affairs of Corporation B pursuant to applicable corporate law.

A conflict of interest can also arise because of specific obligations, such as the obligation to hold information confidential, that the lawyer has assumed to a nonclient.

Illustration:

10. Lawyer represents Association, a trade association in which Corporation C is a member, in supporting legislation to protect Association's industry against foreign imports. Lawyer does not represent any individual members of Association, including Corporation C, but at the request of Association and Lawyer, Corporation C has given Lawyer confidential information about Corporation C's cost of production. Plaintiff has asked Lawyer to sue Corporation C for unfair competition based on Corporation C's alleged pricing below the cost of production. Although Corporation C is not Lawyer's client, unless both Plaintiff and Corporation C consent to the representation under the limitations and conditions provided in § 122, Lawyer may not represent Plaintiff against Corporation C in the matter because of the serious risk of material adverse use of Corporation C's confidential information against Corporation C.

e. *Withdrawal from conflicting representations—in general.* A conflict can be avoided by declining to represent a new client or, when appropriate, by obtaining effective consent (see § 122). However, a lawyer might undertake representation before realizing that a conflict exists. In addition, subsequent events might create conflicts. For example, a merger of law firms or a merger of a corporate client with a nonclient enterprise might create conflicts after the representation begins (see Comment *e(v)* hereto). The appropriate course of action in such situations might vary with the circumstances, as indicated in the following Comments.

e(i). Withdrawal or consent in typical cases of postrepresentation conflict. If a lawyer withdraws from representation of multiple clients because of a conflict of interest (or for any other reason), the rule stated in § 132 prohibits representation in the same or a substantially related matter of a remaining client whose interests in the matter are materially adverse to the interests of a now-former client. For example, two clients previously represented by lawyers in a firm in the same transaction pursuant to effective consent might thereafter have a falling out such that litigation is in prospect (see §§ 130 & 128). The firm may not withdraw from representing one client and take an adversary position against that client in behalf of the other in the subsequent litigation (see § 132, Comment *c*). The firm must obtain informed consent from both clients (see § 122) or withdraw entirely. Consent in advance to such continued representation may also be provided as stated in § 122, Comment *d*. The fact that neither joint client could assert the attorney-client privilege in subsequent litigation between them (see § 75) does not by itself negate the lawyer's more extensive obligations of confidentiality under § 60 and loyalty under § 16(1).

e(ii). Successive representations involving no conflict. A lawyer or firm might be in a position to withdraw from fewer than all the representations in a joint-client representation and thereby remove a conflict if it is possible after withdrawal for the lawyer to continue representation only with respect to matters not substantially related to the former representation (compare § 132) or with respect to related matters for clients that are not adverse to the now-former client.

Illustration:

11. The same facts as in Illustration 5, except that Law Firm represented Bank in negotiating the loan agreement. That was done after Law Firm obtained the effective consent of Manufacturer, although the consent did not extend to representation of Bank in possible future litigation concerning the agreement (see § 122, Comments *d–f*). The clients have now reached a point of serious difference over the agreement. Law Firm must cure the resulting conflict by renewed informed consents or by withdrawal. If either Bank or Manufacturer is unwilling to consent, Law Firm must withdraw from further representing Bank in the dispute over the agreement. However, Law Firm may continue to represent Bank and Manufacturer in their unrelated, separate matters because in those matters, as in Illustration 5, there is no conflict of interest between the clients.

e(iii). Withdrawal due to revocation of consent. On the effect of one client's revocation of consent on a lawyer's ability to continue representing other clients, see § 122, Comment *f*.

e(iv). Withdrawal from representing an "accommodation" client. On representing a regular client after withdrawal from representation of another client undertaken for a limited purpose and as an accommodation to the clients, see § 132, Comment *i*.

e(v). Withdrawal to cure a conflict created by a business transaction of a client. On continuing to represent a client after that client's opponent in litigation has been acquired by another of the lawyer's clients, see § 132, Comment *j*.

f. Sanctions and remedies for conflicts of interest. In addition to the sanction of professional discipline, disqualifying a lawyer from further participation in a pending matter is a common remedy for conflicts of interest in litigation (§ 6, Comment *i*). For matters not before a tribunal where disqualification can be sought, an injunction against a lawyer's further participation in the matter is a comparable remedy (§ 6, Comment *c*).

When a conflict of interest has caused injury to a client, the remedy of legal malpractice is available (§§ 48 and following). Availability of the sanction of fee forfeiture is considered in § 37. If the result in a matter was affected prejudicially by conflicting loyalties or misuse of confidential information by the lawyer, the result will sometimes be reversed or set aside. Some conflicts of interest subject a lawyer to criminal sanctions.

In general, whether a particular sanction or remedy is appropriate in a specific instance depends on the relationship between the lawyer and client or clients involved, the nature and seriousness of the conflict, the circumstances giving rise to the conflict and its avoidability, and the consequences of the particular remedy sought. In some situations, even an appropriate process for determining conflicts of interest could result in a conflict going undetected for a period of time. For example, the fact that someone in a law firm possesses confidential information that would be material in a pending matter (see § 132) might be difficult to ascertain in some cases. When a lawyer undertakes a representation that is later determined to involve a conflict of interest that could not reasonably have been and in fact was not identified at an earlier point (see Comment *g*), the lawyer is not liable for damages or subject to discipline.

g. Detecting conflicts. For the purpose of identifying conflicts of interest, a lawyer should have reasonable procedures, appropriate for the size and type of firm and practice, to detect conflicts of interest, including procedures to determine in both litigation and nonlitigation matters the parties and interests involved in each representation.

Based on concern about a conflict of interest under self-imposed standards more exacting than those of this Section, a lawyer ordinarily may decline a representation (see § 14) or withdraw as provided in § 32. A client may urge a lawyer to limit practice in conformance with the client's own more-exacting concepts of conflict, but the lawyer is not required to comply. The lawyer must not misrepresent the lawyer's standards to the client, for example by purporting to limit the lawyer's other representations but evading the restriction in secret. Moreover, the lawyer may not agree to such a limitation when doing so would violate applicable professional prohibitions against restricting by agreement a lawyer's right to practice law.

The reasonableness of a lawyer's initial determination concerning a conflict is subject to later review by a tribunal to the extent indicated in Comment *f*. When a lawyer is or should reasonably be aware that there is a substantial risk that the lawyer's representation of the client will be challenged on conflicts grounds and thus delay the representation to the client's material disadvantage or make it otherwise more expensive or burdensome for the client, the lawyer must either decline representation or consult with the client concerning the risk (see § 20) and proceed only with the informed consent of the client. If the representation has already commenced when an issue of conflict arises, the lawyer must consult with the client (see § 20) and proceed in the best interests of the client. On withdrawal, see § 32.

§ 122. Client Consent to a Conflict of Interest

(1) A lawyer may represent a client notwithstanding a conflict of interest prohibited by § 121 if each affected client or former client gives informed consent to the lawyer's representation. Informed consent requires that the client or former client have reasonably adequate information about the material risks of such representation to that client or former client.

(2) Notwithstanding the informed consent of each affected client or former client, a lawyer may not represent a client if:

(a) the representation is prohibited by law;

(b) one client will assert a claim against the other in the same litigation; or

(c) in the circumstances, it is not reasonably likely that the lawyer will be able to provide adequate representation to one or more of the clients.

Comment:

* * *

b. Rationale. The prohibition against lawyer conflicts of interest is intended to assure clients that a lawyer's work will be characterized by loyalty, vigor, and confidentiality (see § 121, Comment *b*). The conflict rules are subject to waiver through informed consent by a client who elects less than the full measure of protection that the law otherwise provides. For example, a client in a multiple representation might wish to avoid the added costs that separate representation often entails. Similarly, a client might consent to a conflict where that is necessary in order to obtain the services of a particular law firm.

Other considerations, however, limit the scope of a client's power to consent to a conflicted representation. A client's consent will not be effective if it is based on an inadequate understanding of the nature and severity of the lawyer's conflict (Comment *c* hereto), violates law (Comment *g(i)*), or if the client lacks capacity to consent (Comment *c*). Client consent must also, of course, be free of coercion. Consent will also be insufficient to permit conflicted representation if it is not reasonably likely that the lawyer will be able to provide adequate representation to the affected clients, or when a lawyer undertakes to represent clients who oppose each other in the same litigation (Comment *g(iii)*).

In effect, the consent requirement means that each affected client or former client has the power to preclude the representation by withholding consent. When a client withholds consent, a lawyer's power to withdraw from representation of that client and proceed with the representation of the other client is determined under § 121, Comment *e*.

While a lawyer may elect to proceed with a conflicted representation after effective client consent as stated in this Section, a lawyer is not required to do so (compare § 14, Comment *g* (required representation by order of court)). A lawyer might be unwilling to accept the risk that a consenting client will later become disappointed with the representation and contend that the consent was defective, or the lawyer might conclude for other reasons that the lawyer's own interests do not warrant proceeding. In such an instance, the lawyer also may elect to withdraw if grounds permitting withdrawal are present under § 32. After withdrawal, a lawyer's ability to represent other clients is as described in § 121, Comment *e*.

c(i). The requirement of informed consent—adequate information. Informed consent requires that each affected client be aware of the material respects in which the representation could have adverse effects on the interests of that client. The information required depends on the nature of the conflict and the nature of the risks of the conflicted representation. The client must be aware of information reasonably adequate to make an informed decision.

Information relevant to particular kinds of conflicts is considered in several of the Sections hereafter. In a multiple-client situation, the information normally should address the interests of the lawyer and other client giving rise to the conflict; contingent, optional, and tactical considerations and alternative courses of action that would be foreclosed or made less readily available by the conflict; the effect of the representation or the process of obtaining other clients' informed consent upon confidential information of the client; any material reservations that a disinterested lawyer might reasonably harbor about the arrangement if such a lawyer were representing only the client being advised; and the consequences and effects of a future withdrawal of consent by any client, including, if relevant, the fact that the lawyer would withdraw from representing all clients (see § 121, Comment *e*). Where the conflict arises solely because a proposed representation will be adverse to an existing client in an unrelated matter, knowledge of the general nature and scope of the work being performed for each client normally suffices to enable the clients to decide whether or not to consent.

When the consent relates to a former-client conflict (see § 132), it is necessary that the former client be aware that the consent will allow the former lawyer to proceed adversely to the former client. Beyond that, the former client must have adequate information about the implications (if not readily apparent) of the adverse representation, the fact that the lawyer possesses the former client's confidential information, the measures that the former lawyer might undertake to protect against unwarranted disclosures, and the right of the former client to refuse consent. The former client will often be independently represented by counsel. If so, communication with the former client ordinarily must be through successor counsel (see § 99 and following).

The lawyer is responsible for assuring that each client has the necessary information. A lawyer who does not personally inform the client assumes the risk that the client is inadequately informed and that the consent is invalid. A lawyer's failure to inform the clients might also bear on the motives and good faith of the lawyer. On the other hand, clients differ as to their sophistication and experience, and situations differ in terms of their complexity and the subtlety of the conflicts presented. The requirements of this Section are satisfied if the client already knows the necessary information or learns it from other sources. A client independently represented—for example by inside legal counsel or by other outside counsel—will need less information about the consequences of a conflict but nevertheless may have need of information adequate to reveal its scope and severity. When several lawyers represent the same client, responsibility to make disclosure and obtain informed consent may be delegated to one or more of the lawyers who appears reasonably capable of providing adequate information.

Disclosing information about one client or prospective client to another is precluded if information necessary to be conveyed is confidential (see § 60). The affected clients may consent to disclosure (see § 62), but it also might be possible for the lawyer to explain the nature of undisclosed information in a manner that nonetheless provides an adequate basis for informed consent. If means of adequate disclosure are unavailable, consent to the conflict may not be obtained.

The requirement of consent generally requires an affirmative response by each client. Ambiguities in a client's purported expression of consent should be construed against the lawyer seeking the protection of the consent (cf. § 18). In general, a lawyer may not assume consent from a client's silent acquiescence. However, consent may be inferred from active participation in a representation by a client who has reasonably adequate information about the material risks of the representation after a lawyer's request for consent. Even in the absence of consent, a tribunal applying remedies such as disqualification (see § 121, Comment *f*) will apply concepts of estoppel and waiver when an objecting party has either induced reasonable reliance on the absence of objection or delayed an unreasonable period of time in making objection.

Effective client consent to one conflict is not necessarily effective with respect to other conflicts or other matters. A client's informed consent to simultaneous representation of another client in the same matter despite a conflict of interest (see Topic 3) does not constitute consent to the lawyer's later representation of the other client in a manner that would violate the former-client conflict rule (see § 132; see also § 121, Comment *e(i)*).

Illustration:

1. Client A and Client B give informed consent to a joint representation by Lawyer to prepare a commercial contract. Lawyer's bill for legal services is paid by both clients and the matter is terminated. Client B then retains Lawyer to file a lawsuit against former Client A on the asserted ground that A breached the contract. Lawyer may not represent Client B against Client A in the lawsuit without A's informed consent (see § 132). Client A's earlier consent to Lawyer's joint representation to draft the contract does not itself permit Lawyer's later adversarial representation.

c(ii). The requirement of informed consent—the capacity of the consenting person. Each client whose consent is required must have the legal capacity to give informed consent. Consent purportedly given by a client who lacks legal capacity to do so is ineffective. Consent of a person under a legal disability normally must be obtained from a guardian or conservator appointed for the person. Consent of a minor normally is effective when given by a parent or guardian of the minor. In class actions certification of the class, determination that the interests of its members are congruent, and assessment of the adequacy of representation are typically made by a tribunal.

In some jurisdictions, a governmental unit might lack legal authority under applicable law to give consent to some conflicts of interest (see Comment *g(ii)* below).

When the person who normally would make the decision whether or not to give consent—members of a corporate board of directors, for example—is another interested client of the lawyer, or is otherwise self-interested in the decision whether to consent, special requirements apply to consent (see §§ 131 & 135, Comment *d*). Similarly, an officer of a government agency capable of consenting might be disabled from giving consent when that officer is a lawyer personally interested in consenting to the conflict.

d. Consent to future conflicts. Client consent to conflicts that might arise in the future is subject to special scrutiny, particularly if the consent is general. A client's open-ended agreement to consent to all conflicts normally should be ineffective unless the client possesses sophistication in the matter in question and has had the opportunity to receive independent legal advice about the consent. A client's informed consent to a gift to a lawyer (see § 127) ordinarily should be given contemporaneously with the gift.

On the other hand, particularly in a continuing client-lawyer relationship in which the lawyer is expected to act on behalf of the client without a new engagement for each matter, the gains to both lawyer and client from a system of advance consent to defined future conflicts might be substantial. A client might, for example, give informed consent in advance to types of conflicts that are familiar to the client. Such an agreement could effectively protect the client's interest while assuring that the lawyer did not undertake a potentially disqualifying representation.

Illustrations:

2. Law Firm has represented Client in collecting commercial claims through Law Firm's New York office for many years. Client is a long-established and sizable business corporation that is sophisticated in commercial matters generally and specifically in dealing with lawyers. Law Firm also has a Chicago office that gives tax advice to many companies with which Client has commercial dealings. Law Firm asks for advance consent from Client with respect to conflicts that otherwise would prevent Law Firm from filing commercial claims on behalf of Client against the tax clients of Law Firm's Chicago office (see § 128). If Client gives informed consent the consent should be held to be proper as to Client. Law Firm would also be required to obtain informed consent from any tax client of its Chicago office against whom Client wishes to file a commercial claim, should Law Firm decide to undertake such a representation.

3. The facts being otherwise as stated in Illustration 2, Law Firm seeks advance consent from each of its Chicago-office corporate-tax clients to its representation of any of its other clients in matters involving collection of commercial claims adverse to such tax clients if the matters do not involve information that Law Firm might have learned in the tax representation. To provide further assurance concerning the protection of confidential information, the consent provides that, should Law Firm represent any client in a collection matter adverse to a tax client, a procedure to protect confidential information of the tax client will be established (compare § 124, Comment *d*). Unless such a tax client is shown to be unsophisticated about legal matters and relationships with lawyers, informed consent to the arrangement should be held to be proper.

If a material change occurs in the reasonable expectations that formed the basis of a client's informed consent, the new conditions must be brought to the attention of the client and new informed consent obtained (see also Comment *f* hereto (client revocation of consent)). If the new conflict is not consentable (see Comment *g* hereto), the lawyer may not proceed.

e. Partial or conditional consent. A client's informed consent to a conflict can be qualified or conditional. A client might consent, for example, to joint representation with one co-party but not another. Similarly, the client might condition consent on particular action being taken by the lawyer or law firm. For example, a former client might consent that the conflict of one individually prohibited lawyer should not be imputed (see § 123) to the rest of the firm, but only if the firm takes steps to assure that the prohibited lawyer is not involved in the representation (see § 124; see also Illustration 3 hereto). Such a partial or conditional consent can be valid even if an unconditional consent in the same situation would be invalid. For example, a client might give informed consent to a lawyer serving only in the role of mediator between clients (see § 130, Comment *d*), but not to the lawyer representing those clients opposing each other in litigation if mediation is unavailing (see Comment *g(iii)* hereto).

f. Revocation of consent through client action or a material change of circumstances. A client who has given informed consent to an otherwise conflicted representation may at any time revoke the consent (see § 21(2)). Revoking consent to the client's own representation, however, does not necessarily prevent the lawyer from continuing to represent other clients who had been jointly represented along with the revoking client. Whether the lawyer may continue the other representation depends on whether the client was justified in revoking the consent (such as because of a material change in the factual basis on which the client originally gave informed consent) and whether material detriment to the other client or lawyer would result. In addition, if the client had reserved the prerogative of revoking consent, that agreement controls the lawyer's subsequent ability to continue representation of other clients.

A material change in the factual basis on which the client originally gave informed consent can justify a client in withdrawing consent. For example, in the absence of an agreement to the contrary, the consent of a client to be represented concurrently with another (see Topic 3) normally presupposes that the co-clients will not develop seriously antagonistic positions. If such antagonism develops, it might warrant revoking consent. If the conflict is subject to informed consent (see Comment *(g)(iii)* hereto), the lawyer must thereupon obtain renewed informed consent of the clients, now adequately informed of the change of circumstances. If the conflict is not consentable, or the lawyer cannot obtain informed consent from the other client or decides not to proceed with the representation, the lawyer must withdraw from representing all affected clients adverse to any former client in the matter (see § 121, Comment *e*).

A client who has given informed consent to be represented as a joint client with another would be justified in revoking the consent if the common lawyer failed to represent that client with reasonable loyalty (see Comment *h* hereto). The client would also be justified in revoking consent if a co-client materially violated the express or implied terms of the consent, such as by abusing the first client's confidential information through disclosing important information to third persons without justification. Improper behavior of the other client or the lawyer might indicate that one or both of them cannot be trusted to respect the legitimate interests of the consenting client.

Illustration:

4. Client A and Client B validly consent to be represented by Lawyer in operating a restaurant in a city. After a period of amicable and profitable collaboration, Client A reasonably concludes that Lawyer has begun to take positions against Client A and consistently favoring the interests of Client B in the business. Reasonably concerned that Lawyer is no longer properly serving the interests of both clients, Client A withdraws consent. Withdrawal of consent is effective and justified (see Comment *h* hereto). Lawyer may not thereafter continue representing either Client A or Client B in a matter adverse to the other and substantially related to Lawyer's former representation of the clients (see § 121, Comment *e(i)*).

In the absence of valid reasons for a client's revocation of consent, the ability of the lawyer to continue representing other clients depends on whether material detriment to the other client or lawyer would result and, accordingly, whether the reasonable expectations of those persons would be defeated. Once the client or former client has given informed consent to a lawyer's representing another client, that other client as well as the lawyer might have acted in reliance on the consent. For example, the other client and the lawyer might already have invested time, money, and effort in the representation. The other client might already have disclosed confidential information and developed a relationship of trust and confidence with the lawyer. Or, a client relying on the consent might reasonably have elected to forgo opportunities to take other action.

Illustrations:

5. On Monday, Client A and Client B validly consent to being represented by Lawyer in the same matter despite a conflict of interest. On Wednesday, before either Client B or Lawyer has taken or forgone any significant action in reliance, Client A withdraws consent. Lawyer is no longer justified in continuing with the joint representation. Lawyer also may not continue to represent Client B alone without A's renewed informed consent to Lawyer's representation of B if doing so would violate other Sections of this Chapter, for example because A's and B's interests in the matter would be antagonistic or because Lawyer had learned confidential information from A relevant in the matter (see § 132; see also § 15, Comment *c*, & § 121, Comment *e(i)*). Similarly, if Client A on Wednesday did not unequivocally withdraw consent but stated to Lawyer that on further reflection Client A now had serious doubts about the wisdom of the joint representation, Lawyer could not reasonably take material steps in reliance on the consent. Before proceeding, Lawyer must clarify with Client A whether A indeed gives informed consent and whether the joint representation may thereby continue.

6. Clients A and B validly consent to Lawyer representing them jointly as co-defendants in a breach-of-contract action. On the eve of trial and after months of pretrial discovery on the part of all parties, Client A withdraws consent to the joint representation for reasons not justified by the conduct of Lawyer or Client B and insists that Lawyer cease representing Client B. At this point it would be difficult and expensive for Client B to find separate representation for the impending trial. Client A's withdrawal of consent is ineffective to prevent the continuing representation of B in the absence of compelling considerations such as harmful disloyalty by Lawyer.

7. Client A, who consulted Lawyer about a tax question, gave informed advance consent to Lawyer's representing any of Lawyer's other clients against Client A in matters unrelated to Client A's tax question. Client B, who had not theretofore been a client of Lawyer, wishes to retain Lawyer to file suit against Client A for personal injuries suffered in an automobile accident. After Lawyer informs Client B of the nature of Lawyer's work for Client A, and the nature and risks presented by any conflict that might be produced, Client B consents to the conflict of interest. After Lawyer has undertaken substantial work in preparation of Client B's case, Client A seeks to withdraw the advance consent for reasons not justified by the conduct of Lawyer or Client B. Even though Client A was Lawyer's client before Client B was a client, the material detriment to both Lawyer and Client B would render Client A's attempt to withdraw consent ineffective.

The terms of the consent itself can control the effects of revocation of consent. A client's consent could state that it is conditioned on the client's right to revoke consent at any time for any reason. If so conditioned, the consent would cease to be effective if the client exercised that right.

g. *Nonconsentable conflicts.* Some conflicts of interest preclude adverse representation even if informed consent is obtained.

g(i). Representations prohibited by law. As stated in Subsection (2)(a), informed consent is unavailing when prohibited by applicable law. In some states, for example, the law provides that the same lawyer may not represent more than one defendant in a capital case and that informed consent does not cure the conflict (see § 129, Comment *c*). Under federal criminal statutes, certain representations by a former government lawyer (cf. § 133) are prohibited, and informed consent by the former client is not recognized as a defense.

g(ii). Consent by governmental clients. Decisional law in a minority of states has limited the extent to which a governmental client may consent to a conflict of interest. Subject to local law on the powers of governmental bodies and the requirement that any consenting governmental officer must be disinterested in the issues giving rise to the question of conflict (see Comment *c(ii)* hereto), such questions should otherwise be decided under the customary rules governing conflicts of interest.

g(iii). Conflicts between adversaries in litigation. When clients are aligned directly against each other in the same litigation, the institutional interest in vigorous development of each client's position renders the conflict nonconsentable (see § 128, Comment *c*, & § 129). The rule applies even if the parties themselves believe that the common interests are more significant in the matter than the interests dividing them. While the parties might give informed consent to joint representation for purposes of negotiating their differences (see § 130, Comment *d*), the joint representation may not continue if the parties become opposed to each other in litigation.

Illustration:

8. A and B wish to obtain an amicable dissolution of their marriage. State law treats marriage dissolution as a contested judicial proceeding. Lawyer is asked to represent both A and B in negotiation of the property settlement to be submitted to the court in the proceeding. Informed consent can authorize Lawyer to represent both parties in the property-settlement negotiations (subject to exceptions in some jurisdictions, where interests of children are involved, for example), but consent does not authorize Lawyer to represent both A and B if litigation is necessary to obtain the final decree. The parties may agree that Lawyer will represent only one of them in the judicial proceeding. The other party would either be represented by another lawyer or appear pro se (see §§ 128 & 130).

Whether clients are aligned directly against each other within the meaning of this Comment requires examination of the context of the litigation. In multi-party litigation, a single lawyer might, for example, represent members of a class in a class action, multiple creditors or debtors in a bankruptcy proceeding, or multiple interested parties in environmental clean-up litigation (see § 128). Joint representation is appropriate following effective client consent, together with compliance with applicable statutory or rule requirements, which may require court approval of the representation after disclosure of the conflict. Such joint representation is appropriate, notwithstanding that the co-clients may have conflicting claims against each other in other matters as to which the lawyer is not providing representation. The clients may also give informed consent to joint representation while they negotiate any differences they may have in the matter in litigation, perhaps employing the lawyer as appropriate in such negotiations (see § 130, Comments *c* & *d*), or prior agreement on such negotiated matters may be a condition of the clients' consent (see Comment *e* hereto).Where the alignment of parties, clients, and claims is such that the lawyer will not oppose another client with respect to the matters of dispute between them, as indicated in § 122(2)(b), there is no conflict. Thus, in complex litigation, the same lawyer may represent two defendants with largely congruent positions with respect to their defense, if other counsel are representing the two clients with respect to a dispute between them.

g(iv). Other circumstances rendering a lawyer incapable of providing adequate representation. Concern for client autonomy generally warrants respecting a client's informed consent. In some situations, however, joint representation would be objectively inadequate despite a client's voluntary and informed consent. In criminal cases, for example, joint representation of co-defendants with irreconcilable or unreconciled interests might render their representation constitutionally inadequate and thus require a court to prohibit the joint representation (see § 129, Comment *c*). Similarly, a conflict of interest among class members might render a lawyer's representation in a class action inadequate despite informed consent by the class representatives (see § 128, Comment *d*; see also, e.g., § 131, Comment *f*, Illustration 5).

The general standard stated in Subsection (2)(c) assesses the likelihood that the lawyer will, following consent, be able to provide adequate representation to the clients. The standard includes the requirements both that the consented-to conflict not adversely affect the lawyer's relationship with either client and that it not adversely affect the representation of either client. In general, if a reasonable and disinterested lawyer would conclude that one or more of the affected clients could not consent to the conflicted representation because the representation would likely fall short in either respect, the conflict is nonconsentable.

Decisions holding that a conflict is nonconsentable often involve facts suggesting that the client, who is often unsophisticated in retaining lawyers, was not adequately informed or was incapable of adequately appreciating the risks of the conflict (compare Comments *c(i)* & *c(ii)* hereto). Decisions involving clients sophisticated in the use of lawyers, particularly when advised by independent counsel, such as by inside legal counsel, rarely hold that a conflict is nonconsentable.

The nature of the conflict is also important. The professional rules and court decisions indicate that informed consent will always suffice with respect to a former-client conflict of interest (§ 132). With respect to simultaneous-representation conflicts (Topic 3), when the matters are unrelated it would only be in unusual circumstances that a lawyer could not provide adequate representation with consent of all affected clients. On the other hand, when the representation involves the same matter or the matters are significantly related, it may be more difficult for the lawyer to provide adequate legal assistance to multiple clients (see, e.g., § 131, Comment *e*, Illustration 4).

Illustrations:

9. Lawyer occasionally represents Bank in collection matters and is doing so currently in one lawsuit. Employee requests Lawyer to file an employment-discrimination charge against Bank. Bank, acting through its inside legal counsel, gives informed consent to Lawyer's representation of Employee against Bank with respect to the matter. Employee, following discussion with Lawyer concerning the nature of Lawyer's collection representations of Bank, freely gives informed consent as well. The circumstances indicate no basis for concluding that Lawyer would be unable to provide adequate representation to Bank in the collection matters and to Employee in the discrimination claim against Bank.

10. Lawyer has been asked by Buyer and Seller to represent both of them in negotiating and documenting a complex real-estate transaction. The parties are in sharp disagreement on several important terms of the transaction. Given such differences, Lawyer would be unable to provide adequate representation to both clients.

11. The facts being otherwise as stated in Illustration 10, the parties are both in agreement on terms and possess comparable knowledge and experience in such transactions, but, viewed objectively, the transaction is such that both parties should receive extensive counseling concerning their rights in the transaction and possible optional arrangements, including security interests, guarantees, and other rights against each other and in resisting the claims of the other party for such rights. Given the scope of legal representation that each prospective client should receive, Lawyer would be unable to provide adequate representation to both clients.

A conflict can be rendered nonconsentable because of personal circumstances affecting the lawyer's ability in fact to provide adequate representation. For example, if the lawyer has such strong feelings of friendship toward one of two prospective joint clients that the lawyer could not provide adequate representation to the other client (compare Comment *h* hereto), the lawyer may not proceed with the joint representation.

h. Duties of a lawyer representing a client subject to a conflict consent. When a lawyer undertakes representation despite a conflict and after required disclosure and informed consent, the lawyer must represent all affected clients diligently and competently (see § 16) and must not regard informed consent as a basis for limiting the scope of the representation or favoring the interests of one client over the interests of another, except as expressly agreed under the informed consent. The lawyer must protect the confidential information of all affected clients (see § 60), subject to whatever modifications are warranted pursuant to the informed consent. On communicating information with each client in the absence of a different agreement among co-clients, see § 60, Comment *l*, and § 75, Comment *d*.

§ 123. Imputation of a Conflict of Interest to an Affiliated Lawyer

Unless all affected clients consent to the representation under the limitations and conditions provided in § 122 or unless imputation hereunder is removed as provided in § 124, the restrictions upon a lawyer imposed by §§ 125–135 also restrict other affiliated lawyers who:

(1) are associated with that lawyer in rendering legal services to others through a law partnership, professional corporation, sole proprietorship, or similar association;

(2) are employed with that lawyer by an organization to render legal services either to that organization or to others to advance the interests or objectives of the organization; or

(3) share office facilities without reasonably adequate measures to protect confidential client information so that it will not be available to other lawyers in the shared office.

Comment:

a. Scope and cross-references. This Section prohibits representation or action by lawyers affiliated with a lawyer who is prohibited from representation or action pursuant to §§ 125–135. On the extent of imputation under § 125, see Comment *g* thereto. For example, if a lawyer is prohibited from simultaneously representing two clients with conflicting interests under § 130, this Section also prohibits lawyers affiliated with the conflicted lawyer from representing one of the clients. Imputation under this Section is predicated upon a conflict as defined in § 121, including the absence of valid client consent to the basic conflict under § 122. When a conflict is imputed to an affiliated lawyer under this Section, the imputation can be removed under the conditions stated in § 124. Client consent under the conditions and limitations of § 122 suffices to remove the imputation. The sanctions and remedies described in § 121, Comment/ apply to violations of this Section.

The concepts of imputation stated here are those found in lawyer codes and judicial decisions. The imputation rules are applicable in a disciplinary proceeding against a personally prohibited lawyer or an affiliated lawyer based on a prohibited imputed conflict and in deciding whether to disqualify a lawyer from acting in a matter (see § 6, Comment *i*). Although an imputed conflict might be evidence of negligent breach of duty by each of the lawyers (see § 52), a claimant seeking a civil remedy is required to prove other elements of a tort, including causation and damages (see § 53).

Imputation is imposed in the context of conflicts of interest arising under this Chapter, primarily as a prophylactic measure. In other contexts, the general rule is that knowledge of a lawyer in a firm who is not working on a client matter is not imputed to others who are (see § 28, Comment *b*).

On the extent to which personal interests of associated lawyers preclude representation of a client, see § 125, Comment *g*. On imputation in the instance of client gifts to lawyers, see § 127, Comment *a*.

b. Rationale. Imputation of conflicts of interest to affiliated lawyers reflects three concerns. First, lawyers in a law firm or other affiliation described in this Section ordinarily share each other's interests. A fee for one lawyer hi a partnership, for example, normally benefits all lawyers in the partnership. Where a lawyer's relationship with a client creates an incentive to violate an obligation to another client, an affiliated lawyer will often have similar incentive to favor one client over the other. Second, lawyers affiliated as described in this Section ordinarily have access to files and other confidential information about each other's clients. Indeed, clients might assume that their confidential information will be shared among affiliated lawyers (compare § 60, Comment *f*). Sharing confidential client information among affiliated lawyers might compromise the representation of one or both clients if the representations conflict. Third, a client would often have difficulty proving that the adverse representation by an affiliated lawyer was wholly isolated. Duties of confidentiality on the part of the affiliated lawyers prevents adequate disclosure of the interactions among them. Moreover, to demonstrate that the lawyer misused confidential information the client often would be forced to reveal the very information whose confidentiality the client seeks to protect. However, considerations of free choice of lawyers by clients and the free mobility of lawyers between firms or other employers caution against extending imputation further than necessary (see § 124, Comment *b*).

c. Lawyers associated in a law partnership, professional corporation, sole proprietorship, or similar association. This Section most commonly applies to lawyers associated in various forms of organization engaged in the private practice of law.

c(i). Law-firm members and employees. The rule of imputation applies to both owner-employer and associate-employees of a sole-proprietorship law practice, to partners and associates in a partnership for the practice of law, and to shareholder-principals and nonequity lawyer employees of a professional corporation or similar organization conducting a law practice. The lawyers in all such organizations typically have similar access to confidential client information. Owners, partners, and shareholder-principals have a shared economic interest. Associates and nonequity lawyer employees have both a stake in the continued viability of their employer and an incentive to keep the employer's good will.

Illustration:

1. Lawyer A and Lawyer B are partners in a law firm. Client is considering filing suit against a commercial enterprise in which Lawyer A has a 30 percent ownership interest. Without the informed consent of Client, Lawyer A may not represent Client in the matter (see § 125). Under the rule of imputation described in this Section, Lawyer B also may not represent Client.

A form of lawyer-employee is the lawyer temporary—a lawyer who temporarily works for a firm needing extra professional help. The rules barring representation adverse to a former client (see § 132) and imputing conflicts to all lawyers associated in a firm generally apply to such lawyer temporaries.

c(ii). Of-counsel relationships. The rule of imputation of this Section ordinarily applies due to the association of lawyers who are "of counsel." A lawyer is of counsel if designated as having that relationship with a firm or when the relationship is regular and continuing although the lawyer is neither a partner in the firm nor employed by it on a full-time basis. A lawyer who is of counsel to a firm often has more limited access to confidential client information than firm partners and associates and usually a smaller financial stake in the firm. Nonetheless, the incentive to misuse confidential information, the difficulty of determining when it has been misused, the ostensible professional relationship, as well as the administrative ease of a definite rule, justify extending imputation to lawyers having an of-counsel status. In unusual situations, the relationship between an "of counsel" lawyer and the firm may be shown to be so attenuated, despite typical connotations of the term, that there is no significant risk of compromising client confidentiality or otherwise providing a basis for imputation.

c(iii). Associated lawyers or law firms. Two or more lawyers or law firms might associate for purposes of handling a particular case. A common example is a lawyer who appears as local counsel in litigation principally handled by another firm. Each lawyer must comply with the rules concerning conflict of interest, and other lawyers in their respective firms are governed by the rules of imputation. However, a conflict imputed within a firm does not extend by imputation to lawyers in another firm working on another matter.

Similarly, when a lawyer consults with other lawyers in specialized areas of the law, the consultant lawyer may not personally represent clients with conflicting interests. However, the normal consulting relationship is essentially an association for purposes of the matter in question between lawyers otherwise practicing separately. Hence, the rule of this Comment applies.

Illustration:

2. Firm X is about to file a patent-infringement action on behalf of Client against Opponent. Firm X has no patent lawyers in its office, so it wishes to affiliate with Firm Y, a patent firm, to handle the representation. Firm Y has had no connection with Opponent but Lawyer A in Firm Y represents P against D, another of Firm X's clients, in an unrelated matter. Lawyer A's adverse representation of P is not imputed to Firm X, nor is Firm X's relationship with D imputed to Firm Y. The fact that Firms X and Y represent opposing clients in a different matter would not prevent their affiliation in the patent matter.

d. Lawyers employed by an organization to render legal services to it. Section 123(2) applies the rule of imputation to certain situations in which lawyers are employed by an organization.

d(i). Corporate legal offices. Lawyers employed by the legal department of a corporation or similar organization commonly represent only the organization as a client. However, such a lawyer might sometimes be asked to represent officers, directors, or employees of the organization. A lawyer so employed might also have continuing obligations to clients formerly represented in previous employment. Furthermore, lawyers in corporate legal offices will often have access to confidential information in the possession of other lawyers in the same office. The possibility of misuse of information in such situations can be as great as in private law firms. The lawyer-employees are to that extent comparable to partners and associates in a private law firm. Thus, as provided in this Section, the principles of imputed prohibition apply.

Illustration:

3. Lawyer A and Lawyer B are employed in the corporate legal office of Company. A government agency is conducting an investigation of the activities of Company and is considering whether to initiate criminal charges against Company, some of its employees, or both. The established practice of the agency is not to charge a corporation for offenses committed by corporate employees if the corporation can demonstrate that it actively sought to discourage the offense in question. Such a demonstration would, however, significantly increase the likelihood that an employee would be charged with the offense. Employee is a Company employee upon whose activities the agency has begun to focus. Before Lawyer B's employment by Company, Lawyer B had been in private practice and had advised Employee with respect to conduct that is the subject of the agency investigation.

Because Company's position in the investigation might be adverse to that of Employee, Lawyer B could not represent Company in connection with the investigation (see § 132) without the informed consent of Employee and Company (see § 122). Under the rule of imputation described in this Section, neither Lawyer A nor any other member of Company's corporate legal office may represent Company without obtaining the same informed consent.

Questions concerning the proper scope of imputation can also arise because of inter-organizational relationships. For example, if one corporation owns all of the stock of another, it is ordinarily appropriate to consider lawyers employed by each corporation as part of a single legal office for purposes of imputed prohibition. Likewise, if one corporation exercises substantial control over the actions of another corporation or if such control is exercised by a group of shareholders of two or more corporations, principles of imputed prohibition similarly should be applied to corporate counsel. However, imputation between the legal offices might be inappropriate where, despite common management in other respects, the legal offices of the affiliated organizations are separately operated. On identifying a lawyer's client, see § 121, Comment *d*. With respect to possible conflicts between affiliated organizations, see § 131, Comment *d*.

Consent to conflict affecting a lawyer employed by the legal department of an organization may be obtained as stated in § 122. Such a lawyer acts properly in following the informed direction of senior lawyers or other officers of the organization who reasonably appear to be empowered to give informed consent on behalf of the relevant organizational client.

d(ii). Government legal offices—in general. Government legal offices often present the same potential for access to confidential information and motivation to direct the representations as exist in a corporate legal office or private law firm. Government lawyers thus are subject to imputed prohibition under this Section when they are employed by a government agency to render legal services to that agency as stated in Subsection (2) or are officed in physical proximity to each other as stated in Subsection (3). However, measures taken within a governmental law office can adequately assure that confidential client information will not be shared by various lawyers within the office (see § 124).

d(iii). Prosecutor offices. When one member of a prosecutor's office is personally prohibited from acting because of a conflict of interest, the question arises whether the entire office is disqualified, so that outside counsel must be retained to prosecute the case. If prosecutor staff lawyers commonly discuss cases with each other and have physical access to each other's files, Subsection (3) imputes conflicts to all such prosecutors (see Comment *e* hereto). If there is no such access, the issue under Subsection (2) is whether the lawyers in the prosecutor offices should be said to work for the same "organization." If prosecutor offices are organized by county, for example, the county might be regarded as the common organizational employer, so that if one assistant prosecutor in the county were prohibited from acting, all other prosecutors in that county would be prohibited as well. However, if the office is operated so as to avoid material risk that confidential information will be inadequately safeguarded, the formal organization of the prosecutor's office should not inevitably require imputation. Establishing procedures for removal of imputation like those in § 124 can in appropriate circumstances ameliorate otherwise serious practical problems created by imputation.

Illustration:

4. Assistant Prosecutor A, who has recently joined a county prosecutor's office, represented Defendant at a preliminary hearing in a pending criminal case while in private practice. Because A would be prohibited from prosecuting Defendant at trial in the same matter (see § 132), under the rule of imputation described in this Section, ordinarily no other member of the same county prosecutor's office could conduct the prosecution. A special prosecutor or a prosecutor from an adjoining but jurisdictionally distinct county ordinarily could act. If state law does not permit appointment of such other prosecutors, however, screening measures such as those described in § 124(2) can suffice to permit the prosecution to proceed.

d(iv). Public-defender offices. In a public-defender office, conflict-of-interest questions commonly arise when the interests of two or more defendants so conflict that lawyers in a private-practice defense firm could not represent both or all the defendants (see § 129). The rules on imputed conflicts and screening of this Section apply to a public-defender organization as they do to a law firm in private practice in a similar situation.

d(v). Nonprofit legal-services agencies. Lawyers in some nonprofit legal-services agencies might be affected by conflicting interests in much the same manner as lawyers in any other legal office. As with a public defender (see Comment *d(iv)* hereto), the rules on imputed conflicts and screening apply to a nonprofit legal-services organization. If more than one party in such a matter is in need of legal assistance and their interests conflict, either a private lawyer or a lawyer from an autonomous legal-services agency must provide the representation.

e. Lawyers sharing office space. When lawyers share office space, they typically share some common costs such as rent, library, and office salaries, but not income from work on cases. Subsection (3) governs imputation of conflicts in such arrangements. The key inquiry is whether the physical organization and actual operation of the office space is such that the confidential client information of each lawyer is secure from the others. Where such security is provided and where no other plausible risks to confidentiality and loyalty are presented, the conflicts of the lawyers are not imputed to each other by reason of their office-sharing arrangement. On the other hand, lawyers who do associate in a matter, share fee income, or hold themselves out as partners or members of a professional corporation (even if that is not a fact) are held to the stricter rule applicable to members of a firm (see Comment *c(i)* hereto).

f. Imputed conflicts through nonlawyer employees. Nonlawyer employees of a law office owe duties of confidentiality by reason of their employment (see Restatement Second, Agency § 396). However, their duty of confidentiality is not imputed to others so as to prohibit representation of other clients at a subsequent employer. Even if the person learned the information in circumstances that would disqualify a lawyer and the person has become a lawyer, the person should not be regarded as a lawyer for purposes of the imputation rules of this Section.

Law students who clerk in firms, like other nonlawyer employees, typically have limited responsibilities and thus might acquire little sensitive confidential information about matters. Absent special circumstances, they should be considered nonlawyer employees for the purposes of this Section. Persons who have completed their legal education and are awaiting admission to practice at the time of providing services to a client of a law firm typically have duties comparable to admitted lawyers and accordingly should ordinarily be treated as lawyers for purposes of imputation.

Some risk is involved in a rule that does not impute confidential information known by nonlawyers to lawyers in the firm. For example, law students might work in several law offices during their law-school careers and thereby learn client information at Firm A that could be used improperly by Firm B. Experienced legal secretaries and paralegal personnel similarly often understand the significance and value of confidential material with which they work. Incentives exist in many such cases for improper disclosure or use of the information in the new employment.

On the other hand, nonlawyers ordinarily understand less about the legal significance of information they learn in a law firm than lawyers do, and they are often not in a position to articulate to a new employer the nature of the information gained in the previous employment. If strict imputation were applied, employers could protect themselves against unanticipated disqualification risks only by refusing to hire experienced people. Further, nonlawyers have an independent duty as agents to protect confidential information, and firms have a duty to take steps designed to assure that the nonlawyers do so (see § 60, Comment *d*). Adequate protection can be given to clients, consistent with the interest in job mobility for nonlawyers, by prohibiting the nonlawyer from using or disclosing the confidential information (see § 124) but not extending the prohibition on representation to lawyers in the new firm or organization. If a nonlawyer employee in fact conveys confidential information learned about a client in one firm to lawyers in another, a prohibition on representation by the second firm would be warranted.

g. Family relationships among lawyers. The fact that lawyers are related by blood or marriage does not, in itself, require imputation under the rule described in this Section. Like lawyers in the same firm, however, the degree of financial interdependence, sharing of information, and loyalty between spouses, for example, is ordinarily high. Yet, if the rule were that a spouse and the spouse's firm are disqualified from any case in which the other spouse was disqualified, law firms would be reluctant to hire either spouse. Thus, in general, the law does not impute conflicts between firms of lawyers by virtue of family relationship alone. However, in the absence of informed consent by all affected clients (see § 122), lawyers who are married to each other, or lawyers similarly related such as parent-lawyers and their lawyer children-may not personally represent clients adverse to the interests of clients of the other spouse or relative. Each must also observe prohibitions against misuse of confidential client information (see § 60). Conflicts arising out of relationships in which financial resources are pooled and living quarters shared in circumstances closely approximating marriage should be treated in the same way as spousal conflicts.

h. Client consent as an exception to imputation. Client consent under § 122 avoids an imputed conflict. If the client gives informed consent to representation by the personally conflicted lawyer, there is no imputation to associates of that lawyer. A client who refuses to consent to an adverse representation by the personally conflicted lawyer might, however, give informed consent to representation by a lawyer affiliated with that lawyer. In any event, the client can condition the consent, for example by requiring screening (see § 122, Comment *e,* & § 124, Comment *d).*

§ 124. Removing Imputation

(1) Imputation specified in § 123 does not restrict an affiliated lawyer when the affiliation between the affiliated lawyer and the personally prohibited lawyer that required the imputation has been terminated, and no material confidential information of the client, relevant to the matter, has been communicated by the personally prohibited lawyer to the affiliated lawyer or that lawyer's firm.

(2) Imputation specified in § 123 does not restrict an affiliated lawyer with respect to a former-client conflict under § 132, when there is no substantial risk that confidential information of the former client will be used with material adverse effect on the former client because:

(a) any confidential client information communicated to the personally prohibited lawyer is unlikely to be significant in the subsequent matter;

(b) the personally prohibited lawyer is subject to screening measures adequate to eliminate participation by that lawyer in the representation; and

(c) timely and adequate notice of the screening has been provided to all affected clients.

(3) Imputation specified in § 123 does not restrict a lawyer affiliated with a former government lawyer with respect to a conflict under § 133 if:

(a) the personally prohibited lawyer is subject to screening measures adequate to eliminate involvement by that lawyer in the representation; and

(b) timely and adequate notice of the screening has been provided to the appropriate government agency and to affected clients.

Comment:

a. Scope and cross-references. This Section removes the prohibition of § 123 from affiliated lawyers when the justifications for imputation are insignificant. This Section presupposes that a lawyer in an affiliation is personally prohibited from a representation or action pursuant to §§ 125–135; that the affected client or clients have not consented as provided in § 122 to representation despite the conflict; and that applying § 123 would impute the prohibition to affiliated lawyers but for the operation of this Section.

Subsection (1) removes imputation when a lawyer or firm of lawyers possesses no material confidential information relevant to the matter. Subsection (2) removes imputation under § 132 when the confidential information is unlikely to be significant in the matter and an appropriate screen is erected. Subsection (3) removes, also through effective screening, imputation under § 133; it removes imputation even when the confidential information may be significant in the succeeding representation.

A lawyer's general obligation to preserve confidential client information is considered in § 60 and throughout Chapter 5. On limiting conflicts of interest in the case of prospective clients, see § 15.

b. Rationale. Imputation creates burdens both for clients and lawyers. Some clients who wish to be represented by a trusted or highly recommended lawyer or law firm must forgo the engagement. A single personally prohibited lawyer can conflict out literally hundreds of lawyers in a firm. Prospective imputed prohibition inhibits mobility of lawyers from one firm or employer to another. The burden of prohibition should end when material risks to confidentiality and loyalty resulting from shared income and access to information have been avoided by appropriate measures (see Comment *d* hereto).

c. Imputation after the termination of an affiliation.

c(i). Personally prohibited lawyer terminates the affiliation. During the time that a personally prohibited lawyer is associated with another lawyer, law firm, or other organization to which prohibition is imputed under § 123, the lawyer could reveal confidential information to any other lawyer within the organization. Accordingly, imputed prohibition of all lawyers in the firm is appropriately required by § 123. However, after the personally prohibited lawyer has left the firm, an irrebuttable presumption of continued sharing of client confidences or continued disloyalty induced by the affiliation is no longer justified.

The lawyers remaining in the affiliation may rebut the presumption that confidential information was shared during the period of actual affiliation. They have the burden of persuasion concerning three facts: (1) that no material confidential client information relevant to the matter was revealed to any lawyer remaining in the firm; (2) that the firm does not now possess or have access to sources of client confidential information, particularly client documents or files; and (3) that the personally prohibited lawyer will not share fees in the matter so as to have an interest in the representation.

Illustration:

1. Lawyer A is a partner in ABC law firm, and Lawyer B formerly was a partner. Client X has sought to retain Lawyer A to file suit on behalf of X against Y. Before joining the ABC firm, Lawyer B had represented Y at an earlier stage of the current dispute. Lawyer B has now resigned from the ABC firm, disclosed no confidential information about Y relevant to the matter to other lawyers in ABC, left no files at ABC that relate to the proposed suit, and will not share in fees derived by the ABC firm from the representation of X. The limitation governing B, resulting from the proposed representation being substantially related to the prior representation of Y by B (see § 132), is no longer imputed to A. Hence A may represent Client X against Y.

A personally prohibited lawyer who enters a new law firm or other affiliation causes imputed prohibition of all affiliated lawyers as stated in § 123. Such imputation is subject to removal under Subsection (2) or (3).

c(ii). A non-personally-prohibited lawyer terminates the affiliation. When a lawyer leaves a firm or other organization whose lawyers were subject to imputed prohibition owing to presence in the firm of another lawyer, the departed lawyer becomes free of imputation so long as that lawyer obtained no material confidential client information relevant to the matter. Similarly, lawyers in the new affiliation are free of imputed prohibition if they can carry the burden of persuading the finder of fact that the arriving lawyer did not obtain confidential client information about a questioned representation by another lawyer in the former affiliation.

Illustration:

2. Client X has sought to retain Lawyer A, a partner in the firm of ABC, to represent X in a suit against Y. The suit has not yet been filed. Lawyer A is required to decline the representation because Y is also a client of Lawyer B in ABC. Lawyer A resigns from the ABC firm without having learned material confidential information of Y relevant to X's claim. The imputed disqualification is thereby removed, and Lawyer A may now represent Client X.

d. Screening against the risk of misuse of confidential information.

d(i). Screening—in general. Three situations must be distinguished. First, a lawyer's minor involvement in a matter for a former client might have involved no or so little exposure to confidential information that no conflict should be found (see § 132, Comment *h*). Second, the lawyer's involvement might have been more substantial, rendering the lawyer personally prohibited from the representation by reason of a former-client conflict of interest (see § 132), but screening may be appropriate under Subsection (2). A common instance in which this may be true is that of a junior lawyer in a law firm who provides minimal assistance on a peripheral element of a transaction, thereby gaining little confidential information that would be relevant in the later matter. Third, in the circumstances the lawyer's involvement and the nature and relevance of confidential information in the lawyer's possession might be such that screening will not remove imputation under Subsection (2). Determining which result is appropriate requires careful analysis of the particular facts.

If the requirements of either Subsection (2) or (3) are met, imputation is removed and consent to the representation by the former client is not required. The required screening measures must be imposed in the subsequent representation at the time the conflict is discovered or reasonably should have been discovered, and they must be of sufficient scope, continuity, and duration to assure that there will be no substantial risk to confidential client information.

Lawyer codes generally recognize the screening remedy in cases involving former government https://www.facebook.com/lawyers who have returned to private practice (see Comment *e* hereto). Screening to prevent imputation from former private-client representations has similar justification, giving clients wider choice of counsel and making it easier for lawyers to change employers. The rule in Subsection (2) thus permits screening as a remedy in situations in which the information possessed by a personally prohibited lawyer is not likely to be significant. The lawyer or firm seeking to remove imputation has the burden of persuasion that there is no substantial risk that confidential information of the former client will be used with material adverse effect on the former client.

Significance of the information is determined by its probable utility in the later representation, including such factors as the following: (1) whether the value of the information as proof or for tactical purposes is peripheral or tenuous; (2) whether the information in most material respects is now publicly known; (3) whether the information was of only temporary significance; (4) the scope of the second representation; and (5) the duration and degree of responsibility of the personally prohibited lawyer in the earlier representation.

The lawyer codes in most states impose disciplinary responsibility in a wider range of circumstances of former private-client representations. Specifically, most codes do not recognize that screening can preclude disqualification of a law firm by imputation from a personally prohibited lawyer, even if the screening is timely and effective and the client information involved is innocuous. The issue typically arises under motions to disqualify, not in disciplinary proceedings. A tribunal has discretion whether or not to require disqualification. Subsection (2) states a rule to guide exercise of that discretion.

Illustrations:

3. As can readily be shown from contemporaneous time records, when Lawyer was an associate in Law Firm ABC, Lawyer spent one-half hour in conversation with another associate about research strategies involving a narrow issue of venue in federal court in the case of Developer v. Bank, in which the firm represented Bank. The conversation was based entirely on facts pleaded in the complaint and answer, and Lawyer learned no confidential information about the matter. Lawyer then left Firm ABC and became an associate in Firm DEF. Two years later, Lawyer was asked to represent Developer against Bank in a matter substantially related to the matter in which Firm ABC represented Bank. In the circumstances, due to the proven lack of exposure of Lawyer to confidential information of Bank, Bank should not be regarded as the former client of Lawyer for the purpose of applying § 132 (see § 132, Comment *h*). Alternatively, a tribunal may require that Lawyer be screened from participation in the matter as provided in this Section and, on that basis, permit other lawyers affiliated with Lawyer in Firm DEF to represent the client against Bank.

4. The same facts as Illustration 3, except that Lawyer while representing Bank in Firm ABC was principally in charge of developing factual information about the underlying dispute. The dispute involved a loan Bank made to Developer on Tract A in the city in which both conduct business. The dispute was resolved after extensive discovery and a full trial before Lawyer left Firm ABC. An affiliated lawyer in Lawyer's new firm, Firm DEF, has been asked to represent Developer in a dispute with Bank over a loan on Tract B. Because of the similarity of facts in the two disputes—involving both tracts, both loans, and both parties to them—a tribunal finds the matters are substantially related and accordingly that Lawyer is personally prohibited from representing Developer against Bank with respect to Tract B (see § 132). However, the tribunal also finds that, despite that factual overlap, the information Lawyer might have acquired about Bank would have little significance in the later dispute because it concerned only an earlier period of time so that any importance it might have had was significantly diminished by the time of the second dispute, because it mainly involves information already a matter of public record in the earlier trial, and because all factual information will be largely

irrelevant in view of the fact that the pleadings indicate that the only contested issue in the second dispute involves a matter of contract interpretation. In the circumstances, the tribunal should further find that Firm DEF may represent Developer against Bank if Lawyer has been screened as provided in Subsection (2).

5. The same facts as Illustration 4, except that the earlier dispute was settled after Lawyer had conducted extensive examination of Bank's files but without any discovery by Developer's then counsel or trial. Little time has passed since Lawyer acquired the information from Bank, and the information remains highly relevant in the later dispute. The pleadings in the second dispute indicate that a large number of important factual issues similar to those in the earlier dispute remain open. In the circumstances, the likelihood that the information possessed by Lawyer will be significant in the second matter renders screening under this Section inappropriate.

d(ii). Screening—adequacy of measures. Screening must assure that confidential client information will not pass from the personally prohibited lawyer to any other lawyer in the firm. The screened lawyer should be prohibited from talking to other persons in the firm about the matter as to which the lawyer is prohibited, and from sharing documents about the matter and the like. Further, the screened lawyer should receive no direct financial benefit from the firm's representation, based upon the outcome of the matter, such as a financial bonus or a larger share of firm income directly attributable to the matter. However, it is not impermissible that the lawyer receives compensation and benefits under standing arrangements established prior to the representation. An adequate showing of screening ordinarily requires affidavits by the personally prohibited lawyer and by a lawyer responsible for the screening measures. A tribunal can require that other appropriate steps be taken.

If a lawyer in a law firm assertedly observing screening measures in fact breaches the screen and shares confidential information with lawyers proceeding adversely to the former client, the tribunal should take appropriate corrective measures. The screen should no longer be considered adequate to prevent disqualification of affiliated lawyers. Contempt might be an appropriate remedy to the extent that breach of the screen was knowing and deliberate and in violation of direct undertakings to the tribunal. In circumstances involving lesser culpability, lesser sanctions within the court's inherent power may be appropriate.

d(iii). Screening—timely and adequate notice of screening to all affected clients. An affected client will usually have difficulty demonstrating whether screening measures have been honored. Timely and adequate notice of the screening must therefore be given to the affected clients, including description of the screening measures reasonably sufficient to inform the affected client of their adequacy. Notice will give opportunity to protest and to allow arrangements to be made for monitoring compliance.

Notice should ordinarily be given as soon as practical after the lawyer or firm realizes or should realize the need for screening. Obligations of confidentiality to a current client, however, might justify reasonable delay. A firm advising about a possible takeover of a former client of a lawyer now in the firm, for example, need not provide notice until the attempt becomes known to the target client.

e. Screening a former government lawyer. As stated in Comment *d* hereto, avoidance of imputation by screening of former government lawyers is permitted in most lawyer codes. If hiring a former government lawyer would disqualify an entire firm from cases arising before that lawyer's agency, the lawyer would not likely be hired. That, in turn, would make it more difficult for the government to hire able lawyers at the outset.

The personally prohibited lawyer must be screened from any participation in the matter and should receive no direct financial benefit from the firm's representation as stated in Comment *d(ii)*. Written notice must be given to the appropriate government agency so that it can ascertain compliance with the screening requirement. Those precautions prevent imputation even if the confidential information communicated to the lawyer in the prior matter is significant (see § 74 & § 133, Comment *b*).

In appropriate cases, the government may challenge screening as inadequate to protect the government's interest. For example, where a former prosecutor who personally knows the strengths and weaknesses of a criminal case has become affiliated with defense counsel, disqualification of defense counsel may be required despite screening. Similarly, where the lawyer acquires while in the government highly confidential information about a person whom an affiliated lawyer's client now opposes in a substantially related matter, a court has discretion to disqualify the entire firm to protect the confidentiality of the information.

TOPIC 2. CONFLICTS OF INTEREST BETWEEN A LAWYER AND A CLIENT

§ 125. A Lawyer's Personal Interest Affecting the Representation of a Client

Unless the affected client consents to the representation under the limitations and conditions provided in § 122, a lawyer may not represent a client if there is a substantial risk that the lawyer's representation of the client would be materially and adversely affected by the lawyer's financial or other personal interests.

Comment:

a. *Scope and cross-references.* This Section is a specific application of the general conflicts standard expressed in § 121. Conflicts arising under this Section are imputed to affiliated lawyers pursuant to § 123, except as provided in Comment *g* hereto. Economic incentives created by particular forms of fee agreements are analogous to the conflicts raised in this Section, but they are separately considered. See, e.g., § 38 (agreements for contingent fee, hourly rates, and fixed fees); § 36(1) (lawyer acquisition of an interest in the subject matter of litigation); and § 36(3) (arrangements to secure media rights to a client's story). Issues presented when a third person pays a client's fee are considered in § 134. Section 135 addresses conflicts created by a lawyer's fiduciary or similar obligations to a nonclient.

Conflicts arising under this Section are subject to client consent to the extent and in the manner stated in § 122. Often only one client will be affected by a conflict under this Section, and only that client's informed consent is required.

Sanctions and remedies for violation of this Section are outlined in § 121, Comment *f*. Disqualification is ordinarily not a relevant remedy because the harm is suffered by the lawyer's client who may terminate the lawyer at any time (see § 32(1)). If the lawyer's personal interest is the proximate cause of harm to the client, the remedy of professional malpractice is available (see § 48 and following). If the breach of the lawyer's duty to the client is sufficiently serious, the lawyer can be required to forfeit the fee otherwise due (see § 37).

b. *Rationale.* Personal interests of a lawyer that are inconsistent with those of a client might significantly limit the lawyer's ability to pursue the client's interest. Even if a lawyer could subordinate significant personal interests to the interests of clients, it is difficult to determine after the fact whether a lawyer had succeeded in keeping a client's interests foremost.

c. *A lawyer with a personal or financial interest adverse to an interest of a client.* Client interests include all those that a reasonable lawyer, unaffected by a conflicting personal interest, would protect or advance. Perhaps the clearest case of a conflict is where the lawyer has a significant adverse financial interest in the object of the representation. Such a financial interest, other than one so insignificant that a person of normal sensibility would be unaffected by it, ordinarily constitutes a conflict of interest. A lawyer having such an interest is prohibited from accepting or continuing the representation unless the affected client gives informed consent.

A conflict under this Section need not be created by a financial interest. Included are interests that might be altruistic, such as an interest in furthering a charity favored by the lawyer, and matters of personal relationship, for example where the opposing party is the lawyer's spouse or a long-time friend or an institution with which the lawyer has a special relationship of loyalty. Such a conflict may also result from a lawyer's deeply held religious, philosophical, political, or public-policy beliefs. (On the limited imputation of such conflicts, see Comment *g* hereto.) A conflict exists if such an interest would materially impair the lawyer's ability to consider alternative courses of action that otherwise might be available to a client, to discuss all relevant aspects of the subject matter of the representation with the client, or otherwise to provide effective representation to the client. In some cases, a conflict between the personal or financial interests of a lawyer and those of a client will be so substantial that client consent will not suffice to remove the disability (see § 122, Comment *g*).

Illustrations:

1. Lawyer owns a 25 percent interest in a restaurant. Client was a customer at the restaurant and suffered severe food poisoning. Client has asked Lawyer to file suit against the restaurant for damages substantially in excess of insurance coverage. Lawyer's interest as investor in the restaurant might materially and adversely affect Lawyer's representation of Client. Because Client's recovery could significantly affect the value of Lawyer's investment interest, Lawyer may not represent Client even if Client were to give informed consent (see § 122(2)).

2. Same facts as in Illustration 1, except that Lawyer's child owns a five percent interest in the restaurant. Even though Lawyer owns no interest personally, concern about injuring the financial position or reputation of Lawyer's child might materially and adversely affect Lawyer's representation of Client. If Lawyer concludes that Lawyer can overcome the personal concerns involved and represent Client effectively, the representation may proceed if Client gives informed consent to the representation (see § 122).

3. Lawyer owns stock in a publicly held mutual fund that, in turn, carries in its diversified portfolio an interest of less than one percent in the common stock of Ajax Corporation, a publicly held corporation that produces frozen foods. The value of Lawyer's indirect interest in Ajax Corporation is less than $25.00. Client developed food poisoning after eating frozen peas that had been processed by Ajax Corporation and has asked Lawyer to file suit for damages against it. The described interest is so small, and the possibility of an effect on Lawyer's representation is so remote, that Lawyer need not raise the possibility of a conflict of interest with Client.

A representation that commences with no prospect of a conflict might, because of a change of circumstances, require the lawyer thereupon to cease the representation or to obtain the client's informed consent. A lawyer who becomes aware of such a change must call the circumstances to the attention of the client and permit the client to determine whether the lawyer may continue the representation after client provides informed consent (see § 121, Comment *e(i)*).

d. A lawyer seeking employment with an opposing party or law firm. This Section applies when a lawyer seeks to discuss the possibility of the lawyer's future employment with an adversary or an adversary's law firm. The conflict arises whether the discussions about future employment are initiated by the lawyer or by the other side. If discussion of employment has become concrete and the interest in such employment is mutual, the lawyer must promptly inform the client. Without effective client consent (see § 122), the lawyer must terminate all further discussions concerning the employment, or withdraw from representing the client (see § 32(2) & (3)). The same protocol is required with respect to a merger of law firms or similar change (see § 123).

Illustration:

4. Lawyer has been employed by Law Firm ABC for three years. For the last two of those years, Lawyer has worked on a case on behalf of Client against a company represented by Law Firm DEF. Lawyer decided to explore leaving Law Firm ABC. Lawyer wrote letters to 10 firms, including Law Firm DEF, to determine if they had any openings. Law Firm DEF indicated that it has an opening and encouraged Lawyer to come for an interview. This Section does not require Lawyer, at the time of sending the initial letters, to inform Client of the possible relationship to Law Firm DEF. However, when Firm DEF responded favorably, the possibility of employment became both concrete and mutual. At that point, Lawyer must promptly notify Client, fully inform Client of the nature and consequences of the conflict, and obtain Client's voluntary consent before continuing the representation.

e. A lawyer openly expressing public-policy views inconsistent with a client's position. In general, a lawyer may publicly take personal positions on controversial issues without regard to whether the positions are consistent with those of some or all of the lawyer's clients. Consent of the lawyer's clients is not required. Lawyers usually represent many clients, and professional detachment is one of the qualities a lawyer brings to each client. Moreover, it is a tradition that a lawyer's advocacy for a client should not be construed as an expression of the lawyer's personal views. Resolution of many public questions is benefited when independent legal minds are brought to bear on them. For example, if tax lawyers advocating positions about tax reform were obliged to advocate only positions that would serve the positions of their present clients, the public would lose the objective contributions to policy making of some persons most able to help.

However, a lawyer's right to freedom of expression is modified by the lawyer's duties to clients. Thus, a lawyer may not publicly take a policy position that is adverse to the position of a client that the lawyer is currently representing if doing so would materially and adversely affect the lawyer's representation of the client in the matter. The requirement that a lawyer not misuse a client's confidential information (see § 60) similarly applies to discussion of public issues. On the right of a lawyer to withdraw from a representation because of disagreement with a client's views, see § 32.

Illustrations:

5. Lawyer currently represents Client, a large mining company with mining operations in Lawyer's state. Lawyer's work for Client includes lobbying before government agencies concerning restoration of strip-mined land. Lawyer has also been a long-time member of Seed, an organization with an interest in preserving the environment. Seed has proposed legislation that would require mining companies to restore strip-mined land to a fertile condition, legislation that Lawyer's work for Client will require Lawyer to oppose. Unless Lawyer obtains Client's informed consent (see § 122), Lawyer may not personally take a public position supporting the legislation.

6. Lawyer represents Corporation in negotiating with the Internal Revenue Service to permit Corporation to employ accelerated depreciation methods for machinery purchased in a prior tax year. At the same time, Lawyer believes that the accelerated depreciation laws for manufacturing equipment reflect unwise public policy. Lawyer has been working with a bar-association committee to develop a policy statement against the allowance, and the committee chair has requested Lawyer to testify in favor of the report and its proposal to repeal all such depreciation allowances. Any new legislation, as is true generally of such tax enactments, would apply only for current and future tax years, thus not directly affecting Corporation's matter before the IRS. Although the proposed legislation would be against Corporation's economic interests, Lawyer may, without Corporation's consent, continue the representation of Corporation while working to repeal the allowance.

Whether a lawyer's interest in furthering the objectives of a client requires the lawyer to abstain from participating in professional forums is to be determined by the rules of those forums or the groups sponsoring them and is beyond the scope of the Restatement.

f. Initiation and settlement of class actions and other multiple-client representations. Class actions and similar proceedings can raise a number of personal-interest conflict-of-interest questions. A class action can transform a modest claim into a set of claims of large consequence and often has potential for magnifying attorney's fees. An individual plaintiff usually begins with a concern about an individual wrong, and prompt and complete redress of that wrong is often the client's goal. A class action might be the only practical means of vindicating the client interest. However, a class action can substitute a longer, more complex proceeding for one more beneficial for the client's individual interests. Where bringing a claim as a class action might materially and adversely affect the interests of the individual client, that possibility must be disclosed to that client. On the determination of client-lawyer relationships in class actions, see § 14, Comment *f*.

Settlement of a class action or similar suit can also create a conflict concerning the lawyer's fee. The defendant, for example, might offer to settle the matter for an amount or kind of relief that is relatively generous to the lawyer's client if the lawyer will agree to accept a low fee award. Conversely, the defendant might acquiesce in a generous award of attorney's fees in exchange for relatively modest relief for the client's substantive claim. The latter arrangement must be rejected by the class lawyer as subordinating the interests of the lawyer's client to the lawyer's own interest.

The lawyer should make reasonable effort to separate settlement of the substantive claim from determination of the amount of attorney's fees. Some decisions have attempted to effectuate that requirement by forbidding settlement discussions to address the fee that the lawyer is to receive. Some commentators have urged that a court refuse to approve a settlement unless award of reasonable attorney's fees is to be judicially determined rather than negotiated. Neither of those suggestions gives adequate effect to the interests of the client in all cases.

A more appropriate arrangement, where possible, is for the lawyer's fee to be negotiated initially by the client and lawyer at the outset of the relationship, it being understood and disclosed to the client that the ultimate award may be scrutinized by the opposing party and approved by the court (compare § 22, Comment *c*). On interpretation of agreements between client and lawyer concerning fee awards, see § 38,

Comment *f*. On aggregate settlement of claims involving multiple clients who are not class members, see § 128, Comment *d(i)*.

g. Effect of personal-interest conflicts of associated lawyers. The stated rule of the lawyer codes, followed in the Section and in § 123, is that personal-interest conflicts of a lawyer such as those described in this Section are imputed to affiliated lawyers. It may be appropriate not to impose any sanction if the personal-interest conflict was not known to the lawyer handling the matter and could not have been determined by use of a reasonable conflict-checking system. In addition, personal interests of a lawyer may be idiosyncratic or otherwise of such a kind that it is improbable that affiliated lawyers would be impaired in their representation of clients due to such interests. Consequently, one affiliated lawyer's personal interests that produce personal prohibition disable an affiliated lawyer from representing the same client only when there is a significant risk that the interests of the first lawyer would materially and adversely impair the second lawyer's representation. Whether such a risk exists requires examination of such facts as the magnitude of the interest of the personally prohibited lawyer, the extent to which pursuing the client's interests would threaten that interest, and the other circumstances that might indicate the described significant risk.

Illustration:

7. Lawyer A has a strong philosophical or political aversion to the objectives of Landlord, whom Lawyer B in the same firm represents in eviction proceedings. Lawyer A's feelings are sufficiently strong that they would disable Lawyer A from providing effective representation to Landlord. Lawyer A therefore may not represent Landlord under the rule of this Section (see Comment *c* hereto). So long as Lawyer A has no part in the representation and no supervisory or other control over Lawyer B, there is no adequate basis for concluding that Lawyer A's personal interests should preclude Lawyer B from the representation.

§ 126. Business Transactions Between a Lawyer and a Client

A lawyer may not participate in a business or financial transaction with a client, except a standard commercial transaction in which the lawyer does not render legal services, unless:

(1) the client has adequate information about the terms of the transaction and the risks presented by the lawyer's involvement in it;

(2) the terms and circumstances of the transaction are fair and reasonable to the client; and

(3) the client consents to the lawyer's role in the transaction under the limitations and conditions provided in § 122 after being encouraged, and given a reasonable opportunity, to seek independent legal advice concerning the transaction.

Comment:

a. Scope and cross-references. This Section is a specific application of the general prohibition of conflicts of interest in § 121. Conduct that violates this Section is presumed to cause the material and adverse effect on representation that creates a conflict of interest under § 121. Accordingly, additional conditions for consent to a conflict are required beyond those specified by § 122, in particular that the transaction be objectively fair and reasonable and that the client have opportunity to obtain independent counsel. In contrast to § 125, there is no requirement that business transactions addressed in this Section have any adverse effect on any aspect of the client's representation aside from the transaction itself.

The prohibition in this Section is imputed to affiliated lawyers pursuant to § 123. Imputation is not provided for under the ABA Model Rules of Professional Conduct (1983) but is provided for in several jurisdictions following the ABA Model Code of Professional Responsibility (1969), which this Section follows. In all jurisdictions, a lawyer who enters into a business transaction—other than a standard commercial transaction in which the lawyer does not render legal services—with a client of an affiliated lawyer without complying with this Section does so at the risk that the transaction is voidable by the client and subject to other appropriate remedies (see § 121, Comment *f*).

The requirements of this Section do not apply to ordinary client-lawyer fee agreements providing, for example, for hourly, lump-sum, or contingent fees. They do apply when a lawyer takes an interest in the client's business as payment of all or part of a legal fee. Other financial arrangements are examined in Chapter 3, including the reasonableness of legal fees (see § 34; see also § 135 (acting as officer or director of a client)). With respect to conflict-of-interest issues that arise out of transactions involving a client and a business in which a lawyer has an interest, see § 125, Comment *c*.

In any civil proceeding between a lawyer and a client or their successors, the lawyer has the burden of persuading the tribunal that requirements stated in this Section have been satisfied. In a disciplinary, criminal, or similar proceeding, the burden of persuasion rests on the prosecution (see § 5 (lawyer discipline)). In a discipline case, once proof has been introduced that the lawyer entered into a business transaction with a client, the burden of persuasion is on the lawyer to show that the transaction was fair and reasonable and that the client was adequately informed.

b. *Rationale.* A lawyer's legal skill and training, together with the relationship of trust that arises between client and lawyer, create the possibility of overreaching when a lawyer enters into a business transaction with a client. Furthermore, a lawyer who engages in a business transaction with a client is in a position to arrange the form of the transaction or give legal advice to protect the lawyer's interests rather than advancing the client's interests. Proving fraud or actual overreaching might be difficult. Hence, the law does not require such a showing on the part of a client.

Illustration:

1. Lawyer, Investor, and Developer agree to form a corporation for the purpose of developing a residential subdivision. At the time, Lawyer represents both Investor and Developer as clients in other matters. Stock allocations are to be based on the agreed value of Investor's contributed land, the value of Developer's design and development services, and the value of Lawyer's legal services in organizing the enterprise and representing it thereafter. The arrangement constitutes a business transaction with a client and is subject to the requirements of this Section throughout the period during which the parties continue the arrangement.

This Section applies only to transactions of a lawyer with a client of the lawyer or of the lawyer's firm (see § 123). Transactions of a lawyer with a nonclient are not covered. While this Section does not apply to a lawyer's transaction with a former client, such a transaction is subject to challenge if the lawyer takes advantage of the lawyer's former position (see Restatement Second, Trusts § 170, Comment *g*).

c. *Standard commercial transactions.* The requirements of informed consent and objective fairness are satisfied when lawyer and client enter into standard commercial transactions in the regular course of business of the client, involving a product or service as to which the lawyer provides no legal services. This Section therefore does not apply to such transactions. Standard commercial transactions are those regularly entered into between the client and the general public, typically in which the terms and conditions are the same for all customers. In such circumstances, the client's interests in the transaction with the lawyer need no special protection. On the other hand, where a lawyer engages in the sale of goods or services ancillary to the practice of law, for example, the sale of title insurance, the requirements of this Section do apply.

d. *A client's knowledge of the terms and the lawyer's role.* A lawyer violates the standard of candor by entering into a transaction with a client as undisclosed principal, or without disclosing information or terms that might materially affect the client's bargain (see Restatement Second, Trusts § 170(2)).

Illustrations:

2. Lawyer represents the surviving Spouse of a long-time client. Lawyer advises Spouse that farmland owned by the estate should be sold to pay taxes. Using the name of a business associate as purported buyer, Lawyer purchases the land from Spouse without disclosing Lawyer's involvement in the purchase. Even if the price is objectively fair, Lawyer has violated the requirement that Lawyer's identity be disclosed to the client.

3. Lawyer has been helping Client negotiate the terms for the purchase of a boat. Client has experienced difficulties arranging financing and will lose a substantial deposit on the boat if Client cannot raise $30,000 by the end of the day. Lawyer has $30,000 in available cash. Lawyer agrees to lend the money to Client and, without explaining the agreement, has Client sign a security agreement

in favor of Lawyer in properties owned by Client. When Client defaults on the loan, Lawyer files suit against Client to foreclose on the properties. Lawyer has violated this Section by failing to explain to Client the terms of the transaction. Client can, for example, rescind the transaction and prevent the foreclosure (see § 121, Comment *f*).

e. The requirement that the terms of the transaction be fair. The requirement that the transaction be fair from the perspective of an objective observer derives from the general fiduciary requirement of fair dealing with a client (see § 16(3); Restatement Second, Trusts § 170(2) & Comment *w* thereto). Unintended overreaching is a possibility in transactions involving lawyers and their clients. Accordingly a lawyer must overcome a presumption that overreaching occurred by demonstrating the fairness of the transaction. Fairness is determined based on facts that reasonably could be known at the time of the transaction, not as the facts later develop. The relative ability of lawyer and client to foresee how the facts might develop, however, is relevant in determining fairness. An appropriate test is whether a disinterested lawyer would have advised the client not to enter the transaction with some other party.

Illustration:

4. Lawyer and Client agree to purchase a parcel of land together. Because Client lacks sufficient cash, Client borrows the money from Lawyer at an interest rate of 10 percent. That was the general market rate of interest on the date of the loan, but Lawyer knew from discussions with another client, Banker, that Client would be able to borrow the same amount from several financial institutions at a lower rate of interest. Lawyer violated Lawyer's obligations to deal fairly with Client. Lawyer had reliable information, relevant to a material element of the transaction, that Lawyer failed to convey to Client.

f. Consent only after encouragement and opportunity to obtain independent legal advice. The client must be encouraged and have a reasonable opportunity to obtain independent legal advice before entering into the transaction. There is no requirement that the client actually consult another lawyer. A client might determine to consult another trusted adviser, such as an accountant, a tax adviser, or a business person, or to consult no one at all.

An opportunity to obtain competent independent advice tends to assure that the client has time to consider the transaction and that the lawyer is not applying undue pressure on the client. By the same token, evidence that a lawyer has not allowed the client opportunity to obtain independent counsel is evidence of overreaching. An independent adviser also can bring an objective eye to the proposed arrangement.

Illustration:

5. Lawyer helped negotiate for Client a sale of Client's family business for $1 million. Client, who was inexperienced in business or investments, asked Lawyer for help in investing the proceeds. Lawyer offered to borrow the money from Client at an interest rate of 15 percent. Lawyer prepared and signed a note evidencing the loan. Lawyer afforded Client no encouragement or opportunity to obtain independent advice before entering into the transaction. Lawyer has violated this Section.

g. The requirement of written notice and consent. Lawyer codes commonly require that notice to the client and the client's consent to a business transaction with the client's lawyer be in writing. When required by law, disclosure to the client of the terms of the transaction must also be in writing. Absence of the required writing renders the transaction voidable at the client's option. Written notice focuses the client's attention upon the right to withhold consent and has important evidentiary value if a dispute later arises concerning the client's consent. The notice should provide the client sufficient time to enable the client to study the transaction and obtain independent advice.

§ 127. A Client Gift to a Lawyer

(1) A lawyer may not prepare any instrument effecting any gift from a client to the lawyer, including a testamentary gift, unless the lawyer is a relative or other natural object of the client's generosity and the gift is not significantly disproportionate to those given other donees similarly related to the donor.

(2) A lawyer may not accept a gift from a client, including a testamentary gift, unless:

(a) the lawyer is a relative or other natural object of the client's generosity;

(b) the value conferred by the client and the benefit to the lawyer are insubstantial in amount; or

(c) the client, before making the gift, has received independent advice or has been encouraged, and given a reasonable opportunity, to seek such advice.

Comment:

a. Scope and cross-references. This Section is a specific application of the general prohibition of conflicts of interest in § 121. The conduct defined in this Section is presumed to have a material and adverse effect on the client. Consent under § 122 is ineffective if the lawyer's conduct violates this Section. The prohibition set forth in this Section is imputed to affiliated lawyers pursuant to § 123. That is, a lawyer may not receive a gift from a client of an affiliated lawyer (see § 123) in circumstances inconsistent with the standards in this Section.

Sanctions for violation of this rule include those in § 121, Comment *f*. A client can rescind a gift to the client's lawyer, for example, and a testamentary gift can be set aside as the product of undue influence. The lawyer might also be subject to the sanctions of professional discipline (see § 5) and fee forfeiture (see § 37).

The law of undue influence treats client gifts as presumptively fraudulent, so that the lawyer-donee bears a heavy burden of persuasion that the gift is fair and not the product of overreaching or otherwise an imposition upon the client. See Restatement Second, Trusts § 343, Comments *l* and *m* (voidability of gifts from beneficiary to trustee); cf. Restatement Second, Contracts § 177 (contracts voidable on ground of undue influence). This Section assumes, but does not restate fully, the law of undue influence. The Section is stricter than the general law of undue influence in some jurisdictions. For example, the Section prohibits a lawyer from accepting a gift from a client (apart from the three stated exceptions) even if the lawyer has not engaged in undue influence.

b. Rationale. A client's valuable gift to a lawyer invites suspicion that the lawyer overreached or used undue influence. It would be difficult to reach any other conclusion when a lawyer has solicited the gift. Testamentary gifts are a subject of particular concern, both because the client is often of advanced age at the time the will is written and because it will often be difficult to establish the client's true intentions after the client's death. At the same time, the client-lawyer relationship in which a gift is made is often extended and personal. A genuine feeling of gratitude and admiration can motivate a client to confer a gift on the lawyer. The rule of this Section respects such genuine wishes while guarding against overreaching by lawyers.

c. Gifts subject to this Section. For the purposes of this Section, a gift is any transfer by the client to the lawyer of a thing of value made without consideration (compare § 126). A client's gift to a member of the lawyer's family, or to a person or institution designated by the lawyer, is treated as a gift to the lawyer if it was made under circumstances manifesting an intent to evade the rule of this Section.

d. Solicitation of a client gift. Even with respect to a gift not otherwise in violation of the lawyer's duty to the client under Subsection (2), a lawyer may not improperly induce the gift to the lawyer or to a spouse, child, or similar beneficiary of the lawyer (see generally Restatement Second, Property (Donative Transfers) 34.7). Even bargain exchanges between lawyer and client are subject to a high level of scrutiny (see § 126, Comment *b*); it follows that gratuitous transfers conferring benefits on the lawyer are at least as subject to scrutiny. Accordingly, a client may void the client's gift to a lawyer or to the lawyer's beneficiary, unless the lawyer can demonstrate that the gift was not improperly induced by undue influence or otherwise. A lawyer's suggestion that a client make a gift to a charity favored by a lawyer would not ordinarily be improper, so long as the lawyer informs the client that the lawyer favors the charity and employs no improper means such as misrepresentation or other means of overreaching. A lawyer's suggestion to a client that the client employ the lawyer's services in the future does not constitute the solicitation of a gift.

e. A lawyer as a relative or other natural object of a client-donor's generosity. The general prohibition against a lawyer's receipt of a gift from a client is subject to exception when the lawyer is so related to the client that the gift should not cause suspicion (Subsection (2)(a)). Thus, a client-parent's gift to a lawyer-child is permissible. Such gifts are permissible even in the absence of independent legal advice (compare

Subsection (2)(c)). In many families, one of whose members is a lawyer, it would be thought unusual for a family member to go outside the family for legal advice, for example, to write a will or create a trust for a family member. That the lawyer receives a gift under such a will or trust would, in context, ordinarily not indicate overreaching. However, if the lawyer receives significantly more benefit from a donative transfer of the family-member client than others in the family who are similarly related to the client, in the event of a challenge the lawyer bears the burden of persuading the tribunal that the gift was not the product of overreaching.

Illustration:

1. Lawyer is one of Mother's five children. At Mother's instruction, Lawyer prepares her will leaving one-fifth of the estate to each of the children, including Lawyer. Lawyer's preparation of such an instrument is within the exceptions in § 127(2). However, if Lawyer received one-third of the estate, and the other four children each received one-sixth, in the event of a challenge, Lawyer would be required to persuade the tribunal that Lawyer did not overreach Mother.

f. *Substantial gifts.* In determining whether a gift to a lawyer is substantial within the meaning of Subsection (2)(b), the means of both the lawyer and the client must be considered. To a poor client, a gift of $100 might be substantial, suggesting that such an extraordinary act was the result of the lawyer's overreaching. To a wealthy client, a gift of $1,000 might seem insubstantial in relation to the client's assets, but if substantial in relation to the lawyer's assets, it suggests a motivation on the part of the lawyer to overreach the client-donor, or at least not to have fully advised the client of the client's rights and interests. Under either set of circumstances, the lawyer violates the client's rights by accepting such a gift.

Illustration:

2. Client, who has a longstanding professional relationship with Lawyer, presents Lawyer with an antique locket, with a market value of under $50, that had belonged to Client's deceased sister. "My sister always wanted to be a lawyer," Client says to Lawyer, "but that was difficult in her generation. I like to think she would have been as good a lawyer as you now are, and I think she would like you to have this." Lawyer may accept the Client's gift.

g. *The effect of the client's opportunity to obtain independent advice.* When a competent and independent person other than the lawyer-donee acts as the client's adviser with respect to a particular gift, there is less reason to be concerned with overreaching by the lawyer. A lawyer's encouragement to a client to seek independent advice also evidences concern for fairness on the lawyer's part. Whether the lawyer may prepare an instrument effecting the gift from the client to the lawyer is determined by Subsection (1), under which independent advice is irrelevant. If the lawyer does not prepare such an instrument, the lawyer is not precluded from receiving a gift subject to the limitations of Subsection (2)(c), including that of independent advice. Such a gift also remains subject to invalidation if the circumstances warrant under the law of fraud, duress, undue influence, or mistake (see Restatement Second, Trusts § 141 & § 343, Comments *l* & *m*).

Illustrations:

3. Client has come to Lawyer for preparation of Client's will. "I do not have living relatives and you have been my trusted friend and adviser for most of my adult life," Client tells Lawyer. "I want you to have a bequest of $50,000 from my estate." Lawyer urges Client to ask another lawyer to advise Client about such a gift and prepare any will effecting it. Client refuses, saying "I do not want anyone else to know my business." Lawyer may not draft Client's will containing the proposed gift to Lawyer.

4. The same facts as in Illustration 3, except that Client, professing the same wish to benefit Lawyer, tells Lawyer that Client is going to make a $50,000 cash gift to Lawyer. Lawyer encourages and gives Client a reasonable opportunity to seek independent advice about making a gift to Lawyer. Client does not do so. Lawyer may accept the inter vivos gift of $50,000 from Client, so long as Lawyer did not solicit the gift or prepare an instrument effecting the gift from Client.

5. On behalf of Client, a corporation assisted in the matter by Inside Legal Counsel, Lawyer has obtained satisfaction of a judgment in an amount significantly surpassing what Client and Inside Legal Counsel thought possible. Lawyer receives payment of Lawyer's final statement with a covering letter from Inside Legal Counsel stating that Client, on the recommendation of Inside Legal Counsel,

was also enclosing an additional check in a substantial amount in gratitude for the outstanding result obtained by Lawyer. Lawyer may accept the gift of the additional check, reasonably assuming that Client has been appropriately advised in the matter by Inside Legal Counsel.

The recommendation of independent advice must be more than perfunctory. The independent adviser may not be affiliated with the lawyer-donee. It is not necessary that the person consulted as adviser be a lawyer. Any person qualifies who is mature and appropriately experienced in personal financial matters, trusted by the client, not a beneficiary of the gift, and not selected by or affiliated with the lawyer.

A lawyer-donee bears the burden of showing that reasonable effort was made to persuade the client to obtain independent advice and that the lawyer did not otherwise unduly influence or overreach the client. If the lawyer-donee has tried but failed to persuade the client to seek such help, or if the client rejects the independent adviser's counsel, the presumption of overreaching can be overcome and the gift upheld.

TOPIC 3. CONFLICTS OF INTEREST AMONG CURRENT CLIENTS

§ 128. Representing Clients with Conflicting Interests in Civil Litigation

Unless all affected clients consent to the representation under the limitations and conditions provided in § 122, a lawyer in civil litigation may not:

(1) represent two or more clients in a matter if there is a substantial risk that the lawyer's representation of one client would be materially and adversely affected by the lawyer's duties to another client in the matter; or

(2) represent one client to assert or defend a claim against or brought by another client currently represented by the lawyer, even if the matters are not related.

Comment:

a. Scope and cross-references. This Section applies the general conflicts standard in § 121 to situations in which a lawyer represents two or more parties in civil litigation. On identifying who is the lawyer's client within the meaning of this rule, see § 121, Comment *d.* Conflicts under this Section are subject to consent under the limitations and conditions provided in § 122. The conflicts are imputed to affiliated lawyers by § 123, and the imputation can be removed as described in § 124. On limiting conflicts of interest in the case of a prospective client, see § 15.

Multiple representation in criminal litigation is considered in § 129 and, in matters not involving litigation, in § 130. Conflicts arising when a lawyer represents both an entity and one or more of its officers, employees, or other associated persons are considered in § 131. Conflicts in filing and settling class actions are examined in § 125, as well as in this Section.

Remedies for violation of this Section include those set forth in § 121, Comment *f.* The most common remedy is the lawyer's disqualification from further representation of one or more clients in a matter (see § 6, Comment *i*). A suit for professional malpractice is available if a client has suffered damage as a result of a lawyer's conflict of interest (see § 48 and following). In appropriate cases, the lawyer is also subject to professional discipline (see § 5) or fee forfeiture (see § 37).

b. Rationale. Dealing with a conflict of interest among current clients requires reconciling four fundamental and sometimes competing values. First, confidential information of one client must not be used, intentionally or inadvertently, on behalf of another client in ways that would have material and adverse consequences for the disadvantaged client. Although such use violates the requirement of § 60(1), the fact of use will often be difficult to detect and therefore requires preventive measures. Second, the client's faith in the lawyer's loyalty to the client's interests will be severely tried whenever the lawyer must be loyal to another client whose interests are materially adverse. Third, a tribunal properly wishes assurance that its own processes not be compromised by less than vigorous advocacy, delayed by a necessary change of counsel in the course of the proceeding, or later reversed because a litigant was inadequately represented. Even if the parties would give informed consent to being represented by one lawyer, in some cases the parties' positions cannot be effectively presented through the same advocate (see § 122(2)(b) & Comment *g(iii)* thereto). Fourth, clients might want to reduce the costs of litigation and achieve the benefits of a coordinated position in their cases. Clients normally are allowed to give informed consent to a representation that otherwise would violate this Section.

c(i). Clients aligned in opposition to each other—in general. Fundamental conflicts of loyalty and threats to client confidentiality would be inevitable if a lawyer were to represent clients opposing each other in the same litigation. Many actions that the lawyer took on behalf of one client would have the potential for being at the expense of the other. Furthermore, the public interest in the orderly management of litigation could be seriously compromised. Thus, the same lawyer may not represent both plaintiff and defendant in a breach-of-contract lawsuit, for example. A similar rule applies, as stated in Subsection (2), when the clients are involved in two or more lawsuits that are otherwise unrelated. The rule of Subsection (2) applies without regard to the specific inquiries relevant in assessing a conflict under Subsection (1). See Comment *e* hereto.

c(ii). Opposing clients in multiparty litigation. Certain types of civil proceedings may involve multiple parties and disputes, such as bankruptcy cases and proceedings involving environmental liability for alleged polluted conditions. In general, in all multiparty situations the lawyer must comply with Subsection (1) and § 121 generally, both before and after the filing of a formal proceeding.

With respect to bankruptcy, there is substantial disagreement whether certain types of cases or proceedings should be considered under the automatic rule of Subsection (2) or under the general rule of § 121 and, in general, whether general conflict-of-interest rules should be changed in some instances. Tribunals must resolve such questions in light of a body of decisions developed in the specific context of bankruptcy, and often the issues are controlled by statute. The Restatement takes no position on the applicability of Subsection (2) in the many situations that may arise in bankruptcy.

d. Clients nominally aligned on the same side in the litigation. Multiple representation is precluded when the clients, although nominally on the same side of a lawsuit, in fact have such different interests that representation of one will have a material and adverse effect on the lawyer's representation of the other. Such conflicts can occur whether the clients are aligned as co-plaintiffs or co-defendants, as well as in complex and multiparty litigation.

d(i). Clients aligned as co-plaintiffs. No conflict of interest is ordinarily presented when two or more of a lawyer's clients assert claims against a defendant. However, sometimes two parties aligned on the same side of a case as co-claimants might wish to characterize the facts differently. The client-claimants might also have a potential lawsuit against each other. For example, a passenger in an automobile damage action might be a co-plaintiff with the driver of the car in a suit alleging negligence of the driver of the other car, but also be able to contend that the driver of the passenger's car was negligent as well, a conclusion that the driver would be motivated to deny. Where there are such possible claims, the lawyer must warn clients about the possibilities of such differences and obtain the consent of each before agreeing to represent them as co-claimants (see § 122).

When multiple claimants assert claims against a defendant who lacks sufficient assets to meet all of the damage claims, a conflict of interest might also be presented. Indeed, whether or not the defendant has assets sufficient to pay all claims, a proposed settlement might create conflicts because the plaintiffs differ in their willingness to accept the settlement. Before any settlement is accepted on behalf of multiple clients, their lawyer must inform each of them about all of the terms of the settlement, including the amounts that each of the other claimants will receive if the settlement is accepted. A similar conflict of interest can arise for a lawyer representing multiple defending parties.

Illustrations:

1. Lawyer represents A and B, pedestrians struck by an automobile as they stood at a street corner. Each has sued C, the owner-driver, for $150,000. C has $100,000 in liability insurance coverage and no other assets with which to satisfy a judgment. Neither A nor B can be paid the full amount of their claims and any sum recovered by one will reduce the assets available to pay the other's claim. Because of the conflict of interest, Lawyer can continue to represent both A and B only with the informed consent of each (see § 122).

2. The same facts as in Illustration 1, except that C offers to settle A's claim for $60,000 and B's claim for $40,000. Lawyer must inform both A and B of all of the terms of the proposed settlement, including the amounts offered to each client. If one client wishes to accept and the other wishes to

reject the proposed settlement, Lawyer may continue to represent both A and B only after a renewal of informed consent by each.

d(ii). Clients aligned as co-defendants in civil case. Clients aligned as co-defendants also can have conflicting interests. Each would usually prefer to see the plaintiff defeated altogether, but if the plaintiff succeeds, each will often prefer to see liability deflected mainly or entirely upon other defendants. Indeed, a plaintiff often sues multiple defendants in the hope that each of the defendants will take the position that another of them is responsible, thus enhancing the likelihood of the plaintiff's recovering. Such conflicts preclude joint representation, absent each co-defendant's informed consent (see § 122).

A contract between the parties can eliminate the conflict. When an employee injures someone in an incident arising out of the employment, for example, an employer that is capable of paying the judgment might agree in advance to hold the employee harmless in the matter so that only the employer will bear any judgment ultimately entered. If only one of the parties will ultimately be liable to the plaintiff, there is little reason to incur the expense of separate counsel. However, the initial conflict must be understood by both defendants and each must consent, particularly if the clients must negotiate an agreement governing who will bear ultimate liability (see § 130).

d(iii). Complex and multiparty litigation. Not all possibly differing interests of co-clients in complex and multiparty litigation involve material interests creating conflict. Determination whether a conflict of material interests exists requires careful attention to the context and other circumstances of the representation and in general should be based on whether (1) issues common to the clients' interests predominate, (2) circumstances such as the size of each client's interest make separate representation impracticable, and (3) the extent of active judicial supervision of the representation. For example, a lawyer might represent several unsecured creditors in a bankruptcy proceeding. In addition to general conflict-of-interest rules that may apply, a lawyer representing such multiple clients must also comply with statutory regulations if more stringent.

Similar considerations apply in representing multiple co-parties in class-action proceedings, due to the possible existence of different objectives or other interests of class members (see also § 125 on creation and settlement of class actions). A plaintiff class might agree, for example, that the local school system discriminates against a racial or ethnic minority, but there might be important differences within the class over what remedy is appropriate (see § 14, Comment *f*). As one possible corrective, under procedural law a class may be subdivided. Through that process objecting members of the class may be heard. However, such differences within the class do not necessarily produce conflicts requiring that the lawyer for the class not represent some or all members of the class or necessitate creation of subclasses. The tasks of a lawyer for a class may include monitoring and mediating such differences. In instances of intractable difference, the lawyer may proceed in what the lawyer reasonably concludes to be the best interests of the class as a whole, for example urging the tribunal to accept an appropriate settlement even if it is not accepted by class representatives or members of the class. In such instances, of course, the lawyer must inform the tribunal of the differing views within the class or on the part of a class representative.

e. Suing a present client in an unrelated matter. A lawyer's representation of Client A might require the lawyer to file a lawsuit against Client B whom the lawyer represents in an unrelated matter. Because the matters are unrelated, no confidential information is likely to be used improperly, nor will the lawyer take both sides in a single proceeding. However, the lawyer has a duty of loyalty to the client being sued. Moreover, the client on whose behalf suit is filed might fear that the lawyer would pursue that client's case less effectively out of deference to the other client. Thus, a lawyer may not sue a current client on behalf of another client, even in an unrelated matter, unless consent is obtained under the conditions and limitations of § 122. On identifying who is a present client, see § 14 and § 121, Comment *d*. On the possibility of informed consent in advance to such suits in certain cases, see § 122, Comment *d*.

Illustrations:

3. Lawyer represents Client B in seeking a tax refund. Client A wishes to file suit against Client B in a contract action unrelated to the tax claim. Lawyer may not represent Client A in the suit against Client B as long as Lawyer represents Client B in the tax case, unless both clients give informed consent. On withdrawal, see § 121, Comment *e*.

4. The same facts as in Illustration 3, except that Client A's contract action is against corporation C, which is not Lawyer's client. After A's suit has been filed, C is acquired by and merged into Lawyer's client B, thus creating the conflict. Unauthorized use of confidential information would not be an issue in such a case, and any remedy imposed by a tribunal should minimize adverse impact on the parties. Because the action of B created the conflict, Lawyer might be permitted to withdraw from pursuing the tax claim on behalf of B, for example, but continue to pursue the contract action. Compare the discussion at § 132, Comment *e*.

f. *Concurrently taking adverse legal positions on behalf of different clients.* A lawyer ordinarily may take inconsistent legal positions in different courts at different times. While each client is entitled to the lawyer's effective advocacy of that client's position, if the rule were otherwise law firms would have to specialize in a single side of legal issues.

However, a conflict is presented when there is a substantial risk that a lawyer's action in Case A will materially and adversely affect another of the lawyer's clients in Case B. Factors relevant in determining the risk of such an effect include whether the issue is before a trial court or an appellate court; whether the issue is substantive or procedural; the temporal relationship between the matters; the practical significance of the issue to the immediate and long-run interests of the clients involved; and the clients' reasonable expectations in retaining the lawyer. If a conflict of interest exists, absent informed consent of the affected clients under § 122, the lawyer must withdraw from one or both of the matters. Informed client consent is provided for in § 122. On circumstances in which informed client consent would not allow the lawyer to proceed with representation of both clients, see § 122(2)(c) and Comment *g(iv)* thereto.

Illustrations:

5. Lawyer represents two clients in damage actions pending in different United States District Courts. In one case, representing the plaintiff, Lawyer will attempt to introduce certain evidence at trial and argue there for its admissibility. In the other case, representing a defendant, Lawyer will object to an anticipated attempt by the plaintiff to introduce similar evidence. Even if there is some possibility that one court's ruling might be published and cited as authority in the other proceeding, Lawyer may proceed with both representations without obtaining the consent of the clients involved.

6. The same facts as in Illustration 5, except that the cases have proceeded to the point where certiorari has been granted in each by the United States Supreme Court to consider the common evidentiary question. Any position that Lawyer would assert on behalf of either client on the legal issue common to each case would have a material and adverse impact on the interests of the other client. Thus, a conflict of interest is presented. Even the informed consent of both Client A and Client B would be insufficient to permit Lawyer to represent each before the Supreme Court.

§ 129. Conflicts of Interest in Criminal Litigation

Unless all affected clients consent to the representation under the limitations and conditions provided in § 122, a lawyer in a criminal matter may not represent:

(1) two or more defendants or potential defendants in the same matter; or

(2) a single defendant, if the representation would involve a conflict of interest as defined in § 121.

Comment:

a. *Scope and cross-references.* This Section addresses the analogues in criminal litigation to the issues raised in § 128. The Section is a specific application of the conflicts standard expressed in § 121, as interpreted and applied in light of the constitutional issues that arise in criminal cases. It is subject to consent under the limitations and conditions provided in § 122. See Comment *c* hereto. The conflict is imputed to affiliated lawyers under § 123, an imputation that can be removed as described in § 124.

Section 131 considers conflicts arising when a criminal-defense lawyer represents both an organization and employees or other persons associated with the organization. Conflicts arising from duties that a criminal-defense lawyer owes to a former client are examined in § 132. Conflict issues arising from third-person payment of a criminal-defense lawyer's fee are considered in § 134. Conflicts of a prosecuting attorney are analyzed in § 135. A lawyer's obligation to preserve the confidential information of a client is discussed in § 60 and other Sections in Chapter 5.

The remedies for conflicts of interest (see § 121, Comment *f*) available in a civil case (see § 128) are also generally available in a criminal case. In addition, courts sometimes exercise judicial supervisory power to disqualify lawyers for prophylactic reasons in instances in which the lawyer is otherwise permissibly representing multiple clients. A lawyer's ability to obtain effective consents (see § 122(2)) to conflicts in criminal representations is, to that extent, less than in comparable civil cases.

b. Rationale. The rules in this Section, like those examined in § 128, seek to protect confidential client information, enhance clients' sense of lawyers' loyalty, assist a court's effort to assure fairness and the finality of results, and minimize the cost of legal assistance for clients. In addition, criminal litigation is governed by constitutional protections not applicable in civil litigation. The Sixth Amendment, for example, guarantees that "In all criminal prosecutions, the accused shall enjoy the right . . . to have the Assistance of Counsel for his defense." That guarantee and its implied right to the effective assistance of counsel impose special constraints on the representation of multiple clients in criminal matters. However, the same guarantee cautions that a tribunal not disturb a fully informed selection of counsel absent compelling circumstances.

This Section applies to all stages of the criminal-justice process from initial investigation, whether or not before a grand jury, through final appeal. In some situations, rules stated in other Sections can also apply because of parallel administrative or other civil proceedings. Whether or not a conflict is presented in any given stage of the process depends in part on what the lawyer has undertaken to do in that particular stage. A lawyer for two or more targets of a grand-jury investigation might be able to represent them jointly, for example, if there were little risk of abuse of confidential information or breach of the duty of loyalty while awaiting the decision of the grand jury whether to indict. On the other hand, if plea negotiations allow the possibility of testimony on behalf of the government, joint representation without informed consent ordinarily would be improper (see Comment *c* hereto).

c. Multiple criminal-defense representations. Subsection (1) recognizes that the representation of co-defendants in criminal cases involves at least the potential for conflicts of interest. For example, if one defendant is offered favorable treatment in return for testimony against a co-defendant, a single lawyer could not give advice favorable to one defendant's interests while adhering to the duty of loyalty to the other. Similarly, individual defendants might have had different motives for and understandings of events, so that establishing a common position among them is difficult. Witnesses who would be favorable to one defendant might be subject to cross-examination that would be unfavorable to another defendant. In closing argument, counsel must choose which facts to stress. For example, stressing the minor role of one defendant might imply the major role of another.

Because of such potential conflicts and the constitutional significance of the issues they raise, joint representation in criminal cases often has a material and adverse effect on the representation of each defendant and thus cannot be undertaken in the absence of client consent under the limitations and conditions stated in § 122.

Criminal defendants might nonetheless consider it in their interest to be represented by a single lawyer even when the financial cost of separate counsel is not a factor. A single lawyer can help assure a common position and increase the likelihood that none of the co-defendants will cooperate with the prosecution against the others. For such reasons, a criminal conviction involving joint representation ordinarily is not impeachable absent a showing of timely objection and actual prejudice. Were the rule otherwise, defendants could avoid raising a conflict issue before trial so as to create an issue for later appeal.

On the other hand, both the prosecutor and the trial judge have a responsibility to assure a fair trial for each defendant. When a defense lawyer would be required to assume an adverse position with respect to one or more of the clients, the conflict is nonconsentable (see § 122(2)(b) & Comment *g(iii)* thereto). Efficient operation of the judicial system requires that a verdict not be vulnerable to contentions that a defendant was disadvantaged by an undisclosed conflict of interest. A prosecutor might object to joint-representation arrangements to assure that a conflict possibility is resolved before trial. Even without objection by the prosecutor or defendant, the tribunal may raise the issue on its own initiative and refuse to permit joint representation where there is a significant threat to the interest in the finality of judgments.

Illustrations:

1. A and B are co-defendants charged with a felony offense of armed robbery. They are both represented by Lawyer. The prosecutor believes that A planned the crime and was the only one carrying a weapon. The prosecutor offers to accept B's plea of guilty to a misdemeanor if B will testify against A. Lawyer's loyalty to A causes Lawyer to persuade B that the prosecutor's proposal should be rejected. Following a trial, both A and B are convicted of the felony. When plea negotiations involving B's separate interests began, B should have received independent counsel. In the circumstances, Lawyer could not properly represent A and B even with the informed consent of both clients (see § 122, Comment *g(iii))*.

2. The same facts as in Illustration 1, except that the evidence at trial is highly damaging to Defendant A but less so to Defendant B. Both defendants were represented by Lawyer, who did not consult with A and B concerning their conflicting interests. Lawyer spent most of the closing argument explaining away A's guilt and did not mention the weak case against B, because doing so would invite the jury to consider the greater likelihood of A's guilt. Lawyer could represent B only with the informed consent of B (see § 122).

d. A criminal-defense lawyer with conflicting duties to other clients. As required in Subsection (2), a conflict exists when a defense lawyer in a criminal matter has duties to clients in other matters that might conflict. A conflict exists, for example, if the lawyer also represents either a prosecutor or a prosecution witness in an unrelated matter. The conflict could lead the lawyer to be less vigorous in defending the criminal case in order to avoid offending the other client, or the lawyer might be constrained in cross-examining the other client (see § 60(1)). A lawyer who represents a criminal defendant may not represent the state in unrelated civil matters when such representation would have a material and adverse effect on the lawyer's handling of the criminal case.

Ordinarily, these conflicts may be waived by client consent under the limitations and conditions in § 122. Because the defendant's constitutional rights are implicated, court procedures often require that consent be made part of the formal record in the criminal case (see Comment *c* hereto).

§ 130. Multiple Representation in Nonlitigated Matter

Unless all affected clients consent to the representation under the limitations and conditions provided in § 122, a lawyer may not represent two or more clients in a matter not involving litigation if there is a substantial risk that the lawyer's representation of one or more of the clients would be materially and adversely affected by the lawyer's duties to one or more of the other clients.

Comment:

a. Scope and cross-references. This Section is a specific application of the general conflicts standard expressed in § 121. Whereas §§ 128 and 129 consider conflicts of interest among current clients in litigation, this Section addresses situations not involving litigation. Representation can progress from one setting to the other or otherwise involve more than one setting, thus making relevant more than one Section. The conflicts identified in this Section are subject to consent under the limitations and conditions provided in § 122. The conflicts are imputed to affiliated lawyers by § 123, and the imputation can be removed as described in § 124. Identification of the lawyer's clients is addressed in § 14 and § 121, Comment *d*.

The conflicts considered in this Section generally arise in two contexts. The multiple clients might seek the lawyer's assistance on achieving a common goal, such as forming a corporation, recognizing that they have common interests with respect to major elements of the relationship but also interests concerning which there might be differences and potential for conflict. Second, multiple clients might seek the lawyer's assistance to resolve a recognized area of difference, such as the settlement outside litigation of a business dispute. The latter conflicts include those considered under the heading of "intermediation" in ABA Model Rules of Professional Conduct, Rule 2.2 (1983). Although its terminology might be thought to imply otherwise, Rule 2.2 addresses a particular setting for applying the general rules governing conflicts. "Intermediation" is a term that has not passed into general professional usage and is not employed here.

Clients represented by the lawyer under the terms of this Section are "co-clients"; the communications of each with the lawyer are not privileged from disclosure to the other co-clients unless the co-clients have agreed otherwise (see § 75). On confidentiality in co-client representations, see § 60, Comment *l*. Counseling clients is considered generally in § 94.

Remedies for a violation of this Section include those set forth for conflicts generally in § 121, Comment *f*. Ordinarily, a remedy for a violation of this Section causing actionable damage to a client is a suit for professional malpractice (see § 48 and following). In appropriate cases, the lawyer is subject to professional discipline (see § 5) or fee forfeiture (see § 37).

b. *Rationale.* As in litigated cases, multiple representation not involving litigation requires a lawyer to remain loyal to clients and protect their confidential information (see § 60(1)). Providing economical legal services is also a relevant concern (see § 128 & § 129, Comment *b*). The orderly administration of tribunals is, by definition, not a relevant factor for the issues in this Section.

Whether a lawyer can function in a situation of conflict (see § 121) depends on whether the conflict is consentable (see § 122(2)), which in turn depends on whether it is "reasonably likely that the lawyer will be able to provide adequate representation" to all affected clients (see § 122(2)). Conflicted but unconsented representation of multiple clients, for example of the buyer and seller of property, is sometimes defended with the argument that the lawyer was performing the role of mere "scrivener" or a similarly mechanical role. The characterization is usually inappropriate. A lawyer must accept responsibility to give customary advice and customary range of legal services, unless the clients have given their informed consent to a narrower range of the lawyer's responsibilities. On limitations of a lawyer's responsibilities, see § 19(1).

c. *Assisting multiple clients with common objectives, but conflicting interests.* When multiple clients have generally common interests, the role of the lawyer is to advise on relevant legal considerations, suggest alternative ways of meeting common objectives, and draft instruments necessary to accomplish the desired results. Multiple representations do not always present a conflict of interest requiring client consent (see § 121). For example, in representing spouses jointly in the purchase of property as co-owners, the lawyer would reasonably assume that such a representation does not involve a conflict of interest. A conflict could be involved, however, if the lawyer knew that one spouse's objectives in the acquisition were materially at variance with those of the other spouse.

Illustrations:

1. Husband and Wife consult Lawyer for estate-planning advice about a will for each of them. Lawyer has had professional dealings with the spouses, both separately and together, on several prior occasions. Lawyer knows them to be knowledgeable about their respective rights and interests, competent to make independent decisions if called for, and in accord on their common and individual objectives. Lawyer may represent both clients in the matter without obtaining consent (see § 121). While each spouse theoretically could make a distribution different from the other's, including a less generous bequest to each other, those possibilities do not create a conflict of interest, and none reasonably appears to exist in the circumstances.

2. The same facts as in Illustration 1, except that Lawyer has not previously met the spouses. Spouse A does most of the talking in the initial discussions with Lawyer. Spouse B, who owns significantly more property than Spouse A, appears to disagree with important positions of Spouse A but to be uncomfortable in expressing that disagreement and does not pursue them when Spouse A appears impatient and peremptory. Representation of both spouses would involve a conflict of interest. Lawyer may proceed to provide the requested legal assistance only with consent given under the limitations and conditions provided in § 122.

3. The same facts as in Illustration 1, except that Lawyer has not previously met the spouses. But in this instance, unlike in Illustration 2, in discussions with the spouses, Lawyer asks questions and suggests options that reveal both Spouse A and Spouse B to be knowledgeable about their respective rights and interests, competent to make independent decisions if called for, and in accord on their common and individual objectives. Lawyer has adequately verified the absence of a conflict of interest and thus may represent both clients in the matter without obtaining consent (see § 122).

Clients might not fully understand the potential for conflict in their interests as the result of ignorance about their legal rights, about possible alternatives to those that the clients have considered prior to retaining the lawyer, or about the uncommunicated plans or objectives of another client. In other situations, prospective clients might agree on objectives when they first approach the common lawyer, but it should be reasonably apparent that a conflict is likely to develop as the representation proceeds. A client's right to communicate in confidence with the attorney should not be constrained by concern that discord might result (cf. § 75). A lawyer is not required to suggest or assume discord where none exists, but when a conflict is reasonably apparent or foreseeable, the lawyer may proceed with multiple representation only after all affected clients have consented as provided in § 122.

Illustration:

4. A, B, and C are interested in forming a partnership in which A is to provide the capital, B the basic patent, and C the management skill. Only C will spend significant amounts of time operating the business. A, B, and C jointly request Lawyer to represent them in creating the partnership. The different contributions to be made to the partnership alone indicate that the prospective partners have conflicts of interest with respect to the structure and governance of the partnership (see § 121). With the informed consent of each (see § 122), Lawyer may represent all three clients in forming the business. Lawyer may assist the clients in valuing their respective contributions and suggest arrangements to protect their respective interests. With respect to conflicts and informed consent in representing the partnership as well as the partners once the business is established, see § 131, Comment *e*.

d. Clients with known differences to be resolved. Multiple prospective clients might already be aware that their interests and objectives are antagonistic to some degree. The lawyer must ascertain at the outset what kind of assistance the clients require. Service by the lawyer or another person as an arbitrator or mediator (and not as a lawyer representing clients), for example, might well serve the clients' interests.

When circumstances reasonably indicate that the prospective clients might be able to reach a reasonable reconciliation of their differences by agreement and with the lawyer's assistance, the lawyer may represent them after obtaining informed consent (see § 122). In particular, the lawyer should explain the effect of joint representation on the lawyer's ability to protect each client's confidential information (see § 75). If the joint representation is undertaken, the lawyer should help the clients reach agreement on outstanding issues but should not advance the interests of one of the clients to the detriment of another (see § 122, Comment *h*).

Relations among multiple clients can develop into adversarial, even litigated, matters. Even if the possibility of litigation is substantial and even though the consent does not permit the lawyer to represent one client against the other if litigation does ensue (see § 122(2)(b) & § 128), with informed consent a lawyer could accept multiple representation in an effort to reconcile the differences of the clients short of litigation. The lawyer should inform the clients that the effort to overcome differences might ultimately fail and require the lawyer's complete withdrawal from the matter, unless the clients agreed that the lawyer thereafter could continue to represent less than all clients (see § 121, Comment *e(i)*). The lawyer is not required to encourage each client to obtain independent advice about being jointly represented, but the lawyer should honor any client request for such an opportunity.

Illustrations:

5. The same facts as in Illustration 4, except that the partnership of A, B, and C is formed and commences business. The business encounters difficulty in securing customers and controlling costs, and it shortly appears that the business will fail unless additional funding is obtained. No outside funds are available, and A announces unwillingness to provide additional capital unless B and C agree to increase A's interest in the business. B and C believe that A is requesting an unreasonably large additional share. A, B, and C seek Lawyer's assistance in resolving their disagreements. A conflict clearly exists between the clients (§ 121). Lawyer may agree to represent the three clients in seeking to arrive at a mutually satisfactory resolution, but only after Lawyer obtains the informed consent of each client and there is a clear definition of the services that Lawyer will provide. In representing the clients, Lawyer may not favor the position of any client over the others (see § 122, Comment *h*).

6. Husband and Wife have agreed to obtain an uncontested dissolution of their marriage. They have consulted Lawyer to help them reach an agreement on disposition of their property. A conflict of interest clearly exists between the prospective clients (§ 121). If reasonable prospects of an agreement

exist, Lawyer may accept the joint representation with the effective consent of both (see § 122). However, in the later dissolution proceeding, Lawyer may represent only one of the parties (see § 128, Comment c), and Lawyer must withdraw from representing both clients if their efforts to reach an agreement fail (see § 121, Comment *e(i)*).

§ 131. Conflicts of Interest in Representing an Organization

Unless all affected clients consent to the representation under the limitations and conditions provided in § 122, a lawyer may not represent both an organization and a director, officer, employee, shareholder, owner, partner, member, or other individual or organization associated with the organization if there is a substantial risk that the lawyer's representation of either would be materially and adversely affected by the lawyer's duties to the other.

Comment:

a. *Scope and cross-references.* This Section concerns conflict-of-interest issues involving a lawyer for an organization. For the purpose of this Section, an organization includes a corporation (whether for-profit or not-for-profit), limited or general partnership (whether formal or informal), labor union, unincorporated association, joint venture, trust, estate, or similar entity with a recognizable form, internal organization, and relative permanence. Many organizations are recognized as entities for other legal purposes, but such recognition is not invariably required for the purposes of this Section (see, e.g., Comment *f* hereto, Illustration 5).

This Section is a particular application of the general conflicts standard expressed in § 121. The conflict is subject to consent under the limitations and conditions provided in § 122. The conflict is imputed to affiliated lawyers by § 123, an imputation that can be removed as described in § 124. Remedies for violation of the Section include those set forth in § 121, Comment *f*. A lawyer's violation of this Section that injures the organization renders the lawyer liable to the organization for professional malpractice (see § 48 and following).

Issues of who constitutes a lawyer's client are addressed in § 14 and § 121, Comment *d*. This Section presupposes that the lawyer has a client-lawyer relationship with an organization. On the power of authorized agents of the organization to instruct the lawyer on behalf of the client, see § 96, Comment *d*.

The duty to preserve confidential client information of organizational clients is described in § 60 and the attorney-client privilege for organizations in § 73. A lawyer's role in counseling organizational clients is addressed in § 96; on a lawyer's duties when a person associated with an organizational client threatens to harm the organization, see § 96(2). A lawyer's ownership of an interest in an organizational client is considered in § 126. Representation of two or more individuals who are forming an organization is examined in § 130, Comment *c*. Payment by an organization of the legal expenses of one or more directors, officers, employees, or other individuals, is considered in § 134. Conflicts of interest created by a lawyer's duties as a corporate director or officer is discussed in § 135, Comment *d*.

b. *Rationale.* An organization with more than a single owner-employee is an aggregation of multiple interests, if only because it is made up of multiple persons or entities. Persons initially forming an organization are linked by a common interest that partly transcends their individual interests. The individuals might have separate lawyers for their other activities and for negotiating the question of their shares or other forms of control in the organization. However, a lawyer might be retained for representation relating to the organization separate from that of any individual associated with the enterprise. An organization's lawyer thus is said to represent the entity and not the elements that make it up. A lawyer for an organization serves whatever lawful interest the organization defines as its interest, acting through its responsible agents and in accordance with its decision making procedures (see § 96(1) and Comment *d* thereto).

c. *A challenge to the policy of a client organization.* Individuals having responsible roles in an organization can disagree about the definition of its interests. However, that does not by itself indicate that a lawyer representing the organization has a conflict of interest within the meaning of § 121. If conduct of the organization is challenged as unlawful, the lawyer for the organization generally may defend at least until it is ruled upon by the tribunal or changed pursuant to the procedures of the organization. Such a change can occur, for example, because the lawyer is directed to settle the controversy as instructed by the agent (see § 21).

Illustration:

1. The Board of Directors of Corporation, acting pursuant to its articles and by-laws, votes not to declare a preferred stock dividend because of a perceived shortage of working capital. This is done contrary to the recommendation of Lawyer for Corporation, who believes that there is a reasonable argument that the dividend can be omitted but that a tribunal would probably order the dividend declared. Thereafter, Lawyer implements the decision of Board, memorializing its decision in a resolution. Several shareholders file suit to compel Corporation to issue a dividend. Neither Lawyer's earlier advice nor the lawsuit itself creates a conflict of interest that would prevent Lawyer from defending against the suit.

On the lawyer's duty if the responsible agent is acting in violation of a duty to the organization, see § 96(2). On the lawyer's duty if the organization engages in a crime or fraud, see § 67. On the lawyer's right to withdraw from representation because of disagreement with the organizational policy, see § 32. On the lawyer's right to take public positions inconsistent with those of the lawyer's client, see § 125, Comment *e*.

d. Conflicting interests of affiliated organizations. Whether a lawyer represents affiliated organizations as clients is a question of fact determined under § 14 (see Comment *f* thereto). When a lawyer represents two or more organizations with some common ownership or membership, whether a conflict exists is determined primarily on the basis of formal organizational distinctions. If a single business corporation has established two divisions within the corporate structure, for example, conflicting interests or objectives of those divisions do not create a conflict of interest for a lawyer representing the corporation. Differences within the organization are to be resolved through the organization's decisionmaking procedures.

If an enterprise consists of two or more organizations and ownership of the organizations is identical, the lawyer's obligation is ordinarily to respond according to the decisionmaking procedures of the enterprise, subject to any special limitations that might be validly imposed by regulatory regimes such as those governing financial institutions and insurance companies.

On the other hand, when ownership or membership of two or more organizations is not identical, the lawyer must respect the organizational boundaries of each and analyze possible conflicts of interest on the basis that the organizations are separate entities. That is true even when a single individual or organization has sufficient ownership or influence to exercise working control of the organizations (cf. § 123, Comment *d(i)*).

Illustration:

2. A Corporation owns 60 percent of the stock of B Corporation. All of the stock of A Corporation is publicly owned, as is the remainder of the stock in B Corporation. Lawyer has been asked by the President of A Corporation to act as attorney for B in causing B to make a proposed transfer of certain real property to A at a price whose fairness cannot readily be determined by reference to the general real-estate market. Lawyer may do so only with effective informed consent of the management of B (as well as that of A). The ownership of A and B is not identical and their interests materially differ in the proposed transaction.

e. Representation of an organization and an individual constituent. Representation of a client organization often is facilitated by a close working relationship between the lawyer and the organization's officers, directors, and employees. However, unless the lawyer and such an individual person enter into a client-lawyer relationship (see § 14, Comment *f*), the individual is not a client of the lawyer (see § 121, Comment *d*). With respect to the attorney-client privilege attaching to communications with a person affiliated with an organization, see § 73, Comment *j*.

When a lawyer proposes to represent both an organization and a person associated with it, such as an officer, director, or employee, whether a conflict exists is determined by an analysis of the interests of the organization as an entity and those of the individuals involved. That is true whether the multiple representation involves civil (see § 128) or criminal (see § 129) litigation or a nonlitigated matter (see § 130). The interests of the organization are those defined by its agents authorized to act in the matter (see § 96,

Comment *d*). For example, when an organization is accused of wrongdoing, an individual such as a director, officer, or other agent will sometimes be charged as well, and the lawyer representing the organization might be asked also to represent the individual. Such representation would constitute a conflict of interest when the individual's interests are materially adverse to the interests of the organization (see § 121). When there is no material adversity of interest, such as when the individual owns all of the equity in the organization or played a routine role in the underlying transaction, no conflict exists. In instances of adversity, concurrent representation would be permissible with the consent of all affected clients under the limitations and conditions stated in § 122.

Consent by an organization can be given in any manner consistent with the organization's lawful decision making procedures. Applicable corporate law may provide that an officer who is personally interested in the matter may not provide consent in the matter. In deciding whether to consent to multiple representation by outside counsel, the organization might rely upon the advice of inside legal counsel. Issues concerning informed consent by public organizations to otherwise conflicted representations are discussed in § 122, Comment *c*.

Illustrations:

3. President, the chief executive officer of Corporation, has been charged with discussing prices with the president of a competing firm. If found guilty, both President and Corporation will be subject to civil and criminal penalties. Lawyer, who is representing Corporation, has concluded after a thorough investigation that no such pricing discussions occurred. Both Corporation and President plan to defend on that ground. President has asked Lawyer to represent President as well as Corporation in the proceedings. Although the factual and legal defenses of President and Corporation appear to be consistent at the outset, the likelihood of conflicting positions in such matters as plea bargaining requires Lawyer to obtain the informed consent of both clients before proceeding with the representation (see § 129, Comment *c*).

4. The same facts as in Illustration 3, except that after further factual investigation both President and Corporation now concede that the pricing discussions took place. One of President's defenses will be that the former general counsel of Corporation told President that discussion of general pricing practices with a competitor was not illegal. Corporation denies that such was the advice given and asserts that President acted without authority. The conflict between President and Corporation is so great that the same lawyer could not provide adequate legal services to both in the matter. Thus, continued representation of both is not subject to consent (see § 122, Comment *g(iii)*, & §§ 128 & 129).

If a person affiliated with an organization makes an unsolicited disclosure of information to a lawyer who represents only the organization, indicating the person's erroneous expectation that the lawyer will keep the information confidential from the organization, the lawyer must inform the person that the lawyer does not represent the person (see § 103, Comment *e*). The lawyer generally is not prohibited from sharing the communication with the organization. However, the requirements stated in § 15, Comment *c*, with respect to safeguarding confidential information of a prospective client may apply. That would occur when the person reasonably appeared to be consulting the lawyer as present or prospective client with respect to the person's individual interests, and the lawyer failed to warn the associated person that the lawyer represents only the organization and could act against the person's interests as a result (see § 103, Comment *e*). With respect to a lawyer's duties when a person associated with the organization expressed an intent to act wrongfully and thereby threatens harm to the organization client, see § 96(2) and Comment *f* thereto.

Issues considered in this Comment may be particularly acute in the case of close corporations, small partnerships, and similar organizations in which, for example, one person with substantial ownership interests also manages. Such a manager may have a corresponding tendency to treat corporate and similar entity distinctions as mere formalities. In such instances, when ownership is so concentrated that no nonmanaging owner exists and in the absence of material impact on the interests of other nonclients (such as creditors in the case of an insolvent corporation), a lawyer acts reasonably in accepting in good faith a controlling manager's position that the interests of all controlling persons and the entity should be treated as if they were the same. Similar considerations apply when a close corporation or similar organization is owned and managed by a small number of owner-managers whose interests are not materially in conflict.

f. A challenge by a client organization to the action of an associated person. Both Subsections of this Section can be applicable when the organization challenges the action of one or more of its associated persons, such as an officer, director, or employee. The policy of the organization in the matter will be that established according to the organization's decision making procedures (see § 96(1)(a)). Because the interests of the organization and the associated person are necessarily adverse, the conflict of interest ordinarily will not be subject to consent (see § 122(2)(c)). On the lawyer's dealing with threatened wrongdoing by a person associated with an organizational client, see § 96(2); see also §§ 66–67.

Illustration:

5. Treasurer, the chief financial officer of Club, a private investment trust, has been accused of converting $25,000 of Club's assets for personal use. Responsible other officers of Club, acting on Club's behalf, retain Lawyer to recover the money from Treasurer. They direct Lawyer not to reveal the loss or file suit until other collection efforts have been exhausted. Lawyer may properly represent Club and in doing so must proceed in the manner directed. Further, although the matter is not yet in litigation, the interests of Club and Treasurer are so adverse that even informed consent of both would not permit their common representation by Lawyer in the matter (see § 122, Comment *g*).

g. *Derivative action.* When an organization such as a business corporation is sued in a derivative action, the organization is ordinarily aligned as an involuntary plaintiff. Persons associated with the organization who are accused of breaching a duty to the organization, typically officers and directors of the organization, are ordinarily named as defendants. The theory of a derivative action is that relief is sought from the individuals for the benefit of the organization. Even with informed consent of all affected clients, the lawyer for the organization ordinarily may not represent an individual defendant as well (see § 128, Comment *c*). If, however, the disinterested directors conclude that no basis exists for the claim that the defending officers and directors have acted against the interests of the organization, the lawyer may, with the effective consent of all clients, represent both the organization and the officers and directors in defending the suit (see § 122).

In a derivative action, if the advice of the lawyer acting for the organization was an important factor in the action of the officers and directors that gave rise to the suit, it is appropriate for the lawyer to represent, if anyone, the officers and directors and for the organization to obtain new counsel. Because the lawyer would be representing clients with interests adverse to the corporation, consent of the corporation would be required. That would be true even if the lawyer withdrew from representing the corporation in order to represent the individuals (see § 132, Comment *c*). Whom the lawyer should represent in the matter, if anyone, should be determined by responsible agents of the organization. Ordinarily, those will be persons who are not named and are not likely to be named parties in the case.

If an action challenging an act of an organization is not a derivative action, whether a conflict exists is determined under § 128, Comment *d(ii).*

h. *Proxy fights and takeover attempts.* Outsiders or insiders might challenge incumbent management for control of organizations. Incumbent management, shareholders, creditors, and employees will all be affected by such a contest in various ways. When the challenge to incumbent management comes from outside the management group, the role of the lawyer representing the organization must be to follow policies adopted by the organization, in accordance with the organization's decision making procedures. Persons authorized to act on behalf of the organization determine the organization's interest in responding to the challenge (see § 96(1)).

When all or part of incumbent management seeks to obtain control of the organization, typically by restructuring ownership of and authority in the organization, a conflict of interest is presented between the individual interests of those members of management and the holders of ownership and authority. Because of their personal interests, those members of management ordinarily would not be appropriate agents to direct the work of a lawyer for the organization with respect to the takeover attempt. Whether a lawyer's personal interests, for example, those based on longtime association with incumbent management, preclude the lawyer from representing the organization or the managers seeking control depends on whether the lawyer's personal interests create a substantial risk of material and adverse effect on the representation (see § 125).

Illustrations:

6. The Board of Directors of Company A expects soon to receive a letter from Company B offering to purchase a controlling interest in Company A at a price 20 percent above current market

value of the stock. The Board of Directors decides to resist the takeover attempt and directs Lawyer, the general counsel of Company A, to prepare a by-law amendment making it more difficult for Company B to gain control. In such circumstances, the Board of Directors, not Lawyer, has the legal responsibility to determine whether or not the by-law change is in the best interests of Company A. Lawyer may advise the Board of Directors concerning the proposed by-law.

7. The same facts as in Illustration 6, except that President and Treasurer of Company A have proposed to transform Company A into a privately held corporation in which they would hold all the shares. Without effective consent, Lawyer's responsibilities to Company A would not permit Lawyer to represent President and Treasurer in the transaction. If Lawyer participates in the matter at all, it should be to represent Company A's interest as defined by the members of Company A's Board of Directors who are empowered to act.

Similar considerations apply when a contest over ownership or control arises within a closely held corporation or similar small organization such as a two-person partnership. If the lawyer also represents a principal in such an enterprise personally, the possibility of conflict is increased if the lawyer undertakes to represent that person in such a contest. When it reasonably appears that the lawyer can serve effectively in the role of conciliator between contending factions, the lawyer may undertake to do so with effective consent of all affected clients (see § 130, Comment *d*). In other cases, however, the lawyer will be required to withdraw from representing all of the individual interests (see § 132).

TOPIC 4. CONFLICTS OF INTEREST WITH A FORMER CLIENT

§ 132. A Representation Adverse to the Interests of a Former Client

Unless both the affected present and former clients consent to the representation under the limitations and conditions provided in § 122, a lawyer who has represented a client in a matter may not thereafter represent another client in the same or a substantially related matter in which the interests of the former client are materially adverse. The current matter is substantially related to the earlier matter if:

(1) the current matter involves the work the lawyer performed for the former client; or

(2) there is a substantial risk that representation of the present client will involve the use of information acquired in the course of representing the former client, unless that information has become generally known.

Comment:

a. Scope and cross-references. This Section applies the general conflicts principles of § 121 to situations in which a lawyer represents a present client in a matter in which there is a substantial risk of material and adverse effect on the interests of the present or a former client. Such a risk can arise from the threat to that client's confidential information, to the interests of the present client because of the lawyer's continuing duties to a former client, or to the interests of both clients because of confusion of the lawyer's role. A lawyer formerly employed by the government is subject to the similar provisions of § 133. Imputation to affiliated lawyers of a conflict identified by this Section is addressed in § 123. Circumstances under which imputation can be removed are addressed in § 124(1) and (2). Conflicts of interest arising out of dealings with a prospective client are addressed in § 15, Comment *c*.

In light of the confidentiality requirements of Chapter 5, a lawyer representing a client in a matter may not use confidential client information if doing so will adversely affect a material interest of the former client, even though that matter is not substantially related to a former representation (see Comments *f* & *g* hereto).

The conflict described in this Section is subject to consent of the present and former clients under the limitations and conditions provided in § 122. Conditional consent might be especially relevant in situations arising under this Section (see § 122, Comment *e*). For example, a client might give informed consent on the condition that a law firm employ screening measures such as those described in § 124.

Remedies discussed in § 121, Comment *f*, can be invoked for a violation of this Section. Because the issues raised by this Section often arise in litigation against or negotiations with a former client, the remedies of disqualification and injunction are commonly invoked. The sanction of professional discipline is also available (see § 5). If a violation of this Section causes injury to a present or former client, the remedy of professional malpractice might be available (see § 48 and following). When a lawyer has undertaken a representation that is later determined to involve a conflict of interest, but could not reasonably have identified the conflict, that should be given substantial weight in determining what sanction, if any, is appropriate.

b. *Rationale.* The rule described in this Section accommodates four policies. First, absent the rule, a lawyer's incentive to serve a present client might cause the lawyer to compromise the lawyer's continuing duties to the former client (see § 33). Specifically, the lawyer might use confidential information of the former client contrary to that client's interest and in violation of § 60. The second policy consideration is the converse of the first. The lawyer's obligations to the former client might constrain the lawyer in representing the present client effectively, for example, by limiting the questions the lawyer could ask the former client in testimony. Third, at the time the lawyer represented the former client, the lawyer should have no incentive to lay the basis for subsequent representation against that client, such as by drafting provisions in a contract that could later be construed against the former client. Fourth, and pointing the other way, because much law practice is transactional, clients often retain lawyers for service only on specific cases or issues. A rule that would transform each engagement into a lifetime commitment would make lawyers reluctant to take new, relatively modest matters.

c. *The relationship between current-client and former-client conflicts rules.* The difference between a former-client conflict under this Section and a present-client conflict considered in Topic 3 (§§ 128–130) is that this Section applies only to representation in the same or a substantially related matter. The present-client conflict rules prohibit adverse representation regardless of the lack of any other relationship between them. If the two representations overlap in time, the rules of §§ 128–130 apply.

Withdrawal is effective to render a representation "former" for the purposes of this Section if it occurs at a point that the client and lawyer had contemplated as the end of the representation (see § 32, Comment *c*). The representation will also be at an end for purposes of this Section if the existing client discharges the lawyer (other than for cause arising from the improper representation) or if other grounds for mandatory or permissive withdrawal by the lawyer exist (see § 32), and the lawyer is not motivated primarily by a desire to represent the new client.

If a lawyer is approached by a prospective client seeking representation in a matter adverse to an existing client, the present-client conflict may not be transformed into a former-client conflict by the lawyer's withdrawal from the representation of the existing client. A premature withdrawal violates the lawyer's obligation of loyalty to the existing client and can constitute a breach of the client-lawyer contract of employment (see § 32, Comment *c*). On withdrawal when a dispute arises between two or more of the lawyer's clients, see § 121, Comment *e(i)*. On advance consent, see id. and § 122, especially Comment *d*.

d. *The same or a substantially related matter.* As indicated in the Section, three types of former-client conflicts are prohibited.

d(i). Switching sides in the same matter. Representing one side and then switching to represent the other in the same matter clearly implicates loyalty to the first client and protection of that client's confidences. Similar considerations apply in nonlitigated matters. For example, a lawyer negotiating a complex agreement on behalf of Seller could not withdraw and represent Buyer against the interests of Seller in the same transaction. Switching sides in a litigated matter can also risk confusing the trier of fact. Just as a lawyer may not represent both sides concurrently in the same case (see §§ 128–130), the lawyer also may not represent them consecutively.

d(ii). Attacking a lawyer's own former work. Beyond switching sides in the same matter, the concept of substantial relationship applies to later developments out of the original matter. A matter is substantially related if it involves the work the lawyer performed for the former client. For example, a lawyer may not on behalf of a later client attack the validity of a document that the lawyer drafted if doing so would materially and adversely affect the former client. Similarly, a lawyer may not represent a debtor in bankruptcy in seeking to set aside a security interest of a creditor that is embodied in a document that the lawyer previously drafted for the creditor.

Illustration:

1. Lawyer has represented Husband in a successful effort to have Wife removed as beneficiary of his life insurance policy. After Husband's death, Wife seeks to retain Lawyer to negotiate with the insurance company to set aside the change of beneficiary and obtain the proceeds of the policy for Wife. The subsequent representation would require that Lawyer attack the work Lawyer performed for Husband. Accordingly, Lawyer may not accept Wife as a client in the matter.

d(iii). The substantial-relationship test and the protection of confidential information of a former client. The substantial-relationship standard is employed most frequently to protect the confidential information of the former client obtained in the course of the representation. A subsequent matter is substantially related to an earlier matter within the meaning of Subsection (2) if there is a substantial risk that the subsequent representation will involve the use of confidential information of the former client obtained in the course of the representation in violation of § 60. "Confidential information" is defined in § 59. Substantial risk exists where it is reasonable to conclude that it would materially advance the client's position in the subsequent matter to use confidential information obtained in the prior representation.

A concern to protect a former client's confidential information would be self-defeating if, in order to obtain its protection, the former client were required to reveal in a public proceeding the particular communication or other confidential information that could be used in the subsequent representation. The interests of subsequent clients also militate against extensive inquiry into the precise nature of the lawyer's representation of the subsequent client and the nature of exchanges between them.

The substantial-relationship test avoids requiring disclosure of confidential information by focusing upon the general features of the matters involved and inferences as to the likelihood that confidences were imparted by the former client that could be used to adverse effect in the subsequent representation. The inquiry into the issues involved in the prior representation should be as specific as possible without thereby revealing the confidential client information itself or confidential information concerning the second client. When the prior matter involved litigation, it will be conclusively presumed that the lawyer obtained confidential information about the issues involved in the litigation. When the prior matter did not involve litigation, its scope is assessed by reference to the work that the lawyer undertook and the array of information that a lawyer ordinarily would have obtained to carry out that work. The information obtained by the lawyer might also be proved by inferences from redacted documents, for example. On the use of in camera procedures to disclose confidential material to the tribunal but not to an opposing party, see § 86, Comment *f*.

Illustrations:

2. Lawyer represented Client A for a period of five years lobbying on environmental issues relating to uranium production. In the course of the representation in one matter, Lawyer learned the basis for Client A's uranium-production decisions. Lawyer now has been asked to represent Client B, a purchaser of uranium, in an antitrust action against A and others alleging a conspiracy to impose limits on production. It is likely that Client B's claims against A would include addressing the same production decisions about which Lawyer earlier learned. Use of confidential information concerning A's production decisions learned in the earlier representation would materially advance the position of Client B in the antitrust matter. The matters are substantially related, and Lawyer may not represent Client B without effective consent of both A and B (see § 122).

3. Lawyer was general inside legal counsel to Company A for many years, dealing with all aspects of corporate affairs and management. Lawyer was dismissed from that position when Company A hired a new president. Company B has asked Lawyer to represent it in an antitrust suit against Company A based on facts arising after Lawyer left Company A's employ but involving broad charges of anti-competitive practices of Company A that, if true, were occurring at the time that Lawyer represented Company A. Lawyer may not represent Company B in the antitrust action. Because of the breadth of confidential client information of Company A to which Lawyer is likely to have had access during the earlier representation and the breadth of issues open in the antitrust claim of Company B, a substantial risk exists that use of that information would materially advance Company B's position in the later representation.

4. Lawyer represented Client A, a home builder, at the closings of the sales of several homes Client A had built in Tract X. Lawyers performing such work normally might encounter issues relating to marketability of title. A is now represented by other counsel. Client B has asked Lawyer to represent him in a suit against A in connection with B's sale to A of Tract Y, a parcel of land owned by Client B on which A plans to build homes. The present suit involves the marketability of the title to Tract Y. Although both representations involve marketability of title, it is unlikely that Lawyer's knowledge of marketability of Tract X would be relevant to the litigation involving the marketability of title to Tract Y. Accordingly, the matters are not substantially related. Lawyer may represent Client B against A without informed consent of A.

As used in this Section, the term "matter" includes not only representation in a litigated case, but also any representation involving a contract, claim, charge, or other subject of legal advice (compare § 133, Comment *e*). The term "matter" ordinarily does not include a legal position taken on behalf of a former client unless the underlying facts are also related. For example, a lawyer who successfully argued that a statute is constitutional on behalf of a former client may later argue that the statute is unconstitutional on behalf of a present client in a case not involving the former client, even though the lawyer's success on behalf of the present client might adversely affect the former client (compare § 128, Comment *f*).

Information that is confidential for some purposes under § 59 (so that, for example, a lawyer would not be free to discuss it publicly (see § 60)) might nonetheless be so general, readily observable, or of little value in the subsequent representation that it should not by itself result in a substantial relationship. Thus, a lawyer may master a particular substantive area of the law while representing a client, but that does not preclude the lawyer from later representing another client adversely to the first in a matter involving the same legal issues, if the matters factually are not substantially related. A lawyer might also have learned a former client's preferred approach to bargaining in settlement discussions or negotiating business points in a transaction, willingness or unwillingness to be deposed by an adversary, and financial ability to withstand extended litigation or contract negotiations. Only when such information will be directly in issue or of unusual value in the subsequent matter will it be independently relevant in assessing a substantial relationship.

e. A subsequent client with interests "materially adverse" to the interests of a former client. A later representation is prohibited if the second client's interests are materially adverse to those of the former client (see § 121, Comments *c(i)* (adverseness) & *c(ii)* (materiality)). The scope of a client's interests is normally determined by the scope of work that the lawyer undertook in the former representation. Thus, a lawyer who undertakes to represent a corporation with respect to the defense of a personal-injury claim involving only issues of causation and damages does not represent the corporation with respect to other interests. The lawyer may limit the scope of representation specifically for the purpose of avoiding a future conflict (see § 16). Similarly, the lawyer may limit the scope of representation of a later client so as to avoid representation substantially related to that undertaken for a previous client.

Illustration:

5. Lawyer formerly represented Client A in obtaining FDA approval to market prescription drug X for treating diseases of the eye. Client B has now asked Lawyer for legal assistance to obtain FDA approval for sale of prescription drug Y for treating diseases of the skin. Client B is also interested in possibly later application for FDA approval to market a different form of drug Y to treat diseases of the eye, thus significantly reducing the profitability of Client A's drug X. Confidential information that Lawyer gained in representing Client A in the earlier matter would be substantially related to work that Lawyer would do with respect to any future application by Client B for use of drug Y for eye diseases (although the information would not relate to the use of drug Y for treating diseases of the skin). Client B and Lawyer agree that Lawyer's work will relate only to FDA approval for use of drug Y to treat diseases of the skin. Thus limited, Lawyer's work for Client B does not involve representation adverse to former Client A on a substantially related matter.

f. A lawyer's subsequent use of confidential information. Even if a subsequent representation does not involve the same or a substantially related matter, a lawyer may not disclose or use confidential information of a former client in violation of § 60.

Illustration:

6. Lawyer, now a prosecutor, had formerly represented Client in defending against a felony charge. During the course of a confidential interview, Client related to Lawyer a willingness to commit perjury. Lawyer is now prosecuting another person, Defendant, for a matter not substantially related to the former prosecution. In the jurisdiction, a defendant is not required to serve notice of defense witnesses that will be called. During the defense case, Defendant's lawyer calls Client as an alibi witness. Lawyer could not reasonably have known previously that Client would be called. Because of the lack of substantial relationship between the matters, Lawyer was not prohibited from undertaking the prosecution. Because Lawyer's knowledge of Client's statement about willingness to lie is confidential client information under § 59, Lawyer may not use that information in cross-examining Client, but otherwise Lawyer may cross-examine Client vigorously.

g. A lawyer's duties of confidentiality other than to a former client. The principles in this Section presuppose that the lawyer in question has previously represented the person adversely affected by the present representation. Whether a client-lawyer relationship exists is considered in § 14 and § 121, Comment *d*. Two situations present analogous problems—communications with a prospective client and confidential information about a nonclient learned in representing a former client.

g(i). Duties to a prospective client. A lawyer's obligation of confidentiality with respect to information revealed during an initial consultation prior to the decision about formation of a lawyer-client relationship is considered in § 15, Comment *c*.

g(ii). Duties to a person about whom a lawyer learned confidential information while representing a former client. A lawyer might have obligations to persons who were not the lawyer's clients but about whom information was revealed to the lawyer under circumstances obligating the lawyer not to use or disclose the information. Those obligations arise under other law, particularly under the law of agency. For example, a lawyer might incur obligations of confidentiality as the subagent of a principal whom the lawyer's client serves as an agent (see Restatement Second, Agency §§ 5, 241, & 396). An important difference between general agency law and the law governing lawyers is that general agency law does not normally impute a restriction to other persons. Thus, when a lawyer's relationship to a nonclient is not that of lawyer-client but that, for example, of subagent-principal, imputation might not be required under the law governing subagents.

Illustrations:

7. Lawyer has represented Hospital in several medical-malpractice cases. In the course of preparing to defend one such case, Lawyer reviewed the confidential medical file of Patient who was not a party in the action. From the file, Lawyer learned that Patient had been convicted of a narcotics offense in another jurisdiction. Patient is now a material witness for the defense in an unrelated case that Lawyer has filed on behalf of Plaintiff. Adequate representation of Plaintiff would require Lawyer to cross-examine Patient about the narcotics conviction in an effort to undermine Patient's credibility. Lawyer may not reveal information about Patient that Hospital has an obligation to keep confidential. That limitation in turn may preclude effective representation of Plaintiff in the pending case. However if, without violating the obligation to Patient, Lawyer can adequately reveal to Plaintiff the nature of the conflict of interest and the likely effect of restricted cross-examination, Lawyer may represent Plaintiff with Plaintiff's informed consent (see § 122, Comment *c*).

8. Lawyer represents Underwriter in preparing to sell an issue of Company's bonds; Lawyer does not represent Company. Several questions concerning facts have arisen in drafting disclosure documents pertaining to the issue. Under applicable law, Underwriter must be satisfied that the facts are not material. Lawyer obtains confidential information from Company in the course of preparing Lawyer's opinion for Underwriter. Among the information learned is that Company might be liable to A for breach of contract. Unless the information has become generally known (see § 59), Lawyer may not represent A in a breach of contract action against Company because the information was learned from Company in confidence.

In the circumstances described in Illustration 8, standards of agency law or other law might permit the underwriter to provide services to another customer in a subsequent transaction so long as the underwriter takes appropriate steps to screen its employees. A lawyer affiliated with the disqualified lawyer could represent the underwriter in the second transaction after appropriate screening of the disqualified lawyer (compare § 124).

A lawyer's duties as fiduciary to nonclient third persons might create a conflict of interest with clients of the lawyer (see § 135).

A lawyer who learns confidential information from a person represented by another lawyer pursuant to a common-interest sharing arrangement (see § 76) is precluded from a later representation adverse to the former sharing person when information actually shared by that person with the lawyer or the lawyer's client is material and relevant to the later matter (see Illustration 8, above). Such a threatened use of shared information is inconsistent with the undertaking of confidentiality that is part of such an arrangement.

h. A lawyer with only a minor role in a prior representation. The specific tasks in which a lawyer was engaged might make the access to confidential client information insignificant. The lawyer bears the burden of persuasion as to that issue and as to the absence of opportunity to acquire confidential information. When such a burden has been met, the lawyer is not precluded from proceeding adversely to the former client (see § 124, Comment *d*, Illustration 3).

i. Withdrawal from representing an "accommodation" client. With the informed consent of each client as provided in § 122, a lawyer might undertake representation of another client as an accommodation to the lawyer's regular client, typically for a limited purpose in order to avoid duplication of services and consequent higher fees. If adverse interests later develop between the clients, even if the adversity relates to the matter involved in the common representation, circumstances might warrant the inference that the "accommodation" client understood and impliedly consented to the lawyer's continuing to represent the regular client in the matter. Circumstances most likely to evidence such an understanding are that the lawyer has represented the regular client for a long period of time before undertaking representation of the other client, that the representation was to be of limited scope and duration, and that the lawyer was not expected to keep confidential from the regular client any information provided to the lawyer by the other client. On obtaining express consent in advance to later representation of the regular client in such circumstances, see § 122, Comment *d*. The lawyer bears the burden of showing that circumstances exist to warrant an inference of understanding and implied consent. On other situations of withdrawal, see § 121, Comment *e*.

Illustrations:

9. Law Firm has represented Financial Corporation for many years as outside general counsel. Financial Corporation, represented by Law Firm, and Client Two, represented by separate counsel, entered into an agreement to operate a business. A shareholder derivative suit was later filed against both Financial Corporation and Client Two on a claim related to the agreement. Client Two by this point had become hard-pressed financially. Financial Corporation and Client Two had potential claims against each other arising out of the transaction but did not assert them so as to present a united front to the plaintiffs in the shareholder suit. Although separately represented in the shareholder derivative action, Financial Corporation and Client Two exchanged information in that action for the common purpose of defending against it (see § 76). During pretrial, Law Firm, with the informed consent of Financial Corporation and Client Two, filed motions in the action in behalf of both Financial Corporation and Client Two. Later, Client Two filed for bankruptcy, and the Trustee in bankruptcy brought suit against Financial Corporation, seeking to recover damages based on the same underlying agreement. Notwithstanding Trustee's objection (compare Comment *c* hereto), Law Firm may withdraw from representing Client Two in the derivative action and represent Financial Corporation in defending against Trustee's suit. Circumstances warrant the inference that Client Two understood that Law Firm would continue to represent Financial Corporation in any such action.

10. The same facts as in Illustration 9, except that Law Firm withdraws from representing Financial Corporation and seeks to represent Trustee in the claims filed against Financial Corporation by Client Two. Even if withdrawal is permissible in the circumstances (compare § 32), Law Firm's representation of Trustee without the informed consent of Financial Corporation would violate this Section (see Comment *c* hereto).

j. Cure of conflicts created by transactions of a client. A lawyer may withdraw in order to continue an adverse representation against a theretofore existing client when the matter giving rise to the conflict and requiring withdrawal comes about through initiative of the clients. An example is a client's acquisition of an interest in an enterprise against which the lawyer is proceeding on behalf of another client. However, if the client's acquisition of the other enterprise was reasonably foreseeable by the lawyer when the lawyer undertook representation of the client, withdrawal will not cure the conflict. In any event, continuing the representation must be otherwise consistent with the former-client conflict rules.

Illustration:

11. Law Firm represents Client One in litigation against X Corporation. At the same time, Law Firm represents Client Two in an unrelated matter. Client Two, assisted by other counsel, acquires X Corporation as a wholly owned subsidiary. The circumstances are such that a conflict would exist in Law Firm's continued representation of Client One against the subsidiary (X Corporation) of Client Two (compare § 131, Comment *d*). Law Firm may withdraw from representing Client Two in order to continue representing Client One in the suit against X Corporation, and must do so unless the affected clients provided consent (see § 121). Law Firm may not represent X Corporation in the suit by Client One by withdrawing from representing Client One (see § 121, Comment *e(i)*).

§ 133. A Former Government Lawyer or Officer

(1) A lawyer may not act on behalf of a client with respect to a matter in which the lawyer participated personally and substantially while acting as a government lawyer or officer unless both the government and the client consent to the representation under the limitations and conditions provided in § 122.

(2) A lawyer who acquires confidential information while acting as a government lawyer or officer may not:

(a) if the information concerns a person, represent a client whose interests are materially adverse to that person in a matter in which the information could be used to the material disadvantage of that person; or

(b) if the information concerns the governmental client or employer, represent another public or private client in circumstances described in § 132(2).

Comment:

a. Scope and cross-references. This Section deals with a lawyer who leaves government employment and then undertakes private representation in the matter on which the lawyer was employed while in government or is otherwise in a position to use confidential information gained while in public employment. This Section applies whether the lawyer was formerly employed by a governmental agency as a lawyer or in some other capacity, such as an officer of the agency. If conflicts involving a government agency are governed by more stringent statutory or regulatory requirements, they also apply.

This Section is a special application of the general prohibition set forth in § 121 and is subject to consent under the limitations and conditions described in § 122. The law in some jurisdictions limits the extent to which governmental officials can waive the rights of the government (see § 122, Comment *g(ii)*). In addition, under 18 U.S.C. § 207, a criminal statute governing, among other kinds of conflicts, the conflicts of a former employee of the federal government, there is no provision for government consent.

The prohibition of this Section is imputed to affiliated lawyers by § 123. Removing the imputed prohibition is governed by § 124(3). The application of the attorney-client privilege to governmental clients is addressed in § 74; a lawyer's general duty of confidentiality, applicable to both governmental and nongovernmental clients, is considered in § 60.

The remedies for violation of this Section are those in § 121, Comment *f*. Criminal penalties are provided for in some statutes on conflicts of interest by former government employees.

b. Rationale. Prohibitions on the activities of former government lawyers are based on concerns similar to those protecting former private clients. Because those concerns apply somewhat differently to government clients, however, the rule of this Section is both broader and narrower than that of § 132.

First, the protection accorded government confidential information is parallel to that for confidential information of private clients. As discussed in § 74, however, statutes requiring openness in government operations might limit the government information that is given protection. Second, since government agencies have special powers to allocate public benefits and burdens, it is reasonable to prohibit a lawyer while in government from taking action designed to improve the lawyer's opportunities upon leaving government service.

On the other hand, government agencies must be able to recruit able lawyers. If the experience gained could not be used after lawyers left government service, recruiting lawyers would be more difficult. There is also a public interest in having lawyers in private practice who have served in government and understand both the substance and rationale of government policy. The experience of such lawyers might sometimes enable clients to achieve higher levels of compliance with law. Thus, this Section protects three government functions, those of client, recruiter of able employees, and law enforcer.

c. Personal and substantial involvement. This Section forbids former government lawyers or officers from taking on matters on which they worked personally and substantially while in government. Former government lawyers are not forbidden to work on matters solely because the matters were pending in the agency during the period of their employment.

The standard of "substantiality" is both formal and functional. A lawyer who signed a complaint on behalf of the government is substantially involved in the matter even if the lawyer knew few of the underlying facts. An action undertaken by a lawyer in the name of a superior is also within the rule.

Illustrations:

1. While acting as special assistant to the Governor of a state, Lawyer participated in negotiation of the purchase of a new computer system for state government. Lawyer is now in the private practice of law. Lawyer may not represent the computer contractor in a dispute arising under the contract.

2. While Lawyer was serving as general counsel of a government agency with many branch offices, a staff attorney in one branch office wrote a letter to X, a private citizen, initiating an official inquiry into a transaction involving X. The letter bore the stamped signature of Lawyer, but Lawyer had no personal involvement in the matter. After leaving government service, Lawyer is asked to represent X in resisting the inquiry. Lawyer may do so under this Section, unless an applicable statute or regulation prohibits the representation.

d. Adverse involvement is not required. The rule of this Section differs from § 132 in that prohibition applies even though the subsequent representation is not adverse to the interests of the former government client. There are three justifications for this distinction. First, prohibiting representation in a matter, even where consistent with the government's interest, diminishes the risk of subsequent misuse of information obtained by the government. If a former government lawyer could make use of confidential reports to an agency, for example, even in a cause that was consistent with the government position, it would go beyond the original purpose for making the reports and make it more difficult for the government to obtain voluntary disclosures from members of the public. Second, the rule removes an incentive to gain later advantages through methods of gathering information that are available only to the government, such as a grand-jury investigation. Third, the rule removes an incentive to begin proceedings as a government agent with a view to obtaining a subsequent advantage in private practice, such as by filing a complementary action for a subsequent private client. Because the rationale for this rule is in part to prevent misconduct by government officials while still in government, in some circumstances the government should not be permitted to consent to the subsequent representation (see § 122(2)(c)).

Illustration:

3. While working for the Securities and Exchange Commission, Lawyer participated in development of a case of securities fraud against a securities dealer. After leaving the Commission, Lawyer may not represent a private person victimized by the fraud in a suit for damages against the dealer, even though the representation is not adverse to the government.

e. Definition of a "matter." The term "matter," as applied to former government employees, is often defined as a judicial or other proceeding, application, request for a ruling or other determination, contract, claim, controversy, investigation, charge, accusation, arrest, or other particular matter involving a specific party or parties. Drafting of a statute or regulation of general applicability is not included under that definition, nor is work on a case of the same type (but not the same parties) as the one in which the lawyer seeks to be involved. The definition is narrower than that governing former-client conflicts of interest under § 132 (see id., Comment *d(iii)*).

Illustrations:

4. While serving in the general counsel's office of the state revenue department, Lawyer was involved in the drafting of regulations to implement new amendments to the state tax law. The regulations affected a large number of taxpayers. When Lawyer returns to private practice, Lawyer may advise taxpayers seeking to determine how the regulations apply, suing to have the regulations construed or challenging the constitutionality of the statute or regulations.

5. In the capacity of city corporation counsel, Lawyer participated in drafting and negotiating the terms of an ordinance to rezone a specific tract of land of a major developer. Now that Lawyer has returned to private practice, the developer has sought to retain Lawyer in a lawsuit to construe the ordinance to permit more housing density than the city asserts the ordinance permits. Lawyer may not accept the case. The work by Lawyer on behalf of city was not of general application and was analogous to representation of the city in a case involving a particular party and parcel of land.

f. Possession of confidential information. Even if a lawyer was not personally and substantially involved in a matter while in government service, there can still be a risk that the lawyer will either misuse governmental authority and power against a citizen or misuse confidential information of the former governmental client against its interests. To protect against such misuse, Subsection (2) imposes two additional prohibitions.

f(i). A risk of misuse of confidential information. Subsection (2)(a), following ABA Model Rules of Professional Conduct, Rule 1.11(b) (1983), imposes limitations on representations after return to private practice of a former government lawyer or officer who learned confidential government information about a person while employed in government service. It prohibits private-practice representation against the interests of that person when the information could be used to the person's material disadvantage. The prohibition reflects two concerns. The first parallels the restriction against use of confidential information of a nonclient that has been obtained in representing a client, in this case the government to whom the third person provided confidential information (see § 132, Comment *g(ii)*). A second concern reflects the government's unique coercive powers to collect information. If a former government lawyer were free to use such information against the provider, the cooperative instincts to provide such information to the government would be chilled, and there would be legitimate indignation at misuse of powers of a public agency to benefit a private client (see Comment *d*). Such confidential information includes all information obtained under governmental authority (whether of the particular governmental employer or some other agency) which, at the time Subsection (2)(a) is applied, either the government is prohibited by law from disclosing to the public or has a privilege not to disclose, and which is not otherwise available to the public (compare § 131 (broader definition of confidential client information for purposes of the prohibitions stated in § 60)).

f(ii). A risk of misuse of information against a former governmental client or employer. Even if not personally and substantially participating in a matter, a government lawyer or employee might overhear or otherwise learn of confidential information of the employing agency. Its subsequent use against the interests of the agency is prohibited to the extent provided in § 132, Comment *f*.

g. Screening a former government lawyer. Screening of a former government lawyer will remove the imputed effects of the personally prohibited former government lawyer as provided in § 124(3) and Comment *e* thereto.

TOPIC 5. CONFLICTS OF INTEREST DUE TO A LAWYER'S OBLIGATION TO A THIRD PERSON

§ 134. Compensation or Direction of a Lawyer by a Third Person

(1) A lawyer may not represent a client if someone other than the client will wholly or partly compensate the lawyer for the representation, unless the client consents under the limitations and conditions provided in § 122 and knows of the circumstances and conditions of the payment.

(2) A lawyer's professional conduct on behalf of a client may be directed by someone other than the client if:

(a) the direction does not interfere with the lawyer's independence of professional judgment;

(b) the direction is reasonable in scope and character, such as by reflecting obligations borne by the person directing the lawyer; and

(c) the client consents to the direction under the limitations and conditions provided in § 122.

Comment:

a. Scope and cross-references. This Section applies the general conflicts prohibition of § 121 to the various situations in which a third person pays a lawyer's fee for representing a client or directs a lawyer's work for a client. The third person might be interested as a relative or friend or have obligations to the client because of indemnification or similar arrangements, or be interested directly in the matter because of a co-client, such as a corporation sued along with one or more of its employees (see § 131, Comment *e*). The risk of adverse effect on representation of the client is inherent in any such payment or direction. Accordingly, this Section, following the standard rule of the lawyer codes, requires informed consent of the client and imposes limitations on the control that a third person may exercise over the lawyer's work.

While discussion in the following Comments (see Comment *f*) will consider issues of the law governing a lawyer representing an insured person, the relationship between the insured person and the insurer or indemnitor will be controlled by other law, such as the law of insurance or of contract. Similarly, other law may govern other relationships between a client and a third person who pays or directs the lawyer, such as when the government pays a lawyer to represent a client in a criminal or civil matter (see Comment *g*). Issues relating to all such other relationships are beyond the scope of the Restatement.

The prohibition imposed by this Section applies to all affiliated lawyers (see § 123). Sanctions and remedies listed in § 6, are available for violation of this Section. Where a violation of this Section has caused actionable harm to a client, the remedy of legal malpractice (see Chapter 4) is available.

Issues relating to payment of legal fees generally are considered in Chapter 3. Chapter 5 examines a lawyer's duty to protect confidential information of a client.

b. Initial client consent. As stated in the Section, under § 122 a client must consent to a lawyer's accepting either a third person's payment of the fee for a client or a third person's direction in a matter. In particular, the client must have knowledge of the circumstances and conditions under which the fee payment or direction is to be provided and any substantial risks to the client thereby created (see § 122, Comment *c*). On consent in insurance-defense representations, see Comment *f* hereto. In an emergency situation in which the lawyer must take action to protect the interests of the client, as in filing an answer to avoid default, the lawyer may take such action even if a conflict appears to exist, but must also promptly take action to address the conflict.

c. Third-person fee payment. This Section accommodates two values implicated by third-person payment of legal fees. First, it requires that a lawyer's loyalty to the client not be compromised by the third-person source of payment. The lawyer's duty of loyalty is to the client alone, although it may also extend to any co-client when that relationship is either consistent with the duty owing to each co-client or is consented to in accordance with § 122. Second, however, the Section acknowledges that it is often in the client's interest to have legal representation paid for by another. Most liability-insurance contracts, for example, provide that the insurer will provide legal representation for an insured who is charged with responsibility for harm to another (see also Comment *f* hereto). Lawyers paid by civil-rights organizations have helped citizens pursue their individual rights and establish legal principles of general importance. Similarly, lawyers in private practice or in a legal-services organization may be appointed or otherwise come to represent indigent persons pursuant to arrangements under which their fees will be paid by a governmental body (see Comment *g*).

d. Third-person direction of a representation. The principle that a lawyer must exercise independent professional judgment on behalf of the client (Subsection (2)(a)) is reflected in the requirement of the lawyer codes that no third person control or direct a lawyer's professional judgment on behalf of a client. Consistent with that requirement, a third person may, with the client's consent and otherwise in the circumstances and to the extent stated in Subsection (2), direct the lawyer's representation of the client. When the conditions of the Subsection are satisfied, the client has, in effect, transferred to the designated third person the client's prerogatives of directing the lawyer's activities (see § 21(2)). The third person's directions must allow for effective representation of the client, and the client must give informed consent to the exercise of the power of direction by the third person. The direction must be reasonable in scope and character, such as by reflecting obligations borne by the person directing the lawyer. Such directions are reasonable in scope and character if, for example, the third party will pay any judgment rendered against the client and makes a decision that defense costs beyond those designated by the third party would not significantly change the likely outcome. Informed client consent may be effective with respect to many forms of direction, ranging from informed consent to particular instances of direction, such as in a representation in which the client otherwise directs the lawyer, to informed consent to general direction of the lawyer by another, such as an insurer or indemnitor on whom the client has contractually conferred the power of direction (see Comment *f*).

Illustration:

1. Resettle, a nonprofit organization, works to secure better living conditions for refugees. Resettle's board of directors believes that a case should be filed to test whether a federal policy of detaining certain refugees is legally justified. Client is a refugee who has recently been detained under the federal policy, and Resettle has offered to pay Lawyer to seek Client's release from detention. With the informed consent of Client, Lawyer may accept payment by Resettle and may agree to make contentions that Resettle wishes to have tested by the litigation.

Just as there are limits to client consent in § 122, there are limits to the restrictions on scope of the representation permitted under this Section. See § 122, Comment *g* (nonconsentable conflicts).

Illustrations:

2. Client is charged with the crime of illegally selling securities. Client's employer, Brokerage, has offered to pay Lawyer to defend Client on the condition that Client agree not to implicate Brokerage or any of its other employees in the crimes charged against Client. Lawyer may not accept the representation on those terms. Whether to accept a plea bargain, for example, and whether to implicate others in the wrongdoing are matters about which the client, not the person paying for the defense, must have the authority to make decisions (see § 22).

3. Same facts as stated in Illustration 2, except that there is no substantial factual or legal basis for implicating Brokerage or any of its other employees and Client consents to accept Lawyer's representation on the condition stated by Brokerage under the limitations and conditions provided in § 122, including knowledge that Brokerage has stated the condition. Under such circumstances, Client's consent authorizes Lawyer to accept payment from Brokerage and adhere to the described conditions.

e. Preserving confidential client information. Although a legal fee may be paid or direction given by a third person, a lawyer must protect the confidential information of the client. Informed client consent to the third-person payment or direction does not by itself constitute informed consent to the lawyer's revealing such information to that person. Consent to reveal confidential client information must meet the separate requirements of § 62.

Illustration:

4. Employer has agreed to pay for representation of Employee in defending a claim involving facts arguably arising out of pursuit of Employer's business. Employer asks Lawyer what Employee intends to testify about the circumstances of Employee's actions. Without consent of Employee as provided in § 62, Lawyer may not give Employer that information.

On a lawyer's discretion to disclose confidential information of a client to a co-client in the representation, see § 60, Comment *l*.

f. Representing an insured. A lawyer might be designated by an insurer to represent the insured under a liability-insurance policy in which the insurer undertakes to indemnify the insured and to provide a defense. The law governing the relationship between the insured and the insurer is, as stated in Comment *a*, beyond the scope of the Restatement. Certain practices of designated insurance-defense counsel have become customary and, in any event, involve primarily standardized protection afforded by a regulated entity in recurring situations. Thus a particular practice permissible for counsel representing an insured may not be permissible under this Section for a lawyer in noninsurance arrangements with significantly different characteristics.

It is clear in an insurance situation that a lawyer designated to defend the insured has a client-lawyer relationship with the insured. The insurer is not, simply by the fact that it designates the lawyer, a client of the lawyer. Whether a client-lawyer relationship also exists between the lawyer and the insurer is determined under § 14. Whether or not such a relationship exists, communications between the lawyer and representatives of the insurer concerning such matters as progress reports, case evaluations, and settlement should be regarded as privileged and otherwise immune from discovery by the claimant or another party to the proceeding. Similarly, communications between counsel retained by an insurer to coordinate the efforts of multiple counsel for insureds in multiple suits and such coordinating counsel are subject to the privilege. Because and to the extent that the insurer is directly concerned in the matter financially, the insurer should be accorded standing to assert a claim for appropriate relief from the lawyer for financial loss proximately caused by professional negligence or other wrongful act of the lawyer. Compare § 51, Comment *g*.

The lawyer's acceptance of direction from the insurer is considered in Subsection (2) and Comment *d* hereto. With respect to client consent (see Comment *b* hereto) in insurance representations, when there appears to be no substantial risk that a claim against a client-insured will not be fully covered by an insurance policy pursuant to which the lawyer is appointed and is to be paid, consent in the form of the acquiescence of the client-insured to an informative letter to the client-insured at the outset of the representation should be all that is required. The lawyer should either withdraw or consult with the client-insured (see § 122) when a substantial risk that the client-insured will not be fully covered becomes apparent (see § 121, Comment *c(iii)*).

Illustration:

5. Insurer, a liability-insurance company, has issued a policy to Policyholder under which Insurer is to provide a defense and otherwise insure Policyholder against claims covered under the insurance policy. A suit filed against Policyholder alleges that Policyholder is liable for a covered act and for an amount within the policy's monetary limits. Pursuant to the policy's terms, Insurer designates Lawyer to defend Policyholder. Lawyer believes that doubling the number of depositions taken, at a cost of $5,000, would somewhat increase Policyholder's chances of prevailing and Lawyer so informs Insurer and Policyholder. If the insurance contract confers authority on Insurer to make such decisions about expense of defense, and Lawyer reasonably believes that the additional depositions can be forgone without violating the duty of competent representation owed by Lawyer to Policyholder (see § 52), Lawyer may comply with Insurer's direction that taking depositions would not be worth the cost.

Material divergence of interest might exist between a liability insurer and an insured, for example, when a claim substantially in excess of policy limits is asserted against an insured. If the lawyer knows or should be aware of such an excess claim, the lawyer may not follow directions of the insurer if doing so would put the insured at significantly increased risk of liability in excess of the policy coverage. Such occasions for conflict may exist at the outset of the representation or may be created by events that occur thereafter. The lawyer must address a conflict whenever presented. To the extent that such a conflict is subject to client consent (see § 122(2)(c)), the lawyer may proceed after obtaining client consent under the limitations and conditions stated in § 122.

When there is a question whether a claim against the insured is within the coverage of the policy, a lawyer designated to defend the insured may not reveal adverse confidential client information of the insured to the insurer concerning that question (see § 60) without explicit informed consent of the insured (see § 62). That follows whether or not the lawyer also represents the insurer as co-client and whether or not the insurer has asserted a "reservation of rights" with respect to its defense of the insured (compare § 60, Comment *l* (confidentiality in representation of co-clients in general)).

With respect to events or information that create a conflict of interest between insured and insurer, the lawyer must proceed in the best interests of the insured, consistent with the lawyer's duty not to assist client fraud (see § 94) and, if applicable, consistent with the lawyer's duties to the insurer as co-client (see § 60, Comment *l*). If the designated lawyer finds it impossible so to proceed, the lawyer must withdraw from representation of both clients as provided in § 32 (see also § 60, Comment *l*). The designated lawyer may be precluded by duties to the insurer from providing advice and other legal services to the insured concerning such matters as coverage under the policy, claims against other persons insured by the same insurer, and the advisability of asserting other claims against the insurer. In such instances, the lawyer must inform the insured in an adequate and timely manner of the limitation on the scope of the lawyer's services and the importance of obtaining assistance of other counsel with respect to such matters. Liability of the insurer with respect to such matters is regulated under statutory and common-law rules such as those governing liability for bad-faith refusal to defend or settle. Those rules are beyond the scope of this Restatement (see Comment *a* hereto).

g. Legal service and similarly funded representations. Lawyers who provide representation to indigent persons may do so pursuant to various arrangements under which their fees or other compensation will be paid by a governmental agency or similar funding organization. For example, a lawyer may represent clients as a staff attorney of a legal aid, military legal assistance, or similar organization, with compensation in the form of a salary paid by the organization. Lawyers in private practice may be appointed by a court, defender or legal-service organization, or bar association to represent a person accused of crime or a person involved in a civil matter (see § 14, Comment *g*), with the lawyer's fee to be paid by the government or organization, often pursuant to a schedule of fees. Certain for-profit legal-service arrangements have also been approved, under which individual private practitioners provide assistance to participants who pay a flat charge to the legal-service organization for limited legal services. Regardless of the method of appointment, the form of compensation, or the nature of the paying organization (for example, whether governmental or private or whether nonprofit or for-profit), the lawyer's representation of and relationship with the individual client must proceed as provided for in this Section.

§ 135. A Lawyer with a Fiduciary or Other Legal Obligation to a Nonclient

Unless the affected client consents to the representation under the limitations and conditions provided in § 122, a lawyer may not represent a client in any matter with respect to which the lawyer has a fiduciary or other legal obligation to another if there is a substantial risk that the lawyer's representation of the client would be materially and adversely affected by the lawyer's obligation.

Comment:

a. Scope and cross-references. This Section applies the general conflicts prohibition of § 121 to situations in which a lawyer has legal duties to persons or organizations in a capacity other than that of lawyer. The considerations in §§ 128–130 on representation of multiple clients are analogous to those in this Section, as are conflicts addressed in § 125 involving a lawyer's personal interests. Related issues can arise regarding a former-client conflict (see § 132, Comment g(ii)).

The prohibition of this Section can be waived by client consent as provided in § 122. Whether and on what terms the other beneficiaries or obligees of the lawyer may consent is beyond the scope of this Section (compare, e.g., Restatement Second, Agency § 392 (acting for adverse party with principal's consent)). Where the fiduciary responsibility may not be waived by the beneficiary, the lawyer will have a conflict that is not subject to consent by the client alone (see § 122, Comment c). The prohibition imposed by this Section is imputed to affiliated lawyers under § 123 (see Comment a thereto).

Sanctions and remedies described in § 121, Comment f, can be imposed for violation of this Section. The sanction of professional discipline (see § 5) and the remedy of professional malpractice (see § 48 and following) are available. The nonclient to whom the lawyer owes duty may have a remedy of disqualification of the lawyer (see § 6, Comment i) or an injunction (id. Comment c) against further representation in order to protect its interests. The law governing the lawyer's other role—for example, the law governing members of a legislative body—may also provide both substantive requirements and remedies in addition to those stated in this Restatement.

b. Rationale. Legal duties to nonclients other than those owed as a lawyer can create conflicting loyalties for a lawyer. If those duties restrict the lawyer's representation of the client, they require informed client consent. The duties of the lawyer arising from law external to the law governing lawyers as such can enhance or otherwise alter the responsibilities of a lawyer-fiduciary (see generally Restatement Second, Trusts).

c. A lawyer as executor or trustee. A lawyer's service as executor of a will or trustee of a trust can create conflicts between the duties of the lawyer as such a fiduciary and the interests of clients whom the lawyer represents. When those duties would materially and adversely affect the lawyer's representation of the client, the lawyer must either withdraw from the representation, withdraw from the conflicting office, or, after making suitable adjustments in order to provide adequate legal services to the client (see § 122, Comment *h*), obtain the informed consent of the client.

Illustrations:

1. Lawyer is outside counsel to Company, a business corporation. Lawyer is also executor of the estate of Boss, the former president of Company. From examining Boss's papers, Lawyer knows that Company has plausible claims against the estate for the return of Company assets taken by Boss for personal use. Lawyer may not represent Company in seeking compensation for the assets because Lawyer's obligation as executor would be to resist the claims of Company. Whether Lawyer may inform Company of the existence of the claims depends on whether the law applicable to executors imposes a duty of confidentiality on Lawyer as executor.

2. The same facts as in Illustration 1, except that Company through another lawyer asserts the claim against Boss's estate. Because of the antagonistic positions between Company and Lawyer as executor, Lawyer must withdraw from representing Company on unrelated matters, unless Company gives informed consent to Lawyer's continued representation (see § 122 & § 128, Comment *e*). Whether, due to Lawyer's relationship with Company, Lawyer may continue as executor after Company asserts its claim is determined under the law governing executors.

d. A lawyer as corporate director or officer. A lawyer's duties as counsel can conflict with the lawyer's duties arising from the lawyer's service as a director or officer of a corporate client. Simultaneous service as corporate lawyer and corporate director or officer is not forbidden by this Section. The requirement that a lawyer for an organization serve the interests of the entity (see § 96(1)(a)) is generally consistent with the duties of a director or officer. However, when the obligations or personal interests as director are materially adverse to those of the lawyer as corporate counsel, the lawyer may not continue to serve as corporate counsel without the informed consent of the corporate client. The lawyer may not participate as director or officer in the decision to grant consent (see § 122, Comment *c(ii)*).

Illustration:

3. Lawyer serves on the board of directors of Company and is also employed by Company as corporate secretary and inside legal counsel. Company proposes to give bonuses to its five highest-paid officers, including Lawyer. Authority to pay such bonuses presents a close legal question. The directors have requested Lawyer to render an opinion as counsel concerning the legality of the payments. Lawyer's status as recipient of the bonus and role as a director to whom the opinion will be addressed create a substantial risk that Lawyer's opinion for Company will be materially and adversely affected. The conflict would not be cured by having the opinion prepared by a partner of Lawyer, because conflicts under this Section are imputed to affiliated lawyers. Both Lawyer's personal conflict and the imputed conflict are subject to effective consent by agents of Company authorized to do so (see § 122).

A second type of conflict that can be occasioned by a lawyer's service as director or officer of an organization occurs when a client asks the lawyer for representation in a matter adverse to the organization. Because of the lawyer's duties to the organization, a conflict of interest is present, requiring the consent of the clients under the limitations and conditions provided in § 122.

Illustration:

4. Lawyer has been asked to file a medical-malpractice action against Doctor and Hospital on behalf of Client. Hospital is operated by University, on whose Board of Trustees Lawyer serves. While Lawyer would not personally be liable for the judgment if Client prevails (compare § 125, Comment *c*), the close relationship between Lawyer and University requires that Lawyer not undertake the representation unless Client's consent is obtained pursuant to § 122.

e. A lawyer as director of a legal-services organization. Service of a private-practice lawyer on the board of directors of a legal-services organization can usefully support the delivery of legal services to persons unable to pay for them. However, the agency's clients might from time to time have interests opposed to those of the lawyer's clients. Such service does not constitute an inherent conflict of interest with the lawyer's private clients, but the lawyer must be alert to the possibility of a conflict with respect to particular decisions. In general, if there is a risk that the lawyer-director's performance of functions as a director with respect to a particular decision would materially and adversely affect the lawyer's representation of private clients, the lawyer may not participate in that decision without the informed consent of affected clients.

Illustration:

5. A significant part of Lawyer's practice consists of enforcing the claims of banks against borrowers. Lawyer is also on the board of directors of the local Legal Services Agency (LSA). LSA is considering a proposal that it bring an action to challenge the use of certain clauses in consumer sales contracts that facilitate collection of bank claims. Such litigation would materially and adversely affect the interests of Lawyer's bank clients. Accordingly, Lawyer may not participate in the LSA board's consideration of the proposal.

f(i). A lawyer as public official—in general. Service by a lawyer as an official in local, state, or federal government carries fiduciary duties within the meaning of this Section. In many jurisdictions, private practice is permitted on the part of public officials in smaller communities and in certain offices, such as part-time judge and as legislator. Public duties can impair the lawyer's effective representation of private clients, requiring that the lawyer-official not represent the affected client, withdraw from the representation, or obtain effective consent (see § 122; cf. also § 122, Comment *g(ii)* (limits in minority of states on power of public agencies to consent to conflicted representation)).

A lawyer-official's obligations as public official are defined by public law outside the law governing lawyers. For example, a lawyer might be required to abstain on any matter in which a client of the lawyer was interested even if an unaffiliated lawyer represented the client in the particular matter. In general, an official's responsibilities as such require that the lawyer seek to serve the public interest and not the interests of private-practice clients.

Illustration:

6. Lawyer is a member of the city council of a town. The council is considering the mayor's proposal to raise the property tax rate by five percent. Some of Lawyer's private clients favor the proposal and some oppose it. Whether Lawyer may vote on the proposal is determined by public law. However, Company, one of Lawyer's private clients, seeks to retain Lawyer to persuade the city council to exempt Company's large and valuable tract of land from the tax increase. Lawyer may not accept the representation. Lawyer's responsibility as public official to vote on the merits of Company's planned exemption creates a risk that Lawyer's representation of Company would be materially and adversely affected. Public law would also likely prohibit Lawyer from participating in the matter of Client's exemption.

f(ii). Functioning as a lawyer in a part-time public office. A lawyer serving as a public official may perform the role of lawyer in that office. Such exercise of official duties is subject to the law governing lawyers when not overridden by other law. For example, a part-time prosecutor exercises wide discretion over the decision whether to prosecute, what charges to file, and what criminal sanctions to seek (see § 97). Where proper exercise of the prosecutor's discretion creates the risk of material and adverse effect on the lawyer-prosecutor's representation of a private client, it is improper for the prosecutor to represent the client without effective consents. Similarly, where there is a substantial risk that proper functioning as a prosecuting official will be materially and adversely affected by the interests of private clients, a conflict of interest requires that the prosecutor not function in the public office unless effective consent of all affected clients is obtained. The informed consent of affected nonclients may be necessary, and such consent may be required to comply with standards different from those stated in § 122, such as those of due process.

Illustration:

7. Prosecutor, who has a part-time private law practice, represents Client in a divorce case. Client alleges that she was the victim of an assault by her Husband. Prosecutor may neither prosecute Husband nor take part in such decisions as whether to prosecute or what charge to file. Another prosecutor must decide whether to charge Husband. Consent to the conflict by Client and an appropriate official of the state would be unavailing without the effective consent of Husband.

PART FIVE

STATUTES THAT AFFECT THE LEGAL PROFESSION

TABLE OF CONTENTS

Introduction

This part includes several selected federal statutes that affect the legal profession.

SELECTED FEDERAL STATUTES

---

5 U.S.C.A.

CHAPTER 73. SUITABILITY, SECURITY, AND CONDUCT

§ 7301. Presidential Regulations

* * *

Executive Order No. 12731: Principles of Ethical Conduct for Government Officers and Employees

By virtue of the authority vested in me as President by the Constitution and the laws of the United States of America, and in order to establish fair and exacting standards of ethical conduct for all executive branch employees, it is hereby ordered that Executive Order 12674 of April 12, 1989, is henceforth modified to read as follows:

"PRINCIPLES OF ETHICAL CONDUCT FOR GOVERNMENT OFFICERS AND EMPLOYEES

"By virtue of the authority vested in me as President by the Constitution and the laws of the United States of America, and in order to establish fair and exacting standards of ethical conduct for all executive branch employees, it is hereby ordered as follows:

Part I—Principles Of Ethical Conduct

Section 101. Principles of Ethical Conduct. To ensure that every citizen can have complete confidence in the integrity of the Federal Government, each Federal employee shall respect and adhere to the fundamental principles of ethical service as implemented in regulations promulgated under sections 201 and 301 of this order:

(a) Public service is a public trust, requiring employees to place loyalty to the Constitution, the laws, and ethical principles above private gain.

(b) Employees shall not hold financial interests that conflict with the conscientious performance of duty.

(c) Employees shall not engage in financial transactions using nonpublic Government information or allow the improper use of such information to further any private interest.

(d) An employee shall not, except pursuant to such reasonable exceptions as are provided by regulation, solicit or accept any gift or other item of monetary value from any person or entity seeking official action from, doing business with, or conducting activities regulated by the employee's agency, or whose interests may be substantially affected by the performance or nonperformance of the employee's duties.

(e) Employees shall put forth honest effort in the performance of their duties.

(f) Employees shall make no unauthorized commitments or promises of any kind purporting to bind the Government.

(g) Employees shall not use public office for private gain.

(h) Employees shall act impartially and not give preferential treatment to any private organization or individual.

(i) Employees shall protect and conserve Federal property and shall not use it for other than authorized activities.

(j) Employees shall not engage in outside employment or activities, including seeking or negotiating for employment, that conflict with official Government duties and responsibilities.

(k) Employees shall disclose waste, fraud, abuse, and corruption to appropriate authorities.

(*l*) Employees shall satisfy in good faith their obligations as citizens, including all just financial obligations, especially those—such as Federal, State, or local taxes—that are imposed by law.

(m) Employees shall adhere to all laws and regulations that provide equal opportunity for all Americans regardless of race, color, religion, sex, national origin, age, or handicap.

(n) Employees shall endeavor to avoid any actions creating the appearance that they are violating the law or the ethical standards promulgated pursuant to this order.

Sec. 102. Limitations on Outside Earned Income.

(a) No employee who is appointed by the President to a full-time noncareer position in the executive branch (including full-time noncareer employees in the White House Office, the Office of Policy Development, and the Office of Cabinet Affairs), shall receive any earned income for any outside employment or activity performed during that Presidential appointment.

(b) The prohibition set forth in subsection (a) shall not apply to any full-time noncareer employees employed pursuant to 3 U.S.C. 105 [section 105 of Title 3, The President] and 3 U.S.C. 107(a) [section 107(a) of Title 3] at salaries below the minimum rate of basic pay then paid for GS-9 of the General Schedule. Any outside employment must comply with relevant agency standards of conduct, including any requirements for approval of outside employment.

Part II—Office Of Government Ethics Authority

Sec. 201. The Office of Government Ethics. The Office of Government Ethics shall be responsible for administering this order by:

(a) Promulgating, in consultation with the Attorney General and the Office of Personnel Management, regulations that establish a single, comprehensive, and clear set of executive-branch standards of conduct that shall be objective, reasonable, and enforceable.

(b) Developing, disseminating, and periodically updating an ethics manual for employees of the executive branch describing the applicable statutes, rules, decisions, and policies.

(c) Promulgating, with the concurrence of the Attorney General, regulations interpreting the provisions of the post-employment statute, section 207 of title 18, United States Code [section 207 of Title 18, Crimes and Criminal Procedure]; the general conflict-of-interest statute, section 208 of title 18, United States Code [section 208 of Title 18]; and the statute prohibiting supplementation of salaries, section 209 of title 18, United States Code [section 209 of Title 18].

(d) Promulgating, in consultation with the Attorney General and the Office of Personnel Management, regulations establishing a system of nonpublic (confidential) financial disclosure by executive branch employees to complement the system of public disclosure under the Ethics in Government Act of 1978. Such regulations shall include criteria to guide agencies in determining which employees shall submit these reports.

(e) Ensuring that any implementing regulations issued by agencies under this order are consistent with and promulgated in accordance with this order.

Sec. 202. Executive Office of the President. In that the agencies within the Executive Office of the President (EOP) currently exercise functions that are not distinct and separate from each other within the meaning and for the purposes of section 207(e) of title 18, United States Code [section 207(e) of Title 18], those agencies shall be treated as one agency under section 207(c) of title 18, United States Code [section 207(c) of Title 18].

Part III—Agency Responsibilities

Sec. 301. Agency Responsibilities. Each agency head is directed to:

(a) Supplement, as necessary and appropriate, the comprehensive executive branch-wide regulations of the Office of Government Ethics, with regulations of special applicability to the particular functions and activities of that agency. Any supplementary agency regulations shall be prepared as addenda to the branch-wide regulations and promulgated jointly with the Office of Government Ethics, at the agency's expense, for inclusion in Title 5 of the Code of Federal Regulations.

(b) Ensure the review by all employees of this order and regulations promulgated pursuant to the order.

(c) Coordinate with the Office of Government Ethics in developing annual agency ethics training plans. Such training shall include mandatory annual briefings on ethics and standards of conduct for all employees appointed by the President, all employees in the Executive Office of the President, all officials required to file public or nonpublic financial disclosure reports, all employees who are contracting officers and procurement officials, and any other employees designated by the agency head.

(d) Where practicable, consult formally or informally with the Office of Government Ethics prior to granting any exemption under section 208 of title 18, United States Code [section 208 of Title 18], and provide the Director of the Office of Government Ethics a copy of any exemption granted.

(e) Ensure that the rank, responsibilities, authority, staffing, and resources of the Designated Agency Ethics Official are sufficient to ensure the effectiveness of the agency ethics program. Support should include the provision of a separate budget line item for ethics activities, where practicable.

* * *

18 U.S.C.A.

CHAPTER 11. BRIBERY AND GRAFT

§ 201. Bribery of public officials and witnesses

(a) For the purpose of this section—

(1) the term "public official" means Member of Congress, Delegate, or Resident Commissioner, either before or after such official has qualified, or an officer or employee or person acting for or on behalf of the United States, or any department, agency or branch of Government thereof, including the District of Columbia, in any official function, under or by authority of any such department, agency, or branch of Government, or a juror;

(2) the term "person who has been selected to be a public official" means any person who has been nominated or appointed to be a public official, or has been officially informed that such person will be so nominated or appointed; and

(3) the term "official act" means any decision or action on any question, matter, cause, suit, proceeding or controversy, which may at any time be pending, or which may by law be brought before any public official, in such official's official capacity, or in such official's place of trust or profit.

(b) Whoever—

(1) directly or indirectly, corruptly gives, offers or promises anything of value to any public official or person who has been selected to be a public official, or offers or promises any public official or any person who has been selected to be a public official to give anything of value to any other person or entity, with intent—

(A) to influence any official act; or

(B) to influence such public official or person who has been selected to be a public official to commit or aid in committing, or collude in, or allow, any fraud, or make opportunity for the commission of any fraud, on the United States; or

(C) to induce such public official or such person who has been selected to be a public official to do or omit to do any act in violation of the lawful duty of such official or person;

(2) being a public official or person selected to be a public official, directly or indirectly, corruptly demands, seeks, receives, accepts, or agrees to receive or accept anything of value personally or for any other person or entity, in return for:

(A) being influenced in the performance of any official act;

(B) being influenced to commit or aid in committing, or to collude in, or allow, any fraud, or make opportunity for the commission of any fraud, on the United States; or

(C) being induced to do or omit to do any act in violation of the official duty of such official or person;

(3) directly or indirectly, corruptly gives, offers, or promises anything of value to any person, or offers or promises such person to give anything of value to any other person or entity, with intent to influence the testimony under oath or affirmation of such first-mentioned person as a witness upon a trial, hearing, or other proceeding, before any court, any committee of either House or both Houses of Congress, or any agency, commission, or officer authorized by the laws of the United States to hear evidence or take testimony, or with intent to influence such person to absent himself therefrom;

(4) directly or indirectly, corruptly demands, seeks, receives, accepts, or agrees to receive or accept anything of value personally or for any other person or entity in return for being influenced in testimony under oath or affirmation as a witness upon any such trial, hearing, or other proceeding, or in return for absenting himself therefrom;

shall be fined under this title or not more than three times the monetary equivalent of the thing of value, whichever is greater, or imprisoned for not more than fifteen years, or both, and may be disqualified from holding any office of honor, trust, or profit under the United States.

(c) Whoever—

(1) otherwise than as provided by law for the proper discharge of official duty—

(A) directly or indirectly gives, offers, or promises anything of value to any public official, former public official, or person selected to be a public official, for or because of any official act performed or to be performed by such public official, former public official, or person selected to be a public official; or

(B) being a public official, former public official, or person selected to be a public official, otherwise than as provided by law for the proper discharge of official duty, directly or indirectly demands, seeks, receives, accepts, or agrees to receive or accept anything of value personally for or because of any official act performed or to be performed by such official or person;

(2) directly or indirectly, gives, offers, or promises anything of value to any person, for or because of the testimony under oath or affirmation given or to be given by such person as a witness upon a trial, hearing, or other proceeding, before any court, any committee of either House or both Houses of Congress, or any agency, commission, or officer authorized by the laws of the United States to hear evidence or take testimony, or for or because of such person's absence therefrom;

(3) directly or indirectly demands, seeks, receives, accepts, or agrees to receive or accept anything of value personally for or because of the testimony under oath or affirmation given or to be given by such person as a witness upon any such trial, hearing, or other proceeding, or for or because of such person's absence therefrom;

shall be fined under this title or imprisoned for not more than two years, or both.

(d) Paragraphs (3) and (4) of subsection (b) and paragraphs (2) and (3) of subsection (c) shall not be construed to prohibit the payment or receipt of witness fees provided by law, or the payment, by the party upon whose behalf a witness is called and receipt by a witness, of the reasonable cost of travel and subsistence incurred and the reasonable value of time lost in attendance at any such trial, hearing, or proceeding, or in the case of expert witnesses, a reasonable fee for time spent in the preparation of such opinion, and in appearing and testifying.

(e) The offenses and penalties prescribed in this section are separate from and in addition to those prescribed in sections 1503, 1504, and 1505 of this title.

§ 202. Definitions

(a) For the purpose of sections 203, 205, 207, 208, and 209 of this title the term "special Government employee" shall mean an officer or employee of the executive or legislative branch of the

United States Government, of any independent agency of the United States or of the District of Columbia, who is retained, designated, appointed, or employed to perform, with or without compensation, for not to exceed one hundred and thirty days during any period of three hundred and sixty-five consecutive days, temporary duties either on a full-time or intermittent basis, a part-time United States commissioner, a part-time United States magistrate, or, regardless of the number of days of appointment, an independent counsel appointed under chapter 40 of title 28 and any person appointed by that independent counsel under section 594(c) of title 28. Notwithstanding the next preceding sentence, every person serving as a part-time local representative of a Member of Congress in the Member's home district or State shall be classified as a special Government employee. . . .

(b) For the purposes of sections 205 and 207 of this title, the term "official responsibility" means the direct administrative or operating authority, whether intermediate or final, and either exercisable alone or with others, and either personally or through subordinates, to approve, disapprove, or otherwise direct Government action.

(c) Except as otherwise provided in such sections, the terms "officer" and "employee" in sections 203, 205, 207 through 209 and 218 of this title, mean those individuals defined in sections 2104 and 2105 of title 5. The terms "officer" and "employee" shall not include the President, the Vice President, a Member of Congress, or a Federal judge.

(d) The term "Member of Congress" in sections 204 and 207 means—

(1) a United States Senator; and

(2) a Representative in, or a Delegate or Resident Commissioner to, the House of Representatives.

(e) As used in this chapter, the term—

(1) "executive branch" includes each executive agency as defined in title 5, and any other entity or administrative unit in the executive branch;

(2) "judicial branch" means the Supreme Court of the United States; the United States courts of appeals; the United States district courts; the Court of International Trade; the United States bankruptcy courts; any court created pursuant to article I of the United States Constitution, including the Court of Appeals for the Armed Forces, the United States Claims Court, and the United States Tax Court, but not including a court of a territory or possession of the United States; the Federal Judicial Center; and any other agency, office, or entity in the judicial branch; and

(3) "legislative branch" means—

(A) the Congress; and

(B) the Office of the Architect of the Capitol, the United States Botanic Garden, the General Accountability Office, the Government Printing Office, the Library of Congress, the Office of Technology Assessment, the Congressional Budget Office, the United States Capitol Police, and any other agency, entity, office, or commission established in the legislative branch.

§ 203. Compensation to Members of Congress, officers, and others in matters affecting the Government

(a) Whoever, otherwise than as provided by law for the proper discharge of official duties, directly or indirectly—

(1) demands, seeks, receives, accepts, or agrees to receive or accept any compensation for any representational services, as agent or attorney or otherwise, rendered or to be rendered either personally or by another—

(A) at a time when such person is a Member of Congress, Member of Congress Elect, Delegate, Delegate Elect, Resident Commissioner, or Resident Commissioner Elect; or

(B) at a time when such person is an officer or employee or Federal Judge of the United States in the executive, legislative, or judicial branch of the Government, or

in any agency of the United States, in relation to any proceeding, application, request for a ruling or other determination, contract, claim, controversy, charge, accusation, arrest, or other particular matter in which the United States is a party or has a direct and substantial interest, before any department, agency, court, court-martial, officer, or any civil, military, or naval commission; or

(2) knowingly gives, promises, or offers any compensation for any such representational services rendered or to be rendered at a time when the person to whom the compensation is given, promised, or offered, is or was such a Member, Member Elect, Delegate, Delegate Elect, Commissioner, Commissioner Elect, Federal Judge, officer, or employee;

shall be subject to the penalties set forth in section 216 of this title.

(b) Whoever, otherwise than as provided by law for the proper discharge of official duties, directly or indirectly—

(1) demands, seeks, receives, accepts, or agrees to receive or accept any compensation for any representational services, as agent or attorney or otherwise, rendered or to be rendered either personally or by another, at a time when such person is an officer or employee of the District of Columbia, in relation to any proceeding, application, request for a ruling or other determination, contract, claim, controversy, charge, accusation, arrest, or other particular matter in which the District of Columbia is a party or has a direct and substantial interest, before any department, agency, court, officer, or commission; or

(2) knowingly gives, promises, or offers any compensation for any such representational services rendered or to be rendered at a time when the person to whom the compensation is given, promised, or offered, is or was an officer or employee of the District of Columbia;

shall be subject to the penalties set forth in section 216 of this title; and

(c) A special Government employee shall be subject to subsections (a) and (b) only in relation to a particular matter involving a specific party or parties—

(1) in which such employee has at any time participated personally and substantially as a Government employee or as a special Government employee or as a special Government employee through decision, approval, disapproval, recommendation, the rendering of advice, investigation or otherwise; or

(2) which is pending in the department or agency of the Government in which such employee is serving except that paragraph (2) of this subsection shall not apply in the case of a special Government employee who has served in such department or agency no more than sixty days during the immediately preceding period of three hundred and sixty-five consecutive days.

(d) Nothing in this section prevents an officer or employee, including a special Government employee, from acting, with or without compensation, as agent or attorney for or otherwise representing his parents, spouse, child, or any person for whom, or for any estate for which, he is serving as guardian, executor, administrator, trustee, or other personal fiduciary except—

(1) in those matters in which he has participated personally and substantially as a Government employee or as a special Government employee through decision, approval, disapproval, recommendation, the rendering of advice, investigation, or otherwise; or

(2) in those matters that are the subject of his official responsibility,

subject to approval by the Government official responsible for appointment to his position.

(e) Nothing in this section prevents a special Government employee from acting as agent or attorney for another person in the performance of work under a grant by, or a contract with or for the benefit of, the United States if the head of the department or agency concerned with the grant or contract certifies in writing that the national interest so requires and publishes such certification in the Federal Register.

(f) Nothing in this section prevents an individual from giving testimony under oath or from making statements required to be made under penalty of perjury.

§ 204. Practice in United States Claims Court or the United States Court of Appeals for the Federal Circuit by Members of Congress

Whoever, being a Member of Congress or Member of Congress Elect, practices in the United States Claims Court or the United States Court of Appeals for the Federal Circuit shall be subject to the penalties set forth in section 216 of this title.

§ 205. Activities of officers and employees in claims against and other matters affecting the Government

(a) Whoever, being an officer or employee of the United States in the executive, legislative, or judicial branch of the Government or in any agency of the United States, otherwise than in the proper discharge of his official duties—

(1) acts as agent or attorney for prosecuting any claim against the United States, or receives any gratuity, or any share of or interest in any such claim in consideration of assistance in the prosecution of such claim, or

(2) acts as agent or attorney for anyone before any department, agency, court, court-martial, officer, or civil, military, or naval commission in connection with any covered matter in which the United States is a party or has a direct and substantial interest—

shall be subject to the penalties set forth in section 216 of this title.

(b) Whoever, being an officer or employee of the District of Columbia or an officer or employee of the Office of the United States Attorney for the District of Columbia, otherwise than in the proper discharge of official duties—

(1) acts as agent or attorney for prosecuting any claim against the District of Columbia, or receives any gratuity, or any share of or interest in any such claim in consideration of assistance in the prosecution of such claim; or

(2) acts as agent or attorney for anyone before any department, agency, court, officer, or commission in connection with any covered matter in which the District of Columbia is a party or has a direct and substantial interest;

shall be subject to the penalties set forth in section 216 of this title.

(c) A special Government employee shall be subject to subsections (a) and (b) only in relation to a covered matter involving a specific party or parties—

(1) in which he has at any time participated personally and substantially as a Government employee or special Government employee through decision, approval, disapproval, recommendation, the rendering of advice, investigation, or otherwise; or

(2) which is pending in the department or agency of the Government in which he is serving.

Paragraph (2) shall not apply in the case of a special Government employee who has served in such department or agency no more than sixty days during the immediately preceding period of three hundred and sixty-five consecutive days.

(d)(1) Nothing in subsection (a) or (b) prevents an officer or employee, if not inconsistent with the faithful performance of that officer's or employee's duties, from acting without compensation as agent or attorney for, or otherwise representing—

(A) any person who is the subject of disciplinary, loyalty, or other personnel administration proceedings in connection with those proceedings; or

(B) except as provided in paragraph (2), any cooperative, voluntary, professional, recreational, or similar organization or group not established or operated for profit, if a majority of the organization's or group's members are current officers or employees of the United States or of the District of Columbia, or their spouses or dependent children.

(2) Paragraph (1)(B) does not apply with respect to a covered matter that—

(A) is a claim under subsection (a)(1) or (b)(1);

(B) is a judicial or administrative proceeding where the organization or group is a party; or

(C) involves a grant, contract, or other agreement (including a request for any such grant, contract, or agreement) providing for the disbursement of Federal funds to the organization or group.

(e) Nothing in subsection (a) or (b) prevents an officer or employee, including a special Government employee, from acting, with or without compensation, as agent or attorney for, or otherwise representing, his parents, spouse, child, or any person for whom, or for any estate for which, he is serving as guardian, executor, administrator, trustee, or other personal fiduciary except—

(1) in those matters in which he has participated personally and substantially as a Government employee or special Government employee through decision, approval, disapproval, recommendation, the rendering of advice, investigation, or otherwise, or

(2) in those matters which are the subject of his official responsibility,

subject to approval by the Government official responsible for appointment to his position.

(f) Nothing in subsection (a) or (b) prevents a special Government employee from acting as agent or attorney for another person in the performance of work under a grant by, or a contract with or for the benefit of, the United States if the head of the department or agency concerned with the grant or contract certifies in writing that the national interest so requires and publishes such certification in the Federal Register.

(g) Nothing in this section prevents an officer or employee from giving testimony under oath or from making statements required to be made under penalty for perjury or contempt.

(h) For the purpose of this section, the term "covered matter" means any judicial or other proceeding, application, request for a ruling or other determination, contract, claim, controversy, investigation, charge, accusation, arrest, or other particular matter.

(i) Nothing in this section prevents an employee from acting pursuant to—

(1) chapter 71 of title 5;

(2) section 1004 or chapter 12 of title 39;

(3) section 3 of the Tennessee Valley Authority Act of 1933 (16 U.S.C. 831b);

(4) chapter 10 of title I of the Foreign Service Act of 1980 (22 U.S.C. 4104 et seq.); or

(5) any provision of any other Federal or District of Columbia law that authorizes labor-management relations between an agency or instrumentality of the United States or the District of Columbia and any labor organization that represents its employees.

§ 207. Restrictions on former officers, employees, and elected officials of the executive and legislative branches

(a) Restrictions on all officers and employees of the executive branch and certain other agencies.—

(1) Permanent restrictions on representation on particular matters.—Any person who is an officer or employee (including any special Government employee) of the executive branch of the United States (including any independent agency of the United States), or of the District of Columbia, and who, after the termination of his or her service or employment with the United States or the District of Columbia, knowingly makes, with the intent to influence, any communication to or appearance before any officer or employee of any department, agency, court, or court-martial of the United States or the District of Columbia, on behalf of any other person (except the United States or the District of Columbia) in connection with a particular matter—

(A) in which the United States or the District of Columbia is a party or has a direct and substantial interest,

(B) in which the person participated personally and substantially as such officer or employee, and

(C) which involved a specific party or specific parties at the time of such participation,

shall be punished as provided in section 216 of this title.

(2) Two-year restrictions concerning particular matters under official responsibility.—Any person subject to the restrictions contained in paragraph (1) who, within 2 years after the termination of his or her service or employment with the United States or the District of Columbia, knowingly makes, with the intent to influence, any communication to or appearance before any officer or employee of any department, agency, court, or court-martial of the United States or the District of Columbia, on behalf of any other person (except the United States or the District of Columbia), in connection with a particular matter—

(A) in which the United States or the District of Columbia is a party or has a direct and substantial interest,

(B) which such person knows or reasonably should know was actually pending under his or her official responsibility as such officer or employee within a period of 1 year before the termination of his or her service or employment with the United States or the District of Columbia, and

(C) which involved a specific party or specific parties at the time it was so pending,

shall be punished as provided in section 216 of this title.

(3) Clarification of restrictions.—The restrictions contained in paragraphs (1) and (2) shall apply—

(A) in the case of an officer or employee of the executive branch of the United States (including any independent agency), only with respect to communications to or appearances before any officer or employee of any department, agency, court, or court-martial of the United States on behalf of any other person (except the United States), and only with respect to a matter in which the United States is a party or has a direct and substantial interest; and

(B) in the case of an officer or employee of the District of Columbia, only with respect to communications to or appearances before any officer or employee of any department, agency, or court of the District of Columbia on behalf of any other person (except the District of Columbia), and only with respect to a matter in which the District of Columbia is a party or has a direct and substantial interest.

(b) One-year restrictions on aiding or advising.—

(1) In general.—Any person who is a former officer or employee of the executive branch of the United States (including any independent agency) and is subject to the restrictions contained in subsection (a)(1), or any person who is a former officer or employee of the legislative branch or a former Member of Congress, who personally and substantially participated in any ongoing trade or treaty negotiation on behalf of the United States within the 1-year period preceding the date on which his or her service or employment with the United States terminated, and who had access to information concerning such trade or treaty negotiation which is exempt from disclosure under section 552 of title 5, which is so designated by the appropriate department or agency, and which the person knew or should have known was so designated, shall not, on the basis of that information, knowingly represent, aid, or advise any other person (except the United States) concerning such ongoing trade or treaty negotiation for a period of 1 year after his or her service or employment with the United States terminates. Any person who violates this subsection shall be punished as provided in section 216 of this title.

(2) Definition.—For purposes of this paragraph—

(A) the term "trade negotiation" means negotiations which the President determines to undertake to enter into a trade agreement pursuant to section 1102 of the Omnibus Trade and Competitiveness Act of 1988, and does not include any action taken before that determination is made; and

(B) the term "treaty" means an international agreement made by the President that requires the advice and consent of the Senate.

(c) One-year restrictions on certain senior personnel of the executive branch and independent agencies.—

(1) Restrictions.—In addition to the restrictions set forth in subsections (a) and (b), any person who is an officer or employee (including any special Government employee) of the executive branch of the United States (including an independent agency), who is referred to in paragraph (2), and who, within 1 year after the termination of his or her service or employment as such officer or employee, knowingly makes, with the intent to influence, any communication to or appearance before any officer or employee of the department or agency in which such person served within 1 year before such termination, on behalf of any other person (except the United States), in connection with any matter on which such person seeks official action by any officer or employee of such department or agency, shall be punished as provided in section 216 of this title.

(2) Persons to whom restrictions apply.—(A) Paragraph (1) shall apply to a person (other than a person subject to the restrictions of subsection (d))—

(i) employed at a rate of pay specified in or fixed according to subchapter II of chapter 53 of title 5,

(ii) employed in a position which is not referred to in clause (i) and for which that person is paid at a rate of basic pay which is equal to or greater than 86.5 percent of the rate of basic pay for level II of the Executive Schedule, or, for a period of 2 years following the enactment of the National Defense Authorization Act for Fiscal Year 2004, a person who, on the day prior to the enactment of that Act, was employed in a position which is not referred to in clause (i) and for which the rate of basic pay, exclusive of any locality-based pay adjustment under section 5304 or section 5304a of title 5, was equal to or greater than the rate of basic pay payable for level 5 of the Senior Executive Service on the day prior to the enactment of that Act,

(iii) appointed by the President to a position under section 105(a)(2)(B) of title 3 or by the Vice President to a position under section 106(a)(1)(B) of title 3, or

(iv) employed in a position which is held by an active duty commissioned officer of the uniformed services who is serving in a grade or rank for which the pay grade (as specified in section 201 of title 37) is pay grade 0–7 or above.

(v) assigned from a private sector organization to an agency under chapter 37 of title 5.

(B) Paragraph (1) shall not apply to a special Government employee who serves less than 60 days in the 1-year period before his or her service or employment as such employee terminates.

(C) At the request of a department or agency, the Director of the Office of Government Ethics may waive the restrictions contained in paragraph (1) with respect to any position, or category of positions, referred to in clause (ii) or (iv) of subparagraph (A), in such department or agency if the Director determines that—

(i) the imposition of the restrictions with respect to such position or positions would create an undue hardship on the department or agency in obtaining qualified personnel to fill such position or positions, and

(ii) granting the waiver would not create the potential for use of undue influence or unfair advantage.

(d) Restrictions on very senior personnel of the executive branch and independent agencies.—

(1) Restrictions.—In addition to the restrictions set forth in subsections (a) and (b), any person who—

(A) serves in the position of Vice President of the United States,

(B) is employed in a position in the executive branch of the United States (including any independent agency) at a rate of pay payable for level I of the Executive Schedule or employed in a position in the Executive Office of the President at a rate of pay payable for level II of the Executive Schedule, or

(C) is appointed by the President to a position under section 105(a)(2)(A) of title 3 or by the Vice President to a position under section 106(a)(1)(A) of title 3,

and who, within 2 years after the termination of that person's service in that position, knowingly makes, with the intent to influence, any communication to or appearance before any person described in paragraph (2), on behalf of any other person (except the United States), in connection with any matter on which such person seeks official action by any officer or employee of the executive branch of the United States, shall be punished as provided in section 216 of this title.

(2) Persons who may not be contacted.—The persons referred to in paragraph (1) with respect to appearances or communications by a person in a position described in subparagraph (A), (B), or (C) of paragraph (1) are—

(A) any officer or employee of any department or agency in which such person served in such position within a period of 1 year before such person's service or employment with the United States Government terminated, and

(B) any person appointed to a position in the executive branch which is listed in sections 5312, 5313, 5314, 5315, or 5316 of title 5.

(e) Restrictions on Members of Congress and officers and employees of the legislative branch.—

(1) Members of Congress and elected officers of the house.—

(A) Senators.—Any person who is a Senator and who, within 2 years after that person leaves office, knowingly makes, with the intent to influence, any communication to or appearance before any Member, officer, or employee of either House of Congress or any employee of any other legislative office of the Congress, on behalf of any other person (except the United States) in connection with any matter on which such former Senator seeks action by a Member, officer, or employee of either House of Congress, in his or her official capacity, shall be punished as provided in section 216 of this title.

(B) Members and officers of the House of Representatives.—(i) Any person who is a Member of the House of Representatives or an elected officer of the House of Representatives and who, within 1 year after that person leaves office, knowingly makes, with the intent to influence, any communication to or appearance before any of the persons described in clause (ii) or (iii), on behalf of any other person (except the United States) in connection with any matter on which such former Member of Congress or elected officer seeks action by a Member, officer, or employee of either House of Congress, in his or her official capacity, shall be punished as provided in section 216 of this title.

(ii) The persons referred to in clause (i) with respect to appearances or communications by a former Member of the House of Representatives are any Member, officer, or employee of either House of Congress and any employee of any other legislative office of the Congress.

(iii) The persons referred to in clause (i) with respect to appearances or communications by a former elected officer are any Member, officer, or employee of the House of Representatives.

(2) Officers and staff of the Senate.—Any person who is an elected officer of the Senate, or an employee of the Senate to whom paragraph (7)(A) applies, and who, within 1 year after that person leaves office or employment, knowingly makes, with the intent to influence, any communication to or appearance before any Senator or any officer or employee of the Senate, on behalf of any other person (except the United States) in connection with any matter on which such former elected officer or former employee seeks action by a Senator or an officer or employee of the Senate, in his or her official capacity, shall be punished as provided in section 216 of this title.

(3) Personal staff.—(A) Any person who is an employee of a Member of the House of Representatives to whom paragraph (7)(A) applies and who, within 1 year after the termination of that employment, knowingly makes, with the intent to influence, any communication to or appearance before any of the persons described in subparagraph (B), on behalf of any other person (except the United States) in connection with any matter on which such former employee seeks action by a Member, officer, or employee of either House of Congress, in his or her official capacity, shall be punished as provided in section 216 of this title.

(B) The persons referred to in subparagraph (A) with respect to appearances or communications by a person who is a former employee are the following:

(i) the Member of the House of Representatives for whom that person was an employee; and

(ii) any employee of that Member of the House of Representatives.

(4) Committee staff.—Any person who is an employee of a committee of the House of Representatives, or an employee of a joint committee of the Congress whose pay is disbursed by the Clerk of the House of Representatives, to whom paragraph (7)(A) applies and who, within 1 year after the termination of that person's employment on such committee or joint committee (as the case may be), knowingly makes, with the intent to influence, any communication to or appearance before any person who is a Member or an employee of that committee or joint committee (as the case may be) or who was a Member of the committee or joint committee (as the case may be) in the year immediately prior to the termination of such person's employment by the committee or joint committee (as the case may be), on behalf of any other person (except the

United States) in connection with any matter on which such former employee seeks action by a Member, officer, or employee of either House of Congress, in his or her official capacity, shall be punished as provided in section 216 of this title.

(5) Leadership staff.—(A) Any person who is an employee on the leadership staff of the House of Representatives to whom paragraph (7)(A) applies and who, within 1 year after the termination of that person's employment on such staff, knowingly makes, with the intent to influence, any communication to or appearance before any of the persons described in subparagraph (B), on behalf of any other person (except the United States) in connection with any matter on which such former employee seeks action by a Member, officer, or employee of either House of Congress, in his or her official capacity, shall be punished as provided in section 216 of this title.

(B) The persons referred to in subparagraph (A) with respect to appearances or communications by a former employee are any Member of the leadership of the House of Representatives and any employee on the leadership staff of the House of Representatives.

(6) Other legislative offices.—(A) Any person who is an employee of any other legislative office of the Congress to whom paragraph (7)(B) applies and who, within 1 year after the termination of that person's employment in such office, knowingly makes, with the intent to influence, any communication to or appearance before any of the persons described in subparagraph (B), on behalf of any other person (except the United States) in connection with any matter on which such former employee seeks action by any officer or employee of such office, in his or her official capacity, shall be punished as provided in section 216 of this title.

(B) The persons referred to in subparagraph (A) with respect to appearances or communications by a former employee are the employees and officers of the former legislative office of the Congress of the former employee.

(7) Limitation on restrictions.—(A) The restrictions contained in paragraphs (2), (3), (4), and (5) apply only to acts by a former employee who, for at least 60 days, in the aggregate, during the 1-year period before that former employee's service as such employee terminated, was paid a rate of basic pay equal to or greater than an amount which is 75 percent of the basic rate of pay payable for a Member of the House of Congress in which such employee was employed.

(B) The restrictions contained in paragraph (6) apply only to acts by a former employee who, for at least 60 days, in the aggregate, during the 1-year period before that former employee's service as such employee terminated, was employed in a position for which the rate of basic pay, exclusive of any locality-based pay adjustment under section 5302 of title 5, is equal to or greater than the basic rate of pay payable for level IV of the Executive Schedule.

(8) Exception.—This subsection shall not apply to contacts with the staff of the Secretary of the Senate or the Clerk of the House of Representatives regarding compliance with lobbying disclosure requirements under the Lobbying Disclosure Act of 1995.

(9) Definitions.—As used in this subsection—

(A) the term "committee of Congress" includes standing committees, joint committees, and select committees;

(B) a person is an employee of a House of Congress if that person is an employee of the Senate or an employee of the House of Representatives;

(C) the term "employee of the House of Representatives" means an employee of a Member of the House of Representatives, an employee of a committee of the House of Representatives, an employee of a joint committee of the Congress whose pay is disbursed by the Clerk of the House of Representatives, and an employee on the leadership staff of the House of Representatives;

(D) the term "employee of the Senate" means an employee of a Senator, an employee of a committee of the Senate, an employee of a joint committee of the Congress whose pay is disbursed by the Secretary of the Senate, and an employee on the leadership staff of the Senate;

(E) a person is an employee of a Member of the House of Representatives if that person is an employee of a Member of the House of Representatives under the clerk hire allowance;

(F) a person is an employee of a Senator if that person is an employee in a position in the office of a Senator;

(G) the term "employee of any other legislative office of the Congress" means an officer or employee of the Architect of the Capitol, the United States Botanic Garden, the Government Accountability Office, the Government Printing Office, the Library of Congress, the Office of Technology Assessment, the Congressional Budget Office, the United States Capitol Police, and any other agency, entity, or office in the legislative branch not covered by paragraph (1), (2), (3), (4), or (5) of this subsection;

(H) the term "employee on the leadership staff of the House of Representatives" means an employee of the office of a Member of the leadership of the House of Representatives described in subparagraph (L), and any elected minority employee of the House of Representatives;

(I) the term "employee on the leadership staff of the Senate" means an employee of the office of a Member of the leadership of the Senate described in subparagraph (M);

(J) the term "Member of Congress" means a Senator or a Member of the House of Representatives;

(K) the term "Member of the House of Representatives" means a Representative in, or a Delegate or Resident Commissioner to, the Congress;

(L) the term "Member of the leadership of the House of Representatives" means the Speaker, majority leader, minority leader, majority whip, minority whip, chief deputy majority whip, chief deputy minority whip, chairman of the Democratic Steering Committee, chairman and vice chairman of the Democratic Caucus, chairman, vice chairman, and secretary of the Republican Conference, chairman of the Republican Research Committee, and chairman of the Republican Policy Committee, of the House of Representatives (or any similar position created on or after the effective date set forth in section 102(a) of the Ethics Reform Act of 1989);

(M) the term "Member of the leadership of the Senate" means the Vice President, and the President pro tempore, Deputy President pro tempore, majority leader, minority leader, majority whip, minority whip, chairman and secretary of the Conference of the Majority, chairman and secretary of the Conference of the Minority, chairman and co-chairman of the Majority Policy Committee, and chairman of the Minority Policy Committee, of the Senate (or any similar position created on or after the effective date set forth in section 102(a) of the Ethics Reform Act of 1989).

(f) Restrictions relating to foreign entities.—

(1) Restrictions.—Any person who is subject to the restrictions contained in subsection (c), (d), or (e) and who knowingly, within 1 year after leaving the position, office, or employment referred to in such subsection—

(A) represents a foreign entity before any officer or employee of any department or agency of the United States with the intent to influence a decision of such officer or employee in carrying out his or her official duties, or

(B) aids or advises a foreign entity with the intent to influence a decision of any officer or employee of any department or agency of the United States, in carrying out his or her official duties,

shall be punished as provided in section 216 of this title.

(2) Special rule for Trade Representative.—With respect to a person who is the United States Trade Representative or Deputy United States Trade Representative, the restrictions described in paragraph (1) shall apply to representing, aiding, or advising foreign entities at any time after the termination of that person's service as the United States Trade Representative.

(3) Definition.—For purposes of this subsection, the term "foreign entity" means the government of a foreign country as defined in section 1(e) of the Foreign Agents Registration Act of 1938, as amended, or a foreign political party as defined in section 1(f) of that Act.

(g) Special rules for detailees.—For purposes of this section, a person who is detailed from one department, agency, or other entity to another department, agency, or other entity shall, during the period such person is detailed, be deemed to be an officer or employee of both departments, agencies, or such entities.

(h) Designations of separate statutory agencies and bureaus.—

(1) Designations.—For purposes of subsection (c) and except as provided in paragraph (2), whenever the Director of the Office of Government Ethics determines that an agency or bureau within a department or agency in the executive branch exercises functions which are distinct and separate from the remaining functions of the department or agency and that there exists no potential for use of undue influence or unfair advantage based on past Government service, the Director shall by rule designate such agency or bureau as a separate department or agency. On an annual basis the Director of the Office of Government Ethics shall review the designations and determinations made under this subparagraph and, in consultation with the department or agency concerned, make such additions and deletions as are necessary. Departments and agencies shall cooperate to the fullest extent with the Director of the Office of Government Ethics in the exercise of his or her responsibilities under this paragraph.

(2) Inapplicability of designations.—No agency or bureau within the Executive Office of the President may be designated under paragraph (1) as a separate department or agency. No designation under paragraph (1) shall apply to persons referred to in subsection (c)(2)(A)(i) or (iii).

(i) Definitions.—For purposes of this section—

(1) the term "officer or employee", when used to describe the person to whom a communication is made or before whom an appearance is made, with the intent to influence, shall include—

(A) in subsections (a), (c), and (d), the President and the Vice President; and

(B) in subsection (f), the President, the Vice President, and Members of Congress;

(2) the term "participated" means an action taken as an officer or employee through decision, approval, disapproval, recommendation, the rendering of advice, investigation, or other such action; and

(3) the term "particular matter" includes any investigation, application, request for a ruling or determination, rulemaking, contract, controversy, claim, charge, accusation, arrest, or judicial or other proceeding.

(j) Exceptions.—

(1) Official government duties.—

(A) In general.—The restrictions contained in this section shall not apply to acts done in carrying out official duties on behalf of the United States or the District of Columbia or as an elected official of a State or local government.

(B) Tribal organizations and inter-tribal consortiums.—The restrictions contained in this section shall not apply to acts authorized by section 104(j) of the Indian Self-Determination and Education Assistance Act (25 U.S.C. 450i(j)).

(2) State and local governments and institutions, hospitals, and organizations.—The restrictions contained in subsections (c), (d), and (e) shall not apply to acts done in carrying out official duties as an employee of—

(A) an agency or instrumentality of a State or local government if the appearance, communication, or representation is on behalf of such government, or

(B) an accredited, degree-granting institution of higher education, as defined in section 101 of the Higher Education Act of 1965, or a hospital or medical research organization, exempted and defined under section 501(c)(3) of the Internal Revenue Code of 1986, if the appearance, communication, or representation is on behalf of such institution, hospital, or organization.

(3) International organizations.—The restrictions contained in this section shall not apply to an appearance or communication on behalf of, or advice or aid to, an international organization in which the United States participates, if the Secretary of State certifies in advance that such activity is in the interests of the United States.

(4) Special knowledge.—The restrictions contained in subsections (c), (d), and (e) shall not prevent an individual from making or providing a statement, which is based on the individual's own special knowledge in the particular area that is the subject of the statement, if no compensation is thereby received.

(5) Exception for scientific or technological information.—The restrictions contained in subsections (a), (c), and (d) shall not apply with respect to the making of communications solely for the purpose of furnishing scientific or technological information, if such communications are made under procedures acceptable to the department or agency concerned or if the head of the department or agency concerned with the particular matter, in consultation with the Director of the Office of Government Ethics, makes a certification, published in the Federal Register, that the former officer or employee has outstanding qualifications in a scientific, technological, or other technical discipline, and is acting with respect to a particular matter which requires such qualifications, and that the national interest would be served by the participation of the former officer or employee. For purposes of this paragraph, the term "officer or employee" includes the Vice President.

(6) Exception for testimony.—Nothing in this section shall prevent an individual from giving testimony under oath, or from making statements required to be made under penalty of perjury. Notwithstanding the preceding sentence—

(A) a former officer or employee of the executive branch of the United States (including any independent agency) who is subject to the restrictions contained in subsection (a)(1) with respect to a particular matter may not, except pursuant to court order, serve as an expert witness for any other person (except the United States) in that matter; and

(B) a former officer or employee of the District of Columbia who is subject to the restrictions contained in subsection (a)(1) with respect to a particular matter may not, except pursuant to court order, serve as an expert witness for any other person (except the District of Columbia) in that matter.

(7) Political parties and campaign committees.—(A) Except as provided in subparagraph (B), the restrictions contained in subsections (c), (d), and (e) shall not apply to a communication or appearance made solely on behalf of a candidate in his or her capacity as a candidate, an authorized committee, a national committee, a national Federal campaign committee, a State committee, or a political party.

(B) Subparagraph (A) shall not apply to—

(i) any communication to, or appearance before, the Federal Election Commission by a former officer or employee of the Federal Election Commission; or

(ii) a communication or appearance made by a person who is subject to the restrictions contained in subsections [FN1] (c), (d), or (e) if, at the time of the communication or appearance, the person is employed by a person or entity other than—

(I) a candidate, an authorized committee, a national committee, a national Federal campaign committee, a State committee, or a political party; or

(II) a person or entity who represents, aids, or advises only persons or entities described in subclause (I).

(C) For purposes of this paragraph—

(i) the term "candidate" means any person who seeks nomination for election, or election, to Federal or State office or who has authorized others to explore on his or her behalf the possibility of seeking nomination for election, or election, to Federal or State office;

(ii) the term "authorized committee" means any political committee designated in writing by a candidate as authorized to receive contributions or make expenditures to promote the nomination for election, or the election, of such candidate, or to explore the possibility of seeking nomination for election, or the election, of such candidate, except that a political committee that receives contributions or makes expenditures to promote more than 1 candidate may not be designated as an authorized committee for purposes of subparagraph (A);

(iii) the term "national committee" means the organization which, by virtue of the bylaws of a political party, is responsible for the day-to-day operation of such political party at the national level;

(iv) the term "national Federal campaign committee" means an organization that, by virtue of the bylaws of a political party, is established primarily for the purpose of providing assistance, at the national level, to candidates nominated by that party for election to the office of Senator or Representative in, or Delegate or Resident Commissioner to, the Congress;

(v) the term "State committee" means the organization which, by virtue of the bylaws of a political party, is responsible for the day-to-day operation of such political party at the State level;

(vi) the term "political party" means an association, committee, or organization that nominates a candidate for election to any Federal or State elected office whose name appears on the election ballot as the candidate of such association, committee, or organization; and

(vii) the term "State" means a State of the United States, the District of Columbia, the Commonwealth of Puerto Rico, and any territory or possession of the United States.

(k)(1)(A) The President may grant a waiver of a restriction imposed by this section to any officer or employee described in paragraph (2) if the President determines and certifies in writing that it is in the public interest to grant the waiver and that the services of the officer or employee are critically needed for the benefit of the Federal Government. Not more than 25 officers and employees currently employed by the Federal Government at any one time may have been granted waivers under this paragraph.

(B)(i) A waiver granted under this paragraph to any person shall apply only with respect to activities engaged in by that person after that person's Federal Government employment is terminated and only to that person's employment at a Government-owned, contractor operated entity with which the person served as an officer or employee immediately before the person's Federal Government employment began.

(ii) Notwithstanding clause (i), a waiver granted under this paragraph to any person who was an officer or employee of Lawrence Livermore National Laboratory, Los Alamos National Laboratory, or Sandia National Laboratory immediately before the person's Federal Government employment began shall apply to that person's employment by any such national laboratory after the person's employment by the Federal Government is terminated.

(2) Waivers under paragraph (1) may be granted only to civilian officers and employees of the executive branch, other than officers and employees in the Executive Office of the President.

(3) A certification under paragraph (1) shall take effect upon its publication in the Federal Register and shall identify—

(A) the officer or employee covered by the waiver by name and by position, and

(B) the reasons for granting the waiver.

A copy of the certification shall also be provided to the Director of the Office of Government Ethics.

(4) The President may not delegate the authority provided by this subsection.

(5)(A) Each person granted a waiver under this subsection shall prepare reports, in accordance with subparagraph (B), stating whether the person has engaged in activities otherwise prohibited by this section for each six-month period described in subparagraph (B), and if so, what those activities were.

(B) A report under subparagraph (A) shall cover each six-month period beginning on the date of the termination of the person's Federal Government employment (with respect to which the waiver under this subsection was granted) and ending two years after that date. Such report shall be filed with the President and the Director of the Office of Government Ethics not later than 60 days after the end of the six-month period covered by the report. All reports filed with the Director under this paragraph shall be made available for public inspection and copying.

(C) If a person fails to file any report in accordance with subparagraphs (A) and (B), the President shall revoke the waiver and shall notify the person of the revocation. The revocation shall take effect upon the person's receipt of the notification and shall remain in effect until the report is filed.

(D) Any person who is granted a waiver under this subsection shall be ineligible for appointment in the civil service unless all reports required of such person by subparagraphs (A) and (B) have been filed.

(E) As used in this subsection, the term "civil service" has the meaning given that term in section 2101 of title 5.

(l) **Contract advice by former details.**—Whoever, being an employee of a private sector organization assigned to an agency under chapter 37 of title 5, within one year after the end of that assignment, knowingly represents or aids, counsels, or assists in representing any other person (except the United States) in connection with any contract with that agency shall be punished as provided in section 216 of this title.

§ 208. Acts affecting a personal financial interest

(a) Except as permitted by subsection (b) hereof, whoever, being an officer or employee of the executive branch of the United States Government, or of any independent agency of the United States, a Federal Reserve bank director, officer, or employee, or an officer or employee of the District of Columbia, including a special Government employee, participates personally and substantially as a Government officer or employee, through decision, approval, disapproval, recommendation, the rendering of advice, investigation, or otherwise, in a judicial or other proceeding, application, request for a ruling or other determination, contract, claim, controversy, charge, accusation, arrest, or other particular matter in which, to his knowledge, he, his spouse, minor child, general partner, organization in which he is serving as officer, director, trustee, general partner or employee, or any person or organization with whom he is negotiating or has any arrangement concerning prospective employment, has a financial interest—

Shall be subject to the penalties set forth in section 216 of this title.

(b) Subsection (a) shall not apply—

(1) if the officer or employee first advises the Government official responsible for appointment to his or her position of the nature and circumstances of the judicial or other proceeding, application, request for a ruling or other determination, contract, claim, controversy, charge, accusation, arrest, or other particular matter and makes full disclosure of the financial interest and receives in advance a written determination made by such official that the interest is not so substantial as to be deemed likely to affect the integrity of the services which the Government may expect from such officer or employee;

(2) if, by regulation issued by the Director of the Office of Government Ethics, applicable to all or a portion of all officers and employees covered by this section, and published in the Federal Register, the financial interest has been exempted from the requirements of subsection (a) as being too remote or too inconsequential to affect the integrity of the services of the Government officers or employees to which such regulation applies;

(3) in the case of a special Government employee serving on an advisory committee within the meaning of the Federal Advisory Committee Act (including an individual being considered for an appointment to such a position), the official responsible for the employee's appointment, after review of the financial disclosure report filed by the individual pursuant to the Ethics in Government Act of 1978, certifies in writing that the need for the individual's services outweighs the potential for a conflict of interest created by the financial interest involved; or

(4) if the financial interest that would be affected by the particular matter involved is that resulting solely from the interest of the officer or employee, or his or her spouse or minor child, in birthrights—

(A) in an Indian tribe, band, nation, or other organized group or community, including any Alaska Native village corporation as defined in or established pursuant to the Alaska Native Claims Settlement Act, which is recognized as eligible for the special programs and services provided by the United States to Indians because of their status as Indians,

(B) in an Indian allotment the title to which is held in trust by the United States or which is inalienable by the allottee without the consent of the United States, or

(C) in an Indian claims fund held in trust or administered by the United States,

if the particular matter does not involve the Indian allotment or claims fund or the Indian tribe, band, nation, organized group or community, or Alaska Native village corporation as a specific party or parties.

(c)(1) For the purpose of paragraph (1) of subsection (b), in the case of class A and B directors of Federal Reserve Banks, the Board of Governors of the Federal Reserve System shall be deemed to be the Government official responsible for appointment.

(2) The potential availability of an exemption under any particular paragraph of subsection (b) does not preclude an exemption being granted pursuant to another paragraph of subsection (b).

(d)(1) Upon request, a copy of any determination granting an exemption under subsection (b)(1) or (b)(3) shall be made available to the public by the agency granting the exemption pursuant to the procedures set forth in section 105 of the Ethics in Government Act of 1978. In making such determination available, the agency may withhold from disclosure any information contained in the determination that would be exempt from disclosure under section 552 of title 5. For purposes of determinations under subsection (b)(3), the information describing each financial interest shall be no more extensive than that required of the individual in his or her financial disclosure report under the Ethics in Government Act of 1978.

(2) The Office of Government Ethics, after consultation with the Attorney General, shall issue uniform regulations for the issuance of waivers and exemptions under subsection (b) which shall—

(A) list and describe exemptions; and

(B) provide guidance with respect to the types of interests that are not so substantial as to be deemed likely to affect the integrity of the services the Government may expect from the employee.

§ 209. Salary of Government officials and employees payable only by United States

(a) Whoever receives any salary, or any contribution to or supplementation of salary, as compensation for his services as an officer or employee of the executive branch of the United States Government, of any independent agency of the United States, or of the District of Columbia, from any source other than the Government of the United States, except as may be contributed out of the treasury of any State, county, or municipality; or

Whoever, whether an individual, partnership, association, corporation, or other organization pays, makes any contribution to, or in any way supplements the salary of any such officer or employee under circumstances which would make its receipt a violation of this subsection—

Shall be subject to the penalties set forth in section 216 of this title.

(b) Nothing herein prevents an officer or employee of the executive branch of the United States Government, or of any independent agency of the United States, or of the District of Columbia, from continuing to participate in a bona fide pension, retirement, group life, health or accident insurance, profit-sharing, stock bonus, or other employee welfare or benefit plan maintained by a former employer.

(c) This section does not apply to a special Government employee or to an officer or employee of the Government serving without compensation, whether or not he is a special Government employee, or to any person paying, contributing to, or supplementing his salary as such.

(d) This section does not prohibit payment or acceptance of contributions, awards, or other expenses under the terms of chapter 41 of title 5.

(e) This section does not prohibit the payment of actual relocation expenses incident to participation, or the acceptance of same by a participant in an executive exchange or fellowship program in an executive agency: *Provided*, That such program has been established by statute or Executive order of the President, offers appointments not to exceed three hundred and sixty-five days, and permits no extensions in excess of ninety additional days or, in the case of participants in overseas assignments, in excess of three hundred and sixty-five days.

(f) This section does not prohibit acceptance or receipt, by any officer or employee injured during the commission of an offense described in section 351 or 1751 of this title, of contributions or payments from an organization which is described in section 501(c)(3) of the Internal Revenue Code of 1954 and which is exempt from taxation under section 501(a) of such Code.

(g)(1) This section does not prohibit an employee of a private sector organization, while assigned to an agency under chapter 37 of title 5, from continuing to receive pay and benefits from such organization in accordance with such chapter.

(2) For purposes of this subsection, the term "agency" means an agency (as defined by section 3701 of title 5) and the Office of the Chief Technology Officer of the District of Columbia.

§ 216. Penalties and injunctions

(a) The punishment for an offense under sections 203, 204, 205, 207, 208, or 209 of this title is the following:

(1) Whoever engages in the conduct constituting the offense shall be imprisoned for not more than one year or fined in the amount set forth in this title, or both.

(2) Whoever willfully engages in the conduct constituting the offense shall be imprisoned for not more than five years or fined in the amount set forth in this title, or both.

(b) The Attorney General may bring a civil action in the appropriate United States district court against any person who engages in conduct constituting an offense under sections 203, 204, 205, 207, 208, or 209 of this title and, upon proof of such conduct by a preponderance of the evidence, such person shall be subject to a civil penalty of not more than $50,000 for each violation or the amount of compensation which the person received or offered for the prohibited conduct, whichever amount is greater. The imposition of a civil penalty under this subsection does not preclude any other criminal or civil statutory, common law, or administrative remedy, which is available by law to the United States or any other person.

(c) If the Attorney General has reason to believe that a person is engaging in conduct constituting an offense under section 203, 204, 205, 207, 208, or 209 of this title, the Attorney General may petition an appropriate United States district court for an order prohibiting that person from engaging in such conduct. The court may issue an order prohibiting that person from engaging in such conduct if the court finds that the conduct constitutes such an offense. The filing of a petition under this section does not preclude any other remedy which is available by law to the United States or any other person.

§ 218. Voiding transactions in violation of chapter; recovery by the United States

In addition to any other remedies provided by law the President or, under regulations prescribed by him, the head of any department or agency involved, may declare void and rescind any contract, loan, grant, subsidy, license, right, permit, franchise, use, authority, privilege, benefit, certificate, ruling, decision, opinion, or rate schedule awarded, granted, paid, furnished, or published, or the performance of any service or transfer or delivery of any thing to, by or for any agency of the United States or officer or employee of the United States or person acting on behalf thereof, in relation to which there has been a final conviction for any violation of this chapter, and the United States shall be entitled to recover in addition to any penalty prescribed by law or in a contract the amount expended or the thing transferred or delivered on its behalf, or the reasonable value thereof.

CHAPTER 21. CONTEMPTS

§ 401. Power of court

A court of the United States shall have power to punish by fine or imprisonment, or both, at its discretion, such contempt of its authority, and none other, as—

(1) Misbehavior of any person in its presence or so near thereto as to obstruct the administration of justice;

(2) Misbehavior of any of its officers in their official transactions;

(3) Disobedience or resistance to its lawful writ, process, order, rule, decree, or command.

§ 402. Contempts constituting crimes

Any person, corporation or association willfully disobeying any lawful writ, process, order, rule, decree, or command of any district court of the United States or any court of the District of Columbia, by doing any act or thing therein, or thereby forbidden, if the act or thing so done be of such character as to constitute also a criminal offense under any statute of the United States or under the laws of any State in which the act was committed, shall be prosecuted for such contempt as provided in section 3691 of this title and shall be punished by a fine under this title or imprisonment, or both.

Such fine shall be paid to the United States or to the complainant or other party injured by the act constituting the contempt, or may, where more than one is so damaged, be divided or apportioned among them as the court may direct, but in no case shall the fine to be paid to the United States exceed, in case the accused is a natural person, the sum of $1,000, nor shall such imprisonment exceed the term of six months.

This section shall not be construed to relate to contempts committed in the presence of the court, or so near thereto as to obstruct the administration of justice, nor to contempts committed in disobedience of any lawful writ, process, order, rule, decree, or command entered in any suit or action brought or prosecuted in the name of, or on behalf of, the United States, but the same, and all other cases of contempt not specifically embraced in this section may be punished in conformity to the prevailing usages at law.

For purposes of this section, the term "State" includes a State of the United States, the District of Columbia, and any commonwealth, territory, or possession of the United States.

CHAPTER 49. FUGITIVES FROM JUSTICE

§ 1074. Flight to avoid prosecution for damaging or destroying any building or other real or personal property

(a) Whoever moves or travels in interstate or foreign commerce with intent either (1) to avoid prosecution, or custody, or confinement after conviction, under the laws of the place from which he flees, for willfully attempting to or damaging or destroying by fire or explosive any building, structure, facility, vehicle, dwelling house, synagogue, church, religious center or educational institution, public or private, or (2) to avoid giving testimony in any criminal proceeding relating to any such offense shall be fined under this title or imprisoned not more than five years, or both.

(b) Violations of this section may be prosecuted in the Federal judicial district in which the original crime was alleged to have been committed or in which the person was held in custody or confinement: *Provided, however*, That this section shall not be construed as indicating an intent on the part of Congress to prevent any State, Territory, Commonwealth, or possession of the United States of any jurisdiction over any offense over which they would have jurisdiction in the absence of such section.

CHAPTER 63. MAIL FRAUD

§ 1341. Frauds and swindles

Whoever, having devised or intending to devise any scheme or artifice to defraud, or for obtaining money or property by means of false or fraudulent pretenses, representations, or promises, or to sell, dispose of, loan, exchange, alter, give away, distribute, supply, or furnish or procure for unlawful use any counterfeit or spurious coin, obligation, security, or other article, or anything represented to be or intimated or held out to be such counterfeit or spurious article, for the purpose of executing such scheme or artifice or attempting so to do, places in any post office or authorized depository for mail matter, any matter or thing whatever to be sent or delivered by the Postal Service, or deposits or causes to be deposited any matter or thing whatever to be sent or delivered by any private or commercial interstate carrier, or takes or receives therefrom, any such matter or thing, or knowingly causes to be delivered by mail or such carrier according to the direction thereon, or at the place at which it is directed to be delivered by the person to whom it is addressed, any such matter or thing, shall be fined under this title or imprisoned not more than 20 years, or both. If the violation occurs in relation to, or involving any benefit authorized, transported, transmitted, transferred, disbursed, or paid in connection with, a presidentially declared major disaster or emergency (as those terms are defined in section 102 of the Robert T. Stafford Disaster Relief and Emergency Assistance Act (42 U.S.C. 5122)), or affects a financial institution, such person shall be fined not more than $1,000,000 or imprisoned not more than 30 years, or both.

§ 1348. Securities and commodities fraud

Whoever knowingly executes, or attempts to execute, a scheme or artifice—

(1) to defraud any person in connection with any commodity for future delivery, or any option on a commodity for future delivery, or any security of an issuer with a class of securities registered under section 12 of the Securities Exchange Act of 1934 (15 U.S.C. 78l) or that is required to file reports under section 15(d) of the Securities Exchange Act of 1934 (15 U.S.C. 78o(d)); or

(2) to obtain, by means of false or fraudulent pretenses, representations, or promises, any money or property in connection with the purchase or sale of any commodity for future delivery, or any option on a commodity for future delivery, or any security of an issuer with a class of securities registered under section 12 of the Securities Exchange Act of 1934 (15 U.S.C. 78l) or that is required to file reports under section 15(d) of the Securities Exchange Act of 1934 (15 U.S.C. 78o(d));

shall be fined under this title, or imprisoned not more than 25 years, or both.

CHAPTER 73. OBSTRUCTION OF JUSTICE

§ 1501. Assault on process server

Whoever knowingly and willfully obstructs, resists, or opposes any officer of the United States, or other person duly authorized, in serving, or attempting to serve or execute, any legal or judicial writ or process of any court of the United States, or United States magistrate judge; or

Whoever assaults, beats, or wounds any officer or other person duly authorized, knowing him to be such officer, or other person so duly authorized, in serving or executing any such writ, rule, order, process, warrant, or other legal or judicial writ or process—

Shall, except as otherwise provided by law, be fined under this title or imprisoned not more than one year, or both.

§ 1502. Resistance to extradition agent

Whoever knowingly and willfully obstructs, resists, or opposes an extradition agent of the United States in the execution of his duties, shall be fined under this title or imprisoned not more than one year, or both.

§ 1503. Influencing or injuring officer or juror generally

(a) Whoever corruptly, or by threats or force, or by any threatening letter or communication, endeavors to influence, intimidate, or impede any grand or petit juror, or officer in or of any court of the United States, or officer who may be serving at any examination or other proceeding before any

United States commissioner or other committing magistrate, in the discharge of his duty, or injures any such grand or petit juror in his person or property on account of any verdict or indictment assented to by him, or on account of his being or having been such juror, or injures any such officer, commissioner, or other committing magistrate in his person or property on account of the performance of his official duties, or corruptly or by threats or force, or by any threatening letter or communication, influences, obstructs, or impedes, or endeavors to influence, obstruct, or impede, the due administration of justice, shall be punished as provided in subsection (b).

(b) The punishment for an offense under this section is—

(1) in the case of a killing, the punishment provided in sections 1111 and 1112;

(2) in the case of an attempted killing, or a case in which the offense was committed against a petit juror and in which a class A or B felony was charged, imprisonment for not more than 20 years, a fine under this title, or both; and

(3) in any other case, imprisonment for not more than 10 years, a fine under this title, or both.

§ 1504. Influencing juror by writing

Whoever attempts to influence the action or decision of any grand or petit juror of any court of the United States upon any issue or matter pending before such juror, or before the jury of which he is a member, or pertaining to his duties, by writing or sending to him any written communication, in relation to such issue or matter, shall be fined under this title or imprisoned not more than six months, or both.

Nothing in this section shall be construed to prohibit the communication of a request to appear before the grand jury.

§ 1505. Obstruction of proceedings before departments, agencies, and committees

Whoever, with intent to avoid, evade, prevent, or obstruct compliance, in whole or in part, with any civil investigative demand duly and properly made under the Antitrust Civil Process Act, willfully withholds, misrepresents, removes from any place, conceals, covers up, destroys, mutilates, alters, or by other means falsifies any documentary material, answers to written interrogatories, or oral testimony, which is the subject of such demand; or attempts to do so or solicits another to do so; or

Whoever corruptly, or by threats or force, or by any threatening letter or communication influences, obstructs, or impedes or endeavors to influence, obstruct, or impede the due and proper administration of the law under which any pending proceeding is being had before any department or agency of the United States, or the due and proper exercise of the power of inquiry under which any inquiry or investigation is being had by either House, or any committee of either House or any joint committee of the Congress—

Shall be fined under this title, imprisoned not more than 5 years or if the offense involves international or domestic terrorism (as defined in section 2331), imprisoned not more than 8 years or both.

§ 1506. Theft or alteration of record or process; false bail

Whoever feloniously steals, takes away, alters, falsifies, or otherwise avoids any record, writ, process, or other proceeding, in any court of the United States, whereby any judgment is reversed, made void, or does not take effect; or

Whoever acknowledges, or procures to be acknowledged in any such court, any recognizance, bail, or judgment, in the name of any other person not privy or consenting to the same—

Shall be fined under this title or imprisoned not more than five years, or both.

§ 1507. Picketing or parading

Whoever, with the intent of interfering with, obstructing, or impeding the administration of justice, or with the intent of influencing any judge, juror, witness, or court officer, in the discharge of his duty, pickets or parades in or near a building housing a court of the United States, or in or near a building or residence occupied or used by such judge, juror, witness, or court officer, or with such intent uses any sound-truck or similar device or resorts to any other demonstration in or near any such building or residence, shall be fined under this title or imprisoned not more than one year, or both.

Nothing in this section shall interfere with or prevent the exercise by any court of the United States of its power to punish for contempt.

§ 1508. Recording, listening to, or observing proceedings of grand or petit juries while deliberating or voting

Whoever knowingly and willfully, by any means or device whatsoever—

(a) records, or attempts to record, the proceedings of any grand or petit jury in any court of the United States while such jury is deliberating or voting; or

(b) listens to or observes, or attempts to listen to or observe, the proceedings of any grand or petit jury of which he is not a member in any court of the United States while such jury is deliberating or voting—

shall be fined under this title or imprisoned not more than one year, or both.

Nothing in paragraph (a) of this section shall be construed to prohibit the taking of notes by a grand or petit juror in any court of the United States in connection with and solely for the purpose of assisting him in the performance of his duties as such juror.

§ 1509. Obstruction of court orders

Whoever, by threats or force, willfully prevents, obstructs, impedes, or interferes with, or willfully attempts to prevent, obstruct, impede, or interfere with, the due exercise of rights or the performance of duties under any order, judgment, or decree of a court of the United States, shall be fined under this title or imprisoned not more than one year, or both.

No injunctive or other civil relief against the conduct made criminal by this section shall be denied on the ground that such conduct is a crime.

§ 1510. Obstruction of criminal investigations

(a) Whoever willfully endeavors by means of bribery to obstruct, delay, or prevent the communication of information relating to a violation of any criminal statute of the United States by any person to a criminal investigator shall be fined under this title, or imprisoned not more than five years, or both.

(b)(1) Whoever, being an officer of a financial institution, with the intent to obstruct a judicial proceeding, directly or indirectly notifies any other person about the existence or contents of a subpoena for records of that financial institution, or information that has been furnished in response to that subpoena, shall be fined under this title or imprisoned not more than 5 years, or both.

(2) Whoever, being an officer of a financial institution, directly or indirectly notifies—

(A) a customer of that financial institution whose records are sought by a subpoena for records; or

(B) any other person named in that subpoena;

about the existence or contents of that subpoena or information that has been furnished in response to that subpoena, shall be fined under this title or imprisoned not more than one year, or both.

(3) As used in this subsection—

(A) the term "an officer of a financial institution" means an officer, director, partner, employee, agent, or attorney of or for a financial institution; and

(B) the term "subpoena for records" means a Federal grand jury subpoena or a Department of Justice subpoena (issued under section 3486 of title 18) for customer records that has been served relating to a violation of, or a conspiracy to violate—

(i) section 215, 656, 657, 1005, 1006, 1007, 1014, or 1344, 1956, 1957, or chapter 53 of title 31; or

(ii) section 1341 or 1343 affecting a financial institution.

(c) As used in this section, the term "criminal investigator" means any individual duly authorized by a department, agency, or armed force of the United States to conduct or engage in investigations of or prosecutions for violations of the criminal laws of the United States.

(d)(1) Whoever—

(A) acting as, or being, an officer, director, agent or employee of a person engaged in the business of insurance whose activities affect interstate commerce, or

(B) is engaged in the business of insurance whose activities affect interstate commerce or is involved (other than as an insured or beneficiary under a policy of insurance) in a transaction relating to the conduct of affairs of such a business,

with intent to obstruct a judicial proceeding, directly or indirectly notifies any other person about the existence or contents of a subpoena for records of that person engaged in such business or information that has been furnished to a Federal grand jury in response to that subpoena, shall be fined as provided by this title or imprisoned not more than 5 years, or both.

(2) As used in paragraph (1), the term "subpoena for records" means a Federal grand jury subpoena for records that has been served relating to a violation of, or a conspiracy to violate, section 1033 of this title.

(e) Whoever, having been notified of the applicable disclosure prohibitions or confidentiality requirements of section 2709(c)(1) of this title, section 626(d)(1) or 627(c)(1) of the Fair Credit Reporting Act (15 U. S.C. 1681u(d)(1) or 1681v(c)(1)), section 1114(a)(3)(A) or 1114(a)(5)(D)(i) of the Right to Financial Privacy Act (12 U.S.C. 3414(a)(3)(A) or 3414(a)(5)(D)(i)), or section 802(b)(1) of the National Security Act of 1947 (50 U.S.C. 436(b)(1)), knowingly and with the intent to obstruct an investigation or judicial proceeding violates such prohibitions or requirements applicable by law to such person shall be imprisoned for not more than five years, fined under this title, or both.

§ 1511. Obstruction of State or local law enforcement

(a) It shall be unlawful for two or more persons to conspire to obstruct the enforcement of the criminal laws of a State or political subdivision thereof, with the intent to facilitate an illegal gambling business if—

(1) one or more of such persons does any act to effect the object of such a conspiracy;

(2) one or more of such persons is an official or employee, elected, appointed, or otherwise, of such State or political subdivision; and

(3) one or more of such persons conducts, finances, manages, supervises, directs, or owns all or part of an illegal gambling business.

(b) As used in this section—

(1) "illegal gambling business" means a gambling business which—

(i) is a violation of the law of a State or political subdivision in which it is conducted;

(ii) involves five or more persons who conduct, finance, manage, supervise, direct, or own all or part of such business; and

(iii) has been or remains in substantially continuous operation for a period in excess of thirty days or has a gross revenue of $2,000 in any single day.

(2) "gambling" includes but is not limited to pool-selling, bookmaking, maintaining slot machines, roulette wheels, or dice tables, and conducting lotteries, policy, bolita or numbers games, or selling chances therein.

(3) "State" means any State of the United States, the District of Columbia, the Commonwealth of Puerto Rico, and any territory or possession of the United States.

(c) This section shall not apply to any bingo game, lottery, or similar game of chance conducted by an organization exempt from tax under paragraph (3) of subsection (c) of section 501 of the Internal Revenue Code of 1954, as amended, if no part of the gross receipts derived from such activity inures to the benefit of any private shareholder, member, or employee of such organization, except as compensation for actual expenses incurred by him in the conduct of such activity.

(d) Whoever violates this section shall be punished by a fine under this title or imprisonment for not more than five years, or both.

§ 1512. Tampering with a witness, victim, or an informant

(a)(1) Whoever kills or attempts to kill another person, with intent to—

(A) prevent the attendance or testimony of any person in an official proceeding;

(B) prevent the production of a record, document, or other object, in an official proceeding; or

(C) prevent the communication by any person to a law enforcement officer or judge of the United States of information relating to the commission or possible commission of a Federal offense or a violation of conditions of probation, parole, or release pending judicial proceedings;

shall be punished as provided in paragraph (3).

(2) Whoever uses physical force or the threat of physical force against any person, or attempts to do so, with intent to—

(A) influence, delay, or prevent the testimony of any person in an official proceeding;

(B) cause or induce any person to—

(i) withhold testimony, or withhold a record, document, or other object, from an official proceeding;

(ii) alter, destroy, mutilate, or conceal an object with intent to impair the integrity or availability of the object for use in an official proceeding;

(iii) evade legal process summoning that person to appear as a witness, or to produce a record, document, or other object, in an official proceeding; or

(iv) be absent from an official proceeding to which that person has been summoned by legal process; or

(C) hinder, delay, or prevent the communication to a law enforcement officer or judge of the United States of information relating to the commission or possible commission of a Federal offense or a violation of conditions of probation, supervised release, parole, or release pending judicial proceedings;

shall be punished as provided in paragraph (3).

(3) The punishment for an offense under this subsection is—

(A) in the case of a killing, the punishment provided in sections 1111 and 1112;

(B) in the case of—

(i) an attempt to murder; or

(ii) the use or attempted use of physical force against any person, imprisonment for not more than 30 years; and

(C) in the case of the threat of use of physical force against any person, imprisonment for not more than 20 years.

(b) Whoever knowingly uses intimidation, threatens, or corruptly persuades another person, or attempts to do so, or engages in misleading conduct toward another person, with intent to—

(1) influence, delay, or prevent the testimony of any person in an official proceeding;

(2) cause or induce any person to—

(A) withhold testimony, or withhold a record, document, or other object, from an official proceeding;

(B) alter, destroy, mutilate, or conceal an object with intent to impair the object's integrity or availability for use in an official proceeding;

(C) evade legal process summoning that person to appear as a witness, or to produce a record, document, or other object, in an official proceeding; or

(D) be absent from an official proceeding to which such person has been summoned by legal process; or

(3) hinder, delay, or prevent the communication to a law enforcement officer or judge of the United States of information relating to the commission or possible commission of a Federal offense or a violation of conditions of probation, supervised release, parole, or release pending judicial proceedings;

shall be fined under this title or imprisoned not more than 20 years, or both.

(c) Whoever corruptly—

(1) alters, destroys, mutilates, or conceals a record, document, or other object, or attempts to do so, with the intent to impair the object's integrity or availability for use in an official proceeding; or

(2) otherwise obstructs, influences, or impedes any official proceeding, or attempts to do so,

shall be fined under this title or imprisoned not more than 20 years, or both.

(d) Whoever intentionally harasses another person and thereby hinders, delays, prevents, or dissuades any person from—

(1) attending or testifying in an official proceeding;

(2) reporting to a law enforcement officer or judge of the United States the commission or possible commission of a Federal offense or a violation of conditions of probation, supervised release, parole, or release pending judicial proceedings;

(3) arresting or seeking the arrest of another person in connection with a Federal offense; or

(4) causing a criminal prosecution, or a parole or probation revocation proceeding, to be sought or instituted, or assisting in such prosecution or proceeding;

or attempts to do so, shall be fined under this title or imprisoned not more than 3 years, or both.

(e) In a prosecution for an offense under this section, it is an affirmative defense, as to which the defendant has the burden of proof by a preponderance of the evidence, that the conduct consisted solely of lawful conduct and that the defendant's sole intention was to encourage, induce, or cause the other person to testify truthfully.

(f) For the purposes of this section—

(1) an official proceeding need not be pending or about to be instituted at the time of the offense; and

(2) the testimony, or the record, document, or other object need not be admissible in evidence or free of a claim of privilege.

(g) In a prosecution for an offense under this section, no state of mind need be proved with respect to the circumstance—

(1) that the official proceeding before a judge, court, magistrate judge, grand jury, or government agency is before a judge or court of the United States, a United States magistrate judge, a bankruptcy judge, a Federal grand jury, or a Federal Government agency; or

(2) that the judge is a judge of the United States or that the law enforcement officer is an officer or employee of the Federal Government or a person authorized to act for or on behalf of the Federal Government or serving the Federal Government as an adviser or consultant.

(h) There is extraterritorial Federal jurisdiction over an offense under this section.

(i) A prosecution under this section or section 1503 may be brought in the district in which the official proceeding (whether or not pending or about to be instituted) was intended to be affected or in the district in which the conduct constituting the alleged offense occurred.

(j) If the offense under this section occurs in connection with a trial of a criminal case, the maximum term of imprisonment which may be imposed for the offense shall be the higher of that otherwise provided by law or the maximum term that could have been imposed for any offense charged in such case.

(k) Whoever conspires to commit any offense under this section shall be subject to the same penalties as those prescribed for the offense the commission of which was the object of the conspiracy.

§ 1514A. Civil action to protect against retaliation in fraud cases

(a) Whistleblower protection for employees of publicly traded companies.—No company with a class of securities registered under section 12 of the Securities Exchange Act of 1934 (15 U.S.C. 78l), or that is required to file reports under section 15(d) of the Securities Exchange Act of 1934 (15 U.S.C. 78o(d)) including any subsidiary or affiliate whose financial information is included in the consolidated financial statements of such company, or nationally recognized statistical rating organization (as defined in section 3(a) of the Securities Exchange Act of 1934 15 U.S.C. 78c), or any officer, employee, contractor, subcontractor, or agent of such company or nationally recognized statistical rating organization, may discharge, demote, suspend, threaten, harass, or in any other manner discriminate against an employee in the terms and conditions of employment because of any lawful act done by the employee—

(1) to provide information, cause information to be provided, or otherwise assist in an investigation regarding any conduct which the employee reasonably believes constitutes a violation of section 1341, 1343, 1344, or 1348, any rule or regulation of the Securities and Exchange Commission, or any provision of Federal law relating to fraud against shareholders, when the information or assistance is provided to or the investigation is conducted by—

(A) a Federal regulatory or law enforcement agency;

(B) any Member of Congress or any committee of Congress; or

(C) a person with supervisory authority over the employee (or such other person working for the employer who has the authority to investigate, discover, or terminate misconduct); or

(2) to file, cause to be filed, testify, participate in, or otherwise assist in a proceeding filed or about to be filed (with any knowledge of the employer) relating to an alleged violation of section 1341, 1343, 1344, or 1348, any rule or regulation of the Securities and Exchange Commission, or any provision of Federal law relating to fraud against shareholders.

(b) Enforcement action.—

(1) In general.—A person who alleges discharge or other discrimination by any person in violation of subsection (a) may seek relief under subsection (c), by—

(A) filing a complaint with the Secretary of Labor; or

(B) if the Secretary has not issued a final decision within 180 days of the filing of the complaint and there is no showing that such delay is due to the bad faith of the claimant, bringing an action at law or equity for de novo review in the appropriate district court of the United States, which shall have jurisdiction over such an action without regard to the amount in controversy.

(2) Procedure.—

(A) In general.—An action under paragraph (1)(A) shall be governed under the rules and procedures set forth in section 42121(b) of title 49, United States Code.

(B) Exception.—Notification made under section 42121(b)(1) of title 49, United States Code, shall be made to the person named in the complaint and to the employer.

(C) Burdens of proof.—An action brought under paragraph (1)(B) shall be governed by the legal burdens of proof set forth in section 42121(b) of title 49, United States Code.

(D) Statute of limitations.—An action under paragraph (1) shall be commenced not later than 180 days after the date on which the violation occurs, or after the date on which the employee became aware of the violation.

(E) Jury trial.—A party to an action brought under paragraph (1)(B) shall be entitled to trial by jury.

(c) Remedies.—

(1) In general.—An employee prevailing in any action under subsection (b)(1) shall be entitled to all relief necessary to make the employee whole.

(2) Compensatory damages.—Relief for any action under paragraph (1) shall include—

(A) reinstatement with the same seniority status that the employee would have had, but for the discrimination;

(B) the amount of back pay, with interest; and

(C) compensation for any special damages sustained as a result of the discrimination, including litigation costs, expert witness fees, and reasonable attorney fees.

(d) Rights retained by employee.—Nothing in this section shall be deemed to diminish the rights, privileges, or remedies of any employee under any Federal or State law, or under any collective bargaining agreement.

(e) Nonenforceability of certain provisions waiving rights and remedies or requiring arbitration of disputes.—

(1) Waiver of rights and remedies.—The rights and remedies provided for in this section may not be waived by any agreement, policy form, or condition of employment, including by a predispute arbitration agreement.

(2) Predispute arbitration agreements.—No predispute arbitration agreement shall be valid or enforceable, if the agreement requires arbitration of a dispute arising under this section.

§ 1519. Destruction, alteration, or falsification of records in Federal investigations and bankruptcy

Whoever knowingly alters, destroys, mutilates, conceals, covers up, falsifies, or makes a false entry in any record, document, or tangible object with the intent to impede, obstruct, or influence the investigation or proper administration of any matter within the jurisdiction of any department or agency of the United States or any case filed under title 11, or in relation to or contemplation of any such matter or case, shall be fined under this title, imprisoned not more than 20 years, or both.

§ 1520. Destruction of corporate audit records

(a)(1) Any accountant who conducts an audit of an issuer of securities to which section 10A(a) of the Securities Exchange Act of 1934 (15 U.S.C. 78j–1(a)) applies, shall maintain all audit or review workpapers for a period of 5 years from the end of the fiscal period in which the audit or review was concluded.

(2) The Securities and Exchange Commission shall promulgate, within 180 days, after adequate notice and an opportunity for comment, such rules and regulations, as are reasonably necessary, relating to the retention of relevant records such as workpapers, documents that form the basis of an audit or review, memoranda, correspondence, communications, other documents, and records (including electronic records) which are created, sent, or received in connection with an audit or review and contain conclusions, opinions, analyses, or financial data relating to such an audit or review, which is conducted by any accountant who conducts an audit of an issuer of securities to which section 10A(a) of the Securities Exchange Act of 1934 (15 U.S.C. 78j–1(a)) applies. The Commission may, from time to time, amend or supplement the rules and regulations that it is required to promulgate under this section, after adequate notice and an opportunity for comment, in order to ensure that such rules and regulations adequately comport with the purposes of this section.

(b) Whoever knowingly and willfully violates subsection (a)(1), or any rule or regulation promulgated by the Securities and Exchange Commission under subsection (a)(2), shall be fined under this title, imprisoned not more than 10 years, or both.

(c) Nothing in this section shall be deemed to diminish or relieve any person of any other duty or obligation imposed by Federal or State law or regulation to maintain, or refrain from destroying, any document.

CHAPTER 93. PUBLIC OFFICERS AND EMPLOYEES

§ 1905. Disclosure of confidential information generally

Whoever, being an officer or employee of the United States or of any department or agency thereof, any person acting on behalf of the Federal Housing Finance Agency, or agent of the Department of Justice as defined in the Antitrust Civil Process Act (15 U.S.C. 1311–1314), or being an employee of a private sector organization who is or was assigned to an agency under chapter 37 of title 5, publishes, divulges, discloses, or makes known in any manner or to any extent not authorized by law any information coming to him in the course of his employment or official duties or by reason of any examination or investigation made by, or return, report or record made to or filed with, such department or agency or officer or employee thereof, which information concerns or relates to the trade secrets, processes, operations, style of work, or apparatus, or to the identity, confidential statistical data, amount or source of any income, profits, losses, or expenditures of any person, firm, partnership, corporation, or association; or permits any income return or copy thereof or any book containing any abstract or particulars thereof to be seen or examined by any person except as provided by law; shall be fined under this title or imprisoned not more than one year, or both; and shall be removed from office or employment.

CHAPTER 201. CRIMINAL PROCEDURE—GENERAL PROVISIONS

§ 3004. Decorum in court room—(Rule)

SEE FEDERAL RULES OF CRIMINAL PROCEDURE

Photographing or radio broadcasting prohibited, Rule 53.

§ 3005. Counsel and witnesses in capital cases

Whoever is indicted for treason or other capital crime shall be allowed to make his full defense by counsel; and the court before which the defendant is to be tried, or a judge thereof, shall promptly, upon the defendant's request, assign 2 such counsel, of whom at least 1 shall be learned in the law applicable to capital cases, and who shall have free access to the accused at all reasonable hours. In assigning counsel under this section, the court shall consider the recommendation of the Federal Public Defender organization, or, if no such organization exists in the district, of the Administrative Office of the United States Courts. The defendant shall be allowed, in his defense to make any proof that he can produce by lawful witnesses, and shall have the like process of the court to compel his witnesses to appear at his trial, as is usually granted to compel witnesses to appear on behalf of the prosecution.

§ 3006. Assignment of counsel—(Rule)

SEE FEDERAL RULES OF CRIMINAL PROCEDURE

Appointment by court, Rule 44.

Accused to be informed of right to counsel, Rules 5 and 44.

§ 3006A. Adequate representation of defendants

(a) Choice of plan.—Each United States district court, with the approval of the judicial council of the circuit, shall place in operation throughout the district a plan for furnishing representation for any person financially unable to obtain adequate representation in accordance with this section. Representation under each plan shall include counsel and investigative, expert, and other services necessary for adequate representation. Each plan shall provide the following:

(1) Representation shall be provided for any financially eligible person who—

(A) is charged with a felony or a Class A misdemeanor;

(B) is a juvenile alleged to have committed an act of juvenile delinquency as defined in section 5031 of this title;

(C) is charged with a violation of probation;

(D) is under arrest, when such representation is required by law;

(E) is charged with a violation of supervised release or faces modification, reduction, or enlargement of a condition, or extension or revocation of a term of supervised release;

(F) is subject to a mental condition hearing under chapter 313 of this title;

(G) is in custody as a material witness;

(H) is entitled to appointment of counsel under the sixth amendment to the Constitution; or

(I) faces loss of liberty in a case, and Federal law requires the appointment of counsel.

(2) Whenever the United States magistrate or the court determines that the interests of justice so require, representation may be provided for any financially eligible person who—

(A) is charged with a Class B or C misdemeanor, or an infraction for which a sentence to confinement is authorized; or

(B) is seeking relief under section 2241, 2254, or 2255 of title 28.

(3) Private attorneys shall be appointed in a substantial proportion of the cases. Each plan may include, in addition to the provisions for private attorneys, either of the following or both:

(A) Attorneys furnished by a bar association or a legal aid agency.

(B) Attorneys furnished by a defender organization established in accordance with the provisions of subsection (g).

Prior to approving the plan for a district, the judicial council of the circuit shall supplement the plan with provisions for representation on appeal. The district court may modify the plan at any time with the approval of the judicial council of the circuit. It shall modify the plan when directed by the judicial council of the circuit. The district court shall notify the Administrative Office of the United States Courts of any modification of its plan.

(b) Appointment of counsel.—Counsel furnishing representation under the plan shall be selected from a panel of attorneys designated or approved by the court, or from a bar association, legal aid agency, or defender organization furnishing representation pursuant to the plan. In every case in which a person entitled to representation under a plan approved under subsection (a) appears without counsel, the United States magistrate or the court shall advise the person that he has the right to be represented by counsel and that counsel will be appointed to represent him if he is financially unable to obtain counsel. Unless the person waives representation by counsel, the United States magistrate or the court, if satisfied after appropriate inquiry that the person is financially unable to obtain counsel, shall appoint counsel to represent him. Such appointment may be made retroactive to include any representation furnished pursuant to the plan prior to appointment. The United States magistrate or the court shall appoint separate counsel for persons having interests that cannot properly be represented by the same counsel, or when other good cause is shown.

(c) Duration and substitution of appointments.—A person for whom counsel is appointed shall be represented at every stage of the proceedings from his initial appearance before the United States magistrate or the court through appeal, including ancillary matters appropriate to the proceedings. If at any time after the appointment of counsel the United States magistrate or the court finds that the person is financially able to obtain counsel or to make partial payment for the representation, it may terminate the appointment of counsel or authorize payment as provided in subsection (f), as the interests of justice may dictate. If at any stage of the proceedings, including an appeal, the United States magistrate or the court finds that the person is financially unable to pay counsel whom he had retained, it may appoint counsel as provided in subsection (b) and authorize payment as provided in subsection (d), as the interests of justice may dictate. The United States magistrate or the court may, in the interests of justice, substitute one appointed counsel for another at any stage of the proceedings.

(d) Payment for representation.—

(1) Hourly rate.—Any attorney appointed pursuant to this section or a bar association or legal aid agency or community defender organization which has provided the appointed attorney shall, at the conclusion of the representation or any segment thereof, be compensated at a rate not exceeding $60 per hour for time expended in court or before a United States magistrate and $40 per hour for time reasonably expended out of court, unless the Judicial Conference determines that a higher rate of not in excess of $75 per hour is justified for a circuit or for particular districts within a circuit, for time expended in court or before a United States magistrate and for time expended out of court. The Judicial Conference shall develop guidelines for determining the maximum hourly rates for each circuit in accordance with the preceding sentence, with variations by district, where appropriate, taking into account such factors as the minimum range of the prevailing hourly rates for qualified attorneys in the district in which the representation is provided and the recommendations of the judicial councils of the circuits. Not less than 3 years after the effective date of the Criminal Justice Act Revision of 1986, the Judicial Conference is authorized to raise the maximum hourly rates specified in this paragraph up to the aggregate of the overall average percentages of the adjustments in the rates of pay under the General Schedule made pursuant to section 5305 of title 5 on or after such effective date. After the rates are raised under the preceding sentence, such maximum hourly rates may be raised at intervals of not less than 1 year each, up to the aggregate of the overall average percentages of such adjustments made since the last raise was made under this paragraph. Attorneys may be reimbursed for expenses reasonably incurred, including the costs of transcripts authorized by the United States magistrate or the court, and the costs of defending actions alleging malpractice of counsel in furnishing representational services under this section. No reimbursement for expenses in defending against malpractice claims shall be made if a judgment of malpractice is rendered against the counsel furnishing representational services under this section. The United States magistrate or the court shall make determinations relating to reimbursement of expenses under this paragraph.

(2) Maximum amounts.—For representation of a defendant before the United States magistrate or the district court, or both, the compensation to be paid to an attorney or to a bar association or legal aid agency or community defender organization shall not exceed $7,000 for each attorney in a case in which one or more felonies are charged, and $2,000 for each attorney in a case in which only misdemeanors are charged. For representation of a defendant in an appellate court, the compensation to be paid to an attorney or to a bar association or legal aid agency or community defender organization shall not exceed $5,000 for each attorney in each court. For representation of a petitioner in a non-capital habeas corpus proceeding, the compensation for each attorney shall not exceed the amount applicable to a felony in this paragraph for representation of a defendant before a judicial officer of the district court. For representation of such petitioner in an appellate court, the compensation for each attorney shall not exceed the amount applicable for representation of a defendant in an appellate court. For representation of an offender before the United States Parole Commission in a proceeding under section 4106A of this title, the compensation shall not exceed $1,500 for each attorney in each proceeding; for representation of an offender in an appeal from a determination of such Commission under such section, the compensation shall not exceed $5,000 for each attorney in each court. For any other representation required or authorized by this section, the compensation shall not exceed $1,500 for each attorney in each proceeding. The compensation maximum amounts provided in this paragraph shall increase simultaneously by the same percentage, rounded to the nearest multiple of $100, as the aggregate percentage increases in the maximum hourly compensation rate paid pursuant to paragraph (1) for time expended since the case maximum amounts last adjusted.

(3) Waiving maximum amounts.—Payment in excess of any maximum amount provided in paragraph (2) of this subsection may be made for extended or complex representation whenever the court in which the representation was rendered, or the United States magistrate if the representation was furnished exclusively before him, certifies that the amount of the excess payment is necessary to provide fair compensation and the payment is approved by the chief judge of the circuit. The chief judge of the circuit may delegate such approval authority to an active or senior circuit judge.

(4) Disclosure of fees.—

(A) In general.—Subject to subparagraphs (B) through (E), the amounts paid under this subsection for services in any case shall be made available to the public by the court upon the court's approval of the payment.

(B) Pre-trial or trial in progress.—If a trial is in pre-trial status or still in progress and after considering the defendant's interests as set forth in subparagraph (D), the court shall—

(i) redact any detailed information on the payment voucher provided by defense counsel to justify the expenses to the court; and

(ii) make public only the amounts approved for payment to defense counsel by dividing those amounts into the following categories:

(I) Arraignment and or plea.

(II) Bail and detention hearings.

(III) Motions.

(IV) Hearings.

(V) Interviews and conferences.

(VI) Obtaining and reviewing records.

(VII) Legal research and brief writing.

(VIII) Travel time.

(IX) Investigative work.

(X) Experts.

(XI) Trial and appeals.

(XII) Other.

(C) Trial completed.—

(i) In general.—If a request for payment is not submitted until after the completion of the trial and subject to consideration of the defendant's interests as set forth in subparagraph (D), the court shall make available to the public an unredacted copy of the expense voucher.

(ii) Protection of the rights of the defendant.—If the court determines that defendant's interests as set forth in subparagraph (D) require a limited disclosure, the court shall disclose amounts as provided in subparagraph (B).

(D) Considerations.—The interests referred to in subparagraphs (B) and (C) are—

(i) to protect any person's 5th amendment right against self-incrimination;

(ii) to protect the defendant's 6th amendment rights to effective assistance of counsel;

(iii) the defendant's attorney-client privilege;

(iv) the work product privilege of the defendant's counsel;

(v) the safety of any person; and

(vi) any other interest that justice may require, except that the amount of the fees shall not be considered a reason justifying any limited disclosure under section 3006A(d)(4) of title 18, United States Code.

(E) Notice.—The court shall provide reasonable notice of disclosure to the counsel of the defendant prior to the approval of the payments in order to allow the counsel to request redaction based on the considerations set forth in subparagraph (D). Upon completion of the trial, the court shall release unredacted copies of the vouchers provided by defense counsel to justify the expenses to the court. If there is an appeal, the court shall not release unredacted copies of the vouchers provided by defense counsel to justify the expenses to the court until such time as the appeals process is completed, unless the court determines that none of the defendant's interests set forth in subparagraph (D) will be compromised.

(F) Effective date.—The amendment made by paragraph (4) shall become effective 60 days after enactment of this Act, will apply only to cases filed on or after the effective date, and shall be in effect for no longer than 24 months after the effective date.

(5) Filing claims.—A separate claim for compensation and reimbursement shall be made to the district court for representation before the United States magistrate and the court, and to each appellate court before which the attorney provided representation to the person involved. Each claim shall be supported by a sworn written statement specifying the time expended, services rendered, and expenses incurred while the case was pending before the United States magistrate and the court, and the compensation and reimbursement applied for or received in the same case from any other source. The court shall fix the compensation and reimbursement to be paid to the attorney or to the bar association or legal aid agency or community defender organization which provided the appointed attorney. In cases where representation is furnished exclusively before a United States magistrate, the claim shall be submitted to him and he shall fix the compensation and reimbursement to be paid. In cases where representation is furnished other than before the United States magistrate, the district court, or an appellate court, claims shall be submitted to the district court which shall fix the compensation and reimbursement to be paid.

(6) New trials.—For purposes of compensation and other payments authorized by this section, an order by a court granting a new trial shall be deemed to initiate a new case.

(7) Proceedings before appellate courts.—If a person for whom counsel is appointed under this section appeals to an appellate court or petitions for a writ of certiorari, he may do so without prepayment of fees and costs or security therefor and without filing the affidavit required by section 1915(a) of title 28.

(e) Services other than counsel.—

(1) Upon request.—Counsel for a person who is financially unable to obtain investigative, expert, or other services necessary for adequate representation may request them in an ex parte application. Upon finding, after appropriate inquiry in an ex parte proceeding, that the services are necessary and that the person is financially unable to obtain them, the court, or the United States magistrate if the services are required in connection with a matter over which he has jurisdiction, shall authorize counsel to obtain the services.

(2) Without prior request.—(A) Counsel appointed under this section may obtain, subject to later review, investigative, expert, and other services without prior authorization if necessary for adequate representation. Except as provided in subparagraph (B) of this paragraph, the total cost of services obtained without prior authorization may not exceed $800 and expenses reasonably incurred.

(B) The court, or the United States magistrate (if the services were rendered in a case disposed of entirely before the United States magistrate), may, in the interest of justice, and upon the finding that timely procurement of necessary services could not await prior authorization, approve payment for such services after they have been obtained, even if the cost of such services exceeds $800.

(3) Maximum amounts.—Compensation to be paid to a person for services rendered by him to a person under this subsection, or to be paid to an organization for services rendered by an employee thereof, shall not exceed $2,400, exclusive of reimbursement for expenses reasonably incurred, unless payment in excess of that limit is certified by the court, or by the United States magistrate if the services were rendered in connection with a case disposed of entirely before him, as necessary to provide fair compensation for services of an unusual character or duration, and the amount of the excess payment is approved by the chief judge of the circuit. The chief judge of the circuit may delegate such approval authority to an active or senior circuit judge.

(4) Disclosure of fees.—The amounts paid under this subsection for services in any case shall be made available to the public.

(5) The dollar amounts provided in paragraphs (2) and (3) shall be adjusted simultaneously by an amount, rounded to the nearest multiple of $100, equal to the percentage of the cumulative adjustments taking effect under section 5303 of title 5 in the rates of pay under the General Schedule since the date the dollar amounts provided in paragraphs (2) and (3), respectively, were last enacted or adjusted by statute.

(f) Receipt of other payments.—Whenever the United States magistrate or the court finds that funds are available for payment from or on behalf of a person furnished representation, it may authorize or direct that such funds be paid to the appointed attorney, to the bar association or legal aid agency or community defender organization which provided the appointed attorney, to any person or organization authorized pursuant to subsection (e) to render investigative, expert, or other services, or to the court for deposit in the Treasury as a reimbursement to the appropriation, current at the time of payment, to carry out the provisions of this section. Except as so authorized or directed, no such person or organization may request or accept any payment or promise of payment for representing a defendant.

(g) Defender organization.—

(1) Qualifications.—A district or a part of a district in which at least two hundred persons annually require the appointment of counsel may establish a defender organization as provided for either under subparagraphs (A) or (B) of paragraph (2) of this subsection or both. Two adjacent districts or parts of districts may aggregate the number of persons required to be represented to establish eligibility for a defender organization to serve both areas. In the event that adjacent districts or parts of districts are located in different circuits, the plan for furnishing representation shall be approved by the judicial council of each circuit.

(2) Types of defender organizations.—

(A) Federal Public Defender Organization.—A Federal Public Defender Organization shall consist of one or more full-time salaried attorneys. An organization for a district or part of a district or two adjacent districts or parts of districts shall be supervised by a Federal Public Defender appointed by the court of appeals of the circuit, without regard to the provisions of title 5 governing appointments in the competitive service, after considering recommendations from the district court or courts to be served. Nothing contained herein shall be deemed to authorize more than one Federal Public Defender within a single judicial district. The Federal Public Defender shall be appointed for a term of four years, unless sooner removed by the court of appeals of the circuit for incompetency, misconduct in office, or neglect of duty. Upon the expiration of his term, a Federal Public Defender may, by a majority vote of the judges of the court of appeals, continue to perform the duties of his office until his successor is appointed, or until one year after the expiration of such Defender's term, whichever is earlier. The compensation of the Federal Public Defender shall be fixed by the court of appeals of the circuit at a rate not to exceed the compensation received by the United States attorney for the district where representation is furnished or, if two districts or parts of districts are involved, the compensation of the higher paid United States attorney of the districts. The Federal Public Defender may appoint, without regard to the provisions of title 5 governing appointments in the competitive service, full-time attorneys in such number as may be approved by the court of appeals of the circuit and other personnel in such number as may be approved by the

Director of the Administrative Office of the United States Courts. Compensation paid to such attorneys and other personnel of the organization shall be fixed by the Federal Public Defender at a rate not to exceed that paid to attorneys and other personnel of similar qualifications and experience in the Office of the United States attorney in the district where representation is furnished or, if two districts or parts of districts are involved, the higher compensation paid to persons of similar qualifications and experience in the districts. Neither the Federal Public Defender nor any attorney so appointed by him may engage in the private practice of law. Each organization shall submit to the Director of the Administrative Office of the United States Courts, at the time and in the form prescribed by him, reports of its activities and financial position and its proposed budget. The Director of the Administrative Office shall submit, in accordance with section 605 of title 28, a budget for each organization for each fiscal year and shall out of the appropriations therefor make payments to and on behalf of each organization. Payments under this subparagraph to an organization shall be in lieu of payments under subsection (d) or (e).

(B) Community Defender Organization.—A Community Defender Organization shall be a non-profit defense counsel service established and administered by any group authorized by the plan to provide representation. The organization shall be eligible to furnish attorneys and receive payments under this section if its bylaws are set forth in the plan of the district or districts in which it will serve. Each organization shall submit to the Judicial Conference of the United States an annual report setting forth its activities and financial position and the anticipated caseload and expenses for the next fiscal year. Upon application an organization may, to the extent approved by the Judicial Conference of the United States:

(i) receive an initial grant for expenses necessary to establish the organization; and

(ii) in lieu of payments under subsection (d) or (e), receive periodic sustaining grants to provide representation and other expenses pursuant to this section.

(3) Malpractice and negligence suits.—The Director of the Administrative Office of the United States Courts shall, to the extent the Director considers appropriate, provide representation for and hold harmless, or provide liability insurance for, any person who is an officer or employee of a Federal Public Defender Organization established under this subsection, or a Community Defender Organization established under this subsection which is receiving periodic sustaining grants, for money damages for injury, loss of liberty, loss of property, or personal injury or death arising from malpractice or negligence of any such officer or employee in furnishing representational services under this section while acting within the scope of that person's office or employment.

(h) Rules and reports.—Each district court and court of appeals of a circuit shall submit a report on the appointment of counsel within its jurisdiction to the Administrative Office of the United States Courts in such form and at such times as the Judicial Conference of the United States may specify. The Judicial Conference of the United States may, from time to time, issue rules and regulations governing the operation of plans formulated under this section.

(i) Appropriations.—There are authorized to be appropriated to the United States courts, out of any money in the Treasury not otherwise appropriated, sums necessary to carry out the provisions of this section, including funds for the continuing education and training of persons providing representational services under this section. When so specified in appropriation acts, such appropriations shall remain available until expended. Payments from such appropriations shall be made under the supervision of the Director of the Administrative Office of the United States Courts.

(j) Districts included.—As used in this section, the term "district court" means each district court of the United States created by chapter 5 of title 28, the District Court of the Virgin Islands, the District Court for the Northern Mariana Islands, and the District Court of Guam.

(k) Applicability in the District of Columbia.—The provisions of this section shall apply in the United States District Court for the District of Columbia and the United States Court of Appeals for the District of Columbia Circuit. The provisions of this section shall not apply to the Superior Court of the District of Columbia and the District of Columbia Court of Appeals.

28 U.S.C.A.

CHAPTER 5. DISTRICT COURTS

§ 144. Bias or prejudice of judge

Whenever a party to any proceeding in a district court makes and files a timely and sufficient affidavit that the judge before whom the matter is pending has a personal bias or prejudice either against him or in favor of any adverse party, such judge shall proceed no further therein, but another judge shall be assigned to hear such proceeding.

The affidavit shall state the facts and the reasons for the belief that bias or prejudice exists, and shall be filed not less than ten days before the beginning of the term at which the proceeding is to be heard, or good cause shall be shown for failure to file it within such time. A party may file only one such affidavit in any case. It shall be accompanied by a certificate of counsel of record stating that it is made in good faith.

CHAPTER 16. COMPLAINTS AGAINST JUDGES AND JUDICIAL DISCIPLINE

§ 351. Complaints; judge defined

(a) Filing of complaint by any person.—Any person alleging that a judge has engaged in conduct prejudicial to the effective and expeditious administration of the business of the courts, or alleging that such judge is unable to discharge all the duties of office by reason of mental or physical disability, may file with the clerk of the court of appeals for the circuit a written complaint containing a brief statement of the facts constituting such conduct.

(b) Identifying complaint by chief judge.—In the interests of the effective and expeditious administration of the business of the courts and on the basis of information available to the chief judge of the circuit, the chief judge may, by written order stating reasons therefor, identify a complaint for purposes of this chapter and thereby dispense with filing of a written complaint.

(c) Transmittal of complaint.—Upon receipt of a complaint filed under subsection (a), the clerk shall promptly transmit the complaint to the chief judge of the circuit, or, if the conduct complained of is that of the chief judge, to that circuit judge in regular active service next senior in date of commission (hereafter, for purposes of this chapter only, included in the term "chief judge"). The clerk shall simultaneously transmit a copy of the complaint to the judge whose conduct is the subject of the complaint. The clerk shall also transmit a copy of any complaint identified under subsection (b) to the judge whose conduct is the subject of the complaint.

(d) Definitions.—In this chapter—

(1) the term "judge" means a circuit judge, district judge, bankruptcy judge, or magistrate judge; and

(2) the term "complainant" means the person filing a complaint under subsection (a) of this section.

§ 352. Review of complaint by chief judge

(a) Expeditious review; limited inquiry.—The chief judge shall expeditiously review any complaint received under section 351(a) or identified under section 351(b). In determining what action to take, the chief judge may conduct a limited inquiry for the purpose of determining—

(1) whether appropriate corrective action has been or can be taken without the necessity for a formal investigation; and

(2) whether the facts stated in the complaint are either plainly untrue or are incapable of being established through investigation.

For this purpose, the chief judge may request the judge whose conduct is complained of to file a written response to the complaint. Such response shall not be made available to the complainant unless authorized by the judge filing the response. The chief judge or his or her designee may also communicate orally or in writing with the complainant, the judge whose conduct is complained of, and any other person who may have knowledge of the matter, and may review any transcripts or other relevant documents. The chief judge shall not undertake to make findings of fact about any matter that is reasonably in dispute.

(b) Action by chief judge following review.—After expeditiously reviewing a complaint under subsection (a), the chief judge, by written order stating his or her reasons, may—

(1) dismiss the complaint—

(A) if the chief judge finds the complaint to be—

(i) not in conformity with section 351(a);

(ii) directly related to the merits of a decision or procedural ruling; or

(iii) frivolous, lacking sufficient evidence to raise an inference that misconduct has occurred, or containing allegations which are incapable of being established through investigation; or

(B) when a limited inquiry conducted under subsection (a) demonstrates that the allegations in the complaint lack any factual foundation or are conclusively refuted by objective evidence; or

(2) conclude the proceeding if the chief judge finds that appropriate corrective action has been taken or that action on the complaint is no longer necessary because of intervening events.

The chief judge shall transmit copies of the written order to the complainant and to the judge whose conduct is the subject of the complaint.

(c) Review of orders of chief judge.—A complainant or judge aggrieved by a final order of the chief judge under this section may petition the judicial council of the circuit for review thereof. The denial of a petition for review of the chief judge's order shall be final and conclusive and shall not be judicially reviewable on appeal or otherwise.

(d) Referral of petitions for review to panels of the judicial council.—Each judicial council may, pursuant to rules prescribed under section 358, refer a petition for review filed under subsection (c) to a panel of no fewer than 5 members of the council, at least 2 of whom shall be district judges.

§ 353. Special committees

(a) Appointment.—If the chief judge does not enter an order under section 352(b), the chief judge shall promptly—

(1) appoint himself or herself and equal numbers of circuit and district judges of the circuit to a special committee to investigate the facts and allegations contained in the complaint;

(2) certify the complaint and any other documents pertaining thereto to each member of such committee; and

(3) provide written notice to the complainant and the judge whose conduct is the subject of the complaint of the action taken under this subsection.

(b) Change in status or death of judges.—A judge appointed to a special committee under subsection (a) may continue to serve on that committee after becoming a senior judge or, in the case of the chief judge of the circuit, after his or her term as chief judge terminates under subsection (a)(3) or (c) of section 45. If a judge appointed to a committee under subsection (a) dies, or retires from office under section 371(a), while serving on the committee, the chief judge of the circuit may appoint another circuit or district judge, as the case may be, to the committee.

(c) Investigation by special committee.—Each committee appointed under subsection (a) shall conduct an investigation as extensive as it considers necessary, and shall expeditiously file a comprehensive written report thereon with the judicial council of the circuit. Such report shall present both the findings of the investigation and the committee's recommendations for necessary and appropriate action by the judicial council of the circuit.

CHAPTER 17. JUDGES—RESIGNATION—RETIREMENT

§ 372. Retirement for disability; substitute judge on failure to retire

(a) Any justice or judge of the United States appointed to hold office during good behavior who becomes permanently disabled from performing his duties may retire from regular active service, and the President shall, by and with the advice and consent of the Senate, appoint a successor.

Any justice or judge of the United States desiring to retire under this section shall certify to the President his disability in writing.

Whenever an associate justice of the Supreme Court, a chief judge of a circuit or the chief judge of the Court of International Trade, desires to retire under this section, he shall furnish to the President a certificate of disability signed by the Chief Justice of the United States.

A circuit or district judge, desiring to retire under this section, shall furnish to the President a certificate of disability signed by the chief judge of his circuit.

A judge of the Court of International Trade desiring to retire under this section, shall furnish to the President a certificate of disability signed by the chief judge of his court.

Each justice or judge retiring under this section after serving ten years continuously or otherwise shall, during the remainder of his lifetime, receive the salary of the office. A justice or judge retiring under this section who has served less than ten years in all shall, during the remainder of his lifetime, receive one-half the salary of the office.

(b) Whenever any judge of the United States appointed to hold office during good behavior who is eligible to retire under this section does not do so and a certificate of his disability signed by a majority of the members of the Judicial Council of his circuit in the case of a circuit or district judge, or by the Chief Justice of the United States in the case of the Chief Judge of the Court of International Trade, or by the chief judge of his court in the case of a judge of the Court of International Trade, is presented to the President and the President finds that such judge is unable to discharge efficiently all the duties of his office by reason of permanent mental or physical disability and that the appointment of an additional judge is necessary for the efficient dispatch of business, the President may make such appointment by and with the advice and consent of the Senate. Whenever any such additional judge is appointed, the vacancy subsequently caused by the death, resignation, or retirement of the disabled judge shall not be filled. Any judge whose disability causes the appointment of an additional judge shall, for purpose of precedence, service as chief judge, or temporary performance of the duties of that office, be treated as junior in commission to the other judges of the circuit, district, or court.

CHAPTER 21. COURTS AND JUDGES

§ 454. Practice of law by justices and judges

Any justice or judge appointed under the authority of the United States who engages in the practice of law is guilty of a high misdemeanor.

§ 455. Disqualification of justice, judge, or magistrate

(a) Any justice, judge, or magistrate of the United States shall disqualify himself in any proceeding in which his impartiality might reasonably be questioned.

(b) He shall also disqualify himself in the following circumstances:

(1) Where he has a personal bias or prejudice concerning a party, or personal knowledge of disputed evidentiary facts concerning the proceeding;

(2) Where in private practice he served as lawyer in the matter in controversy, or a lawyer with whom he previously practiced law served during such association as a lawyer concerning the matter, or the judge or such lawyer has been a material witness concerning it;

(3) Where he has served in governmental employment and in such capacity participated as counsel, adviser or material witness concerning the proceeding or expressed an opinion concerning the merits of the particular case in controversy;

(4) He knows that he, individually or as a fiduciary, or his spouse or minor child residing in his household, has a financial interest in the subject matter in controversy or in a party to the proceeding, or any other interest that could be substantially affected by the outcome of the proceeding;

(5) He or his spouse, or a person within the third degree of relationship to either of them, or the spouse of such a person:

(i) Is a party to the proceeding, or an officer, director, or trustee of a party;

(ii) Is acting as a lawyer in the proceeding;

(iii) Is known by the judge to have an interest that could be substantially affected by the outcome of the proceeding;

(iv) Is to the judge's knowledge likely to be a material witness in the proceeding.

(c) A judge should inform himself about his personal and fiduciary financial interests, and make a reasonable effort to inform himself about the personal financial interests of his spouse and minor children residing in his household.

(d) For the purposes of this section the following words or phrases shall have the meaning indicated:

(1) "proceeding" includes pretrial, trial, appellate review, or other stages of litigation;

(2) the degree of relationship is calculated according to the civil law system;

(3) "fiduciary" includes such relationships as executor, administrator, trustee, and guardian;

(4) "financial interest" means ownership of a legal or equitable interest, however small, or a relationship as director, adviser, or other active participant in the affairs of a party, except that:

(i) Ownership in a mutual or common investment fund that holds securities is not a "financial interest" in such securities unless the judge participates in the management of the fund;

(ii) An office in an educational, religious, charitable, fraternal, or civic organization is not a "financial interest" in securities held by the organization;

(iii) The proprietary interest of a policyholder in a mutual insurance company, of a depositor in a mutual savings association, or a similar proprietary interest, is a "financial interest" in the organization only if the outcome of the proceeding could substantially affect the value of the interest;

(iv) Ownership of government securities is a "financial interest" in the issuer only if the outcome of the proceeding could substantially affect the value of the securities.

(e) No justice, judge, or magistrate shall accept from the parties to the proceeding a waiver of any ground for disqualification enumerated in subsection (b). Where the ground for disqualification arises only under subsection (a), waiver may be accepted provided it is preceded by a full disclosure on the record of the basis for disqualification.

(f) Notwithstanding the preceding provisions of this section, if any justice, judge, magistrate, or bankruptcy judge to whom a matter has been assigned would be disqualified, after substantial judicial time has been devoted to the matter, because of the appearance or discovery, after the matter was assigned to him or her, that he or she individually or as a fiduciary, or his or her spouse or minor child residing in his or her household, has a financial interest in a party (other than an interest that could be substantially affected by the outcome), disqualification is not required if the justice, judge, magistrate, bankruptcy judge, spouse or minor child, as the case may be, divests himself or herself of the interest that provides the grounds for the disqualification.

CHAPTER 31. THE ATTORNEY GENERAL

§ 530B. Ethical standards for attorneys for the Government

(a) An attorney for the Government shall be subject to State laws and rules, and local Federal court rules, governing attorneys in each State where such attorney engages in that attorney's duties, to the same extent and in the same manner as other attorneys in that State.

(b) The Attorney General shall make and amend rules of the Department of Justice to assure compliance with this section.

(c) As used in this section, the term "attorney for the Government" includes any attorney described in section 77.2(a) of part 77 of title 28 of the Code of Federal Regulations and also includes any independent counsel, or employee of such a counsel, appointed under chapter 40.

PART SIX

STANDARDS FOR SPECIALIZED AREAS OF PRACTICE

TABLE OF CONTENTS

Introduction

Although the ABA has sought to regulate all lawyers' conduct through one general code of conduct, certain groups of lawyers who practice in a specialized area have sought to promulgate their own codes of conduct. On one level, such efforts have been justified on the grounds that a specific area of practice needs its own code of conduct because of unique characteristics that cannot be taken into account in the general code. On another level, such efforts may be viewed as a struggle between the general governing group of the bar and the governing groups of certain specialized areas of practice. By promulgating a special code for an area of practice, lawyers can control conduct and entry in a small area of practice. Although the future of such codes is not entirely clear, one can gain an appreciation for the different attempts to draft rules for a specialized area of practice. Thus, this part examines several standards for specialized areas of practice.

The first two standards, one dealing with criminal law and the other with family law, were drafted by groups within the ABA and are intended as supplements to the general codes of conduct. The third standard illustrates the regulation of one area of practice by a governmental agency, the Treasury of the United States. All lawyers who practice before the Internal Revenue Service must comply with these regulations. The fourth document involves the regulation of attorneys who practice before the Securities and Exchange Commission. This document represents the SEC's implementation of the Sarbanes Oxley legislation passed by Congress to curb corporate fraud. The fifth set of standards collects several examples of efforts to control abuse in litigation practice. These codes of professionalism and courtesy in litigation seek to temper the traditional view of the lawyer as a zealous advocate for the client. The final document sets forth guidelines for ethical conduct in settlement negotiations.

AMERICAN BAR ASSOCIATION STANDARDS RELATING TO THE ADMINISTRATION OF CRIMINAL JUSTICE

The Prosecution Function

The Defense Function

THE PROSECUTION FUNCTION

PART I. GENERAL STANDARDS

Standard 3–1.1 The Scope and Function of These Standards

(a) As used in these standards, "prosecutor" means any attorney, regardless of agency, title, or full or part-time assignment, who acts as an attorney to investigate or prosecute criminal cases or who provides legal advice regarding a criminal matter to government lawyers, agents, or offices participating in the investigation or prosecution of criminal cases. These Standards are intended to apply in any context in which a lawyer would reasonably understand that a criminal prosecution could result.

(b) These Standards are intended to provide guidance for the professional conduct and performance of prosecutors. They are written and intended to be entirely consistent with the ABA's Model Rules of Professional Conduct, and are not intended to modify a prosecutor's obligations under applicable rules, statutes, or the constitution. They are aspirational or describe "best practices," and are not intended to serve as the basis for the imposition of professional discipline, to create substantive or procedural rights for accused or convicted persons, to create a standard of care for civil liability, or to serve as a predicate for a motion to suppress evidence or dismiss a charge. For purposes of consistency, these Standards sometimes include language taken from the Model Rules of Professional Conduct; but the Standards often address conduct or provide details beyond that governed by the Model Rules of Professional Conduct. No inconsistency is ever intended; and in any case a lawyer should always read and comply with the rules of professional conduct and other authorities that are binding in the specific jurisdiction or matter, including choice of law principles that may regulate the lawyer's ethical conduct.

(c) Because the Standards for Criminal Justice are aspirational, the words "should" or "should not" are used in these Standards, rather than mandatory phrases such as "shall" or "shall not," to describe the conduct of lawyers that is expected or recommended under these Standards. The Standards are not intended to suggest any lesser standard of conduct than may be required by applicable mandatory rules, statutes, or other binding authorities.

(d) These Standards are intended to address the performance of prosecutors in all stages of their professional work. Other ABA Criminal Justice Standards should also be consulted for more detailed consideration of the performance of prosecutors in specific areas.

Standard 3–1.2 Functions and Duties of the Prosecutor

(a) The prosecutor is an administrator of justice, a zealous advocate, and an officer of the court. The prosecutor's office should exercise sound discretion and independent judgment in the performance of the prosecution function.

(b) The primary duty of the prosecutor is to seek justice within the bounds of the law, not merely to convict. The prosecutor serves the public interest and should act with integrity and balanced judgment to increase public safety both by pursuing appropriate criminal charges of appropriate severity, and by exercising discretion to not pursue criminal charges in appropriate circumstances. The prosecutor should seek to protect the innocent and convict the guilty, consider the interests of victims and witnesses, and respect the constitutional and legal rights of all persons, including suspects and defendants.

(c) The prosecutor should know and abide by the standards of professional conduct as expressed in applicable law and ethical codes and opinions in the applicable jurisdiction. The prosecutor should avoid an appearance of impropriety in performing the prosecution function. A prosecutor should seek out, and the prosecutor's office should provide, supervisory advice and ethical guidance when the proper course of prosecutorial conduct seems unclear. A prosecutor who disagrees with a governing ethical rule should seek its change if appropriate, and directly challenge it if necessary, but should comply with it unless relieved by court order.

(d) The prosecutor should make use of ethical guidance offered by existing organizations, and should seek to establish and make use of an ethics advisory group akin to that described in Defense Function Standard 4–1.11.

(e) The prosecutor should be knowledgeable about, consider, and where appropriate develop or assist in developing alternatives to prosecution or conviction that may be applicable in individual cases or classes of cases. The prosecutor's office should be available to assist community efforts addressing problems that lead to, or result from, criminal activity or perceived flaws in the criminal justice system.

(f) The prosecutor is not merely a case-processor but also a problem-solver responsible for considering broad goals of the criminal justice system. The prosecutor should seek to reform and improve the administration of criminal justice, and when inadequacies or injustices in the substantive or procedural law come to the prosecutor's attention, the prosecutor should stimulate and support efforts for remedial action. The prosecutor should provide service to the community, including involvement in public service and Bar activities, public education, community service activities, and Bar leadership positions. A prosecutorial office should support such activities, and the office's budget should include funding and paid release time for such activities.

Standard 3–1.3 The Client of the Prosecutor

The prosecutor generally serves the public and not any particular government agency, law enforcement officer or unit, witness or victim. When investigating or prosecuting a criminal matter, the prosecutor does not represent law enforcement personnel who have worked on the matter and such law enforcement personnel are not the prosecutor's clients. The public's interests and views are should be determined by the chief prosecutor and designated assistants in the jurisdiction.

Standard 3–1.4 The Prosecutor's Heightened Duty of Candor

(a) In light of the prosecutor's public responsibilities, broad authority and discretion, the prosecutor has a heightened duty of candor to the courts and in fulfilling other professional obligations. However, the prosecutor should be circumspect in publicly commenting on specific cases or aspects of the business of the office.

(b) The prosecutor should not make a statement of fact or law, or offer evidence, that the prosecutor does not reasonably believe to be true, to a court, lawyer, witness, or third party, except for lawfully authorized investigative purposes. In addition, while seeking to accommodate legitimate confidentiality, safety or security concerns, a prosecutor should correct a prosecutor's representation of material fact or law that the prosecutor reasonably believes is, or later learns was, false, and should disclose a material fact or facts when necessary to avoid assisting a fraudulent or criminal act or to avoid misleading a judge or factfinder.

(c) The prosecutor should disclose to a court legal authority in the controlling jurisdiction known to the prosecutor to be directly adverse to the prosecution's position and not disclosed by others.

Standard 3–1.5 Preserving the Record

At every stage of representation, the prosecutor should take steps necessary to make a clear and complete record for potential review. Such steps may include: filing motions including motions for reconsideration, and exhibits; making objections and placing explanations on the record; requesting evidentiary hearings; requesting or objecting to jury instructions; and making offers of proof and proffers of excluded evidence.

Standard 3–1.6 Improper Bias Prohibited

(a) The prosecutor should not manifest or exercise, by words or conduct, bias or prejudice based upon race, sex, religion, national origin, disability, age, sexual orientation, gender identity, or socioeconomic status. A prosecutor should not use other improper considerations, such as partisan or political or personal considerations, in exercising prosecutorial discretion. A prosecutor should strive to eliminate implicit biases, and act to mitigate any improper bias or prejudice when credibly informed that it exists within the scope of the prosecutor's authority.

(b) A prosecutor's office should be proactive in efforts to detect, investigate, and eliminate improper biases, with particular attention to historically persistent biases like race, in all of its work. A prosecutor's office should regularly assess the potential for biased or unfairly disparate impacts of its policies on communities within the prosecutor's jurisdiction, and eliminate those impacts that cannot be properly justified.

Standard 3–1.7 Conflicts of Interest

(a) The prosecutor should know and abide by the ethical rules regarding conflicts of interest that apply in the jurisdiction, and be sensitive to facts that may raise conflict issues. When a conflict requiring recusal exists and is non-waivable, or informed consent has not been obtained, the prosecutor should recuse from further participation in the matter. The office should not go forward until a non-conflicted prosecutor, or an adequate waiver, is in place.

(b) The prosecutor should not represent a defendant in criminal proceedings in the prosecutor's jurisdiction.

(c) The prosecutor should not participate in a matter in which the prosecutor previously participated, personally and substantially, as a non-prosecutor, unless the appropriate government office, and when necessary a former client, gives informed consent confirmed in writing.

(d) The prosecutor should not be involved in the prosecution of a former client. A prosecutor who has formerly represented a client should not use information obtained from that representation to the disadvantage of the former client.

(e) The prosecutor should not negotiate for private employment with an accused or the target of an investigation, in a matter in which the prosecutor is participating personally and substantially, or with an attorney or agent for such accused or target

(f) The prosecutor should not permit the prosecutor's professional judgment or obligations to be affected by the prosecutor's personal, political, financial, professional, business, property, or other interests or relationships. A prosecutor should not allow interests in personal advancement or aggrandizement to affect judgments regarding what is in the best interests of justice in any case.

(g) The prosecutor should disclose to appropriate supervisory personnel any facts or interests that could reasonably be viewed as raising a potential conflict of interest. If it is determined that the prosecutor should nevertheless continue to act in the matter, the prosecutor and supervisors should consider whether any disclosure to a court or defense counsel should be made, and make such disclosure if appropriate. Close cases should be resolved in favor of disclosure to the court and the defense.

(h) The prosecutor whose current relationship to another lawyer is parent, child, sibling, spouse or sexual partner should not participate in the prosecution of a person who the prosecutor knows is represented by the other lawyer. A prosecutor who has a significant personal, political, financial, professional, business, property, or other relationship with another lawyer should not participate in the prosecution of a person who is represented by the other lawyer, unless the relationship is disclosed to the prosecutor's supervisor and supervisory approval is given, or unless there is no other prosecutor who can be authorized to act in the prosecutor's stead. In the latter rare case, full disclosure should be made to the defense and to the court.

(i) The prosecutor should not recommend the services of particular defense counsel to accused persons or witnesses in cases being handled by the prosecutor's office. If requested to make such a recommendation, the prosecutor should consider instead referring the person to the public defender, or to a panel of available criminal defense attorneys such as a bar association lawyer-referral service, or to the court. In the rare case where a specific recommendation is made by the prosecutor, the recommendation should be to an independent and competent attorney, and the prosecutor should not make a referral that embodies, creates or is likely to create a conflict of interest. A prosecutor should not comment negatively upon the reputation or abilities of a defense counsel to an accused person or witness who is seeking counsel in a case being handled by the prosecutor's office.

(j) The prosecutor should promptly report to a supervisor all but the most obviously frivolous misconduct allegations made, publicly or privately, against the prosecutor. If a supervisor or judge initially determines that an allegation is serious enough to warrant official investigation, reasonable measures, including possible recusal, should be instituted to ensure that the prosecution function is fairly and effectively carried out. A mere allegation of misconduct is not a sufficient basis for prosecutorial recusal, and should not deter a prosecutor from attending to the prosecutor's duties.

Standard 3–1.8 Appropriate Workload

(a) The prosecutor should not carry a workload that, by reason of its excessive size or complexity, interferes with providing quality representation, endangers the interests of justice in fairness, accuracy, or the timely disposition of charges, or has a significant potential to lead to the breach of professional obligations. A prosecutor whose workload prevents competent representation should not accept additional matters until the workload is reduced, and should work to ensure competent representation in existing matters. A prosecutor within a supervisory structure should notify supervisors when counsel's workload is approaching or exceeds professionally appropriate levels.

(b) The prosecutor's office should regularly review the workload of individual prosecutors, as well as the workload of the entire office, and adjust workloads (including intake) when necessary to ensure the effective and ethical conduct of the prosecution function.

(c) The chief prosecutor for a jurisdiction should inform governmental officials of the workload of the prosecutor's office, and request funding and personnel that are adequate to meet the criminal caseload. The prosecutor should consider seeking such funding from all appropriate sources. If workload exceeds the appropriate professional capacity of a prosecutor or prosecutor's office, that office or counsel should also alert the court(s) in its jurisdiction and seek judicial relief.

Standard 3–1.9 Diligence, Promptness and Punctuality

(a) The prosecutor should act with diligence and promptness to investigate, litigate, and dispose of criminal charges, consistent with the interests of justice and with due regard for fairness, accuracy, and rights of the defendant, victims, and witnesses. The prosecutor's office should be organized and supported with adequate staff and facilities to enable it to process and resolve criminal charges with fairness and efficiency.

(b) When providing reasons for seeking delay, the prosecutor should not knowingly misrepresent facts or otherwise mislead. The prosecutor should use procedures that will cause delay only when there is a legitimate basis for such use, and not to secure an unfair tactical advantage.

(c) The prosecutor should not unreasonably oppose requests for continuances from defense counsel.

(d) The prosecutor should know and comply with timing requirements applicable to a criminal investigation and prosecution, so as to not prejudice a criminal matter.

(e) The prosecutor should be punctual in attendance in court, in the submission of motions, briefs, and other papers, and in dealings with opposing counsel, witnesses and others. The prosecutor should emphasize to assistants and prosecution witnesses the importance of punctuality in court attendance.

Standard 3–1.10 Relationship with the Media

(a) For purposes of this Standard, a "public statement" is any extrajudicial statement that a reasonable person would expect to be disseminated by means of public communication or media, including social media. An extrajudicial statement is any oral, written, or visual presentation not made either in a courtroom during criminal proceedings or in court filings or correspondence with the court or counsel regarding criminal proceedings.

(b) The prosecutor's public statements about the judiciary, jurors, other lawyers, or the criminal justice system should be respectful even if expressing disagreement.

(c) The prosecutor should not make, cause to be made, or authorize or condone the making of, a public statement that the prosecutor knows or reasonably should know will have a substantial likelihood of materially prejudicing a criminal proceeding or heightening public condemnation of the accused, but the prosecutor may make statements that inform the public of the nature and extent of the prosecutor's or law enforcement actions and serve a legitimate law enforcement purpose. The prosecutor may make a public statement explaining why criminal charges have been declined or dismissed, but must take care not to imply guilt or otherwise prejudice the interests of victims, witnesses or subjects of an investigation. A prosecutor's public statements should otherwise be consistent with the ABA Standards on Fair Trial and Public Discourse.

(d) A prosecutor should not place statements or evidence into the court record to circumvent this Standard.

(e) The prosecutor should exercise reasonable care to prevent investigators, law enforcement personnel, employees, or other persons assisting or associated with the prosecutor from making an extrajudicial statement or providing non-public information that the prosecutor would be prohibited from making or providing under this Standard or other applicable rules or law.

(f) The prosecutor may respond to public statements from any source in order to protect the prosecution's legitimate official interests, unless there is a substantial likelihood of materially prejudicing a criminal proceeding, in which case the prosecutor should approach defense counsel or a court for relief. A statement made pursuant to this paragraph shall be limited to such information as is necessary to mitigate the recent adverse publicity.

(g) The prosecutor has duties of confidentiality and loyalty, and should not secretly or anonymously provide non-public information to the media, on or off the record, without appropriate authorization.

(h) The prosecutor should not allow prosecutorial judgment to be influenced by a personal interest in potential media contacts or attention.

(i) A prosecutor uninvolved in a matter who is commenting as a media source may offer generalized commentary concerning a specific criminal matter that serves to educate the public about the criminal justice system and does not risk prejudicing a specific criminal proceeding. A prosecutor acting as such a media commentator should make reasonable efforts to be well-informed about the facts of the matter and the governing law. The prosecutor should not offer commentary regarding the specific merits of an ongoing criminal prosecution or investigation, except in a rare case to address a manifest injustice and the prosecutor is reasonably well-informed about the relevant facts and law.

(j) During the pendency of a criminal matter, the prosecutor should not re-enact, or assist law enforcement in re-enacting, law enforcement events for the media. Absent a legitimate law enforcement purpose, the prosecutor should not display the accused for the media, nor should the prosecutor invite media presence during investigative actions without careful consideration of the interests of all involved, including suspects, defendants, and the public. However, a prosecutor may reasonably accommodate media requests for access to public information and events.

Standard 3–1.11 Literary or Media Rights Agreements Prohibited

(a) Before the conclusion of all aspects of a matter in which a prosecutor participates, the prosecutor should not enter into any agreement or informal understanding by which the prosecutor acquires an interest in a literary or media portrayal or account based on or arising out of the prosecutor's involvement in the matter.

(b) The prosecutor should not allow prosecutorial judgment to be influenced by the possibility of future personal literary or other media rights.

(c) In creating or participating in any literary or other media account of a matter in which the prosecutor was involved, the prosecutor's duty of confidentiality must be respected even after government service is concluded. When protected confidences are involved, a prosecutor or former prosecutor should not make disclosure without consent from the prosecutor's office. Such consent should not be unreasonably withheld, and the public's interest in accurate historical accounts of significant events after a lengthy passage of time should be considered.

Standard 3–1.12 Duty to Report and Respond to Prosecutorial Misconduct

(a) The prosecutor's office should adopt policies to address allegations of professional misconduct, including violations of law, by prosecutors. At a minimum such policies should require internal reporting of reasonably suspected misconduct to supervisory staff within the office, and authorize supervisory staff to quickly address the allegations. Investigations of allegations of professional misconduct within the prosecutor's office should be handled in an independent and conflict-free manner.

(b) When a prosecutor reasonably believes that another person associated with the prosecutor's office intends or is about to engage in misconduct, the prosecutor should attempt to dissuade the person. If such attempt fails or is not possible, and the prosecutor reasonably believes that misconduct is ongoing, will occur, or has occurred, the prosecutor should promptly refer the matter to higher authority in the prosecutor's office including, if warranted by the seriousness of the matter, to the chief prosecutor.

(c) If, despite the prosecutor's efforts in accordance with sections (a) and (b) above, the chief prosecutor permits, fails to address, or insists upon an action or omission that is clearly a violation of law, the prosecutor should take further remedial action, including revealing information necessary to address, remedy, or prevent the violation to appropriate judicial, regulatory, or other government officials not in the prosecutor's office.

Standard 3–1.13 Training Programs

(a) The prosecutor's office should develop and maintain programs of training and continuing education for both new and experienced prosecutors and staff. The prosecutor's office, as well as the organized Bar or courts, should require that current and aspiring prosecutors attend a reasonable number of hours of such training and education.

(b) In addition to knowledge of substantive legal doctrine and courtroom procedures, a prosecutor's core training curriculum should address the overall mission of the criminal justice system. A core training curriculum should also seek to address: investigation, negotiation, and litigation skills; compliance with applicable discovery procedures; knowledge of the development, use, and testing of forensic evidence; available conviction and sentencing alternatives, reentry, effective conditions of probation, and collateral consequences; civility, and a commitment to professionalism; relevant office, court, and defense policies and procedures and their proper application; exercises in the use of prosecutorial discretion; civility and professionalism; appreciation of diversity and elimination of improper bias; and available technology and the ability to use it. Some training programs might usefully be open to, and taught by, persons outside the prosecutor's office such as defense counsel, court staff, and members of the judiciary.

(c) A prosecution office's training program should include periodic review of the office's policies and procedures, which should be amended when necessary. Specialized prosecutors should receive training in their specialized areas. Individuals who will supervise attorneys or staff should receive training in how effectively to supervise.

(d) The prosecutor's office should also make available opportunities for training and continuing education programs outside the office, including training for non-attorney staff.

(e) Adequate funding for continuing training and education, within and outside the office, should be requested and provided by funding sources.

PART II. ORGANIZATION OF THE PROSECUTION FUNCTION

Standard 3–2.1 Prosecution Authority to be Vested in Full-time, Public-Official Attorneys

(a) The prosecution function should be performed by a lawyer who is

(i) a public official,

(ii) authorized to practice law in the jurisdiction, and

(iii) subject to rules of attorney professional conduct and discipline.

Prosecutors whose professional obligations are devoted full-time and exclusively to the prosecution function are preferable to part-time prosecutors who have other potentially conflicting professional responsibilities.

(b) A prosecutor's office should have open, effective, and well-publicized methods for communicating with, and receiving communications from, the pubic in the jurisdiction that it serves.

(c) If a particular matter requires the appointment of a special prosecutor from outside the office, adequate funding for this purpose should be made available. Such special prosecutors should know and are governed by applicable conflict of interest standards for prosecutors. A private attorney who is paid by, or who has an attorney-client relationship with, an individual or entity that is a victim of the charged crime, or who has a personal or financial interest in the prosecution of particular charges, or who has demonstrated any impermissible bias relevant to the particular matter, should not be permitted to serve as prosecutor in that matter.

(d) Unless impractical or unlawful, the prosecutor's office should implement a system for allowing qualified law students, cross-designated prosecutors from other offices, and private attorneys temporarily assigned to the prosecutor's office, to learn about and assist with the prosecution function.

Standard 3–2.2 Assuring Excellence and Diversity in the Hiring, Retention, and Compensation of Prosecutors

(a) Strong professional qualifications and performance should be the basis for selection and retention for prosecutor positions. Effective measures to retain excellent prosecutors should be encouraged, while recognizing the benefits of some turnover. Supervisory prosecutors should select and promote personnel based on merit and expertise, without regard to partisan, personal or political factors or influence.

(b) In selecting personnel, the prosecutor's office should also consider the diverse interests and makeup of the community it serves, and seek to recruit, hire, promote and retain a diverse group of prosecutors and staff that reflect that community.

(c) The function of public prosecution requires highly developed professional skills and a variety of backgrounds, talents and experience. The prosecutor's office should promote continuing professional development and continuity of service, while providing prosecutors the opportunity to gain experience in all aspects of the prosecution function.

(d) Compensation and benefits for prosecutors and their staffs should be commensurate with the high responsibilities of the office, sufficient to compete with the private sector, and regularly adjusted to attract and retain well-qualified personnel. Compensation for prosecutors should be adequate and also comparable to that of public defense counsel in the jurisdiction.

Standard 3–2.3 Investigative Resources and Experts

The prosecutor should be provided with funds for qualified experts as needed for particular matters. When warranted by the responsibilities of the office, funds should be available to the prosecutor's office to employ professional investigators and other necessary support personnel, as well as to secure access to forensic and other experts.

Standard 3–2.4 Office Policies and Procedures

(a) Each prosecutor's office should seek to develop general policies to guide the exercise of prosecutorial discretion, and standard operating procedures for the office. The objectives of such policies and procedures should be to achieve fair, efficient, and effective enforcement of the criminal law within the prosecutor's jurisdiction.

(b) In the interest of continuity and clarity, the prosecution office's policies and procedures should be memorialized and accessible to relevant staff. The office policies and procedures should be regularly reviewed and revised. The office policies and procedures should be augmented by instruction and training, and are not a substitute for regular training programs.

(c) Prosecution office policies and procedures whose disclosure would not adversely affect the prosecution function should be made available to the public.

(d) The prosecutor's office should have a system in place to regularly review compliance with office policies.

Standard 3–2.5 Removal or Suspension and Substitution of Chief Prosecutor

(a) Fair and objective procedures should be established by appropriate legislation that empowers the governor or other public official or body to suspend or remove, and supersede, a chief prosecutor for a jurisdiction and designate a replacement, upon making a public finding after reasonable notice and hearing that the prosecutor is incapable of fulfilling the duties of office due to physical or mental incapacity or for gross deviation from professional norms.

(b) The governor or other public official or body should be similarly empowered by law to substitute, in a particular matter or category of cases, special counsel in the place of the chief prosecutor, by consent or upon making a finding after fair process that substitution is required due to a serious conflict of interest or a gross deviation from professional norms.

(c) Removal, suspension or substitution of a prosecutor should not be permitted for improper or irrelevant partisan or personal reasons.

PART III. PROSECUTORIAL RELATIONSHIPS

Standard 3–3.1 Structure of, and Relationships Among, Prosecution Offices

(a) When possible, the geographic jurisdiction of a prosecution office should be determined on the basis of population, caseload, and other relevant factors sufficient to warrant at least one full-time prosecutor and necessary support staff.

(b) In all States, there should be coordination of the prosecution policies of local prosecution offices to improve the administration and consistency of justice throughout the State. To the extent needed, a central pool of supporting resources, forensic laboratories, and personnel such as investigators, additional prosecutors, accountants and other experts, should be maintained by the state government and should be available to assist local prosecutors. A coordinated forum for prosecutors to discuss issues of professional responsibility should also be available. In some jurisdictions, it may be appropriate to create a unified statewide system of prosecution, in which the state attorney general is the chief prosecutor and district or county or other local prosecutors are the attorney general's deputies.

(c) Regardless of the statewide structure of prosecution offices, a state-wide association of prosecutors should be established. When questions or issues arise that could create important state-wide precedents, local prosecutors should advise and consult with the attorney general, the state-wide association, and the prosecutors in other local prosecution offices.

(d) Federal, state, and local prosecution offices should develop practices and procedures that encourage useful coordination with prosecutors within the jurisdiction and in other jurisdictions. Prosecutors should work to identify potential issues of conflict, coordinate with other prosecution offices in advance, and resolve inter-office disputes amicably and in the public interest.

Standard 3–3.2 Relationships With Law Enforcement

(a) The prosecutor should maintain respectful yet independent judgment when interacting with law enforcement personnel.

(b) The prosecutor may provide independent legal advice to law enforcement about actions in specific criminal matters and about law enforcement practices in general.

(c) The prosecutor should become familiar with and respect the experience and specialized expertise of law enforcement personnel. The prosecutor should promote compliance by law enforcement personnel with applicable legal rules, including rules against improper bias. The prosecutor's office should keep law enforcement personnel informed of relevant legal and legal ethics issues and developments as they relate to prosecution matters, and advise law enforcement personnel of relevant prosecution policies and procedures. Prosecutors may exercise supervision over law enforcement personnel involved in particular prosecutions when in the best interests of justice and the public.

(d) Representatives of the prosecutor's office should meet and confer regularly with law enforcement agencies regarding prosecution as well as law enforcement policies. The prosecutor's office should assist in developing and administering training programs for law enforcement personnel regarding matters and cases being investigated, matters submitted for charging, and the law related to law enforcement activities.

Standard 3–3.3 Relationship With Courts, Defense Counsel and Others

(a) In all contacts with judges, the prosecutor should maintain a professional and independent relationship. A prosecutor should not engage in unauthorized *ex parte* discussions with, or submission of material to, a judge relating to a particular matter which is, or is likely to be, before the judge. With regard to generalized matters requiring judicial discussion (for example, case-management or administrative matters), the prosecutor should invite a representative defense counsel to join in the discussion to the extent practicable.

(b) When *ex parte* communications or submissions are authorized, the prosecutor should inform the court of material facts known to the prosecutor, including facts that are adverse, sufficient to enable the court to make a fair and informed decision. Except when non-disclosure is authorized, counsel should notify opposing counsel that an *ex parte* contact has occurred, without disclosing its content unless permitted.

(c) In written filings, the prosecutor should respectfully evaluate and respond as appropriate to opposing counsel's arguments and representations, and avoid unnecessary personalized disparagement.

(d) The prosecutor should develop and maintain courteous and civil working relationships with judges and defense counsel, and should cooperate with them in developing solutions to address ethical, scheduling, or other issues that may arise in particular cases or generally in the criminal justice system. Prosecutors should cooperate with courts and organized bar associations in developing codes of professionalism and civility, and should abide by such codes that apply in their jurisdiction.

Standard 3–3.4 Relationship With Victims and Witnesses

(a) "Witness" in this Standard means any person who has or might have information about a matter, including victims.

(b) The prosecutor should know and follow the law and rules of the jurisdiction regarding victims and witnesses. In communicating with witnesses, the prosecutor should know and abide by law and ethics rules regarding the use of deceit and engaging in communications with represented, unrepresented, and organizational persons.

(c) The prosecutor or the prosecutor's agents should seek to interview all witnesses, and should not act to intimidate or unduly influence any witness.

(d) The prosecutor should not use means that have no substantial purpose other than to embarrass, delay, or burden, and not use methods of obtaining evidence that violate legal rights. The prosecutor and prosecution agents should not misrepresent their status, identity or interests when communicating with a witness.

(e) The prosecutor should be permitted to compensate a witness for reasonable expenses such as costs of attending court, depositions pursuant to statute or court rule, and pretrial interviews, including transportation and loss of income. No other benefits should be provided to witnesses unless authorized by law, regulation, or well-accepted practice. All benefits provided to witnesses should be documented and disclosed to the defense. A prosecutor should not pay or provide a benefit to a witness in order to, or in an amount that is likely to, affect the substance or truthfulness of the witness's testimony.

(f) A prosecutor should avoid the prospect of having to testify personally about the content of a witness interview. The prosecutor's interview of most routine or government witnesses (for example, custodians of records or law enforcement agents) should not require a third-party observer. But when the need for corroboration of an interview is reasonably anticipated, the prosecutor should be accompanied by another trusted and credible person during the interview. The prosecutor should avoid being alone with any witness who the prosecutor reasonably believes has potential or actual criminal liability, or foreseeably hostile witnesses.

(g) The prosecutor should advise a witness who is to be interviewed of his or her rights against self-incrimination and the right to independent counsel when the law so requires. Even if the law does not require it, a prosecutor should consider so advising a witness if the prosecutor reasonably believes the witness may provide self-incriminating information and the witness appears not to know his or her rights. However, a prosecutor should not so advise, or discuss or exaggerate the potential criminal liability of, a witness with a purpose, or in a manner likely, to intimidate the witness, to influence the truthfulness or completeness of the witness's testimony, or to change the witness's decision about whether to provide information.

(h) The prosecutor should not discourage or obstruct communication between witnesses and the defense counsel, other than the government's employees or agents if consistent with applicable ethical rules. The prosecutor should not advise any person, or cause any person to be advised, to decline to provide defense counsel with information which such person has a right to give. The prosecutor may, however, fairly and accurately advise witnesses as to the likely consequences of their providing information, but only if done in a manner that does not discourage communication.

(i) Consistent with any specific laws or rules governing victims, the prosecutor should provide victims of serious crimes, or their representatives, an opportunity to consult with and to provide information to the prosecutor, prior to making significant decisions such as whether or not to prosecute, to pursue a disposition by plea, or to dismiss charges. The prosecutor should seek to ensure that victims of serious crimes, or their representatives, are given timely notice of:

(i) judicial proceedings relating to the victims' case;

(ii) proposed dispositions of the case;

(iii) sentencing proceedings; and

(iv) any decision or action in the case that could result in the defendant's provisional or final release from custody, or change of sentence.

(j) The prosecutor should ensure that victims and witnesses who may need protections against intimidation or retaliation are advised of and afforded protections where feasible.

(k) Subject to ethical rules and the confidentiality that criminal matters sometimes require, and unless prohibited by law or court order, the prosecutor should information about the status of matters in which they are involved to victims and witnesses who request it.

(*l*) The prosecutor should give witnesses reasonable notice of when their testimony at a proceeding is expected, and should not require witnesses to attend judicial proceedings unless their testimony is reasonably expected at that time, or their presence is required by law. When witnesses' attendance is required, the prosecutor should seek to reduce to a minimum the time witnesses must spend waiting at the proceedings. The prosecutor should ensure that witnesses are given notice as soon as practicable of scheduling changes which will affect their required attendance at judicial proceedings.

(m) The prosecutor should not engage in any inappropriate personal relationship with any victim or other witness.

Standard 3–3.5 Relationship with Expert Witnesses

(a) An expert may be engaged for consultation only, or to prepare an evidentiary report or testimony. The prosecutor should know relevant rules governing expert witnesses, including possibly different disclosure rules governing experts who are engaged for consultation only.

(b) A prosecutor should evaluate all expert advice, opinions, or testimony independently, and not simply accept the opinion of a government or other expert based on employer, affiliation or prominence alone.

(c) Before engaging an expert, the prosecutor should investigate the expert's credentials, relevant professional experience, and reputation in the field. The prosecutor should also examine a testifying expert's background and credentials for potential impeachment issues. Before offering an expert as a witness, the prosecutor should investigate the scientific acceptance of the particular theory, method, or conclusions about which the expert would testify.

(d) A prosecutor who engages an expert to provide a testimonial opinion should respect the independence of the expert and should not seek to dictate the substance of the expert's opinion on the relevant subject.

(e) Before offering an expert as a witness, the prosecutor should seek to learn enough about the substantive area of the expert's expertise, including ethical rules that may be applicable in the expert's field, to enable effective preparation of the expert, as well as effective cross-examination of any defense expert on the same topic. The prosecutor should explain to the expert that the expert's role in the proceeding will be as an impartial witness called to aid the fact-finders, explain the manner in which the examination of the expert is likely to be conducted, and suggest likely impeachment questions the expert may be asked.

(f) The prosecutor should not pay or withhold any fee or provide or withhold a benefit for the purpose of influencing the substance of an expert's testimony. The prosecutor should not fix the amount of the fee contingent upon the expert's testimony or the result in the case. Nor should the prosecutor promise or imply the prospect of future work for the expert based on the expert's testimony.

(g) The prosecutor should provide the expert with all information reasonably necessary to support a full and fair opinion. The prosecutor should be aware, and explain to the expert, that all communications with, and documents shared with, a testifying expert may be subject to disclosure to opposing counsel. The prosecutor should be aware of expert discovery rules and act to protect confidentiality and the public interest, for example by not sharing with the expert confidences and work product that the prosecutor does not want disclosed.

(h) The prosecutor should timely disclose to the defense all evidence or information learned from an expert that tends to negate the guilt of the accused or mitigate the offense, even if the prosecutor does not intend to call the expert as a witness.

Standard 3–3.6 When Physical Evidence With Incriminating Implications is Disclosed by the Defense

When physical evidence is delivered to the prosecutor consistent with Defense Function Standard 4–4.7, the prosecutor should not offer the fact of delivery as evidence before a fact-finder for purposes of establishing the culpability of defense counsel's client. The prosecutor may, however, offer evidence of the fact of such delivery in response to a foundational objection to the evidence based on chain-of-custody concerns, or in a subsequent proceeding for the purpose of proving a crime or fraud regarding the evidence.

PART IV. INVESTIGATION; DECISIONS TO CHARGE, NOT CHARGE, OR DISMISS; AND GRAND JURY

Standard 3–4.1 Investigative Function of the Prosecutor

(a) When performing an investigative function, prosecutors should be familiar with and follow the ABA Standards on Prosecutorial Investigations.

(b) A prosecutor should not use illegal or unethical means to obtain evidence or information, or employ, instruct, or encourage others to do so. Prosecutors should research and know the law in this regard before acting, understanding that in some circumstances a prosecutor's ethical obligations may be different from those of other lawyers.

Standard 3–4.2 Decisions to Charge Are the Prosecutor's

(a) While the decision to arrest is often the responsibility of law enforcement personnel, the decision to institute formal criminal proceedings is the responsibility of the prosecutor. Where the law permits a law enforcement officer or other person to initiate proceedings by complaining directly to a judicial officer or the grand jury, the complainant should be required to present the complaint for prior review by the prosecutor, and the prosecutor's recommendation regarding the complaint should be communicated to the judicial officer or grand jury.

(b) The prosecutor's office should establish standards and procedures for evaluating complaints to determine whether formal criminal proceedings should be instituted.

(c) In determining whether formal criminal charges should be filed, prosecutors should consider whether further investigation should be undertaken. After charges are filed the prosecutor should oversee law enforcement investigative activity related to the case.

(d) If the defendant is not in custody when charged, the prosecutor should consider whether a voluntary appearance rather than a custodial arrest would suffice to protect the public and ensure the defendant's presence at court proceedings.

Standard 3–4.3 Minimum Requirements for Filing and Maintaining Criminal Charges

(a) A prosecutor should seek or file criminal charges only if the prosecutor reasonably believes that the charges are supported by probable cause, that admissible evidence will be sufficient to support conviction beyond a reasonable doubt, and that the decision to charge is in the interests of justice.

(b) After criminal charges are filed, a prosecutor should maintain them only if the prosecutor continues to reasonably believe that probable cause exists and that admissible evidence will be sufficient to support conviction beyond a reasonable doubt.

(c) If a prosecutor has significant doubt about the guilt of the accused or the quality, truthfulness, or sufficiency of the evidence in any criminal case assigned to the prosecutor, the prosecutor should disclose those doubts to supervisory staff. The prosecutor's office should then determine whether it is appropriate to proceed with the case.

(d) A prosecutor's office should not file or maintain charges if it believes the defendant is innocent, no matter what the state of the evidence.

Standard 3–4.4 Discretion in Filing, Declining, Maintaining, and Dismissing Criminal Charges

(a) In order to fully implement the prosecutor's functions and duties, including the obligation to enforce the law while exercising sound discretion, the prosecutor is not obliged to file or maintain all criminal charges which the evidence might support. Among the factors which the prosecutor may properly consider in exercising discretion to initiate, decline, or dismiss a criminal charge, even though it meets the requirements of Standard 3–4.3, are:

(i) the strength of the case;

(ii) the prosecutor's doubt that the accused is in fact guilty;

(iii) the extent or absence of harm caused by the offense;

(iv) the impact of prosecution or non-prosecution on the public welfare;

(v) the background and characteristics of the offender, including any voluntary restitution or efforts at rehabilitation;

(vi) whether the authorized or likely punishment or collateral consequences are disproportionate in relation to the particular offense or the offender;

(vii) the views and motives of the victim or complainant;

(viii) any improper conduct by law enforcement;

(ix) unwarranted disparate treatment of similarly situated persons;

(x) potential collateral impact on third parties, including witnesses or victims;

(xi) cooperation of the offender in the apprehension or conviction of others;

(xii) the possible influence of any cultural, ethnic, socioeconomic or other improper biases;

(xiii) changes in law or policy;

(xiv) the fair and efficient distribution of limited prosecutorial resources;

(xv) the likelihood of prosecution by another jurisdiction; and

(xvi) whether the public's interests in the matter might be appropriately vindicated by available civil, regulatory, administrative, or private remedies.

(b) In exercising discretion to file and maintain charges, the prosecutor should not consider:

(i) partisan or other improper political or personal considerations;

(ii) hostility or personal animus towards a potential subject, or any other improper motive of the prosecutor; or

(iii) the impermissible criteria described in Standard 1.6 above.

(c) A prosecutor may file and maintain charges even if juries in the jurisdiction have tended to acquit persons accused of the particular kind of criminal act in question.

(d) The prosecutor should not file or maintain charges greater in number or degree than can reasonably be supported with evidence at trial and are necessary to fairly reflect the gravity of the offense or deter similar conduct.

(e) A prosecutor may condition a dismissal of charges, *nolle prosequi*, or similar action on the accused's relinquishment of a right to seek civil redress only if the accused has given informed consent, and such consent is disclosed to the court. A prosecutor should not use a civil waiver to avoid a bona fide claim of improper law enforcement actions, and a decision not to file criminal charges should be made on its merits and not for the purpose of obtaining a civil waiver.

(f) The prosecutor should consider the possibility of a noncriminal disposition, formal or informal, or a deferred prosecution or other diversionary disposition, when deciding whether to initiate or prosecute criminal charges. The prosecutor should be familiar with the services and resources of other agencies, public or private, that might assist in the evaluation of cases for diversion or deferral from the criminal process.

Standard 3–4.5 Relationship with a Grand Jury

(a) In presenting a matter to a criminal grand jury, and in light of its *ex parte* character, the prosecutor should respect the independence of the grand jury and should not preempt a function of the grand jury, mislead the grand jury, or abuse the processes of the grand jury.

(b) Where the prosecutor is authorized to act as a legal advisor to the grand jury, the prosecutor should appropriately explain the law and may, if permitted by law, express an opinion on the legal significance of the evidence, but should give due deference to the grand jury as an independent legal body.

(c) The prosecutor should not make statements or arguments to a grand jury in an effort to influence grand jury action in a manner that would be impermissible in a trial.

(d) The entirety of the proceedings occurring before a grand jury, including the prosecutor's communications with and presentations and instructions to the grand jury, should be recorded in some manner, and that record should be preserved. The prosecutor should avoid off-the-record communications with the grand jury and with individual grand jurors.

Standard 3–4.6 Quality and Scope of Evidence Before a Grand Jury

(a) A prosecutor should not seek an indictment unless the prosecutor reasonably believes the charges are supported by probable cause and that there will be admissible evidence sufficient to support the charges beyond reasonable doubt at trial. A prosecutor should advise a grand jury of the prosecutor's opinion that it should not indict if the prosecutor believes the evidence presented does not warrant an indictment.

(b) In addition to determining what criminal charges to file, a grand jury may properly be used to investigate potential criminal conduct, and also to determine the sense of the community regarding potential charges.

(c) A prosecutor should present to a grand jury only evidence which the prosecutor believes is appropriate and authorized by law for presentation to a grand jury. The prosecutor should be familiar with the law of the jurisdiction regarding grand juries, and may present witnesses to summarize relevant evidence to the extent the law permits.

(d) When a new grand jury is empanelled, a prosecutor should ensure that the grand jurors are appropriately instructed, consistent with the law of the jurisdiction, on the grand jury's right and ability to seek evidence, ask questions, and hear directly from any available witnesses, including eyewitnesses.

(e) A prosecutor with personal knowledge of evidence that directly negates the guilt of a subject of the investigation should present or otherwise disclose that evidence to the grand jury. The prosecutor should relay to the grand jury any request by the subject or target of an investigation to testify before the grand jury, or present other non-frivolous evidence claimed to be exculpatory.

(f) If the prosecutor concludes that a witness is a target of a criminal investigation, the prosecutor should not seek to compel the witness's testimony before the grand jury absent immunity. The prosecutor should honor, however, a reasonable request from a target or subject who wishes to testify before the grand jury.

(g) Unless there is a reasonable possibility that it will facilitate flight of the target, endanger other persons, interfere with an ongoing investigation, or obstruct justice, the prosecutor should give notice to a target of a grand jury investigation, and offer the target an opportunity to testify before the grand jury. Prior to taking a target's testimony, the prosecutor should advise the target of the privilege against self-incrimination and obtain a voluntary waiver of that right.

(h) The prosecutor should not seek to compel the appearance of a witness whose activities are the subject of the grand jury's inquiry, if the witness states in advance that if called the witness will claim the constitutional privilege not to testify, and provides a reasonable basis for such claim. If warranted, the prosecutor may judicially challenge such a claim of privilege or seek a grant of immunity according to the law.

(i) The prosecutor should not issue a grand jury subpoena to a criminal defense attorney or defense team member, or other witness whose testimony reasonably might be protected by a recognized privilege, without considering the applicable law and rules of professional responsibility in the jurisdiction.

(j) Except where permitted by law, a prosecutor should not use the grand jury in order to obtain evidence to assist the prosecution's preparation for trial of a defendant who has already been charged. A prosecutor may, however, use the grand jury to investigate additional or new charges against a defendant who has already been charged.

(k) Except where permitted by law, a prosecutor should not use a criminal grand jury solely or primarily for the purpose of aiding or assisting in an administrative or civil inquiry.

PART V. PRETRIAL ACTIVITIES AND NEGOTIATED DISPOSITIONS

Standard 3–5.1 Role in First Appearance and Preliminary Hearing

(a) A prosecutor should be present at any first appearance of the accused before a judicial officer, and at any preliminary hearing.

(b) At or before the first appearance, the prosecutor should consider:

(i) whether the accused has counsel, and if not, whether and when counsel will be made available or waived;

(ii) whether the accused appears to be mentally competent, and if not, whether to seek an evaluation;

(iii) whether the accused should be released or detained pending further proceedings and, if released, whether supervisory conditions should be imposed; and

(iv) what further proceedings should be scheduled to move the matter toward timely resolution.

(c) The prosecutor handling the first appearance should ensure that the charges are consistent with the conduct described in the available law enforcement reports and any other information the prosecutor possesses.

(d) If the accused does not yet have counsel and has not waived counsel, the prosecutor should ask the court not to engage in substantive proceedings, other than a decision to release the accused. The prosecutor should not obtain a waiver of other important pretrial rights, such as the right to a preliminary hearing, from an unrepresented accused unless that person has been judicially authorized to proceed *pro se*.

(e) The prosecutor should not approach or communicate with an accused unless a voluntary waiver of counsel has been entered or the accused's counsel consents. If the accused does not have counsel, the prosecutor should make reasonable efforts to assure that the accused has been advised of the right to, and the procedure for obtaining, counsel, and is given reasonable opportunity to obtain counsel.

(f) If the prosecutor believes pretrial release is appropriate, or it is ordered, the prosecutor should cooperate in arrangements for release under the prevailing pretrial release system.

(g) If the prosecutor has reasonable concerns about the accused's mental competence, the prosecutor should bring those concerns to the attention of defense counsel and, if necessary, the judicial officer.

(h) The prosecutor should not seek to delay a prompt judicial determination of probable cause for criminal charges without good cause, particularly if the accused is in custody.

Standard 3–5.2 The Decision to Recommend Release or Seek Detention

(a) The prosecutor should favor pretrial release of a criminally accused, unless detention is necessary to protect individuals or the community or to ensure the return of the defendant for future proceedings.

(b) The prosecutor's decision to recommend pretrial release or seek detention should be based on the facts and circumstances of the defendant and the offense, rather than made categorically. The prosecutor should consider information relevant to these decisions from all sources, including the defendant.

(c) The prosecutor should cooperate with pretrial services or other personnel who review or assemble information to be provided to the court regarding pretrial release determinations.

(d) The prosecutor should be open to reconsideration of pretrial detention or release decisions based on changed circumstances, including an unexpectedly lengthy period of detention.

Standard 3–5.3 Preparation for Court Proceedings, and Recording and Transmitting Information

(a) The prosecutor should prepare in advance for court proceedings unless that is impossible. Adequate preparation depends on the nature of the proceeding and the time available, and will often include: reviewing available documents; considering what issues are likely to arise and the prosecution's position regarding those issues; how best to present the issues and what solutions might be offered; relevant legal research and factual investigation; and contacting other persons who might be of assistance in addressing the anticipated issues. If the prosecutor has not had adequate time to prepare and is unsure of the relevant facts or law, the prosecutor should communicate to the court the limits of the prosecutor's knowledge or preparation.

(b) The prosecutor should make effort to appear at all hearings in cases assigned to the prosecutor. A prosecutor who substitutes at a court proceeding for another prosecutor assigned to the case should make reasonable efforts to be adequately informed about the case and issues likely to come up at the proceeding, and to adequately prepare.

(c) The prosecutor handling any court appearance should document what happens at the proceeding, to aid the prosecutor's later memory and so that necessary information will be available to other prosecutors who may handle the case in the future.

(d) The prosecutor should take steps to ensure that any court order issued to the prosecution is transmitted to the appropriate persons necessary to effectuate the order.

(e) The prosecutor's office should be provided sufficient resources and be organized to permit adequate preparation for court proceedings.

Standard 3–5.4 Identification and Disclosure of Information and Evidence

(a) After charges are filed if not before, the prosecutor should diligently seek to identify all information in the possession of the prosecution or its agents that tends to negate the guilt of the accused, mitigate the offense charged, impeach the government's witnesses or evidence, or reduce the likely punishment of the accused if convicted.

(b) The prosecutor should diligently advise other governmental agencies involved in the case of their continuing duty to identify, preserve, and disclose to the prosecutor information described in (a) above.

(c) Before trial of a criminal case, a prosecutor should make timely disclosure to the defense of information described in (a) above that is known to the prosecutor, regardless of whether the prosecutor believes it is likely to change the result of the proceeding, unless relieved of this responsibility by a court's protective order. (Regarding discovery prior to a guilty plea, see Standard 3–5.6(f) below.) A prosecutor should not intentionally attempt to obscure information disclosed pursuant to this standard by including it without identification within a larger volume of materials.

(d) The obligations to identify and disclose such information continue throughout the prosecution of a criminal case.

(e) A prosecutor should timely respond to legally proper discovery requests, and make a diligent effort to comply with legally proper disclosure obligations, unless otherwise authorized by a court. When the defense makes requests for specific information, the prosecutor should provide specific responses rather than merely a general acknowledgement of discovery obligations. Requests and responses should be tailored to the case and "boilerplate" requests and responses should be disfavored.

(f) The prosecutor should make prompt efforts to identify and disclose to the defense any physical evidence that has been gathered in the investigation, and provide the defense a reasonable opportunity to examine it.

(g) A prosecutor should not avoid pursuit of information or evidence because the prosecutor believes it will damage the prosecution's case or aid the accused.

(h) A prosecutor should determine whether additional statutes, rules or caselaw may govern or restrict the disclosure of information, and comply with these authorities absent court order.

Standard 3–5.5 Preservation of Information and Evidence

(a) The prosecutor should make reasonable efforts to preserve, and direct the prosecutor's agents to preserve, relevant materials during and after a criminal case, including

(i) evidence relevant to investigations as well as prosecutions, whether or not admitted at trial;

(ii) information identified pursuant to Standard 3–5.4(a); and

(iii) other materials necessary to support significant decisions made and conclusions reached by the prosecution in the course of an investigation and prosecution.

(b) The prosecutor's office should develop policies regarding the method and duration of preservation of such materials. Such policies should be consistent with applicable rules and laws (such as public records laws) in the jurisdiction. These policies, and individual preservation decisions, should consider the character and seriousness of each case, the character of the particular evidence or information, the likelihood of further challenges to judgments following conviction, and the resources available for preservation. Physical evidence should be preserved so as to reasonably preserve its forensic characteristics and utility.

(c) Materials should be preserved at least until a criminal case is finally resolved or is final on appeal and the time for further appeal has expired. In felony cases, materials should be preserved until post-conviction litigation is concluded or time-limits have expired. In death penalty cases, information should be preserved until the penalty is carried out or is precluded.

(d) The prosecutor should comply with additional statutes, rules or caselaw that may govern the preservation of evidence.

Standard 3–5.6 Conduct of Negotiated Disposition Discussions

(a) The prosecutor should be open, at every stage of a criminal matter, to discussions with defense counsel concerning disposition of charges by guilty plea or other negotiated disposition.

(b) A prosecutor should not engage in disposition discussions directly with a represented defendant, except with defense counsel's approval. Where a defendant has properly waived counsel, the prosecutor may engage in disposition discussions with the defendant, and should make and preserve a record of such discussions.

(c) The prosecutor should not enter into a disposition agreement before having information sufficient to assess the defendant's actual culpability. The prosecutor should consider collateral consequences of a conviction before entering into a disposition agreement. The prosecutor should consider factors listed in Standard 3–4.4(a), and not be influenced in disposition discussions by inappropriate factors such as those listed in Standards 3–1.6 and 3–4.4(b).

(d) The prosecutor should not set unreasonably short deadlines, or demand conditions for a disposition, that are so coercive that the voluntariness of a plea or the effectiveness of defense counsel is put into question. A prosecutor may, however, set a reasonable deadline before trial or hearing for acceptance of a disposition offer.

(e) A prosecutor should not knowingly make false statements of fact or law in the course of disposition discussions.

(f) Before entering into a disposition agreement, the prosecutor should disclose to the defense a factual basis sufficient to support the charges in the proposed agreement, and information currently known to the prosecutor that tends to negate guilt, mitigates the offense or is likely to reduce punishment.

(g) A prosecutor should not agree to a guilty plea if the prosecutor reasonably believes that sufficient admissible evidence to support conviction beyond reasonable doubt would be lacking if the matter went to trial.

Standard 3–5.7 Establishing and Fulfilling Conditions of Negotiated Dispositions

(a) A prosecutor should not demand terms in a negotiated disposition agreement that are unlawful or in violation of public policy.

(b) The prosecutor may properly promise the defense that the prosecutor will or will not take a particular position concerning sentence and conditions. The prosecutor should not, however, imply a greater power to influence the disposition of a case than is actually possessed.

(c) The prosecutor should memorialize all promises and conditions that are part of the agreement, and ensure that any written disposition agreement accurately and completely reflects the precise terms of the agreement including the prosecutor's promises and the defendant's obligations. At any court hearing to finalize a negotiated disposition, the prosecutor should ensure that all relevant details of the agreement have been placed on the record. The presumption is that the hearing and record will be public, but in some cases the hearing or record (or a portion) may be sealed for good cause.

(d) Once a disposition agreement is final and accepted by the court, the prosecutor should comply with, and make good faith efforts to have carried out, the government's obligations. The prosecutor should construe agreement conditions, and evaluate the defendant's performance including any cooperation, in a good-faith and reasonable manner.

(e) If the prosecutor believes that a defendant has breached an agreement that has been accepted by the court, the prosecutor should notify the defense regarding the prosecutor's belief and any intended adverse action. If the defense presents a good-faith disagreement and the parties cannot quickly resolve it, the prosecutor should not act before judicial resolution.

(f) If the prosecutor reasonably believes that a court is acting inconsistently with any term of a negotiated disposition, the prosecutor should raise the matter with the court.

Standard 3–5.8 Waiver of Rights as Condition of Disposition Agreements

(a) A prosecutor should not condition a disposition agreement on a waiver of the right to appeal the terms of a sentence which exceeds an agreed-upon or reasonably anticipated sentence. Any waiver of appeal of sentence should be comparably binding on the defendant and the prosecution.

(b) A prosecutor should not suggest or require, as a condition of a disposition agreement, any waiver of post-conviction claims addressing ineffective assistance of counsel, prosecutorial misconduct, or destruction of evidence, unless such claims are based on past instances of such conduct that are specifically identified in the agreement or in the transcript of proceedings that address the agreement. If a proposed disposition agreement contains such a waiver regarding ineffective assistance of counsel, the prosecutor should ensure that the defendant has been provided the opportunity to consult with independent counsel regarding the waiver before agreeing to the disposition.

(c) A prosecutor may propose or require other sorts of waivers on an individualized basis if the defendant's agreement is knowing and voluntary. No waivers of any kind should be accepted without an exception for manifest injustice based on newly-discovered evidence, or actual innocence.

(d) Although certain claims may have been waived, a prosecutor should not condition a disposition agreement on a complete waiver of the right to file a habeas corpus or other comparable post-conviction petition.

(e) A prosecutor should not request or rely on waivers to hide an injustice or material flaw in the case which is undisclosed to the defense.

Standard 3–5.9 Record of Reasons for Dismissal of Charges

When criminal charges are dismissed on the prosecution's motion, including by plea of *nolle prosequi*or its equivalent, the prosecutor should make and retain an appropriate record of the reasons for the dismissal, and indicate on the record whether the dismissal was with or without prejudice.

PART VI. COURT HEARINGS AND TRIAL

Standard 3–6.1 Scheduling Court Hearings

Final control over the scheduling of court appearances, hearings and trials in criminal matters should rest with the court rather than the parties. When the prosecutor is aware of facts that would affect scheduling, the prosecutor should advise the court and, if the facts are case-specific, defense counsel.

Standard 3–6.2 Civility With Courts, Opposing Counsel, and Others

(a) As an officer of the court, the prosecutor should support the authority of the court and the dignity of the courtroom by adherence to codes of professionalism and civility, and by manifesting a professional and courteous attitude toward the judge, opposing counsel, witnesses, defendants, jurors, court staff and others. In court as elsewhere, the prosecutor should not display or act out of any improper or unlawful bias.

(b) When court is in session, unless otherwise permitted by the court, the prosecutor should address the court and not address other counsel or the defendant directly on any matter related to the case.

(c) The prosecutor should comply promptly and civilly with a court's orders or seek appropriate relief from such order. If the prosecutor considers an order to be significantly erroneous or prejudicial, the prosecutor should ensure that the record adequately reflects the events. The prosecutor has a right to make respectful objections and reasonable requests for reconsideration, and to seek other relief as the law permits. If a judge prohibits making an adequate objection, proffer, or record, the prosecutor may take other lawful steps to protect the public interest.

Standard 3–6.3 Selection of Jurors

(a) The prosecutor's office should be aware of legal standards that govern the selection of jurors, and train prosecutors to comply. The prosecutor should prepare to effectively discharge the prosecution function in the selection of the jury, including exercising challenges for cause and peremptory challenges. The prosecutor's office should also be aware of the process used to select and summon the jury pool and bring legal deficiencies to the attention of the court.

(b) The prosecutor should not strike jurors based on any criteria rendered impermissible by the constitution, statutes, applicable rules of the jurisdiction, or these standards, including race, sex, religion, national origin, disability, sexual orientation or gender identity. The prosecutor should consider contesting a defense counsel's peremptory challenges that appear to be based upon such criteria.

(c) In cases in which the prosecutor conducts a pretrial investigation of the background of potential jurors, the investigative methods used should not harass, intimidate, or unduly embarrass or invade the privacy of potential jurors. Absent special circumstances, such investigation should be restricted to review of records and sources of information already in existence and to which access is lawfully allowed. If the prosecutor uses record searches that are unavailable to the defense, such as criminal record databases, the prosecutor should share the results with defense counsel or seek a judicial protective order.

(d) The opportunity to question jurors personally should be used solely to obtain information relevant to the well-informed exercise of challenges. The prosecutor should not seek to commit jurors on factual issues likely to arise in the case, and should not intentionally present arguments, facts or evidence which the prosecutor reasonably should know will not be admissible at trial. Voir dire should not be used to argue the prosecutor's case to the jury, or to unduly ingratiate counsel with the jurors.

(e) During voir dire, the prosecutor should seek to minimize any undue embarrassment or invasion of privacy of potential jurors, for example by seeking to inquire into sensitive matters outside the presence of other potential jurors, while still enabling fair and efficient juror selection.

(f) If the court does not permit voir dire by counsel, the prosecutor should provide the court with suggested questions in advance, and request specific follow-up questions during the selection process when necessary to ensure fair juror selection.

(g) If the prosecutor has reliable information that conflicts with a potential juror's responses, or that reasonably would support a "for cause" challenge by any party, the prosecutor should inform the court and, unless the court orders otherwise, defense counsel.

Standard 3–6.4 Relationship With Jurors

(a) The prosecutor should not communicate with persons the prosecutor knows to be summoned for jury duty or impaneled as jurors, before or during trial, other than in the lawful conduct of courtroom proceedings. The prosecutor should avoid even the appearance of improper communications with jurors, and minimize any out-of-court proximity to or contact with jurors. Where out-of-court contact cannot be avoided, the prosecutor should not communicate about or refer to the specific case.

(b) The prosecutor should treat jurors with courtesy and respect, while avoiding a show of undue solicitude for their comfort or convenience.

(c) After discharge of a juror, a prosecutor should avoid contacts that may harass or embarrass the juror, that criticize the jury's actions or verdict, or that express views that could otherwise adversely influence the juror's future jury service. The prosecutor should know and comply with applicable rules and law governing the subject.

(d) After a jury is discharged, the prosecutor may, if no statute, rule, or order prohibits such action, communicate with jurors to investigate whether a verdict may be subject to legal challenge, or to evaluate the prosecution's performance for improvement in the future. The prosecutor should consider requesting the court to instruct the jury that, if it is not prohibited by law, it is not improper for jurors to discuss the case with the lawyers, although they are not required to do so. Any post-discharge communication with a juror should not disparage the criminal justice system and the jury trial process, and should not express criticism of the jury's actions or verdict.

(e) A prosecutor who learns reasonably reliable information that there was a problem with jury deliberations or conduct that could support an attack on a judgment of conviction and that is recognized as potentially valid in the jurisdiction, should promptly report that information to the appropriate judicial officer and, unless the court orders otherwise, defense counsel.

Standard 3–6.5 Opening Statement at Trial

(a) The prosecutor should give an opening statement before the presentation of evidence begins.

(b) The prosecutor's opening statement at trial should be confined to a fair statement of the case from the prosecutor's perspective, and discussion of evidence that the prosecutor reasonably believes will be available, offered and admitted to support the prosecution case. The prosecutor's opening should avoid speculating about what defenses might be raised by the defense unless the prosecutor knows they will be raised.

(c) The prosecutor's opening statement should be made without expressions of personal opinion, vouching for witnesses, inappropriate appeals to emotion or personal attacks on opposing counsel. The prosecutor should scrupulously avoid any comment on a defendant's right to remain silent.

(d) When the prosecutor has reason to believe that a portion of the opening statement may be objectionable, the prosecutor should raise that point with defense counsel and, if necessary, the court, in advance. Similarly, visual aids or exhibits that the prosecutor intends to use during opening statement should be shown to defense counsel in advance.

Standard 3–6.6 Presentation of Evidence

(a) The prosecutor should not offer evidence that the prosecutor does not reasonably believe to be true, whether by documents, tangible evidence, or the testimony of witnesses. When a prosecutor has reason to doubt the truth or accuracy of particular evidence, the prosecutor should take reasonable steps to determine that the evidence is reliable, or not present it.

(b) If the prosecutor reasonably believes there has been misconduct by opposing counsel, a witness, the court or other persons that affects the fair presentation of the evidence, the prosecutor should challenge the perceived misconduct by appealing or objecting to the court or through other appropriate avenues, and not by engaging in retaliatory conduct that the prosecutor knows to be improper.

(c) During the trial, if the prosecutor discovers that false evidence or testimony has been introduced by the prosecution, the prosecutor should take reasonable remedial steps. If the witness is still on the stand, the prosecutor should attempt to correct the error through further examination. If the falsity remains uncorrected or is not discovered until the witness is off the stand, the prosecutor should notify the court and opposing counsel for determination of an appropriate remedy.

(d) The prosecutor should not bring to the attention of the trier of fact matters that the prosecutor knows to be inadmissible, whether by offering or displaying inadmissible evidence, asking legally objectionable questions, or making impermissible comments or arguments. If the prosecutor is uncertain about the admissibility of evidence, the prosecutor should seek and obtain resolution from the court before the hearing or trial if possible, and reasonably in advance of the time for proffering the evidence before a jury.

(e) The prosecutor should exercise strategic judgment regarding whether to object or take exception to evidentiary rulings that are materially adverse to the prosecution, and not make every possible objection. The prosecutor should not make objections without a reasonable basis, or for improper reasons such as to harass or to break the flow of opposing counsel's presentation. The prosecutor should make an adequate record for appeal, and consider the possibility of an interlocutory appeal regarding significant adverse rulings if available.

(f) The prosecutor should not display tangible evidence (and should object to such display by the defense) until it is admitted into evidence, except insofar as its display is necessarily incidental to its tender, although the prosecutor may seek permission to display admissible evidence during opening statement. The prosecutor should avoid displaying even admitted evidence in a manner that is unduly prejudicial.

Standard 3–6.7 Examination of Witnesses in Court

(a) The prosecutor should conduct the examination of witnesses fairly and with due regard for dignity and legitimate privacy concerns, and without seeking to intimidate or humiliate a witness unnecessarily.

(b) The prosecutor should not use cross-examination to discredit or undermine a witness's testimony, if the prosecutor knows the testimony to be truthful and accurate.

(c) The prosecutor should not call a witness to testify in the presence of the jury, or require the defense to do so, when the prosecutor knows the witness will claim a valid privilege not to testify. If the prosecutor is unsure whether a particular witness will claim a privilege to not testify, the prosecutor should alert the court and defense counsel in advance and outside the presence of the jury.

(d) The prosecutor should not ask a question that implies the existence of a factual predicate for which a good faith belief is lacking.

Standard 3–6.8 Closing Argument to the Trier of Fact

(a) In closing argument to a jury (or to a judge sitting as trier of fact), the prosecutor should present arguments and a fair summary of the evidence that proves the defendant guilty beyond reasonable doubt. The prosecutor may argue all reasonable inferences from the evidence in the record, unless the prosecutor knows an inference to be false. The prosecutor should, to the extent time permits, review the evidence in the record before presenting closing argument. The prosecutor should not knowingly misstate the evidence in the record, or argue inferences that the prosecutor knows have no good-faith support in the record. The prosecutor should scrupulously avoid any reference to a defendant's decision not to testify.

(b) The prosecutor should not argue in terms of counsel's personal opinion, and should not imply special or secret knowledge of the truth or of witness credibility.

(c) The prosecutor should not make arguments calculated to appeal to improper prejudices of the trier of fact. The prosecutor should make only those arguments that are consistent with the trier's duty to decide the case on the evidence, and should not seek to divert the trier from that duty.

(d) If the prosecutor presents rebuttal argument, the prosecutor may respond fairly to arguments made in the defense closing argument, but should not present or raise new issues. If the prosecutor believes the defense closing argument is or was improper, the prosecutor should timely object and request relief from the court, rather than respond with arguments that the prosecutor knows are improper.

Standard 3–6.9 Facts Outside the Record

When before a jury, the prosecutor should not knowingly refer to, or argue on the basis of, facts outside the record, unless such facts are matters of common public knowledge based on ordinary human experience, or are matters of which a court clearly may take judicial notice, or are facts the prosecutor reasonably believes will be entered into the record at that proceeding. In a nonjury context the prosecutor may refer to extra-record facts relevant to issues about which the court specifically inquires, but should note that they are outside the record.

Standard 3–6.10 Comments by Prosecutor After Verdict or Ruling

(a) The prosecutor should respectfully accept acquittals. Regarding other adverse rulings (including the rare acquittal by a judge that is appealable), while the prosecutor may publicly express respectful disagreement and an intention to pursue lawful options for review, the prosecutor should refrain from public criticism of any participant. Public comments after a verdict or ruling should be respectful of the legal system and process.

(b) The prosecutor may publicly praise a jury verdict or court ruling, compliment government agents or others who aided in the matter, and note the social value of the ruling or event. The prosecutor should not publicly gloat or seek personal aggrandizement regarding a verdict or ruling.

PART VII. POST-TRIAL MOTIONS AND SENTENCING

Standard 3–7.1 Post-trial Motions

The prosecutor should conduct a fair evaluation of post-trial motions, determine their merit, and respond accordingly and respectfully. The prosecutor should not oppose motions at any stage without a reasonable basis for doing so.

Standard 3–7.2 Sentencing

(a) The severity of sentences imposed should not be used as a measure of a prosecutor's effectiveness.

(b) The prosecutor should be familiar with relevant sentencing laws, rules, consequences and options, including alternative non-imprisonment sentences. Before or soon after charges are filed, and throughout the pendency of the case, the prosecutor should evaluate potential consequences of the prosecution and available sentencing options, such as forfeiture, restitution, and immigration effects, and be prepared to actively advise the court in sentencing.

(c) The prosecutor should seek to assure that a fair and informed sentencing judgment is made, and to avoid unfair sentences and disparities.

(d) In the interests of uniformity, the prosecutor's office should develop consistent policies for evaluating and making sentencing recommendations, and not leave complete discretion for sentencing policy to individual prosecutors.

(e) The prosecutor should know the relevant laws and rules regarding victims' rights, and facilitate victim participation in the sentencing process as the law requires or permits.

Standard 3–7.3 Information Relevant to Sentencing

(a) The prosecutor should assist the court in obtaining complete and accurate information for use in sentencing, and should cooperate fully with the court's and staff's presentence investigations. The prosecutor should provide any information that the prosecution believes is relevant to the sentencing to the court and to defense counsel. A record of such information provided to the court and counsel should be made, so that it may be reviewed later if necessary. If material incompleteness or inaccuracy in a presentence report comes to the prosecutor's attention, the prosecutor should take steps to present the complete and correct information to the court and defense counsel.

(b) The prosecutor should disclose to the defense and to the court, at or before the sentencing proceeding, all information that tends to mitigate the sentence and is known to the prosecutor, unless the prosecutor is relieved of this responsibility by a court order.

(c) Prior to sentencing, the prosecutor should disclose to the defense any evidence or information it provides, whether by document or orally, to the court or presentence investigator in aid of sentencing, unless contrary to law or rule in the jurisdiction or a protective order has been sought.

PART VIII. APPEALS AND OTHER CONVICTION CHALLENGES

Standard 3–8.1 Duty To Defend Conviction Not Absolute

The prosecutor has a duty to defend convictions obtained after fair process. This duty is not absolute, however, and the prosecutor should temper the duty to defend with independent professional judgment and discretion. The prosecutor should not defend a conviction if the prosecutor believes the defendant is innocent or was wrongfully convicted, or that a miscarriage of justice associated with the conviction has occurred.

Standard 3–8.2 Appeals—General Principles

(a) All prosecutors should be sufficiently knowledgeable about appellate practice to be able to make a record sufficient to preserve issues and arguments for appeal, and should make such a record at the trial court level.

(b) When the prosecutor receives an adverse ruling, the prosecutor should consider whether it may be appealed. If the ruling may be appealed, the prosecutor should consider whether an appeal should be filed, and refer it to an appellate prosecutor if appropriate for decision.

(c) When considering whether an adverse ruling should be appealed, the prosecutor should evaluate not only the legal merits, but also whether it is in the interests of justice to pursue such an appeal, taking into account the benefits to the prosecution, the judicial system, and the public, as well as the costs of the appellate process and of delay to the prosecution, defendant, victims and witnesses.

(d) A prosecutor handling a criminal appeal should know the specific rules, practices and procedures that govern appeals in the jurisdiction.

(e) The prosecutor's office should designate one or more prosecutors in the office to develop expertise regarding appellate law and procedure, and should develop contacts with other offices' prosecutors who have such expertise. The prosecutor's office should develop consistent policies and positions regarding issues that are common or recurring in the appellate process or court. The prosecutor's office should regularly notify its prosecutors and law enforcement agents about new developments in the law or judicial decisions, and should provide regular training to such personnel on such topics.

(f) A prosecutor handling a criminal appeal who was not counsel in the trial court should consult with the trial prosecutor, but should exercise independent judgment in reviewing the record and the defense arguments. The appellate prosecutor should not make or oppose arguments in an appeal without a reasonable legal basis.

Standard 3–8.3 Responses to New or Newly-Discovered Evidence or Law

If a prosecutor learns of credible and material information creating a reasonable likelihood that a defendant was wrongfully convicted or sentenced or is actually innocent, the prosecutor should comply with ABA Model Rules of Professional Conduct 3.8(g) and (h). The prosecutor's office should develop policies and procedures to address such information, and take actions that are consistent with applicable law, rules, and the duty to pursue justice.

Standard 3–8.4 Challenges to the Effectiveness of Defense Counsel

(a) In any post-conviction challenge to the effectiveness of defense counsel, the prosecutor should be cognizant of the defendant's potential attorney-client privilege with former defense counsel as well as former defense counsel's other ethical or legal obligations, and not seek to abrogate such privileges or obligations without an unambiguous legal basis, or court order.

(b) If a prosecutor observes, at any stage of a criminal proceeding, defense counsel conduct or omission that might reasonably constitute ineffective assistance of counsel, the prosecutor should take reasonable steps to preserve the defendant's right to effective assistance as well as the public's interest in obtaining a valid conviction, while not intruding on a defendant's constitutional right to counsel. During an ongoing defense representation, the prosecutor should not express concerns regarding possible ineffective assistance on the public record without an unambiguous legal basis or court order, and should not communicate any such concerns directly to the defendant.

Standard 3–8.5 Collateral Attacks on Conviction

If required to respond to a collateral attack on a conviction, the prosecutor should consider all lawful responses, including applicable procedural or other defenses. The prosecutor need not, however, invoke every possible defense to a collateral attack, and should consider potential negotiated dispositions or other remedies, if the prosecutor and the prosecutor's office reasonably conclude that the interests of justice are thereby served.

THE DEFENSE FUNCTION

PART I. GENERAL STANDARDS

Standard 4–1.1 The Scope and Function of these Standards

(a) As used in these Standards, "defense counsel" means any attorney—including privately retained, assigned by the court, acting *pro bono* or serving indigent defendants in a legal aid or public defender's office—who acts as an attorney on behalf of a client being investigated or prosecuted for alleged criminal conduct, or a client seeking legal advice regarding a potential, ongoing or past criminal matter or subpoena, including as a witness. These Standards are intended to apply in any context in which a lawyer would reasonably understand that a criminal prosecution could result. The Standards are intended to serve the best interests of clients, and should not be relied upon to justify any decision that is counter to the client's best interests. The burden to justify any exception should rest with the lawyer seeking it.

(b) These Standards are intended to provide guidance for the professional conduct and performance of defense counsel. They are not intended to modify a defense attorney's obligations under applicable rules, statutes or the constitution. They are aspirational or describe "best practices," and are not intended to serve as the basis for the imposition of professional discipline, to create substantive or procedural rights for clients, or to create a standard of care for civil liability. They may be relevant in judicial evaluation of constitutional claims regarding the right to counsel. For purposes of consistency, these Standards sometimes include language taken from the Model Rules of Professional Conduct; but the Standards often address conduct or provide details beyond that governed by the Model Rules of Professional Conduct. No inconsistency is ever intended; and in any case a lawyer should always read and comply with the rules of professional conduct and other authorities that are binding in the specific jurisdiction or matter, including choice of law principles that may regulate the lawyer's ethical conduct.

(c) Because the Standards for Criminal Justice are aspirational, the words "should" or "should not" are used in these Standards, rather than mandatory phrases such as "shall" or "shall not," to describe the conduct of lawyers that is expected or recommended under these Standards. The Standards are not intended to suggest any lesser standard of conduct than may be required by applicable mandatory rules, statutes, or other binding authorities.

(d) These Standards are intended to address the performance of criminal defense counsel in all stages of their professional work. Other ABA Criminal Justice Standards should also be consulted for more detailed consideration of the performance of criminal defense counsel in specific areas.

Standard 4–1.2 Functions and Duties of Defense Counsel

(a) Defense counsel is essential to the administration of criminal justice. A court properly constituted to hear a criminal case should be viewed as an entity consisting of the court (including judge, jury, and other court personnel), counsel for the prosecution, and counsel for the defense.

(b) Defense counsel have the difficult task of serving both as officers of the court and as loyal and zealous advocates for their clients. The primary duties that defense counsel owe to their clients, to the administration of justice, and as officers of the court, are to serve as their clients' counselor and advocate with courage and devotion; to ensure that constitutional and other legal rights of their clients are protected; and to render effective, high-quality legal representation with integrity.

(c) Defense counsel should know and abide by the standards of professional conduct as expressed in applicable law and ethical codes and opinions in the applicable jurisdiction. Defense counsel should seek out supervisory advice when available, and defense counsel organizations as well as others should provide ethical guidance when the proper course of conduct seems unclear. Defense counsel who disagrees with a governing ethical rule should seek its change if appropriate, and directly challenge it if necessary, but should comply with it unless relieved by court order.

(d) Defense counsel is the client's professional representative, not the client's alter-ego. Defense counsel should act zealously within the bounds of the law and standards on behalf of their clients, but have no duty to, and may not, execute any directive of the client which violates the law or such standards. In representing a client, defense counsel may engage in a good faith challenge to the validity of such laws or standards if done openly.

(e) Defense counsel should seek to reform and improve the administration of criminal justice. When inadequacies or injustices in the substantive or procedural law come to defense counsel's attention, counsel should stimulate and support efforts for remedial action. Defense counsel should provide services to the community, including involvement in public service and Bar activities, public education, community service activities, and Bar leadership positions. A public defense organization should support such activities, and the office's budget should include funding and paid release time for such activities.

(f) Defense counsel should be knowledgeable about, and consider, alternatives to prosecution or conviction that may be applicable in individual cases, and communicate them to the client. Defense counsel should be available to assist other groups in the community in addressing problems that lead to, or result from, criminal activity or perceived flaws in the criminal justice system.

(g) Because the death penalty differs from other criminal penalties, defense counsel in a capital case should make extraordinary efforts on behalf of the accused and, more specifically, review and comply with the ABA Guidelines for the Appointment and Performance of Defense Counsel in Death Penalty Cases.

Standard 4–1.3 Continuing Duties of Defense Counsel

Some duties of defense counsel run throughout the period of representation, and even beyond. Defense counsel should consider the impact of these duties at all stages of a criminal representation and on all decisions and actions that arise in the course of performing the defense function. These duties include:

(a) a duty of confidentiality regarding information relevant to the client's representation which duty continues after the representation ends;

(b) a duty of loyalty toward the client;

(c) a duty of candor toward the court and others, tempered by the duties of confidentiality and loyalty;

(d) a duty to communicate and keep the client informed and advised of significant developments and potential options and outcomes;

(e) a duty to be well-informed regarding the legal options and developments that can affect a client's interests during a criminal representation;

(f) a duty to continually evaluate the impact that each decision or action may have at later stages, including trial, sentencing, and post-conviction review;

(g) a duty to be open to possible negotiated dispositions of the matter, including the possible benefits and disadvantages of cooperating with the prosecution;

(h) a duty to consider the collateral consequences of decisions and actions, including but not limited to the collateral consequences of conviction.

Standard 4–1.4 Defense Counsel's Tempered Duty of Candor

(a) In light of criminal defense counsel's constitutionally recognized role in the criminal process, defense counsel's duty of candor may be tempered by competing ethical and constitutional obligations. Defense counsel must act zealously within the bounds of the law and applicable rules to protect the client's confidences and the unique liberty interests that are at stake in criminal prosecution.

(b) Defense counsel should not knowingly make a false statement of fact or law or offer false evidence, to a court, lawyer, witnesses, or third party. It is not a false statement for defense counsel to suggest inferences that may reasonably be drawn from the evidence. In addition, while acting to accommodate legitimate confidentiality, privilege, or other defense concerns, defense counsel should correct a defense representation of material fact or law that defense counsel knows is, or later learns was, false.

(c) Defense counsel should disclose to a court legal authority in the controlling jurisdiction known to defense counsel to be directly adverse to the position of the client and not disclosed by others.

Standard 4–1.5 Preserving the Record

At every stage of representation, defense counsel should take steps necessary to make a clear and complete record for potential review. Such steps may include: filing motions, including motions for reconsideration, and exhibits; making objections and placing explanations on the record; requesting evidentiary hearings; requesting or objecting to jury instructions; and making offers of proof and proffers of excluded evidence.

Standard 4–1.6 Improper Bias Prohibited

(a) Defense counsel should not manifest or exercise, by words or conduct, bias or prejudice based upon race, sex, religion, national origin, disability, age, sexual orientation, gender identity, or socioeconomic status. Defense counsel should strive to eliminate implicit biases, and act to mitigate any improper bias or prejudice when credibly informed that it exists within the scope of defense counsel's authority.

(b) Defense counsel should be proactive in efforts to detect, investigate, and eliminate improper biases, with particular attention to historically persistent biases like race, in all of counsel's work. A public defense office should regularly assess the potential for biased or unfairly disparate impacts of its policies on communities within the defense office's jurisdiction, and eliminate those impacts that cannot be properly justified.

Standard 4–1.7 Conflicts of Interest

(a) Defense counsel should know and abide by the ethical rules regarding conflicts of interest that apply in the jurisdiction, and be sensitive to facts that may raise conflict issues. When a conflict requiring withdrawal exists and is non-waivable, or informed consent has not been obtained, defense counsel should decline to proceed further, or take only minimal actions necessary to protect the client's interests, until an adequate waiver or new counsel is in place, or a court orders continued representation.

(b) Defense counsel should not permit their professional judgment or obligations regarding the representation of a client to be adversely affected by loyalties or obligations to other, former, or potential clients; by client obligations of their law partners; or by their personal political, financial, business, property, or other interests or relationships.

(c) Defense counsel should disclose to the client at the earliest feasible opportunity any information, including any interest in or connection to the matter or to other persons involved in the matter, that would reasonably be relevant to the client's selection of unconflicted counsel or decision to continue counsel's representation. The disclosure of conflicts of interest that would otherwise be prohibited by applicable rules or law should be in writing, and should be disclosed on the record to any court that the matter comes before. Disclosures to the client should include communication of information sufficient to permit the client to appreciate the material risks involved and available alternatives. Defense counsel should obtain informed consent from a client before proceeding with any representation where an actual or realistically potential conflict is present.

(d) Except where necessary to secure counsel for preliminary matters such as initial hearings or applications for bail, a defense counsel (or multiple counsel associated in practice) should not undertake to represent more than one client in the same criminal case. When there is not yet a criminal case, such multiple representation should be engaged in only when, after careful investigation and consideration, it is clear either that no conflict is likely to develop at any stage of the matter, or that multiple representation will be advantageous to each of the clients represented and that foreseeable conflicts can be waived.

(e) In instances of permissible multiple representation:

(i) the clients should be fully advised that the lawyer may be unable to continue if a conflict develops, and that confidentiality may not exist between the clients;

(ii) informed written consent should be obtained from each of the clients, and

(iii) if the matter is before a tribunal, such consent should be made on the record with appropriate inquiries by counsel and the court.

(f) Defense counsel who has formerly represented a client should not thereafter use information related to the former representation to the disadvantage of the former client, unless the information has become generally known or the ethical obligations of confidentiality and loyalty otherwise do not apply, and should not take legal positions that are substantially adverse to a former client.

(g) In accepting payment of fees by one person for the representation of another, defense counsel should explain to the payor that counsel's loyalty and confidentiality obligations are owed entirely to the person being represented and not to the payor, and that counsel may not release client information to the payor unless applicable ethics rules allow. Defense counsel should not permit a person who recommends, employs, or pays defense counsel to render legal services for another to direct or regulate counsel's professional judgment in rendering such legal services. In addition, defense counsel should not accept such third-party compensation unless:

(i) the client gives informed consent after full disclosure and explanation;

(ii) defense counsel is confident there will be no interference with defense counsel's independence or professional judgment or with the client-lawyer relationship; and

(iii) defense counsel is reasonably confident that information relating to the representation of the client will be protected from disclosure as required by counsel's ethical duty of confidentiality.

(h) Defense counsel should not represent a client in a criminal matter in which counsel, or counsel's partner or other lawyer in counsel's law office or firm, is the prosecutor in the same or a substantially related matter, or is a prosecutor in the same jurisdiction.

(i) If defense counsel's partner or other lawyer in counsel's law office was formerly a prosecutor in the same or substantially related matter or was a prosecutor in the same jurisdiction, defense counsel should not take on representation in that matter unless appropriate screening and consent measures under applicable ethics rules are undertaken, and no confidential information of the client or of the government has actually been exchanged between defense counsel and the former prosecutor.

(j) If defense counsel is a candidate for a position, or seeking employment, as a prosecutor or judge, this should be promptly disclosed to the client, and informed consent to continue be obtained.

(k) Defense counsel who formerly participated personally and substantially in the prosecution or criminal investigation of a defendant should not thereafter represent any person in the same or a substantially related matter, unless waiver is obtained from both the client and the government. Defense counsel who acquired confidential information about a person when counsel was formerly a prosecutor should not use such information in the representation of a client whose interests are adverse to that other person, unless the information has become generally known or the ethical obligations of confidentiality and loyalty otherwise do not apply.

(*l*) Defense counsel whose current relationship to a prosecutor is parent, child, sibling, spouse, or sexual partner should not represent a client in a criminal matter in which defense counsel knows the government is represented by that prosecutor. Nor should defense counsel who has a significant personal or financial relationship with a prosecutor represent a client in a criminal matter in which defense counsel knows the government is represented in the matter by such prosecutor, except upon informed consent by the client regarding the relationship.

(m) Defense counsel should not act as surety on a bond either for a client whom counsel represents or for any other client in the same or a related case, unless it is required by law or it is clear that there is no risk that counsel's judgment could be materially limited by counsel's interest in recovering the amount ensured.

(n) Except as law may otherwise permit, defense counsel should not negotiate to employ any person who is significantly involved as an attorney, employee, or agent of the prosecution in a matter in which defense counsel is participating personally and substantially.

Standard 4–1.8 Appropriate Workload

(a) Defense counsel should not carry a workload that, by reason of its excessive size or complexity, interferes with providing quality representation, endangers a client's interest in independent, thorough, or speedy representation, or has a significant potential to lead to the breach of professional obligations. A defense counsel whose workload prevents competent representation should not accept additional matters until the workload is reduced, and should work to ensure competent representation in counsel's existing matters. Defense counsel within a supervisory structure should notify supervisors when counsel's workload is approaching or exceeds professionally appropriate levels.

(b) Defense organizations and offices should regularly review the workload of individual attorneys, as well as the workload of the entire office, and adjust workloads (including intake) when necessary and as permitted by law to ensure the effective and ethical conduct of the defense function.

(c) Publicly-funded defense entities should inform governmental officials of the workload of their offices, and request funding and personnel that are adequate to meet the defense caseload. Defense counsel should consider seeking such funding from all appropriate sources. If workload exceeds the appropriate professional capacity of a publicly-funded defense office or other defense counsel, that office or counsel should also alert the court(s) in its jurisdiction and seek judicial relief.

Standard 4–1.9 Diligence, Promptness and Punctuality

(a) Defense counsel should act with diligence and promptness in representing a client, and should avoid unnecessary delay in the disposition of cases. But defense counsel should not act with such haste that quality representation is compromised. Defense counsel and publically-funded defense entities should be organized and supported with adequate staff and facilities to enable them to represent clients effectively and efficiently.

(b) When providing reasons for seeking delay, defense counsel should not knowingly misrepresent facts or otherwise mislead. Defense counsel should use procedural devices that will cause delay only when there is a legitimate basis for their use. Defense counsel should not accept a representation for the purpose of delaying a trial or hearing.

(c) Defense counsel should not unreasonably oppose requests for continuances from the prosecutor.

(d) Defense counsel should know and comply with timing requirements applicable to a criminal representation so as to not prejudice the client's rights.

(e) Defense counsel should be punctual in attendance at court, in the submission of motions, briefs, and other papers, and in dealings with opposing counsel, witnesses and others. Defense counsel should emphasize to the client, assistants, and defense witnesses the importance of punctuality in court attendance.

Standard 4–1.10 Relationship With Media

(a) For purposes of this Standard, a "public statement" is any extrajudicial statement that a reasonable person would expect to be disseminated by means of public communication or media, including social media. An extrajudicial statement is any oral, written, or visual presentation not made either in a courtroom during the criminal proceedings or in court filings or correspondence with the court or counsel regarding the criminal proceedings.

(b) Defense counsel's public statements about the judiciary, jurors, other lawyers, or the criminal justice system should be respectful even if expressing disagreement.

(c) Defense counsel should not make, cause to be made, or authorize or condone the making of, a public statement that counsel knows or reasonably should know will have a substantial likelihood of materially prejudicing a criminal proceeding. Defense counsel's public statements should otherwise be consistent with the ABA Standards on Fair Trial and Public Discourse.

(d) Defense counsel should not place statements or evidence into the court record to circumvent this Standard.

(e) Defense counsel should exercise reasonable care to prevent investigators, employees, or other persons assisting or associated with the defense from making an extrajudicial statement or providing non-public information that defense counsel would be prohibited from making or providing under this Standard or other applicable rules or law.

(f) Defense counsel may respond to public statements from any source in order to protect a client's legitimate interests, unless there is a substantial likelihood of materially prejudicing a criminal proceeding, in which case defense counsel should approach the prosecutor or the Court for relief. A statement made pursuant to this paragraph shall be limited to such information as is necessary to mitigate the recent adverse publicity.

(g) In making any public statement regarding a representation, defense counsel should comply with ethical rules governing client confidentiality and loyalty, and should not provide confidential information to the media, on or off the record, without authorization from the client.

(h) Defense counsel should not allow the client's representation to be adversely affected by counsel's personal interest in potential media contacts or attention.

(i) A defense attorney uninvolved in a matter who is commenting as a media source may offer generalized media commentary concerning a specific criminal matter that serves to educate the public about the criminal justice system and does not risk prejudicing a specific criminal proceeding. Counsel acting as such a media commentator should make reasonable efforts to be well-informed about the facts of the matter and the governing law. Counsel should not offer commentary regarding the specific merits of an ongoing prosecution or investigation, except in a rare case to address a manifest injustice and counsel is reasonably well-informed about the relevant facts and law.

Standard 4–1.11 Advisory Groups and Communications for Guidance on Issues of Professional Conduct

(a) In every jurisdiction, a group of lawyers with recognized experience, integrity, and standing in the criminal defense bar should be established to consider issues of professional conduct for defense attorneys in criminal matters. Members of this group should provide prompt and confidential guidance and advice to defense counsel seeking assistance in the application of standards of professional conduct in criminal representations.

(b) Defense counsel should initially take steps to ensure that the member from whom advice is sought does not have any conflicting interests, and the advisory group should establish procedures to avoid such conflicts.

(c) Communications between a defense lawyer and an advisory group member, and the seeking of advice itself, should be treated as confidential, and such communications should be afforded the same attorney-client privilege and other protections of the client's confidences as exists between any other lawyer and client. A group member should be bound by statute or rule of court in the same manner as a lawyer is otherwise bound in that jurisdiction not to reveal confidences of the client of the consulting lawyer.

(d) In seeking advice from a group member, defense counsel should take steps to protect the client's confidences (for example, by the use of anonymous hypotheticals), and reveal only such confidential information as may be necessary.

(e) Defense counsel should employ the foregoing confidentiality measures even when informally seeking advice from any other lawyer, and such informal consultations should be afforded confidentiality to the extent the law permits. Defense counsel should be cautious and protect confidences when seeking advice outside the advisory group context.

(f) Confidences regarding a consultation may later be revealed to the extent necessary if:

(i) defense counsel's client challenges the effectiveness of counsel's conduct of the matter and counsel has relied on the guidance received from an advisory group member, and the information is subpoenaed or otherwise judicially supervised; or

(ii) the defense counsel's conduct is called into question in a disciplinary inquiry or other proceeding against which counsel must defend.

Standard 4–1.12 Training Programs

(a) The community of criminal defense attorneys, including public defense offices and State and local Bar Associations, should develop and maintain programs of training and continuing education for both new and experienced defense counsel. Defense offices, as well as the organized Bar or courts, should require that current and aspiring criminal defense counsel attend a reasonable number of hours of such training and education.

(b) In addition to knowledge of substantive legal doctrine and courtroom procedures, a core training curriculum for criminal defense counsel should seek to address: investigation, negotiation and litigation skills; knowledge of the development, use, and testing of forensic evidence; available sentencing structures including non-conviction and non-imprisonment alternatives and collateral consequences; professional responsibility, civility, and a commitment to professionalism; relevant office, court, and prosecution policies and procedures and their proper application; appreciation of diversity and elimination of improper bias; and available technology and the ability to use it. Some training programs might usefully be open to, and taught by, persons outside the criminal defense community, such as prosecutors, law enforcement agencies, court staff, and members of the judiciary.

(c) A public defense office's training program should include periodic review of the office's policies and procedures, which should be amended when necessary. Counsel defending in specialized subject areas should receive training in those specialized areas. Individuals who will supervise attorneys or staff should receive training in how effectively to supervise.

(d) A public criminal defense organization should also make available opportunities for training and continuing education programs outside the office, including training for non-attorney staff.

(e) Adequate funding for continuing training and education programs, within and outside of public defense offices, should be requested and provided by funding sources.

Standard 4–1.13 Assuring Excellence and Diversity in the Hiring, Retention, and Compensation of Public Defense Counsel

(a) Strong professional qualifications and performance should be the basis for selection and retention for public defense positions. Effective measures to retain excellent defenders should be encouraged, while recognizing the benefits of some turnover. Supervisory defenders should select and promote personnel based on merit and expertise, without regard to partisan, personal or political factors or influence.

(b) In selecting personnel, a public defense office should also consider the diverse interests and makeup of the community it serves, and seek to recruit, hire, promote and retain a diverse group of defenders and staff that reflect that community.

(c) The function of public criminal defense requires highly developed professional skills and a variety of backgrounds, talents and experience. A defender's office should promote continuing professional development and continuity of service, while providing defenders the opportunity to gain experience in all aspects of the defense function.

(d) Compensation and benefits for public defense counsel and their staffs should be commensurate with the high responsibilities of the office, sufficient to compete with the private sector, and regularly adjusted to attract and retain well-qualified personnel. Compensation for public defense counsel should be adequate and also comparable to that of prosecutors in the same jurisdiction.

PART II. ACCESS TO DEFENSE COUNSEL

Standard 4–2.1 Duty to Make Qualified Criminal Defense Representation Available

(a) The government has an obligation to provide, and fully fund, services of qualified defense counsel for indigent criminal defendants. In addition, the organized Bar of all lawyers in a jurisdiction has a duty to make qualified criminal defense counsel available, including for the indigent, and to make lawyers' expertise available in support of a fair and effective criminal justice system.

(b) The Bar should encourage the widest possible participation in the defense of criminal cases by qualified lawyers. Unqualified lawyers should not be assigned the primary role in criminal representation, but interested lawyers should be encouraged to qualify themselves for participation in criminal cases by formal training and by experience as associate counsel. Law firms should encourage and support efforts by their interested attorneys to become qualified and then take on criminal representations.

(c) Qualified defense counsel should be willing and ready to undertake the defense of a suspect or an accused regardless of public hostility or personal distaste for the offense or the client.

(d) Qualified defense counsel should not seek to avoid appointment by a tribunal to represent an accused except for good cause, such as: representing the accused is likely to result in violation of applicable ethical codes or other law; representing the accused is likely to result in an unreasonable financial burden on the lawyer; or the client or crime is so repugnant to the lawyer that it will likely prejudicially impair the lawyer's ability to provide quality representation.

(e) Lawyers who are not qualified to serve as criminal defense counsel should

(i) be encouraged to seek qualification;

(ii) make their legal skills and expertise available to assist qualified counsel in providing indigent criminal defense; and

(iii) provide or assist in obtaining financial assistance and political support for indigent criminal defense budgets and resources.

Standard 4–2.2 Confidential Defense Communication with Detained Persons

(a) Every jurisdiction should guarantee by statute or rule the right of a criminally-detained or confined person to prompt, confidential, affordable and effective communication with a defense lawyer throughout a criminal investigation, prosecution, appeal, or other quasi-criminal proceedings such as habeas corpus.

(b) All detention or imprisonment institutions should provide reasonable, affordable access to confidential and unmonitored telephonic and other communication facilities to allow effective confidential communication between defense counsel and their detained clients. This should include providing or allowing access to language translation or other communication services when necessary.

(c) All detention or imprisonment institutions should provide adequate facilities for private, unmonitored meetings between defense counsel and an accused. Private facilities should also be provided for the review of evidence and discovery materials by counsel together with their detained clients.

(d) Absent a credible threat of immediate danger or violence, or advance judicial authorization, persons working in detention or imprisonment institutions should be prohibited from examining, monitoring, recording, or interfering with confidential communications between defense counsel and their detained clients.

Standard 4–2.3 Right to Counsel at First and Subsequent Judicial Appearances

A defense counsel should be made available in person to a criminally-accused person for consultation at or before any appearance before a judicial officer, including the first appearance.

Standard 4–2.4 Referral Service for Criminal Cases

(a) To assist persons who wish to retain defense counsel, every jurisdiction should have a referral service for qualified criminal defense counsel. The referral service should maintain a list of qualified counsel willing to undertake the defense of a criminal case, for a fee as well as pro bono, and should be organized so that it can provide prompt service at all times.

(b) A defense referral service should employ an objective set of standards for defense attorneys to qualify for placement on the referral list, and should employ fair and neutral criteria for admitting qualified attorneys to the list, making referrals, and striking counsel from the list. Such standards, criteria, and procedures concerning referral lists should be published and readily available.

(c) The availability of the referral service should be publicized, and information regarding fees should be included. Notices containing the essential information about the referral service and how to contact it should be posted in police stations, jails, and wherever else it is likely to give effective notice to criminally-accused persons, including the internet.

Standard 4–2.5 Referrals for Representation

(a) Defense counsel should not give anything of more than nominal value to a person for recommending the lawyer's services, except that

(i) counsel may pay reasonable costs of advertisements, or the usual charges for a legal services plan or qualified lawyer referral service, as described in ABA Model Rule 7.2; and

(ii) counsel may maintain nonexclusive reciprocal referral arrangements with other lawyers, if the client is fully informed of the arrangement and the arrangement does not constrain defense counsel's independent professional judgment regarding the client's best interests.

(b) Defense counsel should not have an ongoing or regular referral relationship with any source (such as prosecutors, public defender programs, law enforcement personnel, bondsmen, or court personnel) when such an ongoing relationship is likely to create conflicting loyalties for the lawyers involved or an appearance of impropriety. Defense counsel's relationship with a referral source should be disclosed to the client.

(c) Referrals by one defense counsel to another should be based on merit, experience, competence for the particular matter, and other appropriate considerations.

PART III. LAWYER-CLIENT RELATIONSHIP

Standard 4–3.1 Establishing and Maintaining An Effective Client Relationship

(a) Immediately upon appointment or retention, defense counsel should work to establish a relationship of trust and confidence with each client. Defense counsel should explain, at an appropriate time, the necessity for frank and honest discussion of all facts known to the client in order to provide an effective defense. Defense counsel should explain that the attorney-client privilege protects the confidentiality of communications with counsel except in exceptional and well-defined circumstances, and explain what the client can do to help preserve confidentiality.

(b) At an early stage, counsel should discuss with the client the objectives of the representation and through what stages of a criminal matter the defense counsel will continue to represent the accused. An engagement letter as described in Standard 4–3.5 should also be provided.

(c) Counsel should consider whether the client appears to have a mental impairment or other disability that could adversely affect the representation. Even if a client appears to have such a condition, this does not diminish defense counsel's obligations to the client, including maintaining a normal attorney-client relationship in so far as possible. In such an instance, defense counsel should also consider whether a mental examination or other protective measures are in the client's best interest.

(d) In communicating with a client, defense counsel should use language and means that the client is able to understand, which may require special attention when the client is a minor, elderly, or suffering from a mental impairment or other disability.

(e) Defense counsel should ensure that space is available and adequate for confidential client consultations.

(f) Defense counsel should actively work to maintain an effective and regular relationship with all clients. The obligation to maintain an effective client relationship is not diminished by the fact that the client is in custody.

Standard 4–3.2 Seeking a Detained Client's Release from Custody, or Reduction in Custodial Conditions

(a) In every case where the client is detained, defense counsel should discuss with the client, as promptly as possible, the client's custodial or release status and determine whether release, a change in release conditions, or less restrictive custodial conditions, should be sought. Counsel should be aware of applicable statutes and rules, and all alternatives less restrictive than full institutional detention. Counsel should investigate community and family resources that might be available to assist in implementing such alternatives.

(b) Counsel should investigate the factual predicate that has been advanced to support detention and custodial conditions, and not assume its accuracy.

(c) Once counsel has sufficient command of the facts, counsel should approach the prosecutor to see if agreement to release or a change in release or custodial conditions can be negotiated and submitted for approval by the court.

(d) If the prosecutor does not agree, counsel should submit to the court a statement of facts, legal argument, and proposed conditions if necessary, to support the client's release or a reduction in release or custodial conditions.

(e) If a court orders release, counsel should fully explain all conditions of release to the client, as well as the consequences of their violation. Counsel should assist the client and others acting for the client in properly implementing the release conditions.

(f) If counsel is unable to secure the client's release, counsel should, after discussion with the client and with due regard to any relevant confidentiality concerns, alert the court and institutional personnel to any special medical, psychiatric, religious, dietary, or security needs of the client while in government custody, and request that the court order the appropriate officials to take steps to meet such special needs.

(g) Counsel should reevaluate the client's eligibility for release, or for reduced release or custodial conditions, at all significant stages of a criminal matter and when there is any relevant change in facts or circumstances. Counsel should request reconsideration of detention or modification of conditions whenever it is in the client's best interests.

Standard 4–3.3 Interviewing the Client

(a) In the initial meeting with a client, defense counsel should begin the process of establishing an effective attorney-client relationship. This includes assuring the client of confidentiality, establishing trust, explaining the posture of the matter, discussing fees if applicable, and inquiring about the client's objectives for the representation. Counsel may also discuss available evidentiary materials with the client, seek information from the client as to the facts and other potential sources of information, and ask what the client's immediate objectives and needs are and how to fulfill them.

(b) Counsel should interview the client as many times as necessary for effective representation, which in all but the most simple and routine cases will mean more than once. Defense counsel should make every reasonable effort to meet in person with the client. Consultation with the client regarding available options, immediately necessary decisions, and next steps, should be a part of every meeting.

(c) As early as practicable in the representation, defense counsel should also discuss:

(i) and share with the client evidentiary materials relevant to the matter (consistent with the terms of any applicable protective order), and determine in depth the client's view of the facts and other relevant facts known to the client;

(ii) the likely length and course of the pending proceedings;

(iii) potential sources of helpful information, evidence, and investigation;

(iv) the client's wishes regarding, and the likelihood of and steps necessary to gain, release or reduction of supervisory conditions;

(v) likely legal options such as motions, trial, and potential negotiated dispositions;

(vi) the range of potential outcomes and alternatives, and if convicted, possible punishments;

(vii) if appropriate, the possibility and potential costs and benefits of a negotiated disposition, including one that might include cooperation with the government; and

(viii) relevant collateral consequences resulting from the current situation as well as from possible resolutions of the matter.

(d) When asking the client for information and discussing possible options and strategies with the client, defense counsel should not seek to induce the client to make factual responses that are not true. Defense counsel should encourage candid disclosure by the client to counsel and not seek to maintain a calculated ignorance.

Standard 4–3.4 Fees

(a) Counsel should be familiar with statutes and rules regarding fees and costs that govern in the jurisdiction(s) in which counsel practices. Before or within a reasonably short time after commencing a representation, defense counsel should discuss with the client:

(i) the likely cost of the representation including the attorney's fees, billing structure, and likely expenses;

(ii) how fees and costs will be paid, and any available options regarding the fee structure;

(iii) what services and expenses the fees will cover;

(iv) what stages of the matter the fee covers, such as pre-charge investigation, preliminary hearing, negotiated disposition or trial, sentencing or appeal; and

(v) whether the fee extends to addressing any related matters.

(b) In determining the amount of the fee in a criminal case, it is proper to consider the time and effort required, the responsibility assumed by counsel, the novelty and difficulty of the issues involved, the skill requisite to proper representation, the need for any special technology, experts, investigators, or other unusual expenses, the likelihood that other employment will be precluded, the fee customarily charged in the locality for similar services, the gravity of the charge, the experience, reputation, and expertise of defense counsel, and the ability of the client to pay the fee.

(c) Once agreed upon, the amount, rate, and terms of the fee should be promptly communicated to the client, in clear terms and in writing, as part of the Engagement Letter.

(d) Defense counsel should not enter into an agreement for, charge, or collect an illegal or unreasonable fee. Defense counsel should be aware that accepting a fee comprised of assets that are contraband or proceeds of crime may be a crime and may also subject those fee assets to seizure and forfeiture.

(e) Defense counsel should not permit a dispute or unhappiness regarding compensation to interfere with providing competent and zealous representation. A competent defense does not require all possible expenditures, and counsel is not required to spend out of counsel's own pocket. If funding becomes an issue, counsel should discuss other possible sources of funds with the client and pursue those that are appropriate. If funding is inadequate, counsel may seek withdrawal in accordance with applicable laws, including court and ethics rules.

(f) A publically-paid defense counsel should not request or accept additional money or other compensation from non-public sources to represent a client in an appointed criminal case, unless permitted by rules of the jurisdiction.

(g) Retained defense counsel may accept compensation from third parties for the representation of a client, subject to counsel's duties of loyalty and confidentiality to the client and the criteria in Standard 4–1.5(f) above.

(h) Defense counsel should not state or imply that their compensation is for any unethical or secret influence.

(i) Defense counsel should not divide a fee with a nonlawyer, except as permitted by applicable ethics rules.

(j) Defense counsel not in the same firm should not divide fees in a criminal matter among lawyers unless consistent with the rules of the jurisdiction and the division is in reasonable proportion to the experience, ability, and services performed by each counsel and is disclosed to the client; or by written agreement with the client each counsel assumes joint responsibility for the representation, the client is advised of and does not object to the participation of all counsel involved, and the total fee is reasonable.

(k) Defense counsel should not enter into an arrangement for, charge, or collect a contingent fee for representing a defendant in a criminal case or in a criminal forfeiture action.

(*l*) Defense counsel may charge a non-refundable "flat rate" fee if such is permitted by the law of the jurisdiction and the arrangement is fully explained in advance, but defense counsel should refund any part of such a fee that constitutes an undeserved windfall if exceptional and unanticipated developments arise such that a significant amount of anticipated work is not done by counsel.

(m) When a representation ends, counsel should offer to return any unearned fee.

Standard 4–3.5 Engagement Letter

(a) Upon agreeing or being appointed to take on a criminal representation, defense counsel should promptly provide a new client with an engagement letter, email, or other written communication, as described below, written in plain language that the particular client can understand. If material conditions of the representation change during the representation, counsel should, after consultation with the client, promptly and specifically communicate the changes in writing to the client. Counsel should also provide an engagement letter to clients who have been previously-represented by the same counsel but have now engaged counsel on a new matter, explaining the scope of and any material changes in the terms of the new representation.

(b) While the content and level of detail may vary depending on the context, an engagement letter should include a description of:

(i) the identity of the client and the scope of, and limitations on, the representation;

(ii) the fee arrangement (including costs and expenses);

(iii) the fact that counsel's duties of confidentiality and loyalty are owed to the client;

(iv) materials that counsel may retain although related to the representation (*e.g.*, legal research for use in future cases);

(v) any other information that is particularly relevant to the specific representation.

Standard 4–3.6 Literary or Media Rights Agreements Prohibited

(a) Before the conclusion of all aspects of a criminal representation in which defense counsel participates, defense counsel should not enter into any agreement or informal understanding by which the defense counsel acquires an interest in a literary or media portrayal or account based on or arising out of defense counsel's involvement in the matter.

(b) Defense counsel should not allow the client's representation to be adversely affected by the possibility of future personal literary or other media rights.

(c) In creating or participating in any literary or other media account of a matter in which defense counsel was involved, counsel's duty of confidentiality must be respected even after a matter is concluded or the client is deceased. When protected confidences are involved, defense counsel should not make disclosure without consent from the client or the client's authorized representative.

Standard 4–3.7 Prompt and Thorough Actions to Protect the Client

(a) Many important rights of a criminal client can be protected and preserved only by prompt legal action. Defense counsel should inform the client of his or her rights in the criminal process at the earliest opportunity, and timely plan and take necessary actions to vindicate such rights within the scope of the representation.

(b) Defense counsel should promptly seek to obtain and review all information relevant to the criminal matter, including but not limited to requesting materials from the prosecution. Defense counsel should, when relevant, take prompt steps to ensure that the government's physical evidence is preserved at least until the defense can examine or evaluate it.

(c) Defense counsel should work diligently to develop, in consultation with the client, an investigative and legal defense strategy, including a theory of the case. As the matter progresses, counsel should refine or alter the theory of the case as necessary, and similarly adjust the investigative or defense strategy.

(d) Not all defense actions need to be taken immediately. If counsel has evidence of innocence, mitigation, or other favorable information, defense counsel should discuss with the client and decide whether, going to the prosecution with such evidence is in the client's best interest, and if so, when and how.

(e) Defense counsel should consider whether an opportunity to benefit from cooperation with the prosecution will be lost if not pursued quickly, and if so, promptly discuss with the client and decide whether such cooperation is in the client's interest. Counsel should timely act in accordance with such decisions.

(f) For each matter, defense counsel should consider what procedural and investigative steps to take and motions to file, and not simply follow rote procedures learned from prior matters. Defense counsel should not be deterred from sensible action merely because counsel has not previously seen a tactic used, or because such action might incur criticism or disfavor. Before acting, defense counsel should discuss novel or unfamiliar matters or issues with colleagues or other experienced counsel, employing safeguards to protect confidentiality and avoid conflicts of interest.

(g) Whenever defense counsel is confronted with specialized factual or legal issues with which counsel is unfamiliar, counsel should, in addition to researching and learning about the issue personally, consider engaging or consulting with an expert in the specialized area.

(h) Defense counsel should always consider interlocutory appeals or other collateral proceedings as one option in response to any materially adverse ruling.

Standard 4–3.8 Anticipated Unlawful Conduct

(a) If defense counsel anticipates that a client may engage in unlawful conduct, defense counsel should advise the client concerning the meaning, scope and validity of the law and the possible consequences of violating the law, and should advise the client to comply with the law.

(b) Defense counsel should not knowingly propose, advise, or assist in a course of conduct which defense counsel knows to be criminal or fraudulent, but defense counsel may discuss the legal consequences of a proposed course of conduct with a client, and may counsel or assist a client in a good faith effort to determine the validity, scope, meaning, or application of the law.

(c) Defense counsel should not enter into an arrangement with persons or organizations counsel knows to be engaged in ongoing criminal conduct, to provide representation on a regular basis to the participants, if the legal services will knowingly assist the ongoing criminal conduct. Counsel may agree in advance to represent clients as part of a good faith effort to determine the validity, scope, meaning, or application of the law, or incident to a general retainer for providing legal services to a person or enterprise engaged in primarily legitimate activities, or if counsel's services are intended to bring conduct into conformance with the law.

(d) When unlawful conduct by a client is anticipated or has taken place, defense counsel should be aware of and follow applicable ethical rules, including provisions that require confidentiality and provisions that mandate or permit disclosures.

Standard 4–3.9 Duty to Keep Client Informed and Advised About the Representation

(a) Defense counsel should keep the client reasonably and currently informed about developments in and the progress of the lawyer's services, including developments in pretrial investigation, discovery, disposition negotiations, and preparing a defense. Information should be sufficiently detailed so that the client can meaningfully participate in the representation.

(b) Defense counsel should promptly comply with the client's reasonable requests for information about the matter and for copies of or access to relevant documents, unless the client's access to such information is restricted by law or court order. Counsel should challenge such restrictions on the client's access to information unless, after consultation with the client, there is good reason not to do so.

Standard 4–3.10 Maintaining Continuity of Representation; Relationship with Successor Counsel

(a) Defense counsel who withdraws from a representation at any stage of a criminal matter before its resolution should make reasonable efforts to assist the client in securing competent defense counsel as successor counsel, and to not leave the client unrepresented, unless the client otherwise directs.

(b) Defense counsel should make reasonable efforts to establish and maintain a cooperative relationship with any prior, or successor, defense counsel in the representation.

(c) When successor counsel enters a representation, prior counsel should still act to protect the client's privileges, confidences and secrets, and obtain consent (express or implied) from the client before providing such information to the new counsel.

Standard 4–3.11 The Client's File

(a) When a representation ends, if the client requests the client's file, defense counsel should provide it to the client or, with the client's consent, to successor counsel or other authorized representative. Defense counsel should provide the client with notice of the file's disposition. Unless rules or statutes in the jurisdiction require otherwise, defense offices may retain clients' files unless a client requests the file. If the client's file remains with defense counsel, counsel should retain copies of essential portions until the client provides further instructions or for at least the length of time consistent with statutes and rules of the jurisdiction.

(b) During a representation, defense counsel should provide the client with the client's file upon request, even if fees or costs are disputed or unpaid in whole or in part.

(c) Not everything in defense counsel's files on a matter is the client's, and the definition of the contents of "the client's file" may vary among jurisdictions. Original documents and property delivered to the attorney by the client are part of the client's file, as are correspondence and court filings in the client's matter.

(d) When a representation ends, defense counsel may seek a release from the client regarding the representation, but may not unreasonably withhold the client's file pending such release.

PART IV. INVESTIGATION AND PREPARATION

Standard 4–4.1 Duty to Investigate and Engage Investigators

(a) Defense counsel has a duty to investigate in all cases, and to determine whether there is a sufficient factual basis for criminal charges.

(b) The duty to investigate is not terminated by factors such as the apparent force of the prosecution's evidence, a client's alleged admissions to others of facts suggesting guilt, a client's expressed desire to plead guilty or that there should be no investigation, or statements to defense counsel supporting guilt.

(c) Defense counsel's investigative efforts should commence promptly and should explore appropriate avenues that reasonably might lead to information relevant to the merits of the matter, consequences of the criminal proceedings, and potential dispositions and penalties. Although investigation will vary depending on the circumstances, it should always be shaped by what is in the client's best interests, after consultation with the client. Defense counsel's investigation of the merits of the criminal charges should include efforts to secure relevant information in the possession of the prosecution, law enforcement authorities, and others, as well as independent investigation. Counsel's investigation should also include evaluation of the prosecution's evidence (including possible re-testing or re-evaluation of physical, forensic, and expert evidence) and consideration of inconsistencies, potential avenues of impeachment of prosecution witnesses, and other possible suspects and alternative theories that the evidence may raise.

(d) Defense counsel should determine whether the client's interests would be served by engaging fact investigators, forensic, accounting or other experts, or other professional witnesses such as sentencing specialists or social workers, and if so, consider, in consultation with the client, whether to engage them. Counsel should regularly re-evaluate the need for such services throughout the representation.

(e) If the client lacks sufficient resources to pay for necessary investigation, counsel should seek resources from the court, the government, or donors. Application to the court should be made *ex parte* if appropriate to protect the client's confidentiality. Publicly funded defense offices should advocate for resources sufficient to fund such investigative expert services on a regular basis. If adequate investigative funding is not provided, counsel may advise the court that the lack of resources for investigation may render legal representation ineffective.

Standard 4–4.2 Illegal and Unethical Investigation Prohibited

Defense counsel should not use illegal or unethical means to obtain evidence or information, or employ, instruct, or encourage others to do so.

Standard 4–4.3 Relationship With Witnesses

(a) "Witness" in this Standard means any person who has or might have information about a matter, including victims and the client.

(b) Defense counsel should know and follow the law and rules of the jurisdiction regarding victims and witnesses. In communicating with witnesses, counsel should know and abide by law and ethics rules regarding the use of deceit and engaging in communications with represented, unrepresented, and organizational persons.

(c) Defense counsel or counsel's agents should seek to interview all witnesses, including seeking to interview the victim or victims, and should not act to intimidate or unduly influence any witness.

(d) Defense counsel should not use means that have no substantial purpose other than to embarrass, delay, or burden, and not use methods of obtaining evidence that violate legal rights. Defense counsel and their agents should not misrepresent their status, identity or interests when communicating with a witness.

(e) Defense counsel should be permitted to compensate a witness for reasonable expenses such as costs of attending court, depositions pursuant to statute or court rule, and pretrial interviews, including transportation and loss of income. No other benefits should be provided to witnesses, other than expert witnesses, unless authorized by law, regulation, or well-accepted practice. All benefits provided to witnesses should be documented so that they may be disclosed if required by law or court order. Defense counsel should not pay or provide a benefit to a witness in order to, or in an amount that is likely to, affect the substance or truthfulness of the witness's testimony.

(f) Defense counsel should avoid the prospect of having to testify personally about the content of a witness interview. An interview of routine witnesses (for example, custodians of records) should not require a third-party observer. But when the need for corroboration of an interview is reasonably anticipated, counsel should be accompanied by another trusted and credible person during the interview. Defense counsel should avoid being alone with foreseeably hostile witnesses.

(g) It is not necessary for defense counsel or defense counsel's agents, when interviewing a witness, to caution the witness concerning possible self-incrimination or a right to independent counsel. Defense counsel should, however, follow applicable ethical rules that address dealing with unrepresented persons. Defense counsel should not discuss or exaggerate the potential criminal liability of a witness with a purpose, or in a manner likely, to intimidate the witness, to intimidate the witness, or to influence the truthfulness or completeness of the witness's testimony, or to change the witness's decision about whether to provide information.

(h) Defense counsel should not discourage or obstruct communication between witnesses and the prosecution, other than a client's employees, agents or relatives if consistent with app0licable ethical rules. Defense counsel should not advise any person, or cause any person to be advised, to decline to provide the prosecution with information which such person has a right to give. Defense counsel may, however, fairly and accurately advise witnesses as to the likely consequences of their providing information, but only if done in a manner that does not discourage communication.

(i) Defense counsel should give their witnesses reasonable notice of when their testimony at a proceeding is expected, and should not require witnesses to attend judicial proceedings unless their testimony is reasonably expected at that time, or their presence is required by law. When witnesses' attendance is required, defense counsel should seek to reduce to a minimum the time witnesses must spend waiting at the proceedings. Defense counsel should ensure that defense witnesses are given notice as soon as practicable of scheduling changes which will affect their required attendance at judicial proceedings.

(j) Defense counsel should not engage in any inappropriate personal relationship with any victim or other witness.

Standard 4–4.4 Relationship With Expert Witnesses

(a) An expert may be engaged to prepare an evidentiary report or testimony, or for consultation only. Defense counsel should know relevant rules governing expert witnesses, including possibly different disclosure rules governing experts who are engaged for consultation only.

(b) Defense counsel should evaluate all expert advice, opinions, or testimony independently, and not simply accept the opinion of an expert based on employer, affiliation or prominence alone.

(c) Before engaging an expert, defense counsel should investigate the expert's credentials, relevant professional experience, and reputation in the field. Defense counsel should also examine a testifying expert's background and credentials for potential impeachment issues. Before offering an expert as a witness, defense counsel should investigate the scientific acceptance of the particular theory, method, or conclusions about which the expert would testify.

(d) Defense counsel who engages an expert to provide a testimonial opinion should respect the independence of the expert and should not seek to dictate the substance of the expert's opinion on the relevant subject.

(e) Before offering an expert as a witness, defense counsel should seek to learn enough about the substantive area of the expert's expertise, including ethical rules that may be applicable in the expert's field, to enable effective preparation of the expert, as well as to cross-examine any prosecution expert on the same topic. Defense counsel should explain to the expert that the expert's role in the proceeding will be as an impartial witness called to aid the fact-finders, explain the manner in which the examination of the expert is likely to be conducted, and suggest likely impeachment questions the expert may be asked.

(f) Defense counsel should not pay or withhold a fee, or provide or withhold a benefit, for the purpose of influencing an expert's testimony. Defense counsel should not fix the amount of the fee contingent upon the substance of an expert's testimony or the result in the case. Nor should defense counsel promise or imply the prospect of future work for the expert based on the expert's testimony.

(g) Subject to client confidentiality interests, defense counsel should provide the expert with all information reasonably necessary to support a full and fair opinion. Defense counsel should be aware, and explain to the expert, that all communications with, and documents shared with, a testifying expert may be subject to disclosure to opposing counsel. Defense counsel should be aware of expert discovery rules and act to protect confidentiality, for example by not sharing with the expert client confidences and work product that counsel does not want disclosed.

Standard 4–4.5 Compliance With Discovery Procedures

Defense counsel should timely respond to legally proper discovery requests, and make a diligent effort to comply with legally proper disclosure obligations, unless otherwise authorized by a court. When the prosecution makes requests for specific information, defense counsel should provide specific responses rather than merely a general acknowledgement of discovery obligations. Requests and responses should be tailored to the case, and "boilerplate" requests and responses should be disfavored.

Standard 4–4.6 Preparation for Court Proceedings, and Recording and Transmitting Information

(a) Defense counsel should prepare in advance for court proceedings. Adequate preparation depends on the nature of the proceeding and the time available, and will often include: reviewing available documents; considering what issues are likely to arise and the client's position regarding those issues; how best to present the issues and what solutions might be offered; relevant legal research and factual investigation; and contacting other persons who might be of assistance in addressing the anticipated issues. If defense counsel has not had adequate time to prepare and is unsure of the relevant facts or law, counsel should communicate to the court the limits of the defense counsel's knowledge or preparation.

(b) Defense counsel should appear at all hearings in cases assigned to them, unless with good cause a substitute counsel is arranged. A defense attorney who substitutes at a court proceeding for another attorney should be adequately informed about the case and issues likely to come up at the proceeding and should adequately prepare.

(c) Defense counsel handling any court appearance should document what happens at the proceeding, to aid counsel's own memory and the client's future reference, and so that necessary information will be available to counsel who may handle the case in the future.

(d) Defense counsel should take steps to ensure that any court order issued to the defense is transmitted to the appropriate persons necessary to effectuate the order.

(e) A public criminal defense office should be provided sufficient resources and be organized to permit adequate preparation for court proceedings.

Standard 4–4.7 Handling Physical Evidence With Incriminating Implications

(a) *Counseling the client:* If defense counsel knows that the client possesses physical evidence that the client may not legally possess (such as contraband or stolen property) or evidence that might be used to incriminate the client, counsel should examine and comply with the law and rules of the jurisdiction on topics such as obstruction of justice, tampering with evidence, and protection for the client's confidentiality and against self-incrimination. Counsel should then competently advise the client about lawful options and obligations.

(b) *Permissible actions of the client*: If requested or legally required, defense counsel may assist the client in lawfully disclosing such physical evidence to law enforcement authorities. Counsel may advise destruction of a physical item if its destruction would not obstruct justice or otherwise violate the law or ethical obligations. Counsel may not assist the client in conduct that counsel knows is unlawful, and should not knowingly and unlawfully impede efforts of law enforcement authorities to obtain evidence.

(c) *Confidentiality:* Defense counsel should act in accordance with applicable confidentiality laws and rules. In some circumstances, applicable law or rules may permit or require defense counsel to disclose the existence of, or the client's possession or disposition of, such physical evidence.

(d) *Receipt of physical evidence:* Defense counsel should not take possession of such physical evidence, personally or through third parties, and should advise the client not to give such evidence to defense counsel, except in circumstances in which defense counsel may lawfully take possession of the evidence. Such circumstances may include:

(i) when counsel reasonably believes the client intends to unlawfully destroy or conceal such evidence;

(ii) when counsel reasonably believes that taking possession is necessary to prevent physical harm to someone;

(iii) when counsel takes possession in order to produce such evidence, with the client's informed consent, to its lawful owner or to law enforcement authorities;

(iv) when such evidence is contraband and counsel may lawfully take possession of it in order to destroy it; and

(v) when defense counsel reasonably believes that examining or testing such evidence is necessary for effective representation of the client.

(e) *Compliance with legal obligations to produce physical evidence:* If defense counsel receives physical evidence that might implicate a client in criminal conduct, counsel should determine whether there is a legal obligation to return the evidence to its source or owner, or to deliver it to law enforcement or a court, and comply with any such legal obligations. A lawyer who is legally obligated to turn over such physical evidence should do so in a lawful manner that will minimize prejudice to the client.

(f) *Retention of producible item for examination.* Unless defense counsel has a legal obligation to disclose, produce, or dispose of such physical evidence, defense counsel may retain such physical evidence for a reasonable time for a legitimate purpose. Legitimate purposes for temporarily obtaining or retaining physical evidence may include: preventing its destruction; arranging for its production to relevant authorities; arranging for its return to the source or owner; preventing its use to harm others; and examining or testing the evidence in order to effectively represent the client.

(g) *Testing physical evidence.* If defense counsel determines that effective representation of the client requires that such physical evidence be submitted for forensic examination and testing, counsel should observe the following practices:

(i) The item should be properly handled, packaged, labeled and stored, in a manner designed to document its identity and ensure its integrity.

(ii) Any testing or examination should avoid, when possible, consumption of the item, and a portion of the item should be preserved and retained to permit further testing or examination.

(iii) Any person conducting such testing or examination should not, without prior approval of defense counsel, conduct testing or examination in any manner that will consume the item or otherwise destroy the ability for independent re-testing or examination by the prosecution.

(iv) Before approving a test or examination that will entirely consume the item or destroy the prosecution's opportunity and ability to re-test the item, defense counsel should provide the prosecution with notice and an opportunity to object and seek an appropriate court order.

(v) If a motion objecting to consumptive testing or examination is filed, the court should consider ordering procedures that will permit independent evaluation of the defense's analysis, including but not limited to:

(A) permitting a prosecution expert to be present during preparation and testing of the evidence;

(B) video recording the preparation and testing of the evidence;

(C) still photography of the preparation and testing of evidence; and

(D) access to all raw data, notes and other documentation relating to the defense preparation and testing of the evidence.

(h) *Client consent to accept a physical item.* Before voluntarily taking possession from the client of physical evidence that defense counsel may have a legal obligation to disclose, defense counsel should advise the client of potential legal implications of the proposed conduct and possible lawful alternatives, and obtain the client's informed consent.

(i) *Retention or return of item when law permits.* If defense counsel reasonably determines that there is no legal obligation to disclose physical evidence in counsel's possession to law enforcement authorities or others, the lawyer should deal with the physical evidence consistently with ethical and other rules and law. If defense counsel retains the evidence for use in the client's representation, the lawyer should comply with applicable law and rules, including rules on safekeeping property, which may require notification to third parties with an interest in the property. Counsel should maintain the evidence separately from privileged materials of other clients, and preserve it in a manner that will not impair its evidentiary value. Alternatively, counsel may deliver the evidence to a third-party lawyer who is also representing the client and will be obligated to maintain the confidences of the client as well as defense counsel.

(j) *Adoption of judicial and legislated procedures for handling physical evidence.* Courts and legislatures, as appropriate, should adopt procedures regarding defense handling of such physical evidence, as follows:

(i) When defense counsel notifies the prosecution of the possession of such evidence or produces such evidence to the prosecution, the prosecution should be prohibited from presenting testimony or argument identifying or implying the defense as the source of the evidence, except as provided in Standard 3–3.6;

(ii) When defense counsel reasonably believes that contraband does not relate to a pending criminal investigation or prosecution, counsel may take possession of the contraband and destroy it.

PART V. CONTROL AND DIRECTION OF LITIGATION

Standard 4–5.1 Advising the Client

(a) Defense counsel should exercise independent professional judgment when advising a client.

(b) Defense counsel should keep the client reasonably and regularly informed about the status of the case. Before significant decision-points, and at other times if requested, defense counsel should advise the client with candor concerning all aspects of the case, including an assessment of possible strategies and likely as well as possible outcomes. Such advisement should take place after counsel is as fully informed as is reasonably possible in the time available about the relevant facts and law. Counsel should act diligently and, unless time does not permit, advise the client of what more needs to be done or considered before final decisions are made.

(c) Defense counsel should promptly communicate to the client every plea offer and all significant developments, motions, and court actions or rulings, and provide advice as outlined in this Standard.

(d) In rendering advice to the client, counsel should consider the client's desires and views, and may refer not only to law but also to other considerations such as moral, economic, social or political factors that may be relevant to the client's situation. Counsel should attempt to distinguish for the client between legal advice and advice based on such other considerations.

(e) Defense counsel should provide the client with advice sufficiently in advance of decisions to allow the client to consider available options, and avoid unnecessarily rushing the accused into decisions.

(f) Defense counsel should not intentionally understate or overstate the risks, hazards, or prospects of the case or exert undue influence on the client's decisions regarding a plea.

(g) Defense counsel should advise the client to avoid communication about the case with anyone, including victims or other possible witnesses, persons in custody, family, friends, and any government personnel, except with defense counsel's approval, although where the client is a minor consultation with parents or guardians may be useful. Counsel should advise the client to avoid any contact with jurors or persons called for jury duty; and to avoid either the reality or the appearance of any other improper activity.

(h) Defense counsel should consider and advise the client of potential benefits as well as negative aspects of cooperating with law enforcement or the prosecution.

(i) After advising the client, defense counsel should aid the client in deciding on the best course of action and how best to pursue and implement that course of action.

Standard 4–5.2 Control and Direction of the Case

(a) Certain decisions relating to the conduct of the case are for the accused; others are for defense counsel. Determining whether a decision is ultimately to be made by the client or by counsel is highly contextual, and counsel should give great weight to strongly held views of a competent client regarding decisions of all kinds.

(b) The decisions ultimately to be made by a competent client, after full consultation with defense counsel, include:

- (i) whether to proceed without counsel;
- (ii) what pleas to enter;
- (iii) whether to accept a plea offer;
- (iv) whether to cooperate with or provide substantial assistance to the government;
- (v) whether to waive jury trial;
- (vi) whether to testify in his or her own behalf;
- (vii) whether to speak at sentencing;
- (viii) whether to appeal; and
- (ix) any other decision that has been determined in the jurisdiction to belong to the client.

(c) If defense counsel has a good faith doubt regarding the client's competence to make important decisions, counsel should consider seeking an expert evaluation from a mental health professional, within the protection of confidentiality and privilege rules if applicable.

(d) Strategic and tactical decisions should be made by defense counsel, after consultation with the client where feasible and appropriate. Such decisions include how to pursue plea negotiations, how to craft and respond to motions and, at hearing or trial, what witnesses to call, whether and how to conduct cross-examination, what jurors to accept or strike, what motions and objections should be made, what stipulations if any to agree to, and what and how evidence should be introduced.

(e) If a disagreement on a significant matter arises between defense counsel and the client, and counsel resolves it differently than the client prefers, defense counsel should consider memorializing the disagreement and its resolution, showing that record to the client, and preserving it in the file.

Standard 4–5.3 Obligations of Stand-By Counsel

(a) An attorney whose assigned duty is to actively assist a *pro se* criminally accused person should permit the accused to make the final decisions on all matters, including strategic and tactical matters relating to the conduct of the case, while still providing the attorney's best advice.

(b) An attorney whose assigned duty is to assist a *pro se* criminally accused person only when the accused requests assistance may bring to the attention of the accused steps that could be potentially beneficial or dangerous to the accused, but should not actively participate in the conduct of the defense unless requested by the accused or as directed by the court.

(c) In either case, the assigned attorney should respect the accused's right to develop and present the accused's own case, while still advising the accused of potential benefits and dangers the attorney perceives in the course of the litigation. Such an attorney should be fully prepared about the matter, in order to offer such advice and in case the court and the accused determine that the full representation role should be transferred to defense counsel at some point during the criminal proceedings.

Standard 4–5.4 Consideration of Collateral Consequences

(a) Defense counsel should identify, and advise the client of, collateral consequences that may arise from charge, plea or conviction. Counsel should investigate consequences under applicable federal, state, and local laws, and seek assistance from others with greater knowledge in specialized areas in order to be adequately informed as to the existence and details of relevant collateral consequences. Such advice should be provided sufficiently in advance that it may be fairly considered in a decision to pursue trial, plea, or other dispositions.

(b) When defense counsel knows that a consequence is particularly important to the client, counsel should advise the client as to whether there are procedures for avoiding, mitigating or later removing the consequence, and if so, how to best pursue or prepare for them.

(c) Defense counsel should include consideration of potential collateral consequences in negotiations with the prosecutor regarding possible dispositions, and in communications with the judge or court personnel regarding the appropriate sentence or conditions, if any, to be imposed.

Standard 4–5.5 Special Attention to Immigration Status and Consequences

(a) Defense counsel should determine a client's citizenship and immigration status, assuring the client that such information is important for effective legal representation and that it should be protected by the attorney-client privilege. Counsel should avoid any actions that might alert the government to information that could adversely affect the client.

(b) If defense counsel determines that a client may not be a United States citizen, counsel should investigate and identify particular immigration consequences that might follow possible criminal dispositions. Consultation or association with an immigration law expert or knowledgeable advocate is advisable in these circumstances. Public and appointed defenders should develop, or seek funding for, such immigration expertise within their offices.

(c) After determining the client's immigration status and potential adverse consequences from the criminal proceedings, including removal, exclusion, bars to relief from removal, immigration detention, denial of citizenship, and adverse consequences to the client's immediate family, counsel should advise the client of all such potential consequences and determine with the client the best course of action for the client's interests and how to pursue it.

(d) If a client is convicted of a removable offense, defense counsel should advise the client of the serious consequences if the client illegally returns to the United States.

PART VI. DISPOSITION WITHOUT TRIAL

Standard 4–6.1 Duty to Explore Disposition Without Trial

(a) Defense counsel should be open, at every stage of a criminal matter and after consultation with the client, to discussions with the prosecutor concerning disposition of charges by guilty plea or other negotiated disposition. Counsel should be knowledgeable about possible dispositions that are alternatives to trial or imprisonment, including diversion from the criminal process.

(b) In every criminal matter, defense counsel should consider the individual circumstances of the case and of the client, and should not recommend to a client acceptance of a disposition offer unless and until appropriate investigation and study of the matter has been completed. Such study should include discussion with the client and an analysis of relevant law, the prosecution's evidence, and potential dispositions and relevant collateral consequences. Defense counsel should advise against a guilty plea at the first appearance, unless, after discussion with the client, a speedy disposition is clearly in the client's best interest.

Standard 4–6.2 Negotiated Disposition Discussions

(a) As early as practicable, and preferably before engaging in disposition discussions with the prosecutor, defense counsel should discuss with and advise the client about possible disposition options.

(b) Once discussions with the prosecutor begin, defense counsel should keep the accused advised of relevant developments. Defense counsel should promptly communicate and explain to the client any disposition proposals made by the prosecutor, while explaining that presenting the prosecution's offer does not indicate counsel's unwillingness to go to trial.

(c) Defense counsel should ensure that the client understands any proposed disposition agreement, including its direct and possible collateral consequences.

(d) Defense counsel should not recommend to a defendant acceptance of a disposition without appropriate investigation. Before accepting or advising a disposition, defense counsel should request that the prosecution disclose any information that tends to negate guilt, mitigates the offense or is likely to reduce punishment.

(e) Defense counsel may make a recommendation to the client regarding disposition proposals, but should not unduly pressure the client to make any particular decision.

(f) Defense counsel should not knowingly make false statements of fact or law in the course of disposition discussions.

(g) Defense counsel should be aware of possible benefits from early cooperation with the government, but should also consider possible disadvantages. Counsel should fully advise the client about the client's overall interests before recommending any cooperation-dependent disposition.

(h) Defense counsel should not negotiate an aggregate disposition for multiple clients, even if joint representation was initially appropriate under applicable conflict provisions.

(i) Defense counsel should not recommend concessions favorable to one client by any agreement which is detrimental to the legitimate interests of a client in another case, unless both clients give their fully-informed consent.

Standard 4–6.3 Plea Agreements and Other Negotiated Dispositions

(a) Defense counsel should ensure that any written disposition agreement accurately and completely reflects the precise terms of the agreement, including the prosecution's promises and the client's obligations and whether any dismissal of charges will be with or without prejudice to later reinstatement.

(b) During any court hearing regarding a negotiated disposition, defense counsel should ensure that all relevant details of the negotiated agreement are placed on the record, and that the record fully reflects any factors necessary to protect the client's best interests. Although the presumption is that the record will be public, in some cases the record (or a portion) may be sealed for good cause or as required by applicable rule or statute.

(c) Defense counsel should fully prepare the client for any hearing before a court related to entering or accepting a negotiated disposition, and for any pre-disposition or post-disposition interview conducted by the prosecution or by court agents such as presentence investigators or probation officers. Counsel should ordinarily be present at any such interview to protect the client's interests there.

(d) In appropriate cases counsel should consider, and with the consent of the client seek, entry of a disposition and immediate sentencing without a presentence investigation.

(e) Defense counsel should investigate and be knowledgeable about sentencing procedures, law, and alternatives, collateral consequences and likely outcomes, and the practices of the sentencing judge, and advise the client on these topics before permitting the client to enter a negotiated disposition. Counsel should also consider and explain to the client how specific terms of an agreement are likely to be implemented.

(f) If defense counsel believes that prosecutorial conduct or conditions (such as unreasonably speedy deadlines or refusal to provide discovery) have unfairly influenced the client's disposition decision, defense counsel should bring the circumstances to the attention of the court on the record, unless after consultation with the client, it is agreed that the risk of losing the negotiated disposition outweighs other considerations.

Standard 4–6.4 Opposing Waivers of Rights in Disposition Agreements

(a) Defense counsel should not accept disposition agreement waivers of post-conviction claims addressing ineffective assistance of counsel, prosecutorial misconduct, or destruction of evidence, unless such claims are based on past instances of such conduct that are specifically identified in the agreement or in the transcript of proceedings that address the agreement. If a proposed disposition agreement contains such a waiver regarding ineffective assistance of counsel, defense counsel should ensure that the defendant has consulted with independent counsel regarding the waiver before agreeing to the disposition.

(b) In addition to claims addressed in (a), defense counsel should not agree to waivers of any other important defense rights such as the right to appeal (including sentencing appeals), to receive *Brady* discovery, or to contest the conviction or sentence in collateral proceedings, unless after consultation with the client it is agreed that the risk of losing the negotiated disposition outweighs other considerations. In negotiations, counsel should request the prosecution to provide specific, individualized reasons for the inclusion of such waivers. Counsel should also consult with the client about whether to object to such waivers in court.

(c) Counsel should not recommend acceptance of any disposition agreement waivers without fully assessing and discussing with the client the impact of any waiver on the defendant's individualized circumstances. Defense counsel should demand that any such waiver include at the very least an exception for a subsequent showing of manifest injustice based on newly discovered evidence, or actual innocence.

(d) Even if the client wishes to agree to such waivers after fully informed consultation, defense counsel should consider challenging the legitimacy of any such waiver if the challenge can be made without harming the client's interests.

PART VII. COURT HEARINGS AND TRIAL

Standard 4–7.1 Scheduling Court Hearings

Final control over the scheduling of court appearances, hearings and trials in criminal matters should rest with the court rather than the parties. When defense counsel is aware of facts that would affect scheduling, defense counsel should advise the court and, if the facts are case-specific, the prosecutor.

Standard 4–7.2 Civility with Courts, Prosecutors, and Others

(a) As an officer of the court, defense counsel should support the authority and dignity of the court by adherence to codes of professionalism and by manifesting a courteous and professional attitude toward the judge, opposing counsel, witnesses, jurors, courtroom staff and others. In court as elsewhere, the defense counsel should not display or act out of any improper or unlawful bias.

(b) In all contacts with judges, defense counsel should maintain a professional and independent relationship. Defense counsel should not engage in unauthorized *ex parte* discussions with, or submission of material to, a judge relating to a particular matter which is, or is likely to be, before the judge. With regard to generalized matters requiring judicial discussion (for example, case-management or administrative matters), defense counsel should invite a representative prosecutor to join in the discussion to the extent practicable.

(c) When *ex parte* communications or submissions are authorized, defense counsel should inform the court of material facts known to counsel (other than those protected by a valid privilege), including facts that are adverse, sufficient to enable the court to make an informed decision. Except when non-disclosure is authorized, counsel should notify opposing counsel that an *ex parte* contact has occurred, without disclosing its content unless permitted.

(d) When court is in session, unless otherwise permitted by the court, defense counsel should address the court and should not address other counsel directly on any matter relating to the case.

(e) In written filings, defense counsel should respectfully evaluate and respond as appropriate to opposing counsel's arguments and representations, and avoid unnecessary personalized disparagement.

(f) Defense counsel should comply promptly and civilly with a court's orders or seek appropriate relief from such order. If defense counsel considers an order to be significantly erroneous or prejudicial, counsel should ensure that the record adequately reflects the events. Defense counsel has a right to make respectful objections and reasonable requests for reconsideration, and to seek other relief as the law permits. If a judge prohibits making an adequate objection, proffer, or record, counsel may take other lawful steps to protect the client's rights.

(g) Defense counsel should develop and maintain courteous and civil working relationships with judges and prosecutors, and should cooperate with them in developing solutions to address ethical, scheduling, or other issues that may arise in particular cases or generally in the criminal justice system. Defense counsel should cooperate with courts and organized bar associations in developing codes of professionalism and civility, and should abide by such codes that apply in their jurisdiction.

Standard 4–7.3 Selection of Jurors

(a) Defense counsel should be aware of legal standards that govern the selection of jurors, and be prepared to discharge effectively the defense function in the selection of the jury, including raising appropriate issues concerning the method by which the jury panel was selected and exercising challenges for cause and peremptory challenges.

(b) Defense counsel should not strike jurors based on any criteria rendered impermissible by the constitution, statutes, or applicable rules of the jurisdiction or these standards, including race, sex, religion, national origin, disability, sexual orientation or gender identity. Defense counsel should consider challenging a prosecutor's peremptory challenges that appear to be based on such criteria.

(c) In cases in which defense counsel conducts a pretrial investigation of the background of potential jurors, the investigative methods used should not harass, intimidate, unduly embarrass, or invade the privacy of potential jurors. Absent special circumstances, such investigation should be restricted to review of records and sources of information already in existence and to which access is lawfully allowed.

(d) The opportunity to question jurors personally should be used solely to obtain information relevant to the well-informed exercise of challenges. Defense counsel should not seek to commit jurors on factual issues likely to arise in the case, or to suggest facts or arguments that the defense counsel reasonably should know are likely to be barred at trial. Voir dire should not be used to argue counsel's case to the jury, or to unduly ingratiate counsel with the jurors.

(e) During voir dire, defense counsel should seek to minimize any undue embarrassment or invasion of privacy of potential jurors, for example by seeking to inquire into sensitive matters outside the presence of other potential jurors, while still enabling fair and efficient juror selection.

(f) If the court does not permit voir dire by counsel, defense counsel should provide the court with suggested questions in advance if possible, and request specific follow-up questions during the selection process when necessary to ensure fair juror selection.

(g) If defense counsel has reliable information that conflicts with a potential juror's responses, or that reasonably would support a "for cause" challenge by any party, defense counsel should inform the court and, unless the court orders otherwise, the prosecutor.

Standard 4–7.4 Relationship With Jurors

(a) Defense counsel should not communicate with persons counsel knows to be summoned for jury duty or impaneled as jurors, prior to or during trial, other than in the lawful conduct of courtroom proceedings. Defense counsel should avoid even the appearance of improper communications with jurors, and minimize any out-of-court proximity to or contact with jurors. Where out-of-court contact cannot be avoided, counsel should not communicate about or refer to the specific case.

(b) Defense counsel should treat jurors with courtesy and respect, while avoiding a show of undue solicitude for their comfort or convenience.

(c) After discharge of a juror, defense counsel should avoid contacts that may harass or embarrass the juror, that criticize the jury's actions or verdict, or that express views that could otherwise adversely influence a juror's future jury service. Defense counsel should know and comply with applicable rules and law governing the subject.

(d) After a jury is discharged, defense counsel may, if no statute, rule or order prohibits such action, communicate with jurors to investigate whether a verdict may be subject to legal challenge, or to evaluate counsel's performance for improvements in the future. Counsel should consider requesting the court to instruct the jury that, if it is not prohibited by law, it is not improper for jurors to discuss the case with the lawyers, although they are not required to do so. Any post-discharge communication with a juror should not disparage the criminal justice system and the jury trial process, and should not express criticism of the jury's actions or verdict.

(e) Defense counsel who learns reasonably reliable information that there was a problem with jury deliberations or conduct that could support an attack on the client's judgment of conviction and that is recognized as potentially valid in the jurisdiction, should promptly report that information to the appropriate judicial officer and, unless the court orders otherwise, to the prosecution.

Standard 4–7.5 Opening Statement at Trial

(a) Defense counsel should be aware of the importance of an opening statement and, except in unusual cases, give an opening statement immediately after the prosecution's, before the presentation of evidence begins. Any decision to defer the opening statement should be fully discussed with the client, and a record of the reasons for such decision should be made for the file.

(b) Defense counsel's opening statement at trial should be confined to a fair statement of the case from defense counsel's perspective, and discussion of evidence that defense counsel reasonably believes in good faith will be available, offered, and admitted. A deferred opening should focus on the defense evidence and theory of the case and not be a closing argument.

(c) Defense counsel's opening statement should be made without expressions of personal opinion, vouching for witnesses, inappropriate appeals to emotion, or personal attacks on opposing counsel.

(d) When defense counsel has reason to believe that a portion of the opening statement may be objectionable, counsel should raise that point with opposing counsel and, if necessary, the court, in advance. Similarly, visual aids or exhibits that defense counsel intends to use during opening statement should be shown to the prosecutor in advance.

Standard 4–7.6 Presentation of Evidence

(a) Defense counsel has no obligation to present evidence, and should always consider, in consultation with the client, whether a decision not to present evidence may be in the client's best interest. In making this decision, defense counsel should consider the impact of any evidence the defense would present and the potential damage that prosecution cross-examination or a rebuttal case could do, as well as the quality of the prosecution's evidence.

(b) Defense counsel should not knowingly offer false evidence for its truth, whether by documents, tangible evidence, or the testimony of witnesses, or fail to take reasonable remedial measures upon discovery of material falsity in evidence offered by the defense, unless the court or specific authority in the jurisdiction otherwise permits.

(c) If defense counsel reasonably believes that there has been misconduct by opposing counsel, a witness, the court or other persons that affects the fair presentation of the evidence, defense counsel should challenge the perceived misconduct by appealing or objecting to the court or through other appropriate avenues, and not by engaging in retaliatory conduct that defense counsel knows is improper.

(d) Defense counsel should not bring to the attention of the trier of fact matters that defense counsel knows to be inadmissible, whether by offering or displaying inadmissible evidence, asking legally objectionable questions, or making impermissible comments or arguments. If defense counsel is uncertain about the admissibility of evidence, counsel should seek and obtain resolution from the court before the hearing or trial if possible, and reasonably in advance of the time for proffering the evidence before a jury.

(e) Defense counsel should exercise strategic judgment regarding whether to object or take exception to evidentiary rulings that are materially adverse to the client, and not make every possible objection. Defense counsel should not make objections without a reasonable basis, or for improper reasons such as to harass or to break the flow of opposing counsel's presentation. Defense counsel should make an adequate record for appeal, and consider the possibility of an interlocutory appeal regarding significant adverse rulings if available.

(f) Defense counsel should not display tangible evidence (and should object to such display by the prosecutor), until it is admitted into evidence, except insofar as its display is necessarily incidental to its tender, although counsel may seek permission to display admissible evidence during opening statement. Defense counsel should avoid displaying even admitted evidence in a manner that is unduly prejudicial.

Standard 4–7.7 Examination of Witnesses in Court

(a) Defense counsel should conduct the examination of witnesses fairly and with due regard for dignity and legitimate privacy concerns, and without seeking to intimidate or humiliate a witness unnecessarily.

(b) Defense counsel's belief or knowledge that a witness is telling the truth does not preclude vigorous cross-examination, even though defense counsel's cross-examination may cast doubt on the testimony.

(c) Defense counsel should not call a witness in the presence of the jury when counsel knows the witness will claim a valid privilege not to testify. If defense counsel is unsure whether a particular witness will claim a privilege to not testify, counsel should alert the court and the prosecutor in advance and outside the presence of the jury.

(d) Defense counsel should not ask a question which implies the existence of a factual predicate for which a good faith belief is lacking.

Standard 4–7.8 Closing Argument to the Trier of Fact

(a) In closing argument to a jury (or to a judge sitting as trier of fact), defense counsel may argue all reasonable inferences from the evidence in the record. Defense counsel should, to the extent time permits, review the evidence in the record before presenting closing argument. Defense counsel should not knowingly misstate the evidence in the record, or argue inferences that counsel knows have no good-faith support in the record.

(b) Defense counsel should not argue in terms of counsel's personal opinion, and should not imply special or secret knowledge of the truth or of witness credibility.

(c) Defense counsel should not make arguments calculated to appeal to improper prejudices of the jury.

(d) Defense counsel should not argue to the jury that the jury should not follow its oath to consider the evidence and follow the law.

(e) Defense counsel may respond fairly to arguments made in the prosecution's initial closing argument. Defense counsel should object and request relief from the court regarding prosecution arguments it believes are improper, rather than responding with arguments that counsel knows are improper.

(f) If the prosecution is permitted a rebuttal argument, defense counsel should craft the defense closing argument to anticipate the government's rebuttal. If defense counsel believes the prosecution's rebuttal closing argument is or was improper, defense counsel should timely object and consider requesting relief from the court, including an instruction that the jury disregard the improper portion of the argument or an opportunity to reopen argument and respond before the factfinder.

Standard 4–7.9 Facts Outside the Record

When before a jury, defense counsel should not knowingly refer to, or argue on the basis of, facts outside the record, unless such facts are matters of common public knowledge based on ordinary human experience or are matters of which a court clearly may take judicial notice, or are facts that counsel reasonably believes will be entered into the record at that proceeding. In a nonjury context counsel may refer to extra-record facts relevant to issues about which the court specifically inquires, but should note that they are outside the record.

Standard 4–7.10 Comments by Defense Counsel After Verdict or Ruling

(a) Defense counsel may publicly express respectful disagreement with an adverse court ruling or jury verdict, and may indicate that the defendant maintains innocence and intends to pursue lawful options for review. Defense counsel should refrain from public criticism of any participant. Public comments after a verdict or ruling should be respectful of the legal system and process.

(b) Defense counsel may publicly praise a favorable court verdict or ruling, compliment participants, supporters, and others who aided in the matter, and note the social value of the ruling or event. Defense counsel should not publicly gloat or seek personal aggrandizement regarding a verdict or ruling.

Standard 4–7.11 Motions For Acquittal During Trial

Defense counsel should move, outside the presence of the jury, for acquittal after the close of the prosecution's evidence and at the close of all evidence, and be aware of applicable rules regarding waiver and preservation of issues when no or an inadequate motion is made.

PART VIII. POST-TRIAL MOTIONS AND SENTENCING

Standard 4–8.1 Post-Trial Motions

(a) Defense counsel should know the relevant rules governing post-trial motions and, if the trier of fact renders a judgment of guilty, timely present all motions necessary to protect the client's rights, including the defendant's right to appeal all aspects of the case. A motion for acquittal notwithstanding a verdict should be filed absent rare and unusual circumstances, and counsel should consider the strategic value of a motion for a new trial. Defense counsel should file only those motions that have a non-frivolous legal basis.

(b) Unless contrary to the client's best interests or otherwise agreed or provided by law, defense counsel should ordinarily to represent the client in post-trial proceedings in the trial court. Defense counsel should consider, however, whether the client's best interests would be served by substitution of new counsel for post-trial motions.

(c) If a post-trial motion is based on ineffective assistance of counsel, defense counsel should seek to withdraw in accordance with the law regarding withdrawal and aid the client in obtaining substitute counsel.

Standard 4–8.2 Reassessment of Options After Trial

After a guilty verdict and before sentencing, defense counsel should, in consultation with the client, reassess prior decisions made in the case, whether by counsel or others, in light of all changed circumstances, and pursue options that now seem appropriate, including possible motions to set or reduce bail or conditions, and possible cooperation with the prosecution if in the client's best interests.

Standard 4–8.3 Sentencing

(a) Early in the representation, and throughout the pendency of the case, defense counsel should consider potential issues that might affect sentencing. Defense counsel should become familiar with the client's background, applicable sentencing laws and rules, and what options might be available as well as what consequences might arise if the client is convicted. Defense counsel should be fully informed regarding available sentencing alternatives and with community and other resources which may be of assistance in formulating a plan for meeting the client's needs. Defense counsel should also consider whether consultation with an expert specializing in sentencing options or other sentencing issues is appropriate.

(b) Defense counsel's preparation before sentencing should include learning the court's practices in exercising sentencing discretion; the collateral consequences of different sentences; and the normal pattern of sentences for the offense involved, including any guidelines applicable for either sentencing and, where applicable, parole. The consequences (including reasonably foreseeable collateral consequences) of potential dispositions should be explained fully by defense counsel to the client.

(c) Defense counsel should present all arguments or evidence which will assist the court or its agents in reaching a sentencing disposition favorable to the accused. Defense counsel should ensure that the accused understands the nature of the presentence investigation process, and in particular the significance of statements made by the accused to probation officers and related personnel. Defense counsel should cooperate with court presentence officers unless, after consideration and consultation, it appears not to be in the best interests of the client. Unless prohibited, defense counsel should attend the probation officer's presentence interview with the accused and meet in person with the probation officer to discuss the case.

(d) Defense counsel should gather and submit to the presentence officers, prosecution, and court as much mitigating information relevant to sentencing as reasonably possible; and in an appropriate case, with the consent of the accused, counsel should suggest alternative programs of service or rehabilitation or other non-imprisonment options, based on defense counsel's exploration of employment, educational, and other opportunities made available by community services.

(e) If a presentence report is made available to defense counsel, counsel should seek to verify the information contained in it, and should supplement or challenge it if necessary. Defense counsel should either provide the client with a copy or (if copying is not allowed) discuss counsel's knowledge of its contents with the client. In many cases, defense counsel should independently investigate the facts relevant to sentencing, rather than relying on the court's presentence report, and should seek discovery or relevant information from governmental agencies or other third-parties if necessary.

(f) Defense counsel should alert the accused to the right of allocution. Counsel should consider with the client the potential benefits of the judge hearing a personal statement from the defendants as contrasted with the possible dangers of making a statement that could adversely impact the sentencing judge's decision or the merits of an appeal.

(g) If a sentence of imprisonment is imposed, defense counsel should seek the court's assistance, including an on-the-record statement by the court if possible, recommending the appropriate place of confinement and types of treatment, programming and counseling that should be provided for the defendant in confinement.

(h) Once the sentence has been announced, defense counsel should make any objections necessary for the record, seek clarification of any unclear terms, and advise the client of the meaning and effects of the judgment, including any known collateral consequences. Counsel should also note on the record the intention to appeal, if that decision has already been made with the client.

(i) If the client has received an imprisonment sentence and an appeal will be taken, defense counsel should determine whether bail pending appeal is appropriate and, if so, request it.

PART IX. APPEALS AND POST-CONVICTION REMEDIES

Standard 4–9.1 Preparing to Appeal

(a) If a client is convicted, defense counsel should explain to the client the meaning and consequences of the court's judgment and the client's rights regarding appeal. Defense counsel should provide the client with counsel's professional judgment as to whether there are meritorious grounds for appeal and the possible, and likely, results of an appeal. Defense counsel should also explain to the client the advantages and disadvantages of an appeal including the possibility that the government might cross-appeal, and the possibility that if the client prevails on appeal, a remand could result in a less favorable disposition. Counsel should also be familiar with, and discuss with the client, possible interactions with other post-conviction procedures such as habeas corpus rules and actions.

(b) The ultimate decision whether to appeal should be the client's. Defense counsel should consider engaging or consulting with an expert in criminal appeals in order to determine issues related to making a decision to appeal.

(c) Defense counsel should take whatever steps are necessary to protect the client's rights of appeal, including filing a timely notice of appeal in the trial court, even if counsel does not expect to continue as counsel on appeal.

(d) Defense counsel should explain to the client that the client has a right to counsel on appeal (appointed, if the client is indigent), and that there are lawyers who specialize in criminal appeals. Defense counsel should candidly explore with the client whether trial counsel is the appropriate lawyer to represent the client on appeal, or whether a lawyer specializing in appellate work should be consulted, added or substituted.

Standard 4–9.2 Counsel on Appeal

(a) Appellate defense counsel should seek the cooperation of the client's trial counsel in the evaluation of potential appellate issues. A client's trial counsel should provide such assistance as is possible, including promptly providing the file of the case to appellate counsel.

(b) When evaluating the case for appeal, appellate defense counsel should consider all issues that might affect the validity of the judgment of conviction and sentence, including any that might require initial presentation in a trial court. Counsel should consider raising on appeal even issues not objected to below or waived or forfeited, if in the best interests of the client.

(c) After examining the record and the relevant law, counsel should provide counsel's best professional evaluation of the issues that might be presented on appeal. Counsel should advise the client about the probable and possible outcomes and consequences of a challenge to the conviction or sentence.

(d) Even if a client has agreed to a waiver of appeal, counsel should follow a client's direction to file an appeal if there are non-frivolous grounds to argue that the waiver is not binding or that the appeal should otherwise be heard.

(e) Appellate defense counsel should not file a brief that counsel reasonably believes is devoid of merit. However, counsel should not conclude that a defense appeal lacks merit until counsel has fully examined the trial court record and the relevant legal authorities. If appellate counsel does so conclude, counsel should fully discuss that conclusion with the client, and explain the "no merit" briefing process applicable in the jurisdiction if available. Counsel should endeavor to persuade the client to abandon a frivolous appeal, and to eliminate appellate contentions lacking in substance. If the client ultimately demands that a no-merit brief not be filed, defense counsel should seek to withdraw.

(f) If the client chooses to proceed with a non-frivolous appeal against the advice of counsel, counsel should present the appeal. When counsel cannot continue without misleading the court, counsel may request permission to withdraw.

(g) Appellate counsel should discuss with the client the arguments to present in appellate briefing and at argument, and should diligently attempt to accommodate the client's wishes. If the client desires to raise an argument that is colorable, counsel should work with the client to an acceptable resolution regarding the argument. If appellate counsel decides not to brief all of the issues that the client wishes to include, appellate counsel should inform the client of *pro se* briefing rights and consider providing the appellate court with a list of additional issues the client would like to present.

(h) In a jurisdiction that has an intermediate appellate court, appellate defense counsel should ordinarily continue to represent the client after the intermediate court renders a decision if further appeals are likely, unless a retainer agreement provides otherwise, new counsel is substituted, or a court permits counsel to withdraw. Similarly, unless a retainer agreement provides otherwise, new counsel is substituted, or a court permits counsel to withdraw, appellate counsel should ordinarily continue to represent the client through all stages of a direct appeal, including review in the United States Supreme Court.

(i) If trial defense counsel will not remain as appellate counsel, trial counsel should notify the client of any applicable time limits, act to preserve the client's appellate rights if possible, and cooperate and assist in securing qualified appellate counsel. If appellate counsel's representation ends but further appellate review is possible, appellate counsel should advise the client of further options and deadlines, such as for a petition for *certiorari*.

(j) When the prosecution appeals a ruling that was favorable to the client, defense counsel should analyze the issues and possible implications for the client and act to zealously protect the client's interests. If the prosecution is appealing, defense counsel should consider adding or consulting with an appellate expert about the matter.

(k) When the law permits the filing of interlocutory appeals or writs to challenge adverse trial court rulings, defense counsel should consider whether to file an interlocutory appeal and, after consultation with the client, vigorously pursue such an appeal if in the client's interest. If the prosecution files an interlocutory appeal, defense counsel should act in accordance with the foregoing paragraphs.

Standard 4–9.3 Conduct of Appeal

(a) Before filing an appellate brief, appellate defense counsel should consult with the client about the appeal, and seek to meet with the client unless impractical.

(b) Appellate counsel should be aware of opportunities to favorably affect or resolve a defendant's appeal by motions filed in the appellate court, before filing a merits brief.

(c) Counsel should understand the complex rules that govern whether arguments listed or omitted on direct appeal can limit issues available in later collateral proceedings, and not unnecessarily or unknowingly abandon arguments that should be preserved. Counsel should explicitly label federal constitutional arguments as such, in order to preserve later federal litigation options.

(d) Appellate counsel should be aware of applicable rules relating to securing all necessary record documents, transcripts, and exhibits, and ensure that all such items necessary to effectively prosecute the appeal are properly and timely ordered. Before filing the brief, appellate counsel should ordinarily examine the docket sheet, all transcripts, trial exhibits and record documents, not just those designated by another lawyer or the client. Counsel should consider whether, and how appropriately, to augment the record with any other matters, documents or evidence relevant to effective prosecution of the client's appeal. Appellate counsel should seek by appropriate motion, filed in either the trial or the appellate court, to make available for the appeal any necessary, relevant extra-record matters.

(e) Appellate counsel should be diligent in perfecting appeals and expediting their prompt submission to appellate courts, and be familiar with and follow all applicable appellate rules, while also protecting the client's best interests on appeal.

(f) Appellate counsel should be accurate in referring to the record and the authorities upon which counsel relies in the presentation to the court of briefs and oral argument. Appellate counsel should present directly adverse authority in the controlling jurisdiction of which counsel is aware and that has not been presented by other counsel in the appeal.

(g) Appellate counsel should not intentionally refer to or argue on the basis of facts outside the record on appeal, unless such facts are matters of common public knowledge based on ordinary human experience or are other matters of which the court properly may take judicial notice.

(h) If the appeal is set for oral argument, appellate counsel should explain to an out-of-custody client that the client is permitted to attend, and that attending the argument may have certain strategic advantages and disadvantages. If after consultation the client desires to attend the argument, counsel should help the client to be present. If the client is in custody, counsel should request a tape or transcript of the oral argument, and consider filing a motion for the government to transport client to the argument.

(i) Appellate counsel should be aware of local rules and practices that may apply to oral arguments, including, for example, rules that apply to the submission of subsequent authorities or the use of demonstrative aids or exhibits during argument.

(j) If appellate counsel's study of the record reveals that an ineffective assistance of trial counsel claim should be made, appellate counsel should weigh the advantages and disadvantages of raising an ineffective assistance claim on the existing record versus pursuing such a claim in the trial court either before, or after, the appeal is heard. Counsel should also learn the rules, if any, of the particular jurisdiction regarding this issue.

(k) Appellate counsel should consider, in preparing the appellate briefing, whether there might be any potential grounds for relief using other post-conviction remedies (such as habeas corpus), and consult with the client regarding timing and who might represent the client in such actions.

Standard 4–9.4 New or Newly-Discovered Law or Evidence of Innocence or Wrongful Conviction or Sentence

(a) When defense counsel becomes aware of credible and material evidence or law creating a reasonable likelihood that a client or former client was wrongfully convicted or sentenced or was actually innocent, counsel has some duty to act. This duty applies even after counsel's representation is ended. Counsel must consider, and act in accordance with, duties of confidentiality. If such a former client currently has counsel, former counsel may discharge the duty by alerting the client's current counsel.

(b) If such newly discovered evidence or law (whether due to a change in the law or not) relevant to the validity of the client's conviction or sentence, or evidence or law tending to show actual innocence of the client, comes to the attention of the client's current defense counsel at any time after conviction, counsel should promptly:

(i) evaluate the information, investigate if necessary, and determine what potential remedies are available;

(ii) advise and consult with the client; and

(iii) determine what action if any to take.

(c) Counsel should determine applicable deadlines for the effective use of such evidence or law, including federal habeas corpus deadlines, and timely act to preserve the client's rights. Counsel should determine whether—and if so, how best—to notify the prosecution and court of such evidence.

Standard 4–9.5 Post-Appellate Remedies

(a) Once a defendant's direct appellate avenues have been exhausted, appellate counsel is not obligated to represent the defendant in a post-appellate collateral proceeding unless counsel has agreed, or has been appointed, to do so. But counsel should still reasonably advise and act to protect the client's possible collateral options.

(b) If appellate counsel believes there is a reasonable prospect of a favorable result if collateral proceedings are pursued, counsel should explain to the client the advantages and disadvantages of pursuing collateral proceedings, and any timing deadlines that apply. Appellate defense counsel should assist the client to the extent practicable in locating competent counsel for any post-appellate collateral proceedings.

(c) Post-appellate counsel should seek the cooperation of the client's prior counsel in the evaluation and briefing of potential post-conviction issues. Prior counsel should provide such assistance as is possible, including providing the file or copies of the file to post-appellate counsel.

Standard 4–9.6 Challenges to the Effectiveness of Counsel

(a) If appellate or post-appellate counsel is satisfied after appropriate investigation and legal research that another defense counsel who served in an earlier phase of the case did not provide effective assistance, new counsel should not hesitate to seek relief for the client.

(b) If defense counsel concludes that he or she did not provide effective assistance in an earlier phase of the case, counsel should explain this conclusion to the client. Unless the client clearly wants counsel to continue, counsel in this situation should seek to withdraw from further representation of the client with an explanation to the court of the reason, consistent with the duty of confidentiality to the client. Counsel should recommend that the client consult with independent counsel if the client desires counsel to continue with the representation. Counsel should continue with the representation only if the client so desires after informed consent and such further representation is consistent with applicable conflict of interest rules.

(c) Defense counsel whose conduct in a criminal case is drawn into question is permitted to testify concerning the matters at issue, and is not precluded from disclosing the truth concerning the matters raised by his former client, even though this involves revealing matters which were given in confidence. Former counsel must act consistently with applicable confidentiality rules, and ordinarily may not reveal confidences unless necessary for the purposes of the proceeding and under judicial supervision.

(d) In a proceeding challenging counsel's performance, counsel should not rely on the prosecutor to act as counsel's lawyer in the proceeding, and should continue to consider the former client's best interests.

ABA CRIMINAL JUSTICE STANDARDS ON PROSECUTORIAL INVESTIGATIONS

The Standards on Prosecutorial Investigations were adopted by the ABA House of Delegates in 2008.

Preamble

A prosecutor's investigative role, responsibilities and potential liability are different from the prosecutor's role and responsibilities as a courtroom advocate. These Standards are intended as a guide to conduct for a prosecutor actively engaged in a criminal investigation or performing a legally mandated investigative responsibility, e.g., serving as legal advisor to an investigative grand jury or as an applicant for a warrant to intercept communications. These Standards are intended to supplement the Prosecution Function Standards, not to supplant them. These Standards may not be applicable to a prosecutor serving in a minor supporting role to an investigation undertaken and directed by law enforcement agents.

PART 1. GENERAL STANDARDS

Standard 1.1 The Function of These Standards

(a) These Standards address the investigative stage of the criminal justice process. They address the charge or post-charge stages of the criminal justice process only when those stages overlap with the investigative stage.

(b) Standards are not intended to serve as the basis for the imposition of professional discipline, nor to create substantive or procedural rights for accused or convicted persons. These Standards do not modify a prosecutor's ethical obligations under applicable rule of professional conduct. These Standards are not intended to create a standard of care for civil liability, nor to serve as a predicate for a motion to suppress evidence or dismiss a charge.

(c) The use of the term "prosecutor" in these Standards applies to any prosecutor or other attorney, regardless of agency or title, who serves as an attorney in a governmental criminal investigation.

Standard 1.2 General Principles

(a) An individual prosecutor is not an independent agent but is a member of an independent institution the primary duty of which is to seek justice.

(b) The prosecutor's client is the public, not particular government agencies or victims.

(c) The purposes of a criminal investigation are to:

(i) develop sufficient factual information to enable the prosecutor to make a fair and objective determination of whether and what charges should be brought and to guard against prosecution of the innocent, and

(ii) develop legally admissible evidence sufficient to obtain and sustain a conviction of those who are guilty and warrant prosecution.

(d) The prosecutor should:

(i) ensure that criminal investigations are not based upon premature beliefs or conclusions as to guilt or innocence but are guided by the facts;

(ii) ensure that criminal investigations are not based upon partisan or other improper political or personal considerations and do not invidiously discriminate against, nor wrongly favor, persons on the basis of race, ethnicity, religion, gender, sexual orientation, political beliefs, age, or social or economic status;

(iii) consider whether an investigation would be in the public interest and what the potential impacts of a criminal investigation might be on subjects, targets and witnesses; and

(iv) seek in most circumstances to maintain the secrecy and confidentiality of criminal investigations.

(e) Generally, the prosecutor engaged in an investigation should not be the sole decision-maker regarding the decision to prosecute matters arising out of that investigation.

(f) The prosecutor should be aware of and comply with the ethical rules and other legal standards applicable to the prosecutor's conduct during an investigation.

(g) The prosecutor should cooperate with other governmental authorities regarding matters that are of legitimate concern to such authorities when doing so is permitted by law and would not compromise an investigation or other criminal justice goals.

(h) The prosecutor's office should provide organizational structure to guide its members' investigative work.

Standard 1.3 Working With Police and Other Law Enforcement Agents

(a) The prosecutor should respect the investigative role of police and other law enforcement agents by:

(i) working cooperatively with them to develop investigative policies; and

(ii) providing independent legal advice regarding their investigative decisions.

(b) The prosecutor should take steps to promote compliance by law enforcement agents with relevant legal rules.

(c) The prosecutor should be aware of the experience, skills and professional abilities of police and other law enforcement agents assigned to an investigation.

(d) The prosecutor's office should assist in providing training to police and other law enforcement agents concerning potential legal issues and best practices in criminal investigations.

(e) Before and throughout the course of complex or non-routine investigations, the prosecutor should work with the police and other participating agencies and experts to develop an investigative plan that analyzes:

(i) the investigative predicate or information concerning the matter that is then known;

(ii) the goals of the investigation;

(iii) the potential investigative techniques and the advantages of each, singularly and in combination, in producing relevant information and admissible evidence; and

(iv) the legal issues likely to arise during the investigation.

(f) The prosecutor should promote timely communications with police and other law enforcement agents about material developments in the investigation.

(g) The prosecutor should not seek to circumvent ethical rules by instructing or recommending that others use means that the prosecutor is ethically prohibited from using. The prosecutor may provide legal advice to law enforcement agents regarding the use of investigative techniques that law enforcement agents are authorized to use.

Standard 1.4 Victims, Potential Witnesses, and Targets During the Investigative Process

(a) Throughout the course of the investigation as new information emerges, the prosecutor should reevaluate:

(i) judgments or beliefs as to the culpability or status of persons or entities identified as "witnesses," "victims," "subjects" and "targets," and recognize that the status of such persons or entities may change; and

(ii) the veracity of witnesses and confidential informants and assess the accuracy and completeness of the information that each provides.

(b) Upon request and if known, the prosecutor should inform a person or the person's counsel, whether the person is considered to be a target, subject, witness or victim, including whether their status has changed, unless doing so would compromise a continuing investigation.

(c) The prosecutor should know the law of the jurisdiction regarding the rights of victims and witnesses and should respect those rights.

(d) Absent a law or court order to the contrary, the prosecutor should not imply or state that it is unlawful for potential witnesses to disclose information related to or discovered during an investigation. The prosecutor may ask potential witnesses not to disclose information, and in doing so, the prosecutor may explain to them the adverse consequences that might result from disclosure (such as compromising the investigation or endangering others). The prosecutor also may alert an individual who has entered into a cooperation agreement that certain disclosures might result in violation of the agreement.

(e) The prosecutor should not imply the existence of legal authority to interview an individual or compel the attendance of a witness if the prosecutor does not have such authority.

(f) The prosecutor should comply with applicable rules and case law that may restrict communications with persons represented by counsel.

(g) The prosecutor should not take into consideration any of the following factors in making a determination of whether an organization has been cooperative in the context of a government investigation unless the specified conduct of the organization would constitute a violation of law or court order:

(i) that the organization has provided, or agreed to provide counsel to, or advanced, reimbursed or indemnified the legal fees and expenses of, an employee;

(ii) that the organization entered into or continues to operate under a joint defense or information sharing and common interest agreement with regard to the investigation;

(iii) that the organization shared its records or other historical information relating to the matter under investigation with an employee; or

(iv) that the organization did not sanction or discharge an employee who invoked his or her Fifth Amendment privilege against self-incrimination in response to government questioning of the employee.

(h) The prosecutor should not interfere with, threaten, or seek to punish persons or entities seeking counsel in connection with an investigation, nor should the prosecutor interfere with, threaten or seek to punish those who provide such counsel unless by doing so such conduct would constitute a violation of law or court order. A good faith basis for raising a conflict of interest, or for investigating possible criminal conduct by the defense attorney, is not "interference" within the meaning of this Standard.

Standard 1.5 Contacts With the Public During the Investigative Process

(a) The prosecutor should neither confirm nor deny the existence of an investigation, or reveal the status of the investigation, nor release information concerning the investigation, with the following exceptions:

(i) releasing information reasonably necessary to obtain public assistance in solving a crime, apprehending a suspect, or calming public fears;

(ii) responding to a widely disseminated public call for an investigation by stating that the prosecutor will investigate, or decline to investigate the matter;

(iii) responding to a law enforcement or regulatory matter of significant public safety concern, by stating that the prosecutor will begin an investigation or begin a special initiative to address the issue, or by releasing information reasonably necessary to protect public safety, subject to restrictions in the law of the jurisdiction;

(iv) announcing future investigative plans in order to deter criminal activity;

(v) stating in an already publicized matter and where justice so requires, that the prosecutor will not initiate, will not continue, or has concluded an investigation of a person, entity, or matter and, if applicable, has informed the subject or potential subject of the decision not to file charges;

(vi) responding to widely disseminated false statements that the prosecutor is, or is not, investigating a person, entity, or matter;

(vii) stating whether and when, if court rules so permit, an event open to the public is scheduled to occur;

(viii) offering limited comment when public attention is generated by an event in the investigation (e.g., arrests, the execution of search warrants, the filing of charges, or convictions), subject to governing legal standards and court rules; and

(ix) making reasonable and fair responses to comments of defense counsel or others.

(b) Except as a proper part of a court proceeding and in accordance with applicable rules, the prosecutor should not publicly make the following types of statements or publicly disclose the following information about an investigation:

(i) statements of belief about the guilt or innocence, character or reputation of subjects or targets of the investigation;

(ii) statements that have a substantial likelihood of materially prejudicing a jury or jury panel;

(iii) information about the character or reputation of a person or entity under investigation, a prospective witness, or victim;

(iv) admissions, confessions, or the contents of a statement or alibi attributable to a person or entity under investigation;

(v) the performance or results of tests or the refusal or agreement of a suspect to take a test;

(vi) statements concerning the credibility or anticipated testimony of prospective witnesses; and

(vii) the possibility or likelihood of a plea of guilty or other disposition.

(c) The prosecutor should endeavor to dissuade police and other law enforcement agents and law enforcement personnel from making public information that the prosecutor would be prohibited from making public, or that may have an adverse impact on the investigation or any potential prosecution.

PART 2. STANDARDS FOR SPECIFIC INVESTIGATIVE FUNCTIONS OF THE PROSECUTOR

Standard 2.1 The Decision to Initiate or to Continue an Investigation

(a) The prosecutor should have wide discretion to select matters for investigation. Thus, unless required by statute or policy:

(i) the prosecutor should have no absolute duty to investigate any particular matter; and

(ii) a particularized suspicion or predicate is not required prior to initiating a criminal investigation.

(b) In deciding whether an investigation would be in the public interest, the prosecutor should consider, but not necessarily be dissuaded by, the following:

(i) a lack of police interest;

(ii) a lack of public or political support;

(iii) a lack of identifiable victims;

(iv) fear or reluctance by potential or actual witnesses; or

(v) unusually complex factual or legal issues.

(c) When deciding whether to initiate or continue an investigation, the prosecutor should consider:

(i) whether there is evidence of the existence of criminal conduct;

(ii) the nature and seriousness of the problem or alleged offense, including the risk or degree of harm from ongoing criminal conduct;

(iii) a history of prior violations of the same or similar laws and whether those violations have previously been addressed through law enforcement or other means;

(iv) the motive, interest, bias or other improper factors that may influence those seeking to initiate or cause the initiation of a criminal investigation;

(v) the need for, and expected impact of, criminal enforcement to:

(A) punish blameworthy behavior;

(B) provide specific and/or general deterrence;

(C) provide protection to the community;

(D) reinforce norms embodied in the criminal law;

(E) prevent unauthorized private action to enforce the law;

(F) preserve the credibility of the criminal justice system; and

(G) other legitimate public interests.

(vi) whether the costs and benefits of the investigation and of particular investigative tools and techniques are justified in consideration of, among other things, the nature of the criminal activity as well as the impact of conducting the investigation on other enforcement priorities and resources

(vii) the collateral effects of the investigation on witnesses, subjects, targets and non-culpable third parties, including financial damage and harm to reputation

(viii) the probability of obtaining sufficient evidence for a successful prosecution of the matter in question, including, if there is a trial, the probability of obtaining a conviction and having the conviction upheld upon appellate review; and

(ix) whether society's interest in the matter might be better or equally vindicated by available civil, regulatory, administrative, or private remedies.

(d) When deciding whether to initiate or continue an investigation, the prosecutor should not be influenced by:

(i) partisan or other improper political or personal considerations, or by the race, ethnicity, religion, gender, sexual orientation, political beliefs or affiliations, age, or social or economic status of the potential subject or victim, unless they are elements of the crime or are relevant to the motive of the perpetrator; or

(ii) hostility or personal animus towards a potential subject, or any other improper motive of the prosecutor.

(e) The prosecutor's office should have an internal procedure to document the reason(s) for declining to pursue prosecution following a criminal investigation.

Standard 2.2 Selecting Investigative Techniques

(a) The prosecutor should be familiar with routine investigative techniques and the best practices to be employed in using them.

(b) The prosecutor should consider the use of costlier, riskier, or more intrusive means of investigation only if routine investigative techniques would be inappropriate, ineffective, or dangerous, or if their use would impair the ability to take other desirable investigative steps. If non-routine techniques are used, the prosecutor should regularly reevaluate the need for them and whether the use of routine investigative techniques will suffice.

(c) The prosecutor should consider, in consultation with police and other law enforcement agents involved in the investigation, the following factors:

(i) the likely effectiveness of a particular technique;

(ii) whether the investigative means and resources to be utilized are appropriate to the seriousness of the offense;

(iii) the risk of physical danger to law enforcement officers and others;

(iv) the costs involved with various investigative techniques and the impact such costs may have on other efforts within the prosecutor's office;

(v) the possibility of lost opportunity if an investigative technique is detected and reveals the investigation;

(vi) means of avoiding unnecessary intrusions or invasions into personal privacy;

(vii) the potential entrapment of otherwise innocent persons;

(viii) the risk of property damage, financial loss to persons or businesses, damage to reputation or other harm to persons;

(ix) interference with privileged or confidential communication;

(x) interference with or intrusion upon constitutionally protected rights; and

(xi) the risk of civil liability or other loss to the government.

(d) The prosecutor should consider the views of experienced police and other law enforcement agents about safety and technical and strategic considerations in the use of investigative techniques.

(e) The prosecutor may consider that the use of certain investigative techniques could cause the subject of the investigation to retain legal counsel and thereby limit the use of some otherwise permissible investigative techniques.

(f) The prosecutor should avoid being the sole interviewer of a witness, being alone with a witness, or otherwise becoming an essential witness to any aspect of the investigation.

(g) While the prosecutor may, and sometimes should, seek changes in law and policy, the prosecutor should abide by existing legal restraints, even if the prosecutor believes that they unjustifiably inhibit the effective investigation of criminal conduct.

Standard 2.3 Use of Undercover Law Enforcement Agents and Undercover Operations

(a) For the purpose of these Standards, an "undercover law enforcement agent" is an employee of a government agency working under the direction and control of a government agency in a criminal investigation, whose true identity as a law enforcement agent involved in the investigation is concealed from third parties.

(b) For the purpose of these Standards, an "undercover operation" means an investigation in which undercover law enforcement agents or other persons working with law enforcement conceal their purpose of detecting crime or obtaining evidence to prosecute those engaged in illegal activities.

(c) In deciding whether to use or to advise the use of undercover law enforcement agents or undercover operations, the prosecutor should consider potential benefits, including:

(i) the character and quality of evidence likely to be obtained; and

(ii) the ability to prevent or solve crimes where obtaining reliable and admissible evidence to do so would otherwise be difficult or impossible to obtain.

(d) In deciding whether to use or to advise the use of undercover law enforcement agents or undercover operations, the prosecutor should consider potential risks, including:

(i) physical injury to law enforcement agents and others;

(ii) lost opportunity if the operation is revealed;

(iii) unnecessary intrusions or invasions into personal privacy;

(iv) entrapment of otherwise innocent persons;

(v) property damage, financial loss to persons or businesses, damage to reputation or other harm to persons;

(vi) interference with privileged or confidential communications;

(vii) interference with or intrusion upon constitutionally protected rights;

(viii) civil liability or other adverse impact on the government;

(ix) personal liability of the law enforcement agents;

(x) involvement in illegal conduct by undercover law enforcement agents or government participation in activity that would be considered unsuitable and highly offensive to public values and that may adversely impact a jury's view of a case; and

(xi) the possibility that the undercover operation will unintentionally cause an increase in criminal activity.

(e) The prosecutor advising an undercover investigation should:

(i) consult with appropriate police or law enforcement agents on a regular basis about the continued propriety of the operation and the legal sufficiency and quality of the evidence that is being produced by the operation;

(ii) seek periodic internal review of the investigation to determine whether the operation's benefits continue to outweigh its risks and costs, including the extent to which:

(A) the goals of the investigation have been accomplished;

(B) there is potential for the acquisition of additional useful and non-duplicative information;

(iii) the investigation can continue without exposing the undercover operation; and

(iv) continuation of the investigation may cause financial or other injury to innocent parties.

(f) The prosecutor should seek to avoid or minimize the risks involved in the active participation of undercover police or law enforcement agents in illegal activity, and provide such agents guidance about authorized participation in otherwise criminal conduct.

(g) Records of funds expended and generated by undercover activity should be retained and accounted for in a manner that facilitates a comprehensive and accurate audit.

Standard 2.4 Use of Confidential Informants

(a) As used in these Standards, a "confidential informant" is a person who supplies information to police or law enforcement agents pursuant to an agreement that the police or investigative agency will seek not to disclose the person's identity. The identity of a confidential informant may also be unknown to the prosecutor. A confidential informant may in some instances become a cooperator, and in such circumstances reference should be made to Standard 2.5.

(b) The prosecutor should consider possible benefits from the use of a confidential informant, including whether the confidential informant might enable the government to obtain:

(i) first-hand, eyewitness accounts of criminal activity;

(ii) critical background information about the criminal activity or criminal organization under investigation;

(iii) information necessary to provide a basis for additional investigative techniques or court-ordered means of investigation such as a search warrant; and

(iv) identification of witnesses or leads to witnesses who can provide direction to further the investigation or valuable testimony to a grand jury or at trial.

(c) The prosecutor should consider possible risks from the use of a confidential informant. These include risks that the confidential informant will:

(i) be untruthful, or provide misleading or incomplete information;

(ii) compromise the criminal investigation by revealing information to others, including the subjects or targets of the investigation;

(iii) engage in behavior constituting entrapment;

(iv) commit or continue to commit crimes;

(v) be subject, or subject others, to serious risk of physical harm as a result of cooperating with law enforcement; and

(vi) interfere with privileged or confidential relationships or communications or violate the rights of the investigation's subject.

(d) The prosecutor should avoid being alone with a confidential informant, even for a brief period of time.

(e) Before deciding to rely upon the information provided by a confidential informant for significant investigative steps, the prosecutor should review the following with the police or law enforcement agents:

(i) the ability of the confidential informant to provide or obtain information relevant to the criminal investigation;

(ii) means of corroborating information received from the confidential informant;

(iii) the possible motives or biases of the confidential informant, including the motive to gain a competitive advantage over others in either criminal or legitimate enterprises;

(iv) the nature of any and all promises made to the prospective confidential informant by other prosecutors, police or law enforcement agents, including promises related to the treatment of associates or relatives of the confidential informant;

(v) the prior history of the confidential informant, including prior criminal activity and other information, including the informant's true identity if necessary for the prosecutor's review;

(vi) whether the prospective confidential informant is represented by an attorney or is party to a joint defense agreement with other targets of the investigation and, if so, how best to address potential legal or ethical issues related to the representation or agreement;

(vii) if reasonably available, the experience other prosecutors and law enforcement agents have had with the confidential informant;

(viii) whether the proposed compensation or benefits to be received by the confidential informant are reasonable under the circumstances;

(ix) the risk that the prospective confidential informant may be an agent of the subjects of the investigation or of other criminal groups and individuals, or may reveal investigative information to them; and

(x) the risk that the prospective confidential informant will engage in criminal activity not authorized by the prosecutor, and the seriousness of that unauthorized criminal activity.

(f) The prosecutor's office should work with police and law enforcement agents to develop best practices and policies for the use of confidential informants that include:

(i) a rule that investigative information obtained from other sources should not be provided to the confidential informant unless doing so would materially advance the investigation;

(ii) prohibitions on making promises of compensation or other benefits that would shock the conscience of a moral society or would risk compromising the credibility of the informant in any proceeding in which the informant's testimony may be important;

(iii) prohibitions on making promises that the police or law enforcement agents are unlikely to be able to keep;

(iv) routine instructions to confidential informants to refrain from criminal conduct other than as directed by law enforcement; and

(v) the routine use of standard form agreements when such agreements are entered into by law enforcement officers without the involvement of the prosecutor.

Standard 2.5 Cooperation Agreements and Cooperating Individuals and Organizational Witnesses

(a) As used in these Standards, "cooperation agreements" are agreements between the prosecutor and otherwise culpable individuals or entities ("cooperators") who provide the government with assistance useful to an investigation in exchange for benefits. A cooperator may have been a confidential informant earlier in the investigation.

(b) The prosecutor should ordinarily seek to have the cooperator plead guilty to an appropriate criminal charge rather than provide the cooperator immunity for culpable conduct.

(c) In deciding whether to offer a cooperator significant benefits, including a limit on criminal liability, immunity, or a recommendation for reduction of sentence, the prosecutor should consider whether:

(i) the cooperator is able and willing to provide valuable assistance to the investigation;

(ii) the cooperator will maintain the confidentiality or secrecy of the investigation;

(iii) the cooperator has biases or personal motives that might result in false, incomplete, or misleading information;

(iv) leniency or immunity for the criminal activity of the cooperator is warranted by the goals of the investigation and the public interest, including appropriate consideration for victim(s) interests;

(v) providing leniency, immunity or other benefits would be seen as offensive by the public or cause a reasonable juror to doubt the veracity of the cooperator's testimony;

(vi) information that has been provided (such as through an attorney proffer or by a debriefing of the cooperator) has been corroborated or can otherwise shown to be accurate;

(vii) the culpability of other participants in the criminal activity relative to the cooperator's culpability has been determined as accurately as possible;

(viii) there is a likelihood that the cooperator will provide useful information only if given leniency or immunity;

(ix) the case could be successfully prosecuted without the cooperator's assistance; and

(x) the cooperator could be successfully prosecuted without the admissions of the cooperator made pursuant to the agreement.

(d) The cooperation agreement should not:

(i) promise to forego prosecution for future criminal activity, except where such activity is necessary as part of an officially supervised investigative and enforcement program; or

(ii) adversely affect third parties' legal rights.

(e) The prosecutor should:

(i) be aware that anything said to the cooperator might be repeated to the cooperator's criminal associates or in open court; and

(ii) be aware of the disclosure requirements under relevant law if a cooperator ultimately testifies at trial, including disclosure of any and all agreements and promises made to the cooperator and evidence which could impact the cooperator's credibility, including the complete criminal history of the cooperator. The prosecutor should take steps to assure the preservation of such evidence.

(f) The prosecutor should recognize and respect the role of the cooperator's attorney in the decision to cooperate and in the disposition of significant legal rights.

(g) Ordinarily, a prosecutor who offers leniency in exchange for cooperation should not withdraw or threaten to withdraw the offer because of the potential cooperator's request to consult with counsel prior to deciding whether to accept it. However, if the time required for the potential cooperator to consult with counsel would render the agreement ineffective, the prosecutor may withdraw or threaten to withdraw the offer before there is opportunity for such consultation. In that event, the prosecutor may condition cooperation on an immediate and uncounseled decision to proceed.

(h) The prosecutor should reduce a cooperation agreement to writing as soon as practicable. An agreement should only cover those crimes known to the government at the time it is made, and should specify:

(i) the specific details of all benefits and obligations agreed upon;

(ii) the specific activities to be performed by the cooperator;

(iii) the requirement that the cooperator be truthful in dealing with the government and in all legal proceedings;

(iv) the prohibition against the cooperator's engaging in any criminal conduct other than as directed by law enforcement;

(v) the extent of the disposition of the potential criminal and civil claims against the cooperator;

(vi) a complete list of any other promises, financial benefits or understandings;

(vii) the limitations of the agreement with respect to the terms it contains and to the identified jurisdiction or jurisdictions; and

(viii) the remedy in the event the cooperator breaches the agreement.

(i) The prosecutor should avoid being alone with a cooperator even for a brief period of time.

(j) The prosecutor should guard against the cooperator obtaining information from others that invades the attorney-client or work product privileges or violates the Sixth Amendment right to counsel.

(k) Prior to relying on the cooperator's information in undertaking an investigative step that could cause adverse consequences to the investigation or to a third party, the prosecutor should be satisfied as to the truthfulness of the cooperator.

(*l*) If an investigative step involves an application to a court or other official body, the prosecutor should make appropriate and required disclosures about the cooperator to the court or other body.

(m) If the prosecutor suspects that the cooperator is not being truthful, the prosecutor should take reasonable steps to address such concerns and seek further corroboration of the cooperator's information.

(n) If the prosecutor determines that a cooperator has knowingly provided false information or otherwise breached the cooperation agreement, the prosecutor should:

(i) seek guidance from a supervisor;

(ii) undertake or request the initiation of an investigation into the circumstances;

(iii) consider the possible prosecution of the cooperator, and;

(iv) carefully reevaluate the investigation.

Standard 2.6 The Decision to Arrest During a Continuing Criminal Investigation

(a) In making a tactical decision whether, when or where to arrest a subject during a continuing investigation, the prosecutor should consider the potential benefits of the arrest, including:

(i) protecting the public from a person known to present an imminent danger;

(ii) reducing the likelihood of flight;

(iii) preventing the destruction of evidence and providing an opportunity to obtain evidence of a crime pursuant to a search incident to arrest;

(iv) stopping or deterring the harassment or coercion of witnesses or other acts of obstruction of justice;

(v) creating an opportunity to ask questions about an unrelated crime;

(vi) encouraging other culpable individuals or witnesses to surrender to law enforcement and to cooperate with the investigation;

(vii) inducing relevant conversation or other communication likely to be intercepted by law enforcement; and

(viii) protecting the existence of an undercover agent or confidential informant, a cooperator or an undercover operation.

(b) In deciding whether, when or where to arrest a subject during a continuing investigation, the prosecutor should consider the potential risks of the arrest, including:

(i) limiting the continued conduct of a criminal investigation by alerting others involved in continuing criminal activity;

(ii) restricting the use of some investigative techniques;

(iii) triggering speedy charge and speedy trial rules;

(iv) triggering disclosure obligations that have been subject to delayed notice;

(v) appearing to be illegitimate or pre-textual and thus adversely affecting community support for police and prosecution efforts; and

(vi) causing significant shame, embarrassment or prejudice to the arrestee or innocent third parties and unintended and unfair financial impacts.

(c) The prosecutor should be aware that Sixth Amendment right to counsel issues raised by the filing of criminal charges may limit the availability of some investigative options, including:

(i) use of the grand jury as an investigative technique;

(ii) soliciting incriminating information from a charged individual; and

(iii) contacts with the individuals or entities who have been charged.

Standard 2.7 Use of Subpoenas

(a) As used in these Standards, a "subpoena," however named or designated, is a written command for a person or entity to provide physical evidence, testimony or documents. A subpoena may be issued by a prosecutor, a court, a grand jury or a law enforcement agency, as provided by the law of the jurisdiction.

(b) In deciding whether to use a subpoena, the prosecutor should consider potential benefits including:

(i) the conservation of law enforcement resources by requiring others to search for and provide factual information and physical evidence needed for an investigation;

(ii) the imposition of an obligation on the subject of the subpoena to provide factual information or physical evidence;

(iii) the fact that no predicate or less of a showing is required to issue a subpoena, as compared to a search warrant;

(iv) the ability to delay or prevent a third party from voluntarily or compulsorily disclosing information about the subpoena (including the disclosure of either the fact of the subpoena itself or of any information provided in response) as a means to preserve the secrecy of the investigation if authorized by law; and

(v) voluntary disclosures or cooperation by witnesses and subjects prompted by receipt of the subpoena.

(c) In deciding whether to use a subpoena, the prosecutor should consider the following potential risks and ways to mitigate them:

(i) that evidence will be destroyed or altered in between receipt and production;

(ii) that information responsive to the subpoena will be improperly withheld or that the request will be interpreted narrowly; and

(iii) that knowledge of the subpoena will cause the subjects of the investigation to disguise criminal activity, or take actions to impede or obstruct the investigation.

(d) The prosecutor using a subpoena should:

(i) seek to limit the scope of the subpoena to the needs of the investigation, avoid overbroad requests, and avoid seeking the production of attorney-client privileged material; and

(ii) provide reasonable accommodations based on factors such as the size or nature of the request, the impact of the request on legitimate business operations, or the time reasonably needed to perform a review for privileged or other legally protected fact information, unless doing so would be outweighed by the government's interest in avoiding delay.

(e) The prosecutor should ensure that materials received pursuant to a subpoena are properly stored, logged or indexed, and are readily retrievable.

(f) The prosecutor should accept copies of documents subject to a subpoena unless there is a specific need for original documents that outweighs the producing party's need and right to retain its original materials.

(g) The prosecutor should provide copies, or if necessary, reasonable access to copies or original documents to the person or entity who has produced the copies or originals.

(h) The prosecutor should seek to minimize the cost and dislocation suffered by a person or entity to whom a subpoena is issued and, where applicable, should inform the person or entity of any right to compensation allowed by law.

(i) The prosecutor should arrange for the return of subpoenaed documents and materials when the purpose for which they were subpoenaed has ended.

(j) The prosecutor involved in an investigation where police or law enforcement agents have legal authority to issue written requests for various records and data without probable cause or judicial oversight, should provide advice as to whether the proposed use of such authority is consistent with the limits of the applicable law, the Constitution, and the circumstances of the investigation.

Standard 2.8 Search Warrants

(a) As used in these Standards a "search warrant" is a written command issued by a judge or magistrate that permits law enforcement agents to search specified persons or premises and seize specified effects and information.

(b) The prosecutor should consider the following potential benefits associated with using a search warrant:

(i) securing evidence that might otherwise be removed, hidden, altered or destroyed;

(ii) removing contraband from commerce before it is transferred or used;

(iii) seeing and documenting the precise location of the items to be seized in their natural or unaltered state or location;

(iv) obtaining statements by individuals at the scene of the search that might further the investigation;

(v) observing and recording the presence of individuals found together at the scene of the search as evidence of their coordination; and

(vi) encouraging other culpable individuals or witnesses to come forward and provide information to the investigation.

(c) The prosecutor should consider the following potential costs and risks before applying for a search warrant:

(i) the extensive utilization of limited government resources during the preparation and execution of a search warrant, as compared with other means of gathering information, such as a subpoena;

(ii) the intrusive nature of the execution of the warrant and its impact on personal privacy or on legitimate business operations;

(iii) the impact of execution of the warrant on innocent third parties who may be on the premises at the time the warrant is executed; and

(iv) the potential danger or harm to third parties.

(d) When the prosecutor is involved in an investigation, the prosecutor should review search warrant applications prior to their submission to a judicial officer. In all other cases, the prosecutor should encourage police and law enforcement agents to seek prosecutorial review and approval of search warrants prior to their submission to a judicial officer.

(e) In jurisdictions that authorize telephonic warrants, the prosecutor should be familiar with the rules governing the use of such warrants and should be available to confer with law enforcement agents about them.

(f) In reviewing a search warrant application, the prosecutor should:

(i) seek to assure the affidavit is complete, accurate and legally sufficient;

(ii) seek to determine the veracity of the affiant and the accuracy of the information, especially when the application is based on information from a confidential informant; and

(iii) seek to ensure that the affidavit is not misleading and does not omit material information which has a significant bearing on probable cause.

(g) The prosecutor involved in the investigation should:

(i) generally, if time permits, meet in advance with all law enforcement and other personnel who will participate in the execution of the warrant to explain the scope of the warrant, including the area(s) to be searched and the items to be seized;

(ii) consistent with the goals of the investigation, provide legitimate business operations and third parties reasonable access to seized records;

(iii) avoid becoming a necessary percipient witness at the scene of the execution of the warrant but be readily available and accessible to respond to immediate questions or to assist in the preparation of additional warrant applications;

(iv) seek to ensure that an inventory is filed as required by relevant rules; and

(v) seek to preserve exculpatory evidence obtained during a search and consider the impact of such evidence on the criminal investigation.

(h) When searching an attorney's office, or any place where attorney-client or other privileged material is likely to be located or is discovered, the prosecutor should arrange for evidence to be recovered in such manner as to prevent or minimize any unauthorized intrusion into confidential relationships or information privileged under law.

(i) The prosecutor should seek to prevent or minimize the disclosure of information to the public which a person or entity may consider private or proprietary.

(j) The prosecutor should consider seeking to delay notice about the execution of a search warrant if such delay is authorized by law and if prompt disclosure of the execution of the warrant could reasonably be expected to result in:

(i) the endangerment of life or physical safety of an individual;

(ii) the intimidation of potential witnesses;

(iii) the flight from prosecution by a target of any investigation;

(iv) the destruction of or tampering with evidence in any investigation; or

(v) any other serious jeopardy to an investigation.

(k) The prosecutor should not notify media representatives of a search before it occurs and should advise law enforcement agents acting with the prosecutor in the investigation not to do so.

(*l*) The prosecutor should consider whether the papers supporting the search warrant should be sealed after the warrant is executed and should make application to do so only when the prosecutor believes that the public's interest in knowing of the warrant is outweighed by the need to maintain secrecy of the investigation or to prevent unfair publicity to the persons or organizations whose premises were searched.

Standard 2.9 Use of the Investigative Powers of the Grand Jury

(a) In deciding whether to use a grand jury, the prosecutor should consider the potential benefits of the power of the grand jury to compel testimony or elicit other evidence by:

(i) conferring immunity upon witnesses;

(ii) obtaining evidence in a confidential forum;

(iii) obtaining evidence from a witness who elects not to speak voluntarily to the police or prosecutor;

(iv) obtaining documentary or testimonial evidence with the added reliability provided by the oath and the secrecy requirements of the grand jury;

(v) obtaining documentary evidence from a third party that may be difficult to obtain from a target; and

(vi) preserving witnesses' accounts in the form of sworn testimony where the jurisdiction provides for recording or transcription of the proceedings.

(b) In deciding whether to use a grand jury, the prosecutor should consider the potential risks including:

(i) revealing the existence or direction of an investigation;

(ii) obtaining evasive or untruthful testimony from witnesses who are loyal to targets or fearful of them;

(iii) relying on witnesses to obey the commands of subpoenas directing them to produce documents or physical evidence;

(iv) granting immunity to witnesses:

(A) who are not believed culpable at the time of the grant but are later found to be culpable; or

(B) who are later found to be more culpable than the prosecutor believed at the time of the grant;

(v) exposing grand jury witnesses to reputational, economic or physical reprisal; and

(vi) exposing grand jury witnesses to collateral consequences such as lost time from employment or family obligations, financial costs of compliance, and potential damage to their reputation from association with a criminal investigation.

(c) In pursuing an investigation through the grand jury, the prosecutor should:

(i) only bring a matter before the grand jury with the primary purpose of seeking justice and to be mindful of the ex parte nature of proceedings;

(ii) prepare adequately before conducting grand jury examinations;

(iii) know and follow the laws of the jurisdiction and the rules, practices, and policies of the prosecutor's office;

(iv) pose only legal and proper questions and, if within the knowledge of the prosecutor questioning may elicit a privileged or self-incriminating response, advise the witness of the existence of the applicable privilege; and

(v) unless prohibited by the law of the jurisdiction, ensure that grand jury proceedings are recorded.

(d) The prosecutor should use grand jury processes fairly and should:

(i) treat grand jurors with courtesy and give them the opportunity to have appropriate questions answered; however, the prosecutor should not allow questions that:

(A) elicit facts about the investigation that should not become known to the witness; or

(B) call for privileged, prejudicial, misleading or irrelevant evidence;

(ii) issue a subpoena ad testificandum only if the prosecutor intends to bring the witness before the grand jury;

(iii) refrain from issuing a subpoena that is excessively broad or immaterial to the legitimate scope of the grand jury's inquiry;

(iv) make reasonable efforts before a witness appears at the grand jury to determine that the testimony is needed, including offering the witness or witness' counsel a voluntary pre-appearance conference;

(v) grant reasonable requests for extensions of dates for appearance and production of documents when doing so does not impede the grand jury's investigation; and

(vi) resist dilatory tactics by witnesses that undermine the grand jury's investigation, authority, or credibility.

(e) The prosecutor should examine witnesses with courtesy and in a manner designed to elicit truthful testimony, and should:

(i) consider warning a witness suspected of perjury of the obligations to tell the truth;

(ii) insist upon definite answers that will:

(A) fully inform the members of grand jury; and

(B) establish a clear record so that a witness committing perjury or contempt can be held responsible for such actions;

(iii) inform grand jury witnesses of their right to consult with their attorneys to the extent provided by the policy, procedure or law of the jurisdiction; and

(iv) seek a compulsion order only when the testimony sought is in the public interest, there is no other reasonable way to elicit such testimony, and the witness has refused to testify or has indicated an intent to invoke the privilege against self-incrimination.

(f) In determining whether obtaining testimony from a culpable witness will outweigh the cost of granting immunity, a prosecutor should consider the following factors:

(i) the relative culpability of the witness to be immunized as compared with the person against whom the testimony will be offered;

(ii) the gravity of the crime(s) being investigated;

(iii) the probability that the testimony would advance the investigation or an eventual prosecution;

(iv) the gravity of the crime(s) for which the witness would be granted immunity;

(v) the character and history of the witness being considered for immunity, including how these factors might affect the witness's credibility;

(vi) the scope of the immunity that the witness would receive;

(vii) the risk that the immunized witness would lie or feign lack of memory;

(viii) the risk that the immunized witness would falsely claim responsibility for criminal acts committed by another; and

(ix) the potential for the grand jury testimony to enhance truthful testimony by hostile or reluctant witnesses at trial or provide evidence to prove perjury if a witness lies at trial.

(g) Ordinarily, the prosecutor should not seek to compel testimony from a close relative of a target of an investigation by threatening prosecution or offering immunity, unless:

(i) the relative participated criminally in an offense or criminal enterprise with the target and the testimony sought would relate to that enterprise's activities;

(ii) the testimony sought relates to a crime involving overriding prosecutorial concerns; or

(iii) comparable testimony is not readily available from other sources.

(h) Ordinarily, the prosecutor should give notice to a target of a grand jury investigation and offer the opportunity for the target to testify without immunity before the grand jury. However, notice need not be provided if there is a reasonable possibility it will result in flight of the target, endanger other persons, or obstruct justice. Prior to taking a target's testimony, the prosecutor should advise the target of the privilege against self-incrimination and obtain a waiver of that right.

(i) A prosecutor with personal knowledge of non-frivolous evidence that directly negates the guilt of a subject of the investigation should present or otherwise disclose that evidence to the grand jury. If evidence is provided to the prosecutor by the subject or target of the investigation and the prosecutor decides not to provide the evidence to the grand jury, the prosecutor should notify the subject, target or their counsel of that decision without delay, so long as doing so would not jeopardize the investigation or prosecution or endanger others.

Standard 2.10 Technologically-Assisted Physical Surveillance

(a) As used in these Standards, "technologically-assisted physical surveillance" includes: video surveillance, tracking devices, illumination devices, telescopic devices, and detection devices.

(b) In deciding whether to use technologically-assisted physical surveillance, the prosecutor should consider the potential benefits, including:

(i) detecting the criminal possession of objects that are dangerous or difficult to locate; and

(ii) seeing or tracing criminal activity by means that are minimally intrusive and limiting the risks posed to the public and law enforcement personnel.

(c) In deciding whether to use technologically-assisted physical surveillance, the prosecutor should consider the legal and privacy implications for subjects, victims and third parties. The prosecutor should seek to use such surveillance techniques in proportion to the seriousness of the criminal activity being investigated and the needs of the particular investigation and in a manner designed to be minimally intrusive.

(d) In deciding whether to use technologically-assisted physical surveillance, the prosecutor should consider the legal requirements applicable to the technique under consideration, and whether those requirements have been met.

Standard 2.11 Consensual Interception, Transmission and Recording of Communications

(a) As used in these Standards "consensual interception" is an electronic, digital, audio or video interception and recording of communications to which one or more but not all participants in the communications has consented.

(b) In deciding whether to use consensual interception, the prosecutor should consider the potential benefits, including obtaining direct, incriminating, and credible evidence that can be used alone or to corroborate other information.

(c) In deciding whether to use consensual interception, the prosecutor should consider the potential risks, including:

(i) problems of audibility and admissibility;

(ii) the danger of detection, including physical risk to those participating, and the risk of disclosure of the investigation;

(iii) selective recording of communications by the cooperating party;

(iv) the danger of obtaining false, misleading or self-serving statements by a party to the conversation who is aware or suspects that the conversation is being recorded;

(v) the risk that the consenting individual will conspire with the subject of the investigation to create false or misleading statements; and

(vi) the risk that the import of a conversation will be distorted by the cooperating party.

(d) To maximize the benefits and to minimize the risks of using consensual interception, the prosecutor should:

(i) obtain written or recorded consent from the consenting individual; and minimize to the extent practicable recording outside the presence of law enforcement agents and, if such a recording occurs or will occur:

(A) have law enforcement agents test and activate the recording equipment before the cooperating party meets with the subject; and

(B) minimize the necessity for the cooperating party to operate the recording equipment and, if it is necessary for the cooperating party to operate the equipment, provide that individual specific directions on how to operate the equipment and strict instruction to be present with it during such operation.

(e) The prosecutor, in consultation with the law enforcement agents, should regularly review all or selected recordings obtained during consensual interceptions.

(f) The prosecutor should take steps to ensure law enforcement agents comply with procedures relating to the acquisition of, custody of, and access to electronic equipment and recording media and to the secure preservation of any recordings produced whether they are obtained by consenting individuals or by law enforcement agents.

Standard 2.12 Non-Consensual Electronic Surveillance

(a) As used in these Standards "non-consensual electronic surveillance" is the court-ordered interception of communications, actions, or events.

(b) In deciding whether to request a court order for non-consensual electronic surveillance, the prosecutor should consider the potential benefit of obtaining direct, incriminating, and credible evidence that can be used alone or to corroborate other information.

(c) In deciding whether to request a court order for non-consensual electronic surveillance, the prosecutor should consider the potential costs and risks, including:

(i) whether the suspected criminal activity being investigated is sufficiently serious and persistent to justify:

(A) the significant intrusion on the privacy interests of targets and innocent third parties;

(B) the need to obtain periodic reauthorization for electronic surveillance; and

(C) the financial and resource costs associated with such surveillance.

(ii) whether all requirements of the law are met.

(d) The prosecutor, including an applicant, should be aware of the reporting requirements under federal and state law and heightened obligations and accountability to the court in connection with the application and use of non-consensual electronic surveillance.

(e) Prior to the initiation of non-consensual electronic surveillance, the prosecutor should review the following with the law enforcement agents and contract personnel such as interpreters who will assist in the execution of the order:

(i) the scope of the order;

(ii) obligations of the monitoring law enforcement agents and monitoring personnel to minimize the interception of privileged conversations and other conversations outside the scope of the order and to alert the prosecutor promptly when recording evidence of new crimes;

(iii) the prohibition on listening without recording;

(iv) rules related to protecting the integrity and chain of custody of recordings;

(v) instructions to contact the prosecutor whenever a noteworthy event occurs, or there is a question regarding the execution of the order; and

(vi) the need to adhere to non-disclosure requirements.

(f) The prosecutor should stay informed of actions of law enforcement agents and contract personnel throughout the use of non-consensual electronic surveillance and should take appropriate steps to determine whether the required procedures are being followed by those carrying out the surveillance.

Standard 2.13 Conducting Parallel Civil and Criminal Investigations

(a) In deciding whether to conduct a criminal investigation and throughout any such investigation that is undertaken, the prosecutor should consider whether society's interest in the matter might be better or equally vindicated by available civil, regulatory, administrative, or private remedies.

(b) When doing so would not compromise a proper prosecutorial interest, and to the degree permitted by law, the prosecutor should cooperate with other governmental authorities regarding their investigations for the purpose of instituting remedial actions that are of legitimate concern to such entities. In the course of such cooperation, the prosecutor:

(i) should retain sole control of the criminal investigation and maintain independent judgment at all times;

(ii) should be aware of rules that prohibit or restrict the sharing or disclosure of information or material gathered through certain criminal investigative techniques;

(iii) should not be a party to nor allow the continuation of efforts by civil investigative agencies or attorneys to use the criminal process for the purpose of obtaining a civil settlement; and

(iv) may, in order to preserve the integrity of a criminal investigation or prosecution, ask a civil investigative agency to refrain from taking an investigative step or bringing an action but, in considering whether to do so, should consider the detriment to the public that may result from such forbearance.

(c) A prosecutor should consider the appropriateness of non-criminal or global (civil and criminal resolutions) dispositions suggested by subjects or targets, whether or not they choose to cooperate, and may consider proposals by them to include civil or regulatory sanctions as part of a disposition or cooperation agreement.

Standard 2.14 Terminating the Investigation, Retention of Evidence and Post-Investigation Analysis

(a) The prosecutor should diligently pursue the timely conclusion of criminal investigations.

(b) The prosecutor's office should periodically review matters under investigation in the office and determine whether the interests of justice would be served by terminating the investigation.

(c) The prosecutor should determine whether information obtained in investigations should be made available for civil enforcement purposes, administrative remedies, or for other purposes consistent with law and the public interest.

(d) To the extent feasible, the prosecutor and members of the investigative agencies should analyze investigations retrospectively, to evaluate techniques and steps that worked well or that proved to be deficient.

(e) Post-investigation analysis by the prosecutor's office should include seeking to identify ways other than prosecution to prevent, minimize or deter similar crimes from occurring in the future.

(f) Prosecutors should be aware of the requirements and office practices regarding the preservation of investigative records and of their compliance obligations with regard to information access and privacy law provisions.

(g) To the extent practicable, the prosecutor should, upon request, provide notice of termination of the investigation to subjects who became aware of the investigation.

(h) Upon termination of the investigation and related proceedings, physical evidence other than contraband should be returned promptly to the person from whom it was obtained, absent an agreement, court order or requirement of law to the contrary.

Standard 2.15 Guidance and Training for Line Prosecutors

(a) A prosecutor's office should be organized in a manner to provide line prosecutors guidance consistent with these Standards.

(b) To guide the exercise of discretion, a prosecutor's office should:

(i) encourage consultation and collaboration among prosecutors;

(ii) appoint supervisors with appropriate experience, strong skills and a commitment to justice and ethical behavior;

(iii) require consultation and approval at appropriate supervisory levels for investigative methods of different levels of intrusiveness, risk and costs;

(iv) provide regular supervisory review throughout the course of investigations;

(v) regularly review investigative techniques and promote best practices to reflect changes in law and policy;

(vi) create and implement internal policies, procedures, and standard practices that teach and reinforce standards of excellence in performance, professionalism, and ethics;

(vii) create and implement policies and procedures that protect against practices that could result in unfair hardships, the pursuit of baseless investigations, and the bringing of charges against the innocent;

(viii) develop and support practices designed to prevent and to rectify conviction of the innocent.

(ix) determine what types of investigative steps require formal supervisory approval, and at what supervisory level, and

(x) require line attorneys to consult with supervisors or experienced colleagues when making significant investigative decisions absent exigent circumstances.

(c) A prosecutor's office should provide guidance and training by:

(i) strongly encouraging consultation and collaboration among line assistants;

(ii) appointing supervisors with appropriate experience and strong commitments to justice, and fostering close working relationships between supervisors and those they supervise;

(iii) providing formal training programs on investigative techniques and the ethical choices implicated in using them; and

(iv) creating internal policies and standard practices regarding investigations that memorialize and reinforce standards of excellence, professionalism, and ethics. In doing so:

(A) policy and practice materials should be regularly reviewed and updated and should allow flexibility for the exercise of prosecutorial discretion, and

(B) written policies and procedures should not be a substitute for regular training for all office members and a commitment to mentoring less-experienced attorneys.

(d) When a line prosecutor believes the needs of an investigation or some extraordinary circumstance require actions that are contrary to or outside of existing policies, the prosecutor should seek prior approval before taking such actions.

(e) A prosecutor's office should develop policies and procedures that address the initiation and implementation of the investigative tools discussed in these Standards in advance of the specific needs of an investigation.

Standard 2.16 Special Prosecutors, Independent Counsel and Special Prosecution Units

(a) As used in these Standards, a "special prosecutor" or an "independent counsel" is a prosecutor serving independently from the general prosecution office under a particularized appointment and whose service in that role typically ends after the purpose of the appointment is completed. A "special prosecution unit" is typically a unit that focuses on a particular type of crime, criminal activity, or victim.

(b) Although the special prosecutor and the special prosecution unit are removed from the responsibilities of a general prosecution office, a prosecutor in this role should:

(i) be bound by the same policies and procedures as regular prosecutors in their jurisdiction, unless to do so would be incompatible with their duties;

(ii) base judgments about the merits of pursuing a particular investigation upon the same factors that should guide a regular prosecutor, including the seriousness of the offense, the harm to the public, and the expenditure of public resources; and

(iii) in choosing matters to investigate, consider the danger that the narrow focus or limited jurisdiction of the prosecutor or the unit will lead to the pursuit of what would, in a general prosecution office, be considered an insubstantial violation, or one more appropriately resolved by civil or administrative actions.

Standard 2.17 Use of Information, Money, or Resources Provided by Non-Governmental Sources

(a) The prosecutor may use information provided by non-governmental sources that is pertinent to a potential or existing criminal investigation. However, consistent with the principles in Standard 2.1, the prosecutor should make an independent evaluation of the information and make an independent decision as to whether to allocate or continue to allocate resources to investigating the matter.

(b) If the law of the jurisdiction permits the acceptance of financial or resource assistance from non-governmental sources, the decision to accept such assistance should be made with caution by the chief public prosecutor or an accountable designee after careful consideration of:

(i) the extent to which the law of the jurisdiction permits the acceptance of financial or resource assistance;

(ii) the extent to which the offer is in the public interest, as opposed to an effort to achieve the limited private interests of the non-governmental sources;

(iii) the extent to which acceptance may result in foregoing other cases;

(iv) the potential adverse impact on the equal administration of the criminal law;

(v) the extent to which the character and magnitude of the assistance might unduly influence the prosecutor's subsequent exercise of investigative and prosecutorial discretion;

(vi) the likelihood that the community may view accepting the assistance as inconsistent with the fair and equal administration of criminal justice;

(vii) the likelihood that accepting assistance from private sources may create an appearance of undue influence over law enforcement; and

(viii) the extent to which financial or resource assistance would enhance or enable the investigation of criminal activity;

(c) The prosecutor should consider the risk that encouraging information gathering from non-governmental sources may lead to abusive, dangerous or even criminal actions by private parties.

(d) The office of the prosecutor should have procedures designed to protect the independent exercise of investigative discretion from being influenced by the receipt of outside financial or resource assistance, including careful accounting and recordkeeping of the amounts and terms of such assistance and clear disclosure that providing assistance will not guide the exercise of investigative or prosecutorial discretion.

(e) The prosecutor, consistent with the law of the jurisdiction, should disclose significant non-governmental assistance to relevant legislative or public bodies having oversight over the prosecutor's office and, when appropriate, the public.

(f) Non-governmental assistance should be disclosed to affected parties as part of the discovery process.

Standard 2.18 Use of Sensitive, Classified or Other Information Implicating Investigative Privileges

(a) The prosecutor should be alert to the need to balance the government's legitimate interests in protecting certain information from disclosure, and the legitimate interests and Constitutional rights of the public and of defendants favoring disclosure.

(b) When appropriate, the prosecutor should request court orders designed to protect the disclosure of law enforcement means and methods, informant identities, observation posts, and such other information that might jeopardize future investigations or the safety or reputation of persons directly or indirectly involved in an investigation.

(c) In investigations believed to have the potential to include classified or sensitive information, prosecutors should seek to obtain the relevant information and consult laws, regulations and other requirements for handling such information before making any charging decisions.

PART 3. PROSECUTOR'S ROLE IN RESOLVING INVESTIGATION PROBLEMS

Standard 3.1 Prosecutor's Role in Addressing Suspected Law Enforcement Misconduct

(a) If the prosecutor has reason to suspect misconduct or unauthorized illegal activity at any level of the prosecutor's office or in any agency or department engaged in a criminal investigation, the prosecutor should promptly report the suspicion and the reason for it to appropriate supervisory personnel in the prosecutor's office who have authority to address the problem, or to the appropriate inspector general's office, or similar agency, if reporting within the prosecutor's own office is problematic. Reporting may also be required to comply with requirements of the applicable rules of professional conduct, the Model Rules and the law of the jurisdiction.

(b) If the prosecutor has reason to believe that a criminal investigation or prosecution is, or is likely to be, adversely affected by incompetence, lack of skilled personnel or inadequate resources in the prosecutor's office or in any other relevant agency or department, the prosecutor should promptly report that belief and the reason for it to supervisory personnel in the prosecutor's office.

(c) A supervisory prosecutor who receives an allegation of misconduct, unauthorized illegal conduct, or who receives an allegation of incompetence, inadequate resources, or lack of skilled personnel that is, or is likely to, adversely affect a criminal investigation, should undertake a prompt and objective review of the facts and circumstances or refer the matter to an appropriate agency or component responsible for addressing such allegations. When practicable, the line prosecutor making any such allegations should not be involved in subsequent investigation(s) relating to the allegation(s).

(d) If the prosecutor's office concludes that there is a reasonable belief that personnel in any agency or department have engaged in unauthorized illegal conduct, the prosecutor's office should initiate a criminal investigation into the conduct or seek the initiation of such an investigation by an appropriate outside agency or office.

(e) If the prosecutor's office concludes that there was not unauthorized illegal conduct, but concludes that there was incompetence or non-criminal misconduct, the prosecutor's office should take appropriate action to notify the relevant agency or department, and if within the prosecutor's own office, to impose sanctions for the conduct.

(f) Decisions on how to respond to allegations of unauthorized illegal conduct, misconduct, or significant incompetence should generally be made without regard to adverse consequences on pending cases or investigations.

Standard 3.2 Prosecutor's Role in Addressing Suspected Judicial Misconduct

(a) Although judges are not exempt from criminal investigation, the prosecutor's office should protect against the use of false allegations as a means of harassment or abuse that may impact the independence of the judiciary.

(b) If a line prosecutor has reason to believe that there is significant misconduct or illegal activity by a member of the judiciary, the line prosecutor should promptly report that belief and the reasons for it to supervisory personnel in the prosecutor's office.

(c) Upon receiving from a line prosecutor, or from any source, an allegation of significant misconduct or illegal conduct by a member of the judiciary, a supervisory prosecutor should undertake a prompt and objective review of the facts and circumstances.

(d) If the prosecutor's office has a reasonable belief that a member of the judiciary has engaged in criminal conduct, the prosecutor's office should initiate, or seek the initiation of, a criminal investigation.

(e) If the prosecutor's office concludes that a member of the judiciary has not engaged in illegal conduct, but has engaged in non-criminal misconduct, the prosecutor's office should take appropriate action to inform the relevant officer of the judicial authorities. Reporting may also be required to comply with requirements of the applicable rules of professional conduct, the Model Rules and the law of the jurisdiction.

(f) The prosecutor's office should take reasonable steps to assure the independence of any investigation of a judge before whom the prosecutor's office practices. In some instances, this may require the appointment of a "pro tem" or "special" prosecutor or use of a "fire-wall" within the prosecutor's office.

Standard 3.3 Prosecutor's Role in Addressing Suspected Misconduct by Defense Counsel

(a) Although defense counsel are not exempt from criminal investigation, the prosecutor's office should protect against the use of false allegations as a means of harassment or abuse that may impact the independence of the defense counsel or the Constitutionally protected right to counsel.

(b) If a line prosecutor has reason to believe that defense counsel is engaging in criminal conduct, is violating the duty to protect a client, or is engaging in unethical behavior or misconduct, the prosecutor should promptly report that belief and the reasons for it to supervisory personnel in the prosecutor's office.

(c) Upon receiving from a line prosecutor, or from any source, an allegation of misconduct or illegal conduct by defense counsel, a supervisory prosecutor should undertake a prompt and objective review of the facts and circumstances.

(d) If the prosecutor's office has a reasonable belief that defense counsel has engaged in illegal conduct, the prosecutor's office should initiate, or seek the initiation of, an investigation into the conduct.

(e) If the prosecutor's office concludes that defense counsel has not engaged in illegal conduct, but has engaged in non-criminal misconduct as defined by the governing ethical code and the rules of the jurisdiction, the prosecutor's office should take appropriate action to inform the appropriate disciplinary authority.

(f) The prosecutor's office should take reasonable steps to assure the independence of any investigation of a defense counsel including, if appropriate, the appointment of a pro tem or special prosecutor or use of a "fire-wall" within the prosecutor's office. At a minimum, an investigation of defense counsel's conduct should be conducted by a prosecutor who has not been involved in the initial matter or in ongoing matters with that defense counsel.

(g) The prosecutor investigating defense counsel should consider whether information regarding conduct by defense counsel should be provided to a judicial officer involved in overseeing aspects of the investigation in which the misconduct occurred.

(h) The prosecutor investigating defense counsel who is representing a client in a criminal matter under the jurisdiction of the prosecutor's office ordinarily should notify the attorney and the court in a timely manner about the possibility that potential charges against the attorney may create a conflict of interest.

Standard 3.4 Prosecutor's Role in Addressing Suspected Misconduct by Witnesses, Informants or Jurors

(a) If a line prosecutor has reason to believe that there has been illegal conduct or non-criminal misconduct by witnesses, informants, or jurors, the prosecutor should seek supervisory review of the matter.

(b) Upon receiving an allegation of unauthorized illegal conduct or non-criminal misconduct by witnesses, informants or jurors, the prosecutor's office should undertake a prompt and objective review. If there is a reasonable belief that there has been illegal conduct or non-criminal misconduct, the prosecutor's office should initiate an investigation into the conduct. All relevant evidence should be preserved in the event it must be disclosed if criminal charges are filed against the individual alleged to have engaged in the conduct.

(c) If the misconduct relates to the official duties of a juror or witness, it must also be reported to an appropriate judicial officer.

Standard 3.5 Illegally Obtained Evidence

(a) If a prosecutor reasonably believes that evidence has been illegally obtained, the prosecutor should consider whether there are potential criminal acts that should be investigated or misconduct that should be addressed or reported. The prosecutor should be familiar with the laws of their jurisdiction regarding the admissibility of illegally obtained evidence.

(b) The prosecutor should take appropriate steps to limit the taint, if any, from the illegally obtained evidence and determine if the evidence may still be lawfully used.

(c) The prosecutor should notify the parties affected by the illegal conduct at the earliest time that will not compromise the investigation or subsequent investigation, or at an earlier time if required by law.

Standard 3.6 Responding to Political Pressure and Consideration of the Impact of Criminal Investigations on the Political Process

(a) The prosecutor should resist political pressure intended to influence the conduct, focus, duration or outcome of a criminal investigation.

(b) The prosecutor should generally not make decisions related to a criminal investigation based upon their impact on the political process.

(c) When, due to the nature of the investigation or the identity of investigative targets, any decision will have some impact on the political process (such as an impending election), the prosecutor should make decisions and use discretion in a principled manner and in a manner designed to limit the political impact without regard to the prosecutor's personal political beliefs or affiliations.

(d) The prosecutor should carefully consider the language in Standard 1.5 ("Contacts with the Public During the Investigative Process") when making any statements or reports regarding a decision to prosecute, or to decline to prosecute, in a matter that may have some impact on the political process.

Standard 3.7 Review and Oversight of Criminal Investigations by Government Agencies and Officials

(a) Prosecutors' offices should attempt to respond in a timely, open, and candid manner to requests from public officials for general information about the enforcement of laws under their jurisdiction or about law reform matters. However, if public officials seek information about ongoing or impending investigations, the prosecutors' offices should consider the potential negative impact of providing such information and should inform public officials about such concerns.

(b) Generally, responses to public officials should be made by high-ranking officials in the prosecutor's office who have policy-making authority. Prosecutors' offices should resist allowing line-attorneys to respond to requests for information by public officials.

(c) Generally, responses to information requests by public officials should be through testimony or by providing pertinent statistics and descriptive and analytical reports, and not by providing information about particular matters. Prosecutors' offices should resist requests for materials that are subject to deliberative process or work product privileges related to pending criminal investigations or closed investigations whose materials have not otherwise been made public, and should oppose disclosure of information that would adversely affect a person or entity.

(d) Prosecutor's offices may respond to requests about the handling of fully adjudicated cases. Absent unusual circumstances, information about adjudicated cases should be provided by high-ranking officials with policy-making authority, and not by line attorneys.

(e) The Prosecutor's office should establish clear and consistent policies to address its responsibilities under public disclosure laws and with regard to the public's potential access to closed matters. The Prosecutor's office should provide sufficient resources to make prompt and appropriate replies to any public disclosure requests.

CIRCULAR 230 REGULATING PRACTICE BEFORE THE TREASURY

31 C.F.R. §§ 10.0–10.97 (2019)

Table of Contents

PART 10. PRACTICE BEFORE THE INTERNAL REVENUE SERVICE

* Sections 10.5, 10.6, 10.9, 10.38, 10.90, 10.91, 10.92, and 10.93 have been omitted.—Ed.

PART 10. PRACTICE BEFORE THE INTERNAL REVENUE SERVICE

§ 10.0 Scope of Part.

(a) This part contains rules governing the recognition of attorneys, certified public accountants, enrolled agents, enrolled retirement plan agents, registered tax return preparers, and other persons representing taxpayers before the Internal Revenue Service. Subpart A of this part sets forth rules relating to the authority to practice before the Internal Revenue Service; subpart B of this part prescribes the duties and restrictions relating to such practice; subpart C of this part prescribes the sanctions for violating the regulations; subpart D of this part contains the rules applicable to disciplinary proceedings; and subpart E of this part contains general provisions relating to the availability of official records.

(b) Effective/applicability date. This section is applicable beginning August 2, 2011.

§ 10.1 Offices.

(a) Establishment of office(s). The Commissioner shall establish the Office of Professional Responsibility and any other office(s) within the Internal Revenue Service necessary to administer and enforce this part. The Commissioner shall appoint the Director of the Office of Professional Responsibility and any other Internal Revenue official(s) to manage and direct any office(s) established to administer or enforce this part. Offices established under this part include, but are not limited to:

(1) The Office of Professional Responsibility, which shall generally have responsibility for matters related to practitioner conduct and shall have exclusive responsibility for discipline, including disciplinary proceedings and sanctions; and

(2) An office with responsibility for matters related to authority to practice before the Internal Revenue Service, including acting on applications for enrollment to practice before the Internal Revenue Service and administering competency testing and continuing education.

(b) Officers and employees within any office established under this part may perform acts necessary or appropriate to carry out the responsibilities of their office(s) under this part or as otherwise prescribed by the Commissioner.

(c) Acting. The Commissioner will designate an officer or employee of the Internal Revenue Service to perform the duties of an individual appointed under paragraph (a) of this section in the absence of that officer or employee or during a vacancy in that office.

(d) Effective/applicability date. This section is applicable beginning August 2, 2011, except that paragraph (a)(1) is applicable beginning June 12, 2014.

§ 10.2 Definitions.

(a) As used in this part, except where the text provides otherwise—

(1) Attorney means any person who is a member in good standing of the bar of the highest court of any state, territory, or possession of the United States, including a Commonwealth, or the District of Columbia.

(2) Certified public accountant means any person who is duly qualified to practice as a certified public accountant in any state, territory, or possession of the United States, including a Commonwealth, or the District of Columbia.

(3) Commissioner refers to the Commissioner of Internal Revenue.

(4) Practice before the Internal Revenue Service comprehends all matters connected with a presentation to the Internal Revenue Service or any of its officers or employees relating to a taxpayer's rights, privileges, or liabilities under laws or regulations administered by the Internal Revenue Service. Such presentations include, but are not limited to, preparing documents; filing documents; corresponding and communicating with the Internal Revenue Service; rendering written advice with respect to any entity, transaction, plan or arrangement, or other plan or arrangement having a potential for tax avoidance or evasion; and representing a client at conferences, hearings, and meetings.

(5) Practitioner means any individual described in paragraphs (a), (b), (c), (d), (e), or (f) of § 10.3.

(6) A **tax return** includes an amended tax return and a claim for refund.

(7) Service means the Internal Revenue Service.

(8) Tax return preparer means any individual within the meaning of section 7701(a)(36) and 26 CFR 301.7701–15.

(b) Effective/applicability date. This section is applicable beginning August 2, 2011.

SUBPART A. RULES GOVERNING AUTHORITY TO PRACTICE

§ 10.3 Who May Practice.

(a) Attorneys. Any attorney who is not currently under suspension or disbarment from practice before the Internal Revenue Service may practice before the Internal Revenue Service by filing with the Internal Revenue Service a written declaration that the attorney is currently qualified as an attorney and is authorized to represent the party or parties. Notwithstanding the preceding sentence, attorneys who are not currently under suspension or disbarment from practice before the Internal Revenue Service are not required to file a written declaration with the IRS before rendering written advice covered under § 10.37, but their rendering of this advice is practice before the Internal Revenue Service.

(b) Certified public accountants. Any certified public accountant who is not currently under suspension or disbarment from practice before the Internal Revenue Service may practice before the Internal Revenue Service by filing with the Internal Revenue Service a written declaration that the certified public accountant is currently qualified as a certified public accountant and is authorized to represent the party or parties. Notwithstanding the preceding sentence, certified public accountants who are not currently under suspension or disbarment from practice before the Internal Revenue Service are not required to file a written declaration with the IRS before rendering written advice covered under § 10.37, but their rendering of this advice is practice before the Internal Revenue Service.

(c) Enrolled agents. Any individual enrolled as an agent pursuant to this part who is not currently under suspension or disbarment from practice before the Internal Revenue Service may practice before the Internal Revenue Service.

(d) Enrolled actuaries. (1) Any individual who is enrolled as an actuary by the Joint Board for the Enrollment of Actuaries pursuant to 29 U.S.C. 1242 who is not currently under suspension or disbarment from practice before the Internal Revenue Service may practice before the Internal Revenue Service by filing with the Internal Revenue Service a written declaration stating that he or she is currently qualified as an enrolled actuary and is authorized to represent the party or parties on whose behalf he or she acts.

(2) Practice as an enrolled actuary is limited to representation with respect to issues involving the following statutory provisions in title 26 of the United States Code: sections 401 (relating to qualification of employee plans), 403(a) (relating to whether an annuity plan meets the requirements of section 404(a)(2)), 404 (relating to deductibility of employer contributions), 405 (relating to qualification of bond purchase plans), 412 (relating to funding requirements for certain employee plans), 413 (relating to application of qualification requirements to collectively bargained plans and to plans maintained by more than one employer), 414 (relating to definitions and special rules with respect to the employee plan area), 419 (relating to treatment of funded welfare benefits), 419A (relating to qualified asset accounts), 420 (relating to transfers of excess pension assets to retiree health accounts), 4971 (relating to excise taxes payable as a result of an accumulated funding deficiency under section 412), 4972 (relating to tax on nondeductible contributions to qualified employer plans), 4976 (relating to taxes with respect to funded welfare benefit plans), 4980 (relating to tax on reversion of qualified plan assets to employer), 6057 (relating to annual registration of plans), 6058 (relating to information required in connection with certain plans of deferred compensation), 6059 (relating to periodic report of actuary), 6652(e) (relating to the failure to file annual registration and other notifications by pension plan), 6652(f) (relating to the failure to file information required in connection with certain plans of deferred compensation), 6692 (relating to the failure to file actuarial report), 7805(b) (relating to the extent to which an Internal Revenue Service ruling or determination letter coming under the statutory provisions listed here will be applied without retroactive effect); and 29 U.S.C. 1083 (relating to the waiver of funding for nonqualified plans).

(3) An individual who practices before the Internal Revenue Service pursuant to paragraph (d)(1) of this section is subject to the provisions of this part in the same manner as attorneys, certified public accountants, enrolled agents, enrolled retirement plan agents, and registered tax return preparers.

(e) Enrolled Retirement Plan Agents—(1) Any individual enrolled as a retirement plan agent pursuant to this part who is not currently under suspension or disbarment from practice before the Internal Revenue Service may practice before the Internal Revenue Service.

(2) Practice as an enrolled retirement plan agent is limited to representation with respect to issues involving the following programs: Employee Plans Determination Letter program;

Employee Plans Compliance Resolution System; and Employee Plans Master and Prototype and Volume Submitter program. In addition, enrolled retirement plan agents are generally permitted to represent taxpayers with respect to IRS forms under the 5300 and 5500 series which are filed by retirement plans and plan sponsors, but not with respect to actuarial forms or schedules.

(3) An individual who practices before the Internal Revenue Service pursuant to paragraph (e)(1) of this section is subject to the provisions of this part in the same manner as attorneys, certified public accountants, enrolled agents, enrolled actuaries, and registered tax return preparers.

(f) Registered tax return preparers. (1) Any individual who is designated as a registered tax return preparer pursuant to § 10.4(c) of this part who is not currently under suspension or disbarment from practice before the Internal Revenue Service may practice before the Internal Revenue Service.

(2) Practice as a registered tax return preparer is limited to preparing and signing tax returns and claims for refund, and other documents for submission to the Internal Revenue Service. A registered tax return preparer may prepare all or substantially all of a tax return or claim for refund of tax. The Internal Revenue Service will prescribe by forms, instructions, or other appropriate guidance the tax returns and claims for refund that a registered tax return preparer may prepare and sign.

(3) A registered tax return preparer may represent taxpayers before revenue agents, customer service representatives, or similar officers and employees of the Internal Revenue Service (including the Taxpayer Advocate Service) during an examination if the registered tax return preparer signed the tax return or claim for refund for the taxable year or period under examination. Unless otherwise prescribed by regulation or notice, this right does not permit such individual to represent the taxpayer, regardless of the circumstances requiring representation, before appeals officers, revenue officers, Counsel or similar officers or employees of the Internal Revenue Service or the Treasury Department. A registered tax return preparer's authorization to practice under this part also does not include the authority to provide tax advice to a client or another person except as necessary to prepare a tax return, claim for refund, or other document intended to be submitted to the Internal Revenue Service.

(4) An individual who practices before the Internal Revenue Service pursuant to paragraph (f)(1) of this section is subject to the provisions of this part in the same manner as attorneys, certified public accountants, enrolled agents, enrolled retirement plan agents, and enrolled actuaries.

(g) Others. Any individual qualifying under § 10.5(e) or § 10.7 is eligible to practice before the Internal Revenue Service to the extent provided in those sections.

(h) Government officers and employees, and others. An individual, who is an officer or employee of the executive, legislative, or judicial branch of the United States Government; an officer or employee of the District of Columbia; a Member of Congress; or a Resident Commissioner may not practice before the Internal Revenue Service if such practice violates 18 U.S.C. 203 or 205.

(i) State officers and employees. No officer or employee of any State, or subdivision of any State, whose duties require him or her to pass upon, investigate, or deal with tax matters for such State or subdivision, may practice before the Internal Revenue Service, if such employment may disclose facts or information applicable to Federal tax matters.

(j) Effective/applicability date. Paragraphs (a), (b), and (g) of this section are applicable beginning June 12, 2014. Paragraphs (c) through (f), (h), and (i) of this section are applicable beginning August 2, 2011.

§ 10.4 Eligibility to become an Enrolled Agent, Enrolled Retirement Plan Agent, or Registered Tax Return Preparer.

(a) Enrollment as an enrolled agent upon examination. The Commissioner, or delegate, will grant enrollment as an enrolled agent to an applicant eighteen years of age or older who demonstrates special competence in tax matters by written examination administered by, or administered under the oversight of, the Internal Revenue Service, who possesses a current or otherwise valid preparer tax identification number or other prescribed identifying number, and who has not engaged in any conduct that would justify the suspension or disbarment of any practitioner under the provisions of this part.

(b) Enrollment as a retirement plan agent upon examination. The Commissioner, or delegate, will grant enrollment as an enrolled retirement plan agent to an applicant eighteen years of age or older who demonstrates special competence in qualified retirement plan matters by written examination administered by, or administered under the oversight of, the Internal Revenue Service, who possesses a current or otherwise valid preparer tax identification number or other prescribed identifying number, and who has not engaged in any conduct that would justify the suspension or disbarment of any practitioner under the provisions of this part.

(c) Designation as a registered tax return preparer. The Commissioner, or delegate, may designate an individual eighteen years of age or older as a registered tax return preparer provided an applicant demonstrates competence in Federal tax return preparation matters by written examination administered by, or administered under the oversight of, the Internal Revenue Service, or otherwise meets the requisite standards prescribed by the Internal Revenue Service, possesses a current or otherwise valid preparer tax identification number or other prescribed identifying number, and has not engaged in any conduct that would justify the suspension or disbarment of any practitioner under the provisions of this part.

(d) Enrollment of former Internal Revenue Service employees. The Commissioner, or delegate, may grant enrollment as an enrolled agent or enrolled retirement plan agent to an applicant who, by virtue of past service and technical experience in the Internal Revenue Service, has qualified for such enrollment and who has not engaged in any conduct that would justify the suspension or disbarment of any practitioner under the provisions of this part, under the following circumstances:

(1) The former employee applies for enrollment on an Internal Revenue Service form and supplies the information requested on the form and such other information regarding the experience and training of the applicant as may be relevant.

(2) The appropriate office of the Internal Revenue Service provides a detailed report of the nature and rating of the applicant's work while employed by the Internal Revenue Service and a recommendation whether such employment qualifies the applicant technically or otherwise for the desired authorization.

(3) Enrollment as an enrolled agent based on an applicant's former employment with the Internal Revenue Service may be of unlimited scope or it may be limited to permit the presentation of matters only of the particular specialty or only before the particular unit or division of the Internal Revenue Service for which the applicant's former employment has qualified the applicant. Enrollment as an enrolled retirement plan agent based on an applicant's former employment with the Internal Revenue Service will be limited to permit the presentation of matters only with respect to qualified retirement plan matters.

(4) Application for enrollment as an enrolled agent or enrolled retirement plan agent based on an applicant's former employment with the Internal Revenue Service must be made within three years from the date of separation from such employment.

(5) An applicant for enrollment as an enrolled agent who is requesting such enrollment based on former employment with the Internal Revenue Service must have had a minimum of five years continuous employment with the Internal Revenue Service during which the applicant must have been regularly engaged in applying and interpreting the provisions of the Internal Revenue Code and the regulations relating to income, estate, gift, employment, or excise taxes.

(6) An applicant for enrollment as an enrolled retirement plan agent who is requesting such enrollment based on former employment with the Internal Revenue Service must have had a minimum of five years continuous employment with the Internal Revenue Service during which the applicant must have been regularly engaged in applying and interpreting the provisions of the Internal Revenue Code and the regulations relating to qualified retirement plan matters.

(7) For the purposes of paragraphs (d)(5) and (6) of this section, an aggregate of 10 or more years of employment in positions involving the application and interpretation of the provisions of the Internal Revenue Code, at least three of which occurred within the five years preceding the date of application, is the equivalent of five years continuous employment.

(e) Natural persons. Enrollment or authorization to practice may be granted only to natural persons.

(f) Effective/applicability date. This section is applicable beginning August 2, 2011.

* * *

§ 10.7 Representing Oneself; Participating in Rulemaking; Limited Practice; and Special Appearances.

(a) Representing oneself. Individuals may appear on their own behalf before the Internal Revenue Service provided they present satisfactory identification.

(b) Participating in rulemaking. Individuals may participate in rulemaking as provided by the Administrative Procedure Act. See 5 U.S.C. 553.

(c) Limited practice—(1) In general. Subject to the limitations in paragraph (c)(2) of this section, an individual who is not a practitioner may represent a taxpayer before the Internal Revenue Service in the circumstances described in this paragraph (c)(1), even if the taxpayer is not present, provided the individual presents satisfactory identification and proof of his or her authority to represent the taxpayer. The circumstances described in this paragraph (c)(1) are as follows:

(i) An individual may represent a member of his or her immediate family.

(ii) A regular full-time employee of an individual employer may represent the employer.

(iii) A general partner or a regular full-time employee of a partnership may represent the partnership.

(iv) A bona fide officer or a regular full-time employee of a corporation (including a parent, subsidiary, or other affiliated corporation), association, or organized group may represent the corporation, association, or organized group.

(v) A regular full-time employee of a trust, receivership, guardianship, or estate may represent the trust, receivership, guardianship, or estate.

(vi) An officer or a regular employee of a governmental unit, agency, or authority may represent the governmental unit, agency, or authority in the course of his or her official duties.

(vii) An individual may represent any individual or entity, who is outside the United States, before personnel of the Internal Revenue Service when such representation takes place outside the United States.

(2) Limitations. (i) An individual who is under suspension or disbarment from practice before the Internal Revenue Service may not engage in limited practice before the Internal Revenue Service under paragraph (c)(1) of this section.

(ii) The Commissioner, or delegate, may, after notice and opportunity for a conference, deny eligibility to engage in limited practice before the Internal Revenue Service under paragraph (c)(1) of this section to any individual who has engaged in conduct that would justify a sanction under § 10.50.

(iii) An individual who represents a taxpayer under the authority of paragraph (c)(1) of this section is subject, to the extent of his or her authority, to such rules of general applicability regarding standards of conduct and other matters as prescribed by the Internal Revenue Service.

(d) Special appearances. The Commissioner, or delegate, may, subject to conditions deemed appropriate, authorize an individual who is not otherwise eligible to practice before the Internal Revenue Service to represent another person in a particular matter.

(e) Fiduciaries. For purposes of this part, a fiduciary (for example, a trustee, receiver, guardian, personal representative, administrator, or executor) is considered to be the taxpayer and not a representative of the taxpayer.

(f) Effective/applicability date. This section is applicable beginning August 2, 2011.

§ 10.8 Return preparation and application of rules to other individuals.

(a) Preparing all or substantially all of a tax return. Any individual who for compensation prepares or assists with the preparation of all or substantially all of a tax return or claim for refund must have a preparer tax identification number. Except as otherwise prescribed in forms, instructions, or other appropriate guidance, an individual must be an attorney, certified public accountant, enrolled agent, or registered tax return preparer to obtain a preparer tax identification number. Any individual who for compensation prepares or assists with the preparation of all or substantially all of a tax return or claim for refund is subject to the duties and restrictions relating to practice in subpart B, as well as subject to the sanctions for violation of the regulations in subpart C.

(b) Preparing a tax return and furnishing information. Any individual may for compensation prepare or assist with the preparation of a tax return or claim for refund (provided the individual prepares less than substantially all of the tax return or claim for refund), appear as a witness for the taxpayer before the Internal Revenue Service, or furnish information at the request of the Internal Revenue Service or any of its officers or employees.

(c) Application of rules to other individuals. Any individual who for compensation prepares, or assists in the preparation of, all or a substantial portion of a document pertaining to any taxpayer's tax liability for submission to the Internal Revenue Service is subject to the duties and restrictions relating to practice in subpart B, as well as subject to the sanctions for violation of the regulations in subpart C. Unless otherwise a practitioner, however, an individual may not for compensation prepare, or assist in the preparation of, all or substantially all of a tax return or claim for refund, or sign tax returns and claims for refund. For purposes of this paragraph, an individual described in 26 CFR 301.7701–15(f) is not treated as having prepared all or a substantial portion of the document by reason of such assistance.

(d) Effective/applicability date. This section is applicable beginning August 2, 2011.

* * *

SUBPART B. DUTIES AND RESTRICTIONS RELATING TO PRACTICE BEFORE THE INTERNATIONAL REVENUE SERVICE

§ 10.20 Information to Be Furnished.

(a) To the Internal Revenue Service. (1) A practitioner must, on a proper and lawful request by a duly authorized officer or employee of the Internal Revenue Service, promptly submit records or information in any matter before the Internal Revenue Service unless the practitioner believes in good faith and on reasonable grounds that the records or information are privileged.

(2) Where the requested records or information are not in the possession of, or subject to the control of, the practitioner or the practitioner's client, the practitioner must promptly notify the requesting Internal Revenue Service officer or employee and the practitioner must provide any information that the practitioner has regarding the identity of any person who the practitioner believes may have possession or control of the requested records or information. The practitioner must make reasonable inquiry of his or her client regarding the identity of any person who may have possession or control of the requested records or information, but the practitioner is not required to make inquiry of any other person or independently verify any information provided by the practitioner's client regarding the identity of such persons.

(3) When a proper and lawful request is made by a duly authorized officer or employee of the Internal Revenue Service, concerning an inquiry into an alleged violation of the regulations in this part, a practitioner must provide any information the practitioner has concerning the alleged violation and testify regarding this information in any proceeding instituted under this part, unless the practitioner believes in good faith and on reasonable grounds that the information is privileged.

(b) Interference with a proper and lawful request for records or information. A practitioner may not interfere, or attempt to interfere, with any proper and lawful effort by the Internal Revenue Service, its officers or employees, to obtain any record or information unless the practitioner believes in good faith and on reasonable grounds that the record or information is privileged.

(c) Effective/applicability date. This section is applicable beginning August 2, 2011.

§ 10.21 Knowledge of Client's Omission.

A practitioner who, having been retained by a client with respect to a matter administered by the Internal Revenue Service, knows that the client has not complied with the revenue laws of the United States or has made an error in or omission from any return, document, affidavit, or other paper which the client submitted or executed under the revenue laws of the United States, must advise the client promptly of the fact of such noncompliance, error, or omission. The practitioner must advise the client of the consequences as provided under the Code and regulations of such noncompliance, error, or omission.

§ 10.22 Diligence as to Accuracy.

(a) In general. A practitioner must exercise due diligence—

(1) In preparing or assisting in the preparation of, approving, and filing tax returns, documents, affidavits, and other papers relating to Internal Revenue Service matters;

(2) In determining the correctness of oral or written representations made by the practitioner to the Department of the Treasury; and

(3) In determining the correctness of oral or written representations made by the practitioner to clients with reference to any matter administered by the Internal Revenue Service.

(b) Reliance on others. Except as provided in §§ 10.34 and 10.37, a practitioner will be presumed to have exercised due diligence for purposes of this section if the practitioner relies on the work product of another person and the practitioner used reasonable care in engaging, supervising, training, and evaluating the person, taking proper account of the nature of the relationship between the practitioner and the person.

(c) Effective/applicability date. Paragraph (a) of this section is applicable on September 26, 2007. Paragraph (b) of this section is applicable beginning June 12, 2014.

§ 10.23 Prompt Disposition of Pending Matters.

A practitioner may not unreasonably delay the prompt disposition of any matter before the Internal Revenue Service.

§ 10.24 Assistance From or to Disbarred or Suspended Persons and Former Internal Revenue Service Employees.

A practitioner may not, knowingly and directly or indirectly:

(a) Accept assistance from or assist any person who is under disbarment or suspension from practice before the Internal Revenue Service if the assistance relates to a matter or matters constituting practice before the Internal Revenue Service.

(b) Accept assistance from any former government employee where the provisions of § 10.25 or any Federal law would be violated.

§ 10.25 Practice by Former Government Employees, Their Partners and Their Associates.

(a) Definitions. For purposes of this section—

(1) Assist means to act in such a way as to advise, furnish information to, or otherwise aid another person, directly, or indirectly.

(2) Government employee is an officer or employee of the United States or any agency of the United States, including a special Government employee as defined in 18 U.S.C. 202(a), or of the District of Columbia, or of any State, or a member of Congress or of any State legislature.

(3) Member of a firm is a sole practitioner or an employee or associate thereof, or a partner, stockholder, associate, affiliate or employee of a partnership, joint venture, corporation, professional association or other affiliation of two or more practitioners who represent nongovernmental parties.

(4) Particular matter involving specific parties is defined at 5 CFR 2637.201(c), or superseding post-employment regulations issued by the U.S. Office of Government Ethics.

(5) Rule includes Treasury regulations, whether issued or under preparation for issuance as notices of proposed rulemaking or as Treasury decisions, revenue rulings, and revenue procedures published in the Internal Revenue Bulletin (see 26 CFR 601.601(d)(2)(ii)(b)).

(b) General rules—(1) No former Government employee may, subsequent to Government employment, represent anyone in any matter administered by the Internal Revenue Service if the representation would violate 18 U.S.C. 207 or any other laws of the United States.

(2) No former Government employee who personally and substantially participated in a particular matter involving specific parties may, subsequent to Government employment, represent or knowingly assist, in that particular matter, any person who is or was a specific party to that particular matter.

(3) A former Government employee who within a period of one year prior to the termination of Government employment had official responsibility for a particular matter involving specific parties may not, within two years after Government employment is ended, represent in that particular matter any person who is or was a specific party to that particular matter.

(4) No former Government employee may, within one year after Government employment is ended, communicate with or appear before, with the intent to influence, any employee of the Treasury Department in connection with the publication, withdrawal, amendment, modification, or interpretation of a rule the development of which the former Government employee participated in, or for which, within a period of one year prior to the termination of Government employment, the former government employee had official responsibility. This paragraph (b)(4) does not, however, preclude any former employee from appearing on one's own behalf or from representing a taxpayer before the Internal Revenue Service in connection with a particular matter involving specific parties involving the application or interpretation of a rule with respect to that particular matter, provided that the representation is otherwise consistent with the other provisions of this section and the former employee does not utilize or disclose any confidential information acquired by the former employee in the development of the rule.

(c) Firm representation—(1) No member of a firm of which a former Government employee is a member may represent or knowingly assist a person who was or is a specific party in any particular matter with respect to which the restrictions of paragraph (b)(2) of this section apply to the former Government employee, in that particular matter, unless the firm isolates the former Government employee in such a way to ensure that the former Government employee cannot assist in the representation.

(2) When isolation of a former Government employee is required under paragraph (c)(1) of this section, a statement affirming the fact of such isolation must be executed under oath by the former Government employee and by another member of the firm acting on behalf of the firm. The statement must clearly identify the firm, the former Government employee, and the particular matter(s) requiring isolation. The statement must be retained by the firm and, upon request, provided to the office(s) of the Internal Revenue Service administering or enforcing this part.

(d) Pending representation. The provisions of this regulation will govern practice by former Government employees, their partners and associates with respect to representation in particular matters involving specific parties where actual representation commenced before the effective date of this regulation.

(e) Effective/applicability date. This section is applicable beginning August 2, 2011.

§ 10.26 Notaries.

A practitioner may not take acknowledgments, administer oaths, certify papers, or perform any official act as a notary public with respect to any matter administered by the Internal Revenue Service and for which he or she is employed as counsel, attorney, or agent, or in which he or she may be in any way interested.

§ 10.27 Fees.

(a) In general. A practitioner may not charge an unconscionable fee in connection with any matter before the Internal Revenue Service.

(b) Contingent fees—(1) Except as provided in paragraphs (b)(2), (3), and (4) of this section, a practitioner may not charge a contingent fee for services rendered in connection with any matter before the Internal Revenue Service.

(2) A practitioner may charge a contingent fee for services rendered in connection with the Service's examination of, or challenge to—

(i) An original tax return; or

(ii) An amended return or claim for refund or credit where the amended return or claim for refund or credit was filed within 120 days of the taxpayer receiving a written notice of the examination of, or a written challenge to the original tax return.

(3) A practitioner may charge a contingent fee for services rendered in connection with a claim for credit or refund filed solely in connection with the determination of statutory interest or penalties assessed by the Internal Revenue Service.

(4) A practitioner may charge a contingent fee for services rendered in connection with any judicial proceeding arising under the Internal Revenue Code.

(c) Definitions. For purposes of this section—

(1) Contingent fee is any fee that is based, in whole or in part, on whether or not a position taken on a tax return or other filing avoids challenge by the Internal Revenue Service or is sustained either by the Internal Revenue Service or in litigation. A contingent fee includes a fee that is based on a percentage of the refund reported on a return, that is based on a percentage of the taxes saved, or that otherwise depends on the specific result attained. A contingent fee also includes any fee arrangement in which the practitioner will reimburse the client for all or a portion of the client's fee in the event that a position taken on a tax return or other filing is challenged by the Internal Revenue Service or is not sustained, whether pursuant to an indemnity agreement, a guarantee, rescission rights, or any other arrangement with a similar effect.

(2) Matter before the Internal Revenue Service includes tax planning and advice, preparing or filing or assisting in preparing or filing returns or claims for refund or credit, and all matters connected with a presentation to the Internal Revenue Service or any of its officers or employees relating to a taxpayer's rights, privileges, or liabilities under laws or regulations administered by the Internal Revenue Service. Such presentations include, but are not limited to, preparing and filing documents, corresponding and communicating with the Internal Revenue Service, rendering written advice with respect to any entity, transaction, plan or arrangement, and representing a client at conferences, hearings, and meetings.

(d) Effective/applicability date. This section is applicable for fee arrangements entered into after March 26, 2008.

§ 10.28 Return of Client's Records.

(a) In general, a practitioner must, at the request of a client, promptly return any and all records of the client that are necessary for the client to comply with his or her Federal tax obligations. The practitioner may retain copies of the records returned to a client. The existence of a dispute over fees generally does not relieve the practitioner of his or her responsibility under this section. Nevertheless, if applicable state law allows or permits the retention of a client's records by a practitioner in the case of a dispute over fees for services rendered, the practitioner need only return those records that must be attached to the taxpayer's return. The practitioner, however, must provide the client with reasonable access to review and copy any additional records of the client retained by the practitioner under state law that are necessary for the client to comply with his or her Federal tax obligations.

(b) For purposes of this section, Records of the client include all documents or written or electronic materials provided to the practitioner, or obtained by the practitioner in the course of the practitioner's representation of the client, that preexisted the retention of the practitioner by the client. The term also includes materials that were prepared by the client or a third party (not including an employee or agent of the practitioner) at any time and provided to the practitioner with respect to the subject matter of the representation. The term also includes any return, claim for refund, schedule, affidavit, appraisal or any other document prepared by the practitioner, or his or her employee or agent, that was presented to the client with respect to a prior representation if such document is necessary for the taxpayer to comply with his or her current Federal tax obligations. The term does not include any return, claim for refund, schedule, affidavit, appraisal or any other document prepared by the practitioner or the practitioner's firm, employees or agents if the practitioner is withholding such document pending the client's performance of its contractual obligation to pay fees with respect to such document.

§ 10.29 Conflicting Interests.

(a) Except as provided by paragraph (b) of this section, a practitioner shall not represent a client before the Internal Revenue Service if the representation involves a conflict of interest. A conflict of interest exists if—

(1) The representation of one client will be directly adverse to another client; or

(2) There is a significant risk that the representation of one or more clients will be materially limited by the practitioner's responsibilities to another client, a former client or a third person, or by a personal interest of the practitioner.

(b) Notwithstanding the existence of a conflict of interest under paragraph (a) of this section, the practitioner may represent a client if—

(1) The practitioner reasonably believes that the practitioner will be able to provide competent and diligent representation to each affected client;

(2) The representation is not prohibited by law; and

(3) Each affected client waives the conflict of interest and gives informed consent, confirmed in writing by each affected client, at the time the existence of the conflict of interest is known by the practitioner. The confirmation may be made within a reasonable period after the informed consent, but in no event later than 30 days.

(c) Copies of the written consents must be retained by the practitioner for at least 36 months from the date of the conclusion of the representation of the affected clients, and the written consents must be provided to any officer or employee of the Internal Revenue Service on request.

(d) Effective/applicability date. This section is applicable on September 26, 2007.

§ 10.30 Solicitation.

(a) Advertising and solicitation restrictions.

(1) A practitioner may not, with respect to any Internal Revenue Service matter, in any way use or participate in the use of any form of public communication or private solicitation containing a false, fraudulent, or coercive statement or claim; or a misleading or deceptive statement or claim. Enrolled agents, enrolled retirement plan agents, or registered tax return preparers, in describing their professional designation, may not utilize the term "certified" or imply an employer/employee relationship with the Internal Revenue Service. Examples of acceptable descriptions for enrolled agents are "enrolled to represent taxpayers before the Internal Revenue Service," "enrolled to practice before the Internal Revenue Service," and "admitted to practice before the Internal Revenue Service." Similarly, examples of acceptable descriptions for enrolled retirement plan agents are "enrolled to represent taxpayers before the Internal Revenue Service as a retirement plan agent" and "enrolled to practice before the Internal Revenue Service as a retirement plan agent." An example of an acceptable description for registered tax return preparers is "designated as a registered tax return preparer by the Internal Revenue Service."

(2) A practitioner may not make, directly or indirectly, an uninvited written or oral solicitation of employment in matters related to the Internal Revenue Service if the solicitation violates Federal or State law or other applicable rule, e.g., attorneys are precluded from making a solicitation that is prohibited by conduct rules applicable to all attorneys in their State(s) of licensure. Any lawful solicitation made by or on behalf of a practitioner eligible to practice before the Internal Revenue Service must, nevertheless, clearly identify the solicitation as such and, if applicable, identify the source of the information used in choosing the recipient.

(b) Fee information. (1)(i) A practitioner may publish the availability of a written schedule of fees and disseminate the following fee information—

(A) Fixed fees for specific routine services.

(B) Hourly rates.

(C) Range of fees for particular services.

(D) Fee charged for an initial consultation.

(ii) Any statement of fee information concerning matters in which costs may be incurred must include a statement disclosing whether clients will be responsible for such costs.

(2) A practitioner may charge no more than the rate(s) published under paragraph (b)(1) of this section for at least 30 calendar days after the last date on which the schedule of fees was published.

(c) Communication of fee information. Fee information may be communicated in professional lists, telephone directories, print media, mailings, electronic mail, facsimile, hand delivered flyers, radio, television, and any other method. The method chosen, however, must not cause the communication to become untruthful, deceptive, or otherwise in violation of this part. A practitioner may not persist in attempting to contact a prospective client if the prospective client has made it known to the practitioner that he or she does not desire to be solicited. In the case of radio and television broadcasting, the broadcast must be recorded and the practitioner must retain a recording of the actual transmission. In the case of direct mail and e-commerce communications, the practitioner must retain a copy of the actual communication, along with a list or other description of persons to whom the communication was mailed or otherwise distributed. The copy must be retained by the practitioner for a period of at least 36 months from the date of the last transmission or use.

(d) Improper associations. A practitioner may not, in matters related to the Internal Revenue Service, assist, or accept assistance from, any person or entity who, to the knowledge of the practitioner, obtains clients or otherwise practices in a manner forbidden under this section.

(e) Effective/applicability date. This section is applicable beginning August 2, 2011.

§ 10.31 Negotiation of Taxpayer Checks.

(a) A practitioner may not endorse or otherwise negotiate any check (including directing or accepting payment by any means, electronic or otherwise, into an account owned or controlled by the practitioner or any firm or other entity with whom the practitioner is associated) issued to a client by the government in respect of a Federal tax liability.

(b) Effective/applicability date. This section is applicable beginning June 12, 2014.

§ 10.32 Practice of Law.

Nothing in the regulations in this part may be construed as authorizing persons not members of the bar to practice law.

§ 10.33 Best Practices for Tax Advisors.

(a) Best practices. Tax advisors should provide clients with the highest quality representation concerning Federal tax issues by adhering to best practices in providing advice and in preparing or assisting in the preparation of a submission to the Internal Revenue Service. In addition to compliance with the standards of practice provided elsewhere in this part, best practices include the following:

(1) Communicating clearly with the client regarding the terms of the engagement. For example, the advisor should determine the client's expected purpose for and use of the advice and should have a clear understanding with the client regarding the form and scope of the advice or assistance to be rendered.

(2) Establishing the facts, determining which facts are relevant, evaluating the reasonableness of any assumptions or representations, relating the applicable law (including potentially applicable judicial doctrines) to the relevant facts, and arriving at a conclusion supported by the law and the facts.

(3) Advising the client regarding the import of the conclusions reached, including, for example, whether a taxpayer may avoid accuracy-related penalties under the Internal Revenue Code if a taxpayer acts in reliance on the advice.

(4) Acting fairly and with integrity in practice before the Internal Revenue Service.

(b) Procedures to ensure best practices for tax advisors. Tax advisors with responsibility for overseeing a firm's practice of providing advice concerning Federal tax issues or of preparing or assisting in the preparation of submissions to the Internal Revenue Service should take reasonable steps to ensure that the firm's procedures for all members, associates, and employees are consistent with the best practices set forth in paragraph (a) of this section.

(c) Applicability date. This section is effective after June 20, 2005.

10.34 Standards With Respect to Tax Returns and Documents, Affidavits and Other Papers.

(a) Tax returns. (1) A practitioner may not willfully, recklessly, or through gross incompetence—

(i) Sign a tax return or claim for refund that the practitioner knows or reasonably should know contains a position that—

(A) Lacks a reasonable basis;

(B) Is an unreasonable position as described in section 6694(a)(2) of the Internal Revenue code (Code) (including the related regulations and other published guidance); or

(C) Is a willful attempted by the practitioner to understate the liability for tax or a reckless or intentional disregard of rules or regulations by the practitioner as described in section 6694(b)(2) of the Code (including the related regulations and other published guidance).

(ii) Advise a client to take a position on a tax return or claim for refund, or prepare a portion off a tax return or claim for refund containing a position, that—

(A) Lacks a reasonable basis;

(B) Is an unreasonable position as described in section 6694(a)(2) of the Code (including the related regulations and other published guidance); or

(C) Is a willful attempt by the practitioner to understate the liability for tax or a reckless or intentional disregard of rules or regulations by the practitioner as described in section 6694(b)(2) of the Code (including the related regulations and other published guidance).

(2) A pattern of conduct is a factor that will be taken into account in determining whether a practitioner acted willfully, recklessly, or through gross incompetence.

(b) Documents, affidavits and other papers—(1) A practitioner may not advise a client to take a position on a document, affidavit or other paper submitted to the Internal Revenue Service unless the position is not frivolous.

(2) A practitioner may not advise a client to submit a document, affidavit or other paper to the Internal Revenue Service—

(i) The purpose of which is to delay or impede the administration of the Federal tax laws;

(ii) That is frivolous; or

(iii) That contains or omits information in a manner that demonstrates an intentional disregard of a rule or regulation unless the practitioner also advises the client to submit a document that evidences a good faith challenge to the rule or regulation.

(c) Advising clients on potential penalties—(1) A practitioner must inform a client of any penalties that are reasonably likely to apply to the client with respect to—

(i) A position taken on a tax return if—

(A) The practitioner advised the client with respect to the position; or

(B) The practitioner prepared or signed the tax return; and

(ii) Any document, affidavit or other paper submitted to the Internal Revenue Service.

(2) The practitioner also must inform the client of any opportunity to avoid any such penalties by disclosure, if relevant, and of the requirements for adequate disclosure.

(3) This paragraph (c) applies even if the practitioner is not subject to a penalty under the Internal Revenue Code with respect to the position or with respect to the document, affidavit or other paper submitted.

(d) Relying on information furnished by clients. A practitioner advising a client to take a position on a tax return, document, affidavit or other paper submitted to the Internal Revenue Service, or preparing or signing a tax return as a preparer, generally may rely in good faith without verification upon information furnished by the client. The practitioner may not, however, ignore the implications of information furnished to, or actually known by, the practitioner, and must make reasonable inquiries if the information as furnished appears to be incorrect, inconsistent with an important fact or another factual assumption, or incomplete.

(e) Effective/applicability date. Paragraph (a) of this section is applicable for returns or claims for refund filed, or advice provided, beginning August 2, 2011. Paragraphs (b) through (d) of this section are applicable to tax returns, documents, affidavits, and other papers filed on or after September 26, 2007.

§ 10.35 Competence.

(a) A practitioner must possess the necessary competence to engage in practice before the Internal Revenue Service. Competent practice requires the appropriate level of knowledge, skill, thoroughness, and preparation necessary for the matter for which the practitioner is engaged. A practitioner may become competent for the matter for which the practitioner has been engaged through various methods, such as consulting with experts in the relevant area or studying the relevant law.

(b) Effective/applicability date. This section is applicable beginning June 12, 2014.

§ 10.36 Procedures to Ensure Compliance.

(a) Any individual subject to the provisions of this part who has (or individuals who have or share) principal authority and responsibility for overseeing a firm's practice governed by this part, including the provision of advice concerning Federal tax matters and preparation of tax returns, claims for refund, or other documents for submission to the Internal Revenue Service, must take reasonable steps to ensure that the firm has adequate procedures in effect for all members, associates, and employees for purposes of complying with subparts A, B, and C of this part, as applicable. In the absence of a person or persons identified by the firm as having the principal authority and responsibility described in this paragraph, the Internal Revenue Service may identify one or more individuals subject to the provisions of this part responsible for compliance with the requirements of this section.

(b) Any such individual who has (or such individuals who have or share) principal authority as described in paragraph (a) of this section will be subject to discipline for failing to comply with the requirements of this section if—

(1) The individual through willfulness, recklessness, or gross incompetence does not take reasonable steps to ensure that the firm has adequate procedures to comply with this part, as applicable, and one or more individuals who are members of, associated with, or employed by, the firm are, or have, engaged in a pattern or practice, in connection with their practice with the firm, of failing to comply with this part, as applicable;

(2) The individual through willfulness, recklessness, or gross incompetence does not take reasonable steps to ensure that firm procedures in effect are properly followed, and one or more individuals who are members of, associated with, or employed by, the firm are, or have, engaged in a pattern or practice, in connection with their practice with the firm, of failing to comply with this part, as applicable; or

(3) The individual knows or should know that one or more individuals who are members of, associated with, or employed by, the firm are, or have, engaged in a pattern or practice, in connection with their practice with the firm, that does not comply with this part, as applicable, and the individual, through willfulness, recklessness, or gross incompetence fails to take prompt action to correct the noncompliance.

(c) Effective/applicability date. This section is applicable beginning June 12, 2014.

§ 10.37 Requirements for Written Advice.

(a) Requirements. (1) A practitioner may give written advice (including by means of electronic communication) concerning one or more Federal tax matters subject to the requirements in paragraph (a)(2) of this section. Government submissions on matters of general policy are not considered written advice on a Federal tax matter for purposes of this section. Continuing education presentations provided to an audience solely for the purpose of enhancing practitioners' professional knowledge on Federal tax matters are not considered written advice on a Federal tax matter for purposes of this section. The preceding sentence does not apply to presentations marketing or promoting transactions.

(2) The practitioner must—

(i) Base the written advice on reasonable factual and legal assumptions (including assumptions as to future events);

(ii) Reasonably consider all relevant facts and circumstances that the practitioner knows or reasonably should know;

(iii) Use reasonable efforts to identify and ascertain the facts relevant to written advice on each Federal tax matter;

(iv) Not rely upon representations, statements, findings, or agreements (including projections, financial forecasts, or appraisals) of the taxpayer or any other person if reliance on them would be unreasonable;

(v) Relate applicable law and authorities to facts; and

(vi) Not, in evaluating a Federal tax matter, take into account the possibility that a tax return will not be audited or that a matter will not be raised on audit.

(3) Reliance on representations, statements, findings, or agreements is unreasonable if the practitioner knows or reasonably should know that one or more representations or assumptions on which any representation is based are incorrect, incomplete, or inconsistent.

(b) Reliance on advice of others. A practitioner may only rely on the advice of another person if the advice was reasonable and the reliance is in good faith considering all the facts and circumstances. Reliance is not reasonable when—

(1) The practitioner knows or reasonably should know that the opinion of the other person should not be relied on;

(2) The practitioner knows or reasonably should know that the other person is not competent or lacks the necessary qualifications to provide the advice; or

(3) The practitioner knows or reasonably should know that the other person has a conflict of interest in violation of the rules described in this part.

(c) Standard of review. (1) In evaluating whether a practitioner giving written advice concerning one or more Federal tax matters complied with the requirements of this section, the Commissioner, or delegate, will apply a reasonable practitioner standard, considering all facts and circumstances, including, but not limited to, the scope of the engagement and the type and specificity of the advice sought by the client.

(2) In the case of an opinion the practitioner knows or has reason to know will be used or referred to by a person other than the practitioner (or a person who is a member of, associated with, or employed by the practitioner's firm) in promoting, marketing, or recommending to one or more taxpayers a partnership or other entity, investment plan or arrangement a significant purpose of which is the avoidance or evasion of any tax imposed by the Internal Revenue Code, the Commissioner, or delegate, will apply a reasonable practitioner standard, considering all facts and circumstances, with emphasis given to the additional risk caused by the practitioner's lack of knowledge of the taxpayer's particular circumstances, when determining whether a practitioner has failed to comply with this section.

(d) Federal tax matter. A Federal tax matter, as used in this section, is any matter concerning the application or interpretation of—

(1) A revenue provision as defined in section 6110(i)(1)(B) of the Internal Revenue Code;

(2) Any provision of law impacting a person's obligations under the internal revenue laws and regulations, including but not limited to the person's liability to pay tax or obligation to file returns; or

(3) Any other law or regulation administered by the Internal Revenue Service.

(e) Effective/applicability date. This section is applicable to written advice rendered after June 12, 2014.

SUBPART C. SANCTIONS FOR VIOLATION OF THE REGULATIONS

§ 10.50 Sanctions.

(a) Authority to censure, suspend, or disbar. The Secretary of the Treasury, or delegate, after notice and an opportunity for a proceeding, may censure, suspend, or disbar any practitioner from practice before the Internal Revenue Service if the practitioner is shown to be incompetent or disreputable (within the meaning of § 10.51), fails to comply with any regulation in this part (under the prohibited conduct standards of § 10.52), or with intent to defraud, willfully and knowingly misleads or threatens a client or prospective client. Censure is a public reprimand.

(b) Authority to disqualify. The Secretary of the Treasury, or delegate, after due notice and opportunity for hearing, may disqualify any appraiser for a violation of these rules as applicable to appraisers.

(1) If any appraiser is disqualified pursuant to this subpart C, the appraiser is barred from presenting evidence or testimony in any administrative proceeding before the Department of Treasury or the Internal Revenue Service, unless and until authorized to do so by the Internal Revenue Service pursuant to § 10.81, regardless of whether the evidence or testimony would pertain to an appraisal made prior to or after the effective date of disqualification.

(2) Any appraisal made by a disqualified appraiser after the effective date of disqualification will not have any probative effect in any administrative proceeding before the Department of the Treasury or the Internal Revenue Service. An appraisal otherwise barred from admission into evidence pursuant to this section may be admitted into evidence solely for the purpose of determining the taxpayer's reliance in good faith on such appraisal.

(c) Authority to impose monetary penalty—(1) In general. (i) The Secretary of the Treasury, or delegate, after notice and an opportunity for a proceeding, may impose a monetary penalty on any practitioner who engages in conduct subject to sanction under paragraph (a) of this section.

(ii) If the practitioner described in paragraph (c)(1)(i) of this section was acting on behalf of an employer or any firm or other entity in connection with the conduct giving rise to the penalty, the Secretary of the Treasury, or delegate, may impose a monetary penalty on the employer, firm, or entity if it knew, or reasonably should have known, of such conduct.

(2) Amount of penalty. The amount of the penalty shall not exceed the gross income derived (or to be derived) from the conduct giving rise to the penalty.

(3) Coordination with other sanctions. Subject to paragraph (c)(2) of this section—

(i) Any monetary penalty imposed on a practitioner under this paragraph (c) may be in addition to or in lieu of any suspension, disbarment or censure and may be in addition to a penalty imposed on an employer, firm or other entity under paragraph (c)(1)(ii) of this section.

(ii) Any monetary penalty imposed on an employer, firm or other entity may be in addition to or in lieu of penalties imposed under paragraph (c)(1)(i) of this section.

(d) Authority to accept a practitioner's consent to sanction. The Internal Revenue Service may accept a practitioner's offer of consent to be sanctioned under § 10.50 in lieu of instituting or continuing a proceeding under § 10.60(a).

(e) Sanctions to be imposed. The sanctions imposed by this section shall take into account all relevant facts and circumstances.

(f) Effective/applicability date. This section is applicable to conduct occurring on or after August 2, 2011, except that paragraphs (a), (b)(2), and (e) apply to conduct occurring on or after September 26, 2007, and paragraph (c) applies to prohibited conduct that occurs after October 22, 2004.

§ 10.51 Incompetence and Disreputable Conduct.

(a) Incompetence and disreputable conduct. Incompetence and disreputable conduct for which a practitioner may be sanctioned under § 10.50 includes, but is not limited to—

(1) Conviction of any criminal offense under the Federal tax laws.

(2) Conviction of any criminal offense involving dishonesty or breach of trust.

(3) Conviction of any felony under Federal or State law for which the conduct involved renders the practitioner unfit to practice before the Internal Revenue Service.

(4) Giving false or misleading information, or participating in any way in the giving of false or misleading information to the Department of the Treasury or any officer or employee thereof, or to any tribunal authorized to pass upon Federal tax matters, in connection with any matter pending or likely to be pending before them, knowing the information to be false or misleading. Facts or other matters contained in testimony, Federal tax returns, financial statements, applications for enrollment, affidavits, declarations, and any other document or statement, written or oral, are included in the term "information."

(5) Solicitation of employment as prohibited under § 10.30, the use of false or misleading representations with intent to deceive a client or prospective client in order to procure employment, or intimating that the practitioner is able improperly to obtain special consideration or action from the Internal Revenue Service or any officer or employee thereof.

(6) Willfully failing to make a Federal tax return in violation of the Federal tax laws, or willfully evading, attempting to evade, or participating in any way in evading or attempting to evade any assessment or payment of any Federal tax.

(7) Willfully assisting, counseling, encouraging a client or prospective client in violating, or suggesting to a client or prospective client to violate, any Federal tax law, or knowingly counseling or suggesting to a client or prospective client an illegal plan to evade Federal taxes or payment thereof.

(8) Misappropriation of, or failure properly or promptly to remit, funds received from a client for the purpose of payment of taxes or other obligations due the United States.

(9) Directly or indirectly attempting to influence, or offering or agreeing to attempt to influence, the official action of any officer or employee of the Internal Revenue Service by the use of threats, false accusations, duress or coercion, by the offer of any special inducement or promise of an advantage, or by the bestowing of any gift, favor or thing of value.

(10) Disbarment or suspension from practice as an attorney, certified public accountant, public accountant or actuary by any duly constituted authority of any State, territory, or possession of the United States, including a Commonwealth, or the District of Columbia, any Federal court of record or any Federal agency, body or board.

(11) Knowingly aiding and abetting another person to practice before the Internal Revenue Service during a period of suspension, disbarment or ineligibility of such other person.

(12) Contemptuous conduct in connection with practice before the Internal Revenue Service, including the use of abusive language, making false accusations or statements, knowing them to be false or circulating or publishing malicious or libelous matter.

(13) Giving a false opinion, knowingly, recklessly, or through gross incompetence, including an opinion which is intentionally or recklessly misleading, or engaging in a pattern of providing incompetent opinions on questions arising under the Federal tax laws. False opinions described in this paragraph (a)(13) include those which reflect or result from a knowing misstatement of fact or law, from an assertion of a position known to be unwarranted under existing law, from counseling or assisting in conduct known to be illegal or fraudulent, from concealing matters required by law to be revealed, or from consciously disregarding information indicating that material facts expressed in the opinion or offering material are false or misleading. For purposes of this paragraph (a)(13), reckless conduct is a highly unreasonable omission or misrepresentation involving an extreme departure from the standards of ordinary care that a practitioner should observe under the circumstances. A pattern of conduct is a factor that will be taken into account in determining whether a practitioner acted knowingly, recklessly, or through gross incompetence. Gross incompetence includes conduct that reflects gross indifference, preparation which is grossly inadequate under the circumstances, and a consistent failure to perform obligations to the client.

(14) Willfully failing to sign a tax return prepared by the practitioner when the practitioner's signature is required by the Federal tax laws unless the failure is due to reasonable cause and not due to willful neglect.

(15) Willfully disclosing or otherwise using a tax return or tax return information in a manner not authorized by the Internal Revenue Code, contrary to the order of a court of competent jurisdiction, or contrary to the order of an administrative law judge in a proceeding instituted under § 10.60.

(16) Willfully failing to file on magnetic or other electronic media a tax return prepared by the practitioner when the practitioner is required to do so by the Federal tax laws unless the failure is due to reasonable cause and not due to willful neglect.

(17) Willfully preparing all or substantially all of, or signing, a tax return or claim for refund when the practitioner does not possess a current or otherwise valid preparer tax identification number or other prescribed identifying number.

(18) Willfully representing a taxpayer before an officer or employee of the Internal Revenue Service unless the practitioner is authorized to do so pursuant to this part.

(b) Effective/applicability date. This section is applicable beginning August 2, 2011.

§ 10.52 Violations Subject to Sanction.

(a) A practitioner may be sanctioned under § 10.50 if the practitioner—

(1) Willfully violates any of the regulations (other than § 10.33) contained in this part; or

(2) Recklessly or through gross incompetence (within the meaning of § 10.51(a)(13)) violates §§ 10.34, 10.35, 10.36 or 10.37.

(b) Effective/applicability date. This section is applicable to conduct occurring on or after September 26, 2007.

§ 10.53 Receipt of Information Concerning Practitioner.

(a) Officer or employee of the Internal Revenue Service. If an officer or employee of the Internal Revenue Service has reason to believe a practitioner has violated any provision of this part, the officer or employee will promptly make a written report of the suspected violation. The report will explain the facts and reasons upon which the officer's or employee's belief rests and must be submitted to the office(s) of the Internal Revenue Service responsible for administering or enforcing this part.

(b) Other persons. Any person other than an officer or employee of the Internal Revenue Service having information of a violation of any provision of this part may make an oral or written report of the alleged violation to the office(s) of the Internal Revenue Service responsible for administering or enforcing this part or any officer or employee of the Internal Revenue Service. If the report is made to an officer or employee of the Internal Revenue Service, the officer or employee will make a written report of the suspected violation and submit the report to the office(s) of the Internal Revenue Service responsible for administering or enforcing this part.

(c) Destruction of report. No report made under paragraph (a) or (b) of this section shall be maintained unless retention of the report is permissible under the applicable records control schedule as approved by the National Archives and Records Administration and designated in the Internal Revenue Manual. Reports must be destroyed as soon as permissible under the applicable records control schedule.

(d) Effect on proceedings under subpart D. The destruction of any report will not bar any proceeding under subpart D of this part, but will preclude the use of a copy of the report in a proceeding under subpart D of this part.

(e) Effective/applicability date. This section is applicable beginning August 2, 2011.

SUBPART D. RULES APPLICABLE TO DISCIPLINARY PROCEEDINGS

§ 10.60 Institution of Proceeding.

(a) Whenever it is determined that a practitioner (or employer, firm or other entity, if applicable) violated any provision of the laws governing practice before the Internal Revenue Service or the regulations in this part, the practitioner may be reprimanded or, in accordance with § 10.62, subject to a proceeding for sanctions described in § 10.50.

(b) Whenever a penalty has been assessed against an appraiser under the Internal Revenue Code and an appropriate officer or employee in an office established to enforce this part determines that the appraiser acted willfully, recklessly, or through gross incompetence with respect to the proscribed conduct, the appraiser may be reprimanded or, in accordance with § 10.62, subject to a proceeding for disqualification. A proceeding for disqualification of an appraiser is instituted by the filing of a complaint, the contents of which are more fully described in § 10.62.

(c) Except as provided in § 10.82, a proceeding will not be instituted under this section unless the proposed respondent previously has been advised in writing of the law, facts and conduct warranting such action and has been accorded an opportunity to dispute facts, assert additional facts, and make arguments (including an explanation or description of mitigating circumstances).

(d) Effective/applicability date. This section is applicable beginning August 2, 2011.

§ 10.61 Conferences.

(a) In general. The Commissioner, or delegate, may confer with a practitioner, employer, firm or other entity, or an appraiser concerning allegations of misconduct irrespective of whether a proceeding has been instituted. If the conference results in a stipulation in connection with an ongoing proceeding in which the practitioner, employer, firm or other entity, or appraiser is the respondent, the stipulation may be entered in the record by either party to the proceeding.

(b) Voluntary sanction—(1) In general. In lieu of a proceeding being instituted or continued under § 10.60(a), a practitioner or appraiser (or employer, firm or other entity, if applicable) may offer a consent to be sanctioned under § 10.50.

(2) Discretion; acceptance or declination. The Commissioner, or delegate, may accept or decline the offer described in paragraph (b)(1) of this section. When the decision is to decline the offer, the written notice of declination may state that the offer described in paragraph (b)(1) of this section would be accepted if it contained different terms. The Commissioner, or delegate, has the discretion to accept or reject a revised offer submitted in response to the declination or may counteroffer and act upon any accepted counteroffer.

(c) Effective/applicability date. This section is applicable beginning August 2, 2011.

§ 10.62 Contents of complaint.

(a) Charges. A complaint must name the respondent, provide a clear and concise description of the facts and law that constitute the basis for the proceeding, and be signed by an authorized representative of the Internal Revenue Service under § 10.69(a)(1). A complaint is sufficient if it fairly informs the respondent of the charges brought so that the respondent is able to prepare a defense.

(b) Specification of sanction. The complaint must specify the sanction sought against the practitioner or appraiser. If the sanction sought is a suspension, the duration of the suspension sought must be specified.

(c) Demand for answer. The respondent must be notified in the complaint or in a separate paper attached to the complaint of the time for answering the complaint, which may not be less than 30 days from the date of service of the complaint, the name and address of the Administrative Law Judge with whom the answer must be filed, the name and address of the person representing the Internal Revenue Service to whom a copy of the answer must be served, and that a decision by default may be rendered against the respondent in the event an answer is not filed as required.

(d) Effective/applicability date. This section is applicable beginning August 2, 2011.

§ 10.63 Service of complaint; service of other papers; service of evidence in support of complaint; filing of papers.

(a) Service of complaint—

(1) In general. The complaint or a copy of the complaint must be served on the respondent by any manner described in paragraphs (a)(2) or (3) of this section.

(2) Service by certified or first class mail. (i) Service of the complaint may be made on the respondent by mailing the complaint by certified mail to the last known address (as determined under section 6212 of the Internal Revenue Code and the regulations thereunder) of the respondent. Where service is by certified mail, the returned post office receipt duly signed by the respondent will be proof of service.

(ii) If the certified mail is not claimed or accepted by the respondent, or is returned undelivered, service may be made on the respondent, by mailing the complaint to the respondent by first class mail. Service by this method will be considered complete upon mailing, provided the complaint is addressed to the respondent at the respondent's last known address as determined under section 6212 of the Internal Revenue Code and the regulations thereunder.

(3) Service by other than certified or first class mail. (i) Service of the complaint may be made on the respondent by delivery by a private delivery service designated pursuant to section 7502(f) of the Internal Revenue Code to the last known address (as determined under section 6212 of the Internal Revenue Code and the regulations thereunder) of the respondent. Service by this method will be considered complete, provided the complaint is addressed to the respondent at the respondent's last known address as determined under section 6212 of the Internal Revenue Code and the regulations thereunder.

(ii) Service of the complaint may be made in person on, or by leaving the complaint at the office or place of business of, the respondent. Service by this method will be considered complete and proof of service will be a written statement, sworn or affirmed by the person who served the complaint, identifying the manner of service, including the recipient, relationship of recipient to respondent, place, date and time of service.

(iii) Service may be made by any other means agreed to by the respondent. Proof of service will be a written statement, sworn or affirmed by the person who served the complaint, identifying the manner of service, including the recipient, relationship of recipient to respondent, place, date and time of service.

(4) For purposes of this section, respondent means the practitioner, employer, firm or other entity, or appraiser named in the complaint or any other person having the authority to accept mail on behalf of the practitioner, employer, firm or other entity, or appraiser.

(b) Service of papers other than complaint. Any paper other than the complaint may be served on the respondent, or his or her authorized representative under § 10.69(a)(2) by:

(1) Mailing the paper by first class mail to the last known address (as determined under section 6212 of the Internal Revenue Code and the regulations thereunder) of the respondent or the respondent's authorized representative,

(2) Delivery by a private delivery service designated pursuant to section 7502(f) of the Internal Revenue Code to the last known address (as determined under section 6212 of the Internal Revenue Code and the regulations thereunder) of the respondent or the respondent's authorized representative, or

(3) As provided in paragraphs (a)(3)(ii) and (a)(3)(iii) of this section.

(c) Service of papers on the Internal Revenue Service. Whenever a paper is required or permitted to be served on the Internal Revenue Service in connection with a proceeding under this part, the paper will be served on the Internal Revenue Service's authorized representative under § 10.69(a)(1) at the address designated in the complaint, or at an address provided in a notice of appearance. If no address is designated in the complaint or provided in a notice of appearance, service will be made on the office(s) established to enforce this part under the authority of § 10.1, Internal Revenue Service, 1111 Constitution Avenue, NW., Washington, DC 20224.

(d) Service of evidence in support of complaint. Within 10 days of serving the complaint, copies of the evidence in support of the complaint must be served on the respondent in any manner described in paragraphs (a)(2) and (3) of this section.

(e) Filing of papers. Whenever the filing of a paper is required or permitted in connection with a proceeding under this part, the original paper, plus one additional copy, must be filed with the Administrative Law Judge at the address specified in the complaint or at an address otherwise specified by the Administrative Law Judge. All papers filed in connection with a proceeding under this part must be served on the other party, unless the Administrative Law Judge directs otherwise. A certificate evidencing such must be attached to the original paper filed with the Administrative Law Judge.

(f) Effective/applicability date. This section is applicable beginning August 2, 2011.

§ 10.64 Answer; default.

(a) Filing. The respondent's answer must be filed with the Administrative Law Judge, and served on the Internal Revenue Service, within the time specified in the complaint unless, on request or application of the respondent, the time is extended by the Administrative Law Judge.

(b) Contents. The answer must be written and contain a statement of facts that constitute the respondent's grounds of defense. General denials are not permitted. The respondent must specifically admit or deny each allegation set forth in the complaint, except that the respondent may state that the respondent is without sufficient information to admit or deny a specific allegation. The respondent, nevertheless, may not deny a material allegation in the complaint that the respondent knows to be true, or state that the respondent is without sufficient information to form a belief, when the respondent possesses the required information. The respondent also must state affirmatively any special matters of defense on which he or she relies.

(c) Failure to deny or answer allegations in the complaint. Every allegation in the complaint that is not denied in the answer is deemed admitted and will be considered proved; no further evidence in respect of such allegation need be adduced at a hearing.

(d) Default. Failure to file an answer within the time prescribed (or within the time for answer as extended by the Administrative Law Judge), constitutes an admission of the allegations of the complaint and a waiver of hearing, and the Administrative Law Judge may make the decision by default without a hearing or further procedure. A decision by default constitutes a decision under § 10.76.

(e) Signature. The answer must be signed by the respondent or the respondent's authorized representative under § 10.69(a)(2) and must include a statement directly above the signature acknowledging that the statements made in the answer are true and correct and that knowing and willful false statements may be punishable under 18 U.S.C. 1001.

(f) Effective/applicability date. This section is applicable beginning August 2, 2011.

§ 10.65 Supplemental charges.

(a) In general. Supplemental charges may be filed against the respondent by amending the complaint with the permission of the Administrative Law Judge if, for example—

(1) It appears that the respondent, in the answer, falsely and in bad faith, denies a material allegation of fact in the complaint or states that the respondent has insufficient knowledge to form a belief, when the respondent possesses such information; or

(2) It appears that the respondent has knowingly introduced false testimony during the proceedings against the respondent.

(b) Hearing. The supplemental charges may be heard with other charges in the case, provided the respondent is given due notice of the charges and is afforded a reasonable opportunity to prepare a defense to the supplemental charges.

(c) Effective/applicability date. This section is applicable beginning August 2, 2011.

§ 10.66 Reply to answer.

(a) The Internal Revenue Service may file a reply to the respondent's answer, but unless otherwise ordered by the Administrative Law Judge, no reply to the respondent's answer is required. If a reply is not filed, new matter in the answer is deemed denied.

(b) Effective/applicability date. This section is applicable beginning August 2, 2011.

§ 10.67 Proof; variance; amendment of pleadings.

In the case of a variance between the allegations in pleadings and the evidence adduced in support of the pleadings, the Administrative Law Judge, at any time before decision, may order or authorize amendment of the pleadings to conform to the evidence. The party who would otherwise be prejudiced by the amendment must be given a reasonable opportunity to address the allegations of the pleadings as amended and the Administrative Law Judge must make findings on any issue presented by the pleadings as amended.

§ 10.68 Motions and requests.

(a) Motions—(1) In general. At any time after the filing of the complaint, any party may file a motion with the Administrative Law Judge. Unless otherwise ordered by the Administrative Law Judge, motions must be in writing and must be served on the opposing party as provided in § 10.63(b). A motion must concisely specify its grounds and the relief sought, and, if appropriate, must contain a memorandum of facts and law in support.

(2) Summary adjudication. Either party may move for a summary adjudication upon all or any part of the legal issues in controversy. If the non-moving party opposes summary adjudication in the moving party's favor, the non-moving party must file a written response within 30 days unless ordered otherwise by the Administrative Law Judge.

(3) Good Faith. A party filing a motion for extension of time, a motion for postponement of a hearing, or any other non-dispositive or procedural motion must first contact the other party to determine whether there is any objection to the motion, and must state in the motion whether the other party has an objection.

(b) Response. Unless otherwise ordered by the Administrative Law Judge, the nonmoving party is not required to file a response to a motion. If the Administrative Law Judge does not order the nonmoving party to file a response, and the nonmoving party files no response, the nonmoving party is deemed to oppose the motion. If a nonmoving party does not respond within 30 days of the filing of a motion for decision by default for failure to file a timely answer or for failure to prosecute, the nonmoving party is deemed not to oppose the motion.

(c) Oral motions; oral argument—(1) The Administrative Law Judge may, for good cause and with notice to the parties, permit oral motions and oral opposition to motions.

(2) The Administrative Law Judge may, within his or her discretion, permit oral argument on any motion.

(d) Orders. The Administrative Law Judge should issue written orders disposing of any motion or request and any response thereto.

(e) Effective/applicability date. This section is applicable on September 26, 2007.

§ 10.69 Representation; ex parte communication.

(a) Representation. (1) The Internal Revenue Service may be represented in proceedings under this part by an attorney or other employee of the Internal Revenue Service. An attorney or an employee of the Internal Revenue Service representing the Internal Revenue Service in a proceeding under this part may sign the complaint or any document required to be filed in the proceeding on behalf of the Internal Revenue Service.

(2) A respondent may appear in person, be represented by a practitioner, or be represented by an attorney who has not filed a declaration with the Internal Revenue Service pursuant to § 10.3. A practitioner or an attorney representing a respondent or proposed respondent may sign the answer or any document required to be filed in the proceeding on behalf of the respondent.

(b) Ex parte communication. The Internal Revenue Service, the respondent, and any representatives of either party, may not attempt to initiate or participate in ex parte discussions concerning a proceeding or potential proceeding with the Administrative Law Judge (or any person who is likely to advise the Administrative Law Judge on a ruling or decision) in the proceeding before or during the pendency of the proceeding. Any memorandum, letter or other communication concerning the merits of the proceeding, addressed to the Administrative Law Judge, by or on behalf of any party shall be regarded as an argument in the proceeding and shall be served on the other party.

(c) Effective/applicability date. This section is applicable beginning August 2, 2011.

§ 10.70 Administrative Law Judge.

(a) Appointment. Proceedings on complaints for the sanction (as described in § 10.50) of a practitioner, employer, firm or other entity, or appraiser will be conducted by an Administrative Law Judge appointed as provided by 5 U.S.C. 3105.

(b) Powers of the Administrative Law Judge. The Administrative Law Judge, among other powers, has the authority, in connection with any proceeding under § 10.60 assigned or referred to him or her, to do the following:

(1) Administer oaths and affirmations;

(2) Make rulings on motions and requests, which rulings may not be appealed prior to the close of a hearing except in extraordinary circumstances and at the discretion of the Administrative Law Judge;

(3) Determine the time and place of hearing and regulate its course and conduct;

(4) Adopt rules of procedure and modify the same from time to time as needed for the orderly disposition of proceedings;

(5) Rule on offers of proof, receive relevant evidence, and examine witnesses;

(6) Take or authorize the taking of depositions or answers to requests for admission;

(7) Receive and consider oral or written argument on facts or law;

(8) Hold or provide for the holding of conferences for the settlement or simplification of the issues with the consent of the parties;

(9) Perform such acts and take such measures as are necessary or appropriate to the efficient conduct of any proceeding; and

(10) Make decisions.

(c) Effective/applicability date. This section is applicable on September 26, 2007.

§ 10.71 Discovery.

(a) In general. Discovery may be permitted, at the discretion of the Administrative Law Judge, only upon written motion demonstrating the relevance, materiality and reasonableness of the requested discovery and subject to the requirements of § 10.72(d)(2) and (3). Within 10 days of receipt of the answer, the Administrative Law Judge will notify the parties of the right to request discovery and the timeframes for filing a request. A request for discovery, and objections, must be filed in accordance with § 10.68. In response to a request for discovery, the Administrative Law Judge may order—

(1) Depositions upon oral examination; or

(2) Answers to requests for admission.

(b) Depositions upon oral examination—(1) A deposition must be taken before an officer duly authorized to administer an oath for general purposes or before an officer or employee of the Internal Revenue Service who is authorized to administer an oath in Federal tax law matters.

(2) In ordering a deposition, the Administrative Law Judge will require reasonable notice to the opposing party as to the time and place of the deposition. The opposing party, if attending, will be provided the opportunity for full examination and cross-examination of any witness.

(3) Expenses in the reporting of depositions shall be borne by the party at whose instance the deposition is taken. Travel expenses of the deponent shall be borne by the party requesting the deposition, unless otherwise authorized by Federal law or regulation.

(c) Requests for admission. Any party may serve on any other party a written request for admission of the truth of any matters which are not privileged and are relevant to the subject matter of this proceeding. Requests for admission shall not exceed a total of 30 (including any subparts within a specific request) without the approval from the Administrative Law Judge.

(d) Limitations. Discovery shall not be authorized if—

(1) The request fails to meet any requirement set forth in paragraph (a) of this section;

(2) It will unduly delay the proceeding;

(3) It will place an undue burden on the party required to produce the discovery sought;

(4) It is frivolous or abusive;

(5) It is cumulative or duplicative;

(6) The material sought is privileged or otherwise protected from disclosure by law;

(7) The material sought relates to mental impressions, conclusions, or legal theories of any party, attorney, or other representative, of a party prepared in anticipation of a proceeding; or

(8) The material sought is available generally to the public, equally to the parties, or to the party seeking the discovery through another source.

(e) Failure to comply. Where a party fails to comply with an order of the Administrative Law Judge under this section, the Administrative Law Judge may, among other things, infer that the information would be adverse to the party failing to provide it, exclude the information from evidence or issue a decision by default.

(f) Other discovery. No discovery other than that specifically provided for in this section is permitted.

(g) Effective/applicability date. This section is applicable to proceedings initiated on or after September 26, 2007.

§ 10.72 Hearings.

(a) In general—(1) Presiding officer. An Administrative Law Judge will preside at the hearing on a complaint filed under § 10.60 for the sanction of a practitioner, employer, firm or other entity, or appraiser.

(2) Time for hearing. Absent a determination by the Administrative Law Judge that, in the interest of justice, a hearing must be held at a later time, the Administrative Law Judge should, on notice sufficient to allow proper preparation, schedule the hearing to occur no later than 180 days after the time for filing the answer.

(3) Procedural requirements. (i) Hearings will be stenographically recorded and transcribed and the testimony of witnesses will be taken under oath or affirmation.

(ii) Hearings will be conducted pursuant to 5 U.S.C. 556.

(iii) A hearing in a proceeding requested under § 10.82(g) will be conducted de novo.

(iv) An evidentiary hearing must be held in all proceedings prior to the issuance of a decision by the Administrative Law Judge unless—

(A) The Internal Revenue Service withdraws the complaint;

(B) A decision is issued by default pursuant to § 10.64(d);

(C) A decision is issued under § 10.82(e);

(D) The respondent requests a decision on the written record without a hearing; or

(E) The Administrative Law Judge issues a decision under § 10.68(d) or rules on another motion that disposes of the case prior to the hearing.

(b) Cross-examination. A party is entitled to present his or her case or defense by oral or documentary evidence, to submit rebuttal evidence, and to conduct cross-examination, in the presence of the Administrative Law Judge, as may be required for a full and true disclosure of the facts. This paragraph (b) does not limit a party from presenting evidence contained within a deposition when the Administrative Law Judge determines that the deposition has been obtained in compliance with the rules of this subpart D.

(c) Prehearing memorandum. Unless otherwise ordered by the Administrative Law Judge, each party shall file, and serve on the opposing party or the opposing party's representative, prior to any hearing, a prehearing memorandum containing—

(1) A list (together with a copy) of all proposed exhibits to be used in the party's case in chief;

(2) A list of proposed witnesses, including a synopsis of their expected testimony, or a statement that no witnesses will be called;

(3) Identification of any proposed expert witnesses, including a synopsis of their expected testimony and a copy of any report prepared by the expert or at his or her direction; and

(4) A list of undisputed facts.

(d) Publicity—(1) In general. All reports and decisions of the Secretary of the Treasury, or delegate, including any reports and decisions of the Administrative Law Judge, under this subpart D are, subject to the protective measures in paragraph (d)(4) of this section, public and open to inspection within 30 days after the agency's decision becomes final.

(2) Request for additional publicity. The Administrative Law Judge may grant a request by a practitioner or appraiser that all the pleadings and evidence of the disciplinary proceeding be made available for inspection where the parties stipulate in advance to adopt the protective measures in paragraph (d)(4) of this section.

(3) Returns and return information—(i) Disclosure to practitioner or appraiser. Pursuant to section 6103(*l*)(4) of the Internal Revenue Code, the Secretary of the Treasury, or delegate, may disclose returns and return information to any practitioner or appraiser, or to the authorized representative of the practitioner or appraiser, whose rights are or may be affected by an administrative action or proceeding under this subpart D, but solely for use in the action or proceeding and only to the extent that the Secretary of the Treasury, or delegate, determines that the returns or return information are or may be relevant and material to the action or proceeding.

(ii) Disclosure to officers and employees of the Department of the Treasury. Pursuant to section 6103(*l*)(4)(B) of the Internal Revenue Code, the Secretary of the Treasury, or delegate, may disclose returns and return information to officers and employees of the Department of the Treasury for use in any action or proceeding under this subpart D, to the extent necessary to advance or protect the interests of the United States.

(iii) Use of returns and return information. Recipients of returns and return information under this paragraph (d)(3) may use the returns or return information solely in the action or proceeding, or in preparation for the action or proceeding, with respect to which the disclosure was made.

(iv) Procedures for disclosure of returns and return information. When providing returns or return information to the practitioner or appraiser, or authorized representative, the Secretary of the Treasury, or delegate, will—

(A) Redact identifying information of any third party taxpayers and replace it with a code;

(B) Provide a key to the coded information; and

(C) Notify the practitioner or appraiser, or authorized representative, of the restrictions on the use and disclosure of the returns and return information, the applicable damages remedy under section 7431 of the Internal Revenue Code, and that unauthorized disclosure of information provided by the Internal Revenue Service under this paragraph (d)(3) is also a violation of this part.

(4) Protective measures—(i) Mandatory protective order. If redaction of names, addresses, and other identifying information of third party taxpayers may still permit indirect identification of any third party taxpayer, the Administrative Law Judge will issue a protective order to ensure that the identifying information is available to the parties and the Administrative Law Judge for purposes of the proceeding, but is not disclosed to, or open to inspection by, the public.

(ii) Authorized orders. (A) Upon motion by a party or any other affected person, and for good cause shown, the Administrative Law Judge may make any order which justice requires to protect any person in the event disclosure of information is prohibited by law, privileged, confidential, or sensitive in some other way, including, but not limited to, one or more of the following—

(*1*) That disclosure of information be made only on specified terms and conditions, including a designation of the time or place;

(*2*) That a trade secret or other information not be disclosed, or be disclosed only in a designated way.

(iii) Denials. If a motion for a protective order is denied in whole or in part, the Administrative Law Judge may, on such terms or conditions as the Administrative Law

Judge deems just, order any party or person to comply with, or respond in accordance with, the procedure involved.

(iv) Public inspection of documents. The Secretary of the Treasury, or delegate, shall ensure that all names, addresses or other identifying details of third party taxpayers are redacted and replaced with the code assigned to the corresponding taxpayer in all documents prior to public inspection of such documents.

(e) Location. The location of the hearing will be determined by the agreement of the parties with the approval of the Administrative Law Judge, but, in the absence of such agreement and approval, the hearing will be held in Washington, D.C.

(f) Failure to appear. If either party to the proceeding fails to appear at the hearing, after notice of the proceeding has been sent to him or her, the party will be deemed to have waived the right to a hearing and the Administrative Law Judge may make his or her decision against the absent party by default.

(g) Effective/applicability date. This section is applicable beginning August 2, 2011.

§ 10.73 Evidence.

(a) In general. The rules of evidence prevailing in courts of law and equity are not controlling in hearings or proceedings conducted under this part. The Administrative Law Judge may, however, exclude evidence that is irrelevant, immaterial, or unduly repetitious,

(b) Depositions. The deposition of any witness taken pursuant to § 10.71 may be admitted into evidence in any proceeding instituted under § 10.60.

(c) Requests for admission. Any matter admitted in response to a request for admission under § 10.71 is conclusively established unless the Administrative Law Judge on motion permits withdrawal or modification of the admission. Any admission made by a party is for the purposes of the pending action only and is not an admission by a party for any other purpose, nor may it be used against a party in any other proceeding.

(d) Proof of documents. Official documents, records, and papers of the Internal Revenue Service and the Office of Professional Responsibility are admissible in evidence without the production of an officer or employee to authenticate them. Any documents, records, and papers may be evidenced by a copy attested to or identified by an officer or employee of the Internal Revenue Service or the Treasury Department, as the case may be.

(e) Withdrawal of exhibits. If any document, record, or other paper is introduced in evidence as an exhibit, the Administrative Law Judge may authorize the withdrawal of the exhibit subject to any conditions that he or she deems proper.

(f) Objections. Objections to evidence are to be made in short form, stating the grounds for the objection. Except as ordered by the Administrative Law Judge, argument on objections will not be recorded or transcribed. Rulings on objections are to be a part of the record, but no exception to a ruling is necessary to preserve the rights of the parties.

(g) Effective/applicability date. This section is applicable on September 26, 2007.

§ 10.74 Transcript.

In cases where the hearing is stenographically reported by a Government contract reporter, copies of the transcript may be obtained from the reporter at rates not to exceed the maximum rates fixed by contract between the Government and the reporter. Where the hearing is stenographically reported by a regular employee of the Internal Revenue Service, a copy will be supplied to the respondent either without charge or upon the payment of a reasonable fee. Copies of exhibits introduced at the hearing or at the taking of depositions will be supplied to the parties upon the payment of a reasonable fee (Sec. 501, Public Law 82–137) (65 Stat. 290) (31 U.S.C. 483a).

§ 10.75 Proposed findings and conclusions.

Except in cases where the respondent has failed to answer the complaint or where a party has failed to appear at the hearing, the parties must be afforded a reasonable opportunity to submit proposed findings and conclusions and their supporting reasons to the Administrative Law Judge.

§ 10.76 Decision of Administrative Law Judge.

(a) In general—(1) Hearings. Within 180 days after the conclusion of a hearing and the receipt of any proposed findings and conclusions timely submitted by the parties, the Administrative Law Judge should enter a decision in the case. The decision must include a statement of findings and conclusions, as well as the reasons or basis for making such findings and conclusions, and an order of censure, suspension, disbarment, monetary penalty, disqualification, or dismissal of the complaint.

(2) Summary adjudication. In the event that a motion for summary adjudication is filed, the Administrative Law Judge should rule on the motion for summary adjudication within 60 days after the party in opposition files a written response, or if no written response is filed, within 90 days after the motion for summary adjudication is filed. A decision shall thereafter be rendered if the pleadings, depositions, admissions, and any other admissible evidence show that there is no genuine issue of material fact and that a decision may be rendered as a matter of law. The decision must include a statement of conclusions, as well as the reasons or basis for making such conclusions, and an order of censure, suspension, disbarment, monetary penalty, disqualification, or dismissal of the complaint.

(3) Returns and return information. In the decision, the Administrative Law Judge should use the code assigned to third party taxpayers (described in § 10.72(d)).

(b) Standard of proof. If the sanction is censure or a suspension of less than six months' duration, the Administrative Law Judge, in rendering findings and conclusions, will consider an allegation of fact to be proven if it is established by the party who is alleging the fact by a preponderance of the evidence in the record. If the sanction is a monetary penalty, disbarment or a suspension of six months or longer duration, an allegation of fact that is necessary for a finding against the practitioner must be proven by clear and convincing evidence in the record. An allegation of fact that is necessary for a finding of disqualification against an appraiser must be proven by clear and convincing evidence in the record.

(c) Copy of decision. The Administrative Law Judge will provide the decision to the Internal Revenue Service's authorized representative, and a copy of the decision to the respondent or the respondent's authorized representative.

(d) When final. In the absence of an appeal to the Secretary of the Treasury or delegate, the decision of the Administrative Law Judge will, without further proceedings, become the decision of the agency 30 days after the date of the Administrative Law Judge's decision.

(e) Effective/applicability date. This section is applicable beginning August 2, 2011.

§ 10.77 Appeal of decision of Administrative Law Judge.

(a) Appeal. Any party to the proceeding under this subpart D may appeal the decision of the Administrative Law Judge by filing a notice of appeal with the Secretary of the Treasury, or delegate deciding appeals. The notice of appeal must include a brief that states exceptions to the decision of Administrative Law Judge and supporting reasons for such exceptions.

(b) Time and place for filing of appeal. The notice of appeal and brief must be filed, in duplicate, with the Secretary of the Treasury, or delegate deciding appeals, at an address for appeals that is identified to the parties with the decision of the Administrative Law Judge. The notice of appeal and brief must be filed within 30 days of the date that the decision of the Administrative Law Judge is served on the parties. The appealing party must serve a copy of the notice of appeal and the brief to any non-appealing party or, if the party is represented, the non-appealing party's representative.

(c) Response. Within 30 days of receiving the copy of the appellant's brief, the other party may file a response brief with the Secretary of the Treasury, or delegate deciding appeals, using the address identified for appeals. A copy of the response brief must be served at the same time on the opposing party or, if the party is represented, the opposing party's representative.

(d) No other briefs, responses or motions as of right. Other than the appeal brief and response brief, the parties are not permitted to file any other briefs, responses or motions, except on a grant of leave to do so after a motion demonstrating sufficient cause, or unless otherwise ordered by the Secretary of the Treasury, or delegate deciding appeals.

(e) Additional time for briefs and responses. Notwithstanding the time for filing briefs and responses provided in paragraphs (b) and (c) of this section, the Secretary of the Treasury, or delegate deciding appeals, may, for good cause, authorize additional time for filing briefs and responses upon a motion of a party or upon the initiative of the Secretary of the Treasury, or delegate deciding appeals.

(f) Effective/applicability date. This section is applicable beginning August 2, 2011.

§ 10.78 Decision on review.

(a) Decision on review. On appeal from or review of the decision of the Administrative Law Judge, the Secretary of the Treasury, or delegate, will make the agency decision. The Secretary of the Treasury, or delegate, should make the agency decision within 180 days after receipt of the appeal.

(b) Standard of review. The decision of the Administrative Law Judge will not be reversed unless the appellant establishes that the decision is clearly erroneous in light of the evidence in the record and applicable law. Issues that are exclusively matters of law will be reviewed de novo. In the event that the Secretary of the Treasury, or delegate, determines that there are unresolved issues raised by the record, the case may be remanded to the Administrative Law Judge to elicit additional testimony or evidence.

(c) Copy of decision on review. The Secretary of the Treasury, or delegate, will provide copies of the agency decision to the authorized representative of the Internal Revenue Service and the respondent or the respondent's authorized representative.

(d) Effective/applicability date. This section is applicable beginning August 2, 2011.

§ 10.79 Effect of disbarment, suspension, or censure.

(a) Disbarment. When the final decision in a case is against the respondent (or the respondent has offered his or her consent and such consent has been accepted by the Internal Revenue Service) and such decision is for disbarment, the respondent will not be permitted to practice before the Internal Revenue Service unless and until authorized to do so by the Internal Revenue Service pursuant to § 10.81.

(b) Suspension. When the final decision in a case is against the respondent (or the respondent has offered his or her consent and such consent has been accepted by the Internal Revenue Service) and such decision is for suspension, the respondent will not be permitted to practice before the Internal Revenue Service during the period of suspension. For periods after the suspension, the practitioner's future representations may be subject to conditions as authorized by paragraph (d) of this section.

(c) Censure. When the final decision in the case is against the respondent (or the Internal Revenue Service has accepted the respondent's offer to consent, if such offer was made) and such decision is for censure, the respondent will be permitted to practice before the Internal Revenue Service, but the respondent's future representations may be subject to conditions as authorized by paragraph (d) of this section.

(d) Conditions. After being subject to the sanction of either suspension or censure, the future representations of a practitioner so sanctioned shall be subject to specified conditions designed to promote high standards of conduct. These conditions can be imposed for a reasonable period in light of the gravity of the practitioner's violations. For example, where a practitioner is censured because the practitioner failed to advise the practitioner's clients about a potential conflict of interest or failed to obtain the clients' written consents, the practitioner may be required to provide the Internal Revenue Service with a copy of all consents obtained by the practitioner for an appropriate period following censure, whether or not such consents are specifically requested.

(e) Effective/applicability date. This section is applicable beginning August 2, 2011.

§ 10.80 Notice of disbarment, suspension, censure, or disqualification.

(a) In general. On the issuance of a final order censuring, suspending, or disbarring a practitioner or a final order disqualifying an appraiser, notification of the censure, suspension, disbarment or disqualification will be given to appropriate officers and employees of the Internal Revenue Service and interested departments and agencies of the Federal government. The Internal Revenue Service may determine the manner of giving notice to the proper authorities of the State by which the censured, suspended, or disbarred person was licensed to practice.

(b) Effective/applicability date. This section is applicable beginning August 2, 2011.

§ 10.81 Petition for reinstatement.

(a) In general. A practitioner disbarred or suspended under § 10.60, or suspended under § 10.82, or a disqualified appraiser may petition for reinstatement before the Internal Revenue Service after the expiration of 5 years following such disbarment, suspension, or disqualification (or immediately following the expiration of the suspension or disqualification period, if shorter than 5 years). Reinstatement will not be granted unless the Internal Revenue Service is satisfied that the petitioner is not likely to engage thereafter in conduct contrary to the regulations in this part, and that granting such reinstatement would not be contrary to the public interest.

(b) Effective/applicability date. This section is applicable beginning June 12, 2014.

§ 10.82 Expedited suspension.

(a) When applicable. Whenever the Commissioner, or delegate, determines that a practitioner is described in paragraph (b) of this section, expedited proceedings described in this section may be used to suspend the practitioner from practice before the Internal Revenue Service.

(b) To whom applicable. This section applies to any practitioner who, within 5 years prior to the date that a show cause order under this section's expedited suspension procedures is served:

(1) Has had a license to practice as an attorney, certified public accountant, or actuary suspended or revoked for cause (not including failure to pay a professional licensing fee) by any authority or court, agency, body, or board described in § 10.51(a)(10).

(2) Has, irrespective of whether an appeal has been taken, been convicted of any crime under title 26 of the United States Code, any crime involving dishonesty or breach of trust, or any felony for which the conduct involved renders the practitioner unfit to practice before the Internal Revenue Service.

(3) Has violated conditions imposed on the practitioner pursuant to § 10.79(d).

(4) Has been sanctioned by a court of competent jurisdiction, whether in a civil or criminal proceeding (including suits for injunctive relief), relating to any taxpayer's tax liability or relating to the practitioner's own tax liability, for—

(i) Instituting or maintaining proceedings primarily for delay;

(ii) Advancing frivolous or groundless arguments; or

(iii) Failing to pursue available administrative remedies.

(5) Has demonstrated a pattern of willful disreputable conduct by—

(i) Failing to make an annual Federal tax return, in violation of the Federal tax laws, during 4 of the 5 tax years immediately preceding the institution of a proceeding under paragraph (c) of this section and remains noncompliant with any of the practitioner's Federal tax filing obligations at the time the notice of suspension is issued under paragraph (f) of this section; or

(ii) Failing to make a return required more frequently than annually, in violation of the Federal tax laws, during 5 of the 7 tax periods immediately preceding the institution of a proceeding under paragraph (c) of this section and remains noncompliant with any of the practitioner's Federal tax filing obligations at the time the notice of suspension is issued under paragraph (f) of this section.

(c) Expedited suspension procedures. A suspension under this section will be proposed by a show cause order that names the respondent, is signed by an authorized representative of the Internal Revenue Service under § 10.69(a)(1), and served according to the rules set forth in § 10.63(a). The show cause order must give a plain and concise description of the allegations that constitute the basis for the proposed suspension. The show cause order must notify the respondent—

(1) Of the place and due date for filing a response;

(2) That an expedited suspension decision by default may be rendered if the respondent fails to file a response as required;

(3) That the respondent may request a conference to address the merits of the show cause order and that any such request must be made in the response; and

(4) That the respondent may be suspended either immediately following the expiration of the period within which a response must be filed or, if a conference is requested, immediately following the conference.

(d) Response. The response to the show cause order described in this section must be filed no later than 30 calendar days following the date the show cause order is served, unless the time for filing is extended. The response must be filed in accordance with the rules set forth for answers to a complaint in § 10.64, except as otherwise provided in this section. The response must include a request for a conference, if a conference is desired. The respondent is entitled to the conference only if the request is made in a timely filed response.

(e) Conference. An authorized representative of the Internal Revenue Service will preside at a conference described in this section. The conference will be held at a place and time selected by the Internal Revenue Service, but no sooner than 14 calendar days after the date by which the response must be filed with the Internal Revenue Service, unless the respondent agrees to an earlier date. An authorized representative may represent the respondent at the conference.

(f) Suspension—(1) In general. The Commissioner, or delegate, may suspend the respondent from practice before the Internal Revenue Service by a written notice of expedited suspension immediately following:

(i) The expiration of the period within which a response to a show cause order must be filed if the respondent does not file a response as required by paragraph (d) of this section;

(ii) The conference described in paragraph (e) of this section if the Internal Revenue Service finds that the respondent is described in paragraph (b) of this section; or

(iii) The respondent's failure to appear, either personally or through an authorized representative, at a conference scheduled by the Internal Revenue Service under paragraph (e) of this section.

(2) Duration of suspension. A suspension under this section will commence on the date that the written notice of expedited suspension is served on the practitioner, either personally or through an authorized representative. The suspension will remain effective until the earlier of:

(i) The date the Internal Revenue Service lifts the suspension after determining that the practitioner is no longer described in paragraph (b) of this section or for any other reason; or

(ii) The date the suspension is lifted or otherwise modified by an Administrative Law Judge or the Secretary of the Treasury, or delegate deciding appeals, in a proceeding referred to in paragraph (g) of this section and instituted under § 10.60.

(g) Practitioner demand for § 10.60 proceeding. If the Internal Revenue Service suspends a practitioner under the expedited suspension procedures described in this section, the practitioner may demand that the Internal Revenue Service institute a proceeding under § 10.60 and issue the complaint described in § 10.62. The demand must be in writing, specifically reference the suspension action under § 10.82, and be made within 2 years from the date on which the practitioner's suspension commenced. The Internal Revenue Service must issue a complaint demanded under this paragraph (g) within 60 calendar days of receiving the demand. If the Internal Revenue Service does not issue such complaint within 60 days of receiving the demand, the suspension is lifted automatically. The preceding sentence does not, however, preclude the Commissioner, or delegate, from instituting a regular proceeding under § 10.60 of this part.

(h) Effective/applicability date. This section is generally applicable beginning June 12, 2014, except that paragraphs (b)(1) through (4) of this section are applicable beginning August 2, 2011.

STANDARDS OF PROFESSIONAL CONDUCT FOR ATTORNEYS APPEARING AND PRACTICING BEFORE THE SECURITIES AND EXCHANGE COMMISSION IN THE REPRESENTATION OF AN ISSUER

CONTENTS

---

§ 205.1 Purpose and scope

This part sets forth minimum standards of professional conduct for attorneys appearing and practicing before the Commission in the representation of an issuer. These standards supplement applicable standards of any jurisdiction where an attorney is admitted or practices and are not intended to limit the ability of any jurisdiction to impose additional obligations on an attorney not inconsistent with the application of this part. Where the standards of a state or other United States jurisdiction where an attorney is admitted or practices conflict with this part, this part shall govern.

§ 205.2 Definitions

For purposes of this part, the following definitions apply:

(a) *Appearing and practicing before the Commission:*

(1) Means:

(i) Transacting any business with the Commission, including communications in any form;

(ii) Representing an issuer in a Commission administrative proceeding or in connection with any Commission investigation, inquiry, information request, or subpoena;

(iii) Providing advice in respect of the United States securities laws or the Commission's rules or regulations thereunder regarding any document that the attorney has notice will be filed with or submitted to, or incorporated into any document that will be filed with or submitted to, the Commission, including the provision of such advice in the context of preparing, or participating in the preparation of, any such document; or

(iv) Advising an issuer as to whether information or a statement, opinion, or other writing is required under the United States securities laws or the Commission's rules or regulations thereunder to be filed with or submitted to, or incorporated into any document that will be filed with or submitted to, the Commission; but

(2) Does not include an attorney who:

(i) Conducts the activities in paragraphs (a)(1)(i) through (a)(1)(iv) of this section other than in the context of providing legal services to an issuer with whom the attorney has an attorney-client relationship; or

(ii) Is a non-appearing foreign attorney.

(b) *Appropriate response* means a response to an attorney regarding reported evidence of a material violation as a result of which the attorney reasonably believes:

(1) That no material violation, as defined in paragraph (i) of this section, has occurred, is ongoing, or is about to occur;

(2) That the issuer has, as necessary, adopted appropriate remedial measures, including appropriate steps or sanctions to stop any material violations that are ongoing, to prevent any material violation that has yet to occur, and to remedy or otherwise appropriately address any material violation that has already occurred and to minimize the likelihood of its recurrence; or

(3) That the issuer, with the consent of the issuer's board of directors, a committee thereof to whom a report could be made pursuant to § 205.3(b)(3), or a qualified legal compliance committee, has retained or directed an attorney to review the reported evidence of a material violation and either:

(i) Has substantially implemented any remedial recommendations made by such attorney after a reasonable investigation and evaluation of the reported evidence; or

(ii) Has been advised that such attorney may, consistent with his or her professional obligations, assert a colorable defense on behalf of the issuer (or the issuer's officer, director, employee, or agent, as the case may be) in any investigation or judicial or administrative proceeding relating to the reported evidence of a material violation.

(c) *Attorney* means any person who is admitted, licensed, or otherwise qualified to practice law in any jurisdiction, domestic or foreign, or who holds himself or herself out as admitted, licensed, or otherwise qualified to practice law.

(d) *Breach of fiduciary duty* refers to any breach of fiduciary or similar duty to the issuer recognized under an applicable Federal or State statute or at common law, including but not limited to misfeasance, nonfeasance, abdication of duty, abuse of trust, and approval of unlawful transactions.

(e) *Evidence of a material violation* means credible evidence, based upon which it would be unreasonable, under the circumstances, for a prudent and competent attorney not to conclude that it is reasonably likely that a material violation has occurred, is ongoing, or is about to occur.

(f) *Foreign government issuer* means a foreign issuer as defined in 17 CFR 230.405 eligible to register securities on Schedule B of the Securities Act of 1933 (15 U.S.C. 77a et seq., Schedule B).

(g) *In the representation of an issuer* means providing legal services as an attorney for an issuer, regardless of whether the attorney is employed or retained by the issuer.

(h) *Issuer* means an issuer (as defined in section 3 of the Securities Exchange Act of 1934 (15 U.S.C. 78c)), the securities of which are registered under section 12 of that Act (15 U.S.C. 78l), or that is required to file reports under section 15(d) of that Act (15 U.S.C. 78o(d)), or that files or has filed a registration statement that has not yet become effective under the Securities Act of 1933 (15 U.S.C. 77a et seq.), and that it has not withdrawn, but does not include a foreign government issuer. For purposes of paragraphs (a) and (g) of this section, the term "issuer" includes any person controlled by an issuer, where an attorney provides legal services to such person on behalf of, or at the behest, or for the benefit of the issuer, regardless of whether the attorney is employed or retained by the issuer.

(i) *Material violation* means a material violation of an applicable United States federal or state securities law, a material breach of fiduciary duty arising under United States federal or state law, or a similar material violation of any United States federal or state law.

(j) *Non-appearing foreign attorney* means an attorney:

(1) Who is admitted to practice law in a jurisdiction outside the United States;

(2) Who does not hold himself or herself out as practicing, and does not give legal advice regarding, United States federal or state securities or other laws (except as provided in paragraph (j)(3)(ii) of this section); and

(3) Who:

(i) Conducts activities that would constitute appearing and practicing before the Commission only incidentally to, and in the ordinary course of, the practice of law in a jurisdiction outside the United States; or

(ii) Is appearing and practicing before the Commission only in consultation with counsel, other than a non-appearing foreign attorney, admitted or licensed to practice in a state or other United States jurisdiction.

(k) *Qualified legal compliance committee* means a committee of an issuer (which also may be an audit or other committee of the issuer) that:

(1) Consists of at least one member of the issuer's audit committee (or, if the issuer has no audit committee, one member from an equivalent committee of independent directors) and two or more members of the issuer's board of directors who are not employed, directly or indirectly, by the issuer and who are not, in the case of a registered investment company, "interested persons" as defined in section 2(a)(19) of the Investment Company Act of 1940 (15 U.S.C. 80a–2(a)(19));

(2) Has adopted written procedures for the confidential receipt, retention, and consideration of any report of evidence of a material violation under § 205.3;

(3) Has been duly established by the issuer's board of directors, with the authority and responsibility:

(i) To inform the issuer's chief legal officer and chief executive officer (or the equivalents thereof) of any report of evidence of a material violation (except in the circumstances described in § 205.3(b)(4));

(ii) To determine whether an investigation is necessary regarding any report of evidence of a material violation by the issuer, its officers, directors, employees or agents and, if it determines an investigation is necessary or appropriate, to:

(A) Notify the audit committee or the full board of directors;

(B) Initiate an investigation, which may be conducted either by the chief legal officer (or the equivalent thereof) or by outside attorneys; and

(C) Retain such additional expert personnel as the committee deems necessary; and

(iii) At the conclusion of any such investigation, to:

(A) Recommend, by majority vote, that the issuer implement an appropriate response to evidence of a material violation; and

(B) Inform the chief legal officer and the chief executive officer (or the equivalents thereof) and the board of directors of the results of any such investigation under this section and the appropriate remedial measures to be adopted; and

(4) Has the authority and responsibility, acting by majority vote, to take all other appropriate action, including the authority to notify the Commission in the event that the issuer fails in any material respect to implement an appropriate response that the qualified legal compliance committee has recommended the issuer to take.

(*l*) *Reasonable* or *reasonably* denotes, with respect to the actions of an attorney, conduct that would not be unreasonable for a prudent and competent attorney.

(m) *Reasonably believes* means that an attorney believes the matter in question and that the circumstances are such that the belief is not unreasonable.

(n) *Report* means to make known to directly, either in person, by telephone, by e-mail, electronically, or in writing.

§ 205.3 Issuer as client

(a) *Representing an issuer.* An attorney appearing and practicing before the Commission in the representation of an issuer owes his or her professional and ethical duties to the issuer as an organization. That the attorney may work with and advise the issuer's officers, directors, or employees in the course of representing the issuer does not make such individuals the attorney's clients.

(b) *Duty to report evidence of a material violation.* (1) If an attorney, appearing and practicing before the Commission in the representation of an issuer, becomes aware of evidence of a material violation by the issuer or by any officer, director, employee, or agent of the issuer, the attorney shall report such evidence to the issuer's chief legal officer (or the equivalent thereof) or to both the issuer's chief legal officer and its chief executive officer (or the equivalents thereof) forthwith. By communicating such information to the issuer's officers or directors, an attorney does not reveal client confidences or secrets or privileged or otherwise protected information related to the attorney's representation of an issuer.

(2) The chief legal officer (or the equivalent thereof) shall cause such inquiry into the evidence of a material violation as he or she reasonably believes is appropriate to determine whether the material violation described in the report has occurred, is ongoing, or is about to occur. If the chief legal officer (or the equivalent thereof) determines no material violation has occurred, is ongoing, or is about to occur, he or she shall notify the reporting attorney and advise the reporting attorney of the basis for such determination. Unless the chief legal officer (or the equivalent thereof) reasonably believes that no material violation has occurred, is ongoing, or is about to occur, he or she shall take all reasonable steps to cause the issuer to adopt an appropriate response, and shall advise the reporting attorney thereof. In lieu of causing an inquiry under this paragraph (b), a chief legal officer (or the equivalent thereof) may refer a report of evidence of a material violation to a qualified legal compliance committee under paragraph (c)(2) of this section if the issuer has duly established a qualified legal compliance committee prior to the report of evidence of a material violation.

(3) Unless an attorney who has made a report under paragraph (b)(1) of this section reasonably believes that the chief legal officer or the chief executive officer of the issuer (or the equivalent thereof) has provided an appropriate response within a reasonable time, the attorney shall report the evidence of a material violation to:

(i) The audit committee of the issuer's board of directors;

(ii) Another committee of the issuer's board of directors consisting solely of directors who are not employed, directly or indirectly, by the issuer and are not, in the case of a registered investment company, "interested persons" as defined in section 2(a)(19) of the Investment Company Act of 1940 (15 U.S.C. 80a–2(a)(19)) if the issuer's board of directors has no audit committee; or

(iii) The issuer's board of directors, if the issuer's board of directors has no committee consisting solely of directors who are not employed, directly or indirectly, by the issuer and are not, in the case of a registered investment company, "interested persons" as defined in section 2(a)(19) of the Investment Company Act of 1940 (15 U.S.C. 80a–2(a)(19)).

(4) If an attorney reasonably believes that it would be futile to report evidence of a material violation to the issuer's chief legal officer and chief executive officer (or the equivalents thereof)

under paragraph (b)(1) of this section, the attorney may report such evidence as provided under paragraph (b)(3) of this section.

(5) An attorney retained or directed by an issuer to investigate evidence of a material violation reported under paragraph (b)(1), (b)(3), or (b)(4) of this section shall be deemed to be appearing and practicing before the Commission. Directing or retaining an attorney to investigate reported evidence of a material violation does not relieve an officer or director of the issuer to whom such evidence has been reported under paragraph (b)(1), (b)(3), or (b)(4) of this section from a duty to respond to the reporting attorney.

(6) An attorney shall not have any obligation to report evidence of a material violation under this paragraph (b) if:

(i) The attorney was retained or directed by the issuer's chief legal officer (or the equivalent thereof) to investigate such evidence of a material violation and:

(A) The attorney reports the results of such investigation to the chief legal officer (or the equivalent thereof); and

(B) Except where the attorney and the chief legal officer (or the equivalent thereof) each reasonably believes that no material violation has occurred, is ongoing, or is about to occur, the chief legal officer (or the equivalent thereof) reports the results of the investigation to the issuer's board of directors, a committee thereof to whom a report could be made pursuant to paragraph (b)(3) of this section, or a qualified legal compliance committee; or

(ii) The attorney was retained or directed by the chief legal officer (or the equivalent thereof) to assert, consistent with his or her professional obligations, a colorable defense on behalf of the issuer (or the issuer's officer, director, employee, or agent, as the case may be) in any investigation or judicial or administrative proceeding relating to such evidence of a material violation, and the chief legal officer (or the equivalent thereof) provides reasonable and timely reports on the progress and outcome of such proceeding to the issuer's board of directors, a committee thereof to whom a report could be made pursuant to paragraph (b)(3) of this section, or a qualified legal compliance committee.

(7) An attorney shall not have any obligation to report evidence of a material violation under this paragraph (b) if such attorney was retained or directed by a qualified legal compliance committee:

(i) To investigate such evidence of a material violation; or

(ii) To assert, consistent with his or her professional obligations, a colorable defense on behalf of the issuer (or the issuer's officer, director, employee, or agent, as the case may be) in any investigation or judicial or administrative proceeding relating to such evidence of a material violation.

(8) An attorney who receives what he or she reasonably believes is an appropriate and timely response to a report he or she has made pursuant to paragraph (b)(1), (b)(3), or (b)(4) of this section need do nothing more under this section with respect to his or her report.

(9) An attorney who does not reasonably believe that the issuer has made an appropriate response within a reasonable time to the report or reports made pursuant to paragraph (b)(1), (b)(3), or (b)(4) of this section shall explain his or her reasons therefor to the chief legal officer (or the equivalent thereof), the chief executive officer (or the equivalent thereof), and directors to whom the attorney reported the evidence of a material violation pursuant to paragraph (b)(1), (b)(3), or (b)(4) of this section.

(10) An attorney formerly employed or retained by an issuer who has reported evidence of a material violation under this part and reasonably believes that he or she has been discharged for so doing may notify the issuer's board of directors or any committee thereof that he or she believes

that he or she has been discharged for reporting evidence of a material violation under this section.

(c) *Alternative reporting procedures for attorneys retained or employed by an issuer that has established a qualified legal compliance committee.* (1) If an attorney, appearing and practicing before the Commission in the representation of an issuer, becomes aware of evidence of a material violation by the issuer or by any officer, director, employee, or agent of the issuer, the attorney may, as an alternative to the reporting requirements of paragraph (b) of this section, report such evidence to a qualified legal compliance committee, if the issuer has previously formed such a committee. An attorney who reports evidence of a material violation to such a qualified legal compliance committee has satisfied his or her obligation to report such evidence and is not required to assess the issuer's response to the reported evidence of a material violation.

(2) A chief legal officer (or the equivalent thereof) may refer a report of evidence of a material violation to a previously established qualified legal compliance committee in lieu of causing an inquiry to be conducted under paragraph (b)(2) of this section. The chief legal officer (or the equivalent thereof) shall inform the reporting attorney that the report has been referred to a qualified legal compliance committee. Thereafter, pursuant to the requirements under § 205.2(k), the qualified legal compliance committee shall be responsible for responding to the evidence of a material violation reported to it under this paragraph (c).

(d) *Issuer confidences.* (1) Any report under this section (or the contemporaneous record thereof) or any response thereto (or the contemporaneous record thereof) may be used by an attorney in connection with any investigation, proceeding, or litigation in which the attorney's compliance with this part is in issue.

(2) An attorney appearing and practicing before the Commission in the representation of an issuer may reveal to the Commission, without the issuer's consent, confidential information related to the representation to the extent the attorney reasonably believes necessary:

(i) To prevent the issuer from committing a material violation that is likely to cause substantial injury to the financial interest or property of the issuer or investors;

(ii) To prevent the issuer, in a Commission investigation or administrative proceeding from committing perjury, proscribed in 18 U.S.C. 1621; suborning perjury, proscribed in 18 U.S.C. 1622; or committing any act proscribed in 18 U.S.C. 1001 that is likely to perpetrate a fraud upon the Commission; or

(iii) To rectify the consequences of a material violation by the issuer that caused, or may cause, substantial injury to the financial interest or property of the issuer or investors in the furtherance of which the attorney's services were used.

§ 205.4 Responsibilities of supervisory attorneys

(a) An attorney supervising or directing another attorney who is appearing and practicing before the Commission in the representation of an issuer is a supervisory attorney. An issuer's chief legal officer (or the equivalent thereof) is a supervisory attorney under this section.

(b) A supervisory attorney shall make reasonable efforts to ensure that a subordinate attorney, as defined in § 205.5(a), that he or she supervises or directs conforms to this part. To the extent a subordinate attorney appears and practices before the Commission in the representation of an issuer, that subordinate attorney's supervisory attorneys also appear and practice before the Commission.

(c) A supervisory attorney is responsible for complying with the reporting requirements in § 205.3 when a subordinate attorney has reported to the supervisory attorney evidence of a material violation.

(d) A supervisory attorney who has received a report of evidence of a material violation from a subordinate attorney under § 205.3 may report such evidence to the issuer's qualified legal compliance committee if the issuer has duly formed such a committee.

§ 205.5 Responsibilities of a subordinate attorney

(a) An attorney who appears and practices before the Commission in the representation of an issuer on a matter under the supervision or direction of another attorney (other than under the direct supervision or direction of the issuer's chief legal officer (or the equivalent thereof)) is a subordinate attorney.

(b) A subordinate attorney shall comply with this part notwithstanding that the subordinate attorney acted at the direction of or under the supervision of another person.

(c) A subordinate attorney complies with § 205.3 if the subordinate attorney reports to his or her supervising attorney under § 205.3(b) evidence of a material violation of which the subordinate attorney has become aware in appearing and practicing before the Commission.

(d) A subordinate attorney may take the steps permitted or required by § 205.3(b) or (c) if the subordinate attorney reasonably believes that a supervisory attorney to whom he or she has reported evidence of a material violation under § 205.3(b) has failed to comply with § 205.3.

§ 205.6 Sanctions and discipline

(a) A violation of this part by any attorney appearing and practicing before the Commission in the representation of an issuer shall subject such attorney to the civil penalties and remedies for a violation of the federal securities laws available to the Commission in an action brought by the Commission thereunder.

(b) An attorney appearing and practicing before the Commission who violates any provision of this part is subject to the disciplinary authority of the Commission, regardless of whether the attorney may also be subject to discipline for the same conduct in a jurisdiction where the attorney is admitted or practices. An administrative disciplinary proceeding initiated by the Commission for violation of this part may result in an attorney being censured, or being temporarily or permanently denied the privilege of appearing or practicing before the Commission.

(c) An attorney who complies in good faith with the provisions of this part shall not be subject to discipline or otherwise liable under inconsistent standards imposed by any state or other United States jurisdiction where the attorney is admitted or practices.

(d) An attorney practicing outside the United States shall not be required to comply with the requirements of this part to the extent that such compliance is prohibited by applicable foreign law.

§ 205.7 No private right of action

(a) Nothing in this part is intended to, or does, create a private right of action against any attorney, law firm, or issuer based upon compliance or noncompliance with its provisions.

(b) Authority to enforce compliance with this part is vested exclusively in the Commission.

SELECTED STANDARDS FOR PROFESSIONALISM AND COURTESY IN LITIGATION

PROFESSIONALISM STANDARDS IN THE NORTHERN DISTRICT OF TEXAS

121 F.R.D. 287, 88 (N.D.Tex.1988) (en banc)

* * *

B.

We next set out the standards to which we expect litigation counsel to adhere.

The Dallas Bar Association recently adopted "Guidelines of Professional Courtesy" and a "Lawyer's Creed" that are both sensible and pertinent to the problems we address here. From them we adopt the following as standards of practice[8] to be observed by attorneys appearing in civil actions in this district:

(A) In fulfilling his or her primary duty to the client, a lawyer must be ever conscious of the broader duty to the judicial system that serves both attorney and client.

(B) A lawyer owes, to the judiciary, candor, diligence and utmost respect.

(C) A lawyer owes, to opposing counsel, a duty of courtesy and cooperation, the observance of which is necessary for the efficient administration of our system of justice and the respect of the public it serves.

(D) A lawyer unquestionably owes, to the administration of justice, the fundamental duties of personal dignity and professional integrity.

(E) Lawyers should treat each other, the opposing party, the court, and members of the court staff with courtesy and civility and conduct themselves in a professional manner at all times.

(F) A client has no right to demand that counsel abuse the opposite party or indulge in offensive conduct. A lawyer shall always treat adverse witnesses and suitors with fairness and due consideration.

(G) In adversary proceedings, clients are litigants and though ill feeling may exist between clients, such ill feeling should not influence a lawyer's conduct, attitude, or demeanor towards opposing lawyers.

(H) A lawyer should not use any form of discovery, or the scheduling of discovery, as a means of harassing opposing counsel or counsel's client.

(I) Lawyers will be punctual in communications with others and in honoring scheduled appearances, and will recognize that neglect and tardiness are demeaning to the lawyer and to the judicial system.

(J) If a fellow member of the Bar makes a just request for cooperation, or seeks scheduling accommodation, a lawyer will not arbitrarily or unreasonably withhold consent.

(K) Effective advocacy does not require antagonistic or obnoxious behavior and members of the Bar will adhere to the higher standard of conduct which judges, lawyers, clients, and the public may rightfully expect.

---

8 We also commend to counsel the American College of Trial Lawyers' Code of Trial Conduct (rev. 1987). Those portions of the Code that are applicable to our decision today are set out in the appendix.

SELECTED STANDARDS FOR PROFESSIONALISM

Attorneys who abide faithfully by the standards we adopt should have little difficulty conducting themselves as members of a learned profession whose unswerving duty is to the public they serve and to the system of justice in which they practice. Those litigators who persist in viewing themselves solely as combatants, or who perceive that they are retained to win at all costs without regard to fundamental principles of justice, will find that their conduct does not square with the practices we expect of them. Malfeasant counsel can expect instead that their conduct will prompt an appropriate response from the court, including the range of sanctions the Fifth Circuit suggests in the Rule 11 context: "a warm friendly discussion on the record, a hard-nosed reprimand in open court, compulsory legal education, monetary sanctions, or other measures appropriate to the circumstances." *Thomas,* 836 F.2d at 878.

ABA GUIDELINES FOR CONDUCT (1998)

[The ABA Section of Litigation developed these rules of civility based upon the Standards for Professional Conduct adopted by the Seventh Circuit Court of Appeals. These rules are desgined to articulate the duties of civility that lawyers should follow in representing clients. Ed.]

Preamble

A lawyer's conduct should be characterized at all times by personal courtesy and professional integrity in the fullest sense of those terms. In fulfilling our duty to represent a client vigorously as lawyers, we will be mindful of our obligations to the administration of justice, which is a truth-seeking process designed to resolve human and societal problems in a rational, peaceful, and efficient manner.

A judge's conduct should be characterized at all times by courtesy and patience toward all participants. As judges we owe to all participants in a legal proceeding respect, diligence, punctuality, and protection against unjust and improper criticism or attack.

Conduct that may be characterized as uncivil, abrasive, abusive, hostile, or obstructive impedes the fundamental goal of resolving disputes rationally, peacefully, and efficiently. Such conduct tends to delay and often to deny justice. The following Guidelines are designed to encourage us, judges and lawyers, to meet our obligations to each other, to litigants and to the system of justice, and thereby achieve the twin goals of civility and professionalism, both of which are hallmarks of a learned profession dedicated to public service. We encourage judges, lawyers and clients to make a mutual and firm commitment to these Guidelines. We support the principles espoused in the following Guidelines, but under no circumstances should these Guidelines be used as a basis for litigation or for sanctions or penalties.

Lawyers' Duties to Other Counsel

1. We will practice our profession with a continuing awareness that our role is to zealously advance the legitimate interests of our clients. In our dealings with others we will not reflect the ill feelings of our clients. We will treat all other counsel, parties, and witnesses in a civil and courteous manner, not only in court, but also in all other written and oral communications.

2. We will not, even when called upon by a client to do so, abuse or indulge in offensive conduct directed to other counsel, parties, or witnesses. We will abstain from disparaging personal remarks or acrimony toward other counsel, parties, or witnesses. We will treat adverse witnesses and parties with fair consideration.

3. We will not encourage or knowingly authorize any person under our control to engage in conduct that would be improper if we were to engage in such conduct.

4. We will not, absent good cause, attribute bad motives or improper conduct to other counsel.

5. We will not lightly seek court sanctions.

6. We will in good faith adhere to all express promises and to agreements with other counsel, whether oral or in writing, and to all agreements implied by the circumstances or local customs.

7. When we reach an oral understanding on a proposed agreement or a stipulation and decide to commit it to writing, the drafter will endeavor in good faith to state the oral understanding accurately and completely. The drafter will provide other counsel the opportunity to review the writing. As drafts are exchanged between or among counsel, changes from prior drafts will be identified in the draft or otherwise explicitly brought to other counsel's attention. We will not include in a draft matters to which there has been no agreement without explicitly advising other counsel in writing of the addition.

8. We will endeavor to confer early with other counsel to assess settlement possibilities. We will not falsely hold out the possibility of settlement to obtain unfair advantage.

GUIDELINES FOR CONDUCT

9. In civil actions, we will stipulate to relevant matters if they are undisputed and if no good faith advocacy basis exists for not stipulating.

10. We will not use any form of discovery or discovery scheduling as a means of harassment.

11. Whenever circumstances allow, we will make good faith efforts to resolve by agreement objections before presenting them to the court.

12. We will not time the filing or service of motions or pleadings in any way that unfairly limits another party's opportunity to respond.

13. We will not request an extension of time solely for the purpose of unjustified delay or to obtain unfair advantage.

14. We will consult other counsel regarding scheduling matters in a good faith effort to avoid scheduling conflicts.

15. We will endeavor to accommodate previously scheduled dates for hearings, depositions, meetings, conferences, vacations, seminars, or other functions that produce good faith calendar conflicts on the part of other counsel.

16. We will promptly notify other counsel and, if appropriate, the court or other persons, when hearings, depositions, meetings, or conferences are to be canceled or postponed.

17. We will agree to reasonable requests for extensions of time and for waiver of procedural formalities, provided our clients' legitimate rights will not be materially or adversely affected.

18. We will not cause any default or dismissal to be entered without first notifying opposing counsel, when we know his or her identity.

19. We will take depositions only when actually needed. We will not take depositions for the purposes of harassment or other improper purpose.

20. We will not engage in any conduct during a deposition that would not be appropriate in the presence of a judge.

21. We will not obstruct questioning during a deposition or object to deposition questions unless permitted under applicable law.

22. During depositions we will ask only those questions we reasonably believe are necessary, and appropriate, for the prosecution or defense of an action.

23. We will carefully craft document production requests so they are limited to those documents we reasonably believe are necessary, and appropriate, for the prosecution or defense of an action. We will not design production requests to place an undue burden or expense on a party, or for any other improper purpose.

24. We will respond to document requests reasonably and not strain to interpret requests in an artificially restrictive manner to avoid disclosure of relevant and non-privileged documents. We will not produce documents in a manner designed to hide or obscure the existence of particular documents, or to accomplish any other improper purpose.

25. We will carefully craft interrogatories so they are limited to those matters we reasonably believe are necessary, and appropriate, for the prosecution or defense of an action, and we will not design them to place an undue burden or expense on a party, or for any other improper purpose.

26. We will respond to interrogatories reasonably and will not strain to interpret them in an artificially restrictive manner to avoid disclosure of relevant and non-privileged information, or for any other improper purpose.

27. We will base our discovery objections on a good faith belief in their merit and will not object solely for the purpose of withholding or delaying the disclosure of relevant information, or for any other improper purpose.

28. When a draft order is to be prepared by counsel to reflect a court ruling, we will draft an order that accurately and completely reflects the court's ruling, We will promptly prepare and submit a proposed order to other counsel and attempt to reconcile any differences before the draft order is presented to the court.

29. We will not ascribe a position to another counsel that counsel has not taken.

30. Unless permitted or invited by the court, we will not send copies of correspondence between counsel to the court.

31. Nothing contained in these Guidelines is intended or shall be construed to inhibit vigorous advocacy, including vigorous cross-examination.

Lawyers' Duties to the Court

1. We will speak and write civilly and respectfully in all communications with the court.

2. We will be punctual and prepared for all court appearances so that all hearings, conferences, and trials may commence on time; if delayed, we will notify the court and counsel, if possible.

3. We will be considerate of the time constraints and pressures on the court and court staff inherent in their efforts to administer justice.

4. We will not engage in any conduct that brings disorder or disruption to the courtroom. We will advise our clients and witnesses appearing in court of the proper conduct expected and required there and, to the best of our ability, prevent our clients and witnesses from creating disorder or disruption.

5. We will not knowingly misrepresent, mischaracterize, misquote, or mis-cite facts or authorities in any oral or written communication to the court.

6. We will not write letters to the court in connection with a pending action, unless invited or permitted by the court.

7. Before dates for hearings or trials are set, or if that is not feasible, immediately after such date has been set, we will attempt to verify the availability of necessary participants and witnesses so we can promptly notify the court of any likely problems.

8. We will act and speak civilly to court marshals, clerks, court reporters, secretaries, and law clerks with an awareness that they, too, are an integral part of the judicial system.

Courts' Duties to Lawyers

1. We will be courteous, respectful, and civil to lawyers, parties, and witnesses. We will maintain control of the proceedings, recognizing that judges have both the obligation and the authority to insure that all litigation proceedings are conducted in a civil manner.

2. We will not employ hostile, demeaning, or humiliating words in opinions or in written or oral communications with lawyers, parties, or witnesses.

3. We will be punctual in convening all hearings, meetings, and conferences; if delayed, we will notify counsel, if possible.

4. In scheduling all hearings, meetings and conferences we will be considerate of time schedules of lawyers, parties, and witnesses.

5. We will make all reasonable efforts to decide promptly all matters presented to us for decision.

6. We will give the issues in controversy deliberate, impartial, and studied analysis and consideration.

7. While endeavoring to resolve disputes efficiently, we will be considerate of the time constraints and pressures imposed on lawyers by the exigencies of litigation practice.

8. We recognize that a lawyer has a right and a duty to present a cause fully and properly, and that a litigant has a right to a fair and impartial hearing. Within the practical limits of time, we will allow lawyers to present proper arguments and to make a complete and accurate record.

9. We will not impugn the integrity or professionalism of any lawyer on the basis of the clients whom or the causes which a lawyer represents.

10. We will do our best to insure that court personnel act civilly toward lawyers, parties, and witnesses.

11. We will not adopt procedures that needlessly increase litigation expense.

12. We will bring to lawyers' attention uncivil conduct which we observe.

Judges' Duties to Each Other

1. We will be courteous, respectful, and civil in opinions, ever mindful that a position articulated by another judge is the result of that judge's earnest effort to interpret the law and the facts correctly.

2. In all written and oral communications, we will abstain from disparaging personal remarks or criticisms, or sarcastic or demeaning comments about another judge.

3. We will endeavor to work with other judges in an effort to foster a spirit of cooperation in our mutual goal of enhancing the administration of justice.

ABA ETHICAL GUIDELINES FOR SETTLEMENT NEGOTIATIONS

Approved as Guidelines by the ABA House of Delegates in August 2002

[The Section of Litigation in 1999 began to develop ethical guidelines for settlement negotiation. This project produced an 80 page draft of rules and commentary on this topic. In August 2002, the ABA House of Delegates voted on the rules as guidelines for settlement ethics and not as an adoption of these rules as official policy of the ABA. They are not designed to preempt the Model Rules, nor are they designed to be used in court as setting a standard. They are to be used by lawyers as guidelines consistent with the other sources of ethics rules. Ed.]

TABLE OF CONTENTS

Section 1 Preface

Settlement negotiations are an essential part of litigation. In light of the courts' encouragement of alternative dispute resolution and in light of the ever increasing cost of litigation, the majority of cases are resolved through settlement. The settlement process necessarily implicates many ethical issues. Resolving these issues and determining a lawyer's professional responsibilities are important aspects of the settlement process and justify special attention to lawyers' ethical duties as they relate to negotiation of settlements.

These Guidelines are written for lawyers who represent private parties in settlement negotiations in civil cases. The Guidelines should apply to settlement discussions whether or not a third party neutral is involved. To the extent there may be ethical issues specific to mediation and non-binding arbitration proceedings, the Guidelines may provide guidance, but these specific issues deserve particularized treatment and are beyond the scope of these Guidelines. As a general rule, however, the involvement of a third party neutral in the settlement process does not change the attorneys' ethical obligations.

The Guidelines are intended to be a practical, user-friendly guide for lawyers who seek advice on ethical issues arising in settlement negotiations. Generally, the Guidelines set forth existing ABA policy as stated in the *Model Rules of Professional Conduct* ("the *Model Rules*") and ABA Opinions and should be interpreted accordingly. The Guidelines also identify some of the significant conflicts between ABA policy and other rules or law. Counsel should consult not only these Guidelines, but also the applicable rules, codes, ethics opinions, and governing law in the jurisdiction of concern and should be alert for amendments to the *Model Rules* in connection with the work of the ABA Ethics 2000 Commission. References in this work are to the *Model Rules* and comments as amended by the ABA in February 2002. Such amendments may be found at the ABA website.

This compendium is limited to the negotiations phase of settlements (which includes client counseling). These Guidelines do not address the enforcement of settlement agreements or requests for sanctions for conduct in settlement negotiations.

These Guidelines are designed to assist counsel in ensuring that conduct in the settlement context is ethical. They are *not* intended to replace existing law or rules or to provide a basis for civil liability, sanctions, or disciplinary action.

Section 2 Settlement Negotiations Generally

2.1 The Purpose of Settlement Negotiations

The purpose of settlement negotiations is to arrive at agreements satisfactory to those whom a lawyer represents and consistent with law and relevant rules of professional responsibility. During settlement negotiations and in concluding a settlement, a lawyer is the client's representative and fiduciary, and should act in the client's best interest and in furtherance of the client's lawful goals.

2.2 Duty of Competence

A lawyer must provide a client with competent representation in negotiating a settlement.

2.3 Duty of Fair-Dealing

A lawyer's conduct in negotiating a settlement should be characterized by honor and fair-dealing.

2.4 Restrictions on Disclosure to Third Parties of Information Relating to Settlement Negotiations

With client consent, a lawyer may use or disclose to third parties information learned during settlement negotiations, except when some law, rule, court order, or local custom prohibits disclosure or the lawyer agrees not to disclose.

2.5 Required Disclosure to Court of Information Relating to Settlement Negotiations

When seeking court approval of a settlement agreement or describing in court matters relating to settlement, a lawyer shall not knowingly make a false statement of fact or law to the court, fail to correct a false statement of material fact or law previously made to the court by the lawyer, or fail to make disclosure to the court, if necessary as a remedial measure, when the lawyer knows criminal or fraudulent conduct related to the proceeding is implicated. Failure to make such disclosure is not excused by the lawyer's ethical duty otherwise to preserve the client's confidences.

Section 3 Issues Relating to Lawyers and Their Clients

3.1 The Client's Ultimate Authority Over Settlement Negotiations

3.1.1 Prompt Discussion of Possibility of Settlement

A lawyer should consider and should discuss with the client, promptly after retention in a dispute, and thereafter, possible alternatives to conventional litigation, including settlement.

3.1.2 Client's Authority Over Initiation of Settlement Discussions

The decision whether to pursue settlement discussions belongs to the client. A lawyer should not initiate settlement discussions without authorization from the client.

3.1.3 Consultation Respecting Means of Negotiating Settlement

A lawyer must consult with the client respecting the means of negotiation of settlement, including whether and how to present or request specific terms. The lawyer should pursue settlement discussions with a measure of diligence corresponding with the client's goals. The degree of independence with which the lawyer pursues the negotiation process should reflect the client's wishes, as expressed after the lawyer's discussion with the client.

3.1.4 Keeping Client Informed About Settlement Negotiations

A lawyer must keep the client informed about settlement discussions, and must promptly and fairly report settlement offers, except when the client has directed otherwise.

3.2 The Client's Authority Over the Ultimate Settlement Decision

3.2.1 Acting Within the Scope of Delegated Authority

A lawyer can exercise broad general authority from a client to pursue a settlement if the client grants such authority, but a lawyer must not enter into a final settlement agreement unless either (a) all of the agreement's terms unquestionably fall within the scope of that authority, or (b) the client specifically consents to the agreement.

3.2.2 Revocability of Authorization to Settle

A lawyer should advise a client who has authorized the lawyer to pursue settlement that the client can revoke authorization to settle a claim at any time prior to acceptance of the settlement. If the client does revoke authorization, the lawyer must abide by the client's decision.

3.2.3 Avoiding Limitations on Client's Ultimate Settlement Authority

A lawyer should not seek the client's consent to, or enter into, a retainer or other agreement that purports to (a) grant the lawyer irrevocable authorization to settle; (b) authorize the lawyer to withdraw if the client refuses the lawyer's recommendation to settle; (c) require the lawyer's assent before the client can settle; or (d) otherwise attempt to relieve the lawyer of ethical obligations respecting settlement. A lawyer may apprise the client in a retainer or other agreement of the scope of the lawyer's right to withdraw or take other steps based on the client's approach to settlement under the applicable ethics rules and law, but any such disclosure should be accurate and complete.

3.2.4 Assisting Client Without Impairing Client's Decisionmaking Authority

A lawyer should provide a client with a professional assessment of the advantages and disadvantages of a proposed settlement, so that the client can make a fully-informed decision about settlement. Any effort to assist the client in reaching a decision should avoid interference with the client's ultimate decisionmaking authority.

3.3 Preserving the Integrity of the Settlement Process; Restrictions on Client Settlement Authority

3.3.1 Adherence to Ethical and Legal Rules

A lawyer must comply with the rules of professional conduct and the applicable law during the course of settlement negotiations and in concluding a settlement, and must not knowingly assist or counsel the client to violate the law or the client's fiduciary or other legal duties owed to others.

3.3.2 Client Directions Contrary to Ethical or Legal Rules

If a client directs the lawyer to act, in the context of settlement negotiations or in concluding a settlement, in a manner the lawyer reasonably believes is contrary to the attorney's ethical obligations or applicable law, the lawyer should counsel the client to pursue a different and lawful course of conduct. If a mutually agreeable and proper course of action does not arise from the consultation, the lawyer should determine whether withdrawal from representing the client is mandatory or discretionary, and should consider whether the circumstances activate ethical obligations in addition to withdrawal, such as disclosure obligations to a tribunal or to higher decisionmaking authorities in an organization.

3.3.3 Disagreement With or Repugnant Client Strategies

If a lawyer finds a client's proposed strategy or goal regarding settlement to be repugnant, but not contrary to applicable law or rules, or if the lawyer has a fundamental disagreement with the client's strategy or goal, the lawyer may continue the representation on the condition that the lawyer will not be required to perform acts in furtherance of the repugnant strategy or goal, or may withdraw from the representation.

3.4 Clients With Diminished Capacity or Special Needs

A lawyer's general obligations when representing a client with diminished capacity or special needs—the obligations to maintain to the extent possible a normal client-lawyer relationship, and to protect the client when a normal relationship is impossible—apply equally to decisions respecting whether, how and on what terms to settle a dispute. If the client lacks the requisite capacity to make an adequately considered decision, but a guardian or other individual is legally authorized to make decisions in the representation on the client's behalf, the lawyer should abide by the guardian's lawful decisions concerning settlement. If the client lacks the requisite capacity and no one else is legally authorized to make decisions respecting settlement on the client's behalf, a lawyer should take measures to protect the client's interests which may include seeking appointment of a guardian, guardian *ad litem*, or other court-approved representative.

3.5 Multiple Clients Represented by the Same Counsel

A lawyer who represents two or more clients shall not counsel the clients about the possibility of settlement or negotiate a settlement on their behalf if the representation of one client may be materially limited by the lawyer's responsibilities to another client, unless the lawyer reasonably believes the lawyer will be able to provide competent and diligent representation to each affected client, the representation is not prohibited by law and does not involve assertion of a claim by one client against another, and each client gives informed consent in writing.

3.6 Class Actions

An attorney representing a class in settlement of a class action must not only satisfy applicable procedural and legal requirements associated with submission of any proposed class settlement for judicial approval, but also should insure during class settlement negotiations that any agreement providing different recoveries to different categories of class members is grounded upon materially distinct circumstances supporting such different recoveries, and is supported by the attorney's good faith belief that the settlement is fair to each group. An attorney should not represent class members whose interests have become adverse in connection with settlement of class actions.

3.7 Clients With Insured Claims/Dealing With Insurers

The ordinary principles governing an attorney's obligations in connection with settlements apply to clients covered by insurance. Unless the insurance contract provides otherwise, a lawyer should treat the insured as the sole client without regard to any contractual obligations of the insurer to pay the attorney's fees and to indemnify the insured. If the contract provides that both the insured and the insurer are the lawyer's clients, the lawyer should be governed by the rules respecting representation of multiple clients.

3.8 Organizational Clients

A lawyer representing a client that is an organization should generally obtain settlement authority, and take direction concerning settlement, from the representative authorized to act on the organization's behalf.

Section 4 Issues Relating to a Lawyer's Negotiations With Opposing Parties

4.1 Representations and Omissions

4.1.1 False Statements of Material Fact

In the course of negotiating or concluding a settlement, a lawyer must not knowingly make a false statement of material fact (or law) to a third person.

4.1.2 Silence, Omission, and the Duty to Disclose Material Facts

In the course of negotiating or concluding a settlement, a lawyer must disclose a material fact to a third person when doing so is necessary to avoid assisting a criminal or fraudulent act by a client, unless such disclosure is prohibited by the ethical duty of confidentiality.

4.1.3 Withdrawal in Situations Involving Misrepresentations of Material Fact

If a lawyer discovers that a client will use the lawyer's services or work product to further a course of criminal or fraudulent conduct, the lawyer must withdraw from representing the client and in certain circumstances may do so "noisily" by disaffirming any opinion, document or other prior affirmation by the lawyer. If a lawyer discovers that a client has used a lawyer's services in the past to perpetuate a fraud, now ceased, the lawyer may, but is not required to, withdraw, but a "noisy withdrawal" is not permitted in such circumstances.

4.2 Agreements With Opposing Parties Relating to Settlement

4.2.1 Provisions Restricting Lawyer's Right to Practice Law

A lawyer may not propose, negotiate or agree upon a provision of a settlement agreement that precludes one party's lawyer from representing clients in future litigation against another party.

4.2.2 Provisions Relating to the Lawyer's Fee

When an attorney's fee is a subject of settlement negotiations, a lawyer may not subordinate the client's interest in a favorable settlement to the lawyer's interest in the fee.

4.2.3 Agreements Not to Report Opposing Counsel's Misconduct

A lawyer must not agree to refrain from reporting opposing counsel's misconduct as a condition of a settlement in contravention of the lawyer's reporting obligation under the applicable ethics rules.

4.2.4 Agreements on Return or Destruction of Tangible Evidence

Unless otherwise unlawful, a lawyer may agree, as part of a settlement, to return or dispose of documents and other items produced in discovery.

4.2.5 Agreements Containing Illegal or Unconscionable Terms

A lawyer should not negotiate a settlement provision that the lawyer knows to be illegal or unconscionable.

4.2.6 Agreement to Keep Settlement Terms and Other Information Confidential

Except where forbidden by law or disciplinary rule, a lawyer may negotiate and be bound by an agreement to keep settlement terms and other information relating to the litigation confidential.

4.3 Fairness Issues

4.3.1 Bad Faith in the Settlement Process

An attorney may not employ the settlement process in bad faith.

4.3.2 Extortionate Tactics in Negotiations

A lawyer may not attempt to obtain a settlement by extortionate means, such as by making extortionate or otherwise unlawful threats.

4.3.3 Dealing With Represented Persons

A lawyer must not attempt to negotiate a settlement or otherwise communicate about a settlement with a person the lawyer knows to be represented in the lawsuit, except with the permission of the represented person's counsel or where authorized by law or a court order.

4.3.4 Dealing with Unrepresented Persons

A lawyer who negotiates a settlement with an unrepresented person must (a) clarify whom the lawyer represents and that the lawyer is not disinterested, (b) make reasonable efforts to correct any misunderstanding about the lawyer's role in the matter, (c) avoid giving advice to an unrepresented person whose interests are in conflict with those of the lawyer's client, other than advice to obtain counsel, and (d) avoid making inaccurate or misleading statements of law or material fact.

4.3.5 Exploiting Opponent's Mistake

In the settlement context, a lawyer should not exploit an opposing party's material mistake of fact that was induced by the lawyer or the lawyer's client and, in such circumstances, should disclose information to the extent necessary to prevent the opposing party's reliance on the material mistake of fact.

PART SEVEN

STANDARDS FOR THE ORGANIZED REGULATION OF LAWYERS

TABLE OF CONTENTS

Although the legal profession has sought to exercise self regulation over its members through the promulgation of codes of conduct, true self regulation will not result unless the profession has implemented a mechanism for enforcing the codes. In other words, violations of the codes of conduct must in some manner be identified and prosecuted with some degree of effectiveness and fairness. Sanctions must be assessed against violators to deter others from violating the rules and to ensure that the violating lawyer does not commit future violations.

Initially, the ABA had not focused its efforts on the disciplinary mechanism and sanctions; instead, its efforts were placed in defining the substantive aspect of the codes of conduct. In 1970, former Justice Tom Clark chaired a commission on evaluating disciplinary enforcement. The Commission's Report concluded that state bars needed model standards on which to base their systems of discipline. In 1979, the ABA adopted Standards for Lawyer Discipline and Disability Proceedings. In 1985, the ABA adopted the Model Rules for Lawyer Disciplinary Enforcement. These early codes for developing disciplinary systems proved to be inadequate and they have been replaced in 1986 by the Standards for Imposing Lawyer Standards and in 1989 by the Model Rules of Disciplinary Enforcement. In 1992, the ABA House of Delegates adopted 21 recommendations for the evaluation of a system of disciplinary enforcement. These standards are reproduced in this part. In 1993, the ABA amended the Model Rules for Lawyer Disciplinary Enforcement to reflect policies in the recommendations adopted in 1992. And, in 1996, the ABA again amended these rules to reflect the use of alternative discipline programs such as mediation and arbitration in cases of lesser misconduct. In 1998, the ABA approved Model Rules for Mediation of Client-Lawyer Disputes to guide the states in the implementation of alternative dispute resolution in disputes between clients and lawyers. In 2004, the ABA House of Delegates adopted a Model Court Rule on Insurance Disclosure for adoption by the states' highest courts.

One of the most significant areas for concern in professional discipline has been the area of fee disputes. For several years, the ABA has encouraged the use of alternative dispute resolution techniques in this area. In 1995, the ABA approved the Model Rules for Fee Arbitration.

Another significant area of concern to bar authorities is the regulation of trust funds for clients. In 2010, the ABA adopted the Model Rules for Client Trust Account Records.

In July 2000, the President of the American Bar Association appointed a commission to study problems related to the multijurisdictional practice of law in the United States. The MJP Commission was formed at roughly the same time that the ABA House of Delegates rejected the proposals from the Multidisciplinary Practice of Law (MDP) commission that non-lawyers be allowed to practice together with lawyers. See John. S. Dzienkowski & Robert J. Peroni, Multidisciplinary Practice and the American Legal Profession: A Market Approach to the Delivery of Legal Services in the Twenty-First Century, 69 Fordham 83 (2000). Thus, the MJP Commission was asked to deal with many of the same issues relating to the modernization of the legal profession that were the subject of the MDP Commission.

The MJP Commission was a complete success as the vast majority of its proposals were eventually adopted by the House of Delegates. In August 2002, the commission proposed the following recommendations to the ABA:

1. The ABA affirm its support for the principle of state judicial regulation of the practice of law.

2. The ABA re-title Rule 5.5 of the Model Rules of Professional Conduct as "Unauthorized Practice of Law; Multijurisdictional Practice of Law".

The ABA amend Rule 5.5(a) of the ABA *Model Rules of Professional Conduct* to provide that a lawyer may not practice law in a jurisdiction, or assist another in doing so, in violation of the regulations of the legal profession in that jurisdiction.

The ABA adopt proposed Rule 5.5(b) to prohibit a lawyer from establishing an office or other systematic and continuous presence in a jurisdiction, unless permitted to do so by law, or another provision of Rule 5.5; or holding out to the public or otherwise representing that the lawyer is admitted to practice law in a jurisdiction in which the lawyer is not admitted.

The ABA adopt proposed Rule 5.5(c) to identify circumstances in which a lawyer who is admitted in a United States jurisdiction, and not disbarred or suspended from practice in any jurisdiction, may practice law on a temporary basis in another jurisdiction. These would include:

- Work on a temporary basis in association with a lawyer admitted to practice law in the jurisdiction, who actively participates in the representation;
- Services ancillary to pending or prospective litigation or administrative agency proceedings in a state where the lawyer is admitted or expects to be admitted *pro hac vice* or is otherwise authorized to appear;
- Representation of clients in, or ancillary to, an alternative dispute resolution ("ADR") setting, such as arbitration or mediation; and
- Non-litigation work that arises out of or is reasonably related to the lawyer's practice in a jurisdiction in which the lawyer is admitted to practice.

The ABA adopt proposed Rule 5.5(d) to identify multijurisdictional practice standards relating to (i) legal services by a lawyer who is an employee of a client and (ii) legal services that the lawyer is authorized by federal or other law to render in a jurisdiction in which the lawyer is not licensed to practice law.

3. The ABA amend Rule 8.5 of the ABA *Model Rules of Professional Conduct* in order to clarify the authority of a jurisdiction to discipline lawyers licensed in another jurisdiction who practice law within their jurisdiction pursuant to the provisions of Rule 5.5 or other law.

4. The ABA amend Rules 6 and 22 of the ABA *Model Rules for Lawyer Disciplinary Enforcement* to promote effective disciplinary enforcement with respect to lawyers who engage in

the multijurisdictional practice of law and to renew efforts to encourage states to adopt Rule 22, which provides for reciprocal discipline.

5. The ABA should encourage the use of the National Lawyer Regulatory Data Bank to promote interstate disciplinary enforcement mechanisms and urge jurisdictions to adopt the International Standard Lawyer Numbering System®. The ABA should also urge jurisdictions to require lawyers to report to the lawyer regulatory agency in the jurisdiction in which they are licensed, all other jurisdictions in which they are licensed and any status changes in those other jurisdictions.

6. The ABA adopt the proposed *Model Rule on Pro Hac Vice Admission* to govern the admission of lawyers to practice law before courts and administrative agencies *pro hac vice* in jurisdictions in which the lawyer is not admitted to practice.

7. With regard to the establishment of a law practice on a permanent basis in a jurisdiction in which a lawyer is not admitted to practice, the ABA adopt the proposed *Model Rule on Admission by Motion* to facilitate the licensing of the lawyer, if the lawyer is admitted to practice in another United States jurisdiction, has been engaged in the active practice of law for a significant period of time and is in good standing in all jurisdictions where admitted.

8. With regard to lawyers admitted to practice only in non-United States jurisdictions, the ABA encourage United States jurisdictions to adopt the ABA *Model Rule for the Licensing of Legal Consultants* or to conform their already existing rule to the Model Rule.

9. With regard to lawyers who seek to provide legal services in the United States and are admitted to practice law only in non-United States jurisdictions, the ABA adopt the proposed *Model Rule on Temporary Practice by Foreign Lawyers* to identify circumstances where it is not the unauthorized practice of law for a lawyer admitted in a non-United States jurisdiction to provide legal services on a temporary basis for a client in a United States jurisdiction.

American Bar Association, Report of the Commission on Multijurisdictional Practice 5–6 (2002). In August 2002, the ABA House of Delegates adopted these recommendations.

The amendments to the Model Rules of Disciplinary Enforcement are also reflected in the following document. In this section, we also reproduce the Model Rule on Pro Hac Vice Admission, the Model Rule on Admission by Motion, the Model Rule for the Licensing of Legal Consultants, and the Model Rule on Temporary Practice by Foreign Lawyers.

Despite the breadth of the four exceptions for temporary practice under Model Rule 5.5, the exceptions proved to be too narrow to address the out-of-state practice problems created by Hurricane Katrina. After this natural disaster, the ABA formed a Task Force on Hurricane Katrina. The Task Force recommended that the unauthorized practice of law rules be suspended to allow lawyers to help the many organizations that were trying to assist the affected public and to rebuild the damaged areas. Initially, the Task Force proposed a new Model Rule 5.8, but it later refocused its efforts on drafting a Model Court rule that could be implemented by the courts of the affected jurisdiction. In February 2007, the ABA House of Delegates adopted a one sentence addition to Comment 14 of Model Rule 5.5 and a Model Court Rule on the Provision of Legal Services Following a Determination of a Major Disaster.

In February 2016, the ABA House of Delegates adopted the ABA Model Regulatory Objectives for the Provision of Legal Services, a document drafted by the ABA Commission on the Future of Legal Services. The list of regulatory objectives is designed to guide state bars in the creation of rules and regulations relating to provision of legal services by all providers including non-traditional legal service providers. The debate over this proposal was significant with opposition, but an amendment that reinforced the profession's ban on nonlawyer ownership of law firms helped to gain the votes for passage.

ABA MODEL RULES FOR LAWYER DISCIPLINARY ENFORCEMENT

[The Model Rules for Lawyer Disciplinary Enforcement, adopted by the ABA House of Delegates in August 1989, replace the Standards for Lawyer Discipline and Disability Proceedings (adopted in February 1979) and the Model Rules for Lawyer Disciplinary Enforcement (adopted in July 1985). In 1993, the ABA amended the Model Rules to reflect the policies recommended in 1992. In 1996, the ABA amended several provisions relating to lesser misconduct to encourage the use of alternatives to a discipline program. The new Model Rules for Lawyer Disciplinary Enforcement combine into a single policy document the contents of these two documents which, though formatted in different styles, concerned the same subject matter, i.e., model operating procedures for lawyer disciplinary matters. In 1999, the ABA amended Rules 14, 19, and 25 to reflect comments from bar counsel and other members of the ABA. In 2002, the ABA amended Rules 6 and 22 based upon a recommendation of the Commission on Multijurisdictional Practice. The Rules are reprinted in full; however, we have omitted some of the commentary due to space considerations. Ed.]

TABLE OF CONTENTS

Abatement:

A diminution of conditions in an order of discipline, readmission, or reinstatement pursuant to Rule 26.

Advisory Opinion:

The interpretation of law as applied to an assumed set of facts, whether written or oral.

Central Intake Office:

The office established by Rule 1 that is responsible for the receipt, coordination, processing and disposition of information and complaints regarding the conduct of lawyers.

Expunction or Expungement:

Process by which records or other evidence of the existence of complaints terminated by dismissals are destroyed after a period of time, pursuant to Rule 4(B)(12).

Fraud:

Conduct having a purpose to deceive but not merely negligent misrepresentation.

Interim:

Temporary.

Lesser Misconduct:

Conduct that does not warrant a sanction restricting the respondent's right to practice law, as determined pursuant to Rule 9(B).

Official of the State Bar:

Any person who is elected or appointed to any governing office or board of the state bar, or employed by the state bar.

Respondent:

A lawyer who is subject to a complaint.

Serious Crime:

Any felony or any lesser crime that reflects adversely on the lawyer's honesty, trustworthiness or fitness as a lawyer in other respects or any crime a necessary element of which, as determined by the statutory or common law definition of the crime, involves interference with the administration of justice, false swearing, misrepresentation, fraud, deceit, bribery, extortion, misappropriation, theft, or an attempt, conspiracy, or solicitation of another to commit one of the above.

Substantial:

When used in reference to degree or extent, it denotes a material matter of clear and weighty importance.

PREAMBLE: AUTHORITY OF THE COURT

This court declares that it has exclusive responsibility within this state for the structure and administration of the lawyer discipline and disability system and that it has inherent power to maintain appropriate standards of professional conduct and to dispose of individual cases of lawyer discipline and disability in a manner that does not discriminate by race, creed, color, sex, sexual orientation or national origin. In order to effectuate this declaration, the following rules for lawyer discipline and disability proceedings are hereby promulgated.

I. STRUCTURE AND SCOPE

RULE 1. Comprehensive Lawyer Regulatory System

A. *Component Agencies.* There is hereby established a comprehensive system of regulation of the legal profession that includes, but is not limited to a lawyer discipline and disability system, a client protection fund, mandatory arbitration of fee disputes, voluntary arbitration of lawyer malpractice claims and other disputes, mediation, lawyer practice assistance, and lawyer substance abuse counseling.

B. *Central Intake.* There is hereby established a central intake office, which shall:

(1) receive information and complaints regarding the conduct of lawyers over whom the court has jurisdiction, provided this rule shall not be construed to limit the authority of any authorized agency to institute proceedings;

(2) provide assistance to complainants in stating their complaints;

(3) provide information to complainants about the remedies available under the rules of the court, the operations and procedures of agencies designated by the court under Rule 1(A), and the status of their complaints;

(4) determine whether the facts stated in a complaint or other information regarding the conduct of a lawyer provide grounds for further action by any agency designated by the court under Rule 1(A) and:

(a) dismiss the complaint; or

(b) forward it to the appropriate agency or agencies;

(5) provide to the complainant, if a complaint is dismissed or referred to an agency other than the disciplinary agency:

(a) a copy of the written guidelines for dismissal of complaints;

(b) a concise written statement of the facts and reasons for referral of the complaint to an agency other than the disciplinary agency; and

(c) a notice of complainant's right of appeal pursuant to Rule 31; and

(6) record and, when a complaint involves more than one agency, coordinate the processing and disposition of all complaints by designated agencies.

C. [*Disciplinary Districts.* Disciplinary jurisdiction in this state shall be divided into the following districts: If necessary, provisions dividing the state into two or more disciplinary districts].

Commentary

A simple and direct procedure for making a complaint is needed. Complainants should not be expected to know the distinctions among component agencies. They need a central intake office—one clearly designated agency to which to take any type of complaint regarding lawyer conduct. The skilled lawyers of this office should provide the expertise needed to determine where prima facie valid complaints should be directed. It also emphasizes the importance of accountability.

Providing a regulatory system to deter unethical behavior should remain the highest priority of the judicial branch. The central intake office should screen all complaints for allegations of conduct that is a ground for discipline under Rule 9. It should forward those complaints to the disciplinary agency and to any other relevant agency, so that misconduct is not overlooked.

Lawyer discipline should be directly and exclusively controlled by the highest court in the jurisdiction. However, it may be appropriate for bar associations to administer other components of the system, such as arbitration, mediation, lawyer practice assistance, etc., under the court's authority. Therefore, the disciplinary agency should not be the administrative entity for other component agencies.

A fee dispute arbitration system that is mandatory for the lawyer eliminates the overwhelming advantage lawyers have over the majority of clients who are of modest means and have only the most rudimentary knowledge of the law. These programs can work without being unduly burdensome on the profession. Complaints that do not state legitimate grounds for dispute should be screened out. In cases of valid disputes, mandated fee adjustments can provide the incentive to reform for lawyers who do substandard work.

Providing an additional, voluntary arbitration mechanism for lawyers and clients can greatly benefit both lawyers and clients. Disputes to be considered could include contractual, non-disciplinary, and inadequate representation claims.

Mediation services are useful in preserving ongoing lawyer-client relationships when disputes arise or in matters where a lawyer has placed a lien on a client's file. When handled by a skilled mediator, the process can be simple and efficient, saving time and money for both parties. The lawyer's willingness to have a third party assist in resolving the dispute can demonstrate to the client that the lawyer's intention is to act in the client's best interest.

RULE 2. The Disciplinary Board of the Supreme Court [*State Bar*] of [*State Name*]

A. *Agency*. There is hereby established one permanent statewide agency to administer the lawyer discipline and disability system. The agency consists of a statewide board as provided in this Rule 2, hearing committees as provided for in Rule 3, disciplinary counsel as provided for in Rule 4, and staff appointed by the board and counsel. The agency is a unitary entity. While it performs both prosecutorial and adjudicative functions, these functions shall be separated within the agency insofar as practicable in order to avoid unfairness. The prosecutorial functions shall be directed by a lawyer employed full-time by the agency and performed, insofar as practicable, by employees of the agency. The adjudicative functions shall be performed by practicing lawyers and public members. No official of the [state bar] shall have the right to appoint any members or serve in any ex officio capacity.

B. *Appointment*. A board shall be appointed by the court with the requisite authority and responsibility to administer the lawyer discipline and disability system. The board shall consist of [nine] members to serve for fixed, staggered terms, and to be referred to as the "board," which shall consist of:

(1) [Two] members of the bar of this state and [one] public member appointed for an initial term of three years;

(2) [Two] members of the bar of this state and [one] public member appointed for an initial term of two years; and

(3) [Two] members of the bar of this state and [one] public member appointed for an initial term of one year.

Subsequent terms of all members shall be for three years. No member shall serve more than two consecutive three-year terms. The members of the board shall not be subject to removal by the court during their terms of office except for cause.

C. *Election of Officers.* The members of the board shall annually elect [the Court shall annually appoint] lawyer members as chair and vice-chair. The chair, and in the chair's absence the vice-chair, shall perform the duties normally associated with that office and shall preside over all meetings of the full board, ruling on all motions, objections, and evidence.

D. *Quorum.* [Five] members shall constitute a quorum. The board shall act only with the concurrence of a majority of the whole board except as to administrative matters, which shall only require a majority of those present and voting.

E. *Compensation and Expenses.* Members shall receive no compensation for their services, but may be reimbursed for travel and other expenses incidental to the performance of their duties.

F. *Abstention and Disqualification of Board Members[; Alternate Members].*

(1) Board members shall refrain from taking part in any proceeding in which a judge, similarly situated, would be required to abstain.

(2) In addition to complying with the Rules of Professional Conduct regarding a former judge or arbitrator (Model Rule of Professional Conduct 1.12), a former member of the board shall not personally represent a lawyer in any proceeding as provided in these Rules for a period of one year following completion of the member's service.

(3) [The court shall maintain current rosters of lawyer and nonlawyer alternates. If a board member becomes incapacitated or disqualified, the next alternate on the appropriate roster shall take the place of the board member in the matter.]

G. *Powers and Duties.* The board shall have the following powers and duties:

(1) To propose rules of procedure for lawyer discipline and disability proceedings for promulgation by the court, and to comment on the enforceability of existing and proposed [Rules of Professional Conduct];

(2) To review periodically the operation of the system with the court;

(3) To appoint three or more hearing committees [within each disciplinary district] and

(i) establish the rotation by which they will be assigned formal hearings,

(ii) designate the chair for each, and

(iii) assign the chair to review in rotation dispositions by the central intake office, recommendations of counsel for disposition of disciplinary matters and petitions for transfer to and from disability inactive status pursuant to Rule 3(E)(1);[1]

(4) To perform appellate review functions, consisting of review of the findings of fact, conclusions of law and recommendations of adjudicators in hearings on lesser misconduct pursuant to Rule 18(H) and of hearing committees with respect to formal charges, petitions for transfer to and from disability inactive status, and petitions for reinstatement, and prepare and forward to the court its own findings, if any, and recommendations, together with the record of the proceedings before the hearing committee;

(5) To administer reprimands;

(6) To impose probation for a specified period with the consent of the respondent;

(7) To appoint and supervise its staff, separate from the prosecutorial staff, to assist the board in its functions;

---

1 See Appendix for alternative provisions.

(8) To inform the public about the existence and operation of the system and the disposition of each matter in which public discipline has been imposed, a lawyer has been transferred to or from disability inactive status, or a lawyer has been reinstated or readmitted;

(9) To delegate, in its discretion, to the chair or vice-chair the power to act for the board on administrative and procedural matters.

Commentary

With more than 700,000 lawyers licensed to practice in the United States, the highest courts of the states cannot handle discipline and disability matters directly by themselves. The agency assists the court in the exercise of its inherent power to supervise the bar, inquiring into all matters assigned to its jurisdiction by the court's rules of disciplinary enforcement. The agency performs prosecutorial and adjudicative functions, and reports its findings and recommendations to the court.

A statewide system provides the greatest degree of structural impartiality since it minimizes the adverse effects of local bias. Moreover, a statewide structure provides uniformity, since only a single statewide court and a single statewide agency are involved in the process. In a decentralized structure, complaints in one community may be governed by one set of standards and those in a different community by another. Consequently, lawyers admitted to practice in the same state may receive radically different discipline for the same misconduct.

A single statewide agency avoids these problems by imposing a single standard of conduct throughout the state.

In a unitary system, both prosecution and adjudication are the responsibility of a single agency. Nevertheless, prosecutorial and adjudicative functions should be separated as much as possible within the unitary system to avoid unfairness and any appearance of unfairness. Persons who perform prosecutorial functions should neither perform nor supervise persons who perform adjudicative functions, and vice versa. In addition, persons who perform adjudicative functions in a particular matter at a preliminary stage should not thereafter perform nor have control over persons who must later perform ultimate adjudicative functions in the same matter.

The disciplinary system should be controlled and managed exclusively by the state's highest court and not by state or local bar associations for these compelling reasons. First, the disciplinary process should be directed solely by the disciplinary policy of the court and its appointees and not influenced by the internal politics of bar associations. Second, the disciplinary system should be free from even the appearance of conflicts of interest or impropriety. When elected bar officials control all or parts of the disciplinary process, these appearances are created, regardless of the actual fairness and impartiality of the system. This is true whether the bar is unified or not.[9]

It is of course desirable, and in the larger states essential, for the board to have available the assistance of staff to carry out its functions. Staff responsible directly to the board, totally separate from counsel, should be hired for that purpose to further the separation of the prosecutorial and adjudicative functions within the unitary agency.

In the appointment process, there should be appropriate representation of all segments of the public and the profession, including minority members, women, and solo or small firm practitioners. A combination of lawyers and nonlawyers on the board results in a more balanced evaluation of complaints. Currently more than two-thirds of all jurisdictions involve public members in their disciplinary structure. Participation by nonlawyers increases the credibility of the discipline and disability process in the eyes of the public. There is a human tendency to suspect the objectivity of a discipline body composed solely of members of the respondent's professional colleagues. Involving public members helps allay that suspicion.

* * *

---

[9] Rec. 5.

RULE 3. Hearing Committees[14]

A. *Appointment.* The board shall appoint three or more hearing committees [within each disciplinary district]. Each hearing committee shall consist of two members of the bar of this state and one public member. A lawyer member of each hearing committee shall be appointed chair by the board. No official of the [state bar] shall have the right to appoint any members or serve in an ex officio capacity.

B. *Terms of Office.* The chair and other members of the hearing committee shall serve for fixed, staggered terms. One member shall be appointed for an initial term of one year, another member for an initial term of two years and the third member for an initial term of three years. Thereafter all regular terms shall be three years and no member shall serve for more than two consecutive three-year terms. A member whose term has expired may continue to serve on any case that was commenced before the expiration of the member's term. A member who has served two consecutive three-year terms may not be reappointed before the expiration of at least one year. The members shall not be subject to removal by the board during their terms of office except for cause.

C. *Quorum.* Except in hearings alleging lesser misconduct as defined in Rule 9(B) and conduct under Rule 18(H), three members shall constitute a quorum. The committee shall act only with the concurrence of two. The chair of the board may appoint alternate members to a hearing committee as necessary to meet the requirements of this subsection.

D. *Powers and Duties.* Hearing committees shall have the following powers and duties:

(1) To conduct hearings into formal charges of misconduct, petitions for reinstatement or readmission, and petitions for transfer to and from disability inactive status upon assignment; and

(2) To submit to the board written findings of fact, conclusions of law, and recommendations, together with the record of the hearing.

E. *Powers and Duties of Hearing Committee Chair.* Each hearing committee chair shall have the following powers and duties:

(1) To review dispositions by the central intake office or recommendations of disciplinary counsel following investigation for disposition of disciplinary matters, dismissals by disciplinary counsel upon a request for review by complainant, and petitions for transfer to and from disability inactive status. The hearing committee chair may approve, modify, or disapprove the recommendations of disciplinary counsel, or direct that the matter be investigated further. If the hearing committee chair modifies or disapproves the recommendation, or directs that the matter be investigated further, disciplinary counsel may appeal that action to the chair of another hearing committee designated by the board, who shall approve either disciplinary counsel's recommendation or the action of the first hearing committee chair. The decision of the second hearing committee chair shall be final within the agency.

(2) To conduct prehearing conferences regarding formal charges of misconduct, petitions for reinstatement or readmission, and petitions for transfer to and from disability inactive status; and

(3) To consider and decide prehearing motions.

F. *Abstention and Disqualification of Hearing Committee Members.*

(1) Hearing committee members shall refrain from taking part in any proceeding in which a judge, similarly situated, would be required to abstain.

(2) In addition to complying with the Rules of Professional Conduct regarding a former judge or arbitrator (Model Rule of Professional Conduct 1.12), a former member of a hearing

[14] See Appendix for alternative provisions.

committee shall not personally represent a lawyer in any proceeding as provided in these Rules for a period of one year following completion of the member's service.

Commentary

If any member of a hearing committee has a conflict of interest, the entire committee is disqualified and another committee must be appointed in its place. If that is not practicable, the individual member of the committee should be replaced for that particular matter only.

The creation of hearing committees for specific cases should be avoided. Hearing committees should have fixed membership. The committees should sit on a pre-established rotating schedule and cases should be assigned on the basis of which is the next committee to sit. Each committee should have one alternate member scheduled to sit in case of illness, emergency, or conflicts of interest.

* * *

RULE 4. Disciplinary Counsel

A. *Appointment.* The court shall appoint a lawyer admitted to practice in the state to serve as disciplinary counsel. Neither the chief disciplinary counsel nor full-time staff disciplinary counsel shall engage in private practice. No official of the [state bar] shall serve as disciplinary counsel or investigator.

B. *Powers and Duties.* Disciplinary counsel shall perform all prosecutorial functions and have the following powers and duties:

(1) To evaluate all information coming to the attention of the agency to determine whether it concerns a lawyer subject to the jurisdiction of the agency because it relates to misconduct by the lawyer or to the incapacity of the lawyer;

(2) To investigate all information coming to the attention of the agency which, if true, would be grounds for discipline or transfer to disability inactive status and investigate all facts pertaining to petitions for reinstatement or readmission;

(3) To dismiss or recommend probation, informal admonition, a stay, the filing of formal charges, or the petitioning for transfer to disability inactive status with respect to each matter brought to the attention of the agency;

(4) To prosecute before hearing committees, the board, and the court discipline, reinstatement and readmission proceedings, and proceedings for transfer to or from disability inactive status;

(5) To employ and supervise staff needed for the performance of prosecutorial functions [and, when circumstances necessitate their use, appoint and supervise volunteer assistant counsel];

(6) To notify promptly the complainant and the respondent of the status and the disposition of each matter including but not limited to providing to the complainant:

(a) a copy of any notice, motion, or order sent to respondent;

(b) a copy of any written communication from the respondent to the disciplinary counsel relating to the matter except information that is subject to the privilege of one other than the complainant;

(c) a concise written statement of the facts and reasons a matter has been dismissed prior to a hearing and a copy of the written guidelines for dismissal issued pursuant to Rule 4(B)(7), provided that the complainant shall be given a reasonable opportunity to rebut statements of the respondent before the complaint is dismissed; and

(d) a notice of the date, time, and location of the hearing;[19]

(7) To issue written guidelines for use by the central intake office and disciplinary counsel to determine which matters shall be dismissed for failing to allege facts that, if true, would constitute grounds for disciplinary action.[20]

(8) To notify each jurisdiction in which a lawyer is admitted of a transfer to or from disability inactive status, reinstatement, readmission, or any public discipline imposed in this state;

(9) To seek reciprocal discipline when informed of any public discipline imposed in any other jurisdiction;

(10) To forward a certified copy of the judgment of conviction to the disciplinary agency in each jurisdiction in which a lawyer is admitted when the lawyer is convicted of a serious crime (as hereinafter defined) in this state;

(11) To maintain permanent records of discipline and disability matters, subject to the expunction requirements of Rule 4(B)(12), and compile statistics to aid in the administration of the system, including but not limited to a single log of all complaints received, investigative files, statistical summaries of docket processing and case dispositions, transcripts of all proceedings (or the reporter's notes if not transcribed), and other records as the board or court requires to be maintained. Statistical summaries shall contain, at a minimum:

(a) time records for all counsel and investigators, tracked by case or other task including time spent on non-disciplinary functions;

(b) the number of pending cases at each stage in the disciplinary process for each counsel and for the agency;

(c) the number of new cases assigned to each counsel during the year and the total for the agency;

(d) the number of cases carried over from the prior year for each counsel and the total for the agency;

(e) the number of cases closed by each counsel during the year and the total for the agency;

(f) the number of cases of special difficulty or complexity at each stage in the proceedings; and

(g) the ratio of staff turnover.[21]

(12) To expunge (i.e. destroy) after [three] years all records or other evidence of the existence of complaints terminated by dismissals or referrals to other component agencies pursuant to Rule 1(B)(4), except that upon disciplinary counsel's application, notice to respondent, and a showing of good cause, the board may permit disciplinary counsel to retain such records for one additional period of time not to exceed [three] years.

(i) Notice to Respondent. If the respondent was contacted by the agency concerning the complaint, or the agency otherwise knows that the respondent is aware of the existence of the complaint, the respondent shall be given prompt written notice of the expunction.

(ii) Effect of Expunction. After a file has been expunged, any agency response to an inquiry requiring a reference to the matter shall state that there is no record of such matter.

---

[19] Rec. 8.1, 8.2, 8.3, and 8.5.

[20] Rec. 8.4.

[21] Rec. 14.1.

The respondent may answer any inquiry requiring a reference to an expunged matter by stating that no complaint was made.

(13) To make referrals to the Alternatives to Discipline Program pursuant to Rule 11(G), to the central intake office or to any of the component agencies of the comprehensive system of lawyer regulation established by Rule 1; and

(14) To prepare an annual budget for the disciplinary counsel's office and submit it to the court for approval and to make reasonable and necessary expenditures pursuant to the approved budget to perform the duties of the office;[24]

C. *Advisory Opinions Prohibited.* Disciplinary counsel shall not render advisory opinions, either orally or in writing.[25]

D. *Ex Parte Communication With Disciplinary Counsel.*

(1) Members of a hearing committee, the board, or the court shall not communicate ex parte with disciplinary counsel regarding a pending or impending investigation or disciplinary matter except as explicitly provided for by law or for scheduling, administrative purposes or emergencies that do not deal with substantive matters or issues on the merits provided that:

(a) it is reasonable to believe that no party will gain a procedural or tactical advantage as a result of the ex parte communication; and

(b) provision is promptly made to notify all other parties of the substance of the ex parte communication and an opportunity to respond is allowed.

(2) A violation of this rule shall be a ground for lawyer or judicial discipline, as appropriate, and cause for removal from the hearing committee or the board.[26]

E. *Disqualification.* In addition to complying with the Rules of Professional Conduct regarding successive government and private employment (Model Rule of Professional Conduct 1.11), a former disciplinary counsel shall not personally represent a lawyer in any proceeding as provided in these Rules for a period of one year following completion of the disciplinary counsel's service.

Commentary

The court should appoint a permanent, full-time disciplinary counsel. The court should consider recommendations from many sources, including the board, state bar, civic groups, and other interested parties. The power to appoint should not be restricted by limiting the pool of potential candidates only to nominees from specific sources. Alternatively, instead of appointing disciplinary counsel directly, the court may wish to appoint a Commission on Lawyer Regulation, which would have the responsibility of appointing disciplinary counsel, as discussed in the Commentary to Rule 1.[29]

Volunteers should be avoided if possible. They cannot devote the same time and attention to processing complaints as paid counsel, nor can they investigate complicated matters as thoroughly as one professionally trained to do so.

Disciplinary counsel may be allowed a reasonable amount of time for transition from private practice following appointment to phase out his or her private practice.

Since the court has the responsibility for the efficient operation of the agency, the court should appoint the board and disciplinary counsel. However, the court should not allow itself to become involved in the internal personnel management of the agency. The board and disciplinary counsel should have full authority to hire and fire their respective staffs.

---

[24] Rec. 6.1(a).

[25] Rec. 6.1(e). The language "except upon the request of the court" is suggested to permit disciplinary counsel to provide opinions to, e.g., a court appointed committee drafting ethics or disciplinary procedural rules.

[26] Rec. 6.2.

[29] Rec. 6.1 and commentary.

Vesting all prosecutorial responsibility in disciplinary counsel is necessary if there is to be a separation of prosecutorial and adjudicative functions within a unitary agency.

Disciplinary counsel has the responsibility for investigating and prosecuting all matters. Disciplinary counsel must therefore have the authority to hire, compensate, and fire the staff necessary to carry out that responsibility in conformity with the applicable limits established by the board in the budget it has approved for the operation of the agency. All personnel assigned prosecutorial functions, whether lawyer or nonlawyer, full-time, part-time, or volunteer, should be appointed by and responsible to counsel. Full-time lawyer personnel hired by counsel should not be permitted to engage in the private practice of law.

Members of the public who come to the agency seeking its services are entitled to be advised of the disposition of their complaints. Fairness requires that no recommendation adverse to the respondent be made without providing an opportunity to be heard.

The clerk of the court in which the lawyer is convicted should send a certified copy of the judgment of conviction to counsel for the agency of the state in which the lawyer is admitted to practice. The certified copy of the judgment should be filed with the court to support the proposed order for immediate interim suspension.

Meaningful statistics can most effectively be recorded by using uniform terminology. The following terms are adopted to identify available sanctions in disciplinary matters: disbarment, suspension, reprimand, admonition, probation, and discipline by consent. The term adopted to indicate removal from practice on grounds of disability is transfer to disability inactive status.

* * *

RULE 5. Expenses

The salaries of disciplinary counsel and staff and their expenses, shall be paid by the court out of the funds collected under the provisions of Rule 8. Costs, and the expenses of the members of the board and of hearing committees shall be paid by the board [out of the funds collected under the provisions of Rule 8]. The board and disciplinary counsel shall annually obtain an independent audit by a certified public accountant of the funds entrusted to them and the disposition thereof and shall file a copy of the audit with this court.

Commentary

Disciplinary counsel and the board should be accountable for the expenditure of funds only to the court, except that unified bars may provide accounting and other financial services that do not impair the independence of disciplinary officials.

RULE 6. Jurisdiction*

A. *Lawyers Admitted to Practice.* Any lawyer admitted to practice law in this state, jurisdiction, including any formerly admitted lawyer with respect to acts committed prior to resignation, suspension, disbarment, or transfer to inactive status, or with respect to acts subsequent thereto which amount to the practice of law or constitute a violation of these Rules or of the Rules of Professional Conduct [Code of Professional Responsibility] or any Rules or Code subsequently adopted by the court in lieu thereof, and any lawyer specially admitted by a court of this state jurisdiction for a particular proceeding [, and any lawyer not admitted in this state jurisdiction who practices law or renders or offers to render any legal services in this state] jurisdiction, is subject to the disciplinary jurisdiction of this court and the board.

B. *Former Judges.* A former judge who has resumed the status of a lawyer is subject to the jurisdiction of the board not only for conduct as a lawyer but also for misconduct that occurred while the lawyer was a judge and would have been grounds for lawyer discipline, provided that the misconduct was not the subject of a judicial disciplinary proceeding as to which there has been a final

* In 2002, the ABA House of Delegates amended Rule 6 to change the word "state" to the word "jurisdiction."

determination by the court. Misconduct by a judge that is not finally adjudicated before the judge leaves office falls within the jurisdiction of the lawyer disciplinary agency.

C. *Incumbent Judges.* Incumbent judges shall not be subject to the jurisdiction of the agency; however, if an incumbent judge is to be removed from office in the course of a judicial discipline or disability proceeding, the court shall first afford the board and the respondent an opportunity to submit a recommendation whether lawyer discipline should be imposed, and if so, the extent thereof.

D. *Powers Not Assumed.* These rules shall not be construed to deny to any court the powers necessary to maintain control over its proceedings.

Commentary

Admission to practice triggers the jurisdiction of the disciplinary authority, regardless of the location of the lawyer, the place where the act occurred, or whether the lawyer is qualified to practice; the court has the right and the obligation to inquire into any facts bearing upon the lawyer's fitness to practice.

A lawyer specially admitted in a state has a license for that limited appearance and is subject to the disciplinary authority of that jurisdiction. In the same way that the motorist has given his implied consent to be bound by the traffic laws of the states he travels, the lawyer admitted for a limited purpose subjects himself or herself to the rules of conduct in the jurisdiction.

It is inappropriate for the state in which the lawyer is specially admitted to rely exclusively upon the lawyer's home jurisdiction to enforce ethical standards. The witnesses and other evidence of misconduct are likely to be located in the adopted jurisdiction. Moreover, the jurisdiction in which the misconduct occurred will be far more interested in pursuing the matter. Finally, misconduct should in the first instance be judged by the ethical standards of the jurisdiction where it occurred.

If at the time a judge leaves office the entity responsible for bringing judicial disciplinary proceedings has an investigation in progress against him or her, the matter should be immediately transferred to the lawyer disciplinary agency. The only issue in that circumstance is the lawyer's fitness to continue to practice in light of the alleged misconduct. Since a judge may be subject to discipline as a judge for conduct that does not constitute misconduct as a lawyer, the allegations giving rise to the jurisdiction of the agency under paragraph B must cite conduct violating the Code of Judicial Conduct which also constitutes grounds for lawyer discipline.

The judicial discipline and disability retirement commission has special expertise to evaluate the conduct of sitting judges and to determine how that conduct reflects upon their continued ability to hold office. The status of a judge as a judge and discipline to be imposed during the judge's tenure should be determined by judicial discipline and disability retirement proceedings.

Consequently, even if the misconduct occurred prior to the judge's assumption of office, the commission should have jurisdiction since the judge's status as a judge is at issue. If a lawyer disciplinary agency has an investigation in progress against a judge at the time the judge takes office, it should immediately transfer the file to the commission. If the judge is to be removed from office and thus returned to the practice of law, the court should afford the lawyer disciplinary agency the opportunity to be heard on the issue of what lawyer discipline, if any, should be imposed. The agency has the special expertise to determine how conduct reflects upon a lawyer's continued qualification to practice law.

Affording the agency an opportunity to be heard on the subject of lawyer discipline protects the right of the profession to preserve the high standards of conduct that it maintains in the public interest.

RULE 7. Roster of Lawyers

Disciplinary counsel shall maintain or have ready access to current information relating to all lawyers subject to the jurisdiction of the board including:

(a) full name and all names under which the lawyer has been admitted or practiced;

(b) date of birth;

(c) current law office address and telephone number;

(d) current residence address;

(e) date of admission in the state;

(f) date of any transfer to or from inactive status;

(g) all specialties in which certified;

(h) other jurisdictions in which the lawyer is admitted and date of admission;

(i) location and account numbers in which clients' funds are held by the lawyer;

(j) nature, date, and place of any discipline imposed and any reinstatements in any other jurisdiction;

(k) date of death; and

(*l*) the universal lawyer identification number [together with the jurisdiction's prefix, if any, issued by the court].

Commentary

A permanent registration system should be established from which the agency can determine whether an individual is licensed to practice in the state, is living or deceased, and where the individual is located. The registration records may be maintained by the court, a court-designated agency, or in unified bar states by the state bar. Disciplinary counsel should have ready access to the records.

The individual lawyer has the responsibility of keeping his or her registration information current, and should be required to promptly inform the registration agency of any change. Generally, the address listed in the roster is the lawyer's legal address for purposes of service of process and any other notices. See Rule 13.

* * *

RULE 8. Periodic Assessment of Lawyers

A. *Requirement.* Every lawyer admitted to practice before this court shall pay to the clerk of this court [*state bar*] an annual fee for each fiscal year beginning [*date*] to be set by the court [*state bar*] from time to time. The fee shall be used to defray the costs of disciplinary administration and enforcement under these rules, other components of the system of lawyer regulation under other rules established by the court and for those other purposes the court shall from time to time designate. The annual fee until further order of the court shall be:

After Date of Admission to Practice Law	Annual fee
Up to five years:	$
Five years or more:	$

B. *Exemption of Judges.* Full-time judges shall be exempt from the payment of the fee during the time they serve in office.

C. *Suspension for Nonpayment.* Unless excused on grounds of financial hardship pursuant to procedures to be established by the board, any lawyer who fails to timely pay the fee required under paragraph A shall be summarily suspended, provided that a notice of delinquency, addressed to the lawyer's last known business address, has been forwarded to the lawyer by certified mail, return receipt requested, at least [thirty] days prior to such suspension.

D. *Reinstatement After Payment.* Any lawyer suspended under paragraph C shall be reinstated without further order if, within five years of the effective date of the suspension for nonpayment, the lawyer makes payment of all arrears and a penalty of 20% of the amount due from the date of the last payment to the date of the request for reinstatement. Any lawyer who fails to make these complete payments within five years of the effective date of the suspension for nonpayment may, in the discretion of the court, be required to petition for reinstatement under Rule 25.

E. *Registration Statement.* To facilitate the collection of the annual fee provided for in paragraph A and the regulation of lawyers, each lawyer required by this rule to pay an annual fee shall, on or before [*date*] of every year, commencing [*date*] file with the clerk of this court a registration statement, on a form prescribed by this court, setting forth the lawyer's residence and office addresses, other jurisdictions in which the lawyer is admitted to practice, the imposition of any public sanction or transfer to or from inactive status in any other jurisdiction, and such other information as this court may from time to time direct. Each lawyer shall file with the clerk of this court a supplemental statement of any change in the information previously submitted within [thirty] days of the change. All persons first becoming subject to these rules by admission to the practice of law before the courts of this state after [*date*] shall file the statement required by this rule at the time of admission, but no annual fee shall be payable until [*date*] next following such date of admission.

F. *Receipt Demonstrating Filing of Registration Statement.* Within [thirty] days of the receipt of a statement or supplement thereto filed by the lawyer in accordance with paragraph E, the clerk of this court shall acknowledge receipt on a form prescribed by the court in order to enable the lawyer on request to demonstrate compliance with the requirements of paragraphs A and E.

G. *Suspension for Failure to File Registration Statements.* Any lawyer who fails to file the statement or supplement in accordance with paragraph E shall be summarily suspended, provided a notice of delinquency has been forwarded to the lawyer by certified mail, return receipt requested, addressed to the lawyer's last known business address at least [thirty] days prior to the suspension. The lawyer shall remain suspended until compliance is demonstrated, whereupon the lawyer shall be reinstated without further order.

H. *Application for Transfer to Inactive Status.* A lawyer who has retired or is not engaged in practice shall advise the clerk of this court in writing that the lawyer desires to assume inactive status and discontinue the practice of law. Upon the filing of the notice, the lawyer shall no longer be eligible to practice law. A lawyer who is retired or on inactive status shall not be obligated to pay the annual fee imposed by this rule upon active practitioners. A lawyer on inactive status shall be removed from the roll of those classified as active until and unless the lawyer requests and is granted reinstatement to the active rolls.

I. *Reinstatement From Inactive Status.* Any lawyer on inactive status under paragraph H shall be reinstated without further order if the lawyer makes application within five years of the effective date of transfer to inactive status. Any lawyer who fails to make application for reinstatement within five years of the effective date of transfer to inactive status may, in the discretion of the court, be required to petition for reinstatement under Rule 25.

Any lawyer who is under an order of discipline in any other jurisdiction shall be required to petition for reinstatement under Rule 25.

Commentary

In some jurisdictions, statutory provisions vest ultimate authority and control over disciplinary agency budgets with the legislature. Within state constitutional constraints, the court should assert its inherent power to regulate the profession to provide for adequate funding of the disciplinary system. Lawyer discipline and other regulatory functions such as client protection funds, mandatory fee arbitration, voluntary arbitration, mediation, lawyer practice assistance, and lawyer substance abuse counseling should be funded by fees assessed on lawyers admitted to practice in the state. Funds collected by this assessment and disbursements made for lawyer discipline and other regulatory activities (such as mandatory fee arbitration, client protection funds, and lawyer practice assistance) should be controlled exclusively by the highest court in the jurisdiction. The court may choose to exercise these functions through a unified bar.

Inadequate funding is the major cause of inadequate enforcement. The availability of adequate funds for personnel and expenses will enable an agency to perform all essential duties and not just unavoidable tasks.

The profession recognizes that the creation and maintenance of an effective structure for discipline and disability proceedings is one of its primary responsibilities.

The level of funding for the agency will determine whether it can hire experienced, full-time lawyers as counsel, or whether it can rely upon volunteers, part-time participants and clerks. Adequate funding will enable the agency to unravel a complex or obscure fact situation with which it might not otherwise be able to cope. The level of funding will determine how promptly allegations can be resolved, thereby affecting the length of time the lawyer remains uncertain about his future, the extent to which clients are exposed to further harm, and the amount of public confidence in the system.

Disciplinary counsel should have sufficient staff and resources to: (1) fully investigate complaints by such means as sending investigators into the field to interview witnesses and examine records and evidence; and (2) regularly monitor sources of public information such as news reports and court decisions likely to contain information about lawyer misconduct.

* * *

RULE 9. Grounds for Discipline/Lesser Misconduct

A. *Grounds for Discipline.* It shall be a ground for discipline for a lawyer to:

(a) violate or attempt to violate the [State Rules of Professional Conduct], or any other rules of this jurisdiction regarding professional conduct of lawyers;

(b) engage in conduct violating applicable rules of professional conduct of another jurisdiction;

(c) willfully violate a valid order of the court or the board imposing discipline, willfully fail to appear before disciplinary counsel for admonition pursuant to Rule 10(A)(5), willfully fail to comply with a subpoena validly issued under Rule 14, or knowingly fail to respond to a lawful demand from a disciplinary authority, except that this rule does not require disclosure of information otherwise protected by applicable rules relating to confidentiality.

B. *Lesser Misconduct.* Lesser misconduct is conduct that does not warrant a sanction restricting the respondent's license to practice law. Conduct shall not be considered lesser misconduct if any of the following considerations apply:

(1) the misconduct involves the misappropriation of funds;

(2) the misconduct results in or is likely to result in substantial prejudice to a client or other person;

(3) the respondent has been publicly disciplined in the last three years;

(4) the misconduct is of the same nature as misconduct for which the respondent has been disciplined in the last five years;

(5) the misconduct involves dishonesty, deceit, fraud, or misrepresentation by the respondent;

(6) the misconduct constitutes a "serious crime" as defined in Rule 19(C); or

(7) the misconduct is part of a pattern of similar misconduct.

Commentary

When a lawyer is admitted to practice he or she becomes subject to rules of conduct in effect in that jurisdiction. A violation of those rules triggers the jurisdiction of the agency. This does not mean that every violation necessarily requires the imposition of a sanction, but merely that the agency can investigate the matter.

The agency's jurisdiction to investigate and to take whatever action is deemed to be appropriate is triggered by discipline imposed in another state. The imposition of discipline in one jurisdiction does not mean that every other jurisdiction in which the lawyer is admitted must necessarily impose discipline, but the burden is on the respondent to demonstrate that the imposition of the same discipline is inappropriate. See Rule 22.

All lawyers have an affirmative duty to cooperate, including keeping disciplinary counsel advised of current address for service of process, cooperating with disciplinary investigations, and appearing at disciplinary hearings.

This rule establishes the proper policy for the relationship of the disciplinary system to the bar. Respondents are entitled to due process in disciplinary proceedings and are protected by fifth amendment rights against self-incrimination. However, disciplinary proceedings are not criminal proceedings; respondents are not entitled to "stonewall."

* * *

RULE 10. Sanctions

A. *Types of Sanctions.* Misconduct shall be grounds for one or more of the following sanctions:

(1) Disbarment by the court.

(2) Suspension by the court for an appropriate fixed period of time not in excess of three years.

(3) Probation imposed by the court not in excess of two years, or imposed by the board or counsel with the consent of the respondent not in excess of two years; provided, however, that probation may be renewed for an additional [two year] period by consent or after a hearing to determine if there is a continued need for supervision. If the respondent objects to the board or counsel's imposition of probation, the misconduct must either be made the subject of formal charges or a recommendation that probation be imposed must be filed with the court. The conditions of probation should be stated in writing. Probation shall be used only in cases where there is little likelihood that the respondent will harm the public during the period of rehabilitation and the conditions of probation can be adequately supervised. Probation shall be terminated upon the filing of an affidavit by respondent showing compliance with the conditions and an affidavit by the probation monitor stating that probation is no longer necessary and summarizing the basis for that statement.

(4) Reprimand by the court or the board. A reprimand shall be in writing and either imposed in person or served upon the respondent by certified mail. A reprimand issued by the court shall be published in the official reports for the guidance of other lawyers. A reprimand imposed by the board shall be published in the journal of the state bar and in a newspaper of general circulation in each judicial district in which the lawyer maintained an office for the practice of law.

(5) Admonition by disciplinary counsel imposed with the consent of the respondent and the approval of the chair of a hearing committee. An admonition cannot be imposed after formal charges have been issued. Admonitions shall be in writing and served upon the respondent. They constitute private discipline since they are imposed before the filing of formal charges. Only in cases of minor misconduct, when there is little or no injury to a client, the public, the legal system, or the profession, and when there is little likelihood of repetition by the lawyer, should an admonition be imposed. A summary of the conduct for which an admonition was imposed may be published in a bar publication for the education of the profession, but the lawyer shall not be identified. An admonition may be used in subsequent proceedings in which the respondent has been found guilty of misconduct as evidence of prior misconduct bearing upon the issue of the sanction to be imposed in the subsequent proceeding.

(6) Upon order of the court or the board, or upon stipulation, restitution to persons financially injured and reimbursement to the client security fund.

(7) Upon order of the court or the board, or upon stipulation, assessment of the costs of the proceedings, including the costs of investigations, service of process, witness fees, and a court reporter's services, in any case where discipline is imposed or there is a transfer to disability inactive status.

(8) Limitation by the court on the nature or extent of the respondent's future practice.

B. *Conditions.* Written conditions may be attached to an admonition or a reprimand. Failure to comply with such conditions shall be grounds for reconsideration of the matter and prosecution of formal charges against the respondent.

C. *Factors to Be Considered in Imposing Sanctions.* In imposing a sanction after a finding of lawyer misconduct, the court or board shall consider the following factors as enumerated in the ABA Standards for Imposing Lawyer Sanctions:

(1) whether the lawyer has violated a duty owed to a client, to the public, to the legal system, or to the profession;

(2) whether the lawyer acted intentionally, knowingly, or negligently;

(3) the amount of the actual or potential injury caused by the lawyer's misconduct; and

(4) the existence of any aggravating or mitigating factors.

D. *Public Nature of Sanctions.* Disposition of lawyer discipline shall be public in cases of disbarment, suspension, probation, and reprimand. In all cases of public discipline by the court, the court shall issue a written opinion setting forth its justification for imposing the sanction in that particular case.

Commentary

* * *

The *Standards for Imposing Lawyer Sanctions* were adopted by the ABA in 1986. These standards provide a framework to guide the courts in imposing sanctions, thereby giving the courts the flexibility to select the appropriate sanction in each particular case of lawyer misconduct. . . . The *Standards for Imposing Lawyer Sanctions* set forth a comprehensive system for determining sanctions, permitting flexibility and creativity in assigning sanctions in particular cases of lawyer misconduct. Use of the *Standards* will help achieve the degree of consistency in the imposition of lawyer discipline necessary for fairness to the public and the bar.

II. PROCEDURE FOR DISCIPLINARY PROCEEDINGS

RULE 11. Generally

A. *Evaluation.* The disciplinary counsel shall evaluate all information coming to his or her attention by complaint or from other sources alleging lawyer misconduct or incapacity. If the lawyer is not subject to the jurisdiction of the court, the matter shall be referred to the appropriate entity in any jurisdiction in which the lawyer is admitted. If the information, if true, would not constitute misconduct or incapacity, the matter may be referred to the central intake office or dismissed. If the lawyer is subject to the jurisdiction of the court and the information alleges facts which, if true, would constitute misconduct or incapacity, disciplinary counsel shall conduct an investigation.

B. *Investigation.*

(1) All investigations shall be conducted by disciplinary counsel. Upon the conclusion of an investigation, disciplinary counsel may dismiss or may recommend probation, admonition, the filing of formal charges, the petitioning for transfer to disability inactive status, participation in those programs listed in Rule 21(F), or a stay.

(2) Notice to Respondent. Disciplinary counsel shall not recommend a disposition other than dismissal or stay without first notifying the respondent in writing of the substance of the matter and affording him or her an opportunity to be heard. Notice to the respondent at his or her last known address is sufficient.

(3) Disciplinary counsel's recommended disposition shall not be subject to review upon the respondent's request for review. Disciplinary counsel's recommended disposition other than a

dismissal or a referral to the Alternatives to Discipline Program shall be reviewed by the chair of a hearing committee selected in order from the roster established by the board. The complainant shall be notified of the disposition of a matter following investigation. The complainant may file a written request for review of counsel's dismissal within [thirty] days of receipt of notice of disposition pursuant to Rule 4(B)(6). Disciplinary counsel's dismissal shall be reviewed by the chair upon the complainant's request for review. The chair may approve, disapprove, or modify the recommendation or appealed dismissal. Disciplinary counsel may appeal a decision to disapprove or modify his or her recommendation to a reviewing chair of a second hearing committee also selected in order from the roster established by the board who shall approve either disciplinary counsel's recommendation or the action of the first reviewer, but the decision of the second reviewing chair shall not be appealable. Any hearing committee whose chair reviews a recommendation of disciplinary counsel is disqualified from participating in further consideration of the matter.

C. *Admonition or Probation—Imposition.*

(1) If a matter is recommended to be concluded by admonition or by probation, disciplinary counsel shall notify the respondent in writing of the proposed disposition and of the right to demand in writing within [fourteen] days that the matter be disposed of by a formal proceeding. Failure of the respondent to so demand within [fourteen] days after written notice of the proposed admonition or probation constitutes consent to the admonition or probation.

(2) If the respondent within [fourteen] days demands a formal hearing, formal charges may be instituted.

D. *Formal Charges.* If a matter is to be resolved by a formal proceeding, disciplinary counsel shall prepare formal charges in writing that give fair and adequate notice of the nature of the alleged misconduct.

(1) Disciplinary counsel shall file the charges with the board.

(2) Disciplinary counsel shall cause a copy of the formal charges to be served upon the respondent and proof of service to be filed with the board.

(3) The respondent shall file a written answer with the board and serve a copy on disciplinary counsel within [twenty] days after service of the formal charges, unless the time is extended by the chair of the hearing committee. In the event the respondent fails to answer within the prescribed time, or the time as extended, the factual allegations shall be deemed admitted as provided in Rule 33(A).

(4) If there are any material issues of fact raised by the pleadings or if the respondent requests the opportunity to be heard in mitigation, the [hearing committee] [board] shall serve a notice of hearing upon disciplinary counsel and the respondent, stating the date and place of hearing at least [twenty-five] days in advance thereof. The notice of hearing shall advise the respondent of the right to be represented by a lawyer, to cross-examine witnesses and to present evidence. The complainant, if any, shall have the right to make a statement to the [hearing committee] [board] concerning the respondent's alleged misconduct and the effect of the alleged misconduct on the complainant. The hearing shall be recorded. The [hearing committee] [board] shall promptly submit its report containing its findings and decision on dismissal or sanction to the [board] [court] and shall serve the report on disciplinary counsel and respondent.

(5) Information concerning prior discipline of the respondent shall not be divulged to the hearing committee until after the committee has made a finding of misconduct unless said information is probative of issues pending in the present matter.[47]

E. *Review by Board.* Review by the board shall be limited to a review of the report from the hearing committee and the record below. The board shall not review a matter unless (a) the respondent or disciplinary counsel files objections with the board within [20] days of the date of service of the report, or (b) a majority of the full board, at its next meeting after submission of the report, votes to

[47] Standard 8.39 of the 1979 Standards for Lawyer Discipline and Disability Proceedings.

review the matter. If the board does not review the matter and the hearing committee has decided to dismiss the matter, the matter shall be dismissed. If the board does not review the matter and the sanction recommended by the hearing committee is not disbarment or suspension, the board shall impose the sanction upon the respondent. If the board does not review the matter and the sanction recommended by the hearing committee is disbarment or suspension, the board shall transmit the report of the hearing committee to the court with a statement that the parties have waived objections and the board has declined to review the matter. If the matter is to be reviewed by the board, the respondent and disciplinary counsel should be afforded an opportunity to file briefs and present oral argument during the review by the board. The board shall adopt rules establishing a timetable and procedure for the filing of briefs and presentation of argument.

(1) Decision by Board. Following its review, the board may approve, modify, or disapprove the recommendation of the hearing committee. The board shall prepare a written report containing its findings and decision on sanction or decision to dismiss the matter. A copy of the report shall promptly be submitted to the court and served on disciplinary counsel and the respondent. If the board determines that the matter shall be dismissed or that a sanction other than disbarment or suspension shall be imposed, and the court does not vote to review the matter, then the board shall dismiss the matter or impose the sanction upon respondent.

(2) During its review, the board shall not receive or consider any evidence that was not presented to the hearing committee, except upon notice to the respondent and disciplinary counsel and opportunity to respond. The hearing committee is the initial trier of fact; the board serves an appellate review function. If new evidence warranting a reopening of the proceeding is discovered, the case should be remanded to the hearing committee.

F. *Review by the Court.* The court may, within its discretion, review a matter if the respondent or disciplinary counsel files objections to the report of the board or if a majority of the court, within the time for filing objections, votes to review the matter. If the court does not review the matter and the sanction decided upon by the board or by the hearing committee with review declined by the board is suspension or disbarment, the court shall impose the sanction.

(1) The respondent and disciplinary counsel may file objections to the report of the board within [twenty] days from the date of service. Within [sixty] days after the court grants review, the respondent and disciplinary counsel may file briefs and present oral arguments pursuant to the rules governing civil appeals. Upon conclusion of the proceedings, the court shall promptly enter an appropriate order. The decision of the court shall be in writing and state the reasons for the decision. Upon final disposition at any stage of the proceedings, the written findings shall be published in an appropriate journal or reporter and a copy shall be mailed to the respondent and the complainant and to the ABA National Discipline Data Bank.[53]

(2) During its review, the court shall not receive or consider any evidence that was not presented to the hearing committee, except upon notice to the respondent and disciplinary counsel and opportunity to respond.

(3) If new evidence warranting a reopening of the proceeding is discovered, the case shall be remanded to the hearing committee.

G. *Alternatives to Discipline Program*

(1) Referral to Program. In a matter involving lesser misconduct as defined in Rule 9(B), prior to the filing of formal charges, disciplinary counsel may refer respondent to the Alternatives to Discipline Program. The Alternatives to Discipline Program may include fee arbitration, arbitration, mediation, law office management assistance, lawyer assistance programs, psychological counseling, continuing legal education programs, ethics school or any other program authorized by the court.

---

[53] See also Rule 16(H).

(2) Notice to Complainant. Pursuant to Rule 4(B)(6), the complainant, if any, shall be notified of the decision to refer the respondent to the Alternatives to Discipline Program, and shall have a reasonable opportunity to submit a statement offering any new information regarding the respondent. This statement shall be made part of the record.

(3) Factors. The following factors shall be considered in determining whether to refer a respondent to the program:

(a) whether the presumptive sanction under the *ABA Standards for Imposing Lawyer Sanctions* for the violations listed in the complaint is likely to be no more severe than reprimand or admonition;

(b) whether participation in the program is likely to benefit the respondent and accomplish the goals set forth by the program;

(c) whether aggravating or mitigating factors exist; and

(d) whether diversion was already tried.

(4) Contract. Disciplinary counsel and the respondent shall negotiate a contract, the terms of which shall be tailored to the individual circumstances. In each case, the contract shall be signed by the respondent and the disciplinary counsel. The contract shall set forth the terms and conditions of the plan for the respondent and, if appropriate, shall identify the use of a practice monitor and/or a recovery monitor and the responsibilities of the monitor(s). The contract shall provide for oversight of fulfillment of the contract terms. Oversight includes reporting of any alleged breach of contract to the disciplinary counsel. The contract shall also provide that the respondent will pay all costs incurred in connection with the contract. The contract shall include a specific acknowledgment that a material violation of a term of the contract renders voidable the respondent's participation in the program for the original charge(s) filed. The contract may be amended upon agreement of the respondent and disciplinary counsel. If a recovery monitor is assigned, the contract shall include respondent's waiver of confidentiality so that the recovery monitor may make necessary disclosures in order to fulfill the monitor's duties under the contract.

(5) Effect of Non-participation in the Program. The respondent has the right not to participate in the Alternatives to Discipline Program. If the respondent does not participate, the matter will proceed as though no referral to the program had been made.

(6) Status of Complaint. After an agreement is reached, the disciplinary complaint shall be held in abeyance [dismissed] pending successful completion of the terms of the contract.

(7) Termination.

(a) Fulfillment of the Contract: The contract is automatically terminated when the terms of the contract have been fulfilled. Successful completion of the contract constitutes a bar to any further disciplinary proceedings based upon the same allegations.

(b) Material Breach: A material breach of the contract shall be cause for termination of the respondent's participation in the program. After a material breach, disciplinary proceedings may be resumed or reinstituted.

Commentary

The evaluation process eliminates those matters over which the agency has no jurisdiction. It precedes investigation, which is reserved for those matters determined to involve a lawyer subject to the jurisdiction of the agency and allegations which, if true, would constitute misconduct.

If the matter is terminated at this stage because the matter does not involve allegations of misconduct, disciplinary counsel should notify the complainant and refer him or her to the central intake office. Disciplinary counsel may refer matters to the central intake office or directly to any of the component agencies included in the comprehensive lawyer regulation system established by Rule 1, such as the lawyer assistance program (which provides assistance for impairment problems) or the fee arbitration program.

Matters terminated at the evaluation stage because they concern a lawyer not admitted to practice in the jurisdiction should be forwarded by disciplinary counsel to the agency for the jurisdiction in which the lawyer is admitted. The complainant should be notified of the disposition if a matter is concluded at the screening stage.

A stay is appropriate only in extraordinary circumstances. Disciplinary counsel must determine whether the complainant or the respondent will suffer prejudice in the pending proceeding should the disciplinary action proceed immediately. In some cases, witnesses and evidence pertinent to both cases might not be obtainable at a later date; in other cases, the disciplinary action may be expedited by waiting for evidence to be adduced in another proceeding.

Fairness requires that no recommendation adverse to the respondent be made without providing him or her an opportunity to be heard. This does not mean that the respondent is entitled to notice immediately upon receipt of a complaint. In some instances, early notice would be harmful to the investigation. It does mean that the respondent has a right to be heard before the investigation is concluded and an adverse disposition formulated. If the matter is dismissed or stayed following investigation, respondent has no reason to appeal.

The review process preserves elements of bifurcation within the unitary system, because the recommendation of disciplinary counsel is subject to review and approval by a representative of the adjudicative body. The approval of counsel's recommendation to file formal charges by the reviewing member amounts to a finding of probable cause to proceed.

In order to prevent any possibility of forum shopping by disciplinary counsel, the hearing committee chairperson should be designated by the board. The hearing committee of which the reviewing chair is a member should be disqualified from any future consideration of the matter, in order to avoid being placed in the position of passing upon the correctness of his or her approval of the recommendation to prosecute formal charges.

The board supervises the operations of the agency. Any person dissatisfied with the action of the agency may complain to the board. The complaint should be submitted to a panel of the board, rather than the entire board, so that those members not serving on the panel will be available to participate in any future proceedings involving the matter.

If the first reviewing chairperson does not approve the recommendation, disciplinary counsel may submit the matter to a second reviewing chairperson who shall decide the issue by approving either the recommendation of disciplinary counsel or the modification thereon made by the first reviewer. The decision of the second reviewing chair shall be final within the agency.

The court, the board, or disciplinary counsel may impose probation. If probation is imposed by the board or by counsel, the consent of the respondent is required. The terms of the probation should specify periodic review of the order of probation, and provide a means to supervise the progress of the respondent.

Admonitions should be in writing and served upon the respondent. If the respondent does not consent to the admonition or probation, formal charges are instituted. The procedure is similar to the rejection of a settlement offer in a civil case or a plea bargain in a criminal case, which results in a trial.

The fact that refusal to consent to the admonition or probation subjects the respondent to formal charges and potentially more serious discipline does not violate due process any more than does the fact that a person charged with a crime is subject to conviction of a more serious offense when he or she refuses to plead to a lesser crime.

Prior discipline is relevant and material to the issue of the sanction to be imposed for the conduct which is the subject of the pending charges. Prior discipline is, except in unusual circumstances, not relevant or material to the issue of whether the conduct alleged has occurred. Consequently, introduction of evidence of prior discipline before a finding that the present charges have been sustained is prejudicial. Such records should not ordinarily be introduced until a finding of guilt has been made.

If evidence of prior discipline is necessary to prove the present charges (e.g. an allegation that the respondent continued to practice despite suspension) or to impeach (e.g. false testimony by respondent as to lack of prior discipline), it may be offered. However, it should not be used as a substitute for proving the allegations at issue.

The hearing may be recorded by any method authorized in the jurisdiction. The record will assist the hearing committee in the preparation and presentation of its report.

If the matter ultimately results in a recommendation for discipline, the record should be forwarded with the findings and recommendation. The recording should be available to the respondent upon request, and a transcript provided at cost.

The hearing committee is the initial trier of fact; the board serves an appellate review function. If new evidence warranting a reopening of the proceeding is discovered, the case should be remanded to the hearing committee.

Unless the decision of the hearing committee or the board is appealed or unless the board or court affirmatively decides to review a matter, cases should be disposed at the earliest possible stage. Of course, the court must retain ultimate responsibility for all disciplinary matters and, thus, must reserve the right to review any matter or even hold a *de novo* hearing if it so determines. This should occur only in extraordinary cases involving significant questions of law. In all other cases, the court should rely on its disciplinary counsel, the hearing committee, and the board to dispose of matters in accordance with established disciplinary law. This will both speed up the process and reduce the burden on the court.[54] If new evidence warranting a reopening of the proceeding is discovered, the case should be remanded to the hearing committee.

Written opinions of the court not only serve to educate members of the profession about ethical behavior, but also provide precedent for subsequent cases. Moreover, this requirement is manageable; the courts in the jurisdictions with the heaviest caseloads currently write opinions in every contested disciplinary case they decide. If a matter is concluded without review by the court, the report of the board or hearing committee should be published in the official reporter.

* * *

The overwhelming majority of complaints made against lawyers allege instances of lesser misconduct. Single instances of minor neglect or minor incompetence, while technically violations of the rules of professional conduct, are seldom treated as such. These complaints are almost always dismissed. Summary dismissal of these complaints is one of the chief sources of public dissatisfaction with the system.

These cases seldom justify the resources needed to conduct formal disciplinary proceedings. In most of these cases, the respondent's conduct does not justify imposing a disciplinary sanction. Therefore, these matters should be removed from the disciplinary system and handled administratively. It may be appropriate to compensate the client for the respondent's substandard performance by a fee adjustment or other arbitrated or mediated settlement. The respondent may need guidance to improve his or her skills or to overcome a problem with substance abuse.

A respondent has the right to refuse to participate in the Alternatives to Discipline Program. The only adverse consequence of a respondent's refusal to participate shall be that it is a factor to be considered by disciplinary counsel in determining whether to recommend the filing of formal charges. Disciplinary counsel may recommend formal charges even if the original complaint alleged lesser misconduct as defined in Rule 9(B). Disciplinary counsel, of course, retains the discretion to dismiss the complaint. If fee arbitration is mandatory in the jurisdiction, there is obviously no need for respondent's consent.

Participation in the program is not intended as an alternative to discipline in cases of serious misconduct or in cases that factually present little hope that participation will achieve program goals. In addition, the program will only be considered in cases where, assuming all the allegations against the respondent are true, the presumptive sanctions would be less than suspension or disbarment or other restrictions on the right to practice. See Rule 9(B). After the filing and service of formal charges, a referral to any of the component agencies included in the comprehensive lawyer regulation system established by Rule 1 shall be made as written conditions pursuant to Rule 10(B).

The existence of one or more aggravating factors does not necessarily exclude participation in the program. For example, neglect cases often include a pattern of misconduct and multiple offenses, but do not involve dishonesty, bad faith, or a breach of fiduciary obligation. Thus, the existence of "a pattern of

[54] Rec. 11.

misconduct" and/or "multiple offenses" should not make a respondent ineligible for the program. A pattern of lesser misconduct may be a strong indication that office management is the real problem and that this program is the best way to address that underlying problem.

Factors that may indicate ineligibility for participation in the program include evidence of a dishonest or selfish motive, bad faith in, or the obstruction of, the disciplinary process, the submission of false evidence, or an indifference to making restitution. Both mitigating and aggravating factors should also be considered. The presence of one or more mitigating factors may qualify an otherwise ineligible respondent for the program.

The existence of prior disciplinary offenses would not necessarily make a respondent ineligible for referral to the Alternatives to Discipline Program. Consideration should be given to whether the respondent's prior offenses are of the same or similar nature, whether the respondent has previously been placed in the Alternatives to Discipline Program for similar conduct and whether it is reasonably foreseeable that the respondent's participation in the program will be successful.

Each participant in the program will become a party to a contract that is specifically designed to address the alleged violations. It will be the respondent's responsibility to carry out the contract provisions. The contract provisions will indicate who is responsible to oversee the fulfillment of the terms of the contract. The person overseeing the contract must report to the disciplinary counsel any non-compliance with the contract provisions.

In order to encourage voluntary participation in lawyer assistance programs, such programs provide confidentiality. Rule 8.3(c) of the ABA Model Rules of Professional Conduct states: "This Rule does not require disclosure of information . . . gained by a lawyer or judge while serving as a member of an approved lawyers assistance program to the extent that such information would be confidential if it were communicated subject to the attorney-client privilege." However, participation in the Alternatives to Discipline Program differs from voluntary participation in a LAP program. The Alternatives to Discipline Rule recognizes this difference and requires the recovery monitor to make necessary disclosures in order to fulfill his or her duties under the contract.

RULE 12. Immunity

A. *From Civil Suits.* Communications to the board, hearing committees, or disciplinary counsel relating to lawyer misconduct or disability and testimony given in the proceedings shall be absolutely privileged, and no lawsuit predicated thereon may be instituted against any complainant or witness. Members of the board, members of hearing committees, disciplinary counsel, probation monitors, or any person acting on their behalf and staff shall be immune from suit for any conduct in the course of their official duties.

B. *From Criminal Prosecution.* Upon application by disciplinary counsel and notice to [appropriate prosecuting authority], the court may grant immunity from criminal prosecution to a witness in a discipline or disability proceeding.

Commentary

Agency personnel are an integral part of the judicial process and are entitled to the same immunity which is afforded to prosecuting lawyers. Immunity protects the independent judgment of the agency and avoids diverting the attention of its personnel as well as its resources toward resisting collateral attack and harassment.

The Rule recommends absolute privilege rather than qualified privilege; qualified privilege may not protect against harassment made possible by simply alleging malice in a lawsuit. Conduct on the part of agency personnel which is not authorized or exceeds assigned duties is not protected.

* * *

RULE 13. Service

A. *Service of Petition.* Service upon the respondent of the petition in any disciplinary or disability proceeding shall be made by personal service, by any person authorized by the chair of the board, or by registered or certified mail at an address shown in the current information roster filed by respondent pursuant to Rule 7 or other last known address.

B. *Service of Other Papers.* Service of any other papers or notices required by these rules may be made upon respondent or respondent's counsel and shall, unless otherwise provided by these rules, be made in accordance with Rule ______ of the [*state rules of civil procedure*].

RULE 14. Subpoena Power

A. *Oaths.* Any member of the board or of a hearing committee in matters before it, disciplinary counsel in matters under investigation by him or her, and any person authorized by law may administer oaths and affirmations.

B. *Investigatory Subpoenas.* Before formal charges have been filed, disciplinary counsel may, with the approval of the chairperson of a hearing committee, compel by subpoena the attendance of witnesses, and the production of pertinent books, papers, and documents, in accordance with [appropriate state rule of civil procedure].

C. *Subpoenas for Deposition or Hearing.* After formal charges are filed, disciplinary counsel or respondent may, in accordance with [appropriate state rule of civil procedure], compel by subpoena the attendance of witnesses and the production of pertinent books, papers, and documents at a deposition or hearing under these rules.

D. *Enforcement of Subpoenas.* The [appropriate court of general jurisdiction of the circuit, county, or city] in which the attendance or production is required may, upon proper application, enforce the attendance and testimony of any witnesses and the production of any documents subpoenaed.

E. *Quashing Subpoena.* Any attack on the validity of a subpoena so issued shall be heard and determined by the chair of the hearing committee before which the matter is pending or by the court wherein enforcement of the subpoena is being sought. Any resulting order is not appealable prior to entry of a final order in the proceeding.

F. *Witnesses and Fees.* Subpoena and witness fees and mileage shall be the same as those provided for proceedings in the [appropriate state court of general jurisdiction].

G. *Subpoena Pursuant to Law of Another Jurisdiction.* Whenever a subpoena is sought in this state pursuant to the law of another jurisdiction for use in lawyer discipline or disability proceedings, and where the issuance of the subpoena has been duly approved under the law of the other jurisdiction, the chair of the board, upon petition for good cause, may issue a subpoena as provided in this section to compel the attendance of witnesses and production of documents in the county where the witness resides or is employed or elsewhere as agreed by the witness. Service, enforcement, or challenges to this subpoena shall be as provided in these rules.

Commentary

If the complainant cannot furnish adequate evidence to substantiate his or her allegations and the respondent will not cooperate, counsel must seek independent evidence. If this evidence consists of testimony of a potential witness who does not want to get involved or the records of a third party, such as a bank that will not disclose the transcripts of its depositors' accounts voluntarily, disciplinary counsel without subpoena power will be unable to dispose of the complaint on the merits. Disciplinary counsel thus denied an indispensable investigatory tool can neither be effective nor command public confidence.

RULE 15. Discovery

A. *Scope.* Within [twenty] days following the filing of an answer, disciplinary counsel and respondent shall exchange the names and addresses of all persons having knowledge of relevant facts. Within [sixty] days following the filing of an answer, disciplinary counsel and the respondent may take depositions in accordance with [appropriate state rule of civil procedure], and shall comply with reasonable requests for (1) non-privileged information and evidence relevant to the charges or the respondent, and (2) other material upon good cause shown to the chair of the hearing committee [board].

B. *Resolution of Disputes.* Disputes concerning discovery shall be determined by the chair of the hearing committee [board] before which the matter is pending. All discovery orders by the chair are interlocutory and may not be appealed prior to the entry of the final order.

C. *Civil Rules Not Applicable.* Proceedings under these rules are not subject to the [state rules of civil procedure] regarding discovery except those relating to depositions and subpoenas.

Commentary

Liberal exchanges of non-privileged information should be encouraged, since they facilitate the trial of the charges. However, because a skillful advocate can convert unlimited discovery into a tool for delay, the time for discovery should be limited. An order regarding discovery should be interlocutory and should not be appealable prior to entry of a final order in the proceeding.

RULE 16. Access to Disciplinary Information

A. *Availability of Information.* All records of the agency, except the work product of disciplinary counsel or the hearing committee or the board, shall be available to the public after a determination that probable cause exists to believe that misconduct occurred and after the filing and service of formal charges, unless the complainant or respondent obtains a protective order for specific testimony, documents or records.

B. *Confidentiality.* Prior to the filing and service of formal charges in a discipline matter, the proceeding is confidential within the agency, except that the pendency, subject matter, and status of an investigation may be disclosed by disciplinary counsel if:

(1) the respondent has waived confidentiality;

(2) the proceeding is based upon allegations that include either the conviction of a crime or reciprocal discipline;

(3) the proceeding is based upon allegations that have become generally known to the public; or

(4) there is a need to notify another person or organization, including the clients' security fund, in order to protect the public, the administration of justice, or the legal profession.

C. *Public Proceedings.* Upon a determination that probable cause exists to believe that misconduct occurred and the filing and service of formal charges in a discipline matter, or filing of a petition for reinstatement, the proceeding is public, except for:

(1) deliberations of the hearing committee, board, or court; or

(2) information with respect to which the hearing committee has issued a protective order.

D. *Proceedings Alleging Disability.* Proceedings for transfer to or from disability inactive status are confidential. All orders transferring a lawyer to or from disability inactive status are public.

E. *Protective Orders.* In order to protect the interests of a complainant, witness, third party, or respondent, the [hearing committee to which a matter is assigned] [board] may, upon application of any person and for good cause shown, issue a protective order prohibiting the disclosure of specific information otherwise privileged or confidential and direct that the proceedings be conducted so as to implement the order, including requiring that the hearing be conducted in such a way as to preserve the confidentiality of the information that is the subject of the application.

F. *Request for Nonpublic Information.* A request for nonpublic information other than that authorized for disclosure under paragraph B above shall be denied unless the request is from one of the following agencies:

(1) [*names of agencies authorized to investigate qualifications for admission to practice;*]

(2) lawyer disciplinary enforcement agencies;

(3) [*other agencies, if any, designated by the court.*]

G. *Notice to Lawyer.* Except as provided in paragraph H, if the board or counsel decides to provide nonpublic information requested, and if the lawyer has not signed a waiver permitting the requesting agency to obtain nonpublic information, the lawyer shall be notified in writing at his or her last known address of that information which has been requested and by whom, together with a copy of the information proposed to be released to the requesting agency. The notice shall advise the lawyer that the information shall be released at the end of [twenty-one] days following mailing of the notice unless the lawyer objects to the disclosure. If the lawyer timely objects to the disclosure, the information shall remain confidential unless the requesting agency obtains a court order requiring its release.

H. *Release Without Notice.* If an otherwise authorized requesting agency has not obtained a waiver from the lawyer to obtain nonpublic information, and requests that the information be released without giving notice to the lawyer, the requesting agency shall certify that:

(1) the request is made in furtherance of an ongoing investigation into misconduct by the lawyer;

(2) the information is essential to that investigation; and

(3) disclosure of the existence of the investigation to the lawyer would seriously prejudice that investigation.

I. *Notice to National Discipline Data Bank.* The board shall transmit notice of all public discipline imposed against a lawyer, transfers to or from disability inactive status, and reinstatements to the National Discipline Data Bank maintained by the American Bar Association.

J. *Duty of Officials and Employees of the Agency.* All officials and employees of the agency in a proceeding under these rules shall conduct themselves so as to maintain the confidentiality mandated by this rule.

Commentary

The confidentiality that attaches prior to a finding of probable cause and the filing of formal charges is primarily for the benefit of the respondent, and protects against publicity predicated upon unfounded accusations.

If the respondent waives confidentiality or if the nature of the accusation is already known to the public, the basis for confidentiality no longer exists. Where information has become widely known, interested individuals and particularly the media often seek comment from the disciplinary agency involved. The existence of privacy requirements places the disciplinary agency in the awkward position of being unable to acknowledge the existence of an investigation. This could lead to a mistaken notion that the agency is unaware of or uninterested in allegations of misconduct, without in any way protecting the reputation of the lawyer.

Once a finding of probable cause has been made, there is no longer a danger that the allegations against the respondent are frivolous. The need to assure the integrity of the disciplinary process in the eyes of the public requires that at this point further proceedings be open to the public. An announcement that a lawyer accused of serious misconduct has been exonerated after a hearing behind closed doors will be suspect. The same disposition will command respect if the public has had access to the evidence.

Disability proceedings remain confidential until the final order of the court, because medical evidence or other peculiarly personal information relating to the lawyer is often involved. An order of the court transferring the lawyer to disability inactive status is public. When a lawyer's license to practice has been limited in any way, public disclosure is necessary. Failure to reveal the fact of transfer to disability inactive status would mislead the public and others likely to come into contact with the lawyer into believing that he or she remains eligible to practice.

The order transferring the lawyer to disability inactive status should clearly state the conditions that must be met for the lawyer to be reinstated to active status. Orders of reinstatement to active status should be published in the journal of the state bar and in a newspaper of general circulation in each judicial district in which the lawyer maintained an office for the practice of law.

In most instances, requests to the agency for nonpublic information relating to a specific lawyer should be denied. The court in its discretion may direct that the agency cooperate with specific entities by providing them with nonpublic information. These will usually be entities charged with a public responsibility requiring that they investigate specific individuals, such as bar admissions committees, committees on judicial appointments, or law enforcement agencies.

Many of these agencies require the lawyer to sign a waiver authorizing the release of information. If the lawyer does not know what the file contains, he or she cannot knowingly authorize the disclosure of its contents. Therefore, if the lawyer requests it, a copy of any information which the agency proposes to disclose to the requesting entity should be furnished before a waiver is signed.

If the agency is asked to release information without a waiver from the lawyer, and is prepared to do so, it should first notify the lawyer of the request and furnish the lawyer with a copy of the information it proposes to release. This should be done sufficiently in advance of the release of the information to the requesting party to permit the lawyer to object to the release. The lawyer's timely objection places upon the requesting agency the burden of seeking a court order to release the information involved.

The requirement of notice to the lawyer prior to release does not apply to requests for information about a lawyer which are made in furtherance of an ongoing investigation into alleged misconduct on the part of the lawyer by an entity authorized to engage in such investigation. Before the agency releases information to an authorized entity without notice to the lawyer, the entity must provide the certification required by the rule.

Exchange of public information between agencies contributes to more effective enforcement. It is absurd for one agency to struggle with a substantive or procedural problem completely unaware that the same problem has been faced and resolved by an agency in another state. Nor should cases involving fundamental questions in disciplinary enforcement be litigated through the courts in the state in which they arise without agencies in other states which are likely to be vitally affected by the outcome being made aware of the existence of the proceeding until the Supreme Court of the United States renders a decision disposing of the issue.

The ABA Center for Professional Responsibility has full-time legal and administrative staff trained and educated in the discipline and disability field available to provide research information and consulting services. The Center maintains a file of the current rules of disciplinary enforcement of each jurisdiction, periodically updates an Index of case law, and operates the National Discipline Data Bank. Current information relating to the handling of particular problems or approaches to specific situations throughout the country is available.

RULE 17. Dissemination of Disciplinary Information

A. *Notice to Disciplinary Agencies.* Disciplinary counsel shall transmit notice of public discipline, transfers to or from disability inactive status, reinstatements, readmissions, and certified copies of judgments of conviction to the disciplinary enforcement agency of every other jurisdiction in which the respondent is admitted.

B. *Public Notice of Discipline Imposed.* Disciplinary counsel shall cause notices of suspension, disbarment, reinstatement, readmission, and transfers to or from disability inactive status to be published in the journal of the state bar and in a newspaper of general circulation in each judicial district in which the lawyer maintained an office for the practice of law.

C. *Notice to the Courts.* Disciplinary counsel shall promptly transmit a certified copy of the order of suspension, disbarment, reinstatement, and transfer to or from disability inactive status to all courts in this state. In addition, disciplinary counsel shall request the presiding judge of the court of the judicial district in which a respondent transferred to disability inactive status or otherwise unable to comply with the requirement of Rule 27 maintained an office for the practice of law to take such action under the provision of Rule 28 as may be indicated in order to protect the interests of the respondent and the respondent's clients.

Commentary

Broad dissemination of information concerning public discipline serves several important purposes. Notification to disciplinary agencies outside the jurisdiction where a sanction has been imposed facilitates appropriate action, such as reciprocal discipline, in jurisdictions where the lawyer is admitted or is seeking admission to practice. Transmittal of notice concerning criminal convictions provides disciplinary agencies with information that may form the basis of a petition for interim suspension. Publication in state bar journals and newspapers of general circulation helps protect the public and the legal community from being misled concerning the lawyer's eligibility to provide representation. In addition, public awareness of sanctions also enhances confidence in the disciplinary system as an effective means of responding to lawyer misconduct.

When a limitation on a lawyer's license has been removed through reinstatement, readmission or transfer to active status, publication and notification help the lawyer avoid a potential burden involved in correcting misunderstandings concerning his or her eligibility to practice. It is fair and reasonable to give notice of reinstatements, readmissions, and transfers to active status in the same manner as notice of public sanctions.

RULE 18. Additional Rules of Procedure

A. *Nature of Proceedings.* Disciplinary proceedings are neither civil nor criminal but are *sui generis.*

B. *Proceedings Governed by Rules of Civil Procedure and Evidence.* Except as otherwise provided in these rules, the [state rules of civil procedure] and the [state rules of evidence in civil nonjury matters] apply in discipline and disability cases.

C. *Standard of Proof.* Formal charges of misconduct, lesser misconduct, petitions for reinstatement and readmission, and petitions for transfer to and from disability inactive status shall be established by clear and convincing evidence.

D. *Burden of Proof.* The burden of proof in proceedings seeking discipline or transfer to disability inactive status is on disciplinary counsel. The burden of proof in proceedings seeking reinstatement, readmission, or transfer from disability inactive status is on the respondent.

E. *Prehearing Conference.* At the discretion of the [hearing committee] [board] or upon request of either party, a conference may be ordered for the purpose of obtaining admissions or otherwise narrowing the issues presented by the pleadings. The conference shall be held before the chair of the [hearing committee] [board] or another member of the [committee] [board] designated by the chair.

F. *Hearings Recorded.* The hearing should be recorded. Upon request, the board shall make the record of a hearing available.

G. *Related Pending Litigation.* Upon a showing of good cause to the board, the processing of a disciplinary matter may be stayed because of substantial similarity to the material allegations of pending criminal or civil litigation or disciplinary action.

H. *Hearings on Lesser Misconduct.* Hearings to adjudicate formal charges alleging lesser misconduct as defined in Rule 9(B) shall proceed in accordance with these rules except as follows:

(1) The hearing shall be held by a single adjudicator [member of a hearing committee] who shall be a lawyer and shall make written findings of fact and conclusions of law and shall:

(a) dismiss;

(b) recommend the imposition of no sanction other than reprimand, costs, restitution, probation not to exceed one year, or a combination thereof; or

(c) remand to a hearing committee if the misconduct is not lesser misconduct as defined in Rule 9(B).

(2) A prehearing conference need not be held. If no prehearing conference is held, the hearing shall commence within [30] days after the hearing committee member is designated.

(3) Respondent, complainant and disciplinary counsel shall have the right to seek review of the decision by a three member panel of the board, which shall either adopt the decision of the single adjudicator or make written findings. The panel shall either dismiss the case or impose a sanction that does not constitute a restriction on the respondent's right to practice.

(4) The decision of the appellate adjudicator may be reviewed at the discretion of the court upon application by respondent, complainant or disciplinary counsel. The court shall grant review only in cases involving significant issues of law or upon a showing that the decision constituted an abuse of discretion. The court shall either adopt the decision or reject it. If the court rejects the decision, it shall make written findings and either dismiss the case or impose a sanction that does not constitute a restriction on the respondent's right to practice.

(5) Upon final disposition of the case, the written findings and conclusions of the final adjudicator shall be published in an appropriate journal or reporter and a copy shall be mailed to the respondent and to the complainant and to the ABA National Discipline Data Bank.

I. *Delay Caused by Complainant.* Neither unwillingness or neglect of the complainant to sign a complaint or prosecute a charge or settlement or compromise between the complainant and the lawyer or restitution by the lawyer, shall, in itself, justify abatement of the processing of any complaint.

J. *Effect of Time Limitations.* Except as is otherwise provided in these rules, time is directory and not jurisdictional. Failure to observe prescribed time intervals may result in sanctions against the violator but does not justify abatement of any discipline or disability investigation or proceeding.

K. *Complaints Against Disciplinary Agency Members.* If a complaint is filed against disciplinary counsel or disciplinary counsel's staff, a member of a hearing committee, or a member of the board, the matter shall proceed in accordance with these rules except that:

(1) If the respondent is disciplinary counsel or a member of the staff, the board shall appoint a special counsel to present the case;

(2) If the respondent is a member of a hearing committee, the chair of the board shall appoint a special hearing committee for the case; or

(3) If the respondent is a member of the board, the chief justice shall appoint a special board for the case.

Commentary

The holder of a license to practice law is subject to discipline for breaches of the standards of professional conduct; the license must not be arbitrarily taken away and the holder is entitled to procedural due process in any proceeding relating to such conduct. Such due process rights include fair notice of the charges, right to counsel, right to cross-examine witnesses, right to present arguments to the adjudicators, right of appeal (Rule 11); and right to subpoena and discovery (Rules 14 and 15).

The standard of proof for misconduct is higher than "preponderance of the weight of credible evidence" which is usually deemed sufficient in civil proceedings, yet not as stringent as "beyond a reasonable doubt" required in criminal cases.

A prehearing conference may be held by the chairman *sua sponte,* or upon request of counsel, the respondent (or respondent's counsel), or another hearing committee member. Prehearing conferences need not be held in lesser misconduct cases.

The hearing may be recorded by any method authorized in the jurisdiction. The record will assist the hearing committee in the preparation and presentation of its report. If the matter ultimately results in a recommendation for discipline, the record should be forwarded with the findings and recommendation. The recording should be available to the respondent upon request, and a transcript provided at cost.

Statutes of limitation are wholly inappropriate in lawyer disciplinary proceedings. Conduct of a lawyer, no matter when it has occurred, is always relevant to the question of fitness to practice. The time between the commission of the alleged misconduct and the filing of a complaint predicated thereon may be pertinent to whether and to what extent discipline should be imposed, but should not limit the agency's power to investigate.

This rule provides a rational basis for appointment of special counsel, special hearing committee, or special board by the next higher entity in the adjudicative process.

* * *

Lawyer discipline actions are in fact licensing proceedings. Due process accorded to respondent lawyers should be commensurate with the rights and privileges under review. Where the alleged misconduct would not warrant a sanction restricting the lawyer's right to practice, there is no justification for more elaborate procedures. The recommended expedited procedures preserve the rights to notice and hearing, to present evidence and confront witnesses, and to seek review.

At first, a respondent facing a possible reprimand or probation might think that full formal hearing and appeal procedures would provide more protection to his or her professional reputation. A more realistic assessment will show that the recommended expedited procedures are fair and equitable and offer sufficient protection, while full formal procedures are burdensome emotionally and financially compared to the rights at stake.

* * *

RULE 19. Lawyers Found Guilty of a Crime

A. *Transmittal of Proof of Determination of Guilt by Clerk of Trial Court.* The clerk of any court in this state in which a lawyer is found guilty of a crime shall within [ten] days after the finding of guilt transmit a certified copy of the proof of the finding of guilt to counsel for the lawyer disciplinary agency of every state in which the lawyer is admitted to practice.

B. *Determination of "Serious Crime."* Upon being advised that a lawyer subject to the disciplinary jurisdiction of this court has been found guilty of a crime, disciplinary counsel shall determine whether the crime constitutes a "serious crime" warranting immediate interim suspension. If the crime is a "serious crime," disciplinary counsel shall prepare an order for interim suspension and forward it to the court and the respondent with proof of finding of guilt. Disciplinary counsel shall in addition file formal charges against the respondent predicated upon the finding of guilt. On or before the date established for the entry of the order of interim suspension the lawyer may assert any jurisdictional deficiency that establishes that the suspension may not properly be ordered, such as that the crime did not constitute a "serious crime" or that the lawyer is not the individual found guilty. If the crime is not a "serious crime," counsel shall process the matter in the same manner as any other information coming to the attention of the agency.

C. *Definition of "Serious Crime."* A "serious crime" is any felony or any lesser crime that reflects adversely on the lawyer's honesty, trustworthiness or fitness as a lawyer in other respects, or any crime a necessary element of which, as determined by the statutory or common law definition of the crime, involves interference with the administration of justice, false swearing, misrepresentation, fraud, deceit, bribery, extortion, misappropriation, theft, or an attempt, conspiracy or solicitation of another to commit a "serious crime."

D. *Immediate Interim Suspension.* The court has exclusive power to place a lawyer on interim suspension.

(1) Imposition. The court shall place a lawyer on interim suspension immediately upon proof that the lawyer has been found guilty of a serious crime regardless of the pendency of any appeal.

(2) Termination. The court has exclusive power to terminate an interim suspension. In the interest of justice, the court may terminate an interim suspension at any time upon a showing of extraordinary circumstances, after affording disciplinary counsel notice and an opportunity to be heard.

E. *Conviction as Conclusive Evidence.* For purposes of a hearing on formal charges filed as a result of a finding of guilt, a certified copy of a judgment of conviction constitutes conclusive evidence that the lawyer committed the crime, and the sole issue in any such hearing shall be the nature and extent of the discipline to be imposed.

F. *Automatic Reinstatement From Interim Suspension Upon Reversal of Conviction.* If a lawyer suspended solely under the provisions of paragraph D demonstrates that the underlying finding of guilt or conviction has been reversed or vacated, the order for interim suspension shall be vacated and the lawyer placed on active status. The vacating of the interim suspension will not automatically terminate any formal proceeding then pending against the lawyer, the disposition of which shall be determined by the hearing committee and the board on the basis of the available evidence other than the finding of guilt or conviction.

G. *Notice to Clients and Others on Interim Suspension.* An interim suspension under this rule shall constitute a suspension of the lawyer for the purpose of Rule 27.

Commentary

Interim suspension is necessary both to protect members of the public and to maintain public confidence in the legal profession. The interim suspension not only removes any danger to clients and the public which the respondent may pose, but also serves to protect the profession and the administration of justice from the specter created where an individual found guilty of a "serious crime" continues to serve as an officer of the court in good standing.

Interim suspension is not final discipline; therefore counsel must proceed to file formal charges based upon the finding of guilt and subsequent conviction. Formal proceedings should not be conducted until all appeals from the conviction have been exhausted, unless the respondent requests that the hearing not be deferred.

Continued practice by a lawyer found guilty of a "serious crime" undermines the public confidence in the profession and the administration of justice. Because there may be delay between a determination of guilt and entry of a judgment of conviction, the disciplinary agency should seek interim suspension upon a finding of guilt. It is difficult to understand why a lawyer found guilty of stealing funds from a client can continue to handle client funds, why a lawyer found guilty of securities fraud can continue to prepare and certify registration statements, or why a lawyer found guilty of conspiracy to suborn perjury can continue to try cases and present witnesses. Immediate suspension of a lawyer so convicted, regardless of the pendency of any appeal, is essential to preserve public confidence.

* * *

RULE 20. Interim Suspension for Threat of Harm

A. *Transmittal of Evidence.* Upon receipt of sufficient evidence demonstrating that a lawyer subject to the disciplinary jurisdiction of this court has committed a violation of the [state Rules of Professional Conduct] or is under a disability as herein defined and poses a substantial threat of serious harm to the public, disciplinary counsel shall:

(i) transmit the evidence to the court together with a proposed order for interim suspension; and

(ii) contemporaneously make a reasonable attempt to provide the lawyer with notice, which may include notice by telephone, that a proposed order for immediate interim suspension has been transmitted to the court.

B. *Immediate Interim Suspension.* Upon examination of the evidence transmitted to the court by disciplinary counsel and of rebuttal evidence, if any, which the lawyer has transmitted to the court prior to the court's ruling, the court may enter an order immediately suspending the lawyer, pending final disposition of a disciplinary proceeding predicated upon the conduct causing the harm, or may order such other action as it deems appropriate. In the event the order is entered, the court may appoint a trustee pursuant to Rule 28 to protect clients' interests.

C. *Notice to Clients.* A lawyer suspended pursuant to paragraph B shall comply with the notice requirements in Rule 27.

D. *Motion for Dissolution of Interim Suspension.* On [two] days notice to disciplinary counsel, a lawyer suspended pursuant to paragraph B may appear and move for dissolution or modification of the order of suspension, and in that event the motion shall be heard and determined as expeditiously as the ends of justice require.

Commentary

Certain misconduct poses such an immediate threat to the public and the administration of justice that the lawyer should be suspended from the practice of law immediately pending a final determination of the ultimate discipline to be imposed. Interim suspension is also appropriate when the lawyer's continuing conduct is causing or is likely to cause serious injury to a client or the public, as, for example, where a lawyer abandons the practice of law or is engaged in an ongoing conversion of trust funds.

The procedures set forth in Rule 20 are similar to those applicable to civil temporary restraining orders, except that an immediate interim suspension order does not expire automatically, but requires a motion for dissolution or modification. Since immediate interim suspension may be imposed *ex parte* following reasonable efforts to notify the lawyer, a lawyer suspended without a hearing should be afforded an opportunity to seek dissolution or modification of the suspension order on an expedited basis.

RULE 21. Discipline by Consent

A. *Board Approval of Tendered Admission.* A lawyer against whom formal charges have been made may tender to disciplinary counsel a conditional admission to the petition or to a particular count thereof in exchange for a stated form of discipline. The tendered conditional admission shall be approved or rejected by the board [considering the recommendation of the hearing committee if the matter has already been assigned for hearing, and] subject to final approval or rejection by the court if the stated form of discipline includes disbarment, suspension or transfer to disability inactive status pursuant to Rule 11(F). If the stated form of discipline is rejected by the [adjudicative body] [board], the admission shall be withdrawn and cannot be used against the respondent in any subsequent proceedings.

B. *Review of Discipline by Consent.* The extent of discipline to be imposed is subject to review. If an agreement providing for admonition or probation is reached prior to the filing of formal charges, the agreement must be approved by the chair of a hearing committee [board].

C. *Discontinuance of Jurisdiction.* Approval of the discipline proposed by the board and, if required, by the court, shall divest the hearing committee of further jurisdiction and no report need be prepared in such cases. The final order of discipline shall be predicated upon the petition and the conditional admission tendered.

D. *Affidavit of Consent.* A lawyer who consents to a stated form of discipline shall present to the board an affidavit stating that he or she consents to the discipline and that:

(1) The consent is freely and voluntarily rendered; the lawyer is not being subjected to coercion or duress; the lawyer is fully aware of the implications of submitting the consent;

(2) The lawyer is aware that there is presently pending an investigation into, or proceeding involving, allegations that there exist grounds for discipline, the nature of which shall be specifically set forth;

(3) The lawyer acknowledges that the material facts so alleged are true; and

(4) The lawyer consents because the lawyer knows that if charges predicated upon the matters under investigation were filed, or if the pending proceeding were prosecuted, the lawyer could not successfully defend against them.

E. *Order of Discipline.* The board shall file the affidavit with the court. If the discipline by consent is a reprimand, the board shall enter the order. In all other instances in which proposed discipline has been approved the court shall enter the order disciplining the lawyer on consent. Whether the sanction is made public shall be governed by Rule 10(D).

Commentary

If an agreement provides for reprimand, suspension or disbarment, or if any agreement is reached after formal charges have been filed, the agreement must be approved by a panel of the board. Members of the panel are disqualified from any future consideration of the matter in the event the stipulated discipline is for any reason not imposed. If the stipulated discipline provides for suspension or disbarment, it must also be approved by the court.

Acceptance of stipulated discipline by a lawyer who has been guilty of misconduct and desires to avoid the trauma and expense of a proceeding is in the interest of the public and the agency. The public is immediately protected from further misconduct by the lawyer, who otherwise might continue to practice until a formal proceeding is concluded. The agency is relieved of the time-consuming and expensive necessity of prosecuting a formal proceeding.

The respondent should be required to admit the charges before discipline is stipulated, so that evidence of guilt will be available if the respondent later claims that he or she was not, in fact, guilty. Petitions for reinstatement are often filed years after discipline has been imposed, and if there is no admission it may be difficult for the agency to establish the misconduct because relevant evidence and witnesses may no longer be available.

Discipline by consent which results in the lawyer withdrawing from the practice of law should be recorded and treated as disbarment, not as resignation. An agreement made when the charges are before the board shall be reviewed by the court. In the event that proposed stipulated discipline is disapproved by the reviewing entity, or the matter is returned to formal proceedings for any reason, the respondent's admission of the charges cannot be used against the respondent.

RULE 22. Reciprocal Discipline and Reciprocal Disability Inactive Status*

A. *Disciplinary Counsel Duty to Obtain Order of Discipline or Disability Inactive Status From Other Jurisdiction.* Upon being disciplined or transferred to disability inactive status in another jurisdiction, a lawyer admitted to practice in [this jurisdiction] shall promptly inform disciplinary counsel of the discipline or transfer. Upon notification from any source that a lawyer within the jurisdiction of the agency has been disciplined or transferred to disability inactive status in another jurisdiction, disciplinary counsel shall obtain a certified copy of the disciplinary order and file it with the board and with the court.

B. *Notice Served Upon Respondent.* Upon receipt of a certified copy of an order demonstrating that a lawyer admitted to practice in [name of jurisdiction] has been disciplined or transferred to disability inactive status in another jurisdiction, the court shall forthwith issue a notice directed to the lawyer and to disciplinary counsel containing:

(1) A copy of the order from the other jurisdiction; and

(2) An order directing that the lawyer or disciplinary counsel inform the court, within [thirty] days from service of the notice, of any claim by the lawyer or disciplinary counsel predicated upon the grounds set forth in paragraph D, that the imposition of the identical discipline or disability inactive status in this jurisdiction would be unwarranted and the reasons for that claim.

---

* In 2002, the ABA House of Delegates amended Rule 22 based upon a recommendation of the Commission on Multijurisdictional Practice.

C. *Effect of Stay in Other Jurisdiction.* In the event the discipline or transfer imposed in the other jurisdiction has been stayed there, any reciprocal discipline or transfer imposed in this jurisdiction shall be deferred until the stay expires.

D. *Discipline to Be Imposed.* Upon the expiration of [thirty] days from service of the notice pursuant to the provisions of paragraph B, this court shall impose the identical discipline or disability inactive status unless disciplinary counsel or the lawyer demonstrates, or this court finds that it clearly appears upon the face of the record from which the discipline is predicated, that:

(1) The procedure was so lacking in notice or opportunity to be heard as to constitute a deprivation of due process; or

(2) There was such infirmity of proof establishing the misconduct as to give rise to the clear conviction that the court could not, consistent with its duty, accept as final the conclusion on that subject; or

(3) The discipline imposed would result in grave injustice; or be offensive to the public policy of the jurisdiction; or

(4) The reason for the original transfer to disability inactive status no longer exists.

If this court determines that any of those elements exists, this court shall enter such other order as it deems appropriate. The burden is on the party seeking different discipline in this jurisdiction to demonstrate that the imposition of the same discipline is not appropriate.

E. *Conclusiveness of Adjudication in Other Jurisdictions.* In all other aspects, a final adjudication in another jurisdiction that a lawyer, whether or not admitted in that jurisdiction, has been guilty of misconduct or should be transferred to disability inactive status shall establish conclusively the misconduct or the disability for purposes of a disciplinary or disability proceeding in this state.

Commentary

If a lawyer suspended or disbarred in one jurisdiction is also admitted in another jurisdiction and no action can be taken against the lawyer until a new disciplinary proceeding is instituted, tried, and concluded, the public in the second jurisdiction is left unprotected against a lawyer who has been judicially determined to be unfit. Any procedure which so exposes innocent clients to harm cannot be justified. The spectacle of a lawyer disbarred in one jurisdiction yet permitted to practice elsewhere exposes the profession to criticism and undermines public confidence in the administration of justice.

Disciplinary counsel in the forum jurisdiction should be notified by disciplinary counsel of the jurisdiction where the original discipline or disability inactive status was imposed. Upon receipt of such information, disciplinary counsel should promptly obtain and serve upon the lawyer an order to show cause why identical discipline or disability inactive status should not be imposed in the forum jurisdiction. The certified copy of the order in the original jurisdiction should be incorporated into the order to show cause.

The imposition of discipline or disability inactive status in one jurisdiction does not mean that every other jurisdiction in which the lawyer is admitted must necessarily impose discipline or disability inactive status. The agency has jurisdiction to recommend reciprocal discipline or disability inactive status on the basis of public discipline or disability inactive status imposed by a jurisdiction in which the respondent is licensed.

A judicial determination of misconduct or disability by the respondent in another jurisdiction is conclusive, and not subject to relitigation in the forum jurisdiction. The court should impose identical discipline or disability inactive status unless it determines, after review limited to the record of the proceedings in the foreign jurisdiction, that one of the grounds specified in paragraph D exists. This Rule applies whether or not the respondent is admitted to practice in that jurisdiction. See also, Model Rule 8.5, Comment [1], Model Rules of Professional Conduct.

RULE 23. Proceedings in Which Lawyer Is Declared to Be Incompetent or Alleged to Be Incapacitated

A. *Involuntary Commitment or Adjudication of Incompetency.* If a lawyer has been judicially declared incompetent or is involuntarily committed on the grounds of incompetency or disability, the court, upon proper proof of the fact, shall enter an order immediately transferring the lawyer to disability inactive status for an indefinite period until the further order of the court. A copy of the order shall be served, in the manner the court may direct, upon the lawyer, his or her guardian, or the director of the institution to which the lawyer has been committed.

B. *Inability to Properly Defend.* If a respondent alleges in the course of a disciplinary proceeding an inability to assist in the defense due to mental or physical incapacity, the court shall immediately transfer the lawyer to disability inactive status pending determination of the incapacity.

(1) If the court determines the claim of inability to defend is valid, the disciplinary proceeding shall be deferred and the respondent retained on disability inactive status until the court subsequently considers a petition for transfer of the respondent to active status. If the court considering the petition for transfer to active status determines the petition shall be granted, the court shall also determine the disposition of the interrupted disciplinary proceedings.

(2) If the court determines the claim of incapacity to defend to be invalid, the disciplinary proceeding shall resume and the respondent shall immediately be placed on interim suspension pending the final disposition of the matter.

C. *Proceedings to Determine Incapacity.* Information relating to a lawyer's physical or mental condition which adversely affects the lawyer's ability to practice law shall be investigated, and where warranted, shall be the subject of formal proceedings to determine whether the lawyer shall be transferred to disability inactive status. The hearings shall be conducted in the same manner as disciplinary proceedings, except that all of the proceedings shall be confidential. The court shall provide for such notice to the respondent of proceedings in the matter as it deems proper and advisable and may appoint a lawyer to represent the respondent if the respondent is without adequate representation. The court may take or direct whatever action it deems necessary or proper to determine whether the respondent is so incapacitated, including the examination of the respondent by qualified medical experts designated by the court. If, upon due consideration of the matter, the court concludes that the respondent is incapacitated from continuing to practice law, it shall enter an order transferring the respondent to disability inactive status for an indefinite period and until the further order of the court. Any pending disciplinary proceedings against the respondent shall be held in abeyance.

D. *Public Notice of Transfer to Disability Inactive Status.* The board shall cause a notice of transfer to disability inactive status to be published in the journal of the state bar and in a newspaper of general circulation in each judicial district in which the lawyer maintained an office for the practice of law.

E. *Reinstatement From Disability Inactive Status.*

(1) Generally. No respondent transferred to disability inactive status may resume active status except by order of this court.

(2) Petition. Any respondent transferred to disability inactive status shall be entitled to petition for transfer to active status once a year, or at whatever shorter intervals the court may direct in the order transferring the respondent to disability inactive status or any modifications thereof.

(3) Examination. Upon the filing of a petition for transfer to active status, the court may take or direct whatever action it deems necessary or proper to determine whether the disability has been removed, including a direction for an examination of the respondent by qualified medical experts designated by the court. In its discretion, the court may direct that the expense of the examination be paid by the respondent.

(4) Waiver of Doctor-Patient Privilege. With the filing of a petition for reinstatement to active status, the respondent shall be required to disclose the name of each psychiatrist, psychologist, physician and hospital or other institution by whom or in which the respondent has been examined or treated since the transfer to disability inactive status. The respondent shall furnish to this court written consent to the release of information and records relating to the disability if requested by the court or court-appointed medical experts.

(5) Learning in Law; Bar Examination. The court may also direct that the respondent establish proof of competence and learning in law, which proof may include certification by the bar examiners of successful completion of an examination for admission to practice.

(6) Granting Petition for Transfer to Active Status. The court shall grant the petition for transfer to active status upon a showing by clear and convincing evidence that the disability has been removed.

(7) Judicial Declaration of Competence. If a respondent transferred to disability inactive status on the basis of a judicial determination of incompetence has been judicially declared to be competent, the court may dispense with further evidence that his disability has been removed and may immediately direct his reinstatement to active status upon terms as are deemed proper and advisable.

Commentary

Since the principal responsibility of the agency is to protect the public, it must concern itself with disabled lawyers who endanger the interests of clients, even if no misconduct has been committed. It is important that incapacity not be treated as misconduct, and to clearly distinguish willful conduct from conduct beyond the control of the lawyer.

* * *

RULE 24. Reinstatement Following a Suspension of Six Months or Less

A lawyer who has been suspended for six months or less pursuant to disciplinary proceedings shall be reinstated at the end of the period of suspension by filing with the court and serving upon disciplinary counsel an affidavit stating that he or she has fully complied with the requirements of the suspension order and has paid any required fees and costs.

Commentary

Reinstatement proceedings may take months to complete. Requiring a proceeding before a lawyer can be reinstated after a suspension of six months or less would unfairly prolong the period of suspension. Consequently, reinstatement following a suspension for six months or less should be automatic upon the expiration of the prescribed period of time, a filing of an affidavit alleging compliance with the terms of the order of suspension and the payment of fees and costs.

RULE 25. Reinstatement After Suspension for More Than Six Months and Readmission

A. *Generally.* A lawyer suspended for more than six months or a disbarred lawyer shall be reinstated or readmitted only upon order of the court. No lawyer may petition for reinstatement until [six months before] the period of suspension has expired. No lawyer may petition for readmission until [five] years after the effective date of disbarment. A lawyer who has been placed on interim suspension and is then disbarred for the same misconduct that was the ground for the interim suspension may petition for readmission at the expiration of [five] years from the time of the effective date of the interim suspension.

B. *Petition.* A petition for reinstatement or readmission must be under oath or affirmation under penalty of perjury and shall specify with particularity the manner in which the lawyer meets each of the criteria specified in paragraph E or, if not, why there is good and sufficient reason for reinstatement or readmission. [Unless abated under Rule 26] the petition must be accompanied by an advance cost deposit in the amount set from time to time by the board to cover anticipated costs of the proceeding.

C. *Service of Petition.* The lawyer shall file a copy of the petition with disciplinary counsel and disciplinary counsel shall serve a copy of the petition upon each complainant in the disciplinary proceeding that led to the suspension or disbarment.

D. *Publication of Notice of Petition.* At the same time that a lawyer files a petition for reinstatement or readmission, the lawyer shall also publish a notice of the petition in the journal of the state bar and in a newspaper of general circulation in each judicial district in which the lawyer maintained an office for the practice of law when the lawyer was suspended or disbarred. The notice shall inform members of the bar and the public about the application for reinstatement or readmission, and shall request that any individuals file notice of their opposition or concurrence with the board within [sixty] days. In addition, the lawyer shall notify the complainant(s) in the disciplinary proceeding that led to the lawyer's suspension or disbarment that the lawyer is applying for reinstatement or readmission, and shall inform each complainant that he or she has [sixty] days to raise objections to or to support the lawyer's petition.

E. *Criteria for Reinstatement and Readmission.* A lawyer may be reinstated or readmitted only if the lawyer meets each of the following criteria, or, if not, presents good and sufficient reason why the lawyer should nevertheless be reinstated or readmitted:

(1) The lawyer has fully complied with the terms and conditions of all prior disciplinary orders except to the extent that they are abated under Rule 26.

(2) The lawyer has not engaged nor attempted to engage in the unauthorized practice of law during the period of suspension or disbarment.

(3) If the lawyer was suffering under a physical or mental disability or infirmity at the time of suspension or disbarment, including alcohol or other drug abuse, the disability or infirmity has been removed. Where alcohol or other drug abuse was a causative factor in the lawyer's misconduct, the lawyer shall not be reinstated or readmitted unless:

(a) the lawyer has pursued appropriate rehabilitative treatment;

(b) the lawyer has abstained from the use of alcohol or other drugs for at least [one year]; and

(c) the lawyer is likely to continue to abstain from alcohol or other drugs.

(4) The lawyer recognizes the wrongfulness and seriousness of the misconduct for which the lawyer was suspended or disbarred.

(5) The lawyer has not engaged in any other professional misconduct since suspension or disbarment.

(6) Notwithstanding the conduct for which the lawyer was disciplined, the lawyer has the requisite honesty and integrity to practice law.

(7) The lawyer has kept informed about recent developments in the law and is competent to practice.

(8) In addition, a lawyer who has been disbarred must pass the bar examination and the character and fitness examination.

F. *Review of Petition.* Within [ninety] days after receiving a lawyer's petition for reinstatement or readmission, disciplinary counsel shall either: (1) advise the lawyer and the [board] court that disciplinary counsel will stipulate to the lawyer's reinstatement or readmission, or (2) advise the lawyer and the [board] court that disciplinary counsel opposes reinstatement or readmission and request the [board] court to set a hearing.

G. *Hearing; Report.* Upon receipt of disciplinary counsel's request for a hearing, the [board] court shall promptly refer the matter to a hearing committee. Within [ninety] days of the request, the hearing committee shall conduct a hearing at which the lawyer shall have the burden of demonstrating by clear and convincing evidence that he or she has met each of the criteria in paragraph E or, if not, that there is good and sufficient reason why the lawyer should nevertheless be reinstated or readmitted. The hearing committee shall file a report with the [board] court containing its findings and recommendations. [The board shall promptly review the report of the hearing committee and the record and shall file its own findings and recommendations with the court.]

H. *Decision as to Reinstatement or Readmission.* The court shall review the report filed by the [hearing committee] [board] or any stipulation agreed to by the lawyer and disciplinary counsel. If the court finds that the lawyer has complied with each of the criteria of paragraph E, or has presented good and sufficient reason for failure to comply, the court shall reinstate or readmit the lawyer. If the court reinstates or readmits the lawyer, the court shall issue a written opinion setting forth the grounds for its decision; if the court denies reinstatement or readmission, the court shall issue a written opinion setting forth the ground for its decision and shall identify the period after which the lawyer may reapply. Generally, no lawyer should be permitted to reapply for reinstatement or readmission within one year following an adverse judgment upon a petition for reinstatement or readmission.

I. *Conditions of Reinstatement or Readmission.* The court may impose conditions on a lawyer's reinstatement or readmission. The conditions shall be imposed in cases where the lawyer has met the burden of proof justifying reinstatement or readmission, but the court reasonably believes that further precautions should be taken to insure that the public will be protected upon the lawyer's return to practice.

The court may impose any conditions that are reasonably related to the grounds for the lawyer's original suspension or disbarment, or to evidence presented at the hearing regarding the lawyer's failure to meet the criteria for reinstatement or readmission. Passing the bar examination and the character and fitness examination shall be conditions to readmission following disbarment. The conditions may also include any of the following: limitation upon practice (to one area of law or through association with an experienced supervising lawyer); participation in continuing legal education courses; monitoring of the lawyer's practice (for compliance with trust account rules, accounting procedures, or office management procedures); abstention from the use of drugs or alcohol; active participation in Alcoholics Anonymous or other alcohol or drug rehabilitation program; monitoring of the lawyer's compliance with any other orders (such as abstinence from alcohol or drugs, or participation in alcohol or drug rehabilitation programs). If the monitoring lawyer determines that the reinstated or readmitted lawyer's compliance with any condition of reinstatement or readmission is unsatisfactory and that there exists a potential for harm to the public, the monitoring lawyer shall notify the court and, where necessary to protect the public, the lawyer may be suspended from practice under Rule 20(B).

J. *Reciprocal Reinstatement or Readmission.* Where the court has imposed a suspension or disbarment solely on the basis of imposition of discipline in another jurisdiction, and where the lawyer gives notice to the court that he or she has been reinstated or readmitted in the other jurisdiction, the court shall determine whether the lawyer should be reinstated or readmitted. Unless disciplinary counsel presents evidence demonstrating procedural irregularities in the other jurisdiction's proceeding or presents other compelling reasons, the court shall reinstate or readmit a lawyer who has been reinstated or readmitted in the jurisdiction where the misconduct occurred.

Commentary

Readmission occurs when a disbarred lawyer is returned to practice. Since the purpose of lawyer discipline is not to punish, readmission may be appropriate; the presumption, though, should be against readmission. In no event should a lawyer be considered for readmission until at least five years after the effective date of disbarment.

Reinstatement occurs when a suspended lawyer is returned to practice. Reinstatement is appropriate when a lawyer shows rehabilitation. Application for reinstatement should be permitted at the expiration of the ordered period of suspension. While reinstatement should not be ordered prior to the expiration of the ordered period of suspension, application for reinstatement may be allowed up to six months preceding the expiration so that the time required for a decision on the application does not unfairly prolong the suspension.

As a condition of readmission or reinstatement, a disbarred or suspended lawyer is usually required to establish rehabilitation, fitness to practice and competence, and may be required to pay the costs of the disciplinary proceedings, to make restitution, to disgorge all or part to the lawyer's or law firm's fee, to pass an examination in professional responsibility, and to comply with court orders.

There is a compelling reason not to grant reciprocal reinstatement under paragraph J if the forum jurisdiction imposed a longer suspension than the original jurisdiction or if there was a delay between the imposition of the original discipline and the imposition of the reciprocal discipline.

RULE 26. Abatement or Modification of Conditions of Discipline, Reinstatement, or Readmission

Where the court has imposed conditions in an order of discipline or in an order of reinstatement or readmission, the lawyer may request of the court an order of abatement discharging the lawyer from the obligation to comply with the conditions, or an order modifying the conditions. The lawyer may so request either prior to or as part of lawyer's petition for reinstatement or readmission. The court may grant the request if the lawyer shows by clear and convincing evidence that the lawyer has made a timely, good faith effort to meet the condition(s) but it is impossible to fulfill the condition(s).

Commentary

A jurisdiction adopting this Rule should also adopt the bracketed language in Rule 25(B).

RULE 27. Notice to Clients, Adverse Parties, and Other Counsel

A. *Recipients of Notice; Contents.* Within [ten] days after the date of the court order imposing discipline or transfer to disability inactive status, a respondent disbarred, transferred to disability inactive status, placed on interim suspension, or suspended for more than [six months] shall notify or cause to be notified by registered or certified mail, return receipt requested,

(1) all clients being represented in pending matters;

(2) any co-counsel in pending matters; and

(3) any opposing counsel in pending matters, or in the absence of opposing counsel, the adverse parties, of the order of the court and that the lawyer is therefore disqualified to act as lawyer after the effective date of the order.

The notice to be given to the lawyer(s) for an adverse party, or, in the absence of opposing counsel, the adverse parties, shall state the place of residence of the client of the respondent.

B. *Special Notice.* The court may direct the issuance of notice to such financial institutions or others as may be necessary to protect the interests of clients or other members of the public.

C. *Duty to Maintain Records.* The respondent shall keep and maintain records of the steps taken to accomplish the requirements of paragraphs A and B, and shall make those records available to the disciplinary counsel on request.

D. *Return of Client Property.* The respondent shall deliver to all clients being represented in pending matters any papers or other property to which they are entitled and shall notify them and any counsel representing them of a suitable time and place where the papers and other property may be obtained, calling attention to any urgency for obtaining the papers or other property.

E. *Effective Date of Order; Refund of Fees.* Orders imposing disbarment, suspension, or transfers to disability inactive status are effective on a date [15] days after the date of the order except where the court finds that immediate disbarment or suspension is necessary to protect the public. The respondent shall refund within [ten] days after entry of the order any part of any fees paid in advance that has not been earned.

F. *Withdrawal From Representation.* In the event the client does not obtain another lawyer before the effective date of the disbarment or suspension, it shall be the responsibility of the respondent to move in the court or agency in which the proceeding is pending for leave to withdraw. The respondent shall in that event file with the court, agency or tribunal before which the litigation is pending a copy of the notice to opposing counsel or adverse parties.

G. *New Representation Prohibited.* Prior to the effective date of the order, if not immediate, the respondent shall agree not to undertake any new legal matters between service of the order and the effective date of the discipline. Upon the effective date of the order, the respondent shall not maintain a presence or occupy an office where the practice of law is conducted. The respondent shall take such action as is necessary to cause the removal of any indicia of lawyer, counselor at law, legal assistant, law clerk or similar title.

H. *Affidavit Filed With Court.* Within [ten] days after the effective date of the disbarment or suspension order, or order of transfer to disability inactive status, the respondent shall file with this court an affidavit showing:

(1) Compliance with the provisions of the order and with these rules;

(2) All other state, federal and administrative jurisdictions to which the lawyer is admitted to practice;

(3) Residence or other addresses where communications may thereafter be directed; and

(4) Service of a copy of the affidavit upon disciplinary counsel.

Commentary

These notice provisions are necessary to ensure that the respondent's inability to practice does not prejudice the rights of existing clients or other parties, and that those who might otherwise have occasion to deal with the lawyer are made aware of the lawyer's suspension or disbarment. Compliance with the notice provision is an absolute precondition for reinstatement or readmission, and failure to comply may be grounds for further discipline.

Usually the effective date of discipline or transfer to disability inactive status should be the end of the period during which the final order may be appealed but at least fifteen days, unless the court finds immediate suspension or disbarment is necessary. The interval between the entry of the order and its effective date permits the respondent to wind up his or her practice in an orderly manner. The respondent should not accept new retainers during this period since it is unlikely he or she can adequately represent new clients before the effective date when practice must be discontinued.

RULE 28. Appointment of Counsel to Protect Clients' Interests When Respondent Is Transferred to Disability Inactive Status, Suspended, Disbarred, Disappears, or Dies

A. *Inventory of Lawyer Files.* If a respondent has been transferred to disability inactive status, or has disappeared or died, or has been suspended or disbarred and there is evidence that he or she has not complied with Rule 27, and no partner, executor or other responsible party capable of conducting the respondent's affairs is known to exist, the presiding judge in the judicial district in which the respondent maintained a practice, upon proper proof of the fact, shall appoint a lawyer or lawyers to inventory the files of the respondent, and to take such action as seems indicated to protect the interests of the respondent and his or her clients.

B. *Protection for Records Subject to Inventory.* Any lawyer so appointed shall not be permitted to disclose any information contained in any files inventoried without the consent of the client to whom the file relates, except as necessary to carry out the order of the court which appointed the lawyer to make the inventory.

Commentary

In any situation in which the lawyer is not available to protect clients, the agency has an obligation to protect them. When such information comes to the attention of the agency, it need not await the determination that misconduct has occurred before acting.

The cost of the inventory may be paid from the fees owing to the lawyer whose files are inventoried. The cost may also be paid by funds made available for that purpose by state and local bar associations. Often the lawyer appointed as trustee will waive all or part of his or her fee as a public service.

The trustee is appointed to inventory the files of the lawyer's clients, not to represent them. The trustee should review each file and recommend to the judge who appointed him or her a proposed disposition. The trustee may take only such action with respect to each client's file as is authorized by the judge who appointed him or her.

The lawyer-client privilege must be extended so that review of the file by the trustee is not deemed to be disclosure to a third party, which would waive the privilege.

RULE 29. Maintenance of Trust Funds in Approved Financial Institutions; Overdraft Notification

A. *Clearly Identified Trust Accounts in Approved Financial Institutions Required.*

(1) Lawyers who practice law in [name of state] shall deposit all funds held in trust in this jurisdiction [in accordance with Rule 1.15(a) of the Model Rules of Professional Conduct] in accounts clearly identified as "trust" or "escrow" accounts, referred to herein as "trust accounts," and shall take all steps necessary to inform the depository institution of the purpose and identity of the accounts. Funds held in trust include funds held in any fiduciary capacity in connection with a representation, whether as trustee, agent, guardian, executor or otherwise. Lawyer trust accounts shall be maintained only in financial institutions approved by the court [the board].

(2) Every lawyer engaged in the practice of law in [name of state] shall maintain and preserve for a period of at least five years, after final disposition of the underlying matter, the records of the accounts, including checkbooks, cancelled checks, check stubs, vouchers, ledgers, journals, closing statements, accountings or other statements of disbursements rendered to clients or other parties with regard to trust funds or similar equivalent records clearly and expressly reflecting the date, amount, source, and explanation for all receipts, withdrawals, deliveries and disbursements of the funds or other property of a client.

B. *Overdraft Notification Agreement Required.* A financial institution shall be approved as a depository for lawyer trust accounts if it files with the court an agreement, in a form provided by the court [board] to report to the disciplinary agency whenever any properly payable instrument is presented against a lawyer trust account containing insufficient funds, irrespective of whether or not the instrument is honored. The court [board] shall establish rules governing approval and termination of approved status for financial institutions, and shall annually publish a list of approved financial institutions. No trust account shall be maintained in any financial institution that does not agree to so report. Any such agreement shall apply to all branches of the financial institution and shall not be cancelled except upon [thirty] days notice in writing to the court [board].

C. *Overdraft Reports.* The overdraft notification agreement shall provide that all reports made by the financial institution shall be in the following format:

(1) In the case of a dishonored instrument, the report shall be identical to the overdraft notice customarily forwarded to the depositor, and should include a copy of the dishonored instrument, if such a copy is normally provided to depositors;

(2) In the case of instruments that are presented against insufficient funds but which instruments are honored, the report shall identify the financial institution, the lawyer or law firm, the account number, the date of presentation for payment, and the date paid, as well as the amount of overdraft created thereby.

D. *Timing of Reports.* Reports under paragraph C shall be made simultaneously with, and within the time provided by law for notice of dishonor, if any. If an instrument presented against insufficient funds is honored, then the report shall be made within [five] banking days of the date of presentation for payment against insufficient funds.

E. *Consent by Lawyers.* Every lawyer practicing or admitted to practice in this jurisdiction shall, as a condition thereof, be conclusively deemed to have consented to the reporting and production requirements mandated by this rule.

F. *Costs.* Nothing herein shall preclude a financial institution from charging a particular lawyer or law firm for the reasonable cost of producing the reports and records required by this rule.

G. *Definitions.* For purposes of this Rule:

(1) "Financial institution" includes a bank, savings and loan association, credit union, savings bank, and any other business or person that accepts for deposit funds held in trust by lawyers.

(2) "Properly payable" refers to an instrument which, if presented in the normal course of business, is in a form requiring payment under the laws of this jurisdiction.

(3) "Notice of dishonor" refers to the notice that a financial institution is required to give, under the laws of this jurisdiction, upon presentation of an instrument that the institution dishonors.

Commentary

Paragraph A sets forth the requirements for deposit of trust funds in clearly identified trust accounts in approved financial institutions. Funds held not in connection with a representation, such as a trust fund for a lawyer's own spouse or minor child, do not fall under the rule. The rule also does not concern a lawyer's own funds properly held in a non-fiduciary capacity, such as funds in a business or personal account.

Under Rule 1.15(a) of the Model Rules of Professional Conduct, trust property may be held outside the lawyer's home jurisdiction upon consent of the client. The overdraft notification rule governs funds held within the adopting state. A lawyer's obligation to deposit trust funds in an approved institution will arise upon adoption of the overdraft notification rule in a state where the lawyer deposits trust funds, whether that state is the state wherein the lawyer's office is situated or some other state.

The overdraft notification agreement requires that all overdrafts be reported, irrespective of whether the instrument is honored. In light of the purposes of Rule 29, and in view of ethical proscriptions concerning the preservation of client funds and commingling of client and lawyer funds, it would be improper for a lawyer to accept overdraft privileges or any other arrangement for a personal loan on a client trust account in exchange for the institution's promise to delay or not to report an overdraft.

Absence of discretion makes notification by a financial institution an administratively simple matter. An institution which receives an instrument for payment against insufficient funds need not evaluate whether circumstances require that notification be given; it merely provides notice. It then becomes the responsibility of the disciplinary agency to determine whether further action is necessary. In cases where an overdraft is a result of an accounting error (caused by either the lawyer or the institution), but notification has already been sent to the state agency, the institution should provide the lawyer with a written explanation (preferably, an affidavit from an officer of the institution) that the lawyer can then submit to the agency to verify the error.

The rule provides the proper format for overdraft reports. In so doing, the rule distinguishes between dishonored instruments and instruments that are presented against insufficient funds but honored. Where instruments are presented against insufficient funds but paid, the rule specifies the information that the institution should provide.

Ordinarily, within 24 hours of dishonor an institution gives notice of an overdraft to a depositor whose account is charged. See Uniform Commercial Code, Section 3–508. This is the same time period in which overdraft notification is given to the state disciplinary agency.

Where an instrument presented against insufficient funds is honored, the financial institution should send overdraft notification to the agency within five days of the date of presentation.

Upon receipt of an overdraft notification, Rule 29 contemplates that the state agency will contact the lawyer or firm by telephone and request an explanation for the overdraft. A letter requesting a documented explanation may also be sent. If the overdraft is an accounting error, the lawyer or firm submits a written explanation, including any documents to substantiate the claim. Where the lawyer or firm cannot supply an adequate or complete explanation for the overdraft, other action may be generated, including an audit or a demand for production of the lawyer's books and records.

The rule establishes that consent to the reporting and production requirements mandated by the rule is a condition of the privilege to practice law in a jurisdiction that has adopted the rule. This condition is intended to protect financial institutions from claims by lawyer-depositors based on disclosures made by financial institutions, provided that the disclosures are in accordance with the rule. Parties to an overdraft notification agreement are the court and a financial institution. The consent provision in the rule avoids the necessity for financial institutions to draft separate agreements with lawyers to establish consent to overdraft notification.

In addition to normal monthly maintenance fees on each account, a lawyer or firm can anticipate additional fees to be charged by the financial institutions for reporting overdrafts in accordance with this rule. However, because financial institutions already flag overdrafts and returned checks, it appears only slightly more burdensome for the institution to forward a copy to the local disciplinary agency. As a result, the additional cost to the lawyer should not be exorbitant.

Paragraph F should not be interpreted to allow a lawyer to permit trust account funds to be reduced through deductions made by a financial institution to cover costs of overdraft notification. Such costs should not be borne by clients.

Under the laws of most jurisdictions, the definition of "properly payable" will be contained in section 4–104 of the Uniform Commercial Code.

Under the laws of most jurisdictions, the definition of "notice of dishonor" will be determined by reference to section 3–508 of the Uniform Commercial Code, under which notice must be given by a bank before its midnight deadline and by any other person or institution before midnight on the third business day after dishonor or receipt of notice of dishonor.

RULE 30. Verification of Bank Accounts

A. *Generally.* Whenever disciplinary counsel has probable cause to believe that bank accounts of a lawyer that contain, should contain or have contained funds belonging to clients have not been properly maintained or that the funds have not been properly handled, disciplinary counsel shall request the approval of the chair of a hearing committee selected in order from the roster established by the board to initiate an investigation for the purpose of verifying the accuracy and integrity of all bank accounts maintained by the lawyer. If the reviewing member approves, counsel shall proceed to verify the accuracy of the bank accounts. If the reviewing member denies approval, counsel may submit the request for approval to one other chair of a hearing committee selected in order from the roster established by the board.

B. *Confidentiality.* Investigations, examinations, and verifications shall be conducted so as to preserve the private and confidential nature of the lawyer's records insofar as is consistent with these rules and the lawyer-client privilege.

Commentary

Evidence that one account of a lawyer has not been properly maintained or that funds of one client have not been properly handled should constitute cause for verifying the accuracy of all accounts containing the funds of any client maintained by the lawyer.

Examples of cause warranting audit include a check drawn on a client trust account returned for insufficient funds, failure to timely distribute funds to a client, or failure to file a certificate of compliance with the jurisdiction's audit rule.

RULE 31. Appeal by Complainant

A. *From Disposition by Central Intake Office.* A complainant who is not satisfied with the disposition of a matter by the central intake office may appeal, within [thirty] days of receipt of notice pursuant to Rule 1(B)(5), to a hearing committee chair, who may approve, modify or disapprove the dismissal, or direct that the matter be investigated by disciplinary counsel.

B. *From Disposition by Disciplinary Agency.* Except in matters involving lesser misconduct, which are governed by Rule 18(H)(3) and (4),[68] the determination of the board may be the subject of a petition for leave to appeal to the court, but leave shall not be granted unless the complainant shows that the board acted arbitrarily, capriciously, or unreasonably.

Commentary

It is very important that the disciplinary system be structured not only to actually protect the public, but also to inspire confidence in the public that the profession is acting to regulate itself. Thus it is important that complainants have the right to appeal a dismissal of their complaints.

It is important that complainants feel they have had their day in court on the basis for their complaint. Disciplinary hearings are neither civil nor criminal but *sui generis.* It is incorrect to assume that, as in a criminal proceeding, the complainant has no rights in regard to case disposition. It is also incorrect to assume that, as in a civil proceeding, a complainant has full participation in the litigation.

Without a limited right of appeal, complainants may feel that their grievances were not given sufficient consideration by the disciplinary system as a whole. Public sentiments of "lawyers protecting their own" can stem from this misunderstanding.

* * *

RULE 32. Statute of Limitations

Proceedings under these rules shall be exempt from all statutes of limitations.

Commentary

Statutes of limitation are wholly inappropriate in lawyer disciplinary proceedings. Conduct of a lawyer, no matter when it has occurred, is always relevant to the question of fitness to practice. The time between the commission of the alleged misconduct and the filing of a complaint predicated thereon may be pertinent to whether and to what extent discipline should be imposed, but should not limit the agency's power to investigate. An unreasonable delay in the presentation of a charge of misconduct might make it impossible for an attorney to procure witnesses or the testimony available at an earlier time to meet such a charge.

Discipline and disability proceedings serve to protect the public from lawyers who are unfit to practice; they measure the lawyer's qualifications in light of certain conduct, rather than punish for specific transgressions. Misconduct by a lawyer whenever it occurs reflects upon the lawyer's fitness.

EFFECTIVE DATE

These rules shall become effective on [*date*], and any discipline or disability investigation pending on that date shall be transferred to the board. Any matter then pending with respect to which a formal hearing has been commenced shall be concluded under the procedure existing prior to the effective date of these rules.

---

[68] Rec. 8.

RULE 33. Failure to Answer/Failure to Appear

A. *Failure to Answer.* Failure to answer charges filed shall constitute an admission of the factual allegations.

B. *Failure to Appear.* If respondent should fail to appear when specifically so ordered by the committee or the board, the respondent shall have been deemed to have admitted the factual allegations which were to be the subject of such appearance and/or a concession to any motion or recommendations to be considered at such appearance. The committee or board shall not, absent good cause, continue or delay proceedings due to the respondent's failure to appear.

Commentary

This rule provides remedies for a lawyer's disregard of the duty to respond to a lawful demand for information from a disciplinary authority. Failure by respondents to answer or to appear in disciplinary matters is a significant problem. Rule 9(A)(3) applies if the court finds that the respondent has failed to answer or to appear.

Rule 18(B) provides that the rules of civil procedure apply unless otherwise provided; Rule 11(D)(3) provides that the respondent shall answer within [twenty] days after service of the formal charges unless the time is extended by the hearing committee chair.

RULE 34. Counsel for Indigent Respondent

Upon receipt of satisfactory proof of a respondent's indigency, the board may request a lawyer to serve as counsel for the respondent upon such terms and subject to such provisions as justice and equity may require. The respondent shall file with the board an affidavit demonstrating financial inability to retain counsel. The board's determination of indigency shall be based upon its review of the financial circumstances of the respondent. The board shall not consider a request for counsel if the respondent refuses to furnish proof of indigency.

Commentary

Upon satisfactory demonstration of a respondent's indigency, the board may request that a lawyer represent the respondent. While no simple formula can be devised for determining eligibility for representation by counsel based on indigency, the board should consider such factors as the respondent's income, fixed monthly expenditures, assets, fixed liabilities, borrowing capacity, and good faith efforts to secure representation.

The board may reserve the right to approve the rate of compensation for counsel who represents an indigent respondent. In any event, the fee for services rendered shall be supported by documentation of the time spent on the matter.

APPENDIX

A system in which inquiry officers, rather than hearing committees, are used may be established by adoption of the following two alternative provisions in place of Rules 2(G)(4), 2(G)(5), and 3:

AS AN ALTERNATIVE TO RULES 2(G)(4) AND (5), THE FOLLOWING SUBPARAGRAPH MAY BE ADOPTED:

(4) To conduct hearings into formal charges of misconduct, petitions for reinstatement, and petitions for transfer to and from disability inactive status, and prepare and forward to the court its own findings, if any, and recommendations together with the record of the hearing;

AS AN ALTERNATIVE TO RULE 3, THE FOLLOWING MAY BE ADOPTED: RULE 3. INQUIRY OFFICERS.

A. *Appointment.* The board shall appoint three or more inquiry officers [within each disciplinary district].

B. *Terms of Office.* All terms shall be three years and no inquiry officer shall serve for more than two consecutive three-year terms. An inquiry officer who has served two consecutive three-year terms may not be reappointed before the expiration of at least one year.

C. *Powers and Duties.* Inquiry officers shall review recommendations of counsel following investigation for disposition of disciplinary matters and petitions for transfer to and from disability inactive status.

ABA STANDARDS FOR IMPOSING LAWYER SANCTIONS

[In 1970, an ABA Report chaired by former Supreme Court Justice Tom Clark recognized that lawyers and judges needed standards for the enforcement of professional discipline. This report prompted the ABA to create a special commission to draft Standards for Lawyer Discipline and Disability Proceedings (1979). These standards, however, did not provide much guidance on the particular sanction that should be imposed upon a lawyer in a disciplinary proceeding. In 1980, the ABA commissioned another committee to study lawyer sanctions and to draft guidelines for imposing sanctions so that variations in punishment for the same offenses could be avoided. This committee studied all published disciplinary cases between 1980 and 1984 and developed Standards for Imposing Lawyer Sanctions. The ABA adopted these standards in 1986. They were amended in 1992 and in 2012. In 2015, the ABA published a 600 page annotated version of this document to help state courts apply the standards in their disciplinary process. Ed.]

CONTENTS

I. PREFACE

A. BACKGROUND

In 1979, the American Bar Association published the Standards for Lawyer Discipline and Disability Proceedings. [The Standards for Lawyer Discipline and Disability Proceedings have been superseded by the ABA Model Rules for Lawyer Disciplinary Enforcement (MRLDE)][1] That book [the Standards] was a result of work by the Joint Committee on Professional Discipline of the American Bar Association. The Joint Committee was composed of members of the Judicial Administration Division and the Standing Committee on Professional Discipline of the American Bar Association. The task of the Joint Committee was to prepare standards for enforcement of discipline in the legal community.

The 1979 standards have been most helpful, and have been used by numerous jurisdictions as a frame of reference against which to compare their own disciplinary systems. Many jurisdictions have modified their procedures to comport with these suggested standards, and the Standing Committee on Professional Discipline of the American Bar Association has assisted state disciplinary systems in evaluating their programs in light of the approved standards.

It became evident that additional analysis was necessary in one important area—that of appropriate sanctions for lawyer misconduct. The American Bar Association Standards for Lawyer Discipline and Disability Proceedings (hereinafter "Standards for Lawyer Discipline") do not attempt to recommend the type of discipline to be imposed in any particular case. The Standards merely state that the discipline to be imposed "should depend upon the facts and circumstances of the case, should be fashioned in light of the purpose of lawyer discipline, and may take into account aggravating or mitigating circumstances" (Standard 7.1) [See generally Rule 10, ABA MRLDE].

For lawyer discipline to be truly effective, sanctions must be based on clearly developed standards. Inappropriate sanctions can undermine the goals of lawyer discipline: sanctions which are too lenient fail to adequately deter misconduct and thus lower public confidence in the profession;

---

1 Model Rules for Lawyer Disciplinary Enforcement (American Bar Association Standing Committee on Professional Discipline, 1989).

sanctions which are too onerous may impair confidence in the system and deter lawyers from reporting ethical violations on the part of other lawyers. Inconsistent sanctions, either within a jurisdiction or among jurisdictions, cast doubt on the efficiency and the basic fairness of all disciplinary systems.

As an example of this problem of inconsistent sanctions, consider the range in levels of sanctions imposed for a conviction for failure to file federal income taxes. In one jurisdiction, in 1979, a lawyer who failed to file income tax returns for one year was suspended for one year,[2] while, in 1980, a lawyer who failed to file income tax returns for two years was merely censured.[3] Within a two-year period, the sanctions imposed on lawyers who converted their clients' funds included disbarment,[4] suspension,[5] and censure.[6] The inconsistency of sanctions imposed by different jurisdictions for the same misconduct is even greater.

An examination of these cases illustrates the need for a comprehensive system of sanctions. In many cases, different sanctions are imposed for the same acts of misconduct, and the courts rarely provide any explanation for the selection of sanctions. In other cases, the courts may give reasons for their decisions, but their statements are too general to be useful. In still other cases, the courts may list specific factors to support a certain result, but they do not state whether these factors must be considered in every discipline case, nor do they explain whether these factors are entitled to equal weight.

The Joint Committee on Professional Sanctions (hereinafter "Sanctions Committee") was formed to address these problems by formulating standards to be used in imposing sanctions for lawyer misconduct. The Sanctions Committee was composed of members from the Judicial Administration Division and the Standing Committee on Professional Discipline. The mandate given was ambitious: the Committee was to examine the current range of sanctions imposed and to formulate standards for the imposition of appropriate sanctions.

In addressing this task, the Sanctions Committee recognized that any proposed standards should serve as a model which sets forth a comprehensive system of sanctions, but which leaves room for flexibility and creativity in assigning sanctions in particular cases of lawyer misconduct. These standards are designed to promote thorough, rational consideration of all factors relevant to imposing a sanction in an individual case. The standards attempt to ensure that such factors are given appropriate weight in light of the stated goals of lawyer discipline, and that only relevant aggravating and mitigating circumstances are considered at the appropriate time. Finally, the standards should help achieve the degree of consistency in the imposition of lawyer discipline necessary for fairness to the public and the bar.

While these standards will improve the operation of lawyer discipline systems, there is an additional factor which, though not the focus of this report, cannot be overlooked. In discussing sanctions for lawyer misconduct, this report assumes that all instances of unethical conduct will be brought to the attention of the disciplinary system. Experience indicates that such is not the case. In 1970, the ABA Special Committee on Evaluation of Disciplinary Enforcement (the Clark Committee), was charged with the responsibility for evaluating the effectiveness of disciplinary enforcement systems. The Clark Committee concluded that one of the most significant problems in lawyer discipline was the reluctance of lawyers and judges to report misconduct.[7] That same problem exists today. It cannot be emphasized strongly enough that lawyers and judges must report unethical conduct to the

2 In re Gold, 77 Ill. 2d 224, 396 N.E.2d 25 (1979).

3 In re Oliver, M.R. 2454, 79–CH–6 (1980).

4 In re Smith, 63 Ill. 2d 250, 347 N.E.2d 133 (1976).

5 In re DiBella, 58 Ill. 2d 5, 316 N.E.2d 771 (1974).

6 In re Sherman, 60 Ill. 2d 590, 328 N.E.2d 553 (1975).

7 Problems and Recommendations in Disciplinary Enforcement (Chicago: American Bar Association, Special Committee on Evaluation of Disciplinary Enforcement, 1970), at 167.

appropriate disciplinary agency.[8] Failure to render such reports is a disservice to the public and the legal profession.

Judges in particular should be reminded of their obligation to report unethical conduct to the disciplinary agencies. Under [Canon 3(D)(1) and (2)] of the ABA Model Code of Judicial Conduct, a judge [who receives information indicating a substantial likelihood that that another judge or a lawyer has violated the applicable rules of professional conduct] is obligated to [take appropriate action. This action includes making a report of the violation to the appropriate authority when the violation raises a substantial question about the judge's fitness or the lawyer's honesty trustworthiness or fitness.][9] Frequently, judges take the position that there is no such need and that errant behavior of lawyers can be remedied solely by use of contempt proceedings and other alternative means. It must be emphasized that the goals of lawyer discipline are not properly and fully served if the judge who observes unethical conduct simply deals with it on an ad hoc basis. It may be proper and wise for a judge to use contempt powers in order to assure that the court maintains control of the proceeding and punishes a lawyer for abusive or obstreperous conduct in the court's presence. However, the lawyer discipline system is in addition to and serves purposes different from contempt powers and other mechanisms available to the judge. Only if all lawyer misconduct is in fact reported to the appropriate disciplinary agency can the legal profession have confidence that consistent sanctions are imposed for similar misconduct.

Consistency of sanctions depends on reporting of other types as well. The American Bar Association Center for Professional Responsibility has established a "National Lawyer Regulatory Data Bank" which collects statistics on the nature of ethical violations and sanctions imposed in lawyer discipline cases in all jurisdictions. The information available from the Data Bank is only as good as the reports which reach it. It is vital that the Data Bank promptly receive complete, accurate and detailed information with regard to all discipline cases.

Finally, the purposes of lawyer sanctions can best be served, and the consistency of those sanctions enhanced, if courts and disciplinary agencies throughout the country articulate the reasons for sanctions imposed. Courts of record that impose lawyer discipline do a valuable service to the legal profession and the public when they issue opinions in lawyer discipline cases that explain the imposition of a specific sanction. The effort of the Sanctions Committee was made easier by the well-reasoned judicial opinions that were available. At the same time, the Sanctions Committee was frustrated by the fact that many jurisdictions do not publish lawyer discipline decisions, and that even published decisions are often summary in nature, failing to articulate the justification for the sanctions imposed.

[The Standards for Imposing Lawyer Sanctions were amended by the ABA House of Delegates on February 4, 1992 and in 2012. The amendments were proposed by the ABA Standing Committee on Professional Discipline as a result of its ongoing review of the courts' use of the Standards in lawyer disciplinary cases to assure their consistency with the developing case law.]

B. METHODOLOGY

The Standards for Imposing Lawyer Sanctions have been developed after an examination of all reported lawyer discipline cases from 1980 to June, 1984, where public discipline was imposed.[10] In

[8] Lawyers have a duty to report ethical misconduct of other lawyers under Rule 8.3 of the Model Rules of Professional Conduct (American Bar Association, 1983) and under DR1–103 of the Model Code of Professional Responsibility (American Bar Association, 1981). Judges have a similar duty under the Model Code of Judicial Conduct, Canon 3(D)(2) (American Bar Association, 1990).

[9] *Id.*, Model Code of Judicial Conduct, [Canon 3(D)(1)].

[10] See Appendix 3 for a listing of the actual number of reported cases from each jurisdiction. The differences in the number of reported cases among the jurisdictions is a function not only of the differences in lawyer populations, but in the operation of the state discipline systems. States differ dramatically in the sophistication of their disciplinary systems; most importantly for this study, states vary in the extent to which disciplinary orders are published. In those jurisdictions where disciplinary decisions are not published in the regional reporters, summaries in state bar publications or unreported cases (supplied by bar counsel) were examined. (To obtain copies of unreported decisions, contact the ABA

addition, eight jurisdictions, which represent a variety of disciplinary systems as well as diversity in geography and population size, were examined in depth. In these jurisdictions—Arizona, California, the District of Columbia, Florida, Illinois, New Jersey, North Dakota, and Utah—all published disciplinary cases from January, 1974 through June, 1984, were analyzed. In each case, data were collected concerning the type of offense, the sanction imposed, the policy considerations identified, and aggravating or mitigating circumstances noted by the court.[11]

These data were examined to identify the patterns that currently exist among courts imposing sanctions and the policy considerations that guide the courts. In general, the courts were consistent in identifying the following policy considerations: protecting the public, ensuring the administration of justice, and maintaining the integrity of the profession. In the words of the California Supreme Court: "The purpose of a disciplinary proceeding is not punitive but to inquire into the fitness of the lawyer to continue in that capacity for the protection of the public, the courts, and the legal profession."[12] However, the courts failed to articulate any theoretical framework for use in imposing sanctions.

In attempting to develop such a framework, the Sanctions Committee considered a number of options. The Committee considered the obvious possibility of identifying each and every type of misconduct in which a lawyer could engage, then suggesting either a recommended sanction or a range of recommended sanctions to deal with that particular misconduct. The Sanctions Committee unanimously rejected that option as being both theoretically simplistic and administratively cumbersome.[13]

The Sanctions Committee next considered an approach that dealt with general categories of lawyer misconduct and applied recommended sanctions to those types of misconduct depending on whether or not—and to what extent—the misconduct resulted from intentional or malicious acts of the lawyer. There is some merit in that approach; certainly, the intentional or unintentional conduct of the lawyer is a relevant factor. Nonetheless, that approach was also abandoned after the Sanctions Committee carefully reviewed the purposes of lawyer sanctions. Solely focusing on the intent of the lawyer is not sufficient, and proposed standards must also consider the damage which the lawyer's misconduct causes to the client, the public, the legal system, and the profession. An approach which looked only at the extent of injury was also rejected as being too narrow.

The Committee adopted a model that looks first at the ethical duty and to whom it is owed, and then at the lawyer's mental state and the amount of injury caused by the lawyer's misconduct. (See Theoretical Framework, p. 5, for a detailed discussion of this approach.) Thus, one will look in vain for

Center for Professional Responsibility.) The states in which only reported cases were examined were: Alabama, Alaska, Arkansas, Colorado, Connecticut, Delaware, Georgia, Hawaii, Idaho, Indiana, Iowa, Kansas, Louisiana, Maryland, Minnesota, Mississippi, Missouri, Montana, Nebraska, Nevada, New Jersey, New Mexico, North Carolina, South Dakota, Ohio, Oklahoma, Oregon, Rhode Island, South Carolina, South Dakota, Utah, Vermont, Washington, West Virginia, and Wisconsin. In the following jurisdictions both reported and unreported cases were examined: Arizona, California, District of Columbia, Florida, Illinois, Kentucky, Massachusetts, New York, Pennsylvania, Tennessee, Virginia, and Wyoming. In the following jurisdictions, all data were collected from unreported decisions (supplied by bar counsel or taken from case summaries in bar publications): Maine, Michigan, New Hampshire, and Texas.

[11] Because of the difficulty in getting complete factual statements, the report does not include cases which were the result of consent orders, or cases in which reciprocal discipline was imposed.

[12] Ballard v. State Bar of California, 35 Cal. 3d 274, 673 P.2d 226 197 Cal. Rptr. 556 (1983).

[13] An example of the problems which would be encountered in such an approach will suffice to demonstrate why that approach was rejected. It is improper for a lawyer to neglect a legal matter entrusted to him (Rule 1.3/DR 6–101(A)(3)). Sanctions which are imposed for violations of this ethical rule vary dramatically. Such conduct may be an intentional violation of the rule (as where a lawyer takes a client's money never intending to perform the services requested), or it may result from negligence (as where an overworked or inexperienced lawyer does not meet a deadline relating to some aspect of the representation). The Sanctions Committee felt that a listing of sanctions based merely on the type of lawyer misconduct would not adequately differentiate between conduct which has an extremely deleterious effect on the client, the public, the legal system, and the profession, and conduct which has only a minimal effect. In short, the Sanctions Committee concluded that an approach that reviewed each type of misconduct would result in nothing more than a general statement that the individual circumstances of a case dictate the type of sanction which ought to be imposed.

a section of this report which recommends a specific sanction for, say, improper contact with opposing parties who are represented by counsel [Rule 4.2/DR 7–104(A)(1)],[14] or for any other specific misconduct. What one will find, however, is an organizational framework that provides recommendations as to the type of sanction that should be imposed based on violations of duties owed to clients, the public, the legal system, and the profession.

To provide support for this approach, the Sanctions Committee has offered as much specific data and guidance as possible from reported cases.[15] Thus, with regard to each category of misconduct, the report provides the following:

—discussion of what types of sanctions have been imposed for similar misconduct in reported cases;

—discussion of policy reasons which are articulated in reported cases to support such sanctions; and,

—finally, a recommendation as to the level of sanction imposed for the given misconduct, absent aggravating or mitigating circumstances.

While it is recognized that any individual case may present aggravating or mitigating factors which would lead to the imposition of a sanction different from that recommended, these standards present a model which can be used initially to categorize misconduct and to identify the appropriate sanction. The decision as to the effect of any aggravating or mitigating factors should come only after this initial determination of the sanction.

The Sanctions Committee also recognized that the imposition of a sanction of suspension or disbarment does not conclude the matter. Typically, disciplined lawyers will request reinstatement or readmission. While this report does not include an in-depth study of reinstatement and readmission cases, a general recommendation concerning standards for reinstatement and readmission appears as Standard 2.10.

II. THEORETICAL FRAMEWORK

These standards are based on an analysis of the nature of the professional relationship. Historically, being a member of a profession has meant that an individual is some type of expert, possessing knowledge of high instrumental value such that the members of the community give the professional the power to make decisions for them. In the legal profession, the community has allowed the profession the right of self-regulation. As stated in the Preamble to the ABA Model Rules of Professional Conduct (hereinafter "Model Rules"), "[t]he legal profession's relative autonomy carries with it special responsibilities of self-government. The profession has a responsibility to assure that its regulations are conceived in the public interest and not in furtherance of parochial or self-interested concerns of the bar."[16]

This view of the professional relationship requires lawyers to observe the ethical requirements that are set out in the Model Rules (or applicable standard in the jurisdiction where the lawyer is licensed). While the Model Rules define the ethical guidelines for lawyers, they do not provide any method for assigning sanctions for ethical violations. The Committee developed a model which requires a court imposing sanctions to answer each of the following questions:

(1) What ethical duty did the lawyer violate? (A duty to a client, the public, the legal system, or the profession?)

---

[14] Although the House of Delegates of the American Bar Association adopted the Model Rules of Professional Conduct on August 2, 1983, as the ethical standards for the legal profession, references to the Code of Professional Responsibility are included here because some states' ethical standards still follow the Code in both form and substance.

[15] While it is not possible to discuss in detail each of the 2,991 cases which have been examined in preparing this report, statistical summaries are available from the American Bar Association Center for Professional Responsibility.

[16] Preamble to Model Rules, paragraph 11, *supra* n.8.

(2) What was the lawyer's mental state? (Did the lawyer act intentionally, knowingly, or negligently?)

(3) What was the extent of the actual or potential injury caused by the lawyer's misconduct? (Was there a serious or potentially serious injury?) and

(4) Are there any aggravating or mitigating circumstances?

In determining the nature of the ethical duty violated, the standards assume that the most important ethical duties are those obligations which a lawyer owes to clients. These include:

(a) the duty of loyalty which (in the terms of the Model Rules and Code of Professional Responsibility) includes the duties to:

 (i) preserve the property of a client [Rule 1.15/DR9–102],

 (ii) maintain client confidences [Rule 1.6/DR4–101], and

 (iii) avoid conflicts of interest [Rules 1.7 through 1.13, 2.2, 3.7, 5.4(c) and 6.3/ DR5–101 through DR 5–105, DR9–101];

(b) the duty of diligence [Rules 1.2, 1.3, 1.4/DR6–101(A)(3)];

(c) the duty of competence [Rule 1.1/DR6–101(A)(1) & (2)]; and

(d) the duty of candor [Rule 8.4(c)/DR 1–102(A)(4) & DR7–101(A)(3)].

In addition to duties owed to clients, the lawyer also owes duties to the general public. Members of the public are entitled to be able to trust lawyers to protect their property, liberty, and their lives. The community expects lawyers to exhibit the highest standards of honesty and integrity, and lawyers have a duty not to engage in conduct involving dishonesty, fraud, or interference with the administration of justice [Rules 8.2, 8.4(b) & (c)/DR 1–102(A)(3)(4) & (5), DR 8–101 through DR 8–103, DR 9–101(c)].

Lawyers also owe duties to the legal system. Lawyers are officers of the court, and must abide by the rules of substance and procedure which shape the administration of justice. Lawyers must always operate within the bounds of the law, and cannot create or use false evidence, or engage in any other illegal or improper conduct [Rules 3.1 through 3.6, 3.9, 4.1 through 4.4, 8.2, 8.4(d)(e) & (f)/DR7–102 through DR7–110].

Finally, lawyers owe duties to the legal profession. Unlike the obligations mentioned above, these duties are not inherent in the relationship between the professional and the community. These duties do not concern the lawyer's basic responsibilities in representing clients, serving as an officer of the court, or maintaining the public trust, but include other duties relating to the profession. These ethical rules concern:

(a) restrictions on advertising and recommending employment [Rules 7.1 through 7.5/DR2–101 through 2–104];

(b) fees [Rules 1.5, 5.4 and 5.6/DR2–106, DR2–107, and DR3–102];

(c) assisting unauthorized practice [Rule 5.5/DR3–101 through DR3–103];

(d) accepting, declining, or terminating representation [Rules 1.2, 1.14, 1.16/DR2–110]; and

(e) maintaining the integrity of the profession [Rules 8.1 & 8.3/DR1–101 and DR 1–103].

The mental states used in this model are defined as follows. The most culpable mental state is that of intent, when the lawyer acts with the conscious objective or purpose to accomplish a particular result. The next most culpable mental state is that of knowledge, when the lawyer acts with conscious awareness of the nature or attendant circumstances of his or her conduct both without the conscious objective or purpose to accomplish a particular result. The least culpable mental state is negligence, when a lawyer fails to be aware of a substantial risk that circumstances exist or that a result will follow, which failure is a deviation from the standard of care that a reasonable lawyer would exercise in the situation.

The extent of the *injury* is defined by the type of duty violated and the extent of actual or potential harm. For example, in a conversion case, the injury is determined by examining the extent of the client's actual or potential loss. In a case where a lawyer tampers with a witness, the injury is measured by evaluating the level of interference or potential interference with the legal proceeding. In this model, the standards refer to various levels of injury: "serious injury," "injury," and "little or no injury." A reference to "injury" alone indicates any level of injury greater than "little or no" injury.

As an example of how this model works, consider two cases of conversion of a client's property. After concluding that the lawyers engaged in ethical misconduct, it is necessary to determine what duties were breached. In these cases, each lawyer breached the duty of loyalty owed to clients. To assign a sanction, however, it is necessary to go further, and to examine each lawyer's mental state and the extent of the injuries caused by the lawyers' actions.

In the first case, assume that the client gave the lawyer $100 as an advance against the costs of investigation. The lawyer took the money, deposited it in a personal checking account, and used it for personal expenses. In this case, where the lawyer acted intentionally and the client actually suffered an injury, the most severe sanction—disbarment—would be appropriate.

Contrast this with the case of a second lawyer, whose client delivered $100 to be held in a trust account. The lawyer, in a hurry to get to court, neglected to inform the secretary what to do with these funds and they were erroneously deposited into the lawyer's general office account. When the lawyer needed additional funds he drew against the general account. The lawyer discovered the mistake, and immediately replaced the money. In this case, where there was no actual injury and a potential for only minor injury, and where the lawyer was merely negligent, a less serious sanction should be imposed. The appropriate sanction would be either reprimand or admonition.

In each case, after making the initial determination as to the appropriate sanction, the court would then consider any relevant aggravating or mitigating factors (Standard 9). For example, the presence of aggravating factors, such as vulnerability of the victim or refusal to comply with an order to appear before the disciplinary agency, could increase the appropriate sanction. The presence of mitigating factors, such as absence of prior discipline or inexperience in the practice of law, could make a lesser sanction appropriate.

While there may be particular cases of lawyer misconduct that are not easily categorized, the standards are not designed to propose a specific sanction for each of the myriad of fact patterns in cases of lawyer misconduct. Rather, the standards provide a theoretical framework to guide the courts in imposing sanctions. The ultimate sanction imposed will depend on the presence of any aggravating or mitigating factors in that particular situation. The standards thus are not analogous to criminal determinate sentences, but are guidelines which give courts the flexibility to select the appropriate sanction in each particular case of lawyer misconduct.

The standards do not account for multiple charges of misconduct. The ultimate sanction imposed should at least be consistent with the sanction for the most serious instance of misconduct among a number of violations; it might well be and generally should be greater than the sanction for the most serious misconduct. Either a pattern of misconduct or multiple instances of misconduct should be considered as aggravating factors (see Standard 9.22).

III. STANDARDS FOR IMPOSING LAWYER SANCTIONS: BLACK LETTER RULES

For reference purposes, a list of the black letter rules is set out below.

DEFINITIONS

"Injury" is harm to a client, the public, the legal system, or the profession which results from a lawyer's misconduct. The level of injury can range from "serious" injury to "little or no" injury; a reference to "injury" alone indicates any level of injury greater than "little or no" injury.

"Intent" is the conscious objective or purpose to accomplish a particular result.

"Knowledge" is the conscious awareness of the nature or attendant circumstances of the conduct but without the conscious objective or purpose to accomplish a particular result.

"Negligence" is the failure of a lawyer to heed a substantial risk that circumstances exist or that a result will follow, which failure is a deviation from the standard of care that a reasonable lawyer would exercise in the situation.

"Potential injury" is the harm to a client, the public, the legal system or the profession that is reasonably foreseeable at the time of the lawyer's misconduct, and which, but for some intervening factor or event, would probably have resulted from the lawyer's misconduct.

A. PURPOSE AND NATURE OF SANCTIONS

1.1 Purpose of Lawyer Discipline Proceedings.

The purpose of lawyer discipline proceedings is to protect the public and the administration of justice from lawyers who have not discharged, will not discharge, or are unlikely properly to discharge their professional duties to clients, the public, the legal system, and the legal profession.

1.2 Public Nature of Lawyer Discipline.

Upon the filing and service of formal charges, lawyer discipline proceedings should be public, and disposition of lawyer discipline should be public in cases of disbarment, suspension, and reprimand. Only in cases of minor misconduct, when there is little or no injury to a client, the public, the legal system, or the profession, and when there is little likelihood of repetition by the lawyer, should private discipline be imposed.

1.3 Purpose of These Standards.

These standards are designed for use in imposing a sanction or sanctions following a determination by clear and convincing evidence that a member of the legal profession has violated a provision of the Model Rules of Professional Conduct (or applicable standard under the laws of the jurisdiction where the proceeding is brought). Descriptions in these standards of substantive disciplinary offenses are not intended to create grounds for determining culpability independent of the Model Rules. The Standards constitute a model, setting forth a comprehensive system for determining sanctions, permitting flexibility and creativity in assigning sanctions in particular cases of lawyer misconduct. They are designed to promote: (1) consideration of all factors relevant to imposing the appropriate level of sanction in an individual case; (2) consideration of the appropriate weight of such factors in light of the stated goals of lawyer discipline; (3) consistency in the imposition of disciplinary sanctions for the same or similar offenses within and among jurisdictions.

B. SANCTIONS

2.1 Scope

A disciplinary sanction is imposed on a lawyer upon a finding or acknowledgement that the lawyer has engaged in professional misconduct.

2.2 Disbarment

Disbarment terminates the individual's status as a lawyer. Where disbarment is not permanent, procedures should be established for a lawyer who has been disbarred to apply for readmission, provided that:

(1) no application should be considered for five years from the effective date of disbarment; and

(2) the petitioner must show by clear and convincing evidence:

- (a) successful completion of the bar examination,
- (b) compliance with all applicable discipline or disability orders or rules; and
- (c) rehabilitation and fitness to practice law.

2.3 Suspension

Suspension is the removal of a lawyer from the practice of law for a specified minimum period of time. Generally, suspension should be for a period of time equal to or greater than six months, but in no event should the time period prior to application for reinstatement be more than three years. Procedures should be established to allow a suspended lawyer to apply for reinstatement, but a lawyer who has been suspended should not be permitted to return to practice until he has completed a reinstatement process demonstrating rehabilitation, compliance with all applicable discipline or disability orders and rules, and fitness to practice law.

2.4 Interim Suspension

Interim suspension is the temporary suspension of a lawyer from the practice of law pending imposition of final discipline. Interim suspension includes:

(a) suspension upon conviction of a "serious crime" or,

(b) suspension when the lawyer's continuing conduct is or is likely to cause immediate and serious injury to a client or the public.

2.5 Reprimand

Reprimand, also known as censure or public censure, is a form of public discipline which declares the conduct of the lawyer improper, but does not limit the lawyer's right to practice.

2.6 Admonition

Admonition, also known as private reprimand, is a form of non-public discipline which declares the conduct of the lawyer improper, but does not limit the lawyer's right to practice.

2.7 Probation

Probation is a sanction that allows a lawyer to practice law under specified conditions. Probation can be imposed alone or in conjunction with a reprimand, an admonition or immediately following a suspension. Probation can also be imposed as a condition of readmission or reinstatement.

2.8 Other Sanctions and Remedies

Other sanctions and remedies which may be imposed include:

(a) restitution,

(b) assessment of costs,

(c) limitation upon practice,

(d) appointment of a receiver,

(e) requirement that the lawyer take the bar examination or professional responsibility examination,

(f) requirement that the lawyer attend continuing education courses, and

(g) other requirements that the state's highest court or disciplinary board deems consistent with the purposes of lawyer sanctions.

2.9 Reciprocal Discipline

Reciprocal discipline is the imposition of a disciplinary sanction on a lawyer who has been disciplined in another jurisdiction.

2.10 Readmission and Reinstatement

In jurisdictions where disbarment is not permanent, procedures should be established to allow a disbarred lawyer to apply for readmission. Procedures should be established to allow a suspended lawyer to apply for reinstatement.

C. FACTORS TO BE CONSIDERED IN IMPOSING SANCTIONS

3.0 Generally

In imposing a sanction after a finding of lawyer misconduct, a court should consider the following factors:

(a) the duty violated;

(b) the lawyer's mental state;

(c) the potential or actual injury caused by the lawyer's misconduct; and

(d) the existence of aggravating or mitigating factors.

4.0 Violations of Duties Owed to Clients

4.1 Failure to Preserve the Client's Property

Absent aggravating or mitigating circumstances, upon application of the factors set out in 3.0, the following sanctions are generally appropriate in cases involving the failure to preserve client property:

4.11 Disbarment is generally appropriate when a lawyer knowingly converts client property and causes injury or potential injury to a client.

4.12 Suspension is generally appropriate when a lawyer knows or should know that he is dealing improperly with client property and causes injury or potential injury to a client.

4.13 Reprimand is generally appropriate when a lawyer is negligent in dealing with client property and causes injury or potential injury to a client.

4.14 Admonition is generally appropriate when a lawyer is negligent in dealing with client property and causes little or no actual or potential injury to a client.

4.2 Failure to Preserve the Client's Confidences

Absent aggravating or mitigating circumstances, upon application of the factors set out in 3.0, the following sanctions are generally appropriate in cases involving improper revelation of information relating to representation of a client:

4.21 Disbarment is generally appropriate when a lawyer, with the intent to benefit the lawyer or another, knowingly reveals information relating to representation of a client not otherwise lawfully permitted to be disclosed, and this disclosure causes injury or potential injury to a client.

4.22 Suspension is generally appropriate when a lawyer knowingly reveals information relating to the representation of a client not otherwise lawfully permitted to be disclosed, and this disclosure causes injury or potential injury to a client.

4.23 Reprimand is generally appropriate when a lawyer negligently reveals information relating to representation of a client not otherwise lawfully permitted to be disclosed and this disclosure causes injury or potential injury to a client.

4.24 Admonition is generally appropriate when a lawyer negligently reveals information relating to representation of a client not otherwise lawfully permitted to be disclosed and this disclosure causes little or no actual or potential injury to a client.

4.3 Failure to Avoid Conflicts of Interest

Absent aggravating or mitigating circumstances, upon application of the factors set out in Standard 3.0, the following sanctions are generally appropriate in cases involving conflicts of interest:

4.31 Disbarment is generally appropriate when a lawyer, without the informed consent of client(s):

(a) engages in representation of a client knowing that the lawyer's interests are adverse to the client's with the intent to benefit the lawyer or another, and causes serious or potentially serious injury to the client; or

(b) simultaneously represents clients that the lawyer knows have adverse interests with the intent to benefit the lawyer or another, and causes serious or potentially serious injury to a client; or

(c) represents a client in a matter substantially related to a matter in which the interests of a present or former client are materially adverse, and knowingly uses information relating to the representation of a client with the intent to benefit the lawyer or another, and causes serious or potentially serious injury to a client.

4.32 Suspension is generally appropriate when a lawyer knows of a conflict of interest and does not fully disclose to a client the possible effect of that conflict, and causes injury or potential injury to a client.

4.33 Reprimand is generally appropriate when a lawyer is negligent in determining whether the representation of a client may be materially affected by the lawyer's own interests, or whether the representation will adversely affect another client, and causes injury or potential injury to a client.

4.34 Admonition is generally appropriate when a lawyer engages in an isolated instance of negligence in determining whether the representation of a client may be materially affected by the lawyer's own interests, or whether the representation will adversely affect another client, and causes little or no actual or potential injury to a client.

4.4 Lack of Diligence

Absent aggravating or mitigating circumstances, upon application of the factors set out in Standard 3.0, the following sanctions are generally appropriate in cases involving a failure to act with reasonable diligence and promptness in representing a client:

4.41 Disbarment is generally appropriate when:

(a) a lawyer abandons the practice and causes serious or potentially serious injury to a client; or

(b) a lawyer knowingly fails to perform services for a client and causes serious or potentially serious injury to a client; or

(c) a lawyer engages in a pattern of neglect with respect to client matters and causes serious or potentially serious injury to a client.

4.42 Suspension is generally appropriate when:

(a) a lawyer knowingly fails to perform services for a client and causes injury or potential injury to a client, or

(b) a lawyer engages in a pattern of neglect causes injury or potential injury to a client.

4.43 Reprimand is generally appropriate when a lawyer is negligent and does not act with reasonable diligence in representing a client, and causes injury or potential injury to a client.

4.44 Admonition is generally appropriate when a lawyer is negligent and does not act with reasonable diligence in representing a client, and causes little or no actual or potential injury to a client.

4.5 Lack of Competence

Absent aggravating or mitigating circumstances, upon application of the factors set out in Standard 3.0, the following sanctions are generally appropriate in cases involving failure to provide competent representation to a client:

4.51 Disbarment is generally appropriate when a lawyer's course of conduct demonstrates that the lawyer does not understand the most fundamental legal doctrines or procedures, and the lawyer's conduct causes injury or potential injury to a client.

4.52 Suspension is generally appropriate when a lawyer engages in an area of practice in which the lawyer knows he or she is not competent, and causes injury or potential injury to a client.

4.53 Reprimand is generally appropriate when a lawyer:

(a) demonstrates failure to understand relevant legal doctrines or procedures and causes injury or potential injury to a client; or

(b) is negligent in determining whether he or she is competent to handle a legal matter and causes injury or potential injury to a client.

4.54 Admonition is generally appropriate when a lawyer engages in an isolated instance of negligence in determining whether he or she is competent to handle a legal matter, and causes little or no actual or potential injury to a client.

4.6 Lack of Candor

Absent aggravating or mitigating circumstances, upon application of the factors set out in Standard 3.0, the following sanctions are generally appropriate in cases where the lawyer engages in fraud, deceit, or misrepresentation directed toward a client:

4.61 Disbarment is generally appropriate when a lawyer knowingly deceives a client with the intent to benefit the lawyer or another, and causes serious injury or potential serious injury to a client.

4.62 Suspension is generally appropriate when a lawyer knowingly deceives a client, and causes injury or potential injury to the client.

4.63 Reprimand is generally appropriate when a lawyer negligently fails to provide a client with accurate or complete information, and causes injury or potential injury to the client.

4.64 Admonition is generally appropriate when a lawyer engages in an isolated instance of negligence in failing to provide a client with accurate or complete information, and causes little or no actual or potential injury to the client.

5.0 Violations of Duties Owed to the Public

5.1 Failure to Maintain Personal Integrity

Absent aggravating or mitigating circumstances, upon application of the factors set out in Standard 3.0, the following sanctions are generally appropriate in cases involving commission of a criminal act that reflects adversely on the lawyer's honesty, trustworthiness, or fitness as a lawyer in other respects, or in cases with conduct involving dishonesty, fraud, deceit, or misrepresentation:

5.11 Disbarment is generally appropriate when:

(a) a lawyer engages in serious criminal conduct a necessary element of which includes intentional interference with the administration of justice, false swearing, misrepresentation, fraud, extortion, misappropriation, or theft; or the sale, distribution or importation of controlled substances; or the intentional killing of another; or an attempt or conspiracy or solicitation of another to commit any of these offenses; or

(b) a lawyer engages in any other intentional conduct involving dishonesty, fraud, deceit, or misrepresentation that seriously adversely reflects on the lawyer's fitness to practice.

5.12 Suspension is generally appropriate when a lawyer knowingly engages in criminal conduct which does not contain the elements listed in Standard 5.11 and that seriously adversely reflects on the lawyer's fitness to practice.

5.13 Reprimand is generally appropriate when a lawyer knowingly engages in any other conduct that involves dishonesty, fraud, deceit, or misrepresentation and that adversely reflects on the lawyer's fitness to practice law.

5.14 Admonition is generally appropriate when a lawyer engages in any other conduct that reflects adversely on the lawyer's fitness to practice law.

5.2 Failure to Maintain the Public Trust

Absent aggravating or mitigating circumstances, upon application of the factors set out in Standard 3.0, the following sanctions are generally appropriate in cases involving public officials who engage in conduct that is prejudicial to the administration of justice or who state or imply an ability to influence improperly a government agency or official:

5.21 Disbarment is generally appropriate when a lawyer in an official or governmental position knowingly misuses the position with the intent to obtain a significant benefit or advantage for himself or another, or with the intent to cause serious or potentially serious injury to a party or to the integrity of the legal process.

5.22 Suspension is generally appropriate when a lawyer in an official or governmental position knowingly fails to follow proper procedures or rules, and causes injury or potential injury to a party or to the integrity of the legal process.

5.23 Reprimand is generally appropriate when a lawyer in an official or governmental position negligently fails to follow proper procedures or rules, and causes injury or potential injury to a party or to the integrity of the legal process.

5.24 Admonition is generally appropriate when a lawyer in an official or governmental position engages in an isolated instance of negligence in not following proper procedures or rules, and causes little or no actual or potential injury to a party or to the integrity of the legal process.

6.0 Violations of Duties Owed to the Legal System

6.1 False Statements, Fraud, and Misrepresentation

Absent aggravating or mitigating circumstances, upon application of the factors set out in Standard 3.0, the following sanctions are generally appropriate in cases involving conduct that is prejudicial to the administration of justice or that involves dishonesty, fraud, deceit, or misrepresentation to a court:

6.11 Disbarment is generally appropriate when a lawyer, with the intent to deceive the court, makes a false statement, submits a false document, or improperly withholds material information, and causes serious or potentially serious injury to a party, or causes a significant or potentially significant adverse effect on the legal proceeding.

6.12 Suspension is generally appropriate when a lawyer knows that false statements or documents are being submitted to the court or that material information is improperly being withheld, and takes no remedial action, and causes injury or potential injury to a party to the legal proceeding, or causes an adverse or potentially adverse effect on the legal proceeding.

6.13 Reprimand is generally appropriate when a lawyer is negligent either in determining whether statements or documents are false or in taking remedial action when material information is being withheld, and causes injury or potential injury to a party to the legal proceeding, or causes an adverse or potentially adverse effect on the legal proceeding.

6.14 Admonition is generally appropriate when a lawyer engages in an isolated instance of neglect in determining whether submitted statements or documents are false or in failing to disclose material information upon learning of its falsity, and causes little or no actual or potential injury to a party, or causes little or no adverse or potentially adverse effect on the legal proceeding.

6.2 Abuse of the Legal Process

Absent aggravating or mitigating circumstances, upon application of the factors set out in Standard 3.0, the following sanctions are generally appropriate in cases involving failure to expedite litigation or bring a meritorious claim, or failure to obey any obligation under the rules of a tribunal except for an open refusal based on an assertion that no valid obligation exists:

6.21 Disbarment is generally appropriate when a lawyer knowingly violates a court order or rule with the intent to obtain a benefit for the lawyer or another, and causes serious injury or potentially serious injury to a party or causes serious or potentially serious interference with a legal proceeding.

6.22 Suspension is generally appropriate when a lawyer knows that he or she is violating a court order or rule, and causes injury or potential injury to a client or a party, or causes interference or potential interference with a legal proceeding.

6.23 Reprimand is generally appropriate when a lawyer negligently fails to comply with a court order or rule, and causes injury or potential injury to a client or other party, or causes interference or potential interference with a legal proceeding.

6.24 Admonition is generally appropriate when a lawyer engages in an isolated instance of negligence in complying with a court order or rule, and causes little or no actual or potential injury to a party, or causes little or no actual or potential interference with a legal proceeding.

6.3 Improper Communications With Individuals in the Legal System

Absent aggravating or mitigating circumstances, upon application of the factors set out in Standard 3.0, the following sanctions are generally appropriate in cases involving attempts to influence a judge, juror, prospective juror or other official by means prohibited by law:

6.31 Disbarment is generally appropriate when a lawyer:

(a) intentionally tampers with a witness and causes serious or potentially serious injury to a party, or causes significant or potentially significant interference with the outcome of the legal proceeding; or

(b) makes an ex parte communication with a judge or juror with intent to affect the outcome of the proceeding, and causes serious or potentially serious injury to a party, or causes significant or potentially significant interference with the outcome of the legal proceeding; or

(c) improperly communicates with someone in the legal system other than a witness, judge, or juror with the intent to influence or affect the outcome of the proceeding, and causes significant or potentially significant interference with the outcome of the legal proceeding.

6.32 Suspension is generally appropriate when a lawyer engages in communication with an individual in the legal system when the lawyer knows that such communication is improper, and causes injury or potential injury to a party or causes interference or potential interference with the outcome of the legal proceeding.

6.33 Reprimand is generally appropriate when a lawyer is negligent in determining whether it is proper to engage in communication with an individual in the legal system, and causes injury or potential injury to a party or interference or potential interference with the outcome of the legal proceeding.

6.34 Admonition is generally appropriate when a lawyer engages in an isolated instance of negligence in improperly communicating with an individual in the legal system, and causes little or no actual or potential injury to a party, or causes little or no actual or potential interference with the outcome of the legal proceeding.

7.0 Violations of Other Duties Owed as a Profession

Absent aggravating or mitigating circumstances, upon application of the factors set out in Standard 3.0, the following sanctions are generally appropriate in cases involving false or misleading communication about the lawyer or the lawyer's services, improper communication of fields of practice, improper solicitation of professional employment from a prospective client, unreasonable or improper fees, unauthorized practice of law, improper withdrawal from representation, or failure to report professional misconduct.

7.1 Disbarment is generally appropriate when a lawyer knowingly engages in conduct that is a violation of a duty owed as a professional with the intent to obtain a benefit for the lawyer or another, and causes serious or potentially serious injury to a client, the public, or the legal system.

7.2 Suspension is generally appropriate when a lawyer knowingly engages in conduct that is a violation of a duty owed as a professional and causes injury or potential injury to a client, the public, or the legal system.

7.3 Reprimand is generally appropriate when a lawyer negligently engages in conduct that is a violation of a duty owed as a professional and causes injury or potential injury to a client, the public, or the legal system.

7.4 Admonition is generally appropriate when a lawyer engages in an isolated instance of negligence that is a violation of a duty owed as a professional, and causes little or no actual or potential injury to a client, the public, or the legal system.

8.0 Prior Discipline Orders

Absent aggravating or mitigating circumstances, upon application of the factors set out in Standard 3.0, the following sanctions are generally appropriate in cases involving prior discipline.

8.1 Disbarment is Generally Appropriate When a Lawyer:

(a) intentionally or knowingly violates the terms of a prior disciplinary order and such violation causes injury or potential injury to a client, the public, the legal system, or the profession; or

(b) has been suspended for the same or similar misconduct, and intentionally or knowingly engages in further similar acts of misconduct that cause injury or potential injury to a client, the public, the legal system, or the profession.

8.2 Suspension is generally appropriate when a lawyer has been reprimanded for the same or similar misconduct and engages in further similar acts of misconduct that cause injury or potential injury to a client, the public, the legal system, or the profession.

8.3 Reprimand is generally appropriate when a lawyer:

(a) negligently violates the terms of a prior disciplinary order and such violation causes injury or potential injury to a client, the public, the legal system, or the profession; or

(b) has received an admonition for the same or similar misconduct and engages in further similar acts of misconduct that cause injury or potential injury to a client, the public, the legal system, or the profession.

8.4 An admonition is generally not an appropriate sanction when a lawyer violates the terms of a prior disciplinary order or when a lawyer has engaged in the same or similar misconduct in the past.

9.0 Aggravation and Mitigation

9.1 Generally

After misconduct has been established, aggravating and mitigating circumstances may be considered in deciding what sanction to impose.

9.2 Aggravation

9.21 Definition. Aggravation or aggravating circumstances are any considerations or factors that may justify an increase in the degree of discipline to be imposed.

9.22 Factors which may be considered in aggravation.

Aggravating factors include:

(a) prior disciplinary offenses;

(b) dishonest or selfish motive;

(c) a pattern of misconduct;

(d) multiple offenses;

(e) bad faith obstruction of the disciplinary proceeding by intentionally failing to comply with rules or orders of the disciplinary agency;

(f) submission of false evidence, false statements, or other deceptive practices during the disciplinary process;

(g) refusal to acknowledge wrongful nature of conduct;

(h) vulnerability of victim;

(i) substantial experience in the practice of law;

(j) indifference to making restitution;

(k) illegal conduct, including that involving the use of controlled substances.

9.3 Mitigation

9.31 Definition. Mitigation or mitigating circumstances are any considerations or factors that may justify a reduction in the degree of discipline to be imposed.

9.32 Factors which may be considered in mitigation.

Mitigating factors include:

(a) absence of a prior disciplinary record;

(b) absence of a dishonest or selfish motive;

(c) personal or emotional problems;

(d) timely good faith effort to make restitution or to rectify consequences of misconduct;

(e) full and free disclosure to disciplinary board or cooperative attitude toward proceedings;

(f) inexperience in the practice of law;

(g) character or reputation;

(h) physical disability;

(i) mental disability or chemical dependency including alcoholism or drug abuse when:

(1) there is medical evidence that the respondent is affected by a chemical dependency or mental disability;

(2) the chemical dependency or mental disability caused the misconduct;

(3) the respondent's recovery from the chemical dependency or mental disability is demonstrated by a meaningful and sustained period of successful rehabilitation; and

(4) the recovery arrested the misconduct and recurrence of that misconduct is unlikely.

(j) delay in disciplinary proceedings;

(k) imposition of other penalties or sanctions;

(*l*) remorse;

(m) remoteness of prior offenses.

9.4 Factors Which Are Neither Aggravating Nor Mitigating

The following factors should not be considered as either aggravating or mitigating:

(a) forced or compelled restitution;

(b) agreeing to the client's demand for certain improper behavior or result;

(c) withdrawal of complaint against the lawyer;

(d) resignation prior to completion of disciplinary proceedings;

(e) complainant's recommendation as to sanction;

(f) failure of injured client to complain.

APPENDIX 1

Cross-Reference Table: ABA Model Rules of Professional Conduct and Standards for Imposing Sanctions

ABA Model Rules of Professional Conduct	*Standards for Imposing Sanctions*
Competence	
Rule 1.1	Standard 4.5
Scope of Representation	
Rule 1.2(a), (b), (c), (e)	Standard 4.4
Rule 1.2(d)	Standard 6.1
Diligence	
Rule 1.3	Standard 4.4
Communication	
Rule 1.4	Standard 4.4
Fees	
Rule 1.5	Standards 4.6 & 7.0
Confidentiality of Information	
Rule 1.6	Standard 4.2
Conflict of Interest	
Rule 1.7	Standard 4.3
Prohibited Transactions	
Rule 1.8	Standard 4.3
Former Client	
Rule 1.9	Standard 4.3
Imputed Disqualification	
Rule 1.10	Standard 4.3
Successive Government and Private Employment	
Rule 1.11	Standard 4.3
Former Judge or Arbitrator	
Rule 1.12	Standard 4.3
Organization as Client	
Rule 1.13	Standard 4.3
Disabled Client	
Rule 1.14	Standard 7.0
Safekeeping Property	
Rule 1.15	Standard 4.1
Declining or Terminating Representation	
Rule 1.16	Standard 7.0
Advisor	
Rule 2.1	Standard 7.0
Intermediary	
Rule 2.2	Standard 4.3

APPENDIX 1

ABA Model Rules of Professional Conduct	*Standards for Imposing Sanctions*
Evaluation for Use by Third Persons	
Rule 2.3	Standard 7.0
Meritorious Claims and Contentions	
Rule 3.1	Standard 6.2
Expediting Litigation	
Rule 3.2	Standard 6.2
Candor Toward the Tribunal	
Rule 3.3	Standard 6.1
Fairness to Opposing Party and Counsel	
Rule 3.4	Standard 6.2
Impartiality and Decorum	
Rule 3.5	Standard 6.3
Trial Publicity	
Rule 3.6	Standard 6.2
Lawyer as Witness	
Rule 3.7	Standard 4.3
Special Responsibilities of a Prosecutor	
Rule 3.8	Standard 5.2
Advocate in Nonadjudicative Proceedings	
Rule 3.9	Standard 6.2
Truthfulness to Others	
Rule 4.1	Standard 6.1
Communication with Represented Persons	
Rule 4.2	Standard 6.3
Dealing with Unrepresented Persons	
Rule 4.3	Standard 6.3
Respect for Rights of Third Persons	
Rule 4.4	Standard 6.2
Responsibilities of a Partner or Supervisory Lawyer	
Rule 5.1	Standard 7.0
Responsibilities of a Subordinate Lawyer	
Rule 5.2	Standard 7.0
Responsibilities Regarding Nonlawyer Assistants	
Rule 5.3	Standard 7.0
Professional Independence of Lawyer	
Rule 5.4(a) & (b)	Standard 7.0
Rule 5.4(c)	Standard 4.3
Rule 5.4(d)	Standard 7.0
Unauthorized Practice of Law	
Rule 5.5	Standard 7.0
Restrictions on Right to Practice	
Rule 5.6	Standard 7.0

APPENDIX 1

ABA Model Rules of Professional Conduct	*Standards for Imposing Sanctions*
Pro Bono Publico Service	
Rule 6.1	No Applicable Standard
Accepting Appointments	
Rule 6.2	Standard 7.0
Membership in Legal Services Organization	
Rule 6.3	Standard 4.3
Law Reform Activities Affecting Client Interests	
Rule 6.4	Standard 5.2
Communication Concerning Lawyer's Services	
Rule 7.1	Standard 7.0
Advertising	
Rule 7.2	Standard 7.0
Direct Contact with Prospective Clients	
Rule 7.3	Standard 7.0
Communication of Fields of Practice	
Rule 7.4	Standard 7.0
Firm Names and Letterheads	
Rule 7.5	Standard 7.0
Bar Admission and Disciplinary Matters	
Rule 8.1	Standards 5.1 & 7.0
Judges and Legal Officials	
Rule 8.2	Standard 6.1
Reporting Professional Misconduct	
Rule 8.3	Standard 7.0
Misconduct	
Rule 8.4(a)	Standards 4.0, 5.0, 6.0, & 7.0
Rule 8.4(b)	Standard 5.1
Rule 8.4(c)	Standards 4.6 & 5.1
Rule 8.4(d)	Standard 6.0
Rule 8.4(e) & (f)	Standard 6.2
Jurisdiction	
Rule 8.5	None

[Deleted Appendices 2 and 3]

ABA MODEL RULES FOR MEDIATION OF CLIENT-LAWYER DISPUTES (1998)

[In August 1998, the ABA House of Delegates adopted a set of Model Rules for Mediation of Client-Lawyer Disputes.]

PREFACE

Mediation is a process by which those who have a dispute, misunderstanding or conflict come together and, with the assistance of a trained neutral mediator, resolve the issues and problems in a way that meets the needs and interests of both parties. The mediation process is an alternative to litigation or other more formal and expensive dispute resolution mechanisms.

The *Model Rules for Mediation of Client-Lawyer Disputes* implement Recommendation 3 of the 1992 Report of the Commission on Evaluation of Disciplinary Enforcement (the "McKay Commission,") in which the American Bar Association called for jurisdictions to expand their systems of lawyer regulation by establishing mechanisms to resolve disputes between lawyers and clients and to handle nondisciplinary complaints about lawyers. The McKay Commission included a mediation program among its court-established dispute resolution mechanisms. Comments do not add obligations to the Rules but provide guidance for conducting a mediation program in compliance with the Rules.

Rule 1. GENERAL PRINCIPLES AND JURISDICTION

A. Definitions.

(1) "Client" means a person or entity who directly or through an authorized representative consults or retains a lawyer in the lawyer's professional capacity.

(2) "Commission" means the Client-Lawyer Mediation Commission.

(3) "Lawyer" means any lawyer admitted to practice law in [name of jurisdiction], including any formerly admitted lawyer, any lawyer specially admitted by a court of this jurisdiction for a particular proceeding and any lawyer not admitted in this jurisdiction who practices law or renders or offers to render any legal services in this jurisdiction.

B. Establishment; Purpose. It is the policy of the [highest court of the jurisdiction] to encourage the Informal resolution of disputes between lawyers who practice law in [name of Jurisdiction] and their clients. To that end, She [highest court of the jurisdiction] hereby establishes through adoption of these rules, a program for mediation of client-lawyer disputes. The program Includes mediations referred by [the lawyer disciplinary agency] and voluntary mediation requests made by the client or by the lawyer, if both the client and the lawyer agree to mediate.

C. Jurisdiction.

(1) Any lawyer is subject to these rules for mediation.

(2) The Commission has jurisdiction over disputes which Involve lesser misconduct or no misconduct on the part of the lawyer and appear to be resolvable by mediation.

(3) The Commission has jurisdiction over disputes referred by [the lawyer disciplinary agency] and voluntary mediations in which a lawyer or client requests mediation and the other party agrees.

Comment

The mediation program described in these rules is part of this jurisdiction's comprehensive lawyer regulatory system. The comprehensive system includes: [a lawyer discipline and disability system, a client protection fund, mandatory arbitration of fee disputes, mediation, law office management assistance, and lawyer assistance programs].

Since mediation is a process that works by building consensus and agreement, the mediation process can preserve existing client-lawyer or other fiduciary relationships by allowing both sides to air their grievances and work together on a solution agreeable to all parties. When handled by a skilled mediator, the process can be simple and efficient, saving time and money for both parties. The lawyer's willingness to have a third party assist in resolving the dispute can demonstrate to the client that the lawyer's intention is to act in the client's best interest.

Mediation is not suitable when the dispute involves an allegation of lawyer misconduct which, if true, would warrant a sanction restricting the lawyer's license to practice law. Mediation is appropriate when the dispute involves no allegation of lawyer misconduct or an allegation of lesser misconduct as defined in [jurisdiction's rules of disciplinary enforcement]. It is appropriate because there is little or no injury to a client, the public, the legal system, or the profession, and there is little likelihood of repetition by the lawyer.

Examples of disputes that might be referred to mediation include allegations of a lawyer's failure or refusal to return a client's file based on a fee dispute with the client, release a lien on a client's recovery in a case in which the lawyer has been succeeded by another lawyer, withdraw from representation upon being discharged by the client, conclude a legal representation by preparing an essential dispositive document, such as the findings of fact and conclusions of law in a divorce or the final account in an estate, return an unearned fee or a portion of the fee, comply with his or her agreement with a medical provider on the client's behalf or communicate concerning the status of a matter.

Other examples of situations in which the parties might agree to voluntary mediation could include allegations of a client's failure to pay or fulfill the contract, pay for costs (including future costs) or communicate with the lawyer.

The primary purpose of the program is to resolve complaints referred from the jurisdiction's lawyer disciplinary agency. Therefore, such referrals should be given priority over voluntary mediations. Mediation can be used to complement fee arbitration proceedings. The Commission may accept jurisdiction in a dispute in which a fee arbitration proceeding is pending but has not yet begun. The intention is to solve the dispute in a less formal way, if possible, not to refer complainants back and forth between the two programs.

Rule 2. MEDIATION COMMISSION

A. Appointment of Commission. The [highest court of the jurisdiction] shall appoint a Mediation Commission to administer the Mediation Program. The [highest court of the jurisdiction] shall designate one member to serve as Chair of the Commission.

B. Composition. The Commission shall consist of [six] members, of whom at least one-third shall be nonlawyers. Members shall be appointed for terms of three years except where a vacancy has occurred in which event appointments shall be for the unexpired portion of the term being filled. Appointments shall be on a staggered basis so that the number of terms expiring shall be approximately the same each year. No members shall be appointed for more than two consecutive full terms, but members appointed for less than a full term (either originally or to fill a vacancy) may serve two full terms in addition to such part of a term.

C. Duties of the Commission. The Commission shall have the following powers and duties to:

(1) appoint and remove mediators and provide appropriate training;

(2) interpret these rules;

(3) establish written procedures not inconsistent with these rules;

(4) issue an annual report and periodic policy recommendations, as needed, to the [state's highest court] regarding the program;

(5) maintain all records of the Mediation Program;

(6) determine challenges for cause where a mediator has not voluntarily acceded to a challenge;

(7) educate the public and the bar about the Mediation Program;

(8) perform all acts necessary for the effective operation of the program; and

(9) establish fee schedules and oversee financial matters.

Comment

Overall authority to administer the Mediation Program is delegated by [the highest court of the jurisdiction] to the Commission. The court should ensure diversity in the membership of the Commission.

The Commission has authority to limit the types of matters accepted for mediation. Personal disputes and business matters where one of the parties is a lawyer but the allegations do not involve the practice of law are not appropriate for mediation under these rules. Mediation of disputes between lawyers is not precluded by these rules where the complaint otherwise meets the guidelines of matters that are appropriate for mediation.

The Commission has the authority to establish reasonable fees for the program and also to waive fees in cases of hardship. No fee should be charged a client if the charging of the fee would unduly restrict the client's access to the mediation process. Additionally, in mediations referred by [the lawyer disciplinary agency], the client should not be charged a fee for participating in the mediation.

With respect to the funding of the mediation program, it is envisioned that there will be minimal costs involved: lawyer and nonlawyer volunteers will be serving as mediators. The Commission may delegate the day-to-day administration of the Mediation Program to staff assigned to the lawyer disciplinary agency. However, a state or local bar association could administer this component of the lawyer regulation system.

Rule 3. MEDIATORS

A. **List of Approved Mediators.** The Commission shall maintain a list of approved mediators, both lawyers and nonlawyers, and shall adopt written standards for the appointment of the mediators. Mediators should represent all segments of the profession and the general population, including diversity on the basis of race, gender, and practice setting. Mediators shall be appointed for terms of [three] years and may be reappointed. The Commission may remove a mediator from the list of approved mediators for good cause, and may appoint a replacement member to serve the balance of the term of the removed member.

B. **Conflicts of Interest.** Within [20] days of the notification of appointment as a mediator, and prior to the initiation of the mediation, the mediator shall notify the Commission if he or she has previously acted as a mediator in the proceeding or in any other related proceeding or of any conflict of interest with a party to the mediation as defined in the [Code of Judicial Conduct] with respect to part-time judges. Upon notification of the conflict, the Commission shall appoint a replacement from the list of approved mediators.

C. **Challenges for Cause.** If either party has cause to object to participation by a mediator, a substitute shall be appointed by the Commission. A challenge for cause shall be filed within [15] days after service of the notice of appointment. A mediator shall accede to a reasonable challenge and the Commission shall appoint a replacement. If a mediator does not voluntarily accede, the Commission shall decide whether to appoint a replacement. The decision of the Commission on challenges shall be final.

D. **Duties.** The mediator shall have powers and duties to:

(1) grant extensions of time as deemed appropriate;

(2) reschedule or terminate the mediation if a party fails to appear; and

(3) perform all acts necessary to conduct an effective mediation conference.

Comment

Written standards for the appointment of mediators should ensure appropriate training and experience for mediators as well as diversity in the background and experience of the mediators. Mediators should also be dispersed throughout the jurisdiction to Increase access to the mediation process.

Mediators should be required to attend an appropriate training course, as determined by the Commission, which should include training in mediation theory, skills and the applicable provisions of the rules of professional conduct.

Mediators exercise a quasi-judicial role and should, therefore, be disqualified upon the same grounds and conditions applicable to part-time judges, The decisions of the mediators should be free from any appearance of outside influence.

Rule 4. THE PROCESS

A. Commencement of Mediation.

(1) Referral from Lawyer Disciplinary Agency. Within [15] calendar days after receipt by the Commission of a mediation referral from [the lawyer disciplinary agency], the Commission shall mail to both the lawyer and the complainant a copy of these rules and an agreement to mediate, together with a notice that shall Include the name, address and telephone number of the mediation program and the date on which the referral for mediation was received. If the signed agreement to mediate is not returned to the Commission by both parties within [30] calendar days of mailing, the Commission shall close the file, notify the parties that it is closing the file because one or both parties failed to return the agreement, and inform the [lawyer disciplinary agency] of the identity of the party or parties who did not consent to mediation.

(2) Voluntary Mediation. Within [15] calendar days after receipt by the Commission of the approved written application for voluntary mediation of a dispute and a signed agreement to mediate, the Commission shall notify the other party of the request and shall forward to that party an agreement to mediate, together with a copy of these Rules and a copy of the written application. If the signed agreement is not returned to the program by the other party within [30] calendar days of mailing, the Commission shall close the file and notify the requestor that the other party did not consent to mediation.

B. Assignment of Mediators. The Commission shall notify the parties of the assignment of a mediator within [15] calendar days after receipt of the fully executed agreement to mediate. The notice shall include the name, address and telephone number of the mediator assigned. The mediator shall be assigned at random from the available pool of qualified individuals. Upon withdrawal or removal of a mediator, the Commission shall notify the parties within [10] calendar days of the name, address and telephone number of a new mediator.

C. Mediation Hearing Date. Within [15] calendar days after the date of mailing of the notice of the assignment of a mediator, the mediator shall arrange a mediation conference date which shall be scheduled to take place within [30] calendar days after the assignment notice mailing date, unless both parties to the mediation agree to a longer date. The mediator shall promptly notify the parties and the Commission of the place, date and time of the conference.

D. The Conference.

(1) Only the parties to the mediation, their lawyers, if any, and the mediator are required to be present during the mediation, but the mediator shall have authority to determine if others may be present at and participate in the mediation.

(2) The mediator shall have the authority to meet separately with the parties.

(3) If all parties and the mediator agree, the mediation may be conducted by telephone. In cases of hardship, the mediation may be conducted by telephone at the discretion of the mediator even if all parties do not agree.

(4) If upon completion of the mediation, the parties have an agreement, the mediator shall reduce the agreement of the parties to writing. The parties shall sign as many originals as there are parties to the mediation. A copy of the signed agreement shall be made for the Commission's records. The mediator shall report to the Commission on the Mediation Summary Report form, which will indicate if the dispute was resolved, was not resolved, or did not proceed because a party did not appear (with an indication of which party did not appear). Such agreement and/or report shall be submitted within [15] calendar days after the conclusion of the mediation.

(5) In the case of any mediation referred from the disciplinary agency, the following materials shall be transmitted to the [lawyer disciplinary agency] at the conclusion of the mediation:

a. A duplicate original of the signed mediation agreement described in Rule 4.D.4 above; and

b. the completed Mediation Summary Report form.

Comment

The overwhelming majority of complaints made against lawyers allege instances of lesser misconduct. Summary dismissal of these complaints is one of the chief sources of public dissatisfaction with the lawyer regulation system. These cases seldom justify the resources needed to conduct formal disciplinary proceedings and should be removed from the disciplinary system and handled administratively.

The mediation program established by these rules is designed to receive cases from a number of sources: the central intake office; the disciplinary agency; other agencies within the lawyer regulation system; the courts; or directly from the parties. Referrals from the disciplinary agency will usually be part of a diversion program or an agreement in lieu of discipline, in which a lawyer agrees to mediate a dispute with the understanding that the disciplinary matter will be dismissed upon successful completion of the mediation. Agreement of both the client and the lawyer is required for a matter to be referred to mediation from the disciplinary agency. Matters that come to the mediation program from the central intake office, other agencies, or directly from the parties are voluntary as described in these rules. The mediator is authorized to determine the rules by which the mediation will proceed. The mediator should conduct the conference informally. At the outset, the mediator should make clear to the parties that the mediator is serving as a mediator and not a judge. The mediators role is to facilitate communication and suggest ways of resolving the dispute; the mediator is not to impose a settlement on the parties. The mediator should make every effort to hear all the relevant facts, review all the relevant documents, become familiar with any controlling legal principles and seek to bring about an acceptable compromise between the parties. The mediator should make sure that any proposal offered for resolution of the matter is clearly understood by the parties and perceived to be fair.

Rule 5. CONFIDENTIALITY

A. Except as provided in Rule 4.D.5 above, and Rule 5.B below, all communications, negotiations or settlement discussions by and between participants and/or mediators in the mediation shall remain confidential. All parties attending a mediation shall sign a written agreement that the proceeding will be confidential.

B. Notwithstanding Rule 5.A above, lawyer mediators have a duty to, and nonlawyer mediators should, report conduct that would be reportable under the applicable rules of professional conduct or other applicable statutes or rules.

Comment

Confidentiality in a mediation hearing Is of paramount importance. Nevertheless, the need to report lawyer misconduct takes precedence. Lawyer mediators have a duty to, and nonlawyer mediators should, report conduct that would be reportable under the state's applicable rules or statutes. A lawyer having knowledge that another lawyer has committed a violation of the [rules of professional conduct] that raises a substantial question as to that lawyer's honesty, trustworthiness or fitness as a lawyer in other respects, must inform the appropriate professional authority. Nonlawyer mediators should refer to this standard in determining their responsibility to report lawyer misconduct. The fact that mediators have a duty to report lawyer misconduct should not have a chilling effect on those parties who are sincere in availing themselves of the benefits of mediation. All mediators may also be required by the laws in their jurisdiction to report to the appropriate agency evidence of other types of misconduct, i.e., child abuse or criminal conduct, that comes to light during a mediation.

Rule 6. IMMUNITY

Communications to the Commission, mediators, or disciplinary counsel relating to lawyer misconduct or disability and testimony given in the proceedings shall be absolutely privileged, and no lawsuit predicated thereon may be instituted against any client or witness. Members of the Commission, mediators, disciplinary counsel, or any person acting on their behalf, and staff shall be immune from suit for any conduct in the course of their official duties.

Comment

The personnel involved in the mediation process are an Integral part of the judicial process and are entitled to the same immunity, which is afforded prosecuting lawyers. Immunity protects the independent judgment of the mediation personnel and avoids diverting the attention of its personnel as well as its resources toward resisting collateral attack and harassment. A policy of conferring absolute immunity encourages those who have some doubt about a lawyer's conduct to submit the matter to the proper agency, where it may be examined and determined.

ABA MODEL COURT RULE ON INSURANCE DISCLOSURE

[In August 2004, the ABA House of Delegates approved the Model Court Rule on Insurance Disclosure for adoption by highest courts of the states.]

PREFACE

The ABA *Model Court Rule on Insurance Disclosure* requires lawyers to disclose on their annual registration statements whether they maintain professional liability insurance. The Model Court Rule excludes from the Rule's reporting requirement those lawyers who are not engaged in the active practice of law and those who are engaged in the practice of law as full-time government lawyers or as counsel employed by an organizational client and do not represent clients outside that capacity. The Model Court Rule places an affirmative duty upon lawyers to notify the highest court whenever the insurance policy covering the lawyer's conduct lapses or is terminated. This ensures that the information reported to the highest court is accurate during the entire reporting period. Lawyers who do not comply with the Model Court Rule are not unauthorized to practice law until they comply.

The purpose of the Model Court Rule is to provide a potential client with access to relevant information related to a lawyer's representation in order to make an informed decision about whether to hire a particular lawyer. The Model Court Rule is a balanced standard that allows potential clients to obtain relevant information about a lawyer if they initiate an inquiry, while placing a modest annual reporting requirement on lawyers. The information submitted by lawyers will be made available by such means as designated by the highest court in the jurisdiction.

Rule ___. Insurance Disclosure

A. Each lawyer admitted to the active practice of law shall certify to the [highest court of the jurisdiction] on or before [December 31 of each year]: 1) whether the lawyer is engaged in the private practice of law; 2) if engaged in the private practice of law, whether the lawyer is currently covered by professional liability insurance; 3) whether the lawyer intends to maintain insurance during the period of time the lawyer is engaged in the private practice of law; and 4) whether the lawyer is exempt from the provisions of this Rule because the lawyer is engaged in the practice of law as a full-time government lawyer or is counsel employed by an organizational client and does not represent clients outside that capacity. Each lawyer admitted to the active practice of law in this jurisdiction who reports being covered by professional liability insurance shall notify [the highest court in the jurisdiction] in writing within 30 days if the insurance policy providing coverage lapses, is no longer in effect or terminates for any reason.

B. The foregoing shall be certified by each lawyer admitted to the active practice of law in this jurisdiction in such form as may be prescribed by the [highest court of the jurisdiction]. The information submitted pursuant to this Rule will be made available to the public by such means as may be designated by the [highest court of the jurisdiction].

C. Any lawyer admitted to the active practice of law who fails to comply with this Rule in a timely fashion, as defined by the [highest court in the jurisdiction], may be suspended from the practice of law until such time as the lawyer complies. Supplying false information in response to this Rule shall subject the lawyer to appropriate disciplinary action.

ABA MODEL RULES FOR FEE ARBITRATION

[In February 1995, the ABA House of Delegates adopted the Model Rules for Fee Arbitration as a model system for states to use in the resolution of fee disputes. In February 2012, the ABA House of Delegates amended these provisions to reflect changes in arbitration practice.]

Rule 1. GENERAL PRINCIPLES AND JURISDICTION

(A) Definitions. The following definitions shall apply in all fee arbitration proceedings:

(1) "Client" means a person or entity who directly or through an authorized representative consults, retains or secures legal service or advice from a lawyer in the lawyer's professional capacity.

(2) "Commission" means the Fee Arbitration Commission.

(3) "Decision" means the determination made by the panel in a fee arbitration proceeding.

(4) "Lawyer" means:

(a) a person admitted to practice law in this jurisdiction;

(b) a person formerly admitted to practice law in this jurisdiction or any other jurisdiction with respect to acts committed prior to resignation, suspension, disbarment or transfer to inactive status, or with respect to acts subsequent thereto that amount to the practice of law;

(c) a person admitted to practice law in another jurisdiction who is specially admitted by a court in this jurisdiction for a particular proceeding;

(d) a person admitted to practice law in another jurisdiction who practices law or renders any legal services in this jurisdiction; and

(e) the assignee of any of the above-named persons in regard to rights or responsibilities related to the fees or costs that are the subject of the arbitration.

(5) "Panel" means the arbitrator(s) assigned to hear a fee dispute and to issue a decision.

(6) "Party" means the client, the lawyer(s) responsible for the representation, the lawyer's assignee, and any third person or entity who may be liable for payment of, or entitled to a refund of lawyer's fees.

(7) "Petition" means a written request for fee arbitration in a form approved by the Commission.

(8) "Petitioner" means the party requesting fee arbitration.

(9) "Respondent" means the party with whom the petitioner has a fee dispute.

(B) Establishment; Purpose. It is the policy of the [highest court of appellate jurisdiction] to encourage the informal resolution of fee disputes between lawyers who practice law in [name of jurisdiction] and their clients. In the event such informal resolution cannot be achieved, [highest court of appellate jurisdiction] hereby establishes through adoption of these Rules, a program and procedures for the arbitration of disputes

concerning any and all fees and/or costs paid, charged, or claimed for professional services by lawyers.

(C) Commission Authority. A lawyer admitted to practice in this jurisdiction is subject to the authority of the Fee Arbitration Commission in this jurisdiction, regardless of where the conduct occurs. A lawyer not admitted in this jurisdiction is also subject to the authority of the Fee Arbitration Commission of this jurisdiction if the lawyer provides any legal services related to the matter that is the subject of the arbitration in this jurisdiction.

(D) Choice of Law. In any exercise of the authority of the Fee Arbitration Commission of this jurisdiction, the rules of professional conduct to be applied shall be as follows:

(1) for conduct in connection with a matter pending before a tribunal, the rules of the tribunal shall apply; and

(2) for any other conduct, the rules of the jurisdiction in which the conduct occurred, or, if the predominant effect of the conduct is in a different jurisdiction, the rules of that jurisdiction shall be applied to the conduct.

(E) Arbitration Mandatory for Lawyers. Fee arbitration pursuant to these Rules is voluntary for clients and mandatory for lawyers if commenced by a client. If at any time the parties have agreed, in writing, to submit fee disputes to Mandatory Fee Arbitration, arbitration is mandatory for both the lawyer and the client.

(F) Binding and Nonbinding Arbitration.

(1) Fee arbitration is only binding if,

(a) all parties have agreed in writing, after the dispute has arisen, that it will be binding, or

(b) none of the parties have sought a *trial de novo* within 30 days after service of the decision. This period shall not be extended by an application for modification of decision as permitted under Rule 6(C).

(2) A party who is found to have willfully failed to appear for the arbitration hearing is not entitled to a *trial de novo.* The determination of whether the party's non-appearance at hearing was willful shall be made by the court determining a motion for *trial de novo.* The arbitrator's finding on the issue of willful non-appearance is admissible in the court proceeding.

(3) After all parties have agreed in writing to be bound by an arbitration decision in accordance with Rule 1(F)(1), a party may not withdraw from that agreement unless all parties consent to the withdrawal in writing. At any time during the proceedings, the parties may agree in writing to be bound by the decision.

(G) Disputes Covered. Disputes concerning fees, costs, or both paid, charged, or claimed for professional services by a lawyer are subject to these Rules, except:

(1) disputes where the lawyer is also admitted to practice in another jurisdiction, the lawyer maintains no office in this jurisdiction, and no material portion of the legal services was rendered in this jurisdiction;

(2) claims for affirmative relief for damages against the lawyer based upon alleged malpractice or professional misconduct, except as provided in Rule 5(T);

(3) disputes where entitlement to and the amount of the fees and/or costs charged, claimed, or paid to a lawyer by the client or on the client's behalf have been authorized by statute or are determinable by court order; and

(4) disputes where the request for arbitration is filed more than [four] year(s) after the client-lawyer relationship has been terminated or more than [four] year(s)

after the final billing has been received by the client, whichever is later, unless a civil action concerning the disputed amount is not barred by the statute of limitations.

(H) Notice of Right to Arbitration; Stay of Proceedings; Waiver by Client.

(1) Prior to or at the time of service of a summons in a civil action against his or her client for the recovery of fees, costs, or both for professional services rendered, a lawyer shall deliver to the client or the person liable for payment of the lawyer's fees if other than the client, a written notice of the client's right to arbitrate under the fee arbitration program. The notice, in a form approved by the Commission, shall include a provision advising the client that failure to file a Petition for Fee Arbitration within 30 days of receipt of notice of the right to arbitrate shall constitute a waiver of the right to arbitrate. Failure to give this notice shall be grounds for dismissal of the civil action without prejudice.

(2) If a lawyer commences a fee collection action in any court or other tribunal, the lawyer must notify the court or other appropriate authority that a Petition for Arbitration was filed with the Commission within [thirty] days of service of the notice of the right to arbitrate.

(3) After a client files a timely Petition, the lawyer shall refrain from any judicial or non-judicial collection activities related to the fees and/or costs in dispute pending the outcome of the arbitration.

(4) Unless all parties agree in writing to the arbitration, the right of the client to petition for an arbitration is waived if:

(a) the client fails to file a Petition for Arbitration within [thirty] days of service of the notice of right to arbitrate; or

(b) the client commences an action or files any pleading seeking judicial resolution of the fee dispute, or seeks affirmative relief against the lawyer for damages based upon alleged malpractice or professional misconduct; or

(c) the client files an answer or equivalent response in an action or other proceeding prior to filing a petition for fee arbitration, if notice of the client's right to fee arbitration was properly given pursuant to this Rule, unless the client can show good cause for filing the answer or equivalent response after receiving notice of the right to arbitration.

Comment

[1] A fee arbitration system provides lawyers and clients with an out-of-court method of resolving disputes regarding lawyer's fees, costs, or both that is expeditious, confidential, inexpensive, and impartial. The court should ensure adequate funding for an effective program.

[2] For the purpose of these Rules, "assignee" refers to a person to whom the lawyer has transferred any interest in or right to the fees or costs that are the subject of the arbitration.

[3] The scope of these Rules includes costs charged by the lawyer as well as fees, because in many cases, fees and costs are inextricably linked. The fee arbitration process should be able to resolve both issues in one process.

[4] A client who believes he or she may have been overcharged by a lawyer may have the lawyer's fee reviewed without incurring the expense of formal litigation. Participation in the Fee Arbitration Program is mandatory for lawyers if the request for arbitration is commenced by a client. Because the inherent regulatory authority of the highest court of appellate jurisdiction extends only to lawyers, fee arbitration is not mandatory for clients unless agreed to pursuant to these Rules. If the parties agreed, in writing, to submit their disputes over fees and costs to the Fee Arbitration Program, then arbitration is also mandatory for the client. The parties may enter into such an agreement at any time.

[5] The fee arbitration decision is binding only upon written agreement of the parties entered into after the fee dispute has arisen. While the lawyer and client may agree to enter into fee arbitration to settle a potential fee dispute before a dispute arises, the client should not be asked to surrender the right to challenge the fee arbitration decision before the dispute arises. This distinction acknowledges the fact that a client's considerations at the onset of the client-lawyer relationship may change if the relationship becomes adversarial. In the absence of a written agreement to be bound by the arbitration decision, any party may seek a trial de novo within 30 days after service of the decision. If the parties have an existing private arbitration agreement to resolve the fee dispute outside of the Fee Arbitration Program, then private arbitration would substitute for a trial de novo. The decision becomes binding if neither party seeks a trial de novo within the 30-day period. However, a party who is found to have willfully failed to appear for the arbitration hearing is not entitled to a trial de novo following nonbinding arbitration.

[6] An alternative approach, which currently works effectively in those jurisdictions where it has been adopted, is to provide for arbitration that is both mandatory and binding in all cases. Under such a system, the arbitration decision is binding on the parties, subject to appeal only in cases of demonstrable and fundamental unfairness in the procedures utilized in deciding the matter.

[7] A lawyer should notify a client of the right to participate in the Fee Arbitration Program prior to or at the time of service of a summons in a civil action against the client to recover fees and/or costs for professional services. Notice is accomplished by delivery, to the client, in accordance with Rule 10(A), of the Notice form approved by the Commission. The client should file a Petition for Fee Arbitration within [thirty] days of receipt of service of such notice or the client waives the right to petition or maintain an arbitration proceeding under these rules. If all parties agree to set aside any purported waiver, the fee arbitration can proceed even if the client did not file the Petition for Fee Arbitration within the [thirty] day period.

[8] A third person who is not the client, but who the lawyer believes is liable for or who claims an entitlement to a refund of lawyer's fees or costs, is entitled to receive notice of the right to arbitration and to appear as a party in fee arbitration. Fee arbitration between a lawyer and a non-client is not intended to abrogate the requirement that the lawyer exercise independence of professional judgment on behalf of the client. Absent the client's written consent to disclosure of confidential information, a fee arbitration is not intended to abrogate the lawyer's duty to maintain the confidentiality of information relating to the representation of the client, unless such disclosure is otherwise permitted by law, applicable rules, or court order. Absent the client's signature on the request for arbitration, when an arbitration with a non-client is initiated, notice of the request should be sent to the client at the client's last known address.

[9] If the parties have not entered into a written fee agreement that provides for fee arbitration, the client may waives the right to the fee arbitration program by: commencing a civil action, filing any pleading seeking judicial resolution of the fee dispute, seeking affirmative relief against the lawyer for damages based on alleged malpractice, or by filing an answer to a civil action or equivalent pleading after having received notice of the client's right to arbitration from the lawyer, unless the client can show good cause why the answer was filed after receiving notice of the right to fee arbitration. This provision assumes that notice was properly given. Waiving the right to the fee arbitration program in these limited circumstances prevents the same facts from being the subject matter of the arbitration and a civil action, and discourages forum shopping. Nothing herein precludes a client from filing a complaint with the disciplinary authority. Nothing in these Rules prevents the filing of a malpractice action after a decision is rendered in the fee arbitration proceeding if the malpractice action is otherwise permitted under the applicable statute of limitations. In accordance with Rule 7(B)(4), a decision under these Rules is not admissible in a subsequent malpractice action or trial de novo following nonbinding arbitration except as provided in these Rules.

[10] The Fee Arbitration Program can be expanded by the Commission with applicable rules to arbitrate fee disputes between lawyers provided the petitioning lawyer gives notice to the client and the client joins the request for arbitration as a party.

[11] The Commission is not authorized to impose or require an automatic stay of any civil action or other judicial or administrative proceeding. It is the responsibility of the lawyer who commenced an action or other proceeding to collect fees to notify the court or program administering the other proceeding that a timely request for arbitration was filed. The lawyer should also agree to refrain from judicial or non-judicial collection pending the outcome of the fee arbitration.

Rule 2. FEE ARBITRATION COMMISSION

(A) Appointment of Commission. The [highest court of appellate jurisdiction] shall appoint a Fee Arbitration Commission to administer the Fee Arbitration Program. The [highest court of appellate jurisdiction] shall designate one member to serve as Chair of the Commission.

(B) Composition. The Commission shall consist of [nine] members of whom one-third shall be nonlawyers. Members shall be appointed for terms of three years or until a successor has been appointed. Appointments shall be on a staggered basis so that the number of terms expiring shall be approximately the same each year. No members shall be appointed for more than two consecutive full terms, but members appointed for less than a full term (either originally or to fill a vacancy) may serve two full terms in addition to such part of a term.

(C) Duties of the Commission. The Commission shall have the following powers and duties:

(1) to appoint, remove and provide appropriate training for lawyer and nonlawyer arbitrators and arbitration panels;

(2) to interpret these Rules;

(3) to approve forms, and decision form language;

(4) to establish written procedures that afford a full and equal opportunity to all parties to present relevant evidence;

(5) to issue an annual report and periodic policy recommendations, as needed, to the [highest court of appellate jurisdiction] regarding the program;

(6) to maintain all records of the Fee Arbitration Program;

(7) to determine challenges for cause where an arbitrator has not voluntarily acceded to a challenge;

(8) to determine challenges to the Fee Arbitration Program's jurisdiction to arbitrate a dispute, including claims that the client has waived the right to arbitration or that the dispute is not subject to the Fee Arbitration Program;

(9) to educate the public and the bar about the Fee Arbitration Program; and

(10) to perform all acts necessary for the effective operation of the Fee Arbitration Program.

Comment

[1] Overall authority to administer the Fee Arbitration Program is delegated by the [highest court of appellate jurisdiction] to the Commission. Both lawyers and nonlawyers serve on the Commission. Commission members are appointed by the court for a three year terms. The court should ensure diversity in the membership of the Commission.

[2] Members may be appointed for a period not to exceed two consecutive full terms and a portion of an additional term, if appointed originally to less than a full term. A rotation system is employed in the appointment of members so that, generally, the terms of one-third of the members expire annually. This procedure preserves continuity while inviting the fresh ideas that new personnel inevitably bring to a task.

[3] The Commission has the duty to inform the bar and the public about the Fee Arbitration Program through such means as brochures, public service announcements, and any other means available. There should be a central place where the public can call with questions about lawyers and which can refer appropriate matters to the Fee Arbitration Program. Members of the bar should be encouraged to inform any member of the public known to have a fee dispute with a lawyer about the right to seek fee arbitration or to pursue other available means to resolve the dispute, such as mediation.

[4] Depending on funding, pro bono requirements, and other considerations, the Commission may authorize the reimbursement of reasonable costs and expenses to its members and to arbitrators. the Commission may employ staff to perform functions delegated by the Commission. The Commission can authorize local bar associations to sponsor and conduct fee arbitration programs. However, a client who believes he or she may not be able to obtain a fair resolution at the local level should be permitted to utilize the statewide program.

Rule 3. ARBITRATORS

(A) List of Approved Arbitrators. The Commission shall maintain a list of approved arbitrators and shall adopt written standards for the appointment of the arbitrators. Such standards should ensure appropriate training and experience for arbitrators as well as diversity in the background and experience of the arbitrators. Arbitrators shall be appointed for terms of [three] years and may be reappointed. For good cause, the Commission may remove an arbitrator from the list of approved arbitrators, and may appoint a replacement member to serve the balance of the term of the removed member.

(B) Panels. The Commission shall appoint panels from the list of approved arbitrators. For disputes involving [$7,500] or more, the panel shall consist of three arbitrators of whom one shall be a nonlawyer member. For disputes involving less than [$7,500], or in any case if the parties so stipulate, the panel shall consist of a sole arbitrator who shall be a lawyer. If the panel consists of three members, the Commission shall designate one lawyer member to act as Chair of the panel and to preside at the arbitration hearing. When a three-member panel is appointed, all panel members must be present for the panel to proceed, except, the parties may agree, in writing, to accept a single lawyer arbitrator in lieu of a three member panel.

(C) Area of Practice. At the option of the client, one member of a three-member panel or the sole arbitrator shall be a lawyer with significant experience in the same area of law as the underlying matter that gave rise to the dispute. The client shall be informed of this option (as part of the notice of the right to arbitration).

(D) Impartiality. Within [five] days of the notification of appointment to a panel, an arbitrator shall notify the Commission of any reason **why the arbitrator's impartiality might reasonably be questioned, including, but not limited to the circumstances listed in ABA Model Code of Judicial Conduct Rule 2.11(A). Upon notification of the conflict, the Commission shall appoint a replacement from the list of approved arbitrators.**

(E) Challenges. Each party may disqualify one arbitrator without cause and may challenge any arbitrator for cause. A challenge for cause must include the reason for the challenge. Any challenge or request for disqualification shall be filed within [fifteen] days after service of the notice of appointment. If the challenge or request for disqualification is not timely filed, it will be ineffective, unless good cause is shown why the request was not timely filed. An arbitrator shall accede to a reasonable challenge and the Commission shall appoint a replacement. If an arbitrator does not voluntarily accede, the Commission shall decide whether to appoint a replacement. The decision of the Commission on challenges shall be final.

(F) Prohibited Contact with Arbitrators. A party or a lawyer or representative acting for a party shall not directly or indirectly communicate with an arbitrator regarding a matter pending before such arbitrator, except:

(1) at scheduled hearings;

(2) in writing with a copy to all other parties, or their representative counsel, if any, and the Commission;

(3) for the sole purpose of scheduling a hearing date or other administrative procedure with notice of same to other parties;

(4) for the purpose of obtaining the issuance of a subpoena as set forth in these Rules; or

(5) in the event of an emergency.

(G) Duties. The panel shall have the following powers and duties:

(1) to take and hear evidence pertaining to the proceeding;

(2) to administer oaths and affirmations;

(3) to compel, by subpoena, the attendance of witnesses and the production of books, papers, and documents pertaining to the proceeding

(4) to consider challenges to the validity of subpoenas;

(5) to issue decisions; and

(6) to perform all acts necessary to conduct an effective arbitration hearing.

Comment

[1] The Commission appoints both lawyers and nonlawyers to serve as arbitrators for [three] year renewable terms, and maintains a list of approved arbitrators. An arbitration panel composed of lawyers and nonlawyers results in a more balanced evaluation of fee disputes and enhances the credibility of the fee arbitration program for clients. When a Petition is received, the Commission appoints from the list of approved arbitrators a panel of one or three arbitrators to hear the matter, depending on the amount in dispute. The Commission may hire staff or designate a presiding arbitrator to handle the appointment of panels or other administrative tasks as delegated by the Commission. The number of people on the list of approved arbitrators should not be so large as to prevent the participating arbitrators from obtaining sufficient experience in the program.

[2] Appointments to the list of approved arbitrators should represent all segments of the profession and the general population, including diversity on the basis of race, gender and practice setting. Arbitrators should also be dispersed throughout the state to increase access to the fee arbitration process.

[3] The Commission should adopt written standards for appointment of arbitrators which should include compliance with training requirements, ability to meet minimum time and case commitments, years in practice, and experience. All panels of more than one arbitrator should include one nonlawyer member.

[4] Members of panels exercise a quasi-judicial role and should, therefore, be disqualified upon the same grounds and conditions applicable to judges. The Commission should provide that within [fifteen] days after service of the notice of appointment, any party may file one peremptory challenge. In the event of a peremptory challenge, the Commission should relieve the challenged arbitrator and appoint a replacement.

[5] Panels do not render advisory opinions but, rather, adjudicate fee controversies between lawyers and clients.

[6] In jurisdictions with a high volume of arbitration cases, consideration should be given to having pre-set arbitration panels that meet at specified times to simplify the scheduling of hearings.

Rule 4. COMMENCEMENT OF PROCEEDINGS

(A) Petition to Arbitrate. A fee arbitration proceeding shall commence with the filing of a Petition for Arbitration on a form approved by the Commission and by paying the appropriate filing fee as established by the [highest court of appellate jurisdiction]. Any person who is not the client of the lawyer, but who has paid or may be liable for the lawyer's fees, may commence or join the arbitration as a party to the arbitration. The Petition for Arbitration must be signed by the client and/or any other proper party seeking fee arbitration.

(B) Commission Review. The Commission shall review the Petition to determine if it is properly completed and if the Commission has jurisdiction. If the Petition is not properly completed, the Commission will return it to the petitioner and specify what clarification

or additional information is required. If the Commission believes, based on the face of the Petition, that the fee arbitration program does not have jurisdiction, the petitioner shall be so advised. The parties shall be given an opportunity to submit written statements supporting their respective positions. The Commission will make a determination of whether jurisdiction should be accepted based on these Rules and the written materials submitted.

(C) Service of Petition; Response. Within [five] days of the receipt of a properly completed Petition, the Commission shall serve a copy of the Petition, along with a Fee Arbitration Response Form on the respondent, and provide notice to the law firm, if any, with which a lawyer-party is associated that a petition for arbitration has been filed. Within [twenty] days after service, the respondent shall file the completed Fee Arbitration Response Form with the Commission, which shall forward a copy to all other parties. If the respondent is a lawyer, the respondent shall set forth in the response the name of any other lawyer or law firm who the lawyer claims is responsible for all or part of the client's claim. Within [five] days of receipt of the response, the Commission shall serve on the lawyer(s) named in the response a copy of the Petition for Arbitration and a Fee Arbitration Response Form for completion, with a copy to the law firm, if any, with which a lawyer-party is associated. Within [twenty] days after service, the lawyer(s) may file the completed Fee Arbitration Response Form with the Commission which shall forward a copy to all other parties.

(D) Failure of a Lawyer Respondent to Respond. Failure of a lawyer respondent to file the Fee Arbitration Response Form shall not delay the scheduling of a hearing; however, in any such case the panel may, in its discretion, refuse to consider evidence offered by the lawyer that would reasonably be expected to have been disclosed in the response.

(E) Client Consent Required. If a lawyer files a Petition for Arbitration, the arbitration shall proceed only if the client files a written consent within [thirty] days of service of the Petition.

(F) Settlement of Disputes. If the dispute giving rise to the Petition for Arbitration has been settled, upon reasonable confirmation of that settlement, the matter shall be dismissed by the Commission or by the panel if one has been assigned.

(G) Appointment of Panel. The Commission shall, within [ten] days after receipt of the Petition for Arbitration, appoint a panel and mail to the parties written notification of the name(s) of the panel member(s) assigned to hear the matter.

Comment

[1] The fee arbitration process begins with the filing of a Petition for Arbitration on a form approved by the Commission. The respondent has twenty days after service to return the Fee Arbitration Response Form. The process is commenced either unilaterally by a client or by the lawyer with the client's consent. If it is initiated by the client, participation is mandatory on the part of the lawyer.

[2] The Fee Arbitration Program is designed to be simple and fast. Consequently, most cases should be concluded within six months.

[3] The respondent lawyer(s) named by the client as being the person(s) responsible for refunding an unearned fee is entitled to identify another lawyer(s) as being responsible for providing such refund to the client. The client must be notified that another lawyer(s) has been so named and that the client has the right to join that named individual in the fee arbitration.

[4] Nothing in these Rules precludes a client from naming more than one lawyer in a fee arbitration if each named lawyer has either had direct or actual responsibility for the underlying representation or is named as the billing lawyer for the underlying representation.

[5] If a respondent lawyer fails to timely file a Fee Arbitration Response Form, the hearing will nonetheless be held in the normal course and the panel may, in its discretion, refuse to consider evidence

offered by the respondent lawyer that would reasonably be expected to have been disclosed in the Response. This is not intended as a default procedure. It will still be necessary for the panel to assess the evidence presented and issue a decision.

[6] The Commission must serve a copy of the Petition and the Fee Response Form on the law firm, if any, of which a lawyer is a member. The purpose of this rule is to assure that where a law firm is due a fee, or is obligated therefore, the law firm will have notice of the arbitration and an opportunity to participate. Notice of the fee arbitration proceeding also allows the associated law firm the opportunity to identity and address problematic billing patterns in a timelier manner.

Rule 5. HEARING

(A) Notice of Hearing. The panel shall set the date, time and place for the hearing. The panel shall send written notice of the hearing to the parties not less than [thirty], but no more than [sixty], days in advance of the hearing date, unless otherwise agreed by the parties.

(B) Representation by Counsel. Any party, at their expense, may be represented by counsel.

(C) Recording of Proceedings. No stenographic, audio, or video recording of the hearing is permissible.

(D) Continuances. For good cause shown, a panel may continue a hearing upon the request of a party or upon the panel's own motion.

(E) Oaths and Affirmations. The testimony of witnesses shall be by oath or affirmation administered by the sole arbitrator or panel Chair.

(F) Panel Quorums. All three arbitrators shall be required for a quorum where the panel consists of three members. A panel of three arbitrators shall act with the concurrence of at least two arbitrators. Any dissenting positions must be filed with the majority decision.

(G) Appearance; Failure of a Party to Appear. Appearance by a party at a scheduled hearing shall constitute waiver by said party of any deficiency with respect to the giving of notice of hearing. The panel shall proceed in the absence of any party or representative who, after due notice, fails either to be present or to obtain a continuance. A decision shall be made on the basis of the petition, response, testimony of the party in attendance and other materials presented, and not based on the default of a party. The panel shall require parties who are present to submit such evidence as the panel may require to issue a decision. A decision may be made in favor of a party who is absent if the evidence so warrants. If neither party appears, the panel will issue a decision based on the petition, response, and other materials presented prior to the arbitration.

(H) Waiver of Personal Appearance. Any party may waive personal appearance and designate a lawyer or nonlawyer representative to appear at the hearing to submit the client's written testimony and exhibits with the client's written declaration under oath to the panel. Such declarations shall be filed with the panel at least [ten] days prior to the hearing. If all parties, in writing, waive appearances at a hearing, the matter may be decided on the basis of written submissions. If the panel concludes that oral presentations are necessary, the panel may schedule a hearing.

(I) Telephonic Hearings. In its discretion, a panel may permit a party to appear or present witness testimony at the hearing by telephonic conference call.

(J) Stipulations. Agreements between the parties as to issues not in dispute and the voluntary exchange of documents prior to the hearing are encouraged.

(K) Evidence. The panel shall accept such evidence as is relevant and material to the dispute and request additional evidence as necessary to understand and resolve the dispute. The rules of evidence [of the jurisdiction] need not be strictly followed. The parties shall be entitled to be heard, to present evidence and to cross-examine parties and witnesses. The panel shall judge the relevance and materiality of the evidence.

(L) Subpoenas. Upon request of a party the panel shall issue in blank subpoenas for witnesses or documents necessary to a resolution of the dispute. The requesting party shall be responsible for service of the subpoenas.

(M) Reopening of Hearing. For good cause shown, the panel may reopen the hearing at any time before a decision is issued.

(N) Death or Incompetency of a Party. In the event of death or incompetency of a party, the personal representative of the deceased party or the guardian or conservator of the incompetent may be substituted.

(O) Burden of Proof. The burden of proof shall be on the lawyer to prove the reasonableness of the fee by a preponderance of the evidence.

(P) Order of Proof. The parties shall present their proof in a manner determined by the panel.

(Q) The Commission shall not lose jurisdiction, nor shall any arbitration be dismissed or any decision invalidated or modified in any way, solely because of the Commission's or panel's failure to comply with time requirements set forth in these Rules.

(R) Upon request, the panel may permit the client to be accompanied by a person for personal assistance or support. Any such person shall be subject to the confidentiality of the arbitration proceedings.

(S) No discovery is allowable except as specifically set forth in these Rules.

(T) Evidence relating to claims of malpractice and final orders of professional misconduct shall be admissible only to the extent that those claims bear upon the fees, costs, or both, to which the lawyer claims to be entitled. The arbitrators shall not award affirmative relief, in the form of damages or offset or otherwise, for injuries underlying any such claim. Nothing in these Rules shall be construed to prevent the arbitrators from awarding the client a refund of unearned fees, costs, or both previously paid to lawyer.

Comment

[1] The goal of these Rules is to provide a setting for hearings that is informal yet fair. To that end, the panel has discretion to grant postponements but need not permit the process to be subverted by unexcused absences. The panel will receive the evidence and testimony offered and judge its relevance and materiality. While the hearing may be conducted informally, witnesses should be required to testify under oath. Support persons are permitted to provide support or assistance to the client.

[2] Clients may be hesitant to participate in the fee arbitration program or pursue other civil remedies to settle a fee dispute for fear that confidential information may be disclosed by the lawyer as permitted under Rule 1.6 of the *Model Rules of Professional Conduct*. The prohibition against recordings in fee arbitration proceedings helps to ensure that any disclosure of the client's confidential information is limited to the fee arbitration proceedings.

[3] There is no provision for formal discovery; however, the panel has the power of subpoena, subject to rules of relevancy and materiality.

[4] The burden of proof in fee arbitration is on the lawyer to prove the reasonableness of the fee by a preponderance of the evidence. See, Rule 1.5 of the ABA *Model Rules of Professional Conduct*. Rule 1.5 which provides that a lawyer's fee shall be reasonable.

[5] The panel should admit evidence relating to claims of malpractice and professional misconduct, but only to the extent that those claims bear upon the fees, costs, or both to which the lawyer claims to be entitled. The panel may not award affirmative relief in the form of damages for injuries underlying any such claim.

Rule 6. DECISION

(A) Form of Decision. The panel's decision shall be in writing and shall include the names of the responsible lawyer(s), a clear statement of the amount in dispute, all questions submitted to the panel, whether and to whom monies are due, and a brief explanation of the decision. The panel shall be authorized to include an allocation of the filing fee in the arbitration decision; however, it shall not include an award for any other costs of the arbitration, including lawyer's fees resulting from the arbitration proceeding, notwithstanding any contract between the parties providing for such an award of costs or lawyer's fees.

(B) Issuance of Decision. The decision should be rendered within [thirty] days of the close of the hearing or from the end of any time period permitted by the panel for the filing of supplemental briefs or other materials. No decision is final or is to be served until the decision is approved for procedural compliance by the Commission or its designee. The arbitrator or panel Chair shall forward the decision to the Commission, which shall serve a copy of the decision on each party to the arbitration. At the time of service of the decision on the parties, the parties shall also be provided with notice of post-arbitration rights, on a form approved by the Commission.

(C) Modification of Decision.

(1) On application to the panel by a party to a fee dispute, the panel may modify or correct a decision if:

(a) there was an error in the computation of figures or a mistake in the description of a person, thing, or property referred to in the decision;

(b) the decision is imperfect in a matter of form not affecting the merits of the proceeding; or

(c) the decision needs clarification.

(2) Any party may file an application for modification with the panel within [twenty] days after service of the decision and shall serve a copy of the application on all other parties. An objection to the application must be filed with the panel within [ten] days after service of the application for modification.

(3) An application for modification shall not extend the thirty day time period to seek trial de novo under these Rules.

(4) Any corrected or amended decision shall be served by the Commission. The time for filing a petition to correct, amend, or vacate the decision begins from the date of service of the amended or corrected decision or the date of denial of the request for correction or amendment of the decision.

(D) Retention of Files. The Commission shall maintain all fee arbitration files for a period of [three] years from the date a decision is issued.

Comment

[1] In order to bring a final and speedy conclusion to fee disputes, the decision of the panel is required to be in writing and should be rendered within thirty days. Discretion to extend the time period for unusually complicated or difficult matters should be provided.

[2] Where the petitioner has paid a filing fee for fee arbitration, the arbitrator(s) may allocate the filing fee between both parties. Contracts between the parties providing for lawyer's fees and costs should not be enforced as part of the fee arbitration decision.

[3] The decision should be accompanied by a notice on a form approved by the Commission advising the parties of their rights to judicial relief subsequent to the arbitration proceeding.

Rule 7. EFFECT OF DECISION; ENFORCEMENT

(A) Compliance with Decision.

(1) Where the parties have agreed to be bound by the arbitration or have settled the dispute, the parties shall have [thirty] days from service of the written decision or the date the stipulation of settlement is signed by the parties to comply with the decision or settlement.

(2) Where there is no agreement to be bound by the arbitration, any party is entitled to a trial de novo if sought within thirty days from service of the written decision, except that if a party willfully fails to appear at the arbitration hearing, that party shall not be entitled to a trial de novo. The determination of willfulness shall be made by the court. The party who failed to appear at the arbitration shall have the burden of proving that the failure to appear was not willful. In making its determination, the court may consider any findings made by the arbitrators on the subject of a party's failure to appear. If a trial de novo is not sought within 30 days, the decision becomes binding.

(B) Trial De Novo.

(1) If there is an action pending, the trial de novo shall be initiated by filing a rejection of arbitration decision and request for trial in that action within 30 days from service of the written decision.

(2) If no action is pending, the trial de novo shall be initiated by the commencement of an action in the court having jurisdiction over the amount in controversy within thirty days from the service of the written decision.

(3) The party seeking a trial de novo shall be the prevailing party if that party obtains a judgment more favorable than that provided by the arbitration decision, and in all other cases the other party shall be the prevailing party. The prevailing party may, in the discretion of the court, be entitled to an allowance for reasonable attorney's fees and costs incurred in the trial de novo, which allowance shall be fixed by the court. In determining the lawyer's fees, the court shall consider the decision and determinations of the arbitrators, in addition to any other relevant evidence.

(4) Except as provided in this Rule, the decision and determinations of the arbitrators shall not be admissible in any action or proceeding and shall not operate as collateral estoppel or res judicata.

(C) Petition to Confirm, Correct, or Vacate the Decision.

(1) If a civil action has been stayed pursuant to these Rules, any petition to confirm, correct, or vacate the decision shall be filed with the court in which the action is pending, and shall be served in accordance with the [jurisdiction's statutes or rules of civil procedure.]

(2) If no action is pending in any court, the decision may be confirmed, corrected, or vacated by petition to the court having jurisdiction over the amount of the decision, in accordance with the [jurisdiction's statutes or rules of civil procedure].

(3) A court confirming, correcting or vacating a decision under these rules may award to the prevailing party reasonable fees and costs including, if applicable, fees

or costs on appeal, incurred in obtaining confirmation, correction or vacation of the decision. The party obtaining judgment confirming, correcting, or vacating the decision shall be the prevailing party except that, without regard or consideration of who the prevailing party may be, if a party did not appear at the arbitration hearing in the matter provided by these Rules, that party shall not be entitled to lawyer's fees or costs upon confirmation, correction, or vacation of the decision. In determining the lawyer's fees, the court shall consider the fee arbitration decision and determinations of the arbitrator(s), in addition to any other relevant evidence.

Comment

[1] Thirty days is considered a reasonable time period in which to expect the parties to comply with the decision. The thirty days begins to run when the decision in the fee arbitration process is served on the parties or when a settlement agreement is signed.

[2] The Commission itself has no authority to enforce a decision. Either party may use the summary action mechanisms that are provided by the jurisdiction to obtain a judgment consistent with the panel's decision as expeditiously as possible.

[3] Reasonable fees and costs may be awarded to the prevailing party in an action to confirm, correct or vacate a panel decision, unless the prevailing party failed to appear at the arbitration hearing in the manner provided in these Rules. This exception should encourage full participation of the parties in the arbitration proceeding.

[4] Every jurisdiction is encouraged to consider developing means of assisting clients in enforcing decisions. Some jurisdictions use a panel of pro bono lawyers to assist the clients in obtaining civil judgments. Some jurisdictions refer lawyers who fail to comply with a decision or judgment to an appropriate agency for administrative, non-disciplinary action such as that used in the jurisdiction for failure to comply with mandatory continuing legal education requirements or failure to pay registration fees.

Rule 8. CONFIDENTIALITY

(A) Confidentiality of Proceedings. Except as may be otherwise necessary for compliance with these Rules or to take ancillary legal action with respect thereto, all records, documents, files, proceedings and hearings pertaining to the arbitration of any dispute under these Rules shall be confidential and closed to the public, unless ordered open by a [court of general jurisdiction] upon good cause shown, except that a summary of the facts, without reference to the parties by name, may be publicized in all cases once the proceeding has been formally closed.

Confidentiality of Information. A lawyer may reveal information relating to the representation of the client to the extent necessary to establish his or her fee claim. In no event shall such disclosure be deemed a waiver of the confidential character of such information for any other purpose.

Confidentiality and Non-Clients. A fee arbitration between a lawyer and a non-client does not limit the lawyer's duty to exercise independence of professional judgment on behalf of the client.

Comment

[1] Rule 8(B) is consistent with Rule 1.6(b)(5) of the ABA *Model Rules of Professional Conduct*, which permits limited disclosure of otherwise confidential information "to the extent the lawyer reasonably believes necessary to establish a claim or defense . . . in a controversy between the lawyer and the client. . . ."

[2] Fee arbitration may proceed between a non-client and the lawyer. In arbitrations where the client is neither a party nor a witness and is not present at the arbitration hearing, the lawyer should exercise care to avoid abrogating the lawyer's duty to maintain the confidentiality of information relating to the representation of the client. See also Rule 1, Comment [4].

Rule 9. IMMUNITY

(A) Parties and Witnesses. Parties and witnesses shall have such immunity as is applicable in a civil action in the jurisdiction.

(B) Commissioners; Arbitrators; Staff. Members of the Commission, panels and staff shall be immune from suit for any conduct in the course and scope of their official duties.

Rule 10: SERVICE

(A) Method. Service on any party other than a lawyer shall be by personal delivery, by any person authorized by the Chair of the Commission, or by deposit in the United States mail, postage paid, addressed to the person on whom it is to be served at his or her office or home address as last given to the Commission.

(B) Official Address of Lawyer. Service on an individual lawyer shall be at the latest address shown on the official membership records of the [highest court of appellate jurisdiction or state bar association.] Notice to a law firm shall be at the address as shown in the Petition for Arbitration Form unless the law firm designates a lawyer to be responsible for the arbitration, in which case, service shall be at the designee's latest address shown on the official membership records of the [highest court or state bar association.] The method of service shall be in accordance with section 10(A) above.

(C) Service on Represented Parties. If either party is represented by counsel, service shall be on the party as indicated in Rules 10(A) and 10(B), and on the counsel at the latest address shown on the official membership records of the [highest court of appellate jurisdiction or state bar association.]

(D) Completion of Service. The service is complete at the time of deposit. The time for performing any act shall commence on the date service is complete and shall not be extended by reason of service by mail.

ABA MODEL RULES FOR CLIENT TRUST ACCOUNT RECORDS

[On August 9, 2010, the ABA House of Delegates adopted the Model Rules for Client Trust Account Records. This document replaces the ABA Model Rule on Financial Recordkeeping (Feb. 9, 1993).]

RULE 1: RECORDKEEPING GENERALLY

A lawyer who practices in this jurisdiction shall maintain current financial records as provided in these Rules and required by [Rule 1.15 of the Model Rules of Professional Conduct], and shall retain the following records for a period of [five years] after termination of the representation:

(a) receipt and disbursement journals containing a record of deposits to and withdrawals from client trust accounts, specifically identifying the date, source, and description of each item deposited, as well as the date, payee and purpose of each disbursement;

(b) ledger records for all client trust accounts showing, for each separate trust client or beneficiary, the source of all funds deposited, the names of all persons for whom the funds are or were held, the amount of such funds, the descriptions and amounts of charges or withdrawals, and the names of all persons or entities to whom such funds were disbursed;

(c) copies of retainer and compensation agreements with clients [as required by Rule 1.5 of the Model Rules of Professional Conduct];

(d) copies of accountings to clients or third persons showing the disbursement of funds to them or on their behalf;

(e) copies of bills for legal fees and expenses rendered to clients;

(f) copies of records showing disbursements on behalf of clients;

(g) the physical or electronic equivalents of all checkbook registers, bank statements, records of deposit, pre-numbered canceled checks, and substitute checks provided by a financial institution;

(h) records of all electronic transfers from client trust accounts, including the name of the person authorizing transfer, the date of transfer, the name of the recipient and confirmation from the financial institution of the trust account number from which money was withdrawn and the date and the time the transfer was completed;

(i) copies of [monthly] trial balances and [quarterly] reconciliations of the client trust accounts maintained by the lawyer; and

(j) copies of those portions of client files that are reasonably related to client trust account transactions.

Comment

[1] Rule 1 enumerates the basic financial records that a lawyer must maintain with regard to all trust accounts of a law firm. These include the standard books of account, and the supporting records that are necessary to safeguard and account for the receipt and disbursement of client or third person funds as required by Rule 1.15 of the Model Rules of Professional Conduct or its equivalent. Consistent with Rule

1.15, this Rule proposes that lawyers maintain client trust account records for a period of five years after termination of each particular legal engagement or representation. Although these Model Rules address the accepted use of a client trust account by a lawyer when holding client or third person funds, some jurisdictions may permit a lawyer to deposit certain advance fees for legal services into the lawyer's business or operating account. In those situations, the lawyer should still be guided by the standards contained in these Model Rules.

[2] Rule 1(g) requires that the physical or electronic equivalents of all checkbook registers, bank statements, records of deposit, pre-numbered canceled checks, and substitute checks be maintained for a period of five years after termination of each legal engagement or representation. The "Check Clearing for the 21**st** Century Act" or "Check 21 Act", codified at 12 U.S.C. § 5001 *et. seq.*, recognizes "substitute checks" as the legal equivalent of an original check. A "substitute check" is defined at 12 U.S.C. § 5002(16) as "paper reproduction of the original check that contains an image of the front and back of the original check; bears a magnetic ink character recognition ("MICR") line containing all the information appearing on the MICR line of the original check; conforms with generally applicable industry standards for substitute checks; and is suitable for automated processing in the same manner as the original check. Banks, as defined in 12 U.S.C. § 5002(2), are not required to return to customers the original canceled checks. Most banks now provide electronic images of checks to customers who have access to their accounts on internet-based websites. It is the lawyer's responsibility to download electronic images. Electronic images shall be maintained for the requisite number of years and shall be readily available for printing upon request or shall be printed and maintained for the requisite number of years.

[3] The ACH (Automated Clearing House) Network is an electronic funds transfer or payment system that primarily provides for the inter-bank clearing of electronic payments between originating and receiving participating financial institutions. ACH transactions are payment instructions to either debit or credit a deposit account. ACH payments are used in a variety of payment environments including bill payments, business-to-business payments, and government payments (e.g. tax refunds.) In addition to the primary use of ACH transactions, retailers and third parties use the ACH system for other types of transactions including electronic check conversion (ECC). ECC is the process of transmitting MICR information from the bottom of a check, converting check payments to ACH transactions depending upon the authorization given by the account holder at the point-of-purchase. In this type of transaction, the lawyer should be careful to comply with the requirements of Rule 1(h).

[4] There are five types of check conversions where a lawyer should be careful to comply with the requirements of Rule 1(h). First, in a "point-of-purchase conversion," a paper check is converted into a debit at the point of purchase and the paper check is returned to the issuer. Second, in a "back-office conversion," a paper check is presented at the point of purchase and is later converted into a debit and the paper check is destroyed. Third, in an "account-receivable conversion," a paper check is converted into a debit and the paper check is destroyed. Fourth, in a "telephone-initiated debit" or "check-by-phone" conversion, bank account information is provided via the telephone and the information is converted to a debit. Fifth, in a "web-initiated debit," an electronic payment is initiated through a secure web environment. Rule 1(h) applies to each of the type of electronic funds transfers described. All electronic funds transfers shall be recorded and a lawyer should not re-use a check number which has been previously used in an electronic transfer transaction.

[5] The potential of these records to serve as safeguards is realized only if the procedures set forth in Rule 1(i) are regularly performed. The trial balance is the sum of balances of each client's ledger card (or the electronic equivalent). Its value lies in comparing it on a monthly basis to a control balance. The control balance starts with the previous month's balance, then adds receipts from the Trust Receipts Journal and subtracts disbursements from the Trust Disbursements Journal. Once the total matches the trial balance, the reconciliation readily follows by adding amounts of any outstanding checks and subtracting any deposits not credited by the bank at month's end. This balance should agree with the bank statement. Quarterly reconciliation is recommended only as a minimum requirement; monthly reconciliation is the preferred practice given the difficulty of identifying an error (whether by the lawyer or the bank) among three months' transactions.

[6] In some situations, documentation in addition to that listed in paragraphs (a) through (i) of Rule 1 is necessary for a complete understanding of a trust account transaction. The type of document that a lawyer must retain under paragraph (j) because it is "reasonably related" to a client trust transaction will

vary depending on the nature of the transaction and the significance of the document in shedding light on the transaction. Examples of documents that typically must be retained under this paragraph include correspondence between the client and lawyer relating to a disagreement over fees or costs or the distribution of proceeds, settlement agreements contemplating payment of funds, settlement statements issued to the client, documentation relating to sharing litigation costs and attorney fees for subrogated claims, agreements for division of fees between lawyers, guarantees of payment to third parties out of proceeds recovered on behalf of a client, and copies of bills, receipts or correspondence related to any payments to third parties on behalf of a client (whether made from the client's funds or from the lawyer's funds advanced for the benefit of the client).

RULE 2: CLIENT TRUST ACCOUNT SAFEGUARDS

With respect to client trust accounts required by [Rule 1.15 of the Model Rules of Professional Conduct]:

(a) only a lawyer admitted to practice law in this jurisdiction or a person under the direct supervision of the lawyer shall be an authorized signatory or authorize transfers from a client trust account;

(b) receipts shall be deposited intact and records of deposit should be sufficiently detailed to identify each item; and

(c) withdrawals shall be made only by check payable to a named payee and not to cash, or by authorized electronic transfer.

Comment

[1] Rule 2 enumerates minimal accounting controls for client trust accounts. It also enunciates the requirement that only a lawyer admitted to the practice of law in the jurisdiction or a person who is under the direct supervision of the lawyer shall be the authorized signatory or authorize electronic transfers from a client trust account. While it is permissible to grant limited nonlawyer access to a client trust account, such access should be limited and closely monitored by the lawyer. The lawyer has a non-delegable duty to protect and preserve the funds in a client trust account and can be disciplined for failure to supervise subordinates who misappropriate client funds. See, Rules 5.1 and 5.3 of the Model Rules of Professional Conduct.

[2] Authorized electronic transfers shall be limited to (1) money required for payment to a client or third person on behalf of a client; (2) expenses properly incurred on behalf of a client, such as filing fees or payment to third persons for services rendered in connection with the representation; or (3) money transferred to the lawyer for fees that are earned in connection with the representation and are not in dispute; or (4) money transferred from one client trust account to another client trust account.

[3] The requirements in paragraph (b) that receipts shall be deposited intact mean that a lawyer cannot deposit one check or negotiable instrument into two or more accounts at the same time, a practice commonly known as a split deposit.

RULE 3: AVAILABILITY OF RECORDS

Records required by Rule 1 may be maintained by electronic, photographic, or other media provided that they otherwise comply with these Rules and that printed copies can be produced. These records shall be readily accessible to the lawyer.

Comment

[1] Rule 3 allows the use of alternative media for the maintenance of client trust account records if printed copies of necessary reports can be produced. If trust records are computerized, a system of regular and frequent (preferably daily) back-up procedures is essential. If a lawyer uses third-party electronic or internet based file storage, the lawyer must make reasonable efforts to ensure that the company has in place, or will establish reasonable procedures to protect the confidentiality of client information. See, ABA Formal Ethics Opinion 398 (1995). Records required by Rule 1 shall be readily accessible and shall be readily available to be produced upon request by the client or third person who has an interest as provided in Model

Rule 1.15, or by the official request of a disciplinary authority, including but not limited to, a subpoena duces tecum. Personally identifying information in records produced upon request by the client or third person or by disciplinary authority shall remain confidential and shall be disclosed only in a manner to ensure client confidentiality as otherwise required by law or court rule.

[2] Rule 28 of the Model Rules for Lawyer Disciplinary Enforcement provides for the preservation of a lawyer's client trust account records in the event that the lawyer is transferred to disability inactive status, suspended, disbarred, disappears, or dies.

RULE 4: DISSOLUTION OF LAW FIRM

Upon dissolution of a law firm or of any legal professional corporation, the partners shall make reasonable arrangements for the maintenance of client trust account records specified in Rule 1.

Comment

[1] Rules 4 and 5 provide for the preservation of a lawyer's client trust account records in the event of dissolution or sale of a law practice. Regardless of the arrangements the partners or shareholders make among themselves for maintenance of the client trust records, each partner may be held responsible for ensuring the availability of these records. For the purposes of these Rules, the terms "law firm," "partner," and "reasonable" are defined in accordance with Rules 1.0(c),(g), and (h) of the Model Rules of Professional Conduct

RULE 5: SALE OF LAW PRACTICE

Upon the sale of a law practice, the seller shall make reasonable arrangements for the maintenance of records specified in Rule 1.

ABA MODEL RULE ON PRO HAC VICE ADMISSION

[In August 2002, the ABA House of Delegates approved the Model Rule on Pro Hac Vice Admission. In February 2013, the House of Delegates amended this rule to reflect changes proposed by the Ethics 20/20 Commission.]

I. Admission In Pending Litigation Before A Court Or Agency

A. Definitions

1. An "out-of-state" lawyer is a person not admitted to practice law in this state but who is admitted in another state or territory of the United States or of the District of Columbia and not disbarred or suspended from practice in any jurisdiction.
2. An out-of-state lawyer is "eligible" for admission pro hac vice if that lawyer:
   a. lawfully practices solely on behalf of the lawyer's employer and its commonly owned organizational affiliates, regardless of where such lawyer may reside or work; or
   b. neither resides nor is regularly employed at an office in this state; or
   c. resides in this state but (i) lawfully practices from offices in one or more other states and (ii) practices no more than temporarily in this state, whether pursuant to admission pro hac vice or in other lawful ways.
3. A "client" is a person or entity for whom the out-of-state lawyer has rendered services or by whom the lawyer has been retained prior to the lawyer's performance of services in this state.
4. An "alternative dispute resolution" ("ADR") proceeding includes all types of arbitration or mediation, and all other forms of alternative dispute resolution, whether arranged by the parties or otherwise.
5. "This state" refers to [state or other U.S. jurisdiction promulgating this Rule]. This Rule does not govern proceedings before a federal court or federal agency located in this state unless that body adopts or incorporates this Rule.

B. Authority of Court or Agency To Permit Appearance By Out-of-State Lawyer

1. Court Proceeding. A court of this state may, in its discretion, admit an eligible out-of-state lawyer retained to appear in a particular proceeding pending before such court to appear pro hac vice as counsel in that proceeding.
2. Administrative Agency Proceeding. If practice before an agency of this state is limited to lawyers, the agency may, using the same standards and procedures as a court, admit an eligible out-of-state lawyer who has been retained to appear in a particular agency proceeding to appear as counsel in that proceeding pro hac vice.

C. **In-State Lawyer's Duties.** When an out-of-state lawyer appears for a client in a proceeding pending in this state, either in the role of co-counsel of record with the in-state lawyer, or in an advisory or consultative role, the in-state lawyer who is co-counsel or counsel of record for that client in the proceeding remains responsible to the client and responsible for the conduct of the proceeding before the court or agency. It is the duty of the in-state lawyer to advise the client of the in-state lawyer's independent judgment on contemplated actions in the proceeding if that judgment differs from that of the out-of-state lawyer.

D. Application Procedure

1. Verified Application. An eligible out-of-state lawyer seeking to appear in a proceeding pending in this state as counsel pro hac vice shall file a verified application with the court where the proceeding is filed. The application shall be served on all parties who have appeared in the case and the [Disciplinary Counsel]. The application shall include proof of service. The court has the discretion to grant or deny the application summarily if there is no opposition.

2. Objection to Application. The [Disciplinary Counsel] or a party to the proceeding may file an objection to the application or seek the court's imposition of conditions to its being granted. The [Disciplinary Counsel] or objecting party must file with its objection a verified affidavit containing or describing information establishing a factual basis for the objection. The [Disciplinary Counsel] or objecting party may seek denial of the application or modification of it. If the application has already been granted, the [Disciplinary Counsel] or objecting party may move that the pro hac vice admission be withdrawn.

3. Standard for Admission and Revocation of Admission. The courts and agencies of this state have discretion as to whether to grant applications for admission pro hac vice. An application ordinarily should be granted unless the court or agency finds reason to believe that such admission:

    a. may be detrimental to the prompt, fair and efficient administration of justice,

    b. may be detrimental to legitimate interests of parties to the proceedings other than the client(s) the applicant proposes to represent,

    c. one or more of the clients the applicant proposes to represent may be at risk of receiving inadequate representation and cannot adequately appreciate that risk, or

    d. the applicant has engaged in such frequent appearances as to constitute regular practice in this state.

4. Revocation of Admission. Admission to appear as counsel pro hac vice in a proceeding may be revoked for any of the reasons listed in Section I.D.3 above.

E. Verified Application and Fees

1. Required Information. An application shall state the information listed on Appendix A to this Rule. The applicant may also include any other matters supporting admission pro hac vice.

2. Application Fee. An applicant for permission to appear as counsel pro hac vice under this Rule shall pay a non-refundable fee as set by the [court or other proper authority] at the time of filing the application. The [court or other proper authority] shall determine for what purpose or purposes these fees shall be used.

3. Exemption for Pro Bono Representation. An applicant shall not be required to pay the fee established by I.E.2 above if the applicant will not charge an attorney fee to the client(s) and is:

    a. employed or associated with a pro bono project or nonprofit legal services organization in a civil case involving the client(s) of such programs; or

    b. involved in a criminal case or a habeas proceeding for an indigent defendant.

4. Lawyers' Fund for Client Protection. Upon the granting of a request to appear as counsel pro hac vice under this Rule, the lawyer shall pay any required assessments to the lawyers' fund for client protection. This assessment is in addition to the application fee referred to in Section (E)(2) above.

F. Authority of the [Disciplinary Counsel], the Court: Application of Rules of Disciplinary Enforcement, Contempt, and Sanctions

1. Authority Over Out-of-State Lawyer and Applicant.

   a. During pendency of an application for admission pro hac vice and upon the granting of such application, an out-of-state lawyer submits to the authority of the courts and the jurisdiction of [Disciplinary Counsel] of this state for all conduct arising out of or relating in any way to the application or proceeding in which the out-of-state lawyer seeks to appear, regardless of where the conduct occurs. An applicant or out-of-state lawyer who has pro hac vice authority for a proceeding may be disciplined in the same manner as an in-state lawyer.

   b. The court's and the [Disciplinary Counsel's] authority includes, without limitation, the court's and [Disciplinary Counsel's] rules of professional conduct, rules of disciplinary enforcement, contempt and sanctions orders, local court rules, and court policies and procedures.

2. Familiarity With Rules. An applicant shall become familiar with all applicable rules of professional conduct, rules of disciplinary enforcement, local court rules, and policies and procedures of the court before which the applicant seeks to practice.

II. Out-of-State Proceedings, Potential In-State and Out-of-State Proceedings, and All ADR

A. In-State Ancillary Proceeding Related to Pending Out-of-State Proceeding. In connection with proceedings pending outside this state, an out-of-state lawyer admitted to appear in that proceeding may render in this state legal services regarding or in aid of such proceeding.

B. Consultation by Out-of-State Lawyer

1. Consultation with In-State Lawyer. An out-of-state lawyer may consult in this state with an in-state lawyer concerning the in-state's lawyer's client's pending or potential proceeding in this state.

2. Consultation with Potential Client. At the request of a person in this state contemplating a proceeding or involved in a pending proceeding, irrespective of where the proceeding is located, an out-of-state lawyer may consult in this state with that person about that person's possible retention of the out-of-state lawyer in connection with the proceeding.

C. Preparation for In-State Proceeding. On behalf of a client in this state or elsewhere, the out-of-state lawyer may render legal services in this state in preparation for a potential proceeding to be filed in this state, provided that the out-of-state lawyer reasonably believes he is eligible for admission pro hac vice in this state.

D. Preparation for Out-of-State Proceeding. In connection with a potential proceeding to be filed outside this state, an out-of-state lawyer may render legal services in this state for a client or potential client located in this state, provided that the out-of-state lawyer is admitted or reasonably believes the lawyer is eligible for admission generally or pro hac vice in the jurisdiction where the proceeding is anticipated to be filed.

E. Services Rendered Outside This State for In-State Client. An out-of-state lawyer may render legal services while the lawyer is physically outside this state when requested by a client located within this state in connection with a potential or pending proceeding filed in or outside this state.

F. **Alternative Dispute Resolution ("ADR") Procedures.** An out-of-state lawyer may render legal services in this state to prepare for and participate in an ADR procedure regardless of where the ADR procedure is expected to take or actually takes place.

G. **No Solicitation.** An out-of-state lawyer rendering services in this state in compliance with this Rule or here for other reasons is not authorized by anything in this Rule to hold out to the public or otherwise represent that the lawyer is admitted to practice in this jurisdiction. Nothing in this Rule authorizes out-of-state lawyers to solicit, advertise, or otherwise hold themselves out in publications as available to assist in litigation in this state.

H. **Temporary Practice.** An out-of-state lawyer will only be eligible for admission pro hac vice or to practice in another lawful way only on a temporary basis.

I. **Authorized Services.** The foregoing services may be undertaken by the out-of-state lawyer in connection with a potential proceeding in which the lawyer reasonably expects to be admitted pro hac vice, even if ultimately no proceeding is filed or if pro hac vice admission is denied.

III. Admission of Foreign Lawyer in Pending Litigation Before a Court or Agency

A. A foreign lawyer is a person admitted in a non-United States jurisdiction and who is a member of a recognized legal profession in that jurisdiction, the members of which are admitted to practice as lawyers or counselors at law or the equivalent and are subject to effective regulation and discipline by a duly constituted professional body or a public authority, and who is not disbarred, suspended or the equivalent thereof from practice in any jurisdiction.

B. The definitions of "client" and "state" in paragraphs I(A)(3) and (5) are incorporated by reference in this Paragraph III.

C. A court or agency of this state may, in its discretion, admit a foreign lawyer in a particular proceeding pending before such court or agency to appear pro hac vice in a defined role as a lawyer, advisor or consultant in that proceeding with an in-state lawyer, provided that the in-state lawyer is responsible to the client, responsible for the conduct of the proceeding, responsible for independently advising the client on the substantive law of a United States jurisdiction and procedural issues in the proceeding, and for advising the client whether the instate lawyer's judgment differs from that of the foreign lawyer. See paragraph III(E).

D. In addition to the factors listed in paragraph I(D)(3) above, a court or agency in ruling on an application to admit a foreign lawyer pro hac vice, as a lawyer, advisor, or consultant, or in an advisory or consultative role, shall weigh factors, including:

1. the legal training and experience of the foreign lawyer including in matters similar to the matter before the court or agency;
2. the extent to which the matter will include the application of: a. the law of the jurisdiction in which the foreign lawyer is admitted or b. international law or other law with which the foreign lawyer has a demonstrated expertise;
3. the foreign lawyer's familiarity with the law of a United States jurisdiction applicable to the matter before the court or agency;
4. the extent to which the foreign lawyer's relationship and familiarity with the client or with the facts and circumstances of the matter will facilitate the fair and efficient resolution of the matter;
5. the foreign lawyer's English language ability; and
6. the extent to which it is possible to define the scope of the foreign lawyer's authority in the matter as described in paragraph III(F) so as to facilitate its fair and efficient

resolution, including by a limitation on the foreign lawyer's authority to advise the client on the law of a United States jurisdiction except in consultation with the in-state lawyer.

E. The court or agency shall limit the activities of the foreign lawyer or require further action by the in-state lawyer, as appropriate in its discretion in light of paragraph III(D). It may, for example, require the in-state lawyer to sign all pleadings and other documents submitted to the court or to other parties, to be present at all depositions and conferences among counsel, or to attend all proceedings before the court or agency.

APPENDIX A

The out-of-state or foreign lawyer's verified application for admission pro hac vice shall include:

1. the applicant's residence and business address, telephone number(s), and e-mail address(es);
2. the name, address, telephone number(s), and e-mail address(es) of each client sought to be represented;
3. the U.S. and foreign jurisdictions in, and agencies and courts before which the applicant has been admitted to practice, the contact information for each, and the respective period(s) of admission;
4. the name and address of each court or agency and a full identification of each proceeding in which the applicant has filed an application to appear pro hac vice in this state within the preceding two years and the date of each application;
5. a statement as to whether the applicant (a) within the last [five (5)] years has been denied admission pro hac vice in any jurisdiction, U.S. or foreign, including this state, (b) has ever had admission pro hac vice revoked in any jurisdiction, U.S. or foreign, including this state, or (c) has ever been disciplined or sanctioned by any court or agency in any jurisdiction, U.S. or foreign, including this state. If so, specify the nature of the allegations; the name of the authority bringing such proceedings; the caption of the proceedings, the date filed, and what findings were made and what action was taken in connection with those proceedings. A certified copy of the written finding or order shall be attached to the application. If the written finding or order is not in English, the applicant shall submit an English translation and satisfactory proof of the accuracy of the translation;
6. whether any disciplinary proceeding has ever been brought against the applicant by a disciplinary counsel or analogous foreign regulatory authority in any jurisdiction within the last [five (5)] years and, as to each such proceeding: the nature of the allegations; the date the proceedings were initiated, which, if any, of the proceedings are still pending, and, for those proceedings that are not still pending, the dates upon which the proceedings were concluded; the caption of the proceedings; and the findings made and actions taken in connection with those proceedings;, including exoneration from any charges. A certified copy of any written finding or order shall be attached to the application. If the written order or findings is not in English, the applicant shall submit an English translation and satisfactory proof of the accuracy of the translation.
7. whether the applicant has been held in contempt by any court in a written order in the last [five (5)] years, and, if so: the nature of the allegations; the name of the court before which such proceedings were conducted; the date of the contempt order, the caption of the proceedings, and the substance of the court's rulings. A copy of the written order or transcript of the oral rulings shall be attached to the application. If the written finding or order is not in English, the applicant shall submit an English translation and satisfactory proof of the accuracy of the translation;

8. an averment as to the applicant's familiarity with the rules of professional conduct, rules of disciplinary enforcement, local or agency rules, and policies and procedures of the court or agency before which the applicant seeks to practice;

9. the name, address, telephone number(s), e-mail address(es), and bar number of the active member in good standing of the bar of this state who supports the applicant's pro hac vice request, who shall appear of record together with the out-of-state lawyer, and who shall remain ultimately responsible to the client as set forth in Paragraph C of this Rule; and

10. for applicants admitted in a foreign jurisdiction, an averment by the in-state lawyer referred to in Paragraph 9 above and by the lawyer admitted in a foreign jurisdiction that, if the application for pro hac vice admission is granted, service of any documents by a party or Disciplinary Counsel upon that foreign lawyer shall be accomplished by service upon the in-state lawyer or that in-state lawyer's agent.

11. Optional: the applicant's prior or continuing representation in other matters of one or more of the clients the applicant proposes to represent and any relationship between such other matter(s) and the proceeding for which applicant seeks admission.

12. Optional: any special experience, expertise, or other factor deemed to make it particularly desirable that the applicant be permitted to represent the client(s) the applicant proposes to represent in the particular cause.

ABA MODEL RULE ON ADMISSION BY MOTION

[In August 2002, the ABA House of Delegates approved the Model Rule on Admission by Motion. In August 2012, the ABA House of Delegates amended this rule to reflect changes proposed by the Ethics 20/20 Commission.]

---

1. An applicant who meets the requirements of (a) through (h) of this Rule may, upon motion, be admitted to the practice of law in this jurisdiction.

The applicant shall:

(a) have been admitted to practice law in another state, territory, or the District of Columbia;

(b) hold a first professional degree in law (J.D. or LL.B.) from a law school approved by the Council of the Section of Legal Education and Admissions to the Bar of the American Bar Association at the time the graduate matriculated;

(c) have been primarily engaged in the active practice of law in one or more states, territories or the District of Columbia for three of the five years immediately preceding the date upon which the application is filed;

(d) establish that the applicant is currently a member in good standing in all jurisdictions where admitted;

(e) establish that the applicant is not currently subject to lawyer discipline or the subject of a pending disciplinary matter in any other jurisdiction;

(f) establish that the applicant possesses the character and fitness to practice law in this jurisdiction; and

(g) designate the Clerk of the jurisdiction's highest court for service of process.

2. For the purposes of this Rule, the "active practice of law" shall include the following activities, if performed in a jurisdiction in which the applicant is admitted, or if performed in a jurisdiction that affirmatively permits such activity by a lawyer not admitted to practice; however, in no event shall activities listed under (2)(e) and (f) that were performed pursuant to the Model Rule on Practice Pending Admission or in advance of bar admission in the jurisdiction to which application is being made be accepted toward the durational requirement:

(a) Representation of one or more clients in the practice of law;

(b) Service as a lawyer with a local, state, territorial or federal agency, including military service;

(c) Teaching law at a law school approved by the Council of the Section of Legal Education and Admissions to the Bar of the American Bar Association;

(d) Service as a judge in a federal, state, territorial or local court of record;

(e) Service as a judicial law clerk; or

(f) Service as corporate counsel.

3. For the purposes of this Rule, the active practice of law shall not include work that, as undertaken, constituted the unauthorized practice of law in the jurisdiction in which it was performed or in the jurisdiction in which the clients receiving the unauthorized services were located.

4. An applicant who has failed a bar examination administered in this jurisdiction within five years of the date of filing an application under this Rule shall not be eligible for admission on motion.

ABA MODEL RULE ON PRACTICE PENDING ADMISSION

[In August 2012, the ABA House of Delegates adopted a Model Rule on Practice Pending Admission.]

1. A lawyer currently holding an active license to practice law in another U.S. jurisdiction and who has been engaged in the active practice of law for three of the last five years, may provide legal services in this jurisdiction through an office or other systematic and continuous presence for no more than [365] days, provided that the lawyer:

a. is not disbarred or suspended from practice in any jurisdiction and is not currently subject to discipline or a pending disciplinary matter in any jurisdiction;

b. has not previously been denied admission to practice in this jurisdiction or failed this jurisdiction's bar examination;

c. notifies Disciplinary Counsel and the Admissions Authority in writing prior to initiating practice in this jurisdiction that the lawyer will be doing so pursuant to the authority in this Rule;

d. submits within [45] days of first establishing an office or other systematic and continuous presence for the practice of law in this jurisdiction a complete application for admission by motion or by examination;

e. reasonably expects to fulfill all of this jurisdiction's requirements for that form of admission;

f. associates with a lawyer who is admitted to practice in this jurisdiction;

g. complies with Rules 7.1 and 7.5 of the Model Rules of Professional Conduct [or jurisdictional equivalent] in all communications with the public and clients regarding the nature and scope of the lawyer's practice authority in this jurisdiction; and

h. pays any annual client protection fund assessment.

2. A lawyer currently licensed as a foreign legal consultant in another U.S. jurisdiction may provide legal services in this jurisdiction through an office or other systematic and continuous presence for no more than [365] days, provided that the lawyer:

a. provides services that are limited to those that may be provided in this jurisdiction by foreign legal consultants;

b. is a member in good standing of a recognized legal profession in the foreign jurisdiction, the members of which are admitted to practice as lawyers or counselors at law or the equivalent, and are subject to effective regulation and discipline by a duly constituted professional body or a public authority;

c. submits within [45] days of first establishing an office or other systematic and continuous presence for the practice of law in this jurisdiction a complete application for admission to practice as a foreign legal consultant;

d. reasonably expects to fulfill all of this jurisdiction's requirements for admission as a foreign legal consultant; and

e. meets the requirements of paragraphs 1(a), (b), (c), (f), (g), and (h) of this Rule.

3. Prior to admission by motion, through examination, or as a foreign legal consultant, the lawyer may not appear before a tribunal in this jurisdiction that requires *pro hac vice* admission unless the lawyer is granted such admission.

4. The lawyer must immediately notify Disciplinary Counsel and the Admissions Authority in this jurisdiction if the lawyer becomes subject to a disciplinary matter or disciplinary sanctions in any other jurisdiction at any time during the [365] days of practice authorized by this Rule. The Admissions

Authority shall take into account such information in determining whether to grant the lawyer's application for admission to this jurisdiction.

5. The authority in this Rule shall terminate immediately if:

a. the lawyer withdraws the application for admission by motion, by examination, or as a foreign legal consultant, or if such application is denied, prior to the expiration of [365] days;

b. the lawyer fails to file the application for admission within [45] days of first establishing an office or other systematic and continuous presence for the practice of law in this jurisdiction;

c. the lawyer fails to remain in compliance with Paragraph 1 of this Rule;

d. the lawyer is disbarred or suspended in any other jurisdiction in which the lawyer is licensed to practice law; or

e. the lawyer has not complied with the notification requirements of Paragraph 4 of this Rule.

6. Upon the termination of authority pursuant to Paragraph 5, the lawyer, within [30] days, shall:

a. cease to occupy an office or other systematic and continuous presence for the practice of law in this jurisdiction unless authorized to do so pursuant to another Rule;

b. notify all clients being represented in pending matters, and opposing counsel or co-counsel of the termination of the lawyer's authority to practice pursuant to this Rule;

c. not undertake any new representation that would require the lawyer to be admitted to practice law in this jurisdiction; and

d. take all other necessary steps to protect the interests of the lawyer's clients.

7. Upon the denial of the lawyer's application for admission by motion, by examination, or as a foreign legal consultant, the Admissions Authority shall immediately notify Disciplinary Counsel that the authority granted by this Rule has terminated.

8. The Court, in its discretion, may extend the time limits set forth in this Rule for good cause shown.

Comment

[1] This Rule recognizes that a lawyer admitted in another jurisdiction may need to relocate to or commence practice in this jurisdiction, sometimes on short notice. The admissions process can take considerable time, thus placing a lawyer at risk of engaging in the unauthorized practice of law and leaving the lawyer's clients without the benefit of their chosen counsel. This Rule closes this gap by authorizing the lawyer to practice in this jurisdiction for a limited period of time, up to 365 days, subject to restrictions, while the lawyer diligently seeks admission. The practice authority provided pursuant to this Rule commences immediately upon the lawyer's establishment of an office or other systematic and continuous presence for the practice of law.

[2] Paragraph 1(f) requires a lawyer practicing in this jurisdiction pursuant to the authority granted under this Rule to associate with a lawyer who is admitted to practice law in this jurisdiction. The association between the incoming lawyer and the lawyer licensed in this jurisdiction is akin to that between a local lawyer and a lawyer practicing in a jurisdiction on a temporary basis pursuant to Model Rule of Professional Conduct 5.5(c)(1).

[3] While exercising practice authority pursuant to this Rule, a lawyer cannot hold out to the public or otherwise represent that the lawyer is admitted to practice in this jurisdiction. See Model Rule of Professional Conduct 5.5(b)(2). Because such a lawyer will typically be assumed to be admitted to practice in this jurisdiction, that lawyer must disclose the limited practice authority and jurisdiction of licensure in all communications with potential clients, such as on business cards, websites, and letterhead. Further, the lawyer must disclose the limited practice authority to all potential clients before agreeing to represent them. See Model Rules 7.1 and 7.5(b).

PRACTICE PENDING ADMISSION

[4] The provisions of paragraph 5 (a) through (d) of this Rule are necessary to avoid prejudicing the rights of existing clients or other parties. Thirty days should be sufficient for the lawyer to wind up his or her practice in this jurisdiction in an orderly manner.

ABA MODEL RULE FOR THE LICENSING AND PRACTICE OF FOREIGN LEGAL CONSULTANTS

[In August 2002, the ABA House of Delegates approved the Model Rule for Licensing of Legal Consultants. This Model Rule was amended in 2006.]

---

§ 1. General Regulation as to Licensing

In its discretion, the [name of court] may license to practice in this United States jurisdiction as a foreign legal consultant, without examination, an applicant who:

(a) is, and for at least five years has been, a member in good standing of a recognized legal profession in a foreign country, the members of which are admitted to practice as lawyers or counselors at law or the equivalent and are subject to effective regulation and discipline by a duly constituted professional body or a public authority;

(b) for at least five years preceding his or her application has been a member in good standing of such legal profession and has been lawfully engaged in the practice of law in the foreign country or elsewhere substantially involving or relating to the rendering of advice or the provision of legal services concerning the law of the foreign country;[1]

(c) possesses the good moral character and general fitness requisite for a member of the bar of this jurisdiction; and

(d) intends to practice as a foreign legal consultant in this jurisdiction and to maintain an office in this jurisdiction for that purpose.

§ 2. Application

An applicant under this Rule shall file an application for a foreign legal consultant license, which shall include all of the following:

(a) a certificate from the professional body or public authority having final jurisdiction over professional discipline in the foreign country in which the applicant is admitted, certifying the applicant's admission to practice, date of admission, and good standing as a lawyer or counselor at law or the equivalent;

(b) a letter of recommendation from one of the members of the executive body of such professional body or public authority or from one of the judges of the highest law court or court of original jurisdiction in the foreign country in which the applicant is admitted;

(c) duly authenticated English translations of the certificate required by Section 2(a) of this Rule and the letter required by Section 2(b) of this Rule if they are not in English;

(d) other evidence as the [name of court] may require regarding the applicant's educational and professional qualifications, good moral character and general fitness, and compliance with the requirements of Section 1 of this Rule;

(e) an application fee as set by the [name of court].

---

[1] Section 1(b) is optional; it may be included as written, modified through the substitution of shorter periods than five and seven years, respectively, or omitted entirely.

§ 3. Scope of Practice

A person licensed to practice as a foreign legal consultant under this Rule may render legal services in this jurisdiction but shall not be considered admitted to practice law in this jurisdiction, or in any way hold himself or herself out as a member of the bar of this jurisdiction, or do any of the following:

(a) appear as a lawyer on behalf of another person in any court, or before any magistrate or other judicial officer, in this jurisdiction (except when admitted *pro hac vice* pursuant to [citation of applicable rule]);

(b) prepare any instrument effecting the transfer or registration of title to real estate located in the United States of America;

(c) prepare:

(i) any will or trust instrument effecting the disposition on death of any property located in and owned by a resident of the United States of America, or

(ii) any instrument relating to the administration of a decedent's estate in the United States of America;

(d) prepare any instrument in respect of the marital or parental relations, rights or duties of a resident of the United States of America, or the custody or care of the children of such a resident;

(e) render professional legal advice on the law of this jurisdiction or of the United States of America (whether rendered incident to the preparation of legal instruments or otherwise) except on the basis of advice from a person duly qualified and entitled (other than by virtue of having been licensed under this Rule) to render professional legal advice in this jurisdiction;

(f) carry on a practice under, or utilize in connection with such practice, any name, title, or designation other than one or more of the following:

(i) the foreign legal consultant's own name;

(ii) the name of the law firm with which the foreign legal consultant is affiliated;

(iii) the foreign legal consultant's authorized title in the foreign country of his or her admission to practice, which may be used in conjunction with the name of that country; and

(iv) the title "foreign legal consultant," which may be used in conjunction with the words "admitted to the practice of law in [name of the foreign country of his or her admission to practice]".

[(g) render legal services in this State pursuant to the *Model Rule for Temporary Practice by Foreign Lawyers.*]

§ 4. Practice by a Foreign Legal Consultant Licensed in Another United States Jurisdiction

[A person licensed as a foreign legal consultant in another United States jurisdiction may provide legal services in this State on a temporary basis pursuant to the *Model Rule for Temporary Practice by Foreign Lawyers*. A person licensed as a foreign legal consultant in another United States jurisdiction shall not establish an office or otherwise engage in a systematic and continuous practice in this jurisdiction or hold out to the public or otherwise represent that the foreign legal consultant is licensed as a foreign legal consultant in this jurisdiction.]

§ 5. Rights and Obligations

Subject to the limitations listed in Section 3 of this Rule, a person licensed under this Rule shall be considered a foreign legal consultant affiliated with the bar of this State and shall be entitled and subject to:

(a) the rights and obligations set forth in the [Rules] [Code] of Professional [Conduct] [Responsibility] of [citation] or arising from the other conditions and requirements that apply to a member of the bar of this jurisdiction under the [rules of court governing members of the bar, including ethics]; and

(b) the rights and obligations of a member of the bar of this jurisdiction with respect to:

(i) affiliation in the same law firm with one or more members of the bar of this jurisdiction, including by:

(A) employing one or more members of the bar of this jurisdiction;

(B) being employed by one or more members of the bar of this jurisdiction or by any partnership [or professional corporation] that includes members of the bar of this jurisdiction or that maintains an office in this jurisdiction; and

(C) being a partner in any partnership [or shareholder in any professional corporation] that includes members of the bar of this jurisdiction or that maintains an office in this jurisdiction; and

(ii) attorney-client privilege, work-product privilege, and similar professional privileges.

§ 6. Discipline

A person licensed to practice as a foreign legal consultant under this Rule shall be subject to professional discipline in the same manner and to the same extent as members of the bar of this jurisdiction. To this end:

(a) Every person licensed to practice as a legal consultant under this Rule:

(i) shall be subject to the jurisdiction of [name of court] and to censure, suspension, removal, or revocation of his or her license to practice by the [name of court] and shall otherwise be governed by [citation of applicable rules]; and

(ii) shall execute and file with the [name of court], in the form and manner as the court may prescribe:

(A) a commitment to observe the [Rules] [Code] of Professional [Conduct] [Responsibility] of [citation] and the [rules of court governing members of the bar] to the extent applicable to the legal services authorized under Section 3 of this Rule;

(B) an undertaking or appropriate evidence of professional liability insurance, in an amount as the court may prescribe, to assure the foreign legal consultant's proper professional conduct and responsibility;

(C) a written undertaking to notify the court of any change in the foreign legal consultant's good standing as a member of the foreign legal profession referred to in Section 1(a) of this Rule and of any final action of the professional body or public authority referred to in Section 2(a) of this Rule imposing any disciplinary censure, suspension, or other sanction upon the foreign legal consultant; and

(D) a duly acknowledged instrument in writing, providing the foreign legal consultant's address in this jurisdiction and designating the clerk of [name of court] as his or her agent for service of process. The foreign legal consultant shall keep the clerk advised in writing of any changes of address in this jurisdiction. In any action or proceeding brought against the foreign legal consultant and arising out of or based upon any legal services rendered or offered to be rendered by the foreign legal consultant within or to residents of this jurisdiction, service shall first be attempted upon the foreign legal consultant at the most recent address filed with the clerk. Whenever after due diligence service cannot be made upon the foreign legal consultant at that address, service may be made upon the clerk. Service made upon the clerk in accordance with this provision is effective as if service had been made personally upon the foreign legal consultant.

(b) Service of process on the clerk under Section 5(a)(ii)(D) of this Rule shall be made by personally delivering to the clerk's office, and leaving with the clerk or with a deputy or assistant authorized by the clerk to receive service, duplicate copies of the process together with a fee as set by the [name of court]. The clerk shall promptly send one copy of the process to the foreign legal consultant to whom the process is directed, by certified mail, return receipt requested, addressed to the foreign legal consultant at the most recent address provided in accordance with Section 5(a)(ii)(D).

§ 7. Annual Fee

A person licensed as a foreign legal consultant shall pay an annual fee as set by the [name of court].

§ 8. Revocation of License

If the [name of court] determines that a person licensed as a foreign legal consultant under this Rule no longer meets the requirements for licensure set forth in Section 1(a) or Section 1(b) of this Rule, it shall revoke the foreign legal consultant's license.

§ 9. Admission to Bar

If a person licensed as a foreign legal consultant under this Rule is subsequently admitted as a member of the bar of this jurisdiction under the Rules governing admission, that person's foreign legal consultant license shall be deemed superseded by the license to practice law as a member of the bar of this jurisdiction.

§ 10. Application for Waiver of Provisions

The [name of court], upon written application, may waive any provision or vary the application of this Rule where strict compliance will cause undue hardship to the applicant. An application for waiver shall be in the form of a verified petition setting forth the applicant's name, age, and residence address; the facts relied upon; and a prayer for relief.

ABA MODEL RULE ON TEMPORARY PRACTICE BY FOREIGN LAWYERS

[In August 2002, the ABA House of Delegates approved the Model Rule on Temporary Practice by Foreign Lawyers.]

(a). A lawyer who is admitted only in a non-United States jurisdiction shall not, except as authorized by this Rule or other law, establish an office or other systematic and continuous presence in this jurisdiction for the practice of law, or hold out to the public or otherwise represent that the lawyer is admitted to practice law in this jurisdiction. Such a lawyer does not engage in the unauthorized practice of law in this jurisdiction when on a temporary basis the lawyer performs services in this jurisdiction that:

1. are undertaken in association with a lawyer who is admitted to practice in this jurisdiction and who actively participates in the matter;
2. are in or reasonably related to a pending or potential proceeding before a tribunal held or to be held in a jurisdiction outside the United States if the lawyer, or a person the lawyer is assisting, is authorized by law or by order of the tribunal to appear in such proceeding or reasonably expects to be so authorized;
3. are in or reasonably related to a pending or potential arbitration, mediation or other alternative dispute resolution proceeding held or to be held in this or another jurisdiction, if the services arise out of or are reasonably related to the lawyer's practice in a jurisdiction in which the lawyer is admitted to practice;
4. are not within paragraphs (2) or (3) and
   i. are performed for a client who resides or has an office in a jurisdiction in which the lawyer is authorized to practice to the extent of that authorization; or
   ii. arise out of or are reasonably related to a matter that has a substantial connection to a jurisdiction in which the lawyer is authorized to practice to the extent of that authorization; or
5. are governed primarily by international law or the law of a non-United States jurisdiction.

(b). For purposes of this grant of authority, the lawyer must be a member in good standing of a recognized legal profession in a foreign jurisdiction, the members of which are admitted to practice as lawyers or counselors at law or the equivalent and subject to effective regulation and discipline by a duly constituted professional body or a public authority.

ABA MODEL COURT RULE ON PROVISION OF LEGAL SERVICES FOLLOWING DETERMINATION OF A MAJOR DISASTER

[In February 2007, after Hurricane Katrina, the ABA House of Delegates approved the Model Rule on Provision of Legal Services Following Determination of a Major Disaster.]

RULE ____. PROVISION OF LEGAL SERVICES FOLLOWING DETERMINATION OF MAJOR DISASTER

(a) *Determination of existence of major disaster.* Solely for purposes of this Rule, this Court shall determine when an emergency affecting the justice system, as a result of a natural or other major disaster has occurred in:

(1) this jurisdiction and whether the emergency caused by the major disaster affects the entirety or only a part of this jurisdiction, or

(2) another jurisdiction but only after such a determination and its geographical scope have been made by the highest court of that jurisdiction. The authority to engage in the temporary practice of law in this jurisdiction pursuant to paragraph (c) shall extend only to lawyers who principally practice in the area of such other jurisdiction determined to have suffered a major disaster causing an emergency affecting the justice system and the provision of legal services.

(b) *Temporary practice in this jurisdiction following major disaster.* Following the determination of an emergency affecting the justice system in this jurisdiction pursuant to paragraph (a) of this Rule, or a determination that persons displaced by a major disaster in another jurisdiction and residing in this jurisdiction are in need of pro bono services and the assistance of lawyers from outside of this jurisdiction is required to help provide such assistance, a lawyer authorized to practice law in another United States jurisdiction, and not disbarred, suspended from practice or otherwise restricted from practice in any jurisdiction, may provide legal services in this jurisdiction on a temporary basis. Such legal services must be provided on a *pro bono* basis without compensation, expectation of compensation or other direct or indirect pecuniary gain to the lawyer. Such legal services shall be assigned and supervised through an established not-for-profit bar association, *pro bono* program or legal services program or through such organization(s) specifically designated by this Court.

(c) *Temporary practice in this jurisdiction following major disaster in another jurisdiction.* Following the determination of a major disaster in another United States jurisdiction, a lawyer who is authorized to practice law and who principally practices in that affected jurisdiction, and who is not disbarred, suspended from practice or otherwise restricted from practice in any jurisdiction, may provide legal services in this jurisdiction on a temporary basis. Those legal services must arise out of and be reasonably related to that lawyer's practice of law in the jurisdiction, or area of such other jurisdiction, where the major disaster occurred.

(d) *Duration of authority for temporary practice.* The authority to practice law in this jurisdiction granted by paragraph (b) of this Rule shall end when this Court determines that the conditions caused by the major disaster in this jurisdiction have ended except that a lawyer then representing clients in this jurisdiction pursuant to paragraph (b) is authorized to continue the provision of legal services for such time as is reasonably

necessary to complete the representation, but the lawyer shall not thereafter accept new clients. The authority to practice law in this jurisdiction granted by paragraph (c) of this Rule shall end [60] days after this Court declares that the conditions caused by the major disaster in the affected jurisdiction have ended.

(e) Court appearances. The authority granted by this Rule does not include appearances in court except:

(1) pursuant to that court's *pro hoc vice* admission rule and, if such authority is granted, any fees for such admission shall be waived; or

(2) if this Court, in any determination made under paragraph (a), grants blanket permission to appear in all or designated courts of this jurisdiction to lawyers providing legal services pursuant to paragraph (b). If such an authorization is included, any *pro hac vice* admission fees shall be waived.

(f) *Disciplinary authority and registration requirement.* Lawyers providing legal services in this jurisdiction pursuant to paragraphs (b) or (c) are subject to this Court's disciplinary authority and the *Rules of Professional Conduct* of this jurisdiction as provided in Rule 8.5 of the *Rules of Professional Conduct.* Lawyers providing legal services in this jurisdiction under paragraphs (b) or (c) shall, within 30 days from the commencement of the provision of legal services, file a registration statement with the Clerk of this Court. The registration statement shall be in a form prescribed by this Court. Any lawyer who provides legal services pursuant to this Rule shall not be considered to be engaged in the unlawful practice of law in this jurisdiction.

(g) *Notification to clients.* Lawyers authorized to practice law in another United States jurisdiction who provide legal services pursuant to this Rule shall inform clients in this jurisdiction of the jurisdiction in which they are authorized to practice law, any limits of that authorization, and that they are not authorized to practice law in this jurisdiction except as permitted by this Rule. They shall not state or imply to any person that they are otherwise authorized to practice law in this jurisdiction.

Comment

[1] A major disaster in this or another jurisdiction may cause an emergency affecting the justice system with respect to the provision of legal services for a sustained period of time interfering with the ability of lawyers admitted and practicing in the affected jurisdiction to continue to represent clients until the disaster has ended. When this happens, lawyers from the affected jurisdiction may need to provide legal services to their clients, on a temporary basis, from an office outside their home jurisdiction. In addition, lawyers in an unaffected jurisdiction may be willing to serve residents of the affected jurisdiction who have unmet legal needs as a result of the disaster or, though independent of the disaster, whose legal needs temporarily are unmet because of disruption to the practices of local lawyers. Lawyers from unaffected jurisdictions may offer to provide these legal services either by traveling to the affected jurisdiction or from their own offices or both, provided the legal services are provided on a *pro bono* basis through an authorized not-for-profit entity or such other organization(s) specifically designated by this Court. A major disaster includes, for example, a hurricane, earthquake, flood, wildfire, tornado, public health emergency or an event caused by terrorists or acts of war.

[2] Under paragraph (a)(*l*), this Court shall determine whether a major disaster causing an emergency affecting the justice system has occurred in this jurisdiction, or in a part of this jurisdiction, for purposes of triggering paragraph (b) of this Rule. This Court may, for example, determine that the entirety of this jurisdiction has suffered a disruption in the provision of legal services or that only certain areas have suffered such an event. The authority granted by paragraph (b) shall extend only to lawyers authorized to practice law and not disbarred, suspended from practice or otherwise restricted from practice in any other manner in any other jurisdiction.

[3] Paragraph (b) permits lawyers authorized to practice law in an unaffected jurisdiction, and not disbarred, suspended from practice or otherwise restricted from practicing law in any other manner in any

other jurisdiction, to provide pro bono legal services to residents of the affected jurisdiction following determination of an emergency caused by a major disaster; notwithstanding that they are not otherwise authorized to practice law in the affected jurisdiction. Other restrictions on a lawyer's license to practice law that would prohibit that lawyer from providing legal services pursuant to this Rule include, but are not limited to, probation, inactive status, disability inactive status or a non-disciplinary administrative suspension for failure to complete continuing legal education or other requirements. Lawyers on probation may be subject to monitoring and specific limitations on their practices. Lawyers on inactive status, despite being characterized in many jurisdictions as being "in good standing," and lawyers on disability inactive status are not permitted to practice law. Public protection warrants exclusion of these lawyers from the authority to provide legal services as defined in this Rule. Lawyers permitted to provide legal services pursuant to this Rule must do so without fee or other compensation, or expectation thereof. Their service must be provided through an established not-for-profit organization that is authorized to provide legal services either in its own name or that provides representation of clients through employed or cooperating lawyers. Alternatively, this court may instead designate other specific organization(s) through which these legal services may be rendered. Under paragraph (b), an *emeritus* lawyer from another United State jurisdiction may provide *pro bono* legal services on a temporary basis in this jurisdiction provided that the *emeritus* lawyer is authorized to provide *pro bono* legal services in that jurisdiction pursuant to that jurisdiction's *emeritus or pro bono* practice rule. Lawyers may also be authorized to provide legal services in this jurisdiction on a temporary basis under Rule 5.5(c) of the *Rules of Professional Conduct.*

[4] Lawyers authorized to practice law in another jurisdiction, who principally practice in the area of such other jurisdiction determined by this Court to have suffered a major disaster, and whose practices are disrupted by a major disaster there, and who are not disbarred, suspended from practice or otherwise restricted from practicing law in any other manner in any other jurisdiction, are authorized under paragraph (c) to provide legal services on a temporary basis in this jurisdiction. Those legal services must arise out of and be reasonably related to the lawyer's practice of law in the affected jurisdiction. For purposes of this Rule, the determination of a major disaster in another jurisdiction should first be made by the highest court of appellate jurisdiction in that jurisdiction. For the meaning of "arise out of and reasonably related to," see Rule 5.5 Comment [14], *Rules of Professional Conduct.*

[5] Emergency conditions created by major disasters end, and when they do, the authority created by paragraphs (b) and (c) also ends with appropriate notice to enable lawyers to plan and to complete pending legal matters. Under paragraph (d), this Court determines when those conditions end only for purposes of this Rule. The authority granted under paragraph (b) shall end upon such determination except that lawyers assisting residents of this jurisdiction under paragraph (b) may continue to do so for such longer period as is reasonably necessary to complete the representation. The authority created by paragraph (c) will end [60] days after this Court makes such a determination with regard to an affected jurisdiction.

[6] Paragraphs (b) and (c) do not authorize lawyers to appear in the courts of this jurisdiction. Court appearances are subject to the *pro hoc vice* admission rules of the particular court. This Court may, in a determination made under paragraph (e)(2), include authorization for lawyers who provide legal services in this jurisdiction under paragraph (b) to appear in all or designated courts of this jurisdiction without need for such *pro hoc vice* admission. If such an authorization is included, any *pro hac vice* admission fees shall be waived. A lawyer who has appeared in the courts of this jurisdiction pursuant to paragraph (e) may continue to appear in any such matter notwithstanding a declaration under paragraph (d) that the conditions created by major disaster have ended. Furthermore, withdrawal from a court appearance is subject to Rule 1.16 of the *Rules of Professional Conduct.*

[7] Authorization to practice law as a foreign legal consultant or in-house counsel in a United States jurisdiction offers lawyers a limited scope of permitted practice and may therefore restrict that person's ability to provide legal services under this Rule.

[8] The ABA National Lawyer Regulatory Data Bank is available to help determine whether any lawyer seeking to practice in this jurisdiction pursuant to paragraphs (b) or (c) of this Rule is disbarred, suspended from practice or otherwise subject to a public disciplinary sanction that would restrict the lawyer's ability to practice law in any other jurisdiction.

ABA MODEL REGULATORY OBJECTIVES FOR THE PROVISION OF LEGAL SERVICES

[In February 2016, the ABA House of Delegates approved the Model Regulatory Objectives for the Provision of Legal Services.]

A. Protection of the public

B. Advancement of the administration of justice and the rule of law

C. Meaningful access to justice and information about the law, legal issues, and the civil and criminal justice systems

D. Transparency regarding the nature and scope of legal services to be provided, the credentials of those who provide them, and the availability of regulatory protections

E. Delivery of affordable and accessible legal services

F. Efficient, competent, and ethical delivery of legal services

G. Protection of privileged and confidential information

H. Independence of professional judgment

I. Accessible civil remedies for negligence and breach of other duties owed, disciplinary sanctions for misconduct, and advancement of appropriate preventive or wellness programs

J. Diversity and inclusion among legal services providers and freedom from discrimination for those receiving legal services and in the justice system

FURTHER RESOLVED, That the American Bar Association urges that each state's highest court, and those of each territory and tribe, be guided by the ABA Model Regulatory Objectives for the Provision of Legal Services when they assess the court's existing regulatory framework and any other regulations they may choose to develop concerning non-traditional legal service providers.

FURTHER RESOLVED, that nothing contained in this Resolution abrogates in any manner existing ABA policy prohibiting non lawyer ownership of law firms or the core values adopted by the House of Delegates.

PART EIGHT

PRIOR VERSIONS OF THE ABA MODEL RULES AND THE ABA CODE OF JUDICIAL CONDUCT

TABLE OF CONTENTS

The full edition of this supplement contains the prior versions of the Model Rules and the Code of Judicial Conduct for those who wish to consult these provisions that are retained in many state ethics codes.

PART EIGHT

PRIOR VERSIONS OF THE ABA MODEL RULES AND THE ABA CODE OF JUDICIAL CONDUCT

2001 VERSION OF THE AMERICAN BAR ASSOCIATION MODEL RULES OF PROFESSIONAL CONDUCT

Annotated to Reflect Amendments and Prior Text of the Model Rules in Footnotes.

Adopted August 1983, as Amended to February 2001.

NOTE: The 2001 version has been completely replaced by the 2002 version as of February 2002.

[Less than a decade after the Model Code of Professional Responsibility was promulgated in 1969, the ABA established a commission to create another code of ethics for the legal profession. Between 1977 to 1983 the Kutak Commission, named after its chairman Robert Kutak, proceeded to write several drafts of a new code of conduct for lawyers. In 1983, the ABA enacted the Model Rules of Professional Conduct based upon the work of the Kutak Commission. The Model Rules were a response to criticisms about the Model Code's focus on litigation and its three tier structure of Canons, Ethical Considerations, and Disciplinary Rules. The Model Rules follow a UCC or restatement-like approach by placing the rule of professional responsibility in text and including elaborative material in the comments. Since its adoption in 1983, the ABA has amended the Model Rules several times, and thus this version of the Model Rules is annotated to indicate in footnotes the manner in which the ABA has amended the Model Rules since the original adoption in 1983. Ed.]

CONTENTS

2.3 Evaluation for Use by Third Persons.

ADVOCATE

3.1 Meritorious Claims and Contentions.
3.2 Expediting Litigation.
3.3 Candor Toward the Tribunal.
3.4 Fairness to Opposing Party and Counsel.
3.5 Impartiality and Decorum of the Tribunal.
3.6 Trial Publicity.
3.7 Lawyer as Witness.
3.8 Special Responsibilities of a Prosecutor.
3.9 Advocate in Nonadjudicative Proceedings.

TRANSACTIONS WITH PERSONS OTHER THAN CLIENTS

4.1 Truthfulness in Statements to Others.
4.2 Communication With Person Represented by Counsel.
4.3 Dealing With Unrepresented Person.
4.4 Respect for Rights of Third Persons.

LAW FIRMS AND ASSOCIATIONS

5.1 Responsibilities of a Partner or Supervisory Lawyer.
5.2 Responsibilities of a Subordinate Lawyer.
5.3 Responsibilities Regarding Nonlawyer Assistants.
5.4 Professional Independence of a Lawyer.
5.5 Unauthorized Practice of Law.
5.6 Restrictions on Right to Practice.
5.7 Responsibilities Regarding Law-Related Services.

PUBLIC SERVICE

6.1 Voluntary Pro Bono Publico Service.
6.2 Accepting Appointments.
6.3 Membership in Legal Services Organization.
6.4 Law Reform Activities Affecting Client Interests.

INFORMATION ABOUT LEGAL SERVICES

7.1 Communications Concerning a Lawyer's Services.
7.2 Advertising.
7.3 Direct Contact With Prospective Clients.
7.4 Communication of Fields of Practice.
7.5 Firm Names and Letterheads.
7.6 Political Contributions to Obtain Government Legal Engagements or Appointments by Judges.

MAINTAINING THE INTEGRITY OF THE PROFESSION

8.1 Bar Admission and Disciplinary Matters.
8.2 Judicial and Legal Officials.
8.3 Reporting Professional Misconduct.
8.4 Misconduct.
8.5 Disciplinary Authority; Choice of Law.

PROFESSIONAL CONDUCT

PREAMBLE, SCOPE, AND TERMINOLOGY

Preamble: A Lawyer's Responsibilities

[1] A lawyer is a representative of clients, an officer of the legal system and a public citizen having special responsibility for the quality of justice.

[2] As a representative of clients, a lawyer performs various functions. As advisor, a lawyer provides a client with an informed understanding of the client's legal rights and obligations and explains their practical implications. As advocate, a lawyer zealously asserts the client's position under the rules of the adversary system. As negotiator, a lawyer seeks a result advantageous to the client but consistent with requirements of honest dealing with others. As intermediary between clients, a lawyer seeks to reconcile their divergent interests as an advisor and, to a limited extent, as a spokesperson for each client. A lawyer acts as evaluator by examining a client's legal affairs and reporting about them to the client or to others.

[3] In all professional functions a lawyer should be competent, prompt and diligent. A lawyer should maintain communication with a client concerning the representation. A lawyer should keep in confidence information relating to representation of a client except so far as disclosure is required or permitted by the Rules of Professional Conduct or other law.

[4] A lawyer's conduct should conform to the requirements of the law, both in professional service to clients and in the lawyer's business and personal affairs. A lawyer should use the law's procedures only for legitimate purposes and not to harass or intimidate others. A lawyer should demonstrate respect for the legal system and for those who serve it, including judges, other lawyers and public officials. While it is a lawyer's duty, when necessary, to challenge the rectitude of official action, it is also a lawyer's duty to uphold legal process.

[5] As a public citizen, a lawyer should seek improvement of the law, the administration of justice and the quality of service rendered by the legal profession. As a member of a learned profession, a lawyer should cultivate knowledge of the law beyond its use for clients, employ that knowledge in reform of the law and work to strengthen legal education. A lawyer should be mindful of deficiencies in the administration of justice and of the fact that the poor, and sometimes persons who are not poor, cannot afford adequate legal assistance, and should therefore devote professional time and civic influence in their behalf. A lawyer should aid the legal profession in pursuing these objectives and should help the bar regulate itself in the public interest.

[6] Many of a lawyer's professional responsibilities are prescribed in the Rules of Professional Conduct, as well as substantive and procedural law. However, a lawyer is also guided by personal conscience and the approbation of professional peers. A lawyer should strive to attain the highest level of skill, to improve the law and the legal profession and to exemplify the legal profession's ideals of public service.

[7] A lawyer's responsibilities as a representative of clients, an officer of the legal system and a public citizen are usually harmonious. Thus, when an opposing party is well represented, a lawyer can be a zealous advocate on behalf of a client and at the same time assume that justice is being done. So also, a lawyer can be sure that preserving client confidences ordinarily serves the public interest because people are more likely to seek legal advice, and thereby heed their legal obligations, when they know their communications will be private.

[8] In the nature of law practice, however, conflicting responsibilities are encountered. Virtually all difficult ethical problems arise from conflict between a lawyer's responsibilities to clients, to the legal system and to the lawyer's own interest in remaining an upright person while earning a satisfactory living. The Rules of Professional Conduct prescribe terms for resolving such conflicts. Within the framework of these Rules many difficult issues of professional discretion can arise. Such issues must be resolved through the exercise of sensitive professional and moral judgment guided by the basic principles underlying the Rules.

[9] The legal profession is largely self-governing. Although other professions also have been granted powers of self-government, the legal profession is unique in this respect because of the close relationship between the profession and the processes of government and law enforcement. This connection is manifested in the fact that ultimate authority over the legal profession is vested largely in the courts.

[10] To the extent that lawyers meet the obligations of their professional calling, the occasion for government regulation is obviated. Self-regulation also helps maintain the legal profession's independence from government domination. An independent legal profession is an important force in preserving government under law, for abuse of legal authority is more readily challenged by a profession whose members are not dependent on government for the right to practice.

[11] The legal profession's relative autonomy carries with it special responsibilities of self-government. The profession has a responsibility to assure that its regulations are conceived in the public interest and not in furtherance of parochial or self-interested concerns of the bar. Every lawyer is responsible for observance of the Rules of Professional Conduct. A lawyer should also aid in securing their observance by other lawyers. Neglect of these responsibilities compromises the independence of the profession and the public interest which it serves.

[12] Lawyers play a vital role in the preservation of society. The fulfillment of this role requires an understanding by lawyers of their relationship to our legal system. The Rules of Professional Conduct, when properly applied, serve to define that relationship.

Scope

[1] The Rules of Professional Conduct are rules of reason. They should be interpreted with reference to the purposes of legal representation and of the law itself. Some of the Rules are imperatives, cast in the terms "shall" or "shall not." These define proper conduct for purposes of professional discipline. Others, generally cast in the term "may," are permissive and define areas under the Rules in which the lawyer has professional discretion. No disciplinary action should be taken when the lawyer chooses not to act or acts within the bounds of such discretion. Other Rules define the nature of relationships between the lawyer and others. The Rules are thus partly obligatory and disciplinary and partly constitutive and descriptive in that they define a lawyer's professional role. Many of the Comments use the term "should." Comments do not add obligations to the Rules but provide guidance for practicing in compliance with the Rules.

[2] The Rules presuppose a larger legal context shaping the lawyer's role. That context includes court rules and statutes relating to matters of licensure, laws defining specific obligations of lawyers and substantive and procedural law in general. Compliance with the Rules, as with all law in an open society, depends primarily upon understanding and voluntary compliance, secondarily upon reinforcement by peer and public opinion and finally, when necessary, upon enforcement through disciplinary proceedings. The Rules do not, however, exhaust the moral and ethical considerations that should inform a lawyer, for no worthwhile human activity can be completely defined by legal rules. The Rules simply provide a framework for the ethical practice of law.

[3] Furthermore, for purposes of determining the lawyer's authority and responsibility, principles of substantive law external to these Rules determine whether a client-lawyer relationship exists. Most of the duties flowing from the client-lawyer relationship attach only after the client has requested the lawyer to render legal services and the lawyer has agreed to do so. But there are some duties, such as that of confidentiality under Rule 1.6, that may attach when the lawyer agrees to consider whether a client-lawyer relationship shall be established. Whether a client-lawyer relationship exists for any specific purpose can depend on the circumstances and may be a question of fact.

[4] Under various legal provisions, including constitutional, statutory and common law, the responsibilities of government lawyers may include authority concerning legal matters that ordinarily reposes in the client in private client-lawyer relationships. For example, a lawyer for a government agency may have authority on behalf of the government to decide upon settlement or whether to appeal from an adverse judgment. Such authority in various respects is generally vested in the attorney general and the state's attorney in state government, and their federal counterparts, and the same may be true of other government law officers. Also, lawyers under the supervision of these officers may be authorized to represent several government agencies in intragovernmental legal controversies in circumstances where a private lawyer could not represent multiple private clients. They also may have authority to represent the "public interest" in circumstances where a private lawyer would not be authorized to do so. These Rules do not abrogate any such authority.

[5] Failure to comply with an obligation or prohibition imposed by a Rule is a basis for invoking the disciplinary process. The Rules presuppose that disciplinary assessment of a lawyer's conduct will be made

on the basis of the facts and circumstances as they existed at the time of the conduct in question and in recognition of the fact that a lawyer often has to act upon uncertain or incomplete evidence of the situation. Moreover, the Rules presuppose that whether or not discipline should be imposed for a violation, and the severity of a sanction, depend on all the circumstances, such as the willfulness and seriousness of the violation, extenuating factors and whether there have been previous violations.

[6] Violation of a Rule should not give rise to a cause of action nor should it create any presumption that a legal duty has been breached. The Rules are designed to provide guidance to lawyers and to provide a structure for regulating conduct through disciplinary agencies. They are not designed to be a basis for civil liability. Furthermore, the purpose of the Rules can be subverted when they are invoked by opposing parties as procedural weapons. The fact that a Rule is a just basis for a lawyer's self-assessment, or for sanctioning a lawyer under the administration of a disciplinary authority, does not imply that an antagonist in a collateral proceeding or transaction has standing to seek enforcement of the Rule. Accordingly, nothing in the Rules should be deemed to augment any substantive legal duty of lawyers or the extra-disciplinary consequences of violating such a duty.

[7] Moreover, these Rules are not intended to govern or affect judicial application of either the attorney-client or work product privilege. Those privileges were developed to promote compliance with law and fairness in litigation. In reliance on the attorney-client privilege, clients are entitled to expect that communications within the scope of the privilege will be protected against compelled disclosure. The attorney-client privilege is that of the client and not of the lawyer. The fact that in exceptional situations the lawyer under the Rules has a limited discretion to disclose a client confidence does not vitiate the proposition that, as a general matter, the client has a reasonable expectation that information relating to the client will not be voluntarily disclosed and that disclosure of such information may be judicially compelled only in accordance with recognized exceptions to the attorney-client and work product privileges.

[8] The lawyer's exercise of discretion not to disclose information under Rule 1.6 should not be subject to reexamination. Permitting such reexamination would be incompatible with the general policy of promoting compliance with law through assurances that communications will be protected against disclosure.

[9] The Comment accompanying each Rule explains and illustrates the meaning and purpose of the Rule. The Preamble and this note on Scope provide general orientation. The Comments are intended as guides to interpretation, but the text of each Rule is authoritative. Research notes were prepared to compare counterparts in the ABA Model Code of Professional Responsibility (adopted 1969, as amended) and to provide selected references to other authorities. The notes have not been adopted, do not constitute part of the Model Rules, and are not intended to affect the application or interpretation of the Rules and Comments.

Terminology

[1] "Belief" or "Believes" denotes that the person involved actually supposed the fact in question to be true. A person's belief may be inferred from circumstances.

[2] "Consult" or "Consultation" denotes communication of information reasonably sufficient to permit the client to appreciate the significance of the matter in question.

[3] "Firm" or "Law firm" denotes a lawyer or lawyers in a private firm, lawyers employed in the legal department of a corporation or other organization and lawyers employed in a legal services organization. See Comment, Rule 1.10.

[4] "Fraud" or "Fraudulent" denotes conduct having a purpose to deceive and not merely negligent misrepresentation or failure to apprise another of relevant information.

[5] "Knowingly," "Known," or "Knows" denotes actual knowledge of the fact in question. A person's knowledge may be inferred from circumstances.

[6] "Partner" denotes a member of a partnership and a shareholder in a law firm organized as a professional corporation.

[7] "Reasonable" or "Reasonably" when used in relation to conduct by a lawyer denotes the conduct of a reasonably prudent and competent lawyer.

[8] "Reasonable belief" or "Reasonably believes" when used in reference to a lawyer denotes that the lawyer believes the matter in question and that the circumstances are such that the belief is reasonable.

[9] "Reasonably should know" when used in reference to a lawyer denotes that a lawyer of reasonable prudence and competence would ascertain the matter in question.

[10] "Substantial" when used in reference to degree or extent denotes a material matter of clear and weighty importance.

CLIENT-LAWYER RELATIONSHIP

RULE 1.1 Competence

A Lawyer shall provide competent representation to a client. Competent representation requires the legal knowledge, skill, thoroughness and preparation reasonably necessary for the representation.

COMMENT:

Legal Knowledge and Skill

[1] In determining whether a lawyer employs the requisite knowledge and skill in a particular matter, relevant factors include the relative complexity and specialized nature of the matter, the lawyer's general experience, the lawyer's training and experience in the field in question, the preparation and study the lawyer is able to give the matter and whether it is feasible to refer the matter to, or associate or consult with, a lawyer of established competence in the field in question. In many instances, the required proficiency is that of a general practitioner. Expertise in a particular field of law may be required in some circumstances.

[2] A lawyer need not necessarily have special training or prior experience to handle legal problems of a type with which the lawyer is unfamiliar. A newly admitted lawyer can be as competent as a practitioner with long experience. Some important legal skills, such as the analysis of precedent, the evaluation of evidence and legal drafting, are required in all legal problems. Perhaps the most fundamental legal skill consists of determining what kind of legal problems a situation may involve, a skill that necessarily transcends any particular specialized knowledge. A lawyer can provide adequate representation in a wholly novel field through necessary study. Competent representation can also be provided through the association of a lawyer of established competence in the field in question.

[3] In an emergency a lawyer may give advice or assistance in a matter in which the lawyer does not have the skill ordinarily required where referral to or consultation or association with another lawyer would be impractical. Even in an emergency, however, assistance should be limited to that reasonably necessary in the circumstances, for ill considered action under emergency conditions can jeopardize the client's interest.

[4] A lawyer may accept representation where the requisite level of competence can be achieved by reasonable preparation. This applies as well to a lawyer who is appointed as counsel for an unrepresented person. See also Rule 6.2.

Thoroughness and Preparation

[5] Competent handling of a particular matter includes inquiry into and analysis of the factual and legal elements of the problem, and use of methods and procedures meeting the standards of competent practitioners. It also includes adequate preparation. The required attention and preparation are determined in part by what is at stake; major litigation and complex transactions ordinarily require more elaborate treatment than matters of lesser consequence.

Maintaining Competence

[6] To maintain the requisite knowledge and skill, a lawyer should engage in continuing study and education. If a system of peer review has been established, the lawyer should consider making use of it in appropriate circumstances.

MODEL CODE COMPARISON:

DR 6–101(A)(1) provided that a lawyer shall not handle a matter "which he knows or should know that he is not competent to handle, without associating himself with a lawyer who is competent to handle it"; DR 6–101(A)(2) requires "preparation adequate in the circumstances." Rule 1.1 more fully particularizes the elements of competence. Whereas DR 6–101(A)(3) prohibited the "[N]eglect of a legal matter," Rule 1.1 does not contain such a prohibition. Instead, Rule 1.1 affirmatively requires the lawyer to be competent.

RULE 1.2 Scope of Representation

(a) A lawyer shall abide by a client's decisions concerning the objectives of representation, subject to paragraphs (c), (d) and (e), and shall consult with the client as to the means by which they are to be pursued. A lawyer shall abide by a client's decision whether to accept an offer of settlement of a matter. In a criminal case, the lawyer shall abide by the client's decision, after consultation with the lawyer, as to a plea to be entered, whether to waive jury trial and whether the client will testify.

(b) A lawyer's representation of a client, including representation by appointment, does not constitute an endorsement of the client's political, economic, social or moral views or activities.

(c) A lawyer may limit the objectives of the representation if the client consents after consultation.

(d) A lawyer shall not counsel a client to engage, or assist a client, in conduct that the lawyer knows is criminal or fraudulent, but a lawyer may discuss the legal consequences of any proposed course of conduct with a client and may counsel or assist a client to make a good faith effort to determine the validity, scope, meaning or application of the law.

(e) When a lawyer knows that a client expects assistance not permitted by the rules of professional conduct or other law, the lawyer shall consult with the client regarding the relevant limitations on the lawyer's conduct.

COMMENT:

Scope of Representation

[1] Both lawyer and client have authority and responsibility in the objectives and means of representation. The client has ultimate authority to determine the purposes to be served by legal representation, within the limits imposed by law and the lawyer's professional obligations. Within those limits, a client also has a right to consult with the lawyer about the means to be used in pursuing those objectives. At the same time, a lawyer is not required to pursue objectives or employ means simply because a client may wish that the lawyer do so. A clear distinction between objectives and means sometimes cannot be drawn, and in many cases the client-lawyer relationship partakes of a joint undertaking. In questions of means, the lawyer should assume responsibility for technical and legal tactical issues, but should defer to the client regarding such questions as the expense to be incurred and concern for third persons who might be adversely affected. Law defining the lawyer's scope of authority in litigation varies among jurisdictions.

[2] In a case in which the client appears to be suffering mental disability, the lawyer's duty to abide by the client's decisions is to be guided by reference to Rule 1.14.

Independence from Client's Views or Activities

[3] Legal representation should not be denied to people who are unable to afford legal services, or whose cause is controversial or the subject of popular disapproval. By the same token, representing a client does not constitute approval of the client's views or activities.

Services Limited in Objectives or Means

[4] The objectives or scope of services provided by a lawyer may be limited by agreement with the client or by the terms under which the lawyer's services are made available to the client. For example, a retainer may be for a specifically defined purpose. Representation provided through a legal aid agency may

be subject to limitations on the types of cases the agency handles. When a lawyer has been retained by an insurer to represent an insured, the representation may be limited to matters related to the insurance coverage. The terms upon which representation is undertaken may exclude specific objectives or means. Such limitations may exclude objectives or means that the lawyer regards as repugnant or imprudent.

[5] An agreement concerning the scope of representation must accord with the Rules of Professional Conduct and other law. Thus, the client may not be asked to agree to representation so limited in scope as to violate Rule 1.1, or to surrender the right to terminate the lawyer's services or the right to settle litigation that the lawyer might wish to continue.

Criminal, Fraudulent and Prohibited Transactions

[6] A lawyer is required to give an honest opinion about the actual consequences that appear likely to result from a client's conduct. The fact that a client uses advice in a course of action that is criminal or fraudulent does not, of itself, make a lawyer a party to the course of action. However, a lawyer may not knowingly assist a client in criminal or fraudulent conduct. There is a critical distinction between presenting an analysis of legal aspects of questionable conduct and recommending the means by which a crime or fraud might be committed with impunity.

[7] When the client's course of action has already begun and is continuing, the lawyer's responsibility is especially delicate. The lawyer is not permitted to reveal the client's wrongdoing, except where permitted by Rule 1.6. However, the lawyer is required to avoid furthering the purpose, for example, by suggesting how it might be concealed. A lawyer may not continue assisting a client in conduct that the lawyer originally supposes is legally proper but then discovers is criminal or fraudulent. Withdrawal from the representation, therefore, may be required.

[8] Where the client is a fiduciary, the lawyer may be charged with special obligations in dealings with a beneficiary.

[9] Paragraph (d) applies whether or not the defrauded party is a party to the transaction. Hence, a lawyer should not participate in a sham transaction; for example, a transaction to effectuate criminal or fraudulent escape of tax liability. Paragraph (d) does not preclude undertaking a criminal defense incident to a general retainer for legal services to a lawful enterprise. The last clause of paragraph (d) recognizes that determining the validity or interpretation of a statute or regulation may require a course of action involving disobedience of the statute or regulation or of the interpretation placed upon it by governmental authorities.

MODEL CODE COMPARISON:

Paragraph (a) has no counterpart in the Disciplinary Rules of the Model Code. EC 7–7 stated: "In certain areas of legal representation not affecting the merits of the cause or substantially prejudicing the rights of a client, a lawyer is entitled to make decisions on his own. But otherwise the authority to make decisions is exclusively that of the client. . . ." EC 7–8 stated that "[I]n the final analysis, however, the . . . decision whether to forego legally available objectives or methods because of nonlegal factors is ultimately for the client. . . . In the event that the client in a nonadjudicatory matter insists upon a course of conduct that is contrary to the judgment and advice of the lawyer but not prohibited by Disciplinary Rules, the lawyer may withdraw from the employment." DR 7–101(A)(1) provided that a lawyer "shall not intentionally . . . fail to seek the lawful objectives of his client through reasonably available means permitted by law. . . . A lawyer does not violate this Disciplinary Rule, however, by . . . avoiding offensive tactics. . . ."

Paragraph (b) has no counterpart in the Model Code.

With regard to paragraph (c), DR 7–101(B)(1) provided that a lawyer may, "where permissible, exercise his professional judgment to waive or fail to assert a right or position of his client."

With regard to paragraph (d), DR 7–102(A)(7) provided that a lawyer shall not "counsel or assist his client in conduct that the lawyer knows to be illegal or fraudulent." DR 7–102(A)(6) provided that a lawyer shall not "participate in the creation or preservation of evidence when he knows or it is obvious that the evidence is false." DR 7–106 provided that a lawyer shall not "advise his client to disregard a standing rule of a tribunal or a ruling of a tribunal . . . but he may take appropriate steps in good faith to test the validity of such rule or ruling." EC 7–5 stated that a lawyer "should never encourage or aid his client to commit criminal acts or counsel his client on how to violate the law and avoid punishment therefor."

With regard to Rule 1.2(e), DR 2–110(C)(1)(c) provided that a lawyer may withdraw from representation if a client "insists" that the lawyer engage in "conduct that is illegal or that is prohibited under the Disciplinary Rules." DR 9–101(C) provided that "a lawyer shall not state or imply that he is able to influence improperly . . . any tribunal, legislative body or public official."

RULE 1.3 Diligence

A lawyer shall act with reasonable diligence and promptness in representing a client.

COMMENT:

[1] A lawyer should pursue a matter on behalf of a client despite opposition, obstruction or personal inconvenience to the lawyer, and may take whatever lawful and ethical measures are required to vindicate a client's cause or endeavor. A lawyer should act with commitment and dedication to the interests of the client and with zeal in advocacy upon the client's behalf. However, a lawyer is not bound to press for every advantage that might be realized for a client. A lawyer has professional discretion in determining the means by which a matter should be pursued. See Rule 1.2. A lawyer's workload should be controlled so that each matter can be handled adequately.

[2] Perhaps no professional shortcoming is more widely resented than procrastination. A client's interests often can be adversely affected by the passage of time or the change of conditions; in extreme instances, as when a lawyer overlooks a statute of limitations, the client's legal position may be destroyed. Even when the client's interests are not affected in substance, however, unreasonable delay can cause a client needless anxiety and undermine confidence in the lawyer's trustworthiness.

[3] Unless the relationship is terminated as provided in Rule 1.16, a lawyer should carry through to conclusion all matters undertaken for a client. If a lawyer's employment is limited to a specific matter, the relationship terminates when the matter has been resolved. If a lawyer has served a client over a substantial period in a variety of matters, the client sometimes may assume that the lawyer will continue to serve on a continuing basis unless the lawyer gives notice of withdrawal. Doubt about whether a client-lawyer relationship still exists should be clarified by the lawyer, preferably in writing, so that the client will not mistakenly suppose the lawyer is looking after the client's affairs when the lawyer has ceased to do so. For example, if a lawyer has handled a judicial or administrative proceeding that produced a result adverse to the client but has not been specifically instructed concerning pursuit of an appeal, the lawyer should advise the client of the possibility of appeal before relinquishing responsibility for the matter.

MODEL CODE COMPARISON:

DR 6–101(A)(3) required that a lawyer not "[n]eglect a legal matter entrusted to him." EC 6–4 stated that a lawyer should "give appropriate attention to his legal work." Canon 7 stated that "a lawyer should represent a client zealously within the bounds of the law." DR 7–101(A)(1) provided that a lawyer "shall not intentionally . . . fail to seek the lawful objectives of his client through reasonably available means permitted by law and the Disciplinary Rules. . . ." DR 7–101(A)(3) provided that a lawyer "shall not intentionally . . . [p]rejudice or damage his client during the course of the relationship. . . ."

RULE 1.4 Communication

(a) A lawyer shall keep a client reasonably informed about the status of a matter and promptly comply with reasonable requests for information.

(b) A lawyer shall explain a matter to the extent reasonably necessary to permit the client to make informed decisions regarding the representation.

COMMENT:

[1] The client should have sufficient information to participate intelligently in decisions concerning the objectives of the representation and the means by which they are to be pursued, to the extent the client is willing and able to do so. For example, a lawyer negotiating on behalf of a client should provide the client with facts relevant to the matter, inform the client of communications from another party and take other reasonable steps that permit the client to make a decision regarding a serious offer from another party. A lawyer who receives from opposing counsel an offer of settlement in a civil controversy or a proffered plea

bargain in a criminal case should promptly inform the client of its substance unless prior discussions with the client have left it clear that the proposal will be unacceptable. See Rule 1.2(a). Even when a client delegates authority to the lawyer, the client should be kept advised of the status of the matter.

[2] Adequacy of communication depends in part on the kind of advice or assistance involved. For example, in negotiations where there is time to explain a proposal the lawyer should review all important provisions with the client before proceeding to an agreement. In litigation a lawyer should explain the general strategy and prospects of success and ordinarily should consult the client on tactics that might injure or coerce others. On the other hand, a lawyer ordinarily cannot be expected to describe trial or negotiation strategy in detail. The guiding principle is that the lawyer should fulfill reasonable client expectations for information consistent with the duty to act in the client's best interests, and the client's overall requirements as to the character of representation.

[3] Ordinarily, the information to be provided is that appropriate for a client who is a comprehending and responsible adult. However, fully informing the client according to this standard may be impracticable, for example, where the client is a child or suffers from mental disability. See Rule 1.14. When the client is an organization or group, it is often impossible or inappropriate to inform every one of its members about its legal affairs; ordinarily, the lawyer should address communications to the appropriate officials of the organization. See Rule 1.13. Where many routine matters are involved, a system of limited or occasional reporting may be arranged with the client. Practical exigency may also require a lawyer to act for a client without prior consultation.

Withholding Information

[4] In some circumstances, a lawyer may be justified in delaying transmission of information when the client would be likely to react imprudently to an immediate communication. Thus, a lawyer might withhold a psychiatric diagnosis of a client when the examining psychiatrist indicates that disclosure would harm the client. A lawyer may not withhold information to serve the lawyer's own interest or convenience. Rules or court orders governing litigation may provide that information supplied to a lawyer may not be disclosed to the client. Rule 3.4(c) directs compliance with such rules or orders.

MODEL CODE COMPARISON:

Rule 1.4 has no direct counterpart in the Disciplinary Rules of the Model Code. DR 6–101(A)(3) provided that a lawyer shall not "[n]eglect a legal matter entrusted to him." DR 9–102(B)(1) provided that a lawyer shall "[p]romptly notify a client of the receipt of his funds, securities, or other properties." EC 7–8 stated that a lawyer "should exert his best efforts to insure that decisions of his client are made only after the client has been informed of relevant considerations." EC 9–2 stated that "a lawyer should fully and promptly inform his client of material developments in the matters being handled for the client."

RULE 1.5 Fees

(a) A lawyer's fee shall be reasonable. The factors to be considered in determining the reasonableness of a fee include the following:

(1) the time and labor required, the novelty and difficulty of the questions involved, and the skill requisite to perform the legal service properly;

(2) the likelihood, if apparent to the client, that the acceptance of the particular employment will preclude other employment by the lawyer;

(3) the fee customarily charged in the locality for similar legal services;

(4) the amount involved and the results obtained;

(5) the time limitations imposed by the client or by the circumstances;

(6) the nature and length of the professional relationship with the client;

(7) the experience, reputation, and ability of the lawyer or lawyers performing the services; and

(8) whether the fee is fixed or contingent.

(b) When the lawyer has not regularly represented the client, the basis or rate of the fee shall be communicated to the client, preferably in writing, before or within a reasonable time after commencing the representation.

(c) A fee may be contingent on the outcome of the matter for which the service is rendered, except in a matter in which a contingent fee is prohibited by paragraph (d) or other law. A contingent fee agreement shall be in writing and shall state the method by which the fee is to be determined, including the percentage or percentages that shall accrue to the lawyer in the event of settlement, trial or appeal, litigation and other expenses to be deducted from the recovery, and whether such expenses are to be deducted before or after the contingent fee is calculated. Upon conclusion of a contingent fee matter, the lawyer shall provide the client with a written statement stating the outcome of the matter and, if there is a recovery, showing the remittance to the client and the method of its determination.

(d) A lawyer shall not enter into an arrangement for, charge, or collect:

(1) any fee in a domestic relations matter, the payment or amount of which is contingent upon the securing of a divorce or upon the amount of alimony or support, or property settlement in lieu thereof; or

(2) a contingent fee for representing a defendant in a criminal case.

(e) A division of fee between lawyers who are not in the same firm may be made only if:

(1) the division is in proportion to the services performed by each lawyer or, by written agreement with the client, each lawyer assumes joint responsibility for the representation;

(2) the client is advised of and does not object to the participation of all the lawyers involved; and

(3) the total fee is reasonable.

COMMENT:

Basis or Rate of Fee

[1] When the lawyer has regularly represented a client, they ordinarily will have evolved an understanding concerning the basis or rate of the fee. In a new client-lawyer relationship, however, an understanding as to the fee should be promptly established. It is not necessary to recite all the factors that underlie the basis of the fee, but only those that are directly involved in its computation. It is sufficient, for example, to state that the basic rate is an hourly charge or a fixed amount or an estimated amount, or to identify the factors that may be taken into account in finally fixing the fee. When developments occur during the representation that render an earlier estimate substantially inaccurate, a revised estimate should be provided to the client. A written statement concerning the fee reduces the possibility of misunderstanding. Furnishing the client with a simple memorandum or a copy of the lawyer's customary fee schedule is sufficient if the basis or rate of the fee is set forth.

Terms of Payment

[2] A lawyer may require advance payment of a fee, but is obliged to return any unearned portion. See Rule 1.16(d). A lawyer may accept property in payment for services, such as an ownership interest in an enterprise, providing this does not involve acquisition of a proprietary interest in the cause of action or subject matter of the litigation contrary to Rule 1.8(j).* However, a fee paid in property instead of money may be subject to special scrutiny because it involves questions concerning both the value of the services and the lawyer's special knowledge of the value of the property.

---

* In 1987, the ABA added the following clause to the 1983 version of the Model Rules: "providing this does not involve acquisition of a proprietary interest in the cause of action or subject matter of the litigation contrary to Rule 1.8(j)."

[3] An agreement may not be made whose terms might induce the lawyer improperly to curtail services for the client or perform them in a way contrary to the client's interest. For example, a lawyer should not enter into an agreement whereby services are to be provided only up to a stated amount when it is foreseeable that more extensive services probably will be required, unless the situation is adequately explained to the client. Otherwise, the client might have to bargain for further assistance in the midst of a proceeding or transaction. However, it is proper to define the extent of services in light of the client's ability to pay. A lawyer should not exploit a fee arrangement based primarily on hourly charges by using wasteful procedures. When there is doubt whether a contingent fee is consistent with the client's best interest, the lawyer should offer the client alternative bases for the fee and explain their implications. Applicable law may impose limitations on contingent fees, such as a ceiling on the percentage.

Division of Fee

[4] A division of fee is a single billing to a client covering the fee of two or more lawyers who are not in the same firm. A division of fee facilitates association of more than one lawyer in a matter in which neither alone could serve the client as well, and most often is used when the fee is contingent and the division is between a referring lawyer and a trial specialist. Paragraph (e) permits the lawyers to divide a fee on either the basis of the proportion of services they render or by agreement between the participating lawyers if all assume responsibility for the representation as a whole and the client is advised and does not object. It does not require disclosure to the client of the share that each lawyer is to receive. Joint responsibility for the representation entails the obligations stated in Rule 5.1 for purposes of the matter involved.

Disputes Over Fees

[5] If a procedure has been established for resolution of fee disputes, such as an arbitration or mediation procedure established by the bar, the lawyer should conscientiously consider submitting to it. Law may prescribe a procedure for determining a lawyer's fee, for example, in representation of an executor or administrator, a class or a person entitled to a reasonable fee as part of the measure of damages. The lawyer entitled to such a fee and a lawyer representing another party concerned with the fee should comply with the prescribed procedure.

MODEL CODE COMPARISON:

DR 2–106(A) provided that a lawyer "shall not enter into an agreement for, charge, or collect an illegal or clearly excessive fee." DR 2–106(B) provided that a fee is "clearly excessive when, after a review of the facts, a lawyer of ordinary prudence would be left with a definite and firm conviction that the fee is in excess of a reasonable fee." The factors of a reasonable fee in Rule 1.5(a) are substantially identical to those listed in DR 2–106(B). EC 2–17 states that a lawyer "should not charge more than a reasonable fee. . . ."

There was no counterpart to Rule 1.5(b) in the Disciplinary Rules of the Model Code. EC 2–19 stated that it is "usually beneficial to reduce to writing the understanding of the parties regarding the fee, particularly when it is contingent."

There was no counterpart to paragraph (c) in the Disciplinary Rules of the Model Code. EC 2–20 provided that "[c]ontingent fee arrangements in civil cases have long been commonly accepted in the United States," but that "a lawyer generally should decline to accept employment on a contingent fee basis by one who is able to pay a reasonable fixed fee. . . ."

With regard to paragraph (d), DR 2–106(C) prohibited "a contingent fee in a criminal case." EC 2–20 provided that "contingent fee arrangements in domestic relation cases are rarely justified."

With regard to paragraph (e), DR 2–107(A) permitted division of fees only if: "(1) The client consents to employment of the other lawyer after a full disclosure that a division of fees will be made. (2) The division is in proportion to the services performed and responsibility assumed by each. (3) The total fee does not exceed clearly reasonable compensation. . . ." Paragraph (e) permits division without regard to the services rendered by each lawyer if they assume joint responsibility for the representation.

RULE 1.6 Confidentiality of Information*

(a) A lawyer shall not reveal information relating to representation of a client unless the client consents after consultation, except for disclosures that are impliedly authorized in order to carry out the representation, and except as stated in paragraph (b).

(b) A lawyer may reveal such information to the extent the lawyer reasonably believes necessary:

(1) to prevent the client from committing a criminal act that the lawyer believes is likely to result in imminent death or substantial bodily harm; or

(2) to establish a claim or defense on behalf of the lawyer in a controversy between the lawyer and the client, to establish a defense to a criminal charge or civil claim against the lawyer based upon conduct in which the client was involved, or to respond to allegations in any proceeding concerning the lawyer's representation of the client.

COMMENT:

[1] The lawyer is part of a judicial system charged with upholding the law. One of the lawyer's functions is to advise clients so that they avoid any violation of the law in the proper exercise of their rights.

[2] The observance of the ethical obligation of a lawyer to hold inviolate confidential information of the client not only facilitates the full development of facts essential to proper representation of the client but also encourages people to seek early legal assistance.

[3] Almost without exception, clients come to lawyers in order to determine what their rights are and what is, in the maze of laws and regulations, deemed to be legal and correct. The common law recognizes that the client's confidences must be protected from disclosure. Based upon experience, lawyers know that almost all clients follow the advice given, and the law is upheld.

[4] A fundamental principle in the client-lawyer relationship is that the lawyer maintain confidentiality of information relating to the representation. The client is thereby encouraged to communicate fully and frankly with the lawyer even as to embarrassing or legally damaging subject matter.

[5] The principle of confidentiality is given effect in two related bodies of law, the attorney-client privilege (which includes the work product doctrine) in the law of evidence and the rule of confidentiality established in professional ethics. The attorney-client privilege applies in judicial and other proceedings in which a lawyer may be called as a witness or otherwise required to produce evidence concerning a client. The rule of client-lawyer confidentiality applies in situations other than those where evidence is sought from the lawyer through compulsion of law. The confidentiality rule applies not merely to matters communicated in confidence by the client but also to all information relating to the representation, whatever its source. A lawyer may not disclose such information except as authorized or required by the Rules of Professional Conduct or other law. See also Scope.

---

* In 1991, The ABA House of Delegates rejected the ethics committee recommendation that it modify Model Rule 1.6. The rejected language would have inserted the following exception to the general rule of confidentiality under Model Rule 1.6(b): "to rectify the consequences of a client's criminal or fraudulent act in the furtherance of which the lawyer's services had been used." This language is identical to an exception listed in the Kutak Commission's 1982 Final Revised Draft of Model Rule 1.6. The proposed Kutak Rule 1.6(b) would have contained the following exceptions:

(1) to prevent the client from committing a criminal or fraudulent act that the lawyer reasonably believes is likely to result in death or substantial bodily harm, or in substantial injury to the financial interests or property of another;

(2) to rectify the consequences of a client's criminal or fraudulent act in the furtherance of which the lawyer's financial services had been used;

(3) to establish a claim or defense on behalf of the lawyer in a controversy between the lawyer and the client, or to establish a defense to a criminal charge, civil claim or disciplinary complaint against the lawyer based upon conduct in which the client was involved; or

(4) to comply with other law.

Proposed Model Rule 1.6(b) (Revised Final Draft) (June 20, 1982).

[6] The requirement of maintaining confidentiality of information relating to representation applies to government lawyers who may disagree with the policy goals that their representation is designed to advance.

Authorized Disclosure

[7] A lawyer is impliedly authorized to make disclosures about a client when appropriate in carrying out the representation, except to the extent that the client's instructions or special circumstances limit that authority. In litigation, for example, a lawyer may disclose information by admitting a fact that cannot properly be disputed, or in negotiation by making a disclosure that facilitates a satisfactory conclusion.

[8] Lawyers in a firm may, in the course of the firm's practice, disclose to each other information relating to a client of the firm, unless the client has instructed that particular information be confined to specified lawyers.

Disclosure Adverse to Client

[9] The confidentiality rule is subject to limited exceptions. In becoming privy to information about a client, a lawyer may foresee that the client intends serious harm to another person. However, to the extent a lawyer is required or permitted to disclose a client's purposes, the client will be inhibited from revealing facts which would enable the lawyer to counsel against a wrongful course of action. The public is better protected if full and open communication by the client is encouraged than if it is inhibited.

Several situations must be distinguished.

[10] First, the lawyer may not counsel or assist a client in conduct that is criminal or fraudulent. See Rule 1.2(d). Similarly, a lawyer has a duty under Rule 3.3(a)(4) not to use false evidence. This duty is essentially a special instance of the duty prescribed in Rule 1.2(d) to avoid assisting a client in criminal or fraudulent conduct.

[11] Second, the lawyer may have been innocently involved in past conduct by the client that was criminal or fraudulent. In such a situation the lawyer has not violated Rule 1.2(d), because to "counsel or assist" criminal or fraudulent conduct requires knowing that the conduct is of that character.

[12] Third, the lawyer may learn that a client intends prospective conduct that is criminal and likely to result in imminent death or substantial bodily harm. As stated in paragraph (b)(1), the lawyer has professional discretion to reveal information in order to prevent such consequences. The lawyer may make a disclosure in order to prevent homicide or serious bodily injury which the lawyer reasonable believes is intended by a client. It is very difficult for a lawyer to "know" when such a heinous purpose will actually be carried out, for the client may have a change of mind.

[13] The lawyer's exercise of discretion requires consideration of such factors as the nature of the lawyer's relationship with the client and with those who might be injured by the client, the lawyer's own involvement in the transaction and factors that may extenuate the conduct in question. Where practical, the lawyer should seek to persuade the client to take suitable action. In any case, a disclosure adverse to the client's interest should be no greater than the lawyer reasonably believes necessary to the purpose. A lawyer's decision not to take preventive action permitted by paragraph (b)(1) does not violate this Rule.

Withdrawal

[14] If the lawyer's services will be used by the client in materially furthering a course of criminal or fraudulent conduct, the lawyer must withdraw, as stated in Rule 1.16(a)(1).

[15] After withdrawal the lawyer is required to refrain from making disclosure of the clients' confidences, except as otherwise provided in Rule 1.6. Neither this Rule nor Rule 1.8(b) nor Rule 1.16(d) prevents the lawyer from giving notice of the fact of withdrawal, and the lawyer may also withdraw or disaffirm any opinion, document, affirmation, or the like.

[16] Where the client is an organization, the lawyer may be in doubt whether contemplated conduct will actually be carried out by the organization. Where necessary to guide conduct in connection with this Rule, the lawyer may make inquiry within the organization as indicated in Rule 1.13(b).

Dispute Concerning Lawyer's Conduct

[17] Where a legal claim or disciplinary charge alleges complicity of the lawyer in a client's conduct or other misconduct of the lawyer involving representation of the client, the lawyer may respond to the extent the lawyer reasonably believes necessary to establish a defense. The same is true with respect to a claim involving the conduct or representation of a former client. The lawyer's right to respond arises when an assertion of such complicity has been made. Paragraph (b)(2) does not require the lawyer to await the commencement of an action or proceeding that charges such complicity, so that the defense may be established by responding directly to a third party who has made such an assertion. The right to defend, of course, applies where a proceeding has been commenced. Where practicable and not prejudicial to the lawyer's ability to establish the defense, the lawyer should advise the client of the third party's assertion and request that the client respond appropriately. In any event, disclosure should be no greater than the lawyer reasonably believes is necessary to vindicate innocence, the disclosure should be made in a manner which limits access to the information to the tribunal or other persons having a need to know it, and appropriate protective orders or other arrangements should be sought by the lawyer to the fullest extent practicable.

[18] If the lawyer is charged with wrongdoing in which the client's conduct is implicated, the rule of confidentiality should not prevent the lawyer from defending against the charge. Such a charge can arise in a civil, criminal or professional disciplinary proceeding, and can be based on a wrong allegedly committed by the lawyer against the client, or on a wrong alleged by a third person; for example, a person claiming to have been defrauded by the lawyer and client acting together. A lawyer entitled to a fee is permitted by paragraph (b)(2) to prove the services rendered in an action to collect it. This aspect of the rule expresses the principle that the beneficiary of a fiduciary relationship may not exploit it to the detriment of the fiduciary. As stated above, the lawyer must make every effort practicable to avoid unnecessary disclosure of information relating to a representation, to limit disclosure to those having the need to know it, and to obtain protective orders or make other arrangements minimizing the risk of disclosure.

Disclosures Otherwise Required or Authorized

[19] The attorney-client privilege is differently defined in various jurisdictions. If a lawyer is called as a witness to give testimony concerning a client, absent waiver by the client, Rule 1.6(a) requires the lawyer to invoke the privilege when it is applicable. The lawyer must comply with the final orders of a court or other tribunal of competent jurisdiction requiring the lawyer to give information about the client.

[20] The Rules of Professional Conduct in various circumstances permit or require a lawyer to disclose information relating to the representation. See Rules 2.2, 2.3, 3.3 and 4.1. In addition to these provisions, a lawyer may be obligated or permitted by other provisions of law to give information about a client. Whether another provision of law supersedes Rule 1.6 is a matter of interpretation beyond the scope of these Rules, but a presumption should exist against such a supersession.

Former Client

[21] The duty of confidentiality continues after the client-lawyer relationship has terminated.

MODEL CODE COMPARISON:

Rule 1.6 eliminates the two-pronged duty under the Model Code in favor of a single standard protecting all information about a client "relating to the representation." Under DR 4–101, the requirement applied only to information protected by the attorney-client privilege and to information "gained in" the professional relationship that "the client has requested be held inviolate or the disclosure of which would be embarrassing or would be likely to be detrimental to the client." EC 4–4 added that the duty differed from the evidentiary privilege in that it existed "without regard to the nature or source of information or the fact that others share the knowledge." Rule 1.6 imposes confidentiality on information relating to the representation even if it is acquired before or after the relationship existed. It does not require the client to indicate information that is to be confidential, or permit the lawyer to speculate whether particular information might be embarrassing or detrimental.

Paragraph (a) permits a lawyer to disclose information where impliedly authorized to do so in order to carry out the representation. Under DR 4–101(B) and (C), a lawyer was not permitted to reveal "confidences" unless the client first consented after disclosure.

Paragraph (b) redefines the exceptions to the requirement of confidentiality. Regarding paragraph (b)(1), DR 4–101(C)(3) provided that a lawyer "may reveal . . . [t]he intention of his client to commit a crime and the information necessary to prevent the crime." This option existed regardless of the seriousness of the proposed crime.

With regard to paragraph (b)(2), DR 4–101(C)(4) provided that a lawyer may reveal "[c]onfidences or secrets necessary to establish or collect his fee or to defend himself or his employers or associates against an accusation of wrongful conduct." Paragraph (b)(2) enlarges the exception to include disclosure of information relating to claims by the lawyer other than for the lawyer's fee; for example, recovery of property from the client.

RULE 1.7 Conflict of Interest: General Rule

(a) A lawyer shall not represent a client if the representation of that client will be directly adverse to another client, unless:

(1) the lawyer reasonably believes the representation will not adversely affect the relationship with the other client; and

(2) each client consents after consultation.

(b) A lawyer shall not represent a client if the representation of that client may be materially limited by the lawyer's responsibilities to another client or to a third person, or by the lawyer's own interests, unless:

(1) the lawyer reasonably believes the representation will not be adversely affected; and

(2) the client consents after consultation. When representation of multiple clients in a single matter is undertaken, the consultation shall include explanation of the implications of the common representation and the advantages and risks involved.

COMMENT:

Loyalty to a Client

[1] Loyalty is an essential element in the lawyer's relationship to a client. An impermissible conflict of interest may exist before representation is undertaken, in which event the representation should be declined. The lawyer should adopt reasonable procedures, appropriate for the size and type of firm and practice, to determine in both litigation and non-litigation matters the parties and issues involved and to determine whether there are actual or potential conflicts of interest.*

[2] If such a conflict arises after representation has been undertaken, the lawyer should withdraw from the representation. See Rule 1.16. Where more than one client is involved and the lawyer withdraws because a conflict arises after representation, whether the lawyer may continue to represent any of the clients is determined by Rule 1.9. See also Rule 2.2(c). As to whether a client-lawyer relationship exists or, having once been established, is continuing, see Comment to Rule 1.3 and Scope.

[3] As a general proposition, loyalty to a client prohibits undertaking representation directly adverse to that client without that client's consent. Paragraph (a) expresses that general rule. Thus, a lawyer ordinarily may not act as advocate against a person the lawyer represents in some other matter, even if it is wholly unrelated. On the other hand, simultaneous representation in unrelated matters of clients whose interests are only generally adverse, such as competing economic enterprises, does not require consent of the respective clients. Paragraph (a) applies only when the representation of one client would be directly adverse to the other.

[4] Loyalty to a client is also impaired when a lawyer cannot consider, recommend or carry out an appropriate course of action for the client because of the lawyer's other responsibilities or interests. The conflict in effect forecloses alternatives that would otherwise be available to the client. Paragraph (b)

---

* The ABA added this sentence in the comments to the Model Rules in 1987. The remainder of paragraph 1 in the original version of this comment now appears in the current paragraph 2.

addresses such situations. A possible conflict does not itself preclude the representation. The critical questions are the likelihood that a conflict will eventuate and, if it does, whether it will materially interfere with the lawyer's independent professional judgment in considering alternatives or foreclose courses of action that reasonably should be pursued on behalf of the client. Consideration should be given to whether the client wishes to accommodate the other interest involved.

Consultation and Consent

[5] A client may consent to representation notwithstanding a conflict. However, as indicated in paragraph (a)(1) with respect to representation directly adverse to a client, and paragraph (b)(1) with respect to material limitations on representation of a client, when a disinterested lawyer would conclude that the client should not agree to the representation under the circumstances, the lawyer involved cannot properly ask for such agreement or provide representation on the basis of the client's consent. When more than once client is involved, the question of conflict must be resolved as to each client. Moreover, there may be circumstances where it is impossible to make the disclosure necessary to obtain consent. For example, when the lawyer represents different clients in related matters and one of the clients refuses to consent to the disclosure necessary to permit the other client to make an informed decision, the lawyer cannot properly ask the latter to consent.

Lawyer's Interests

[6] The lawyer's own interests should not be permitted to have adverse effect on representation of a client. For example, a lawyer's need for income should not lead the lawyer to undertake matters that cannot be handled competently and at a reasonable fee. See Rules 1.1 and 1.5. If the probity of a lawyer's own conduct in a transaction is in serious question, it may be difficult or impossible for the lawyer to give a client detached advice. A lawyer may not allow related business interests to affect representation, for example, by referring clients to an enterprise in which the lawyer has an undisclosed interest.

Conflicts in Litigation

[7] Paragraph (a) prohibits representation of opposing parties in litigation. Simultaneous representation of parties whose interests in litigation may conflict, such as co-plaintiffs or co-defendants, is governed by paragraph (b). An impermissible conflict may exist by reason of substantial discrepancy in the parties' testimony, incompatibility in positions in relation to an opposing party or the fact that there are substantially different possibilities of settlement of the claims or liabilities in question. Such conflicts can arise in criminal cases as well as civil. The potential for conflict of interest in representing multiple defendants in a criminal case is so grave that ordinarily a lawyer should decline to represent more than one codefendant. On the other hand, common representation of persons having similar interests is proper if the risk of adverse effect is minimal and the requirements of paragraph (b) are met. Compare Rule 2.2 involving intermediation between clients.

[8] Ordinarily, a lawyer may not act as advocate against a client the lawyer represents in some other matter, even if the other matter is wholly unrelated. However, there are circumstances in which a lawyer may act as advocate against a client. For example, a lawyer representing an enterprise with diverse operations may accept employment as an advocate against the enterprise in an unrelated matter if doing so will not adversely affect the lawyer's relationship with the enterprise or conduct of the suit and if both clients consent upon consultation. By the same token, government lawyers in some circumstances may represent government employees in proceedings in which a government agency is the opposing party. The propriety of concurrent representation can depend on the nature of the litigation. For example, a suit charging fraud entails conflict to a degree not involved in a suit for a declaratory judgment concerning statutory interpretation.

[9] A lawyer may represent parties having antagonistic positions on a legal question that has arisen in different cases, unless representation of either client would be adversely affected. Thus, it is ordinarily not improper to assert such positions in cases pending in different trial courts, but it may be improper to do so in cases pending at the same time in an appellate court.

Interest of Person Paying for a Lawyer's Service

[10] A lawyer may be paid from a source other than the client, if the client is informed of that fact and consents and the arrangement does not compromise the lawyer's duty of loyalty to the client. See Rule 1.8(f).

For example, when an insurer and its insured have conflicting interests in a matter arising from a liability insurance agreement, and the insurer is required to provide special counsel for the insured, the arrangement should assure the special counsel's professional independence. So also, when a corporation and its directors or employees are involved in a controversy in which they have conflicting interests, the corporation may provide funds for separate legal representation of the directors or employees, if the clients consent after consultation and the arrangement ensures the lawyer's professional independence.

Other Conflict Situations

[11] Conflicts of interest in contexts other than litigation sometimes may be difficult to assess. Relevant factors in determining whether there is potential for adverse effect include the duration and intimacy of the lawyer's relationship with the client or clients involved, the functions being performed by the lawyer, the likelihood that actual conflict will arise and the likely prejudice to the client from the conflict if it does arise. The question is often one of proximity and degree.

[12] For example, a lawyer may not represent multiple parties to a negotiation whose interests are fundamentally antagonistic to each other, but common representation is permissible where the clients are generally aligned in interest even though there is some difference of interest among them.

[13] Conflict questions may also arise in estate planning and estate administration. A lawyer may be called upon to prepare wills for several family members, such as husband and wife, and, depending upon the circumstances, a conflict of interest may arise. In estate administration the identity of the client may be unclear under the law of a particular jurisdiction. Under one view, the client is the fiduciary; under another view the client is the estate or trust, including its beneficiaries. The lawyer should make clear the relationship to the parties involved.

[14] A lawyer for a corporation or other organization who is also a member of its board of directors should determine whether the responsibilities of the two roles may conflict. The lawyer may be called on to advise the corporation in matters involving actions of the directors. Consideration should be given to the frequency with which such situations may arise, the potential intensity of the conflict, the effect of the lawyer's resignation from the board and the possibility of the corporation's obtaining legal advice from another lawyer in such situations. If there is material risk that the dual role will compromise the lawyer's independence of professional judgment, the lawyer should not serve as a director.

Conflict Charged by an Opposing Party

[15] Resolving questions of conflict of interest is primarily the responsibility of the lawyer undertaking the representation. In litigation, a court may raise the question when there is reason to infer that the lawyer has neglected the responsibility. In a criminal case, inquiry by the court is generally required when a lawyer represents multiple defendants. Where the conflict is such as clearly to call in question the fair or efficient administration of justice, opposing counsel may properly raise the question. Such an objection should be viewed with caution, however, for it can be misused as a technique of harassment. See Scope.

MODEL CODE COMPARISON:

DR 5–101(A) provided that "[e]xcept with the consent of his client after full disclosure, a lawyer shall not accept employment if the exercise of his professional judgment on behalf of the client will be or reasonably may be affected by his own financial, business, property, or personal interests." DR 5–105(A) provided that a lawyer "shall decline proffered employment if the exercise of his independent professional judgment in behalf of a client will be or is likely to be adversely affected by the acceptance of the proffered employment, or if it would be likely to involve him in representing differing interests, except to the extent permitted under DR 5–105(C)." DR 5–105(C) provided that "a lawyer may represent multiple clients if it is obvious that he can adequately represent the interest of each and if each consents to the representation after full disclosure of the possible effect of such representation on the exercise of his independent professional judgment on behalf of each." DR 5–107(B) provided that a lawyer "shall not permit a person who recommends, employs, or pays him to render legal services for another to direct or regulate his professional judgment in rendering such services."

Rule 1.7 clarifies DR 5–105(A) by requiring that, when the lawyer's other interests are involved, not only must the client consent after consultation but also that, independent of such consent, the representation reasonably appears not to be adversely affected by the lawyer's other interests. This requirement appears to be the intended meaning of the provision in DR 5–105(C) that "it is obvious that he can adequately represent" the client, and was implicit in EC 5–2, which stated that a lawyer "should not accept proffered employment if his personal interests or desires will, or there is a reasonable probability that they will, affect adversely the advice to be given or services to be rendered the prospective client."

RULE 1.8 Conflict of Interest: Prohibited Transactions

(a) A lawyer shall not enter into a business transaction with a client or knowingly acquire an ownership, possessory, security or other pecuniary interest adverse to a client unless:

(1) the transaction and terms on which the lawyer acquires the interest are fair and reasonable to the client and are fully disclosed and transmitted in writing to the client in a manner which can be reasonably understood by the client;

(2) the client is given a reasonable opportunity to seek the advice of independent counsel in the transaction; and

(3) the client consents in writing thereto.

(b) A lawyer shall not use information relating to representation of a client to the disadvantage of the client unless the client consents after consultation, except as permitted or required by Rule 1.6 or Rule 3.3.

(c) A lawyer shall not prepare an instrument giving the lawyer or a person related to the lawyer as parent, child, sibling, or spouse any substantial gift from a client, including a testamentary gift, except where the client is related to the donee.

(d) Prior to the conclusion of representation of a client, a lawyer shall not make or negotiate an agreement giving the lawyer literary or media rights to a portrayal or account based in substantial part on information relating to the representation.

(e) A lawyer shall not provide financial assistance to a client in connection with pending or contemplated litigation, except that:

(1) a lawyer may advance court costs and expenses of litigation, the repayment of which may be contingent on the outcome of the matter; and

(2) a lawyer representing an indigent client may pay court costs and expenses of litigation on behalf of the client.

(f) A lawyer shall not accept compensation for representing a client from one other than the client unless:

(1) the client consents after consultation;

(2) there is no interference with the lawyer's independence of professional judgment or with the client-lawyer relationship; and

(3) Information relating to representation of a client is protected as required by rule 1.6.

(g) A lawyer who represents two or more clients shall not participate in making an aggregate settlement of the claims of or against the clients, or in a criminal case an aggregated agreement as to guilty or nolo contendere pleas, unless each client consents after consultation, including disclosure of the existence and nature of all the claims or pleas involved and of the participation of each person in the settlement.

(h) A lawyer shall not make an agreement prospectively limiting the lawyer's liability to a client for malpractice unless permitted by law and the client is independently represented in making the agreement, or settle a claim for such liability with an

unrepresented client or former client without first advising that person in writing that independent representation is appropriate in connection therewith.

(i) A lawyer related to another lawyer as parent, child, sibling or spouse shall not represent a client in a representation directly adverse to a person who the lawyer knows is represented by the other lawyer except upon consent by the client after consultation regarding the relationship.

(j) A lawyer shall not acquire a proprietary interest in the cause of action or subject matter of litigation the lawyer is conducting for a client, except that the lawyer may:

(1) acquire a lien granted by law to secure the lawyer's fee or expenses; and

(2) contract with a client for a reasonable contingent fee in a civil case.

COMMENT:

Transactions Between Client and Lawyer

[1] As a general principle, all transactions between client and lawyer should be fair and reasonable to the client. In such transactions a review by independent counsel on behalf of the client is often advisable. Furthermore, a lawyer may not exploit information relating to the representation to the client's disadvantage. For example, a lawyer who has learned that the client is investing in specific real estate may not, without the client's consent, seek to acquire nearby property where doing so would adversely affect the client's plan for investment. Paragraph (a) does not, however, apply to standard commercial transactions between the lawyer and the client for products or services that the client generally markets to others, for example, banking or brokerage services, medical services, products manufactured or distributed by the client, and utilities services. In such transactions, the lawyer has no advantage in dealing with the client, and the restrictions in paragraph (a) are unnecessary and impracticable.

[2] A lawyer may accept a gift from a client, if the transaction meets general standards of fairness. For example, a simple gift such as a present given at a holiday or as a token of appreciation is permitted. If effectuation of a substantial gift requires preparing a legal instrument such as a will or conveyance, however, the client should have the detached advice that another lawyer can provide. Paragraph (c) recognizes an exception where the client is a relative of the donee or the gift is not substantial.

Literary Rights

[3] An agreement by which a lawyer acquires literary or media rights concerning the conduct of the representation creates a conflict between the interests of the client and the personal interests of the lawyer. Measures suitable in the representation of the client may detract from the publication value of an account of the representation. Paragraph (d) does not prohibit a lawyer representing a client in a transaction concerning literary property from agreeing that the lawyer's fee shall consist of a share in ownership in the property, if the arrangement conforms to Rule 1.5 and paragraph (j).

Person Paying for Lawyer's Services

[4] Rule 1.8(f) requires disclosure of the fact that the lawyer's services are being paid for by a third party. Such an arrangement must also conform to the requirements of Rule 1.6 concerning confidentiality and Rule 1.7 concerning conflict of interest. Where the client is a class, consent may be obtained on behalf of the class by court-supervised procedure.

Family Relationships Between Lawyers

[5] Rule 1.8(i) applies to related lawyers who are in different firms. Related lawyers in the same firm are governed by Rules 1.7, 1.9, and 1.10. The disqualification stated in Rule 1.8(i) is personal and is not imputed to members of firms with whom the lawyers are associated.

Acquisition of Interest in Litigation

[6] Paragraph (j) states the traditional general rule that lawyers are prohibited from acquiring a proprietary interest in litigation. This general rule, which has its basis in common law champerty and maintenance, is subject to specific exceptions developed in decisional law and continued in these Rules, such

as the exception for reasonable contingent fees set forth in Rule 1.5 and the exception for certain advances of the costs of litigation set forth in paragraph (e).

[7] This Rule is not intended to apply to customary qualification and limitations in legal opinions and memoranda.

MODEL CODE COMPARISON:

With regard to paragraph (a), DR 5–104(A) provided that a lawyer "shall not enter into a business transaction with a client if they have differing interests therein and if the client expects the lawyer to exercise his professional judgment therein for the protection of the client, unless the client has consented after full disclosure." EC 5–3 stated that a lawyer "should not seek to persuade his client to permit him to invest in an undertaking of his client nor make improper use of his professional relationship to influence his client to invest in an enterprise in which the lawyer is interested."

With regard to paragraph (b), DR 4–101(B)(3) provided that a lawyer should not use "a confidence or secret of his client for the advantage of himself, or of a third person, unless the client consents after full disclosure."

There was no counterpart to paragraph (c) in the Disciplinary Rules of the Model Code. EC 5–5 stated that a lawyer "should not suggest to his client that a gift be made to himself or for his benefit. If a lawyer accepts a gift from his client, he is peculiarly susceptible to the charge that he unduly influenced or overreached the client. If a client voluntarily offers to make a gift to his lawyer, the lawyer may accept the gift, but before doing so, he should urge that the client secure disinterested advice from an independent, competent person who is cognizant of all the circumstances. Other than in exceptional circumstances, a lawyer should insist that an instrument in which his client desires to name him beneficially be prepared by another lawyer selected by the client."

Paragraph (d) is substantially similar to DR 5–104(B), but refers to "literary or media" rights, a more generally inclusive term than "publication" rights.

Paragraph (e)(1) is similar to DR 5–103(B), but eliminates the requirement that "the client remains ultimately liable for such expenses."

Paragraph (e)(2) has no counterpart in the Model Code.

Paragraph (f) is substantially identical to DR 5–107(A)(1).

Paragraph (g) is substantially identical to DR 5–106.

The first clause of paragraph (h) is similar to DR 6–102(A). There was no counterpart in the Model Code to the second clause of paragraph (h).

Paragraph (i) has no counterpart in the Model Code.

Paragraph (j) is substantially identical to DR 5–103(A).

RULE 1.9 Conflict of Interest: Former Client*

(a) A lawyer who has formerly represented a client in a matter shall not thereafter represent another person in the same or a substantially related matter in which that

* In 1989, the ABA amended Model Rule 1.9 by moving some of the text in original Model Rule 1.10(b) into current Model Rule 1.9(b). The original Model Rule 1.9(b) was moved to Model Rule 1.9(c). The impetus behind this change was to clarify an overlap between Model Rule 1.9 and 1.10 and to address the question of duties to former clients when a lawyer changes firms and did not represent the former client but may have acquired confidential information about a former client of the old firm. The following represents Model Rule 1.9 as adopted in 1983:

RULE 1.9 Conflict of Interest: Former Client

A Lawyer who has formerly represented a client in a matter shall not thereafter:

(a) Represent another person in the same or a substantially related matter in which that person's interests are materially adverse to the interests of the former client unless the former client consents after consultation; or

(b) Use information relating to the representation to the disadvantage of the former client except as Rule 1.6 would permit with respect to a client or when the information has become generally known.

person's interests are materially adverse to the interests of the former client unless the former client consents after consultation.

(b) A lawyer shall not knowingly represent a person in the same or a substantially related matter in which a firm with which the lawyer formerly was associated had previously represented a client,

(1) whose interests are materially adverse to that person; and

(2) about whom the lawyer had acquired information protected by Rules 1.6 and 1.9(c) that is material to the matter;

unless the former client consents after consultation.

(c) A lawyer who has formerly represented a client in a matter or whose present or former firm has formerly represented a client in a matter shall not thereafter:

(1) use information relating to the representation to the disadvantage of the former client except as Rule 1.6 or Rule 3.3 would permit or require with respect to a client, or when the information has become generally known; or

(2) reveal information relating to the representation except as Rule 1.6 or Rule 3.3 would permit or require with respect to a client.

COMMENT:

[1] After termination of a client-lawyer relationship, a lawyer may not represent another client except in conformity with this Rule. The principles in Rule 1.7 determine whether the interests of the present and former client are adverse. Thus, a lawyer could not properly seek to rescind on behalf of a new client a contract drafted on behalf of the former client. So also a lawyer who has prosecuted an accused person could not properly represent the accused in a subsequent civil action against the government concerning the same transaction.

[2] The scope of a "matter" for purposes of this Rule may depend on the facts of a particular situation or transaction. The lawyer's involvement in a matter can also be a question of degree. When a lawyer has been directly involved in a specific transaction, subsequent representation of other clients with materially adverse interests clearly is prohibited. On the other hand, a lawyer who recurrently handled a type of problem for a former client is not precluded from later representing another client in a wholly distinct problem of that type even though the subsequent representation involves a position adverse to the prior client. Similar considerations can apply to the reassignment of military lawyers between defense and prosecution functions within the same military jurisdiction. The underlying question is whether the lawyer was so involved in the matter that the subsequent representation can be justly regarded as a changing of sides in the matter in question.

*Lawyers Moving Between Firms**

[3] When lawyers have been associated within a firm but then end their association, the question of whether a lawyer should undertake representation is more complicated. There are several competing considerations. First, the client previously represented by the former firm must be reasonably assured that the principle of loyalty to the client is not compromised. Second, the rule should not be so broadly cast as to preclude other persons from having reasonable choice of legal counsel. Third, the rule should not unreasonably hamper lawyers from forming new associations and taking on new clients after having left a previous association. In this connection, it should be recognized that today many lawyers practice in firms, that many lawyers to some degree limit their practice to one field or another, and that many move from one association to another several times in their careers. If the concept of imputation were applied with unqualified rigor, the result would be radical curtailment of the opportunity of lawyers to move from one practice setting to another and of the opportunity of clients to change counsel.

* The comments under this topic originally appeared under Model Rule 1.10. With the modification of Model Rule 1.9, the ABA moved these comments under Model Rule 1.9 without significant change.

[4] Reconciliation of these competing principles in the past has been attempted under two rubrics. One approach has been to seek per se rules of disqualification. For example, it has been held that a partner in a law firm is conclusively presumed to have access to all confidences concerning all clients of the firm. Under this analysis, if a lawyer has been a partner in one law firm and then becomes a partner in another law firm, there may be a presumption that all confidences known by the partner in the first firm are known to all partners in the second firm. This presumption might properly be applied in some circumstances, especially where the client has been extensively represented, but may be unrealistic where the client was represented only for limited purposes. Furthermore, such a rigid rule exaggerates the difference between a partner and an associate in modern law firms.

[5] The other rubric formerly used for dealing with disqualification is the appearance of impropriety proscribed in Canon 9 of the ABA Model Code of Professional Responsibility. This rubric has a two fold problem. First, the appearance of impropriety can be taken to include any new client-lawyer relationship that might make a former client feel anxious. If that meaning were adopted, disqualification would become little more than a question of subjective judgment by the former client. Second, since "impropriety" is undefined, the term "appearance of impropriety" is question-begging. It therefore has to be recognized that the problem of disqualification cannot be properly resolved either by simple analogy to a lawyer practicing alone or by the very general concept of appearance of impropriety.

*Confidentiality**

[6] Preserving confidentiality is a question of access to information. Access to information, in turn, is essentially a question of fact in particular circumstances, aided by inferences, deductions or working presumptions that reasonably may be made about the way in which lawyers work together. A lawyer may have general access to files of all clients of a law firm and may regularly participate in discussions of their affairs; it should be inferred that such a lawyer in fact is privy to all information about all the firm's clients. In contrast, another lawyer may have access to the files of only a limited number of clients and participate in discussions of the affairs of no other clients; in the absence of information to the contrary, it should be inferred that such a lawyer in fact is privy to information about the clients actually served but not those of other clients.

[7] Application of paragraph (b) depends on a situation's particular facts. In such an inquiry, the burden of proof should rest upon the firm whose disqualification is sought.

[8] Paragraph (b) operates to disqualify the lawyer only when the lawyer involved has actual knowledge of information protected by Rules 1.6 and 1.9(b). Thus, if a lawyer while with one firm acquired no knowledge or information relating to a particular client of the firm, and that lawyer later joined another firm, neither the lawyer individually nor the second firm is disqualified from representing another client in the same or a related matter even though the interests of the two clients conflict. See Rule 1.10(b) for the restrictions on a firm once a lawyer has terminated association with the firm.

[9] Independent of the question of disqualification of a firm, a lawyer changing professional association has a continuing duty to preserve confidentiality of information about a client formerly represented. See Rules 1.6 and 1.9.

*Adverse Positions**

[10] The second aspect of loyalty to a client is the lawyer's obligation to decline subsequent representations involving positions adverse to a former client arising in substantially related matters. This obligation requires abstention from adverse representation by the individual lawyer involved, but does not properly entail abstention of other lawyers through imputed disqualification. Hence, this aspect of the problem is governed by Rule 1.9(a). Thus, if a lawyer left one firm for another, the new affiliation would not preclude the firms involved from continuing to represent clients with adverse interests in the same or related matters, so long as the conditions of paragraphs (b) and (c) concerning confidentiality have been met.

[11] Information acquired by the lawyer in the course of representing a client may not subsequently be used or revealed by the lawyer to the disadvantage of the client. However, the fact that a lawyer has once

* The comments under this topic originally appeared under Model Rule 1.10. With the modification of Model Rule 1.9, the ABA moved these comments under Model Rule 1.9 without significant change.

served a client does not preclude the lawyer from using generally known information about that client when later representing another client.

[12] Disqualification from subsequent representation is for the protection of former clients and can be waived by them. A waiver is effective only if there is disclosure of the circumstances, including the lawyer's intended role in behalf of the new client.

[13] With regard to an opposing party's raising a question of conflict of interest, see Comment to Rule 1.7. With regard to disqualification of a firm with which a lawyer is or was formerly associated, see Rule 1.10.

MODEL CODE COMPARISON:*

There was no counterpart to this Rule in the Disciplinary Rules of the Model Code. Representation adverse to a former client was sometimes dealt with under the rubric of Canon 9 of the Model Code, which provided: "A lawyer should avoid even the appearance of impropriety." Also applicable were EC 4–6 which stated that the "obligation of a lawyer to preserve the confidences and secrets of his client continues after the termination of his employment" and Canon 5 which stated that "[a] lawyer should exercise independent professional judgment on behalf of a client."

The provision in paragraph (a) for waiver by the former client is similar to DR 5–105(C).

The exception in the last clause of paragraph (c)(1) permits a lawyer to use information relating to a former client that is in the "public domain," a use that was also not prohibited by the Model Code, which protected only "confidences and secrets." Since the scope of paragraph (a) is much broader than "confidences and secrets," it is necessary to define when a lawyer may make use of information about a client after the client-lawyer relationship has terminated.

RULE 1.10 Imputed Disqualification: General Rule**

(a) While lawyers are associated in a firm, none of them shall knowingly represent a client when any one of them practicing alone would be prohibited from doing so by Rules 1.7, 1.8(c), 1.9 or 2.2.

---

* When ABA modified Model Rule 1.9 in 1989, it did not change the text of the Model Code Comparison. Thus, the current Model Code Comparison only refers to the Model Rule 1.9 as originally enacted. To understand the amended Model Rule 1.9, one must read the following text quoted from the Code Comparison to Model Rule 1.10: "DR 5–105(D) provided that '[i]f a lawyer is required to decline or to withdraw from employment under a Disciplinary Rule, no partner, or associate, or any other lawyer affiliated with him or his firm, may accept or continue such employment.' "

** In 1989, the ABA amended Model Rule 1.10 to remove original Rule 1.10(b) and move it to Model Rule 1.9(b). The ABA thus renumbered original Model Rule 1.10(c) and 1.10(d) as new Model Rule 1.10(b) and 1.10(c). The impetus behind this change was to clarify an overlap between Model Rule 1.9 and 1.10 and to address the question of duties to former clients when a lawyer changes firms and did not represent the former client but may have acquired confidential information about a former client of the old firm. Also, the ABA added the words "and, not currently represented by the firm" to current Model Rule 1.10(b). This was added to clarify the problem that when a lawyer leaves a firm, Model Rule 1.7's general prohibition of a directly adverse conflict still applies to the situation. The original version of Model Rule 1.10 is reproduced below:

RULE 1.10 Imputed Disqualification: General Rule

(a) While lawyers are associated in a firm, none of them shall knowingly represent a client when any one of them practicing alone would be prohibited from doing so by Rules 1.7, 1.8(c), 1.9 or 2.2.

(b) When a lawyer becomes associated with a firm, the firm may not knowingly represent a person in the same or a substantially related matter in which that lawyer, or a firm with which the lawyer was associated, had previously represented a client whose interests are materially adverse to that person and about whom the lawyer had acquired information protected by Rules 1.6 and 1.9(b) that is material to the matter.

(c) When a lawyer has terminated an association with a firm, the firm is not prohibited from thereafter representing a person with interests materially adverse to those of a client represented by the formerly associated lawyer unless:

(1) the matter is the same or substantially related to that in which the formerly associated lawyer represented the client; and

(2) any lawyer remaining in the firm has information protected by Rules 1.6 and 1.9(b) that is material to the matter.

(b) When a lawyer has terminated an association with a firm, the firm is not prohibited from thereafter representing a person with interests materially adverse to those of a client represented by the formerly associated lawyer and not currently represented by the firm, unless:

(1) the matter is the same or substantially related to that in which the formerly associated lawyer represented the client; and

(2) any lawyer remaining in the firm has information protected by Rules 1.6 and 1.9(c) that is material to the matter.

(c) A disqualification prescribed by this rule may be waived by the affected client under the conditions stated in Rule 1.7.

COMMENT:*

Definition of "Firm"

[1] For purposes of the Rules of Professional Conduct, the term "firm" includes lawyers in a private firm, and lawyers in the legal department of a corporation or other organization, or in a legal services

---

(d) A disqualification prescribed by this rule may be waived by the affected client under the conditions stated in Rule 1.7.

* When the ABA amended Model Rule 1.10 in 1989, it moved several paragraphs of comments from Model Rule 1.10 to Model Rule 1.9. The paragraphs which appeared in the original version of the Model Rules are reproduced below:

Lawyers Moving Between Firms

When lawyers have been associated in a firm but then end their association, however, the problem is more complicated. The fiction that the law firm is the same as a single lawyer is no longer wholly realistic. There are several competing considerations. First, the client previously represented must be reasonably assured that the principle of loyalty to the client is not compromised. Second, the rule of disqualification should not be so broadly cast as to preclude other persons from having reasonable choice of legal counsel. Third, the rule of disqualification should not unreasonably hamper lawyers from forming new associations and taking on new clients after having left a previous association. In this connection, it should be recognized that today many lawyers practice in firms, that many to some degree limit their practice to one field or another, and that many move from one association to another several times in their careers. If the concept of imputed disqualification were defined with unqualified rigor, the result would be radical curtailment of the opportunity of lawyers to move from one practice setting to another and of the opportunity of clients to change counsel.

Reconciliation of these competing principles in the past has been attempted under two rubrics. One approach has been to seek per se rules of disqualification. For example, it has been held that a partner in a law firm is conclusively presumed to have access to all confidences concerning all clients of the firm. Under this analysis, if a lawyer has been a partner in one law firm and then becomes a partner in another law firm, there is a presumption that all confidences known by a partner in the first firm are known to all partners in the second firm. This presumption might properly be applied in some circumstances, especially where the client has been extensively represented, but may be unrealistic where the client was represented only for limited purposes. Furthermore, such a rigid rule exaggerates the difference between a partner and an associate in modern law firms.

The other rubric formerly used for dealing with vicarious disqualification is the appearance of impropriety proscribed in Canon 9 of the ABA Model Code of Professional Responsibility. This rubric has a twofold problem. First, the appearance of impropriety can be taken to include any new client-lawyer relationship that might make a former client feel anxious. If that meaning were adopted, disqualification would become little more than a question of subjective judgment by the former client. Second, since "impropriety" is undefined, the term "appearance of impropriety" is question-begging. It therefore has to be recognized that the problem of imputed disqualification cannot be properly resolved either by simple analogy to a lawyer practicing alone or by the very general concept of appearance of impropriety.

A rule based on a functional analysis is more appropriate for determining the question of vicarious disqualification. Two functions are involved: preserving confidentiality and avoiding positions adverse to a client.

Confidentiality

Preserving confidentiality is a question of access to information. Access to information, in turn, is essentially a question of fact in particular circumstances, aided by inferences, deductions or working presumptions that reasonably may be made about the way in which lawyers work together. A lawyer may have general access to files of all clients of a law firm and may regularly participate in discussions of their affairs; it should be inferred that such a lawyer in fact is privy to all information about all the firm's clients. In contrast, another lawyer may have access to the files of only a limited number of clients and participate in discussion of the affairs of no other clients; in the

organization. Whether two or more lawyers constitute a firm within this definition can depend on the specific facts. For example, two practitioners who share office space and occasionally consult or assist each other ordinarily would not be regarded as constituting a firm. However, if they present themselves to the public in a way suggesting that they are a firm or conduct themselves as a firm, they should be regarded as a firm for the purposes of the Rules. The terms of any formal agreement between associated lawyers are relevant in determining whether they are a firm, as is the fact that they have mutual access to information concerning the clients they serve. Furthermore, it is relevant in doubtful cases to consider the underlying purpose of the Rule that is involved. A group of lawyers could be regarded as a firm for purposes of the rule that the same lawyer should not represent opposing parties in litigation, while it might not be so regarded for purposes of the rule that information acquired by one lawyer is attributed to the other.

[2] With respect to the law department of an organization, there is ordinarily no question that the members of the department constitute a firm within the meaning of the Rules of Professional Conduct. However, there can be uncertainty as to the identity of the client. For example, it may not be clear whether the law department of a corporation represents a subsidiary or an affiliated corporation, as well as the corporation by which the members of the department are directly employed. A similar question can arise concerning an unincorporated association and its local affiliates.

[3] Similar questions can also arise with respect to lawyers in legal aid. Lawyers employed in the same unit of a legal service organization constitute a firm, but not necessarily those employed in separate units. As in the case of independent practitioners, whether the lawyers should be treated as associated with each other can depend on the particular rule that is involved, and on the specific facts of the situation.

[4] Where a lawyer has joined a private firm after having represented the government, the situation is governed by Rule 1.11(a) and (b); where a lawyer represents the government after having served private clients, the situation is governed by Rule 1.11(c)(1). The individual lawyer involved is bound by the Rules generally, including Rules 1.6, 1.7 and 1.9.

[5] Different provisions are thus made for movement of a lawyer from one private firm to another and for movement of a lawyer between a private firm and the government. The government is entitled to protection of its client confidences and, therefore, to the protections provided in Rules 1.6, 1.9 and 1.11. However, if the more extensive disqualification in Rule 1.10 were applied to former government lawyers, the potential effect on the government would be unduly burdensome. The government deals with all private citizens and organizations and, thus, has a much wider circle of adverse legal interests than does any private law firm. In these circumstances, the government's recruitment of lawyers would be seriously impaired if Rule 1.10 were applied to the government. On balance, therefore, the government is better served in the long run by the protections stated in Rule 1.11.

---

absence of information to the contrary, it should be inferred that such a lawyer in fact is privy to information about the clients actually served but not those of other clients.

Application of paragraphs (b) and (c) depends on a situation's particular facts. In any such inquiry, the burden of proof should rest upon the firm whose disqualification is sought.

Paragraphs (b) and (c) operate to disqualify the firm only when the lawyer involved has actual knowledge of information protected by Rules 1.6 and 1.9(b). Thus, if a lawyer while with one firm acquired no knowledge of information relating to a particular client of the firm, and that lawyer later joined another firm, neither the lawyer individually nor the second firm is disqualified from representing another client in the same or a related matter even though the interests of the two clients conflict.

Independent of the question of disqualification of a firm, a lawyer changing professional association has a continuing duty to preserve confidentiality of information about a client formerly represented. See Rules 1.6 and 1.9.

Adverse Positions

The second aspect of loyalty to client is the lawyer's obligation to decline subsequent representations involving positions adverse to a former client arising in substantially related matters. This obligation requires abstention from adverse representation by the individual lawyer involved, but does not properly entail abstention of other lawyers through imputed disqualification. Hence, this aspect of the problem is governed by Rule 1.9(a). Thus, if a lawyer left one firm for another, the new affiliation would not preclude the firms involved from continuing to represent clients with adverse interests in the same or related matters, so long as the conditions of Rule 1.10(b) and (c) concerning confidentiality have been met.

Principles of Imputed Disqualification

[6] The rule of imputed disqualification stated in paragraph (a) gives effect to the principle of loyalty to the client as it applies to lawyers who practice in a law firm. Such situations can be considered from the premise that a firm of lawyers is essentially one lawyer for purposes of the rules governing loyalty to the client, or from the premise that each lawyer is vicariously bound by the obligation of loyalty owed by each lawyer with whom the lawyer is associated. Paragraph (a) operates only among the lawyers currently associated in a firm. When a lawyer moves from one firm to another, the situation is governed by Rules 1.9(b) and 1.10(b).

[7]* Rule 1.10(b) operates to permit a law firm, under certain circumstances, to represent a person with interests directly adverse to those of a client represented by a lawyer who formerly was associated with the firm. The Rule applies regardless of when the formerly associated lawyer represented the client. However, the law firm may not represent a person with interests adverse to those of a present client of the firm, which would violate Rule 1.7. Moreover, the firm may not represent the person where the matter is the same or substantially related to that in which the formerly associated lawyer represented the client and any other lawyer currently in the firm has material information protected by Rules 1.6 and 1.9(c).

MODEL CODE COMPARISON:

DR 5–105(D) provided that "[i]f a lawyer is required to decline or to withdraw from employment under a Disciplinary Rule, no partner, or associate, or any other lawyer affiliated with him or his firm, may accept or continue such employment."

RULE 1.11 Successive Government and Private Employment

(a) Except as law may otherwise expressly permit, a lawyer shall not represent a private client in connection with a matter in which the lawyer participated personally and substantially as a public officer or employee, unless the appropriate government agency consents after consultation. No lawyer in a firm with which that lawyer is associated may knowingly undertake or continue representation in such a matter unless:

(1) the disqualified lawyer is screened from any participation in the matter and is apportioned no part of the fee therefrom; and

(2) written notice is promptly given to the appropriate government agency to enable it to ascertain compliance with the provisions of this rule.

(b) Except as law may otherwise expressly permit, a lawyer having information that the lawyer knows is confidential government information about a person acquired when the lawyer was a public officer or employee, may not represent a private client whose interests are adverse to that person in a matter in which the information could be used to the material disadvantage of that person. A firm with which that lawyer is associated may undertake or continue representation in the matter only if the disqualified lawyer is screened from any participation in the matter and is apportioned no part of the fee therefrom.

(c) Except as law may otherwise expressly permit, a lawyer serving as a public officer or employee shall not:

(1) participate in a matter in which the lawyer participated personally and substantially while in private practice or nongovernmental employment, unless under applicable law no one is, or by lawful delegation may be, authorized to act in the lawyer's stead in the matter; or

(2) negotiate for private employment with any person who is involved as a party or as attorney for a party in a matter in which the lawyer is participating personally and substantially, except that a lawyer serving as a law clerk to a judge, other

* The ABA added this entire paragraph to the comments to Model Rule 1.10 in 1989. Thus, this language does not appear in the original version of the Model Rules.

adjudicative officer or arbitrator may negotiate for private employment as permitted by Rule 1.12(b) and subject to the conditions stated in Rule 1.12(b).

(d) As used in this rule, the term "matter" includes:

(1) any judicial or other proceeding, application, request for a ruling or other determination, contract, claim, controversy, investigation, charge, accusation, arrest or other particular matter involving a specific party or parties; and

(2) any other matter covered by the conflict of interest rules of the appropriate government agency.

(e) As used in this rule, the term "confidential government information" means information which has been obtained under governmental authority and which, at the time this rule is applied, the government is prohibited by law from disclosing to the public or has a legal privilege not to disclose, and which is not otherwise available to the public.

COMMENT:

[1] This Rule prevents a lawyer from exploiting public office for the advantage of a private client. It is a counterpart of Rule 1.10(b), which applies to lawyers moving from one firm to another.

[2] A lawyer representing a government agency, whether employed or specially retained by the government, is subject to the Rules of Professional Conduct, including the prohibition against representing adverse interests stated in Rule 1.7 and the protections afforded former clients in Rule 1.9. In addition, such a lawyer is subject to Rule 1.11 and to statutes and government regulations regarding conflict of interest. Such statutes and regulations may circumscribe the extent to which the government agency may give consent under this Rule.

[3] Where the successive clients are a public agency and a private client, the risk exists that power or discretion vested in public authority might be used for the special benefit of a private client. A lawyer should not be in a position where benefit to a private client might affect performance of the lawyer's professional functions on behalf of public authority. Also, unfair advantage could accrue to the private client by reason of access to confidential government information about the client's adversary obtainable only through the lawyer's government service. However, the rules governing lawyers presently or formerly employed by a government agency should not be so restrictive as to inhibit transfer of employment to and from the government. The government has a legitimate need to attract qualified lawyers as well as to maintain high ethical standards. The provisions for screening and waiver are necessary to prevent the disqualification rule from imposing too severe a deterrent against entering public service.

[4] When the client is an agency of one government, that agency should be treated as a private client for purposes of this Rule if the lawyer thereafter represents an agency of another government, as when a lawyer represents a city and subsequently is employed by a federal agency.

[5] Paragraphs (a)(1) and (b) do not prohibit a lawyer from receiving a salary or partnership share established by prior independent agreement. They prohibit directly relating the attorney's compensation to the fee in the matter in which the lawyer is disqualified.

[6] Paragraph (a)(2) does not require that a lawyer give notice to the government agency at a time when premature disclosure would injure the client; a requirement for premature disclosure might preclude engagement of the lawyer. Such notice is, however, required to be given as soon as practicable in order that the government agency will have a reasonable opportunity to ascertain that the lawyer is complying with Rule 1.11 and to take appropriate action if it believes the lawyer is not complying.

[7] Paragraph (b) operates only when the lawyer in question has knowledge of the information, which means actual knowledge; it does not operate with respect to information that merely could be imputed to the lawyer.

[8] Paragraphs (a) and (c) do not prohibit a lawyer from jointly representing a private party and a government agency when doing so is permitted by Rule 1.7 and is not otherwise prohibited by law.

[9] Paragraph (c) does not disqualify other lawyers in the agency with which the lawyer in question has become associated.

MODEL CODE COMPARISON:

Paragraph (a) is similar to DR 9–101(B), except that the latter used the terms "in which he had substantial responsibility while he was a public employee."

Paragraphs (b), (c), (d) and (e) have no counterparts in the Model Code.

RULE 1.12 Former Judge or Arbitrator

(a) Except as stated in paragraph (d), a lawyer shall not represent anyone in connection with a matter in which the lawyer participated personally and substantially as a judge or other adjudicative officer, arbitrator or law clerk to such a person, unless all parties to the proceeding consent after consultation.

(b) A lawyer shall not negotiate for employment with any person who is involved as a party or as attorney for a party in a matter in which the lawyer is participating personally and substantially as a judge or other adjudicative officer, or arbitrator. A lawyer serving as a law clerk to a judge, other adjudicative officer or arbitrator may negotiate for employment with a party or attorney involved in a matter in which the clerk is participating personally and substantially, but only after the lawyer has notified the judge, other adjudicative officer or arbitrator.

(c) If a lawyer is disqualified by paragraph (a), no lawyer in a firm with which that lawyer is associated may knowingly undertake or continue representation in the matter unless:

(1) the disqualified lawyer is screened from any participation in the matter and is apportioned no part of the fee therefrom; and

(2) written notice is promptly given to the appropriate tribunal to enable it to ascertain compliance with the provisions of this rule.

(d) An arbitrator selected as a partisan of a party in a multi-member arbitration panel is not prohibited from subsequently representing that party.

COMMENT:

This Rule generally parallels Rule 1.11. The term "personally and substantially" signifies that a judge who was a member of a multi-member court, and thereafter left judicial office to practice law, is not prohibited from representing a client in a matter pending in the court, but in which the former judge did not participate. So also the fact that a former judge exercised administrative responsibility in a court does not prevent the former judge from acting as a lawyer in a matter where the judge had previously exercised remote or incidental administrative responsibility that did not affect the merits. Compare the Comment to Rule 1.11. The term "adjudicative officer" includes such officials as judges pro tempore, referees, special masters, hearing officers and other parajudicial officers, and also lawyers who serve as part-time judges. Compliance Canons A(2), B(2) and C of the Model Code of Judicial Conduct provide that a part-time judge, judge pro tempore or retired judge recalled to active service, may not "act as a lawyer in any proceeding in which he served as a judge or in any other proceeding related thereto." Although phrased differently from this Rule, those Rules correspond in meaning.

MODEL CODE COMPARISON:

Paragraph (a) is substantially similar to DR 9–101(A), which provided that a lawyer "shall not accept private employment in a matter upon the merits of which he has acted in a judicial capacity." Paragraph (a) differs, however, in that it is broader in scope and states more specifically the persons to whom it applies. There was no counterpart in the Model Code to paragraphs (b), (c) or (d).

With regard to arbitrators, EC 5–20 stated that "a lawyer [who] has undertaken to act as an impartial arbitrator or mediator, . . . should not thereafter represent in the dispute any of the parties involved." DR 9–101(A) did not permit a waiver of the disqualification applied to former judges by consent of the parties. However, DR 5–105(C) was similar in effect and could be construed to permit waiver.

RULE 1.13 Organization as Client*

(a) A lawyer employed or retained by an organization represents the organization acting through its duly authorized constituents.

(b) If a lawyer for an organization knows that an officer, employee or other person associated with the organization is engaged in action, intends to act or refuses to act in a matter related to the representation that is a violation of a legal obligation to the organization, or a violation of law which reasonably might be imputed to the organization, and is likely to result in substantial injury to the organization, the lawyer shall proceed as is reasonably necessary in the best interest of the organization. In determining how to proceed, the lawyer shall give due consideration to the seriousness of the violation and its consequences, the scope and nature of the lawyer's representation, the responsibility in the organization and the apparent motivation of the person involved, the policies of the organization concerning such matters and any other relevant considerations. Any measures taken shall be designed to minimize disruption of the organization and the risk of revealing information relating to the representation to persons outside the organization. Such measures may include among others:

(1) asking reconsideration of the matter;

(2) advising that a separate legal opinion on the matter be sought for presentation to appropriate authority in the organization; and

(3) referring the matter to higher authority in the organization, including, if warranted by the seriousness of the matter, referral to the highest authority that can act in behalf of the organization as determined by applicable law.

(c) If, despite the lawyer's efforts in accordance with paragraph (b), the highest authority that can act on behalf of the organization insists upon action, or a refusal to act, that is clearly a violation of law and is likely to result in substantial injury to the organization, the lawyer may resign in accordance with rule 1.16.

(d) In dealing with an organization's directors, officers, employees, members, shareholders or other constituents, a lawyer shall explain the identity of the client when it is apparent that the organization's interests are adverse to those of the constituents with whom the lawyer is dealing.

(e) A lawyer representing an organization may also represent any of its directors, officers, employees, members, shareholders or other constituents, subject to the provisions of rule 1.7. If the organization's consent to the dual representation is required by rule 1.7,

---

* The Kutak Commission's Revised Final Draft contained substantially different language on the lawyer's duty to rectify third party acts which are likely to result in substantial injury to the corporation. Proposed Rule 1.13(a) and (c) are reproduced below. Proposed provision (b) of 1.13 was substantially similar to the final version.

Rule 1.13 Organization as Client

(a) A lawyer employed or retained to represent an organization represents the organization as distinct from its directors, officers, employees, members, shareholders or other constituents.

. . .

(c) When the organization's highest authority insists upon action, or refuses to take action, that is clearly a violation of a legal obligation to the organization, or a violation of law which reasonably might be imputed to the organization, and is likely to result in substantial injury to the organization, the lawyer may take further remedial action that the lawyer reasonably believes to be in the best interest of the organization. Such action may include revealing information otherwise protected by Rule 1.6 only if the lawyer reasonably believes that:

(1) the highest authority in the organization has acted to further the personal or financial interests of members of that authority which are in conflict with the interests of the organization; and

(2) revealing the information is necessary in the best interest of the organization.

Proposed Model Rule 1.13(a), (c) (Revised Final Draft) (June 20, 1982).

the consent shall be given by an appropriate official of the organization other than the individual who is to be represented, or by the shareholders.

COMMENT:

The Entity as the Client

[1] An organizational client is a legal entity, but it cannot act except through its officers, directors, employees, shareholders and other constituents.

[2] Officers, directors, employees and shareholders are the constituents of the corporate organizational client. The duties defined in this Comment apply equally to unincorporated associations. "Other constituents" as used in this Comment means the positions equivalent to officers, directors, employees and shareholders held by persons acting for organizational clients that are not corporations.

[3] When one of the constituents of an organizational client communicates with the organization's lawyer in that person's organizational capacity, the communication is protected by Rule 1.6. Thus, by way of example, if an organizational client requests its lawyer to investigate allegations of wrongdoing, interviews made in the course of that investigation between the lawyer and the client's employees or other constituents are covered by Rule 1.6. This does not mean, however, that constituents of an organizational client are the clients of the lawyer. The lawyer may not disclose to such constituents information relating to the representation except for disclosures explicitly or impliedly authorized by the organizational client in order to carry out the representation or as otherwise permitted by Rule 1.6.

[4] When constituents of the organization make decisions for it, the decisions ordinarily must be accepted by the lawyer even if their utility or prudence is doubtful. Decisions concerning policy and operations, including ones entailing serious risk, are not as such in the lawyer's province. However, different considerations arise when the lawyer knows that the organization may be substantially injured by action of [a] constituent that is in violation of law. In such a circumstance, it may be reasonably necessary for the lawyer to ask the constituent to reconsider the matter. If that fails, or if the matter is of sufficient seriousness and importance to the organization, it may be reasonably necessary for the lawyer to take steps to have the matter reviewed by a higher authority in the organization. Clear justification should exist for seeking review over the head of the constituent normally responsible for it. The stated policy of the organization may define circumstances and prescribe channels for such review, and a lawyer should encourage the formulation of such a policy. Even in the absence of organization policy, however, the lawyer may have an obligation to refer a matter to higher authority, depending on the seriousness of the matter and whether the constituent in question has apparent motives to act at variance with the organization's interest. Review by the chief executive officer or by the board of directors may be required when the matter is of importance commensurate with their authority. At some point it may be useful or essential to obtain an independent legal opinion.

[5] In an extreme case, it may be reasonably necessary for the lawyer to refer the matter to the organization's highest authority. Ordinarily, that is the board of directors or similar governing body. However, applicable law may prescribe that under certain conditions highest authority reposes elsewhere; for example, in the independent directors of a corporation.

Relation to Other Rules

[6] The authority and responsibility provided in paragraph (b) are concurrent with the authority and responsibility provided in other Rules. In particular, this Rule does not limit or expand the lawyer's responsibility under Rules 1.6, 1.8, and 1.16, 3.3 or 4.1. If the lawyer's services are being used by an organization to further a crime or fraud by the organization, Rule 1.2(d) can be applicable.

Government Agency

[7] The duty defined in this Rule applies to governmental organizations. However, when the client is a governmental organization, a different balance may be appropriate between maintaining confidentiality and assuring that the wrongful official act is prevented or rectified, for public business is involved. In addition, duties of lawyers employed by the government or lawyers in military service may be defined by statutes and regulation. Therefore, defining precisely the identity of the client and prescribing the resulting obligations of such lawyers may be more difficult in the government context. Although in some circumstances the client may be a specific agency, it is generally the government as a whole. For example,

if the action or failure to act involves the head of a bureau, either the department of which the bureau is a part or the government as a whole may be the client for purpose of this Rule. Moreover, in a matter involving the conduct of government officials, a government lawyer may have authority to question such conduct more extensively than that of a lawyer for a private organization in similar circumstances. This Rule does not limit that authority. See note on Scope.

Clarifying the Lawyer's Role

[8] There are times when the organization's interest may be or become adverse to those of one or more of its constituents. In such circumstances the lawyer should advise any constituent, whose interest the lawyer finds adverse to that of the organization of the conflict or potential conflict of interest, that the lawyer cannot represent such constituent, and that such person may wish to obtain independent representation. Care must be taken to assure that the individual understands that, when there is such adversity of interest, the lawyer for the organization cannot provide legal representation for that constituent individual, and that discussions between the lawyer for the organization and the individual may not be privileged.

[9] Whether such a warning should be given by the lawyer for the organization to any constituent individual may turn on the facts of each case.

Dual Representation

[10] Paragraph (e) recognizes that a lawyer for an organization may also represent a principal officer or major shareholder.

Derivative Actions

[11] Under generally prevailing law, the shareholders or members of a corporation may bring suit to compel the directors to perform their legal obligations in the supervision of the organization. Members of unincorporated associations have essentially the same right. Such an action may be brought nominally by the organization, but usually is, in fact, a legal controversy over management of the organization.

[12] The question can arise whether counsel for the organization may defend such an action. The proposition that the organization is the lawyer's client does not alone resolve the issue. Most derivative actions are a normal incident of an organization's affairs, to be defended by the organization's lawyer like any other suit. However, if the claim involves serious charges of wrongdoing by those in control of the organization, a conflict may arise between the lawyer's duty to the organization and the lawyer's relationship with the board. In those circumstances, Rule 1.7 governs who should represent the directors and the organization.

MODEL CODE COMPARISON:

There was no counterpart to this Rule in the Disciplinary Rules of the Model Code. EC 5–18 stated that a "lawyer employed or retained by a corporation or similar entity owes his allegiance to the entity and not to a stockholder, director, officer, employee, representative, or other person connected with the entity. In advising the entity, a lawyer should keep paramount its interests and his professional judgment should not be influenced by the personal desires of any person or organization. Occasionally, a lawyer for an entity is requested by a stockholder, director, officer, employee, representative, or other person connected with the entity to represent him in an individual capacity; in such case the lawyer may serve the individual only if the lawyer is convinced that differing interests are not present." EC 5–24 stated that although a lawyer "may be employed by a business corporation with non-lawyers serving as directors or officers, and they necessarily have the right to make decisions of business policy, a lawyer must decline to accept direction of his professional judgment from any layman." DR 5–107(B) provided that a lawyer "shall not permit a person who . . . employs . . . him to render legal services for another to direct or regulate his professional judgment in rendering such legal services."

RULE 1.14 Client Under a Disability

(a) When a client's ability to make adequately considered decisions in connection with the representation is impaired, whether because of minority, mental disability or for

some other reason, the lawyer shall, as far as reasonably possible, maintain a normal client-lawyer relationship with the client.

(b) A lawyer may seek the appointment of a guardian or take other protective action with respect to a client, only when the lawyer reasonably believes that the client cannot adequately act in the client's own interest.

COMMENT:

[1] The normal client-lawyer relationship is based on the assumption that the client, when properly advised and assisted, is capable of making decisions about important matters. When the client is a minor or suffers from a mental disorder or disability, however, maintaining the ordinary client-lawyer relationship may not be possible in all respects. In particular, an incapacitated person may have no power to make legally binding decisions. Nevertheless, a client lacking legal competence often has the ability to understand, deliberate upon, and reach conclusions about matters affecting the client's own well-being. Furthermore, to an increasing extent the law recognizes intermediate degrees of competence. For example, children as young as five or six years of age, and certainly those of ten or twelve, are regarded as having opinions that are entitled to weight in legal proceedings concerning their custody. So also, it is recognized that some persons of advanced age can be quite capable of handling routine financial matters while needing special legal protection concerning major transactions.

[2] The fact that a client suffers a disability does not diminish the lawyer's obligation to treat the client with attention and respect. If the person has no guardian or legal representative, the lawyer often must act as de facto guardian. Even if the person does have a legal representative, the lawyer should as far as possible accord the represented person the status of client, particularly in maintaining communication.

[3] If a legal representative has already been appointed for the client, the lawyer should ordinarily look to the representative for decisions on behalf of the client. If a legal representative has not been appointed, the lawyer should see to such an appointment where it would serve the client's best interests. Thus, if a disabled client has substantial property that should be sold for the client's benefit, effective completion of the transaction ordinarily requires appointment of a legal representative. In many circumstances, however, appointment of a legal representative may be expensive or traumatic for the client. Evaluation of these considerations is a matter of professional judgment on the lawyer's part.

[4] If the lawyer represents the guardian as distinct from the ward, and is aware that the guardian is acting adversely to the ward's interest, the lawyer may have an obligation to prevent or rectify the guardian's misconduct. See Rule 1.2(d).

Disclosure of the Client's Condition

[5] Rules of procedure in litigation generally provide that minors or persons suffering mental disability shall be represented by a guardian or next friend if they do not have a general guardian. However, disclosure of the client's disability can adversely affect the client's interests. For example, raising the question of disability could, in some circumstances, lead to proceedings for involuntary commitment. The lawyer's position in such cases is an unavoidably difficult one. The lawyer may seek guidance from an appropriate diagnostician.

Emergency Legal Assistance *

[6] In an emergency where the health, safety or a financial interest of a person under a disability is threatened with imminent and irreparable harm, a lawyer may take legal action on behalf of such a person even though the person is unable to establish a client-lawyer relationship or to make or express considered judgments about the matter, when the disabled person or another acting in good faith on that person's behalf has consulted the lawyer. Even in such an emergency, however, the lawyer should not act unless the lawyer reasonably believes that the person has no other lawyer, agent or other representative available. The lawyer should take legal action on behalf of the disabled person only to the extent reasonably necessary to maintain the status quo or otherwise avoid imminent and irreparable harm. A lawyer who undertakes to represent a

* In 1997, the ABA House of Delegates added comments 6 and 7 to Model Rule 1.14 in order to clarify a lawyer's role when a disabled person is in need of emergency legal services.

person in such an exigent situation has the same duties under these Rules as the lawyer would with respect to a client.

[7] A lawyer who acts on behalf of a disabled person in an emergency should keep the confidences of the disabled person as if dealing with a client, disclosing them only to the extent necessary to accomplish the intended protective action. The lawyer should disclose to any tribunal involved and to any other counsel involved the nature of his or her relationship with the disabled person. The lawyer should take steps to regularize the relationship or implement other protective solutions as soon as possible. Normally, a lawyer would not seek compensation for such emergency actions taken on behalf of a disabled person.

MODEL CODE COMPARISON:

There was no counterpart to this Rule in the Disciplinary Rules of the Model Code. EC 7–11 stated that the "responsibilities of a lawyer may vary according to the intelligence, experience, mental condition or age of a client. . . . Examples include the representation of an illiterate or an incompetent." EC 7–12 stated that "[a]ny mental or physical condition of a client that renders him incapable of making a considered judgment on his own behalf casts additional responsibilities upon his lawyer. Where an incompetent is acting through a guardian or other legal representative, a lawyer must look to such representative for those decisions which are normally the prerogative of the client to make. If a client under disability has no legal representative, his lawyer may be compelled in court proceedings to make decisions on behalf of the client. If the client is capable of understanding the matter in question or of contributing to the advancement of his interests, regardless of whether he is legally disqualified from performing certain acts, the lawyer should obtain from him all possible aid. If the disability of a client and the lack of a legal representative compel the lawyer to make decisions for his client, the lawyer should consider all circumstances then prevailing and act with care to safeguard and advance the interests of his client. But obviously a lawyer cannot perform any act or make any decision which the law requires his client to perform or make, either acting for himself if competent, or by a duly constituted representative if legally incompetent."

RULE 1.15 Safekeeping Property

(a) A lawyer shall hold property of clients or third persons that is in a lawyer's possession in connection with a representation separate from the lawyer's own property. Funds shall be kept in a separate account maintained in the state where the lawyer's office is situated, or elsewhere with the consent of the client or third person. Other property shall be identified as such and appropriately safeguarded. Complete records of such account funds and other property shall be kept by the lawyer and shall be preserved for a period of [five years] after termination of the representation.

(b) Upon receiving funds or other property in which a client or third person has an interest, a lawyer shall promptly notify the client or third person. Except as stated in this rule or otherwise permitted by law or by agreement with the client, a lawyer shall promptly deliver to the client or third person any funds or other property that the client or third person is entitled to receive and, upon request by the client or third person, shall promptly render a full accounting regarding such property.

(c) When in the course of representation a lawyer is in possession of property in which both the lawyer and another person claim interests, the property shall be kept separate by the lawyer until there is an accounting and severance of their interest. If a dispute arises concerning their respective interests, the portion in dispute shall be kept separate by the lawyer until the dispute is resolved.

COMMENT:

[1] A lawyer should hold property of others with the care required of a professional fiduciary. Securities should be kept in a safe deposit box, except when some other form of safekeeping is warranted by special circumstances. All property which is the property of clients or third persons should be kept separate from the lawyer's business and personal property and, if monies, in one or more trust accounts. Separate trust accounts may be warranted when administering estate monies or acting in similar fiduciary capacities.

[2] Lawyers often receive funds from third parties from which the lawyer's fee will be paid. If there is risk that the client may divert the funds without paying the fee, the lawyer is not required to remit the portion from which the fee is to be paid. However, a lawyer may not hold funds to coerce a client into accepting the lawyer's contention. The disputed portion of the funds should be kept in trust and the lawyer should suggest means for prompt resolution of the dispute, such as arbitration. The undisputed portion of the funds shall be promptly distributed.

[3] Third parties, such as a client's creditors, may have just claims against funds or other property in a lawyer's custody. A lawyer may have a duty under applicable law to protect such third-party claims against wrongful interference by the client, and accordingly may refuse to surrender the property to the client. However, a lawyer should not unilaterally assume to arbitrate a dispute between the client and the third party.

[4] The obligations of a lawyer under this Rule are independent of those arising from activity other than rendering legal services. For example, a lawyer who serves as an escrow agent is governed by the applicable law relating to fiduciaries even though the lawyer does not render legal services in the transaction.

[5] A "client's security fund" provides a means through the collective efforts of the bar to reimburse persons who have lost money or property as a result of dishonest conduct of a lawyer. Where such a fund has been established, a lawyer should participate.

MODEL CODE COMPARISON:

With regard to paragraph (a), DR 9–102(A) provided that "funds of clients" are to be kept in an identifiable bank account in the state in which the lawyer's office is situated. DR 9–102(B)(2) provided that a lawyer shall "identify and label securities and properties of a client . . . and place them in . . . safekeeping. . . ." DR 9–102(B)(3) required that a lawyer "[m]aintain complete records of all funds, securities, and other properties of a client. . . ." Paragraph (a) extends these requirements to property of a third person that is in the lawyer's possession in connection with the representation.

Paragraph (b) is substantially similar to DR 9–102(B)(1), (3) and (4).

Paragraph (c) is similar to DR 9–102(A)(2), except that the requirement regarding disputes applies to property concerning which an interest is claimed by a third person as well as by a client.

RULE 1.16 Declining or Terminating Representation

(a) Except as stated in paragraph (c), a lawyer shall not represent a client or, where representation has commenced, shall withdraw from the representation of a client if:

(1) the representation will result in violation of the rules of professional conduct or other law;

(2) the lawyer's physical or mental condition materially impairs the lawyer's ability to represent the client; or

(3) the lawyer is discharged.

(b) Except as stated in paragraph (c), a lawyer may withdraw from representing a client if withdrawal can be accomplished without material adverse effect on the interests of the client, or if:

(1) the client persists in a course of action involving the lawyer's services that the lawyer reasonably believes is criminal or fraudulent;

(2) the client has used the lawyer's services to perpetrate a crime or fraud;

(3) a client insists upon pursuing an objective that the lawyer considers repugnant or imprudent;

(4) the client fails substantially to fulfill an obligation to the lawyer regarding the lawyer's services and has been given reasonable warning that the lawyer will withdraw unless the obligation is fulfilled;

(5) the representation will result in an unreasonable financial burden on the lawyer or has been rendered unreasonably difficult by the client; or

(6) other good cause for withdrawal exists.

(c) When ordered to do so by a tribunal, a lawyer shall continue representation notwithstanding good cause for terminating the representation.

(d) Upon termination of representation, a lawyer shall take steps to the extent reasonably practicable to protect a client's interests, such as giving reasonable notice to the client, allowing time for employment of other counsel, surrendering papers and property to which the client is entitled and refunding any advance payment of fee that has not been earned. The lawyer may retain papers relating to the client to the extent permitted by other law.

COMMENT:

[1] A lawyer should not accept representation in a matter unless it can be performed competently, promptly, without improper conflict of interest and to completion.

Mandatory Withdrawal

[2] A lawyer ordinarily must decline or withdraw from representation if the client demands that the lawyer engage in conduct that is illegal or violates the Rules of Professional Conduct or other law. The lawyer is not obliged to decline or withdraw simply because the client suggests such a course of conduct; a client may make such a suggestion in the hope that a lawyer will not be constrained by a professional obligation.

[3] When a lawyer has been appointed to represent a client, withdrawal ordinarily requires approval of the appointing authority. See also Rule 6.2. Difficulty may be encountered if withdrawal is based on the client's demand that the lawyer engage in unprofessional conduct. The court may wish an explanation for the withdrawal, while the lawyer may be bound to keep confidential the facts that would constitute such an explanation. The lawyer's statement that professional considerations require termination of the representation ordinarily should be accepted as sufficient.

Discharge

[4] A client has a right to discharge a lawyer at any time, with or without cause, subject to liability for payment for the lawyer's services. Where future dispute about the withdrawal may be anticipated, it may be advisable to prepare a written statement reciting the circumstances.

[5] Whether a client can discharge appointed counsel may depend on applicable law. A client seeking to do so should be given a full explanation of the consequences. These consequences may include a decision by the appointing authority that appointment of successor counsel is unjustified, thus requiring the client to represent himself.

[6] If the client is mentally incompetent, the client may lack the legal capacity to discharge the lawyer, and in any event the discharge may be seriously adverse to the client's interests. The lawyer should make special effort to help the client consider the consequences and, in an extreme case, may initiate proceedings for a conservatorship or similar protection of the client. See Rule 1.14.

Optional Withdrawal

[7] A lawyer may withdraw from representation in some circumstances. The lawyer has the option to withdraw if it can be accomplished without material adverse effect on the client's interests. Withdrawal is also justified if the client persists in a course of action that the lawyer reasonably believes is criminal or fraudulent, for a lawyer is not required to be associated with such conduct even if the lawyer does not further it. Withdrawal is also permitted if the lawyer's services were misused in the past even if that would

materially prejudice the client. The lawyer also may withdraw where the client insists on a repugnant or imprudent objective.

[8] A lawyer may withdraw if the client refuses to abide by the terms of an agreement relating to the representation, such as an agreement concerning fees or court costs or an agreement limiting the objectives of the representation.

Assisting the Client Upon Withdrawal

[9] Even if the lawyer has been unfairly discharged by the client, a lawyer must take all reasonable steps to mitigate the consequences to the client. The lawyer may retain papers as security for a fee only to the extent permitted by law.

[10] Whether or not a lawyer for an organization may under certain unusual circumstances have a legal obligation to the organization after withdrawing or being discharged by the organization's highest authority is beyond the scope of these Rules.

MODEL CODE COMPARISON:

With regard to paragraph (a), DR 2–109(A) provided that a lawyer "shall not accept employment . . . if he knows or it is obvious that [the prospective client] wishes to . . . [b]ring a legal action . . . or otherwise have steps taken for him, merely for the purpose of harassing or maliciously injuring any person. . . ." Nor may a lawyer accept employment if the lawyer is aware that the prospective client wishes to "[p]resent a claim or defense . . . that is not warranted under existing law, unless it can be supported by good faith argument for an extension, modification, or reversal of existing law." DR 2–110(B) provided that a lawyer "shall withdraw from employment . . . if:

"(1) He knows or it is obvious that his client is bringing the legal action . . . or is otherwise having steps taken for him, merely for the purpose of harassing or maliciously injuring any person.

"(2) He knows or it is obvious that his continued employment will result in violation of a Disciplinary Rule.

"(3) His mental or physical condition renders it unreasonably difficult for him to carry out the employment effectively.

"(4) He is discharged by his client."

With regard to paragraph (b), DR 2–110(C) permitted withdrawal regardless of the effect on the client if:

"(1) His client: (a) Insists upon presenting a claim or defense that is not warranted under existing law and cannot be supported by good faith argument for an extension, modification, or reversal of existing law; (b) Personally seeks to pursue an illegal course of conduct; (c) Insists that the lawyer pursue a course of conduct that is illegal or that is prohibited under the Disciplinary Rules; (d) By other conduct renders it unreasonably difficult for the lawyer to carry out his employment effectively; (e) Insists, in a matter not pending before a tribunal, that the lawyer engage in conduct that is contrary to the judgment and advice of the lawyer but not prohibited under the Disciplinary Rules; (f) Deliberately disregards an agreement or obligation to the lawyer as to expenses and fees.

"(2) His continued employment is likely to result in a violation of a Disciplinary Rule.

"(3) His inability to work with co-counsel indicates that the best interest of the client likely will be served by withdrawal.

"(4) His mental or physical condition renders it difficult for him to carry out the employment effectively.

"(5) His client knowingly and freely assents to termination of his employment.

"(6) He believes in good faith, in a proceeding pending before a tribunal, that the tribunal will find the existence of other good cause for withdrawal."

With regard to paragraph (c), DR 2–110(A)(1) provided: "If permission for withdrawal from employment is required by the rules of a tribunal, the lawyer shall not withdraw . . . without its permission."

RULE 1.17 Sale of Law Practice*

A lawyer or a law firm may sell or purchase a law practice, including good will, if the following conditions are satisfied:

(a) The seller ceases to engage in the private practice of law [in the geographic area] [in the jurisdiction] (a jurisdiction may elect either version) in which the practice has been conducted;

(b) The practice is sold as an entirety to another lawyer or law firm;

(c) Actual written notice is given to each of the seller's clients regarding:

(1) the proposed sale;

(2) the terms of any proposed change in the fee arrangement authorized by paragraph (d);

(3) the client's right to retain other counsel or to take possession of the file; and

(4) the fact that the client's consent to the sale will be presumed if the client does not take any action or does not otherwise object within ninety (90) days of receipt of the notice.

If a client cannot be given notice, the representation of that client may be transferred to the purchaser only upon entry of an order so authorizing by a court having jurisdiction. The seller may disclose to the court *in camera* information relating to the representation only to the extent necessary to obtain an order authorizing the transfer of a file.

(d) The fees charged clients shall not be increased by reason of the sale. The purchaser may, however, refuse to undertake the representation unless the client consents to pay the purchaser fees at a rate not exceeding the fees charged by the purchaser for rendering substantially similar services prior to the initiation of the purchase negotiations.

COMMENT:

[1] The practice of law is a profession, not merely a business. Clients are not commodities that can be purchased and sold at will. Pursuant to this Rule, when a lawyer or an entire firm ceases to practice and another lawyer or firm takes over the representation, the selling lawyer or firm may obtain compensation for the reasonable value of the practice as may withdrawing partners of law firms. See Rules 5.4 and 5.6.

Termination of Practice by the Seller

[2] The requirement that all of the private practice be sold is satisfied if the seller in good faith makes the entire practice available for sale to the purchaser. The fact that a number of the seller's clients decide not to be represented by the purchaser but take their matters elsewhere, therefore, does not result in a violation. Neither does a return to private practice as a result of an unanticipated change in circumstances result in a violation. For example, a lawyer who has sold the practice to accept an appointment to judicial office does not violate the requirement that the sale be attendant to cessation of practice if the lawyer later resumes private practice upon being defeated in a contested or a retention election for the office.

[3] The requirement that the seller cease to engage in the private practice of law does not prohibit employment as a lawyer on the staff of a public agency or a legal services entity which provides legal services to the poor, or as in-house counsel to a business.

[4] The Rule permits a sale attendant upon retirement from the private practice of law within the jurisdiction. Its provisions, therefore, accommodate the lawyer who sells the practice upon the occasion of moving to another state. Some states are so large that a move from one locale therein to another is tantamount to leaving the jurisdiction in which the lawyer has engaged in the practice of law. To also

* Model Rule 1.17 did not appear in the original version of the Model Rules. This provision and its comments were added by the ABA in 1990.

accommodate lawyers so situated, states may permit the sale of the practice when the lawyer leaves the geographic area rather than the jurisdiction. The alternative desired should be indicated by selecting one of the two provided for in Rule 1.17(a).

Single Purchaser

[5] The Rule requires a single purchaser. The prohibition against piecemeal sale of a practice protects those clients whose matters are less lucrative and who might find it difficult to secure other counsel if a sale could be limited to substantial fee-generating matters. The purchaser is required to undertake all client matters in the practice, subject to client consent. If, however, the purchaser is unable to undertake all client matters because of a conflict of interest in a specific matter respecting which the purchaser is not permitted by Rule 1.7 or another rule to represent the client, the requirement that there be a single purchaser is nevertheless satisfied.

Client Confidences, Consent and Notice

[6] Negotiations between seller and prospective purchaser prior to disclosure of information relating to a specific representation of an identifiable client no more violate the confidentiality provisions of Model Rule 1.6 than do preliminary discussions concerning the possible association of another lawyer or mergers between firms, with respect to which client consent is not required. Providing the purchaser access to client-specific information relating to the representation and to the file, however, requires client consent. The Rule provides that before such information can be disclosed by the seller to the purchaser the client must be given actual written notice of the contemplated sale, including the identity of the purchaser and any proposed change in the terms of future representation, and must be told that the decision to consent or make other arrangements must be made within 90 days. If nothing is heard from the client within that time, consent to the sale is presumed.

[7] A lawyer or law firm ceasing to practice cannot be required to remain in practice because some clients cannot be given actual notice of the proposed purchase. Since these clients cannot themselves consent to the purchase or direct any other disposition of their files, the Rule requires an order from a court having jurisdiction authorizing their transfer or other disposition. The Court can be expected to determine whether reasonable efforts to locate the client have been exhausted, and whether the absent client's legitimate interests will be served by authorizing the transfer of the file so that the purchaser may continue the representation. Preservation of client confidences requires that the petition for a court order be considered *in camera.* (A procedure by which such an order can be obtained needs to be established in jurisdictions in which it presently does not exist.)

[8] All the elements of client autonomy, including the client's absolute right to discharge a lawyer and transfer the representation to another, survive the sale of the practice.

Fee Arrangements Between Client and Purchaser

[9] The sale may not be financed by increases in fees charged the clients of the practice. Existing agreements between the seller and the client as to fees and the scope of the work must be honored by the purchaser, unless the client consents after consultation. The purchaser may, however, advise the client that the purchaser will not undertake the representation unless the client consents to pay the higher fees the purchaser usually charges. To prevent client financing of the sale, the higher fee the purchaser may charge must not exceed the fees charged by the purchaser for substantially similar service rendered prior to the initiation of the purchase negotiations.

[10] The purchaser may not intentionally fragment the practice which is the subject of the sale by charging significantly different fees in substantially similar matters. Doing so would make it possible for the purchaser to avoid the obligation to take over the entire practice by charging arbitrarily higher fees for less lucrative matters, thereby increasing the likelihood that those clients would not consent to the new representation.

Other Applicable Ethical Standards

[11] Lawyers participating in the sale of a law practice are subject to the ethical standards applicable to involving another lawyer in the representation of a client. These include, for example, the seller's obligation to exercise competence in identifying a purchaser qualified to assume the practice and the purchaser's obligation to undertake the representation competently (see Rule 1.1); the obligation to avoid

disqualifying conflicts, and to secure client consent after consultation for those conflicts which can be agreed to (see Rule 1.7); and the obligation to protect information relating to the representation (see Rules 1.6 and 1.9).

[12] If approval of the substitution of the purchasing attorney for the selling attorney is required by the rules of any tribunal in which a matter is pending, such approval must be obtained before the matter can be included in the sale (see Rule 1.16).

Applicability of the Rule

[13] This Rule applies to the sale of a law practice by representatives of a deceased, disabled or disappeared lawyer. Thus, the seller may be represented by a non-lawyer representative not subject to these Rules. Since, however, no lawyer may participate in a sale of a law practice which does not conform to the requirements of this Rule, the representatives of the seller as well as the purchasing lawyer can be expected to see to it that they are met.

[14] Admission to or retirement from a law partnership or professional association, retirement plans and similar arrangements, and a sale of tangible assets of a law practice, do not constitute a sale or purchase governed by this Rule.

[15] This Rule does not apply to the transfers of legal representation between lawyers when such transfers are unrelated to the sale of a practice.

MODEL CODE COMPARISON:

There was no counterpart to this Rule in the Model Code.

COUNSELOR

RULE 2.1 Advisor

In representing a client, a lawyer shall exercise independent professional judgment and render candid advice. In rendering advice, a lawyer may refer not only to law but to other considerations such as moral, economic, social and political factors, that may be relevant to the client's situation.

COMMENT:

Scope of Advice

[1] A client is entitled to straightforward advice expressing the lawyer's honest assessment. Legal advice often involves unpleasant facts and alternatives that a client may be disinclined to confront. In presenting advice, a lawyer endeavors to sustain the client's morale and may put advice in as acceptable a form as honesty permits. However, a lawyer should not be deterred from giving candid advice by the prospect that the advice will be unpalatable to the client.

[2] Advice couched in narrowly legal terms may be of little value to a client, especially where practical considerations, such as cost or effects on other people, are predominant. Purely technical legal advice, therefore, can sometimes be inadequate. It is proper for a lawyer to refer to relevant moral and ethical considerations in giving advice. Although a lawyer is not a moral advisor as such, moral and ethical considerations impinge upon most legal questions and may decisively influence how the law will be applied.

[3] A client may expressly or impliedly ask the lawyer for purely technical advice. When such a request is made by a client experienced in legal matters, the lawyer may accept it at face value. When such a request is made by a client inexperienced in legal matters, however, the lawyer's responsibility as advisor may include indicating that more may be involved than strictly legal considerations.

[4] Matters that go beyond strictly legal questions may also be in the domain of another profession. Family matters can involve problems within the professional competence of psychiatry, clinical psychology or social work; business matters can involve problems within the competence of the accounting profession or of financial specialists. Where consultation with a professional in another field is itself something a competent lawyer would recommend, the lawyer should make such a recommendation. At the same time, a

lawyer's advice at its best often consists of recommending a course of action in the face of conflicting recommendations of experts.

Offering Advice

[5] In general, a lawyer is not expected to give advice until asked by the client. However, when a lawyer knows that a client proposes a course of action that is likely to result in substantial adverse legal consequences to the client, duty to the client under Rule 1.4 may require that the lawyer act if the client's course of action is related to the representation. A lawyer ordinarily has no duty to initiate investigation of a client's affairs or to give advice that the client has indicated is unwanted, but a lawyer may initiate advice to a client when doing so appears to be in the client's interest.

MODEL CODE COMPARISON:

There was no direct counterpart to this Rule in the Disciplinary Rules of the Model Code. DR 5–107(B) provided that a lawyer "shall not permit a person who recommends, employs, or pays him to render legal services for another to direct or regulate his professional judgment in rendering such legal services." EC 7–8 stated that "[a]dvice of a lawyer to his client need not be confined to purely legal considerations. . . . In assisting his client to reach a proper decision, it is often desirable for a lawyer to point out those factors which may lead to a decision that is morally just as well as legally permissible. . . . In the final analysis, however, . . . the decision whether to forego legally available objectives or methods because of nonlegal factors is ultimately for the client. . . ."

RULE 2.2 Intermediary

(a) A lawyer may act as intermediary between clients if:

(1) the lawyer consults with each client concerning the implications of the common representation, including the advantages and risks involved, and the effect on the attorney-client privileges, and obtains each client's consent to the common representation;

(2) the lawyer reasonably believes that the matter can be resolved on terms compatible with the clients' best interests, that each client will be able to make adequately informed decisions in the matter and that there is little risk of material prejudice to the interest of any of the clients if the contemplated resolution is unsuccessful; and

(3) the lawyer reasonably believes that the common representation can be undertaken impartially and without improper effect on other responsibilities the lawyer has to any of the clients.

(b) While acting as intermediary, the lawyer shall consult with each client concerning the decisions to be made and the considerations relevant in making them, so that each client can make adequately informed decisions.

(c) A lawyer shall withdraw as intermediary if any of the clients so request, or if any of the conditions stated in paragraph (a) is no longer satisfied. Upon withdrawal, the lawyer shall not continue to represent any of the clients in the matter that was the subject of the intermediation.

COMMENT:

[1] A lawyer acts as intermediary under this Rule when the lawyer represents two or more parties with potentially conflicting interests. A key factor in defining the relationship is whether the parties share responsibility for the lawyer's fee, but the common representation may be inferred from other circumstances. Because confusion can arise as to the lawyer's role where each party is not separately represented, it is important that the lawyer make clear the relationship.

[2] The Rule does not apply to a lawyer acting as arbitrator or mediator between or among parties who are not clients of the lawyer, even where the lawyer has been appointed with the concurrence of the parties. In performing such a role the lawyer may be subject to applicable codes of ethics, such as the Code

of Ethics for Arbitration in Commercial Disputes prepared by a joint Committee of the American Bar Association and the American Arbitration Association.

[3] A lawyer acts as intermediary in seeking to establish or adjust a relationship between clients on an amicable and mutually advantageous basis; for example, in helping to organize a business in which two or more clients are entrepreneurs, working out the financial reorganization of an enterprise in which two or more clients have an interest, arranging a property distribution in settlement of an estate or mediating a dispute between clients. The lawyer seeks to resolve potentially conflicting interests by developing the parties' mutual interests. The alternative can be that each party may have to obtain separate representation, with the possibility in some situations of incurring additional cost, complication or even litigation. Given these and other relevant factors, all the clients may prefer that the lawyer act as intermediary.

[4] In considering whether to act as intermediary between clients, a lawyer should be mindful that if the intermediation fails the result can be additional cost, embarrassment and recrimination. In some situations the risk of failure is so great that intermediation is plainly impossible. For example, a lawyer cannot undertake common representation of clients between whom contentious litigation is imminent or who contemplate contentious negotiations. More generally, if the relationship between the parties has already assumed definite antagonism, the possibility that the clients' interests can be adjusted by intermediation ordinarily is not very good.

[5] The appropriateness of intermediation can depend on its form. Forms of intermediation range from informal arbitration, where each client's case is presented by the respective client and the lawyer decides the outcome, to mediation, to common representation where the clients' interests are substantially though not entirely compatible. One form may be appropriate in circumstances where another would not. Other relevant factors are whether the lawyer subsequently will represent both parties on a continuing basis and whether the situation involves creating a relationship between the parties or terminating one.

Confidentiality and Privilege

[6] A particularly important factor in determining the appropriateness of intermediation is the effect on client-lawyer confidentiality and the attorney-client privilege. In a common representation, the lawyer is still required both to keep each client adequately informed and to maintain confidentiality of information relating to the representation. See Rules 1.4 and 1.6. Complying with both requirements while acting as intermediary requires a delicate balance. If the balance cannot be maintained, the common representation is improper. With regard to the attorney-client privilege, the prevailing rule is that as between commonly represented clients the privilege does not attach. Hence, it must be assumed that if litigation eventuates between the clients, the privilege will not protect any such communications, and the clients should be so advised.

[7] Since the lawyer is required to be impartial between commonly represented clients, intermediation is improper when that impartiality cannot be maintained. For example, a lawyer who has represented one of the clients for a long period and in a variety of matters might have difficulty being impartial between that client and one to whom the lawyer has only recently been introduced.

Consultation

[8] In acting as intermediary between clients, the lawyer is required to consult with the clients on the implications of doing so, and proceed only upon consent based on such a consultation. The consultation should make clear that the lawyer's role is not that of partisanship normally expected in other circumstances.

[9] Paragraph (b) is an application of the principle expressed in Rule 1.4. Where the lawyer is intermediary, the clients ordinarily must assume greater responsibility for decisions than when each client is independently represented.

Withdrawal

[10] Common representation does not diminish the rights of each client in the client-lawyer relationship. Each has the right to loyal and diligent representation, the right to discharge the lawyer as stated in Rule 1.16, and the protection of Rule 1.9 concerning obligations to a former client.

MODEL CODE COMPARISON:

There was no direct counterpart to this Rule in the Disciplinary Rules of the Model Code. EC 5–20 stated that a "lawyer is often asked to serve as an impartial arbitrator or mediator in matters which involve present or former clients. He may serve in either capacity if he first discloses such present or former relationships." DR 5–105(B) provided that a lawyer "shall not continue multiple employment if the exercise of his independent judgment in behalf of a client will be or is likely to be adversely affected by his representation of another client, or if it would be likely to involve him in representation of differing interests, except to the extent permitted under DR 5–105(C)." DR 5–105(C) provided that "a lawyer may represent multiple clients if it is obvious that he can adequately represent the interests of each and if each consents to the representation after full disclosure of the possible effect of such representation on the exercise of his independent professional judgment on behalf of each."

RULE 2.3 Evaluation for Use by Third Persons

(a) A lawyer may undertake an evaluation of a matter affecting a client for the use of someone other than the client if:

(1) the lawyer reasonably believes that making the evaluation is compatible with other aspects of the lawyer's relationship with the client; and

(2) the client consents after consultation.

(b) Except as disclosure is required in connection with a report of an evaluation, information relating to the evaluation is otherwise protected by rule 1.6.

COMMENT:

Definition

[1] An evaluation may be performed at the client's direction but for the primary purpose of establishing information for the benefit of third parties; for example, an opinion concerning the title of property rendered at the behest of a vendor for the information of a prospective purchaser, or at the behest of a borrower for the information of a prospective lender. In some situations, the evaluation may be required by a government agency; for example, an opinion concerning the legality of the securities registered for sale under the securities laws. In other instances, the evaluation may be required by a third person, such as a purchaser of a business.

[2] Lawyers for the government may be called upon to give a formal opinion on the legality of contemplated government agency action. In making such an evaluation, the government lawyer acts at the behest of the government as the client but for the purpose of establishing the limits of the agency's authorized activity. Such an opinion is to be distinguished from confidential legal advice given agency officials. The critical question is whether the opinion is to be made public.

[3] A legal evaluation should be distinguished from an investigation of a person with whom the lawyer does not have a client-lawyer relationship. For example, a lawyer retained by a purchaser to analyze a vendor's title to property does not have a client-lawyer relationship with the vendor. So also, an investigation into a person's affairs by a government lawyer, or by special counsel employed by the government, is not an evaluation as that term is used in this Rule. The question is whether the lawyer is retained by the person whose affairs are being examined. When the lawyer is retained by that person, the general rules concerning loyalty to client and preservation of confidences apply, which is not the case if the lawyer is retained by someone else. For this reason, it is essential to identify the person by whom the lawyer is retained. This should be made clear not only to the person under examination, but also to others to whom the results are to be made available.

Duty to Third Person

[4] When the evaluation is intended for the information or use of a third person, a legal duty to that person may or may not arise. That legal question is beyond the scope of this Rule. However, since such an evaluation involves a departure from the normal client-lawyer relationship, careful analysis of the situation is required. The lawyer must be satisfied as a matter of professional judgment that making the evaluation is compatible with other functions undertaken in behalf of the client. For example, if the lawyer is acting as

advocate in defending the client against charges of fraud, it would normally be incompatible with that responsibility for the lawyer to perform an evaluation for others concerning the same or a related transaction. Assuming no such impediment is apparent, however, the lawyer should advise the client of the implications of the evaluation, particularly the lawyer's responsibilities to third persons and the duty to disseminate the findings.

Access to and Disclosure of Information

[5] The quality of an evaluation depends on the freedom and extent of the investigation upon which it is based. Ordinarily a lawyer should have whatever latitude of investigation seems necessary as a matter of professional judgment. Under some circumstances, however, the terms of the evaluation may be limited. For example, certain issues or sources may be categorically excluded, or the scope of search may be limited by time constraints or the noncooperation of persons having relevant information. Any such limitations which are material to the evaluation should be described in the report. If after a lawyer has commenced an evaluation, the client refuses to comply with the terms upon which it was understood the evaluation was to have been made, the lawyer's obligations are determined by law, having reference to the terms of the client's agreement and the surrounding circumstances.

Financial Auditors' Requests for Information

[6] When a question concerning the legal situation of a client arises at the instance of the client's financial auditor and the question is referred to the lawyer, the lawyer's response may be made in accordance with procedures recognized in the legal profession. Such a procedure is set forth in the American Bar Association Statement of Policy Regarding Lawyers' Responses to Auditors' Requests for Information, adopted in 1975.

MODEL CODE COMPARISON:

There was no counterpart to this Rule in the Model Code.

ADVOCATE

RULE 3.1 Meritorious Claims and Contentions

A lawyer shall not bring or defend a proceeding, or assert or controvert an issue therein, unless there is a basis for doing so that is not frivolous, which includes a good faith argument for an extension, modification or reversal of existing law. A lawyer for the defendant in a criminal proceeding, or the respondent in a proceeding that could result in incarceration, may nevertheless so defend the proceeding as to require that every element of the case be established.

COMMENT:

[1] The advocate has a duty to use legal procedure for the fullest benefit of the client's cause, but also a duty not to abuse legal procedure. The law, both procedural and substantive, establishes the limits within which an advocate may proceed. However, the law is not always clear and never is static. Accordingly, in determining the proper scope of advocacy, account must be taken of the law's ambiguities and potential for change.

[2] The filing of an action or defense or similar action taken for a client is not frivolous merely because the facts have not first been fully substantiated or because the lawyer expects to develop vital evidence only by discovery. Such action is not frivolous even though the lawyer believes that the client's position ultimately will not prevail. The action is frivolous, however, if the client desires to have the action taken primarily for the purpose of harassing or maliciously injuring a person or if the lawyer is unable either to make a good faith argument on the merits of the action taken or to support the action taken by a good faith argument for an extension, modification or reversal of existing law.

MODEL CODE COMPARISON:

DR 7–102(A)(1) provided that a lawyer may not "[f]ile a suit, assert a position, conduct a defense, delay a trial, or take other action on behalf of his client when he knows or when it is obvious that such action would serve merely to harass or maliciously injure another." Rule 3.1 is to the same general effect as DR 7–

102(A)(1), with three qualifications. First, the test of improper conduct is changed from "merely to harass or maliciously injure another" to the requirement that there be a basis for the litigation measure involved that is "not frivolous." This includes the concept stated in DR 7–102(A)(2) that a lawyer may advance a claim or defense unwarranted by existing law if "it can be supported by good faith argument for an extension, modification, or reversal of existing law." Second, the test in Rule 3.1 is an objective test, whereas DR 7–102(A)(1) applied only if the lawyer "knows or when it is obvious" that the litigation is frivolous. Third, Rule 3.1 has an exception that in a criminal case, or a case in which incarceration of the client may result (for example, certain juvenile proceedings), the lawyer may put the prosecution to its proof even if there is no nonfrivolous basis for defense.

RULE 3.2 Expediting Litigation

A lawyer shall make reasonable efforts to expedite litigation consistent with the interests of the client.

COMMENT:

Dilatory practices bring the administration of justice into disrepute. Delay should not be indulged merely for the convenience of the advocates, or for the purpose of frustrating an opposing party's attempt to obtain rightful redress or repose. It is not a justification that similar conduct is often tolerated by the bench and bar. The question is whether a competent lawyer acting in good faith would regard the course of action as having some substantial purpose other than delay. Realizing financial or other benefit from otherwise improper delay in litigation it not a legitimate interest of the client.

MODEL CODE COMPARISON:

DR 7–101(A)(1) stated that a lawyer does not violate the duty to represent a client zealously "by being punctual in fulfilling all professional commitments." DR 7–102(A)(1) provided that a lawyer "shall not . . . file a suit, assert a position, conduct a defense [or] delay a trial . . . when he knows or when it is obvious that such action would serve merely to harass or maliciously injure another."

RULE 3.3 Candor Toward the Tribunal

(a) A lawyer shall not knowingly:

(1) make a false statement of material fact or law to a tribunal;

(2) fail to disclose a material fact to a tribunal when disclosure is necessary to avoid assisting a criminal or fraudulent act by the client;

(3) fail to disclose to the tribunal legal authority in the controlling jurisdiction known to the lawyer to be directly adverse to the position of the client and not disclosed by opposing counsel; or

(4) offer evidence that the lawyer knows to be false. If a lawyer has offered material evidence and comes to know of its falsity, the lawyer shall take reasonable remedial measures.

(b) The duties stated in paragraph (a) continue to the conclusion of the proceeding, and apply even if compliance requires disclosure of information otherwise protected by rule 1.6.

(c) A lawyer may refuse to offer evidence that the lawyer reasonably believes is false.

(d) In an ex parte proceeding, a lawyer shall inform the tribunal of all material facts known to the lawyer which will enable the tribunal to make an informed decision, whether or not the facts are adverse.

COMMENT:

[1] The advocate's task is to present the client's case with persuasive force. Performance of that duty while maintaining confidences of the client is qualified by the advocate's duty of candor to the tribunal.

However, an advocate does not vouch for the evidence submitted in a cause; the tribunal is responsible for assessing its probative value.

Representations by a Lawyer

[2] An advocate is responsible for pleadings and other documents prepared for litigation, but is usually not required to have personal knowledge of matters asserted therein, for litigation documents ordinarily present assertions by the client, or by someone on the client's behalf, and not assertions by the lawyer. Compare Rule 3.1. However, an assertion purporting to be on the lawyer's own knowledge, as in an affidavit by the lawyer or in a statement in open court, may properly be made only when the lawyer knows the assertion is true or believes it to be true on the basis of a reasonably diligent inquiry. There are circumstances where failure to make a disclosure is the equivalent of an affirmative misrepresentation. The obligation prescribed in Rule 1.2(d) not to counsel a client to commit or assist the client in committing a fraud applies in litigation. Regarding compliance with Rule 1.2(d), see the Comment to that Rule. See also the Comment to Rule 8.4(b).

Misleading Legal Argument

[3] Legal argument based on a knowingly false representation of law constitutes dishonesty toward the tribunal. A lawyer is not required to make a disinterested exposition of the law, but must recognize the existence of pertinent legal authorities. Furthermore, as stated in paragraph (a)(3), an advocate has a duty to disclose directly adverse authority in the controlling jurisdiction which has not been disclosed by the opposing party. The underlying concept is that legal argument is a discussion seeking to determine the legal premises properly applicable to the case.

False Evidence

[4] When evidence that a lawyer knows to be false is provided by a person who is not the client, the lawyer must refuse to offer it regardless of the client's wishes.

[5] When false evidence is offered by the client, however, a conflict may arise between the lawyer's duty to keep the client's revelations confidential and the duty of candor to the court. Upon ascertaining that material evidence is false, the lawyer should seek to persuade the client that the evidence should not be offered or, if it has been offered, that its false character should immediately be disclosed. If the persuasion is ineffective, the lawyer must take reasonable remedial measures.

[6] Except in the defense of a criminal accused, the rule generally recognized is that, if necessary to rectify the situation, an advocate must disclose the existence of the client's deception to the court or to the other party. Such a disclosure can result in grave consequences to the client, including not only a sense of betrayal but also loss of the case and perhaps a prosecution for perjury. But the alternative is that the lawyer cooperate in deceiving the court, thereby subverting the truth-finding process which the adversary system is designed to implement. See Rule 1.2(d). Furthermore, unless it is clearly understood that the lawyer will act upon the duty to disclose the existence of false evidence, the client can simply reject the lawyer's advice to reveal the false evidence and insist that the lawyer keep silent. Thus the client could in effect coerce the lawyer into being a party to fraud on the court.

Perjury by a Criminal Defendant

[7] Whether an advocate for a criminally accused has the same duty of disclosure has been intensely debated. While it is agreed that the lawyer should seek to persuade the client to refrain from perjurious testimony, there has been dispute concerning the lawyer's duty when that persuasion fails. If the confrontation with the client occurs before trial, the lawyer ordinarily can withdraw. Withdrawal before trial may not be possible, however, either because trial is imminent, or because the confrontation with the client does not take place until the trial itself, or because no other counsel is available.

[8] The most difficult situation, therefore, arises in a criminal case where the accused insists on testifying when the lawyer knows that the testimony is perjurious. The lawyer's effort to rectify the situation can increase the likelihood of the client's being convicted as well as opening the possibility of a prosecution for perjury. On the other hand, if the lawyer does not exercise control over the proof, the lawyer participates, although in a merely passive way, in deception of the court.

[9] Three resolutions of this dilemma have been proposed. One is to permit the accused to testify by a narrative without guidance through the lawyer's questioning. This compromises both contending principles; it exempts the lawyer from the duty to disclose false evidence but subjects the client to an implicit disclosure of information imparted to counsel. Another suggested resolution, of relatively recent origin, is that the advocate be entirely excused from the duty to reveal perjury if the perjury is that of the client. This is a coherent solution but makes the advocate a knowing instrument of perjury.

[10] The other resolution of the dilemma is that the lawyer must reveal the client's perjury if necessary to rectify the situation. A criminal accused has a right to the assistance of an advocate, a right to testify and a right of confidential communication with counsel. However, an accused should not have a right to assistance of counsel in committing perjury. Furthermore, an advocate has an obligation, not only in professional ethics but under the law as well, to avoid implication in the commission of perjury or other falsification of evidence. See Rule 1.2(d).

Remedial Measures

[11] If perjured testimony or false evidence has been offered, the advocate's proper course ordinarily is to remonstrate with the client confidentially. If that fails, the advocate should seek to withdraw if that will remedy the situation. If withdrawal will not remedy the situation or is impossible, the advocate should make disclosure to the court. It is for the court then to determine what should be done—making a statement about the matter to the trier of fact, ordering a mistrial or perhaps nothing. If the false testimony was that of the client, the client may controvert the lawyer's version of their communication when the lawyer discloses the situation to the court. If there is an issue whether the client has committed perjury, the lawyer cannot represent the client in resolution of the issue and a mistrial may be unavoidable. An unscrupulous client might in this way attempt to produce a series of mistrials and thus escape prosecution. However, a second such encounter could be construed as a deliberate abuse of the right to counsel and as such a waiver of the right to further representation.

Constitutional Requirements

[12] The general rule—that an advocate must disclose the existence of perjury with respect to a material fact, even that of a client—applies to defense counsel in criminal cases, as well as in other instances. However, the definition of the lawyer's ethical duty in such a situation may be qualified by constitutional provisions for due process and the right to counsel in criminal cases. In some jurisdictions these provisions have been construed to require that counsel present an accused as a witness if the accused wishes to testify, even if counsel knows the testimony will be false. The obligation of the advocate under these Rules is subordinate to such a constitutional requirement.

Duration of Obligation

[13] A practical time limit on the obligation to rectify the presentation of false evidence has to be established. The conclusion of the proceeding is a reasonably definite point for the termination of the obligation.

Refusing to Offer Proof Believed to be False

[14] Generally speaking, a lawyer has authority to refuse to offer testimony or other proof that the lawyer believes is untrustworthy. Offering such proof may reflect adversely on the lawyer's ability to discriminate in the quality of evidence and thus impair the lawyer's effectiveness as an advocate. In criminal cases, however, a lawyer may, in some jurisdictions, be denied this authority by constitutional requirements governing the right to counsel.

Ex Parte Proceedings

[15] Ordinarily, an advocate has the limited responsibility of presenting one side of the matters that a tribunal should consider in reaching a decision; the conflicting position is expected to be presented by the opposing party. However, in an ex parte proceeding, such as an application for a temporary restraining order, there is no balance of presentation by opposing advocates. The object of an ex parte proceeding is nevertheless to yield a substantially just result. The judge has an affirmative responsibility to accord the absent party just consideration. The lawyer for the represented party has the correlative duty to make disclosures of material facts known to the lawyer and that the lawyer reasonably believes are necessary to an informed decision.

MODEL CODE COMPARISON:

Paragraph (a)(1) is substantially identical to DR 7–102(A)(5), which provided that a lawyer shall not "knowingly make a false statement of law or fact."

Paragraph (a)(2) is implicit in DR 7–102(A)(3), which provided that "a lawyer shall not . . . knowingly fail to disclose that which he is required by law to reveal."

Paragraph (a)(3) is substantially identical to DR 7–106(B)(1).

With regard to paragraph (a)(4), the first sentence of this subparagraph is similar to DR 7–102(A)(4), which provided that a lawyer shall not "knowingly use" perjured testimony or false evidence. The second sentence of paragraph (a)(4) resolves an ambiguity in the Model Code concerning the action required of a lawyer who discovers that the lawyer has offered perjured testimony or false evidence. DR 7–102(A)(4), quoted above, did not expressly deal with this situation, but the prohibition against "use" of false evidence can be construed to preclude carrying through with a case based on such evidence when that fact has become known during the trial. DR 7–102(B)(1), also noted in connection with Rule 1.6, provided that a lawyer "who receives information clearly establishing that . . . [h]is client has . . . perpetrated a fraud upon . . . a tribunal shall [if the client does not rectify the situation] . . . reveal the fraud to the . . . tribunal. . . ." Since use of perjured testimony or false evidence is usually regarded as "fraud" upon the court, DR 7–102(B)(1) apparently required disclosure by the lawyer in such circumstances. However, some states have amended DR 7–102(B)(1) in conformity with an ABA-recommended amendment to provide that the duty of disclosure does not apply when the "information is protected as a privileged communication." This qualification may be empty, for the rule of attorney-client privilege has been construed to exclude communications that further a crime, including the crime of perjury. On this interpretation of DR 7–102(B)(1), the lawyer has a duty to disclose the perjury.

Paragraph (c) confers discretion on the lawyer to refuse to offer evidence that the lawyer "reasonably believes" is false. This gives the lawyer more latitude than DR 7–102(A)(4), which prohibited the lawyer from offering evidence the lawyer "knows" is false.

There was no counterpart in the Model Code to paragraph (d).

RULE 3.4 Fairness to Opposing Party and Counsel

A lawyer shall not:

(a) unlawfully obstruct another party's access to evidence or unlawfully alter, destroy or conceal a document or other material having potential evidentiary value. A lawyer shall not counsel or assist another person to do any such act;

(b) falsify evidence, counsel or assist a witness to testify falsely, or offer an inducement to a witness that is prohibited by law;

(c) knowingly disobey an obligation under the rules of a tribunal except for an open refusal based on an assertion that no valid obligation exists;

(d) in pretrial procedure, make a frivolous discovery request or fail to make reasonably diligent effort to comply with a legally proper discovery request by an opposing party;

(e) in trial, allude to any matter that the lawyer does not reasonably believe is relevant or that will not be supported by admissible evidence, assert personal knowledge of facts in issue except when testifying as a witness, or state a personal opinion as to the justness of a cause, the credibility of a witness, the culpability of a civil litigant or the guilt or innocence of an accused; or

(f) request a person other than a client to refrain from voluntarily giving relevant information to another party unless:

(1) the person is a relative or an employee or other agent of a client; and

(2) the lawyer reasonably believes that the person's interests will not be adversely affected by refraining from giving such information.

COMMENT:

[1] The procedure of the adversary system contemplates that the evidence in a case is to be marshalled competitively by the contending parties. Fair competition in the adversary system is secured by prohibitions against destruction or concealment of evidence, improperly influencing witnesses, obstructive tactics in discovery procedure, and the like.

[2] Documents and other items of evidence are often essential to establish a claim or defense. Subject to evidentiary privileges, the right of an opposing party, including the government, to obtain evidence through discovery or subpoena is an important procedural right. The exercise of that right can be frustrated if relevant material is altered, concealed or destroyed. Applicable law in many jurisdictions makes it an offense to destroy material for purpose of impairing its availability in a pending proceeding or one whose commencement can be foreseen. Falsifying evidence is also generally a criminal offense. Paragraph (a) applies to evidentiary material generally, including computerized information.

[3] With regard to paragraph (b), it is not improper to pay a witness's expenses or to compensate an expert witness on terms permitted by law. The common law rule in most jurisdictions is that it is improper to pay an occurrence witness any fee for testifying and that it is improper to pay an expert witness a contingent fee.

[4] Paragraph (f) permits a lawyer to advise employees of a client to refrain from giving information to another party, for the employees may identify their interests with those of the client. See also Rule 4.2.

MODEL CODE COMPARISON:

With regard to paragraph (a), DR 7–109(A) provided that a lawyer "shall not suppress any evidence that he or his client has a legal obligation to reveal." DR 7–109(B) provided that a lawyer "shall not advise or cause a person to secrete himself . . . for the purpose of making him unavailable as a witness. . . ." DR 7–106(C)(7) provided that a lawyer shall not "[i]ntentionally or habitually violate any established rule of procedure or of evidence."

With regard to paragraph (b), DR 7–102(A)(6) provided that a lawyer shall not participate "in the creation or preservation of evidence when he knows or it is obvious that the evidence is false." DR 7–109(C) provided that a lawyer "shall not pay, offer to pay, or acquiesce in the payment of compensation to a witness contingent upon the content of his testimony or the outcome of the case. But a lawyer may advance, guarantee or acquiesce in the payment of: (1) Expenses reasonably incurred by a witness in attending or testifying; (2) Reasonable compensation to a witness for his loss of time in attending or testifying; [or] (3) A reasonable fee for the professional services of an expert witness." EC 7–28 stated that witnesses "should always testify truthfully and should be free from any financial inducements that might tempt them to do otherwise."

Paragraph (c) is substantially similar to DR 7–106(A), which provided that "A lawyer shall not disregard . . . a standing rule of a tribunal or a ruling of a tribunal made in the course of a proceeding, but he may take appropriate steps in good faith to test the validity of such rule or ruling."

Paragraph (d) has no counterpart in the Model Code.

Paragraph (e) substantially incorporates DR 7–106(C)(1), (2), (3) and (4). DR 7–106(C)(2) proscribed asking a question "intended to degrade a witness or other person," a matter dealt with in Rule 4.4. DR 7–106(C)(5), providing that a lawyer shall not "fail to comply with known local customs of courtesy or practice," was too vague to be a rule of conduct enforceable as law.

With regard to paragraph (f), DR 7–104(A)(2) provided that a lawyer shall not "give advice to a person who is not represented . . . other than the advice to secure counsel, if the interests of such person are or have a reasonable possibility of being in conflict with the interests of his client."

RULE 3.5 Impartiality and Decorum of the Tribunal

A lawyer shall not:

(a) seek to influence a judge, juror, prospective juror or other official by means prohibited by law;

(b) communicate ex parte with such a person except as permitted by law; or

(c) engage in conduct intended to disrupt a tribunal.

COMMENT:

[1] Many forms of improper influence upon a tribunal are proscribed by criminal law. Others are specified in the ABA Model Code of Judicial Conduct, with which an advocate should be familiar. A lawyer is required to avoid contributing to a violation of such provisions.

[2] The advocate's function is to present evidence and argument so that the cause may be decided according to law. Refraining from abusive or obstreperous conduct is a corollary of the advocate's right to speak on behalf of litigants. A lawyer may stand firm against abuse by a judge but should avoid reciprocation; the judge's default is no justification for similar dereliction by an advocate. An advocate can present the cause, protect the record for subsequent review and preserve professional integrity by patient firmness no less effectively than by belligerence or theatrics.

MODEL CODE COMPARISON:

With regard to paragraphs (a) and (b), DR 7–108(A) provided that "[b]efore the trial of a case a lawyer . . . shall not communicate with . . . anyone he knows to be a member of the venire. . . ." DR 7–108(B) provided that during the trial of a case a lawyer "shall not communicate with . . . any member of the jury." DR 7–110(B) provided that a lawyer shall not "communicate . . . as to the merits of the cause with a judge or an official before whom the proceeding is pending, except . . . upon adequate notice to opposing counsel," or as "otherwise authorized by law."

With regard to paragraph (c), DR 7–106(C)(6) provided that a lawyer shall not engage in "undignified or discourteous conduct which is degrading to a tribunal."

RULE 3.6 Trial Publicity*

(a) A lawyer who is participating or has participated in the investigation or litigation of a matter shall not make an extrajudicial statement that a reasonable person would

* In August 1994, the ABA House of Delegates amended Model Rule 3.6 to reflect the Supreme Court's decision in Gentile v. Nevada State Bar, 501 U.S. 1030 (1991). The original version of Model Rule 3.6 read as follows:

(a) A lawyer shall not make an extrajudicial statement that a reasonable person would expect to be disseminated by means of public communication if the lawyer knows or reasonably should know that it will have a substantial likelihood of materially prejudicing an adjudicative proceeding.

(b) A statement referred to in paragraph (a) ordinarily is likely to have such an effect when it refers to a civil matter triable to a jury, a criminal matter, or any other proceeding that could result in incarceration, and the statement relates to:

(1) the character, credibility, reputation or criminal record of a party, suspect in a criminal investigation or witness, or the identity of a witness, or the expected testimony of a party or witness;

(2) in a criminal case or proceeding that could result in incarceration, the possibility of a plea of guilty to the offense or the existence or contents of any confession, admission, or statement given by a defendant or suspect or that person's refusal or failure to make a statement;

(3) the performance or results of any examination or test or the refusal or failure of a person to submit to an examination or test, or the identity or nature of physical evidence expected to be presented;

(4) any opinion as to the guilt or innocence of a defendant or suspect in a criminal case or proceeding that could result in incarceration;

(5) information the lawyer knows or reasonably should know is likely to be inadmissible as evidence in a trial and would if disclosed create a substantial risk of prejudicing an impartial trial; or

expect to be disseminated by means of public communication if the lawyer knows or reasonably should know that it will have a substantial likelihood of materially prejudicing an adjudicative proceeding in the matter.

(b) Notwithstanding paragraph (a), a lawyer may state:

(1) the claim, offense or defense involved and, except when prohibited by law, the identity of the persons involved;

(2) information contained in a public record;

(3) that an investigation of a matter is in progress;

(4) the scheduling or result of any step in litigation;

(5) a request for assistance in obtaining evidence and information necessary thereto;

(6) a warning of danger concerning the behavior of a person involved, when there is reason to believe that there exists the likelihood of substantial harm to an individual or to the public interest; and

(7) in a criminal case, in addition to subparagraphs (1) through (6):

(i) the identity, residence, occupation and family status of the accused;

(ii) if the accused has not been apprehended, information necessary to aid in apprehension of that person;

(iii) the fact, time and place of arrest; and

(iv) the identity of investigating and arresting officers or agencies and the length of the investigation.

(c) Notwithstanding paragraph (a), a lawyer may make a statement that a reasonable lawyer would believe is required to protect a client from the substantial undue prejudicial effect of recent publicity not initiated by the lawyer or the lawyer's client. A statement made pursuant to this paragraph shall be limited to such information as is necessary to mitigate the recent adverse publicity.

---

(6) the fact that a defendant has been charged with a crime, unless there is included therein a statement explaining that the charge is merely an accusation and that the defendant is presumed innocent until and unless proven guilty.

(c) Notwithstanding paragraph (a) and (b)(1–5), a lawyer involved in the investigation or litigation of a matter may state without elaboration:

(1) the general nature of the claim or defense;

(2) the information contained in a public record;

(3) that an investigation of the matter is in progress, including the general scope of the investigation, the offense or claim or defense involved and, except when prohibited by law, the identity of the persons involved;

(4) the scheduling or result of any step in litigation;

(5) a request for assistance in obtaining evidence and information necessary thereto;

(6) a warning of danger concerning the behavior of a person involved, when there is reason to believe that there exists the likelihood of substantial harm to an individual or to the public interest; and

(7) in a criminal case:

(i) the identity, residence, occupation and family status of the accused;

(ii) if the accused has not been apprehended, information necessary to aid in apprehension of that person;

(iii) the fact, time and place of arrest; and

(iv) the identity of investigating and arresting officers or agencies and the length of the investigation.

(d) No lawyer associated in a firm or government agency with a lawyer subject to paragraph (a) shall make a statement prohibited by paragraph (a).

COMMENT:*

[1] It is difficult to strike a balance between protecting the right to a fair trial and safeguarding the right of free expression. Preserving the right to a fair trial necessarily entails some curtailment of the information that may be disseminated about a party prior to trial, particularly where trial by jury is involved. If there were no such limits, the result would be the practical nullification of the protective effect of the rules of forensic decorum and the exclusionary rules of evidence. On the other hand, there are vital social interests served by the free dissemination of information about events having legal consequences and about legal proceedings themselves. The public has a right to know about threats to its safety and measures aimed at assuring its security. It also has a legitimate interest in the conduct of judicial proceedings, particularly in matters of general public concern. Furthermore, the subject matter of legal proceedings is often of direct significance in debate and deliberation over questions of public policy.

[2] Special rules of confidentiality may validly govern proceedings in juvenile, domestic relations and mental disability proceedings, and perhaps other types of litigation. Rule 3.4(c) requires compliance with such Rules.

[3] The Rule sets forth a basic general prohibition against a lawyer's making statements that the lawyer knows or should know will have a substantial likelihood of materially prejudicing an adjudicative proceeding. Recognizing that the public value of informed commentary is great and the likelihood of prejudice to a proceeding by the commentary of a lawyer who is not involved in the proceeding is small, the rule applies only to lawyers who are, or who have been involved in the investigation or litigation of a case, and their associates.

[4] Paragraph (b) identifies specific matters about which a lawyer's statements would not ordinarily be considered to present a substantial likelihood of material prejudice, and should not in any event be considered prohibited by the general prohibition of paragraph (a). Paragraph (b) is not intended to be an exhaustive listing of the subjects upon which a lawyer may make a statement, but statements on other matters may be subject to paragraph (a).

[5] There are, on the other hand, certain subjects which are more likely than not to have a material prejudicial effect on a proceeding, particularly when they refer to a civil matter triable to a jury, a criminal matter, or any other proceeding that could result in incarceration. These subjects relate to:

(1) the character, credibility, reputation or criminal record of a party, suspect in a criminal investigation or witness, or the identity of a witness, or the expected testimony of a party or witness;

(2) in a criminal case or proceeding that could result in incarceration, the possibility of a plea of guilty to the offense or the existence or contents of any confession, admission, or statement given by a defendant or suspect or that person's refusal or failure to make a statement;

(3) the performance or results of any examination or test or the refusal or failure of a person to submit to an examination or test, or the identity or nature of physical evidence expected to be presented;

(4) any opinion as to the guilt or innocence of a defendant or suspect in a criminal case or proceeding that could result in incarceration;

(5) information that the lawyer knows or reasonably should know is likely to be inadmissible as evidence in a trial and that would, if disclosed, create a substantial risk of prejudicing an impartial trial; or

---

* The ABA's amendment of Model Rule 3.6 in August 1994 deleted the original comment 2 and renumbered comment 3 as comment 2 and added comments 3, 4, 5, 6 and 7. The deleted comment 2 read as follows:

[2] No body of rules can simultaneously satisfy all interests of fair trial and all those of free expression. The formula in this Rule is based upon the ABA Model Code of Professional Responsibility and the ABA Standards Relating to Fair Trial and Free Press, as amended in 1978.

(6) the fact that a defendant has been charged with a crime, unless there is included therein a statement explaining that the charge is merely an accusation and that the defendant is presumed innocent until and unless proven guilty.

[6] Another relevant factor in determining prejudice is the nature of the proceeding involved. Criminal jury trials will be most sensitive to extrajudicial speech. Civil trials may be less sensitive. Non-jury hearings and arbitration proceedings may be even less affected. The Rule will still place limitations on prejudicial comments in these cases, but the likelihood of prejudice may be different depending on the type of proceeding.

[7] Finally, extrajudicial statements that might otherwise raise a question under this Rule may be permissible when they are made in response to statements made publicly by another party, another party's lawyer, or third persons, where a reasonable lawyer would believe a public response is required in order to avoid prejudice to the lawyer's client. When prejudicial statements have been publicly made by others, responsive statements may have the salutary effect of lessening any resulting adverse impact on the adjudicative proceeding. Such responsive statements should be limited to contain only such information as is necessary to mitigate undue prejudice created by the statements made by others.

MODEL CODE COMPARISON:

Rule 3.6 is similar to DR 7–107, except as follows: First, Rule 3.6 adopts the general criteria of "substantial likelihood of materially prejudicing an adjudicative proceeding" to describe impermissible conduct. Second, Rule 3.6 makes clear that only attorneys who are, or have been involved in a proceeding, or their associates, are subject to the Rule. Third, Rule 3.6 omits the particulars in DR 7–107(b), transforming them instead into an illustrative compilation as part of the Rule's commentary that is intended to give fair notice of the kinds of statements that are generally thought to be more likely than other kinds of statements to pose unacceptable dangers to the fair administration of justice. Whether any statement will have a substantial likelihood of materially prejudicing an adjudicatory proceeding will depend upon the facts of each case. The particulars of DR 7–107(c) are retained in Rule 3.6(b), except DR 7–107(C)(7), which provided that a lawyer may reveal "[a]t the time of seizure, a description of the physical evidence seized, other than a confession, admission or statement." Such revelations may be substantially prejudicial and are frequently the subject of pretrial suppression motions whose success would be undermined by disclosure of the suppressed evidence to the press. Finally, Rule 3.6 authorizes a lawyer to protect a client by making a limited reply to adverse publicity substantially prejudicial to the client.

RULE 3.7 Lawyer as Witness

(a) A lawyer shall not act as advocate at a trial in which the lawyer is likely to be a necessary witness except where:

(1) the testimony relates to an uncontested issue;

(2) the testimony relates to the nature and value of legal services rendered in the case; or

(3) disqualification of the lawyer would work substantial hardship on the client.

(b) A lawyer may act as advocate in a trial in which another lawyer in the lawyer's firm is likely to be called as a witness unless precluded from doing so by rule 1.7 or rule 1.9.

COMMENT:

[1] Combining the roles of advocate and witness can prejudice the opposing party and can involve a conflict of interest between the lawyer and client.

[2] The opposing party has proper objection where the combination of roles may prejudice that party's rights in the litigation. A witness is required to testify on the basis of personal knowledge, while an advocate is expected to explain and comment on evidence given by others. It may not be clear whether a statement by an advocate-witness should be taken as proof or as an analysis of the proof.

[3] Paragraph (a)(1) recognizes that if the testimony will be uncontested, the ambiguities in the dual role are purely theoretical. Paragraph (a)(2) recognizes that where the testimony concerns the extent and value of legal services rendered in the action in which the testimony is offered, permitting the lawyers to

testify avoids the need for a second trial with new counsel to resolve that issue. Moreover, in such a situation the judge has first hand knowledge of the matter in issue; hence, there is less dependence on the adversary process to test the credibility of the testimony.

[4] Apart from these two exceptions, paragraph (a)(3) recognizes that a balancing is required between the interests of the client and those of the opposing party. Whether the opposing party is likely to suffer prejudice depends on the nature of the case, the importance and probable tenor of the lawyer's testimony, and the probability that the lawyer's testimony will conflict with that of other witnesses. Even if there is risk of such prejudice, in determining whether the lawyer should be disqualified due regard must be given to the effect of disqualification on the lawyer's client. It is relevant that one or both parties could reasonably foresee that the lawyer would probably be a witness. The principle of imputed disqualification stated in Rule 1.10 has no application to this aspect of the problem.

[5] Whether the combination of roles involves an improper conflict of interest with respect to the client is determined by Rule 1.7 or 1.9. For example, if there is likely to be substantial conflict between the testimony of the client and that of the lawyer or a member of the lawyer's firm, the representation is improper. The problem can arise whether the lawyer is called as a witness on behalf of the client or is called by the opposing party. Determining whether or not such a conflict exists is primarily the responsibility of the lawyer involved. See Comment to Rule 1.7. If a lawyer who is a member of a firm may not act as both advocate and witness by reason of conflict of interest, Rule 1.10 disqualifies the firm also.

MODEL CODE COMPARISON:

DR 5–102(A) prohibited a lawyer, or the lawyer's firm, from serving as advocate if the lawyer "learns or it is obvious that he or a lawyer in his firm ought to be called as a witness on behalf of his client." DR 5–102(B) provided that a lawyer, and the lawyer's firm, may continue representation if the "lawyer learns or it is obvious that he or a lawyer in his firm may be called as a witness other than on behalf of his client . . . until it is apparent that his testimony is or may be prejudicial to his client." DR 5–101(B) permitted a lawyer to testify while representing a client: "(1) If the testimony will relate solely to an uncontested matter; (2) If the testimony will relate solely to a matter of formality and there is no reason to believe that substantial evidence will be offered in opposition to the testimony; (3) If the testimony will relate solely to the nature and value of legal services rendered in the case by the lawyer or his firm to the client; (4) As to any matter if refusal would work a substantial hardship on the client because of the distinctive value of the lawyer or his firm as counsel in the particular case."

The exception stated in paragraph (a)(1) consolidates provisions of DR 5–101(B)(1) and (2). Testimony relating to a formality, referred to in DR 5–101(B)(2), in effect defines the phrase "uncontested issue," and is redundant.

RULE 3.8 Special Responsibilities of a Prosecutor*

The prosecutor in a criminal case shall:

(a) refrain from prosecuting a charge that the prosecutor knows is not supported by probable cause;

(b) make reasonable efforts to assure that the accused has been advised of the right to, and the procedure for obtaining, counsel and has been given reasonable opportunity to obtain counsel;

* In 1990, the ABA House of Delegates added subparagraph (f) to Model Rule 3.8 to address the profession's concerns over the increased use of subpoenas by prosecutors towards attorneys for information about their clients. The original amendment included a statement limiting the situations in which a prosecutor may subpoena a lawyer in a grand jury or criminal proceeding to cases in which "the prosecutor obtains prior judicial approval after an opportunity for an adversarial hearing." This statement was removed by the House of Delegates in August 1995, because several judicial decisions had invalidated this ABA requirement. Thus, under the current rule, a prosecutor must continue to meet the remaining standards in subparagraph (f) to obtain a subpoena against a criminal defense lawyer; however, the prosecutor does not need to obtain prior court approval.

In August 1994, the ABA added the text in subparagraph (g) to the original Model Rule 3.8. This amendment reflects the changes that the ABA made to Model Rule 3.6 as it applies to prosecutors.

(c) not seek to obtain from an unrepresented accused a waiver of important pretrial rights, such as the right to a preliminary hearing;

(d) make timely disclosure to the defense of all evidence or information known to the prosecutor that tends to negate the guilt of the accused or mitigates the offense, and, in connection with sentencing, disclose to the defense and to the tribunal all unprivileged mitigating information known to the prosecutor, except when the prosecutor is relieved of this responsibility by a protective order of the tribunal; and

(e) exercise reasonable care to prevent investigators, law enforcement personnel, employees or other persons assisting or associated with the prosecutor in a criminal case from making an extrajudicial statement that the prosecutor would be prohibited from making under rule 3.6.

(f) not subpoena a lawyer in a grand jury or other criminal proceeding to present evidence about a past or present client unless:

(i) the prosecutor reasonably believes:

(1) the information sought is not protected from disclosure by any applicable privilege;

(2) the evidence sought is essential to the successful completion of an ongoing investigation or prosecution;

(3) there is no other feasible alternative to obtain the information.

(g) except for statements that are necessary to inform the public of the nature and extent of the prosecutor's action and that serve a legitimate law enforcement purpose, refrain from making extrajudicial comments that have a substantial likelihood of heightening public condemnation of the accused.

COMMENT:

[1] A prosecutor has the responsibility of a minister of justice and not simply that of an advocate. This responsibility carries with it specific obligations to see that the defendant is accorded procedural justice and that guilt is decided upon the basis of sufficient evidence. Precisely how far the prosecutor is required to go in this direction is a matter of debate and varies in different jurisdictions. Many jurisdictions have adopted the ABA Standards of Criminal Justice Relating to Prosecution Function, which in turn are the product of prolonged and careful deliberation by lawyers experienced in both criminal prosecution and defense. See also Rule 3.3(d), governing ex parte proceedings, among which grand jury proceedings are included. Applicable law may require other measures by the prosecutor and knowing disregard of those obligations or a systematic abuse of prosecutorial discretion could constitute a violation of Rule 8.4.

[2] Paragraph (c) does not apply to an accused appearing pro se with the approval of the tribunal. Nor does it forbid the lawful questioning of a suspect who has knowingly waived the rights to counsel and silence.

[3] The exception in paragraph (d) recognizes that a prosecutor may seek an appropriate protective order from the tribunal if disclosure of information to the defense could result in substantial harm to an individual or to the public interest.

[4]* Paragraph (f) is intended to limit the issuance of lawyer subpoenas in grand jury and other criminal proceedings to those situations in which there is a genuine need to intrude into the client-lawyer relationship.

---

* The ABA added paragraph [4] in 1990 when it amended Model Rule 3.8 by adding subparagraph (f). The 1995 amendment to subparagraph (f) deleted the following sentence: "The prosecutor is required to obtain court approval for the issuance of the subpoena after an opportunity for an adversarial hearing is afforded in order to assure an independent determination that the applicable standards are met."

[5]* Paragraph (g) supplements Rule 3.6, which prohibits extrajudicial statements that have a substantial likelihood of prejudicing an adjudicatory proceeding. In the context of a criminal prosecution, a prosecutor's extrajudicial statement can create the additional problem of increasing public condemnation of the accused. Although the announcement of an indictment, for example, will necessarily have severe consequences for the accused, a prosecutor can, and should, avoid comments which have no legitimate law enforcement purpose and have a substantial likelihood of increasing public opprobrium of the accused. Nothing in this Comment is intended to restrict the statements which a prosecutor may make which comply with Rule 3.6(b) or 3.6(c).

MODEL CODE COMPARISON:

DR 7–103(A) provided that a "public prosecutor . . . shall not institute . . . criminal charges when he knows or it is obvious that the charges are not supported by probable cause." DR 7–103(B) provided that "[a] public prosecutor . . . shall make timely disclosure . . . of the existence of evidence, known to the prosecutor . . . that tends to negate the guilt of the accused, mitigate the degree of the offense, or reduce the punishment."

RULE 3.9 Advocate in Nonadjudicative Proceedings

A lawyer representing a client before a legislative or administrative tribunal in a nonadjudicative proceeding shall disclose that the appearance is in a representative capacity and shall conform to the provisions of rules 3.3(a) through (c), 3.4(a) through (c), and 3.5.

COMMENT:

[1] In representation before bodies such as legislatures, municipal councils, and executive and administrative agencies acting in a rule-making or policy-making capacity, lawyers present facts, formulate issues and advance argument in the matters under consideration. The decision-making body, like a court, should be able to rely on the integrity of the submissions made to it. A lawyer appearing before such a body should deal with the tribunal honestly and in conformity with applicable rules of procedure.

[2] Lawyers have no exclusive right to appear before nonadjudicative bodies, as they do before a court. The requirements of this Rule therefore may subject lawyers to regulations inapplicable to advocates who are not lawyers. However, legislatures and administrative agencies have a right to expect lawyers to deal with them as they deal with courts.

[3] This Rule does not apply to representation of a client in a negotiation or other bilateral transaction with a governmental agency; representation in such a transaction is governed by Rules 4.1 through 4.4.

MODEL CODE COMPARISON:

EC 7–15 stated that a lawyer "appearing before an administrative agency, regardless of the nature of the proceeding it is conducting, has the continuing duty to advance the cause of his client within the bounds of the law." EC 7–16 stated that "[w]hen a lawyer appears in connection with proposed legislation, he . . . should comply with applicable laws and legislative rules." EC 8–5 stated that "[f]raudulent, deceptive, or otherwise illegal conduct by a participant in a proceeding before a . . . legislative body . . . should never be participated in . . . by lawyers." DR 7–106(B)(1) provided that "[i]n presenting a matter to a tribunal, a lawyer shall disclose . . . [u]nless privileged or irrelevant, the identity of the clients he represents and of the persons who employed him."

---

* The ABA added paragraph [5] in 1994 when it amended Model Rule 3.8 by adding subparagraph (g).

TRANSACTIONS WITH PERSONS OTHER THAN CLIENTS

RULE 4.1 Truthfulness in Statements to Others*

In the course of representing a client a lawyer shall not knowingly:

(a) make a false statement of material fact or law to a third person; or

(b) fail to disclose a material fact to a third person when disclosure is necessary to avoid assisting a criminal or fraudulent act by a client, unless disclosure is prohibited by rule 1.6.

COMMENT:

Misrepresentation

[1] A lawyer is required to be truthful when dealing with others on a client's behalf, but generally has no affirmative duty to inform an opposing party of relevant facts. A misrepresentation can occur if the lawyer incorporates or affirms a statement of another person that the lawyer knows is false. Misrepresentations can also occur by failure to act.

Statements of Fact

[2] This Rule refers to statements of fact. Whether a particular statement should be regarded as one of fact can depend on the circumstances. Under generally accepted conventions in negotiation, certain types of statements ordinarily are not taken as statements of material fact. Estimates of price or value placed on the subject of a transaction and a party's intentions as to an acceptable settlement of a claim are in this category, and so is the existence of an undisclosed principal except where nondisclosure of the principal would constitute fraud.

Fraud by Client

[3] Paragraph (b) recognizes that substantive law may require a lawyer to disclose certain information to avoid being deemed to have assisted the client's crime or fraud. The requirement of disclosure created by this paragraph is, however, subject to the obligations created by Rule 1.6.

MODEL CODE COMPARISON:

Paragraph (a) is substantially similar to DR 7–102(A)(5), which stated that "[i]n his representation of a client, a lawyer shall not . . . [k]nowingly make a false statement of law or fact."

With regard to paragraph (b), DR 7–102(A)(3) provided that a lawyer shall not "[c]onceal or knowingly fail to disclose that which he is required by law to reveal."

RULE 4.2 Communication With Person Represented by Counsel**

In representing a client, a lawyer shall not communicate about the subject of the representation with a person the lawyer knows to be represented by another lawyer in the matter, unless the lawyer has the consent of the other lawyer or is authorized by law to do so.

---

* The Kutak Commission's Revised Final Draft contained substantially different language on the interaction of Rules 1.6 and 4.1: "The duties stated in this Rule apply even if compliance requires disclosure of information otherwise protected by Rule 1.6." Proposed Model Rule 4.1(b) (Revised Final Draft) (June 20, 1982).

** In August 1995, the ABA House of Delegates amended Model Rule 4.2 to substitute the word "person" for the word "party" so as to clarify that the rule applies to situations where a lawyer seeks to contact a represented individual in pre-litigation or pre-custodial settings as well or when a lawyer seeks to contact a non-party such as an informant or undercover agent who is represented by counsel.

COMMENT:†

[1] This Rule does not prohibit communication with a represented person, or an employee or agent of such a person, concerning matters outside the representation. For example, the existence of a controversy between a government agency and a private party, or between two organizations, does not prohibit a lawyer for either from communicating with nonlawyer representatives of the other regarding a separate matter. Also, parties to a matter may communicate directly with each other and a lawyer having independent justification for communicating with the other party is permitted to do so. Communications authorized by law include, for example, the right of a party to a controversy with a government agency to speak with government officials about the matter.

[2] Communications authorized by law also include constitutionally permissible investigative activities of lawyers representing governmental entities, directly or through investigative agents, prior to the commencement of criminal or civil enforcement proceedings, when there is applicable judicial precedent that either has found the activity permissible under this Rule or has found this Rule inapplicable. However, the Rule imposes ethical restrictions that go beyond those imposed by constitutional provisions.

[3] This rule applies to communications with any person, whether or not a party to a formal adjudicative proceeding, contract or negotiation, who is represented by counsel concerning the matter to which the communication relates.

[4] In the case of an organization, this Rule prohibits communications by a lawyer for another person or entity concerning the matter in representation with persons having a managerial responsibility on behalf of the organization, and with any other person whose act or omission in connection with that matter may be imputed to the organization for purposes of civil or criminal liability or whose statement may constitute an admission on the part of the organization. If an agent or employee of the organization is represented in the matter by his or her own counsel, the consent by that counsel to a communication will be sufficient for purposes of this Rule. Compare Rule 3.4(f).

[5] The prohibition on communications with a represented person only applies, however, in circumstances where the lawyer knows that the person is in fact represented in the matter to be discussed. This means that the lawyer has actual knowledge of the fact of the representation; but such actual knowledge may be inferred from the circumstances. See Terminology. Such an inference may arise in circumstances where there is substantial reason to believe that the person with whom communication is sought is represented in the matter to be discussed. Thus, a lawyer cannot evade the requirement of obtaining the consent of counsel by closing eyes to the obvious.

[6] In the event the person with whom the lawyer communicates is not known to be represented by counsel in the matter, the lawyer's communications are subject to Rule 4.3.

MODEL CODE COMPARISON:

This Rule is substantially identical to DR 7–104(A)(1).

RULE 4.3 Dealing With Unrepresented Person

In dealing on behalf of a client with a person who is not represented by counsel, a lawyer shall not state or imply that the lawyer is disinterested. When the lawyer knows or reasonably should know that the unrepresented person misunderstands the lawyer's role in the matter, the lawyer shall make reasonable efforts to correct the misunderstanding.

† The ABA's amendment of Rule 4.2 in August 1995 included a substantial revision of the comments: (1) to clarify that knowledge of the fact that a person is represented by counsel may be inferred from the circumstances; (2) to elaborate on the situations in which the communication with represented persons is authorized by law; (3) to make clear that the rule applies to persons represented by counsel in all matters (for example, contract or negotiation matters) and not just to parties in formal proceedings; and (4) to cross reference discussions of situations where the person is not represented by counsel to Model Rule 4.3. Comments 2, 5, and 6 are added in this amendment. Comments 1, 3, and 4 are based upon prior comments and rewritten to reflect the clarifications discussed above.

COMMENT:

An unrepresented person, particularly one not experienced in dealing with legal matters, might assume that a lawyer is disinterested in loyalties or is a disinterested authority on the law even when the lawyer represents a client. During the course of a lawyer's representation of a client, the lawyer should not give advice to an unrepresented person other than the advice to obtain counsel.

MODEL CODE COMPARISON:

There was no direct counterpart to this Rule in the Model Code. DR 7–104(A)(2) provided that a lawyer shall not "[g]ive advice to a person who is not represented by a lawyer, other than the advice to secure counsel. . . ."

RULE 4.4 Respect for Rights of Third Persons

In representing a client, a lawyer shall not use means that have no substantial purpose other than to embarrass, delay, or burden a third person, or use methods of obtaining evidence that violate the legal rights of such a person.

COMMENT:

Responsibility to a client requires a lawyer to subordinate the interests of others to those of the client, but that responsibility does not imply that a lawyer may disregard the rights of third persons. It is impractical to catalogue all such rights, but they include legal restrictions on methods of obtaining evidence from third persons.

MODEL CODE COMPARISON:

DR 7–106(C)(2) provided that a lawyer shall not "[a]sk any question that he has no reasonable basis to believe is relevant to the case and that is intended to degrade a witness or other person." DR 7–102(A)(1) provided that a lawyer shall not "take . . . action on behalf of his client when he knows or when it is obvious that such action would serve merely to harass or maliciously injure another." DR 7–108(D) provided that "[a]fter discharge of the jury . . . the lawyer shall not ask questions or make comments to a member of that jury that are calculated merely to harass or embarrass the juror. . . ." DR 7–108(E) provided that a lawyer "shall not conduct . . . a vexatious or harassing investigation of either a venireman or a juror."

LAW FIRMS AND ASSOCIATIONS

RULE 5.1 Responsibilities of a Partner or Supervisory Lawyer

(a) A partner in a law firm shall make reasonable efforts to ensure that the firm has in effect measures giving reasonable assurance that all lawyers in the firm conform to the rules of professional conduct.

(b) A lawyer having direct supervisory authority over another lawyer shall make reasonable efforts to ensure that the other lawyer conforms to the rules of professional conduct.

(c) A lawyer shall be responsible for another lawyer's violation of the rules of professional conduct if:

(1) the lawyer orders or, with knowledge of the specific conduct, ratifies the conduct involved; or

(2) the lawyer is a partner in the law firm in which the other lawyer practices, or has direct supervisory authority over the other lawyer, and knows of the conduct at a time when its consequences can be avoided or mitigated but fails to take reasonable remedial action.

COMMENT:

[1] Paragraphs (a) and (b) refer to lawyers who have supervisory authority over the professional work of a firm or legal department of a government agency. This includes members of a partnership and the

shareholders in a law firm organized as a professional corporation; lawyers having supervisory authority in the law department of an enterprise or government agency; and lawyers who have intermediate managerial responsibilities in a firm.

[2] The measures required to fulfill the responsibility prescribed in paragraphs (a) and (b) can depend on the firm's structure and the nature of its practice. In a small firm, informal supervision and occasional admonition ordinarily might be sufficient. In a large firm, or in practice situations in which intensely difficult ethical problems frequently arise, more elaborate procedures may be necessary. Some firms, for example, have a procedure whereby junior lawyers can make confidential referral of ethical problems directly to a designated senior partner or special committee. See Rule 5.2. Firms, whether large or small, may also rely on continuing legal education in professional ethics. In any event, the ethical atmosphere of a firm can influence the conduct of all its members and a lawyer having authority over the work of another may not assume that the subordinate lawyer will inevitably conform to the Rules.

[3] Paragraph (c)(1) expresses a general principle of responsibility for acts of another. See also Rule 8.4(a).

[4] Paragraph (c)(2) defines the duty of a lawyer having direct supervisory authority over performance of specific legal work by another lawyer. Whether a lawyer has such supervisory authority in particular circumstances is a question of fact. Partners of a private firm have at least indirect responsibility for all work being done by the firm, while a partner in charge of a particular matter ordinarily has direct authority over other firm lawyers engaged in the matter. Appropriate remedial action by a partner would depend on the immediacy of the partner's involvement and the seriousness of the misconduct. The supervisor is required to intervene to prevent avoidable consequences of misconduct if the supervisor knows that the misconduct occurred. Thus, if a supervising lawyer knows that a subordinate misrepresented a matter to an opposing party in negotiation, the supervisor as well as the subordinate has a duty to correct the resulting misapprehension.

[5] Professional misconduct by a lawyer under supervision could reveal a violation of paragraph (b) on the part of the supervisory lawyer even though it does not entail a violation of paragraph (c) because there was no direction, ratification or knowledge or the violation.

[6] Apart from this Rule and Rule 8.4(a), a lawyer does not have disciplinary liability for the conduct of a partner, associate or subordinate. Whether a lawyer may be liable civilly or criminally for another lawyer's conduct is a question of law beyond the scope of these Rules.

MODEL CODE COMPARISON:

There was no direct counterpart to this Rule in the Model Code. DR 1–103(A) provided that a lawyer "possessing unprivileged knowledge of a violation of DR 1–102 shall report such knowledge to . . . authority empowered to investigate or act upon such violation."

RULE 5.2 Responsibilities of a Subordinate Lawyer

(a) A lawyer is bound by the rules of professional conduct notwithstanding that the lawyer acted at the direction of another person.

(b) A subordinate lawyer does not violate the rules of professional conduct if that lawyer acts in accordance with a supervisory lawyer's reasonable resolution of an arguable question of professional duty.

COMMENT:

[1] Although a lawyer is not relieved of responsibility for a violation by the fact that the lawyer acted at the direction of a supervisor, that fact may be relevant in determining whether a lawyer had the knowledge required to render conduct a violation of the Rules. For example, if a subordinate filed a frivolous pleading at the direction of a supervisor, the subordinate would not be guilty of a professional violation unless the subordinate knew of the document's frivolous character.

[2] When lawyers in a supervisor-subordinate relationship encounter a matter involving professional judgment as to ethical duty, the supervisor may assume responsibility for making the judgment. Otherwise a consistent course of action or position could not be taken. If the question can reasonably be answered only

one way, the duty of both lawyers is clear and they are equally responsible for fulfilling it. However, if the question is reasonably arguable, someone has to decide upon the course of action. That authority ordinarily reposes in the supervisor, and a subordinate may be guided accordingly. For example, if a question arises whether the interests of two clients conflict under Rule 1.7, the supervisor's reasonable resolution of the question should protect the subordinate professionally if the resolution is subsequently challenged.

MODEL CODE COMPARISON:

There was no counterpart to this Rule in the Model Code.

RULE 5.3 Responsibilities Regarding Nonlawyer Assistants

With respect to a nonlawyer employed or retained by or associated with a lawyer:

(a) a partner in a law firm shall make reasonable efforts to ensure that the firm has in effect measures giving reasonable assurance that the person's conduct is compatible with the professional obligations of the lawyer;

(b) a lawyer having direct supervisory authority over the nonlawyer shall make reasonable efforts to ensure that the person's conduct is compatible with the professional obligations of the lawyer; and

(c) a lawyer shall be responsible for conduct of such a person that would be a violation of the rules of professional conduct if engaged in by a lawyer if:

(1) the lawyer orders or, with the knowledge of the specific conduct, ratifies the conduct involved; or

(2) the lawyer is a partner in the law firm in which the person is employed, or has direct supervisory authority over the person, and knows of the conduct at a time when its consequences can be avoided or mitigated but fails to take reasonable remedial action.

COMMENT:

Lawyers generally employ assistants in their practice, including secretaries, investigators, law student interns, and paraprofessionals. Such assistants, whether employees or independent contractors, act for the lawyer in rendition of the lawyer's professional services. A lawyer should give such assistants appropriate instruction and supervision concerning the ethical aspects of their employment, particularly regarding the obligation not to disclose information relating to representation of the client, and should be responsible for their work product. The measures employed in supervising nonlawyers should take account of the fact that they do not have legal training and are not subject to professional discipline.

MODEL CODE COMPARISON:

There was no direct counterpart to this Rule in the Model Code. DR 4–101(D) provided that a lawyer "shall exercise reasonable care to prevent his employees, associates, and others whose services are utilized by him from disclosing or using confidences or secrets of a client. . . ." DR 7–107(J) provided that "[a] lawyer shall exercise reasonable care to prevent his employees and associates from making an extrajudicial statement that he would be prohibited from making under DR 7–107."

RULE 5.4 Professional Independence of a Lawyer*

(a) A lawyer or law firm shall not share legal fees with a nonlawyer, except that:

(1) an agreement by a lawyer with the lawyer's firm, partner, or associate may provide for the payment of money, over a reasonable period of time after the lawyer's death, to the lawyer's estate or to one or more specified persons;

* In 1990, the ABA amended the text of Model Rule 5.4(a)(2) to recognize the addition of Model Rule 1.17 on the sale of a law practice. The original Model Rule 5.4(a)(2) read as follows:

(2) a lawyer who purchases the practice of a deceased, disabled, or disappeared lawyer may, pursuant to the provisions of Rule 1.17, pay to the estate or other representative of that lawyer the agreed-upon purchase price; and

(3) a lawyer or law firm may include nonlawyer employees in a compensation or retirement plan, even though the plan is based in whole or in part on a profit-sharing arrangement.

(b) A lawyer shall not form a partnership with a nonlawyer if any of the activities of the partnership consist of the practice of law.

(c) A lawyer shall not permit a person who recommends, employs, or pays the lawyer to render legal services for another to direct or regulate the lawyer's professional judgment in rendering such legal services.

(d) A lawyer shall not practice with or in the form of a professional corporation or association authorized to practice law for a profit, if:

(1) a nonlawyer owns any interest therein, except that a fiduciary representative of the estate of a lawyer may hold the stock or interest of the lawyer for a reasonable time during administration;

(2) a nonlawyer is a corporate director or officer thereof; or

(3) a nonlawyer has the right to direct or control the professional judgment of a lawyer.

COMMENT:

The provisions of this Rule express traditional limitations on sharing fees. These limitations are to protect the lawyer's professional independence of judgment. Where someone other than the client pays the lawyer's fee or salary, or recommends employment of the lawyer, that arrangement does not modify the lawyer's obligation to the client. As stated in paragraph (c), such arrangements should not interfere with the lawyer's professional judgment.

MODEL CODE COMPARISON:

Paragraph (a) is substantially identical to DR 3–102(A).

Paragraph (b) is substantially identical to DR 3–103(A).

Paragraph (c) is substantially identical to DR 5–107(B).

Paragraph (d) is substantially identical to DR 5–107(C).

RULE 5.5 Unauthorized Practice of Law

A lawyer shall not:

(a) practice law in a jurisdiction where doing so violates the regulation of the legal profession in that jurisdiction; or

(b) assist a person who is not a member of the bar in the performance of activity that constitutes the unauthorized practice of law.

RULE 5.4 **Professional Independence of a Lawyer**

(a) A lawyer or law firm shall not share legal fees with a nonlawyer, except that:

* * *

(2) a lawyer who undertakes to complete unfinished legal business of a deceased lawyer may pay to the estate of the deceased lawyer that proportion of the total compensation which fairly represents the services rendered by the deceased lawyer; and

* * *

COMMENT:

The definition of the practice of law is established by law and varies from one jurisdiction to another. Whatever the definition, limiting the practice of law to members of the bar protects the public against rendition of legal services by unqualified persons. Paragraph (b) does not prohibit a lawyer from employing the services of paraprofessionals and delegating functions to them, so long as the lawyer supervises the delegated work and retains responsibility for their work. See Rule 5.3. Likewise, it does not prohibit lawyers from providing professional advice and instruction to nonlawyers whose employment requires knowledge of law; for example, claims adjusters, employees of financial or commercial institutions, social workers, accountants and persons employed in government agencies. In addition, a lawyer may counsel nonlawyers who wish to proceed pro se.

MODEL CODE COMPARISON:

With regard to paragraph (a), DR 3–101(B) of the Model Code provided that "[a] lawyer shall not practice law in a jurisdiction where to do so would be in violation of regulations of the profession in that jurisdiction."

With regard to paragraph (b), DR 3–101(A) of the Model Code provided that "[a] lawyer shall not aid a non-lawyer in the unauthorized practice of law."

RULE 5.6 Restrictions on Right to Practice

A lawyer shall not participate in offering or making:

(a) a partnership or employment agreement that restricts the rights of a lawyer to practice after termination of the relationship, except an agreement concerning benefits upon retirement; or

(b) an agreement in which a restriction on the lawyer's right to practice is part of the settlement of a controversy between private parties.

COMMENT:

[1] An agreement restricting the right of partners or associates to practice after leaving a firm not only limits their professional autonomy but also limits the freedom of clients to choose a lawyer. Paragraph (a) prohibits such agreements except for restrictions incident to provisions concerning retirement benefits for service with the firm.

[2] Paragraph (b) prohibits a lawyer from agreeing not to represent other persons in connection with settling a claim on behalf of a client.

[3]* This Rule does not apply to prohibit restrictions that may be included in the terms of the sale of a law practice pursuant to Rule 1.17.

MODEL CODE COMPARISON:

This Rule is substantially similar to DR 2–108.

RULE 5.7 Responsibilities Regarding Law-Related Services†

(a) A lawyer shall be subject to the Rules of Professional Conduct with respect to the provision of law-related services, as defined in paragraph (b), if the law-related services are provided:

(1) by the lawyer in circumstances that are not distinct from the lawyer's provision of legal services to clients; or

* This paragraph was added by the ABA in 1990 to resolve the potential overlap between this provision and the restrictions placed in Model Rule 1.17 regarding the sale of a law practice.

† See footnote a, page 1183 infra, for text and comment to former Rule 5.7, Provision of Ancillary Services (Repealed).

(2) by a separate entity controlled by the lawyer individually or with others if the lawyer fails to take reasonable measures to assure that a person obtaining the law-related services knows that the services of the separate entity are not legal services and that the protections of the client-lawyer relationship do not exist.

(b) The term "law-related services" denotes services that might reasonably be performed in conjunction with and in substance are related to the provision of legal services, and that are not prohibited as unauthorized practice of law when provided by a nonlawyer.

COMMENT:

[1] When a lawyer performs law-related services or controls an organization that does so, there exists the potential for ethical problems. Principal among these is the possibility that the person for whom the law-related services are performed fails to understand that the services may not carry with them the protections normally afforded as part of the client-lawyer relationship. The recipient of the law-related services may expect, for example, that the protection of client confidences, prohibitions against representation of persons with conflicting interests, and obligations of a lawyer to maintain professional independence apply to the provision of law-related services when that may not be the case. Rule 5.7 applies to the provision of law-related services by a lawyer even when the lawyer does not provide any legal services to the person for whom the law-related services are performed. The Rule identifies the circumstances in which all of the Rules of Professional Conduct apply to the provision of law-related services. Even when those circumstances do not exist, however, the conduct of a lawyer involved in the provision of law-related services is subject to those Rules that apply generally to lawyer conduct, regardless of whether the conduct involves the provision of legal services. See, e.g., Rule 8.4.

[2] When law-related services are provided by a lawyer under circumstances that are not distinct from the lawyer's provision of legal services to clients, the lawyer in providing the law-related services must adhere to the requirements of the Rules of Professional Conduct as provided in Rule 5.7(a)(1).

[3] Law-related services also may be provided through an entity that is distinct from that through which the lawyer provides legal services. If the lawyer individually or with others has control of such an entity's operations, the Rule requires the lawyer to take reasonable measures to assure that each person using the services of the entity knows that the services provided by the entity are not legal services and that the Rules of Professional Conduct that relate to the client-lawyer relationship do not apply. A lawyer's control of an entity extends to the ability to direct its operation. Whether a lawyer has such control will depend upon the circumstances of the particular case.

[4] When a client-lawyer relationship exists with a person who is referred by a lawyer to a separate law-related service entity controlled by the lawyer, individually or with others, the lawyer must comply with Rule 1.8(a).

[5] In taking the reasonable measures referred to in paragraph (a)(2) to assure that a person using law-related services understands the practical effect or significance of the inapplicability of the Rules of Professional Conduct, the lawyer should communicate to the person receiving the law-related services, in a manner sufficient to assure that the person understands the significance of the fact, that the relationship of the person to the business entity will not be a client-lawyer relationship. The communication should be made before entering into an agreement for provision of or providing law-related services, and preferably should be in writing.

[6] The burden is upon the lawyer to show that the lawyer has taken reasonable measures under the circumstances to communicate the desired understanding. For instance, a sophisticated user of law-related services, such as a publicly held corporation, may require a lesser explanation than someone unaccustomed to making distinctions between legal services and law-related services, such as an individual seeking tax advice from a lawyer-accountant or investigative services in connection with a lawsuit.

[7] Regardless of the sophistication of potential recipients of law-related services, a lawyer should take special care to keep separate the provision of law-related and legal services in order to minimize the risk that the recipient will assume that the law-related services are legal services. The risk of such confusion is especially acute when the lawyer renders both types of services with respect to the same matter. Under

some circumstances the legal and law-related services may be so closely entwined that they cannot be distinguished from each other, and the requirement of disclosure and consultation imposed by paragraph (a)(2) of the Rule cannot be met. In such a case a lawyer will be responsible for assuring that both the lawyer's conduct and, to the extent required by Rule 5.3, that of nonlawyer employees in the distinct entity which the lawyer controls complies in all respects with the Rules of Professional Conduct.

[8] A broad range of economic and other interests of clients may be served by lawyers' engaging in the delivery of law-related services. Examples of law-related services include providing title insurance, financial planning, accounting, trust services, real estate counseling, legislative lobbying, economic analysis social work, psychological counseling, tax return preparation, and patient, medical or environmental consulting. When a lawyer is obliged to accord the recipients of such services the protections of those Rules that apply to the client-lawyer relationship, the lawyer must take special care to heed the proscriptions of the Rules addressing conflict of interest (Rules 1.7 through 1.11, especially Rules 1.7(b) and 1.8(a), (b) and (f)), and to scrupulously adhere to the requirements of Rule 1.6 relating to disclosure of confidential information. The promotion of the law-related services must also in all respects comply with Rules 7.1 through 7.3, dealing with advertising and solicitation. In that regard, lawyers should take special care to identify the obligations that may be imposed as a result of a jurisdiction's decisional law.

[9] When the full protections of all of the Rules of Professional Conduct do not apply to the provision of law-related services, principles of law external to the Rules, for example, the law of principal and agent, govern the legal duties owed to those receiving the services. Those other legal principles may establish a different degree of protection for the recipient with respect to confidentiality of information, conflicts of interest and permissible business relationships with clients. See also Rule 8.4 (Misconduct).

a. Model Rule 5.7 did not appear in the original version of the Model Rules. In 1991, the ABA added the provision reproduced in this footnote and its comments in response to the debate created by the adoption of the District of Columbia rule that allows lawyers and non-lawyers to practice together in the same law firm. D.C. Rule 5.4 is contained on pages 252–54. Model Rule 5.7 was passed by a vote of 197 to 186 in the House of Delegates.

In the August 1992 ABA meeting, the House of Delegates voted 190 to 183 to repeal the provision reproduced in this footnote. In February 1994, the ABA passed a new rule dealing with ancillary services. The short-lived Model Rule 5.7 text and comment are reprinted below:

(a) A lawyer shall not practice law in a law firm which owns a controlling interest in, or operates, an entity which provides non-legal services which are ancillary to the practice of law, or otherwise provides such ancillary non-legal services, except as provided in paragraph (b).

(b) A lawyer may practice law in a law firm which provides non-legal services which are ancillary to the practice of law if:

(1) The ancillary services are provided solely to clients of the law firm and are incidental to, in connection with and concurrent to, the provision of legal services by the law firm to such clients;

(2) Such ancillary services are provided solely by employees of the law firm itself and not by a subsidiary or other affiliate of the law firm;

(3) The law firm makes appropriate disclosure in writing to its clients; and

(4) The law firm does not hold itself out as engaging in any non-legal activities except in conjunction with the provision of legal services, as provided in this rule.

(c) One or more lawyers who engage in the practice of law in a law firm shall neither own a controlling interest in, nor operate, an entity which provides non-legal services which are ancillary to the practice of law, nor otherwise provide such ancillary non-legal services, except that their firms may provide such services as provided in paragraph (b).

(d) Two or more lawyers who engage in the practice of law in separate law firms shall neither own a controlling interest in, nor operate, an entity which provides non-legal services which are ancillary to the practice of law, nor otherwise provide such ancillary non-legal services.

COMMENT:

General

[1] For many years, lawyers have provided to their clients non-legal services which are ancillary to the practice of law. Such services included title insurance, trust services and patent consulting. In most instances, these ancillary nonlegal services were provided to law firm clients in connection with, and concurrent to, the provision of legal services by the lawyer or law firm. The provision of such services afforded benefits to clients, including making available a greater range of services from one source and maintaining technical expertise in various fields within a law firm. However, the provision of both legal and ancillary nonlegal services raises ethical concerns, including conflicts of interest, confusion on the part of clients and possible loss (or inapplicability) of the attorney-client privilege, which may not have been addressed adequately by the other Model Rules of Professional Conduct.

[2] Eventually, law firms began to form affiliates, largely staffed by nonlawyers, to provide ancillary nonlegal services to both clients and customers who were not clients for legal services. In addition to exacerbating the ethical problems of conflicts of interest, confusion and threats to confidentiality, the large-scale movement of law firms into ancillary nonlegal businesses raised serious professionalism concerns, including compromising lawyers' independent judgment, the loss of the bar's right to self-regulation and the provision of legal services by entities controlled by nonlawyers.

[3] Rule 5.7 addresses both the ethical and professionalism concerns implicated by the provision of ancillary nonlegal services by lawyers and law firms. It preserves the ability of lawyers to provide additional services to their clients and maintain within the law firm a broad range of technical expertise. However, Rule 5.7 restricts the ability of law firms to provide ancillary nonlegal services through affiliates to nonclient customers and clients alike, the rendition of which raises serious ethical and professionalism concerns.

Limitations on the Provision of Nonlegal Services Which Are Ancillary to the Practice of Law

[4] Paragraph (a) attempts to forestall the ethical and professional concerns which are raised when law firms own or operate nonlegal businesses which are ancillary to the practice of law or otherwise provide such services. The provision of such ancillary services by law firms has the potential of compromising a lawyer's independent professional judgment and otherwise causing harm to law firm clients (*e.g.*, creating conflicts of interest, jeopardizing clients' expectations of confidentiality and causing confusion on the part of clients). Additionally, serious threats to lawyers' professionalism are also posed when law firms own or operate ancillary businesses which provide services to persons who are not concurrently seeking legal services from the law firm.

[5] Paragraph (a) prohibits lawyers from practicing in a law firm which owns a controlling interest in, or operates, an entity which provides nonlegal services which are ancillary to the practice of law, or which provides such ancillary services from within the law firm, unless such services are incidental to the law firm's provision of legal services as set forth in Paragraph (b).

[6] The term "nonlegal services which are ancillary to the practice of law" refers to those services which satisfy all or most of the following indicia: (1) are provided to clients of a law firm (or customers of a business owned or controlled by a law firm); (2) clearly do not constitute the practice of law; (3) are readily available from those not licensed to practice law; (4) are functionally connected to the provision of legal services, i.e., services which are often sought or needed in connection with (and in addition to) legal services; (5) involve intellectual ability or learning; and (6) have the potential for creating serious ethical problems in the lawyer-client relationship, such as compromising the independent professional judgment of lawyers; creating conflicts of interest; threatening the clients' (or customers') expectations of confidentiality and/or causing confusion on the part of clients or customers.

[7] Among those activities which are not included in the term "nonlegal services which are ancillary to the practice of law" because they do not pose serious ethical problems in the lawyer-client relationship are:

(1) law firms or lawyers owning, for example, restaurants, shops or taxi services (since these services are not functionally connected to the practice of law);

(2) law firms providing copying services or other clerical services incidental to the practice of law;

(3) law firms owning and managing the buildings in which their offices are located or other property (since owning and managing property—even through a subsidiary or affiliate—is not functionally connected to the provision of legal services to clients);

(4) a law firm providing services or products intended for use by other lawyers, such as publications, software programs, or legal malpractice insurance (since such services or products are not functionally connected to the provision of legal services to clients);

(5) lawyers serving as fiduciaries of trusts or corporate directors or lawyers serving in quasi-judicial positions such as mediators or arbitrators.

[8] When services provided by a law firm are performed by nonlawyers, there should be an initial presumption that the services do not constitute the practice of law and may be a "nonlegal service which is ancillary to the practice of law." In addition, a presumption that a service is "ancillary to the practice of law" should exist if the service is normally provided by nonlawyers in discrete professions or occupations, e.g., doctors, architects, engineers, real estate brokers, investment bankers or financial consultants.

[9] Note that Paragraph (a) does not prohibit a lawyer from practicing in a law firm which acquires a passive financial interest in an entity which provides nonlegal ancillary services (i.e., purchasing shares of an investment banking firm or a consulting company), provided that the interest is not a controlling one. This rule does not define the concept of control, which is generally a fact-based inquiry dependent on the particular facts and circumstances. However, the existence of an ownership interest by lawyers in other entities (especially clients) may implicate conflict of interest concerns (see Model Rules of Professional Conduct 1.7 and 1.8) and may require disclosure by the lawyers pursuant to these rules.

Connection Between the Provision of Legal and Ancillary Nonlegal Services

[10] Paragraph (b) preserves the ability of law firms to provide nonlegal services which are ancillary to the practice of law, but under conditions designed to ensure that such services are closely related to the firms' provision of legal services and not independent of, and unrelated to, such legal services.

[11] Subsection (1) of Paragraph (b) requires that ancillary nonlegal services be provided solely to law firm clients (as opposed to persons who are not currently seeking legal services from a law firm) and be incidental to, in connection with, and concurrent to, the provision of legal services by the law firm. The requirement that ancillary services be "incidental to" and "in connection with" the firm's provision of legal services seeks to ensure that any nonlegal services be secondary to, strictly related to, and under the supervision of those responsible for, the provision of legal services.

[12] Paragraph (b) permits law firms to employ the services of other professionals if their services are connected to the firm's provision of legal services. For example, an architect on staff at a law firm would be permitted to help clients and lawyers understand the technical issues in a construction contract negotiation, a building accident litigation or the like. However, the requirement in Paragraph (b) that such services be "incidental to" and "in connection with" the provision of legal services would proscribe a law firm from employing architects to design buildings for law firm clients or for nonclient customers who do not use the law firm's legal services. Similarly, an investment banker on staff at a law firm would be permitted to assist lawyers in the negotiation of a transaction or the litigation of valuation issues or the like, as well as to consult with law firm clients when the firm is providing legal services to them, but a law firm would be prohibited from employing investment bankers to seek out acquisitions, sell securities (or otherwise secure financing) or perform other investment banking services unrelated to a pending legal representation. Likewise, a corporation pursuing an acquisition might need the assistance of nonlawyer lobbyists before a state legislature considering anti-takeover legislation. Such lobbying designed to forestall (or attain) a change in the law, if provided by nonlawyers within a law firm, could reasonably be construed to be incidental to the firm's provision of legal services.

[13] Paragraph (b) also requires that the provision of nonlegal services be concurrent with the provision of legal services. In essence, law firm clients (like nonlegal services customers generally) may not obtain ancillary nonlegal services from the law firm (e.g., investment banking services or medical tests), and the firm may not provide them, at a time when the client is not obtaining legal services from the law firm on a related matter.

Provision of Ancillary Nonlegal Services by Employees of Law Firms

[14] Subsection (2) of Paragraph (b), in an effort to vitiate risks of compromise to lawyers' professional judgment, conflicts of interest, client confusion and potential loss of confidentiality, provides that any ancillary services provided by a law firm must be performed within the law firm by employees of the law firm itself (who work together with, and are supervised by, the firm's lawyers), and not through a subsidiary or affiliate of the law firm. This requirement closely unites the provision of legal and nonlegal services under the supervision of lawyers and thereby affords lawyers the opportunity to ensure that their nonlawyer employees are acting responsibly and in accordance with the rules of legal ethics. Such a requirement minimizes the risks of nonlegal employees either providing advice with which the firm's lawyers will disagree and/or engaging in improper behavior for which the firm's lawyers would be responsible. In addition, structuring the provision of nonlegal services in such a way forestalls confusion on the part of clients as to whether the nonlegal services are provided subject to the limitations of the Model Rules (and will prevent lawyers from seeking to provide services outside of the protections afforded to clients by the Model Rules). Finally, if lawyers are present (or otherwise involved) in the provision of nonlegal services ancillary to the practice of law, there is a greater likelihood that client confidences will be protected and a client will be able to maintain evidentiary privileges with respect to communications made by the client to the providers of nonlegal ancillary services. Paragraph (b)(2) is not designed to limit the ability of lawyers to retain outside (*i.e.,* nonaffiliated) consultants such as experts, private investigators or accountants to help them provide legal services to clients.

Disclosure Requirements Relating to the Provision of Ancillary Nonlegal Services

[15] Subsection (3) of Paragraph (b) requires that before providing ancillary services to a client, a law firm must comply with appropriate disclosure requirements (as mandated in Model Rule of Professional Conduct 1.8, relevant case law and other authorities) and fully disclose in writing the firm's interest in the providers of nonlegal services employed by the firm and the potential conflicts of interest inherent in the provision of such services. The law firm should also consider, in appropriate circumstances, recommending that the client seek the advice of independent counsel (or independent providers of nonlegal services) before obtaining nonlegal services from the firm.

Representations Concerning Ancillary and Nonlegal Services

[16] Subsection (4) of Paragraph (b) ensures that when law firms deal with clients (whether prospective or actual) or the public, they do not represent themselves as providing any ancillary nonlegal services independent of the firm's provision of legal services. This proscription attempts to obviate the risks of confusion on the part of clients and the public, actual or apparent overreaching by attorneys and improper solicitation. It ensures that clients and the public are aware that they are dealing with a law firm and can therefore assume that representatives of the firm are bound by the rules of legal ethics; prospective or actual clients do not feel compelled to use the firm's ancillary services; and law firms do not engage in improper solicitation by seeking business for the firm's nonlegal services with an expectation that these nonlegal services will serve as a "feeder" for the firm's legal services. Paragraph (b)(4) also seeks to preserve the unique and independent status of the legal profession in the public's perception by preventing law firms from representing themselves to clients and the public as multidisciplinary conglomerates or otherwise emphasizing their nonlegal activities.

[17] Paragraph (b)(4) is not intended to preclude law firms from making the existence of their nonlegal business known to clients who have retained the firm for legal services, and who, in the attorney's opinion, might have a need for the firm's ancillary services in addition to legal services (subject to appropriate disclosure requirements). In addition, Paragraph (b)(4) is not intended to prevent individual lawyers from indicating that they are qualified or licensed in other professions, e.g., accounting, where relevant jurisdictions so permit.

Provision of Ancillary Nonlegal Services By One or More Lawyers in a Law Firm

[18] Paragraph (c) prevents one or more lawyers in a single law firm from owning or operating an entity which provides nonlegal services which are ancillary to the practice of law. Paragraph (c) attempts to prevent lawyers or law firms from circumventing the restrictions on law firm ownership and operation of ancillary businesses by vesting ownership not in the entire law firm, but in one or more of the attorneys in a law firm. The ethical and professional concerns inherent in the ownership of ancillary businesses are not

vitiated when ownership or operation is vested in several partners in a law firm (as opposed to an entire law firm). However, a law firm itself may provide such ancillary nonlegal services in accordance with Paragraph (b).

Provision of Ancillary Nonlegal Services by Lawyers from Different Law Firms

[19] Paragraph (d) addresses the concerns which may result when lawyers in separate law firms own or operate an entity which provides nonlegal services which are ancillary to the practice of law. The ethical and professional concerns inherent in the ownership and operation of such ancillary businesses by law firms (or one or more lawyers in a firm) are also present (or may be exacerbated) when lawyers in different firms own or operate such businesses.

MODEL CODE COMPARISON:

There was no counterpart to this Rule in the Model Code.

PUBLIC SERVICE

RULE 6.1 Voluntary Pro Bono Publico Service*

A lawyer should aspire to render at least (50) hours of pro bono publico legal services per year. In fulfilling this responsibility, the lawyer should:

(a) provide a substantial majority of the (50) hours of legal services without fee or expectation of fee to:

(1) persons of limited means or

(2) charitable, religious, civic, community, governmental and educational organizations in matters which are designed primarily to address the needs of persons of limited means; and

* In February 1993, the ABA House of Delegates replaced the original version of Model Rule 6.1 with an aspirational plea for 50 hours a year from each lawyer. The amended language also seeks to direct lawyers to provide pro bono services to the economically disadvantaged rather than to charitable and nonprofit organizations. The new rule was adopted by a vote of 228 to 215. The following represents the original text of Model Rule 6.1 and its comments:

RULE 6.1 Pro Bono Publico Service

A lawyer should render public interest legal service. A lawyer may discharge this responsibility by providing professional services at no fee or a reduced fee to persons of limited means or to public service or charitable groups or organizations, by service in activities for improving the law, the legal system or the legal profession, and by financial support for organizations that provide legal services to persons of limited means.

COMMENT:

[1] The ABA House of Delegates has formally acknowledged "the basic responsibility of each lawyer engaged in the practice of law to provide public interest legal services" without fee, or at a substantially reduced fee, in one or more of the following areas: poverty law, civil rights law, public rights law, charitable organization representation and the administration of justice. This Rule expresses that policy but is not intended to be enforced through disciplinary process.

[2] The rights and responsibilities of individuals and organizations in the United States are increasingly defined in legal terms. As a consequence, legal assistance in coping with the web of statutes, rules and regulations is imperative for persons of modest and limited means, as well as for the relatively well-to-do.

[3] The basic responsibility for providing legal services for those unable to pay ultimately rests upon the individual lawyer, and personal involvement in the problems of the disadvantaged can be one of the most rewarding experiences in the life of a lawyer. Every lawyer, regardless of professional prominence or professional workload, should find time to participate in or otherwise support the provision of legal services to the disadvantaged. The provision of free legal services to those unable to pay reasonable fees continues to be an obligation of each lawyer as well as the profession generally, but the efforts of individual lawyers are often not enough to meet the need. Thus, it has been necessary for the profession and government to institute additional programs to provide legal services. Accordingly, legal aid offices, lawyer referral services and other related programs have been developed, and others will be developed by the profession and government. Every lawyer should support all proper efforts to meet this need for legal services.

(b) provide any additional services through:

(1) delivery of legal services at no fee or substantially reduced fee to individuals, groups or organizations seeking to secure or protect civil rights, civil liberties or public rights, or charitable, religious, civic, community, governmental and educational organizations in matters in furtherance of their organizational purposes, where the payment of standard legal fees would significantly deplete the organization's economic resources or would be otherwise inappropriate;

(2) delivery of legal services at a substantially reduced fee to persons of limited means; or

(3) participation in activities for improving the law, the legal system or the legal profession.

In addition, a lawyer should voluntarily contribute financial support to organizations that provide legal services to persons of limited means.

COMMENT:

[1] Every lawyer, regardless of professional prominence or professional work load, has a responsibility to provide legal services to those unable to pay, and personal involvement in the problems of the disadvantaged can be one of the most rewarding experiences in the life of a lawyer. The American Bar Association urges all lawyers to provide a minimum of 50 hours of pro bono services annually. States, however, may decide to choose a higher or lower number of hours of annual service (which may be expressed as a percentage of a lawyer's professional time) depending upon local needs and local conditions. It is recognized that in some years a lawyer may render greater or fewer hours than the annual standard specified, but during the course of his or her legal career, each lawyer should render on average per year, the number of hours set forth in this Rule. Services can be performed in civil matters or in criminal or quasi-criminal matters for which there is no government obligation to provide funds for legal representation, such as post-conviction death penalty appeal cases.

[2] Paragraphs (a)(1) and (2) recognize the critical need for legal services that exists among persons of limited means by providing that a substantial majority of the legal services rendered annually to the disadvantaged be furnished without fee or expectation of fee. Legal services under these paragraphs consist of a full range of activities, including individual and class representation, the provision of legal advice, legislative lobbying, administrative rule making and the provision of free training or mentoring to those who represent persons of limited means. The variety of these activities should facilitate participation by government attorneys, even when restrictions exist on their engaging in the outside practice of law.

[3] Persons eligible for legal services under paragraphs (a)(1) and (2) are those who qualify for participation in programs funded by the Legal Services Corporation and those whose incomes and financial resources are slightly above the guidelines utilized by such programs but nevertheless, cannot afford counsel. Legal services can be rendered to individuals or to organizations such as homeless shelters, battered women's centers and food pantries that serve those of limited means. The term "governmental organizations" includes, but is not limited to, public protection programs and sections of governmental or public sector agencies.

[4] Because service must be provided without fee or expectation of fee, the intent of the lawyer to render free legal services is essential for the work performed to fall within the meaning of paragraphs (a)(1) and (2). Accordingly, services rendered cannot be considered pro bono if an anticipated fee is uncollected, but the award of statutory attorneys' fees in a case originally accepted as pro bono would not disqualify such services from inclusion under this section. Lawyers who do receive fees in such cases are encouraged to contribute an appropriate portion of such fees to organizations or projects that benefit persons of limited means.

[5] While it is possible for a lawyer to fulfill the annual responsibility to perform pro bono services exclusively through activities described in paragraphs (a)(1) and (2), to the extent that any hours of service remained unfulfilled, the remaining commitment can be met in a variety of ways as set forth in paragraph (b). Constitutional, statutory or regulatory restrictions may prohibit or impede government and public sector lawyers and judges from performing the pro bono services outlined in paragraphs (a)(1) and (2). Accordingly,

where those restrictions apply, government and public sector lawyers and judges may fulfill their pro bono responsibility by performing services outlined in paragraph (b).

[6] Paragraph (b)(1) includes the provision of certain types of legal services to those whose incomes and financial resources place them above limited means. It also permits the pro bono attorney to accept a substantially reduced fee for services. Example of the types of issues that may be addressed under this paragraph include First Amendment claims, Title VII claims and environmental protection claims. Additionally, a wide range of organizations may be represented, including social service, medical research, cultural and religious groups.

[7] Paragraph (b)(2) covers instances in which attorneys agree to and receive a modest fee for furnishing legal services to persons of limited means. Participation in judicare programs and acceptance of court appointments in which the fee is substantially below a lawyer's usual rate are encouraged under this section.

[8] Paragraph (b)(3) recognizes the value of lawyers engaging in activities that improve the law, the legal system or the legal profession. Serving on bar association committees, serving on boards of pro bono or legal services programs, taking part in Law Day activities, acting as a continuing legal education instructor, a mediator or an arbitrator and engaging in legislative lobbying to improve the law, the legal system or the profession are a few examples of the many activities that fall within this paragraph.

[9] Because the provision of pro bono services is a professional responsibility, it is the individual ethical commitment of each lawyer. Nevertheless, there may be times when it is not feasible for a lawyer to engage in pro bono services. At such times a lawyer may discharge the pro bono responsibility by providing financial support to organizations providing free legal services to persons of limited means. Such financial support should be reasonably equivalent to the value of the hours of service that would have otherwise been provided. In addition, at times it may be more feasible to satisfy the pro bono responsibility collectively, as by a firm's aggregate pro bono activities.

[10] Because the efforts of individual lawyers are not enough to meet the need for free legal services that exists among persons of limited means, the government and the profession have instituted additional programs to provide those services. Every lawyer should financially support such programs, in addition to either providing direct pro bono services or making financial contributions when pro bono service is not feasible.

[11] The responsibility set forth in this Rule is not intended to be enforced through disciplinary process.

MODEL CODE COMPARISON:

There was no counterpart of this Rule in the Disciplinary Rules of the Model Code. EC 2–25 stated that the "basic responsibility for providing legal services for those unable to pay ultimately rests upon the individual lawyer. . . . Every lawyer, regardless of professional prominence or professional work load, should find time to participate in serving the disadvantaged." EC 8–9 stated that "[t]he advancement of our legal system is of vital importance in maintaining the rule of law . . . [and] lawyers should encourage, and should aid in making, needed changes and improvements." EC 8–3 stated that "[t]hose persons unable to pay for legal services should be provided needed services."

RULE 6.2 Accepting Appointments

A lawyer shall not seek to avoid appointment by a tribunal to represent a person except for good cause, such as:

(a) representing the client is likely to result in violation of the rules of professional conduct or other law;

(b) representing the client is likely to result in an unreasonable financial burden on the lawyer; or

(c) the client or the cause is so repugnant to the lawyer as to be likely to impair the client-lawyer relationship or the lawyer's ability to represent the client.

COMMENT:

[1] A lawyer ordinarily is not obliged to accept a client whose character or cause the lawyer regards as repugnant. The lawyer's freedom to select clients is, however, qualified. All lawyers have a responsibility to assist in providing pro bono publico service. See Rule 6.1. An individual lawyer fulfills this responsibility by accepting a fair share of unpopular matters or indigent or unpopular clients. A lawyer may also be subject to appointment by a court to serve unpopular clients or persons unable to afford legal services.

Appointed Counsel

[2] For good cause a lawyer may seek to decline an appointment to represent a person who cannot afford to retain counsel or whose cause is unpopular. Good cause exists if the lawyer could not handle the matter competently, see Rule 1.1, or if undertaking the representation would result in an improper conflict of interest, for example, when the client or the cause is so repugnant to the lawyer as to be likely to impair the client-lawyer relationship or the lawyer's ability to represent the client. A lawyer may also seek to decline an appointment if acceptance would be unreasonably burdensome, for example, when it would impose a financial sacrifice so great as to be unjust.

[3] An appointed lawyer has the same obligations to the client as retained counsel, including the obligations of loyalty and confidentiality, and is subject to the same limitations on the client-lawyer relationship, such as the obligation to refrain from assisting the client in violation of the Rules.

MODEL CODE COMPARISON:

There was no counterpart to this Rule in the Disciplinary Rules of the Model Code. EC 2–29 stated that when a lawyer is "appointed by a court or requested by a bar association to undertake representation of a person unable to obtain counsel, whether for financial or other reasons, he should not seek to be excused from undertaking the representation except for compelling reasons. Compelling reasons do not include such factors as the repugnance of the subject matter of the proceeding, the identity or position of a person involved in the case, the belief of the lawyer that the defendant in a criminal proceeding is guilty, or the belief of the lawyer regarding the merits of the civil case." EC 2–30 stated that "a lawyer should decline employment if the intensity of his personal feelings, as distinguished from a community attitude, may impair his effective representation of a prospective client."

RULE 6.3 Membership in Legal Services Organization

A lawyer may serve as a director, officer or member of a legal services organization, apart from the law firm in which the lawyer practices, notwithstanding that the organization serves persons having interests adverse to a client of the lawyer. The lawyer shall not knowingly participate in a decision or action of the organization:

(a) if participating in the decision or action would be incompatible with the lawyer's obligations to a client under rule 1.7; or

(b) where the decision or action could have a material adverse effect on the representation of a client of the organization whose interests are adverse to a client of the lawyer.

COMMENT:

[1] Lawyers should be encouraged to support and participate in legal service organizations. A lawyer who is an officer or a member of such an organization does not thereby have a client-lawyer relationship with persons served by the organization. However, there is potential conflict between the interests of such persons and the interests of the lawyer's clients. If the possibility of such conflict disqualified a lawyer from serving on the board of a legal services organization, the profession's involvement in such organizations would be severely curtailed.

[2] It may be necessary in appropriate cases to reassure a client of the organization that the representation will not be affected by conflicting loyalties of a member of the board. Established, written policies in this respect can enhance the credibility of such assurances.

MODEL CODE COMPARISON:

There was no counterpart to this Rule in the Model Code.

RULE 6.4 Law Reform Activities Affecting Client Interests

A lawyer may serve as a director, officer or member of an organization involved in reform of the law or its administration notwithstanding that the reform may affect the interests of a client of the lawyer. When the lawyer knows that the interests of a client may be materially benefitted by a decision in which the lawyer participates, the lawyer shall disclose that fact but need not identify the client.

COMMENT:

Lawyers involved in organizations seeking law reform generally do not have a client-lawyer relationship with the organization. Otherwise, it might follow that a lawyer could not be involved in a bar association law reform program that might indirectly affect a client. See also Rule 1.2(b). For example, a lawyer specializing in antitrust litigation might be regarded as disqualified from participating in drafting revisions of rules governing that subject. In determining the nature and scope of participation in such activities, a lawyer should be mindful of obligations to clients under other Rules, particularly Rule 1.7. A lawyer is professionally obligated to protect the integrity of the program by making an appropriate disclosure within the organization when the lawyer knows a private client might be materially benefitted.

MODEL CODE COMPARISON:

There was no counterpart to this Rule in the Model Code.

INFORMATION ABOUT LEGAL SERVICES

RULE 7.1 Communications Concerning a Lawyer's Services

A lawyer shall not make a false or misleading communication about the lawyer or the lawyer's services. A communication is false or misleading if it:

(a) contains a material misrepresentation of fact or law, or omits a fact necessary to make the statement considered as a whole not materially misleading;

(b) is likely to create an unjustified expectation about results the lawyer can achieve, or states or implies that the lawyer can achieve results by means that violate the rules of professional conduct or other law; or

(c) compares the lawyer's services with other lawyers' services, unless the comparison can be factually substantiated.

COMMENT:

This Rule governs all communications about a lawyer's services, including advertising permitted by Rule 7.2. Whatever means are used to make known a lawyer's services, statements about them should be truthful. The prohibition in paragraph (b) of statements that may create "unjustified expectations" would ordinarily preclude advertisements about results obtained on behalf of a client, such as the amount of a damage award or the lawyer's record in obtaining favorable verdicts, and advertisements containing client endorsements. Such information may create the unjustified expectation that similar results can be obtained for others without reference to the specific factual and legal circumstances.

MODEL CODE COMPARISON:

DR 2–101 provided that "[a] lawyer shall not . . . use . . . any form of public communication containing a false, fraudulent, misleading, deceptive, self-laudatory or unfair statement or claim." DR 2–101(B) provided that a lawyer "may publish or broadcast . . . the following information . . . in the geographic area or areas in which the lawyer resides or maintains offices or in which a significant part of the lawyer's clientele resides, provided that the information . . . complies with DR 2–101(A), and is presented in a dignified manner. . . ." DR 2–101(B) then specified twenty-five categories of information that may be disseminated. DR 2–101(C) provided that "[a]ny person desiring to expand the information authorized for disclosure in DR 2–101(B), or to provide for its dissemination through other forums may apply to [the agency having jurisdiction under state law]. . . . The relief granted in response to any such application shall be promulgated as an amendment to DR 2–101(B), universally applicable to all lawyers."

RULE 7.2 Advertising*

(a) Subject to the requirements of rule 7.1 and 7.3, a lawyer may advertise services through public media, such as a telephone directory, legal directory, newspaper or other periodical, outdoor advertising, radio or television, or through written or recorded communication.

(b) A copy or recording of an advertisement or written communication shall be kept for two years after its last dissemination along with a record of when and where it was used.

(c) A lawyer shall not give anything of value to a person for recommending the lawyer's services, except that a lawyer may

(1) pay the reasonable costs of advertisements or communications permitted by this Rule;

(2) pay the usual charges of a not-for-profit lawyer referral service or legal service organization; and

(3) pay for a law practice in accordance with Rule 1.17.

(d) Any communication made pursuant to this rule shall include the name of at least one lawyer responsible for its content.

COMMENT:

[1] To assist the public in obtaining legal services, lawyers should be allowed to make known their services not only through reputation but also through organized information campaigns in the form of advertising. Advertising involves an active quest for clients, contrary to the tradition that a lawyer should not seek clientele. However, the public's need to know about legal services can be fulfilled in part through advertising. This need is particularly acute in the case of persons of moderate means who have not made extensive use of legal services. The interest in expanding public information about legal services ought to prevail over considerations of tradition. Nevertheless, advertising by lawyers entails the risk of practices that are misleading or overreaching.

[2] This Rule permits public dissemination of information concerning a lawyer's name or firm name, address and telephone number; the kinds of services the lawyer will undertake; the basis on which the lawyer's fees are determined, including prices for specific services and payment and credit arrangements; a lawyer's foreign language ability; names of references and, with their consent, names of clients regularly represented; and other information that might invite the attention of those seeking legal assistance.

---

* The ABA amended Model Rule 7.2 in 1989 to conform to the holding in Shapero v. Kentucky Bar Ass'n, 486 U.S. 466 (1988) and in 1990 to reflect the addition of Model Rule 1.17 on the sale of a law practice. The original version of Model Rule 7.2 read as follows:

RULE 7.2 Advertising

(a) Subject to the requirements of Rules 7.1, a lawyer may advertise services through public media, such as a telephone directory, legal directory, newspaper or other periodical, outdoor, radio or television, or through written communication not involving solicitation as defined in Rule 7.3.

(b) A copy or recording of an advertisement or written communication shall be kept for two years after its last dissemination along with a record of when and where it was used.

(c) A lawyer shall not give anything of value to a person for recommending the lawyer's services, except that a lawyer may pay the reasonable cost of advertising or written communication permitted by this rule and may pay the usual charges of a not-for-profit lawyer referral service or other legal service organization.

(d) Any communication made pursuant to this rule shall include the name of at least one lawyer responsible for its content.

[3] Questions of effectiveness and taste in advertising are matters of speculation and subjective judgment. Some jurisdictions have had extensive prohibitions against television advertising, against advertising going beyond specified facts about a lawyer, or against "undignified" advertising. Television is now one of the most powerful media for getting information to the public, particularly persons of low and moderate income; prohibiting television advertising, therefore, would impede the flow of information about legal services to many sectors of the public. Limiting the information that may be advertised has a similar effect and assumes that the bar can accurately forecast the kind of information that the public would regard as relevant.

[4] Neither this Rule nor Rule 7.3 prohibits communications authorized by law, such as notice to members of a class in class action litigation.

Record of Advertising

[5] Paragraph (b) requires that a record of the content and use of advertising be kept in order to facilitate enforcement of this Rule. It does not require that advertising be subject to review prior to dissemination. Such a requirement would be burdensome and expensive relative to its possible benefits, and may be of doubtful constitutionality.

*Paying Others to Recommend a Lawyer**

[6] A lawyer is allowed to pay for advertising permitted by this Rule and for the purchase of a law practice in accordance with the provisions of Rule 1.17, but otherwise is not permitted to pay another person for channeling professional work. This restriction does not prevent an organization or person other than the lawyer from advertising or recommending the lawyer's services. Thus, a legal aid agency or prepaid legal services plan may pay to advertise legal services provided under its auspices. Likewise, a lawyer may participate in not-for-profit lawyer referral programs and pay the usual fees charged by such programs. Paragraph (c) does not prohibit paying regular compensation to an assistant, such as a secretary, to prepare communications permitted by this Rule.

MODEL CODE COMPARISON:

With regard to paragraph (a), DR 2–101(B) provided that a lawyer "may publish or broadcast, subject to DR 2–103, . . . in print media . . . or television or radio. . . ."

With regard to paragraph (b), DR 2–101(D) provided that if the advertisement is "communicated to the public over television or radio, . . . a recording of the actual transmission shall be retained by the lawyer."

With regard to paragraph (c), DR 2–103(B) provided that a lawyer "shall not compensate or give anything of value to a person or organization to recommend or secure his employment . . . except that he may pay the usual and reasonable fees or dues charged by any of the organizations listed in DR 2–103(D)." (DR 2–103(D) referred to legal aid and other legal services organizations.) DR 2–101(I) provided that a lawyer "shall not compensate or give anything of value to representatives of the press, radio, television, or other communication medium in anticipation of or in return for professional publicity in a news item."

There was no counterpart to paragraph (d) in the Model Code.

RULE 7.3 Direct Contact With Prospective Clients**

(a) A lawyer shall not by in-person or live telephone contact solicit professional employment from a prospective client with whom the lawyer has no family or prior

* In 1990, the ABA added the clause "and for the purchase of a law practice in accordance with the provisions of Rule 1.17" to reflect the addition of this provision to the Model Rules.

** The ABA amended the original version of Model Rule 7.3 in 1989 because in 1988 the Supreme Court had declared a blanket restriction on targeted mailings unconstitutional under the First Amendment. See Shapero v. Kentucky Bar Ass'n, 486 U.S. 466 (1988). The Kentucky rule which was the subject of the Supreme Court decision was identical to the original Model Rule 7.3. This provision read as follows:

RULE 7.3 Direct Contact With Prospective Clients

A lawyer may not solicit professional employment from a prospective client with whom the lawyer has no family or prior professional relationship, by mail, in-person or otherwise, when a significant motive for the lawyer's doing so is the lawyer's pecuniary gain. The term "solicit" includes contact in person, by telephone or telegraph, by letter or other writing or by other communication directed to a specific recipient,

professional relationship when a significant motive for the lawyer's doing so is the lawyer's pecuniary gain.

(b) A lawyer shall not solicit professional employment from a prospective client by written or recorded communication or by in-person or telephone contact even when not otherwise prohibited by paragraph (a), if:

(1) the prospective client has made known to the lawyer a desire not to be solicited by the lawyer; or

(2) the solicitation involves coercion, duress or harassment.

(c) Every written or recorded communication from a lawyer soliciting professional employment from a prospective client known to be in need of legal services in a particular matter, and with whom the lawyer has no family or prior professional relationship, shall include the words "Advertising Material" on the outside envelope and at the beginning and ending of any recorded communication.

(d) Notwithstanding the prohibitions in paragraph (a), a lawyer may participate with a prepaid or group legal service plan operated by an organization not owned or directed by the lawyer which uses in-person or telephone contact to solicit memberships or subscriptions for the plan from persons who are not known to need legal services in a particular matter covered by the plan.

COMMENT:*

[1] There is a potential for abuse inherent in direct in-person or live telephone contact by a lawyer with a prospective client known to need legal services. These forms of contact between a lawyer and a

---

but does not include letters addressed or advertising circulars distributed generally to persons not known to need legal services of the kind provided by the lawyer in a particular matter, but who are so situated that they might in general find such services useful.

* The ABA amended the comments to Model Rule 7.3 in 1989 to reflect changes made in the text of the Rule brought about by the *Shapero* decision. The text of the original comment reads as follows:

COMMENT:

There is a potential for abuse inherent in direct solicitation by a lawyer of prospective clients known to need legal services. It subjects the lay person to the private importuning of a trained advocate, in a direct interpersonal encounter. A prospective client often feels overwhelmed by the situation giving rise to the need for legal services, and may have an impaired capacity for reason, judgment and protective self-interest. Furthermore, the lawyer seeking the retainer is faced with a conflict stemming from the lawyer's own interest, which may color the advice and representation offered the vulnerable prospect.

The situation is therefore fraught with the possibility of undue influence, intimidation, and over-reaching. This potential for abuse inherent in direct solicitation of prospective clients justifies its prohibition, particularly since lawyer advertising permitted under Rule 7.2 offers an alternative means of communicating necessary information to those who may be in need of legal services.

Advertising makes it possible for a prospective client to be informed about the need for legal services, and about the qualifications of available lawyers and law firms, without subjecting the prospective client to direct personal persuasion that may overwhelm the client's judgment.

The use of general advertising to transmit information from lawyer to prospective client, rather than direct private contact, will help to assure that the information flows cleanly as well as freely. Advertising is out in public view, thus subject to scrutiny by those who know the lawyer. This informal review is itself likely to help guard against statements and claims that might constitute false or misleading communications, in violation of Rule 7.1. Direct, private communications from a lawyer to a prospective client are not subject to such third-scrutiny and consequently are much more likely to approach (and occasionally cross) the dividing line between accurate representations and those that are false and misleading.

These dangers attend direct solicitation whether in-person or by mail. Direct mail solicitation cannot be effectively regulated by means less drastic than outright prohibition. One proposed safeguard is to require that the designation "Advertising" be stamped on any envelope containing a solicitation letter. This would do nothing to assure the accuracy and reliability of the contents. Another suggestion is that solicitation letters be filed with a state regulatory agency. This would be ineffective as a practical matter. State lawyer discipline agencies struggle for resources to investigate specific complaints, much less for those necessary to screen lawyers' mail solicitation material. Even if they could examine such materials, agency staff members are unlikely to know anything about the lawyer or about the prospective client's underlying problem. Without such knowledge they cannot determine whether the lawyer's

prospective client subject the layperson to the private importuning of the trained advocate in a direct interpersonal encounter. The prospective client, who may already feel overwhelmed by the circumstances giving rise to the need for legal services, may find it difficult fully to evaluate all available alternatives with reasoned judgment and appropriate self-interest in the face of the lawyer's presence and insistence upon being retained immediately. The situation is fraught with the possibility of undue influence, intimidation, and over-reaching.

[2] This potential for abuse inherent in direct in-person or live telephone solicitation of prospective clients justifies its prohibition, particularly since lawyer advertising and written and recorded communication permitted under Rule 7.2 offer alternative means of conveying necessary information to those who may be in need of legal services. Advertising and written and recorded communications which may be mailed or autodialed make it possible for a prospective client to be informed about the need for legal services, and about the qualifications of available lawyers and law firms, without subjecting the prospective client to direct in-person or telephone persuasion that may overwhelm the client's judgment.

[3] The use of general advertising and written and recorded communications to transmit information from lawyer to prospective client, rather than direct in-person or live telephone contact, will help to assure that the information flows cleanly as well as freely. The contents of advertisements and communications permitted under Rule 7.2 are permanently recorded so that they cannot be disputed and may be shared with others who know the lawyer. This potential for informal review is itself likely to help guard against statements and claims that might constitute false and misleading communications, in violation of Rule 7.1. The contents of direct in-person or live telephone conversations between a lawyer to a prospective client can be disputed and are not subject to third-party scrutiny. Consequently, they are much more likely to approach (and occasionally cross) the dividing line between accurate representations and those that are false and misleading.

[4] There is far less likelihood that a lawyer would engage in abusive practices against an individual with whom the lawyer has a prior personal or professional relationship or where the lawyer is motivated by considerations other than the lawyer's pecuniary gain. Consequently, the general prohibition in Rule 7.3(a) and the requirements of Rule 7.3(c) are not applicable in those situations.

[5] But even permitted forms of solicitation can be abused. Thus, any solicitation which contains information which is false or misleading within the meaning of Rule 7.1, which involves coercion, duress or harassment within the meaning of Rule 7.3(b)(2), or which involves contact with a prospective client who has made known to the lawyer a desire not to be solicited by the lawyer within the meaning of Rule 7.3(b)(1) is prohibited. Moreover, if after sending a letter or other communication to a client as permitted by Rule 7.2 the lawyer receives no response, any further effort to communicate with the prospective client may violate the provisions of Rule 7.3(b).

[6] This Rule is not intended to prohibit a lawyer from contacting representatives of organizations or groups that may be interested in establishing a group or prepaid legal plan for their members, insureds, beneficiaries or other third parties for the purpose of informing such entities of the availability of and details concerning the plan or arrangement which the lawyer or lawyer's firm is willing to offer. This form of

---

representations are misleading. In any event, such review would be after the fact, potentially too late to avert the undesirable consequences of disseminating false and misleading material.

General mailings not speaking to a specific matter do not pose the same danger of abuse as targeted mailings, and therefore are not prohibited by this Rule. The representations made in such mailings are necessarily general rather than tailored, less importuning than informative. They are addressed to recipients unlikely to be specially vulnerable at the time, hence who are likely to be more skeptical about unsubstantiated claims. General mailings not addressed to recipients involved in a specific legal matter or incident, therefore, more closely resemble permissible advertising rather than prohibited solicitation.

Similarly, this Rule would not prohibit a lawyer from contacting representatives of organizations or groups that may be interested in establishing a group or prepaid legal plan for its members, insureds, beneficiaries or other third parties for the purpose of informing such entities of the availability of and details concerning the plan or arrangement which he or his firm is willing to offer. This form of communication is not directed to a specific prospective client known to need legal services related to a particular matter. Rather, it is usually addressed to an individual acting in a fiduciary capacity seeking a supplier of legal services for others who may, if they choose, become prospective clients of the lawyer. Under these circumstances, the activity which the lawyer undertakes in communicating with such representatives and the type of information transmitted to the individual are functionally similar to and serve the same purpose as advertising permitted under Rule 7.2.

communication is not directed to a prospective client. Rather, it is usually addressed to an individual acting in a fiduciary capacity seeking a supplier of legal services for others who may, if they choose, become prospective clients of the lawyer. Under these circumstances, the activity which the lawyer undertakes in communicating with such representatives and the type of information transmitted to the individual are functionally similar to and serve the same purpose as advertising permitted under Rule 7.2.

[7] The requirement in Rule 7.3(c) that certain communications be marked "Advertising Material" does not apply to communications sent in response to requests of potential clients or their spokespersons or sponsors. General announcements by lawyers, including changes in personnel or office location, do not constitute communications soliciting professional employment from a client known to be in need of legal services within the meaning of this Rule.

[8] Paragraph (d) of this Rule would permit an attorney to participate with an organization which uses personal contact to solicit members for its group or prepaid legal service plan, provided that the personal contact is not undertaken by any lawyer who would be a provider of legal services through the plan. The organization referred to in paragraph (d) must not be owned by or directed (whether as manager or otherwise) by any lawyer or law firm that participates in the plan. For example, paragraph (d) would not permit a lawyer to create an organization controlled directly or indirectly by the lawyer and use the organization for the in-person or telephone solicitation of legal employment of the lawyer through memberships in the plan or otherwise. The communication permitted by these organizations also must not be directed to a person known to need legal services in a particular matter, but is to be designed to inform potential plan members generally of another means of affordable legal services. Lawyers who participate in a legal service plan must reasonably assure that the plan sponsors are in compliance with Rules 7.1, 7.2 and 7.3(a). See 8.4(a).

MODEL CODE COMPARISON:

DR 2–104(A) provided with certain exceptions that "[a] lawyer who has given in-person unsolicited advice to a layperson that he should obtain counsel or take legal action shall not accept employment resulting from that advice. . . ." The exceptions include DR 2–104(A)(1), which provided that a lawyer "may accept employment by a close friend, relative, former client (if the advice is germane to the former employment), or one whom the lawyer reasonably believes to be a client." DR 2–104(A)(2) through DR 2–104(A)(5) provided other exceptions relating, respectively, to employment resulting from public educational programs, recommendation by a legal assistance organization, public speaking or writing and representing members of a class in class action litigation.

RULE 7.4 Communication of Fields of Practice*

A lawyer may communicate the fact that the lawyer does or does not practice in particular fields of law. A lawyer shall not state or imply that the lawyer is a specialist in a particular field of law except as follows:

---

* In August 1992, the ABA House of Delegates modified Model Rule 7.4(c) as a reaction to the Supreme Court's decision in Peel v. Attorney Registration and Disciplinary Commission, 496 U.S. 91 (1990). The 1983 version of 7.4(c) read as follows: "(c) (provisions on designation of specialization of the particular state)." The original intent of the rule was to limit the right of lawyers to state or imply that they are specialists except when a state has an organized plan of specialization or in the two well defined area of law (admiralty and patent) in which a long tradition of specialization exists. In *Peel*, the Supreme Court held that a state could not prohibit a lawyer from stating that he or she is a civil trial specialist certified by the National Board of Trial Advocacy. The revised rule encourages the states to create organizations to certify organizations that seek to qualify lawyers as specialists and requires lawyers who wish to advertise specialties by organizations that have either been denied or not approved to disclose such information in the advertisement. In its February 1993 meeting, the ABA adopted "Standards for Accreditation of Specialty Certification Programs for Lawyers." These standards seek to ensure that certification programs ensure that the lawyer has a special proficiency in the specialty and devotes a substantial amount of time to this type of work. They also require that certifying organizations be made up primarily of lawyer members.

In August 1994, the ABA House of Delegates added the last line to alternative paragraph (c): "If, however, the named organization has been accredited by the American Bar Association to certify lawyers as specialists in a particular field of law, the communication need not contain such a statement."

This line reflects the new role of the ABA committee on specialization to accredit organizations.

(a) a lawyer admitted to engage in patent practice before the United States Patent and Trademark Office may use the designation "Patent Attorney" or a substantially similar designation;

(b) a lawyer engaged in admiralty practice may use the designation "Admiralty," "Proctor in Admiralty" or a substantially similar designation; and

(c) [for jurisdictions where there is a regulatory authority granting certification or approving organizations that grant certification] a lawyer may communicate the fact that the lawyer has been certified as a specialist in a field of law by a named organization or authority, but only if:

(1) such certification is granted by the appropriate regulatory authority or by an organization which has been approved by the appropriate regulatory authority to grant such certification; or

(2) such certification is granted by an organization that has not yet been approved by, or has been denied the approval available from, the appropriate regulatory authority, and the absence or denial of approval is clearly stated in the communication, and in any advertisement subject to Rule 7.2, such statement appears in the same sentence that communicates the certification.

(c) [for jurisdictions where there is no procedure either for certification of specialties or for approval of organizations granting certification] a lawyer may communicate the fact that the lawyer has been certified as a specialist in a field of law by a named organization, provided that the communication clearly states that there is no procedure in this jurisdiction for approving certifying organizations. If, however, the named organization has been accredited by the American Bar Association to certify lawyers as specialists in a particular field of law, the communication need not contain such a statement.

COMMENT:*

[1] This Rule permits a lawyer to indicate areas of practice in communications about the lawyer's services. If a lawyer practices only in certain fields, or will not accept matters in a specified field or fields, the lawyer is permitted to so indicate. A lawyer is generally permitted to state that the lawyer is a "specialist," practices a "specialty," or "specializes in" particular fields, but such communications are subject to the "false and misleading" standard applied in Rule 7.1 to communications concerning a lawyer's services.

---

* In 1989, the ABA amended the comment to Model Rule 7.3 to reflect concerns that the language in the original comment may violate the Supreme Court's legal advertising decisions. The original language read as follows:

COMMENT:

This Rule permits a lawyer to indicate areas of practice in communications about the lawyer's services; for example, in a telephone directory or other advertising. If a lawyer practices only in certain fields, or will not accept matters except in such fields, the lawyer is permitted so to indicate. However, stating that the lawyer is a "specialist" or that the lawyer's practice "is limited to" or "concentrated in" particular fields is not permitted. These terms have acquired a secondary meaning implying formal recognition as a specialist. Hence, use of these terms may be misleading unless the lawyer is certified or recognized in accordance with procedures in the state where the lawyer is licensed to practice.

The 1989 amendment adopted the following language:

COMMENT:

[1] This Rule permits a lawyer to indicate areas of practice in communications about the lawyer's services; for example, in a telephone directory or other advertising. If a lawyer practices only in certain fields, or will not accept matters except in such fields, the lawyer is permitted so to indicate. However, a lawyer is not permitted to state that the lawyer is a "specialist," practices a "specialty," or "specializes in" particular fields. These terms have acquired a secondary meaning implying formal recognition as a specialist and therefore, use of these terms is misleading. [An exception would apply in those states which provide procedures for certification or recognition of specialization and the lawyer has complied with such procedures.]

[2] Recognition of specialization in patent matters is a matter of long-established policy of the Patent and Trademark Office. Designation of admiralty practice has a long historical tradition associated with maritime commerce and the federal courts.

[2] However, a lawyer may not communicate that the lawyer has been recognized or certified as a specialist in a particular field of law, except as provided by this Rule. Recognition of specialization in patent matters is a matter of long-established policy of the Patent and Trademark Office, as reflected in paragraph (a). Paragraph (b) recognizes that designation of admiralty practice has a long historical tradition associated with maritime commerce and the federal courts.

[3] Paragraph (c) provides for certification as a specialist in a field of law when a state authorizes an appropriate regulatory authority to grant such certification or when the state grants other organizations the right to grant certification. Certification procedures imply that an objective entity has recognized a lawyer's higher degree of specialized ability than is suggested by general licensure to practice law. Those objective entities may be expected to apply standards of competence, experience and knowledge to insure that a lawyer's recognition as a specialist is meaningful and reliable. In order to insure that consumers can obtain access to useful information about an organization granting certification, the name of the certifying organization or agency must be included in any communication regarding the certification.

[4] Lawyers may also be certified as specialists by organizations that either have not yet been approved to grant such certification or have been disapproved. In such instances, the consumer may be misled as to the significance of the lawyer's status as a certified specialist. The Rule therefore requires that a lawyer who chooses to communicate recognition by such an organization also clearly state the absence or denial of the organization's authority to grant such certification. Since lawyer advertising through public media and written or recorded communications invites the greatest danger of misleading consumers, the absence or denial of the organization's authority to grant certification must be clearly stated in such advertising in the same sentence that communicates the certification.

[5]* In jurisdictions where no appropriate regulatory authority has a procedure for approving organizations granting certification, the Rule requires that a lawyer clearly state such lack of procedure.

If, however, the named organization has been accredited by the American Bar Association to certify lawyers as specialists in a particular field of law, the communication need not contain such a statement.

MODEL CODE COMPARISON:

DR 2–105(A) provided that a lawyer "shall not hold himself out publicly as a specialist, as practicing in certain areas of law or as limiting his practice . . . except as follows:

> "(1) A lawyer admitted to practice before the United States Patent and Trademark Office may use the designation 'Patents,' 'Patent Attorney,' 'Patent Lawyer,' or 'Registered Patent Attorney' or any combination of those terms, on his letterhead and office sign.
>
> "(2) A lawyer who publicly discloses fields of law in which the lawyer . . . practices or states that his practice is limited to one or more fields of law shall do so by using designations and definitions authorized and approved by [the agency having jurisdiction of the subject under state law].
>
> "(3) A lawyer who is certified as a specialist in a particular field of law or law practice by [the authority having jurisdiction under state law over the subject of specialization by lawyers] may hold himself out as such, but only in accordance with the rules prescribed by that authority."

EC 2–14 stated that "In the absence of state controls to insure the existence of special competence, a lawyer should not be permitted to hold himself out as a specialist, . . . other than in the fields of admiralty, trademark, and patent law where a holding out as a specialist historically has been permitted."

RULE 7.5 Firm Names and Letterheads

(a) A lawyer shall not use a firm name, letterhead or other professional designation that violates rule 7.1. A trade name may be used by a lawyer in private practice if it does not imply a connection with a government agency or with a public or charitable legal services organization and is not otherwise in violation of rule 7.1.

(b) A law firm with offices in more than one jurisdiction may use the same name in each jurisdiction, but identification of the lawyers in an office of the firm shall indicate the

* The ABA added the last line in this paragraph when it amended alternative paragraph (c).

jurisdictional limitations on those not licensed to practice in the jurisdiction where the office is located.

(c) The name of a lawyer holding a public office shall not be used in the name of a law firm, or in communications on its behalf, during any substantial period in which the lawyer is not actively and regularly practicing with the firm.

(d) Lawyers may state or imply that they practice in a partnership or other organization only when that is the fact.

COMMENT:

[1] A firm may be designated by the names of all or some of its members, by the names of deceased members where there has been a continuing succession in the firm's identity or by a trade name such as the "ABC Legal Clinic." Although the United States Supreme Court has held that legislation may prohibit the use of trade names in professional practice, use of such names in law practice is acceptable so long as it is not misleading. If a private firm uses a trade name that includes a geographical name such as "Springfield Legal Clinic," an express disclaimer that it is a public legal aid agency may be required to avoid a misleading implication. It may be observed that any firm name including the name of a deceased partner is, strictly speaking, a trade name. The use of such names to designate law firms has proven a useful means of identification. However, it is misleading to use the name of a lawyer not associated with the firm or a predecessor of the firm.

[2] With regard to paragraph (d), lawyers sharing office facilities, but who are not in fact partners, may not denominate themselves as, for example, "Smith and Jones," for that title suggests partnership in the practice of law.

MODEL CODE COMPARISON:

With regard to paragraph (a), DR 2–102(A) provided that "[a] lawyer . . . shall not use . . . professional announcement cards . . . letterheads, or similar professional notices or devices, except . . . if they are in dignified form. . . ." DR 2–102(B) provided that "[a] lawyer in private practice shall not practice under a trade name, a name that is misleading as to the identity of the lawyer or lawyers practicing under such name, or a firm name containing names other than those of one or more of the lawyers in the firm, except that . . . a firm may use as . . . its name the name or names of one or more deceased or retired members of the firm or of a predecessor firm in a continuing line of succession."

With regard to paragraph (b), DR 2–102(D) provided that a partnership "shall not be formed or continued between or among lawyers licensed in different jurisdictions unless all enumerations of the members and associates of the firm on its letterhead and in other permissible listings make clear the jurisdictional limitations on those members and associates of the firm not licensed to practice in all listed jurisdictions; however, the same firm name may be used in each jurisdiction."

With regard to paragraph (c), DR 2–102(B) provided that "[a] lawyer who assumes a judicial, legislative, or public executive or administrative post or office shall not permit his name to remain in the name of a law firm . . . during any significant period in which he is not actively and regularly practicing law as a member of the firm. . . ."

Paragraph (d) is substantially identical to DR 2–102(C).

RULE 7.6 Political Contributions to Obtain Government Legal Engagements or Appointments by Judges*

A lawyer or law firm shall not accept a government legal engagement or an appointment by a judge if the lawyer or law firm makes a political contribution or solicits political contributions for the purpose of obtaining or being considered for that type of legal engagement or appointment.

* In February 2000, the ABA enacted the new Model Rule 7.6 to address ethical problems with the "pay to play" practice in effect in some jurisdictions.

COMMENT:

[1] Lawyers have a right to participate fully in the political process, which includes making and soliciting political contributions to candidates for judicial and other public office. Nevertheless, when lawyers make or solicit political contributions in order to obtain an engagement for legal work awarded by a government agency, or to obtain appointment by a judge, the public may legitimately question whether the lawyers engaged to perform the work are selected on the basis of competence and merit. In such a circumstance, the integrity of the profession is undermined.

[2] The term "political contribution" denotes any gift, subscription, loan, advance or deposit of anything of value made directly or indirectly to a candidate, incumbent, political party or campaign committee to influence or provide financial support for election to or retention in judicial or other government office. Political contributions in initiative and referendum elections are not included. For purposes of this Rule, the term "political contribution" does not include uncompensated services.

[3] Subject to the exceptions below, (i) the term "government legal engagement" denotes any engagement to provide legal services that a public official has the direct or indirect power to award; and (ii) the term "appointment by a judge" denotes an appointment to a position such as referee, commissioner, special master, receiver, guardian or other similar position that is made by a judge. Those terms do not, however, include (a) substantially uncompensated services; (b) engagements or appointments made on the basis of experience, expertise, professional qualifications and cost following a request for proposal or other process that is free from influence based upon political contributions; and (c) engagements or appointments made on a rotational basis from a list compiled without regard to political contributions.

[4] The term "lawyer or law firm" includes a political action committee or other entity owned or controlled by a lawyer or law firm.

[5] Political contributions are for the purpose of obtaining or being considered for a government legal engagement or appointment by a judge if, but for the desire to be considered for the legal engagement or appointment, the lawyer or law firm would not have made or solicited the contributions. The purpose may be determined by an examination of the circumstances in which the contributions occur. For example, one or more contributions that in the aggregate are substantial in relation to other contributions by lawyers or law firms, made for the benefit of an official in a position to influence award of a government legal engagement, and followed by an award of the legal engagement to the contributing or soliciting lawyer or the lawyer's firm would support an inference that the purpose of the contributions was to obtain the engagement, absent other factors that weigh against existence of the proscribed purpose. Those factors may include among others that the contribution or solicitation was made to further a political, social, or economic interest or because of an existing personal, family, or professional relationship with a candidate.

[6] If a lawyer makes or solicits a political contribution under circumstances that constitute bribery or another crime, Rule 8.4(b) is implicated.

MAINTAINING THE INTEGRITY OF THE PROFESSION

RULE 8.1 Bar Admission and Disciplinary Matters

An applicant for admission to the bar, or a lawyer in connection with a bar admission application or in connection with a disciplinary matter, shall not:

(a) knowingly make a false statement of material fact; or

(b) fail to disclose a fact necessary to correct a misapprehension known by the person to have arisen in the matter, or knowingly fail to respond to a lawful demand for information from an admission or disciplinary authority, except that this rule does not require disclosure of information otherwise protected by rule 1.6.

COMMENT:

[1] The duty imposed by this Rule extends to persons seeking admission to the bar as well as to lawyers. Hence, if a person makes a material false statement in connection with an application for admission, it may be the basis for subsequent disciplinary action if the person is admitted, and in any event

may be relevant in a subsequent admission application. The duty imposed by this Rule applies to a lawyer's own admission or discipline as well as that of others. Thus, it is a separate professional offense for a lawyer to knowingly make a misrepresentation or omission in connection with a disciplinary investigation of the lawyer's own conduct. This Rule also requires affirmative clarification of any misunderstanding on the part of the admissions or disciplinary authority of which the person involved becomes aware.

[2] This Rule is subject to the provisions of the Fifth Amendment of the United States Constitution and corresponding provisions of state constitutions. A person relying on such a provision in response to a question, however, should do so openly and not use the right of nondisclosure as a justification for failure to comply with this Rule.

[3] A lawyer representing an applicant for admission to the bar, or representing a lawyer who is the subject of a disciplinary inquiry or proceeding, is governed by the rules applicable to the client-lawyer relationship.

MODEL CODE COMPARISON:

DR 1–101(A) provided that a lawyer is "subject to discipline if he has made a materially false statement in, or if he has deliberately failed to disclose a material fact requested in connection with, his application for admission to the bar." DR 1–101(B) provided that a lawyer "shall not further the application for admission to the bar of another person known by him to be unqualified in respect to character, education, or other relevant attribute." With respect to paragraph (b), DR 1–102(A)(5) provided that a lawyer shall not engage in "conduct that is prejudicial to the administration of justice."

RULE 8.2 Judicial and Legal Officials

(a) A lawyer shall not make a statement that the lawyer knows to be false or with reckless disregard as to its truth or falsity concerning the qualifications or integrity of a judge, adjudicatory officer or public legal officer, or of a candidate for election or appointment to judicial or legal office.

(b) A lawyer who is a candidate for judicial office shall comply with the applicable provisions of the code of judicial conduct.

COMMENT:

[1] Assessments by lawyers are relied on in evaluating the professional or personal fitness of persons being considered for election or appointment to judicial office and to public legal offices, such as attorney general, prosecuting attorney and public defender. Expressing honest and candid opinions on such matters contributes to improving the administration of justice. Conversely, false statements by a lawyer can unfairly undermine public confidence in the administration of justice.

[2] When a lawyer seeks judicial office, the lawyer should be bound by applicable limitations on political activity.

[3] To maintain the fair and independent administration of justice, lawyers are encouraged to continue traditional efforts to defend judges and courts unjustly criticized.

MODEL CODE COMPARISON:

With regard to paragraph (a), DR 8–102(A) provided that a lawyer "shall not knowingly make false statements of fact concerning the qualifications of a candidate for election or appointment to a judicial office." DR 8–102(B) provided that a lawyer "shall not knowingly make false accusations against a judge or other adjudicatory officer."

Paragraph (b) is substantially identical to DR 8–103.

RULE 8.3 Reporting Professional Misconduct*

(a) A lawyer having knowledge that another lawyer has committed a violation of the rules of professional conduct that raises a substantial question as to that lawyer's honesty, trustworthiness or fitness as a lawyer in other respects, shall inform the appropriate professional authority.

(b) A lawyer having knowledge that a judge has committed a violation of applicable rules of judicial conduct that raises a substantial question as to the judge's fitness for office shall inform the appropriate authority.

(c) This rule does not require disclosure of information otherwise protected by Rule 1.6 or information gained by a lawyer or judge while serving as a member of an approved lawyers assistance program to the extent that such information would be confidential if it were communicated subject to the attorney-client privilege.

COMMENT:

[1] Self-regulation of the legal profession requires that members of the profession initiate disciplinary investigation when they know of a violation of the Rules of Professional Conduct. Lawyers have a similar obligation with respect to judicial misconduct. An apparently isolated violation may indicate a pattern of misconduct that only a disciplinary investigation can uncover. Reporting a violation is especially important where the victim is unlikely to discover the offense.

[2] A report about misconduct is not required where it would involve violation of Rule 1.6. However, a lawyer should encourage a client to consent to disclosure where prosecution would not substantially prejudice the client's interests.

[3] If a lawyer were obliged to report every violation of the Rules, the failure to report any violation would itself be a professional offense. Such a requirement existed in many jurisdictions but proved to be unenforceable. This Rule limits the reporting obligation to those offenses that a self-regulating profession must vigorously endeavor to prevent. A measure of judgment is, therefore, required in complying with the provisions of this Rule. The term "substantial" refers to the seriousness of the possible offense and not the quantum of evidence of which the lawyer is aware. A report should be made to the bar disciplinary agency unless some other agency, such as a peer review agency, is more appropriate in the circumstances. Similar considerations apply to the reporting of judicial misconduct.

[4] The duty to report professional misconduct does not apply to a lawyer retained to represent a lawyer whose professional conduct is in question. Such a situation is governed by the rules applicable to the client-lawyer relationship.

[5] Information about a lawyer's or judge's misconduct or fitness may be received by a lawyer in the course of that lawyer's participation in an approved lawyers' or judges' assistance program. In that circumstance, providing for the confidentiality of such information encourages lawyers and judges to seek treatment through such program. Conversely, without such confidentiality, lawyers and judges may hesitate to seek assistance from these programs, which may then result in additional harm to their professional careers and additional injury to the welfare of clients and the public. The Rule therefore exempts the lawyer from the reporting requirements of paragraphs (a) and (b) with respect to information that would be privileged if the relationship between the impaired lawyer or judge and the recipient of the information were that of a client and a lawyer. On the other hand, a lawyer who receives such information would nevertheless be required to comply with the Rule 8.3 reporting provisions to report misconduct if the impaired lawyer or judge indicates an intent to engage in illegal activity, for example, the conversion of client funds to his or her use.

---

* In 1991, the ABA amended Model Rule 8.3(c) to include the reference to the protection of certain information obtained in lawyer assistance programs. The original version of 8.3(c) read as follows: "This rule does not require disclosure of information otherwise protected by Rule 1.6."

MODEL CODE COMPARISON:

DR 1–103(A) provided that "[a] lawyer possessing unprivileged knowledge of a violation of [a Disciplinary Rule] shall report such knowledge to . . . authority empowered to investigate or act upon such violation."

RULE 8.4 Misconduct

It is professional misconduct for a lawyer to:

(a) violate or attempt to violate the rules of professional conduct, knowingly assist or induce another to do so, or do so through the acts of another;

(b) commit a criminal act that reflects adversely on the lawyer's honesty, trustworthiness or fitness as a lawyer in other respects;

(c) engage in conduct involving dishonesty, fraud, deceit or misrepresentation;

(d) engage in conduct that is prejudicial to the administration of justice;

(e) state or imply an ability to influence improperly a government agency or official; or

(f) knowingly assist a judge or judicial officer in conduct that is a violation of applicable rules of judicial conduct or other law.

COMMENT:

[1] Many kinds of illegal conduct reflect adversely on fitness to practice law, such as offenses involving fraud and the offense of willful failure to file an income tax return. However, some kinds of offense carry no such implication. Traditionally, the distinction was drawn in terms of offenses involving "moral turpitude." That concept can be construed to include offenses concerning some matters of personal morality, such as adultery and comparable offenses, that have no specific connection to fitness for the practice of law. Although a lawyer is personally answerable to the entire criminal law, a lawyer should be professionally answerable only for offenses that indicate lack of those characteristics relevant to law practice. Offenses involving violence, dishonesty or breach of trust, or serious interference with the administration of justice are in that category. A pattern of repeated offenses, even ones of minor significance when considered separately, can indicate indifference to legal obligation.

[2] * A lawyer who, in the course of representing a client, knowingly manifests by words or conduct, bias or prejudice based upon race, sex, religion, national origin, disability, age, sexual orientation or socioeconomic status, violates paragraph (d) when such actions are prejudicial to the administration of justice. Legitimate advocacy respecting the foregoing factors does not violate paragraph (d). A trial judge's finding that peremptory challenges were exercised on a discriminatory basis does not alone establish a violation of this rule.

[3] A lawyer may refuse to comply with an obligation imposed by law upon a good faith belief that no valid obligation exists. The provisions of Rule 1.2(d) concerning a good faith challenge to the validity, scope, meaning or application of the law apply to challenges of legal regulation of the practice of law.

[4] Lawyers holding public office assume legal responsibilities going beyond those of other citizens. A lawyer's abuse of public office can suggest an inability to fulfill the professional role of attorney. The same is true of abuse of positions of private trust such as trustee, executor, administrator, guardian, agent and officer, director or manager of a corporation or other organization.

MODEL CODE COMPARISON:

With regard to paragraphs (a) through (d) DR 1–102(A) provided that a lawyer shall not:

"(1) Violate a Disciplinary Rule.

---

* The ABA House of Delegates added this comment to Model Rule 8.4 in 1998 after pressure from many groups to amend the text of the rule to prohibit attorney conduct or words based upon bias or prejudice unrelated to the merits of the representation.

"(2) Circumvent a Disciplinary Rule through actions of another.

"(3) Engage in illegal conduct involving moral turpitude.

"(4) Engage in conduct involving dishonesty, fraud, deceit, or misrepresentation.

"(5) Engage in conduct that is prejudicial to the administration of justice.

"(6) Engage in any other conduct that adversely reflects on his fitness to practice law."

Paragraph (e) is substantially similar to DR 9–101(C).

There was no direct counterpart to paragraph (f) in the Disciplinary Rules of the Model Code. EC 7–34 stated in part that "[a] lawyer . . . is never justified in making a gift or a loan to a [judicial officer] except as permitted by . . . the Code of Judicial Conduct." EC 9–1 stated that a lawyer "should promote public confidence in our [legal] system and in the legal profession."

RULE 8.5 Disciplinary Authority; Choice of Law*

(a) Disciplinary Authority. A lawyer admitted to practice in this jurisdiction is subject to the disciplinary authority of this jurisdiction, regardless of where the lawyer's conduct occurs. A lawyer may be subject to the disciplinary authority of both this jurisdiction and another jurisdiction where the lawyer is admitted for the same conduct.

(b) Choice of Law. In any exercise of the disciplinary authority of this jurisdiction, the rules of professional conduct to be applied shall be as follows:

(1) for conduct in connection with a proceeding in a court before which a lawyer has been admitted to practice (either generally or for purposes of that proceeding), the rules to be applied shall be the rules of the jurisdiction in which the court sits, unless the rules of the court provide otherwise; and

(2) for any other conduct,

(i) if the lawyer is licensed to practice only in this jurisdiction, the rules to be applied shall be the rules of this jurisdiction, and

(ii) if the lawyer is licensed to practice in this and another jurisdiction, the rules to be applied shall be the rules of the admitting jurisdiction in which the lawyer principally practices; provided, however, that if particular conduct clearly has its predominant effect in another jurisdiction in which the lawyer is licensed to practice, the rules of that jurisdiction shall be applied to that conduct.

---

* In August 1993, the ABA amended Model Rule 8.5 to more clearly address the problem of choice of professional responsibility rules when more than one jurisdiction's rules may potentially apply to the lawyer's conduct. The original Model Rule 8.5 text and comments are reprinted below:

RULE 8.5 Jurisdiction

A lawyer admitted to practice in this jurisdiction is subject to the disciplinary authority of this jurisdiction although engaged in practice elsewhere.

COMMENT:

[1] In modern practice lawyers frequently act outside the territorial limits of the jurisdiction in which they are licensed to practice, either in another state or outside the United States. In doing so, they remain subject to the governing authority of the jurisdiction in which they are licensed to practice. If their activity in another jurisdiction is substantial and continuous, it may constitute practice of law in that jurisdiction. See Rule 5.5.

[2] If the rules of professional conduct in the two jurisdictions differ, principles of conflict of laws may apply. Similar problems can arise when a lawyer is licensed to practice in more than one jurisdiction.

[3] Where the lawyer is licensed to practice law in two jurisdictions which impose conflicting obligations, applicable rules of choice of law may govern the situation. A related problem arises with respect to practice before a federal tribunal, where the general authority of the states to regulate the practice of law must be reconciled with such authority as federal tribunals may have to regulate practice before them.

COMMENT:

Disciplinary Authority

[1] Paragraph (a) restates longstanding law.

Choice of Law

[2] A lawyer may be potentially subject to more than one set of rules of professional conduct which impose different obligations. The lawyer may be licensed to practice in more than one jurisdiction with differing rules, or may be admitted to practice before a particular court with rules that differ from those of the jurisdiction or jurisdictions in which the lawyer is licensed to practice. In the past, decisions have not developed clear or consistent guidance as to which rules apply in such circumstances.

[3] Paragraph (b) seeks to resolve such potential conflicts. Its premise is that minimizing conflicts between rules, as well as uncertainty about which rules are applicable, is in the best interest of both clients and the profession (as well as the bodies having authority to regulate the profession). Accordingly, it takes the approach of (i) providing that any particular conduct of an attorney shall be subject to only one set of rules of professional conduct, and (ii) making the determination of which set of rules applies to particular conduct as straightforward as possible, consistent with recognition of appropriate regulatory interests of relevant jurisdictions.

[4] Paragraph (b) provides that as to a lawyer's conduct relating to a proceeding in a court before which the lawyer is admitted to practice (either generally or pro hac vice), the lawyer shall be subject only to the rules of professional conduct of that court. As to all other conduct, paragraph (b) provides that a lawyer licensed to practice only in this jurisdiction shall be subject to the rules of professional conduct of this jurisdiction, and that a lawyer licensed in multiple jurisdictions shall be subject only to the rules of the jurisdiction where he or she (as an individual, not his or her firm) principally practices, but with one exception: if particular conduct clearly has its predominant effect in another admitting jurisdiction, then only the rules of that jurisdiction shall apply. The intention is for the latter exception to be a narrow one. It would be appropriately applied, for example, to a situation in which a lawyer admitted in, and principally practicing in, State A, but also admitted in State B, handled an acquisition by a company whose headquarters and operations were in State B of another, similar such company. The exception would not appropriately be applied, on the other hand, if the lawyer handled an acquisition by a company whose headquarters and operations were in State A of a company whose headquarters and main operations were in State A, but which also had some operations in State B.

[5] If two admitting jurisdictions were to proceed against a lawyer for the same conduct, they should, applying this rule, identify the same governing ethics rules. They should take all appropriate steps to see that they do apply the same rule to the same conduct, and in all events should avoid proceeding against a lawyer on the basis of two inconsistent rules.

[6] The choice of law provision is not intended to apply to transnational practice. Choice of law in this context should be the subject of agreements between jurisdictions or of appropriate international law.

MODEL CODE COMPARISON:

There was no counterpart to this Rule in the Model Code.

1990 VERSION OF THE ABA MODEL CODE OF JUDICIAL CONDUCT

Adopted August 1990, as Amended to August 2003.

NOTE: The 1990 version has been completely replaced by the 2008 version as of February 2008.

TABLE OF CONTENTS

PREAMBLE

[1] Our legal system is based on the principle that an independent, fair and competent judiciary will interpret and apply the laws that govern us. The role of the judiciary is central to American concepts of justice and the rule of law. Intrinsic to all sections of this Code are the precepts that judges, individually and collectively, must respect and honor the judicial office as a public trust and strive to enhance and maintain confidence in our legal system. The judge is an arbiter of facts and law for the resolution of disputes and a highly visible symbol of government under the rule of law.

[2] The Code of Judicial Conduct is intended to establish standards for ethical conduct of judges. It consists of broad statements called Canons, specific rules set forth in Sections under each Canon, a Terminology Section, an Application Section and Commentary. The text of the Canons and the Sections, including the Terminology and Application Sections, is authoritative. The Commentary, by explanation and example, provides guidance with respect to the purpose and meaning of the Canons and Sections. The Commentary is not intended as a statement of additional rules. When the text uses "shall" or "shall not," it is intended to impose binding obligations the violation of which can result in disciplinary action. When "should" or "should not" is used, the text is intended as hortatory and as a statement of what is or is not appropriate conduct but not as a binding rule under which a judge may be disciplined. When "may" is used, it denotes permissible discretion or, depending on the context, it refers to action that is not covered by specific proscriptions.

[3] The Canons and Sections are rules of reason. They should be applied consistent with constitutional requirements, statutes, other court rules and decisional law and in the context of all relevant circumstances. The Code is to be construed so as not to impinge on the essential independence of judges in making judicial decisions.

[4] The Code is designed to provide guidance to judges and candidates for judicial office and to provide a structure for regulating conduct through disciplinary agencies. It is not designed or intended as a basis

for civil liability or criminal prosecution. Furthermore, the purpose of the Code would be subverted if the Code were invoked by lawyers for mere tactical advantage in a proceeding.

[5] The text of the Canons and Sections is intended to govern conduct of judges and to be binding upon them. It is not intended, however, that every transgression will result in disciplinary action. Whether disciplinary action is appropriate, and the degree of discipline to be imposed, should be determined through a reasonable and reasoned application of the text and should depend on such factors as the seriousness of the transgression, whether there is a pattern of improper activity and the effect of the improper activity on others or on the judicial system. See ABA Standards Relating to Judicial Discipline and Disability Retirement.[1]

[6] The Code of Judicial Conduct is not intended as an exhaustive guide for the conduct of judges. They should also be governed in their judicial and personal conduct by general ethical standards. The Code is intended, however, to state basic standards which should govern the conduct of all judges and to provide guidance to assist judges in establishing and maintaining high standards of judicial and personal conduct.

TERMINOLOGY

Terms explained below are noted with an asterisk (*) in the Sections where they appear. In addition, the Sections where terms appear are referred to after the explanation of each term below.

"Appropriate authority" denotes the authority with responsibility for initiation of disciplinary process with respect to the violation to be reported. See Sections 3D(1) and 3D(2).

"Candidate." A candidate is a person seeking selection for or retention in judicial office by election or appointment. A person becomes a candidate for judicial office as soon as he or she makes a public announcement of candidacy, declares or files as a candidate with the election or appointment authority, or authorizes solicitation or acceptance of contributions or support. The term "candidate" has the same meaning when applied to a judge seeking election or appointment to non-judicial office. See Preamble and Sections 5A, 5B, 5C and 5E.

"Continuing part-time judge." A continuing part-time judge is a judge who serves repeatedly on a part-time basis by election or under a continuing appointment, including a retired judge subject to recall who is permitted to practice law. See Application Section C.

"Court personnel" does not include the lawyers in a proceeding before a judge. See Sections 3B(7)(c) and 3B(9).

"De minimis" denotes an insignificant interest that could not raise reasonable question as to a judge's impartiality. See Sections 3E(1)(c) and 3E(1)(d).

"Economic interest" denotes ownership of a more than de minimis legal or equitable interest, or a relationship as officer, director, advisor or other active participant in the affairs of a party, except that:

(i) ownership of an interest in a mutual or common investment fund that holds securities is not an economic interest in such securities unless the judge participates in the management of the fund or a proceeding pending or impending before the judge could substantially affect the value of the interest;

(ii) service by a judge as an officer, director, advisor or other active participant in an educational, religious, charitable, fraternal or civic organization, or service by a judge's spouse, parent or child as an officer, director, advisor or other active participant in any organization does not create an economic interest in securities held by that organization;

(iii) a deposit in a financial institution, the proprietary interest of a policy holder in a mutual insurance company, of a depositor in a mutual savings association or of a member in a credit union, or a similar proprietary interest, is not an economic interest in the

---

[1] Judicial disciplinary procedures adopted in the jurisdictions should comport with the requirements of due process. The ABA Standards Relating to Judicial Discipline and Disability Retirement are cited as an example of how these due process requirements may be satisfied.

organization unless a proceeding pending or impending before the judge could substantially affect the value of the interest;

(iv) ownership of government securities is not an economic interest in the issuer unless a proceeding pending or impending before the judge could substantially affect the value of the securities.

See Sections 3E(1)(c) and 3E(2).

"Fiduciary" includes such relationships as executor, administrator, trustee, and guardian. See Sections 3E(2) and 4E.

"Impartiality" or "impartial" denotes absence of bias or prejudice in favor of, or against, particular parties or classes of parties, as well as maintaining an open mind in considering issues that may come before the judge. See Sections 2A, 3B(10), 3E(1), 5A(3)(a) and 5A(3)(d)(i).*

"Knowingly," "knowledge," "known" or "knows" denotes actual knowledge of the fact in question. A person's knowledge may be inferred from circumstances. See Sections 3D, 3E(1), and 5A(3).

"Law" denotes court rules as well as statutes, constitutional provisions and decisional law. See Sections 2A, 3A, 3B(2), 3B(6), 4B, 4C, 4D(5), 4F, 4I, 5A(2), 5A(3), 5B(2), 5C(1), 5C(3) and 5D.

"Member of the candidate's family" denotes a spouse, child, grandchild, parent, grandparent or other relative or person with whom the candidate maintains a close familial relationship. See Section 5A(3)(a).

"Member of the judge's family" denotes a spouse, child, grandchild, parent, grandparent, or other relative or person with whom the judge maintains a close familial relationship. See Sections 4D(3), 4E and 4G.

"Member of the judge's family residing in the judge's household" denotes any relative of a judge by blood or marriage, or a person treated by a judge as a member of the judge's family, who resides in the judge's household. See Sections 3E(1) and 4D(5).

"Nonpublic information" denotes information that, by law, is not available to the public. Nonpublic information may include but is not limited to: information that is sealed by statute or court order, impounded or communicated in camera; and information offered in grand jury proceedings, presentencing reports, dependency cases or psychiatric reports. See Section 3B(11).

"Periodic part-time judge." A periodic part-time judge is a judge who serves or expects to serve repeatedly on a part-time basis but under a separate appointment for each limited period of service or for each matter. See Application Section D.

"Political organization" denotes a political party or other group, the principal purpose of which is to further the election or appointment of candidates to political office. See Sections 5A(1), 5B(2) and 5C(1).

"Pro tempore part-time judge." A pro tempore part-time judge is a judge who serves or expects to serve once or only sporadically on a part-time basis under a separate appointment for each period of service or for each case heard. See Application Section E.

"Public election." This term includes primary and general elections; it includes partisan elections, nonpartisan elections and retention elections. See Section 5C.

"Require." The rules prescribing that a judge "require" certain conduct of others are, like all of the rules in this Code, rules of reason. The use of the term "require" in that context means a judge is to exercise reasonable direction and control over the conduct of those persons subject to the judge's direction and control. See Sections 3B(3), 3B(4), 3B(6), 3B(9) and 3C(2).

* The definition of the terms "impartiality" and "impartial" were added by the ABA House of Delegates in August 2003.

"Third degree of relationship." The following persons are relatives within the third degree of relationship: great-grandparent, grandparent, parent, uncle, aunt, brother, sister, child, grandchild, great-grandchild, nephew or niece. See Section 3E(1)(d).

CANON 1

A Judge Shall Uphold the Integrity and Independence of the Judiciary

A. An independent and honorable judiciary is indispensable to justice in our society. A judge should participate in establishing, maintaining and enforcing high standards of conduct, and shall personally observe those standards so that the integrity and independence of the judiciary will be preserved. The provisions of this Code are to be construed and applied to further that objective.

Commentary

[1] Deference to the judgments and rulings of courts depends upon public confidence in the integrity and independence of judges. The integrity and independence of judges depends in turn upon their acting without fear or favor. A judiciary of integrity is one in which judges are known for their probity, fairness, honesty, uprightness, and soundness of character. An independent judiciary is one free of inappropriate outside influences.† Although judges should be independent, they must comply with the law, including the provisions of this Code. Public confidence in the impartiality of the judiciary is maintained by the adherence of each judge to this responsibility. Conversely, violation of this Code diminishes public confidence in the judiciary and thereby does injury to the system of government under law.

CANON 2

A Judge Shall Avoid Impropriety and the Appearance of Impropriety in All of the Judge's Activities

A. A judge shall respect and comply with the law* and shall act at all times in a manner that promotes public confidence in the integrity and impartiality* of the judiciary.

Commentary

[1] Public confidence in the judiciary is eroded by irresponsible or improper conduct by judges. A judge must avoid all impropriety and appearance of impropriety. A judge must expect to be the subject of constant public scrutiny. A judge must therefore accept restrictions on the judge's conduct that might be viewed as burdensome by the ordinary citizen and should do so freely and willingly. Examples are the restrictions on judicial speech imposed by Sections 3(B)(9) and (10) that are indispensable to the maintenance of the integrity, impartiality, and independence of the judiciary.

[2] The prohibition against behaving with impropriety or the appearance of impropriety applies to both the professional and personal conduct of a judge. Because it is not practicable to list all prohibited acts, the proscription is necessarily cast in general terms that extend to conduct by judges that is harmful although not specifically mentioned in the Code. Actual improprieties under this standard include violations of law, court rules or other specific provisions of this Code. The test for appearance of impropriety is whether the conduct would create in reasonable minds a perception that the judge's ability to carry out judicial responsibilities with integrity, impartiality and competence is impaired.

See also Commentary under Section 2C.

B. A judge shall not allow family, social, political or other relationships to influence the judge's judicial conduct or judgment. A judge shall not lend the prestige of judicial office to advance the private interests of the judge or others; nor shall a judge convey or

---

† The definition of the terms "impartiality" and "impartial" were added by the ABA House of Delegates in August 2003.

* See Terminology.

permit others to convey the impression that they are in a special position to influence the judge. A judge shall not testify voluntarily as a character witness.

Commentary

[1] Maintaining the prestige of judicial office is essential to a system of government in which the judiciary functions independently of the executive and legislative branches. Respect for the judicial office facilitates the orderly conduct of legitimate judicial functions. Judges should distinguish between proper and improper use of the prestige of office in all of their activities. For example, it would be improper for a judge to allude to his or her judgeship to gain a personal advantage such as deferential treatment when stopped by a police officer for a traffic offense. Similarly, judicial letterhead must not be used for conducting a judge's personal business.

[2] A judge must avoid lending the prestige of judicial office for the advancement of the private interests of others. For example, a judge must not use the judge's judicial position to gain advantage in a civil suit involving a member of the judge's family. In contracts for publication of a judge's writings, a judge should retain control over the advertising to avoid exploitation of the judge's office. As to the acceptance of awards, see Section 4D(5)(a) and Commentary.

[3] Although a judge should be sensitive to possible abuse of the prestige of office, a judge may, based on the judge's personal knowledge, serve as a reference or provide a letter of recommendation. However, a judge must not initiate the communication of information to a sentencing judge or a probation or corrections officer but may provide to such persons information for the record in response to a formal request.

[4] Judges may participate in the process of judicial selection by cooperating with appointing authorities and screening committees seeking names for consideration, and by responding to official inquiries concerning a person being considered for a judgeship. See also Canon 5 regarding use of a judge's name in political activities.

[5] A judge must not testify voluntarily as a character witness because to do so may lend the prestige of the judicial office in support of the party for whom the judge testifies. Moreover, when a judge testifies as a witness, a lawyer who regularly appears before the judge may be placed in the awkward position of cross-examining the judge. A judge may, however, testify when properly summoned. Except in unusual circumstances where the demands of justice require, a judge should discourage a party from requiring the judge to testify as a character witness.

C. A judge shall not hold membership in any organization that practices invidious discrimination on the basis of race, sex, religion or national origin.

Commentary

[1] Membership of a judge in an organization that practices invidious discrimination gives rise to perceptions that the judge's impartiality is impaired. Section 2C refers to the current practices of the organization. Whether an organization practices invidious discrimination is often a complex question to which judges should be sensitive. The answer cannot be determined from a mere examination of an organization's current membership rolls but rather depends on how the organization selects members and other relevant factors, such as that the organization is dedicated to the preservation of religious, ethnic or cultural values of legitimate common interest to its members, or that it is in fact and effect an intimate, purely private organization whose membership limitations could not be constitutionally prohibited. Absent such factors, an organization is generally said to discriminate invidiously if it arbitrarily excludes from membership on the basis of race, religion, sex or national origin persons who would otherwise be admitted to membership. *See New York State Club Ass'n. Inc. v. City of New York,* 108 S.Ct. 2225, 101 L.Ed.2d 1 (1988); *Board of Directors of Rotary International v. Rotary Club of Duarte,* 481 U.S. 537, 107 S.Ct. 1940, 95 L.Ed.2d 474 (1987); *Roberts v. United States Jaycees,* 468 U.S. 609, 104 S.Ct. 3244, 82 L.Ed.2d 462 (1984).

[2] Although Section 2C relates only to membership in organizations that invidiously discriminate on the basis of race, sex, religion or national origin, a judge's membership in an organization that engages in any discriminatory membership practices prohibited by the law of the jurisdiction also violates Canon 2 and Section 2A and gives the appearance of impropriety. In addition, it would be a violation of Canon 2 and Section 2A for a judge to arrange a meeting at a club that the judge knows practices invidious discrimination on the basis of race, sex, religion or national origin in its membership or other policies, or for the judge to

regularly use such a club. Moreover, public manifestation by a judge of the judge's knowing approval of invidious discrimination on any basis gives the appearance of impropriety under Canon 2 and diminishes public confidence in the integrity and impartiality of the judiciary, in violation of Section 2A.

[3] When a person who is a judge on the date this Code becomes effective [in the jurisdiction in which the person is a judge][2] learns that an organization to which the judge belongs engages in invidious discrimination that would preclude membership under Section 2C or under Canon 2 and Section 2A, the judge is permitted, in lieu of resigning, to make immediate efforts to have the organization discontinue its invidiously discriminatory practices, but is required to suspend participation in any other activities of the organization. If the organization fails to discontinue its invidiously discriminatory practices as promptly as possible (and in all events within a year of the judge's first learning of the practices), the judge is required to resign immediately from the organization.

CANON 3

A Judge Shall Perform the Duties of Judicial Office Impartially and Diligently

A. Judicial Duties in General. The judicial duties of a judge take precedence over all the judge's other activities. The judge's judicial duties include all the duties of the judge's office prescribed by law.* In the performance of these duties, the following standards apply.

B. Adjudicative Responsibilities.

(1) A judge shall hear and decide matters assigned to the judge except those in which disqualification is required.

(2) A judge shall be faithful to the law* and maintain professional competence in it. A judge shall not be swayed by partisan interests, public clamor or fear of criticism.

(3) A judge shall require* order and decorum in proceedings before the judge.

(4) A judge shall be patient, dignified and courteous to litigants, jurors, witnesses, lawyers and others with whom the judge deals in an official capacity, and shall require* similar conduct of lawyers, and of staff, court officials and others subject to the judge's direction and control.

Commentary

[1] The duty to hear all proceedings fairly and with patience is not inconsistent with the duty to dispose promptly of the business of the court. Judges can be efficient and businesslike while being patient and deliberate.

(5) A judge shall perform judicial duties without bias or prejudice. A judge shall not, in the performance of judicial duties, by words or conduct manifest bias or prejudice, including but not limited to bias or prejudice based upon race, sex, religion, national origin, disability, age, sexual orientation or socioeconomic status, and shall not permit staff, court officials and others subject to the judge's direction and control to do so.

Commentary

[1] A judge must refrain from speech, gestures or other conduct that could reasonably be perceived as sexual harassment and must require the same standard of conduct of others subject to the judge's direction and control.

[2] A judge must perform judicial duties impartially and fairly. A judge who manifests bias on any basis in a proceeding impairs the fairness of the proceeding and brings the judiciary into disrepute. Facial expression and body language, in addition to oral communication, can give to parties or lawyers in the

---

[2] The language within the brackets should be deleted when the jurisdiction adopts this provision.

* See Terminology.

proceeding, jurors, the media and others an appearance of judicial bias. A judge must be alert to avoid behavior that may be perceived as prejudicial.

(6) A judge shall require* lawyers in proceedings before the judge to refrain from manifesting, by words or conduct, bias or prejudice based upon race, sex, religion, national origin, disability, age, sexual orientation or socioeconomic status, against parties, witnesses, counsel or others. This Section 3B(6) does not preclude legitimate advocacy when race, sex, religion, national origin, disability, age, sexual orientation or socioeconomic status, or other similar factors, are issues in the proceeding.

(7) A judge shall accord to every person who has a legal interest in a proceeding, or that person's lawyer, the right to be heard according to law.* A judge shall not initiate, permit, or consider ex parte communications, or consider other communications made to the judge outside the presence of the parties concerning a pending or impending proceeding except that:

(a) Where circumstances require, ex parte communications for scheduling, administrative purposes or emergencies that do not deal with substantive matters or issues on the merits are authorized; provided:

(i) the judge reasonably believes that no party will gain a procedural or tactical advantage as a result of the ex parte communication, and

(ii) the judge makes provision promptly to notify all other parties of the substance of the ex parte communication and allows an opportunity to respond.

(b) A judge may obtain the advice of a disinterested expert on the law* applicable to a proceeding before the judge if the judge gives notice to the parties of the person consulted and the substance of the advice, and affords the parties reasonable opportunity to respond.

(c) A judge may consult with court personnel* whose function is to aid the judge in carrying out the judge's adjudicative responsibilities or with other judges.

(d) A judge may, with the consent of the parties, confer separately with the parties and their lawyers in an effort to mediate or settle matters pending before the judge.

(e) A judge may initiate or consider any ex parte communications when expressly authorized by law* to do so.

Commentary

[1] The proscription against communications concerning a proceeding includes communications from lawyers, law teachers, and other persons who are not participants in the proceeding, except to the limited extent permitted.

[2] To the extent reasonably possible, all parties or their lawyers shall be included in communications with a judge.

[3] Whenever presence of a party or notice to a party is required by Section 3B(7), it is the party's lawyer, or if the party is unrepresented the party, who is to be present or to whom notice is to be given.

[4] An appropriate and often desirable procedure for a court to obtain the advice of a disinterested expert on legal issues is to invite the expert to file a brief amicus curiae.

[5] Certain ex parte communication is approved by Section 3B(7) to facilitate scheduling and other administrative purposes and to accommodate emergencies. In general, however, a judge must discourage ex parte communication and allow it only if all the criteria stated in Section 3B(7) are clearly met. A judge

* See Terminology.

must disclose to all parties all ex parte communications described in Sections 3B(7)(a) and 3B(7)(b) regarding a proceeding pending or impending before the judge.

[6] A judge must not independently investigate facts in a case and must consider only the evidence presented.

[7] A judge may request a party to submit proposed findings of fact and conclusions of law, so long as the other parties are apprised of the request and are given an opportunity to respond to the proposed findings and conclusions.

[8] A judge must make reasonable efforts, including the provision of appropriate supervision, to ensure that Section 3B(7) is not violated through law clerks or other personnel on the judge's staff.

[9] If communication between the trial judge and the appellate court with respect to a proceeding is permitted, a copy of any written communication or the substance of any oral communication should be provided to all parties.

(8) A judge shall dispose of all judicial matters promptly, efficiently and fairly.

Commentary

[1] In disposing of matters promptly, efficiently and fairly, a judge must demonstrate due regard for the rights of the parties to be heard and to have issues resolved without unnecessary cost or delay. Containing costs while preserving fundamental rights of parties also protects the interests of witnesses and the general public. A judge should monitor and supervise cases so as to reduce or eliminate dilatory practices, avoidable delays and unnecessary costs. A judge should encourage and seek to facilitate settlement, but parties should not feel coerced into surrendering the right to have their controversy resolved by the courts.

[2] Prompt disposition of the court's business requires a judge to devote adequate time to judicial duties, to be punctual in attending court and expeditious in determining matters under submission, and to insist that court officials, litigants and their lawyers cooperate with the judge to that end.

(9) A judge shall not, while a proceeding is pending or impending in any court, make any public comment that might reasonably be expected to affect its outcome or impair its fairness or make any nonpublic comment that might substantially interfere with a fair trial or hearing. The judge shall require* similar abstention on the part of court personnel* subject to the judge's direction and control. This Section does not prohibit judges from making public statements in the course of their official duties or from explaining for public information the procedures of the court. This Section does not apply to proceedings in which the judge is a litigant in a personal capacity.

(10) A judge shall not, with respect to cases, controversies or issues that are likely to come before the court, make pledges, promises or commitments that are inconsistent with the impartial* performance of the adjudicative duties of the office.†

Commentary

[1] Sections 3B(9) and (10) restrictions on judicial speech are essential to the maintenance of the integrity, impartiality, and independence of the judiciary. A pending proceeding is one that has begun but not yet reached final disposition. An impending proceeding is one that is anticipated but not yet begun. The requirement that judges abstain from public comment regarding a pending or impending proceeding continues during any appellate process and until final disposition. Sections 3B(9) and (10) do not prohibit a judge from commenting on proceedings in which the judge is a litigant in a personal capacity, but in cases such as a writ of mandamus where the judge is a litigant in an official capacity, the judge must not comment publicly. The conduct of lawyers relating to trial publicity is governed by [Rule 3.6 of the ABA Model Rules of Professional Conduct.] (Each jurisdiction should substitute an appropriate reference to its rule.)

* See Terminology.

† The ABA House of Delegates in August 2003 added a new subsection 10 and modified the commentary to reflect the change. The remaining subsections were also renumbered.

(11) A judge shall not commend or criticize jurors for their verdict other than in a court order or opinion in a proceeding, but may express appreciation to jurors for their service to the judicial system and the community.

Commentary

[1] Commending or criticizing jurors for their verdict may imply a judicial expectation in future cases and may impair a juror's ability to be fair and impartial in a subsequent case.

(12) A judge shall not disclose or use, for any purpose unrelated to judicial duties, nonpublic information* acquired in a judicial capacity.

C. Administrative Responsibilities.

(1) A judge shall diligently discharge the judge's administrative responsibilities without bias or prejudice and maintain professional competence in judicial administration, and should cooperate with other judges and court officials in the administration of court business.

(2) A judge shall require staff, court officials and others subject to the judge's direction and control to observe the standards of fidelity and diligence that apply to the judge and to refrain from manifesting bias or prejudice in the performance of their official duties.

(3) A judge with supervisory authority for the judicial performance of other judges shall take reasonable measures to assure the prompt disposition of matters before them and the proper performance of their other judicial responsibilities.

(4) A judge shall not make unnecessary appointments. A judge shall exercise the power of appointment impartially and on the basis of merit. A judge shall avoid nepotism and favoritism. A judge shall not approve compensation of appointees beyond the fair value of services rendered.

Commentary

[1] Appointees of a judge include assigned counsel, officials such as referees, commissioners, special masters, receivers and guardians and personnel such as clerks, secretaries and bailiffs. Consent by the parties to an appointment or an award of compensation does not relieve the judge of the obligation prescribed by Section 3C(4).

(5)[††] A judge shall not appoint a lawyer to a position if the judge either knows that the lawyer has contributed more than [$] within the prior [ ] years to the judges's election campaign,[3] or learns of such a contribution by means of a timely motion by a party or other person properly interested in the matter, unless

(a) the position is substantially uncompensated;

(b) the lawyer has been selected in rotation from a list of a qualified and available lawyers compiled without regard to their having made political contributions; or

(c) the judge or another presiding or administrative judge affirmatively finds that no other lawyer is willing, competent and able to accept the position.

D. Disciplinary Responsibilities.

(1) A judge who receives information indicating a substantial likelihood that another judge has committed a violation of this Code should take appropriate action. A judge having knowledge* that another judge has committed a violation of this Code that raises a

---

†† [Editor's Note: This language was added by the ABA House of Delegates in 1999.]

3 This provision is meant to be applicable wherever judges are subject to public election; specific amount and time limitations, to be determined based on circumstances within the jurisdiction, should be inserted in the brackets.

substantial question as to the other judge's fitness for office shall inform the appropriate authority.*

(2) A judge who receives information indicating a substantial likelihood that a lawyer has committed a violation of the Rules of Professional Conduct [substitute correct title if the applicable rules of lawyer conduct have a different title] should take appropriate action. A judge having knowledge* that a lawyer has committed a violation of the Rules of Professional Conduct [substitute correct title if the applicable rules of lawyer conduct have a different title] that raises a substantial question as to the lawyer's honesty, trustworthiness or fitness as a lawyer in other respects shall inform the appropriate authority.*

(3) Acts of a judge, in the discharge of disciplinary responsibilities, required or permitted by Sections 3D(1) and 3D(2) are part of a judge's judicial duties and shall be absolutely privileged, and no civil action predicated thereon may be instituted against the judge.

Commentary

[1] Appropriate action may include direct communication with the judge or lawyer who has committed the violation, other direct action if available, and reporting the violation to the appropriate authority or other agency or body.

E. Disqualification.

(1) A judge shall disqualify himself or herself in a proceeding in which the judge's impartiality* might reasonably be questioned, including but not limited to instances where:

Commentary

[1] Under this rule, a judge is disqualified whenever the judge's impartiality might reasonably be questioned, regardless whether any of the specific rules in Section 3E(1) apply. For example, if a judge were in the process of negotiating for employment with a law firm, the judge would be disqualified from any matters in which that law firm appeared, unless the disqualification was waived by the parties after disclosure by the judge.

[2] A judge should disclose on the record information that the judge believes the parties or their lawyers might consider relevant to the question of disqualification, even if the judge believes there is no real basis for disqualification.

[3] By decisional law, the rule of necessity may override the rule of disqualification. For example, a judge might be required to participate in judicial review of a judicial salary statute, or might be the only judge available in a matter requiring immediate judicial action, such as a hearing on probable cause or a temporary restraining order. In the latter case, the judge must disclose on the record the basis for possible disqualification and use reasonable efforts to transfer the matter to another judge as soon as practicable.

(a) the judge has a personal bias or prejudice concerning a party or a party's lawyer, or personal knowledge* of disputed evidentiary facts concerning the proceeding;

(b) the judge served as a lawyer in the matter in controversy, or a lawyer with whom the judge previously practiced law served during such association as a lawyer concerning the matter, or the judge has been a material witness concerning it;

Commentary

[1] A lawyer in a government agency does not ordinarily have an association with other lawyers employed by that agency within the meaning of Section 3E(1)(b); a judge formerly employed by a government agency, however, should disqualify himself or herself in a proceeding if the judge's impartiality might reasonably be questioned because of such association.

---

* See Terminology.

(c) the judge knows* that he or she, individually or as a fiduciary, or the judge's spouse, parent or child wherever residing, or any other member of the judge's family residing in the judge's household,* has an economic interest* in the subject matter in controversy or in a party to the proceeding or has any other more than de minimis* interest that could be substantially affected by the proceeding;

(d) the judge or the judge's spouse, or a person within the third degree of relationship* to either of them, or the spouse of such a person:

(i) is a party to the proceeding, or an officer, director or trustee of a party;

(ii) is acting as a lawyer in the proceeding;

(iii) is known* by the judge to have a more than de minimis* interest that could be substantially affected by the proceeding;

(iv) is to the judge's knowledge* likely to be a material witness in the proceeding.

(e)† the judge knows or learns by means of a timely motion that a party or a party's lawyer has within the previous [ ] year[s] made aggregate* contributions to the judge's campaign in an amount that is greater than [[[$] for an individual or [$] for an entity]] [[is reasonable and appropriate for an individual or an entity]].[4]

Commentary

[1] The fact that a lawyer in a proceeding is affiliated with a law firm with which a relative of the judge is affiliated does not of itself disqualify the judge. Under appropriate circumstances, the fact that "the judge's impartiality might reasonably be questioned" under Section 3E(1), or that the relative is known by the judge to have an interest in the law firm that could be "substantially affected by the outcome of the proceeding" under Section 3E(1)(d)(iii) may require the judge's disqualification.

(f)†† the judge, while a judge or a candidate* for judicial office, has made a public statement that commits, or appears to commit, the judge with respect to

(i) an issue in the proceeding; or

(ii) the controversy in the proceeding.

(2) A judge shall keep informed about the judge's personal and fiduciary* economic interests,* and make a reasonable effort to keep informed about the personal economic interests of the judge's spouse and minor children residing in the judge's household.

F. Remittal of Disqualification. A judge disqualified by the terms of Section 3E may disclose on the record the basis of the judge's disqualification and may ask the parties and their lawyers to consider, out of the presence of the judge, whether to waive disqualification. If following disclosure of any basis for disqualification other than personal bias or prejudice concerning a party, the parties and lawyers, without participation by the judge, all agree that the judge should not be disqualified, and the judge is then willing to participate, the judge may participate in the proceeding. The agreement shall be incorporated in the record of the proceeding.

Commentary

[1] A remittal procedure provides the parties an opportunity to proceed without delay if they wish to waive the disqualification. To assure that consideration of the question of remittal is made independently

---

* See Terminology.

† [Editor's Note: This language was added by the ABA House of Delegates in 1999.]

4 This provision is meant to be applicable wherever judges are subject to public election. Where specific dollar amounts determined by local circumstances are not used, the "reasonable and appropriate" language should be used.

†† The ABA House of Delegates added the new (f) in August 2003.

of the judge, a judge must not solicit, seek or hear comment on possible remittal or waiver of the disqualification unless the lawyers jointly propose remittal after consultation as provided in the rule. A party may act through counsel if counsel represents on the record that the party has been consulted and consents. As a practical matter, a judge may wish to have all parties and their lawyers sign the remittal agreement.

CANON 4

A Judge Shall So Conduct the Judge's Extra-Judicial Activities as to Minimize the Risk of Conflict With Judicial Obligations

A. Extra-judicial Activities in General. A judge shall conduct all of the judge's extra-judicial activities so that they do not:

(1) cast reasonable doubt on the judge's capacity to act impartially as a judge;

(2) demean the judicial office; or

(3) interfere with the proper performance of judicial duties.

Commentary

[1] Complete separation of a judge from extra-judicial activities is neither possible nor wise; a judge should not become isolated from the community in which the judge lives.

[2] Expressions of bias or prejudice by a judge, even outside the judge's judicial activities, may cast reasonable doubt on the judge's capacity to act impartially as a judge. Expressions which may do so include jokes or other remarks demeaning individuals on the basis of their race, sex, religion, national origin, disability, age, sexual orientation or socioeconomic status. See Section 2C and accompanying Commentary.

B. Avocational Activities. A judge may speak, write, lecture, teach and participate in other extra-judicial activities concerning the law,* the legal system, the administration of justice and non-legal subjects, subject to the requirements of this Code.

Commentary

[1] As a judicial officer and person specially learned in the law, a judge is in a unique position to contribute to the improvement of the law, the legal system, and the administration of justice, including revision of substantive and procedural law and improvement of criminal and juvenile justice. To the extent that time permits, a judge is encouraged to do so, either independently or through a bar association, judicial conference or other organization dedicated to the improvement of the law. Judges may participate in efforts to promote the fair administration of justice, the independence of the judiciary and the integrity of the legal profession and may express opposition to the persecution of lawyers and judges in other countries because of their professional activities.

[2] In this and other Sections of Canon 4, the phrase "subject to the requirements of this Code" is used, notably in connection with a judge's governmental, civic or charitable activities. This phrase is included to remind judges that the use of permissive language in various Sections of the Code does not relieve a judge from the other requirements of the Code that apply to the specific conduct.

C. Governmental, Civic or Charitable Activities.

(1) A judge shall not appear at a public hearing before, or otherwise consult with, an executive or legislative body or official except on matters concerning the law,* the legal system or the administration of justice or except when acting pro se in a matter involving the judge or the judge's interests.

Commentary

[1] See Section 2B regarding the obligation to avoid improper influence.

---

* See Terminology.

(2) A judge shall not accept appointment to a governmental committee or commission or other governmental position that is concerned with issues of fact or policy on matters other than the improvement of the law,* the legal system or the administration of justice. A judge may, however, represent a country, state or locality on ceremonial occasions or in connection with historical, educational or cultural activities.

Commentary

[1] Section 4C(2) prohibits a judge from accepting any governmental position except one relating to the law, legal system or administration of justice as authorized by Section 4C(3). The appropriateness of accepting extra-judicial assignments must be assessed in light of the demands on judicial resources created by crowded dockets and the need to protect the courts from involvement in extra-judicial matters that may prove to be controversial. Judges should not accept governmental appointments that are likely to interfere with the effectiveness and independence of the judiciary.

[2] Section 4C(2) does not govern a judge's service in a nongovernmental position. See Section 4C(3) permitting service by a judge with organizations devoted to the improvement of the law, the legal system or the administration of justice and with educational, religious, charitable, fraternal or civic organizations not conducted for profit. For example, service on the board of a public educational institution, unless it were a law school, would be prohibited under Section 4C(2), but service on the board of a public law school or any private educational institution would generally be permitted under Section 4C(3).

(3) A judge may serve as an officer, director, trustee or non-legal advisor of an organization or governmental agency devoted to the improvement of the law,* the legal system or the administration of justice or of an educational, religious, charitable, fraternal or civic organization not conducted for profit, subject to the following limitations and the other requirements of this Code.

Commentary

[1] Section 4C(3) does not apply to a judge's service in a governmental position unconnected with the improvement of the law, the legal system or the administration of justice; see Section 4C(2).

[2] See Commentary to Section 4B regarding use of the phrase "subject to the following limitations and the other requirements of this Code." As an example of the meaning of the phrase, a judge permitted by Section 4C(3) to serve on the board of a fraternal institution may be prohibited from such service by Sections 2C or 4A if the institution practices invidious discrimination or if service on the board otherwise casts reasonable doubt on the judge's capacity to act impartially as a judge.

[3] Service by a judge on behalf of a civic or charitable organization may be governed by other provisions of Canon 4 in addition to Section 4C. For example, a judge is prohibited by Section 4G from serving as a legal advisor to a civic or charitable organization.

(a) A judge shall not serve as an officer, director, trustee or non-legal advisor if it is likely that the organization

(i) will be engaged in proceedings that would ordinarily come before the judge, or

(ii) will be engaged frequently in adversary proceedings in the court of which the judge is a member or in any court subject to the appellate jurisdiction of the court of which the judge is a member.

Commentary

[1] The changing nature of some organizations and of their relationship to the law makes it necessary for a judge regularly to reexamine the activities of each organization with which the judge is affiliated to determine if it is proper for the judge to continue the affiliation. For example, in many jurisdictions charitable hospitals are now more frequently in court than in the past. Similarly, the boards of some legal aid organizations now make policy decisions that may have political significance or imply commitment to causes that may come before the courts for adjudication.

(b) A judge as an officer, director, trustee or non-legal advisor, or as a member or otherwise:

(i) may assist such an organization in planning fund-raising and may participate in the management and investment of the organization's funds, but shall not personally participate in the solicitation of funds or other fund-raising activities, except that a judge may solicit funds from other judges over whom the judge does not exercise supervisory or appellate authority;

(ii) may make recommendations to public and private fund-granting organizations on projects and programs concerning the law,* the legal system or the administration of justice;

(iii) shall not personally participate in membership solicitation if the solicitation might reasonably be perceived as coercive or, except as permitted in Section 4C(3)(b)(i), if the membership solicitation is essentially a fund-raising mechanism;

(iv) shall not use or permit the use of the prestige of judicial office for fund-raising or membership solicitation.

Commentary

[1] A judge may solicit membership or endorse or encourage membership efforts for an organization devoted to the improvement of the law, the legal system or the administration of justice or a nonprofit educational, religious, charitable, fraternal or civic organization as long as the solicitation cannot reasonably be perceived as coercive and is not essentially a fund-raising mechanism. Solicitation of funds for an organization and solicitation of memberships similarly involve the danger that the person solicited will feel obligated to respond favorably to the solicitor if the solicitor is in a position of influence or control. A judge must not engage in direct, individual solicitation of funds or memberships in person, in writing or by telephone except in the following cases: 1) a judge may solicit for funds or memberships other judges over whom the judge does not exercise supervisory or appellate authority, 2) a judge may solicit other persons for membership in the organizations described above if neither those persons nor persons with whom they are affiliated are likely ever to appear before the court on which the judge serves and 3) a judge who is an officer of such an organization may send a general membership solicitation mailing over the judge's signature.

[2] Use of an organization letterhead for fund-raising or membership solicitation does not violate Section 4C(3)(b) provided the letterhead lists only the judge's name and office or other position in the organization, and, if comparable designations are listed for other persons, the judge's judicial designation. In addition, a judge must also make reasonable efforts to ensure that the judge's staff, court officials and others subject to the judge's direction and control do not solicit funds on the judge's behalf for any purpose, charitable or otherwise.

[3] A judge must not be a speaker or guest of honor at an organization's fund-raising event, but mere attendance at such an event is permissible if otherwise consistent with this Code.

D. Financial Activities.

(1) A judge shall not engage in financial and business dealings that:

(a) may reasonably be perceived to exploit the judge's judicial position, or

(b) involve the judge in frequent transactions or continuing business relationships with those lawyers or other persons likely to come before the court on which the judge serves.

* See Terminology.

Commentary

[1] The Time for Compliance provision of this Code (Application, Section F) postpones the time for compliance with certain provisions of this Section in some cases.

[2] When a judge acquires in a judicial capacity information, such as material contained in filings with the court, that is not yet generally known, the judge must not use the information for private gain. See Section 2B; see also Section 3B(11).

[3] A judge must avoid financial and business dealings that involve the judge in frequent transactions or continuing business relationships with persons likely to come either before the judge personally or before other judges on the judge's court. In addition, a judge should discourage members of the judge's family from engaging in dealings that would reasonably appear to exploit the judge's judicial position. This rule is necessary to avoid creating an appearance of exploitation of office or favoritism and to minimize the potential for disqualification. With respect to affiliation of relatives of judge with law firms appearing before the judge, see Commentary to Section 3E(1) relating to disqualification.

[4] Participation by a judge in financial and business dealings is subject to the general prohibitions in Section 4A against activities that tend to reflect adversely on impartiality, demean the judicial office, or interfere with the proper performance of judicial duties. Such participation is also subject to the general prohibition in Canon 2 against activities involving impropriety or the appearance of impropriety and the prohibition in Section 2B against the misuse of the prestige of judicial office. In addition, a judge must maintain high standards of conduct in all of the judge's activities, as set forth in Canon 1. See Commentary for Section 4B regarding use of the phrase "subject to the requirements of this Code."

(2) A judge may, subject to the requirements of this Code, hold and manage investments of the judge and members of the judge's family,* including real estate, and engage in other remunerative activity.

Commentary

[1] This Section provides that, subject to the requirements of this Code, a judge may hold and manage investments owned solely by the judge, investments owned solely by a member or members of the judge's family, and investments owned jointly by the judge and members of the judge's family.

(3) A judge shall not serve as an officer, director, manager, general partner, advisor or employee of any business entity except that a judge may, subject to the requirements of this Code, manage and participate in:

(a) a business closely held by the judge or members of the judge's family,* or

(b) a business entity primarily engaged in investment of the financial resources of the judge or members of the judge's family.

Commentary

[1] Subject to the requirements of this Code, a judge may participate in a business that is closely held either by the judge alone, by members of the judge's family, or by the judge and members of the judge's family.

[2] Although participation by a judge in a closely-held family business might otherwise be permitted by Section 4D(3), a judge may be prohibited from participation by other provisions of this Code when, for example, the business entity frequently appears before the judge's court or the participation requires significant time away from judicial duties. Similarly, a judge must avoid participating in a closely-held family business if the judge's participation would involve misuse of the prestige of judicial office.

(4) A judge shall manage the judge's investments and other financial interests to minimize the number of cases in which the judge is disqualified. As soon as the judge can do so without serious financial detriment, the judge shall divest himself or herself of investments and other financial interests that might require frequent disqualification.

---

* See Terminology.

(5) A judge shall not accept, and shall urge members of the judge's family residing in the judge's household,* not to accept, a gift, bequest, favor or loan from anyone except for:

Commentary

[1] Section 4D(5) does not apply to contributions to a judge's campaign for judicial office, a matter governed by Canon 5.

[2] Because a gift, bequest, favor or loan to a member of the judge's family residing in the judge's household might be viewed as intended to influence the judge, a judge must inform those family members of the relevant ethical constraints upon the judge in this regard and discourage those family members from violating them. A judge cannot, however, reasonably be expected to know or control all of the financial or business activities of all family members residing in the judge's household.

(a) a gift incident to a public testimonial, books, tapes and other resource materials supplied by publishers on a complimentary basis for official use, or an invitation to the judge and the judge's spouse or guest to attend a bar-related function or an activity devoted to the improvement of the law,* the legal system or the administration of justice;

Commentary

[1] Acceptance of an invitation to a law-related function is governed by Section 4D(5)(a); acceptance of an invitation paid for by an individual lawyer or group of lawyers is governed by Section 4D(5)(h).

[2] A judge may accept a public testimonial or a gift incident thereto only if the donor organization is not an organization whose members comprise or frequently represent the same side in litigation, and the testimonial and gift are otherwise in compliance with other provisions of this Code. See Sections 4A(1) and 2B.

(b) a gift, award or benefit incident to the business, profession or other separate activity of a spouse or other family member of a judge residing in the judge's household, including gifts, awards and benefits for the use of both the spouse or other family member and the judge (as spouse or family member), provided the gift, award or benefit could not reasonably be perceived as intended to influence the judge in the performance of judicial duties;

(c) ordinary social hospitality;

(d) a gift from a relative or friend, for a special occasion, such as a wedding, anniversary or birthday, if the gift is fairly commensurate with the occasion and the relationship;

Commentary

[1] A gift to a judge, or to a member of the judge's family living in the judge's household, that is excessive in value raises questions about the judge's impartiality and the integrity of the judicial office and might require disqualification of the judge where disqualification would not otherwise be required. See, however, Section 4D(5)(e).

(e) a gift, bequest, favor or loan from a relative or close personal friend whose appearance or interest in a case would in any event require disqualification under Section 3E;

(f) a loan from a lending institution in its regular course of business on the same terms generally available to persons who are not judges;

(g) a scholarship or fellowship awarded on the same terms and based on the same criteria applied to other applicants; or

(h) any other gift, bequest, favor or loan, only if: the donor is not a party or other person who has come or is likely to come or whose interests have come or are likely to

come before the judge; and, if its value exceeds $150.00, the judge reports it in the same manner as the judge reports compensation in Section 4H.

Commentary

[1] Section 4D(5)(h) prohibits judges from accepting gifts, favors, bequests or loans from lawyers or their firms if they have come or are likely to come before the judge; it also prohibits gifts, favors, bequests or loans from clients of lawyers or their firms when the clients' interests have come or are likely to come before the judge.

E. Fiduciary Activities.

(1) A judge shall not serve as executor, administrator or other personal representative, trustee, guardian, attorney in fact or other fiduciary,* except for the estate, trust or person of a member of the judge's family,* and then only if such service will not interfere with the proper performance of judicial duties.

(2) A judge shall not serve as a fiduciary* if it is likely that the judge as a fiduciary will be engaged in proceedings that would ordinarily come before the judge, or if the estate, trust or ward becomes involved in adversary proceedings in the court on which the judge serves or one under its appellate jurisdiction.

(3) The same restrictions on financial activities that apply to a judge personally also apply to the judge while acting in a fiduciary* capacity.

Commentary

[1] The Time for Compliance provision of this Code (Application, Section F) postpones the time for compliance with certain provisions of this Section in some cases.

[2] The restrictions imposed by this Canon may conflict with the judge's obligation as a fiduciary. For example, a judge should resign as trustee if detriment to the trust would result from divestiture of holdings the retention of which would place the judge in violation of Section 4D(4).

F. Service as Arbitrator or Mediator. A judge shall not act as an arbitrator or mediator or otherwise perform judicial functions in a private capacity unless expressly authorized by law.*

Commentary

[1] Section 4F does not prohibit a judge from participating in arbitration, mediation or settlement conferences performed as part of judicial duties.

G. Practice of Law. A judge shall not practice law. Notwithstanding this prohibition, a judge may act pro se and may, without compensation, give legal advice to and draft or review documents for a member of the judge's family.*

Commentary

[1] This prohibition refers to the practice of law in a representative capacity and not in a pro se capacity. A judge may act for himself or herself in all legal matters, including matters involving litigation and matters involving appearances before or other dealings with legislative and other governmental bodies. However, in so doing, a judge must not abuse the prestige of office to advance the interests of the judge or the judge's family. See Section 2(B).

[2] The Code allows a judge to give legal advice to and draft legal documents for members of the judge's family, so long as the judge receives no compensation. A judge must not, however, act as an advocate or negotiator for a member of the judge's family in a legal matter.

[3] Canon 6, new in the 1972 Code, reflected concerns about conflicts of interest and appearances of impropriety arising from compensation for off-the-bench activities. Since 1972, however, reporting requirements that are much more comprehensive with respect to what must be reported and with whom

* See Terminology.

reports must be filed have been adopted by many jurisdictions. The Committee believes that although reports of compensation for extra-judicial activities should be required, reporting requirements preferably should be developed to suit the respective jurisdictions, not simply adopted as set forth in a national model code of judicial conduct. Because of the Committee's concern that deletion of this Canon might lead to the misconception that reporting compensation for extra-judicial activities is no longer important, the substance of Canon 6 is carried forward as Section 4H in this Code for adoption in those jurisdictions that do not have other reporting requirements. In jurisdictions that have separately established reporting requirements, Section 4H(2) (Public Reporting) may be deleted and the caption for Section 4H modified appropriately.

H. Compensation, Reimbursement and Reporting.

(1) Compensation and Reimbursement. A judge may receive compensation and reimbursement of expenses for the extra-judicial activities permitted by this Code, if the source of such payments does not give the appearance of influencing the judge's performance of judicial duties or otherwise give the appearance of impropriety.

(a) Compensation shall not exceed a reasonable amount nor shall it exceed what a person who is not a judge would receive for the same activity.

(b) Expense reimbursement shall be limited to the actual cost of travel, food and lodging reasonably incurred by the judge and, where appropriate to the occasion, by the judge's spouse or guest. Any payment in excess of such an amount is compensation.

(2) Public Reports. A judge shall report the date, place and nature of any activity for which the judge received compensation, and the name of the payor and the amount of compensation so received. Compensation or income of a spouse attributed to the judge by operation of a community property law is not extra-judicial compensation to the judge. The judge's report shall be made at least annually and shall be filed as a public document in the office of the clerk of the court on which the judge serves or other office designated by law.*

Commentary

[1] See Section 4D(5) regarding reporting of gifts, bequests and loans.

[2] The Code does not prohibit a judge from accepting honoraria or speaking fees provided that the compensation is reasonable and commensurate with the task performed. A judge should ensure, however, that no conflicts are created by the arrangement. A judge must not appear to trade on the judicial position for personal advantage. Nor should a judge spend significant time away from court duties to meet speaking or writing commitments for compensation. In addition, the source of the payment must not raise any question of undue influence or the judge's ability or willingness to be impartial.

I. Disclosure of a judge's income, debts, investments or other assets is required only to the extent provided in this Canon and in Sections 3E and 3F, or as otherwise required by law.*

Commentary

[1] Section 3E requires a judge to disqualify himself or herself in any proceeding in which the judge has an economic interest. See "economic interest" as explained in the Terminology Section. Section 4D requires a judge to refrain from engaging in business and from financial activities that might interfere with the impartial performance of judicial duties; Section 4H requires a judge to report all compensation the judge received for activities outside judicial office. A judge has the rights of any other citizen, including the right to privacy of the judge's financial affairs, except to the extent that limitations established by law are required to safeguard the proper performance of the judge's duties.

* See Terminology.

CANON 5[5]

A Judge or Judicial Candidate Shall Refrain From Inappropriate Political Activity†

A. All Judges and Candidates.

(1) Except as authorized in Sections 5B(2), 5C(1) and 5C(3), a judge or a candidate* for election or appointment to judicial office shall not:

(a) act as a leader or hold an office in a political organization*;

(b) publicly endorse or publicly oppose another candidate for public office;

(c) make speeches on behalf of a political organization;

(d) attend political gatherings; or

(e) solicit funds for, pay an assessment to or make a contribution to a political organization or candidate, or purchase tickets for political party dinners or other functions.

Commentary

[1] A judge or candidate for judicial office retains the right to participate in the political process as a voter.

[2] Where false information concerning a judicial candidate is made public, a judge or another judicial candidate having knowledge of the facts is not prohibited by Section 5A(1) from making the facts public.

[3] Section 5A(1)(a) does not prohibit a candidate for elective judicial office from retaining during candidacy a public office such as county prosecutor, which is not "an office in a political organization."

[4] Section 5A(1)(b) does not prohibit a judge or judicial candidate from privately expressing his or her views on judicial candidates or other candidates for public office.

[5] A candidate does not publicly endorse another candidate for public office by having that candidate's name on the same ticket.

(2) A judge shall resign from judicial office upon becoming a candidate* for a non-judicial office either in a primary or in a general election, except that the judge may continue to hold judicial office while being a candidate for election to or serving as a delegate in a state constitutional convention if the judge is otherwise permitted by law* to do so.

---

[5] Introductory Note to Canon 5: There is wide variation in the methods of judicial selection used, both among jurisdictions and within the jurisdictions themselves. In a given state, judges may be selected by one method initially, retained by a different method, and selected by still another method to fill interim vacancies.

According to figures compiled in 1987 by the National Center for State Courts, 32 states and the District of Columbia use a merit selection method (in which an executive such as a governor appoints a judge from a group of nominees selected by a judicial nominating commission) to select judges in the state either initially or to fill an interim vacancy. Of those 33 jurisdictions, a merit selection method is used in 18 jurisdictions to choose judges of courts of last resort, in 13 jurisdictions to choose judges of intermediate appellate courts, in 12 jurisdictions to choose judges of general jurisdiction courts and in 5 jurisdictions to choose judges of limited jurisdiction courts.

Methods of judicial selection other than merit selection include nonpartisan election (10 states use it for initial selection at all court levels, another 10 states use it for initial selection for at least one court level) and partisan election (8 states use it for initial selection at all court levels, another 7 states use it for initial selection for at least one level). In a small minority of the states, judicial selection methods include executive or legislative appointment (without nomination of a group of potential appointees by a judicial nominating commission) and court selection. In addition, the federal judicial system utilizes an executive appointment method. See State Court Organization 1987 (National Center for State Courts, 1988).

† The Supreme Court's decision in the Republican Party of Minnesota v. White case may call into question Canon 5's attempt to restrict judicial freedom of speech.

(3) A candidate* for a judicial office:

(a) shall maintain the dignity appropriate to judicial office and act in a manner consistent with the impartiality,* integrity and independence of the judiciary, and shall encourage members of the candidate's family* to adhere to the same standards of political conduct in support of the candidate as apply to the candidate;

Commentary

[1] Although a judicial candidate must encourage members of his or her family to adhere to the same standards of political conduct in support of the candidate that apply to the candidate, family members are free to participate in other political activity.

(b) shall prohibit employees and officials who serve at the pleasure of the candidate,* and shall discourage other employees and officials subject to the candidate's direction and control from doing on the candidate's behalf what the candidate is prohibited from doing under the Sections of this Canon;

(c) except to the extent permitted by Section 5C(2), shall not authorize or knowingly permit any other person to do for the candidate what the candidate is prohibited from doing under the Sections of this Canon;

(d) shall not:

(i) with respect to cases, controversies, or issues that are likely to come before the court, make pledges promises or commitments that are inconsistent with the impartial performance of the adjudicative duties of the office; or**

(ii) knowingly* misrepresent the identity, qualifications, present position or other fact concerning the candidate or an opponent;

Commentary

[1] Section 5A(3)(d) prohibits a candidate for judicial office from making statements that commit the candidate regarding cases, controversies or issues likely to come before the court. As a corollary, a candidate should emphasize in any public statement the candidate's duty to uphold the law regardless of his or her personal views. See also Section 3B(9) and (10), the general rule on public comment by judges. Section 5A(3)(d) does not prohibit a candidate from making pledges or promises respecting improvements in court administration. Nor does this Section prohibit an incumbent judge from making private statements to other judges or court personnel in the performance of judicial duties. This Section applies to any statement made in the process of securing judicial office, such as statements to commissions charged with judicial selection and tenure and legislative bodies confirming appointment. See also Rule 8.2 of the ABA Model Rules of Professional Conduct.

(e) may respond to personal attacks or attacks on the candidate's record as long as the response does not violate Section 5A(3)(d).

B. Candidates Seeking Appointment to Judicial or Other Governmental Office.

(1) A candidate* for appointment to judicial office or a judge seeking other governmental office shall not solicit or accept funds, personally or through a committee or otherwise, to support his or her candidacy.

(2) A candidate* for appointment to judicial office or a judge seeking other governmental office shall not engage in any political activity to secure the appointment except that:

(a) such persons may:

* See Terminology.

** The ABA House of Delegates amended (d) in August 2003.

(i) communicate with the appointing authority, including any selection or nominating commission or other agency designated to screen candidates;

(ii) seek support or endorsement for the appointment from organizations that regularly make recommendations for reappointment or appointment to the office, and from individuals to the extent requested or required by those specified in Section 5B(2)(a); and

(iii) provide to those specified in Sections 5B(2)(a)(i) and 5B(2)(a)(ii) information as to his or her qualifications for the office;

(b) a non-judge candidate* for appointment to judicial office may, in addition, unless otherwise prohibited by law*;

(i) retain an office in a political organization,*

(ii) attend political gatherings, and

(iii) continue to pay ordinary assessments and ordinary contributions to a political organization or candidate and purchase tickets for political party dinners or other functions.

Commentary

[1] Section 5B(2) provides a limited exception to the restrictions imposed by Sections 5A(1) and 5D. Under Section 5B(2), candidates seeking reappointment to the same judicial office or appointment to another judicial office or other governmental office may apply for the appointment and seek appropriate support.

[2] Although under Section 5B(2) non-judge candidates seeking appointment to judicial office are permitted during candidacy to retain office in a political organization, attend political gatherings and pay ordinary dues and assessments, they remain subject to other provisions of this Code during candidacy. See Sections 5B(1), 5B(2)(a), 5E and Application Section.

C. Judges and Candidates Subject to Public Election.

(1) A judge or a candidate* subject to public election* may, except as prohibited by law:*

(a) at any time

(i) purchase tickets for and attend political gatherings;

(ii) identify himself or herself as a member of a political party; and

(iii) contribute to a political organization*;

(b) when a candidate for election

(i) speak to gatherings on his or her own behalf;

(ii) appear in newspaper, television and other media advertisements supporting his or her candidacy;

(iii) distribute pamphlets and other promotional campaign literature supporting his or her candidacy; and

(iv) publicly endorse or publicly oppose other candidates for the same judicial office in a public election in which the judge or judicial candidate is running.

* See Terminology.

Commentary

[1] Section 5C(1) permits judges subject to election at any time to be involved in limited political activity. Section 5D, applicable solely to incumbent judges, would otherwise bar this activity.

(2) A candidate* shall not personally solicit or accept campaign contributions or personally solicit publicly stated support. A candidate may, however, establish committees of responsible persons to conduct campaigns for the candidate through media advertisements, brochures, mailings, candidate forums and other means not prohibited by law. Such committees may solicit and accept reasonable campaign contributions, manage the expenditure of funds for the candidate's campaign and obtain public statements of support for his or her candidacy. Such committees are not prohibited from soliciting and accepting reasonable campaign contributions and public support from lawyers. A candidate's committees may solicit contributions and public support for the candidate's campaign no earlier than [one year] before an election and no later than [90] days after the last election in which the candidate participates during the election year. A candidate shall not use or permit the use of campaign contributions for the private benefit of the candidate or others.

Commentary†

[1] There is legitimate concern about a judge's impartiality when parties whose interests may come before a judge, or the lawyers who represent such parties, are known to have made contributions to the election campaigns of judicial candidates. This is among the reasons that merit selection of judges is a preferable manner in which to select the judiciary. Notwithstanding that preference, Section 5C(2) recognizes that in many jurisdictions judicial candidates must raise funds to support their candidates for election to judicial office. It therefore permits a candidate, other than a candidate for appointment, to establish campaign committees to solicit and accept public support and reasonable financial contributions. In order to guard against the possibility that conflicts of interest will arise, the candidate must instruct his or her campaign committees at the start of the campaign to solicit or accept only contributions that are reasonable and appropriate under the circumstances. Though not prohibited, campaign contributions of which a judge has knowledge, made by lawyers or others who appear before the judge may, by virtue of their size or source, raise questions about a judge's impartiality and be cause for disqualification as provided under Section 3(E).

[2] Campaign committees established under Section 5C(2) should manage campaign finances responsibly, avoiding deficits that might necessitate post-election fund-raising, to the extent possible. Such committees must at all times comply with applicable statutory provisions governing their conduct.

[3] Section 5C(2) does not prohibit a candidate from initiating an evaluation by a judicial selection commission or bar association, or, subject to the requirements of this Code, from responding to a request for information from any organization.

(3)†† A candidate shall instruct his or her campaign committees(s) at the start of the campaign not to accept campaign contributions for any election that exceed, in the aggregate*, $[ ] from an individual or $[ ] from an entity. This limitations is in addition to the limitations provided in Section 5C(2).[6]

(4)†† In addition to complying with all applicable statutory requirements for disclosure of campaign contributions, campaign committees established by a candidate shall file with

† In 1997, the ABA amended the Commentary to Canon 5C(2).

†† [Editor's Note: The language in (3) and (4) was added in 1999 by the ABA House of Delegates. The language in (5) was originally numbered as (3) and moved down when the two prior sections were added.]

* See Terminology.

6 Jurisdictions wishing to adopt campaign contribution limits that are lower than generally applicable campaign finance regulations provide should adopt this provision, inserting appropriate dollar amounts where brackets appear.

[ ][7] a report stating the name, address, occupation and employer of each person who has made campaign contributions to the committee whose value in the aggregate* exceed [$].[8] The report must be filed within [ ][9] days following the election.

(5) Except as prohibited by law,* a candidate* for judicial office in a public election* may permit the candidate's name: (a) to be listed on election materials along with the names of other candidates for elective public office, and (b) to appear in promotions of the ticket.

Commentary

[1] Section 5C(5) provides a limited exception to the restrictions imposed by Section 5A(1).

D. Incumbent Judges. A judge shall not engage in any political activity except (i) as authorized under any other Section of this Code, (ii) on behalf of measures to improve the law,* the legal system or the administration of justice, or (iii) as expressly authorized by law.

Commentary

[1] Neither Section 5D nor any other section of the Code prohibits a judge in the exercise of administrative functions from engaging in planning and other official activities with members of the executive and legislative branches of government. With respect to a judge's activity on behalf of measures to improve the law, the legal system and the administration of justice, see Commentary to Section 4B and Section 4C(1) and its Commentary.

E. Applicability. Canon 5 generally applies to all incumbent judges and judicial candidates.* A successful candidate, whether or not an incumbent, is subject to judicial discipline for his or her campaign conduct; an unsuccessful candidate who is a lawyer is subject to lawyer discipline for his or her campaign conduct. A lawyer who is a candidate for judicial office is subject to [Rule 8.2(b) of the ABA Model Rules of Professional Conduct]. (An adopting jurisdiction should substitute a reference to its applicable rule.)

APPLICATION OF THE CODE OF JUDICIAL CONDUCT

A. Anyone, whether or not a lawyer, who is an officer of a judicial system[10] and who performs judicial functions, including an officer such as a magistrate, court commissioner, special master or referee, is a judge within the meaning of this Code. All judges shall comply with this Code except as provided below.

Commentary

[1] The four categories of judicial service in other than a full-time capacity are necessarily defined in general terms because of the widely varying forms of judicial service. For the purposes of this Section, as long as a retired judge is subject to recall the judge is considered to "perform judicial functions." The determination of which category and, accordingly, which specific Code provisions apply to an individual judicial officer, depend upon the facts of the particular judicial service.

---

7 Each jurisdiction should identify an appropriate depository for the information required under this provision, giving consideration to this public's need for convenient and timely access to the information. Electronic filing is to be preferred.

8 Jurisdictions wishing to adopt campaign contribution disclosure levels lower than those set in generally applicable campaign finance regulations should adopt this provision, inserting appropriate dollar amounts where brackets appear.

9 A time period chosen by the adopting jurisdiction should appear in the bracketed space.

10 Applicability of this Code to administrative law judges should be determined by each adopting jurisdiction. Administrative law judges generally are affiliated with the executive branch of government rather than the judicial branch and each adopting jurisdiction should consider the unique characteristics of particular administrative law judge positions in adopting and adapting the Code for administrative law judges. See, e.g., Model Code of Judicial Conduct for Federal Administrative Law Judges, endorsed by the National Conference of Administrative Law Judges in February 1989.

B. Retired Judge Subject to Recall. A retired judge subject to recall who by law is not permitted to practice law is not required to comply:

(1) except while serving as a judge, with Section 4F; and

(2) at any time with Section 4E.

C. Continuing Part-time Judge. A continuing part-time judge*:

(1) is not required to comply:

(a) except while serving as a judge, with Section 3B(9); and

(b) at any time with Sections 4C(2), 4D(3), 4E(1), 4F, 4G, 4H, 5A(1), 5B(2) and 5D.

(2) shall not practice law in the court on which the judge serves or in any court subject to the appellate jurisdiction of the court on which the judge serves, and shall not act as a lawyer in a proceeding in which the judge has served as a judge or in any other proceeding related thereto.

Commentary

[1] When a person who has been a continuing part-time judge is no longer a continuing part-time judge, including a retired judge no longer subject to recall, that person may act as a lawyer in a proceeding in which he or she has served as a judge or in any other proceeding related thereto only with the express consent of all parties pursuant to [Rule 1.12(a) of the ABA Model Rules of Professional Conduct]. (An adopting jurisdiction should substitute a reference to its applicable rule).

D. Periodic Part-time Judge. A periodic part-time judge*:

(1) is not required to comply

(a) except while serving as a judge, with Section 3B(9);

(b) at any time, with Sections 4C(2), 4C(3)(a), 4D(1)(b), 4D(3), 4D(4), 4D(5), 4E, 4F, 4G, 4H, 5A(1), 5B(2) and 5D.

(2) shall not practice law in the court on which the judge serves or in any court subject to the appellate jurisdiction of the court on which the judge serves, and shall not act as a lawyer in a proceeding in which the judge has served as a judge or in any other proceeding related thereto.

Commentary

[1] When a person who has been a periodic part-time judge is no longer a periodic part-time judge (no longer accepts appointments), that person may act as a lawyer in a proceeding in which he or she has served as a judge or in any other proceeding related thereto only with the express consent of all parties pursuant to [Rule 1.12(a) of the ABA Model Rules of Professional Conduct]. (An adopting jurisdiction should substitute a reference to its applicable rule).

E. Pro Tempore Part-Time Judge. A pro tempore part-time judge*:

(1) is not required to comply:

(a) except while serving as a judge, with Sections 2A, 2B, 3B(9) and 4C(1);

(b) at any time with Sections 2C, 4C(2), 4C(3)(a), 4C(3)(b), 4D(1)(b), 4D(3), 4D(4), 4D(5), 4E, 4F, 4G, 4H, 5A(1), 5A(2), 5B(2) and 5D.

(2) A person who has been a pro tempore part-time judge shall not act as a lawyer in a proceeding in which the judge has served as a judge or in any other proceeding related thereto except as otherwise permitted by [Rule 1.12(a) of the ABA Model Rules of**

* See Terminology.

** See Terminology.

Professional Conduct]. (An adopting jurisdiction should substitute a reference to its applicable rule.)

F. Time for Compliance. A person to whom this Code becomes applicable shall comply immediately with all provisions of this Code except Sections 4D(2), 4D(3) and 4E and shall comply with these Sections as soon as reasonably possible and shall do so in any event within the period of one year.

Commentary

[1] If serving as a fiduciary when selected as judge, a new judge may, notwithstanding the prohibitions in Section 4E, continue to serve as fiduciary but only for that period of time necessary to avoid serious adverse consequences to the beneficiary of the fiduciary relationship and in no event longer than one year. Similarly, if engaged at the time of judicial selection in a business activity, a new judge may, notwithstanding the prohibitions in Section 4D(3), continue in that activity for a reasonable period but in no event longer than one year.